The Columbia History of Chinese Literature

The Columbia History of Chinese Literature

Victor H. Mair
EDITOR

COLUMBIA UNIVERSITY PRESS
NEW YORK

Columbia University Press
Publishers Since 1893
New York, Chichester, West Sussex

Columbia University Press wishes to express its
appreciation for assistance given by the
Chiang Ching-kuo Foundation for International Scholarly Exchange,
the Pushkin Fund, and the
Center for East Asian Studies of the University of Pennsylvania
toward the cost of publishing this book.

Library of Congress Cataloging-in-Publication Data

The Columbia history of Chinese literature / Victor H. Mair, editor.
p. cm.
Includes bibliographical references and index.
ISBN 0-231-10984-9 (alk. paper)
1. Chinese literature—History and criticism. I. Mair, Victor H., 1943–

PL2265 .C65 2001
895.1'09—dc21
2001028236
∞

Cover art: Juan Chi (210–263) and Sung/Chin-period actor whistling
Woodcuts by Daniel Heitkamp

Casebound editions of Columbia University Press books
are printed on permanent and durable acid-free paper.
Printed in the United States of America
c 10 9 8 7 6 5 4 3 2 1

To the people of China—be they Han or non-Han, be they literate or illiterate. They have all contributed, each in his or her own way, to making Chinese civilization what it is today.

CONTENTS

Prolegomenon xi
Preface xv
Acknowledgments xix
Abbreviations xxi
Map of China xxii

Introduction: The Origins and Impact of Literati Culture 1

I. FOUNDATIONS

1. Language and Script, VICTOR H. MAIR 19
2. Myth, ANNE BIRRELL 58
3. Philosophy and Literature in Early China, MICHAEL PUETT 70
4. The Thirteen Classics, PAUL RAKITA GOLDIN 86
5. *Shih-ching* Poetry and Didacticism in Ancient Chinese Literature, JEFFREY RIEGEL 97
6. The Supernatural, RANIA HUNTINGTON 110
7. Wit and Humor, KARIN MYHRE 132
8. Proverbs, JOHN S. ROHSENOW 149
9. Buddhist Literature, HELWIG SCHMIDT-GLINTZER AND VICTOR H. MAIR 160
10. Taoist Heritage, JUDITH MAGEE BOLTZ 173
11. Women in Literature, ANNE BIRRELL 194

II. POETRY

12. *Sao, Fu*, Parallel Prose, and Related Genres, CHRISTOPHER LEIGH CONNERY 223
13. Poetry from 200 B.C.E. to 600 C.E., ROBERT JOE CUTTER 248
14. Poetry of the T'ang Dynasty, PAUL W. KROLL 274
15. *Tz'u*, STUART SARGENT 314
16. Sung Dynasty *Shih* Poetry, MICHAEL A. FULLER 337
17. Yüan *San-ch'ü*, WAYNE SCHLEPP 370
18. Mongol-Yüan Classical Verse (*Shih*), RICHARD JOHN LYNN 383
19. Poetry of the Fourteenth Century, JOHN TIMOTHY WIXTED 390
20. Poetry of the Fifteenth and Sixteenth Centuries, DANIEL BRYANT 399
21. Poetry of the Seventeenth Century, RICHARD JOHN LYNN 410
22. Poetry of the Eighteenth to Early Twentieth Centuries, DANIEL BRYANT 429
23. Ch'ing Lyric, DAVID MCCRAW 444
24. Modern Poetry, MICHELLE YEH 453
25. Poetry and Painting, CHARLES HARTMAN 466

III. PROSE

26. The Literary Features of Historical Writing, STEPHEN DURRANT 493
27. Early Biography, WILLIAM H. NIENHAUSER, JR. 511
28. Expository Prose, RONALD EGAN 527
29. Records of Anomalies, HU YING 542
30. Travel Literature, JAMES M. HARGETT 555
31. Sketches, JAMES M. HARGETT 560
32. Twentieth-Century Prose, PHILIP F. C. WILLIAMS 566

IV. FICTION

33. T'ang Tales, WILLIAM H. NIENHAUSER, JR. 579
34. Vernacular Stories, YENNA WU 595
35. Full-Length Vernacular Fiction, WAI-YEE LI 620
36. Traditional Vernacular Novels: Some Lesser-Known Works, DARIA BERG 659
37. The Later Classical Tale, ALLAN H. BARR 675
38. Fiction from the End of the Empire to the Beginning of the Republic (1897–1916), MILENA DOLEŽELOVÁ-VELINGEROVÁ 697
39. Twentieth-Century Fiction, PHILIP F. C. WILLIAMS 732
40. China, Hong Kong, and Taiwan During the 1980s and 1990s, HELMUT MARTIN 758

V. DRAMA

41. Traditional Dramatic Literature, WILT L. IDEMA 785
42. Twentieth-Century Spoken Drama, XIAOMEI CHEN 848

VI. COMMENTARY, CRITICISM, AND INTERPRETATION

43. The Rhetoric of Premodern Prose Style, CHRISTOPH HARBSMEIER 881
44. Classical Exegesis, HAUN SAUSSY 909
45. Literary Theory and Criticism, DORE J. LEVY 916
46. Traditional Fiction Commentary, DAVID L. ROLSTON 940

VII. POPULAR AND PERIPHERAL MANIFESTATIONS

47. Balladry and Popular Song, ANNE BIRRELL 953
48. Tun-huang Literature, NEIL SCHMID 964
49. The Oral-Formulaic Tradition, ANNE E. MCLAREN 989
50. Regional Literatures, MARK BENDER 1015
51. Ethnic Minority Literature, MARK BENDER 1032
52. The Translator's Turn: The Birth of Modern Chinese Language and Fiction, LYDIA H. LIU 1055
53. The Reception of Chinese Literature in Korea, EMANUEL PASTREICH 1067
54. The Reception of Chinese Literature in Japan, EMANUEL PASTREICH 1079
55. The Reception of Chinese Literature in Vietnam, EMANUEL PASTREICH 1096

Suggestions for Further Reading 1105
Principal Chinese Dynasties and Periods 1153
Romanization Schemes for Modern Standard Mandarin 1155
Glossary of Terms 1161
Glossary of Names 1179
Glossary of Titles 1213
Index 1241
Contributors 1335

PROLEGOMENON

It was only about a century ago that the first histories of Chinese literature began to be written in any language. These earliest attempts at writing the history of Chinese literature were often little more than glorified anthologies. In many instances, they were essentially collections of translated chestnuts with scarcely any explanation or commentary. Seldom was there an attempt to construct a systematic account of the development of genres, styles, and themes or to analyze the relationship of literature to society, political institutions, or even the other arts. Around half a century later, it became possible to write general introductions to the history of Chinese literature, and several dozen of these indeed appeared in Chinese, Japanese, English, French, and German. For the most part, however, such histories were still filled largely with translations and excerpts, and offered only minimal interpretation. Of course, all the while scores of monographs and hundreds of articles were being written on various specific authors, works, movements, and periods.

In the 1960s, 1970s, 1980s, and 1990s, however, secondary studies on virtually all aspects of Chinese literature mushroomed to the point that bibliographical control became a genuine problem. Simply keeping up with the flood of new research was a challenge that occupied many specialists who compiled bibliographies, guides, and encyclopedias. The outpouring of scholarly investigations, many of them of very high quality, was both a blessing and a curse. It was a blessing because valuable insights and materials were being made available, but it was a curse because no one person could possibly stay abreast of everything that was appearing, as had been possible in the first half of the twentieth century. The superabundance of new studies proved to be so intimidating that some of the best minds in Chinese literary studies declared that it was no longer possible to write a history of Chinese literature–not even by committee, much less by a single person. Collectively, there was simply too much known about the subject to compress it into a single volume or even into several volumes. Furthermore, it was felt that, as more was learned about the complexities of Chinese literature, it became virtually impossible to make sense of them.

Pessimism over the propriety of attempting a comprehensive history of Chinese literature also arose as a result of changing perceptions and paradigms. Whereas it used to be taken for granted that the history of Chinese literature should be chronologically divided up by dynasties and topically arranged according to genres, these once comfortable assumptions have now become subjected to such severe scrutiny that they can no longer be relied on. Critical analysis and skeptical hermeneutics have called into question even the most basic premises about Chinese literature. Periodization no longer follows a dynastic approach; traditional categories and rankings are shown to be faulty; and hitherto ignored literary realms are brought to the fore.

Despite these daunting obstacles to the creation of a viable history of Chinese literature for our time, the need for such a work is so compelling that we have gone forward, fully aware of the difficulties. What *The Columbia History of Chinese Literature* attempts to do is to weave together the latest findings of critical scholarship in a framework that is simultaneously chronological and topical. The chronology used here is far from strictly dynastic, but it does not eschew dynastic divisions altogether when they are warranted. As for topics covered, this volume by no means subscribes to the view that Chinese literature can be neatly broken up according to traditional genres. Since many of the old genre categories are problematic, they are referred to but not regarded as restrictions. Above all, the history of Chinese literature is seen through entirely new prisms that transcend both time and genre. These unaccustomed lenses for looking at Chinese literature may be found in a number of specific chapters (e.g., chapters 43 and 49), but are also spread throughout the book.

The scope of this work is the entire history of Chinese literature from its inception to the present day. Most attention is naturally devoted to the premodern period, because it is so vast by itself and because postimperial (after 1911) literature in China has increasingly become international, in both themes and form. By the same token, however, the twentieth century is covered to show the extent to which traditions persist and the degree to which they have changed. The primary aim throughout this volume is to illuminate essential features of the history of Chinese literature so that those who are completely unacquainted with it will be able to gain a foothold, and so that those who are minimally acquainted with the subject as a whole or who are familiar with one facet of it will gain a deeper understanding and a more comprehensive grasp.

Some of the issues and themes that run throughout the volume can be enumerated here. A primary concern is with the way that thought (broadly construed) and religion have conditioned the growth of literature. Confucianism, Buddhism, Taoism, and folk religion have all played decisive roles in the unfolding of literature in China. The permutations and combinations of these various strands of Chinese secular and sacred discourse are extraordinarily complicated, yet coming to grips with them is essential for an accurate and adequate understanding of Chinese literature. This work also endeavors to clarify the importance of the relationship between the elite and the popular for Chinese literature, by no means a simple task. Similarly, a special effort has been made to account for the intricate interaction between the Han (Sinitic) and non-Han (non-Sinitic) as it is manifested in literary works that have survived. Linked to this is a serious examination of the role of language (both literary and vernacular) in determining the nature of particular texts. This, in turn, leads to the matter of written versus oral, and national versus regional and local, in the Chinese literary landscape.

In general, Chinese literature is seen here as intimately associated with the society in which it was nurtured and manifested. Literature is not a thing unto itself but, rather, the product of an infinite array of sociopolitical forces and cultural factors. In each chapter, the purpose is to illuminate as many of these interconnections as possible. Obviously, it would be impossible to mention every author and every work written in the long history of Chinese literature. Instead, representative figures and titles have been selected, in an effort not to miss anything essential; yet we also introduce some authors and works that have hitherto been ignored for one reason or another despite their significance. Although the volume aims to be comprehensive, it would be folly to believe it could be exhaustive. For a history of literature to be genuine, it is more important for it to be enlightening than to be all-inclusive. Therefore, this history touches on such matters as the fuzzy interface between prose and poetry, the uncertain boundary between fiction and drama, and the ineffable interplay between spoken and written language. In the end, what this history has helped the contributors to see—and what we hope it helps our readers to see—is the varied nature of Chinese literature, its shifting contours and kaleidoscopic transformations, its subtle lineaments and lasting verities. If, on the completion of this volume, one can say anything with conviction about the history of Chinese literature, perhaps it would be that it is long, abundant, and vibrant. May some such recognition stand as a much-needed corrective to customary notions of Chinese literature as effete, exotic, and monotonous. Quite the contrary, the history of Chinese literature is as multifarious and vital as that of any other literary tradition on earth.

Victor H. Mair
Peking
May 25, 2000

PREFACE

As Chinese culture becomes more familiar to the general public and as increasing numbers of citizens of East Asian descent with an interest in their heritage fill our nation's classrooms, many individuals feel the need for a multipurpose, comprehensive history of Chinese literature. Ideally, this should be a work to which specialists and nonspecialists alike can turn when they require background on Chinese literary genres, texts, figures, and movements. From its very conception, *The Columbia History of Chinese Literature* was designed to meet the needs of such users.

Unlike several earlier histories of Chinese literature (none of which remains in print), this book eschews extensive quotation of specific texts. There now exist so many good translations of Chinese literature from all periods, and so many fine anthologies presenting either the whole sweep of the tradition or various pertinent slices thereof, that the interested reader can turn directly to integral texts if that is desired. It would make inefficient use of the space available in this history to pad it with lengthy translated passages. Instead, the aim is to pack its pages with as much basic information as possible. Thus the serious student of Chinese literature has available in this single volume a reliable resource for finding out essential facts about Chinese authors and works in historical context.

Its contextual and conceptual framework distinguishes this history from various handbooks, guides, dictionaries, and encyclopedias of Chinese literature, some of which are excellent in their own ways, that the reader may also wish to consult. The organization of *The Columbia History of Chinese Literature* is intended to complement that of *The Columbia Anthology of Traditional Chinese Literature* (1994) and *The Shorter Columbia Anthology of Traditional Chinese Literature* (2000). It begins with the linguistic and intellectual foundations, moves successively through verse, prose, fiction, drama, and commentary and criticism, then closes with popular and peripheral manifestations. Particular emphasis is placed on certain aspects of Chinese literature that are frequently slighted or overlooked entirely but that are essential for a full understanding of the subject. For example, a great deal of attention is devoted to the supernatural (see chapters 6 and 29) because it is one of the most powerful sources of literary inspiration in China. Similarly, folk and regional styles and genres are brought to the fore, as is Sinitic interaction with non-Sinitic peoples, inasmuch as these were also potent forces in the development of Chinese literature (see, for example, chapters 50 and 51). Proportionally greater attention is also paid to certain key periods and personages, such as the seventeenth century, Wang Shih-chen (1634–1711), the end of the nineteenth and the beginning of the twentieth century, Lu Hsün, and the 1980s and 1990s (see chapters 21–23, 38, and 40), because major transitions and transformations are associated with them. Like the *Columbia Anthology*, the *Columbia History* strives to combine a thematic approach with an overall chronological framework. No single formula has been applied to all the chapters. Rather, the authors of the individual chapters have been encouraged to let the materials therein take their own specific shape and course.

In a volume as large as this, in which more than forty authors are engaged with a subject as complex as that of the entire history of Chinese literature, some differences of opinion or interpretation are unavoidable. For instance, how should one explain the apparent cultural wasteland of the fifteenth century? Was it the result of the paranoid depredations of the Ming dynasty founder, Chu Yüan-chang? The aftereffects of the Mongol occupation? Internal inertia? A combination of all these factors? Or was the fifteenth century not such a literary and artistic lacuna after all? Various authors interpret the fifteenth-century cultural scene differently. This may actually be a blessing in disguise, since they may all illuminate one or more aspects of a complicated, multifaceted problem. For this reason, I have not insisted on absolute uniformity of opinion, only on rigorous marshalling of evidence.

As editor, I have reviewed all fifty-five chapters carefully and have added portions to most of them, while subtracting sections from others. With an eye toward consistency, I have also made stylistic revisions where they seemed appropriate. Fortunately, because I gave the authors explicit guidelines when the project to create this history first began in June 1996, most of the chapters did not have to be extensively modified.

Inasmuch as this is a *history*, hundreds of dates appear in this volume. For some events, the exact days on which they occurred are known. For others, only the years in which they took place can be established with confidence. The fact that the traditional Chinese calendar was lunar (with periodic intercalary months)—whereas the current international standard is solar—occasionally makes references to the exact time when something transpired (e.g., the beginning or end of a ruler's reign, the birth or death of a poet) a challenge. In addition, sometimes scholarly interpretations of data relating to the timing of a historical event differ. Despite these difficulties concerning dating, an effort has been made to be as consistent and precise as possible.

Several special usages are employed herein, which recur in many of the chapters and consequently require explanation at the outset. First is the problem of the multiplicity of names for Chinese individuals. Except in rare cases, a person is normally referred to by his or her given name (*ming*). It needs to be pointed out, however, that many writers often went by alternative names, such as house names (*shih-ming*), studio names (*chai-ming*), and numerous other types of nicknames and sobriquets. Aside from a writer's given name, the most frequently cited type of name in this volume is the *tzu*, which was assumed upon coming of age.

An asterisk appearing before an italicized transcription (e.g., **tiawk*) indicates that it is a tentative reconstruction of an ancient pronunciation.

Two terms relating to the parts of books must be introduced here. Ubiquitous in discussions of Chinese texts is the word *chüan*. Literally, it means "scroll," and that is what it actually signified as well until around the eleventh century, when it became increasingly common to print books with woodblocks and bind them in pages at the spine, rather than writing them out by hand on long strips of paper wrapped around a wooden stick or roller, as was the earlier practice. Even when books were no longer written on sets of scrolls, the long-established usage of *chüan* persisted. The word *chüan* is commonly translated as "chapter," "volume," and "fascicle." The latter two English words designate units that are usually of much greater length than a *chüan*, so the reader should not imagine that a book consisting of eight *chüan*, for example, consisted of eight volumes or even eight fascicles. In reality, it more likely may only have been made up of one volume and a couple of fascicles. The English word "fascicle" (from a Latin word designating a small bundle) is actually better suited as a translation for another frequently encountered bibliographical term, the *ts'e*, which indicates those parts of a book that are separately stitched together.

This volume employs two terms that have already found fairly broad acceptance among specialists in Chinese studies: "tricent" (three hundred paces) for *li*, which is equal to approximately a third of a mile ("one thousand paces"), and "topolect" (language of a place) for *fang-yen*, which is generally translated as "dialect," giving rise to tremendous misunderstanding and confusion about the nature of the Sinitic group of languages (see chapter 1 and *The American Heritage Dictionary of the English Language*, 4th ed., p.1822a.).

Next, the lamentably vexed question of romanization must be addressed. The primary romanization employed in this volume is a slightly modified version of the Wade-Giles system (e.g., the usual *i* in strict Wade-Giles is here rendered as *yi*). The reasons for making this choice are numerous. First (aside from the fact that it is much closer to the International Phonetic Alphabet [IPA] than any other system currently in use), the Wade-Giles system has been the standard of English-language sinology for over a century, and so a vast body of translation and scholarship uses it. Second, the overwhelming majority of libraries (especially the best research libraries) continued to use Wade-Giles until very recently and have accumulated millions of records in this system. Third, many of the most useful research tools for the study of Chinese language, literature, and history (such as the magnificent new Ricci Institute dictionaries; *The Indiana Companion to Traditional Chinese Literature*, edited by William H. Nienhauser, Jr.; and *A Dictionary of Official Titles in Imperial China*, by Charles O. Hucker) use Wade-Giles. Fourth, nearly all the publications on traditional China from Columbia University Press, which has the strongest offerings in this field of any press in the United States, use Wade-Giles. At the same time, in recognition of the fact that pinyin is the official romanized orthography of the People's Republic of China and has gained increasing ground as a pedagogical device in recent years, a conversion chart from Wade-Giles to pinyin is provided at the back of the book (pp. 1155–1160).

For several authors from mainland China who are well known by the pinyin spelling of their names, the pinyin is given along with the Wade-Giles.

Finally, for those who would like access to the best scholarship and the most important primary texts concerning Chinese history in general, recommended titles include Endymion Wilkinson, *Chinese History: A Manual*, rev. and enlarged (Cambridge: Harvard University Asia Center, 2000), and Wm. Theodore de Bary, Irene Bloom, and Richard Lufrano, comp., *Sources of Chinese Tradition*, 2d ed. (New York: Columbia University Press, 1999–2000).

Victor H. Mair
Swarthmore, Pennsylvania
January 15, 2000

ACKNOWLEDGMENTS

The editor thanks the following individuals and institutions:

The authors of the various chapters, without which this history would not exist, and to each of whom is due his heartfelt gratitude for their scholarship and for staying with him all these years.

Jennifer Crewe, Publisher for the Humanities at Columbia University Press, for suggesting to him the project of writing a history of Chinese literature in the first place and for sagely guiding him through every step of the way in making it a reality.

Ron Harris, assistant managing editor at Columbia University Press, for answering all manner of technical questions swiftly and surely, and for taking care of endless details during production.

Debra E. Soled, for her meticulous copy-editing of a conspicuously unruly manuscript.

The two anonymous readers of the manuscript for Columbia University Press. They offered numerous insightful suggestions for improvement; my only regret is that it was impossible for me to adopt every one of them. Their generous praise of this *History*, at a time when it was still in a rather chaotic state, served as welcome encouragement to carry on with the seemingly endless editorial tasks.

Patricia Ebrey, Ronald Egan, Patrick Hanan, Stephen Owen, Evelyn Rawski, Haun Saussy, and John E. Wills, Jr., for reading and commenting on the introduction; W. South Coblin, S. Robert Ramsey, Charles N. Li, John DeFrancis,

David Prager Branner, William C. Hannas, Axel Schuessler, Benjamin Ao, Wolfgang Behr, Peter Daniels, James A. Matisoff, Denis C. Mair, and Michael Carr, for reading and commenting on chapter 1; Daniel Boucher, Stephen F. Teiser, and Chun-fang Yu, for reading and commenting on chapter 9; Li-ching Chang, for detailed information about the life and works of Lu Hsün; Sara Davis, for reading and commenting on chapter 51; and Keith Taylor, G. Cameron Hurst III, William C. Hannas, and Linda Chance, for reading and commenting on the last three chapters. None of them should be held responsible for errors or infelicities that remain.

Perry Link, Jeffrey Kinkley, Jidong Yang, Philip F. C. Williams, David Derwei Wang, Julia F. Andrews, Bert Scruggs, and Patricia Schiaffini, for tracking down missing dates and characters in chapter 40, which was left in a semifinished state by our deceased colleague Helmut Martin.

Rick Fields, Brian Catillo, and Mayuma Oda, for four lines from *The Turquoise Bee: Love Songs of the Sixth Dalai Lama* (San Francisco: Harper, 1998; 1993; excerpts available at www.tricycle.com).

Kayhan Kalhor, for interesting discussions about Iranian musical instruments.

Bert Scruggs, for building and maintaining the bibliography Web site, and Vasu Renganathan, Mark Wilhelm, Jay Treat, Phil Miraglia, Laura Geller, Eli Alberts, and all the others who have contributed to its construction, enlargement, and refinement.

Jidong Yang, for assistance in preparing the glossaries of Chinese characters and for many other favors large and small.

Anne Holmes and Rob Rudnick, for help in compiling the index.

Timothy Connor, Helen Greenberg, Denis Mair, and Paula Roberts, for reading the proofs.

The Institute for Advanced Study, Princeton, New Jersey, for providing the perfect intellectual atmosphere and natural environment in which to put the finishing touches on the manuscript.

His students, colleagues (including staff members), and dedicated librarians at the University of Pennsylvania, for stimulating, sustaining, and supporting him for the two decades leading up to publication of this work.

His research assistant, Conán Carey, for checking fine points, retyping whole chapters, and exercising his eagle-eyed vigilance throughout.

His good friends Justine Snow, Carol Conti-Entin, and Xu Wenkan, for their enthusiastic appreciation and constant kindness.

Julie Lee Wei, for asking so many good questions and for making so many keen observations.

His siblings (Joe, Dave, Sue, Tom, Denis, and Heidi), one and all, for their limitless love and infinite inspiration.

His wife, Li-ching Chang, and son, Thomas Krishna Mair, for their understanding and encouragement.

ABBREVIATIONS

b.	born
B.C.E.	Before the Common Era
BHSi	Buddhist Hybrid Sinitic (also referred to as BHC [Buddhist Hybrid Chinese])
c.	circa
C.E.	Common Era
c.s.	*chin-shih* (Presented Scholar or Metropolitan Graduate)
d.	died
fl.	flourished
LS	Literary Sinitic (often referred to as Classical Chinese)
MSM	Modern Standard Mandarin
OS	Old Sinitic
r.	reigned
VS	Vernacular Sinitic

Most of the above abbreviations are used in two or more chapters. Other abbreviations, which are found in only one chapter, are noted upon their first occurrence.

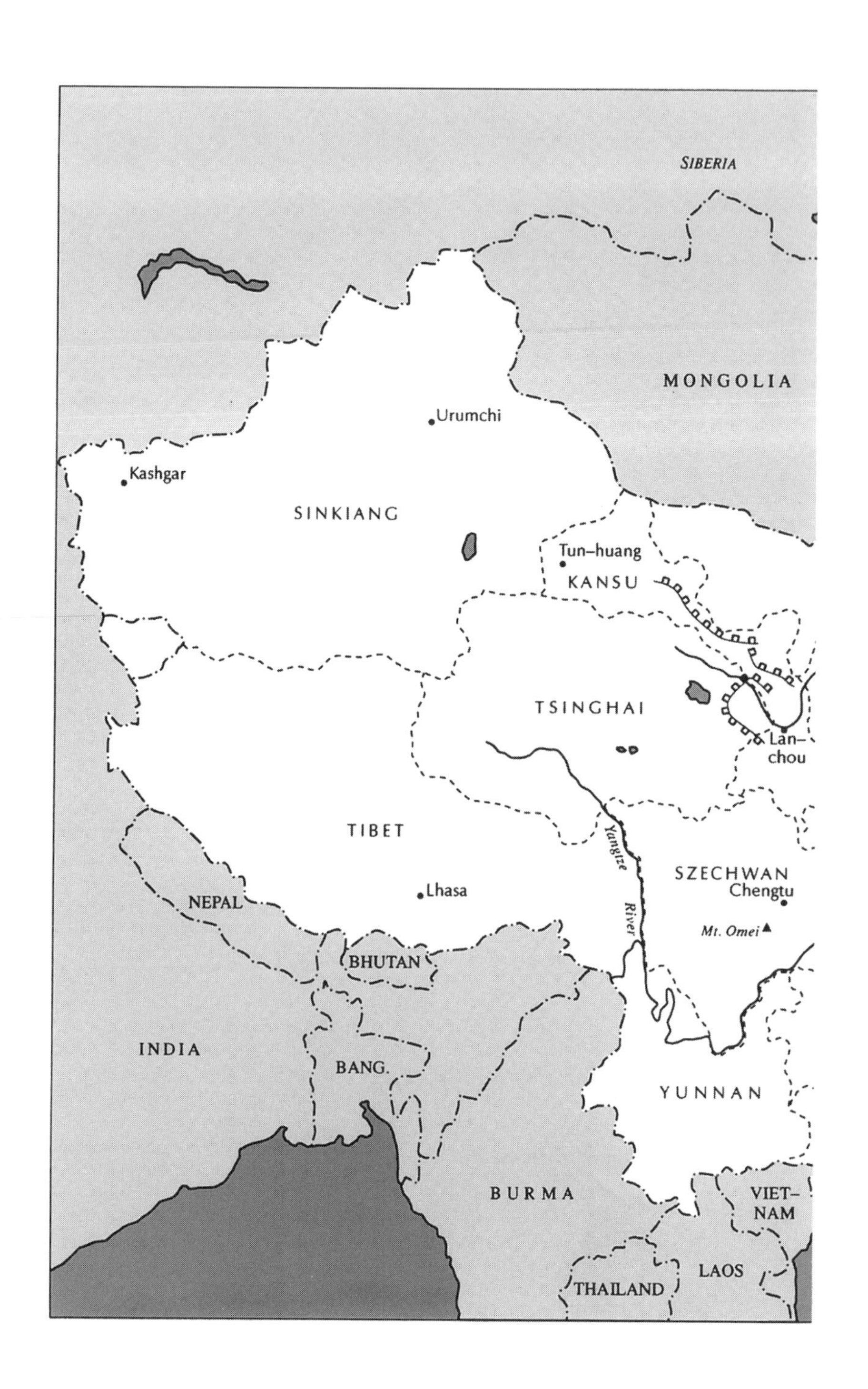
SIBERIA
MONGOLIA
Urumchi
Kashgar
SINKIANG
Tun-huang
KANSU
TSINGHAI
Lan-
chou
TIBET
Yangtze
River
SZECHWAN
Chengtu
Mt. Omei
Lhasa
NEPAL
BHUTAN
INDIA
BANG.
YUNNAN
BURMA
VIET-
NAM
LAOS
THAILAND

HEILUNGKIANG
KIRIN
LIAONING
INNER MONGOLIA
KOREA
JAPAN
Yellow River
Peking
Tientsin
HOPEI
Taiyuan
SHANSI
NINGHSIA
Tsinan
Tsingtao
Mt. T'ai
SHANTUNG
Yellow
Kaifeng
Loyang
Chengchow
Sian
(Ch'ang-an)
SHENSI
HONAN
KIANGSU
Huai R.
Yangchow
Nanking
Soochow
Shanghai
HUPEI
ANHWEI
Ch'ien-t'ang R.
Hangchow
Yangtze River
Chungking
Tung-t'ing Lake
Mt. Lu
P'o-yang Lake
CHEKIANG
Changsha
KIANGSI
KWEI-CHOW
HUNAN
FUKIEN
Chuanchow
TAIWAN
KWANGSI
KWANGTUNG
Canton
HAINAN
CHINA
Long Walls
Grand Canal

The Columbia History of Chinese Literature

INTRODUCTION: THE ORIGINS AND IMPACT OF LITERATI CULTURE

From the Sui dynasty (581–618) onward, the chief aspiration of highly literate young men in China was to pass the *chin-shih* (Presented Scholar or Metropolitan Graduate) examination. With this degree came power, prestige, and privilege. The *chin-shih* degree was conferred upon successful candidates in the top level of the civil service recruitment examinations, and it qualified them for office in the imperial bureaucracy. Often the only biographical datum available about a historical personage is the year that he passed the *chin-shih* examination.

Why was this particular degree so coveted in China? The most straightforward answer to this question is that it certified that the holder of the degree possessed superlative skill in reading and writing Literary Sinitic (i.e., Classical Chinese). This was not a test of one's political acumen or practical knowledge. Rather, it emphasized above all else the candidate's talent in literary composition or fine writing (*wen-chang*). This was truly a *docteur ès lettres*. Even the lesser *hsiu-ts'ai* (Cultivated Talent or Licentiate) degree, which qualified one to participate in the provincial examinations, was much sought after, and there are countless sad tales of old men with white, disheveled hair taking (and failing) the *hsiu-ts'ai* examinations over and over again for most of their adult lives.

Another highly popular and very competitive examination was known as *ming-ching* (Elucidating the Classics). Local authorities would nominate candidates to participate in the regular civil service recruitment system. However, whereas the *chin-shih* examination emphasized literary composition, the *ming-ching* required a greater command of the classics.

Passage of these examinations proclaimed to one and all that the holder of the degree was a master of written Sinitic. This was no mean feat, for the writing system was difficult and the texts that had to be memorized were numerous. Preparations for the examinations were both prolonged and intense. Consequently, they required a substantial economic investment, one that was normally available only to individuals from families of considerable wealth.

Even before the institution of the *hsiu-ts'ai* and *chin-shih* degrees, going back to the Western (or Former) Han dynasty (206 B.C.E.–8 C.E.) and before, officials possessing vast learning and outstanding writerly skills, such as the *po-shih* (Erudites), were greatly respected. Thus, in traditional China, a tremendous premium was placed on advanced literary ability, but only a minuscule proportion of the population, perhaps one or two per cent, could attain it. The relatively tiny numbers of advanced scholar-officials, in turn, contributed to the aura of awesomeness that surrounded them. Gradually, a literati culture centered on refined compositional competence developed; we may refer to it as an ethos of *wen*.

To understand Chinese intellectual life of the past two thousand or more years, then, one must grasp the significance and the importance of *wen*. A modern dictionary might give the following main definitions of *wen*: writing; literary composition, article; literature; culture; refined, elegant, urbane; civilized; education; civil (as opposed to military [*wu*]). The root meaning of all these derivatives is "(elegant) pattern." *Wen*, then, is the sum of everything that is esthetically refined, but above all of literature. This is evident from the types of bisyllabic words into which it enters: *wen-hua* (culture), *wen-ming* (civilization), *wen-yi* (the arts [especially belles lettres]), *wen-hsüeh* (literature), and *wen-tzu* ([simple and compound] graphs [i.e., script]). *Wen* applied particularly to writing, above all fine writing, to such a degree that it—in the minds of most Chinese—has become closely identified with literature. Yet it is worthwhile to search deeper into the origins of *wen* in order to understand this quintessentially Chinese term still more fully.

Paleographers are in general agreement that the earliest known form of the graph (c. 1200 B.C.E.) used to write the word *wen* depicts a man with a tattoo on his chest. This may seem incongruous in light of the fact that, throughout most of later Chinese history, tattooing became a kind of stigma associated with barbarians and prisoners. But it is actually not at all surprising that the Chinese of the Bronze Age would have considered tattooing a mark of beauty and goodness, for in many early cultures it had strongly positive connotations. For example, among the Thracians, the Scythians, and other Central Asian peoples, and the Maori, tattooing was restricted to chieftains and other kinds of leading personages. Indeed, the fundamental meaning of *wen* is preserved in an old Chinese expression that is still current—*wen-shen* (tattoo the body).

The path from tattooing to (elegant) patterning and thence to script, writing, and culture is a long one. Furthermore, the process of evolution from tattooing to literature and culture was so utterly transformative that the results can barely be recognized in light of *wen*'s apparent genesis. It is interesting to observe, however, that some of the Bronze Age mummies of the Tarim Basin in Eastern Central Asia (now part of China) sport tattoos in the shape of the letters *E* and *S*, and other scriptlike signs.

Whatever the relationship between Bronze Age tattooing as personal adornment and the public practice of writing may ultimately prove to be, *wen* emerged as the key feature of elite culture in historical times. Chinese intellectuals themselves clearly comprehended the centrality of *wen* and even customarily referred to it as *ssu-wen* (this culture [of ours]), an expression that can be traced back to the Confucian *Lun-yü* ([Analects] 9.5, in a passage dating to the early fifth century B.C.E.): "If Heaven were going to destroy this culture, the one who will die [after the sages, that is, Confucius speaking of himself] would not have been enabled to come into association with this culture." "This culture [of ours]" came to be perceived as the precious politicocultural heritage bequeathed by Confucius and his predecessors, the founding fathers of the Chou dynasty (c. 1027–246 B.C.E.) and the mythical sages before them.

The central notion of *wen* in the literati culture of China took on a new life when it passed into the hands of Western literary theorists and estheticians. Prime among them was Ernest Fenollosa (d. 1908), who wrote a small but extremely influential book on the subject, *The Chinese Written Character as a Medium for Poetry* (first published posthumously in 1919). Ezra Pound and several Imagist poets came under the powerful spell of this tiny tract, and critics are still energetically debating whether its effect has been harmful (because it has such a distorted idea of how the characters work) or beneficial (because it introduced basic concepts of Chinese poetry to Western poets).

Writing was the essence of the *ju* (Confucianists) and their most distinctive characteristic. The *ju* were a group of scholars who espoused the way of Confucius (K'ung Tzu) and were first active during the Warring States period (481/403–221 B.C.E.). The word *ju* signifies gentleness, weakness, and meekness and is actually a cognate of words conveying these meanings as well as of words with meanings like "suckling child." The antecedents of the *ju* lay within the *shih* (scholar) class. To be sure, they were a particular type of *shih*, as indicated by their fuller designation, *ju-shih* (Confucian scholars). And who were the *shih*? At the beginning of the Western Chou dynasty (c. 1045–771 B.C.E.), the *shih* were samurai-like warriors, the lowest aristocratic class of early feudal society. During the subsequent Spring and Autumn (722–481/463 B.C.E.) and Warring States periods, they slowly evolved into the scholar class of late feudal society. It is both ironic and intriguing that the *ju*, who became the dominant group of *shih*, were distinguished for their gentleness, weakness, and meekness. Confucius himself best exemplifies the warrior who turns into a literatus.

Confucius was heir to a military landholding and consequently liable for military service. Indeed, he served as a member of the guard of Duke Chao

(r. 541–510) of Lu, but his heart was not in chariotry or archery (*Analects* 9.2). Instead, he gravitated toward a career of political persuasion. After Duke Chao's unsuccessful coup against the Chi, an antagonistic collateral clan in the state of Lu, Confucius turned increasingly to the role of teacher who attracted a devoted band of disciples. In this capacity, he transmitted what he considered the way of the ancient sages, shaped the canon of texts (including *Shih-ching* [Classic of Poetry, or Classic of Odes, or Classic of Songs] and *Yi-ching* [Classic of Change]) that supposedly embodied their doctrines, and strove to convince the government to adopt policies consonant with those doctrines. This established for all time the Confucian espousal of moral principles, devotion to the classics, and sociopolitical activism.

Because the core Confucian texts were not divinely inspired, they cannot readily be considered scriptures. Nonetheless, for the *ju*, the texts promulgated by Confucius and his followers functioned in a capacity similar to that of scripture in religion. Just as scriptures are the sources of authority in Judaism, Christianity, Buddhism, and Islam, so are the classical texts of the *ju* sources of authority for Confucianism. So revered was the written text in early China that writing itself became cloaked in authority. Thus the very foundations of imperial government were intimately intertwined with the technology and craft of writing.

The prominence given to literati culture by the Chinese state found expression in specific government institutions. Already during the second century B.C.E., there was founded a "Supreme School" (*t'ai-hsüeh*) or "School for the Scions of State" (*kuo-tzu hsüeh*), which, in effect, functioned as a national academy. Here, a select body of students gathered to study under Erudites (*po-shih*), who specialized in various texts. Upon graduation, the young scholars were often drafted as members of officialdom. From the T'ang dynasty (618–907) until the end of the Ch'ing dynasty (1644–1911), the most prestigious group of scholars were located in the (Academy of the) Grove of Writing-Brushes (Han-lin [yüan]—commonly referred to as the Han-lin Academy), an explicit reference to their mastery of writing skills. These Han-lin academicians performed drafting and editorial tasks on behalf of the emperor, and they often held—either concurrent with or subsequent to their appointment to the Han-lin Academy—some of the highest positions in the imperial government. The Han-lin Academy represented the pinnacle of success in officialdom, and its single most defining characteristic—its very emblem—was the writing brush.

A PROLIFERATION OF GENRES

Traditional Chinese literature can be divided into many different categories. In one section of his preface to the celebrated anthology *Wen hsüan* (Literary Selections), Hsiao T'ung (501–531; Prince Chao-ming of the Liang dynasty [502–557]) rattles off the following: *chen* (admonition), *chieh* (warning), *lun* (disquisition), *ming* (inscription), *lei* (dirge), *tsan* (appreciation), *chao* (proclamation), *kao* (announcement), *chiao* (instruction), *ling* (command), *piao* (memorial), *tsou* (proposal), *chien* (report), *chi* (memorandum), *shu* (letter), *shih* (address), *fu* (commission), *chi* (charge), *tiao* (condolence), *chi* (requiem), *pei* (threnody), *ai* (lament), *ta k'o* (replies to opponents), *chih shih* (evinced examples), *san yen* (three-word text), *pa tzu* (eight-character text), *p'ien* (ode), *tz'u* (elegy), *yin* (ditty), *hsü* (preface), *pei* (epitaph), *chieh* (columnar inscription), *chih* (necrology), and *chuang* (obituary). It is striking how many of these literary forms are directly or indirectly related to the lives and activities of officials. Many other genres not mentioned by Hsiao T'ung were employed by literati in their capacity as officials of the government. Throughout the history of Chinese literature, this intimate linkage between fine writing and officialdom has persisted. As such, writers were under constant pressure to make their works relevant to the moral and political needs of the state, whether directly or indirectly. The concepts of "pure literature" or "literature for literature's sake" emerged slowly in China. Only with the advent of Buddhist esthetics did the nonutilitarian aspects of literature begin to be systematically appreciated, examined, and propagated. Even as late as the middle of the twentieth century, there was a strong resurgence—under Communist aegis—of the old habit of insisting that literature fulfill a didactic, edifying function (*wen yi tsai tao*). The most notable instance of such ideological invocation concerning the role of literature in society is the famous "Tsai Yen-an wen-yi tso-t'an-hui shang te chiang-hua" (Talks at the Yenan Forum on Literature and Art; 1942) of Mao Tse-tung (1893–1976).

An illustration of the delicate balance between the public, pragmatic mission of literature and the private, personal desire for creative expression can be seen in the evolution of the *fu* (rhymeprose, rhapsody). Among the earliest usages of the word *fu* in a literary context is as one of the six modes of expression employed in the *Classic of Poetry*: *feng* (instruction), *fu* (description), *pi* (simile), *hsing* (metaphor), *ya* (ode), and *sung* (hymn). This particular formulation dates from the late Western Han, that is, the latter part of the first century B.C.E., but it has its roots in the previous centuries and it continued to flourish in subsequent centuries.

One of the most frequent statements concerning the Grand Master (*ta-fu*; an honorific title for exalted officials) or, indeed, concerning the gentleman (*chün-tzu*) was that "ascending on high, he can / must *fu*" (*teng kao neng / pi fu*). In other words, when he climbs to an elevation, the eminent or cultivated person cannot help but express himself in a refined manner. The variant wording of the statement reveals that the superior person, by virtue of his character, not only is capable of brilliantly expounding his lofty perceptions, but is compelled by the circumstances to do so. Describing one's vision from a lofty vantage is incumbent upon a cultivated, responsible person.

During the course of the Han dynasty, however, some authors became enamored of their powers of description and began to write epideictic *fu*. Their lush verbiage and emotion-laden, excessive elaboration (or so it seemed to more staid and sober individuals) showed a lack of restraint that made them liable to criticism. For all the sheer beauty of this newly found literary artifice, at least one of the most outstanding authors of the rhapsody professed a sense of shame at what he had written in that genre. Others even went so far as to attach retractions to the conclusions of some of their best pieces. Yet the *fu* continued to prosper and evolve, experiencing a renaissance during the Six Dynasties (220–581), when it came to be applied to a much wider variety of topics (whistling, lamentation, parrots, snow, and so forth). By the T'ang dynasty, the *fu* had bifurcated into a crude type of folkish rhapsody (*su-fu*), with its roots in the Chin dynasty (265–420), and the regulated prose-poem (*lü-fu*), in which the author had to follow a particular rhyme pattern and employ strictly parallel lines. Although the old Han-style rhapsody and other varieties of the *fu* were also sporadically composed during the T'ang era, the genre was already in decline and, after the prose rhapsody (*wen-fu*) of the Sung period (960–1279), it was seldom utilized as a vehicle of literary expression again throughout the succeeding ages.

In brief, such are the vagaries of a single genre from inception to demise over a period of more than a thousand years. A full appreciation of Chinese literature demands exposure to a burgeoning array of genres, from the most euphuistic and mannered to the most energetic and unrestrained. In investigating the wide range of Chinese genres, one encounters whole categories of literary treasures that are barely known except to the specialist, yet are rich beyond measure. For example, during the late Ming dynasty (1368–1644) and into the early Ch'ing period (i.e., approximately the sixteenth and seventeenth centuries), there flourished a species of prose called *hsiao-p'in(-wen)* (brief/informal essay). A glance at this single genre, out of hundreds that might be considered, offers a good example of the inexhaustible storehouse of Chinese literature when viewed through the multifaceted prism of its diverse genres.

The earliest occurrence of the term *hsiao-p'in* is in the title of the abbreviated translation of the *Prajñāpāramitā-sūtra* (*Hsiao-p'in po-je po-lo-mi ching*), where it stands in contrast to the full translation of the same text, the *Ta-p'in po-je po-lo-mi ching*. Here it is very clear that *p'in* signifies "chapter," a standard Buddhist usage. Liu Yi-ch'ing (403–444) makes reference to *Hsiao-p'in po-je po-lo-mi ching* in the thirtieth, forty-third, and forty-fifth sections of the chapter entitled "Wen-hsüeh" (Letters and Scholarship) of his celebrated *Shih-shuo hsin-yü* (A New Account of Tales of the World). It is noteworthy that most of the anecdotes recounted by Liu Yi-ch'ing in this chapter are Buddhistic in nature and (as seen in chapter 1) that the modern Sinitic word for "literature" (*wen-hsüeh*) was calqued during the nineteenth century upon the title of Liu Yi-ch'ing's chapter (its roots lay in the *wen-hsüeh* [civil learning] of the Confucians, which appears already in the *Analects*), via Japan. Hence, not only does *hsiao-p'in* possess deep Buddhist resonances, but even the nascent concept of literature was nourished in a fifth-century atmosphere that was redolent with Buddhist discourse. Yet the *hsiao-p'in* of the late Ming certainly cannot be comprehended by applying merely the signification of the term in early Buddhist usage.

Hsiao-p'in are not easy to characterize in formal terms. In length, they range from a couple of sentences to three or more pages in English translation. They are usually nonfictional, but some of them are highly imaginative. They are often exclusively in prose, but it is not rare for verse to creep in. And so on. What is common to all of the *hsiao-p'in* is their style of informality. The experience of reading *hsiao-p'in* is frequently like that of reading the *Tsurezuregusa* (Essays in Idleness; c. 1330) of the Japanese Buddhist monk Yoshida Kenkō (c. 1283–c. 1350/1352), although not quite so mind-altering.

Among the most noted practitioners of *hsiao-p'in* are Kuei Yu-kuang (1506–1571), Lu Shu-sheng (1509–1605), Hsü Wei (1521–1593), Li Chih (1527–1602), T'u Lung (1542–1605), Ch'en Chi-ju (1558–1639), Yüan Tsung-tao (1569–1600), Yüan Hung-tao (1568–1610), Yüan Chung-tao (1570–1624), Chung Hsing (1574–1624), Li Liu-fang (1575–1629), Wang Ssu-jen (1575–1646), T'an Yüan-ch'un (1585–1637), and Chang Tai (1597–1684?), the last and greatest of them all. These men wrote about such topics as wars, temples, belvederes, gazebos, huts, scholars, maids, courtesans, actors, storytellers, ventriloquists, dogs, calligraphy, stationery, bamboo, canes, trips to the countryside, attendants, fools, paintings, portraits, poetry, retirement, old age, death, dreams, the mind of a child, peach blossoms, flowers, excursions, brooks, lakes, ponds, mountains, drinking, and all manner of books. Reading *hsiao-p'in* collections is a pleasant invitation not only to the world of the late Ming but also to the capacious landscape of Chinese literature as a whole.

Certain monuments of Chinese literature can scarcely be considered as belonging to a specific, well-defined literary genre, and yet they are broadly recognized for their memorable qualities. For example, many immortal letters exist that were originally intended only for a single recipient, but are now appreciated by countless readers as epistolary exemplars. These stem from many different ages, places, and persons: Ssu-ma Ch'ien's (c. 145–c. 85 B.C.E.) poignant letter to his friend Jen An in which he explains why he submitted to castration, rather than commit suicide or face execution, so that he could finish the writing of China's first history, *Shih-chi* (Records of the [Grand] Historian, or Records of the Scribe), which had been begun by his father; the bohemian Chi K'ang's (Hsi K'ang; 223–262) bittersweet, witty letter to Shan T'ao (205–283) telling him why he no longer wished to be his friend; and the poet-official Po Chü-yi's (772–846) sad missive written from his southern exile to his dear friend Yüan Chen (779–831), whom he had not seen for three years. The Chinese fascination with and appreciation of eloquent, impassioned epistolary writing has persisted to the present. The disclosure of personal letters by literary figures like Lu Hsün (Chou Shu-jen; 1881–1936), Ch'en Yin-ch'üeh/k'o (1890–1969), and Hu Shih (1891–1962) has often served either to provoke or to resolve scholarly controversies. It is in the letters of luminaries such as Su Shih (Su Tung-p'o; 1037–1101) and Yüan Mei (1716–1798) that one can glimpse autobiography, evaluations of contemporary events, revelations of personal experience, development of sustained argumentation concerning all sorts of topics, concerns over daily life, relations with kin, and moral or political advocacy. In short, in their personal letters Chinese authors bared their inmost thoughts and feelings. Hence, many were memorable, not merely because they were beautifully expressed, but because of the sheer openness of their sentiments. The letter occupies such an exalted place in the literary culture of China that numerous anthologies of preserved specimens were compiled as models for schoolchildren's recitation and emulation. The variety of different names used for letters in China—*shu, chien, cha, tu, ch'ih-tu, ch'ih-han, hsin*—indicates not only how prevalent they were but how seriously they were taken by literary arbiters.

Another noteworthy characteristic of Chinese literature, especially of fiction and drama, is that the same material can be reworked in many different genres, both in the literary language and in the vernacular language. One of the most productive subjects was the incorruptible Judge Pao (Pao Kung), who ingeniously solved countless criminal cases (Pao Kung an). Based on an actual historical figure from the Sung period, Pao Cheng (999–1062), Judge Pao became the legendary champion of justice and righteousness in an impressive variety of stories and plays.

Finally, the unpredictability of Chinese literature can be gauged by the amplitude of its rhetorical pitch. Although the normal rhetorical desideratum of literati writing is to express oneself subtly (see chapter 43), this disposition was tempered by explicitness when the occasion demanded. The tremendous quantity of documents related to court activities (underlying a great deal of Liu Hsieh's [465?–520?] classifications of genres in *Wen-hsin tiao-lung* [The Literary Mind and Carving of Dragons]), such as admonitions, remonstrations, and memorials (for example, Wang An-shih's [1021–1086] renowned "Wan yen shu" [Ten Thousand Word Document] and K'ang Yu-wei's [1858–1927] seismic series of petitions to the Manchu throne arguing in favor of fundamental reform), was created in an environment of sustained attempts to achieve maximal ethicopolitical persuasion. In such cases, one could scarcely afford to be overly indirect and subtle. Furthermore, this environment was constantly reinforced by the imperially supervised civil examination system, which demanded precisely worded and intricately structured statements on specific topics.

The same impetus for clear explanation in bureaucratic, office-holding contexts was fostered by the tradition of classical exegesis founded in the Han dynasty (see chapter 44). Here, too, genres multiplied: *chu* (commentary), *shu* (subcommentary), *p'i* (annotation), *p'ing* (appraisal), *p'an* (judgement), *chu* (note), *chiao* (collation), *k'an* (comparison), *chieh* (explanation), *shih-yi* (exegesis), *hsi* (analysis), and so forth. In view of all the commentary and criticism that has been lavished on poetry, fiction, and drama in China (see chapters 45 and 46), it is clear that the exegetical impulse was broadened still further. Thus, whether in terms of genres or the commentarial and exegetical strategies applied to them, literature in China was not only unmonotonous, it was positively overwhelming in its multifariousness.

A MULTIPLICITY OF IDEOLOGIES AND PEOPLES

If China had a multitude of literary genres, styles, and rhetorical positions, so too did it have a plethora of doctrines, ethnicities, and local folklore. It is a commonplace to speak of China as an "empire of uniformity": a billion or more people all sharing the same ethnicity, language, script, cuisine, clothing, customs, and the like. Nothing could be further from the truth. Chinese population, society, and culture are as diverse as those of any other country in the world. Even Chinese elite society and culture demonstrate great variety. To take systems of thought, for instance, Buddhism and Taoism both have extremely elaborate doctrines and canons that are of even more enormous scope than that of the Confucians. And the "Confucians" themselves are not all of a piece. Already in pre-Han times (i.e., before 206 B.C.E.), the views of Hsün Tzu (300?–219? B.C.E.) and Mencius (372–289 B.C.E.) on how to interpret the teachings of Confucius diverged radically. Moreover, among the neo-Confucians nearly two millennia later, the followers of Chu Hsi (1130–1200) and Wang Yang-ming (Wang Shou-jen; 1472–1529) differed so markedly in their approach to basic issues that it is hard to conceive of them as belonging to the same school of thought. (This is not to deny the ideal of doctrinal uniformity voiced by some protagonists. While never achieved, it certainly did have an effect upon the lives and fortunes of intellectuals, causing them to reinterpret earlier teachings anachronistically, or even add to them, in light of later teachings.) In addition, the spectrum of Chinese intellectual orientations can by no means be limited to Buddhism, Taoism, and Confucianism. Also to be taken into account are Magianism, shamanism, Legalism, hedonism, eremitism, utilitarianism, naturalism, technocracy, rationalism, Nestorian Christianity, Manicheism, Zoroastrianism, Judaism, Islam, Hinduism, Catholicism, Protestantism, and many other assorted teachings and practices that have existed in China for longer or shorter periods of time. While not all these groups had a designated succession of leaders and an authoritative corpus of texts, they all did have an impact on various segments of Chinese society. Traditional Chinese culture, like contemporary Chinese culture, consisted of a virtually infinite number of separate strands and fibers, such that the fabric of society as a whole was exceedingly complex in its structure and in its nature.

These doctrinal dispositions influenced literature in various ways and to varying degrees. It is easy to identify inscriptions, poems, essays, stories, novels, and plays that embody each of these ideological approaches. Two of the most fecund sources of Chinese literature are Buddhism and Taoism. Merely to speak of "Buddhism" and "Taoism" as though they were two discrete entities is, of course, simplistic, for there were many different types of Buddhism and Taoism, not to mention numerous Buddho-Taoist blends. Certain sects, such as Zen (Ch'an; Sanskrit, *dhyāna* [meditation]) and Pure Land, were particularly fertile fields for authors and critics to cultivate. The literary influence of just one Taoist thinker—Chuang Tzu (355?–275 B.C.E.)—is incalculable. To take merely a single example, in Chia Yi's (200–168 B.C.E.) "Fu niao fu" (Rhapsody on an Owl), the first specimen of this genre whose authorship and date are reasonably certain, nine out of fifty-four lines (one-sixth of the total) derive directly from the *Chuang Tzu*, while two lines may be said to derive from the *Tao te ching* (Classic of the Way and Integrity) and one other line occurs both in the *Huainan Tzu*, a heterogeneous Taoist text dating to the second century B.C.E., and in the *Lü-shih ch'un-ch'iu* (Springs and Autumns of Master Lü), a legalistic compendium from the third century B.C.E. It would be tedious to recite all the echoes of the *Chuang Tzu* in later works. Suffice it to say that one simply cannot imagine what Chinese literature would have been like had there never been a Chuang Tzu.

Although two separate chapters (9 and 10) are devoted to Buddhism and Taoism in this *History*, it is necessary to point out in the most emphatic terms that it is utterly impossible—and wrong—to isolate Buddhism and Taoism from any phase of the development of Chinese literature during the past two thousand years. Consequently, Buddhism and Taoism are touched upon in many different chapters. The two designated chapters on Buddhism and Taoism treat mainly scriptural writings produced or translated by the religious communities themselves. Although the corpora of such writings are manifestly quite large and composed of an impressive variety of different types of texts (biographies, narratives, histories, and so forth) aside from scriptures per se, they cannot exhaust the significance of Buddhism and Taoism and the degree to which they have shaped and fashioned literary developments in terms of diction, images, symbols, structures, allegorical techniques, prosodic features, and the creation of entirely new genres and styles.

With respect to Taoism, the pioneering research of scholars such as Rolf Stein, Edward Schafer, Kristofer Schipper, Nathan Sivin, Anna Seidel, Michel Strickmann, Michael Saso, Isabelle Robinet, John Lagerwey, Paul Kroll, Livia Kohn, Stephen Bokenkamp, Kenneth Dean, Terry Kleeman, and Lowell Skar has shown how this protean way of thinking and believing has shaped vast stretches of Chinese imaginative writing. The works of Schafer and Kroll have been especially valuable in bringing to light the Taoistic dimensions of a great deal of Chinese poetry. In equal or even greater measure, Taoist notions of ritual, alchemy, cultivation, and sex have profoundly affected the writing of Chinese fiction. Recent scholarship has focused in particular on the impact of the Ch'üan-chen and Cheng-yi schools of Taoism on diverse major and minor Ming novels, including several important works of erotic fiction from that period (see chapters 35–37).

As for the effects of Buddhism, particularly noteworthy are the Indian linguistic influence it had on Chinese phonology and prosody, systems of logical argumentation, the elaborate taxonomical schemes exemplified in such works of literary criticism as *The Literary Mind and Carving of Dragons,* and the formation and standardization of Buddhist Hybrid Sinitic (a unique blend of elements from Literary Sinitic, Vernacular Sinitic, Sanskrit, and various Central Asian languages) in scriptures and the legitimation of a national semivernacular style of writing in the secular realm. Individual Buddhist monks, such as Hui-yüan (334–416) and Hsüan-tsang (c. 600–664), assumed awesome stature in legend and lore, the former for his critique of imperial politics and pretensions, among other things, and the latter for his fabled pilgrimage to India and his advanced skills as a translator of sutras and teacher of abstruse doctrines.

By the T'ang dynasty, if not before, Buddhism had permeated Chinese society to such an extent that it was virtually impossible to remain immune to it. Even the great Confucian literatus Han Yü (768–824), who wrote sharply worded memorials inveighing against Buddhism, had close associations with Buddhist monks and, perhaps unwittingly, displayed Buddhist sentiments in his prose and poetry from time to time. So pervasive was Buddhism in T'ang society, which was ruled by an ostensibly pro-Taoist imperial house, that, of the approximately 48,000 poems in the *Ch'üan T'ang shih* (Complete T'ang Poems), nearly 10 percent have explicit references to Buddhism in their titles. The number with explicit references to Buddhism in the body of the poem is, of course, far greater, while the number of poems with implicit references to Buddhism through image, metaphor, diction, and values is so large as to be uncountable. The oeuvre of major T'ang poets such as Po Chü-yi, Wang Wei (Vimalakīrti Wang; 701–761), Han-shan (Cold Mountain), and Wang Fan-chih (Brahmacārin Wang) cannot be comprehended without knowledge of basic Buddhist concepts and terms. This Buddhistic permeation of T'ang poetry is a perfect example of why it is difficult to draw a line between Buddhism and secular culture.

Among the most fruitful avenues of twentieth-century research on Chinese literature has been the work of scholars such as Cheng Chen-to (1898–1958) and Jaroslav Průšek (1906–1980) on so-called *chiang-ch'ang wen-hsüeh* or *shuo-ch'ang wen-hsüeh* (spoken-sung literature). The primary impetus for this research resulted from the recovery of the Tun-huang manuscripts (see chapter 48), among which were found the earliest examples of this type of text; but it soon broadened to a systematic investigation of the prosimetric or chantefable form in Chinese popular literature during the last millennium and more. The role of Buddhism in the rise of prosimetric literature was crucial, since prosimetrum is typical of many genres of Indian religious and secular literature and was introduced to China through Buddhist texts. Buddhism was equally essential for the creation of fundamental concepts in Chinese literary theory, for example, the notion of poetic inspiration as being a kind of Zenlike "knack" or enlightenment proposed by the Sung period critic Yen Yü (c. 1195–c. 1245) in his *Ts'ang-lang shih-hua* (Poetry Talks by [the Hermit of] the Ts'ang-lang River) and the notion of *ching-chieh* (Sanskrit, *viṣaya, gocara*) as a poetic realm proposed by the brilliant, tragic polymath Wang Kuo-wei (1877–1927). These and other fundamental contributions of Buddhism to the growth of Chinese literature have been brought to light by such outstanding twentieth-century scholars as Chi Hsien-lin, Jao Tsung-yi, Huo Shih-hsiu, Wu Hsiao-ling, Chou Shao-liang, Hsiang Ch'u, Sun Ch'ang-wu, Fujieda Akira, Iriya Yoshitaka, Kawaguchi Hisao, Makita Tairyō, Kanaoka Shōkō, and Fukui Fumimasa (Bunga).

Although Buddhism and Taoism each individually had an incalculable effect upon the development of Chinese literature, it is often difficult to distinguish Buddhist influences from Taoist influences. For example, certain *tz'u* (song lyric) tunes emerged within Taoist communities at the same time that other tunes became associated with specifically Buddhist tendencies. Both religious traditions helped generate and perpetuate such a genre from the late imperial period as *pao-chüan* (precious scrolls). Two of the most famous Chinese novels, *Hsi-yu chi* (Journey to the West, or Monkey) and *Hung-lou meng* (A Dream of Red Towers; also known as *Shih-t'ou chi* [Story of the Stone]), are so infused with Buddhist *and* Taoist ideas and images that they make little sense to anyone who is completely ignorant of these two religions. This phenomenon underscores the close interrelationship between Buddhism and Taoism, which began almost from the moment representatives of the former faith set foot on Chinese soil.

If it is hard to separate out Buddhism, Taoism, and all the other previously mentioned systems of thought from the tapestry of Chinese society and culture, it is even more difficult to set aside the so-called non-Chinese or non-Han peoples from the rest of the population. The contributions of the minority nationalities to Chinese civilization go beyond exotic filigree. In a word, were it not for the "barbarians," there would be no China.

The supposed "nuclear area" of Chinese civilization, the confluence of the Yellow River and the Wei River in Shensi province (alternatively, and somewhat later, the vicinity of Mount T'ai in Shantung province), was surrounded in all directions by non-Chinese (those outside the ruling polity and its subjects). Several factors have called into question the concept of a nuclear area from which all of Chinese civilization spread. Among these are the fact that ruling groups kept coming from beyond the supposed nuclear area to the north and northwest, the clear presence of strong, coexisting centers of Bronze Age cultures in other parts of what is now China, and the survival of non-Sinitic groups across the length and breadth of China, including the Yellow River Valley itself, in historic times.

It is customary to speak of *chung* (central; Chinese) and *wai* (external; foreign)—these adjectives are applied culturally as well as spatially—as if the world of China were strictly dichotomous. Yet the dividing line between *chung* and *wai* is so vague that any attempt to separate the two becomes an exercise in futility. Throughout history, so many of the greatest generals, politicians, artists, architects, authors, mathematicians, physicians, and even members of royalty have come wholly or partly from the *wai* segments of the Chinese world that it seems meaningless to maintain such a dualistic worldview.

Nor will the outmoded notion of Sinicization suffice to explain the intricate dynamics of the relationship between *chung* and *wai* in the Chinese cultural sphere. According to this once-prevalent model, supposedly external, non-Han elements (peoples and their cultures) became internal and Han through a process of transformation. The fallacy of such an approach can be demonstrated by enumerating all the untransformed or partially transformed components of Chinese civilization. We need mention only the fact that horses and chariots came from "outside" the original Chinese cultural sphere, and yet they both became central features of imperial ceremony and military might. Indeed, were it not for horse-riding nomads in trousers, the king of the state of Chao would not have been prompted in 307 B.C.E. to order his own people to wear pants so that they too could ride horses. The simultaneous identification of horses with the nomads and their exalted centrality in ritual and strategy persisted from the late second millennium B.C.E. through to the end of the empire. Such examples as the horse could be multiplied endlessly, with the result that one seriously begins to wonder whether it might be more accurate to speak of "barbarization" (Tabgatchization, Mongolization, Manchuization, etc.) than of "Sinicization." The best course is to avoid reductionist, bipolar explanations and, instead, to recognize the intricacy of the origins and nature of Chinese civilization. The same, after all, is true of virtually all other civilizations on earth, so there is no reason to expect that the civilization of China would be any different, especially in light of its huge extent and long history, both of which would have made it natural for the Chinese people to interact with their neighbors on all sides.

APPROACHES TO CHINESE LITERATURE

Given China's demographic and cultural complexity, it is unsurprising that Chinese literature cannot be subsumed solely under the rubric of elite, Confucian writing. This introduction began with a discussion of the origins and importance of literati writing in China. However, it soon became evident that, although Confucian texts and authors may have been the most prestigious models for aspiring bureaucrats, they were by no means the only arena of literary expression for the populace as a whole, nor were they ultimately able to prevent themselves from being tainted by un-Confucian or even anti-Confucian sentiments and styles.

The rise of *tz'u* during the T'ang dynasty and its flowering during the Sung dynasty attest to the subtle sociocultural nuances inherent in the history of Chinese literature (see chapter 15). *Tz'u* have their background in the aggressively open, cosmopolitan society of the T'ang period. They stem from the culture of the so-called Silk Roads in Central Asia, South Asia, and Southeast Asia. The milieu of their earliest composition and performance was in the caravanserais, inns, and ports of the open road and in the entertainment centers of the cities. Thus, in large measure, the earliest inspiration for *tz'u* was culturally alien and sociologically low. Nonetheless, this did not preclude the literati from being attracted to *tz'u* and trying their own hand at it. Eventually, the prosodic patterns for *tz'u* became standardized and the diction more refined. Still, traces of the popular heritage of the genre remained and the same pattern was repeated under the Mongols with *ch'ü* (arias; see chapter 17). This process of the adoption of popular materials, motifs, and modes by the literati recurred again and again throughout Chinese literary history. This is a paradigm that was first clearly delineated by the great twentieth-century scholar Hu Shih in his *Pai-hua wen-hsüeh shih* (History of Vernacular Literature).

At the same time, from the medieval period onward, those who were not literate in Literary Sinitic took it upon themselves to write stories, poems, and plays in Vernacular Sinitic. This unprecedented type of written Sinitic opened hitherto-unimagined avenues of expression. The early stages of writing in the vernacular have now been documented by the accidental discovery of the Tun-huang manuscripts. Here again, although an entire chapter is devoted to this topic, the Tun-huang manuscripts are of such importance that they are mentioned in other chapters as well. Although they are "popular," they can hardly be considered "peripheral" except in a purely geographical sense.

Another exciting event in Chinese literary studies is the reinterpretation of women's literature and women's place in literature (see chapter 11). A major initiative, led by K'ang-i Sun Chang and Haun Saussy in collaboration with dozens of associates, has uncovered, translated, and commented on hundreds of previously overlooked poems by women. Journals focusing wholly or largely on gender studies in China have been founded, and conferences on sex and society have been held. All these activities have made possible a much more sophisticated understanding of women in Chinese literature and society. To take but a single example, the celebrated poem of Po Chü-yi entitled "Ch'ang-hen ko" (The Song of Everlasting Regret) is normally read by Confucian-minded or Confucian-influenced interpreters as being about the female consort as a stereotypical symbol of evil. A more sensitive interpretation of the poem shows how Po Chü-yi departs from history in an attempt to fashion a relationship based on mutual love between emperor and consort. The last part of the poem dwells at some length on Yang Kuei-fei's genuine regard for the emperor and her attempt—even from beyond the grave—to reciprocate his inconsolable longing by sending back a part of her hairpin and reminding him of their secret pledge of undying love. The irony of such an aspiration, if sincere, seems to challenge the venerable Confucian and patriarchal verdict on "the calamity of a beautiful woman" (*mei-jen huo-shui*) or simply "the calamity of women" (*nü-*

huo). If the poet errs, as feminist critics have charged, he has erred in making the emperor and consort far too sentimental and idealized, a vision nonetheless wrought with the completely tacit approval of the poetic narrator.

Because of these processes (the interplay of the vernacular and the literary, the interaction of the Han and non-Han, the exchange among various regions, the tension between male and female voices), Chinese literature has remained vital to this day. Considering the enormous array of internal and external forces at play, it is impossible to predict with any degree of accuracy what will happen on the Chinese literary scene during the twenty-first century. One thing is certain, however: there will continue to be exciting, new manifestations of this old tradition, including, perhaps, the emergence of regional vernacular literatures. The implications of such a development would be profound, but not entirely unexpected, considering the trajectory of events in the history of Chinese literature during its last 3,200 years—from oracular pronouncements to inscriptional vows; from classical prose and verse to elliptical, euphuistic, epideictic parallel rhymeprose; from literary-language tales of the "strange" to semivernacular narratives; from prosodically and dictionally innovative song lyrics and arias to proto-drama; from prosimetric storytelling and oral performing arts (*ch'ü-yi*) to full-blown vernacular fiction and operatic drama; from vernacular short stories to spoken drama; from Soviet-style reportage (*pao-kao wen-hsüeh*, Russian *ocherkovaia literatura*) to "scar literature" (*shang-hen wen-hsüeh*), "exposure literature" (*pao-lu wen-hsüeh*), "misty/obscure poetry" (*meng-lung shih*), avant-garde fiction, theater of the absurd, postmodern and postcontemporary criticism, and anarchist disillusion of the New Cultural Revolution (see chapters 24, 32, 39, 40, and 42). The next stage remains to be seen—and read with gusto!

Victor H. Mair
Princeton, New Jersey
March 25, 1999

PART I

Foundations

Chapter 1

LANGUAGE AND SCRIPT

Without language, there would be no literature. Hence, we must begin our history of Chinese literature with a description of the Sinitic languages and the sinographic script in which they were written. Unfortunately, there are popular myths and misconceptions about Chinese characters and, in turn, about the languages they were used to write. Consequently, this chapter proceeds slowly, deliberately, and cautiously to introduce the basic elements and features of the Chinese writing system, because a firm grasp of the essential nature of the sinographic script and the Sinitic group of languages serves as a solid foundation for accurately understanding and truly appreciating Chinese literature.

The most important point to start with is to stress that there is not now, nor has there ever been (except at the very earliest beginnings some four thousand years ago), a single Sinitic ("Chinese") language. Like all other languages that have been spoken in human history, Sinitic languages have changed through time and varied across space. One of the most widespread misconceptions encountered in dealing with China is that all its people (excluding the so-called minority nationalities) speak the same language with only minor differences in "accent" or "dialect." The second great misunderstanding about the linguistic situation in China is that somehow language and script are identical: that the script is the language. This notion is patently fallacious, though nearly universal in the popular imagination. Again, as is true of all other tongues used on earth, language is primary and prior to script. Scripts are secondary devices for recording languages. There is always a gap between spoken language and writing.

This is especially true of Sinitic languages and the Chinese script, for the gulf between them is enormous and has been conspicuous for at least the past two thousand years.

Nonetheless, until modern times, which witnessed the invention of various mechanical, electronic, and notational devices that can more or less faithfully record speech, our knowledge of languages depends on written records. This is particularly true of ancient China's spoken languages, which are filtered through, and to a certain extent distorted by, the Chinese script, comprising thousands of sinographs (*han-tzu*) or, as they are commonly called, "characters."

Any attempt to assess the impact of the script/speech dichotomy on the development of Chinese literature must keep in the forefront the bifurcation between literary (classical) styles, on the one hand, and vernacular (or common) styles, on the other hand. In more familiar terms, the difference between the literary and the vernacular is like that between Classical Greek and Demotic Greek, between Classical Latin and Modern Italian, between Sanskrit and Hindi. The division between these two stylistic registers of writing in China is seldom absolute, but it is usually marked and almost always obvious to the linguist who is sensitive to nuances of grammar, syntax, morphology, phonology, and lexicon. The differences between the literary and vernacular registers of Sinitic are so great that they may be said to constitute two different linguistic systems. Basically, Literary Sinitic (LS) is a book language, whereas written Vernacular Sinitic (VS) is a type of *koine* (or demotic standard) that has ambiguous ties to the numerous spoken languages of China, especially to those of the north. Normally, the *koine* was most closely associated with the language of the national capital, wherever that might be at a particular time. The problem is that the division between the vernacular and the literary in China is never a neat one, since the two systems frequently borrow from each other. Thus a poem written by a celebrated T'ang (618–907) poet such as Tu Fu (712–770) may have a few vernacular expressions in it, while the supposedly vernacular verse of the T'ang Buddhist eccentric Han-shan (Cold Mountain [a collective persona]; ninth century) is constructed essentially within a classical matrix.

One of the most striking facts about the history of literature in China is that, unlike what happened in Europe, India, and elsewhere, the many spoken Sinitic languages never developed vernacular literatures of their own. Throughout Chinese history, there have basically been only two types of written Sinitic, the national literary language (LS) and the national *koine* (VS). Furthermore, the national *koine* has always been more or less permeated with classical elements and has seldom been a close approximation of the actual speech of any particular place.

This chapter begins by discussing the origins, classification, and characteristics of Sinitic languages. It then examines the history and cultural implications of Chinese characters. Finally, the chapter concludes with a look at the present status of language and literature in China, together with a peek into the future.

A full, monographic treatment of Sinitic languages and the Chinese script would include other subjects, such as the role and notation of tones, the influence of the writing system in other East Asian cultures, and writing materials and tools. But these topics are of a specialized nature and do not have a direct bearing on the main theoretical and practical issues being discussed here; hence there are no sections devoted exclusively to them, although some of them are touched upon in passing and many are discussed elsewhere in this volume.

ORIGINS AND AFFILIATIONS

The genetic affinities of the Sinitic group of languages remain in doubt. Many scholars believe that Sinitic has some relationship to Tibeto-Burman (hence the frequently heard denomination "Sino-Tibetan"), because of claims of close to a thousand cognates having been discovered, but the precise nature and extent of their relatedness have not been conclusively demonstrated. Other scholars see a connection between Austronesian (also called Malayo-Polynesian, a family of languages spoken in the Malay Peninsula, Indonesia, the Philippines, Vietnam, Taiwan, Oceania, and Madagascar) or other language families and Sinitic (i.e., Han). In fact, the more we learn about the complex origins of Chinese civilization during the Neolithic period, the rise of the first states during the Bronze Age, and the unification of the empire during the Iron Age, it has become increasingly clear that the beginnings of the Sinitic group of languages are associated with interaction among half a dozen or more distinct archeological cultures, which—judging from their locations and the autochthonous languages (many of which survive in significant populations) that characterized these regions—constituted separate linguistic entities. In this sense, the germs of what later grew or coalesced into the Sinitic group of languages may have been the result of a combination of elements from the various languages of the regional cultures that were absorbed into the emerging Chinese civilization.

The Shang people, who lived in the eastern half of the Yellow River Valley and adjoining areas during the middle to late second millennium B.C.E., principally spoke one language, whereas the Chou people, who displaced them as rulers over the north China heartland around the middle of the eleventh century B.C.E., came from the distant northwest and may have originally spoken another language, whose precise identity has not been determined. (Apparently, the Chou rulers initiated the pattern of the conquerors of China adopting the language and script of the people whom they conquered. This was a pattern that would be repeated in China again and again throughout its history.) The founders of the Ch'in dynasty (221–207 B.C.E.), which succeeded the Chou, represent yet another wave of militarily powerful peoples from the northwest who encroached upon the Central Plains; it was the Ch'in who established there the imperial system that lasted essentially unchanged until 1911. Thus there seems to have been a complex layering of linguistic elements in the final solidification of Sinitic as a distinct group. By the time of the Han dynasty (206 B.C.E.–220 C.E.), the basic foundations of the Sinitic language group as we know it today had apparently been laid, so it is no accident that the usual way to refer to Sinitic in Modern Standard Mandarin (MSM, the current national language of China) is *Han-yü* (literally, "Han language"). Indeed, it has been suggested that the group might well be designated as Hannic. After a century of dedicated efforts to reconstruct the sounds of Old Sinitic (that is, Sinitic from pre-Ch'in and earlier times), some historical phonologists (e.g., South Coblin and Jerry Norman) have come to the realization that there is a watershed or horizon at the Han period, beyond which opinions differ widely. In other words, whereas there is rough agreement concerning the main features in the reconstruction of post-Han phonology, the recovery of pre-Han phonology presents seemingly insurmountable obstacles. This appears to be true not only of Sinitic as a whole but also of its constituent branches.

It is certain that before and during the Han period, Sinitic had already borrowed many Indo-European words (particularly from the Iranian group, but also from Tocharian, Indic, and other groups), among them (in MSM pronunciation) *ku-lu* (wheel), *shan-hu* (coral), *mai* (wheat), *wu* (mage), *shih-tzu* (lion), *p'i-p'a* (balloon lute), and *mi* (honey). The usual view is that, as Sinitic speakers expanded southward in historic times, they absorbed words from the non–Sinitic-speaking indigenes of the Yangtze Valley and farther south, including the word *chiang* for the Yangtze itself (*Ch'ang chiang*; literally, Long River), the word *nu* for "crossbow," and the word *sheng* for a quintessentially southern type of multiple-piped mouth organ. Thus lexical and other types of evidence for substrate (i.e., underlying) Austroasiatic and Austronesian elements is identifiable in the southern branches of Sinitic. This linguistic evidence is corroborated by different kinds of data (e.g., genetics, tooth structure, fingerprints, surnames, clan structures, and ethnic practices) indicating a major north-south ethnic, social, and cultural division in China.

After the Han period, a new set of massive linguistic influences spread over China from the north, such that what certain scholars (e.g., David Prager Branner) recognize as a process of creolization occurred during the Eastern Chin (317–420) and Northern and Southern Dynasties (420–589), when the heartland of China was ruled by peoples who were speakers of Altaic (modern members of this Central and Inner Asian language family—not accepted in toto by all linguists—are Turkic, Mongolic, and Manchu). This process, which included relexification, morphological restructuring, and phonological shifts, has been referred to as Altaicization. To a lesser extent (as observed by the historical linguists Mantarō Hashimoto and Charles N. Li), it continued when the Chin (Jurchen) (1115–1234), Liao (Khitan) (916–1125), Yüan (Mongol) (1260–1368), and Ch'ing (Manchu) (1644–1911) dynasties, all of which were Altaic rather than Han, controlled the whole of China or at least the northern part.

During this same post-Han period, thousands of Indic words (both as transcriptions and as translations) flooded into China with the arrival of Buddhism, but Indic languages have had only a minimal impact on the structure and phonology of Sinitic. Similarly, since the arrival of the Jesuits around the middle of the sixteenth century and the diverse Westerners who followed them, Sinitic has borrowed thousands more Indo-European words. Again, however, the impact on the grammar and syntax of Sinitic languages, though detectable, has generally been slight.

CLASSIFICATION

It is a commonplace to talk of Chinese "dialects" as though there were only a single language in China with a dozen or so mutually intelligible varieties. In reality, if the usual yardstick of mutual intelligibility is applied to the linguistic situation in China, a rough estimate would be that there are scores of different Sinitic languages, which may be divided into hundreds of dialects and thousands of subdialects. (This discussion does not include the numerous languages and dialects of China [such as Mongolian, Manchu, Uyghur, Kazakh, Kirghiz, Chuang, Tai, Hmong/Miao, Pai, Lolo/Yi, and Korean] which belong to other linguistic groups and families.) Despite linguistic reality, however, it is customary to refer to the "eight major dialects" (*pa ta fang-yen*) of Sinitic. (This number has recently been increased to ten or eleven by some authorities.) How can we account for this enormous discrepancy between linguistic reality and common usage?

Part of the problem lies in the meaning of the term *fang-yen*, which most dictionaries simply define as "dialect." Literally, however, it merely means "speech of a place" and has been used to designate linguistic entities as disparate as Uyghur, Tibetan, Pekingese, Shanghainese, Taiwanese, Amoyese, Hokkien, Hoklo, Hakka, Cantonese, and Toishan (a variety of Cantonese spoken by many Chinese Americans). (Even Italian and German were called *fang-yen* by early Chinese travelers to Europe.) Obviously, the notion of place can be large or small, far or near, hence the extreme heterogeneity of the languages enumerated. Consequently, some scientifically minded scholars have begun to translate *fang-yen* as "topolect" to ensure that its original meaning is preserved in English and to dissociate it from the word "dialect," which normally signifies mutual intelligibility when employed in linguistic parlance. Furthermore, the fourth edition of the *American Heritage Dictionary of the English Language* has included "topolect" among its entries. Nonetheless, since "dialect" is so deeply entrenched as a translation of *fang-yen*, for the sake of clarity in discussions of the linguistic situation in China, it is necessary to compare and contrast "language" and "dialect" more fully. The following discussion of languages and dialects distinguishes between politically motivated definitions and those determined by linguistic criteria.

"Language" and "dialect" are difficult to define individually, because each is capable of multiple definitions, depending on the theoretical concepts, level of abstraction, and degree of specificity brought to bear. Yet, there is universal agreement that, when these two terms are considered in mutual relationship to each other, a dialect is a smaller subset of a language. The problem is that the dividing line between what constitutes a language and what constitutes a dialect is hazy.

It has often been facetiously remarked and widely quoted that "a language is a dialect with an army/navy" and that, since Cantonese, Shanghainese, Szechwanese, and so forth do not have their own armies/navies, they cannot be considered separate languages. Disregarding the tortured logic of the second half of the sentence, the oft-repeated claim of the first half of the sentence (the part within quotation marks) is itself not true. The falsity of this quip can be demonstrated by pointing out that the United States, Canada, Great Britain, and Australia all have their own sizable armies and navies, yet it is recognized everywhere that the vast majority of their populations all speak a single language, namely English (albeit in various dialects). Conversely, although Switzerland has only one army, its inhabitants speak at least four languages: German, French, Italian, and Romans(c)h (also called Rhaeto-Romanic). And Navajo, which is accepted by all as a language, is totally devoid of an army to back it up. Of course, there are thousands of other languages like Navajo that lack an army or navy. It is evident that the question of what is a language and what is a dialect cannot be determined by wit or military might and organization alone.

It must be admitted that the distinction between "dialect" and "language" can be an extremely subtle matter. For example, spoken Yorkshire dialect may be difficult for someone from the American Midwest to understand, yet it is still accepted as belonging to the English language, and literate persons from Yorkshire customarily speak and write standard British English. Furthermore, dialects on the periphery of one language can merge with dialects on the periphery of another language, as is the case with certain patois of French and Italian. Such marginal phenomena, of course, are the exceptions that prove the rule: "dialect" does not equal "language."

Despite these complexities, the best test of the difference between a dialect and a language is normally still the tried and true standard of mutual intelligibility. If we apply this test to the Sinitic (Hannic) group, we discover that there are scores of mutually unintelligible languages in China. Let us just take the case of Mandarin, for example, which is supposed to be spoken by approximately 800 million people, from the far northeast to the far southwest, all using the same language with only minor differences of "accent." Despite tremendous actual differences in pronunciation (including tones) and colloquial usages across the vast regions where Mandarin is spoken, the urban populations from these regions can, more or less, converse with one another. It is another matter altogether when one goes out into the rural and mountainous hinterlands. Here one swiftly discovers that one's standard Mandarin frequently will not suffice, and it becomes quite difficult, often even impossible, to sustain a conversation with local denizens who are using their own (supposedly Mandarin) tongue.

One of the biggest sources of confusion in dealing with the problem of languages and dialects in China is the persistent perception that all Sinitic expressions, when written down, represent the same linguistic entity. This is evident in the nearly unanimous claim that, although Sinitic topolects may be mutually unintelligible when spoken, when written down they magically become mutually intelligible. In other words, it is somehow thought that the sinographic script has the power to transmute mutually unintelligible spoken language into mutually intelligible written language: the famous notion that "the Chinese characters function as a bridge between the various 'dialects.'" In reality, the sinographs are not capable of performing such magic. Except in extremely rare instances, sinographically written Sinitic is either *wen-yen* (LS) or Mandarin. In the past, if one wished to be sinographically literate—no matter where one was from or what one's mother tongue was—one learned to write *wen-yen* or the national *koine*; one did not write one's *fang-yen*. Since there were no communities of *wen-yen* speakers and since the national *koine* was not the spoken language of the overwhelming majority of the Chinese population, this meant that customarily one had to learn a new language (or two new languages—*wen-yen* and the *koine*) to become sinographically literate in China. *Wen-yen* was strictly a *shu-mien-yü* (book language), never a *k'ou-yü* (spoken language).

We can draw a parallel with the linguistic situation in India. For the past two millennia, Sanskrit has played a role in India quite similar to that of *wen-yen* in China. Although highly educated individuals could actually speak Sanskrit (just as in Europe, where highly educated persons could speak Latin), it was not the native tongue of anyone, so it had to be learned as a separate, classical language. The major Indian regional vernaculars, however, came to be written down—most of them in their own distinctive scripts—and to develop their own extensive literatures. As such, they are recognized as separate languages. In China, the regional Sinitic vernaculars were not committed to writing, neither in their own scripts nor in sinographs, and they did not develop their own literatures. In trying to come to grips with the contentious issue of "language" versus "dialect" in China, the key thing to keep in mind is that the degree of linguistic difference (in terms of phonology, grammar, lexicon, syntax, idiomatic usages, and so forth) among the regional Indic vernaculars is probably smaller (and certainly no greater) than that among the regional Sinitic vernaculars. Consequently, it would seem to be illogical or, at least, inconsistent to refer to the regional Indic vernaculars as "languages" and the regional Sinitic vernaculars as "dialects," yet that is exactly what most people continue to do. Some would justify this discrepant usage on the grounds of shared culture, but cultural diversity among the Sinitic speakers of China is surely as great as or greater than that among the Indic speakers of India. Others would champion the incongruous application of the term "dialect" to the regional Sinitic vernaculars by virtue of their all belonging to the same political entity, but the same is true of the regional Indic vernaculars. The final, fallback argument for the special usage of "dialect" with regard to the regional Sinitic vernaculars is that they are all written with the same script. As mentioned above, however, the regional Sinitic vernaculars have historically not been written in sinographs. Even if they had been, that by itself would not justify calling them "dialects" for, by the same logic, all of the hundreds of languages around the world that are now written in the Roman script (e.g., Turkish, Indonesian, Malaysian, Vietnamese, Finnish, Hungarian, Czech, and Romanian) would have to be considered "dialects" of some single language. This, of course, is a ludicrous proposition. In sum, then, the continuing reference to the regional Sinitic vernaculars as "dialects" rather than as "languages" cannot be defended on the grounds of linguistics, culture, politics, or script. Rather, it is primarily the result of the misunderstanding and mistranslation of the term *fang-yen* (topolect) and sheer habit. Whatever its sources, the use of the word "dialect" to designate the regional Sinitic vernaculars of China plays havoc with linguistic classification.

Yet another part of the problem concerning the classification of Sinitic languages is what exactly is meant by terms like *Han-yü* (Han language), *Chung-kuo-hua* (literally, "speech of China"), and *Chung-wen* (literally, "Chinese writing"), all of which are vaguely translated into English as "Chinese." Sometimes they are used to designate all the Sinitic languages collectively, but sometimes they are used rather more restrictively to refer specifically to MSM.

The most sensible solution to the taxonomy of Sinitic is to start afresh and apply to the group the same sort of rules and standards that are applied to other language groups. According to such taxonomic principles, *Han-yü* (i.e., Sinitic or Hannic) must be viewed as a group of languages (comparable to Indo-Iranian or Germanic within the Indo-European family). As pointed out above, it has still not been conclusively determined to which family the Sinitic group belongs, although many historical linguists believe that it is related in some fashion primarily to the Tibeto-Burman family. The most authoritative statements in Chinese reference works implicitly admit that *Han-yü* is not a single language when they refer to it as *hsiang-tang yü yi ke yü-tsu* ("equivalent to a language group"). Once we accept that Sinitic is a group of languages, this means that the "eight (or ten or eleven) major 'dialects'" are actually branches (*yü-chih*). (If Sinitic cannot ultimately be convincingly linked up with Tibeto-Burman or another language family, then it may have to be considered a family [*yü-hsi*] unto itself. However, since at present the jury is still out on the relationship of Sinitic to Tibeto-Burman, Austronesian, and several other families, it is best to refrain from designating Sinitic as a language family.) As is true of all other language groups in the world, within the branches of Sinitic there are generally several languages, and within the languages there are dialects, under which there are subdialects. Only when we follow such a rigorous and systematic taxonomical scheme do the interrelationships among the various types of Sinitic become clear.

VERNACULAR VERSUS LITERARY

Linguistically, as seen above, the most distinctive feature of Chinese literature is the division between texts written in the vernacular and those written in a literary or classical style. The border between these two realms is blurred because they tend to borrow from each other. However, while most literary texts approach a pure form in the sense of being nearly or wholly uncontaminated by vernacular elements, exceedingly few vernacular texts are free of literary elements, and, to be sure, many texts that are referred to as vernacular are actually laced with literary elements or consist of a sprinkling of vernacular elements in a basically literary matrix.

From the very earliest stage of writing in China, there was such an emphasis on concision that many parts of spoken language were omitted. This may initially have been due to the intractable nature of the media (bones and shells that had to be scratched with a sharp instrument) and the highly particularized function of the texts. After the practice got started, however, it became a *sine qua non* for writing in the literary style. Anaphora and elision were invoked to such an extreme degree that it became a sort of game between author and reader; the challenge was to see how much the former could leave out without losing the latter. If one could possibly get by without a grammatical subject, then by all means drop it. If one syllable of a two- or three-syllable term would suffice, why go to all the crude bother of including the extra sounds? This paradigm of pared-down writing having been established, it became the norm and was considered the height of elegance (*ya*). Vernacular writing, in which all the elements of speech were "spelled out," came to be considered vulgar (*su*) and was to be ruthlessly expunged from texts. Consequently, there developed a deep chasm between the vernacular and the literary, such that eventually they became two different types of language altogether, with distinct grammars and distinct lexicons.

These phenomena are not unique to the writing of Old Sinitic (OS) and its derivative, LS. On the contrary, they are quite common in "logographic" writing systems, where the morphology (and even parts of the phonology) get chronically under- or misrepresented. For example, Sumerian was once believed to be almost entirely monosyllabic (as LS is still erroneously thought to be in the popular imagination), or at least only moderately agglutinating, and to have a relatively simple phonology. Yet recent research has revealed that the spoken language that underlay written Sumerian was actually highly flectional (inflected) and as phonologically complex as the northwest Caucasian language known as Circassian, which is thought to have more distinct phonemes than any other extant language in the world.

To call attention to the large gulf between LS and VS in China is by no means to claim that the former is unrelated to the latter. Of course, even in its most abbreviated form and in its earliest attested stages, the writing system revealed remnants of its derivation from spoken language: lento and allegro forms, fusion words, (unconscious) use of wrong characters because of homophony and tone sandhi (morphophonemic alternation as determined by phonetic environment) effects, dialectal phonetic loans, and so forth. Indeed, the process of loss of a once rather intricate morphology was neither instantaneous nor total, since enough traces of prefixation, infixation, suffixation, quantitative and qualitative ablaut (regular alternation of internal phonological structure, usually to express grammatical function), and so on remained in the latter-day spoken and written languages to enable historical linguists to establish that Proto-Sinitic (the earliest stage of Sinitic) was not simply a strictly monosyllabic, isolating (using few or no bound forms and indicating grammatical relationship chiefly through word order), uninflected language.

The epigrammatic terseness of the literary style was compensated for in part by copious use of allusion. By hinting with a word or two an entire sentence, poem, or essay of an earlier writer, one could—by metalinguistic means—communicate a tremendous amount of (old) information without actually stating it wholly and straightforwardly, provided that one's reader was learned enough to catch the hint and to recall accurately the original text to which one was referring. Many of the most revered texts in the canon of classical literature consist almost entirely of allusions and quotations from earlier texts. Far from being looked down upon as imitative or uncreative, this sort of intentional (but usually not overt) referencing was held to be the mark of excellence and erudition. Conversely, the reader who was incapable of recognizing all the allusions and quotations in such works was considered insufficiently learned. LS thus put a double premium on memorization: not only did the large number of discrete units of the script (i.e., the thousands of characters) have to be recalled, but a huge corpus of classical literature had to be controlled. Since neither the script nor the classical corpus was based directly on the native spoken languages of those who strove to command them, they required heroic feats of rote memorization and prodigious powers of association.

Literary language, quite naturally, was the written language of the literati, and the vernaculars, just as inevitably, were the spoken languages of the illiterate plebes (and of the literati when they had to speak to anyone). One had to be explicit when one was talking or one ran the risk of not being understood. (In war or at work, this could be a dangerous proposition.) Writing was an entirely different matter. Here, the very possibility that one might be misconstrued if one left out too much offered a kind of excitement to authors. It was as though one were asking, "Where is that sympathetic reader who will know what I mean even when I don't say it altogether straightforwardly?" Furthermore, both writing and reading permit virtually unlimited reflection and reconsideration, whereas speech is a matter of the moment. Once a speaker makes an utterance, the listener either catches it or does not. Although the listener may ruminate upon the words he or she has heard, the act of communication itself is instantaneous. Finally, the nature of the Chinese writing system (as detailed below) accentuates the gulf between speech and writing because of its phonetically poor, semantically rich, and highly visual qualities.

Similar gaps between the vernacular and the literary exist elsewhere among the world's languages, notably in Arabic. There are many parallels between the diglossia (employing two sharply divergent, formal and informal varieties of language within a society for different functions) of China and that of the Arabic-speaking world, where all writing is done in a sort of Koranic (Qur'anic) literary medium called *fusha* ("eloquent"; cf. LS as *ya* [elegant]), whereas speech is carried out in one of the many more or less mutually unintelligible national and regional vernaculars. A more thorough examination of the reasons for this uncanny similarity between Sinitic and Arabic, despite their complete lack of linguistic relatedness, may reveal corresponding sociological and ideological factors that contribute to the dichotomy between the vernacular and the literary. Conversely, it would appear that a different set of sociological and ideological (the two leading to political and economic) factors have ensured that the vernacular and literary realms of Europe and India, for example, are not so remote from each other. For all languages, there are admittedly stylistic differences between speaking and writing. For English, French, German, Hindi, and Bengali, the differences are relatively slight; for Arabic, they are great; and, for Sinitic (especially in premodern times, but even today), they are enormous.

There was a keen awareness of topolectal differences among a few outstanding Chinese scholars, such as Yang Hsiung (53 B.C.E–18 C.E), in his monumental *Fang-yen* [Topolects], and Kuo P'u (276–324), in his insightful and incisive commentaries on difficult terms in early texts. Unfortunately, their data collection and particular observations have only limited value for research because they were hampered by the lack of precise, convenient, and reliable means for making phonological notations. Nonetheless, the work of these scholars lends strong support to claims about the complexity of the linguistic landscape in ancient China.

In China, writing in the vernacular was unthinkable before the Buddhists came along. Prior to the advent of Buddhism, we find only a few traces of the vernacular that managed to slip through the rigorously antivernacular redactional processes that were in place for more than two millennia. A few of these relics of pre-Buddhist vernacular may be gleaned from literary texts, and others are found in texts that have been archeologically recovered in recent years. The paucity of the vernacular in pre-Buddhist China indicates that writing in this linguistic register simply was not meant to be.

The reasons why Buddhism fostered the use of the vernacular in China are numerous and complicated. First is the injunction of the Buddha himself, as recorded in the *vinaya* (rules of discipline governing the community of monks) to transmit his *dharma* (doctrine) throughout the world in the languages of various regions, rather than in the preclassical language of the Vedas. Thus, right from the founding of the religion in India, Buddhism strongly sanctioned the vernacular ahead of the classical. Second, Indian tradition has always stressed the memorization and recitation of texts over their transmission through writing. This emphasis on oral expression promoted the vernacular at the expense of the literary. Third, Indian linguistic science, going back to the celebrated grammarians Pāṇini (c. 500 B.C.E.) and Patañjali (c. second century B.C.E.), was extraordinarily sophisticated. The analysis of the sounds of language in India was far more advanced than it was in China. When Indian phonological concepts and practices were introduced to China, they heightened Chinese scholars' awareness of the importance of speech, which had hitherto been grossly devalued relative to the sinographic script toward which traditional scholars displayed a fascination that amounted to a linguistically distracting fixation. Fourth, philosophically Buddhism has downplayed the significance of written texts as being capable of capturing or conveying enlightened insights about the human condition. Fifth, Buddhism fundamentally adheres to egalitarian social values that favor demotic forms of language over elitist, hieratic forms. A sixth factor was the process of translation of Indic texts into Sinitic. Since in the early stages this was almost always done by foreign monks who had a limited command of LS but who would have possessed some fluency in the vernacular, it was inevitable that elements of the latter would end up in their translations. This was true even later, when large teams of translators, including Chinese assistants and collaborators, were assembled. The discussions over the meanings of various passages and the mechanisms for writing them down led to the incorporation of bits of vernacular in the final product.

For all the above reasons and more, the result of the arrival of Buddhism in China was the gradual legitimization of writing in vernacular. There can be no doubt that it was Buddhism that initially triggered vernacular writing in China. The first extended, semivernacular narratives in China are the eighth- to tenth-century transformation texts (*pien-wen*) preserved at Tun-huang (see chapter 48), and the overwhelming majority of all evidence for written vernacular before that time is found in Buddhist texts or in Buddhist contexts.

Despite the limited legitimization of writing in the vernacular brought about by the spread of Buddhism in China, the full implications of the vernacular revolution have never come to fruition. As reiterated below, most of the vernacular languages of China have never been reduced to writing throughout their entire history. And even standard written Mandarin is usually peppered with LS elements to such an extent that it can hardly be thought of grammatically, syntactically, or lexically as vernacular in the true sense of the word. The continual backsliding from vernacular to literary is due to several factors that are explored in greater detail below, the chief two being (1) the inertia of the multimillennial attachment to literary styles; and (2) the nature (or genius) of the script, which, on the one hand, is perfectly suited to and naturally reinforces literary styles of writing and, on the other hand, is inimical to and consequently discourages writing in the vernacular.

NONDEVELOPMENT OF WRITTEN REGIONAL VERNACULARS

One of the most striking features of the linguistic situation in China is that, although there are countless different Sinitic languages spoken by the Han and Hui (Muslim) populations, throughout history only two different types of written language have ever developed to any appreciable extent: LS (Literary Sinitic) and what is now known as MSM (Modern Standard Mandarin). (Here we refer only to speakers of Sinitic languages, not to speakers of languages belonging to other groups and families, such as Tibetan, Mongolian, Manchu, and Uyghur, many of which did develop written literary traditions.) Thus, even though there are tens of millions of speakers of Cantonese, Shanghainese, Szechwanese, and other Sinitic languages, all of which have their own oral traditions, they have never developed independent written traditions. This is quite unlike the situation in Europe and in India, where numerous national and regional vernacular literatures have flourished for hundreds of years.

When, starting in the late sixteenth century, the Jesuits and then other European and American missionaries came to China, they created written forms of many local and regional vernaculars using the Roman alphabet. During the late nineteenth and early twentieth centuries, Chinese language reformers emulated them and invented various schemes for writing their local and regional languages. None of these caught on, however, with the result that today the only non-Mandarin vernaculars being written in China are romanized Taiwanese (until recently restricted largely to adherents of the Presbyterian Church) and occasionally Colloquial Cantonese, using a mixture of standard, semistandard, and nonce sinographs, plus some romanized native and borrowed (particularly English) words.

We may state unequivocally: one of the chief reasons for the nondevelopment of the written regional vernaculars in China is that the sinographic script, although perfectly suited to writing LS, was (and still is) unfortunately ill-suited to writing the vernaculars (the reasons why this is so may be gleaned from the other sections of this chapter). Robert Cheng, an authority on Taiwanese language and writing, has spoken of "Taiwanese morphemes in search of Chinese characters" that they simply cannot find. And Lao She (1899–1966), the preeminent author of fiction and drama in Pekingese, complained bitterly of having to forgo many of his favorite expressions because it was impossible to write them in Chinese characters.

Even after the partial legitimization of the vernacular under Buddhist influence, the only written vernacular that developed in China was the *koine* of the T'ang period. Of obscure origins (scholars are still debating whether it was originally based on the language of Loyang or some other city and to what extent it incorporated southern elements [by this time Hannic had long since solidified in the north]), usage of the written *koine* continued to expand during the Sung period (960–1279), and by the Mongol Yüan dynasty it had unmistakably solidified as a national vernacular. This is not to say that it was yet a true *lingua franca* (that would not emerge until the twentieth century), but it was at least the common spoken language of the officials at the district and higher levels of government. This can be seen in its Chinese name, *kuan-hua* (literally, "officials' speech" = Mandarin < Spanish *mandarín* < Portuguese *mandarim* < Malay *mẽntẽri* < Hindi *mantrī* < Sanskrit *mantrin-* [counselor] < *mantraḥ* [counsel]).

Mandarin was also the basis of a flourishing vernacular literature, especially in fiction, drama, and in various genres derived from oral performance (see chapters 41 and 49). Although the vernacular by no means displaced LS even in the latter realms, its role grew steadily during the Sung, Yüan, Ming, and Ch'ing dynasties, paving the way for more widespread acceptance of written demotic language after the Republic of China was established in 1912. Except for the song lyric (*tz'u*; see chapter 15), the aria/canto (*ch'ü*; see chapter 17), and some popular ballads (*yüeh-fu*, etc.; see chapter 47), before the twentieth century the vernacular made little headway in poetry, much less in prose in all its nonfictional manifestations.

The *koine* began as the common spoken language of the officials from various parts of China whose native tongues were more or less mutually unintelligible, even though all but the tiniest fraction of these were speakers of one variety or another of Sinitic (Hannic). Soon, however, it also came to be used by merchants and monks, whose mobility was even greater than that of the officials. It was among the bourgeoisie that written vernacular literature flourished, not among the peasantry and the proletariat, who were totally illiterate and so poor that they could not afford even the cheapest printed material anyway.

The *koine* of the successive dynasties varied somewhat, depending in part on the shifting locations of the capital (Ch'ang-an, Loyang, Peking, Nanking) and in part because the dominant cliques of intellectuals under the different dynasties came from different regions. Both factors led to modifications, but not total transformation, of the *koine*.

Given its original background in bureaucratic circles, Mandarin (i.e., *kuan-hua*) is an appropriate name for the *koine* as it developed in the Ming and Ch'ing periods. Now, however, it goes by different names in various places: in China it is called *p'u-t'ung-hua* (common speech), in Singapore it is called *hua-yü* ("[culturally] florescent [i.e., Chinese] language"), and in Taiwan it is called *kuo-yü* (national language < Japanese *kokugo*), although rising consciousness and nationalism among the native Taiwanese are causing the latter term to be questioned as an appropriate designation for the language that was imposed on the island's population as a whole only from the 1950s on.

During the Yüan period, standard Mandarin was based on the language of the capital of the Mongols (Ta-tu, i.e., Peking). By the late Ming dynasty (1368–1644), the locus of standard Mandarin had shifted to Nanking, but under the Manchus it shifted back to Peking again. It is clear from the history of Mandarin that it is fundamentally a northern language with close ties to Altaic ruling peoples. It is not surprising, therefore, that—of all the Sinitic languages—in many respects (e.g., phonologically and lexically) Mandarin is least like earlier forms of Sinitic, insofar as they can be reconstructed.

A rare exception to the nondevelopment of written local and regional vernaculars in China is the now celebrated "Women's Script" (*nü-shu*) of Chiang-yung county in Hunan province. Discovered by the outside world only in the 1970s, this intriguing form of writing was probably invented sometime during the Manchu (Ch'ing) period, although local legends attempt to trace it back to the Sung dynasty. Regardless of when it came into being and the fact that it was probably never used by more than a few hundred people at any given time, this script is theoretically of the utmost significance. Fundamentally, it was an unstandardized syllabary consisting of some seven hundred different graphs to represent the approximately five hundred basic syllables (i.e., disregarding tones, consideration of which would increase the number of syllables to more than thirteen hundred). The individual graphs were formed mostly through rhomboidal deformation of sinographs. (Attempts to link Women's Script with archaic forms of the sinographs are completely without historical foundation.) In other words, a single Chinese character was essentially made to fit inside a diamond-shaped space rather than within a square, and, furthermore, it stood for all the morphemes in the language that were pronounced in roughly the same fashion. This is quite unlike typical Chinese morphosyllabic writing, in which each morpheme (meaningful linguistic unit) is usually indicated by a separate graph that is one syllable long. For example, standard Chinese writing has hundreds of different semantic/syllabic sinographs to write the single syllable *yi* (disregarding tones), whereas in the Women's Script, although some syllables are represented by two to five graphs, only one purely syllabic graph is normally used to write all the morphemes in question. Obviously, this constitutes a stupendous simplification of the complicated Chinese script, and it is what made the acquisition of literacy relatively easy for the women of Chiang-yung county, unlike their sisters elsewhere in China. The men, however, did not know the secret (which was intentionally kept from them), and so they were illiterate in the script. Consequently, the women used it to write laments and complaints (often about their husbands!) or simply to write letters to their female friends.

The only other more or less well-known exception to the nondevelopment of vernacular writing for Sinitic languages is the case of Dungan script. The Dungans were Muslims (Hui) of northwest China who escaped from persecution at the hands of the Ch'ing government during the late nineteenth century and fled to the parts of imperial Russia that are now Kyrgyzstan and Kazakhstan. The majority of these peasants and villagers were illiterate when they left China, but eventually they began to write their language in an alphabetic script, using first Roman letters and later the Cyrillic script. The fact that they were using an alphabetic script enabled them to borrow words freely from Persian, Arabic, Russian, and other languages without the syllabic distortion necessarily imposed by the Chinese script. Hence, the word for "tractor" in Dungan is simply *traktor*, not *t'o-la-chi*, as it is in MSM. And the surname of one of the most famous Dungan poets of this century, Mohamud Sushanlo, reportedly was constructed from what would have been—if written in Chinese characters—Su San-lao ("Old Number Three Su"). The Dungans have used their highly flexible alphabetic script to write plays, short stories, novels, essays, and poems. The Dungan literary tradition is proof positive that Sinitic languages can be written with facility in an alphabetic script. There are no particular linguistic limitations to writing any spoken Chinese language with a simple phonetic script. After all, hundreds of millions of people speak the Sinitic vernaculars fluently and effectively every day without recourse to Chinese characters. It is a straightforward matter to transcribe their speech in such a script.

Despite Chinese acquaintance (albeit highly restricted) with syllabaries and alphabets acquired over a period of nearly two thousand years (since the introduction of Buddhism and contact with Japan as well as with various non-Sinitic peoples within China who had their own writing systems), and despite the demonstration by the Women's Script and the Dungan script that it is possible to write Sinitic vernaculars with syllabaries and alphabets, the Chinese people as a whole (following the lead of the intellectuals, of course) have consistently rejected such scripts and declined to commit their local and regional vernaculars to writing. Although many scholars have been mystified by this persistent rejection of phonetic scripts, the reasons for it are not too far to seek. First, the sinographic script carries with it prodigious prestige, even among those who are totally illiterate in it. Second, the sinographic literary tradition has the enormous weight of 3,200 years of history, which makes it difficult even to contemplate any other form of writing. Third, "vulgar" (i.e., vernacular) writing has continually been discouraged by the Chinese literati, backed by the totalitarian power of successive governments that perpetuate an elitist approach in this area.

Fourth, there has been a dearth of competing script systems in East Asia that would have posed a serious challenge to the deeply entrenched Chinese characters. There are other historical and cultural reasons why phonetic scripts, and with them local and regional vernacular writing, have not prospered in China. For example, romanized Min (which was actually used during the second quarter of the twentieth century by tens of thousands of individuals in the provinces of Fukien and Taiwan) was ruthlessly suppressed by the Kuomintang (Nationalist) authorities during the 1950s and 1960s in Taiwan, where they had fled—taking their Mandarin proclivities with them—from the mainland in 1949 after their defeat at the hands of the Communists. And it would have been a very risky business to attempt to publish anything in Cantonese outside of Hong Kong (since Hong Kong reverted to Chinese control in 1997, this is increasingly the case there as well, although the limits of expression in written Cantonese are being tested on an almost daily basis). In just the past few decades, however, the social, political, economic, and cultural conditions of China have changed tremendously. These transformations, coupled with revolutionary new information technologies, may well result in the proliferation of the written vernaculars in the future. That, in turn, will lead to unexpected developments in the ancient and heretofore largely monolithic Chinese literary tradition.

A BRIEF HISTORY OF THE SCRIPT

The earliest writing in China is the one found on the "oracle bones" (*chia-ku-wen;* literally, "shell and bone inscriptions" [SBIs], but this is a modern term) dating to around 1200 B.C.E. There are occasional, isolated pottery marks and symbols found on other artifacts dating to as much as three to four thousand years earlier, but they do not constitute a system of writing that can record syntactically explicit language, and there is no evidence of a connection between them and the later developments. Thus, based on extant records, writing in China first appears nearly two thousand years after it did in Mesopotamia and Egypt (both around 3000 B.C.E., the former apparently slightly ahead of the latter). This naturally leads to the question whether Chinese writing arose entirely independently. The following considerations would seem to indicate that some sort of stimulus diffusion may have been operative: 1. the Chinese script appears essentially full-blown, without the long process of gradual evolution that can be documented locally for writing in Southwest Asia; 2. it is attested shortly after bronze metallurgy and at almost exactly the same time as the chariot, both of which are generally acknowledged by archeologists and historians of science to have come from the West; 3. the nature of the writing systems (fundamentally morphosyllabic with semantic determinatives and phonophoric [sound-bearing] elements but also containing pictographic and ideographic elements, etc.) is remarkably similar in ancient Mesopotamia, Egypt, and China; 4. it has been repeatedly and independently observed by many researchers that certain subsets of the earliest sinographic writing visually resemble equivalent groups of symbols in the West (viz., the twenty-two "heavenly stems" and "earthly branches" [*t'ien-kan ti-chih*] used for counting and calendrical purposes in China, compared to the twenty-two-letter Phoenician alphabet and the Ugaritic alphabet in its various guises [particularly its shortest form], which preceded it) and, to the extent that we have any idea about how they would have been pronounced more than three thousand years ago, appear to share phonetic correspondences (this would by no means necessitate direct contact between the Levant and China but could have been due to indirect transmission, or the stimulus might have originated somewhere between East and West, traveling in both directions outward from the center); 5. numerous individual sinographs (Chinese characters) resemble their Western counterparts in shape, meaning, and occasionally even in sound; 6. embedded in the earliest forms of the characters is tantalizing evidence that the sinographic writing system derives from an earlier stage, unknown within the borders of China for the second millennium B.C.E., when writing was done on strips or leaves bound together with thread; 7. the script, though already fully developed, was for the first several hundred years of its attested existence used only for a single, highly specialized purpose (the recording of royal divinations) and then for several hundred more years was employed for only one other highly specialized purpose (inscriptions on aristocratic bronze vessels), implying that it may have functioned as the restricted preserve of a very small group of aristocratic or priestly scribes and their successors, who jealously guarded their ability to write with it. No single one of these factors by itself would be sufficient to call into question the pristine indigenousness of the sinographic script, but their collectivity requires that the possibility of external influence should not be dismissed out of hand.

Regardless of how it came into being, the Chinese script as we know it was initially employed solely to record the questions posed and answers received during divination. These are the SBIs mentioned above. Writing on oracle shells and bones was closely associated with the Shang dynasty kings, especially starting with Wu-ting (r. c. 1200?–1181? B.C.E.), and their close advisers, who were specialists in divination and its interpretation. Thus the earliest writing in China was a royal prerogative delegated almost exclusively to designated, largely sacerdotal scribes. In the Near East (southwest Asia and northeast Africa), however, writing in its early stages was used for a greater variety of purposes, ranging from economic and administrative to literary and religious subjects.

The SBIs may not be said to have been written with a literary intent, and they address only a narrow range of subjects of prime interest to the king, but they occasionally evince a literary effect or presage the literary qualities of later Chinese writing. The same can be said of the next stage of writing in China: inscriptions on bronze vessels or other bronze implements. Such inscriptions are identified chiefly with the Chou dynasty, but it is significant that—with bronze inscriptions—access to the script has broadened to the feudal lords and great families. Moreover, in the two longest texts known, the length of inscriptions grew from tens or scores of graphs to nearly five hundred.

As the length of Chinese texts grew, the number of sinographs proliferated. The number of different characters on the oracle shells and bones totals approximately forty-five hundred (including approximately a thousand variant forms), only about a thousand to fifteen hundred of which can be equated more or less confidently with later forms. In Chou dynasty bronze inscriptions, there are roughly four thousand different graphs, of which a little over twenty-four hundred are recognizable. Because of the fragmentary, scattered quality of the evidence, it is difficult to determine the number of different graphs employed on silk, bamboo strips, bronze and stone inscriptions, and so on during the Warring States period (403–221 B.C.E.), but there were surely more than five thousand, including many variants restricted to certain regions. When the first emperor of the Ch'in dynasty unified the empire in the latter part of the third century B.C.E., he standardized the script by eliminating regional variants and duplicate forms, but soon the number of graphs began to rise rapidly once again. Thus lexicographical works from succeeding centuries include the following total numbers of graphs: 9,353 (100 C.E.), 11,520 (c. 227–239), 12,824 (in 400), 13,734 (in 500), 22,726 (in 534), 26,911 (in 753), 31,319 (in 1066), 33,179 (in 1615), and 47,043 (in 1716). Recent character dictionaries contain more than sixty thousand sinographs and two even have more than eighty thousand, while a couple of Peking University professors are planning to produce a dictionary that lists more than a hundred thousand different graphs. Such gargantuan numbers of discrete elements in the Chinese script are unimaginable for users of alphabets, whose individual letters usually total between twenty and forty.

In fact, the sinographic script is open-ended and consequently still growing. Any of its users is free to invent new characters (and many do—as for their own names or when scientists discover a hitherto-unknown element). After a character has been invented, it becomes a part of the total inventory of the script forever. This is quite unlike alphabetic writing, in which lexical items are created by rearranging the letters of the alphabet (Shakespeare alone coined nearly seventeen hundred words, among them "barefaced," "castigate," "countless," "critical," "dwindle," "excellent," "fretful," "frugal," "gust," "hint," "hurry," "leapfrog," "lonely," "majestic," "monumental," "obscene," "pedant," "radiance," "submerged," and "summit") but do not add to the total number of letters. That is, no matter how many hundreds of thousands of words are added to the English language, the number of basic elements in the script (twenty-six) remains constant. Of course, Sinitic languages can expand their vocabularies by combining morphemes, and they do this all the time. For example, in Mandarin, *t'ien* means "heaven/sky," *hua* means "flower," *fen* means "powder," and *pan* means "board." These may be combined as follows: *t'ien-hua* (diphtheria), *t'ien-hua-fen* (tricosanthes root [a medicinal preparation]), *t'ien-hua-pan* (ceiling), and so forth. In fact, this is the normal way to create new words in Sinitic languages, but it has not stopped the proliferation of new graphs, in part because totally new morphemes arise from time to time, but also simply because people want to be different and one of the ways of expressing difference is to invent a new character.

Obviously, no human being could possibly keep in mind more than a relatively small fraction of these stupefyingly large numbers of different characters. A thousand characters are required to provide the most rudimentary so-called basic literacy, two to three thousand characters enable one to scrape by in most circumstances, and some four thousand characters are needed for full literacy (including the ability to read a newspaper and exchange written communication on all sorts of topics). Mastery of six thousand characters, the approximate number provided in most computer programs for processing Chinese and in typical desk dictionaries, would be an extraordinary feat, and it is questionable whether anyone could actively command ten thousand or more characters. The customary restriction of most writing to a few thousand different characters is true not only today but even for T'ang poetry, the glory of Chinese literature. As for the other tens of thousands of sinographs, many of them have been used only once or twice in the whole of history, and either their pronunciation or meaning (or both) is not known for sure. Nevertheless, font-makers must take them into account because they do occasionally show up in writing. Information-processing specialists must be prepared to cope with at least twenty-five thousand separate sinographs on a fairly regular basis, even though most of them occur with a frequency of less than one one-thousandth of one percent in the majority of texts; they still show up from time to time in names, historical references, lexicographical discussions, and so forth.

Large as the number of different characters may be, it is obviously not equal to the total number of words in any one of the Sinitic languages, much less is it equal to the total number of words in the collectivity of all Sinitic languages. Indeed, the average length of words in MSM is almost exactly two syllables, and even in LS many frequently used words and terms consist of two or more syllables (including so-called *lien-mien-tzu*, *fu-ho-tz'u* or *fu-yin-tz'u*, onomatopoetic expressions, tightly bound synonyms or near-synonyms, and other types of common lexical items). Thus, although it is widely claimed that Sinitic languages are monosyllabic (consist of words having only one syllable), careful analysis of actual usage reveals that this is surely not the case. While the majority of morphemes in Sinitic are monosyllabic, that is also true of most other languages, including English, and, furthermore, there are numerous morphemes (even in LS) that consist of more than a single syllable, such as those for "butterfly" (*hu-tieh*), "spider" (*chih-chu*), "mosquito larvae" (*chieh-chüeh*), "pear-shaped lute" (*p'i-p'a*), "kumquat" (*p'i-p'a*), "coral" (*shan-hu*), "unicorn" (*ch'i-lin*), "phoenix" (*feng-huang*), "indecisive" (*t'an-t'e*), "winding, meandering" (*wei-yi*), and "awkward" (*kan-ka*). Some of these words may anciently have consisted of only a single syllable containing consonant clusters, but phonological evolution and the resultant phonotactics (phonemic sequential patterning) have led to the breakup of all consonant clusters in Sinitic. When the clustered consonants are redistributed in two successive syllables, this is called dimidiation, a phenomenon that seems to have been quite common in late Old Sinitic. Furthermore, some scholars believe that the breakup of consonant clusters and the loss of certain final consonants led to the origin of tones (tonogenesis) in Sinitic as a sort of compensation. Others maintain that these processes also resulted in a sharp increase in the number of bisyllabic words to ensure lexical differentiation in speech in the face of rising homophony, especially when the number of tones was later reduced in some Sinitic languages (it is now four in Mandarin [level, rising, low dipping, falling], but the number of tones is larger in such conservative branches as Min and Cantonese).

A study of parallel terms in Tibeto-Burman languages and a comparison with very old loans to and from Indo-European, Austroasiatic, Austronesian, and other language families indicate that Sinitic originally possessed consonant clusters. Aside from the phonological processes mentioned above, the syllabic nature of the script itself may have reinforced the breakup of consonant clusters, since syllabic scripts worldwide display a tendency toward the combination of single consonants plus vowels in their construction. Similar phonological constraints, plus the propensity toward extreme concision noted above, have also resulted in the loss of morphological elements (affixes, suffixes, inflections, etc.) that were present in Old Sinitic. Subsequently, in Middle Sinitic and even in Modern Sinitic, these losses were restored through the processes of Altaicization and vernacularization discussed above, with the difference that grammatical elements were no longer expressed as changes made to roots and stems themselves, but as separate syllables (characters when written) added to the beginnings or endings of morphosyllables.

THE NATURE OF THE SCRIPT

Recall that, as mentioned above, scripts are not languages and languages are not scripts. A given script can be used to write many different, unrelated languages (e.g., English, Turkish, Vietnamese, and Indonesian are all written with the Roman alphabet), and a given language can be written with various scripts (e.g., Uyghur, which was written in the following scripts: runes, Old Uyghur [Aramaic-derived, via Sogdian cursive, and the predecessor of the Mongolian and Manchu scripts], Arabic, Cyrillic, Roman, and then again Arabic—in chronological order). Therefore, the classification of scripts is irrelevant to the classification of languages, and vice versa. The classification of Sinitic languages is discussed above; this section aims to classify the sinographic script.

There is much disagreement over how to designate the Chinese script. Although it is often referred to in nonspecialist literature as "pictographic," this is certainly incorrect since only a very small proportion of sinographs, such as those for words meaning "mountain," "sun," "horse," "bird," "fish," and "turtle," were originally intended to represent the appearance of the things in question. Even these few originally pictographic characters have become totally unrecognizable in their current forms to those who have not been schooled in the script. Similarly, only a tiny proportion of all sinographs, such as those for words meaning "above," "below," and "middle," have an ideographic basis, and these too are recognizable only to those who have received special training, so it is likewise improper to refer to the Chinese script as "ideographic." Many authorities prefer the designation "logographic," implying that each syllabic unit of the script is equal to a word and that, therefore, Sinitic languages are monosyllabic. Yet, as seen above, this has surely not been the case for at least the past two millennia, inasmuch as most words in vernacular Sinitic languages consist of two or more syllables, and even in texts from earlier periods numerous frequently recurring words and expressions are longer than one syllable. A more precise designation for the Chinese script is "morphosyllabic," which signifies that each unit of the script is one syllable in length and conveys a basic meaning. It must be reiterated that the fundamentally syllabic nature of the script cannot be used to claim that all Sinitic words consist of only one syllable. Using grammatical analysis, psycholinguistics, and other methods, scholars have conclusively demonstrated that Mandarin speakers have an unmistakable sense of words of various syllabic lengths apart from the script.

While it is true that the Chinese script is overwhelmingly morphosyllabic, even here there are exceptions, since there exist quite a few sinographs (several of which go back to the T'ang period and even earlier) that actually express more than one syllable. Among this type of so-called *ho-wen* (compound graphs) are those for "bodhisattva" (*p'u-sa*), "enlightenment" (*p'u-t'i;* Sanskrit, *bodhi*), "nirvana" (*nieh-p'an*), "so-and-so" (*mou-yi*), "agricultural [commissioner]" (*ying-t'ien*[*-shih*]), "kilowatt" (*ch'ien-wa*), "question" (*wen-t'i*), "Shantung" (Shan-tung), "cadre" (*kan-pu*), "international" (*kuo-chi*), "socialism" (*she-hui-chu-yi*), and "library" (*t'u-shu-kuan*) (these words may also, of course, be written with multiple characters), some of which are so widely used as still to be found in standard dictionaries. During the twentieth century, more than a thousand such polysyllabic characters were used, often quite widely, clearly indicating that Sinitic speakers possess an innate recognition that their languages are not entirely monosyllabic. Since these polysyllabic graphs were often created for very high-frequency terms, this also indicates a recurrent desire to simplify the script.

Another related phenomenon, which lasted from at least the latter part of the tenth century until the end of the nineteenth century, was the practice of writing *fan-ch'ieh* (countertomy or reverse cutting), Buddhist-inspired pseudo-spellings as one graph instead of as three. Normally, such pseudo-spellings were written as X Y *fan*, which indicates that one was to take the initial (beginning sound) of graph X and the final (ending sound) of graph Y to determine the sound of a third graph, Z. Occasionally, X Y *fan* (three graphs) is written simply as XY (one graph). In this practice, both graphs—in their entirety—are fused to form a single graph. Once again, this shows not only that late imperial Chinese scholars were capable of phonological analysis that had the potential to evolve into true spelling but also that the sinographic writing system—much less Sinitic languages—was not ineradicably monosyllabic and monomorphemic.

In fact, at the earliest known stage of the Chinese script, that of the SBIs, it was not at all uncommon for two or even three syllables to be written together as a single graph, for example, Yi-tsu (a name), *san-wan* (thirty thousand), and *shih-wu-fa* (fifteen expeditions). Bisyllabic graphs are also often found in bronze inscriptions from the Chou period, for instance, *hsiao-tzu* (little son), *hsiao-ch'en* (lesser vassal), Wu Wang (King Wu), and Wen Wang (King Wen). Thus, it is evident that, at the earliest known stage of Chinese writing, there was still a clear understanding that graphs (and apparently lexical units as well) could have more than one syllable. By the Ch'in and Han periods, however, the monosyllabicizing tendencies of the script had eliminated nearly all bisyllabic and trisyllabic graphs from the texts that were deemed worthy of preservation and transmission. But the intuitive sense that lexical items could be polysyllabic persisted, and so graphs of more than one syllable continued to be created, such as *pu-yung* (don't), *erh-shih* (twenty), *san-shih* (thirty), and *ssu-shih* (forty). Yet the pressure to conform to the monosyllabic constraints of the script was so compelling that fusion and other special pronunciations for these expressions soon arose (respectively *peng*, *nien*, *sa*, and *hsi*). Nonetheless, the bisyllabic and polysyllabic nature of much of the Sinitic lexicon is undeniable. Furthermore, as seen above, many Sinitic morphemes consist of more than one syllable. Consequently, it is probably best to think of the script as morphophonetic or semantophonetic (rather than simply as morphosyllabic) in the sense that its basic units convey both sound and meaning, but that the length of the units is not necessarily always a single syllable.

Whether we agree to call the script as a whole logographic, morphosyllabic, or morphophonetic/semantophonetic, most sinographs (roughly 85 percent) consist of a component that conveys sound (the phonophore) and a component that conveys meaning (the radical or semantic classifier). Neither component, however, tells the reader exactly what the character means or precisely how it sounds but only gives a more or less vague approximation of the meaning and the sound. For example, the reader may encounter a character whose semantic classifier consists of three dots vertically stacked on the left side. This indicates that the graph in all likelihood (but not necessarily) has something to do with water or liquid substances, hence we might guess that the graph means "wave," "splash," "shallow," and so forth. But, judging from this "water" radical alone, we cannot be sure exactly what the graph means, only that it probably has something vaguely to do with aqueousness or liquidity. More than two thousand graphs share the "water" radical, with meanings running the gamut from "eternal" to "pure," "stream," "islet," "the Milky Way," "mercury," "float," "swim," "basket for catching fish," "bubbles," "varnish," "sap," "juice," "gravy," "oil," "wine," "briny," "drench," "drivel," "diarrhea," "spit," "damp," "stagnant," "mud," "licentious," "tears," and "Macao"; merely recognizing the semantic classifier of a character is not necessarily of much use in determining its meaning. Similarly, the reader may encounter a character whose phonophore may be variously pronounced in tonal variations of *fang, pang, p'ang,* and *peng* (with meanings ranging from "square" to "boat," "loosen," "neglect," "banish," "fragrant," "dike," "a kind of pottery," "the name of a place," "a surname," "heavy snowfall," "side," "oar," and "voluminous flow [of rain, tears, etc.]") and whose semantic classifier indicates that it has something to do with "door." Only through the combination of its two components, the phonophore and the semantic classifier, does the practiced reader realize that this particular character stands for a morpheme pronounced *fang* in the second tone and meaning "house, building." This morpheme can occur in LS as a word by itself, but in MSM it usually occurs in combination with noun suffixes or near synonyms to form bisyllabic words, for example, *fang-tzu* (house), *fang-chien* (room), and *lou-fang* (multistory building). In addition, in trying to determine the meaning of the graph in question, we have for the moment ignored the fact that this same phonophore (pronounced in tonal variations of *fang, pang, p'ang,* and *peng*) may itself serve as a semantic classifier in characters pronounced *yü* (in, at, on, by, from), *shih* (act, do, make, bestow, grant), *yu* (swim, rove about freely), and so on and in characters with a bewildering variety of pronunciations that mean "flag, banner, flutter," and so forth. In one character pronounced *p'ang* (most commonly: side), *pang, peng,* and *p'eng,* it simultaneously functions as both phonophore and semantic classifier.

Moreover, many characters of this basic type (those consisting of a phonophore and a semantic classifier) have multiple readings that cannot be explained by simple processes of phonological derivation. For example, the character pronounced *shih,* mentioned above as meaning "act, do, make, bestow, grant," actually has the following specific readings (the superscript numbers signify different tones): *shih*^{1} (with the verbal meanings given), *yi*^{2} (an adverb meaning "[follow] furtively"), *yi*^{4} (an adjective meaning "extended [continuously/lengthily]"), and *shi*^{3} (in mostly colloquial bisyllabic or quadrisyllabic words with a wide range of meanings such as "abandon," "release," and "indecisive"). In such cases (and there are thousands of such characters with more than a single pronunciation—one of these "split sound" [*p'o-yin*] or "multiple sound" [*to-yin*] characters has as many as eleven different pronunciations), the reader must depend on context and intuition to decide how to pronounce the character and what it means.

This type of character consisting of semantic classifier plus phonophore, it should be pointed out, is the relatively easier type of character to process. To read the remaining 15 to 20 percent of characters, the reader must rely totally on memorization to extract sound and meaning from shape.

Regardless of the complexities just mentioned in the category of characters consisting of semantic classifier plus phonophore, their preponderance amply justifies labeling the writing system as morphosyllabic or morphophonetic. Furthermore, since the phonetic half of this term is by far the more important, the Chinese script can be viewed as basically a syllabic or phonetic system of writing with secondary accretions of semantic elements. It comprises an unstandardized syllabary that, if standardized, would make it possible to present the syllables of MSM with only about four hundred graphs without tonal indication or thirteen hundred graphs with indication of tones. Instead of this simple 1:1 correspondence, in the common database of some sixty-five hundred characters in computer usage, the ratio of written characters to spoken syllables is either 5:1 or 16:1, depending on whether tones are indicated. This may be compared to estimates ranging from 15:1 to 40:1 for the forty or so phonemes of the similarly unstandardized English system of writing, in which semantic-phonetic spellings like sent, cent, and scent suggest a parallel label for English as a morphophonemic system of writing.

When we comprehend that we are dealing with a writing system consisting of well over fifty thousand discrete units conveying both sound and meaning, it becomes readily apparent that the Chinese characters (to put it daintily) constitute a high-maintenance script. Only those who devote great amounts of time to the sinographs can achieve a reasonable degree of proficiency with them. Even such a common word as "sneeze" (*ta-p'en-t'i*) is unexpectedly difficult to write in characters, to the point that few Chinese (including those with advanced degrees) are capable of committing it to paper. The graph used to write the second syllable of Hsin-chiang/Sinkiang (literally, "New Frontier"; the far western Uyghur Autonomous Region, which occupies approximately one-sixth of the territory of China) has nineteen strokes and is so annoying to write that many people, out of pure frustration, either chop off the top half of the phonophore on the right side or substitute the homophonic graph used to write "Yangtze" (*chiang*), which only has six strokes, although it is "illegal" to do so. Similarly, the graph used to write the character for "dance" (*wu*) has fourteen strokes, leading those who frequent discothèques to replace it with the homophonous character for "noon," which has only four strokes. Another very common character, that for "street" (*chieh*), has twelve strokes; since it has to be written so often, it is tempting for those in a hurry to discard all but a few of the six strokes in the central portion of the graph. None of these three graphs (*chiang, wu, chieh*) has an officially recognized simplified form, but with the average graph in the Chinese writing system consisting of more than twelve strokes, one can readily see that the incentive to coin them is high and always has been. The most widely used phonetic writing systems (e.g., the Roman alphabet and Japanese *kana*) ultimately derive from much more complicated forms, so the natural tendency for Chinese informally to reduce the number of strokes in the characters could lead to phonetic writing for Chinese. However, the strong resistance by the government and the intellectuals has so far prevented that from happening.

The graph used to write what is by far the most frequent morpheme in Mandarin, *te*, deserves special attention. It signifies, among other things, the possessive case, adjectival endings, relative clauses, prepositional phrases, and nouns made from verbs and adjectives. This graph occurs approximately once out of every twenty characters in an average text (!), consists of eight strokes, and is so troublesome to write, even in cursive script, that some people—in private communications—now insert the Roman letter "d" as a substitute (abbreviating the spelling of the morpheme as *de* in the pinyin system of romanization). No acceptable simplified form of the graph has yet been devised, much less officially sanctioned. An even greater irony is that the graph used to write the ubiquitous morpheme *te* also still carries its original meaning of "bright, brilliant; target" with the pronunciation *ti*^{2} (pronounced *tiek* over a thousand years ago and perhaps **tiawk* more than two thousand years ago).

Many writers now privately pepper their compositions with the letter "d," which stands for the frequently used morpheme *te* (pronounced *duh*). This enormously multivalent morpheme is actually at least three separate homophonic morphemes collapsed into one, but formally written with three separate characters. It is interesting that none of the three characters used to write these three extremely high-frequency morphemes originally meant what the morphemes signify but each was adapted: 1. as seen above, the *te* marking possession and relative clauses is written with a graph that really means "target"; 2. the *te* marking verbal complements is written with a character that originally meant "get, obtain": and 3. the *te* for adverbial endings is written with a character that originally meant "land, ground" and was pronounced *ti.* The fact that three of the highest-frequency morphemes in Mandarin (together they account for roughly 6.5 percent of the characters in a typical text!) are written with semantically "bleached" graphs that originally had totally different meanings underscores the gulf between the sinographic writing system and vernacular language addressed earlier in this chapter. It is no wonder, then, that some writers resort to "d," which can be written with one stroke (i.e., without taking one's pen, pencil, or brush off the writing surface), instead of characters that require eight, ten, and six strokes respectively.

The extraordinarily intricate and difficult nature of the script inevitably had important consequences for literacy and literature. Some of the social, linguistic, and esthetic implications of the script will become obvious in the following discussion and throughout the rest of this book.

TRADITIONAL LANGUAGE STUDIES IN CHINA

It is revealing that traditional Chinese language studies are called *hsiao-hsüeh* (literally, "minor learning"), in contrast to *ta-hsüeh* ("major learning"), which was held to be more substantial and dealt with moral and political issues. Pre-Buddhist Chinese *hsiao-hsüeh*—starting from the early centuries of the Common Era—dealt almost exclusively with the writing system and had very little to say about language per se. (In MSM, under the influence of Japanese, *ta-hsüeh* has come to mean "university" and *hsiao-hsüeh* has come to signify "primary school.") It was Buddhism that coaxed the reluctant Chinese intelligentsia to pay token attention to spoken language in addition to their cherished script. But, until well into the twentieth century, traditional language studies in China focused largely on the characters and paid scant attention to speech.

The fact that *hsiao-hsüeh* has come to mean "primary school" and *ta-hsüeh* has come to mean "university," in emulation of Japanese *shōgaku* and *daigaku*, which are written with the same sinographs, points to an interesting aspect of the formation of the modern Sinitic lexicon. Namely, hundreds of important words (especially in the fields of science, culture, sociology, economics, and education) were originally borrowed by Japanese from Chinese in premodern times with one meaning, then fitted with a new (usually Western-inspired) meaning by Japanese, and finally borrowed back into Sinitic with the newly attached meaning. Among these lexical items, which can be called "roundtrip words," are those for "literature," "culture," "civilization," "grammar," "analysis," "physics," "(graphite) pencil," "speech, oration, lecture, address," "satire," "B.A.," "Ph.D.," "art," "pass a resolution," "concrete" (opposite of abstract), "insurance, safe, sure," "feudal," "aspect," "law," "model," "guarantee," "expression," "idea" (in psychology), "meaning, significance, implication," "freedom, liberty," "residence, domicile," "accounting," "(social) class," "reconstruct, reform," "revolution," "environment," "course, curriculum," "plan," "manager," "economics, economical," "right(s)," "self-criticism," "mechanical," "opportunity," "mechanism, gear, office, organ, body" (the last three in the political or institutional sense), "rule, regulation," "protest," "(mimeographed or printed) teaching materials, lecture notes," "intentionally," "association, social intercourse, communication," "negotiate," "structure," "education," "professor," "republican (form of government)," "labor," "comprehend, grasp," "popular," "politics," "society," "progress," "credit," "support," "thought," "nature," "means, measure," "religion," "chairman," "staple food," "speculator, opportunist," "movement," "budget," "guerrilla," and "unique, sole." (A particularly interesting word of this type is the Sinitic equivalent of the English word "China." This derives from the predynastic name Ch'in, which was borrowed into Sanskrit as *Cīna*, then passed back into Sinitic in transcribed form already by at least the T'ang period as *Chih-na*, whence it traveled to Japan as *Shina*. Thus *Chih-na* is essentially a "double-round-trip" word. The Mandarin name *Chih-na* is now generally avoided in China itself because of the experience of World War II, when it became tainted in the mouths of Japanese soldiers and officials, although some writers still use it occasionally for special historical effect.) A much larger subset of modern Sinitic words (including those equivalent to English words ending in "—ology" and "—ism") were initially devised by the Japanese to match Western concepts and then borrowed by the Chinese. Unlike the roundtrip words enumerated above, this type of word did not originally exist in Sinitic with other meanings.

The first thorough examination of the Chinese script, one that is still quoted virtually as gospel for matters relating to the characters, is Hsü Shen's *Shuo-wen chieh-tzu* (Explanation of Simple and Compound Graphs), completed in 100 C.E. Hsü divided up all Chinese characters into six types:

1. *Chih-shih* (indicative), which are ideographs.
2. *Hsiang-hsing* (representational), which are pictographs.
3. *Hsing-sheng* (pictophonetic), consisting of a meaning-bearing classifier and a sound-bearing component; the majority of characters belong to this category.
4. *Hui-yi* (conjunct), whose meanings are allegedly derived from the combined meanings of their components (e.g., *jen* [person] + *yen* [speech] = *hsin* [trust]); this is a fallacious category, since no character actually evolved in this manner.
5. *Chuan-chu* (transferred), an obscure category that is intended to explain supposedly related words written with visually similar, though slightly transformed, graphs; pairs of characters differentiated by minimal diacritical changes.
6. *Chia-chieh* (borrowed), a category for dealing with homophones that was relatively prominent in bronze inscriptional writing.

The kind of graphic analysis exemplified by Hsü's six categories of characters is what usually passes for "etymology" in China. In fact, there has never been a rigorous, systematic etymological science for Sinitic languages. Genuine etymology deals with the origin and historical development of words, as evinced by the study of their basic elements, earliest known use, and changes in form and meaning. It involves the phonological and semantic analysis of the roots of basic lexical items and morphological components, together with their combination in words consisting of more than one such element. Etymology is concerned with the origins and evolution of words, not with the development of script(s). An etymological dictionary of Sinitic is finally being compiled by an international team of scholars and should be available early in the twenty-first century.

Another drawback of *Shuo-wen chieh-tzu* is that even its graphic analysis is based on the small seal script dating to around the end of the third century

B.C.E. The small seal script was already very different from the bronze and oracle shell-bone inscriptional forms that preceded it by as much as a millennium. As a result, Hsü's explanations of the visual forms of the graphs are often seriously flawed. Similarly, being unaware of the tremendous phonological transformations that had occurred between the time of the origins of the script and his own day, Hsü is often far from the mark when he analyzes the sounds conveyed by the characters. Despite these deficiencies, Hsü Shen is recognized as the founder of language (more accurately, "script") studies in China, and his *Shuowen chieh-tzu* established a benchmark for all later work in this area.

One of Hsü Shen's greatest contributions is that he grappled with the monumental problem of how to order the thousands of characters, a problem that still haunts information specialists. Hsü's solution was to isolate 540 elements of the script that he designated as semantic classifiers. He then proceeded to group all extant characters under one of the 540 classifiers or "radicals," as they are commonly called. Later, this number was reduced to 214, as in the famous K'ang-hsi dictionary of the early Ch'ing dynasty (an ordering that was actually already established in 1615 by Mei Ying-tso). The formidable nature of such a system can readily be grasped when one considers the following realities: 1. a single character may include two, three, or more classifiers, making it hard to choose the correct one (*chang* [emblem, statute, chapter] has only eleven strokes but no fewer than five possible classifiers); 2. the classifier may appear in a distorted form because of the procrustean manner in which it is made to fit into the square shape of all characters; 3. even after one successfully identifies the "correct" classifier, there may still be hundreds of characters that share that same key, raising the intimidating question of how to order logically the characters grouped under it (usually this is done by counting the number of residual strokes that remain after subtracting the strokes of the classifier, though the actual number of strokes is itself frequently ambiguous and there may yet be well over a hundred characters with, for example, the "tree" or "heart" radical plus eight residual strokes). Apart from the difficulty of locating specific characters by means of the system of classifiers devised by Hsü Shen, after this system was securely in place, it more or less precluded the gradual evolution of the script into a purely phonetic syllabary because it insisted that all characters consisting of more than one element (the overwhelming majority) be analyzed in such a manner that they could be thought of as bearing a semantic component—whether or not the designated semantic component was truly operative in the etymological development of the word signified by the graph in question.

The mind-boggling challenge of how to order (and, conversely, how to locate) the tens of thousands of Chinese characters led to the creation of many other methods. Traditional Chinese encyclopedias were often organized according to thesaurus-like concepts (such as "heaven," "earth," "man," "weather," "animals," or "plants"). After the assimilation and elaboration of

Indian phonology, characters were grouped according to a highly technical system of rhyme categories. Hundreds of additional methods have been devised for ordering and finding Chinese characters (types of strokes at all four corners, types of strokes at top left and bottom right, types of strokes in succession, and so forth). Most of these schemes were invented during the fiercely efficiency-minded twentieth century under the pressure of international economic and cultural competition formerly not encountered by Chinese lexicographers. Increasingly, speakers of Sinitic languages are finding it simplest and fastest to locate characters by the romanization of their sounds. (This is proved by the tattered and soiled alphabetical indices at the back of library dictionaries as well as by the most prevalent computer input methods used by those who are not professional typists.) And, for whole words (monosyllabic, bisyllabic, and polysyllabic), a single-sort alphabetical order is becoming the preferred method over an ordering by head (initial) characters. This is as true of lexicography as it is of information and computer sciences.

Aside from *Shuo-wen chieh-tzu*, another landmark work in traditional Chinese language studies is *Shih-ming* (Explanation of Terms), written by Liu Hsi around 200 C.E. Its chief analytical technique is to use homophones or near-homophones to explain words. Thus, in essence, it attempts to explain the origins and relations of words through paronomasia (punning). Although this makes *Shih-ming* somewhat valuable for phonological research, it is hardly reliable for semantic and etymological studies.

To summarize the main thrust of this section and the two sections that went before it, Chinese characters constitute a script that is neither fully phonetic nor fully semantic. The script works only through the combination of its partially phonetic and partially semantic properties. This quintessentially dual nature of the sinographs makes them unique among the world's extant functioning scripts and has important implications for art and for literature.

ESTHETIC ASPECTS OF CHINESE CHARACTERS

The preceding sections aim to clear up several serious misconceptions concerning the sinographs, but one widely held view about them is indisputable: they are beautiful. Furthermore, the fact that even those who are totally illiterate in the script generally consider it esthetically pleasing is a collective recognition of its beauty. As shown above, the script is not pictographic, but it is nonetheless highly visual; thus the characters readily lend themselves to calligraphic treatment. When a calligrapher writes a series of characters having to do with trees, water, and mountains, he may impart to them wooden, splashing, and rockily soaring effects. Even when the visual aspect is less overt, the emotions of the calligrapher can readily find outlet in the proliferation of forms that make up the Chinese script. Such expression of emotion is, of course, also possible with Arabic, Roman, and other scripts, but not to such a seemingly unlimited extent.

The importance of calligraphy in the world of the Chinese scholar and statesman can scarcely be overstated. From the oracle shell and bone inscriptions, to bronze inscriptions, the development of numerous regional variants during the Spring and Autumn period (722–481/463 B.C.E.) and the Warring States period, and the (re)unification of the script under the first emperor of the Ch'in (Ch'in Shih Huang-ti), and then through the evolution of the major calligraphic styles—great seal (*ta-chuan*), small seal (*hsiao-chuan*), clerical style (*li-shu*), regular style (*k'ai-shu*), running style (*hsing-shu*), and grass style (*ts'ao-shu*)—each stage of the Chinese script was practiced and preserved as a type of calligraphy long after the time of its initial currency. Calligraphy was central to the life of the literatus, hence the expression "Four Treasures of a [Scholar's] Study" (*wen-fang ssu-pao*): paper, ink stick, ink slab, and writing brush. Even today, the gift of a piece of calligraphy from a famous personage is much esteemed, and talented calligraphers are avidly sought after to provide their brushwork for book titles, store signs, and other public displays of writing. This great love of the Chinese for their script spread to the rest of East Asia—Japan, Korea, and Vietnam—and, indeed, the earliest known writing in all three of these countries was done with Chinese characters (see chapters 53, 54, and 55).

The highly visual nature of the Chinese script tends to blur the boundary between literature and art. A poet who wrote his verse on a wall (and many did) was doing something quite different from someone who merely chanted his lines aloud. Inevitably, he was expressing himself both visually and literarily. Likewise, a calligrapher who wrote a poem on a hanging scroll could not escape conveying the verbal sentiments of the verse at the same time as he expressed himself through the thickness of strokes, the density of the ink, the placement of the characters, and so forth.

Because the dividing line between art and literature in China was not always firm, it became common to illustrate poems with paintings and to cover paintings with written comments, flamboyant signatures, and the impressions of elaborately engraved seals. The appreciation of such hybrid works of literature and art transcends either the verbal or the visual alone.

The conjoining of poetry and painting thus became a characteristic feature of Chinese culture (see chapter 25) in a way that is almost unthinkable for cultures that use alphabets or syllabaries. The purely phonetic qualities of alphabets and syllabaries lead to a dichotomy between the verbal and the visual. Conversely, the semiphonetic, semisemantic nature of the Chinese script bridges that dichotomy and naturally lends itself to subtle intermediary forms of art and literature: palindromes, anagrams, visual puns and riddles, sculptures that are also steles with inscriptions, maps that are paintings, drawings that are maps, characters or groups of characters that are figures, and so forth. Whereas critics, both in the East and in the West, have often argued that the nature of the Chinese script may have inhibited the development of certain modes of abstract and analytical thought to which those in the West are accustomed (epistemology, ontology, linear logic, Cartesian realism, hypothetical propositions, etc.) and may have been inimical to the full flowering of vernacular literatures, its greatest strength lay in its tremendous concreteness. Those who are familiar with the script realize that it opens up vistas of seeing, feeling, and thinking that are not so readily available to users of purely phonetic scripts.

Implications for Literature

The special features of the sinographic script have had an enormous impact on Chinese literature. The influences of the Chinese script on literature range from technical, linguistic aspects of writing to sociological and attitudinal matters.

First, the sinographic script enjoyed tremendous prestige in China. Those who mastered it possessed unparalleled power. Even those who were totally illiterate held the script in awe. This almost numinous quality of the characters is brought home powerfully in the 1984 film *Huang t'u-ti* (Yellow Earth). In this film, peasants who know no characters, and cannot afford to hire a scribe, paste auspicious couplets on their doorframes in hopes that they will bring good fortune. What is shocking, however, is that the couplets consist of empty circles meant to stand for characters.

It is worth pondering what it was about the script that made it so exalted. Undoubtedly, many facets could be listed: innate qualities, monumental heritage, religious and ideological associations, and so on. However numerous such factors may be, they were all undergirded by the paramount sociopolitical authority of those few individuals who were capable of wielding the script with proficiency (roughly 2 percent of the population), that is, being able to write polished LS in approved styles. For more than two thousand years (starting with the texts called *tui-ts'e* [topical replies] inaugurated in 178 B.C.E. during the reign of the Han emperor Wen-ti [r. 180–157 B.C.E.] and continuing sporadically until 1905, particularly from the seventh century on), such proficiency was measured by performance on the celebrated civil service examinations (usually called *k'o-chü*). Those who demonstrated advanced writing ability on the higher examinations were all but assured posts in the upper ranks of officialdom. With such appointments almost invariably came wealth and power. Consequently, virtually anyone of ability aspired to pass the examinations because it meant that not only would he himself be honored but his entire extended family would likely experience prosperity for generations.

The prestige of the script was so great that it clearly privileged writing over speech. This is the opposite of the experience in India, Greece, and other ancient cultures, where the priest, the seer, the orator, and the bard were respected because they carried wisdom and beauty in their minds and could flawlessly recite the texts that embodied them when called upon to do so. The dominance of writing over speech in China was the result of the unquestioned authority of the literati, who were proficient in the esoteric script and, in turn, produced a particular configuration of literary forms. Ranked at the top of the hierarchy were history (which recorded the affairs of the rulers and their officials), moral disquisitions (which reinforced the sociopolitical order), and lyric verse (which expressed the deepest aspirations of the literati). Thus the complicated writing system and the literati-dominated sociopolitical order buttressed each other and resisted alternative possibilities.

Historians of Chinese literature have often been puzzled by the fragmentary state of ancient Chinese myth and the lack of great epics comparable to the *Mahābhārata* and *Rāmāyaṇa*, the *Iliad* and the *Odyssey*. Myths and epics are essentially narratives, originally the preserve of oral "singers of tales," and were naturally ranked low on the scale of genres in ancient China. Eventually narrative genres did develop, but they had to do so, first, under the guise of history (see chapter 26), especially historical biography (see chapter 27), and, second, but more unabashedly, on the coattails of Buddhism, which brought to China the unfettered and exuberant Indian love of good stories.

The second salient feature of Chinese characters, obvious to anyone who looks at them, is that each one fits within the confines of a square. Whether a character has two strokes or forty-two (one character actually has sixty-four strokes!), it is supposed to fit neatly in the same size box; hence the characters have also been called *fang-k'uai-tzu* (square-graphs or tetragraphs). Furthermore, the majority of characters are morphemes (or are viewed as morphemes) with a strong semantic carrying capacity in and of themselves. Finally, the characters have traditionally been written in continuous strings (limited only by the length of the surface on which they were written), without any breaks or spaces and without any punctuation. The implications of these facts about the script for language and literature are profound. Relevant phenomena that were complemented by the special qualities of the Chinese script can be listed as follows: 1. dropping of inflectional affixes, 2. ellipsis of many parts of words and sentences that are not absolutely essential for conveying the gist of meaning, 3. extreme emphasis on parallelism (lexical, grammatical, and syntactical), both in poetry and in prose, 4. strong preference for bisyllabic pairing and structuring, 5. obligatory word order (subject-verb-object, modifer preceding the modified) with inversion only in the most extraordinary circumstances (unlike Latin and other inflected languages, in which it is both customary and easy to move elements of the sentence around for dramatic effect). It is obvious that these phenomena would all color Chinese literature in various ways.

The history of Chinese literature is full of specific instances of the effect these qualities (and other characteristics of the script mentioned in this chapter) had on writing. In general, they put a premium on brevity; valued the expression of emotions, feelings, and impressions over logical and analytical thought; and evoked concrete images over abstract concepts. When Chinese authors, lexicographers, and commentators wished to define something, they often resorted to paronomasia. When one character sounded like another character, the two characters could be used to explain each other, regardless of the actual origins of the words represented by the characters. Although this is a perilous method of conducting etymological investigations, nearly all premodern Chinese scholars believed in it implicitly and resorted to it frequently. To indulge in a small pun of our own, this is a graphic demonstration of the power and prestige of the Chinese script. Such substantial power and prestige allowed the sinographic script to shape not only literature but even—to a certain extent—language itself.

CURRENT SITUATION AND FUTURE PROSPECTS

The Sinitic language group has probably been in existence for at least four thousand years; the sinographic script has been in use for more than thirty-two hundred years; Chinese literary texts have been composed for approximately twenty-six hundred years. Thus the Chinese literary tradition is of great antiquity. Although, like the Chinese political and ideological system, it exhibited great overall stability and continuity throughout its long history, it was not without significant change. The script was transformed, the languages evolved, genres came and went, literary trends waxed and waned. In the twentieth century, however, the magnitude of the changes undergone by the script and the languages, together with the impact of these changes on literature, was so great that one can legitimately ponder whether future changes of similar magnitude will result in entirely new forms of language and literature in China.

When the Ch'ing dynasty was overthrown in 1911, along with it collapsed the bureaucratic institutions and imperial structures that had been in place for more than two thousand years. As the literati-bureaucrats disappeared, the Confucian-oriented examination system that had selected them was dismantled and the by then moribund literary language that sustained them was rejected. Although the promise of the democratic institutions and vernacular language (both advocated by Chinese reformers of the 1920s and 1930s) that were to have replaced them has not yet been completely fulfilled, it is extremely unlikely that the imperial state, the Confucian bureaucracy, and the literary language will ever be revived—regardless of the agitation for a "New Confucianism" (*Hsin ju-chiao*) among a few overseas scholars and their associates within China.

Even before the overthrow of the Ch'ing government and inspired at least in part by the alphabetical initiatives of the Jesuit scholars Matteo Ricci (1522–1610) and Nicolas Trigault (1577–1628), Chinese language reformers had been arguing in favor of a script that would be easier for China's masses to master. The defects of the Chinese characters were wittily examined in the twelve sections of *Men-wai wen-t'an* (An Outsider's Chats on Script), a small book written in 1934 by Lu Hsün (1881–1936), China's most renowned twentieth-century author. Near the end of his life, Lu Hsün is widely reported to have declared from his sickbed, "If the Chinese characters are not eradicated, China will certainly perish!" (*Han-tzu pu mieh, Chung-kuo pi wang!*). Even if Lu Hsün did not really say these exact words, there were those in the late 1930s who wished to represent him as having done so. Regardless of how it came into circulation, such an extreme statement shows the depth of feelings that the characters are capable of evoking.

The Republican government that followed the Ch'ing dynasty actually went part way toward realizing the aims of the Chinese script reformers in devising two auxiliary phonetic scripts, the National Phonetic Symbols (also informally referred to as *po-p'o-mo-fo*) and National Romanization (Gwoyeu Romatzyh), an ingenious system of tonal spelling. The custodians of the Republican government took both of these systems to Taiwan in 1949 when they were defeated by Communist forces. The latter, for their part, wasted little time in carrying out even more radical language reform policies. Rather than using the National Phonetic Symbols and National Romanization, the Communists established a romanization called pinyin (literally, "spelling"—written *p'in-yin* in Wade-Giles transcription). Pinyin is now recognized by the United Nations and the International Standards Organization as the official standard for the transcription of MSM. In China, it is (or, at different times, has been) widely used on signage and for semaphore, telegraphy, archeological notation, scientific terminology and formulations, and computer applications. (Chinese Braille has always used one or another phonetically based system of spelling and does not indicate significs.) All schoolchildren in China learn to read and write with pinyin and, in some experimental school districts, students are permitted to continue to use pinyin until the sixth grade. In addition, the government has now issued orthographic rules for pinyin, specifying how and when to leave spaces between words, capitalization, italicization, and so forth, none of which was a concern for those who wrote only in characters. (Some specialists, among them the prominent information scientist Feng Chih-wei [Zhiwei], have even seriously proposed the adoption of word division in character texts.) Although originally intended as a type of phonetic annotation and auxiliary script for specialized applications, pinyin is now gradually assuming the status of a full partner in a de facto digraphia. The other partner in this emerging digraphia, the sinographic script, has itself changed so remarkably as to cause problems of recognition and production for those who have not been living in the People's Republic of China for the past thirty or forty years. Literally thousands of common characters have been subjected to drastic simplification or elimination. The simplified characters used in mainland China and the traditional/"complex" characters used on Taiwan are so dissimilar as to constitute two separate sets, each with a different look and a different feel. Furthermore, when premodern texts are printed in simplified characters, as is now standard practice in China, it often leads to ambiguity and confusion, since one simplified character may stand for several traditional characters. In simplifying the characters, the PRC government aimed to reduce illiteracy by making the complicated, time-consuming script easier to learn and use. Since most Chinese citizens seem to agree and are quite happy to go on using the simplified characters, ultimately a trigraphia might develop: simplified characters for most normal purposes including modern literature, traditional characters for classical and historical studies, and pinyin for technical and international purposes. In fact, such a trigraphia to a certain extent already reflects the present state of affairs. Consequently, one might argue that "the Chinese writing system," taken as a whole at the beginning of the twenty-first century, is composed of all three subsystems: simplified characters, traditional characters, and the Roman alphabet.

While some authors may regard this complicated situation with dismay as depressingly chaotic, others have welcomed it as a challenge and have begun to experiment with new forms of writing that confront the complexity head-on. The contemporary artist Hsü Ping (b. 1955) has created numerous works consisting of what he calls *t'ien-shu* (heavenly writing). Hsü's books and installations consist of thousands of carefully executed characters that look like traditional forms, but not one of them is real. What Hsü has done is to juggle the components of the traditional characters and rearrange them in their customary square shape. Viewers sometimes puzzle and strain for hours to "read" Hsü's art/literature, but few of them are able to make any "sense" of it. Hsü's amazing achievement has been to deconstruct simultaneously both traditional Chinese literature and traditional Chinese art, while reaffirming the close bond between them.

Some writers have begun to play with pinyin mixed in among Chinese characters. A notorious example was the 1980s spoken drama "Wo-men" (Us), which had its title written only in pinyin ("Women") and used pinyin for the first-person plural pronoun *wo-men* (we, us) throughout in some versions of the script. It is difficult to determine precisely what the authors (a collective from a military unit, no less!) meant by this usage (perhaps a subtle pun on the English word written with the same letters?—a so-called *faux ami*), but the government was sufficiently incensed to ban the play before it actually opened.

The use of Roman letters in modern Chinese literature extends even further to the insertion of whole words and sentences from European languages. The Taiwan poet Tu Yeh (b. 1953) skillfully plays on how the English word "love" fits snugly inside the word "glove" like a hand. Mainland authors write about the glory of *Zhina*, the pinyin romanization of *Chih-na* (in Wade-Giles romanization). Indeed, the Latin alphabet unequivocally has already become an integral part of the Chinese writing system. There is, of course, Lu Hsün's famous story about "Ah Q" (see chapter 39), which has made it necessary to include the letter "Q" in Chinese dictionaries. And there are *X-kuang* (x-rays), *T-hsü* (T-shirt; Cantonese, *T-shoet*), *BP-chi* (beeper), and so forth, with endless new terms of this sort being borrowed or coined year after year. The permutations and combinations of Chinese characters and Roman letters will continue to grow.

Some émigré authors and overseas Chinese have begun to write about Chinese subjects in English and other foreign languages (e.g., Ha Chin [Ha Jin]).

Indeed, Asian-American novelists such as Amy Tan and Maxine Hong Kingston have broken into the bestseller ranks by writing about their Chinese heritage. And there are countless overseas authors, such as the science fiction writer Chang Hsi-kuo (b. 1944), who use Chinese characters to write about non-Chinese subjects. In such instances, we can speak of the internationalization of Chinese literature. As the Chinese diaspora increases, the international dimensions of Chinese literature will expand.

More than anything, however, the Internet will transform Chinese writing and Chinese literature beyond recognition. This is already happening at an unbelievably rapid pace. Why? First, some fundamentals. It is technically feasible to transmit and receive Chinese characters over the Internet. There are many commercially available software programs that permit sinographic access to the Internet. However, compared to programs using alphabetic transmission, those allowing sinographic access are relatively costly and cumbersome. In terms of information science, the Chinese script is semantically redundant but phonetically deficient, whereas electronic language-processing systems thrive on phonetic redundancy and are relatively unfussy about the semantic deficiency of the individual components of a writing system. The cybernetics of the sinographic script are such that each unit or graph requires two bytes of memory instead of one byte, as for the letters of the alphabet. Whereas 2^8 (= 256) characters are sufficient to represent all the letters (upper- and lowercase), numerals, and punctuation marks of an alphabetic script, 2^{16} (= 65,536) characters are necessary to represent most, but by no means all, of the sinographs. The colossal cybernetic dimensions of the Chinese script can be grasped by recognizing that a streamlined version of it takes up roughly 75 percent of the total code-space allocation of Unicode, which is designed to accommodate all the scripts and symbols in the world that are employed in electronic information processing. Inputting alone presents challenges so major that many people are unwilling to face them. As discussed above, there are hundreds of ways to order (and hence look up) Chinese characters in dictionaries. Similarly, there are hundreds of ways to identify specific characters for inputting in computers. Most nonprofessional users in China, Japan, and elsewhere are opting for some sort of romanized inputting with more or less automatic conversion to characters. But problems of word division and homophony, and especially a predilection for literary (i.e., classical) styles of writing, render even romanized inputting of characters extremely frustrating and time-consuming. Consequently, many Chinese Internet users are turning directly to Roman letters without conversion to characters.

There are two main ways to use Roman letters on the Internet. The first, and most prevalent, way is simply to write in English. The number of Chinese who have learned English primarily to gain access to the Internet is breathtaking. The second, whose adherents are much fewer and increasing at a much slower rate, is to write in the romanized form of one of the Sinitic languages. Mandarin is undoubtedly the most popular of these romanized Sinitic languages on the Internet, but Cantonese, Shanghainese, and Taiwanese are also used. Taiwanese, in particular, has a number of active Web sites and many individuals who exchange letters using romanization. As these languages are being applied to real-life functions and for practical purposes, they are developing conventions that can enable them to become full-fledged written vernaculars. Already, Internet authors are experimenting with poems, essays, and other genres. It may seem paradoxical that this modern, foreign technology is enabling the ancient, regional vernaculars of China to acquire the written voice they never had. Yet, when we recall that it was another foreign intermediary (Buddhism) that prompted the initial development of the written vernacular *koine* nearly two thousand years ago, the current situation is not so odd after all.

CONCLUSION

First came Proto-Sinitic, which eventually evolved into a group of languages with various branches, dialects, and subdialects. Then came the sinographic script, which was first used for recording the laconic oracle texts of the Shang diviners, was then adapted for use on bronze inscriptions, and eventually was elaborated into a script that was sufficiently flexible for writing on virtually any subject. However, because of the rather refractory media on which it was first written (bone, shell, and metal) and because of the lack of competing scripts in East Asia and surrounding regions, once the highly elliptical style of LS and the somewhat awkward semantosyllabic, tetragraphic properties of the script were established, they survived essentially intact.

Its literary language and sinographic script in place, China proceeded to produce a wealth of literature. The early literature dealt mostly with ethical and political thought, history, and lyrical impulses. Already by Western Han times, though, authors were striving to create new, more belletristic types of writing. Notable among these was the *fu* (rhapsody, rhyme-prose), which makes a pretense of being purely a beautiful catalog of lush verbiage, complete with moralistic retractions tacked on at the end of individual pieces and, indeed, retrospective denials of whole oeuvres by authors who wished to ensure that no one would condemn them for having written mere frivolous literature.

With the advent of Buddhism in China, however, a sea change occurred in language and literature. The remarkable linguistic and literary transformations precipitated by Buddhism can be subsumed under the following rubrics: 1. partial legitimization of the vernacular; 2. enlargement of the lexicon by at least thirty-five thousand words, including many that are still in common use (e.g., *fang-pien* [convenient; from Sanskrit, *upāya*, skill-in-means] and *ch'a-na* [instant; from Sanskrit, *kṣaṇa*, instant]); 3. sanctioning of literature for its own sake; 4. promotion of literary theory and criticism; 5. advancement of phonology as a type of linguistic science and as applied to prosody (e.g., direct involvement in the rise of *lü-shih* [regulated verse]); 6. promotion of new modes of thought, in particular, ontological presuppositions that permitted unabashed fictionalizing; 7. the prosimetric (chantefable) narrative form; and 8. stage conventions that became pervasive in the theater.

The impact of Buddhism on Chinese language and literature was rivaled only by the influence of the West, another paradigmatic change that began with the Jesuits and the evidential learning (*k'ao-cheng-hsüeh*) they inspired during the seventeenth and eighteenth centuries, continued with the Protestant missionaries of the nineteenth century, and accelerated with the flood of Chinese students going overseas for training during the twentieth century. Now, at the dawn of the third millennium, China is poised to become a member of the global community. The award of a Nobel Prize for literature in 2000 to Kao Hsing-chien (Gao Xingjian, 1940–), the modernist playwright, novelist, and artist—the first time in its century-long history that the literature prize had been given to a Chinese author—signaled that Chinese literature had come of age in the eyes of the world. Although the People's Republic of China was quick to point out that Kao is a French citizen, the fact that all his works are written in Mandarin is a source of pride to speakers of Chinese languages everywhere.

The Great Wall is no longer a symbol of China's isolation from the rest of the world (a state of affairs that never really existed). Instead, it is now a symbol of an outmoded mentality, trenchantly satirized in another great cultural event of the 1980s: the broadcasting of the "Ho-shang" (River Elegy) series on Chinese television with its barbed criticism of orthodoxy and authority, one of the main factors leading to the monumental confrontation between the government and the people that occurred at T'ien-an-men Square during May and June 1989. Far above the hugely diminished Great Wall fly aircraft transporting people reading Amy Tan's novels translated into Chinese and Li Po's poetry translated into English. High in space, satellites beam e-mail messages and radio signals to and from every corner of China and the world—totally oblivious to the pathetic Great Wall and all other imagined barriers. In those messages and signals are the seeds of China's future languages and literatures.

Victor H. Mair

Chapter 2

MYTH

The study of Chinese myth has made significant advances in the past half century, both in East Asian scholarship and in Western research. This chapter surveys the subject, focusing on the scope of the discipline, the nature of its source material, methodological problems, the major concerns of mythic narratives, and the relationship between myth and literature.

DEFINITION OF TERMS

The modern Chinese term for myth, *shen-hua*, is almost identical to one of the many contemporary Western definitions of myth as "sacred narrative." *Shen* means "divinity, sacred, holy"; *hua* means "speech, oral tale, oral narrative." *Hua* is equivalent to the original meaning of the word *mythology:* the root of the word *myth* contains the Proto-Indo-European root **mu* (to mutter or murmur), from which the Greek stem *my* and the noun *mythos* (word, oral story) are derived; the Greek noun *logos* denotes "word," but also "ordered discourse, doctrine." Although most specialists of mythology today agree that the basic definition of myth is "an oral tale, narrative," there is considerable disagreement as to whether myth is necessarily always sacred or limited to the deities and the divine. It is clear from reading the texts of world mythologies that other elements, such as natural phenomena and fabulous creatures, and other basic concerns, such as eating, drought, flood, soil pollution, modes of procreation, gender conflict, survival techniques, and emblems of power all belong to the corpus of myth. So, although the terms *shen-hua* and *sacred narrative* are used and will continue to be used, it should be recognized that their basic definitions are of limited use and should be extended to encompass the wider application of the term "mythology" in the contemporary study of world mythological systems.

It is necessary, moreover, to draw a distinction between myth and legend, although the term "legend" is not readily defined. Legend is most certainly present in a text in which biographical data, hagiographical features, topographical identification, magical agency, secret symbols, words, and documents, as well as transformational display and similar effects are attached to figures who are quasi-historical, historical, or imaginary. When such effects are seen to be attached to a mythical figure of the early written tradition, this is termed "mythopoeia," or a late manipulative invention of a philosophical school or literary genre. In general, myth does not observe human chronology or geographic or topographical localization. Myth is timeless and placeless. Its meaning has both symbolic and literal value, and its symbolic valorizations change according to the perception of successive historical periods. The potency of mythic images and meanings reverberates through the continuity of the cultural history of a people.

Since it is accepted that mythology, the study of myth, has its own autonomy, which distinguishes it from other human sciences, such as philosophy and religion, large exclusions have been made in the context of Chinese mythology. They are the systems of Confucianism (Ju-chiao or K'ung-chiao), Taoism (Tao-chiao), and Buddhism (Fo-chiao), in addition to the network of local and regional cults. These systems of belief have generated immensely complex mythologies and pantheons of their own, which still remain to be fully codified and interpreted.

PERIODIZATION OF CHINESE MYTH

The scope and period of Chinese myth are defined by the prolific repertoire of mythic texts to be found in classical writings, both poetry and prose, that date from between the sixth century B.C.E. and the second century C.E. Apart from Bernhard Karlgren's informal scheme, which is sociological in orientation and focuses on the founding myths of clans in ancient China, no standard model exists for the periodization of the classical Chinese mythographic record. The following new four-part model is proposed. The first mythographic phase, c. 600–c. 100 B.C.E., includes literary anthologies, chronicles, philosophical treatises, and other writings. The second mythographic phase, c. 100 B.C.E.–c. 100 C.E., includes the first imperial histories, late classical philosophy, eclectic essays, treatises, and miscellaneous texts. The third mythographic phase, c. 100–c. 600 C.E., includes encyclopedias, anthologies, commentaries on classical texts, early fiction, travel notes, regional history, geographical treatises, and miscellanies of prose works. The fourth mythographic phase, c. 600–eleventh century C.E., includes imperial encyclopedias, commentaries on the classics, prototype novels, essays, travel diaries, and antiquarian writings. The first phase constitutes the earliest stratum of mythic texts; the second comprises mythopoeic writings and fugitive mythic versions; and the third and fourth phases may be termed the "conservationist era."

Although most sinologists accept the periodization of mythic texts proposed by Karlgren, that is, his chronological organizing principle, there is no general acceptance of his substantive organizing principle. His substantive principle distinguished between early texts of the pre-Han era, which he termed "free texts," and "sources of fundamentally different purport" written by scholars whose "goal was to create a system," which he termed "systematizing texts." Sinologists find it difficult to reconcile certain terminological problems inherent in Karlgren's model. For example, it could be argued that some of his so-called free texts, such as *Shang-shu* (Classic of Documents; also called *Shu-ching*), *Kuo-yü* (Discourses of the States), and so forth, reveal a considerable distortion, amplification, and reorganization of early mythic material into a new ideological construct.

Sources

The most important early classical texts of the first phase that have preserved valuable mythic material are *Shih-ching* (Classic of Poetry), *Mo Tzu*, *Meng Tzu* (Mencius), *Shih Tzu*, *Kuan Tzu*, *Chuang Tzu*, *Ch'u tz'u* (Elegies of Ch'u), *Tso chuan* (Tso Commentary), *Hsün Tzu*, *Lü-shih ch'un-ch'iu* (The Springs and Autumns of Master Lü), *Huai-nan Tzu*, *Han Fei Tzu*, *Shang-shu*, *Kuo-yü*, and *Shan hai ching* (Classic of Mountains and Seas).

The *Classic of Poetry* is the earliest text in the mythological tradition. It contains poems narrating several major mythic themes (or mythemes): the flood myth, the etiological myth of cereal agriculture, the divine origin of the Shang as a people, and the foundation of the Chou dynasty by a deity (see chapter 5).

The *Chuang Tzu*, which dates from about the fourth century B.C.E., contains references to numerous mythic figures and themes: fabulous creatures, metamorphoses, lists of divine beings, and fugitive references to mythic episodes. Its most extended narrative concerns the myth of chaos. Numerous passages feature the mythical figure of Huang Ti (the great god Yellow) and the figure of Yao (Lofty), but they clearly contain mythopoeic material reflecting early Taoist ideology.

Huai-nan Tzu, compiled c. 139 B.C.E. by the king of Huai-nan (Huai-nan Wang), Liu An (c. 179–122 B.C.E.), is an important source for cosmological myth and for variant mythic versions.

Two significant texts constitute the only surviving examples of a corpus of mythic narratives in classical writings: chapter 3 of *Elegies of Ch'u*, called "T'ien wen" (Heavenly Questions), and the eighteen-chapter *Classic of Mountains and Seas*. "Heavenly Questions" is one of the most valuable documents of the first mythographic phase. Written in about the fourth century B.C.E., its 186 verses present an account of the main myths of ancient Ch'u. The account opens with a narrative of the creation of the world and proceeds to the acts of the deities and suprahumans and of mythical figures of the prehistorical era, ending with the deeds of historical personages up to the kings of Ch'u in the late sixth century B.C.E. This is a rich store of ancient myth: it constitutes the earliest repertoire of most primary and some minor myths, and it serves as a control text, because of its antiquity, through which to compare and contrast other mythic texts, whether earlier fragments, contemporary accounts, or later narratives. It is a unique mythic record because it contains in its brief confines the totality of deeply held beliefs at a single point in the mythological tradition.

The *Classic of Mountains and Seas* (c. 300 B.C.E.–200 C.E.)is the most important source for the repertoire of classical myth. The *locus classicus* for many myths, it contains a valuable collection of mythic variants. A total of 204 mythical figures are represented; most of them are obscure in terms of location, attribute, and function, but many feature in partial or fuller narratives that are unique to the *Classic*. The first five chapters are more important for their religious ritual than for their mythological content. The myths recounted there are mostly interfaces between formulaic accounts of the natural world and the religious sphere. Most of the important myths are related in chapters 6 to 18: the cosmogonic solar and lunar myths of the birth of the ten suns and the twelve moons by two goddesses (Hsi-ho and Ch'ang-hsi); the marplot myth of a titan, Kung-kung, who damages the cosmos; references to the myth of the world flood and the world conflagration; and the world-measuring myth. Numerous etiological myths are narrated: the origins of archery, of musical instruments, of agriculture and agricultural tools, of vehicles and transport. There are several divine foundation myths of peoples and countries inaugurated by deities. The mythic content of the last chapter is divine genealogies and culture benefits brought to humans from sky deities.

The mythological content of the *Classic* represents but one stratum of the myths preserved in classical writings. This stratum, which relates myths in a different mode from other works, is distinct and unique. Its narratives and their symbolic meaning, central concern, and mythic variants diverge considerably from those in other works. Its myths have close affinities with the mythological tradition of texts such as *Chuang Tzu*, "Heavenly Questions," and *Huai-nan Tzu*, but without the philosophical strategies and the historical imperative of these texts. The clearest line of demarcation is most noticeable between the manner of presenting myth in the *Classic of Mountains and Seas* and a group of texts with a strongly historicizing and humanizing ethos, such as *Classic of Documents*, *Discourses of the States*, and *Mencius*. In these texts, certain mythical figures who have a recognizably mythological role in the *Chuang Tzu*,

"Heavenly Questions," and the *Classic of Mountains and Seas* are selected from the repertoire and have their role and function rewritten. In the general mythological tradition these figures are positioned last in the divine pantheon, some are shadowy with few known myths (such as Yao), and all are shorn of their original mythic significance. The most famous examples of this rewriting of myth are Yao, Shun, and Yü. The shadowy figure of Yao assumes a prominent role in the historicizing texts as an idealized human ruler. Shun acquires moral virtues. Yü's major role as savior of the world in the flood myth is rewritten so that his function is bureaucratized as the superintendant of Water Works. Moreover, whereas mythological narratives are timeless and placeless, historicizing texts transpose the action to human time, beginning with Yao, and the place to Yao's imperial court. This rewriting of the mythological tradition creates new myths of the etiology of human time, of human government, and of perfect human society. These texts, especially the two "canons" ("Yao tien" and "Shun tien") of the *Classic of Documents*, may therefore be read as later mythopoeic inventions of the historicizing wing of the Confucian school of moral philosophy.

Thus it can be seen that in the context of mythology, classical texts may be subsumed into two distinct categories: (1) texts that present mythological material with minimal doctrinal distortion and (2) texts that significantly rewrite existing mythic narratives and remold existing mythic roles and functions on the basis of doctrinal belief in order to express new ideological propositions.

THE NATURE OF MYTHIC NARRATIVE

Classical authors incorporated mythic material into their writings in order to illustrate their diverse philosophical and intellectual concepts through analogue, symbolic language, and archaic authority. Mencius, for example, used the flood myth in his deliberations on the decline of civilized values. Chuang Tzu employed the metamorphosis myth of a fabled bird to project ideas of relative values and subjectivity. Mythic narratives have been preserved in the contexts of history, philosophy, literature, political theory, and intellectual essays. The piecemeal manner of their recording in classical texts is compensated for by the fact that they were preserved in the texts during the shaping of the scriptural canon from the fourth century B.C.E. to the third century C.E. This means that modern readers encounter Chinese mythic narratives in their original written context. When one speaks of a corpus of classical Chinese myth, what is meant is the preserved repertoire of an amorphous, untidy, lapidary, fragmentary, and scattered congeries of archaic expression. Yet, to the extent that this repertoire was not extrapolated from its written text and reworked in the style of a Hesiod, Homer, or Ovid, the Chinese repertoire of myth retains a measure of authenticity.

MAJOR THEMES

Scattered and fragmentary though the mythic narratives are, they can be organized into thematic categories that correlate with world mythologies, such as cosmogony (the creation of the universe), the creation of humankind, the etiology of culture and civilization, foundation myth, and catastrophe myth.

Cosmogonic Myth

Four main traditions of the creation of the world survive in early texts. There is the world picture of the square earth canopied by the sky, with pillars propping up the sky that is recorded in "Heavenly Questions." Second, there is the cosmogonic model of matter forming out of a shapeless vapor, represented in *Huai-nan Tzu.* Third, there is the myth of the separation of the sky and the earth, the primeval moment of creation, out of which the universe was formed, that is narrated in the comparatively late text, *San wu li chi* (Historical Records of the Three Sovereign Divinities and Five Gods; third century C.E.). Fourth, there is the myth of the cosmological human body, the figure of P'an-ku—the dying god whose body forms the universe and bears striking resemblances to the cosmogonic man, Puruṣa, of Indian myth. P'an-ku's myth is narrated in *Wu yün li-nien chi* (Chronicle of the Five Cycles of Time; third century C.E.).

Myths of the Creation of Humankind

There are four mythological traditions regarding the creation of humankind. There is the creation of humans from pure vapor, narrated in *Huai-nan Tzu.* Second, there is the creation of humans from mites on the body of the dying god P'an-ku, narrated in *Chronicle of the Five Cycles of Time.* Third, there is the creation of the first human, the divinely born P'an-ku, who was created from the separation of sky and earth, which is narrated in *Historical Records of the Three Sovereign Divinities and Five Gods.* Fourth, there is a female-gendered creation myth, in which the goddess Nü-wa (older pronunciation, Nü-kua), created humans out of yellow earth and mud, narrated in *Feng-su t'ung-yi* (Explanations of Social Customs; second century C.E.).

Concept of a Creator

Within the mythological tradition two concepts of a creator are evident. One is the mechanistic concept of a primal generator, the *Tao* or Way, which is related in *Huai-nan Tzu.* The other, older tradition narrates the myth of the creatrix figure Nü-wa, whose transformations formed the world, who made humans out of clay, and who restored the cosmos.

Etiological Myths of Culture and Civilization

Central to cosmogonic myth is a sequence of myths that recount the origin of plants, fire, medicine, animals, and human institutions. All these were revealed *ab origine* by deities or suprahuman heroes. Their value lay not so much in the cultural benefit itself as in the fact that it was deities who first invented and then taught humans how to use these cultural gifts.

The text that relates most myths of divinely bestowed cultural benefits is the *Classic of Mountains and Seas*, especially the last chapters. These benefits are grain, agricultural tools like the plow, and techniques such as the ox-drawn plow, the carriage, weapons (bows and arrows), plants and herbal medicines, fire, metal weapons, the domestication of animals and birds, boats, music, writing, record keeping, prediction, and the method of worshiping the deities, as in Yü's creation of a terrace to the deities after the flood abated. The myth of the creation of the first human government has been discussed in reference to texts that transform existing myth into an historicized, humanized narrative.

Catastrophe Myths

The most enduring and widespread of all mythic themes is the catastrophe myth, which constitutes a fundamental and recurring topic in classical Chinese writings. The most prominent theme is the catastrophe of a world deluge, but that of a world conflagration is also a major theme.

The myth of a world conflagration is expressed through two mythical figures, the female deity Nü-wa and the male god Yi the Archer. The Nü-wa conflagration myth is linked to the Nü-wa flood-myth, which is related in *Huai-nan Tzu* and is the only surviving text of this myth. The text shows clear signs of Taoist philosophical influence in its patriarchal treatment of the gender issue. The Yi conflagration myth occurs in several versions, the main texts being from the *Classic of Mountains and Seas* and *Huai-nan Tzu*. These two texts reveal considerable mythic variation; in the *Classic* the myth centers on the command of the great god Chün that the world fire is to be controlled to save humankind, whereas in *Huai-nan Tzu* it is Yao in his humanized representation who gives Yi the command. The Nü-wa conflagration myth is cosmos-centered, whereas the Yi myth is centered on the human world.

The numerous narrative texts relating the classical flood myth form four distinct, basically discrete mythological traditions. First there is the Nü-wa flood myth, retold in *Huai-nan Tzu*. Second, there is the Kung-kung flood myth, which relates that this god is the cause of the flood, in contrast to the other flood protagonists, who are world saviors. This myth is recounted in several texts; the most mythological account is given in *Huai-nan Tzu*, in which Kung-kung's marplot role is clearly shown, and a humanized, historicized version occurs in *Discourses of the States* as "Discourses of Chou" (Chou yü). Third, there is the Kun flood-myth tradition, which receives both mythological treatment and historicized rewriting, with several versions of each mode of representation. The oldest mythic account occurs in "Heavenly Questions," which tells how Kun so pitied humans suffering from the world deluge that he stole the great god's cosmic soil to restore the world, but he was executed for this sacrilege. The historicized version describes how Kun rebelled against his ruler, Yao, who reluctantly allowed Kun to control the flood and then punished him for failing. The versions that depict Kun in a criminalized role, rather than a soteriological role, include those in the "Canon of Yao" and "Hung fan" (The Glorious Plan) of the *Classic of Documents* and in "Discourses of Chou." Fourth, there is the Yü flood-myth tradition, which is included in most classical texts, receiving both mythological and historicized treatment. In this tradition, Yü, the son of Kun, succeeds in controlling the flood.

These four traditions of the classical flood myth are replete with potent mythic motifs and deal with numerous central concerns. The Yü flood myth came to form the dominant tradition, in part because this mythical figure attracted a cluster of major mythic attributes aside from those engendered by the flood myth: his heroic labors, his soteriological role, his exemplary conduct in line with newly emerging Confucian values, and his crucial function in inaugurating the Second Creation after the world deluge. His other mythic functions are those of World Measurer (Yü liang ta-ti), maker of the Nine Cauldrons (Chiu Ting), Warrior, former of the First Assembly of the Gods (Ta K'uai-chi), Establisher of the House of the Hsia, and Divinely Ordained Founder of the Hsia Dynasty (Yü Hsia), with its fundamental concept of hereditary succession.

Foundation Myths

Classical texts narrate many foundation myths, of a people, a dynasty, a country, or a city. The *Classic of Poetry* relates the two foundation myths of the Shang and the Chou. The most prolific source for myths of divine foundation is the *Classic of Mountains and Seas.* These myths also constitute divine genealogies, which end with accounts of the divine origin of various peoples, lands, and countries, many of them lying beyond the frontiers of ancient Chinese civilization. The myths mostly appear in the last five chapters of that *Classic.*

THE DEITIES: ATTRIBUTE, FUNCTION, TERMINOLOGY

Mythic narratives in many classical works feature some recurring figures who are represented as major deities or demigods. Some of these narratives constitute divine chronologies and divine pantheons. A typical chronology, one that became standardized in the historicizing texts, lists Fu-hsi, Shen Nung (Farmer God), Yen Ti (Flame or Fire God), Huang Ti, Shao-hao (God of Light),

Chuan-hsü (the sky god), and Ti K'u (the great god K'u), followed by the trinity of Yao, Shun, and Yü. The striking aspect of this chronology is the absence of female deities; even the cosmogonic creatrix Nü-wa and the sun goddess Hsi-ho are not visible here. A second feature is the privileged position given to Yao, Shun, and Yü, whose myths underwent a transformational process in the humanizing texts of the Confucian school. A third feature, implicit in the existence of other pantheons, is that there is no fixed pantheon in the classical texts relating myths, but a plurality of divine chronologies. The *Classic of Mountains and Seas*, for example, features as many as 204 mythical figures, mostly divine, but the pantheon implicit in this *Classic* differs fundamentally from that of other texts. Its divine hierarchy, arrived at by counting the number of mythic episodes for each mythical figure, gives the great god Chün, the great god Chuan-hsü, and the great god Shun as its major deities.

The physical attributes and symbolic emblems of mythical figures are not frequently portrayed in the earliest classical texts. Yet some clues are given concerning their appearance. For example, the god of war (Ch'ih Yu) has a horned head, denoting belligerence. The portrayal of the Queen Mother of the West (Hsi Wang-mu) appears in the longest descriptive passage in the *Classic of Mountains and Seas;* she is given therianthropic features, part feline, part human, with wild hair, conveying the idea of untamed savagery, which coincides with her function of bringing pestilence and punishment to the human world. The appearance of some figures is suggested through their names; for example, Kun = Hugefish, Yü = Animal-pawprint, and Shun = Hibiscus. Reptilian features and snake emblems are most characteristic of deities portrayed in the *Classic of Mountains and Seas.* Teeth and ears, in various shapes and sizes, sometimes mark the special attributes of deities.

Flora and fauna also serve as divine emblems. For example, the three green birds, the panther, and the nine-tailed fox are animal attributes of the Queen Mother of the West. The bear is emblematic of Kun and Yü, through their divine metamorphoses. In general, divine creatures in classical Chinese mythology, such as dragons, serpents, the tortoise, and birds of paradise, are the attributes of different mythical figures and impart no specific symbolic meaning in their relation to individual figures.

The terminology of deities defines their gender and their position in the divine hierarchy. The term *Ti,* translated as "the great god" in the mythological context, may appear before or after a deity's own name, such as the great god K'u (Ti K'u) or the great god Yellow (Huang Ti). This term almost always applies to male deities. In historicizing texts the meaning of the term shades into "ideal human ruler." In imperial histories, the emperor's title became Huang-ti (August Thearch). The term *shen,* translated as "deity, god, divine, holy," also appears in these nominal positions. It is usually applied to male deities, such as Shen Nung (the Farmer God, or Divine Farmer). The term *kuei* (ghost) usually appears with a defining attribute, such as Exhausted Ghosts

(*Ch'iung-kuei*). The term *shih* (corpse) is attached to the name of a dead mythical figure who has been apotheosized, such as the Corpse of Wang-tzu Yeh (Prince Night). There is also the term *shen-jen* (divine being).

The stopgap names of Nü, O, and Pa occur only with female deities, to mean Girl/Woman, Sublime, and Droughtghoul, respectively. These prefixes make the gender of some mythical figures identifiable. But it would be unsafe to assume that the remainder of the list of mythical figures is male-gendered. This is especially the case in a mythological system such as that represented in the *Classic of Mountains and Seas,* in which gendered functions are contrary to expectations, and that represented in the "Canon of Yao," in which the female-gendered sun goddess Hsi-ho of the old mythology has her role rewritten as two male bureaucrats, Hsi and Ho, at Yao's court. (Her bisyllabic name is simply split in half to come up with their names, a linguistic phenomenon that would be repeated countless times throughout Chinese history, leading to endless confusion over the origins of deities, mythological creatures, toponyms, and so forth.) Moreover, there is an ambiguity in the title of the grain and earth deities, Hou Chi (Sovereign Millet) and Hou T'u (Sovereign Earth), first in comparison with cereal and earth deities in world mythologies, which tend toward female gender, and second in consideration of the functional application of the title *Hou* to human empresses in the early imperial era.

A great deal of research remains to be done on the question of the relationship between the function and gender of mythical figures as these are represented in different classical texts. In contrast to many texts, the *Classic of Mountains and Seas,* for example, consistently assigns major cosmological and calendrical functions to female figures, while male figures are assigned the role of procreation through parthenogenesis.

APPROACHES TO THE STUDY OF CHINESE MYTH

It is fortunate for Chinese mythology as a discipline that for two millennia traditional Chinese scholars not only accorded classical texts preserving valuable mythic fragments the status of canonical authority, but also respected the classics themselves as their heritage of scriptural orthodoxy. Only in the first half of the twentieth century did the scribal role of conservation and preservation make the transition to that of investigative research and disciplinary analysis. At first, modern Chinese scholars approached the classical canon from the perspective of the discipline of history. They faced a multiplicity of intellectual and academic challenges: to demarcate the disciplinary boundaries between history and mythology, to discriminate between authentic and spurious historical sources, to debunk age-old fallacies and misconceptions, and to identify the pseudo-historical texts among verifiable historiographic material. Their methodological advance was achieved in the field of mythology when they shifted their focus from anecdotal material labeled as historical tradition (*ch'uan-shuo*), fictional story (*ku-shih*), or rhetorical anecdote (*shuo*) and reconceptualized it as mythological, renaming it *shen-hua*. The great contributions of the scholars Ku Chieh-kang, Yang K'uan, T'ung Shu-yeh, and Lü Ssu-mien are found in the pages of the seven-volume opus *Ku-shih pien* (Critiques of Ancient History). At about the same time, Chinese writers of fiction, such as Shen Yen-ping (pseudonym, Mao Tun) and Wen Yi-to, opened up the study of the Chinese mythological tradition by embarking on the first comparative study of world mythologies.

Recent research has included a plurality of approaches to myth: myth-ritual, nature myth theory, structuralism, structural symbolism, ethnology, gender analysis, concepts of "otherness" and "difference," and the oral-textual approach. The crucial tasks of collating mythic data and of translating and annotating classical texts containing mythic passages continue apace.

MYTH IN LITERATURE

Although China's first great historian, Ssu-ma Ch'ien (c. 145–c. 86 B.C.E.), voiced his skepticism toward mythic material when he stated, "I do not presume to discuss the monstrosities in the *Classic of Mountains and Seas*" (Shan hai ching *so yu kuai wu yü bu kan yen yeh*), he made creative use of the existing mythical tradition in the opening section of his comprehensive history of Chinese civilization. Enshrining the story of the Chinese people in the concept of divine origin, he posited a chronology of divinities from the beginning of time to the commencement of human history, interlacing his construct with the idea that the first human rulers of China were descended from the gods. His newly reconstituted pantheon, selected from the mythical repertoire, was a pentiad: Huang-ti (the Yellow Emperor, later to become the supreme god of the Taoist religion), Chuan-hsü, Ti K'u, Yao, and Shun.

The continuity of the mythological tradition is mainly expressed, however, through the diverse genres and modes of literature. Kuo P'u's "T'u tsan" (Verse Captions for the Illustrations) of the *Classic of Mountains and Seas* serve as an early, if trite, example. Of greater literary interest is T'ao Ch'ien's (or T'ao Yüan-ming; 365–427) long poem, "Tu *Shan hai ching* shih-san shou" (On Reading the *Classic of Mountains and Seas*, Thirteen Poems). In early medieval love poetry, epitomized by the anthology *Yü-t'ai hsin-yung* (New Songs from a Jade Terrace), numerous mythic motifs are allusively utilized by poets, such as fabulous creatures, the divine terrace, the tragic figures of Shun's two wives metamorphosed into river goddesses, and especially the figure of Weaver Girl (Chih-nü) of stellar myth. From the same period the theme of gender transposition is represented in "Mu-lan shih" (The Ballad of Mulan), which has its mythic counterpart in the goddesses of sacral violence encountered in the *Classic of Mountains and Seas*. The semivernacular medieval tale from Tun-huang,

"Shun-tzu chih-hsiao pien-wen" (The Boy Shun's Great Filial Piety), develops latent mythemes of classical mythology. In the sixteenth-century traditional novel *Hsi-yu chi* (Journey to the West), the representation of the monkey Sun Wu-k'ung (The Monkey Who Is Enlightened to Emptiness [Sanskrit, *śūnyatā*]) as the embodiment of the Monkey of the Mind reveals affinities with the simian divinities portrayed in the *Classic of Mountains and Seas* and with the supernatural monkey Hanumat of the Indian epic *Rāmāyaṇa*. Some Ming novels used mythic themes as a frame for historical fiction. Among them are novels on the cosmogonic myth *P'an-ku* and *K'ai-p'i* (The Beginning of the World) and the dynastic myth *Yü Hsia* (Yü of the Hsia). *Feng-shen yen-yi* (Investiture of the Gods) is another example of an enormously rich assemblage of mythic themes, including a number of Iranian motifs, as demonstrated by Sir J. C. Coyajee in *Cults and Legends of Ancient Iran and China* (1936).

The porcine attributes of numerous deities in the *Classic of Mountains and Seas*, such as Han Liu, with his pig's snout, trotters, and wheel-high thighs, who married a beautiful girl (she gave birth to the sky god Chuan-hsü), prefigure Chu Pa-chieh (Pig of the Eight Precepts [Sanskrit, *śīla*]; Pigsy in the translation by Arthur Waley) in *Journey to the West*. In his eighteenth-century novel *Hung-lou meng* (A Dream of Red Towers), Ts'ao Hsüeh-ch'in (c. 1724–1764) creates a cosmological dimension for his story of blighted romance and failed hopes by invoking the myth of Nü-wa, creatrix restorer of the cosmos, in the opening passages: in her role of Divine Smith she made 36,501 stones to repair the world after the catastrophes of flood and fire, but threw away the odd one, which was to become the metaphysical hero of his story, Pao-yü (Precious Jade). Perhaps the most famous example of the literary use of mythic material, and certainly the most artistically consistent, is Li Ju-chen's *Ching hua yüan* (Flowers in the Mirror, A Romance) of the early nineteenth century. Li brilliantly subverted the mythic attributes and motifs of the *Classic of Mountains and Seas* in his allegorical story of a voyage around strange lands and peoples in order to voice a satirical critique of his own country and his Chinese contemporaries.

Anne Birrell

Chapter 3

PHILOSOPHY AND LITERATURE IN EARLY CHINA

From the fifth through the second centuries B.C.E., a set of widespread philosophical debates flourished in China. Many of the positions taken during this time concerning such issues as authorship, the nature of the cosmos, and the purpose of literature were to have a major impact on the development of Chinese literary thought. This chapter surveys the history of philosophical debates concerning these issues and explicates the ways in which the positions taken during these debates influenced the later tradition.

THE EMERGENCE AND MAJOR CHARACTERISTICS OF CHINESE PHILOSOPHY DURING THE EASTERN CHOU PERIOD

During the second half of the first millennium B.C.E., several societies in Eurasia witnessed the emergence of intellectual debates. The most notable of these included Greece, India, and China. Indeed, the florescence of philosophical thought in these cultures led Karl Jaspers in the middle of the twentieth century to pronounce this period of Eurasian history the "Axial Age."

In all these cultures, the emergence of philosophical debate was produced by a comparable set of social and political circumstances. At the end of the second millennium and the beginning of the first millennium B.C.E., the settled agricultural civilizations of Eurasia were dominated by aristocratic societies that utilized bronze metallurgy and were characterized by forms of chariot warfare. From roughly the eighth century B.C.E. onward, however, aristocratic dominance gradually declined, and social mobility increased. Part of this process can be seen in the fact that the use of iron spread throughout Eurasia during this period, gradually replacing bronze in most societies within a few centuries. Since iron was much easier to produce than bronze, it allowed for mass production that undercut the aristocratic domination of metallurgy seen during the earlier Bronze Age. In warfare, mass infantry armies gradually replaced the aristocratic form of chariot warfare. Since infantry armies inevitably involved large numbers of people born below the aristocracy, such forms of organization broke the aristocratic control of warfare and opened an avenue of social mobility for the lower-born. Moreover, market economies began to emerge in many of these societies, and this provided yet another avenue of social mobility.

This emergence of social mobility and the concurrent breakdown of aristocratic control in the major agricultural civilizations of Eurasia led to significant cultural crises as well. In India, Greece, and China, many of the lower-born figures who came to prominence during this period began reflecting on and questioning the ideas of the earlier Bronze Age. In all three of these societies, this led to the emergence of philosophical debates.

In China, these broad trends took specific forms that would have a lasting influence. The Bronze Age societies in the North China plain consisted of the Shang dynasty, which had, according to later texts, overthrown an earlier Hsia dynasty, and which was in turn replaced by the feudalistic state of the Western Chou. The Western Chou ruled from the eleventh century to 771 B.C.E., when the Western Chou capital was overrun.

The ensuing period, known as the Eastern Chou (770–256 B.C.E.), was one of enormous political, social, and technological changes. Politically, the period can be characterized in terms of the interplay of competing states, many of which had originated during the Western Chou through enfeoffment by the Chou kings. These states became increasingly independent from the Chou rulers, to the point that, by the fourth century B.C.E., many of the leaders of the various states usurped the Chou title and began calling themselves "kings." Although the state of Chou would not actually be extinguished until the third century B.C.E., such a usurpation of the royal title was clearly meant to symbolize the complete autonomy of the states from the Chou rulers. Indeed, many of these rulers had ambitions of once again unifying China and beginning a new dynasty to replace the Chou.

Administratively, the states began engaging in a general policy of centralization, a process involving the creation of bureaucracies based on merit rather than birth, the promulgation of written legal statutes, and the large-scale mobilization of peasants for mass infantry armies. All these policies led to a gradual breakdown of the power and privileges associated with the old aristocracy of the Bronze Age. In their place there rose to prominence the *shih* class: men born below the aristocracy who had been retainers and knights during the Bronze Age but became the primary officeholders of the developing bureaucracies in the Eastern Chou.

Another aspect of this process of centralization was territorial expansion: in order to increase their resources, the larger states engaged in a policy of annexing surrounding smaller states. Indeed, the ferocity of the wars of annexation led later historians to refer to the latter part of the Eastern Chou as the period of the Warring States (403–221 B.C.E.).

It was out of this sociopolitical context that intellectual debates emerged in early China. The majority of the figures involved belonged to the *shih* class, and many of the debates in which they engaged concerned the nature of these new states—states that were clearly recognized at the time as moving further and further away from the institutions of the Western Chou. The debates accordingly came to focus on questions such as the legitimacy of these new states, the degree to which it was acceptable to break from the aristocratic culture of the Western Chou, and the degree to which kings should follow the examples of statecraft from the past or base their rule on other criteria. The fact that merit, rather than birth, was becoming the dominant means of political access also meant that much of the intellectual debate came to focus on issues of self-cultivation: how one should cultivate oneself and how one should live one's life.

This practical orientation in early Chinese thought also had important ramifications for the development of rhetoric and logic. The Platonic distinction between philosophical discourses that aim at a correct representation of the Ideas and literary and rhetorical discourses that do not is entirely absent in early Chinese thought. Indeed, the terms "philosophy" and "literature" have no equivalents in early Chinese texts, nor was there a concern at the time with the issue of representing Truth. Instead, the concern was with convincing one's intellectual opponent, or ultimately in convincing the rulers of the day, to accept one's own view, rather than with defining a correct form of representation. Storytelling and poetry thus became a major aspect of philosophical writing during the Warring States period; there was never an attempt to prevent a "philosophical" discourse from utilizing "literary" techniques of persuasion. Consequently, it is common to find in texts that would now be classified as philosophical a frequent utilization of poetry, narratives, and other so-called literary techniques.

However, because so much intellectual discussion was concerned with the relevance of past exemplars of statecraft, many of the arguments came to focus on analyses of the actions of the significant kings and ministers from the Bronze Age. Indeed, a great deal of the intellectual debate involved telling various stories and poems about the exemplary figures of the past, with the philosophical disagreements being phrased in terms of offering different versions and interpretations of what these figures in the past had said and done. And, insofar as the historical events of the past came to be so strongly emphasized, conscious fictionality was rarely regarded in the early texts as a laudable activity. The concern tended to focus much more on debating what had in fact happened in the past and what should happen in the future. Accordingly, although stories and poems were frequently utilized, both were presented as revealing factual accounts of what had occurred in the past.

With these general statements in mind, a survey of the intellectual discussions follows, beginning with the teachings of the Confucian school.

EARLY CONFUCIANISM

One of the earliest and most influential figures in early Chinese intellectual life was Confucius (550–479 B.C.E.). The primary text devoted to Confucius's teachings is the *Lun-yü* (Analects), a set of sayings attributed to Confucius by his later disciples. The sayings themselves were written down over the course of the Warring States period. According to the *Analects,* Confucius viewed the early Western Chou as a fully moral culture, guided by kings and ministers who correctly followed the ethical dictates of righteousness and benevolence. However, he argued, the morals and ritual traditions of the Chou had slowly decayed, resulting ultimately in a loss of sovereign authority for the Chou kings and a full breakdown in morality throughout society at large. Confucius saw his own world of the Eastern Chou as in a state of decline, and he called upon his contemporaries to put in place once again the moral and ritual traditions of the Chou. This would involve everything from, at the highest level, a recognition of the Chou king as the one proper ruler for all of China to, at a lower level, an attempt by the elites of society to cultivate themselves through practicing the rituals of the Chou. In short, the ideal society for Confucius was not located in an afterlife or in a distant mythical past; he believed that an ideal moral society had been realized by humans only a few generations earlier and that it could be realized once again simply through acts of proper moral cultivation. The ideal society, in other words, was realizable here and now.

Confucius's vision of history reinforced this notion. Following earlier Chou political ideology, Confucius argued that history was cyclical, consisting of the rise and fall of dynasties. When a moral ruler arose, Heaven, a moral deity, would confer upon him the Mandate of Heaven, thus starting a new dynasty. The kingship would then be passed down from generation to generation. When an immoral ruler inherited the kingship, however, Heaven would take away the mandate and confer it upon a worthy person, thus beginning a fresh dynasty.

The Chou was thought to be so moral because it had built upon the culture handed down from earlier antiquity. According to several passages in the *Analects*, the sages of earlier antiquity patterned themselves after Heaven and then brought these cultural patterns, *wen,* to the world of humanity. The patterns were thereafter passed down throughout history, finally being brought to their most refined state by the Chou. Confucius presented himself as simply transmitting these patterns to the people of his own day. From such a perspective, a true sage was one who was able to recognize the proper patterns in the universe and bring them to humanity.

The educational curriculum favored by Confucius involved a study of these patterns from the past, patterns that included both the ritual traditions themselves and the early texts written by or about the early sages, namely, the *Shih-ching* (Classic of Poetry) and the *Shu-ching* (Classic of Documents). The view was that these texts, if understood properly, would explicate the views of the early sages. In other words, one had to learn to read the words correctly so as to reveal the inner meaning that the sages had given them.

Later Confucians claimed that Confucius himself, despite his disclaimers, was a sage, not a transmitter. Thus they attributed to Confucius the authorship of *Ch'un-ch'iu* (Springs and Autumns), a text that chronicles events in the state of Lu from 722 to 481 B.C.E. Since a sage wrote the text, however, the argument was that the work was not a simple chronicle at all: instead, it was interpreted as a subtle critique of the rulers' actions during that period and thus a guide to any future ruler. In short, it was a work that distilled patterns of morality from the events that occurred in the state of Lu, and any proper reading of the text must involve an attempt to recover these patterns distilled by Confucius.

There were several consequences of these views of sagehood. First, early Confucians strongly advocated a didactic function for writing. The goal of writing was to guide moral activity, and this was to be accomplished by distilling proper patterns of morality. Accordingly, moral patterning, rather than representation, became the cornerstone of Confucian hermeneutics. The criterion for evaluating writing was thus the issue whether a given work was moral or immoral. For example, Confucius condemned particular poems in the *Classic of Poetry* that he deemed licentious, that is, promoting immoral behavior. This was not a claim of poor representation. On the contrary: the argument was precisely that the poems did manifest the views of the authors and that such views were to be condemned.

Second, Confucians were strongly committed to the notion that only a true sage ought to compose a work, for only a sage would be able to write in morally edifying ways. For example, Mencius (372–289 B.C.E.), the leading Confucian of the fourth century B.C.E., explicitly criticized his intellectual opponents for inventing new ideas that would only turn people away from the correct moral path. Only a true sage, Mencius argued, would be able to compose in the proper way. Thus, he claimed, Confucius's composition of the *Springs and Autumns* was an example of a correct form of authoring. For anyone other than a sage to invent, however, was not only an act of hubris but in fact a socially dangerous act.

Finally, there was a strong emphasis on reading proper texts in order to discover the ideas and actions of the sages of antiquity. Thus, for example, by the Han dynasty (202 B.C.E.–220 C.E.), a lengthy commentarial tradition had emerged in which the acceptable poems of the *Classic of Poetry* were interpreted as referring to historical figures in the past. Even love poems were read as allegories of virtuous conduct between particular ministers and rulers. Literature, therefore, was appreciated only insofar as it provided a morally efficacious pattern for the reader, and this emphasis led in turn to a strong tendency to read even poems as referring to the historical actions of the past.

MOHISTS

The school of Mohism grew out of the teachings of Mo Tzu (480?–400? B.C.E.), a strong critic of the early Confucian schools. Although the Mohists would have little direct impact on later literary thought, many of their ideas were to spark a strong reaction among other, highly influential, Warring States thinkers. Accordingly, a few of their ideas are worth mentioning here.

One of the central doctrines of the Mohists concerned the importance of the spiritual world. The Mohists were strongly committed to the idea that natural phenomena were governed by individual deities who rewarded the worthy and punished the unworthy. At the top of the celestial hierarchy was Heaven. Like the early Confucians, the Mohists regarded Heaven as a moral deity who granted and withdrew a mandate to rule. But the Mohists viewed Heaven as actively intervening in everyday affairs to a far greater extent than the early Confucians allowed. Moreover, the Mohists presented spirits and ghosts as equally involved in actively rewarding and punishing the behavior of humans.

Just as the spiritual world of the Mohists was theistic, so did the Mohist vision of sages reflect a comparably activist vision. For the Mohists, the sages were innovators, creators of the artifice of material culture that brought humanity away from the world of nature. Whereas the early Confucian texts emphasize how sages brought ritual and textual patterns (*wen*) to humanity, the Mohist texts claim that the crucial act of the sages consisted in giving humans material inventions, such as housing, clothing, agriculture, boats, and chariots. The sages, in short, were creators of artifice.

Although such a view could have been taken over by later literary theorists to argue for a notion of literature as a created artifice, this in fact rarely occurred. Instead, the Mohist vision both of the spirit world and of sagely creation became increasingly suspect in Warring States intellectual culture, as these notions came to be rejected in favor of naturalistic interpretations. This shift would have profound implications for later literary theory in China.

SELF-CULTIVATION TECHNIQUES

Some of the earliest shifts toward a naturalistic interpretation of human action can be seen in the early literature on self-cultivation. One of the clearest examples is in the "Nei yeh" (Inner Workings) chapter of the *Kuan Tzu,* a chapter probably written in the fourth century B.C.E.

A key notion in the chapter is that the universe is composed of *ch'i,* a term that can mean matter, breath, air, or energy. "Inner Workings" uses this notion to criticize some of the theistic views found in popular religion and supported by the Mohists. A widespread religious belief of the time held that natural phenomena were under the direct control of spirits. Thus particular spirits controlled the rain, the wind, and more general aspects of change in the world. The claim of "Inner Workings," however, is that change is not controlled by single spirits but is, rather, simply a product of the alterations and transformation of *ch'i.* Therefore the universe changes according to spontaneous, natural processes, instead of being controlled by anthropomorphic spirits.

Moreover, the text argues, spirits are simply highly refined *ch'i.* Because they are made of refined aspects of the same substance that pervades the rest of the cosmos, spirits are able to understand fully the movements and changes of the universe. However, humans also have such aspects of *ch'i* within themselves. So, humans, if they cultivate themselves properly, can refine the *ch'i* within themselves and ultimately gain the powers of the spirits.

Crucial in this argument are the claims that any human, through proper cultivation, can attain sagehood and that the path to sagehood cannot be found in the patterns passed down from antiquity. In such a philosophy, studying early texts and following the example of past sages become increasingly irrelevant. Moreover, the result of such an attainment is the achievement of an intuitive understanding of the universe comparable to what the spirits themselves possess. Such claims, which rejected several of the dominant strands of both early Confucian and Mohist thought, would become crucial in the later development of literary thought in China.

CHUANG TZU AND LAO TZU

Many of these ideas concerning self-cultivation and the cosmos were taken to even greater extremes in the texts attributed to Chuang Tzu and Lao Tzu. Although these two texts are quite different, they were, several centuries later, classified together as "Taoist." Despite their many differences, both texts argue for a nontheistic interpretation of the universe—that the universe changes spontaneously, without a conscious will driving it—and both texts argue that the goal of the sage should be to act in accordance with these spontaneous changes. Moreover, both explicitly state opposition to the moral vision of the Confucian and Mohist schools.

Chuang Tzu, a figure who lived in the fourth century B.C.E. and probably wrote the first seven chapters of the work attributed to him, argued that the moral patterns advocated by both the Confucians and the Mohists were artificial constructs of humans and thus should not be followed. Since the universe operates according to spontaneous processes, the goal of humans should be to act spontaneously as well, thus according with the natural way. However, Chuang Tzu argued, humans, because of their cognitive faculties, have a tendency to make artificial distinctions, thus removing themselves from the spontaneous processes of the natural world. Confucian morality, Chuang Tzu argues, was one such artificial construct.

Chuang Tzu writes in a highly playful style, attempting to break his readers out of the habitual, and artificial, distinctions to which they had become accustomed. In direct contrast to the early Confucian view of writing, Chuang Tzu tells clearly fictive stories with patently fictive characters, many of whom are invented out of puns and word plays. And when he does refer to the earlier sages mentioned in other texts of the time, he utilizes them in ways that overtly contradict the normal associations of the figures. Early sage kings are thus described as renouncing their positions, Confucius is presented as opposing rituals, and so on. It is important to note, however, that such fictional play was not an attempt to celebrate the ability of humans to create artifice but, rather, the exact opposite. It was, in short, written to oppose any notion of creation and artifice and instead to support an emphasis on natural spontaneity.

This commitment to spontaneity was further developed in the *Tao te ching* (Classic of the Way and Integrity), the text attributed to Lao Tzu. Lao Tzu is probably a fictitious name (it means "Old Master"), and the exact date of the composition of the *Tao te ching* is unclear. The *Tao te ching* shows some vestiges of oral composition and is probably a collection of wise sayings of *rishi*-like sages. The text did, however, begin to achieve a great deal of influence by around 270 B.C.E. Like the *Chuang Tzu*, the *Tao te ching* argues that any attempt to break from natural processes, any attempt to impose one's own conscious will upon the world, will only result in failure.

However, Lao Tzu subscribed to a very different definition of nature from the one found in the *Chuang Tzu*. Lao Tzu's argument was that the universe operated through a constant process of generation and decay: things are naturally born, and then they naturally die. Everything emerges from oneness and, ultimately, returns to it. The act of differentiation, although perfectly natural, is thus a movement away from oneness, from stillness, from emptiness. The goal of the true sage, therefore, is to become still and empty and thus achieve a state of returning to this oneness. Such a state was referred to as attaining the way, or *tao*. Insofar as the text places a higher value on the undifferentiated than on the differentiated world, it is not surprising that the additional creation of anything artificial by humans is strongly opposed. A true sage instead acts without conscious deliberation and without the introduction of artifice. Moreover, he is amoral, for the *tao* itself is amoral: like Chuang Tzu, Lao Tzu held that morality is an artificial human construct and should thus be opposed.

The text also casts a great deal of suspicion upon the use of language. Insofar as language concerns differentiation, and hence cannot refer to the *tao*, it was presented as an inaccurate medium for conveying ideas. Accordingly, the text itself is written as a series of highly elusive aphorisms and poems, with constantly changing terminology. Even the term "oneness" is described differently in different passages—at times as a root, at other times as a gate, and at other times as the mother. Because of this suspicion of stable categories, the text also avoids the emphasis found in other Warring States texts on referring to exemplary figures from the past. Indeed, the *Tao te ching* utilizes no stories of past sages and does not mention personal names at all. Still, along with the Hindu philosophical dialog known as the *Bhagavad-Gita* (Song of the Blessed One), the deeply mystical *Tao te ching* is one of the most popular non-Western works of antiquity, with new translations of widely varying quality appearing in an unending stream.

REACTIONS AGAINST "TAOISTIC" THOUGHT

Such claims that nature was a spontaneous process on which humans should model their behavior provoked a strong reaction among other thinkers in the third century B.C.E. One of these responses was from Hsün Tzu (c. 300–c. 219 B.C.E.), a Confucian who accepted the definition of nature as an amoral, spontaneous, self-generating process but argued that humans should not attempt to accord with it. On the contrary, Hsün Tzu argued, human culture was indeed an artificial construct of the early sages, morality was merely a creation of the sages, and following morality actually involved an overcoming of man's spontaneous nature. Nonetheless, Hsün Tzu claimed, such artifice should be embraced.

One of Hsün Tzu's students, Han Fei Tzu, took this valorization of artifice to even greater lengths. Han Fei Tzu (d. 233 B.C.E.), who would later be classified as a "Legalist" thinker, accepted the Mohist notion that human culture consisted of the artificial constructs invented by sages to raise humanity away from nature. Moreover, he argued, times change, so that even the artifice invented by the earlier sages need not be followed. Sages must be willing to create new institutions of governance whenever they are necessary. Han Fei Tzu conceded to the Confucians the claim that the Chou dynasty ruled with righteousness and benevolence, but he argued that times had once again changed, and that the proper form of governance for the Warring States period was one based on strong bureaucratic structures, a full use of uniform laws, and a lack of concern for morality. Unlike most intellectuals of the time, in other words, Han Fei Tzu fully supported the bureaucratic and legalistic institutions that were appearing in the Warring States period, and he believed that the only problem was that such policies needed to be pursued more consistently.

COSMOLOGICAL MODELS

Despite these reactions, by the mid-third century B.C.E. most intellectuals were moving in a very different direction. Claims concerning the spontaneity of the universe became increasingly common in the latter part of the Warring States period, from roughly 250 B.C.E. on. By this time, the growth of centralized states had progressed to such a point that a simple return to the Western Chou seemed increasingly idealistic and impracticable. As a result, calls for rulers to follow past exemplars seemed less persuasive. However, many intellectuals were uncomfortable with the kind of support that Legalist figures like Han Fei Tzu were willing to grant to the institutions of the day. Accordingly, they began searching for ways to legitimate the centralizing states of the time while providing a means to limit and direct their development. Some of these intellectuals started using versions of the definitions of nature first developed in the self-cultivation literature. They argued that political states should attempt to accord with the spontaneous processes of nature, and they then defined these spontaneous processes so as to limit the states in specific ways.

In particular, many intellectuals defined nature in such a way as to encompass the political teachings of several earlier schools of thought. Their argument was that a successful political ideology would include earlier intellectual positions but would limit each of them. Thus, for example, aspects of the political teachings of Legalism would be granted a place in the natural model, but it would be only one of several ideologies included.

A clear example of such a cosmological and syncretistic approach was the theory of *yin* and *yang*. Although these terms had appeared earlier in Chinese philosophy, it was only during the third century B.C.E. that they achieved a great deal of influence. *Yin* and *yang* were thought of as distinctive, but complementary, forces in the universe. *Yin* was associated with inactivity, *yang* with activity. *Yin* was female, night, winter, the lower, earth; *yang* was male, day, summer, the higher, Heaven. Although *yang* was usually associated with the superior, *yin* was seen as crucial as well: unlike an opposition such as "good/evil," neither *yin* nor *yang* was expected to win out ultimately over the other. On the contrary, each was necessary and complementary to the other, and there were proper times when each would be in the ascendancy.

For example, one of the arguments provided in the eclectic work by Lü Pu-wei (d. 235 B.C.E.) entitled *Lü-shih ch'un-ch'iu* (The Springs and Autumns of Master Lü; c. 239 B.C.E.) is that the actions of the ruler should accord with the natural movement of the seasons, which are themselves a product of the spontaneous mixing of *yin* and *yang*. The height of winter is pure *yin*; spring is the rebirth of *yang*; the height of summer is pure *yang*; and autumn is the gradual growth of *yin* again. Thus the ruler should promulgate self-cultivation techniques during the spring, Confucian policies for maturation in the summer and Legalist policies during the autumn, and then reserve winter for warfare and executions. In short, the ruler is called upon to model himself upon the natural world, and the natural world is then defined such that many of the major intellectual positions taken during the earlier Warring States period are assigned a proper time for implementation. The argument, then, is that many of the earlier intellectual positions were correct but limited: the proper vision would be comprehensive, encompassing earlier views and wedding them all to a general cosmological model.

Another crucial cosmological idea that came to the forefront in the late Warring States period was the theory of *wu-hsing* (five phases), later attributed to Tsou Yen (305–240 B.C.E.) but articulated in late Warring States texts like *The Springs and Autumns of Master Lü*. The argument held that all processes of nature go through a cycle, in which certain phases of *ch'i* would, in succession, come into ascendancy. There were supposedly five such phases or elements: fire, water, earth, wood, and metal. Moreover, each phase was correlated with particular colors, numbers, and features.

For a ruler to start a new dynasty successfully, he would have to rule according to the characteristics of the proper phase in ascendancy at that time: of the three earliest dynasties, the Hsia was said to have ruled by the phase of wood, the Shang by the phase of metal, and the Chou by the phase of fire. At the time these ideas were being propounded (the second half of the third century B.C.E.), it was thought that, were a ruler to arise who could unify the states and begin a new dynasty, he would be ruling under the phase of water, since water is the phase that extinguishes fire. Moreover, fire was correlated in this system with moral rule, and water was associated with law, harsh punishments, and warfare. Thus the cosmological theory was articulated so as to support the policies of the centralizing states of the day, while arguing that, at the proper time, there existed cosmological justification for the policies advocated by other schools of thought.

In different ways, therefore, both theories emphasized the importance of according with the spontaneous movement of nature, and both defined the natural world so as to encompass several competing notions of statecraft.

THE "TA CHUAN" (GREAT TREATISE) CHAPTER IN *YI-CHING* (CLASSIC OF CHANGE)

In terms of the later development of literary thought, perhaps the most influential work from the late Warring States period to develop such a comprehensive cosmological theory was the "Great Treatise" of the *Classic of Change*. The "Great Treatise" was an attempt to develop a cosmological interpretation of the universe by means of the *Classic of Change*, a divinational text written during the Western Chou period. Moreover, the text tried to link this cosmological viewpoint with a generally Confucian vision. The particular way in which the text did this was to have a lasting influence not only on the Confucian movement but on much of later Chinese thought as well.

The general cosmology presented by the author is quite common in many late Warring States texts. The basic components of the universe are described in terms of pairs of opposites (Heaven and earth, hardness and softness, *yang* and *yin*). These opposites are seen as spontaneously interacting, thus generating the various changes and movements of the universe. The universe, in other words, is a spontaneously generated process that transforms of its own accord, without a guiding will.

Humans are then called upon in the text to model their behavior on these spontaneous changes in the universe, learning to act at the appropriate moment in accordance with the processual movement of nature. In order to help humans achieve this, the text argues, the sages of antiquity wrote the *Classic of Change* as a guide for all later generations. The first stage in this process began with Fu-hsi, the earliest sage recognized in the text. Fu-hsi, the "Great Treatise" argues, studied the images in Heaven, the models on earth, and the patterns of the birds and beasts. The sage then took these patterns and used them to make eight trigrams. Each trigram consisted of three lines, each of which could be either broken or unbroken. The trigrams were then combined into hexagrams, consisting of six lines apiece. The total number of possible combinations was sixty-four hexagrams. The claim of the "Great Treatise," then, is that these combinations were originally patterns in the natural world and that Fu-hsi simply brought these into the realm of humanity.

The "Great Treatise" goes on to describe how the early sages were inspired by the hexagrams to invent cultural implements (including nets and snares for hunting, plowshares, plow handles, markets, boats, oars, domesticated oxen and horses, mortars and pestles, bows and arrows, palaces and houses, coffins, and writing). Thus human culture was itself a product of the patterns brought from the natural world by the ancient sages. In opposition to those figures, like the Mohists or Han Fei Tzu—who presented the inventions of material culture as artificial constructs of the sages—the "Great Treatise" reads them as having been inspired by the hexagrams, which were themselves inspired by patterns of the natural world.

Moreover, the "Great Treatise" argues, the hexagrams can be used to divine the future precisely because they replicate the changes in the universe itself: the shifting lines in the hexagrams form a microcosm of the shifting patterns in the universe at large. The changes in the hexagram lines of the *Classic of Change* thus mirror the changes that occur in the natural world. However, since only a sage can understand how to interpret the hexagrams, the sages of antiquity appended statements to each line so that any human can divine and thus understand what actions are proper for each situation.

The view in the "Great Treatise," in short, is a cosmological version of the ideas found in early Confucian texts: the sages brought patterns from nature to the world of humanity and then invented human culture from these patterns. Unlike Hsün Tzu, the "Great Treatise" argues that culture is not an artifice at all; it is instead a product of the patterns of nature as distilled by the early sages.

The sages transmitted these patterns through textual traditions, so that later generations could understand the workings of the universe and how to act. Unlike the ideas in the *Tao te ching*, for example, those in the "Great Treatise" hold that writing can express the intentions of the author, that it can be an accurate guide to behavior, and that it can express the workings of the universe. This view of writing as an act of both manifesting the patterns of nature and manifesting the intentions of the author was to have a tremendous influence on later theories of literature in China.

EARLY HAN IDEAS

The Warring States period ended in 221 B.C.E., when the state of Ch'in completed its conquests and thereafter created the first unified imperial state in Chinese history. Its policies were unapologetically Legalist. However, the empire of Ch'in lasted until only 207 B.C.E., whereupon a civil war erupted. When a new empire, the Han, was finally proclaimed in 206 B.C.E., one of the pressing concerns was to develop an ideology that could legitimate imperial rule more successfully than the Ch'in had been able to do.

The main theoretical formulations to which intellectuals turned to forge such an imperial ideology were the cosmological systems of the late Warring States period. As a consequence, the various claims that had been made during the Warring States period by figures as diverse as the Mohists and Han Fei Tzu concerning the sages as inventors of artifice were fully rejected and the naturalistic and cosmological philosophies from the late Warring States period emerged into full prominence.

HUAI-NAN TZU AND CORRELATIVE COSMOLOGY

One of the more influential of these texts was *Huai-nan Tzu*, a text submitted to the Han court in 139 B.C.E. *Huai-nan Tzu* was compiled by Liu An (c. 179–122 B.C.E.), a local king who was calling for a more decentralized form of empire. Many of the chapters of the text involve an attempt to develop a full cosmological system out of ideas found in earlier texts like the *Tao te ching*.

"T'ien wen hsün" (Treatise on the Patterns of Heaven), chapter 3 of *Huai-nan Tzu*, provides a cosmogony of the universe. The text posits that initially there was formlessness, which then gave birth to *ch'i*. The more refined parts of *ch'i* then drifted upward and formed Heaven, and the less refined parts drifted downward and formed the earth. The essences of Heaven and earth became *yang* and *yin*, which in turn gave rise to the four seasons, fire and water, and so on. The universe, in this argument, came into being solely through spontaneous processes. There was no external will, no demiurge, directing it at all. Indeed, in such a cosmology Heaven itself is simply a product and part of the ongoing spontaneity of the universe.

Moreover, the cosmology given here is fully monistic and fully correlated: everything in the universe, including human beings, consists of *ch'i*, and everything is inherently linked and in constant interaction with everything else. Thus, for example, an action in one part of the universe will, spontaneously, stimulate a response in another part. This relationship, called *kan-ying*—literally "stimulus and response" but often translated as "cosmic resonance"—was characteristic of most Han systems of thought: things that are correlated, whether that be through *yin* and *yang* categories or five phases categories, were seen as sympathetically linked and hence as resonating with one another.

Therefore the true sage is one who acts spontaneously, in accordance with natural processes, and is thus able to resonate harmony throughout the cosmos. The chapter thus provides a cosmological version of the types of arguments given in the Warring States texts that would later be classified as "Taoist": the sage acts spontaneously and so need not follow past exemplars or textual precedents. Such a philosophical position granted individuals an enormous amount of autonomy from reading ancient texts and following the teachings of ancient sages.

HAN CONFUCIANISM

Partly in reaction to ideas found in texts like *Huai-nan Tzu*, several Confucian scholars began to develop fully syncretistic and cosmological models that would define man's role in the universe while still advocating the importance of following the moral teachings of the past sages. The most influential figure in this movement was Tung Chung-shu (c. 179–104 B.C.E.). While using the correlative system of cosmic resonance found in *Huai-nan Tzu*, Tung and his followers argued that the correspondences in the universe are fully moral. So, if the emperor does anything immoral, negative portents will spontaneously develop in Heaven. Similarly, if the emperor acts morally, there will spontaneously develop positive signs in Heaven as well as harmony throughout his realm.

A further argument of these scholars was that the proper guide to moral development was in the texts that recorded the actions and statements of the ancient sages. Thus the Western Han Confucians advocated the creation of a standard canon of early texts that should be studied. There were five of these "classics": the *Classic of Poetry*, the *Classic of Documents*, the *Classic of Change*, the *Springs and Autumns*, and the *Li-chi* (Record of Ritual), a text devoted to the nature of ritual. Confucius was credited not only with having written the *Springs and Autumns* but with having had a crucial role in transmitting or editing the other four. Indeed, Confucius was credited with having written the "Great Treatise" in the *Classic of Change* itself.

The consequence of this position was that the earlier Confucian emphasis on reading texts as a method of gaining an understanding of the ancient sages came to be combined with the cosmological systems that had become dominant by the early Han. This synthesis of early Confucian teachings with correlative cosmology proved highly influential. The Han ultimately made this synthesis into its imperial ideology, and this form of cosmological Confucianism was to predominate throughout the Western Han (206 B.C.E.–8 C.E.).

IMPLICATIONS

The above survey of some of the most important philosophical positions in early China allows us now to discuss how some of these ideas played out in the development of Chinese literary thought. The various claims made in the early philosophical texts provided many of the themes, images, and views around which literary theory would later revolve and to which it would respond.

Several early texts, as seen above, presented natural phenomena as being under the direct control of specific gods and spirits, and this view prevailed in the world of popular religion. However, for the historical reasons outlined earlier, much of the intellectual culture of the late Warring States and early Han periods came instead to embrace a vision of the natural world as a spontaneous, correlative system. In such a cosmos, there could be no directing will and certainly no demiurge or creator-deity of any kind. Similarly, although several early texts had emphasized the notion of the sage as a creator of artifice, much of the intellectual culture of early China ultimately came to oppose such a view and instead to embrace a definition of the sage as one who acted in accordance with the spontaneous movement of the universe.

These intellectual choices had tremendous implications for the development of Chinese literary thought. Although it would have been possible for later writers to draw on certain early Chinese philosophical statements to develop literary theories based on notions of artifice, much of Chinese literary thought developed out of the cosmological notions that had become predominant by the late Warring States and early Han periods. Therefore, rather than building on Mohist ideas of deities as imposing their will on natural phenomena and of sages as creators of artificial constructs, later literary thought much more frequently spoke of literature in terms of the issues seen in the other strands of thought from early China—issues such as manifesting natural patterns, manifesting the natural inclinations and feelings of the author, or distilling the moral and didactic patterns of the world. Debates continued to rage over such basic questions as whether writing should serve a didactic function, or whether past exemplars should be followed. But only rarely would literary writings be discussed in terms of a conscious creation of artifice. Thus, for example, the image that became so prevalent in early modern Europe, of the author as a demiurge creating a fictional world of his own, has no clear analog in Chinese literary thought: notions of constructed artifice tended to be strongly downplayed.

The nature of intellectual discourse in early China, as well as the specific ideological choices made therein, had a tremendous impact on the later tradition of Chinese literary thought. It is perhaps not going too far to suggest that some of the distinctiveness of that tradition derives in part from the particular directions that the intellectual debates took in early China.

Michael Puett

Chapter 4

THE THIRTEEN CLASSICS

The study of traditional Chinese literature must begin with the so-called *Shih-san ching* (Thirteen Classics), since writers of Literary Sinitic or Classical Chinese could safely assume that their educated readers would be intimately familiar with them. These are the writings that generations of Chinese intellectuals regarded as the foundation of their civilization. They were taught in public and private schools, by tutors to the scions of the mightiest; they were memorized character by character; the verses they contain were cited meticulously by judges, government ministers, scholars, and teachers. The classics occupied a position in China analogous to that held for centuries in the West by the Bible as the basis for moral disquisition. Learned men wrote commentaries on the classics and expounded the principles that they believed to inhere in them, while polemicists endeavored to find scriptural justification for whatever enterprise they happened to be recommending. Even a man's interpretation of a particular passage often served as a pretext for his ouster from political power—although in traditional China dogma led far less often than in Europe to institutional violence or warfare.

What are the Chinese classics? The Chinese term that we render as "classic" and occasionally as "canon" is *ching*, literally "warp," as in weaving. "Text" (i.e., "woven thing") might complete the metaphor; and indeed early medieval translators of Buddhist texts typically used *ching* to render the Sanskrit *sūtra* (thread), echoing the textile image. But *ching* carries another shade of meaning; the *ching* is the warp and, hence, the regulator. What is *ching* is normative; and this sense informs the expressions *ching-shih* (literally "warp-generation"), "regulate the world," and *yüeh-ching,* (literally "moon-warp"), the "regular [cycle] of the moon," "menses." To call a work *ching* therefore implies not only that it is woven together like a text but that it can be taken as the foundation for a weave to be made around it. Weave your tapestry in accordance with the warp: live by the classics.

Many texts have enjoyed the epithet *ching* over the course of history; whether a particular work qualifies as a *ching* generally depends on whom one asks. The *Chuang Tzu,* for example, an irreverent and often anti-Confucian anthology of the pre-imperial and early imperial periods, is sometimes called by its devotees *Nan-hua ching* (Classic of Southern Florescence), Nan-hua being the honorary title granted the supposed author approximately one millennium after his death. But most orthodox intellectuals would not have considered the *Chuang Tzu* a *ching,* because *ching* tend to be Confucian texts. At the beginning of the empire (the Ch'in-Han period), it was the Confucians who emerged with the most political power of any philosophical group or school, having survived a competition lasting two or three centuries with several different parties, most notably the so-called Mohists (*Mo-che* or *Mo-chia*) and Legalists (*fa-chia*). The rise of early Confucianism is too intricate a topic to deal with in detail here (see chapter 3); suffice it to say that over the years, the Confucians persuaded court and state to accept their *ching* as the empire's *ching* and award them a position of pre-eminence that they then retained, except for rare interludes, until the very end of the empire in 1911.

The governments of several dynasties issued orthodox versions of the classics at various times, in monumental gestures intended to solidify their own position as ultimate arbiter in matters pertaining to the intellectual tradition. Thus in 175 C.E., in the midst of massive domestic and foreign problems that would soon cause the collapse of the Han empire, Emperor Ling (r. 168–189) of the Later Han dynasty (25–220 C.E.) commissioned a recension of the classics to be carved in stone. The bulk of the editorial task fell to the scholar Ts'ai Yung (133–192), under whose direction the work was finished in 183. Fragments of these Stone Classics actually survive to this day. Similarly, in 638, the usurper Li Shih-min—who killed his brother and was honored posthumously with the title Emperor T'ai-tsung (r. 626–649) of the T'ang dynasty—appointed a committee to compile authoritative subcommentaries (*shu*) to five of the classics, under the grand title *Wu-ching cheng-yi* (Correct Meanings of the Five Classics). By that time the standard commentaries (*chu*) had already long since been determined. The project was headed by a direct descendant of Confucius (551–479 B.C.E.) named K'ung Ying-ta (574–648 C.E.) but was not completed until after his death in 653. This edition of the classics survives complete; it constitutes one of the bases of the entire subsequent commentarial tradition.

The ongoing and conspicuous marriage of Confucian orthodoxy and imperial autocracy did much to elevate the position of the Confucian lineage but alienated the many parties whom the arrangement did not benefit. Some Confucian intellectuals such as Chu Hsi (1130–1200) decried what they perceived as the pollution of the ancient teachings by those interested only in glory and profit. In 1313 the court appropriated even Chu Hsi's legacy by adopting his interpretations of the classics as the basis of the civil service examinations. The doctrinal supremacy of the Confucians was thereby assured—but, almost immediately thereafter, a new movement of dissent emerged, culminating in the explicit rejection of Chu Hsi and his followers in the Ming and Ch'ing dynasties. In a sense, the figure of Chu Hsi came to stand for everything that he had found repugnant in his own day.

It is not entirely clear when the canon attained its present form, but several of the accepted classics have been recognized as authoritative for more than two thousand years. There were at various times different lists of the canonical classics, numbering two, three, four, five, six, seven, nine, ten, eleven, twelve, thirteen, and fourteen. The received collection is known as the *Shih-san ching* (Thirteen Classics), a name supposedly first used by the great bibliophile Wang Ying-lin (1223–1296). The *Thirteen Classics* are made up of the following texts:

1. *Chou-yi* (Changes of Chou), or *Yi-ching* (Classic of Change).
2. *Shang-shu*, or *Shu-ching* (Classic of Documents or History).
3. *Mao-shih*, or *Shih-ching* (Classic of Odes/Songs/Poetry).
4. *Chou-li* (Rites of Chou).
5. *Yi-li* (Ceremonies and Rites).
6. *Li-chi* (Record of Ritual).

7.–9. *Ch'un-ch'iu* (Springs and Autumns)—with three commentaries:
    Tso chuan (Tso Commentary).
    Kung-yang chuan (Kung-yang Commentary).
    Ku-liang chuan (Ku-liang Commentary).

10. *Lun-yü* (Analects [of Confucius]).
11. *Hsiao-ching* (Classic of Filial Piety).
12. *Erh-ya* (Approaching Elegance); this text usually goes by the Chinese name.
13. *Meng Tzu* (Mencius).

The *Yi-ching* is a divination manual. The core of the text—attributed to the primeval sage Fu-hsi—is a list of sixty-four "hexagrams" composed of six horizontal lines, each either unbroken or broken once in the middle. These sixty-four hexagrams represent all the possible results of a divination procedure in which stalks of the milfoil plant (*Achillea millefolium*), known as "yarrow stalks," were cast and the results recorded. Each hexagram is accompanied by a "hexagram statement" (*kua-tz'u*) revealing, in archaic language inscrutable even to ancient readers, the import of the result. The hexagram statements are attributed to King Wen, who founded the Chou dynasty in the mid-eleventh century B.C.E. (The traditional date of 1122 B.C.E. is not likely.) Recent research indicates that the original senses of the hexagram statements appear to refer to results of divination in an idiom reminiscent of the inscriptions (known as "charges") on the oracle bones of the Shang dynasty (c. 1600–c. 1028 B.C.E.). The famous statement *yüan heng li chen*, for example—understood since even the Spring and Autumn period as the enumeration of four virtues—is now translated by Edward L. Shaughnessy in its older sense: "primary receipt: beneficial to divine." The implication is that the *Yi-ching* had undergone a series of reinterpretations long before the imperial era.

After the hexagram statement come the six "line statements" (*yao-tz'u*), one for each line of the hexagram. These are attributed to the Duke of Chou, King Wen's son. While few scholars believe today that the hexagram and line statements come down to us from the hands of King Wen and the Duke of Chou, the text is nevertheless one of the oldest in all Chinese literature and may have already coalesced by the middle of the Western Chou dynasty. Citations of the *Yi-ching* in early narratives such as the *Tso chuan* and *Kuo-yü* (Discourses of the States) match very well with the text as it appears today.

It would not be evident why later thinkers took the *Yi-ching* so seriously were it not for the fascinating appendices to the text, known as the "Shih yi" (Ten Wings) and for centuries accepted as the work of Confucius himself. By far the most influential is the "Hsi-tz'u chuan" (Tradition of the Appended Statements), which includes a mythologized account of the *Yi-ching*'s origins and an explanation of the ways in which it takes into account the interrelated movements of the cosmos. This implied view of the text as a guide to the workings of Heaven and earth proved foundational to the metaphysical speculation of several eleventh-century thinkers, especially Shao Yung (1011–1077) and Ch'eng Yi (1033–1107)—after whom their adherents considered an intimate knowledge of the *Yi-ching* to be essential. Shao's and Ch'eng's contemporary Ou-yang Hsiu (1007–1072) was probably the first to doubt the traditional attribution of the appendices; in this matter, contemporary scholarship concurs. Nevertheless, the *Yi-ching* manuscript discovered at Ma-wang-tui (see chapter 5) in 1973—dated by Shaughnessy to c. 190 B.C.E.—includes at the end a number of commentaries, including the "Hsi-tz'u," indicating that appendices to the text already existed at the beginning of the empire.

The transmission of the *Shu-ching* is one of the most notorious cases in Chinese literature. At the time of the bibliocaust under the first emperor of Ch'in (r. 221–210 B.C.E.), a scholar named Fu Sheng is said to have hidden a copy of the text in the wall of his house. Of this manuscript, however, Fu Sheng was able to salvage only twenty-eight chapters after the fall of the dynasty; these formed the basis of the "New Text" recension of the *Shu-ching* during the Han dynasty. Later, in the first half of the first century B.C.E., another manuscript was supposedly discovered in the wall of someone's house. This was the very long and celebrated chapter known as "T'ai-shih" (Great Declaration), which was subsequently combined with Fu Sheng's text to make a "New Text" recension in twenty-nine chapters. The received text of "T'ai-shih" is known to be spurious.

Around the same time, Prince Kung of Lu (r. 153–128 B.C.E.) ordered the demolition of Confucius's ancestral home in order to make way for the expansion of his palace. Manuscripts of four classics were found in a wall of the house—including yet a third edition of the *Shu-ching*, which K'ung An-kuo (c. 130–c. 90 B.C.E.), a direct descendant of the Master, copied into the contemporary script and presented to the throne. (The other three texts were the *Analects*, *Hsiao-ching*, and *Yi-li*.) K'ung's text, known as the "Old Text" *Shu-ching*, contained sixteen new documents in addition to the twenty-nine chapters of the "New Text" version, for a total of forty-five items. For many reasons, this larger recension gained popularity during the first three centuries of the Common Era, becoming orthodox by the time of the *San-t'i shih-ching* (Three-Font Stone Classics) of the 240s. In 317 C.E., the imperial court made a general appeal for contributions to the imperial library, which had been destroyed three years earlier. Mei Tse (fl. 317–322) presented a text called *K'ung An-kuo Shang-shu* (K'ung An-kuo's Classic of Documents), which was accepted as a reliable edition of the "Old Text" *Shu-ching* and ultimately incorporated into *Wu-ching cheng-yi*.

Yen Jo-ch'ü (1636–1704) was one of the first scholars to demonstrate that Mei Tse's text must have been a forgery. His conclusion is undisputed today, and most critics consider the forger to have been Mei Tse himself. It is now clear that many chapters in the "New Text" version also cannot be as old as they pretend to be. Specialists continue to debate the dating of the "New Text" chapters, and a final consensus has yet to be reached.

The *Shih-ching* is said to be the compilation of a group of officials who were specially charged by the Chou court with the task of roaming the countryside and recording the songs sung by the people. This collection was subsequently edited, so the story goes, by Confucius himself. The legend about the poetry-gathering officials may even contain a kernel of truth. The tradition of Confucius's involvement was probably inspired by the fact that he and other teachers in his school were fond of illustrating their points with relevant citations from the *Classic of Poetry*. In any case, the text must have coalesced fairly early; Hsün Tzu (c. 300–c. 219 B.C.E.), who quotes the *Classic of Poetry* dozens of times, seems to have followed a recension substantially the same as our own. Hsün Tzu's student Mao Heng (with his son, Mao Ch'ang) transmitted the received text, which has come to be known as *Mao-shih* (Mao Odes). There were originally at least three other textual traditions (Lu, Ch'i, and Han), but these are now all lost. (A text known as *Han shih wai-chuan* [External Commentary to the Han Odes], attributed to Han Ying [fl. mid-second century B.C.E.], has survived; this is a collection of anecdotes intended to illustrate the multivalent verses of the *Classic of Poetry*.) Some skeptical writers have alleged that the whole of the text underwent a massive revision at the hands of Han editors in order to bring the already antiquated rhymes in line with contemporary pronunciation. Advances in Old Chinese phonology have made it possible to identify a few such instances, but they remain rare enough to be noteworthy.

The *Classic of Poetry* has 305 poems, divided into four parts: (1) the "Feng" (Airs), with 160 poems; (2) the "Hsiao-ya" (Lesser Odes, or Lesser Elegantiae), with 74; (3) the "Ta-ya" (Greater Odes, or Greater Elegantiae), with 31; (4) and the "Sung" (ritual Hymns), with 40 poems. The last three sections deal with lofty themes, including the Chou conquest and the proper invocations for various rituals. The "airs" include a number of songs that celebrate in unadorned language the pleasures of carnal love. Generations of interpreters have attributed to these items a secondary layer of meaning in the more spiritual realm of ethical and political philosophy. Many early Western sinologists (such as Herbert A. Giles) were unpersuaded by what they perceived as ridiculous sobriety on the part of the commentators, but recent studies suggest that these figurative senses of the text may have been intended from the very beginning. An analogy may be drawn with the biblical "Song of Songs," in which the union between Solomon and the queen of Sheba can easily be read in the context of the Old Testament as a metaphor for the union between Israel and God.

The next three classics, *Chou-li*, *Yi-li*, and *Li-chi*, are collectively known as the *San-li* (Three Ritual [Texts]). *Chou-li*—originally called *Chou-kuan* (Offices of Chou)—is a long text purporting to describe the government of the Chou state, with tables of organization and descriptions of the various officials' duties. The text was attributed to the Duke of Chou, but there are no references to *Chou-li* from before the end of the Former Han dynasty (206 B.C.E.–8 C.E.). It is said to have been presented, with the final section missing, to Emperor Wu (r. 141–87 B.C.E.) by his younger brother, Prince Hsien of Ho-chien (r. 155–129 B.C.E.)—but we have no record of this event until centuries after the fact. (The final section of the received text is a treatise on craftsmen and their art intended to replace the original chapter, which apparently was never found.)

Liu Hsin (46 B.C.E.–23 C.E.), the palace librarian in the service of the usurper Wang Mang (33 B.C.E.–23 C.E.; r. 9–23 C.E.), vigorously promoted the text as the blueprint for Wang Mang's new government. Because several apocryphal texts "presaging" Wang Mang's rule are known to have appeared out of thin air at this time, Liu Hsin has been accused by generations of scholars of having fabricated the work out of whole cloth. However, these indictments were themselves usually politically motivated, since they came from the camp of the so-called New Text scholars, who for their own reasons wished to disparage *Chou-li* and other "Old Text" classics. In a famous article pioneering the technique of analyzing classical Chinese grammar, Bernhard Karlgren demonstrated that the received *Chou-li* must come from a time well before that of Liu Hsin. Still, there is no question that the text paints an idealized picture of Chou government, and is unreliable—at best—as a source on the Western Chou.

Yi-li may be the only extant volume of a large set of materials discussing the rituals pertaining to each level of the ancient aristocracy. *Yi-li*, which was originally known by the name *Shih-li* (and sometimes—confusingly enough—

Li-chi, which now denotes an entirely separate classic), deals with the rituals of the *shih*, the lowest noble class. We know that *Yi-li* was already in circulation during the Former Han dynasty, because three manuscripts of the text were discovered in a tomb in Wu-wei, Kansu province, which has been dated to the end of that period. But the origin and transmission of *Yi-li* is still unclear. There were originally both "New Text" and "Old Text" recensions. The "Old Text" version included previously lost chapters that were allegedly discovered in Confucius's house (the details of this event were related above) and was presented to the emperor by the same Prince Hsien of Ho-chien. The received text is edited by Cheng Hsüan (127–200 C.E.); it is a critical edition taking into account both the "Old Text" and "New Text" readings of each passage, but including only those seventeen chapters common to both recensions.

It is somewhat unfortunate that by far the most interesting of the three ritual classics, *Li-chi*, also has the most unclear origins. The text is of a diverse nature: some chapters are made up of ritual prescriptions similar to what is found in *Yi-li*; some contain further "information" (most of it romanticized) on Confucius and his school; and another whole section of the text is devoted to definitions of ritual terms appearing in *Yi-li* and similar books. None of the accounts of the compilation of *Li-chi* are believable, and the collection may not have circulated as such until the first century C.E. or later—although individual chapters are sometimes cited before then by their own titles. There is another text called *Ta Tai Li-chi* (Record of Ritual of Tai the Elder), attributed to Tai Te (fl. first century B.C.E.). This work pretends to be an older version of *Li-chi* and actually includes some similar material, but its origins are highly questionable, as it includes whole tracts that are clearly culled from earlier works.

Despite its obscure provenance, *Li-chi* contains many chapters of supreme importance for the study of Chinese philosophy. Two of these, "Chung-yung" (Application of the Mean) and "Ta-hsüeh" (Great Learning), were anointed during the Confucian revival of the Middle Ages as two of the highest expressions of the sages' teachings; they were combined by Chu Hsi with the *Analects* and *Mencius* to form the most essential canon, the *Ssu shu* (Four Books). Other chapters, such as "Yüeh-chi" (Record of Music) and "Yüeh-ling" (Monthly Ordinances), are essential to understanding the correlative thinking of the Han period. "Yüeh-chi," like certain other chapters in the collection, seems to be derivative of Hsün Tzu.

Among the texts recently excavated from a tomb at Kuo-tien was a recension of the "Tzu yi" chapter of the *Li-chi*. This demonstrates that at least some of the *Li-chi* goes back to c. 300 B.C.E.

Ch'un-ch'iu (Springs and Autumns) has been incorporated into the canon with three ancient commentaries. *Ch'un-ch'iu san chuan* (Springs and Autumns with Three Commentaries) should therefore actually be counted as *four* classics, although together they take up only three places in the total of thirteen. There were originally at least two other commentaries (those by "Mr. Tsou" and "Mr. Chia"), but these have long been lost. The *Springs and Autumns* is a terse chronicle from the state of Lu, covering the important events in the period 722–481 B.C.E. The fact that the record ends just two years before Confucius's death led to the traditional belief that the Master himself edited the text, indicating his approval or disapproval through his subtle choice of words. Mencius's testimony to this effect bolstered the theory. Whether or not Confucius really had any hand in its compilation, the text has resisted several efforts to prove it spurious. Apparently, every major court during the Eastern Chou period kept an annalistic record like the *Springs and Autumns*, and the received text is the only one that has survived—because it came from Lu, the home state of Confucius. The only possible exceptions are the *Chu-shu chi-nien* (Bamboo Annals), a text allegedly discovered in a tomb around 280 C.E. that may—if genuine—be a court history from the state of Wei; and the records of the state of Ch'in, which form, according to Fang Pao (1668–1749) and others, the basis of the fifth chapter of *Shih-chi* (Records of the Historian). It is not surprising, therefore, that among the manuscripts recovered in 1975 from the late Ch'in period (c. 217 B.C.E.) tombs at Shui-hu-ti in Hupei was a chronicle from the state of Ch'in.

During the Former Han, the most important commentary to the *Springs and Autumns* was the *Kung-yang Commentary*, which is said to have been transmitted by Kung-yang Kao and finally written down by his descendant Kung-yang Shou during the reign of Emperor Ching (r. 157–141 B.C.E.). The scholar-official Tung Chung-shu (c. 179–c. 104 B.C.E.) was an influential supporter of this text; he is famous for having based his decisions in court cases on precedents in the *Kung-yang*. The *Ku-liang Commentary* (named after its author, Ku-liang Hsi) is thought to be later than the *Kung-yang*, in part because of its frequent citations of that work.

The peculiar commentary is the *Tso*, attributed to Tso Ch'iu-ming, a disciple of Confucius mentioned in the *Analects*. Like *Chou-li*, *Tso chuan* was denounced by K'ang Yu-wei (1858–1927) as a forgery from the hand of Liu Hsin. Since Karlgren, most scholars accept *Tso chuan* as an "authentic" text from the fourth century B.C.E., incorporating material that is probably even older. The *Tso* chronicle continues for eighteen years after the end of the *Ch'un-ch'iu*, down to 463 B.C.E. This discrepancy and other stylistic anomalies in the text imply that *Tso chuan* was not originally written as a commentary on the *Springs and Autumns*, but was arranged—perhaps by Tu Yü (222–284 C.E.), the first important commentator on the text—for that purpose.

Tso chuan is far longer and richer than the other two commentaries and has enjoyed much wider readership for centuries. Many famous Eastern Chou legends—for example, the peregrinations of Ch'ung-erh (Double-Ears), the future Duke Wen of Chin (r. 636–628 B.C.E.); and the life and death of Wu Tzu-hsü (d. 484 B.C.E.)—are recorded first, and often most fully, in *Tso chuan*. This was the most influential text in molding the imperial Chinese reader's sense of his civilization's ancient history. Therefore *Tso chuan* is essential to understanding every period of Chinese history, even though it cannot itself be taken as a pristine account of events as they actually transpired. The authors of the *Tso* were primarily interested in producing a didactic work illustrating the transcendent principles *governing* history—the just deserts awaiting the wicked and the virtuous. There is not a single story in *Tso chuan* that does not end as it "should." Wars, for example, are waged over breaches of ritual rather than for riches and conquest: more often than not, the victor decides to return the greater part of the spoils—especially if he is convinced of his opponent's contrition—in a gesture designed to express his own unwillingness to upset the ancient and inviolable balance of power. A seasoned reader can predict the outcome of every armed conflict: victory will go to the side that has acted more honorably and has shown the higher esteem for the rituals and the Way.

Lun-yü is known in English by the name *Analects*, after the Latin *analecta*, meaning the selected writings of an author—though the Latin word is itself borrowed from the Greek. This rendering, attributable to the early Jesuit missionaries, is felicitous in that the Chinese title means precisely *Selected Sayings*, that is, of Confucius. Since *Lun-yü* is regarded as the most authoritative source on Confucius and his discussions with his disciples, the veneration that has been accorded this text is immense. After the Master's death, according to the legend, several of his disciples compared their private records of his sayings and anthologized his most important sayings in the collection entitled *Lun-yü*. The remaining material was supposedly preserved in a companion volume, *Chia-yü* (School Sayings). There is indeed an extant text called *K'ung Tzu chia-yü* (School Sayings of Confucius), but most scholars believe that it was forged.

There are several problems with the above account of the composition of the *Analects*. First, critics—such as Ts'ui Shu (1740–1816)—have observed for centuries that there are significant stylistic differences, and often outright inconsistencies, among many of the twenty chapters in the book; furthermore, certain references to persons and events—such as the use of Duke Ai of Lu's (r. 494–468 B.C.E.) posthumous name in *Analects* 6.3—provide for those chapters more or less definite *termini a quo* that are later than Confucius's death in 479 B.C.E. An ancient solution to these difficulties was to suggest that the variant traditions represent the teachings of different disciples. More recently, some scholars have attempted to date each chapter—and, in extreme cases, each verse—independently; E. Bruce Brooks and A. Taeko Brooks, for example, date the oldest chapter to 479 B.C.E. and the latest to 249 B.C.E.

The issue is not trivial, especially given the weight that Confucius's opinions carried in traditional China and throughout East Asia. Serious students of Confucian philosophy need to know how reliable the *Analects* really are, and a chapter composed in 249 B.C.E. can hardly be accepted as the veritable words of the Sage. However, while it is true that the *Analects* may not have taken their present shape until Han times, there has been a tendency, in the current revisionist mood, to overlook ancient testimony. For example, an unmistakable reference to *Analects* 13.16 can be found in chapter 46 of the *Mo Tzu,* in a section that forms part of what are sometimes called the "Mohist Analects," or records of discussions between Mo Ti (480?–400? B.C.E.) and his own disciples. Most scholars consider the "Mohist Analects" a reliable collection of material dating from the turn of the fifth century B.C.E. and earlier; indeed, it is by far the least problematic part of the entire *Mo Tzu.* This is especially important because chapter 13 of the *Analects* is usually thought to be relatively *late* (the Brookses date it to 321 B.C.E., more than 150 years after Confucius's death). The consequence is that sayings now included in the *Analects* were already in circulation during the century between the death of Confucius and the death of Mo Tzu. Thus, while the final verdict on the dating of the *Analects* is still not in, we must keep open the possibility that much of the text is actually genuine.

The next classic, *Hsiao-ching,* is a short work composed of a lecture by Confucius to his disciple Tseng Tzu or Tseng Shen (505–436 B.C.E.?) on the ideal of *hsiao.* Chu Hsi observed that there seem to be two distinct strata in the received text: one consisting of the discussion between the Master and his disciple, which may have been transmitted by Tseng Tzu or his own followers; and another including citations from *Tso chuan* and *Kuo-yü,* which consequently cannot date from before c. 300 B.C.E. Two lengthy quotations from *Hsiao-ching* in *Lü-shih ch'un-ch'iu* (The Springs and Autumns of Master Lü, an encyclopedic work dated to approximately 240 B.C.E.), however, indicate that the classic was already in circulation by the end of the third century. The *Classic of Filial Piety* was particularly influential during the Han dynasty and remained a respected text throughout the imperial era. The classic was the center of a great controversy after the massive cultural reassessment known as the May Fourth movement (1919), however; thinkers like Wu Yü (1871–1949) saw in *hsiao* the root of what they perceived as China's social and technological backwardness, since that "virtue" required children to sacrifice everything for their parents when circumstances dictated.

The twelfth classic, *Erh-ya,* is an ancient lexicon containing entries on flora and fauna, as well as glosses on terms to be found in the older classics. The text has been attributed to the Duke of Chou since at least the time of Chang Yi (fl. 227–233 C.E.), but the presence of numerous citations dating from the middle and late Chou period refutes that suggestion. Karlgren believes that the compilation dates to the third century B.C.E., and most scholars today are apt to agree. *Erh-ya* is of some value to specialists, since its testimony can be helpful when it happens to contain a gloss on an obscure phrase encountered in another text; otherwise, the work is rarely read and is, in any case, virtually impossible to use without a concordance.

The last classic is the *Mencius,* or the collected works of the philosopher Meng K'o (372–289 B.C.E.), which was not included in the canon until the Sung period. It is clear from such compilations as *Li-chi, Ta Tai Li-chi,* and *Han shih wai-chuan* that the most influential teacher and transmitter in early imperial times was not Mencius but Hsün Tzu. After the rise of Neo-Confucianism, however, Mencius was acknowledged as the last ancient sage (relegating Hsün Tzu to secondary or even tertiary status). The received text of the *Mencius* consists of seven of the original eleven books in the collection, the other four having been excised by the commentator Chao Ch'i (d. 201 C.E.) because he thought them spurious and inferior. The text includes isolated sayings by Mencius, records of audiences with various dignitaries, discussions between Mencius and his disciples, and debates between Mencius and representatives of other philosophical schools. Chu Hsi, as mentioned above, considered the *Mencius* one of the four most important books in the entire literature.

Many twentieth-century critics—such as Wu Yü and Max Weber (1864–1920)—have suggested that the unquestioned prestige of the Confucian classics and slavish adherence to their precepts without any adaptation to the times were to blame for many of modern China's problems. What such arguments overlook is that, for much of China's two-thousand-year history, there was no more desirable place on earth for an intellectual or aristocrat to be born. The Middle Kingdom was arguably more advanced technologically, economically, and socially than most other civilizations on earth until the middle of the past millennium. It is important to keep in mind that at least part of the reason for China's cultural and intellectual excellence lies in the teachings of the Thirteen Classics.

To take only one example, the doctrine of *t'ien-ming* (Mandate of Heaven), as expounded in the *Classic of Documents* and *Mencius*, holds that the ruler of men is but Heaven's vice-gerent and is allowed to maintain his exalted status only on the condition of his virtuous governance of the realm. This was the justification that King Wen of Chou and his representatives supposedly presented to the subjugated people of Shang: Heaven had decreed that the Shang king, who was given to licentiousness and dissipation, be removed justly and forcibly by King Wen and his army. The ramifications of this theory in Chinese history are inestimable. The emperors of the Sung dynasty (960–1279), one of the most glorious, surely did not believe that a vengeful Heaven would strike them down if they abused their power, and yet document after document reveals how assiduously policymakers debated the consequences that prospective legislation would have on the welfare of their lowliest subjects. Parties often disagreed, and if the peasants themselves had had a say in political affairs, they might not have endorsed any of the ministers' proposals. But the concern for humanity displayed by the emperor and his cabinet was evident. Such sentiments informed much of the literature of China inspired by Confucianism.

Paul Rakita Goldin

Chapter 5

SHIH-CHING POETRY AND DIDACTICISM IN ANCIENT CHINESE LITERATURE

The 305 songs of the *Shih-ching* (Classic of Poetry or Songs) date, by rough estimation, to the first four hundred years of the first millennium B.C.E. This was the period that encompassed the initial flourishing of the newly founded Chou dynasty in the valley of the Wei River, the destruction of the Chou capital in 771 B.C.E. and the subsequent dislocation of the Chou kings to Lo-yi in the east, and, finally, in 679 B.C.E., to protect the Chou realm against encroachments from Ch'u in the south, the royal recognition of Duke Huan of Ch'i (r. 685–643 B.C.E.) as protector of the king and hence de facto overlord of all the vassal states. In literary terms, the period may be identified as that of the archaic or preclassical texts, among which were the *Shih-ching*, parts of the *Shang-shu* (*Shu-ching*; Classic of Documents), the oracle-book *Chou-yi* (Changes of Chou), as well as inscriptions on bronze vessels recording royal donations, investitures, and other events that took place at the Chou court and its dependencies.

Much of this preclassical literature was composed out of a desire by early authors to preserve and transmit, both orally and in writing, the accumulated wisdom of their culture. A similar desire to instruct can be readily recognized in the famous works of philosophy and historical narrative that have been transmitted to us from the classical period of Chinese literature, a time known in political terms as that of the late Spring and Autumn period (722–481/463 B.C.E.) and Warring States (c. 403–221 B.C.E.). The *Lun-yü* (Analects) of Confucius teaches the moral principles necessary to self-cultivation and governing others;

the *Tso chuan* (Tso Commentary) richly illustrates the complex workings of reciprocity in human history; the *Lao Tzu* urges us to forget the attachments born of conventional sentimentality in order to reveal the forces hidden deep within that give leverage over the challenges of life. Chou literature was thus permeated by the will of the literary pedagogue to instruct and to improve through the power of words. While ancient Chinese literature may also occasionally have been intended to entertain, lurking not far beneath its diverting surface was a lesson that gave meaning and purpose to its art.

Thanks to the discoveries of Chinese archeology made in the past twenty-five years, previously lost ancient works that enhance our understanding of the instructional purposes of literature are also available. From such famous ancient tombs as those at Ma-wang-tui, Yin-ch'üeh-shan, Kuo-tien, and other sites of pre-Han and Han dynasty date, most of them located in what was once the southern state of Ch'u, a whole library of handbooks and guides have been recovered. These manuals and textbooks for the afterlife provide lessons in such practical matters as how to cure illness, select a suitable horse, or engage in passionate sex, the lofty skills of governing states and winning crucial military battles, and the esoteric techniques of worshiping the spirits and divining their will.

Of all the early forms of literary expression, poetry perhaps best embodies the didactic purposes of ancient Chinese authors and the capacity of artful language to accomplish them. To read the lyrics preserved in the *Shih-ching* is both to learn the wisdom that the ancients held dear and to hear the preaching voice of the poet, instructing one to do this and not that, reminding one of the right course and warning against straying into evil ways.

THE *SHIH-CHING* AND CONFUCIANISM

Because Confucius (551–479 B.C.E.) appreciated its didactic essence, he recommended the poetry of the *Shih-ching* to his disciples and relied on it to illustrate the principles and methods of moral cultivation he was trying to impart. It is thus of enormous importance that the Shanghai Museum has announced officially that it has acquired a manuscript—written on bamboo strips excavated from a c. 300 B.C.E. tomb in the area of ancient Ch'u (south-central China)—that records early Confucian interpretations of the moral significance of *Shih-ching* poetry. While publication of the manuscript is perhaps years in the future and thus information about its contents is still incomplete, it appears that it represents the *Shih-ching* teachings of Confucius's disciple Tzu Hsia, or Master Hsia (also known as Pu Shang or Pu Tzu). Master Hsia is credited in early sources with the transmission of the *Shih-ching*, which he had received from Confucius, and with having been the author of the "Ta hsü" (Major Preface) and "Hsiao hsü" (Minor Preface), important parts of the Mao school text of the *Shih-ching*. The publication of the Shanghai Museum manuscript will, without doubt, occasion a full reevaluation and revision of what has been said (here and elsewhere) about the nature of early poetry and the role of Confucius and his followers in preserving, transmitting, and interpreting the *Shih-ching.*

Confucius's use of the ancient collection of poetry effectively made it a text of the Confucian school. From his time on, it became increasingly difficult to separate *Shih-ching* poetry from the moral lessons of Confucius's philosophy. Later generations of Confucian thinkers, such as Confucius's grandson Tzu Ssu, as well as Mencius and Hsün Tzu, emulated the Master by frequently quoting from *Shih-ching* to cap off philosophical arguments. Dramatic new proof of the early assimilation of the songs into Confucian moral philosophy is provided by a text excavated in 1993 from a Ch'u tomb at Kuo-tien, Hupei province. The text is one of eleven ancient Confucian documents buried in what seems to have been the tomb of a royal tutor who served in the Ch'u court at the end of the fourth century B.C.E. It is almost identical to the "Tzu yi" chapter of the Han ritual compendium *Li-chi* (Record of Ritual)—a chapter that has been traditionally ascribed to Tzu Ssu. The Kuo-tien find suggests that many of the diverse chapters that make up *Li-chi* are more ancient than modern scholars have believed. Like its counterpart in *Li-chi,* the Kuo-tien "Tzu yi" frequently quotes from the *Shih-ching* and the *Shang-shu* in order to provide archaic precedents for its philosophy. It thus provides our earliest text versions of many lines of ancient Chinese poetry and shows how thinkers in the fourth century B.C.E. manipulated these lines to suit their philosophical purposes.

THE EARLY SCHOOLS OF INTERPRETATION

Confucian interest in the moral meaning of the *Classic of Poetry* produced, by the Western Han dynasty, formal schools of interpretation. In spite of the fact that the *Shih-ching* had suffered from the same Ch'in-dynasty proscription that led to the burning of other ancient classics, because memorizing poetry was a common practice in antiquity, the work survived to become a subject of intense scholarly interest during the Han. Although, at the beginning of the Han, no one scholar knew the whole collection, nevertheless, through a collective effort of transcription and collation, there emerged over the first few decades of Han rule several more or less full versions complete with their own interpretations.

The most prominent of the Han schools of *Shih-ching* interpretation were the Lu, Han, and Ch'i—the *San chia shih* (Three Schools of the *Shih-ching*)—all of which first received imperial recognition during the successive reigns of the Han emperors Wen-ti (r. 179–157 B.C.E.) and Ching-ti (r. 156–141 B.C.E.). It is to be presumed that the versions of other schools, which never received official recognition, were lost. Among the better attested of those that disappeared very early was the version of King Yüan of Ch'u (d. 178 B.C.). Together with Shen P'ei, the founder of the Lu school, the king of the Han kingdom of

Ch'u was a student of the *Shih-ching* master Fou-ch'iu Po of Ch'i, who, in turn, claimed Hsün Tzu as his teacher. In the late 1970s, an extremely damaged *Shih-ching* manuscript was excavated near Fu-yang, in northwestern Anhui province, in the burial of Hsia-hou Tsao, a minor nobleman who died in 165 B.C.E. The southern provenance of the manuscript has led scholars who have closely examined its fragments to propose that it may be a remnant of the *Shih-ching* studied in the school of King Yüan of Ch'u.

The Three Schools were eventually displaced by the Mao school (see chapter 4), the sole ancient tradition of *Shih-ching* interpretation extant in its entirety. The Mao school first appeared at the court of Liu Te (d. 133 B.C.E.), Prince Hsien of Ho-chien. Like the Three Schools it finally overshadowed, the Mao school reads the songs as records of historical events, supplying the names and details of time and place to which it believes the obscure metaphors, analogies, and other figurative speech allude.

There are several elements in the Mao school text that, taken together, constitute the school's readings of the ancient poems. First there is the "Major Preface" traditionally ascribed to Master Hsia. This treatise describes the process by which poetry was first created and also defines the most important poetical terms, including the words for poetry and song and the names for the different divisions of the Mao school text. Each poem is introduced by a "Minor Preface." The opening of each "Minor Preface" is traditionally attributed to Master Hsia and, among scholars of the *Shih-ching*, is referred to as the "Shang hsü" (Upper Preface). Such an opening, seldom longer than two or three words and ending with the particle *yeh*, usually characterizes the moral purpose of the poem it introduces. (The Shanghai Museum manuscript mentioned above contains quotations identified by name as Master Hsia's teachings on the *Shih-ching*. This will no doubt cause scholars to reexamine the authenticity and significance of both the "Major Preface" and "Minor Prefaces" of the Mao school text.) The brief interpretation found in the "Upper Preface" is linked to the poems themselves in the "Mao chuan" (Mao Commentary), composed c. 150 B.C.E. The commentary also provides brief glosses on difficult terms and occasionally dangles a line or two of interpretation. Chronologically, the "Upper Preface" and the "Mao Commentary" are followed by elaborations on Master Hsia's comments, written sometime during the first century C.E., that are incorporated into a "Minor Preface" and referred to as the "Hsia hsü" (Lower Preface). Such a "Lower Preface" reconstructs, sometimes at great length, the historical circumstances in which it supposes the poem was composed. The most extensive remarks and a definitive summation of the Mao school reading are found in the comprehensive commentary of Cheng Hsüan (127–200). Here the historical interpretations of the "Lower Preface" are embraced, elaborated upon, and made to fit with what the "Upper Preface" and "Mao Commentary" say.

A close comparison of differences between the text readings of the Mao school and those preserved in the Fu-yang exemplar suggests that the Mao school may have triumphed over competitors because its renderings of the songs more closely represented contemporary Han dynasty pronunciation, rather than the more archaic readings of the other schools, and supplied cues for performance missing in other versions.

Study of the emergence of the various *Shih-ching* commentaries and interpretations has also greatly benefited from the text discoveries of Chinese archeologists. A manuscript excavated in 1973 from a Han dynasty tomb at Ma-wang-tui, near Ch'ang-sha, Hunan province, provides evidence of a previously undocumented stage in the hermeneutic shift from the moral interpretations found in the pre-Han Confucian philosophers to the explicit commentary of the Han dynasty schools of *Shih-ching* interpretation. The text, assigned the title "Wu-hsing-p'ien" (Essay on the Five Behaviors) by its discoverers, is a fourth-century B.C.E. work that has been identified by many scholars as a product of Tzu Ssu's school of moral cultivation. Proof of the text's early date was confirmed recently when an even earlier exemplar of *Wu-hsing-p'ien* was discovered in the same Ch'u tomb at Kuo-tien that yielded the earliest version of "Tzu yi." Attached to the Ma-wang-tui exemplar (but not found in the Kuo-tien text) is an early commentary that was probably composed by a mid-third-century B.C.E. member of the school of Shih Tzu, who is quoted by name in the commentary and who, according to the *Han shu* (History of the Han Dynasty) bibliographic catalogue, wrote a now-lost work of Confucian philosophy. Among its explanations of terms like "benevolence" and "propriety" and its references to virtuous paragons, the *Wu-hsing-p'ien* commentary provides important glosses and interpretations of selected lines from Mao 1 ("Kuan-chü"), Mao 28 ("Yen-yen"), and other *Shih-ching* verses. When the Shanghai Museum manuscript is published, the evidence it supplies should also shed light on the birth of *Shih-ching* commentaries.

THE TEXT AND ITS DIVISIONS

In part because of the layers of commentary accreted on its elliptical lines of verse, it is now difficult to determine with precision or certainty under what circumstances, and for what purposes, the poetry of the *Classic of Poetry* was first created. By reviewing all the songs that survive in the *Shih-ching*, however, it is possible to suggest how they evolved and are related to one another as well as to identify points of similarity and difference among them. When the songs were compiled and when they were written down are also unknown. The *Shih-ching* appears to have existed as an entity by no later than the end of the sixth century B.C.E., since Confucius and his contemporaries referred to the "Three Hundred Songs." *Chou-li* (Rites of Chou), a highly schematic fourth-century B.C.E. outline of the early Chou court, describes a corps of musicians, led by a grand master, who knew the six forms of poetical composition (*liu shih*), which they taught to the blind men who sang at the court of the Chou dynasty kings.

It may be that official musicians like these were responsible for compiling and editing the songs and perhaps for creating many of them as well.

The 305 songs in *Shih-ching* are divided into four groups: 160 "Kuo-feng" (Airs of the States), 74 "Hsiao ya" (conventionally rendered as Lesser Elegantiae), 31 "Ta ya" (conventionally rendered as Greater Elegantiae), and 40 "Sung" (Temple Hymns). This division of the text perhaps predates the orthodox Mao school version in which it is preserved. It is already hinted at in the *Analects* of Confucius and attested to in detail in a remarkable *Tso chuan* passage that recounts how, in 544 B.C.E., Sire Hsiang of Lu had his musicians sing all 305 songs for the entertainment of a visitor from Wu. Most authorities agree that the "Sung" are the oldest songs in the collection and the "Kuo-feng" the youngest. It is possible, however, that the disparities of grammatical usage and style upon which conclusions about the dates of the poems are based are the reflections of the different purposes the song types served rather than diachronic change. Thus the "Sung," "Hsiao ya," and "Ta ya" may be somewhat younger than has usually been thought.

"SUNG" (TEMPLE HYMNS)

The "Sung" are the most solemn of the songs. They appear to have been based largely on the liturgies recited to accompany the sacred rites of worship that took place in the ancestral temples of the Chou (Mao 266–296). The Chou hymns praise the accomplishments of the dynastic founders Wen and Wu (Mao 267–274) and Hou Chi (Lord Millet), the mythical ancestor of the Chou people and inventor of agriculture (Mao 275). Most typical of the hymns is Mao 280, a poetical description of the temple music played for the enjoyment of the ancestors. The sophisticated artfulness of the piece, which prefigured and inspired the treatises on music found in *Lü-shih ch'un-ch'iu* (The Annals of Lü Pu-wei) and the *Li-chi*, reminds us that none of the temple hymns is a simple record of the liturgies sung in the ancestral temples. All use the devices of poetry to memorialize how rituals were performed so that later generations would remember and emulate their forebears.

Also preserved among the "Sung" are chants of the state of Lu (Mao 297–300), Confucius's native state, and of Sung (Mao 301–305), where worship of the Shang ancestors was continued after the Chou defeated the Shang around the middle of the eleventh century B.C.E. The inclusion of the Lu hymns is further proof of the active role the Confucian school played in the early transmission of *Shih-ching*. The most splendid of the Lu hymns and perhaps of all the "Sung" is Mao 300, a long paean to Duke Hsi of Lu (r. 659–627) that describes his thankful worship of the duke of Chou, the founder of the Lu lineage, for helping him with his conquests and securing the state for all time. Of the five hymns sung to celebrate the Shang ancestors, the most important is Mao 303 ("Hsüan niao"), which recalls the myth of the "dark bird" that gave birth to the Shang lineage and celebrates the conquests of King Wu-ting (r. c. 1200?–1181?B.C.E.) and his descendants.

Because the Mao school text uses the term "Sung" to entitle this section, it is common to understand the songs that constitute it to have been "hymns" or "odes" of praise. But it is worth noting that the term used by the Mao school may have been particular to that school. If one keeps in mind words cognate with "Sung," written with related graphs, then it is possible to envision alternative ways of approaching these hymns. For example, the cognate term *sung* (reproach, dispute) suggests that these pieces, while they praised ancestors and founders, may also have been thought of as critical of the rulers and other prominent figures whose lives and deeds did not measure up to their predecessors'.

"TA YA" (GREATER YA)

Although it is common to claim that the "Ta ya," along with the "Hsiao ya," take their name from the fact that they were regarded as *ya* or "elegant," this is in fact a doubtful understanding of the name. It has been observed, by authorities as diverse as Wang Yin-chih and Arthur Waley, that *ya* (**ngragx*) is phonologically related to *Hsia* (**gragx*), the ethnic term the peoples of the Central States (the states of the central plains) used to distinguish themselves from the peoples of Ch'u, Wu, Yüeh, and other outlying (particularly southern) states. Thus the names "Ta ya" and "Hsiao ya" were meant to suggest that these songs represented Hsia culture and traditions and should thus be intoned with strict observation of the Hsia standards of pronunciation. The conventional understanding of "Ta ya" as "Greater Elegantiae" and "Hsiao ya" as "Lesser Elegantiae" is thus a makeshift means of referring to the songs in these sections of the *Classic of Poetry* as "Hsia-like" (hence "elegant").

Several of the so-called Greater Elegantiae verses are concerned with preserving the memory of the great rulers of antiquity and with ensuring that the traditions of proper ritual performance are continued. Thus, to cite but a few examples, Mao 235, a poem often cited by Mencius and Hsün Tzu, lists the virtues of King Wen to remind a later ruler of the examples he must study and emulate; Mao 245 gives a glowing account of the miraculous birth of "Lord Millet" and of his invention of agriculture, but concludes with a lesson on which foods are properly offered to the ancestors.

Others of the "Greater Ya" explore subjects not found in the "Sung." Mao 253, for example, is a memorial in verse that cautions an unnamed king to rid himself of his "wily and obsequious" servants and thus allow the weary subjects they victimize with their robbery and tyranny to rest. While thankfully much shorter, the piece is of a kind with "Li sao" (Encountering Sorrow; see chapter 12). Mao 256 is a lengthy, and somewhat carping, address to a presumably young king that sets forth all the lessons he needs to learn to be a wise and respected ruler. Its philosophical message—that the ruler should cultivate himself and rely on his own counsel—greatly influenced Hsün Tzu and the author of "Chung yung" (Application of the Mean; see chapters 3 and 4).

"HSIAO YA" (LESSER YA)

Several important pieces in the "Lesser Ya"—for example, Mao 209, 210, and 220—recite the details of ritual performance and thus seem intended to preserve the traditions of proper worship of the ancestors and spirits. Still others, like Mao 191, resemble Mao 253 and complain about the behavior of a king from the perspective of one of his close advisers. Otherwise, the poems in this section move away from the solemn surroundings of the temple and the innermost circles at the royal court toward the events that filled the everyday life of the larger society of aristocrats, including their loves and their hardships. Perhaps most typical of the "Lesser Ya" are the songs, like Mao 170–176, that memorialize happy occasions of companionship and shared drunkenness with lords and "lucky guests" from other states, and those, like Mao 177–180, that boast of the bravery and military exploits of comrades-in-arms.

"KUO FENG" (AIRS OF THE STATES)

The "Kuo feng" are divided into fifteen parts according to the names of ancient states or regions, a rubric whose antiquity is also attested to by the *Tso chuan* passage referred to above. This division of the songs was meant to reflect their geographical provenance, an identification supported to some extent by geographical and historical allusions in the songs themselves. How songs from such diverse regions were gathered together is explained by an old tradition, first recorded in Han dynasty sources, that, upon visiting a state, the Chou king ordered his grand master to gather its songs so that he could learn its popular customs and complaints. The antiquity of this practice cannot be determined, and it is possible that the Han dynasty accounts of it were meant to provide a precedent for the Han practice of collecting popular songs critical of the emperor and his court.

Regardless of whether the songs did in fact come from different states, it is striking that those attributed to the lands of Chou Nan and Shao Nan, identified as a southern region that is elsewhere deprecated as barbaric, are placed at the very beginning of the anthology, while those from the royal Chou are relegated to a later position. This sequence was explained by the claim that the Chou Nan and Shao Nan songs are older than the others in "Kuo-feng." The prominent position given them may in fact be an early reflection of the notion that the southern states of Ch'u and Wu had displaced the Chou as the geographical center of China, an idea that also influenced the order of the contents in *Shan hai ching* (Classic of Mountains and Seas; see chapter 2) and some other ancient sources.

Many of the "Kuo feng" continue themes found in the "Sung" and "Ya" sections of *Shih-ching*. We still find, in somewhat shorter form in the "Kuo-feng," songs apparently intended to preserve for posterity important cultural wisdom. For example, Mao 25 ("Tsou-yü") seems to be an abbreviated account of archery rites performed to encourage the new growth of springtime vegetation. The purpose of the piece might be missed were it not made much more explicit in an elaboration on Mao 25 found in "Tung ching fu" (Eastern Capital Rhapsody), by Chang Heng (78–139). Mao 8 provides a brief lesson for young women on how to gather and use a fertility herb, punningly named "babes-in-a pot." Mao 154 ("Ch'i-yüeh" [Seventh Month]) is a remarkable poetical almanac that echoes the agriculture wisdom of Mao 245 but is much closer in intent to the "Almanac" chapters of *Lü-shih ch'un-ch'iu*. The song also may have influenced the rhymed and metrically regular treatises on agronomy found in chapter 26 of that comprehensive synthesis of imperial philosophy compiled under the patronage of the Ch'in prime minister Lü Pu-wei in c. 239 B.C.E.

It is doubtful, however, that other "Kuo-feng" pieces, similarly concerned with traditional customs and practices, should be understood narrowly and literally as mere records of how things are done. For example, Mao 158 emphasizes the need to use a good matchmaker when seeking a bride and compares that with using a good axe handle as a model for cutting a new one. This song should not be taken simply as a note on how to go about getting betrothed. The images of taking a bride and cutting an axe handle should be interpreted as metaphorical elements in a larger lesson that the song teaches: in making crucial decisions, follow existing models and proceed systematically. Similarly, the sketch, found in Mao 64, of a courtship ritual in which fruit is exchanged for girdle pendants can be read as metaphorical teaching on the need for reciprocity in all forms of hierarchical relationships.

Unique to the "Kuo-feng" section of the *Shih-ching* are songs that narrate, in the elliptical, redundant, and circuitous fashion of poetry, tales and vignettes of everyday life in the countryside and in other locales far removed from the activities of court and temple memorialized in other songs. These songs, in sharp contrast to those of the "Ya" and "Sung" sections, are reminiscent of the persuader's tales or "persuasions" (*shuo*) that provided itinerant philosophers with illustrations to entertain their listeners as well as instruct them. Perhaps the verse tales were precursors to these rhetorical devices; it may be that the well-known chapters of the *Han Fei Tzu* and the *Huai-nan Tzu* (see chapters 2 and 3) that collect and comment on the *shuo* were modeled after the "Kuo-feng" compendium of poetical vignettes.

Examples of verse tales in "Kuo-feng" are too numerous to list. A few examples should suffice to identify the genre and define its chief characteristics. Mao 39 provides an almost comical account of a young woman who goes to her maiden aunts and unmarried sisters for advice on how to proceed with her marriage. Mao 43 sketches the parable of a ruler who craves beauty but finds himself surrounded by ugliness instead. Mao 58 recounts the tale of a wife who devotes herself to her husband, only to be abandoned by him when he no longer finds her beautiful. Mao 76 tells of a girl who cannot restrain her lover's advances because he knows that her protests are hollow.

Frequently, the plot of a short story is obscured by the orthodox commentaries. The historicizing tendencies of the Mao school make it almost impossible to recognize Mao 28 as a tale of profound grief for a dead ruler. Mao 1's story of a young man who is deep in the throes of passion but nevertheless manages to contain himself is similarly obscured by the commentaries of the Mao school. Fortunately, the discovery of the "Wu-hsing-p'ien" commentary described above helps us to read these songs in a way that is truer to their original intent. In the case of the very famous Mao 1 ("Kuan-chü"), which begins with the cry of an osprey, reading it as the story of a man sorely tempted by love who nevertheless manages to control his erotic desires enables us to recognize the poem as the direct ancestor of the much more elaborate versions of this theme found in "Mei-jen fu" (Rhapsody on a Beautiful Woman) of the pseudo-Ssu-ma Hsiang-ju and "Teng-t'u tzu hao-se fu" (Rhapsody on the Lechery of Master Teng-t'u), attributed to Sung Yü (290?–222? B.C.E.).

THE LANGUAGE OF ANCIENT POETRY

The language of the *Shih-ching*, and in particular that of the "Airs of the States," is extraordinarily figurative and allusive. Metaphors and other forms of figurative language are so common in *Shih-ching* poetry that it is often difficult for an interpreter to distinguish between the lines that are allusive and those that are part of the "concrete" and immediate narrative of a song. Some pieces, for instance Mao 9, appear to be composed entirely of metaphorical allusions, and the song's import can be guessed at only by identifying the references that lie behind these allusions and inducing from them an overall meaning or message. Other songs, like Mao 42, embed in their narratives figures of speech derived from extremely diverse sources.

The most crucial figure of speech—and an important characteristic of the "Airs of the States"—is the *hsing*. The *locus classicus* of the term *hsing* is the "Wu-hsing-p'ien" commentary excavated at the Han site of Ma-wang-tui. Use of the term is also a prominent and much-discussed feature of the *Mao Commentary* of c. 150 B.C.E. Both *Wu-hsing-p'ien* and the *Mao Commentary* apply the term to the opening imagery of *Shih-ching* poetry. No metaphor that occurs elsewhere in a song, no matter how close in form and content it may be to a *hsing*, is ever labeled *hsing* by either source. Their use of the term suggests that we should understand the term as "initiate" or "prompt," a meaning it has elsewhere. Studying how the lines identified as *hsing* work within a song suggests that the *hsing* should be considered a metaphorical allusion quoted by a poet to introduce a song and to serve as a unifying element that determines the choice of figurative and narrative imagery that appears in the remainder of the piece. Although almost 70 percent of "Kuo-feng" begin with lines identified in the *Mao Commentary* as *hsing*, only a third of the "Lesser Ya" do. The poetic device is extremely rare in the "Greater Ya" and "Temple Hymns."

The imagery of the *hsing* most often involves birds, plants, mountains, and rivers. For example, the *Mao Commentary* identifies the allusions to the ospreys in Mao 1 and to the kudzu in Mao 2 as *hsing*. Other metaphorical allusions refer to the wind, animals, fish, boats, the stars, and articles of clothing. The metaphorical images identified as *hsing* in the context of *Shih-ching* poetry appear in divinatory poetry as the signs and portents that reveal the future and prefigure human fate. Examples of this mantic poetry are found in the *yao tz'u* in *Chou-yi*; the *t'ung yao* or portentous "Songs of Young Boys" quoted in *Tso chuan*; and the large number of prophetic verses collected in *Yi-lin*, a divinatory work attributed to Ts'ui Chuan (early first century C.E.). The discovery of a *Chou-yi* manuscript at Ma-wang-tui has contributed greatly to our understanding of the text's mantic poetry and its role in the arts of divination.

THE *SHIH* STYLE

Among the 160 poems in "Kuo-feng" are examples of what can be called mature *shih*-style poetry. Numerous formal elements, including rhyme patterns, metrical length, and the regular division of songs into stanzas characterize this *shih* style. The number of stanzas and lines appears almost random throughout "Hsiao ya" and "Ta ya," and all but six of the "Sung" consist solely of one long stanza. In contrast, the "Kuo-feng" verses present a nearly consistent standard of three stanzas (*chang*), which are usually repetitive and consist of four lines. In "Kuo-feng," songs identified with the states of Ts'ao and Pin usually have more than three stanzas, while those from Cheng clearly favor two stanzas; moreover, the stanzas of Wei, T'ang, and Ch'in songs are consistently longer than four lines.

Most "Kuo-feng" lines form couplets, each line of which usually consists of four syllables; metrically irregular lines of three or five syllables occur in the "Ya" and "Sung" sections, though not often. The lines of a couplet are seldom independent; most form a single syntactic and semantic unit. Moreover, line-sharing among songs frequently involves couplets. This suggests that what are usually taken to be couplets should be read as a single eight-syllable line consisting of two four-syllable half-lines, or hemistichs.

All the songs of *Shih-ching* rhyme, with the exception of six pieces in the "Sung" section and the last two stanzas of one piece in "Ta ya." Head-rhyme (beginning rhyme or alliteration) and internal rhyme occur occasionally, but only end-rhymes are used systematically. They mark the end of a line and, since the rhyme usually remains constant for an entire stanza, also mark the division of a song into stanzas. Although individual quatrains might have an AABB rhyme pattern, songs arranged as a series of rhyming couplets occur infrequently. In a standard "Kuo-feng" quatrain, the second and fourth lines must rhyme, and the most common rhyme patterns are AAOA and OAAA. Another standard pattern is ABAB.

Formal features such as the aforementioned were not the exclusive property of poetry, distinguishing it from other forms of literary expression. Contemporary prose employed the same organizing devices: metrical regularity and division into *chang* or similar units. Even pieces as prosaic as bronze inscriptions were often rhymed. The ancients did not mention rhyme and metrical regularity in defining what they meant by poetical expression. In their minds what was prominent was that poetry was sung to a melody and accompanied by music. Equally, if not more, important was the idea that poetry was the expression of innermost thoughts and feelings, a personal and emotional revelation, couched in epigrams, usually not communicated to others and never expressed in the forms of ordinary discourse.

These definitive characteristics of verse are summarized in a *Classic of Documents* version of the myth of how the hero Shun summoned the one-legged dragon K'uei to temper the character of his son and to harmonize the relations of men and spirits by singing songs.

> Sovereign Shun declared, "K'uei, I command you to take charge of music and to teach my heir. Warm his strictness and cool his gentleness. Make his resoluteness unoppressive and his ambitiousness humble. With poetry put your thoughts into words. Prolong the words in song. Have musical tones accompany the prolonging and use pitch-pipes to harmonize the tones. Let the sounds of the eight instruments blend and not interfere with one another. Then will there be harmony among spirits and men." K'uei replied, "O, I strike the stone chimes! I beat the stone chimes! The hundred beasts lead one another in a dance."

The "Major Preface," a first- or second-century C.E. Mao school collection of traditional sayings and definitions related to *Shih-ching*, repeats the substance of the myth in an oft-quoted passage:

> Poetry is the extension of thought. What is thought in the heart becomes a poem when words issue forth. When emotions stir one within, they take shape in his words. When his words are insufficient, then he exclaims and sighs; when exclamations and sighs are insufficient, he chants and sings; when chant and song are insufficient, without thinking, he automatically gestures with his hands and stamps his feet.

Among the exclusive characteristics of poetry mentioned in the "Major Preface" are the *chieh* (exclamations) and *t'an* (sighs) used to enhance the capacity of ordinary language to communicate deep emotions. They are interjections, sounds without specific meanings, and there are numerous examples of them in *Shih-ching*. The graph used to write the word *shih* itself has as its phonophore one of these utterances, read *ssu* in modern pronunciation. In the Kuo-tien "Tzu yi," the *ssu* phonophore alone, rather than the usual graph for *shih* that combines the *ssu* phonophore and the semantic classifier for speech (*yen*), stands for the word *shih* (poetry) when the canonical source is quoted in the ancient manuscript.

The numerous *Shih-ching* interjections can be divided into two categories according to reconstructions of their pronunciation in Old Chinese: the larger number have dental or similar palatal initials; the remainder are made up of gutturals or laryngeals. How the ancient poets and performers actually pronounced them is another matter entirely. Just as our "sigh" only approximates the actual sound we make to express sadness or longing, it is doubtful that the Chinese sounds were as meek as the "Oh!" or "Alas!" with which they are frequently translated. What are reconstructed as dentals and palatals may have been whistles and hisses, while the gutturals and laryngeals were howls, sighs, snorts, or groans. Such were the sounds exploited to enhance the language of poetry and to make its diverse messages and meanings more compelling.

Jeffrey Riegel

Chapter 6

THE SUPERNATURAL

A discussion of the supernatural in Chinese literature must begin by defining terms. There is no premodern Chinese term that directly translates as "supernatural"; the modern *ch'ao-tzu-jan* is derived from English. Content that we would now describe as supernatural is labeled either with varying words for "strange" or with names of classes of extraordinary beings. "Supernatural" implies another realm distinct from the natural, but in premodern China such events and creatures are not beyond or apart from nature; instead the odd and exceptional is an inherent part of the natural system. Yet these phenomena were perceived as a category in premodern Chinese literature. While the word "supernatural" can be used for convenience's sake, this inherent difference in definition should be kept in mind.

The following discussion includes the literature in which extraordinary beings figure and the literature of the strange. It is impossible to exclude the supernatural visions of Buddhism and Taoism from this survey; however, scriptures and temple inscriptions as such are omitted, and early Chinese mythology is discussed in chapter 2. This is an essay on literature of the supernatural, not beliefs in the supernatural, although the two are inextricably connected: received lore about the supernatural provides material for literature, and literature is instrumental in its transmission. Although it is impossible to ascertain whether an author believed what he wrote, premodern authors themselves problematized the question of belief. Belief in some level of supernatural interaction with the human world was the mainstream view throughout the history of premodern China, but at the same time it was acknowledged that these were particularly fertile grounds for fabrication and delusion. Another distinction frequently applied by traditional critics, and closely related to belief, is that between the strange for its own sake and the strange as a means to raise other issues. It would seem that the supernatural may be employed for divergent purposes but derives its power from fascination with the supernatural itself; the mask is never entirely meaningless.

Elements of the supernatural are found throughout the history of Chinese literature, cutting across genres. It has differing importance in different genres: it is the preeminent topic of the classical tale, one important topic of vernacular fiction and drama, and a specific mode in poetry. Each genre explores different territory of the supernatural.

The discussion begins with an introduction to the categories that make up the supernatural in China and follows with a chronological treatment of different works. This opening thematic section is not meant to imply that these concepts were ahistorical and unchanging; it should be regarded instead as an extended definition of terms, while acknowledging that meanings shift over time.

TERRITORY OF THE SUPERNATURAL

One of the principal concerns of literature of the supernatural is the revelation of startling but still comprehensible patterns in the universe: this is seen in tales of omens and prophecy, destined retribution and reward. The correspondences are startling because of their distance in time or space; the supernatural is expressed in the nonlinear, causal link between them. The crucial terms are *chao* (omens), *ming* (fate), *kan-ying* (stimulus-response), *yin-kuo* (karmic cause and effect), and *pao* (retribution). Omens were seen as an indication of the condition of a kingdom; aberrations in human affairs would cause anomalies in nature as well, and these strange events in turn foretold the downfall of a state, although the initial cause of both omen and disaster lay in this world. The concept of omens as responses to human events is described in pre-Ch'in texts, but omens were systematized with the centralization of the empire. Imperial gathering of omens is one of the earliest forms of writing about the supernatural. Relevant omens included natural disasters and monstrous births, but also popular phenomena not normally categorized as supernatural, like children's rhymes and changes in fashion.

The pre-Buddhist concept of fate allows for injustice: man's life span, wealth, or success is predetermined through no fault or virtue of his own. This concept of unjust fate survives into later periods alongside schemes of moral justice. Yet in the crucial matter of national fate, the Mandate of Heaven that grants a dynasty its right to rule contains a strong component of moral judgment. The concept of different elements in the universe, man and nature or Heaven and earth, responding to each other like strings resounding to the same note, is ancient; later *kan-ying* is used more specifically to refer to the response of supernatural beings to human actions. The Buddhist concept of karmic retribution replaced an apparently arbitrary fate with a karmic sense that current circumstances were earned by one's behavior in former lives; the range of moral correspondences in time and space is increased dramatically. Buddhism supplied the vocabulary and clear mechanisms for discussing rewards for the good and punishment for the wicked, but these ideas became shared cultural property. Narrative is more interested in retribution that takes place within the same lifetime; retribution remains one of the central subjects and organizing principles of both classical and vernacular fiction up until late in the Ch'ing dynasty (1644–1911). These correspondences are usually depicted as the work of an impersonal "Heaven," although divinities and other creatures may work to fulfill the ordained pattern.

Dreams can be another means of linking worlds and bringing the supernatural into personal experience. Although there exist from early times theories explaining dreams in psychological and medical terms, literature is more concerned with dreams having a source outside the self. On the simplest level, dreams foretell the future or reveal the present at a distant place (most commonly the death of a distant loved one is revealed in a dream). A dream can also be an experience of another real world. In both stories of prophecy and accounts of dream travel, there is a need to demonstrate the correspondence between the worlds inside and outside the prophecy and the dream. Buddhist ideas about the illusory nature of all human existence gave dream narratives new range, allowing for the creation of elaborate illusory worlds.

Much of the literature of the supernatural deals with human interaction with nonhuman creatures, not all of which will be familiar to readers of other traditions. In rough descending order, there are gods (*shen*), *hsien*, ghosts (*kuei*), *yao* (specters), and supernatural animals like the dragon. The Chinese word *shen* can mean the spirit that animates a living being, a positive spiritual force, or a divinity. The world of Chinese literature is uninhibitedly polytheistic. On the whole, the more abstract and general gods, while theoretically the most powerful, do not receive as much attention in literature as those of more moderate rank and more local appeal. Divinity is a status accessible to exceptional humans as well, often a reward for extraordinary deeds. By the same token, there is emphasis on the humanlike needs and desires of the divinities; interactions with the gods can be much more personal than simple reward and punishment. The Chinese tradition emphasizes the symbiotic relationship between gods and their worshippers: humans' devotion grants deities their power, and humans worship divinities because of their power. The divine system as a whole is frequently imagined as a bureaucracy, but there is a fascination with the individual divinities that defy the system.

Hsien defies exact translation. It has been rendered variously as immortal, transcendent, and fairy; each translation seems to capture different aspects of the *hsien*. In one of its principal meanings, *hsien* describes humans who, through Taoist self-cultivation (whether alchemical, physical, or chemical), transcend their human status and achieve agelessness. For that sense of *hsien*, both immortal and transcendent seem appropriate, the latter expressing the idea of ascent more clearly. Yet some *hsien* occupy the lower ranks of divine hierarchies in the heavens, enchanted islands, mountains, and caves without ever having been human. Those who have ascended are of both sexes, but primarily male; those who are themselves aspects of paradise are primarily young, beautiful females. For the latter kind of *hsien*, fairy is a more appropriate translation. Although there can be some blurring between the concepts of *shen* and *hsien*, as in the common compound *shen-hsien*, differences remain. Becoming a *hsien* is a goal to which one can aspire, while becoming a *shen* is an unsought reward for worldly accomplishments. *Hsien* appear in the literature as elusive figures, associated with lightness and flight, promising a realm of pleasure and detachment from worldly care that is hidden but alluringly accessible to humans. Taoist hagiography provides a vivid range of images: figures riding cranes or deer, swooping through the clouds, or lurking in the woods. Their relationship to humanity differs from that of the gods. The exchange of worship and the demand for recognition are not as crucial to their identity, and in their emotional detachment they seem less human than many gods. They relate to humans as enigmatic teachers inspiring humans to fly off following them. The female *hsien* are objects of desire, the most sensuous embodiment of paradise.

Kuei (ghosts) have a similar ambiguity in meaning to *shen:* they can be the souls of deceased humans; demonic figures that never had a human past; or the negative embodiment of universal forces, the malevolent opposite of *shen*. Horror is one of the possible tones of ghost tales, but it is not necessarily the predominant one: melancholy, romance, and comedy are also possible and more prevalent than in the West. Early texts like *Tso chuan* (Tso Commentary; third century B.C.E.) describe those untimely or wrongly killed as becoming ghosts, remaining in this world partly through their own strength of mind; in Buddhism the ghost is one of the orders of being to which one might be condemned for a period of time, one of the lower moral tiers of the system. Some ghosts are vengeful, but many are simply unsettled, seeking a proper burial. For a young woman to have died unmarried is often enough of a source of instability for her to remain on earth as a ghost; the young female ghost is a focus of literary and erotic interest. There is strong emphasis on the continuity of human feelings and relationships beyond the grave. Ghosts are also a means of interacting with the national past; an encounter with a historical ghost often takes on an elegiac tone. There are stories that look at the world of the dead from the inside, often as a mirror for the human world; its bureaucracy is treated more satirically than the heavenly equivalent. Under exceptional circumstances, ghosts, particularly passionate and loyal lovers, can return to life, reanimating their own corpses or the bodies of others recently deceased. Souls can travel in circumstances other than death: the most beloved narrative device is the woman whose soul follows her lover while her body remains behind.

Yao are in a sense the negative reflection of *hsien*; in this case progression from one state to another is threatening to the human order since creatures below human status intrude on human identity and space. *Yao* originally meant any kind of anomaly, particularly sinister omens, but after the Ch'in and Han dynasties it came to have the specific association of a nonhuman creature attaining the ability to assume human form and deceive men. It is also used as a general term for anything monstrous or spectral. Transformation is possible for all animals, with certain species far more adept than others: the shape-shifting fox, snake, and ape have their own independent narrative traditions stretching into the Ch'ing. Plants, especially trees and flowers, can also transform, if less frequently than animals; even inanimate objects, particularly if tainted with human contact or attention, attain this power. In the Six Dynasties period (220–589) these transformations were viewed as threats to order; the creature in question was to be eliminated once exposed. In Ming and Ch'ing fiction, these animals' self-advancement is rationalized as a curriculum or ladder of promotion, advancement depending on either sexual parasitism or virtuous self-cultivation. Overall, such creatures, especially the commonly depicted species like foxes and snakes, become more human and less like beasts as time goes on.

Human descent into nonhuman form is not nearly so common as the opposite trajectory, but it does occur. Reincarnation renders the boundaries between species permeable, but rebirth as another species is not the same as metamorphosis. Voluntary transformations into animal form are a playful power granted to Taoist adepts; they seem to be chiefly an entertaining spectacle, without the threat of the witch who can move in the shape of a cat. Most often men turn into man-eating tigers; this is very similar to European lycanthropy, a descent into bloodthirsty madness. Other transformations seem to be more direct moral punishments (the form of a pig being particularly humiliating). There are occasional stories of humans using sorcery to transform others into beasts against their will, but again, this is much more rare than in European literature, and some argue for an Indian origin of such stories.

As for animals beyond the range of mundane zoology, dragons can be both a raw elemental force and anthropomorphic divinities. Their chief association is with water, dwelling under the seas or lakes and rising into the heavens to produce storms. They are certainly more than animals, able to assume human form at will, and in either guise their power can be beneficial or destructive. Their underwater palaces, complete with fish and crustacean minions, are a favorite site of imaginary geography in many tales. The distinction between Chinese dragon and Indian *Nāga* is blurred after the arrival of the latter with Buddhism, in part because they are similar creatures and also because in Chinese they are both referred to as *lung*. Other supernatural creatures, like the *feng-huang* (phoenix) or *ch'i-lin* (unicorn), though both decidedly auspicious, do not have as broad a range of narrative possibilities; they remain decorative images or symbols rather than characters with whom humans interact.

This introduction of terms makes plain that boundaries are more permeable than in some other traditions: all humans might become ghosts; the extraordinary few can become gods or *hsien*; animals can become *yao* (attempting to be human but not accepted as human) or even *hsien*; humans can be reborn as animals. Similarly, interactions with alien beings are charged with interest precisely because of difference, but are often ruled by fundamental similarities. Yet quite often there is reciprocity between the realms; both sides avenge wrongs, repay debts, and contract relationships according to the same rules.

Perhaps because the interaction across boundaries is so vital, the most intimate possible contact between two realms is particularly fascinating. An erotic encounter with an alien woman, in its two aspects as a desired encounter with a goddess and a perilous encounter with a demon, is one of the central topics in Chinese tales of the supernatural, developing in both poetry and fiction. This theme has great power both in its own right and as a vehicle for allegorical expression.

As these creatures enter the human world, humans stray into other realms. All the major religious traditions contribute fantastic geographies, which are freely combined in literary works. Buddhism bequeaths an elaborate architecture of heavens and hells, as well as the idea of a western paradise. Taoist-inspired paradises can be located not only in the literal heavens but in a variety of sites contained within the terrestrial world, mountain peaks, caves, or immortal islands. Journeys to paradise tend to be temporary sojourns; journeys to hell a graphic illustration of the punishment awaiting evildoers. The fantastic geography of the edges of the world bears considerable resemblance to the borders of the maps in other cultures: there are distortions and exaggerations of human shape or society, kingdoms of giants, of women, and of dwarfs.

Another territory of the supernatural is that of human beings becoming strange by the acquisition of magic arts, the supernatural as deed rather than identity. There is a distinction between magical powers that are the results of merit (whether inherent or acquired in study) and amoral skills that can be learned by anyone. Taoist adepts and Buddhist monks displaying the former kind of power can often be "marvelous people," standing on the borders between humanity and their respective states of transcendence. Both can amaze ordinary mortals with their powers and eccentricities, but for the Taoists there is more emphasis on enigma than on the moral clarity displayed in Buddhist miracles. There is a sense of Buddhist miracles as the by-product of advanced spiritual states, while Taoist arts are more deliberately learned and blur more easily with other forms of sorcery. The Taoist pursuit of immortality through discipline or alchemy is a distinct tradition; the *tan*, the elixir of distilled life force that embodies a Taoist's achievement, is a focus of particular interest, as it can be toyed with and lost. *Fang-shih* (mountebanks) or *shu-shih* (adepts) seem closer to being technicians; they understand secret knowledge without the glamor of transcendence.

Sorcery falls into familiar categories: magic of creation, of illusion, or of influence over one's fellow man. Arts such as divination, physiognomy, and medicine straddle the borders between scientific discipline and the supernatural. The written word is crucial: written amulets are the most powerful means of exorcism or protection, especially among Taoist practitioners.

There are more sinister arts, which involve poisons and the stealing of souls. Negative portrayals of sorcery are colored by the ambivalence felt toward popular religion. Much of this sorcery has associations with illicit religious practitioners; the image of a sorcerer is often an evil Taoist or monk. Sorcery is strongly associated with plotting rebellion. One of the most constantly recurring tricks is the animation of paper cutouts of soldiers or horses to generate armies. The most unsympathetic portrayals of sorcery shade over into descriptions of chicanery and fraud, but false sorcery has just as much power to stir up rebellion and is also feared.

It is the nature of the strange that not everything fits neatly into categories; there are, of course, anomalies that defy the classification scheme outlined above.

EARLY PHILOSOPHICAL AND HISTORICAL WORKS

In the period before the Han dynasty, there are records of the supernatural in both historical and philosophical works, but not a literature devoted exclusively to the supernatural. Historical works, especially *Tso chuan*, already offer narratives of ghosts and omens, as well as explanations of their origins and meaning.

The philosophical works of the pre-Han and Han illustrate a debate on the existence of spirits that lays the basis for later ideas about ghosts and gods. The famous comment in the *Analects* of Confucius—"The Master did not speak of anomalies, acts of violence, rebellions, or gods"—necessitated self-justifications for generations of authors of such material but did not silence them; Confucius's own remark recognized these as topics about which most others did speak. Mo Ti (480?–400? B.C.E.) justified belief in ghosts both by listing evidence from earlier history, including tales of vengeful ghosts, and by pointing out their utility as a means of social control. Later the rationalist Wang Ch'ung (27–c. 97 C.E.) presented the skeptical position with a decisive clarity that was not surpassed in the following centuries. Yet, while Wang Ch'ung argued that ghosts are products of the human mind and the pursuit of immortality is a falsehood, he did believe in *yao* in the sense of omens; there is *ch'i* (energy), which creates images and forms to foretell the future. Dragons are also an accepted part of his world.

Chuang Tzu (355–275 B.C.E. is the earliest author to whom the word "fantastic" (in the sense of fanciful) applies; he does not take a documentary or argumentative approach to the supernatural. He creates a world of conversing animals, river gods, shadows, giant birds, and skulls; but they are just part of his palette, alongside historical figures, bandits, and craftsmen. Upending divisions between strange and ordinary, real and unreal was Chuang Tzu's purpose, quite the opposite of most other sources, which strove to distinguish the supernatural from the natural. He is considered the inventor of *yü-yen* (lodged words, or parables), but those who followed in that tradition never used quite as outrageous a range of creatures and dialogues. His model, with the idea of an additional layer of meaning justifying dubious surface content, became one of the major justifications for writing about the supernatural. Chuang Tzu was also the first to use the terms *hsiao-shuo* (literally "small talk"; later a term for fiction) and *chih-kuai* (tales of the strange), so on the level of these individual words he was the founding ancestor of writing about the supernatural. Indeed, the seminal influence of Chuang Tzu on all subsequent fictive literature may be readily gauged by the ubiquitous references to him, whether explicit or inexplicit, in later works.

Many of the philosophical works loosely categorized as Taoist include relevant ideas: *Lieh Tzu* (including materials dating from as early as 300 B.C.E., and as late as 300 C.E.) is roughly similar to the *Chuang Tzu*, but it presents supernatural material in a more coherent and somewhat more earnest manner, including discussion of the difference between reality and illusion, theories on the origins of dreams, and descriptions of the weird kingdoms beyond China. *Huai-nan Tzu* (by Liu An, c. 179–122 B.C.E.) elucidates the concept of *kan-ying*. Ko Hung's (283–343) *Pao-p'u Tzu* (The Master Who Embraces Simplicity) is a vital source for ideas about attainment of immortality and animals' capacity for transformation and sorcery.

CH'U TZ'U AND THE SUPERNATURAL IN PRE-T'ANG POETRY AND RHAPSODIES

Ch'u tz'u (Elegies of Ch'u; 300 B.C.E.–200 C.E.) is a poetic corpus from the southern state of Ch'u in which many kinds of writing about the supernatural intersect. "T'ien wen" (Heavenly Questions) is a set of unanswered questions offering a glimpse of an entire mythical system; "Chiu ko" (Nine Songs) and "Chao hun" (Summons of the Soul) appear to be devotional or ritual songs, and "Li sao" (Encountering Sorrow) and later poems use the divinities and devotees of the "Nine Songs" world as allegory. This is a world of worshippers and shamans longing for distant deities, bedecking themselves with flowers to attract them, being ecstatically possessed, and following those divinities on dizzying tours of the cosmos. The shifting perspectives of possession and ritual performance allow the possibility of speaking in the voice of the divinity, looking on the world from outside. Although this religious system becomes inaccessible to later readers, the *Elegies of Ch'u* bequeath a vivid and expansive vision of the cosmos and an individual human's relation to it, particularly the tie between a human and a divine lover. The *Elegies of Ch'u* is the most important influence on later poetic treatments of the supernatural.

Although there are both male and female divine lovers in the "Nine Songs," it is the female lovers of the "Shan kuei" (Mountain Goddess) and the "Hsiang chün" (Goddess of the Hsiang River) who live on in the tradition. The divine lover of the *Elegies of Ch'u* is elusive and fickle, hovering at the edges of perception and strongly identified with the natural scenery in which she dwells, a river or a mountain. Consummation, if possible at all, is brief and always returns to desperate longing.

The journey through the cosmos (treated briefly in some of the "Nine Songs" but more extensively in "Encountering Sorrow") takes place in alternating flashes of light and dark; at dawn the sojourner is at one extreme of the universe, at dusk at another. Supernatural creatures appear as steeds and an entourage. The world has exotic, mythical points at the extremes, peaks or constellations, but not a coherent geography; it is a world of constant motion and upward flight. "Summons of the Soul" and the poems in its tradition also draw a cosmos through which the individual soul wanders, but it is a much more threatening vision, as all the cardinal directions are populated by soul-destroying monsters, and the emphasis is on the lost soul finding its way back home rather than on the desire to fly.

Aside from the *Chuang Tzu*, "Encountering Sorrow" is the most important early text using supernatural imagery for allegorical purposes. Its quest for the divine lover is traditionally read as political, the fickle goddess becoming a figure for the ruler who spurns Ch'ü Yüan (340–278 B.C.E.), the putative author of the *Elegies of Ch'u*, and the fantastic journey a search for a virtuous ruler. The continuation of the journey tradition becomes strongly associated with the Taoist quest for immortality and transcendence (as in "Yüan yu" [Far Roaming]) or with the glorious progress of a divine ruler through the cosmos (in "Ta jen fu" [Rhapsody on the Great Man], by Ssu-ma Hsiang-ju [179–117 B.C.E.]). The journey theme evolves into the *yu-hsien shih* (poems of wandering immortals) of the Six Dynasties (for example, Kuo P'u's [276–324]). In Chung Jung's *Shih-p'in* (An Evaluation of Poetry; c. 513–517), an influential work of literary criticism, a distinction is made between *yu-hsien shih,* in which the authors use the immortals to express their own discontent, and poems celebrating the immortals, with both possibilities leading back to the *Elegies of Ch'u.*

The figure of the goddess continues to be developed in Han rhapsodies. In "Kao-t'ang fu" (Rhapsody on Mount Kao-t'ang, attributed to Sung Yü [290?–222? B.C.E.]), she presents herself to a king in an erotic dream, but then reveals her identity as the ever-changing morning clouds and evening rain; she is still literally the stuff of the natural world. In "Shen-nü fu" (Rhapsody on the Goddess, also attributed to Sung Yü), the poet who had earlier given an account of the king's experience himself dreams of the goddess. She is given much more detailed, human flesh, but consummation is denied. Already she approaches in dreams, at one remove from literal experience. The goddess who is "the clouds and the rain" not only provides the standard euphemism for sexual intercourse but remains the embodiment of desire, equal parts temptation and frustration. In the later poetic tradition, the physical figure of the goddess vanishes and becomes latent in the landscape; she is a tantalizing illusion as much as an actual presence.

CHIH-KUAI (TALES OF THE STRANGE)

It was in the Han and Six Dynasties that the supernatural became set apart as a topic for literary works. The term *chih-kuai* was not used as a term for a genre until the late T'ang (618–907) (and more clearly in the Ming), but was used as the title of several books in the Six Dynasties. Today these works are often considered the ancestors of Chinese fiction; although this is true to the extent that the subject matter and motifs of the *chih-kuai* are developed further in later fictional genres, there is disagreement over how they should be regarded in their own context. Some critics argue that they were intended as historical works; some that they are primarily persuasive texts; and others that they do involve an element of entertainment and esthetic pleasure. Authorial prefaces positioned themselves in the context of historical or expository writing; *chih* literally means "to record." These works are presented as having definite sources, whether in personal experience, other written sources, or oral narrative. In form, *chih-kuai* are generally assemblies of short, simple prose anecdotes; some collections are topically or geographically organized, but others are not. Many of the entries take the form of mini-biographies, beginning "So and so was a person from such and such a place . . . ," starting out firmly grounded in this world and in the experience of a single, named individual who confronts an intrusion of the strange. The combination of bizarre content with a matter-of-fact presentation provides for the particular pleasure of this genre. Although the literature of the supernatural continued to evolve throughout the premodern period, most of its topical territory was established in the Six Dynasties *chih-kuai.*

One of the founding works in this genre, representative of supernatural geography, is *Shan hai ching* (Classic of Mountains and Seas). It is arranged according to the cardinal directions and distance from the center, describing the geographical features, flora, fauna, and inhabitants of distant lands and seas. Its date of composition is disputed; current scholarship argues that it contains many different strata, with *chüan* (scrolls) 1–5 dating approximately to the Warring States period (403–221 B.C.E.) and the later portions to the Han (206 B.C.E.–220 C.E.) or perhaps the Wei-Chin dynasties (220–420). The entries are short and often cryptic, sometimes containing fragments of mythology. These distant realms are populated with chimerical creatures, assemblies of the limbs and heads of many different species. Eating or wearing the flora or fauna of these exotic places often has medicinal or magical effects. The *Shan hai ching* is one of the most visual of the *chih-kuai* collections and was associated early on with a set of illustrations of its creatures, subsequently lost, but it was reillustrated later. Although most of the creatures are restricted to this work, the book as a whole remains influential, standing on the borderline of geography and fiction to provide an appealingly imaginative space through which to journey. The parallels to Western bestiaries and geographies from around the same time are striking and merit further investigation. T'ao Ch'ien (365–427) uses it to make his own kind of circuit of the cosmos through pleasure-reading in his series of poems, "Tu *Shan hai ching* shih-san shou" (On Reading the *Classic of Mountains and Seas*, Thirteen Poems). Much later, when the voyagers of the Ch'ing novel *Ching hua yüan* (Flowers in the Mirror, A Romance, by Li Ju-chen [c. 1763–1830]) leave Chinese waters, they journey through the lands of *Shan hai ching*.

Chang Hua's (232–300) *Po-wu chih* (A Treatise on Curiosities) represents a part of the genre focusing more on marvelous objects than on narrative and on *chih-kuai* as a source of scarce information. Chang Hua as the expert on oddities becomes a character in *chih-kuai* as well as a collector himself. Serving its encyclopedic project, the collection is topically arranged, beginning with geography, mountains and waters, continuing through oddities of foreign nations, strange animals and plants, and ending with miscellaneous tales and legends. Although there were further continuations of this subgenre, overall it dwindled in later periods.

The most prominent work of the genre is Kan Pao's (fl. 320) *Sou-shen chi* (Search for the Supernatural). Kan Pao was a historian himself, and in his preface he defends his work in those terms: despite the difficulties of being entirely accurate in historical writing, historians proceed in their endeavor. Should there be errors in what he records, he takes solace that others share in his faults. He moves from a historical to a persuasive justification: he wishes to "make it clear that the spirit world is not a lie." This purpose does not, however, exclude pleasure in storytelling. There is a general scholarly consensus that the current version of *Sou-shen chi* is a late Ming recompilation from compendia. Its loose topical arrangement, starting with immortals and working down to animals, may date from this period. It owes its appeal to a rich variety of contents and mood, as well as an accessible writing style. There are many omens, monstrous births, freaks of nature, and even changes of fashion, with and without explanation. Yet the most influential stories are well-developed narratives, ranging from romantic liaisons with female ghosts to horrific confrontations with demons, from origin myths to heroic tales of monster-slaying. The perspective of *Sou-shen chi* is founded on the encounters of a broad range of ordinary people with the weird; that individual perspective remains influential in the later tradition.

Some *chih-kuai* collections are more clearly affiliated with particular religious or philosophical positions, most prominently Taoist or Buddhist. The most obvious of these are the collections concentrating on biographies of Taoist *hsien*, for example, *Lieh-hsien chuan* (Biographies of Transcendents), attributed to Liu Hsiang (79–8 B.C.E., but the work is probably later). This hagiographical tradition continues into subsequent dynasties; later popular publications are frequently illustrated, suggesting a guide to iconography as well as narrative. These collections focus on the experiences of the *hsien* more than on the ordinary mortal who encounters them. There are also collections of Buddhist miracle tales, such as *Hsüan-yen chi* (Records in Proclamation of Manifestations), attributed to Liu Yi-ch'ing (403–444). The moral values of miracles are more overt than those of the *hsien*'s mysteries; there are many stories of bodhisattvas or their images rescuing believers or, at the other extreme, illustrations of the punishments of hell. Buddhist tales allow for personal rescue by and contact with the major figures of the pantheon. This tradition later led to pure hagiographies in a series of biographies of eminent monks from various dynasties.

Although the collections from the Six Dynasties are the most famous, the *chih-kuai* tradition continues into the early twentieth century. After the rise of *ch'uan-ch'i*, the longer and more elaborate classical-language narrative form, the question of which works count as *chih-kuai* becomes more problematic; it is best to see *chih-kuai* and *ch'uan-ch'i* as a continuum along which one can place various works, rather than as absolutely distinct. In later periods *chih-kuai* material is often contained in miscellanies, *pi-chi*, such as Shen Kua's *Meng-hsi pi-t'an* (Brush Talks from Dream Brook), mixed together with other topics and subject matter.

Most of this kind of writing from the T'ang dynasty and earlier has been preserved in the great encyclopedia *T'ai-p'ing kuang-chi* (Extensive Records from the Reign of Great Tranquility; 977). *T'ai-p'ing kuang-chi* was the companion work to the other imperial encyclopedia, *T'ai-p'ing yü-lan* (Imperial Digest of the Reign of Great Tranquility), including material from sources too informal or dubious to meet the latter's standards. Aside from the sheer amount of valuable material that it preserves, *T'ai-p'ing kuang-chi* always carefully notes the works on which it draws, many of which are now lost. It is arranged by topic, beginning with the gods, *hsien*, and the human world, working its way through categories of human beings, character traits, and then on to strange phenomena: ghosts, foreknowledge, reincarnation, retribution, dreams, monsters, and foreign peoples. *T'ai-p'ing kuang-chi* not only saved a great volume of unorthodox material from loss but also provided the framework in which later readers imagined it. The categories listed above are also strongly influenced by its structure. The republication of *T'ai-p'ing kuang-chi* in 1566, along with republication of selections from it under a variety of titles in the latter half of the Ming dynasty (1368–1644), played a central role in reawaking interest in *chih-kuai* and was extremely influential on later works in the genre.

Hung Mai's (1123–1202) *Yi-chien chih* (Records of the Listener) is a personal *chih-kuai* collection of unprecedented scope. Hung collected anecdotes from a wide variety of informants and some earlier written collections; once he acquired a reputation for collecting weird anecdotes, people sent them to him in great numbers, and he filled volume after volume, with no topical organization. In his prefaces Hung emphasizes the oral nature of his anecdote gathering. Hung positioned himself as a historian, in his prefaces criticizing anecdotes that were too implausible (yet there are hints of playfulness at other points in the prefaces). Some changes in content relative to earlier collections reflect historical change: more merchants are characters, relations with the supernatural are often depicted as litigious, and the examination system has become a preoccupation of tales of prophecy and accurate dreams. Divinities play a larger role than in Ming-Ch'ing collections.

Throughout the tradition, there is a strong identification with informal, oral storytelling; although this can be a conventional pose, in general many *chih-kuai* collections are assemblies of a multitude of voices and can be fruitfully read as portrayals of a variety of views of the supernatural, mediated by the male literatus author. The strong association of this subject matter with informal exchanges gives some idea of the prevalence of these topics in society.

CH'UAN-CH'I

The distinctions between *ch'uan-ch'i* and *chih-kuai* have been discussed elsewhere. In terms of depiction of supernatural beings, *ch'uan-ch'i* brought several kinds of innovation. Supernatural beings could become psychologically complex and sympathetic characters, notably the fox spirit Miss Jen in Shen Chi-chi's (c. 740–c. 800) "Jen-shih chuan" (The Story of Miss Jen). Miss Jen's lover is willing to continue his relationship with her after discovering her true identity and thus for a time spares her the fated end of fox stories. In the end, however, she is slain by hunting dogs and becomes a tragic figure. The romance with a nonhuman woman was particularly suited to *chuan-ch'i*'s combination of the emotional with the marvelous. Inclusion of poetry allowed the romance of the divine woman that had been developed in poetic genres to be brought into narrative; this is most obvious in Shen Ya-chih's (781–832) work. In "Hsiang-chung yüan chieh" (An Explanation of the Laments Written in Hsiang), the hero literally encounters a goddess of the *Elegies of Ch'u*, speaking that language herself. In Li Ch'ao-wei's (fl. 790) "Liu Yi," a human man is drawn into the complicated dynamics of a dragon clan. At the same time that the dragon maiden becomes a damsel in distress and her father a dignified, human-seeming sovereign, an uncle contains the violence of the elemental side of the dragon's nature. In this case the supernatural marriage is allowed a happy resolution.

Dreams as complex illusory worlds in their own right were portrayed in elaborate narratives, such as Li Kung-tso's (c. 770–c. 848) "Nan-k'o t'ai-shou chuan" (The Story of the Prefect of South Branch) and Shen Chi-chi's "Chen-chung chi" (Record of the World Within a Pillow). Here the dream takes up the bulk of the narrative, rather than simply being a prophecy or sign referring to the waking world. "The Story of the Prefect of South Branch" is the more complex story, with the dream of wealth and glory revealed not as a pure fabrication, but with exact correspondences between the dream and a miniature world in an actual anthill. This more elaborate construction and exposure of illusion is closely related to Buddhist ideas about life as illusion and illusions as means of enlightenment.

PIEN-WEN

The earliest extant semivernacular narratives, a prosimetric form called *pien-wen* (transformation texts), also expanded new possibilities for portrayal of the supernatural. As Buddhist sutras had done earlier, some *pien-wen* with Buddhist subject matter excel at portraying vast mandalas of fantastic beings, divinities or demons, surrounding the central Buddha, and panoramas of other worlds, whether the Buddha's paradise or hell. This aspect is not surprising if one considers *pien-wen*'s probable origins as picture storytelling: the verse sections often particularly dwell on the visual spectacle. "Mu-lien pien-wen" (the Mu-lien story, "Ta-mu-ch'ien-lien ming-chien chiu-mu pien-wen" [Transformation Text on Mahāmaudgalyāyana's Rescue of His Mother from the Underworld]; eighth–ninth century) combines this spectacular cosmos with a basic human relationship. Unlike the hapless travelers to hell in earlier *chih-kuai*, Mu-lien is not only a witness to suffering in hell but an actor who can leap from hell to paradise at will and change that suffering with divine assistance. By presenting a world populated largely by supernatural beings, rather than the brief intersection of the human and nonhuman worlds, it lays a basis for the depiction of the supernatural in vernacular fiction. "Hsiang-mo pien-wen" (Transformation Text on the Subduing of Demons) contains a vivid description of a battle of supernatural transformations or manifestations between a heretic and one of the Buddha's disciples, prefiguring the exuberant displays of transformation in *Hsi-yu chi* (Journey to the West).

T'ANG POETRY

Although the poetic and narrative traditions of the supernatural share some themes and vocabulary, there is a markedly different emphasis between marvels of the senses and of incident, between the personal journey and a third-person account. The influence of the *Elegies of Ch'u* is all the more strongly felt in poetic engagements with the supernatural.

Poems about temples or popular religion can be points of contact with the supernatural. Wang Wei (701–761) wrote poems about popular rites in which the divinity worshipped is almost present. For example, in "Yü-shan shen-nü tz'u ko erh shou: sung shen ch'ü" (Second Song for the Worship of the Goddess at Yü Mountain: Bidding the Goddess Farewell), he evokes the world of the *Elegies of Ch'u* while remaining on the outside. The frenzied devotion of the believers and the actual goddess seem equally strange and marvelous.

Han Yü (768–824) has an ambivalent attitude toward the supernatural, wavering between a fascination with divinities and suspicion of the human representatives of supernatural forces. The focus of tension is often a young, lower-class woman with access to the world of the supernatural. "Hua-shan nü" (The Girl of Mount Hua) casts aspersions on the sexual interest of worshippers in a female religious figure. In "Hsieh Tzu-jan," Han Yü portrays a young woman's apotheosis as an actual event, but nonetheless misguided. He extols the values of home and family, staying in this world, making her an exile to be pitied. Elsewhere Han Yü invents his own supernatural stories: in "T'iao Chang Chi" (Written Playfully to Chang Chi), he recasts Li Po's (701–762) and Tu Fu's (712–770) poetry as the myth of Yü controlling the flood; in the end, through contact with their poetry, he ascends to the heavens in his own vision of the spirit journey.

The vocabulary of Taoist transcendence and spirit journeys remains a living one, deployed by different poets to different effect. Wu Yün (d. 778) is one of the poets most devoted to this subject matter. His "Yu-hsien shih" (Apotheosis, or Roaming to Transcendence) renders the ascent to the heavens in highly visual terms, beginning with losing the human world, obscured by dust, and the glittering lights of the immortal world. Wu's friend Li Po claimed the tradition of spirit journeys for himself. The conventions seem in his hands more the work of an individual personality than a shared cultural vocabulary; his own figure, making spirited claims on the supernatural world, looms large. His poems on these subjects often present a colorful vision of the otherworldly, which dramatically vanishes; Li Po is left frustrated, but making a bold statement of his determination to achieve immortality, as in his "Ku feng" (Old Style) Poems 5 and 7. Li Po is often imagined by later dynasties as the drunken *hsien* of poetry, reeling beyond this world, but that image is largely self-invented.

Li Ho (790–816) was called the "spectral talent" (*kuei-ts'ai*) for his poems of disjointed and fantastic worlds. The dissolution of the scene into hallucinatory images adds to the uncanny effect, suggesting haunting even when nothing overtly supernatural is described (as in "Hsi wan liang" [Ravine on a Cold Evening]). "Kung wu ch'u men" (Don't Go Out the Gate) is an even more horrible revisiting of the devouring cosmos of the "Summons of the Soul"; the order of the cardinal directions and the safe place back home has broken down.

In his visions of heaven, such as "Ti-tzu ko" (Song of the Child of the God) or "T'ien shang yao" (In Heaven), he notices the individual actions of particular supernatural beings, rather than simply making them part of a static, dazzling tableau.

The last pages of *Ch'üan T'ang shih* (Complete T'ang Poems) contain poems attributed to supernatural beings or acquired by supernatural means. Many of these are gleaned from narratives, with the narrative context retained as a preface. Most common are ghost poems, which turn on a body of imagery suggesting gloom and loss.

DRAMA

Supernatural elements are well represented in Chinese drama; there seems to be more overlap between the supernatural topics in drama and vernacular fiction than between either and the classical tale. For some dramas, the tie to religion is closer than for other genres, because the performance can itself occur at a temple or in a ritual context. Portrayals of gods or demons can serve as exorcism or as devotion. The supernatural is acknowledged early as one of the subjects of *tsa-chü* drama; a Ming list gives three supernatural subject categories: "gods and Buddhas," "gods, immortals, and Taoist transcendence," and "spirit-heads and ghostly faces" (Chu Ch'üan; 1378–1448; *T'ai-ho cheng-yin p'u* [A Formulary for the Correct Sounds of Great Harmony]). The Mu-lien story was one of the most commonly enacted. Immortals also appeared frequently, among other contexts, in longevity plays for birthdays.

On stage, the supernatural could be conveyed through special effects and spectacular acrobatics, with large numbers of acrobats as minor demons or battling immortals. This kind of spectacle is the territory the drama shares with vernacular fiction; riotous divinities like the monkey Sun Wu-k'ung from *Journey to the West* and Ne-cha (Naṭa) from *Feng-shen yen-yi* (Investiture of the Gods) figured prominently in both genres. At the other extreme, the poetic language of arias could conjure up otherworldly landscapes without stage business.

The structural nature of the drama, demanding resolution, excludes some of the inexplicable oddities of *chih-kuai*. Supernatural justice is a favorite structuring principle. The wronged or vengeful ghost makes a frequent appearance in the drama, often exposing crimes and leading to the conclusion, as in "Kan t'ien tung ti: Tou Ŏ yüan tsa-chü" (Moving Heaven and Earth: Injustice to Tou Ŏ), by Kuan Han-ch'ing (c. 1220–c. 1307). The supernatural demonstrations of Tou Ŏ's innocence—snow in the midst of summer, the innocent's blood flying up to a silk banner without a drop falling to the ground—are the climax of the play.

Chinese drama's focus on romance leads to differing treatments of liaisons with nonhuman women. The supernatural plot material best developed in the drama is the amorous ghost or wandering soul, beginning with Cheng Kuang-tsu's (c. 1260–c. 1320) "Ch'ien-nü li-hun" (Ch'ien-nü's Soul Leaves Her Body) and reaching its apogee in T'ang Hsien-tsu's (1550–1616) "Mu-tan t'ing" (The Peony Pavilion). The combination of narrative and lyric allows these women to be desiring, sympathetic selves rather than simply the objects of desire, as the female ghosts of the classical tale were. "The Peony Pavilion"'s Tu Li-niang, who meets her lover in a dream and pursues him as a ghost, seems one of the very few supernatural females with whom female readers personally identified. Both women allow their desires to lead them out of the human state, and as disembodied souls they can pursue their desires more directly than they could in human form.

Hung Sheng's (1645–1704) "Ch'ang-sheng tien" (Palace of Eternal Life) clothes the story of the ill-fated love between the T'ang emperor Hsüan-tsung and his concubine Yang Kuei-fei with the trappings of immortal destiny; they were immortal lovers in their previous lives. This is a common means of linking supernatural and mundane material in both the drama and vernacular fiction. The alternation of scenes in different worlds is one of the strengths of the long *ch'uan-ch'i* form of drama. This glamor makes an even starker contrast with the violence of the An Lu-shan (703–757) rebellion (755–757/763) and the ruler's unwitting cruelty at the same time as it validates their love. They are allowed final reunion in the supernatural world; as in "The Peony Pavilion," human passion is granted supernatural power.

While romances with ghosts, immortals, and dragon maidens are retold in the drama, *yao* are almost entirely absent. The one exception is the snake spirit Miss Pai (Pai niang-tzu). One of her earliest notable appearances is in one of Feng Meng-lung's *hua-pen*, which seems to waver between treating her as a demon and as a loyal, love-struck woman. Her story is developed in all the vernacular genres, including more than one *chuan-ch'i* drama (both called "Lei-feng t'a" [Thunderpeak Pagoda], one in 1738 and the other in 1771), more than one novel (one in 1806), a *tan-tz'u* (see chapter 50), and other popular storytelling forms. Her redemption is completed in the later plays and novels: she becomes an entirely sympathetic heroine, and her son is allowed to rescue his mother from the consequences of exorcism. Although this happy ending may be related to the generic requirements of the drama, this is the most prominent role ever given the offspring of a liaison with an animal spirit.

VERNACULAR FICTION

Lu Hsün (1881–1936) in his *Chung-kuo hsiao-shuo shih-lüeh* (Brief History of Chinese Fiction) defines *shen-mo hsiao-shuo* (novels of gods and demons) as a subgenre, but supernatural elements are not limited to those novels. Novels that contain no hint of supernatural elements are instead a rarity. The uses of the supernatural discussed below are arranged in roughly chronological order.

There is often a difference of theme and emphasis in its treatment in vernacular and classical fiction. The vernacular concentrates on a panoramic display of the supernatural, or large structural systems, rather than an individual encounter with the uncanny. The vernacular can represent the point of view of a nonhuman protagonist, which remained very rare in the classical.

Supernatural elements appear in the vernacular short story, although they are not as predominant an element as in the classical tale. (One sign of the differing importance of supernatural subject matter in classical and vernacular fiction is that when stories from *Liao-chai chih-yi* [Strange Tales from Make-Do Studio; see below] were adapted as vernacular fiction, primarily those works with human main characters were selected.) Many of the *hua-pen* that deal with such topics are reworkings of classical-language stories. The most common intervention of the supernatural in these stories, as in the drama, is the consequence of moral retribution. A distinctive story type in the earlier vernacular short story is the "demon" story, in which the male protagonist meets a deadly woman and is saved by the intervention of an exorcist. A tone of horror seems more central to the early *hua-pen* ghost stories than to the classical tale in general. For example, "Yi-k'u kuei lai tao-jen ch'u kuai" (A Den of Ghosts, by Feng Meng-lung [1574–1646], in *Ching-shih t'ung-yen* [Common Words to Warn the World], story number 14) describes a man stumbling in a single horrific night into the recognition that not only his new bride and her maid but also the matchmaker, her godmother, and a wine seller are all ghosts.

One of the principal uses of the supernatural in vernacular fiction is structural: a supernatural background provides a frame for the events of a novel's plot. Often the first few chapters of a novel will be set in another world, explaining how extraterrestrial spirits come to be reborn in the human world and enact most of the plot of the book. For example, in *Shui-hu chuan* (Outlaws of the Marsh, or Water Margin, the earliest edition dating to the early fifteenth century), the 108 bandits are 108 stars who are released by accident. This frame is largely unmentioned throughout much of the novel, but emerges again to justify the union of the bandits and Sung Chiang's leadership. The same sort of frame of previous lives is present in *Hsing-shih yin-yüan chuan* (Marriage Destinies to Awaken the World, or The Bonds of Matrimony, from the early Ch'ing) and *Ching hua yüan*, and used more ironically in *Ju-lin wai-shih* (The Scholars, from the mid-eighteenth century). *Hung-lou meng* (A Dream of Red Towers; c. 1763) uses the frame of another world, but makes the link between the two worlds far more complex. The supernatural frame can give mundane events an added sense of meaning and purpose or ironically undercut them.

Vernacular fiction is more interested than the classical in sorcery as a weapon and a means of rebellion, although the actual arts portrayed are the same. This is a means of overlaying supernatural material on historical plots. For many novels, sorcery is simply an additional weapon in the arsenals of opposing armies. Chu-ko Liang's strategies in *San-kuo yen-yi* (Romance of the Three Kingdoms) cross the boundaries between the brilliant and the supernatural, and some of the heroes in *Shui-hu chuan* have magical skills as their special weapon, just as another figure might be very good with the slingshot. In *P'ing-yao chuan* (The Quelling of Demons), the supernatural skills are more central, as the focus for most of the novel is on the *yao* who are subdued, rather than the conquerors. The two texts of *P'ing-yao chuan* treat the supernatural in different ways. In the twenty-chapter version attributed to Lo Kuan-chung (which probably dates from the early decades of the Ming), one of the central elements is a "sorcerer's apprentice" plot in which a young girl has imperfect control of her newly learned magic, with comic results. In his 1620 edition, Feng Meng-lung attempted to pull the disparate supernatural elements together by adding still another, converting the main characters into foxes. This novel draws on the historical association of rebellions with millennial cults and sorcery. The supernatural enhancement of historical armies takes place on the largest scale in *Feng-shen yen-yi* (Investiture of the Gods, attributed to Hsü Chung-lin [d. c. 1566]). Vernacular genres, both fiction and drama, thrive on elaborately choreographed battles of magical skill. Later the occasional supernatural villain adds variety to martial-arts novels.

Another common means of blending the supernatural and the historical in early vernacular fiction was the demonization of nation-destroying imperial concubines. The largest cycle of stories of this type was focused on Ta Chi, the concubine of the last Shang emperor (middle of the eleventh century B.C.E.). Her story was related in *Wu wang fa Chou p'ing-hua* (Expository Tale on King Wu's Expedition Against Chou; 1321–1323), *Lieh-kuo chih-chuan* (A Fictionalized History of the States, sixteenth century), and *Investiture of the Gods*. The real Ta Chi's soul was sucked away by a fox, which then took her place. Replacing the human woman with a demon is a means of inserting the supernatural into this world that seems as contrived as plots involving earlier lives. The notorious Empress Wu, who established her own dynasty (the Chou [684–705]), shared the same associations; in both Feng Meng-lung's version of *P'ing-yao chuan* and *Ching hua yüan* she is described as a fox. While the vixen in the later classical tale could become a more sympathetic character, in the vernacular she became the embodiment of destructive female sexuality.

The supernatural novel par excellence is *Hsi-yu chi* (Journey to the West, or Monkey, attributed to Wu Ch'eng-en [c. 1500–1582]). It is the preeminent example of a story playing overwhelmingly in a supernatural world, with a supernatural figure as the main character. Sun Wu-k'ung's (Monkey's) development and steady increase in powers is an influential model for the more systematic pursuit of magical powers by animal spirits in other vernacular fiction. He is a unique protagonist in his resemblance to and yet essential difference from humanity, which derives from the special status of our close primate relatives; his monkey nature adds to his license for mischief. This is in marked contrast to the development of fox and snake women whose original form becomes more and more remote. Chu Pa-chieh's (Pigsy's) nature as a pig is even less concealed and more comic. Pig-human hybrids represent descent and the grotesque, a capitulation to the basest appetites, rather than self-improvement or deception, as is the case for other creatures.

Monkey moves through a syncretic cosmos that incorporates the entire range of Chinese divinities in an apparently bureaucratic order, with the bodhisattva Kuan-yin (Avalokiteśvara), the Buddha, and Lao Tzu communicating with full civil, diplomatic protocol. However, display of divinity, like Sun Wu-k'ung's failing to jump out of the Buddha's palm, though he thought he had journeyed to the end of the world, makes the Buddha seem to transcend this order. On the other side of this celestial order are the pilgrims' erstwhile kin, the demons, a colorful variety of beasts aspiring to improvement of their powers. Some of the demons have their humanlike family entanglements, notably the Bull Demon King. Monkey himself was once a demon, so the reader gets to tour the cosmos in two directions, with two different dynamics: Monkey's upward struggle bringing chaos to the heavens and the trip to outer realms bringing figures like his former self under control.

Supernatural combat and weaponry are brought to new heights, with emphasis on transformation and containment. Monkey's transformations are the most exuberant use of the theme in all of Chinese literature; he can be both a sky-spanning, many-headed monster and an insect that can fly into the body of his foes. In this most famous work of supernatural literature, these pyrotechnic and acrobatic displays can serve both as pure entertainment and as allegory for the struggles of the self.

Journey to the West can also be placed in the context of religious novels. It furthers the cult of Kuan-yin, and Sun Wu-k'ung himself becomes a transcendent god. Other Ming novels of gods and magic were more clearly related to established cults, although there is similarly a blend of entertainment spectacle with the religious content. Examples include the derivatively titled works of journeys to the other cardinal directions: *Tung-yu chi* (Journey to the East, about the eight *hsien* of popular legend), *Nan-yu chi* (Journey to the South, about Hua Kuang [Flower Light]), and *Pei-yu chi* (Journey to the North, about Chen-wu [True Martiality]). All three are associated with the Fukien publisher Yü Hsiang-tou (late sixteenth and early seventeenth centuries), and all represent a more popular level of the Ming novel. Vernacular fiction tends to concentrate on the more rebellious and unconventional divinities, which fit the strengths of the genre for description of action and comedy. These novels often serve as the most unified records for story cycles about divinities that clearly developed earlier. Full-length vernacular novels can contain the long story cycles of major popular divinities, as opposed to the more local and private encounter with the supernatural in the classical tale.

Tung Yüeh's (1620–1686) sequel to *Journey to the West*, *"Hsi-yu" pu* (Supplement to *Journey to the West*; some think it is the work of Tung and his father) inserts its plot in the middle of the earlier novel, as the entire plot is Monkey's dream. This novel is a unique exploration of the theme of dream, the only Chinese novel that actually imitates the dizzying, illogical shifts of a dream.

Another category of supernatural fiction is that of satirical works. *Chan-kuei chuan* (Tale of Beheading Ghosts, by Liu Chang, published 1701) depicts the legendary demon slayer Chung K'uei; his foes are the ghosts that populate the human world, rather than those from the underworld. Demonic disguise allows for caricature of human vice and the satisfaction of seeing it destroyed. The first half of *Ching hua yüan*, as we have seen above, uses the strange nations of the *Shan hai ching* for satirical purposes, while the later chapters of the novel instead use the supernatural as an allegory for vice.

LIAO-CHAI AND OTHERS

After *Journey to the West*, P'u Sung-ling's (1640–1715) *Liao-chai chih-yi* (Strange Tales from Make-Do Studio) is the most celebrated work of literature of the supernatural in the Chinese tradition; it is viewed as the pinnacle of the *chih-kuai* and *ch'uan-ch'i* traditions. *Liao-chai chih-yi* has antecedents in the *chih-kuai* revival of the second half of the Ming, discussed in chapter 37. In terms of the subject matter on the simplest level, one can usually find comparable material in earlier collections; but P'u Sung-ling always gives it his own twist. P'u is not interested in establishing clear rules for the behavior of the supernatural, but allows each story to be its own fictional universe.

P'u Sung-ling continues the T'ang *ch'uan-ch'i* innovation of combining the marvel with psychological depth. He is particularly fascinated with the supernatural romance, allowing female ghosts and foxes to be integrated into the human family. He is just as interested in the variations of human domesticity as he is in the strange; the two are combined in startling patterns. Psychological interests also lead to a subtle understanding of the relationship between human desire and its manifestation in magical creatures, as well as the power of human desire to alter reality. Wishes do come true in P'u's world, but never as the wisher would have imagined.

P'u Sung-ling's work was widely imitated, but not entirely successfully, with both romantic fulfillment and moral retribution becoming rote. More interesting is the work of those who disagreed with him on a deep level, especially Chi Yün (1724–1805). His *Yüeh-wei ts'ao-t'ang pi-chi* (Sketches from the Cottage for the Contemplation of Subtleties) is distinguished by an effort to make the supernatural make sense and obey certain explicable rules. The principle he seeks in the world is above all moral, with many of his stories having moral purposes. He can be seen as an extreme example of a compulsion in the Ch'ing dynasty to explain the supernatural, but he will occasionally admit he is baffled. He eschews creatures with any claim of superiority over the human world, concentrating instead on the ghosts and foxes who are close to our status, acting as both our mirrors and acerbic observers of our foibles. His world of the supernatural consists largely of conversation: exorcisms are decided by verbal argument, foxes and ghosts lecture on their condition, and he records his own social circle's debate on the meaning of the anecdotes they share.

The tradition of writing about the supernatural continues in the late Ch'ing; Western-style periodicals such as the daily newspaper *Shen pao* (Shanghai News) and the illustrated magazine *Tien-shih-chai hua-pao* (Lithography Studio Illustrated) also contain familiar *chih-kuai* material, tales of haunting foxes or moral retribution, in that new framework. Both vernacular and classical fiction of the supernatural continued to be composed into the Republican period, and traditional supernatural themes and motifs continue to be evoked in the literature and the films of the People's Republic.

Rania Huntington

Chapter 7

WIT AND HUMOR

Humor is pervasive in traditional Chinese literature, evident not only in jokes and humorous anecdotes but also in poetry, drama, fiction, and works of history and philosophy. However, humor is notoriously difficult to define, and people frequently disagree about what is funny. Recognizing humor does not depend only on objective criteria; it is also a matter of taste and judgment. While other types of literature may be identified by formal generic characteristics or historical period, the boundaries of humorous literature are comparatively indistinct. Incongruous things may induce laughter, but the ability to perceive humorous incongruity is often determined by cultural background. To the extent that one shares assumptions and experience of the human condition, one will find traditional Chinese humor amusing. But humor depends at least in part on details and complexities of life that may be peculiar to a given place and time. If we do not fully understand these details, what might have been funny to someone else will pass us by. Thus some jokes transfer effortlessly from traditional China, while others need extensive commentary and explanation. When a quack doctor comes on stage in a Chinese drama and recalls the people he has sent to the grave with his medical practices, we all get the grim joke. When comic players dressed up as officials mime tripping over stones in a garden (a reference to those in the know that some of the highest government officials had cheated in an imperial poetry writing contest), the humor may elude us.

What is distinctive about humor in Chinese literature is not the form it takes, the range of topics it covers, or the mechanisms by which it functions but, instead, the kinds of moral restraint imposed on comic expression, especially jokes, by guardians of the cultural orthodoxy. These judgments are most clearly articulated in the first systematic analysis of literary genres, *Wen-hsin tiao-lung* (The Literary Mind and Carving of Dragons), written at the turn of the sixth century by Liu Hsieh (465?–520?). Liu Hsieh's assessment of humor is decidedly ambivalent. While acknowledging the value of some kinds of humor, Liu roundly attacks the literary style associated with jocose writings and condemns the notion that laughing or joking might have any intrinsic value. Liu's quarrel with humorous expression centers on the indirection and subversion of jests and riddles, though he also criticizes their common and inelegant use of language. Thus humor is "wandering and devious," hiding the main point in overstatement, obfuscation, analogy, or puns. That words should mean what they say is a tenet central to the thinking of the Confucian traditionalists. Comic literature presents a persistent problem precisely because its most important message is not expressed directly.

The sense that language should and did reflect reality runs through many strains of Chinese literary culture. The logical extension of this idea—that circumstances will conform to linguistic descriptions of them and thus that language may have the power to influence events—is evident in comments about an importune jest in Ou-yang Hsiu's (1007–1072) *Liu-yi shih-hua* (Remarks on Poetry). Ou-yang Hsiu reports that at a party someone quipped to the poet Mei Yao-ch'en (1002–1060), who late in life had been appointed to a position on the prison board, that the writings of a former officer of the prison board, Cheng Ku (*chin-shih* 887), were not long in circulation. Cheng's poems, though once popular, were later judged to be simple and fit only for teaching children. Mei was displeased by the comment linking him to Cheng Ku and, according to this account, died not long afterward. Ou-yang Hsiu thought highly of Mei's poems and wrote a preface to his volume of poetry, *Wan-ling chi* (The Wan-ling Collection). Despite this, Mei's work soon became known as the "poems of Mei of the Prison Board," echoing the common title of Cheng's works and confirming an association between the two men's literary productions. Ou-yang Hsiu writes of these events in part to redress an unfair appraisal of Mei's work, but the joke seemed to have had a powerful influence. The account concludes with Ou-yang Hsiu's lament that words spoken in jest can determine the course of later events.

Although the inappropriate use of humor is understood to be dangerous or destructive, Liu Hsieh gives a balanced assessment, noting that the derisive popular ditties recorded in *Li-chi* (Book of Rites) can serve as warnings and the jocular remonstrations of court humorists may save rulers from foolish or immoral actions. At the same time, by their very form, jokes and riddles are intrinsically transgressive, and in the wrong hands unfairly manipulate opinions and serve to benefit the undeserving. In sum, in traditional China humor was understood to be tremendously powerful, and its power could be used for either moral or immoral ends.

The idea that humor was always somehow transgressive was connected to the notion that inappropriately indirect use of language was common or inferior, a form of expression suitable only to casual occasions or to people of lower social standing. These judgments long kept jokes and humorous writings at the margins of official Chinese discourse and letters. Jokes, jests, and other kinds of humor were included in dynastic histories, imperially sponsored anthologies of literature, and officially sponsored entertainment. In the dynastic histories that include them, however, biographies of court entertainers come after biographies of people of status and even after biographies of some more peripheral individuals. For instance, in *Liao-shih* (History of the Liao) the section on entertainers follows the biographies of virtuous women (*lieh-nü*) and magicians (*fang-shih*), though it precedes accounts of eunuchs and traitors. In the voluminous Ch'ing collection of T'ang poetry, *Chüan T'ang shih* (Complete T'ang Poems), three chapters of poetic jokes and jests follow the poetry said to have been written by transcendents, spirits, and ghosts. At official banquets in the capital, jokes and humorous skits were performed by actors who, by virtue of physical deformity or legally inferior status, were marked as members of a lower class than their official audiences. It is clear from many sources—including Liu Hsieh's comments, bibliographies listing works of humor, and the *pi-chi* (occasional jottings) of literati and officials (see chapter 31)—that people often told and even wrote down and circulated collections of jokes and riddles. In general, however, humorous writings, like other popular and oral literatures, were not recorded and preserved with the same care given to other genres. Many of the writings that once existed are now lost. It was only in the Ming and Ch'ing periods, as popular literature became more acceptable and the audience for written versions of these age-old forms grew, that jokes and humorous drama and fiction were conscientiously collected, published, and preserved.

An investigation of the semantic range of words used for humor in traditional China can shed some further light on the ways humor might have been understood. While the range of meaning of these terms reflected to some degree the double-edged moral assessment of humor by the central tradition, other semantic associations of the words for joke, jest, and buffoonery indicate that fun, play, and social cohesion were also part of the appeal of humor. The term in common use today, *yu-mo*, occurs in some of the earliest Chinese texts (with the meaning "somber, dark, silent, reserved"), though it only began to be used as a transcription for the English word "humor" in the twentieth century. However, early on the Chinese language already had a fine supply of words for joke, jest, jape, satire, wordplay, and other humor-filled types of language and behavior.

One of the common terms with a fairly broad meaning is *hua-chi* (traditional pronunciation: *ku-chi*). Ssu-ma Ch'ien (c. 145–c. 86 B.C.E.) used this word in the title for the biographies of court jesters included in *Shih-chi* (Records of the Historian). The word also appears in *Ch'u tz'u* (Elegies of Chu) to refer to accommodating or ingratiating behavior. Other glosses of the term identify it as a word for a kind of large-bellied flask from which wine could nearly endlessly pour out. The two words *ku* and *chi* used by themselves can indicate movement. *Ku* can mean slippery, and *chi* can indicate a kind of bobbing motion. These words and other terms with semantic relations to movement suggest that humor was understood to shift meanings or the usual associations of verbal expression. The notion that words might be slippery or undependable is reflected in Ssu-ma Chen's early-eighth-century commentary on the *Elegies of Ch'u*, which notes that *ku* means "chaos," as does *chi*, and that those who use words in this manner say that what is true is false and what is false is true, confusing things that are similar with those that are different. The semantic association of other words used to refer to humorous speech or actions also includes movement, especially of air or water, as well as confusion, dissembling, both positive and negative value judgments, both unification and division, and the sound of laughing. Thus meanings associated with words for humor in ancient China mirror verbal methods of constructing jokes, the conceptual functioning of jokes and humor, and the social and cultural effects of joking, which can create both harmony and division.

COLLECTIONS OF JOKES

Books of jokes have been compiled in China for centuries and the titles of these collections make use of some of the common terms for humor, most frequently *hsiao* (laugh) and *hsieh* (jest), though *hsüeh* (joke) and *ch'ao* (laugh at or ridicule) also occur frequently. The earliest volume of jokes, *Hsiao-lin* (Forest of Laughs), was compiled by Han-tan Ch'un (fl. c. 221). The book itself is no longer extant, but survives in a few items collected in later anthologies of humor and in T'ang and Sung encyclopedias. Joke books continued to be compiled through the centuries and are still published today. Some collections of jokes are arranged by topic, as though one might study them in advance in order to enliven casual conversation. Joke collections proliferated during the Ming and Ch'ing dynasties, a period of increasing interest in popular and oral literary forms when more economical printing methods made books available to a wider reading audience. There are twice as many joke books extant from the five hundred odd years between the beginning of the Ming dynasty and the end of the Ch'ing as there are from the period of more than one thousand years from Han-tan Ch'un's volume to the beginning of the Ming dynasty. However, as is the case with much popular literature, the few existing records indicate that the great portion of what was once known or printed has now been lost. The table of contents for the vast early Ming encyclopedia *Yung-le ta-tien* (Yung-le Encyclopedia) notes that 18,890 items were included in the compilation of jokes in fascicle 44. The encyclopedia, produced in 1408, has mostly been lost to time; had more of it survived, it would have greatly increased our collection of early jokes. Many of the selections from joke books of early periods that do survive are collected in later encyclopedias, including Ou-yang Hsün's (557–641) *Yi-wen lei-chü* (Categorical Medley of Literary Texts), Li Fang's (925–996) *T'ai-p'ing kuang-chi* (Extensive Records from the Reign of Great Tranquility), and T'ao Tsung-yi's (1316–1403) *Shuo-fu* (The Environs of Fiction).

As if to underline the consistent ambivalence of the central Confucian tradition's assessment of humor and humorous writings, the names associated with joke collections span the social and literary registers. Some joke books are ascribed to well-known writers, while others have anonymous compilers. Although some volumes were collected by unknown historical figures, others have notes and prefaces attributed to obvious and often funny pseudonyms. Names of literary luminaries associated with joke collections include the T'ai-k'ang (280–289) era poet Lu Yün (262–303), the Sung poet Su Tung-p'o (Su Shih; 1037–1101), the prolific Ming critic and historian Wang Shih-chen (1526–1590), the Ming antitraditional philosopher Li Chih (1527–1602), the Ming writer and popular-literature enthusiast Feng Meng-lung (1574–1646), the fiction writer, dramatist, and critic Li Yü (1610/11–1680), and the Ch'ing classicist Yü Yüeh (1821–1907). Some of these attributions are disputed. In particular, doubt has been cast on Su Tung-p'o's editing of the volume of jokes *Ai-tzu tsa-shuo* (Master Mugwort's Miscellany). Obvious pseudonyms include the commentators on Li Chih's book of jokes *Shan-chung yi-hsi* (One Night in the Mountains), Hsiao-hsiao Hsien-sheng (Mr. Laughs) and Ha-ha Tao-shih (Taoist Master Ha-ha); the compiler of the *Hsi-t'an lu* (Record of Jovial Talk), Hsiao-shih Tao-jen (Man of the Way from Smallstone); and the editor of *Hsiao-lin kuang-chi* (Expanded Forest of Laughs), Yu-hsi Chu-jen (Master of Diversion).

Feng Meng-lung's *Hsiao-fu* (Treasury of Laughs) is the best-known of these collections of jokes. Although lost for a time in China, it was preserved in Japan and later formed the basis of the Ch'ing compilation *Expanded Forest of Laughs*, first published in 1899 and still frequently reprinted today. Feng Meng-lung also edited another collection of jokes, *Kuang hsiao-fu* (Expanded Treasury of Laughs) and other anthologies of classical-language stories and anecdotes. One of these, *Ku-chin t'an-kai* (Talks Old and New), includes several jokes and humorous stories from classical sources.

The themes in these collections of jokes tend to have a wide appeal to a fairly broad audience; recurring characters include doltish sons, henpecked husbands, incompetent doctors, idiotic officials, venal judges, immoral monks, and a cast of braggarts, thieves, flatterers, tricksters, and fools. Ravenous and thoughtless guests are regularly found in the homes of stingy and resentful hosts. Many of the jokes in these collections make fun of religious dogma or practitioners. Foolish Taoist masters and corrupt Buddhist monks are often the butt of ridicule in popular drama and short fiction, but some of the jokes on religious practitioners are frankly vicious. While some jokes that reflect social mores or details of cultural life are peculiar to traditional China, others have broad enough appeal that they continue to be enjoyed today both in China and abroad. Reflecting a common theme in humor worldwide, the punch lines of many jokes center on the failure of mental capacities, such as perception, memory, and reasoning; and the tenuousness of our communicative capacities revealed in linguistic problems of double meaning or the breach of understanding caused by a clash of cultures or social status. The broader themes of these jokes focus on the basic human needs to be competent and to communicate and on our fear of not being able to understand our fellows or cope with our environment.

Because jokes belong at least as much to an oral as to a written tradition, themes and punch lines as well as jokes themselves circulate through various collections. As in other popular literature, fragments tend to be borrowed and repeated in different contexts and publications. Thus it is common to find several jokes on a similar theme or jokes with slightly different themes or characters but a similar pattern. Sometimes the same jokes are repeated in different volumes. Alternatively, jokes with different elements but a similar set of premises may address, for example, the perceptual problem of confusing the dream world with the waking world. Feng Meng-lung's *Hsiao-fu* includes a selection about a lover of drink who laments that he has awakened from his dream before he had time to enjoy the wine that he had ordered to be warmed. "If I had known I was about to wake up, I would have just drunk it cold!" Addressing the same mental slip with a different joke, Fu-pai Chu-jen's (Master Bottoms Up) *Hsiao-lin* (Grove of Laughter) tells of a man who hurls insults at his wife when she wakes him up from a dream in which theatricals are to be given. In response she tells him to go back to sleep, as the play cannot be more than half over.

Jokes circulate not only through different joke collections but also through other genres of writing. Jokes can usually be distinguished from humorous historical anecdotes inasmuch as the latter make some claim, at least, to be reporting a real incident about a specific individual. By contrast, jokes tend to refer to types of people or to give clearly apocryphal stories of famous figures. Recognizable names in jokes include the Three Kingdoms general and cultural hero Kuan Kung (Kuan Yü; d. 219), the Sung statesman Wang An-shih (1021–1086), and the mythical ghost catcher Chung K'uei. But while some jokes focus on stereotyped characteristics of well-known historical or cultural figures, just as many begin with the words "one person," "one family," or "there was a person of such and such a place." Anecdotes, however, give titles and the specific time, location, and audience present during the events reported. The distinction between these two forms is not absolute; as the example below shows, sometimes nearly identical items appear in different kinds of collections.

An Hung-chien is identified as an actor in Wen Ying's mid-eleventh-century collection of historical anecdotes *Yü-hu ch'ing-hua* (Elegant Sayings in Yü-hu).

The volume includes one of An Hung-chien's ill-considered quips to a man who would later become his superior. Ou-yang Hsiu's *Remarks on Poetry* includes another jibe An made to a Buddhist monk as well as the monk's witty retort. The Sung compilation of jokes *Fu-chang lu* (Record of Clapping Hands) has a joke featuring An Hung-chien, who, warned by his wife that he must cry before his father-in-law's funeral, puts a wet kerchief under his hat to produce the requisite moisture. The ruse is, of course, quickly discovered by An's wife. These items appear in three different kinds of collections, the first in a volume of occasional jottings, the second in a book focusing on poetry criticism, and the third in a collection of jokes. Yet all three seem to be referring to the same historical person, thus blurring the expected line between jokes, which are usually not based on recognizable past events, and historical anecdotes, which are.

EARLY WORKS OF PHILOSOPHY AND HISTORY

Both jokes and humorous anecdotes are included in works from the Han and pre-Han periods. While these passages may evoke laughter, just as jokes in joke collections do, humor in histories and philosophies serves a didactic purpose as well as providing amusement. Anecdotes illustrate points of rhetoric, and tales of fools warn against thoughtless or wrong-headed action. The "person from Sung" was a favorite butt of jokes, especially in these early texts. There are more than twenty examples of jokes poking fun at the foolish Sung citizens from texts central to the Confucian, Taoist, and Legalist schools including *Mencius, Chuang Tzu, Han Fei Tzu, Huai-nan Tzu,* and *Lieh Tzu.* Well-known examples include the impatient Sung farmer who one day goes out into the field to pull on each of his seedlings just a bit, thinking that this will encourage them to grow faster. The seedlings have all withered by the end of the day, and Mencius uses this story as an illustration of a common but improper approach to moral development. Another story, included in *Han Fei Tzu,* relates how a Sung farmer notices that a rabbit has run headlong into a stump in his field, broken its neck, and died. The farmer gives up plowing and sits by the stump to wait for more rabbits. *Han Fei Tzu* uses this tale to criticize Confucians who advocate adhering to the outworn rules and methods of ancient kingdoms.

Although the benighted Sung fools seem to have been a favorite target of jokes, there were also quips and funny stories about people from almost every other state in Chou-era China, including Ch'u, Ch'i, Yen, Cheng, Ch'in, Chou, and Chin. *Lü-shih ch'un-ch'iu* (The Springs and Autumns of Master Lü) relates the tale of a citizen of Ch'u who marks the spot on his boat where he has dropped his sword overboard so that he can look for it when the boat stops at the far bank of the river. Some of these early jokes appear in other works of nearly the same time, suggesting an oral tradition from which philosophers, historians, and other writers could draw for illustration of their arguments. For instance, both *Han Fei Tzu* and *Chan-kuo ts'e* (Intrigues of the Warring States) include an oddly amusing anecdote about an elixir of immortality presented to Prince Ching. This valuable gift is consumed by an underling in the prince's employ, but the man escapes without punishment when one of the prince's attendants points out certain logical contradictions in the case of lese majesty brought against him. The defense hinges on two double meanings. The attendant argues that, first, the person who presented the gift said it *could* be eaten, and, second, that to kill the man after he has consumed an elixir of life would turn the potion into an "elixir of death." Essentially this same story is included in the Ming collection of jokes *Ya-hsüeh* (Elegant Banter), though the main characters are changed to Emperor Wu of the Han (r. 141–87 B.C.E.) and the jester Tung-fang Shuo (c. 140–87 B.C.E.). Other early jokes also persist in the later tradition, circulating either unchanged or modified only slightly in later joke collections. In another example, *Han Fei Tzu* includes a story about a man from Cheng, who, on arriving at the shoe stall, discovers that he has forgotten the measurement he made of his foot. He goes back home to get the measurement, only to find on his return that the shoe stall had closed. The same joke is included in the Sung collection *K'ai-yen lu* (Record of Cracking Smiles). A quip about a man from Ch'u who lost his sword overboard is included in a collection of humorous writings from the Ming, Feng Meng-lung's *Talks Old and New*. This episode is also one of many that survive in a *ch'eng-yü* (set phrase), pithy four-character sayings used both to preserve the sense of a complex point in classical writings and to deftly identify and categorize a current situation.

Although the scatterbrains of foreign lands are used in many Han and pre-Han works as a way of illustrating a point in an argument, philosophers also employed humor to poke fun at and discredit one another. Mencius's rhetorical one-upmanship turns the ruler of many a state into the fool, effectively trouncing (at least in the context of his dialogs) political assumptions about the necessity of such things as warfare and heavy taxation. The Taoist text *Chuang Tzu* includes funny and sometimes insulting anecdotes aimed at wrong-headed thinking or thinkers. In one of these, Duke Huan (r. 685–643 B.C.E.) of the state of Ch'i, who believes that he has seen a ghost and has become ill, is visited by a Huang-tzu Kao-ao. The clairvoyant Huang-tzu Kao-ao names all the different types of demonic creatures, ending with one that serves as an omen that the person who sees it will become a powerful ruler. Duke Huan determines that this last kind of ghost is what he has seen and immediately feels better. The anecdote subtly ridicules both political aspirations and the belief in ghosts. *Chuang Tzu* also includes passages poking fun at the Taoist's philosophical rival, Confucius; tales in this volume place the revered philosopher in compromising or embarrassing situations.

Even one of the most esteemed philosophical works, the Confucian *Analects*, has an informal conversational style that allows for more moments of humor than generally appear in synthetic philosophical argument. Although the *Analects* does not contain jokes as such, it does offer examples of good-natured banter between the teacher and his pupils; some scholars have argued that the information available about Confucius from the *Analects* and other works indicates that Confucius was endowed with a good sense of humor and enjoyed making jokes. The Confucius of the *Analects* occasionally uses what appear to be humorous rebukes in response to pride, lack of insight, or overbearing moral piety. Confucius quips at one point that his disciple Hui is not useful because "he agrees with everything I say" (11.4). On hearing that the overly conscientious Chi Wen-tzu always thinks thrice before acting, Confucius responds, "Twice is quite enough" (5.20). Lines from the *Analects* are used as punch lines in some later jokes and are thus made comic. The comment about Chi Wen-tzu is taken up in a joking way in the Yüan play "Hu-tieh meng" (Butterfly Dream), as other lines and characters from the *Analects* are also used in other works.

DYNASTIC HISTORIES AND "UNOFFICIAL" HISTORY

Humorous remonstrance and political jibes appear in a variety of history texts, beginning in pre-Han and continuing down to the present day in sources such as dynastic histories, *pi-chi* (occasional jottings), and *yeh-shih* (unofficial histories). Books as early as *Tso chuan* (Tso Commentary) and *Yen Tzu ch'un-ch'iu* (The Springs and Autumns of Master Yen) include anecdotes of ministers who keep their rulers from immoral or ill-considered action through well-placed jokes or sarcasm. Ssu-ma Ch'ien's collective biography of jesters in *Shih-chi* (Records of the Historian) has a passage recounting the ironic persuasions and humorous admonitions of entertainers in royal courts of the Warring States period. Unofficial histories and occasional jottings also contain humorous anecdotes about historical figures, accounts of political jokes told at official government functions, and examples of popular rumor.

Ssu-ma Ch'ien relates the successful remonstrative jests of three different counselors who lived in periods before his own. In many cases the jester's method was to twist or exaggerate the inappropriate actions of the ruler so as to induce him to see the error of his ways. In one of these, the actor Meng joked with King Chuang of Ch'u (r. 613–591 B.C.E.) about his favorite horse. The king was exceedingly fond of this horse, which he clothed in patterned brocade and fed jujube fruits. King Chuang had previously threatened that anyone who remonstrated with him on the subject would be put to death. When the horse died of obesity, Meng went to the king and suggested burial plans for the horse that included employing the rites due the ruler of a state, the production of coffins made of carved jade and catalpa wood, a temple with sacrifices for the deceased, and rewarding the animal with a district of ten thousand households. In Ssu-ma Ch'ien's rendition of this debacle, the king, on hearing the jester's absurd suggestions, immediately realizes his mistake and has the horse carcass quietly given to his cook.

Dynastic histories contain jokes and funny stories, and some, including *Shih-chi*, *Han shu* (History of the Han Dynasty), *Hsin Wu-tai shih* (New History of the Five Dynasties), and *History of the Liao*, have biographies of quick-witted performers and counselors along with renditions of some of their humorous jests and antics. These accounts may be of strikingly different character, however. In some cases an intelligent and morally minded minister provides effective, if funny, remonstrance and keeps a ruler from inappropriate action, but other anecdotes depict joke tellers who operate with very different intentions and produce quite different results. The divide between virtuous and destructive uses of humor articulated by Liu Hsieh at the turn of the sixth century is reflected in the two-part collective biography of humorists in *Records of the Historian*. Appended to Ssu-ma Ch'ien's collective biography of humorists is another section written about fifty years after Ssu-ma Ch'ien's death by a man named Ch'u Shao-sun. Possibly Ch'u's purpose was to bring the chapter up-to-date by adding accounts of court entertainers from the Former Han, whom Ssu-ma Ch'ien had not included. But the two sets of anecdotes are quite different in character. Jesters in Ssu-ma Ch'ien's half of the chapter all give righteous and effective remonstrance and thus, despite their comparatively low status and verbal indirection, provide last-resort protection from mistaken government and national chaos. In the biographies in the second half of the chapter appended by Ch'u Shao-sun, jokes and humorous antics are simply a means by which unscrupulous court retainers advance their own causes and serve their own greed, providing no benefit to the ruler or the state. The well-known jokester Tung-fang Shuo first appears in Ch'u Shao-sun's section of *Shih-chi*. Some of Tung-fang Shuo's antics include refusing to answer a question until he is given a feast, taking home meat from the imperial table in the folds of his robes, and spending the money he received from the emperor on a yearly changing of wives. On being called to apologize for his gaffes, Tung-fang Shuo regularly wriggles out of punishment by saying something witty and ends by being granted a pardon, and sometimes even a reward, from Emperor Wu of the Han. Clearly humor, especially in political circles, could be either beneficial or harmful, and the power of humor as a political tool could be used to advance righteous causes or simply to benefit those who were skilled at wielding it. The debate illustrated in the collective biography of humorists continues into later centuries, evinced by strong statements on either the improving or destructive effects of jokes. Ts'ai T'ao (d. after 1147) includes an anecdote about the jester Ting Hsien-hsien's (late eleventh century) regular criticisms of Wang An-shih's policies in his *T'ieh-wei shan ts'ung-t'an* (Collection of Talks from the Iron Mountains Surrounding This Mundane World), concluding with a line he identifies as a common saying of the day: "Having an investigating censor is not as good as having an entertainment official."

Accounts from occasional jottings show more clearly the political dimensions of humor and the kinds of power struggles in which humor was used as a weapon. Some accounts note that officials would pay court entertainers to tell jokes critical of their political opponents during government-sponsored gatherings. In at least one case, an entertainer who told such a joke was himself punished. The profusion of jokes poking fun at Wang An-shih in occasional jottings from the Northern Sung indicate a political backlash to the power Wang enjoyed. Although in many cases these historical anecdotes appear to report some real historical information, in other cases tales were repeated in variant form, with the names of the characters or other details shifted only slightly. At times historical anecdotes look very much like jokes in joke collections. Certainly the urge to write something funny may override any interest in giving an accurate report, particularly if the quip is also somehow fitting to the situation. In one especially rich example, a joke based on a historical anecdote appears to have become so thoroughly a part of daily speech that for a time it became a common saying and part of a children's game.

Shen Te-fu (c. late sixteenth century) recounts in *Pi-chou hsüan sheng-yü* (Left-Over Talk from Broken Broom Studio) that, during his childhood in the metropolitan capital, groups of children would shout out at people coming out of side doors "False Ssu-ma, Duke of Wen!" in sarcastic reference to the Sung statesman Ssu-ma Kuang's (1019–1086) reputation for upright, honest behavior. This game can be traced to a joke recounted in Shao Po-wen's (1057–1134) *Shao-shih chien-wen lu* (Record of Things Seen and Heard by Master Shao). According to Shao, Wen Yen-po (1006–1094) reported to Ssu-ma Kuang that one of his men spying on the Liao (Khitans) described a humorous skit that the players performed at a banquet. In this skit, an actor dressed up as a Confucian would snatch away any object at hand and hide it in the folds of his robe. Another actor followed behind with a stick asking, "Is this the bright and luminous commander Ssu-ma?" Ssu-ma Kuang is supposed to have been pleased at this, as the joke indicated that, while other government officials might engage in corrupt activity, there was a common perception that he was above such behavior. There are numerous other references in period texts to what must have been for a time a fairly common habit of speech. Chou Mi (1232–1299/1308) also mentions this usage in *Ch'i-tung yeh-yü* (Words of a Retired Scholar from the East of Ch'i), as do Chao Shan-liao (*chin-shih* 1208) and Hsü Hsien (*chin-shih* c. 1506–1522) in their works. The righteous and insightful judge Pao Cheng (999–1062) is subject to the same treatment in the colloquial language of the Sung. Chao Shan-liao reports that people would point and laugh at those accused of nepotism and shout out, "You're a Paoist!" Thus the names of the two most famously principled government officials of the Sung, Ssu-ma Kuang and Judge Pao, are used in inverted sarcastic reference to criticize those whose grasp of ethics or uprightness of character did not match their own.

HUMOR IN DRAMA

Humor in historical accounts often involves actors and performers, in part because there was an understanding, noted by Liu Hsieh and amply illustrated by Ssu-ma Ch'ien in his accounts of jesters in pre-Han courts, that joking remonstrance was in some cases the only effective way to get a powerful ruler to mend his ways and entertainers were acknowledged to be in the best position to accomplish this. Certainly humor was always an integral part of the entertainer's art, and in some cases quick wit seems to have been considered sufficient in its own right to qualify someone as a member of the entertainment profession. One anecdote in Ssu-ma Ch'ien's collective biography of humorists makes clear that acting could also be integral to humorous remonstrance. The passage recounts how the actor Meng, mentioned above, pretended to be one of the king's deceased advisers in order to awaken the ruler's conscience to his responsibility in supporting his former retainer's family. The king mistakes the actor for his former adviser and asks that he return to his position at court, but Meng, continuing the ruse, refuses on the grounds that there will be no benefit to his family. The king is made the fool in this episode, and his failing is, for a moment, funny. Later accounts of court entertainment in a long tradition of *pi-chi* materials show that actors commonly told jokes and took on roles as part of humorous entertainments.

Although information tracing the origins and development of drama in China is incomplete, by the T'ang dynasty records arise of at least two distinct kinds of dramatic performance. One of these, *ko-wu-chü* (singing and dancing play), involved dancing, singing, and perhaps also acrobatics or simple dialog connected to a narrative story line. The other, *ts'an-chün-hsi* (adjutant play) was a comedic performance usually involving two actors, one playing the comic or butt (the *ts'an-chün* [adjutant]) and the other playing a straight man (the *ts'ang-ku* [gray hawk]). There is more than one explanation of the origins of this latter form, which, according to early sources on drama, date back to at least the beginning of the fourth century. One account traces the form back even further, to a magistrate at the turn of the first century who was found accepting bribes. Since his services were deemed too valuable for the court simply to dismiss him, as punishment he was forced to attend banquets at which he would participate in skits and be ridiculed. Whether or not there is truth in this explanation of the origins of the form, there was certainly a close connection between the various kinds of humorous performances at court, including ironical remonstrance and political jibing, and the butt-and-knave comic duo.

This comic duo is also cited as the forebear of different kinds of verbally based humorous performances, culminating in *hsiang-sheng*[a] (cross-talk), a popular type of comic dialog still in existence today. Like the adjutant play, cross-talk performances usually feature two people, though there may sometimes be only one, or three or more. The origins of cross-talk are disputed. Some scholars believe that the form derives from another kind of popular dialog that was present across China during the Ming, called by different names in different places but referred to as *hsiang-sheng*[b] (seeming-sounds) in the area of modern Peking. Other researchers suggest that modern cross-talk originated in the north, primarily in Peking and Tientsin, only during the latter part of the nineteenth century and spread throughout China in the early part of the twentieth century. Whichever is the case, there is ample evidence that humorous verbal arts existed in China from as early as there is recording of any such matters, and, despite fragmentary historical records, they have continued in some form to the present.

The two stock characters in comic dialogs are central to the structure of more complex narrative dramas. Chinese traditional drama is organized by role-types, which are sometimes compared to the masked types in *commedia dell'arte*. In each troupe one actor would be responsible for the roles assigned to the male lead, another for female roles, another for comic parts, and another for the roles of officials. The two earliest role types were the adjutant and the gray hawk, which over time developed into a male role (*fu-mo*) and a clown role (*ching*). The names and number of role types changed as popular tastes shifted and different styles of drama developed, but there were always characters that specialized in jokes, slapstick, and bawdy humor. Role types were distinguished by makeup and costume as well as by styles of speech and movement. Thus an audience would know as soon as a character came on stage what kind of behavior to expect from a clown role (*ching* or *ch'ou*) and what kinds of interactions were likely to take place between a butt and a jape.

The multiple references of the word *tsa-chü* also indicate a relationship between humor and dramatic performance. In the Chin and Sung dynasties, the term *tsa-chü* referred to short farce skits, as well as to the newly emergent northern-style musical dramas and performances in the entertainment quarters in general. During this period, although dramatic productions regularly included farcical or humorous skits and a more serious dramatic piece, the comedic actors were the stars of the troupe. While records indicate that there was variation in the arrangement of the elements of a production, in some cases, the one nonhumorous dramatic piece was sandwiched between groups of funny skits and comic dialog. In the longer musical dramas that developed in the Yüan and Ming periods, narrative plots become more complex, but stock bits of comedy or even entire farce skits (called *tsa-chü* in the Sung and *yüan-pen* in the Chin) were sometimes borrowed from earlier dramas and functioned as a kind of backdrop or occasional relief from the more demanding language and emotional expression of the serious parts of the play. Even in the full-fledged musical dramas produced in the Yüan, Ming, and Ch'ing periods, regardless of the topic of the play there were always some comical sections.

One type of comic bit that was preserved in later dramatic forms was the humorous characterization of certain professions. Early habits of joking seem to have defined the dramatic possibilities of particular vocations for centuries.

Thus a doctor who appears on stage is most probably one who kills his patients, and almost any magistrate other than the famously upright Judge Pao bows to the plaintiffs who have bribed him because "They support me; they are my mother and father." Stock comic bits circulate intact through very different dramas, with poems and sets of dialog repeated verbatim.

Although some humor and clowning can be found in any traditional Chinese play regardless of theme, certain subjects involve more humor and joking than others. Tales of life in the entertainment quarters and the mishaps of prostitutes and young wastrels are usually funnier than the depictions of serious historical subjects. In addition, the plays associated with story cycles later written up into long novels, particularly *Hsi-yu chi* (Journey to the West, or Monkey) and *Shui-hu chuan* (Outlaws of the Marsh, or Water Margin), often include substantial doses of humor. In some cases, however, the humorous element takes over a play on a more serious theme. The Yüan play "P'en-erh kuei" (Ghost in the Pot) involves a grisly murder at an inn, but comic scenes of an old man engaging with the ghost in a chamber pot overshadow the more perfunctory investigation and solution of the murder case. Moreover, earlier scripts tend to preserve more humor and, in particular, include more bawdy bits. The Ch'eng-hua period (1465–1487; see chapter 49) text of one of the "white rabbit" plays, which recount the parting and reuniting of Liu Chih-yüan and his devoted wife Li San-niang, has the heroine's illiterate evil sister making the equivalent of a thumb print with her backside. This and other bits of roguish clowning are excised from later Ming versions of the drama. The more polished literati texts favored fine poetry and the characterization of moral models rather than good laughs.

Particularly humorous Yüan dramas include Kuan Han-ch'ing's "Chiu Feng-ch'en" (The Rescue of a Courtesan), the tale of a prostitute rescuing her friend from a bad marriage, and "Butterfly Dream," a parody of the usually infallible and far-seeing Judge Pao. Some quite serious and well-known plays also have hilarious sections. Cheng Kuang-tsu is criticized in *Lu kuei pu* (The Register of Ghosts, a handbook for Yüan drama; 1330) for being overly fond of humor in his plays, and his *tsa-chü* "Ch'ien-nü li-hun" (Ch'ien-nü's Soul Leaves Her Body) includes some lovely irony. Chu K'ai's "Meng Liang tao ku" (Meng Liang Steals the Bones) or "Hao-t'ien t'a" (Pagoda of the Vast Heaven) has a section of high verbal humor precisely at the military and moral climax of the plot. In the celebrated romantic drama "Hsi-hsiang chi" (Romance of the Western Chamber), the maid "Red" is the center of much of the comic dialog and adds refreshing earthy sarcasm to the interactions of the two less-experienced and very self-involved romantic leads.

Humorous Ming plays include Chu Yu-tun's *tsa-chü* "Fu-lo ch'ang" (Becoming a Singsong Girl Again), a farce about a former prostitute who leaves successive husbands as soon as they run out of money and eventually returns to her original profession. A *yüan-pen* (farce play) is part of Chu's play "Shen-hsien hui" (A Meeting of Immortals). There is also satire in Wang Chiu-ssu's (1468–1551) plays and wit in some of Hsü Wei's (1521–1593) dramatic works. Among the famous humorists of later periods are Li Yü, whose voluminous contributions to Chinese letters include a group of funny plays as well as dramatic criticism and works of fiction.

FICTION: TALES AND STORIES

Humor is evident in narrative works of philosophy and history at least as early as the Warring States period. Among the narrative genres with comic sections are *chih-kuai* (tales of the strange), *ch'uan-chi* (tales, classical-language stories), *hua-pen* (vernacular stories), and *hsiao-shuo* (novels). Records of anomalies flourished during the Six Dynasties and continued to be written in later periods. Although the primary intention of *chih-kuai* was ostensibly the preservation of knowledge about strange happenings, the form of these accounts was well suited to humor, and a few examples are quite funny. Many records of anomalies are frankly persuasive in intent and are collected into volumes that advocate one or another philosophical or religious viewpoint. Rhetorically, these pieces function somewhat like a joke, often tricking the reader into a new perspective by incorporating an unexpected twist of plot. In one often-anthologized example, a man named Sung meets a ghost on his way to the market. Sung allows that he too is a ghost, though a new one, and, on learning some of the ways of ghosts and what ghosts most heartily detest, he tricks his traveling companion into changing into a sheep and sells him at the market for a profit.

In the longer *ch'uan-ch'i* (classical-language stories) that developed during the eighth century, the jokelike character of some *chih-kuai* is less evident. Instead, tales tend to be more concerned with the motivations and moral qualities of human protagonists. In famous examples of this genre such as "Jen-shih chuan" (The Story of Miss Jen), "Nan-k'o t'ai-shou chuan" (The Story of the Prefect of South Branch), and "Ying-ying chuan" (Story of Ying-ying), the humor, rather than being an abrupt joke on the reader or one of the central characters, is instead more subtle or poignant irony on mishaps of fate and moral misconceptions. In the hands of later Ming and Ch'ing writers, the classical-language tale is more self-conscious and often wittier. Examples in collections such as P'u Sung-ling's (1640–1715) *Liao-chai chih-yi* (Strange Tales from Make-Do Studio) provide healthy doses of irony and parody.

Vernacular stories (*hua-pen*) begin to appear during the Sung and Yüan periods. Many of these also include humor in the form of ironic or unforeseen shifts of plot. "K'uai-tsui Li Ts'ui-lien chi" (The Shrew: Sharp-Tongued Li Ts'ui-lien), a hilarious early work by an anonymous author, provides a fine illustration of this. Ts'ui-lien is a fast and inveterate talker who manages repeatedly to have her way, exhausting everyone in her family, getting out of a bad marriage, and talking her way into a monastery simply by the constant and inexhaustible wagging of her tongue. During the Ming, vernacular stories became more popular and were collected, imitated, and published by such well-known figures as Feng Meng-lung and Ling Meng-ch'u (1580–1644). Ling Meng-ch'u's works in particular are known for their humorous sarcasm. The famous Ch'ing humorist and dramatist Li Yü produced vernacular stories, including the collections *Wu-sheng hsi* (Silent Operas) and *Shih-erh lou* (Twelve Towers). A few comic vernacular stories are also included in the Ch'ing collection *Chao-shih pei* (The Cup That Reflects the World).

FICTION: NOVELS

Like the longer narrative plays of the Ming and Ch'ing, episodic Chinese novels all contain at least some comic aspects, regardless of their overarching themes. Two of the best-known humorous novels are *Journey to the West* and *Ju-lin wai-shih* (The Scholars). *Journey to the West,* ascribed to Wu Ch'eng-en (c. 1500–1582), is a fanciful account of the monk Tripiṭaka's long and treacherous journey from the T'ang capital of Ch'ang-an to India to collect Buddhist scriptures. Accompanying Tripiṭaka on his novelistic journey are an irascible Monkey, the gluttonous half-pig, half-human Chu Pa-chieh (Pigsy), the sorrowful, once-cannibalistic Sandy, and a white horse that in a former incarnation had been a dragon prince. Monkey has extraordinary powers but limited control of his impulses, and is a central character throughout the novel; his antics and Tripiṭaka's struggles to tame him form one of the main themes of the story. Humorous incidents focus primarily on the rapacious and fallible Pigsy and the escapades of the magical Monkey, who has the ability to change size and travel though space and can transform his hairs into an army of little monkeys to do his bidding.

Wu Ching-tzu's (1701–1754) novel *The Scholars* is a satirical treatment of social ills, rampant abuses of the examination system, and the pedantry and hypocrisy of many Confucian scholars of the day. Although Wu's book is critical of the scholar-characters he invents, his own ideal is a purer version of Confucianism. In a sense Wu's work can be seen as jester's remonstrations, an attempt to correct moral decay through humorous parody.

There are bawdy aspects to *The Water Margin*, especially in the scenes including Lu Chih-shen, the brigand who becomes a monk and yet cannot keep himself from climbing over the monastery wall for a drinking bout. Sexual humor and braggadocio abound in *Jou p'u-t'uan* (The Prayer Mat of Flesh), an erotic novel ascribed by some to Li Yü, the well-known Ch'ing writer and critic. In *Ching hua yüan* (Flowers in the Mirror, A Romance), by Li Ju-chen (c. 1763–1830), a scholar, a merchant, and a mariner travel together through strange foreign lands, each with satirical import. In the improbable land of gentlemen, buyers try to pay more while merchants demand that their customers part with as little money as possible. In busy-people country, no time can be spared for tilling the soil, harvesting, or cooking and the population subsists on an abundance of fruit. In the land of women, men must undergo the agonies of footbinding while women participate in the imperial exams.

CONCLUSION

Humor pervaded traditional Chinese writings and played an integral role in social, cultural, and political affairs in traditional China. Many different forms of comedy, lighthearted joking, and bawdy farce were prevalent over centuries in a variety of different genres. In some cases, imperfect preservation, particularly of popular literatures, may make the full range of humor somewhat difficult to trace. In other cases, such as the sayings of Confucius collected in the *Analects* or some traditional poetry, the lack of context characteristic of the genres themselves makes it harder to confirm comic passages. A survey of humor in traditional Chinese literature makes clear both that jokes serve a social function and that at least some of what is funny in writing comes from what is amusing in conversation. Jokes are passed from person to person, and the telling of jokes establishes cohesion in social groups with similar experience and perceptions while separating those who do not have the same cultural or educational background.

For the orthodox Confucian tradition, the importance of accurate use of language (related to the doctrine of *cheng-ming* [rectification of names]) meant that the single appropriate function of humor was admonishment of moral impropriety. Thus from a conservative Confucian standpoint, the inverted or exaggerated uses of humorous remonstration could be sanctioned only when affairs, in particular government affairs, were disordered. The powerful uses of joking are also evident in the political sphere, where jests and jibes were used to gain advantage in argument for both principled and self-seeking purposes. There is a vast array of humorous writing in traditional Chinese literature of almost every period and genre, yet humor in traditional Chinese literature was rarely included in the primary canon. In some circles humor and clowning were understood to be powerful, perhaps even capable of influencing the material reality of the subjects of their jokes, while at the same time they were considered inferior forms of expression. Thus humor, while abundant in Chinese writings, was regularly confined to the margins of official discourse and canonical literature.

Karin Myhre

Chapter 8

PROVERBS

The Chinese are famous for their proverbs. Although it is true that proverbs and proverbial wisdom play a large part in most illiterate, orally based peasant cultures, the Chinese perhaps more than any other people are world renowned for their proverbs, and proverbs have long played and continue to play an important part in Chinese *written* culture up to and through the twentieth century.

The topic of proverbs and proverbial expressions in Chinese literature must first be related to the basic distinctions made by the Chinese literati between the written style of language, which was considered "elegant" (*ya*), and the colloquial, spoken language, which was viewed as "vulgar" (*su*). In literature this contrast ultimately came to be reflected in the modern distinction between works written in "classical-language style" (*wen-yen-wen*) and those written in colloquial or "unadorned" style (*pai-hua-wen*; see chapter 1).

Proverbs are at base an *oral* form, encapsulating the experiences, observations, and wisdom of ordinary people into short, pithy, colloquial statements and judgments phrased in easily memorized forms. Proverbs employ familiar images and tropes to capture the experience and values shared by successive generations, and are repeatedly quoted and appealed to for persuasion, in argumentation, and as guides for daily living. In the mouths of ordinary peasant farmers, craftspeople, and tradespeople, they are "minitexts" of a commonly shared "oral literature" that possess authority by virtue of their constant repetition and use.

Thus, on the one hand, their "vulgar" origins and phrasing seem to make them "unfit for the sophisticated salons" of literature (*pu teng ta-ya chih t'ang*);

on the other hand, their pithy insights and formulations seem constantly to admit them through the "back door" into literary works, where they usually appear wearing such "scare quote" markers as *ku-jen yün* ("the ancients said"), *yen yün* or *yen yüeh* ("the proverb says"), or *su-yü yün* ("the proverbial expression says"). Just as ancient works such as *Shih-ching* (Classic of Poetry) and *Yi-ching* (Classic of Change) represent collections of much older orally transmitted values and traditions, so over the centuries have the values and utterances of the common people continued to find their way into the written works of the literate "great tradition," while many of the concepts and phrases of that literate tradition have also been borrowed or reborrowed into the oral "little tradition" of the peasantry. Thus the incorporation of proverbs and other "familiar expressions" into Chinese literature represents merely one more step in an ongoing interchange and intertextuality between the language and values of China's literate great tradition and the age-old, orally transmitted beliefs and values of its common people.

In his comprehensive evaluation of the history of literary theory and criticism up to his own time entitled *Wen-hsin tiao-lung* (The Literary Mind and the Carving of Dragons; see chapter 45), the sixth-century Liang dynasty scholar Liu Hsieh (465?–520? C.E.), in his chapter "Shu chi" (Epistolary Writing), noted: "Proverbs [*yen*] are direct statements. . . . A commonplace proverb[ial expression] is: 'fruit without flowers.' Duke Mu of [the kingdom of] Tsou said: 'A leaky bag can still hold things.' . . . The 'T'ai-shih' [Great Vow] [in *Li-chi* (Record of Ritual)] says: 'The ancients had a saying: "A hen should not crow at dawn." And in 'Ta ya' [Greater Elegantiae; a section of the *Shih-ching*], it is said: 'Through grief one grows old.' Both of these are proverbs from antiquity that are quoted in the classics." After citing additional examples of "proverbs employed in literary writings" found in these two ancient works, Liu concludes: "In literature there is nothing more vulgar than proverbs, but they were used by the sages in [these] classic works, so how can one ignore them?"

PROVERBS AND OTHER FAMILIAR EXPRESSIONS

Another major problem in addressing the history of proverbs in Chinese literature is that of definition and differentiation. This is evident in the passage from Liu Hsieh quoted above, where the first example he cites ("fruit without flowers") is in fact a *proverbial expression* (*su-yü*) rather than, as in his second example, a *proverb* proper—that is, a complete sentence expressing (directly or indirectly) an observation or judgment. Although the Chinese usage, both past and present, of the various terms discussed below has never been consistent, for present-day purposes, a distinction should be drawn between *yen-yü* (proverbs), *su-yü* (proverbial expressions), *ko-yen* (maxims), *hsieh-hou-yü* (enigmatic folk similes or truncated witticisms), and the ubiquitous *ch'eng-yü* (fused-phrase [literary] idioms or "four-character expressions" or simply "set/fixed phrases"), all of which can be collectively referred to under the general heading of *shu-yü* (familiar expressions).

As noted above, proverbs are an oral form consisting of complete sentences that express observations, judgments, or wisdom about commonly shared experience and values, using familiar images and tropes. For example, *ch'iao fu nan wei wu mi chih ts'ui* ("[Even] the cleverest housewife cannot cook [a meal] without rice") is equivalent to the English proverb "One cannot make bricks without straw." *Su-yü* are equally familiar colloquial set phrases, images or tropes, but consist only of sentence fragments used for description, such as the "fruits without flowers" expression quoted by Liu Hsieh above; they are *not* complete sentences or judgments.

Ko-yen are usually also complete statements, likewise expressing judgments or values, but they differ in being "quotations," guides for behavior taken from the writings of some famous author or work of the past, and thus have a decidedly written flavor in lexical choice, grammar, and style, even if they have become "proverbial" in use. Thus, from the "Shu-erh" chapter of the *Lun-yü* (Analects) of Confucius comes the famous quotation attributed to the Master: "If three of us are walking together, at least one must be able to be my teacher." The famous line from the *Tao te ching* (Classic of the Way and Integrity), attributed to Lao Tzu ("the Old Master")—"The longest journey begins with a single step"—is thought by some to be a quotation itself of an even older oral proverb, but in any case has gone on to become "proverbial," not only for those Chinese who may not know its (written) source, but even (in translation) for many others around the world.

Another basically written form is the *ch'eng-yü*. *Ch'eng-yü* are also fixed (usually four-character) literary expressions, employing the vocabulary and structures of Classical Chinese or Literary Sinitic (*wen-yen*), often taken from or containing allusions (*tien-ku*) to situations in classical written works. *T'ou shu chi ch'i*—literally "to [hesitate to] pelt a rat [for fear of] smashing the vase [near it]," meaning "to hold back from taking action against evildoers for fear of also harming others"—is a *ch'eng-yü* that alludes to an ancient fable in which something thrown at a rat accidentally destroyed a valuable vase. *Ch'eng-yü* are included along with the other terms under the general rubric of *shu-yü* because many have passed into common use and are widely employed, even in contemporary vernacular (*pai-hua*) writing, as well as in the speech of educated people.

Lastly, in modern writings and even in some older works, one encounters another primarily spoken form, *hsieh-hou-yü*. A true *hsieh-hou-yü* is a two-part allegorical saying consisting of a descriptive phrase, always stated and more often than not preceded by a verb of explicit comparison (e.g., *hao pi* . . . [it's just like . . .]; thus it is a kind of simile). This is then followed by a pause, followed by a second phrase that, either directly or indirectly, resolves and explains the relevance of the simile to which the first part of the *hsieh-hou-yü* has been applied metaphorically. For example, so-and-so's lecture was (just like) "an old [Chinese] woman's foot-binding bandages—[i.e.,] both long and stinky!" Often the resolution of the metaphor involves a double entendre or pun on the superficial meaning of the second part of the *hsieh-hou-yü*, as when Mao Tse-tung (1893–1976) described himself to Edgar Snow as (being like) "a [tonsured Buddhist] monk under an umbrella" (*ho-shang ta san*). Not knowing the second part of the simile, *wu fa, wu t'ien* (literally, "having neither hair nor heaven [above]"), Snow could only take Mao's image literally, but the literal meaning of the resolution of the simile is not sufficient. *Wu fa, wu t'ien* is in fact homophonous with the *truly* intended meaning, the *ch'eng-yü* "[bound by] neither [earthly] law (*fa* [hair] / *fa* [law]) nor heaven [above]," which was what Mao really intended to say.

These popular enigmatic folk similes may be seen as a kind of spoken "linguistic game," in which the speaker pauses momentarily to see if his listener knows the *hsieh-hou-yü* and then supplies the resolution, unless the listener, already familiar with the expression, completes it for him (which is usually the case, hence the characterization "truncated"). These folk similes have also been incorporated into literature, nowadays often written with a long dash to indicate the separation of the two parts of the simile, and—in the case of puns—often with the characters for the "true," alternative reading of the homophonous punning reading given next to the literal meaning in parentheses. In the past, neither the truncated second part nor still less the explanation of the pun would have been supplied, since it was assumed that the listener was fully aware of both, which were implicit in the speaker's utterance of just the first part. (Because these enigmatic folk similes are often used humorously, they are sometimes mistakenly referred to by the more general term *ch'iao-p'i-hua*, or simply "witticisms.")

PROVERBS IN EARLY WRITTEN WORKS

Proverbs, along with many of the other related forms discussed above, being primarily popular, orally based forms, doubtless have a long, unwritten history as one of the "little traditions" of China's common people, which is reflected in the "great tradition" of Chinese written literature only much later. Two of the oldest recorded types of proverb are the "agricultural proverbs" (*nung-yen*) and "weather proverbs" (*ch'i-hsiang yen-yü*), which encapsulate traditional observations and advice concerning the weather and various agricultural practices in different parts of China over the centuries. If these are included, the extant examples of collections of such agricultural and weather proverbs date back as far as eighteen hundred years ago, in the Eastern Han, when Ts'ui Shih first collected agricultural proverbs as part of his *Ssu-min yüeh-ling* (Monthly Guidance for the Four Classes of People). Similar collections of these *nung-yen* are found in works on agriculture in the Three Kingdoms (220–265), Northern Wei (386–534), Sung (960–1279), Yüan (1260–1368), Ming (1368–1644), and Ch'ing (1644–1911) dynasties. Not until the Sung dynasty were there works devoted purely to the collection of proverbs per se; Kung Yi-cheng's *Shih ch'ang t'an* (Explanations of Common Sayings) and Chou Shou-chung's *Ku-chin yen* (Ancient and Contemporary Proverbs) are the first two such collections known, followed by similar works in the Ming and Ch'ing dynasties. At the same time, general, agricultural, and weather proverbs peculiar to a particular locality were also often included in local gazetteers (*fang-chih* or *ti-fang-chih*). In the twentieth century, collections devoted specifically to proverbs, often to certain types of proverbs or to the proverbs of a certain province or locality, became more numerous.

As examples of their quotation in ancient writings, there are proverbs from pre-Ch'in dynasty times in many classic works. The third-century B.C.E. *Kuo-yü* (Discourses of the States) includes: "To follow goodness is to ascend; to follow evil is to plummet"; *Chan-kuo ts'e* (Intrigues of the Warring States) contains: "Better to be the head of a chicken than the tail of an ox"; and *Han Fei Tzu* warns: "[Just as] distant water cannot extinguish nearby fires, [so] distant relatives are not as good as close neighbors"—all of which are pairs of balanced, rhymed couplets. The Former Han dynasty (206 B.C.E.–8 C.E.) classic work *Shih-chi* (Records of the Historian), by Ssu-ma Ch'ien, contains proverbs that are still in use today, such as: "Honest advice, though unpleasant to the ear, benefits one's conduct, [just as] good medicine, though bitter to the taste, benefits one's health," and "Sometimes an inch may be too long, or a foot too short," meaning that everyone has both strong and weak points.

As is true in many literate cultures, in Chinese literature, fiction consciously separated from myth/legend/history, poetry, and drama is a relatively recent development. Just as the written record indicates that proverbs have a long, primarily oral history in China, so does it reveal that for hundreds of years storytelling was as popular among the illiterate peasantry and city dwellers of China as it was in other illiterate premodern cultures around the world, and that—then as later—proverbs played an important part in introducing, advancing, and summarizing the common wisdom contained in this popular form of "oral literature." In the Sui (581–618) and early T'ang (618–907) dynasties, Buddhist monks became storytellers to convert the uneducated laity to Buddhism. As can be discerned from manuscripts of transformation texts (*pien-wen*) and other narrative genres dating from roughly the eighth through the tenth centuries preserved in the Tun-huang caves of northwestern China (see chapter 48), not only do these stories contain highly romanticized accounts of such personages as Confucius, the legendary sage-king Shun, and other famous figures of Chinese history and legend, but, even in their recounting of Buddhist legends, traditional Chinese moral values are stressed, often by the use of Chinese proverbs, proverbial expressions, and allusions.

In the succeeding Sung dynasty, especially after the prohibition of public storytelling by Buddhist monks, other types of storytellers flourished and were organized into guilds, each group specializing in telling a different type of story, such as short love stories, ghost stories, crime stories, and recitations of early dynastic histories. Although the basic facts, characters, and story lines were often written down in script outlines or prompt books, these were sketchy at best, and the art of the storyteller (many were blind) obviously resided in his or her skill in reifying, elaborating, and commenting in his or her development of these sketchy plot summaries, relying on such rhetorical devices as well-known proverbs, proverbial expressions, and allusions familiar to his or her textually illiterate, yet "orally literate," audience.

Even as these tales, stories, and histories were captured and transformed into what was to become written fiction of the Yüan, Ming, and Ch'ing eras, because the majority of China's population remained illiterate, this centuries-old tradition of storytelling and the use of such rhetorical devices as proverbs continued well into the twentieth century and, in some sense, carries on not only in traditional Chinese opera but also in the written versions of these stories and histories, which evolved out of them over the succeeding centuries and continue to evolve today.

THE INCORPORATION OF PROVERBS INTO WRITTEN LITERATURE

As discussed above, the incorporation of proverbs, proverbial expressions, and the other more vernacular, orally based forms of "familiar expressions" (*shu-yü*) into written literature is tied to the sharp distinction between "vulgar" (*su*) and "elegant" (*ya*) maintained by the Chinese literati. Because of the growth of agriculture and manufacturing enterprises in the T'ang and Sung dynasties, China's population and urban areas continued to expand, and with them the demand from illiterate and literate city dwellers for popular entertainment. As noted above, for the first group storytelling expanded, while for the more literate group there developed deliberately invented written prose narrative romances about ghosts, marvels, love, and swordsmen derogatorily referred to as "strange transmissions" (*ch'uan-ch'i*), still written in the more classical literary Chinese style of language familiar to educated readers. With continued economic improvement and urban growth under the succeeding Sung dynasty, these prose romances died out and were gradually replaced by short stories, which, as noted above, were often ultimately based on storytellers' tales (whether transmitted purely orally or in the form of sketches and outlines), enlarged and polished into written stories, but in a far more colloquial style than the T'ang *ch'uan-ch'i*. These vernacular short stories in many ways followed the storyteller's original organization and—like the earlier oral versions—are interspersed with verses, proverbs, and comments to the reader, as well as incorporating proverbs and proverbial expressions in both the dialog and commentary, in keeping with the colloquial style of this new literary form. (Although the extant written record preserves such vernacular works as *p'ing-hua* and *hua-pen* [see chapter 34] only from the Yüan era and later, it would appear that they have their roots in developments that took place during the Sung era, especially the Southern Sung.)

After the fall of the Sung dynasty, storytelling in the cities declined in popularity, but later writers perpetuated this style and the short-story form flourished as popular written literature for several hundred years through the occupation of China by the non-Chinese Mongol (Yüan dynasty) rulers and on into the restored Chinese Ming dynasty, when various Sung short stories were collected and edited into impressive multivolume works. At the same time, the earliest forms of the Chinese novel began to emerge out of the popular folktales transmitted through the earlier storytelling scripts and the colloquial short stories derived therefrom. These longer novels derive from and in many respects follow the overall format of the popular tales and histories of the earlier storytellers and thus, not surprisingly, incorporate proverbs, proverbial sayings, and other such oral forms into the more colloquial language of the novel, particularly in the dialog but also in the author's commentary. To give but one example, in the Ming dynasty novel version of the famous storytellers' tale now known as *Shui-hu chuan* (Outlaws of the Marsh, or Water Margin, or—in Pearl Buck's borrowing of the old Confucian maxim—All Men Are Brothers), when her pandering neighbor, Mistress Wang, describes the beautiful P'an Chin-lien and her dwarf husband, Wu Ta-lang, to the rich seducer Hsi-men Ch'ing, she cites the proverb "A magnificent steed gets a dolt for a rider; a charming wife sleeps with an oaf of a husband" and then explains her easy discernment of his lustful desires by quoting "the old saying 'One look at a man's face will tell you whether he is prospering or suffering.'" After their adulterous liaison is established, the author comments in the style of an oral narrator, "As the proverb has it, 'Good news never gets past the door, but scandal is heard a thousand miles away.' In less than half a month, all the neighbors knew; only [her husband] Wu Ta-lang remained in ignorance."

As a clear indication of just how important proverbial language is in *Shui-hu chuan* and other Ming-Ch'ing fiction, Wolfram Eberhard identified 119 proverbs in this famous Ming dynasty adventure novel; the sixteenth-century Ming dynasty novel *Feng-shen yen-yi* (The Investiture of the Gods, or, more literally, The Romance of the Deification of the Gods), a mythological history of the end of the Shang dynasty and the beginning of the Chou dynasty, contains 276 proverbs; the late Ming erotic masterpiece *Chin P'ing Mei* (The Golden Lotus, or Gold Vase Plum) quotes 136 proverbs; the Ch'ing dynasty novella *Ju-lin wai-shih* (The Scholars, or The Unofficial History of Officialdom) has 44 proverbs; and the famous Ch'ing dynasty novel *Hung-lou meng* (A Dream of Red Towers), generally recognized as China's greatest novel, includes 110 proverbs.

PROVERBS IN TWENTIETH-CENTURY LITERATURE

After the founding of the Republic of China in 1912, the New Literature movement associated with the "May Fourth movement" (see chapter 39) sought to vernacularize the Chinese written language in order to facilitate the promotion of widespread literacy and democratize China's "feudal" culture. "Official speech" (*kuan-hua*) in the form of "Mandarin" was actively promoted as the "national language" (*kuo-yü*) by the new government, and democratic writers such as Hu Shih (1891–1962) and Lu Hsün (1881–1936) worked hard to encourage writing in a new vernacular style (*pai-hua-wen*) more closely approximating this "standard" national spoken language instead of the traditional "literary Chinese" style (*wen-yen-wen*), the standard educated way of writing through the end of the Ch'ing dynasty. Authors and scholars educated abroad in Japan, Europe, and North America, or in the new, Western-influenced missionary universities in China, deliberately abandoned literary Chinese and experimented with this new vernacular *pai-hua-wen*, trying to create a modern literary style unique to the new China they hoped to build. Writers espousing liberal, democratic, and "progressive" ideals, such as Lu Hsün, Hu Shih, Pa Chin (pseudonym of Li Fei-kan; b. 1904), Ts'ao Yü (1910–1996), Mao Tun (pseudonym of Shen Yen-ping; 1896–1981), and Lao She (pseudonym of Shu Ch'ing-ch'un; 1899–1966), in their attempts to capture the ideas, concerns, and actual language of ordinary people in this new medium, naturally included such colloquial forms as proverbs, proverbial expressions, enigmatic folk similes, and "ballads and sayings" (*yao-yen*) of the common people in their essays, articles, short stories, novels, and plays. Hu Shih, in his pioneering and influential 1917 article "Wen-hsüeh kai-liang ch'u-yi" (Tentative Suggestions for Literary Reform), while urging writers to eschew the *wen-yen* language and style of the "ancients," to "discard stale, timeworn [i.e., *wen-yen*] phrases" and "classical allusions," concluded by stating: "Do not avoid popular expressions." He particularly stressed the importance of such popular oral expressions as proverbs, proverbial expressions, and *hsieh-hou-yü* because of his belief that vernacular literature, in both language and content, should be the primary literature of the new democracy, available to *all* readers, especially those newly literate in the more orally based *pai-hua-wen* writings. Regardless of their political leanings, the various groups of young Chinese writers who advanced different philosophies and goals for literature during the turbulent 1920s and 1930s generally shared the same basic attitude toward the creation of a new vernacular language and style, which would include all these popular forms in writing, albeit sometimes as examples of out-of-date traditional thinking that some of them wished to criticize.

By 1932, the pioneering rhetorician of the new *pai-hua-wen*, Ch'en Wang-tao, in the chapter on quotations in his influential *Hsiu-tz'u-hsüeh fa-fan* (Introduction to Rhetoric), cited not only famous proverbs from the classics but also anonymous popular proverbs, used both with and without quotation marks, as well as devoting a section to the history and structure of *hsieh-hou-yü* (enigmatic folk similes).

The historical struggle that dominated China in the second quarter of the twentieth century was primarily between the urban-based Kuomintang (Nationalist party) led by Chiang K'ai-shek (1887–1975), who had succeeded Sun Yat-sen (1866–1925), the founder of the Republic, and the Soviet-supported Communist Party, founded in Shanghai in 1921. After the failure of the Communist-led uprising among the urban workers in Shanghai in 1927 (dramatized in André Malraux's novel *La Condition humaine* [Man's Fate; 1933]), the Communists fled to the countryside and shifted their focus to organizing the peasant "masses" according to the revolutionary theories and tactics of their new leader, a self-educated peasant named Mao Tse-tung.

The roots of the propagandistic fiction, poetry, and drama that became widespread in the People's Republic of China from the time of its founding in 1949 until around 1976 can also be traced back to the Marxist influence of the Soviet Union, beginning with the "proletarian literature" of the 1920s. After the Long March of 1934–1936, the Chinese Communists relocated to the remote northwest mountain caves of Yenan for the duration of the War of Resistance Against Japan and continued to devote themselves to Mao Tse-tung's new strategy of mobilizing China's peasantry. In Yenan, Mao lectured to largely illiterate cadres and troops, deliberately employing a popular vernacular style, rich with proverbs and other familiar expressions, allusions to folklore, traditional stories and operas, including many of the popular works cited above. Most important for the rise and dominance of Chinese literature by the prescriptions of "socialist realism" were Mao's talks at the 1942 Forum on Art and Literature. In addition to emphasizing the political and propaganda functions of literature, Mao stressed to writers the importance of recognizing the mass audience and of employing a populist language and style accessible to the majority of that audience, including proverbs, folk idioms, and other such familiar expressions, as he himself often did.

Perhaps the single most influential author to implement Mao's dicta in the 1940s and 1950s was Chao Shu-li (1906–1970), best known for his 1943 work *Li Yu-ts'ai pan-hua* (The Rhymes of Li Yu-ts'ai), whose work deliberately employed folk idioms and vernacular speech in its characterizations of peasant life and led to the formation of the so-called Potato school (*shan-yao[-tan] p'ai*) of Communist Chinese literature. In these works, the proverbs, proverbial expressions, and *ch'eng-yü* that had already passed into popular usage in northern (Mandarin) Chinese became required elements of this new style. In this way, many originally regional, familiar sayings gained wider currency and passed into the emerging standard of the new national language and style. These basic directions—stemming from the literary reform associated with the May Fourth movement, from Mao Tse-tung's pronouncements in his Yenan talks, and from the resultant Potato school of literature—all continued to guarantee the currency of proverbs and other familiar expressions in Chinese fiction, drama, and other writings past the end of the Maoist era with his death in 1976 and into the last quarter of the twentieth century. Although most of China's population is still agricultural and rural (and many of those still either illiterate or only minimally literate), it remains to be seen whether the result of China's rapid industrialization and "modernization" will be to decrease the currency of these traditional expressions in society and literature, as it has in the West, or whether they will survive as bearers of traditional peasant wisdom and humor.

THE FORMS OF CHINESE PROVERBS

As noted above, a Chinese proverb is, strictly speaking, a grammatically complete sentence expressing an observation or judgment based on experience. In form, it consists of one or two lines of four or more syllables each, using either colloquial (*pai-hua*) or literary (*wen-yen*) language. Agricultural proverbs (*nung-yen*) and weather proverbs (*ch'i hsiang yen-yü*) usually refer to local conditions and do not gain national currency, with the exception of a few general ones such as *Chao-hsia ch'u yü; wan-hsia ch'u ch'ing* (equivalent to "Red sky at night, sailor's/shepherd's delight; red sky in the morning, sailor/shepherd take warning").

Like proverbs all over the world, many Chinese proverbs are meant to be understood metaphorically. Thus the colloquial proverb *Chen chin pu p'a huo lien* (literally, "True gold fears not the fire") is understood metaphorically to mean that a person of integrity can stand severe testing.

Proverbs that happen to comprise four characters must be distinguished from *ch'eng-yü* such as the *t'ou shu chi ch'i* example cited above, which is merely a descriptive literary phrase alluding to an ancient fable. Four-character colloquial sentences such as *Hao shih to mo* ("The road to happiness is strewn with setbacks"), often equated with Shakespeare's "The course of true love never did run smooth," and the more literary *Neng-che to lao* ("Able persons have to do more work") do fulfill the criteria for proverbs and should not be misclassified as *ch'eng-yü*.

Proverbs often follow fixed formulae, such as the comparative "A *pu-ju* (is not equal to) B" single-line pattern, as in *Pai wen pu-ju yi chien* ("Better to see once than to hear a hundred times") or the two-line "*ning* (*k'o*) (is preferable) A . . . , *pu* (not) B . . ." comparative pattern, for example, *Ning wei yü sui, pu wei wa ch'üan* ("Better to be a shattered jade vessel than an unbroken earthenware tile"), meaning that it is better to die in glory than to live in dishonor.

The grammar of Chinese proverbs is determined largely by the basic "topic-comment" structure of Chinese sentences, which—unlike in poetry—outweighs formal considerations of parallelism. Thus in *Ch'ien li sung o mao; li ch'ing, jen-yi chung* ("[When] a goose feather is sent a thousand miles, [although] the gift [itself] is light, the [accompanying] sentiment is weighty," or "It's the thought that counts"), the two lines of five syllables each together form one sentence, but without the strict grammatical parallelism and rhyme required by classical Chinese poetry. This is true even when the two lines do end-rhyme, as proverbs often do for ease of memorization, for example, the extremely colloquial doggerel proverb *Hao chieh, hao huan; tsai chieh pu nan* ("Well borrowed and well returned, borrowing again will not be spurned"). Formal grammatical parallelism usually occurs when the same structure is repeated for contrast or comparison, as in the now-proverbial citation from *Discourses of the States*: *Ts'ung shan ju teng; ts'ung o ju peng* ("To follow goodness is to ascend; to follow evil is to plummet"). The second structurally parallel line may be an explicit metaphorical comparison, for example, *Chung yen ni erh, li yü hsing; liang yao k'u k'ou, li yü ping* ("Sincere advice, [although] unpleasant to the ear, is beneficial to [one's] conduct, [just as] good medicine, [though] bitter to the taste, is beneficial to [one's] health"). Often only one of the two lines of such familiar proverbs is stated, the other being implied.

These two examples also illustrate that, given the "topic-comment" structure of Chinese sentences and the generally monosyllabic nature of many words in Chinese, proverbs with lines of seven or eight syllables generally fall into a "four-plus-three" or "four-plus-four" pattern, respectively, for each line, with the topic introduced in the first four syllables and the comment in the remaining syllables. Another example of a seven-syllable sentence is *Ch'e tao shan ch'ien, pi yu lu* ("When the cart gets to the mountain, there must be a way [through]"), meaning that things always work themselves out; the now-proverbial quotation attributed to Confucius, *San jen t'ung hsing, pi yu wo shih* ("[When] three [of us] persons are walking together, [one of them] must be my teacher"—"One can always learn something from others"), illustrates the "four-plus-four" syllable pattern.

CONCLUSION

Although proverbs were neither well documented nor well studied in traditional China, sufficient evidence exists to confirm that, in premodern times as in the first half of the twentieth century, they played an important role in speech, particularly that of peasants and workers. With the advent of the vernacular language movement, they were also consciously adopted by demotically minded authors. However, during the second half of the twentieth century, because of increasing urbanization, national guidelines for education, and mass communication, proverbs have become less and less an integral part of daily speech. They are still frequently employed in certain types of written literature, however, if only as a nostalgic hearkening back to earlier days.

John S. Rohsenow

Chapter 9

BUDDHIST LITERATURE

INTRODUCTION

After Buddhism was introduced to China, this Indian religion and philosophy permeated all levels of Chinese culture and society, a lengthy process that began during the earliest centuries of the Common Era. The first Buddhists in China were not Indian missionaries, but Central Asian and Iranian traders who happened to be Buddhists but made no particular effort to proselytize the local population. Missionary monks, apparently first from Parthia (southeast of the Caspian sea) and other parts of Central Asia, then later by land and by sea from India itself, were either summoned by lay merchant communities living in China or embarked upon the dangerous passage themselves. They began trickling into China from the first century C.E. onward. As they strove to translate sometimes highly abstruse Buddhist concepts into Chinese, there was much interchange with preexisting philosophical Taoism and nascent religious Taoism, the latter of which, in some sense, may itself be viewed as a response to the newly imported religion.

Therefore, in some early Buddhist translations Taoist expressions were occasionally used to translate Sanskrit or Prakrit (the latter being vernacular Indic languages of the ancient or medieval period) terminology, especially numerical categories (this later came to be called *ko-yi* [matching terms]), while Buddhist concepts, practices, and institutions were grafted onto Taoism. As time passed, more philologically accurate translations were devised. Transcription was often employed, especially for proper nouns, although individual translators varied in their preferences regarding transcription vis-à-vis translation and the degree to which the two techniques should be mixed.

The preaching of the Buddhist law and the performance of narratives about the Buddha's lives in previous reincarnations (birth stories; Sanskrit, *jātaka*) or other Indian legends influenced and even in many ways inspired stage performances, and thus became the starting point of the Chinese theater. In particular, the Buddhist tradition of discipline, which required strict adherence to the rules for recitation and hymnody, had a certain impact on lyric theory and the establishment of regulated verse prosody. Furthermore, Buddhist esthetics played a large role in the rise of theories about literature, art, and music, while Buddhist ontological presuppositions strongly stimulated the fictive impulse among Chinese authors and also had a great influence on Chinese thought (especially Neo-Confucianism).

Thus Buddhism had a significant impact on nearly every aspect of Chinese literary, intellectual, and cultural life. Even the development of printing techniques was at least promoted, if not initiated, by the interest of Buddhists in multiplying holy texts. Indeed, the fundamental importance of Buddhism for the Chinese literary tradition throughout the past two millennia is so enormous that it is also touched on in many other chapters of this book. This chapter concentrates primarily on Buddhist literature per se and presents a few of the highlights of Buddhism in secular literature.

THE BUDDHIST CANON

The Buddhist canon in Chinese is not merely a collection of a few major texts. It covers more than a hundred thousand densely packed pages in its printed form and is perhaps more adequately described as a library in its own right. The Buddhist canon represents translations into Chinese from just before the middle of the second century through about 1000 C.E. and thus can be regarded as a mirror of intellectual, philosophical, and linguistic continuity and change, development, and stagnation during that long, formative period of medieval Chinese culture. In India, the Buddhist canon is traditionally divided into three sections; hence it is called the *Tripiṭaka* ("Three Baskets"; *San-tsang*), which the Taoists took as a model in forming their own canon consisting of "Three Caves" (*San-tung*).

The first section of the canon is that containing sūtras (scriptures) conveying the words attributed to the Buddha himself as they were transmitted orally by his pupils. "Sūtra" comes from the Sanskrit and literally means "thread," probably in reference to the stitching together of the leaves of manuscripts. The term was translated into Chinese as *ching* (literally, "warp"), a designation previously applied to the Confucian classics (see chapter 4). The second section comprises the rules on conduct (Sanskrit, *vinaya*; Chinese, *lü*), including texts on monastic and general discipline for the followers, plus legends and biographies of the Buddha. The third section, called Abhidharma or "high" *dharma* (moral law, fundamental principle, or doctrine; Chinese, *lun*), consists largely of advanced exegetical literature, philosophy, and metaphysics. In actual practice, however, Chinese Buddhist bibliographers did not observe this tripartite scheme rigidly.

Canonicity in China was established largely through the compilation of catalogs and eventually through the intervention of the rulers. During the T'ang (618–907) and earlier dynasties, many versions of the canon were compiled, controlled, and distributed by various state and monastic authorities, a practice that continued into later times. The Chinese Buddhist canon in the form (more or less) as we know it today, however, with its thousands of scrolls, was not produced in its entirety until the Sung dynasty (960–1279) officially decided to sponsor its production and distribution.

In 972 C.E., the carving of wooden printing blocks for the whole canon was commissioned by the court in Chengtu, Szechwan province, at that time the Chinese wood-carving center. In 983, a total of 130,000 blocks were carved, and from this time on manuscript copying was replaced by xylographic (woodblock) reproduction techniques. In Korea, another version of the Chinese canon was realized between 1010 and 1030. After this edition was destroyed, the Korean monk Sugi produced a new version between 1236 and 1251 in more than 81,000 blocks, which are still stored at the Hae-in monastery in southern Korea and remain the basis for all modern critical editions. There have been further block-print editions of the canon in China since Sung times. The canon, in addition to being copied by hand and printed by woodblock, was also carved in stone. The most important of such epigraphical canons, the earliest of which dates from the early seventh century C.E., was executed at Fang-shan district (southwest of Peking).

TRANSLATED TEXTS

Many Buddhist miracle tales became known to Chinese audiences because they were part of Buddhist sūtras that had been translated since the second century C.E. The earliest prominent translator was the Parthian missionary An Shih-kao (fl. 148–170), who is said in later catalogs to have translated more than a hundred sūtras (accurate counts put the number at closer to sixteen). But his most sought-after work was the translation of the *Mahānāpanānusmṛti-sūtra* (*Ta-an-pan shou-yi ching; Taishō Tripiṭaka* [hereafter *T*], text no. 602), a manual devoted to breathing techniques to be used during contemplation. It is an open question whether An Shih-kao's translation of this sūtra indicates that he was connected with an early Yogācāra tradition—that of meditation practitioners within the Sarvāstivādin school. Other important translators were Chih-ch'ien (fl. latter part of the third century), Chu Fa-hu (or Dharmarakṣa; fl. 265–291), and Chu Shu-lan (fl. 291), as well as Chiu-mo-lo-shih (Kumārajīva; active in Ch'ang-an from 402 to 413), and the famous pilgrim Hsüan-tsang (c. 600–664). A native tradition of exegesis soon arose, with such outstanding representatives as Hui-yüan (334–416) and Tao-an (c. 313–c. 385). It is significant that Buddhism was introduced to China at a time when Mahāyāna (*Ta-sheng*) Buddhism arose as a newly conceived path to liberation centered on the figure of the bodhisattva (one who aspires to enlightenment). The doctrinal orientation and social praxis of the early Mahāyāna community helped to accustom this foreign creed to the upper layers of Chinese society, which led to the formation of what was labeled "gentry Buddhism." The prominence and ultimate success of the Mahāyāna in China, however, should not obscure the fact that early translators were interested in a variety of texts and that they made an interesting range and mix of materials available to Chinese readers.

Among the most influential texts translated into Chinese were the Perfection of Wisdom scriptures (*Prajñāpāramitā*). The *Prajñāpāramitā Sūtra in Eight Thousand Lines* was translated into Chinese six times, and the text in twenty-five thousand lines was translated four times. A short extract (only 260 characters, making it twenty times smaller than the *Tao te ching* [Classic of the Way and Integrity; see chapter 10]) from the *prajñāpāramitā* literature that evolved during the T'ang period (618–907) and later came to be known as the *Hsin ching* (Heart/Mind Sūtra; *T* 250–255) was phenomenally popular and is still probably the most widely read Buddhist text in East Asia. Another important translated text was the *Vimalakīrtinirdeśa-sūtra* (*Wei-mo-chieh ching; T* 474–476). Of the several translations of this text with the ideal Buddhist layman Vimalakīrti at its center, the one by Kumārajīva (*T* 475) was the most influential. It had a substantial and long-lasting impact on Chinese poetry, storytelling, and painting.

Another group is the Pure Land (Ching-t'u) literature, consisting of texts that describe the Buddha Amitābha's power to save sentient beings, for example, the *O-mi-t'o* [or *A-mi-t'o*] *ching* (*Amitābha-sūtra; T* 366; translated in the early fifth century C.E. by Kumārajīva), the *Wu-liang-shou ching* (*Sukhāvativyūha, Amitābhavyūha, A[pari]mitāyuḥ-sūtra; T* 360; translated in the mid-third century C.E. by K'ang Seng-hui), the *Kuan wu-liang-shou Fo ching* (Sūtra of Contemplation on the Buddha of Infinite Life; *T* 365; translated between 424 and 442), and three or four other works focusing on the Paradise of the West and its presiding Buddha.

Arguably the most important text translated from Sanskrit into Chinese, in terms of sheer literary influence, was the *Saddharmapuṇḍarīka-sūtra* (*Miao-fa lien-hua ching* [Lotus Sūtra]), translated in 286 C.E. by the Yüeh-chih monk Dharmarakṣa (*T* 263) and translated a second time in 406 by Kumārajīva (*T* 262), it was again translated into Chinese in 601 C.E. The doctrines contained in this sūtra became the foundation for several Chinese and Japanese Buddhist schools. Parts of it, such as the parables of the "Burning House" and the "Prodigal Son," became well-known pieces of literature in their own right. The sūtra deals at length with the merciful and compassionate deity Avalokiteśvara (Kuan [-shih]-yin or Kuang[-shih]-yin). A collection of texts on this particular deity entitled *Kuang-shih-yin ying-yen chi* (Accounts of Miracles by Avalokiteśvara) from 399 C.E. had long been lost. With the help of discoveries in Japanese libraries, it was reconstructed by the Buddhist scholars Tsukamoto Zenryū and Makita Tairyō during the second half of the twentieth century. The *Abhidharma-mahāvibhāṣā-śāstra* (*A-p'i-ta-mo-p'i-p'o-sha lun; T* 1545), translated by Hsüan-tsang, also gained widespread acceptance.

In many translated sūtras and śāstras (treatises), the Mahāyāna teaching on the powers of Mañjuśrī (Kumārabhūta Bodhisattva) to save sentient beings is discussed. Mañjuśrī's sacred mountain in China was Wu-t'ai shan (Five Terraces Mountain; Sanskrit, Pañcaśīrṣa or Pañcaśikhā). Located near the northeastern border of Shansi province, it became an international pilgrimage site and spawned a vast amount of legend, lore, and poetry by ardent devotees and pilgrims.

Another very important source of inspiration for Buddhist (and secular) literature was the translations of *vinaya* texts, especially those done in the fifth century. Although these ostensibly deal with such boring subjects as the rules governing the community of monks, they are filled with illustrative material that is often colorful and memorable. There were also many Tantric Buddhist works translated into Chinese, especially by Amoghavajra (705–774). Tantrism is an esoteric tradition that emphasizes the recitation of mystical formulas known as *dhāraṇīs* and mantras, as well as highly nuanced postures and gestures called *mūdras.* The formulas, which can be fairly long and elaborate, usually contain only a few syllables that are intelligible, even in Sanskrit. When rendered as transcriptions in Chinese characters, they are even more difficult to understand. What becomes important is the incantatory effect of their recitation, their function as meditative devices, and the elaboration of their hidden meanings by initiates and teachers.

DOCTRINAL, HISTORICAL, APOLOGETIC, AND SYNCRETISTIC LITERATURE

In the course of the canonization of the Buddhist scriptures, bibliographies and collections of canonical scriptures were compiled. The earliest extant bibliography is the *Ch'u san-tsang chi chi* (Collection of Records on the Translated Tripiṭaka; *T* 2145), by Seng-yu (445–518), containing numerous prefaces to Buddhist texts that are full of vital historical information. Compilations of biographies of monks became a standard form of Chinese Buddhist historiography, of which the *Kao-seng chuan* (Lives of Eminent Monks; *T* 2059), by Hui-chiao (497–554), who was a specialist in the *vinaya*, became the model. This work can be regarded as one of the masterpieces of Six Dynasties (220–589) prose style in which purely factual biographical material is interwoven with a hagiographic narrative aimed at propagating the Buddhist faith by telling the life stories of eminent monks, both Chinese and foreign. This collection of biographies became the model for a series of further collections of monks' biographies such as Tao-hsüan's (596–667) *Hsü-kao-seng chuan* (Continuation of Lives of Eminent Monks; *T* 2060) and Tsan-ning's (919–1002?) *Sung kao-seng chuan* (Lives of Eminent Monks Compiled Under the Sung; *T* 2061; dated 988 C.E.). There is also an early collection of biographies of nuns entitled *Pi-ch'iu-ni chuan* (Biographies of Nuns; *T* 2063), compiled by Pao-ch'ang (sixth century C.E.). Many of the biographies of famous Buddhists contain miracles that captivated even those who did not subscribe to the religion.

Related to Buddhist historiography are the records of Buddhist countries and travelogs by Chinese monks. Arduous journeys were undertaken for a number of purposes: to see the traces and homeland of the Buddha; to visit other important Buddhist sites; to study with Indian teachers; and, above all, to bring back new scriptures of the faith from India. In some cases, upon their return the pilgrims were requested to provide the Chinese emperors with reports on neighboring countries and on the travel routes they took. The most prominent of the Chinese pilgrims' reports are the following: *Fo-kuo chi* (Record of Buddhist Kingdoms; *T* 2085), by the monk Fa-hsien, who traveled to India and Ceylon (Sri Lanka) between 399 and 414; the report on Sung Yün's and Hui-sheng's travel to Udyāna and Gandhāra in 518 C.E., which is contained in Yang Hsüan-chih's *Lo-yang ch'ieh-lan chi* (Account of Monasteries and Temples of Loyang; *T* 2092, dated 547 C.E.), itself a masterpiece of urban architectural description; *Ta-T'ang hsi-yü chi* (Accounts of the Western Regions Under the Great T'ang; *T* 2087), which contains autobiographical experiences of Hsüan-tsang, written down by his disciple Pien-chi (Hsüan-tsang was not only the founder of the Fa-hsiang [Sanskrit, Dharmalakṣana] school of Yogācāra Buddhism in China but also the greatest Chinese Buddhist translator); and *Nan-hai chi-kuei nei-fa chuan* (Account of Buddhist Practices Sent Home from the Southern Sea; *T* 2125), by the monk Yi-ching (633–713), which reports on his travels between 671 and 695 C.E. in India and the Malay archipelago. These accounts became essential sources for the early history and geography of the regions visited by the Chinese monks.

APOLOGETIC LITERATURE

Another genre that flourished during the period of accommodation of Buddhism to Chinese circumstances is the polemical literature on Buddhism or on the relationship between Buddhism, Taoism, and Confucianism. The first collection of this type of discourse is the *Hung-ming chi* (Collection on Propagating and Illuminating Buddhism; *T* 2102), compiled by the Buddhist monk Seng-yu. "Li-huo lun" (Discourse Resolving Doubts), by a Chinese layman known as Mou Tzu (Master Mou), at the beginning of this collection is regarded as one of the earliest extant native Chinese Buddhist texts. A subsequent collection of such texts, *Kuang hung-ming chi* (Expanded Collection on Propagating and Illuminating Buddhism; *T* 2103), by the monk Tao-hsüan, is much larger than Seng-yu's *Hung-ming chi.*

The debates documented in these and several other collections provide insight into the intellectual climate stimulated by the introduction of Buddhist ideas, values, and practices to China, especially during the period from the fifth to the seventh centuries. Buddhist convictions as well as anti-Buddhist attitudes prompted many of the most outstanding texts in Chinese literary history, such as Han Yü's (768–824) "Lun Fo-ku piao" (Memorial on the Buddha Bone) and Tsung-mi's (780–841) "Yüan jen lun" (On the Origin of Humanity). A satire on such debates was launched under the title "Ch'a-chiu lun" (Discourse Between Tea and Wine), by an otherwise unknown Wang Fu (eighth or ninth century C.E.). This text was found in several versions among the tens of thousands of manuscripts discovered in the Tun-huang caves at the beginning of the twentieth century (see chapter 48).

Treatises on Buddhist doctrinal subjects had the side effect of augmenting new expressions, motifs, plots, and narratives in the Chinese cultural sphere. Among these were treatises on the immortality of the soul, on the Buddha-nature of every living being, on the Pure Land (e.g., T'an-luan's [b. 476] *Ching-t'u lun-chu* [Commentary and Discourses Regarding the Pure Land; *T* 1819]), on paradise, and so forth. Such texts were not limited to any particular school or sect. These lively doctrinal discussions and debates often spilled outside Buddhism and became a part of intellectual discourse among Confucians, Taoists, and others. Consequently, although Buddhism proper was periodically subject to major persecutions and suppressions in China, Buddhist discourse had already been appropriated by Chinese society and adopted into common parlance by the eighth century. Thus it continued at all times to exert an influence on modes of thought and belief in Chinese society, albeit sometimes cloaked in the guise of a "native" tradition (but one that had borrowed extensively from Buddhist phraseology with the express purpose of elaborating a rival cosmology).

CHRONICLES

In the context of rivalries between different Buddhist schools and lineages, chronicles of the transmission of the dharma emerged (for example, Tsung-mi's *Ch'an-yüan chu-ch'üan-chi tu-hsü*[General Preface to the Collected Explanations of the Origins of the Zen Sect; *T* 2015]), which in turn became the point of departure for Buddhist universal histories. One such universal history was the *Lung-hsing Fo-chiao pien-nien t'ung-lun* (Comprehensive Chronicle of Buddha's Teaching from the Lung-hsing Period), by the monk Tsu-hsiu, dated 1164, which follows the example of Ssu-ma Kuang's (1019–1086) phenomenally influential history entitled *Tzu-chih t'ung-chien* (A Comprehensive Mirror for Aid in Government). Another work in this style is the *Shih-shih t'ung-chien* (Comprehensive Mirror of the Śākya Clan), by the monk Pen-chüeh, from 1270 C.E., which stands in the tradition of the T'ien-t'ai school represented by *Shih-men cheng-t'ung* (Correct Sequence of the Buddhist Schools; dated 1237), by the layman Wu K'o-chi (1195–1214) and the monk Tsung-chien (d. 1206), and by the *Fo-tsu t'ung-chi* (Comprehensive History of Buddha and the Patriarchs; *T* 2035; dated 1269), by Chih-p'an (c. 1220–1275). *Fo tsu li-tai t'ung tsai* (Comprehensive Accounts of the Buddha and the Patriarchs Under Successive Dynasties; *T* 2036; dated 1333), by the monk Nien-ch'ang, is one of several Buddhist universal histories compiled in China during the time of Mongol rule.

ORAL AND PERFORMED LITERATURE

The Buddhist scriptures were used as a basis for practicing as well as for propagating the *dharma*. Out of this emerged a certain variety of sermonizing texts called *chiang-ching-wen* (sūtra lecture texts), which were used to explain the content of certain scriptures to a broader audience. These preachings originally took place only on festival days but were later performed at the demand of laypersons who would pay for this service.

The practice of visualizing Buddhas and bodhisattvas, together with the recitation of their names, as well as the making of pictures showing heavens and hells and of texts describing such realms in great detail, had a tremendous impact on Chinese popular literature and art. The vivid portrayals of these kinds of Buddhist texts and illustrations did much to heighten the imagination and spark the creativity of Chinese authors. Especially significant are "transformation texts" (*pien-wen*), many of which were found in the Tun-huang caves (see chapter 48). These texts were performed with the intent of representing a miraculous event in order to enlighten the audience by exemplifying Buddhist teachings. These extraordinary events were presented in the vernacular in a prosimetric style. The written semivernacular texts are to a certain extent related to "popular sermons" (*su-chiang*) expounded by Chinese Buddhists as early as the fourth century, but evolve more directly out of the Indian tradition of storytelling with pictures, which flourished in many genres and ultimately spread over much of Europe and Asia.

Only about twenty of the roughly eighty texts gathered in the first comprehensive collection under the title *Tun-huang pien-wen chi* (Collection of *pien-wen* from Tun-huang), by Wang Chung-min (1903–1975) et al., are actually transformation texts in the strictest sense. Since some of the genuine *pien-wen* manuscripts present one and the same text, there remain only between eight and twelve—depending on the exactness of one's definition—transformation texts. Among the most important are "Hsiang-mo pien" (Transformation on the

Subduing of Demons), "Ta-mu-ch'ien-lien ming-chien chiu-mu pien-wen" (Transformation Text on Mahāmaudgalyāyana's Rescue of His Mother from the Underworld), and "Chang Yi-ch'ao [pien-wen]" ([Transformation Text on] Chang Yi-ch'ao).

The Buddhist imagery and underlying ideology of early Chinese novels like *Hsi-yu chi* (Journey to the West), *Jou p'u-t'uan* (Prayer Mat of Flesh), and *Feng-shen yen-yi* (Investiture of the Gods) are evident (see chapters 35, 36, and 37). Among the frequent Buddhist topoi in Chinese fiction are abstinence (or the lack thereof), karmic retribution, rebirth, heavens and hells, and miraculous transformations and manifestations. The same is true of some of the most enduring monuments of Chinese drama, though to a lesser extent, since Taoism appears to have had a greater impact on the full-blown theater than did Buddhism (see chapter 41). Buddhist influence on the theater in China (and Indian influence generally) comes at the earliest stages of development and has more to do with form and conventions (role types, makeup, gestures, prosimetric alternation between sung and spoken parts, structure by acts and interludes, etc.) than with content, although such Buddhist themes as renunciation, asceticism, transmigration, and emptiness (*śūnyatā*) are often alluded to.

THE *YÜ-LU*

One of the many indigenous Chinese contributions to Buddhism is the development of Ch'an (Japanese, Zen; from Sanskrit *dhyāna* [meditation]) Buddhism. Ch'an Buddhism makes what appears to be a rather contradictory claim: enlightenment is immediate in that it entails no mediation and cannot be expressed in symbols or words, yet this insight is uniquely available in Ch'an. Here the teachings of Ch'an masters and dialogs with their students play a prominent role. The genre of the particular Ch'an Buddhist textual transmission called *yü-lu* (records of sayings) took shape with the Ch'an master Ma-tsu Tao-yi (709–788), who addressed not only a few adepts but a broader audience. Naturally, however, *yü-lu* had indigenous literary antecedents stretching all the way back to the *Lun-yü* (Analects) attributed to Confucius (see chapter 4). During the Sung dynasty, this genre was adopted to publish the recorded sayings of prominent Neo-Confucians such as Ch'eng Yi (1033–1107), Chang Chiu-ch'eng (1092–1159), and Chu Hsi (1130–1200).

Of utmost importance for the transmission of Ch'an teaching is that the masters' sayings were not taken out of the context in which they were uttered, nor were they rendered in Literary Sinitic. Instead, the quoted portions of these records represent a language that is very close to the vernacular of the period to which they supposedly pertain (aside from a few texts preserved at Tun-huang and dating to the T'ang and Five Dynasties [907–960] periods [starting from the early eighth century], extant *yü-lu* date to the Sung and later periods, even though many of them are associated with T'ang masters). *Yü-lu* that played a major role in later times were *Ma-tsu yü-lu* (Recorded Sayings of Master Ma-tsu); *Tung-shan yü-lu* (Recorded Sayings of Master Tung-shan), recording the teachings of Tung-shan Liang-chieh (807–867), the patriarch of the Ts'ao-tung (Japanese, Sōtō) line of Ch'an teaching; the *Lin-chi lu* (Recorded Sayings of Master Lin-chi) of Lin-chi Yi-hsüan (d. 867 C.E.); and *Tsu-t'ang chi* (Collection from the Hall of the Patriarchs; published 952). Others were *Pi-yen lu* (Records from the Emerald Cliff; *T* 2003), compiled by K'o-ch'in (1064–1136), and *Wu-men kuan* (Doorless Gate; *T* 2005), by Wu-men Hui-k'ai (1182–1260). *Ching-te ch'uan-teng lu* (Records of the Transmission of the Lamp from the Ching-te Period; *T* 2076; dated 1006), compiled by Tao-yüan (dates unknown), is a combination of genealogy and records of the teachings of many Ch'an masters. Full of the masters' inexplicable antics and mind-shattering puzzlers (called *kung-an*; Japanese, *kōan*; literally "public case record") such as "What is the meaning of Bodhidharma's coming from the West?", "What was your original face before your parents were born?", and "What is the color of the red-bearded barbarian's beard?", the *yü-lu* still hold a tremendous fascination. The *yü-lu* were not all so intentionally difficult to comprehend, many of them being accompanied by commentaries and poems to explain their logic.

Among the many sectarian writings by the followers of the Ch'an Buddhist schools, *Liu-tsu t'an-ching* (Platform Sūtra of the Sixth Patriarch; *T* 2007), attributed to Hui-neng (d. 713), has become one of the most authoritative scriptures of Ch'an in China, perhaps partly because it survived in a Tun-huang manuscript. Some Ch'an Buddhists wrote hymns and poetry, and Ch'an ideas were absorbed into literary theory and appreciation. But Buddhist teachings also had great influence on Chinese poetry and literature in general, especially Pure Land teachings, which constituted the doctrine of the greatest popular faith among the Chinese masses. Buddhist ideas and concepts—like emptiness (*śūnyatā*), impermanence (*anitya*), suffering (*duḥkha*), illusion (*māyā*), the cycle of births and rebirths (*saṃsāra*), karma, and concepts such as paradises and hells—permeated all layers of society.

BUDDHISM IN THE WORLD OF THE LITERATI

Many texts, prefaces, treatises, confessions, letters, and so forth written by literati demonstrate the great influence of Buddhist doctrines on Chinese cultural and literary life, even among the elite, who were not always exclusively Confucian in their ideological orientation. There were as well several highly original thinkers among the Chinese Buddhist clergy, the top levels of which were, at least in the earlier centuries, largely part of the aristocracy or mingled closely with them. Authors like Chih-tun (314–366), Hui-yüan, Tsung-ping (375–443), and Seng-chao (c. 374–414) must be mentioned here for having forged a distinctly Buddhist style in Literary Sinitic, as well as outstanding clerical and Buddhistically inclined lay poets like Hsieh Ling-yün (385–433), Wang Wei (701–761), Chiao-jan (720–805?), Meng Hao-jan (689–740), and Po Chü-yi (772–846). The highly vernacular poetry of Wang Fan-chih (Brahmacārin Wang, eighth or ninth century C.E.) was preserved among the Tun-huang manuscripts. Ch'an Buddhists were authors of evocative hymns and poetry, for example, "Hsin-hsin ming" (Inscription of Faith in Mind, *T* 2010), attributed to Seng-ts'an (?–606; third patriarch of the Ch'an school); "Cheng-tao ko" (Song of Realization of the Way), attributed to the Master of Yung-chia, Hsüan-chüeh (665–713); and various pieces assigned to Kuan-hsiu (832–912). The poetry of Han-shan (Cold Mountain) was not the work of a single author but, rather, a compilation of lyric poetry from different periods of the T'ang dynasty. Like the work of Wang Fan-chih, it is full of vernacularisms but even more eccentric.

Among the later Buddhist poets, Te-hung (1071–1128) and Ch'i-sung (1107–1172) are outstanding, but the long-neglected Buddhist side of otherwise well-known authors has been traced only recently, as in the case of Su Shih (Su Tung-p'o; 1037–1101). The lasting effect of Buddhism on Chinese poetry and literary criticism can already be seen in Liu Hsieh's (465?–520?) *Wen-hsin tiao-lung* (The Literary Mind and the Carving of Dragons) and, in a more complex way, in the crucial role played by Yen Yü's (c. 1195–1245) *Ts'ang-lang shih-hua* (Ts'ang-lang's Remarks on Poetry), which was deeply influenced by Ch'an thinking (see chapter 45), and still later in Wang Kuo-wei's (1877–1927) literary theories.

The Buddhist concept of "mind" (*hsin*) became extremely important in intellectual and literary circles during the Six Dynasties. "Mind" (Sanskrit, *hṛd[aya], citta, manas,* etc.) was contrasted with "form" (*se;* Sanskrit, *rūpa*), dividing all phenomena into physical and mental, material and immaterial. The clear delineation of abstract states of mind enabled Chinese literary theorists and critics to elaborate esthetic concepts of previously unimagined complexity and subtlety. Thus Buddhism became one of the determining forces of Chinese literature, although its influence cannot always be traced in detail.

The founders or central figures of the greater Chinese Buddhist schools—such as Chih-yi (538–597), founder of T'ien-t'ai and author of an important set of lectures delivered in the year 594 and published under the title *Mo-ho chih-kuan* (The Great Cessation and Contemplation; *T* 1911) by his disciple Kuan-ting (561–627)—deserve mention as authors introducing new ideas, coining new words and expressions, and inspiring later literary activities. Indeed, one of the main reasons Buddhism was able to survive and prosper in China (unlike other foreign religions, such as Zoroastrianism, Manichaeism, and Nestorian Christianity—all of which were present by the T'ang period) was its intellectual vitality. Chinese scholars, poets, and essayists had to take Buddhism seriously, because the Buddhists were learned, skillful writers.

STRANGE STORIES

Stories of strange events and about experiences of supernatural things, which have a long autochthonous tradition in China (see chapters 6 and 29), merged with Buddhist tales to such a degree that the elements sometimes became nearly indistinguishable. Such stories of anomalies (*chih-kuai hsiao-shuo*), among others collected in Buddhist encyclopedias like the *Fa-yüan chu-lin* (Pearl Grove of the Garden of the Law; *T* 2122; dated 668 C.E.), often depend on older Chinese narrative traditions, which assume in them a Buddhist guise, for example, materials from *Yüan-hun chih* (Accounts of Ghosts with Grievances), compiled by Yen Chih-t'ui (531–591). Since these stories deal to a great extent with retribution for evil deeds, they could also be understood as exemplifications of the teaching of karma. These Buddhist tales of the supernatural are mainly of the following three kinds: accounts of supernatural powers, usually wielded by Avalokiteśvara to help those who call out in difficult situations; examples of piety and sincere belief; and remarkable deeds of monks and laymen indicating particular spiritual powers. Among the many collections of Buddhist miracle tales are *Kuang-shih-yin ying-yen chi*, by Fu Liang (374–426); *Hsüan-yen chi* (Records in Proclamation of Manifestations), by Liu Yi-ch'ing (author of *Shih-shuo hsin-yü* [New Account of Tales of the World]; 403–444; see chapter 29); *Hsü Kuang-shih-yin ying-yen chi* (Further Accounts of Miracles by Avalokiteśvara; first half of the fifth century), by Chang Yen (dates unknown); *Hsü Kuan-shih-yin ying-yen chi* (Continued Records of Kuan-shih-yin's Responsive Manifestations), by Lu Kao (459–532); and *Ming-hsiang chi* (Accounts of Mysterious Revelations), by Wang Yen (around 500 C.E.), with 131 tales, the largest of these collections.

AVADĀNA, JĀTAKA, AND BIOGRAPHIES OF THE BUDDHA

Distinguishable from these miracle tales and strange stories is the large quantity of stories relating the earlier existences of Gautama Buddha, the "Buddha's Birth Stories," or *Jātakas*. The earliest Chinese collection of *Jātakas*, containing ninety-one stories, is *Liu-tu chi-ching* (Canonical Scripture on the Six Perfections; *T* 152), by the Sogdian monk K'ang Seng-hui (d. 280 C.E.). There were allegedly earlier translations of parables (Sanskrit, *avadāna*) into Chinese, of which the most important are *Tsa p'i-yü ching* (Canonical Scripture of Miscellaneous Parables; *T* 204), containing twelve stories; and *P'u-sa tu-jen ching* (Canonical Scripture on Bodhisattvas Leading Men to the Truth; *T* 205), with thirty-two parables. Other *avadāna* collections are *Chiu tsa p'i-yü ching* (Old Canonical Scripture of Miscellaneous Parables; *T* 206), containing sixty-one stories translated by K'ang Seng-hui (between 251 and 280 C.E.); and *Canonical Scripture of Miscellaneous Parables*, with thirty-nine stories (around 400 C.E.). Another collection, under the title *Chung-ching chuan tsa p'i-yü* (Various Parables from All Sūtras; *T* 208), contains forty-four pieces from translations of sūtras by Kumārajīva. The most comprehensive *avadāna* collection, however, is *Pai-yü ching* (Canonical Scripture of a Hundred Parables; *T* 209), attributed to the Indian author Gunavṛddhi (fl. c. 480 C.E.). It is not just a collection of earlier *avadānas* but rather a polished and revised version showing the hand of an author who wished to craft excellent narratives that would provide the reader with a prologue and an epilogue attached to the main story. All these Buddhist story collections greatly enriched the fund of themes and motifs available to later Chinese writers of fiction. None, however, was more influential than *Hsien-yü ching* (The Sūtra of the Wise and the Foolish; *T* 202), which was composed of stories heard by eight Chinese monks in the Central Asian city of Khotan in 445.

Finally, any discussion of Buddhist literature in China that overlooked the *Buddhacarita* would be grossly remiss. This is a poetic life of Śākyamuni Buddha composed by Aśvaghoṣa (in Chinese, Ma-ming; second century C.E.), who is widely regarded as the most prominent predecessor of the peerless Kālidāsa (fl. fifth century) as well as a distinguished creator of epic, dramatic, and lyrical compositions. Variants of the *Buddhacarita* were translated by Dharmarakṣa in 412–421 as *Fo so hsing tsan ching* (*Buddhacarita-kāvya-sūtra*) and by Jñānagupta in 587 as *Fo pen-hsing chi ching*. The Buddha's biography is also related in the *T'ai-tzu jui-ying pen-ch'i ching* (Sūtra on the Auspicious Responses of the Prince; *T* 185; translated by Chih-ch'ien) and in *P'u-yao ching* (*Lalitavistara*; *T* 186, translated by Fa-hu).

CONCLUSION

The advent of Buddhism in China from around the middle of the first century C.E. wrought enormous social and cultural change. The significance of Buddhism was not restricted to religion but cut across all levels and facets of secular life as well. Bringing with it Indian learning in numerous fields, Buddhism had a profound effect on philosophy, linguistics, medicine, astronomy, mathematics, architecture, and virtually every other area of human endeavor.

Since literature broadly reflects the whole of human experience, the Buddhist impact on all these activities showed up in canonical and noncanonical writings almost from the moment the new religion took root in China. In literature, aside from the overt reflections of the Indian faith, such as descriptions of monks, temples, religious rituals, statues, and paintings, there were countless subtler—yet equally or perhaps even more transformative—aspects brought by Buddhism, among them the prosimetric form, sophisticated prosodic rules, esthetic standards, specific genres, dramatic conventions, and, above all, the acceptance and affirmation of fictive, imaginary realms.

Helwig Schmidt-Glintzer and Victor H. Mair

Chapter 10

TAOIST HERITAGE

EARLY TEXTS AND TERMINOLOGY

The term "Taoist" first of all brings to mind Lao Tzu (c. 250 B.C.E.?) and Chuang Chou or Chuang Tzu (355?–275 B.C.E.) of Meng (Honan). Little is known about Chuang Tzu beyond his origins, and no one has ever been able to determine with any certainty just who Lao Tzu was. This has not diminished and may have even enhanced the popularity of the texts transmitted in their names. The eponymous *Lao Tzu,* also known as the *Tao te ching* (Classic of the Way and Integrity), has been translated into more languages more times than any other book in Chinese. The appeal of this concise treatise derives in part from the way its intrinsic ambiguity openly invites multiple interpretations. No less complex and considerably more voluminous, the *Chuang Tzu,* also known as the *Nan-hua ching* (Classic of Southern Florescence), has stymied all but the most intrepid translators. It is nonetheless widely familiar because of the sheer good humor and thus popularity of many of its stories, as well as its recognized influence on Chinese Buddhism, poetry, and painting.

Neither the *Lao Tzu* nor the *Chuang Tzu* in any of their extant forms can be considered the work of a single author. In each case, what survives is a collaborative work of later generations. All editions of the *Chuang Tzu* are based on the thirty-three-unit recension by the commentator Kuo Hsiang (d. 312). The seven "Nei-p'ien" (Inner Chapters) display a remarkable consistency in language and substance and are thus regarded as the earliest core of the text. The fifteen "Wai-p'ien" (Outer Chapters) and eleven "Tsa-p'ien" (Miscellaneous Chapters) are, by contrast, more heterogeneous and are thought to voice competing schools of thought dating at least a century later. The textual history of the *Lao Tzu* is more complicated, in part because of its uncertain provenance. The two best-known editions come with a commentary, one by a Ho-shang Kung and another by an apparent contemporary, Wang Pi (226–249). The 1973 recovery of two nearly complete copies of the text inscribed on silk from a tomb dating to 168 B.C.E. at Ma-wang-tui (Hunan) has led to a resurgence of new translations. These two copies of the text differ from all other known versions in their reversal of the two major components, with the *Te ching* unit preceding the *Tao ching* unit in both cases. New research on the *Lao Tzu* now also takes into account the recent recovery at Kuo-tien (Hupei) of numerous bamboo strips inscribed with corresponding passages.

Like the terms "Buddhism" and "Buddhist," the two words "Taoism" and "Taoist" are anglicized forms. The contrast between the roots "Buddha" and "Tao" marks a significant difference between the two major religious traditions of China. The understanding that the *tao* (the Way or Track) is the fount of all creation clearly took precedence over any perception of a historic figure in the formulation of what is known as Taoism. Had dominance been given to a personnage called Lao Tzu, the higher indigenous religion of China might easily have been dubbed Laoism instead of Taoism. The fact that Lao Tzu came to be regarded ex post facto as the founding father of Taoism does not mean that the teachings transmitted in his name stood alone. Many writings of comparable antiquity offer interpretations of the Tao. But there is no evidence that anyone behind such writings considered himself a "Taoist" at the time, just as anyone known as Lao Tzu was no Taoist in his time.

The term "Taoism" defies ready definition. A common source of confusion rests in the tendency to distinguish "philosophical" from "religious" Taoism. This false dichotomy derives from a narrow view of the ultimately interchangeable terms "Tao-chia" and "Tao-chiao." The designation "Tao-chia," or "Taoist school," is often used to specify a school of thought based on writings dating to the Spring and Autumn and Warring States periods. The term "Tao-chiao" popularly denotes the Taoist religious tradition, in counterpart thus to Fo-chiao, or Buddhism. Both "Tao-chia" and "Tao-chiao" have been applied over time to a broad, sometimes conflicting corpus of teachings. Tao-chia, moreover, is a bibliographic category of long standing that eventually grew to accommodate not only the formative body of texts considered Taoist but also the wide variety of texts arising from diverse schools of Taoism.

The earliest known use of the term "Tao-chia" comes in an idiosyncratic discourse on Six Schools by Ssu-ma T'an (d. 110 B.C.E.). It is recorded in the innovative history of China that he left behind at his death for his son Ssu-ma Ch'ien (c. 145–c. 86 B.C.E.) to complete, known as the *Shih-chi* (Records of the Historian). To Ssu-ma T'an's way of thinking, the Taoist school drew on the assets of the Yin-yang, Ju(ist), Mo(ist), Logician, and Legalist schools. He concluded that Tao-chia was highly adaptable to changing times, readily applicable and easily grasped, and brought results with minimal exertion.

The collaborative effort of another father-son team led to the compilation of the first list of texts to be categorized as Tao-chia. This category is introduced in *Ch'i lüeh* (Seven Summaries), a descriptive catalog of the Han imperial library initiated by Liu Hsiang (79–8 B.C.E.) and finished in 6 B.C.E. by his son Liu Hsin (46 B.C.E.–23 C.E.). Although the catalog itself is lost, the list of titles is incorporated in *Han shu* (History of the Han Dynasty), compiled by Pan Ku (32–92 C.E.). Among notable bodies of texts cited are four transmissions or interpretations of the *Lao Tzu*, the *Chuang Tzu* in fifty-two units, and four titles in the name of Huang-ti (Yellow Emperor). The last is significant to a fairly new field of research seeking to identify a Huang-Lao legacy based on teachings ascribed to Huang-ti and Lao Tzu.

By the time of the Northern Sung (960–1127), catalogers saw the need to reclassify titles that the *Han shu* bibliography and its successors listed under subheadings within the class of prescriptive arts or medicine. The bibliographic staff working on *Kuo shih* (State History), completed in 1030, took a special interest in the subheading Shen-hsien (Divine Transcendence). According to a surviving postface, these catalogers were also compelled to take into account a growing body of scriptural writings that had begun to appear with the ascendance of Tao-chia after the Eastern Han. They concluded it was essential to establish Shen-hsien as a distinct bibliographic class in order to accommodate a range of texts on self-cultivation, dietary practice, exercise, alchemy, talismanic registers, and petitionary fêtes.

The compilers of the *Hsin T'ang shu* (New T'ang History), completed in 1060, further refined this organizational system by setting up Shen-hsien as a subheading under the category Tao-chia. And under this subheading they added works of hagiography that previously had been listed in the biography class of imperial catalogs. This more comprehensive approach set the standard for generations to come, including the mammoth imperial library catalog of the reign of the Emperor Ch'ien-lung (1736–1795), the *Ssu-k'u ch'üan-shu tsung-mu t'i-yao* (Annotated General Catalog of the Complete Library of the Four Treasuries).

FUNDAMENTAL SCHOOLS AND COLLECTIONS OF TEXTS

The Taoist legacy, like that of Buddhism in China, encompasses a wide range of teachings representing different lineages or schools. The two most enduring schools are Ch'üan-chen (Complete Perfection) and T'ien-shih (Celestial Master), also known as the covenant of Cheng-yi (Authentic Unity). Ch'üan-chen is now the dominant school, with headquarters at the Pai-yün Kuan (White

Cloud Abbey) in Peking, home of the nationally registered Chung-kuo Tao-chiao hsieh-hui (Chinese Association of Taoism). The seat of the Celestial Master patriarchy is located at Mount Lung-hu (Dragon-Tiger) in northern Kiangsi province.

Early teachings of what came to be designated as Ch'üan-chen originated in the Shantung peninsular region following the collapse of the Northern Sung empire in 1127. It evolved as a synthesis of the so-called *san-chiao* (Three Teachings) of Taoism, Buddhism, and Juism (i.e., doctrine of the literati, or Confucianism). An immigrant to the peninsula from the central plains named Wang Che (1112–1170) is considered the founder of Ch'üan-chen. His most prominent disciple, Ch'iu Ch'u-chi (1148–1227), gained the support of Chinggis Khan (i.e., Genghis Khan; 1162–1227) and ended up in charge of what is now the Pai-yün Kuan in Peking.

The origins of the Celestial Master lineage are traced back a millennium earlier than Ch'üan-chen, in the remote mountainous area of western China. Historical and hagiographic accounts differ in detail but generally report that Lao Tzu as the deity T'ai-shang Lao-chün (Lord Lao the Most High) appeared in 142 C.E. before an elderly recluse named Chang Tao-ling (d. 156 C.E.) and conveyed to him the sacred writ of Cheng-yi and the title of T'ien-shih (Heavenly Teacher or Celestial Master). The network of twenty-four parishes set up thereafter in central Szechwan province marks the beginning of a communal form of Taoism based on confession, penance, and talismanic healing practice, as well as public works.

The influence of both the Cheng-yi and the Ch'üan-chen lineages spread far beyond their home communities, leading eventually to the establishment of monastic compounds throughout China, frequently with the support of the royal house. Imperial patronage also proved to be an important force behind the canonization of Taoist writings. The history of the compilation of the Taoist canon itself is closely tied to the rise of variant schools of teachings.

Early inventories of texts did much to pave the way toward the formulation of a Taoist canon. One important list appears in the well-known *Pao-p'u Tzu* (The Master Who Embraces Simplicity), compiled by Ko Hung (283–343), a member of the aristocracy in the area of present-day Nanking. In putting together a compendium of local religious practices, Ko sought to provide an exhaustive record of his teacher Cheng Yin's private library, including the titles of texts he had never seen. Cheng Yin had inherited the textual legacy of Ko Hung's great-uncle, Ko Hsüan (164–224). By the end of the fourth century, Ko Hung's grand-nephew Ko Ch'ao-fu codified the scriptural corpus of the Ling-pao (Numinous Treasure) school. He traced its origins to his ancestor Ko Hsüan, presumably so as to claim a greater antiquity for his family's heritage than that of the roughly contemporary lineage called Shang-ch'ing (Supreme Clarity). Both the Shang-ch'ing and Ling-pao schools, endorsed by well-established families in the southeastern Chiang-nan region of the fourth century, drew on an extensive body of prevailing teachings, including those of Mahāyāna Buddhism.

The Shang-ch'ing school evolved from the divine communications that a visionary named Yang Hsi (330–386) received at Mao shan (Mount Mao, in Kiangsu) and then conveyed to his patrons Hsü Mi (303–373) and son Hsü Hui (334–c. 370). The teachings of these revelations expanded on the macrobiotic texts associated with the so-called *fang-shih* (technocrats), whose pursuit of a transcendent state of immortality was especially well received in court circles. Shang-ch'ing adepts were primarily concerned with visualizing their bodies as hosts to ranks of deities. The sense of corporeal refinement they tried to cultivate also depended on the notion that the radiant vitality of the sun, moon, and stars could be ingested. Ultimately, they viewed themselves as destined for the celestial realm of Shang-ch'ing, which was considered more exalted than the T'ai-ch'ing (Grand Clarity) realm at the heart of an earlier school of texts. An eschatological component of the Shang-ch'ing revelations fed expectations of messianic movements for centuries thereafter.

The major teachings of the Shang-ch'ing school survive largely because of the assiduous editorial work of the devotee T'ao Hung-ching (456–536) of Tan-yang (Kiangsu). His encyclopedic *Chen kao* (Declarations of the Perfected; HY* 1010) supplies a detailed record of how Yang Hsi came to receive divine instruction. T'ao also took the responsibility of cataloging and transmitting the fundamental corpus of Shang-ch'ing texts. An encyclopedic work, moreover, the *Wu-shang pi-yao* (The Essentials of Unsurpassed Arcana; HY 1130), compiled c. 580, preserves numerous excerpts from not only early Shang-ch'ing writings but also contemporary Cheng-yi and Ling-pao texts as well. The *Yün-chi ch'i-ch'ien* (Seven Lots from the Bookbag of the Clouds; HY 1026), compiled c. 1028 by Chang Chün-fang (961?–1042?), is an equally important resource for texts at the heart of the various early schools of Taoism.

The Shang-ch'ing legacy dominated early canonizations of Taoist writings. But the origins of the Taoist canon date back somewhat anachronistically to the editorial work of a preeminent Ling-pao devotee named Lu Hsiu-ching (406–477). A native of Wu-hsing (Chekiang), Lu undertook the compilation of a catalog of altogether twenty-seven scriptures that he determined to be the original Ling-pao corpus. Putatively traced to Ko Hsüan, the Ling-pao scriptural legacy offered a new promise of salvation for all humankind. Clearly derived in part from contemporary Buddhist teachings, the Ling-pao codification informs a wide range of Taoist liturgy even today, from mourning ritual to annual commemorative celebrations.

---

*For the abbreviation "HY," see the last entry of the section on Taoism in the "Suggestions for Further Reading" at the back of this volume.

Imperial interest in the compilation of a comprehensive catalog of Taoist writings began with the Liu Sung ruler Ming-ti (r. 465–472). He sought the expertise of none other than Lu Hsiu-ching. In 471 Lu presented the emperor with a copy of the *San-tung ching-shu mu-lu* (A Catalog of the Scriptural Writings of the Three Caverns), listing a variety of scriptural, pharmaceutical, and talismanic texts adding up to more than 1,200 *chüan*. Two centuries later the T'ang emperor Kao-tsung (r. 649–683), as the perceived heir of Lao Tzu, ordered a systematic collection of all writings reflecting his ancestry. The T'ang emperor Hsüan-tsung (r. 712–756) went even further. He authorized not only a comprehensive search for all pertinent texts but also the copying and distribution of what came to be known as the Taoist canon of the K'ai-yüan era (713–741).

Emperors of the Sung followed suit. The Sung emperor Chen-tsung (r. 998–1022) put Wang Ch'in-jo (962–1025) in charge of compiling a catalog and ordered Chang Chün-fang to oversee the copying of *Ta Sung t'ien-kung pao-tsang* (Precious Canon of the Celestial Palace of the Great Sung) for dispersal to major temples. A century later the Sung emperor Hui-tsung (r. 1101–1125) authorized the compilation of a new canon. The *Cheng-ho wan-shou Tao-tsang* (Taoist Canon of Cheng-ho Era Longevity) that resulted was the first canon to be issued in a woodcut printing. It served as the foundation for a new canon produced by order of the Jurchen ruler, the Chin emperor Chang-tsung (r. 1189–1208). By 1244 the largest canon yet was completed under the direction of a renowned disciple of Ch'iu Ch'u-chi named Sung Te-fang (1183–1247). This monumental canon of the Yüan regime was all but lost after Khubilai Khan's (Qubilai; 1215–1294; r. 1260–1294) decree in 1281 to have it destroyed, sparing only the *Tao te ching*. Remnants of the Sung, Jurchen, and Yüan canons ultimately found their way into the *Ta Ming Tao-tsang ching* (Scriptures of the Taoist Canon of the Great Ming), the editorship of which the Ming emperor Ch'eng-tsu (r. 1403–1424) assigned to Chang Yü-ch'u (1361–1410), Celestial Master patriarch of the forty-third generation. Published in 1445 during the Cheng-t'ung reign-period (1436–1449) of the Ming emperor Ying-tsung, this canon is popularly known as *Cheng-t'ung Tao-tsang*. In 1607 the fiftieth Celestial Master, Chang Kuo-hsiang (d. 1611), produced an addendum by imperial decree, known as the *Hsü Tao-tsang ching* (Scriptures in Supplement to the Taoist Canon). Encompassing approximately 1,500 titles, the Ming canon of 1445, together with the supplement of 1607, remains the fundamental resource for the study of Taoism before the Ch'ing dynasty.

A number of subsidiary collections of Taoist texts has been published since the Ming. The best known is the *Tao-tsang chi-yao* (Collected Essentials of the Taoist Canon), initially compiled by P'eng Ting-ch'iu (1656–1719). An expanded edition prepared by Ho Lung-hsiang, first published in 1906 at the Erh-hsien An (Retreat of Two Transcendents) in Chengtu (Szechwan), is available in both thread-bound and reduced-print editions. Another collection, the *Tao-chiao wen-hsien* (Literary Resources on Taoism), includes facsimile reproductions of rare topographic and hagiographic texts. A more diverse selection of important works may be found in a large collectaneum entitled *Tsang-wai Tao-shu* (Extracanonical Taoist Texts). Manuscript collections include discoveries at Ma-wang-tui and Tun-huang and the Taoist ritual texts gathered in Taiwan by Michael Saso and published as *Chuang Lin hsü Tao-tsang* (Supplementary Taoist Canon of Chuang and Lin). *Tao-chia chin-shih lüeh* (A Collection of Taoist Epigraphy), initiated by Ch'en Yüan and completed by Ch'en Chih-ch'ao and Tseng Ch'ing-ying, moreover, is an invaluable resource for all facets of Taoist studies.

CELESTIAL MASTER LINEAGE

The mark of the Celestial Master lineage on the Ming Taoist canon goes far beyond an editorial role. Two works of special literary interest come from the forty-third patriarch, Chang Yü-ch'u, himself. One anthology, compiled in 1395, is based on his retrieval of the writings of the thirtieth patriarch, Chang Chi-hsien (1092–1126), prominent at the court of the Sung emperor Hui-tsung. *San-shih tai t'ien-shih Hsü-ching chen-chün yü-lu* (Discourse Record of the Thirtieth Generation Celestial Master Perfected Lord of Vacant Tranquility; HY 1239) is a rich collection of his letters and diverse forms of prosody. Much may be gained from this work on not only Taoist teachings and practice but also the close ties established between clergy and government officials during the Northern Sung. The second, larger anthology to which Chang Yü-ch'u's name is attached is a collection of his own compositions. *Hsien-ch'üan chi* (Anthology of Alpine Spring; HY 1300) takes its title from the name of the patriarch's private retreat at Mount Lung-hu. Outstanding features of this text include Chang's accounts of the history of Taoism, from Lord Lao's revelations to the emergence of Ling-pao and later ritual codifications. Numerous writings also contribute details on life at the Celestial Master headquarters of Mount Lung-hu as well as at neighboring temple sites honoring local deities.

A historical overview of the T'ien-shih lineage may be gained from two complementary texts conveyed with Chang Yü-ch'u's help. Copies of different editions of the *Lung-hu shan chih* (Topography of Mount Lung-hu) are included in the *Tao-chiao wen-hsien* and *Tsang-wai Tao-shu*. Its hagiographic counterpart, *Han t'ien-shih shih-chia* (Lineage of the Han Celestial Masters; HY 1451) falls in the 1607 supplement to the Ming canon. It is an amplification of the work of Chang Yü-ch'u's father, Chang Cheng-ch'ang (1335–1377), and encompasses biographies for altogether forty-nine generations. Expanded editions covering later heirs to the patriarchy are widely available.

Further evidence of the abiding presence of the Celestial Master lineage may be detected in a broad range of texts arising from sites beyond Mount Lung-hu. Of special note is a voluminous tribute to the sacred mountain of the

East, T'ai-shan, *Tai-shih* (A History of Tai; HY 1460) that Chang Kuo-hsiang endorsed for incorporation into the 1607 supplement. Additional treatises on local shrines closely regulated by the patriarchy and state alike include a Sung compilation dedicated to a site southwest of Mount Lung-hu, *Hua-kai shan Fou-ch'iu Wang Kuo san chen-chün shih-shih* (A Case History of the Three Perfected Lords Fou-ch'iu, Wang, and Kuo of Mount Hua-kai; HY 777). Across the Yangtze to the northwest stands Mount Wu-tang (Hupei), reputed home of the powerful guardian Hsüan-wu (Dark Warrior). Credited with aiding in the establishment of the Ming royal house, this deity was honored with new shrines under clergy appointed by the T'ien-shih patriarchy, as documented in the *Ta Ming Hsüan-t'ien shang-ti jui-ying t'u-lu* (An Illustrated Account of Auspicious Responses to the Great Ming from the Supreme Sovereign of the Dark Celestial Realm; HY 958).

Three Sung hagiographies celebrate the careers of figures with links to the Cheng-yi mandate in the coastal provinces. A set of talismans from Chang Tao-ling allegedly lies behind Yeh Fa-shan's (616–720/722?) ritual prowess in Kua-ts'ang (Chekiang), as recounted in *T'ang Yeh chen-jen chuan* (A Biography of Perfected Yeh of the T'ang; HY 778). The story of a T'ai-shan guardian named Wen Ch'iung (b. 702) is told in *Ti-ch'i shang-chiang Wen t'ai-pao chuan* (A Biography of Grand Guardian Wen, Supreme Commander of the Tutelary Deities; HY 779). He reportedly refused to be honored with a shrine in his hometown of P'ing-yang (present-day Wenchow, Chekiang) after answering prayers for rain and subsequently gained commendation from the thirtieth Celestial, Master Chang Chi-hsien, in the form of new talismans. Chang Chi-hsien is also said to have had close ties with the acclaimed prognosticator from T'ai-chou (Kiangsu) named Hsü Shou-hsin (1033–1108), whose prophecies are chronicled in *Hsü-ching ch'ung-ho hsien-sheng Hsü shen-weng yü-lu* (Discourse Record of Divine Elder Hsü, Master of Piercing Harmony and Vacant Tranquility; HY 1241).

SHANG-CH'ING AND LING-PAO LEGACIES

The organization of the Taoist canon reflects the prominence of the fourth-century revelations of Shang-ch'ing and Ling-pao. The canon is divided into seven components, the San-tung (Three Caverns) and Ssu-fu (Four Supplements). This arrangement is thought to reflect levels of ordination, from the highest ranks of Shang-ch'ing and Ling-pao down to Cheng-yi. The contents of the Ming canon, however, are not wholly in accord with this long-established classification system. The initial text in the first so-called Tung-chen (Caverned Perfection) unit, traditionally reserved for Shang-ch'ing writings, is in fact a sixty-one-*chüan* copy of *Ling-pao wu-liang tu-jen shang-p'in miao-ching* (Wondrous Scripture of Supreme Rank on the Infinite Salvation of Ling-pao; i.e., Scripture on Salvation; HY 1), which is central to the Ling-pao legacy. The primacy of this text in the canon may be due to the preeminence during the Northern Sung of the Shen-hsiao (Divine Empyrean) school, which conveyed a copy of the scripture with matching subheadings. Or it may actually be linked to a derivative Ch'ing-wei (Clarified Tenuity) school prominent during the Ming. In any case, the significance of the *Scripture on Salvation* cannot be overestimated. The faithful have recited it for centuries, and it is at the heart of variant liturgies that continue to be performed to this day. Its vision of the deity Yüan-shih t'ien-tsun (Celestial Worthy of Primordial Commencement), lighting the way for deliverance of all, has also evoked numerous commentaries and interpretative studies. Another early Ling-pao codification of equal weight, *Pu-hsü ching* (Scripture on Pacing the Void; HY 1427), has likewise inspired centuries of poetic simulations by writers envisioning journeys into the celestial realm.

Scriptures central to the Shang-ch'ing school include the *Huang-t'ing ching* (Yellow Court Scripture), a prosodic guide in variant forms that locates the spirits inhabiting one's body. By reciting this scripture repeatedly while visualizing the corporeal spirit realm, adepts sought to maintain a youthful state of health and to ward off malign forces. Even more exalted claims accompany the predominant Shang-ch'ing codification, *Ta-tung chen-ching* (True Scripture of the Great Cavern; HY 6). Like the *Yellow Court Scripture*, this sacred text is said to have been conveyed by the goddess Wei Hua-ts'un, one of Yang Hsi's transcendent mentors. Adepts who took up recitation of the *Great Cavern Scripture* strove to envision a harmonious internalization of the spirit realm on high so as ultimately to achieve a sense of unity with the cosmos.

Shang-ch'ing followers also took solace in the anticipated arrival of a messiah named Li Hung, as promised in the *Shang-ch'ing hou-sheng tao-chün lieh-chi* (Annals of the Lord of the Tao, the Sage-to-Come of Shang-ch'ing; HY 442). This eschatological vision of an incarnation of Lao Tzu come to bring order from chaos led to many highly syncretic formulations like *Shen-chou ching* (Scripture of Spirit Spells; HY 335), compiled in the fifth to sixth centuries. The Shang-ch'ing legacy also figures prominently in several other hagiographic works, from the *Han Wu-ti nei-chuan* (Esoteric Biography of Emperor Wu of Han; HY 292) of the late Six Dynasties (220–589) to the *Hsüan-p'in lu* (Record of Arcane Ranks; HY 780), compiled in 1335 by a denizen of Mount Mao named Chang Yü (1283–1356+). Overall, however, the most comprehensive resource on the Shang-ch'ing legacy in the canon is *Mao shan chih* (Treatise on Mount Mao; HY 304), completed in 1328 by Liu Ta-pin (fl. 1313–1333), Shang-ch'ing Lineal Master (*tsung-shih*) of the forty-fifth generation. Produced during a time of marked royal patronage, this account of Mount Mao includes substantial hagiographic, narrative, and prosodic writings in addition to abundant data on the topography of the site, its temple compounds, and various folk shrines.

The Ling-pao counterpart to Mount Mao is a site just west of Mount Lung-hu called Mount Ko-tsao (Kiangsi). It was from this hub of the Ling-pao school that an early hagiography reportedly made its way east and ended up serving as the foundation for *T'ai-chi Ko hsien-kung chuan* (A Biography of Transcendent Lord Ko of the Grand Ultimate; HY 450). Chu Ch'o (fl. 1377) of Chiang-ning (present-day Nanking, Kiangsu) compiled this tribute to the putative founder Ko Hsüan at the request of clergymen from a hometown temple established to commemorate Ko's ascent. Aside from this hagiography, the later textual legacy of the Ling-pao school is primarily represented in the Ming canon by large compendia of ritual practice. Important liturgical anthologies of the Sung and Yüan with Ming addenda include *Wu-shang huang-lu ta-chai li-ch'eng yi* (Straightforward Protocols on the Great Fête of the Incomparable Yellow Register; HY 508), edited by Chiang Shu-yü (1162–1223) of Yung-chia (present-day Wenchow, Chekiang), and *Ling-pao ling-chiao chi-tu chin-shu* (Golden Script on Salvation Based on the Conveyed Teachings of Ling-pao; HY 466), compiled by Lin Wei-fu (1239–1302) from the same locale. These and analogous compendia offer varying syntheses of competing schools of ritual practice. All claim as a common thread the Ling-pao codification first achieved by Lu Hsiu-ching and later refined by the renowned cleric Tu Kuang-t'ing (850–933), who was also the author of the remarkable T'ang *ch'uan-ch'i* story "Ch'iu-jan k'o chuan" (An Account of the Curly-Bearded Stranger; see chapter 33).

LAO TZU LORE

All schools of Taoism in one way or another trace their lineage back to Lao Tzu. Thus recitation of the *Tao te ching* came to serve as an anchor for a wide variety of contemplative and liturgical practice. The full text has been inscribed on stelae all across China and has evoked a diverse range of commentary, especially during periods of ardent imperial patronage. The fiftieth Celestial Master, Chang Yü-ch'u, went so far as to declare that Cheng-yi, Ling-pao, and Shang-ch'ing were just different names for teachings transmitted by Lord Lao the Most High. This claim appears in the invaluable guide *Tao-men shih-kuei* (Ten Guidelines on the Taoist Lineage; HY 1222) that he submitted to the Ming emperor Ch'eng-tsu in 1406. As the unifying force behind variant scriptural codifications, Lao Tzu is thought to have revealed himself in many forms and to have spoken in many voices. Those who perceived themselves to be graced with his presence came up with differing views on what they saw and heard. Some sense of these varying perceptions may be detected in the statuary and narrative temple paintings that have survived centuries of religious persecution.

Although some vision of Lao Tzu may be said to reside in every Taoist shrine, there are three temple compounds of particular note devoted to his memory. Each is supported by a significant textual legacy. Best known perhaps is the T'ai-ch'ing Kung (Palace of Grand Clarity) located in Lu-yi (Honan) at Lao Tzu's putative birthplace. In the last years of his reign, the Eastern Han emperor Huan (r. 147–167) is known to have sanctioned offerings to Lao Tzu at this very site. The local magistrate, Pien Shao (fl. 155–166), commemorated the imperial gifts by composing *Lao Tzu ming* (Inscription on Lao Tzu). His tribute projects an image of Lao Tzu as the incarnation of a cosmic force come to serve as mentor of the royal house and as savior of all humankind. A Taoist master named Chia Shan-hsiang (fl. 1086), affiliated with the T'ai-ch'ing Kung, produced an account that documents not only Lao Tzu's many manifestations but also the history of the shrine itself. The title of his *Yu-lung chuan* (Like unto a Dragon; HY 773) is derived from the way Confucius allegedly characterized Lao Tzu when he told his disciples about their meeting. Chia's compilation includes descriptions of Lao Tzu born as Li Erh that recall the life of the Buddha. He also chronicles Lao Tzu's service to successive generations of Chinese sovereigns and enumerates all the teachings thereby revealed. A century later, a Taoist master at Hsi shan (West Mountain), across the Kan River from Mount Lung-hu, sought to improve upon Chia's work. Originally from Yung-chia (present-day Wenchow), Hsieh Shou-hao (1134–1212) submitted his *Hun-yüan sheng-chi* (A Chronicle of the Sage from the Primordiality of Chaos; HY 769) to the Sung emperor Kuang-tsung (r. 1190–1194) in 1191. His lengthy account, titled in accordance with the imperial designation granted Lao Tzu in 1014, is especially noteworthy for numerous passages cited from texts that are no longer extant.

Two temple compounds in the far west honor variant legends concerning Gatekeeper Yin Hsi's discipleship under Lao Tzu. The Ch'ing-yang Kung (Blue Goat Palace) in Chengtu marks the site where Lao Tzu reportedly told Yin Hsi they would meet again. An early chronicle compiled by the eminent Tu Kuang-t'ing, *Li-tai ch'ung-tao chi* (A Record of Revering the Tao Throughout the Ages; HY 593), takes up a history of the shrine following a concise survey of imperial patronage of Taoism with emphasis on the T'ang royal house. Tu reports in detail on Lord Lao's guardianship during the uprising of 880–884, which forced the T'ang emperor Hsi-tsung (r. 873–888) to take refuge in Chengtu. His account culminates with the story of how a brick fell from the sky during a fête at the Hsüan-chung Kuan (Abbey of Sublime Focus) in Blue Goat Market. An inscription on the brick prophesied that Lord Lao would bring peace to the turbulent age. Tu presented his chronicle to the emperor in 885, following victory over the rebel Huang Ch'ao (d. 884) and imperial authorization to enlarge the abbey and rename it Blue Goat Palace.

The Lou Kuan (Tiered Abbey) located at Yin Hsi's putative residence at Mount Chung-nan outside present-day Sian (Shensi) is the northern counterpart to the Blue Goat Palace. A Taoist master from Mount Mao named Chu Hsiang-hsien (fl. 1279–1315) compiled two works concerning this site. After a pilgrimage to the shrine in 1279, Chu examined early hagiographies he found in the temple library. *Chung-nan shan Shuo-ching T'ai li-tai chen-hsien pei-chi* (An Epigraphic Record of Successive Generations of Perfected Transcendents at the Pavilion for Explaining Scripture on Mount Chung-nan; HY 955) is his enlargement of the latest account that he discovered, ascribed to a putative heir named Yin Wen-ts'ao (d. 688). Chu's rendition in prose and verse traces the history of the shrine to the dominion of the Ch'üan-chen abbot Li Chih-jou (1189–1266). The second work regarding the site produced by Chu Hsiang-hsien is the *Ku Lou Kuan tzu-yün yen-ch'ing chi* (Anthology from the Abundant Felicity of Purple Clouds at the Ancient Tiered Abbey; HY 956). Like the complementary hagiographic text, the title of this compilation alludes to a specific structure in the temple compound. It includes a wealth of poetry by well-known literati and Ch'üan-chen clergy in addition to the texts of stele inscriptions documenting state support of the shrine from the seventh to the fourteenth centuries.

CH'ÜAN-CHEN SCHOOL

The abundance of texts in the Ming canon regarding the Ch'üan-chen lineage attests to its strength not only as a school of Taoism but also as a significant literary force in China. A rich body of Ch'üan-chen hagiographic lore, moreover, conveys a sense of the profound interest many followers had in documenting their faith. *Chin-lien cheng-tsung hsien-yüan hsiang-chuan* (An Illustrated Biographical Account of the Transcendent Origins of the True Lineage of the Golden Lotus; HY 174) is a prime example of such devotion. In a preface dated 1326, Taoist Master Liu Chih-hsüan writes that he sought to compile a definitive resource on Ch'üan-chen and with the help of his colleague Hsieh Kuei collected data from a wide range of written texts, including stele inscriptions. Their efforts are highly praised in a preface composed in 1327 by the thirty-ninth Celestial Master, Chang Ssu-ch'eng (d. 1344). The text includes thirteen biographies, beginning with the so-called Five Patriarchs (*wu-tsu*): Hun-yüan Lao Tzu, Tung-hua ti-chün (Sovereign Lord of Eastern Florescence), Chung-li Ch'üan (eighth century?), Lü Yen (b. 798?), and Liu Ts'ao (fl. 1031). The biography of the founding father, Wang Che, that follows reports on his visionary encounters in the Kan-ho (Shensi) region and subsequent migration in 1167 to Ning-hai (Shantung). Ma Yü (1123–1183) and his wife, Sun Pu-erh (1119–1183), took him in and became his first disciples. The remaining biographies concern the so-called Seven Perfected (*ch'i-chen*), Wang's two hosts and five additional disciples living on the Shantung peninsula: T'an Ch'u-tuan (1123–1185), Liu Ch'u-hsüan (1147–1203), Ch'iu Ch'u-chi, Wang Ch'u-yi (1142–1217), and Hao Ta-t'ung (1140–1212).

An analogous, substantially larger hagiography, the *Chin-lien cheng-tsung chi* (An Account of the True Lineage of the Golden Lotus; HY 173), dates to 1241. The Taoist Master Ch'in Chih-an (1188–1244) of P'ing-yang (Shansi) compiled this text while helping his mentor, Sung Te-fang, prepare the canon of 1244. Like the later hagiography by Liu Chih-hsüan, Ch'in's work includes remarkable testimony on the various oral and written expressions by which

Wang was able to evoke a state of awareness in his disciples. Both texts similarly make note of all writings emerging from the Ch'üan-chen leadership, in some cases listing titles that cannot be traced. The two hagiographies also cite several exemplary prosodic compositions, complete with background explanations of how they came to be inscribed or recited.

Indispensable supporting reference works include three anthologies compiled by the most prominent archivist of the early Ch'üan-chen school, the Taoist Master Li Tao-ch'ien (1219–1296) of Yi-shan (Honan). His concise *Ch'i-chen nien-p'u* (A Chronicle of the Seven Perfected; HY 175) spans a century and a quarter, from the birth of Wang Che in 1112 to the demise of Ch'iu Ch'u-chi in 1227. A hagiographic anthology compiled by Li, *Chung-nan shan tsu-t'ing hsien-chen nei-chuan* (An Inside Account of the Transcendent Perfected of the Ancestral Hall of Mount Chung-nan; HY 954), contains thirty-seven biographies of Ch'üan-chen disciples associated with the site, dedicated to Wang's memory. Li also brought together a voluminous body of texts copied from stele inscriptions and other sources for *Kan-shui hsien-yüan lu* (A Record of the Transcendent Wellsprings at Kan-shui; HY 971). The title alludes to the Kan-ho Garrison (Shensi), where a transcendent encounter led Wang to devote himself to a cultivation of the Tao. The texts shed considerable light on the Ch'üan-chen way of life in word and deed, as pursued within the temple of the body and the monastic compound alike.

Three highly entertaining works in the Ming canon take up the lives of three figures associated with the early Ch'üan-chen school. *Ch'un-yang ti-chün shen-hua miao-t'ung chi* (Annals of the Wondrous Communications and Divine Transformations of the Sovereign Lord Ch'un-yang; HY 305), by Taoist Master Miao Shan-shih (fl. 1288–1324) of Chin-ling (present-day Nanking, Kiangsu), traces the life of Lü Yen from his birth in 798 to his appearance before Wang Che in 1149. Wang Ch'u-yi's activities as healer and rainmaker in the Shantung peninsular region are narrated in an anonymously compiled *T'i-hsüan chen-jen hsien-yi lu* (A Record of the Striking Marvels of the Perfected Who Embodies Sublimity; HY 594). Best known of all is *Ch'ang-ch'un chen-jen hsi-yu chi* (The Journey to the West of the Perfected Ch'ang-ch'un; HY 1418), a record of Ch'iu Ch'u-chi's life with emphasis on his trek into Central Asia at the summons of Chinggis Khan. Li Chih-ch'ang (1193–1256) of K'ai-chou (Hopei), a member of Ch'iu's entourage, produced this firsthand account of events culminating with the momentous meeting of clergyman and Mongolian warlord.

The Taoist canon preserves many of the collected writings from the formative era of the Ch'üan-chen school. Although provenance often remains vague, all such anthologies are clearly the work of later generations. A vast amount of poetry is ascribed to Lü Yen alone. One of the members of the editorial team compiling the canon of 1244, Ho Chih-yüan (1189–1279), brought together a collection of Lü's writings in 1251. His *Ch'un-yang chen-jen hun-ch'eng chi* (Anthology of the Perfected Ch'un-yang on Arising from Turbulence; HY 1048) is superseded by an anonymously compiled late-sixteenth-century anthology entitled *Lü Tsu chih* (A Treatise on Patriarch Lü; HY 1473). The texts ascribed to Lü Yen in both collections reveal more about the convictions of his devotees than about any historically authentic figure of that name.

The textual history of anthologies arising from Wang Che and his disciples is no less problematic. Altogether six titles in the Taoist canon are purportedly derived from Wang's teachings. Three of the compilations bear prefaces that Fan Yi (fl. 1183–1188), superintendent of schools in Ning-hai, contributed at the request of various disciples. The largest collection of writings attributed to Wang, *Ch'ung-yang ch'üan-chen chi* (Ch'ung-yang's Anthology of Complete Perfection; HY 1145), includes numerous *shih* (poems), *tz'u* (lyrics), and *ko* (songs). Addressed to a wide range of acquaintances, this body of verse yields an eloquent articulation of early Ch'üan-chen guidelines. "Wild and Crazy" (Hai-feng) Wang, as he was known, counseled abstinence from what he deemed the four obstructions: drink (*chiu*), lust (*se*), riches (*ts'ai*), and hostility (*ch'i*). Two additional anthologies endorsed by Fan Yi pay tribute to Ma Yü's discipleship. *Ch'ung-yang fen-li shih-hua chi* (Anthology of Ch'ung-yang on the Ten Transformations of Sectioning a Pear; HY 1147) takes its title from the manner in which Wang tutored his hosts, Ma and wife, Sun Pu-erh, bite by bite. A companion text, *Ch'ung-yang chiao-hua chi* (Anthology on the Proselytism of Ch'ung-yang; HY 1146), is devoted largely to an extensive exchange of verse between Wang and Ma. The two texts provide rare insight into the literary and intellectual demands of this quintessential Ch'üan-chen master-disciple relationship. Finally, three other works in Wang's name are completely devoid of supporting prefaces but uniformly display an eclectic assimilation of the rudiments of the "Three Teachings": *Ch'ung-yang chen-jen chin-kuan yü-so chüeh* (Lessons of the Perfected Ch'ung-yang on the Jade Lock of the Golden Gateway; HY 1148), *Ch'ung-yang shou Tan-yang erh-shih-ssu chüeh* (Twenty-four Lessons Conveyed to Tan-yang by Ch'ung-yang; HY 1149), and *Ch'ung-yang li-chiao shih-wu lun* (Fifteen Discourses on the Teachings Set Forth by Ch'ung-yang; HY 1223).

The literary prowess of Ma Yü is further demonstrated by three anthologies of verse and two of prose. By far the richest is *Tung-hsüan chin-yü chi* (Anthology of the Gold-Jade of Caverned Sublimity; HY 1141), compiled between 1269 and 1310. The title alludes to the origin of his name as well as that of his retreat and ultimately harks back to the symbolic lexicon of the contemplative practice known as *nei-tan* (Inner, or Physiological, Alchemy). Dominated by the heptasyllabic quatrain and *tz'u* form of verse, this anthology documents Ma's passage from husband and father to ascetic devotee of the Tao and eventually clergyman in service to communities of the central plains.

Ma Yü's pedagogical approach is also lucidly expressed in a collection of one hundred lyrics to the *tz'u* tune "Man-t'ing fang" (Fragrance Filling the Courtyard), appearing under the title *Tan-yang shen-kuang ts'an* (Tan-yang's

Luster of Hallowed Radiance; HY 1142). As a disciple named Ning Shih-ch'ang explains in a preface dated 1175, his master achieved a state of purification through kindling and channeling the radiance of his heart into his cortex. Many of the lyrics themselves take up the *nei-tan* vision of creating an enchymoma or "inner macrobiogen." Another anthology of *tz'u* lyrics, *Chien-wu chi* (Anthology of Gradual Awakening; HY 1134), finds Ma often conveying his message by means of a heavily repetitive onomatopoeia. The lyrics in this undated compilation offer a vivid portrait of the austere training that led him to advocate control over the *yi-ma hsin-yüan* (horse of the will and monkey of the mind) in order to gain a sense of *ch'ing-ching* (pure quiescence). The rigors of taking up a discipline of contemplative practice are further explained in the transcript of a sermon Ma delivered to disciples at Mount Lung-men (Shansi) in 1179, the *Tan-yang chen-jen chih-yen* (Forthright Discourse of the Perfected Tan-yang; HY 1224). Wang Yi-chung of Tung-wu (Hopei), after less than a year's discipleship, compiled an invaluable guide to Master Ma's final reflections back home at Ning-hai. His *Tan-yang chen-jen yü-lu* (Discourse Record of the Perfected Tan-yang; HY 1050) is a remarkable testament to the enduring wit and wisdom of an early Ch'üan-chen devotee with consummate skill in communicating through the written and spoken word.

The literary output of Ma's wife, Sun Pu-erh, is less easily assessed. Lyrics to *tz'u* tunes may be found in early hagiographies as well as a mid-fourteenth-century anthology entitled *Ming-ho yü-yin* (Lingering Reverberations of the Calling Crane; HY 1092). Collections of writings in her name found outside the Taoist canon, however, do not date before the Ch'ing and are therefore open to questions of authenticity.

Regrettably few compilations of the remaining Seven Perfected are extant. *Shui-yün chi* (Anthology of Clouds and Water; HY 1152) contains but a small portion of T'an Ch'u-tuan's writings. An introduction of 1187 by his personal friend Fan Yi reviews T'an's discipleship under Wang Che and subsequent ministry in the Loyang area. As Fan indicates, the selections demonstrate T'an's ability to inspire in blunt and subtle language alike through a variety of prosodic forms. The only collection of Wang Ch'u-yi's writings to survive is *Yün-kuang chi* (Anthology of Cloud Radiance; HY 1144), titled for the name of the cavern where he took refuge on Wang Che's command. This remarkable collection of verse conveys a personal side of Wang Ch'u-yi that complements *A Record of the Striking Marvels.* Hao Ta-t'ung, who like Wang gave top priority to his mother's welfare, came to Wang Che as a successful diviner. The *T'ai-ku chi* (Anthology of Grand Antiquity; HY 1153) is but a vestige of Hao's legacy as an expert on the *Yi-ching* (Classic of Change), master of *nei-tan* practice, and outstanding orator capable of enthralling huge crowds. Among those captivated by his preaching was Wang Chih-chin (1178–1263) of Tung-ming (Honan). Wang's own skill in communication is reflected in *P'an shan yü-lu* (Discourse Record of Mount P'an; HY 1052), compiled from the notes of a devout disciple named Liu. Chi Yi (1193–1268) of Ch'ang-an (Shensi), Wang's most accomplished disciple, left behind, moreover, *Yün-shan chi* (Anthology of Cloudy Mountains; HY 1132). A superb range of texts, from *fu* (rhapsodies) to stele inscriptions, make this collection one of the most comprehensive tributes to the spread of the Ch'üan-chen mission.

One anthology and one treatise are all that remain of Liu Ch'u-hsüan's literary works. *Hsien-le chi* (Anthology of Transcendent Joy; HY 1133) suggests a preference for succinct if sometimes abstruse quatrains. His responses to fundamental questions on matters of life and death, as recorded in *Chih-chen yü-lu* (Discourse Record on Ultimate Perfection; HY 1051), were reportedly picked up and recited by anyone who heard him preach. Liu's best-known disciple, Yü Tao-hsien (1168–1232) of Wen-teng (Shantung), is said to have learned how to read and write through recitation of texts like the *Lao Tzu* and *Chuang Tzu*. *Li-feng lao-jen chi* (Anthology of Old Man Li-feng; HY 1254) shows that he, too, became adept at expressing his thoughts in writing.

The youngest and ultimately most influential of the Seven Perfected, Ch'iu Ch'u-chi, is credited with several works of prose and prosody. Nearly five hundred poems fill *P'an-hsi chi* (Anthology from P'an Tributary; HY 1151), named for the site where Ch'iu took refuge after Wang Che's interment at Mount Chung-nan in 1173. Regulated verses in both pentasyllabic and heptasyllabic meter, the predominant genre, celebrate Ch'iu's activities in the central plains as well as back home serving communities in the Ch'i-hsia (Shantung) region. Quatrains largely take up less personal, more didactic concerns. Another anthology, *Hsüan-feng ch'ing-hui lu* (Record of a Felicitous Convocation on Sublime Practice; HY 176), compiled by Yeh-lü Ch'u-ts'ai (1190–1244), supplements the *Journey to the West*. It purports to be a verbatim transcript of the counsel Ch'iu offered Chinggis Khan in 1222.

Posthumously honored as patriarch of the Lung-men (Dragon Gate) branch of the Ch'üan-chen school, Ch'iu was succeeded as pre-eminent abbot of the Mongol empire by his devoted follower Yin Chih-p'ing (1169–1251) of Lai-chou (Shantung). A disciple named Tuan Chih-chien brought Yin's prosody together in *Pao-kuang chi* (Anthology of Concealed Radiance; HY 1138). *Tz'u* lyrics outnumber all other forms of verse and often include Yin's explanation on how he came to compose a particular epistle or commemoration. Tuan also supervised the compilation of *Ch'ing-ho chen-jen pei-yu yü-lu* (Discourse Record on the Northern Journeys of the Perfected Ch'ing-ho; HY 1299), based on the notes of disciples who attended Yin's talks at various abbeys in 1233. It includes not only Yin's responses to specific questions but also spontaneous comments on a wide range of subjects, revealing his talent as both an exegete and a storyteller. The governor of Ch'in-chou (Shansi), Tu Te-k'ang, is identified as the person responsible for overseeing the publication of both tributes to Yin's memory, proof again of the elite patronage that Ch'üan-chen clergy attracted.

SOUTHERN LEGACIES

The *nei-tan* contemplative practice to which the Ch'üan-chen teachings subscribe is also closely associated with a textual legacy given the name Nan-tsung (Southern Lineage). Although the precise origins of *nei-tan* procedures remain unclear, proponents of the Southern Lineage commonly trace it to Ch'en T'uan (d. 989), Liu Ts'ao, or Chang Po-tuan (d. 1082?). By the thirteenth century, five generations of the Southern Lineage came to be identified, perhaps on the model of the Five Patriarchs of the Ch'üan-chen legacy: Liu Ts'ao, Chang Po-tuan, Shih T'ai (d. 1158), Hsüeh Tzu-hsien (d. 1191), and Ch'en Nan (d. 1213). Southern exegetes readily acknowledge Liu Ts'ao's role as the mentor of both Chang Po-tuan and Wang Che.

Chang Po-tuan of T'ien-t'ai (Chekiang) is the earliest Nan-tsung patriarch to whom any substantial body of writings is ascribed. Early studies of these texts mistook them as the teachings of *wai-tan* (Outer, or Laboratory, Alchemy) because of a confusing similarity in terminology. The primary work associated with Chang is *Wu-chen p'ien* (Folios on Apprehending Perfection), an anthology of enigmatic verse available in many editions. One version of the text is included with other Nan-tsung writings in an anthology of diverse *nei-tan* teachings entitled *Tao shu* (Pivot of the Tao; HY 1011). The renowned literatus Tseng Ts'ao (d. 1155) of Chin-chiang (Fukien) compiled this vast compendium, adding extensive commentary throughout.

An even more comprehensive body of Nan-tsung writings is recorded in an anonymous thirteenth-century anthology entitled *Hsiu-chen shih-shu* (Ten Texts on the Cultivation of Perfection; HY 263). This eclectic body of texts includes not only compositions attributed to the early Nan-tsung patriarchs but also the major compilations of Ch'en Nan's heirs, Pai Yü-ch'an (fl. 1209–1224) and a second-generation disciple named Hsiao T'ing-chih (fl. 1260). The latter is represented by *Chin-tan ta-ch'eng chi* (Anthology on the Great Completion of the Golden Enchymoma), modeled in part on *Folios on Apprehending Perfection*. Even more prominent is a set of three anthologies ascribed to Pai Yü-ch'an alone, occupying over one-third of the *Ten Texts on the Cultivation of Perfection*. Two of the anthologies include many writings attesting to Pai's practice of Five Thunder Rites (*wu-lei-fa*) around Mount Wu-yi (Fukien) in 1215–1216. The third anthology is dedicated to the enshrining of Hsü Hsün (239–292/374?) at the Yü-lung Kuan (Abbey of Jade Beneficence) located on West Mountain. Pai chronicles the history of Hsü as healer, dragon-slayer, paragon of filiality, and ultimately national guardian.

A number of comparable testimonials to the devout following of Hsü Hsün are included in the Ming canon. By far the most exceptional is *Hsü t'ai-shih chen-chün t'u-chuan* (An Illustrated Hagiography of the Perfected Lord, Grand Scribe Hsü; HY 440). This illustrated narrative account is a product of the era when Hsü Hsün was honored as the exemplar of both filiality and loyalty by a movement known as the Ching-ming Tao (Way of Purity and Radiance). A disciple of the founder, Liu Yü (1257–1308), named Huang Yüan-chi (1270–1324) compiled *Ching-ming chung-hsiao ch'üan-shu* (Complete Writings on the Loyalty and Filiality of Ching-ming; HY 1102). Half of this encyclopedic document on the Ching-ming movement supplements the earlier hagiographic works and half is dedicated to the teachings of Liu and Huang. As characterized in transcripts of master-disciple dialogues, the Way of Purity and Radiance fostered a code of behavior benefiting both family and state in lieu of pursuing a contemplative life.

The force of Pai Yü-ch'an's legacy is also discernible in a variety of additional texts in the Ming canon. Three compilations by his disciples augment the *Ten Texts on the Cultivation of Perfection*: *Hai-ch'iung Pai chen-jen yü-lu* (Discourse Record of the Perfected Pai Hai-ch'iung; HY 1296), *Hai-ch'iung wen-tao chi* (Anthology of Hai-ch'iung's Inquiries into the Tao; HY 1297), and *Hai-ch'iung ch'uan-tao chi* (Anthology of Hai-ch'iung's Transmission of the Tao; HY 1298). Among the outstanding components of these works are some of Pai's best-known songs, such as "K'uai-huo ko" (Song of Joy) and "Wan-fa kuei-yi ko" (Song on the Unity Back to Which All Creeds Hearken).

The works of a prominent heir to Pai's legacy, the syncretist Li Tao-ch'un (fl. 1288–1299) of Yi-chen (Kiangsu), are also well represented in the Taoist canon. Several exegeses convey a pedagogical approach in harmony with the Ch'üan-chen school, showing equal respect for writings from all facets of the so-called Three Teachings. An invaluable record of Li's ability to convey instruction through repartee and impromptu verse, moreover, is provided in *Ch'ing-an Ying-ch'an-tzu yü-lu* (Discourse Record of Ying-ch'an-tzu, [Li] Ch'ing-an; HY 1053). A disciple named Ch'ai Yüan-kao compiled this text from notes that he and five other students had taken during their sessions with the master. One of his peers, Ts'ai Chih-yi, also put together *Chung-ho chi* (Anthology of Focused Harmony; HY 249), based on Li's oral and written communications. The first half of this text is dominated by a diagrammatic discourse on the fundamental concepts of *nei-tan* practice, and the second half follows up with a selection of Li's exemplary prosodic compositions.

Another preeminent exegete, Ch'en Chih-hsü (b. 1290) of Lu-ling (Kiangsi), demonstrates an assimilation of both Nan-tsung and Ch'üan-chen legacies. In his magnum opus, *Shang-yang-tzu chin-tan ta-yao* (Great Principles of the Golden Enchymoma According to Shang-yang-tzu; HY 1059) of 1335, Ch'en identifies his mentor as a Ch'üan-chen master named Chao Yu-ch'in (fl. 1329). A series of Ch'an (or Zen)-inspired epigrams recasting the *Tao te ching* into eighty-one heptasyllabic quatrains offers a rare glimpse of the influence of Ch'en's teacher, whose own writings do not survive. Three supplements to the *Great Principles* provide a diagrammatic survey of *nei-tan* practice, hagiographies of Ch'üan-chen figures, and the formulary for a ritual commemorating the birthdays of Chung-li Ch'üan and Lü Yen. A variant version of the latter text in the *Tao-tsang chi-yao* envisions a substantially larger procession, with Buddha and Bodhidharma among those joining the ranks of Nan-tsung and Ch'üan-chen patriarchs led by Lord Lao the Most High.

Two compilations in the name of Wang Wei-yi (d. 1326) of Sung-chiang (Kiangsu) attest to the enduring legacy of Pai Yü-ch'an as a *nei-tan* adept who applied his expertise to the exorcistic practice of Thunder Rites. Wang writes in his preface to the *Ming-tao p'ien* (Folios on Illuminating the Tao; HY 273) that he was inspired by the *Lao Tzu* to engage in a comprehensive search for *nei-tan* instruction. Organized on the model of the *Folios on Apprehending Perfection*, this anthology closes with Wang's tribute to Chang Po-tuan and a "Te Tao ko" (Song on Attaining the Tao). In his preface to the *Tao-fa hsin-chuan* (Core Teachings on the Rites of the Tao; HY 1243), Wang reveals his debt to practitioners of Thunder Rites, which he characterizes as an external manifestation of *nei-tan*. Here he identifies as his master the founder of Thunderclap Rites (*lei-t'ing fa*), Mo Ch'i-yen (1226–1294) of Hu-chou (Chekiang). His utter faith in the superiority of his training is articulated in a range of prose and prosodic compositions.

Finally, a late-fourteenth-century anthology, the *Tao-fa hui-yüan* (Collective Sources on Taoist Rites; HY 1210), includes copious ritual formularies on Thunder Rites (*lei-fa*) in the name of renowned experts like Pai Yü-ch'an and Mo Ch'i-yen. This immense compilation is dominated foremost by manuals on the rituals of Ch'ing-wei, many of which are the contributions of the leading syncretist Chao Yi-chen (d. 1382) of Chi-chou (Kiangsi). It also contains a diverse selection of ritual codes traced to schools prominent during the Sung, such as Shen-hsiao and T'ien-hsin (Celestial Heart). The merit of this resource as a canon of the prayers of invocation and therapeutic incantation cannot be overstated. The lives of many adepts of Thunder Rites featured in *Collective Sources on Taoist Rites* are taken up in the largest work of its kind in the Ming canon, *Li-shih chen-hsien t'i-tao t'ung-chien* (Comprehensive Mirror of Successive Generations of Perfected Transcendents and Those Who Embody the Tao; HY 296). Printed with two supplements, this hagiographic resource is the achievement of Taoist Master Chao Tao-yi (fl. 1294–1307) of Mount Fou-yün (Chekiang). Chao was himself a practitioner of Thunder Rites and very much aware of Pai Yü-ch'an's legacy.

EPILOG

Aspects of the Taoist heritage have for centuries infused all levels of Chinese society. And like the Judeo-Christian legacy in Western culture, Taoist lore has in some way or other found expression in virtually all Chinese literary genres.

Myriad poems, songs, stories, dramatic works, and novels bear the mark of some exposure to the Taoist legacy of China. Writings that find their way into the *Taoist Canon* and subsidiary collections clearly reflect a sympathetic if not devout frame of mind. Many texts preserved outside such compendia also convey an empathetic view of the Taoist heritage. Some writers may embrace the values and ideals of a certain school. Others may express sympathy toward specific teachings without necessarily counting themselves among the faithful. Still others may exhibit profound respect for figures, institutions, or sites associated with a particular lineage, again without claiming affiliation.

Just as some—but by no means all—pilgrims to Mount Lung-hu would identify themselves as followers of the Celestial Master school, so, too, are there diverse motivations behind any tribute to a site sacred to a Taoist lineage. Similarly, a composition displaying familiarity with the concepts and notions of a Taoist school could just as easily be the product of erudition as conviction. In addition, a poem extolling the merits of seclusion or a contemplative life, for example, cannot automatically be designated as a "Taoist poem." Nor can poets who seek tranquility in nature, moreover, justifiably sustain the label "Taoist poet." Readers who come across labels like this should ask if they have been or can be applied with any meaning.

At the heart of such quandaries lies the fundamental question of what it means to be considered in any way Taoist. As indicated in the discussion above, there is no one answer to this question because the Taoist heritage is represented by many different schools, emphasizing variant practices and codes of behavior. Thus, the only way to ascertain the degree to which a piece of writing bears on any Taoist teaching is to ask when, where, and at what age or station in life it arose. First, it is essential to find out what can be determined about the precise context of the writing at issue. In addition to concrete data concerning time and place, readers should investigate what can be known about the particular circumstances behind the composition under consideration. The questions to be asked in this regard, for example, are what teachers, texts, or experiences can be said to have helped shape a text suggesting more than a passing acquaintance with some facet of the Taoist heritage. An author's frame of mind may be more difficult to assess. First, unlike in Western society, no member of any Chinese community conventionally subscribed to one and only one belief system or way of life. According to the pluralistic approach to religion characterizing traditional Chinese society, different ways were called upon to serve different needs. Second, what may at first appear to be an expression in consonance with an identifiable school of Taoism may prove in the end to be simply a reflection of the wisdom that comes with life's journey. A mature level of reflection concerning matters of life and death, in other words, may or may not have been discernibly formulated through an assimilation of recognizable Taoist teachings.

Finally, it is important to realize that labels can be helpful and misleading at the same time. Readers ultimately need to ask who is applying the designation "Taoist" to any given text and for what reasons. In the end, the question to ask is whether it is a designation the author in question would have used or even accepted and why or why not. What needs to be kept in mind above all is that a writer who talks the talk does not inevitably walk the Way.

Judith Magee Boltz

Chapter 11

WOMEN IN LITERATURE

Among the most dynamic and stimulating conceptual approaches in modern literary criticism are the inclusion of gender as a category of literary analysis and the utilization of the idea of woman to create a new rhetorical mode for exploring language and logic in all forms of literature. This chapter, employing a chronological and thematic approach, examines the continuity of Chinese literature from these modernist critical perspectives, focusing on the dual topics of male-authored representations of woman and the self-representation of women in female-authored literature. Within the broad periodizations of literature adopted in this volume, four key aspects will be discussed: first, representations of women in antiquity in male-authored works; second, male-authored representations of women in the medieval era; third, the self-representation of women in works written by women from the classical to the modern era; and fourth, male representations of women in drama and fiction. This survey is followed by a summary discussion of the emerging awareness of issues relating to literary women in traditional China and reasons for the relative invisibility of women in the literary canon. The chapter concludes with an assessment of the role of male authors in promoting women's literature and the visibility of gendered equality in works by male and female authors. The discussion is supported by citation from or reference to significant texts in the literary tradition.

REPRESENTATIONS OF WOMEN IN ANTIQUITY IN MALE-AUTHORED WORKS (I)

Woman as Social Construct in the Classic of Poetry *and Other Works*

The earliest representation of woman occurs in the first literary anthology, *Shih-ching* (Classic of Poetry; c. 600 B.C.E.). This text constitutes a valuable document on the theme of gender for several reasons. First, it forms the literary summation of the successful Chou civilization centered in north China, in the Wei River Valley, just before the historical process of dynastic decline and fragmentation. Second, it reflects, especially in its hymns and odes, the cultural concept of the Chou as a divinely founded people, conscious of the integral institutions of their society and enacting their social roles through bonding ritual and self-identifying festivals.

Among the numerous representations of woman in the *Classic of Poetry*, two are singled out for special significance in gender analysis: woman as subject at the center of society and woman as subject at the boundary of society.

The finest example of the first case is poem no. 57, the famous "Shih jen" (That Stately Person), which describes a woman on a ritual excursion accompanied by her family and retinue. The identity and social position of this unnamed female are projected through her male relations: her father, husband, brother, and brothers-in-law. Her social role is conveyed through her representation as an object of rank and wealth, a prestige object in the powerful clan system of the Ch'i and Wei states. From the perspective of the anonymous poet, probably male, she is a desirable object, but inaccessible because she belongs to the topmost echelon of Chou society. The representation of this woman's physical beauty constitutes the earliest in male-authored approaches to the female body. The use of natural similes, while appearing unsophisticated on the surface, constructs specific feminine concepts: the marital bed and procreation through the "reeds," fecundity and youth through the "congealed fat" (*ning chih*), fertility through the "melon seeds" (*hu hsi*), and longevity through the "cicada" (*ch'in*). Her "cunning smile" (*ch'iao-hsiao*) denotes her awareness of her high social position and her gendered success. The representation of this woman expresses her material worth and her reproductive value to the clan, rather than a valorization of her individuated self.

By contrast, the second example dramatically represents woman at the margins of society. Poem no. 58, "Meng" (Vulgar!), presents the verse autobiography of a woman deserted by her husband, who had once courted her with elegant, fine-mannered grace. Like the poem discussed above, it is probably a male-authored poem. The subtext of this poem demonstrates that, without a husband or male protector, a woman is condemned to exist at the edge of society, an object of pity and scorn.

Even more liminal is the representation of woman waiting uselessly to get married, of which many examples occur in the *Classic of Poetry*. These situate woman in isolation, picking and gathering crops in fields and lanes. In such poems, woman is physically and metonymically marginalized from the center of society. Their subtexts, especially in poem nos. 69, 72, 125, and 226, reinforce the idea that woman without a male is a social failure. This type of poem forms the reverse or negative image of the positive concept of woman as a social construct.

Woman as Social Construct in the Tso Commentary

The application of gender as a category of analysis to the prose work of the fourth-century B.C.E., *Tso chuan* (Tso Commentary), provides episodic examples of the male-authored representation of woman. In this early genre of fictionalized history, woman is typically represented as the catalyst of domestic drama, in episodes of marital infidelity, incest, attempted murder, sexual jealousy, wife swapping, and sexual freedom. Yet the narratives also represent woman as the empowered gender in episodes that relate events turning on the politics of hereditary succession or episodes enacting female solidarity and self-preservation through female resourcefulness and independent judgment.

Philosophical Foundations of Gender Relations

Beginning in the fourth century B.C.E., approaches to gender relations altered radically with the formulation of the concept of social relationships by philosophers of the Confucian school. The text of the *Mencius* (c. 300 B.C.E.), for example, enunciates a predominantly male scale of social values in the five ethico-social relationships of father : son, ruler : minister, husband : wife, the elderly : the young, and friend : friend. This system, known as the Five Human Relationships (*wu lun*), is both hierarchical and gender exclusive. Woman is mentioned as the inferior gender in the marital relationship. She appears in her biological role as a mother, and as a subordinate, in the new patriarchal system that evolved from doctrines of moral philosophy and informed gender relations for two millennia.

Records of the Historian

Gender exclusiveness is immediately apparent in the opening of the first history of the Chinese people, *Shih-chi* (Historical Records, or Records of the Historian), by Ssu-ma Ch'ien (c. 145–c. 86 B.C.E.). The historian reaches back to mythological time to posit a divine origin of the Chinese people from a pentiad of male deities. Although earlier texts relate the myths of two major female deities, the cosmogonic creatrix Nü-wa (older pronunciation Nü-kua; Woman

Wa/Kua) and the sun-mother Hsi-ho, these goddesses are excluded from the historian's new gender construct, which privileges the male in a masculine pantheon.

A similar diminution of the female gender is apparent in his negative account of woman's historical role in palace politics. The collective biography of the empresses opens with a list of the faults of some Han empresses, followed by a list of the transgressions of female consorts in antiquity, which the historian states to have been the cause of the failure of former dynasties. The misogyny implicit in this monocausal analysis of dynastic decline is accentuated in the historian's representation of one of only three female rulers in Chinese history, Empress Lü (Lü-hou). Her biography in chapter 9 culminates in a scene of dehumanized depravity that is equaled in the annals of Chinese literature only by the scene of male ritual brutality performed on a woman's body that is described a millennium and a half later in the novel *Shui-hu chuan* (Water Margin). The Han historian's treatment of his female subject constitutes the demonization of a woman who dared to aspire to political power, which was the preserve of males.

Although the concept of sexual politics could be applied to the role of women in power relationships in antiquity, the term conceals more than it explains. Early historical accounts show that female sexuality was instrumental in facilitating an ambitious woman's career. Yet the real issue confronting women in power politics, localized in the palace harem, was less sexual than biological. The problem of the control of power centered on procreation, with its inherent problems of actual paternity, infertility (always ascribed to the female), infant mortality, death in childbirth, and permanent loss of sexual attraction during pregnancy as well as postpartum disease. These biological issues are latent in the subtext of early historical narratives, but they are rendered almost invisible by male-authored representations of woman in power politics.

Biographies of Women

From the extreme position of political woman as demonized subject, the important Han text *Lieh-nü chuan* (Biographies of Women) represents women at the other extreme of exemplary female model, usually in their roles as mother and wife. Of the total 125 biographies of 130 women, 92 represent woman as moral exemplar, 16 as examples of immorality, and 22 in the final, later chapter as paragons of virtue or as examples of depravity. Although the text is attributed to Liu Hsiang (79–8 B.C.E.), its author is probably better characterized as anonymous.

In this work woman is elevated to the position of an intelligent, diplomatic, judicious, virtuous, rational social being, who is well versed in oratory and classical rhetoric. Much of the substance of the biographies is taken up with extended and uninterrupted speeches that women deliver to argue their case or prove their point. The rhetorical strategy is to conserve and uphold the moral fabric of society. The authorial device of putting sophisticated rhetoric, traditionally practiced by educated males, into the mouths of women (who are not otherwise known in antiquity for their literacy or scholarship) constitutes a major break with the patristic moral code, which silences and subjugates woman in society. More than a rupture with tradition, this rhetorical device can be read as a subversive gendered tactic. In the war of words recorded in this text, women invariably win the moral argument. The subtext may be read as a male-authored plea for a greater degree of involvement of women in society. Examples of this exemplary female tradition are seen in biographies entitled "Tsou Meng K'o mu" (The Mother of Meng K'o of Tsou; i.e., Mencius's mother), "Liang kua Kao Hsing" (Kao Hsing, the Widow of Liang), and "Lu Ch'iu chieh-fu" (The Chaste Wife of Ch'iu [Hu] of Lu), in books 1–5.

The representation of exemplary women alters with book 6 and conveys different literary values. Whereas the biographies in the first books are written in a serious mode with a high moral purpose, the later biographies exhibit more interesting authorial strategies. For example, there is subversive humor in the account of a concubine defeating the illustrious statesman Kuan Chung in debate; there is gender competition in a woman's excellence in the aristocratic masculine art of archery and in a woman's successful performance of a man's function as a state diplomat. There is grotesque humor in the marital success of ugly or deformed women; and there is bathos in the account of females competing to submit to a punishment inflicted by a male official. When these biographies are read within the rhetorical tradition of male-authored works such as *Chan-kuo ts'e* (Intrigues of the Warring States), the subversive intent of *Biographies of Women* becomes more evident. Women in this text have been empowered by male authors through the masculine techniques of rational discourse.

That the text was traditionally read as a manual for women on exemplary standards of social and moral conduct, which enshrines virtues ascribed to females of chastity and obedience, as much as wisdom and right thinking, is clear from the number of updated versions of the text and the imitations it inspired through the centuries. It also generated successive illustrated versions, of which the set based on Ku K'ai-chih's (c. 348–c. 409) "Nü-shih chen t'u" (Admonitions of the Instructress to the Court Ladies) and that of "Hui-t'u *Lieh-nü chuan*" (Illustrations of the *Biographies of Women*) are the most famous examples.

Early Ballads and the Gender Debate

The indomitable spirit of the moral matriarchs represented in the Han *Biographies of Illustrious Women* also finds expression in early anonymous Han ballads on domestic themes. But although the women of the biographies and the women of domestic ballads share the same expressions of moral exemplariness, they differ in the way they are represented in situations of social control. The women in the biographies usually take control of their own lives, whereas the women in the ballads are defeated by social conditions that are shown to be beyond their control. This is seen in "Fu ping hsing" (Ballad of the Ailing Wife).

In the late and post-Han period, the role of some leading male literary figures was crucial in ensuring that the issue of woman's low social status was foregrounded in contemporary literary debate. The genre chosen for male expressions of social protest on this issue was the narrative ballad. These poets boldly adopted the female voice and used the autobiographical mode. Ts'ao Chih's (192–232) ballad "Ch'i fu p'ien" (The Discarded Wife) and Fu Hsüan's (217–278) "K'u hsiang p'ien" (Bitter Fate) go to the very heart of the gender question. The former represents a woman who is discarded for not producing an heir, and the latter represents a woman who experiences gender inequality throughout her life, especially in her marital relationship. Fu Hsüan's ballad, in particular, can be read as an intertextual development of the patristic gender proposition expressed in poem no. 189 in the *Classic of Poetry*, "Ssu Kan" (This Mountain Stream), stanzas 8 and 9.

REPRESENTATIONS OF WOMEN IN ANTIQUITY IN MALE-AUTHORED WORKS (II)

Woman as Idealized Goddess in the Elegies of Ch'u *and Other Works*

The very different cognitive values in the literature of the southern state of Ch'u offer alternative perspectives on the question of gender and the representation of woman. This southern tradition revolved around the Yangtze River. Its early literature has been preserved in a verse anthology, *Ch'u tz'u* (Elegies of Ch'u), which contains several pieces dating from about 400 B.C.E. Three of its major pieces, "T'ien wen" (Heavenly Questions), "Chiu ko" (Nine Songs), and "Li sao" (Encountering Sorrow), reveal a common cultural indicator: Ch'u culture in antiquity privileges the female.

In the mythological text "Heavenly Questions," two major cosmogonic goddesses are included in the ancient Ch'u pantheon and are given a prestige position in its divine hierarchy. They are Nü-wa and Hsi-ho, both of whom are mentioned above. In two of the pieces that make up the "Nine Songs" (nine is a numerological motif denoting the sky, or heaven), the titles are overtly gendered: "Hsiang chün" (The Goddess of Hsiang River) and "Hsiang fu-jen" (The Lady of Hsiang River [the Hsiang is a tributary of the Yangtze]). These songs are shamanistic incantations in which a male human ritually performs a mimesis of the courtship of a goddess and attempted sexual union with her. The songs may be read as a form of supplications used in ancient fertility rites.

In the more complex poem, "Encountering Sorrow," the anonymous male author uses the mode of autobiographical narrative to relate how his male subject exiles himself from human society in quest of an ideal goddess. He is represented as a marginalized male, who belongs neither to human society nor to the divine world. This representation dramatizes the irreconcilable aspects of the divine and the human experience, and creates a conflict between feminine superiority and masculine subordination. In this gender hierarchy, woman is represented as the embodiment of spiritual and physical perfection and as the conceptualized object of unattainable desire. In these literary works from ancient Ch'u, the female is accorded the dominant role in gender relations, and her privileged position is informed by a pro-female bias in Ch'u mythology.

In the late Han, this literary mode of representing woman was transposed from the Ch'u elegy, song, and mythic narrative to the genre of the rhapsody (*fu*; see chapter 12). Its earliest authenticated expression by a named poet occurs in Ts'ao Chih's "Lo-shen fu" (Rhapsody on the Goddess of the Lo River), in which the royal poet tempers Ch'u eroticism with courtly protestations of sexual control. The idealized theme of woman as goddess is also seen in two anonymous rhapsodies, "Shen-nü fu" (Rhapsody on the Goddess) and "Kao-t'ang fu" (Rhapsody on Mount Kao-t'ang), pseudepigraphically ascribed to Sung Yü of Ch'u but dating more nearly to the third–fourth century C.E. The mode becomes transposed to the balladic genre with Lu Chi's (261–303) "Yen-ko hsing" (Song of Glamorous Beauty) of the third century C.E., in which the poet uses the device of *effictio* (detailed description) to represent the idealized human beauty of palace ladies imagined on an excursion to a river from the harem. The concept of unattainability shifts from female divinity to a palace lady. Gendered poems in the Ch'u tradition create a dialectic of desire that forms a discourse in numerous male-authored works and culminates in the complex eighteenth-century novel *Hung-lou meng* (A Dream of Red Towers).

MALE-AUTHORED REPRESENTATIONS OF WOMAN IN THE MEDIEVAL ERA

Woman as Ludic Construct

The major literary form of the early medieval era, the fourth to the sixth centuries C.E., is a love lyric known as Palace-Style Poetry (*kung-t'i-shih*). Five hundred examples are preserved in the mid-sixth-century anthology *Yü-t'ai hsin-yung* (New Songs from a Jade Terrace). These love poems, mostly by male authors, place woman in the foreground in five major ways. First, woman is their subject. Second, male poets wrote in the feminine voice. Third, the poems treat the themes of gender relations and gender hierarchy, which privilege the male over the female. Fourth, some poems are by women. Fifth, in his preface to this imperial anthology, the male compiler addresses a female readership.

In this love poetry, woman is typically represented by male poets as someone rejected by or separated from her lover. In their representations, they objectify woman as immured in opulent solitude, glamorously helpless, emotionally dependent, physically weak, and consumed by a desire for the male that is so obsessive that it threatens to destroy her. In this male poetic representation, woman suffers from a paralysis of will, from mental confusion, anorexia nervosa, boredom, despair, and a neurotic fear of aging. Such a representation constitutes the poetics of male fantasy. Two examples drawn from the collection in the anthology illustrate this mode. The first piece, "Yung wu chi" (Poem on an Object: The Dancer), by Ho Hsün (d. 517 C.E.), presents the gender issue through the erotic relationship between a male guest at a lavish entertainment and a female entertainer. A gender hierarchy is established in the poem, first, through its title, which classifies the female as an object and, second, through the epithet given to the male: "honored guest" (*chia k'o*). This hierarchy of gender roles is reinforced by the gesture in the poem whereby the male throws the female/object an earring. This is an erotic code of sexual invitation; if the woman accepts, she will pick the jewel up. But, to do so, she must stoop to the floor in a coded gesture of female subordination.

The second example is the third in a set of six poems by Wu Chün (469–520), "Ho Hsiao Hsi-ma Tzu-hsien 'Ku yi' liu shou" (Six Poems Harmonizing with the Royal Equerry Hsiao Tzu-hsien's "Poem on an Old Theme"). In this poem Wu depicts humorously the slow disintegration of a woman's elaborate makeup, in which rouge-stained tears are "pearls turned to blood" (*chu ch'eng hsüeh*). The representation of woman is achieved by the male poet through the approach to the female body: the thick facial mask of cosmetics becomes the woman, and its messy obliteration becomes the erosion of her female self.

The frequent occurrence of this mode of representing woman in the role of victim in a gendered power play, and as the object of male ridicule, exposes a decoratively concealed misogyny. This mode of male-authored fantasy is an expression of poetic rhetoric: Woman is a ludic construct in early medieval love lyrics. Yet through their imaginative strategies, male poets also began to explore the gendered power relationship that is central to the theme of love and concepts of masculinity and femininity beyond the patriarchal gender structure.

Woman as Mediator of Pleasure

The late T'ang poetry anthology *Hua chien chi* (Among the Flowers; preface dated 940 C.E.) to some extent marks the continuity of the Palace-Style Poetry mode. It comprises five hundred contemporary love poems by eighteen male authors, who mostly project a feminine world of courtesans, palace favorites, and female entertainers. This feminine literary construct is controlled by males, and it proclaims the notion that woman exists as the mediator of male sexual pleasure. Although money is not mentioned, this type of pleasure can only be bought: desire is a function of finance.

Woman is represented as an entertainer in most of the poems. Although her role is accepted in the urban society of this period, she has no status in the social hierarchy. She is not shown as seeking or finding a way out of this liminal world through marriage. She is an unnamed marginal figure who has no individual personality beyond the stereotypical woman of pleasure. Her client relationship with the male inhibits the poetic exploration of a realistically observed love affair.

The reiterated use of key words in many poems in this anthology creates a linguistic code that enables a deeper reading of their subtexts. The male-authored representations of woman describe her as lazy, dull, weary, sad, slumped, tipsy, tearful, heavy, weak, slow, idle, broken-hearted, and motionless. This woman who mediates pleasure for the male is represented as a maudlin luxury object anesthetized by sleep, drink, and sexual exhaustion. Her perception of reality, projected through the poets' imaginings, is shown as distorted by dreams, mist, dust, rain, incense, and smoke.

The gendered construct formulated in these poems can be read as analogous to the paralysis of the male will and of the male refusal to engage with the immediacy of the real world. Certainly, traditional literary critics have drawn a political analogy between the world of the anthology, with its comfort sex in a curtained feminine space, and the failure of male poets, whose primary sociopolitical function was official and administrative, to confront the crisis of a divided and war-torn nation.

The Condemnation of History

When the great T'ang poet Po Chü-yi (772–846) addressed the historical question of the causes of national collapse resulting from the recent An Lu-shan (703–757) rebellion (755–757/763; see chapter 14), he structured his literary analysis by using four distinct strategies. First, he chose as his vehicle for this historical theme the genre of the song. "Ch'ang-hen ko" (Song of Everlasting Regret), his most famous work, was written not in the prestige traditional form of the ode (*shih*), but in a form that is closely linked to the ballad (*yüeh-fu*; see chapter 47). Anonymous Han songs in the balladic genre that provided a prototype for Po Chü-yi were thematically diverse: a lament for a lovers' parting, death in nature, departure from home, and the brevity of human life, besides the rough satire of political broadside. Thus the older balladic song form served as a literary model for the thirty-five-year-old poet as he attempted to combine form and content to maximum effect.

His second strategy was to posit his poetic argument on the premise of traditional history—that woman is the cause of dynastic decline. Thus the poet begins his narrative poem with the clichéd metaphor of *ch'ing-kuo* ([beauty who] topples the state). His third strategic ploy supported his thesis by situating his narrative in the intimate female quarters of the imperial T'ang palace. Fourth, he employed the poetic mode of Palace-Style Poetry, which he developed into a long narrative on the relationship between the T'ang emperor Hsüan-tsung (r. 712–756) and his concubine and consort, Yang Kuei-fei.

Because of the poet's choice of earlier literary and historical models for his verse narrative, a negative view of woman is imprinted on the story. These models prevented him from constructing a convincing historical narrative. Also, his attachment to the romantic rather than the historical aspect of the episode determines that his poem is marked by a gendered ambiguity. The poet has formed a sentimental attachment to the doomed female victim, Yang Kuei-fei, yet he seeks ultimately to pursue the line of moralistic condemnation of the figure of the female consort as a stereotypical symbol of evil.

The Appeal to Reason in Gender Relations

The love story of a young girl and a graduate student, "Ts'ui Ying-ying" (The Story of Oriole; c. 800), marks a new departure in the representation of gender relations in traditional literature. It relates the awakening of first love between Oriole and Chang, their complicated courtship and sexual fulfillment, and their eventual separation (see chapter 33). Their relationship appears initially to express a perfect complementarity of two equals: they are both well-born, literary, good-looking virgins. The enduring popularity of the story is explained in part by its enigmatic closure, which allows multiple readings.

If the main narrative is Oriole's story its closure belongs to the graduate student Chang. In this section he explains to his friends his reasons for breaking off relations with Oriole, presented in a coolly logical manner that is unprecedented in the earlier tradition of romantic love. His main argument is that Oriole is the sort of woman who has the psychological power to destroy those whom she loves, including himself. The subtext suggests several other readings of his argument. There is the recognition that humans cannot sustain a love relationship at the same white heat of passion that comes with first arousal. There is also an admission that love requires a social context if the gendered relationship is to endure. In fact, both lovers make good, if unremarkable, marriages with other partners in the story. There is also an acknowledgment that the deepest love creates the psychological need for the partners to contend for power in the sexual relationship. Finally, there is the realization that a love that is too passionate excludes the ordinary business of life. In the story, the graduate student fails his examinations, but goes on to pick up the pieces of his life and settle down.

Although it could be claimed that the model on which the student's argument is based derives from the older misogynistic view of woman's role in history, his rational discourse moves far beyond any literary or historical models. It voices a psychological pragmatism and emotional realism that mark this male-authored story in the classical language as a quintessential literary work of the medieval T'ang period. While many modern readers of the story who are sympathetic to Oriole consider student Chang crass, cold, and calculating, his approach to love is actually quite sophisticated and might be seen as resonant with certain features of postmodernity.

The Psychology of the Couple

Three early poetic forms are central to the development of the theme of conjugal love: linked verse, the lyrical ballad, and the letter-poem. An early example of the theme has been noted in the ballad by Fu Hsüan, "Bitter Fate." Written in the female voice and in an autobiographical mode, it expresses a wife's sense of oppression within marriage. An example of the theme in the linked-verse form is found in the couplets of Chia Ch'ung and his wife, Lady Li (third century C.E.), in which the wife expresses anxiety about their uneasy alliance as a couple, while the husband voices reassurance. An early example of the third form is seen in Ch'in Chia's three letter-poems (second century C.E.) addressed to his wife, in which the young poet voices courteous expressions of gallantry and tender love while they are apart.

The most interesting psychological treatment of the uneasy alliance between the couple within the traditional institution of marriage occurs in the epistolary verse of Lu Yün (262–303 C.E.). Four male-authored poems are written alternately in the female voice and the male voice, representing an exchange between a husband and wife at a critical point in their marital relationship. While the husband maintains a courtly, urbane tone in his affectionate expression of marital fidelity, the wife displays feelings of jealousy mingled with pathos and low self-esteem.

It is perhaps not surprising to discover that the male subject is given the higher position in the gender hierarchy in terms of self-control and worldly bonhomie. But the sequence of poems written in the female voice is of great literary and social significance. They express for the first time a woman's rejection of some aspects of a wife's behavior toward her husband that are prescribed by traditional patriarchal family values. Whereas she should be submissive, obedient, and reverent toward her husband, she is instead high-spirited, independent, and argumentative. The silence of woman in early medieval society is shattered by her articulate repartee. Yet, at the social level, this literary figuration of the wife represented by the male author remains inferior to that of her husband. Her social inferiority is measured by the psychological interplay between the couple, in which the wife expresses her low self-esteem with her identification of her female self as ugly and worthless.

The later narrative poem by Tu Fu (712–770), "Pei cheng" (The Journey North), indicates a turning of literary attention from the theme of conjugal complementarity and psychological insight to the representation of the poet's wife and family at a time of civil war. In the famous domestic passage of this narrative, when the poet reaches home after a dangerous journey from the besieged capital, he presents a realistic cameo of his impoverished family existing on the margins of society. The destitution Tu Fu describes suggests the earlier literary model of anonymous Han ballads on the domestic theme. Yet a crucial distinction is seen between the voice of the wife in the Han ballad, which combines moral rigor with courageous realism, and the wife in Tu Fu's poem, who is given no voice. The poet's representation of the female gender is mediated through his own masculine perspective. In this respect at least, the poet looks backward to the tradition, rather than shaping the new conceptual idiom.

IN THE VOICE OF WOMEN: FROM EARLY EMPIRE TO THE LATE IMPERIAL ERA

China's first woman of letters is Pan Chao (45–120? C.E.), the sister and collaborator of Pan Ku (32–92 C.E.), author of *Han shu* (History of the Han Dynasty). When she was sixty-one, she wrote a booklet of advice, ostensibly for her own daughters, on how to conduct themselves in married life. However, since her daughters would have been in their forties at that time, 106 C.E., it is likely that she actually addressed her book to young women of marriageable age. The social class of her intended readership is limited to well-born girls. Her aim in "Nü chieh" (Lessons for Women) was to prescribe a set of easily understood rules for a wife's behavior toward her husband and his family in the wife's new home. It was based on an earlier manual, "Nü tse" (A Model for Women).

Although Pan Chao implicitly endorses the patriarchal code in her prescriptions for young women, her advice is rescued from authoritarianism by several key characteristics in her writing that reflect her personality. While she upholds the theoretical position of male privilege and female subservience in marital relations, the rationale she offers for the rigid patriarchal code is humanized by her pragmatism, common sense, moderation, realism, and intuitive perceptions about the psychology of social relationships. She even injects much-needed humor into her advice. For example, she warns loving newlyweds not to follow each other around or else they will become besotted and eventually bored with each other. She also advises young widows not to relax the high standards of married life by not keeping up appearances.

Nevertheless, "Lessons for Women" is basically a female writer's public statement on woman's inferior, secondary role in society, rather than a real attempt by a female writer to explore her own individual response to the patriarchal code or the psychological workings of marital relations in a social context.

The first example of a woman's conscious self-representation in the literary tradition is in an autobiographical verse narrative by Ts'ai Yen (b. 177 C.E.), the daughter of the learned scholar Ts'ai Yung (133–192). Her narrative relates her experiences in the civil war at the end of the Han dynasty, when she was captured by non-Chinese invaders and married off to their tribal chief in a foreign country. After twelve years, she was ransomed back to China but had to leave behind her two boys. She later remarried. Her account appears in three poetic versions, of which the first is the 108-line "Pei-fen shih" (Poem of Grief and Anger).

The stark choices confronting Ts'ai Yen throughout her life in exile relate to the theme of the cultural other. She had to overcome traditional sinocentric racial prejudice by living among foreigners and accepting them as superior to herself. She also had to come to terms with a sexual relationship for more than a decade with two enemy men. Moreover, she had to enter marriage with them even though she was a widow. She had also to endure maternal loss at having to leave her sons behind when she was ransomed and returned to her home territory.

Ts'ai Yen's self-representation in the verse narrative reflects the moral dilemma of a woman who has to deny her own cultural values in order to survive. In this respect, her autobiographical account links her to the writing of Pan Chao, whose precepts are based on the premise of female survival in the hostile world of power politics. It is possible to read in the subtext of her impassioned poem a confessional plea, which serves to explain why she did not commit suicide. Traditional readers, however, have interpreted Ts'ai Yen's poem as the story of the archetypal patriotic heroine who endures shameful indignities at the hand of the foreign enemy, yet maintains to the last her own cultural identity.

A different form of female self-representation is seen in the song-texts of five professional female singers who lived in the fourth and fifth centuries. During this period, the cultural divide was between northern China, which was ruled by non-Sinitic military powers, and south China, which was the seat of the government in exile beginning in 317 C.E. The Chin court fled north China and settled in the southeastern region of the ancient kingdom of Wu in the Yangtze River delta. At this time, southeastern urban centers were witnessing an explosion of popular song and music, especially a radically new form of love song that derived from a local entertainment culture (see chapter 47). Originating in the pleasure quarters of the Yangtze River Valley towns, these love songs take the form of a female singer's direct address to her rich male client. As the product of a commercial culture, the songs voice mercantile values. Yet the subtext expresses the dubious worth of a love based on sexual favors that can be bought and sold, discarded and replaced like a commodity. The female voice in the songs is intimate with a playful eroticism and a seductive charm that disguises her encouragement to the male client to spend money on her. She seeks a permanence in their relationship, but marriage is usually denied her, and she must settle for the short-lived role of favored girl-entertainer or concubine.

Five singers in the popular tradition of southern song are named, and some biographical data are given for them in contemporary documents. Peach Leaf (T'ao-yeh) was the fourth-century concubine of the painter and scholar Wang Hsien-chih. The Pearl of Meng (Meng Chu) was from the Tan-yang region (Kiangsu province) in the fifth century. Little Su (Su Hsiao[-hsiao]) was from the southern city of Ch'ien-t'ang (modern-day Hangchow). Her surviving song and her legend inspired later poets to write graveyard love poetry. The Fairy of Wu-hsing, who was from the region of modern Chekiang province, lived in the early sixth century. The fifth is the most famous, Girl of the Night (Tzu-yeh), of the fourth century, from the southern capital Chien-k'ang (modern-day Nanking). Several traditions are attached to her name, which occurs in the title of two large groups of southern love songs. These women were all professional singers who probably composed the songs they performed before audiences, either in towns or at court.

The years of exile mark a liminal moment in the development of women's literature. It is significant that this change occurred during the Northern and Southern Dynasties (420–589), when the central plains were ruled over by mostly non-Sinitic peoples, and hundreds of thousands of Chinese, together with their court, moved to the Yangtze region and farther south. For a number of complex reasons, perhaps mainly due to the privileged position accorded to professional female singers in southern society, several educated, literary women became more visible in southern literary life and made their voices heard. Three women poets of the fifth and sixth centuries emerged from this new cultural environment: Pao Ling-hui (fl. c. 464), Liu Ling-hsien (late fifth to early sixth century), and Shen Man-yüan (c. 540). They were all female writers who had connections with the southern court, and their poems are preserved in the contemporary anthology of love poetry, Hsü Ling's (507–583) *New Songs from a Jade Terrace*, whose patron was the crown prince of the southern Liang dynasty, Hsiao Kang (Emperor Chien-wen; 503–551; r. 550–551). It is noteworthy that the other major anthology of this period, *Wen hsüan* (Literary Selections), whose patron was the previous crown prince and Hsiao Kang's brother, Hsiao T'ung (501–531), contains not a single literary work by a female writer.

Since the anthology preserving the poems of these three women constitutes the major repertoire of the new literary form of Palace-Style Poetry, which was a masculine creation and a masculine mode of expression, the question arises as to what extent these literary women voiced their individual female expression and inscribed their female experience into their own poems. It is evident that Pao Ling-hui's self-representation was limited by the genre she adopted. She imitated earlier balladic models in a sophisticated and nuanced manner. Shen Man-yüan broke with tradition and inscribed her feminine issues into poems such as "Hsi Hsiao Niang" (Parody of Hsiao Niang), which raised the question of a loving wife's obligatory acceptance of her husband's more alluring, younger mistress, the Hsiao Niang of her poem. Liu Ling-hsien developed a mature literary voice in letter-poems, such as the second poem of "Ta wai shih erh shou" (Two Poems in Reply to My Husband Who Is Away). Her poem reveals a new way of conceptualizing the female self as an equal partner in a reciprocal marital relationship. It demonstrates a perfect complementarity between husband and wife in a shared life of affection and ludic literariness.

A further question arises with respect to these three female writers: why were they in particular rescued from oblivion? Fortunately, their biographical data, however scant, provide some answers to this question. All three had vertical and lateral lines of personal and familial communication in their literary network. Pao Ling-hui had access to literary life through her older brother, the famous ballad writer Pao Chao (414–466), who had a royal patron. Shen Man-yüan was the granddaughter of the illustrious poet and historian Shen Yüeh (441–513), who also enjoyed royal patronage in his day, and she was the wife of a courtier-official. Liu Ling-hsien was doubly lucky, because both of her husbands served at court, and she also belonged to the famous literary Liu family; her three brothers all enjoyed royal patronage. Moreover, the compiler of the anthology that preserved their poems, however few, was particularly sympathetic to the position of literary women. Thus it can be seen that the intervention of male authors was crucial to the advancement of female writers and to the preservation of their literary work.

Although women authors must have used other genres for self-expression, at least experimentally, their work in these genres has not survived. It was only because they wrote in the prestige form of the Palace-Style Poem, in their woman's voice, that their work in this form was preserved. Their skill in this form, in addition to the factors of literary influence, indirect royal patronage, and sympathetic male sponsorship, makes this a period when the voice of some literary women was not completely silent.

During the T'ang period, the literary status of female writers improved, as seen in the careers of three distinguished poets: Hsüeh T'ao (770–830), Yü Hsüan-chi (840–868), and Lady Hua-jui (fl. c. 960–970). These three writers produced relatively large collections of verse, of which a significant percentage has been preserved. Of the five hundred poems originally attributed to Hsüeh T'ao, ninety are extant in her *Hung-tu chi* (Hung-tu Collection [Hung-tu was Hsüeh T'ao's literary style], also known as Brocade River Collection). Fifty of Yü Hsüan-chi's pieces have survived. Lady Hua-jui's extant corpus of one hundred poems represents about a third of her literary opus.

Male literary intervention was crucial to the careers of these writers. Hsüeh T'ao exchanged poems with twenty male poets of the metropolitan literary world who were famous in their day, such as Po Chü-yi, and especially his friend Yüan Chen, with whom she had a long-standing affair. Yü Hsüan-chi's career was aided by her association with a government official, as his concubine, and her freedom to receive literary men at her residential quarters in a medieval convent enabled her to conduct extensive literary friendships with male authors in the artistic life of the capital. Lady Hua-jui's career was sponsored by her husband, Meng Hsü, emperor of Shu in the Five Dynasties era (907–960). These three women were connected to metropolitan literary life in Ch'ang-an and Ch'eng-tu, and they were also free to travel, thus enriching their personal and literary experience.

The poetry of Hsüeh T'ao and Yü Hsüan-chi contains several progressive features. In the case of the former, her wit sparkles in works like her "Shih li" (Ten Parting) poems—for example, one on the pet parrot who repeated indiscreet pillow talk. The erotic punning and innuendo of southern love songs are elegantly developed in her verse. In the compositions of Yü Hsüan-chi, literary innovation is primarily thematic and metrical. Her verse includes themes of travel, history, love, parties, friendship, and literary subjects. By contrast, Lady Hua-jui's poetry looks back to Palace-Style Poetry, miming its form in stereotypical love plaints rather than emulating its experimental modernist spirit.

Both Hsüeh and Yü inscribed their feminine experience into their verse, reflecting their worlds, their poetics, and their interior life, each in her own idiom. In their self-representation, they raise similar issues concerning the status of literary women. Hsüeh's poem "Ch'ou Chu shih-san hsiu-ts'ai" (In Response to Graduate Chu) privileges literary fame but questions the relevance of a civil service career. Yü goes much further in her female aspiration for a career in public life when she voices her opposition to gender inequality as it is manifested in female exclusion from the civil service examinations. In her poem "Yu Ch'ung-chen kuan nan-lou tu hsin chi-ti t'i-ming ch'u" (Visiting the South Hall of Ch'ung-chen Temple, I Look at the Names of Recent Examination Graduates), the title proclaims her agenda: she protests in a muted, but not silent, way her lack of empowerment as a woman who is barred from entry to public life.

Of the later voices in the female literary tradition, the most famous is the lyricist Li Ch'ing-chao (1084–c. 1151). Her literary career was nurtured by her outstanding literary family and developed by her marriage to Chao Ming-ch'eng, with whom she shared a relationship of almost complete gender equality. Li broke with tradition by entering the field of literary theory, previously a male preserve, in her "Tz'u lun" (Discourse on the Lyric). Although the *tz'u* lyric was written predominantly by male authors in the female voice, a lyrical style in the masculine voice also existed, one that was usually used by male poets. Li used the form to experiment with female-authored verse in the male voice. In her extant corpus of fifty lyrics, the contrasting periods of her career are seen: the young literary woman sharing her life with her cultured husband and her later widowhood when she mourns her personal loss in a war-torn country.

Another celebrated female lyric writer is Chu Shu-chen (fl. c. 1100), who also wrote notable poems in the ode (*shih*) genre. In her own day, her melodic style of verse and her particular expression of distress and misery were very popular. Her literary career illustrates the factors that contributed to the exclusion of women from literary life and from the literary canon. Chu's uncultured husband was hostile to her literary career, and so she lacked the literary society enjoyed by writers such as Liu Ling-hsien and Li Ch'ing-chao. Moreover, after her death, her literary output was destroyed by her parents in a gesture of uncomprehending piety. Yet, again through male literary intervention, her poems were collected from among friends by Wei Chung-kung (Tuan-li) and published in 1182. Chu's direct mode of self-representation is seen in her poem "Tzu tse" (I Blame Myself), in which she ironically subverts conventional notions that women should not and do not write literature. Women's writing, in the tradition, is called "dabbling in literature" and an "evil" practice; her ability is called into question—"How could she?"—a woman's "business" is needlework; and a woman is said "to be mad" from involvement in literature. Chu's self-referential poem, in which she mockingly censures herself as a female author, reads as one of the most modern statements on the ambivalent role of female writers in society.

Female self-representation in later literature is circumscribed by generic considerations. Nevertheless, women become increasingly outspoken on the subject of gender issues. Whereas women had channeled their creative expression into prestige genres like the ode (*shih*) and the lyric (*tz'u*), female writers in the later tradition found themselves excluded from using the prevalent genres of drama and fiction from the sixteenth to the nineteenth centuries. Because of this failure to come to terms with these major contemporary genres, female writers became even more marginalized in literary life, and their work in the increasingly outmoded poetry genres meant that they were not able to become involved with progressive literary culture during those crucial centuries of creative activity.

Still, some female writers overcame the problems of genre and managed to exploit familiar genres, experimented with other minor genres, and succeeded in inscribing women's issues into their work. During the Ming period (1368–1644), Huang O (1498–1569) broke with gender conventions when she adopted the hitherto-masculine theme of eroticism in her poem on orgasm. Her imaginative code risks becoming mere pornography, but her poem is rescued from sensationalism by the fact that modern readers have learned to interpret the theme of female orgasm as a woman's fundamental right to pleasure; her woman's *jouissance* is a biological expression of cultural independence.

During the Ch'ing dynasty (1644–1911), Wang Tuan (early eighteenth century), besides writing conventional verse, experimented with two genres formerly inaccessible to women when she wrote an historical novel in the vernacular and compiled an anthology of Ming verse, in which she introduced her own scale of literary values. Since compiling anthologies requires critical judgment, Wang is seen as having entered the field of literary criticism.

Wu Tsao (1799–1862), besides being an acclaimed writer of southern songs and a practitioner of the *tz'u* and operatic aria (*san-ch'ü*; see chapter 17), experimented with writing drama. Her play, "Yin chiu tu 'Sao'" (As I Drink Wine, I Read "Encountering Sorrow"), can be considered an example of self-representation by gender substitution. That is, the woman author transposes her lack of empowerment to episodes of liminality and powerlessness in the fictionalized life of the ancient Ch'u poet Ch'ü Yüan.

The literary career of the remarkable writer Ku T'ai-ch'ing (1799–c. 1875), like that of Li Ch'ing-chao, can be divided into a period of brilliant success, in which she shared common cultural interests with a Manchu nobleman, and a period of personal loss. Her literary recognition is due to the sympathetic intervention of K'uang Chou-yi (1859–1926), who had her collected works published and promoted her to the reading public in the early twentieth century.

The early Ch'ing writers Wang Yün, T'ao Chen-huai, Ch'en Tuan-sheng, and Ch'iu Hsin-ju all used the genre of drama to inscribe their female aspirations at the personal and career level. Wang Yün's play, with its socially explicit title, "Fan-hua meng" (A Dream of Splendor), voices regret that a woman is denied access to the career options open to males in society. T'ao Chen-huai (nineteenth century) used the subgenre of melodious dramatic storytelling known as "strummed lyric" (*t'an-tz'u*) to express her protest against the double standards of traditional gender roles. This popular performance art form originated in southern China and is defined as a woman's genre, or feminine literature (see chapter 50). In her play "T'ien yü hua" (Flowers Under the Rain of Heaven), T'ao advocated full gender equality in the institution of marriage and called for dual monogamy. The work of Ch'en Tuan-sheng (1751–1796?) and Ch'iu Hsin-ju (nineteenth century) adopted the same agenda, but they employed the strategy of gender transposition to dramatize the issue of gender equality. They both used the performance art form of the strummed lyric. Through the device of cross-dressing, their heroines pose as male candidates in the civil service examinations and pass with flying colors. In Ch'en's play "Tsai-sheng yüan" (Love Reincarnate), the heroine, Meng Li-chün, reaches the top of the social ladder and becomes prime minister. By empowering their heroines, these two authors inscribed their own career aspirations into their writing. It is significant that, in presenting the issue of gender equality to the public, they chose as their medium a distinctively feminine literary genre.

MALE-AUTHORED REPRESENTATIONS OF WOMAN IN DRAMA AND FICTION

By the thirteenth century, the prestige literary genres of the ode and the lyric had been superseded by the emergent genre of drama, with new patrons in the form of the Yüan (Mongol) conquerors. Later, beginning in the sixteenth century, fiction evolved as the main literary genre from its popular, oral origins in urban areas of public entertainment. Neither genre belonged to the salon literary environment, and both genres retained the stigma of plebeian unrespectability until the twentieth century. The creative sources for drama and fiction were situated in the middle and lower echelons of society.

Kuan Han-ch'ing: Woman as Abstract Concept, Woman as Dominant Role Model

China's first, and arguably finest, playwright, Kuan Han-ch'ing (c. 1220–c. 1307), humorously declared his special sympathy for women in two verses in the southern song style, "Han-ch'ing pu fu lao" (I Refuse to Grow Old) and "Huang-chung sha/wei" (Yellow Bell, Coda). In his extant repertoire of eighteen plays, most of his main characters are female. His representation of woman is most clearly observed in two gender constructs: woman as abstract concept and woman as dominant role model.

The first occurs in his representation of an idealistic young girl called Tou Ŏ, who is beheaded for a crime she did not commit, in the play "Kan t'ien tung ti: Tou Ŏ yüan tsa-chü" (Moving Heaven and Earth: Injustice to Tou Ŏ). The primary concepts given dramatic expression through her characterization are filiality and chastity. Tou Ŏ sets criminal proceedings in motion by refusing to marry a bullying lout and then substitutes herself in court for her foster mother, who unwittingly caused a man's death. The important issues raised in this play are a woman's right to choose her own husband and the individual's right to justice. To enable his contemporary female character to voice these radical social issues, Kuan empowers her as the symbolic embodiment of the abstract concepts of independence and justice. For this female enablement, Kuan drew on traditional models, especially the model of the fiercely confrontational and idealistic heroines represented in *Biographies of Women* of the Han period.

Kuan's representation of the second gender construct is more securely positioned in the modes of realism and humor. The dominant role he assigned to the déclassé woman in his play "Chao P'an-erh feng-yüeh chiu feng-ch'en tsa-chü" (Chao P'an-erh's Sexy Ploy to Rescue a Whore) is unprecedented in the literary tradition. The main issue again is a woman's right to choose her own husband. In this play, however, the female lead's dramatic function is to rescue her brothel friend from a disastrous forced marriage. The subtext of the play suggests that it is preferable for a woman to remain within the relative freedom of the brothel than to risk the imprisonment of marriage. Kuan's female lead, Chao P'an-erh, is a streetwise woman. She is dynamic, resourceful, and pragmatic, and she exhibits an astute understanding of the way of the world, rather than displaying a hidebound moral virtue. The sharp-edged comedy arises from her energetic manipulation of other characters, both male and female, through promises, threats, and foulmouthed curses, to do what she thinks is best for them. Her vital, colorful language forms one of the mainsprings of the play, rather than slowing the action down with overly long monologues or speeches. Characters like Chao P'an-erh are not derived from dehumanized abstract concepts or based on earlier literary stereotypes. Their representation is informed by the playwright's knowledge of the real world, his understanding of human motivation, and his observation of human behavior. Chao P'an-erh, and others like her, are represented as women who live at the nadir of medieval society. Yet because they are women who take charge of their own lives instead of being passively manipulated, they prefigure more modern female role models.

The Treatment of Gender Relations in Fiction

In the genre of fiction, the question of gender and gender relations receives uniquely varied and creative treatment. In the hands of the short story writer Feng Meng-lung (1574–1646), women become key players in paradigms of satire. For example, the brothel madam, the greedy and garrulous Mama Tu (Tu Ma-ma), is a target of satire in the story "Tu Shih-niang nu ch'en pai-pao-hsiang" (Tu Shih-niang Angrily Sinks Her Jewel-Box), while the idealized young girl of the title serves as a foil for her mercenary personality.

The lengthy *Water Margin* contains several passages that demonstrate the attitude of its anonymous author toward women. The narrative is an account of a band of outlaws who follow a rigid code of sworn brotherhood. They constitute an almost exclusively male group that exists beyond the boundaries of society and that exacts primitive punishments on those who break the code. Four women who violate the masculine code are brutally tortured, humiliated, and slaughtered: Yen P'o-hsi for blackmail, P'an Chin-lien for murdering her husband (an outlaw brother), Mrs. Lu (Lu Chün-yi's wife) for informing, and P'an Ch'iao-yün for slander—and all four for adultery. The account of the brothers' ritual execution of P'an Ch'iao-yün is unrivaled in the annals of sadistic literature. The misogyny of the brotherhood is expressed through their physical violence against the traditionally weaker sex. These women demonstrate their superiority to the male through their mental agility. Thus the male body functions in binary opposition to the female mind. The women are punished in the end not so much for their immorality or their violation of the brotherhood's code as for daring to act independently and to move beyond the roles prescribed for women in a male-dominated society, of which the brotherhood is a reflection of the lowest point. Existing on the margins of society, it represents a male organization that militantly privileges the male. Women represent the outsider, the cultural other. Thus the ritual aspect of their punishment is not just an enforcement strategy, but a male response designed to reinforce the masculine identity of the brotherhood. Episodes of brutalized misogyny form a significant component of the culture of violence that is written into the subtext of this popular sixteenth-century novel.

The theme of gender transposition and its subtheme of cross-dressing are given comic expression in a long section of the novel *Ching hua yüan* (Flowers in the Mirror, A Romance; published 1825), by Li Ju-chen (c. 1763–1830). Li derived his literary model for this novel from chapters 6–18 of the anonymous Han work *Shan hai ching* (Classic of Mountains and Seas; third century B.C.E.–c. 200 C.E.). This anonymous prose classic relates, inter alia, the strange customs, manners, and appearance of foreign peoples on the frontiers of ancient China (see chapter 2). Its brief narratives project a sinocentric perspective that emerges from the dialectic between the cultural self and the uncivilized other.

Li Ju-chen uses this ancient text as his model, but he subverts its message by establishing a different cultural paradigm: he represents the strange lands as inhabited by peoples who exhibit Chinese cultural characteristics that are targets of his inventive satire. The hero of the novel, Lin Chih-yang ("Lin Who Traverses the Ocean"), visits one of these lands, the Kingdom of Women, and he is kidnapped. This is a country where women rule and men play feminine roles. As a male, Lin has to submit to a gender transposition in the form of footbinding, primping, and cross-dressing, and he is then presented as a woman to the masculinized female emperor, who displays an obvious sexual interest in him (*qua* her). In addition to this sexually transgressive strategy, the novel also presents the subversive theme of women's participating in the Chinese civil service examination system and eventually achieving full representation in the male bureaucratic system. For added irony, the novel is set during the reign of one of the few historical female rulers of China, the T'ang empress Wu (Wuhou, Wu Tse-t'ien; r. 684–704). In contrast to her representation in traditional male-authored histories, which demonize this female ruler, in the novel she receives more positive treatment by Li Ju-chen. His transgressive and subversive authorial strategies compel contemporary readers, mostly male, to confront these social issues and to reconceptualize the misogynistic practices and attitudes of ritualized female subordination in late imperial society.

Chin P'ing Mei (Gold Vase Plum) is a domestic novel of the late sixteenth century by an anonymous author. It is a study of the sociopsychological relationships between a husband and his six legal wives in a wealthy household. Because the husband is frequently absent, the focus also turns on the relations between the six women in the traditional hierarchy of the main wife, junior wives, and concubines. Since one of the lesser concubines in this marital hierarchy, Golden Lotus (Chin-lien), is socially ambitious, the narrative action revolves around her determination to become the mistress of the household. In this sense, the novel can be read as a study of female behavior in the context of career competition. The strategy of the concubine is to secure sexual domination over the master, who has what proves to be a fatal preoccupation with sex, ranging through gradations of normal, deviant, and pornographic.

The novel's closure, however, remains unevenly balanced between dual authorial strategies: the overreliance on pornographic passages, which do not always contribute to the structure of the plot, and the continual moralistic interfacing in the form of authorial asides. Despite its ambivalence, this domestic novel exposes for the first time, in intimate detail, the competition among women, and between the male and the female, to gain matrimonial power through psychological and sexual control.

Ju-lin wai-shih (The Scholars), a satirical novel by Wu Ching-tzu (1701–1754), targets institutional and behavioral weaknesses in the academic community, the bureaucratic machine, and the examination system in the mid-Ch'ing dynasty. Although these authorial concerns relate to masculine areas of activity, the novel presents several episodes relating to gender. Two in particular that point up contrasting aspects of conjugal relations deserve special mention. One episode constitutes a caricature of marital relations and the institution of marriage. It concerns the issue of woman's socially sanctioned ignorance of the actual circumstances and personality of her future husband. In the novel, a rich widow with social pretensions discovers too late that her new husband is an actor, a profession ranked lower than the bottom stratum of the social classes. The widow goes completely out of her mind when she finds this out. The episode is presented comedically, and the representation of the duped widow receives unsympathetic treatment by the author. One of the reasons for his negative approach is that it is founded on entrenched male prejudice against the remarriage of widows in that period.

The second example occurs in a brief episode that resonates with the rare theme of the complementarity of the couple within marriage. Although this relationship, between the nobly born scholar Tu Shao-ch'ing and his wife, is not developed in the novel, it remains a remarkable vignette of the social display of happily married love.

The eighteenth-century novel *Hung-lou meng* (A Dream of Red Towers; also known as *Shih-t'ou chi* [The Story of the Stone]), by Ts'ao Hsüeh-ch'in (c. 1724–1764), is an eighty-chapter narrative that relates the transformation of a powerful clan from its preeminent socioeconomic position to one of irreversible decline. It is a domestic novel in the sense that most of its action revolves around several important households. But its ethos and esthetic differ fundamentally from those represented in *Gold Vase Plum.* In this, his only novel, the author addresses many issues relating to gender.

First, the novel privileges the female through the number of female characters in proportion to males and, more important, through the significance the author attaches to representations of women.

Second, the author also privileges the feminine by situating his narrative in a feminine environment of refined domesticity in such a significant way that his subtext implicitly argues for the superiority of this feminine world over that of public and social life. This authorial bias is even embodied in the male character of the young hero, Chia Pao-yü, who has many feminine traits.

Third, the author uses the female gender to represent symbolically the idealized period of his youth, projected as an age of innocence and esthetic enchantment, that exists before the male's necessary entry into the harsh world of masculine decision-making and social responsibilities. At the psychological level, the novel's feminized subjectivity translates into the adolescent male fear of puberty and sexual maturity and the later refusal to envisage a rupture with desexualized childhood.

Fourth, the novel presents the issue of gender through the theme of desire. Its major symbolic representation is seen in the form of the goddess of Disenchantment, K'o-ching, and her sister, Perfect Beauty (Chien-mei), the models for whom derive from the ancient Ch'u evocation of the female divine and from the ancient female figures of the White Girl (Su Nü) and the Dark Girl (Hsüan Nü) with their mythic function of sexual arousal and erotic instruction. The theme of desire runs as a leitmotif through this long novel at the philosophical, psychological, and romantic levels. Its clearest manifestation occurs in the complex relationship between the two main characters of the first part, Pao-yü and his cousin Lin Tai-yü. They are able to express their love only through a contradictory symbolic code, which the author resolves by rupturing the relationship and pairing the hero with a more subdued, moderate girl in the traditional mold.

The most dynamic and realistic representation of the gender issue is seen in the figure of Phoenix (Wang Hsi-feng), the acting head of the Chia household. In her complex psychological makeup are combined both feminine and masculine characteristics. Her superb administrative abilities are countered by her ruthless bullying of her social inferiors. Through the novel her personality is seen gradually to disintegrate as she loses touch with her own humanity.

APPROACHES TO THE FEMALE BODY

Recent studies have focused on the body, especially the female body, as the symbolic object around which strategies of power and dominance are played out. In literary representations of woman, male-authored approaches to the female body offer a significant means of understanding questions of gender. In this discussion of Chinese literature and its relationship to gender analysis, numerous examples of this literary mode are seen: the portrayal of woman in her reproductive and clan-maintaining roles through natural images; the "exemplary" action of a virtuous widow who slices off her own nose to avoid an unworthy marriage; the male thrashing of the nude female; group male mutilation and ritual execution of a female; self-induced anorexia nervosa in male-authored representations of women in romantic despair; the comatose condition of women of pleasure; the cosmetic mask; and the mutilation of women through the practice of foot-binding, whereby female distress and agony are dismissed in the male pursuit of fetishistic stimulation.

LITERARY WOMEN: PREREQUISITES AND ISSUES

It is clear from this discussion that, if a female author wants to have her voice represented in the canonical tradition, she must meet certain requirements.

First, literacy is required. Although girls were not formally admitted to the educational system, they were often able to become literate through informal means, namely, the practice of educating male siblings in the home, as was the case with Pan Chao.

Second, literariness is required. If a woman's literary ideas and techniques were to develop, she required access to literary life. Sometimes this was achieved through the literary accomplishments of her extended family, especially on the mother's side, as guide and role model. These two prerequisites in the formation of literary women are satisfied in the case of most female writers, of whom Pan Chao, Ts'ai Yen, Liu Ling-hsien, and Li Ch'ing-chao are notable examples.

Third, if a female writer wanted her literary work to mature and remain contemporary, she had to be admitted to a literary circle or salon, which would provide the stimulus of competition, the discipline of peer criticism, and the companionship of colleagues. Most women did not achieve this. However, writers such as Hsüeh T'ao and Yü Hsüan-chi maintained literary friendships with a wide circle of male authors, who provided encouragement, competition, and critical readings of their work. Moreover, female authors like Liu Ling-hsien, Shen Man-yüan, and Lady Hua-jui had indirect access to literary authors through male members of their families and thus to the mainstream of literary activity at court.

Fourth, her work had to be sponsored by a male patron of high social and literary standing. Usually this was achieved through family connections, especially male siblings and husbands or lovers. The literary life of Liu Ling-hsien indicates evidence of indirect patronage of this kind, while direct patronage is seen in the career of Hsüeh T'ao, through Yüan Chen, and with Yü Hsüan-chi, through numerous influential male authors, and especially with Lady Hua-jui, the royal consort. A negative example of this factor occurs in the career of Chu Shu-chen, whose literary work survived despite the obstructiveness of her husband and the literary ignorance of her family.

Fifth, a female writer needed access to the means of literary production. In traditional society, this could take the form of private circulation among influential friends through correspondence and family readings but, most important, through the mediation of literary editors and compilers who were sympathetic to the position of women in literature. For example, Hsü Ling preserved the work of literary women and the song texts of female song makers in his anthology. In addition, more than four hundred southern song texts were preserved through the intervention of men who recorded the songs in performance and deposited the texts in palace libraries in the same early medieval era.

Yet the documentary evidence of women's writing for two millennia reveals how much literary work by women authors was destroyed, lost, or preserved only in fragments. Although this phenomenon also applies to male authors, it played a more significant part in the fragmentation or loss of a female oeuvre. This factor is partly due to the marginal role of women in society in general.

Their liminality is evinced by the scant biographical data available for the majority of female writers, especially in comparison with male authors, the most famous of whom received relatively detailed official biographical notices in the dynastic histories.

An index of the numerical representation of notable female authors may be gleaned from the following figures for the main historical periods: two in the Han dynasty; three in the early medieval era (plus five song-makers); three in the T'ang dynasty; two in the Sung dynasty; one in the Ming dynasty; and eight in the Ch'ing dynasty—a total of nineteen noteworthy female authors for the two millennia from the first century C.E. through the nineteenth century.

The low incidence of female writers in the six-hundred-year period covering the Yüan, Ming, and Ch'ing dynasties, with a representation of nine women authors, is explained in part by the choice of literary genres available to both genders. The genres of drama and fiction in this period attracted the finest male writers, but these genres were not an option for women. First, women in general lacked the means to enter fully into public life and, cut off from this vital creative source, their work had no contact with the literary material of these genres, which derived from the public arena of the marketplace and the pleasure quarters of urban centers. Second, being excluded from public life, women were not free to move among the social classes and groups that formed the inspiration for most plays and novels. Third, although the subgenre of the domestic novel might have been a literary option, women lacked a proficiency and fluency in the vernacular medium in which these genres were increasingly being written. Fourth, the literary and political establishments viewed drama and fiction as plebeian genres, in comparison with the more prestigious literary forms of poetry and classical prose. Male playwrights and novelists risked the opprobrium of the literary establishment in pursuing their craft. Female writers chose to remain silent in drama and fiction.

By the time women did begin to write in these genres, a time lag had developed between the heyday of the genre and their adoption of it. In the writing of drama, there was a time lag of four hundred years between the successful plays of Kuan Han-ch'ing and those of the female dramatist Liang Yi-su. By the time she began to employ it, the form was outmoded. In the case of fiction, Wang Tuan's historical novel in the vernacular, though it dealt with contemporary history, followed two hundred years after the literary model for the historical novel *San-kuo yen-yi* (Romance of the Three Kingdoms; c. 1400–1500).

Apart from the later major genres of drama and fiction, limited female representation is seen in the following masculine genres: the classics, philosophy, the rhapsody, history, anecdotes in prose, the elegy, and thematic poems on feasting, hunting, reclusion, religion, frontier warfare, connoisseurship, and others.

Despite the limitations of genre, women's self-representation made a significant contribution to the literature of the past two millennia. Women did not, in general, merely mime the predominant masculine code in the literary tradition, but raised issues central to their own gender, each in her own age. The main issues they raised were education for women, the inequities of marriage, the need for gender equality in society, the right to enter public life, the right to take the civil service examinations, the need for monogamy by women and men in marriage, and the right to practice literature at the same professional level as male writers. Most female authors perceived the problem of women in literature and society to be one of gender conflict and gender inequality. Although they were circumscribed by generic limitations, linguistic mode, and creative source material, women were empowered through the nascent feminine code to inscribe the female self into their own literature.

WOMEN IN LITERATURE: THE ROLE OF MALE AUTHORS

Although the exclusions and limitations imposed on female writers are a reflection of the patriarchal tradition, this does not mean that individual male authors were opposed to the idea of women's literature. On the contrary, it has been shown that in almost every case literary men actively promoted women's writing and facilitated its publication and its preservation in the literary canon. Inclusion in anthologies, the recording of oral performance in song texts, posthumous collection of scattered copies of verse, critical literary correspondence, editing of texts, preparation of manuscripts for publication, and promoting literary work to the reading public are just some of the major examples of male literary intervention in the transmission of women's literature.

Male-authored approaches to woman, however, reveal an ambivalence toward the female gender as well as numerous conceptual and ludic strategies in the use of woman as a gender construct. There is the utilitarian view of procreative woman as the perpetuator of the clan and its prestige. There is the materialistic view of woman as an expensive, desirable adjunct to and gendered trophy of the successful male. There is also the concept of woman as a metaphysical, or religio-ritualized, construct, ambiguously represented as the unattainable object and subject of male desire.

A recurring model in the male representation of woman is the negative idea of the female gender as a destructive, aggressive, and evil force. Some male authors, especially the early historians writing in a moralistic mode, implicitly endorse this negative perspective. Others make self-conscious literary use of this view as a polemical premise to their argument. In its extreme manifestation, the negative attitude toward women is transposed to the psychological expression of misogyny, seen in narratives of wife abuse and the ritual killing of the female.

Ludic misogyny is liminally present in some poems in the Palace-Style Poetry mode. In the early medieval era, ludic misogyny generated subversive strategies, which enabled male writers to adopt the female voice in love poetry in order to investigate the nature of masculinity and femininity in gender relations. Their poems foregrounded the concept of a gender hierarchy, the use of Woman as rhetorical subject, the mercenary aspect of gendered power relationships, and the relationship between power and desire. In this form of literature, male authors inscribed their own male anxieties and vulnerability in ways that differed fundamentally from more traditional literary forms.

The positive representation of woman in male-authored writing is seen in four main ways. First, there is the evocation of woman as a superior being, sublimated as a goddess. Second, there are poems and prose works that raise women's issues sympathetically, in the form of social protest against the unequal position of women in society, especially in marital relations. Third, there is the representation of female role models, whether at the center or on the margins of society, who are strong-minded and independent and who resolve problems and take control of their own lives. Fourth, there is the literary representation of the couple, in which male authors celebrate the idea that in a symmetrical conjugality there is an affectionate, mutual respect and an equality of gender that transcends the patriarchal code of female subordination and male privilege. In this more humane code, both male authors and female authors perceive a new way of expressing the love relationship through true reciprocity. The more repressive attitudes toward women reflected in traditional literature can be judged in comparison with male literary interventions and in the light of the fragile new gender construct that is informed by this emergent humanism.

Anne Birrell

PART II

Poetry

Chapter 12

SAO, FU, PARALLEL PROSE, AND RELATED GENRES

GENRES AND GENERIC DIVISION

It is appropriate to begin this first genre-related chapter of *The Columbia History of Chinese Literature* with a group of literary genres that straddle the boundary between prose and poetry. This serves as a cautionary note against taking such divisions too seriously, particularly when dealing with Chinese literature, where poetry often blends with prose and prose with poetry in a continuum of styles and combinations. With some significant exceptions, the genres treated in this chapter—*sao, fu,* and the various parallel prose forms—are of less interest to the average Western reader than *shih* poetry, philosophical texts, classical or vernacular fiction, essays, or historiographical writing—all of whose translations have shaped the ways in which international readers have conceived of Chinese writing. Even in China, a host of pre-T'ang parallel prose forms, as well as Western Han–style *fu,* have been subject to periodic and frequent excoriation for obscurantism, for frivolous, empty, or excessive formalism, and for stylized vacuity. In twentieth-century China, with the important exception of the poems from the Ch'u anthology *Ch'u tz'u* (Elegies of Ch'u), these genres came to stand for the least appealing features of Literary Sinitic writing. They were described as excessively bureaucratic, formulaic, and verbose as well as insufficiently personal, subtle, or meaningful. Individual readers will doubtless form their own judgments, but whatever one's esthetic reaction to these works, they are important objects of study for several reasons, among which is that they offer insights into the nature and boundaries of the literary and into the character of official writing.

Generic boundaries, as readers of this volume are aware, are never absolutely fixed. Suprageneric categories like fiction and nonfiction, poetry and prose, or original and copy are themselves rarely constant across different writing systems or within a single writing system through history. The genres discussed in this chapter pose particular problems for suprageneric categorization. *Fu* is variously translated as "rhapsody," "rhyme-prose," or "prose-poem"; "parallel prose" is the common translation for *p'ien-wen* or *p'ien-t'i-wen* (parallelistic writing), Ch'ing dynasty terms for a style that flourished before the T'ang dynasty (618–907). *Sao* presents a special case, since it is a style commonly associated with a particular anthology—the *Elegies of Ch'u*—and its imitations. Situated as they are somewhere between poetry and prose, *fu* are made closer to one or the other, as these two suprageneric terms are understood in English, only by the absence or occasional presence of rhyme. But both *fu* and *sao* differ sufficiently from the central Chinese literary genres commonly identified with "poetry"—*shih* poetry and *yüeh-fu* (ballad) poetry, for example—to warrant some suprageneric differentiation, and it is not therefore unreasonable to use the term "prose," if we do so to distinguish it from other types of "poetic" genres, rather than to suggest affinity with the medieval and postmedieval European forms that would bear that designation. The student of Chinese literature should always bear in mind the culturally specific character of all generic and suprageneric categories. For most of the Chinese imperial period, the scope of the "literary" itself was far wider than it is today. During the Han dynasty (206 B.C.E.–220 C.E.), it included declarations of war, edicts, commands, memorials, and obituaries. The pre-T'ang Chinese counterparts to European bureaucratic or legalistic texts written in a dry colonial shorthand, which most contemporary historians would read and study only for their informational content, might in China have been written in elegant, allusive parallel prose.

PROTO-*FU* AND *SAO*-STYLE VERSE

Only toward the end of the Later Han dynasty (25–220) do we begin to find evidence of some codification of generic boundaries. Before this time, even the distinction between a genre and an anthology was not a clear one: the word *shih*, for example, generally referred to *Shih-ching* (Classic of Poetry, or Book of Songs). *Sao* referred to the pieces collected in *The Elegies of Ch'u*. The term *fu* became tentatively identified with a specific, identifiable literary practice only in the works of Ssu-ma Hsiang-ju (179–117 B.C.E.), acknowledged as the master of the Former Han *fu*, and his contemporaries. Until this period, there were no clear delineations between *sao* and *fu*: the *fu* of Chia Yi (c. 200–168 B.C.E.) show close thematic affiliation with *The Elegies of Ch'u*, and the Han bibliographers Liu Hsiang (79–8 B.C.E.) and his son Liu Hsin (46 B.C.E.–23 C.E.)

call the poem "Li sao" (Encountering Sorrow) a *fu*. *Fu* in *sao* style, in fact, continued to be written through the T'ang and Sung (960–1279) dynasties. *Fu*, for most of its history, was a remarkably broad term. Its earliest use, in *Tso chuan* (Tso Commentary) and in other texts, suggests simply the presentation of literary material, usually in an official or ritualistic context. This presentation seems commonly to have consisted of oral recitation of poems from the *Classic of Poetry*, and only rarely does the term seem to refer to original composition or even adaptation. Internal evidence such as rhyme and the presence of what may have been exclamatory, interjectional, or caesural (breath-mark) particles, as well as documentary evidence in the historical record, suggests that much early "literary" writing was circulated through recitation—that "presentation" was recitation. This is not to suggest an "oral" character to official writing: recitation was a ritualized and bureaucratized event, and there is no indication that it allowed for genuinely spontaneous or improvisatory oral recitation.

Since *fu* was to become a central court genre in the Former Han dynasty (206 B.C.E.–8 C.E.), it is possible that this character of formal, official presentation was a determining feature of the genre. Various writings have been adduced as the precursors to the Former Han *fu*. *The Elegies of Ch'u*, discussed below, is most commonly cited as the source of the genre. Other proto-*fu* include the highly polished suasory pieces that are found throughout *Chan-kuo ts'e* (Intrigues of the Warring States), arranged and compiled by Liu Hsiang between 26 B.C.E. and 8 C.E. but purporting to consist of documents from 454 to 209 B.C.E. These are in mixed form. Typically, unrhymed "prose" sections frame a longer middle section in rhymed tetrasyllabic lines. Throughout, the use of formal rhetoric for persuasion is clear. Both the suasory character and the mixture of regular and irregular prosodic elements suggest affinities with Former Han *fu*. Chapter 18 of the *Hsün Tzu* (attributed to Hsün Ch'ing/K'uang, c. 300–c. 219 B.C.E.) is called "Fu," a title that was probably a later compiler's addition. The chapter consists of five rhymed riddles with one-word topics and two poems. The riddles each have one section in rhymed four-character verse, which enumerates the qualities of the topic (ritual, wisdom, clouds, silkworms, and needles) followed by a section in a *sao*-style line, which asks and answers a series of questions about the topic, finally naming it. These riddles' enumeration of qualities was also a common rhetorical feature of the fully developed Former Han *fu*. In the two hundred years before the Han dynasty, then, there was clearly a variety of court writing that had rhetorical, thematic, and stylistic affinities with the *fu* at its apogee. Ssu-ma Hsiang-ju's *fu* were not sui generis. The indistinct character of generic division, however, and the unreliability of many of the key pre-Han texts make the direct precursors of the Former Han *fu* somewhat difficult to delineate.

The Elegies of Ch'u was compiled and edited by Wang Yi (c. 89–158) during the reign of the Later Han emperor Shun (125–144 C.E.). It consists of seventeen titled sections, several of which contain from seven to eleven individual pieces.

About half the pieces are attributed to Han authors, and the rest are ascribed to pre-Ch'in nobles primarily from the southern state of Ch'u. The oldest pieces in the anthology are certainly no earlier than the late fourth century B.C.E., and some scholars maintain that the entire anthology dates from the Han. The *Elegies*, particularly "Encountering Sorrow" and "Chiu ko" (Nine Songs), occupy a central position in Chinese literary history and, with the *Classic of Poetry*, serve as foundational texts for the Chinese poetic tradition. The pathos of their subject matter, revealed both in the content of the works and in their biographical accretions, the exotic and magical character of the imagery, and the distinctiveness of their formal features combine to produce a striking impression on the reader. The *Elegies* served as a primary source for images, quotations, allusions, and literary modalities for hundreds of years after the anthology was compiled, and the Chinese poetic tradition would have been vastly different had it not existed.

One of the *Elegies'* primary distinguishing features is formal. In "Encountering Sorrow" and several other works in the anthology, each couplet is divided by the meaningless particle *hsi*, which may have functioned like a caesura. Each line of the couplet consists of a three-syllable and a two-syllable unit, broken by a grammatical particle (possessive, locative, preposition, etc.). In the scheme that follows, X equals a single graph:

X X X particle XX *hsi*
X X X particle X X

The couplets in "Encountering Sorrow" show occasional and irregular syntactic parallelism. Later adaptations of this form show occasional variety in line length. The "Nine Songs" style consists of couplets six syllables long, with the particle *hsi* as the fourth syllable of each line:

X X X *hsi* X X
X X X *hsi* X X

This "Nine Songs" style, too, would be commonly adopted in Han writing, with some variation in the number of syllables. Line length, it must be noted, is an important feature in this chapter. In Chinese, each graph represents a single syllable. The term "tetrameter," for the present purposes, refers to a four-graph, and thus four-syllable, line. "T'ien wen" (Heavenly Questions), surely the most cryptic part of the *Elegies* and perhaps in all of Chinese literature, is written largely in the tetrameter line that stemmed from the *Classic of Poetry* as the Han standard for poetry, and several other pieces in the anthology use a variant of the tetrameter, where the fourth syllable of the second couplet is a meaningless particle like *hsi*. Some scholars believe that the formal characteristics of many pieces in the Ch'u anthology, particularly the use of what appear to be "sound" particles, are clear proof of an originally musical or oral compositional character. There is no reason to think that this was actually the case, although it is not unlikely that many of the Ch'u texts were presented in recitation form, as discussed above. The term "*sao* style" is used in varying ways: it can refer to any of the various styles in the *Elegies*, to "Encountering Sorrow" in particular, or to any writing that uses the particle *hsi* as a recurrent element. The most common reference is to "Encountering Sorrow" or "Nine Songs"-style lines.

Aside from their common metrical features, the Ch'u texts show considerable thematic, imagistic, and stylistic similarities. Many of them have rich and exotic descriptive passages, often drawn from the flora, fauna, and rituals of the Ch'u region. There is also more supernaturalism in the Ch'u poems than in any other Ch'in–Han anthology: the reader is transported into the realm of mediums, wandering souls, extraterrestrial journeys, Taoist and cult deities, and spirit landscapes. Time itself becomes a subject, as *memento mori* or as a life element plastic in its malleability: time is stretched, collapsed, doubled, struggled against, and opened out. Journeys are quest journeys, where the poem's persona seeks and reaches a definite goal, or they are quests without end or resolution, spirals of redoubling within a maelstrom of disjunctive time.

Certain critics consider the "Nine Songs" the oldest texts in the anthology, and the standard story about them is that they are literati reworkings of verses from shamanic rituals. There is as yet no firm basis for either of these claims. The poems do center largely on union, ritualized or not, with a set of deities, and touch on themes of the evanescence of time, the difficulty of being together, and the sadness of separation. Unlike "Encountering Sorrow" and related poems, the "Nine Songs" are not unified by a single poetic voice. Shifts in viewpoint are frequent—from participant to observer, from suitor to the one sought after. Unions pass in a flash or are veiled in such mystery that it is not clear that they have occurred at all. The "Nine Songs" share with "Encountering Sorrow" a rich and exotic botanical image bank. Although most of the poems in the anthology use this imagery in the manner of "Encountering Sorrow," where flowers and gems stand for the outer adornment of an inner cultivation, the rich accretion of botanical excess also works to create a specific imagistic quality. "Shan kuei" (Mountain Goddess), for example, is full of dark, shade-dwelling medicinal plants. The image systems, shamanic references, shift of voice, and manipulation of time give the "Nine Songs" considerable power, and readers can return to them again and again for a brush with the otherworldly.

"Encountering Sorrow" reaches such an affective pitch that the linearity of the quest narrative is subsumed into a riot of emotions, visions, and sensory abandonment. Its hero, Ch'ü Yüan the poet, is slandered by court enemies and banished. In the course of the poem's nearly two hundred couplets, the poet embarks on a series of metaphorical journeys, to woo the "fair one" and regain her/his favor. The poem is full of fantastic imagery: plants, gems, supernatural creatures. At several points, the journey itself seems more important than its goal. The poet wants to linger and dally, in an absorption with the moment that could stand for the poetic vocation itself. The poem ends after several unions have been made and broken. Homesickness calls the poet back to the earth, to his home, and the fate of his quest is uncertain. The poem has some narrative elements—it is, after all, a kind of quest poem—but familiar narrative elements like progressive time, causality, and resolution are so attenuated that it is unclear whether the poem should be called a narrative at all. An extraordinary feature of the poem, and doubtless a feature that has contributed to its popularity, is the pathos of its hero. The character Ch'ü Yüan, the earliest poet-hero in the literature, served for centuries as a model scholar-official: cultivated, pure, accomplished, steadfast, and loyal, but vulnerable to the slanders and attacks of venal contemporaries at court, as well as to the ravages of fleeting time.

"Pu chü" (Divination) and "Yü fu" (The Fisherman) are extensions of the Ch'ü Yüan story in the form of short parables. "Yüan yu" (Distant Journey), which has been attributed to the Western Han *fu* master Ssu-ma Hsiang-ju, is a Taoist re-casting of "Encountering Sorrow," tracing the path of an adept from worldly frustrations to the attainment of mystical union. Sung Yü, supposedly a third-century B.C.E. disciple of Ch'ü Yüan's at the Ch'u court, to whom a variety of *fu* and other compositions are mistakenly attributed, is the purported author of the "Chiu pien" (Nine Changes), a multisection work in nearly three hundred lines. "Nine Changes" likewise contains a quest journey for a Fair One prompted both by frustrations at court and by grief over the passing of time. Many critics find the autumn lamentation that forms the first quarter of the "Nine Changes" to be among the anthology's most outstanding sections. It established a motif to which generations of later poets would turn. "Chao hun" (Summons of the Soul) and "Ta chao" (The Great Summons) are full of "Encountering Sorrow"–style imagery and exhort the soul not to journey into the nether world, replete with gruesome scenes and practices, but to remain in the luxurious and resplendent present. It has been suggested that these works were based on ritual healing poems. The nine works in "Chiu chang" (Nine Pieces), also usually attributed to Ch'ü Yüan, include some of the anthology's best-known and imagistically richest selections. "Chü sung" (In Praise of the Orange Tree) is typical of the pre- and early-imperial encomia on objects whose outstanding qualities mirror the human virtues. "Huai sha" (Embracing Sands), quoted in its entirety in Ssu-ma Ch'ien's biography of Ch'ü Yüan, is the work that expresses Ch'ü Yüan's resolve to commit suicide. Several of the "Nine Pieces" share "Encountering Sorrow" 's time-obsessed journey; "Pei hui feng" (Grieving at the Eddying Wind) includes several lines from "Encountering Sorrow" and in some ways surpasses it in affective pathos. One anomalous element in the *Elegies* is "Heavenly Questions," a series of questions about early history and mythology. Like other early texts of the "riddle" form, they are predominantly tetrasyllabic and show little formal or thematic affinity with the other Ch'u works.

Wang Yi and most subsequent critics held that the works from the *Elegies* discussed above, with the exception of Ssu-ma Hsiang-ju's poem, predate the

Han dynasty, a dating some contemporary critics find too early. About half the remaining pieces in the anthology are attributed to Han authors, including Wang Yi himself and the bibliographer Liu Hsiang, whose earlier work as compiler Wang Yi claims as the basis for his own. One of these pieces is "Chao yin-shih" (Summoning the Recluse), attributed to a member of the court of Liu An (c. 179–122 B.C.E.), prince of Huai-nan, uncle of Emperor Wu, and patron of a host of literary activities and compilations, of which *Huai-nan Tzu* is the best known. Records of literary activity at the court of Liu An are not wholly reliable, but many scholars believe that Ch'u-style verse enjoyed a kind of official status there and that the consolidation of literary activity around that genre contributed to the semiofficial character of Ch'u-style verse in Emperor Wu's court and in subsequent periods. It is likely that group composition and presentation was a widespread activity throughout the Han. Although there is reliable evidence for this only in the Later Han, for which see below, there are references to multiple *fu* compositions on single themes as far back as the second century B.C.E. The reader should always be alert to the possibility of group composition, since it suggests, among other things, notions of authorship and voice that differ from modern ones. In group and official composition, one would expect an attenuation of an individual author's persona and an emphasis on stylistic or rhetorical mastery.

The *sao* forms seem to have been prevalent during the reign of the Han emperor Hsüan (73–48 B.C.E.) and subsequent emperors, which was broadly the era of Liu Hsiang, supposed compiler of an earlier collection of Ch'u texts and the author of one of the works in the anthology, "Chiu t'an" (Nine Laments). Wang Pao (d. c. 49 B.C.E.) was a prominent literatus in Emperor Hsüan's court, famous for *fu* and other compositions. His "Chiu huai" (Nine Regrets) are also found in Wang Yi's *Elegies*. These two works are recastings of "Encountering Sorrow," consisting largely of an alienated official's spirit journey. Wang Pao's composition is in "Nine Songs" style; Liu Hsiang's is predominantly in "Encountering Sorrow" style and mixes a first-person Ch'ü Yüan persona with another commentarial voice, presumably Liu Hsiang's own. Wang Pao was a courtier of high renown who enjoyed considerable imperial favor. The disjuncture between his own circumstances and that of the "Encountering Sorrow" persona demonstrates the conventionality of the Ch'ü Yüan voice and suggests that we should be wary about reading the poetry in a biographically literal way, as an expression of frustration in personal or official life.

Many of the Han texts in the *Elegies* assume the voice of Ch'ü Yüan, which has undoubtedly contributed to the difficulties in dating and authorial identification. To identify a historical Ch'ü Yüan with any of the pieces, even "Encountering Sorrow" and the "Nine Songs," is of course problematic. It might be best to think of Ch'ü Yüan not as an author or as a historical figure, though he certainly could have existed, but as a rhetorical stance, one that had stylistic, as well as emotional and political, signification. From Liu Hsiang's era onward,

"Encountering Sorrow" has functioned something like a classic. This was the poet Yang Hsiung's (53 B.C.E.–18 C.E.) judgment and was certainly a factor in the widespread adaptation of the Ch'ü Yüan rhetorical stance throughout the Han. The *Elegies'* semiclassic status also likely accounted for the canonical status of the *sao* form. For most of the Han dynasty, there was little poetic writing that did not take the form of *sao*-style lines or of tetrasyllables in the *Classic of Poetry* mode. A wide range of Han *fu*, from Ssu-ma Hsiang-ju to Wang Ts'an and Ts'ao Chih at the end of the Later Han, were composed in *sao* style as well. Beginning with Wang Yi's own "Chiu ssu" (Nine Longings), another multisegmented retelling of the "Encountering Sorrow" plaint and journey, which is the last piece in the *Elegies*, however, the simple rewriting of "Encountering Sorrow" seems to have become less common. From Ssu-ma Hsiang-ju's time onward, *sao* forms were used in a variety of compositions that had little to do with *Elegies* thematics or image systems.

The use of *sao*-style lines declined after the Han, as the *fu* evolved in the direction of the mixed tetrameter and hexameter that became the dominant line in Six Dynasties (220–589) parallel prose. Poets took occasional recourse to the *sao* line, however, in *fu* and in other genres, for centuries after the Han. The T'ang poet Wang Wei (701–761), for example, has several poems in *sao* style. The "ancient style" masters Liu Tsung-yüan and Han Yü, also from the T'ang period, used the *sao* form in poetry, *fu*, and in essays (*wen*). Several of Han Yü's best known *fu* are in the *sao* style, and Liu Tsung-yüan wrote "Tiao Ch'ü Yüan wen" (Lament for Ch'ü Yüan), a title first used in a *fu* by Chia Yi in the Han dynasty. Sung dynasty writers in the "ancient style" tradition also wrote in *sao* style. Huang T'ing-chien (1045–1105) has several poems in the *sao* style, and both Wang An-shih (1021–1086) and Su Shih (Su Tung-p'o; 1037–1101) used *sao* lines in *fu* and other prose compositions. Throughout the Han dynasty, the *sao* style was one of the primary compositional modes; by the T'ang and Sung eras, though, the form was clearly used quite consciously as a statement of affinity and of principle, and as a protest against those literary tendencies its authors opposed. The figure of the alienated, principled poet that the *Elegies* introduced into Chinese literature, however, became central to Chinese literary history, and it would not be unreasonable to call Ch'ü Yüan, whether or not he actually existed, China's originary poetic voice. The supernatural journeys and fantastic visions that filled the *Elegies* would also become an important minor key in literary writing throughout the imperial period.

HAN *FU*

The reign of Emperor Wu (141–87 B.C.E.) marked the consolidation of the *fu* as a central court genre, a position it would hold throughout the Former and Later Han. Emperor Wu's reign was also the era of the genre's first acknowledged master, Ssu-ma Hsiang-ju, who set the stylistic parameters for Han *fu* and with whom subsequent readers and critics have most intimately associated Former Han *fu*. Ssu-ma Hsiang-ju's biography in Ssu-ma Ch'ien's (c. 145–c. 86 B.C.E.) *Shih-chi* (Records of the Historian) is one of the earliest historiographical records of a prototypical "writer's" life. Several of Ssu-ma Hsiang-ju's *fu* compositions are reproduced in it, and his life course contained the romantic ups and downs of an artiste: he won advancement for his literary talent, was reduced to wine-shopkeeper status after a love marriage by elopement, and was elevated to the center of Emperor Wu's court on re-recognition of his literary talent.

The eminent modern scholar of the *fu* genre David Knechtges used the term "epideictic rhapsody" to describe the ornate, hyperbolic, eloquent, and enumerative style of Former Han *fu*. It is an apt term; no reader can fail to be struck by the sheer verbal excess in the *fu* of Ssu-ma Hsiang-ju and his contemporaries. A section of Ssu-ma's "Shang-lin fu" (Imperial Park Rhapsody) describing the vegetation in Emperor Wu's hunting park contains a list of twenty plants: "selenium . . . , peonies . . . , knot-thread . . . , galingale, car-halt, wild ginger, thoroughwort, nothosmyrnium, blackberry lily, purple ginger, mioga ginger, winter cherry, ground cherry, pollia, sweet flag, malabar nightshade, virgin's bower, water bamboo, chufa, and green sedge." The Ch'ing literatus Yüan Mei (1716–1797) was perhaps the first to suggest that these early *fu* functioned as encyclopedias or lexicographies, that they were records of Literary Sinitic vocabulary as much as "descriptions" of real or imagined places or things. Former Han *fu* were long: most ran more than two hundred lines, and *fu* of more than five hundred lines, exceeding even "Encountering Sorrow," were not uncommon. The enumerative character of so many Former Han *fu* suggests that the genre's dominant esthetic principles were completeness and exhaustiveness rather than specificity or precision. Indeed, it might be inaccurate to see in *fu* image systems anything like "description" as we know it, for the rhetorical density seems to exceed by far the texts' referential capacity. Early genre critics such as Ts'ao P'i (187–226) and Liu Hsieh (465?–520?) characterized the *fu* as centered primarily on objective, material phenomena, and the sheer number of nouns in the long Former Han *fu* certainly adds to this impression. However one is to judge its referential capacity, this "objective" character was generally less amenable to philosophical argument, historical or other kinds of narrative, or emotional expression than was writing in other genres, but an admixture of suasory or admonitory rhetoric also characterized most Former Han *fu*. This frequently took the form of anti-ostentation, a criticism, both direct and implied, of the material excess that the *fu* itself took most of its lines to delineate and glorify. Yang Hsiung, probably the most renowned *fu* writer of the two Han dynasties after Ssu-ma Hsiang-ju, criticized the *fu* later in his life for its own verbal ostentation and the inappropriateness of its verbal excess for admonitory or suasory writing.

The *fu* of Ssu-ma Hsiang-ju, court composer par excellence, seem to have taken shape in the literary milieu of Liu Wu, who reigned as Prince Hsiao of Liang from 168 to 144 B.C.E. and whose court also included the *fu* writers

Mei Ch'eng (d. 140 B.C.E., author of the famous "Ch'i fa" [Seven Stimuli]), Chuang Chi, and Tsou Yang (c. 206–129 B.C.E.). Ssu-ma's "Tzu hsü fu" (Master Void Rhapsody) dates from this period; it is one of the Former Han's best-known *fu*, said to have been the work that gained him Emperor Wu's favor. Both the *Han shu* (History of the Han Dynasty) and *Hsi-ching tsa-chi* (Miscellanies of the Western Capital) note the concentration of literary activity at Prince Hsiao's court; and the latter text, composed more than four hundred years after the events it described, identifies the prince's court as the first scene of group *fu* composition on prescribed topics, a practice that would become common in the Later Han. Ssu-ma Hsiang-ju probably emerged as a poet, then, in a court milieu, where composition on command, group composition, and official composition marked literary activity. The primary function of these compositions would have been to add luster to the court.

Formally, Ssu-ma Hsiang-ju's *fu*, which set the norm for the longer Former Han *fu*, are somewhat varied. He does not always follow the tripartite division into short narrative introduction, long central exposition, and short, rhymed envoi (*luan*, which sometimes served as a sort of retraction), a structure that characterized several compositions in the *Elegies*. Narrative sections, which either describe actions and conversations or introduce longer descriptive sections, are generally unrhymed lines of varied length, differing little from Former Han essay writing style. They frequently reproduce conversation or otherwise introduce circumstances of composition. In the descriptive sections, which constitute the bulk of the *fu*, tetrametric lines predominate, and these often take the form of a two-syllable noun and a two-syllable modifier. Descriptive, reduplicative binomials are an outstanding characteristic of Ssu-ma Hsiang-ju's *fu*; as with their counterparts in the *Classic of Poetry*, their meaning is often unclear and often seems to suggest an essential quality of the object or action described. Some may have been in the text primarily for sheer sound quality. The long sections in tetrameter are frequently broken by lines of varied length, including sustained sections of trimeters. There seems to have been no pattern for rhyme. Often, the tetrameter descriptive sections rhymed on even-numbered lines, but frequently they did not, and the rhyme class seemed to shift according to no particular pattern. As explained above, many Han *fu* were composed in *sao* style; authors did not seem to specialize in one style or the other. With the exception of the *sao*-style *fu*, the tetrameter was the most common line length, followed by the hexameter and the trimeter. Neither Ssu-ma Hsiang-ju nor Yang Hsiung used much parallelism in their *fu*, although the descriptive tetrameters were often quite similar syntactically. Strict formal requirements for *fu*, then, were few. Rather, formal features were used irregularly to contribute to the desired rhetorical effect. Technical excellence was judged not by adherence to a formal generic norm, but by overall effect and by specific passages of brilliance.

The Former Han emperors who followed Emperor Wu continued the custom of literary patronage, inviting *fu* composers of renown to their courts and commanding the fruits of their literary talents during hunting expeditions and other activities. Mei Kao (fl. 128 B.C.E.), Tung-fang Shuo (c. 140–87 B.C.E.), Wang Pao, Chang Tzu-ch'iao (fl. c. 60 B.C.E.), and Liu Hsiang were among the outstanding *fu* composers of the Former Han court; they all composed epideictic *fu* in *sao* and other modes. Taking subsequent literary practice as a guide, it is possible that compositions like Liu Hsiang's *fu* "Wei-ch'i fu" (Encirclement Chess) were part of group compositions, where several poets would write on assigned topics. Epideictic rhapsodies were typical in the era of the *fu*'s earlier status as official court genre, and it is only beginning with Yang Hsiung, who lived at the end of the Former Han and into the Wang Mang interregnum (9–23 C.E., the period between the Former Han and Later Han dynasties), that the *fu* began to be used for philosophical, emotional, or otherwise expressive writing. With Yang Hsiung, the thematic scope of the *fu* expanded, although epideictic rhapsodies continued to be composed throughout the Later Han and afterward. Most of Yang Hsiung's own early *fu* compositions, including "Kan ch'üan fu" (Sweet Springs Rhapsody), perhaps his best-known work in this genre, are very close to Ssu-ma Hsiang-ju's in style. Although it has been argued that Yang Hsiung's are less supernatural but more narrative and specific, they differ little in form and general content from the Former Han orthodoxy as Ssu-ma Hsiang-ju had codified it. In later philosophical writings, particularly *Fa-yen* (Discourses on Method), Yang Hsiung rejected the *fu* and epideictic writing in general, criticizing court *fu* as ostentatious and insignificant "worm carving." Yang's poem "Chieh ch'ao" (Dissolving Ridicule), which did not have the word *fu* in its title but was structurally similar to a *fu*, was an early example of a type of piece that would grow more common in the Later Han: the essay of rejection. One of Yang's last works, "Chu p'in fu" (Rhapsody on Expelling Poverty), continued this mode and signified, in its hortatory tone, in its verbal austerity, and in its tetrameter classicism, the moral seriousness and philosophical didacticism that Yang's "Discourses on Method" had found lacking in the court *fu*.

The number of Former Han *fu* that survive is only a fraction of the number listed in early bibliographies, and it is difficult to draw conclusions on the limited evidence available. Still, it seems reasonable to conclude that *fu* of the Later Han contained more philosophically oriented, expressive pieces than did those of the Former Han. Pan Ku's (32–92) "Yu t'ung fu" (Rhapsody on Communicating with the Hidden) is written in *sao* style and makes extensive use of *Elegies* imagery and, like the Ch'u poems, centers on lessons for a moral life. Chang Heng's (78–139) "Ssu hsüan fu" (Rhapsody on the Contemplation of Mystery) uses *sao*-style lines to describe a scholar's frustration similar to Ch'ü Yüan's own. Chang's short "Kuei-t'ien fu" (Rhapsody on Returning to the Fields) uses "Nine Songs"–derived lines (various particles replace *hsi*) to celebrate his retirement from officialdom. Through the end of the Han and beyond, the *fu* continued to be used for such expressions of moral seriousness. Pan Ku and Chang Heng are best known for their *fu* on the western and eastern capitals.

In lexicographic and enumerative reach, these *fu* are more like Former Han epideictic rhapsodies, but with a greater admixture of historical detail and allusion. Pan Ku's and Chang Heng's *fu* on the capitals were models for the Chin dynasty courtier Tso Ssu's (c. 253–c. 307) "San tu fu" (Rhapsody on the Three Capitals), which was perhaps the best-known *fu* from the post-Han period. Through the middle of the second century, then, *fu* remained a central court genre and were composed in a variety of modes and styles, several of them squarely within the parameters established by Ssu-ma Hsiang-ju. As the Han drew to a close, however, a new kind of *fu* appeared on the scene, which, along with other changes in literary fashion, significantly changed the nature and position of the genre.

As the Han dynasty neared its collapse, and as conditions in the capital became precarious and unstable, regional or quasi-imperial centers of political and cultural authority arose, where systems of regional court patronage similar to those at the beginning of the Former Han dynasty stimulated another resurgence of belletristic activity. There is ample evidence of group composition on specified themes, extemporaneous *fu* composition, *fu* on command, and *fu* on shared topics exchanged between fellow authors at two courts: Liu Piao's (d. 208) court in Ching-chou (central Yangtze region) in the last decade of the second century, and Ts'ao Tsao's (155–220) court in the north in the first two decades of the third century. The Chien-an reign-period, from 196 until 220, the end of the Later Han dynasty, the period during which Ts'ao Ts'ao had control of the imperial government, has gone down in history as a period of flourishing literary activity (see chapter 13). Occasions for group composition in the final thirty years of the dynasty included military campaigns, excursions to the newly popular country residences, hunts, and banquets. *Fu* on objects are common, and Ts'ao P'i's preface to his "Ma-nao lei fu" (Rhapsody on an Agate [a.k.a. Horse-brain] Bridle) reads, in part,

> Agate is a type of jade. It comes from the Western Regions. Its decussated veins resemble a horse's brains, so that's what the locals call it. It can be worn around the neck or used to adorn bridles. I have that kind of bridle. Admiring it, I composed a *fu* on it. I ordered Wang Ts'an and Ch'en Lin to do likewise.

Ch'en Lin's (c. 157–217) and Wang Ts'an's *fu* of that title both survive as well. Wang Ts'an's is in *sao* style, and Ch'en Lin's is largely in tetrameter; there is no indication that group composition involved prescribed formal elements in addition to the common topics.

Readers generally associate the Han *fu* with the period from Ssu-ma Hsiang-ju to Yang Hsiung, but bibliographic evidence makes it clear that the *fu* remained the prominent literary genre in these closing years of the Han dynasty as well. The Chien-an reign-period is best known in literary history for the birth of a new "lyricism" in *shih* poetry, and there are indeed many affectively expressive literati compositions of *shih*, letters, dirges, and other genres as well as *fu*. At the end of the Han, however, belletristic composition still referred primarily to *fu*, which extended across a broad range of topics: they could be descriptions and elucidations of single objects, expressions of feeling, philosophical discussions, and narratives. Several late Later Han writers wrote on capitals and metropolises in a style somewhat reminiscent of Pan Ku and Chang Heng from the earlier period. In formal terms, the *fu* from the last years of the Han dynasty are noteworthy for their shorter length and a use of syntactic parallelism exceeding that of earlier periods of *fu* composition. Compared to *shih* poetry, parallelism in late Han *fu* was far more varied. Poets wrote, for example, syntactically parallel texts, where each parallel section consisted of several lines, or wrote sections of text in which alternate lines were syntactically parallel. Rhyme was used much more frequently than it was in the longer *fu*, though single rhymes would rarely be maintained throughout an entire composition. Several well-known *fu* of this period were composed in *sao*-style lines, and poets also mixed in *sao*-style lines with other styles. The ornate, excessively descriptive language of earlier *fu* was replaced by a lexical register that differed little from compositions in other genres.

Two of the best-known *fu* of the early third century are Wang Ts'an's (177–217) "Teng-lou fu" (Rhapsody on Climbing the Tower) and Ts'ao Chih's (192–232) "Lo-shen fu" (Rhapsody on the Goddess of the Lo River). A brief examination of their qualities helps illustrate the changed nature of the genre at the end of the Han dynasty. Wang Ts'an's *fu*, in tone, language, subject matter, and affective positioning, could easily have been written in *shih* form. It adopts the familiar topos of the ascent of a height, contemplation of a forlorn situation, and expression of grief. Wang's *fu* is fifty-two lines long and is written mostly in "Encountering Sorrow"–style lines. Syntactic parallelism is common, accounting for around one-quarter of the whole. There are references to contemporary political events and restrained use of allusion, mostly to the *Tso Commentary* and the *Records of the Historian*, which served as common source texts in a variety of late Later Han genres. The tone of personal immediacy conveyed in the *fu* is not atypical of the literature of the period, but marks a new mode in the *fu* genre. Ts'ao Chih's *fu* owes some of its fame to the apocryphal legend that it is a disguised address to his brother Ts'ao P'i's wife, with whom Ts'ao Chih was reportedly in love. But it is also renowned for its expressive reach, sustained imagery, and stylistic brilliance. It is written in mixed lines—*sao*, tetrameter, and other line lengths—and contains all varieties of parallelism available to the late Han *fu* composer. As one would expect from a *fu* with this title, it draws significantly on *Elegies*-style imagery and thematics. The description of the goddess, though, is far more focused and complete than in the earlier period and indicates the level of sustained accumulation of image qualities that had become normative by Ts'ao Chih's time. The narrative of failed encounter and spirit journey is pared down as well, so that its essential affective character is expressed with great economy. Allusions are few, and although descriptive passages take up the bulk of the poem's 166 lines, the language is fairly straightforward. Compared to the Western Han *fu* typified by Ssu-ma Hsiang-ju and Yang Hsiung, the *fu* of the Eastern (or Later) Han–Wei period was a genre that allowed for a great variety of expressive styles and forms. Its formal sophistication set the parameters of the genre for the next several hundred years.

PARALLEL PROSE AND *FU* FROM HAN TO T'ANG

At the end of the Han dynasty, literary forms beame more codified, and formal criteria entered into the evaluative process in various ways. In critical writings such as Ts'ao P'i's "Lun wen" (Essay on Literature), in *Tien lun* (Normative Essays), and in evidence from the literary texts themselves, the reader can observe greater regularity in a variety of formal elements, such as line length, rhyme, use and position of parallel lines, and prosody. Beginning at this time, and gathering strength throughout the Six Dynasties and into the T'ang dynasty, parallel prose genres account for the great majority of literary output in a wide range of styles and situations of composition. The basic formal elements of parallel prose are use of parallel lines; an embellished allusive language; some form of prosodic regularity, including rhyme; and, late in the period, a system of tonal alternation. The rules for parallel prose composition were considerably more flexible than those for poetry genres such as *shih* but considerably more rigid than those for nonparallel prose. Parallel prose could be used for short pieces, such as *fu*, letters, tomb inscriptions, or prefaces, or for works in multiple volumes. Liu Hsieh's *Wen-hsin tiao-lung* (The Literary Mind and the Carving of Dragons), the central pre–Sung dynasty work of literary criticism and theory, is composed in parallel prose. There is virtually no literary genre in the period that does not contain examples of composition in parallel prose. The prefaces to many *shih* poems are written in parallel prose and even the dynastic histories after that of the Han, written largely in common prose, contain passages of parallel prose. So ubiquitous is parallel prose in the Six Dynasties, in fact, that there is no term for it. *P'ien-wen,* or *p'ien-t'i-wen,* the Chinese originals of the English expression "parallel prose," came into common use during the Ch'ing dynasty (1644–1911), when the terms were adopted by critics and anthologists as the form underwent a revival. Parallel prose is also sometimes known in Chinese as "Four-Six prose" (*ssu-liu-wen*) because it consists primarily of paired lines of these lengths, but this too is a later appellation and refers primarily to the more highly regulated parallel prose of the post-T'ang period. As a specialized term in literary classification, parallel prose is used primarily to differentiate texts from those written in "prose" (*san-wen* or *ku-wen*) or in "poetry" (*shih, yüeh-fu, tz'u, ch'ü*). Even this tripartite division is not clear-cut: the eight-legged essay (*pa-ku-wen*), for example, shares characteristics of prose and parallel prose; the prosimetric story-telling genres, such as chantefable or opera, share qualities of prose and poetry. In the T'ang dynasty, literati such as Han Yü and Liu Tsung-yüan instituted a campaign for a "return to the ancient style" that favored straight prose, particularly in the style of Ssu-ma Ch'ien and the pre-Ch'in philosophers, over parallel prose. The divisions become somewhat more distinct, and the esthetic and ideological stakes in suprageneric choice become more clear. In the eyes of ancient-style partisans, Six Dynasties parallel prose, excepting that of a small group of widely respected masters, came to stand for excessive artifice, complexity, and formalism.

The formal components of parallel prose grew steadily more regular over the course of the Six Dynasties. Parallelism itself was of course the main requirement, and this referred to both grammatical and lexical parallelism. Parallel couplets were the most common form, but, as seen in the *fu*, alternate lines could also be parallel. Unlike *shih* poetry, parallel prose had no formal taboo against repeating the same graph in the same position in two parallel lines. Tetrametric and hexametric lines constituted the vast majority of all parallel prose compositions. Although five- and seven-character lines were not uncommon, these lines were based on tetrametric or hexametric syntax and almost never used the syntactic structures found in pentametric or septametric *shih* poetry. Not infrequently, a section of tetrametric text would have a one- or two-word introductory adverb or particle that would not count, metrically speaking, as part of the line. This was exceedingly rare in *shih* poetry, where line-length strictures were far more rigorous.

It is important for readers of other languages and writing systems to grasp the importance of line length, which has been such an important part of the description here. Line length referred to syllabic and semantic units and had little similarity to measured meter in European languages. What distinguished different line lengths—and lines from three to seven graphs long constituted the vast bulk of the poetic and rhymed genres—was both their syntactic qualities and their intertextual possibilities. Particular line lengths also allowed for a variety of references to specific texts. Over the generations, specific sets of esthetic criteria developed for specific line lengths, and a writer's achievement in hexameter or pentameter would be measured against the hexameters and pentameters of his predecessors. Late in the Six Dynasties, antithetical metrics (where level- and deflected-tone words alternate) became firmly established, as it had in *shih* poetry, and it worked in similar ways. Rhyme never became a regularized formal element in the parallel prose genres until the regulated *fu* of the T'ang and Sung, though rhyme was quite commonly used. Sometimes writers had a section of text completely in tetrameter, followed by a section in alternating hexameter and tetrameter, and used a single rhyme in each section of text. Some compositions were almost wholly unrhymed.

Many critics in and out of China who have written on parallelism in literature trace its roots to the structure of the cosmos itself: parallelism is structurally activated by binaries of the physical and human world such as light and dark, male and female, or above and below. One could also argue, of course, that binarism itself is very much a human and linguistic category, rather than one that inheres as such in the physical world, although it also exists in magnetism, atomic particles, biology, and other natural phenomena. As a compositional principle, however, parallelism permits a variety of expressive modes that became central to Chinese writing. For example, parallelism makes the phrase as a whole more prominent than individual words. This, as indicated above, puts a great weight on syntactic strategies and makes the genre extremely conducive to intertextual strategies such as allusion and quotation. When interrelation itself is the primary compositional principle, the range of interrelation can be multilayered. Accretion of parallel qualities, in which description is at once specific and generalized, is also abetted by parallel construction. As a technique that could appear stale and banal or illuminating and masterful, it lent itself well to the evaluative function, which was important in the many official uses of the genre. Some critics have asserted that parallelism is suited to a literary milieu where texts were commonly recited or memorized. There is no reason, however, to think that this was necessarily the case; parallel prose lends itself no better to memorization or recitation than does common prose. With its dense, allusive texture and often exotic lexicon, it is perhaps the most literary of Literary Sinitic's expressive modalities.

As genre theory took shape at the end of the Han and into the Six Dynasties, particular genres were identified not only by function and formal character but also by the degree of expressivity that the genres permitted. Expressivity was not restricted to private genres; many of the memorial genres demanded a high degree of personal expression. Parallel prose was the favored medium for a number of both semiofficial and "personal" expressive genres; *fu* was only one of many parallel prose genres in the Six Dynasties. Several of the best-known examples of late Han and Six Dynasties *p'ien-wen* were in official memorial genres, including the shorter and somewhat informal *ch'i*, the longer and more official *piao* and *tsou*, and the admonition (*chen*). Dirges, stele biographies, grave memoirs, and other funerary genres had, over the course of the Later Han–Wei period, become central literary genres in parallel prose; the blending of ritual, solemnity, and grief made them appropriate mixtures of the official and the expressive. Letters (*shu*) and disquisitions (*lun*) were more miscellaneous in content, ranging from statements of philosophical, political, or moral principle to expressions of intimate friendship, but both became central parallel prose genres during the Six Dynasties period. With the exception of some work in *fu* form, these were not genres of group composition, although several of the better-known parallel prose works from the period are memorials commissioned by officials and written by court literati "on behalf of" their patrons. *Shih* poetry, in fact, became a more common genre for group composition throughout the southern courts. Many of the Six Dynasties parallel prose genres were court genres, however, and, like Han dynasty court *fu*, flourished in a milieu where epideictic, euphuistic ornament was welcome and appreciated.

By the Chin dynasty (265–420), many of the central features of parallel prose were beginning to fall into place. Lu Chi (261–303), best known to readers as author of "Wen fu" (Rhapsody on Literature), was a prominent official in the Western Chin (265–316) and composed in a variety of genres. His "Ta-jen fu hsü" (Preface to the "Rhapsody on the Great Man") is written in mixed line length, but tetrameter and hexameter predominate, indicating that what later came to be known as the "Four-Six" style was being consolidated and codified. Rhetorical flourishes such as regular alternation of four- and six-character lines show a formal agility that marks a more advanced state of structural development. His "Pien wang lun" (Treatise on the Fall of a State) and "Wu teng lun" (Treatise on the Five Classes of Officials) show the ability of parallel prose to handle both philosophical discussion and historical narrative, an expansion of the mode's thematic and generic scope that would prove important for its subsequent history and that would earn Lu Chi a central place in the history of the genre.

The Chin dynasty was fairly decentralized politically, and there were centers of literary activity at the courts of various princes. The political intrigues in the Chin made these patterns of association both necessary and dangerous, and it was not uncommon for writers to meet bad ends because of the misfortunes of a patron. As in the late Han, regional courts were interested in attracting literary talent, who congregated in various salonlike groups. One such group was the "twenty-four friends of Chia Mi," which included two other prominent literati of the period, Tso Ssu and P'an Yüeh (247–300). Both of them are renowned for work in *shih* poetry and in the parallel prose genres. Tso Ssu's "Rhapsody on the Three Capitals," which consists of a preface and three *fu*, are among the best known and most highly acclaimed *fu* of all time. Tso Ssu's preface explains that he modeled his *fu* after Chang Heng's *fu* on the capitals, mentioned above. The comparison is apt: Tso's are long *fu*, ranging from four hundred to more than eight hundred lines. Tetrameter predominates, but Tso also makes frequent use of hexametric and septametric lines based on *sao* style: X X X particle X X or X X X X particle X X, the former being a common Chin dynasty hexameter form. Tso's parallelism also shows Han influence: several tetrametric or trimetric lines in a row will all be parallel, for example. Rhyme is irregular and shifting. Thematically, Tso's poems differ from his predecessor's in their descriptive detail: Chang Heng's *fu* focus far more on the court and the emperor; Tso's are simultaneously more encyclopedic and more descriptively precise. Tso makes considerable reference to historical events, as did Chang, but Tso puts a greater emphasis on daily life. The language of Tso's *fu* is less embellished and allusion-laden, however, than the *fu* of later generations, one reason that Tso's *fu* were generally not cited as examples of the excessive rhetoric of Six Dynasties parallel prose. P'an Yüeh's literary reputation comes largely from his *fu* and *shih* poetry, which have been judged more "personal" and expressive, and less weighty, than those of his near-contemporary Lu Chi. The bulk of P'an's parallel prose is in the *fu* or in the funerary genres; his dirges (*lei*) are especially noteworthy for the inclusion of the author's personal grief, which was more rarely the case in earlier dirges. Many of P'an's *fu* are shorter pieces on objects. These are usually under one hundred lines and treat topics such as the mouth-organ, the orange, and the hibiscus. They are reminiscent of the shorter *fu* at the end of the Later Han and could have been composed in similar group milieus.

By the end of the Chin dynasty, parallel prose had developed many of the characteristics with which the category was subsequently associated. However, certain of the mode's best-known writers continued to write in a fairly unadorned style that belied the effusive, elaborate, highly ornamental reputation of Six Dynasties parallel prose. In the (Liu) Sung dynasty (420–479), parallel prose became more ornate, more allusive, more intertextual, and technically more regular and more complex. Several Sung emperors were acclaimed for their literary production, and many of the aristocratic families of the period, like Hsieh Ling-yün's (385–433), included prominent writers. By the time of the Chin and Sung dynasties, *shih* poetry had also become a central literati genre, and certain writers were better known for their *shih*.

Yen Yen-chih (384–456) was acknowledged as the master of Sung parallel prose, with Hsieh Ling-yün closely following him. Yen Yen-chih excelled in a variety of parallel prose genres. His "San yüeh san jih Ch'ü shui shih hsü" (Preface to the Winding Stream Poems, Composed on the Festival of the Third Day of the Third Month), written on imperial command, is far more intricate and regular in its parallelism than were Chin dynasty compositions. Tetrameter and hexameter predominate, and parallelism ranges from single to multiple lines per unit. The *sao*-style hexameter is a less dominant syntactic structure in Yen's prose. The strictness of Yen's parallelism and the marked regularity of his antithetical prosody suggest that a new level of technical exactitude had been reached. Among his other well-known compositions are dirges, including one for his friend T'ao Ch'ien and a lament for Ch'ü Yüan, letters, and memorials. His work was densely allusive, and his source texts were primarily the classics, but also histories, pre-Ch'in philosophy, and other Han and pre-Han miscellanea. With Yen Yen-chih, all the elements of Six Dynasties parallel prose, including tonal prosody, are finally assembled.

Under the Ch'i (479–502) and Liang (502–557) dynasties, imperial patronage of literature continued to flourish. Members of the imperial family were themselves among the period's foremost composers of parallel prose: Hsiao T'ung (501–531), compiler of *Wen hsüan* (Literary Selections), and Hsiao Kang (503–551), Emperor Chien-wen of the Liang, are two examples. The Ch'i-Liang period was also the era of poetry groups, such as the famous Eight Masters of Chin-ling, and of the phonetic regularization of *shih* poetry advocated by its members—the Yung-ming style, as it was then called. This was also the age of Liu Hsieh's *Literary Mind and the Carving of Dragons* and of that major codification of Six Dynasties literary taste and canonicity, *Literary Selections*. The tonal and prosodic regularity established in poetry was also used in parallel prose; tonal antiphony was much more regularly followed in the Ch'i-Liang and afterward. Indeed, one of the masters of Ch'i-Liang parallel prose was Shen Yüeh, with whom the new *shih* prosody is most closely associated. The various parallel prose genres gave greater opportunity for allusive density and intertextuality than did even *shih* poetry, which in this period was confined largely to the Palace Style. Because of all these phenomena, critics and literary historians from the T'ang onward have referred to the Ch'i-Liang period as the height of bellettrism in China. As readers of this volume are well aware, this is not a compliment: mainstream esthetic taste in the imperial period generally regarded excessive verbal elegance and formal exactitude as threats to moral and ethical substance.

The parallel prose masters of the first half of this period—including Wang Jung (468–493), Hsieh T'iao (464–499), Shen Yüeh (441–513), Chiang Yen (444–505), Wu Chün (469–520), and Jen Fang (460–508)—were masters of many parallel prose genres, and most were also acclaimed *shih* poets as well. Several, like Wang Jung and Shen Yüeh, were among the first to experiment with prosodic rules in *shih* poetry by adopting Sanskritic practices brought to China with Buddhism. Shen Yüeh, probably the single foremost literatus of the period, has left a substantial body of parallel prose, which is spread among a great variety of genres, including official ones like edicts and the various memorial genres. Among Wang Jung's most renowned parallel prose pieces are his "Preface to the Winding Stream Poems," modeled after Yen Yen-chih's preface of the same title and also written on command, and his "Yung-ming chiu nien ts'e hsiu-ts'ai wen" (Five Topics for the 491 C.E. Hsiu-ts'ai [Licentiate] Examination). This latter set of pieces was composed on imperial command as topics for imperial examination. The topics are written in highly allusive language and are in complex and elegant parallel prose lines, with tetrameter predominating. It would have been quite a challenge for a candidate's essays to match the topics themselves in allusive density and verbal complexity.

In the judgment of later critics, the apotheosis of the Ch'i-Liang parallel prose esthetic was reached in the work of Hsü Ling (507–583) and Yü Hsin (513–581), who, while at the Liang court, gave their names to a style of palace poetry that literary historians view as the direct antecedent of T'ang dynasty court poetry. Hsü Ling, a central figure in Hsiao Kang's court, is now best known as the compiler of the *Yü-t'ai hsin-yung* (New Songs from a Jade Terrace). As a powerful and influential courtier, Yü produced work in all genres, including perhaps the best-known piece of Six Dynasties *fu:* "Ai Chiang-nan fu" (Rhapsody Lamenting the South). This piece, composed during a period of northern exile which lent a melancholy tone to much of his later work, has been judged as unsurpassed in its ability to combine typical Ch'i-Liang figural density, formal regularity and control, and depth of feeling. This piece is largely responsible for the way the two writers are distinguished: Hsü's prose is said to be more philosophical, more narrative; Yü's more expressive and emotional. Both writers' prose showed greater prosodic regularity than the work of the earlier Ch'i-Liang authors and a wider allusive range, with more reference to late Han and early Six Dynasties literary work. Similarly, both authors show a mastery of literary history and a sense of historically determined style that surpassed their predecessors'.

The dominance of tetrametric and hexametric lines complemented the pentametric dominance in poetry. When writers wrote pentametric lines in parallel prose, they avoided the standard two-three syntactical division of *shih* poetry and wrote pentametric lines that divided differently. Antiphonal tonal alternation in parallel lines was most rigorously observed in two graphs per line, the positions of which were dependent on syntax and caesura placement, which were naturally more flexible in the hexameters than in the tetrameters. In the work of Yü Hsin and Hsü Ling, the Four-Six style reaches a recognizable stylistic maturity. Parallelism is used with greater variety and sophistication, particularly the alternating tetrametric-hexametric line couplets for which Yü Hsin is so famous. The complex and varied ways in which Yü and Hsü alternate tetrameter and hexameter reinvigorated the forms. Although Ch'i-Liang *fu* included other longer and more expressive pieces, such as Yü Hsin's "Rhapsody Lamenting the South," the dominant mode for *fu* continued to be the shorter *fu* on objects, which arose at the end of the Later Han. These also became more regular prosodically and were the source for the T'ang dynasty development of the regulated *fu*, which were to be used in examinations.

The allusive density of Ch'i-Liang parallel prose is one component of the period's pervasive tropological density. A fundamental esthetic of the early Han *fu*—accumulation and enumeration of qualities—had transformed itself, in parallel prose, into an esthetic of resonant accretion: allusions and other tropes linked the prose to a limitless range of writing, where a single piece could contain a volume of textual history within it. Allusion was a perfect trope through which an author could inscribe into the surface texture of a composition—the words themselves—a canonized body of civilizational content. Allusions were of many kinds, and frequently a seemingly inconsequential line or two-graph expression would be an allusion, a trope seemed designed to build into the text a variety of different readings, some more sophisticated and perceptive than others. Occasionally, a writer would allude to a version of the source text that he had rearranged. Liu Hsieh's line in the *Literary Mind and the Carving of Dragons*—"Words travel far due to their literary quality" (*yen yi wen yüan*)—is a contracted version of the famous *Tso Commentary* lines "words without literary qualities will not travel far" (*yen chih wu wen, hsing erh pu yüan*). Yü Hsin's allusions were not only to words, but even to the tone and diction of his literary predecessors, such as Juan Chi (210–263) of the Wei period (220–265). In Yü Hsin's parallel prose, particularly the *fu*, a varied stylistic vocabulary complements the intertextual range, and all contribute to the affective unity of his compositions.

PARALLEL PROSE AND THE REGULATED *FU* OF THE T'ANG-SUNG PERIOD

The literary landscape at the end of the Six Dynasties was quite different from that at the end of the Han. During the Han, *shih* poetry was a nascent and minor genre, and nonparallel prose was common in official and nonofficial writing. By the time of *Literary Selections*'s compilation, *shih* and *fu* were the two central belletristic genres, and parallel prose was pervasive in court literary production. Beginning in the early T'ang, *shih* poetry grew in importance, in official and in unofficial contexts, and parallel prose retained its central position as an official form. After Yü Hsin and Hsü Ling's time, however, with the exception of the regulated *fu*, innovation within parallel prose genres came about primarily through the admixture of syntax and esthetics from the "ancient style." The polemics of the "revive antiquity" (*fu-ku*) movement and the rise of ancient-style (*ku-wen*) prose, a mode that reached fruition in the work of Han Yü (768–824) and Liu Tsung-yüan (773–819), criticized Six Dynasties court parallel prose as artificial and overelaborate, a criticism that recurred over several centuries. To judge parallel prose as artificial and elaborate is, of course, to use the language of the antiquity partisans. In fact, parallel prose and ancient-style prose had considerable areas of overlap and mutual influence. There are examples of Han Yü's ancient-style prose that are full of parallelism, tetrameter and hexameter, and other formal features associated with parallel prose genres. The ancient-style movement referred more to tone and content than to form, and its ascendancy was concurrent with changes in the nature of literati life and practice, both of which had become far more diverse than in the early T'ang. From the T'ang through the Ch'ing, parallel prose and its related modes enjoyed varying degrees of official recognition. In the T'ang and beyond, a highly regulated parallel prose was the required mode for examinations, but after the mid-T'ang, parallel prose ceased to be the central and all-pervasive mode of Literary Sinitic.

The first stylists credited with bringing about a major change in T'ang parallel prose were the officials Chang Yüeh (667–731) and Su T'ing (670–727), who were literary arbiters in the first part of Emperor Hsüan-tsung's reign (712–756). Their work has much less of the performative accretion of qualities that typified the Ch'i-Liang and more of the directness and communicative versatility of Han-Wei parallel prose, which they took as a model. Their greatest prose achievements are their prefaces and their work in the funerary genres. Tetrameter and hexameter predominate, but allusions and diction stick more closely to the classics than did early T'ang writings. Lu Chih (754–805), a member of the Han-lin Academy who made the rare transition from the academy to the official bureaucracy, serving as Chief Minister to Emperor Te-tsung (r. 780–805), used parallel prose in such a broad way, for narrative and argument rather than the strictly expressive genres, and with so much admixture of ancient-style diction, style, and tone that he is given a low ranking in appraisals of parallel prose based on formal qualities alone. Still, his was certainly the apotheosis of the parallel prose—ancient-style admixture, and his influence on later developments in the mode was decisive. The final innovation in T'ang parallel prose—that of Li Shang-yin (811?–859) and his contemporaries—continued the expansion of scope that Lu Chih had given the form, but added a greater variety of linguistic registers and greatly increased the level of formal complexity. Li Shang-yin used the form in many official and personal expressive genres and surpassed many of his T'ang predecessors in affective depth. His parallel lines occasionally formed syntactic units of great length; the complication of the relation between line and syntax added a level of technical complexity that some later critics condemned as hyperesthetic excess but that also led directly to the Sung dynasty Four-Six style.

Regulated *fu* were a special kind of rhapsody used in examinations throughout the T'ang and Sung. Formally, regulated *fu* continued the main tradition of the parallel *fu* that had developed in the Six Dynasties, but insisted on adherence to strict parallelism and added a new strictness in rhyme scheme. A four- to eight-graph quotation from antiquity—usually the classics—would supply both the rhyme scheme and the essay topic. Toward the end of the T'ang, regulated *fu* were composed with multiline parallel constructions, a practice that continued into the Sung. Regulated *fu* were fairly short and followed tonal antiphony fairly rigorously. Since the genre was used as an examination form, it had something of the taint of the hyperformal, but it was canonical enough that the poet Po Chü-yi was well known for his regulated *fu*. Po's regulated *fu*, written in a clear, plain style, often touched on quite personal expressive themes. A more palpable organizational logic was beginning to be evident in late T'ang and Sung regulated *fu*, one that many critics saw as the precursor to the eight-legged essay. The connective phrases—one- or two-graph elements that meant things like "thereby," "therefore," or "and then"—acquired greater importance in logical construction. The Sung regulated *fu* differed little from those of the T'ang, but they did show more influence from the prose *fu* (*wen-fu*), a major revision of the genre that began in the T'ang and became very popular among Sung ancient-style prose stylists like Ou-yang Hsiu (1007–1072) and Su Shih. Su Shih and Ou-yang Hsiu were also acclaimed stylists in regulated *fu* and were known for their clarity, brilliant parallelism, and sophisticated admixture of ancient-style and parallel prose elements.

Sung period parallel prose usually goes by the name of Four-Six style, which represented the last major stylistic shift in parallel prose, with the possible exception of the eight-legged essay. Four-Six refers to the common phrase length, and it was mostly restricted to the memorial genres: *chao, chih, piao,* and *ch'i,* which were distinguished by the relative ranks of writer and addressee. By the Sung, ancient-style prose and prose *fu* were already the common modes for personal expressive pieces. What distinguished Sung Four-Six style, though, was the length of the syntactic elements, which sometimes extended through tens of tetrametric or hexametric couplets to form larger syntactic units in the ancient style. This practice was not wholly new—it was seen in the T'ang—but the Sung carried it to greater length than previously. The greater length of the syntactic unit meant that the couplets within could display considerable craft: quotations from the classics would be parallel to other quotations from the classics, historical allusion would be parallel to historical allusion, and so on. Quotations and allusions, in fact, were a hallmark of the style. The generic scope of the Four-Six style generally emphasized argument and logic. Sung Four-Six parallel prose is often criticized for the elaborateness and length of its segments, but even its critics acknowledge the genre's capacity for logical exposition.

THE "PROSE *FU*" OF THE T'ANG AND SUNG DYNASTIES

The ancient-style prose movement that began in the T'ang dynasty often makes critics and literary historians draw too rigid distinctions between the parallel and nonparallel prose forms. Even at their most rigid, the parallel prose genres were far looser in line length, parallelism itself, and rhyme than the poetic genres were. As passages above indicate, parallel prose and ancient-style prose existed on a continuum, rather than on two sides of a great divide. The prose *fu,* which most critics trace to Tu Mu (803–852), reaches its height in the Sung, in the work of Ou-yang Hsiu, Su Shih, and Yang Wan-li (1124–1206). Su Shih's "Ch'ih-pi fu" (Rhapsody on the Red Cliff, parts 1 and 2) are arguably the best-known *fu* in the world, having been widely anthologized in the original and in translation. Prose *fu* are generally in mixed tetrameter and hexameter, with considerable admixture of lines of irregular length. Rhyme is loose, though common, and parallelism itself is generally restricted to lines of heightened evocative force. Some critics have remarked that Later Han and Wei *fu* could be said to satisfy all the formal requirements of Sung prose *fu.* The social and official character of the two *fu* modes are, however, completely different. Sung prose *fu* were primarily private, expressive genres. They could be used for philosophical argument, but also for travel pieces and other narratives or lyrical expression, as in Ou-yang Hsiu's famous "Ch'iu-sheng fu" (Rhapsody on the Sounds of Autumn). What made these pieces *fu,* as opposed to simple prose, was the use of rhyme and of parallelism, which, while not predominant, were clearly positioned for expressive and rhetorical effect.

MING-CH'ING PARALLEL PROSE AND *FU*

With limited exceptions, parallel prose lost its official sanction in the Chin-Yüan period. In that period and after, official and nonofficial prose tended to be written in ancient style. Prose *fu* all but disappeared. Regulated *fu* survived in the examinations, and parallel prose was required in a restricted number of official documentary genres in the Ming dynasty (1368–1644). The Ch'ing dynasty saw a great revival of parallel prose. Its outstanding practitioners were concentrated in the eighteenth century and consciously modeled their own styles after a study and internalization of period styles from the Sung and earlier. Although it is common in literary histories to describe Ch'ing parallel prose writers as being of the Han-Wei school, or the Ch'i-Liang school, or the Sung Four-Six school, Ch'ing writers were considerably more versatile than such labels suggest. The work of the most acclaimed Ch'ing parallel prose stylists, such as poet and calligrapher Wang Chung (1745–1794), Wu Hsi-ch'i (1746–1818), compiler of *Ch'üan T'ang wen* (Complete T'ang Prose), and Hung Liang-chi (1746–1809), showed an internalization of the entire history of the genre, with only the syntactic elaboration of the Sung Four-Six style being absent. They wrote in a variety of genres, and some of their best-known pieces are in the prefatory and funerary genres. Juan Yüan (1764–1849), the well-known lexicographer, classicist, editor, philologist, mathematician, and historian, was a champion of parallel prose against the ancient-style hegemony that had been achieved by the T'ung-ch'eng school (an eighteenth-century group of prose stylists based in Anhwei province). Juan Yüan, who was a scholar of parallel prose as well as an author, made the argument that, for writing to be called "literary" or "patterned" (*wen*), as opposed to mere words or speech, it had to have a pattern and that parallel prose was the pattern most expressive of the genius of the Chinese language.

The examination essays of the Ming and Ch'ing dynasties, the famous eight-legged essays, derive ultimately from the regulated *fu* examination form of the T'ang and Sung periods. By the end of the fifteenth century, the eight-legged essay assumed its mature form and, because of its position as the official examination genre, achieved a stylistic and expressive hegemony that put it in a class of its own. Books of examination essays were very popular throughout the period and were used for examination preparation and stylistic refinement. The topics of eight-legged essays were quotations from the classics, and the length was set at anywhere from three hundred to six hundred graphs. The rhetoric, organization, and scholarly orientation of the essays were strictly prescribed, as were sections where parallelism was obligatory or optional. Neither rhyme nor tonal antiphony was expected. The bare format is straightforward: introduction, main body, and conclusion, but the argument does not "progress" in a linear way. Since all explications followed the Neo-Confucian Ch'eng-Chu orthodoxy that had its foundations in the eleventh and twelfth centuries, what was valued in the eight-legged essay was not argumentative logic, but evidence of the candidate's wide learning as revealed in verbal and referential patterns, intertextual reference, and exegetical resonance—all tropes to which parallel construction was eminently suited. In certain sections of the essay, the author was required to speak in his own voice; in others in the voice of the sage. References to the topic were also prescribed, in different sections, as to degree of directness or paraphrase. The middle sections of the essay—the "legs"—contained obligatory parallel lines, with the number of lines usually unfixed. Here, the candidate's learning was most on display.

The absence of rhyme is one reason not to include eight-legged essays within the parallel prose mode, and some critics follow that criterion. But since the form is seen in its nascent state in several parallel prose styles, and since its fundamental logic is the logic of parallelism, it makes sense to include it here. None of the parallel prose genres translates particularly well into English, and eight-legged essay translations tend to be nearly unreadable. Still, the reader will understand much about late imperial logic, narrative, and thought through a consideration of the patterned, reticulated logic of argumentation and reference, the suggestive elaboration, and the intertextual linkages that give structure to the eight-legged essay. In this sense, the eight-legged essay represented a bureaucratized apotheosis of what we would understand as the entire parallel prose project: an official architecture of expression through an emphasis on what were perceived to be the writing system's fundamental linguistic, textual, cosmo-political, and social patterns.

Christopher Leigh Connery

Chapter 13

POETRY FROM 200 B.C.E. TO 600 C.E.

During the long period covered by this chapter, crucial developments took place in Chinese poetry, and extraordinary poets composed works that left a lasting mark on all subsequent verse. These were the centuries when Chinese poetry developed many of its constitutive characteristics. One of the principal problems in attempting to write about so long and fundamental a period in so limited a space is the need to speak in generalities, to characterize periods and writers in a few strokes without letting them speak with the full range of their voices. In some cases this may actually be a blessing, but in most it is an injustice. Furthermore, some poets and types of poetry simply have to be omitted. Many deserving human poets find no place here, much less divine beings like those of Shang-ch'ing Taoism, who purportedly recited verses to their earthly amanuensis Yang Hsi (330–386) in the fourth century (see chapter 10).

Despite the dictates of chronology and the tyranny of space, several important threads will become apparent, among them the evolution of the pentasyllabic line; the gradual recognition of the tonal nature of Chinese and the manipulation and codification of tonal sequences in the march toward regulated verse; the prominence of imitation and intertextuality; the shift from a more direct, public, and universal poetry to a more ornate, elite, and court-centered one; the tension between old values and new; the conspicuous roles of patronage and literary coteries in the development of poetic styles; the unfolding and growth of new poetic subgenres; and above all the extraordinary richness and exuberance of poetry during these centuries.

THE HAN DYNASTY: *CH'U KO* (CH'U SONGS)

Han dynasty (206 B.C.E.–220 C.E.) poetry consists mainly of tetrasyllabic-line poems, poems in the Ch'u *ko* or Ch'u *sheng* (Ch'u Song) form, and pentasyllabic-line poems. At the beginning of the Han, poetry remained metrically close to the *Shih-ching* (Classic of Poetry) in its continued use of the tetrasyllabic line, particularly for ritual hymns, and to the *Ch'u tz'u* (Elegies of Ch'u) tradition through the literary form called Ch'u Songs. These Ch'u Songs are short pieces, metrically similar to the "Chiu ko" (Nine Songs), and were probably sung to music associated with the Ch'u region in southern China. The fundamental pattern is a line of two hemistiches of three characters each separated by the syllable *hsi* (which functions like a breath-mark or caesura), though there are variations. Ch'u Songs tend to have a melancholy air, and they are often presented as having been improvised at moments of peak emotion. Thus there are elements of orality and lyricism associated with them. Two of the best known are connected with the principal rivals for control of China at the end of the Ch'in dynasty (221–207 B.C.E.)—Hsiang Yü (233–202 B.C.E.) and Liu Pang (247–195 B.C.E.), the eventual Han founder. Hsiang Yü's poem, entitled "Kai-hsia ko" (Song of Kai-hsia), is supposed to have been composed spontaneously when he realized that his defeat was at hand. Liu Pang's "Ta feng ko" (Song of the Great Wind) is reported to have been extemporized at a banquet in P'ei, his hometown. Even in triumph and celebration a note of anxiety haunts Liu Pang's piece: "A great wind arose, and clouds scudded and flew. / With might that bears on all the world, I return to my native home. / From whence will come brave men to secure the four directions?" Emperor Wu (r. 141–87 B.C.E.) of the Han also composed a famous Ch'u Song entitled "Ch'iu feng tz'u" (Autumn Wind) that expresses sadness over the impermanence of things. Ch'u Songs continued to be written throughout the Han, and some of the Han ritual *yüeh-fu* (Music Bureau, or ballad) poems can prosodically, if not contextually, be viewed as Ch'u Songs.

THE HAN DYNASTY: PENTASYLLABIC- AND HEPTASYLLABIC-LINE *SHIH* POETRY

The poetic line of five syllables, one of the most fundamental prosodic units in the Chinese literary tradition, is already found among the Han *yüeh-fu*. While those pieces are not datable, this line length does appear in works that are clearly from the Former Han (206 B.C.E.–8 C.E.). One famous example is Li Yen-nien's *yüeh-fu* in six lines "Li fu-jen ko" (Song of Lady Li), which has one heptasyllabic line. There is controversy over the authenticity of some pentasyllabic-line poems credited to Former Han poets. The *yüeh-fu* "Yüan ko hsing" (Song of Complaint), attributed to Favorite Beauty Pan, a consort of Emperor Ch'eng

(r. 32–7 B.C.E.), is one of them, for it does not appear in any text before the sixth century. The song was supposedly composed after she fell out of favor with the emperor. If authentic, it would be an early example of a poem on an object (*yung-wu shih*), a type of poem describing a thing that was popular in later times. "Song of Complaint" is constructed around the metaphor of a fan, which may be used and then put aside. Whether or not this and other pentasyllabic-line poems linked to the Former Han by various sources are authentic, this sort of poetry did not have any great currency among the top writers of the time.

Some pentasyllabic-line poems traditionally ascribed to the Former Han are not *yüeh-fu* at all but *ku-shih* (old poems), a rubric applied to untitled old poems whose authorship was unknown or uncertain. *Shih*, a general name for poetry, also designates non-*yüeh-fu* poetry. The distinction between *ku-shih* and *yüeh-fu* is not always clear, and the same poem may be designated one or the other in different sources. One way of looking at the problem is to view poems classified as Han *ku-shih* as dissociated from the musical and performance context originally important to songs called *yüeh-fu*. An example of this is the poem known as "Shih-wu ts'ung-chün cheng" (At Fifteen I Went for a Soldier), which is about a man returning home after long years at war, only to find his family dead and his homestead in ruins. This piece, which can be considered a *ku-shih*, is found embedded in a *yüeh-fu* poem that was clearly meant to be performed.

Among the most famous of the *ku-shih* are the Su Wu–Li Ling poems. Li Ling (d. 74 B.C.E.), the Han general that the historian Ssu-ma Ch'ien was castrated for defending (see chapter 26), had surrendered to the non-Chinese Hsiung-nu confederation (northern nomads linked with the Huns who later threatened Europe). Su Wu (140–60 B.C.E.) was a Han envoy who was also held by the Hsiung-nu. After nearly twenty years, Su returned to China proper in 81 B.C.E., while Li remained with the Hsiung-nu. *Wen hsüan* (Literary Selections), compiled by Hsiao T'ung (501–531), contains three poems attributed to Li and four attributed to Su that they supposedly wrote to each other. These poems seem quite developed, and their authorship was in doubt as early as the fourth century. Modern scholarship generally places them no earlier than Later Han. Other poems attributed to the pair are found in other sources, and there were still more that exist only in fragments. Probably the story of their famous friendship simply provided material for unidentified later poets, who wrote *about* them. It is because of the highly dubious authenticity of these poems that they can be called *ku-shih*, but, given the existence of a Ch'u song purportedly extemporized by Li at a farewell banquet for Su and preserved in Su's biography in the *Han shu* (History of the Han Dynasty), it is not impossible that parts of the poems extant today are in fact his words or versions of them from some unknown source.

The most renowned and influential *ku-shih* is the grouping found in *Literary Selections* under the title "Ku-shih shih-chiu shou" (Nineteen Old Poems).

These pieces treat many common themes, such as the absent lover, *carpe diem*, and the brevity of life, and they address these themes in a generic fashion, so the poems are not tied to any particular person or context. It is not known when they were written or who wrote them. Many scholars believe that they were composed during the second century C.E., but attempts to link them to specific authors have not been convincing. They are quite similar to the anonymous *yüeh-fu* of Han, and at least ten of them have been so classified at times. Number 15, with some differences, even appears as part of the *yüeh-fu* "Hsi men hsing" (West Gate). The equivocal status of the "Nineteen Old Poems" and "At Fifteen I Went for a Soldier" hints that *ku-shih* may have had their origins in *yüeh-fu*.

The first reliable attributions of pentasyllabic-line poems to known poets are to Later Han figures. The poem often mentioned as the first true pentasyllabic-line poem by such a writer is "Yung-shih shih" (Poem on History) by the Han historian and rhapsodist Pan Ku. It is a rather plain piece recounting in verse the story of a daughter's rescue of her father from official punishment. Another famous rhapsodist who has left a pentasyllabic-line poem is the great polymath Chang Heng (78–139). The poem is an epithalamium entitled "T'ung sheng ko" (Song of Harmonious Sounds). On leaving to assume a post in Loyang, Ch'in Chia (mid-second century) wrote four "Tseng fu shih" (Poems for My Wife), three pentasyllabic and one tetrasyllabic. There are two "Hsien chih shih" (Poems Expressing My Aims) by Li Yen (150–177), and two pentasyllabic-line poems are contained in Chao Yi's (d. c. 185) satirical rhapsody "Tz'u shih chi hsieh fu" (Rhapsody on Satirizing the World and Denouncing Evil). A further pentasyllabic-line poem by a literatus poet, "Ts'ui niao shih" (Kingfisher), comes from Ts'ai Yung (133–192), the leading scholar and writer of his day. This piece on the kingfisher is a poem on an object. Ts'ai Yung is known in part for writing *fu* on small objects, so although the heyday of poems on objects was still three centuries away, their indebtedness to *fu* on objects (*yung-wu fu*) is already adumbrated here.

Chang Heng was also responsible for one of the earliest heptasyllabic-line poems. This line form, which derives from Ch'u song and *Elegies of Ch'u* prosody, would eventually take its place alongside the five-syllable line as one of the most common prosodic frameworks in Chinese poetry. Chang used it in his "Ssu ch'ou shih" (Poem of Four Sorrows), a possibly allegorical poem in which the speaker fails at wooing four beauties.

DISINTEGRATION

The years from about 184 to 205 constitute a turning point in Chinese literary life. The Yellow Turban Uprising of 184 (a millenarian rebellious movement whose adherents wore yellow headgear) weakened the central government, and a struggle between eunuchs and imperial relatives in the late 180s shattered both groups and drove them from the political stage, leaving military leaders as the main holders of power. Soon Ts'ao Ts'ao (155–220) became the most powerful single figure in China. In 196 he took the last Han emperor under his protection, and by 205 he had gained control of a significant part of northern China and set up his base of power in the city of Yeh, where writers of distinction gathered for security and patronage. His son Ts'ao P'i (187–226) eventually forced the abdication of the Han sovereign and founded the Wei dynasty (220–265). Since Wei was unable to conquer its chief rivals, China split into the three contending states of Wei, Wu (222–280), and Shu (221–263).

With the initial division of the empire into three states (the so-called San kuo or "Three Kingdoms"), China embarked upon a long period of disunion, turmoil, and instability. Except for the brief Chin (or Western Chin, 265–316) period, this fragmentation was to last for the next three and a half centuries. The Chin, beset by external pressure from the Hsiung-nu confederation to the north and its own internal difficulties, was forced to relinquish control of north China and withdraw to the south to continue its existence as the Eastern Chin (317–420). While a succession of alien states occupied north China, Chinese rule continued in the south, where the Eastern Chin maintained itself for some time. But, taking advantage of rebellion and turmoil, an Eastern Chin general, Liu Yü (d. 422), eventually became strong enough to proclaim himself emperor of the Liu Sung dynasty in 420. In 479, a powerful Liu Sung subject, Hsiao Tao-ch'eng, set aside the reigning Sung emperor and took the throne as ruler of a new dynasty, Ch'i, which lasted until 502. Ch'i was supplanted by Liang (502–557), which in turn succumbed to Ch'en (557–589). In 589, the Sui dynasty reunified China under Chinese control and opened the way for the T'ang (618–907).

North China, too, saw the rise of a succession of mostly non-Sinitic states. The Altaic T'o-pa (Tabgatch) people moved into northern China in the wake of the Hsiung-nu push south. They declared their state of Wei (Northern Wei, 386–534) in 386 and subdued their rivals in the north by 439. The T'o-pa underwent gradual sinicization until the late fifth century, when Emperor Wen made it a deliberate policy. He moved his capital from present-day Ta-t'ung in northern Shansi to Loyang, a traditional Chinese capital, and made Chinese the exclusive court language. Revolts in 524 led to the formation a decade later of the Eastern and Western Wei, which gave way to the Northern Ch'i in 550 and the Northern Chou in 557.

This period of disunion from the end of the Han to the T'ang is known as the early medieval period. The term Six Dynasties (Liu-ch'ao) is most commonly used to refer to the six southern dynasties that had their capital at Chien-k'ang (modern-day Nanking): Wu, Eastern Chin, Sung, Ch'i, Liang, and Ch'en. It is also customary to refer to the whole period as the Wei, Chin, and Southern and Northern Dynasties (Nan-pei-ch'ao). Literary studies have tended to focus on the writers of the South, although studies of northern literature are increasing.

During the political instability and upheavals of the early medieval period, major cultural developments occurred. Celestial Master Taoism (T'ien-shih tao), which had grown up in the region of modern-day Szechwan and Shensi, spread to Loyang when the leader of the sect, Chang Lu, surrendered to Ts'ao Ts'ao in 215. From there it spread south in the great migrations of the first two decades of the fourth century, where it contributed to the growth of the Shang-ch'ing and Ling-pao scriptural and liturgical traditions of Taoism (see chapter 10). At the same time, Buddhism was establishing itself in China and became important in both north and south, finding adherents among the royal houses, undergoing translation and transformation, and working its influence on autochthonous Chinese religion and literature (see chapter 9). The arts of painting, calligraphy, sculpture, and literature all reached a high level of achievement, and poetry in particular enjoyed great esteem. Well before the end of the early medieval period, poetic achievement had a definite cachet, both for individuals and for aristocratic families. Literary circles were important, and contact among poets, often in a court setting, strongly influenced the development of themes and styles. Although coteries of writers existed earlier, the Chien-an period, at the very beginning of the early medieval age, provides the first true example of a close-knit literary group.

THE CHIEN-AN PERIOD

Chien-an refers to the final reign-period (196–220) of the Han dynasty, but the literary period of that name both begins earlier and ends later. The dates 184–240 are about right, but perhaps it is best simply to understand that Chien-an literature refers to the works of a specific group of writers active around the end of the second century and the beginning of the third. Thus the Chien-an period overlaps the end of the Han and the beginning of the Wei.

Works of great and enduring value in a variety of genres exist in significant numbers from the Han and earlier periods, but the end of the Han marks the beginning of an unprecedented burst of literary activity. As the initial phase of this early medieval period, Chien-an was a time of important developments and innovations in poetic genres and an age dominated by a circle of talented writers who were keenly conscious of one another's work. Leading Chien-an poets include Ts'ao Ts'ao, who was the chief political and military leader of his day, and his sons Ts'ao P'i (Emperor Wen of Wei; r. 220–226) and Ts'ao Chih (192–232), as well as the Seven Masters of the Chien-an Period (Chien-an ch'i tzu): K'ung Jung (153–208), Ch'en Lin (c. 157–217), Wang Ts'an (177–217), Hsü Kan (171–218), Juan Yü (c. 165–212), Ying Yang (d. 217), and Liu Chen (d. 217).

The corpus of surviving Chien-an poems is not large. Only four poems by Ch'en Lin survive and about seventy by Ts'ao Chih. But Chien-an poetry is held in high esteem and has had a powerful influence on subsequent Chinese verse. Literature was clearly important to the Ts'aos and their followers.

Collecting, compiling, and editing were serious undertakings. Ts'ao P'i was a leader in this area, having personally worked on a collection of the works of Hsü Kan, Ch'en Lin, Ying Yang, and Liu Chen, all of whom passed away in the great epidemic of 217. He also collected the writings of K'ung Jung. And, after Ts'ao Chih died, his nephew Ts'ao Jui (Emperor Ming; r. 227–239) ordered the collection of his works.

With textual conservation came new ideas about literature. The pre-Han and Han pragmatic view of literature, which tended to view poetry as a moral and didactic medium, gradually gave way with the failure of the Han polity. Although ideas about the didactic function of literature never died out, and were voiced even late in the early medieval period by some critics, literature as literature came into its own in Chien-an times. Lu Hsün (see chapter 39) called it the Age of Literary Self-Awareness (*wen-hsüeh tzu-chüeh te shih-tai*) and linked it to the concept of "art for art's sake." The old axiom from the *Tso chuan* (Tso Commentary) that the three ways to immortal fame were, in descending order of preference, through virtue, deeds, and words still held true. But literature had gained ground.

The Chien-an poets established subgenres and themes that were to endure throughout much of subsequent Chinese literary history. Unlike the "Nineteen Old Poems," their poetry tends to be closely tied to the events of their age and to their lives, although their *yüeh-fu* are sometimes less so than their *shih*. They wrote poems on history, feast poems (*yen-hui shih*), sightseeing poems (*yu-lan shi*), poems of presentation and response (*tseng-ta shih*), poems on roaming into the world of immortals (*yu-hsien shih*), and poems on lonely or abandoned women (*yüan-nü shih* or *ch'i-fu shih*). Topics included separation, political turmoil, personal aspirations and frustrations, praise for superiors, the hardships of the times and the plight of the dispossessed, the plight of women, and military campaigns. Poems on widows, cockfighting, and the depiction of beautiful women reveal interaction with the *fu* genre.

Poets used a variety of forms. They continued to employ the tetrasyllabic line, which remained fairly common and was the forte of Ts'ao Ts'ao in particular; they wrote poems in mixed-length lines; and they even employed the hexasyllabic line. But their major achievement in prosodic form was unquestionably the pentasyllabic line. Frequent and practiced use by these poets assured that meter its place as one of the most important Chinese verse forms. The significance of their role in the history of Chinese poetry can scarcely be overstated. If the Chien-an period is excluded, there are very few surviving *shih* and *yüeh-fu* from identifiable Han poets.

A few poems on history exist from Chien-an times. While it is sometimes difficult to know just when Chien-an poems acquired the titles they have today, it does not appear that the "Yung-shih shih" (Poem on History) title attached to Pan Ku's old piece was common then. Juan Yü and Wang Ts'an each have a piece by that name about the three courtiers who went to the grave with Duke

Mu of Ch'in about 620 B.C.E., but it is more usual for poems dealing with historical events to bear other kinds of titles, and Ts'ao Chih's poem on the Duke Mu incident is entitled "San liang" (Three Good Men).

Similar to poems on history are those that treat contemporary events or near-contemporary events. Both *yüeh-fu* and *shih* forms are used. Ts'ao Ts'ao, whose extant poems are all *yüeh-fu*, did sometimes use that form to write about events in his life. Among the most famous Chien-an poems on the times are such highly circumstantial pieces as Ts'ao Ts'ao's "Hsieh lu hsing" (Dew on the Shallots), a *yüeh-fu* describing the fall of the Han and castigating those responsible, and his "Hao-li hsing" (Wormwood Hamlet), which depicts the destruction that attended the failure of a military alliance against Tung Cho, the commander who took control of the ruler after a disastrous struggle between the court eunuchs and important families and officials in 189. Ts'ao Ts'ao also wrote a *yüeh-fu* entitled "Shan tsai hsing" (Good!), in which he contrasts his anguish over his father's murder with the joy he feels at the emperor's return to Loyang under his protection. For his part, Wang Ts'an has a famous series of five "Ts'ung-chün shih" (Poems on Accompanying the Army) written on the occasion of military campaigns in 215 and 216. These poems—with the exception of the third in the series, which looks more like a typical soldier's plaint—eulogize Ts'ao Ts'ao. Fifth- and sixth-century sources identify these as *shih* poems, but they are sometimes designated as *yüeh-fu* and are included in Kuo Mao-ch'ien's *Yüeh-fu shih chi* (Collection of Ballad Poetry; see chapter 47). It is tempting to speculate that imitations of an old *yüeh-fu* title, "Ts'ung-chün hsing" (Accompanying the Army), by Lu Chi (261–303), and other early medieval poets may have retroactively drawn Wang's poems into the *yüeh-fu* genre.

The interaction of Chien-an poets with the Ts'aos and with one another is most immediately seen in various kinds of social or occasional poetry they wrote—feast poems and poems of presentation and response, for example. The feast poems, which several poets wrote and which sometimes go by the title "Kung-yen shih" (Feast Poem), typically describe the scene and express gratitude for the host's devotion to his guests. Sometimes the poems contain an indication that such pleasures cannot last, which may have to do with the turbulent and dangerous times. This apprehensiveness seems to underlie the *carpe diem* mentality of the young revelers in Ts'ao Chih's "Ming tu p'ien" (Famous Cities), one of the many *yüeh-fu* titles Ts'ao Chih originated and one alluded to in the T'ang poet Li Po's (701–762) even more famous "Chiang chin chiu" (Bring On the Drink).

One aspect of Chien-an poetry that has sometimes been singled out for praise is its so-called realism. By this is meant its depiction of the harsher realities of life during the turbulent years of war and dislocation that attended the end of the Han. This overly simple view of Chien-an verse is related to the genuinely close connection between the speaker in the poem and the Chien-an poet himself in many poems—especially in *shih* poems but also in *yüeh-fu*—and, therefore, between the poem and historical circumstance. This is not to say that such a relationship obtains in every poem or that the speaker is necessarily identical to the poet, but the observation holds in general nonetheless. It is apparent on reading certain poems by Wang Ts'an and Ts'ao Chih, for instance. One example is the first of three pentasyllabic-line poems entitled "Ch'i ai shih" (Seven Sadnesses) that Wang Ts'an wrote around 192. It depicts his escape from the chaos in Ch'ang-an after the death of the warlord Tung Cho. One part says: "Once out the gate, nothing to see, / Just white bones covering the plain. / A starving woman on the road, / Embraces a child and abandons it in the grass." Ts'ao Chih's "Sung Ying shih" (Sending Off Mr. Ying), which depicts Loyang after it had been destroyed by Tung Cho, says, "The outlands, how bleak and desolate! / A thousand *li* [tricents] without smoke of man. / Remembering my old life here, / My breath catches and I cannot speak."

Sadness informs many Chien-an poems. In one of the best Chien-an poems, "Tseng Pai-ma wang Piao" (Presented to Piao, Prince of Pai-ma), his long, seven-part poem of presentation on parting from his half-brother Ts'ao Piao, Ts'ao Chih uses conventional images of obstruction, along with language from a classical text transformed to fit new prosodic needs. The references here to the horses being black with sweat and yellow with dust echo the *Classic of Poetry*: "Torrential rains muddy my road, / Running waters spread far and wide. / The crossroad is cut, there is no track, / I change my route and climb a high ridge. / The long slope stretches to the clouds and sun, / My horses turn black and yellow." But the melancholy in Chien-an poetry is often tempered by a quality traditional critics called *k'ang-k'ai*, which connotes strength in the face of adversity, a kind of fortitude even when one's innermost desires or heroic ambitions are frustrated. "Presented to Piao, Prince of Pai-ma" is an example, as is the sixth of Ts'ao Chih's "Tsa shih" (Miscellaneous Poems), which expresses a strong desire to sacrifice his life in battle with the enemy.

A similar heroic tone is also heard in Ts'ao Chih's "Pai ma p'ien" (White Horse), a poem depicting a hero. Ts'ao Chih's *yüeh-fu* are not generally first-person narratives, so there is some danger in reading this as an expression of Ts'ao's desire to serve his state, but this is a perennial problem of interpretation hardly unique to Ts'ao Chih. In any case, this influential poem is also notable for its demonstration of Ts'ao's control over parallel couplets in the lines "He draws the bowstring, breaks the left bull's-eye, / Shooting right, smashes a moon target, / Lifts a hand, snags a flying gibbon, / Bends his body, scatters horse-hoof targets." Other Chien-an poets exploited parallelism as well. In his "Kung-yen shih" (Lord's Feast), for example, Liu Chen writes: "A pure stream courses a stone canal, / The flowing waves become a fish weir. / Lotus plants strew their blossoms, / Lotus flowers fill the golden pond. / Numinous birds occupy the water's edge, / Marvelous beasts roam the arching bridge."

Who is the principal poet of the Chien-an period? The easy answer is Ts'ao Chih; he is one of China's great poets and has left more poems than any other

Chien-an writer. Furthermore, his influence on later poetry was strong. In his works are the seeds of the increased embellishment and higher level of diction of poets who come later in the period of disunion. Note his verbal parallelism, accompanied in the original by tonal parallelism, in these lines from "Shih t'ai-tzu tso" (Seated in Attendance on the Heir Apparent): "The white sun lights the verdant spring, / A timely rain settles the flying dust." But Wang Ts'an was also important to the development of poetry during this phase of Chinese literary history. Of his talent and intelligence, there is no doubt. In addition, he was roughly fifteen years older than Ts'ao Chih and was already producing powerful poetry in Ching-chou well before political and military events brought about his association with the Ts'aos. For his part, as heir apparent to Ts'ao Ts'ao, Ts'ao P'i was important mainly as a focal point of literary activities. He is the author of one of the seminal works of literary theory of the early medieval period, "Lun wen" (Essay on Literature), in *Tien lun* (Normative Essays), but his poetry is usually not so highly regarded as Ts'ao Chih's. His most cited poems are two heptasyllabic-line pieces in the voice of a lonely woman pining for her absent lover, both entitled "Yen ko hsing" (Song of Yen). Ts'ao Ts'ao's own poetry is generally underrated because of his preference for the tetrasyllabic line and for his role in the fall of the Han. While it does not match Ts'ao Chih's works, some see in its immediacy and ruggedness the qualities that underlie the best Chien-an poems.

One final name linked to the Chien-an period requires mention. Ts'ai Yen (b. 177) was the daughter of Ts'ai Yung. She was captured by the Hsiung-nu and married to one of their leaders. When he died, she was by custom then married to his son. She spent twelve years among the Hsiung-nu, during which time she bore two sons, until Ts'ao Ts'ao ransomed her back. Two poems entitled "Pei-fen shih" (Poem of Grief and Indignation) are attributed to her. The longer one, which is a good narrative poem, is in 108 pentasyllabic lines; the other is in the Ch'u Song form. Both deal with her capture, her life among the Hsiung-nu, her ransom by Ts'ao Ts'ao, her wrenching parting from her children, and her return to China. But it is doubtful that either of these pieces is by Ts'ai Yen; they are, instead, later works about her. Another long poem often attributed to Ts'ai Yen is "Hu chia shih-pa p'ai" (Eighteen Cadences for the Barbarian Flute). Judging from its late appearance, factual errors, and anachronistic style, it is even less likely that this poem is by her. Thus, although Ts'ai Yen is often mentioned as an important writer of the Chien-an period, it is not clear that any authentic works of hers survive.

THE CHENG-SHIH PERIOD

In 239 Emperor Ming (Ts'ao Jui) died and was succeeded by his eight-year-old adopted son Ts'ao Fang. Ts'ao Fang reigned until 254, mainly under the domination of his regents Ts'ao Shuang (d. 249) and Ssu-ma Yi (179–251). The

Ssu-ma family ultimately took full control of the Ts'ao court, and in 254 Ts'ao Fang was removed as emperor and replaced with Ts'ao Mao (241–260). In 260 Ts'ao Mao tried to dismantle the authority of the Ssu-ma family but was killed. The Wei carried on in name only until 265, when Ssu-ma Yen (r. 265–290) ascended the throne as Emperor Wu of Chin.

Cheng-shih was the name of Ts'ao Fang's first reign-period (239–248). Once again, the literary period does not coincide precisely with the reign-period; this one lasted roughly until the Wei dynasty came to an end in 265. Beginning in this age and continuing through the Western Chin, poetry became a deadly business. Many leading poets met violent deaths at the hands of the state during the years the Ssu-ma family was in power. Involvement in government was so risky that many people went to extraordinary lengths to avoid it. But that could be dangerous, too, for refusing to serve might also be taken as criticism. The literary theorist and critic Liu Hsieh (465?–520?) pointed to the Taoist proclivities of the age in his *Wen-hsin tiao-lung* (The Literary Mind and Carving of Dragons), no doubt reflecting on the escapism and interest in immortality prevalent among Cheng-shih writers. The most famous poets of the period are Juan Chi (210–263) and Hsi K'ang (also pronounced Chi K'ang; 223–262).

Juan Chi was the son of Juan Yü, a Chien-an writer. Juan Chi was known for bizarre and antiritualistic behavior that sometimes shocked people, but the leading political figures of the day repeatedly tried to employ him thanks to his fame. Juan was wary of the danger that might attend slighting the Ssu-mas or their followers, so his strategy for avoiding appointment to office was to try to beg off, and if that didn't work, to quit as soon as possible by pleading illness. He seems to have enjoyed goodwill within the Ssu-ma leadership, and that probably afforded him a measure of protection. Even so, when Ssu-ma Chao (211–265) reportedly tried to arrange a marriage between his son, the future Emperor Wu of Chin, and Juan's daughter, Juan supposedly stayed drunk for sixty days to avoid it. Juan's affection for drink is legendary—he is said to have taken one post solely because it came with an assistant who was clever at distilling spirits. Juan's name is also associated with the so-called Seven Sages of the Bamboo Grove (Chu-lin ch'i hsien), a famous group of nonconformists. Whatever attitudes or eccentricities the seven may initially have had in common, different opinions regarding Ssu-ma rule eventually caused rifts among them.

Juan is best known for his eighty-two "Yung-huai shih" (Poems Expressing My Heart, or Songs of My Soul), which, except for thirteen tetrasyllabic pieces, are all pentasyllabic. These are mainly lyric poems expressing sentiments like melancholy, anguish, and frustration. They are exceedingly elliptical and frequently allude to legendary and historical persons and events. Because of their vagueness, and because of the strength of feeling they convey, it is widely assumed that they contain hidden references to contemporary matters. Such a reading is further encouraged by the confessional side of the Chien-an poets, who wrote about their lives in many poems. Ts'ao Chih, who was often truly, and perhaps justifiably, unhappy with his treatment at the hands of his brother and nephew, Emperors Wen and Ming, respectively, wrote plainly in prose and in poetry of his dissatisfaction. This dissatisfaction has then been read back into poems that do not contain obvious references to particular circumstances, as in the case of his poems on lonely and abandoned women, including his "Miscellaneous Poems" on the subject, which are commonly read as allegories for his relationship with his brother or nephew.

Juan Chi's friend Hsi K'ang was a Taoist and a proponent of alchemical practices for prolonging life. One of his most famous works is the prose essay "Yang-sheng lun" (On Nourishing Life). There was a close relationship between alchemy and the forge, and Hsi K'ang knew blacksmithing. A famous anecdote has him ignoring a powerful official who had come to see him by continuing to attend to his forge, an insult that may have been one of the reasons for his execution. Hsi had also married into the Ts'ao family, which put him on dangerous ground with the Ssu-mas. Since he was reluctant to serve them, he spent most of his time at his family estate at Shan-yang, north of Loyang, where the Seven Sages of the Bamboo Grove are supposed to have gathered.

Hsi's contempt for government service can be detected in his eighteen tetrasyllabic-line poems of presentation bearing the title "Tseng hsiung hsiu-ts'ai ju chün" (Presented to My Elder Brother the Flourishing Talent on His Entering the Army). But the best statement of his opinion of officialdom and of social niceties is seen in a letter he wrote in 261 to break off relations with Shan T'ao (205–283), a member of the Seven Sages who had accepted employment in the Ssu-ma government, after Shan had recommended Hsi K'ang for a post. In the letter Hsi explained in a highly entertaining way how utterly unsuited he was for officialdom.

Hsi K'ang was friendly with a man mentioned in passing in his letter, Lü An. In 262, Lü An was involved in a dispute with his elder brother, who had apparently had an affair with Lü An's wife. Hsi K'ang advised his friend to do nothing, but Lü An's brother soon accused Lü An of being unfilial. Lü An was arrested, as was Hsi K'ang for trying to help him, and both were executed. Hsi's end is described in several places. He had a reputation as a zither player, and he asked to play again just before his execution. One source says that thousands of students appealed for his life to be spared, but to no avail.

Hsi K'ang's reputation as a poet is overshadowed by that of the Chien-an poets, especially Ts'ao Chih, and by that of his friend Juan Chi. His best poems, however, are very good. Just as he was unconventional in life, so he was in his poetry. He is something of a throwback in his use of the tetrasyllabic line—about half of his approximately sixty extant poems are in that meter. But in his hands this somewhat archaic form becomes a natural and expressive medium. To his brother he writes, perhaps chiding, "Your fine horse seasoned, / Your handsome uniform ablaze" and "Wetland fowl, though starving, / Want not royal parks."

Another poet deserving mention is Fu Hsüan (217–278). Fu was born in the Chien-an era, lived through the Cheng-shih era, and died in the literary T'ai-k'ang era (if we take T'ai-k'ang to run from around 270 to the early fourth century—see below), yet seldom is his name associated with any of these. He is best known for his *yüeh-fu*—more than eighty of his surviving one hundred or so poems are in this genre, more than from any other writer of his time. Many of them are ritual pieces of dynastic accomplishment and virtue in praise of the Ssu-mas, but the remainder show his facility for creating new poems from old themes. In fact, his thematic imitations of earlier pieces set the tone for much of the subsequent history of the *yüeh-fu* and surely played a role in creating the genre as we know it. He writes on many topics that indicate social concern. Often he writes of women, sometimes assuming the voice of a woman in his poems. He was not the first to do this, for such poems, both *shih* and *yüeh-fu*, are also characteristic of the Chien-an period. But some think Fu was particularly sensitive to women's plight in traditional society. An example is his most famous poem, "Yü-chang hsing: K'u hsiang p'ien" (Yü-chang Ballad: Bitter Fate), which begins, "A bitter fate to take a woman's form, / So low and base beyond repeating," then goes on to speak of inequality and the ultimate alienation of husband and wife. In this poetic treatment of such topics as the plight of women, and in the more literary style he employs, there is a thread that connects him with Ts'ao Chih and with the still more ornate poets to come. A good example of his manipulation of earlier, more folklike materials is seen in his poem "Hsi Ch'ang-an hsing" (Western Ch'ang-an), which is modeled on the Han anonymous *yüeh-fu* "Yu so ssu" (There Is One for Whom I Long). He also has a well-known lyrical "Tsa shih" (Miscellaneous Poem) beginning "A man of will regrets the days are short, / A man of sorrow perceives the nights are long," in which the cause for the speaker's unease is obscure in the manner of much *yung-huai* poetry.

THE T'AI-K'ANG PERIOD

The poetry of the Western Chin is often referred to as T'ai-k'ang poetry after the T'ai-k'ang reign-period of Emperor Wu of Chin. The reign lasted from 280 to 289, but the literary period runs from about 270 to the early fourth century. In his *Shih-p'in* (An Evaluation of Poetry), Chung Jung (469?–518) talks about this as the age of the three Changs, two Lus, two P'ans, and one Tso. He is referring to Chang Hua (232–300), the brothers Chang Tsai (fl. 280) and Chang Hsieh (255?–307), the brothers Lu Chi and Lu Yün (262–303), P'an Yüeh (247–300) and his nephew P'an Ni (d. c. 310), and Tso Ssu (c. 253–c. 307). Any such formulation is bound to be artificial, and in this case some of the poets may be omitted from a general discussion, while others, namely, Liu K'un (271–317) and Kuo P'u (276–324), should be added. As indicated above, the Western Chin was a dangerous time for poet-officials. In 300, five of the most prominent poets of the time were executed, including Chang Hua and P'an Yüeh. Lu Chi and Lu Yün were executed in 303 (along with their families), Liu K'un in 318, and Kuo P'u in 324.

Liu Hsieh characterized the poetry of this period as somewhat trivial and ornate. A strong tendency toward imitation of earlier works was already seen in Fu Hsüan, but this was the age when imitative verse became very common. That does not diminish its importance, however, for while adopting the themes of Han and Wei poems, these poets produced new, highly wrought pieces with more refined diction, which ultimately led to the still more elegant poetry of the eras to follow. Although there was some loss of vitality, some of the best poems on history and roaming into immortality date from this period, and new subgenres, such as summoning the recluse (*chao-yin shih*), emerged and became popular.

P'an Yüeh was from a family of prominent officials and was something of a child prodigy. He is also reputed to have been one of the most handsome men in Chinese history. P'an began serving in office around 266 and thereafter held many posts, both in and out of the capital. In about 293, he returned to the capital, Loyang, and was one of the Twenty-four Companions of the Duke of Lu (Lu kung erh-shih-ssu yu), meaning he was in the salon of the Empress Chia's nephew Chia Mi. He held an official post but soon resigned because of his mother's illness. In 297 he returned to office, and in 298 his wife died. In 300 Chia Mi was assassinated in a coup staged by Ssu-ma Lun (d. 301). An old enemy falsely accused P'an of plotting rebellion with rival Ssu-ma family members, and P'an and his entire family, including his aged mother, were all executed. This is not to say that P'an was entirely innocent. He seems to have had an active, perhaps even unscrupulous, desire to get ahead and may have forged a document that would allow Empress Chia to replace the heir apparent with Chia Mi.

The prevailing emotion in the twenty or so surviving poems from P'an Yüeh is grief. His most famous pieces are undoubtedly three poems entitled "Tao wang shih" (Mourning the Deceased), written to lament the death of his wife. This title thenceforth became the name of a poetic subgenre. Most cited as an example of P'an's art is the first of the three, in the usual order. This moving pentasyllabic poem uses a good deal of parallelism, but the language is relatively unornamented. In the final lines there is an allusion to the story of Chuang Tzu beating on a vessel after his wife's death. P'an writes: "I suppose someday this grief will fade, / And Chuang Tzu's pot will get pounded again."

Chang Hua was one of the leading political and literary figures of his day. He is known as much for *Po-wu chih* (A Treatise on Curiosities), a collection of recorded marvels (*chih-kuai*), as for his poetry. He was also a sponsor of other scholar-writers, including Lu Chi, Lu Yün, and the historian Ch'en Shou (233–297), author of *San-kuo chih* (History of the Three Kingdoms). Not originally a follower of the Chia family, he eventually switched his allegiance to them.

As in the case of P'an Yüeh, this association cost him his life when Ssu-ma Lun rose against them.

Chang wrote some poems of social comment, the most famous being the *yüeh-fu* "Ch'ing po p'ien" (Frivolity), an exposé of the extravagance and profligacy of aristocratic life. His *shih* poem "Yu-lieh shih" (Hunting), which shows some influence from the *fu* genre, criticizes a clearly aristocratic activity. He also has several love poems to his credit, but they seem somewhat detached. These pieces sometimes rely on objects (curtains, beds, quilts) to express such feelings as they can be said to contain, a tendency that becomes even more pronounced in later Palace-Style Poetry (*kung-t'i shih*). One of Chang's most famous "Ch'ing shih" (Love Poems) is about a woman longing for her absent lover; it concludes, "Striking the pillow, I wail and sigh alone, / Wracked with emotion, an ache in my heart."

Chang also wrote on heroic themes. Examples are his *yüeh-fu* "Chuang shih p'ien" (Braveheart) and "Yu-hsia p'ien" (Wandering Hero). The former is in the style of Ts'ao Chih's "White Horse." "Wandering Hero" is also apparently inspired by Ts'ao's piece, for the title seems to come from a line in "White Horse," but otherwise the two poems are quite dissimilar. The contrast is an example of the embellishment of an earlier theme by a Chin poet. Ts'ao's poem is a description of a hero, employing parallelism but not allusions. Chang's poem, by contrast, is full of allusions. Chang was not alone in this, for other poets of the period, such as Liu K'un and Tso Ssu, also wrote highly allusive verse.

One of the three most famous works of literary theory from the early medieval period is Lu Chi's "Wen fu" (Rhapsody on Literature), the other two being Ts'ao P'i's "Essay on Literature" and Liu Hsieh's *The Literary Mind and Carving of Dragons* (see chapter 45). Like Ts'ao P'i, and unlike Liu Hsieh, Lu Chi was a leading poet of his day. He was from a family of officials, and in 289 he and his brother went north to Loyang to serve in the Chin government, a journey that led to two of his most famous pieces, both entitled "Fu Lo-yang tao chung tso" (Written on the Road to Loyang). In the first of these, which employs a great deal of parallelism, he expresses his sadness over having to leave his home to take up an official post. Although the poem implies that taking up office was something beyond his control, Lu Chi appears to have been an active participant in government and politics, perhaps motivated by both a strong sense of his own self-worth and a desire to perform great service. Beginning in about 299, during the time of the Insurrections of the Eight Kings (a violent jostling for power among the regional rulers of the Western Chin), he confidently served first one king and then another, until his luck ran out and he was executed in 303.

Like P'an Yüeh, Tso Ssu, Shih Ch'ung (249–300), Liu K'un, and other well-known men of his day, Lu was a member of the Twenty-four Companions of Chia Mi, and he addressed several poems of presentation to Chia. He was also one of the originators of poems summoning the recluse. This subgenre of *shih* poetry is traceable to the "Chao yin-shih" (Summoning the Recluse) poem of the *Elegies of Ch'u*, but there the goal is to lure the recluse out of reclusion. In the summoning the recluse poems by Lu and others, reclusion is depicted as an attractive alternative to social and political involvement. Eremitism (espousing the life of a hermit) was an ideal during much of the early medieval period, but for most it remained a literary pose, since few poet-officials were willing or able to separate themselves from active engagement in worldly affairs. Chang Hua, Chang Tsai, Tso Ssu, and Wang K'ang-chü all composed such poems, and Wang even wrote "Fan chao-yin" (Contra Summoning the Recluse), which satirizes the subgenre.

Lu has also left many feast poems. But a major part of his poetic reputation comes from his many imitations of anonymous poems, both *yüeh-fu* and *ku-shih* alike, and of Chien-an poetry. He has a large number of such pieces in the important anthology *Literary Selections*. More than even Fu Hsüan or Chang Hua, Lu seems to have taken the act of imitation as a goal in itself, as a way to show what he could do with words.

According to an anecdote, Lu Chi was planning to write a *fu* on the capitals of Wei, Wu, and Shu. When he heard that Tso Ssu was already composing such a work, he wrote disparagingly to his brother about it. But once Tso's rhapsody appeared, its brilliance made Lu give up his project. Thus Tso Ssu's reputation, too, is based in part on a *fu*, but a very different one from Lu's "Rhapsody on Literature." Tso's "San tu fu" (Rhapsody on the Three Capitals) is a long and learned rhapsody in the tradition of *fu* on capitals and metropolises epitomized by the grand Han dynasty works of Pan Ku and Chang Heng.

Very little is known of Tso's life. He was not from an old, influential family, but he did have a sister, Tso Fen, who wrote poetry and was taken into the palace in 272, perhaps because of her literary talents. Although only fourteen of Tso Ssu's poems survive, he is considered one of the better poets of early medieval times. He has two pieces entitled "Poem Summoning the Recluse," the first of which (in the *Literary Selections* order) is excellent. But more unusual is Tso's "Chiao nü shih" (Darling Daughters), a sweet and humorous description of his two daughters. Although there are some earlier pieces dealing with daughters, they are often laments or threnodies for deceased children. Thus a tradition of poems about adorable daughters—which licensed poems about dim-witted sons, as in T'ao Ch'ien's (365–427) "Tse tzu shih" (Chiding Sons)—originated with Tso.

Tso's most famous works, however, are eight pentasyllabic "Poems on History," in which he uses ancient persons and events to express his feelings and comment on society. Naturally, these pieces contain historical references and allusions, and the seventh of them contains nearly an allusion per line. Although Tso Ssu was associated with Chia Mi, he escaped the slaughter of poets that marked the first years of the fourth century. He had ambition, but not the social background that might have allowed him to achieve high office, and the injustice of this is one of the messages of his "Poems on History." In the end, he knew when to get out. With the fall of the Chia clan, he left the capital and died several years later of illness.

Invasion and internal problems ended the Western Chin. Large numbers of refugees went south, and the Chin was reestablished (Eastern Chin) at Chien-k'ang. In poetry the names Liu K'un and Kuo P'u are connected with this period of transition. Liu K'un was from an influential family and was one of Chia Mi's Twenty-four Companions. He served as a Chin military leader and in the Yung-chia period (307–312) led troops against the Hsiung-nu. In 315 he was put in charge of military affairs for three northern provinces and, after suffering defeat in battle with Hsiung-nu forces, formed an alliance with the Hsien-pei (Särbi; another tribe whose descendants in the T'o-pa [Tabgatch] clan later founded the Northern Wei [386–534]) to support the Chin. He was later executed because his son betrayed a Hsien-pei leader.

Liu has only three extant poems, so there is little from which to judge his merit as a poet. What does remain reveals certain similarities of style and outlook to Chien-an poetry. His best-known poem is the patriotic *yüeh-fu* "Fu-feng ko" (Song of Fu-feng), usually dated 307; it is a good example of the use of parallelism that had become so popular by his time. It begins: "In the morning I left through Kuang-mo Gate, / In the evening I rested at Tan-shui mountain. / With my left hand I bend a Fan-jo bow, / With my right hand I brandish a Lung-yüan sword." There are allusions in "Song of Fu-feng," to Confucius and to the Han general Li Ling. Liu's "Ch'ung tseng Lu Ch'en" (Again, Presented to Lu Ch'en), usually dated 317 or 318, when the poet was in prison awaiting execution, is essentially constructed of a series of allusions to several historical figures who aided their rulers. It also laments what he has left undone and contains the traditional topos of anxiety over the swift passage of time, which takes on an added edge in light of his imminent demise.

Whereas Liu K'un remained in the north, Kuo P'u was a native of northern China who moved south in the large migrations that took place as a result of the gradual loss of the north to non-Chinese invaders in the early years of the fourth century. He reached the south sometime before 311. Kuo was an outstanding scholar and the last important writer before T'ao Ch'ien. He wrote commentaries on many texts, and the ones he prepared for *Shan hai ching* (Classic of Mountains and Seas), *Mu t'ien-tzu chuan* (Travels of Emperor Mu), *Erh-ya* (Approaching Elegance), and *Fang-yen* (Topolects) are still standard. Kuo was versed in the occult and was famous as a diviner, a skill that ultimately cost him his life when he found himself trapped in the service of the insurgent Wang Tun (266–324). He produced a divination that predicted failure for Wang's mutiny, so Wang had him executed.

As a poet Kuo is best known by far for his "Yu-hsien shih" (Poems on Roaming into Immortality). Fourteen of these survive, along with four fragments. The genre has its origins in the *Elegies of Ch'u* and was practiced during the Chien-an period, most notably by Ts'ao Chih, who has left several such pieces. Other poets, including Juan Chi, Hsi K'ang, and Lu Chi, wrote such poems after Ts'ao, but Kuo's are considered the epitome of all of the early medieval poems on Taoist escape and immortality. Clearly there is an ideological connection between poems on roaming into immortality and summoning-the-recluse poems, but summoning-the-recluse poems show more interest in mountain landscapes than in the other-worldly imagery of poems on roaming into immortality. Some of Kuo's poems show a desire to flee the entanglements of this world, while others are more narrowly focused on the ideas and conventions of the immortal world. No doubt because of these pieces and because of Kuo's reputation for possessing acroamatic knowledge, he became a subject of Taoist hagiography and is depicted in some sources as having attained true immortality by magical means. There is always a question regarding the poet's belief in the possibility of actually becoming a *hsien*, or transcendent immortal. Although belief in immortality was already a strain in Chinese thought long before the early medieval period, not everyone was a believer. Often poets who wrote poems on roaming into immortality were skeptical, or simply wanted to believe, or believed but thought *hsien*-hood was exceedingly elusive. Although Kuo actually believed in immortals, what really matters is what he did with the subgenre. Ts'ao Chih is the best writer of poems on roaming into immortality before Kuo, but Kuo invested more of himself in the poems, using them to convey personal anxieties and frustrations.

EASTERN CHIN AND SUNG DYNASTY POETRY

Chien-an poetry had been intensely concerned with the personal lives and historical circumstances of the poets. It was often a poetry of involvement that more or less candidly and clearly expressed the authors' hopes, aspirations, feelings, and frustrations with regard to their roles in society and government. But in the Cheng-shih and T'ai-k'ang periods, for political, philosophical, and social reasons, poetry generally had become somewhat less plainspoken and new subgenres were emphasized that paid less overt attention to worldly matters. In general, this detachment increased in the second half of the early medieval period, when Chinese poetry was practiced mainly on the smaller stage of a highly cultured south—and there, frequently, in a courtly environment.

The poetry of the Eastern Chin is often held in low esteem because of the popularity then of metaphysical verse (*hsüan-yen shih*). Such poetry derived from the broader interest in Taoism and metaphysical topics that marked the Wei and Chin, which resulted in rather abstract poems of dubious appeal on the nature of the Tao. Representative poets of this subgenre are Sun Ch'o (320–377) and Hsü Hsün (fl. c. 358?). Sun is perhaps better remembered for his rhapsody "Yu T'ien-t'ai shan fu" (Rhapsody on Roaming Mount T'ien-t'ai), which in some ways foreshadows the development of landscape poetry (*shan-shui shih*).

There were poets who straddled the Eastern Chin and Sung periods whose poetry escaped the limitations of metaphysical verse. The most renowned of these poets were T'ao Ch'ien (or T'ao Yüan-ming; 365–427) and Hsieh Ling-yün (385–433). Many consider T'ao the finest pre-T'ang poet. Although he had admirers, T'ao was not widely considered a great poet during the Southern Dynasties, for tastes ran to more elaborate phrasing and diction than he typically used. It is, in fact, his poetry's relative lack of ornament that makes it appealing to modern readers, even in translation. T'ao is not quite the stylistic maverick he is sometimes made out to be, however. Other, less well-known poets of his region, like Chan Fang-sheng, wrote in a similarly unlabored style, and T'ao himself sometimes shows traces of the metaphysical in his writing. Nor was he as isolated as is sometimes imagined. He was on good terms with Yen Yen-chih (384–456), one of the leading poets of the Yüan-chia period (424–453) and a very different sort of writer.

T'ao's great-grandfather and grandfather had been prominent officials, but by his time the family was relatively poor and undistinguished. Although T'ao served briefly in office, he is much more famous for his withdrawal to the life of a farmer. He seems to have felt that he had an obligation to accomplish great things, yet he also wished to avoid official involvement and be free to live a simple life. In the end, the attractions of the simple life won out, and he lived his last twenty-two years in retirement. The inner tension in his life, which is often posited in terms of Confucian versus Taoist values, was not unusual in those days. The topos of reclusion was pervasive within scholar-official culture, and those who could not bring themselves to give up the trappings of officialdom often affected disengagement in their writings. T'ao's ability to withdraw, both in word and in deed, is noteworthy. Shen Yüeh (441–513), for one, had an intimate involvement with both Taoism and Buddhism, yet his writings and his life merely exhibit a wistful distance from actualized disengagement.

T'ao Ch'ien's poetry is often called bucolic poetry (*t'ien-yüan shih*) and is compared to the landscape poetry of Hsieh Ling-yün. Both write about nature, but T'ao's is more a poetry of the farmstead, though not, of course, addressed to farmers. T'ao is largely an autobiographical poet; much of his poetry is closely related to the events, both large and small, of his life. Although earlier poets, notably those of the Chien-an period, had written of their experiences, they did not generally reflect on diurnal life quite as T'ao did.

T'ao could write highly structured poems, as in the three-part allegory "Hsing ying shen" (Form, Shadow, Spirit), which draws on the old debate form seen in the *fu* genre, or he could compose more spontaneously, as in the group of twenty poems entitled "Yin chiu" (Tippling). A preface to the latter emphasizes how much he liked getting drunk and dashing off these poems for his own amusement, but the existence of the preface suggests his awareness of an audience and a certain self-consciousness. He seems to have wanted to be understood as a particular kind of person. He projects this image in various ways—through his poems, his *fu*, his "Wu-liu hsien-sheng chuan" (Biography of Mr. Five Willows). His poems on history also serve this purpose by allowing him to identify with certain famous figures from the past. His "Yung Ching K'o shih" (Poem on Ching K'o) is an example, as is his "Yung erh Shu" (Poem on the Two Shus). Shu Kuang and his nephew Shu Shou were eminently respected Former Han officials who retired happily to their old home at the peak of their success. Chang Hsieh had earlier written a "Poem on History" about them, but his treatment follows their biography in the *History of the Han Dynasty* rather closely. T'ao's has a more complex structure and is more subjective in its approach.

T'ao naturally often wrote on the theme of withdrawal and reclusion. The famous fifth poem of the "Tippling" group exemplifies this tendency. It begins: "I built my hut where people dwell, / But there is no clamor of horse or carriage. / 'May I ask how this can be?' / If the mind is distant, the place is of itself remote." Works of later, politically engaged poets like Shen Yüeh and Hsieh T'iao (464–499) employ a similar conceit but lack T'ao's conviction. Some of T'ao Ch'ien's works—the prose depiction of an agrarian utopia entitled "T'ao-hua yüan chi" (Record of a Peach Blossom Spring) and the first of his pentasyllabic "Kuei yüan t'ien chü" (Returning to Live in Garden and Field) as well as the celebrated rhapsody "Kuei-ch'ü-lai tz'u" (Let's Return!) on the same theme, for example—echo images and language found in *Lao Tzu*, and the major source of allusions in T'ao's poetry is another Taoist text, the *Chuang Tzu*. After the *Chuang Tzu*, the second source of allusions in his works is the Confucian *Lun-yü* (Analects), perhaps a further sign of the tension in T'ao Ch'ien's personality.

In contrast to T'ao Ch'ien, Hsieh Ling-yün was the leading literary figure of the fifth century and a scion of one of the most aristocratic and cultured families of the south. His grandfather was the Duke of K'ang-le, a title Hsieh Ling-yün inherited at about age eighteen. Hsieh was a lionized poet, an accomplished, stylish, headstrong man who happened to love scenic landscapes.

Hsieh Ling-yün served in various official positions under both the Eastern Chin and the Sung, but under the Sung his noble rank was reduced to marquis, with a significant reduction in income. In 422 he was dispatched to be administrator of Yung-chia, near modern-day Wenchow. There he ignored the duties of his office and spent much of his time roaming the countryside, enjoying its scenery, and composing poetry. After a year or so, he resigned and returned to his family estate at Shih-ning in Kuei-chi (in Chekiang province), where he engaged in landscape gardening and continued his sightseeing excursions. When Emperor Wen ascended the throne, he summoned Hsieh to return to court, but Hsieh again neglected his duties and soon withdrew to the pleasures of his estate and the companionship of friends and family, which cost him his post. In 431 he was sent to take up a distant minor post in Lin-ch'uan, near modern-day Fuchow. Again he ignored his work, and when he was impeached and the government tried to arrest him, he took up arms in rebellion against the dynasty. Because of his actions, he was first exiled still farther south to Kuangchow (Canton) and then executed there.

Hsieh's name is synonymous with landscape poetry. Among the factors in the growth of such poetry were the strong contemporary interest in reclusion and the finely honed esthetic sensibilities of the elite. The intense literary activity that characterized the latter half of the early medieval period took place against an inspiring southern landscape of mountains, rivers, and exuberant vegetation; and what nature didn't provide, wealthy aristocrats did on their own landscaped estates. The highly descriptive *fu* tradition—along with the landscape elements and philosophical reflections present in various *shih* subgenres, such as feast poems, metaphysical verse, poems summoning the recluse, and poems on roaming into immortality—also provided a literary basis on which to build. But while description is essential to landscape poetry, that is not to say that such poetry is devoid of emotional or philosophical content. Indeed, Hsieh was a profoundly learned lay Buddhist who wrote commentaries on scripture and had an interest in Indian phonological principles. Such concerns preoccupied him and naturally informed his writing. Thus, landscape poems by Hsieh and others commonly contain a substantial expressive component.

Hsieh was not necessarily the first landscape poet. Chang Hsieh is often viewed as Hsieh Ling-yün's forerunner in this subgenre. Like Hsieh Ling-yün, Chang employed parallelism and detailed description, and he, too, linked external scenes with his inner thoughts. But Chang's descriptions of landscapes are generally limited to mountains, whereas the southerner Hsieh was more expansive. Hsieh liked mountains and was drawn to high ground. But Hsieh carried landscape poetry to new heights by his addition of watery scenes. Parallelism, extremely important in his works, is often constructed around alternating images of mountains and water as he passes through a landscape. For example, in "Yu Nan-shan wang Pei-shan ching hu chung chan-t'iao" (Gazing About as I Cross the Lake from South Mountain to North Mountain), he writes: "I look down and see tips of the tall trees, / I look up and hear rapids in a deep ravine." Hsieh's poems also contain allusions, personification, and evidence of sensitivity to tonal values in prosody.

Although his social background and career were much different, Pao Chao (414–466) was clearly influenced by Hsieh Ling-yün, and, despite a relatively undistinguished official life, Pao achieved recognition for his writing. Some of the twenty or so "landscape poems" he wrote actually have relatively little scenic description. Among his most celebrated pieces in the subgenre are those dealing with Mount Lu. But one of his most interesting landscape poems is "Shan hsing chien ku t'ung" (Traveling in the Mountains I See a Solitary Paulownia). Landscape poems, with their concentrated descriptive passages, are in a sense a manifestation of a trend toward description that grew progressively stronger in the early medieval period, and this piece, which focuses on a single tree, can be viewed as a precursor of the kind of poems on objects that would become popular in the Ch'i (479–502) and Liang (502–557) periods.

Pao is better known for his *yüeh-fu* than for his landscape verse. More than eighty survive, written on a wide variety of themes, including the military frontier, separation and travel, the ephemeral nature of existence, social and political criticism, and lonely and abandoned women. Like other poets of the age, Pao often composed *yüeh-fu* inspired by earlier anonymous and literati poems, sometimes in difficult or startling language. Although he is imitating Ts'ao Chih's "K'u je hsing" (Suffering from Heat), of which only a fragment survives, it is unlikely that any Chien-an poet could have written lines like this almost surrealistic vision from Pao's "Tai 'K'u je hsing'" ("Suffering from Heat," Surrogate Version): "Miasmal vapors mornings smoke our bodies, / Toxic dews nights soak our clothes. / Hungry apes will not descend to eat, / Morning birds do not dare to fly. / At the poisonous Ching even many died, / Crossing the Lu, won't everyone succumb?" But in a sense it is an outgrowth of the kind of transformation of poetry that Ts'ao Chih began with unusual lines like "A startling wind sets the white sun flying" from his "Tseng Hsü Kan" (Presented to Hsü Kan).

Some of Pao's works are, in fact, characterized by a boldness and vigor more reminiscent of the Han and Wei than of his own time. Sometimes he imitated Han-Wei poets, as in his "Hsüeh Liu Kung-kan t'i wu shou" (Five Poems Imitating the Style of Liu Kung-kan), which are modeled on Liu Chen's style but seem to express personal feelings of isolated integrity. He also wrote an imitation of T'ao Ch'ien—his "Hsüeh T'ao P'eng-tse t'i" (Imitating T'ao P'eng-tse's Style) ably captures T'ao's outlook on life and simple style. Pao's most famous poems, however, are his eighteen "Ni 'Hsing lu nan'" (Imitating "The Road Is Hard"). These mainly heptasyllabic-line poems helped form the common image of Pao as an aggrieved, low-level military official of talent frustrated in his desire to get ahead by his modest origins. The pieces are innovative in their use of rhyme in even-numbered lines. Earlier heptasyllabic-line poems had, almost without exception, rhymed every line. Pao's "Yeh t'ing chi" (Listening to Geishas at Night) makes a similar contribution to the quatrain form by using the rhyme scheme *aaba*, which would become predominant in *chüeh-chü* (regulated-verse quatrains; see chapter 14) poetry. The quatrain appealed to Pao, who wrote many poems in the manner of popular southern *yüeh-fu*, making him one of the first literati to adopt this poetic style that was later important in the courts and salons of Ch'i and Liang.

FROM CH'I AND LIANG TO REUNIFICATION

During the entire period of disunion, salons and coteries—close-knit groups of poets acutely aware of one another's work—influenced the development of poetry. Less formal poetic and social relationships, whose inner dynamics are not so clear, also existed, so that poets were well informed about the writings of their contemporaries and predecessors. The influence of literary salons in the formulation of acceptable styles, themes, and forms is particularly associated with the Ch'i and Liang dynasties. Many of the developments that would come to be associated with Ch'i and Liang verse began to take shape at the court of Hsiao Tzu-liang (460–494), who was the prince of Ching-ling and patron of the most important salon of Ch'i. The leading members of his salon were the Eight Companions of Ching-ling (Ching-ling pa yu): Hsiao Yen (464–549); Shen Yüeh; Hsieh T'iao; Wang Jung (468–493); Hsiao Ch'en (478–529); Fan Yün (451–503); Jen Fang (460–508); and Lu Ch'ui (470–526). The poetry that originated in the prince's salon is called both Yung-ming Style (Yung-ming *t'i*), after the Yung-ming reign-period (483–494), and New-Style Verse (*hsin t'i shih*). Yung-ming poems tend to be either eight-line poems (octaves) or quatrains; parallel couplets are common, and some follow the prosodic rules established by Shen Yüeh and others. Poems on objects, often composed at social gatherings, were a major subgenre for salon poets, who wrote such pieces about everything from musical instruments to birds and insects. Other types of poetry were written as well, but poems on objects, along with such poetic games and oddments as palindromes, were staples of the salon.

The gradual evolution of tonal rules, born of an increased sensitivity to the tonal nature of the Chinese language, was a major Yung-ming development. Although mature regulated verse does not appear by design until T'ang times, by the time of Hsiao Kang, Emperor Chien-wen of Liang (503–551; r. 550–551), many of the rules had already taken form. Shen Yüeh played an important role in this process. Although Chou Yung (d. 485) probably initially theorized about the four tones, Shen wrote one of the first works on tones in Chinese, the *Ssu sheng p'u* (Manual on the Four Tones). It no longer exists, but parts are preserved in *Bunkyō hifuron* (Treatise on the Secret Treasury of the Literary Mirror), by the Japanese Buddhist monk Kūkai, who was in China from 804 to 806. During this time, Kūkai collected many important works on prosody that were subsequently lost in China, making *Bunkyō hifuron* an extremely important repository for research on poetics of the late Six Dynasties, Sui, and early T'ang. Hsiao Tzu-liang was a patron of Buddhism and had sutras recited for his courtiers, and it has been shown that the principles and terms Shen uses to explain the four tones derived from a system current in the late Six Dynasties for explaining Sanskrit phonology. Shen applied the ideas about tones to poetry, and he and Wang Jung are credited with formulating rules regarding tonal distribution, rhyme, and alliteration. This is not to say that earlier poets did not manipulate the sounds of the language for artistic ends, but it does mean that in Ch'i and Liang times new rules for doing so began to be codified based on Sanskrit models. Breaking these rules would result in one of the Eight Defects (*pa-ping*, cf. Sanskrit *doṣa*). Shen does not himself always follow the rules he was creating, but, *yüeh-fu* aside, Shen's own verse does show increasing adherence to tonal prosody after about 487.

Shen Yüeh served under the Sung, Ch'i, and Liang dynasties, a remarkable feat of survival, and was the leading intellectual of his time. He was responsible for *Sung shu* (History of the [Liu] Sung Dynasty), generally regarded as one of the better dynastic histories—and one that is very important for the history of *yüeh-fu*. A man with lifelong Taoist beliefs, Shen converted to Buddhism as an adult and often expressed guilt over his excesses, including sexual encounters with both men and women. He wrote some love poems, including "Liu yi shih" (Six Recollections), a poem of four mildly erotic reminiscences about a lover that clearly augurs the impending popularity of Palace-Style Poetry, a subgenre more immediately associated with the court of the Liang heir apparent Hsiao Kang.

One of the best of the Yung-ming poets was Hsieh T'iao, who was highly admired in T'ang times. Hsieh was a member of the same family as Hsieh Ling-yün, and so is sometimes referred to as Little Hsieh (Hsiao Hsieh). He served as a commandery administrator, but after a time he was transferred back to the capital, where he was eventually implicated in a plot and executed.

About a third of Hsieh T'iao's extant 130 poems are octaves, a sign of the increasing popularity of this form in court circles. Like his famous forebear, he wrote landscape poetry, but in his landscape verse there is often a blending of cityscapes with natural scenes. His reputation rests in part on memorable couplets, such as "Fish sport, and new lotuses stir, / Birds scatter, and belated blossoms fall" from "Yu Tung-t'ien" (Roaming Tung-t'ien). Many of Hsieh's works are poems on objects. Perhaps most noteworthy are the quatrains he wrote. His pentasyllabic quatrains are very similar to the mature *chüeh-chü* of the T'ang dynasty. The best known of these may be his "Yü chieh yüan" (Jade Steps Plaint), a poem about a lonely woman that inspired another, more famous poem by Li Po. Hsieh's reads: "In the evening palace she lowers the pearl curtains, / Drifting fireflies flit then rest again. / Through the long night she sews the gauze garment. / This thinking of you, when will it end?"

Salons continued to be important under the Liang dynasty. The Liang founder, Hsiao Yen (Emperor Wu of Liang; r. 502–549), had been one of the Eight Companions of Ching-ling. After becoming emperor, he invited writers to his court and continued his long association with Shen Yüeh and others. Having lived both in the capital and in Ching-chou, he was strongly influenced by the "Wu sheng ko" (Songs to Wu Music) and "Hsi ch'ü ko" (Songs to Western Tunes) he heard in these places and composed his own poems in the popular style. His poems focus on women and love, and they often emphasize the sort of delicate, objectified depiction of women that was typical of the period. Despite the attention to tonal prosody espoused by some of his fellow poets, Hsiao Yen was not interested in this aspect of versification. In his later years he is believed to have turned more to Buddhism, and the many poems he wrote on Buddhist themes are often presumed to reflect that stage of his life.

Hsiao Yen's sons were even more enthusiastic supporters of literature and had salons of their own, where two of the most important anthologies of early

Chinese literature—*Literary Selections* and *Yü-t'ai hsin-yung* (New Songs from a Jade Terrace)—were produced. These two works are very different, each reflecting a specific attitude toward literature. *Literary Selections*, which includes works in a wide range of genres, was compiled under the direction of the heir apparent Hsiao T'ung. This great anthology represents what has been called a moderate or compromise notion of literature—one that reflects the more traditional view that literature has a public function and ought to have moral and didactic value, without excluding more personal works of an expressive nature. *Literary Selections* has little poetry from Ch'i and Liang dynasty poets, except for Shen Yüeh and Hsieh T'iao, preferring instead the works of those of the Wei, Western Chin, and Sung. Nor does it include any poems on objects or Palace-Style Poetry from the courts and salons of Ch'i and Liang. These latter find their place in *New Songs from a Jade Terrace*, compiled by Hsü Ling (507–583) under the patronage of Hsiao T'ung's younger brother Hsiao Kang.

After Hsiao T'ung's untimely death in 531, Hsiao Kang replaced him as heir apparent. Hsiao Kang became a focal point of literary values quite different from those represented in Hsiao T'ung's anthology. Hsiao Kang was himself a prolific poet, with more than two hundred pieces still extant, and, like his father, he felt the influence of the popular *yüeh-fu* of the south. As did many other Six Dynasties poets, he wrote some pieces on martial themes, including frontier poetry (*pien-sai shih*), a martial subgenre in which even southerners deploy the imagery of traditional northern border areas. But he is more famous by far as an advocate of what is called, because of its connection with the Eastern Palace (the heir apparent's residence), Palace-Style Poetry. Palace-Style Poetry deals largely with the material and sensual aspects of court life. Poems on objects figure prominently, as do poems on women and love and, occasionally, homosexual relationships between men. The poems on women are closely related to the poems on objects in that the women are objectified in such poems, which have little or no emotional content. Although there was already a strong tendency toward Palace-Style Poetry before this time, it may have been imitation of the works of Hsü Ling's father, Hsü Ch'ih (472–549), at Hsiao's court that finally established the style. Just how far advanced it already was by Hsü Ch'ih's time, however, is shown by the fact that many Palace-Style poems by Ch'i and early Liang period poets like Ho Hsün (c. 472–c. 519), Shen Yüeh, Wang Jung, and Wu Chün (469–520) are collected in *New Songs from a Jade Terrace*. Oddly enough, none by Hsü Ch'ih are included, whereas Hsiao Kang's other tutor, Yü Chien-wu (c. 487–c. 552), is well represented.

Yü Chien-wu was the father of the finest poet of the late sixth century, Yü Hsin (513–581). Yü Hsin began in Hsiao Kang's salon, where he composed Palace-Style Poetry and absorbed the evolving principles of tonal prosody. In the aftermath of the terrible rebellion of Hou Ching (502–552), which cost Hsiao Kang and countless others their lives, Yü was sent north as an envoy to the Western Wei and was prevented by that regime from returning south. Soon the Liang collapsed, to be replaced by the Ch'en dynasty.

Yü Hsin was treated with honor in the north, where he had long been famous as a poet. He served as an official there, first under the Western Wei (535–556) and then under the Northern Chou (557–581). Although he continued to write court poetry, he also wrote pieces about the hardships he had encountered and his longing for his old homeland. His major piece in this regard is "Ai Chiang-nan fu" (Rhapsody Lamenting the South), a long rhapsody both lyrical and historical in nature that tells of Hou Ching's rebellion, the fall of the Liang, and the usurpation by the Ch'en, attaching blame to the Liang rulers, describing the plight of southern captives in the north, and relating his own difficult lot. Yü Hsin's experience was not unique. Large numbers of southerners found themselves in the north, most no doubt in much worse circumstances. Other poets wound up there, too, including Hsü Ling and Wang Pao (513?–577?). Their poetry, too, underwent a thematic and emotional shift in the north.

Most of Yü's extant two hundred fifty poems date from his years in the north. Illustrative of his works is a celebrated cycle of twenty-seven pieces entitled "Ni 'Yung-huai'" (Imitating "Songs of My Soul"), ostensibly modeled on the works of Juan Chi. These poems rely heavily on allusions. The twenty-sixth of the group, for example, is a frontier poem. The first four lines of the octave consist of frontier imagery, but the last four contain three allusions—first to Su Wu, the Western Han envoy to the Hsiung-nu; then to the heroic would-be assassin Ching K'o (d. 227 B.C.E.); and finally, by means of the "Song of Kai-hsia," to the Ch'u commander Hsiang Yü.

In a sense, then, we end where we began—a late-sixth-century poet returns to Hsiang Yü's late-third-century B.C.E. Ch'u Song in a very nearly perfect example of T'ang regulated verse. Yü Hsin was the last great poet of the early medieval period. He represents in his person what had not been attained politically for three hundred years and more—a fusion of north and south. After the brief interlude of the Sui dynasty (581–618), that fusion was to come soon and would lead the way to the consummate writers of the T'ang, who continued to look back to their predecessors as a source in creating their own poetry.

Robert Joe Cutter

Chapter 14

POETRY OF THE T'ANG DYNASTY

The three centuries of the T'ang dynasty (618–907) are traditionally seen as the time of the fullest flowering and highest excellence of Chinese poetry. "Poetry" in this context refers only to verse in the *shih* form, sometimes identified as "lyric poetry." In the orthodox allotment of generic "golden ages" in Chinese literary history, the *shih* is assigned to the T'ang as that dynasty's consummate form of poetic expression, just as the *fu* (see chapter 12) stands as cynosure for the Han dynasty, the *tz'u* (see chapter 15) for the Sung, and the *ch'ü*[1] (see chapter 17) for the Yüan. However, the *fu* (rhapsody) remained in T'ang times an important genre of poetry, and it must be taken into account in any survey of T'ang poetry that is not willfully restricted. The T'ang also witnessed the first definite stirrings of the *tz'u* form, but that subject will be dealt with in a separate chapter.

In any discussion of T'ang poetry, the reader should keep in mind that the presumed unity of this subject is a scholarly construct, dependent mainly on the political duration of the dynastic house. The T'ang enjoyed a reign comparable in length to the entire period from the accession of Elizabeth I to that of Victoria in England; from the birth of Benjamin Franklin to the present day in the United States; or, to use a Chinese example, the centuries of disunion from the fall of the Western Chin in 316 to the founding of the T'ang itself in 618. When we realize this and think how formidable it would be to characterize the verse of such times as a uniform phenomenon, we may better appreciate the variety of different aspects and emphases that T'ang poetry comprises.

PERIODIZATION

With regard to T'ang *shih*, later scholars have sought to organize the tangles of literary history by means of periodization. The Ming dynasty scholar Kao Ping (1350–1423) detailed in the general preface to his large anthology of T'ang poetry (*T'ang-shih p'in-hui* [Graded Collocation of T'ang Poetry]) a periodization scheme that, with some quibbling, has enjoyed widespread acceptance among scholars for the past five hundred years. Kao's scheme builds on the earlier suggestions of the Sung critic Yen Yü (c. 1195–c. 1245) and the opinions of Kao Ping's contemporary Lin Hung (c. 1340–c. 1400). This fourfold periodization divides T'ang *shih* into (1) an "early" (*ch'u*) stage, lasting from the founding of the dynasty to 705, followed by a transitional stage of seven years that leads to (2) a time of "fullness" (*sheng*), often referred to in English as the "High T'ang," comprising the forty-four-year reign of the great Emperor Hsüan-tsung (712–756), followed by a transitional decade that in turn ushers in (3) the "middle" (*chung*) era of T'ang poetry, stretching from 766 to 806 and representing a time of second fullness (*tsai-ṣheng*), which modulates during a gradual fifteen-year changeover into (4) a "late" (*wan*) age, spanning the years from 821 to the end of the T'ang in 907.

This standard periodization is not objective but evaluative and owes at least as much to considerations of political and moral history as it does to the complex realities of literary history. In particular, the elevated position it awards to the poets of Hsüan-tsung's reign both reflects and contributes to the tendency to think of the "High T'ang" as the apex of T'ang verse, if not its only salience. There is also an organic hint to this perspective on T'ang *shih*. Thus the "early" period is a time of weakness, still in thrall to the influence of the preceding Six Dynasties era, but it gradually develops distinctive traits that prepare the way for the mature and vigorous style of the time of "fullness," a ripeness that—despite occasional jolts of renewed vitality—lapses during the "middle" and "late" stages into progressive decline and eventual decadence. The following discussion shows that this view of T'ang *shih* is often belied by the facts. The question of periodizing the T'ang *fu* is addressed in the subsection below on the forms of the rhapsody.

FORMS OF T'ANG POETRY

The T'ang *shih* includes assorted forms. The staple was verse in pentasyllabic lines. Since the second century C.E. this had been the most favored form for *shih* poetry, and it remained so through the T'ang, although verse in heptasyllabic lines became increasingly popular from the eighth century onward. The number of lines in a poem, or, more accurately (from the viewpoint of the creating poet), the number of couplets, was not prescribed. However, there is a pronounced preference for poems made up of multiples of four lines, the quatrain (*chüeh-chü*) being the lower limit and two hundred lines (i.e., one hundred rhymes) being the rarely achieved upper limit. When attention to the tonal qualities of the language as well as the use of syntactic parallelism between the lines of couplets is lacking, sporadic, or not strictly patterned, we have what is called in the T'ang "Old-Style" (*ku-t'i*) verse. Poems designated as *ko* (songs) also fall under this general rubric but do not seem to have as strong a penchant as other *ku-t'i* poems for resolving themselves in multiples of four lines; indeed the shortest "songs" typically consist of six lines. Finally, the *ku-t'i* category also includes poems in the *sao* style, recalling the works attributed to Ch'ü Yüan in the *Ch'u tz'u* (Elegies of Ch'u) anthology. It is sometimes just as reasonable to include such works under the heading of *fu*.

The contrasting "Recent-Style" (*chin-t'i*) verse of the T'ang requires observance of euphonic strictures throughout the poem and of parallelism in designated couplets. Recent-Style verse builds on the theories and occasional practice of Shen Yüeh (441–513) and his followers, who sought to reproduce by means of tonal prosody in Chinese the auditory effects realized by use of the *śloka* meter in Buddhist Sanskrit poetry. This important development in Chinese poetry led eventually to the creation of the T'ang *lü-shih* (regulated verse). For this purpose, the four tone-classes (*p'ing*, level; *shang*, rising; *ch'ü*[2], departing; *ju*, entering) of Middle Chinese were disposed in a binary opposition of "level" (*p'ing*) and "deflected" (*tse*, comprising the three nonlevel classes). In ideal form, the pentametric *lü-shih* demanded a mirror-image balancing of level and deflected tones in the words occupying the second and fourth position in the opposing lines of a couplet, thus: xAxBx/xBxAx. For heptasyllabic lines the significant words are the second, fourth, and sixth: xAxBxAx/xBxAxBx. The *lü-shih* was restricted in length to eight lines, with syntactic parallelism expected both between the lines of the second couplet and between those of the third couplet. Additional rules, deriving from the "eight defects" (*pa ping*) identified by Shen Yüeh, where tonal and other prosodic infelicities fall elsewhere, were elaborated during the T'ang into a full twenty-eight faults to be avoided; but many of these points have more theoretical than practical consequence, to judge from the frequency with which they were ignored by the poets themselves. The first decade of the eighth century saw the codification of the *lü-shih* into its now-standard form. The composition of *shih* poetry as an occasional requirement in the civil service examination likely played a role here.

Also included in the category of "Recent-Style" verse is the *p'ai-lü*. A *p'ai-lü* is essentially an extended sequence of couplets displaying the traits of the middle (i.e., second and third) couplets of a *lü-shih*. The final couplet of a *p'ai-lü*, as sometimes the opening couplet, is usually free of syntactic parallelism. Although a *p'ai-lü* may run to whatever length the poet desires, compositions in multiples of eight lines are most common. Lastly, quatrains (*chüeh-chü*) that adhere to the rules of tonal euphony and in which at least one couplet exhibits parallelism may also be classified among *chin-t'i shih*.

Yüeh-fu (ballad) verse is formally a kind of *ku-t'i* poetry but is usually treated separately. The most familiar sort adopts titles and affiliated themes from earlier *yüeh-fu*, producing (in the best case) individual variations or (in less satisfying cases) literary exercises on traditional topics. Most *yüeh-fu* are written in standard pentasyllabic or heptasyllabic lines, but some poets—most notably Li Po—also make use of mixed line lengths, ranging from trisyllabic to enneasyllabic and even decasyllabic, in a single poem. The so-called new (*hsin*) *yüeh-fu* created by Po Chü-yi and others in the early ninth century was an attempt to reinvigorate the tradition by introducing into it topics of contemporary social and political concern. Another type of *yüeh-fu* is that commissioned for performance at designated official and court rituals. These poems were typically accompanied by music (now lost), thus continuing in the tradition of the original *yüeh-fu* of Han times. The most often employed meter in such ceremonial lyrics is tetrasyllabic, presumably because of the archaic and classical associations of the four-beat line. Performative *yüeh-fu* verse from the T'ang has been largely ignored by scholars, but it offers insights into the more formal productions of court poets as well as into the workings of court ritual itself.

Although the T'ang *fu* has not been studied as intensively or continually as T'ang *shih* poetry, some scholars, such as Wang Ch'i-sun (1755–1818), have characterized it as occupying a place of importance in the long history of the *fu* genre comparable to that held by the T'ang *shih* in the history of that genre. Like the *shih*, the *fu* embraces a variety of forms. In all of them the "Four-Six style" (*ssu-liu t'i*), referring to lines of primarily tetra- or hexasyllabic length with frequent parallelism, predominates.

The large-scale display, or epideictic, *fu* characteristic of the Han dynasty was still occasionally written during the T'ang. But the efforts of *fu* poets mostly took a different direction from the seventh through the ninth centuries. Continuing a trend evident during the Six Dynasties period (317–589), T'ang rhapsodists were partial to the "smaller [*hsiao*] *fu*." The adjective must be understood in a relative sense, for it is not unusual for such pieces to run more than fifty lines—small when compared with the display *fu* but still larger than most *shih*. This form was used in celebrating single objects in detail (*yung-wu*), in expressing one's own feelings (*shu-ch'ing*), and in commenting on contemporary topics and satirizing or indirectly criticizing government practices (*feng-tz'u*), the last a focus that—although inherent in the earliest examples of the *fu*—was more fully exploited during the T'ang than in any preceding era.

The *lü-fu*, or "regulated *fu*," made its appearance as a distinct form during the early eighth century, becoming the usual kind of rhapsody required for the *chin-shih* examination as well as for various special or "decree" examinations. It was gradually employed by writers for more personal expression as well. Except for its rhyming imperative, the regulated *fu* is similar to parallel prose (*p'ien-t'i wen*) in its employment of syntactic parity between the lines of every couplet. The fact that most official documents produced by the T'ang government were composed in the parallel style made the *lü-fu* an effective form with which to test the writing skill of potential bureaucrats—and also their command of literary tradition, since an examination *fu* would have a set topic, usually historical or philosophical in nature, and a stipulated sequence of rhymes the paradigms of which, read as a complete sentence, would deliver an interpretive comment on the topic of the *fu* itself.

The *su-fu*, or "*fu* in common speech," appeared late in the ninth century, making abundant use of vernacular and oral elements in its diction and syntax. Examples, by anonymous writers, are found among the Tun-huang materials (see chapter 48). But, as the *su-fu* usually leans more toward prose in its presentation, rhyming only loosely and sometimes not at all, it falls beyond the bounds of this chapter. The same is true of the so-called *wen-fu*, or "prose *fu*," experimented with by a few ninth-century writers, which was to become popular during the Sung dynasty. The oral qualities of the *su-fu*, however, recall in a somewhat altered way the original performative nature of the early *fu*.

There is no recognized periodization for the T'ang *fu*. One that might be suggested on purely stylistic grounds would include three divisions. The "early" period extends, as is the case with the *shih*, to the first decade of the eighth century. The "middle" period, marked by the rise of the *lü-fu*, lasts from the beginning of Hsüan-tsung's reign in 712 to the mid-820s, a century or more during which the topics of such rhapsodies are generally of an "official" or court-oriented temper. The "late" period, from the mid-820s onward, corresponds with the increasing use of the *lü-fu* in writing of less public, more privately pertinent subjects. Although *fu* in the older forms were, of course, written throughout the T'ang, the development of the regulated rhapsody is a convenient phenomenon by which to periodize the T'ang *fu*.

Because of space limitations and the fact that *fu* cannot be properly appreciated in brief excerpts, examples from such works are not included here. The few examples of verse to be presented in this chapter are perforce restricted to couplets or short poems in the *shih* form. But it would be wrong to conclude from this that *fu* were less prized in the T'ang than *shih* or of minor concern to the poets of that time.

THE SOURCES AND THEIR LIMITATIONS

When studying T'ang *shih* and *fu*, it is normal first to consult, respectively, the *Ch'üan T'ang shih* (Complete T'ang Poems, or *CTS*) and *Ch'üan T'ang wen* (Complete T'ang Prose, or *CTW*). The former, which contains more than 48,900 poems by more than 2,200 individuals, was compiled during the years 1705–1707; the latter, which contains more than 18,400 compositions (including more than fifteen hundred *fu*—it is interesting to observe that *fu* were treated by the editors as a type of prose) by more than 3,000 individuals, was compiled during 1808–1814. Both were court-sponsored projects that aimed to be more comprehensive than previous such compilations, upon which they drew heavily. However, it must be remembered that neither is a primary source and that neither justifies its editorial decisions when choosing between variant readings of a text. Hence, despite their size and the convenience with which they may be consulted, these two compendia do not always present the most reliable recension of a given text. Nor do they constitute the complete corpus of T'ang poetry. The Tun-huang materials have added a large number of *shih* and some *fu*, plus many variant readings, to the works found in *CTS* and *CTW*. And further additions have been made to the corpus from other sources either not available to or ignored by the Ch'ing dynasty compilers. For *shih*, most such stray pieces are now collected in the *CTS pu-pien* (Supplements to the Complete T'ang Poems).

Editions of individual poets' works, at least those that include text-critical information and full variora, are more reliable sources than the *CTS* and *CTW*. However, only about a hundred T'ang poets are actually represented by an individual edition today, and few of these can be traced back with any authority to even the eleventh century, much less the T'ang itself. The despoilment and wasting of the T'ang imperial library, after the ravaging of the capital at Ch'ang-an during 756–757, 762, and 881–882, caused a heavy loss to posterity of writings of all kinds—as did the dissolution of numerous private libraries in times of trouble. Thus, although far more specimens (more than 50,000) of verse survive from the T'ang than from any preceding period in Chinese history, what remains is but a small fraction of the contemporary output. This is especially so for the seventh century. It is not uncommon to find scholar-officials from the dynasty's first three reigns (618–684) noted in the imperial library catalog of 721 as having left behind collections of forty or more *chüan*, collections that had disintegrated or been lost, however, by the tenth century and that today exist as merely one or two reconstructed *chüan* and only a dozen or so poems. There are known gaps even in the extant works of Li Po and Tu Fu, the two most famous and therefore most comprehensively edited T'ang poets. In view of the practice of individual writers' preparing collections of their own works, as Yüan Chen and Po Chü-yi did in the ninth century, the odds for relatively more complete preservation, at least at the first stage, increase—but this was by no means the norm during T'ang times.

Anthologies furnish another source of T'ang poetry, starting most importantly with those compiled during the T'ang itself. More than 130 contemporary T'ang anthologies of *shih*, arranged in various fashions—some by subject matter, some by a delimited time, others by poetic form or by the geographical provenance of the authors—are known to scholars today. The *CTS* and the *CTW* and their precursors made much use of such works. Alas, only thirteen of these exist today in full or partial recensions: 1. the misnamed *Han-lin hsüeh-shih chi* (Anthology of Han-lin Academicians), which includes sets of matching poems by Emperor T'ai-tsung (r. 626–649) and members of his court, possibly collected by Hsü Ching-tsung; 2. the fragmentary *Sou-yü hsiao-chi* (Little Collection of Discovered Jade), compiled by an anonymous scholar in the late 730s or early 740s, containing poems by court poets of the preceding ninety years, its one extant *chüan* (of an original ten) including sixty-one works by thirty-seven writers; 3. the fragmentary *Chu-ying hsüeh-shih chi* (Anthology of the "Choice-Gem" Academicians), recovered from Tun-huang, consisting of poems composed by those courtiers charged with compiling the mammoth *San-chiao chu-ying* (Choice Gems of the Three Teachings) encyclopedia in 699–701, collected by Ts'ui Jung; 4. *Tan-yang chi* (A Tan-yang Anthology), a small collection of poems by writers hailing from the Wu area (lower Yangtze River valley), compiled by Yin Fan between 735 and 741; 5. *Ho-yüeh ying-ling chi* (The Finest Souls of River and Alp), the most important extant T'ang anthology, being a collection of more than 230 poems dating from 714 to 753 by twenty-four of the most prominent writers of Emperor Hsüan-tsung's reign, also compiled by Yin Fan; 6. *Kuo-hsiu chi* (Fullest Flowers of the State), including 220 poems by eighty-eight writers from the beginning of the T'ang until 744, compiled by Jui T'ing-chang; 7. *Ch'ieh-chung chi* (Out of the Book-Bin), a little anthology, made in 760, of twenty-four poems by seven writers contemporary with the compiler, Yüan Chieh, who admired their moral temper and lamented their lack of official position; 8. *Yü-t'ai hou-chi* (Another Jade Terrace Anthology), a fragment of an originally larger collection of poems on romantic and erotic themes, meant to be a continuation of the Liang dynasty (502–557) anthology *Yü-t'ai hsin-yung* (New Songs from a Jade Terrace) and including works dating from the end of the Liang until the 760s (counting fourteen pre-T'ang and forty-five T'ang writers), compiled by Li K'ang-ch'eng; 9. *Chung-hsing chien-ch'i chi* (The Interjacent Spirit of the Restoration), consisting of 130-some poems by twenty-six writers active in the period immediately after the quelling of the An Lu-shan rebellion from approximately 760 to 780, compiled by Kao Chung-wu in the mid-780s; 10. *Yü-lan shih* (Poems for Imperial Perusal), including 286 "Recent-Style" poems by thirty writers active during the four decades from 765 to 805, compiled by Ling-hu Ch'u between 814 and 817; 11. *Chi-hsüan chi* (Collection of the Superlatively Mysterious), comprising exactly one hundred poems, mostly pentametric *lü-shih*, by twenty-one writers dating from the 740s to the early 800s, compiled by Yao Ho; 12. *Yu-hsüan chi* (Collection of the Even More Mysterious), not merely, as the title would suggest, a continuation of the preceding anthology but, rather, of much larger scope, including poems (often only one and never more than a few) by 150 writers from all decades of the eighth and ninth centuries, compiled by Wei Chuang in 900; 13. *Ts'ai-tiao chi* (Collection of the Melodies of Genius), the last and largest of contemporary anthologies, comprising a thousand poems by writers from all periods of the T'ang but with most emphasis on the ninth century, compiled by Wei Hu sometime between 910 and 925, although now badly disordered.

The most important Sung dynasty repositories of T'ang verse are the *Wen-yüan ying-hua* (Finest Flowers from the Preserve of Letters; completed by a team of court scholars in 987) and *T'ang wen ts'ui* (The Pure Sum of T'ang

Literature; completed 1011, edited by Yao Hsüan), both of which include capacious selections of T'ang *shih* and *fu* as well as compositions in prose genres. Restricted to *shih* are two other influential collections. These are *T'ang-shih chi-shih* (Recorded Occasions of T'ang Poetry; compiled by Chi Yu-kung in the first half of the twelfth century), an anthology of more than eleven hundred T'ang poets with accompanying biographical and anecdotal information, and *Yüeh-fu shih-chi* (Collection of Ballad Poetry; compiled by Kuo Mao-ch'ien in the twelfth century), a comprehensive collection of *yüeh-fu* verse from the very beginnings of the genre but especially rich in T'ang compositions. All four of these works were drawn on heavily by the compilers of *Ch'üan T'ang shih* and *Ch'üan T'ang wen.*

Among Ming dynasty collections of T'ang *shih,* two, of enormous size, also contributed importantly to the eventual production of the *CTS.* The *T'ang-shih p'in-hui,* completed 1393, of Kao Ping (noted above as codifying the four-fold periodization of T'ang *shih*) includes more than 6,700 poems by 681 poets in one hundred *chüan,* arranged according to form. Many times larger still was the *T'ang-yin t'ung-ch'ien* (Comprehensive Inventory of T'ang Lyrics), an immense compendium assembled by Hu Chen-heng in the early seventeenth century. This contained (no complete text remains today) a full thousand *chüan* of poems from the T'ang and the succeeding Five Dynasties, plus thirty-three *chüan* of critical remarks. Hu's collection in fact formed the direct basis of the *CTS,* along with the equally massive and anticipatorily named *Ch'üan T'ang shih* compiled in the late Ming or early Ch'ing period by Ch'ien Ch'ien-yi and Chi Chen-yi. The Ch'ien/Chi *CTS,* which exists today only in one rare edition held in the National Central Library of Taipei, contains 42,931 poems by 1,895 T'ang authors. Important supplements to the *CTS* corpus derive most notably from the Tun-huang materials and from manuscripts previously lost in China but recovered in Japan.

The final collection of T'ang *shih* that needs to be cited reverses the trend toward inclusiveness tracked here. This is the ubiquitously famous *T'ang-shih san-pai-shou* (Three Hundred T'ang Poems), published by Sun Chu in 1764. One of many such Ch'ing anthologies, its selection of three hundred poems representing its compiler's view of the best models in the various *shih* forms has achieved great popularity in the past two centuries. It has also exerted significant influence, for it is now typically one's first introduction to T'ang *shih.* The negative effect of this is the degree to which general readers and, too often, scholars have in recent times accepted unquestioningly the evaluations implied in Sun's selection of poets and of poems. One's understanding of T'ang *shih* is thereby hastily and stiffly circumscribed. Another drawback to this anthology is its capricious and often demonstrably incorrect handling of textual variants.

With regard to *fu,* there is not a similarly extensive history of compilations and anthologies focusing on T'ang works. Besides the collections of individual authors, and grouped collections such as *T'ang wu-shih-chia shih-chi* (Collected Works of Fifty T'ang Poets), the main repositories of T'ang *fu*—after *Wen-yüan ying-hua* and *T'ang wen ts'ui*—are encyclopedias such as *Yü-hai* (Sea of Jade; completed 1252, first published 1337), *Yüan-chien lei-han* (Classified Repository of the Profound Mirror; 1701), and *Ku-chin t'u-shu chi-ch'eng* (Collection of Ancient and Modern Books and Charts; 1725), all of which were exploited by the *CTW* compilers. Thus, the surviving texts of all T'ang verse are the result of various and sometimes uncertain paths of filiation. Problems and questions remain in countless instances. But a general survey of T'ang verse need not delve into the finer points of textual criticism. To this survey we now turn.

For the sake of convenience, and also to avoid being confined too strictly by post-T'ang interpretive systems, this discussion organizes the subject by centuries, acknowledging that such a division into three parts must be somewhat loose. The history of T'ang verse in the main fits such a structure at least as well as any other.

THE SEVENTH CENTURY

The establishment of the T'ang dynasty in June 618 does not mark an abrupt break or new direction in belles lettres. However, the first T'ang emperors, Kao-tsu (r. 618–626) and his son T'ai-tsung, drew together at court the most learned scholar-officials of the first half of the seventh century, including some whose renown reached back to the early Sui (581–618). There was keen interest in establishing for the new dynasty a reputation for court-sponsored official scholarship. This was partly intended as a contrast with the Sui, who had done little in this area. Indeed the fondness of the last Sui emperor, Yang-ti, for poetry composition in the "southern" style, especially when placed next to the absence of orthodox (particularly historiographic) scholarly projects during the Sui, was taken as a sign of that regime's moral failing.

Accordingly, in 622, Emperor Kao-tsu ordered the compilation of a literary encyclopedia, the *Yi-wen lei-chü* (Categorical Medley of Literary Texts), which was completed two years later in one hundred *chüan* by a team headed by Ou-yang Hsün (557–641). This was the only project finished before Kao-tsu's forced abdication to T'ai-tsung in September 626, but the founding emperor was also responsible for the commissioning of official histories for the dynasties of the Northern Wei, Liang, Ch'en, Northern Ch'i, Northern Chou, and Sui. Begun in 623, this project was completed in 636 (except for the monographs, which were added to the *Sui shu* [History of the Sui Dynasty] alone in 656, and the Wei history, which was finally omitted), after T'ai-tsung replaced the original team in 629 with a new group headed by Fang Hsüan-ling (578–648) and Wei Cheng (see below). The establishment of a set of fixed texts for the Confucian canon and the promulgation of imperially sanctioned commentaries claimed the participation of many scholars during T'ai-tsung's reign and resulted in the publication in 631 of definitive versions (*ting-pen*) of the Five Classics, due to

Yen Shih-ku (581–645), and in 654 of orthodox interpretations (*cheng-yi*) of the Five Classics, the joint work of two successive commissions, headed respectively by K'ung Ying-ta (578–648) and Chang-sun Wu-chi (c. 600–659). Founded in early 621 was the Hsiu-wen kuan (College for the Cultivation of Literature), which included a separate library ancillary to the imperial collection (now being built up assiduously after the inevitable depredations of wartime following the Sui's downfall) and whose members were on call for consultation with the emperor. The institution's name was changed in 626 to Hung-wen kuan (College for the Enhancement of Literature) and remained so throughout most of the dynasty.

Well before he ascended the throne, Emperor T'ai-tsung had sought to surround himself with men both learned and politically astute, beginning in 621 with the creation of his own advisory brain trust called the Wen-hsüeh kuan (College of Literary Studies). Counted among its original eighteen members were the historian Fang Hsüan-ling and the classicist K'ung Ying-ta, both mentioned above, and Lu Te-ming (556–627), author of the phonological dictionary *Ching-tien shih-wen* (Textual Explications for the Classical Canon), the historian Yao Ssu-lien (?–637), principal compiler of the *Liang shu* (History of the Liang Dynasty) and *Ch'en shu* (History of the Ch'en Dynasty), as well as several individuals who were or would become famous for their poetry.

Among the last the most senior was Yü Shih-nan (558–638), a southerner who had already served at the Ch'en and Sui courts. Only four of his *fu* and thirty-odd *shih* remain, but they show his skill in several styles. Like the work of most court poets for at least the first sixty years of the T'ang, the majority of Yü's extant poetry consists of pieces written on command, to set topics or set rhymes, at gatherings and banquets. These exhibit the rich diction associated with the sixth century and at times surprisingly fresh, uncluttered images. Yü Shih-nan's long rhapsodies on a lion (*shih-tzu*, which had been presented to the court by an embassy from Samarkand in 635) and on the lute (*p'i-p'a*), two objects of foreign provenance, merit reading. His *shih* depicting soldiers' hardships in the far northwest are often viewed as prototypes of T'ang "frontier" poetry. Yü Shih-nan was, as much as anyone, the emperor's own preceptor of poetry. A famous anecdote tells that once, when T'ai-tsung showed the eminent writer a Palace-Style (*kung-t'i*) poem he had composed, thinking to use it as the base-text for a round of matching verses to be written by his courtiers, Yü stopped him by saying that, although the composition itself was skillful, this style of poetry was not proper (*ya-cheng*) and that, if the emperor's liking for such verse were widely known, it would surely provoke an imitative mania for this impolitic style among his subjects. Yü's critique is meant to evoke the censures of the Liang, Ch'en, and Sui rulers who lost their empires while fostering overly precious styles in literature.

T'ai-tsung himself, as the preceding story suggests, was no mere bystander when it came to literary activities. Nearly a hundred of his *shih* and five *fu* remain, one of the largest corpora of any T'ang poet before the end of the century, no doubt owing to the solicitude with which a monarch's works would be preserved. The majority of T'ai-tsung's poems, in spite of Yü Shih-nan's admonition, are in the "Palace Style," and they rarely stand out from those of his vassals. This is most apparent when one compares T'ai-tsung's poems with theirs on occasions when he and various courtiers participated in writing matching poems; examples from eight such occasions can be found in the *Han-lin hsüeh-shih chi* anthology. A charming couplet, such as "The shade of the pine-tree turns with the sun on its back; / Shadows of the bamboo slue before the wind," is more the exception than the rule. Some sense of the man's own voice comes through most clearly in his verses on hunts and outings and in those that celebrate his past martial successes.

Wei Cheng (580–643), T'ai-tsung's most trusted and candid court minister, is the author of several stolid sequences of ceremonial *yüeh-fu* for ritual use. However, of his handful of other efforts, one, called "Shu huai" (Expressing Heart-held Thoughts), is usually pointed to as a forerunner of the cleaner, more sinewy style of the eighth century. This is a twenty-line contemplation of the poet's political convictions and personal feelings upon setting out on a diplomatic mission; it is most strongly reminiscent of some of the verse of Ts'ao Chih (192–232). His lone remaining *fu*, on "Tao-kuan nei po-shu fu" (A Cypress Tree at a Taoist Abbey), has some similar flashes. Wei Cheng's other important piece of writing, from the standpoint of literary history, is his preface to the chapter on men of letters in the *Sui shu*. This lays out the traditional dichotomy between the ornate southern style of poetry (tending to finickiness) and the sturdy northern style (tending to plainness) and states that the strengths of both are now being combined under the T'ang, with their excesses avoided. Echoes of this document, especially its characterizations of southern verse, will resound in various manifestoes and critical pronouncements into the eighth century.

Notable poets of Kao-tsu's and T'ai-tsung's reigns worth at least a mention here include Ch'u Liang (560–647) and Li Pai-yao (565–648), both southerners who had earlier served at the Sui court; Yang Shih-tao (?–647), who was affiliated with the Sui royal line but married to a T'ang princess and among whose works is one of the earliest specimens of a formally perfect *p'ai-lü*, "Huan shan-chai" (Returning to My Mountain Studio); and Ch'en Tzu-liang (?–632). The last deserves more study than he usually receives, for his thirteen extant *shih* display a liveliness and bright tone that is striking. Particularly worth noting is his poem "Ju Shu ch'iu-yeh su chiang-chu" (Passing an Autumn Night on a River Islet on the Way to Shu), which bears comparison to any landscape/travel verse thought typical of the High T'ang: "I travel on till I meet the sun's setting; / Stilling the oars, I tie the boat up alone. / Mist rises over the water from one side, / While the woods are all autumn in the breeze on both shores. / The darkness of mountains throws black across the shingles, / And moonlight shadows show pale in the chill current. / My own home is a thousand miles behind— / What is there that can soothe a wayfarer's sadness?" Before considering Hsü Ching-tsung and Shang-kuan Yi, two court poets whose work and influence lasted well into the next reign, we must briefly step outside the court.

A poet who stands apart from the others of his day is Wang Chi (590–644). Younger half-brother of the Confucian teacher Wang T'ung and of the scholar-official Wang Tu (author of the famous tale "Ku-ching chi" [Record of an Ancient Mirror]), Wang Chi is best known as a self-conscious recluse who seems never to have felt comfortable at court. Although he was at the Sui court as a young man and twice had positions (623–627 and 637–638) in Ch'ang-an during the T'ang, he resigned both offices, preferring to be unfettered by obligation. His poetic remains include four *fu*, more than fifty *shih*, and stray fragments. Unlike the work of his contemporaries, his *shih* contain no "on command" or matching poems. Instead poem after poem sings the pleasures of rustic life, the natural scene, and full measures of wine. These often contain deliberate traces of poems by T'ao Ch'ien (365–427) on similar themes, though Wang's verse is sometimes less genial than his model's. Wang's rhapsodies are quite interesting. His *fu* on the swallow is actually an allegorical disquisition on dynastic change; the "Yüan-cheng fu" (New Year's Rhapsody; recovered from Tun-huang) includes valuable descriptions of T'ang holiday practices, as does the early and rather less successful *fu* on the festival of the third day of the third month. "Yu pei-shan fu" (Wandering on North Mountain) is a prodigious composition written in 640, late in Wang's life, combining personal recollection with philosophical speculation and much beautiful description of landscape. While it is tempting to look at Wang Chi as an outsider, it may be more accurate to see in his works the complementary—not opposed—portion of a scholar's personality, in this case purposely restricted to a few chosen themes. The narrowed focus of his *shih* poetry is not necessarily a positive attribute, though it is often regarded as such by those who see the poetry produced at court as morally demeaning.

Probably the two most influential poets of their time were Hsü Ching-tsung (592–672) and Shang-kuan Yi (c. 608–665), both of whom carried the literary practices of the first quarter-century of T'ang rule into the reign of Emperor Kao-tsung (649–683). The former's reputation suffered in later centuries because of the supposed taint adhering to him as a supporter of Wu Tse-t'ien, the capable and ruthless empress who held complete sway at court from approximately 660 to 705, ruling in her own name as monarch of a new Chou dynasty beginning in October 690. Shang-kuan Yi, however, as an antagonist and eventual victim of the empress (executed in January 665 for urging her removal), has enjoyed a better posthumous press than his quondam colleague. But the struggles for power in which they were engaged are not our concern. As a poet, Hsü Ching-tsung is consistently dexterous, handling with grace and erudition a range of topics in the nearly fifty court poems of his that have survived. Attention to the effects of light and radiance is a primary quality of his imagery.

His technical virtuosity is especially apparent in a pentametric eight-line palindrome verse, included in the *Han-lin hsüeh-shih chi* anthology. Because he is far better represented in this anthology than any other poet and penned the preface for one of the poem-sets preserved there, it has even been suggested that Hsü himself or one of his family members may have been the compiler.

Although Shang-kuan Yi's poems, like those of Hsü Ching-tsung, do not reveal the secrets of his heart, they exhibit an even more aureate gloss and polish. Here, for instance, is an eight-line "Ode on a Painted Screen" (Yung hua-chang), sketching in its balanced, somewhat arch diction scenes involving two different women painted on this *objet d'art,* making reference to several literary allusions: "Scented morn and beauteous sun at the Cove of the Peach Blossoms; / Curtains of pearls, drapes of halcyon feathers, in the Tower of the Phoenixes. / A girl from Ts'ai sings a song for picking caltrop, pulls at the brocaded tie-rope; / The paramour from Yen gazes out on springtime as she hangs a carnelian hook. / Fresh in her make-up, in a clepsydra's reflections the light fan of this one floats; / Wafting fragrance from that one's alluring sleeves falls into the shallow current. / One not inferior to the moving clouds descending to the terrace in Ching; / The other like the skimmer of waves roving by the banks of the Lo." It is worth underlining here that we are dealing with literary art that is highly traditional, in which disclosure of the author's personal history is not prized so much as mastery of conventional form: individuality emerges in the choice and precision of one's diction, the aptness of one's tectonic and phonetic structuring. Craft is more important than emotion. Indeed, there seems, during the second half of the seventh century, to be an increasing emphasis on formal aesthetics, a trend that was retrospectively designated by the reign-name of the years 661–664 as the "Lung-shuo transformation." This also reveals itself in heightened attention to the intricacies of parallelism and antithesis. Shang-kuan Yi himself wrote an analysis, including examples, of the six types of parison used in poetry; he followed this with a discussion, from a slightly different angle, of eight types. Phonetic patterning was subsumed under this subject as well. All this and more is to be found in Shang-kuan Yi's monograph on poetics, *Pi-cha hua-liang* (The Ornamented Ridgepole of Written Tablets), which exists today in remnants quoted in the important compendium of T'ang poetics and prosody, *Wen-ching mi-fu lun* (Treatise on the Secret Treasury of the Literary Mirror; in Japanese, *Bunkyō hifuron*), assembled in 819 by the Japanese Buddhist monk Kūkai (774–835) from materials gathered during his visit to China in 804–806. Shang-kuan Yi did not simply theorize but put his ideas into practice in his poetry. In due course, other writers began to adopt features of his verse, and the "Shang-kuan style" became a mode of composition central to court poetry until the end of the century.

Another monograph from this period concentrating on poetic theory is Yüan Ching's (fl. 661–684) *Shih sui-nao* (The Nous and Pith of Poetry). Also quoted in Kūkai's *Wen-ching mi-fu lun,* Yüan's work is a tighter refinement of the Ch'i-

Liang precepts on tonal euphony advocated by Shen Yüeh and his circle. It is interesting, however, that in his preface (also cited by Kūkai) to the *Ku-chin shih-jen hsiu-chü* (Outstanding Lines from Poets Ancient and Modern), an anthology he compiled, Yüan Ching states that feeling must come first in poetry, technique second.

The most conspicuous poets of the last quarter of the seventh century are Lo Pin-wang (c. 619–c. 687), Lu Chao-lin (c. 630–c. 685), Wang Po (649–676), and Yang Chiung (650–695?), traditionally referred to as the "Four Elites of Early T'ang" (Ch'u-T'ang ssu-chieh). Although they are usually spoken of as a group, these four poets belong to two different generations—Lu and Lo being older, Wang and Yang younger—and their personal contacts with one another were sporadic at best. It is a mistake to think of them as a coterie. The fact that each of them, in some fashion, reacted against or moved beyond the stiffening glitter of court poetry (even though they could and sometimes did write in this style) has led to their being viewed collectively. Unlike the major poets of the preceding decades, none of the four succeeded in climbing far up the official ladder; except for Yang Chiung, they all spent large portions of their life outside the capital. This is a significant change. Although poetry would remain throughout the T'ang an expected activity at court, the careers of the *ssu-chieh* are a convenient indicator of its beginning to flow in larger channels, which will increase henceforth. The broadening of the scope and venue of verse has some relation to the inevitable growth of the bureaucracy needed to fill the provincial posts of the expanding T'ang empire. In this process the lives and writings of an increasing number of persons who did not figure prominently in central government politics are revealed. The life of a Wang Chi, for example, will no longer seem as unusual as it did in the early years of the dynasty. Life in the capital is primary in one's desires for fame and honor and is clearly most helpful in circulating one's writings, but the spread of T'ang culture throughout the fifteen hundred prefectures that would constitute the mature empire brings into play other opportunities for professional and personal expression.

The "Four Elites" were conspicuous not only for their literary talent but also for their behavior. While Lo Pin-wang, Lu Chao-lin, and Wang Po had early in life found positions as retainers in the capital establishments of princes, and Yang Chiung had come to court as a child prodigy, they all encountered difficult times afterward. Lo and Lu were each incarcerated for brief periods, and Wang was convicted of murdering a slave girl whose escape from jail he had effected. Earlier, at the age of twenty, Wang was dismissed by order of the emperor himself from the retinue of Prince P'ei: an elaborate "call-to-arms" (*hsi*, usually reserved for detailing the faults of a ruler against whom one is mounting an assault) he had written in jest for a cockfight between the champion gallerines of Prince P'ei and Prince Chou was proof of his impropriety and presumption. Neither he nor Lo Pin-wang nor Lu Chao-lin ever reached the rank of even a district magistrate. Lo's life was forfeited in the unsuccessful rebellion of 684 against Empress Wu; Lu committed suicide after years of debilitating illness; Wang, though younger, predeceased them both, dying, perhaps by drowning, on his way back from Vietnam, where he had gone to join his exiled father. Yang was a quieter figure, but even he was rusticated because of family involvement in the 684 uprising; he eventually was called back to the capital and later given provincial appointment as magistrate of a small district, dying in unremarkable circumstances, the only one of the four to do so.

These were learned poets and they were not afraid to show, some would say flaunt, their learning. Thus Lo Pin-wang's two-hundred-line autobiographical poem "Ch'ou-hsi p'ien" (Times of Yesteryear), written in a mixture of parallel pentasyllabic and heptasyllabic lines, teems with allusions that fairly choke the vigor of the narrative, recalling in this respect Yü Hsin's (513–581) "Ai Chiang-nan fu" (Rhapsody Lamenting the South). This is a feature common to much of Lo's poetry, whether *shih* or *fu*, obviously more appealing to his contemporaries than to those who came later. Many of Lo's eight-line *shih*, especially those on natural objects or written as farewell pieces, are easier going. His longer *ku-t'i* poems, particularly those written entirely in heptasyllabic lines, contributed to a growing appreciation of verse done in a more swiftly moving and effusive "song" style.

Lu Chao-lin was a chief contributor to this vogue also, his two most famous efforts of this sort being his "Ch'ang-an ku-yi" (Old-time Thoughts of Ch'ang-an), set in the Han dynasty (206 B.C.E.–220 C.E.), and "Hsing lu nan" (Traveling the Road Is Hard), a quite original variation on an old *yüeh-fu* theme. Lu is a consistently interesting poet whose range of forms and topics is greater than those of the three men usually associated with him. All five of his remaining *fu* are masterpieces, and his *shih* are filled with surprising and satisfying turns of phrase. Witness, for example, these lines from "Chiang-chung wang yüeh" (Gazing at the Moon in the [Yangtze] Kiang): "Here the Kiang's waters turn toward Ts'en-yang, / Clear and limpid, transcribing the light of the moon. / The mirror now is round—a pearl translucent in the current; / The bowstring has filled out—arrows lengthen in the waves," in which, along with the more familiar image of the reflected moon-mirror as a submerged glowing pearl, we see with fresh eyes the ripples of the river transcribing (*hsieh*) the moonlight's water-borne flickerings and the latter themselves as bright-tipped arrows in the water, sent forth from the moon's seeming bow that is now full-drawn. Lu Chao-lin's most memorable works are those composed during his last tormented years, when, crippled by what seems to have been progressive rheumatoid arthritis, he sought with increasing desperation a cure for the disease that had rendered him lame of foot and palsied of hand. A significant portion of his poems are allegories of solitary or trapped birds, stranded fish, and blighted trees, containing harsh, cutting images played off against a tone of frustration and distress. Near the end of his life he created two lengthy and remarkable works, called "Wu pei" (Five Grievings) and "Shih-chi wen" (Text to Dispel Illness). These are multipart *sao*-style compositions, using prosodic schemes borrowed from the *Elegies of Ch'u*, and are artfully contrived, intensely personal meditations on the author's life that are deeply moving and at times painful to read. In them Lu Chao-lin becomes the only medieval poet to succeed in renewing the *sao* idiom and investing it with his own personality instead of a pale semblance of Ch'ü Yüan's. He finally chose to put an end to his physical agony by drowning himself in the Ying River, recalling his tragic predecessor's death in the Mi-lo River.

As a youth Lu Chao-lin had studied with Ts'ao Hsien (fl. 605–649), master philologist and doyen of *Wen hsüan* (Literary Selections) studies, and with Wang Yi-fang (615–669), an "old-text" scholar of the classics. Special study of the Liang anthology *Literary Selections* came into its own during the seventh century, capped by the important commentary of Li Shan (?–689), who was also a student of Ts'ao Hsien. Thorough knowledge of the *Wen hsüan* was, by the last half of the seventh century, added to knowledge of "classical" texts as indispensable for a cultivated education. This helped to shape what one may think of as an expanded canon, with increased emphasis on literary art, that would be *de rigueur* throughout the T'ang. The achievement of Lu Chao-lin and, to a lesser degree, Lo Pin-wang, Wang Po, and Yang Chiung lies in the extent to which they brought together in their poems lyricism, technique, and learning, without accenting one element to the detriment of the others.

Despite Wang Po's early death, more than ninety of his *shih* and a dozen *fu* are extant. Among his prose writings more than forty "prefaces" (*hsü*) are preserved, this being a genre that he virtually invented, or at least refitted as a vehicle for personal reflection. His famous "'Ch'iu-jih teng Hung-fu T'eng-wang ko chien-pieh hsü'" (Preface to "Ascending the Gallery of Prince T'eng of Hung-fu for a Parting Feast on an Autumn Day"), written in 675, is recognized as a bravura masterwork of parallel prose, but its style is not typical of most of Wang's prefaces. In his *shih* Wang shows a preference for the smaller format, octave and quatrain, and his best work presages the *chin-t'i* excellence of the celebrated poets of the eighth century. This is evident, for example, in his "Chung-ch'un chiao-wai" (Outside the Suburbs in Mid-Spring): "In the eastern garden, a path through dangling willows; / By the western embankment, a ford of fallen blossoms. / The look of things blends into the third month, / And a bright breeze wraps through all four environs. / Birds fly, and the village senses dawnglow; / Fishes sport, and the river knows it is spring. / Soft light early in a mountain cloister— / No place sullied by dust and din." His *fu* often resemble in their freshness and momentum the narrative, song-style *shih* of Lu Chao-lin and Lo Pin-wang. Wang Po's large-scale rhapsodies on "Springtime Longings" (Ch'un-ssu fu), which begins in Szechwan and then moves in thought to Ch'ang-an, the northwest frontier, Loyang, and Chin-ling, and on "Lotus-Picking" (Ts'ai-lien fu), an avowed attempt to improve on the verse treatment of the lotus by previous poets, are particularly engaging. A *fu* devoted to Śākyamuni Buddha ("Shih-chia Fo fu") is noteworthy for purposes of religious history. Had Wang Po lived to old or even middle age, he might well have become one of the greatest of all T'ang poets.

His reputation was burnished posthumously by a laudatory preface that Yang Chiung wrote in the early 680s for his collected works, in which Yang denigrates the "aberrant style" of poetry associated with the Lung-shuo era and extols Wang for his classicism. In this document Lu Chao-lin is credited with being the hero who, "discerning the clear guidelines, checked the ninefold exactions" of the overformalized court style. Although Yang Chiung's criticisms of the poetry of the preceding generation have been largely accepted by traditional scholars, they should be recognized as an attempt to create a discrete space for the poets and poetry that he values from his own time. Immediate literary antecedents are always hardest to dissociate oneself from and so come in for the roughest appraisal. As for Yang Chiung's own verse, while his *shih* are insignificant, his eight remaining *fu* are rich confections of scholarly lore and wordplay. Prominent among them are rhapsodies on "The Enveloping Sky" (Hun-t'ien fu) and on "The Old Man Star (designating our Canopus)" (Lao-jen hsing fu), both of which contain much fascinating information about T'ang astral beliefs, and that on the Buddhist Ullambana festival (Yü-lan-p'en fu) held in 692 at Empress Wu's behest in Loyang.

Yang Chiung received his first official appointment, to the prestigious Hung-wen College, when he was but a lad of nine years in 659, after passing the special civil service examination reserved for boys in their first decade of life. This was an unusual achievement. The more normal approach to the exam system was to sit for either the *ming-ching* (canonical expositor) or *chin-shih* (presented scholar) degree as a young man. This was the approach taken by Ch'en Tzu-ang (659–700?). Ch'en passed the *chin-shih* exam in 682 after failing once before. By his day the *chin-shih* had become the most difficult and hence most coveted of the degrees to attain, in contrast to the less demanding examination it had been in the first fifty years of the dynasty. Henceforth the *chin-shih* would be the gate by which many men who rank among the most famous T'ang poets entered public service.

Ch'en Tzu-ang is often regarded as the leading critic of ornate verse in the reprobate Ch'i-Liang style and the herald of a conscious return to the stronger Han-Wei style. This is due to statements he wrote in a brief preface (Ch'en was fond of providing prose introductions to his works) to a poem called "Hsiu-chu p'ien" (The Tapering Bamboo), probably composed in 698. As seen above, condemnation of sixth-century Palace-Style verse and its lingering effect on poetry of the present day was standard rhetoric from at least the time of Emperor T'ai-tsung. Ch'en Tzu-ang's declaration was neither novel nor more forcefully put than those of other writers, and it did not spark a "movement." The singular attention that has been paid to it in this regard is misplaced. Ch'en is more interesting as a poet than as a critic. More than a hundred of his *shih* have survived. Those most worthy of acclaim are the set of thirty-eight poems titled

"Kan-yü" (Empathetic Experiences). Written over a period of years, these are largely allegorical poems on a variety of topics ranging from plants and animals to cosmology, contemporary politics, and alchemy. They are in the tradition of the "Yung-huai" (Songs of My Soul) poems of Juan Chi (210–263), and, like them, many of Ch'en's poems have generated ongoing debate over their veiled references and meaning.

In 681, a year before Ch'en Tzu-ang passed the *chin-shih* exam, an exam section on literary composition was added to the requirements for this civil service degree. Although at first bureaucratically oriented genres such as memorials, inscriptions, and admonitions were the expectation for this section, soon the more esthetically elegant *fu* and *p'ai-lü* became the favored genres. Later, during the reign of Emperor Hsüan-tsung, they would come virtually to monopolize this part of the exam. By the end of the seventh century and the start of the eighth, this emphasis was already beginning to be apparent, in response to current fashions of court composition. We shall need to consider these issues further as we look at eighth-century verse.

THE EIGHTH CENTURY

The first decade of the eighth century saw the establishment of regulated verse (*lü-shih*) as a form of poetry attaining widespread use. Although the prosodic patterns of *lü-shih* had been worked out previously in theory and many seventh-century poets occasionally wrote in a form that comes close to *lü-shih*, it is only at this time that regulated verse assumes a prime position in practice and the tonal rules, in particular, are employed with enough prevalence to suggest acceptance of a "perfect" form. The increasing use and mastery of this form in court circles is evident in a comparison of the poems found in remaining fragments of the *Chu-ying hsüeh-shih chi* anthology, compiled around 702, with those in the *Ching-lung wen-kuan chi* (a record of the activities of the scholars associated with Chung-tsung's court; see below) compiled around a decade later. Both works reflect developments in poetry in the few years prior to their completion, and they are comparable in many respects; but barely a quarter of the *shih* included in the former satisfy all the strictures of regulated verse, while nearly three-quarters of the latter's do. Also apparent is an increase in the frequency of *lü-shih* in heptasyllabic lines and of the extended, *p'ai-lü* form, which soon becomes a staple of the *chin-shih* exam. Much of the credit for the *lü-shih*'s attaining its majority is usually given to Shen Ch'üan-ch'i (?–713) and Sung Chih-wen (c. 656–712), not only as exemplary practitioners but also as promoters of the form in their role as chief examiners for the *chin-shih* degree in 702 (Shen) and 708 (Sung).

The reigns of Chung-tsung (705–710) and Jui-tsung (710–712), following and building upon literary practices in Empress Wu's era, are a critical period in the history of T'ang poetry, as of T'ang culture in general. The restoration of the T'ang in early 705, in consequence of Empress Wu's deposition and the demise of her temporary Chou dynasty, indicated that the T'ang was indeed a more stable and lasting regime than all those that had preceded it since Han times. The great days to come of Hsüan-tsung's reign were to furnish the undeniable proof of this. But the years from 705 to 712 were themselves a celebration of T'ang security in the poetic arena.

In May 708, during the Ching-lung reign-period, Emperor Chung-tsung summoned to the Hung-wen College (which had retaken its original name of Hsiu-wen kuan) the most famous poets of the day, installing them as Academicians (*hsüeh-shih*) and making the college no longer an advisory institute but a literary salon. The members included such writers as Li Chiao (c. 645–714), Wei Ssu-li (654–719), Tu Shen-yen (c. 645–708), Li Shih (663–711), Liu Hsien (?–711), Ts'ui Shih (?–712), Hsü Yen-po (?–714), Li Yi[1] (657–716), and Lu Ts'ang-yung (?–713), along with Shen Ch'üan-ch'i and Sung Chih-wen.

Poetry competitions, whose rewards were gold and silk, were common at court banquets and on outings to temples, scenic spots, and manorial residences in Ch'ang-an and its suburbs. Chung-tsung was an enthusiastic participant in these activities, as were Empress Wei and the princesses An-le and Ch'ang-ning. Most often serving as arbiter of the poetry contests was Shang-kuan Wan-erh (c. 664–710), a granddaughter of Shang-kuan Yi. When the latter, along with most of his family and descendants, was executed by Empress Wu in 665, the infant Wan-erh and her mother were sent to the palace as slaves. The girl grew to be quick-witted and smooth-spoken, eventually gaining the empress' favor. From 697 on, the empress relied on Shang-kuan Wan-erh to draft most imperial decrees, and she became deeply involved in court politics. After the T'ang restoration in 705, she maintained and even advanced her status under Chung-tsung, who promoted her to the second rank of palace ladies. More important, she became a confidante of Empress Wei, who during these years exercised the real power of the throne. A famous anecdote of one poetry competition tells of Wan-erh's measured elimination of the entries of all contestants except Shen Ch'üan-ch'i and Sung Chih-wen and records the details of her astute appraisal in judging Shen's composition to be superior on this occasion. More than thirty of Shang-kuan Wan-erh's own *shih* remain, the majority of them quatrains done with a careful technique and diction worthy of her grandfather's approval. Indeed, self-consciousness and self-confidence are two characteristics of all of the poets of this period. Among others meriting special mention is Li Chiao, who has left more than two hundred *shih*, over half of which are odes on objects (*yung-wu*); he had a marked preference for regulated verse and in his mastery of this form yields nothing to the greater names of the next generation.

The forty-four-year reign of Hsüan-tsung, comprising the Hsien-t'ien (712–713), K'ai-yüan (713–742), and T'ien-pao (742–756) periods, represents the cultural high-water mark of the T'ang, with the dynasty at its height of political power and economic prosperity. This is the so-called High T'ang, whose literary arena is crowded with poets, some of them among the most illustrious in China's long history. The quantity of works extant from the writers of this time also increases dramatically, and it is not unusual to find several hundred compositions surviving for individual poets.

Chang Yüeh (667–731), although also active earlier, is really the first major poet of the "High T'ang" period. The most appealing of his 350 surviving *shih*, the majority of which are pentametric *lü-shih* or *p'ai-lü*, are those written during his various official postings to the provinces. In many of these the literary refinement of the courtier is blended in a supple manner with the sounds and sights confronting the poet in less aristocratic environments, often admitting an attractive emotional coloring absent in his compositions written while holding high position in the capital. The ceremonial *yüeh-fu* that Chang composed for various sacrificial and celebratory occasions are, however, among the most agreeable of the entire dynasty. The preface that he wrote for the collected works of Shang-kuan Wan-erh, upon imperial request in 711, is an important document of literary history and criticism. Chang Yüeh was also one of the compilers of the *Ch'u-hsüeh chi* (Records for Elementary Studies), a commonplace book commissioned by the emperor as a literary aid for his young sons; a special feature of this still-useful encyclopedia is its inclusion under each entry of appropriately matched parallel phrases culled from earlier texts, which serve as examples of syntactic and imagistic balance.

Chang Chiu-ling (678–740), who hailed from Kwangtung in the far south, placed second in the *chin-shih* exam of 702 (when Shen Ch'üan-ch'i was one of the chief examiners) and later became a protégé of Chang Yüeh. The most conspicuous example of a southerner rising to fame and high influence in T'ang times, he eventually served as prime minister in 734–736. His poetry was no less notable than his political success. The greater part of Chang Chiu-ling's 250 extant *shih*, all but a handful of which are in pentasyllabic meter, are devoted to depictions of natural scenes. At his best, he has a flair for capturing precise visualizations of natural objects, particularly in parallel couplets containing unexpected juxtapositions of elements in the landscape. For instance, describing a waterfall: "Its spewing flow wets the moving clouds, / And the swashing froth startles flying birds," or the scene near a forest pavilion: "Lichens deepen the oldness of the mountain's markings, / And a pool swells the freshness of air near bamboo," or while stopping overnight in travel: "The darkened plants now set forth flowers of frost, / And by the empty inn shadows of wild geese pass." An especially large number of Chang's poems are "ascent" verses, depicting views from atop hills, many-storied buildings, city walls, and towers. Above all, he excels in compositions, such as his wonderful *fu* on the lichee ("Li-chih fu"), in which he celebrates the unappreciated (by northerners) glories of his native region and attempts to redress traditional geographic prejudice. Thus, in the preface to his "Rhapsody on the Lichee," he claims that the fruit's "shape is uncommonly, even perfectly round and its taste peculiarly sweet and succulent; among all the hundred fruits there is none to compare with it," and he is surprised that, "when I once enthused about it while working in the imperial secretariat, I discovered that none of the gentlemen there had ever heard of it and they refused to believe what I told them." Or, to take another example, in several of his poems the mournful cry of the southern gibbon, traditionally an image of lonely gloom, is welcomed as the sound of a familiar, indigenous companion.

Meng Hao-jan (689–740) is normally classified as a "nature poet." Of course, all labels that seek to delimit poets in such exclusive fashion are suspect. But it is true that the most memorable of Meng Hao-jan's *shih* (he has left no *fu*) picture natural scenes. This he does in fairly detailed fashion, usually including in his poems a notable human presence or at least an unmistakable persona (contrast the imagery of Wang Wei, below). Many of Meng Hao-jan's "signature" works focus on the area around his hometown of Hsiang-yang in north-central Hupei province, although his travel verses are also very fine. His quatrain "Ch'un hsiao" (Daybreak in Spring)—"Dozing in spring and unaware of daybreak— / Till all around one hears the chittering of birds! / During the night, the sound of wind and rain— / But of the blossoms' falling, how much do we know?"—is one of the best known of all T'ang poems, partly because of its inclusion as the opening selection in the *Ch'ien-chia shih* (Poems of a Thousand Authors), a beginner's anthology of verse much used from late Sung times on. It bears mentioning that this poem is not just a lyrical vignette of waking up late in the morning to the raucous cries of birds and dimly recalling the preceding night's storm that is sure to have battered in the dark many of the season's young flowers (although it *is* primarily this); it is also a portrait in miniature of our human, merely superficial, and uncertain perception of the ways of life in this world: we know as much, and as little, about our own existence and passing away as about the falling of nature's blooms. A warm poet who does not often lose himself in his scenes, Meng is a moody writer and perhaps the most erratic of the major poets of the period. Although he failed in his only attempt at the *chin-shih* exam and only once, late in his life, held even a low-ranking provincial post (this thanks to Chang Chiu-ling's patronage), he knew and was admired by most of the younger poets, such as Wang Wei and Li Po, whose work represents the height of T'ang poetic art.

Wang Wei (701–761), who took the *chin-shih* degree at the age of twenty in 721, is one of the four or five most famous of all Chinese poets. His reputation now rests mainly on the serene and seemingly depersonalized nature poetry that has come to be most associated with him, of quiet landscapes immanent with final truths of cosmic consonance. Perhaps best known among these are the poems written at his Wang-ch'uan estate in the foothills south of Ch'ang-an, which had previously been owned by Sung Chih-wen. Most famous of these are twenty pentametric quatrains on particular spots, to which his friend P'ei Ti wrote accompanying pieces. Wang's "Mu-lan chai" (Enclosure for Viewing

Magnolia) serves as an example: "Autumn's mountains garner the lingering daylight, / As birds aloft follow after their mates. / Flashes of bright blue come distinct at times and clear, / But evening's hilltop-mists are without place or home." Nature, in Wang Wei's poems, is rarely seen in specific close-in view; it is more often suggested by large-scale generic images that effectively suggest *every* landscape. The simple diction of such poems (one of the reasons Wang Wei attracts so many translators) is inviting but is only apparently artless, often masking interesting complexities in tonal patterns. Wang Wei's mid-life turn toward Buddhism, prompting him to adopt the sobriquet Mo-chieh—which, when added to his given name, yields the Chinese transcription for Vimalakīrti, the ideal Buddhist layman and focus of a popular *sūtra*—is evident in many of these poems. Wang Wei is also the author of a commemorative inscription, famous among Buddhologists, on the renowned sixth patriarch of the Ch'an (Zen) school, Hui-neng. In his own day Wang Wei was not categorized as a nature poet; his repute owed as much if not more to his *yüeh-fu* verse. He composed in all forms of *shih* poetry (four hundred poems remain), though it is his *lü-shih* and quatrains that are most read today. During his lifetime he was equally acclaimed as a musician and as a painter. In the latter field he is regarded as one of the fathers of Chinese landscape painting. Despite his professed inclinations toward reclusion, Wang Wei had a full official career. His forced collaboration with An Lu-shan's rebel government in 756–757, which foreclosed further service under the T'ang when the capital was retaken, has led certain later scholars to question his moral courage even while appreciating his poetry.

The wonderful flowering of verse during the first half of the eighth century is perhaps best reflected in Yin Fan's *Ho-yüeh ying-ling chi* anthology, completed in 753, which gives us a contemporary selection by a knowledgeable critic of the finest poets of Hsüan-tsung's reign. Most of these men entered officialdom by passing the *chin-shih* (*c.s.*) exam in the 720s or 730s and many of them knew one another. Their names form a roster of "silver" poets of the High T'ang, including such figures as Wang Ch'ang-ling (c. 690–c. 756, *c.s.* 727), Ch'ang Chien (c. 708–c.754, *c.s.* 727), Li Ch'i (?–c. 751, *c.s.* 735), Ts'ui Kuo-fu (c. 678–754, *c.s.* 725), Ch'u Kuang-hsi (709–759?, *c.s.* 726), Liu Shen-hsü (*c.s.* 733), T'ao Han (*c.s.* 730), Ts'ui Hao (c. 700–754?, *c.s.* 723), Ho-lan Chin-ming (?–c. 761, *c.s.* 728), and Ch'i-wu Ch'ien (c. 692–c. 749, *c.s.* 726). Wang Ch'ang-ling, who is better represented than any other poet in Yin Fan's anthology, is today the best known of this group. His poetry displays a fluent sureness, especially in his *chin-t'i* verse. He is also the author of an important work of literary criticism, entitled *Shih-ko* (The Framework of Poetry), which uses critical metaphors adopted from Buddhism; this text, like several other T'ang works of literary criticism, is preserved in Kūkai's *Wen-ching mi-fu lun*.

Kao Shih (716–765, *c.s.* 749) and Ts'en Shen (715–770, *c.s.* 744) are the youngest poets included in the *Ho-yüeh ying-ling chi*. In the same way that

Wang Wei and Meng Hao-jan are often, despite their differences, yoked together as exemplars of a school of nature poetry, so Kao Shih and Ts'en Shen are usually considered the leading pair of T'ang "frontier" poets. Poems centering on the isolation and hardships of soldiers on the northwest marches of the T'ang empire in Central Asia had been written from at least the mid-seventh century and constitute an identifiable subgenre of T'ang *shih*. Both Kao Shih and Ts'en Shen had extensive personal experience of these haunting, desolate landscapes while serving as literary adjutants to various generals. The works they composed out of these experiences, especially those in heptametric *ku-t'i* style, are paramount among T'ang "frontier" verse. However, such poems are but a small part of Kao's and Ts'en's surviving works, and it does not seem that their contemporary reputations depended on them: none of Ts'en Shen's poems included in Yin Fan's anthology are frontier verse, and only three of Kao Shih's (most notably his celebrated "Yen ko hsing" [Song of Yen]) are.

In the long sweep of Chinese literary history, the two most famous poets are Li Po (701–762?) and Tu Fu (712–770). Li Po, the older of the two by eleven years, was raised in Szechwan, descending from obscure origins but probably with Serindian (eastern central Asian) background in the preceding two or three generations (though he asserted descent from a distant branch of the imperial family), and became known and acclaimed early on for his poetry. Tu Fu hailed from a pedigreed, though somewhat diminished, family of the capital area—including among his ancestors the great third-century scholar-official Tu Yü (222–284) and the late-eighth-century poet Tu Shen-yen as grandfather—and gained high repute for his own poetry only posthumously. Tu Fu is not among the poets of the *Ho-yüeh ying-ling chi*: he was still unknown or not well regarded at the time of its completion. Li Po, however, is one of the most prominently represented poets in the anthology.

The genius of Li Po lies at once in his total command of the literary tradition before him and his ingenuity in bending (without breaking) it to discover a uniquely personal idiom. This much might be said of all great poets. More specifically, Li Po shows a willingness, indeed eagerness, to play with language and form in exuberant, sometimes audacious, ways. While much of this is evident in his diction, more of it is revealed in the special felicity with which he exploits the untranslatable interplay between sense and sound. Li Po is the most musical, most versatile, and most engaging of Chinese poets, a Mozart of words. His verbal genius, coupled with, by all accounts, an irresistibly gallant—if at times impudent and imprudent—personality, ensured for him an early and continuing notoriety as the Byron of T'ang China. Li Po shunned the examination system as a path to official service, preferring the freer uncertainty of individual patronage. His one brief stint as a capital courtier, in the role of an on-call scholar and littérateur in 742–744, ended badly, and his naive involvement in Prince Yung's ill-advised uprising against the newly enthroned Su-tsung in 757 nearly cost him his life.

The thousand *shih* and eight *fu* of Li Po that survive testify amply to his excellence in all poetic forms. His *yüeh-fu* verse, offering the most extensive canvas of topics and titles of any T'ang poet, is especially notable for its deepening and turning of traditional motifs: in some cases, Li Po's treatment of a theme effectively culminates the variations of all previous poets, while, in other cases, his handling spins a heretofore unimagined facet into view. His *yüeh-fu* teem with highly varied rhythmical and metrical schemes, often exhibiting a superabundance of rhyme and assonance; two famous examples are "Shu tao nan" (The Way to Shu Is Hard) and "Yüan pieh-li" (Distantly Parting). These poems are too long to cite in full here, but we cannot refrain from quoting at least part of the former, in which Li Po limns in lines of varying length and breathless velocity the perils of the route to Shu ("Triaster" and "Well" are constellations):

Above is the high bough where six dragons reversed the sun's course;
Below, a backflow of waters where crashing waves swirl and recoil.
Even the flight of the yellow crane cannot push on beyond this place;
 Long-armed monkeys who wish to cross over fear to swing up here.
  Twisted so and tortuous is the Blue Mud Pass—
 Nine turnings for every hundred paces to wind round the rugged crest.
 Grab onto Triaster! Pass through the Well! Look up and gasp in alarm!
 Hold your hand against your panting chest—sit down, catch your breath.
 I ask you, sir, as you travel west, when is it you'll come back?
 I dread the craggy steeps of the route, impossible to scale.
 There you'll see only disheartened birds, calling in age-old trees;
 The male takes wing, trailing his mate, circling amid the grove.
  And too, you'll hear the cuckoo's crying—
  In moonlight, sorrowing in empty hills.
   The hardships of the way to Shu—
  much harder than climbing the blue sky.
 It will waste the ruddy features of all who hear of it!

Many of the stylistic traits just mentioned—which sometimes remind one of *fu*—are manifest as well in Li Po's "Old-Style" verse, into which he often infuses surprising tonal designs to enhance the poem's semantic freight. His "Yüan Tan-ch'iu ko" (Song of Yüan Tan-ch'iu), heralding the otherworldly aspirations of a Taoist friend, in which an unusual preponderance of level-tone words (forty-one out of fifty-four) contributes to the fast pace and "altitude" of the poem, while a patterned metrical irregularity imparts a distinctiveness to the subject, is representative of some of these qualities: "Cinnabar-Hill Yüan— / He loves divine transcendence, / At dawn drinking from a clear current of the River Ying, / At sunset returns to the purple haze of Mount Sung's crags, / Of whose six-and-thirty peaks he is wont to make a full circuit! / Wont to make a full circuit— / He treads the starry rainbow, / Himself mounted on a flying dragon, with the winds born from his ears, / Athwart the river, bestride the sea, now in touch with Heaven, / And what *I* know myself of these travels gives thought no end on earth!"

A bit more sedate is Li Po's celebrated set of fifty-nine pentametric "Ku feng" (Olden Airs), written on different occasions throughout his life, which follow in the meditative, frequently allegorical, introspective tradition of Juan Chi's "Yung-huai" and Ch'en Tzu-ang's "Kan-yü." The first of this set is often regarded as expressing Li Po's poetic ethos, in characteristically self-confident style—as in the opening couplet's statement that "Greater Elegantiae [Ta ya] for so long were not composed; / When I wane, who will bring them forth again?" and the later announcement that "My resolve lies in editing and transmitting [as did Confucius], / To let a radiance trail shining for a thousand springtimes," with a selective and fairly traditional survey of Chinese poetic history condensed in the lines between. But it is better not to overinterpret this momentarily pious poem or attempt to apply its assertions to all the poet's work.

Another important element in a large portion of Li Po's poetry is his profound use of Taoist imagery, often deriving from canonical texts of the Shang-ch'ing and Ling-pao scriptures (see chapter 10). This was a lifelong interest of Li Po's (a "banished immortal," in the keen words of the unconventional statesman-poet Ho Chih-chang [659–744]), leading in 744 to his first-level ordination in the Taoist priesthood. His spiritual attainments may even have played a part in his earlier summons to court, and he continued to pursue Taoist teachings into his final years. The literary influences on Li Po were clearly manifold, and he is generous in his appreciation of earlier writers. In particular, he learned much from the poetry of Pao Chao (414–466) about *yüeh-fu* phrasing, from Hsieh T'iao (464–499) about stylistic grace, and from the Taoist—and also Buddhist—scriptures about potent imagery.

Li Po's *fu*, though neglected in comparison with his *shih*, are marvels. The rhapsodies "Ming-t'ang fu" (The Hall of Light) and "Ta-lieh fu" (The Great Hunt) are in the grand manner of the Han epideictic *fu*. So is that on "The Great *P'eng*-bird" (Ta p'eng-niao fu), in which the gigantic bird of the *Chuang Tzu*'s opening passage is personalized into a symbol of the self-assured Li Po himself, who is then ultimately humbled upon meeting the "rarely held bird" that images the revered Shang-ch'ing prelate Ssu-ma Ch'eng-chen (647–735). This kind of daring, even arrant, self-portrayal is habitual in Li Po's writing but, somehow, never offends. His other *fu* are smaller, more lyrical compositions that are similar in form and style to some of his *ku-t'i* poems (compare, e.g., his *fu* on the Sword Gallery mountain pass [Chien-ko fu] with his "Shu tao nan"), suggesting that neat "generic" distinctions were not always of great import to him. To add that Li Po is also hailed as an uncommon master of the briefest form of verse, the quatrain, is to emphasize the ease with which he moves between all types of poetry.

Although Tu Fu, as noted above, was not widely esteemed during his lifetime, the critical appreciation that began within two generations of his death and crested in the eleventh century, rolling on unabated to the present day, was of such magnitude as to make him into a cultural icon. For several centuries, it has been difficult to speak of Tu Fu the masterful poet without implicating Tu Fu the paragon of moral integrity, and vice versa. One of the ironies of literary history is that Tu Fu, who wished above all for a career in government service and contemned himself for this failures in this area, should ultimately have been the person whose life most served to legitimize poetry as a vocation in its own right. He came up short in the *chin-shih* exam of 736 and was unsuccessful in a special examination decreed by the emperor in 747. He caught the monarch's attention in 751 through direct submission of three *fu* on state ceremonies carried out by Hsüan-tsung earlier that year, but several years passed before he was offered even a minor provincial post. In 756–757 he (along with many more-important figures) was detained in rebel-held Ch'ang-an by An Lu-shan's forces, but he escaped at last to join Su-tsung at the new emperor's military headquarters. As a reward for his loyalty, he received a court appointment but within a year was dismissed. The final twelve years of his life were spent in dependence on various friends and local officials, first near Chengtu, then at spots along the upper and middle Yangtze River. It is the poems written during and after the An Lu-shan rebellion that constitute the bulk of Tu Fu's nearly fifteen hundred remaining *shih*, including almost all of his most famous works.

It is often said that only in Tu Fu's poetry does one find a contemporary reflection in literature of the great rebellion that shattered the T'ang world at its height. This is an exaggeration; other poets who lived through the period had their say as well, but no one captured the human pathos of the events as memorably as Tu Fu. Poems such as the *lü-shih* "Ch'un wang" (Spring Prospects) and "Yüeh yeh" (Moonlit Night), and the Old-Style "Ai chiang-t'ou" (Lament by the Stream), "Ai wang-sun" (Lament for a Royal Scion), "Pei cheng" (The Journey North), and the "Ch'iang-ts'un" (Ch'iang Village) triptych show the poet in the roles of faithful subject, staunch official, and devoted husband and father that have become emblematic of him. The first of the "Ch'iang Village" set depicts with intense tenderness the poet's unlooked-for return in late September 757 to his family, whom he had placed out of harm's way more than a year earlier:

> Lofted and lifted, west of the clouds of red,
> The trek of the sun descends to the level earth.
> By the brushwood gate songbirds and sparrows chaffer,
> And the homebound stranger from a thousand *li* arrives.
> Wife and children marvel that I am here;
> When the shock wears off, still they wipe away tears.

In the disorders of the age was I tossed and flung;
That I return alive is a happening of chance.
Neighbors swarm up to the tops of the walls,
Touched and sighing, even they sob and weep.
The night wastes on, and still we hold the candle,
Across from one another, as if asleep and in a dream.

The three "officer" poems (Hsin-an li, T'ung-kuan li, Shih-hao li) and three "parting" poems (of the newly married [Hsin-hun pieh], the aged [Ch'ui-lao pieh], and the homeless [Wu-chia pieh]) of 759 movingly evoke the effects of war at the level of the unprotected, vulnerable individual. Here the poet adopts the viewpoint of the common folk, those who suffered the most during the years of upheaval. Tu Fu's compassion for all suffering creatures—animals as well as human beings (see, e.g., his poems on an ailing horse or on trussed chickens)—is one of his most appealing traits, as is his willingness to poke fun at his too-serious self on occasion.

As Tu Fu resigned himself in his later years to a life centered on writing, his concern with exploring intricacies of technique deepened. As he said in a famous line from this period, "If my words don't surprise others, death will bring me no rest"—which reminds one curiously of Keats' dictum that "Poetry must surprise by a fine excess." Whereas the great poems of the years before 760 were most often *ku-t'i* verse, the rich technical achievements of his last decade were most often disposed in *chin-t'i* poems. In these *lü-shih* and *chüeh-chü*, particularly those in heptasyllabic lines, Tu Fu presents a sometimes astounding, if not daunting, complexity of diction, symbol, consonance, and emotion—an involved inwardness that resembles the late sonnets of Gerard Manley Hopkins. Among these his eight-poem suite "Ch'iu hsing" (Autumn Sentiments) is the most famous example. There is in Tu Fu a deep-lying recognition of the bittersweet earnestness of life that is matched by no other Chinese poet. Although Tu Fu created powerful works in all forms of *shih* poetry, he did not excel in the composition of *fu:* his seven extant rhapsodies are rather crabbed and overdone.

Several mid-century poets contemporaneous with Tu Fu—notably, as mentioned above, Li Po—were attracted to and adept in writing *fu.* In this context one might also include Ts'en Shen for his autobiographical *fu* on his early years ("Kan-chiu fu" [Remembering Old Times]), written in 743, and his lengthy "Chao pei-k'o wen" (Text to Summon Back a Visitor from the North), written in 769, a gorgeously frightening depiction of the hazards of travel in Szechwan that blends expanded elements of Li Po's "Shu tao nan" and "Chien-ko fu" with echoes of "Chao hun" (Summons of the Soul) from the *Elegies of Ch'u.* A particularly interesting poet of this period, much esteemed by his peers, is Ch'ien Ch'i (c. 720–c. 783, *c.s.* 750), who was something of a virtuoso in the regulated *fu.* His thirteen surviving compositions in this form, on topics ranging from constellations to the crunkling of cranes, from an ivory bracelet to the dancing of the hundred trained horses that performed annually at Hsüan-tsung's birthday celebration, complement his prodigious output of more than four hundred *shih.* Ch'ien Ch'i's *lü-shih* were especially admired. As an official in Lant'ien (near Ch'ang-an), the district that included Wang Wei's Wang-ch'uan estate, he came to know Wang Wei well in the older poet's late years. He even composed a set of twenty-two quatrains on Wang-ch'uan scenes in tribute to the famous sets that Wang Wei and his friend P'ei Ti had written a decade or more before.

The *fu* of Hsiao Ying-shih (707–759) and Li Hua (?–774), both *chin-shih* graduates of 735, are more engrossing than their *shih.* Hsiao Ying-shih's rhapsodies emphasize narrative records of his experiences as well as ruminations on current issues. Thus, in "Fa ying-t'ao shu fu" (Felling a Cherry Tree), written in 749, Hsiao shows his scorn for the dictatorial prime minister Li Lin-fu, and, in "Teng Yi-ch'eng ku-ch'eng fu" (Atop the Olden Walls of Yi-ch'eng), written in 756 during the worst period of the An Lu-shan rebellion, when Hsiao was posted in the territory of the old Ch'u kingdom in Hupei and heard that Ch'ang-an had fallen and the emperor had fled, he presents on a sweeping scale the background of the insurrection while voicing his own frustrations and resolutions. Li Hua's truly stupendous *fu* on the Han-yüan Basilica (Han-yüan tien fu), describing Ch'ang-an's main hall of state, is one of the longest of T'ang *fu* and bears comparison with the two famous "architectural" rhapsodies of Wang Yen-shou (144–164) and Ho Yen (?–249) in *Wen hsüan.*

Yüan Chieh (719–772, *c.s.* 753) is often mentioned with Hsiao Ying-shih and Li Hua as one of the forerunners of the *ku-wen* (ancient prose) movement (see chapter 28). The poems for which he is best known, written during his magistracies in the south in the mid-760s, speak in straightforward language of his efforts to relieve the suffering of common people whose lives were rent by the disorder of the great rebellion and its aftermath. These works had an influence on poets of the ninth century who were to write even more pointedly of social concerns. Yüan's *fu* are moralistic and rather plodding in style. Yüan Chieh, Hsiao Ying-shih, and Li Hua shared the view that Hsüan-tsung's reign, in which they passed their youth, had been a time when literary excess and gaudiness increasingly came to outweigh right-principled content. As seen above, this is a standard, virtually constant criticism of the writers of one generation against their predecessors; here it is charged even against what came to be the so-called golden age of Chinese poetry. Interestingly, it is only at this time that the reputation of Ch'en Tzu-ang (two generations removed) as the first T'ang figure to seek to call poetry back to its moral foundations was solidified, largely through the determined praise of these writers and their followers. Yüan Chieh's anthology of verse, *Ch'ieh-chung chi,* compiled in 760, is a miniature manifestation of Yüan's critical program: it consists of twenty-four *ku-t'i* poems by seven writers little known in their day and unsuccessful in official life but whose poems, according to Yüan, breathe a classical sincerity instead of being constricted by tonal rules and verbal refinements.

Space permits only passing mention of a few other poets of the mid- and late eighth century. The most important of these are Liu Chang-ch'ing (c. 710–c. 790, *c.s.* 733) and Wei Ying-wu (737–792?). Liu's life almost spans the century, but he did not find his own voice as a poet until the time of the rebellion. More than five hundred of his *shih* remain. The most moving of them concern the grievous effects of the war; the most pleasing are landscape verses that present farm and country scenes reminiscent of T'ao Ch'ien. The preceding applies just as well to Wei Ying-wu, but Wei, almost thirty years Liu's junior, is remarkable also for his vividly acute poems of nostalgia for the vanished days of Hsüan-tsung's splendor. These poems anticipate the fondness for this subject that reached a peak in the first half of the ninth century. His poems mourning the death of his wife are also deeply touching. One of these latter poems, "Shang shih" (Aching for the Departed), begins with the following bleak lines: "What is dyed white will all at once turn black, / And burnt wood become ashes in the end. / I recall her who lived within my rooms, / Gone and departed now, never to come back." The traditional appraisal of Wei Ying-wu as an epigone of Wang Wei and Meng Hao-jan is unfair to him and the many-sided merits of his poetry. Writers such as Li Chia-yu (c. 728–c. 783, *c.s.* 748), Tai Shu-lun (732–789), Lu Lun (c. 737–c. 798), and Li Tuan (?–785, *c.s.* 770), though not of the first rank, are competent craftsmen and agreeable in their own ways.

Wu Yün (?–778) was a poet and Taoist priest, honored by Hsüan-tsung and a friend of Li Po, who wrote some of the eighth century's most striking verse on spiritual themes. His sets of twenty-four "Yu-hsien" (Roaming to Transcendence) and ten "Pu-hsü" (Pacing the Void) *shih* are dazzling explorations of mystical experience and ecstasy. Even more impressive are his eight extant *fu*, especially "Ssu huan ch'un fu" (Longing to Return to Incorruptibility), "Hsi hsin fu" (Cleansing the Heart), and "Teng chen fu" (The Ascent to Perfection). Of poets among the Buddhist clergy, Chiao-jan (720–805?; named Hsieh Chou at birth) is preeminent. Besides his poems on Buddhist subjects, Chiao-jan wrote widely on secular themes and was very active in literary circles along the lower Yangtze during the last decades of the eighth century. He also wrote three valuable works of poetry criticism and theory, the *Shih-shih* (The Designs of Poetry), *Shih-p'ing* (A Critique of Poetry), and *Shih-yi* (Deliberations on Poetry).

This is perhaps a fitting place to mention the two most famous collections of Buddhist-inspired verse of the T'ang, those associated with the names Han-shan (Cold Mountain; see chapter 48) and Wang Fan-chih (Wang "the Brahmacārin"). Approximately three hundred poems have been attributed to the former and four hundred (most of which are quatrains) to the latter. Despite the fanciful accounts that have become attached to the eponymous personae of the collections, it is clear that both comprise blocs of poems composed at various times—from the seventh century to the ninth—by various hands. The Wang corpus consists of texts recovered from the Tun-huang hoard. The human interest of both the Han Shan and Wang Fan-chih collections rests in their unpretentious, sometimes quizzical, or edgy, or mocking, expressions of Ch'an disdain for worldly passions and mundane ties—witness this from Wang: "Life and death are like shooting stars, / Rushing and gushing onward and away. / Those that die first, after some myriad years, / Then merge with the sum of imperceptible dust!" Their linguistic importance lies in their extensive use of elements deriving from vernacular speech, providing us with some of the best available examples of T'ang "popular" poetry.

THE NINTH CENTURY

A poet who can best be viewed as a transitional figure between the eighth and ninth centuries is Li Yi[2] (748–829, *c.s.* 769). A stripling at the time of An Lu-shan's rebellion, he lived for seventy years afterward, well into the new age that looked back to the K'ai-yüan/T'ien-pao epoch with an awe born from distance. Li Yi spent most of the last quarter of the eighth century in subaltern posts on the northern borders. Approximately one-third of his extant poems are "frontier" verses from that period. These are the works for which he is remembered. They represent the capstone of this thematic category, even though later poets continued to try their hand at this well-established topic. An example is the quatrain "Yeh shang Shou-hsiang ch'eng wen ti" (Hearing a Barbarian Flute from Atop the Walls of Shou-hsiang Citadel at Night): "In front of Returning-to-Joy [Hui-le] Peak, the sands seem as snow; / Below Accepting-Surrender [Shou-hsiang] Citadel, moonlight is like frost. / I cannot tell from where that reed-pipe is blowing, / But all this night the troops gaze endlessly toward home." Li Yi's ninth-century verses inhabit a comfortable mid-range of facility, lacking the vitality of his frontier poetry. He is recognized as one of the finest of T'ang poets to write in the quatrain form.

Meng Chiao (751–814, *c.s.* 796) might also be considered a transitional figure, according to chronology. But, unlike the works of Li Yi, his most important works were penned during the final, not the middle, decades of his life; he thus more truly belongs to the ninth century. Regardless of time, however, Meng Chiao could only be a marginal poet. A *chin-shih* graduate quite late, in his mid-forties (after failing twice previously), he felt himself set apart from most of his fellows by straits of adversity and privation. He found a kindred soul and supporter in Han Yü (see below). Meng Chiao's poetry, the bulk of which is "Old-Style" verse, is marked largely by its tone of personal hurt, carried in a vocabulary consciously severe, acutely thorny. Sometimes this even extends to suggestions of cosmic malevolence. The most distinctive of his poems are also the most disturbing. Reading his work is usually an intense rather than an exhilarating experience. Meng Chiao is not the friend you invite home but the one whose darker moods you understand too well and prefer to keep at bay.

Han Yü (768–824, *c.s.* 792) seems to have been stung all his life that he did not pass the *chin-shih* exam until his fourth attempt and that he soon thereafter failed three times at decree exams. The righteousness of the underappreciated genius colored his writing and pushed him to extremes of both pride and controversy. There is no question that he became the chief literary—and intellectual—figure of the ninth century's opening decades. His friends and disciples were many, but his influence on them flowed mainly from his prose compositions, which are discussed elsewhere in this volume (see chapter 28). It may be said of Han Yü, as it was of Jonathan Swift, that his poetry has the merits of his prose but not many other merits. He studied Li Po and Tu Fu with profit, but acquired neither the deftness of the one nor the discipline of the other. He is less a poet than a personality. A native itch to stand forth and be different, more than any logical consequence of his moral and philosophical (Confucian) advocacy, led him to play with unusual diction and prosody in his *shih*. Sometimes the effects increase one's enjoyment; at other times they are merely clever. Finding the requirements of "Recent-Style" verse uncongenial, he concentrated on *ku-t'i* compositions. His serious poems are well meant but only rarely impressive. The poems on intentionally humorous topics, an interest for which he was criticized on occasion, frequently succeed in raising a smile. Few of his *shih* stand up well to rereading. His *fu*, however, being less contrived for effect, have a certain charm. The four rhapsodies titled as such were written during the years 795 to 803 and express his early frustrations over official life and separation from friends. Their language is direct: feeling dominates form, and, but for their rhymes, they have much in common with the author's prose style. Some other, later works, such as "Chin-hsüeh chieh" (Analysis of Advancing in Learning), "Sung ch'iung wen" (Text to Send Off Poverty, or Farewell to Misfortune), and "Sung feng-po" (Denouncing the Lord of the Wind), though not called *fu*, are best regarded as such. They include some of his most satisfying poetic works. Han Yü seems to have had no patience for the regulated *fu* that by now prevailed in this genre of writing, declaring his shame over writing a creditable piece in this style to pass the *chin-shih* examination.

Liu Tsung-yüan (773–819, *c.s.* 793), usually paired with Han Yü as a leading representative of the *ku-wen* prose movement, was an excellent poet. In *shih* and especially in *fu*, he claims high standing. Liu's initially heady but ultimately unfortunate involvement in dynastic politics led in late 805, after the forced abdication of Shun-tsung, who had ruled for barely six months, to exile in the far south. For Liu, exile turned out to be lifelong: after ten years in Yung-chou (Hunan province), he was recalled to the capital, only to be reassigned even farther south to Liu-chou (Kwangsi province), where he died four years later. As a writer of descriptive poetry, which was his forte, Liu Tsung-yüan has a precise eye for the individual properties of the world around him. Natural objects, even when used for symbolic effect, are keenly observed and closely drawn. His poems focusing on various plants and birds, for example, are a delight to read, capturing vital quiddities of his subjects as few other poets do. Here is a portion of a poem on a goshawk: "Autumn's cold wind blows and blusters, setting sharp frost flying— / The gray goshawk ramps above, wheeling in the fresh light of dawn. / Clouds are cloven, the haze is rent, the nimbus cut in twain, / As *its* drawn lightning, dartling, flashing, lifts over the level ridge. / With tearing *thwook* its sturdy pinions clip the brambly bosk, / Down to pounce on fox or hare, racing over open terrain. / Talons and feathers dripping blood—every other bird has fled; / Alone it perches, glaring all about, proud and redoubtable for now." Later in the poem this hawk is caught and caged, suffering the fate of all creatures (like the poet himself) who become too conspicuous. Liu Tsung-yüan's years away from the cultural center made him more than usually sensitive to what the margins of empire lacked and offered. Distant banishment, even in the role of a local magistrate, was no trivial sentence in premodern times (think of Ovid by the Black Sea), and grief and loneliness also find their outlet in Liu's *shih*, but fitly so and in moderate measure.

Liu Tsung-yüan is one of the most important figures in the history of the *fu* during the T'ang centuries. Besides twelve *fu* so titled, which include outstanding examples of "Old-Style," *sao*-style, and regulated types, he has many works that, although not designated *fu*, can be regarded at least as hybrid rhapsodies. Among the former, "The Ox" (Niu fu) and "The Wine-Jar" (P'ing fu), which depict these objects in their actual and their allegorical significance, and "Ch'iu-shan fu" (The Imprisoning Hills), as well as the longer "Min sheng fu" (Despairing Over Life) and "Ch'eng chiu fu" (Reprehending My Faults), which address the author's physical and emotional circumstances in his banishment, are masterly compositions. Among the latter, pieces such as "Ma shih-ch'ung wen" (Reviling the Corporeal Worms) and "Ai ni wen" (Lamenting a Death by Drowning) show Liu Tsung-yüan restoring to the *fu* a full mixture of narrative, satire, and social philosophy that had become rare by the ninth century. No matter the topic or the style, his rhapsodies do not tarry for virtuoso arias but run with pace and momentum, impelling the reader onward. Although Liu Tsung-yüan is an acknowledged master of prose and the great majority of his extant writings are in prose, he is also one of his generation's most gifted and engaging writers of verse.

Liu Yü-hsi (772–842, c.s. 793) took the *chin-shih* exam the same year that Liu Tsung-yüan did. A member of the same ill-starred political faction, he too was banished in 805, to Hunan. Ten years later he was recalled to the capital, traveling much of the way with Liu Tsung-yüan, and then was likewise sent farther south—in his case, to Lien-chou in Kwangtung. In 819, the year Liu Tsung-yüan died, Liu Yü-hsi was allowed to return north to see to the obsequies for his recently deceased mother. This began his rehabilitation, and during his final two decades of life he was gradually able to regain official success. (One wonders how Liu Tsung-yüan might have fared had he survived his years in the wilderness.) Liu Yü-hsi, also an esteemed prose stylist, was a prolific poet, leaving behind more than seven hundred *shih* and eleven *fu*. Noteworthy among his *shih* are poems of social protest and political satire. He is especially praised for his poems done in imitation of folk songs of the southwest and southern regions. The most famous of these are his nine "Chu-chih tz'u"

(Bamboo-Branch Lyrics), composed in heptametric quatrains, in the preface to which Liu describes the popular songs of the Szechwan area that were his inspiration, and the nine "Yang-liu-chih tz'u" (Willow-Branch Lyrics), also in heptametric quatrains. The numerous other examples of such joyfully lilting songs scattered through his works possess a pure gaiety in mood and rhythm. Also deserving mention is Liu's two-hundred-line poem "Yu T'ao-yüan" (Roaming to Peach Blossom Spring), the longest and most elaborate T'ang version of T'ao Ch'ien's fabled hidden haven in Wu-ling, supposedly located in present-day Ch'ang-te district, Hunan province. Of special interest among Liu Yü-hsi's *fu* are "Ti-shih fu" (The Whetstone), which neatly applies the care one must give a sword to keep it sharp as an analogy for the sovereign's need to keep worthy men in use and not let them rust in the provinces; "Che chiu-nien fu" (Being Banished Nine Years), a brief and surprisingly straightforward account of what might easily be a most lugubrious topic; and "Ch'iu-sheng fu" (The Sounds of Autumn). The last composition, written in 841, the year before Liu died, to reply to a like-titled rhapsody by Li Te-yü, puts its final emphasis not on the traditional melancholy of autumn but, rather, on the season's potential to rouse an aging man's nature to action once more.

Li Te-yü (787–850), leader of one of the two major factions that dominated official politics during the second quarter of the century, had a special fondness for the *fu*. Thirty-two of his rhapsodies, all with prefaces telling the motive behind their composition, are preserved. Most of these deal with physical objects—plants or animals, for which Li Te-yü had a consuming appreciation: he went to great effort to stock his grand P'ing-ch'üan estate near Loyang with rare and beautiful specimens encountered on his official travels. His *fu* are both lively and elegant, even when the topic is historical, as is true of his rhapsody "Chih-chih fu" (Knowing Where to Stop), in which he sings the praises of men from the Spring and Autumn period to Western Han times who combined an appropriate commitment to government service with intervals of deliberate reclusion. Li Te-yü's *shih* poems are equally felicitous. Most interesting are the two sets (one of twenty poems, the other of ten) describing objects at his P'ing-ch'üan grounds and also a long poem with self-commentary reconstructing from remembered fragments lines he composed in a dream (shades of Coleridge).

In contrast to Li Te-yü and the three preceding poets, Chia Tao (779–843) was a political back bencher, but someone who poured great energy into his verse. As a young man, Chia Tao was ordained a Buddhist monk, with the religious name Wu-pen ("Rootless"). He was, however, equally devoted to poetry, and, after becoming acquainted with Han Yü in 801, he chose to return to the secular world and cultivate his literary skills. Chia Tao eventually entered the bureaucracy through appointed office (having failed at the *chin-shih* exam), but it was always about poetry that he was most zealous, one might almost say pious. For him it was a matter of scrupulous discipline and hard work, not simple inspiration. Excess, alas, is often a counterpart of diligence, and

Chia Tao can at times deliver unfortunate, even risible, appositions in parallel couplets. His forte is the pentametric *lü-shih,* in which form he particularly favors quotidian subjects invested by him with lyric dignity. Chia's best verse exerted much influence on poets late in the century, and into the Sung period, who sought a more approachable model for their writing than titans like Li Po or Tu Fu.

Yao Ho (781–c. 859, *c.s.* 816) is usually associated with Chia Tao, for they share some similarities in tenor and tone. However, where Chia Tao sometimes leans toward the "rough" style promoted by Meng Chiao and Han Yü, Yao Ho makes no overtures in that direction. Yao's famous poem "Hsin huai shuang" (The Heart Harbors Frost), in twelve pentametric lines, gives an especially vivid picture of how he conceived the mental process of making poetry. He compiled an anthology, *Chi-hsüan chi,* of a hundred poems (mostly pentametric *lü-shih*) by twenty-one writers (mainly from the second half of the eighth century) to showcase what he considered works of extreme perfection.

The foremost poet of the ninth century is Po Chü-yi (772–846, *c.s.* 800). Although Chinese tradition does not place him alongside the inimitable Li Po and Tu Fu, his work probably elicits a more consistent response of sympathetic affection than that of any other T'ang poet. Nearly twenty-eight hundred of Po Chü-yi's *shih* survive as well as sixteen *fu,* testimony to what he called his "obsession" with writing poems. Although Po wrote profusely and agreeably in all forms and styles of verse, he is most lauded for his long narrative poems and for his poems of social criticism. Chief among the latter are the fifty "new *yüeh-fu*" that Po Chü-yi gathered into a set in 809. The poems describe and denounce matters of official extravagance, malfeasance, and misuse of power, along with their effects on the state and especially the common people. Po uses the heptasyllabic line as standard throughout, intermingled with occasional lines of different meter to avoid monotony. In the preface to the whole series, Po Chü-yi speaks of how he has purposely composed these poems in plain language so that their meaning will be easily understood, in fluently cadenced style so that they may be circulated by song, and for the sake of bettering real people and events in the world rather than for the sake of literature. The poems are arranged in careful order, the first twenty focusing on historical incidents dating mostly from the preceding two centuries of T'ang rule, the second thirty poems focusing on contemporary issues. Within these two large divisions are several subgroupings, including an introductory lot comprising the first four poems and a clinching set made up of the final two. The complete series is the most integrated and rigorously constructed composite work in all of T'ang poetry; its cumulative impact is formidable. Po himself regarded these poems as his most significant work.

Poems of this kind, if not of this organizational complexity, had been written earlier by Tu Fu, Yüan Chieh, Wei Ying-wu, and Liu Chang-ch'ing, among others. In Po Chü-yi's own day Yüan Chen (see below), Chang Chi (768–830?, *c.s.* 799), Wang Chien (766–831?), and Li Shen (772–846, *c.s.* 806) all wrote important works of "new *yüeh-fu*" before the appearance of Po Chü-yi's series so designated in 809. During the first decade of the ninth century, particularly in the opening years of Emperor Hsien-tsung's (r. 805–820) reign, there was increased interest in exploring the limits of socially concerned verse. Po Chü-yi praised highly the poems done in this vein before 809 by Chang Chi and Wang Chien, whose work still deserves attention. The idea for Po's set of fifty poems seems to have been triggered by a group of twenty "newly titled" (*hsin-t'i*) *yüeh-fu* written by Li Shen, to twelve of which Yüan Chen had written matching poems. It is unfortunate that these poems are not among the surviving 130 *shih* of Li Shen; we have only the titles of the twelve that Yüan Chen took up and, in seven cases, Yüan's quotation of Li Shen's own remarks on the incidents engendering the poems. All twelve of Li's "new *yüeh-fu*" whose titles we know of also have identically titled counterparts in Po Chü-yi's set of fifty. Within a year or two of completing his fifty political ballads, Po composed a set of ten "Ch'in-chung yin" (Odes from Ch'in), treating social injustices in the capital. These are done in regular pentametric verse and are somewhat less boisterous, though no less forthright, than the ballads. There are approximately a hundred other poems by Po Chü-yi that may be classified as political or social criticism.

Many of Po's socially oriented poems contain a narrative element. Although there is a "message" in poems such as "Ch'ang-hen ko" (The Song of Everlasting Regret), "P'i-p'a hsing" (Ballad of the Balloon Lute), and "Chiang-nan yü T'ien-pao yüeh-sou" (Meeting an Old Musician from the T'ien-pao Era in Chiang-nan), it is the story that holds center stage. Appreciation of the narrative drama (or melodrama) is the objective here. The fact that "Ch'ang-hen ko" has become the most famous of all Chinese poems suggests Po Chü-yi's knack for such composition.

Written in early 807, this romanticized retelling of the ill-starred love affair between the Emperor Hsüan-tsung and "Precious Consort" Yang (Yang Kuei-fei) is not a historical but a sentimental tale, freely embroidered with scenes contrary to fact or purely imaginary. The poem is composed in 120 heptasyllabic lines, organized in a series of vignettes set forth in rhyming couplets and in quatrains. One example of the latter is his description of the scene after Lady Yang's forced execution at the Ma-wei post station: "Floriform filigrees were strewn on the ground, to be retrieved by no one, / Halcyon tailfeathers, an aigrette of gold, and hairpins made of jade. / The sovereign king covered his face—he could not save her; / When he looked back, it was with tears of blood that mingled in their flow." These short, lilting units are framed by octets at the beginning of the work: "Monarch of Han, he doted on beauty, yearned for a bewitching temptress; / Through the dominions of his sway, for many years he sought but did not find her. / There was in the family of Yang a maiden just then reaching fullness, / Raised in the women's quarters protected, unacquainted yet with others. / Heaven had given her a ravishing form, impossible for her to hide, / And one morning she was chosen for placement at the side of the sovereign king. / When she glanced behind with a single smile, a hundred seductions were quickened; / All the powdered and painted ones in the Six Palaces now seemed without beauty of face"; and at the end: "As the envoy [from Hsüan-tsung grieving on earth below, to Lady Yang in her posthumous paradise] was to depart, she entrusted poignantly to him words as well, / Words in which there was a vow that only two hearts would know: / 'On the seventh day of the seventh month, in the Hall of Protracted Life, / At the night's midpoint, when we spoke alone, with no one else around— / "In heaven, would that we might become birds of coupled wings!/ On earth, would that we might be trees of intertwining limbs! . . . "' / Heaven is lasting, earth long-standing, but there is a season for their end; / *This* regret stretches on and farther, with no ending time." Po Chü-yi later grumbled over the poem's extraordinary popularity, expressing chagrin that it was preferred to his more serious poems.

Indeed it is because of the frankly facile nature of that style that Po Chü-yi is sometimes found wanting by traditional critics, although the very ease of his style helped make him by far the favorite Chinese poet in Heian Japan and contributes to his broad appeal even today. As a writer of *fu*, Po Chü-yi excelled in the regulated form. He was well represented with examples of his work in contemporary handbooks, like the recently rediscovered *Fu-p'u* (Ledger for the Rhapsody), that sought to teach proper compositional technique in the *lü-fu*. Perhaps most interesting among his rhapsodies is a *fu* on *fu*, rhyming to the words of Pan Ku's (32–92) famous statement "*fu che ku-shih chih liu*" (the *fu* is a technique of the ancient *Songs*), which Po here prefers to interpret as "The *fu* is the mainstream of ancient poetry."

Yüan Chen (779–831, *ming-ching* 793) is now quite overshadowed as a poet by his friend Po Chü-yi. However, much of his *yüeh-fu* verse—to old and new titles—is fully comparable with that of Po in artistic merit and moral content. Both Yüan Chen and Po Chü-yi pronounced often in prose about matters of literary theory and history. In such contexts Yüan was one of Tu Fu's early and most vociferous champions, frequently advancing Tu Fu's superiority over Li Po. Yüan Chen's best-known poem is his ninety-line heptametric "Lien-ch'ang kung tz'u" (Lyric on the Lien-ch'ang Palace), written c. 816. This centers on the reminiscences purportedly spoken by an aged peasant who had in his boyhood served food at the Lien-ch'ang compound—an imperial "traveling palace" on the route between Ch'ang-an and Loyang—when it was visited by Hsüan-tsung and Yang Kuei-fei in T'ien-pao times (742–756). These memories, combined with description of the site's present sad dilapidation and an imperial command to raze the palace, conclude with a paean to the military strength and good government of the reigning monarch. Although the closing panegyric is a bald political maneuver, the poem is an effective comment on the transience of worldly glory.

As noted above, the sweet and sunlit but forever-vanished days of Hsüan-tsung's reign had become a subject for poetic treatment within decades of their passing. Whether one focused on the theme of dynastic fortunes sliding from the peak of pomp and prosperity to the pit of dethronement and civil war or on the overweening pleasures of the court as opposed to the crushing miseries of the plebs or on Hsüan-tsung's besotted infatuation with his voluptuous Lady Yang, this was a tale impossible to ignore. Edged with varying degrees of nostalgia and admonition, history soon became legend and nearly myth, to be evoked in all forms of *shih* from simple quatrain to lengthy narrative and in *fu* as well. Wei Ying-wu's half-dozen or so compositions on this subject are more influential than is usually realized, but it is the poets of the ninth century who exploited the subject to the full in more than a hundred extant works. Besides Po Chü-yi's "Song of Everlasting Regret" and several other related poems, and Yüan Chen's "Lien-ch'ang Palace," remarkable poems on the topic were written by Li Yi[2], Liu Yü-hsi, Tu Mu, and Li Shang-yin (see below for the latter two poets). Chang Hu (fl. 820–845), who specialized in writing quatrains on historical themes, reverted to the subject a dozen times. Two sites were favored by the poets as the geographic focus of such works—either the Palace of Floriate Clarity (Hua-ch'ing kung) on Blackhorse Mountain (Li Shan) 25 miles east of Ch'ang-an, including the famous hot springs, where Hsüan-tsung and Lady Yang usually spent the beginning of winter, or the Ma-wei post station 30 miles west of the capital, where, on 15 July 756, Yang Kuei-fei was put to death by extorted command of the emperor. The grandest of all such poems is Cheng Yü's (*c.s.* 851) "Chin-yang men" (The Chin-yang Gate; denoting the Hua-ch'ing gateway that faced the road to the capital). This superbly crafted poem comprises two hundred heptametric lines and a copious interlinear commentary by the author himself. It is a historically accurate but still poignant (without being histrionic) supplement to "Ch'ang-hen ko."

The most eccentric poet of the T'ang, perhaps in all of Chinese poetry, is the short-lived Li Ho (790–816). His most striking poems, notorious for their charged and overstrained imagery, are bizarre mosaics of hallucinatory vision and personalized allusion. Li Ho's uniquely hermetic use of symbols derived from the *Elegies of Ch'u* and from his own spiritual interests sometimes results in a nearly impenetrable screen of language, as in the concluding six lines of his "Shen-hsien ch'ü" (Tune for Unearthly Strings): "Cassia leaves are scoured by wind and cassia sheds its seeds, / As a blue raccoon-dog weeps blood and the cold fox dies. / A gaudy spirax from an ancient mural, tail of gold trailing, / Is ridden by the Lord of Rain into waters of an autumn tarn. / An owl aged a hundred years now turns into a wood-ghoul, / Cyan flames and the sound of laughter rising out of its nest." Transitions and connections between couplets, lines, even single images, can be enigmatic. Li Ho is the Chinese Mallarmé. Two of the most famous poets of the next generation, Tu Mu and Li Shang-yin, commemorated him in their prose, the former with a preface to Li Ho's collected poems, the latter with a short account of his life.

Tu Mu (803–852, *c.s.* 828) is the author of one of the most, perhaps the most, celebrated *fu* of the ninth century: "The O-p'ang Palace" (O-p'ang kung fu). Done in regulated fashion, Tu Mu's exuberant description of this largest and most costly of the capital constructions of the First Emperor of Ch'in is meant analogously to criticize Ching-tsung's (r. 824–827) plan to refurbish and expand the palace resort complex on Mount Li, infamous for its association with the revels of Hsüan-tsung and Yang Kuei-fei. As a writer of *shih*, Tu Mu excels in cleanly fitted placements of image and allusion. Although he is most lauded for his heptametric quatrains, it is a mistake to consider him, as do many traditional scholars, as skilled only in "New-Style" verse. He is proficient and graceful in all forms of *shih*.

Li Shang-yin (811?–859, *c.s.* 837) was more than competent in writing the various types of verse expected of a T'ang scholar-official. A characteristic ninth-century topic—a survey of T'ang history concluding with contemporary social concerns, voiced mainly in the person of a rustic—is treated convincingly in his "Hsing-tz'u hsi-chiao tso yi-pai yün" (One Hundred Rhymes Composed While Traveling Through the Western Suburbs), a *tour de force* written shortly after he passed the *chin-shih* exam. But he came to develop a style unmistakably his own, eventually becoming a poet of great originality. The works for which he is best known contain densely packed imagery presented in diction that glitters with rich sensuality. In one of his quatrains, "Ou t'i" (Inscribed Perfunctorily), an afternoon's open-air liaison between the poet and a lover is revealed by the scene itself—entwined azalea ("mountain pomegranate") and cypress branches, along with the unseen lady's dropped hair ornaments: "In the little kiosk lazing drowsily—a faint drunkenness dissolves; / Mountain pomegranate and lake cypress—limbs of both entangled. / On bamboo mat of rippled design, a pillow made of amber, / And next to it a fallen hairpin, a pair of halcyon plumes." Hidden allusions in certain phrases here may even hint—but merely hint—at imperial indiscretions past and possibly present. Many of these poems seem, on the surface, to be about the tortures and passions of love. But their lexical glitter, like the glare of the sun when viewed directly, blinds the querying eye. A wealth of allusive reference also brings into play dizzying counterpoints of literary echoes. The difficulties and ambiguities of Li Shang-yin's verse, whether consciously intended or not, often produce unresolvable differences in interpretation: is the once dear but now distant inamorata a Taoist priestess, a palace lady, a metaphor for a political patron? Poems such as the many that are called "Wu-t'i" (Untitled) or the mysterious trio called "Pi-ch'eng" (The Walls of Cyan-Blue) are peculiarly fascinating, almost hypnotically involving. Like Tu Fu in his later years and Li Ho, Li Shang-yin favored *chin-t'i* poetry for his more intricate experiments.

Minor poets of interest from the first three-quarters of the ninth century who merit at least some mention include Shih Chien-wu (*c.s.* 820), whose remaining poems are almost entirely in *chüeh-chü* form and largely on Taoist themes; Hsü Hun (c. 791–c. 858, *c.s.* 832), who was especially adept in *lü-shih*; Ma Tai (*c.s.*

844), a friend of Chia Tao and Yao Ho, whose reputation climbed in the Sung dynasty; Li Ch'ün-yü (813–861), who shunned an official career and wrote handsomely on historical and lyric themes and in *yüeh-fu* verse that has more than the normal air of folk songs; and Ts'ao Yeh (816–875?, *c.s.* 850), who was most comfortable with "Old-Style" verse and also composed admirable *yüeh-fu*, including "new" *yüeh-fu* on unwonted subjects. Two celebrated women poets call for notice here: Hsüeh T'ao (770–830) and Yü Hsüan-chi (840–868). The former, a geisha from Shu who enjoyed the favor of successive governors in Ch'eng-tu, writes with moderate grace in quatrains about nature and on the inconstant course of relations between men and women. The latter, a more considerable and more volatile poet, also concentrates on emotional matters but is capable on occasion of taking well-founded umbrage at being treated as a mere ornament in a man's world. Her murder of a servant girl brought her own life to an early end. Wen T'ing-yün (812?–866), a sometime companion of Yü Hsüan-chi, is a dextrous but not a distinctive voice in the *shih* genre; he is, however, the earliest poet to devote a large portion of his poetic output to the writing of *tz'u* (see chapter 15). Two collections of his languorous *tz'u* poetry, in which he often adopts a feminine persona, were in circulation during his lifetime.

P'i Jih-hsiu (834?–883?, *c.s.* 867) and Lu Kuei-meng (?–c. 881) are usually regarded as the most eminent poets of the mid- to late ninth century. In some ways their lives are a study in contrasts: P'i was a seeker of political prestige, mostly unsuccessful, and in 878 joined the devastating rebellion of Huang Ch'ao, ultimately dying in the latter's service (possibly executed for affronting the great man), while Lu steered clear of official entanglements after failing the *chin-shih* exam, instead cultivating the life of a country gentleman with a decided taste for tea and pursuing a deep interest in Taoist rites and texts. Nevertheless, in 869–871 the two became close friends during P'i's bureaucratic tenure in the area of Lu's estate (near Soochow); they wrote several hundred *shih* on shared topics, mostly in praise of the flora and fauna of the Wu region. These works are perhaps the best of P'i Jih-hsiu's poetry and are among the best of Lu Kuei-meng. However, Lu wrote equally excellent verse on, for instance, religious topics, and his *fu* (nineteen of which survive) are unrivaled for their quick spirit in the T'ang's final fifty years. Lo Yin (833–909), a contemporary of P'i and Lu who lived to see the fall of the dynasty, is known for *chin-t'i* verse that denounced the corruption of court officials and the pusillanimity of Emperors Hsi-tsung (r. 873–888) and Chao-tsung (r. 888–904) in the most unsparing terms. Lo's refusal to cast such criticism in indirect fashion was both a cause and, eventually, a result of his failing the *chin-shih* exam ten times over. His five extant *fu* are likewise vehicles of straight-out reproach.

Two Buddhist monks, Kuan-hsiu (birth-name Chiang Te-yin; 832–912) and Ch'i-chi (birth-name Hu Te-sheng; fl. 870–890) were both expert practitioners of "Recent-Style" verse who wrote with freshness and fervor on Buddhist themes, often exploiting images that are as closely associated with Taoist texts. On other subjects, such as poems on objects, farewell pieces, and scenic depictions, which account for the bulk of their voluminous *oeuvres*, they equal the finest of their contemporaries. Fang Kan (fl. 830–860), Li P'in (?–876, *c.s.* 854), Tu Hsün-ho (846–907, *c.s.* 891), Cheng Ku (c. 851–c. 911, *c.s.* 896), and Han Wo (844–923, *c.s.* 889) are poets who each contributed a chorus to the teeming symphony of the ninth century.

The last T'ang poet we shall mention here is Wei Chuang (836?–910, *c.s.* 894). A fourth-generation descendant of Wei Ying-wu, Wei Chuang is a poet of seemly facility in both *shih* and *tz'u*. As one of the leading lights in the maturing of *tz'u* poetry, he is traditionally paired with Wen T'ing-yün. This, and the compilation of the *Yu-hsüan chi* anthology, was Wei's main repute until early in the twentieth century. Then the unsealed library at Tun-huang yielded among its treasures no fewer than nine manuscript copies of Wei's long-lost poem "Ch'in-fu yin" (The Lament of the Lady of Ch'in). This is the last and the longest (some 238 heptasyllabic lines) of the great T'ang narrative poems. It tells in horrifying, sometimes sickening, detail of the rape and plunder of Ch'ang-an and its people in 881 by Huang Ch'ao's rebel forces. The real speaker of the poem, once the poet sets the scene, is a noblewoman who witnessed it all and has finally escaped, making her way on foot to Loyang, where the poet discovers her cowering unkempt beneath a willow tree. No longer rehearsing the ruin of T'ien-pao resplendence, Wei Chuang now offers us a powerful narrative of present terror and catastrophe. History here catches up with the current moment. The poem, written sometime between 883 and 886, was an immediate sensation. As the Tun-huang manuscripts show, it was well known even on the outskirts of the empire within a short time. For political reasons Wei Chuang disowned the poem in the late 890s and eliminated it from his collected works. Only a two-line fragment filtered down through the centuries until the Tun-huang finds revealed the whole monumental poem to the world once more.

The fickle fate of Wei Chuang's masterpiece—lost for a thousand years and then recovered by chance in an abundance of manuscripts from a distant Central Asian cave—is an eerie reminder of the incompleteness of any account of the history of Chinese literature, but it also serves as a challenge to retrieve by various means as much of China's literary heritage as possible. All of these strictures apply in full measure to the subject of chapter 15, on *tz'u* (song lyrics).

Paul W. Kroll

Chapter 15

TZ'U

What is a *tz'u?* If you had posed this question to a popular entertainer in one of the thriving commercial centers on the route into T'ang China from Central Asia in 900 C.E., she might have replied, "Well, *tz'u* means 'the words,' that is, 'the words to a song.' It's a poem in Chinese that we sing with music to entertain the visitors from China. The people love it, and I'll tell you why: the music is interesting and the songs are great for banquets, where everyone is feeling romantic after a few cups of wine." She might then study your face a moment, take a sip of grape wine, and confide, "You know, the Chinese were never a great musical people. The music they perform in their state temple rituals—they call it 'elegant' or 'orthodox music' [*ya-yüeh*] and claim it is at least eleven hundred years old—is terribly boring. From Han times, through the southern courts and until the Sui and T'ang reasserted Chinese control over north and northwest China three centuries ago, the Chinese managed to come up with music that was slightly better. Although it gave them tunes they could sing songs to, it was unexciting by our standards. Whether that is because or in spite of the fact that it had some of its roots in Chinese folk music, I couldn't say. . . . Since they now dignify it with the name 'pure music' [*ch'ing-yüeh*], you *know* it is a fossil. Of course it is now largely forgotten: the T'ang people finally caught up with the rest of the world! By that I mean that they started participating in the culture that stretches all the way across Central Asia, from Persia to Japan, and they discovered what real music can be. Now they don't want to hear anything but international tunes, with a few of the more charming Chinese folk songs thrown in for variety.

"I see you want to know more about the 'words.' Well, then: often we sing quatrains that everyone knows written by famous poets in simple Classical Chinese; there's definitely an audience for that. But you see, my fellow singers and I also know how to write songs, and we make the rhythm a lot more interesting by squeezing more syllables into the same number of beats. (We also put in quite a bit of ordinary, everyday language.) A lot of those poets are trying to catch up with us: they also are getting away from the uniform seven-syllable line, and they even experiment with using stanzas to fit our music."

You would get a similar answer from those who were at the top of this woman's profession, the musicians who entertained the court in Ch'ang-an with the same pan-Asian music. During the eighth century, when they were driven by the tides of war out to the metropolitan centers elsewhere in China, these men and women brought their high standards into the growing urban culture, ensuring that performances of *tz'u* and its associated music would appeal even to the most elite classes.

Some of our interviewee's contemporaries, however, would have found her account incomplete. The performers, merchants, or novice monks whose transcriptions of *tz'u* lay sealed for nine hundred years in a cave at Tun-huang (see chapter 48) until they were unearthed a century ago would have added, "Yes, but there are other kinds of *tz'u*, such as the long stories told in song with pictures, the song sequences about the twelve hours of Buddhist mediation or the five watches of the night, and sets of songs to go with dances. OK, so maybe we don't *call* all of them *tz'u*—but you will note that some of them use the music you recognize as *tz'u* melodies. The point is that there is a lot going on besides poets who write in classical Chinese taking the old romantic themes and imagery of the Palace-Style poems and folksongs of the southern courts and dressing them up with the new music."

The complexity of these answers shows that *tz'u* (which this chapter calls "lyrics"; also called "song lyrics" and "lyric meters") was an amorphous genre in its formative years, one whose boundaries and definitions are still subject to debate. The picture becomes somewhat clearer in the Sung dynasty (960–1279), although it remains a diverse and changing one.

Our view of the evolving genre in the early eleventh century is captured in this line from a lyric by the poet Yen Chi-tao (1030?–1106?): "Longing told on the strings of the *p'i-p'a*." The typical theme of the lyric is love (almost always love-longing), and the typical musical accompaniment is by stringed instruments (the *p'i-p'a* being a plucked and strummed instrument of presumed Central Asian origin, shaped like an elongated lute and held vertically on the lap). Moreover, Yen Chi-tao is typical of the men who wrote most of the lyrics that have come down to us from the Northern Sung (960–1127): he was a member of the educated elite who made it their mission to define the culture of their empire as well as its administrative policies. That such serious-minded and prominent leaders should compose songs about love, that they should have them sung at banquets or even sing them personally with their friends, and that they should allow these songs to be preserved are puzzling matters. As might be expected, there were many among their peers who frowned on the composition of "trifling lyrics" (*hsiao tz'u*) as unworthy. Yen Chi-tao himself was criticized by an eminent friend of his father's for revealing in the act of composing lyrics "a surplus of talent and a deficiency in virtue." Yet Yen saw no harm in lyrics, as long as they were composed well—which to most writers of lyrics meant "elegantly." In a well-known anecdote, Yen's father, Yen Shu (991–1055), distinguished sharply between his own songs (*ch'ü-tzu*) and those of Liu Yung (987?–1053), whose depictions of romantic behavior were too direct and hence coarse or "vulgar." Although the recorded conversation between Yen Shu and Liu Yung makes no mention of form, Liu also violated contemporary decorum by adopting what was apparently a popular form of lyric, the *man-tz'u*, characterized by long stanzas and organizational techniques that are described in more detail below. Elite poets eventually followed suit, but in the time of Yen Shu and Liu Yung themselves the "acceptable" form was the *hsiao-ling*, usually consisting of a pair of stanzas, each four or five lines long. Yen's scorn for Liu's coarseness may or may not account for the fact that Liu never made much headway in the bureaucracy (Yen Shu, a child prodigy, had risen to the highest possible posts).

If Yen Chi-tao and men of his station wrote lyrics as an elegant pastime, they collected and preserved them for several reasons. First, the lyrics they and their friends wrote on informal occasions served as mementos of those friends and those occasions. The romantic content of the lyrics may or may not have reflected the content of the conversation at those gatherings, but Yen states specifically that lyrics kept people from getting too serious or too drunk and in this were far superior to "song words that find fault with the times" (*ping-shih chih ko-tz'u*).

Another motive for making written records of lyrics was to fix an uncorrupted text of the words. Once a song started circulating, it could be altered in accordance with more plebeian tastes, much to the frustration of the original composer. Recorded on paper, however, the lyric was guarded against debasement. Most of the lyric writers whose names are known to us were always conscious of a need to differentiate their work from that of the common musicians, who undoubtedly were responsible for most of the lyrics written in the centuries when *tz'u* performance was a living, popular art. The preface (dated 940) to the earliest securely dated major anthology of lyrics, *Hua chien chi* (Among the Flowers), expresses the hope that the lyrics therein will not only be used by talented and intelligent men to aid in the pleasure of their gatherings of "feather-parasoled chariots" but also that "beauties of the southern states will cease to sing the 'lotus-boat' songs." In making this dual justification for the writing and collecting of lyrics, Ou-yang Chiung (896–971) called upon the elite writer of lyrics to resist the expanding hegemony of the popular lyric and even to indoctrinate the "beauties" who controlled the oral media marketplace with a superior standard. Yen Chi-tao appears to have had less faith in the receptivity of the popular entertainment scene to the uplifting influence of his works; he committed his texts to paper to keep popular entertainers from changing them, from making them "common" or "vulgar."

While Yen Chi-tao's "P'i-p'a hsien shang shuo hsiang-ssu" (Longing Told on the Strings of the *P'i-p'a*) does index what has come down to us as the dominant style of the early Sung lyric, it does not tell the whole story. Some tunes apparently called for no more than the human voice and the beating of time with a small drum, the hands, or—in some anecdotes—an oar on the side of a boat. Buddhist monks sometimes fit simple sermons to these tunes, a preaching technique that had precedents in Indian Buddhism, according to one contemporary account. Ou-yang Hsiu (1007–1072) used the tune "Yü-chia ao" (Fisherman's Pride) to write a dozen lyrics on the twelve months of the year to be performed with a small drum; Wang An-shih (1021–1086) used this tune to compose lyrics on rustic scenes and quiet thoughts, and he listened to a monk friend sing "Fisherman's Pride" songs as the two walked in the countryside, where the clap of hands or the thump of a walking stick must have been the only accompaniment. All this may seem to indicate that Ou-yang and Wang were not so constrained by their roles as major cultural and political leaders that they could not participate in a little middlebrow recreation now and then; but while that is undoubtedly true, there is evidence that "Fisherman's Pride" could be performed in an elegant manner. This can be deduced from the fact that Yen Shu used this tune fourteen times, more than any other in his surviving works. Moreover, Li Ch'ing-chao (1084–c. 1151) used it for two lyrics, one of which is justifiably among her most famous compositions and by no means a simple folk song. Noting that every line of the lyrics written to this tune ends in a rhyme and there is no change of rhyme throughout, we can infer that in performance these lyrics had an insistent beat that could serve a variety of stylistic purposes.

At any given time during the development of the genre, people experienced the lyric through a variety of performance styles, whether in the context of popular culture, elite culture, or something between. This tells us much about why lyrics flourished in the tenth and early eleventh centuries despite what often strikes us (since we can no longer *hear* them) as a stifling monotony. However, changes in the form, content, and uses of the lyric across time also kept it vital, and these are aspects of the genre that we can appreciate if we read lyrics with care and study the critical literature that gradually came to flourish around them.

The most critical formal innovation was Liu Yung's production of a significant number of lyrics in the *man* form, which had hitherto been confined to popular lyrics. Isolated *man-tz'u* by such writers as Tu Mu (803–852) had failed to have any impact on the elite practice of lyric writing, but more than 90 percent of the 204 lyrics in Liu's collection were in this longer format (a *man* averages fifty syllables per stanza, whereas the *hsiao-ling* averages thirty), sufficient as a body of work to have an influence on other writers (despite Liu's offenses against contemporary decorum).

The older *hsiao-ling* and the newly elevated *man* were alike in that the favored topic was love—flirtatious love or bald complaints about infidelity for the "vulgar" lyric and discreetly wistful love-longing for the "elegant" style—and writers in either form fit their words to pre-existing melodies. In form, however, the *hsiao-ling* remained close to the quatrain (see *chüeh-chü* in chapter 14) of seven syllables per line. The seven-syllable line had historically been associated with popular culture: originally used only for satirical or prophetic "ditties in the lanes," it eventually was taken up by T'ang poets for their more exuberant songs and gradually became an option for important poetry. Although both pentasyllabic and heptasyllabic poems could be and were sung throughout the T'ang dynasty, it was the heptasyllabic poem that was destined to bridge the gap between literati culture and popular culture in such a way as to lead to the rise of the *tz'u*. Wen T'ing-yün (812?–866) wrote a significant number of heptasyllabic *shih* (see chapters 13 and 14) that resemble in form and content the lyrics for which he became famous later. They can be read as single poems divided into stanzas by rhyme change or as suites of quatrains under a single title, and they were probably sung. Li Ho (790–816) also provided precedent, but Wen T'ing-yün's poems more typically feature a generalized persona or situation—precisely as found in most lyrics until Liu Yung. This suggests that, for Wen at least, the differences between these songs and his lyrics were minor details of music.

The refinement of sung stanzaic poetry into the *hsiao-ling* was a major step, however, in the birth of *tz'u* as we know it. It gave poets the potential for a new kind of emotional complexity: one stanza might tell of the past, another of the present; or one might relate an event and the other focus on simple imagery. Even when a poet (such as Wei Chuang [836?–910]) typically wrote "across" the gap, with no disjunction in time frame or in style of language, the musical structure (whether it involved a repeated melody or an instrumental bridge passage) would have broken the depicted event into two parts. (Refrain lines typical of stanzaic poetry in the West were avoided in the lyrics, though the music probably involved repeated phrases.) The result is the creation of an unspoken relationship between the stanzas, which fosters the sense that private emotions infuse the whole. Paradoxically, the conventionality of diction in the lyric supports this sense of individual feeling, because the reader or listener pays little attention to the smaller units of language within each line or to reconstituting the logical relationships between these units (relationships that would be complex and of major interest in the *shih* that lent themselves less to singing and more to reading or chanting) and instead looks for emotive links or shifts between the stanzas of the lyric. The resultant tendency of the lyric to present itself as an exploration of feeling reaches its full potential as a result of the innovations of Liu Yung.

To understand what the introduction of the *man* form into the literary realm brought, it is useful to review the relationship between the rhythm of music and the rhythm of poetry in the eleventh century, as it can be extrapolated from a few isolated scores and comments by specialists in the following century. In the traditional seven-syllable line of poetry, there are eight beats: the seventh syllable is either followed by a pause, or, if it is a rhyming syllable, it is prolonged to two beats to fill the eighth unit. Only notes of two durations, one beat and two beats, are needed. The *hsiao-ling* stanza (averaging only two more syllables than a quatrain) required little or no adjustment to match this eight-beat measure. Where there were eight or more syllables in an eight-unit measure, notes of half-beat duration would be used. In the *man-tz'u*, however, one encounters large numbers of lines of three, four, five, and six syllables, some ending in rhyme, some not. Analysis has shown that these lines were probably squeezed into four-beat measures, with more half-beat syllables being used. When one of these short lines seems to correspond to a line of eight beats in another stanza, as long as it has at least five or six syllables it could be slowed down to make an eight-beat measure without having to exceed the two-beat maximum for any syllable. Once a singer noticed whether a line ended in rhyme (a two-beat syllable) or did not end in rhyme (which meant it would be a single-beat syllable or, if there were only three syllables in the line, a pause on the fourth beat), she had a limited number of patterns of single- and half-beat syllables from which to choose.

In the longer *man* form, then, Liu Yung not only had more room to tell a story—and he is known for filling that room with extended reminiscences of love affairs and travels that we take to be his own—he had space within stanzas to create a variety of units bound by rhyme and comprising one, two, three, or four lines, most of which were shorter than seven syllables. From popular lyrics he adopted the use of "line-leading words" (*ling-chü tzu*) that helped frame these units. (We can illustrate by italicizing the "line-leading words" in the first stanza of the translation of Liu's "Pa-sheng Kan-chou" [Eight Beats of a Kan-chou Song]: "*Facing me*, the blustering evening rain . . . *Gradually*, the frosty wind . . . The landscape . . . The fading sun . . . *Everywhere* . . .") Like the discontinuities already created by stanzaic form, the shifts of rhythm between and within these substanza units and the tensions between the regular beat and the more complicated combinations of note durations in the *man-tz'u* created even more of a feeling that the lyric self behind the composition (the "speaker" of the poem) was engaged in the process of experiencing and reflecting on emotion. As Stephen Owen once put it, "*Tz'u* could isolate a phrase, add a single long line as if an afterthought; it could formally enact a sudden shift, an odd association, a flashback, an image left hanging." This was especially true of the *man-tz'u*.

From then on, most lyric writers used both forms, choosing as they thought appropriate. Ch'in Kuan (1049–1100) combined the structural techniques that

Liu Yung introduced with the more imagistic and suggestive language of the tradition Liu rejected to produce a style of refined purity, which he employed to celebrate true love, rather than coquettish charm, and to describe skillfully landscapes imbued with feeling. (His personification of natural objects is often quite striking: one poem states: "Rain *sets* more flowers *blooming*.") In this, he not only returned the lyric to its standard of elegance but gave it a tone more acceptable to the scholar-officials of his time than could be found either in the lyrics of the Five Dynasties (907–960) or in Liu Yung's works.

Su Shih (1037–1101) was also heir to Liu Yung's innovations, but he took the genre in entirely new directions: he made the lyric a vehicle for personal expression, blurring the boundary between *t'zu* and *shih*, at least where theme and diction were concerned. From the time he began writing lyrics (in his early twenties), Su used them as farewell poems to friends and associates, a function formerly limited to *shih* poetry. He even once answered a request for a poem by sending a lyric instead. It is as if Su Shih made it his mission to upset genre distinctions. Perhaps he would smile smugly if he knew that there are ten compositions of his whose classification is so problematic that they have been included among both his *shih* and his *tz'u*.

When, as he does with 43 percent of his lyrics, Su Shih adds a preface to a lyric indicating the circumstances of its composition (as was common with other forms of poetry), he changes the way we read the lyric: even the more conventional songs become a direct statement of Su Shih's sentiment in response to a specific situation, and we are discouraged from reading them as the emotions of a generalized persona, as one would with earlier banquet lyrics. His best and most famous lyrics date from his period of exile (1080–1084) in Huang-chou (in modern-day Hupei province). By this time, as his letters and prefaces indicate, his musical know-how had advanced far beyond that of his earlier years. Moreover, Su Shih could express himself in the lyric with less anxiety than he could in prose or *shih*; the lyric was not considered a serious, public form of writing. Whereas Su Shih usually considered emotion an impediment to enlightenment and found ways of transcending his feelings, in the genre that was, above all, a genre of emotion he could be content simply to express his feelings and leave it at that. (This is not to say that he did not philosophize in his lyrics, of course: one can see his typical intellectual deconstruction of sorrow, for example, in the early lyric on the moon that he wrote to his brother.)

Ever since the early sixteenth century, Su Shih has been regarded as the epitome of the "bold and unfettered" (*hao-fang*) style and Ch'in Kuan as the leading example of the "delicate and suggestive" (*wan-yüeh*) mode. This division is the framework within which most people read the lyric in China, although sometimes it is most interesting to look closely at the times when this bifurcation breaks down. For example, one characteristic of Su Shih's lyrics that contributes to the impression of boldness and freedom is the loose way he plays with chronological time within a lyric, jumping backward and forward without warning. Su Shih's view that good writing moves naturally and shapes itself to the particular situation certainly seems applicable to his lyrics. Now, if we say that this is part of his "unfettered" style, we have to ask whether a similar complication of time in the lyrics of a "delicate and suggestive" poet such as Chou Pang-yen (1056–1121) has a different effect. As Hsia Ching-kuan (1875–1953) put it, "Liu Yung's depiction of scene was always well done, though he did not put effort into cutting and polishing his lines. Chou Pang-yen imitated him . . . [but] Liu usually laid out his material straight, whereas Chou changed the technique: in a single composition he would turn in circles, go one way and return, so that one sang it through once and then savored its subtlety over and over. Thus it is that *man* lyrics had their first flowering with Liu Yung but came into full maturity with Chou Pang-yen."

Chou Pang-yen brought the lyric to its full maturity in two other ways. The first was by refining its musical qualities by being more particular about the match between the quality of each syllable and the corresponding note of the melody. It is usually noted that Chou was the first poet to go beyond distinctions between the "even" and "deflected" tones of the syllables in a line (the patterns of these two categories of tones defined the "meter" of Chinese poetry); by comparing different lyrics he wrote to the same tune, we can see that his tone patterns included discriminations between the three "deflected" tones as well. Since it would be nearly impossible to sing Chinese words with the tones they have in ordinary speech and still follow a melody, these tonal discriminations could have had little to do with pitch per se; instead, they must have involved a mapping of tones against note length and front/back vowel positions and voiced/unvoiced initial distinctions against note length or pitch. Whatever the details, Chou certainly knew them: an excellent scholar of music, he was appointed to the Imperial Music Bureau that was founded to research ancient music and provide court music during the period 1103–1120.

The full impact of Chou's finer musical discriminations was not felt for many decades. As for the second important characteristic of Chou's lyrics, the incorporation of extensive quotations, he was not atypical of his generation of writers, simply more skillful. Ch'in Kuan and Ho Chu (1052–1125), who were better known both in their own generation and in the next one, may have been more influential in the short term for their practice of borrowing lines. (Ho boasted of "driving Li Shang-yin [811?–859] and Wen T'ing-yün before my brush-tip, scurrying on without a moment's rest.") Moreover, these poets were not unique in quoting others; the poets of the *Among the Flowers* anthology had traded diction long before. In the case of Chou Pang-yen and his contemporaries, however, the quotations usually came from *shih* poetry, especially from the lines of Li Ho, Li Shang-yin, Wen T'ing-yün, and other late-T'ang figures. What excited the admiration of later generations about Chou was his ability to find lines and parts of lines in famous and not-so-famous poets that would fit his melodies to a high degree of tonal precision.

Quotations and allusions appear in all genres of Chinese writing, of course. There is a sense, however, in which they are almost intrinsic to the lyric. We have mentioned "conventionality of diction" as characteristic of most lyrics, we have noted that love-longing is the dominant theme, and we have related how the lyric grew out of and maintained a tradition within *shih* poetry in which the writer presented a universal situation in a generalized voice. Granted that a high degree of conventionality supports the intelligibility of a poem meant to be presented in song, it is hard to imagine how the finest literary minds of a civilization not only would continue to read such works with genuine pleasure century after century but would even write their own compositions in such a limited genre. The answer to this puzzle lies in the structural characteristics of the lyric as discussed above: its changes of pace, its asymmetry, the "line-leading words" that frame blocks of language. What is thus framed becomes the object of reflection or of "rediscovery." As Stephen Owen puts it, the lyric "quotes and comments on the received images of poetry, changing them in the process and making them animate again." For Chou Pang-yen and other lyricists, "received language" was a special subset of "received images": by quoting from earlier poets, they asserted that the old language could be applied to the speaker's present feelings and was therefore true and alive. This assertion and the reanimation of old language implied some kind of mental processing, perhaps in the form of an emotional experience by the speaker of the poem or maybe as an intellectual game by the implied author of the poem—or both, depending on the style of the poem.

("Implied author" is used here because we are talking about the author as imagined by the reader of the work. With supporting anecdotal information we may get closer to the real author and his intentions, but the flesh-and-blood author is forever unknowable. The distance between the speaker of the poem and the implied author can be greater in the lyric than in other traditions of Chinese poetry, as when the speaker is a lonely young lady and the author is a middle-aged man, or it can be as minimal as in most *shih* poetry, where we find a plausible overlap between the persona whose thoughts are related in the lyric and the author as we know him. The Chinese expectation that a literary work must express the character of the author encouraged a double-level reading in which the plaint of the young lady is considered an analog for the concerns of the male author; as seen below, later lyric writers *wrote* within the framework of this manner of reading.)

Perhaps the most interesting examples of quotation are to be found in the works of Hsin Ch'i-chi (1140–1207), whose 626 surviving lyrics constitute the largest corpus for an individual Sung lyricist. Hsin is known not only for the frequency with which he alludes to other texts but also for the manner with which he does so: from earlier poets, he quotes entire lines verbatim; he also lifts language from prose texts, complete with all the grammatical particles of classical Chinese that are unnecessary in poetry and almost always avoided.

("Sentences"—grammatically complete strings—are generally shorter in poetry [in *shih:* one line, with enjambment rare and usually confined to the last couplet of a poem; in *tz'u:* the space between rhymes]; instead of particles, rhythm does the work of organizing the poetic line into topic, comment, and other meaningful units; and relationships between units or between lines are inferable or purposely ambiguous.) In several famous lyrics, Hsin Ch'i-chi actually takes a complete argument from an ancient text such as the *Chuang Tzu* and rewrites it in the form of a lyric. In part, this is intellectual wit and bravado, merely an extreme example of the play with the ocean of texts that characterizes so much Sung dynasty writing.

It may also reflect an evolving attitude toward texts that can be associated with the fact that by Hsin Ch'i-chi's time printing had been flourishing for two centuries. The manuscript culture that had supported the preservation of information since paper came into widespread use in the third century had now given way to print culture. The new technology brought about a situation in which virtually all knowledge vital to the continuation of the civilization had been stored in multiple copies: by the middle of the twelfth century, information was less something to be memorized with the help of texts than something to be retrieved from texts. Although in certain situations one still read to memorize (the civil service examinations being the most critical occasion for verbatim recall), the fact that information was now stored in multiple identical texts enabled cross-referencing and indexing to replace brute memorization. When Hsin Ch'i-chi was five years old, *Shih-shih lei-yüan* (Garden of Contemporary Events Arranged by Category), in which citations of sources included not only book titles but also *chüan* number, was published. In a print culture, one does not assume the reader has memorized a few books but, rather, that he will look information up in many books, and telling which part of the book contains the information becomes a useful service. Within decades, vast numbers of books appeared that rearranged information by category, abstracted texts, provided glosses, and appended examples and evidence. This suggests that the Chinese were reading in a new way, one that resembles in many respects the way in which Europeans read texts at a similar stage in the evolution of print culture in the late sixteenth and early seventeenth centuries: the format of the books themselves tells us that people looked for maxims, for precedents, for bits of diction that could be reassembled into persuasive new texts. Writers used allusions and borrowed diction with the expectation that they would be recognized and that this recognition was part of reading or hearing a text. The early champion of the lyric in English, Robert Herrick (1591–1674), was as given to quotation and borrowing as Hsin, though his sources were ancient Latin texts and therefore veiled by translation into English.

Herrick and Hsin shared another characteristic as lyricists: they were faced with the difficult task of raising the prestige of their chosen genre. Bringing respected predecessors into one's text through quotation was one defense against scorn. Among the people Hsin quoted was Su Shih; he also followed Su's precedent in taking a composition by T'ao Ch'ien (see chapter 13) and rewriting it as a lyric. Thus claiming comparability with the greatest intellectual and literary figure of the Northern Sung, Hsin reminded people that the *tz'u* had a respectable literary tradition. The printing of lyrics, common by his time, also helped. Just as the form of the lyric translates familiar feelings and common images into a specific emotional experience—gives them reality—so print makes them and the lyric literally and permanently visible.

Another way to raise the prestige of the form was to write a great deal and write well, both of which Hsin succeeded in doing. Although he wrote in all genres, Hsin Ch'i-chi is remembered chiefly for his lyrics, which he made a vehicle for serious self-expression. It must be admitted that Hsin (like Herrick and his predecessor Horace) devoted a large number of lyrics to the description of a rather idyllic country life; the majority of Hsin's *tz'u* were written during two decades of withdrawal from public life. Nevertheless, his most important lyrics voiced his feelings over the loss of the north to the Jurchen, the treacheries of political slander, and the onset of weak old age. He knew from experience that nothing was permanent, including his refuge in retirement. This awareness is found also in Herrick and Horace, although Hsin led a more active life than they did. Born in Jurchen territory (in modern-day Shantung province, occupied since 1027), the young Hsin Ch'i-chi had raised troops and joined an ongoing revolt. When the revolt was betrayed, he and fifty horsemen snatched the traitor from his camp and delivered him to Southern Sung territory. Hsin was then twenty-three. From then until he retired at age forty-three, he applied his energies to a variety of posts at the prefectural and circuit level. He came out of retirement from age sixty-four until his death four years later, but experienced many setbacks because of his aggressive advocacy of expeditions into northern territory against the Jurchen forces.

It could be argued that Hsin Ch'i-chi found a certain kind of psychological distancing in the writing of lyrics, a distancing that reconciled his strong ambition to change the world with the fact that the world would not change. More than most lyric writers, Hsin tells us that the familiar images are only borrowed; the words of Chuang Tzu, the phrases and poetic techniques of Su Shih and his generation, do not belong to them alone. The more aware one becomes of this, the more detached one becomes from words—some say printing encourages a similar liberation—and, rather than looking for the new words to say what he means, the poet reanimates old words through his skill and the framing power of the lyric and makes them mean what he says.

From Hsin Ch'i-chi's time through the end of the Southern Sung dynasty, major and minor figures who admired his integrity and agreed with his ideas wrote lyrics using his rhymes or showing the influence of his style. Writers who used the lyric to declare their frustration with what they considered a foreign policy of appeasement and to express nostalgia for the north include Hu Ch'üan

(1102–1180), Chang Hsiao-hsiang (1132–1170), Liu Kuo (1150–1206), Ch'en Liang (an important and innovative thinker in the Confucian tradition; 1143–1194), Liu K'o-chuang (1187–1269), Liu Ch'en-weng (a strong critic of Chia Ssu-tao, mentioned below; 1239–1315), and Wen T'ien-hsiang (1236–1283; his death date is often given as 1282, but his execution by the Mongols actually took place in the twelfth month of the Chinese year, January 1283 in the Western calendar). This Hsin Ch'i-chi tradition also includes Su Shih as a forebear: most notably, Chang Hsiao-hsiang (who had distinguished himself in the third war with the Jurchen in 1161) looked to Su Shih as the standard against which to measure his achievement.

Much later, a few poets in the Ch'ing dynasty, such as Wu Wei-yeh (1609–1672) and Ch'en Wei-sung (1625–1682), patterned lyrics after those of Hsin and Su Shih. It must also be emphasized that lyrics were also being written in Jurchen-held territory and that the influence of Su Shih had never waned in the north. The works of Ts'ai Sung-nien (1107–1159) are early evidence of this, but the great lyric poet Yüan Hao-wen (1190–1257) expanded the genre even further: his heroic lyric on the might of the Yellow River and his lament over the love suicide of a young couple who were not allowed to marry are without precedent.

Meanwhile, there had been major developments in the Southern Sung that owed much less to Su Shih. Let us backtrack to Li Ch'ing-chao, another of China's finest poets.

A native of the same town as Hsin Ch'i-chi, Li would have been about sixty years old when he was born, had she still been alive in 1145. She had fled south in 1127 after rioting troops made it dangerous for her to continue guarding the family property in Shantung (her husband had preceded her five months earlier to what is now the Nanking area, where his mother had just passed away). Jurchen troops sacked the city a few months after she left, and most of the fifteen carts of books and antiques her husband had taken with him had already been jettisoned in the course of his journey. On top of this cultural and financial catastrophe, Li lost her husband to illness in 1128.

The conventional picture of Li Ch'ing-chao is that she and her husband led an ideal life of shared intellectual pursuits while they lived in the north and that her lot was one of unrelieved misery after he died. (Whether or not she remarried became a subject of intense interest several centuries later, when widow chastity was promoted as a virtue.) Leaving aside the question whether we can judge the quality of a marriage so long ago and with as little evidence as we have in this case, we take note of the strange effect this storyline has had on the reading of Li's lyrics. While a few of her *tz'u* explicitly refer to preinvasion days of innocence in the "central province" or otherwise provide internal evidence that would allow us to place them in time and space, most cannot be dated. Nevertheless, readers in recent centuries have assumed that any of her lyrics expressing unhappiness and loneliness must have been written after her flight south, with the rest presumed to date from her happy years in the north.

Similar assumptions have been made about a superb early lyric writer, Li Yü (937–978), who, as the last ruler of the Southern T'ang dynasty, saved his kingdom from social and economic ruin by submitting to the emerging Sung power without military resistance. Faced with the undated lyrics of these writers whose fortunes changed radically at a clearly identifiable point in their lives, readers have assigned them to different periods of the writers' lives based on their idea of how the writers must have felt during those periods. Once that is done, of course, the lyrics become "evidence" for how the writer felt.

This is a textbook example of circular reasoning; it also disregards the unique quality of this genre of literature: lyrics historically sang of generalized situations not assumed to be connected in any direct way with the author's life. (Su Shih, whom Li Ch'ing-chao dismissed as someone who did not truly understand the genre, is one notable exception; Hsin Ch'i-chi and some Ch'ing dynasty lyricists are others, but they come later.) Ideally, then, the enlightened reader should disregard the classification of the lyrics of Li Ch'ing-chao and Li Yü as happy = early and sad = late and read them simply as successful creations of mood by gifted poets who could use all the resources of the lyric genre to make emotion seem real. However, we must also acknowledge that in China any literary writing was thought to reflect, at least in a general way, a person's character and experiences; thus, Liu Yung's lyrics purporting to sing of his own experiences with love are read as if they came out of his affairs with the *demimonde*; a set of romantic lyrics attributed to Ou-yang Hsiu excited a controversy within or very close to his lifetime over whether they indicated moral failings on his part—or even gave evidence of inappropriate relations with a younger relative. In neither case do the lyrics come with the specificity of autobiographical reference that we have already noted in Su Shih, but that does not matter. The Chinese notion that literature is intimately connected with the character of the writer (if literature reflects the Tao or the universe, it still requires the *capacity* of the writer to encompass the Tao) is so deep that the rising quality and prestige of the lyric as genuine poetry guaranteed that the lyric would come to be read as derived from the experiences of the author, and no longer as an exercise in pure invention for banquet entertainment.

Fitting the lyrics of Li Ch'ing-chao into a simplified life plot also has the appeal of making them more poignant: the sadness of a woman struggling through "An unending night / A full moon flooding an empty bed" is more moving if we believe this to be the real experience of a widow and refugee. Regardless of whether it is intellectually defensible, the "autobiographical" aspect of Li's lyrics has become part of them.

Let us suppose that we succeed in separating Li's artistry from her biography, that we do not care whether she had personally tasted the sorrow of "An unending night / A full moon flooding an empty bed" when she wrote the lyric in which these lines appear, as long as she gives us the full flavor of the feeling. We will still find it hard to separate her artistry from her sex. That is to say, we cannot dismiss from our minds the fact that, while countless lyrics down to Li Ch'ing-chao's time had presented the feelings of lonely or amorous women, hers is the first significant corpus of lyrics that we know with certainty to have been written by a woman. Moreover, unlike the fictional singer "interviewed" at the beginning of this chapter, Li was not writing for an audience of men expecting to be entertained. We grant her voice authenticity: these are the true thoughts of a woman. Liu Yung had given us much more of the "psychology" of the women he wrote about than had his contemporaries, who still confined themselves to describing the material surroundings and stereotypical actions of their subjects, but he was a man. Moreover, the women he wrote about were courtesans: their concerns are hardly more elevated than those of the women who speak frankly about their hopes and frustrations in the anonymous lyrics from Tun-huang—which may be one reason Li Ch'ing-chao disparaged his diction as "dusty and low." Li does not claim to speak "for women," but we are aware that she, not a man, is the maker of the voice in her poems—and we are aware that it is the voice of a consummate artist.

It seems clear that male and female writers operated within the same tradition at this time. Li Ch'ing-chao never identifies herself as continuing a heritage of writing by or for women, nor will later female lyric writers declare her the founder of any such tradition, although critics could praise a female writer by declaring her comparable to Li.

Critical writing on *tz'u* begins with Li Ch'ing-chao and a few of her contemporaries. Her "Tz'u lun" (Discourse on the Lyric) is generally considered the most interesting. Though short, it surveys the genre from its beginnings as a popular form of entertainment in the T'ang to the generation of writers who preceded her. Her aim is less history than the definition of the genre as it *should* be practiced. Her first criterion of judgment appears to be the performability of a writer's lyrics. Writers who do not understand that distinctions between all five tones and between voiced and unvoiced consonants are crucial in composition will produce "unsingable" lyrics. It is interesting that she does not cite Chou Pang-yen as a model to follow. Perhaps this was because she was unacquainted with his work, or maybe because she found nothing to criticize about him—in this essay she never mentions a writer without finding fault. Those who pass the musical test—Yen Chi-tao, Ho Chu, Ch'in Kuan, and Huang T'ing-chien (1045–1105)—come up short when measured by other criteria, such as those concerning style and structure. Yen, for example, lacks narrative or discursive structure (*p'u-hsü*), while Ho is deficient in classical weightiness (*tien-chung*). In view of what we have observed about Ch'in Kuan, it is puzzling to see Li criticize him for insufficient "precedents" (*ku-shih*); perhaps she was looking for a specific kind of allusiveness. Whatever the case, it seems she was trying to define this genre not only by what it should be but also by what it was not, and these writers provided the necessary negative examples.

Between Li and the end of the Southern Sung, the lyric continued to flourish: even if we ignore all lyricists in the north under the Jurchen Chin dynasty and all Southern Sung lyricists for whom fewer than twenty lyrics have survived, there are still more than a hundred lyricists after her time whose names are known to us. Li Ch'ing-chao's careful structure, her continuation of the push beyond normative diction while yet remaining within the general style of the "indirect and suggestive," and her attention to phonological patterning place her within the dominant lyric tradition as it was to develop in the Southern Sung. As mentioned, Hsin Ch'i-chi's influence was also important. There was, in addition, a widespread knowledge of lyric composition among ordinary people. Several stories that provide evidence of this have been handed down from the time of the Jurchen incursion and from that of the Mongol retaliation against the Southern Sung for treaty violations in the third quarter of the thirteenth century. In these accounts, women inscribe lyrics on walls as they are about to commit suicide to preserve their honor when they have been captured by enemy forces or marauding troops. Clearly, there would be no time under such horrific circumstances for a nonmusician to compose a metrically polished lyric to the standards of a Li Ch'ing-chao. We can conclude that some melodies not requiring a precise match between music and language were still current. Indeed, for two of the melodies that figure in these stories, patterns of even and deflected tones were sufficient to define the meter, with no further discriminations.

In contrast, however, some lyricists developed the genre along the lines prescribed by Li Ch'ing-chao and exemplified by Chou Pang-yen, bringing it to new heights of musical sophistication. The prime example is Chiang K'uei (1155–1221), who sometimes composed music first and then added the lyrics and sometimes wrote lyrics for which he then composed the music. The flute was replacing strings as the instrumental accompaniment for lyrics in the Southern Sung, and Chiang used a flute to play the melody as he composed; it came closer to the sound of the human voice. (Note that Su Shih had caused one of his lyrics to be performed with a flute, but it was paired with a drum, and he says specifically that they reinforced the beat for a "robust" effect. In fact, the singer was a stalwart man clapping his hands and stamping his feet.) Chiang K'uei also left musical notations for several of his lyrics that, with some interpretation, can be converted into modern scores. He did not see lyrics solely as a performance art, however. It would scarcely have been possible to do so in an age when printed collections of lyrics were so common. Eighty (out of eighty-four) of Chiang's lyrics carry prefaces that are often as carefully worded and expressive as his lyrics themselves—almost to the point that either the preface or the lyrics could have stood alone. Clearly, he was producing texts for reading as well as lyrics for hearing.

The musician-poets Chiang K'uei and Chou Pang-yen were not scholar-officials like most of the poets discussed up to this point. Chou had worked within the framework of the Imperial Music Bureau, of course; Chiang was a poet-recluse who sought private patronage. Perhaps for this reason, he is even less concerned with expressing his values and his feelings in poetry than the most "delicate and suggestive" poets before him; instead of writing about his own experiences or lonely women, he focuses on objects. Naturally, a lyric that merely presented the qualities of an object without some reference to human values would have been found lacking in his tradition, and most of the objects one would write a lyric about carried rich cultural associations. Chiang's two most famous lyrics are on the plum blossom, which had become by then an important theme in poetry and painting, representing everything from reclusive purity to toughness in the face of adversity. He uses the rhythms and "line-leading words" discussed above to create a "morphology of feeling" around the lyric speaker's experience of the object or the emotions imputed to the object.

Wu Wen-ying (c. 1200–c. 1260), like Chiang K'uei, betrays the influence of print culture. The "density" of language for which Wu has been famous since the end of the thirteenth century can be seen as an extreme development of Chou Pang-yen's style of indirection, but whereas Chou had usually mentioned, however briefly, the occasion or situation that forms the putative starting point for the feelings expressed, Wu rarely tells us what is going on, where we are, and why we are there. He also creates new and difficult language. For these reasons, critics have complained that one cannot tell—at first glance, at least—what Wu Wen-ying is writing about. Ch'en T'ing-cho (1853–1892) assures us that, once we grasp the theme, the difficulties dissolve, and this may be so. However, the point is that one would have to hear the lyric many times or, especially to grasp the unfamiliar expressions that Wu uses, *read* the lyric over and over to find the thread that ties everything together.

Wu Wen-ying wrote the longest lyrics in the Sung, one being 240 syllables in 4 stanzas. That is exceptional even in his corpus, but he did prefer the *man tz'u* over the *hsiao-ling*. It clearly gave him the space he required to build up the layers of complexity necessary to create an artistic whole.

Through Wu Wen-ying we can also glimpse a custom that accounted for many lyrics written in the Southern Sung: birthday lyrics. Powerful officials such as Chia Ssu-tao (1213–1275) might receive several thousand such lyrics at a time; thirteenth-century books on the lyric find birthday lyrics so important that they devote space to the writer's problem of being appropriate to the occasion without falling into trite and nonliterary language. Wu Wen-ying wrote several of these lyrics for prominent political figures and for an imperial prince, his wife, and sons. These lyrics too appear to have been designed to be read (or collected unread) as well as performed.

Wu is another lyricist whose livelihood seems to have depended largely on his friendships with the rich and powerful. For reasons that remain unclear, he never attempted the simplified civil service examinations of the time, although men from his district had great advantages over candidates from the areas torn by war and his own brothers were successful in the examinations. His devotion to art rather than politics is reflected in his lyrics: the genre was by now a vehicle for the direct or indirect expression of frustration over one's being unable to influence the times or meet with appreciation for one's abilities, but Wu does not use it that way. When presenting lyrics to the rich and powerful, he hints at no ambitions; when writing to men whose status is similar to his own, he voices no complaints.

An interesting question is the degree to which Wu Wen-ying's literary reputation has been affected by his association with people like Chia Ssu-tao. Chia's success, as grand councilor, in raising government revenues and reducing tax evasion by what amounted to government expropriation of a portion of the holdings of big landlords in 1263–1275 earned him powerful enemies. After Chia's failure to hold a critical position against superior Mongol artillery as they advanced toward the Southern Sung capital in 1275, his political enemies had him exiled. He was murdered by his escort en route to his place of banishment. The official historical record heaps blame on Chia for fatally weakening the Sung—and, to the extent that he alienated powerful interests whose loyalty the court could not afford to lose, he may have done just that. Any literary person associated with him was branded a sycophant, and this has cast something of a cloud over Wu Wen-ying.

There were many other lyric writers in the shrinking territory of the Southern Sung. Some were officials; most were connoisseurs of fine living. They painted, designed gardens, exchanged poems, and wrote critical works about literature. They were heir to the entire tradition and learned from one another; as a result, they wrote in many styles. Later critics have assigned eclectic lyricists such as Chou Mi (1232–1299/1308) to a bewildering variety of contradictory affiliations. Exercises in lineage-making are an important part of past and present writing about the lyric. In Chinese, if a critic can sum up a writer—say, Chiang K'uei—with a phrase such as *ch'ing-hsü sao-ya* (pure and empty; poetic and elegant) and then say that another writer has the *ch'ing-hsü sao-ya* of Chiang, one can take satisfaction in establishing both a stylistic judgment and a historical connection. Translated into English, of course, these descriptive phrases lose all their rich connotations and appear much more vapid than they really are. For Chou Mi and many of his fellows, it is simply fruitless to reduce their influences to a single forebear. Some say Chou is in the tradition of one predecessor, some say he resembles another predecessor, and some try to solve the problem by placing him "between Chiang K'uei and Wu Wen-ying."

After the Mongols established a government, some of these late lyricists refused to participate in it at all, and others defended local interests by accepting low-level appointments as education officials. (The political goals of office holders had already shifted measurably from the national level to the regional level in the Southern Sung, and they used the same strategy under the Yüan dynasty founded by the Mongols.) In response to the desecration of the Sung royal tombs at the direction of the Mongols, fourteen of these loyalists compiled a collection of thirty-seven lyrics in 1279 called *Yüeh-fu pu-t'i* (Additional Themes for "Ballads"). In this we see lyric composition as a kind of ceremony, but also as an act of bearing witness for the ages. Although the ostensible topics were such things as incense and flowers, the lyricists made use of images of substitution (for example, the image of white birds floating down through the air *substitutes* for white flowers waving above a pond—the flowers are never mentioned directly), allusions to earlier poems, and historical allusions to build up a recurring pattern of references that covertly point to objects associated with the imperial corpses and their fate. At the same time, there is a theme of constancy or continuity in the imagery and in the awareness of historical precedents.

The use of such disguised language for the purpose of expressing moral outrage was to influence greatly the revival of the lyric in the Ch'ing dynasty (see chapter 23), especially after this collection was rescued from obscurity and published by Chu Yi-tsun (1629–1709).

Fashions change, especially with social upheavals that come with events on the scale of the reunification of China under Mongol administration. A new kind of poetry, the *ch'ü* (aria; see chapter 17), had been developing in northern China, and it now offered such great competition to the lyric that the latter was to fall into dormancy for several centuries. New developments (described elsewhere in this volume) now would take place "above" the lyric in the still-prestigious *shih* genre of the Yüan dynasty and "below" it in the *ch'ü*, with its vernacular language and new structural possibilities; the middle ground occupied by the *tz'u* was drained of its vitality, especially as the music for it was replaced by new styles suited for different kinds of songs.

People did not entirely stop writing lyrics, though the range of themes was limited to the typical themes of the aria: eremitism, enjoyment of landscape, and laments for the past, perhaps predictable in the face of limited opportunities for the subjects of the fallen Southern Sung in the Mongol administration. Some of these Yüan lyrics are of remarkable power and quality, and there are a few lyrics on locust disasters, drought, and the rapacity of officials that break new ground. However, the influences of *ch'ü* diction on lyric vocabulary and of *ch'ü* music on attempts to continue composing melodies for lyrics led to a "pollution" of the genre—at least in the eyes of later critics.

The Ming dynasty (1368–1644) saw two and a half centuries of repression of the literati who might have been expected to produce high-quality lyrics. Although there was a certain interest in collecting, copying, and printing old *tz'u* anthologies and individual collections, a significant revival of the lyric came only in the early seventeenth century, during the closing decades of the Ming dynasty. Part of the revival can be explained by a rising infatuation with antiquity—not high antiquity in this case, but definitely earlier times than the decadent Ming dynasty; part can be traced to the growing stress on authentic feeling as a value in Chinese literature and philosophy—the lyric, as seen, excels in the evocation of an emotional experience.

Women played a pivotal role in the revival. Social life in the flourishing commercial centers guaranteed a continuing market for romantic lyrics, and it is no surprise that collections such as *Among the Flowers* remained in circulation. When late Ming courtesans and gentrywomen began producing an increasing quantity of lyrics that looked back beyond current fashions in music to the roots of the genre, literary men returned to the genre with enthusiasm. Courtesans who displayed talent in the arts enjoyed remarkably high status in the Ming; their relationships—and marriages—with eminent scholars and poets were celebrated by society as perfect love affairs. Moreover, in the transition period from the Ming to the Ch'ing, some courtesans and their partners risked their lives in acts of sabotage and resistance against the Manchu (Ch'ing) forces. Thus, these talented women achieved a degree of moral stature that, despite growing hostility from men and women who believed that literature was an immoral pursuit for "proper" women, was never entirely erased in the ensuing years.

Poetry, including the lyric, was a medium through which these relationships were conducted and celebrated. One of the most significant partnerships in the revival of the lyric in the seventeenth century was that between Liu Shih (1618–1664) and her lover Ch'en Tzu-lung (1608–1647). Taking their lead from Ch'in Kuan but exceeding him in tender emotion (perhaps the reader, aware that their lyrics were exchanged in the course of a love affair involving real people with known identities, grants them a greater authenticity) and introducing certain themes from Ming drama (such as lovesickness—stressed by Ch'en more than Liu), the pair produced an important body of lyrics. Love was not the only theme of their lyrics. Loyalty to the fallen Ming dynasty was expressed in many compositions. Ch'en, in particular, was intensely moved by the events surrounding the composition of *Additional Themes for "Ballads,"* mentioned above: he followed the example of those fourteen Sung loyalists in writing lyrics on objects, giving them a hidden symbolic meaning. In the case of Ch'en's poems on such things as fallen apricot blossoms, there seems to be a recurrent association with the palace ladies of a lost dynasty; poems on willows can be read in the light of similar associations or as purely romantic poems (and we cannot forget that the surname of his lover, Liu, is a homograph and homophone of the Chinese word for "willow").

A more openly heroic style characterizes the early Ch'ing lyricist Ch'en Wei-sung—the first of his age known chiefly for his lyrics (which number more than sixteen hundred, written to more than four hundred melodies), rather than for other genres or philosophical writings. Ch'en's forceful feelings and desolate landscapes are often encompassed within the shorter *hsiao-ling* form—one scholar has recently compared him to a man taking command of a narrow lane with hand-to-hand fighting, in contrast to Hsin Ch'i-chi, who arrayed his troops across the plains of the *man* form.

Another poet who worked within the *hsiao-ling* form was Nalan Singde (1655–1685), a Manchu poet who in his brief life wrote unrelievedly melancholy lyrics.

Nalan Singde did not found a movement, and the influence of Ch'en Wei-sung grew dim with the passing decades. Of more lasting significance were Ch'en Tzu-lung's poems on objects: the lack of a clear indication of whether they are to be read as lyrics on lost love or a lost dynasty affected the way Ch'en Tzu-lung's love lyrics were read in succeeding generations: it was assumed that they had a hidden loyalist theme. This reflects a strong trend throughout the Ch'ing dynasty to read romantic lyrics as indirect expressions of serious moral feelings about the state of society; moreover, when writing lyrics, one employed all the romantic images of loneliness and ennui with the expectation that they would be read as encoded yearning for some kind of lost ideal. Chu Yi-tsun, who printed the 1279 *Additional Themes for "Ballads,"* wrote romantic lyrics and lyrics on objects in the Southern Sung style that might have been read this way, although most critics have found them deficient in implied feelings. Perhaps it is the fact that some of his most passionate lyrics are connected with an affair he had with his wife's younger sister that limits their appeal.

This trend is more strongly exemplified in Chang Hui-yen (1761–1802) and his Ch'ang-chou school (named after his native place in Kiangsu province). In evaluating the lyrics of the past, Chang and his fellows preferred the early *tz'u* of the Five Dynasties and the first half of the eleventh century. The normative language and stereotypical situations in the lyrics of those times ("longing told on the strings of the *p'i-p'a*") gave one the space to look for "deeper" meanings—indeed, they challenged one to do so because, from the perspective of the Ch'ing intellectual, they *had to* contain something of the upright character of their authors, authors who, after all, were either witnesses to the downfall of a dynasty (Wen T'ing-yün et al. at the end of the T'ang) or serious and prominent officials (Ou-yang Hsiu, Yen Shu, and others in the Sung) and would be expected to have morally valuable feelings. Since the "proper and harmonious" expression of righteous views was, in the minds of Chang and others, the essence of the *Shih-ching* (Classic of Poetry; see chapter 5) and all such canonical poetic texts in the Chinese tradition, they granted lyrics the status of serious literature by reading Confucian values into them.

It is interesting that these critics had slightly less respect for the works of Hsin Ch'i-chi and others whose lyrics overtly expressed patriotic sentiments. It may be that the conflation of love and loyalism that Ch'en Tzu-lung and Liu Shih and their contemporaries had achieved in their lives and works continued its hold on the Ch'ing imagination. (Ironically, that conflation also provided the code that could be used to *disguise* a writer's anxieties over the state of the world so that he would not be forced to follow Ch'en and so many other

Ming loyalists into martyrdom; the Ch'ing government vigilantly combated anti-Manchu sentiments.) However, this is not enough to account for the relative disapproval of Hsin Ch'i-chi's style. In the minds of Chang Hui-yen and other intellectuals, Hsin's style violated the true spirit of poetry precisely because it was direct in expression, rather than indirect; therefore it failed to conform to the true Chinese tradition as embodied in the *Classic of Poetry* (as they read it) and the "delicate and indirect" style of lyric.

Ultimately, this leads to the extreme position articulated by Chou Chi (1781–1839): "When one first begins to learn the lyric, he strives to have 'lodging' in it; when there is this lodging, the outer and the inner make each other apparent and the result is a striking composition. Once one has attained the right mode, he seeks to have no lodging; when there is no lodging, one 'designates affairs and draws categorical correspondences between situations.' The benevolent [reader] will see benevolence in it and the wise [reader] will see wisdom in it." This is a difficult passage, but the ideas are so interesting that it is worth quoting and glossing. The last sentence simply means that each reader will see his or her own nature and values reflected in the lyrics of the accomplished writer. The meaning of the text is for the reader, not the author, to determine. Chou would have been intrigued to learn that he was anticipating certain twentieth-century theories, as was a contemporary of his in distant Germany—Novalis, whose declaration that the reader and the reader alone decided how to read a text and what he would make of a book is remarkably similar. However, in Chou Chi's view this retreat of the author is not part of a general theory of the text but a sign of the author's mastery of the "mode" (*ko-tiao*; the term can refer either to music or to the style of a genre or a person).

What he devalues is *chi-t'o*, here translated as "lodging." *Chi-t'o* refers to the writer's "entrusting to" a text the feelings and values that arise from within a larger context. It is because of that implied larger context that translators often use "allegory" to render *chi-t'o*. This seems appropriate, and one might gain further precision by using the term "topical allegory" to describe situations such as *Additional Themes for "Ballads"* of 1279, where a very specific incident was the context for the lyrics. However, the term "allegory" obscures the fact that, in Chinese poetry and lyrics at least, no attempt is made to construct a *narrative* with an implied meaning. The work evokes a series of events in the mind of the knowledgeable reader, but the plot of that series is nowhere reflected in the structure of the work.

In view of this, it is difficult to interpret the phrase "designate affairs [and] draw categorical correspondences between situations." These words (*chih-shih lei-ch'ing*) are used in *Shih-chi* (Records of the Historian; see chapter 26) to tell us what Chuang Tzu did. Chuang Tzu, of course, is known and loved for his parables and allegories, but Chou cannot be advocating allegorical poetry here. Not only was true allegory not an option that he would have considered; Chou disapproved even Chang Hui-yen's attempts to find specific hidden references (without a narrative plot) in each line of the lyrics on which he wrote commentaries. The key to understanding Chou's use of this phrase is to note that he is talking about the *reading* process.

The parallel passage applied to lyrics *with* "lodging" states that if it is too easy for the reader to make the connections between the lyricist's life and the lyric ("the inner and the outer illuminate each other"), although the reader reconstitutes a "splendid work" in his mind, the lyricist has still not reached the highest level. When there is no "lodging," in contrast, the lyric still contains events (*shih*) and "aspects" of events (note that *ch'ing* means "manner of being" and can be applied to both feelings—the active mode of our human being—and the way in which events and objects present themselves to us) to which the reader responds by finding analogs in his own experience. *Lei*, translated here as "find categorical correspondences," is an important concept in Chinese cosmology. One theory to explain the tides, for example, held that the ocean responds to the moon because both the moon and water are *yin* (in the familiar yin-yang categories); they are of the same *lei*, or category. Chou Chi's idea seems to be that certain feelings and experiences (which differ from reader to reader) are aroused in the mind of the reader of the lyric in correspondence to what the lyricist puts into the text, but ideally these feelings and experiences *will not be limited by what inspired the lyricist originally.*

This is not the place for a complete account of the Chang Hui-yen–Chou Chi line of thought with all its variations—this tradition is known as the Ch'ang-chou school, and it has been explored in more detail by fine scholars such as Chia-ying Yeh Chao. Suffice it to say that this school had a tremendous influence on our perception of the lyric well into the twentieth century through its anthologizing and commentarial activities.

The Ch'ang-chou school was not the only voice in the late lyric tradition, however. Teng T'ing-chen (1776–1846) and Lin Tse-hsü (1785–1850), the officials whose resistance against British importation of opium precipitated the Opium War (1839–1842), used the lyric to declare their determination to fight foreign aggression to the bitter end. Wen T'ing-shih (1856–1904) and others found lyrics one medium in which to criticize the Ch'ing Empress Dowager Tz'u-hsi (1835–1908) for her perfidy and weakness in the face of Japanese pressures in Manchuria, the homeland of her people. When European troops occupied Peking in 1900, Wang P'eng-yün (1849–1904) and Chu Tsu-mou (compiler of a major collection of T'ang, Sung, Chin, and Yüan lyrics; 1857–1931) wrote allegorical lyrics in a gesture reminiscent of the *Additional Themes* collection by Chou Mi and his fellows six centuries before. Finally, mention must be made of the revolutionary martyr Ch'iu Chin (1875–1907), a woman who did everything imaginable to reject the traditional roles assigned to her sex and left a stunning collection of lyrics that range from the "delicate and indirect" to fierce and "masculine" declarations of yearning for a better world.

Mao Tse-tung's lyrics must be seen as a continuation of this late Ch'ing heroic tradition, with the difference that he wrote more in triumph and exultation than out of frustrated ambition. Today, lyrics are still written by those with an interest in classical culture. Typical themes include the recent struggles of the nation against foreign and domestic enemies and the natural beauty of scenic districts visited by the writers. Whether any works are being produced that will continue the vitality of the lyric tradition is for future ages to determine.

Stuart Sargent

Chapter 16

SUNG DYNASTY *SHIH* POETRY

AN INITIAL CONSIDERATION: SOURCES FOR THE STUDY OF SUNG DYNASTY POETRY

Block printing already was a refined art by the time the founder of the Sung reunited the empire in 960. As scholars of the later development of printing in Europe are beginning to reveal, this transition from a manuscript to a print culture is of epochal importance. Although the full implications of this technology have yet to be explored for China, one result of the increasingly broad availability of printing was the survival of an unprecedented variety and quantity of writings for the Sung dynasty (960–1279). These texts allow us to develop a much fuller picture of the culture and society of the Sung dynasty than was available for the T'ang. Consequently, for the Sung, it is not necessary to rely on a few anthologies of poetry to the same extent as for the T'ang. The collected works of most major writers have survived reasonably well, as have those of a large cast of secondary figures. As a result, the number of extant poems and poets is extraordinary. *Ch'üan Sung shih* (Complete Sung Poems), now being compiled in China, will comprise works by more than nine thousand authors, compared to the approximately twenty-two hundred poets in *Ch'üan T'ang shih* (Complete T'ang Poems). Given this abundance of writings—and the same is as true of Sung period prose as it is of poetry—it is possible to construct an integrated account of poetry in the culture of the Sung dynasty, which is not the case for previous dynasties. What follows is a preliminary account, which will be refined as our understanding of Sung dynasty social and cultural history deepens.

As seen in chapter 14, the anthologizing process from the Ming period onward has largely shaped our tastes as well as that of the literati concerning T'ang poetry. Moreover, the few available T'ang anthologies provide important clues about contemporary tastes and reputations. Finally, literati of all periods—from Wang An-shih in the Sung to the compiler of *T'ang-shih san-pai shou* (Three Hundred T'ang Poems) in the Ch'ing dynasty—used the anthologizing of T'ang poetry to make arguments about proper contemporary poetic practice.

The role of anthologies in Sung dynasty poetry is quite different. A few Sung anthologies became iconic representations of particular styles, and these are discussed below. Because of the flourishing publishing industry, however, individual collections survived reasonably well. Moreover, since Ming dynasty arbiters of poetic values considered Sung poetry inferior to that of the T'ang, there is less concern by literary historians to shape a particular story about the Sung. Thus, in a sense, scholars have less to unlearn about Sung poetry than about T'ang poetry. The two great anthologies of Sung poetry—*Sung-shih ch'ao* and *Sung-shih chi shih*—are from the early Ch'ing period, when interest in poetry once again turned toward values of creativity and individuality. Thus they tell us less about Sung poetry than about Ch'ing cultural values.

OVERVIEW

Poetry flourished in the Sung dynasty. During this period of cultural renaissance, a new social stratum—the literati/official elite—replaced the aristocratic lineages that had dominated T'ang society and culture. The literati learned to compose *shih* poetry, the classical form of verse with roots stretching back to the Chou dynasty, not only to pass the examinations qualifying them for government service but for all manner of social occasions as well as for quieter moments of reflection. With the widespread adoption of woodblock printing, the literati bought and sold poetry, and discussed it and wrote about it with great knowledge and enthusiasm. Yet, by the end of the Sung dynasty, the vitality of *shih* poetry seems to have ebbed. This chapter traces the vicissitudes of the *shih* poetic genre through the Sung dynasty, from its growing importance early in the dynasty to its distinctive features at its height, to its gradual marginalization as literati culture began to fragment before the Mongols brought the dynasty to an end.

In 959 the ambitious emperor Shih-tsung of the Later Chou (951–960) died, leaving his hapless seven-year-old son to inherit the throne. Six months later, Chao K'uang-yin, commander of the palace army, deposed the boy and established the Sung dynasty, reigning as Emperor T'ai-tsu (r. 960–976). Five years later, in 965, the Sung defeated Shu (in modern-day Szechwan). The Southern Han surrendered the next year. The Southern T'ang, ruled by the esthete Li

Yü (937–978; r. 961–975), lasted longer than anticipated and was not swallowed up for another ten years. With the fall of the Southern T'ang and the surrender of the state of Wu-Yüeh in the Yangtze region, however, the Sung had largely reunified China and imposed centralized control, which had eluded rulers since the An Lu-shan rebellion (755–763) during the T'ang dynasty two hundred years earlier. T'ai-tsu and his younger brother Chao K'uang-yi, who would reign as Emperor T'ai-tsung from his succession in 976 until 997, made sure that others could not repeat their own rise to power. They lavishly rewarded their loyal generals but took their armies away. They also began to build a centralized civil bureaucracy by recruiting officials who had served the various small splinter states of the Five Dynasties and Ten Kingdoms period (907–979).

Yet the Sung dynasty continually felt the threat of two formidable "barbarian" kingdoms to the north: the Hsi-hsia of the Tanguts and the Liao of the Khitans. As the dynasty flourished, the literati who staffed its government attempted to perpetuate their clans' power at both the local and national levels. Their efforts gave rise to various institutional reforms to keep government service open and effective. However, the most radical reform, the "New Policies" (*hsin-fa*) of the great statesman Wang An-shih (1021–1086), sought to shore up the dynasty's finances in order to buy peace on the frontier through annual payments to the Liao and to maintain the border garrisons. Wang aimed to raise revenue through intervention in many aspects of the private economy. His policies, supported by the Emperor Shen-tsung (Chao Hsü, r. 1068–1086), created intense factional disputes. The opposition was driven out of the central government, and some were exiled. When Shen-tsung died, the conservatives gained power. They in turn exiled the reformers and attempted to dismantle Wang's innovations. Their regime, however, only lasted until Shen-tsung's son Che-tsung (r. 1086–1101) came of age and began to rule on his own, when he banished the conservatives once more. After Che-tsung died at the beginning of 1101, his younger brother Hui-tsung (r. 1101–1125) ascended the throne. Although he initially attempted to curb the harshness of the factional strife, in the end he sided with the reformers. During his reign, Ts'ai Ching (1046–1126), who has been damned as a rapacious minister who led his artistically accomplished but ineffective ruler to disaster, rose to power. Hui-tsung had helped the Jurchen in Manchuria defeat their overlords, the Khitan Liao dynasty. In the process, however, the Jurchen also discovered the Sung's military weakness. After establishing the Chin dynasty in the north, the Jurchen attacked the Sung and quickly conquered northern China in 1126. They captured Hui-tsung and much of the imperial court. One son who escaped managed to rally the military, regroup the civil bureaucracy, and reestablish the (Southern) Sung dynasty with its "temporary capital" at Hangchow. Reigning as Emperor Kao-tsung (r. 1127–1163), he shrewdly let his minister Ch'in Kui do the dirty work of suppressing the "War Faction" that wanted to retake the north. The Chin and the Southern Sung maintained an uneasy peace—punctuated by fruitless campaigns—for the next hundred years. The imperial government increasingly fell into the hands of powerful prime ministers who sought to dominate the bureaucracy and silence criticism of their regimes. In Inner Asia, however, the Mongols were growing into a powerful military force and increasingly threatened the Chin. In 1233 the Southern Sung allied itself with the Mongols: together, they destroyed the Chin dynasty the following year. However, the Southern Sung overstepped the terms of its agreement with the Mongols and soon had a new, far more dangerous enemy attacking its western territories. For a time, however, the Mongols turned their attention to other regions, allowing the Sung a brief respite. In the 1250s, the Mongol ruler Möngke renewed the campaign. By 1258 he had captured Ch'eng-tu and most of Szechwan, only to die in an epidemic. The new ruler, Möngke's younger brother Khubilai (Qubilai; 1215–1294; r. 1260–1294), hastened back to the Mongol homeland to fight to secure his elevation as khan (or *qaghan*). By 1268, however, he was ready for an assault on the Southern Sung heartland.

In 1276 his general Bayan captured the Southern Sung capital. Sung loyalists fled with the young emperor and put up a spirited but futile resistance. On November 19, 1279, the last ruler of the Southern Sung, a child of seven, drowned when a loyal minister jumped into the sea with him to prevent their capture. All of these historical events had a direct bearing on the development of poetry during the Sung period.

During the Sung dynasty the changes in poetry's functions, status, and formal features were intimately connected to the transformations of a larger cultural category, that of *wen*. *Wen*, at its most literal level, means a pattern of stripes, but by extension it refers to surface adornment, as opposed to the substance below. It means the cultured as opposed to the vulgar, the civil as opposed to the martial, and the literary as opposed to the philosophical or moralistic. A writer's individual compositions were *wen-chang*; his collected writings were his *wen-chi*. The Sung dynasty, perhaps more than any other, has been considered a reign of *wen*. The founding Sung emperors emphasized civil rule even at the expense of military strength. The Sung saw a renaissance of Confucianism, a broad commitment in the literati/official stratum to recover and live by the models embodied in the texts (*wen*) written by the Confucian sages of antiquity. Sung emperors recruited their officials by written examinations intended to demonstrate a mastery of the inherited textual traditions. Yet, by the end of the Sung, *wen* proved inadequate to serve as a basis for society. The classical tradition said too much and led in too many conflicting directions. Reading the canonical tradition proved difficult and lacked any final source for the validity of interpretation. Neo-Confucianism—*tao-hsüeh* (learning of the Way), also often referred to as *li-hsüeh* (learning about principle)—arose within the gradual fragmentation of the broader Confucian interpretive enterprise.

Poetry and *wen* are linked in a complex way: the evolution of poetry as traced in this chapter demonstrates the deeper implication of the common observation that Sung writers "used *wen* to make poems" (*yi wen wei shih*).

EARLY SUNG POETRY

Literature and the Origins of the Sung Literati Stratum

Sung civil officials could not repeat the T'ang model, which had relied on the great aristocratic clans to provide suitable candidates who could weather the uncertainties of a bureaucratic career by relying on their clan's independent wealth and social status. In the two hundred years since the An Lu-shan rebellion, the aristocratic structure had largely collapsed through warfare in the northeast—which was the economic basis of many of the most important clans—and migrations southward. The shapers of the Sung bureaucracy sought potential candidates in a world very different from that of the T'ang, and they needed a different rationale in their recruitment.

The writings of Hsü Hsüan (917–992), who had served as Minister of Personnel in the Southern T'ang and as an auxiliary Han-lin academician for Emperor T'ai-tsung, explain why evaluating the "literary" ability of a candidate was an appropriate part of the selection process. At issue were three questions: *who* are the "noble men" (*chün-tzu*), *what* makes them noble, and *how* can they make use of their noble nature? Hsü Hsüan explains: "The Way of the noble man comes from his self and is applied to objects [in the world]. It starts within and reaches the external, and that by which one enacts [the Way] is language. That by which language reaches far is *wen* [well-structured writing]." The Way of the noble man must be properly manifest in the world if it is to have any effect. Literariness (*wen*) aids in the manifestation of the Way. Yet *wen* as the representation of patterns in the world has an important objective quality: "A gentleman reserves his capabilities within himself and responds to things as an echo. What one [thereby] accomplishes in one's duty to the realm remains as one's vocation. Penetrating the situations [*ch'ing*] of all things is in one's literary expressions." Centrally, the Way of humane governance lies in right response. The noble man relies on his own reactions to respond effectively, and poetry in particular has the unique ability to articulate these reactions.

> That by which Man is spiritually effective [*ling*] is his feelings [*ch'ing*]. That by which feelings are communicated is language. Yet on occasion, the depth of his feelings, the scope of his thoughts accumulate within and cannot be fully expressed in words. Then one expresses it through poetry.

Thus Hsü Hsüan concludes that poetry is different from mere words and reveals the depths of a man's ability to respond; it is therefore a useful way to select men for office.

From the very beginning of the dynasty, a connection between governance (*cheng*), emotional response (*ch'ing*), and the literary (*wen*) profoundly shaped the role of poetry in the culture. *Ch'ing* became not a mark of private subjective experience that isolates the self from others but, instead, the bridge by which meaningful communication became possible. A noble man used his own responses in order to understand those of others. Thus the goal was to "respond to things as an echo" and not allow one's private concerns to distort the response. The poetry of the early Sung dynasty that embodies these values is public, written as a gesture of communication, and therefore transparent in its language and unburdened in its response to its occasion.

Transition from the Poetic Practices of the Five Dynasties

The poetry that survives from the reigns of the first two Sung emperors reflects the cultural values of transparency and ease. The preeminent writer of the early Sung was Hsü Hsüan. His poetry is mostly regulated verse written either for public formal occasions—farewells, visits, inscriptions, and so on—or for more quiet moments of reflection, such as those sent to friends, on gazing at the moon or watching snow. It maintains a posture of calm dignity and strives for a style that is well crafted but simple. Most histories of Sung poetry filiate Hsü Hsüan to a "Po Chü-yi" style, in contrast to a "Late T'ang" style that arose in reaction to the overly easy manner of the "Po" style (*Po-t'i*). This distinction, however, is probably overworked and not very helpful. Early Northern Sung poets like Hsü Hsüan, Li Fang (925–996), and T'ien Hsi (940–1004) leaned either toward Po's ease or toward Late T'ang crafting, but all showed a rather broad catholicity of taste.

After the initial period of rebuilding a civil elite, more complicated cultural commitments came to the fore. First, the process of sorting out what to assimilate from the cultural heritage in defining the Sung ethos brought differing visions into conflict. T'ien Hsi, for example, warned against a narrowing of sensibility in which only explicitly morally committed literature was acceptable. Second, since the practice of poetry became a measure of a man's potential for office and acquired all but inescapable political overtones, some writers sought to free themselves from these connections and developed a counter-poetics of Late T'ang estheticism.

Wang Yü-ch'eng (954–1001) was an important spokesman for the restrictive view of "literature based on the Five Confucian Classics." The child of a humble family, Wang attracted the attention of the local prefect. He passed the *chin-shih* examination in 983 and spent the rest of his life as an official. His early poetry follows the norms of the time, with many leisurely regulated-verse compositions written to fulfill social obligations. After Wang was demoted to local office (for raising charges of slander against a Taoist nun who had the emperor's support), his poetry began to reveal a growing commitment to the Confucian project of "rectifying the times." He wrote more old-style poems of social protest like "Kan liu-wang" (Moved by the Refugees). Wang Yü-ch'eng often is considered the first

"Sung dynasty poet" in his attempt both to restore a sense of the seriousness of the everyday and to fuse craftsmanship with Confucian commitments.

The Early Northern Sung Styles

The founders of the Sung state forged links between civil rule, the Confucian textual tradition, and literary production. The generation of writers born after the establishment of the dynasty could not avoid confronting these relationships, and they shaped their poetry in response to them. The writers who came to be regarded as the most important poets of the early Northern Sung all addressed the social and political implications of their status as poets. The reclusive outsiders Wei Yeh (960–1020) and Lin Pu (968–1028), for example, explicitly rejected any link between poetry and politics (even though the Sung state honored them for preserving their right to be free of any government entanglements). Their poetry mirrors the rejection of imposed commitments in the ease and purity of its Late T'ang style. Yang Yi (974–1020), in contrast, was a high official whose *Hsi-k'un ch'ou-ch'ang chi* (Collection of Exchanged Poems at Hsi-k'un) came to represent the work of ultimate cultural insiders.

Lin Pu was the best writer among a group of poets who wrote in the Late T'ang manner and poetically asserted their independence from government service. P'an Lang (d. 1009), Wei Yeh, and the so-called Nine Monks (Chiu seng: Hui-ch'ung, Chien-ch'ang, Pao-hsien, Wei-feng, Hsi-chou, Yü-chao, Wen-chao, Huai-ku, and Hsing-chao) all preceded him. Not all, however, succeeded in maintaining their aloofness: P'an Lang, for example, was granted the status of a *chin-shih* and eventually served as a local official. Wei Yeh, in contrast, managed to extricate himself when he was summoned to court by Emperor Chen-tsung (Chao Te-ch'ang; r. 998–1022). Lin Pu, a native of Hangchow, spent most of his life on Hangchow's Ku-shan, a beautiful secluded hill overlooking West Lake. It was said that, although he lived on Ku-shan for twenty years, he was so reclusive that he never set foot in Hangchow itself. He never married but, because he raised cranes and grew plum trees on Ku-shan, he was said to have "plums for a wife and cranes for children." Much of his poetry describes the scenery of Ku-shan and West Lake, as seen in "Su Tung-hsiao Kung" (Spending the Night at Cave Mist Temple).

> The autumn hills are without end:
> Autumn longings also have no mooring.
> In the emerald ravines float red leaves.
> The green forests are dotted with white clouds.
> In the cool shade a single bird descends.
> As the sun sets, a profusion of cicadas calls out clear.
> Tonight's rain on the banana leaves:
> Who hears it on his pillow?

Lin Pu's poetry captures small scenes with highly crafted simplicity. He became well known for the purity of his language and for poetic conceptions that perfectly matched the simple independence of his life on Ku-shan. Yet this independence could not escape becoming a role played within a larger cultural framework. The Emperor Chen-tsung, for example, honored Lin Pu's reclusive purity with presents of silk and grain and sent a messenger to inquire every New Year. After Lin Pu's death, the Emperor Jen-tsung (r. 1022–1063) presented him with the honorary title "Tranquil Gentleman."

Although Late T'ang regulated verse was the mainstay of contemporary poetic practice, Lin Pu's intense, exclusive commitment to it presented one possible model for the emerging literati stratum in which self-cultivation through broadly esteemed cultural practices transcended the claims of service. The openness of the Late T'ang style established this model as a possibility for all practitioners. The opposite of this open simplicity is the recondite, densely allusive and often cryptic style of Li Shang-yin (813?–858) that served as the model for poetry of the *Hsi-k'un Collection.* The latter volume records 250 regulated-verse poems by Yang Yi (seventy-five poems), Liu Yün (970–1030; seventy poems), Ch'ien Wei-yen (977–1034; fifty-five poems), and fourteen other contributors, written while they served as editors for various compilation projects in the capital. The poems' allusiveness is a display of erudition beyond the means of many who sought entry into the scholar-official stratum. Their cryptic quality, their opacity of reference, suggests poetic exclusivity and the creation of a small, elite group. Only those with inside knowledge could either read or write such poems. These links between style and status made the *Hsi-k'un Collection* a perennial target for later Confucian attacks. In any case, the Hsi-k'un style enjoyed only a brief vogue and quietly disappeared until Shih Chieh (1005–1045) attacked it as part of his polemic against contemporary writing. In place of the ornate, difficult Hsi-k'un style, writers of both high and low status returned to variants on the Late T'ang style. Some, like K'ou Chun (961–1023), reflect the increasing influence of Wang Wei (701–761) and Wei Ying-wu (737–792) as High T'ang models for landscape poetry. Still, poetry remained backward-looking. Change came only as part of the broader cultural transformations of the next generation.

THE HEIGHT OF THE NORTHERN SUNG CONFUCIAN RENAISSANCE (1040–1100)

Sung Poetry Finds Its Voice

Early Sung writers already had asserted the relationship between writing, suppleness of response, and rulership. Ou-yang Hsiu's (1007–1072) generation discovered the particular relevance of the Confucian texts as guides in shaping those relations. Their approach was radical in its egalitarian and rationalist impulse. Status as a "noble man" (*chün-tzu*) came not from hereditary birthright but from insight into the Confucian canon. Those texts, printed and widely distributed by the government, were open to careful analysis and reflection: the Sung Confucian literati believed that many layers of encrusted traditional interpretation could be stripped away to gain fresh understanding of the Way of the Former Kings. The canonical texts, moreover, provided principles for policy at both the central and local levels. Many of the reforms that the Confucian statesman and poet-essayist Fan Chung-yen (989–1052) advocated at the beginning of the Ch'ing-li reign-period (1040–1048) aimed to increase the quality and responsibilities of local officials. He and his colleagues sought to limit the privileged access to government positions available to already established bureaucratic clans. They sought to make the recruitment examinations focus on the ability to apply canonical texts to practical problems, and they sought to tighten the oversight of local administration.

What we know as "Sung poetry" was created largely by writers associated with that Ch'ing-li reform effort. Among these, Ou-yang Hsiu was the central figure even if not the best poet. A great polymathic writer, scholar, and official, Ou-yang most fully represents the Confucian renaissance of the Northern Sung. Of humble origin, he rose to prominence as a leader in the Ch'ing-li reforms. Nonetheless, he argued that the humane values he found in the texts of early Confucianism dealt with more than simply the art of rulership. The faith that "the Way of the Former Kings was necessarily based on human feelings" gave him and his fellow reformers great confidence in their ability to understand the sage texts of the past, to enact the intentions of the sages in the contemporary world, and to participate in a living Confucian tradition through their own writings and actions. The centrality of human feelings as the basis of sagely action reaffirmed the importance of the ordinary as both the locus of moral action and the object of poetic reflection. The writings of the major poets of the reform group—Ou-yang Hsiu, Mei Yao-ch'en (1002–1060), Su Shun-ch'in (1008–1048), and Shih Yen-nien (994–1041)—all reflect the values of this emerging Confucian humanism and its concern for the ordinary. Their poetry expanded the range of topics for composition, stressed simplicity and directness of style, and sought to capture the broader implications of the events that occasioned its writing.

Ou-yang Hsiu's most significant and representative poems are free-flowing, old-style verse that use uneven line lengths and prosy grammatical particles pointing back to Li Po (701–762) and Han Yü (768–824). "Ming-fei ch'ü ho Wang Chieh-fu tso" (Song of Bright Consort, Matching Wang Chieh-fu [An-shih]) suggests these qualities. Its shifting perspectives that frame and mediate the rather standard set of emotional responses are typical of his poetry.

> Tatars take horse and saddle as home, shooting and hunting as their
> custom.
> Wherever springs are sweet and grass fine: no fixed abode.
> Birds startle, animals take fright as they vie in galloping pursuit.

4 Who would make a Han woman marry a Tatar man?
Wind and sand have no compassion: her face is like jade.
Where she travels she meets no Chinese people.
On horseback she wrote herself a tune of longing to return:
8 Strumming down is a *p'i*, pulling up a *p'a*.*
The Tatars all listened, and they too sighed.
Her jade countenance drifted away, died at Heaven's edge,
But the *p'i-p'a* was conveyed to Han households.
12 In the Han palace they vied to follow the new music score.
The lingering regret was deep; given voice, it is yet more bitter.
Long and slim a girl's hands, born in the secluded chamber.
Having mastered the *p'i-p'a*, she does not descend to the hall.
16 She has no acquaintance with the yellow dust on the road leaving
the passes:
How can she know that this sound can break one's heart?

The juxtaposing of frame after frame is part of the bravura performance on a well-worn theme (that of the Han dynasty heroine Wang Chao-chün) in this poem. In other compositions, however, the framing becomes a form of emotional and intellectual self-discipline. Strongly influenced by the canonical understanding of the poetry of the *Shih-ching* (Classic of Poetry), Ou-yang discovered that he could write poetry not only to represent but to contextualize, complicate, and ultimately shape his responses to things. There is a consistent, even if not entirely successful, effort in Ou-yang Hsiu's poems to recast intense emotion, to channel it in manageable directions. This quality that stands out in Ou-yang's verse gives Sung dynasty poetry its intellectualized, "dry" character.

Just as Ou-yang Hsiu revealed new esthetic possibilities for old-style verse, his friend Mei Yao-ch'en restored a high seriousness to regulated forms. Landscape poetry in regulated verse had been the most common form of occasional poetry in the early Sung. Mei reshaped the expectations and terms of judgment for this form as he defined its "even and bland" (*p'ing-tan*) quality. Mei insisted poets should think about exactly what they want to capture when they write,

---

*This formulation draws on a false but old and frequently repeated etymology of the Sinitic word *p'i-p'a* (>Japanese, *biwa*). The real origins of the "balloon guitar" are West Asian, and the Chinese word *p'i-p'a* ultimately derives from the Iranian expression *barbaṭ*, perhaps meaning "chest" (*bar*) and "duck" (*bat*), from the shape of the instrument when turned upside down; cf. the name of the outstanding Sassanian musician Bārbad (fl. c. 250 C.E.), which is apparently related to that of the "balloon guitar" on which he was an epochal virtuoso. The same instrument, when it was transmitted to Arabic-speaking peoples, was called by them *al 'ūd* (the wood), the derivation—via medieval French—of the English word "lute." Greek *barbita/barbitos/barbiton* was probably borrowed from the same Central Asian sources as Iranian *barbaṭ*, but it is a very different type of instrument, being a lyre with many strings (VHM).

about the poem's language and structure, and about the broader implications of the experience they record.

Like Ou-yang Hsiu, Mei Yao-ch'en took contemporary poetry's origins in the *Classic of Poetry* seriously. He believed that poetry was worthy of deep thought and that it captured important aspects of experience not easily recorded in other modes of composition. Although he could write in the more raucous old-style forms at which Ou-yang Hsiu excelled, his best poems are in the quiet, thoughtful regulated-verse styles that he championed. "Lu-shan shan hsing" (Traveling in the Mountains on Mount Lu) suggests these qualities.

> Now so suiting my outland mood:
> A thousand mountains, high and also low.
> Fine peaks change following my position.
> Secluded paths: I stray as I walk along.
> Frost descends, and the bears climb trees.
> The forest is empty: deer drink from the creek.
> A farmstead: where?
> Beyond the clouds, one cry of a rooster.

Mei's commenting on his mood and on the role of his position in shaping his response is characteristic of the intellectualizing tendencies that Ou-yang Hsiu, Mei Yao-ch'en, and their generation brought to Sung poetry. They saw experience as complex and sought a poetry to shape that complexity into compelling new forms.

Su Shun-ch'in in particular used poetry to explore the intellectual contours of experience. He was not a great poet: his use of language and form could not match the quality of either Ou-yang Hsiu's old-style or Mei Yao-ch'en's regulated verse. Still, his poetry has an idiosyncratic intellectual energy. In such poems as "Ch'eng-nan kuei chih ta feng hsüeh" (Returning from South of the City Wall, Encountering Heavy Snow and Strong Wind), "Ch'eng-nan kan-huai ch'eng Yung-shu" (South of the City Wall, Stirred Thoughts, Shown to Yung-shu [Ou-yang Hsiu]), and "Sheng-yang tien ku-chih" (Old Site of the Sheng-yang Palace), he traces the logic by which the events he records arose and imagines where they might lead. In his poetry, he captures an unflinching yet reflective sensibility in its process of ordering experience. The modern scholar Hsü Tsung points out that Su Shun-ch'in wrote well in many T'ang styles, so increasing the range of models available for composition.

The phrase *yi wen wei shih*, usually rendered "turning prose into poetry," refers to all the changes in poetry wrought by Ou-yang Hsiu's group. In terms of form, it points to the loose, prosy structure of their old-style verse. In terms of content, it points not simply to their more argumentative poems and enthusiastic incorporation of "unpoetic" topics but also to the broader transformations suggested above. Their inclusion of speculative thought and self-reflection attenuated the "feelings" (*ch'ing*), as did the assertion of an objective, inherently moral, socially situated component in the "feeling." Poetry, for Ou-yang Hsiu, Mei Yao-ch'en, Su Shun-ch'in, and their friends, was not just about poetry anymore. It was about all that could be accommodated within the category of *wen* (ordered human pattern).

Maturation of the Style: Wang An-shih and Su Shih

It is easy to take the longevity of Chinese dynasties for granted. Yet the resources available to the central authority to control the widespread population of China were relatively meager. Survival called for successful institutions, appropriate technologies, and the absence of overwhelming external pressures. It was not at all clear, at its founding, that the Sung dynasty would succeed. Emperors T'ai-tsu and T'ai-tsung worked to diminish the power of regional commanders, but their structure for civil rule was still an evolving experiment. Indeed, even three generations after the founding, the model was not yet secure: Ou-yang Hsiu and the other reformers sought to implement changes to keep the central institutions flexible and responsive to local concerns and to avoid the creation of a narrow, quasi-hereditary elite. By the generation after Ou-yang Hsiu, however, the political institutions implemented early in the dynasty had helped to reshape the cultural and economic life of China. Meritocratic recruitment into government service—still the most prestigious role in society—was real even if imperfect. To implement this ideal, the government had encouraged broad literacy and fostered the rapid growth of a literati stratum in the society. It ordered the widespread dissemination of woodblock prints of the classics, and schools were established at the local level. These changes, plus decades of relative peace, encouraged the local elites to participate in—and be integrated into—the larger national economic, political, and cultural systems. It gave the local elites a role in the national polity as they trained their children in the Confucian canon that was the entrance to government service.

The evolution of this literati/official stratum created tensions that grew precisely because both the literati and the dynasty flourished. When Ou-yang Hsiu was demoted to an insignificant post in the countryside, he discovered that, if his legitimacy was bound to state service, then being deprived of that role also took away his moral authority. Yet the Confucian canon strongly suggests that the state's authority comes from its willingness to uphold the Confucian Way, not the other way around. So issues of authority began to multiply. Which Confucian texts are most authoritative? What is the scope of individual action outside the state? What is the scope of state action within society? With these questions, the Confucian renaissance began to fragment. Since poetry was part of the Confucian synthesis of the ordering of the human realm, it too registered these strains.

The two best poets of the Northern Sung—Wang An-shih and Su Shih (1037–1101)—were members of the new literati stratum whose writings were deepened by the strengths and strains in the Confucian cultural institutions that brought them both to prominence. Wang was from Lin-ch'uan (in modern-day Kiangsi province). His great-grandfather's generation had been farmers, but his grandfather's and father's generations reached literati status through the examination system and service to the state. As a young man, he quickly attracted the attention and patronage of Ou-yang Hsiu. He went on to become prime minister under Emperor Shen-tsung and implemented an extremely controversial set of reforms aimed at shoring up government finances.

Su Shih, sixteen years younger than Wang, was from Szechwan province. His family had just begun to enter government service in his father's generation. Su Shih established himself through a brilliant performance on the *chin-shih* and a special imperial examination. He is the best writer in the Sung dynasty and indeed one of the most important in the entire Chinese tradition. Unfortunately he did not fit well in his own time: not only did he oppose Wang An-shih's reforms, but he also opposed the counterreforms of the conservatives who sought to dismantle Wang An-shih's innovations.

Wang An-shih was a fine writer who did not believe in fine writing: "Now what is called writing [*wen*] is to endeavor to be of use to the age and that is all. What we call elaboration is like a vessel's having carvings or painting." His pragmatic statecraft set aside the former arguments about the connection between flexibility in action, acuteness of affective response, and the ability to write. Consequently, during his reforms he removed the composing of poetry from the recruitment examinations. His own verse reflects this stripping away of the inherently moral dimension from poetry. His early writings were explicitly political: the moral component was in the manifest content. During the period of his reforms, he largely stopped writing, but when he retired from office, he returned to poetry. This poetry set politics aside and was profoundly estheticized. It was concerned with its own technique.

Wang An-shih is best known for the poetry he wrote after his retirement, for it is indeed masterly. He concentrated primarily on regulated verse, and quatrains in particular. Rather than returning to the Late T'ang style, however, Wang drew broadly from the entire T'ang heritage and especially admired Tu Fu. "Nan p'u" (South Bank) is a frequently cited quatrain.

> South Bank and East Knoll in the Second Month:
> The flourishing scene compels me to write new verse.
> Holding the wind, mallard-green [water] rises in clear ripples.
> Sporting with sunlight, goose-yellow [branches] hang in fine wisps.

The second, very well-known couplet describes green river water and yellow early-spring willow branches. It is a *tour de force* of couplet crafting that, in context, attains the character of a quotation. The couplet is precisely the "new verse" that Wang claims the scene has forced him to write. Wang An-shih was intensely concerned with technique (*fa*) and with emulating the poets he admired. He reflected on and used their language in his own writings in a way that proved extremely influential for the next generation of poets.

Su Shih, by contrast, openly affirmed poetry's fundamental importance. His writing was the culmination of the Northern Sung Confucian renaissance perspective just as that perspective was fragmenting. Su Shih was at home in most poetic forms, from his monumental old-style "Shih ku ko" (Song of the Stone Drums) to witty quatrains like "Yin hu-shang ch'u ch'ing hou yü" (Drinking on the Lake: At First It Was Clear, Then It Rained).

> The gleam on the water as it ripples is at its best on clear days.
> The appearance of the mountains, empty and hazy, is also remarkable in the rain.
> I would like to compare West Lake to Lady West:
> Light makeup or heavy powder, both are becoming.

Su Shih's using the chance events of his outing on West Lake to link together the lake and Hsi Shih, the legendary beauty, reveals great bravado and wit. The poem makes a further point: Su Shih in his poetry enthusiastically welcomed the variety of experience. Poetry allowed Su Shih, particularly during his periods of increasingly remote exile, to bring to bear a prodigious intelligence and broad eclectic learning to recast experience into wonderful new forms. This interpretative quality—sometimes meditative, sometimes joyous, and often restless—assimilates and extends the innovations of Ou-yang Hsiu's generation. His best poems probably are his old-style verse filled with twists and turns as he explores the complex contours of an experience. "Chou-chung yeh ch'i" (Aboard Boat, Rising at Night) shows the subtlety and economy with which Su Shih integrates many layers of a meditative late-night mood.

> A light breeze, rustling, blows the reeds.
> I opened the door to look at the rain: the moon filled the lake.
> The boatmen and the waterbirds shared the same dreams.
> 4 A large fish, startled, took cover like a fleeing fox.
> Night grew late—man and creatures had no concern for each other.
> I alone with my form and shadow amused myself.
> The unseen high waters rose on the islets; I pitied the cold earthworms.
> 8 Where the setting moon hung among the willows, I saw the suspended spiders.
> In this life, rushing on amid grief and calamity,
> Pure scenes pass before one's eyes—can they be for more than a moment?
> The rooster crows, the bell rings, the many birds scatter.
> 12 At the boat's prow, they strike the drum and shout to one another.

Su Shih establishes the framing mood of the poem in the first, quite dazzling couplet. He expected rain because he misidentified the reeds' rustling, but the mistake suggests that his thoughts were elsewhere. The poem reveals that in the back of Su Shih's mind is the question of what his role, in a very broad sense, ought to be. He was heading to a new post and knew that his political future was not promising. How should he respond to what the future might bring? The poem answers that unspoken question by situating Su Shih and all his thoughts amid a larger world of transformation. The poem shifts between close observations of the landscape—with each detail chosen to stress issues of transformation and connection—and reflections that reveal an abstracted sense of self that is, in fact, a form of freedom. This mix of abstraction and connection to the particular imbues the final couplet with a strong sense of affirmation: the active day here partakes of the same "pure" patterns as the quiet night. All the elements of the poem—the framing subjectivity, the abstraction, and the concern for concrete detail—already were part of the poetry of the former generation: Su Shih simply integrated them with particular brilliance.

In his writings Su Shih was fighting the same fight against the narrowing of *wen* already seen in T'ien Hsi's protest against Confucian dogmatism. Su Shih, however, confronted two separate threats. The first was the interpretative debate about which texts best represented the intentions of the Sages, which texts were heterodox, and what sort of writing best served the sage tradition. Su Shih was a Confucian, but he loved the writings of Chuang Tzu, knew the Buddhist canon well, and included references to both traditions in his poetry. He was a liberal in the old debate about books.

However, a second debate grew ever louder during Su Shih's lifetime, an argument that writing—concerned as it was with *wen* and the ordering of externals—is categorically a distraction that impedes one's cultivation of the Way. Factional strife produced competing theories of rule equally well supported by the Confucian canon, and it increasingly made government service an exercise in frustration. Men of the literati/official stratum maintained a commitment to Confucian self-realization, but they increasingly directed their efforts away from service to the search for a more internalized sagehood. At a time when the competing interpretations made textual understanding ever more problematic, the goal of sagehood held out the promise of direct, authoritative apprehension of the Way. Su Shih, whose poetry still insisted on the meaningfulness and interpretability of experience in the world, became the object of systematic attack by later generations of Neo-Confucian teachers.

Fragmentation of Poetry: Su Shih's Four Students

Su Shih could—for one last time—hold the manifold possibilities for poetry together. His followers—Ch'in Kuan (1049–1100), Chang Lei (1054–1114), Ch'ao Pu-chih (1053–1110), and Huang T'ing-chien—could not. They were buffeted strongly by the political and intellectual winds of their day. They participated in Su Shih's brief period of high office in the capital, but they were exiled and had their writings proscribed along with his during the subsequent return to power of the New Policies faction of the radical reformist Chancellor Ts'ai Ching. Moreover, they felt keenly the need to justify their literary writings in the face of Neo-Confucian distrust of alluring surfaces. They specialized their writings and defended their endeavor on one front rather than many.

Ch'in Kuan, for example, established a reputation as a writer of *tz'u* (see chapter 15), a poetic form that explores the subjective realm of love relations. His *shih* poetry largely shares the qualities of delicacy and circumscribed refinement of his *tz'u*. Still, Ch'in Kuan's poetry retains characteristically "Sung" traits, in particular his careful reflection on the details of the physical world and an objectification of the process of perception.

Su Shih reportedly said that Ch'in Kuan inherited his crafting, but Chang Lei inherited his ease. Chang returned to Po Chü-yi (772–846) and Chang Chi (768–830?) as his models for old-style verse composition. Chang outlived the other three of the "Four Scholars of Mr. Su's Gate" (i.e., Su Shih's followers) and attracted a large following of students. His poetry—largely forgotten today—remained popular and influential throughout the remainder of the Sung dynasty. It captures one aspect of Su Shih's style well: the sort of reflective engagement with life, from more intense political poems to casual renderings of the everyday. The quatrain "Yeh tso" (Sitting at Night) suggests these qualities.

> Out the courtyard door no people: the autumn moon is bright.
> As the night frost is about to fall, the air first grows clear.
> The *wu-t'ung* tree truly does not willingly wither:
> Several leaves, greeting the wind, still sound out.

The quatrain sets out images emblematic of the poet's situation and mood, but it is not allegorical. Instead, Chang Lei with a well-trained eye finds correspondences in the night scene.

The act of reading a scene, seemingly so simple, was strongly debated in the late Northern Sung. The impact of *tao-hsüeh* (Neo-Confucianist) attacks on literary crafting of meaning is clear in the defense that Chang offers for writing (*wen-chang*) in his preface to Ho Chu's (1052–1125) *tz'u* poetry:

> Writing's relationship to people is that, when one's heart is full, it is produced; it takes form relying on one's mouth. Not waiting for reflection, it is well crafted; not waiting for embellishment, it is beautiful. This is all the spontaneity of Heavenly Pattern and the utmost Way of Nature [*hsing*] and Feelings.

Chang Lei, in this very sweeping affirmation, adopts the language of *tao-hsüeh*—especially in the last two sentences—to defend the naturalness of writing. Ironically, but perhaps not coincidentally, many commentaries find Chang Lei's most glaring fault as a poet precisely in his spontaneity, his unwillingness to go over poems and fix deficiencies of language and conception.

Ch'ao Pu-chih, the youngest of Su Shih's students, was an exceptional prose stylist. He ranked first in the *chin-shih* and palace examinations of 1079 and had a good, but not brilliant, career before being caught in the downfall of the conservative regime in the Yüan-yu reign-period (1086–1094). His old-style poetry—the largest part of his extant collection—preserves some of the more radical aspects of Ou-yang Hsiu's and Su Shih's style: their prosy argumentation and irregularities in line length. Later critics singled out his poems in *yüeh-fu* (ballad) manner for particular praise. Ch'ao's poetry reveals an interest in T'ao Ch'ien (365–427) as a model both in poetry and in life. In part Ch'ao was following Su Shih's lead: during his various exiles, Su Shih wrote poems to match the rhymes of all of T'ao Ch'ien's poems. Moreover, writers whose careers had been halted quite frequently turned to the themes of retirement and the simple life that are part of T'ao Ch'ien's persona. Nonetheless, Ch'ao Pu-chih's interests reveal a shift in the culture away from a commitment to government service and a reconception of what it meant to be a literatus. *Wen-shih* (scholar-officials) were becoming *wen-jen* (literati) in a more modern Western sense. "Li sao" (Encountering Sorrow) and other works from the lush ancient southern collection of verse called *Ch'u tz'u* (Elegies of Ch'u; see chapter 12), for example, appear in both the art and the scholarship of the period. Ch'ao Pu-chih himself compiled a *Hsü Ch'u tz'u* (Continued *Elegies of Ch'u*) and a "Pien Li sao" (Transformed "Encountering Sorrow"), anthologies of poems after the Han that continue the highly expressive *sao* tradition. This growing interest in the eremitic further eroded the triangular relationship among writing, responsiveness, and right action that had shaped the public character of *wen* in the early Sung dynasty.

Huang T'ing-chien and Ch'en Shih-tao

Huang T'ing-chien (1045–1105) is the most important of Su Shih's "Four Scholars." He and Su Shih often are paired as the two greatest poets of the late Northern Sung. Like Su Shih, he was an important calligrapher and respected writer of *tz'u* song lyrics. He was broadly learned in Taoist and Buddhist traditions as well as the Confucian and literary canons. He passed the *chin-shih* examination at twenty-three, was an instructor at the imperial university (*kuo-tzu-chien*), and served in a variety of local positions. Like Su Shih's other students, however, he was exiled on the return to power of the New Policies faction.

Above all else, Huang T'ing-chien was a poet. He thought deeply about the craft and about his own relationship to the poetic tradition. His poetry is notoriously difficult because of its multifaceted engagement with prior texts and because Huang's poetic sensibility is perhaps the most complex in the Sung dynasty. Like Wang An-shih, he was concerned with technique and with Tu

Fu's technique in particular, although he drew inspiration from the entirety of the earlier poetic tradition. Concern over technique, however, almost inevitably raises the question of transcending it, and Huang T'ing-chien discussed liberation from literary self-consciousness through the language of Ch'an (Zen) Buddhist enlightenment. He also introduced the Taoist transformative images of "exchanging the bones, snatching the embryo" (*huan ku to t'ai*) and "changing iron into gold" (*tien t'ieh ch'eng chin*) to explain his relationship to past poetry. As Huang explained,

> When Tu Fu wrote poetry and Han Yü wrote prose, there was not a single expression without earlier usage. It's just that people's reading was limited, so they said Tu and Han made up these phrases. Those of old skilled in composition truly were able to shape and refine the myriad phenomena. Even when the common sayings of former times flowed from their brushes, they added a speck of spirit cinnabar, touching the iron to make gold.

This sort of transformation of the inherited resources for writing was his goal and proved a very influential model for later generations. Although the complexity of Huang T'ing-chien's relationship to the past is difficult to convey in English, the following quatrain may suggest his approach:

SSU-CHAI SHUI CH'I (WAKING FROM SLEEP AT THE TEMPLE PURIFICATION HALL)

Small cleverness and great foolishness: the mantis catching the cicada.
Excess and inadequacy: the one-footed *k'uei* envies the millipede.
Retiring to eat, coming back, a north-window dream:
On a river of spring moon, to ride a fishing boat.

Huang wrote this poem in 1089 while he served in the Secretariat (an important organ of the central government) in the capital and was living in rooms in a temple complex. The first two lines refer to two well-known allusions from the *Chuang Tzu*. A mantis about to seize a cicada ignores the bird about to eat it, and the bird in turn ignores the boy hunting it. In another series, the *k'uei* (a strange creature with one foot) envies the millipede, while the millipede envies the snake with no feet at all. The third line is also allusive: the initial phrase "retiring to eat" comes from the *Classic of Poetry*, while "north-window dream" refers to T'ao Ch'ien's search for the simple, retired life. The phrase, "coming back" also echoes the title of T'ao Ch'ien's famous poem "Kuei ch'ü lai tz'u" (Let's Return!). Yet the point is not that the language here embellishes a simple wish to escape strife and envy, but that Huang's state of mind as he looks at the river on waking is complex precisely because it echoes with all these inflections from the earlier tradition. The poem captures a real but highly nuanced experience. Huang T'ing-chien's craftsmanship still preserves the central commitment of earlier Sung poetry—a thoughtful articulation of experience—but the task was growing increasingly complex and meeting greater opposition.

Ch'en Shih-tao's (1053–1101) career as an official and a poet marks a transition to the patterns that characterize the second half of the Sung dynasty. He was from a Hsü-chou (in Kiangsu province) literati clan. His father entered government service through *yin* (protection) privilege (i.e., without having to take the examinations),* and his mother was from a yet more prestigious family. Coming of age during the New Policies period, Ch'en did not seek government service. Instead, he studied under the scholar-official Tseng Kung (1019–1083) and worked on his prose style. Tseng attempted to have Ch'en join his staff when he was appointed to the History Bureau, but Ch'en's lack of an official degree raised objections. Through various other contretemps and seemingly a lack of enthusiasm for political maneuvering, Ch'en failed to find a post until 1087, when he became a school instructor in his hometown. Soon thereafter he was appointed as an erudite at the imperial university, but the posting was canceled. He spent many years as a local school instructor. He did not suffer greatly from the suppression of his fellow Yüan-yu conservatives, in part because he spent much of the worst period in mourning for his father, who had died in 1076 (followed by his mother the same year) and in part because he was too minor a figure to persecute severely. The wariness of the dangers of high official position expressed in his poetry, his record of local service near his home, and his desire to establish his reputation through writing (rather than through accomplishments) were part of a new trend in literati culture.

Ch'en Shih-tao as a poet is equally a harbinger of what was to follow. Though determined to make his name through writing, his relationship to past models was complex. Like Huang T'ing-chien, Ch'en esteemed Tu Fu (712–770) above all other poets and emulated Tu Fu's method in his own poetry. Ch'en Shih-tao was fastidious in his manner of composing. By one account, when he was working on a poem, he would lie in bed with the covers over his head; all the children would be sent to the neighbors and the dogs and cats driven out of the house so that he would not be disturbed. Nonetheless, Ch'en Shih-tao's poetry is less intellectualized than Huang T'ing-chien's, and he sought in it to return to the powerful emotional resonances of Tu Fu. One intensifying

---

*Officials above a certain rank could nominate relatives (or dependents) to become eligible for government office. The number of names one could submit depended upon one's rank. The recommended person still had to study for two years in the Directorate of Public Education and pass an examination. Even at its most competitive, however, half of the students who took this special examination passed, and so this route was simpler and less arduous than the regular route to officialdom through the *chin-shih* examination system.

technique is compression of images and language, the sort of couplet crafting implied by the image of Ch'en chanting in bed. This mode includes the artful reworking of couplets from earlier poets to invoke overtones from the tradition. Another mode counterbalances the intensity of composition with the seeming directness of "clumsiness." Ch'en, like Huang, saw the need to roughen the texture of poetry and attempted to match the simplicity of emotionally powerful but familiar experiences to a correspondingly immediate and "unworked" simplicity of language and form. However, the simplicity Ch'en achieves is a "return to simplicity" rather than the thing itself. In general, the self-consciousness of crafting in both Huang T'ing-chien and Ch'en Shih-tao creates a poetry always "in quotation marks." Yet the model for poetry that Huang and Ch'en offered their students was elegant and demanding, and provided a sense of continuity and community. They offered techniques that aspiring poets could master with proper practice and study. Thus they proved extremely influential in a way that the inimitable genius of Ou-yang Hsiu and Su Shih did not.

The Late Northern Sung: the "Kiangsi School" and Ch'en Yü-yi

Lü Pen-chung (1084–1145), a self-conscious inheritor of Huang T'ing-chien's style, declared it the basis of the "Kiangsi school." Ever since he published the "Chiang-hsi shih she tsung-p'ai t'u" (Chart of the Branches of the Kiangsi Poetic Community), however, its list of names has been surrounded by controversy. Although the original text is lost, extant records allowed later scholars to reconstruct a list of twenty-five names, starting with Ch'en Shih-tao and including mainly poets from the early years of the twelfth century. Critics have objected that the list represents no single style and that it has nothing to do with Kiangsi. Some have protested that it includes people arbitrarily, and others have decided that the list is too short. Still, the creation of the list and the attention paid to it were important cultural events that require some explanation.

One noteworthy aspect of the Kiangsi school chart is its use of the phrase "poetic community." By the early twelfth century, poetry clubs were beginning to appear in the larger cities. After a century of peace, the monetarized economy had created flourishing metropolitan centers. Printed books, including poetry by contemporary authors, were widely available, and writing poetry on shared themes as well as the more formally organized poetry clubs was a part of the evolving local literati culture. Most of the "members" of the Kiangsi group were part of this milieu: educated, locally connected men who could not get or did not seek official appointment. (Since Huang T'ing-chien and Ch'en Shih-tao were part of the proscribed Yüan-yu faction, their followers and sympathizers felt disinclined to cooperate with Ts'ai Ching's New Policies regime in any case.)

A second aspect of the historical significance of Lü Pen-chung's Kiangsi school chart is that, although many men from the literati elite—and some women as well—wrote poetry during the early twelfth century, the Kiangsi school broadly defines a style that was judged the most significant both at the time and in retrospect. The major poets of the late Northern Sung and early Southern Sung—Lü Pen-chung himself, Han Chü (d. 1135), Tseng Chi (1084–1166), and Ch'en Yü-yi (1090–1139)—all wrote in the style. Moreover, the major poets of the Southern Sung all shaped their poetry through confrontation with the Kiangsi legacy. What, then, is the Kiangsi style? As noted above, it largely followed the models provided by Huang T'ing-chien and Ch'en Shih-tao. Its broad features are:

- Reflective poetry of "ordinary" experience;
- Poetry separated from experience by concerns for form, language, and the "poetic";
- Concern for a "poetic method" derived from Tu Fu's late poetry;
- Transformation of earlier poetic material made possible through a form of "poetic enlightenment."

Later critics of the style added two more traits:

- Difficult language based on obscure allusion, deriving from Huang T'ing-chien's assertion that every phrase in Tu Fu's poetry has a prior source;
- Arid intellectualizing.

Rather than attempting to present samples of a style that cannot be easily explained through English translation, it is perhaps more useful to explore the power of the Kiangsi style through its influence on Ch'en Yü-yi, the best poet of the emperors Hui-tsung's (r. 1100–1126) and Kao-tsung's (r. 1127–1162) reigns. His transformations of the style illustrate both its strengths and its weaknesses. Ch'en was from Lo-yang. His great-grandfather, having risen to high rank, moved his family to that ancient cultural center. Ch'en's grandfather and father also held official rank. Ch'en Yü-yi passed the examinations for entrance to officialdom as an imperial student but ran into trouble with Ts'ai Ching's regime. After the collapse of the north in 1126, however, he became an important official in Kao-tsung's government and rose to the position of Grand Master of the Palace. As a young writer, he admired Su Shih, Huang T'ing-chien, and Ch'en Shih-tao, and from them he learned to consider Tu Fu the preeminent model for poetry. In Kiangsi fashion, he reworked couplets from these models into his own carefully crafted verse. After the fall of the north, however, Ch'en regretted that in his youth he had failed to understand Tu Fu thoroughly. Only the bitter experience of the dislocations of war could teach him the meaning of Tu Fu's late poetry. Ch'en Yü-yi, with Tu Fu as his model, wrote of the warfare and has been honored as an important patriotic poet. Critics have praised poems like "Teng Yüeh-yang lou" (Climbing Yüeh-yang Tower) and "Lei yü hsing" (Song of the Thunderstorm) for capturing the mood and sensibility of Tu Fu's writings on the An Lu-shan rebellion. The problem in Ch'en's verse, however, is to escape the self-consciousness of literary construction. The artifice, intellectualizing, and display of the poet's subjectivity that typify the Kiangsi style continue to dog Ch'en's poetry. "Mu-tan" (Peonies) is one of Ch'en Yü-yi's best-known quatrains: it is a simple, direct, evocative poem about a flower for which Lo-yang—part of the territory captured by the Chin—was famous. Nonetheless, the poem cannot escape the frame of an ironic self-presentation:

> Ever since the border dust entered the Han passes,
> For ten years, the road to Lo-yang has been so long and distant.
> On the bank of Greenmound Ravine, a wan weary traveler,
> Standing alone in the east wind, looks at the peony.

The writer's self-portrayal in the last couplet as the weary traveler is a standard element of Tu Fu's late poetry that highlights the particular circumstances shaping the poet's perspective. Here the mildly ironic objectification succeeds—as it does in Tu Fu—in presenting the poet's concerns as part of a larger historical process. Yet Tu Fu had a profound faith in the universal order that corresponded to the political order of the T'ang. His poetry located him in this compelling, larger vision. With the continuing development of *tao-hsüeh*, the intellectual world of late Northern Sung writers was far more complicated, skeptical, and inward looking. Li P'eng, one of the authors Lü Pen-chung listed in his chart, proclaimed: "I take that limited scene [*ching*] / To depict my limitless mind." The mind here increasingly becomes the locus of meaning. Ou-yang Hsiu's and Su Shih's poetry of exile already had shown that sorrow was largely a failure of the imagination and of perspective. Ch'en Yü-yi retains this quality of perspectivism even in his late poetry. He suggests that, although the north is lost, the catastrophe nonetheless allowed him to see new places. He does not seem to be ironic when he writes: "The world in chaos does not prevent these pines from growing gnarled. / The village being empty, I'm more aware of the rippling of the water." The mix of intense intellectual and poetic self-consciousness that is part of the Kiangsi mode and the impulse to retain poise through the philosophic refusal to mourn inherited from early-Sung Confucian humanism pull Ch'en Yü-yi's poetry toward estheticism and solipsism. Experience in the external world threatens to collapse into a Self that entirely determines the meaning of what it encounters. The history of Southern Sung poetry is largely the story of the attempt to escape this inward spiral.

SOUTHERN SUNG DYNASTY POETRY

After the fall of the north, southern China continued to flourish. The major cities of the Yangtze valley, having become even more important as centers of the economy and culture, were the grandest cities in the world at the time. Yet the society was uneasy and divided. The south's humiliating failure to retake the north and the threat of renewed warfare cast long shadows. Military expenditures and tribute payments to the Jurchen Chin dynasty that occupied the north put pressure on the state to increase revenues. The government was dominated by a succession of prime ministers who raised ruthless expediency to a high art. Meanwhile, the literati were busy consolidating their control of the local economy by accumulating large landholdings. Yet the prime ministers' impatience with principles and precedents helped to polarize literati discourse, and *tao-hsüeh* became both a call for individual moral self-renewal and the effective center of political opposition. The *tao-hsüeh* fellowship in turn was highly partisan and sought to discredit most of the major cultural figures of the Northern Sung in order to establish their own legitimacy as the spokesmen for the true transmission of the sage Way. They distrusted skilled writing as alluring surfaces in the service of false notions: it "harmed the Way."

Most of the elements of the Northern Sung Confucian humanistic synthesis had unraveled. First, commitment to *wen* no longer demanded commitment to service. Second, one's responses to the world were no longer the basis for action: *tao-hsüeh* theorizing preferred the stillness and purity of the inborn Nature *before* it was provoked to activity by the world. Finally, *wen* as "writing" came close to Plato's imitation of an imitation: it was the artful manipulation of responses that were all too easily mired in the personal—rather than the universal—and in desire rather than in disinterested concern.

These changes that contracted the range of meaning for *wen* correspondingly changed poetry. The Kiangsi style was both a symptom of and a response to the fragmentation of the larger culture. Grounding meaning in the poetic tradition (validating a poem through reference to earlier poetry) and in the self (exploring the controlling subject behind the vagaries of experience) reflects a desire for certainty and community shared by both poets and *tao-hsüeh* partisans within the literati culture. Moreover, poetry's withdrawal from immediacy to more inward meanings held out the possibilities for purity and self-sufficiency that *tao-hsüeh* advocates also sought. Yet the major poets of the Southern Sung rejected such a model as inadequate and sought once again to open the Kiangsi style to the contours of the world of experience. Lu Yu, Yang Wan-li, and Fan Ch'eng-ta all reshaped the Kiangsi legacy, but in significantly different ways.

Lu Yu

Lu Yu (1125–1210) came from a well-established Shan-yin (Shao-hsing, in Chekiang province) clan with a record of service going back to the early Northern Sung. In his teens, he went to the capital to make the right connections and prepare for the *chin-shih* examinations. There he met Tseng Chi, the most prominent poet of his day, and studied with him. Tseng is considered an important Kiangsi school poet and was said to have told Lu Yu that his poetry resembled that of Lü Pen-chung, the creator of the Kiangsi school chart. Lu Yu seems to have run afoul of Emperor Kao-tsung's Prime Minister, Ch'in Kuei (1090–1155), and failed the *chin-shih* examination. He returned to his family's estate in Shan-yin and finally took a minor post through *yin* privilege when he was thirty-four. His prospects brightened when Chao Po-ts'ung ascended the throne, to reign as Emperor Hsiao-tsung (r. 1162–1189), and those who had opposed Ch'in Kuei and his policy of seeking peace with the Chin came into favor. After a northern campaign failed, the war faction was again demoted. Lu Yu went back to a career of minor posts punctuated by time spent at the family estate. When Lu Yu was forty-eight, however, Wang Yen (b. 1113), the Pacification Commissioner of Szechwan, invited him to join his staff. Lu Yu remained in the southwestern province of Szechwan serving in various capacities—including a period on the staff of the famous poet Fan Ch'eng-ta—for the next six years. He then returned to a life divided between official positions and semiretirement at his estate. He retired in 1189 at age sixty-five and spent his last twenty years at home.

Lu Yu's career was typical of that of many prominent writers of the Southern Sung. Like Lu Yu, they were members of the local literati elite who opposed the policies of the central government. When they were called to serve, they usually ran into trouble over their continued criticism and so found themselves back home fairly soon. Because the central government always needed to demonstrate its inclusiveness and its ability to recruit men of proven integrity, it in turn called them back into service, and so the cycle repeated itself.

The details of Lu Yu's career are also important because they powerfully shaped his poetry. His service in Szechwan especially transformed his style. He himself explained that in his youth he sought the perfection of crafting typical of the Kiangsi school. After he arrived in Szechwan, however, Lu Yu found that the Kiangsi style could no longer accommodate the experiences and strongly held beliefs about which he sought to write. From his youth, Lu Yu had argued in favor of going to war to retake the north, but Szechwan provided a particularity of images to embody that commitment from which he drew for the rest of his life, thus broadening the scope of his vision. That is, Lu Yu did not abandon his training in couplet crafting but used it with tremendous effect to encompass a new and wider range of material. The resulting corpus of poems in which Lu Yu powerfully expresses his unrelenting anguish over the Sung dynasty's failure to retake the north has made him one of China's great patriotic poets.

Lu Yu's poetic oeuvre is the largest of any Sung poet, totaling an astonishing 9,300 poems. Yet even this does not represent his total output, for when he compiled his poems for printing, he removed most of his early verse as still under the sway of the Kiangsi school. His extant collection is divided uneasily between his poems of patriotic anguish and what amounts to a diaristic account of his daily life. His genial mode, however, can be seen as a method of resistance like Su Shih's that subtly complements his patriotic verse. When Lu Yu was serving in the retinue of Fan Ch'eng-ta in Szechwan, he was criticized for being unrestrained. Taking up the challenge, he used "unrestrained" in his literary style name, "Fang-weng" (The Unrestrained Old Man), to insist on his right to independent views.

Although Lu Yu had no use for the obsessive concern for origins that haunted the Kiangsi style at its worst, even in his old age he used Kiangsi school terms (as well as some obvious Taoist imagery) to describe the poetic process, as seen in a poem entitled "Yeh yin" (Chanting at Night):

> For more than sixty years I've foolishly studied poetry;
> The depths of my effort I alone know in my thoughts.
> Since nightfall, I laugh that below this lamp giving no warmth,
> Now starts the time of gold-making cinnabar and exchanging the bone.

Lu Yu did not stop crafting his couplets: he became better at it than any of his contemporaries. He has an eye for detail, broad reading, long practice, and a keen structuring intelligence. A famous early poem, "Yu Shan-hsi ts'un" (An Excursion to Shan-hsi Village), suggests these qualities:

> Don't laugh that the farmers' late-year wine is cloudy:
> In this fruitful year they entertain guests with plenty of chicken and pork.
> Mountain after mountain, waters twist and turn: it seems there is no path:
> 4 The willows are dark, the flowers bright—again a village.
> With flute and drum they follow along: the spring altar day nears.
> Their clothes and hats are simple: the old ways remain.
> From this time, if you allow, at leisure following the moonlight,
> 8 With staff in hand, I'll come unannounced to knock at your gate.

The second couplet is particularly famous. It reworks earlier poems that had described such scenery, but the sequencing of natural images and the simplicity of the language hide the "effort" and make the couplet a particularly successful realization. Lu Yu's casual poetry charms with this deceptive ease.

Fan Ch'eng-ta

The same year that Lu Yu unexpectedly failed the *chin-shih* examination, both Yang Wan-li (1124–1206) and Fan Ch'eng-ta (1126–1193) passed it. They all knew one another and in later years wrote poems to one another. Although their initial training in poetry seems to have been similar and based on late Kiangsi school crafting, their subsequent development reflects significantly different interests.

Fan Ch'eng-ta was self-disciplined in his commitments. He rose to high positions in government, while Lu Yu spent his energy fuming at bad policies from lowly posts. Fan accepted a mission as ambassador to the Chin (Jurchen) court in 1170. The assignment was awkward and ill-defined and required a mix of diplomacy and a willingness to affront. His completing the task without humiliation established his reputation for loyalty, determination, and competence and aided his rise to key military administrative posts. His poetry shows the same mix of qualities. On his embassy to the Chin court, for example, he wrote a perceptive series of heptasyllabic quatrains about the landscape through which he traveled, not unexpected for one of the most celebrated travel diarists of Chinese history (see chapter 30). There is wry, sometimes biting wit, veiled criticism, and patriotic fervor. The series, however, is strongly crafted, and its intensity is deflected through an objectivity of gaze, an eye for fresh detail.

Writing to Lu Yu, Fan observed, "A poet has many matters to disturb his ease, / [Yet] you close your gate and create sorrows like this!" Fan here addresses an important difference between the two poets. Lu Yu tends to assume the naturalness of his intentions; all should feel his fervor and outrage about the Chin conquest of the north. Lu's later poetry is a more complex diffusion of his sense of the appropriate through the entire range of human experience. There is never a loss of the sense of ordering—there is a consciousness that the poems themselves are constructed—but his ordering, Lu Yu implies, captures the very nature of human experience. In "Tsai t'i Po fu shih" (Again Writing About Master Po [Chü-yi]'s Poetry), however, Fan Ch'eng-ta is far more circumspect: his intentions are not part of the world:

> Lieh Tzu, riding the wind, still had to wait.
> Master Tsou blowing the pitch-pipe forced spring to arise:
> If one lets external things control ease and sorrow,
> Then I'm afraid along the way one has mixed up guest and host.

Here Fan clearly reflects the eclectic Southern Sung intellectual milieu, with Taoist, Confucian, and Buddhist ideas smoothly fused into a coherent whole. Even by the time of the late Northern Sung, "intentions" were part of a technical vocabulary shared by Buddhism and *tao-hsüeh:* they were within the mind, interior to the subject rather than a part of the external world. Part of the power of the Kiangsi school style was that it made this distinction explicit. These poets explored the inwardness of intention and the manner in which it shaped the poet's encounter with the world. In seeking to articulate this shaping process, both in form and in content, Kiangsi school writers created a larger context for the writing of poetry to compensate for the failure of the integrating power of *wen* as a category. The problem was that the larger context was not very large. Because they distrusted any inherent meaning in the phenomenal, they drew their material and their ordering of it from a circumscribed human realm—a mix of the poetic tradition and current philosophy—that gave them canonically sanctioned readings of the world which they were free to reorganize. The Southern Sung writers preserved the Kiangsi style's larger project of articulating inward intentions but sought to situate these poetic intentions within yet larger social and cultural orderings. Indeed, Fan Ch'eng-ta's most famous and influential compositions are two sets of quatrains in which he locates his own poetic effort within a larger set of shared values. First is the series written on his embassy to Chin discussed above. The second is a set of sixty poems entitled "Ssu-shih t'ien-yüan tsa-hsing" (Impromptu Verses on the Four Seasons of the Countryside). The "Four Seasons" is successful because it incorporates a multiplicity of views—the peasants are not always happy or always sad—and it avoids the clichéd stances of earlier agrarian poetry. The series is about the larger collective effort of life in the countryside rather than a self-portrait of Fan as the nobly reclusive gentleman farmer:

> Butterflies in pairs enter the vegetable blossoms.
> The day is long; no travelers come to the farmstead.
> Chickens fly across the hedge; a dog barks in his hollow:
> I know there is a traveling peddler coming to sell tea.

Chickens and dogs have been part of the theme of rural seclusion since the *Lao Tzu*, but Fan Ch'eng-ta here incorporates them into a fresh, believable vignette of early summer in the countryside. The scene is from his perspective, but his gaze is calm and clear.

Yang Wan-li

Lu Yu, Fan Ch'eng-ta, and Yang Wan-li were friends, but even Lu Yu conceded that Yang Wan-li was the best poet. Yang had the greatest contemporary fame; he was the poets' poet, who transformed the Kiangsi school style from within.

Yang explains, in a preface to *Ching-hsi chi* (Ching Stream Collection), that he started with the Kiangsi poets but then progressed to Ch'en Shih-tao's regulated verse, Wang An-shih's heptasyllabic quatrains, and then T'ang dynasty quatrains. Yet, he continues, the more he studied, the fewer poems he wrote. Then he had to put poetry aside because local administrative tasks took all his time. Over one New Year's holiday, however, he had "what seemed an enlightenment," and, once he left his models behind, poetry just flowed from his brush. Wherever he went, the "ten thousand images" (*wan hsiang*) provided "material for poetry." Kiangsi poets starting with Huang T'ing-chien had talked of poetic breakthroughs as akin to Ch'an (Zen) enlightenment and of the goal of an effortless transformation of poetic materials. Yang Wan-li claimed to have achieved this breakthrough and used his spontaneity as proof. It is significant that, even after this realization, however, Yang continued to frame his relationship to the world of experience much as had Fan Ch'eng-tao: the external was "material" for his creation. Yang once wrote, "I initially had no intention of writing this poem, but I happened to encounter this thing, this event. My intention happened to be stirred by this thing, this event. The encounter was first, then the stirring, and then the poem comes out of it." Although the process Yang describes here relies on the canonical model of the *Classic of Poetry*, he is very much part of the intellectual world of the Southern Sung, with its specific concerns. His vocabulary—"things" and "intentions"—participates in the *tao-hsüeh* analysis of the phenomenal realm. Indeed, as a young man Yang Wan-li was deeply influenced by the general and scholar Chang Chün (1086–1154), who inspired Yang to take the style name Ch'eng-chai (Studio of Sincerity). Yang Wan-li knew many of the important *tao-hsüeh* thinkers of his day and wrote a commentary on the *Yi-ching* (Classic of Change) that during the Southern Sung was printed as a companion to the commentary of the Ch'eng brothers (the Neo-Confucian thinkers Ch'eng Hao [1032–1085] and Ch'eng Yi [1033–1107]). The style of poetry that Yang Wan-li developed out of his breakthrough preserves the *tao-hsüeh* distinction between the self and the phenomenal world. The so-called Ch'eng-chai style in fact thematizes the comparative, category-making processes by which the self makes sense of experience:

YEH SU TUNG-CHU FANG KO (SPENDING THE NIGHT AT EAST ISLE: WILD SONG), THIRD OF THREE

The Lord of Heaven wishes to sate the poet's eye:
He greatly grieves that autumn mountains are too sere and pale.
He then cuts out Shu brocade and spreads out Wu mists,
Placing them low, low, halfway up the autumn mountains.
Next the red brocade becomes kingfisher silk:
On the loom he weaves in crows returning at dusk.
The sunset crows and kingfisher silk suddenly disappear:
I only see a "clear river pure as white silk."

Yang Wan-li here brilliantly uses the extended conceit of sunset as godly weaving both to describe the shifts in the scene (evoking southwestern Szechwan and southeastern Kiangsu in the third line) and to set up the final line. The line directly quotes Hsieh T'iao (464–499; see chapter 13) and, in quoting, also points to two other poets before him—Li Po and Huang T'ing-chien—who already had incorporated this line into their own work. Yang's particular wit here is to restore the cloth image in Hsieh's line to its full force. Yang turned this witty technique of literary, metaphorical framing on a wide range of experience and thus kept alive the earlier Sung impulse to expand the range of materials incorporated into poetry. Like Huang T'ing-chien, however, he mixed erudite, complex couplet-crafting with anti-esthetic elements, most notably vernacular speech patterns. Also like Huang and the early Kiangsi poets, Yang in his poetry largely turned away from the social concerns that occupied Lu Yu. A poetry that explores how the phenomenal impinges on the self cannot take events—as phenomena—too seriously.

LATE SOUTHERN SUNG POETRY

During the Southern Sung the national elite slowly evolved into a system of local elites. Ever more candidates were qualified to serve as officials, but because of the loss of half the empire, official posts decreased in number. The central government was increasingly under the control of strong prime ministers who sought to silence the opposition. The local elites, disaffected from the central government, increasingly turned to *tao-hsüeh* to provide models for moral action and authority at the local level. The sort of integration of self, society, and state implicit in the Northern Sung ideas of *wen* failed. By the late Southern Sung, *wen* had been relegated to the realm of private sensibility and the merely esthetic. In writing poetry, the literati increasingly rejected the breadth of topics, language, material, and styles of earlier Sung poetry as well as its intellectualizing, analytic tendencies. They condemned what they called "turning prose into poetry" and "turning discursive analysis into poetry." They turned back to Late T'ang models of poetry as vignettes of sensibility.

The Four Lings of Yung-chia

The most important proponents of Late T'ang verse were four writers from the Yung-chia district (Wenchow, in modern-day Chekiang): Hsü Chi (style name Ling-yün; 1162–1214), Hsü Chao (style name Ling-hui; d. 1211), Weng Chüan (style name Ling-shu; n.d.) and Chao Shih-hsiu (style name Ling-hsiu; d. 1219). Because each had a "Ling" (numinous) in his public name, they were called the "Four Lings of Yung-chia." Yeh Shih (1150–1223), an important cultural figure and leader of the Yung-chia branch of *tao-hsüeh*, sufficiently praised their small corpus of poetry to establish their contemporary fame. They emphasized intense crafting of couplets in the manner of Chia Tao (779–843) and Yao Ho (781–c. 859). Chao Shih-hsiu, the best of the four, once exclaimed, "Luckily a poem has just forty characters. If it had just one more, I wouldn't know what to do." Although on occasion they touched on social themes, their poems are mostly regulated verse depicting quiet, secluded, pure scenes. Buddhist images—temples, incense, bells—often appear.

CHAO SHIH-HSIU, "YÜEH K'O"
(APPOINTMENT WITH A GUEST)

In the season of yellow plums, rain on house after house.
Green grass by ponds and dikes, frogs calling everywhere.

> We had an appointment, but he didn't come—now past midnight:
> Idly rapping a *go* stone knocks a flicker from the lamp.

The late critic Ch'ien Chung-shu (see chapter 32) noted that many poets had used the image of sparks flying from the falling wick of a candle (here precipitated by the tapping of a Chinese chess piece) as part of a late-night scene of solitude and disappointed anticipation, but that this poem captured the ambience and mood especially well.

Liu K'o-chuang and the "Rivers and Lakes" Poets

The Neo-Confucian thinker Yeh Shih stated that the Four Lings' verse transformed the poetry of the time, rescuing it from moribund Kiangsi bookishness. However, he also lamented the Late T'ang style's narrowness and suggested to Liu K'o-chuang that he could do better. Liu K'o-chuang (1187–1269) is the most important writer of a group known as the "Rivers and Lakes" poets. The group is named after an anthology of their poems put together by the commercial bookseller Ch'en Ch'i (c. 1190–1251) in Hangchow, the "temporary" capital of the Southern Sung. The current regime was still smarting from criticism of the brutal tactics by which the new emperor, Li-tsung (Chao Yü-chü; r. 1224–1264), had ascended the throne: when the emperor noticed yet more criticism in the poems of the anthology, he demoted and exiled the poets and banned the writing of poetry in the capital. The *Chiang-hu chi* (Rivers and Lakes) collection points to a role for poetry quite different from that suggested by the success of the Four Lings. Writing polite poetry was part of the social world of Southern Sung literati. But they also used poetry for one of Chinese poetry's oldest functions: to voice social criticism. The relationship between the ruling cliques and the local elites was one of constant tension, not mutual indifference. Central policies had an impact on local conditions, and the central government needed the cooperation of the local elites to implement its policies. The literati elite expressed their opinions through protests by the students at the imperial universities, memorials by low-ranking officials, and the publicly disseminated writings of morally committed literati. Poetry, with its ancient canonical right to express grievances, played an important role in this process.

Liu K'o-chuang was perhaps more successful and prominent than most of the authors in the *Rivers and Lakes* anthology, but his career and poetry followed the same general pattern as theirs. Like Lu Yu, he was from an important local clan, began his government career through *yin* privilege, and spent some time on the staff of a military administrator. Like Yang Wan-li, he had strong connections to the *tao-hsüeh* circles of his day. He spent most of his life moving between low-level positions in government and the sinecure of a temple guardianship in his home town. When appointed to a rank that allowed him to write memorials, he usually wasted little time before submitting his criticisms of current policies. As a poet, Liu never stopped writing critical verse even though it directly harmed his career. Even so, he was opposed to topical poems that were no more than political squibs. Liu, like most of the "Rivers and Lakes" poets, is usually associated with the Late T'ang manner, but the picture is more complex. He began as an admirer of Lu Yu but was also strongly affected by Yang Wan-li. His poetry had a dry wit and well-crafted couplets mixed with an intentionally prosaic counter-esthetic. He had a good sense of the limitations of both the Late T'ang and the Kiangsi styles. Similarly, he knew better than to yoke his poetry to his moral commitments, but he also did not give it over entirely to fragmentary sensibility. In the end, his verse was adrift: the intellectual universe of *tao-hsüeh* could offer no compelling role for poetry. He decided that if he had failed at all else, he would at least write *more* poems than Lu Yu. He failed at that, too.

Wen T'ien-hsiang, the Loyalists, and the End of Sung Poetry

By the final decades of the Sung dynasty, the rationale for writing poetry—its connection with any larger order of meaning—had largely collapsed. The end of the dynasty, however, provided one last flurry of creativity.

The most famous writer of the debacle (the total collapse of the Sung dynasty) was Wen T'ien-hsiang (1236–1282), an extraordinary patriot who turned poetry into brilliant propaganda. As a young man, Wen did not differ markedly from many other children of the local literati elite. He had a strong sense of his local traditions and was well educated in one contemporary version of *tao-hsüeh*. He also had little real interest in poetry. When the Mongols invaded, however, he used poetry to document his escape from captivity (since 1275) and his campaign of organizing resistance. *Chih-nan lu* (Record of the Compass) is an autobiographical account of this period that intersperses prose narration and poetry. After a valiant but doomed effort by Wen and other loyalists to save the child emperor from enemy forces, Wen was recaptured and taken north to the Yüan capital at Peking. In captivity he completed *Chih-nan hou lu* (Latter Record of the Compass), which includes his famous "Cheng ch'i ko" (Song of the Rectifying Force), a stirring, heroic declaration of his patriotic sentiments. The Yüan emperor, Khubilai Khan (1271–1368), eventually decided that Wen T'ien-hsiang would never submit to Yüan rule and had him executed.

Wen T'ien-hsiang had an extremely good sense of Tu Fu's grand style, which imbued the landscape with great symbolic density. In his youth he had experimented with the style but lacked a content to match the rhetoric. In the poetry of the two *Compass* collections, however, the high rhetoric and momentous events come together to produce some remarkable verse. He wrote "Chin-ling yi" (Chin-ling Post-Station), for example, while a prisoner on his way north:

> Grasses enclose the old palaces as waning sunlight shifts.
> A lone wind-tossed cloud stops briefly: on what can it depend?
> The view here, mountains and rivers, has never changed,

Yet the people within the city wall already are half gone.
The reed flowers that fill the land have grown old with me,
But into whose eaves have the swallows of my former home flown?
Now I depart on the road out of Kiang-nan;
Transformed into a weeping cuckoo, reeking of blood, I shall return.

The physical scene becomes complex symbolic portents. The poem raises the question of nature's relation to human loss: although the fall of the dynasty threatens to be swallowed up in nature's ceaseless ebb, Wen insists—calling upon old cultural lore—that he will transform himself into part of the natural world of the poem and still protest forever the defeat of the Sung.

After the end of the dynasty, some who had served the Sung dynasty refused to cooperate with the Yüan. The poets Wang Yüan-liang (n.d.), Hsieh Fang-te (1226–1289), Hsieh Ao (1249–1295), and Cheng Ssu-hsiao (1241–1318) were their spokesmen. The most interesting aspect of their poetry is the renewed interest in the Late T'ang poets Meng Chiao (751–814) and Li Ho (790–816) and the spirit-haunted world. The imagined persistence of sorrow in the landscape compensates for the failure of history to protect the Sung.

CHENG SSU-HSIAO, "CH'IU YÜ" (AUTUMN RAIN)

Clouds fill the long void; rain fills the mountains.
With biting chill, the wind turns newly cold.
Since nightfall, the White Emperor has taken away the autumn:
Ten thousand trees drenched, their crying will not dry.

The reference to the White Emperor in the penultimate line superficially signifies the snow of winter, but it also evokes myths and legends of ancient conquerors from the west and north, a not-so-veiled allusion to the Mongols.

RETROSPECTIVE

Poetry, of course, did not die with the passing of the last Sung loyalist, nor did "Sung poetry" entirely disappear. Although the Ming dynasty (1368–1644) saw a return to T'ang models, the writings of the major Sung authors continued to be printed and circulated. At the beginning of the Ch'ing dynasty (1644–1911), many scholars grew interested in Sung dynasty poetry as a whole, and we owe much to their diligence for our understanding of the period. Their resurrection of the Sung, however, was to help them find answers to their own cultural crises. They looked back on the earlier poetry from a perspective profoundly different from that of the world in which the poems were actually created. We today are even further away from that world. To understand Sung poetry and its esthetic qualities, we need to restore some of the social and intellectual contexts that shaped the poetry and its transformations throughout the dynasty. After all, the history of poetry is not just a list of styles. At its best, poetry powerfully shapes our understanding of experience, yet these moments when poets of particular brilliance integrate the available formal and conceptual orderings into great poetry are rare. The effort to shape poetry's relationship to *wen*—and then to define and defend *wen* itself—underlies the larger transformations in Sung poetry. These historical and cultural issues are dauntingly complex, but understanding them helps us to appreciate what is truly great in poets like Su Shih, to admire the sad but noble failure of Liu K'o-chuang, and to listen attentively to all the Sung poets as they shape their world on the page.

Michael A. Fuller

Chapter 17

YÜAN *SAN-CH'Ü*

The poetry called *san-ch'ü* occupies a place of its own in the tradition of song verse. Verse written to the music of the times was a part of the literature of any period, but occasionally it rose to such prominence that it characterized for later generations the literary excellence of an age; this is so with the *yüeh-fu* of the Han (206 B.C.E.–220 C.E.) and the *tz'u* of the Sung dynasty (960–1279), the latter of which is usually seen as the epitome of literary song. The *san-ch'ü* have come to be known as the poetry of the Yüan (1279–1368), and regardless of whether this is historically accurate, these songs are certainly one of the rich treasures in Chinese literature.

Yüan *san-ch'ü* has distinctive characteristics that set it apart in the tradition of writing verses to music. It is perhaps the drama with its many arias (*ch'ü*) that gave impetus to the spread of *san-ch'ü* (separate or "dispersed" songs, i.e., not woven into a drama). Indeed, many of the tunes were the same and could be used both in arias of the drama and for separate songs. Moreover, *san-ch'ü* writers often wrote song sets (*t'ao-shu*), the basic form of a scene in the drama, as a separate group and, although sets were not unique to the Yüan, never before were they so well developed in the song tradition or so intrinsic a part of composing verse.

Like the *tz'u* (song verse or lyric) of the late T'ang and Sung, *san-ch'ü* takes its form from a melody. All tunes belonged to a key or mode and, though it may be of little interest to the modern reader, the modes and their tunes likely dictated the content of the verse to some extent, since the music probably had a specific mood. Single songs (*hsiao-ling,* i.e., a single tune standing by itself, as opposed to sets of songs) comprise the majority of *san-ch'ü* that have survived. They were a lyrical form relatively easily executed even for the casual writer. Songs in sets had to be in the same mode and have the same rhyme throughout, which required considerable skill in versification, though set phrases, clichés, and conventional subject matter made composition less arduous.

Rhythm and the meters were also based on the music. Because Yüan music is lost, it is sometimes difficult to know what the rhythmic divisions of a line might have been. One of the features of *san-ch'ü* is the use of extrametric syllables, that is, syllables that probably were sung rapidly or otherwise executed outside the basic meter of a line. Sometimes they make a line sound awkward to a modern reader, though it was not necessarily so in original performance. This feature attracted later critical attention, where it is often seen as throwing off the yoke of conventional versification. The conventions of *san-ch'ü* are rigorous, and the view of this genre as a vehicle of iconoclasm is a distortion of our own age.

Perhaps one of the main reasons *san-ch'ü* is now seen as a separate branch of literary song is that it developed, as the music and verse of the drama had, along a relatively independent course in the north. If the Northern Sung dynasty had carried on without interruption from 1127 to the beginning of the Yüan dynasty in 1279, the developments in the song forms brought about by the influx of foreign music and linguistic change in the north would have been seen as a matter of differing local styles rather than as a new genre. It is worth considering that Yen-ching (modern-day Peking) was in a "foreign" land from shortly after the fall of the T'ang to the beginning of the Yüan, some 375 years, and the Chinese people of the Yellow River basin, including the cities of Kaifeng, Tsinan, Taiyuan, and P'ing-yang, were not directly in touch with the south for roughly the latter half of that time, about 150 years. Therefore, while the north was governed by the Chin (1115–1234), certain centers of Chinese culture were separated from the Sung, now confined to the south, and though there were cultural exchanges between the Chin and the Southern Sung, it was mostly formal from south to north; the local and folk culture largely did not travel. When China was reunited in 1279, the northern dialect, or the language of the Central Plain, became predominant for political reasons. Had the Chinese capital remained in Kaifeng, northern speech, and the culture related to it, would have developed gradually *within* the general culture of the whole and very likely would not have had the same influence on the history of Chinese literature.

The earliest stages of the *san-ch'ü* are difficult to know, because the extant corpus was collected mostly during the last generations of the Yüan, and the material produced in the north during the Liao (916–1125) and Chin dynasties is rather spare. The best information derives from studies on the development of the drama. It is good to remember that the practice of setting words to songs is a continuing process and that the place of songs in the greater scheme of literature will often be influenced by nonliterary circumstances, and so seeking direct lines to previous forms may not be useful. To be sure, there were songs from Sung times, found in the collected works of Yüan writers, but perhaps the most important point to consider is that most of what are now called *san-ch'ü* were new songs, which had not yet been heard in the south.

One must consider the language differences that became a fact of life after the reunification in 1279. Very few southern writers could know firsthand the patois of which northern writers could so easily make use in their *san-ch'ü*. One might ask why southern writers would want to write northern songs in the first place; it was not as though they had suddenly lost their own very rich tradition. It might simply have been that the northern songs and the dramas were so fresh and attractive that many writers wanted to make them part of their own repertoire. There is a possibility that, since the language of the Central Plain had become the prestige topolect, knowledge of it might have been an asset.

A hint of this is found in a work by Chou Te-ch'ing (fl. 1324), who was from Kao-an in the northern part of present-day Kiangsi (a southern province). His interesting book *Chung yüan yin-yün* (The Sounds and Rhymes of the Central Plain) was essentially a manual for composing northern songs. It discusses matters of style and verse form, but most of it is devoted to giving the "right" pronunciations of words. The tonal contours of words had undergone changes that resulted in differences as radical as that, for example, between "e" and "i" in English. This meant that if a southerner were keen to write in the northern style, he could make unintended mistakes such that singing "heavy mist" might sound to the northern ear like "we sink in feasting." For Chou, this work might have been more than a guidebook for colleagues writing songs. As is suggested in the preface by Yü Chi (1272–1348), generally considered the best prose writer of the Yüan and also a major poet, it showed his worthiness for government service. If that was the case, however, it did him little practical good, for, aside from his authorship of *Chung Yüan yin-yün*, virtually nothing is known about him.

Modern histories of literature commonly represent *san-ch'ü* as the only poetry of the Yüan era. This ignores the many Yüan poets who produced creditable poetry of the kind written in the T'ang and Sung dynasties (see chapters 18 and 19); indeed the collected works of such writers during the Yüan outnumber the collected works of *san-ch'ü* writers. This bias likely owes much to the early Ming critics, who maintained that no worthwhile *shih* poetry was written after the T'ang, and to the May Fourth movement, which held that major literary developments occurred only in "colloquial" or other nonestablishment types of writing. Therefore, if it is true that "the literary vitality of the time went into writing colloquial songs, song-suites, plays, and stories," as Arthur Waley has remarked, then we must admit that this was a limited effort, as the *san-ch'ü* corpus is relatively small. Allowing for the longer duration of the T'ang and Sung periods, the number of extant Yüan *san-ch'ü* is about one-fifth that of verses in the *Ch'üan T'ang shih* (Complete T'ang Poems) and half that in the *Ch'üan Sung tz'u* (Complete Lyrics of the Sung Dynasty). Such facts notwithstanding, the vitality of *san-ch'ü* is refreshing and attractive, while its subtle and refined side bears comparison with the poetry of any period. The refinement was given added impetus after the unification at the end of the thirteenth century, when, less often by merchants and common folk than by the free movement of officials, the songs were introduced in the south, where they were taken up by some members of the literary community there.

Besides the collected *san-ch'ü* of three writers—Chang Yang-hao (1269–1329), Ch'iao Chi (d. 1345), and Chang K'o-chiu (fl. 1317)—the *san-ch'ü* have been preserved mainly in four anthologies of Yüan times: two, *Yang-ch'un pai-hsüeh* (The Snows of Sunny Spring) and *T'ai-p'ing yüeh-fu* (The Ballads of the Pax Magnifica), were collected by Yang Chao-ying (fl. 1300); the other two, *Yüeh-fu hsin-sheng* (Ballads of the New Music) and *Yüeh-fu ch'un-yü* (Treasury of Ballads), are by unknown editors. Of these, *Yüeh-fu ch'un-yü* is thought to be the earliest; *Yang-ch'un pai-hsüeh*, in one form or another, appeared before 1324 and *T'ai-ping yüeh-fu* was published in the mid-fourteenth century. Least is known about *Yüeh-fu hsin-sheng*. Ming anthologies have preserved many songs as well.

The Yüan anthologies reflect the tastes of aficionados, so that an outer circle of *ch'ü* enthusiasts, as may have existed, certainly did not get collected. This is most evident with verse written by women. Furthermore, nearly a third of the single songs preserved are from the collected poems of the three writers mentioned above. This suggests that the best writers are not necessarily the ones that are best represented. For example, Chang K'o-chiu, although a master versifier, is perhaps not a great poet, nor was he one who made the best use of the genius of the *san-ch'ü*; yet the most numerous songs preserved of one author, 855 single songs, are his—about four times those of Ch'iao Chi, with the next largest number. Kuan Han-ch'ing (c. 1220–c. 1307) was the acknowledged master of the times and very likely produced as much verse during his lifetime; yet the number of single songs attributed to him is only fifty-seven, a small quantity even compared to the output of less well-known writers. Ma Chih-yüan (c. 1260–1325), perhaps the best *san-ch'ü* writer, left 115 single songs. An excellent writer like Ch'iao Chi, who (like most *san-ch'ü* poets) never held office of any kind, tried but failed to publish his works before his death. His 209 songs and 11 sets were preserved by others.

Prefaces to the two major collections of the period offer a glimpse of the status of *san-ch'ü* in the contemporary view. Yang Chao-ying's *Yang-ch'un pai-hsüeh* takes its name from a collection of the best songs in the ancient state of Ch'u. In his preface to it, the Uyghur *san-ch'ü* poet Kuan Yün-shih (Sewinch Qaya; 1286–1324) praised contemporary writers highly but then added, almost in surprise, that this collection could be considered of the same order as the ancient one, which must have been a daring thing to say. Teng Tzu-chin (fl.

1351), in his preface to *T'ai-p'ing yüeh-fu*, also attempted to set *san-ch'ü* in the grand tradition of Chinese poetry, particularly the *yüeh-fu* and, by implication, even so exalted a work as the *Shih-ching* (Classic of Poetry). Although on the surface this seems exaggerated, seen in the light of the song tradition, the contribution of the *san-ch'ü* was considerable, and as a form it continued to be used after the Yüan era and was admired by many writers in the Ming and Ch'ing periods, as well as down to the present. A remark by Chou Te-ch'ing indicates the scope of the form's popularity in his time:

> Everyone sings it, from the gentry to the common folk. . . . [T]he rhymes all conform to natural language, the vocabulary is compatible with the language of the [whole] empire, the diction is lucid and the phrasing is elegant, the rhymes are brisk and the sounds are harmonious; what they write about is sincere and filial and a remedy to the world.

Hyperbole though this may be, it is perhaps true enough in general, especially in the north. Whether *san-ch'ü* ever functioned as a remedy to the world is debatable, but it is clear that the form was held in high regard. The Ming writer Wang Chi-te (1560–1623) considers it a most accommodating type of verse, far superior in his estimation to T'ang and Sung poetry. Although this also is an extreme view, *san-ch'ü* does have its admirable qualities as regards both form and uses of theme.

Histories of *san-ch'ü* divide the Yüan period roughly in half, the first period being more robust (*hao-fang*) and the second more refined (*ch'ing-li*). The majority of the authors of the early period are characterized as having a free, forthright attitude and as being not much concerned with the niceties of form. The second-period authors are more meticulous in the approach to their craft. This is a good distinction, though it describes individuals better than it does the period.

For some the Yüan era is characterized by protest against domination by a barbaric foreign power. There is no doubt that certain kinds of corruption in government increased and that the best people were perhaps less often employed in public service than before, in the Sung, for example. Several excellent verses deplore the state of affairs. Among these is an anonymous song referring explicitly to instances of government ineptitude such as the Yellow River canal project of 1351, which led to the uprising of the anti-Confucian rebel Red Turbans, who strove for the restoration of the Sung dynasty; it condemns the severe exactions imposed by the law of the land, starvation, paper money and the hardships it was seen to have caused, government corruption, and the lack of good statesmen (*Ch'üan Yüan san-ch'ü* [Complete Yüan *san-ch'ü*; hereafter CYSC] 1664). According to T'ao Tsung-yi (1316–1403), who chronicled his times in *Ch'o keng lu* (Records After Plowing), this song was known from the capital all the way to the south. Similar, though less vehement, are two anonymous songs and a third by Chang Ming-shan (fl. 1354), which complain that learning does not bring success; though these may be read as a commentary on deteriorating social values, they can easily be taken as antigovernment protest as well (CYSC 1688, 1282). Chang Ming-shan was one of the most outspoken critics of his day; it appears there was little he would not say. In one of his songs, he addresses the snow, saying: "You are the one who freezes the people of Wu to death! / Must be a lucky thing for the government" (CYSC 1283).

However, poems like this hardly characterize the genre, for there were political poems of various kinds, including paeans to the government. Representative of several celebrating the inauguration of the Ta-te reign-period (1297–1307), for example, is a song composed by Wu Hung-tao (fl. 1310), with lavish praise of the emperor and a concluding verse expressing the hope that his glorious reign will go on forever (CYSC 736–737).

Along with protest verse were subtler poems such as those by T'ang Shih (fl. 1383), in which he laments the passing of a better time as reflected in poems on places he visited, especially his "Hsi-hu kan chiu" (Mulling over the Past at West Lake; CYSC 1559). Such verse, of which there is a great deal, might also be considered a kind of veiled protest, but insofar as it is about place, it is also related to the landscape theme a part of which is reminiscence poetry and another part of which extols the simple and contemplative life. This latter theme, usually called *tao-ch'ing* (literally, "expressing emotions/feelings/sentiments," but sometimes also interpreted as "Taoist sentiments," etc.), implies that rejecting the world is the best method of survival, whether physical or spiritual. Because it became quite popular, especially among those who had no desire to give up their lives in the urban centers, *tao-ch'ing* poetry became highly conventionalized, but those songs that are fresh and have insight and the bite of social criticism are among the great *san-ch'ü* delights. Writers like Teng Yü-pin (fl. 1194) and Ch'en Ts'ao-an (1275?) make especially good use of *tao-ch'ing*, avoiding the trivial banter of the "wine and women" writers. Nor is the theme confined to the Taoist world of escape; Jen Yü (fl. 1331) wrote in one of a place that sounds like a Confucian utopia (CYSC 1008).

Perhaps the largest class of all is love poetry. Some of it, one can imagine, relates an actual situation, as when it is written to a named person. Most, however, is cliché-ridden and focused on a limited number of themes. There are the innumerable poems written by men in the voice of a lovesick girl waiting for an errant lover, a tradition that long predates the *san-ch'ü*. Another set piece seems to be "Shu so chien" (Writing of Something I Have Seen), which always describes a chance encounter with a nubile young girl. Many poems describe trysts; these can be quite good if the poet is able to elicit the innocence of young love or a sense of sincere affection. Such a moment can be made unique through special language and unusual imagery, but most *san-ch'ü* poets sought to legitimize it through repetition of clichés and allusions to famous affairs of the past; though this does not necessarily result in bad verse, it does take a poet of some skill to rise above the mediocre.

Among the many references to lovers of the past, none has as great a fascination for poets of this period as the elopement of the poor scholar Shuang Chien and his beloved Su Ch'ing. Su Ch'ing was the unfortunate inmate of a brothel; her escape with Shuang Chien outwitted a rich merchant who wanted to ransom her. The mere mention of their names or even the town to which the lovers fled is enough to set the tone for a poem or a whole song set.

Much of the extant verse amounts to clever displays of great ingenuity. This comes from the general use of *san-ch'ü* as a pastime. There is the banter one finds in songs written for the amusement of friends drinking together, which usually revolves around clever turns of phrase, variations on a theme, or verses using the rhymes of another poem. There were also technical challenges, such as using three rhyming words in the same line, for example, the third line of a song by Wang Ho-ch'ing (fl. 1246): "Shen shou P'an ch'ou ho jih hsiu?" (Pining and sorrow, when will they end?; *CYSC* 41). Some poems were written with the same word in every line, one of the best examples of which is a pair of verses by Liu Shih-chung (fl. 1302) using the word "spring" (*CYSC* 659–660). Besides being a metaphor for "love," it was also the name of a singing girl, which gives each line double and triple meanings.

One of the favorite pastimes among writers, and of very long standing in China, was writing a poem matching someone else's using not only the sound but the very rhyme words of the original poem. Usually one was satisfied to write just a single matching verse, but on one such occasion a poem by Pai Pi (fl. 1297) was taken up by Feng Tzu-chen (1257–1327?), who produced no fewer than forty-two different matching versions (*CYSC* 340–353). Most of them, like the original, describe bucolic scenes with a tinge of retreat from the world, but there are other subjects such as parting. The poem by Pai Pi was much admired but somewhat overpowered by the forty-two that Feng wrote, each with the very same rhyme words.

Humor overlaps all categories, even protest, as seen in one of Chang Ming-shan's songs. Most *san-ch'ü* humor is raucous satire. Much of it celebrates a curiosity of some kind or a bizarre imagining, like Wang Ho-ch'ing's "Yung ta hu-tieh" (The Great Butterfly; *CYSC* 41), "Ta yü" (The Great Fish; *CYSC* 45), "Lü-mao-pieh" (The Tortoise with Algae on Its Back; *CYSC* 45), and "Ch'ang mao hsiao kou" (The Little Dog with Long Hair; *CYSC* 46). Typical of his wit is the reference to the little dog as "a dust mop that can bite." One of the earliest and most famous humorous pieces is Tu Jen-chieh's (fl. 1234) song set recounting a theatrical performance as seen through the eyes of a peasant who is amused by the strange speech and costumes; he laughs so hard that he nearly wets himself (*CYSC* 31–32). Another is by Sui Ching-ch'en (fl. 1302) on the return of Liu Pang to his home county after establishing the Han dynasty, only to find that everyone still sees him as the nobody they knew years before (*CYSC* 543–545). Much satire in the *san-ch'ü*, however, is humor at someone's expense. Although it can be gentle and very funny—as seen in the last line of an anonymous song about a tall girl: "I'm only afraid that next year you'll be taller still!" (CYSC 1726)—there are others that appear less playful, for instance, the deliberations on "T'o-pei chi" (The Hunchbacked Whore; CYSC 1666).

There are perhaps a dozen or so major writers of *san-ch'ü*, the most outstanding among whom are Ma Chih-yüan, Kuan Han-ch'ing, Ch'iao Chi, and Chang K'o-chiu. Although the fact that Chang K'o-chiu left behind the most songs accounts in part for the considerable attention he is paid, certainly his exceptionally polished style and mastery of allusion were greatly admired in later times, leading Li K'ai-hsien (1501–1568) of the Ming dynasty to call him the Tu Fu of *san-ch'ü*. Given the large corpus of his work, one finds less variety in themes and subjects than expected. The strongest characteristics of his verse are the descriptive power of his lines and his ability to evoke a subtle mood. His use of classical phraseology and allusion is more like that of earlier poets in the *shih* or *t'zu* forms. Some argue that, because of this, he fails to represent the genius of *san-ch'ü*. Still, it was his refined style that made his poems so popular among Ming and Ch'ing writers.

If Chang K'o-chiu is the Tu Fu of *san-ch'ü*, then Ch'iao Chi was their Li Po. He was in the entertainment world for forty years, "a scholar of the mists and clouds, the drunken sage of the lakes and streams" ("Tzu shu" [Of Myself; CYSC 575]). A long-standing friendship with a certain Li Ch'u-yi inspired many poems, and his relationship with her invested these works with special significance. His well-practiced hand, which could turn a verse on any subject, often used language in unconventional or experimental ways, as in one of his verses in which each syllable is doubled, a device made famous by Li Ch'ing-chao, a poet of the Sung (CYSC 592). But more subtle, for example, is his verse "Yung shou" (On Hands), where slightly conflicting imagery becomes beautifully evocative in "[they] secretly give rise to spring [i.e., feelings of love]" in an otherwise innocent and casual scene and, as they reach up to adjust the hair, are "painfully lovely" (CYSC 575). In a comparison of his verse to the work of Chang K'o-chiu, it is often easier to discover a voice behind his lines and to envision the individual in them.

Kuan Han-ch'ing, one of the four great Yüan dramatists, is best known for his plays; however, his stylistic excellence carries over to fifty-seven separate songs and thirteen song sets. In these, he writes mainly about the sadness of parting or the longing of love. He is capable of evoking vivid emotions, as in the last three lines of "Pieh ch'ing" (Parting): "The stream winds away, / The hill screens the view, / And you are gone" (CYSC 156). In a set of nine songs he recounts a clandestine tryst of two young lovers (CYSC 180–181). The first four songs describe a young man who waits outside the window as agreed, sees no sign of the one he desires, and is afraid someone will discover him standing under the shadows of the flowers. Just as he is about to give up, she appears, looking as beautiful as he had dreamed. As their passions rise, the earth becomes their couch, the moon their lamp: "A pleasant breeze opens the peony. / . . .

And all in a moment, shuddering, they lie languid." In the last song, the young lady straightens her hair and, as she is about to return to her boudoir, she suggests, "Maybe you could come a bit earlier tomorrow." Perhaps one of his best-known song sets is "Pu fu lao" (Refusal to Get Old; *CYSC* 172–173). He portrays himself as someone who is still able to do all that the young can do, and even better, and he vows never to stop his drinking, singing, and loving women until the god of hell, Yama, orders his souls to be drawn out of him and consigned to oblivion.

Critics are divided as to whether Kuan Han-ch'ing or Ma Chih-yüan is the best of the Yüan songwriters. Very little is known of Ma Chih-yüan's life except that he was from Ta-tu (the Yüan capital, near modern-day Peking). He wrote fifteen plays, of which seven survive, but he also left 115 songs and 16 song sets. In these there are two exceptional poems, both called "Ch'iu ssu" (Autumn Thoughts). One is a short descriptive poem composed as a tour de force almost entirely in noun phrases, expressing a sentiment of perennial interest to the Chinese: a traveler looking at a pleasant and tranquil evening scene and thinking of home (*CYSC* 242). Many poems can be compared to this, the best-known *san-ch'ü*, but few surpass it. There is some question whether it was actually written by Ma, which in itself is an interesting commentary on the casual way even this most famous and admired poem was recorded and an insight into the informal status of the *san-ch'ü* itself.

In Ma's "Autumn Thoughts" song set, the world-weary poet sets forth questions about life and fame, concluding that seclusion is best. He begins by remarking how life passes as if in a dream: spring is here today and flowers wither tomorrow, so we should drink quickly—"it is getting late and the lamp is dying." What becomes of the great, he asks, and their palaces? What good is wealth if one must be a slave to it? Now he too has reached the end of life, his hair is white, and his days are few; if others laugh, then he has played the fool well in his time. But now there is no time for fame and "the world no longer vexes me here"; his life is simple, nature is his domain, and his days are filled by it. If anyone asks, he is drunk beneath the east hedge (*CYSC* 268–270). His thought and his reading of the universal conditions of man earn this poem its just renown.

Some of his best descriptive songs are like scenes from paintings. For example, "Yüan p'u fan kuei" (Returning Sails) includes the usual static tableau: an evening scene, the sun setting, the flag drooping outside a wineshop, boats slowly coming to shore, and evening settling over the rooftops. In the last line, "At the old bridge, fishmongers leave for home," one almost hears, as if in the distance, the quiet gathering up of things and a few words of farewell (*CYSC* 245). Or where he describes the warm weather, which brings with it spring fever, even the butterflies are too lazy to play and the birds are too tired to sing. "No wonder the fallen petals hardly stir, the evening breezes lack the strength" (*CYSC* 284).

Another important writer of the period is Pai P'u (1226–after 1306). Two of his plays survive; his extant thirty-seven songs and four song sets are barely representative of his best talents. "Chia jen lien shang hei chih" (To a Pretty Girl with a Mole on Her Cheek) is especially charming, but "Chih chi" (Knowing Things to Come) comprises sincere and convincing poems of the world-weary and *tao-ch'ing* type using fresh imagery (CYSC 193, 194).

Kuan Yün-shih is the best of several sinicized foreign writers of *san-ch'ü* and indeed holds a secure place among all who applied themselves to this genre. His themes tend toward romantic love and parting; some verses expound on the carefree life, though these tend to be more conventional exercises. His mastery of language is perhaps his strongest quality. Although he has much of the smoothness of Chang K'o-chiu, his phrasing is sometimes more colorful and imaginative, for example, the nine terse verb phrases in three lines of a song describing two blissful lovers who forget time and are surprised by the sounding of the dawn watch (CYSC 363–364). He was an acquaintance of Hsü Tsai-ssu (fl. 1320), and their poems have been collected together in one volume. Some say that Hsü was a better writer than Kuan. Certainly Hsü's themes are no more varied than Kuan's, since they are mostly conventional (romantic love, scenic descriptions, a few occasional pieces), but in them can often be found imaginative phrasing and some playful ideas, as well as exceptional expression of emotion.

Chang Yang-hao was one of the *san-ch'ü* writers whose 161 songs and 2 song sets were preserved in a separate anthology. He wrote most of his songs after retiring from a succession of high-ranking government appointments. Overshadowing these, however, are ones he wrote in the final years of his life, when he emerged from retirement to take up a post once again, this time in Kuan-chung (in Shensi province), which was then in the midst of drought and famine. His poems and songs from this period are deeply moving. He witnessed the helplessness of human beings at the hands of fate as well as unnecessary trouble caused by bad government: "Kingdoms rise, the people suffer. / Kingdoms fall, the people suffer" (CYSC 437).

Yao Sui (1239–1314) was a Han-lin academician and a teacher of Pai P'u. He left a small corpus of pleasant verses. They contain comments on life such as: "The sea of life is wide; / And there are storms upon it every day" (CYSC 211). Another typical theme was his caution to friends as they enjoy themselves: "Sing softly the old songs of Yang Kuan,* / Or you might break the heart of a passing traveler" (CYSC 210). His contemporary was Lu Chih (1234–1300), one of the

---

*Sunny/Southern Pass, established during the Han dynasty, which lay to the south of Jade Gate Pass (Yü-men kuan) and led to the harsh deserts of Central Asia; this line is probably an allusion to a very famous verse by the T'ang poet Wang Wei: "Once you go out of the Yang Kuan to the west, there are no more old friends."

poets mentioned in the preface to *Yang-ch'un pai-hsüeh*. Lu wrote in both the heroic and the elegant styles, though most classify him among the practitioners of the latter. For themes, he tends toward landscapes and escapism, but in a way that is contemplative rather than remonstrative. His exchanges with Chu Lien-hsiu, a courtesan, are affectionate, demonstrating the gentle character one perceives behind his verse.

Tseng Jui (fl. 1294) moved to Hangchow and spent his life there as an eccentric, living on the gifts of local notables. He was a talented painter and wrote a play that is still extant. The collection of his verse has been lost, but ninety-five songs and seventeen sets survive in other Yüan anthologies. Many poets wrote in disdain of the public life, but perhaps none from so genuine a position as Tseng Jui nor so well: "The talent of an age, / Great plans of state; / All useless. / . . . If there is one who can leap out of the struggle . . . , / To him is a name that lives forever" (*CYSC* 472). Tseng Jui is certainly one of the most interesting among the lesser poets.

T'ang Shih, who lived at the end of the Yüan and into the Ming, is not frequently considered among the major writers of *san-ch'ü*, but his corpus of songs is larger than those of any others but Chang K'o-chiu and Ch'iao Chi. His works display a mastery of style to match a variety of themes. These include many satirical pieces as well as some very effective love songs and pensive poems. It was suggested that the comments in his poem on West Lake might be read as censure of society, but his treatment makes it also a work of deep personal feeling. Among his most sensitive are four poems titled "Tao ling nü" (Mourning the Death of an Actress; *CYSC* 1580–1581). He is another of the minor poets well worth our attention.

Wang Yüan-heng (fl. 1354), another poet who lived late in the Yüan, was fond of writing what one might call a "song series," that is, the same tune repeated many times, perhaps twenty or more, all to the same theme and often, but not necessarily, with a single refrain. His "Ching shih" (Cautionary Verses) are a good example of this and are superior poems as well; the refrain at the end is used skillfully both for humor and for the thoughtful message that underlies these verses (*CYSC* 1377–1380).

Besides Kuan Yün-shih, who is the best-known among the non-Han writers, there were many others, such as Hsieh Ang-fu (fl. 1302), like Kuan of Uyghur origin; Ah-li Hsi-ying (fl. 1320) and Hsien-yü Pi-jen (fl. 1323), both from the western reaches of the empire; Ah-lu Wei (fl. 1302), a Mongol; and Pu-hu-mu (1255–1300), from the K'ang-li people, whose homeland was to the west of the Urals and north of the Caspian Sea. Ah-li Hsi-ying wrote three songs on the carefree life in his "Lan yün wo" (Lazy Cloud Grotto), which were very popular and prompted many responses in the same verse form using the same rhymes (*CYSC* 339). Hsieh Ang-fu, the most notable of this group, was an excellent writer, some think better than Kuan Yün-shih; he left sixty-five songs and three sets, wrote *shih* as well, and was an acquaintance of Sa-tu-la (Sadula), one of the better *shih* poets of the Yüan (see chapter 18). He has a series of twenty-two songs of the world-weary type, some alluding to historical personages, some to the trials of holding office, and so on, which give scope to a certain wit and irony (*CYSC* 704–707).

Among the women of the brothels and the performance troupes there must have been good writers. Unfortunately, few examples of their verse have been preserved. There is one song and one song set by Chu Lien-hsiu (fl. 1279), the famous singer and acquaintance of Lu Chih; several poets, including Kuan Han-ch'ing and Hu Chih-yü (1227–1293), dedicated poems to her (*CYSC* 354–355). There is also one song each by Liu P'o-hsi (fl. 1360) and Yi Fen-erh (fl. 1368) that has survived (*CYSC* 1412, 1409). Chen Shih (née Chen; dates unknown) complained of her life and probably spoke for other prostitutes when she wrote, "Before others I pretend, but by myself I shed a thousand tears" (CYSC 1144). This song is not in the usual anthologies, but was preserved by T'ao Tsung-yi in his notes on the times. Wang Shih, of whom we know nothing, wrote a song set "Chi ch'ing-jen" (To My Beloved); though it alludes to the Su Ch'ing story, the unpretentious language and use of extra syllables in the lines give a sense of sincerity to her writing that is very moving. It was much admired, and there were versions of it in several of the anthologies (CYSC 1274–1276).

There are dozens of noteworthy minor poets in this genre. The poems of Liu Ping-chung (1211–1274) and Hu Chih-yü are good examples of the genre as a casual pursuit in its earlier stages. Although the *san-ch'ü* never entirely lost this nonchalant quality, the anthologies of Yang Chao-ying and the work of Chou Te-ch'ing, both writers of *san-ch'ü* themselves, went far toward setting trends, especially in the south, where at the turn of the fourteenth century the songs of the Central Plain were a novelty. Despite the "enlarged scope of themes" that some writers brought to the *san-ch'ü*, much of the verse betrayed few concerns in the world other than a young maiden's thoughts in her boudoir and appeared to indicate that a versifier had only to ring the changes on the time-honored formulas to satisfy his audience. But it is hardly fair to judge these pieces against the high literature. High literary standards were probably not the prime consideration for most songwriters in the Yüan, as is true even now. Certainly this did not prevent excellence, but it was of a distinct kind with its own standards. It is important to remember that the ability of a modern audience to grasp certain verses and not others is a question of the modern cultural context; *san-ch'ü* should be considered in the context of the era in which it was written.

This is not, of course, to say that *san-ch'ü* immediately and irrevocably perished at the close of the Yüan dynasty. Although the genre did suffer a decline at the beginning of the Ming dynasty, this was part of the general literary and cultural malaise of the times (see chapters 18–20). During the fifteenth century, *san-ch'ü* experienced a revival of sorts through its association with the Archaist movement of men like Li Meng-yang (1475–1529), K'ang Hai (1475–1541), Wang

Chiu-ssu (1468–1551), and Li K'ai-hsien. Perhaps the greatest Ming period advocate and practitioner of *san-ch'ü* was Feng Wei-min (1511–1578?). In his hands, however, this lighthearted, personal verse underwent what has been called a process of Confucianization, making it more serious and society-oriented. Since little is heard of *san-ch'ü* after the sixteenth century, it would appear that its essential spirit—so in keeping with the *Zeitgeist* of the Yüan—had indeed finally been exhausted.

Wayne Schlepp

Chapter 18

MONGOL-YÜAN CLASSICAL VERSE (*SHIH*)

The classical verse (*shih*) of the Mongol Yüan era (1260–1368) is one of the least-studied areas of Chinese literary history and, as such, is virtually unknown today. In fact, Yüan *shih* seems to have enjoyed a period of high esteem only during the Ch'ing dynasty, from about 1690 until the end of the nineteenth century. It was between 1664 and 1720 that the four collections (*chi*) of Ku Ssu-li's (1665–1722) *Yüan-shih hsüan* (Anthology of Yüan Verse) appeared, with a supplementary (*kuei*) collection published after Ku's death during the reign of the Chia-ch'ing emperor (1796–1820). This four-part collection is the single most important source for the study of Yüan *shih*, without which the works of many a Yüan *shih* poet would have been lost. However, the *Anthology of Yüan Verse* was not itself an accident of literary history but the inevitable product both of the general trends of *shih* development during the Ming and early Ch'ing eras and of the historical and political views of Ku's own age. It was a product of literary and political culture. The age that produced it, the mid-Ch'ing, was intensely concerned with legitimacy and orthodoxy, and Yüan *shih* poetry provided an important ingredient in the constitution of both.

The Manchus, inaugurating another era of non-Chinese rule, looked to the Mongols for precedents to enhance the legitimacy of their own rule, and Chinese scholar-officials looked to the Yüan for precedents to help rationalize life under the Manchus. As part of this joint effort, Ku's *Anthology of Yüan Verse* can be viewed as a monumental attempt to prove that Chinese high culture flourished during the Yüan and, similarly, could do so again under the Manchus. After it appeared, the *Anthology of Yüan Verse* was widely read, and it remained a popular work throughout the rest of the eighteenth century, stimulating several smaller, more compact anthologies of Yüan verse, and Yüan *shih* for a time enjoyed a popularity that it had never known since its own time. However, with the growth of anti-Manchu sentiment during the period of dynastic decline in the nineteenth and early twentieth centuries, all attempts to justify Manchu rule in terms of Mongol precedents became unpleasant for the Manchus and superfluous for the Chinese: the Manchus found any comparison between their rule and the short-lived Yüan odious; and the Chinese, reformers and revolutionaries alike, ignored the Yüan and looked for inspiration to earlier periods of native Chinese rule, especially the Ming (1368–1644), which had crushed the Mongols and driven them out of China. The distortions and oversimplifications of the Chinese literary tradition that resulted from the polemics of the vernacular literary movement (*pai-hua yün-tung*) after 1919 (see chapters 32 and 39) also helped to bury Yüan *shih* poetry, along with most other *shih* poetry written after the T'ang. Only the verse of a few Sung era poets was spared condemnation as "lifeless imitation" in a relentless harangue against supposedly effete literati writing "divorced from the people." In such a context, Yüan *shih* had no historical or cultural role to play, and the utter eclipse of interest in it by the 1920s and 1930s was inevitable.

The history of interest in Yüan classical verse can also be explained in different terms: as a course shaped by intrinsic literary forces within the tradition of *shih* poetry itself. Most of the Ming era was dominated by the theory and practice of archaism (*fu-ku*), which devalued any *shih* composed after the T'ang era, whether it was from the Sung or the Yüan (curiously anticipating the conclusions of the vernacular literature polemicists of the twentieth century, but for very different reasons), and most archaist critics, if they looked at Sung and Yüan verse at all, judged it solely in terms of how it succeeded or failed to equal the work of the T'ang masters. When this view was challenged toward the end of the Ming by anti-archaists such as the Yüan brothers from Kung-an in Hupei province—in particular Yüan Hung-tao (1568–1610), who condemned the slavish imitation of T'ang poets and what he saw as a lack of real expression and individuality in poetry written by archaists—attention began to be focused on Sung-era poetry (and that of the mid-T'ang poet Po Chü-yi, who anticipated much of the Sung style) that exhibited different features, among which the casual, offhand atmosphere, loose narrative structure, prosy description of everyday life, and explicit and easily accessible diction contrast sharply with the articulation of intense moments of insight and sensibility and the dense, elliptical, and connotative diction often associated with the T'ang "style." The Kung-an school was very fond of Sung *shih*, especially that of Su Shih (1037–1101), and it is likely that the appearance of several anthologies of Sung and Yüan *shih* during the late Ming can be attributed to the influence of the literary circle revolving around the Yüan brothers. This circle and the anthologies generated by it did not distinguish between Sung and Yüan *shih* but simply, and erroneously, viewed the Yüan as a continuation of the Sung. Nevertheless, the Kung-an school helped to emancipate Yüan verse from almost total obscurity and stimulate the more sophisticated critical attention addressed to it during the Ch'ing era that followed.

With the appearance in 1671 of Wu Chih-chen's (1640–1717) immensely popular and influential anthology of Sung poetry, the *Sung-shih ch'ao*, many poets began to emulate Sung instead of T'ang models, and attitudes toward the entire earlier tradition of verse became more pliant. At the same time, interest in Yüan *shih* began to increase, now not in terms of the erroneous view that it was simply an extension of that of the Sung but in a context of the new realization that Yüan *shih*, in both technique and spirit, was very close to the *shih* of the T'ang masters. The Ming archaists knew this, but their total commitment to the T'ang allowed them to admit only that Yüan *shih* was more "orthodox" (*cheng*) than that of the Sung; this marked the limit of their interest in it. Of them, only Hu Ying-lin (1551–1602) devoted much critical attention to Yüan *shih*, which he praised for having reversed the pernicious tendency of Sung poets to depart from the correct path established by the T'ang masters. However, Hu was not really a champion of Yüan *shih*, since he regarded it—"orthodox" though it may have been—as decidedly inferior to the *shih* of the T'ang itself. But, whatever its failings, it was in his view superior to that of the Sung, which he dismissed categorically as nothing more than "rhymed prose."

Critics of the seventeenth century took a much closer look at Yüan *shih* than did the Ming archaists, Hu Ying-lin included. What they saw convinced them that a revival of Yüan *shih* was in order, both to combat the growing interest in Sung verse, which the *Sung-shih ch'ao* was generating, and to revitalize current poetic practice: the study of Yüan *shih* could help to recover the best features of T'ang verse. In a preface he wrote to the *Anthology of Yüan Verse*, Sung Lo (1634–1713), one of the major poets and critics of the seventeenth century, had this to say:

> In my opinion, poetry in this present age has reached a juncture where it must undergo a change. It must change by going back to the T'ang. It must also change by keeping up with the flow, that is, by going back to the Yüan.

Ku Ssu-li was more explicit:

> The great flow of the tradition of poetry has its source in two ancestors: the "Feng" [Airs; in *Shih-ching* (Classic of Poetry)] and "[Li] sao" [Encountering Sorrow, in *Ch'u tzu* (Elegies of Ch'u)]. Poets who came after the composers of the [Li sao] went through successive transformations. For example, pentasyllabic verse reached its apogee with the T'ang, and

> its transformations went as far as they could go with the Sung. By the time it came down to the Yüan, since *shih* had exhausted all the possibilities open to it, it turned away from what the Sung had done and returned to the T'ang, and, at this, all possible variations were complete with it.

Although little attention is paid to Yüan *shih* nowadays, this neglect would have struck eighteenth-century writers and editors as decidedly odd and thoroughly unjustified. It is significant that the compilers of the *Ssu-k'u ch'üan-shu tsung-mu t'i-yao* (Annotated General Catalog of the Complete Library of the Four Treasuries), first published in 1782, devote almost two hundred pages to critiques of 170 individual collections of Yüan *shih* poets. Many of these poets are well worth reading, for real gems can be found among their works.

Yüan *shih* pursued trends that already existed at the end of the Sung, most of which were related to T'ang verse in one way or another; but some actually harked back to other periods, including the Sung. Yüan Hao-wen (1190–1257), who lived his younger years under the Chin dynasty, is usually thought of as the first significant Yüan *shih* poet, and he wrote verse in the grand, individualistic manner of Su Shih, from whom he obviously derived much inspiration and whose amateur scholar/literati (*wen-jen*) ideals he clearly shared. Hao Ching (1223–1275), Wang Yün (1236–1304), and Liu Yin (1247–1293) acknowledged Yüan Hao-wen as their teacher and continued his tradition of verse into the later thirteenth century—a "northeastern" tradition that emphasized straightforward and intense personal expressionism and an exalted Confucian idealism—though Liu generally stayed closer to High T'ang models. Yüan verse in the southeast, in the early period after the Mongol conquest of the south, begins with Chao Meng-fu (1254–1322), a descendant of the Sung imperial family who agonized over his decision to serve the Yüan court. Chao is also famous as a painter and is considered the best calligrapher of the entire Yüan era. He rejected the innovations of Sung *shih* and emulated the High T'ang style so well that he was thought by his contemporaries to have equaled the very best poets of that era. Chao is often grouped with several other poets of the first quarter of the fourteenth century: Yüan Chüeh (1267–1327), Teng Wen-yüan (dates unknown), Kung K'uei (1268–1329), Yü Chi (1272–1348), Yang Tsai (1271–1323), Fan P'eng (1272–1330), Chieh Hsi-ssu (1274–1344), and, slightly later, Ma Tsu-ch'ang (1279–1338) and the two brothers Sung Pen (1281–1334) and Sung Chiung (1294–1346) for their common interest in emulating the T'ang, for their success in representing the one brief age of stability and relative prosperity during the entire Yüan, and for their excellence as poets endowed with sublime sensitivity and insight and the highest powers of articulation. Thus they are considered the great classic poets of the Yüan era, though sometimes Liu Yin and Yü Chi are singled out as the very best of them. Some poets tried to continue this classic tradition based on the T'ang masters in later years, the most creative of whom were Ch'en Lü (1288–1343), Li Hsiao-kuang (1296–1348), Chang Chu (1287–1367), and Chang Hsien, who lived into the early Ming.

Another group of poets from Kiangsu and Chekiang in the southeast—Sung Wu (1260–1340), Ch'eng T'ing-kuei (fl. c. 1338), and Ch'en Ch'iao (1278–1365)—were close students of the *shih* of the Six Dynasties era (220–589). They tried to discover the fundamental principles that the T'ang masters—especially those of the late T'ang—had derived from the work of Six Dynasties poets in order to employ them in their own *shih*. The results are often quite engaging, for they excelled at transforming common expressions into startling and animated passages. Like many Yüan *shih* poets, Sung emulated Li Ho and Wen T'ing-yün; Ch'eng is noted for the forceful beauty (*ch'iu-li*) he achieved in his septasyllabic ancient-style verse; and Ch'en strove for a mysterious voluptuousness (*yu-yen*) after the manner of Wen T'ing-yün.

Many *shih* poets of the Yüan are of such singular character that they defy all attempts at classification, except that their extraordinary individual talents and success at bringing off unusual effects seem to give them a kind of group identity. Ku Ssu-li collectively characterizes their *shih* as "aiming at the unusual yet striving for the utmost grace" (*piao ch'i ching hsiu*) and observes that "the demonic transformations over which they have natural control" (*k'ai-ho pien-kuai*) can so "shock the sight and hearing that they defy comprehension." Here we find the sinicized Uyghur Kuan Yün-shih (Sewinch Qaya; 1286–1324) and Feng Tzu-chen (1257–1327?) (both now better known as *san-ch'ü* poets), Ch'en Fu (1240–1303), the sinicized Mongol Sa-tu-la (b. 1308), Wu Lai (1301–1341; teacher of the prominent early Ming Neo-Confucian and writer Sung Lien [1310–1381], who edited his works), and, most important, the late Yüan poet Yang Wei-chen (1296–1370). Yang is known for his success at emulating the ancient ballad form (*yüeh-fu*) of the Han and Wei eras and for his brilliant adaptations of the styles of the T'ang poets Tu Fu, Li Po, Li Ho, and Wen T'ing-yün. Yang had hundreds of followers, the most important of whom were Chang Hsien (mentioned above), Yüan K'ai, and Yang Chi (all active during the last years of Yüan rule and the early Ming). Yang Wei-chen's sobriquet (*hao*) was T'ieh-ya (Iron Cliff), so his followers constituted a tradition of poetry called the "iron style" (*t'ieh-t'i*). The main stream of the early Ming *shih* that followed in the next generation was initially a reaction against this kind of "heterodox" verse, which early Ming archaist critics (i.e., champions of the High T'ang such as Kao Ping [1350–1423]) often characterized as "extravagant and decadent," "reckless with the rules," and too "bitingly sarcastic."

Not many significant *shih* poets of the late Yüan worked outside Yang Wei-chen's tradition, and the few who did were almost all well-known painters of the day—fully realized literati in avocation. Foremost among them was Ni Tsan (1301–1374), whose verse, often inscribed to enhance the overall esthetic effect of his paintings, has been favorably compared to the landscape verse of Wei Ying-wu (737–792). Other painter-poets (see chapter 25) include K'o Chiu-ssu (1290–1343), to whose collected verse Yü Chi and Ch'en Lü wrote prefaces; Wang Mien (1287–1359; the mysterious hermit-hero of the opening chapter of the mid-eighteenth-century novel *Ju-lin wai-shih* [The Scholars], on which see chapter 35), whose verse reveals a highly individual and unrestrained expressiveness, worlds apart from the exquisite craft of Yang Wei-chen; and Ku Ssu-li's ancestor, Ku Ying (1310–1369), who made a fortune in his youth as a merchant, then retired from business to pursue a life devoted to learning, art collecting, and the patronage of painters and poets (including Yang Wei-chen and Ni Tsan). Ku retired to an elegant country retreat in Kiangsu province, where he cultivated his own painting, calligraphy, and poetry, all of which was highly regarded by critics and connoisseurs in his own day. His *shih* largely emulated the style of Li Ho.

So-called commoner poetry (*pu-yi shih*), a significant literary phenomenon that first arose along with poetry societies (*shih-she*, *yin-shih-she*, or *yin-she*) in the Southern Sung era, continued to thrive throughout the Yüan. The suspension of the civil service examinations until 1315 effectively frustrated most attempts by members of the scholar-official class to attain government office for generations. This had many important repercussions for Chinese society as a whole, but, particularly germane for our purposes here, it meant that—with the blurring of traditional cultural distinctions between degree and non–degree holders—membership in poetry societies often included poets from a wide variety of social backgrounds: Sung loyalists who had served in high office during the prior regime; mid-career officials, both those who served the new government and those who refused office; younger scholars who now pursued different careers as teachers in private and public local academies; rural landowners; and urban merchants who had strong interests in high literati culture, among others. As such, the poetry society under the Yüan became a significant civil institution that helped to maintain the fabric of intellectual culture in the absence of official patronage of the educational-scholarly establishment once connected with the now-defunct examination system. One such society, the Yüeh-ch'üan yin-she (Moon Spring Poetry Society), whose center was a local school, the Moon Spring Academy, in P'u-chiang, Chekiang province, is well documented, thanks to surviving records of a poetry competition that it held in 1286–1287. Such records and the publication during the Yüan of several poetry composition manuals, designed for a popular but highly literate audience, combine to suggest that a trend begun under the Sung still continued and even intensified during the Yüan: the writing and appreciation of classical verse (*shih*) was spreading throughout all literate sections of Chinese society and could no longer be considered an activity associated exclusively with a scholar-official elite. In fact, a case can be made that the *shih* was probably the main vehicle for literary expression for most writers during the Yüan—and not the newly developed drama (*tsa-chü*), dramatic lyrics (*san-ch'ü*), or vernacular fiction (*hsiao-shuo*) for which the period is famous—the conventional view of most modern literary histories of China. However, although an enormous amount of creative energy was undoubtedly poured into the *shih* of Yüan times, it remains to be seen whether enough quality resulted to justify a major reappraisal of the literature of this era.

Richard John Lynn

Chapter 19

POETRY OF THE FOURTEENTH CENTURY

The fourteenth century marks the end of alien rule under the Mongol Yüan dynasty and the reinstitution of Chinese rule under the Ming dynasty. In terms of poetry, it is very much a period of transition. Three closely related tendencies are noteworthy. First, the proliferation of poetry writing, especially among urban nonofficials, which was already in evidence in the Southern Sung and early Yüan, becomes more pronounced during the period. Second, the development of the idea of the *wen-jen* as an "independent artist," free of political responsibility, devoted to literature and art, and often unfettered by societal convention, comes to the fore. Third, the use of poetic models of the past, which was to become so much a defining feature (indeed, obsession) of poetry later in the Ming, and throughout the Ch'ing dynasty as well, is established in this period.

As viewed by later ages, the poetry of the fourteenth century was something very much "in between," as shown by the contrasting, contradictory labels applied to it. The century's poetry was said to retrieve the best features of T'ang poetry, or to be an extension of Sung poetry; to be the poetry of an alien dynasty, or to prove how Chinese culture could survive and flourish under non-Chinese rule; to be a key to the "truth" of the heart of earlier Chinese poetry, or part of the confining baggage of later "antiquarian" archaists. The poetry of the period was to become far more important for the polemical uses to which it could be put than for any value it might have in its own right. A cursory awareness of these competing interpretations is helpful for understanding developments in

Chinese poetry of the remaining five centuries of the imperial period, until 1911. In all these senses, the poetry of the fourteenth century represents an in-between stage.

The Yüan dynasty of the Mongols is more famous for the development of drama (chapter 41) and of *ch'ü* popular song (chapter 17) than it is for *shih* (standard, traditional) poetry, the subject of this chapter. During most of the twentieth century, the comparatively new genres of the Yüan period, drama and *ch'ü* song, were accorded far more attention than was traditional poetry. This new interest was prompted in part by the literary revolution, the post-1918 cultural and political movement that promoted the use of vernacular Chinese as a written language in place of the classical language, which, although far removed from the spoken language, was still considered the only serious medium of written expression. (It is as if as late as 1900 Latin had still been considered the only serious written medium in Italy, and a movement to promote "Italian" as the written language emerged only in recent times.) In reaction to the neglect that drama and *ch'ü* song were earlier accorded (having been tainted by their "low" vernacular language and "low" social origins), the undeniable literary importance and value of these genres were discovered and touted. As a consequence, the study and appreciation of traditional poetry of the fourteenth and later centuries have been slighted. Although an understanding of the developments in the newer genres is important, and in the vernacular short story and novel as well, one should keep in mind that classical Chinese poetry and classical Chinese prose were nearly always considered more important and more central by writers of the time when they were written, even by vernacular-language writers. (This is true for the entire Yüan–Ming–Ch'ing period.) Although the argument has been made that the newer genres reflect the changed social realities of the period, the counterargument has also been made that traditional poetry does so even more. In either case, much of the poetry is of high quality. Very little of it has been studied in detail.

TOWNSMAN POETRY

Chinese poetry had long been monopolized by officials: would-be, current, and former officials. The development of poetry among nonofficials, specifically those living in the urban centers that were burgeoning so remarkably in the Sung, is a distinguishing feature of the latter part of the dynasty. The suspension of the examination system under the Mongols (notwithstanding its reinstatement in 1315), while cutting off that route to an official career as a bureaucrat, accentuated the tendency (already operative) for poetry to be written by a broad stratum of what might be called "townsmen": namely, commoners (those "dressed in white"), such as shopkeepers, merchants, and landlords. The unhappy circumstances that China for the first time was completely under an alien regime also fueled the *wen-jen* ideal of the "independent artist," gave crucial impetus to the development of vernacular song (*ch'ü*), and spurred interest in drama, a genre that had already been developing under the previous dynasty.

Two groups of poets of the first half of the thirteenth century, the Four Lings of Yung-chia (Yung-chia ssu Ling) and the Chiang-hu, or River and Lakes school poets, had all been ordinary nonofficials. (They were minor poets who imitated the minor verse of the late T'ang that was descriptive of everyday life.) Poetry-writing societies proliferated in the thirteenth century, especially in South China. (It is as if the Lions Clubs and Kiwanis Clubs of countless American communities had been organized for the purpose of writing poetry, while serving as a mechanism of social intercourse for such "townsmen.") The compilation of four important poetry-writing manuals—"how-to" books—between 1240 and 1300 reflects the proliferation of poetry-writing among a broader social stratum. The full flowering of poetry-writing societies took place in the first half of the fourteenth century. By midcentury, the number of societies was enormous, as attested to by references in the prose writings of the senior figure of many poetry-writing societies, Yang Wei-chen.

THE *WEN-JEN* IDEAL

An eccentric figure, Yang Wei-chen illustrates how the burgeoning of poetry-writing among nonofficials was intertwined with the development of the *wen-jen* ideal, which was to prove central to the later history of the arts in China.

In the Northern Sung, the ideal of the tripartite unity of literature, philosophy, and political affairs reached its zenith in figures like Ou-yang Hsiu, Wang An-shih, and Su Shih, who were outstanding in all three areas. The ideal continued into the Southern Sung; "commoner"-poets such as those of the Chiang-hu school were an exception. Under Mongol rule, the concept was undermined; earlier tendencies away from such unity intensified, and many Chinese retreated into their respective worlds. Yang Wei-chen and others, like the famous painter Ni Tsan, had no ties to philosophy or statecraft. Instead, they made their lives as artists supreme, divorced from politics and manifesting varying degrees of eccentricity or deviation from accepted norms. Society of the time accorded them respect. And their elevation of literature or art, which was new to Chinese society (where, if anything, literature had been viewed as *less important* than statecraft and philosophy), became a pattern. The *wen-jen* ideal also carried the expectation of simultaneous proficiency, at least to some degree, in poetry-writing, painting, and calligraphy. (The literary dimension of this ideal has generally not received the attention it deserves in later Chinese art history.)

YANG WEI-CHEN

Yang Wei-chen (1296–1370) is the most prominent "townsman poet" of the age. His character as a poet of the ordinary citizen is partly reflected in poems he presented to such diverse individuals as a fortuneteller, a physiognomist, the blacksmith who cast his beloved iron flute, a writing brush craftsman, a physician, and a cauterizer. It is also seen in prose pieces that he gave to a female storyteller, a puppeteer, and a comb-maker.

Dressed in unusual garb, his iron flute always to hand, Yang Wei-chen traveled back and forth throughout the lower Yangtze area, visiting the various poetry societies that he headed. His lifestyle of at least superficial eccentricity was consistent with the *wen-jen* ideal that was developing, one insistent on the special place of the artist and his work. Displaying skill in more than one art form, Yang wrote in a truly eccentric calligraphic style and showed immense interest in painting, writing many poems on paintings. Equally, his poetry went off in an unfettered direction—one rich in imagination and beautiful in language—being modeled on verse that had been largely ignored since Northern Sung times: *yüeh-fu* ballads of the Han and Six Dynasties, and the late T'ang poetry of Li Ho, Li Shang-yin, and Han Wo.

Yang Wei-chen's collection of more than four hundred *yüeh-fu* ballads appeared when he was fifty. With their imaginative evocations of mythic moments set in a narrative frame, many are intensely lyrical. But his boldest work appeared when he was past seventy. Many treat the theme of a young woman's sensuality. The following poem, the second in a series entitled "Hsü lien chi erh-shih yung" (Twenty Supplementary Toilette Box Songs), is called "Ch'eng p'ei" (Mating):

> Eyebrow mounds dark, facing the spluttering lamp,
> Her billowy half-bun spills over pillow's edge.
> Arms and legs joined with another's, fetchingly about to sob,
> She grasps the fine silk, nearly kneading it to pieces.

Such poems illustrate a lack of restraint that reflects how townsman poetry had grown from its origins, when it was confined to descriptions of the ordinary and everyday.

Yang Wei-chen wrote series of poems on history, women, immortals, filial piety, and other diverse topics. As a poet so indebted to ninth-century models that were considered decadent, Yang was himself criticized for being a "literary devil" (*wen-yao*) by his contemporary, Wang Wei (1323–1374). Nonetheless, he was very popular in his own time; in his work and in his persona he seems to have united a combination of traits that were greatly favored. Invited to serve the founding emperor of the new Ming dynasty, the poet at his audience jocularly declined, reciting poetic lines of his own to the effect that he was an old lady who had already served one master. Treated with uncharacteristic indulgence by the cruel founder-emperor, Yang Wei-chen was allowed to return home in the white clothes of a nonofficial.

There are parallels in the life of Yang's friend, the immensely famous painter Ni Tsan (1301–1374): a consciously eccentric lifestyle, versatility in poetry and calligraphy as well as painting, and a poetry that (although more understated than Yang's) includes mildly erotic folksong themes.

LATE YÜAN POETRY BY OFFICIALS

In the first half of the fourteenth century, poetry in the Yüan capital of Peking was dominated by former southerners who came to serve in the Han-lin Academy and History Bureau. Notwithstanding Khubilai Khan's (Qubilai; 1215–1294; r. 1260–1294) extraordinary magnanimity, there had been initial reluctance to serve the Mongol regime, which was both new and alien. Chao Meng-fu (1254–1322), who in 1286 arrived in the capital to serve (a quarter-century after the founding of the dynasty in 1260), was considered a turncoat for working for the new regime, especially because he was a distant relative of the imperial Chao family of the Sung rulers. But as the situation of Mongol rule became normalized, such reluctance and the attendant stigma lessened.

Yüan Chüeh (1267–1327) arrived in Peking about fifteen years after Chao Meng-fu, at the turn of the fourteenth century. And Yü Chi (1272–1348), another transplanted southerner, was the most trusted Yüan government official for more than a quarter of a century, until 1329. What distinguishes both is the way they, like many Sung poets, treated previously unused subject matter from contemporary life in their verse, but in a style and diction that were more akin to those of High T'ang poetry.

For example, Yüan Chüeh wrote a marvelous series of old-style poems entitled "Chou chung tsa yung" (Shipboard Songs) describing his trip to Peking by boat. It tells of products and scenes he was seeing for the first time, such as the white reeds on the water's surface that served as the capital's fuel source. Similarly, Yü Chi could write of a visit to his hatmaker, who, like the fisherman or woodcutter of earlier poetry, is depicted as embodying Taoist ideals that put the author to shame. The subject matter in each case—the capital's fuel source, a master hatter—had been previously untreated. Thus, like *tsa-chü* drama earlier in the dynasty, the poems tell us something of the life of the age. But in terms of diction and style, they are different from the poetry of Yang Wei-chen. Using only models from earlier periods of T'ang poetry, these poet-officials in the north were more restrained and conservative than their contemporaries in the south, who wrote in the late T'ang style. In terms of the poetic models they emulated, Yüan Chüeh and Yü Chi had taken the next logical step.

LITERARY MODELS

Like Chinese painters who emulate the style of an earlier master and make it their own by melding themselves into it, eventually developing a related style (or aspect of style) of their own *from* or *out of* the earlier model, Chinese poets would train themselves by imitating earlier poetry. The literary models that were used by townsman-poets and poet-officials shifted over time from the rather stiff, rationalistic poetry of the Northern Sung to T'ang verse that dealt with minor descriptions of daily life. The use of models from the central core of T'ang poetry, that of the High T'ang (associated with Tu Fu, Li Po, and others), was the next step. It was taken by Yü Chi and other late Yüan Han-lin Academy poet-officials. Once they started the practice of using the "heart" of T'ang poetry as a model—a practice also followed in part by Kao Ch'i (1336–1374), a generation their junior—it intensified during the subsequent Ming dynasty.

An important development in literary criticism around the end of the century was to contribute to the practice. In 1393 Kao Ping completed his *T'ang-shih p'in-hui* (Graded Collocation of T'ang Poetry), a work that was to fix T'ang dynasty poetry in period categories that have been used to this day: Early, High, Middle, and Late. Poetry of the fourteenth century was mostly influenced by Late T'ang models, but by the century's end, interest had shifted to the Early and High T'ang periods (as well as earlier *yüeh-fu* ballads). This set the stage for the exclusive use of High T'ang models later in the Ming dynasty.

KAO CH'I

Kao Ch'i is considered the greatest poet not only of the fourteenth century but also of the entire Ming dynasty (1368–1644). This is ironic, because he lived only six years into the Ming period, being executed in his thirties on trumped-up charges brought by the dynasty's founder-emperor; his only extant portrait depicts him wearing the court robes of the new dynasty.

Born and raised in Soochow, Kao Ch'i had a circle of youthful friends called the "Ten Friends near the Northern City-wall" (Pei-kuo shih-yu) or "Ten Talented Ones" (Shih ts'ai-tzu). They included the future poet, painter, and official Hsü Pen; the monk Tao-yen, better known as the prominent official Yao Kuang-hsiao; and the writers Chang Yü and Yang Chi. Their mixed social origins are reflected in one of their number, Wang Hsing, whose father was a seller of Chinese medicines.

Kao Ch'i enjoyed early success as a poet. While young, he married into a prominent family. In his early twenties, he spent the better part of two years traveling in South China on vague business, presumably in search of a patron; it probably was part of maneuvering on his part to avoid too direct association with the region's warlord. Many of his poems of this and other periods speak of an inexplicable melancholy.

Within two years of the fall of Soochow in 1367 to Chu Yüan-chang, the founder-emperor of the Ming, Kao Ch'i was summoned to the early Ming capital at Nanking. Already famous as a writer, he was appointed to the board of sixteen compilers of the *Yüan shih* (History of the Yüan Dynasty). Under the direction of Sung Lien (1310–1381), the work was completed by the end of 1369. A year later Kao Ch'i was granted permission to retire to his native Soochow, where he remained in semiretirement until 1374. Charged with treason for having praised acts of the local prefect that were deemed lèse-majesté, he was executed (sliced in half) along with the prefect and Kao's fellow Yüan-history compiler, Wang Wei.

As a poet, Kao Ch'i illustrates some of the tendencies noted for the century as a whole. For example, he took one step further the tendency of the townsman-poet Yang Wei-chen to give extraordinary flights of mental fancy to his poetry. This is evident in Kao's "signature poem" written when he was twenty-two, "Ch'ing-ch'iu-tzu ko" (Song of the Green Hill Master), wherein he refers to himself by the name of his in-laws' manor; "Green Hill" also had latent exotic associations. The poem opens with Kao referring to himself as "The Green Hill Master / Thin but clean"; the witty, self-deprecatory tone of the second line might be better rendered as "Skinny but squeaky clean" or "Threadbare but well laundered." Kao proceeds to speak of himself as someone from the heavens above who, like the poet Li Po, has been banished to this world. And in reference to his own writing, he says: "Among the Eight Extremes indistinct, his mental wits do roam, / And cause the formless to fashion sound." Kao Ch'i is said to mark the culmination of the preceding century and a half of townsman poetry. But whereas Yang Wei-chen and others dressed up their language with elements from Li Po and the Late T'ang poet Li Ho, Kao integrated these influences better, taking them to a new level. As one of his contemporaries (Wang Wei) wrote: "Kao Ch'i's poetry, in its superb abandon and poetic beauty, is like a hawk soaring through autumn skies. Performing a hundred twisting maneuvers, even if summoned, it will not descend."

Kao Ch'i was a master of many styles. And, by Ming times, there was a wide selection of poetic genres for him and others to emulate: *yüeh-fu* ballads, *sao*-style verse in the manner of *Ch'u tz'u* (Elegies of Ch'u), *shih* poetry of different periods, *tz'u* song-poetry, *ch'ü* arias, and so on, not to mention variations within these. There were, as well, many past poetic greats who could serve as models. What distinguished Kao Ch'i was his creative mastery of many such styles and models. It is one reason why—along with Yüan Hao-wen (1190–1257), Wang Shih-chen (1634–1711; to be distinguished from the sixteenth-century author with a similar name who lived from 1526 to 1590), and Yüan Mei (1716–1797)—he is counted among the giants of later, post-Sung Chinese poetry. (The circumstances of Kao's early death doubtless also contributed to his almost universally high reputation both as a person and as a poet.)

Kao Ch'i shares with the aforementioned greats a place in the history of literary theory. He argued that poetry must have *ko* (framework), *yi* (meaning), and *ch'ü* (atmosphere). These terms were to have their respective analogs in phrases made more famous by later critical theorists: *ko-tiao* (formal style) by Shen Te-ch'ien (1673–1769), *hsing-ling* (native sensibility) by Yüan Mei, and *shen-yün* (ineffable personal tone or flavor) by Wang Shih-chen.

Notwithstanding Kao Ch'i's protean mastery of a variety of styles, his own contemporaries discerned preferences that foreshadow those of later Ming archaists. One contemporary (Li Chih-kuang) spoke of how the poet surveyed the earlier tradition, from the Chien-an period (196–219) to the High T'ang, and ignored later T'ang and Sung poetry. Another contemporary, Chang Yü (1283–1356+), put a similar view into verse, in the first of a three-poem series entitled "Tiao Kao Ch'ing-ch'iu" (Lamenting Kao Ch'i):

> His was the will of a lifetime, and to what end?
> Deprived of salary, deprived of land—most tragic!
> Yet he may rest on fame inextinguishable—
> Ballads in the style of Han and poems à la High T'ang.

The old phraseology (*ku-wen-tz'u*) archaist movement, which developed during the middle years of the Ming and came to dominate the dynasty's poetry, initially focused on precisely these parts of the poetic tradition (see chapter 20). Hence, along with Yü Chi, Kao Ch'i is a forerunner of Ming archaism.

FIN DE SIÈCLE

Much of the direct, unadorned tone of the Ming dynasty was set by its founding emperor. Chu Yüan-chang was a man of plebeian origins who, upon ascending the throne, became increasingly paranoid. He was especially suspicious of generals and officials who served under him, as well as of those who were from areas like Soochow that had resisted his rule. He had thousands killed in a wave of purges. Kao Ch'i was simply one of the more prominent victims.

Chu Yüan-chang instituted a new examination system, an attenuated version of the old one, that he hoped would bring people of a lower social stratum to the fore. In his anti-intellectualism, in his desire to favor rural areas at the expense of towns and cities, and in his draconian social policies, he has been likened to Mao Tse-tung in the twentieth century.

Probably in part because of the very success of his policies (especially the decimation of the intelligentsia), by the end of the fourteenth century, when Chu Yüan-chang's rule ended (1398), cultural life was at a nadir. Scholars speak of the fifty-, seventy-, or one-hundred-year period that encompasses the first half of the fifteenth century as a cultural wasteland.

Kao Ch'i and his generation of early Ming poets were mostly killed or driven to suicide. Of the Four Outstanding Talents of Wu-chung, or Soochow (Wu-chung ssu-chieh), Kao Ch'i was executed, Yang Chi (c. 1334–c. 1383) died doing hard labor, and Chang Yü drowned himself when recalled from exile; only Hsü Pen (1335–1380) died of natural causes. Except for Kao, all were notable as painters as well as poets. Although the poetry of the other three was not of the caliber of Kao Ch'i's, it remains remarkable for its serene tone, quite in contrast with the disquietude they must have felt.

The one additional poet of the period worthy of note is Liu Chi (1311–1375). Although he lived only seven years under the new dynasty, Liu had been in Chu Yüan-chang's service since 1359. He and Sung Lien (1310–1381), who also joined Chu Yüan-chang in 1359, were the only men of literary accomplishment to serve the new regime unscathed. (Even then, the early Ch'ing critic Ch'ien Ch'ien-yi discerns a "rueful and spent" air in Liu Chi's later poetry.) Sung Lien, though famous as a prose writer, has not been admired as a poet. Liu Chi was outstanding as both.

Liu Chi's poetry is the most contemplative of the period. Yet it is not "rationalistic" in the style of much philosophical poetry of the Sung. Rather, it is modeled on the more sober poetic series by Ch'en Tzu-ang and Li Po of the Early and High T'ang periods. Thus—it has been argued—the conscious use of models from the zenith of T'ang poetry was operative not only in early Ming poems full of feeling, such as those by Kao Ch'i, but also in poetry of the period more expressive of thought, such as that of Liu Chi.

In sum, poetry of the fourteenth century, although often "detailed" and "involved" in the manner of Late T'ang poetry, could sometimes be more freewheeling, as when ballad themes were used. Some of the period's best poetry, in its sober and restrained style and diction, is more like that of the High T'ang; yet it has a freshness to it. By the middle of the Ming dynasty, T'ang poetic models had become not only orthodox but *de rigueur*. Regardless of what most later Ming poets thought they were producing when imitating High T'ang models, much of the best of their poetry is "generously open" (*hao-fang*) and "unadornedly 'real'" (*p'u-shih*). In this, it is heir to the early Ming.

Poetry of the fourteenth century has the verve of a literature in flux. Styles are used inventively, through the resuscitation of past models and attempts at their use. But unlike so much of later Ming poetry, fourteenth-century poetry has not become formulaic. It still has the air of possibility.

John Timothy Wixted

Chapter 20

POETRY OF THE FIFTEENTH AND SIXTEENTH CENTURIES

No period in the history of Chinese literature has attracted less attention than the fifteenth century, and the reasons for this are not far to seek. Although a considerable body of poetry has been preserved from this period, there is not a single poet between Kao Ch'i (see chapter 19) and Li Tung-yang (1447–1516) for whom a claim to real greatness can plausibly be made. Moreover, even the vernacular traditions of drama and fiction, on which most historical treatments of post-Sung literature concentrate, seem to pause during this century. The *ch'ü* (see chapter 17), the dramatic form characteristic of the Yüan dynasty, fades after the work of Chu Yu-tun early in the Ming dynasty, to the extent that its "revival" early in the sixteenth century by writers such as K'ang Hai and Wang Chiu-ssu (see below) is best understood as another facet of their archaist interests rather than as the persistence of a living tradition. It may be presumed that some of the storytellers' cycles that later coalesced into such long novels of the later Ming as *Shui-hu chuan* (Water Margin) and *Hsi-yu chi* (Journey to the West) were being elaborated, or at least transmitted, during this century, and the same may be true of some of the shorter tales that later helped constitute the tradition of the Ming short story. What is lacking is much evidence of the process as it was taking place.

Indeed, the same sort of hiatus can be seen in most other areas of cultural activity during the fifteenth century. Confucian philosophy is largely quiescent, except for a few men who appear chiefly as forerunners of Wang Shou-jen (Wang Yang-ming; 1472–1529), such as Wu Yü-pi (1392–1469) and Ch'en Hsien-chang (1428–1500). In painting, while the situation was not so dull as later Ming accounts—chiefly those of Tung Ch'i-ch'ang (1555–1636)—made out, notable painters were few, the most conspicuous being Tai Chin (1388–1462). Even in ceramics there is a hiatus in the record during the years 1436 to 1465, because of a suspension of purchases for the court. Printing too seems to have become less common during this period than it had been earlier; scattered references suggest that printed texts may have been in relatively short supply at this time. Only toward the end of the century do we find a quickening, resulting in new editions of some classic books, including *Shih-chi* (Records of the Historian), and in the publication of contemporary literary works and local histories on a larger scale than before.

If showing the existence of this uniquely dull period in the history of Chinese civilization is not difficult, accounting for it seemingly is. The century is mostly one of remarkable peace and stability. After the usurpation of the throne in 1402 by Chu Ti, a son of Chu Yüan-chang, the founding emperor of the Ming, the only perturbation of note is the battle of T'u-mu in 1449 and its consequences—the capture of a reigning emperor (Ying-tsung; r. 1436–1449, 1457–1464) by the Mongols, his replacement by a brother (Tai-tsung or Ching-ti; r. 1449–1457), and his return and eventual restoration. This event had serious consequences for members of the imperial family and for a limited number of officials at the highest levels of government, but not for society as a whole. Indeed, in many respects the period from 1465 to 1505 can be seen as the high point of Ming government.

The consequences of the collapse of the Yüan dynasty and the founding of the Ming do not appear to provide a sufficient explanation. It is true that, during the dynastic transition, much of the heaviest warfare took place in the lower Yangtze region, which was already the cultural and economic center of China. Moreover, Chu Yüan-chang's last rival had his power base in the Yangtze delta and had enjoyed the support of many among the educated class of the region. Although Chu levied sanctions against the region as a consequence, and they had a direct impact on arts and letters for a considerable period of time, the effect of these began to wear off after several decades. Neither did frontier battles against the Mongols exact a cost sufficient to cripple the world of culture.

One must seek an explanation of the dullness of fifteenth-century poetry above all in the poetry itself. One likely explanation is just the converse of the hypothesis that economic hardship somehow hobbled creativity. Quite the contrary, the fairly rapid recovery of China from the anarchy of the late Yüan and the dynastic transition that followed, coupled with administrative stability and the relatively light burden of taxation characteristic of a dynasty's first century, may have contributed to a sense of ease that encouraged more people to write poetry, though with less training in the craft, and at the same time discouraged any effort to take the activity too seriously.

At the very beginning of the century, a variety of regional centers were active. The most important of these, outside the lower Yangtze, was probably that in

Fukien province. This group of poets was important not so much for its leading figure, Lin Hung (c. 1340–c. 1400), as for Lin's follower, the anthologist Kao Ping (1350–1423), who compiled an anthology of about six thousand T'ang poems graded and classified according to principles partly historical and partly esthetic, the *T'ang-shih p'in-hui* (Graded Collocation of T'ang Poetry). Published at the outset of the fifteenth century, Kao's work remained the most important such compendium for most of the Ming dynasty.

The organizing principles of Kao's anthology were strongly influenced by the ideas of the Southern Sung critic Yen Yü, whose *Ts'ang-lang shih-hua* (Ts'ang-lang's Remarks on Poetry) lies behind much of the history of poetry criticism during the Ming. That Kao chose to anthologize and rank T'ang poetry reflects Yen's values. His division of the T'ang into four periods, Early, High, Middle, and Late, was partly original and has persisted to the present day. His assignment of literary value to writers according to their relationship to the High T'ang period was more controversial but still broadly accepted by many subsequent writers. Kao tended to see Early T'ang poets as valuable to the extent that they led to High T'ang, and later poets declining in value to the extent that they deviated from the style of the High T'ang masters, above all Li Po and Tu Fu.

Kao's ideas come to be very influential only around the end of the fifteenth century, though even then he is not often explicitly cited as their source. The important shift earlier is away from regional centers in favor of the capital, which Chu Ti had returned to Peking (Nanking had been his father's capital, and it remained the "Southern Capital" for ceremonial purposes for the rest of the dynasty). Chu's usurpation had been so troubling an event politically that he depended for the most part on relatively young men to staff even the highest levels of his administration. Because his successors maintained a considerable degree of administrative continuity, most of these men retained political authority for several decades and, in the evident absence of competition from other creative centers, dominated the world of letters as well. They included the "Three Yangs" (Yang Shih-ch'i [1365–1444], Yang Jung [1371–1440], and Yang P'u [1372–1446]), as well as Wang Chih (1379–1462), Chin Yu-tzu (1368–1431), Hsieh Chin (1369–1425), and Tseng Ch'i (1372–1432).

The poetic style associated with these men has come to be called the *t'ai-ko t'i*, usually rendered in English as the "cabinet style." The term may come from a combination of *yü-shih-t'ai* (Censorate) and *nei-ko* (Inner [i.e., "Grand"] Secretariat), but in Ming writings it refers to officials in the Han-lin Academy and related offices, including tutors to the crown prince, and is not limited to the period of the "Three Yangs." These men quite reasonably saw themselves as an educated elite, their broad learning validated by the offices they had achieved. While extensive, their literary expertise was not specifically poetic, and their works, like those of most of their contemporaries, were generally reminiscent of Sung styles in both prose and verse, clear and uncomplicated. The most notable among the generations after the Yangs was perhaps Yü Ch'ien

(1398–1457), but his fame is due less to his poetry than to his decisive role in saving the dynasty after the defeat at T'u-mu. Having driven the Mongols beyond the Great Wall, he refrained from attempting to recover the lost emperor. Consequently, after the defeated emperor regained his throne, Yü's opponents at court had him impeached and executed.

In the meantime, the most significant literary alternative to the capital was once again Soochow. Although, with the economic resurgence of the lower Yangtze region, Soochow had begun once again to supply many of the men who held the highest offices in the government, including Wu K'uan (1436–1504) and Wang Ao (1450–1524), it was their fellow townsmen who stayed home who contributed most to literature. The restoration of Soochow as cultural center was first evident in painting, especially in the person of Shen Chou (1427–1509), a painter of the first rank, if a poet of rather less accomplishment. Shen drew on the long-established preeminence of the south in art, but combined his mastery of this tradition with a strongly personal tension between the conventional and its realization under his brush. His manner of painting ordinary and time-honored scenes in an extraordinary way prefigures much that would develop more slowly in poetry during the years to come.

The fullest flowering of Soochow awaited the maturation of a later generation, including Yang Hsün-chi (1458–1546), Chu Yün-ming (1461–1527), T'ang Yin (1470–1524), and Wen Cheng-ming (1470–1559). None of these men had any significant career as an official. Yang was a book collector and scholar. The other three are known above all as painters and calligraphers, but all four wrote a good deal of poetry as well. It is characteristic of the Soochow milieu both that they became eminent without holding office and that literature was only one among their various accomplishments. Breadth was much respected in Soochow, as was a certain degree of eccentricity. While their poetry, mostly in the Sung-like style also favored in Peking, shows accomplished facility, it is unlikely that it would have attracted the attention of later generations had these men not distinguished themselves in other fields. Indeed, during their own lifetimes, the significant new developments in poetry were taking place away from Soochow, especially in Peking, in the form of what has come to be known as the archaist (*fu-ku;* revive antiquity) movement, to which we now turn.

The reasons for the interest in "antiquity" at this time are not entirely understood. One element may have been reforms in the education system, especially the creation of a new sort of official, the "[Provincial] Education Vice-Commissioner" (*t'i-hsüeh fu-shih*). This placed supervision of education in the provinces in the hands of highly educated men who had served in the central government, with the result that they began to raise standards, revise curricula, and actively search out and nurture talented young men. Such an effort naturally generated an appropriate ideology and a set of standards for judgment. Over the next few decades, some of these men found both in the idea that the great writers of bygone ages had embodied in their work the true principles of literature. Their efforts moved in time from education to poetry and then to philosophy, but central to all was the notion of taking more seriously than had their predecessors the role and responsibility of the educated governing class.

A key figure in the evolution of archaism was Li Tung-yang. Although a southerner, Li came from humble origins and from Kiangsi province, well upstream from the centers of the Yangtze delta region. He attained the *chin-shih* degree while still in his teens, rose to the highest ranks of the civil service, and remained the paramount figure in the administration for well over a decade during both the benevolent reign of the Hung-chih emperor (r. 1487–1505) and the quite horrifying rule of the Cheng-te emperor (r. 1505–1521), from whose service he resigned in disgust a few years before he died.

Although relatively little studied or read in modern times, Li Tung-yang was a fascinating man and the force behind the revival of *shih* poetry in his age. There were two elements to his influence. The first of these was the example of his own work, both his poetry and his "remarks on poetry," in which he commented extensively on his contemporaries and on the works of the great masters of the past. For instance, Li stressed the notion of *shih-tiao* (poetic style), hearkening back to ideas already raised by writers like Lu Kuei-meng (d. c. 881) and Liu Ch'ung-yüan of the Southern T'ang period (937–975). It is noteworthy that he used the term "cabinet style" only in the broad sense of poetry written by high officials, including Po Chü-yi in the T'ang, and found something good to say about Yang Shih-ch'i. In fact, he was not so much a successful opponent of the cabinet style (as he has been portrayed) as its culmination. His own poetic program was deceptively modest in its ambitions. He simply strove to write poetry that would match the greatest work of the past. This meant close attention to all aspects of form, above all to metrical requirements. He did not advocate the imitation of poetry from any particular period exclusively, only the attempt to write poetry as well as the ancients had.

The second element of his influence lay in his nurturing of talented younger men, whom he was in a position to help in both their careers and their study of poetry. For all his political wiles—and they carried him into and through situations that embarrassed some of his more idealistic followers—he seems to have been a man of generous spirit and high civilization who kept the best interests of others in mind and respected talent wherever he found it. (Parallels have been drawn, in modern times, between his career and that of Chou En-lai.) He was responsible for discovering and promoting most of the leading poets and officials of the early decades of the sixteenth century, including both men such as Shao Pao (1460–1527) and Ho Meng-ch'un (1474–1536), who remained most closely associated with Li himself, and those such as Li Meng-yang (1473–1529), who began as his followers but then moved beyond his poetics to take up positions of their own.

Li Tung-yang and those who are identified chiefly with him are referred to as the "Ch'a-ling school" (Ch'a-ling p'ai), after the ancestral home of his family.

The next, and more celebrated, literary grouping found in histories of the period is the "(Earlier) Seven Masters of the Ming" (Ming [ch'ien] ch'i tzu), consisting of Li Meng-yang, Ho Ching-ming (1483–1521), Pien Kung (1476–1532), Wang T'ing-hsiang (1474–1544), K'ang Hai (1475–1541), Wang Chiu-ssu (1468–1551), and Hsü Chen-ch'ing (1479–1511). With the exception of Hsü, a Soochow native who in his youth had associated with Chu Yün-ming, T'ang Yin, and Wen Cheng-ming, these men were all from northern China.

The grouping of just these seven men is, like many of its analogs in other periods, somewhat misleading, but it reflects a real phenomenon all the same. What it actually amounts to is a partial list of men who were closely associated with Li Meng-yang in Peking during the years 1496 to 1505 and who accepted his leadership of a literary coterie. There were only a few months during which it is possible that all seven men were simultaneously in the capital, and there are many other writers, such as Ts'ui Hsien (1478–1541) and Ku Lin (1476–1545), who were also influenced by Li Meng-yang at this time. Li and his colleagues aimed to raise standards in poetry beyond the level of competence that had been Li Tung-yang's goal. They asked where the highest possible standards were to be found, and their answer was in the Han and Wei dynasties for old-style (*ku-t'i*) poetry and in the High T'ang for new-style (*chin-t'i*) poetry; the latter choice no doubt reflected the influence of Yen Yü and Kao Ping.

During their years in Peking, these men met frequently to discuss poetry and criticize one another's work. This was during the latter years of the Hung-chih reign, a time of generally good government, at least by Ming standards. The political ambiance seems to have quickened in the minds of many younger intellectuals the idea that they might take their roles, whether as officials, poets, or Confucian thinkers, more seriously than had their predecessors. One of Li Meng-yang's closest political associates at this time was Wang Shou-jen (Yang-ming), who was to become the most important philosopher in China between the time of Chu Hsi (1130–1200) and the present.

With the death of the Hung-chih emperor in 1505 and the accession of his successor, a teenage boy utterly lacking a sense of his role and its responsibilities, the favorable atmosphere in the capital vanished. Most of the "Seven" were gone from Peking within two years, driven from office by the new emperor's favorites and in many cases persecuted even in retirement. Li Meng-yang never again held office in the capital, and Ho Ching-ming spent the years 1507 to 1511 at home, before being summoned back on the recommendation of Li Tung-yang. The two members of the "Seven" who prospered during the early years of the new reign, K'ang Hai and Wang Chiu-ssu, fell from grace in consequence of its first coup, in 1510. They were sent back to their native Shensi province in disgrace and never recalled. At home, they cultivated music and the theater, reviving to some extent the old forms of the Mongol period (see above). It was they who created the notion of the "Seven Masters" retrospectively, evidently seeking to secure their place in history and to emphasize the group's roots in northern China. In particular, they may have wanted to temper the influence of Ku Lin, a southerner who was actively promoting Li Meng-yang's archaist ideas in his native region (Hsü Chen-ch'ing had died by this time).

Some caution is in order in interpreting the relationships among these men. Although it is clear that they had their differences over politics and poetry, in no case does it appear that they actually rejected, or even neglected, their former friendships. Ho Ching-ming, for example, enjoyed quite a few apparently cordial visits with K'ang Hai and Wang Chiu-ssu while he was in office in Shensi during the years 1518 to 1521. In one case he traveled with them for several days around the noted historic and scenic places of their native districts. He did so in spite of their having enjoyed great favor just at the time when he was in serious difficulty because of his opposition to their sponsor. No doubt he remembered that, in those dangerous days, it had been K'ang Hai who had saved Li Meng-yang's life when Li was in danger of judicial murder.

The most celebrated disagreement among these men, however, was genuinely important and prefigures literary debates that would continue throughout the rest of the Ming and Ch'ing dynasties. In an exchange of letters that took place late in 1515, or perhaps early in the following year, Li Meng-yang and Ho Ching-ming debated the relationship between *fa* (variously translated as "law," "method," and "normative standards") and individual creativity. Ho Ching-ming's position was similar to that taken later by Yüan Hung-tao (see below) and other writers with what might be characterized as "individualist" views of the poet's role. He recognized that it was necessary to learn from the great masters of the past, but added that a great poet would then go on to create his own standards and forms. He likened *fa* to the raft in a Buddhist parable—once the stream was crossed one could leave the raft behind. (Indeed, the fact that *fa* also served as the well-known Chinese translation of the Sanskrit term *dharma* may reveal the partially Buddhistic inspiration for its usage in literary theory.) Li Meng-yang, for his part, defended with great resourcefulness a view that modern readers find much less sympathetic. For Li, the *fa* of poetry were like a carpenter's compass and square; although different men might use them differently and apply them to different materials, the rules that they reflected were unchanging and had, moreover, already been perfectly exemplified in the works of the greatest masters of the past. In addition, Li argued that making the individual primary in literary creation was an error in itself and would lead to inferior writing. As he put it, a poet who could express only his own vision was like an artisan who could make only one kind of door or implement.

The grounds for this disagreement were real and persistent, but this open and, at least on Li's side, sometimes testy debate over them also owed something to the differing circumstances of the two men at the time the letters were written. Li Meng-yang had been cashiered in 1514 and was living at home in Kaifeng, where he associated with prosperous merchants and advised them on poetry. Ho Ching-ming, having been recalled to office in 1511, was a literary figure of increasing celebrity in Peking, already attracting his own associates and followers, including Cheng Shan-fu (1485–1524), Hsüeh Hui (1489–1541), and others. It is thus hard not to see Li's motives—it was he who wrote the first letter—as including an urge to reassert himself in the leader's role that he had enjoyed a decade and more before.

In the event, Li need not have worried about recognition of his part in the archaist movement in sixteenth-century literature. As for the intervention of K'ang Hai and Wang Chiu-ssu, it too made a lasting impression on the historical standing of their role. All the same, the future of archaist poetics lay in the south, both in the medium term, with Ku Lin and such writers as Huang Hsing-tseng (1490–1540), who advised the literary heirs of Ho Ching-ming on the proper way to arrange his collected works, Ho Liang-chün (1506–1573), and the Huang-fu brothers, including Huang-fu Fang (1503–1582), and, later, with Hsieh Chen (1495–1575) and the other "Later Seven Masters" (Hou ch'i tzu), to whom we shall shortly return.

First, however, one other figure merits attention. This is Yang Shen (1488–1559), a son of Yang T'ing-ho (1459–1529), the dominant Grand Secretary during the period after Li Tung-yang's retirement. Yang Shen began his career by taking the highest rank in the *chin-shih* examination of 1511, and this, combined with his father's eminence, seemed to promise him the most brilliant of careers. Instead, for his opposition to the Chia-ching emperor (r. 1521–1567), he was banished to Yunnan in 1524 and never allowed to return, even after he had reached the normal retirement age. Yang was a prolific writer in both poetry and prose, and left not only a large collection of poetry but also voluminous scholarly and critical notes on all manner of subjects, especially those relating to Yunnan. He wrote *tz'u* and *ch'ü* as well, many of which were exchanged with his second wife, Huang O (1498–1569), who was perhaps the best female poet of the Ming period. While Yang was in exile, Huang remained at the family home in Szechwan, managing their property and sending funds for his support. Her poems sometimes express quite frankly her longing for his presence.

Yang Shen had not been particularly close to the circle around Ho Ching-ming in the decade after his *chin-shih* and so stood somewhat aloof from the archaist movement. His own taste in poetry was for the sensuous beauty of Six Dynasties and Late T'ang poetry. Indeed, insofar as it could be considered a movement at all, the archaist impulse did not regain for some years the influence it had enjoyed around the turn of the century. With Li Meng-yang, K'ang Hai, and Wang Chiu-ssu retired to the provinces, Hsü Chen-ch'ing dead, and Pien Kung and Ku Lin pursuing their official careers in the provinces, only Ho Ching-ming and Wang T'ing-hsiang remained active, and by 1518 or so they were both turning their attention to broader questions of scholarship, teaching, and the problems of civil administration (both served as Education Commissioners). Ts'ui Hsien even renounced the writing of poetry altogether in his later years. Their shifting interests to some extent paralleled those of Wang Shou-jen, who had never been greatly intrigued by literary questions and who was now preoccupied with his efforts to reawaken and redefine dedication to Confucian principles in public and private life.

The archaist impulse shifted for a while to the realms of prose and drama, where we shall not follow it in detail. It was, however, at this time that T'ang Shun-chih (1507–1560) and others advocated study of the "old prose" of the T'ang and Sung masters, while the experiments with earlier dramatic forms by K'ang Hai and Wang Chiu-ssu were taken up by Li K'ai-hsien (1502–1568), an indifferent poet who spent a few weeks with K'ang and Wang in 1531 and went on to cultivate dramatic writing. His initiative was subsequently continued by Hsü Wei (1521–1593), who is best known as a painter and dramatist.

The man who gave archaism in poetry its second lease on life, Hsieh Chen, was a figure quite different from Li Meng-yang in several important respects. First, he was from the south; second, unlike all the other "masters," Early and Late alike, he never attained the *chin-shih* degree or held office. Although he stressed the highest standards in poetry in his critical work, the *Shih-chia chih shuo* (Straight Talk from a Poet, now more frequently encountered under the title *Ssu-ming shih-hua* [Remarks on Poetry from Ssu-ming (Mountain, in Chekiang)]), Hsieh's attitude was closer to the individualist and evolutionary ideas of Ho Ching-ming than to the narrower stance of Li Meng-yang. Perhaps for this reason—some say that his lack of success in the official examinations also made him a victim of snobbery—he was eventually edged out of the leadership of the "Later Seven" by Li P'an-lung (1514–1570), whose approach was more rigid. Li had attained the *chin-shih* in 1544 and become preeminent among the "Later Seven," which, in addition to Hsieh and Li, consisted of Wang Shih-chen (1526–1590, *c.s.* 1547), Hsü Chung-hsing (1517–1578), Liang Yu-yü (c. 1520–1556), Tsung Ch'en (1525–1560), and Wu Kuo-lun (1529–1593), the latter four all *chin-shih* of 1550.

Li P'an-lung's poetry has not found great favor with later readers, and, unlike Hsieh Chen, he wrote little in the way of explicit criticism—the *Yi-yüan chih yen* (Apt Words from the Garden of the Arts) that he and Wang Shih-chen collaborated on is mostly Wang's work. Li's influence has been most evident through an anthology of T'ang poetry (*T'ang shih hsüan*) that he compiled. There has been a good deal of confusion over the texts and versions of this work. Three different versions are known, all apparently based on Li's original, which in turn seems to have drawn on Kao Ping's *T'ang-shih p'in-hui*. This collection has been important as a "corpus definer" for Japanese readers as well as Chinese down to the present.

Among the "Later Seven" it is Wang Shih-chen who was the major poet. Not only is his verse interesting, but there is an enormous quantity of it. Wang published his "collected works" (not limited to poetry), the *Yen-chou shan-jen ssu-pu kao* (The Mountain Man of Yen-chou's Manuscripts from the Four

Divisions [of a library, i.e., Classics, History, Thought, and Belles Lettres]), at the age of fifty in no fewer than 174 *chüan*, leaving 207 *chüan* of additional material for posthumous publication as a continuation (*Ssu-pu hsü-kao* [Continued Manuscripts in Four Divisions]) by a grandson. The earlier collection includes *Yi-yüan chih yen*, while the continuation includes a somewhat larger critical work titled *Tu-shu hou* (After Reading) that reflects much broader standards. The same tendency is to be found both in anecdotes about Wang's later years and, more important, in his own later poems, whose sources go far beyond the Han, Wei, and High T'ang models to which Li Meng-yang and Li P'an-lung would have restricted writers. In particular, Wang came to accord a much higher esteem to such writers as Po Chü-yi and Su Shih than his archaist predecessors would have allowed. It seems likely that the essential motive for this was satisfaction of the active and original intelligence that so often appears in Wang's works in all forms. Some, however, have attributed Wang's tolerance, as well as the interest in Buddhism and Taoism that he showed in his later years, to the various difficulties he had endured in the course of his life, including the judicial murder of his father and repeated career reverses, often explained by reference to the jealousy of powerful rivals.

Wang certainly gave his rivals grounds for envy. Although his career as an official was marred by accusations (not necessarily justified) of malfeasance and by several retirements, not all voluntary, he still rose to high rank. More significantly, he came to dominate the literary world of his age in a remarkable way. Most of the poets of the latter decades of the sixteenth century considered themselves his followers, and the archaist doctrines with which he was associated influenced virtually all his contemporaries, especially because of his own prestige.

Sequels, it is said, are rarely as good as the originals, and the "Later Seven," as a group, conform to this pattern. Although one might well regard Wang Shih-chen as a greater writer than any one of the "Earlier Seven" and recognize the importance of Hsieh Chen as a critic and Li P'an-lung as an anthologist, the group itself seems important chiefly as a symptom of the influence that archaist poetics exerted during the latter half of the sixteenth century and as evidence that the notion of the "Earlier Seven" had become well established in literary history. Like the "Earlier" group, the members of the "Later Seven" were all together for only a few years in Peking at the outset of their official careers in the early 1550s. Once they had dispersed to provincial appointments or into retirement, they met only occasionally and in groups of two or three.

Nonetheless, they were far from lacking influence of their own. In the decades to come, there would be additional coteries denominated according the same pattern: "Later Five Masters," "Expanded Five Masters" (*kuang wu tzu*), "Continued Five Masters" (*hsü wu tzu*), and "Concluding Five Masters" (*mo wu tzu*), including the dramatist T'u Lung (1542–1605) and the critic Hu Ying-lin (1551–1602).

Among these writers, the most important was probably Hu Ying-lin. Hu came from a wealthy family, but never attained the *chin-shih* degree or held an official post. His own poetry is not of much interest (*pace* Wang Shih-chen), but he compiled a substantial encyclopedia of poetics, *Shih sou* (Poetry Oasis). Hu's book is a well-organized review of poetic forms, history, and sources from an archaist perspective, and aspects of it have been very influential since its publication. Hu's view of the history of *shih* poetry sees the High T'ang as a high point, but also recognizes a kind of renaissance during the Yüan period, culminating in the "Earlier Seven Masters" and "Later Seven Masters" of his own century.

Hu's interpretation of China's poetic history is out of favor now and indeed was on the verge of revaluation even as it appeared. The very triumph of the archaist mode that the poetry of Wang Shih-chen and Hu's *Shih sou* represented was soon in question. It is nonetheless important to notice that the "anti-archaist" schools that tended to dominate the last decades of the Ming dynasty represented not so much a wholesale rejection of the poetics of the sixteenth century as an evolutionary process in which views first developed by such men as Li Tung-yang, Ho Ching-ming, Hsieh Chen, and Wang Shih-chen himself were further extended.

This is true above all of the "Kung-an school," which revolved around Yüan Hung-tao (1568–1610), along with his older and younger brothers Tsung-tao (1560–1600) and Chung-tao (1570–1624). For much of the twentieth century, these men were portrayed as the arch-opponents of archaism and as partisans of the vernacular fiction and drama of their day. While it is true that they had broad interests—Hung-tao wrote on such subjects as flower arranging, among much else—their poetry was written mostly in the same T'ang modes favored by the archaists. Hung-tao's defense of vernacular literature was based on its ability to express moral truths equivalent to those found in the works of Tu Fu and other classic poets, not on a claim for esthetic parity, much as he enjoyed the theater. The poetry of the Yüan brothers is, as poetry, neither much different from that which preceded it nor of noticeably greater interest. Where they were truly influential was in their foreshadowing of the broadly hedonistic attitude to literature that would characterize the last decades of the Ming dynasty.

Daniel Bryant

Chapter 21

POETRY OF THE SEVENTEENTH CENTURY

It is helpful to view the poetry of the seventeenth century in terms of three general periods: (1) the first four decades of the century under Ming rule (1600–1643), a time of political factionalism and gentry societies, a blurring of distinctions between high and popular culture, the popularity of poetry clubs (including clubs for commoners or women), and the promotion of individual and intense expressionism in literature and art; (2) the four decades that spanned the Manchu conquest and consolidation of Ch'ing rule (1644–1682), a period of stirring resistance by some, ambivalent accommodation by others (both had important implications for writing), and a surge of interest in Sung and Yüan era *shih* poetry, which led to a renovated and expanded archaism (*fu-ku*) and was reflected in new traditions in poetry; and (3) the last two decades of the century, the 1680s and 1690s, which ushered in the long, stable High Ch'ing era (which was to last until the early nineteenth century), an era that saw the first maturation of new and sophisticated critical views (often developed by synthesizing old, sometimes diverse approaches) and the establishment of schools of poetry based more on theoretical principles than on the traditional categories of geographical affiliation or personal master-disciple relationships.

The early years of the seventeenth century saw a continuation of a trend to emphasize the "natural self," individual creativity, intense emotion, and direct expressionism in literature and the arts—a trend whose philosophical underpinnings were articulated with the greatest force and in the most detail by the independent, iconoclastic thinker Li Chih (1527–1602). Li, inspired by Wang

Shou-jen's (Wang Yang-ming; 1472–1529) assertion that the principles of things (*li*) were not to be sought in external things but existed to be recovered in one's individual mind, took Wang's thought a radical step further: everyone has the potential to be a sage, for perfect wisdom resides within the innate, autonomous self, which should be the sole agent and arbiter of morals, taste, and cultural values. Li referred to this autonomous or inner self as the "infant's heart/mind" (*t'ung-hsin*) and declared that the Confucian classics were not sacred authorities but, at their most useful, repositories of insights into how the *t'ung-hsin* can be recovered and applied to enriching life and solving its problems. He was a synthetic thinker and amalgamated much from Buddhism and Taoism in his transformation of orthodox and official Confucianism into a personal credo.

Such ideas were in wide circulation during the second half of the sixteenth century, and so it is difficult to determine how much influence Li exerted on major creative figures of the time who thought in similar ways—for example, T'ang Hsien-tsu (1550–1616), poet, essayist, literary theorist, and dramatist; Hsü Wei (1521–1593), poet, essayist, calligrapher, painter, and dramatist; and T'u Lung (1542–1605), poet, critic, dramatist, art connoisseur, occasional Taoist priest, and bon vivant (that is, when means or opportunity allowed). However, it is known that Li directly influenced the three Yüan brothers of Kung-an (in Hupei province on the Yangtze), Yüan Tsung-tao (1560–1600), Yüan Hung-tao (1568–1610), and Yüan Chung-tao (1570–1624), for they exchanged visits with Li, recorded conversations with him, and praised him in their writings. Chung-tao, in fact, became one of Li's biographers. The influential Kung-an school of writing founded by them obviously owes much to Li, for its anti-archaist theoretical tenets (see chapter 20) include the rejection of the authority of the past, the shunning of imitation (arguing that imitation destroys creativity), the insistence that each writer, above all else, express individual "native sensibilities" (*hsing-ling*), and the promotion of fiction and drama as important, legitimate forms of literature. Nevertheless, in practice the three brothers were rather conventional, and their poetry falls far short of the heterodox and iconoclastic polemics of their theoretical writings. Whereas they went on writing poetry largely as most poets did in the two or more generations before them, they did differ significantly from the archaist poetic practice of the Earlier and Later Seven Masters (see chapter 20), which they often attacked in theoretical statements, by emulating Middle instead of High T'ang poets, especially Po Chü-yi, whom most archaists shunned because of his prosy, casual, and often semi-colloquial style, and the Sung era master Su Shih, the heterodox genius who bent the rules to suit himself, whom the archaists sometimes grudgingly admired as a person but whose works they vehemently condemned as poetic models. The Yüan brothers were also typical of many late-sixteenth- and early-seventeenth-century literati, especially those in Kiangnan (southern lower Yangtze River region), in that they founded and patronized literary societies, promoted the unification of the "Three Teachings" of Confucianism, Taoism, and Buddhism, and were involved in the writing, compilation, editing, or publication of fiction, drama, treatises on Buddhism and Taoism, and a wide variety of other works dealing with topics on the fringe of literati interests that ranged from flower arrangement to pharmacopoeia. It was also significant that they moved in "heterodox" cultural circles that encompassed painters, writers, and calligraphers who made a professional living out of work that expressed "amateur" ideals, merchants who had a taste and pocketbook for high culture, families that encouraged literary and artistic activity among their women, some of whom achieved regional and even national fame, and talented courtesans who were establishing prominent literary reputations of their own. Such circles were becoming an increasingly significant part of literary history as the Ming moved on to its end a generation or so later.

Another tradition of poetry that flourished briefly but was soon absorbed into more lasting trends was that of T'an Yüan-ch'un (1585–1637) and Chung Hsing (1574–1624), who headed the Ching-ling school, named after their native place in Hupei. T'an and Chung agreed with the Kung-an school that the expression of "native sensibilities" (*hsing-ling*) was the core of great poetry but took issue with it for promoting the emulation of Po Chü-yi and Su Shih, for the results, they judged, made current poetry so "vulgar and crude" that it had to be steered in a new direction back to "refinement," which they hoped to accomplish through the publication in 1617 of two anthologies, *Ku-shih kuei* (Homecoming to Ancient Verse) and *T'ang-shih kuei* (Homecoming to T'ang Verse). Their own poetry attempted to capture the particular "spirit" (*ling*) of pre-T'ang and T'ang poets as it was revealed in these anthologies, a spirit rich in "profundity and aloofness" (*shen-yu ku-ch'iao*), but their approach proved too piecemeal and erratic, concentrating as it did on emulating individual words and expressions that supposedly embodied this "spirit." The resulting poetry at times achieved a novel and mysterious charm, but the meaning was often so obscure that students and critics soon lost patience with it and began to look elsewhere for inspiration and guidance.

The Ching-ling school tried to carve a new path away from the poetics of both the Earlier and Later Seven Masters and the Kung-an school, but Ch'en Tzu-lung (1608–1647), another Kiangnan poet, attempted to combine the best features of both: influenced by the Earlier and Later Seven Masters, he strove for a gentleness and refinement (*wen-ya*) embedded in a formal sophistication derived from close study of past masters—Ts'ao Chih (192–232), Hsieh Ling-yün (385–433), and Pao Chao (414–466) for ancient-style verse (*ku-shih*) and the High Tang poet Tu Fu for regulated verse (*lü-shih*)—infused with the intense expression of native sensibilities, which for him meant lofty personal ambition (*chih*) and profoundly felt emotion (*ch'ing*); this meant that he also had one foot planted firmly in the Li Chih–Kung-an school camp. Ch'en and several like-minded associates, principally Li Wen (1608–1647), Sung Cheng-yü (1618–1667), and Hsia Wan-ch'un (1631–1647), made up the Yün-chien school of poetry, named after Ch'en's home district, also known as Sung-chiang (Kiangsu province). In several ways Ch'en was the epitome of the late Ming literatus. For instance, he was a founding member of a literary society, a regional branch of the Fu-she (Restoration Society) called the Chi-she (Incipiency Society), devoted to the clarification of philosophical principles and the reformation of both literary standards and ethical standards in officialdom. His affiliation with the Earlier and Later Seven Masters is readily apparent in the anthology of Ming *shih* of which he was the chief editor, *Huang Ming shih-hsüan*, in thirteen *chüan*, whose selection overwhelmingly favors the archaist poets. Ch'en was also deeply involved in the growing world of women's writing and had formed a liaison with the literary courtesan Liu Shih (Ju-shih; 1618–1664), whom he met in 1632 in Sung-chiang. The relationship lasted until 1635, when Ch'en's family forced Liu Shih to leave him, but Ch'en's encouragement of her writing continued, for he later helped with the publication of her first poetry collection, *Wu-yin ts'ao* (Drafts of Poetry from the *Wu-yin* Year [1638]), to which he wrote a preface. A few years later, Liu Shih formed a more lasting union with another famous poet of the day, Ch'ien Ch'ien-yi (1582–1664), who left his own legal wife and married her with proper ceremony in 1641. Ch'ien and Liu are discussed further below.

Ch'en Tzu-lung is remembered principally for his loyalist martyrdom defending the doomed Ming state and for the passionate love poems, both *shih* and *tz'u* (there was a corresponding Yün-chien school of *tz'u* poetry), that he exchanged with Liu Shih. In them, romantic, sensual love (*ch'ing*) is elevated to the status of cultural ideal and the great motivating principle of human existence. This passionate, romantic idealism prevalent in the personal lives of people like Ch'en seems to have been a common denominator of the age. Such idealism spilled over into public life, where it became identified with loyalty to state and emperor, which may help explain the intensity and perseverance of resistance to Manchu rule and the extraordinary number of martyrs—both resistance fighters and suicides among literati families—that mark the Ming–Ch'ing transition.

The Three Talents of Southern Chihli (Chi-nan san-ts'ai-tzu)—Shen Han-kuang (1620–1677), Yin Yüeh (1603–1670), and Chang Kai (dates unknown)—are unheralded today, but their collective role in the history of Ch'ing-era poetry is significant, for they served as one of the links between the Earlier and Later Seven Masters of the Ming and the foremost poet and critic of the seventeenth century (and perhaps the entire Ch'ing), Wang Shih-chen (1634–1711; to be distinguished from the sixteenth-century author with a similar name who lived from 1526 to 1590). Wang apparently coined the school name by which they and several other associates became known, the Ho-shuo (North of the Yellow River) school of *shih* poetry, which he greatly admired. The Ho-shuo school consisted of Ming loyalists (*yi-min*) who refused to serve the Ch'ing (Shen's father had taken his own life as a Ming martyr) and instead devoted their lives to literary and scholarly pursuits. Shen Han-kuang was the principal theoretical spokesman for the school, and the following remarks are gleaned from his *Ts'ung-shan shih-hsüan* (Selected Verse from the Mountain of Acute Hearing) and *Ts'ung-shan wen-chi* (Literary Collection from the Mountain of Acute Hearing). Shen advocated expressionism in poetry in much the same way as did the Kung-an and Ching-ling schools, declaring that the expression of the "spirit that resides in one's personal nature and feeling" (*hsing-ch'ing chih ling*) was essential to poetry, but he condemned the Kung-an school for its "vulgarity" and the Ching-ling school for its "superficiality and obscurity." Shen greatly admired the Earlier and Later Seven Masters, especially Li Meng-yang, Ho Ching-ming, and Li P'an-lung, for their success at leaping back over the heterodox developments of Sung-era verse to achieve great technical virtuosity in the High T'ang style. Nevertheless he thought that they failed to express enough of the "purity and strength" (*ch'ing-kang*) that should characterize the "authenticity" (*chen*) and "personal nature and feeling" (*hsing-ch'ing*) of great poets. For Shen, poetry was the medium of great cultural heroes—the very voice of the Tao itself. He and the other Ho-shuo poets, obviously strong traditionalists, were also advocates of the Ch'eng-Chu (the Ch'eng brothers [Ch'eng Yi and Ch'eng Hao] and Chu Hsi) version of Neo-Confucianism and were among the forerunners of the movement that was soon to discredit Wang Yang-ming and all that his school of mind (*hsin*) stood for, even blaming it for the fall of the Ming. Shen went so far as to declare that poetry (*shih*) and the study of principles (*li-hsüeh*) (Ch'eng-Chu learning) were ultimately the same thing and that one should regard the Ch'eng brothers, Chu Hsi, Li Po, and Tu Fu as "a single person" (*yi-shen*) (see chapters 14 and 16). Although Wang Shih-chen never equated poetry with *li-hsüeh*, his generally high regard for the theory and practice of the Earlier and Later Seven Masters, including their advocacy of the High T'ang, is likely to have come in part from his familiarity with the views of Shen Han-kuang and other members of the Ho-shuo school. These views contrast sharply with those of another figure who played an important role in Wang's earlier literary career—Ch'ien Ch'ien-yi, who had little use for period style as a guide for composing poetry, the High T'ang included, and who attacked the Earlier and Later Seven Masters on various theoretical and practical grounds throughout his career.

Another early Ch'ing regional school was the Hsi-ling (old name for Hangchow) school, which included poets who made reputations in both the *shih* and the *tz'u* forms. These poets were collectively called the "Ten Masters of Hsi-ling," the most important being Mao Hsien-shu (1620–1688), Shen Ch'ien (1620–1670), Ting P'eng (b. 1622), and Chang Tan (b. 1619). They were all heavily influenced by Ch'en Tzu-lung, and their *shih* and *tz'u* are generally similar to the works of the Yün-chien school.

Farther south was the Ling-nan (Kwangtung and Kwangsi) school, the most famous members of which were the "Three Great Masters of Ling-nan": Ch'ü Ta-chün (1630–1696) was a Ming loyalist and for much of his life a peripatetic renegade, for a time even becoming a Buddhist priest. He emulated the heroic, devil-may-care tone of Li Po the wandering swashbuckler in his *shih* and also was fond of writing poems concerned with the plight of "tragic resistance"—imaginative fantasies reminiscent of *Ch'u tzu* (Elegies of Ch'u), attributed to Ch'ü Yüan, whom he considered his ancestor. Ch'en Kung-yin (1631–1700), another Ming loyalist, whose early life resembled Ch'ü's, spent his last twenty years in Canton (Kwangchow) devoted to writing, scholarly pursuits, and calligraphy. Wang Shih-chen was especially fond of Ch'en's *shih,* which he characterized as "pure-and-distant and transcending all vulgarity" (*ch'ing-chiung pa-su*) and as having achieved "enlightenment" (*san-mei;* Sanskrit, *samādhi*) (for a discussion of these terms, see below under Wang Shih-chen). Liang P'ei-lan (1629–1705) was a native of Nan-hai, Kwangtung, and had a career as a minor official under the Ch'ing. Liang founded a local poetry society that achieved national fame for a time, the Lan-hu she (Orchid Lake Society), which also included Ch'en Kung-yin among its members. Liang's *shih,* especially his modern-style verse (*chin-t'i shih*), were widely admired; Wang Shih-chen and Chu Yi-tsun, among many others, sang his praises. He also had a major reputation as a calligrapher.

Ch'ien Ch'ien-yi along with Wu Wei-yeh (1609–1672) and Kung Ting-tzu (1615–1673), a painter as well as a poet, were the "Three Great Masters from Left of the River" (Chiang-tso san-ta-chia) (that is, from Kiangsu) of the Ming–Ch'ing transition era. Ch'ien served in various high offices between 1610 and 1629, including Vice Minister of Rites, but, when dismissed from office after an unsubstantiated charge of corruption had been made against him, he returned to Ch'ang-shu, his native place. There, toward the end of 1640, Liu Shih introduced herself to him, and the next year they married. The couple shared romance, scholarship, and writing in the studio-library Ch'ien had built for her in 1643, the Chiang-yün lou (Puce Gauze Cloud Lodge)—the name combines an allusion to the fourth-century scholar-teacher Madame Sung, mother of Wei Ch'eng, who taught imperial stipendiary students from behind a puce gauze (*chiang*) curtain, with a reference to Liu Shih's personal name, Yün-chüan (Cloud Beauty). Ch'ien returned to a year's service in the court of Prince Fu in Nanking during 1644 and 1645 as Minister of Rites, but when Nanking surrendered to the Manchus, he refused Liu Shih's (an ultra-Ming loyalist herself) call to commit suicide and instead went to Peking to serve briefly in the new Ch'ing government as Senior Vice Minister of Rites. However, by 1647 he was back in retirement in Ch'ang-shu, where he and Liu Shih remained. The marriage lasted until Ch'ien's death in 1664; Liu Shih subsequently hanged herself in the same year, at age forty-six.

The Chiang-yün lou contained Ch'ien's magnificent library, and it was here that the couple carried out various literary projects, among which was the compiling and editing of the massive anthology of Ming poetry, *Lieh-ch'ao shih-chi* (Collection of Poetry from Successive Reigns), with its complementary collection of critique-biographies, *Lieh-ch'ao shih-chi hsiao-chuan* (1646–1649).

It is unknown how much Liu Shih contributed to the overall project, but it is certain that she is responsible for section 4, the *Jun-chi* (The Intercalary Collection) of women poets. Another large project was Ch'ien's *Ming shih kao* (Draft History of the Ming Era) in one hundred *chüan*, but this was lost along with much of the rest of the library in 1650, when the Chiang-yün lou was destroyed by fire. The poems that Ch'ien and Liu Shih exchanged were edited as *Tung-shan ch'ou-ho chi* (Collection of Offer and Response Poems from East Mountain), in three *chüan*, which is preserved in the first series of Ch'ien's own collected works, *Mu-chai ch'u-hsüeh chi* (Literary Collection from the Shepherd's Studio During the First Stages of Learning), published in 1643.

As a young man under the Ming, Wu Wei-yeh, a native of T'ai-ts'ang, Kiangsu, was a member of the Restoration Society, attained the *chin-shih* degree in his early twenties, and was immediately appointed to high office as a Hanlin academician. At the fall of the Ming, his mother dissuaded him from taking his own life, and, after several years as a private teacher and scholar, he accepted office under the Ch'ing as Libationer of the Imperial Academy in 1653 but returned to private life again in 1660. Wu had been a close friend of Ch'en Tzu-lung, with whom he shared similar literary views, and he thought highly of Ch'ien Ch'ien-yi. He also had a special affinity for the mid-T'ang poets Yüan Chen (779–831) and Po Ch'ü-yi as well as the Southern Sung poet Lu Yu (1125–1210). Although Wu wrote in all forms of *shih* poetry and was one of the foremost *tz'u* poets of the seventeenth century, his most remarkable achievement was a number of long narrative poems in the heptasyllabic ancient-verse (*ch'i-yen ku-shih*) form collectively praised ever since as "a poetic history of the age" (*yi-tai shih-shih*). Characterized by realistic portrayal of people and events, these lyrical and evocative poems are detailed accounts in ballad form of the great cataclysm of the Ming–Ch'ing transition era, some titles of which are "Yüan-yüan ch'ü" (Song of Yüan-yüan), "Yung-ho kung tz'u" (Lyric of Yung-ho Palace), "Yüan-hu ch'ü" (Song of Mandarin Ducks Lake), and "P'i-p'a hsing" (Ballad of the Balloon Lute). These and other poems of Wu's, all rich in romantic nostalgia, dramatic intensity, and melancholy, defined a new tradition of poetry for the early Ch'ing, which became known as the Mei-ts'un *t'i* (Mei-ts'un style), after Wu's style-name, or the Lou-tung style (Lou-tung being an old name for T'ai-ts'ang), terms applied to poetry both in the *shih* and *tz'u* forms.

Wu Wei-yeh's principal literary disciples were Wu Chao-ch'ien (1631–1684) and Ch'en Wei-sung (1625–1682), who, like Wu Wei-yeh, was an accomplished *tz'u* poet. Wu Chao-ch'ien had a very strange life. A native of Wu-chiang, Kiangsu, he spent his youth in exceptional scholarly and literary attainment—Wu Wei-yeh called him, along with P'eng Shih-tu (b. 1624) and Ch'en Wei-sung, "Chiang-tso san feng" (Three Phoenixes Left of the River)—but when he passed the *chü-jen* examination in Nanking in 1657, he was implicated in a corruption case involving one of the chief examiners and was banished to Ninguta on the far northeast frontier, where he remained in exile for twenty-two years. He was finally released in 1681, thanks to the great Manchu *tz'u* poet Na-lan Hsing-te (Nara Singde; 1655–1685), patron of many worthy scholars and writers. Hsing-te had been made aware of Wu by a fellow *tz'u* enthusiast, Ku Chen-kuan (b. 1637), to whom Wu had been sending poems, and, impressed by Wu's literary brilliance, Hsing-te took an interest in the case and worked for his release, after which he had him appointed tutor to a younger brother in the home of his father, Na-lan (Nara) Mingju (1635–1708), then Grand Secretary. Wu Chao-ch'ien's collected literary works in eight *chüan* is called *Ch'iu-chia chi* (Collection of Sounds of the Autumn Frontier Woodwind).

Ch'en Wei-sung, a native of Yi-hsing, Kiangsu, started his literary career associated with Wu Wei-yeh and Mao Hsiang (1611–1693), a fellow leader of the Restoration Society and a close friend of Ch'en's father, Ch'en Chen-hui (1605–1656). Repeatedly failing the civil service examinations, Ch'en Wei-sung lived for many years in Mao's home until he was successful in the special *Po-hsüeh hung-tz'u* (For Erudites Whose Writings Carry Far) examination of 1679, in consequence of which he was appointed as a Han-lin academician. (Two such examinations were held during the Ch'ing period, in 1679 and 1736. These special examinations were designed to attract and recruit men of exceptional talent from outside the regular examination system that culminated in the *chin-shih* degree. The 1679 examination was especially directed toward Ming loyalist scholars who had refused to join the new Ch'ing government, and the 1736 examination was designed to attract into government service talented scholars who, for one reason or another, had avoided the examination system or failed to achieve success within it.) Mao Hsiang is remembered for his patronage of the arts, drama, and poetry, for his own poetry, especially in the *tz'u* form, and for his love affair with the literary courtesan Tung Pai (Hsiao-wan) (1625–1651), herself a noted *tz'u* poet, whom he was able to take into his household in 1642 thanks to Ch'ien Ch'ien-yi's help in removing various obstacles. Mao's biography of her, composed after her death, *Ying-mei-an yi-yü* (Reminiscences of Shadow-Cast Plums Cottage), is a touching tribute to her talent and his love for her.

Ch'en is probably the most important *tz'u* poet of the early Ch'ing era, and by far the most prolific. He specialized in long songs rich in metaphor and allegorical meaning, and his works as a whole, which critics assign to the "bold and unrestrained" (*hao-fang*) tradition, have been compared favorably to those of Su Shih and Hsin Ch'i-chi (1140–1207). Ch'en's efforts to invest his *tz'u* with high-minded political and historical allegorical significance were consciously made to re-elevate the *tz'u* form, which during the late Ming and early Ch'ing had become largely a vehicle for individual personal expression, love, nostalgic reminiscence, and even erotic-romantic titillation, to the status of a "serious" form of literature equal to classical forms of poetry and prose. In doing so, he anticipated the efforts of the Ch'ang-chou school (in Kiangsu) of *tz'u* a century and a half later (see chapter 22). Although he also wrote often in the *shih* form, his real forte was the *tz'u*, of which 1,629 are preserved in his *Hu-hai-lou tz'u-chi* (Collection of Lyrics from the Lakes and Seas Lodge [Ch'en's studio]), also called *Chia-ling tz'u ch'üan-chi* (The Complete *Tz'u* of Chia-ling [Ch'en's personal name]), both in thirty *chüan*.

Three other *tz'u* poets of the seventeenth century whose reputations rival that of Ch'en Wei-sung are Nara Singde, Yu T'ung (1618–1704), and P'eng Sun-yü (1631–1700). Singde died at the age of thirty, but even this short span of years allowed him to fill two collections of *tz'u*, *Ts'e-mao tz'u* (Lyrics by One Who Wears His Hat Aslant) and *Yin-shui tz'u* (Lyrics of a Water Drinker). His collected literary works, including much interesting *shih* poetry, is called *T'ung chih t'ang chi* (Literary Works from the Hall of Realized Ambition) in twenty *chüan*. Singde's short lyrics, his favorite mode of composition, bear comparison to those of Li Yü (937–978) for their plain yet evocative diction, melancholic tone, longing for a simple life free of the burdens of responsibility, and intense personal expression. Yu T'ung, a native of Soochow, had a modest earlier official career, twenty years of retirement as a private scholar and writer, a return to official life as a Han-lin academician after passing the *Po-hsüeh hung-tz'u* examination of 1679, and a final twenty years of retirement in Soochow after 1683. Although Yu wrote prolifically in all forms of poetry and prose—including drama in the *tsa-chü* and *ch'uan-ch'i* forms—this *tz'u* collection, the *Pai-mo tz'u* (Powder from Hundreds of Blossoms Lyrics), deserves special attention. Yu's lyrics have a spontaneity and naturalness of diction and tone that are most appealing, and the profound emotional tone of some is quite moving. P'eng Sun-yü, who, among other achievements, placed first in the *Po-hsüeh hung-tz'u* examination of 1679, was an accomplished *tz'u* poet. Wang Shih-chen, who knew him in his Yangchow days, thought him the best of the age and praised him in particular for the "voluptuousness" (*yen*) of his boudoir lyrics.

Mao Hsiang declined to take office under the Ch'ing, but many of the other figures associated with Ch'ien Ch'ien-yi did, for example, Wu Wei-yeh and Ch'en Wei-sung, if only briefly. Many others, of course, took pride in having nothing whatsoever to do with the Ch'ing regime, and some of these were accomplished, even brilliant, poets. These include Ku Yen-wu (1613–1682), geographer, historian, and the great forerunner of the historical and textual criticism movement that was later known as the School of Han Learning (*Han-hsüeh p'ai*) or school of "evidential research" (*k'ao-cheng hsüeh*); Kuei Chuang (1613–1673), great-grandson of the renowned literatus Kuei Yu-kuang (1506–1571), former member of the Restoration Society, friend of Ku Yen-wu, known for his cursive calligraphy and bamboo paintings, and famous as the author of a long narrative poem, "Wan-ku-ch'ou ch'ü" (Song of Everlasting Sorrow), which relates the history of China from its beginnings until the fall of Nanking in 1645; Huang Tsung-hsi (1610–1695), historian, political activist, commentator on the classics, anthologist, critic and chronicler of Neo-Confucianism, and political philosopher; and Wang Fu-chih (1619–1692), Neo-Confucian philosopher, historian, commentator on the Confucian classics, the *Lao Tzu,* the *Chuang Tzu, Ch'u tz'u* (Elegies of Ch'u), essayist, poet, anthologist, and literary critic.

Ku Yen-wu's *shih* are characterized by much apt allusion to history and emulation of the spirit and formal qualities of Tu Fu's verse, about which critics say "he excelled at all the forms" (*ko-t'i chieh shan*). Several annotated editions of Ku's complete poetry, *Ku T'ing-lin shih-chi,* have been published (the earliest in 1897), which greatly assist in reading this highly allusive and densely metaphoric poet.

Huang Tsung-hsi's *shih* poetry combines scholarly erudition with a powerful emotional impact in emulation of the formal style of the High T'ang. His was a highly successful version of archaist-expressionism, which maintains affiliations with both Ch'ien Ch'ien-yi, whose literary disciple he considered himself, and the Earlier and Later Seven Masters. About three hundred poems survived his own careful editing (approximately two in ten of his total output by his reckoning) and are included in his *Nan-lei shih-li* (A Poetic Chronicle from South of Thunder [Peaks]), in four *chüan.* Huang lived in seclusion in Nan-lei village, Yü-yao district, Chekiang, and used Nan-lei as a style name.

Wang Fu-chih was a much more prolific poet than Ku and Huang. He wrote both *shih* and *tz'u,* took the composition of *tz'u* very seriously, and was an innovative literary theorist. After the fall of the Ming, Wang lived in seclusion at Shih-ch'uan shan (Stone Boat Mountain), Heng-yang district, Hunan, and so one of his style names is Ch'uan-shan (Boat Mountain); the other one that he often used was Chiang-chai ([Keeper of the] Ginger Studio). Wang's view of *shih* poetry was similar to that of Ch'ien Ch'ien-yi in that he rejected the largely formulaic practices based on notions of poetic "law," "method," or "dharma" (*fa*) associated with the Earlier and Later Seven Masters and instead advocated individual expressionism inspired by, but not restricted to, achievements of past masters. However, he also developed a theory of poetry that articulated expressionist aims in terms of new and sophisticated principles—something never attempted by Ch'ien, who as a critic did little more than expand on Kung-an school views. As in his historical and philosophical writings, Wang was an independent and original thinker about literary issues. One passage in Wang's *Chiang-chai shih-hua* (Discussions of Poetry from the Ginger Studio) sums up his basic approach:

> Although there are different names for "emotion" [*ch'ing*] and "scene" [*ching*], the two are really inseparable. Those who have divine talent [*shen*] in poetry achieve such a marvelous fusion [*miao-ho*] of them that nothing marks the one off from the other, but those who are merely accomplished poets either incorporate scene into emotional expression or emotion into description of scene.

Wang's writings concerned with poetry include fifteen separate collections of *shih* (the majority consist of just one *chüan*), three of *tz'u*, and a voluminous amount of literary criticism, all of which can be found in the modern reprints of his complete works, entitled either *Ch'uan-shan ch'üan-shu* or *Ch'uan-shan yi-shu*. In his *tz'u*, Wang often adapts a heroic and sorrowful stance reminiscent of Ch'ü Yüan (340–278 B.C.E.) as he was thought to reveal himself in the *Elegies of Ch'u*. His *tz'u* are largely lamentations for the sad times in which he found himself and expressions of his own frustrated hopes—lofty sentiments similar to those of Ch'en Wei-sung in his *tz'u*.

Before moving on to the most important poet of the seventeenth century, Wang Shih-chen, we should take a brief look at two slightly earlier poets whose prominence was summed up in a popular contemporary saying coined by Wang, "Shih in the south and Sung in the north," which refers to Shih Jun-chang (1618–1683), a native of Hsüan-ch'eng, Anhwei, and Sung Wan (1614–1673), a native of Lai-yang, Shantung. Both Wang and Ch'ien Ch'ien-yi praised Shih in the highest possible terms; Wang judged him the best of all contemporary *shih* poets and was especially fond of his pentasyllabic pastoral (*t'ien-yüan*) verse, which he thought was as good as that of Hsieh Ling-yün or Hsieh T'iao (464–499). Shih had a long and distinguished official career, first in the provinces, where he worked hard to alleviate the plight of common folk who had just lived through devastating times, and, later after passing the special *Po-hsüeh hung-tz'u* examination of 1679, in the capital as a Han-lin academician. His experiences as a provincial official are reflected in many *shih* in the ballad form (*yüeh-fu*) reminiscent of Tu Fu, which are filled with realistic description and compassionate feeling. Many little masterpieces can be found throughout the more than fifty *chüan* of his poetry contained in his collected literary works, the *Hsüeh-yü t'ang wen-chi* (Literary Collection from the Hall for Time Extra to Study).

Sung Wan was also a successful provincial official, serving in Anhwei, Kansu, Chih-li, Shao-hsing (Chekiang), and Szechwan. He was outstanding in all forms of *shih* as well as of *tz'u* and was also known as one of the best calligraphers of his time. Sung excelled at several different and distinctive styles. In his early years he stayed close to the High T'ang tradition of the Earlier and Later Seven Masters, but by his middle years he expanded his interests to include a wider range of models, often writing in the style of Lu Yu and, for the ancient pentasyllabic ballad form, Tu Fu and Han Yü (768–824); some of his verses are lengthy narratives. He was a close friend of Wang Shih-chen, whom he once asked to edit his poetic works; Wang did so in 1672, but this edition, to which Wu Wei-yeh had written a preface, was never published and was lost after Sung's death. Wang said that Sung's *shih* revealed a "personal character both profound and sturdy" (*ch'i-ko shen-wen*). Sung's literary collection is called the *An-ya t'ang chi* (Collection from the Hall Where One Finds Solace in Literary Elegance), and most of his extant lyrics are preserved in the *Erh-hsiang t'ing tz'u* (Lyrics from Two Village Hall), in three *chüan*. His early *tz'u* are characterized by an exuberant "lingering sense of beauty" (*mien-li*), but the tone of his later *tz'u*, composed during and after imprisonment on false charges (1661–1664), is often sad and grief-stricken—punctuated, however, by moments of ironic humor and a sense of world-weary wisdom.

Wang Shih-chen, a native of Hsin-ch'eng, Shantung, came from a family that had enjoyed generations of success in officialdom. Although several of his uncles and older cousins, ardent loyalists and serving Ming officials, had committed suicide on the fall of the Ming in 1644, his father did not, probably because his elderly grandfather, eighty-three years old, who had retired from government service in 1637, needed care and because Wang's father had himself never served as a Ming official. Thus this branch of the family survived and continued to produce *chin-shih*; besides Wang Shih-chen, two of his three older brothers also became officials. In addition to his literary attainments, of all major poets during the entire Ch'ing, Wang had perhaps the most illustrious official career, at the peak of which he served successively as Director of the Imperial Censorate (1698–1699), then as Minister of Justice (1699–1704), concurrently serving as Director of the Bureau of Imperial Historiography. He also represented the K'ang-hsi emperor (r. 1662–1722) as Commissioner of Sacrifices to the Spirit of the South Seas (Kwangtung, 1685) and to the Spirit of the West (Szechwan, 1696)—journeys that inspired much poetry. It was toward the beginning of his career, while serving as police magistrate of Yangchow (1660–1665), that he had the opportunity to visit scenic places in Kiangnan and associate with prominent literati there, including Ch'ien Ch'ien-yi.

At the time, Ch'ien Ch'ien-yi (in his late seventies and early eighties) was still considered the foremost poet of his day. He was immensely influential and the "grand old man" of poetry. The two became close friends; as the mature giant of poetry and its most promising student, the two were inevitably drawn together. Writing toward the end of his own life in 1704, Wang declared that Ch'ien had been the best friend that he had ever had. Ch'ien also had the highest regard for Wang and praised him in the preface he wrote to Wang's first major collection of poetry, *Wang Yi-shang shih-chi* (1661). However, the form this praise takes runs counter to the later conventional view of Wang's poetry and poetics, shaped largely by Chao Chih-hsin (1662–1744) and Yüan Mei (1716–1797) in the eighteenth century (and still prevalent today), that would have Wang writing only in a serene and impersonal style in the tradition of Wang Wei and Meng Hao-jan, based exclusively on the so-called Ch'an (Zen) poetics of Yen Yü's (c. 1195–c. 1245) *Ts'ang-lang shih-hua* (Ts'ang-lang's Remarks on Poetry) and the "mystical" poetics of Ssu-k'ung T'u (837–908; see chapter 45). This simplistic and misleading interpretation of Wang's works, his poetics, and his relation to Yen Yü and Ssu-k'ung T'u should be corrected. A good place to start is Ch'ien's preface.

Ch'ien begins evaluating Wang's poetry by saying that his poems "on being moved by the times" (*kan-shih*) are sadder than Tu Fu's and his "love" (*yüan-ch'ing*) poems are more touching than Li Shang-yin's (811?–859), then notes

Wang's profound learning and assimilation of the grand tradition of poetry, and goes on to state with approval Wang's four essential principles of poetry (Wang provides them also in his own preface): classical diction (*tien*), esthetic distance (*yüan*), prosodic harmony (*hsieh*), and esthetic standards (*tse*). Ch'ien adds that Wang's successful incorporation of these principles into his own poetry means that "the 'Hsiao ya' [Lesser Elegantiae, in the *Classic of Poetry*] are now composed again!" Ch'ien probably had two sets of poems by Wang in mind here: the extravagantly allusive "Ch'iu-liu shih" (Autumn Willows Poems) and the "Ch'in-huai tsa-shih" (Miscellaneous Poems on the Ch'in-huai River), both of which are redolent of nostalgia, a feeling for the vicissitudes of time, and an atmosphere of carpe diem. The "Ch'in-huai Poems," on the pleasure quarters of old Nanking, have an additional atmosphere of romance and mild eroticism.

However, for all their appreciation of each other as poets, Ch'ien and Wang were worlds apart when it came to poetic theory. Ch'ien's approach stayed close to the expressionist views of the Kung-an school, and he deplored the works of the Earlier and Later Seven Masters and their affiliation with Yen Yü, because he thought they did not compose "authentic" (*chen*) poetry—the spontaneous expression of real emotion—but only "phony" (*wei*) poetry—imitative expression based on false emotion. Wang's approach, by contrast, comes directly from the tradition of the Earlier and Later Seven Masters, and he adapted much from Yen Yü's poetics into his own. Ch'ien seems to have been unable to grasp what Yen meant when he said he was using "Ch'an [Zen] as an analogy for poetry" (*yi Ch'an yü shih*) and, like so many others before and since, dismissed it as obscurantist nonsense. However, the Earlier and Later Seven Masters and Wang Shih-chen seem to have understood the analogy—apparently correctly—as operating in three different ways: (1) in organizational terms, (2) in operational terms, and (3) in substantive terms. When the analogy expresses itself in *organizational* terms, it means that the truth of Ch'an and the truth of poetry are organized in similar ways. Each has a method or way (*fa*, cf. Sanskrit *dharma*) that the student must assimilate and internalize, and the transmission of this *fa* and its preservation are accomplished through a succession of masters or patriarchs in both organizations or systems. The "masters," of course, are those who have achieved enlightenment (*wu*, cf. Sanskrit *bodhi*): in Ch'an there are Ch'an masters, and in poetry there are masters of poetry. The substances of the respective *fa* may or may not have anything in common; what matters is that their organizations are similar. Within each, truth is one and immutable, and each organization has a tradition that both defines its truth and protects it against the snares and delusions of heterodoxy. When the analogy expresses itself in *operational* terms, it means that the truth of Ch'an and the truth of poetry are learned or acquired in similar ways. This is concerned with *how* truth is transmitted but not with truth *per se*. The way the student of poetry learns poetry is just like the way the student of Ch'an learns Ch'an; their respective organizations offer similar programs or operations for the student to follow. The operation of acquiring enlightenment in poetry, where enlightenment is understood as *spontaneous* control over the *correct* poetic medium, is the same kind of operation of acquiring enlightenment as in Ch'an, where enlightenment is understood as the achievement of pure consciousness, self-transcendence, mystical experience, and so forth. The ends of these two operations may or may not have anything in common, but the operations are similar, since the student in both is advised to go through the same stages: from conscious learning to assimilation and internalization, then to transcendence and sudden enlightenment. When the analogy expresses itself in *substantive* terms, it means that the truth of Ch'an, Ch'an enlightenment, and the truth of poetry, poetic enlightenment, are in some way(s) similar: in formal terms, enlightenment (*wu*) in poetry means the achievement of perfect intuitive control over the poetic medium, but in psychological or spiritual terms it means the attainment of a state of being where subjective self, medium of communication, and objective reality all become one. As such, intuitive control and intuitive cognition are opposite sides of the same coin, the "coin" being the poem *in toto*, the fusion of a spontaneous and effortless poetic act within a poetic medium that perfectly articulates "pure experience." It is here that poetry and Ch'an exhibit substantive or ontological similarity. Thus intuitive control in poetry is analogous to effortlessness in Ch'an, and intuitive cognition *as it is articulated* in poetry is analogous to the transcendence of discriminations in Ch'an enlightenment. However, in poetry the objects of cognition do not necessarily extend to the Absolute or Nirvana. It might be argued that the "transcendental" landscape poetry of a poet such as Wang Wei (701–761) or Meng Hao-jan (689–740) attempts to do just this; but Yan Yü, the Earlier and Later Seven Masters, and Wang Shih-chen did not limit their view of poetic enlightenment to this kind of poetry alone but included in it all poetry that they regarded as embodiments of the true *fa* of poetry, poetry often far removed in subject matter from the landscape poetry of a Wang Wei. In fact, all of them, including Wang Shih-chen (contrary to what is generally thought), believed and declared that Li Po and Tu Fu—not Wang Wei, Wei Ying-wu, or Meng Hao-jan—were the very best poets in the entire tradition.

Ch'ien Ch'ien-yi had no use for the notion of an "orthodox tradition of poetry" that required any "enlightenment" to unlock the secrets of the *fa* of poetry. As he said, "Poetry is where the heart's wishes go. One molds his native sensibilities [*hsing-ling*] and wanders amid scenery. Every person says what he wants to say—that's all there is to it!" He and Wang must have agreed to disagree, for Wang once regretfully said, "Mr. Ch'ien . . . did not approve of Yen's theory of marvelous enlightenment [*miao-wu*]. The chronic shortcoming that bedeviled him his whole life was exactly because of this." However, Ch'ien composed a great deal of very moving verse, filled with subtlety of meaning and fascinating imagery; apparently his genius did not require the sophisticated theory of a Yen Yü or a Wang Shih-chen.

Much of Wang's extensive critical writings on *shih*, which originally appeared either in small collections of *shih-hua* or scattered throughout his prose writings—in prefaces, postfaces, letters, etc.—were collected and published by Chang Tsung-nan (1704–1765) as the *Tai-ching t'ang shih-hua* (Discussions of Poetry from the Hall of the Vademecum Classics Scholar), thirty *chüan*, in 1760. As voluminous as his critical writings are—and as extensive in scope and detailed in analysis—Wang's basic view of poetry can be defined by reference to a few critical terms he often uses: "spirit resonance" (*shen-yün*), "enlightened / heightened concentration / meditation / insight" (*san-mei*, Chinese transcription of Sanskrit *samādhi*), which is roughly equivalent to "enlightened / enlightenment" (*wu*), "poetic method / way" (*fa*), "enter spirit" (*ju shen*) or "enter Ch'an (*ju Ch'an*), and "serenity and distance" (*hsien-yüan*) or "purity and distance" (*ch'ing-yüan*). Perhaps the best introduction to these terms and the concepts they express—as well as to the nature of Wang's affiliations to Yen Yü and Ssu-k'ung T'u—is his preface to the anthology of T'ang verse he edited, *T'ang-hsien san-mei chi* (Collection of Samādhi [Enlightened] Poetry by Bhadras [Virtuous Sages] of the Tang), written in 1688 when he was fifty-three:

> When Yan Yü discussed poetry, he said such things as: "Poets of the High T'ang were only concerned with inspired interest [*hsing-ch'ü*]." "As antelopes that hung by their horns, they left behind no tracks by which they could be found." "As utterly transparent crystals, their poems defy rational analysis [*pu-k'o ts'ou-po*]." "Like a sound in the air, the play of color in the appearance of things, the moon reflected in water, or an image in a mirror, the words come to an end, but the thought [*yi*] is infinite." When Ssu-k'ung T'u discussed poetry he also said that the marvelousness [*miao*] of poetry "lies beyond sourness and saltiness." Toward the end of the spring of the *mao-chen* year of the K'ang-hsi era [1688], when I returned home, . . . I selected poetry by various masters of the K'ai-yüan [713–741] and T'ien-pao [742–756] eras [the High T'ang] to read every day. It was then that I had a separate flash of insight of my own into what these two gentlemen [Yen Yü and Ssu-k'ung T'u] had said. So I set down poems that especially possessed delicious lingering flavor and transcendent profundity [*chün-yung ch'ao-yi*], which, beginning with those of Wang Wei, includes the works of forty-two poets in all; this is *T'ang-hsien san-mei chi*, a work edited in three *chüan*. . . . My not including poems by the two masters Li Po and Tu Fu follows the example of Wang An-shih's [1021–1086] *T'ang pai-chia shih-hsüan* [Anthology of One Hundred T'ang Masters]. Chang Chiu-ling [678–740] initiates the poetry of the High Tang, and Wei Ying-wu concludes it, but I do not include the poetry of these two masters either since I have already done so in my anthology of pentasyllabic verse and do not wish to duplicate that selection here.

Elsewhere Wang explains that Wang An-shih did not include poetry by Li Po and Tu Fu, or by Han Yü, in his anthology because "their poems are so very numerous and commonly circulate in individual collections of their own." The anthology in which Wang Shih-chen included poetry by Chang Chiu-ling and Wei Ying-wu is his *Ku-shih hsüan* (Anthology of Ancient-Style Verse). Wang could have added that another reason for not including works by Li and Tu in *T'ang-hsien san-mei chi* was that he had already included fifty-three poems by Li and sixty-seven by Tu in *Ku-shih hsüan*. In any event, Li Po and Tu Fu are also mentioned scores of times throughout Wang's critical writings—always in positive, laudatory terms—so that Chao Chih-hsin's accusation that Wang had absolutely no liking for Tu Fu's poetry but lacked the courage to attack Tu openly is patently false, and Yüan Mei's assertion that Wang had no taste for "strongly expressive poetry" is utterly without foundation as well. Nevertheless, critics and historians of poetry often cite Chao's and Yüan's remarks to support the claim that Wang's poetry and poetics are never more than latter-day derivations from the Wang Wei tradition of landscape poetry and can be pigeonholed accordingly.

T'ang-hsien san-mei chi certainly contains many "antique-and-placid and serene-and-distant" [*ku-tan hsien-yüan*] landscape poems by Wang Wei and Meng Hao-jan, yet many other poems by them and other T'ang poets included are not at all this kind of poetry but often poems of parting that overflow with the grief of separation and longing for absent friends—full of "powerful expressiveness" [*ch'en-cho t'ung-k'uai*]. Wang, in fact, rejected the claim that "purity and distance" and "powerful expressiveness" were mutually exclusive, polar opposite modes of poetry and believed that truly great poetry was a fusion of both, which he strove to achieve in his own work: "As for 'powerful expressiveness,' this was not something that only Li Po, Tu Fu, and Han Yü had, but that T'ao Ch'ien, Hsieh Ling-yün, Wang Wei, and Meng Hao-jan, as well as their followers, also had without exception."

Similarly, "enlightenment" (*wu*) or *samādhi* (*san-mei*) in Wang's poetics does not simply refer to, as is conventionally assumed, the transcendent landscape tradition of Wang Wei, noted for its attempts to combine flashes of insight into the Tao (Way) of the natural world with metaphoric expressions of Ch'an enlightenment. "Enlightenment" as a term and concept is part of the Ch'an-poetry analogy (analyzed above) that Wang—like Yen Yü—uses throughout his critical writings. Other expressions for poetic "enlightenment" in Wang's writings are "enter spirit" (*ju shen*) and "enter Ch'an" (*ju Ch'an*): to enter the state or realm where one has a grasp of the "undifferentiated marvelous" (*hun-miao chih ching*), that is, the "realm of creativity" (*hua-ching*) where one has perfect intuitive control over the poetic medium, which is the highest attainment in any kind of poetry—and not just in poetry that embodies "spirit resonance" (*shen-yün*), as does some of Wang Wei's or some of Wang Shih-chen's own poetry.

In the light of all this, the *shen* (spirit) in Wang's famous catchword *shen-yün* most likely refers to "perfect intuitive control," and, in the light of Wang's belief that the best poetry fuses "purity and distance" with "powerful expressiveness," it is most likely that the *yün* (resonance) in *shen-yün* refers to the tone of the poet's mood, feeling, and emotions as they resonate at a distance "serenely" (*hsien*) or "purely" (*ch'ing*) in poems. Wang himself never defined what *shen-yün* meant, but the following passage from his *shih-hua* reveals that it does indeed include the concept of "purity and distance":

> [K'ung T'ien-yün (*chin-shih* of 1533)] . . . said that poetry is for expressing personal nature [*shih yi ta hsing*] but to be the best it had to be pure and distant [*ch'ing-yüan*]. When Hsüeh Hui [1489–1541] discussed poetry, he only promoted the works of poets such as Hsieh Ling-yun, Wang Wei, Meng Hao-jan, and Wei Ying-wu. He said: " 'While white clouds embrace hidden rocks, / Green bamboos form eyebrows over a clear brook.' [Hsieh] exemplifies 'purity.' 'The magic revealed—no one appreciates, / The immortals hidden—who tells their tale?' [Hsieh] exemplifies 'distance.' 'Why must one have strings and woodwinds? / Mountains and waters provide their own pure notes' [Tso Ssu (c. 253–c. 307)] and 'Setting sun sets flocks of birds singing, / Water and trees add depth to exquisite beauty' [Hsieh Hun (d. c. 412)] exemplify the conjoining of 'purity' and 'distance.' All the marvelousness of this can be summed up in the one expression 'spirit resonance.' " In the past, when I began to use the term *shen-yün* while discussing poetry with students, I did not realize that it had first appeared here.

Wang Shih-chen often tried to compose this kind of poetry—sometimes succeeding admirably, for which he is justly famous—and he certainly argued that it should be granted a prominent place in the poetic tradition, but it is essential to realize that he recognized that other, more directly emotive and expressive, kinds of poetry deserve prominence as well. Both advocates and opponents of Wang and his theory of *shen-yün* have tended to ignore his wide and varied tastes and practices and focus instead exclusively on his interest in serene landscape poetry. This distorts and devalues his place in the Chinese poetic tradition and does him and his work great injustice.

Wang during his younger years was also an enthusiastic *tz'u* poet. Descriptions of scenery, send-off poems, eulogies to beautiful women, melancholic musings, longing for absent friends—the conventional themes associated with *tz'u*—he did them all. Musical and easy to read, they stand in great contrast to the serious *shih* he was writing at the same time. Wang's lyrics are preserved in two collections, the *Juan-t'ing shih-yü* (Juan-t'ing's Lyrics; 1655–1657) and *Yen-p'o tz'u* (Spreading Waves Lyrics; 1658–1664), which expands on the contents of the first collection. He also compiled a collection of historical, technical, and critical remarks on *tz'u*, *Hua-ts'ao meng-shih* (Blossoming Bushes Plucked by Juvenile Ignorance), material written before 1665, which is a valuable source for the history of the lyric during the Ming–Ch'ing transitional period. Wang's interest in the *tz'u* peaked during the years he served as police magistrate in

Yangchow (1660–1665) and seems to have ended when he was recalled to the capital to take up a post in the Ministry of Rites in 1665. His eldest brother, Wang Shih-lu (1626–1673), a minor *shih* poet, was better known as a fine *tz'u* writer. His lyrics were edited as *Ch'ui-wen chih-yü* (Goblet Words to Hear Around the Cooking Fire), a title later changed to *Ch'ui-wen tz'u* (Lyrics to Hear Around the Cooking Fire) (two *chüan*). His short songs on love and "longing of ladies in boudoirs" (*kuei-ssu*) were highly praised, and he also became well known for "Chiang-ts'un ch'ang-ho tz'u" (River Village Offer and Response Lyrics), which he, Sung Wan, and Ts'ao Erh-k'an (1617–1679) composed together in 1665 at West Lake, Hangchow. After these began to circulate, dozens of other *tz'u* poets all over the country composed matching lyrics. Wang Shih-lu, Sung, and Ts'ao had originally composed eight lyrics to the tune "Man-chiang hung" (River Filled with Red [Blossoms]), and these twenty-four *tz'u*, full of melancholy, nostalgia, and reflection on the vicissitudes of history and the hard times—all obliquely articulated—struck a strong sympathetic chord, especially among the many poets who still harbored Ming-loyalist sympathies.

Other significant *shih* poets of the seventeenth century include Wu Chia-chi (1618–1684), a commoner poet from the Yangchow region. Wu had attracted the attention of Wang Shih-chen, who promoted his works, often sympathetic portrayals of the plight of the common folk during the Ming–Ch'ing transition years; Li Yü (1610/11–1680), better known as a dramatist, fiction writer, critic, and publisher but whose *shih* poetry also deserves attention for its wit, irony, unconventional approach, and often unrestrained expressiveness; Sung Lo (1634–1713), associated with the Ch'ing-era revival of Sung era *shih* poetry (see the reference to Wu Chih-chen in chapter 18), especially that of Su Shih, was himself a *shih* poet of national stature, whose reputation rivaled that of Wang Shih-chen, who nevertheless had nothing but praise for his work; and Chu Yi-tsun (1629–1709), a commoner who passed the special *Po-hsüeh hung-tz'u* examination of 1679 (to have a checkered career for the next twenty years), anthologist, critic, and historian, now better known as a *tz'u* poet and leader of the Che-hsi (western Chekiang) *tz'u* school than for his *shih*. Sung's *shih* were also highly regarded in his day, and he was often associated with Wang Shih-chen and Sung Lo as the three best *shih* poets of the early Ch'ing era. Note should also be taken of Yeh Hsieh (1627–1703), who, while not achieving distinction as a poet, wrote the most comprehensive and systematic treatise on poetry since Yen Yü's *Ts'ang-lang shih-hua*, namely, *Yüan shih* (On the Origin of Poetry). Yeh's theory of poetry was essentially expressionistic, but he also explored the metaphysical foundation of poetry in terms of "principle" (*li*), "event" (*shih*), and "tendency" or "manner" (*ch'ing*).

Painters who were also highly appreciated as *shih* poets include Wan Shou-ch'i (1603–1652), Yün Shou-p'ing (1633–1690), Chu Ta (Pa-ta shan-jen; 1626–1705), Wu Li (1632–1718), and Shih-t'ao (Tao-chi; 1642–1707). These are among the most famous painters of the seventeenth century (see chapter 25). Although their poems are rarely studied except as adjuncts to their paintings, familiarity with these men can be an enriching experience, for they are often highly individualistic—eccentric, even crazy sometimes (as in the case of Chu Ta and Shih-t'ao)—and one of them, Wu Li, both an enthusiast of Sung era *shih* poetry and a close student of Wang Shih-chen's poetics, was not only a convert to Catholicism but an ordained Catholic priest. His *shih* on Christian themes make especially interesting reading.

Another fascinating area of seventeenth-century poetry is the *shih* and *tz'u* of female poets, which have recently been coming to light after long years of neglect. Important new research on this hitherto neglected area of literary history is summarized in chapter 11.

Considering the enormous sweep of time during which Chinese literature has existed and the tremendous variety of its different genres and forms, the present chapter on the poetry and poetics of the seventeenth century may seem to have been granted a disproportionately large amount of space in this volume. Yet it was during this single century that the greatest cultural transformation in Chinese history since the advent of Buddhism began to take place. Not only did the seventeenth century witness the transition from the native Ming dynasty to the foreign-dominated Ch'ing dynasty, it also saw the first stirrings of Westernization, the inception of methods for evidential research (*k'ao-cheng-hsüeh*), an unprecedented degree of religious syncretism, and whole new modes of esthetic consciousness—all set against a background of strong cultural continuity. It was this complex combination of trusted traditions from the past and vibrant challenges from the future that characterized the literary world of the seventeenth century, and nowhere were the changes being wrought more evident than in the tensions expressed over poetry and poetics. China had embarked on the measured march to modernity.

Richard John Lynn

Chapter 22

POETRY OF THE EIGHTEENTH TO EARLY TWENTIETH CENTURIES

For sheer bulk of the surviving corpus of work, there are few if any bodies of literature that can rival the poetry written in the traditional Chinese *shih* and *tz'u* forms during the period from about 1700 to the early twentieth century. Thousands of men, and not a few women, produced verse in these forms daily, many writers leaving to posterity several thousand poems. Any account of this material is bound to be highly selective and to omit much of interest and delight, especially an account as brief as this one necessarily is.

Selection and presentation alike require organizing principles. Chronology can serve to some extent, but the nature of the social and intellectual world of Ch'ing poetry requires that the previous "schools" of poetry and their ideals be kept well in view. The schools of poetry that flourished and contended during this period differed over the locus of literary values. Very broadly considered, the contrast was between those who emphasized formal values and those whose concerns were expressive. The former tended to look to the past, seeking their standards in the existing tradition, while the latter located the source of poetic worth in the individual poet himself. When they looked to the past, the formalists usually valued most the poetry of the T'ang dynasty, while the individualists often saw Sung poetry as the high point of the tradition before their own day.

These differing values were not, of course, new in themselves. Indeed, along with the idea of literature as an encouragement to public morality, they have been present virtually from the origins of the Chinese poetic tradition. Even the almost universal explicitness about poetic values and the tendency to see the contemporary world of letters as embodying an active contention among contradictory views can be traced back continuously at least to the *fu-ku* (revive antiquity, or archaist) movement of the middle of the Ming dynasty (see chapter 20).

What is striking is, rather, the very persistence, during and after the Ch'ing dynasty, of so much that was strictly traditional. Although there was much debate about how poetry should be written, no new forms of verse were introduced, nor were any fundamentally new critical views advanced. The field of play for most of this period consisted, instead, of the entire existing content of the classical tradition in both *shih* and *tz'u* poetry. The questions at issue were matters of emphasis rather than of development or progress. Even the great social and political upheavals of the late Ch'ing and the Republic were reflected more as topical concerns than as occasions for renewed evolution of the traditional forms among the poets thought most influential by their contemporaries. In the end, it was the status of classical poetry that changed, not its content. Late Ch'ing political reformers and conservatives alike cast their poetic works in "classical" Chinese (i.e., Literary Sinitic) and in forms whose origins lay at least a millennium in the past. This perpetuation of early norms and models for such a long period of time and in the face of the increasingly insistent encroachment of modernity (particularly from abroad) is remarkable in the annals of world cultural history.

The economic, military, and, in the end, even cultural pressure on China from the outside world grew from a barely perceptible force in 1700 to one of overwhelming effect by the early twentieth century. This had the result of increasingly skewing the distribution of authority among existing views within the classical tradition and eventually of forcing that tradition toward the margins of Chinese civilization. Foreign influence was, however, of only minor importance inside the tradition itself. The writing of poetry in the *shih* and *tz'u* forms was evidently so inherently Chinese an activity that even the few outsiders (chiefly, Japanese) who wrote in these forms tended to adopt Chinese literary values.

In the discussion below, chronology will be at least roughly observed, but the more fundamental concern will be to articulate literary relationships. For the first century or so of the Ch'ing dynasty, observing a division between formalists and individualists gives a reasonably adequate framework for discussion. Later in the dynasty, however, more complex relationships among ideas and writers tend to blur this distinction.

The greatest poet of the Ch'ing dynasty was probably Wang Shih-chen (discussed at length in chapter 21). The formalist tradition for the rest of the Ch'ing found its central figure in one of Wang's followers, Shen Te-ch'ien (1673–1769), who in the course of an extraordinarily long life not only produced a great deal of poetry but also compiled a series of highly influential anthologies.

Both in his poetry and in the anthologies, Shen attempted to embody the "traditionalist" ideal of poetry that was at once formally perfect and morally improving. The term attached to his literary standard is *ko-tiao* ("form and mode" [in Modern Standard Mandarin, this term has come to signify a literary or artistic "style"]). In practice, this meant poetry entirely in accordance with prescriptive norms, first, based on the practice of T'ang and pre-T'ang poets and, second, with ideals of attitude and behavior appropriate to the public-minded Confucian. The necessary degree of art came both from the accomplishment of an understated personal expression ("gentle and sincere, aggrieved but not angry" was the classic formulation of this ideal) and from the invisible craft required to meet these requirements without leaving any evident traces of the effort expended in doing so.

For a man so influential and eventually so prominent in public life, Shen was remarkably late in achieving success. He was in his sixties before he finally passed the provincial-level civil service examinations, after dozens of attempts. Success came more swiftly in the capital, where he attained the *chin-shih* degree in 1739. He was soon one of the Ch'ien-lung emperor's (1736–1795) closest literary advisers, favor being extended to him right to the end of his long life (though not for long after it, as he was posthumously stripped of his honors when he was found to have written a biographical essay for a man later deemed disloyal).

The first of Shen's anthologies, *T'ang-shih pieh-tsai chi* (Separately Collected Anthology of T'ang Verse), appeared in 1717, followed in 1725 by *Ku-shih yüan* (Source of Old Poetry), a collection of pre-T'ang poetry, excluding the canonical *Shih-ching* (Classic of Poetry) and the all but canonical *Ch'u tz'u* (Elegies of Ch'u) but including many bits of verse traditionally attributed to figures of great antiquity, beginning with the Yellow Emperor. Shen's *Separately Collected Anthologies* of Ming and early Ch'ing poetry appeared in 1739 and 1759. He also compiled several other anthologies of both poetry and prose.

That Shen's anthologies have appeared to modern Chinese readers to reflect a mature and well-balanced, if rather conservative, taste is due at least in part to the anthologies themselves having done much to shape Chinese taste in poetry down to the present. Thus, in the T'ang anthology, pride of place goes to the great figures of the High T'ang: Tu Fu (254 poems), Li Po (139), and Wang Wei (104), with much less space allotted to such poets as Po Chü-yi (61) and Tu Mu (18), favorites of Japanese taste, and very little indeed to the sort of poetry that Western readers have tended to find intriguing, such as the work of Meng Chiao (13), Li Ho (10), and the Buddhist poems attributed to Han-shan (0). It is also significant that, although *Separately Collected Anthologies*, titled by analogy with Shen's compilations, do exist for the poetry of the Sung (published in 1761) and Yüan (1764) dynasties, they were compiled by other hands, since these periods were thought by Shen and like-minded literati to be of less interest.

Li O (1692–1752) is often taken to represent the classicist Che-hsi (western Chekiang) school of *tz'u* poetry (Che-hsi p'ai). This school grew out of the work of Chu Yi-tsun, a seventeenth-century master (discussed in chapter 21). Li is thus seen as following Chu in a way analogous to Shen Te-ch'ien's relationship to Wang Shih-chen. This view does Li less than perfect justice. While he was certainly influenced by Chu, he was a more significant figure than the other men affiliated with this school in the formative anthology *Che-hsi liu-chia tz'u* (Lyric Poems by Six Poets of Western Chekiang), one of the latter being the anthology's compiler, Kung Hsiang-lin.

Although Li passed the provincial-level examination for the *chü-jen* (Recommended Scholar) degree in 1720, his subsequent attempt at the special *po-hsüeh hung-tz'u* (Erudite Literatus) examination held in 1736 failed when his paper was disqualified on a technicality. Throughout his adult life, Li lived not as an official but, rather, as a teacher and scholar hosted by various wealthy patrons, the most important of whom were the Ma brothers of Yangchow. In addition to works on historical subjects, he compiled one of the most important collections of source material on Sung dynasty poetry, the *Sung-shih chi-shih* (Annals of Sung Poetry).

While Li's own *shih* poetry reflects T'ang and earlier models rather than Sung, he found the inspiration for his *tz'u* poetry in the late Southern Sung, among the works of such poets as Chiang K'uei and Chang Yen. This preference, in which he followed Chu Yi-tsun, was based on the view that Southern Sung represented the high point of the *tz'u*, analogous to the High T'ang for *shih* poetry. Such a preference reflected his essentially archaistic orientation, for the excellence of Chiang and Chang was seen to lie in their mastery of the verbal resources of the form rather than in the more direct expression of emotion found in earlier Sung writers such as Su Shih and Hsin Ch'i-chi. It also accounts for his affiliation with the Che-hsi school, as opposed to the Yang-hsien school (Yang-hsien p'ai) of expressive, self-assertive *tz'u* exemplified by Ch'en Wei-sung.

The earliest and most pointed reaction to the influence of Wang Shih-chen is found in the work of Chao Chih-hsin (1662–1744). Chao, related to Wang by marriage, made a brilliant start to his public career, attaining the *chin-shih* degree when he was eighteen and holding offices in both the Han-lin Academy and the provinces, only to be dismissed and barred for life from holding office ten years later when he was found to have been in the audience of an opera performed while the court was in mourning. Evidently a proud and somewhat difficult man by nature, he passed the rest of his long life in bitter retirement, quick to criticize those more fortunate than he.

Chief among his targets was Wang Shih-chen. Wang's delay in providing a promised preface to a collection of Chao's writings is usually cited as the occasion for the rupture between them, but it is likely that Wang's reluctance grew out of a recognition that he and Chao were already very different in their approaches to poetry. Chao eventually made his criticism of Wang explicit in a brief but influential work titled *T'an lung lu* (A Record of Comments on a

Dragon; the "dragon" in question was not Wang Shih-chen himself but a beast introduced by way of analogical argument in one of his comments on poetry).

In *T'an-lung lu*, Chao took Wang to task for making poetry mystical and impersonal. In place of "in a poem there is no 'I'" (*shih chung wu wo*), which he took to be Wang's goal, Chao insisted that "in a poem, 'I' am present" (*shih chung yu wo*). He argued that poetry should be based on personal experience and that its themes should be real things and events. He also opposed "schoolish" narrowness, urging poets to learn from many masters, and insisted that in a poem, sense is primary and language subservient. In spite of this de-emphasis of language, Chao Chih-hsin was also interested in poetic prosody and compiled a large work on the use of tonal patterns by T'ang poets. His interest in formal mastery and his choice of the T'ang era as his reference standard, can both be seen as continuations of the "archaist" tradition of the Ming, while his interest in a poetry of "substance" and in the individual voice look ahead to Weng Fang-kang and Yüan Mei, respectively.

Weng Fang-kang (1733–1818) is the last of our four major representatives of the formalist tradition. Weng, a child prodigy, was awarded the *hsiu-ts'ai* (Cultivated Talent or Licentiate degree, which qualified one to take the provincial examinations) when he was nine years old and attained the *chin-shih*, the highest degree, in his late teens. His subsequent career was spent at the highest levels of the Han-lin Academy, and he was shown frequent marks of esteem by the Ch'ien-lung emperor.

Weng is not an easy poet for modern taste to accommodate. His critical byword, analogous to Wang Shih-chen's *shen-yün* (spirit resonance), was *chi-li*, which translates literally as "flesh and principle" and in practice meant something like "substance and order." A man of the greatest erudition, Weng believed that learning ought to serve as the basis for poetry. His poems draw frequently on his mastery of history and epigraphy, and this has, not surprisingly, made him an easy target for critics both contemporary and modern who see individual expression as the essence of poetry (and also lack the breadth and depth of learning needed to appreciate Weng's work on its own terms). He was lampooned by Yüan Mei (see below) but did not himself deign to respond to Yüan, reserving his critical remarks for poets and schools who represented values closer to his own. A balanced view must recognize that his collected poetry does include poems that individualist critics would call "true poetry," but that most of his works consist of colophons on paintings and antique inscriptions. Both sorts of poems are unfailingly reflective of orthodox social opinions and faithful to traditional formal norms. The former characteristic is the more noticeable, as Weng was an admirer of Sung dynasty poetry, works whose detractors said were merely versified philosophy.

Shen Te-ch'ien, Li O, Chao Chih-hsin, and Weng Fang-kang reflect in their various ways the formalist tradition in Ch'ing poetry. Opposition to them is found among a variety of poets whose ideals stood in distinct contrast to theirs.

This latter group comprises men who differed a great deal among themselves, but who all considered the individual and his sensibility central to poetic creation. Each of the men to be discussed had his own antecedents and followers, some of whom were important poets themselves but most of whom will not be taken up here.

The first is Cha Shen-hsing (1650–1727), who can be considered to some extent a transitional figure between Ch'ien Ch'ien-yi and Yüan Mei. Cha had a varied educational and scholarly career but finally attained the *chin-shih* in his fifties, having come to the attention of the K'ang-hsi emperor (r. 1662–1722) during one of the latter's visits to southern China. After ten years as a court poet and academician, Cha retired, only to be arrested in connection with the prosecution of one of his brothers for suspected disloyalty in one of the dynasty's famous literary persecutions. Although his brother died in prison and another brother was exiled to Shensi province, Cha Shen-hsing was allowed to return home, where he died within a few months of his release.

A participant in the compilation of *P'ei-wen yün-fu* (Storehouse [of Quotations Classified by] Rhyme from the Pendant to Letters [Studio]), a vast compendium of literary extracts still widely used by scholars, and of a number of gazetteers, including *Ta Ch'ing yi-t'ung-chih* (Comprehensive Gazetteer of the Great Ch'ing), Cha left a large body of poetry. In contrast to the orientation toward the *shih* poetry of the T'ang characteristic of most of the formalist writers of Ming and Ch'ing (Weng Fang-kang is an important exception), Cha wrote within a tradition that saw Tu Fu not as the culmination of the *shih* but, rather, as the origin of a line that included Po Chü-yi, Han Yü, Su Shih, Lu Yu, Yüan Hao-wen, and Kao Ch'i. The crucial distinction was that between the "T'ang" concentration on the individual poem as a perfected linguistic artifact and the "Sung" manner of reading a poet's corpus as a cumulative collection of autobiographical poetic documents. Although it is possible to read Tu Fu's works in this way, Po Chü-yi was the first poet to treat his works as a kind of autobiography, ideally read as a corpus and in chronological order. The later and more voluminous example of particular relevance to Cha Shen-hsing was Lu Yu, whose day-by-day response to the complexities of his society and his own character established his standing as a poet by accretion as much as by the success of particular poems.

If a poet's work could cumulatively express his personal character and vision, then the same might be true of individual poems, provided the poet made a point of centering his work on his individual perceptions. The most important Ch'ing poets to take this approach were Cheng Hsieh (1691–1764), Yüan Mei (1716–1797), and Chao Yi (1727–1814). With Yüan, in particular, is associated the name of the "sensibility" or "inspirational" school (*hsing-ling p'ai*). This group is generally considered one of the leading rivals of the *shen-yün* (Wang Shih-chen), *ko-tiao* (Shen Te-ch'ien), and *chi-li* (Weng Fang-kang) schools of the early and middle Ch'ing.

Cheng Hsieh was raised in straitened circumstances, eventually attained the *chin-shih* degree, served meritoriously as a local official, and then retired to relative poverty, in which he supported himself by his calligraphy and painting. As a visual artist, Cheng is counted among the "Eight Eccentrics of Yangchow." His experience of privation, both his own and that of the common people around him, gave his poetry an edge as well as a consolatory quality, epitomized by his recollection of a pastry given him by his wet-nurse at a time when she had more pressing concerns of her own—he said it meant more to him than any official salary.

Cheng, like Wen Cheng-ming, Shen Chou, and Hsü Wei in the Ming dynasty, is known as much for his painting and calligraphy as for his poetry and essays. There is always the danger, especially in the Chinese tradition, that esteem earned by achievements in the visual arts may be too easily extended to one's writings. Cheng Hsieh may be an example of this, but his directness of expression makes him both a pleasure to read and an important forerunner of Yüan Mei in claiming importance for the poetry—and style of life—of the writer indifferent both to the prestige of earlier models and to the often-claimed moral role of literature.

Yüan Mei is the better-known (in his own day even notorious) poet. Having grown up in a prosperous family and distinguished himself by passing the *chin-shih* exam while still in his early twenties, he was assigned to the Grand Secretariat and appeared destined for a brilliant career as an official. His failure to master the Manchu language, required by his duties, led to his relegation to a series of provincial posts beginning in 1742. In 1749 he retired and built his retreat in Nanking, an elaborate garden estate that he named Sui-yüan (Accommodation Garden) and later declared to have been the original of the Ta-kuan (Great Vista) Garden in which much of the famous novel *Hung-lou meng* (A Dream of Red Towers) was set (see chapter 35). He never returned to official life but, instead, alternated extensive travels around China with a life of cultivated and elegant retirement on his estate.

Yüan's major predecessors were Yang Wan-li in the Sung dynasty and Yüan Hung-tao in the Ming. He was not so much opposed to archaism as he was indifferent to its central criterion. For him, the issue was simply one of good poetry versus bad, not of ancient versus contemporary. Good poetry was expressive of individual experience, freshly realized and cast in original language. As he was fond of pointing out, many of the songs in the canonical *Shih-ching* were spontaneous expressions of emotion, with no "antiquity" or formal rules to which they might have referred. Moreover, he argued, were Tu Fu to have been writing in the same age as Yüan himself, his poetry would not be the same as what he had actually written during the T'ang dynasty.

By coincidence, Yüan passed the *chin-shih* exam in the same year as Shen Te-ch'ien, although Shen was already in his sixties at the time. Yüan later wrote a number of letters to Shen in which he criticized, sometimes in quite saucy terms, the latter's poetics. It is possible that part of Yüan's motive was resentment of Shen's success at a time when Yüan, for all his promise, had seen his chances for a career in the capital vanish. In any event, while Yüan's letters are preserved in his collected works, Shen either did not deign to reply or at least left his responses out of his own collected works.

Yüan Mei is often grouped with Chiang Shih-ch'üan (1725–1785) and Chao Yi as one of the three leading writers of southern China in his day. Chiang is most highly regarded as a dramatist and is not discussed here. Chao Yi, however, was a *shih* poet of great interest. Son of a private tutor, he succeeded his father in this profession while still in his teens when the latter died. He eventually traveled to Peking, where his talents were recognized by his employment in the Grand Secretariat even before he passed the *chin-shih* examination of 1762. He served with some distinction in the remote southwestern provinces of Kweichow and Yunnan before retiring in 1773.

A major part of Chao Yi's reputation rests on his historical writings rather than his poetry. He was one of the most significant premodern historians of China, notable for his success in tracing the larger historical patterns ignored by traditional scholarship, which tended to concentrate on detail and on moral evaluation, all within the framework of dynastic periodization.

In fact, the qualities of intellectual alertness and independence from conventional thinking that distinguish his historical work are also evident in his poetry, which consistently displays wit and originality. He was not opposed in principle to the emulation of old masters, but neither did he see doing so as a necessary element of writing poetry. He did not object to a poet's making use of his learning, but he insisted that the resulting poetry be interesting. His own learning, whether historical or exotic—he referred in his works to such Western devices as the microscope and telescope—is often displayed in his poetry, but only as an element in something original. Not concerned with the embodiment of orthodox opinions in his verse, he nonetheless showed an interest in the condition of the common people.

The influence of Yüan Mei continued through the eighteenth century and into the nineteenth, even while the prosperity and social peace that had supported his independence of outlook and his refined hedonism were beginning to wane. Perhaps the most important of his younger followers was Chang Wen-t'ao (1764–1814), who enjoyed a successful career as an official in both the capital and the provinces. Chang's views on poetry were generally similar to Yüan's. He opposed the formalism of Shen Te-ch'ien and the antiquarian approach of Weng Fang-kang and, like Yüan, saw no need to choose between the poetry of T'ang and that of Sung. His poetry, however, introduces themes that Yüan would have had little occasion to treat, most notably in a set of eighteen poems that Chang wrote in 1798, the year of Yüan's death, while traveling in southern Shensi at the time of the White Lotus Rebellion (a religious secret society persecuted by the Ch'ing authorities). The greatness of the Ch'ing was beginning to fray, and poets could hardly ignore the consequences.

On literary grounds too, Yüan's influence was beginning to fade. Among the first to venture a criticism was one of his own followers, Hung Liang-chi (1746–1809), whose extensive training and practice of historical and geographical scholarship had made him realize that poetry was necessarily embedded in history, at least in literary history. Hung compiled some local gazetteers himself, offered far-sighted critiques of court policy (which in one instance almost cost him his life), and even anticipated Malthus's observations on population growth. As a poet, he is a fine and representative figure, but perhaps not one deserving further comment to the extent that his friend Huang Ching-jen (1749–1783) clearly does.

Huang Ching-jen belonged by birth to almost the last generation that could ignore the impending crisis of confrontation with Western imperialism. In a sense, he avoided the crisis only because he died in his early thirties after a life of misfortune (he died before Hung Liang-chi attained the *chin-shih* degree). He responded to his troubles very much as other unfortunate Chinese poets had responded before him, albeit with his own distillation of their tradition and his own impressive mastery of the received resources of poetry. Indeed, his mastery was so evident that he earned the respect even of senior writers whose poetic ideals were quite different from his own. No less unlikely a figure than Weng Fang-kang edited a posthumous edition of Huang's works.

Huang was orphaned at the age of three and subsequently lost his grandfather and a brother. Although recognized for his brilliance by many of the most accomplished men of the age, he failed eight times to pass the *chin-shih* examination and never held an official position of any consequence. Moreover, having acquired some of the expensive habits of the circles in which he traveled, he spent more than he earned and was harassed by debt by the time tuberculosis carried him away.

As a poet, Huang is known above all for having succeeded more extravagantly than any predecessor in reviving the style of the great T'ang master Li Po. The style was in part, as in the case of Li himself, a matter of adopting a poetic persona appropriate to his circumstances. A poor but gifted genius frequently dependent on the generosity of appreciative patrons, he evokes, in his "Li Po" works, both his hardships and the generosity of spirit that he would seek in his associates. His distinction lies in the brilliance with which he does this, questions of motive aside.

There are, moreover, other sides to Huang's work, perhaps less aggressive in their claims on a reader's sympathy but often more successful as poetry. These include both his *shih* poems in modes other than that of Li Po and his *tz'u* lyrics. The *shih* evoke a variety of Late T'ang styles in a way that is convincingly personal and deeply satisfying, while his *tz'u* lyrics are generally more natural in their effect than the formally more complex mode preferred by the Che-hsi school dominant at the time (see above, under Li O).

In fact, *tz'u* poetry was just on the verge of an important development, in the form of what came to be known as the Ch'ang-chou school (Ch'ang-chou p'ai), named after the native place of many of its members in Kiangsi province. Chang Hui-yen (1761–1802) is regarded as the founder of this movement. His reputation depends less on his own verse, of which only a few dozen poems survive, than on his criticism and on the anthologies of early *tz'u* poems, the *Tz'u hsüan* (Anthology of Song Lyrics) and its sequel (*Hsü tz'u-hsüan*), which he and his brother Chang Ch'i (1765–1833) published in 1797 and 1830. In opposition to the artful or self-expressive poems characteristic of the Che-hsi and Yang-hsien schools, Chang Hui-yen advocated poetry that would bear the same kind of analogical interpretation that he was accustomed to practicing on the canonical texts of Confucianism. He, his brother, and their followers found this in the earliest centuries of the *tz'u,* in which, for example, the sentiments of a deserted woman could be interpreted as those of a loyal official ignored by his ruler in the same way that traditional exegeses interpreted the poems of the *Shih-ching* and "Li sao" (Encountering Sorrow) in *Ch'u tz'u* (Elegies of Ch'u).

This allegorical mode of reading and writing *tz'u* was further developed by Chou Chi (1781–1839). In his case too it was criticism, especially the *Chieh-ts'un-chai lun-tz'u tsa-chu* (Miscellaneous Writings on Song Lyrics from the Chieh-ts'un Studio), and an anthology of selected *tz'u* by four late Sung poets (Chou Pang-yen, Hsin Ch'i-chi, Wang Yi-sun, and Wu Wen-ying), the *Sung ssu-chia tz'u-hsüan* (Anthology of Song Lyrics by Four Sung Poets), that established his influence. In addition to developing and refining the allegorical approach of the Chang brothers and their followers, Chou was very interested in *tz'u* prosody. His works on this subject, a technique essential to the composition of *tz'u,* and his concern with the training of poets in general played an important role in making the Ch'ang-chou school influential long after his own time.

The schools and theories that evolved during the first half of the Ch'ing dynasty continued to be influential during its second half as well, but variously combined and modified by individual poets. In the works of Cheng Chen (1806–1864), for example, we find adherence to Weng Fang-kang's ideas about the centrality of learning to the poet's art, but combined with subject matter linked directly to the particular experience of the poet. Cheng was a native of Kweichow, on China's southwestern border, and spent most of his life in the region, where he served as an education official in various localities. This region was racked by ethnic conflict during this period and eventually swept by a Taiping army (part of a massive rebellion that convulsed the Yangtze Valley between 1851 and 1864, leaving millions dead in its wake). Cheng wrote several long narrative poems about these events, works that seem independent of Weng's influence and express Cheng's individual response to what he beheld around him. These poems are among the most important produced in the latter part of the Ch'ing, in spite of the rather narrow views of the poet who composed them.

Another poet who wrote extensively of his experiences in the troubled times of mid-nineteenth-century China was Chin Ho (1818–1885). Chin never succeeded in the official examinations and spent most of his life in the lower Yangtze region earning his living by teaching and holding minor positions in government offices. He witnessed at first hand the activities of both the increasingly active British forces and the tremendously destructive Taiping rebels, writing extensively of what he had seen. Chin's poetry is of interest not only because he reported on his experience of historically significant events but also because he experimented with unusual meters and with a style of poetry much closer to the vernacular than is usually found in *shih*. He is thus a precursor of twentieth-century developments, which broke free of the Literary Sinitic constraints of traditional *shih* and freely adopted the vocabulary and grammar of the vernacular (see chapter 24).

Cheng Chen and Chin Ho attract attention today in part because of the singularity of their subject matter. By virtue of standing somewhat apart from the mainstream, however, they can cast only an oblique light on the literary history of their age. We turn back now to that mainstream, to consider some figures who are interesting for having embodied the existing tradition in spite of the changing conditions around them.

The predicament of China in the nineteenth century becomes manifest in the life and works of Kung Tzu-chen (1792–1841), a man whose political vision was extraordinarily prescient but whose poetry kept, for all its originality of content, well within the bounds of traditional forms.

Kung came from a successful family of officials. His family recognized his precocious talents early and saw to it that he had a thorough education in both intellectual and practical affairs. In spite of his talents, he managed to attain the *chin-shih* degree only on his sixth attempt and even then was barred from high office by his deficiency in calligraphy. He spent more than twenty years in Peking before abandoning his search for a career there and returning to his home in Hangchow. He died only two years later while teaching in Kiangsu province.

Kung's originality of thought was remarkable. Well before the Western powers began their concerted attempts to bring China under their control, Kung foresaw the problems they would create and wrote an essay urging that they be banned from trading in the ports of southern China. He also opposed the importation of opium and the practice of foot-binding. He was, moreover, outspoken in his opinions and believed in the open discussion of controversial issues—attitudes that did not serve to advance his political ambitions.

As a poet, Kung is best known for a set of 315 quatrains that he wrote just after leaving Peking in 1839. Titled *Chi-hai tsa-shih* (Miscellaneous Poems of the Year Chi-hai), they offer a complex, wide-ranging, and forceful account of his concerns, both personal and public, and have been cited ever since for their incisive expression. In addition to this set, Kung left many poems in both the *shih* and *tz'u* forms. Some of the former reflect Kung's turn toward Buddhist quietism later in life (when Kung refers to "Western learning," it is Buddhism he has in mind). Other poems in both forms are in the best tradition of personal, introspective verse. What is not found in Kung's poetry is an originality of formal structure parallel to his independence of mind with respect to content.

Another among the men who were keeping the old traditions in poetry current even while they were immersed in the struggle to save China from a bleak future was Tseng Kuo-fan (1811–1872), best known as the architect of the Ch'ing victory over the Taiping rebels. It is not always remembered that Tseng was a serious scholar and poet who held the *chin-shih* degree and had been pursuing his career in the Han-lin Academy until his early forties, when he was ordered to organize a militia in Hunan to fight the Taipings, an assignment that he undertook with much reluctance. He spent over a decade in his methodical and often troubled suppression of the Taiping rebellion, but even during this period he continued to read and write, producing a body of works by turns poetic and intensely practical.

Tseng was not a major poet, but he illustrates the persistence of old literary concerns in the midst of a rapidly changing environment. As a poet, he was somewhat eclectic, essaying to combine the modes of the two earlier writers whose works he most admired, Li Shang-yin of the T'ang and Huang T'ing-chien of the Sung. He also compiled an anthology of poetry by eighteen poets from Ts'ao Chih of the Wei dynasty to Yüan Hao-wen of the Yüan, thus displaying both his knowledge of the entire tradition and his openness to its various period styles.

Wang K'ai-yün (1832–1916), who served for a time as an official under Tseng Kuo-fan, was perhaps the last of the real archaists, a man whose views on poetry were little different from those associated with the Earlier and Later Seven Masters of the Ming dynasty. Except for extending his taste to include poetry and prose from the Six Dynasties, he kept to the Han and Wei as models for "old-style" verse and to the High T'ang for "new-style" verse just as Li Meng-yang had advocated four hundred years earlier. This remarkable loyalty to the past extended to his public life. Even after the fall of the Ch'ing dynasty in 1911 and the subsequent establishment of the Republic, he regarded himself as a Ch'ing subject and continued to wear the queue as a sign of submission to the Manchus. Unlikely as it might seem, Wang's writings are in fact of considerable interest. Persevering in his cultivation of all but vanished traditions, Wang infused some of his poetry with a touching tension between his world and his vision of what might have been.

Huang Tsun-hsien (1848–1905) has a fair claim to being the last truly outstanding poet in the *shih* form, a claim all the more remarkable for his having had a career almost beyond the imagining of his predecessors. Shortly after attaining the provincial-level *chü-jen* degree in 1876, Huang was sent to join the Chinese diplomatic mission in Tokyo, and this posting was followed by assignments to San Francisco, London, and Singapore. Alert to both China's predicaments and the significance of what he encountered abroad, Huang became an outspoken and well-informed advocate of institutional change in China. His detailed account of Japan's remarkable progress since the 1868 Meiji Restoration of the emperor and the demise of the military government known as the "shogunate," published in 1890, came as a welcome validation of the views of those who believed that a thoroughgoing modernization along Japanese lines was necessary for China's salvation. During an ill-fated attempt at reform in 1898 led by K'ang Yu-wei (1858–1927), who had caught the ear of the Kuang-hsü emperor (r. 1875–1908) and leading officials, such as Li Hung-chang (1823–1901)—the so-called Hundred Days' Reform, which ended in a palace coup—Huang was recalled to office and named minister to Japan, but the reformers were suppressed before he could leave Shanghai, and so he was retired and spent his remaining years at home in Kwangtung province.

In literature, Huang rejected archaism and even advocated poetry written in the vernacular language; he once declared, "My hand writes what my mouth speaks" (*wo shou hsieh wo k'ou*), a famous sentence that proponents of romanization have often cited. Nonetheless, for all his novel experience and openness to innovation, Huang wrote no vernacular poetry himself and remained in essence a traditional poet. His poems are steeped in the resources of earlier masters, even though their subject matter and vocabulary frequently roam far beyond traditional bounds. Indeed, part of the interest in reading his works lies in the novelty of encountering Japanese place names and Western technological terminology worked into the texture of verse forms that had been used almost unchanged for more than a millennium.

This persistence of the old forms had many causes. The sheer difficulty of finding a properly poetic "voice" in the spoken language was to hamper the development of vernacular poetry for many years; some of the first efforts have been shown to have been translations of verse in foreign newspapers. Simple inertia played a part as well, as did the cultural nationalism that persists to the present. For men of Huang's generation and those just a little younger, both the weight of the traditional education curriculum and their eventual satisfaction at having mastered its complexities, including the writing of verse, were conditions that lay very close to the creative self. It is ironic that Huang's clarion call for use of the vernacular quoted above was itself issued in a bastardized form of the literary language (*wu shou shu wu k'ou*). A purer vernacular version would have been *wo yung wo te shou hsieh wo k'ou-t'ou / tsui-li shuo-te hua* or at least *wo te shou hsieh wo te k'ou/tsui*.

Even the abolition of the traditional system of civil service examinations, not long after Huang Tsun-hsien died, and the increasingly radical content of reformist doctrines did not bring an end to the tradition of classical *shih* and *tz'u*. Two of Huang's fellow reformers, K'ang Yu-wei and Liang Ch'i-ch'ao (1874–1930), both of whom lived into the Republican era, continued to write their poetry in the classical forms only. K'ang was in many ways the more backward-looking of the two, identifying himself with the T'ang master Tu Fu as both sage and poet, turning to Taoism and Buddhism as systems of belief, especially in his later years, and, like Liang, proving hostile to the Republican revolution when it finally came.

The problem of maintaining a traditional literary form in a world much changed was perhaps most severe for men such as Huang, K'ang, and Liang, active participants in attempts to bring about far-reaching change in the public sphere. To the extent that men might isolate their literary creation from the uncertain and turbulent world of events, they could continue to write classical poetry as though nothing had happened, for, in a sense, nothing had. True, the imperial institutions of two millennia had crumbled, and busy reformers were setting out to reestablish the literary and educational world on a vernacular basis, but for the very reason that institutional reformers such as Huang Tsun-hsien had continued to use the traditional forms, those forms had not changed or evolved and so remained available to anyone able to use them.

The last Ch'ing master of the *tz'u,* Wang Kuo-wei (1877–1927), embodied the tensions between the old world of the classics and the empire and the new one of Western learning, vernacular literature, and republican institutions. Wang studied Western philosophy intensively, especially the works of Kant, Nietzsche, and Schopenhauer, and might have been expected to reconcile himself to the changing world around him more readily than those classically trained intellectuals whose knowledge was limited to things Chinese. Even in his scholarship, which was of the highest order, he explored newly opened areas of inquiry, such as the tradition of vernacular drama and the recently discovered oracle bones. All the same, he finally took his own life by drowning in a lake at the old Summer Palace, apparently in despair because of the triumph of the Republic over the last vestiges of the imperial order.

Wang's most notable contribution to the poetic tradition was probably his slim volume of *tz'u* criticism, *Jen-chien tz'u-hua* (Remarks on Lyric Poetry from the Human World), in which he set out his idea of poetry as a matter of *ching-chieh* (literally, "boundedness" or "realm"). That is, a poem should have a certain unique existence depending on its expression of a spontaneous and genuine apprehension of reality. In coming to this idea, Wang was influenced not only by his reading in Western philosophy but also by his knowledge of the Chinese traditions of Taoism and Buddhism.

Even as the imperial order was collapsing, new groups of poets were forming, dedicated to the preservation and development of classical verse. The most important of these was the "Southern Society" (Nan-she), whose leading figure was Liu Ya-tzu (1887–1958). Founded by seventeen men in Soochow in 1909, in explicit opposition to the "Northern Court," the Southern Society grew after the fall of the Ch'ing to a membership of more than a thousand. Its members generally shared both a progressive stance in politics and an orientation toward the past in literature. Unlike the various "schools" of poetry during the Ch'ing, however, they differed widely among themselves as to which aspect of the tradition most deserved emulation. Liu Ya-tzu, for example, "honored the T'ang and looked down on the Sung," while another of the society's leading figures, Huang Chieh (1873–1935), most esteemed Sung poetry, even referring to himself as *Hou-shan chih hou* (a descendant of Hou-shan [Ch'en Shih-tao]).

Indeed, from this time on, writing in the classical forms would be sufficient in itself to set one apart from contemporary trends. Few have been thoroughly trained in these traditions since the end of the Ch'ing, but the practice of writing classical poetry persists. The most famous example is, of course, Mao Tse-tung (1893–1976), of whose works in the old forms Arthur Waley is said to have quipped, "Well, they are not as good as Churchill's paintings, but they are better than Hitler's." Other readers have found more value in Mao's poems, but his unique political career still renders a fair assessment difficult. What is more significant is the simple fact of his having written the sort of poetry he did. In any case, Mao's example tends to obscure a phenomenon that may prove of greater importance in the long term, a continuing interest in the writing of classical verse among limited numbers of well-educated city dwellers. From Peking to Kao-hsiung, in Taiwan, more or less formal associations devoted to classical versifying still exist, in some cases flourish, and it is likely that not a day goes by without a few dozen poems at least being added to the enormous corpus accumulated over the past two millennia. As literary forms, the Chinese *shih* and *tz'u* might appear to be as moribund as the English sermon, but the example of the tanka and haiku in modern Japan should discourage hasty judgments on this score. Only time will tell what the future will bring.

Daniel Bryant

Chapter 23

CH'ING LYRIC

The Chinese song lyric (*tz'u*) enjoyed a long heyday from the eighth through the thirteenth centuries, thanks to its lively music, popular lyrics, and the intimate relations between literati and the singing girls/courtesans/geishas who usually sang (or whose voices one imagined singing) the *tz'u*. Eventually, this popular form was eclipsed by a new wave of robust dramatic arias (*ch'ü*), and the song lyric languished for centuries. Oddly, during the seventeenth century the genre underwent a striking revival that continued throughout the Ch'ing dynasty (1644–1911) and even into the twentieth century (see also chapters 21 and 22). This phenomenon, its cultural underpinnings, and its ramifications make up a fascinating chapter in traditional Chinese literary history.

Why did seventeenth-century literati revive the song lyric? First, the antiquarian bent of late imperial literati made such an exhumation more likely. Second, literati expression in more prestigious genres like *shih* poetry was constrained by political repression and government censorship. Subjugation by Manchu troops made literati much more likely to consign their complaints to the confines of a woman's boudoir lament, even as the trauma of yet another alien conquest made them more likely to revive the muted nativist lyric protests of an earlier age. Finally, one notes that relations between literati and singing girls never went out of style; only times and fashions could resolve which sort of popular songs literati would write for their dulcet geishas.

Several poets of the seventeenth century stand out for their relatively distinctive approaches to song lyrics. The earliest, Ch'en Tzu-lung (1608–1647), became legendary as a Ming loyalist martyr. Ch'en led an insurrection against Manchu troops in his native town of Sung-chiang, Kiangsu province. After years of flight and concealment, Ch'en was captured and, en route to Nanking for trial, threw himself into a river and drowned. Such exploits considerably enhanced the appeal of Ch'en's lyrics for later readers, though his songs do not engage politics directly, as do his *shih* poems. An examination of Ch'en's songs reveals characteristics and limitations reminiscent of early ninth- and tenth-century songs: languishing ladies, unhappy love, oblique and concise treatment of emotions (with some more explicit poems on loss that evoke the end of the Ming dynasty), and uniformly elegant, "poetic" diction. His efforts would not seem out of place in the tenth-century *Hua chien chi* (Among the Flowers) anthology, and his style seems close in particular to that of Feng Yen-ssu (903–960), who was also wont to lodge sad emotions within a beautiful, ornate setting. If one wished to epitomize Ch'en's poetic style, one could cite "Helpless against the lightsome madness of the wretched east wind."

Wu Wei-yeh (1609–1672) also returned south when the Ming dynasty collapsed in 1644, but after ten years of retirement he emerged to serve the Ch'ing for several years, a term he later regretted bitterly. Compared with Ch'en's oeuvre, Wu's displays a wider range of poetic realms. Wu more often sketches little romantic dramas and shows a more sensual bent. In his longer tunes, Wu also examines the scars his political misfortunes caused and sometimes essays complex meditations much in the style of Su Shih (1037–1101) or Hsin Ch'i-chi (1140–1207). Wu's customary persona, his frankness, and his discursive style rather recall those of Wei Chuang (836?–910) and evoke a different face of the *Among the Flowers* poets. In taking leave of Wu, one may quote as characteristic his line "Again the west wind rises, I can't control my feelings."

If Wu Wei-yeh's lyrics examined the uncomfortably mixed emotions of a compromised man, Wang Fu-chih's display no such conflict. Wang (1619–1692) became famous as a scholar, historian, philosopher (often called a "materialist skeptic," perhaps more accurately an evolutionary situationalist), literary critic, and patriot. Wang fled the Ch'ing invaders and led a 1648 mutiny in his native Heng-yang, Hunan province. Captured, condemned, and rescued, Wang fled deeper into the Hunan mountains and spent the rest of his life as an untonsured Ming loyalist hermit and one-man literary cottage industry. His lyrics (nearly unknown during the era of Ch'ing censorship and so undeservedly obscure), very like his *shih* poems, lament the fall of the Ming or wax philosophical. Like Su Shih, but unlike Ch'en Tzu-lung or Wu Wei-yeh, Wang's song lyrics appear very much to reveal his personal character and aims. One might describe that character as "volcanic," since Wang seemed half adamantine, half igneous—a passionate stoic. The more complex worlds within his lyrics tell of a loyalist's pain or of mortal intimations, couched often in plainer and yet more graphic language than that employed by Ch'en or Wu. Wang uses what appear to be personal symbols, such as his dying spark of light, his lotus-fibered strands of (uncut) hair, or defeated Titans. Critics have compared his lyrics to those of the Southern Sung lyricist Wang Yi-sun (1241?–1290?), a loyalist who couched his pain within cunningly allusive, indirect "songs on things." Wang Fu-chih, however, also displays the wit, bold directness, and dynamic imagination of Su Shih, though not Su's transcendent affirmations. Wang's distinctive style, which marries moral seriousness with esthetic appeal, makes a considerably greater contribution to the Ch'ing song lyric than that of his predecessors. Although his complexity defies simple epitome, one may end by quoting two typical selections that capture facets of his lyric character: "When stones have rotted, the sea dried up. My lonesome heart, one fleck of loneliness." "The blood in my neck fountainlike, impatient to burst forth!"

All three lyricists described above altogether wrote only half as many songs as Ch'en Wei-sung (1625–1682), who made his reputation almost exclusively as a lyricist and whose oeuvre totaled 1,644 songs. Ch'en, like Wu and Wang, hid away for a time after the Ch'ing conquest, but reemerged in 1655 and eventually was granted an office. He won greater renown or at least notoriety as a partier and as the lyric celebrant of his own homosexual love for the actor-singer Hsü Tzu-yün. "Whiskers" Ch'en Wei-sung was quite the gay blade. His lyrics offer a wide range of poetic realms, but nearly all express his passions and sorrows. Pathos and pathetic fallacy dominate his work. An heir to the "powerful and unrestrained" school of Chinese lyricism, Ch'en fortifies his poems with vehement subjective rhetoric and many words of violence, destruction, and bombast. He is often compared to Su Shih and Hsin Ch'i-chi, though such a yardstick seems unfair. In Chen's lyrics one looks in vain for the ironic wit, profundity, or epiphanies of the great Sung poets. Still, for affective power, if not for intellectual subtlety, Ch'en's oeuvre usually does follow such "powerful and unrestrained" models. Sometimes overrated, for quantity and often for quality, Ch'en remains an indispensable figure in the development of Ch'ing lyrics. As a poetic epitome for his style, one recalls a conclusion where, mirroring the persona's forceful melancholy, "In the little tower bellows up the frosty wind."

Although Ch'en Wei-sung never quite succeeded as a court poet, his friend Chu Yi-tsun (1629–1709) did. The scion of a declining western Chekiang family, Chu parlayed his energy, erudition, and lyric skills into high office. In 1683 he even became imperial tutor to the great K'ang-hsi emperor (r. 1662–1722). An important anthologist and commentator of song lyrics, Chu stressed "orthodox elegance" in his own prescriptions and imitated Southern Sung formalist models. Fortunately, his own praxis displayed more ecumenical borrowings and a rather passionate sensibility. Chu's oeuvre features skillful songs on things, elegant allusive elaborations upon *Among the Flowers* love laments, and songs of travel that include both occasional pieces and musings on ancient sites. Less forceful and less personal than Ch'en Wei-sung's lyrics, Chu's stand out for their intense, vivid involvement with long-dead events and figures. Chu's poetic language, too, impresses not by novelty or distinctively personal tropes but by a thorough mastery of traditional phrases and styles. One cannot pin this versatile pedant down to any one model predecessor, but one does hear often in his work echoes of the elegant, prosodically meticulous, rather impersonal Southern Sung masters, like Chiang K'uei (1155–1221), Chang Yen (1248–c. 1320), and especially Shih Ta-tsu (1154–1207). One cannot help feeling that Chu's own decorum and scholarship inhibited his verse and kept him from the sublime: master of all styles, genius of none. The closing from a song revisiting some ruined temple captures Chu's reticence and his relations to past sources of lyric inspiration and suggests an epitaph: "Profusely as before, the chilly moonlight brims."

The rise of Na-lan Hsing-te (Nara Singde; 1655–1685) astonishes; somehow this young Manchu and imperial guardsman became proficient enough at song-making to win accolades as the finest lyricist since the Sung. Son of a prominent Manchu prince, the precocious Hsing-te joined the K'ang-hsi emperor's retinue on the first of many excursions at the tender age of twenty. Unfortunately, Hsing-te fell ill and died before he could fulfill the early promise of his career as courtier and poet. Perhaps premonitions of an early end (as well as the untimely death of his bride) help account for the passionate pessimism that imbues Hsing-te's verse. Hsing-te's songs mostly explore a narrow poetic realm of grief and loss; his personae pour out their sorrows—lonely, frustrated, or elegiac. Hsing-te couches these in strikingly plain and explicit language. Like his lyric model, Li Yü (937–978), Hsing-te excels at the "plain sketch" style, with few images but much strong subjective rhetoric. Hsing-te himself wrote that poetry must express one's "native sensibility," and most critics have been content to cast him as untutored genius, effortlessly gushing forth a powerful overflow of spontaneous feelings. Actually, Hsing-te studied the lyric tradition carefully; aside from Li Yü's influence, one can easily discern Hsing-te's deep debts to Li Shang-yin and to the lyrics of Yen Chi-tao (1030?–1106?), also famous for heartbreaking songs. Some skeptics consider Hsing-te's oeuvre immature, excessively narrow, and monotonous; the majority, however, rank him above all other seventeenth-century lyricists: Mozart to Chu Yi-tsun's Salieri. One could hardly sum up his lyric style and character better than with this conclusion to an elegy he wrote for his good friend Kung Ting-tzu: "A lovely spirit seared away before the evening light."

One more important seventeenth-century lyric trend demands attention. The number of extant lyrics penned by women increased greatly during the late sixteenth century and afterward. Chinese began looking at literati with new eyes. This apparently stemmed not from any sea change in women's social status but, rather, from several factors that enlivened boudoir life. First, rising literacy rates and publishing volume gave more women a chance to become literate, especially in the poem-crazy southeast, where literary talent could enhance a dowry. Hidebound Neo-Confucians, traditional enemies to female talent, grudgingly allowed that reading morality books could help women become exemplars; they failed to accept that a literate woman could read other, less edifying books and imitate lyric models. The insecurity of elite families in an age of mercantilism, high social mobility, and dynastic upheaval led them to make a fetish of wifely chastity (control within the home, at least). For the boudoir dweller to write and disseminate laments proclaiming how she loyally pines away for an absent husband apparently could enhance the status of her clan. Political factors contributed; as in earlier dynasties of conquest, subjugated Chinese males became somewhat "feminized" (within literary discourse) and relinquished some literary spokesmen's privileges to women, particularly when poetic dissent became too dangerous. During the Ming—Ch'ing transition, talented courtesan-poets played an important role in expressing resentments and veiled loyalist sentiments. Elite men's frustration with the wider world of politics drove them into closer relations with their wives; a common interest in literature helped. The age abounds with famous and rather romantic poetic couples. Two examples illustrate these trends.

Hsü Ts'an (1610–1677 or later) perfected her lyric craft in Soochow's famous salon "Five Poetesses of Plantain Garden." Hsü disapprovingly followed her husband north to office under the Ch'ing, wrote some strong laments with loyalist implications, and lapsed into a chastely loyal widow's silence after his death. Her lyrics, while consisting largely of conventional boudoir laments, display skill and versatility. Her laments for a lost home down south have won high praise from critics who see therein heroically loyalist sentiments.

Liu Shih (Ju-shih; 1618–1664) did Hsü Ts'an one better, managing to combine a flamboyant career as courtesan with a denouement as Ming loyalist and loyally martyred wife. Her relationships with literary patrons had an effect on seventeenth-century verse; she helped her lover Ch'en Tzu-lung learn how to write lyrics and later sheltered her "husband" Ch'ien Ch'ien-yi (1582–1664), a major poet of the era. Liu's lyrics do not, unfortunately, speak of her life and concerns beyond the boudoir lament, but they do suggest her intensity and strength of character. Although the lyrics of Hsü and Liu do not measure up to those of the great Sung female lyricist Li Ch'ing-chao (1084–c. 1151), they provided models and inspiration for thousands of subsequent published Ch'ing lady lyricists, some of whom receive fuller treatment below.

The eighteenth century saw advances in the theory of lyric songs and in the formation of lyric "schools" (loose affiliations based on particular models). The Yang-hsien group, claiming allegiance to Ch'en Wei-sung's "powerful and unrestrained" style, soon ran out of steam, although the artist Cheng Hsieh (1691–1764), one of the "Eight Eccentrics of Yangchow" (Yang-chou pa kuai), wrote some distinctive and untrammeled lyrics about private life and common folks' sufferings. Chu Yi-tsun left a stronger lyric legacy; he influenced a coterie of western Chekiang (Che-hsi) lyricists who continued his espousal of Southern Sung writing in the elegant, refined, and sometimes bloodless style of Chiang K'uei and Chang Yen. The finest songwriter in this school, Li O (1692–1752), does not entirely deserve such pigeonholing, for some of his later, shorter lyrics show the influence of earlier models. A poor orphan, Li parlayed his scholarly talents into a long association with the wealthiest Yangchow salt merchants of the day, a dizzying social ascent. But his most characteristic songs feature a reclusive bent and the "empty [that is, elusive] vitality" highly prized by traditional critics. One might epitomize this facet of his work by his conclusion from a moonlit excursion to the site of an ancient hermit's creek: "White clouds come back to rest deep in the dell."

The most influential "school" of Ch'ing lyrics, however, proved the Ch'ang-chou school, founded largely by Chang Hui-yen (1761–1802). Ch'ang-chou adherents promoted lyrics marked by indirection and especially by serious-minded topical allegory; they wanted to "elevate" and refine the genre. Although this trend took lyrics far from their popular origins, it did find a welcome, especially among poets late in the dynasty who were trying to express their anguish at the waning of a corrupt and oppressive government. Chang's own verse at its best avoids the heaviness and obscurity that mar some doctrinaire Ch'ang-chou songs; his display a deft delicacy, for example in the first of his "Shui-tiao ko-t'ou" (Water Music) series, which ends with a traditional symbol for absent friends:

> Beyond blossoms, a road for Spring's return
> That fragrant grasses never have obscured.

The Chinese believed that poets vibrate in response to the rhythmic frequency of an age; the troubled nineteenth century intensified sociocultural rhythms, and poets answered with more interesting lyrics. Most adhered to Ch'ang-chou school precepts, although Kung Tzu-chen (1792–1841) did keep alive a more personal and more overtly political style of lyric, somewhat in the manner of Cheng Hsieh. Other lyricists followed in the footsteps of Nalan Hsing-te. Hsiang Hung-tso (or T'ing-chi; 1797–1835) achieved great fame as "heartbroken lyricist," though in retrospect he seems narrow and derivative. His emulator Chiang Ch'un-lin (1818–1868), however, remains an important poet. Like Hsiang, Chiang lived a poet's life: early genius, poverty, career disappointments, suffering, unhappy love, and suicide. Chiang is usually filiated to Southern Sung lyricists like Chang Yen, but Chiang's style seems more directly subjective and more strongly imbued with grief. He wrote in many modes, but one salient style evokes Tu Fu or even Hsin Ch'i-chi more than Chang. One might best express the difference between Hsiang and Chiang by quoting a couplet each wrote; the first by Hsiang:

> Cicada brocade secretly worn away by paired-pillow tears;
> Goose-strings sadly locked in by a single zither's dust.

This couplet's cleverness (fancy stationery embroidered with cicada patterns, a mateless zither silenced by loneliness) outweighs its freight of disappointed love.

Compare the conclusion to Chiang's trip along the Yangtze River (the hibernating fish and dragons evoke the ebbing force of a dormant dynasty):

> Silent, still, fish and dragons sleep sound;
> My wounded heart consigned to autumn mists.

At the Ch'ing dynasty's troubled end, many lyricists revived Southern Sung writers' obscurely allegorical expressions of sorrow and distress. Most followed in the footsteps of Ch'ang-chou prescription, but some—particularly the "Four Masters" (see below)—nonetheless wrote distinctive verse. Wang P'eng-yün (1849–1904), the eldest, served as mentor to the "Four Masters." He enjoyed some career success, but as a reformist saw his hopes dashed. Wang's lyrics display the usual thorough study of Southern Sung models, but his songs pulse with an energetic spirit; in this he rather recalls Hsin Ch'i-chi. The complexity, verve, and momentum of his best works elude easy epitomization, but one might offer this couplet from a "Huai-ku" (Meditation on Antiquity) at the Ming tombs. "Golden Grain," incidentally, can refer to pine flowers, Buddha, or imperial tombs:

> Billows swelling in Golden Grain:
> Ancient pines seem to rear up like dragons.

Wen T'ing-shih (1856–1904), not technically one of the "Four Masters," also belonged to the reformist camp. Disgraced after the failure of the 1898 reforms (see chapter 22), Wen fled to Japan and died early, disappointed. His lyrics owe very little to the dominant Southern Sung esthetics; unsurprisingly, Wen himself inveighed against the formalist excesses of the Che-hsi school. His own lyrics feature powerful, mournful emotions, somewhat in the unrestrained manner of many songs by Su Shih and Hsin Ch'i-chi. Wen's songs usually contain more pathos than those of Wang P'eng-yün; this conclusion from Wen's "Shang ch'un" (Spring Lament, to the meter of "Tieh lien hua" [Butterflies in Love with Flowers]) affords a good example:

> Redoubled tearstains seal the brocade letter—
> In life only our feelings just will not die.

Chu Hsiao-tsang (or Tsu-mou; 1857–1931) has a somewhat higher reputation among most critics. Chu rose to become a high minister in the Grand Secretariat and also won fame as a scholar, anthologist, and annotator of lyric songs. His lyrics tend toward the intricate and even obscure, rather in the style of Wu Wen-ying (c. 1200–c. 1260). Under the pressures of the 1898 palace coup, which ended the Hundred Days' Reform led by K'ang Yu-wei (1858–1927), and of the xenophobic 1900 Boxer uprising in north China, however, Chu modulated into a craggier key owing something to Su Shih. All critics have admired his skill, though some find Chu's work (especially the pre-1900 poems) pedantic or contrived. A good example of his style comes from this lyric about a difficult night—the New Year's Eve of the lunar year corresponding to 1900:

> My boozy guts' needle tips bristling like spears;
> My writing brush's icy frost too solemn to bloom.

Chu's friend Cheng Wen-cho (1856–1918), equally talented, failed to match Chu's official triumphs. Cheng spent most of his life as secretary to provincial governors and intendants, who appreciated his profound knowledge of medicine, calligraphy, painting, and lyrics. Cheng's songs range from spare to lush, but usually display a bent for the reclusive or for natural beauty. The malaise of the time also hit Cheng hard, an impact visible in the more anguished lyrics he wrote after 1899. This finds expression, for example, in a three-poem sequence wherein the loyalist turns to his beloved landscape, beginning each stanza: "You cannot leave!" "You cannot stay!" "You cannot return!" The well-known conclusion from the first stanza conveys Cheng's voice:

> Yesterday the master, now a wanderer
> In blue hills not our former land.

One could add other, almost equally skilled lyricists, such as K'uang Chou-yi (1859–1926), last of the "Four Masters." More popular among modern readers, however, has been the scholar Wang Kuo-wei (1877–1927). An important literary critic and the first to try melding Western theories with traditional Chinese approaches, Wang wrote moving songs expressing very pessimistic notions about our "human world," for example:

> In this human world, nothing's dependable
> Except these two words:
> Un—reliable.

For those who consider these late Ch'ing lyrics the last decadent gasp of a dying culture, it seems fitting that Wang forsook lyric poetry. Like Chu Hsiao-tsang (and others), Wang ruefully wrote of his lyrics:

> Fancy phrases such as these can make you want to laugh . . .
> Trivial passions of the heart, and nothing corresponds.

This seems to ring the curtain down on the traditional lyric song just as the dynasty dies, even years before Wang drowned himself in a lake.

But one cannot count out the lyric yet. One more episode—that of women writers—demonstrates its continuing vitality. Oddly, two of the nineteenth century's finest songwriters remained obscure because of their sex. First, Wu Tsao (1799–1862), daughter of a merchant family, who won notoriety as the lyric star of Hangchow's Emerald Citadel Salon, as a lesbian, and especially as a female musical dramatist. Wu's lyrics bear close comparison with those of Li Ch'ing-chao; both alter boudoir conventions with "plain style," vigorous vernacular language, and irony. Wu also explored the "powerful and vigorous" style, enlivening her masculine imitations with a playful sense of self-mockery. Wu's parodic role-playing and ironic complexity offer something distinctive to the history of song lyrics. One may adduce as an example this conclusion from a song that laments (and secretly celebrates her triumph over) the hardships of literary toil: "What's led me Wrong: all this talk of my cleverness." The word "wrong" (*wu*), a pun on her surname, contains the graphic elements *wu* and "talk." Resonating complexly against boudoir convention, Wu thus turns the boudoir topos into a scholar's studio and "wrongfully" rescripts her identity from lonely wife to suffering poet.

Ku T'ai-ch'ing (or Ku Ch'un; 1799–c. 1875) became the distaff Hsing-te—the greatest Manchu poetess, at least. She was a concubine to a cultivated Manchu prince but, when he died young, his wife threw Ku and her children out in the street. Ku spent the rest of her life scraping by, marrying off her children, and writing when she could. Her lyrics hew close to Che-hsi ideals of refined sensibility and aristocratic reserve. She also explored political protest, philosophical speculation, and bitterly ironic reappraisal of her life. One might epitomize Ku's style with the conclusion from her poem inscribed on a fan with ink-sketched gardenias, which celebrates the flowers' plain, unadorned beauty: "Pure scent, even better in the dark."

Wu's and Ku's achievements teach two important lessons. First, genres do not necessarily die like organic creatures; they thrive upon variation, such as the variations in poets' social circumstances typified by a lesbian merchant wench and a hypergamous Manchu dame. Second, they remind us that women did not have to wait for Western intrusion to win a measure of strength and a place to speak within the literary tradition. The song lyric, from its inception a vehicle for "women's voices," never lost that distinctive and thrilling trait.

David McCraw

Chapter 24

MODERN POETRY

If we had to choose one word to describe the history of modern Chinese poetry, it would be "revolution." Compared to other genres, poetry underwent a transformation that is radical, complete, and unprecedented in Chinese literary history. This transformation pertains not only to the linguistic medium and form of poetry but also to its sociocultural foundation and esthetic raison d'être.

Modern Chinese poetry was born in the literary revolution of 1917, as heralded by the two seminal essays: "Wen-hsüeh kai-liang ch'u-yi" (Tentative Suggestions for Literary Reform), by Hu Shih (1891–1962), and "Wen-hsüeh koming lun" (On Literary Revolution), by Ch'en Tu-hsiu (1879–1942), both published in the avant-garde journal *Hsin ch'ing-nien* (New Youth) founded by Ch'en. Hu Shih, who had studied at Cornell and Columbia Universities, would become one of the leading Chinese scholars, philosophers, and literary theorists of the twentieth century and would also later serve as China's ambassador to the United States, representative to the United Nations, and head of Academia Sinica. Ch'en Tu-hsiu, on the other hand, had studied in Japan and France and would later be one of the founding members of the Chinese Communist Party in 1921, serving as its General Secretary until 1927. In his essay (in vol. 2, no. 5), Hu called for a decisive departure from the classical poetic tradition, seeking to change the linguistic medium (vernacular in place of Classical Chinese), form (free verse and new forms instead of traditional forms), content (personal experience rather than conventional themes and stock imagery), and source of creation (genuine feeling, not imitation of ancient masters). Ch'en's essay (in vol. 2, no. 6), by contrast, emphasized the class origin of traditional literature, which he categorized as "aristocratic," "hermetic," and "classical." In pointing out the complicitous relationship between traditional literature and the ruling class, Ch'en envisioned a "national literature" that would be of, for, and by the people. Given Hu's and Ch'en's emphases on the spoken language and common humanity, it is no wonder that modern Chinese poetry was christened "vernacular poetry" in 1917 and, to distinguish it from traditional poetry, was also called *hsin-shih* (new poetry). Other pioneers of the literary revolution include Liu Pan-nung (Liu Fu; 1891–1934), Ch'ien Hsüan-t'ung (1887–1939), Yü P'ing-po (1900–1990), Chou Tso-jen (1885–1967), and K'ang Pai-ch'ing (1896–1945).

However, like any other revolution in literary history, the radical literary reform that Hu, Ch'en, and others called for did not happen overnight. Modern Chinese poetry had precursors in the *shih chieh ko-ming* (Poetry Revolution) of the late Ch'ing period, led by such outstanding intellectuals as Liang Ch'i-ch'ao (1874–1930), T'an Ssu-t'ung (1865–1898), Huang Tsun-hsien (1848–1905), and Hsia Tseng-yu (1863–1924). Although these Ch'ing writers advocated reforms in the diction and content of poetry, their goal was much more limited than that of later proponents of *pai-hua shih* (vernacular poetry) in that they still adhered to traditional forms, into which they only sought to instill modern ideas and feelings. Thus it is important to note the iconoclastic nature of "vernacular poetry" as advocated by Hu and others, which challenged the poetic tradition fundamentally.

The first modern Chinese poems appeared in 1917 in *New Youth*, where more than 130 poems were published between 1918 and 1920. Among the frequent contributors were Hu Shih, Shen Yin-mo (1883–1971), Liu Pan-nung, Lu Hsün (1881–1936), and Chou Tso-jen. The first individual poetry collection, also by Hu Shih, was published in Shanghai in 1920 and was appropriately entitled *Ch'ang-shih chi* (Experiments). During its formative period, which coincided with the culturally iconoclastic May Fourth movement of the 1920s, modern Chinese poetry made remarkable progress. Having renounced the established poetic tradition, modern poets found new resources in folk literature and foreign poetry; they incorporated elements of native folksongs and translated a large amount of poetry from English, French, German, ancient Greek, Japanese, and Russian. The spirit of experiment was inseparable from the ideals of democracy and science championed by the progressive intellectuals of the time and was responsible for the accomplishments of "vernacular poetry" in the May Fourth period, including the popularity of modern-style love poetry, the birth of prose poetry, and a wide variety of poetic forms ranging from the native ballad to the Western-style sonnet.

Further, in view of the irrevocable loss of the traditional role of poetry as a result of the fundamental changes in the political, social, and cultural structures of modern China, many poets engaged in extensive reflections and lively discussions on the nature and purpose of poetry that went beyond mere concerns with form and content. Although no full-fledged theory was produced because of the constant political turmoil and eventual national crisis that plagued China, their discourses touched on themes that were to recur throughout the history of modern Chinese poetry, such as the cultural identity of modern Chinese poetry, the role of the poet, and the relationship between poetry and social reality.

Having renounced the Chinese poetic tradition, how does modern poetry distinguish itself as Chinese? This question first arose in the May Fourth period and has continued to be a concern of poets and critics. The persistence of this kind of reflection shows the immense influence of foreign, particularly Western, literature. Since the late Ch'ing, Western ideas and trends had been pouring into China, often via Japan. Western influence was enhanced through direct and frequent contacts between China and the West. Western writers and scholars, such as George Bernard Shaw, W. H. Auden, I. A. Richards, William Empson, and Harold Acton, visited or taught in China, and almost all the major poets in pre-1949 China studied abroad, whether in France, the United States, Germany, Britain, the Soviet Union (and, before it, Russia), or Japan. In the realm of poetry, romanticism and symbolism were especially popular among modern Chinese poets. For example, Hsü Chih-mo (1897–1931), who studied economics in the United States and traveled in Britain in 1918–1922, and Wen Yi-to (1899–1946), who studied art at several institutions in the United States in 1922–1925, founded the Hsin-yüeh p'ai (Crescent school) in 1923, which leaned heavily toward English romanticism. Their work embodies a quest for freedom, beauty, and love, on the one hand, and bespeaks Gothic gloom, on the other. Kuo Mo-jo (1892–1978), who studied medicine in Japan in 1914–1923, was deeply influenced by Goethe and exulted in the romantic sublime as embodied in the grandeur of nature. The popularity of romanticism declined with the untimely death of Hsü (in a plane crash), Wen's shift of interest from creative writing to classical scholarship, and Kuo's increasing leftist political involvement.

Li Chin-fa ("Golden Hair" Li; 1901–1974), who studied sculpture in France in 1919–1925, was attracted to the symbolists and published the first volume of Chinese symbolist poetry, entitled *Wei yü* (Light Rain), in 1925. His contemporaries, such as Wang Tu-ch'ing (1898–1940), Mu Mu-t'ien (1900–1971), and Feng Nai-ch'ao (1901–1983), also identified with French symbolism. If, by disposition or by chance of access, romanticism had been most influential among the pioneers in the 1910s and 1920s, symbolism and high modernism, including futurism, Dadaism, and surrealism, grew more influential in the 1930s and 1940s. Evocativeness and suggestiveness, central to symbolist poetry, characterized the book *Han-yüan chi* (The Han Garden), published in 1936; it was a joint collection of three young men studying at Peking University: Pien Chih-lin (1910–2000), Ho Ch'i-fang (1912–1977), and Li Kuang-t'ien (1906–1968). In

Shanghai in 1932, Shih Che-ts'un (b. 1905) and Tu Heng (1906–1964) founded the literary magazine *Hsien-tai* (Les Contemporains), which published translations of many symbolist as well as modernist poets, from Rémy de Gourmont, Stéphane Mallarmé, Paul Fort, and Guillaume Apollinaire to W. B. Yeats, T. S. Eliot, Ezra Pound, and other imagists. Before it folded in 1935, *Les Contemporains* was the main venue for symbolist and modernist works by a diverse group of poets including Tai Wang-shu (1905–1950), Ai Ch'ing (Chiang Hai-ch'eng; 1910–1995), Lin Keng (b. 1910), Ho Ch'i-fang, and Lu Yi-shih (later known as Chi Hsien; b. 1913).

However, the avid exploration of foreign literatures—particularly Anglo-European romanticism and symbolism—and applications of these styles to Chinese literary efforts suffered severe setbacks as China was thrown into an unprecedented national crisis. As a full-fledged Japanese invasion became imminent in the mid-1930s, many poets turned their attention to the urgent question of national survival and relinquished their personal visions for a collective one. After Japan invaded China in 1937, these poets de-emphasized their creative freedom and embraced a poetic of social responsibility. In fact, many poets, including Ai Ch'ing, Ho Ch'i-fang, and Pien Chih-lin, went to Yenan, the communist base during the war against Japan, and their poetry took a sharp turn toward social realism and patriotism. Poetry, like the other genres, became part of the "resistance literature" written for the explicit purpose of rousing and uniting the Chinese people against Japanese imperialism. To achieve this purpose, poetry was written in a language easily accessible to common folk, in rhymes so as to make it easy to recite and remember, and often literally taken to the street in public readings. Understandably, political correctness took precedence over art, and the demand for a populist literature overshadowed personal expression.

However, even during the long-drawn-out Sino-Japanese War (1937–1945), poets did not stop experimenting completely. Ou Wai-ou's (b. 1911) futurist poetry was published in a collection in Kweilin in 1942. Avant-garde work was found in such vastly different and unlikely places as Japanese-occupied Shanghai—the largest and most cosmopolitan city in China—and the remote southwestern mountain town of Kunming in Yunnan province, which sheltered refugees from the war-ravaged north, including some of the most accomplished poets in the country, such as Wen Yi-to, Feng Chih (1905–1993), and Chu Tzu-ch'ing (1898–1948). In Japanese-occupied Shanghai, as long as they avoided explicitly political topics, writers had the freedom to engage in literary experiments. This, plus Shanghai's continuing access to Western trends, made it possible for poets to do as they pleased. Lu Yi-shih in 1944 founded the journal *Shih ling-t'u* (Poetry Territory), which emphasized "pure poetry" and creative freedom. Excellent original work was also being written in Kunming. Feng Chih's *Shih-ssu hang chi* (Sonnets), which collected twenty-seven sonnets of Rilkean contemplation, was published there in 1942. Kunming also nurtured a younger generation of fine poets, including Mu Tan (1918–1977), Cheng Min

(b. 1920), Ch'en Ching-jung (1917–1994), Yüan K'o-chia (b. 1921), Hsin Ti (b. 1912), Tu Yün-hsieh (b. 1918), T'ang Shih (b. 1920), T'ang Ch'i (b. 1920), and Hang Yüeh-ho (b. 1917), who were either students at the Southwest United University (the wartime conglomerate of three prestigious universities in China: Peking, Nankai, and Tsinghua) or associated with the magazine *Chung-kuo hsin shih* (New Chinese Poetry). Their work, however, would have to wait more than thirty years before it was rediscovered in the early 1980s under the name of "Chiu yeh p'ai" (School of Nine Leaves).

Overall, however, national crisis and increasing communist influence in the 1930s and 1940s created an environment hostile to explorations of poetic art. The expedient marriage between literature and politics solidified into a creed culminating in 1942 in Mao Tse-tung's "Tsai Yen-an wen-yi tso-t'an-hui shang te chiang-hua" (Talks at the Yenan Forum on Literature and Art), in which he held that literature was to serve the worker, the peasant, and the soldier. Mao's talk dictated cultural policies in mainland China for the next four decades. In essence, it ended all free literary expression, and the situation did not change significantly until the late 1970s, when China opened its door to the Western world.

Thus, for the three decades after 1949, original Chinese poetry was found almost exclusively outside mainland China, in particular in Hong Kong and Taiwan. In the 1940s many poets visited Hong Kong, most notably Tai Wang-shu, who lived there and edited the *Hsing-tao jih-pao* (Hong Kong Daily) from 1938 to 1949. After 1949, Hong Kong served as a haven for many writers who fled the mainland, including such poets as Li K'uang (1927–1991), Ch'i Huan (b. 1930), Huang Ssu-ch'eng, and Lin Yi-liang (Stephen C. Soong; 1919–1996). A poet, literary critic, translator, and editor, Lin was a major contributor to the journal *Jen-jen wen-hsüeh* (Everyman's Literature) in 1952–1955 and exerted a significant influence on the poetry scene of Hong Kong. Like Lin, Ma Lang (Ronald Mar; b. 1936) also came to Hong Kong from Shanghai, where he had published poetry, although Ma belonged to a younger generation. A friend of Lu Yi-shih and Shao Hsün-mei (1898–1968), Ma founded *Wen-yi hsin-ch'ao* (Literary Current) in Hong Kong and from 1956 to 1959 was largely responsible for introducing modernist writers including Wallace Stevens, William Carlos Williams, Marianne Moore, Archibald MacLeish, E. E. Cummings, D. H. Lawrence, Dylan Thomas, Paul Éluard, Max Jacob, Robert Desnos, René Char, André Breton, Octavio Paz, César Vallejo, and Federico García Lorca. Ma was also instrumental in bringing together avant-garde poets in Hong Kong and Taiwan in the 1950s. Not only did *Literary Current* publish poems and translations by many Taiwanese poets, but in 1957 it devoted two special issues to modernist poets in Taiwan, including Lin Ling (b. 1938), Huang Ho-sheng (b. 1938), Lo Ma (better known as Shang Ch'in; b. 1930), Lin Heng-t'ai (b. 1924), Chi Hung (b. 1927), and Hsiu T'ao (b. 1934).

During the Cold War, Hong Kong had the unique advantage of being the back door to China, on the one hand, and a window to the outside world, on the other. In terms of the development of post-1949 modern Chinese poetry, it similarly served as an intermediary between China and Taiwan. Through Hong Kong, some of the poetry of pre-1949 China was made available to poets in Taiwan, sometimes in the form of handwritten copies circulated secretly among friends. The work of such Taiwanese modernists as Ya Hsien (b. 1932) and Yü Kuang-chung (b. 1928) also inspired many in Hong Kong in the 1950s and 1960s. Yü's influence grew even greater when he taught in the Chinese Department at the Chinese University of Hong Kong in 1974–1980, to the extent that his large following was facetiously referred to as "Yü p'ai" (Yü school). The interaction between Hong Kong and Taiwan also became closer as a new generation of Hong Kong poets went to study at Taiwanese universities: Yeh Wei-lien (Wai-lim Yip; b. 1937), who had edited poetry journals in Hong Kong; Tai T'ien (b. 1937); and Ao Ao (later known as Chang Ts'o, Dominic Cheung; b. 1943). Yeh and Ao Ao, in particular, identified with Taiwan rather than Hong Kong as their cultural homeland.

The modern history of Taiwan is no less traumatic than that of China. First exploited by the Portuguese in the sixteenth century, then colonized by the Dutch and the Spanish, successively, in the seventeenth, Taiwan was annexed as a province by the Ch'ing dynasty (1644–1911) in the eighteenth century. When the declining empire was defeated in the Sino-Japanese War of 1895, Taiwan was ceded to Japan, which ruled the island for half a century. During the colonial period, Japanese was made the "national language," and from 1937 until Japan's defeat in 1945 Chinese was banned and only Japanese was allowed.

The literary revolution of 1917 finds its Taiwanese counterpart in 1925, when Chang Wo-chün (1902–1955)—who, after studying in Peking in the early 1920s, returned to Taiwan to edit the *T'ai-wan min pao* (Taiwan People's Daily)—published the essay "Tsao-kao te T'ai-wan wen-hsüeh chieh" (The Terrible Taiwanese Literary Scene) in 1925. In this essay, Chang harshly criticized the traditional poetry clubs and poets in Taiwan, thus touching off a heated debate. In his subsequent essays, Chang introduced Hu Shih and Ch'en Tu-hsiu and was the chief advocate of vernacular literature in Taiwan, publishing in his newspaper works by major May Fourth poets, including Kuo Mo-jo and Liang Tsung-tai (1903–1983). Like Hu Shih, Chang published, in 1925, the first individual collection of modern Chinese poetry in Taiwan, entitled *Luan-tu chih lien* (Love of a City in Chaos). (The earliest modern poems in Taiwan were written by Chui Feng [b. 1902] in 1923, in Japanese, and were published in *T'ai-wan ch'ing-nien* [Taiwanese Youth] in April 1924.) By emphasizing that Taiwanese literature was "a tributary of Chinese literature," Chang expressed implicit resistance to Japanese domination.

Likewise, the campaign for *hsiang-t'u wen-hsüeh* (native literature) led by Huang Shih-hui and Kuo Ch'iu-sheng in 1930–1931 can be viewed as another effort to resist Japanese domination while seeking to establish a Taiwanese cultural identity distinct from that of mainland China. These writers held that the

Taiwanese vernacular, that is, southern Fukienese, should replace Literary Sinitic, Mandarin, and Japanese as the medium to make literature accessible to the common people. Though short-lived, this was the first native literature movement in Taiwan. As the language policy under Japanese rule became more stringent, all Taiwanese literature was written exclusively in Japanese after 1937.

Besides May Fourth literature, Taiwanese writers also drew on Western literature (often via Japanese translation) and Japanese literature (which itself was influenced by the former) as models. Cross-cultural contact was facilitated by the fact that many Taiwanese writers either studied in Japan or were bilingual. For instance, in 1930 Yang Ch'ih-ch'ang (1908–1994) published a book of poetry in Japanese entitled *Nettaigyo* (Tropical Fish) under the pen name Shui-yin-p'ing, then studied Japanese literature in Japan in 1931–1934. After returning to Taiwan, he edited the literary supplement to the *Tainan shimpō / T'ai-nan hsin pao* (T'ainan New Daily) and advocated *un esprit nouveau,* by which he meant surrealism. Yang and six fellow poets, three Taiwanese and three Japanese, also founded the Feng-ch'e shih-she (Le Moulin [Windmill] Poetry Club) in 1935, but their poetry journal by the same name folded after only four issues because of pressure from the literary scene, which considered such radical artistic experiments inappropriate for the colonial reality in Taiwan.

During the Japanese occupation, Taiwanese literature, including poetry, was dominated by realism and often dealt with harsh social and political reality under colonial rule. The poets Lai Ho (1894–1943) and Yang Hua (1906–1936), for instance, depicted the suffering of the oppressed and protested against social injustice. Yang himself was arrested in 1927 for violating the Japanese security law; the fifty-three poems that he wrote in jail were later collected in *Hei ch'ao chi* (Black Tides).

Taiwan was retroceded to China at the end of World War II in 1945. But the early postwar years were far from peaceful. Harsh living conditions grew even harsher as a result of corruption and discrimination, which led to widespread disaffection on the island. A clash between the native Taiwanese people and the Kuomintang (KMT; Nationalist Party) government of the Republic of China (composed almost entirely of mainland Chinese) broke out at a demonstration demanding better treatment on February 28, 1947, followed by a brutal suppression that left a deep wound that took decades to heal. The eagerness with which the Taiwanese people had looked forward to being reunited with the motherland was quickly replaced by a bitter sense of betrayal and disillusionment.

After the Communist victory in the civil war (which had actually started before the Japanese were defeated and broke out in full force after they withdrew) and the Kuomintang's retreat from the mainland to Taiwan after Mao proclaimed the establishment of the People's Republic of China on the mainland in October 1949, the reign of Pai-se k'ung-pu (White Terror; in contrast to the Red Terror that was taking place on the mainland) began. Although carried out on a more limited scale and with less drastic measures than Mao's purges, the repression of free expression in Taiwan was not much different from what occurred in Communist China from the 1950s through the 1970s. Books written by mainland writers—now labeled "leftist"—were peremptorily banned, thus severing the tie between young writers in Taiwan and their mainland predecessors. The postwar generation was similarly uprooted from the native Taiwanese literary tradition. As mentioned earlier, under Japanese rule many Taiwanese writers had written in Japanese. After the retrocession, however, Chinese became the only official written language and Mandarin the only spoken language allowed in Taiwan. Implicit in such a policy is the suppression of the local language and the native literary tradition. This entailed a double deprivation for the writers: prewar Chinese and Taiwanese literature was excluded from the canon and was unavailable to the general public, and older Taiwanese writers had to re-educate themselves in Mandarin in order to continue to write and publish. Although a few made the linguistic transition, many were silenced permanently.

Thus, in the transition period, the mainland poets who moved to Taiwan after 1949 played a leading role on the poetry scene. While many participated in state-sponsored literary activities revolving around the themes of anticommunism and the reclamation of the mainland, some were dissatisfied with the orthodox discourse and sought other avenues for expressing their creativity. Chi Hsien, who had established himself as a promising young poet on the mainland in the 1940s, founded *Hsien-tai shih chi-k'an* (Modern Poetry Quarterly) in 1953 and promoted the avant-garde. In January 1956 he went on to found the Hsien-tai p'ai (Modernist school); in its manifesto he declared that modern Chinese poetry was the result of "horizontal transplants" (*heng te yi-chih*) rather than "vertical inheritance" (*tsung te chi-ch'eng*), and the goal of the Modernist school was to embrace "selectively all new poetic schools since Baudelaire." The manifesto has caused much controversy ever since and continues to draw both criticism and defense from poets and critics.

Other poetry clubs at the time included the Lan-hsing shih-she (Blue Star Poetry Club), founded in March 1954 under the leadership of Ch'in Tzu-hao (1912–1963); Ch'uang-shih-chi shih-she (Epoch Poetry Club), founded in October 1954 by three young military officers: Chang Mo (b. 1931), Ya Hsien, and Lo Fu (b. 1928); Nan-pei ti shih-she (North and South Flute Poetry Club), founded in April 1956 by Yang Ling-yeh (b. 1923) and Yeh Ni (b. 1924); P'u-t'ao-yüan shih-she (Grape Orchard Poetry Club), founded in July 1962 by Wen Hsiao-ts'un (b. 1928); and Hsing-tso shih-she (Constellations Poetry Club), founded in April 1964 by a group of college students, including Wang Jun-hua (b. 1941), Ch'en Hui-hua (b. 1942), Tan Ying (b. 1943), and Ao Ao. Of all the poetry clubs in the 1950s and early 1960s, the Modernist school was undoubtedly the largest (at one point it had more than a hundred members) and most influential, although it was far from a close-knit group that followed the same theories and practices. The lively poetry scene in the 1950s produced many fine works by such poets as Ya Hsien, Shang Ch'in, Lo Fu, Cheng Ch'ou-yü (b. 1933), Yeh Shan (later known as Yang Mu, originally named Wang Ching-hsien; b. 1940), Lin Heng-t'ai, and Pai Ch'iu (b. 1937).

In the early 1970s, a large-scale debate about modern poetry broke out, ignited by two essays by Kuan Chieh-ming (John Kwan Terry), a professor of English at the National Singapore University, published in the literary supplement to the *Chung-kuo shih-pao* (China Times) in February and September 1972. Terry, who had read an anthology of Taiwanese poetry in English translation, criticized it as having lost its Chinese characteristics and as having become a mere slave to Western culture. Terry's essays were followed by many that mounted attacks on modern—especially modernist—poetry, accusing it of being escapist, narcissistic, and completely Westernized. Modernism was equated with irresponsible individualism and decadent estheticism; such poets as Yü Kuang-chung, Yeh Shan, and Chou Meng-tieh (b. 1920) were singled out as examples of modernist malaise. Coming from different angles, critics of modern poetry unanimously faulted modern poetry for having lost its own cultural identity as a result of being colonized by the capitalist, imperialist West, especially the United States. Correlated with such critiques of modern poetry was the fervent call for an awakening of nationalism, a renewed concern for the native land, and the embracing of realism as the preferred mode of writing.

The scale and intensity of the discussions on this subject were so great that they were referred to as the Hsien-tai shih lun-chan (Modern Poetry Debate). From a historical point of view, the Modern Poetry Debate was not an accident or an isolated incident. It resurrected the problem that had divided earlier poets, including the May Fourth generation in mainland China and Taiwanese writers in the 1920s and 1930s. Periodically, the tension between the native and the Western, between Chinese nationalism and Westernization, reached such a height that it triggered debates of varying scope. In poetry, the emphasis on the native land was not new to the modern poetry debate of the 1970s. In 1964 a poetry club called Li shih-she (Bamboo Hat) was founded by Wu Ying-t'ao (1916–1971), Chan Ping (b. 1921), Huan Fu (b. 1922), Lin Heng-t'ai, Chin Lien (b. 1928), Chao T'ien-yi (b. 1935), Pai Ch'iu, Huang Ho-sheng, and Tu Kuo-ch'ing (b. 1941), all native Taiwanese poets. *Bamboo Hat* is also the longest-running poetry journal in the history of Taiwan. Later, in 1970, poets of a younger generation founded the Lung-tsu shih-she (Dragon Race Poetry Club), whose manifesto proclaimed: "We strike our own gongs, beat our own drums, and do our own dragon dance."

Given its emphasis on the native land and its call for realism in place of modernism, the Modern Poetry Debate should be seen as a precursor of the Hsiang-t'u wen-hsüeh yün-tung (Native Literature movement) in 1977–1979. In fact, many of the criticisms of modern poetry were to recur in the latter movement, couched in the same rhetoric of binary opposition: modernism was described as "sick," "effeminate," and "impotent," whereas realism was "healthy" and "masculine"; modernism was identified with the decadent and materialistic bourgeoisie, whereas realism belonged to the masses.

The Native Literature movement ended in 1979, when the democracy movement led by oppositional political forces culminated in the "Beautiful Island [Formosa] Incident"—demonstrations against the KMT that were crushed by the government. Some of the Nativist writers and intellectuals involved in the political movement were either imprisoned or kept temporarily silent. As the political atmosphere became more open in the early 1980s, many poets started writing "political poetry" (*cheng-chih shih*) focusing on the repressed history of Taiwan. Long-standing taboos, such as the February 28 Incident of 1947 and the White Terror, were breached, often in a satiric way, and the historical ironies of being Taiwanese were examined critically. Among the most powerful political poems were those by Liu K'o-hsiang (b. 1957) and K'u Ling (b. 1955).

At the same time, postmodernism began to find its way onto the literary scene in Taiwan. Despite the bafflingly protean nature of the term and the lack of a systematic understanding of it in Taiwan at the time, postmodernism was seen in the work of many younger poets who started writing in the increasingly affluent 1970s. Most notable was Hsia Yü (b. 1956), whose incorporation of elements of popular culture, parodic appropriations of the literary canon, and radical feminist approach to sexuality and sexual relations clearly distinguished her poetry as postmodernist. Others, such as Lo Ch'ing (b. 1948) and Lin Yaote (1962–1996), consciously employed postmodernist elements, including fragmentation, meta-writing, and deconstruction, in their work.

The 1980s also saw an unprecedented rebirth of the poetry scene on the mainland. As the Dark Ages of the decade-long Cultural Revolution drew to a close in 1976 and Teng Hsiao-p'ing launched the Open Door policy in 1978, China experienced a long-awaited "thaw," allowing writers and artists more creative freedom. This social climate led to the birth of underground journals, such as the *Ssu wu lun-t'an* (April Fifth Forum), *T'an-so* (Exploration, cofounded by Wei Ching-sheng [Wei Jingsheng] and Lu Lin), *Ch'i-meng* (Enlightenment), and *Chin-t'ien* (Today). Among these publications, *Today*, founded in December 1978 and closed under political pressure in 1980, was the first underground journal devoted exclusively to literature, publishing fiction, critical essays, translations, and, of course, poetry. Some of the poets who contributed to *Today*, including its cofounders and editors, Pei Tao (Bei Dao; b. 1949) and Mang K'o (Mang Ke; b. 1950), went on to enjoy national and even international fame; among them were To To (Duo Duo; b. 1951), Shu T'ing (Shu Ting; b. 1952), Ku Ch'eng (Gu Cheng; 1957–1994), Chiang Ho (Jiang He; b. 1949), and Yang Lien (Yang Lian; b. 1955).

The history of underground poetry in mainland China can be traced to the late 1950s and early 1960s. During the Cultural Revolution, the work of Kuo Lu-sheng (writing under the pen name Shih Chih; b. 1948) was widely circulated among the youth sent down to the countryside for re-education. Others who also started writing poetry in the 1960s included Huang Hsiang (b. 1941) and Ya Mo (b. 1942). In the 1970s, there were private "salons" in Peking, where aspiring writers and artists gathered to discuss literature and art, especially the Chinese translations of foreign literature that were intended only for higher-level party cadres, from Erenberg and Sartre to Beckett and Salinger. Those so-called yellow-covered books—they were bound in yellow—were circulated secretly among the young poets, who also exchanged their own poetry with one another. The thaw in the political atmosphere allowed their work to be published for the first time.

The emergence of this underground work catapulted the poets associated with *Today* to fame in 1979–1980, but they also became the target of scathing attacks by critics in the cultural establishment, which by now included many rehabilitated poets such as Ai Ch'ing. Their poetry was criticized for its obscurity and other supposedly modernist tendencies and was consequently named *meng-lung shih* (Misty Poetry). Despite the criticisms in the early 1980s, Misty Poetry was immensely popular on college campuses, and by the mid-1980s some examples of the genre even received attention outside China and were translated into foreign languages.

To the extent that it reflected the traumas of the Cultural Revolution, Misty Poetry was related to the *shang-hen wen-hsüeh* (Scar Literature) popular in the late 1970s. But the fact that it was born at the same time as the democracy movement of Peking Spring (there was some contact between *Today* and the other, more politically oriented, groups) meant that Misty Poetry was part of the outpouring of the society's demand for more individual rights and freedom. Moreover, it drew on foreign, especially European and Anglo-American, literature for inspiration; thus Misty Poetry followed in the footsteps of modern Chinese poetry since the May Fourth period. In post-Mao China, Misty Poetry came to symbolize the avant-garde, who courageously rebelled against the official ideology and upheld individualism and human dignity.

The canonization of Misty Poetry outside the establishment happened so fast that, by 1986, it became the target of revolt by a new generation of poets, who were collectively known as Ti-san tai (Third Generation) or Hsin-sheng tai (Newborn Generation). Unlike the Misty Poets, who had been in their teens during the Cultural Revolution, these younger poets were mostly college students (some went on to study in the United States and Europe), better educated, and more familiar with Western literature. Their artistic experiments also went further than those of their immediate predecessors'. Too diverse to be described even as a loose group, the Newborn Generation has produced many fine poets, such as Pai Hua (b. 1956), Yü Chien (b. 1954), Hsi Ch'uan (b. 1963), Hai Tzu (1964–1989), Ou-yang Chiang-ho (b. 1956), Chai Yung-ming (b. 1955), Han Tung (b. 1961), Meng Lang (b. 1961), and Chang Tsao (b. 1962).

Ironically, if creative freedom was no longer an issue for poets in the 1990s, they were faced with problems that they had never before encountered or even dreamed of. As China was becoming more commercialized and consumer-oriented toward the end of the millennium, poets were finding that the readership of serious poetry was shrinking and their status as spokespersons of the society and culture was declining dramatically. While the rapid marginalization of poetry provided some with a new stimulus for writing, others found it a cause for discouragement, even despair. Given the escalating costs of living and the ever-present allure of making money, many avant-garde poets, at least temporarily, stopped writing and became entrepreneurs with varying degrees of success, opening bookstores, publishing houses, advertising agencies, and consulting firms.

Across the Taiwan Strait, the situation was similar but less dramatic. Most poets had long accepted the marginal status of poetry in a postmodern society and were quite content to write for a small audience. Although quantitatively poetry is clearly no match for popular culture or even fiction, the number of neither poets nor readers appeared to suffer a significant decline. In fact, some poets, such as Cheng Ch'ou-yü and Yang Mu, continued to sell well for decades.

In the 1990s, modern Chinese poetry was more diverse than ever before, in terms of geographical scope, stylistic range, and venues of publication. Not only was poetry written in mainland China (including Hong Kong) and Taiwan, but it maintained a vital presence in Chinese communities all over the world, especially in Singapore, Malaysia, the Philippines, the United States, and Europe. At least two journals in North America were devoted exclusively to poetry: *Yi hang* (One Line), founded in New York in 1987 by the painter-poet Yen Li (Yan Li; b. 1954), and *Hsin-ta-lu shih shuang-yüeh-k'an* (New World Poetry Bimonthly), founded in Los Angeles in 1989 by a group of poets, mostly recent immigrants from Taiwan. In addition, poetry was regularly published in Chinese magazines outside China, including *Today* (revived in 1990); *Pei-ching chih ch'un* (Peking Spring); and *Tendency* (Ch'ing-hsiang; originally published on the mainland in the late 1980s as a poetry journal). Finally, poetry started to become available by electronic mail (e.g., *Kan-lan-shu* [Olive Tree: Chinese Poetry Magazine] at editors@wenxue.com) and on the Internet (e.g., *Modern Taiwanese Poetry League* at www.jour.nccu.edu.tw and *Shuang-tzu-hsing jen-wen shih k'an* [Gemini Poetry Journal] at www.gemini.neto.net).

Chinese poetry is becoming more and more international as it is written, published, and read in many parts of the world. Chinese poets in different areas interact with one another more easily and frequently than before, and translations of Chinese poetry are becoming more readily available, although they tend to focus on the contemporary period. Modern Chinese poetry has come a long way since 1917. In retrospect, we see that poetry, more than fiction or any other genre of modern Chinese literature, has struggled long and hard to establish its own identity. In departing from the dominant poetic tradition of three millennia, modern poetry has constantly had to defend itself against extraliterary demands, on the one hand, and repeated criticisms that it is too Westernized and not sufficiently Chinese, on the other. The resolution of this issue will not be reached in debate but must ultimately be discovered in actual practice. In this sense, the diverse group of talented poets and the works they have produced have demonstrated that modern Chinese poetry is truly both *modern* and *Chinese*.

Michelle Yeh

Chapter 25

POETRY AND PAINTING

This chapter explores the relationship between literature and the visual arts in traditional China, with special attention paid to the interaction between poetry and painting. One of the most distinctive achievements of Chinese civilization is the development of an integrated art form that combined text and image. Beginning in the eleventh century, an influential group of Chinese scholar-officials, or literati, asserted that it was esthetically and morally desirable to pursue equal perfection in the practice of poetry, painting, and calligraphy. By the Yüan dynasty (1368–1644), this notion of the "three perfections" (*san-chüeh*) had evolved into a pervasive esthetic standard that most literati accepted in theory and often in practice. The Chinese literati of this period evolved a distinctive approach to painting that incorporated poetic inscriptions executed on the work itself in calligraphic styles calculated to correspond to the esthetic and intellectual contents of the painting. This ideal combination of the three "arts of the brush" had a profound influence both on Chinese painting and on later *shih* poetry, as poems composed for inscriptions on paintings became an important poetic subgenre. The topic also has much to offer those interested in the theoretical implications of the interaction and "convertibility" of textual and visual "signs." Finally, even a modest pursuit of the topic reveals how existing textual material often governed the subject matter of Chinese painting. This influence seems hardly surprising in a society that gave such pride of place to the written text. Yet Western historians of Chinese art have only recently begun to explore these connections between text and image, having previously devoted their efforts, rightly, to matters of style and authenticity in order to compile a chronologically accurate network of authentic and correctly dated works upon which to ground further studies.

The major focus of this chapter is on paintings and related theoretical models that contributed to the development of this integrated expression of text and image, in other words, on works of art that contain a poetic inscription related to the content of the image. Much of the material covered in the chapter falls under the general Chinese rubric of "inscription literature" (*t'i-hua wen-hsüeh*) or, more literally, "writings inscribed on paintings." The great Japanese Sinologist Aoki Masaru divided "inscription literature" into four categories: (1) "picture eulogies" (*hua-tsan*), rhymed inscriptions on portraits first popular during the Han period; (2) "inscription poetry" (*t'i-hua shih*), *shih* poetry inscribed on paintings; (3) "painting records" (*hua chi*), prose accounts usually inscribed by the painter himself on his work; and (4) "colophons" (*t'i-pa*), generally prose notes (although they are sometimes in verse) often inscribed on separate sheets of paper at the end of a handscroll. In terms of content, Aoki's third and fourth categories consist largely of scholarly and technical notes on painting and fall outside the scope of this chapter. Also outside the scope of this chapter, although certainly related to it, is the notion of "poetic painting," the idea that much of the lyrical focus of landscape painting derives in a general way from the overwhelmingly lyrical tendency of traditional Chinese poetry.

The link between text and visual object appears early in Chinese civilization. The inscriptions on early Chou dynasty (1027–256 B.C.E.) bronzes show that their makers already conceived of these texts as a component of the bronze vessel itself. The combined vessel and text played a significant role during the ritual conveyance of the object from patron to subordinate and was a symbol of the political and social relationship between giver and receiver. One may perhaps draw a vague parallel between the Chou sovereigns' ritual presentation of inscribed bronzes that narrated the meritorious exploits of their vassals to the conferral by Sung dynasty (960–1279) emperors of symbolic paintings inscribed with poetry that lauded the promotions or achievements of their officials.

This close connection between text and image continued to develop during the middle and late years of the Chou dynasty. Of the two major writing media then in use, silk lent itself better than did narrow bamboo strips to the recording of visual images. Perhaps the earliest surviving example of an illustrated text is the "Ch'u silk manuscript" dating from the third century B.C.E., a text variously interpreted by modern scholars as either a shamanistic manual or an astronomical treatise. The production of illustrated manuscripts was common in the Warring States period (403–221 B.C.E.) and the Han dynasty (206 B.C.E.–220 C.E.). Han versions of the *Shan hai ching* (Classic of Mountains and Seas) were certainly illustrated, and scholars have long speculated that the original text was composed to accompany a large map that depicted the various regions and creatures discussed in the text. In his "Tu *Shan hai ching* shih-san shou" (On

Reading the *Classic of Mountains and Seas*, Thirteen Poems), T'ao Ch'ien (365–427) was clearly responding to an illustrated text and writes of viewing the pictures and "taking in all the cosmos in a single glance." Traditional Han commentators also held that the text of the "T'ien wen" (Heavenly Questions) section of the *Ch'u tz'u* (Elegies of Ch'u) had been composed as captions for mural paintings of mythological and historical figures on the walls of the ancestral shrines of the Ch'u state. Although now largely discounted, this theory relates to the Han custom of adorning imperial palace halls, provincial offices, and tombs with portraits of past and present cultural heroes that were identified by cartouches and supporting textual passages.

For example, the Han emperor Ming-ti (r. 57–75 C.E.) ordered construction of a pavilion decorated with mural portraits of historical figures culled from the classics and histories by a committee headed by the historian Pan Ku (32–92), who also composed "picture eulogies" (*hua-tsan*) for the figures. These texts were clearly related to the historical eulogies, sometimes in this case also translated "appraisals" (*tsan*), that had by then become a standard feature of Chinese history writing. The "picture eulogy" (or, perhaps better, "eulogy on a portrait") developed into a literary genre whose practice continued in later periods. The influential preface to *Wen hsüan* (Literary Selections), completed about 530, writes that *tsan* were composed to accompany portraits. Among the best-known surviving "picture eulogies" are those the poet Ts'ao Chih (192–232) composed in 214 to accompany illustrations in the "Wen shih" (Warm Chamber) of the Wei dynasty (220–265) palace at Yeh (in modern-day Honan province). Tso Ssu's (c. 253–c. 307) "Wei tu fu" (Wei Capital Rhapsody) describes these murals as "representations of the cosmos, and portraits of ancient worthies and sages . . . drawn with hundreds of lucky signs, embellished with elegant songs of praise." Ts'ao Chih's works contain a series of twenty-nine eulogies, each four couplets of four-character rhymed verse. The series begins with praise for the early mythological figures Fu-hsi and Nü-wa, proceeds through legendary rulers such as Yao, Shun, and the early Chou sovereigns, and culminates with the Western Han emperors.

A particularly interesting example of the Han use of "picture eulogies" concerns the grave shrine of Chao Ch'i (d. 201), who is known today primarily for his commentary on the *Mencius*. The factional struggles of the second century resulted in the execution of Chao Ch'i's entire family and forced him to wander the country incognito. While selling griddle cakes in a market, he attracted the attention of Sun Ch'ung, a young scholar who hid him between the walls of his house for two years, during which time Chao completed his work on the *Mencius*. A subsequent amnesty allowed him to emerge from confinement, and his career was revived. At the end of his life, he planned the memorial hall of his own grave site. He designed a portrait of himself flanked by four worthies of antiquity and composed a "picture eulogy" for each. Visitors understood that the four worthies served as historical analogies for Sun Ch'ung and other friends who had helped Chao during his lifetime. This combination of text and image at Chao Ch'i's grave manifested the political and moral values that marked his life and may be seen as prefiguring the later Sung-Yüan period combination of painting and poetry to articulate political values.

By far the most impressive examples of surviving "picture eulogies" come from the ancestral shrine at the grave of the Confucian scholar Wu Liang (78–151) in Shantung province, a site its modern explicator describes as "the most ambitious representation of human history ever attempted in Chinese art." Wu Liang devised an elaborate program of forty-four distinct pictorial units carved into the stone walls of the shrine. The figures begin with Fu-hsi and Nü-wa leading off the series of ten ancient sovereigns. These are followed by seven eminent women, seventeen filial sons and virtuous men, nine heroes and heroines who demonstrated outstanding political loyalty to their sovereigns, and finally Wu Liang himself. By his selection and positioning of these figures, Wu Liang enshrined for his descendants a version of Chinese history that espoused his Confucian beliefs and placed his own life in the context of those values. Recent scholarship has demonstrated that Wu Liang chose the specific figures for his shrine, especially those in the virtuous women and men series, from a large corpus of illustrated biographies compiled several centuries earlier by Liu Hsiang (79–8 B.C.E.). Although Liu's original compilations survive only in fragments, an early tradition records that the *Lieh-nü chuan* (Biographies of Illustrious Women) was first composed to be displayed on a screen with illustrations of the individual stories and textual explanations. The Ming edition of this work, although extensively reworked in the Sung, still contains a woodblock illustration, followed by a biography and a eulogy for each exemplar. This format is mirrored in the Wu shrine, where each figure is provided with an identifying cartouche; and many have "picture eulogies," whose diction is based on Han Confucian texts.

For example, the first scene in the filial sons series portrays Tseng Shen (505–436 B.C.E.), the kneeling figure to the left and his mother sitting at her loom on the right (see fig. 1). The four-character rhymed "eulogy" above Tseng Shen alludes to his reputed authorship of the *Hsiao-ching* (Classic of Filial Piety) and relates how his piety toward his mother was so great that it moved the gods and spirits to facilitate telepathic communication between them. The inscription at the bottom, however, is contrastive: "But when slanderous words three times arrived, even this kind mother dropped her shuttle." This text summarizes the account of how even Tseng Shen's mother eventually believed her son had murdered a man after hearing three reports that a similarly named "Tseng Shen has killed a man." By choosing to begin his series of filial sons with this example of the destructive effect of calumny on even the strongest of filial relationships, Wu Liang alludes to the equally corrosive effects of slander on the political relationships that are the later focus of his pictorial program. Text and image are here skillfully combined to emphasize this contrast. In visual

FIGURE 1. Illustration of the filial piety of Tseng Shen, ink rubbing of stone carving, Wu Liang Shrine, second century C.E. Photo after Wu Hung, *Monumentality in Early Chinese Art and Architecture*, p. 233.

terms, the kneeling paragon is dramatically separated from his distraught mother, her body twisted away from her work, by the falling shuttle about to hit the ground between them. In textual terms, the elegantly phrased, rhymed eulogy that praises Tseng Shen's filial behavior in glowing but general terms at the top of the frame contrasts with the blunt prosaic force of the concluding line, with a different rhyme, at the bottom of the illustration: in a moment, slander can destroy a lifetime of devotion.

Text and image in the "picture-eulogies" of the Han stone reliefs are mutually reinforcing. The image illustrates existing textual material, but the choice and formulation of the specific text guide the viewer toward the desired interpretation of the image. This relationship between text and image dominated painting through the Six Dynasties period (220–589). It was also applied to other painting formats, such as screens and handscrolls. The works of T'ao Ch'ien contain a "Shan shang hua tsan" (Picture Eulogy on a Fan), a verse text of twenty-four four-character rhymed couplets, which lauds eight recluses who lived from the time of Confucius through the Eastern (or Later) Han (25–220). If text corresponded at all to image, the fan depicted the eight recluses, each with a distinctive implement or motif associated with his biography—fishing, surrounded by tame animals, and so on. In this case, as in the Wu Liang shrine, image was perhaps unintelligible without text; and text was clearly crafted with the image in mind yet drew upon the diction of prior texts. The inscription on the painting thus mediated between past textual tradition and the present visual image. T'ao's work also contains a harbinger of the future. His "Shang Chang Ch'in Ch'ing tsan" (Eulogy on Shang Chang and Ch'in Ch'ing), which celebrates two Han recluses who fled to the mountains to escape service under the usurper Wang Mang (33 B.C.E.–23 C.E.), was almost certainly also composed to accompany a portrait. In this case, T'ao Ch'ien wrote his eulogy in pentasyllabic verse, perhaps the earliest surviving example of this new verse form composed for a painting.

The same relationship between text and image can be seen on the remarkable lacquer screen recovered in 1966 from the tomb of a Northern Wei general who died in 484. The original screen, about a meter high all around, had a back section about three meters long flanked by right and left sections that emerged at right angles and extended about a meter toward the front. When the owner sat in the middle, he was thus surrounded on three sides by painted images. Of the twenty or so lacquered wooden panels that made up the entire screen, only five have survived. These are illustrated with scenes from the biographies of virtuous women, filial sons, political exemplars, and recluses. Female exemplars are on the inside of the screen, men on the outside. The best-preserved panel, illustrated here (see fig. 2), depicts four scenes of virtuous women. Proceeding chronologically from top to bottom, the panel depicts the two queens of the legendary Emperor Shun, three empresses from the beginning of the Chou dynasty, a benevolent mother from the state of Lu, and Lady Pan, a loyal concubine to the Han emperor Ch'eng (r. 32–7 B.C.E.). Each image is provided with identifying cartouches and text inserts, as in the Han reliefs. In this case, the texts derive from Liu Hsiang's *Biographies of Illustrious Women*. And this Northern Wei screen may indeed be much like the original version of Liu Hsiang's "book." Although these are prose texts, their function and use on the screen do not differ from those of illustrations of poetic texts during the same period.

It is not surprising that surviving works associated with Ku K'ai-chih (c. 348–c. 409), the preeminent painter of his time, are handscroll illustrations of Han texts. The earliest of these, probably a T'ang copy of the original, known as "Nü-shih chen t'u" (Admonitions of the Instructress to the Court Ladies), illustrates a text of the same name written by Chang Hua (232–300) preserved in the *Literary Selections*. Chang frames his text as a harangue given by the "instructress," a female court officer charged with the oversight of palace concubines, to her charges. The speech is highly didactic and urges meekness,

FIGURE 2. Scenes of virtuous women, panel from a painted wood and lacquer screen, 484 C.E. Photo after Wu Hung, *Monumentality in Early Chinese Art and Architecture*, p. 232.

modesty, loyalty, and decorum. The T'ang commentators on the *Literary Selections* understood the work as directed against the growing influence of the clan of a Chin dynasty (265–420) empress. Although the beginning of the scroll has been lost, the surviving portion contains alternating sections of text and illustrating images for the final two-thirds of the text, which is reproduced complete. The artist has exercised considerable artistic control in dividing the text into segments for illustration. Like many Chinese didactic works, Chang Hua's "Admonitions" is a combination of conceptual abstraction and concrete example. The artist has followed the Han models to illustrate the concrete examples of admirable female behavior, one of which is the identical scene from the life of Lady Pan depicted on the Northern Wei screen. The genius of the scroll, however, rests in the scenes the artist has devised to illustrate the text's more abstract portions. For example, the most commonly reproduced section of the scroll captures a tense moment between a gentleman sitting on the edge of a bed and its female occupant, at whom he is gazing suspiciously. The scene illustrates the passage: "If your words are true, all for a thousand miles will respond to you; but if you violate this principle, even your bed mate will distrust you." The scroll ends, as does the text, with an image of the instructress recording her admonitions before two concubines, who, in a scroll rich with ironic overtones, seem not to be paying the slightest attention.

Other handscrolls illustrating Ts'ao Chih's "Lo-shen fu" (Rhapsody on the Goddess of the Lo River) are also associated with Ku K'ai-chih. Although all are Sung dynasty (960–1279) or later renditions, and there is wide variety among them concerning the placement of text and image, the version thought to approximate best the original represents the text divided into segments and interspersed with illustrations in the same manner as the "Admonitions" scroll. A particularly interesting feature of the "Lo River Goddess" scrolls is the literal solution the artist has devised to represent metaphor. The poem contains a vivid description of the goddess that compares the movement of her body to the flight of startled swans and roaming dragons, her aura to the moon obscured by clouds, and her luster to the sun and to lotus blossoms. The goddess has been painted surrounded by literal renditions of the things to which she is compared.

Ku K'ai-chih is reported to have painted more than three hundred murals in Buddhist and Taoist temples, including a portrait of the famous Buddhist layman Vimalakīrti. No trace of these survives, but we know that the arrival of Buddhism in China and the institutionalization of the Taoist church that occurred during the same period profoundly affected the earlier Han formats and genres for combining text and image. The eminent monk Chih-tun (314–366) composed an "image eulogy" (*hsiang-tsan*) for a portrait of the Buddha, certainly a wall painting, that greatly enlarged the Han genre by providing a lengthy and detailed biography of the Buddha to accompany the image. Mural artists from Central Asia working in the Indian artistic tradition illustrated complex narrative texts such as the Buddhist *jātaka* (birth stories) by recourse to a continuous series of interlocking "space cells" that framed specific moments of the story. Cave 428 at Tun-huang from the late Northern Wei period (386–534) narrates in three long horizontal registers the story of how the young prince Mahāsattva was reborn as a Buddha after sacrificing himself to a hungry tigress. Similar visual techniques occur in the "Lo River Goddess" scrolls, and the relationship between the horizontal handscroll and such horizontal wall registers at Tun-huang—between Chinese and Indian traditions of textual illustration—has yet to be studied in detail. Although such Buddhist narratives are textually grounded, the murals rarely contain text, possibly because their presumably illiterate viewers either knew the story or had it explained to them as they viewed the paintings.

By the end of the Six Dynasties, the Han "picture eulogy" had already assumed many of the characteristics of the later "inscription poem" (*t'i-hua shih*). Among the earliest evidence for this transformation is the four-poem series by Chiang Yen (445–505) entitled "Hsüeh-shan tsan" (Eulogies on the Snowy Mountain). A short preface explains that the poems, all eight-line pentasyllabic verses, were inscribed next to figures of four Taoist transcendents portrayed in the landscape setting of a Taoist heaven. Chiang writes that he was inspired by the paintings to inscribe them with "these small eulogies." As in previous examples, the diction of the poems is based on earlier texts and mediates between these sources and the image. Viewed from the vantage point of the later development of "inscription poetry," it is most important in the case of Chiang's series that the poems were pentasyllabic verses written and inscribed as personal testament to his emotional response to a previously existing painting.

The development of "inscription poetry" owes much to the combination of the Han "eulogy" and "poems on the description of objects" (*yung-wu shih*), a poetic subgenre popular in the late Six Dynasties that delighted in the precise and elaborate delineation of selected physical objects. Although this tradition had begun with the description of natural objects and phenomena such as wind, rain, snow, plants, and animals, by this period smaller manmade objects such as musical instruments, mirrors, and fans had become favorite choices. Descriptive poems became, in the words of one scholar, "sensuous word-pictures." The object was not simply to describe the object but to evoke in words the mood or feeling associated with the object. Paintings were an especially apt choice for the descriptive treatment, since their intricate and varied subject matters presented possibilities and challenges that simpler objects lacked. Especially appealing were outdoor scenes, where the poet could apply his descriptive powers to a range of natural objects rather than to only one isolated element. Most challenging, however, was the task of recreating the painting's mood or atmosphere in poetic language, in short, of re-creating in words the experience of viewing the painting.

"Yung hua p'ing-feng shih erh-shih-ssu shou" (Twenty-four Poems Describing Painted Screens), by the great poet Yü Hsin (513–581), is among the most famous early examples of the genre. The poems are, like the Chiang Yen poems discussed above, all pentasyllabic octaves. Seven of the poems describe landscapes, one hunting, one washing clothes, one a traveling knight-errant, and the remainder describe pavilions, gardens, and palace women. It is not clear whether the twenty-four scenes were all part of one large screen assembly or, as is more likely, the series represents simply an editor's collection of Yü's unrelated poems on individual screens. Only some of the poems betray a hint of Yü's subjective reaction to the paintings, the vast majority being entirely descriptive. The advent of the T'ang in the early seventh century did little to change this approach, the early T'ang being in this respect, as in so many other aspects of cultural life, a continuation of late Six Dynasties practice. The graph *yung* (describing or, more literally, singing/chanting of/about) occurs frequently in the titles of the handful of seventh-century poems on paintings, the majority of which continue in the purely descriptive mode of earlier times.

The great Ch'ing critic Shen Te-ch'ien (1673–1769) wrote unequivocally that "there was no inscription poetry before the T'ang; the genre started with Tu Fu." The poetry of Tu Fu (712–770) contains about two dozen poems that relate to painting. These poems document a fundamental change in the relationship between text and image in Chinese art and establish Tu Fu as the most important "inscription poet" of the T'ang. In short, the eighth century witnessed the completed transition from "painting eulogy" to "inscription poetry." The text of the Han *tsan*, as explained above, attempted to deliver an objective message to the viewer by mediating between the prior textual tradition and the image. In other words, the text, through its links to previous literature, shaped the viewer's understanding of the image. The *tsan*, in either political or religious usage, was a fully didactic genre. The viewer's "reception" of the work was assumed to be a univocal acceptance of the didactic message that the composite work transmitted. In the hands of Tu Fu, however, "inscription poetry" became an instrument to record the interaction between the image and the poet as viewer. The text now became a vehicle for recording the viewer's subjective reaction to the painting. The older function of the text as a link to past tradition continued to exist and would be reconfigured during the coming Sung dynasty. But the new focus, as seen in Tu Fu's approach to painting, brought the vital relationship between image and viewer to center stage and laid the foundation for the later evolution of both inscribed poetry and prose as vehicles for criticism and scholarship on painting. Symptomatic of this change is the disappearance of the graph *yung* and the increasing frequency of the graph *kuan* (looking at, viewing) in the titles of T'ang poems on paintings.

Central to Tu Fu's approach is the conceit of the painting's "reality" (*chen*). At its most elemental, this myth praises the artist: your painting is so well done that it seems to be real. Sung Chih-wen (c. 656–712) and Li Po (701–762) had earlier used this motif, but Tu Fu developed this simple fiction into a theory of art that linked the experience of viewing the painting to the viewer's experience of the actual world. The fictional "reality" of the painting became a vehicle for Tu Fu to meditate on the real world. For example, in "Chiang Ch'u kung chiao ying ko" (A Song on a Goshawk Painted by Chiang, Duke of Ch'u), written in the poet's old age, Tu Fu marvels that the portrait of a goshawk in the yamen at Mien-chou is so "real" that its viewers fear the hawk will momentarily fly from its master's arm. But this fine quality of the work, done by the painter in happier days before the tumultuous An Lu-shan (703–757) rebellion (755–757/763) that almost destroyed the T'ang dynasty, reminds the poet that the "real bones" of the live hawk "have passed to nothing." Although his "real" image remains, the actual hawk, the real source of the qualities the painting has so well captured, has long since passed away. Tu Fu merges reality and image to shape the contrast between the once live and now painted hawk into a magnificent metaphor for his own failed career: "So the swallows and sparrows in the rafters fear no more, / nor will he ever again stroke the sky and soar to highest heaven." In short, Tu Fu makes the painting a vehicle for memory. In another poem, "Wei Feng lu-shih chai kuan Ts'ao chiang-chün hua ma t'u ko" (In the Residence of Recorder Wei Feng, I View a Painting of Horses by General Ts'ao Pa), a newly painted picture of nine famous T'ang horses is so real that "from the white silk there rises a vast desert of wind and sand." But the lifelike horses in the painting remind the poet of the real, live horses that once graced the court of the former emperor and carried him to his tomb, where now "only the birds cry in the wind." Once again, the contrast between the fictive "reality" of the new painting and the lost reality of the genuine past generates an overwhelming pathos and sense of loss. Or, as the great Sung critic Hung Mai (1123–1202) remarked of Tu Fu's poems on paintings, "Reality is fiction, and fiction is reality, and both are but illusory scenes."

Tu Fu's poetry on painting is filled with admiration for painters. Their power to create "real" images of such stark emotive power rivaled the creative power of nature itself. Tu Fu held that painting, like literature, had the power to reveal the mind of its maker and thus function as a medium for intellectual discourse. Moreover, almost half of Tu Fu's poems on paintings concern images of horses, hawks, or pine trees: all subjects with long-standing metaphorical associations in Chinese literature. By choosing to concentrate his poetic reactions to paintings on these subjects, Tu Fu stressed the common ground of metaphorical assumptions that underlay audience presumptions about the significance of these images in both literature, especially poetry, and painting.

Tu Fu has more poems whose titles begin with the graph *t'i* (inscribed on) than any of his contemporaries. Most probably, some of Tu Fu's poems without *t'i* in the title were also inscribed on the paintings themselves. The graph *t'i* had long been used to designate poems inscribed on walls of houses, structures at scenic locations, or even on trees. Its extension to poems written on paintings no doubt occurred because mural paintings were so common during the T'ang. But there is also no doubt that the practice of writing the poem on or near the painting that had inspired it, and the practice of labeling such poems as *t'i*, reflect the changing eighth-century attitude toward text and image and arose in the hope of preserving the two works together. Just as a poem inscribed on the pavilion at a scenic vista recorded the poet's response to the natural scene, so a poem inscribed on a painting now recorded the poet's response to the painted scene. In all these areas—his estimation of the painter's craft, his focus on selected images of literary value, and his use of the graph *t'i*—Tu Fu was much ahead of his time and both presaged and laid important groundwork for the development of literati painting during the Northern Sung.

Tu Fu's poems on landscape paintings also conform to his notion of the painting as a "real" or, in this case, a "realized" scene. When the reference is to landscape painting, the idea of *chen* relates to the religious significance of *chen* as a realized or perfected state in which the mind unites in harmony with its perceived object. Mountains were long believed to possess distinctive spiritual auras that promoted attainment of this harmony. The earliest Chinese texts on landscape painting, by Ku K'ai-chih and Tsung-ping (375–443), describe the use of landscape images as a substitute for the experience of the actual landscape itself. Meditation, either in front of or about a landscape painting, aided "realization" of the union between the practitioner's mind and the perceived landscape. The painting thus became a functional equivalent to the landscape itself, and the origins of landscape painting in China are closely linked to the cultivation of tray landscapes, rock gardens, and the other manifestations of miniaturized nature. T'ang poems on landscape inherit and develop these notions. The earliest T'ang poem on a landscape painting is a short text by Ch'en Tzu-ang (659–700?) on a landscape mural. The mountains in the painting are compared to the Wu mountains in Szechwan, the waters to the currents surrounding the three isles of the immortals, the Taoist paradise, in the eastern sea. Ch'en holds that the image is a reflection of the mind of the painter who "sought the Way in the solitude of clouds of mountains."

This fiction that painted landscapes depict the mountains and mists of the Taoist paradises of K'un-lun in the west or P'eng-lai in the east became a routine conceit in poetry on landscape painting. And many landscape paintings were indeed understood, either literally or metaphorically, as representations of the land of the immortals. Tu Fu's "Kuan Li Ku ch'ing ssu-ma ti shan-shui t'u san shou" (Three Poems upon Viewing a Landscape Painted by the Adjutant at the Request of His Brother Li Ku) describes a landscape painting populated with Taoist immortals, whom the poet recognizes and names. The series closes with the conceit that the poet wishes to enter the picture, seat himself on a raft portrayed there, and be taken away by the immortals. The conceit that the painting was so real (*chen*) that the viewer/poet wished to enter the picture became a commonplace in later Sung and Yüan inscription poetry. This trope is certainly rooted in the religious origins of landscape painting and in the theoretical identity of the observing mind and the perceived landscape. Several of Li Po's poems on landscapes are based on this identity. "Ying Ch'an-shih fang kuan shan-hai t'u" (Viewing the Painting of Mountains and Seas in the Chamber of the Ch'an [Zen] Master Ying) portrays the "realized monk" meditating in his chamber surrounded by screens that seem to fill the room with landscape, such that "P'eng-hu enters through the window and the seas of Ying flood around the furniture." Distinctions between the landscape and the chamber vanish, and "the vastness merges with the realized mind, / comes into accord to be savored in quietude." This consensus between Tu Fu and Li Po on the religious nature of landscape painting is significant, for in most other ways Li Po's poems on paintings are more conservative than Tu Fu's and reflect Six Dynasties practice. His corpus contains more than a dozen "picture eulogies," many on recently deceased persons that were probably executed as commissions. There is also a long pentasyllabic *hua-tsan* with preface on a Buddhist Pure Land (i.e., heavenly paradise) transformation tableau (*pien-hsiang*) or realized scene that was probably similar to surviving murals found in the Tun-huang caves.

Compared to Tu Fu and Li Po, Wang Wei (701–761), traditionally regarded as the greatest poet-painter of the T'ang, has virtually no surviving poems related to painting. Much of the aura surrounding Wang Wei as the original scholar-painter results from a series of anachronistic projections that began in the Northern Sung, and from the picturelike quality of many of his poetic couplets. However, some evidence does suggest that Wang Wei occasionally allowed his talents as poet and painter to intersect. First, a ninth-century text records that a Ch'ang-an mansion contained a landscape mural by Wang Wei along with his own inscription. Second, Wang's reputation as a poet-painter rests largely on the relationship between *Wang ch'uan chi* (Wang River Collection), a poetic dialog between Wang and his friend P'ei Ti (b. 716) written at twenty named sites on Wang's estate in the mountains south of Ch'ang-an, and some later handscrolls that illustrate these poems. Following his own poetic sequence, Wang Wei apparently painted depictions of these Wang River sites on the walls of a Buddhist monastery that he had constructed on the grounds. The monastery and its murals were destroyed during the persecution of Buddhism in 845, but sometime before this date either Wang or another artist painted a handscroll version of the murals. A plethora of later versions supposedly derives from this first handscroll. But probably none predates the Yüan period, and it is impossible to say how these later scrolls may relate to Wang's original murals. The treatment of the *Wang River* text in these later versions is inconsistent. In some, the text follows the painting; in others the text occurs next to the appropriate image; others indicate only the name of the site; others have no text at all.

Two surviving handscroll versions of a work originally by Lu Hung, a contemporary of Wang Wei, entitled "Ts'ao-t'ang shih chih t'u" (Ten Views from My Thatched Lodge), present a somewhat similar situation. One version of the scroll contains ten scenes of Lu's retreat on Mount Sung, each accompanied by the name of the location and a poem, but the second version omits the poems. This popularity of both the Wang and the Lu scrolls is best understood as post-Sung literati enthusiasm for any hint of a fusion of text and image in earlier periods that would validate and provide a plausible T'ang pedigree for their own practices. In addition, it reflects the popularity in Yüan and Ming painting of portrayals of literati homesteads and retreats, images often accompanied by inscriptions that commended the ideals of reclusion.

The emergence of a mature literati society with unquestioned dominance over political and cultural life in the eleventh century set in motion a series of theoretical and practical changes that eventually resulted in the elevation of painting to a status on a par with literature as an accepted form of literati expression. "Painting is the ultimate expression of culture," wrote Teng Ch'un, a major twelfth-century art historian. This formulation acknowledges the fruition of a new valuation of painting advocated in the preceding century principally by Su Shih (1037–1101) and other members of his circle such as Huang T'ing-chien (1045–1105), Li Kung-lin (1049–1106), and Ch'ao Pu-chih (1053–1110). Expanding Tu Fu's ideas on the relationship of text and image, these Northern Sung scholars and painters developed a sophisticated theoretical model that prepared the way for the subsequent integration of text and image. The practical application of this model on a large scale in the late Sung and Yüan eventually transformed the practice of both painting and poetry, and these changes established the tenor of literati cultural life until the dissolution of that culture in the twentieth century.

Northern Sung ideas that came to define "literati painting" (*shih-jen hua*) can be summarized in two broad categories. First, painting should express the character, personality, and emotions of the artist. Second, the content of painting should relate broadly to the literati's role as political and social leaders. (Evidence in Northern Sung texts for a third category—that painting should form part of the literati program of moral self-cultivation—is ambiguous and is perhaps best understood as a projection of later literati values back to the Sung period.) Each of these categories in its own way altered existing conceptions about the relationship of text and image. Su Shih, when he expressed a preference for Wang Wei over the artisan painter Wu Tao-tzu (c. 710–760), insisted that painting should express the character of the artist. Wu Tao-tzu was a master painter, but because Wang Wei was also a poet, he could see and paint what was "beyond the image." What was beyond the image was in fact the mind of the painter, an idea encapsulated in the formulation that painting is an "image of the mind." This conception has affinities both to Ch'an (Zen) Buddhism and to the earlier idea that landscape painting could unite the mind of the observer or painter with the realized landscape. Su Shih also attacked the notion that "form likeness" (*hsing-ssu*), the degree to which the pictorial image resembled its physical subject, should be a prime esthetic value. He suggested that the "meaning and spirit" (*yi-ch'i*) of the work were more important. He did not disapprove of form-likeness per se, only of painting that sought this quality as its ultimate goal. His "meaning and spirit" were essentially the mind and the intentions of the painter as expressed through his rendering of the objects in the painting.

The parallel to the act of poetic creation was explicit: the literatus painter "leaves the measures and calculations of the artisan painter behind and attains the pure beauty of the poet." The catalog of the Sung imperial painting collection, completed in 1120, relates that the best painter, like the poet, "lodges his emotions" in images of nature, a poetic goal outlined in the classic "Preface to the *Book of Poetry*" (see chapters 5 and 45). Just as bad poetry might contain only flat description, be lacking in emotional and intellectual depth, and so fail to reveal much of the poet's personality, so artisan painting that limited itself to a literal rendering of the image could never reveal the mind of the artist "beyond the image." Comparing Su Shih's ideas to those of Tu Fu, the change in focus is striking. For Tu Fu, the painter may indeed be a master of his craft and worthy of admiration, but the meaning of the work comes ultimately from the observer/poet who brings his mind and experience of the world to reading significance into its images. For Su Shih, the painter/poet uses the images of nature to express his own mind and experience and is thus himself the ultimate shaper of his work's significance.

Although the esthetic theory of painting outlined above has links to Ch'an Buddhism, its social theory is largely Confucian. The significance or "meaning" of a work should relate to the political and social involvement of the painter, an involvement that only the literatus painter would be presumed to have. Politics should be understood here as encompassing not only discrete political events but the entire spectrum of private and public moral issues generated by active participation in traditional Chinese political life. Confucius taught that a major function of poetry was to "observe" (*kuan*) social realities and to serve as a forum for the airing of social policy. The art critic Kuo Jo-hsü, in about 1080, extended this function to painting, writing that painting can "hold a mirror to sage and fool and cast light on order and disorder." A consequence of this extension was that certain subjects long accepted as metaphorical vehicles for discussion of such issues in poetry now came to be preferred images for painting. For example, the dichotomy of the pine versus the deciduous tree provided a wealth of metaphors to portray the eternal conflict between the "gentleman" and the "petty man." And images of plum, bamboo, and orchid used the poetic associations of these plants to advocate a range of positive moral and political values.

This aspect of early literati painting must be considered within the context of the confrontational nature of Northern Sung political life. Su Shih and his circle represented one among three factions contending for political supremacy at the time. His was the least politically powerful, and most of its members suffered ruined careers and long years of confinement or exile, which began in

1079 after Su Shih's trial for writing poetry that slandered the emperor and criticized government policy. The practice of painting among Su Shih's circle provided a sense of solidarity and moral superiority in the face of the increasingly stark consequences of political failure. Some scholars have also suggested that painting may have provided the group with a vehicle for communication that was less subject to government scrutiny than poetry or prose. But there is no doubt that these literati viewed "meaning" in painting as a way for the knowing viewer to commune with the artist: if only the morally superior literati could imbue a work with "meaning," then only the morally superior viewer could discern that "meaning." Much of the inscription writing of Su Shih and his friends aims to document this moral bond between artist and viewer.

Both later Chinese and modern Western scholars have written that literati views on painting amounted to a notion of the "convertibility" of painting and poetry. Most often cited is Su Shih's famous formulation: "If you savor Wang Wei's poetry, there is painting in his poetry; if you contemplate his painting, there is poetry in his painting." A closer reading of this and related texts, however, shows that Northern Sung scholars were well aware of the different media, strengths, and limitations of each art. Painting and poetry were not convertible or identical but complementary. Writers as different in their political and intellectual orientations as Ou-yang Hsiu (1007–1072), Shao Yung (1011–1077), Shen Kua (1030–1094), and the Su Shih group all maintained the distinctiveness of each art, yet realized the potential for each to augment the other. An inchoate vision was emerging of a new art form that would combine painting, calligraphy, and poetry. By the end of the dynasty, when this vision was fully realized, the scholar Wu Lung-han (1233–1293) summarized the Sung relationship between poetry and painting: "One can succeed through poetry in completing the scenes that are most difficult to paint, and one can supplement through painting those parts in the poem that are most difficult to express."

Although the works of Su Shih and his circle were suppressed in the years immediately following his death (no genuine painting of Su Shih survives), other Northern Sung scholars and painters soon recognized the esthetic possibilities to be gained from a complementary coordination of the arts of the brush. As measured by surviving works, court painters attached to the Sung Painting Academy rather than literati painters achieved this coordination of text and image. The Sung imperial clan did much to elevate the social status of painting. Virtually all the Sung emperors after Jen-tsung (r. 1022–1063) were proficient painters or calligraphers. Emperor Hui-tsung (r. 1101–1125) reorganized the court Painting Academy and enhanced the number and status of painters assigned there. An accomplished painter and calligrapher himself, he took immediate steps to develop the possibilities of these recent theoretical models within the artistic life of the Sung court. Among his innovations were examinations for entrance into the Painting Academy. Following the precedent of their literary counterparts, these examinations tested the candidates' ability to interpret fragments of verse. The aspiring court artists were required to execute a painting that would evoke the atmosphere and mood of a given poetic text. In grading, a premium was placed on indirection, subtlety, and allusion—all prime values in Sung poetics. The goal was to reveal the meaning beyond the immediate visual image of the text. For example, one examination posed the couplet "At the wild river, no one to cross over; / a lone skiff moored in the setting sun." Lesser submissions portrayed the obvious image: an empty skiff moored cliffside with egrets perched on the gunwales or crows in the rigging to indicate the boat's disuse and the approaching evening. The first-place candidate, however, painted a boatman reclining in the stern playing a flute. This image focused attention on the forced idleness of the boatman and thus better illustrated the central "meaning" of the text, which is not that there is no boatman but that there is no traveler to cross the river.

Hui-tsung also made lavish use of painting and calligraphy as tokens of recognition, reward, or admonition to his officials, a practice that continued for the remainder of the dynasty. "Fu-jung chin-chi t'u" (Golden Pheasant and Hibiscus; see fig. 3) is a rare surviving example of this art. Attributed to the emperor himself, the painting displays a sophisticated coordination, much in advance of its time, that anticipated the subsequent full-scale integration of text and image. The inscribed poem reads: "His autumn strength wards off the fearsome frost, / with lofty cap, the brocade-feathered fowl; / his knowledge complete, perfect in the Five Virtues, / in ease and rest he surpasses the ducks and widgeons." This complex poem guides the viewer's interpretation of the image by skillful allusions to classic texts. These references establish the pheasant as a figure for a man whose unique moral virtue surpasses that of the common crowd (here, the "ducks and widgeons"). "Lofty cap" refers both to the crest of the pheasant and to the high-topped hats worn by government officials. The inscription fixes the image of the pheasant as a figure of moral perfection, a symbol of the Five Virtues or Five Constants (humaneness or benevolence, justice or righteousness, rites or propriety/civility, wisdom or knowledge, and trust or faith), and makes the entire painting an allegory where the pheasant becomes a substitute image for the living recipient of the work. In spatial terms, the inscription is well integrated into the picture, framed by the butterflies and the pheasant's glance. One may well imagine this painting as a gift from Hui-tsung, painted either by the emperor himself or by an Academy artist, to a high official, perhaps on the occasion of promotion to second-class rank, of which the golden pheasant was the official emblem.

The Sung penchant for illustrating poetic couplets continued in the tradition of the round double-sided fan with matching text and image on opposite sides. The texts were usually T'ang or Northern Sung couplets or quatrains, but surviving fans also contain examples of original compositions. In either case, it seems that the image, as in the examination pictures, was designed to accompany an existing text. A fan (see fig. 4) by the Academy painter Hsia Kuei (fl.

FIGURE 3. Attributed to Emperor Hui-tsung, "Golden Pheasant and Hibiscus," ink and colors on silk. Palace Museum, Beijing.

FIGURE 4. Hsia Kuei, "Sailboat in the Rain." Fan. Ink and light colors on silk. Boston Museum of Fine Arts.

1195–1230) with calligraphy on the reverse by Emperor Hsiao-tsung (r. 1162–1189) illustrates a couplet by Su Shih: "My whole life a weary sleep in rain along the river, / at day's end I travel by boat through wind that tears the banks." This work epitomizes the Sung goal of complementary coordination of text and image. As an illustration of the couplet, the painting well captures the general emotions of a lone traveler on an unending journey across rivers and lakes. But the specificity of the text adds a special poignancy to the image once the observer realizes that the traveler/poet in the boat is Su Shih.

The late Sung and early Yüan periods witnessed the completed realization of the Northern Sung ideal of integration between text and image, of a unified artistic creation in which painting, calligraphy, and poetry would all issue from the same hand. This development was related to the effect of the Mongol invasions on the unemployed former Sung literati and the desire of some for an artistic expression of loyalty to the fallen dynasty. Among the earliest to produce such works was Ch'ien Hsüan (c. 1235–1301+), a Sung literatus who turned to a life of seclusion after the end of the Sung dynasty. A short handscroll known as "Li-hua chüan" (Pear Blossoms), probably completed about 1280, at first sight resembles similar examples of Southern Sung Academy "birds and flowers" painting (see fig. 5). Yet the painter's own poem at the left reveals that Ch'ien Hsüan has used references to earlier literature to shape the image for the expression of his political ideals. The poem reads:

> From her lonely tear-stained face, teardrops fill the branch;
> Though her makeup is washed away, old charms remain.
> In night rain behind closed gates she is overcome with sadness;
> How different she was under golden moonlight before darkness fell.

The first couplet alludes to a passage in Po Chü-yi's poem "Ch'ang-hen ko" (Song of Everlasting Regret), where that poet compares the tears on the face of Yang Kuei-fei, Emperor Hsüan-tsung's favorite consort, whom he was forced to abandon in 756 during the chaos of the An Lu-shan rebellion, to spring raindrops on a pear blossom. In Po's poem, the lost consort stands for loss of the country to invading non-Chinese forces. In Ch'ien's scroll, the pear blossoms represent Yang Kuei-fei, who stands in turn for those Sung officials who, now "behind closed gates" and "overcome with sadness," have lost the security of the Sung dynasty and the happiness of their situation "before darkness fell." The quotation in the text generates a double metaphor that turns the image of the flower into a symbol for the artist himself (pear blossoms = Yang Kuei-fei = Ch'ien Hsüan). Such complex integrations of text and image go far beyond the easy pairings of Southern Sung Academy art and usher in the mature practice of literati painting.

The Yüan dynasty marks a watershed in the history of literati painting and accordingly in the increasingly nuanced relationships between text and image.

FIGURE 5. Ch'ien Hsüan, "Pear Blossoms." Handscroll. Ink and color on paper. Metropolitan Museum of Art, New York.

The practice of inscribing poems on paintings grew dramatically during the Yüan. More than a quarter of the surviving corpus of such major Yüan poets as Yü Chi (1272–1348) and Hsieh Hsi-ssu (1274–1344) are poems inscribed on paintings. Many inscriptions record viewings of the paintings in social gatherings or their transmittals as gifts, and this fact, plus the great number of such poems, testifies to the increasing popularity of paintings as vehicles for social and intellectual discourse during the period. Major Yüan painters such as Chao Meng-fu (1254–1322), Huang Kung-wang (1269–1354), Wu Chen (1280–1354), Ni Tsan (1301–1374), and Wang Meng (1303–1358) were also accomplished poets, whose poetic inscriptions now graced their own paintings and those of their colleagues. These paintings, in turn, were now conceived and designed with the knowledge that they would receive contemporary and future inscriptions.

Generally speaking, scholars have divided Yüan inscription poems into five broad categories, most of which have antecedents that go back to the Sung, if not to the T'ang. First are poems that confine themselves largely to a literal description of the painting. The challenge for the poet is to reproduce as closely as possible the atmosphere of the painting while maintaining his own detachment as an observer. Popular were poems that taxed the poet's descriptive skills, for example, Mei Yao-ch'en's (1002–1060) poem on a temple mural by the Sui dynasty (581–618) painter Chan Tzu-ch'ien that depicted a tug-of-war between twenty-four ghosts. Second were poems that used the painting as a vehicle for discourse on a topic not directly generated by the painted image. A landscape painting of the "Ch'ih-pi" (Red Cliff), site of a famous third-century battle, might prompt the poet to meditate on the shortness of life or the vanity of human struggle. Many poets used paintings as vehicles to express attitudes toward public service and as political satire or criticism. The value of friendship and the solace of political reclusion were especially popular topics. Such poems develop Tu Fu's earlier practice of using the painted image as a springboard for his own private meditations. Third were poems that transformed the painting into an allegory by stating a direct correlation between the image and another person or thing. For example, the poet Yüan Chüeh (1267–1327) wrote a poem on a painting of an escaped horse by Chao Meng-fu and presented it to the Mongol official Qutugdar (1296–1349) when that official departed from the capital to return to his home. The inscription created a direct analogy between the emancipated horse and the official who had just completed a tour of capital service. Such usage continued in the tradition of allegorical paintings such as the "Pheasant and Hibiscus," by the Emperor Hui-tsung, or Ch'ien Hsüan's "Pear Blossoms." Fourth were poems that extolled the skill of the painter, discoursed on theories of painting, or offered remarks on painting history. Fifth were inscriptions that made little or no reference to the painting and that served simply to mark the social occasion of its conveyance from one owner to another.

Ni Tsan's "Liu chün-tzu t'u" (The Six Gentlemen) may serve to show how the artist and his audience attached a specific meaning to the painting through

FIGURE 6. Ni Tsan, "The Six Gentlemen," dated 1345, ink on paper. Shanghai Museum.

inscriptions and how later inscribers reacted to the work (see fig. 6). The painting depicts six trees clustered on a sloping spit of land along a wide river with distant hills across the water. Ni Tsan's own prose inscription to the middle left relates that he executed the work one spring evening in 1345 immediately after arriving by boat at the residence of his friend Lu Heng, where several other guests including the painter Huang Kung-wang were already staying. Ni writes in his inscription that Lu pressed him for a painting whenever they met, and this evening was no exception. Although weary from his travels, Ni has exerted himself to satisfy Lu's request, and he expects that Huang Kung-wang will smile when he sees the painting. By this conclusion, Ni, in a tribute to the elder painter, alludes to the fact that he has executed "The Six Gentlemen" using a style of painting that Huang will identify as his own. Huang apparently saw the painting soon afterward, and he inscribed a poem in the upper-right-hand corner:

> Gaze far away upon clouds and mountains across autumn waters,
> See nearby these old trees that crowd the sloping shore.
> In elegant ease, these Six Gentlemen face one another,
> Free of bias and slant, they stand straight and true.

The Six Gentlemen of Huang's poem, from which the subsequent title of the painting was taken, alludes to a group of Sung dynasty scholar-officials who were banished into political exile for protesting the autocratic actions of a powerful minister.

One cannot know whether Ni intended the six trees to represent the individuals then gathered at Lu's house, or whether he intended to refer to the Six Gentlemen of Sung history, or both. But Huang, who was there, understood the painting as an expression of moral solidarity and principled companionship in the face of political decay and isolation. The second inscription writer, who may have been another guest of Lu Heng, writes that if the painter should decide to add a fishing boat to his work, Ni should use the writer himself as the model for the fisherman. The last inscription, obviously composed sometime later, refers to the passing of Huang Kung-wang and writes that the memory of both Huang and Ni will live on in the painting. Ni Tsan not only has integrated his own inscription at the left into the overall structure and balance of the work but also has left space at the top for Huang and subsequent viewers to record their reactions. Poetic inscriptions on paintings thus enabled the original work to accrue new meanings over time. And among literati connoisseurs, the appropriateness and depth of the later inscriptions could do much to enhance the esthetic reputation of a painting.

The material for the history of the interrelationship of text and image in the Ming (1368–1644) and Ch'ing (1644–1911) periods is both voluminous and complex, but quantity and variety more than innovation distinguish these later periods. The metrical structure of Chinese verse had always focused attention on the couplet, and paintings, either album leaves or hanging scrolls illustrating famous T'ang couplets, became widespread in the seventeenth century. Most popular were couplets from Wang Wei, both because of his now secure status as the founder of literati painting and because Su Shih had declared him the most "picturesque" of the T'ang poets. Such paintings routinely divorced the couplet from its original context and were often chosen because of their vivid natural images. There was often a loose connection between text and image, and couplets were sometimes chosen after the painting had been completed. Reclusion was a favorite theme, and paintings depicting gardens and mountain retreats were especially popular. In late Ming Soochow, for example, artists transformed the imagery of T'ang couplets into the familiar country and urban garden settings of Soochow. Viewed in a positive light, such treatment created for the artists' clients a comfortable sense of connection to the past and an atmosphere of cultural sophistication and refinement. The fusion of text and image was now complete at all levels of esthetic and intellectual expression. A professional Soochow painter might grace a fulsome birthday painting for public display with a Wang Wei couplet on a Taoist paradise, or a highly individual master such as Chu Ta (Pa-ta shan-jen; 1626–1705) might use an arcane fragment of medieval text to create an elaborate visual enigma that expressed his private loyalty to the fallen Ming rulers.

The interactions described above among poetry, painting, and calligraphy created a distinctive art form—the painting-poem—that became the hallmark of literati culture in China as well as in Korea and Japan. These interactions, in turn, created synergies that guided separate developments in each medium. Chinese poetry, always alert for the vivid natural image, was infused with a new, close, and inexhaustible source of that imagery. Painting, especially landscape painting, developed a poetic and lyrical quality that defines its character to this day. And painting and calligraphy were brought into closer contact as the literati generated styles of "calligraphic" brushwork that enabled paintings to be read and appreciated by the same standards as calligraphy.

Charles Hartman

PART III

Prose

Chapter 26

THE LITERARY FEATURES OF HISTORICAL WRITING

Preserving and recalling the past has been an important part of Chinese civilization almost from its beginning. As a result, China has produced an impressive collection of historical writings. No one in traditional China could claim to be educated without ingesting a huge dose of history. In fact, one twentieth-century scholar, Hu Shih (1891–1962), placed the twenty-five dynastic histories (*erh-shih-wu shih*), a collection that runs to approximately thirty-five hundred *chüan* (volumes or chapters), among his list of what one "must read in beginning studies." Most of this body of historical writing, although surely a blessing to the historian, is not of great literary significance. Nevertheless, one certainly does find in this vast storehouse much that deserves to be read for its literary value as well as for its historical content. This is particularly true of the earliest texts, which are our primary focus here. These early writings, much like the writings of the ancient Greek and Roman historians in the West, have special significance because they emerged at a time when a historical consciousness was first taking shape and when the presentations of that consciousness were fresh and had not yet fallen into the repetitive formulae that characterize so much of the later tradition. Moreover, certain historical texts from this early period gained such prestige that they were read and memorized by virtually every educated person and consequently established the parameters that defined and sometimes constrained the later historical tradition.

Before turning to the historiographic tradition in China and a discussion of its considerable literary value, we should briefly mention one particularly problematic issue: the somewhat murky boundary between history and fiction. In China the dominance and prestige of history were such that early Chinese fictional accounts—*chih-kuai* (reports of the strange; see chapter 29) being one noteworthy example—were presented as history and were discussed by serious critics not as fiction per se but as a form of defective history that presumably had emerged from "the gossip of back alleys" and therefore had some minimal historical value. Furthermore, history in China frequently became the "stuff" upon which fiction fed, so that one can sometimes trace a particular historical episode from a rather terse initial account, found in a text widely read as history, through a series of texts until it appears, much later, in a vastly inflated and obviously fictional guise. But it is quite impossible to draw a definitive boundary at any point in this process between what is clearly historical and what is clearly fictional.

Much material that now seems historically doubtful has, of course, insinuated itself into even the soberest historical texts in China, particularly into those that derive from the early period under consideration here. Anxiety about this tendency toward the fictionalization of history appears as early as the Confucian *Lun-yü* (Analects), where the Master Confucius (550–479 B.C.E.) refers to a time, presumably better than his own, when historians did not fill in gaps with their own conjecture (15.26) and also indicates that scribes writing in his age were emphasizing literary style over substance (6.18). The modern literary reader, however, might have much less concern than Confucius about such problems because so many of the sections of Chinese historical texts that are regarded as most literarily significant are precisely those portions of the text that are most historically questionable. But our purpose here is not to engage in the controversies concerning the relative reliability of various historical records. Certainly the ideal of the Chinese historian was that of a courageous official who observed events and recorded them dispassionately. Still, the tendencies to speculate, to amplify, and to stylize surely sometimes overwhelmed the more sober ideal of objectivity, and, from the perspective of the literary reader, such tendencies are often quite welcome.

Historical writing in China emerges from an official, ceremonial context. This original context has continued to shape many of the features of Chinese historiography long after certain writers of history have somewhat distanced themselves from centers of political and ritual control. The earliest forms of the historiographic tradition are associated with ancestral rites, with formalized governmental decrees, with records of the movements and words of the Son of Heaven, and with the portrayal of the verbal exchanges between rulers and ministers. The ancient Chinese *shih* (scribe), who managed this tradition, was attached in the Chou dynasty (c. 1027–256 B.C.E.) bureaucracy to the Ministry of Rites and was responsible for writing with an objectivity and moral discretion that could withstand the scrutiny of both ancestors and descendants. The tensions and contradictions inherent in these duties, as we shall see, spawned a tradition that, despite certain common features, was by no means uniform.

The first clearly attested writing in China, the Shang oracle bones, which date at the earliest from the thirteenth century B.C.E., are historical documents. These records of instances of oracle divination were inscribed on turtle shells and ox bones *after* the act of divination had been completed and were then stored in archives. That is, acts of divination that had been undertaken to foretell the future were meticulously transposed into dated historical records and thereby attested to events of the past. The content of the oracle inscriptions, which were initially the subjects of divination and were only secondarily turned into historical records, were highly circumscribed and consisted entirely of items of concern to the Shang king and his family: should a certain state be attacked? why did the king have a toothache? how should the king dispose of captives seized in battle? when should a particular sacrifice take place? and so forth. While these texts are valuable as historical documents and display the early association of writing and religious ritual, it is difficult to identify significant literary merit in such brief records.

The bronze inscriptions, particularly those of the first centuries of the Chou dynasty, are much more expansive texts than those found on the oracle bones and, at their best, display a crafted poetic grandeur that deserves more literary attention than they have normally been granted. Many of the bronze inscriptions, which were carefully cast on the inner surface of magnificent bronze vessels, register and memorialize noteworthy achievements in the life of some important member of an aristocratic clan. They are, in a very real sense, family history and were intended to be transmitted "from son to son and from grandson to grandson" and read as a means of keeping an ancestor and his virtues alive in the memory of his descendants. Typically, the inscription begins with a date, then records an event in which the person who had commissioned the bronze played a key role, and next commemorates the gifts he received from the king for this loyal service. The inscription concludes with a recognition of the king's beneficence and with a wish that the vessel might be transmitted through the clan of the person who commissioned it. One of the most unusual of these inscriptions, that of the "Shih Ch'iang Basin," describes in the most laudatory terms the early succession of Chou kings and juxtaposes this regal succession with a succession of family ancestors that culminates in the "filial and convivial" Scribe Ch'iang. This inscription has been characterized as the first deliberate effort in China to write history because it does not merely make note of an immediate event, like most of the oracle and bronze inscriptions, but gives a recapitulation of imperial and family history.

While the oracle inscriptions are impersonal accounts of the propositions tested by a diviner-priest, the longer bronze inscriptions, illustrated by the example of the Shih Ch'iang text, are dramatic presentations in which the direct speech of the king, who announces gifts, is juxtaposed with the direct speech of the recipient. The latter typically voices his gratitude for the gifts and expresses hope that his clan will continue to use the vessel and thereby remember him, the person who sponsored its production in the first place. This distinction between recording events (which Chinese critics call *chi shih*)—or, in the case of the oracle bones, anticipated possibilities—and recording ritually spoken words (*chi yen*), which are the substance of most bronze inscriptions, continued to play a critical role in the organization of Chinese historiography.

The difference between texts that record spoken words and those that record events is evident when we turn from these early inscriptional sources to the earliest extensive monuments of Chinese historiography—*Shang-shu* (Classic of Documents) and *Chun-ch'iu* (Springs and Autumns). The first of these works is primarily a record of spoken words and consists largely of announcements, declarations, commands, and dialogs that are ostensibly dated to the first centuries of the Chou era, a time when the new dynastic founders were in the process of articulating a political justification for their conquest of the Shang. Only minimal context is provided for these instances of speech. Consequently, the reader must often reconstruct some plausible scenario from the raw historical documents themselves. As is the case with both the oracle and bronze inscriptions, the documents included in *Shang-shu* obviously emerged from centers of political power and gave voice almost exclusively to the words of kings and high officials. The language, like that of the bronze inscriptions with which they are supposedly contemporary, is lofty in style and often employs highly rhythmic language. However, in many of these documents, unlike in the bronze inscriptions, there is an apologetic tone in which the speaker alternately proclaims his own unworthiness to rule and attempts to awe his audience into obedience.

Ch'un-ch'iu, in contrast to *Shang-shu*, is entirely a record of events and belongs to a tradition of annals that we know was widespread throughout the Spring and Autumn (722–468 B.C.E.) and Warring States periods (403–221 B.C.E.). Unfortunately, most of the annals produced by Chinese states during this time have been lost, but *Ch'un-ch'iu*, which derives from the small eastern state of Lu, was preserved and became the focus of an extraordinary commentarial tradition. The high status of *Ch'un-ch'iu* as well as the richness and imaginativeness of its commentaries almost surely result from a belief, first attested to in *Meng Tzu* (Mencius), that Confucius played an important role in putting this text into its present form. *Ch'un-ch'iu* appears on the surface to be little more than a list of major events taking place in the central Chinese states between 722 and 481 B.C.E., as seen from the perspective of the state of Lu. The entries are so terse and so apparently unadorned as to defy literary discussion. However, the entire commentarial tradition on *Ch'un-ch'iu* is predicated upon the curious notion that the text, though it appears quite simple and direct, actually consisted of extraordinarily subtle language and that, through employing such techniques as word choice, elision, and double meanings, the sage Confucius passes judgment upon the major figures and events of the Spring and Autumn period. What this commentarial tradition proves, more than anything else, is the capacity of interpreters to find impressive levels of subtlety and profundity in any text, however apparently mundane it appears on the surface, where important authorities have declared those qualities to exist.

The two types of history described so far, those that primarily record spoken words and those that record events, converge in *Tso chuan* (Tso Commentary), a text of remarkable literary quality that was probably written in the last decades of the fourth century B.C.E. In all likelihood, *Tso chuan* was originally a work independent of *Ch'un-ch'iu* that was subsequently reconfigured and then transmitted and read throughout later generations as a *Ch'un-ch'iu* commentary. Unlike the rather brief historical documents discussed so far, *Tso chuan* is a lengthy work (four volumes in its most recent, popular edition). This text is still shaped and contained by the year-by-year annalistic format that characterized earlier records of events such as *Ch'un-ch'iu*. Thus events in *Tso chuan* are arranged in a strict chronological order so that interrelated episodes and the actions of individual characters are often broken up by the intrusion of unrelated events that happen to have taken place in the same or intervening years. Certain narrative tactics are employed to mitigate the constraint of this scrupulous and rather mechanical style. Chief among these are the flashback, typically signaled by the Chinese word *ch'u* (in the beginning, or originally), a feature that continued in later histories of an annals format, and the anticipation of outcomes, or the "flash forward," so frequently embedded in the narratives themselves.

As noted above, *Tso chuan* is the first Chinese historical text to unify fully the recording of events and the recording of words. The literary contrast between these two elements of the text, however, is striking. The narration of events is, for the most part, extremely terse and tends toward a paratactic style, which means that clauses are juxtaposed with little verbal indication of causal relationships. Such a narrative style forces the reader to use considerable effort to construct the sequence of episodes into a story, a process some have described as "satori-reading"—that is, after each clause one typically must pause, ponder, and then finally grasp the meaning of the clause and its relationship to what has gone before. The language of these records of events in *Tso chuan* is concrete and unadorned in a way that becomes a model for many later writers who oppose the movement in later ages toward more florid forms of literary expression. However, the style of quoted discourse in *Tso chuan*, or records of words, quite unlike the terse, paratactic records of events, can be lively, ornate, and verbally complex. The speakers in these sections typically are arguing a position before a ruler, sometimes with other speakers who are presenting contrary positions, and they employ a rich array of rhetorical devices. Particularly important in the rhetoric of *Tso chuan* speakers are appeals to historical precedent and to what is deemed ritually and ethically appropriate.

The historian-narrator in *Tso chuan* is largely absent. In contrast to the roughly contemporary Greek historians Herodotus and Thucydides, who repeatedly enter their histories as a first-person "I" to explain the meaning of events or to comment upon the validity of variant accounts, the narrator of *Tso chuan* presents events in an ostensibly objective fashion that puts the narrative beyond question or qualification. Put somewhat differently, the historian implied in this text appears to be a simple recorder, who quite automatically writes down what has actually transpired. This remained the norm in Chinese historical writing. It is as though the past were thought to be a series of concrete events and overt acts that the impersonal scribe simply registered exactly and dispassionately, without coloring them in the slightest. But such absent narrators are never quite so absent as they may first appear. Certainly the narrator in this case is constructing the text with obvious didactic intent. Simply stated, his message is that ritually and ethically improper behavior is sure to be punished, whereas good behavior will eventually gain a deserved reward. Such a message is generally consistent with the somewhat earlier teachings of Confucius and no doubt contributed to the eventual promotion of *Tso chuan* to a place as one of the Confucian classics.

The historian-narrator in *Tso chuan*, who never appears in the text as a first-person presence, employs voices other than his own, or voices that at least appear to be other than his own, to provide judgments on particular episodes or characters. The two most common of these voices are an anonymous "princely man" (*chün-tzu*) and Confucius himself. No one knows precisely who this oft-quoted princely man is, and it may well be that he is nothing more than a hypothetical construct that simultaneously reflects the historian's own judgment while rhetorically distancing that judgment from the historian-author in a way that preserves the latter's status as an objective recorder. Thus, we could perhaps best understand and translate the words "a princely man says," which introduce these authoritarian judgments, as "a princely man *would* say." The sayings and judgments of Confucius included in this text, mostly at the conclusion of particular episodes, are generally not attested elsewhere and presumably represent interpretations of historical incidents that had developed among Confucius's much later followers, of whom the *Tso* historian is almost certainly one.

As is true of so many narratives that come to us from the ancient world, characters in *Tso chuan* tend to be stable and undergo virtually no change or development from one section of the narrative to the next. Once we grasp what kind of a person a particular character is, something that is usually not difficult, he or she will rarely surprise us in subsequent episodes. The reader's sense of character, what literary scholars call "characterization," comes largely from observing what the characters do and listening to what they say rather than from the direct exposition of a narrator telling us how we should understand and respond to particular persons. Moreover, there is virtually no penetration into the psychologically interior worlds of motivation, aspiration, and intention. The quiet inner life of characters must be implied from the sequence of events and from language that is externalized in the form of speeches and dialogs.

Some Chinese scholars have attempted to identify and describe the various basic literary forms from which *Tso chuan* is constructed. Others have tried to derive certain genres of the later tradition from seeds that they believe can be found in this unusually rich and complex text. Chief among the former are argumentations, admonitions, edicts, petitions, persuasions, exultations, descriptions, and quotations and expositions of poetry. Many of these forms derive directly from the relationship between ruler and minister, precisely the official relationship that dominates the text and was of such enduring concern to Confucius and his followers. Among the later genres for which scholars have identified *Tso chuan* antecedents, we might list "reports of the strange" (*chih-kuai*), the historical novel, parallel prose, the ancient prose essay, and the rhapsody (*fu*). While some of these generic connections are rather tenuous, the wealth and variety of material that can be found in *Tso chuan* are striking and have had enormous impact on the later tradition.

Several of the most compelling and famous sections of *Tso chuan* are those that deal with critical battles such as the battle of Han (645 B.C.E.), the battle of Ch'eng-p'u (632 B.C.E.), that of Pi (597 B.C.E.), and others. What is particularly interesting about these narratives is that much more space and care are given to the description of preparations for battle than to a portrayal of the actual fighting itself. Although not without some descriptions of battle and bloodshed, such episodes are far less graphic than those encountered in so many early Western texts. This reticence probably results, at least in part, from the belief that ritual appropriateness and strategic preparation determine the outcome of conflict much more than the martial valor of particular individuals. Such emphasis continued throughout later historical writing and distinguishes this more official, restrained discourse from the sometimes graphic accounts one finds in historical novels such as *San kuo yen-yi* (Romance of the Three Kingdoms) and *Shui-hu chuan* (Water Margin).

Another topic that recurs in several of the most famous sections of *Tso chuan* is that of the succession crisis. Such crises, which seem to have been frequent in Spring and Autumn China, usually involved the tangled affections of political leaders. Consequently, stories of this type were amenable to a highly dramatic portrayal that casts the reader in the coveted role of a voyeur into the lives of the privileged and powerful. In many of these accounts of succession crises, women who have gained the affection of the ruler are portrayed as ever eager to disrupt established principles of succession in order to promote their own favored sons. The first lengthy narrative in *Tso chuan*, the famous and often anthologized account of Duke Chuang of Cheng (r. 743–701 B.C.E.), is an example of just such a narrative and concerns a mother's efforts to make her second son the successor to her husband simply because her first son was born in a manner that "startled" her (often explained as a breech birth). What is important in this story, and what has no doubt made it so popular with generations of Chinese readers, is that the narrative ends with reconciliation between mother and son. Ritual order, although it has been temporarily disrupted by petty sentiment and self-interest, is reestablished, and reestablished in a fashion fully congruent with filial emotion.

Although much of the appeal of *Tso chuan* derives from a dramatic but always somewhat restrained presentation of major affairs of state such as battles, succession struggles, and the diplomacy that attends ever-shifting political alliances, sometimes one finds embedded within the text short narratives of supernatural or, at least, extraordinarily curious events. Confucius, whose teachings are often considered to have profoundly influenced *Tso chuan* and who is quoted so often throughout the text, is said not to have discussed "strange occurrences" and spirits (see *Lun-yü* 7.21). The author of *Tso chuan* does not share the Master's famous discretion on such issues. In one account, a ghost appears to his former chariot driver and is convinced by the driver that his plans for revenge will only hurt his own posterity. In another episode, dragons battle one another outside the main gate of the Cheng capital. And in still another episode, a stone speaks. Particularly skillful are the accounts of several dream sequences, the most famous involving Duke Ching of Chin (r. 599–581 B.C.E.), who dreams first of an ogre chasing him and then of an illness personified in the form of two small boys who inhabit his body. In both cases, the dreams, like several dreams elsewhere in the text, predict the future in a manner not unlike the tortoise shell divination or the milfoil divination that are so common on the pages of *Tso chuan.*

Tso chuan's high status among later Chinese critics derives in part from its intrinsic literary merit and in part no doubt from the fact that it was read *and* memorized as the most attractive expansion and commentary of *Ch'un-ch'iu*, a text almost all traditional readers ascribed to Confucius. Therefore, to some extent, *Tso chuan* becomes one of those works of world literature, like the Bible or Homer, that *defines* good literature in subsequent generations. No later prose writer can escape its shadow, and all will almost inevitably be judged by how their own styles compare to *Tso chuan*'s laconic, hard prose.

The balance between recording affairs and recording words that characterizes *Tso chuan* shifts in the direction of an emphasis on recording words in three other texts deriving either from the same general time period or from somewhat later. These three texts, *Kuo-yü* (Discourses of the States), *Yen Tzu ch'un-ch'iu* (The Springs and Autumns of Master Yen), and *Chan-kuo ts'e* (Intrigues of the Warring States), consist largely of speeches or dialogs, and, as is the case with so many of the speeches in *Tso chuan*, the primary setting for these verbal exchanges is the court, where ministers advise, admonish, and sometimes even cajole their rulers. While none of these three works has been as widely admired as *Tso chuan*, from neither a literary nor a historical perspective, each has moments of significant literary interest.

Kuo-yü, which covers many of the same events as *Tso chuan* and almost surely derives from the same group of traditions, is characterized by elaborate and occasionally tedious speeches. At their best, however, these speeches employ lively analogies, a clever use of historical precedent, and strong verbal parallelism. The narrative frame surrounding these speeches typically does little more than set the scene and then, at the conclusion of the speech, state the outcome. This outcome is usually predictable: a ruler who perceives the merit of an adviser's speech and acts accordingly will succeed, while one who rejects good advice, quite common in *Kuo-yü*, will fail. Many a state was destroyed during the Spring and Autumn period, *Kuo-yü* would have us believe, because an artfully expressed piece of ritually or ethically sound advice went unheeded. The wise minister who usually offers this advice is essentially an astute reader of the subtle signs and meanings that suffuse the political world. Such ministers, as portrayed in *Kuo-yü*, foresee the future and predict outcomes through observing facial features, bodily movements, the way one dresses, the use one makes of quotations from earlier texts such as *Shih-ching* (Classic of Poetry), and, most important, one's conformity to ritual expectations. In short, the man of wisdom, he whose advice must be followed, is a discerning reader of the world and its people.

Yen Tzu ch'un-ch'iu displays some of the characteristics of *Tso chuan* and *Kuo-yü* to such an extreme degree that one is tempted to read it as a satire, which it almost assuredly is not. This text, unlike *Tso chuan* and *Kuo-yü*, is classified by the earliest bibliography, that of the historian Pan Ku (32–92 C.E.), as a philosophical text, literally a text of the "masters," which belongs to the Confucian (Juist) school. *Yen Tzu ch'un-ch'iu* shows how difficult it is in early China to draw a clear line between historical and philosophical works. Many of the admonitions in this text are given a historically concrete setting and, in a few cases, repeat with only slight variations lengthy passages found in *Tso chuan*. But it is the form of *Yen Tzu ch'un-ch'iu*, as much as anything else, that leads us to treat this text here. The protagonist in this lengthy series of courtly admonitions is Yen Tzu, a contemporary of Confucius, who gained renown in early China as a wise and courageous minister to several rulers of the state of Ch'i, primarily Duke Ching (r. 547–490 B.C.E.). The ruler, as he appears in this text, can do little that is right. Fortunately, his faithful minister stands ever ready to correct his numerous political errors and moral failings. But the ruler is a hopeless recidivist and quickly falls back into his old weaknesses—an excessive fondness for drink, a proclivity to be sidetracked by his love for women, a proneness to neglect long-term benefit while thinking only of short-term political gain, and so on. *Yen Tzu ch'un-ch'iu* has the peculiar literary appeal of many forms that are pushed to an extreme: it defines the outer limit of a tendency in Chinese historiography, and many philosophical texts as well, toward the portrayal of feckless rulers encountering articulate and competent ministers who try, usually against impossible odds, to set their superiors upon the proper path. This theme, which is to be so much a part of later Chinese literature, is of course a self-serving one. Historical writing, along with so many other genres of Chinese literature, emerges largely from a class that was dependent upon state service and could only hope that rulers would heed and support them. It was plainly in their interest to portray their own insightful political advice as the ruler's only salvation.

If the precise intent of *Yen Tzu ch'un-ch'iu* is not always easy to determine, this is not so of *Chan-kuo ts'e*. Many of the most engaging pieces in this collection of historical and pseudo-historical episodes are obviously crafted as model examples of clever argument. Indeed, the text, which was compiled by Liu Hsiang (79–8 B.C.E.) from a variety of sources, has sometimes been regarded as a work emanating from a school of Diplomatists (the *tsung-heng chia*, or "School of the Horizontal and Vertical Alliances"). This has led some modern scholars to view *Chan-kuo ts'e* as a sort of handbook of examples for training in rhetoric with *suasoriae* and other forms comparable to those in the Greco-Roman tradition. Although *Chan-kuo ts'e* has been criticized as a particularly untrustworthy historical record, the esteemed historian Ssu-ma Ch'ien (c. 145–c. 86 B.C.E.), discussed below, used the same sources that were eventually to become *Chan-kuo ts'e* as primary material for much of his history of the Warring States period. From a literary perspective, this text is of considerable interest. Cleverness and humor are often more important in the discussions and admonitions of *Chan-kuo ts'e* than ritual or moral appropriateness, a quality that was to provoke many later Confucian scholars to condemn this text as immoral and potentially corrupting. Some of the best sections of *Chan-kuo ts'e* are anecdotes consisting of little more than an extraordinarily clever response to a highly problematic situation. "The Queen of Ch'in and Her Lover" is a splendid example of a humorous persuasion that might have been used as a model of perfect argumentation. The queen in this episode is sick and asks that her lover be buried with her at the time of her own interment. The lover, "troubled" by the queen's decision, enlists a persuader, who cleverly convinces the queen to change her plan by demonstrating to the queen that her intention is entirely inconsistent with her stated belief that there is no life after death. Many of these clever episodes in *Chan-kuo ts'e* have spawned *ch'eng-yü* (set expressions—see chapter 8) that are still employed by almost every speaker of the Chinese language. For example, "a fox borrows the authority of a tiger" (*hu chia hu wei*), which means to behave boldly because someone with real power is supporting you, derives from the humorous tale of "The Tiger and the Fox," in which a fox cleverly tricks a tiger into believing that he, the fox, is the king of the forest.

If *Tso chuan* inaugurates early Chinese narrative history and sets a literary standard that towers over its immediate successors, then surely *Shih-chi* (Records of the Historian) crowns that early tradition and establishes a new standard that almost all subsequent historians will emulate. This vast, 130-chapter masterpiece was the work of Ssu-ma T'an (d. 110 B.C.E.) and his son Ssu-ma Ch'ien, who both served as Prefect Grand Historian (*t'ai-shih ling*) under Emperor Wu (r. 141–87 B.C.E.) of the Han dynasty. It is not always possible to determine precisely how much of this text was written by the father and how much by the son, but it is certain that *Shih-chi*, as extant today, was brought into its final form by Ssu-ma Ch'ien long after his father died, and it is, therefore, with good reason that Chinese have usually identified this text as primarily the younger man's work.

The precise form of *Shih-chi* cannot be discussed here in great detail. Briefly, it is divided into five sections, four of which became common and two *de rigueur* in later Chinese dynastic histories: "basic annals" (*pen-chi*; twelve chapters), organized around the dynastic rulers; tables (*piao*; ten chapters), showing historical events and relationships in table form; topical essays or treatises (*shu*—later called *chih*; eight chapters); "hereditary houses" (*shih-chia*; thirty chapters); and "arrayed traditions" (*lieh-chuan*; seventy chapters), or what we shall hereafter call, somewhat loosely, "biographies." Chinese scholars referred to this organization as "the form of annals and biographies" (*chi-chuan t'i*), for these two sections, unlike the other three, were included in *each* of the twenty-five dynastic histories. Ssu-ma Ch'ien's emphasis on traditions or biographies as a supplement to the year-by-year annals is a significant departure from the historiographic tradition that preceded him. This new form emphasized the role of the individual human being, so some scholars have described Ssu-ma Ch'ien's historical writing as "revolving around the human being." Moreover, the human beings who occupy the center of the stage in *Shih-chi* are not just rulers and ministers, who remained important, to be sure, but also such socially marginal groups as merchants, jesters, assassins, and figures like the philosopher Chuang Tzu, who did his best to remain aloof from the political world.

Despite the structural originality of Ssu-ma Ch'ien's *Shih-chi*, this long text is to a significant degree a digest of all that had preceded it. For example, Ssu-ma Ch'ien adapts much of *Tso chuan*, translating the difficult language of this earlier text into his more expansive Han dynasty idiom, and whole sections of the sources that became *Chan-kuo ts'e* are quoted with only minor variations. Scholars have identified by name more than seventy sources utilized in *Shih-chi*, so one must be careful in ascribing the literary qualities of specific passages to Ssu-ma Ch'ien rather than to the sources, sometimes lost, that he utilized so freely in compiling his vast history. Nevertheless, one comes away from Ssu-ma Ch'ien's work with the sense that he is a literary genius and has made a series of artistic contributions that assure this text, more than any other historical work from ancient China, a continued large and admiring readership. Three literary qualities of *Shih-chi* are particularly significant: first, the complexity and density of Ssu-ma Ch'ien's characters; second, the liveliness of both the narration and quoted discourse; and third, the powerful emotional reactions of the historian Ssu-ma Ch'ien himself, which fashion him into a compelling and interesting character in his own text. Each of these features is discussed briefly below.

Most of the characters in early Chinese historical writing, as noted above, tend to be static and lack subtlety and nuance. The good are wholly good, the bad bad beyond redemption. But in *Shih-chi* one encounters characters who are not so easily classified. This is particularly so of characters who live within a hundred or so years of Ssu-ma Ch'ien's own lifetime, a period when his history presumably draws upon richer sources, including living memory, and therefore contains more detail than for more remote periods of time. Hsiang Yü, the great general who led the overthrow of the Ch'in empire (249–207 B.C.E.) and then struggled, in a losing effort, against Liu Pang (247–195 B.C.E.) for the post-Ch'in hegemony, is a case in point. Hsiang Yü's (233–202 B.C.E.) skill in battle is beyond dispute, and he is, moreover, a character of deep emotion and courage, qualities Ssu-ma Ch'ien obviously admires. But Hsiang Yü is also seriously flawed. He fails to heed the counsel of his best advisers, and at critical junctures he seems inextricably frozen in indecision. Indeed, Hsiang Yü wavers between emotional outbursts and an almost uncanny tendency to hesitate. Ssu-ma Ch'ien portrays this complexity, for the most part, not by directly telling us about Hsiang Yü but by showing us how he behaves in a wide range of situations. When the historian, at the end of the chapter he has devoted to this great general, finally speaks about Hsiang Yü's character, he further complicates the picture with an appraisal that many critics have regarded as surprisingly negative and therefore in sharp contrast with the narrative that precedes it.

General Li Kuang (d. 125 B.C.E.), whom Ssu-ma Ch'ien himself had met, is another excellent example of a fascinating and complex character, and the biography of this important Han dynasty figure is one of the literary high points of Ssu-ma Ch'ien's text. General Li is a man of great daring and is so considerate of his army that soldiers everywhere wish to serve under his command. He also is the one Chinese general the nomadic Hsiung-nu tribes fear most. These virtues notwithstanding, General Li repeatedly makes mistakes and finally commits suicide under duress after one of his more serious miscalculations. In case after case, as these two examples illustrate, Ssu-ma Ch'ien presents characters who, quite unlike those of *Tso chuan*, defy easy categorization. With Ssu-ma Ch'ien, the individual human being, in all his complexity and mystery, has become critical in the narrative of history. This feature of the Han historian, which has endeared him to generations of readers, did not always continue in later official historiography. The biography form that Ssu-ma Ch'ien initiated remained alive, but it came to be filled, at the hands of many subsequent historians, more with stereotypes than with complex individuals and thereby lost much of its literary appeal.

Shih-chi, for the most part, harmoniously integrates the recording of events and the recording of words, to use this traditional Chinese division once again. Part of Ssu-ma Ch'ien's art is to move smoothly between narrative and dialog, improving upon the rather stilted way in which earlier texts like *Tso chuan* use narrative as little more than a means to set up a speech or a court debate. In fact, after *Shih-chi*, it makes little sense to maintain the earlier distinction between recording words and recording events, so comfortably are the two traditions woven together. Some chapters in *Shih-chi* are little more than concatenations of speeches or memorials, but the wooden style of these chapters seems, at least in several cases, to be a comment upon the historian's attitude toward his subject—those whom Ssu-ma Ch'ien dislikes (Generals Huo Ch'ü-ping and Wei Ch'ing being two obvious examples) he renders boring. Much of the dialog in *Shih-chi* is so cleverly constructed and so lively that its veracity has been questioned. Certainly there is a great deal in *Shih-chi* that must be fabricated, either by Ssu-ma Ch'ien himself or by the textual or oral traditions that preceded him; to give one obvious example, who was there in the tent to record the final words between Hsiang Yü and his concubine on that fateful day when he was about to ride off to his death? However, Ssu-ma Ch'ien, unlike the Greek historian Thucydides, does not explain the principles he has used to construct speeches and dialogs. Perhaps the prestige of the historian in China freed him from the necessity of such explanation, or perhaps there was more concern in China with verisimilitude than with the historical "truth" that so concerned a historian like Thucydides, who labored under the shadow of Homer's epics and Herodotus's famous "lies."

What gives Ssu-ma Ch'ien's historical writing an additional layer of depth and literary power, and what distinguishes him from all previous and most subsequent historians, is that he himself becomes one of the most compelling and complex characters in his own text. From some perspectives, this is a remarkable claim because Ssu-ma Ch'ien, much like the earlier writer of *Tso chuan*, remains generally "absent" from his text. That is, he is not constantly at our shoulder, like Thucydides or Herodotus, voicing an opinion about this source or that source or musing with us over the meaning of a particular tale. Instead, Ssu-ma Ch'ien's comments are confined largely to passages at the end of chapters and are clearly introduced with the formula "the Lord Grand Historian says" (*tai-shih kung yüeh*). In these clearly demarcated sections of his text, Ssu-ma Ch'ien, having shouldered the mantle of his official position, steps forward and makes some comment about the content of the chapter. More often than not, these comments are brief and, in an important sense, constitute the first commentary on his own text.

What sets these comments of "the Lord Grand Historian" apart from the comments of "the princely man" in *Tso chuan* is that they are so replete with essentially emotional and, thereby, highly personal reactions to the characters and events of the past. Whether dealing with the topic of frustration and death or with such related issues as the amazing reversals that are so frequent in the lives he studies, Ssu-ma Ch'ien's judgments are filled with emotional effusions and wonderment. After noting that Hsiang Yü blamed heaven for his failure, for example, the Historian asks: "How could this not be absurd?" (7:339); elsewhere he says of Emperor Wen: "Alas, how could he not be considered 'humane'?" (10:437–438); of T'ai-po of Wu, Ssu-ma Ch'ien asks, rhetorically: "Alas, how could he have been a sage of such a vast vision of all things?" (31:1475); visiting the state of Lu and the temple of Confucius, he tells us he was "filled with respect and was unable to depart" (47:1947); and "if Yen Tzu were still alive," Ssu-ma Chi'en says in another judgment, "Even though I were his chariot driver, it is something I would be pleased and filled with admiration to do" (62:2137); "How tragic!" he exclaims in response to the calamities that befell the military strategists Sun Tzu and Wu Ch'i (65:2169); "How tragic!" he exclaims again, reacting to the story of Wu Tzu-hsü (66:2183); "Never," he admits in his judgment of chapter 74, does he read Mencius's comments to King Hui of Liang on the subject of profit without "putting down the book and sighing" (74:2343); "Alas, how tragic!" Ssu-ma Ch'ien says concerning Ch'en Hsi's fall into treason, and "how could it not be sad" that Han Hsin and Lu Wan defected to the Hsiung-nu (93:2642); "Alas, how pitiful," he responds to T'ien Tan's behavior, and "Alas, how pitiful" again in the same chapter that "disaster should come to good men" (107:2856); "Everyone wept at the death of General Li," Ssu-ma Ch'ien tells us, with the clear implication that we should weep too (109:2878); and of Kuo Hsieh, his contemporary, "Alas, how sad that he should meet such an unhappy end" (124:3189). Such examples of the historian's emotional reactions could go on and on. Indeed, Ssu-ma Ch'ien appears in his text as his own first reader, recording how he responds and how we, his subsequent readers, should also respond to the history he transmits.

Through such comments, the historian himself becomes a central character in his own text and inevitably forces us to consider how the narratives themselves are being shaped by this passionate figure. An approach to *Shih-chi* that considers this relationship between Ssu-ma Ch'ien and his history is further encouraged by two fascinating autobiographical texts that derive from Ssu-ma Ch'ien himself: first, the "postface" (T'ai-shih kung tzu-hsü) of *Shih-chi*, chapter 130, in which Ssu-ma Ch'ien tells us something of his own background and how he came to write *Shih-chi*; and, second, a remarkable letter attributed to Ssu-ma Ch'ien and preserved in Pan Ku's subsequent history (see below) that explains why Ssu-ma Ch'ien, after having been accused of "insulting the emperor," submitted to the punishment of castration rather than voluntarily committing suicide. It is possible from these texts to construct Ssu-ma Ch'ien himself as a character and then to read that character into the narratives of *Shih-chi*. One might challenge the validity of such a reading, but it has been a long-standing Chinese literary tradition to understand texts biographically and then to construct, or at least supplement, the biographies of authors from those same texts. Whatever one thinks of such a circular procedure, there is no doubt that one can discern considerable resonance between what we know of Ssu-ma Ch'ien and the way he portrays so many of the important persons of the past; and, furthermore, it is this very resonance that breathes life and power into some of his finest creations—Hsiang Yü, Ch'ü Yüan, General Li, Wu Tzu-hsü, and others.

One example of a historical theme that obviously resonates with Ssu-ma Ch'ien's own experience and recurs throughout the pages of *Shih-chi* is that of the noble figure who faces a moment of supreme crisis. Those who take bold action at such times—Hsiang Yü, General Li, Ching K'o the Assassin, Ch'ü

Yüan, and many others—are vividly and powerfully described. But sycophants and those who seek only personal safety, sacrificing others in order to avoid harming themselves, are portrayed with disdain and derision. There were several prominent political figures of this latter type in Ssu-ma Ch'ien's own time. He suffered terribly at the hands of such men, and he does not hesitate to attack them despite his own political vulnerability. In general, *Shih-chi* is a great literary work precisely because Ssu-ma Ch'ien is so obviously engaged with the material he presents and is so willing to display that engagement.

Ssu-ma Ch'ien's *Shih-chi* lays the foundation for much of the historical writing that followed. Indeed, it stands as the first of the twenty-five dynastic histories. However, in contrast to the other, later works in this collection, Ssu-ma Ch'ien's text is a comprehensive history and spans the long period of time from the legendary Yellow Emperor, who is traditionally dated to sometime around 2500 B.C.E., until midway through the reign of the Han emperor Wu or approximately 100 B.C.E. While the histories that succeed *Shih-chi* in the twenty-five dynastic histories may in general follow Ssu-ma Ch'ien's "annals and traditions form," they are limited to a single dynasty or to a succession of relatively brief dynasties. For a history to present a single dynasty was a tradition initiated by Pan Ku, who, under the inspiration of his father, Pan Piao (3–54), and with the supplementary work after his own execution by his remarkable sister Pan Chao (45–120?), compiled a history of the Former Han dynasty, extending from the fall of the Ch'in in 207 B.C.E. until the end of the Wang Mang usurpation in 23 C.E.

Pan Ku criticized his predecessor, Ssu-ma Ch'ien, for the latter's Taoist leanings and obvious admiration for knights-errant, merchants, and other groups that Confucians considered marginal or unworthy. These reservations notwithstanding, Pan Ku was also a great admirer of Ssu-ma Ch'ien's prose style and paid him the honor of copying almost verbatim much of the history of the first hundred years of the Han dynasty in *Shih-chi.* Thus, for example, Pan Ku's biography of Kuo Hsieh, one of the more swashbuckling figures of the early Han, is drawn with only minor changes in wording from Ssu-ma Ch'ien's earlier account. Still, a critical difference between these two Han historians is demonstrated by the fact that Ssu-ma Ch'ien concludes his account of Kuo Hsieh with a highly personal reaction to this "wandering knight," sighing and expressing pity over Kuo Hsieh's demise, whereas Pan Ku maintains much greater emotional distance from his subject. Pan Ku is more formal and aloof than his great predecessor, an attitude that in some measure reflects the stricter Confucian mood of his time. If such a characteristic has given Pan Ku's work less stature among literary scholars, it has earned him esteem among some historians who prefer his apparent objectivity and formality over Ssu-ma Ch'ien's frequently passionate engagement.

The general trend in much of the historical writing after the time of Ssu-ma Ch'ien, very much in the tradition established by Pan Ku, is toward increased emphasis on a rather rigid Confucian didacticism and on an increasingly court-centered political world. This trend is particularly clear in the biographies of the later dynastic histories, which so often reduce a character to little more than a succession of official positions and political acts, with a few stereotypical comments about personal qualities. It is exceedingly difficult to form a textured picture of an individual from these biographies. Instead, they are meant to convey lessons and illuminate the appropriate relationships that should characterize the political world. This general flattening in the literary quality of later history writing happens in part because of the increasingly professional way these histories were compiled, with the vast resources of government offices being used to make sure that the histories reflected precisely those values the reigning dynasty wished to uphold and promote. Furthermore, the growing compilation of collections of unofficial biographies provided an opportunity for writers to tell of interesting lives, sometimes their own, in highly imaginative or, at the least, unofficial ways. Collections such as *Lieh-nü chuan* (Biographies of Women), attributed to Liu Hsiang, and *Shen-hsien chuan* (Biographies of Divine Transcendents), attributed to Ko Hung (283–343), are two early examples of collections that obviously exist in a large world of Chinese biography occupying a murky realm between history and fiction (cf. chapters 6 and 29). Other soberer, unofficial collections appeared as well, such as Yüan Hung's (328–376) *Ming-shih chuan* (Biographies of Famous Scholars), and individual writers, including Wang Ch'ung (27–c. 97) and Ko Hung, produced brief but fascinating accounts of their own lives.

There are obvious exceptions to the gradual decline in the literary interest of official histories. Ch'en Shou's (233–297) *San-kuo chih* (History of the Three Kingdoms), for example, has some of the liveliest biographies in the entire corpus of Chinese historical writing. Ch'en himself lived through a time of great political turmoil, serving the state of Shu before ultimately entering service in Chin, a career that may have given him a particularly close exposure to living traditions of the events he narrates. His accounts of such figures as Kuan Yü (d. 219), Liu Pei (162–223), and Chu-ko Liang (181–234), although relatively brief, are extremely vivid and spark the growing folklore that surrounded this period and eventually culminated in the great Ming dynasty historical novel *San-kuo yen-yi*. A particularly splendid example of Ch'en Shou's literary skill is his fascinating biography of Hua T'o. This biography not only paints a portrait of a doctor who was medically far ahead of his time, apparently performing operations under general anesthesia, but also exemplifies the clipped and unadorned yet lively style of some of the best early Chinese narrative. Some of the best episodes concerning Hua T'o in *San-kuo chih* are no more than two or three lines in the original Chinese, but they convey a surprising sense of the calm self-assurance of this doctor as he diagnoses and recommends cures for a variety of illnesses.

The folklore element, which gives so much early Chinese history its particular literary appeal, diminishes over time as the writing of history increasingly falls under the purview of the Confucian bureaucracy, but it never entirely disappears from even the official histories. One sees this most dramatically in the accounts of the events surrounding the conception and birth of dynastic founders. There are several such stories in Ssu-ma Ch'ien's *Shih-chi*: the early ancestress of the Shang imperial line conceives when she swallows a bird egg; the early ancestress of the Chou conceives by stepping on the big toe of god's footprint; and so forth. Such accounts continued throughout the later tradition despite their miraculous nature. *Yüan shih* (History of the Yüan Dynasty) tells us that the mother of Chinggis Khan (1162–1227; r. 1206–1227), the "Grand Ancestor" of the Yüan, conceived when she dreamed that a white light came through her window and transformed into "a gold-colored deity" who came and lay upon her bed. According to *Ming shih* (History of the Ming Dynasty), the mother of the founder of the Ming dynasty, Chu Yüan-chang (1328–1398; r. 1368–1398), conceived after she dreamed that a "god gave her a pill," which shone as she held it in the palm of her hand. She swallowed the pill and awoke with a fragrant taste in her mouth and the room full of red light. And, finally, *Man-chou shih-lu* (The Veritable History of the Manchus), a trilingual (i.e., Manchu, Chinese, and Mongolian) official account of the origin of the Ch'ing dynasty (1644–1911), tells of three heavenly maidens who descended from heaven to bathe in a lake near Long White Mountain along the Chinese-Korean border. In this story, obviously related to the much earlier story of the origin of the Shang, one of the maidens swallows an apple that is brought to her by a bird, conceives, and is unable to return to heaven with her two companions. The fact that such stories of the miraculous conception of imperial ancestors can appear in normally staid historical sources indicates that even skeptical Confucian bureaucrats could not resist folklore pertaining to an imperial clan anxious to enhance its own prestige.

While much Chinese historiography, particularly that of the dynastic histories, is dominated by the "annals and traditions form," the older annals style, which follows a strict, dated, chronological format throughout, continued to appear. For example, the late Han dynasty scholar Hsün Yüeh (148–209) produced a digest of Han history entitled *Han chi* (Annals of the Han) that drew almost exclusively upon *Shih-chi* and *Han shu* but rearranged the materials found in these sources into a rigid chronological frame. Perhaps the most broadly acclaimed history of this sort was produced by the Sung statesman Ssu-ma Kuang (1019–1086) and is entitled *Tzu-chih t'ung-chien* (A Comprehensive Mirror for Aid in Government). Ssu-ma Kuang's work is 294 *chüan* long and covers the span from the beginning of the Warring States period in 403 B.C.E. to the beginning of the Sung dynasty in 960 C.E. In a memorial he presented to the throne, Ssu-ma Kuang acknowledged his debt to *Tso chuan*, a fitting tribute to the continuing influence of that text. If anything, *Tzu-chih t'ung-chien* is as sober and cautious an account of the past as one finds in the dynastic histories. For example, almost all episodes that include elements of the miraculous or supernatural are meticulously excluded, even though many of Ssu-ma Kuang's sources are rife with such accounts. Although this work shares the literary limitations of historical works such as *Tso chuan* that are strictly confined within an annalistic straitjacket, and although a clear didactic intent suffuses almost every narrative, Ssu-ma Kuang's prose is so clean and limpid that *Tzu-chih t'ung-chien* stands as one of the most admired works in the Chinese historical tradition.

Another important and revealing feature of Ssu-ma Kuang's work is the inclusion of a section in thirty *chüan* entitled "K'ao-yi" (Investigations into Differences), which goes beyond the normal evaluative comments of the historian, also found in this text, to an investigation of the reliability of different sources. This section confronts head on the problem of variant traditions and therefore marks a significant step forward, at least from the perspective of scientific historiography. However, the impact of this new feature was limited because general histories continued to be compiled without authors feeling the need to cite or examine the evidence presented in them. What this highlights, from a literary point of view, is that Chinese history continued, by and large, as if it were entirely objective, with opinions and evaluations expressed separately and in a clearly demarcated fashion. Such a style, if anything, enhances the stature of history, appearing to raise it above personal expression to a kind of self-evident authority. This enduring aspect of Chinese historiography may have its exceptions, but it gives to history-writing in China much of its distinctive style. To the end, the historian presented himself largely as a scribe who recorded with complete objectivity. His opinion, whether concerning the figures of the past or the sources he used, had to be clearly marked and was regarded as something quite different from history itself.

If the Chinese tradition of historical writing, surely one of the world's richest traditions of this type, tends to be literarily diminished by the heavy political and moral burden it is made to carry, its considerable literary power and interest are never entirely overwhelmed. We must bear in mind that the Chinese historiographical tradition was the product, almost entirely, of men who had undergone a strict education in the Confucian classics, and much of the austere power of their classical learning was to live on in the highly dignified and serious way they wrote of the events of the past and in their careful selection of the subject matter they deemed most appropriate. Put somewhat differently, Chinese historians remained largely within the parameters of the ritual tradition from which they had initially emerged. What they produced belonged mostly to an increasingly conservative tradition, but a tradition that blesses the student of the Chinese past and, on numerous occasions, rewards the literary reader as well.

Stephen Durrant

Chapter 27

EARLY BIOGRAPHY

Traditional Chinese biographies were generally short, stereotyped narratives intended to emphasize the social role of the subject rather than the subject's individuality. The literary importance of the genre lies in its central role in the development of all early narrative. Biographies helped to shape both "fiction" and "history" and also served as a bridge across which these two narrative forms were able to influence each other. In the early 1960s, Western scholars extracted what they claimed was a normative structure for traditional Chinese biography. It required the recording of (1) name(s), (2) ancestry, (3) significant events of childhood or education, (4) official positions, (5) official documents or other writings, (6) the date and details of death, (7) posthumous titles, (8) a eulogy, and (9) posterity. Yet this is a norm that developed over time and is most valid in examining biographies in and about the T'ang dynasty (618–907 C.E.). This structure was an end-product of more than fifteen hundred years of the biography's development (500 B.C.E.–1000 C.E.) and has proved inconsistent with many early biographies.

The study of early biography in China has been hampered because the genre developed at a time when written texts were only emerging. Most of the literature of the Chou dynasty (c. 1045–256 B.C.E.) was oral. Moreover, just as many Hebrew scholars have assumed an immense body of oral traditions drawn on by the earliest compilers of the Bible (c. 1000 B.C.E.), it seems reasonable that a culture like that of the Chinese, in which memorization and oral recitation have played—and continue to play—a major role, would have a similarly large corpus of oral narratives. Some scholars have argued that a "romance" type of biography existed in oral form and that story-cycles of these romances influenced accounts of figures such as Duke Wen of Chin (r. 636–628 B.C.E.) and Duke Chuang of Cheng (r. 743–701 B.C.E.) in the *Tso chuan* (Tso Commentary). If their hypothesis is correct, these tales may have been influenced by intense patriotic or even religious feelings (as were similar works of biography and hagiography in periods like the Six Dynasties [220–589 C.E.]). This oral-literary romance form may represent the earliest type of biographical narrative.

Early biographical development can be traced more reliably, however, through a closer examination of the written record in the *Tso chuan*, which led to speculation about an oral romance. It has been claimed that anecdotes are the basic unit of early Chinese narrative writing. Leaving this larger question aside, it seems that anecdotes were unquestionably the basic unit of early Chinese biography. The first passage in the *Tso chuan* to deal with Duke Chuang of Cheng begins, indeed, with an anecdote about how, because of his difficult breech birth, the duke became estranged from his mother. The text continues through a series of anecdotes and conversations in which time is suspended (the story moves forward in terms of "whens" and "thens") as the duke battles his mother and her favorite, the duke's younger brother, in a power struggle for the state of Cheng. Although the duke attempts to yield to their demands, he must finally drive off his brother and exile his mother. A clever adviser teaches the duke a way to reconcile himself with his mother without breaking a vow that he had made never to set eyes on her again. This exciting story led the most famous translator of the Chinese classics, James Legge, to label Duke Chuang "the hero" of the first part of the *Tso chuan*.

Yet this first passage on the duke is the only one in the *Tso chuan* that lends insight into the duke's personality, made evident when he admits to his adviser that he regrets his vow to avoid seeing his mother or when he reveals his joy on their reconciliation in a song. Moreover, this initial anecdote seems clearly intended to characterize the duke, to show through his actions his personality and morality, while also providing details on his birth and home place. The duke is revealed as a tolerant but capable, sympathetic but perceptive, harsh but forgiving man; the archetypal mother-son relationship is also probed. After this initial encounter, there are a score of descriptions of the duke interspersed throughout early chapters of the *Tso chuan*. All are, however, laconic narrative accounts of how he led an expedition to punish this or that vassal state for the King of Chou or how he was summoned by a hegemon for a covenant, each carefully dated. By 707 B.C.E. the duke was seen as a threat by the Chou court and had to repulse an attack by Chou and allied armies. Yet not a single one of these passages shows Duke Chuang's personal reactions. The technique of showing the reader his personal side regresses to a mere description of his place in the larger sweep of chronological history through a recounting of his career. The reader must bring along knowledge of the duke's character shown in the opening anecdotes to find a deeper understanding of these career developments. Regardless of whether these sketchy narratives were fleshed out by anecdote, dialog, or detail in the oral versions of the duke's life that scholars argue could have existed, it is the written record of this hybrid proto-biography—achronological anecdotes that characterize an individual and give his background, followed by a chronology of his career—which can be seen as having a significant influence on the first consciously conceived biographies in the Han dynasty.

Indeed, other early texts suggest that, for those individuals without a distinguished official career like Duke Chuang, or for whom records of such a career did not exist, the characterizing anecdote(s)—with its possibilities for generalization and didactic application—was the normal biographical record. At least as early as the Warring States period (481/403–221 B.C.), it became common for intellectuals to embellish their speech with anecdotes that emphasized morality rather than humor. These brief, often didactic, accounts can first be found in various philosophical works such as the *Meng Tzu* (Mencius) and later in the allusions that crowd the numerous speeches and letters cited in works like the *Chan-kuo ts'e* (Intrigues of the Warring States) and *Shih-chi* (Records of the Historian, or The Grand Scribe's Records). In chapter 83 of *Shih-chi*, Tsou Yang (c. 206–129 B.C.E.) begins a monolog with a long list of allusions to stories intended to drive home his arguments and at one point says: "Long ago Ssu-ma Hsi's leg was cut off in Sung and in the end he became Prime Minister of Chung-shan. Fan Sui's ribs were fractured and his teeth broken but in the end he became Marquis of Ying." Although the second story is well known (and recorded in chapter 79 of *Shih-chi*), the first has been lost. This is but one example of allusions that now are meaningless because they refer to narratives that no longer exist. The large number of incomplete allusions in extant speeches suggests the vastness of the original corpus of such anecdotes in oral literature. It seems that written versions of these stories, which often made a man synonymous with a certain trait, such as equanimity in the face of political success or failure (like Sun-shu Ao, who was made prime minister three times without showing joy and dismissed three times without exhibiting sorrow), made up the first of what Chinese historians call *lei chuan* (categorized biographies), works that characterized a man by relating one or more events illustrating the most important trait(s) of his personality. Sometimes the stories were told about made-up people, such as the many allegorical accounts of the foolish people of the state of Sung, one of the most famous of whom saw a rabbit run headlong into the stump of a tree and die and then sat down to wait for more rabbits for his cooking pot. More often they told of famous men of antiquity like Ssu-ma Hsi and Fan Sui.

These stories were certainly intended to teach, but their ability to entertain was also well known. When one reads that the rather stiff speeches of men such as Tsou Yang so moved the rulers who listened to them that they reformed, something seems amiss. What is missing is likely that the rulers—like the modern reader—were ignorant of many of these "epithet stories" told to them and that after the speaker finished his harangue he was asked to elaborate further on this or that person.

In contrast to these lost biographies, the materials concerning the life of Wu Tzu-hsü, general and counselor to Ho-lu, King of Wu, are perhaps the most numerous and most often studied. They tell of Wu Tzu-hsü's consuming desire to have revenge on the king of Ch'u, who had murdered his father and elder brother. The several distinct versions of the story may indicate disparate oral sources. Yet this narrative, like the Duke Chuang biography, can be read in a larger context, one that expounds the dangers of unchecked emotions. In this chapter it is an all-consuming revenge that brings down both Wu Tzu-hsü and his king.

Perhaps the most successful account of Wu Tzu-hsü is found in *Shih-chi*, written by Ssu-ma Ch'ien (c. 145–c. 86 B.C.E.) following his father Ssu-ma T'an's (d. 110 B.C.E.) design. *Shih-chi* contains 130 chapters—12 basic annals telling of events closely allied to the royal houses of early China, 10 chronological tables that help to order events, 8 treatises on topics such as astronomy and music, 30 accounts of the hereditary feudal rulers of various vassal states, and 70 *lieh-chuan*, normally translated as "memoirs" or "biographies," which recount primarily the lives of early Chinese individuals of various sorts (see chapter 26). The sixth *lieh-chuan* (chapter 66 overall) depicts Wu Tzu-hsü. Ssu-ma Ch'ien relates that he was a native of the state of Ch'u, that his given name was Yün, that his father was Wu She, his elder brother Wu Shang, and his ancestor the famous minister to King Chuang of Ch'u (r. 613–591 B.C.E.), Wu Chü. Then the reader is presented with a series of anecdotes about Wu Tzu-hsü and his relatives held together by temporal expressions such as "in a short while," "then," "when," "before," "some time later," and so on. Wu Tzu-hsü is shown to watch helplessly as a traitorous minister leads his ruler, King P'ing of Ch'u (r. 528–516 B.C.E.), astray. When his father remonstrates, both Wu She and Wu Shang are executed. Wu Tzu-hsü flees, vowing revenge. After some adventures vividly recounted, Wu Tzu-hsü is helped by an old fisherman to escape across the Yangtze River to the state of Wu, which was then at war with Ch'u. Wu Tzu-hsü becomes a trusted adviser to Ho-lu, the heir, who becomes king of the state of Wu by murdering his father. By this point in the biography, Ssu-ma Ch'ien has clearly shown Wu Tzu-hsü's character through a series of anecdotes. Moreover, Wu Tzu-hsü has gained an official position. Then an exact date is recorded, signaling a change of style and structure as the account of Wu's career begins. What follows is a laconic, year-by-year account of the battles between the states of Wu and Ch'u for the period 512–506 B.C.E. and Wu Tzu-hsü's role in them. Although King P'ing of Ch'u has died, the state of Wu finally conquers Ch'u; Wu Tzu-hsü exhumes King P'ing's corpse and whips it, only to be warned by an old friend that he has gone too far. The plot thickens when Ho-lu is mortally wounded in battle by the King of Yüeh. On his deathbed, Ho-lu enjoins his heir, Fu-ch'ai, to promise to avenge him. Fu-ch'ai promises, but later decides to let the King of Yüeh live after routing his army. Wu Tzu-hsü remonstrates against Fu-ch'ai and is executed not long before the Yüeh forces overrun Wu and kill Fu-ch'ai.

Although the bifurcated structure of this chapter is nearly lost in the complexity of the various subplots and the episodic style, it bears some resemblance to the *Tso chuan* "biography" of Duke Chuang in its alternation of anecdote and annals relating Wu Tzu-hsü's character and career, respectively. One reason Ssu-ma Ch'ien constructed such a complex narrative must have been his desire—evident especially in other biographies of early figures such as Kuan Chung—to attach a life (career) to a theme (represented by the subject's character). Wu Tzu-hsü's story may have been overwhelmed by Ssu-ma Ch'ien's attempts to lend it such an extended rhetorical meaning, since the several subplots, all warning against revenge's power to blind a person (this admonition enhanced by Wu Tzu-hsü's final request to have his eyes dug out from his corpse and hung on the city gate so he can watch as the Yüeh armies eventually conquer Wu), make the basic story difficult to follow. A second reason for the biography's prolixity may have been Ssu-ma Ch'ien's belief that the existing written versions of the Wu Tzu-hsü story placed restrictions on his brush, for, like Confucius, Ssu-ma Ch'ien thought of himself as primarily a transmitter of early history.

When it came to the biographies that Ssu-ma Ch'ien wrote about individuals in his own Han dynasty (206 B.C.E.–220 C.E.), he had a freer hand. In these biographies, his two-part biographical standard is more discernible. The account of the Han dynasty's founder, Liu Pang (247–195 B.C.E.), for example, begins with the future emperor's supernatural conception and birth, then relates a series of stories about his youth and years as the local precinct chief, and finally turns to a chronological account of Liu Pang's official career. This second section begins with the rebellion of the farm laborer Ch'en She against the Ch'in dynasty in 209 B.C.E. Ch'en, leading a group of conscript laborers, established himself as the King of Ch'u. After only half a year, he was killed by his own charioteer, but his revolt weakened the Ch'in enough to pave the way for Liu Pang's more successful rebellion. As in the Wu Tzu-hsü biography discussed above, a precise date acts as a transition from characterizing anecdotes to a chronology of Liu Pang's career. The first part of the biography is driven by the force of his personality and reveals personal traits—brashness, a fondness for wine and women, a superstitious nature, the ability to profit from advice—which are evident in the following chronological portion of the Ssu-ma Ch'ien life of Liu Pang. Although this "biography" is presented in a "basic annals" because Liu Pang became Emperor Kao-tsu, it was clearly modeled on *Tso chuan* accounts such as that of Duke Chuang of Cheng. This structure became a conscious pattern. In Ssu-ma Ch'ien's accounts of the lives of Ch'en P'ing (chapter 56), Chang Erh and Ch'en Yü (chapter 89), Ch'ing Pu (chapter 91), T'ien Tan (chapter 94), Li Shang (chapter 95), and Li Yi-chi (chapter 97), he begins by characterizing his subject, often in one or more anecdotes, before punctuating this opening section with the phrase "when Ch'en She began his uprising," after which follow chronological depictions of the official lives of these associates of Liu Pang. Other biographies, including those of Chang Liang (chapter 55), P'eng Yüeh (chapter 90), Wei Pao (chapter 90), and Han Hsin (chapter 92), are similar in structure but use another easily datable transitional phrase, such as "when Hsiang Liang crossed the Huai River," to switch from personal descriptive anecdotes to the impersonal chronology of official deeds.

This hybrid biographical pattern created by Ssu-ma Ch'ien, which was employed in more than half the *Shih-chi* biographies, combined the rhetorical truth of the anecdotes with the conventional reliability attributed to chronological annals. This personal yet verifiable life should be seen as the first consciously constructed account of an individual that presents a "complete" biography. It became the early standard for official historiography. This type of biography was also a literary form, primarily because of the emphasis Ssu-ma Ch'ien put on the anecdotal opening section. His skill in selecting interesting anecdotes and recasting them in a captivating style has made many of these tales part of basic Chinese cultural knowledge down to modern times. Although these biographies can be seen as having two major parts defined by two distinct styles and approaches, the detailed structure of these lives often included some components similar to what scholars established as a normative biography in the early 1960s. Parallel lives, such as that of Sheng, the magistrate of Pai, which follows the biography of Wu Tzu-hsü in chapter 66, might be considered a sort of epilog, especially when they are obviously added to support the rhetorical impact of the first life.

Aside from this hybrid norm, Ssu-ma Ch'ien constructed a purely rhetorical biographical type employing only an anecdote or two to portray a life. Examples are found most readily in his "collective biographies" such as that on the "Hsün-li" or "Reasonable Officials" (chapter 119). There the life of Sun-shu Ao, the Prime Minister of Ch'u (c. 600 B.C.E.), is told through two stories. The second illustrates his laissez-faire style of governing. The King of Ch'u was upset because the low-slung carriages then popular in his state were overtaxing the horses pulling them. He wanted to promulgate a law forbidding low-slung carriages. Sun-shu Ao dissuaded him and, by simply asking that the sills of village gates be raised so that carriage owners could not get through them without dismounting, he effected the change. The life is made exemplary by Ssu-ma Ch'ien's preface to this chapter, which defines "reasonable officials," and by the closing lines on Sun-shu Ao: "In this way, without instructing them, the people were made to follow the king's influence, those who were near observing and imitating Sun-shu, those who were distant looking up to him from the four directions and taking him as their model." Even independent biographies, like those of Kuan Chung and Yen Ying (chapter 62), employ this epithet biographical style. Ssu-ma Ch'ien was not the first to use anecdotes to characterize an individual, but he was the first to classify this usage as a type of *lieh-chuan*.

The term *lieh-chuan* is not seen in any texts before the *Shih-chi* and appears to be Ssu-ma Ch'ien's creation. Having seen the practical application of the expression, a definition of *lieh-chuan* can now be attempted. *Chuan* refers to a tradition, in this case one related to a specific person. It could be a written tradition or, presumably, an oral one. There could be three basic meanings for *lieh* in this context: (1) to carve or break up, (2) to arrange or put in order, and (3) to oppose or juxtapose. By choosing a word rich with meaning, Ssu-ma Ch'ien belabored interpreters of the term. Yet all three meanings of *lieh* seem to reverberate here—the traditions in the *lieh-chuan* are indeed "broken off" from the larger scheme of chronology as presented in subgenres such as the basic annals or the hereditary houses; they are "arranged" with the character-creating anecdotes coming at the beginning followed by a chronology of the official life; and they are "juxtaposed," one tradition to another, sometimes in collective biographies, sometimes in parallel accounts (reminding us of Plutarch's *Lives*), such as that of Kuan Chung and Yen Ying, mentioned above. "Biography" and "memoir," the two most widely accepted translations in English, are only approximations for this difficult generic label.

Aside from creating the first two types of standard biography, Ssu-ma Ch'ien's lives are important because he was eclectic in his use of early sources, combing archaic manuscripts as well as the imperial archives, and adding to this material the stories he had heard during his extensive travels as a young man. Without the accounts provided in the *Shih-chi*, many of these biographies would be lost. Another important contribution was his attention to a broad cross section of human beings—he wrote lives of assassins as well as generals, told of entertainers and scholars, and admired both kings and rebels, occasionally even providing a glimpse of a memorable woman or lackey. Although the work was not widely circulated for a century or so, the eventual importance of the *Shih-chi* to the development of biography came through the immense popularity that Ssu-ma Ch'ien's accounts soon gained and their influence on a wide spectrum of subsequent biographical writing.

Less than a century after Ssu-ma Ch'ien's death, the indefatigable scholar Liu Hsiang (c. 79–c. 8 B.C.E.) became imperial bibliographer, with access to all the texts and archives in the possession of the Han royal house. He put together several biographical works that seem to have been primarily based on earlier texts: *Hsin hsü* (New Prefaces), *Shuo yüan* (Florilegea of Persuasions), and *Lieh-nü chuan* (Biographies of Illustrious Women). The first two books are collections of illustrative anecdotes of figures, ancient and modern, arranged under subject-titles such as "Fu-en" (Repaying Kindness) and reminiscent of Ssu-ma Ch'ien's collective biographies. *Shuo yüan* contains stories of actual historical figures (such as the account of a mother weeping while General Wu

Ch'i sucked clean the wounds of her son—she had seen Wu Ch'i do the same for her husband, who then fought to the death for his commander) as well as didactic fables. *Lieh-nü chuan* is the first collection of biographies of women, each intended to provide moral examples for its readers. Although later women's biographies often focused solely on chaste widows, Liu Hsiang included many types of model women, such as the mother of the philosopher Meng Tzu (Mencius), who moved their residence three times so that her son could grow up in the proper environment. Liu also arranged these female biographical anecdotes by topic, suggesting that Liu Hsiang may have taken not only his biographical materials but also the categories under which they were filed directly from the imperial archives. Since Ssu-ma Ch'ien also had access to these archives, they may have played a role in the arrangement and naming of his collective biographies as well.

The earliest extant regional biographies, which also date from this era, are those in the *Shu-wang pen-chi* (Basic Annals of the Kings of Shu). Attributed to Yang Hsiung (53 B.C.E.–18 C.E.), this text depicts the lives of the cultural builders of what is now Szechwan. The account of Pieh-ling (Efficacious Turtle) is typical. After he appeared to die in his native state of Ching, his corpse ascended the Yangtze River through the gorges to arrive in Shu. Turtle soon became Prime Minister of Shu, controlled flood waters there, and ordered the waterways. After the emperor seduced his wife (playing on the meaning of another word for turtle, which also means cuckold), he yielded the throne to Pieh-ling, who was then called Emperor K'ai-ming.

In addition to these epithet stories, the standard biographies Ssu-ma Ch'ien had created also developed under the Eastern Han. Pan Ku (32–92 C.E.), continuing the work of his father (as Ssu-ma Ch'ien had), included seventy chapters of biographies in his *Han shu* (History of the Han Dynasty). Pan Ku was critical of Ssu-ma Ch'ien's tendency to take liberties with his sources and intolerant of his predilection for writing lives of people (such as merchants or knights-errant) repugnant to the Confucians. Nevertheless, the *Han shu* is clearly modeled after the *Shih-chi*. Pan Ku's major contributions in the *History of the Han Dynasty* were to restrict the scope to a single dynasty and to attempt to treat historical detail more carefully than had most of his predecessors. Care for detail is evident in the biographies found in the *History of the Han Dynasty*, numbering more than a hundred, but Pan Ku's style may have suffered in the process. One modern scholar characterizes it as laconic and impersonal, presenting a grim realism with an air of brooding grandeur.

There are two other obvious changes in Pan Ku's biographies. First, although nearly all of Pan Ku's biographical chapters contain accounts of several individuals, the relationship between these men is less obvious than in similar biographies in *Shih-chi*. In chapter 34 of the *History of the Han Dynasty*, for example, Pan Ku has included the lives of many of the generals who helped bring the Han to power. These biographies, based largely on parallel accounts in *Shih-chi,* do not underline a single idea or thread. In his comment at the end of the chapter, Pan Ku observes that men like Han Hsin (of Huai-yang in modern-day Honan province), P'eng Yüeh, and Ch'ing Pu used duplicity and deception to attain their stature and were therefore distrustful of Emperor Kao-tsu, who had encouraged such actions. They were anxious that the emperor might take back their lands and titles, and one by one rebelled and were killed. Pan Ku notes, however, that Chang Erh and Wu Jui do not fit this mold, and both were able to escape the fate of their colleagues. Proving the rule or norm by the exception is a technique that Pan Ku also used in other chapters (for example, chapter 67, which grapples with the problem of loyalty in officials); in his presentation of individual differences, moreover, Pan Ku emphasizes the realism of these accounts and thereby removes most of the representative power seen in Ssu-ma Ch'ien's biographies.

A second discrepancy between Pan Ku's biographies and those of Ssu-ma Ch'ien can also be seen in the accounts of Ch'ing Pu and Wu Jui (chapter 34). The *History of the Han Dynasty* account of Ch'ing Pu, adhering to that told in *Shih-chi,* relates, first, how when Ch'ing was young a stranger had examined his face and prognosticated that he would be punished by the law and then become a king. A few years later, when he was indeed involved in an offense and tattooed (*Ch'ing* in his appellation refers to this punishment—his surname was actually Ying), he mocked himself by saying that the soothsayer had at least been half correct. Sent to work on the mausoleum of the First Emperor of Ch'in at Mount Li, he escaped from the work gang and joined a band of robbers. After this story, which lends a human face to the subject of the biography, the text moves to Ch'en She's rebellion and a chronological account of Ch'ing Pu's military exploits, his ascension to the throne of Huai-nan (fulfilling the prophecy), and finally his rebellion against the Han, his flight, and his death. In essence the *History of the Han Dynasty* account of Ch'ing Pu reiterates that in the *Shih-chi.*

For Wu Jui, however, there is no biography in the *Shih-chi.* The following paraphrased accounts from the *History of the Han Dynasty* were Pan Ku's own creation. Wu Jui was a prefect in Fan-yang under the Ch'in dynasty who had gained wide popularity among the common people. When the rebellions against the Ch'in began, Ch'ing Pu and Wu formed an alliance. Wu in return married his daughter to Ch'ing. One of Wu's generals then fought with Liu Pang; Wu himself accompanied Liu Pang's rival, Hsiang Yü, west to Hsien-yang (in Shensi province, just northwest of modern-day Sian). He was rewarded with the kingdom of Heng-shan. After Hsiang Yü was killed and Liu Pang became the first Emperor of Han, Wu was made King (or Prince) of Ch'ang-sha primarily because his general had aided Liu Pang. A year later Wu died. Five of his descendants succeeded to the throne of Ch'ang-sha before the kingdom was abolished in 174 B.C.E.. The text concludes with a brief justification explaining why a nonmember of the Liu family should have been made king.

This biography is closer to the nine-part normative biography outlined at the beginning of this chapter. It leaves the reader with a succinct, highly impersonal account of Wu Jui. All ambiguities—such as why Liu Pang should have looked kindly upon a former supporter of his archenemy, Hsiang Yü—have been removed or facilely explained. Anecdotes, such as those Ssu-ma Ch'ien used to enliven his portraits and to make his biographies works of literature, are missing. But it was Pan Ku and this type of biography—realistic in content, narrative in style, and serious in tone—that provided the model for most subsequent biographies in dynastic histories.

There is also an important collection of biographies found in the dynastic history for the Later Han dynasty written by Fan Yeh (398–446) in the 430s. Fan, in his *Hou Han shu* (History of the Later Han Dynasty), drew on about twenty earlier sources to compile nearly six hundred biographies in the eighty chapters devoted to *lieh-chuan*. Fan himself was more interested in the didactic critiques that made up the introductions, discussions, and eulogies around which he organized many of his biographies. Under such general groupings as *wen-yüan* (literati) and *tu-hsing* (independent spirits), Fan returned to a representative type of biography, influenced by ethical concerns. Thus he compiled more collective biographies than Ssu-ma Ch'ien and Pan Ku combined. Although some of his most impressive lives were devoted to pillars of the state, like his massive biography of Ma Yüan (14 B.C.E.–49 C.E., in chapter 24), and many were closely based on documents dating from the Later Han (such as the biography of Hsiang K'ai in chapter 30), he was fond of stressing unusual characters or lifestyles, or depicting members of court factions, eunuchs, independent spirits, magicians, physicians, and hermits. This reflects as much the taste of his own fourth century as the reality of the Later Han. Attributes of character then in fashion—such as classical learning, filial piety, indifference to material success, and devotion to social codes—also appear often in these lives. Archetypal anecdotes like that of the righteous lad who harangues attacking bandits and thereby saves his entire family are common. The tendency to aim for a larger meaning (beyond the historical) and the interest in unusual figures led Fan Yeh to rely on unorthodox sources such as *chih-kuai* (tales of the strange). This can be seen in his account of Fan Shih (in chapter 81, "Independent Spirits"). Fan Shih studied at the imperial university in his youth and became close friends with a fellow student, Chang Shao. Later, before both men returned to their hometowns, Fan Shih promised to come and pay his respects to Chang's parents two years hence. When the two years had nearly passed, with no further news from Fan, Chang enjoined his mother to prepare for the visit. On the prescribed day, Fan indeed arrived, paid his respects, enjoyed wine and food with Chang, and departed. Later, as Chang lay on his deathbed, his last hope was to see Fan again before he was buried. That night Fan Shih dreamed that Chang had died and, upon waking the next morning, convinced his skeptical superior to give him leave to attend the funeral. Not knowing that

Fan was on his way, the Chang family attempted to entomb Chang. Just as they were about to lower the coffin into the grave, they found that they could not move it the last few feet. Fan then arrived and consoled Chang through the coffin; only then could the coffin be lowered into the ground. The biography goes on to recite other stories of Fan's generosity and loyalty before the concluding sentence (a sort of back-frame) relates that Fan became Governor of Lu-chiang, achieved fame, and died in office. The use of anecdotes to characterize Fan, the inattention to chronological detail, and the didactic purpose of the piece all recall Ssu-ma Ch'ien's biographies.

An unusual juxtaposition of both the realistic and the representative styles of biography is seen in the lives of the fourth of the "Four Histories" (*Ssu shih*): *San-kuo chih* (History of the Three Kingdoms), by Ch'en Shou (233–297). Although the sixty-five-*chüan* work depicting the states of Shu, Wei, and Wu is arranged in the *chi-chuan* (annals and biographies) format, it has been dubbed an essentially biographical text. In the ostensibly biographical chapters alone, nearly five hundred individuals are treated. The biographies are mostly meticulous historical accounts pegged to a chronological structure. Many give details on the individual's youth and areas of study or expertise. The commentary by P'ei Sung-chih (372–451), which has become a fixture in most editions of this history, is almost as long as the text itself (each exceeding three hundred thousand characters) and often presents valuable parallel accounts from *pieh-chuan* (separate or distinct biographies) or other marginally historical works. The account of Chao Yün (d. 229), one of the southwestern kingdom of Shu's most courageous generals, who had rescued Liu Pei's (ruler of Shu; 162–223) son from his archenemy, Ts'ao Ts'ao (ruler of Wei; 155–220), for example, traces Yün's military campaigns against Wei. After a series of successful battles, Chao was defeated by a vastly larger Wei force in 224 and demoted. Five years later he died and was posthumously honored as a Shun-p'ing Hou (Smoothing Pacification Marquis). A brief account of the reasons for and recipients of posthumous titles, along with capsule accounts of two of Chao's sons, complete the biography. In his commentary to Chao Yün's life, P'ei Sung-chih cites a "separate biography" of Chao recounting his great height and martial appearance, recites anecdotes proving Chao's loyalty to Liu Pei and his seriousness of character (such as refusing an especially beautiful woman offered to him as a wife by a general he did not trust), and otherwise enhancing the reader's vision of Chao in story and dialog. The combined result of text and commentary is a figure outlined by the black-and-white reality of Ch'en Shou's stark historical narrative, which comes to life through Pei Sung-chih's commentary.

This bifurcation, however, marks the increasing tendency to restrict anecdotes in formal biographies because the method of representing an individual's life through his words and actions had become suspect. *San-kuo chih* and its commentary show the impact of these stricter historical principles on biography. Chronological accounts of careers were deemed more reliable, while the characterizing anecdotes of Ssu-ma Ch'ien's opening section were considered something outside history proper. Thus it is not a coincidence that at about this time "esoteric" or "outside" biographies (*wai chuan*) and collections of quasi-historical anecdotes such as *Hsi-ching tsa-chi* (Miscellanies of the Western Capital; c. 500) and Liu Yi-ch'ing's (403–444) *Shih-shuo hsin-yü* (New Account of Tales of the World) began to appear. The movement of the literary biography from official histories to heterodox genres of narrative eventually resulted in the development of fictional biographies and classical-language tales.

Over the same centuries that normative official biography was crystallizing, two other related forms were also evolving, both ostensibly modeled after the standard *lieh-chuan:* the religious hagiographies of the Buddhists and Taoists and the biographies written to depict exemplary women. Although Taoist biographies—or more properly hagiographies—developed over time from simple stories of holy men to theogonies, it is primarily two collections of texts that relate to the development of early Chinese biography—*Lieh-hsien chuan* (Tradition of Transcendents), attributed to Liu Hsiang but most likely dating at least a century later, and *Shen-hsien chuan* (Biographies of Divine Transcendents), by Ko Hung (283–343). A typical biography from these collections is that of Lü Shang (also known as T'ai-kung Wang). There are fragmentary records of Lü's role in the establishment of the Chou dynasty in *Tso chuan*, *Chu-shu chi-nien* (Bamboo Annals), and *Chuang Tzu*, as well as an account in the hereditary-houses section of the *Shih-chi* (chapter 32) stressing his role in the early history of the state of Ch'i. But the account in *Lieh-hsien chuan* (Biographies of Transcendents) is the first full biography of Lü. It begins formulaically with his name and native place, then tells of his innate wisdom and his prescience, which allow him to predict the rise and fall of states. Lü's "career" begins with his reclusion during the rule of the evil last king of the Shang dynasty. King Wen, the founder of the Chou, dreamed of meeting a sage, then heard of Lü Shang and sought him out. Lü wrote *Yin mou* (Secret Plans) for the king. He then ate some mushrooms, announcing that he was two hundred years old and was about to pass away. After his death, his coffin could not be buried for a time because of local strife. When it was finally possible to bury him, his coffin was found to contain not his corpse but a book on military strategy. This account varies from Ssu-ma Ch'ien's standard biography more in content than in form. Whereas official acts are depicted in a mainstream biography, ostensibly asocial acts often identify a Taoist. Their "careers" were marked by a solitary life, inattention to personal appearance, unusual eating habits, tolerance of climatic extremes, and so on. Individuals often predicted their own "death" or "transcendence."

These early Taoist accounts utilized the form and even some of the concerns of the orthodox biographies because they often depicted ancient individuals like Lü Shang, about whom there was a considerable non-Taoist literature and because they were compiled by editors like Ko Hung, who, despite Taoist leanings, had received a fairly standard education. Furthermore, men like Lü Shang lived long before either philosophical Taoism or religious Taoism emerged. Even accounts of near contemporaries, such as Tung-fang Shuo (c. 140–87 B.C.E.), in *Lieh-hsien chuan* reflect the difficulties contemporaries had in determining whether he was a philosopher or a Philistine. The Taoist account of his life, recorded in the "Tung-fang Shuo pieh-chuan" (The Esoteric Traditions of Tung-fang Shuo), however, collects a series of about thirty anecdotes in support of the popular belief that Tung-fang was not only a jester with great wisdom and clairvoyance but also the earthly manifestation of the planet Jupiter. This contrasts with Pan Ku's biography of Tung-fang Shuo in the *History of the Han Dynasty* (chapter 65), which is also primarily anecdotal but lacks the focus of the esoteric biography.

As Taoism developed through the Wei, Chin, and Northern and Southern dynasties, however, Taoist hagiographies evolved into scripture-laden, doctrinal texts, many now collected in *Yün-chi ch'i-ch'ien* (The Bookcase of the Clouds with the Seven Labels), compiled in the early eleventh century. Yang Hsi's (330–386) "Wei fu-jen chuan" (Traditions of Lady Wei), which in its present form (*T'ai-p'ing kuang-chi* [Extensive Records from the Reign of Great Tranquility], chapter 58) is nearly three thousand characters long, is typical. Although this hagiography begins with the requisite names and background information, the reader is soon privy to recondite conversations with mortal and immortal alike, making this more of a treatise than a biography. The Ling-pao hagiographic literature differed somewhat, having been influenced by the Buddhist *avadāna* literature as the latter became available in Chinese translations beginning c. 400 C.E. (see chapters 9 and 48).

Buddhist hagiography is best represented in *Kao-seng chuan* (Lives of Eminent Monks), written by the monk Hui-chiao (497–554). Based on earlier biographical collections as well as on monastic records and tales of miracles, the work includes accounts of 250 lives, to which a similar number of very brief notices are appended; all are arranged under topics such as translators, exegetes, theurgists, self-immolators, and cantors. The opening story of Nieh-mo-sheng (Kāśyapa Mātaṅga) from central India may be seen as representative. It begins formulaically with names and origin, then describes Kāśyapa Mātaṅga's personal traits, skills, habits, and experience as they relate to Buddhism. A short account of his decision to "leave the mundane world" completes this opening section.

Then, as in the orthodox biographies, a special set of dates (here the Yung-p'ing reign of the Later Han, 58–75) initiates the account of Kāśyapa Mātaṅga's career. After Emperor Ming's (r. 57–75) dream of a metal golden man flying through the air and alighting in Loyang was interpreted as the imminent arrival of a god named "Buddha," said to be inhabiting the Western Regions (see chapter 12), envoys were sent to India, where they met Kāśyapa Mātaṅga. They invited him to Loyang, where he was received grandly as the first representative of Buddhism in China. His attempts to transmit the faith went badly, however, and shortly after his arrival he passed away. A list of his translations and a story about how his place of residence came to be known as the White Horse Monastery are appended to the biography. This again adheres largely to the normative structure of the standard biography, allowing for the substitution of translations and monasteries as this man's "posterity."

Unlike in the orthodox tradition, in Buddhist accounts like Pao-ch'ang's *Pi-ch'iu-ni chuan* (Biographies of Nuns; c. 516), women received fairly equal treatment. Biographies such as that of the nun Chu Ching-chien (Pure Example; c. 292–c. 361) offer the nuns' secular names, family origins, details about fathers (which in turn connect the text to the orthodox tradition), and a sketch of the woman's traits and study interests. The account of Chu Ching-chien, for example, follows the above pattern closely; then, after introducing chronology to the account with the mention that the monk Fa-shih established a monastery near the West Gate of Loyang during the Chien-hsing reign-period (313–317), it begins a discussion of her "career." Ching-chien went to seek instruction with Fa-shih, was awakened, and borrowed a book from the monk for further study. A conversation between student and master is recounted, in which Fa-shih explains what it means to be a nun, a conversation obviously intended to have propaganda value. Ching-chien then formally accepts Buddhism and becomes mentor to the twenty-odd other women who joined her in casting off the secular. Later, she becomes the first Buddhist nun in China, a marvelous fragrance filling the air at her initiation. After years of faithful service (she was then seventy), the same fragrance was detected again, and a woman descended from the sky on a cloud to take Ching-chien away with her. This biography thus differs little in structure from those of monks.

Other accounts of nuns similarly depict a contented "death" and a legacy of good works such as Ching-chien left. Some, like that of Hui-chan, involve miracles. Hui-chan devoted herself to the simple life. When she was attacked by robbers, however, she invoked the goddess Kuan-yin, who paralyzed their hands. Eventually she went south to spread her good works, living devoutly in a convent.

"Good works" in biographies of women collected in the nonreligious, orthodox tradition are those works males considered appropriate—primarily those that adhered to the strict code of Confucian behavior expected of a woman, emphasizing the qualities of a wise mother, virtuous wife, dutiful daughter-in-law, and chaste widow. Unlike the full accounts of Taoist and Buddhist women, these consist of anecdotes gathered in collective biographies, designed more to edify other women than to portray complete lives. Liu Hsiang's *Lieh-nü chuan* is the earliest anthology of these epithet stories. His account of Nü Tsung of the state of Sung, for example, relates how she attended her mother-in-law diligently while her husband, Pao Su, sojourned in the state of Wei, where he took a "second wife." When news of the affair reached the family in Sung, Nü

Tsung's sister-lin-law gibed her and suggested she leave the Pao family and return home. Nü Tsung's long response rejects her sister-in-law's advice by reiterating Confucian ideas about marriage and divorce. When the Duke of Sung heard the story, he awarded her the honorary title of Nü Tsung (Honored Woman) and ordered the construction of a congratulatory arch at her village gate. The biography concludes with a comment from the *chün-tzu* (noble man), a technique borrowed from the *Tso chuan*, followed by a citation from the *Shih-ching* (Classic of Poetry), intending to reflect her actions in a classical context; a final rhymed envoi summarizes the entire biography and was probably intended to be committed to memory.

Collective biographies of chaste and virtuous women, sometimes called *Lieh-nü chuan*, playing on a cognate of the original *lieh*, which was simply a plural marker, appeared in official histories beginning with the *Hou Han shu*. Although over the years these accounts focused increasingly on widows who defended their chastity, the accounts in the *Hou Han shu* are diverse. Huan Shao-chün's biography tells how Huan's father was so impressed with a poor student named Pao Hsüan that he gave him his daughter in marriage along with an expansive dowry. Pao took offense at the largesse and complained to his bride, who promptly rejected all her father's gifts and journeyed to her husband's home dressed in simple clothing and pulling a small cart. To the approbation of the local populace, she proved a dutiful wife and daughter-in-law. Later, after Pao Hsüan became an official and the family prospered, their grandson inquired whether the story about Shao-chün personally pulling a cart to her new home was true. Shao-chün admonished him that gain could be preserved only by never forgetting the prospect of loss—that times of security could be ensured only by keeping moments of danger firmly in mind.

Huan Shao-chün's biography uses a frame resembling that of the orthodox male biographies. Moreover, the style, as in many other biographies by Fan Yeh, is informal and lively in the tradition of *Shih-chi* and its rhetorical designs. This tradition continued to develop in quasi-historical genres, which eventually gave rise to the T'ang *ch'uan-ch'i* tales (see chapter 33).

Historians in the early T'ang dynasty (618–907), following principles similar to those incorporated a little later in Liu Chih-chi's (661–721) *Shih t'ung* (An Understanding of History), found even greater fault with this style of historical writing. They associated it with the contemned era between the Han dynasty (206 B.C.E.–220 C.E.) and the reunification under the Sui (581–618). To counter the literary biography, an Office of Historiography was set up to prepare all sections of official histories, including re-editions of many manuscript accounts of Six Dynasties regimes as well as the records of the current T'ang rule. This office laid down strict guidelines for preparing materials from which biographies would be compiled, including the submission of *hsing-chuang* (accounts of conduct) as the basis for official lives. Although the diminished effectiveness of the Office of History after the An Lu-shan (703–757) rebellion (755–757/763) allowed more variety in the biographies included in the *Chiu T'ang shu* (Old T'ang History) than was designed or desired, the overall trend toward "biography by committee" standardized and eventually stultified the genre. It became a formulaic cast into which the details of a life were to be poured, resulting in biographies dominated by a series of official documents. The biographies that appealed to a literary audience, containing lively human portrayals, from the Sung dynasty onward belonged to the realms of nonofficial biography and fiction. Of these, there were indeed many, but they normally appeared only sporadically in the collected works of individual authors along with all of their other prose writings. In this sense, the literary biographies of Sung and later periods were a variant form of the essay. That is to say, they were essays about persons rather than normative historiographical or religious productions.

William H. Nienhauser, Jr.

Chapter 28

EXPOSITORY PROSE

This chapter is about the prose of exposition in the Chinese tradition. Other important aspects of prose writing are dealt with in different chapters in this volume, including those on mythology (chapter 2), narrative prose and fiction (chapters 27 and 32–40), historical prose (chapter 26), and parallel prose or prose in the "Four-Six" style (chapter 12). Also excluded here is the prose found in the philosophical tradition (see chapter 3), although early examples of that corpus were an important influence upon the writing treated here.

After eliminating these related topics, we are still left with a huge corpus of writings that spans nearly two millennia. Expository prose outside early philosophy and history first emerges as a recognizable type of writing in the Han dynasty (206 B.C.E.–220 C.E.). It gains in quantity and visibility during the period of division that follows, but does not reach full maturity as a literary tradition until the middle dynasties, that is, the T'ang (618–907) and Sung (960–1279) periods. Every century thereafter, from the thirteenth on, has had its masters of this prose, who variously modeled themselves, usually, on T'ang or Sung writers.

The term "expository prose" is employed here deliberately as an alternative to "essay" because of its useful indeterminacy. There is a particular genre of Chinese prose (the *lun*) roughly equivalent to the English "essay," but it is only one of approximately two dozen generic forms that constitute the entire body of "expository prose." The seminal anthology *Wen hsüan* (Literary Selections, early sixth century) already contains some twenty-five distinct genres of writing that might arguably be considered expository prose, although the distinctions between some of the categories are unclear. The Ch'ing dynasty (1644–1911) scholar Yao Nai (1731–1815) simplified the typology to a scheme of thirteen categories, some with two distinguishable, if related, components: *lun-pien* (essay and disquisition), *hsü-pa* (preface and colophon), *tsou-yi* (memorial), *shu-shuo* (letter and discourse), *tseng-hsü* (farewell), *chao-ling* (edicts and orders), *chuan-chuang* (biography), *pei-chih* (epitaph and grave inscription), *tsa-chi* (descriptive accounts and inscriptions), *chen-ming* (admonition), *sung-tsan* (eulogy and appreciation), *tz'u-fu* (rhapsody), and *ai-chi* (lament and requiem). The genres are distinguished primarily by content and purpose rather than by formal features, although some of the types are distinguished by rhyme or rhyming sections.

The literary collections of individuals from later times generally contain several such genres of expository prose. There is a degree of fluidity between these genre distinctions, and few writers' collected works would represent all the genres listed above. Still, a noteworthy feature of Chinese expository prose is the persistence and ubiquity of these generic types. Prose is not simply uncategorized, free nonverse writing. Rather, in formal writing at least, a prose piece usually belongs to one of the standard genres and is identified as such in its title.

Concerning the disposition and content of this enormous body of writing, considered in its entirety and without regard for chronology, a few gross generalizations may be made. There are two broad types of writing, each consisting of many specific genres, that are particularly abundant and probably distinguish this corpus of material from those produced by other cultures. The first is official documentary prose, that is, writing produced in connection with official service in the huge Chinese civil service bureaucracy. China's premodern government was built upon and sustained by the documentary impulse. Every bureaucratic action required the composition of at least one unique document, and every official opinion or viewpoint was customarily put forward in written form. Moreover, the literate class was the ruling class, or at least the office-holding class. It was hardly accidental that entry into the huge imperial bureaucracy was effected through competitive examinations that, in addition to testing mastery of the canon of Confucian classics, also tested the candidate's ability to produce expository prose. Once someone acquired the coveted official appointment, his ability to produce such prose would occupy a sizable proportion of his time and sustain him in his career.

It was not unusual for the voluminous body of official documents produced during the course of a career in the bureaucracy to become part of an individual's literary collection, a collection often compiled and edited by the individual himself late in life or by his heirs. In some instances, such official writing is the sum total of all prose that survives. More often, a person's "complete prose" consists of a combination of official and unofficial or private compositions. The official writing typically consists of memorials to supervisory officials or to the throne (often grouped together under the rubric of *tsou-yi chi*, *tsou-shu chi*, etc.) as well as pieces required by official protocol. An example of the latter would be the "expressions of gratitude" required to be submitted by the bureaucrat upon the assumption of each new office or arrival at each new place of assignment (including demotions and exiles!). Certainly, the memorials of substance on matters of state policy and governance are the more interesting component of official prose. In the case of some high-ranking officials, the collected memorials to the throne have considerable historical as well as literary value.

One other oddity regarding official documents bears mentioning. Through the centuries, many of China's most eminent men of letters served some portion of their career in one of the several positions at the court (e.g., as a member of the Han-lin Academy) in which their duties included writing imperial decrees or rescripts on behalf of the emperor. The imperial decree would always, of course, be issued in the emperor's name, which meant that the real author was technically considered to have only "drafted" the document. Nevertheless, when it came time to compile a "complete works," the dozens or even hundreds of imperial documents might be included in the official's collection, giving him in effect posthumous credit for something he could not take credit for while alive. It hardly needs to be said that most of these documents are highly formulaic and shed little light on their author's thought or preferences. Yet there they are in his collected works.

The other type of prose that has particular abundance is funerary writing. This consists of several distinct genres, the most important of which appear in the list above (epitaph, grave inscription, eulogy, appreciation, lament, and requiem). Obviously, this writing springs from the culture's keen interest in deceased ancestors, posthumous reputation, and history. There is a eulogistic tendency to this writing; indeed, much of it was commissioned by surviving relatives upon the death of a senior family member. Nevertheless, there was also belief in the value of objective biographical record and unbiased evaluation at the time of death. Consequently, there are stories of principled writers who would not be swayed by the relatives' wishes for a more flattering account. The funerary genres also verge on biography per se, which is more a narrative than an expository form. Biography has always been considered a subtype of historical writing in China, and so lies outside the scope of this chapter (see chapters 26 and 27). Suffice it to say that funerary writing has always been an important primary source for biography. Even the court historians who drafted biographies for the national history (eventually the dynastic history) are known to have relied heavily upon copies of funerary documents forwarded to the capital from the provinces. One last point should be made about funerary writing: authors who became famous in their day as prose stylists were so frequently approached by bereaved families that more than one of them complained of the burden of such fame. Commissioning a prestigious writer to compose a funerary piece such as a grave inscription, which would be inscribed on a stele erected at the grave site, was, after all, one of the last and most visible acts a family could perform to show its devotion to the deceased. The productivity of men who became known as adept at this type of writing suggests the centrality of its place in Chinese culture. It is not unusual to find that such funerary writing constitutes one-third or more of a given author's entire prose output.

As for the style and tone of Chinese prose, the overriding issue that must be addressed is the distinction or even rivalry between the parallel and "ancient" styles. This is a dichotomy that runs throughout the history of Chinese prose from the T'ang dynasty until the May Fourth movement of the twentieth century, when the replacement of literary language by the vernacular rendered it irrelevant.

Parallel prose, often referred to in later times as *ssu-liu wen* (Four-Six style), so named for the syllabic length of its clauses, is prose written in couplets of grammatically and metrically parallel members (see chapter 12). The correspondence of morpheme, syllable, and character in the literary language makes Chinese uniquely suited to a style of such metrical and grammatical regularity, even in prose. But there is more to this style than these features alone. The diction is also distinctive in being highly euphuistic. The parallel style normally cultivates a highly bookish, periphrastic, and allusive vocabulary—one that probes the richness of Chinese lexicography and is about as far removed as possible from ordinary speech.

The ancient style, by contrast, is not written exclusively in couplets of parallel lines, although such couplets may occasionally occur. Prosodically, it is free and unpredictable, with widely varying line and clause lengths. The diction may also contain its share of literary allusions, but it will not be persistently periphrastic or ornate. Indeed, the ancient style typically prides itself on language that is "plain" and "unadorned" or even "coarse," modeling its vocabulary after that of the Confucian classics and early histories. The primary claim of the ancient style, indeed, is that it subordinates considerations of language and style to those of content and purpose. The latter, moreover, are normally conceived along the lines of traditional Confucian values and notions of the moralistic purposes that writing ought to serve.

The conventional understanding of the rivalry between the two styles, typically found in modern literary histories, is summarized below. The parallel style developed during the period of division that followed the collapse of the Han dynasty in 220 C.E. This development is often linked to the estheticism of the era and the drift away from Confucian values. Virtually all the prose from the period of division included in *Literary Selections* is written in the parallel style.

Although some dissatisfaction with this vogue of the parallel style was voiced early in the T'ang dynasty, it was not until the appearance of Han Yü (768–824) toward the end of the dynasty that a significant criticism of the ascendancy of parallel prose was articulated and a plausible alternative presented. Han Yü and his followers are generally credited with overthrowing the dominance of the parallel style during their day and forging a new style based on the classics. Their motivation and accomplishment are best understood as part of their call to "revive antiquity" (*fu-ku*), a call that has literary, philosophical, and ideological dimensions. For these reformers, the change in prose writing was bound up inextricably with an archaizing Confucian revival they sought to effect.

The ancient style of prose championed by Han Yü did not, however, have much staying power. By the end of the T'ang dynasty, the parallel style had regained ascendancy, especially in court circles. A version of the ancient style remained in use by writers of fictional tales and anecdote collections, but for official documents the parallel style was used. The parallel style was promoted further early in the Sung dynasty, when Yang Yi (974–1020) and others cultivated a highly elaborate version of it as a prose complement to the Hsi-k'un school of poetry (derived from the allusive and ornate tendencies of Li Shang-yin's [811?–859] abstruse, mannered verse). Again, there were early Sung dynasty critics of parallel prose, now so widespread that it was called "the current style" (*shih-wen*). But it was only after Ou-yang Hsiu (1007–1072) took up the cause of the ancient style again and, in a dramatic move as administrator of the civil service examinations in 1057, surprised the candidates by requiring the ancient style on their answers that the ancient style once more became widespread. This eleventh-century revival of the ancient style is often referred to as the "second act of the ancient-style prose movement," although it is questionable whether the preferences of a small number of writers deserve to be termed a "movement" or even an "act." As in the case of the T'ang episode, the Sung advocacy of a return to ancient styles must be understood as a literary reform that is inseparable from ideological issues. Indeed, the Sung prose reform should be viewed in the context of the Northern Sung beginnings of what would come to be understood as the Neo-Confucian revival.

The eleventh-century writing reform seems to have had a greater impact than its T'ang counterpart. In Su Shih (Su Tung-p'o; 1037–1101) and his circle, Ou-yang Hsiu was succeeded by a second generation of supporters of his cause that was far more productive and influential than those who came after Han Yü had been. Su and his friends thus served to solidify the change for which Ou-yang had worked. That is not to say that the parallel style died off. It persisted through ensuing centuries and dynasties and periodically found its own supporters. It always remained popular at the court. The infamous *pa-ku wen* (eight-legged essay) of the Ming (1368–1644) and Ch'ing civil service examinations was a particularly prescriptive form of the parallel prose essay. The intellectuals who regularly criticized it used many of the same arguments that had been used by ancient-prose advocates in the T'ang and Sung.

This standard account of this ongoing tension between the two prose styles contains some weaknesses. First, by dividing the literary world into rival camps, it tends to overdramatize and exaggerate their incompatibility. In fact, even the leaders of the ancient-prose revivals regularly acknowledged that the parallel style had its place and that, when properly employed, it did not necessarily undermine the proper purposes of writing. Second, the account obscures the evident appeal of the parallel style, which made it so persistent and difficult to replace. To pay attention only to the criticisms of the style is to overlook the reasons for its tenacity.

The parallel style evolved over several centuries, through the Han and the early Northern and Southern Dynasties period (420–589). Since its initial development was gradual and un-self-conscious (there was no "parallel prose movement"), it probably happened in response to some need. What was that need? The prominence of the parallel style in court documents suggests that the need was to develop a "high" prose style that would befit the pomp, seriousness, and elegance of the imperial court. Several traits of the style make sense in this light. The regular metrical parallelism and predictability make it stately, measured, and euphonious. (Even in archaic Chinese, as in the *Shangshu* [Classic of Documents], phrases arranged in a steady four-beat rhythm are a sign of elevated seriousness.) The allusive and periphrastic diction evokes an air of erudition and elegance. Indirection, after all, is commonly a hallmark of cultural refinement. An uninflected and isolating language like Chinese, moreover, does not have much potential for "honorifics" or other style-level markers in word prefixes or suffixes. In such a language, a high style is more likely to be marked by the development of a specialized vocabulary of elegance to take the place of more ordinary words. For these reasons, as unnatural as it may seem, the parallel prose style was a logical and natural development in a literary culture that felt the need for a distinctively high prose style. It made particularly good sense for use in court and court-related documents. It was because it answered this need that it was resilient and kept returning, despite periodic criticisms of it.

Of course, the parallel style had its drawbacks. It was ill-suited to argumentation, mainly because of the requirement that the writing be done in matching statements—which tends to lead either to flaccid redundancy or, worse still, to misstatement, trapping the writer in parallel assertions or antitheses that lead his logic astray. The elaborate diction of the parallel style likewise interfered with clarity of expression. When the purpose was rhetorical and decorous, as, for example, in imperial decrees and other court communications, parallel prose was well suited to the occasion. That is not to say that there were not skillful uses of the form in which even exposition and argument were aptly molded to the couplet prosody. The Six Dynasties (220–589) writers Hsü Ling (507–583) and Yü Hsin (513–581) are often referred to as authors who could, even within the constraints of the parallel style, craft lucid argumentation. But such successes are exceptions. It was challenging, to say the least, to use the form for reasoning or analysis.

The criticisms of parallel prose, however, were generally not couched in these terms. Rather, like so much of traditional Chinese evaluation and esthetics, they were overwhelmingly phrased in moral terms. Parallel prose was said to be undesirable because it was ornate and shallow. The proper goal of writing was not to present a scintillating stylistic beauty but, rather, to transmit age-old Confucian values and principles. The solution to the depraved tendencies of parallel prose was to return to the ways of "the ancients," who had their priorities straight.

It was seldom if ever acknowledged that ancient-style prose was just as artificial and unnatural as the parallel style. It was artificial in the sense that it too was cut off from the living language. The exact relationship between the spoken language and the "ancient-style prose" of, say, the historian Ssu-ma Ch'ien (c. 145–c. 85 B.C.E.), to say nothing of Mencius or Confucius, remains a matter of speculation and controversy. But certainly by the T'ang dynasty, Han Yü's ancient-style prose was entirely a book language, that is, an artificial construct that mimicked the classics children memorized in the first years of their education. (We know this because of the survival of T'ang dynasty vernacular texts that preserve a semblance of the spoken language, the manuscripts discovered at the Tun-huang caves [see chapter 48].) Yet ancient-style prose was free of the hobbling prosodic demands of the parallel style, and so writers who adopted it were better able to let the logic of their ideas determine the rhythm and flow of their language. As seen below, there were nevertheless important differences between variant versions of the ancient style, and these had much to do with expressiveness and adaptability.

The ancient-style prose of the T'ang and Sung dynasties has long been viewed as a subfield of Chinese literary history. This has been especially so ever since the appearance of several Ming and Ch'ing dynasty anthologies of this writing, which were themselves part of periodic revivals of the style and which culminated in the T'ung-ch'eng school led by Fang Pao (1668–1749), Liu Ta-k'uei (1698–1780), and Yao Nai (mentioned above). The single most influential compilation in this tradition was Mao K'un's (1512–1601) *T'ang Sung pa-ta chia wen-ch'ao* (Anthology of Eight Prose Masters of the T'ang and Sung Dynasties). Space here permits only a brief consideration of the four most important among the eight: Han Yü and Liu Tsung-yüan (773–819) of the T'ang, and Ou-yang Hsiu and Su Shih of the Sung. The other four are Wang An-shih (1021–1086); Su Shih's father, Su Hsün (1009–1066), and brother, Su Ch'e (1039–1112); and Tseng Kung (1019–1083).

Han Yü is best known for his series of essays on Confucian themes and values. He appears in these pieces as a staunch defender of the principles of the school, especially against inroads made upon it by the rival systems of Taoism and Buddhism. His views are as forcefully expressed as they are uncompromising. In separate treatments of such topics as "Shih shuo" (Teachers), "Chin-hsüeh chieh" (Progress in Learning), "Yüan tao" (The Way), "Yüan hsing" (Human Nature), and "Yüan hui" (Slander), he addresses key issues in the life of the individual and the state, including the crucial question of how best morally to cultivate both. Positioning himself as the heir to a "transmission of the Way" (*tao-t'ung*) that had lapsed after the time of Mencius, Han Yü calls for a new commitment to moral education and conduct in both private and public life. While somewhat less abstract, his outspoken "Lun Fo ku piao" (Memorial on the Buddha Bone), which earned him exile to the distant south, is written in the same spirit of high moral outrage.

While these may be his most widely read and anthologized prose essays, there is a second group of pieces that reflects Han Yü in a somewhat different light. This group includes a wide array of grave inscriptions, farewells, prefaces, letters, and short uncategorized pieces. It is not that these more numerous and intellectually varied prose writings are inconsistent with the ideas of his dogmatic and didactic essays. Indeed, the latter may best be understood as a distillation of the values that inform this second group of works. But this larger body of work reveals Han Yü as a writer of broader interests and more wide-ranging and subtle rhetorical skills. Several of these compositions are occasional and are rooted in personal relationships between Han Yü and the recipient. Thus they present an interesting mix of personal familiarity, or even affection, and intellectual discourse. Some of them concern Han Yü's views on the arts. There is his prose farewell to his fellow poet Meng Chiao (751–814), which sets forth the doctrine that poetry is born of emotional distress. Another farewell, to a Buddhist monk, discusses the connection between the emotions and excellence in calligraphy and ends by noting pessimistically that the monk's devotion to passionlessness does not bode well for his development as a calligrapher. Many compositions deal with the problematic choice of official service versus withdrawal or retirement. A particularly effective piece is a farewell addressed to a certain Tung Shao-nan, in which Han Yü manages in just a few lines, using allusions and inference, to twist his opening praise for Tung's decision to abandon his ambitions for a career into oblique criticism of the same. The entire piece is just 151 characters long. Han Yü's grave inscriptions frequently celebrate exceptional actions and qualities in the lives of their subject. The eulogy for Liu Tsung-yüan features Liu's offer to assume the poet-essayist Liu Yü-hsi's (772–842) more severe banishment sentence to mitigate his friend's hardship. The grave inscription for the "unorthodox man Wang Shih" includes a long passage recounting the peculiar strategy he used to secure the betrothal of the woman he wanted for his wife, which included deceiving his future father-in-law about his success in the civil service examinations. In Han Yü's eyes, such a ploy showed not the dishonesty but the ingenuity of the man and his singularity of purpose.

A third group of prose pieces has an interest that is out of proportion to its modest quantitative size. This is a collection of humorous pieces or compositions written in a tone of levity. These include the fanciful "Mao Ying chuan" (Biography of Mao Ying), about a writing brush (*mao*), personified as an official and written about in a mock historiographical style; "Sung ch'iung wen" (Text to Send Off Poverty, or Farewell to Misfortune), in which Misfortune, also personified, debates with the author and persuades him that he is better off not banishing him from his life; "Shih ting lien-chü shih hsü" (Preface to the Linked Verse on a Stone Cauldron), which tells the imaginative story of how a mysterious Taoist thoroughly humiliates in a verse-composing contest two hapless men who happen to have been Han Yü's friends in real life; a mock-serious sacrificial memorial addressed to an alligator that tormented the people of his district; and a parody of Chuang Tzu's views on the ills and destructiveness of human civilization. As welcome as such compositions might be to us today for the relief they provide from the high seriousness of so much of Han Yü's collection, they occasioned a good deal of comment and criticism among his contemporaries. Friends complained that Han Yü liked to indulge in "incongruous, baseless" talk. The notice on him in the dynastic history calls the "Biography of Mao Ying" "a joke that has nothing to do with principle" and "his most misguided composition." The idea that an upright defender of Confucian values might also indulge in humor was clearly troubling to some men of Han Yü's time. Han Yü himself took a larger view, telling his critics that even the sages joked from time to time. "What harm," he asked, "does it do to the Way?"

Liu Tsung-yüan's accomplishment as a prose writer is quite different from Han Yü's and somewhat more narrow in scope, if not in interest. His best-known works are a series of eight short landscape essays written during a ten-year period of exile to Yung-chou (at the confluence of the Hsiao and Hsiang rivers in modern-day Hunan). These are probably the most famous "accounts of excursions into nature" (*yu-chi*) in the language, the prototype of the voluminous later literature in this genre (see chapter 30). It is not that Liu Tsung-yüan invented this type of writing out of nothing. There are precursors to his essays; these are prose counterparts to the type of excursions into the mountains described in the nature poetry of Hsieh Ling-yün (385–433). But Liu transforms the tradition by writing himself into the landscape pieces. He is a strong presence in his "accounts," moving through the landscape, reacting to it, even altering the plantings in one favorite spot, which he had purchased. A dynamic of mutual empathy and identification is established, as Liu celebrates pristine knolls, streams, and grottoes (e.g., Yüan-chia chieh [Yüan Family Slough], Shih-chien [Rocky Gorge], Hsiao ch'iu hsi hsiao shih t'an [Small Rocky Pool West of Little Hillock]), that are, like the author, hidden in obscure corners of the empire. Liu's attitude toward these landscapes is complex. While he delights in their natural beauty and serenity, he can hardly observe them without being reminded of how far he is removed from the capital and, consequently, the injustice he has suffered in his career. There must be a creator after all, he reflects in one of the compositions; otherwise, how could such a perfect assortment of natural features have been arranged here? Yet why would a divine being choose to locate such an idyll in the miserable barbarian wastes of Yung-chou? On second thought, there must be no creator after all. Such musings reflect the ambivalence that beset Liu Tsung-yüan and are in evidence at every turn in his landscape essays. It is this ambivalence that animates the compositions and has given them unresolvable tension and enduring appeal.

Another group of prose pieces for which Liu Tsung-yüan is noted are those dealing with such topics as a snake-catcher, a hump-backed gardener, and dung beetles that betray strong influence from the early Taoist thinker Chuang Tzu. He also wrote well-known allegories on animals like the deer, the ox, and the ass. Finally, Liu authored a number of unusually moving biographical sketches about undistinguished persons.

The eleventh century witnessed the second self-conscious revival of the "ancient style" of prose writing. Yet, as happened so often in Chinese history, the retention of the old name masks some very important divergences between the Northern Sung event and its T'ang dynasty predecessor. The Sung prose stylists did not simply return to the prose of Han Yü and his circle, picking up where they had left off. Ostensibly, they said that they were doing so—the most famous pronouncement on this point is Ou-yang Hsiu's postface to a copy of Han Yü's works that he claims to have "discovered," rescuing them from obscurity and neglect. But in fact the writing style that they developed was new and unprecedented, departing from the T'ang models in several of its features.

Because we do not yet have sophisticated methods by which to analyze or even describe prose style, these differences between the Sung and T'ang versions of ancient-style prose can be characterized only in vague, impressionistic terms. Certainly, the diction employed by the eleventh-century writers is different from that used earlier. There is less evidence of archaizing vocabulary, that is, words and phrases drawn directly from the classics, in the Sung version. There is also less reliance generally on uncommon characters or difficult and strange compounds and phrases (what Chinese writers refer to as "teeth-crunching language"). Instead, the Sung writers settled for a diction that has a high content of ordinary words and repeats them frequently. The overall effect is that of a relatively transparent language that does not call attention to itself. These qualities are entirely consistent with the *p'ing-tan* (calm and plain) esthetic that runs through the literary and artistic expression of the age.

In conjunction with this change in diction, and in part due to it, there is a corresponding shift in the tone affected in much of this Sung dynasty prose. (Obviously, these are generalizations; exceptions to them could certainly be found in particular works.) The high, didactic, or insistent tone of so many signature pieces of the T'ang, verging not infrequently on the polemical, has been lowered or softened. The Sung masters adopted a plainness of tone that matched their ordinary diction. Their range of subject matter broadened correspondingly. Feeling less closely bound to didactic purposes, they explored a great variety of topics and treated for the first time in Chinese history the commonplace and mundane events of daily life as subjects worthy of serious, sustained attention in prose.

This contrast between the styles of the leading prose writers of the successive dynasties is aptly captured in a section of a letter sent from Su Hsün, the father of Su Shih, to Ou-yang Hsiu by way of introduction in 1056. The letter, addressed to a senior official and literatus by an unknown aspirant from the provinces, contains elements of unabashed flattery. Yet its characterization of Han Yü's and Ou-yang's own prose styles is accurate and revealing:

> Han Yü's writing resembles the vast Yangtze or the great Yellow rivers, which flow and twist in mighty torrents and nurture water creatures and scaly dragons—a myriad terrifying monsters. Yet he kept them dimly concealed, not letting them reveal themselves outright. Consequently, when people gaze upon the glow of the murky depths and hoary surface, they shrink back in fear, not daring to look from close at hand. Your own writing, sir, is supple and ample, twisting this way and that a hundred times. Yet its reasoning is clear, and it is free of any gaps or breaks. Even when the spirit and diction rise to a climax, when the words come quickly to clinch a point, they remain leisurely and simple, without any trace of the belabored or difficult.

One would like to know where this new style came from, what its sources were, and what motivated the eleventh-century writers to cultivate it. How conscious were they of doing something new? Su Hsün's statement is one of the few that emphasizes the dissimilarity between Han Yü's prose and Ou-yang's. Much more common are assertions of affinity or similarity between the two. We can only speculate about the explanations of what took place. It seems likely that the minor traditions of prose fiction (mostly short "stories of the strange"), anecdotal collections, and "random notes" (*sui-pi*, *pi-chi*; see chapter 31) that experienced considerable growth in the ninth and tenth centuries were an influence and partial inspiration of the new approach to prose writing in the eleventh century. There was, of course, a significant distinction in seriousness, formality, and prestige between the literary compositions produced by the famous masters and the fiction and anecdotal records written almost entirely by minor or unknown authors. The latter were not even considered "literature" and were rigorously excluded from an individual's "literary collection." Seen in this light, it might seem inherently improbable that the style of these "lower" forms would influence that of those examined above. Yet the appeal of the style that the fiction and anecdotal writers had developed is likely to have been considerable. It was more versatile than anything that the famous T'ang literati had used, and it was precisely what was needed for a further broadening of the essay and other expository forms. We have seen, moreover, that Han Yü himself ventured occasionally into the lower forms, or derivations of them, though not without doing some damage to his reputation. The innovation of the Sung stylists was to appropriate the relatively straightforward language in which stories and anecdotes were recorded and adapt it to the literary forms.

Ou-yang Hsiu produced substantial corpora in all the standard literary forms. While he too left formal essays that are masterpieces of argument and rhetoric (e.g., "Tsung ch'iu lun" [On the Release of Criminals], "P'eng-tang lun" [On Factions]), the real strength of his output is in informal prose writings. His genius was for cultivating a highly personal tone. Whether he is writing a grave inscription, a farewell, a preface, or a letter, he is apt to feature intimate feelings and details from the recipient's life or from his friendship with the recipient. This had never been done before on such a regular basis in prose writings. When he writes about subjects in his own life, as he does in numerous pieces about his studios and possessions (e.g., musical instruments, inkstones, and paintings), he follows a similar course, injecting himself into the writing to an extraordinary degree. The result is a sustained autobiographical presence in prose of the kind that had formerly been seen only in poetry. The much-anthologized "Tsui-weng t'ing chi" (Account of the Drunken Old Man's Pavilion) is a prime example of this autobiographical presence; several other, even more effective, pieces project it as well.

It is often said that Sung dynasty poets "wrote poetry out of prose," meaning that they found a way to invest poetry with the argumentation and intellectuality normally found in prose. But it might just as well be said of Ou-yang Hsiu that he "wrote prose out of poetry," for he managed to turn prose into a vehicle for intensely personal, even lyrical expression. His finest pieces are full of sentiment, albeit tempered by reasoning. Ou-yang has a special gift for writing about real objects in the physical world and endowing them, in the course of his reflections on them, with metaphorical or larger meanings. He does this with, for example, his fish pond, antique zithers he owned, a friend's garden he recalls from his boyhood, a large and oddly shaped rock he finds beside a stream, and his studios. He utilizes these objects, in prose inscriptions and accounts (*chi*), to ruminate on the experiences in his life and their larger significance. The objects in these pieces are not reduced to mere symbols, nor would it be accurate to describe the pieces themselves as parables. The physical reality of the objects always remains viable and important. But Ou-yang ingeniously finds ways to impute to them, suggestively, additional layers of significance. For instance, the different materials used for the inlaid studs or tone markers on his three ancient zithers take on new meaning because of the way Ou-yang elaborates on them in one account. The gold and jade studs used in two of his zithers reflect the light of the lamp placed near them at night, making it hard for the elderly and dim-sighted Ou-yang to focus his eyes clearly on the spots. Stone, with its rich associations of simplicity and naturalness, is used for the studs in the third instrument he owns. The stone studs do not reflect the light to dazzle his eyes. It is only the instrument with stone, he concludes, that befits an old man.

Ou-yang Hsiu also wrote in nonliterary forms. He is credited with China's earliest "Shih hua" (Poetry Talks), or collection of comments, criticism, and anecdotes on poetry. He left other short collections of desultory notes on calligraphy, "Pi shuo" (Remarks on the Brush) and "Shih pi" (Calligraphy Exercises), as well as a collection of mostly court anecdotes written upon retirement from government service, *Kuei t'ien lu* (Notes on Returning to the Farm). His voluminous *Chi-ku lu pa-wei* (Colophons on Ancient Inscriptions) contains scholarly identifications and comments on hundreds of rubbings of inscriptions collected over the years. This work is generally regarded as the beginning of the discipline of epigraphy in China. Aside from their intrinsic interest, these various writings are probably relevant to Ou-yang's innovations in literary prose, described above. In Ou-yang Hsiu, we see a prose stylist actively engaged in the nonliterary forms. This is something that had not occurred in the previous dynasty and makes all the more plausible the notion of the linguistic and stylistic influence on the special traits of Sung prose discussed above.

Su Shih is the most prolific of the "eight prose masters of the T'ang and Sung dynasties" and displays the widest range in subject matter and tone. His collected prose, in a modern typeset edition, fills some six volumes and twenty-five hundred pages. He excelled in all the forms and continued the development of a supple and versatile style, adaptable to virtually any subject.

Although the breadth of Su Shih's achievement in prose makes generalization about his corpus difficult, one characteristic of his works stands out. He is less lyrical than Ou-yang Hsiu in the literary genres as well as more intellectual. He uses the various forms, especially the preface, account, and colophon, to stake out intellectual positions on political, philosophical, literary, and esthetic issues. This is particularly noticeable with regard to his views on the arts, a crucial area of his thought. It is in his prose pieces on his and his friend's studios, on painting collections, and on particular paintings and calligraphic works that Su Shih sets forth his novel ideas on art, connoisseurship, the relationship of painter and calligrapher to the image he produces, and the psychology of artistic creation (see chapter 25).

As with esthetics, so too with issues in other fields. Whether the subject be approaches to learning ("Jih yü" [Parable of the Sun]), the philosophy of accommodation ("Ch'ao-jan t'ai chi" [Tower of Transcendence]), a parodic treatment of Buddhistic epistemology ("Ch'ing feng ko chi" [Pure Winds Pavilion]), or the limitations of literati culture ("Shih-chung-shan chi" [Record of Stone Bell Mountain]), Su Shih's literary prose is distinguished by its highly original and dense texture of thought. One is tempted to say that no writer before him (and few after) packed such a quantity of *thinking* into literary prose. Of course, there is no shortage of political and philosophical writing from earlier centuries. But that is a separate type of writing, which is not literary. Su Shih shows how the short literary forms could also be used to convey viewpoints and argument, and not just on hackneyed moral themes.

An early collection of essays on policy and history deserves special mention. This is a group of fifty essays that Su Shih wrote for the "special decree examination" that he and his younger brother were allowed to take as young men, after distinguishing themselves on the regular advanced examination. Half the fifty essays are on policy issues such as national defense and taxation. The other half are devoted to historical figures (generals, imperial advisers, philosophers, poets), each essay on a different person. These are the writings that, more than any other, made Su Shih's early fame. Copies of them circulated throughout the empire and established their author as a brilliant young thinker and writer. The essays on historical figures are particularly striking for their bold re-evaluations of famous lives. Since they first appeared, selections from this group of fifty essays have regularly been included in anthologies of literary prose.

Su Shih also produced a collection of anecdotes and jottings on diverse subjects, known as *Tung-p'o chih-lin* (East Slope's Forest of Recollections). This collection is remarkable for the interest it shows in the "strange." While it does not belong to the tradition of "stories of the strange," it does favor similar subject matter and includes numerous entries on dreams, divination, longevity techniques (alchemy, elixirs, yoga, etc.), immortals, Buddhists and Taoists, and strange events. The involvement of such a major literary figure with such subjects is frequently invoked as a precedent by later authors of supernatural tales. Thus, in the preface to his *Liao-chai chih-yi* (Strange Tales from Make-Do Studio), the seventeenth-century author P'u Sung-ling claims Su Shih as a kindred soul, even though the gap between Su's *Recollections* and P'u's tales is considerable.

Another form in which Su Shih is of major importance is the rhapsody or prose-poem (*fu*). His achievement in the rhapsody follows on that of his mentor, Ou-yang Hsiu, who first revived the form. Together, the two authors altered the prosody of the form by allowing greater latitude in rhyme and metrical parallelism. Consequently, the version of the genre begun by them is given a special designation: the prose rhapsody (*wen-fu*). Ou-yang's "Ch'iu-sheng fu" (Rhapsody on the Sounds of Autumn) pushes the onomatopoetic limits of the language as the author reflects on the rich store of associations of autumn and mortality. Su Shih's most famous rhapsodies by far are his two pieces on Ch'ih-pi (Red Cliff), the supposed site of the most celebrated naval battle of the Three Kingdoms period (220–265). Combining lyrical imagery with Su's much-admired philosophy of joy, the first piece is endlessly anthologized and reproduced, especially in Su Shih's incomparably affable calligraphy. An unexpected shift in tone and content is found in the odd second piece, which narrates a frenzied climb to the top of the cliff by the author and a frightened descent, followed by a menacing encounter with a large bird and the appearance of a Taoist in a late-night dream. The piece is certainly bizarre and memorable, even though readers continue to disagree on its meaning and intent.

This survey of expository prose in premodern China has merely touched on some of the highlights in an attempt to characterize its major features and overall development. A full treatment of its countless practitioners and their ample production, especially as they flourished in the Ming and Ch'ing dynasties, which have barely been mentioned here, would require volumes.

Ronald Egan

Chapter 29

RECORDS OF ANOMALIES

Inspiring in turn fear and fascination, revulsion and attraction, the supernatural brings us up against the unknown and unaccountable. Perhaps because of its elusive nature, it teases our fancy and has fired the imagination of countless writers through the ages. Elements of the supernatural dot the pages of Chinese literary history, from prehistoric legends to contemporary literature. Whether in the realms of secular or religious writings, popular or elite cultures, we chance upon exotic and bizarre fauna and flora, miraculous deities and demons who dwell in terrestrial, celestial and subterrestrial regions; frequently, we encounter mysterious fox spirits and beautiful ghosts, forever knocking on the door of the lonely scholar.

According to the classification system of official bibliographers in ancient times, records of the supernatural were shelved with histories. Only in the early Sung dynasty (960–1279) were such records purged from history proper and grouped with fictional writing. Even then, writers of supernatural tales continued to refer to their works as "records," "accounts," or "biographies," and at least one of them, the most prominent of all writers of supernatural literature, P'u Sung-ling (1640–1715), referred to himself as "historian of the strange." Extending knowledge of the probable world to the invisible yet sometimes tangible realm of the supernatural, it is as though the very act of collecting and writing about the unfamiliar and the mysterious gave the unknown a structure and, ultimately, a place in the known and familiar world of verifiable history. From the beginning, then, what characterizes literature of the supernatural is its strong ties and ambiguous relationship with historiography.

Indeed, historians in earlier times, especially court historians, were at the same time astrologers, whose job it was to interpret various signs of nature as they bore on acts of government by the emperor. Thus recording such signs, especially anomalous ones, was considered an integral part of the writing of history. Mo Tzu (Mo Ti), a great philosopher of the Warring States period (403–221 B.C.E.), explicitly links manifestations of supernatural beings with human actions and, furthermore, with the fate of states. In his "Ming-kuei" (On Ghosts), Mo Tzu expounds on the ability of ghosts and spirits to reward virtue and punish vice, thus establishing a firm relationship between the world of humans and the world of the supernatural. Following this tradition, the mandate of heaven is believed to be communicated through portents and omens, and esoteric knowledge of things invisible offers special access to political power. Confucius, by contrast, takes a very different stance on the matter. His view on the supernatural is primarily expressed in terms of silence; it is said: "The Master did not speak of prodigies, feats of strength, disorders, and gods." As orthodox Confucianism gradually became the state-sponsored ideology in imperial China, supernatural records increasingly came to be considered "left-over history" or "lesser affairs of the offices of historians"—at best marginal to canonical knowledge, at worst frivolous and useless to society and thus not worthy of a true scholar's attention.

This ambiguous status is directly reflected in the kinds of writers attracted to supernatural tales. Some were well-placed literati officials, such as the Eastern Chin court historian Kan Pao (fl. 320), known as "the Tung Hu [legendary historian] of the ghostly world," and the Ch'ing historian Chi Yün (1724–1805), one of the chief editors of the famous Ch'ing imperial library known as the *Ssu-k'u ch'üan-shu* (Complete Library of the Four Treasuries) as well as the author of a vast collection of supernatural tales entitled *Yüeh-wei ts'ao-t'ang pi-chi* (Sketches from the Cottage for the Contemplation of Subtleties). Others were unsuccessful in official careers and led their lives away from the court in the country, such as the famous "Historian of the Strange" P'u Sung-ling, whose work marked the highest achievement of supernatural fiction. What both kinds of writers share, however, is an eclectic taste and an unusually vast store of knowledge, especially about things that fall outside the purview of the narrow definition of canonical learning. These writers typically had access to a large variety of ancient or rare books, either as a result of their positions as historians, librarians, and archivists or through personal connections.

Through the ages, the supernatural permeates all genres, including poetry, drama, and, most prominently, fiction, both short tales in the classical language and full-length narrative in the vernacular. Many great poets wrote pieces dedicated to river goddesses, for example, and virtually all examples of the full-length vernacular novel, a genre that came to its maturity in the Ming dynasty (1368–1644), contain elements of the supernatural, the best-known and sustained development being *Hsi-yu chi* (Journey to the West). It is, however, in classical-language tales that the supernatural initially became a central concern.

They contained amazing descriptions of outlandish freaks of nature, as well as the most exquisite renditions of a seemingly indefinite range of beautiful fox spirits. During its first high point in the Six Dynasties (220–589), supernatural literature permeated every corner of belles lettres, and the genre known as *chih-kuai* (records of anomalies) was immensely popular. Typically collected in the form of *pi-chi* (short sketches or casual jottings), the *chih-kuai* tale is short and exceedingly flexible; it is strong on description, reminiscent of earlier historical records of portents and omens. In later dynasties, although tales of the supernatural remained popular, they were no longer considered a separate category. In time, the classical supernatural tale grew fuller in plot structure, more complex in characterization of humans and nonhumans alike, and the writers more self-conscious in the wielding of their narrative art, adding parody and satire to the power of description. The Ch'ing dynasty (1644–1911) saw another high point in the development of classical supernatural tales, most notably in the two grand collections *Liao-chai chih-yi* (Strange Tales from Make-Do Studio), by P'u Sung-ling, and *Sketches from the Cottage for the Contemplation of Subtleties*, by Chi Yün.

EARLY PROTOTYPES

Among the many prototypes of fiction writing, two are especially important because they point to the basic sources of supernatural literature: myths and history. They are *Shan hai ching* (Classic of Mountains and Seas), an extensive collection of geographically based myths and legends, and *Mu t'ien-tzu chuan* (Travels of Emperor Mu), the story of a mythologized historical figure.

The *Classic of Mountains and Seas*, a veritable sourcebook of later supernatural stories, consists of eighteen volumes and encompasses the five cardinal directions (east, west, south, north, and center). A fantastic map of a largely imagined universe, it is a collection of strange fauna and flora, gods and goblins, and humans of every imaginable shape (with only one arm, with human face but fish body, with nipples for eyes and navel for mouth, etc.). It is subdivided into the *Classic of Mountains* (written earlier and somewhat more factual) and the *Classic of Seas* (written later and highly fanciful). The original entries may have been gradually collected from the Warring States period to the Han dynasty (206 B.C.E.–220 C.E.). The collection circulated widely among the literati during the Western Han (206 B.C.E.–8 C.E.), especially after the availability of the version edited and redacted by the court scholar Liu Hsin (46 B.C.E.–23 C.E.), son of the famous bibliographer Liu Hsiang (79–8 B.C.E.). Liu Hsin's submission of the eighteen-volume text to the throne signals the first flourishing of interest in things supernatural. In his memorial to the emperor, Liu Hsin traces the origin of the *Classic of Mountains and Seas* to the times of the legendary sage-king Yü. The *Classic*, he says, was composed by Yü's scribe-minister Yi (or Po-yi), who recorded the strange creatures he observed in the new universe while accompanying Yü in his grand efforts to bring order to the lands and waters of this universe. Thus Liu Hsin justifies his interest in the supernatural by invoking the ancient tradition of court-sponsored collection of anomalies from the peripheries of the empire. He further argues that the *Classic of Mountains and Seas* is a product of China's cosmographic tradition and that, as such, it is a repository of esoteric knowledge vital to the ruler.

The *Classic of Mountains and Seas* encompasses all three of the original inspirations for supernatural literature: myths, religious practice (shamanistic rituals related to territorial concerns), and the ancient blend of geography, zoology, botany, mineralogy, and physiology. Because its basic structure is the geographic unit whose boundaries are mountains and seas, any given motif has many versions associated with specific locales, and life therein appears in its infinite varieties and offers rich opportunities for change and transformation. The power of deities, for example, tends not to be omnipotent but is limited to specific regions. Many later collections of supernatural fiction written in the classical language are modeled after the organizational principle of the *Classic of Mountains and Seas.* Following the topographically based structure, these collections also maintain a strong interest in geographic locales and are often encyclopedic in scope, aiming for an exhaustive taxonomy of the unseen and the hidden. Many of the mythical stories from the *Classic of Mountains and Seas* were rewritten by later writers, adding more and more details to the original fragmentary accounts. In the ensuing years, some of them were rewritten so many times and became so well known that later writers refer to them as though they were historical records, if not with factual proof at least having the weight of generations of texts. One-line accounts of a women's kingdom in the *Classic of Seas,* for instance, become full-chapter treatments in later vernacular novels such as *Journey to the West* and *Ching hua yüan* (Flowers in the Mirror, A Romance).

Compared to the spatial imagination of the *Classic of Mountains and Seas, Travels of Emperor Mu* has a more linear narrative structure. It is a fantastic chronicle of Emperor Mu's legendary expedition over several years. Composed during the Warring States period, the text of *Travels of Emperor Mu,* written on bamboo slips, was buried in the tomb of King Hsiang of Wei (318–295 B.C.E.) for more than five hundred years and resurfaced only during the T'ai-k'ang reign-period (280–290) of the Chin dynasty (265–420). Rejected by later historians for its lack of historical reliability, *Travels of Emperor Mu* is often noted for its detailed characterization, fine description of scenery, and epic narrative scope.

In *Travels of Emperor Mu,* the historical figure Emperor Mu (c. 976–c. 921 B.C.E.) of the Chou dynasty (c. 1045–256 B.C.E.) becomes a legendary hero of mythic dimensions. In this epic narrative, Emperor Mu and his large retinue journey to the ends of the earth in a grand hunting and inspection tour. His entourage included the legendary eight steeds—a favorite subject for artists for the next thousand years—steeds whose colored coats represent the eight corners of the earth. In much of his journey, Emperor Mu visited with noble families of remote regions and ritualistically sacrificed to local deities, until his journey turned toward the western regions, a strange and exotic land at whose extremity dwelled the Queen Mother of the West (Hsi Wang-mu). In other ancient texts, such as the *Classic of Mountains and Seas*, this female deity appears rather animal-like, with tiger teeth, a leopard tail, and, remarkably, a jade ornament in her hair. Here, however, the goddess sheds her animal associations and resembles more the head of a foreign country, although she still appears to reside among animals. For forty-four days, Emperor Mu sojourned in her kingdom, "enjoying himself and forgetting to return." When he finally took leave, they exchanged verses and sang of their parting sorrow.

The Queen Mother of the West would see more transformations in later times, as she gradually became a powerful deity specifically associated with the gift of longevity. Two biographies from the Han dynasty tell of a meeting of Emperor Wu (141–87 B.C.E.) and the Queen Mother, in which she offers him the coveted medicine for prolonging life.

HAN AND SIX DYNASTIES: THE *CHIH-KUAI*

Throughout the Han dynasty, there was continued court interest in things supernatural. Emperor Wu sought out one alchemist after another and even married his daughter to one; he commissioned a host of temples for local deities and tried out numerous concoctions for immortality offered by adepts eager for self-promotion. During his reign, "thousands and thousands in the kingdom claimed that they possessed secret recipes and could communicate with deities," as reported by the Grand Historian of the Western Han dynasty, Ssu-ma Ch'ien (c. 145–c. 86 B.C.E.). Not surprisingly, Emperor Wu is featured in several legendary accounts depicting his visit with the Queen Mother of the West. During the reign of the usurper Wang Mang (33 B.C.E.–23 C.E.; r. 9–23 C.E.) and much of the Eastern Han dynasty (25–220) that followed, there was great anxiety over political legitimization, and, as a result, the practice known as "prognosticatory apocrypha" (*ch'an-wei*) became very popular. Following the ancient cosmographical tradition, adept-scholars would present their interpretation of certain portents and omens in support of a prince's claim to legitimate succession; they would further link these portents with the line-by-line hermeneutics of classical texts popular at the time. Thus the heavenly mandate was understood to be communicated through "strange texts" whose correct interpretation would offer special access to political power. In the year 220, the last Han emperor, Hsien-ti, was forced to abdicate the throne, an event that marks the end of unity and the beginning of a long period of political turmoil, economic chaos, and massive dislocation. The following three and a half centuries, known as the Six Dynasties, saw the gradual loss of the northern heartland

and the rapid succession of six short-lived dynasties in the south, all of which had their capitals in Chien-an (modern-day Nanking).

The seeds of supernatural fiction sown earlier in the *Classic of Mountains and Seas* and *Travels of Emperor Mu* started to germinate in the rich soil of the Han. By the time of the Six Dynasties, literature of the supernatural had reached an extraordinary popularity that was never again paralleled in Chinese literary history. This was also an age of glorious literary achievement, when the literati class became well known for its insatiable appetite for reading and prolific output in writing. Individual style became highly valued, as shown in contemporary works of literary criticism that stressed the artistry of writing, with markedly less emphasis on the traditional focus of social utility. In the pages of histories, in numerous biographical accounts, and especially in collection after collection of anecdotes and sketches, there emerges a fantastic world permeated by a mysterious atmosphere. In this world, everything—from a severed hand to the drying skin of a dead horse, from a fish or a conch to a rock or a mulberry tree—appears to possess a spiritual dimension and may become animated at any moment, and communion between humans and the spiritual world—such as a relationship between a woman and her beautiful rainbow-spirit of a husband—seems to be part of the daily routine. This is a world that challenges our assumptions about all kinds of boundaries and stretches our very understanding of time and space.

In the titles and subheadings of many of these collections, the term *chih-kuai* frequently appears, and it later became an explicit designation of supernatural fiction in the hands of the Ming scholar Hu Ying-lin (1551–1602). In its original usage in the "inner chapters" of the *Chuang Tzu* (see chapter 10), the term *chih-kuai* means "to record anomalies." The seven inner chapters of this work are known for containing stories of the unusual and extraordinary, which are meant to expose the limitations of our imagination and point to the dangers of rigid categories and hierarchies. The specific passage in which the term *chih-kuai* appears describes the gigantic mythical fish-cum-bird K'un-P'eng, who, with one sweep of its wings, "spirals upward ninety thousand miles high" and whose enormous size and capability defy the understanding of small birds residing in the bushes.

As a generic label in later usage, "records of anomalies" encompasses a wide range of what is considered unusual or extraordinary, represented by an elaboration of categories: deities (*shen*), adepts (*hsien*), ghosts (*kuei*), the numinous (*ling*), freaks of nature (*kuai*), ominous portents or animal spirits (*yao*), and abnormal or disorderly events (*yi*). As time goes on, these categories overlap more and more in semantic content. For example, when Confucius "did not speak of *kuai*," the term means natural disorders such as earthquakes and floods. Around the time of the Han dynasty, *kuai* began to be mixed with *yao* to mean "animal or plant spirit," a meaning that continues to this day. Over the centuries, some of the writers of *chih-kuai* gathered and interpreted these strange beings/happenings primarily as heavenly portents that parallel human behavior; others collected and classified them into a taxonomy of "dark knowledge," to be part of historical understanding; still others were interested in these tales precisely because they resist neat taxonomy and order and thus offer an opportunity to rethink accepted boundaries, much as Chuang Tzu advocated in the original context of *chih-kuai.*

Judging from extant versions, there were at least eighty collections of *chih-kuai* tales produced during the Six Dynasties alone. Typically, a collection comprises many volumes (*chüan*), from the ten-volume *Po-wu chih* (A Treatise on Curiosities), by Chang Hua (232–300 C.E.), and the twenty-volume *Yu-ming lu* (Records of the Hidden and the Visible Worlds), by Liu Yi-ch'ing (403–444), to the largest collection of all, the thirty-volume *Sou-shen chi* (Search for the Supernatural), by Kan Pao. Most collections have two parts: contemporary stories gleaned from other collections and possibly from oral sources, and ancient myths and legends gathered from earlier texts. Virtually all the collections from this period are lost in their original forms. However, many of them survive in large quantities in commentaries and collectanea written and anthologized during the T'ang and Sung dynasties, most notably in the celebrated 500-volume *T'ai-p'ing kuang-chi* (Extensive Records from the Reign of Great Tranquility), a massive effort sponsored by the court and completed in the year 977. In part as a result of this historical lost-and-found situation, the authorship of many *chih-kuai* collections is in dispute.

In terms of the style of "records of anomalies," the most striking feature is their similarity to historical narrative. Written in simple, even terse, classical prose, the *chih-kuai* tale stands in sharp contrast to the elegant genre most often associated with the Six Dynasties, parallel prose (*p'ien-t'i-wen*), noted for its elaborate imagery and ornate language. In the collections from the Han and the Six Dynasties, a *chih-kuai* tale is typically one hundred to two hundred characters long, with a few exceptions exceeding three hundred characters. There is usually a sentence or two about the origin of the story, stating the name and birthplace of the eyewitness, which is sometimes the same as the birthplace of the author, of the particular supernatural occurrence. Much as later scholars often consider *chih-kuai* tales the origin of fiction writing because of the fantastic imagination shown in them, it is useful to remember that these records were not read as fiction at the time. Indeed, a division was not drawn between "fact" and "fiction," and these records were understood as a branch of history. In terms of language, structure, titles, and narrative techniques, the distinction between anomaly records as miscellaneous history and official dynastic history is, at best, blurred.

In fact, history was a particularly favorite genre of the period. Not only were there many fine court historians, but scholars everywhere compiled private histories, including histories of the dynasty, of specific regions, of various religions, and of particular families. There are, for example, more than twenty different histories of the Chin dynasty, not counting the more than one hundred anecdotal histories. Not surprisingly, as a subgenre of history, biography was very much in vogue, with an ever-widening range that included biographies of the ancients, of hermits and monks, of filial sons and daughters, and of loyal ministers and effective officials. Having always been considered a branch of biography, *chih-kuai* tales then played a vital role in the writing of both private and official histories, providing the stamp of personal witness as well as ample room for creative imagination.

As a testimony to the immense popularity of *chih-kuai* stories, writers, collectors, and avid readers included kings, princes, officials of all ranks, and noted members of the literati. Ts'ao P'i (187–226), who reigned as Emperor Wen of Wei (220–226) and forced the abdication of the last Han emperor, Hsien-ti, is also credited with writing *Lieh-yi chuan* (Records of Marvels), one of the earliest *chih-kuai* collections. A leading figure of the literary circle that comprised his father, Ts'ao Ts'ao (155–220), famed general of the swashbuckling times leading up to the Three Kingdoms (220–265), and his brother, the poet Ts'ao Chih (192–232), Ts'ao P'i is known for his poetry, letters, and an important work of literary criticism (see chapters 13 and 45). According to historical records, Ts'ao P'i prided himself on being knowledgeable on all things imaginable, and his poetry showed a clear interest in tales related to deities and ghosts. Fifty items of *Records of Marvels* survive from later collectanea, among which are perennial favorites such as the story of Sung Ting-po's encounter with a ghost on a night journey. Pretending to be a new ghost himself, Sung asked the ghost what the fatal weakness of ghosts is, to which the ghost answered, "Human spittle." Sung then brought the ghost to the market, spat on it, and sold it as a sheep. Like this story, *Records of Marvels* is noted for its simple language and vivid description and is often drawn upon by later writers.

Many collections of *chih-kuai* tales during the Han and early Six Dynasties bear the clear influence of the tradition of the *Classic of Mountains and Seas* in that they are geographically based in organization and encyclopedic in scope. Another factor also contributed to the popularity of this tradition. During this period, what was known as *ch'ing-t'an* (pure conversation) was exceedingly popular among literati members. It typically covered two subjects: comments on the virtues and talents of contemporaries, and philosophical discussions of Taoism and Buddhism. As an aid to conversation, *chih-kuai* tales provided an opportunity for the well-read scholar to demonstrate his vast knowledge of history and geography, zoology, legends, and so on, all of which were crucial to his intellectual eminence and may even have contributed significantly to his official career. The most famous collection in this tradition is *A Treatise on Curiosities*, by Chang Hua, a Taoist adept who achieved prominence as a statesman, arguably due in part to his reputation in court for having a vast knowledge of history and geography. In the extant version, consisting of ten volumes and 329 items, *A Treatise on Curiosities* devotes the first half to exotic fauna and flora and strange deities specifically associated with geographic locations. Later volumes concern themselves primarily with fairy tales and lives of adepts.

Another rich source of inspiration for *chih-kuai* stories is religion. Buddhism began to spread in the heartland of China early in the Eastern Han dynasty around the beginning of the first millennium C.E. By the period of the Six Dynasties, Buddhism, especially Tantric Buddhism, with its dual promise of enlightenment and worldly benefit, had a large following among the general populace as well as the elite class. In part modeled after the success of Buddhism, Taoism as a religion also became more organized in its canonical texts and practice during this period.

The most important work related to the rise of Taoism is *Lieh-hsien chuan* (Biographies of Transcendents), a two-volume hagiography of the lives of seventy Taoist immortals. The author, Liu Hsiang, was a prominent Han statesman and classical scholar, noted for his finely edited ancient texts, among which is the *Classic of Mountains and Seas*. Liu Hsiang is particularly known today for his fine works of biography, including *Lieh-shih chuan* (Biographies of Scholar-Officials) and *Lieh-nü chuan* (Biographies of Illustrious Women). In his *Biographies of Transcendents*, the majority of the Taoists appear less divine than human in their features and sensibilities, their main claim to fame being their transformative abilities (changing the old to the young, changing themselves into white lambs or giant birds) and their strange life habits (clouds or stones for food, dragons or cranes for steeds). Two particular types of stories have been favorites for later generations: those that detail congress between immortals and humans, spawning many later romantic stories, and those that recount accidental encounters of travelers and Taoist immortals, their vivid descriptions of sacred mountains giving rise to utopian stories such as the famed "T'ao-hua yüan chi" (Record of a Peach Blossom Spring) later on (see below under T'ao Ch'ien).

Another finely written work in the Taoist tradition is the ten-volume *Shih-yi chi* (Uncollected Records), by Wang Chia (d. before 393 C.E.), a Taoist adept who spent much of his time as a recluse in the mountains, writing and teaching. The first nine volumes of *Uncollected Records* consist of chronologically arranged tales of anomalies beginning in the time of the legendary sage kings, with a special focus on how various rulers responded to anomalies. The last volume is a geography of Taoist sacred mountains, with detailed descriptions of magical surroundings and numerous stories of romantic encounters between mortals and adept-immortals, thus further developing a theme latent in Liu Hsiang's work. Compared to that in many contemporary *chih-kuai* tales, Wang Chia's language in *Uncollected Records* is far more elaborate, providing a favorite source of imagery for poets in generations to come.

For clear influence of Buddhist tales, hagiographies, and treatises, we turn to Liu Yi-ch'ing, a prince of the Liu Sung dynasty (420–479) among the Southern Dynasties (420–589). Liu was well known for his deep interest in

Buddhist teachings and had a wide reputation as an enthusiastic patron of belles lettres. He was the author of a fabulously influential collection of contemporary anecdotal tales, *Shih-shuo hsin-yü* (A New Account of Tales of the World), which is endlessly alluded to by later writers and is of great linguistic importance because it is one of the very few texts outside the Buddhist canon proper that allowed a limited number of vernacularisms to slip in at such an early stage (see chapter 1). Liu is also credited with having produced two large *chih-kuai* collections, both of which were most likely composed by his retainers under his guidance. The better-known of the two, *Yu-ming lu*, contains many finely wrought *chih-kuai* tales, about 260 in all, the majority of them from recent or contemporary sources. One perennially favorite comic tale tells of a new ghost who often goes hungry. Following the advice of a ghost friend, he goes to Buddhist families and works hard at their mills. The families believe it is the Buddha answering their prayers, and as a result the ghost does not get fed. He then learns the ropes and only visits non-Buddhist homes, whose inhabitants are so scared of his apparition that they sacrifice lavishly for him. Although a large number of these tales concern such Buddhist concepts of karmic retribution and responsive manifestations to prayers, Liu Yi-ch'ing's next collection, *Hsüan-yen chi* (Records in Proclamation of Manifestations), may be properly called a primer of Buddhist teachings. It is one of the earliest Chinese collections of Buddhist miracle tales, of which thirty-five items survive. In these tales, typically a monk conducts an inquest, which results in a great shock for the audience and convinces the skeptic of the higher authority of Buddhism.

KAN PAO'S *SEARCH FOR THE SUPERNATURAL*

If one were to name a single *chih-kuai* collection as the most important among the eighty-some works that survive from the Six Dynasties, it would be *Sou-shen chi*. The author, Kan Pao, was a court historian of the Eastern Chin dynasty (317–420). Besides his renown for writing official histories, none of which has survived, Kan Pao was known to his contemporaries and later readers as "the Tung Hu of the ghostly world," an allusion to an outstanding legendary historian whom Confucius praised as "not concealing" anything. In stating his purpose for penning this collection, Kan Pao proclaims that he wanted to "make clear that the way of spirits is not a fabrication," thus justifying "ghostly" history as history. As though granting his wish, later official histories such as the *Chin shu* (The History of the Chin Dynasty) and *Sung shu* (The History of Liu Sung Dynasty) contain multiple references to *Search for the Supernatural*, citing Kan Pao's words as valuable historical evidence.

The extant edition of *Search for the Supernatural* contains 464 tales in 30 chapters. Making good use of his position as a court historian, Kan Pao perused an enormous number of earlier as well as contemporary compilations, using them as sources for his own lengthy collection.

Many tales in *Search for the Supernatural* retell ancient myths in more elaborate form, one example being the story of the silkworm horse derived from the *Classic of Mountains and Seas.* In ancient times, the story goes, the father of a family went on a military expedition, leaving behind only a daughter and a stallion. One day, the daughter in her loneliness joked with the stallion that, if it could bring back her father, she would be its wife. The stallion ran off and brought back the father. Learning about the deal between the stallion and his daughter, the father killed the horse, shooting it with an arrow. While playing on the drying horsehide with her young companions, the daughter teased the dead horse: an animal like you and wanting a human wife! See what you have done to yourself. At this point, the horsehide reared up, wrapped the woman in itself, and flew away. Days later, the father found both of them between the branches of a gigantic tree, now fused together and transformed into an enormous silkworm! The rest of the narrative cites several ancient textual sources linking women with silkworms and silkworms with horses, as well as sources that describe mulberry trees of giant proportions in the wild north. Originally intended as an etiology of the silkworm, the ancient legend in Kan Pao's hands was transformed into a romantic story, replete with humorous dialog and tragedy.

About half of *Search for the Supernatural* recounts more recent tales, especially those concerning local deities during the Han dynasty, when innumerable temples were built all over the country to honor a host of newly minted gods and goddesses. One such story tells of a certain young woman, Ting, who was driven to suicide by her cruel mother-in-law. Her ghost then appeared, proclaiming that the day of her death, the seventh day of the ninth month, should be a day of rest for all hard-working young wives. The story goes on to testify to the efficacy of this local deity in rewarding a courteous old man and punishing two young men who dared to harass her. This story illustrates the narrative techniques that Kan Pao introduced. Previously, a *chih-kuai* story typically recorded a single incident, whereas this story, using Miss Ting as both protagonist of the primary tale and linkage to the appended account, features three different episodes linked together to form a more complex narrative structure. This technique would later come to be much used by the authors of vernacular stories in the Ming and Ch'ing periods (see chapter 34).

Known for his cryptic style as a historian, Kan Pao used language that was at the same time elegant and highly expressive. In fact, many of the stories in *Search for the Supernatural* are longer than previous *chih-kuai* tales, the longest being more than five hundred words, with poems and personalized dialog, rather than the bare minimum of utterances attributed to characters in most other examples of this genre. They present richly drawn protagonists and more fully developed plots, some with intricate twists and turns. As a testimony to the lasting popularity of this collection, at least half a dozen later collections would claim to be its sequel and pictorial versions of the work were produced. Many of the stories eventually become the kernels for complete operas and fiction in later dynasties, and poets and essayists continue to use them as a rich source of allusion.

T'AO CH'IEN'S *SEQUEL TO SEARCH FOR THE SUPERNATURAL*

Among the many sequels to *Search for the Supernatural,* the best known is attributed to T'ao Ch'ien (T'ao Yüan-ming; 365–427), a famous hermit-poet. T'ao was born into the family of a minor official, and he himself took various advisory positions, none of which he found satisfying. After a particularly short stint as a local magistrate in 405, T'ao retired permanently to the country and remained a farmer for the remainder of his life. *"Sou-shen" hou-chi* (Sequel to *Search for the Supernatural*) is believed to have been written late in his life, most likely expanded by other writers and completed during the (Former or Liu) Sung dynasty. The ten-volume collection includes 116 stories, among which 24 are also found in other sources.

T'ao Ch'ien was not particularly known for his interest in ghosts and spirits, and so his motivation for compiling this multivolume collection of *chih-kuai* stories is somewhat different from Kan Pao's. T'ao's collection was not aiming to prove the historical verity of the spiritual world; rather, it presents fairy tales and legends then in circulation, which parallels the leisurely and carefree mood of his occasional poems on reading the *Classic of Mountains and Seas.* Nor are his stories actual "sequels" to Kan Pao's. Indeed, few of the more than one hundred tales are related in any way to those in Kan Pao's collection.

Sequel to Search for the Supernatural contains the most famous utopian tale by T'ao Ch'ien, "T'ao-hua yüan chi" (Record of the Peach Blossom Spring). Historians believe that this version may be an earlier draft of the better-known version collected among T'ao's essays, which contains an additional poem and is slightly different in the names of the participants. The story tells of a fisherman who one day rowed up a stream and found an entire grove of peach trees in bloom. The grove led him to a cave, which eventually opened up to a little village perfect in every respect, a utopia existing right in the Middle Kingdom, yet hidden away from the rest of the world. Inhabitants of this world claimed to be descendants of those who fled the Ch'in wars. Much as they were curious about the outside world and played wonderful hosts to the fisherman, they asked him not to reveal this place to outsiders. Later on, despite repeated efforts by the fisherman and numerous others to return, the way there was forever lost. The tale is particularly noted for its poetic description of the scenery on the banks of the stream and for the exquisite details about the world behind the cave.

Although nothing apparently supernatural happens in this tale, T'ao Ch'ien drew on several sources from the *chih-kuai* tradition: myths about mountainous dwellings of Taoist immortals and adepts, and legends about ruins of caves of ancient hermits. The typical topoi that T'ao Ch'ien employed in constructing the tale about a world free from the cares of the outside are readily recognizable: an unsuspecting wanderer chancing upon a wondrous world, a narrow cavelike entrance that leads to a wide-open space, and the impossibility of ever repeating the magical trip. These features combine with contemporary stories about communities that fled the wars and lived in secluded places to produce the microcosmic world at the end of the peach blossom spring.

There are seven other similar stories in *Sequel to* Search for the Supernatural. In one of them, instead of the peach blossoms and the stream, a mysterious man doing an ancient ritual dance leads the protagonist into a utopian world. In these stories, T'ao Ch'ien continues the tradition established by Liu Hsiang in his *Biographies of Transcendents* and further elevates it with the political ideal of a "small country with a small population," first promulgated by Lao Tzu and later expanded into a philosophical system of the "natural society" by poet-philosopher Juan Chi (210–263) and others.

Like the inhabitants of T'ao Ch'ien's "Record of the Peach Blossom Spring," readers and writers of the Six Dynasties longed for a respite from endless warfare and constant social unrest. The *chih-kuai* stories, in their fantastic imagination, may have offered temporary solace to nerves worn thin by the harsh vicissitudes of life as they rendered a creative response to the fear and anxiety of the age.

Hu Ying

Chapter 30

TRAVEL LITERATURE

A substantial number of works dating from the traditional period in China are often called *yu-chi* (travel records) or *yu-chi wen-hsüeh* (travel record literature). These terms, devised by twentieth-century scholars, are used to describe prose works that exhibit the following characteristics. First, they relate a personal account of a journey, whether an afternoon hike to a local scenic spot or a long journey to some remote part of the empire or even to a foreign land. Second, these works are usually structured like a diary, with entries arranged chronologically. Third, authors of travel records in China pay close attention to geography (notable landscapes, famous mountains, and so forth) and historical sites (ancient battlegrounds, well-known temples, tumuli of famous people, and so on). Lastly, *yu-chi* almost always reflect the opinions and interpretations of the author himself regarding the places seen and visited during his journey. Travel records are especially valuable because they serve as repositories of geographic, historical, and literary information that is not generally available elsewhere.

The earliest extant specimen of travel writing in China is *Mu t'ien-tzu chuan* (Travels of Emperor Mu), a work of uncertain authorship probably dating from the late Chou dynasty (c. 1027–256 B.C.E.) (see chapters 2 and 29). This work recounts Emperor Mu's (c. 976–c. 921 B.C.E.) journey to western China in the tenth century B.C.E. Other early travel accounts have also survived. Examples include the Han dynasty envoy Chang Ch'ien's (d. 114 B.C.E.) embassy to Bactria and other parts of Central Asia (138–126, 115–114 B.C.E.); the influential travel accounts of Fa-hsien (337–442; traveling 399–414), Hsüan-tsang (c. 600–664;

traveling 629–645), Yi-ching (633–713; traveling 671–695), and other Buddhist monks who journeyed to India in search of scriptures; the landscape essays of the T'ang writers Yüan Chieh (719–772) and Liu Tsung-yüan (773–819); Li Ao's (c. 772–c. 841) travel account titled *Lai-nan lu* (Register of Coming South); the diaries of Lu Yu (1125–1210) and his friend Fan Ch'eng-ta (1126–1193); and the lengthy chronicles of Hsü Hung-tsu (also known as Hsü Hsia-k'o; 1586–1641). These writers are all major contributors to the travel record tradition in China.

Among the authors mentioned, three merit special attention. The first of these is Liu Tsung-yüan, whose "Yung-chou pa-chi" (Eight Records of Yung Prefecture) was especially significant because it contains China's first landscape essays of literary note in which travel narrative, scenic description, and expression of personal sentiment played key roles. For this reason, many literary historians regard Liu Tsung-yüan as the prose stylist of the traditional period most responsible for creating "travel record literature." The T'ang dynasty (618–907) also witnessed the appearance of the first travel diary of a type that would proliferate later: *Register of Coming South*, which describes a journey from Loyang to Kwangtung in 809 by Li Ao, an official and literatus with a strong affinity for Ch'an (Zen) who laid the foundations for the synthesis of Buddhism and Confucianism that would flourish as Neo-Confucianism a few centuries later. It was not until the Sung dynasty (960–1279), however, that travel writing became a popular literary genre. Two Sung writers, Lu Yu and Fan Ch'eng-ta, are responsible for this development.

Travel writing became widespread during the Sung dynasty for three general reasons. First, people traveled more extensively because communication and transportation lines (especially river travel) were more advanced and convenient than ever before. Second, Sung writers were more inclined than their predecessors to record everyday experiences in their prose and poetry (*shih*). And, third, the size of the government bureaucracy increased dramatically during the Sung dynasty. Since government officials usually rotated (about once every three years) through several administrative posts (in different parts of the empire) throughout their careers, it is no surprise that many of them kept records of their travel experiences. Most Sung dynasty *yu-chi* were written by officials traveling to or from government posts.

Sung travel records fall into one of three general categories. The first is records (*chi*) of incidental trips to specific places, such as a famous mountain or temple. These records are short (usually a few hundred Chinese characters) and describe events surrounding a brief excursion that usually lasted a day. These are the most prevalent type of *yu-chi* found in Sung dynasty literary collections. Practically every major writer of the period tried his hand at the genre. Wang An-shih (1021–1086) and Su Shih (Su Tung-p'o; 1037–1101), both famous politicians and writers, are perhaps the best-known composers of these "day trip" essays. Famous examples include Wang An-shih's "Yu Pao-ch'an-shan chi" (Record of a Trip to Pao-ch'an Mountain) and Su Shih's "Shih-chung shan chi" (Record of Stone Bell Mountain). Such works are similar to the landscape essays of Liu Tsung-yüan in that the occasion of the trip provides a setting or stimulus in response to which the author advances a philosophical or moral argument.

The second variety describes extended excursions, often written by officials on their way to or on their way home from official posts in the provinces. These are the most famous and influential of all Sung travel records. Two of these extended *yu-chi* deserve separate mention: Lu Yu's *Ju Shu chi* (Record of a Trip to Shu) and Fan Ch'eng-ta's *Wu ch'uan lu* (Register of a Boat Trip to Wu). The first of these works describes a lengthy trip up the Yangtze River from Chekiang to Szechwan in 1170, while the second is an account of a journey down the Yangtze from Szechwan to Soochow in 1177.

At various times between the eleventh and thirteenth centuries, the Sung was threatened by the Liao (Khitans), Hsi-hsia (Tanguts), and Chin (Jurchens), three non-Chinese states that occupied territory along China's northern and western frontiers. As a result, the Sung concluded a number of treaties and alliances with two of these powers, the Liao and Chin. One outcome of this was the establishment of formalized diplomatic channels that shuttled Sung and northern envoys back and forth between their respective capitals. In general, there were two types of Sung embassies: the first might be called "ceremonial" in that they were commissioned on specific occasions, such as the New Year's holiday, the emperor's birthday, the adoption of a new reign-title, and so on. The second type of embassy was that charged with dispatching diplomatic documents containing inquiries or requests on specific issues. The first major Sung literary figure to compose a travel record resembling an embassy account was Ou-yang Hsiu (1007–1072), who kept a journal of his trip into political exile in 1036 titled *Yü-yi chih* (Chronicle of Going into Service). Other prominent Sung officials who participated in embassies to the Liao and Chin and kept records of their experiences include Su Ch'e (1039–1112; younger brother of Su Shih) and Hung Mai (1123–1202). Since Sung envoys were recruited almost exclusively from the scholar-official class, it is not surprising that many of them kept written accounts of their embassies. These works constitute the third and final variety of Sung dynasty travel records—the embassy account. Unfortunately, only a few of these texts have survived. Fan Ch'eng-ta's *Lan-p'ei lu* (Register of Grasping the Carriage Reins) is one of the most famous surviving embassy accounts. It describes a diplomatic mission to the Chin capital (modern-day Peking) in 1170.

The most significant of the three varieties of Sung travel records are the so-called river diaries (the second variety described above). Although only a handful of these works survive, they form an essential part of the Sung dynasty *yu-chi* tradition, not only because their literary content is proportionately much greater and qualitatively more significant than the day-trip essay and embassy account but also because they established the prototype for the hundreds of travel diaries written in later periods. Another quality that distinguishes these texts is their length and the detailed descriptions they provide. *Ju Shu chi* and *Wu ch'uan lu*, for instance, each describe journeys of about 1,800 miles, covering periods of travel that extended for months. The extended nature of these trips allowed plenty of time for sightseeing and writing. As a result, the river diaries are the longest and most detailed of all Sung dynasty *yu-chi*. Here is a sample selection, taken from Fan Ch'eng-ta's account (in *Wu ch 'uan lu*) of his ascent of Mount Omei (in Szechwan) in 1177:

> *Twenty-eighth day* (25 July): Again we climbed up to the cliff to view and gaze at the sights. Behind the cliff are the ten thousand folds of the Min Mountains. Not far to the north is [Little] Tile-Roof Mountain [Wa-wu shan], which is in Ya county. Not far to the south is Big Tile-Roof Mountain, which is near Nan-chao. In shape it looks like a single tile-roofed house. On Little Tile-Roof Mountain there is a luminous form called the Pratyeka-Buddha Manifestation. Behind all these mountains are the Snow mountains [that is, the Himalayas and their associated ranges] of the Western Regions. Their jagged and cragged peaks, which seemed carved and pared, in all number in the tens and hundreds. When the first light of day shines on them, their snowy hue is piercing and bright, like glistening silver amid the dazzling and resplendent light of dawn. From ancient times until today, these snows have never melted. The mountains stretch and sweep into India and other alien lands, for who knows how many thousands of tricents [one tricent = a third of a mile or 300 paces]. Gazing at them now, they seem to spread out on a little tea table right before my eyes. This magnificent, surpassing view tops everything I have seen in my life.

In addition to descriptions of famous mountains (such as Mount Omei), spectacular river scenery such as the Three Gorges (San-hsia), and historical sites such as the Yellow Crane Tower (Huang-ho lou), Fan Ch'eng-ta's and Lu Yu's river diaries provide reports on a wide range of topics, such as local economic conditions and folktales associated with a particular place. Other, perhaps more fascinating, topics include the origin of the Yangtze river (in *Wu ch'uan lu*), the activities of grave robbers (in *Ju Shu chi*), and Buddhist "apparitions" (the reference is to the Fo-kuang, or "Buddha Light," seen by Fan Ch'eng-ta on the summit of Mount Omei).

One particularly fascinating aspect of the river diaries is that most of the places visited by Fan and Lu had already been celebrated in the works of China's most renowned writers, among them Li Po (701–762), Tu Fu (712–770), Ou-yang Hsiu, Su Shih, and Huang T'ing-chien (1045–1105). Fan Ch'eng-ta and Lu Yu found themselves in situations where they had to respond in some way to themes, sights, and events that had already been described in the poetry and prose of China's most famous writers. While they do not hesitate to quote directly from a masterpiece of the past, at the same time they do not shy away from offering a comment of their own. On some occasions they even attempt to correct errors or misunderstandings. For instance, in *Wu ch'uan lu* Fan Ch'eng-ta openly disputes a popular Sung dynasty interpretation of a couplet in a poem by Tu Fu. The greatest appeal and value of these works, however, is the intimate glimpse they give into the daily life of a twelfth-century scholar-official. In their river diaries Fan and Lu openly reveal their literary preferences, historical consciousness, and most intimate personal concerns. Very few other types of descriptive prose in traditional China, if any, reveal an equally poignant portrait of the daily activities and concerns of a scholar-official.

In the subsequent Yüan, Ming, and Ch'ing dynasties, travel writing became one of the most widely practiced forms of literary expression. Most major writers in these periods, including Yüan Hung-tao (1568–1610), Ch'ien Ch'ien-yi (1582–1664), Chu Yi-tsun (1629–1709), and Yüan Mei (1716–1797), produced travel records. The most famous and most prolific author of *yu-chi* in China, Hsü Hsia-k'o, lived in the final years of the Ming dynasty (1368–1644). His numerous trips to various parts of the Chinese empire spanned more than thirty years; his many journals describing these journeys contain, according to some estimates, more than four hundred thousand Chinese characters. Driven by a desire to verify his knowledge of China's geography acquired from readings and to solve doubts about some of the accounts in those texts, Hsü spent most of his life engaged in geographical exploration and survey. The diaries describing his travels are significant because they contain reports of firsthand investigations of China's great wealth of geographic resources. Never before had anyone in China spent so many years engaged in travel and investigation or explored so many mountains and rivers as Hsü Hsia-k'o. Indeed, Hsü was probably traditional China's only professional traveler and explorer. As a result, Hsü Hsia-k'o has received more critical attention than any other *yu-chi* writer in China.

The traditional personal and somewhat lyrical Chinese *yu-chi* was gradually eclipsed during the Ch'ing dynasty and Republican period when modern Western explorers, geographers, surveyors, and ethnographers, with their advanced methods of observation and notation, began to crisscross the whole of China (see chapter 38). Among them was Freiherr (Baron) Friedrich von Richthofen (1833–1905), uncle of the celebrated World War I flying ace, the "Red Baron," Freiherr Manfred von Richthofen. Friedrich von Richthofen undertook a series of expeditions to China from 1868 to 1872 and coined the term *die Seidenstrasse* ("Silk Road"). This was soon calqued, and now there are countless Chinese travelogs about the Ssu-ch'ou chih lu. Similar stories could be told about other parts of China and about the persons who visited them.

James M. Hargett

Chapter 31

SKETCHES

Pi-chi is a form of prose writing, popular in China since the Sung dynasty (960–1279). *Pi* literally means "writing brush"; *chi* means "record" or "note" (as a noun) or "to make [records] or take [notes]" (as a verb). Most scholars trace the origin of *pi-chi* to a prose form popular during the Wei-Chin period (third to fourth centuries) called *chih-kuai*, or "records of anomalies" (see chapters 6 and 29). "Anomalies" here means extraordinary persons and events; more specifically, ghosts and fantasies. Use of the word *pi-chi* as a reference to the style of prose writing that concerns us here, however, probably did not begin until the Northern Sung dynasty (960–1127), when a writer named Sung Ch'i (998–1061) adopted the term as a book title.

The generic label *pi-chi* is associated with several other related prose forms, such as *sui-pi, pi-t'an, cha-chi, tsa-ch'ao, ts'ung-t'an,* and *ts'ung-cha.* Precise differences between these forms are not clear. For the sake of convenience, the comments that follow also pertain, in a general way, to *sui-pi, pi-t'an,* and other close "relatives" of the *pi-chi.*

Western Sinologists have translated *pi-chi* in many different ways, such as "random jottings," "note-form literature," "occasional notes," "desultory notes," "brush notes," "miscellanies," "literati miscellanies," and "miscellaneous notes." These various renditions suggest a major problem one faces when attempting to discuss *pi-chi:* it is extremely difficult, if not impossible, to define *pi-chi* in precise terms because there are no hard-and-fast rules governing its style and content. This also explains why *pi-chi* does not fit into any single Chinese bibliographic category. Such works are usually assigned to either the *tsa-chia* (miscellaneous schools) or the *hsiao-shuo* (fiction) sections in the traditional bibliographies. Since there are no strict prosodic or genre rules governing *pi-chi*, the number of extant *pi-chi* collections in China could easily number in the thousands. The total would vary greatly depending on how one defines the form.

So what *can* we say about *pi-chi?* First, we might call it an "informal" prose style. "Informal" means that, unlike many other forms of Chinese prose, *pi-chi* were not usually produced for any formal or special event. It seems that anyone could put together a *pi-chi* collection at any time and for just about any purpose. In this sense, we might describe *pi-chi* as a "random" or "casual" form of writing. Second, most *pi-chi* is written in a register of ancient Chinese prose (*ku-wen*) that is clear, direct, allusion-free, and lacking the kinds of prosodic requirements (such as syntactical and verbal parallelism) that govern other, more formal prose forms. *Pi-chi* writers do not use the genre to show off erudition. Rather, they employ it to report information in a way that suggests that they are providing some sort of "inside information" that may not be available elsewhere. Here is an example, taken from the "Strange Occurrences" section of Shen Kua's (1030–1094) *Meng-hsi pi-t'an* (Brush Talks from Dream Brook), a tenth-century collection that is often cited as a paradigmatic example of the *pi-chi* form:

> During the Chia-yu reign-period [1056–1064] there was a huge "pearl" in Yangchow, seen frequently at night. At first it appeared out of the marshes in T'ien-ch'ang county; later it moved to Pi-she Lake; finally it settled at Hsin-k'ai Lake. For more than ten years residents and travelers saw it often. A friend of mine had a retreat by the lake. One night he noticed that the "pearl" was very nearby. At first, it opened its door just slightly. A bright light emerged from its "shell," like a single ray of golden thread. A moment later the "shell" suddenly opened to about the size of half a mat. Inside there was a white light like silver. The "pearl" was as big as a fist, so bright one could not look at it directly. Shadows cast in the forests for more than ten tricents [one tricent = 300 paces] distant were just like those cast by the first rays of sunshine in the morning. In the distance one could see only a red sky, like a forest fire. Quickly the "pearl" sped far off, as if it were flying, floating above the waves, bright and brilliant as sunlight. In ancient times there was a "bright moon pearl," but its color was different from that of the moon. Sparkling and shimmering with a blazing glare, it looked a little bit like sunlight. Ts'ui Po-yi [or Ts'ui Kung-tu, fl. eleventh century] once wrote a "Rhapsody on the Bright Pearl." Po-yi was a native of Kao-yu, and so he probably saw it often. In recent years the "pearl" has not shown itself again. No one knows where it might have gone. Fan-liang village is located exactly where the "pearl" used to move about. Travelers often moor their boats for a few

> nights there and wait for it to appear. The pavilion there is called Wan-chu (The Playful Pearl).

Most noteworthy about Shen Kua's passage is the "human interest" appeal of its "unusual" subject matter. Could this be a report of a UFO sighting? Perhaps. In any case, Chinese scholars have always taken great delight in reading reports and stories involving anomalies or unusual happenings, and this helps explain the popularity of *pi-chi.* Note also Shen Kua's reportorial tone and the use of dates, place names, and especially informants, which ostensibly boost the credibility and lend verisimilitude to the report.

Where did *pi-chi* writers find their informants? Many Sung writers, Shen Kua among them, gathered their information from relatives and acquaintances. *Pi-chi* writers, especially since the Sung dynasty, often had careers as public officials and so had opportunities to travel (government officials typically held several provincial posts during their careers). Notebooks kept during these sojourns were later edited into *pi-chi.*

Pi-chi collections are usually divided into sections or chapters (*men, chüan, chih,* and so on). While some writers leave their chapters untitled, others provide topical headings. Here is an example, taken from Shen Kua's *Brush Talks from Dream Brook:*

1. Ancient Usage
2. Philological Criticism
3. Music and Mathematical Harmonics
4. Numerological Regularities Underlying Phenomena
5. Human Affairs
6. Civil Service
7. Wisdom in Emergencies
8. Literature
9. Calligraphy and Painting
10. Technical and Artistic Skills
11. Artifacts and Implements
12. Divine Marvels
13. Strange Occurrences
14. Errors
15. Wit and Satire
16. Miscellaneous
17. Deliberations on *Materia Medica*

These sections, in turn, are divided into shorter subsections or items or entries (*t'iao*). For instance, our "UFO report" is an entry in the "Strange Occurrences" section of *Brush Talks from Dream Brook.* The topical entry format is useful when dealing with a wide variety of subject matter, especially those in note form made over time. These entries, unlike more definable prose genres such as verse epitaphs or imperial edicts, do not define issues and make arguments. Most entries relate information, provide reports, and correct errors.

Although some *pi-chi* collections possess a general thematic consistency, most do not. As suggested by the topical variation of Shen Kua's famous collection, virtually anything could be included in a *pi-chi.* This organizational format, however, is not so haphazard as it may seem at first. Modern scholarship has convincingly argued that the organizational and thematic taxonomies of Sung dynasty *pi-chi* closely follow a pattern of organizing knowledge evident in one of the great imperial encyclopedias of the period: the *T'ai-ping yü-lan* (Imperial Digest of the Reign of Great Tranquility). The taxonomy of Shen Kua's *Brush Talks from Dream Brook,* in fact, follows the tradition of *T'ai-p'ing yü-lan.*

Some modern scholars have attempted to classify China's many *pi-chi* works according to general thematic content. Liu Yeh-ch'iu, for instance, defines three general categories of *pi-chi.* The first of these, which might be called "narrative *pi-chi,*" consists primarily of brief prose entries (or very short stories) about extraordinary persons and events, some of which are loosely related to historical figures and events (in other words, the person may be historical, but the events described may not). One of the earliest examples is Kan Pao's (fl. 320) *Sou-shen chi* (Search for the Supernatural), a collection of brief prose entries that discuss "unusual" people and happenings (some modern scholars regard this and similar works as among the origins of Chinese fiction). The second variety might be called "historical *pi-chi.*" This is because such works discuss allusions and include bibliographic notes related to historical persons and events. One example is *Hsi-ching tsa-chi* (Miscellanies of the Western Capital), an anonymous collection in 130 sections, most of which describe events and people in Ch'ang-an during the Former Han dynasty (206–8 B.C.E.). The third category is "critical *pi-chi.*" One famous example is Ts'ui Pao's (fl. 300) *Ku-chin chu* (Commentaries on Antiquity and Today). This useful work is a mini-encyclopedia composed of the author's notes on selected topics, such as carriages and clothes, fish and insects, and music. Ts'ui Pao's notes consist of anecdotes, definitions, and lexical glosses. To this third category we might add collections called *shih-hua* (talks on poetry). These collections, which were popular during the Sung dynasty, consist of the authors' critical comments on various aspects of Chinese poetry (see chapter 45).

While the above classification scheme is a first step in approaching the general thematic threads of *pi-chi,* its usefulness is limited, because few texts fit neatly into one category. In fact, many (if not most) *pi-chi,* especially works dating from the Sung dynasty and thereafter, have chapters that deal with "unusual" people and events, history, and various specialized topics. Shen Kua's *Brush Talks from Dream Brook* is a good example of the tremendous thematic breadth found in *pi-chi.* Another example, Lu Yu's (1125–1210) *Lao-hsüeh-an pi-*

chi (Notes from the Retreat of Venerable Knowledge), generously mixes supernatural tales with entries on Southern Sung dynasty (1127–1279) politics, literary criticism, and much more. Clearly, the defining feature of *pi-chi* collections is their eclectic (*tsa*) content. There seems to be no limitation as far as coverage and contents are concerned.

Beginning in about the middle of the eleventh century, each generation wrote more and more *pi-chi*. Many such collections, for instance, were compiled by the famous Northern Sung writer Su Shih (Su Tung-p'o; 1037–1101) and his friends and followers. Why did *pi-chi* writing become so widespread in the Sung dynasty? One reason is that these collections were popular with readers, which in turn meant commercial success (made possible by the growth of printing and publishing). Hung Mai's (1123–1202) *Yi-chien chih* (Records of the Listener), for instance, which appeared in 1161, was so popular that a second installment was published in 1166. Other installments followed thereafter. The popularity of many Sung *pi-chi* was no doubt related to the often fascinating and curious nature of their reports and anecdotes, which covered the entire spectrum of society. Another reason for the popularity of *pi-chi* in the Sung period is related to the men who produced these works. Learned men of the Northern Sung cultivated what might be called a "leisure" culture: they actively engaged in various activities in their free time, such as painting and antique and book collecting. "Note taking" was also a popular leisure activity. *Pi-chi* works are fun to write and talk about because they are marvelously entertaining and full of surprises. No doubt they supplied material for many witty and learned conversations. In this sense, the content of Sung *pi-chi* is valuable because it tells much about the life, careers, and interests of Sung literati, revealing a great deal about the world in which Shen Kua, Su Shih, and others lived. By the end of the eleventh century, a *pi-chi* tradition was in place. *Pi-chi* writers were now even commenting on entries in earlier *pi-chi*. Chang Lei (1054–1114) in his *Ming-tao tsa-chi* (Ming-tao Miscellany), for instance, comments on entries in Shen Kua's *Meng-hsi pi-t'an*. This *pi-chi* tradition continued to flourish through the Ch'ing dynasty (1644–1911). Indeed, the greatest Chinese writer of the twentieth century, Lu Hsün (1881–1936), was an eminent practitioner of the literary sketch on a wide variety of miscellaneous subjects.

Most *pi-chi* collections are found in collectanea (*ts'ung-shu*), but they are difficult to mine because of their thematic breadth. Published indexes, such as Saeki Tomi's *Chūgoku zuihitsu sakuin* (Index to Chinese Miscellaneous Writings; 1954) and *Chūgoku zuihitsu zatcho sakuin* (Index to Chinese Miscellaneous Writings and Essays; 1961) are limited in the number of *pi-chi* covered (206) and format (chapter headings, key words, and important nouns). Indexes do not tell readers about the nature of the subject matter. For instance, it would be difficult, if not impossible, to determine how many other "UFO" accounts (or entries concerning "special pearls") are found in *pi-chi* without reading all of them entry by entry.

Finally, it should be noted that historians have frequently drawn on *pi-chi*. This is because these works form an important (some might say "corrective") supplement to the dynastic histories and other works of official and Confucian historiography. Thus *pi-chi* entries are often quoted in local gazetteers, other collections of anecdotes, medical works, and encyclopedias. The historian Li T'ao (1115–1184), while compiling his monumental *Hsü tzu-chih t'ung-chien ch'ang-pien* (Continuation of the Extended Version of the Mirror for Aiding Government)—a primary source for the study of Northern Sung institutions—profitably mined numerous *pi-chi* for information that presumably was not available in other sources. Some Western scholars have also made extensive use of *pi-chi*. Jacques Gernet's informative book *Daily Life in China on the Eve of the Mongol Invasion, 1250–1276*, for instance, is based largely on Sung *pi-chi* sources.

Since 1973 the publisher Hsin-hsing shu-chü in Taiwan has produced more than thirty series of *pi-chi* under the title *Pi-chi hsiao-shuo ta-kuan* (The Great Compendium of Pi-chi Fiction). This is probably the largest and most conveniently accessible assembly of *pi-chi*, but it must be used with caution. Many titles therein may not be considered *pi-chi*; moreover, the choice of editions is questionable. More useful and reliable are the numerous individual *pi-chi* titles that have been republished in China since the 1980s, many by Chung-hua shu-chü. These works typically include punctuation and collation notes to other editions. One such work, Hu Tao-ching's *Hsin chiao-cheng "Meng-hsi pi-t'an"* (*Brush Talks from Dream Brook*: New Collations and Corrections), is indispensable to anyone interested in probing the rich contents of Shen Kua's famous *pi-chi* collection.

In general, *pi-chi* and other types of sketches and anecdotal literature constitute a vast treasure trove of obscure and arcane information that is otherwise unavailable in the more mainstream types of texts. They are not always distinguished by felicity of style, but occasionally literary gems or striking insights about literature and its authors turn up among them. Consequently, researchers on the history of Chinese literature will often be handsomely rewarded if they delve into *pi-ch'i* and associated genres.

James M. Hargett

Chapter 32

TWENTIETH-CENTURY PROSE

VERNACULARIZATION IN THE TWENTIETH-CENTURY ESSAY

The prose essay can be considered the most thoroughly vernacularized type of twentieth-century Chinese writing. Few Chinese anthologies of twentieth-century essays contain pieces in the classical idiom, even though vernacular literary essays were virtually unknown at the beginning of the century. Readers of twentieth-century Chinese literature are far less likely to have read many of this period's informal essays in the classical idiom than to have sampled classical-language novels of the 1910s such as Hsü Chen-ya's (1889–1937?) *Yü li hun* (The Soul of the Jade Pear Flowers; 1912). Moreover, some prominent fiction writers of the 1920s like Lu Hsün (1881–1936) and Yü Ta-fu (1896–1945) preferred the classical idiom for their poetry compositions but still used the vernacular for their informal essays. In similar fashion, even though Ch'ien Chung-shu (1910–1999) has written most of his scholarly treatises in classical Chinese, his familiar essays are in the vernacular.

Unlike Chinese drama and fiction, the prose essay was not traditionally a hybrid of classical Chinese and the vernacular, but was decidedly classical in its linguistic orientation. Models of literary excellence such as essays by the Eight Great Prose Masters of the T'ang and Sung dynasties (*T'ang-Sung pa ta chia*; see chapter 28) were invariably in the classical idiom. Moreover, the vast majority of prose writers in traditional China were scholar-officials or aspirants to that status, and they had to compose impromptu essays in Classical Chinese in order to pass the all-important imperial civil service examinations. Notwithstanding the abolition of that time-honored institution system in 1905, early-twentieth-century essay writers who wished to be taken seriously continued to use Classical Chinese until 1919–1920, when the New Culture movement to vernacularize written Chinese swept with astonishing rapidity through government, business, educational institutions, literary circles, journalism, and the publishing world.

At first glance, it might seem odd that the first two key essays (see chapter 24) arguing for the discarding of the classical style in favor of a revitalized vernacular literature were themselves composed in Classical Chinese. Yet at the time these polemics were first published in 1917, the somewhat radical ideas of Hu Shih (1891–1962) and Ch'en Tu-hsiu (1879–1942) would have lacked an air of intellectual gravity if they had been couched in vernacular Chinese. The advocacy of vernacular writing by Hu Shih and Ch'en Tu-hsiu was immensely influential, for, within a few years, both they and almost all their intellectual peers had abandoned Classical Chinese as the medium for essay writing. Of course, the concurrent rapid growth of mass-circulation newspapers and magazines in an expanding urban sector undergirded intellectual arguments in favor of vernacularization; intellectuals did not have to search far to find ample evidence that vernacular writings sold better and garnered more visibility than classical compositions. The success of progressive, elite journals like *Hsin ch'ing-nien* (New Youth) and *Hsien-tai p'ing-lun* (Modern Era Review) that resolutely turned to the vernacular in the mid- to late 1910s provided key sections of the foundation upon which other outstanding vernacular publications were built during subsequent decades.

HISTORICAL OVERVIEW OF THE TWENTIETH-CENTURY VERNACULAR ESSAY

Brief literary forms like the short story dominated Chinese literature during the 1920s, the first major decade of the vernacular essay. The novel, which had enjoyed a meteoric rise in China during the first fifteen years of the twentieth century, did not fully reestablish its former prominence until the late 1920s and early 1930s. Yet even as long forms like the novel flourished throughout most of the 1930s, the essay also achieved one of its peaks of popularity in that decade with the founding of many journals devoted exclusively to this genre, such as Lin Yü-t'ang's (1895–1976) *Lun-yü* (The Analects, 1932–1937), *Jen-chien shih* (The Human World, 1934–1935), and *Yü-chou feng* (Wind of the Universe, 1935–1947).

Left-wing writers (many of whom were sympathetic to the cause of the newly founded [in 1921] Chinese Communist Party) emphasizing *engagé* writing countered the personalistic, apolitical tone of these Lin Yü-t'ang journals with essay-based magazines of their own like *T'ai-po* (named for the style of the great T'ang poet Li Po; 1934–1935). In spite of the left's domination of China's 1930s literary scene, left-leaning essay journals like *T'ai-po* had many difficulties attracting a steady readership. Leftist essays tended to be spread through several literary journals rather than concentrated heavily in a few exclusively essay-based magazines. A special section for essays became the norm for many leading journals of the 1930s such as *Hsien-tai* (Les Contemporains, 1932–1935) and *Tung-fang tsa-chih* (Eastern Miscellany, 1904–1948).

In book form, single-author essay collections predominated during the 1920s and 1930s. Lu Hsün alone produced more than ten volumes of his essays, though in the 1950s scholars discovered that he had included among them, without attribution, twelve essays actually penned by Ch'ü Ch'iu-pai (1899–1935). The coining of many dozens of pseudonyms by each of the two authors has made the determination of authorship difficult in many cases. Admittedly, pseudonyms occasionally had the salutary function of enabling leftist authors to elude sporadic bouts of censorship by the Nationalist government authorities. More often, however, the multiplication of pseudonyms simply allowed a writer to hide under a cloak of anonymity and avoid taking responsibility for a given essay or story, especially when it contained *ad hominem* attacks. The use of merely a few pseudonyms by the typical essayist of the period could be considered an act of harmless self-indulgence, but Lu Hsün's coinage of nearly two hundred pseudonyms is an extreme example of how complicated the determination of authorship could become.

The Japanese military invasion and occupation of eastern China that began in 1937 disrupted the development of the essay and nearly all other genres of Chinese literature, for most prominent writers fled into exile, usually to the Chinese-controlled western interior and sometimes abroad. Chou Tso-jen (1885–1969) and a few less well-known essayists continued to write and publish traditionalistic familiar essays in Japanese-occupied Peking and Shanghai, but the center of gravity of the Chinese literary scene shifted west to the wartime capitals of Chungking (Szechwan province) for the Nationalists and Yenan (Shensi province) for the Communists. A variety of the didactic topical essay that expanded rapidly during wartime in both Yenan and Chungking was reportage literature (*pao-kao wen-hsüeh*), a hybrid of fiction and the reportorial essay. On a grimmer note, Mao Tse-tung (1893–1976) initiated the first of what would be a recurrent pattern of harsh Communist political crackdowns on free literary expression in 1942 when he repudiated the *tsa-wen* (polemical topical essay) as an anachronism in the dawn of the brave new socialist millennium. Half a decade later, Mao's execution of an unrepentant ex-Communist *tsa-wen* satirist, Wang Shih-wei (1906–1947), showed how high the stakes could be for dissident essayists. The assassination of the poet and essayist Wen Yi-to (1899–1946) by a Nationalist agent exemplified a similarly harsh intolerance for essays opposing Nationalist government policies on the civil war between the Communists and the Nationalists.

Relatively apolitical essayists who retreated to Taiwan in 1949 with the Nationalist government of the Republic of China in the wake of the Communist victory, such as Liang Shih-ch'iu (1902–1987) and Lin Yü-t'ang, continued to write and publish familiar essays throughout the middle of the century. However, the intense politicization of practically all cultural realms during this period on the mainland by the government of the People's Republic of China (PRC) formed by the Communists discouraged familiar essayists like Feng Tzu-k'ai (1898–1975) from continuing to write in the basically apolitical vein he had preferred before 1949; the result was a dramatic reduction in the quality and quantity of his essays during the first three decades of the PRC.

Some mainland satirical essayists who were dissatisfied with Mao's de facto ban on *tsa-wen*, such as the Communist bureaucrats Teng T'o (1912–1966) and Wu Han (1909–1969), turned to allegorical essays that indirectly criticized the present by satirizing related phenomena from the imperial past. When the PRC government cracked down mercilessly on these political allegorists during the Cultural Revolution (1966–1976), some followed Teng T'o's lead and committed suicide, while others suffered incarceration or even torture for their political views.

Three decades of harsh political controls on essayists and other writers in the PRC began to slacken over the long term only after Mao's death in 1976. The major turning point in the PRC government's easing of its policies toward literature came with an announcement late in 1978 by the new paramount leader, Teng Hsiao-p'ing (1904–1997), that proclaimed a greater latitude for literary creation and less political interference by the Party. A similar if less dramatic liberalization had taken place under the Nationalists in Taiwan after the death of Chiang K'ai-shek (1887–1975). Under his son and successor, Chiang Ching-kuo (1910–1988), the Taiwan government released many dissident writers from jail, including the essayist Po Yang (1920–), and in 1987 finally rescinded the martial law decrees that had been in place for some four decades. It soon became routine for publishers in both the PRC and Taiwan to print collections incorporating essays written on both sides of the Taiwan Strait, as can be observed in the definitive two-volume anthology of the twentieth-century Chinese essay published in Shenyang, *Chin-wen kuan-chih* (Pinnacles of the Modern Essay; 1993).

FEATURES COMMON TO THE CHINESE VERNACULAR ESSAY

Chinese poets have often adopted different personae, and fiction writers have experimented with pointedly inadequate narrators, but in the twentieth-century Chinese essay the narrator is often identified with the author. Some of Lu Hsün's satirical essays make an initial feint in the direction of a self-contradictory or wrongheaded narration, but as the essay continues the author's own perspective and value judgments serve as a corrective to the initial confusion. For example, in his 1918 essay, "Wo chih chieh-lieh-kuan" (My Views on Chastity), he launches into a bare-bones argument in favor of traditional female chastity before quickly settling down to demolish it and present his conceptual alternative. In contrast, the narrator in some of Lu Hsün's fiction is somewhat untrustworthy and inadequate from beginning to end, as can be observed in the story "Chu fu" (Benediction).

The close connection between the author's voice and the narration of an essay often makes for greater intimacy between author and reader than is typically found in other genres. With good reason, readers assume that the essay recounts snippets of personal reflections, actual incidents, or dreams. Even if this subject matter is sketchily or casually recounted, it is assumed to have originally passed through the author's consciousness in an orderly progression quite similar to that in which the reader apprehends it. The twentieth-century essay writer thus has considerably less opportunity or inclination for contrivance and general tinkering with the original inspiration than is the case with literature operating under more formal constraints, such as poetry, fiction, and drama. Instead, the essay writer directly expresses a spontaneous impression of a given phenomenon, often in a more lyrical manner than in an exhaustively descriptive fashion.

Authors have often taken advantage of the intimacy the essay is liable to establish by revealing aspects of their sensibilities that might be obscured in their more formal writings. Lu Hsün repeatedly insisted that China lacks true humor (cf. chapter 7), and he preferred harshly pungent satire as its nearest equivalent in his fiction and *tsa-wen;* yet in the few essays he published in Lin Yü-t'ang's journals before his ideological denunciation of them, he wrote in as waggishly carefree a humorous style as any other informal essayist for these publications. Like Lu Hsün's stories, the fiction of Yeh Shao-chün (1894–1988) and Wu Tsu-hsiang (1908–1994) and the polemics of Ch'ü Ch'iu-pai greatly emphasize the burdens and bleakness of China's cultural inheritance. Yet a famous essay by Yeh Shao-chün pays a warm and personal tribute to Li Shu-t'ung (1880–1942), a contemporary Westernized esthete who forsook the world of art and music to become a Buddhist monk cloistered in a hermitage. Similarly, Wu Tsu-hsiang has nothing but praise for the traditionalistic way of life of the ancient canal port of Yangchow in a 1934 essay. Finally, many of Ch'ü Ch'iu-pai's last essays before his execution by the Nationalists manifest an unusual sensitivity to the modest and time-honored pleasures of a life at last detached from overt political struggle.

MAJOR GENRES OF THE TWENTIETH-CENTURY ESSAY

Chinese scholars of literary prose commonly make a broad distinction between expository essays with a didactic or persuasive dimension and lyrical essays bent on conveying a series of emotions or impressions to the reader. Rather than making this dichotomy absolute and insisting that every essay is either expository or lyrical, it is more useful to place the two functions of exposition and lyricism at opposite ends of a continuous spectrum. Relatively few essays could be situated exactly at one pole or the other of the spectrum, for essayists rarely eschew either exposition or lyricism in a given work. Most essays gravitate more closely to one pole than the other, while a few that are evenly divided between lyricism and exposition would be situated at the exact center of the spectrum.

Genres of the essay also tend to be more or less expository and more or less lyrical. Lying very close to the pole of exposition and persuasion is the *tsa-wen*, often associated with Lu Hsün. Near the other end of the spectrum are highly lyrical genres like the *huai-chiu* (wistful reverie on the past), as can be found in essays by writers including his brother Chou Tso-jen. The following discussion proceeds from the pole of exposition to the pole of lyricism in characterizing various key genres of the twentieth-century essay and providing an example of each. Although space limitations prevent the inclusion of every worthy twentieth-century essayist, all the essays mentioned below have been widely anthologized and discussed by scholars.

The imperative of persuasion comes forth from the very title of one of Lu Hsün's most famous *tsa-wen*, "Lun fei-o p'o-lai ying-kai huan-hsing" (Fair Play Should Be Deferred), published in 1926. Lu Hsün opens the essay with a brief summary of Lin Yü-t'ang's view that the spirit of fair play has seldom prevailed in China and thus should be encouraged. To buttress his argument for fair play, Lin Yü-t'ang had cited the proverb "Don't beat a dog that has just fallen into the water," using precisely the sort of appeal for mercy that Lu Hsün is most anxious to attack. Just as a dog saved from drowning might eventually turn around and bite the very hand that had saved it, human adversaries who are shown mercy may very well regroup once danger is past and turn against the very person who saved them. Arguing that a drowning dog should ordinarily be beaten soundly, Lu Hsün cites the example of a Chinese revolutionary leader who mercifully refrained from punishing some imperial army officers he had captured in 1911 and yet was later murdered by one of those very officers. Lu Hsün insists that Chinese society and folkways have not advanced to the point at which reformers can safely show their enemies mercy.

Unfortunately, Lu Hsün does not specify the conditions under which tolerance and mercy could eventually be shown to adversaries in political and intellectual life without incurring undue risks, for the core of his argument rests on the assumption that benevolent ends justify harsh means. Admittedly, Lu Hsün could not have known that, three decades after his death in 1936, his argument in favor of beating a drowning dog would be parroted endlessly during the Cultural Revolution to justify rampant brutal violence against a vast number of ordinary citizens and officials alike. Still, his cavalier defense of employing brute force to smash "enemies" lends itself to uses that are incompatible with a modern, liberal social order—and suggests that culturalist social critics may justifiably reach the conclusion that a certain nationality cannot be held to global norms of routinized legal conduct and fair play.

Expository *tsa-wen* essays embodying critical reflections on Chinese culture (*wen-hua fan-ssu*) achieved prominence again in the 1980s, engaging many writers on both sides of the Taiwan strait. Perhaps the most influential was Po Yang, a dissident writer in Taiwan whom Chiang Kai-shek's courts had imprisoned for eight years because of his outspoken political satire. Believing that cultures capable of trenchant self-criticism are also better at revitalizing themselves and adapting to change, Po Yang took his cue from works like *The Ugly American* and *The Ugly Japanese* and wrote a lecture and essay in 1984 entitled "Ch'ou-lou te Chung-kuo-jen" (The Ugly Chinaman [the actual title of the published English translation of this work]), which became the lead essay in a phenomenally controversial book of the same name. Having cataloged some of the negative characteristics he had observed in Taiwan—noisy speech, despoiled public spaces, bitter factionalism, and a shortage of analytical thinking—Po Yang traced these ills to what he saw as the stultifying conformity of thought that had been in place since Confucianism had been made the state orthodoxy twenty-two centuries earlier. For Po Yang, China's golden age had been the preceding era of the pre-Ch'in philosophers, when many schools of philosophy contended without any having achieved truly orthodox status.

Po Yang's historicist variety of cultural criticism differs substantially from Lu Hsün's essentialist variety, in which the earlier essayist repeatedly characterized Chinese culture as cannibalistic in its very essence. Po Yang is also less despondent about China's future than Lu Hsün, for he argues that the influx of Euro-American thought since the nineteenth century promises a possible return to the intellectual plenitude of the pre-Ch'in *pai-chia cheng-ming* (Hundred Schools of Thought Contending), a common characterization of the lively intellectual debates that took place among proponents of the various schools of thought that flourished during the Warring States period (c. 481–246 B.C.E.). Yet, in order for this to happen, according to Po Yang, Chinese need to reflect deeply on the darker side of the cultural inheritance that school textbooks tend to paint in such bright hues—and to develop better habits of critical thinking.

The *yu-chi* (travel essay) has a rich history of more than a millennium in China (see chapter 30), but in the twentieth century its descriptive and lyrical functions were increasingly complemented by social satire. A leading example of the twentieth-century satirical travelog is Wu Tsu-hsiang's *T'ai-shan feng-kuang* (Sights at Mount T'ai; 1935). Instead of describing the natural scenery or temple architecture on China's holiest of holy mountains, Wu Tsu-hsiang's largely autobiographical literatus narrator describes the visitors on religious pilgrimages and the various types of people they attract—mainly well-organized and prosperous beggar troupes, preachers, and peddlers. The visitors are mainly middle-class and lower-middle-class provincials who buy mostly kitsch as mementos of their pilgrimage—and make for a gullible audience around soapbox religious orators at the foot of mountain trails. Yet the narrator's major discovery is the contrast between the wealth of a clan of genteel beggars living in a spacious house on the mountain and the ragged and dusty appearance they make up for themselves before going out to beg for alms every evening. This family of beggars were petty bureaucrats of a sort, for some two centuries earlier the Ch'ien-lung emperor had officially licensed their family to enjoy the exclusive privilege of begging on Mount T'ai, and it had become an unbroken tradition. The narrator at first finds this more amusing than shocking, but he recoils with disgust when one of the beggars mistakes him for an ordinary pilgrim, grabbing his clothing tightly and demanding money. After finally extricating himself from the beggar's clutches, he resolves to observe the pilgrims from a greater distance in the future.

Twentieth-century Chinese writers themselves come under the unflattering light of satirical scrutiny in Ch'ien Chung-shu's "Lun wen-jen" (On Writers; 1941). This essayist is considerably more amused than taken aback by the folly he observes, and so he is closer to the pole of lyricism and emotional expression than to the pole of exposition and persuasion. The essayist's announced attempt to persuade the Chinese government to pay budding writers to abandon the writing profession is amusingly preposterous and suggests a generalized mockery of the solemn didactic tract so often encountered in wartime China, the *k'ang-chan pa-ku* (War of Resistance Eight-legged Essay [the traditional eight-legged essay was the rigidly structured standard civil service examination answer form prescribed from the mid-fifteenth century through the beginning of the twentieth century]). Ch'ien Chung-shu's rationale behind this Swiftian "modest proposal" actually seems quite sensible; since many contemporary Chinese writers feel very insecure about their role in society and tend to throw themselves into politics at any opportunity, they might as well act decisively and abandon literature for politics. In so doing, they will be literally following Shelley's romantic exhortation that poets serve as "the legislators of the world."

Satirical send-ups of the contemporary literary scene were much less common throughout the twentieth century than a type of essay focusing on an individual writer's candid reflections about the writing process itself, the *ch'uang-tso t'an* (discussion of fiction composition). Similar to the English-language *Writers At Work* series, collections of *ch'uang-tso t'an* have been popular for many decades among Chinese readers who want access to firsthand knowledge about the writing process, but who seldom find enough information about it in the articles and treatises of academic literary critics and theorists. The Shanghai writer Wang An-yi's (1954–) "Mien-tui tzu-chi" (Facing Oneself; 1986) argues that an increasing focus on struggles within the self in her writing does not cut her off from the broad societal developments occurring around her. In a seemingly paradoxical way, an intense focus on the self's development can enable a writer to communicate with a larger readership than she might reach if she focused on issues relating mainly to social groups. A vast number of readers are grappling with the problems of making the transition from adolescence to adulthood or from one stage of adulthood to another; these readers often turn to fiction or prose for a private perspective or sensibility that they can compare to their own. However, what Wang An-yi sees as the mainstream PRC literary emphasis on individuals within a group context often fails to provide a compelling enough rendering of any individual self to satisfy the reader groping for a better understanding of the self.

Pursuit of the endless complexities in human character often takes the form of the biographical sketch, such as Feng Tzu-k'ai's elegiac "Huai Li Shu-t'ung Hsien-sheng" (In Memory of Mr. Li Shu-t'ung; 1943). Li Shu-t'ung was an extremely versatile and multifaceted personality who helped found China's first spoken-drama acting troupe while a student in Japan (see chapter 42). After returning to his lower-Yangtze homeland, he excelled in many positions, including that of editor, painting teacher, and music instructor. It was in the last capacity that Feng Tzu-k'ai first met Li Shu-t'ung at a Hangchow academy where the elder scholar was teaching piano. In 1918, Li Shu-t'ung gave Feng and two other of his most conscientious students all his worldly possessions and became a Buddhist monk for the rest of his life. Li handled each of these potentially wrenching transitions in his life with such aplomb that Feng imagined the elder man quite capable of putting on a convincing performance of any traditional character type in Chinese opera. While Li Shu-t'ung could flexibly adapt to a strongly contrasting way of life practically overnight, he was nonetheless steadfast in maintaining a seriousness of purpose in whatever activity he was pursuing at a given time. Mild-mannered and yet serious in demeanor, immensely talented in several arts and yet unhesitant in casting them all aside to become a monk, Li Shu-t'ung emerges from Feng Tzu-k'ai's account as one of the truly eminent and yet enigmatic figures on the early-twentieth-century Chinese literary scene.

A more emotionally evocative biographical sketch with elegiac overtones is Chu Tzu-ch'ing's ubiquitously anthologized "Pei-ying" (With His Back Turned; 1925). The narrator's aging father is seeing off his grown son at a train station, and insists on clambering up the opposite platform to buy his son some fresh fruit to take along on the journey. The difficulty with which the old man strains to climb onto the platform vividly awakens the narrator to how vulnerable his formerly robust father has become, and makes the young man ashamed of his private thoughts of impatience with the excessive fuss his father has made over the son's journey. The narrator forges a strong memory of the image of a weakened old man burdened by financial and familial worries, yet still determined to bring back some fruit for his son's trip. When the father writes the narrator months later about his failing health and the inevitability of death, the narrator's tears once again begin to flow silently. This touching essay of almost pure lyricism completes the spectrum of representative essayists that began with Lu Hsün's expository piece.

Philip F. C. Williams

PART IV

Fiction

Chapter 33

T'ANG TALES

"T'ang tales" is the term often used to describe a genre known for almost a millennium as *ch'uan-ch'i* (transmissions of the strange or transmissions of strange stories). This term was first used for a collection of tales compiled by P'ei Hsing (fl. 865–875). It became a generic term during the Sung dynasty (960–1279) and is sometimes used today to refer generally to longer tales composed in the classical language. The major *ch'uan-ch'i*, however, were written during the T'ang dynasty (618–907) between the last decades of the seventh century and the final years of the ninth century—a period of about two hundred years. These stories mark the acme of classical-language fiction in traditional China. Many of the best tales were composed by the generation of writers who were active between 780 and 820, but a steady record of *ch'uan-ch'i* throughout these two centuries can be documented. Although there are precursors in the biographical writings of previous dynasties and works considered *ch'uan-ch'i* in both the Sung and Ming (1368–1644) eras, these narratives were closer to history in earlier periods and had lost the extended meanings of T'ang tales after the ninth century. (The usage of the term *ch'uan-ch'i* to refer to one of the main types of drama [see chapter 41] during the Ming and Ch'ing [1644–1911] periods is unrelated to its original application to a type of short fiction.)

Besides *ch'uan-ch'i*, three other types of short fiction written during the T'ang dynasty merit attention: (1) *chih-kuai* (records of anomalies), similar to those of the Six Dynasties (220–589) but often more lengthy and slightly more complicated in their plots; (2) *yi-shih* (anecdotes), which often depict private events of well-known figures; and (3) *yü-yen* (allegorical stories), a genre that became especially popular among adherents of the *ku-wen* (ancient prose) movement (see chapter 28).

Before the nature of T'ang tales is explored further, however, some background is needed. It is generally accepted that works like the *Shan hai ching* (Classic of Mountains and Seas) and *Mu t'ien-tzu chuan* (Travels of Emperor Mu) were related to the development of what could be called "early fiction" in China (see chapter 2). But these works, like the *chih-kuai* of the Six Dynasties, were fiction only in the eyes of later readers—fiction by value, not by intent. The actual source of T'ang tales is, rather, the biographical tradition in China (see chapter 27). This tradition includes early official histories, some of which were rife with stories that seem to have been selected from the popular tradition. Although not realistic writing, these stories often conveyed a psychological truth about their subject. They include anecdotal stories like those of Fan Shih and Chang Shao (recounted by Fan Yeh [398–446] in *Hou Han shu* [History of the Later Han Dynasty] and discussed in chapter 27) as well as stories with more complicated plots, like that of how Empress Lü disposed of her rival, Lady Ch'i, and the latter's son, Liu Ju-yi (recorded by Ssu-ma Ch'ien [c. 145–c. 86 B.C.E.] to open his "Basic Annals of Empress Dowager Lü" in the *Shih-chi* [Records of the Historian or The Grand Scribe's Records]).

Beyond these accounts in official histories, Han and Six Dynasties unofficial biographies (variously styled *chuan* [biographies, accounts, or traditions], *wai-chuan* [exoteric biographies], *nei-chuan* [esoteric biographies], or *pieh-chuan* [separate or distinct biographies]) influenced the structure and style of T'ang tales. These works included Taoist writings such as the anonymous *Han Wu-ti nei-chuan* (The Esoteric Biography of Emperor Han Wu-ti); Ko Hung's (283–343) *Shen-hsien chuan* (Biographies of Divine Transcendents); Buddhist biographies; the anonymous *Yen Tan Tzu* (Master Tan of Yen), which tells again how Prince Tan of Yen plotted to have Ching K'o assassinate the King of Ch'in and thereby preserve his own state); and *[Chao] Fei-yen wai-chuan* (The Unofficial Biography of [Chao] Fei-yen; attributed to Ling Hsüan [fl. 6–1 B.C.E.] of the Former Han), which recounts the machinations of the beautiful consort of Emperor Ch'eng (r. 32–7 B.C.E.). Two important precursor narratives were Huang-fu Mi's (215–282) *Kao-shih chuan* (Traditions of Lofty-Minded Scholars) and T'ao Ch'ien's (365–427) "T'ao-hua yüan chi" (Record of the Peach Blossom Spring). The former set the tone for those T'ang tales that praised the hermetic life. The latter was a model for the retelling of a verse narrative in story form, a technique adopted by several important T'ang *ch'uan-ch'i*.

The anecdotal type of T'ang tale evolved from works like the *Hsi-ching tsa-chi* (Miscellanies of the Western Capital), attributed to the Taoist recluse Ko Hung, and Liu Yi-ch'ing's (403–444) *Shih-shuo hsin-yü* (A New Account of Tales of the World). The T'ang *chih-kuai* was a descendant of stories collected by Kan Pao (fl. 320) in the *Sou-shen chi* (Search for the Supernatural;

see chapter 29). Many of these accounts are simple records of a man encountering a demon or ghost. Yet some, such as the narrative relating how Han P'ing's beautiful wife outwitted her captor after being stolen away by Han's lecherous lord, King K'ang of Sung, are accounts similar to *ch'uan-ch'i*, especially when the supernatural, often formulaic, frames of such stories are discounted. T'ang allegorical stories, sometimes called "pseudobiographies," evolved from works like T'ao Ch'ien's "Wu-liu hsien-sheng chuan" (Biography of Mr. Five Willows) and Juan Chi's (210–263) "Ta-jen Hsien-sheng chuan" (Biography of a Great Man).

The major collections of T'ang anecdotes include: *Ch'ao-yeh ch'ien-tsai* (A Complete Record of the Court and the Outlying Areas), by Chang Cho (657–730); *Sui T'ang chia-hua* (Fine Discourses from the Sui and T'ang), by Liu Su (fl. 740; son of the historiographer Liu Chih-chi [661–721]); *Feng-shih wen-chien chi* (A Record of What Mr. Feng Saw and Heard), by Feng Yen (fl. 750); *Ta T'ang hsin-hua* (New Accounts of the Grand T'ang), by Liu Su (fl. 807); *Liu Pin-k'o chia-hua lu* (A Record of the Fine Discourses by the Adviser to the Heir Apparent, Liu [Yü-hsi (772–842)]), by Wei Hsün (c. 802–after 860; son of Wei Chih-yi [d. 806], chief minister to Emperor Shun-tsung [r. 805]); *Yu-yang tsa-tsu* (Miscellaneous Delicacies from the South Slope of Mount Yu), by Tuan Ch'eng-shih (c. 803–863); *Ming-huang tsa-lu* (Miscellaneous Records of [Emperor] Ming-huang), by Cheng Ch'u-hui (fl. 850; grandson of Cheng Yü-ch'ing [746–820], chief minister under Emperor Te-tsung [r. 780–805]); *Pei-li chih* (Record of the Northern Wards), by Sun Ch'i (fl. 885); *K'ai T'ien ch'uan-hsin chi* (Record of Accounts of What Really Happened in the K'ai[-yüan] and T'ien[-pao] Eras), by Cheng Ch'i (d. 899); and *T'ang chih yen* (Picked-Up Tales of the T'ang), by Wang Ting-pao (870–940). The literary elements in these anecdotes are often minimal. A typical narrative is the story recorded in *Ch'ao-yeh ch'ien-tsai* in sixty Chinese characters about the beautiful concubine of P'ei Kuei, a Northern Chou court official. Warned by a fortuneteller in an intricate prognostication against giving rein to her desires, she dismissed his advice. Later, extramarital liaisons led P'ei Kuei to submit her to the imperial harem. Readers, no doubt, took most delight in the verbal skill and wit displayed in the fortuneteller's prophecy. Although most of the pieces in these collections are brief (one hundred to two hundred characters), and some (such as the account of how spinach was introduced from the West to China, in *Liu Pin-k'o chia-hua lu*) have virtually no literary qualities, others (like the story of the immortal "Chang Kuo" in *Ming-huang tsa-lu*) take on the dimensions and style of *ch'uan-ch'i*.

T'ang *chih-kuai* collections are also numerous, but the best known are Niu Seng-ju's (780–848) *Hsüan-kuai lu* (Accounts of the Mysterious and Anomalous) and Li Fu-yen's (c. 780–after 830) *Hsü Hsüan-kuai lu* (Sequel to Accounts of the Mysterious and Anomalous). Some of these accounts, such as "Hou Chiung," are brief and resemble Six Dynasties *chih-kuai*, but many, such as

"Kuo Yüan-chen," evince more evolved plots and might easily be considered *ch'uan-ch'i.*

Related to these records of anomalies are the Buddhist collections of miracle tales. Representative texts include T'ang Lin's (c. 600–c. 659) *Ming-pao chi* (Records of Miraculous Retributions) and Meng Hsien-chung's (fl. 712) *Chin-kang po-je ching chi-yen chi* (Collected Records of Diamond-Wisdom-Sutra Miracles). Although they share some narrative conventions with T'ang *ch'uan-ch'i*, these texts were intended to illustrate the basic tenets of Mahāyāna doctrine.

Taoist hagiographies, such as Tu Kuang-t'ing's (850–933) *Yung-ch'eng chi-hsien lu* (Register of the Transcendents Gathered at Yung-ch'eng), which collects stories of Taoist women, and Hu Hui-ch'ao's (d. 703) *Chin Hung-chou Hsi-shan shih-erh chen-chün chuan* (Traditions of the Twelve True Lords on Western Mountain in Hung-chou During the Chin Dynasty), which registers episodes in the lives of early Taoists), must have had a wide circulation in both written and oral form during the T'ang. "Wu Chen-chün" (True Lord Wu, in *Chin Hung-chou Hsi-shan shih-erh chen-chün chuan*) is typical of these hagiographies. It gives us a "life" of Wu Meng. As a young man he was noted for his filial treatment of his parents. Once grown he served in Nan-hai (Kwangtung province), mastering the Tao while there. He then used his powers to quell raging rivers and roaring winds. When he revived an official named Kan Ch'ing who had just died, the latter's brother, Kan Pao, was so moved by the event that he began to record the *Sou-shen chi.* Meng later mounted a jewel-bedecked carriage pulled by a white deer and disappeared. These "traditions" thus consisted primarily of traditional stories about an immortal, arranged in chronological order. Their plots are minimal and, although they were certainly known to the authors of the lay T'ang stories, probably had only a restricted influence on mainstream T'ang fiction.

This mainstream of T'ang tales is without doubt the *ch'uan-ch'i*, yet the extent of this corpus is sometimes difficult to determine, with longer *chih-kuai* resembling shorter *ch'uan-ch'i* (the average *ch'uan-ch'i* contained between fifteen hundred and two thousand Chinese characters). Wang Pi-chiang's 1929 anthology of more than seventy *ch'uan-ch'i* (called *T'ang-jen hsiao-shuo* [Fiction by T'ang Authors]) has helped somewhat in determining the parameters of the genre. The best-known works generally labeled *ch'uan-ch'i* include:

(1) "Ku-ching chi" (Record of an Ancient Mirror), a narrative that ties together several stories related to a magic mirror with the power to exorcise demons. Although the structure of each tale differs little from that of earlier *chih-kuai*, the attempt to construct a more lengthy text and the use of characters who were actual historical figures (Wang Tu [c. 584–c. 625] and his brother, the philosopher Wang Chi [590–644]) foreshadows later developments in the T'ang tale.

(2) "Pai-yüan chuan" (An Account of the White Monkey; also known as "Hsü Chiang-shih chuan") tells the story of the abduction of Ou-yang Ho's wife by

a huge white gibbon. Impregnated by the beast, she is finally rescued and gives birth to a son; this young man resembles a simian but eventually gains fame for his skill in literary arts. The story is generally considered to have been written as an attack on Ou-yang Ho's son, the famous calligrapher Ou-yang Hsün (557–641).

(3) "Yu-hsien k'u" (Grotto of Playful Transcendents), by Chang Cho (mentioned above as the author of the *Ch'ao-yeh ch'ien-tsai*) is unique in this corpus. The story recounts in a euphuistic parallel prose how a wanderer in an unfamiliar, remote setting comes across two unearthly beautiful women in a cavern dwelling. They entertain him through the night, offering witty comments, poems, and, finally, sexual favors. Perhaps because of the salacious banter bordering on the pornographic, the text was lost in China soon after its composition and was preserved only in Japan. The story is also distinguished by its style (a curious combination of highly colloquial language and sophisticated *p'ien-wen* [parallel prose]) and its length (at eight thousand Chinese characters the longest *ch'uan-ch'i*).

(4) Of several tales written by Chang Yüeh (667–731), "Lü-yi shih-che chuan" (An Account of the Green-Robed Deputy) is the most interesting. It depicts how a Ms. Liu, the wife of a wealthy young man (Yang Ch'ung-yi) living in the capital, and her lover, Li Yen, murder her husband after he comes home drunk one night. Taking care to avoid the scrutiny of servants, they hide the body in a well. A parrot in the courtyard witnesses the crime and reports them to the authorities. For his service, the parrot is formally titled "The Green-Robed Deputy."

(5) Ku K'uang's (c. 725–c. 814) "Yu-hsien chi" (A Record of Immortals) relates how, during the Ta-li era (766–779), Li T'ing and some friends lose their way in the mountains and discover an idyllic society living behind a waterfall. While departing, they chop down trees to mark the way, but later are unable to find the place again. This story is reminiscent of T'ao Ch'ien's "Record of the Peach Blossom Spring" and similar to a tale recorded by Wei Hsün in *Liu Pin-k'o chia-hua lu*.

(6) "Tu Hung-chien chuan" (An Account of Tu Hung-chien) was recorded about 755 by the anchoritic Hsiao Shih-ho. It traces the activities of Tu Hung-chien (709–769), who serves as chief minister under Emperor Tai-tsung (r. 766–799). After Tu suddenly dies one night, he is taken by two men to a huge pit in Mount Mang. There he meets various officials of the underworld who determine that an error has been made and he still has years to live. They also tell him that he is destined to attain a certain high position. He then retraces his steps to his home, gets into bed, and awakes, having been considered "deceased" for two days and three nights. He subsequently attains the very position promised him.

(7) Shen Chi-chi's (c. 740–c. 800) "Chen-chung chi" (Record of the World Within a Pillow, written in 781) is a more typical T'ang tale. It relates how a young man named Lu encounters a Taoist monk and, over wine, tells the monk of his dissatisfaction with life as a farmer. The monk tries to convince him that

he has an ideal life, but the young man avers that he prefers military and political power and fame. When the monk begins to cook a pot of millet, Lu grows sleepy, and the monk lends him a pillow. This pillow leads Lu into a dream of the kind of life he had always longed for. Becoming a famous general and minister, he leads a successful family life. But eventually he grows old, becomes ill, and dies. He awakens to find the monk still cooking the pot of millet, but he is enlightened from the dream experience, no longer craving the lifestyle of the high and mighty.

(8) A second tale written by Shen Chi-chi in 781, "Jen-shih chuan" (The Story of Miss Jen), tells of a certain young stalwart named Cheng who falls in love with a fox-fairy named Jen. Cheng has achieved little previously but now prospers under the guidance of his paramour. Ms. Jen remains loyal to Cheng, despite the advances of Wei Yin, Cheng's cousin and a relative of the T'ang royal family. The story ends with Ms. Jen following Cheng to a position she has helped him secure, despite her foreknowledge that she would put herself in great danger if she traveled westward. Along the way they encounter a hunting party with dogs. Jen panics, turns back into a fox, and is killed.

(9) "Li-hun chi" (Record of the Disembodied Soul), by Ch'en Hsüan-yu (fl. 770), is a love story. Wang Chou grows up in the same town as his cousin, Chang Ch'ien-niang; although not formally betrothed, the couple hopes to marry. When her father promises Ch'ien-niang to a colleague, Wang is angered and leaves for the capital. Before he has gone far, Ch'ien-niang catches up with him and the two elope to Shu (modern-day Szechwan). After five years there, Ch'ien-niang asks to go home to see her parents and the couple travel to her hometown together. Upon arriving, Wang Chou is told that Ch'ien-niang has been ill in bed since Wang left five years earlier. Eventually the two manifestations of Ch'ien-niang meet each other and their bodies meld together. The couple live together for another forty years in happiness.

(10) "Liu-shih chuan" (An Account of Ms. Liu), by Hsü Yao-tso (fl. 790–820), tells the story of an actual poet, Han Yi (c. 725–c. 780), and his much-troubled love affair with a consort named Liu. After a friend gives Ms. Liu to Han, they live happily for a few years. When Han returns home to visit his parents, however, the capital is overrun by rebels. Eventually Ms. Liu is taken into the household of a loyalist general. Han Yi is desperate to get her back. He meets a stalwart named Hsü Chün who is able to help Ms. Liu escape the general and return to Han Yi. The case is then referred to the emperor, who orders that Ms. Liu become Han Yi's concubine and the general be given a cash settlement.

(11) "Liu Yi" (Liu Yi; also known as "Tung-t'ing ling-yin chuan" [An Account of the Auspicious Marriage at Tung-t'ing]), by Li Ch'ao-wei (fl. 790), is one of the longer tales (4,000 characters). It tells of a man from the Hsiang River region in modern-day Hunan province named Liu Yi. Having failed the examinations in the late 670s, he is on his way to visit a man from his home area, then

sojourning near the capital. En route he chances to meet a beautiful girl tending sheep. The girl explains that she is the daughter of the Dragon King who lives in Lake Tung-t'ing near Liu's home. Having been abandoned by her husband, she asks Liu to inform her father of her plight and gives him instructions on how to reach the king's palace in the depths of the lake. Liu Yi follows her instructions and meets both the king and the girl's elder brother, a ferocious dragon in charge of the flood tide at Ch'ien-t'ang (modern-day Hangchow in Chekiang province). The dragons entertain Liu lavishly and send him back to the world of mortals with many treasures, allowing him to live a comfortable life. He marries twice, but both of his wives pass away soon afterward. Finally, he marries a mysterious woman from a good family who turns out to be the Dragon King's daughter. They live for several generations in the south. About 740 Liu Yi receives his cousin Hsüeh Ku, then traveling in the south. When Hsüeh comments on Liu's youthful appearance, Liu tells him the entire story. Although stories concerning supernatural realms existed early in China, the idea of dragon-kings and dragon-women was one introduced from India (where they were called *nāgas*) through Buddhism during the Six Dynasties.

(12) "Huo Hsiao-yü chuan" (An Account of Huo Hsiao-yü), by Chiang Fang (fl. 820), has a familiar opening. A young and talented scholar in the capital, Ch'ang-an, to take the examination—here the famous poet Li Yi (748–829) plays this role—meets a lovely, loyal courtesan, Huo Hsiao-yü, through the efforts of a procuress. After an elaborately described first encounter of elegant feasting, drinking, and repartee—the lavish entertainment and sublimity of feminine beauty in these tales always aimed at levels depicted in "Cavern of the Immortals"—the two fall helplessly in love. Li Yi pledges his eternal fidelity. However, after passing the examinations, Li is sent to a post outside the capital. Then, because his parents have arranged a marriage for him with a girl from a wealthy family, he is called upon to travel about to raise funds for the marriage from various relatives. As a result, he is unable to return to Ch'ang-an and Hsiao-yü by the date promised. Hsiao-yü is first lovesick, then physically ill. Li Yi finally returns to the capital but cannot bring himself to see Hsiao-yü. Finally he is tricked into going to her house, and they have a final meal together before Hsiao-yü collapses and dies. Li later marries, but his relations with his wife, whom he soon divorces, and all subsequent lovers are marred by an unreasonable jealousy.

(13) "Nan-k'o t'ai-shou chuan" (The Story of the Prefect of South Branch), by Li Kung-tso (c. 770–c. 848), is often compared to Shen Chi-chi's "Chen-chung chi." The main character is Ch'un-yü Fen, a military man with a checkered past and a fondness for wine. One day in 791 he is drinking with two friends and passes out beneath a large locust tree near his house. Ch'un-yü Fen then seems to wake up and see two messengers arrive. They take him back to the king of the State of Locust Tranquility. His carriage descends into a hole at the roots of the locust tree, where he finds a world not unlike that of T'ang

China. Fen is married to the king's beautiful daughter and given many honors; finally he is asked to govern an important border region. After initial successes, what seemed an ideal life begins to fall apart. Disgrace in battle is followed by the death of his wife. Finally, the king asks him to return to his home. When he is back in his own bed, he awakes as if from a dream. Then, along with his two friends, he discerns that the many events of his recent life actually transpired in the "kingdom" of an ant colony under the locust tree. Thus enlightened, he tempers himself in a study of the Tao until he dies three years later. Some descriptions of the splendor of the ant kingdom show the influence of the enumerations typical in the *fu* (rhapsody), a genre that these authors knew well since it was required for the examinations.

(14) "Li Wa chuan" (An Account of Li Wa), by Po Hsing-chien (775–826, brother of the famous poet Po Chü-yi), is another of the talented-scholar-meets-courtesan tales: the scholar here remains unnamed and the courtesan is Li Wa. After a formulaic initial meeting, the love affair develops until the young man's money is exhausted. Li Wa's manager, an old woman, then moves Li Wa to an unknown location, in part because Li has fallen in love with the young scholar. The young man is forced to take a job singing at funerals. His father discovers him in that guise and beats him so badly that he almost dies. By chance Li Wa finds him in this state and nurses him back to health. She buys her way out of the profession and strictly supervises his study. Three years later he passes the examination with honors and is appointed to office. His position secured, he wins reconciliation with his family and formally marries Li Wa. His successful career is matched by the honor Li Wa receives when she is named Lady of Ch'ien. The tale is noteworthy for its realistic portrayal of the young man's problems after he is destitute and of the difficulty his family has in accepting his actions.

(15) "'Ch'ang-hen ko' chuan" (An Account of the Story of the "Song of Everlasting Regret"), by Ch'en Hung, tells the tragic love story of Emperor Hsüan-tsung (r. 712–756) and Yang Kuei-fei. The couple lives happily for years, but after An Lu-shan's (703–757) revolt in 755, Yang Kuei-fei is blamed for distracting the emperor. Loyal troops demand her death as the imperial retinue flees the capital for Szechwan, and she is forced to take her own life at Ma-wei (in Shensi). The second part of the story is devoted to the efforts—ultimately successful—by a Taoist priest to contact Lady Yang in the afterworld. Thus this narrative combines the motifs of the scholar-beauty tale with those of the immortal goddess. It is also distinctive because it was written as an introduction to a long narrative poem entitled "Ch'ang-hen ko" (Song of Everlasting Regret), by Po Chü-yi (772–846).

(16) "Ying-ying chuan" (Story of Ying-ying), by Yüan Chen (779–831), is yet another scholar-beauty tale. The protagonist, an antihero to readers, is identified only by his surname, Chang. While visiting in P'u-chou he meets a distant relative, Madame Ts'ui, and finds protection for her during a local revolt. To

repay Chang's kindness, Madame Ts'ui invites him to a feast; there he meets her son and daughter. The daughter, Ying-ying, captivates him with her beauty. After several unsuccessful attempts to visit Ying-ying by night, Chang enlists the help of Ying-ying's maid, Hung-niang, and is finally able to seduce Ying-ying. After a month of secret trysts, Chang returns to Ch'ang-an to take the examinations. He fails in his attempt but remains in the capital, writing a letter to Ying-ying to reassure her of his feelings. However, Chang eventually decides that a beauty like Ying-ying's is dangerous if not wicked and determines to abandon her. Both lovers find other mates and within a year are married to them. Chang then tries to visit Ying-ying and her new husband as "a distant relative," but Ying-ying rebuffs him. The story contains several poems and is known for its elegant style. Many readers have seen the young scholar Chang as a transparent persona for the author, Yüan Chen, a close friend of Po Chü-yi, and read this tale autobiographically. "Ying-ying chuan" is the basis for the prosimetric "Hsi-hsiang chi chu-kung-tiao" (Medley of the "Romance of the Western Chamber"), written by Tung Chieh-yüan (Master Tung; active c. 1190–1208) around the turn of the twelfth century, and for the masterpiece of Yüan drama entitled "Hsi-hsiang chi" (Romance of the Western Chamber), attributed to Wang Shih-fu (c. 1250–1300) (see chapter 41).

(17) "Wu-shuang chuan" (An Account of Peerless), by Hsüeh T'iao (830–872), relates a familiar story. Hsüeh employs two actual figures from history as his main characters—Liu Wu-shuang and Wang Hsien-k'o. Although they did not know each other in real life, in the tale they are cousins who grow up together and hope to marry. The two are separated when violence breaks out in the capital in 783 (connected with the rebellion of Chu Tz'u [742–784]). Wu-shuang's parents are executed for serving the rebels and she is taken into the royal harem. When Wang discovers this, he puts all his hope in a knight-errant named Ku. Wang cultivates Ku's friendship in a fashion that closely resembles Prince Tan of Yen's treatment of Ching K'o as he prepares to send the assassin on a mission against the First Emperor of the Ch'in dynasty. Eventually, Ku is able to smuggle a drug to Wu-shuang that lends her the pallor and appearance of death. When she is returned to her relatives for burial, Ku intercepts the body and reunites the couple. Wang and Wu-shuang flee Ch'ang-an and, under new identities, live a long and happy life together.

(18) "Ch'iu-jan-k'o chuan" (An Account of the Curly-Bearded Stranger), by Tu Kuang-t'ing, a well-known Taoist author, centers on the founding of the T'ang dynasty. The main characters are a youthful Li Ching (571–649), who later becomes a general and helps found the T'ang dynasty, a singing girl named Chang, who runs off from the household of a powerful Sui official to follow Li Ching, and a curly-bearded stranger they meet while fleeing to Taiyuan. After gruffly sharing a meal with the couple, the curly-bearded man asks them to help him get a look at Li Shih-min, then a military leader in Taiyuan but later Emperor T'ai-tsung (r. 626–649). Li Ching arranges this and, after the stranger

has seen him, he tells Li Ching that Shih-min is certain to become emperor. The stranger then invites the couple to his home in the capital. When they arrive, they find the stranger attired regally, attended by a beautiful wife, and in possession of a palatial mansion. He confesses that he had hoped to conquer the empire, but realized when he saw Li Shih-min that destiny would thwart him. He strikes out for the south, leaving all his wealth and possessions to the young couple. Years later, when Li Ching has become a high official, he learns that a southern kingdom has been overthrown and suspects that this is the work of the curly-bearded stranger. The story ends with a moral: states are conquered by means of destiny, not heroic action.

(19) "Ch'i T'ui nü" (Ch'i T'ui's Daughter), by Niu Seng-ju, is a supernatural tale that begins with the death of the daughter of a provincial governor, Ch'i T'ui (fl. 812), at the hands of an evil spirit. Her husband hurries back from the capital and encounters her ghost. Encouraged to redress the wrong done her, he appeals to an old man, who is actually a deity. The evil spirit is punished and her souls molded into a human body (since her original form had decayed by this time), allowing her to live out her allotted span of years.

(20) "Ting-hun tien" (The Inn of Betrothral), by Li Fu-yen, tells of Wei Ku, an orphan, who was unable to find a wife. In 821 while traveling he stops at an inn. Someone there suggests the daughter of an official in the town to which he is going as a possible match. Excited by the prospect, Wei rises early the next day and sets out. He soon encounters an old man reading a strange book. Engaging the man in conversation, Wei learns that it is a book of the netherworld in which all the earthly marriage contracts are recorded. From the book and with the old man's help, Wei finds that his future wife is a child in the care of a peasant woman who lives nearby. Enraged, Wei sends his servant to kill the girl. The servant is only able to stab the girl between the eyes before they flee. For years Wei continues to search for a wife. Finally he finds a provincial position and is offered the governor's daughter in marriage. The girl turns out to be the very one he had ordered killed fourteen years earlier, as proved by the slight scar between her eyes.

(21) "Tu Tzu ch'un," by Li Fu-yen, is a tale out of time, identifying the main character, Tu Tzu-ch'un, only as "a man who probably lived under the Northern Chou and Sui dynasties" (557–618). This matches the allegorical mode of the story. Tu is a young man who squanders the family fortune. Destitute, he encounters a Taoist immortal in the form of an old man who twice gives him large sums of cash to no avail. Tu ends up penniless. He uses a third grant for good works. In reward, the Taoist tries to help him gain immortal status. To do so, he must silently run a gamut of imaginary scenes in which Tu's relatives appear to be tortured. Tu utters not a sound until he observes a man killing his own children, then cries out "No!" With this exclamation he is condemned to a mortal existence as a man incapable of divesting himself of the feelings of love. This tale has an Indian source, which is recorded in *Hsi-yü chi* (Records

of the Western Regions) by the famous pilgrim Hsüan-tsang (c. 600–664). In keeping with their name, many *ch'uan-ch'i* have exotic or alien motifs (e.g., Persians rich as Croesus), reflecting the cosmopolitanism of the T'ang dynasty that may also be vividly seen in the tricolor (*san-ts'ai*) mortuary figurines of the same period.

(22) "Pu Fei-yen" (Pu Fei-yen), by Huang-fu Mei (fl. 910), recounts the tragic story of Pu Fei-yen, the favorite concubine of Wu Kung-yeh, a minor official in the 870s. Wu's neighbor, a young man named Chao Hsiang, is struck by Fei-yen's beauty and initiates an affair with her. When Wu Kung-yeh learns of it, he beats Fei-yen severely and she dies. The story is distinguished by the poems exchanged by the young lovers. In the coda, couplets on the tragedy by two of Wu's companions are cited. Fei-yen's ghost is said to have appeared to both men, thanking the former and cursing the latter, who dies shortly thereafter.

(23) "Hung-hsien" (Hung-hsien), by Yüan Chiao (fl. 860–870), tells of the remarkable young woman Hung-hsien (Red Thread) in the service of Hsüeh Sung (d. 772). In the story, as in history, Hsüeh was a powerful general. Ostensibly a maid, Hung-hsien was well read and talented, so Hsüeh made her his personal secretary. The story hinges on the actual military situation of the eastern region of the T'ang empire in the decade following the An Lu-shan rebellion (755–757/763). At this time the three most important figures in the region were Hsüeh, T'ien Ch'eng-ssu (705–779), and Ling-hu Chang. T'ien eventually decides to build up his forces and overrun Hsüeh's territory. When Hung-hsien learns of this, she uses magical powers to transport herself into T'ien's camp, creeps into his tent, and steals a golden box he keeps under his pillow. When Hsüeh has the box returned to T'ien the following day, T'ien realizes that Hsüeh is served by a potential assassin who could elude even his best guards. Thus he gives up the idea of attacking Hsüeh. When questioned about how she had accomplished the theft, Hung-hsien explains to Hsüeh that she had been a doctor in a former life but accidentally poisoned a patient. As punishment, she was reincarnated as a woman, albeit one with extraordinary powers of stealth. Having prevented further fighting, she hopes to devote herself to cultivating the life of an immortal and attempts to become a man again. Hsüeh gives her a farewell feast and she departs, never to be seen again.

(24) "K'un-lun nu" (The K'un-lun Slave), by P'ei Hsing, tells of a young man named Ts'ui who was the son of an official during the Ta-li period. When, at his father's behest, he goes to look in on "the most eminent minister of the court" (a probable reference to Liu Yen [d. 780]), who is ailing, the minister has three beautiful singing girls attend Ts'ui. As Ts'ui is leaving, one of them subtly signals him with her hands. Ts'ui returns home infatuated with the girl but unable to decipher her gestures. An indentured Negrito family slave named Moleh (Mo-le)—who, like many others of his kind, came from Malaya—is adept at sign language, perhaps because he is not fluent in Chinese. Moleh understands the signals to mean that the girl wants to meet Ts'ui in her cham-

bers the following night. The next night, with Ts'ui on his back, Moleh leaps over several walls with ease, bringing the lovers together. The girl explains that she comes from a good family that has fallen on hard times. Her parents entrusted her to the minister as a ward, but he forced her to serve as a singing girl. Moleh takes the pair on his back and sails over the walls again. The next day, the minister, convinced that his house has been visited by a supernatural being, hushes up the matter. Ts'ui and the girl marry and remain in hiding for several years. Then one of the minister's servants chances to see them. The minister, on learning the whole story, decides to leave the couple alone but to have Moleh killed. He surrounds Ts'ui's house with soldiers, only to see Moleh vault the wall and escape. A decade later Moleh is seen selling herbs at a market in Loyang; he seems not to have aged at all.

(25) "Li Ch'ih chuan" (An Account of "Red" Li), by the renowned poet and essayist Liu Tsung-yüan (773–819), relates how a young traveling literatus named Li Ch'ih is seduced by a privy spirit. Under her influence, he comes to believe that the world inside the privy is idyllic and eventually drowns himself in an outhouse. Liu Tsung-yüan appends a comment in which he argues that Li should not be ridiculed, because most men of the day would easily be deluded by desire or profit. The work is often read as an allegorical attack on Liu's former patron, Wang Shu-wen (d. 805), the head of the faction that exerted strong influence at court in the first years of the ninth century.

All the major authors of *ch'uan-ch'i* but one—Shen Ya-chih (781–832)—are mentioned in the above summary. The remaining author and his career illustrate how these authors created a new genre. In 809, on his way from the southeast to the capital, Shen stopped at a monastery in Hangchow and inquired about the history of a statue of the Buddha that was being moved. He then recorded the story that the monks told him as "Yi Fo chi" (Record of Moving the Buddha). Throughout the rest of his life, Shen would remain interested in listening to and recording stories.

Six years later, in 815, Shen joined the staff of Li Hui (c. 755–c. 820). During the summer Li Hui entertained a group of his subordinates with a story about Hsing Feng. Although Li claimed that Hsing was a former commander and had told him this tale, there are no other records of Hsing. Hsing said that in a dream he had met a beautiful woman who exchanged poems with him. She then danced for him and disappeared. When he awoke and changed his clothes, he found copies of the poems stuck in one of his sleeves. The next day another guest told a similar story. The party agreed that these tales should be written down, so Shen fashioned them into an account of their storytelling. He titled it "Yi-meng lu" (Account of Dreams of the Extraordinary).

A few months later Shen was in Loyang. He stayed with a man named Fang Shu-pao, an acquaintance of his friend Nan Cho (791?–854). While there, he recorded the story of how Fang's concubine had persuaded Fang to give up drinking in favor of study. Shortly thereafter, Shen left Loyang and passed through P'eng-ch'eng (modern-day Hsü-chou in Kiangsu province), visiting an old friend, Ts'ui Chü. Ts'ui had a concubine named Yeh who was a talented singer. Shen had heard her perform a few years earlier. When he asked about her on this visit, he discovered she had just died. Shen believed that an account of her talent should be left for posterity and depicted events from her life in "Ko-che Yeh chi" (Record of the Singer Yeh). The piece is particularly interesting, first, because it uses a traditional story about the ancient singer Ch'in Ch'ing to introduce the account of Ms. Yeh, a technique not unlike the *ju-hua* ("entering words," i.e., prolog story) in the *hua-pen* short stories of later dynasties (see chapter 34) and, second, because the depiction of Yeh's life is cast in language very similar to that of *ch'uan-ch'i* tales.

In 818 he learned from friends of a story told in a *yüeh-fu* (ballad) poem written by Wei Ao. It involved the love affair between a "dragon-lady" and a young scholar (and has been compared to "Liu Yi chuan"). Shen titled it "Hsiang-chung yüan chieh" (An Explanation of the Laments Written in Hsiang) and claimed that he composed his piece to match "Yen-chung chih chih" (A Record of What Happened Midst the Smoke) by his friend Nan Cho.

Yet another story, "Feng Yen chuan" (An Account of Feng Yen), came as the result of a trip east from the capital that Shen made with friends in 819. He revisited Hua-chou (having been there five years earlier) and recorded an account he heard from Liu Yüan-ting (*chin-shih* 789) about a knight-errant named Feng Yen. Feng had served the noted scholar and chief minister Chia Tan (730–805) when the latter was military governor of the area from 786 to 793; he was carrying on an affair with the garrison commander's wife. One day the commander came home from a drinking bout and surprised the adulterous couple. Feng hid behind a door and, when the husband passed out, his wife made signs indicating that Feng should kill him. Feng was outraged by her suggestion and killed her instead, then fled. When he learned that the husband had been charged with the murder, he turned himself in. Chia Tan oversaw the case and petitioned the emperor to pardon Feng. A proclamation was issued granting amnesty to all who had received the death penalty in Hua-chou (located 55 miles north-northwest of Kaifeng in modern-day Honan province). At the end of the story Shen Ya-chih added a personal "historian's comment," imitating the doyen of Chinese historians, Ssu-ma Ch'ien, in which he praised Feng for his righteousness. These events may well have actually happened, but, in his adaptation of the story to create a moral tale, Shen reveals a growing confidence in his narrative skills. The tale may also have been written to flatter a relative or associate of Chia Tan—Li Hui, Shen's commander a few years earlier, had served on Chia's staff—and thereby establish another possible connection for Shen in his search for a position.

Sometime during a sojourn in the southeast (824–826), Shen probably wrote two other "stories." The first, entitled "Hsi-tzu chuan" (Biography of Hsi-tzu), recounts how Hsi-tzu, a concubine of a merchant named Liu Ch'eng, resisted the advances of Liu's neighbor, a Master Wei. This situation had come about after Wei asked for passage on Liu's boat as the merchant was sailing north on a business trip. Caught with contraband on the boat, Liu was arrested. Wei bribed a stranger to tell Hsi-tzu that Liu was to be executed. Then Wei tried to seduce her. But Hsi-tzu resisted and tried to drown herself. She was saved by a passerby, and Liu was finally released. The story is set in 809 and was told to Shen by a Master Ch'eng. Shen wrote it down because he was impressed with Hsi-tzu's upright behavior. This conventional plot recalls other similar stories in Chinese literature but may here have been superimposed upon an actual situation.

The second story, "Piao yi-che Kuo Ch'ang" (In Praise of the Medical Practitioner Kuo Ch'ang), tells of a physician who lived in Jao-chou (near modern-day Po-yang in Kiangsi province). Kuo was so skilled that many foreigners trading in south China sought his advice. Once a merchant was seriously ill and could find no one who knew how to treat his illness. He offered Kuo a huge sum of money if he could save his life. Kuo cured the man but then refused to accept the money because he thought that the man would have a relapse and die if he gave up so much money. This kind of idealized biography with a comment appended—much like an official biography—was probably intended as a means of moral suasion. It finds antecedents in works like Liu Tsung-yüan's "Sung Ch'ing chuan" (Biography of [the Druggist] Sung Ch'ing).

In 827 Shen wrote "Ch'in meng chi" (Record of a Dream of Ch'in), in which he records a dream he claims to have had upon setting out for Pin-chou (modern-day Pin county, Shensi, 65 miles northwest of Sian). Stopping at an inn not far from the capital on the first night, Shen dreamed he awoke in the state of Ch'in during the reign of Duke Mu (r. 659–621 B.C.E.). Favored by the duke, Shen marries his daughter and is truly living a dream life. A year later, however, his wife dies and he decides to return to his own country. After an elaborate description (complete with poems) of the farewell festivities, Shen is accompanied to the Han-ku Pass (in western Honan province), but he wakes up before he can formally take his leave. When Shen and his friend Ts'ui Chiu-wan set out from the inn the next day, he tells Ts'ui about his dream. Ts'ui interprets it by pointing out that the inn where they had stayed was very near the place where Duke Mu was buried more than a millennium earlier. This plot is also familiar—it resembles Li Kung-tso's "Story of the Prefect of South Branch" and Shen Chi-chi's "Record of the World Within a Pillow."

What should interest the modern reader is the variety of narrative in Shen's corpus and the development of his narrative art that can be seen in his tales. Shen began by reporting simple stories like his "Record of Moving the Buddha" (809), next adapted narratives in other genres like "An Explanation of the Laments Written in Hsiang" (from a *yüeh-fu*; 817), was then asked to record stories such as "Account of Dreams of the Extraordinary" (815), adapted popular tales like the "Account of Feng Yen" (819) to didactic purposes, and finally exercised his own unconscious or conscious creativity in works like "Account of a Dream of Ch'in" (827). He also wrote allegories such as "Yi-niao lu" (Account of the Bird of Propriety; undated) which show the influence of the ancient-prose movement. Shen's narrative corpus reflects closely what other T'ang tale writers attempted. He showed interest in all sorts of stories and invested varying amounts of his own talent in recasting them for his own purpose. He wrote of real people or of imaginary events with obvious ties to real people. Thus his career also supports the contention of modern scholars that T'ang tales were the first "consciously created fiction," as well as the traditional reading of *ch'uan-ch'i* as texts that often had extended political meanings. "An Account of Feng Yen" is an ideal example. Although the skillful signals that led to the death of Feng's paramour are probably Shen's own creation, the praise for the actions of Chia Tan seem certain to be an attempt to influence Chia's successors in the government. It has been shown that T'ang tales were not part of the *wen-chüan* (warmup [i.e., practice] scrolls) sent to potential patrons (those normally contained only poetry). Nevertheless, these narratives were circulated with the intention of winning friends and influencing people, as "Feng Yen chuan" illustrates. Since the authors were primarily young men—often aspiring historians—seeking a career, it is not surprising that their writing was narrative centered and politically inspired. Moreover, since these young authors understood the scope of their own potential network of connections, it is understandable that they intended to strengthen them with tales that praised an ally or mentor, jibed a rival or opponent.

This kind of extended meaning can be found in both types of *ch'uan-ch'i*. The first type featured real characters in what were fictionalized or stylized narratives. As noted above, real characters figure in twelve of the twenty-five representative *ch'uan-ch'i* summarized above (these characters figure in the plot itself, not merely in the accounts of how the author learned the story), and two others ("An Account of Ying-ying" and "The K'un-lun Slave") strongly suggest that they were written about a historical figure. These texts were intended not only to entertain but to send an extended topical message. "An Account of Huo Hsiao-yü" is typical. Here the intention is to reveal Li Yi as a disreputable rake. The contamination could also extend to associates of Li Yi. "An Account of Tu Hung-chien" is similar. Although this tale is ostensibly merely a record of a supernatural occurrence in Tu's life, it would have been as impossible to write an "innocent" account of a figure like Tu Hung-chien, who served as chief minister at about the time this story was written, as it would be to portray neutrally one of the Kennedy family in a late-twentieth-century American novel.

The second type of *ch'uan-ch'i* employed an unidentified or fictional character. This affords the author the flexibility for general allegorical reference or, in the case of a topical reference, serves to protect him. "An Account of Li Wa," which has been read as an attack on the Cheng clan of Ying-yang, is an example of this type of tale, as is "The Story of the Prefect of South Branch." This second example is read not only as a philosophical statement on the vanity of striving for happiness through material means, but also as an indirect attack—through the ease with which the king of the State of Locust Tranquility grants his daughter to Ch'un-yü Fen—on the policy in the late eighth century of using imperial princesses to placate and control provincial military satraps.

Finally, although attempts are made to trace the evolution of the tale through the T'ang period, it is difficult to distinguish some works in the mid-seventh century from some in the mid-ninth. There seem to have been two important eras in this evolution. The first was the seventh century, when so many official histories were compiled from drafts left by Six Dynasties historians. This effort culminated (not surprisingly) in one of the great works of Chinese historiography, Liu Chih-chi's *Shih t'ung* (An Understanding of History). This text not only made clear for the historians what good history *was* but also suggested for those who might want to bend the rules of historical narrative how a good story *might be created.*

The second was the late eighth century, when the iconoclastic call for a return to antiquity from members of the *fu-ku* (revive antiquity) movement (see chapter 28) brought into question the scholarship of intervening eras and eventually revived classical allegory in works like Han Yü's (768–824) "Mao Ying chuan" (Biography of Mao Ying), the "biography" of a writing brush, and Liu Tsung-yüan's "Ho-chien chuan" (An Account of Ho-chien), which attacked the amoral minister Wang Shu-wen, who ruined Liu's career through the persona of a chaste widow turned nymphomaniac.

The best tales, all dating from 780 to 820, combined the artistic and the politic. They are distinguished by their refined style (influenced by the currency of the ancient-prose movement), elaborate plots, and powerful characters. Although the plots may have been stories familiar to both literati and the common people, the authors of works like "An Account of Li Wa" had the ability to enliven them with a dialog in the literary language that somehow seemed realistic. These writers first told one another their stories orally, then vied to record the most effective written versions. On more occasions than not, they added an element to their tale that would praise a friend or ally, condemn an enemy or antagonist. If they are read in the spirit in which they were written, these tales become not only the best works of fiction in the classical language but also narrative rivals for the rich and complex heritage of T'ang poetry (see chapter 14).

William H. Nienhauser, Jr.

Chapter 34

VERNACULAR STORIES

The vernacular story (hereafter "story" or "stories"), or *hua-pen* (sometimes *tz'u-hua* or *hsiao-shuo*), refers to a short story from the Sung (960–1279) to the Ch'ing (1644–1911) dynasties that is written in the vernacular. Unlike the classical Chinese tale (see chapters 33 and 37), the story is written primarily in colloquial language occasionally mixed with simple classical language. Shorter than the novel and with a simpler and unitary plot, the story was not issued separately; it has neither preface nor table of contents.

ORIGINS AND INFLUENCES

Like the vernacular novel, the story has its origins in the professional storytelling of the Sung and Yüan (1260–1368) periods, especially in the Northern and Southern Sung capitals, Kaifeng and Hangchow. *Hua-pen,* however, were not storytellers' scripts or promptbooks, as was formerly assumed. While writers imitated some of the stories popular in storytelling, storytellers also imitated popular written stories.

This interaction between the story and other literary genres, and the influences of one on the other, has a long tradition. The story was influenced by classical tales, miscellaneous notes (*pi-chi;* see chapter 31) and anecdotes, drama, novels, and oral literature (e.g., the *pien-wen,* or "transformation text," of the T'ang [618–907] and Five Dynasties [907–960]; see chapter 48), and the *chu-kung-tiao,* a prosimetric form of storytelling (twelfth century; see chapter

49). In turn, many stories were adapted into plays, and the stories of the sixteenth and early seventeenth centuries influenced later classical tales, such as those written by P'u Sung-ling (1640–1715), the "tales of brilliant scholars and beautiful girls" (*ts'ai-tzu chia-jen*) popular in the second half of the seventeenth century, and later satiric novels and novels of manners.

STORY TYPES, PURPOSES, AND FORMAL CHARACTERISTICS

In his *Tsui-weng t'an-lu* (Notes of an Old Tippler), the thirteenth-century writer Lo Yeh classified *hsiao-shuo* ("stories" in the context of storytelling) into eight types: spirits and demons, love, marvels, court cases (*kung-an* [law suits]), sword fights, contests with cudgels, immortals, and sorcery. Although all these types continued to appear in written stories, romances as well as stories of folly and crime gradually became dominant. Many stories dealt with the lives of the middle to lower classes, focusing on down-to-earth concerns like the preservation of family and lineage and the pursuit of worldly success. Some, however, treated Taoist and Buddhist themes, emphasizing the emptiness of mundane glory as well as the pleasure of reclusion and transcendence. Satiric, comic, and even farcical, the stories were intended primarily to entertain but also to caution and admonish. Directed at a wider audience than fiction written in the classical language, these stories exerted considerable influence on Chinese culture and society.

Generally speaking, the stories were composed by the educated elite, employing the established storytelling conventions and imitating the models of professional oral fiction. Thus the stories preserve such oral features as the storyteller's stock phrases and interpolated passages in rhyme. The narrator simulates the storyteller addressing his audience, asking them questions, and sometimes engaging in dialog with them. A story normally has a prolog (in the form of a poem or a series of poems), a prose introduction, and a prolog story. The main story includes the narrator's comments, appearing at intervals in the form of either poetry or prose and offering explanation, evaluation, and prediction. The story ends with an epilog in the form of the narrator's final comment and a final poem.

These formal features underwent changes and modifications in the hands of later writers. Beginning in the seventeenth century, many variations appear in the narratorial stance. Li Yü's (1610/11–1680) narrator assumes the author's several personae. Ai-na chü-shih's (fl. 1668) primary narrator retreats into the background. By contrast, in the stories of Shih Ch'eng-chin (1659–c. 1736) and Tu Kang (b. 1740?), the individual author's personal voice and identity are very pronounced.

THE EARLY PERIOD: YÜAN AND EARLY MING

Because vernacular stories are so closely related to storytelling in the Sung period, scholars used to date many stories from this period. However, since there is neither reliable contemporary documentation nor dependable evidence to corroborate this dating, such theories have been discarded. The modern scholar Patrick Hanan has used stringent stylistic criteria to classify stories as dating from the early period (the Yüan and early Ming dynasties, up to 1450) or from the middle period (between 1400 and 1575, particularly from 1450 to 1550).

Thirty-four existing stories may have been written before about 1450, fourteen of which may date from the Yüan dynasty. These stories survive in the following anthologies: Hung P'ien's *Liu-shih chia hsiao-shuo* (Sixty Stories; also called *Ch'ing-p'ing-shan t'ang hua-pen* [Stories from the Clear and Peaceful Mountain Studio]; c. 1550; cited below as Hung); Feng Meng-lung's *Ku-chin hsiao-shuo* (Stories Old and New; also called *Yü-shih ming-yen* [Clear Words to Instruct the World]; 1620; cited below as KC); *Ching-shih t'ung-yen* (Common Words to Warn the World; 1624; cited below as TY); and *Hsing-shih heng-yen* (Constant Words to Awaken the World; 1627; cited below as HY).

The themes of these early stories include love, demons, ghosts, religion, crime, and fighting. The authors make their stories suspenseful in order to mystify, shock, and entertain the reader. They do not moralize through comments, nor do they put the stories in the context of karmic retribution, as later writers are wont to do.

The love stories are either romances between a talented man and a highly educated courtesan or romantic comedies in which a man of brilliant genius eventually marries a beautiful maiden also of the literati class. In the stories of the "spirits," the ghost of a dead wife or lover appears. For example, in "Ts'ui Tai-chao sheng-ssu yüan-chia" (The Jade Kuan-yin; TY 8), an embroiderer, promised in marriage to a jade carver by the prince she serves, prematurely elopes with the carver during a fire. When the prince finds them, the carver blames the escape on the embroiderer and ends up being beaten and exiled. The embroiderer is killed, but her ghost catches up with the carver and lives with him until she is discovered to be a ghost. In the end, she drags her husband away to become a ghost like herself. The story's introductory chain of poems on spring and its departure, as well as the jade Kuan-yin (an image of a bodhisattva [savior]), is a metaphor for love.

The demon stories normally tell how a young man encounters an animal spirit or a ghost in the guise of a young girl, makes love to her, discovers his danger, and calls an exorcist to subjugate her. A slight variation is found in "Pai niang-tzu yung chen Lei-feng T'a" (Madam White; TY 28), in which a benign snake spirit assumes the form of a woman. In love with a clerk, she does not wish to devour or hurt him, though she inadvertently gets him into trouble by stealing money to buy gifts for him. Finally, she is exorcised by a Buddhist monk and imprisoned under a pagoda, and the clerk becomes a monk.

The court-case stories include the commission of a crime (usually sexual in nature), the detection and solution, and judicial punishment. "K'an p'i-hsüeh tan cheng Erh-lang shen" (The Boot That Reveals the Culprit; HY 13) begins as a love story between a lonely palace lady and a scoundrel disguised as a god; it is notable for the extensive revelation of the palace lady's inner feelings. In the latter half, however, the emphasis shifts to the detection of the crime as well as the final trial and execution of the culprit; this process of detection is complicated and well wrought. The story also satirizes the emperor and high-ranking officials.

Bandit stories and men-of-destiny stories tend to have a linked, rather than unitary, plot. "Sung Ssu-kung ta nao chin-hun Chang" (Sung Four Causes Trouble for Miser Chang; KC 36) stresses how the thieves use clever tactics to steal from a rich miser.

THE MIDDLE PERIOD: MID-MING DYNASTY

The publication of Hung P'ien's *Sixty Stories* was a landmark in the development of the vernacular story. *Sixty Stories* included six groups of stories, each with its own title. The groups may have been originally published separately and then republished together in this collection. Only about half of the sixty stories are extant. One group, entitled *Ch'i-chen chi* (Leaning on the Pillow Collection), appears to have been written by a single author of the literati class. The others seem to have been collected haphazardly; the anthology even includes some classical tales.

There are different versions of eleven of the extant stories. One is in a collection published by Hsiung Lung-feng (fl. 1592), a well-known publisher; seven are in Feng Meng-lung's *Stories Old and New*; and three are in Feng's *Common Words to Warn the World*.

The range of sources for stories written from roughly 1450 to 1550 extends to historical biographies, classical tales, drama, and chantefable. In *Sixty Stories*, some stories are adaptations of biographies of renowned historical figures (e.g., the story on Li Kuang, the Han general) or of classical tales found in collections such as *Yi-chien chih* (Records of the Listener). The stories in *Leaning on the Pillow* focus on the scholar-official class and its morality. The author evokes an ideal age in the ancient past, while frequently evaluating historical figures. Concerned with Confucian values and friendship, he expresses sympathy for frustrated scholars, quotes poetry and history, and writes in a language that is close to classical.

"K'uai-tsui Li Ts'ui-lien chi" (The Shrew: Sharp-Tongued Ts'ui-lien; Hung 7) takes the form of a chantefable. It describes a beautiful and intelligent—but insubordinate—bride who is eventually divorced and becomes a nun. Admonitory in purpose, it also can be read as a delightful story about a prototypical independent woman.

Among these middle-period stories, there are six cautionary stories showing how a seemingly insignificant act may have terrible consequences. Directed at members of the mercantile class, these stories caution them to save themselves and their families. The narrator frequently warns against folly and predicts future calamities. In "Shen Hsiao-kuan yi niao hai ch'i ming" (One Songbird Causes Seven Deaths; KC 26), a profligate, idle young man is murdered by a man who also steals his songbird. More murders, connected to the first death and similarly prompted by greed, are committed. In the end, the crimes are discovered and the culprits duly punished. The story cautions against weak human nature.

"Chieh-chih-erh chi" (The Ring; Hung 20) is a love story about a young woman of a high-ranking official's family who has a secret rendezvous with her lover in a temple. Her lover, the son of a mere merchant, dies during their lovemaking. Finding herself pregnant, the young woman resolves to keep the baby and become a chaste widow. Her son later becomes an official and has her honored for her virtue.

The religious stories combine themes involving the priesthood with that of karmic causation. In some stories, a priest wills his own death because he succumbs, or is falsely accused of succumbing, to sexual temptations; he is then reincarnated to repay his debt or avenge himself. An example is "Wu-chieh ch'an-shih ssu Hung-lien chi" (The Five Abstinences Priest Seduces Red Lotus; Hung 13). In contrast, "Hua-teng chiao Lien-nü ch'eng Fo chi" (Lien-nü Attains Buddhahood on the Way to Her Wedding; Hung 16) is about the rebirth of a pious old woman as a girl who, on her wedding day, wills herself to death in the sedan chair, choosing spiritual attainment and avoiding pollution by marriage and mundane concerns.

The Ming witnessed the appearance of several collections of court case fiction, gathered primarily by professional editors and publishers. The only collection that uses the language and the narrative model of the vernacular story is *Pai-chia kung-an* (The Hundred Cases; 1594), a collection of stories about the incorruptible, Solomonic Judge Pao (Pao-kung).

LATE MING

Of the many collections of stories published in the late Ming, Feng Meng-lung's (1574–1646) three collections and Ling Meng-ch'u's (1580–1644) two are the most influential.

Feng Meng-lung and the "Three Words"

The "Three Words" (*san-yen*) refers to three forty-piece collections compiled by Feng Meng-lung in imitation of the *Sixty Stories*, all of which have "Words" in their titles: *Yü-shih ming-yen* (Clear Words to Instruct the World; originally titled Stories Old and New; 1620); *Ching-shih t'ung-yen* (Common Words to Warn the World; 1624); and *Hsing-shih heng-yen* (Constant Words to Awaken the World; 1627). Produced in elegant, finely illustrated editions, the three collections were very popular and thus highly profitable for the publishers. They present a total of 120 stories, 40 of which are early- and middle-period stories adapted by Feng Meng-lung.

A highly educated writer and dramatist from Soochow, Feng Meng-lung nevertheless repeatedly failed in the examinations until 1630, when he received a tribute studentship (*kung-sheng*) and then eventually secured a position. Loyal to the dynasty, he died while fighting in the war of resistance against the Manchus. Feng adapted stories to suit his tastes and those of his intended readers, an audience that included those in the scholarly as well as the less-lettered classes. He rewrote "The Five Abstinences Priest" as a story that elaborates the life and career of the Sung literatus Su Shih and his friendship with a priest ("Ming-wu ch'an-shih kan Wu-chieh" [The Enlightened Priest Attempts to Save Five Abstinences; KC 30]) and adapted "Ts'o jen shih" (The Wrongly Identified Corpse; Hung 18), such that the victim's ghost possesses and kills the blackmailer ("Ch'iao Yen-chieh yi ch'ieh p'o chia" [One Concubine Destroys a Household; TY 33]).

Feng Meng-lung himself probably wrote nineteen stories in *Stories Old and New*, possibly sixteen in *Common Words to Warn the World*, and one or two stories in *Constant Words to Awaken the World*. The sources of his stories are history, anecdotes, and, most frequently, classical tales. Two of his most celebrated stories are derived from classical tales written by Sung Mao-ch'eng (1569–1622) in the early 1600s. "Chiang Hsing-ko ch'ung-hui chen-chu shan" (Chiang Hsing-ko Re-encounters the Pearl Shirt; KC 1) is based on Sung's "Chu shan" (The Pearl Vest), while "Tu Shih-niang nu ch'en pai-pao hsiang" (Tu Shih-niang Angrily Sinks Her Jewel Box; TY 32) is an adaptation of Sung's "Fu-ch'ing-nung chuan" (The Faithless Lover), a tale inspired by a late-sixteenth-century romance between a scholar and a Soochow courtesan named Tu Wei.

Feng Meng-lung was interested in historical men-of-destiny, heroes, generous leaders, and patriotic officials. "Lin-an li Ch'ien P'o-liu fa-chi" (Ch'ien Liu; KC 21) details the rise of the king of Wu and Yüeh in the late T'ang and Five Dynasties. "Ko Ling-kung sheng yi nung chu-erh" (General Ko; KC 6) and "P'ei Chin-kung yi huan yüan-p'ei" (P'ei Tu; KC 9) depict two leaders who care more about worthy men than about beautiful women and are generous enough to give their women as presents to their subordinates. "Wang Hsin-chih yi ssu chiu ch'üan chia" (Wang Hsin-chih Saves His Whole Family Through His Death; KC 39) tells of a patriotic local leader of the Southern Sung period who is wrongly charged with sedition. He sacrifices his life to save his family and estate. "Shen Hsiao-hsia hsiang hui ch'u-shih piao" (Shen Hsiao-hsia; KC 40) relates the story of an upright official's persecution and wrongful death under a tyrannical prime minister. The official's son escapes and, after many hardships, not only preserves his family lineage but also witnesses the death of his father's enemy.

The lives and careers of scholars and highly learned officials also fascinated Feng Meng-lung. "Wang An-shih san nan Su hsüeh-shih" (Su Shih; TY 3) shows how Su Shih fails when the Sung statesman Wang An-shih checks his learning. "Ao hsiang-kung yin-hen Pan-shan t'ang"(The Stubborn Prime Minister; TY 4) details the curses and humiliations the bigoted Wang An-shih suffered on his way home after resigning from office, as well as Wang's final decision to turn to Buddhism. Feng also wrote stories on famous Taoist figures, such as "Chang Tao-ling ch'i shih Chao Sheng" (Chang Tao-ling; KC 13) and "Ch'en Hsi-yi ssu tz'u ch'ao ming" (Ch'en T'uan; KC 14).

Because of his own experiences, Feng Meng-lung was interested in writing about talented but frustrated men who had no one to recommend them for official positions. "Ch'iung Ma Chou tsao chi mai tui ao" (The Impoverished Ma Chou; KC 5) tells of a frustrated T'ang writer who indulges in drink because his talent is not recognized. Only after the emperor, through a rare chance, reads Ma's writings does Ma obtain the high rank and riches he deserves. In "Tun hsiu-ts'ai yi chao chiao-t'ai" (The Luckless Licentiate; TY 17), a scholar is fated to be abandoned by friends and suffers tribulations for ten years before eventually succeeding. "Lao men-sheng san-shih pao-en" (The Old Protégé; TY 18) is a comedy about an old examination candidate who continuously fails in examinations. By a stroke of luck, he at last passes under an examiner who tries unsuccessfully to fail him. Ironically, the old man, believing that he owes his success to this examiner, attempts to further the careers of the examiner's descendants.

While concerned with Confucian values, Feng Meng-lung was also intrigued by love (*ch'ing*) and fidelity in love. "Yang Chiao-ai she ming ch'üan chiao" (Yang Chiao-ai Gives Up His Life for His Friend; KC 7) and "Wu Pao-an ch'i-chia shu-yu" (Wu Pao-an Abandons His Family to Ransom His Friend; KC 8) eulogize selfless friendship between literati. "T'ang chieh-yüan yi hsiao yin-yüan" (T'ang Yin; TY 26) tells of how the renowned sixteenth-century writer T'ang Yin falls in love with, woos, and marries a rich man's maidservant. Love between scholars and courtesans is explored in "Yü-t'ang-ch'un lo nan feng fu" (Yü-t'ang Ch'un; TY 24) and "Tu Shih-niang Angrily Sinks Her Jewel Box." "Fan Ch'iu-erh shuang ching ch'ung yüan" (Fan Hsi-chou; TY 12), "Yü-t'ang Ch'un," and some others depict faithful lovers who are eventually reunited after many difficulties.

Feng Meng-lung's stories typically are structured on the principle of human and heavenly requital (*pao*). In "Chin Yü-nu pang ta po-ch'ing lang" (Chin Yü-nu; KC 27), the daughter of a rich leader of a beggars' union is married to a poor scholar. When the scholar becomes an official, he tries to murder his wife. Finally, the wife is able to shame him publicly and then reconcile with him. Wise and competent officials serve as agents effecting justice in "T'eng ta-yin kuei tuan chia-ssu" (Prefect T'eng's Ghostly Solution of a Case of Inheritance; KC 10) and "Ch'en yü-shih ch'iao k'an chin ch'ai tien" (Censor Ch'en Ingeniously Solves the Case of the Gold Hairpins; KC 2). In the latter story, a wicked man disguises himself as his cousin and sleeps with his cousin's betrothed. Upon discovering that she has lost her virginity to an imposter, the woman commits suicide. The evil man's wife is so ashamed that she demands a divorce. Censor Ch'en finds out that this man, rather than his cousin, is guilty of causing the young woman's death. The cousin ends up marrying the evil man's divorced wife.

Retributive justice is ingeniously orchestrated in "Chiang Hsing-ko Reencounters the Pearl Shirt": a seducer eventually becomes ill and dies, the cuckolded husband marries the seducer's widow, and the adulterous wife is divorced, remarries, and then finally marries her first husband again—but as his secondary wife. In "Tu Shih-niang Angrily Sinks Her Jewel Box," revenge is achieved by the ghost of a singsong girl who has thrown her jewels and herself into the river. The greedy merchant who engineered the selling of the girl dies from fright and the girl's faithless lover goes mad, but her lover's faithful friend is repaid by the girl's ghost with a small casket of jewels.

In some stories of wish fulfillment, frustrated scholars are commissioned to right wrongs and restore justice. The scholar in "Nao yin-ssu Ssu-ma Mao tuan yü" (Ssu-ma Mao; KC 31) writes down his complaints when drunk. His soul is then taken to the underworld, where he acts as judge for half a day. In "Yu Feng-tu Hu-mu Ti yin-shih" (Hu-mu Ti; KC 32), an unsuccessful student becomes furious when reading about the murder of the patriotic general Yüeh Fei by the Sung traitor Ch'in Kuei. After getting drunk and writing poems expressing his wrath, he visits the underworld and sees how the traitor suffers retribution.

Hsi Lang-hsien

A close associate of Feng Meng-lung in his editing of the "Three Words," Hsi Lang-hsien (usually referred to as Lang-hsien) probably wrote twenty-two of the stories in *Constant Words to Awaken the World*. While Feng's stories emphasize scholars' aspirations for public service, Lang-hsien's stress reclusion and religious beliefs.

Lang-hsien's love of nature and reverence for life are seen in "Kuan-yüan sou wan feng hsien-nü" (The Old Gardener; HY 4) and "Hsiao shui-wan t'ien-hu yi shu" (The Foxes' Revenge; HY 6). The theme of immortality emerges in "The Old Gardener," "Hsüeh lu-shih yü fu cheng hsien" (Magistrate Hsüeh's Metamorphosis into a Fish; HY 26), "Lu t'ai-hsüeh shih chiu ao wang hou" (Lu Nan; HY 29), "Tu Tzu-ch'un san ju Ch'ang-an" (Tu Tzu-ch'un; HY 37), and "Li Tao-jen tu pu Yün-men" (Yün-men Cave; HY 38). "Tu Tzu-ch'un" reveals the conflict between human feeling and the purging of emotions that is necessary for attaining immortality. Aided by a Taoist in his search for immortality, Tu Tzu-ch'un believes he has rid himself of joy and anger, grief and fear, loathing and desire. However, during a dreamlike illusion when he is incarnated as a woman, he cries out upon seeing his son killed. Because this indicates that he is still bound by love, he fails to achieve immortality. However, he and his wife continue to cultivate themselves, donate money, and perform charity, and they are finally apotheosized.

Lang-hsien's interest in transformation and his attention to the characters' inner views are best demonstrated in "Magistrate Hsüeh's Metamorphosis into a Fish" (HY 26). When the virtuous and competent magistrate becomes sick and goes into a coma, his soul is transformed into that of a big golden carp. His wife has a Taoist service performed for his soul and invites his colleagues to his house to share sacrificial food. One of his colleagues obtains the carp—Hsüeh's transformation—and wants to have it cooked and served, while the others suggest freeing the carp in the pond in order to accumulate good karma. Hsüeh tries to participate in his colleagues' debate and implores them to release him, but his urgent pleading goes unheard—his colleagues only see the carp's mouth moving. As soon as the carp's head is chopped off, Hsüeh wakes up and asks his wife to stop his colleagues from eating the fish. Enlightened from this nightmarish experience, Hsüeh decides to relinquish his worldly goods and position. He and his wife eventually leave their families and become immortals. Lang-hsien's detailed narration of Hsüeh's fear of being eaten and his inner conversation with his colleagues is both grotesque and comic.

In addition to Taoist and Buddhist themes, Lang-hsien emphasizes fundamental Confucian morality and ethical relationships. "Yi wen ch'ien hsiao hsi tsao ch'i yüan" (A Single Copper Cash; HY 34) cautions against human greed, wrath, and short-sightedness, illustrating the consequences of violating morality. Lang-hsien's attention to particulars is shown in the many gripping details accompanying the chain of disasters caused by a single copper coin. In "Hsü lao-p'u yi fen ch'eng chia" (Old Servant Hsü; HY 35), a faithful and resourceful servant engages in trading with little capital and eventually helps his mistress, a young widow with five children, build a great fortune. What is particularly remarkable is that he continues to serve his mistress loyally. He is so unconcerned with saving money for himself and his family that, after he dies, his young masters find he has no private hoard at all.

Lang-hsien particularly enjoyed writing about female exemplars of moral heroism that surpass even those in biographies of models of virtue. In "Li Yü-ying yü chung sung yüan" (Li Yü-ying Writes Her Defense in Jail; HY 27), an orphaned girl endures her stepmother's persecution and false accusation, eventually clearing herself of the false charge and avenging her younger brother, who was murdered by the stepmother. "Ts'ai Jui-hung jen ju pao ch'ou" (Ts'ai Jui-hung Bears Humiliation for the Sake of Revenge; HY 36) tells of a beautiful girl determined to avenge her parents' death. She marries several times but is disappointed by one husband after another; she is even abducted and forced to become a prostitute at one point. Finally, however, she marries an upright scholar who helps her achieve her goal of revenge. After her parents' murderers are executed, she commits suicide.

Several stories in the "Three Words," possibly written by another of Feng's associates (not Hsi Lang-hsien), are worth mentioning here. "Mai yu lang tu chan hua k'uei" (The Oil Peddler Courts the Courtesan; HY 3) is a successful comic romance about a humble hero winning the love of the Queen of Courtesans through his single-minded devotion. "Ch'en to-shou sheng-ssu fu-ch'i" (The Couple Bound in Life and Death; HY 9) depicts how a girl's selfless love for her leprous betrothed eventually brings about his cure and their happy marriage. In "K'uang t'ai-shou tuan ssu hai-erh" (Prefect K'uang's Solution of the Case of the Dead Infant; TY 35), a pretty and virtuous widow vows to be chaste, but a scoundrel secretly incites her male servant to seduce her. After she gives birth to a baby boy and drowns him to preserve her reputation, the scoundrel blackmails her. When she finds out about the scheme, she kills the servant and commits suicide. The heroine's psychology and the seduction process are skillfully depicted.

Stylistic analysis indicates that Hsi Lang-hsien may also have written *Shih tien t'ou* (The Rocks Nod Their Heads; 1628?; cited below as *Rocks*), a collection of fourteen stories. Each story has an introductory essay discussing the theme, though there is no prolog story. Lang-hsien intended the stories to be so moving, sensational, and extraordinary that even the rocks would "nod their heads." Many of his protagonists demonstrate exemplary conduct under extreme circumstances. "Wang Pen-li t'ien-ya ch'iu fu" (Wang Pen-li; *Rocks* 3) tells of a filial son who devotes his life to searching for his lost father and eventually finds him after many hardships and supernatural aid. In "Chiang-tu shih hsiao-fu t'u shen" (A Filial Daughter-in-Law Offers Her Body to Be Butchered; *Rocks* 11), a brave woman, when trapped in a besieged city, offers her body to be sold for food so that her husband can travel home to take care of his aged mother. Filial devotion, being incompatible with conjugal love in this situation, takes precedence.

The depiction of this filial daughter-in-law indicates Lang-hsien's great admiration for the moral courage exhibited by virtuous women: she flinches neither in offering her own body for sale in the human flesh market nor in preparing to be killed by the butcher. In "Hou-kuan hsien lieh-nü chien-ch'ou" (The Female Martyr; *Rocks* 12), another incredibly courageous woman avenges her husband's death. She marries the murderer and kills him on their wedding night. She then cuts off his head, sacrifices it on her husband's grave, and hangs herself on a tree. The women in both these stories remain calm and unperturbed while performing their courageous acts.

Lang-hsien also attempted to bring together Confucian morality and human feelings. In "Mang shu-sheng ch'iang t'u yüan-lü" (The Impetuous Student;

Rocks 5), a young scholar meets a girl of respectable family when she visits a temple, makes advances to her, and forces her into having a secret affair and eloping with him. After passing his examinations and becoming an official, he regrets his former impulsive behavior and insists on strict discipline with his children.

Lang-hsien showed that moral heroism and idealistic love can arise even from sordid situations. In "Ch'ü Feng-nu ch'ing ch'ien ssu kai" (Ch'ü Feng-nu; *Rocks* 4), in order to secure her relationship with a young man, a lustful widow arranges to have her daughter marry him. The daughter falls in love with the young man, however worthless he may be, and when he dies, she commits suicide to remain faithful to him. "P'an Wen-tzu ch'i-ho yüan-yang chung" (P'an Wen-tzu; *Rocks* 14) similarly tells about an unusual love. P'an Wen-tzu, a handsome young man, is seduced by a friend and initiated into homosexual love. He retires with his friend to the mountains and refuses to go home to marry his betrothed. Eventually, the homosexual couple dies together, while P'an's betrothed hangs herself to demonstrate her devotion to him.

"Ch'i-kai fu ch'ung p'ei luan ch'ou" (The Beggar Woman; *Rocks* 6) is a comedy of fortune. An uneducated daughter of a poor matmaker suffers as a fisherman's wife. She is divorced upon her father's death and must earn her living as a beggar-singer. But even in her poverty, she retains her purity, rejecting a rich man's advances. Eventually, she marries a humble scholar, who later becomes successful.

"T'an-lan han liu yüan mai feng-liu" (The Brothel Keeper; *Rocks* 8) satirizes a cruel and corrupt official who, after being removed from office, opens a brothel both for profit and personal pleasure. He eventually dies in pain, his daughter becomes a prostitute and runs away with a client, and his son becomes a burglar and dies after judicial punishment.

Ling Meng-ch'u and the "Two Slappings"

Ling Meng-ch'u of Wu-hsing, Chekiang province, was a celebrated writer, dramatist, editor, and publisher. Like Feng Meng-lung, he failed to pass the civil service examinations and did not obtain a post through a *kung-sheng* (tribute studentship or senior licentiate) until late in his life. He was a conscientious official who died in service to the empire. As a writer, Ling was strongly influenced by Feng Meng-lung. Because of the success of Feng's collections, booksellers asked Ling to publish his stories. Ling published *P'ai-an ching-ch'i* (Slapping the Table in Amazement; also called *Ch'u-k'o p'ai-an ching-ch'i* [Slapping the Table in Amazement, First Collection]; 1628; cited below as CK) and *Erh-k'o p'ai-an ching-ch'i* (Slapping the Table in Amazement, Second Collection; 1632; cited below as EK), which were commonly called "Two Slappings" (*erh p'ai* or *liang-p'ai*).

There are forty stories apiece in the two collections, most of which are based on classical tales and anecdotes. Ling wrote a total of seventy-eight stories—

one story ("Ta-chieh hun yu wan su-yüan, hsiao-yi ping ch'i hsü ch'ien-yüan" [The Younger Sister Resumes the Older Sister's Marriage Destinies; CK 23/EK 23]) appears in both the first and second collections, and the last piece is one of Ling's *tsa-chü* plays (see chapter 41).

Ling Meng-ch'u was interested in social types and believed in fate and chance; he used coincidences in constructing plots and treated his characters with detachment. His stories are both witty and admonitory. Readers are urged to accept their fate and avoid excesses or striving for fame and riches beyond their lot. Rather than advocating idealistic, rigid, or extreme moral standards, Ling's stories endorse a pragmatic morality and show that prudence is essential for survival. For example, "Liu Tung-shan k'ua chi Shun ch'eng men, shih-pa hsiung tsung ch'i ts'un chiu ssu" (The Braggart Liu Tung-shan; CK 3) warns against bragging by illustrating the familiar maxim: however strong you are, there is always someone stronger.

According to Patrick Hanan, about a third of Ling's stories are comedies, either romantic comedies such as "Hsiao tao-jen yi chao jao t'ien-hsia, nü ch'i-t'ung liang chü chu chung-shen" (The Chess Champions; EK 2) that end in marriage or comedies of fortune such as "Chuan yün han yü ch'iao Tung-t'ing hung, Po-ssu hu chih p'o t'o-lung k'o" (The Tangerines and the Tortoiseshell; CK 1) that culminate in the attainment of worldly success.

Among romantic comedies, "T'ung-ch'uang yu jen chia tso chen, nü hsiu-ts'ai yi-hua chieh-mu" (Her Classmate Takes the False for Real, the Lady Licentiate Grafts One Twig onto Another; EK 17) is exceptional for its unconventional attitude toward love and morality. A girl studies at school in male guise, intending to find a future husband. She falls in love with one of her classmates and allows him to make love to her. Instead of castigating her, her father joyfully urges her to marry the young man. In "Han hsiu-ts'ai ch'eng luan p'in chiao-ch'i, Wu t'ai-shou lien ts'ai chu yin-pu" (The Imperial Decree; CK 10), an impoverished licentiate is able to be betrothed to a girl only because of a misunderstanding of an imperial decree. Thinking that the emperor is recruiting single women for the palace, many parents hurry to marry their daughters off. When the misunderstanding is cleared up, the girl's parents regret the match and want to back out of it. But a wise magistrate decides in the licentiate's favor, and he ends up having a happy marriage.

Despite Ling's emphasizing ordinary reality, he also resorts occasionally to employing the supernatural in his romances. "Tieh chü ch'i Ch'eng k'o te chu, san chiu o hai-shen hsien ling" (The Sea Goddess; EK 37) concerns a goddess who falls in love with a traveling merchant, helps him make a great deal of money, and three times saves him from disaster. "The Younger Sister Resumes the Older Sister's Marriage Destinies" (CK 23/EK 23) tells of the soul of a deceased girl entering her younger sister's body in order to elope with the older sister's betrothed.

The comedies of fortune often depend on a comic twist of fate as a device. The luckless man in "The Tangerines and the Tortoiseshell" (CK 1), who has failed at every business venture he has undertaken, experiences a change of fortune. On a voyage to the South Seas, he sells his only cargo—a big basket of tangerines—at a good price and the tortoiseshell he accidentally picks up on an island turns out to have huge pearls hidden in it. His fellow travelers had jeered at the man for obtaining such "worthless" goods as tangerines and a tortoiseshell, yet it turns out that they are highly valuable. Another story about the misjudgment of valuable items is "Chin-hsiang k'o mang k'an *Chin-kang ching*, ch'u yü seng ch'iao wan fa hui fen" (The Manuscript of *The Diamond Sutra*; EK 1), in which a precious manuscript is not seized by a covetous magistrate because the title page has been accidentally lost and hence the manuscript appears worthless.

Ling also uses the comedy of fortune to teach his readers about human nature and instruct them in religious enlightenment. In "Meng chiao-kuan ai nü pu shou pao, ch'iung hsiang-sheng chu shih te ling chung" (The Foolish Official Tutor Receives No Returns for Doting on His Daughters; EK 26), an old tutor, after dividing his property among his three married daughters, is rejected by them. He stays with his nephew until a former student—now a censor—comes to visit and hires him as an aide. Returning home with the fortune he has earned, he finds his daughters again warming up to him. However, wise enough now not to trust them, he elects to give the money to his nephew and live with him. In "T'ien-she weng shih-shih ching-li, mu-t'ung erh yeh-yeh tsun-jung" (The Herdboy; EK 19), the hard life a boy leads in the daytime results inversely in wonderful nightly dreams, while success in his dream spells disaster for the following day. Later, when his fortune improves, he starts having nightmares. In the end, he becomes enlightened and goes away with a Taoist.

Changes of fortune can also result in part from good deeds and human effort. In "Ch'eng Yüan-yü tien-ssu tai ch'ang ch'ien, Shih-yi niang Yün-kang tsung T'an hsia" (Wei Eleventh-Maiden; CK 4), a man buys a meal for a female knight-errant and she later saves him from being robbed by bandits. "Wu chiang-chün yi fan pi ch'ou, Ch'en Ta-lang san-jen ch'ung hui" (General Wu; CK 8) tells about a merchant buying a meal for a hungry stalwart with a big beard. Later the stalwart—who turns out to be a bandit chief—repays the merchant's kindness by saving him from danger. In "Wei ch'ao-feng hen-hsin p'an kuei ch'an, Ch'en hsiu-ts'ai ch'iao-chi chuan yüan fang" (Licentiate Ch'en Regains His House with a Ruse; CK 15), a capable wife assists a spendthrift husband in recovering a house previously seized by an avaricious man and helps him rebuild the family fortune. "Shen t'ou chi hsing yi-chih mei, hsia tao kuan hsing san mei hsi" (The Master-Thief Lazy Dragon; EK 39) celebrates the many marvelous tricks of a righteous thief who, despite his stealing, does not commit any other crimes.

Ling wrote ten satires of folly, focusing on obsession. "Ch'ü-t'u Chung-jen k'u sha chung-sheng, Yün-chou ssu-ma ming ch'üan nei-chih" (The Hunter; CK 37) depicts a rich young man's hunting for fun and his violence toward animals. His soul is then taken to the underworld, where the animals demand his life. Upon his return, he repents, becomes a vegetarian, copies sutras in his own blood, and uses himself as an example to warn people against killing animals. As a result of his repentance, he dies peacefully. The narrator of "Shen chiang-shih san-ch'ien mai hsiao ch'ien, Wang ch'ao-yi yi-yeh mi-hun chen" (The Gambler; EK 8) denounces gambling and describes how a wealthy young scholar with a weakness for gambling falls into the trap of confidence men. "Ying k'an an ta-ju cheng hsien-ch'i, kan shou hsing hsia-nü chu fang-ming" (The Great Confucian; EK 12) satirizes the renowned Southern Sung Neo-Confucian scholar Chu Hsi, showing him to be so bigoted and biased that he fails in judgment and falls into a trap set by evildoers.

Ling's best satire of folly is "Tan-k'o pan-shu chiu huan, fu-weng ch'ien-chin yi hsiao" (The Rich Man and the Alchemist; CK 18). Well educated and intelligent, the rich man P'an is nevertheless vulnerable because he is obsessed with the art of alchemy. Unaware that he has been deceived by a swindler alchemist and his "concubine," P'an continues to seek out alchemists. Having squandered his property, P'an is then lured by a group of swindler alchemists into shaving his head, disguising himself as a monk, and deceiving another rich man. In the end, the advice and financial assistance of the first alchemist's "concubine" (who is in fact no more than a singsong girl) enables P'an to return home. Similarly driven by greed though much less likable by comparison, the wealthy man in "Ch'ih ch'ü ch'üan Mao Lieh lai yüan ch'ien, shih huan hun ya k'uai so sheng ming" (The Deceitful Accomplice; EK 16) tries to cheat his three brothers out of their inheritance by mortgaging the family estate to an accomplice. But he in turn is cheated by the accomplice.

While resembling the court case stories, Ling's twenty satires of crime and vice focus more on crime and its consequences than on detection. In some stories, Ling also details the reasons leading to the commission of the crime as well as the protagonists' motivations. In "Ch'eng ch'ao-feng tan yü wu t'ou fu, Wang t'ung-p'an shuang hsüeh pu ming yüan" (The Headless Woman; EK 28) a rich man lusting after a wineseller's wife pays her husband for a rendezvous with her. Entering their house on the appointed night, he is shocked to find a headless woman on the floor; he is subsequently imprisoned for her murder. Although it is discovered later that the woman was killed by a wandering "monk," the rich man has already spent a year in jail and a great deal of money hiring detectives to determine the identity of the real murderer. "Yao Ti-chu pi hsiu je hsiu, Cheng Yüeh-o chiang ts'o chiu ts'o" (The Double; CK 2) depicts the events leading up to a woman's abduction: she resolves to leave her husband's home because she can no longer endure mistreatment at the hands of her in-laws.

In some stories, the victims and their families are encouraged to participate in punishing crimes, rather than relying entirely on law enforcement agencies. In "Chiu hsia chiu Chao ni-ao mi hua, chi chung chi Chia hsiu-ts'ai pao yüan" (The Nun's Trick and Licentiate Chia's Revenge; CK 6), a nun is bribed to trick a married woman into being raped. The woman wants to commit suicide, but her husband dissuades her, and they dare not report the crime for fear of losing face. Then the husband thinks up a ruse: his wife bites off the rapist's tongue, while he kills the nun, making it look as if the rapist has killed her. Thus the scholar bypasses legal avenues, avenges his wife, and keeps their reputation intact. The oldest son in "Chao Wu-hu ho-chi t'iao chia-hsin, Mo Ta-lang li-ti san shen chien" (The "Five Tigers of Chao" Conspire to Provoke a Family Dispute; EK 10) is able to foil blackmailers' schemes and protect the family estate. The supernatural affords revenge in "Chiu mo ts'ai Yü Chiao ssu o, kuei tui an Yang Hua chieh shih" (The Ghost's Possession; CK 14). An intoxicated soldier is robbed and strangled to death. His ghost takes possession of a woman and speaks through her to accuse the murderer. But after the wrong is avenged, the ghost is unwilling to leave the woman's body. It is only after the judge threatens a beating that the ghost leaves and the woman regains consciousness.

A very smart five-year-old boy is a great help to law enforcement in "Hsiang Min-kung yüan-hsiao shih tzu, Shih-san lang wu-sui ch'ao t'ien" (The Kidnapping on the Eve of the Lantern Festival; EK 5). When the son of a high-ranking official realizes that he is being kidnapped for his gemstone-studded hat, he hides the hat in his sleeve. He also marks the kidnapper's collar by sewing it with colorful thread. Seeing a row of palanquins passing by on the streets, he shouts "thief!" and is rescued by a palace eunuch. In the palace, the little boy becomes the favorite of the emperor and the imperial concubines; later he is returned to his family. Because of the clue planted by the boy, detectives are able to track down the group of kidnappers.

In addition to condemning criminals, Ling's satires of vice caution against drunkenness, lust, avarice, and wrath. "O ch'uan-chia chi chuan chia shih yin, hen p'u jen wu t'ou chen ming chuang" (The Ginger Merchant; CK 11) warns against wrath and shows the punishment meted out to a blackmailer. An angry scholar hits a ginger merchant and is later blackmailed by someone who claims the ginger merchant is dead. Then the scholar has a servant beaten for failing to engage a pediatrician in time to prevent his only daughter's death. In revenge, the servant has the scholar imprisoned for killing the ginger merchant. When the ginger merchant visits the scholar's house, his wife realizes that her husband has been falsely accused; she defends him in court and saves his life. In "Liang ts'o jen Mo ta-chieh ssu-pen, tsai ch'eng-chiao Yang erh-lang cheng-pen" (The Wife Who Eloped; EK 38), a lascivious woman, while drunk, reveals to her cousin a planned elopement. Her confidant poses as her lover, but the woman does not discover the mistake until the morning of her elopement and marriage.

Later her lover is charged with her abduction. Sold into prostitution by her cousin, the woman is eventually rescued and returned home; after she is divorced by her husband, she marries her former lover. "Chen chien-sheng lang t'un mi-yao, Ch'un-hua nü wu hsieh feng-ch'ing" (Death by Aphrodisiac; EK 18) details how lust and avarice cause a wealthy student to become obsessed with alchemy. Planning to practice the sexual arts he learned from a Taoist, he dies instead in the middle of the night after inadvertently taking an aphrodisiac.

MING–CH'ING TRANSITION

Influenced by Feng Meng-lung's and Ling Meng-ch'u's story collections, about twenty collections appeared between 1629 and 1650. During this period, works by these two popular writers were also reprinted. For example, the late Ming anthology *Chin-ku ch'i-kuan* (Remarkable Stories New and Old) consists of forty stories selected from Feng Meng-lung's and Ling Meng-ch'u's collections and may have been edited by Feng. While stories in some of the other, original, collections are well written, none can compare with the works of Feng, Ling, and Lang-hsien in terms of literary value and significance.

Penned by a Soochow writer, *Ku-chang chüeh-ch'en* (Clapping Your Hands to Get Rid of Worldly Dust; 1629/1630) is original in structure, with four long, elaborately plotted stories divided into ten chapters apiece. Stories 1 and 3 are influenced by Ling Meng-ch'u's romantic comedies, while story 2 is a comedy mixed with satire of folly. Story 4 is an interesting social satire ridiculing such types as the prodigal son, the shrewish wife, and the henpecked husband. It ends with one of the characters leaving home and becoming a monk.

Contemporaneous with Ling Meng-ch'u's *Slapping the Table in Amazement, Second Collection* (1632) is a fairly important collection of forty stories entitled *Hsing-shih yen* (Tales of the World's Exemplars; 1631/1632). Written by the largely unknown writer Lu Jen-lung of Ch'ien-t'ang in Chekiang province, this collection sank into oblivion during the Ch'ing dynasty and was only recently rediscovered in Korea. Most of the stories either celebrate ethical norms and moral exemplars or else warn against vice; and other works depict anomalies and assorted strange occurrences.

The period of the Ming–Ch'ing transition witnessed the publication of primarily two groups of collections, one group leaning toward the erotic (partly under the guise of comic romance) and the other emphasizing morality, though in some collections the erotic and the moralistic overlap. Their anonymous authors hailed mostly from Hangchow.

An anthology of twenty-four stories, *Huan-hsi yüan-chia* (Antagonists in Love; c. 1640) echoes the theme of "Enmity from Love" (Ch'ing ch'ou) from Feng Meng-lung's *Ch'ing-shih lei-lüeh* (Classified Outline of the Anatomy of Love; compiled sometime between 1626 and 1631). Although the stories are unrelated, the narrator sometimes refers to other stories in the collection. The first twenty-three stories demonstrate how lovers eventually become enemies, with love and tenderness turning into hatred and violence. Each of the stories contains an elaborate description of the lovers' sexual attraction and the pleasures of love. In story 23, a rich student traveling to a provincial capital to take the examinations falls in love with a handsome lad. The student has an affair with the young man and then with the man's sister. Only after the brother and sister have departed does the student discover that they have left behind cobblestones in place of his silver ingots. By contrast, story 24 has no explicit sexual description and ends happily with a potential antagonist changing into a helpful secondary wife.

Poetic justice is a dominant theme in the collection, with villains suffering rightful retribution. The author was apparently fond of composing poetry, for his protagonists frequently write poems to one another. In story 7, through a poem composed by her second husband of eighteen years, a woman discovers that he murdered her first husband and she reports his crime.

Possibly influenced by "P'an Wen-tzu" (*Rocks* 14), *Pien erh ch'ai* (Wearing a Cap but Also Hairpins) is an anthology of four five-chapter stories about homosexual love. *Yi-p'ien ch'ing* (An Expanse of Love) comprises fourteen comic-erotic stories. Five of them are reprinted in *Pa-tuan chin* (Eight Pieces of Brocade), a collection of eight stories. *Eight Pieces* ostensibly warns against lust (stories 1, 2, 4, 5), intimidation by one's wife (story 2), gambling (story 3), drinking (story 6), and slander (story 7). However, the stories emphasize explicit sexual descriptions that sometimes border on the grotesque. Story 2 depicts a lascivious virago's sexual abuse of her husband. In story 8, three lustful widows of the same household all commit adultery with the same young man. One widow tells her four-year-old son, who sleeps with them one night, that the man is a tiger. After the frightened child relates to his grandmother how the "devouring tiger" attacks his mother, the grandmother decides to marry off the three daughters-in-law.

In contrast to these collections of erotic stories, a group of works in the 1640s shows strong concern with the dynasty, focuses on scholars and officials, and advocates returning to basic morality.

Huan-ying (Illusions; preface dated 1643), later published under the title *San-k'o p'ai-an ching-ch'i* (Slapping the Table in Amazement, Third Collection), contained thirty stories, twenty-seven of which have survived. Most of the stories express concern with loyalty, filial piety, and chastity in Ming society. Story 6 portrays a virtuous daughter-in-law who, oppressed by her shameless mother-in-law, commits suicide to demonstrate her purity. In story 7, an extraordinary girl, Wang Ts'ui-ch'iao, sells herself as a concubine in order to save her father. After being sold into prostitution and undergoing many hardships, she is taken by a pirate chief. Although she persuades him to surrender to the government, when he dies she also chooses to die in order to repay his kindness to her.

While exposing the sordid reality of the late Ming, some of the stories either serve admonitory purposes or entertain by their sensationalism. In story 17, because of government exploitation, a hard-working peasant keeps losing money and suffers extreme poverty with his wife. When he and his mother fall ill and his land is laid waste, he has no other alternative but to sell his wife. Local bullies then kill him and his mother for the money from the sale of his wife. But when his wife pleads with heaven for justice, all seven scoundrels are killed by thunderbolts. In story 21, a traveling merchant contracts syphilis in a brothel. His soul, taken to the underworld, learns that he will be transformed into a woman and will marry his traveling companion. Story 29 warns against drinking, lust, greed, and wrath and satirizes monks who are not immune to these temptations.

Chou Chi's *Hsi-hu erh-chi* (Second Collection of West Lake Stories), comprising thirty-four stories, is the first collection to focus on a location. Based on anecdotes and legends of Hangchow, the stories express themes of requital, karma, and retribution. Chou was a well-read, conservative, proud, yet frustrated Hangchow scholar; he used the stories to impart his opinions. Story 4 is a comedy of fortune, expressing the irony of Chou's situation. A stupid but kind man passes the examinations because of a grateful ghost. In another stroke of luck, he goes on to become a high-ranking official, while none of his superiors discovers his lack of learning. Story 15, "Wen-ch'ang ssu lien ts'ai man chu lu-chi" (Lo Yin), warns against arrogance, fickleness, and mockery of others. In story 7, which has a long disquisition about the synthesis of the three doctrines (Buddhism, Taoism, and Confucianism), a monk not entirely insensitive to the temptation of worldly pleasures is reincarnated after death as a wicked prime minister. Story 5, "Li Feng-niang k'u tu tsao t'ien-ch'ien" (Jealous and Cruel, Li Feng-niang Suffers from Divine Retribution), is a satire of vice that vividly portrays Empress Li's cruelty as well as her suffering from self-torture when she is possessed by the ghost of a former victim.

Yüan-yang chen (A Pair of Needles; c. 1644/1645) is a collection of four four-chapter stories written during the Southern Ming regimes (1644–1662) that lingered on in the south for a couple of decades after the establishment of the Ch'ing dynasty in 1644. Intended to be like acupuncture needles used to cure the world's illness, the stories expose the deceit and corruption in the examination system in a manner that anticipates the satiric novel *Ju-lin wai-shih* (The Scholars; c. 1750; see chapter 35).

Of the sixteen stories in *Ch'ing-yeh chung* (Alarum Bell on a Still Night; c. 1645), ten survive. These well-written stories condemn evil, celebrate virtue, and admonish the reader to revive morality. In story 2, browbeaten and shamed by their lascivious and unethical mother-in-law, two virtuous daughters-in-law throw themselves into the river to preserve their chastity. Similarly, in story 7, a woman bullied by her husband's concubine—a former prostitute—attempts suicide. However, her thirteen-year-old son dissuades her and then kills the concubine. Instead of being punished, he is praised for his filial devotion and courage.

Only three stories from *T'ien ts'ou ch'iao* (Predetermined Fortune) have survived. Story 2 satirizes the examination system. Story 3 tells of a remarkable, chaste woman, who not only resists the advances made by her husband's master but threatens to kill him, thereby winning her husband's freedom. Both she and her husband eventually leave home and become Taoists.

Tsui hsing shih (The Sobering Stone) contains fifteen stories written by a Ming loyalist, Tung-Lu Ku-k'uang-sheng (pseud.), soon after the Manchu conquest. The stories focus on scholar-officials and their morality. The first story praises an honest official, showing how his descendants receive divine rewards after his death. In story 11, an official who expects advancement learns, through an old monk's dream, that, because he has yielded to his wife's urging to take bribes, he will be deprived by the gods of the anticipated high-ranking appointment. Story 6 is derived from a T'ang tale about a poet who is transformed into a tiger. In the later version, a haughty poet who serves as a low-ranking official is so arrogant that none of his colleagues wants to recommend him for reappointment. However, his fearful patrons give him money, hoping to stop him from lampooning and vilifying them.

EARLY CH'ING DYNASTY

Li Yü, a famous man of letters as well as a dramatist, was also the greatest story writer of the Ch'ing dynasty; he produced witty and original stories characterized by humor, ingenious plots often involving coincidences, and vivid characterizations. Influenced by Ling Meng-ch'u's, Li's stories enlighten as well as entertain readers, advocating that they accept fate, adopt a pragmatic outlook on life, and use their talents and resources to make life better. Li speaks through the narrator, making many comments and adopting a mixture of tones ranging from serious to risqué. In addition to revitalizing the story genre, Li also established the precedent of making plays out of his own stories.

Li Yü's *Wu-sheng hsi* (Silent Operas; 1656; cited below as *Operas*) presents twelve stories with either comic continuations or inversions of existing stereotypes. The plots of *Operas* 1 and 2 employ comic twists of fate: the protagonists repeatedly try—and fail—to avoid certain circumstances, but the problem is solved through an ingenious solution and all ends happily. "Ch'ou lang-chün p'a chiao p'ien te yen" (An Ugly Husband Fears a Pretty Wife but Marries a Beautiful One; *Operas* 1) parodies the "genius and beauty" fictional convention. The story argues that in real life a beautiful maiden is often married not to a talented, refined scholar but, rather, to an ugly and poorly educated boor. Three pretty women are forced to marry the same ugly, foul-smelling, but rich, man. Because of the clever tactics of one wife, they all end up having an obedient husband, a comfortable life, and handsome sons who become officials. In "Mei nan-tzu pi huo fan sheng yi" (A Handsome Lad Raises Doubts by Trying to Avoid Suspicion; *Operas* 2), Li Yü makes the original argument that an upright but incompetent judge can cause injustice just as a corrupt and venal one can. Because the honest judge is so self-righteous and biased, no one dares criticize him, and he fails to see his own mistakes—until a coincidence shows him his folly.

"Nü Ch'en P'ing chi sheng ch'i ch'u" (The Female Ch'en P'ing Saves Her Life; *Operas* 5) tells of an intelligent and virtuous peasant wife who offers herself to a bandit chief in order to save her husband. Outwitting the bandit, she eventually escapes with her chastity preserved and even manipulates the bandit into testifying to her chastity. In addition, she brings great wealth to her husband.

In "Nan Meng-mu chiao ho san ch'ien" (A Male Mencius's Mother Educates His Son; *Operas* 6), a handsome lad, to repay his homosexual lover's kindness to him and his father, castrates himself. Dressing as a woman for the rest of his life, he brings up his partner's child after his death and remains a chaste "widow." Here, the narrator is deliberately ambivalent in his attitude toward homosexuality. While playfully blaming homosexuality for producing no children and being futile, the narrator also describes an almost ideal homosexual marriage and an exemplary male mother.

"Yi-ch'i huan-ch'ieh kuei shen ch'i" (The Spirits Astonish by Switching Wife and Concubine; *Operas* 10) inverts the literary stereotype of the wife who is jealous of a concubine. It describes how a concubine, desiring to monopolize the husband, tries to harm the wife but eventually suffers divine retribution.

Soon after the publication of *Silent Operas*, Li Yü published *Wu-sheng hsi erh-chi* (Silent Operas, Second Collection; 1656), which is no longer extant. However, six stories from the collection can be found in *Lien-ch'eng pi ch'üan-chi* (Priceless Jade), an anthology with eighteen stories from the two *Operas* collections. "T'an Ch'u-yü hsi-li ch'uan-ch'ing, Liu Miao-ku ch'ü chung ssu-chieh" (An Actress Scorns Wealth and Honor to Preserve Her Chastity) is a romantic comedy about a young scholar who joins an acting troupe to be close to the woman he loves. However, the lovers can express their affection only when acting on stage. Resisting marriage to a rich man, the actress actually throws herself into a river near the stage while acting in a play. The scholar follows her. Rescued by a fisherman, the couple is able to live together. After achieving success in officialdom, the scholar chooses to withdraw from the world together with his wife. The story plays upon the paradoxical relationship between acting and life, the false and the real, and engagement and retirement.

Also in *Priceless Jade*, "Kua-fu she-chi chui hsin-lang, chung mei ch'i-hsin to ts'ai-tzu" (A Widow Hatches a Plot to Receive a Bridegroom) is a wish-fulfillment comedy for scholars. Three beautiful courtesans and a widow all fall in love with a handsome and talented poet. To compete with the widow, the courtesans find the poet an outstanding candidate as a wife. In the end, all five women agree to share the man. In "Tu-ch'i shou yu fu chih kua, no-fu huan pu ssu chih hun" (A Jealous Wife Becomes a Widow While Her Husband Is Still Alive), a lengthy story with a complicated plot, an intelligent and courageous virago fights with her husband's friends to keep him from taking concubines. In the end, she falls into a trap sprung by a certain Master Fei, reforms, and becomes a virtuous wife free of jealousy. Deliberate, authorial complexity can be detected in the depiction of a woman who is shrewish yet also smart and brave.

Li Yü's *Shih-erh lou* (Twelve Towers; preface dated 1658) offers twelve excellent stories. Each story is divided into chapters, some with as many as six. In "Ts'ui ya lou" (House of Gathered Refinements), a story that juxtaposes and contrasts concepts of elegance and vulgarity, gentleness and violence, a handsome lad beloved by his two homosexual partners is drugged and castrated by a tyrannical prime minister. "Sheng wo lou" (The House of My Birth) inverts the usual parent-child relationship by telling the story of a man who adopts a father and mother. The artist-recluse in "Wen kuo lou" (Corrigibility House) is one of Li Yü's personae. The artist renounces both his study and art and moves to the countryside after failing his examinations, but his friends find many ways to lure him back.

"Hsia yi lou" (The Summer Pavilion) is a romantic comedy that entertains the reader with one surprise after another. In "Fu yün lou" (The Cloud-Scraper), a resourceful maidservant succeeds in arranging a marriage between the hero and her young mistress, while simultaneously ensuring her own status as his second wife. Inverting the master-servant and husband-wife relationships, she manipulates her unsuspecting master and mistress and forces her future husband to abide by her conditions. Yet she acts not only out of self-interest but also to achieve good for all involved.

"Ho kuei lou" (Homing Crane Lodge) is a great parody of romance that promotes a prudent philosophical attitude toward love, marriage, and life. It contrasts two male protagonists' attitudes toward their wives when leaving home and their respective outcomes. The romantic couple pines so much for each other that, when the hero returns home, he finds his wife has died and he has aged prematurely. By contrast, the prudent hero, who has incurred his wife's hatred because of his coldness in parting, returns to find her in good health. After she realizes that he is in fact a true romantic, despite his antiromantic attitude, they renew their conjugal bliss.

Cho-yüan-t'ing chu-jen's (pseud.) *Chao-shih pei* (The Cup that Reflects the World; c. 1661) contains four original stories. The second story, "Pai-ho fang chiang wu tso yu" (Deception in the Pai-ho Quarter), satirizes a hanger-on who tries to impress wealthy potential patrons with his learning. It mocks those failed and shameless scholars who will become major targets of satire in *The Scholars*. Story 4, "Chüeh hsin-k'eng ch'ien-kuei ch'eng ts'ai-chu" (The Miser Makes a Fortune from New Pits), caricatures a miser who becomes rich through selling night soil collected in the latrines he builds and allows people to use. Instead of being punished for his actions, the miser becomes very rich and his descendants achieve success as officials.

The Hangchow writer Ai-na chü-shih's (pseud.) *Tou-p'eng hsien-hua* (Idle Talk Under the Bean Arbor; c. 1668 + ?) is a story with twelve embedded stories. The primary story is about the construction and eventual destruction of a bean arbor under which villagers exchange stories. The twelve stories are interconnected through references to the vines' growth, flowering, podding, and final withering. Ai-na's stories use the styles of both vernacular and classical fiction and employ humor and irony to parody philosophical ideas. Supplementing Confucian teaching with Buddhist and Taoist thought, they advocate a return-to-basics pragmatism.

Ai-na enjoyed overturning the myths of legendary heroes. The first story, "Chieh Chih-t'ui huo-feng tu-fu" (Chieh Chih-t'ui Traps His Jealous Wife in an Inferno), condemns jealous wives and demythologizes the Confucian paragon Chieh Chih-t'ui, portraying him as a fearful husband. Story 2 debunks the legend of Hsi Shih, the famed patriotic beauty, assigning her the sad fate of being drowned by her former Yüeh lover. Ai-na's story blames her for betraying her husband and benefactor, the King of Wu, and failing to make peace between the kingdoms of Wu and Yüeh. Story 7, "Shou-yang shan Shu-ch'i pien-chieh" (On Mount Shou-yang, Shu-ch'i Switches Loyalties), rewrites the legend of the loyalist brothers Po-yi and Shu-ch'i, portraying Shu-ch'i as disloyal and Po-yi as rigid and stubborn.

Like many other writers of his time, Ai-na moralized through his stories, emphasizing such virtues as chivalry and selflessness. Story 3 tells of a rich but idiotic young man who generously assists a penniless man and later achieves success through the man's help. Story 4 illustrates the importance of accumulating virtue for the sake of one's descendants. In story 5, an honest beggar devoted to his mother is contrasted with a high-ranking official who fails in his filial duty. Story 6 criticizes abuses in Buddhist religious practices.

Ai-na also criticized contemporary society. Story 9 exposes corruption in the late Ming police force. Story 10 caricatures sycophantic idler-impostors in Soochow. Story 11 tells anecdotes of wartime horrors. In the last story, a rigid and satirized Confucian scholar condemns Taoism and Buddhism. The accidental collapse of the bean arbor, symbolic of the fall of the Ming, appropriately brings the story sequence to an end.

Jen-chung hua (Portraits of Society), possibly published during the Shun-chih reign (1644–1661), contains five elaborately plotted stories. These stories eulogize ideal scholars and officials and illustrate how they are rewarded with successful careers and harmonious marriages with beautiful and talented women. The stories also satirize ungrateful, snobbish people and corrupt officials.

Wu-se shih (Multicolored Stones) and *Pa tung-t'ien* (Eight Fairylands), consisting of eight stories each, were written by an anonymous author, possibly during the late seventeenth century. Intended as moral admonitions, these stories also frequently include romantic comedy similar to that of the "genius and beauty" fiction. In the second tale of *Multicolored Stones*, "Shuang tiao ch'ing" (Celebrating the Shooting of Two Vultures), the ugly, ferocious wife of a scholar forbids him to take a concubine even though he has no heir. Aided by a friend, the scholar takes a concubine and secretly impregnates her. His wife sells the girl, not knowing that the buyer is the scholar's friend. Later in her chase after her husband, the wife is seized and then released by bandits and returns home much chastened. She turns over the day-to-day management of the household to the concubine and becomes a lay Buddhist worshipper who stays at home.

Hsi-hu chia-hua (Charming Stories of West Lake; preface dated 1673) comprises sixteen stories about renowned poets, Taoists, and Buddhists in and around Hangchow. The last story is about the famous late Ming scholar Shen Chu-hung, who gave up striving for worldly success and became a monk. All but story 14 have happy endings. Story 14 tells of the famous Hsiao-ch'ing, a talented beauty taken as a concubine by a rich man but then imprisoned by his jealous wife. She languishes and eventually dies. However, this is not a tragic ending: Hsiao-ch'ing will always be remembered precisely because of her sad fate.

In addition, there are at least seven other collections of stories from the seventeenth century. However, these works have much less literary value than the collections mentioned here.

MID-CH'ING DYNASTY

In 1726, Shih Ch'eng-chin (1659–c. 1736), a prolific writer of didactic works, published under his own name (unlike many of his predecessors) a volume combining the forty-tale *Yü-hua hsiang* (Scent of Flowers from Heaven) and the twelve-tale *T'ung-t'ien le* (Understanding Heavenly Pleasures). Some of the stories describe contemporary events that the author claims to have witnessed or heard about. A devout Buddhist, Shih wrote stories of moral admonition featuring karmic retribution. The first story in the volume, "Chin chüeh lou" (House of Awakening), recalls Li Yü's "Corrigibility House" (both stories build on the theme of reclusion, their protagonists having no interest in seeking office, rank, or wealth) and includes a character similar to one that appears later, in the first chapter of the eighteenth-century novel *The Scholars*, about the painter-scholar Wang Mien. A reclusive painter with few friends lives in the countryside. When a prince invites him to serve in the capital, his friend Lan Ho-shang (Indolence, a Buddhist monk) helps him go into hiding instead. As a result, the painter is able to live in peace until a ripe old age. In the last story in Shih's collection, Indolence reappears as a famous and eminent monk who dies peacefully when he has reached his hundredth year.

Hsing-meng p'ien-yen (Refined Words to Awaken One from Dreams), possibly from the late eighteenth century, includes twelve stories, adaptations of classical tales from P'u Sung-ling's *Liao-chai chih-yi* (Strange Tales from Make-Do Studio). Writing under a pseudonym, the author chooses mostly tales about domestic problems, some of which P'u had developed into colloquial plays. In making his adaptations, the author alters the tales in many ways, retelling them in the story format, using very colloquial diction, changing the names of some of the characters and places, deleting P'u's comments, and adding an introductory disquisition as well as plot details particular to each story. Story 4, an adaptation of P'u's "Ta-nan" (Big Boy), recalls P'an Chin-lien's jealousy of Li P'ing-erh's pregnancy and baby in the classic novel *Chin P'ing Mei* (Gold Vase Plum; c. 1617). A jealous wife attempts to cause a pregnant concubine to miscarry and, when this fails, tries to kill the baby boy. In one grotesque scene, the concubine, while looking for her son, suddenly feels the urge to relieve herself. Upon opening the commode, she is shocked to find her baby, upside down, soaking in the nightsoil, and nearly suffocated to death by urine and feces.

Tu Kang's (b. 1740?) *Yü-mu hsing-hsin pien* (Stories to Delight the Eye and Awaken the Heart; 1792) has sixteen *chüan*. Tu instructs the reader in Confucian virtues through entertaining stories, employing karmic retribution to illustrate how virtue is rewarded and vice punished. His stories are based on history, contemporary social events, or earlier stories. Chapter 1 of *chüan* 14 is taken from Feng Meng-lung's "Wu Pao-an Abandons His Family to Ransom His Friend" (KC 8), while *chüan* 11 is adapted primarily from "The Brothel Keeper" (*Rocks* 8).

Tu's stories demonstrate variations of the prolog and the prolog story. In *chüan* 1, the first chapter is a prolog story about a man who devotes his life to searching for his father's bones, while chapters 2–3 comprise the main story about filial piety. *Chüan* 2 has no prolog story. In a disquisition, the narrator claims that, ordinarily, a widow has done well enough by remaining chaste—one cannot expect her to ensure the continuation of her husband's family line. The story then tells of a daughter-in-law who is not only chaste and filial but also ingenious. After both her only son and her husband (also an only son) die in an epidemic, she arranges an unlikely marriage between her nineteen-year-old younger sister and her seventy-year-old father-in-law. As a result, her father-in-law sires three sons, thus perpetuating the family line.

In *chüan* 4, the prolog story in chapter 1 is reminiscent of "The Female Ch'en P'ing." A woman offers herself to a bandit chief in order to save her husband's family. After living with the bandit for years and completely disarming him, she finds a chance to escape and return to her husband. The main story in chapter 2 is about an even more trying situation. During a famine, a woman sells herself to a rich man for money to feed her husband's starving family. Then, to preserve her chastity, she hangs herself in the palanquin on her wedding day. Before her death, however, she has made arrangements to ensure that the rich man will not be implicated in her death and will receive some land in return for his payment.

Although story 10 of *Idle Talk Under the Bean Arbor* contains snippets of dialog in the language of Soochow, Shao Pin-ju's (also called Shao Chi-t'ang) *Su-hua ch'ing-t'an* (Colloquial Chats) is the first collection written substantially in a language other than Mandarin, namely, Cantonese. It comprises eighteen entertaining stories of moral admonition. "P'i-shuang po" (Arsenic Bowl) tells of a vitriolic daughter-in-law who suffers divine punishment because she has mistreated her blind mother-in-law and eventually strangled her to death.

The vernacular story was in full bloom between the 1620s and the 1660s. Feng Meng-lung, Hsi Lang-hsien, and Ling Meng-ch'u established the norm of the genre. Although under their predecessors' influence, Li Yü, Cho-yüan-t'ing chu-jen, and Ai-na chü-shih continued to be experimental and inventive. The genre began to wither and wilt after the third quarter of the seventeenth century. With the exception of works written by better writers such as Shih Ch'eng-chin and Tu Kang, most stories appearing afterward tended to imitate or repeat the plots and ideas of earlier stories, offering little originality in form, content, or style. By the nineteenth century, the genre had lost much of its vitality. Yet the great stories written by the seventeenth-century masters continued to be read and provided fertile ground for the growth of eighteenth- and nineteenth-century novels as well as twentieth-century novels and short stories.

Yenna Wu

Chapter 35

FULL-LENGTH VERNACULAR FICTION

The modern Chinese language owes much to traditional vernacular fiction. During the literary revolution of the late 1910s and early 1920s, a new written language (*pai-hua*) that purported to be more popular, immediate, and closer to the spoken language drew from traditional vernacular fiction and sought therein its own lineage. The literary revolution canonized vernacular fiction as the "countertradition." As such, its ties with orality, performance, popular culture, and folk memory, and its subversive potential for the sociopolitical order (a more problematic proposition) have often been emphasized in twentieth-century criticism. However, many scholars have noted how the elite shaped the early masterpieces of vernacular fiction in their final stages of evolution. Moreover, from about the seventeenth century on, vernacular fiction became one of the venues through which members of the elite displayed their learning and expressed and defined their ideals, frustrations, and self-understanding.

The copresence of or tension between high and low diction—between literati culture and popular culture—is but one token of the intrinsic hybridity of vernacular fiction. Lyric poetry, songs, descriptive verses, poetic exposition, parallel prose, dramatic arias, doggerels, quotations from and summaries of historical texts and other fictional works, and the rhetoric of oral performance are often woven into the fabric of narrative. The best examples of the genre almost never fail self-consciously to exploit the interplay of different generic traits and stylistic levels to achieve ironic disjunctions or visions of totality based on complementary opposites and balanced juxtapositions. The usual term for full-length vernacular fiction, *chang-hui hsiao-shuo,* suggests division into chapters and episodes, with no built-in injunction for form and unity. Notwithstanding the formidable length and apparent shapelessness of some vernacular fiction, the more attentive reader will notice patterns and meanings emerging from contrast and complementarity within each chapter, between chapters, and between narrative units that comprise clusters of chapters, figural and structural repetitions, the gathering and dispersal of characters, and significant midpoints or middle sections, as well as framing sections that function as extended prologs and epilogs. Traditional commentaries published along with works of fiction are often helpful in delineating the esthetics of fiction (see chapter 46).

Vernacular fiction is also called "unofficial history" (*yeh-shih, pai-shih*). The conceit of recording "what actually happened" and the presumed filiation to the rhetoric and concerns of official historiography are most evident in the genre of historical fiction, of which the preeminent example is *San-kuo yen-yi* (Romance of the Three Kingdoms). The collapse of the Han dynasty, the struggle for supremacy among the states of Wei, Shu, and Wu, and the eventual reunification of the country under the Chin dynasty during the third century had become the stuff of popular storytelling (in a subgenre, "telling of historical stories" [*chiang-shih*]) by the Sung dynasty (960–1279). A stylistically naive *Ch'üan-hsiang San-kuo chih p'ing-hua* (Illustrated Stories from the Records of the Three Kingdoms; c. 1321–1323; a less polished version, dated 1294, was recently discovered in Japan), possibly a promptbook for storytellers, and Yüan plays on the Three Kingdoms indicate that the full-length narrative is the culmination of a long tradition. Several sources mention Lo Kuan-chung (c. fourteenth century) as the author, but there is no definite proof for the attribution. The earliest extant edition dates from 1522 and includes a 1494 preface.

The 1522 edition, consisting of 240 *chüan,* was edited and compressed into 120 chapters by Mao Lun and his son, Mao Tsung-kang (c. 1632–1709+). This 1679 edition remains the most widely read version of the *Three Kingdoms.* The book begins with the disintegration of the Han empire and the sworn brotherhood of Liu Pei, Kuan Yü, and Chang Fei, whose initial cause is the suppression of the popular Taoist, millenarian Yellow Turban Rebels. The first quarter of the book charts the ascendancy of various warlords and the eventual consolidation of military dictator Ts'ao Ts'ao's (155–220) position in the Yellow River plains (later the state of Wei) in north China and that of his rival, Sun Ch'üan (181–252), in the lower Yangtze area (later the state of Wu). Still without a real power base, Liu Pei (162–223), the future ruler of Shu, seeks out the preternaturally crafty Chu-ko Liang (181–234) as his adviser. The defeat of Ts'ao Ts'ao's army by the forces of Sun Ch'üan and Liu Pei in the climactic Battle of the Red Cliff (*San-kuo yen-yi,* chapters 43–50) establishes the de facto tripartite division of the country, with Liu Pei ensconced in the upper Yangtze Valley (later the state of Shu) by the middle section of the book. Several major protagonists (Ts'ao Ts'ao, Kuan Yü, Chang Fei, Liu Pei) die just as the three kingdoms become full-fledged political entities (*San-kuo yen-yi*, chapters 76–85), a reminder of the changeable and ephemeral nature of heroic endeavor. The last third of the book chronicles the decline and fall of the three kingdoms. Chu-ko Liang's military expeditions (*San-kuo yen-yi,* chapters 85–104) fail to turn the tide for Shu. There are insistent repetitions: the incompetent and decadent last rulers of the three kingdoms return us to the final years of the Han dynasty. The Ssu-ma clan, which wins out in the end, employs the same ruthless ploys as the usurpers who brought down the Han.

The title of the book in Chinese, which literally means "The Elaboration of the Meanings of the [*Records of the*] *Three Kingdoms*," implies adherence to or assimilation of official historiography: chiefly Ch'en Shou's (233–297) *San-kuo chih* (Records of the Three Kingdoms) and its commentaries and annotations by P'ei Sung-chih (372–451), but also Fan Yeh's (398–446) *Hou Han shu* (History of the Later Han Dynasty), Ssu-ma Kuang's (1019–1086) *Tzu-chih t'ung-chien* (A Comprehensive Mirror for Aid in Government), and Chu Hsi's (1130–1200) *T'ung-chien kang-mu* (Main Principles of the Comprehensive Mirror). Indeed, some early editions have the words "based on the *Mirror*" (*an-chien*) in their titles. The full-length narrative is formed through fusion of the historiographical tradition with the mythologizing memory preserved in storytelling and dramatic performances. This mixture prompted Chang Hsüeh-ch'eng's (1738–1801) famous judgment that the book is "seven parts historical facts, three parts fictional arrangement." Is historical veracity compromised or fictional imagination consequently fettered?

To answer this question, we need first to examine the vision and artistic effect achieved by the amalgamation of disparate materials. Extant popular works from the fourteenth and fifteenth centuries present a clear dichotomy of good and evil in the confrontation between Shu and Wei, with Wu playing a more neutral and secondary role. Distantly and dubiously related to the Han house, Liu Pei, eventually the Shu ruler, is yet honored as the "royal uncle" with the most legitimate claim to the mandate of rulership. Shu is validated for its presumed loyalty to the Han dynasty, but perhaps even more important for popular appeal are the values attributed to its leaders: the deepest mutual devotion sustains the sworn brotherhood of Liu Pei, Kuan Yü, and Chang Fei; the latter two demonstrate great physical valor; Chu-ko Liang, Liu Pei's chief adviser, has the magical prowess of priests in messianic cults. The aura of secret-society morality is reminiscent of the bandit-heroes from *Shui-hu chuan* (Water Margin). In the *Illustrated Stories from the Records of the Three Kingdoms*, both Kuan Yü and Chang Fei kill government officials at the beginning of their careers. Unrecognized and maligned, the three brothers "became bandits [*lo-ts'ao*] in the T'ai-heng Mountains," (a place also associated with early *Water Margin* stories). The formative period of the "Three Kingdoms" tradition could have spanned traumatic events such as the Chin occupation of north China in the twelfth century, the establishment of Mongol rule in the thirteenth century, and the end of the Yüan dynasty in the fourteenth century. Dispossessed heroes unsanctioned by the social-political system, defying the limits of law, and accomplishing great feats through sheer will and gang solidarity might have seemed especially appealing in such moments of historical crisis, when there was confusion regarding legitimate political authority and foreign rule justified insurrection.

The swearing of the brotherhood oath in the Peach Garden is a key scene at the beginning of the *Three Kingdoms.* But the author here tones down the brothers' defiant transgressions and emphasizes their loyalty to Han, which establishes Shu as the kingdom with the legitimate mandate of rulership (*cheng-t'ung*). This is especially obvious in Mao Lun's and Mao Tsung-kang's recension of the text, which goes further than the 1522 edition in eulogizing Shu-Han and vilifying Ts'ao Ts'ao and Wei. Historiography agrees on the necessity of determining legitimacy but argues over the candidacy: Ch'en Shou implicitly supports Wei's claim to the legitimate mandate, Hsi Tso-ch'ih (c. fourth century) and Ssu-ma Kuang link mandate to unification, and Chu Hsi considers Shu the rightful successor to the Han dynasty. *Three Kingdoms* takes up this concern with Shu-Han's legitimate mandate but augments it, sometimes incongruously, through the bonds of sworn brotherhood, gang morality, and Taoist magic.

Such tensions inform the very term *yen-yi:* it can mean to elaborate the meanings of official historiography, to present principles of righteousness and proper conduct, and to enact the bonds of personal loyalty and group solidarity (*yi-ch'i*). The polyvalence of *yi* defines some memorable dilemmas in the book. After the Battle of the Red Cliff, Kuan Yü "honorably releases" (*yi-shih*) Ts'ao Ts'ao and the remnants of his defeated army at Hua-jung Pass (in chapter 50). In order to repay Ts'ao Ts'ao's earlier recognition and respect, Kuan Yü imperils the Shu-Han cause. When Liu Pei rashly launches a military expedition against Wu to avenge the death of Kuan Yü, he and his ministers debate whether such action is "great righteousness" (*ta-yi*) or "petty righteousness" (*hsiao-yi*), "private vengeance" (*ssu-ch'ou*) or "vengeance for the common good" (*kung-ch'ou*) (chapter 81). In both cases, implicit empathy with personal honor and loyalty nevertheless leaves no doubt that the destiny of Shu-Han is the more momentous cause, even if it is also somewhat more abstract.

The fusion of historiographical and popular traditions produces complexity, depth, and unresolved contradictions in the *Three Kingdoms.* The vilified Ts'ao Ts'ao in the storytelling and dramatic traditions, and Ts'ao Ts'ao the statesman with vision in the historical writings of Ch'en Shou and Ssu-ma Kuang, are creatively conflated as the deviant hero (*chien-hsiung*) in the *Three Kingdoms.* Ts'ao Ts'ao sums up his philosophy epigrammatically: "I would rather betray everyone under heaven than let anyone under heaven betray me" (chapter 4). His ruthlessness is mediated, if not redeemed, through self-understanding, appreciation of talent, and unerring assessment of a situation. Hsü Shao judges him to be "an able minister in times of good government, a deviant hero in times of disorder" (chapter 1). This presumably negative judgment also tacitly acknowledges the perversion of heroism as a product of troubled times. Despite numerous instances of his deceit and unscrupulousness, Ts'ao Ts'ao is never totally denied heroic stature and empathy. (Some passages in the 1522 edition praising Ts'ao Ts'ao's generosity and judiciousness edition were excised by Mao Lun and Mao Tsung-kang.) On the eve of his ignominious defeat at the Battle of the Red Cliff, he recites his most famous poem, which dwells on mutability and the sad fate of pleasure and striving but ends by affirming his political aspiration. This scene of poetic composition, possibly inspired by Su Shih's (Su Tung-p'o; 1037–1101) "Ch'ih-pi fu" (Rhapsody on the Red Cliff), adds tragic and ironic pathos to what could have been presented as a just defeat for a villain.

Kuan Yü's image also becomes more complex. Praised primarily for his valor and courage in popular traditions, he is both further elevated and subtly criticized in the full-length narrative. He becomes an avid reader of the *Ch'un-ch'iu* (Springs and Autumns), a paragon of the Confucian general (*ju-chiang*), a loyal defender of the Han dynasty, and a deity after death. In other words, he becomes the ideal embodiment of the moral principles underlying sociopolitical order. At the same time, by incorporating accounts of his vanity, willfulness, and misjudgments from official historiography, his downfall is shown to be all the more tragic for being rooted in his own flaws. Ch'en Shou's final judgment of Kuan Yü as "hard and willfully vain" is put in the mouth of Chu-ko Liang in the *Three Kingdoms*.

In some ways the hybrid image of Chu-ko Liang has greater inherent contradictions. Ch'en Shou describes Chu-ko Liang as a loyal and capable minister but indifferent strategist. Many of his exploits in the *Three Kingdoms* have no basis in historical records. Popular traditions credit him with prescience perilously close to wizardry—in some ways he answers the messianic longings for a leader with charismatic religious power, a frequent component of popular rebellions in imperial China. In the *Three Kingdoms*, he is at once Confucian sage adviser and founding minister, Taoist recluse and esoteric mentor, master military strategist, erudite diplomat and rhetorician, resourceful manipulator of human relations, and Taoist priest with supernatural powers. His uncanny prescience poses a special problem. How then can one account for his miscalculations and defeats? Indeed, myth-making becomes more insistent as the situation deteriorates. As if to redress the moral balance, Chu-ko Liang's powers become progressively more magical as Shu suffers more and more setbacks. With fantastic exploits he captures and releases the southern aboriginal leader Meng Huo seven times and finally brings him to submission, but such successes do not seem to affect Shu's fortunes in any tangible way. The will of heaven is invoked to reconcile Chu-ko Liang's prescience with the enemy's escape: he lets Kuan Yü guard the Hua-jung Pass, although he knows in advance that Kuan will release Ts'ao Ts'ao, because the latter is not yet destined to die. Mao Tsung-kang justifies Chu-ko Liang's strategic error in failing to launch a surprise attack on Wei, "because he knows that heaven's will cannot be reversed and does not wish to fight against it by risky exploits" (chapter 92).

Chu-ko Liang embodies the tension between Confucian political idealism and Machiavellian maneuvering that also defines Liu Pei as well as the larger vision of the book. Protestations of political disinterestedness and tearful, effusive concern for "the common good" notwithstanding, Liu Pei is ambitious and calculating. Compared to Ts'ao Ts'ao's unabashed deceit, Liu Pei's duplicity invites unmasking because the implied author refrains from any explicit negative judgment of him. In general, *Three Kingdoms* adheres to a rhetoric of moral government and legitimate mandate (based on Han lineage and hence conferred on Liu Pei), but the energy of the narrative derives from the fascination with power politics, military stratagems, deception, and cunning. The insistence on moral interpretations of history is also bracketed by visions of fatuous striving, ultimate emptiness, and relentless repetition, which provide a perspective beyond history. Taoist magicians (Yü Chi in chapter 29, Tso Ch'ih in chapter 68) taunt mighty rulers, transcendent recluses point to eremitic escape from all worldly conflicts (chapter 35), Chu-ko Liang himself espouses the ideal of withdrawal and presents public service as a reluctant sacrifice (chapters 36 and 38), and Kuan Yü's ghost seeks vengeance for his death but finds enlightenment instead when the monk P'u-ching discourses on the insubstantiality of the self and the illusory nature of justice, gain, and loss (chapter 77). There are, strictly speaking, no winners in the *Three Kingdoms*. Defeats often come on the heels of victories, and there is a kind of tragic pathos in ephemeral power and futile striving. The end of the three kingdoms is not the beginning of a great age—the Chin dynasty is weak, divided, and short-lived, and Chin reunification of the country merely returns it to the precarious unity and stasis in the last years of Han. Liu Yi compares Ssu-ma Yen (r. 265–290), Emperor Wu of the Chin, to "(emperors) Huan and Ling of Han." In this sense, the *Three Kingdoms* begins and ends with images of last rulers.

In time almost all periods of Chinese history and numerous historical events—the founding, restoration, and fall of dynasties, plus wars and rebellions—become the subject of historical fiction. There are also fictionalized historical biographies, often in the form of sagas about generations of military heroes. The seventeenth century witnessed the emergence of fiction dealing with contemporary or very recent history, including late Ming dynastic decadence, the traumatic Manchu conquest, and Ming loyalist resistance in south China and Taiwan. One of the best-known fictionalized histories is Feng Menglung's (1574–1646) *Hsin lieh-kuo chih* (New Records of the Various States), derived in part from Yü Shao-yü's (c. sixteenth century) account of the Shang and Chou dynasties and the slightly revised and renamed *Tung Chou lieh-kuo chih* (Records of the Various States During the Eastern Chou), by Ts'ai Yüan-fang (c. eighteenth century). Feng conceives of his project as exegetical vernacularization of canonical historical writings, especially *Tso chuan* (Tso Commentary;

c. fifth to fourth centuries B.C.E.) and Ssu-ma Ch'ien's (c. 145–c. 86 B.C.E.) *Shih-chi* (Records of the Historian). As such, it leaves less room for fictional invention than, say, *Three Kingdoms*.

By contrast, *Sui T'ang yen-yi* (Romance of the Sui and T'ang Dynasties), compiled by Ch'u Jen-huo (c. 1630 to c. 1705), represents an amalgamation of diverse works of classical and vernacular fiction on the history of the Sui and T'ang dynasties, but pays little heed to official historiography. One segment, largely indebted to *Sui shih yi-wen* (Remnants of Writings on Sui History; 1633 preface), by Yüan Yü-ling (c. seventeenth century), links heroic endeavor to popular insurrection and focuses on the exploits of Ch'in Shu-pao and other warrior heroes during the transition from the Sui dynasty (581–618) to the T'ang dynasty (618–907). Their rebellion against authority, legitimized by the pressures of the historical moment, is celebrated again in *Shuo T'ang yen-yi ch'üan-chuan* (Complete Tradition of T'ang Stories, c. eighteenth century), in which one can discern echoes of *Water Margin*. However, whereas in the Sui–T'ang heroic sagas rebels are assimilated to the cause of founding a great dynasty, in *Water Margin* rebellion is more profound and problematic.

The connection with historical writings is more tenuous but nevertheless significant in *Water Margin*, another masterpiece of early vernacular fiction. Its title in Chinese, *Shui-hu chuan*, echoes the "biographies" or "arrayed traditions" (*lieh-chuan*), a standard category in official historiography. Indeed, it is customary to speak of "the ten Wu Sung chapters" (*Wu shih-hui*) or "the ten Sung Chiang chapters" (*Sung shih-hui*), which suggests that narrative attention shifts periodically but remains focused on the biographies and adventures of individual characters. Sung Chiang the bandit-rebel and his followers (active in the early twelfth century) are mentioned in some historical records, although their historical significance bears no comparison with their glorified exploits in the fictive realm.

There are important links between the *Three Kingdoms* and *Water Margin*. The formative periods of the two works overlap significantly; both represent accretions of traditions, among them Sung–Yüan storytelling and Yüan–Ming drama. (Extant sources for *Water Margin* include *Ta-Sung Hsüan-ho yi-shih* [Events of the Hsüan-ho Era of the Great Sung Dynasty; c. thirteenth to fourteenth century] and a handful of *tsa-chü* plays.) The two works are printed together in *Ying-hsiung p'u* (The Exemplary Records of Heroes) from the Ch'ung-chen era (1628–1644). The bandit heroes in *Water Margin* derive names, nicknames, appearance and personality traits, even choice of weapons, from the characters in *Three Kingdoms*, and the influence might also have worked in the opposite direction. There is a common emphasis on secret brotherhood, "loyalty and righteousness" (*chung-yi*), and "great righteousness" (*ta-yi*), whose meanings are even more elliptical in *Water Margin* than in *Three Kingdoms*. However, whereas *Three Kingdoms* purports to uphold Confucian political order and the legitimate mandate, *Water Margin* apparently endorses a countergovernment or counterculture based on secret-society morality and defiance of the existent sociopolitical order.

Water Margin has an extremely complex textual history. The longest (120-chapter) version of the book (1614 preface) consists of the following sections: (a) the escape of 108 evil spirits due to the hubris and vanity of a minor official, the adventures of these reborn spirits, their paths to outlawry, and the eventual congregation of 108 bandit-heroes in the Marshes of Liang-shan (chapters 1–71); (b) the outlaws' military victories over government troops, together with their quest for and acceptance of the imperial decree of pacification (chapters 72–82); (c) military expeditions against the Liao (Khitan) invaders (chapters 82–90); campaigns against other rebels, respectively led by (d) T'ien Hu (chapters 91–100), (e) Wang Ch'ing (chapters 100–110), and (f) Fang La, including the dispersal and death of the Liang-shan bandit-heroes as a result of confrontations with Fang La and subsequent calumny at court, as well as Emperor Hui-tsung's (r. 1100–1125) dream-visit to the Marshes of Liang-shan and meeting with the spirits of the bandits, together with their final vindication in temples devoted to their memory (chapters 111–120).

These various components of the *Water Margin* tradition might have been created in the following sequential order: (a), (b), (f), (c), (d), (e). (There is no scholarly consensus on this subject.) Extant one-hundred-chapter editions that omit (d) through (e) date from the sixteenth century (a 1540 edition exists in fragments, a 1589 edition in its entirety). "Simplified editions" in 115, 110, and 124 chapters contain all the events enumerated but leave out the details and are stylistically far inferior. Designed for a broader and less-educated audience, these editions might have preceded or interacted with, or might have been derived from, the more sophisticated full-length narrative. In the mid-seventeenth century, Chin Sheng-t'an (1608–1661) truncated the text and produced a seventy-chapter version, with his own editorial changes and commentaries. Chin's version takes the first seventy-one chapters, turns chapter 1 into the prolog, and at the end adds Lu Chün-yi's dream, in which all 108 Liang-shan rebels are summarily executed. This became the most widely read version of *Water Margin*.

Most extant 100- and 120-chapter editions from the sixteenth and seventeenth centuries bear the title *Chung-yi "Shui hu chuan"* (Loyal and Righteous *Water Margin*). Sung Chiang renames the main hall of the Liang-shan compound "Hall of Loyalty and Righteousness" in the grand gathering of all 108 rebels (chapter 71). "Loyalty" (*chung*) presumably refers to the process wherein some rebels, especially Sung Chiang, seek and achieve reconciliation with the government. The quest for a "pacification decree" challenges the view that the authors of *Water Margin* radically rethink the nature and basis of the established polity. Having been forced into outlawry by an unjust and corrupt system, the Liang-shan heroes try to rectify their displacement by defending the Sung dynasty against the Liao and other bandit-rebels. Loyalty has also been linked to nationalist yearnings. The famous Sung loyalist poet Kung Sheng-yü (1222–after 1304) wrote thirty-six evaluative poems on Sung Chiang and his followers, implicitly affirming their type of heroism at a moment of historical crisis. (Mount T'ai-heng is mentioned five times in these poems, but not Liang-shan. This may indicate that there was a T'ai-heng branch of the rebels' stories that Kung became familiar with through storytelling.) Wang Tao-k'un in his 1589 preface claims that the Liang-shan rebels, despite their disaffection, "understand well the distinction between Chinese and barbarians" and therefore reject the Liao and Chin (Jurchen) governments. Li Chih in his 1590 preface argues that the putative authors, Shih Nai-an (c. fourteenth century) and Lo Kuan-chung, use the book to express their "anguish and frustration [*fen*] over Sung events," especially the Chin's northward abduction of the emperors Hui-tsung and Ch'in-tsung (r. last month of 1125 through 1126) and the complacent acceptance of compromise in the Southern Sung court.

The section on the military expedition against the Liao might have been inspired by resistance against the Chin and then the Mongols in the Sung–Yüan period or by wars with precursors of the Hou Chin (Later Chin, 1616–1636) and Ch'ing (1644–1911) and with tribes supposedly descended from the Yüan (the An-ta and Wa-la) fought in the fifteenth and sixteenth centuries. Sun Shu-yü points out in *"Shui-hu chuan" te lai-li hsin-t'ai yü yi-shu* (The Origins, Mentality, and Art of *Water Margin*; 1981) that resistance forces against the Chin, made up of disbanded Sung troops, local militias, and bandit-rebels, were designated as "the loyal and righteous" by the Southern Sung court. According to Sun, one early stratum of the *Water Margin* tradition articulates the aspirations and frustrations of the resistance fighters along the Sung-Chin border: these stories function as propaganda literature for outsiders and entertainment for insiders. In the present 120-chapter *Water Margin*, we are told that two rebels (Hu-yen Cho and Chu T'ung) and the son of another (Chang Ch'ing) later become heroes fighting Chin invaders (chapters 110 and 120).

The idea that rebellion may embody loyalty and express nationalist strivings is taken up in several works inspired by *Water Margin*. Ch'en Ch'en's (1614–after 1666) sequel to the book, *Shui-hu hou chuan* (*Water Margin*: Later Traditions; 1664 preface), uses the valiant exploits of the surviving bandit-heroes in fighting Chin invaders, defending the Sung dynasty, and escaping to the distant utopia of Siam to express the hopes and anguish of Ming loyalism following the Manchu conquest of the Ming dynasty in 1644. In *Hou "Shui-hu chuan"* (Sequel to *Water Margin*; c. mid-seventeenth century), by "Master of the Blue Lotus Chamber," reincarnations of the Liang-shan heroes continue their struggle against a corrupt Southern Sung government capitulating to the demands of Chin invaders. Yang Yao, a reincarnation of Sung Chiang, protests his loyalty and remonstrates with Emperor Kao-tsung (r. 1127–1162). In Ch'ien Ts'ai's *Shuo Yüeh ch'üan chuan* (Complete Tradition of Yüeh Fei Stories; 1684 or 1744), Hu-yen Cho also fights the Chin; Yüeh Fei (1103–1141), the national hero who repels the Chin armies, shares a teacher with the Liang-shan rebels and encourages bandit-rebels to join the common cause against the Chin, while descendants of the Liang-shan rebels become leaders in Yüeh Fei's army. Even a "contra *Water Margin*" work like *Chieh "Shui hu chuan"* (Conclusion of *Water Margin*), also called *Tang k'ou chih* (Records of the Elimination of Bandits), by Yü Wan-ch'un (1794–1849), pursues the same theme. Although the Liang-shan rebels are here maligned, ruthlessly eliminated, and denied all claims to loyalty, the protagonists who confront them are themselves persecuted by evil ministers, join up with bandits, and seek to rectify their transgression by fighting the Liang-shan rebels in the same way the latter wage wars against Fang La and other bandits in *Water Margin*.

A recurrent but nebulous word, *yi* (variously translated as "righteousness," "honor," "valor," "solidarity"), defines the values of the Liang-shan world. Bandit-rebels "form bonds of righteousness" (*chieh-yi*) when they become sworn brothers, "gather in righteousness" (*chü-yi*) when they confirm their pact of solidarity, and prepare for or celebrate robbery, raid, and battle. Actions undertaken to honor the ties of sworn brotherhood are "righteous deeds" (*yi-chü*). However, the very translation of the word *yi* as "righteous" is problematic, based as it is on the association with propriety (*yi*) and the compound "upright and righteous" (*cheng-yi*). In *Water Margin*, *yi* refers to the ethos that sustains the survival and prosperity of the bandit-rebels as a group, but often there is scant regard for "righteousness" as such.

Modern criticism tends to eulogize *Water Margin* as an antiauthoritarian saga protesting against the repressive forces in Chinese civilization. It is true that some rebels (most notably Lin Ch'ung) are "forced to go up Liang-shan" by corrupt officials abusing their power. But the book is not deeply interested in victimhood. More often than not, acts of vengeance (e.g., Wu Sung kills P'an Chin-lien and Hsi-men Ch'ing, his adulterous sister-in-law and her lover, who murdered his brother; Yang Hsiung disembowels his adulterous wife, P'an Ch'iao-yün) or violent outbursts of anger (e.g., Sung Chiang kills his "kept woman," Yen P'o-hsi, when she threatens to expose his association with Liang-shan outlaws; Lei Heng kills the singing girl Pai Hsiu-ying with his cangue—which he is wearing for having injured Pai's father—when she curses his mother) drive the characters toward Liang-shan. In many cases, coercion "to go up Liang-shan" comes not from the government but from the rebels themselves. Capable potential members are duped or forced into complicity with the Liang-shan establishment—among the most chilling examples are Hu San-niang, sole survivor of her clan after gory battles with Liang-shan; Ch'in Ming, whose family is executed by the governor when the Liang-shan outlaws stage his rebellion; and Chu T'ung, whose charge, his master's young child, is murdered by Li K'uei.

The slogan of Liang-shan is "to realize the Way on behalf of heaven" (*t'i-t'ien hsing-tao*), and "succor for the people" is intermittently mentioned. However, closer inspection of this world reveals no higher justice. Early on in the book, Lu Ta kills the local bully who persecutes Chin Ts'ui-lien and her father, but such instances of "fighting the powerful to defend the weak" are relatively rare. In the critic Sun Shu-yü's apt words, the *Water Margin* is no pastoral idealization of a Robin Hood–like community. C. T. Hsia (*The Classic Chinese Novel*; 1968), Andrew Plaks (*The Four Masterworks of Ming Fiction*; 1987), Y. W. Ma (*Shui-hu lun-heng* [Discussions on *Water Margin*]; 1992), and others have also delineated the darker aspects of this world. Vengeance, elevated here as the highest justice, degenerates into blood lust, as when Wu Sung massacres the entire household of the prison superintendent who plots to kill him, his knife's blade blunted by the relentless hacking, or when the Liang-shan heroes rescue Sung Chiang at the site of his would-be execution, killing countless people and capturing Huang Wen-ping, Sung's accuser, whom they subsequently execute by flaying. In general, there is much willful, indiscriminate, and random violence and, in some cases, almost pleasure in killing. Between chapters 47 and 70, Liang-shan enters an expansionist phase and launches immensely destructive campaigns against the Chu clan estates, Tseng-t'ou-shih, Peking, and Tung-p'ing and Tung-ch'ang prefectures. There is no clear dichotomy of good and evil: the provocation is trivial or perfunctory, and the avowed purpose is vengeance (often for a minor offense) or to "borrow grain." The consequent carnage renders hollow the Liang-shan claim of being "not greedy for goods and not disturbing the people" (chapter 71).

Gang solidarity has led some critics to suggest egalitarianism and disinterest regarding power, but Liang-shan society is quite hierarchical. As in the world outside, in Liang-shan lust for power is a dominant motive. Despite Sung Chiang's protestations of being unworthy (which remind the reader of Liu Pei), he is undoubtedly ambitious, and his covert bid for the position of leader may have motivated major campaigns between chapters 47 and 70. *Water Margin* is also colored by a deep misogyny. One defining trait of the hero (*hao-han*) is indifference to women (*pu hao-se*), and the memorable female characters here are devious, ruthless adulteresses to whom the Liang-shan heroes mete out gruesome but supposedly just punishments. Two women who join the gang are ugly, fierce, and devoid of all feminine traits. Beautiful, spirited, defiant Hu San-niang becomes silent after the elimination of her clan and her own capitulation. Sung Chiang marries her to the lecherous, petty, and most undeserving Wang Ying; thereafter her presence in the book is at best shadowy. Perhaps her beauty and valor make her somehow too dangerous. Women represent a distraction and, worse still, a potential threat to the solidarity and effectiveness of sworn brotherhood.

According to the "gang morality" (C. T. Hsia's term) of *Water Margin*, personal and group loyalty overrides moral judgment. In the territorial disputes between Shih En and Doorgod Chiang, for example, each is trying to be the reigning local bully collecting dues from the weak. Shih En buys Wu Sung's loyalty and with his help "honorably takes over" (*yi-to*) the coveted woods in question, although honor or justice hardly seems the issue. Shih En's name means literally "conferring beneficence," and his relationship with Wu Sung exemplifies personal loyalty sealed by generous treatment or liberal gifts, a common mode of exchange in the book. Despite the recurrent theme of fierce personal loyalty (*yi-ch'i*), the line between friend and foe is sometimes as tenuous as that between justice and its perversion. Characters fleeing official persecution often fall into the hands of outlaws who turn out to be their future comrades. Mutual recognition in a fight or being recognized on the verge of being robbed and murdered is a standard topos. This ubiquitous violence makes Liang-shan seem the only safe haven. Its material abundance supposedly adds to its appeal—we are constantly reminded of the heroes' gargantuan appetites and capacity for wine.

Water Margin fits as uneasily with late-imperial assertions of its "loyalty and righteousness" as with modern interpretations of "peasant uprising" or antiauthoritarian utopia. Its darker, more disturbing aspects pose special problems for interpretation: do they reflect the limitations of naive authors who fail to note the discrepancy between heroic rhetoric and violent reality (as suggested by C. T. Hsia)? Is it possible that what is distasteful to the modern reader might have served as effective propaganda for organizing gangs and for galvanizing anti-Chin, anti-Mongol, or simply antigovernment popular movements (Sun Shu-yü)? Is there self-conscious reflection on the nature of order and disorder, power and authority, and social and political organization through the ironic deflation of the heroic images of the Liang-shan outlaws in popular traditions (Andrew Plaks)? Is this a realistic portrayal of different sides of human nature in situations of persecution, violent appropriation of power, and alternative sociopolitical organization (Y. W. Ma)? Since this novel offers a layered text, it is also possible to imagine a naive, affirmative stance being modified and questioned by the elite shaping the text in its final stages. A good example is how the fiction commentator Chin Sheng-t'an deflates and undermines Sung Chiang in his revision of the text. It seems safe to assume that moments of unease, anxiety, and cold observation belong to a later stratum of the text. As is the case with *Three Kingdoms*, in *Water Margin* divergent perspectives on heroism are further framed by visions of void, renunciation, and ultimate detachment.

Historical and sociopolitical concerns in *Three Kingdoms* and *Water Margin* accommodate mythic-fantastic elements, such as the depiction of Chu-ko Liang's wizardry or of the Liang-shan heroes' supernatural origins as evil stars. History gives fantasy full rein in fictionalized accounts of popular insurrections, probably inspired by the latter's links to messianic cults. *P'ing-yao chuan* (The Quelling of Demons; twenty-chapter version, c. fourteenth to fifteenth century; forty-chapter version edited by Feng Meng-lung, 1620) deals with the suppression of an uprising led by Wang Tse in 1047, but the historical event is merely an excuse to embroider the supernatural origins and magical powers of the rebels. Likewise, *Nü-hsien wai-shih* (The Unofficial History of the Woman Immortal; c. 1703), by Lu Hsiung (c. 1640–c. 1722), rewrites an early Ming rebellion led by T'ang Sai-erh as the unfolding karmic destiny of contending celestial beings (reborn as T'ang and the Ming emperor Ch'eng-tsu). In the novel T'ang Sai-erh supports the dethroned Emperor Chien-wen against the usurper Emperor Ch'eng-tsu in a struggle replete with magical stratagems and Taoist esoteric knowledge. In Hsü Chung-lin's (d. c. 1566) *Feng-shen yen-yi* (Investiture of the Gods; c. sixteenth century), myth-making reaches encyclopedic proportions. It presents a key event in early Chinese history, the Chou conquest of Shang, as the just insurrection of oppressed subjects against tyranny. Both sides are aided by a plethora of gods, spirits, and religious masters anachronistically spinning Taoist and Buddhist mysteries and Confucian homily. Identified respectively with different esoteric cults, Shang and Chou confront each other in endless magical military formations. Lo Mao-teng's *San-pao t'ai-chien hsi-yang chi t'ung-su yen-yi* (Journey to the Western Ocean; 1597 preface) turns the eunuch Cheng Ho's famous late-fourteenth-century journeys (which reached east Africa) into adventures in fantastic realms. The author's claim of being motivated by frustrations with Ming naval impotence vis-à-vis Japanese pirates is not borne out in the narrative, which is concerned primarily with the magical prowess of the Buddhist monk and Taoist priest accompanying Cheng Ho.

Historical references notwithstanding, such works belong to what Lu Hsün (1881–1936) terms "fiction of gods and demons" (*shen-mo hsiao-shuo*), where religious formulas, magical transformations, and fantastic invention hold sway. The most important example of this subgenre is *Hsi-yu chi* (Journey to the West), attributed to Wu Ch'eng-en (c. 1500–1582). Like *Three Kingdoms* and *Water Margin,* it has many antecedents. Compared to them, however, *Journey to the West* shows more deliberate structural design and greater stylistic consistency. Its sources include the historical kernel of the story, the westward journey of the great monk-scholar-translator Hsüan-tsang (c. 600–664) to obtain Buddhist scriptures and his *Ta T'ang hsi-yü chi* (Accounts of the Western Regions Under the Great T'ang); hagiographic biographies of Hsüan-tsang; a Sung prosimetric account that introduces Hsüan-tsang's monkey disciple and his fantastic exploits; Yüan-Ming dramatic works; and a Yüan version used in storytelling, no longer extant, which apparently contained many of the episodes told in the present hundred-chapter novel. Twentieth-century scholars have also investigated the possible Indian origins of the figure of Sun Wu-k'ung, or Monkey.

The earliest extant edition of the hundred-chapter *Journey to the West* dates from 1592. The first part (chapters 1–7) tells of the Monkey's birth from a stone impregnated by the essences of heaven and earth, his ascension as ruler (Handsome Monkey King) of the monkey kingdom, his acquisition of magical powers and attempt to overcome mortality and mutability, the great havoc he wreaks in heaven and his successive confrontations with the celestial hierarchy, his final subjugation by the Buddha and imprisonment within the Five Phases

Mountain, transformed from the Buddha's hand turned downward. The second part (chapters 8–12) describes the Buddha's intention to impart Buddhist scriptures to the Chinese and the preparatory effort of the Boddhisativa Kuan-yin (Avalokiteśvara) to that end, the life story of Tripiṭaka, and the events that lead to the journey: Emperor T'ai-tsung sojourns in the underworld after he fails to save the dragon king, who disobeyed heaven's command and pleaded for his intercession; he convenes the Grand Mass upon his return to the human world; Tripiṭaka, the presiding priest, is called to the mission of seeking scriptures by Kuan-yin. The third and longest part of the book (chapters 13–100) deals with the gathering of the four disciples: Sun Wu-k'ung (Monkey Awake-to-Vacuity), Chu Pa-chieh (Pig Eight-Abstinences; called Pigsy in Arthur Waley's translation) or Wu-neng (Awake-to-Power), Sand Monk Wu-ching (Awake-to-Purity), and the dragon-horse; the eighty-one ordeals endured by Tripiṭaka during the journey (these trials often involve successive captures of the pilgrims by monsters, demons, and renegade celestial beings and their eventual deliverance); and the final successful completion of the mission.

Even modern readers unschooled in traditional Chinese thought may be tempted to read archetypal human emotions into this story about spontaneous generation, coming into being, attaining self-awareness, founding a society and a kingdom, confronting mortality, rebellion against authority, and reaching enlightenment and salvation. As a group, the pilgrims also seem to represent perennial types: Tripiṭaka's conventional piety, gullibility, and dependence on creature comfort make him Everyman; Monkey's pride and willfulness and Pig's excessive carnal appetites make them obvious complementary opposites and, arguably, facets of the human psyche.

Journey to the West has always invited allegorical interpretations. It contains numerous references to *yin-yang* and five phases (*wu-hsing*) terminology, *Yi-ching* (Classic of Change) and alchemical lore, and various other Taoist, Buddhist, and Confucian ideas and practices. The very topos of a journey suggests spiritual progress, a movement toward resolution or higher understanding. Extant Ch'ing-era commentary editions bear titles including words like "true interpretation" (*chen-ch'üan*), "original meaning" (*yüan-chih*), "illumination of the Way" (*cheng-tao*), and "understanding the *Changes*" (*t'ung-yi*), which show that, for at least three centuries, the prime concern of criticism on the novel has been to unravel the allegory and proceed from narrative surface to moral, religious, and philosophical meanings. Such distilled meanings include Confucian rectification of the mind and moral self-cultivation, Taoist alchemical processes in pursuit of immortality, Buddhist salvation through merit-making, Buddha's mercy, and transcending the dialectics of form and emptiness.

Echoing Monkey's injunction to the ruler of the Cart-Slow Kingdom that he should "bring the three teachings together: respect monks, respect Taoists, and also cultivate talents" (chapter 47), some Ch'ing critics read *Journey to the*

West as an argument for the convergence of the three teachings. Yu T'ung (1618–1704), for example, notes that Confucianism is about "the learning of preserving the mind and nourishing nature" (*ts'un-hsin yang-hsing*); Taoism, "the accomplishment of cultivating the mind and refining nature" (*hsiu-hsin lien-hsing*); Buddhism, "the prime concern of illuminating the mind and seeing nature" (*ming-hsin chien-hsing*). From such overlapping concerns with "mind/heart" (*hsin*) and "nature" (*hsing*), he proceeds to establish the simultaneous filiation of *Journey* to the three teachings.

As a reaction against traditional allegorical readings, twentieth-century scholars (notably Hu Shih [1891–1962] and Lu Hsün) emphasize the humor and buoyant good spirits of *Journey to the West* and dismiss the allegory as overly subtle and ultimately irrelevant. A characteristic judgment is found in Hu Shih's introduction to Waley's translation (1942): "*Monkey* is simply a book of good humor, profound nonsense, good-natured satire and delightful entertainment." In order to reinstate the work's moral seriousness, some critics (e.g., C. T. Hsia in *The Classic Chinese Novel*) have turned to dimensions of human experience embodied by the protagonists, while the more politically inclined readers (especially in the People's Republic of China) interpret Monkey's confrontations, first with the celestial hierarchy and then with numerous monsters during the journey, as allegories of sociopolitical struggles. More recently, there has been renewed emphasis on the Taoist, Confucian, and Buddhist allegorical meanings of the work, most notably in the studies of Anthony Yu (introduction to his translation; 1977, *Yü Kuo-fan "Hsi-yu chi" lun-chi* [Essays on *Journey to the West*]; 1989) and Andrew Plaks (*The Four Masterworks of Ming Fiction*).

Among "allegorical indices" are designations of Monkey as "Lord of Metal" (Chin-kung), Pig as "Wood Mother" (Mu-mu), and Sand Monk as "Yellow Hag" (Huang-p'o) or "Earth Mother" (T'u-mu) in titular couplets and verses in the narrative. The five pilgrims are thus matched with the five phases, although the correspondence lapses with the dragon-horse and Tripiṭaka: while the dragon-horse may still be linked to water by virtue of its provenance, Tripiṭaka would need a connection with fire to complete the picture. The monsters the pilgrims encounter, and the weapons used by both sides, are also often associated with the five phases. In the introduction to his translation, Anthony Yu points out that since, in alchemical literature, "the five phases are further correlated with the energies and breaths (*ch'i*) of the five viscera, these three disciples of Tripiṭaka are thereby made symbols of the interior realities in the human body." Beyond specific alchemical references, such correspondences may also point to visions of harmony and totality (with the five pilgrims forming one whole), and to relations of balance and control among the pilgrims or struggle between pilgrims and monsters, analogous to the mutual production and mutual conquest of the five phases, ideas that are as much the province of Confucianism as of Taoism.

The range of allegorical possibilities for *yin-yang* and five-phases terminology is typical. The ubiquitous metaphors of mind function with even broader ramifications. The idiomatic expression "monkey of the mind, horse of the will" (*hsin-yüan yi-ma*), which refers to the propensity of mind and will for unrestraint, conveniently applies to Monkey and the dragon-horse (the latter more incidentally) in the group of pilgrims. The term "Mind-Monkey" appears twelve times in titular couplets: Monkey's history of rebellion and submission, hubris and self-control thus suggests that the book may be read as an allegory for the cultivation of the mind (*hsiu-hsin*). One Ch'ing critic sees the four-stroke character for "heart/mind" (*hsin*) encoded in the very name of "the Cave of Slanting Moon and Three Stars," where Monkey learns magical transformations from his teacher, Subodhi.

There are liberal references in the work to the causative powers of mind: "When the mind arises, different kinds of monsters arise. When the mind is extinguished, different kinds of monsters are extinguished" (chapter 13); "Buddha is the mind; the mind, Buddha" (chapter 14); "Boddhisattvas and monsters are all one single thought" (chapter 17). C. T. Hsia singles out the episode of the transmission of the *Hsin ching* (Heart/Mind Sutra; in Sanskrit, *Prajñāpāramitā-hṛdaya sūtra*) in chapter 19 as the key to understanding the entire narrative. Enlightenment is thus not to be sought in the distance literally traversed or scriptures actually acquired: "the Spirit Mountain is in your mind" (chapter 85). Plaks delineates how sixteenth-century thought, especially the "School of Mind" (*hsin-hsüeh*), informs *Journey to the West*. Yu T'ung's comment, cited earlier, demonstrates how "cultivation of mind," with varying implications, has become the central concern in all three teachings.

A requisite step in the "cultivation of mind" is that of return to origins (*fan-pen*): in Confucian thought, this refers to the recovery of pristine moral consciousness; in philosophical Taoism, the attainment of original oneness; in alchemical Taoism, the refinement of the "inner cinnabar pill" (*nei-tan*) and nourishment of the "holy embryo" (*sheng-t'ai*) that leads to immortality; in Buddhism, the return to nonself and ultimate transcendence of the opposites, form and emptiness. Monkey's very name, Sun Wu-k'ung, combines Taoist and Buddhist versions of the notion of return to origins. "Sun" is both a homophone of part of the bisyllabic word *hu-sun*, which means "monkey," and the word for "child" or "grandson," hence his teacher Subodhi's claim that it corresponds to "the theory of the baby" (*ying-erh pen-lun*), referring thereby to the idea of "holy embryo"; Wu-k'ung is a standard Buddhist name that means "Awake-to-Vacuity." Another recurrent topos in the "cultivation of mind" is the ordering of multifarious and confusing thoughts and sensory experiences, the progression from disunity and conflict to oneness and harmony. Through an accident of transcription, the *Hsin ching* (Heart/Mind Sutra; *Po-je-po-lo-mi-**to hsin** ching*) can also be punned as *To-hsin ching* (The Sutra of Many Hearts/Minds; *to-hsin* [literally, many hearts/minds] may mean suspiciousness, fickleness, and lack of concentration), thus indicating that overcoming *to-hsin* is key to mind-cultivation and that excessive concern with mind may yet prove an obstacle to ultimate enlightenment. As Plaks points out, the nomenclature of some monsters, such as "Liu-erh mi-hou" (Six-Eared Ape; Monkey's impersonator) or "To-mu kuai" (Monster of Many Eyes), also suggests their association with divided consciousness and excessive sensory experiences. To vanquish these monsters is thus to regain unity and equilibrium of the self. By a similar logic, Monkey's trick of getting inside a monster in order to subdue it can be interpreted as an inward purgatory process in mind cultivation; devices of constraint (the Five Phases Mountain, the gold fillet on Monkey's head) may refer to containment of an expansive ego.

The question remains as to how allegorical meanings are connected to comic surface. Sometimes the two converge seamlessly, as when we laugh at the protagonists: Monkey's hubris invites both laughter and reflections on the boundaries of the self; Pig's gross appetite and unrepentant carnality are both comic and philosophically suggestive. But there are also moments when the comic effect depends on the reader laughing with Monkey and empathizing with his pride, mischievousness, irreverence, rebelliousness, and magical powers, qualities that are restrained and sublimated in allegorical readings. The butts of satire are often the same philosophical and religious systems on which allegorical interpretations are based. The great rebellion of Monkey is so appealing precisely because the celestial authority he is threatening seems neither compelling nor morally superior. The Western Heaven is populated by an array of Taoist deities, buddhas, and boddhisattvas, a mélange that does not respect coherence of philosophical and religious schools. Even as a pilgrim during the journey, the irrepressible Monkey sometimes scoffs at the Boddhisattva Kuanyin. Upon reaching the Western Paradise, the enlightened ones, Ānanda and Kāśyapa, first give the pilgrims "wordless scriptures," apparently out of spite because the pilgrims did not present appropriate gifts.

This last incident is an interesting example of the conflict between surface and meaning. The greed and pettiness of Ānanda and Kāśyapa seem a final joke at the expense of Buddhist deities, yet the "wordless scriptures" also point to key issues and debates: the possibility of truth that transcends language and mediation, salvation with or without agents, sudden or gradual enlightenment. A serious philosophical problem is thus introduced through an aside on corruption in the Buddhist paradise. Allegorical decorum may also be disrupted by violence. Shortly after Monkey becomes Tripiṭaka's disciple, he kills six bandits trying to attack them—they are named Eye That Sees and Delights; Ear That Hears and Is Angry; Nose That Smells and Covets; Tongue That Tastes and Desires; Mind That Conceives and Lusts; and Body That Supports and Suffers. The allegorical significance is obvious. In preparation for the journey Monkey destroys sensual and spiritual temptations. Yet this positive development is achieved through acts of violence and leads to a severance of the ties between Tripiṭaka and Monkey. A step toward enlightenment is at the same time regression; the overcoming of evil is itself evil.

Of course, one could argue that such paradoxes are endemic to thought systems that seek to transcend the logic of either-or and the dialectic of form and emptiness—that incongruity between surface and meaning is but an implicit proposition to bracket fictional illusion and the illusion called life. Yet the comedy is too robust, and *Journey* unfolds gaily on the precarious balance between allegorical meanings and the comedy and energy of the esthetic surface. In this world, celestial beings and demons impersonate each other, monsters are often former attendants or creatures of the gods, and pilgrims are renegade immortals. The liminality of the protagonists of *Journey* makes them comic and fantastic counterparts of the liminal heroes of *Three Kingdoms* and *Water Margin*, defined through tensions between different value systems. Here the oxymoronic term "demonic immortals" (*yao-hsien*), often used to designate the main character, Monkey, reminds the readers of the "deviant heroes" in *Three Kingdoms*.

A much shorter and far inferior version of *Journey to the West* is included in *Ssu-yu chi* (Four Journeys; c. sixteenth century). Motifs of journey or quest are not central to the other three works, despite titles indicating journeys to the east, north, and south. All four narratives show how adventures of gods and demons can become insipid without the complex balance of transcendent and human elements, allegory, and comedy that obtains in *Journey to the West*. By contrast, Tung Yüeh's (1620–1686) *"Hsi-yu" pu* (Supplement to *Journey to the West*), which tells of Monkey's dream, self-consciously manipulates these complexities. This gem of a novella combines involutions of self-doubt, urgent social criticism, philosophical speculations, and the discontinuities and fantastic combinations of dream logic to explore the boundaries of the self and the dialectics of illusion and reality. The social and psychological dimensions of *Journey to the West* and Tung Yüeh's *Supplement* show confluences with novels more concerned with the mundane realm. Indeed, some works that emphasize fantastic themes excel much more in human observations, most notably Li Pai-ch'uan's *Lü-yeh hsien-tsung* (Trails of Immortals in the Green Wilds; eighteenth century). Here the protagonist's quest for immortality is not nearly as interesting as the social and emotional entanglements of the less-enlightened characters.

Extended fascination with the mundane realm begins with *Chin P'ing Mei* (Gold Vase Plum). Despite ambiguities and ironic tensions, the heroes of *Three Kingdoms*, *Water Margin*, and *Journey to the West* are decidedly larger than life. By contrast, *Chin P'ing Mei*, designated with the other three novels as the "four masterworks of Ming fiction" (Plaks's translation of *ssu-ta ch'i-shu*), focuses its steady gaze on banal, evil, weak characters. From the world of problematic heroes, we descend to a world without heroes. Instead of heroic deeds, fantastic exploits, or spiritual grandeur, the reader is plunged into a suffocating and all-too-human world dominated by insatiable greed for power, money, and sexual gratification. *Chin P'ing Mei* also departs significantly from the other three works in textual history: it is not the culmination of a long tradition. Stylistic coherence suggests a single author, and immersion in contemporary reality makes it an unmistakable product of the sixteenth century, notwithstanding its ostensible setting in the twelfth century.

The title *Chin P'ing Mei* is made up of parts of the names of three major female characters (P'an **Chin**-lien, Li **P'ing**-erh, and P'ang Ch'un-**mei**); together it may mean "plum in a golden vase." P'an Chin-lien's adulterous relations with Hsi-men Ch'ing, their murder of P'an's husband, Wu Ta, and his brother Wu Sung's subsequent vengeance against them is told in *Water Margin* (chapters 23–27). *Chin P'ing Mei* begins with this story (chapters 1–9), but here retribution is delayed, and P'an Chin-lien and Hsi-men Ch'ing become protagonists in a hundred-chapter novel about the rise and fall of Hsi-men Ch'ing and his household. First mentioned in the 1590s, *Chin P'ing Mei* was probably written during the second half of the sixteenth century and was published in 1610. The identity of the author, whose pseudonym is Lan-ling hsiao-hsiao sheng (The Laughing Scholar of Lan-ling), has not yet been established. The earliest extant edition, entitled *"Chin P'ing Mei" tz'u-hua* (The Prosimetric *Chin P'ing Mei*), contains a preface dated 1617 and begins with the heroic episode of Wu Sung subduing a tiger. *Yüan-pen "Chin P'ing Mei"* (The Original *Chin P'ing Mei*), also called the T'ien-ch'i or Ch'ung-chen edition (after the names of two Ming dynasty reigns, respectively referring to the years 1621–1627 and 1628–1644), was first published in the 1620s or 1630s. It distances itself from *Water Margin* through changes in chapters 1 and 84. It begins with Hsi-men Ch'ing's sworn brotherhood with his nine cronies, a mockery of the "righteous brotherhood" in *Water Margin* and *Three Kingdoms*. This edition also contains more refined titular couplets, fewer dialect expressions, fewer songs and verses, and changes in chapters 53 and 54. Chang Chu-p'o (1670–1698) added his commentaries during the reign of the K'ang-hsi emperor (r. 1662–1722), making this the most widely read edition (see chapter 46).

Closer inspection of this sprawling narrative reveals subtle symmetry. The first twenty chapters tell of Hsi-men Ching's adultery and marriages with P'an Chin-lien and Li P'ing-erh, while his marriage with Meng Yü-lou and patronage of the prostitute Li Kuei-chieh function as interludes. One fifth into the book, fictional space (Hsi-men's compound) is defined and the major characters have gathered: Hsi-men Ch'ing and his six wives—aside from the three mentioned, there are Wu Yüeh-niang (Moon Lady, his principal wife), Li Chiao-erh (a former prostitute and the aunt of Li Kuei-chieh), and Sun Hsüeh-o (the maid of his diseased first wife); P'an Chin-lien's maid, Ch'un-mei; and the coterie of sycophants surrounding Hsi-men Ch'ing, the most memorable among them being Ying Po-chüeh (whose name is homophonous with "should eat without paying"). Between chapter 21 and chapter 79, in which Hsi-men Ch'ing dies from sexual overindulgence, the novel is dominated by intrigues, jealousies, and power struggles within Hsi-men Ch'ing's household. Li P'ing-erh soon emerges as Hsi-men Ch'ing's favorite wife, especially after she gives birth to his only son up to that point (chapter 30), named Kuan-ko (literally, "Official Brother") because Hsi-men Ch'ing bribes his way to officialdom (*kuan*) at that juncture. Consumed by jealousy, P'an Chin-lien brings about the death of

Kuan-ko (chapter 59). Li P'ing-erh dies of grief and anger shortly thereafter (chapter 62).

In the meantime Hsi-men Ch'ing rises ever higher in his official career, accepting and offering bribes to gain power and influence. At the midpoint of the book, he escapes punishment despite indictment by Tseng Hsiao-hsü, the only righteous official in the story (chapter 48), and receives a special aphrodiasiac from an Indian monk (chapter 49), apparently the personification of a penis (comment in the Ch'ung-chen edition). Sex and power, the private and public domains, are thus inextricably intertwined. The expansion of Hsi-men Ch'ing's power and wealth is matched by numerous sexual escapades involving his male and female servants, the wives of his servants and underlings, prostitutes, Kuan-ko's wet-nurse, and the widow of an official. He finally dies from a series of sexual orgies and an overdose of the Indian monk's aphrodisiac administered by P'an Chin-lien. At the moment of his death, Wu Yüeh-niang gives birth to a son, Hsiao-ko (literally "Filial Brother").

In the last twenty-one chapters, Hsi-men Ch'ing's household disintegrates. The tone of the narrative becomes more hurried and melodramatic. An adulterous dalliance between P'an Chin-lien and Ch'en Ching-chi, Hsi-men Ch'ing's son-in-law, hitherto frustrated, is finally consummated after Hsi-men's death. In part out of loyalty to P'an, Ch'un-mei becomes the complicit third partner. All three are evicted or sold when Wu Yüeh-niang discovers the adultery. P'an Chin-lien eventually falls victim to the avenging fury of her nemesis, Wu Sung (chapter 87). Only Wu Yüeh-niang remains as ineffective head of household: Li Chiao-erh returns to her former brothel, Meng Yü-lou remarries, and Sun Hsüeh-o runs away with a former servant. Underlings vie to steal from Hsi-men's estate. While his household declines, Ch'un-mei's fortune rises drastically and she eventually becomes the principal wife of a military official. She reinstates Ch'en Ching-chi, who has fallen into disrepute and destitution and resumes her relationship with him. Both come to an ignominious end: Ch'en is murdered, and Ch'un-mei dies of sexual excesses. In chapter 100, the invading Chin army brings about the collapse of the Sung dynasty. Wu Yüeh-niang and the fifteen-year-old Hsiao-ko seek refuge in a Buddhist temple. The Buddhist monk P'u-ching performs sacrifices for the dead, and a vision of dead characters heading for rebirth comes to Hsiao-yü, Wu Yüeh-niang's maid. P'u-ching convinces Wu Yüeh-niang that Hsiao-ko is Hsi-men Ching's reincarnation. Hsiao-ko becomes P'u-ching's disciple, and the book concludes provisionally with the vision of Buddhist salvation.

Much of the controversy surrounding *Chin P'ing Mei* focuses on its explicit sexual descriptions. It was banned as pornography during the Ch'ing dynasty (1644–1911), and until recently only expurgated editions were readily available. In this work of about a million sinographs, however, the proportion of sexually explicit passages is relatively insignificant, in stark contrast to such examples of erotic literature as *Ju-yi chün chuan* (The Story of the Ideal Lover; c. early sixteenth century), *Ch'ih p'o-tzu chuan* (The Story of the Deluded Woman; c. sixteenth century), or *Jou p'u-t'uan* (The Prayer Mat of Flesh; c. seventeenth century). Hence Chang Chu-p'o's observation that those who regard *Chin P'ing Mei* as pornography read only the pornographic passages. While some critics (especially in the PRC) regard the explicit sexual descriptions in the novel as moral blemishes, others (including Chang Chu-p'o and modern scholars such as David Roy and Plaks) discern critical intent and moral seriousness. Some praise such passages as integral to the book's project of unflinching realism, others examine ironic disjunctions as signs of moral judgment, while yet others even applaud their "liberating" and subversive potential in undermining conceptions of order and authority. The sexual passages in *Chin P'ing Mei* are scarcely the most original aspect of the book. Many of them use clichés common to late Ming erotic literature. The scandalous chapter 27, for example, seems to have been derived from *The Story of the Ideal Lover* (according to Patrick Hanan and Hsü Shuo-fang). It is with the dark accounts of perversions in the second half of the book, when sex ceases to be playful and becomes mechanical, violent, and purely manipulative, often involving pain and humiliation, that *Chin P'ing Meng* stakes out new territory. Moral homilies and accounts of conversion and repudiation of sexual excesses are common currency in late-imperial erotic literature, but *Chin P'ing Mei* stands alone in linking desire and death in the most graphic and gruesome manner imaginable. Few readers can forget Hsi-men Ch'ing's grotesque end (chapter 79).

The author of *Chin P'ing Mei* has a masterful grasp of the banal infinitude of desire. Toward the end of his life, even as Hsi-men Ch'ing is plunged into a vortex of incessant sexual encounters, he pins his fantasies on two unattainable aristocratic women and on a concubine being sent his way. She is appropriately named "Ch'u-yün" (Clouds of Ch'u), a standard kenning for evanescent objects of desire in classical poetry. Yet infinitude is not romanticized or idealized: pleasure is statistical; excesses are treated in a banal, matter-of-fact manner (*yu-chin teng-k'u* ["when the oil is exhausted, the lamp dries up"]). Limitless desire is rooted in inward lack and the fatuous illusion of infinite power. Hsi-men Ch'ing's female counterpart is the insatiable P'an Chin-lien, who veers between masochistic self-abnegation and an increasingly strident control in her sexual relations with Hsi-men Ch'ing. The banality of desire is underlined through its commodification: women (usually those socially inferior to Hsi-men Ch'ing or financially dependent on him) often seek material favors during sexual intercourse. In this sense, the crude exchange of the brothel invades Hsi-men Ch'ing's household; the two spheres draw even closer when prostitutes seek out Hsi-men's wives as "godmothers." When gratification can be bought, one would assume that the "buyer" has greater power, yet often the reverse is true in *Chin P'ing Mei.* The women cynically seeking material recompense do get it—most notably Wang Liu-erh, the wife of one of Hsi-men Ch'ing's underlings. Their goals are often better defined than Hsi-men Ch'ing's—he always wants and buys more, and in his frantic acquisition he "spends" himself. Unlike Wang Liu-erh, P'an Chin-lien does not view mere material satisfaction as the ultimate goal. Instead, she has a more permanent and existential lack, always wants more to compensate for her feelings of inadequacy, and is ultimately destroyed by desire.

Sex is almost always linked to intrigues and power struggles within the household. The author of *Chin P'ing Mei* has boundless curiosity about domestic politics and, more generally, about the texture of daily existence in this fictional universe. Herein lies the true originality of the novel. His obsession with sensuous details extends well beyond sex—at least as much space is devoted to food, clothing and jewelry, architectural details, wine games and jokes, and monetary transactions. *Chin P'ing Mei* is almost maddening in its commitment to surface: there is not much room left for interiority or "psychological realism." For example, the narrator seems much more interested in the details of the funeral services for Li P'ing-erh (which go on for several chapters) than in Hsi-men Ch'ing's grief. *Chin P'ing Mei*'s reputation in the twentieth century as a realistic masterpiece rests on this untiring enactment of family and social relations within a palpable, credible physical context. The plot does not depend on supernatural elements, especially if black magic, physiognomy, and Buddhist reincarnation are regarded as part of a "consensual reality." The penchant for exhaustive description (in contrast to the traditional lyric esthetics of reticence), the tendency to vulgarize and deromanticize, and the focus on baser human actions and motives recall acknowledged conventions of realism. (Modern Chinese writers and scholars also valorize realism and perceive a kind of telos in the emergence of *Chin P'ing Mei*, parallel to the evolution of the European realistic novel from epic, romance, and allegory.)

However, radical shifts in stylistic levels, lapses into the burlesque or carnivalesque, liberal inclusion of song suites, verses, Buddhist homilies and stories (*pao-chüan* [precious scrolls]), storyteller's rhetoric, and dramatic conventions (e.g., a stock character's self-introduction with comic, derogatory rhymed verse) lead C. T. Hsia to call the book's overarching style flawed realism. (Some scholars have also adduced these traits as evidence of multiple authorship.) Roy defends such heterogeneity as deliberate design, a vision of totality based on polyphony and heteroglossia (borrowing Mikhail Bakhtin's terms). Some scholars (e.g., Plaks, Katherine Carlitz) have emphasized the moral judgment implied in ironic juxtapositions of texts and contexts. For example, to have P'an Chin-lien play the *p'i-p'a* (balloon lute) and sing of her loneliness and pining (chapters 12 and 38) demonstrates the disjunction between the pathos of the abandoned, cloistered woman celebrated in traditional poetry and P'an's indiscriminate lust and vengeful jealousy, and possibly also between her self-image and the reader's perception of her. Similarly, the Buddhist vision based on merit-making and karmic retribution that supposedly informs the recitation of precious scrolls is framed by accounts of the reciting nuns' immorality and of the audience's (the women in Hsi-men Ch'ing's household) somnolence and distractions (chapter 39).

Discussions of *Chin P'ing Mei*'s realism are bound up with debates over the nature and role of its moral vision. Realism is sometimes linked to visions of social justice, especially in studies from the PRC that emphasize the corrupting influence of power and wealth and the victimhood of the dispossessed (including P'an Chin-lien, abused servants, and the host of socially inferior women seeking favors from Hsi-men Ch'ing). However, it would be hard to deny the glaringly callous treatment of some lower-class victims (e.g., Ch'iu-chü, the maid abused by P'an Chin-lien) in *Chin P'ing Mei*.

Some accounts of realism imply dispassionate observation and judgment withheld, if not engagement with or downright wallowing in sensuous existence. Sun Shu-yü observes that, whereas Wu Sung's execution of P'an Chin-lien seems just in *Water Margin*, its horrifying and drawn-out description in *Chin P'ing Mei* dims Wu Sung's heroic stature and leaves the reader with residual sympathy for P'an Chin-lien (*"Chin P'ing Mei" te yi-shu* [The Art of *Chin P'ing Mei*]). Thus even evil or worthless characters are not totally denied empathy—Hsi-men Ch'ing has his genial, generous moments; irrepressible P'an Chin-lien elevates curses and squabbles to appreciable art; shameless Ying Po-chüeh has some good lines as a kind of vulgarized and displaced court jester. The author of *Chin P'ing Mei* has a keen understanding of human weaknesses and contradictions: Li Ping-erh commits adultery and drives her husband, Hua Tzu-hsü, to death, yet there is deep pathos in her blind love for Hsi-men Ch'ing and Kuan-ko; Sung Hui-lien (a servant who has adulterous relations with Hsi-men Ch'ing) is immoral, foolish, and vain, yet capable of genuine attachment to her wronged husband, and her despair and suicide somehow redeem her.

Without denying the claims of realism, some scholars emphasize the primacy of an uncompromising moral vision: Roy ties it with Hsün Tzu's (c. 300?–219? B.C.E.) philosophy that human nature is evil and can be redeemed only through moral transformation; Plaks anchors it to the "Ta-hsüeh" (Great Learning; c. third century B.C.E.), which connects self-cultivation to the well-being of family, society, and polity, and to the moral self-consciousness espoused by the School of the Mind prevalent in the sixteenth century. Such moral visions are much more subtle and sophisticated than that articulated in the rhetoric of moral homily that punctuates the book. Yet, like that rhetoric, and like the scheme of Buddhist redemption, they fail to contain totally the fascination with sensuous existence, motivated variously by empathy, curiosity, cynicism, and an almost disinterested esthetic appreciation.

The "containment" of *Chin P'ing Mei* is also discernible in some literary responses to the book. Ting Yao-k'ang (1599–1669) meticulously metes out retributions to reincarnations of characters from *Chin P'ing Mei* in his *Hsü "Chin P'ing Mei"* (Sequel to *Chin P'ing Mei*). Sexual encounters in this novel are often unsatisfactory or delusional (except perhaps for the lesbian relationship between Li Chin-kuei and K'ung Mei-yü, reincarnations of P'an Chin-lien and P'ang Ch'un-mei): Ting claims that, whereas *Chin P'ing Mei* is about form or sensuous reality, his novel is about emptiness. The stern moral rhetoric here is both reinforced and mitigated by the sense of history. Ting depicts with horror and sympathy the Chin invasion and the collapse of the Northern Sung, which clearly echoes his own experience of the traumatic Manchu conquest of the Ming. Dynastic collapse thus both facilitates a retributory scheme and assimilates it as a random component of a general disaster. *Hsing-shih yin-yüan chuan* (The Bonds of Matrimony, or Marriage Destinies to Awaken the World), by Hsi Chou sheng (The Scholar of Western Chou, identity unknown; c. seventeenth century), inherits *Chin P'ing Mei's* concern with domestic intrigues and power struggles. But here all illusions of male power are relentlessly dispelled in the entanglements between the emasculated Ti Hsi-ch'en and his sadistic, shrewish wives, Hsüeh Su-chih and T'ung Chi-chieh. Ti, Hsüeh, and T'ung reenact enmities from former lives (told in the first twenty chapters). The narrator eschews sexual descriptions, adopts the pedagogical tone of a village schoolmaster, introduces karmic retribution, and inserts morality tales to define a supposedly rigorous moral scheme. Yet it is the undeniable fascination with the intricacies of family and social relationships, women's violence and will to power, as well as the grotesquerie of sadomasochistic relationships that sustain narrative interest.

The concern with social reality and the rhetoric of ironic unmasking in *Chin P'ing Mei* form the basis of satirical consciousness, of which the finest example in Chinese fiction is *Ju-lin wai-shih* (The Scholars), by Wu Ching-tzu (1701–1754). At first glance no two works seem more different: *The Scholars* is not concerned with desire and sexuality, even as *Chin P'ing Mei* does not reflect much on literati and scholar-official ideals; stylistically *Chin P'ing Mei* is rich in dialect expressions (*fang-yen*), whereas *The Scholars* is written in pure, limpid vernacular (*pai-hua*). Nevertheless, the sustained scrutiny and critical representation of social relations mark a deeper continuity between the two works, although they focus on different spheres of experience.

The full title of Wu's book is *The Unofficial History of Scholars*, which is reminiscent of the collected biographies of scholars in official historiography. This is not accidental. In both cases, there is a deep concern with the meanings of becoming a Confucian scholar (*ju*) at different historical moments. Formally, *The Scholars* also moves from one character to another, as in such biographies. Despite its considerable length, it reads more like a series of linked short narratives. Of course, it is also unmistakably tied to the conditions of eighteenth-century China. Here fictional imagination is fired by the perversion, distortion, manipulation, and devaluation of the ideal of the Confucian scholar-official in late imperial China. Wu Ching-tzu was himself the scion of a scholar-official family; both his great-grandfather and his eldest son were distinguished officials. He was obviously talented, yet never advanced beyond the lowest *hsiu-ts'ai* (cultivated talent, or licentiate) degree. His frustrations with and disdain for the civil service examination system and his perception of the literati's disorientation define his vision in the book. Most scholars believe that there is an autobiographical dimension to the work and that the author projects himself as the talented, improvident, and generous Tu Shao-ch'ing. Many other characters are supposedly based on people he knew.

The Scholars was completed around 1750 and was first published between 1768 and 1779. The first extant edition, in fifty-six chapters, dates from 1803, and the last chapter was probably an interpolation. No overarching plot or dominant characters tie the book together. The narrative units have affinities with the anecdote, the short story, and the classical essay. Wu Ching-tzu seems to be more interested in the juxtaposition of moods, images, themes, and arguments than in overall structural unity. One early-nineteenth-century commentator suggests that the book's persistent concern is *kung-ming fu-kuei* (success, fame, wealth, exalted position). Indeed, the narrative includes impressive variations on this theme, from serious deliberation on the choice between commitment and disengagement to its debasement as the dilemma between a shameless or concealed quest for recognition and worldly advancement and a self-indulgent, self-destructive, or self-serving rejection of the rules of the game.

The first chapter is temporally removed from the rest of the book and functions as prolog. It contains a much-idealized portrait of the artist and recluse Wang Mien, a historical personage who lived during the mid-fourteenth-century transition from the Yüan (1260–1368) to the Ming (1368–1644). Totally self-contained in moral-artistic cultivation, he is indifferent to recognition of his talents, even in their most momentous form, as when he is sought to serve as an adviser to the future founder of the Ming dynasty, Chu Yüan-chang (1328–1398; r. 1368–1398). He emblematizes an ideal against which later characters may be measured. Wang chooses withdrawal because he foresees dangers and upheavals, possibly an allusion to the perils of public expression in Wu's times, which witnessed the notorious literary inquisitions (*wen-tzu yü*). His dire prediction that the examination system and the "eight-legged" essay (see chapter 12) will lead to obliviousness to *wen-hsing ch'u-ch'u* (learning, conduct, service, withdrawal) is relentlessly fulfilled in the rest of the book.

Chapters 2 to 55, spanning 1487 to 1595, can be divided into three sections. Chapters 2 to 30 introduce a host of seekers of office, fame, and wealth. Again and again the author reverses our expectation of comforting and edifying stories. The vindication of old, abused, and unsuccessful examination candidates such as Chou Chin and Fan Chin promises poetic justice in vain; the "talents" at long last recognized soon reveal their mediocrity and dubious moral fiber. K'uang Ch'ao-jen, a poor, young, aspiring scholar, and initially a filial son, rises with the help of discerning patrons and friends, but he degenerates into an ingrate and opportunist, again betraying expectations of a story of virtue rewarded. In an apparent reenactment of the *ts'ai-tzu chia-jen* (tales of brilliant scholars and beautiful girls) romance, the young lady (Ms. Lu) turns out to be a pedant whose ambitions are frustrated by a husband intent on playing the role of *ming-shih* (renowned literatus). The pursuit of that coveted appellation is the object of much deft satire in the book, for the hypocrisy and ostentatious unconventionality of those seeking the reputation of literary talent and of disdain for officialdom (e.g., the Lou brothers) invites unmasking even more than the sanctimony of those angling for success within the system—the latter are too obviously pathetic or corrupt. Ubiquitous dissemblance and self-deception, both conscious and unconscious, raise questions on the meaning of being genuine. It is ironic that the only sincere characters delineated at length in the first section of the book are Ma Ch'un-shang, a compiler of model examination essays, and Pao T'ing-hsi, an actor. Both are humble, simple characters not given to self-questioning and unaware of the lies latent in their respective professions.

The second section, chapters 31 to 37, forms the novel's moral core. The aforementioned Tu Shao-ch'ing and his friends, worthy embodiments of literati and scholar-official ideals, gather in Nanking. The climax of their activities is the renovation of T'ai-po Temple and the revival of ancient sacrificial rituals there. That Wu Ching-tzu empathizes with and idealizes these characters is obvious, yet they dramatize the literati's predicament rather than provide viable solutions. Tu Shao-ch'ing comes from a distinguished scholar-official family but wastes his patrimony out of indiscriminate generosity, aristocratic disdain for mundane details, and perhaps a longing for freedom. When summoned to take a special examination for office, he declines, preferring to live more humbly but freely by selling his writings. This autobiographical portrait is apologetic yet tinged with irony. The *hao-chü* (generous acts) that impoverish Tu Shao-ch'ing obviously involve errors of judgment; though based on genuine and spontaneous kindness, these acts are also self-conscious fulfillment of a certain self-image. To the end he remains untainted, yet the choice of withdrawal also seems vaguely self-indulgent: he prefers the literati culture of the Lower Yangtze to an official career in Peking.

Tu's friends are more committed to the Confucian vision of engagement, which yet remains elusive and unrealizable. Chuang Shao-kuang is at a loss for words when a scorpion bites him under his cap during an imperial audience. He interprets this as a sign that "his Way cannot prevail," and indeed he is maligned by evil ministers and excluded from government. Yü Yü-te, praised as *chen-ju* (a true Confucian scholar), holds a minor post overseeing examination candidates in Nanking. He is the only character pursuing a moral mission within the system, albeit merely on a modest scale. He presides over the T'ai-po Temple sacrifice, which is envisioned as an alternative means for the literati to realize their sociopolitical vision. The revival of ancient rites and music is supposed to bring about a subtle moral transformation of the people (a belief at least as old as Confucius), which will be more pervasive and fundamental than what can be achieved through participation in government. Wu T'ai-po of the twelfth century B.C.E., to whom the temple is dedicated, himself embodies this hope of realizing virtue through political disinterest. According to Ssu-ma Ch'ien, he renounces kingship and escapes to the wilderness of the Lower Yangtze, which he calls Wu, so that the throne can be passed to his younger brother Chi Li in accordance with his father's wishes, and after that to the latter's son Ch'ang (later honored as the much-revered King Wen of Chou). Ssu-ma Ch'ien places him at the head of the "Hereditary Families" section of the *Records of the Historian* in recognition of this renunciation of power and his filial and fraternal virtues. The sacrifice is described in chapter 37 in elevated diction, with liturgical sentences of solemn brevity and austere precision reminiscent of ritual texts.

Yet the final section of the book (chapters 38 to 54) shows that the T'ai-po Temple sacrifice, which the novelist is at pains to describe in elaborate detail, has no tangible consequences. The dispersal of characters involved in the sacrificial rites held at the temple is juxtaposed with tirades against further moral degeneration in society (chapter 46). Soon characters look back nostalgically to this ritual enactment of yearning for a lost golden age. Moral and heroic actions in this section are plagued by compromises and contradictions. A memorable representative of such dilemmas is Wang Yü-hui. As author of ritual, philological, and contractual texts, he promises continuity of ritual tradition and moral regeneration. Yet the oppressive, destructive side of this moral order is exposed when he encourages his widowed daughter to follow her husband in death. The sacrifices honoring Wang's daughter as a *lieh-fu* (chaste woman) form a dark, disturbing echo of the T'ai-po episode. Torn by grief despite his professed convictions, Wang goes to Nanking, only to find the promoters of ritual revival disbanded and the T'ai-po Temple, symbol of past glory and moral rectitude, locked up and deserted (chapter 48). Melancholy retrospection in this section is interwoven with somewhat haphazard tales of adventure, knight-errantry, extraordinary virtues, and elaborate hoaxes. Here the author is more dependent on the esthetics of surprise and wonder (*ch'i*)—demonstrative prose matches demonstrative characters (e.g., Shen Ch'iung-chih, Feng Ming-ch'i), whose heroic feats seem overly self-conscious and even morally dubious.

The epilog (chapter 55) recounts that the renowned literati of Nanking have all but disappeared. Four extraordinary characters (*ch'i-jen*), who excel respectively in the literati pursuits of playing the *ch'in* (zither), chess, calligraphy, and painting, emerge among the plebians. (This is consonant with the author's idealization of the integrity of some simple, common people throughout the book.) Defiant, obsessive, and oblivious to worldly recognition, they seem to be the last representatives of genuineness and moral purity in a false and corrupt world. The stubborn hope they emblematize is elegiac and despairing. The painter and poet Kai K'uan, a latter-day Tu Shao-ch'ing who runs a humble teashop, visits the T'ai-po Temple and mourns its dilapidation and oblivion.

Ching Yüan, a master musician and a tailor, plays the *ch'in* for a discerning friend and moves him to bitter tears, thus implying that private communion among like-minded souls is the only mode of communication possible.

Largely pruned of storytelling rhetoric, didactic intrusions, and inset materials, infused with a deeply critical spirit, and written consistently in exemplary *pai-hua* (vernacular), *The Scholars* is the traditional work closest to modern Chinese fiction. Its satire ranges from understatement to caricature, but on the whole it is much more subtle and restrained than the late Ch'ing fiction of strident social criticism (e.g., Wu Chien-jen's [1866–1910] *Erh-shih nien mu-tu chih kuai hsien-chuang* [Strange Scenes Witnessed in the Past Twenty Years] or Li Po-yüan's [Li Pao-chia; 1867–1906] *Kuan-ch'ang hsien-hsing chi* [Exposure of the World of Officials] and *Wen-ming hsiao-shih* [A Brief History of Enlightenment]) that it inspired. This is as much a consequence of Wu Ching-tzu's genius as of his historical situation. He perceives a crisis of culture but does not yet fear the collapse of a civilization. He seems genuinely to believe in moral transformation through revival of ancient rituals, educational mission, and scholarly labor, although he also questions their ultimate efficacy. Esthetic self-cultivation remains a viable escape. Wu Ching-tzu's vision is so compelling precisely because he is not delivering judgments from a position of Olympian superiority. He defines and ponders his ideals, convictions, and predilections as he confronts the malaise of the late imperial literatus, presenting it as deeply personal, yet also collective, dilemmas.

Roughly contemporaneous with *The Scholars* and more obviously indebted to *Chin P'ing Mei* is *Shih-t'ou chi* (The Story of the Stone, hereafter *Stone*), also known as *Hung-lou meng* (A Dream of Red Towers), by Ts'ao Chan (sobriquet Hsüeh-ch'in; 1715?–1763 or 1764), widely acknowledged as the crowning achievement of Chinese vernacular fiction. As in *Chin P'ing Mei*, in *Stone* fictional space is mainly domestic, within the enclosure of family compound and garden. Both works depict in closely observed detail the glory and decline of a rich and powerful family, and the relationships between a male protagonist and several women. In both cases, there is a persistent concern with desire and sexuality, but the cynicism, degradation, and banality of the world in *Chin P'ing Mei* are as different as can be from the idealization of love and the lyrical, nostalgic mode in *Stone*.

Assiduous scholarly research in the twentieth century has established that Ts'ao Hsüeh-ch'in came from a Manchuized Han Chinese family that won the trust and favor of the first two Ch'ing emperors, held important posts, and was rich and powerful for several generations before going into steep decline (probably because of court intrigues) during Ts'ao Hsüeh-ch'in's youth. Ts'ao might have started to write *Stone* in the 1740s. By 1754 drafts of the book, with comments by Chih-yen chai (Red Inkstone Studio), and more sporadically by Chi-hu (Crooked Tablet) and others, began to be circulated among the author's friends and family. The identity of Red Inkstone remains unknown, although he or she was obviously a relative or close friend privy to the author's family history and was well aware of—in some cases even tried to influence—his design and vision. Ts'ao Hsüeh-ch'in died before he finished the book, having completed at least eighty chapters; five or six chapters were unfortunately lost in the late 1760s. There are about ten extant versions, with some divergences and varying degrees of completeness, of the eighty-chapter hand-copied manuscripts. In 1791, Kao O (1763–1815) and Ch'eng Wei-yüan (1745?–1819?) published a 120-chapter version of *Stone* that involved editorial changes in the first 80 chapters and added 40 chapters. A slightly revised edition was published in 1792. The source of the last forty chapters is unknown. There is no definite proof for the common attribution to Kao O. The author of this section seems to know about Ts'ao's family history. It is also possible that fragments of what Ts'ao wrote or intended might have been included.

Stone begins with a myth about flaws and equilibrium. In order to repair a hole in heaven, the goddess Nü-wa refines 36,501 stones, one more than she needs. The superfluous stone, refined into consciousness and spirituality and yet deemed unworthy to repair heaven, is discarded at the foot of a mountain whose name (Ch'ing-keng) is roughly homophonous with "roots of desire" (*ch'ing-ken*). The stone laments its destiny and is taken to the human world by a monk and a Taoist, to be reborn as the protagonist Chia Pao-yü ("Fictive Precious Jade"), scion of a rich, powerful, but declining family. Pao-yü is born with a piece of jade—the transformed stone—in his mouth. This "Jade of Numinous Transcendence" (*t'ung-ling pao-yü*) symbolizes both desire and enlightenment—jade (*yü*) is homophonous with desire (*yü*) but also embodies communion with the spiritual realm (*t'ung-ling*). Eons elapse, and K'ung K'ung Tao-jen (Voiding-the-Void Taoist) passes by the stone, which has returned to its original place with its (his) story—our novel—inscribed on it. In the process of copying and transmitting the story, Voiding-the-Void Taoist undergoes a cycle of conversion—through apprehension of form (*se*; Sanskrit, *rūpa*) and feelings (*ch'ing*), he reaches enlightenment—and renames himself Ch'ing-seng (Monk of Feelings).

The inscription begins with the stories of Chen Shih-yin (homophone of "True Events Hidden") and Chia Yü-ts'un ("Fictive Words Remain"). Chen loses his beloved daughter and all worldly possessions and finally disappears with a lame Taoist. A clear religious solution to attachment and loss is thus introduced by, but also disappears with, Chen Shih-yin. His daughter, Ying-lien ("Worthy of Pity"), is eventually sold into concubinage and becomes one of the ill-fated young women whom Pao-yü cherishes. Chen's worldly and morally dubious friend, Chia Yü-ts'un, introduces us to the Chia household, bringing to it Pao-yü's beautiful and talented female cousins, Lin Tai-yü (chapter 3) and (indirectly) Hsüeh Pao-ch'ai (chapter 4). After becoming engrossed in a dense web of realistic details, the reader is abruptly returned to the mythic realm when the protagonist, Pao-yü, dreams of a visit to the Illusory Realm of Great

Void (chapter 5). In this dream, the goddess Ching-huan (Disenchantment) introduces Pao-yü to the totality and acme of sensual pleasures, culminating in sexual union with Disenchantment's sister, Chien-mei (All Beauties-in-One), and also warns of their dangers and ultimate negation, a message encoded in riddles about the sad fate of all the women loved by Pao-yü. Upon waking, Pao-yü has his first sexual experience with a maid, Hua Hsi-jen (chapter 6).

The visit of a poor, distant relative, Granny Liu (chapter 6), establishes the tempo of the book. (She revisits when the idyllic garden world, in which Pao-yü, his sisters and cousins, and their maids are dwelling, is at its height [chapters 39–41] and when the Chia family declines [chapters 113, 119].) Much of *Stone* is taken up with details of daily existence in the Chia household—in the midst of endless feasts, birthday celebrations, family gatherings, and dramatic performances, intrigues unfold, affections deepen, and jealousies and misunderstandings develop. Narrative focus shifts between the irrevocable decline of the Chia family, explained in part by extravagance, greed, corruption, mismanagement, and abuse of power, and Pao-yü's emotional and spiritual world, his relationships with the girls surrounding him and with his family, his perceptions, loves, disappointments, moments of enlightenment, and final renunciation.

Early on in the book (chapters 9–16), desire is linked to transgression, punishment, and death, as symbolized by the Mirror of Love (*feng-yüeh pao-chien*, chapters 11 and 12). Chia Jui, a distant clansman, is smitten with obsessive lust for Wang Hsi-feng, the wife of one of Pao-yü's male cousins. After being tricked and humiliated by Wang, Chia Jui is given the Mirror of Love by a monk. Wang's image beckons in the mirror, while a skeleton appears on the reverse side. Chia Jui fails to follow the monk's injunction to look only at the reverse side and dies after repeated sexual encounters with an illusory Wang Hsi-feng in the mirror. There are strong hints that Ch'in K'o-ch'ing (the young wife of Pao-yü's nephew), who has figural links with Chien-mei and in whose room Pao-yü dreams of visiting the Illusory Realm in chapter 5, commits adultery with her father-in-law, Chia Chen (Pao-yü's uncle). She dies of a mysterious illness in chapter 13. Chia Chen's extravagance over her funeral shows how money and carnal passion are often linked as primary modes of excess. There are also clear intimations of homosexual relations between Chia Pao-yü and Ch'in K'o-ch'ing's younger brother, Ch'in Chung (chapters 7, 9, and 15). Ch'in Chung dies after his illicit affair with a young nun leads to beatings from his father, and then his father dies from anger (chapter 16). Wang Hsi-feng and, much more briefly, Ch'in K'o-ch'ing run the Chia household, managing its income and expenditure. Their involvement in the symbolic logic of the Mirror of Love thus links sexual transgressions to declining family fortune. We know from the Red Inkstone Studio commentary that Ts'ao Hsüeh-ch'in once wrote a book entitled *Feng-yüeh pao-chien* (Mirror of Love) or perhaps that *Stone* bore that title at one point—Red Inkstone is not entirely clear which. However, by chapter 17, Ch'in K'o-ch'ing and Ch'in Chung are dead, the Mirror of Love has disappeared, and the Ta-kuan yüan (Grand View Garden), into which the cousins will move, is being built. Ts'ao Hsüeh-ch'in has shifted from the simple mutual implication of desire and death, transgression and punishment, to the profound paradox of the more infinite, more innocent, and yet more dangerous "lust of the mind" (*yi-yin*).

Pao-yü apparently knows carnal, perhaps even transgressive, love, as suggested by his relationships with Hua Hsi-jen, Ch'in K'o-ch'ing(?), Ch'in Chung, and the actor Chiang Yü-han, but the author focuses more on his innocence, lack of boundaries, and obsessive yet ineffable longing, what Disenchantment calls "the lust of the mind." The arena for the unfolding of this sensibility is the Grand View Garden, constructed for the visit of the imperial concubine, Pao-yü's older sister Chia Yüan-ch'un (chapters 17 and 18). The Grand View Garden belongs to a tradition of Chinese literary gardens, which provide illuminating comparisons with gardens in Western literature, as Plaks has shown in *Archetype and Allegory in the "Dream of the Red Chamber"* (1976). At the behest of Yüan-ch'un, Pao-yü and his female companions move into the garden (chapter 23), which remains the locus of most action until chapter 78. With vistas named by Pao-yü and the girls, and with abodes fashioned as extensions of their personalities, the garden seems an ideal, pure world of youth and innocence, games and literary gatherings, love and poetry. Yet the garden, like its symbolic counterpart, the Illusory Realm, is a precarious dream. Rivalries and jealousies among the girls (chapters 19, 21, and 22) preface the move into the garden and persist afterward, in Hsi-jen's case disguised as concern for Pao-yü's moral well-being and reputation (chapters 30, 34, and 77). Family intrigues erupt melodramatically as Chao, concubine of Pao-yü's father, Chia Cheng, plots demon possession against Pao-yü and Wang Hsi-feng (chapter 25). Desire becomes transgressive and destructive, as when Pao-yü's flirtation with his mother's maid, Chin-ch'uan, leads to her suicide (chapter 32). This incident, together with Pao-yü's dalliance with the actor Chiang Yü-han, provokes a severe beating by his father (chapter 33). The lust of Chia She and his son Chia Lien (husband of Wang Hsi-feng) highlights the plight of the helpless maids and concubines in the household (chapters 44, 46, and 64–69). The attempt of Chia T'an-ch'un (Pao-yü's half-sister) and Hsüeh Pao-ch'ai to turn the economic resources of the garden to good account leads to unsavory intrusions by older female servants (chapters 56, 58, and 59).

However, in ways more fundamental, ineluctable, and impersonal, the garden world is undermined by the sheer passage of time and the very fragility of love and beauty. The tone is elegiac from the beginning—the first act of Pao-yü and Tai-yü in the garden is to bury fallen blossoms. Inmates of the garden refer intermittently to inevitable separation and dispersal (chapters 26, 36, 57, and 78). In *"Hung-lou meng" te liang-ke shih-chieh* (The Two Worlds of *Hung-lou meng*; 1978), the modern scholar Yü Ying-shih discusses how, apparently set apart from a sordid reality, the garden incorporates Chia She's garden, and its stream comes from the neighboring Gathered Blossoms Garden—both are sites of corruption and transgressive desire. The logic of the world of the Mirror of Love, implicated in carnality, transgression, and death, continues to haunt the Grand View Garden. Garden inmates are blithely oblivious to economic reality, yet the financial ruin of the family spells doom for the garden. The garden world is finally destroyed by the discovery of a sachet embroidered with a pornographic image (chapter 73), whose raw sexuality seems to mock the garden's willful innocence and arbitrary self-containment. Pao-yü's mother, Madame Wang, orders a search of the garden (*ch'ao-yüan*; chapter 74). Two maids are consequently expelled; one of them, Pao-yü's maid Ch'ing-wen, dies shortly thereafter (chapter 78). Pao-ch'ai and others move out, and the garden becomes empty and desolate. These eighty chapters are, unfortunately, all that remain of Ts'ao's book.

The last forty chapters of the book have often been criticized as a betrayal of Ts'ao Hsüeh-ch'in's intention. However, the 120-chapter version as an accomplished literary fact has to be considered on its own terms. Moreover, the sequel, though inferior to the first eighty chapters, has inspired moments. The sequel tells of the Chia family's further decline, which is hastened by the death of the imperial concubine Yüan-ch'un and culminates in the search of the family (*ch'ao-chia*)—symbolically presaged by the search of the garden—when it falls from imperial favor (chapter 105), as well as the deaths of the matriarchal figure Grandmother Chia (chapter 110) and of Wang Hsi-feng (chapter 114). In a way probably unintended by Ts'ao, this author mitigates the tragedy by ending with hopes for the family's revival (chapters 107 and 119). The girls Pao-yü loves and cherishes meet their sad fate—betrayal and early death (Tai-yü), early widowhood (Hsiang-yün [Grandmother Chia's great-niece] and Pao-ch'ai), unhappy marriage and persecution unto death (Ying-ch'un [daughter of Chia She]), demeaning concubinage and death from childbirth (Hsiang-ling [concubine of Hsüeh P'an, Hsüeh Pao-chia's brother]), abduction (Miao-yü [resident nun in the Grand View Garden]), and Buddhist renunciation (Hsi-ch'un [sister of Chia Chen] and Tzu-chüan [Tai-yü's maid]). The sequel reduces the contradictions of love to a marriage intrigue. Wang Hsi-feng masterminds a conspiracy to have Pao-yü marry Pao-ch'ai, all the while deceiving him by allowing him to believe that he is going to marry Tai-yü. Consequently, there occurs the melodramatic juxtaposition of Pao-ch'ai's wedding and Tai-yü's death (chapter 97). This none-too-plausible trick of secret substitution works because Pao-yü has been reduced to a state of semi-idiocy by the mysterious disappearance of his jade (chapters 94–115). A monk returns the jade and leads his spirit in a second visit to the Illusory Realm of Great Void, now renamed Joyous Land of Eternal Truth (chapter 116). With this visit Pao-yü understands karmic causes and consequences (*yin-kuo*) and embraces renunciation. After attaining success in the civil service examination, he disappears (chapter 119) and then fleetingly reappears in monk's garb to make a final bow to his father, Chia Cheng (chapter

120). In chapter 120, Chen Shih-yin, Chia Yü-ts'un, and Voiding-the-Void Taoist reappear, and we learn of the stone's return to its provenance and the transmission of its story.

Stone reached a cult status in the twentieth century, and the amount and range of scholarship on the book are formidable. Analyses of the book as roman-à-clef encoding seventeenth-century history, court politics, and important personages have been largely discredited. The autobiographical theory, first articulated in the Red Inkstone commentary and in the writings by Ts'ao's friends, has become widely accepted since Hu Shih propounded it in 1921. There are also speculations that Pao-yü may be modeled on Red Inkstone, or that he may represent a mixture of the author's and Red Inkstone's reminiscences. It may be safer, however, simply to regard Pao-yü as representing a lyrical ideal shared by Ts'ao Hsüeh-ch'in, Red Inkstone, and, to a certain extent, the entire culture. The only incontrovertible convergence of biography and fiction seems to be the youthful experience of the decline and fall of a rich and powerful family.

The most thorough attempt to draw parallels between the historical Ts'ao family and the fictional Chia clan is Chou Ju-ch'ang's *"Hung-lou meng" hsin-cheng* (New Textual Research on *The Dream of the Red Chamber*; 1976). The stone claims to be a faithful scribe of what he "studied with his own eyes and ears in half a lifetime" (chapter 1): to reconstruct the literal facts behind the fictional illusion is thus closely linked to another project: to explain the palpable illusion of reality in terms of psychological subtlety or richness of details. The fascination with the minutiae of the business of daily living in *Stone* sustains broad assertions of realism. Perhaps more remarkable, however, are the bracketing and disruption of the illusion of reality by a mythic-fantastic realm. What emerges is a metafictional consciousness realized through an interplay of ironic distance and nostalgic urgency, self-mockery and self-approbation, which forces the reader to reflect on the dialectics of reality and illusion, truth and fiction (*chen-chia*).

The dialectics of reality and illusion is coextensive with the paradoxical relationship between love (*ch'ing*) and its transcendence or negation (*pu-ch'ing*). Enlightenment is attained through love (*yi ch'ing wu tao*), even as reality is apprehended through illusion (*chi huan wu chen*). In chapter 1, after a second perusal of the story inscribed on the stone, Voiding-the-Void Taoist concludes that its main theme is love. "Love" is perhaps an inadequate rendering of *ch'ing*, whose range of associations includes desire, affection, feelings, emotions, sentiments, sentience. It is also linked to subjective consciousness, imagination, and esthetic sensibility. Like *Chin P'ing Mei*, *Stone* deals with carnal, transgressive desire and its interplay with money, power, and death, as in the episodes on the sexual escapades and adulterous affairs of Chia Lien, Chia She, Chia Chen, Chia Jui, Hsüeh P'an, Ch'in K'o-ch'ing, Yu Erh-chieh (Chia Lien's secondary wife), her younger sister Yu San-chieh (in some versions of the text), and perhaps Wang Hsi-feng. (There are subtle hints of Wang Hsi-feng's intimacy with Chia Jung. More generally, her sexuality is linked to her greed for power and recognition.) In such cases, the logic of transgression and punishment often obtains, but the author also empathizes with Wang Hsi-feng, Ch'in K'o-ch'ing, the Yu sisters, and even Chia Jui, as helpless victims of their passions and obsessions.

As far as Pao-yü and his female companions are concerned, however, Ts'ao Hsüeh-ch'in idealizes *ch'ing* and raises its transcendent dimension to an almost metaphysical level. Its domain is the Grand View Garden, a world of youth, beauty, play, freedom, innocence, compassion, and poetic and artistic pursuits. It is associated with lyrical self-containment, the power of the mind to dream and imagine a world, and the conception of the romantic-esthetic as an alternate sphere of existence. The idealization of *ch'ing* creates certain contradictions: the author insists on the garden inmates' innocence and purity, yet depth requires understanding of the negativity of existence. Perhaps this explains why Ts'ao hints at Pao-yü's less-than-innocent relationships with Ch'in K'o-ch'ing, Ch'in Chung, and Chiang Yü-han, and underlines the disastrous consequences of his flirtation with his mother's maid, Chin-ch'uan. To achieve the paradoxical combination of innocence and experience, Ts'ao emphasizes imagined loss and literary mediation (both love and enlightenment are experienced through empathy and reading, and expressed through literary responses and allusions). Gestures and events in the garden are made to carry the symbolic weight of poetic images. This is why, although on one level nothing much happens in the garden, the flux, intensity, and totality of experience are nevertheless conveyed. In this sense, the lyrical vision here not only is an articulation of the powers and claims of *ch'ing* but also expresses itself as the formal necessity of symbolic condensation and the esthetics of reticence and suggestion.

Ch'ing and the feminine are romanticized together, even as the creatures of *ch'ing*—the garden's inmates—are female or effeminate, hence Pao-yü's famous assertion that "the bones and flesh of girls are made of water; those of men are made of mud" (chapter 2). Sympathetic male characters, such as Pao-yü, Ch'in Chung, and Chiang Yü-han, have a feminine sensibility. Male attributes or roles become attractive when performed by female characters (e.g., Shih Hsiang-yün, Fang-kuan, and Ou-kuan [two of the twelve actresses brought into the Grand View Garden to form the family theatrical troupe]). We recall Pao-yü's prehuman existence as the stone deemed unfit to repair heaven and as the divine attendant watering the crimson pearl flower (reborn as Lin Tai-yü). The individual resolutely falling outside systems of order (social, political, philosophical, and religious) because of his *ch'ing* finds fulfillment as the giver of love and life. However, the fact that Tai-yü is to "repay a debt of tears" (*huan-lei*) shows the inevitable ties of love with sadness, loss, and death. Ethereal Tai-yü is eventually consumed by the burden of her feelings. Love cannot be told—again and again we see the frustrations of miscommunication and inadequate expression. A moment of perfect (nonverbal) communion, when Pao-yü sends Tai-yü some old handkerchiefs on which she writes of her longing, is immediately followed by intimations of death (Tai-yü stops writing because of consumptive feverishness) (chapter 34). To know love is to apprehend its implacable negation, hence Tai-yü's grief when she listens to arias from "Mu-tan t'ing" (The Peony Pavilion) (chapter 23). In some ways this is the most compelling version of attaining "enlightenment through love" or "detachment through attachment" (*yi-ch'ing wu-tao*), which is Disenchantment's professed aim when she guides Pao-yü through the Illusory Realm (chapter 5). This paradox is apparently borne out by the plot: Pao-yü moves from limitless longing to Buddhist renunciation. (In this, the sequel follows Ts'ao's original design.) In *Rereading the Stone* (1997), Anthony Yu shows how mirrors, dreams, and jades chart the theme of Buddhist enlightenment in *Stone*.

In terms of the involutions of Pao-yü's consciousness, there are indeed moments when Pao-yü approaches self-questioning and self-distancing because of the frustrations of love and attachment (chapters 21, 22, and 36), but his stubborn myth-making when his world crumbles—he turns his dead maid, Ch'ing-wen, into a flower spirit in an elegy (chapter 78)—shows how, even to the bitter end, he affirms the power of consciousness, feelings, and words to create a reality he can live by. The fulfillment of the paradox of "enlightenment through love" is symbolically and structurally, but perhaps not psychologically, inevitable. By the same token, although the identical paradoxical logic is supposed to inform processes of esthetic creation (the author claims to have awakened) and literary communication (as exemplified by the cycle of conversions experienced by Voiding-the-Void Taoist), contradictions remain unresolved. The reader is more likely to have been caught up in illusion and emotions than to have transcended them. Ts'ao Hsüeh-ch'in's story is supposed to redeem "the guilt of half a lifetime wasted and not a single skill acquired" (preface, probably by his cousin Ts'ao T'ang-ts'un), yet this is to be accomplished through memory and fictional creation of "all those remarkable girls in the inner chambers." The paradox of "enlightenment through love" thus conveys Ts'ao Hsüeh-ch'in's mixture of nostalgia and irony toward his own past, the world he creates, and the ideal of lyrical self-containment in the tradition.

In the sequel, the paradoxical opposition and mutual implication of reality and illusion, love and its transcendence or negation, yield pride of place to the problem of reconciling different conceptions of order, namely, Confucian engagement and Buddhist-Taoist renunciation. This is obvious in a comparison of Chia Pao-yü's dream of his double, Chen Pao-yü ("Real Precious Jade"), in chapter 56 and the actual meeting of the two characters in chapter 115. In chapter 56, the dream raises questions concerning the real or illusory nature of the self and of its attachments. In chapter 115, Chen Pao-yü espouses Confucian commitment, while Chia Pao-yü believes in otherworldly freedom and detachment. (There is a parallel argument between Pao-yü and Pao-ch'ai on Confucian and Taoist ideas of return in chapter 118.) Thus formulated, the contradiction becomes more conventional and resolvable. In general, the sequel is more moralistic, sentimental, and melodramatic. It contains many scenes of pedagogy (which betray this author's interest in lessons and messages), dramatizes conflicts between victimized innocence, on the one hand, and unalloyed evil and malice, on the other (so that the moral equation is not in doubt), subsumes *ch'ing* to moral order, and insists on solutions of harmony and equilibrium to the problems posed by Ts'ao Hsüeh-ch'in. In this sense, the sequel represents major preoccupations in the tradition and shows how far ahead of his times Ts'ao Hsüeh-ch'in was. In its encyclopedic inclusiveness, *Stone* in a sense sums up Chinese culture, but the greatness of the book lies more in the ways it asks difficult questions of that culture. It poses as problems the ways systems of order (whether sociopolitical, moral, philosophical, or religious) accommodate or define the self; the meanings of roles and displacement; the claims of emotions, desire, imagination, and artistic creation to coherence, autonomy, and responsibility; reconciliation of contradictions in the name of order and harmony. The nostalgia for and idealization of a lost world in *Stone* capture the modern Chinese reader's feelings about the entire traditional Chinese culture; at the same time, its ironic, critical self-reflexivity intimates the burden of modernity.

Stone spawned a vast number of sequels, imitations, and rebuttals. In some cases, a theme or a type of rhetoric from *Stone* is taken up and put into other contexts. Idealized portraits of female characters, already prevalent in the scholar-beauty romances from the seventeenth and eighteeenth centuries, gain new depth and meaning through an elegiac, confessional tone in *Stone*. Echoing the preface of *Stone*, Li Ju-chen (c. 1763–1830) writes at the beginning of his novel, *Ching hua yüan* (Flowers in the Mirror, A Romance; 1828), that he cannot allow beautiful, distinguished women, no matter how distant and unlikely their stories, to pass into oblivion. The idea comes up again about midway through the hundred-chapter novel: the elegiac gesture of preserving the memory of remarkable women is linked to the implied author's own grief and sense of unfulfillment (chapter 48). Taken as a whole, however, *Flowers in the Mirror* excels not in tragic pathos but in imaginative energy, wit, and erudition.

The novel tells of the demotion of a hundred flower spirits to the human world for having bloomed in winter at the powerful T'ang empress-usurper Wu Tse-t'ien's (r. 684–704) command. In the first half of the book, a frustrated scholar, an astute merchant, and a seasoned mariner undertake a journey to distant, fantastic kingdoms, whose descriptions are often transparently satirical and allegorical. In the course of the journey, some of the flower spirits banished to these strange kingdoms—reincarnated as beautiful, talented young women—are gathered and eventually brought back to China. In the second half of the book, Empress Wu institutes literary examinations for young women. The human incarnations of the flower spirits all pass, and much space is devoted to their erudite gatherings where they compose poems, tell stories, paint, play the *ch'in* (zither), and deliver learned disquisitions on chess, lantern riddles, drinking games, divination, phonology, mathematics, and a host of other subjects. With the defeat of Empress Wu by loyalist forces at the end of the book, they disperse—some marry, some die, and some leave for far-off places.

Flowers in the Mirror has often been praised for its social criticism and protofeminist ideas. In fact, there is no genuine reformist zeal in the book. Satire is directed against human foibles and follies, which are perennial, and not against sociopolitical organization, which can actually be changed. When a man is made to submit to painful foot-binding in the Kingdom of Women (described in chapters 32–37), it is the occasion for comedy rather than for sustained reflection on the irrational practice. A more serious critique of foot-binding by a minister of the Kingdom of Gentlemen (chapter 12) shows how contradictory perspectives are played out: Li Ju-chen is aware of social evils and the plight of women, but his attention is intermittent and he does not consistently pursue alternatives; he glorifies talented women but allows them to flourish only in the interregnum of usurpation by Empress Wu; he preserves a haven for female power and public aspirations in the Kingdom of Women, which is nevertheless relegated to the distant periphery of the Central Kingdom. In general, the spectacle of female talent evokes wonder but does not threaten the status quo: the girls display their abilities in literary gatherings in enclosed gardens, and their success in the examination brings them honor, not the chance for public service. Li Ju-chen is completely enamored of many aspects of Chinese culture, from moral premises such as filial piety, loyalty, and chastity, aspirations for Taoist immortality, classical learning, and esoteric knowledge, to all the ornaments of literati culture. In using the novel as the vehicle for displaying erudition and in his conception of knowledge as encyclopedic miscellany, Li Ju-chen is comparable to Hsia Ching-ch'ü (1705–1787). Hsia's mammoth novel, *Yeh-sou p'u-yen* (An Old Rustic's Idle Talk), is a grand fantasy of wish fulfillment in which the male protagonist, Wen Su-ch'en, parades his accomplishments and adventures as scholar, knight-errant, moralist, lover, minister, and military commander in interminable discourses on miscellaneous subjects. However, while Li Ju-chen continues the tradition of *Stone* in valorizing the feminine, Hsia mythologizes the *yang* (masculine) qualities embodied by Wen Su-ch'en. Roughly contemporaneous with *Stone*, *An Old Rustic's Idle Talk* in some ways represents its opposite—the naive self-aggrandizement and apotheosis of certain wonted moral precepts (sometimes fulfilled through perverse, puerile means) cannot be more different from the ironic self-reflexivity and profound questioning of the values upheld by Chinese civilization in *Stone*. Indeed, even works that echo *Stone* often lack its critical spirit. *Flowers in the Mirror* continues the trend of idealizing female characters but is actually much more conventional. Wen K'ang's (1798–1872) *Erh-nü ying-hsiung chuan* (Tales of Boy and Girl Heroes; 1878?) pointedly repudiates the premises of *Stone* even while presenting idealized women. Wen K'ang uses the figure of Thirteenth

Sister (Shih-san Mei, alias Ho Yü-feng), an unconventional female knight-errant who turns into a perfect traditional woman, to show how *ch'ing* sustains heroism and activism, as well as augments the moral and sociopolitical order.

Flowers in the Mirror eulogizes female talent but is not really concerned with romantic love. By the mid-nineteenth century, the locus of idealized love has moved to courtesan quarters. Lu Hsün explains this as an inevitable displacement, the function of literary possibilities on love in the inner chamber having been exhausted. The marriage of the literary conventions of romantic love with the implied promiscuity and commodification of sex in courtesan life at this juncture, what David Wang terms "edifying depravity" (*Fin-de-siècle Splendor*; 1997), may in part be explained by the importance of courtesan quarters in urban centers (especially Shanghai) in the experience of modernity. Ch'en Sen's (c. 1796–c. 1870) *P'in-hua pao-chien* (A Precious Mirror for Judging Flowers; 1849) describes the homosexual relationships of opera singers (who impersonate women) and their lovers with romantic and sentimental rhetoric. Idealized courtesan figures fill the pages of Yü Ta's (d. 1884) *Ch'ing-lou meng* (Dream of the Blue Chamber; 1878) and Wei Tzu-an's (1819–1874) *Hua-yüeh hen* (Traces of Flowers and the Moon; 1858). The latter tries to capture the tragic pathos of *Stone*, to which it alludes self-consciously, by contrasting loss and death in one scholar-courtesan relationship with "what might have been" in another, more fortunate pair. Han Pang-ch'ing's (1856–1894) *Hai-shang hua-lieh chuan* (Biographies of Shanghai Sing-Song Girls; 1892) is the most outstanding example of this subgenre. Its tragic sense is more subtle, more implacable, and more bound up with a sober, realistic description of courtesan life and the onset of modernity in Shanghai. *Shanghai Sing-Song Girls* reworks the esthetic premises and narrative techniques of *Chin P'ing Mei*, *Stone*, and *The Scholars*. Being much less concerned with "messages" than other late Ch'ing novels, it is also much more successful in its nuanced perception and precise delineation of emotions and human relationships. Tseng P'u's (1872–1935) *Nieh-hai hua* (A Flower in a Sea of Sins; 1905) has a paradoxical fusion of female promiscuity and heroic action. Here the unscrupulous and licentious Fu Ts'ai-yün (based on the famous courtesan Sai Chin-hua) enters the stage of national politics and international diplomacy. The novel is unfinished, but apparently Tseng P'u planned to take up the Sai Chin-hua myth: Fu Ts'ai-yün is to "save China" through her liaison with Count Waldersee, the commander-in-chief of the Allied occupation forces during the stridently xenophobic 1900 Boxer Rebellion, which had been manipulated by factions within the Ch'ing (Manchu) government to prop up its ailing government at the peril of foreign residents in China.

A *Flower in a Sea of Sins* is often classified, along with the aforementioned works by Wu Chien-jen and Li Po-yüan, as well as Liu O's (1857–1909) *Lao Ts'an yu-chi* (The Travels of Lao Ts'an; 1907), as important late Ch'ing "novels of indictment" (*ch'ien-tse hsiao-shuo*). All these works are steeped in a sense of urgency, verging on despair, about the national crisis. They are often more articulate in exposing the moral bankruptcy of society, especially among the ruling classes, than in defining new modes of heroic, effective action. The moral ambiguity of Fu Ts'ai-yün is a case in point. *The Travels of Lao Ts'an* also combines fine-tuned attacks on various ills in society with a deep sense of predicament and confusion. The narrative centers on the travels and adventures of Lao Ts'an, an itinerant doctor-literatus and a somewhat unlikely latter-day knight-errant who echoes the author's own aspirations and preoccupations. Liu O ponders the nature of justice and order by choosing as his target the self-righteous fury and murderous misjudgments of incorruptible officials (*ch'ing-kuan*). The concern with uncorrupt yet harsh officials is as old as Ssu-ma Ch'ien, who devoted a chapter of *Records of the Historian* to "Collected Biographies of Harsh Officials." Liu O's preoccupation with justice is burdened by awareness of impending chaos, as evident in references to poverty, deprivation, and "Boxers in the north and revolutionaries in the south." The book persistently raises unresolved questions: does the solution lie then in knight-errantry (including Lao Ts'an's own altruistic and courageous acts), forms of practical knowledge (e.g., medicine, flood control), philosophical visions transcending the present crisis (which involve esoteric combinations of the three teachings [Buddhism, Confucianism, and Taoism] and miscellaneous thought systems), or simply escape (to eremitism or religious renunciation)? *The Travels of Lao Ts'an* is tied to its historical moment in its sustained and sober reflections on the problem of national survival and the possibility of order and justice. That such reflections are filtered through individual unease and lyrical, precise descriptions of scenes and impressions establishes its affinity with modern fiction and brings us to the next stage in Chinese literary history.

Wai-yee Li

Chapter 36

TRADITIONAL VERNACULAR NOVELS: SOME LESSER-KNOWN WORKS

The era of the Ming (1368–1644) and Ch'ing (1644–1911) dynasties produced vernacular works of fiction on an unprecedented scale. Apart from the most famous Chinese novels such as the "four masterworks" of the Ming dynasty—*San kuo chih yen-yi* (Romance of the Three Kingdoms), *Shui-hu chuan* (Water Margin, Outlaws of the Marsh, or All Men Are Brothers), *Hsi-yu chi* (Journey to the West, or Monkey), and *Chin P'ing Mei* (Gold Vase Plum, The Golden Lotus) from the sixteenth century—and the great Ch'ing dynasty novels *Hung-lou meng* (A Dream of Red Towers) and *Ju-lin wai-shih* (The Scholars) from the eighteenth century, Chinese writers created a variety of fictional narratives, some similar in scope and structure to the famous novels, others shorter or dealing with different themes.

The proliferation of vernacular novels in the late Ming dynasty in particular testifies to a burst of creative energy and activity. Such literary activities coincided with the expansion of cities and urban culture, bearing witness to the urban dwellers' craving for entertainment and amusement. The use of the vernacular language or an idiom approaching the vernacular, as opposed to classical Chinese, made these works of fiction accessible to a wider readership. Their readership may have included not only the highly educated members of the literati elite but also literate merchants and women with some education and enough leisure time to devote to them. Many novels remain anonymous, but the authors would most probably have been scholars or officials, some higher up and others lower down the ladder of success in the imperial examination system for recruitment into the civil service. Their writings give voice to an era that today invites us to explore its many facets of literary creation.

ON A BROAD CANVAS: THE LATE MING WORLD IN FICTION

Marriage Destinies to Awaken the World

Hsing-shih yin-yüan chuan (Marriage Destinies to Awaken the World, Tale of Marriage Destinies That Will Bring Society to Its Senses, or The Bonds of Matrimony), a novel of manners from seventeenth-century China, appears to be one of China's most underrated traditional vernacular novels. Its depiction of local society in Shantung province presents one of the most grand-scale explorations of the world in fiction. The action is set in the fifteenth century, but details and rhetoric refer to the time of writing in the seventeenth century.

The authorship of the novel has been wrongly attributed to P'u Sung-ling (1640–1715), Ting Yao-k'ang (1599–1669), and other famous seventeenth-century literati. The author remains anonymous. He reveals only his pen name, Hsi Chou sheng (Scholar of the Western Chou), an allusion to the Confucian Golden Age of the Western Chou dynasty (c. 1100–771 B.C.E.) in the legendary past.

The text betrays a familiarity with life in Shantung province and the capital, Peking, in the 1630s and early 1640s. The novel must have been composed sometime between 1628 and 1681, the transition period from the Ming to the Ch'ing dynasty. Modern scholars are not yet agreed whether the novel is a product of the Ming or the Ch'ing, but the text reflects voices and visions steeped in the late Ming world.

Marriage Destinies to Awaken the World is a chapter-linked novel and one of the longest pieces of Chinese prose fiction ever written. Its hundred chapters depict the lives of marital partners in two incarnations. The action of the novel divides into two main plot strands that are structurally linked by the theme of reincarnation and karmic retribution. One plot strand deals with the rise and fall of the first hero, Ch'ao Yüan, a young rake who thrives on his father's fortune until his excesses lead to his murder; the other focuses on Ch'ao Yüan's reincarnation as the second hero, Ti Hsi-ch'en, and his family. The story recounts how Ti Hsi-ch'en grows from a mischievous pupil and failed scholar into a successful merchant. He suffers for Ch'ao Yüan's crimes at the hands of his two shrewish wives, who act as his tormentors.

The saga of the two families dramatizes the systematic disintegration of society. A catalog of vices and moral decay conjures up the apocalyptic vision of a doomed nation. The domestic dramas unfold against a panoramic view of provincial society in seventeenth-century China. The dream of a lost Confucian utopia undergoes inversion and turns into an anti-utopian satire on contemporary conditions and affairs in the late Ming era, the time the narrative refers to as "the present." Brimming with irony and shrewd observation, the grotesque spectacle makes the novel an engrossing read.

Lost Tales and *Later Tales of the True Way*

Two other late Ming novels—*Ch'an-chen yi-shih* (Lost Tales of the True Way, The Forgotten History of Buddhists) and *Ch'an-chen hou-shih* (Later Tales of the True Way, The Latter History of Buddhists), written by Fang Ju-hao (fl. 1620s–1630s), probably in the 1620s—recall the four masterworks in their depictions of competing states, adventures involving bandits and rebels, battles with monsters and demons, and erotic encounters. Their explicit eroticism, focus on social classes, use of allegory, realistic description, and attention to detail characterize both works as typical of the late Ming novel. Both novels are also linked by a thematic framework of karmic retribution.

The forty-chapter *Lost Tales* focuses on Lin Shih-mao, a general of the Eastern Wei dynasty (534–550), whom circumstances force to flee and to continue life as a Buddhist monk. He later acquires three disciples, who develop their talents and together lead armies in the wars that result in the founding of the Sui dynasty (581–618). Lin and his disciples obtain high honors under the Sui and T'ang (618–907) emperors before retreating to the mountains, where Lin attains nirvana. The narrative projects the illusion of an ideal society through a series of negative examples. One scene shows how the world turns topsy-turvy when women rule a community, drawing up rules and regulations for their men and inverting social norms in parody of the Confucian classics.

The sixty-chapter *Later Tales* recounts how one of Lin's disciples is reincarnated as a character called Ch'ü Yen, who also turns into a model hero and receives honors under the notorious T'ang dynasty empress Wu Tse-t'ien (r. 684–705). Ch'ü Yen purges the state of evil and also serves as a healer before he, too, attains nirvana. As in other works of late Ming fiction, in this novel the cottage in the countryside to which the hero's father retires emerges as an ideal world and illustrates the dream of an ancient agricultural utopia, in contrast to the hubbub of the city. Dangers lurk not only in the form of urban attractions but also in seductive women, in particular Empress Wu, who also symbolizes moral and political decay. Panoramic and encyclopedic in scope, these two novels share with other works of late Ming fiction a voice that warns of contemporary conditions and airs a didactic concern for social and moral issues.

Not much is known about Fang Ju-hao, except that he wrote another long novel in 1635, the hundred-chapter *Tung-yu chi,* also called *Tung-tu chi* (Journey to the East).

WHAT HAPPENED AFTERWARD: SEQUELS TO THE FOUR MASTERWORKS

The four masterworks of the Ming novel inspired a series of sequels in the late Ming and early Ch'ing eras.

Sequels to Chin P'ing Mei

The earliest sequel to *Chin P'ing Mei,* entitled *Yü Chiao Li*[1] (Jade Charming Plum), was allegedly written by the anonymous author of *Chin P'ing Mei* during the Wan-li reign-period (1573–1620), but it is no longer extant. Another, sixty-four-chapter, sequel, *Hsü* Chin P'ing Mei (Sequel to *Chin P'ing Mei*), was written under a pseudonym by the scholar-official and poet Ting Yao-k'ang around 1660, after the fall of the Ming dynasty.

The story takes up the last chapters of *Chin P'ing Mei,* continuing the story of the survivors and the other characters in their reincarnations. Most characters retain their original names. The action is also set in Ch'ing-ho county, Shantung province. The story focuses on the life of Wu Yüeh-niang (Moon Lady), the virtuous principal wife of Hsi-men Ch'ing, the hero of *Chin P'ing Mei,* and the fate of her son, Hsiao-ko, a purged reincarnation of Hsi-men Ch'ing. The action takes place during the turmoil and bloodbath of the Mongol invasion of Sung China, echoing recent events in the author's life when Manchu forces swept across China and overthrew the Ming.

The narrative presents an ironic and playful game with quotations from Taoist, Buddhist, and Confucian works. It claims to dramatize the workings of karmic retribution while delving into a detailed survey of erotic practices and adventures. The early Ch'ing authorities perceived it as an obscene and immoral work and had the author serve a spell in prison in 1665. The Ch'ing government later listed the novel among the banned books because of its subversive content.

The same sequel has survived in a shorter version, numbering forty-eight chapters, under the title *Ko-lien hua-ying* (Flower Shadows Behind the Curtain), which changes the original names of both characters and places and disposes in part of the philosophical and historical contents while retaining its erotic character. The Ch'ing censors also banned this version. Yet another abridged and expurgated version of the *Sequel,* in sixty chapters, called *Chin wu meng* (Dream of Golden Chambers), appeared after the fall of the Ch'ing dynasty. Thus, neither *Flower Shadows Behind the Curtain* nor *Dream of Golden Chambers* was a new or completely different novel in its own right. In a sense, then, Ting Yao-k'ang was still their author, but it was other and later editors, not Ting, who made the abridgments and expurgations (and, in the case of *Flower Shadows Behind the Curtain,* also changed the names of the characters and places in the novel).

Sequels to Water Margin

The novel *Water Margin* and the lore surrounding it inspired a scholar from Chekiang, Ch'en Ch'en (1614–after 1666), to write a forty-chapter sequel, *Shui-hu hou-chuan* (Water Margin: Later Traditions), after the fall of the Ming dynasty, but he tied the plot into the historical context of the early Ch'ing era. Although Ch'en Ch'en's hopes for a resurrection of the Ming dynasty became frustrated, he described in his novel the flight of the surviving *Water Margin* heroes across the borders of China to a utopian realm overseas, where they set up a flourishing alternative empire. Ch'en first published the novel in 1664, but he dated his preface back into the Ming era in order to preserve his anonymity and to conceal from the new Ch'ing rulers his loyalist attitude toward the Ming. The heroes' entry into an idyll on the model of the ancient Chinese Peach Blossom Spring utopia implies the theme of escape from China's wartime devastation. The creation of a Ming loyalist utopia abroad must have exercised a certain fascination for Ch'en and his contemporaries, whose hopes had been dashed by the Manchu conquest.

Two more sequels to *Water Margin* appeared later: the seventy-chapter *Tang-k'ou chih* (Records of the Elimination of Bandits), by Yü Wan-chun (1794–1849), who condemns the heroes of the original novel as bandits and creates a group of superior heroes who set out to destroy the original ones. An anonymous Ch'ing writer ("Master of the Blue Lotus Chamber") wrote the forty-five-chapter sequel *Hou "Shui-hu chuan"* (Sequel to *Water Margin*), which continues the *Water Margin* story after the death of the hero Sung Chiang, with his reincarnation as another rebel from the early Southern Sung era (1127–1279), thus doubly underscoring the history of peasant rebellions in China.

Continuing the Journey to the West

In 1640, a few years before the fall of the Ming dynasty, the scholar and poet Tung Yüeh (1620–1686), from Chekiang province, wrote the sixteen-chapter novel *"Hsi-yu" pu* (Supplement to *Journey to the West*). Rather than forming a sequel to the sixteenth-century novel *Journey to the West*, the novel inserts additional adventures into the original story of monk Tripitaka and his disciple Monkey. It tells how the spirit of a mackerel lures Monkey away into a world of illusions and strange dreams in order to capture his master, Tripitaka. The complex and artistic structure of the novel allows for multiple levels of meaning, and readers have enjoyed it for its intertextual allusions, mythological and fantastic depictions, religious and psychological insights, playful rhetoric, satire, and surrealism.

When Tung Yüeh failed in the imperial civil service examinations, he turned to Buddhism, which had interested him since childhood. After the fall of the Ming dynasty, he became a monk, traveling widely. He also had links to the

Ming loyalist resistance movement. Tung Yüeh expressly linked the theme of escapism in his writings to political conditions. During the final years of Ming rule, he became increasingly preoccupied with the power and importance of dreams in times of upheaval. He regarded his novel as a dream for the inhabitants of a world in disorder: the dreams in his fiction would impose order, justice, and revelation on a chaotic age.

The extraordinary popularity of *Journey to the West* spawned a series of other sequels around the end of the Ming dynasty. These were *Nan-yu chi* (Journey to the South), *Pei-yu chi* (Journey to the North), and *Tung-yu chi* (Journey to the East). The first two were by a Fukien bookdealer named Yü Hsiang-tou (c. 1550–after 1637; fl. 1588–1609) and the third by Wu Yüan-t'ai. All three of these novels are saturated with popular or esoteric Taoist deities and themes. In the first third of the nineteenth century, they were twice published together with a forty-one-chapter abbreviation of *Journey to the West* by the late Ming author Yang Chih-ho as *Ssu-yu chi* (Records of Four Journeys).

PLAYING WITH EROTICISM: FICTION AND SEDUCTION

The Prayer Mat of Flesh

Eroticism plays a conspicuous role in Ming and Ch'ing fiction. One of the most notorious erotic novels is *Jou p'u-t'uan* (The Prayer Mat of Flesh, or The Carnal Prayer Mat), a sexual comedy in twenty chapters written in 1657 and first published in 1693 under the pseudonym Ch'ing-ch'ih Fan-cheng Tao-jen (Man of the Way Who Turned Over a New Leaf After Being Crazed with Passion). The novel is generally attributed to the playwright, theater critic, and comic writer Li Yü (1610/11–1680) from Chekiang province, who at that time was making a living as a writer in Hangchow. Having passed the first examination for the civil service, Li Yü attained a low-level official position but failed at the higher examinations. His fame as a literary genius, however, spread rapidly; thus he chose art as his alternative career. Although Li Yü spent most of his life struggling with financial problems, he lived in luxury among the rich and famous. He was accused of libertinism and counted among his friends both Ming loyalists and officials under the new Manchu government. He trained and directed his own theatrical troupe, with whom he traveled and performed all across the empire.

Chinese authorities have continually banned the novel since 1810, but this may only have contributed to its notoriety. It relates the sexual exploits of Vesperus, a young student on a quest to marry the most beautiful girl and to seduce the most attractive women in the world. As adultery and seduction entail revenge and tragedy, Vesperus eventually repents, reaches enlightenment, and retreats from the world.

Li Yü pretended that Buddhist purification was the main theme of *The Prayer Mat of Flesh.* The novel illustrates a common theme in the tradition of the Chinese erotic novel: depicting its hero as a libertine who abandons himself to sexual escapades and eventually receives his due punishment. Its ribald imagery; the art of humor; irony, and self-mockery; the peculiar style of summoning the fictional characters like actors onto the stage; and an innovative structure of alternating discourse and narrative give the novel a special literary value.

The more famous erotic novels—*The Prayer Mat of Flesh* and *Chin P'ing Mei*—were often indebted to earlier and relatively unknown erotic novels that had enjoyed wide popularity during the lifetime of their authors. They served later writers as sources, supplying them with sexual motifs and models for erotic verse.

The Unofficial History of the Embroidered Couch

The *Hsiu-t'a yeh-shih* (The Unofficial History of the Embroidered Couch), a late Ming erotic novel in four parts, was composed in about 1600 by the playwright and poet Lü T'ien-ch'eng (c. 1573–1619), from Chekiang province, who lived for most of his life in Soochow and Nanking. The renowned unorthodox Ming scholar Li Chih (1527–1602) later attached his critical comments to the novel, and the short story writer Feng Meng-lung (1574–1646) edited one version. The novel is written in a vigorous colloquial style interspersed with verse and local slang. The plot traces the erotic adventures of a young and promising scholar and libertine called Master Tung-men with his wife, his friend, the friend's young widowed mother, and his maids. Their orgies end with the premature death of all his companions, while Master Tung-men repents his sins and enters a monastery.

The Unofficial History of the Bamboo Grove

The sixteen-chapter *Chu-lin yeh-shih* (The Unofficial History of the Bamboo Grove), by an unknown author, published under the pen name Ch'ih-tao jen (Man of the Crazy Way), has a carefully constructed plot and testifies to the author's interest in the sexual black magic of the Taoist alchemists. The Ch'ing government banned the book in 1810 and 1868.

The action of the novel takes place in about 600 B.C.E. during the Spring and Autumn period (722–468 B.C.E.). The young heroine, Su-o, daughter of Duke Mu in the feudal state of Cheng, dreams that she receives instruction in the art of love from a Taoist adept. Young men, one after another, fall prey to her powers of seduction and lose their lives as she thrives on her sexual vampirism, extracting her lovers' vital essence, until she meets her match, a minister of an enemy state who is another Taoist expert. The couple and Su-o's maid continue their sexual exploits until they attain immortality.

Delightful Stories from the Chao-yang Palace

An anonymous author wrote *Chao-yang ch'ü-shih* (Delightful Stories from the Chao-yang Palace) under the pen name Master Yen-yen of Hangchow. It was first printed in 1621. This story, too, focuses on the Taoist art of love and pursuit of immortality. The heroine, a female fox spirit in the guise of a beautiful young girl, seeks a male victim to extract his vital essence in order to attain immortality. Her lover, however, turns out to be a swallow and Taoist adept on the same quest as the fox spirit. A battle ensues between the foxes and swallows of the mythical world until the Taoist supreme deity punishes both the heroine and her lover by reincarnating them as sisters. They both become imperial concubines during the Han dynasty (206 B.C.–220 C.E.), kill the emperor with an aphrodisiac overdose, and eventually receive their due punishment in the Taoist afterlife.

THE HAPPY WORLD OF SCHOLAR-BEAUTY ROMANCES

From the mid-seventeenth century onward, a new genre of shorter fictional narratives, the "tales of brilliant scholars and beautiful girls" (*ts'ai-tzu chia-jen*), gained popularity. These twelve- to twenty-six-chapter-long novels comprise comedies of errors and romances between talented scholars and beautiful ladies. A reaction against the late Ming erotic novels, these works of fiction celebrate chastity, chivalry, virtue, and wit. They dramatize harmonious marriages and superior morality. Such romances were the first Chinese novels to be taken to Europe in the eighteenth and nineteenth centuries and translated into European languages. Most of their authors, who were probably failed scholars or commercial writers, remain anonymous.

P'ing, Shan, Leng, and Yen

One of the earliest beauty-scholar romances, *P'ing-Shan-Leng-Yen* (P'ing, Shan, Leng, and Yen), sometimes wrongly attributed to Hsü Chen (fl. 1711) but actually by Chang Shao, first appeared in 1680. The title bears the names of the four main characters, two talented scholars and two beautiful female poets. The chancellor's daughter, Miss Shan, receives the emperor's praise for her exquisite poetry. She soon acquires a maid, Miss Leng, who develops similar literary talents. They meet the two brilliant poets and aspiring scholars P'ing and Yen and outdo them in a poetry competition. When all intrigues are resolved, the emperor himself gives his blessings to the marriages of the two girls to the two young men. The twenty-chapter novel extols the ideals of morality, monogamy, and literary talent in both men and women.

The Two Cousins

The plot of *Yü Chiao Li*[2] (Jade Charming Pear, or The Two Cousins), a late-seventeenth-century novel in twenty chapters, also creates the illusion of symmetry and harmony by dramatizing the marriage of a scholar with two beauties who are cousins and the best of friends. A Ming dynasty official searches for the best young poet in the empire to marry his daughter, Hung-yü (Red Jade), a talented and beautiful poet. Her uncle wants to marry her to the brilliant and dashing young poet Su, but Su declines as he mistakes the girl for someone else. Su later meets a boy called Meng-li (Dream Pear), who offers his sister to him in marriage, but when Su returns after passing the official examinations, the boy has disappeared. The father meanwhile decides to offer both his daughter and his niece in marriage to another young scholar called Liu. The two girls are upset at first, but then discover that the man called Liu was in fact Su in disguise. Su in turn finds out that the boy Meng-li was Hung-yü's female cousin. The happy ending to this comedy of errors consists in the double marriage to Su of the two pretty cousins.

The Fortunate Union

Perhaps the best-known beauty-scholar romance is the eighteen-chapter novel *Hao-ch'iu chuan* (The Fortunate Union), from the seventeenth century. It tells the tale of the tough, handsome, and clever son of a censor. The hero, T'ieh Chung-yü (Jade Within Iron), proves his valiance by rescuing maidens in distress. He also helps to protect an exiled minister's daughter, Shui Ping-hsin (Water Pure Heart), and prevents her abduction by an enraged suitor whom she has rejected. The suitor and her conniving, semiliterate uncle (of whom she is the ward) gradually poison T'ieh and cause him to fall gravely ill. Shui, however, removes him from their clutches and nurses him back to health. While she looks after him, they engage in moralistic conversations and fall in love. Their enemies accuse them of having a premarital affair, but a physical examination of the heroine ordered by the emperor and empress prove that she has preserved her chastity, enabling them to marry with due pomp and ceremony.

Other Triangle Love Stories

Triangular love affairs involving beauties and scholars proved particularly popular in the early and mid-Ch'ing era. Most such novels have about sixteen chapters and are of anonymous authorship.

Lin-erh pao (The Son of Good Fortune), written in about 1672, relates the story of a man's marriage to two women. It has a long-winded plot detailing how one heroine falls in love with the hero and disguises herself as a man to escape from an arranged marriage to someone else. In this attire she pretends to marry the hero's first wife, who gave her help and protection. When the ruse is finally discovered, the runaway girl marries the hero, too, and becomes his second wife.

A meeting of hero and heroine in male disguise and the hero's marriage to two women who are almost mirror images of each other also appears in *Wan Ju Yüeh* (The Two Wives Well Met), a narrative from the early Ch'ing.

In the novel *Ting-ch'ing jen* (The Tale of Loyal Love), from the second half of the seventeenth century, the hero first believes his marriage to the heroine thwarted and thus marries her maid instead. Later both the heroine and her maid live with the hero happily ever after, in harmony and without jealousy.

The novel *Fei-hua yung* (The Song of Fluttering Flowers), from the early Ch'ing, gives a romantic story a carefully symmetrical design by dramatizing the lovers' meetings, exchanges of poetry, subsequent separations, and failures to recognize each other at later reunions. They even trade families, as each is adopted by the other's parent. The structural symmetry emphasizes the lovers' intertwined destinies.

Another comedy of cross-dressing in the early-eighteenth-century novel *Feng-huang ch'ih* (The Phoenix Pool) describes how the two heroines disguise themselves as scholars and beauties before marrying the two heroes.

The narrative *Pai-kuei chih* (The Tale of the White Jade Tablet), from the turn of the nineteenth century, features five heroines who cross-dress as men in order to participate in the civil service examinations and to meet their future husbands. The women are found out but receive imperial pardon for their fraud.

In the slightly longer, twenty-four-chapter novel *Chu-ch'un yüan hsiao-shih* (The Garden of Spring Residence), from the second half of the eighteenth century, a boy is betrothed to a girl in childhood, but he later forgets and conducts a romantic exchange of poetry with another. When the two women eventually learn about each other, they become friends and both manage to marry the hero while sharing his love.

The eight-chapter novel *Liao-tu yüan* (The Cure for Jealousy, or Jealousy-Curing Destinies), which probably stems from the eighteenth century, describes how a shrewish wife keeps a close watch on her husband until she has to let him go to the capital to sit for the imperial examinations. On the way he falls prey to bandits in the mountains but is rescued and acquires another wife. Later, bandits capture both his first wife, who set out to follow him, and his new wife from the mountains. The second wife looks after the first wife so well that they become friends. A dream cures the first wife of her jealousy; she reforms and accepts the girl as a co-wife of equal rank.

A POLYGAMIST'S PARADISE

Other novels of similar length depicting romances between scholars and beauties feature heroes with more than two wives while focusing on their erotic adventures and resorting to a more earthy version of the vernacular. Such works from the seventeenth, eighteenth, and nineteenth centuries include *Chin-hsiang t'ing* (Pavilion of Embroidered Fragrance), which depicts a hero and his three wives; *Ch'ing-meng t'o* (Awakened from the Love Dream), a tale of cross-dressing and disguises in which a beauty almost marries two men; *Hu-tieh mei* (The Butterfly Go-Between), an erotic story of a hero, his four wives, and a lover; *Hsiu-p'ing yüan* (Omen of the Illustrated Screen), which recounts five co-wives living together in harmony; *Yü-lou ch'un* (The Cross-Dressed Scholar's Three Wives), a story of a hero who dresses as a woman and his adventures with love, kidnapping, and talented beauties; *Ch'un-teng mi-shih* (Dream Story Under the Spring Lamp), which dramatizes a woman's flirtations and pregnancies before marriage; *T'ao-hua ying* (In the Peach Blossom Shadow), which links the hero's erotic exploits with his wife and five concubines to his rise on the ladder of success in the imperial examination system; and *Hsing-hua t'ien* (The Paradise of Apricot Blossoms), which relates how the hero rejects an official career and acquires a family of twelve wives and a hundred sons.

Another romantic and erotic novel, *Shen-lou chih* (The Mirage of Love), first published around 1804, has a rather unusual setting: the action takes place in the southern province of Kwangtung, and some of the characters are merchants involved in the trade with Europeans in the provincial capital, Canton. The twenty-four chapters relate the romantic affairs of the hero, a merchant's son, while also depicting corruption in government and social unrest.

HEROES FROM THE PAGES OF HISTORY

The sixteenth and seventeenth centuries produced many historical romances dealing with the careers of military generals and emperors. One such historical novel that appeared in 1631, the anonymous *Sui Yang-ti yen-shih* (The Merry Adventures of Emperor Yang of the Sui, or The Romantic History of Emperor Yang of the Sui), dramatizes in forty chapters the theme of the bad last ruler, showing how the Emperor Yang (r. 604–617) of the Sui dynasty brings ruin upon himself and his dynasty by overindulging in pleasure. The novel takes its plot from earlier classical tales. The theme of the debauched hero also recalls *Chin P'ing Mei* while reflecting the excesses and disastrous reign of the late Ming Wan-li emperor (r. 1573–1620).

This novel also inspired Ch'u Jen-huo (c. 1630–c. 1705), from Ch'ang-chou, Kiangsu province, in about 1675 to compose another historical novel, the one-hundred-chapter *Sui T'ang yen-yi* (Romance of the Sui and T'ang Dynasties).

Starting with the reign of Emperor Yang of the Sui, the story covers the rise of the T'ang dynasty until the tragic events involving Emperor Hsüan-tsung (r. 712–756) and his favorite consort, the beautiful Yang Kuei-fei. Their fateful love affair appears as an ominous parallel to the earlier story of Emperor Yang. The novel has an elaborate structural design and uses the technique of panoramic presentation similar to that of the more famous literati novels.

THE QUEST OF THE CONFUCIAN HERO: LONGER NOVELS FROM MID-CH'ING CHINA

An Old Rustic's Idle Talk

Yeh-sou p'u-yen (An Old Rustic's Idle Talk), is a 154-chapter novel from the eighteenth century written by Hsia Ching-ch'ü (1705–1787), an eccentric Confucian scholar, poet, and historian from Kiangsu province whose interests included music, mathematics, astronomy, law, military science, and medicine. A century passed before the novel was published, perhaps because Hsia lived in poverty. He never succeeded in the official examinations, but his work as a secretary to officials enabled him to travel extensively throughout China.

The action is projected back into the mid-Ming era. Many details and events in the novel are autobiographical but the male protagonist, Wen Su-ch'en, a child prodigy and Confucian polymath, succeeds in the imperial examination system, attains high rank, and is singled out for special imperial honors. This Confucian superhero is also endowed with magical powers, physical prowess, and sexual potency. He manages a household of two wives, four concubines, and a multitude of sons, grandsons, and great-grandsons, as would have befitted an emperor. His mother reaches old age and, as a sage Confucian matriarch and chaste widow, she too receives imperial honors. A Confucian moralist, Wen Su-ch'en sets out to eradicate heterodoxy. He conquers evil monsters, subdues rebellious monks and eunuchs, and wins the emperor's confidence. He succeeds not only in eliminating Buddhism and Taoism in China but also in subjugating Europe and converting it to Confucianism.

The narrative celebrates a mild eroticism within marriage, the ideal woman in the role of companion, and the mother figure as the superior woman. It imbues descriptions of erotic scenes and bizarre sexual fantasies with an orthodox Confucian morality. The novel records moral corruption and social decay with detachment but in minute detail—true to the tradition of precise scholarship and evidential research (*k'ao-cheng-hsüeh*) in Ch'ing China—while envisaging a Confucian renaissance and the creation of a Confucian superstate.

The Lamp at the Crossroads

It took Li Hai-kuan (1707–1790), a scholar-official from Honan province, almost thirty years to compose *Ch'i-lu teng* (Lamp at the Crossroads, A Lamp at the

Fork, or Warning Light at the Crossroads). Li wrote this 108-chapter novel in the vernacular with snatches of local Honan dialect between 1748 and 1777. The novel tells the story of the young hero, T'an Shao-wen, in Honan in the mid-Ming dynasty. It traces the hero's life from childhood, focusing on his education and upbringing as a Confucian scholar. T'an is torn between different influences in his life: a stern Confucian father devoted to having his son properly educated, an indulgent mother who prefers money to scholarship, and wastrel friends whose hedonism brings about T'an's gradual ruin. Reading the wrong kind of books, such as vernacular fiction (in particular, *Chin P'ing Mei*), also has a corrupting influence on T'an. The hero's wives fail to save him from disaster, but later he acquires a concubine who helps him to reform. T'an becomes a scholar-official after all, and his son, too, turns into a successful scholar. Although the author doubted the value of Ming dynasty fiction, he stressed the appeal of vernacular prose and its didactic and educational qualities.

The Account of Lin, Lan, and Hsiang

At the turn of the nineteenth century, an anonymous author with the pseudonym Sui-yüan Hsia-shih (An Idiot Following Destiny) wrote *Lin Lan Hsiang* (The Account of Lin, Lan, and Hsiang, or The Six Wives of the Wastrel Keng). The sixty-four-chapter novel takes *Chin P'ing Mei* as a model for its title, characters, and plot. The action centers on an aristocratic household in fifteenth- and sixteenth-century Peking. The hero, Keng Lang, a wealthy and high-ranking playboy and wastrel, acquires six women as his wives and concubines—some of them beautiful, talented, virtuous, and self-sacrificing; others sexy, uneducated, shrewish, and debauched. Like ministers surrounding an emperor, some of whom are of high moral caliber and others of evil intent, the women around Keng Lang play out a tale of intrigue, revenge, and murder. The message remains conservative, condemning those who overstep rank and position while celebrating the ideal of the virtuous wife.

Tales of Boy and Girl Heroes

The forty-one-chapter novel *Erh-nü ying-hsiung chuan* (Tales of Boy and Girl Heroes, or The Gallant Maid), by Wen K'ang (1798–1872), a writer of noble Manchu descent, continues the romantic tales of scholars and beauties while including a woman warrior in the tradition of martial arts fiction. The first printed edition dates to 1878. The story focuses on the valiant girl Ho Yü-feng, also called "Thirteenth Sister," who dedicates her life to taking revenge for the death of her father in prison after he became the victim of a high official's plotting. Thirteenth Sister rescues the young scholar An Chi and a girl called Ms. Chang from the hands of cannibals. An Chi later marries both the warrior girl and Ms. Chang and succeeds in attaining high office. When a new emperor ascends the throne, Thirteenth Sister receives justice for her father's death.

The novel was written in response to the famous eighteenth-century *Shih-t'ou chi* (Story of the Stone; also called *Hung-lou meng* [A Dream of Red Towers]), which featured morally superior heroes in a harmonious Confucian universe. However, it remained largely oblivious to contemporary affairs, such as Western encroachments and internal rebellions that ravaged China in the nineteenth century.

ENTERING THE PLEASURE QUARTERS: BITTERSWEET LOVE AND TRAGEDY

Trails of Immortals in the Green Wilds

Between 1753 and 1762 Li Pai-ch'uan (c. 1720–after 1762), a scholar and failed merchant who earned his living as a secretary to officials, wrote the erotic novel *Lü-yeh hsien-tsung* (Trails of Immortals in the Green Wilds), which exists in an eighty-chapter and a hundred-chapter version. The story of Leng Yü-ping, a scholar who turns into a Taoist immortal, takes place in the mid-sixteenth century. It includes episodes about profligates and prostitutes, shrewish wives, henpecked husbands, and rebellious youths. The novel relates their sexual escapades and search for enlightenment, depicting adventures with mortals, dalliances with demons, battles with bandits and scenes of love, suicide, adultery, and moral reform. This relatively unknown novel appears to have been composed independently of the other long and more famous eighteenth-century works of fiction.

A Precious Mirror for Judging Flowers

The romances of beauties and scholars reappear under a different guise in the novel *P'in-hua pao-chien* (A Precious Mirror for Judging Flowers, or A Mirror of Theatrical Life) as stories of male actors who impersonate women and their affairs with their male patrons. The action is set in Peking during the early nineteenth century. The story focuses on the romantic involvement of a young patron called Mei Tzu-yü with his favorite actor, Tu Ch'in-yen. The author of this sixty-chapter novel, Ch'en Sen (c. 1796–c. 1870), from Ch'ang-chou, Kiangsu province, spent some time in Peking in the circles of artists and actors. Completed in 1849, the novel was first printed in 1852 and gained wide popularity in the nineteenth century.

Traces of Flowers and the Moon

A partly autobiographical story about scholars and courtesans, the fifty-two-chapter *Hua-yüeh hen* (Traces of Flowers and the Moon) was written in the

1850s by the unsuccessful scholar Wei Hsiu-jen (also called Wei Tzu-an; 1819–1874), from Fukien province. The novel dramatizes the tragic and romantic love of two scholars for two courtesans. One couple meets with misfortune and death, while the other marries and attains high rank, honor, and happiness.

Biographies of Shanghai Sing-Song Girls

The world of nineteenth-century Shanghai, with its courtesans, opium addiction, gambling dens, and foreign concessions, features in the scandal stories of *Hai-shang hua-lieh chuan* (Biographies of Shanghai Sing-Song Girls). No longer as romantic as the earlier beauty-scholar or scholar-courtesan love stories, this sixty-four-chapter novel traces the ruin of a young man called Chao P'u-chai in the world of Shanghai's courtesans. He ends up as a rickshaw puller, while his sister who comes to Shanghai to save him becomes a courtesan. The author, Han Pang-ch'ing (1856–1894), from Sung-chiang, Kiangsu province, worked as a journalist and newspaper editor in Shanghai. He first published the novel, which includes some dialogs containing regional vernacular, in serialized form in 1892 and as a book in 1894.

The Sea of Regret

The ten-chapter novel *Hen hai* (The Sea of Regret), written in 1905 by Wu Chien-jen (alias Wu Wo-yao; 1866–1910), from Kwangtung province, sets its action during the anti-foreign Boxer Rebellion in 1900. The novel depicts the fate of two couples who had been betrothed by their parents but are separated in the turmoil of social and political unrest. At their reunion, however, they discover their incompatibility as marital partners. One girl has become a prostitute, while one man has turned into a thief and opium addict.

The author worked in Shanghai as a journalist, novelist, and magazine editor. He also gained fame as the author of *Erh-shih nien mu-tu chih kuai hsien-chuang* (Strange Scenes Witnessed in the Past Twenty Years), serialized between 1903 and 1911. Its 108 chapters, including the innovative use of a first-person narrator, present a systematic survey of social dysfunction.

The Trajectory of Late Imperial Vernacular Fiction

The above discussion offers an overview of some genres and themes in Ming and Ch'ing fiction that are obscure today but were quite popular in their own time. Many other types of fictional narratives were also written, including adventure stories, tales of chivalry, military romances, and detective novels. Some works from the late Ch'ing era express social criticism and a fin-de-siècle mood of anxiety and despondency (see chapter 37). Many narratives at the turn of the twentieth century reflect the increasing influence of European fiction in China, heralding the era of modern Chinese literature (see chapter 38). While the major novels of the Ming and Ch'ing dynasties, the so-called masterworks (see chapter 35), may have set the pace and the parameters for extended vernacular fiction in late imperial China, they by no means exhaust the range of possibilities available to readers during this period. As a result of both internal dynamics and external influences, the growth of vernacular fiction from the fifteenth to the nineteenth century was remarkable. Developments in poetry, drama, and prose were relatively minor in comparison. This would change, however, in the twentieth century, when all types of literature underwent radical transformation.

Daria Berg

Chapter 37

THE LATER CLASSICAL TALE

"Classical tale" (*wen-yen hsiao-shuo*) is a term that has come to be used to denote two strands within the very broad tradition of *hsiao-shuo* (literally, "small talk") in classical Chinese: those concerned primarily with relating a story of some kind, namely, the *chih-kuai* anecdote (see chapter 29) and the *ch'uan-ch'i* tale (see chapter 33). The distinction between them is not always clear-cut, but it remains useful as a way of mapping out the literary landscape during much of the later imperial period.

THE ANECDOTAL TRADITION FROM THE SUNG TO THE MING

By the Sung dynasty (960–1279), exchanging interesting anecdotes was a well-established activity at social gatherings, and there was widespread interest in telling, recording, and reading strange tales. Naturally, then, during its long history the Sung dynasty generated a significant body of anecdotal literature. In some cases, Sung anecdotal collections moved beyond the traditional interest in anomalous supernatural events to encompass extraordinary episodes on a purely human level, such as a fortuitous chain of events that entangles various members of the community in some kind of social sensation. In two representative collections from the mid-twelfth century, Lien Pu's (c. 1095–1170) *Ch'ing-tsun lu* (Records of the Clear and Honorable) and Wang Ming-ch'ing's (1127–1202+) *T'ou-hsia lu* (The Linchpin Tossing Collection), this interest in unusual developments within the urban social context is particularly evident. The inclusion of anecdotes emanating from the more humble levels of society also characterizes the greatest Sung collection of anecdotes, Hung Mai's *Yi-chien chih* (Records of the Listener).

Hung Mai (1123–1202) began to record strange tales in his early twenties and completed his first collection (twenty chapters) in 1161. Encouraged by its favorable reception and possessed by an inexhaustible interest in unusual stories, he thereafter greatly accelerated the pace of his story-collecting. It took him only eight months in 1194–1195 to write the second volume (ten chapters) in his second series. He rattled off another four volumes in the course of the next year and completed the seventh volume (10 chapters, 135 reports) in a mere forty-four days in 1196. At the time of his death in 1202, he was working on the second volume of his fourth series. In its final form, *Records of the Listener* comprised some 420 chapters. The 207 chapters that survive total more than 1,800 pages in the modern typeset edition.

During his career in the capital and the provinces, Hung Mai assiduously recorded stories that he heard, leaving us a rich and varied tapestry of incidents and characters that reveals much about popular beliefs and religious lore of the time. The tales derive from the context of informal storytelling at social gatherings, and Hung's informants (whom he often identifies by name) include such varied representatives of Sung society as government officials, gentry, neighborhood women, clerks, traders, soldiers, Buddhist monks, and Taoist priests. As he notes in one of his prefaces: "Whenever I hear a companion tell a story, I immediately write it down. If I hear it at a dinner and do not have such an opportunity, then I will transcribe it from memory the following morning and quickly show the account to my informant, to make sure that my version does not deviate from his account." Hung thus represents himself not as an author of fiction so much as a faithful recorder and transmitter of oral testimony. His tales draw much of their appeal from their economy—most are no more than a page or so in length—and simple, direct language. Because of its raw and unrefined literary qualities, Hung's work lent itself to adaptation and embellishment, and many tales in *Records of the Listener* were used as source material by later authors working in the vernacular medium.

Hung Mai's work created a model that writers in the following decades often sought to follow, albeit on a smaller scale. Notable examples are *K'uei-ch'e chih* (Record of a Carriage Full of Ghosts), by Kuo T'uan (*chin-shih* 1154), the anonymous *Chih-ch'ing tsa-shuo* (Miscellaneous Stories of Chih-ch'ing; late twelfth century), and *Kuei-tung* (A Treasury of Ghost Stories), probably completed about 1230. Yüan Hao-wen (1190–1257) compiled a *Hsü "Yi-chien chih"* (Sequel to *The Records of the Listener*) late in his life, and another work claiming an affinity with Hung's work, the anonymously compiled *Hu-hai hsin-wen "Yi-chien" hsü-chih* (New Reports from Lake and Sea: Sequel to *The Records of the Listener*) is thought to date from the Yüan period.

By the early Ming dynasty (1368–1644), anecdotal accounts of strange or supernatural events occupied a recognized niche in the literary tradition. Scholars intrigued by the supernatural were, on the whole, undeterred by Confucius's reported reluctance to discuss the subject ("The Master did not talk about anomalies, physical exploits, disorders, and spirits" [*Lun-yü* (Analects), 7.20]), finding in this familiar quotation a tacit admission that the supernatural indeed existed. The incorporation of tales of the fantastic into the imperially commissioned *T'ai-p'ing kuang-chi* (Extensive Records from the Reign of Great Tranquility; 981), a vast compilation of arcane lore, and Hung Mai's dedication to his catalog of strange events in the Sung period endowed the anecdotal tradition with a considerable degree of legitimacy. Although no Ming author attempted to emulate *Records of the Listener* in scale, many drew inspiration and encouragement from it when collecting their own tales of the supernatural. As a result a very rich anecdotal literature was generated during the Ming dynasty.

The first major collection was assembled in the late fifteenth century by the idiosyncratic Soochow scholar Chu Yün-ming (1461–1527). Although only a few chapters of the collection survive, Chu's original work appears to have been much larger, compiled intermittently as four serial anthologies. One of Chu's prefaces, dated 1489, identifies the informative and entertaining aspects of the supernatural anecdote as its two indispensable qualities, a claim that runs consistently through Ming discussions of the genre.

Lu Ts'an (1494–1551), author of *Keng-ssu* (originally, *Keng-chi) pien* (A Decade's Jottings), was another important figure. Lu began recording strange tales in 1510, when he was just sixteen, and continued to do so for another ten years as he competed in the civil-service examinations. The publication of *A Decade's Jottings* some years later assured a wide and appreciative readership for his work. Taking his cue from Hung Mai, Lu Ts'an notes punctiliously the names of many of his informants and presents his material—most of it focused on his native Soochow—with sparse yet evocative detail. His collection includes a romance, "Tung-hsiao chi" (The Story of the Flute), admired by Ming readers for its taut narrative and polished style.

Lu Ts'an's interest in the classical anecdote was shared by other members of his family. His younger brother Lu Ts'ai (1497–1537) was an avid recorder of strange or comic tales, and Lu Ts'an's son Lu Yen-chih carried on the family tradition, assembling in 1556 a collection of anecdotes under the title *Shuo-t'ing* (Accounts of Things Heard). His tales, though generally brief and undeveloped, cast many interesting sidelights on the urban culture of the day.

Many anecdotal collections were published during the Wan-li reign-period (1573–1620). A series of such works was compiled by Wang Chao-yün, a bibliophile from Hupei province, between about 1590 and 1615. Wang explains his modest aims at the beginning of one of his anthologies. His casual jottings are designed simply to "keep at bay the specter of sleep" and have no serious moral intent. There is no place in his work for comment on contemporary issues, nor does it aspire to any linguistic complexity: "This collection was originally commissioned by a bookseller, who expressed a preference for a simple style in order to facilitate wide circulation, so I have not dared to discomfit readers by the use of arcane expressions or difficult characters." Naturally enough, therefore, his tales have few literary pretensions, merely recording notable incidents in the most economical way.

The popularity of the classical anecdote in the Wan-li era is epitomized by the reception accorded to Wang T'ung-kuei's *Erh-t'an* (Hearsay Stories). Wang T'ung-kuei first published a modest five-chapter collection of short tales in Peking in 1597. It circulated widely among officials stationed in the capital and was quickly reprinted by publishers in other provinces. Urged by readers to expand the collection, Wang set to work amplifying and classifying the contents. The revised edition, now entitled *Erh-t'an lei-tseng* (Hearsay Stories, Classified and Expanded) and comprising fifty-four chapters, appeared in 1603. A fifteen-chapter edition also was printed, and an unauthorized sequel entitled *Hsü Erh-t'an* (Continued Hearsay Stories) was published in 1603. Another work completed about the same time was *Chu-yü* (Whisk Remnants), assembled by Hsieh Chao-che (1567–1624) during temporary retirement from officialdom after his father's death in 1605.

K'uai-yüan (Garden of Cunning), the largest late Ming anecdotal collection, is devoted exclusively to tales of the supernatural. Its author, Ch'ien Hsi-yen, spent much of his life in Soochow, where he mingled with prominent intellectuals and established a reputation as a poet. According to Ch'ien Ch'ien-yi (1582–1664), a distant relative, he suffered from overweening self-esteem and was quick to take offense at perceived slights, thereby alienating other scholars. He died in poverty in the 1620s. Like most of his contemporaries, Ch'ien Hsi-yen had modest goals in his own anecdotal fiction. Most of his tales appear to be based on oral accounts related to him; they are organized in neat clusters by subject matter. The best of his work shows a dry, understated humor.

As mentioned above, most of these Ming anecdotal collections were casual records of strange tales, and their authors seldom attached reflections of their own to the stories they were telling. Only in a few rare cases did disaffected scholars begin to see possibilities in the anecdotal form as a vehicle for presenting their own ideas on topics of concern to them.

One example is Chiang Ying-k'o (1553–1605), a scholar-official associated with the Kung-an school of literary criticism (see chapter 20). Chiang devoted the last chapter of his collected works, *Hsüeh-t'ao-ko chi* (Snow Billow Pavilion Collection; 1600), to a set of tales in which he adapted the conventional anecdotal medium into a form of personal expression through which he presented his own views on certain moral issues, philosophical dilemmas, and administrative policies. The engaging tone of these short pieces appealed to many readers, and they were later published separately as a free-standing work entitled *Hsüeh-t'ao hsiao-shuo* (Snow Billow Stories).

THE *CH'UAN-CH'I* ROMANCE FROM THE SUNG TO THE MING

The longer literary tale, so notable a product of the T'ang dynasty (618–907), retained its popularity during the Sung dynasty, and Sung authors produced many works in the *ch'uan-ch'i* vein. A notable example is *Yün-chai kuang-lu* (Expanded Records of Cloud Studio), by Li Hsien-min, whose preface is dated 1111. The later chapters of *Expanded Records* are devoted to carefully crafted romances. The best-known Sung collection is *Ch'ing-so kao-yi* (Lofty Judgments from the Green Lattice), assembled in the late eleventh century by an obscure scholar named Liu Fu, who included his own work and that of other contemporaries in this anthology. These stories mark a shift away from the interest in moral dilemma, psychological complexity, and dramatic incident that characterizes the best of the T'ang tales, in favor of a delight in historical reminiscence and lyrical ornamentation. Some offer fictional embellishments of historical episodes, while others focus on such familiar themes as scholar-courtesan romances. On the whole, they are inspired less by an engagement with the contemporary social and cultural context, preferring instead a retrospective immersion in earlier eras. At their weakest, they tend to be rather lacking in substance, drawing on stock situations and predictable plot developments.

The Yüan dynasty (1260–1368) produced one very influential romance, "Chiao Hung chi" (The Story of Chiao-niang and Fei-hung). This work, attributed to a Yüan scholar named Sung Yüan (*tzu* [style name] Mei-tung; fl. 1300), was inspired by "Ying-ying chuan" (The Story of Ying-ying; see chapter 33), but developed a much more intricate tale of tragic romance in a narrative more than five times the length of the T'ang prototype. The story chronicles the series of trysts, separations, and misunderstandings that punctuate the courtship between a talented young scholar named Shen Ch'un and his beautiful cousin Chiao-niang. The clever and resourceful maidservant Fei-hung, whose central role in the story is reflected by the inclusion of part of her name in the story's title, alternately hinders and helps the couple. At the end of the tale, the lovers die of grief when Chiao-niang is betrothed to another man. "The Story of Chiao-niang and Fei-hung" circulated widely in the early Ming and served as a model for similar romantic tales published over the next two centuries.

Equally popular in the early Ming was a short story collection by Ch'ü Yu (1347–1433), a Hangchow writer, completed in 1378. As a young man, Ch'ü had assembled a forty-chapter collection of strange tales, *Chien-teng lu* (Records by the Trimmed Lamp; now lost), and he named a later collection *Chien-teng hsin-hua* (New Stories for Trimming the Lampwick) to distinguish it from its predecessor. *New Stories* circulated in both printed and manuscript copies during the succeeding decades and won many admiring readers. The book was regularly reprinted during the fifteenth and sixteenth centuries and set the tone for classical fiction for many years.

Ch'ü Yu's work displayed an intimate familiarity with *ch'uan-ch'i* of the T'ang and Sung dynasties. His conception of the classical tale seems not dissimilar to that of scholars of a century or two earlier, such as Chao Yen-wei, who made the following oft-quoted comment on T'ang tales of the supernatural: "Writings of this kind combine a whole range of forms, exhibiting historical acumen, poetic inspiration, and discursive force."

The contemporary setting of Ch'ü Yu's stories would have appealed to his early Ming readers, for they are typically set against the backdrop of the disturbances in the closing years of the Yüan dynasty, involving his characters in the crises and rapid shifts of fortune associated with dynastic change. They are polished pieces of work, studded with delicate descriptions and literary allusions. The tendency toward literary display reaches its apogee perhaps in "Chien-hu yeh-fan chi" (A Night Outing on Mirror Lake), which describes an encounter between a scholar and a goddess. Little happens in the course of the story, which merely provides a framework for lavish descriptions in parallel prose and a discussion studded with literary allusions. In this respect it is reminiscent of virtuoso tales of the T'ang and Sung periods.

Not all of Ch'ü Yu's tales are designed simply to showcase his literary talents. Some appear to present the author's personal views on issues about which he felt strongly. In "Hsiu-wen she-jen chuan" (The Tale of the Drafting Secretary), for example, a lengthy passage in parallel prose denounces corruption and favoritism in contemporary society. The sense of grievance conveyed here and elsewhere has led some critics to conclude that, when Ch'ü copyedited the text of his stories late in life, he may have introduced some new content in order to vent the frustrations that he felt during his long period of disgrace and banishment from 1408 to 1425, following alleged irregularities in the performance of his duties. In any case, it is clear that Ch'ü designed his tales in part as a vehicle for expressing his own views about the society of his day.

Chien-teng yü-hua (Supplementary Tales by the Trimmed Lamp), the first of many sequels to Ch'ü's work, was almost equally influential. Composed by Li Chen (1376–1452; *tzu* Ch'ang-ch'i; *chin-shih* 1404) and introduced by a battery of testimonials from other successful scholars, it confirmed the legitimacy of this variety of fiction. In his preface, dated 1420, Li quotes with obvious pride Tseng Ch'i's (a well-known official in the capital; 1372–1432) praise of his tales as "luxuriant and richly abundant, brilliant in literary talent." Li sought to outdo Ch'ü Yu by interlarding his narratives with even more lavish set pieces, prompting Tseng to comment: "This is what is called making an entertainment out of composition, is it not?" The critical note that lends a piquancy to some of Ch'ü's tales is largely absent from *Supplementary Tales*, replaced instead by a more pronounced tone of levity and artifice. Typical of Li's work is "Wu-p'ing ling-kuai lu" (The Spirit Apparitions of Wu-p'ing), which owes its conception to sources in the late T'ang such as "Tung-yang yeh-kuai lu" (Night Apparitions of Tung-yang). In Li's story, the hero spends a night in an abandoned temple and there encounters a series of visitors, one short and square, one thin and pointy-headed, one with a black hat and a squat body, and several others. As dawn breaks and the guests depart after a night of poetry recitations, the hero realizes he has been consorting with the spirits of an inkstone, a writing brush, a rice steamer, and other such items scattered about the temple. Here, as often in Li's work, character and action are less important to the artistic effect than word-play and versification.

In their titles and themes, many of Li's stories owe a conspicuous debt to Ch'ü Yu's work. A notable exception is the final piece in the collection, "Chia Yün-hua huan-hun chi" (The Return of the Soul of Chia Yün-hua), which was written under the influence of "The Story of Chiao-niang and Fei-hung." Li Chen's imitation of "The Story of Chiao-niang and Fei-hung" encouraged the composition of other romances that followed much the same formula: a long, drawn-out love affair set in the spacious apartments and gardens of a prosperous, educated family, the romance alternately abetted and impeded by an assortment of maids, pages, and relatives. Such tales were to proliferate over the next two centuries, before being supplanted in the early Ch'ing dynasty (1644–1911) by vernacular "scholar-beauty" romances.

Between them, the two *Trimmed Lamp* collections established a fictional model that was imitated, sometimes slavishly, during the succeeding centuries. The model was characterized by the following features: a formal design that encompassed some twenty or so stories, often divided into four chapters; a fondness for the romance and the historical reminiscence; a didactic or discursive tendency; and the frequent insertion into the narrative of sequences of poetry or passages of formal prose—letters, panegyrics, judicial rulings, and the like. For many years Ming publications tended to operate within these parameters. The major sequels are considered below.

The first to appear was *Hsiao-p'in chi* (The Contrived Frown Collection), by Chao Pi, a senior licentiate and local educational official, whose postscript is dated 1428. Some of his tales show the marked influence of Ch'ü Yu's *New Stories*, which he claims as one of his two models (the other is Hung Mai's *Records of the Listener*). Thus "Ch'ing-ch'eng yin-che chi" (The Record of the Ch'ing-ch'eng Recluse) not only borrows the plot of Ch'ü's "T'ien-t'ai fang-yin lu" (Record of a Visit to Exiles in T'ien-t'ai) but reproduces some of Ch'ü's language as well. Where Chao differs, however, is in his comparative indifference to refined style, his deliberate neglect of romantic themes, and his emphatic concern for a a clear moral. His interest in history accounts for the inclusion of biographies of historical figures from the Sung to the early Ming.

T'ao Fu (1441–1523+), the author of what is perhaps the most varied and inventive sequel to the *Trimmed Lamp* collections, also held a minor post before retiring and devoting himself more fully to writing. He acknowledged the influence of all his Ming predecessors on his own collection, *Hua-ying chi* (The Flower Reflection Collection):

> To sum up generally the works of the three gentlemen: [Ch'ü] wrote as his impulse took him, [Li] was ingenious in his efforts to surpass, and [Chao] upheld the just and discarded the fantastic. Although the three authors differ in their assertion of the principles and each has his own view, they all pour out their feelings, and combine essence with beauty. Fragrance and color tantalize the senses, ghosts and illusions abound—not qualities that lesser scholars can attain. Mindless of my own limitations, I have compared the successful and unsuccessful features of the three authors, abridged the verbose parts and supplemented what was left brief.

In keeping with this manifesto, some of T'ao's tales share Chao Pi's historical concerns, recounting, for example, the career of Hua Yün (1322–1360), one of Chu Yüan-chang's (1328–1398; r. 1368–1398) generals, and describing the heroic defense of a Ming outpost in northwest China against numerically superior Mongol forces in 1471. This latter tale, "Yu-t'ing wu-meng" (The Dream at the Courier Post), is notable for its innovative use of colloquial language in direct speech, an unusual touch in this type of fiction. Other stories show more affinity to the *Trimmed Lamp* titles, adopting an allegorical form, providing a setting for an extensive moral or philosophical debate, or introducing romantic themes.

Ping-chu ch'ing-t'an (Idle Talk by Candlelight) was the work of Chou Li, a Hangchow scholar and editor active at the end of the fifteenth century. No longer extant, *Idle Talk* was still in circulation in the late Ming period, for it is mentioned, rather disparagingly, in the preface to the famous novel *Chin P'ing Mei* (Gold Vase Plum). Other works in a similar vein included *Pi-p'o ts'ung-ts'o* (Gleanings from the Field of Letters; 1504), *Hsüeh-ch'uang t'an-yi* (Conversations about the Strange by the Snowy Window; c. 1580), *Mi-teng yin-hua* (Inspired Tales of the Searched Lamp; 1593), and *Yu-kuai shih-t'an* (Poetic Stories of Mysterious Anomalies; 1629). *Ch'ing-t'an wan-hsüan* (Myriad Selections of Casual Talk), published in the final decades of the Ming dynasty, marked the final fling of the virtuoso romance.

As this list of titles suggests, fiction in the *Trimmed Lamp* tradition enjoyed considerable popularity during the Ming period. Although efforts were made in the mid-fifteenth century to ban the work of Ch'ü Yu and Li Chen (on the grounds that their tales distracted scholars from their proper studies), this prohibition was not observed for very long. *Supplementary Tales* was reprinted in 1487; both it and *New Stories* were republished in 1511 and again in the Wan-li period. As late as 1593, Ch'ü Yu's tales were still regarded favorably by some, as seen in an enthusiastic preface to them by the Hangchow scholar Yü Ch'un-hsi (d. 1621).

Nevertheless, the *Trimmed Lamp* model clearly declined in standing as time went on. It is noticeable that Li Chen was the only writer of high official status to engage in composition of this type of fiction. Later exponents of the genre were obscure figures who held no higher degree than that of licentiate. Several declined to publish their work under their own names. This is a reflection of the negative opinion held by the educated elite toward such collections. The *Trimmed Lamp* collections had always aroused a considerable amount of hostile comment as well as admiration, and, as the sixteenth century advanced, critical opinion seems to have hardened against them. Mei Ting-tso (1549–1615), the estimable scholar, poet, and dramatist, while including some selections from Ch'ü's and Li's work in his collection *Ts'ai-kuei chi* (Records of Talented Ghosts), considered them inferior to T'ang stories and rejected the later imitations as unworthy of inclusion. Hu Ying-lin (1551–1602), the renowned late Ming literary archaist, despised the *Trimmed Lamp* collections, likening the poetry in them to the work of "village pedants with a feeble knowledge of tonal rules," and he thought *Idle Talk by Candlelight* unspeakable. In deriding the *Trimmed Lamp* stories as vulgar and common, he seems to have been articulating a view that was becoming increasingly widespread.

New Stories and its sequels may also have suffered from their association with popular prose romances. Long scholar-beauty love stories proliferated during the fifteenth and sixteenth centuries. *Chung-ch'ing li-chi* (A Graceful Account of Profound Love), completed about 1486, is a typical example. Though attributed by some Ming readers to the prominent official Ch'iu Chün, it, like other stories of this kind, is most likely the work of an otherwise unknown author. By 1540, at least half a dozen works of this type were in circulation and more were written in the following decades. One of the surviving titles, *Jung-ch'un chi* (Vignettes of Temperate Spring), illustrates the gradual deterioration in quality of this sort of romance. Lacking the delicacy and subtlety of its models, it seeks to entertain instead with the liberal use of bawdy humor. Sexual badinage is the order of the day throughout much of the story, as in the following exchange between Su Yü-chun and his page, Chih-t'ung, just after Su's seduction of the heroine has been foiled by the intervention of her maid:

> Chih-t'ung said to the young scholar, "Is it true that you laid claim to the central plain today?"
> "Not yet," was the reply. "Reinforcements arrived to prop up the defense."
> "If I had known," said the page, "I should have laid an ambush to intercept the relief column!"

Romances that appeared in the late Ming tended to replace the monogamous hero of the earlier romances with a promiscuous hero, who enters into numerous sexual relationships and marries a whole series of women. Ku Ch'u-lung marries five women in *Wu chin-yü chuan* (The Five Goldfish), and Pai Ching-yün weds a trio of cousins in *San-miao chuan* (The Three Wonders).

Ch'i Yü-ti outdoes them both in *T'ien-yüan ch'i-yü* (Marvelous Assignations Predestined by Heaven), making love to a total of twenty-eight women before he settles down with a bevy of wives known collectively as "The Twelve Hairpins of the Fragrant Terrace." Although regarded by some scholars as acceptable light reading, such works were treated with contempt by most commentators.

In the late sixteenth century, these romances (sometimes in abridged form) and selections from the *Trimmed Lamp* collections were incorporated into popular miscellanies such as *Kuo-se t'ien-hsiang* (Outstanding Beauties and Heavenly Scents; first published in 1587), *Hsiu-ku ch'un-jung* (Spring Complexions from the Embroidered Valley; 1587), and *Wan-chin ch'ing-lin* (The Forest of Passions in Myriad Hues; 1598). The inclusion of *Trimmed Lamp* tales in these miscellanies intended for a general audience acknowledged that the highly educated elite no longer constituted their main readership.

By the middle of the sixteenth century, when some established writers turned their hand to the classical tale, they demonstrated a preference for prose-centered narrative and tended to write a different kind of story. Ts'ai Yü (1470?–1541) is a case in point. A native of the countryside southwest of Soochow, he showed great promise in his youth but found his ambitions constantly thwarted at the provincial level of the civil service examinations, failing fourteen times between 1492 and 1531. "Liao-yang hai-shen chuan" (The Tale of the Liao-yang Sea-Goddess), his sole surviving classical tale, was written just five years before his death. In it, a merchant from Hui-chou, Anhwei province, down on his luck in the remote northeast, is visited by a beautiful sea spirit, who becomes his lover and satisfies his every whim, conjuring up lichees and bayberries, talking parrots and precious stones. As his investment consultant, she enables him to make a fortune through trading in unlikely commodities, and in the closing scenes she rescues him from several crises amid the social and political upheavals of the 1520s.

Hu Ju-chia, a Metropolitan Graduate of 1553, was the author of another celebrated piece, "Wei shih-yi niang chuan" (The Tale of Eleventh Lady Wei). It tells the story of a Hui-chou merchant named Ch'eng Te-yü, who is rescued from highwaymen by a remarkable swordswoman. It soon becomes apparent that the heroine is conceived as an agent of vengeance against the powerful and corrupt officials at whose hands the author felt that he had suffered. Asked to list the sorts of people targeted for assassination, Eleventh Lady Wei responds:

> Those magistrates in the world who mistreat the common people and are greedy for bribes. Those provincial officials who abuse their authority, favoring sycophants and injuring men of integrity. Generals who amass private fortunes, neglect frontier defense, and thereby damage national interests. Ministers who establish their own faction, dismissing those who disagree and appointing the wicked to positions that should be held by the principled.

The tale takes up this theme again in its final scene, set many years after Ch'eng's first encounter with Eleventh Lady Wei. Ch'eng, chancing to meet her maid on the highway, inquires as to her destination but is given no clear answer. A few days later, Ch'eng learns of the sudden death of an unscrupulous official in Szechwan province. The maid, Eleventh Lady's protégée, he suspects, was responsible.

These tales by Ts'ai Yü and Hu Ju-chia reflect a distinct shift toward a plain prose style and show little interest in incorporating poetry into the story. In one respect alone do they recall the *Trimmed Lamp* model: both tales devote space to a question-and-answer session, where the heroine enlightens the inquisitive hero on a range of issues. By the early seventeenth century, even these vestiges of the *Trimmed Lamp* manner had disappeared from the work of such writers of the classical tale as Sung Mao-ch'eng and P'an Chih-heng.

These late Ming authors belonged to a period of intense activity in the transmission and appreciation of T'ang and Sung fiction, an era that encouraged further experimentation in the classical tale. The Chia-ching reign-period (1521–1566) saw the beginning of a concerted effort to republish the major collections of pre-Ming classical tales, thus making available to an eager reading public works that hitherto had enjoyed only limited circulation. During the course of the next century, reprints would circulate of all the most important collections then extant. The appearance of a new version of *Records of the Listener* was the first significant development. By the sixteenth century about half of Hung Mai's monumental compilation had been lost, and this edition introduced a completely different format to the surviving corpus, arranging a selection of stories in thirty-seven main categories of subject matter and further grouping them under 113 subheadings—classification being a compulsive concern for most Ming editors. Published in Hangchow in 1546, the new edition included a foreword by the scholar, poet, essayist, and story writer T'ien Ju-ch'eng (*chin-shih* 1526), whose argument that tales of the supernatural revealed an undeniable aspect of existence and conveyed valuable moral lessons was to be reiterated in countless other Ming prefaces.

The republication in 1566 of the large and influential compilation of T'ang and pre-T'ang literary language tales *Extensive Records from the Reign of Great Tranquility* (981) lent further impetus to the burgeoning interest in the fictional heritage. This edition, prepared by a retired official named T'an K'ai (1503–1568), was warmly received by readers and would soon be eagerly exploited by anthologists, who would frequently cannibalize its contents when assembling their own anecdotal collections. In 1626, Feng Meng-lung (1574–1646) also issued an abridged version of the great Sung work as *"T'ai-p'ing kuang-chi" ch'ao* (Selections from *Extensive Records from the Reign of Great Tranquility*). This eighty-chapter edition carried Feng's own commentary and a preface with a generous appraisal of the compilation. Other important works reprinted in the late Ming included the Sung anthology *Lofty Judgments from the Green Lattice* (in 1595) and the outstanding T'ang miscellany *Yu-yang tsa-tsu* (Miscellaneous Delicacies from the South Slope of Mount Yu; 1608).

The reissue of earlier collections was coupled with the production of new compilations by Ming writers and publishers. The first significant compilation to emerge was *Yü Ch'u chih* (Yü Ch'u's Record), a distillation of the best in T'ang *ch'uan-ch'i.* This book takes its title from the name of a man who held office during the reign of the Han emperor Wu-ti (r. 141–87 B.C.E.) and was said to have been the editor of a collection of narrative accounts. It was possibly edited by the Soochow author Lu Ts'ai. Lu Ts'ai must have had access to what at the time would have been a rare, perhaps fragmentary, copy of the *Extensive Records*, importing wholesale into *Yü Ch'u's Record* the celebrated tales found in chapters 484 to 491 of the Sung compilation—stories like those about Li Wa, Wu-shuang, Huo Hsiao-yü, Ying-ying, and Hsieh Hsiao-o (for these T'ang *ch'uan-ch'i*, see chapter 33). It is unclear to what extent his choice of tales was dictated by the resources available to him or was shaped by his own literary tastes. However, it is worth noting that most of the tales included in *Yü Ch'u's Record* are characterized by a relatively austere narrative style, and there are few examples of the ornamental style favored in late T'ang collections of *ch'uan-ch'i.* In this respect, *Yü Ch'u's Record* appears to be an anthology very much in keeping with the literary fashion of the time, which favored a return to the robust prose values of early historical writing.

Even after the republication of the *Extensive Records*, the selective and compact design of *Yü Ch'u's Record* ensured a lasting appeal, and the book went through numerous printings in the late sixteenth and early seventeenth centuries. In his foreword to an enlarged edition of *Yü Ch'u's Record* published by a Hangchow press, the famous dramatist T'ang Hsien-tsu (1550–1617) argued that these tales deserved serious comparison with traditional models of Chinese narrative:

> This book of Yü Ch'u lays before us an array of biographies by T'ang authors and includes some dozen or so anecdotes by Shen Yüeh of the Liang, relating events that are bizarre and fantastic, obscure and elusive, pleasing and astonishing. To read it opens the heart and releases the soul, stirring the senses to excitement. Although in nobility and strength it falls short of *Shih-chi* (Records of the Historian) and the *Han shu* (History of the Han Dynasty), and in economy and austerity it does not equal *Shih-shuo hsin-yü* (A New Account of Tales of the World), with its subtle delicacy and flowing elegance it truly constitutes a boat of pearls among fiction collections.

In keeping with this appreciation of the artistic qualities of the tales, the editor of this edition incorporated comments both by T'ang and himself that draw attention to the narrative technique of the *ch'uan-ch'i.* T'ang's brief notes wax lyrical on all aspects of the classical tale: its structure and characterization, its use of dialog, detail, and poetry. Commentary on *Yü Ch'u's Record* reached a culmination in Ling Hsing-te's late Ming edition, which incorporates comments ascribed to luminaries such as Li Chih (1527–1602) and Yüan Hung-tao (1568–1610). Their comments, while scattered and unsystematic, reflect a highly sympathetic reading of the T'ang *ch'uan-ch'i*.

The prompt success of *Yü Ch'u's Record* encouraged others to prepare rival anthologies and corner a share of the growing market for classical fiction. Lu Chi (1515–1552) was instrumental in funding the publication of *Ku-chin shuo-hai* (The Ocean of Stories, Past and Present) in 1544. The son of a prominent official from the Shanghai area, Lu Chi had secured the first degree at an early age but, much to the disappointment of himself and his friends, made no further progress in the examination system. *The Ocean of Stories* was the culmination of a collaborative effort between Lu Chi and several other book collectors, each contributing various titles from his private library. Lu's father had built up an extensive collection of books, including many incomplete works that he had been able to purchase at a bargain price. These probably included fragments from the *Extensive Records*, for some sixty T'ang *ch'uan-ch'i* were brought together in *The Ocean of Stories*, along with several Ming stories and a variety of miscellaneous records. Published twenty years before the *Extensive Records* returned to circulation, it made a big impression on the young Hu Ying-lin as the largest collection of T'ang tales then available.

Ku Yüan-ch'ing (1487–1561 +), a Soochow bibliophile, also played an important role in reprinting rare Sung editions of anecdotal collections. The forty titles that constitute his *Ku-shih wen-fang hsiao-shuo* (Tales from Mr. Ku's Library), completed about 1550, include both longer romances and excerpts from T'ang anecdotal collections.

Another very influential Ming compendium was *Yen-yi pien* (Tales of Glamor and Wonder). This anthology, edited by Wang Shih-chen (1526–1590), the influential arbiter of literary taste during the late sixteenth century, appears to have been published no later than 1566. It circulated first in a forty-five-chapter edition, its contents culled from many different volumes in Wang's famous library, but in particular from anecdotal collections and the dynastic histories. In arranging *Tales of Glamor and Wonder*, Wang followed the model of the *Extensive Records*, grouping the contents under thematic headings: "Trysts," "Courtesans," "Demons," and so forth. Wang Shih-chen's editorial formula was so successful and his imprimatur so prestigious that the work was reprinted several times in the late Ming period. The enthusiasm with which the reading public greeted Wang Shih-chen's anthology encouraged further efforts in the same direction and led to the publication of *Kuang Yen-yi pien* (Tales of Glamor and Wonder, Amplified), organized on identical principles by the dramatist Wu Ta-chen in the Wan-li period, and *Yi-chien shang-hsin pien*

(Instantly Appealing Tales), a shorter compilation assembled by a Chien-yang publisher.

As reissues of fiction and general collections of stories found a ready market in the sixteenth century, they were soon followed by specialized anthologies devoted to a particular range of subject matter. One of the first to appear was *Chien-hsia chuan* (Tales of Chivalrous Swordsmen), compiled in the mid-sixteenth century by Wang Shih-chen. Confined exclusively to tales of swordsmanship and chivalry, it borrowed heavily from the *Extensive Records*, with a sprinkling of Sung and Ming tales.

Hu-mei ts'ung-t'an (Collected Tales of Fox Fairies), a Wan-li compilation of fox stories, was likewise much indebted to the relevant chapters of the *Extensive Records*, as was Yang Erh-tseng's *Hsien-yüan chi-shih* (Tales of Immortal Maidens), devoted to female divinities. *Ch'i nü-tzu chuan* (Tales of Remarkable Women) and *Lü-ch'uang nü-shih* (Green Window History of Women) took remarkable women as their editorial theme.

Other major thematic collections resulted from the efforts of two late Ming literati, Mei Ting-tso and Feng Meng-lung. Mei, a poet and dramatist, drew upon his large library of fiction titles in preparing his *Ch'ing-ni lien-hua chi* (Accounts of Lotus Blossoms in the Mire; 1602), a digest of stories about courtesans through the ages, and *Records of Talented Ghosts*, on female ghosts. Better known are Feng's anthologies devoted to wit, intelligence, and love, *Ku-chin t'an-kai* (Talks Old and New), *Chih-nang* (Sack of Wisdom), and *Ch'ing-shih* (Anatomy of Love), which were probably all compiled during the 1620s.

As Chinese scholars in the sixteenth century were reintroduced to all the major highlights of the fictional tradition, they gradually developed their own critical appraisal of earlier works, defining and contrasting the literary qualities of tales of different periods. The most influential of these commentators was Hu Ying-lin. Hu acquired a taste for the classical tale early in life, and as time went on he began to nurture ambitions to make his own mark as an anthologist. The proud owner of a hundred-chapter manuscript of *Records of the Listener*, he had plans to edit a sequel to the *Extensive Records* that would encompass all tales written between the eleventh and the sixteenth centuries. The colossal scale of this project was overambitious, and Hu died with the work uncompleted.

One lasting contribution that Hu did make was his formulation of a critical theory concerning the evolution of the classical tale in the pages of his extensive collection of jottings, *Shao-shih shan-fang pi-ts'ung* (Collected Jottings from the Shao-shih Retreat). Most important, he focused attention on the quality of the T'ang *ch'uan-ch'i* and sought to identify the source of its appeal:

> In tales by T'ang authors and their predecessors, the bulk of the narrative is fictitious, and descriptive embellishment is admirable. In works of the Sung and later, the action stems largely from actual events, and there is a striking lack of color. This is probably because works of the T'ang and

> earlier came from the hand of writers and talented scholars, whereas works of the Sung and later all derived from vulgar scholars and elder writers in retirement.

In another passage, Hu identified the T'ang as the true watershed in the evolution of Chinese fiction:

> Talk of prodigies flourished in the Six Dynasties (220–589), but for the most part it stemmed from confusion in transmission—it is doubtful that such tales were purely creative invention. It was only in the T'ang that writers consciously strove to astonish, making tales a vehicle to convey their purpose.

This view of the literary tradition found wide acceptance in the late Ming.

Hsieh Chao-che was another Wan-li author with a sympathetic attitude toward the classical tale. In his famous miscellany *Wu tsa-tsu* (Five Assorted Offerings), he argued that informal narratives provide readers with indispensable variety and have their own distinctive literary qualities. And he commented on the blending of fact and fiction that lies at the heart of the short story: "All stories and plays are bound to be formed half of fiction, half of fact, for only then will they rank as entertaining. It is also essential that the setting be well depicted. There is no need to question whether or not the events truly occurred." By challenging the conventional assumption that narrative should record only what is known or believed to have happened, Hsieh argued that there was a legitimate place for creative fiction.

It was against this backdrop that some outstanding classical tales were written in the opening decades of the seventeenth century. Sung Mao-ch'eng (1569–1622), an unconventional scholar from Sung-chiang (near Shanghai), wrote several exceptional classical tales, most notably "Chu shan" (The Pearl Vest), about a romantic triangle in a mercantile setting, and "Fu-ch'ing-nung chuan" (The Faithless Lover), about a tragic love affair between a Peking courtesan and a Chekiang scholar. Sung's stories, told economically but with memorable detail, are set against the distinctive social backdrop of his day and address issues of particular interest to his generation, examining human personalities under the stress of conflicting loyalties, emotional tension, or unforeseen misadventure. The quality of Sung's work was recognized immediately by his Ming contemporaries. Sung's friend P'an Chih-heng (1556–1622) went so far as to describe him as "pre-eminent among storytellers of today" and maintained that the accomplished prose technique of Sung's "Liu Tung-shan" surpassed that of the novel *Shui-hu chuan* (Water Margin). What he seems to have particularly admired is the ambiguous and open-ended character of tales such as "Liu Tung-shan," which purposefully leave the identity of certain protagonists unresolved.

P'an Chih-heng was himself a practitioner of the realistic tale. A bohemian personality famous for his luxuriant beard, he shared many of Sung's personal and literary values. Like Sung, P'an enrolled in the National Academy, but after several failures in the examinations he abandoned the notion of an official career, devoting himself to literary and recreational pursuits. P'an's *Ken-shih* (Eternal History) is an enormous compilation of tales, assembled in the latter part of his life and not published until four years after his death. It includes T'ang romances as well as tales by Ming authors such as Hu Ju-chia and Sung Mao-ch'eng, but the vast majority of pieces are P'an's own work. Many take the form of biographical sketches of the actors and actresses with whom he spent so much of his time; a few are realistic tales that bear comparison with those of Sung Mao-ch'eng. *Eternal History* seems to have exerted a considerable influence on the vernacular short story writer Ling Meng-ch'u (1580–1644), who almost certainly read it during his visit to Nanking in 1627 to sit for the provincial examination. P'an's fine tale "Liang Ti-chu" (The Two Ti-chus), which he said was based on an actual incident in his home district in 1604, was adapted by Ling as the second story in his first collection, and *Eternal History* also provided the sources for his third and fourth stories. A good example of P'an's work is "Yü-shan fu" (The Woman of Yü-shan), the first of a set of tales relating to elopement. Like much of P'an's work, it has a strong contemporary flavor. The narrative style is terse, the language generally plain, though punctuated by occasional archaic expressions in the manner of the classicist school that held sway in P'an's formative years. P'an's comments on Sung Mao-ch'eng's work show that he valued suggestive rather than explicit detail, and his own work reflects this preference for a somewhat elliptical treatment.

THE CLASSICAL TALE IN THE EARLY CH'ING PERIOD

Writers of the generation or two after Sung Mao-ch'eng and P'an Chih-heng are known for their well-crafted narratives dealing with remarkable episodes and unusual personalities in the turbulent era of the transition from the Ming dynasty to the Ch'ing (1644–1911). Many of these tales were brought together by Chang Ch'ao (1650–1707+) in his anthology *Yü Ch'u hsin-chih* (New Records of Yü Ch'u), completed in 1704. It was Chang Ch'ao's idea to create a companion volume to the popular *Records of Yü Ch'u* by bringing together outstanding classical tales by seventeenth-century authors. These stories have a strong contemporary flavor, often celebrating the exploits of humble but heroic personalities of the recent past, while at the same time dealing with many of the classic situations of Chinese fiction—tragic romances and miraculous reunions, resurrections and ghostly visitations.

Most of the authors whose work is anthologized in *Yü Ch'u hsin-chih* attached no special priority to the recording of strange tales—their biographies of unusual characters were occasional compositions only. One exception is Niu Hsiu (d. 1704), whose collection *Ku-sheng* (Leftover Tablets) was completed in the last few years of his life, while a magistrate in Kwangtung province. His tales run the gamut from skeleton plots to lengthy romances employing subtle and emotive language that the editors of the massive collectanea *Ssu-k'u ch'üan-shu* (Complete Library of the Four Treasuries; compiled by order of the Ch'ien-lung emperor beginning in 1773) later described as reminiscent of tales by T'ang authors.

Another early Ch'ing figure who devoted particular attention to the classical tale is the Kiangsi scholar Hsü Fang (1619–1671). A Metropolitan Graduate of 1640, Hsü served briefly as a department magistrate under the Ming and took an active role in the Southern Ming resistance. Returning home after the suppression of the loyalist movement in Fukien province in 1647, he declined to serve in the Ch'ing administration, devoting the rest of his life to his writing. The traumatic upheavals of the 1640s leading to the Manchu conquest left him deeply disillusioned, equally critical of the late Ming society into which he was born and of the new regime, to which he felt no allegiance. Consciously distancing himself from the power networks of early Ch'ing society, Hsü adopted a reclusive lifestyle in his home district and eked out a living as a geomancer.

Hsü's collection of tales, *Ts'ang-shan kao wai-pien* (Mountain-Stored Manuscript, Outer Collection), was never published in its entirety and survives only in a manuscript copy, although selections appear in *New Records of Yü Ch'u*. Tales of karmic retribution are a prominent feature of Hsü's work, as they are of other contemporary anecdotal collections published in *Shuo-ling* (The Bell of Stories; preface dated 1705). Some of Hsü's tales focus on the heroic exploits of unusual personalities with low social status. A bandit proves to be a model official when he takes on the job of administering a district in Kwangtung; a beggar shows scrupulous integrity by returning lost property to its owner with no expectation of reward; a hermit forsakes all worldly possessions and takes up residence in the mountains, unperturbed by the company of tigers and snakes; a woman from Kiangsi province, after being abducted by marauding soldiers, engineers her escape by executing a brilliant deception. These and other tales seem to reflect the disillusionment with the educated elite that was common among men of Hsü's generation. In making strange events and remarkable personalities the focus of attention, and by articulating through his postscript remarks a serious and highly individual outlook on contemporary affairs, Hsü Fang demonstrated the potential of the classical tale as a vehicle for social commentary, a potential that P'u Sung-ling and other authors after him were to explore more fully.

STRANGE TALES FROM MAKE-DO STUDIO AND THE MID-CH'ING TALE

The most outstanding collection of classical tales of the late imperial era was the work of P'u Sung-ling (1640–1715). P'u was born in rural Shantung province and spent his life studying for the examinations, teaching, and writing, leaving his native province only for a few months in 1670–1671, when he held an appointment as private secretary to a friend serving as magistrate in Kiangsu province. After a long series of fruitless attempts to pass the provincial examination, he had to content himself with the degree of senior licentiate, granted to him just five years before his death.

Liao-chai chih-yi (Strange Tales from Make-Do Studio) is a collection of almost five hundred tales, probably assembled over a forty-year period. Including materials ranging from brief anecdotes to lengthy and complex narratives, it is an extraordinary achievement, endlessly surprising the reader with its imagination and invention. Central to the collection is the notion of a blurring of boundaries between the supernatural and the mundane as characters and actions move between one realm and the other, with an attention to physical detail and to the psychological dimension that makes these developments seem smooth and natural.

Make-Do Studio is justly celebrated for its character portraits. Through their actions and words, heroes and heroines alike are endowed with memorable personality traits. Sun Tzu-ch'u cuts off a finger to demonstrate his love; Keng Ch'ü-ping drops in on a foxes' dinner party with a cheerful shout of "Here comes a gate-crasher!"; Huo Huan smashes a hole in the wall in order to visit the girl next door; Liu Ho, resentful of his father-in-law's behavior, asks a neighbor, "Is that old swine Huang still alive?" Female characters likewise are highly individualized: the skilled surgeon Chiao-no, the aspiring calligraphers Hsiao-hsieh and Ch'iu-jung, the irrepressible tomboy Hsiao-ts'ui, the naïve but calculating Ying-ning, the jealous rivals Lien-hsiang and Li-shih—these and many more take on distinct personalities of their own in the pages of *Make-Do Studio*.

A notable innovation in P'u Sung-ling's work is the incorporation into the classical tale of features hitherto associated with vernacular fiction. P'u Sung-ling was familiar with the major Ming novels and probably with collections of colloquial short stories such as *Chin-ku ch'i-kuan* (Remarkable Stories New and Old), and he himself devoted some of his energies to writing vernacular plays and ballads in the local Shantung idiom. In *Make-Do Studio*, P'u Sung-ling moves beyond the traditional subject matter of the classical tale to deal with the theme of domestic conflicts, a common concern in colloquial fiction. In his keen observation of the interactions between husbands, wives, and concubines, mothers-in-law and daughters-in-law, brothers and stepbrothers, P'u shares the preoccupations of sixteenth- and seventeenth-century vernacular authors.

Make-Do Studio is also admired for its trenchant social criticism. Some tales highlight the flaws in the examination system, others the fallibility of local administrators; corruption and injustice at the provincial level figure prominently in many stories, while snobbery and inequity within the family context are vividly depicted. One story condemns gambling; another is designed as a protest against policies related to the salt monopoly. Often, in the guise of "The Historian of the Strange," P'u Sung-ling adds a postscript commentary echoing the historian Ssu-ma Ch'ien's (c. 145–c. 86 B.C.E.) remarks at the end of each chapter of *Records of the Historian* (see chapter 26) that emphasizes a particular point he wants to make, and the surprising range of these commentaries—oblique or outspoken, facetious or serious—adds a further level of interest to the book.

In keeping with the literary values of his day, P'u Sung-ling writes in a vigorous but economical prose style, largely eschewing the ornamental flourishes that had been popular in the early Ming. P'u preferred instead a supple, smooth-flowing narrative style somewhat akin to traditional biographical writing, in which the primary aim was to relate action and convey character rather than to convey stylistic refinement and taste. In this durable linguistic surface, P'u then embedded occasional allusions and archaic expressions, used in a refreshingly inventive fashion, and introduced colloquial expressions into dialog to simulate an earthy vernacular exchange. The effect achieved is not one of affectation but of bold spontaneity informed by exceptional erudition.

During P'u Sung-ling's lifetime, and for decades afterward, *Make-Do Studio* circulated in manuscript form and was known only to a few readers. When it was finally published in 1766, it had an enormous impact on the elite reading public. One of its nineteenth-century commentators recalled how avidly he would read it when he came home from school each day; another, writing in 1824, noted: "Wherever I have traveled in the years since I was a child, no matter whether to a major town or a remote hamlet, there is always a copy of this book to be found." By the early nineteenth century, *Make-Do Studio* and the novel *Hung-lou meng* (A Dream of Red Towers) were generally agreed to be the preeminent works of contemporary fiction.

Within a few years of the publication of *Make-Do Studio*, other writers were seeking to emulate P'u Sung-ling's success. The first such author was Ho Pang-o, a provincial graduate of 1774. A Manchu and the grandson of a military commander, Ho grew up among soldiers and officers in the Ch'ing armed forces, and his work draws heavily upon the stories circulating among them. His *Yeh-t'an sui-lu* (Evening Conversations Casually Recorded), completed in 1779, reflects wide-ranging social experience. Less subtle and refined than *Make-Do Studio*, it nonetheless contains an abundance of lively and entertaining episodes, many set evocatively by the walls, gates, and markets of eighteenth-century Peking.

Tzu pu yü (What the Master Did Not Speak Of), published in 1788, was the work of the famous poet and critic Yüan Mei (1716–1797). In his preface, Yüan acknowledged the excellence of *Make-Do Studio* but argued that it relied too much on artifice. His own collection of strange tales confines itself to simple and uncomplicated stories that generally show neither the creative impulse nor the serious purpose of P'u Sung-ling and reflect a general indifference to moral issues. It does, however, bring together an enormous variety of anecdotes, many providing fascinating little vignettes of eighteenth-century life, and occasionally Yüan Mei uses this medium to present some of his own ideas, such as his objections to the practice of foot-binding. *What the Master Did Not Speak Of* (which takes its name from the celebrated quotation of Confucius [*Analects*, 7.20] cited above) was followed, several years later, by a short sequel, *Hsü Tzu pu yü* (What the Master Did Not Speak Of, Continued).

Yüeh-wei ts'ao-t'ang pi-chi (Sketches from the Cottage for the Contemplation of Subtleties) is the collective title of the five collections of tales assembled by the eminent scholar-official Chi Yün (1724–1805) during the years 1789 to 1798. By this time Chi had completed his labors as chief editor of the *Complete Library of the Four Treasuries* and was living in semiretirement. Like Yüan, Chi recognized the extraordinary achievement of *Make-Do Studio*, but, as a veteran bibliographer accustomed to classifying books by established categories, he objected to the innovative and unconventional features of P'u Sung-ling's work, particularly its overt fictionality. His own tales, the culmination of a lifetime's exposure to informal storytelling, are notable for their interest in moral issues, causal relationships, and the principles governing the incursion of the supernatural into human affairs: in Chi Yün's hands, incidents of all kinds serve to pull aside the veil that conceals the moral machinery that shapes the course of people's lives, and to inspire reflections and judgments on human nature. Authorial commentary plays a prominent role, and great importance is attached to the interpretation of the meaning of the events. Chi's work, in its own way, represented a new and original approach to the literary anecdote and had many admirers in the nineteenth century, some of whom, like Yü Hung-chien (1781–1846), professed a preference for it over *Make-Do Studio*. The tales are also admired for their crisp, terse style.

Another distinctive collection is *Hsieh-to* (The Bantering Bell; 1791), by the Soochow scholar Shen Ch'i-feng (1741–1802). Shen passed the provincial examination of 1768, but successive failures to pass the metropolitan examination doomed him to a frustrating life of minor administrative appointments. His stories are elegant little miniatures, inspired by the more sardonic pieces in *Make-Do Studio*, but some are so schematic as to seem contrived and predictable. Satire, irony, and allegory are Shen's favored modes, and the best of his tales display a mordant wit and polished style.

Ying-ch'uang yi-ts'ao (Strange Herbs from Firefly Window), first published in the 1870s, has been attributed to a Manchu writer, Ch'ing-lan (d. 1788), the sixth son of the prominent official Yin-chi-shan (1696–1771). The book is heavily influenced by P'u Sung-ling, some of its contents being explicitly presented as sequels to tales in *Make-Do Studio*. Intricate plots abound, but the stories are weakened by their lack of originality and flawed characterization.

Yüeh Chun (1766–c. 1818), a Kiangsi scholar and provincial graduate of 1801, was the author of *Erh-shih lu* (Record of the Ears' Repast). His first collection was completed in 1792, and a second collection followed two years later. His tales, though uneven in quality, show flashes of creative ambition.

Tseng Yen-tung (1751–c. 1830), a Shantung provincial graduate of 1792, wrote the preface to his *Hsiao tou-p'eng* (Little Bean Arbor) in 1795, adding to the collection in later years, but the book languished unpublished until 1880. Despite its relative obscurity, *Little Bean Arbor* is a book of considerable interest, offering through its diverse contents a kaleidoscope of incidents set in the early and mid-Ch'ing. Though reminiscent in places of *Make-Do Studio*, this collection has sufficient novelty and invention to endow it with its own character.

Other significant collections dating to the reign of the Ch'ien-lung emperor (1736–1795) include *Ch'iu-teng ts'ung-hua* (Collected Tales by the Autumn Lamp; 1791), by a Shantung writer named Wang Hsien, and *Liu-ya wai-pien* (Willow Cliff's Informal Collection; 1792), by the Shansi scholar Hsü K'un (*chin-shih* 1781). A preface to the latter work hails the author as the reincarnation of P'u Sung-ling, a testimony to the preeminence of *Make-Do Studio* in the late eighteenth century.

THE CLASSICAL TALE IN THE LATE CH'ING

The classical tale continued to appeal to both authors and readers in the late nineteenth century. The most significant collection to appear was *Yeh-yü ch'iu-teng lu* (Tales Recorded by Evening Rain and Autumn Lamp), published in two installments, in 1877 and 1880. Its author, Hsüan Ting (1832–1880), had encountered many adversities during the turbulent decades of the mid-nineteenth century, and his tales cover a broad range of themes and situations. They are reminiscent of *Make-Do Studio* in their attention to both character and action, and some of Hsüan's finest tales, like the dramatic and touching "Ma-feng nü Ch'iu Li-yü" (Leper Girl Ch'iu Li-yü), won the popular seal of approval through adaptation for the stage.

Other late Ch'ing collections include *Li-ch'eng* (Neighborhood Gazette; 1874), by the Anhwei scholar Hsü Feng-en (c. 1820–1887); *Tsui-ch'a chih-kuai* (Tea-Tipsy Records of the Strange; 1892), by Li Ching-ch'en, a Tientsin licentiate; and the anecdotal collections *Erh-yü* (Hearsay Reports) and *Yu-t'ai hsien-kuan pi-chi* (Notes from Yu-t'ai Lodge), by the well-known scholar Yü Yüeh (1821–1907). The tales in *Sung-yin man-lu* (Casual Notes by a Shanghai Recluse) originally appeared in a pictorial supplement published by a Shanghai newspaper between 1884 and 1887 and are of more or less uniform length, to suit the publisher's requirements. These stories reflect the familiarity of the author, Wang T'ao (1828–1897), with both the urban Chinese scene and Western culture in the closing years of the nineteenth century: while devoting space to tales of Shanghai courtesans, he also includes accounts of tightrope walkers at Niagara Falls, and one of his heroes goes sightseeing in Edinburgh, London, and Paris. *Casual Notes by a Shanghai Recluse* could be seen as a swan song for the classical tale near the end of the empire, yet it also signals the onset of the tumultuous avalanche of modernity that would transform fiction as one curtain closed on the nineteenth century and another opened on the twentieth century.

Allan H. Barr

Chapter 38

FICTION FROM THE END OF THE EMPIRE TO THE BEGINNING OF THE REPUBLIC (1897–1916)

Until recently, the turn of the twentieth century, which coincided with the final decade of the Ch'ing dynasty (1644–1911), seemed a rather uninteresting period in the long history of Chinese fiction. Lu Hsün (1881–1936), China's foremost modern writer, labeled the literary works of the period "novels of exposure" (*ch'ien-tse hsiao-shuo*) and considered them fairly homogeneous, being unified by a common tendency to expose social abuses and criticize contemporary politics. Implicitly, his appraisal linked late Ch'ing fiction with that of the preceding centuries, likewise concerned with criticism of social ills and carrying a moral message. Yet he did not explain any of the differences between the late Ch'ing novel and fiction from the 1910s, when novels and, in particular, short stories frequently elaborated themes of a less public nature in the form of reminiscences, love stories, narratives in epistolary form, or diaries conveying the author's personal feelings and reflections. Lu Hsün's historical account of Chinese fiction (see chapter 39) entirely omitted the 1910s.

The major reason for viewing late Ch'ing fiction as unchanging and thematically invariant, and in such contrast to the experiment-filled modernism of contemporary European and American literature, seems to have been the concept of the literary work as a historical document from the period in which it was written. Thus, during most of the twentieth century, Chinese literary criticism chose to interpret works in terms of their historical provenance, whereby the task of literary studies remained more or less limited to providing an outline of the historical background and narrative content of these works, considered as direct reflections of the then-prevailing social and political situation.

Late Ch'ing fiction was especially prone to being so presented: thematically, the well-known novels of the era dealt with events in China during the period from 1880 to 1910 and concerned themselves with such social and political events as the abortive 1898 reform movement, the anti-foreign Boxer Rebellion of 1900, the invasion of foreign armies, the emigration of impoverished intellectuals to the Americas, women's struggle for emancipation, and the corruption of the bureaucratic system. The impression of historical veracity provided by these novels was, moreover, enhanced by the striving of their authors for authenticity. In their fiction there was no pretext—customary in traditional fiction—that the events portrayed had occurred in the past or at some unspecified time. Rather, they unabashedly claimed that their texts dealt with the here and now, that what the reader saw was the present as witnessed and experienced by his contemporary, the writer.

No wonder, then, that the *Wan Ch'ing hsiao-shuo shih* (A History of Late Ch'ing Fiction), originally published by Ah Ying (Ch'ien Hsing-ts'un; 1905–1977) in 1937, is a repository of literary works, meticulously divided according to topics, a method of organization strongly reminiscent of that used in traditional Chinese historiography. A pioneering work, the *History* still astonishes because of the author's encyclopedic knowledge. Yet, paradoxically, Ah Ying's historicizing view of literature prevented him, as similar views did other modern scholars (for instance, Hu Shih [1891–1962], Wu Hsiao-ju [1922–], and Ōmura Masuo [1933–]), from seeing late Ch'ing fiction in the framework of an ongoing literary evolution. Since artistry was ignored in considering these works, it was impossible to relate late Ch'ing fiction to either earlier or later literary developments. Moreover, like his two succeeding and equally authoritative reference works—*Wan Ch'ing hsi-ch'ü hsiao-shuo mu* (A Catalog of Late Ch'ing Drama and Fiction; 1954) and *Wan Ch'ing wen-hsüeh ts'ung-ch'ao: hsiao-shuo hsi-ch'ü yen-chiu chüan* (Anthology of Late Ch'ing Literature: Research Materials on Fiction and Drama; 1960)—*History* did not include one important literary genre that emerged in the late Ch'ing period: the short story written in both vernacular and classical language. Whatever the reason for this omission, the exclusion of the short story proved detrimental to the evaluation of late Ch'ing fiction. Our picture of late Ch'ing fiction was to remain for many decades static, one-sided, and historically inaccurate.

A still harsher fate was encountered by the fiction of the early Republican period—the first half of the 1910s. At the beginning of the 1920s, the short stories and the novels of this preceding period were inappropriately and mockingly tagged as *yüan-yang hu-tieh p'ai*, that is, of the school of "mandarin ducks and butterflies," the traditional Chinese symbols for a pair of lovers. The fiction of the early 1910s was thus dismissed as consisting of sentimental, commercial kitsch catering to a conservative audience; and, regrettably, even collections of research materials from this period were selected in such a way as to reinforce this official interpretation. Almost sixty years were to pass before Perry Link in 1981 published the first monograph (*Mandarin Ducks and Butterflies: Popular Fiction in Early Twentieth-Century Chinese Cities*) dealing with the period, which had been altogether omitted by most histories of modern Chinese literature.

NEW APPROACHES, NEW PERSPECTIVES

One of the reasons that research devoted to late Ch'ing and early Republican literary works was so long delayed, even in countries where literary studies were not stifled by acceptance of the official Chinese interpretation of literary history, was the relative inaccessibility of source materials. The fiction of those years had been published mainly in literary journals that began to spring up in China at the turn of the century, which in time became a notable cultural phenomenon. With the decisive shift of interest to May Fourth (referring to a cultural reform movement launched on this date in 1919) literature during the 1920s and 1930s, these literary journals were, as a rule, neither collected by Western libraries nor reprinted in China and Japan. Not only research into the literary works themselves, but also the study of literary theories and of Chinese translations from Western and Japanese literatures, were profoundly affected by the lack of original texts, as these literary journals had been great repositories of novelties arising within the cultural and political life of China as well as of foreign countries.

Undeterred by the paucity of available texts and intrigued by this "black hole" in the history of Chinese literature, from the 1950s and 1960s onward a few scholars launched investigations into the unknown. Some produced brilliant translations, while others studied the surprisingly strong Buddhist elements in late Ch'ing political theory of fiction. Attempts to integrate Chinese literature with the rest of contemporary Asian literatures also bore fruit. Late Ch'ing fiction emerged as an important transitional stage in an evolutionary process—a crucial process of fundamental cultural transformation taking place not only in China, but throughout the whole of Asia.

Thus the image of the Chinese fiction of the first two decades of the twentieth century slowly, but ineluctably, began to change. An understanding of this neglected and belittled period has emerged as instrumental for the modernization of Chinese literature and arts. It is interesting to note that the literature produced during these two decades is by no means uniform and invariant. Rather, it can best be viewed as having developed in three distinct stages. During the initial stage, from 1897 to 1904, the contemporary political novel (*hsiao-shuo*) was regarded by reformist politicians as occupying the very pinnacle of Chinese literature, because fiction of this type was believed to possess properties making it an ideal and essential tool for the dissemination of enlightenment among the politically backward masses. During the next stage, from approximately 1904 to 1910, literary theoreticians and critics shifted their attention from politics to the esthetic qualities of fiction. It was also during this period that several masterpieces of the late Ch'ing novel contributed to the artistic renewal of traditional Chinese fiction. Perhaps most important, however, the short story, now awakened from its centuries-long dormancy, began seriously to challenge the dominant position of the novel, not so much in terms of quantity but, rather, because of an entirely new configuration of the narrative in terms of innovative power.

Whereas late Ch'ing fiction is now most often regarded as being in transition to modernity, some bolder souls assert that, during the third stage of the modernization process, the early 1910s, Chinese literature attained—through its own vitality, but inspired also by firsthand translations of contemporary European, American, and Japanese literary works and by the fortuitous confluence of Chinese cultural phenomena, on the one hand, and their European/American counterparts, on the other—a stage quite akin to European modernism. This assertion seems to be substantiated by current research on the hitherto-neglected theory of fiction that arose during the early Republican period, which arrived at a formulation of the fictional world never before envisaged by Chinese scholars. Similarly, new research on the Chinese short story of the early 1910s has revealed parallel tendencies in Chinese and Western creative writing of this particular era. A new generation of Chinese writers definitely abandoned the traditional role of the transmitter between Heaven and Earth and chose instead, like the European symbolists and American imagists, the role of the creators of their own imaginary universes conceived for the express purpose of manifesting the mind and feelings of the author. Thus, whereas most late Ch'ing writers had strived to capture the multifarious social reality of the time in long, detailed novels, the short story writers of the early 1910s preoccupied themselves with the description of the protagonists' psyche, which, in turn, led to exploration of new narrative strategies: frequent use of the first-person narrative mode; the "slice of life" plot that replaced the plot narrating the character's story from the beginning to the end; flexible narrative time that could freely switch from the past to the future and back to the present; creation of private symbols and imagery, and so on. The strong interest of the early Republican writers in narratives of a private nature seems also to explain the otherwise incomprehensible writers' preference for classical Chinese over the vernacular—the dominant language of the late Ch'ing novel. As is well known, of the two Chinese literary languages used in writing works of literature—vernacular and classical Chinese—it was classical Chinese that, by convention, was used and cultivated in literary genres of a personal nature, such as classical poetry and the essay. The short story writers from the early 1910s therefore found classical Chinese most suitable for writing short stories and novels, which were likewise of a lyrical character.

Several factors are crucial for understanding the nature and historical role of Chinese fiction during the period 1897 to 1916. Foremost among them is the rise of Shanghai and the role played by this city in the development of China's modern urban culture.

SHANGHAI: THE CRADLE OF MODERN CHINESE CULTURE

No Chinese city seemed, during the first decades of the early nineteenth century, less likely than Shanghai to become the birthplace of modern Chinese culture. Taking the European and American experience as an example, centers of modern culture, such as Paris, Berlin, Vienna, Zurich, Moscow, St. Petersburg, New York, and Chicago, had been previously established as political, commercial, or cultural capitals in which, for various historical reasons, cultural activities later exploded, thus furnishing these urban centers with great reputations as centers of intellectual and cultural exchange. In comparison, there was little in Shanghai's origins that promised a spectacular growth of cultural importance in the future. Granted, its location at the confluence of the Whampoa (Huang-p'u) River with the Yangtze River close to the sea facilitated the rapid growth of the small village with swampy banks overgrown by reeds into a modest commercial port—something reflected in the local gazetteers, which, recognizing the town's new status, recorded a change of name sometime during the fifteenth century from Hu-tu (fishing landing) to Shang-hai (up from the sea)—but no explosion of cultural activities took place thereafter, nor did one seem likely.

A turning point, however, in the destiny of Shanghai came at the end of the first Opium War (launched in 1840 by Britain over rights to trade and diplomatic representation) with its designation by the Ch'ing court as a treaty port in accordance with the provisions of the Treaty of Nanking, which concluded the war in 1842. When the British and Americans obtained settlement rights in 1843 and the French concession was established five years later, Shanghai became divided into three interconnected sections—two occupied by the foreign settlements and one by the walled Chinese city, each under different municipal administrations.

From the very start, the foreign settlements thrived economically. Strict hygienic regulations that secured a pure and continuous water supply system as well as sewage disposal converted the unpromising place into a site that was modern even by the standards of contemporary Western cities. Lithographs by well-known painters of the day left telling testimonies to the fact that, at the turn of the twentieth century, electric lights adorned the city, streets were raised, broadened, and paved to accommodate horse-drawn carriages, trams facilitated transportation, and trains pulled by steam engines connected Shanghai with the adjoining hinterland.

Within a relatively brief time, Shanghai drew hundreds of thousands, eventually millions, of Chinese from the back country to populate the city with what are often referred to as "small city dwellers" (*hsiao shih-min*)—shopkeepers, merchants, artisans, servants, cooks, nurses, workers, hawkers, peddlers, and beggars, as well as young women from nearby Soochow, Yangchow, and Hangchow, well known throughout the ages for their beauty and sweetness of speech. Multistory buildings, sprawling mansions, banks, schools, libraries, museums, public parks, horse racing, teahouses, cafés, and French and regional Chinese restaurants, where foreigners mingled with Chinese, made of the prosperous harbor city a busy, noisy, racy metropolis with a cosmopolitan and polyglot atmosphere.

However, nothing distinguished Shanghai more from the hinterland towns than its radically different culture and new way of life. This new lifestyle deeply affected traditional interpersonal relations, Confucian ethical values, and the concept of time: whereas in China's rural areas work ceased only during the great festivals three times a year, new working conditions in the metropolis recognized one day a week for leisure, thereby fostering the increasing commercialization of culture and the emergence of new professions or the transformation of old ones: courtesan entertainment, storytelling, theater performances of classical regional dramas or Western-style "spoken" dramas, and, later, dancing and movies.

Still, it was the printing industry whose significance for modern Chinese culture was to prove unrivaled among the new urban entertainment professions and technologies. Equipped with modern technology that replaced the laborious and time-consuming technique of printing from wooden blocks by simpler and faster lithography, publishing companies, most frequently under foreign management, flooded the city with newly established newspapers and journals, thus creating at the same time the modern salaried professional writer and the modern urban reader willing to pay for the new issue of a newspaper or journal or to spend a small fee to borrow books or journals at the book stalls or libraries. In the late 1890s, more than thirty presses specialized in publishing fiction, and, from the 1870s on, fiction was printed in monthly literary supplements of such newspapers as *Shen pao* (Shanghai News; 1872–1949) and *Ying-huan so-chi* (Random Sketches of the World; 1872–1875). There were also tabloids designed especially for entertainment and leisure. Among the most prestigious fiction magazines in the first decade of the twentieth century were *Hsin hsiao-shuo* (New Fiction; 1902–1906), *Hsiu-hsiang hsiao-shuo* (Fiction Illustrated; 1903–1906), *Yüeh-yüeh hsiao-shuo* (All-Story Monthly; 1906–1908), and *Hsiao-shuo lin* (The Grove of Fiction; 1907–1908).

The new status of print media as mercantile commodities, of course, encouraged the production of worthless pulp fiction, but it also provided space for creative authors. With the abolition of the civil service examination system in 1905, prospective writers were deprived of the possibility of employment in the state bureaucracy—previously the major source of livelihood for the traditional writer. Now the professional writer could freely profit from the "public space" offered by the print media, which enjoyed more political freedom in the foreign concessions, with their extraterritorial rights, than in other Chinese cities. Thus, while Shanghai produced modern fiction, fiction, in turn, created modern Shanghai. This fruitful symbiosis is vividly illustrated by the opening paragraph from the famous turn-of-the-century novel *Erh-shih nien mu-tu chih kuai hsien-chuang* (Strange Phenomena Observed during the Last Twenty Years), by Wu Chien-jen (1866–1910):

> Shanghai—what a bustling hub of trade and commerce! Chinese and foreigners mingle; crowds fill the streets. Ships and junks come and go, goods and materials flow in and out. Fallen beauties from Soochow and Yangchow are drawn to the smell of money and flock to set up shops around Fourth Avenue. To succeed you must attract attention, so they put up their racy signs. The merchant princes find their way to the courtesans of the upper ranks; for gourmandizers of lesser taste willing to sup from a more common pot, there are girls of lower rank. And so, what sixty years ago was a stretch of reedy beach became a bustling spot which has no rival in the whole of China.

Wu Chien-jen was possibly the most talented, versatile, and artistically experimental of the late Ch'ing novelists who imprinted individual styles and language on their work. His life story and his lifestyle are, however, in many respects so similar to those of his famous contemporaries—Li Pao-chia (1867–1906), Liu O (1857–1909), and Tseng P'u (1872–1935)—that it is possible to deduce a composite picture of the first generation of Chinese professional journalists and writers at the turn of the twentieth century. As a rule, the writer, from a southern Chinese town (most often located in present-day Kiangsu province), was born into a gentry family, in which the father had prematurely died, leaving the family in need, but where the mother had somehow managed to provide the son with a classical education. For one reason or another, the young man was attracted to Shanghai, where, in order to support himself, he worked as a clerk or scribe, contributed to various literary journals until he (usually together with a few friends) founded a new one, a business venture that frequently foundered. He was actively involved in the political and social situation of contemporary China, and his literary works, though often drawn from his own experiences, do not disclose this personal provenance. As a rule he was a prolific writer who most frequently wrote novels in the vernacular, though he did not avoid other genres and wrote as well in classical language. Knowledge of a foreign language was the exception, but a rather accurate perception of European literature was facilitated by enormously influential paraphrases of Western literary works from the pen of Lin Shu (1852–1924), who prepared his "translations" with the assistance of others who, unlike himself, were versed in foreign languages. Like other men of letters of his time, the late Ch'ing writer wore a long gown, a short jacket, handmade cotton slippers, and a round cap, and his hair was braided in a long queue (legacy of a tonsorial rule imposed by the Manchus).

Little is known about his private life, but his enterprising spirit (and the availability of electric lighting) entirely changed the lifestyle of the traditional scholar. Unlike his Chinese counterpart of the past, who rose with the sun and retired early, the late Ch'ing writer was capable of combining work with pleasure—at night he became a bohemian who indulged in drinking, frequented pleasure quarters, and enjoyed smoking opium, while returning to his business and writing only in the afternoon to recreate in his novel what he himself witnessed and experienced. No wonder, then, that he was not a solitary man. Although Lin Shu and Liu O kept aloof from collective gatherings, others established literary societies that published journals or managed small publishing houses. Like modern European and American literary coteries, Chinese groupings of the period were held together by common beliefs and ideas, but the members also shared a certain lifestyle, often came from the same home towns, and were bound by personal friendship. Thus, for instance, the members of *New Fiction*, under the direction of Liang Ch'i-ch'ao (1873–1929), were all political activists who had resided for some time in Japan or Southeast Asian countries and believed that the role of literature lay in the dissemination of enlightenment. In contrast, those who wrote for *Fiction Illustrated*, founded by Li Pao-chia, and *All-Story Monthly*, established by Wu Chien-jen and Chou Kuei-sheng (1873–1936), had not studied abroad, and although they too were reformists, their goal was to forward the betterment of the nation by restoration of Confucian moral conduct, as propagated in their novels. What distinguished the group around *The Grove of Fiction*—Tseng P'u, Hsü Nien-tz'u (1875–1908), and Huang Jen (1866–1913)—was their common birthplace, the town of Ch'ang-shu in Kiangsu province, as well as their proficiency in at least one foreign language despite not having lived abroad. All three men were also leading theoreticians and critics of the day.

The premature death by 1910 of three of the outstanding late Ch'ing novelists—Wu Chien-jen, Li Pao-chia, and Liu O—would seem to make it natural to view that year as a dividing line between the writers of the late Ch'ing and the early Republican era. However, no arbitrary line is necessary to perceive visible differences between the writers of the late Ch'ing and those of the early Republican era. The distinction is almost palpable in the vibrant lifestyles and remarkable life stories of the four most prolific writers of the 1910s: Pao T'ien-hsiao (1876–1973), Su Man-shu (1884–1918), Hsü Chen-ya (1889–1937?), and Chou Shou-chüan (1895–1968). Moreover, Yeh Sheng-t'ao (1894–1988) and Lu Hsün, both usually associated with the generation of the May Fourth writers, also began their literary career during this period, contributing short stories in classical language to the best-known periodicals of the period, *Hsiao-shuo yüeh-pao* (Short Story Magazine), *Hsiao-shuo ts'ung-pao* (Collection of Fiction), and *Li-pai-liu* (Saturday).

What links the members of the new and old generations is—with the exception of Su Man-shu, who was born in Japan—a birthplace in Kiangsu province. To both generations of writers, too, Shanghai was a place offering plenty of opportunity to earn one's living as either a journalist or an owner of a bookstore and publisher of such leading literary magazines as *Hsiao-shuo shih-pao* (Fiction Actualities), *Chung-hua hsiao-shuo chieh* (The World of Chinese Fiction), and *Hsiao-shuo ta-kuan* (Fiction Panorama). What distinguished members of the younger generation from their older compeers was not only outward appearance—the younger men all dressed in Western business suits and leather shoes, and they all sported Western haircuts and the obligatory cigarette—but, more important, a proficiency in foreign languages (English, French, Japanese) that frequently led them to the profession of translator. The most distinctive differentiating feature, however, was the ostentatious personal lifestyle of the younger writers, said to be the consequence of their oversensitivity and the natural outpouring of their passionate feelings as writers, but, sometimes, critical voices tell us, rather used as a pose to imprint a particular aura of individuality on their persona. Their aim was to present fiction as authentic life experience, but to meet this end, life had sometimes to follow fiction.

The early 1910s is a period in the history of Chinese fiction hard to comprehend if one holds that literary development must follow a linear pattern of evolutionary change. However, the 1910s were marked by more than a simple reversal of the principles dominant during late Ch'ing. It was also the time when the short story was once again revived and became the most important genre on the Chinese literary scene. Last, but not least, it was a period when nonliterary texts, such as diaries (*jih-chi*), records of travel (*yu-chi*), and personal correspondence, were transformed into literary works, thereby broadening the spectrum of Chinese literature. All this was the result of impulses that either came to Shanghai from the outside or arose within the fecund urban environment provided by the city. In sum, without modern Shanghai modern Chinese literature could not have arisen.

THEORETICAL AND CRITICAL DISCOURSES ON FICTION

The newly discovered vigor and visibility of late Ch'ing critical discourses on fiction come as no surprise once we consider that theoretical discourses on fiction (*hsiao-shuo*)—which in the late Ch'ing period came to deal with the Chinese novel, drama, storyteller's narrative, and foreign fiction—were deeply affected by a general drive for a fundamental restructuring of the whole received concept of literature. This demand did not arise from within the cultural sphere proper. Rather, China's bitter conflicts with the West and the waning of its wealth and power brought about a deep national crisis that political leaders sought to address by pragmatic means summed up in a characteristic phrase:

use the techniques of the West, but preserve China's essence (*kuo-ts'ui*). The edifying role of literature, always conspicuous in China's cultural past, thus once again became a prominent, indeed a central, issue. This time, however, and in marked contrast to much of the past, there was a pronounced willingness to look for models outside China. Groups of Chinese intellectuals, in response to the crisis of Chinese culture and inspired by the examples of the Meiji Restoration of 1868 in Japan and of modern Western countries, attempted to devise various means to restore the lost authority of *wen-hsüeh* (literature in the broad sense) and to mold a new literature that could fill the pressing needs of the nation.

This literary discourse proceeded by several distinct and separate paths, from the advocacy of continuation of traditional *ku-wen* (ancient prose) and *p'ien-wen* (parallel prose) to the creation of a more accessible style of writing, the so-called *hsin wen-t'i* (new-style writing) by the foremost reformer and thinker of the period, Liang Ch'i-ch'ao. Liang was, moreover, involved in the reformers' efforts to resuscitate fiction in order to renew the spirit of the people and the nation. A brief survey of the views of the reformers as well as those of later thinkers illustrates how fictional narrative itself was shaped during the late Ch'ing and the early Republican eras.

The first known published article devoted to the renovation of fiction, "Pen-kuan fu-yin shuo-pu yüan-ch'i" (Announcing Our Policy of Printing a Fiction Supplement), which appeared in 1897 in the sixteenth issue of *Kuo-wen pao* (National News), was published in the port city of Tientsin. The authors of this essay—Yen Fu (1853–1921), an erudite, Western educated scholar and the author of the landmark translation of T. H. Huxley's *Evolution and Ethics*, and Hsia Tseng-yü (1863–1924), an ardent reformer and advocate of *hsin-shih* (new poetry)—proclaimed that, in Europe, the United States, and Japan, fiction, by enlightening the common people, had played a vital role in launching the modern era. Yen and Hsia therefore proposed that Chinese fiction should also be utilized in the important task of enlightening the Chinese people about life in the modern world. Moreover, they supported their proposal by pointing out the greater communicative power of the vernacular—the language of traditional Chinese novels. Yen and Hsia clearly noted the advantages of the capacious, vivacious, and colorful vernacular over the lapidary, suggestive, but emotionally restrained classical language (Literary Sinitic; see chapter 1) in the mission of enlightenment. Thus, they argued, just as traditional novels had kept alive among the common people an unofficial alternative to the official, dynastic historiography, so could modern vernacular fiction carry out the educative task they regarded as essential for the modernization of China.

For all Yen and Hsia's merits in pinpointing the medium of choice for the dissemination of a new ideology among the Chinese people, it was left to Liang Ch'i-ch'ao to formulate a systematic theory of fiction. After his flight to Japan following the collapse of the Hundred Days' Reform of 1898, led by his mentor

K'ang Yu-wei, Liang realized the need for a change in political strategy. In his article "Yi-yin cheng-chih hsiao-shuo hsü" (Foreword to the Publication of Political Novels in Translation), published in the first issue of *Ch'ing-yi pao* (The China Discussion; Yokohama, December 1898), Liang introduced to Chinese literary theory the concept of *cheng-chih hsiao-shuo* (political fiction). Adopted from current Japanese theory, the concept had been taken from the ideas of two leading British novelists, Benjamin Disraeli (1804–1881) and Edward George Bulwer-Lytton (1803–1873). Liang advocated the translation of political novels because he saw in them an entirely new literary genre for Chinese, an edifying analogy to the Confucian classics. Just as the classics had instructed the literati about the moral Way, so now the political novel in vernacular could educate the common people on how to accomplish the tasks that lay before them.

Liang's political theory of the vernacular novel culminated in his treatise "Lun hsiao-shuo yü ch'ün-chih chih kuan-hsi" (Fiction Seen in Relation to the Guidance of Society), published in 1902 in Yokohama in the inaugural issue of *New Fiction,* a literary journal founded, as already noted, by Liang himself. In this essay, Liang embraced previous writers' notion of the emotional power of vernacular narrative but further elaborated the concept. Referring explicitly to Zen (Ch'an) Buddhism as the source of his many ideas and concepts, Liang defined what he called "four powers of fiction," which he believed would gradually lead from mere absorption in a literary work to a desire to imitate its heroes. Liang describes "the highest power of fiction"—*t'i* (lifting)—as corresponding to the most advanced of all Buddhist means of self-transformation. Possessing such emotive power, fiction, he said, has the capacity to renovate the minds of a people, and thus a nation's morality, religion, politics, social customs, learning, and arts.

In this way, Liang, again using a Buddhist metaphor, came to regard fiction as "the greatest of all literary vehicles" (*wen-hsüeh chih tsui shang sheng*) because "it possesses an astonishing potentiality to affect the way of man." But, in order to attain these goals, fiction itself must first be revitalized. Numerous well-known novels of the past, such as *San-kuo chih yen-yi* (Romance of the Three Kingdoms), *Shui-hu chuan* (Water Margin), and *Hung-lou meng* (A Dream of Red Towers), had, Liang felt, "poisoned" the people and the nation by inciting banditry and lust. Liang concluded his essay thus: "If [we] now want to reform the governance of the people, [we] must begin with a revolution in the realm of fiction [*hsiao-shuo chieh ko-ming*]; if [we] wish to renew the people, [we] must begin with a renewal of fiction [*hsin hsiao-shuo*]."

This concept of fiction as "the greatest of all literary vehicles" is an obvious echo of the Neo-Confucian dictum that "writing should convey the way" (*wen yi tsai tao*), formulated by Chou Tun-yi (1017–1073) and promulgated by Chu Hsi (1130–1200), which has been the underlying ideological concept of prose composition since the Sung dynasty (960–1279). Liang Ch'i-ch'ao enriched this theory, however, by imaginatively incorporating into it ideas from different traditions, some associated with classical, high literature, others with vernacular literature; these, moreover, were brought together and reconciled with concepts from foreign literatures and thought. The synthetic character of Liang Ch'i-ch'ao's theory of fiction is a clear manifestation of the late Ch'ing period itself. This electrifying climate, in propitious combination with the emergence of a group of astute, highly educated, and well-informed men of letters, induced an effervescence of critical discourses on fiction rarely seen in the history of Chinese literary criticism.

Telling signs of this new atmosphere, in which fiction was recognized for the first time in China's history as the very core of its literature, were the variety of the formats of critical discourse, the richness of the topics discussed, and the gradual shift of importance from one issue (that of "enlightening the people") to others relating to esthetic concerns.

As for the format, some authors, such as Wu Chien-jen and Liu O, conveyed their ideas on the stylistic and structural properties of fictional works in critical commentaries to their own novels (*Liang Chin yen-yi* [Romance of the Two Chin Dynasties] and *Lao Ts'an yu-chi* [The Travels of Lao Ts'an], respectively), thus following a model well established by several seventeenth-century critics and authors, such as Chin Sheng-t'an (1608–1661), Mao Lun (fl. 1666) and his son Mao Tsung-kang (c. 1632–1709 +), Li Yü (1610/11–1680), and K'ung Shang-jen (1648–1718). Again, as in the past, prefaces to a work or a collection of works were a favorite medium for theoretical ideas, as exemplified by Liang Ch'i-ch'ao's "Foreword to the Publication of Political Novels in Translation," referred to above. An entirely new format, however, was the independent essay, standing alone and published in its own right, that evinced a particular logic of exposition and stylistic composition that, even without revealing the author's true name, bore his signature. To this group of essays belonged the very popular *fa-k'an tz'u* (inaugural announcements), which bear a striking similarity to Western literary manifestos. These announcements include declarations of the intentions, programs, and views of a group of writers who were the founders of a new literary periodical. (It is worth repeating that Yen Fu's and Hsia Tseng-yü's discourses, like Liang Ch'i-ch'ao's, were written on the occasion of the publication of the first issue of their respective journals.)

The rise of the independent essay created in its wake the possibility of establishing a new forum for free discussion in the journals: a regularly published series of discourses on similar topics. The first example of such a forum was "Hsiao-shuo ts'ung-hua" (Colloquy on Fiction), which appeared in *New Fiction* in 1903. Another equally successful forum, "Hsiao-shuo hsiao hua" (Briefly on Fiction), began publication in *The Grove of Fiction* in 1907. About thirty different forums of this type emerged in the journals of the period, and they remain the most valuable source material for the study of late Ch'ing critical discourses on fiction.

Detailed study is still required to uncover the full wealth and range of ideas presented in critical writings of the late Ch'ing and early Republican periods. But it is already possible to see a certain shift of topics and their presentation over time. Immediately after the publication of Liang Ch'i-ch'ao's treatise in 1902, most critics supported or elaborated on Liang's views. In 1903, for instance, Hsia Tseng-yü published under the pen name Pieh-shih a long article in *Fiction Illustrated*, no. 3, "Hsiao-shuo yüan-li" (Principles of Fiction), in which he investigated the differences in the readers' responses to pictures and various kinds of verbal texts; he concluded that all readers, irrespective of their social background or cultural level, preferred pictures to verbal texts and, among the verbal texts, fiction to historical and scientific treatises. As in his earlier article, Hsia explained that the reason for this latter preference rests in the "visuality" of vernacular language and the ability of vernacular fiction to convey the sum and substance of everyday life.

The participants in the debate on contemporary fiction largely agreed that romantic fiction is a legitimate and necessary part of literary production, although most critics took the side of Chin T'ien-ho (better known as Chin Sung-ts'en; 1874–1947), who wrote the first chapters of *Nieh-hai hua* (A Flower in a Sea of Sins). In his article "Lun hsieh-ch'ing hsiao-shuo yü hsin she-hui chih kuan-hsi" (On the Relationship Between Romantic Fiction and the New Society), published in 1905 in *New Fiction*, Chin fiercely castigated the publication in 1904 of Lin Shu's and Pao T'ien-hsiao's translation of *Joan Haste*, by H[enry] Rider Haggard (1856–1925), because the heroine became pregnant by her lover and suffered a miscarriage of her illegitimate child. (In the bowdlerized translation of the novel published in 1901–1902, it was the virtue of the heroine who gave up her lover for the sake of her lover's family that appealed to the Chinese audience.)

Still, the most animated discussion was that initiated not by the favorable response, but by criticism of Liang's article, in particular his view of fiction as a mere tool for political reforms as well as his indiscriminate condemnation of the masterpieces of traditional Chinese vernacular literature. Thus Ch'u Ch'ing (fl. 1902) wrote "Lun wen-hsüeh shang hsiao-shuo chih wei-chih" (The Position of Fiction in Literature), published in *New Fiction*, vol. 1, no. 7, in which he forcefully vindicated fiction as an artistic endeavor, grounded, as he thought, in the contrast of its integral components. He maintained that the writer's creative process was more complex than a mere imitation of reality. A storm of disapproval over Liang's views on fiction of the past raged in the pages of "Colloquy on Fiction" from vol. 1, no. 17, to vol. 2, no. 24.

In this "Colloquy," *New Fiction* offered a forum to some ten intellectuals who shattered previous taboos by writing freely about such "subversive" fiction as *Dream of Red Towers, Water Margin, Liao-chai chih-yi* (Strange Tales from Make-Do Studio), *Ju-lin wai-shih* (The Scholars), and even the proscribed *Chin P'ing Mei* (Gold Vase Plum). The degree of freedom of discussion, in which various conflicting views and concepts met, cannot be overestimated. And the fact that many eminent critics expressed indignation over Liang Ch'i-ch'ao's treatment of traditional vernacular novels in Liang's own journal says much about the academic tolerance of the period. At the time, differences in opinion could result in one critic's decision not to publish in a given journal and to join another colleague in a new literary venture. There were, however, no public recantings and meae culpae.

When Wu Chien-jen, who had served as the editor of Liang Ch'i-ch'ao's "Colloquy on Fiction" from its start in 1903, left this post in 1904, after several other ventures he founded *All-Story Monthly*, in collaboration with the prominent and prolific translator Chou Kuei-sheng. In 1906, in "Yüeh yüeh hsiao-shuo hsü" (Preface to *All-Story Monthly*), published in the first issue of the journal, Wu explained the distinction between his views on fiction and Liang's. To Wu, fiction's greatest strength lay in its ability to convey sentiment, which fitted it for use as a tool of "moral education." Moreover, virtue and morality, and only virtue and morality, could save the country. Therefore, he urged, authors should write not only political novels but social novels, detective stories, family stories, science fiction, and adventures as well.

The founding of *The Grove of Fiction* in 1907, however, signaled not just a divergence but a definite departure from Liang Ch'i-ch'ao's utilitarian concept of literature. This departure meant a significant shift toward the concept of fiction and literature as art, independent of didactic aims—a direction in Chinese literary theory that was to be most important on the literary scene during the first half of the 1910s.

This different direction was not altogether a new one. From the very beginning of literary discussions on fiction, Chinese scholars showed a pronounced and educated interest in the artistic properties and values of fiction. Thus, as early as 1897, despite the condemnation of Chin Sheng-t'an, the ingenious founder of the Chinese theory of fiction, by such a powerful luminary of the day as Chang Chih-tung (1837–1909), the literary critic and well-known poet Ch'iu Wei-ai (1874–1941) included in his collection of essays *Shu yüan chui t'an* (Idle Talk from Pulse Garden) a piece called "Chin Sheng-t'an p'i hsiao-shuo shuo" (On Chin Sheng-t'an's Critical Discourses on Fiction). In this essay he praised Chin Sheng-t'an's detailed textual analysis of *Water Margin* and the drama "Hsi-hsiang chi" (Romance of the Western Chamber) as well as his ranking of these works among such acknowledged *ch'i-shu* (masterpieces) as the poetry of Tu Fu (712–770) and Ssu-ma Ch'ien's (c. 145–c. 86 B.C.E.) *Shih chi* (Records of the Historian). But the voices of Ch'iu and others of his contemporaries, such as Yü Ming-chen (*hao* [alternative name] Ku-an; 1866–1918) in his essay "Ku-an man pi" (Ku-an's Literary Notes) of 1907–1908, were silenced by louder voices and overlooked by later research.

Likewise, the efforts of Japanese scholars at the turn of the twentieth century in the study of Chinese literature and vernacular fiction have remained largely unknown. Even now, few scholars have acknowledged that, seven years before Lin Ch'uan-chia (1877–1921) published China's earliest history of Chinese literature in 1904 (see below), Kojō Tandō (Teikichi; 1866–1949) wrote the voluminous, seven-hundred-page *Shina bungaku shi* (History of Chinese Literature) in 1897 or that Sasagawa Rinpū (also called Sasagawa Taneo [sic]; 1870–1949), the foremost Japanese specialist on Chinese literature, the following year wrote his own *Shina bungaku shi*, using the same title, which included several well-researched chapters devoted to the art of vernacular novels and drama. The latter was published in 1903 in Chinese translation by Translation Publishing House of Western Writing in Shanghai. As Lin Ch'uan-chia wrote in his brief recollection about the genesis of his *Chung-kuo wen-hsüeh shih* (History of Chinese Literature), Sasagawa's *History* inspired him to write his own work.

The essay that brought about the most far-reaching impact with regard to the esthetics of fiction was Wang Kuo-wei's (1877–1927) brilliant "*Hung-lou meng* p'ing-lun" (A Critique of *A Dream of Red Towers*; 1904). Before writing this study, Wang had intensively studied the works of such figures as Immanuel Kant (1724–1804), Arthur Schopenhauer, and Friedrich Nietzsche, and he used his knowledge of Western philosophical esthetics to revitalize Chinese theories of the novel. Because Chinese dramas and novels usually conclude with a reconciliatory denouement, Schopenhauer's concept of tragedy (in his *Die Welt als Wille und Vorstellung* [The World as Intention and Conception] from 1819) as the highest form of literary art was a provocative inspiration for Wang to offer an equally provocative re-evaluation of the *Dream*—it is, he said, precisely because of its tragic denouement that this novel has no artistic equal in Chinese literature. The duty of art is to depict the essentially bitter nature of life and provide catharsis.

The consequences of Wang's critical endeavor reverberated far beyond the study of a single novel. First, that this epitome of the politically conservative scholar had chosen to engage himself in a study of a literary genre disparaged by a majority of his educated contemporaries itself served to enhance the status of fiction. Second, that he, one of the most erudite thinkers of his day, allowed himself to be inspired by Western philosophers was a powerful, albeit more tacit than explicit, message that it was time to break out of the confines of Chinese culture. Finally, by making the art of the novel the center of his study, he signaled the possibility of emancipating Chinese fiction from its ubiquitous edifying mission.

The new path that Wang had pointed out was followed by Hsü Nien-tz'u, writing under the pseudonym Tung-hai chüeh-wo ("Enlightened Ego of the Eastern Sea"). Like many of his renowned contemporaries, he was born in Kiangsu province. In 1901 he had founded a branch of the revolutionary organization T'ung-meng hui (Revolutionary Alliance) and became one of the executive functionaries of a revolutionary pedagogic organization in his native Ch'ang-shu. In 1905, in collaboration with Tseng P'u he founded a publishing company called Hsiao-shuo lin (The Grove of Fiction). Two years later, this time in collaboration with Huang Jen, he began publication of the literary journal of the same name. In his essay "*Hsiao-shuo lin* yüan-ch'i" (Origins of *The Grove of Fiction*), published in the first issue of the journal in 1907, Hsü attributed his approach to literature to the influence of the esthetic views of Kant, Hegel (1770–1831), and J. H. von Kirchmann (1802–1884). Although, like Liang Ch'i-ch'ao, he was still fascinated with the "contagious" emotional power (*kan-jan li*) of fiction, unlike his contemporary, Hsü recognized a need to inquire into the origin of this power. He found its source in "beauty" (*mei*) and he continued his inquiry by asking how beauty was manifested. Utilizing Hegel's concept of unity of being and thought, Hsü recognized fiction's need to express reality through concrete images and ideals, which convey reality by esthetically more satisfying and more effective means than the direct imitation of reality itself. In his 1908 essay "Yü chih hsiao-shuo kuan" (My Views on Fiction), which appeared in nos. 9 and 10 of *The Grove of Fiction*, Hsü addressed some questions about the connections between fiction and society. Here, as would Huang Jen later, Hsü sees this relation differently from Liang Ch'i-ch'ao, in that he views fiction and society as exerting reciprocal effects: not only does fiction exert power over society, but society determines the fate of fiction. Hsü's contribution to *The Grove of Fiction* and to the Chinese literary debate as a whole was brought to an end by his untimely death at the age of thirty-four. Thus, Huang Jen took over as the editor-in-chief of the journal from the time its eleventh issue was published.

Huang, who had already published a perceptive chapter on the Ming novel—"Ming-jen chang-hui hsiao-shuo" (Chaptered Novels by Ming Writers) in his *Chung-kuo wen-hsüeh shih* (A History of Chinese Literature)—brought the late Ch'ing theory of fiction to new heights in the essays he published in *The Grove of Fiction* after Hsü's death. Huang finished writing his *History* in 1904, but the manuscript was used only as a textbook for his course on the history of Chinese literature and was not properly published. The manuscript was published in mimeograph form only in 1911, by the Society for Preservation of National Learning. Named Huang Chen-yüan at his birth, Huang changed his name to Huang Jen ("Yellow Man"), probably in order to display his allegiance to the yellow race, but he preferred to use and is better known by another alternative name (*hao*), Huang Mo-hsi ("Huang in Touch with the West"). Like Hsü, Huang was a native of Ch'ang-shu, Kiangsu province. Of all the members of his group of friends and collaborators, which included such outstanding figures of the day as Chang T'ai-yen (1869–1936), Tseng P'u, and Hsü Nien-tz'u, Huang was probably the best informed about the cultural situation in Europe. In 1901 he was appointed professor of literature at Tung Wu ta-hsüeh (University of the Eastern Wu Region) in Soochow, one of the new private universities in China. His *History of Chinese Literature* was the first modern history of Chinese literature.

Lin Ch'uan-chia's *History of Chinese Literature*, published in 1904, cannot be considered a modern literary history, because Lin's understanding of the term *wen-hsüeh* adheres closely to the meaning of this compound as used in the Imperial Edict of 1903 defining the curriculum at the newly reorganized Peking Pedagogical Institute. The Institute defined *wen-hsüeh* as "humanities" and followed the Japanese model in its conception of what should be taught at the university. Lin tailored his *History*, designed to be a textbook for his newly introduced course on Chinese literature at the Peking Pedagogical Institute, strictly according to the Imperial Edict, that is, he excluded poetry, fiction, and drama—precisely those literary genres that constitute "literature" or belles lettres in the modern sense. It is appropriate to note that Lin, though inspired to write his *History* by Sasagawa Rinpū's *History of Chinese Literature*, eventually rejected the latter work as a model for his own endeavor because it dealt with, among other subjects, Chinese fiction and drama, literary genres Lin considered "morally subversive."

In 1905, the year after he completed his own pathbreaking *History of Chinese Literature*, Huang Jen became director of the famous Kuo-hsüeh fu-lun she (Society for Preservation of National Learning). In 1907, he proclaimed his views on literature and the program of his newly founded journal in the manifesto "*Hsiao-shuo lin* fa-k'an-tz'u" (Inaugural Announcement of *The Grove of Fiction*). Although Huang still saw the importance of the educational function of the novel, he was also decidedly opposed to the unilateral emphasis on the utilitarian aspects of fiction and proclaimed that the "substance of fiction" (*hsiao-shuo chih shih-chih*) lay in its esthetic nature: "Fiction is that kind of literature which strives for beauty." In the series of articles called "Briefly on Fiction," published in the journal from 1907 to 1908, Huang, writing under the pseudonym "Man" ("Barbarian" or "Outlandish"), expounded his views on Chinese historical novels; on the close structural relation between the Chinese novel and *shih-wen*, "the prose of our day" (better known as *pa-ku-wen* [eight-legged essay], required of candidates in the civil service examinations of the Ch'ing dynasty); and, in particular, on the qualities required for a text to be considered "literary."

In his *History*, Huang defined a literary work by three attributes—*chen, shan, mei* (truthfulness, goodness and beauty)—and, in contrast to the then generally accepted view that literature and culture develop in a linear manner (following a misunderstood Darwinian model that regarded evolution as a ladder leading to man and equivalent to progress), Huang wrote that "historical evolution seems to consist of moves forward and backward, as well as of interruptions and circuitous returns." So, historical evolution should be considered *chin-hua* (transformative evolution).

Huang's crowning, though nearly forgotten, work was the compilation of the *P'u-t'ung pai-k'o hsin ta tz'u-tien* (A New General Encyclopedic Dictionary), published in 1911 in Shanghai with support of the Society for Preservation of

National Learning. Possibly the first modern-type reference book compiled in China, it has a traditional outer appearance—two cloth-wrapped cases containing 15 *ts'e* (thread-bound volumes)—that barely hints at the extraordinary treasure found within. Huang's *Dictionary* includes 1,415 double pages, a total of 11,809 entries, 156 illustrations, and 36 tables and charts. By its arrangement and content, it is the diametric opposite of its traditional counterpart—the *lei-shu* (classified reference works), a genre of collectanea of literary and nonliterary materials continuously compiled in China from the end of Han dynasty (206 B.C.E.–220 C.E.) until the eighteenth century in order to preserve the wealth of knowledge transmitted from the past. The *lei-shu* is arranged according to substantive topics in hierarchical order, beginning, for instance, with "Heaven" and "Earth" and then proceeding through geographical and geological features—people, society, and material aspects of life—to utensils, illnesses, barbarians, flora, and fauna. In contrast, Huang's work is arranged according to the number of strokes used to write the Chinese characters, following the model of Western, alphabetically ordered dictionaries or encyclopedias. Entries, often featuring the English equivalent of the Chinese word, moreover, provide information as to the larger and more comprehensive domains under which they are subsumed. For example, entry 386, *fang-yen*, includes the English equivalent "dialect" (though this word is now more precisely and accurately rendered as "topolect") and is subsumed under the category *yen* (language). The most notable feature of the work, however, is the text explaining each entry. Written in clear and concise language, definitions vary in length according to the importance of the topic and invariably include the most essential information available at the time.

The *Dictionary* deals with phenomena from both Chinese and Western cultures, and the treatment of the subject demonstrates a high level of conceptual abstraction. For example, entry 389, *wen-hsüeh*, is subsumed under the category *wen* (writing) and includes the English equivalent "literature." Huang provides a succinct historical overview of the Chinese understanding of the term and compares this with its Western counterpart. His major concern is obviously to explain the difference between "literature" as belles lettres and "literature" as embracing all writing, a distinction that was at that time not fully comprehended by Chinese readers.

> Now let me present for your reference the manner in which literature is defined in Europe and America. In a wider sense, all texts verbally expressing thoughts and sentiment belong to the realm of literature. Literature proper, however, emphasizes the reader's emotional response and an accessibility to a common reader. But if this literature strives to move the reader's feeling, its text must possess esthetic quality. Although literature is related to man's knowledge and will, its principal aspect rests in beauty. As a result, belles lettres [*mei-hsüeh*] form a constituent part of fine arts [*mei-shu*].

Huang Jen's persistent efforts to bring the esthetic value of fiction to the forefront of critical discourse were interrupted by his death, hastened by mental disorders, in 1913. There was, however, no rupture between his ideas and those of the following generation of literary scholars and writers. During the brief period from the 1911 Revolution to 1916, discussions on the nature of fiction continued to thrive. To be sure, many discourses written in traditional style and expressing traditional views still appeared. Yet when two young and previously unknown authors published, independently of each other, extensive essays on *hsiao-shuo* in two of the most prestigious literary journals of the day, *Short Story Magazine* and *The World of Chinese Fiction*, it was a telling sign of substantial advances in the scope and strategy of research on fiction. Whereas previous studies had dealt with a particular literary work, a single aspect of fiction, or a biography of a certain literary personality, these new treatises presented fiction as a complex artistic system; moreover, the articles were well organized and well informed about literary theories at home and abroad.

The first of the two treatises to be published, "Shuo hsiao-shuo" (Discourse on Fiction), by Kuan Ta-ju (1892–1975), appeared serially in 1912 in *Short Story Magazine* (vol. 3, nos. 5, 7, 8, 9, 10, and 11). The second, "Colloquy on Fiction," appeared in 1914 in the inaugural issue of the monthly *The World of Chinese Fiction*. Its author was known for many years only by his pseudonym, Ch'eng-chih. His identity was disclosed only recently, when the brilliant literary theoretician turned out to be the well-known historian of modern China, Lü Ssu-mien (1884–1957).

Kuan Ta-ju was only twenty years old when his treatise entered the Chinese literary scene, but his youth did not prevent him from treating theoretical issues in the study of Chinese fiction with a surprising maturity. Like Huang Jen and Hsü Nien-tz'u, Kuan was born in Wu district (present-day Soochow), Kiangsu province, and, like his two famous predecessors, he earned his living as both a literary scholar and journalist, working first for *Min-ch'üan pao* (People's Rights News) and later for *Min-kuo jih-pao* (Republic Daily). He was noted as a drama critic, in particular for his knowledge of the southern-style drama (*k'un-ch'ü*; see chapter 41).

Kuan Ta-ju's "Discourse on Fiction" must have attracted attention for its scope alone. The essay's six chapters deal with matters ranging from fiction as a literary genre and the author's proposed new classification of fictional categories to the influence exerted by fiction on society, the difference between translated foreign fiction and Chinese fiction, and a concluding discussion on what Kuan saw as the deficiencies of older Chinese fiction and new trends leading to its improvement. The forte of the "Discourse" resides, however, in the elaboration of issues rarely discussed in Chinese theoretical discourse, such as the relationship between the real world and the world of fiction and the delineation of fiction by means of a description of *t'i* (rhymed and unrhymed fictional forms, structural division in chapters), languages (distribution of literary languages, *wen-yen* and *pai-hua*, according to fictional forms), and themes (three among the nine enumerated themes—science fiction, detective stories, and adventures—are said to be new to Chinese literature), as well as by what Kuan calls five "specificities" that distinguish fiction (*hsiao-shuo*) from other literary genres: (1) it uses the vernacular rather than the classical language; (2) it deals with substance and avoids empty talk; (3) it employs illusion rather than precisely describing reality; (4) it is conceptual rather than concrete; and (5) it is complex rather than simple.

Kuan maintains that, of all the fictional forms in China, it is fiction in the vernacular (*pai-hua hsiao-shuo*) that is the "mainstream of fiction" (*hsiao-shuo chih cheng-tsung*), as no other fictional category possesses the same potential to exert power over Chinese society. Kuan ends his essay by stating that the future of Chinese fiction is in vernacular fiction because it is vernacular fiction that has the potential to contribute to the reform of contemporary society.

Lü Ssu-mien's essay seems unrelated to Kuan Ta-ju's work. Rather, its title suggests a link with the series of essays published under the same title a decade earlier in Liang Ch'i-ch'ao's *New Fiction*. The link, however, is one of antithesis. Whereas the earlier series had been written by a group of critics, each of whom had addressed a different subject, Lü Ssu-mien's essay was written by a single author who offered the most comprehensive treatment to date of Chinese fiction as a whole. The *New Fiction* series had been concerned primarily with the reception of fiction and its edifying role in society. Lü, however, was interested in the creative process of the artist, which he saw as proceeding in four stages: from the imitation of reality (*mo-fang*) to selection (*hsüan-tse*) of the beautiful from the nonbeautiful, to a mental transformation (*hsiang-hua*) of the source of inspiration, and, finally, to creation (*ch'uang-tsao*). Lü thus defined fiction as an "esthetic construct" (*mei te chih-tso*), which is not imitation of objects of the external world, but a manifestation of our esthetic imagination. In stark distinction to his predecessors, who engaged mainly in theorizing without referring to concrete examples, Lü Ssu-mien filled his well-informed discourse on the origins and nature of the fictional world, narrative modes, narrative structure, and fictional characters with frequent references to individual works of traditional Chinese fiction. He concluded his essay with a brilliant analysis of *A Dream of Red Towers*.

Kuan Ta-ju's and especially Lü Ssu-mien's works signaled another monumental change taking place in literary discourse. Only some ten years after the turn of the twentieth century, both scholars wrote their essays in a sophisticated vernacular suited to the task of bringing new ideas and new terminology to Chinese literary scholarship. Chinese theory of fiction was on the brink of becoming an integral part of the modern narratology developing at about the same time in Europe and the United States and represented by such works as *Der Roman: Geschichte, Theorie und Technik des Romans und der erzählenden Dichtung* (The Novel: History, Theory, and Technique of the Novel and Narrative Poetry; 1908), by Heinrich Keiter and Tony Keller; *Die Rolle des Erzählers in der Epik* (The Role of the Narrator in the Epic; 1911), by Käte Friedemann; *The Study of the Novel* (1905), by Selden Whitcomb; *The Novels and Tales* (1907–17), by Henry James; and *The Theory of Prose* (1925), by Viktor Shklovskij.

THE NOVEL AND THE SHORT STORY

About three hundred novels were published in China during the first decade of the twentieth century, and an even a larger number, around seven hundred works, were translated into Chinese during this period. This figure, though approximate and exclusive of short stories, represents a significant switch in the traditional Chinese hierarchy of literary genres. In China, as elsewhere, poetry was in the process of losing its privileged position; instead, the novel was swiftly climbing to the top position among literary genres.

Impressive as this large volume of publications is, numbers alone say little about what was, after all, the most important reason for the success of fiction. The large numbers confirm the impact of the innovative theories on the role of the "new" political fiction and the evidently widespread belief current among certain intellectuals that literature alone could save the people. The numbers also demonstrate that printing technology and the new urban environment were eminently instrumental in the rise and rapid development of fiction. Still, only an examination of the transformation of the elaborate artistic system of fiction itself during the last years of the Ch'ing dynasty fully demonstrates the changed role of fiction.

This section therefore focuses on a phenomenon that proved vital in the renewal of Chinese literature during the first two decades of the twentieth century—a continuous crossing of boundaries during which certain cultural constituents encroached upon the spheres of the others. This crossing inevitably gave rise to chaos as previously incompatible elements—foreign and native, literary and nonliterary, "low" and "high"—merged, exchanged positions, and coalesced. Yet this chaotic process, manifested by a disturbance of established esthetic norms, eventually culminated in the renovation of declining and outdated literary and artistic systems. The translation of foreign literatures, the restructuring of the novel, and the emergence of the short story were the central elements of the literary renewal that took place during the late Ch'ing and early Republican eras.

Translation Activities

Despite centuries of contact with the West, Chinese intellectuals became interested in foreign literature relatively recently, after the failed 1898 reform movement, when such figures as Yen Fu, Hsia Tseng-yu, and Liang Ch'i-ch'ao turned their attention to Western and Japanese literature in their search for a tool that could be used to "enlighten the people." Certainly, it is possible to explain the belated nature of this interest by the deeply ingrained and centuries-old belief of Chinese scholars that Chinese culture and literature were superior to all other, "barbarian" cultures, and that foreign things were to be learned only to deal with a pressing practical necessity. The low priority assigned to foreign literature is evident, for instance, in two well-known encyclopedic compilations from the late 1840s, *Ssu chou chih* (Geography of the Four Continents), by the high official Lin Tse-hsü (1785–1850), and *Hai kuo t'u chih* (Maps and Documents on Maritime Countries), by Lin's friend, the specialist on waterways and statecraft Wei Yüan (1794–1856). Although detailed descriptions of the lands of the barbarians (i.e., non-Chinese) and their ways of life are provided in the texts, no references to the literatures of these countries are included. This disinterest in foreign literatures can, of course, be explained also in more mundane terms—before the twentieth century, very few Chinese scholars possessed a command of a foreign language, and this situation improved only slowly: the first modern Chinese school for the study of foreign languages, the T'ung-wen kuan (School of Combined Languages), was established in Peking only in 1862.

Understandably, then, the reformers' interest in *hsiao-shuo* was motivated above all by its inherent qualities, which they saw as suitable for their utilitarian aims. A comment by K'ang Yu-wei (1858–1927), the revered Nestor of the reformers, in his *Jih-pen shu-mu chih* (Records of Japanese Book Catalogs) from 1897, is worth recalling in support of this thesis: "Those who can barely read will not read the Classics, but they will all read fiction. Since they can't be taught by means of the Six Classics, fiction should be used. Dynastic histories won't affect them; fiction can. The records of the disputations of the Sages will not instruct them; fiction can. Law cannot regulate them; fiction can."

In the late 1890s, Chinese translations of foreign fiction took an unexpected course, at least for contemporary intellectuals. At about the same time that Liang Ch'i-ch'ao published his own translation of the Japanese political novel *Kajin no kigū* (Strange Encounters with the Beauty), by Shiba Shirō (1852–1922), in the first issue of his journal *The China Discussion* (1898), the majority of foreign novels translated into Chinese dealt with themes far removed from the political enlightenment advocated by these men. Instead, detective stories, science fiction, and romances were flooding the book market at the turn of the twentieth century, with science fiction taking the lead. The famous English utopian novel *Looking Backward*, by Edward Bellamy (1850–1898), was translated into Chinese, in an abridged version, by the British missionary Timothy Richard (1845–1919). It was serialized under the title *Pai nien yi chiao* (A Hundred Years' Sleep) in the magazine *Wan-kuo kung-pao* (World News) from 1891 to 1892 and published in book form by the Kuang-hsüeh hui (Society to Promote Education) in 1894. By the time the novel, which describes the year 1887 from the vantage of the year 2000, was republished in *Fiction Illustrated* in 1904 under the new title *Hui-t'ou k'an* (A Retrospect), other science fiction novels, notably those by Jules Verne, were exciting the imagination of Chinese readers. In 1900, his novel *Autour du globe en quatre-vingt jours* (Around the World in Eighty Days) was translated by Hsüeh Shao-wei, followed by *Cinq semaines en ballon: voyage de découverte* (Five Weeks in a Balloon: A Voyage of Discovery) and *Les cinq cents millions de la begum* (Five Hundred Million Indian Princesses) in 1903. Moreover, in 1896 the journal *Shih-wu pao* (Actualities) began to serialize Chang K'un-te's translation of Arthur Conan Doyle's Sherlock Holmes stories. None of the works translated, however, surpassed the impact of Alexander Dumas fils's novel *La Dame aux camélias* (Camille), which appeared in 1899 in Lin Shu's celebrated translation as *Pa-li ch'a-hua nü yi-shih* (A Story of a Parisian Woman with Camellias). From then on, advertisements in numerous journals and newspapers announced a flood of translations of foreign books, and Sherlock Holmes and Marguerite from Dumas's novel became the darlings of Chinese readers. The peak of the craze for things foreign was reached between 1906 and 1908.

The translators' choice of foreign fiction with entertainment themes is often interpreted as a result of the commercialization of Chinese fiction at the turn of the twentieth century. This is, indeed, the case. Yet the fact that these themes and not others were chosen is in itself of primary historical importance, since it documents the meeting of two historically unrelated cultures and literatures.

In acculturation processes of this type, the receiving culture first accepts those components from an alien culture that are akin to its own system. For example, Yen Fu believed strongly in the affinities between certain ancient Chinese ideas and modern Western ideas and made his own modification of Huxley's *Evolution and Ethics* in his 1895 translation of this work under the title *T'ien-yen lun* (On Evolution). By analogy, Chinese translators of foreign fiction likewise adhered to domestic models when choosing what to translate. It is worth recalling that, long before modern Western literature became disseminated in China, Chinese literature had had its own detective stories (*kung-an hsiao-shuo*) as well as plenty of traditional dramas and novels about beautiful concubines and fiancées who, like Marguerite, demonstrated their love by sacrificing themselves. As for science fiction, Wu Chien-jen, who later became the most accomplished science fiction writer in the late Ch'ing, pointed out in a short essay, "Tsa-shuo" (Miscellanea; 1907), that Chinese fiction also had had its own works of science fiction (*k'o-hsüeh hsiao-shuo*); he demonstrated his thesis with a reference to the nineteenth-century novel *Ching hua yüan* (Flowers in the Mirror, A Romance).

In the same vein, translators searched for ways to restructure the foreign text in order to assimilate it to Chinese literary practice. Thus, excision of some parts of the original texts in the translations, whether cleverly sinicized European ambiance or bowdlerization of those passages of the original considered vulgar by Chinese standards, proved, by accident or by design, to be precisely those strategies that allowed the recipient Chinese culture to accept the alien texts.

This aspect of the translator's problem is evident in *New Fiction* (vol. 1, no. 8, 1902), in which Chou Kuei-sheng translated a French story as "Tu she chüan" (Coil of Vipers) with an opening that was unfamiliar to the Chinese reader—a dialog between a father and his daughter. Realizing that such a beginning would be rather unsettling for a Chinese audience accustomed to an opening of the novel in which the plot outline of the narrative as well as the principal characters are introduced before the narrative starts, Chou Kuei-sheng apologized for this solecism in the preface to his translation. Thus, when the brothers Chou Tso-jen (1885–1969) and Chou Shu-jen (i.e., Lu Hsün) in their 1909 *Yü-wai hsiao-shuo chi* (Collection of Stories from Abroad) introduced without apologies such avant-garde contemporary European writers as the Russian symbolists L. N. Andreyev (1871–1919) and V. M. Garshin (1855–1888), the eighty or so copies of this publication that sold must be considered a relative success. The pace of change in the habits of readers tends to be much slower than that of writers and translators.

In the second, more advanced stage of translation activities, from around 1908 to 1916, translators—such as Chou Kuei-sheng, Hsü Nien-tz'u, Wu Kuang-chien, Wu Tao, the brothers Chou Shu-jen and Chou Tso-jen, and Tseng P'u—became well versed in the language of the translated text, and the foreign texts selected for translation were, it appears, carefully chosen to introduce renowned oeuvres from world literatures. Thus, for instance, in 1910 Pao T'ien-hsiao translated Anton Chekhov's *Ward No. 6*, in 1913 Tseng P'u published Victor Hugo's *Ninety-three*, L. N. Tolstoy's *Resurrection* appeared in 1916 in Ma Chün-wu's rendition, and so forth. Yet, even at this time, quite famous translators must have thought twice before faithfully translating a foreign literary work whose compositional arrangement was not in harmony with traditional Chinese configurations (see also chapter 52).

The Late Ch'ing Novels

History allotted a mere ten years to the late Ch'ing novel. After a phenomenal success during the first decade of the twentieth century, "new" fiction rapidly declined and, in the 1910s, the position of the novel was taken over by the short story. At the distance of a century, the phenomenon of the late Ch'ing novel invites a query about its position in the history of Chinese fiction.

First, it must be admitted that none of the late Ch'ing novelists attained the heights of artistic excellence reached in the seventeenth and eighteenth centuries by such writers as Li Yü, P'u Sung-ling, Wu Ching-tzu, and Ts'ao Hsüeh-ch'in. Yet the late Ch'ing writers did accomplish tasks that their precursors could not—they led Chinese fiction out of the prison of established convention and confronted it with the world beyond.

The setting of the late Ch'ing novel presents a world very different from that of previous Chinese novels. Horizons are widened, and places are no longer static. Only one of the late Ch'ing novels examined, Liu O's *The Travels of Lao Ts'an,* is set in a single province, Shantung, repeating the pattern of traditional fiction, in which plot is usually localized in one town or one particular area. Even in this novel, however, the main hero—Lao Ts'an—travels from one locality to another, driven by a search for injustice and his determination to rectify it. In the other novels, including Wu Chien-jen's *Strange Phenomena Observed During the Last Twenty Years* and *Hen hai* (The Sea of Regret), Li Pao-chia's *Kuan-ch'ang hsien-hsing chi* (Exposure of the World of Officials) and *Wen-ming hsiao shih* (A Brief History of Enlightenment), as well as Tseng P'u's *A Flower in a Sea of Sins,* the characters travel freely from one province to another, observing or taking part in events concerning China as a whole, reflecting a country in the process of modernization with increasing mobility. Rather than being set in a provincial town of the heartland, the action now takes place most frequently in the big cosmopolitan cities on the maritime east coast, while Peking turns into a place of conservative officialdom, out of step with developments both inside and outside China. And for the first time—if we ignore the imaginary travels in *Hsi-yu chi* (Journey to the West) and *Flowers in the Mirror*—scenes set outside the frontiers of China are included—overseas students in Japan in Li Pao-chia's *Brief History of Enlightenment,* England in his *Officials,* Germany and Russia in Tseng P'u's *Flower*—and even outer space in some of the science fantasy novels, such as *Yüeh-ch'iu chih-min-ti* (Moon Colony; 1905), by Huang-chiang tiao-sou, or *Wu-t'o-pang yu-chi* (A Journey to Utopia; 1906), by Hsiao-jan Yü-sheng.

In order to make their novels more dynamic, the authors people them with characters who are outside the usual repertoire of fictional protagonists. The ubiquitous officials, high and low, with their wives and concubines, are still there, and so are the military, the merchants, and the compradors. But among those who appear for the first time are, for instance, space travelers, inventors, journalists, unemployed intellectuals, students who study overseas, revolutionaries, nihilists, anarchists, poor prostitutes, and foreigners, all with more or less important functions in the development of the plot. Still more unusual than the category to which the characters belong is the description of their mutual relationships, which more often than not are in sharp contradiction to Confucian propriety and ethics and are at times turned upside down. For instance, the world of officialdom is frequently related and compared to the underworld of prostitutes and thieves (*Travels, Officials, Strange Phenomena*); the five classical ethical relations (*wu lun*) between relatives and friends, husband and wives, father and children, master and servant are frequently broken, indeed intentionally violated (*Strange Phenomena, Officials, Sea of Regret, Flower*); and the Chinese engage in warfare with foreigners, who are routinely defeated (e.g.,

Kao-yang pu-ts'ai-tzu, *Tien shih-chieh* [Electric World; 1909], and Pi-ho-kuan chu-jen, *Hsin chi-yüan* [New Era; 1908]).

Finally, it is also necessary to stress that love and sentiment appear quite often in the late Ch'ing novels only to show how the passions of a sensitive individual are crushed by insensitive social forces (*Sea of Regret, Flower*). Thus the late Ch'ing novel seems to capture China's emerging modern society in all its complexity, diversity, mobility, and uncertainty. This thematic range, reminiscent of the contemporaneous European novel, indicates the ability of late Ch'ing fiction to function as a national literature, and the broadness of themes, settings, and range of characters is matched by an astonishing variability of narrative forms, devices, and styles.

This greater willingness by authors and readers to accept foreign fiction and the attempts by the former to utilize its techniques in the writing of Chinese fiction can be explained, at least in part, by the loosening of traditional norms and esthetic rules. Writers found the new possibilities to break out of the confines of the old, chronologically arranged narrative time scheme particularly attractive, as the inverted narrative time of, for example, the Western detective story enhanced tension in the plot and the future time used in Western science fiction novels enabled transportation to hitherto unimaginable visionary worlds (e.g., in Liang Ch'i-ch'ao's *Hsin Chung-kuo wei-lai chi* [The Future of New China] or in *Journey to Utopia*). Most important innovations originated, however, in the individual writer's attempt to diminish or to eliminate the grip of traditional writing conventions and to establish his own control over the final form of the narrative. For instance, remarkable changes took place in the principles of plot structuring, modifying the older types of arrangements in order to accommodate the transfiguration taking place in society. The plot in *Officials*, for example, is arranged as a system of relationships among the various new strata of late Ch'ing society described in the novel. Or, in *Flower*, the plot is conceived precisely in accordance with the cosmological cyclic principles and the Buddhist principle of retribution typical of traditional fiction in order to encode a warning against the inevitable historical penalty for the excesses of beclouded contemporary Chinese society. Most striking, however, is a configuration of the plot that, while conveying the protagonist's search for an explanation of something unexpected and shocking, ends in vain with the defeat of the hero or the heroine (*Strange Phenomena* and *Sea of Regret*). In these novels Wu Chien-jen not only incorporated the inverted time of Western and Chinese detective stories, but also turned the traditional reconciliatory dénouement upside down by ending them in merciless tragedy.

The most surprising discovery has been the detection of individual ideologies and styles in the works of the late Ch'ing novelists. The descriptions of late Ch'ing novels in the historical works of Lu Hsün, Hu Shih, Ah Ying, and other Chinese and Japanese literary critics and historians from the 1920s through the 1960s at first seemed to show that in principle only socially engaged literature was produced during the late Ch'ing. Certainly, social engagement is important in most of the late Ch'ing novels. But this does not mean that the sole intention of the authors was to ridicule, castigate, and expose the evils of society. More recent research has revealed that the range of themes of the novels was actually much broader than previously believed, and the revival of the detective story, science fiction, and romance novels triggered by the translation of Western fiction initiated a restructuring of conventional themes. The novels of the period exhibit a striking diversity of ideological attitudes and strengthening of the subjective vantage point, expressed by means of plot structure, at times through narrative symbolism (particularly in the prolog), and sometimes by affinities between the author and the first-person narrator. Therefore it comes as no surprise that the style of the authors is similarly diverse and unique.

Wu Chien-jen, also known as Wu Wo-yao or Wo Fo-shan jen (I, the Native from Fo-shan [in Nan-hai county, west of Canton]), deserves to be acclaimed as the most versatile and imaginative among the late Ch'ing novelists because, in several of his best novels, he set new trends in late Ch'ing fiction writing. Among his first experiments is the tour de force use of the first-person narrative mode in Chinese vernacular fiction, previously written in the third person. Befittingly, Wu introduced this new narrative technique in the novel *Strange Phenomena*, which relates at least some of the author's own experiences. In particular, the author reveals the true nature of his seemingly caring but in fact morally corrupt uncle, which was crushing his own life and which he transformed into a paradigm of the formal and semantic organization of the novel. The first-person narrator of the novel, serialized with interruptions from 1903 to 1910, observes phenomena at first "strange," repulsive, and immoral to him, but gradually revealed as typical of the time. In his novel *Hsin "Shih-t'ou chi"* (A New *Story of the Stone*), the first eleven chapters of which were originally serialized in the journal *Nan-fang pao* (South) in 1905 and which was published in 1908 as a forty-chapter book, Wu created what turned out to be a curiously attractive amalgam because he did not hesitate to merge the new European fictional genre with the most revered of all traditional Chinese novels, Ts'ao Hsüeh-ch'in's *Shih-t'ou chi* (The Story of the Stone), better known as *Hung-lou meng* (A Dream of Red Towers). In the same vein, Wu broke the conventions of linear, chronological narrative time in the traditional Chinese novel when, in his detective novel *Chiu ming ch'i yüan* (The Strange Case of the Nine Murders), first published serially in *New Fiction* journal between 1904 and 1905, he integrated the inversion of narrative time employed in Western detective stories with a technique similar to that in Cantonese *nan-yin* ballads (see chapter 50). Among Wu's finest artistic achievements belongs his ten-chapter novel *The Sea of Regret*, published in 1906, which was staged as spoken drama in 1912 and made into a film in 1931. The novel tells the fate of two young star-crossed pairs of lovers who are engaged, but then separated in the turmoil of the Boxer Rebellion. The hardships experienced mold them into different persons—one of the young men becomes a thief and opium addict, while his fiancée, originally timid and barely literate, grows into an independent and resolute young woman, who—unable to save her betrothed—decides to become a nun; the other young woman becomes a Shanghai prostitute and her fiancé, out of grief, a hermit. In this slim work, Wu simultaneously included three major innovations. The tightly woven, mirrorlike plot allowed him to forsake the long novel with a complex plot and many characters for a shorter one with a unitary plot, populated by a limited number of characters—a move that, in turn, facilitated a shift of focus from action to characterization. In the prolog to the novel, Wu declared his intention of creating a novel of passion (*hsieh-ch'ing hsiao-shuo*), and his concentration on the intimate theme of love (the main romantic theme coupled with motifs of parental love, filial piety, and loyalty toward one's master and country) is a major feature pointing toward the development of the psychological novel.

Li Pao-chia's novels—best represented by *The Officials*, originally serialized in the journal *Shanghai shih-chieh fan-hua pao* (Shanghai Splendor) from April 1903 to June 1905, and by *A Brief History of Enlightenment*, published serially in the journal *Fiction Illustrated* from 1903 to 1905—complement and contrast with those by Wu Chien-jen. In Li's panoramic pictures of Chinese society, there is no room for complex characterization, because to him characters merely represent social groups. Li patterned each of his novels according to an identical plot, which is organized in thematic cycles and serves as a base for a systematic depiction of particular social strata arranged according to their hierarchical position in society. These new inventions in the structural configuration of the novel made Li Pao-chia an unsurpassed master of the late Ch'ing novel in presenting a broad picture of Chinese society.

While Li Pao-chia's and Wu Chien-jen's novels are written in a vivid, everyday vernacular intended for an audience without a classical education, Tseng P'u's and Liu O's novels appealed to the sophisticated reader because their novels carried a message veiled in symbolism and were written in language that borrowed images and illusions from classical literature. The kinship with Chinese poetic and symbolic tradition is discernible, in particular in Liu O's *The Travels of Lao-ts'an*, whose first thirteen chapters appeared originally in *Fiction Illustrated* (nos. 9–18, March 1903–January 1904) and which was contemporaneously reprinted in a twenty-chapter version with a prolog in *T'ien-chin jih-jih hsin-wen pao* (Tientsin Daily News). The novel opens with a prolog describing a dream of its central figure, Lao-ts'an ("Old Decrepit"), in which he sees China as a sinking ship. This symbolic beginning prefigures the overall symbolic character of the narrative. Enlightened by his dream, Lao-ts'an, an itinerant medical practitioner, sets out on a journey to remedy China's ills by various methods: through a search for examples of injustice and attempts at rectification, through philosophical discussions regarding the China of the future, and through a change of attitudes toward women. What sets this novel apart from the others is just this nonaction discourse, including the famous poetic descriptions of Chinese landscape, which are, however, meant to be understood not merely as images of natural beauty but as metaphorical statements about the condition of society. Yet even in this visionary novel, there is room for integration of an element entirely dissimilar to its lyrical components. Liu O organizes a portion of the plot as a series of mini–crime stories featuring Lao-ts'an as detective. It is this mixture of previously incompatible elements that makes the novel so innovative.

Tseng P'u's novel *A Flower in the Sea of Sins* was begun by Chin Sung-ts'en, who wrote the first six chapters, two of which were published in the magazine *Chiang-su* (Kiangsu; 1903–1904). Tseng P'u took over the project in 1904, and the first two volumes of the novel, ten chapters each, were published in Shanghai in 1905 by the Grove of Fiction publishing company. Four more chapters of the projected third volume were published serially in 1907 in *The Grove of Fiction*, but a complete third volume never appeared. In 1928 Tseng P'u substantially revised his work and published it in a thirty-chapter version. As in the case of Liu O's novel discussed above, the prolog foretells the theme of the whole novel by a synecdoche: the Island of Happy Slaves attached to Shanghai is sinking into the sea, but its reveling, savage, and ignorant inhabitants perish without realizing that the cause of their death is lack of fresh air. The novel vividly describes the life of China's high society in Peking and Shanghai during the last quarter of the nineteenth century, while its destiny is symbolically linked to the fate of Chin Wen-ch'ing, a high official who falls into a fateful liaison with the sing-song girl Fu Ts'ai-yün, later his concubine. The novel is skillfully organized along the pattern of retribution for misdeeds (*nieh*), which permeates several levels of the novel. This repetitive pattern is first introduced by an episode in which Chin breaks a promise of marriage, leading the rejected young woman to commit suicide. When Chin becomes infatuated with Fu Ts'ai-yün twenty years later, she, the image of the dead woman, will inevitably be responsible for his downfall. Chin's life as a successful and enlightened official at the court is one of splendor and riches, but during his diplomatic mission to Europe, he turns into a bungling minister out of step with the world outside China, is cheated by his mistress, makes disastrous diplomatic mistakes, and, shortly after his return to China, falls into disgrace and dies abandoned by all. The title compresses several semantic levels of the novel by the polysemy of the word *hua* (flower), which can be also used for "woman" as well as for "China" (by means of a semantically closely related homophone).

A RETROSPECT

When Liang Ch'i-ch'ao called for a "revolution in fiction" in his 1902 essay, the compound *ko-ming* (originally a predicate-object structure used in the *Yi-ching* [Classic of Change], where it meant "to change the mandate of heaven") had only recently, around 1895, been returned to the Chinese language from the Japanese (*kakumei*), where it had acquired a new connotation—"revolution." Nevertheless, by the time Liang employed the term in his call for a revolution in fiction, it had already been much used, not to say overused, in slogans and speeches, calling for all sorts of revolutions—political revolutions, social revolutions, racial revolutions, and familial revolutions. The word had also invaded the cultural sphere. Before Liang raised his demand for a revolution in fiction, he himself had already called for a "revolution in poetry" (*shih chieh ko-ming*) and a "revolution in culture and literature" (*wen chieh ko-ming*).

Judging from essays of the late Ch'ing political reformers that envision a transformation of contemporary Chinese culture, their aim was, above all, a change of literary themes, as a result of which—so they somewhat naively believed—the new "content" would more or less automatically achieve the desired enlightenment of people. However, Liang Ch'i-ch'ao's failure to complete his visionary novel *The Future of New China*, as well as Ch'ien T'ien-hua's novel *Shih-tzu hou* (The Lion Roars; 1905–1906) and other science fiction novels that also remained unfinished, are telling testimonies to how little the reformers realized that talent and writing "know-how" were as important as goodwill for creating a cultural renaissance.

Yet a "revolution" or, more precisely, a radical change in fiction *was* carried out. This was done through an inversion of the pivotal components of the novels. As seen above, plot dénouement changed from reconciliatory to catastrophic; relationships among characters changed from those patterned on Confucian morality to open moral misconduct; the ubiquitous third-person narrative was replaced for the first time by the first-person narrative; the complex plot developed into a unitary one; and the traditional chronological narrative time setting became open to replacement by an inverted narrative order or a temporal setting a hundred years in the future.

But inversion as an effective device for reviving esthetically exhausted writing conventions had by no means been unknown to Chinese artists of the past. Indeed, modification of preceding models had long been one of the major methods of the evolution of Chinese literature. In the late Ming and early Ch'ing, for example, inversion had proved a primary strategy for cultural revival, and Li Yü, the unrivaled master of literary renovation by inversion, coined a fitting term for this method: *fan-an* ("overturn tables," or "reverse a previous verdict"). Certainly, it cannot be doubted that, just as in the time of the Six Dynasties (220–589), when Buddhism, foreign arts, and architecture from abroad were the most important stimuli for the revival of Chinese culture, so the encounter with the West was equally important for late Ch'ing culture and the novel.

The Novels of the 1910s

The novels of the 1910s are excellent examples of the ability of Chinese fiction to revitalize itself. As before, the method of this revitalization was inversion.

The paradigm to be inverted was now that of the late Ch'ing vernacular novel. In contrast to novels with numerous characters (sometimes numbering in the hundreds), the typical novel written during the 1910s featured no more than two or three main characters with only a few auxiliary figures. Moreover, the social issues so predominant in the late Ch'ing novel were now superseded by an interest in the psyches of an individual hero and heroine and their unyielding, but frequently vain, quest for a relationship based on love. The most important change occurred in the linguistic mode in which the novels of the 1910s were written. Unlike the typical vernacular novels of the past, novels of this period were often rendered in classical language, as the authors apparently found it better suited to the expression of sentiments and psychological states of mind—the major topics of the novels of the 1910s. The shift back to a classical language register was also significant for the further restructuring of the Chinese novel, as it facilitated transgressing boundaries between literary and nonliterary texts. This led, in turn, to the rise of epistolary novels and novels in the form of a literary diary. (In premodern times, Chinese correspondence and diaries were, by convention, written in classical language, and these genres were not considered belles lettres.)

The novel that perhaps best succeeded in portraying subjective, intimate experiences was *Tuan-hung ling-yen chi* (The Lone Swan), first serialized in *T'ai-p'ing-yang pao* (Shanghai Pacific News) in 1912 and later published in book form in 1919. Its author, Su Man-shu, whose literary fame rests on his translations of Byron's poems, in addition to his own poetry and fiction, was a frustrated revolutionary who became a self-styled wandering poet and monk. The protagonist of Su's first-person novel—a young Japanese monk of Chinese origin, whose fate and creed prevent him from fulfilling his search for love—shares many affinities with the author, who, like Byron, produced his best story by creating an enigmatic legend about his own life.

A similar conflation of fiction and reality is achieved by Hsü Chen-ya in another famous novel of the period, *Yü li hun* (The Soul of the Jade Pear Flowers), first published serially in 1911 in *People's Rights* and republished in book form in 1912. Hsü introduced in this novel a topic previously taboo—the emotional turmoil experienced by a young Chinese widow who is expected to maintain her chastity after her husband's death but who falls in love with the young tutor to her child. The novel gained fame less because of this new theme than because of the alluring affinities among the author, the narrator, and the lovelorn tutor-poet, which encouraged speculation that the male protagonist was the author himself. In 1914, Hsü promoted this speculation by rewriting the novel, originally a third-person narrative, as a diary. Hsü's *The Soul of the Jade Pear Flowers* thus became the first Chinese novel in diary form, in the process transforming the nonliterary diary into a new literary genre, frequently employed in modern Chinese fiction.

Despite their having contributed to the renewal of Chinese fiction and their enthusiastic reception by an urban readership, novels written in classical language during the 1910s have, as a rule, been omitted from histories of Chinese fiction. One reason for this exclusion might be a simplistic understanding of literary development. The fiction of the 1910s does not fit neatly into a linear conception of literary development that presupposes that one literary period emerges from, and replaces, the one preceding it. Placed between the late Ch'ing and May Fourth periods (both concerned with pressing social issues and both promoting the use of the vernacular), the fiction of the 1910s, with its emphasis on romantic and introversive themes and written, moreover, in the classical language, could easily be seen as a historical anomaly. It seems likely, however, that the erasure of the novel as well as of the short story of the 1910s from the historical accounts of modern Chinese literature was motivated by ideology rather than by an inadequate understanding of the nature of literary development. In the early 1920s the May Fourth ideologues disparagingly considered fiction of the 1910s worthless, commercial kitsch. In this way, any threat presented by the artistic achievements of the previous decade to the May Fourth figures' claim of primacy in the modernization of Chinese culture could be, and was, successfully averted.

The Revival of the Short Story

As noted above, the term *hsiao-shuo* was used by the late Ch'ing reformers to designate fiction, drama, and storytelling as well as foreign fiction. However, when restricted to Chinese fiction of the day, it came to have only one meaning—the lengthy novel, divided into chapters. The reason for this shift in usage was apparently that, although the short story had flourished during the T'ang, Sung, Ming, and early Ch'ing dynasties, by the eighteenth century it had, for reasons not yet well understood, largely disappeared from the Chinese literary scene and thereby from the field of vision of the reformers.

Nevertheless, without being noticed by these reformers, the rise of the short story was in fact one of the most significant phenomena of the last Ch'ing decade. Many of these short stories were already mature and modern artistic works. Attention started to be paid to this new genre only in 1906, when a special section of *All-Story Monthly* was first reserved for short stories. Before then, short stories had appeared sporadically in various journals, but the fiction published there consisted mostly of serialized novels. The resurgence was closely bound with the forum that became available in regularly published periodicals. Interest in the short story was first manifested by the advertisements in the journals announcing the new genre as well as urging writers to submit manuscripts between two thousand and three thousand characters long (e.g., in *All-Story Monthly*, no. 14, 1908). Later, the length permitted was extended to a maximum of several thousand characters (in *Short Story Magazine*, vol. 3, no. 12, 1912).

It took some time before the short story was recognized as a genre of its own, distinct from the novel. Wu Chien-jen, reviewing several English books, admired the precise English nomenclature for works of fiction, which could distinguish between romance, novelette, story, tale, and fable (in *All-Story Monthly*, vol. 1, no. 5, 1907). Thus, between 1906 and 1907, *All-Story Monthly* introduced a section specially designated for *tuan-p'ien hsiao-shuo* (literally, short tales), which were divided thematically into historical, philosophical, nihilistic, detective, and social stories, as well as stories of passion, humorous tales, and so forth. It is not surprising that Wu Chien-jen, the editor-in-chief of the journal, and Chou Kuei-sheng, its main translator, became the principal contributors of short stories to the *All-Story Monthly*. Between 1906 and 1907, Wu published in the journal at least twelve of his own short stories, now considered the best ones written during the late Ch'ing. Hsü Nien-tz'u, in "My Views on Fiction" (discussed above), offers a detailed description of the differences between the novel and the short story, including statistics concerning the readership of the two genres among those of differing social backgrounds.

However, as the editors of both *All-Story Monthly* and *The Grove of Fiction* frequently emphasized, their interest in the short story was aroused by the artistic quality of the individual works rather than by the novelty of the genre. The choice of foreign short stories for translation confirms this bent toward artistic excellence. Among the early works translated were those by Henrik Sienkiewicz, Mark Twain, L. N. Tolstoy, Alphonse Daudet, and, above all, Guy de Maupassant, whose first work was translated in 1904 and whose popularity did not diminish during the next ten years. Perhaps the two works that contributed most to spreading knowledge of Western short story masterpieces were the *Collection of Stories from Abroad*, edited in 1909 by the Chou brothers, and the three-volume anthology *Ou Mei ming-chia tuan-p'ien hsiao-shuo ts'ung-k'o* (Collection of Short Stories by Renowned European and American Writers), published in 1917 by Chou Shou-chüan, who received special praise from Lu Hsün for this endeavor. In this anthology Chou Shou-chüan gathered together short stories by forty-seven writers from fourteen countries, including Italy, Spain, Sweden, the Netherlands, and Serbia, and each work was prefaced by an insightful biography of the author, along with a photograph. Here we must also mention the collection *Hsiao-shuo ming-hua ta-kuan* (Illustrated Panorama of Short Stories), compiled by Hu Chi-ch'en and published by Wen-ming shu-chü in Shanghai in 1916. It featured three hundred of the best Chinese short stories and translations from abroad that had been published up to that time. This is the most representative collection of short stories from the early Republican era.

Among the journals that specialized in short stories during the 1910s were *Short Story Magazine*, *Saturday*, *The World of Chinese Fiction*, and *Fiction*

Panorama. The most accomplished short story writers in the first half of the 1910s were Su Man-shu, Hsü Chen-ya, Ch'eng Shan-chih, Lin Shu, Chou Shou-chüan, Pao T'ien-hsiao, and Yeh Sheng-t'ao. Although Lu Hsün, writing under the pseudonym Chou Ch'o, published only one short story during this period—"Huai chiu" (Remembrances of the Past; in *Short Story Magazine*, vol. 4, no. 1, 1913)—this work is the harbinger of modernity in Chinese literature because of the author's ability to replace the habitual, chronologically arranged plot with loosely connected lyrical scenes presented from the unusual perspective of the first-person narrator—a child, representing the author himself.

As discussed above, the short story of the 1910s, very much like the Chinese theory of fiction of that period, was on the verge of becoming an integral part of modern world fictional prose because its numerous artistic advances were found strikingly similar to those observed in modern Western prose of the 1910s. These observations are based on the early short stories written in classical Chinese by Lu Hsün, Yeh Sheng-t'ao, Pao T'ien-hsiao, Su Man-shu, and Hsü Chen-ya. Yet, as tempting as it is to proceed here with an overview of the short story from the late Ch'ing to the early Republican era, such an attempt would be both premature and a bit presumptuous. As is the case with other genres from the period, from the early 1920s on, these works "disappeared." Indeed, already in 1918, Hu Shih, in "Lun tuan-p'ien hsiao-shuo" (On the Short Story; in *Hsin ch'ing-nien* [New Youth], vol. 4, no. 5), refrains from mentioning the wealth of Chinese short stories from the immediately preceding period, directing attention instead to Daudet and Maupassant as the most suitable foreign models for the modern Chinese short story. He also refers to several classical Chinese poems, such as Tu Fu's "Shih-hao li" (The Officer from Shih-hao Village) and Po Chü-yi's "Hsin feng che pi weng" (The Old Man with the Broken Arm from Hsin-feng), as excellent examples of short stories. Because materials were difficult to obtain, it was generally considered that the history of the modern Chinese short story started only with Lu Hsün's "K'uang-jen jih-chi" (Diary of a Madman; in *New Youth*, vol. 4, no. 5, April 1918).

Only recently as many as twenty-six short stories from the late Ch'ing period and thirty pieces from the early Republican era, together with a selection of novels and novelettes, were republished in collections such as the seven-volume *Chung-kuo chin-tai wen-hsüeh ta-hsi* (A Treasury of Early Modern Chinese Literature; in The Second Division: Fiction, no. 7; 1991) and *Chung-kuo chin-tai hsiao-shuo ta-hsi* (A Treasury of Early Modern Chinese Fiction; 1993). A still more adequate and balanced picture of the abundance of short stories from the late Ch'ing and early Republic had to await the publication of the monumental ten-volume compendium edited by Yü Jun-ch'i, *Ch'ing-mo min-ch'u hsiao-shuo shu-hsi* (A Compendium of Short Stories from the Late Ch'ing and Early Republican Era; 1997).

THE TRANSFORMATION OF TRADITIONAL FICTION

A careful assessment of the remarkable achievements in fiction that occurred during the waning years of the Ch'ing dynasty and the beginning of the Republican period reveals that fundamental changes occurred in virtually all aspects of both the novel and the short story. The rebirth of fiction in China did not have to wait until the May Fourth movement: it had already begun to take place ten to twenty or more years before.

Although there may have been some unsteady wavering on the matter of linguistic register (classical versus vernacular, and even occasionally some snatches of topolectal color), late Ch'ing and early Republican authors experimented with different forms and formats, first-person narrative, unprecedented subject matter, nonlinear plot development, and virtually all other aspects of the novel and the short story. While many of these changes were stimulated by fiction introduced from abroad, Chinese authors were deeply engaged in making them an integral part of their own literary heritage.

Milena Doleželová-Velingerová

Chapter 39

TWENTIETH-CENTURY FICTION

GENERAL HISTORICAL BACKGROUND

Among the minor branches of Chinese literature at the beginning of the twentieth century was fiction (*hsiao-shuo*; literally, "small talk"). Yet by the 1990s, the modern Chinese fiction scholar Fan Pó-ch'ün was waggishly referring to this indubitably dominant literary form as *ta-shuo* (large talk). Whether measured in terms of the number of novels and short story collections published annually or in terms of the circulation of literary journals that feature fiction rather than poetry or other types of prose, fiction had outstripped rival literary genres by the second decade of the twentieth century and has never lost its lead. Even as film and television narratives made serious inroads into the Chinese fiction readership toward the end of the century, the most successful screenplays have more often been reworkings of novels or stories than writings penned from scratch for the screen.

Chinese fiction's rise from the status of a pleasant but marginally edifying diversion to the dominant genre of serious writing occurred mostly during the final decade of the Ch'ing dynasty (1644–1911) and the first half of the Republican era (1911–1949). Although twentieth-century scholars of literature often pointed to the growth of fiction as the most significant Chinese literary development in both the Ming (1368–1644) and the Ch'ing dynasties, this is a retrospective view that would have struck nearly all the elite literati during the Ming and early to mid-Ch'ing as laughably erroneous. Classical poetry and essays (*shih-wen*) had been the dominant forms of serious literature for many centuries, and the vast majority of literati in the Ming and the Ch'ing would have deemed their epoch no exception to the rule.

The ascendancy of Chinese fiction since the late Ch'ing is due to economic and geopolitical factors as well as cultural trends. Although politicians and pundits have commonly emphasized the negative side of China's closer integration into global economic networks during the nineteenth and twentieth centuries, the impressive rate of ensuing urban economic development created new opportunities in the cultural realm. Late-nineteenth-century Chinese cities witnessed the unprecedented rise of a mass readership for a burgeoning press. Readers of the scores of newspapers, tabloids, and magazines that first emerged in the late nineteenth century thirsted for fiction, including short stories, translations of foreign fiction, and serialized novels. Shanghai emerged as the center of China's publishing industry, landmarks of which include the first indigenous publication of an enduring mass-market Chinese newspaper, *Shen pao* (Shanghai News; 1872), and the first publication of a Chinese literary journal, *Hai-shang ch'i-shu* (Marvelous Writings from Shanghai; 1892).

Even a leading eighteenth-century novelist like Wu Ching-tzu (1701–1754) had to supplement his writing income with funds from other sources, but the economic consequences of an emergent mass readership enabled many successful late Ch'ing novelists to support themselves entirely through writing. The symbiosis between fiction and mass journalism continued during the Republican era, as can be attested by the leap in circulation of the Shanghai newspaper *Hsin-wen pao* (The News) to 150,000 in 1929–1930, in the wake of serializing one of the century's most popular novels, Chang Hen-shui's (1895–1967) *T'i-hsiao yin-yüan* (Fate in Tears and Laughter; 1929–1930). The enduring popularity of hybrid prose genres like "reportage literature" (*pao-kao wen-hsüeh*) later in the century suggests the continuing involvement of mass-readership journalism with fiction.

The various geopolitical setbacks China suffered at the hands of the Western maritime powers and Japan in the late Ch'ing and early Republican period occasioned lamentable suffering and injustice—and yet hastened the end of China's relative isolation and awakened many concerned Chinese to the urgent need for reform in culture, family relations, and politics. The ancient complacent assumption that China was the unrivaled epicenter of world civilization, rather than one country among many peers, did not receive a mortal blow until China lost its last remaining protectorate, Korea, in the course of the Sino-Japanese War of 1894–1895. This trouncing by a neighboring East Asian country long viewed as only semicivilized and too weak to mount a serious threat suggested that China sorely needed thorough institutional reform of the sort that Japan had undergone since the Meiji Restoration of 1868. Moreover, the ceding of Taiwan and the Liaotung Peninsula to Japan under the terms of the 1895 Treaty of Shimonoseki marked a worrisome forfeiture of large and vital territories, not merely the nibbling away of distant sleepy borderlands or the extension of foreigners' extraterritorial privileges to a few more treaty ports.

A remarkable Chinese cultural ferment in the aftermath of the mid-1890s debacle led to widespread demands to overhaul various anachronistic institutions like the impractical "eight-legged" civil service examination essay (*pa-ku-wen*). The Kuang-hsü Emperor responded in 1898 with an ambitious reform program somewhat reminiscent of the Japanese Meiji initiatives, but a palace coup led by the empress dowager soon sequestered him in house arrest and put a brutal stop to the reforms, driving many progressive literati, such as Liang Ch'i-ch'ao (1873–1929), into exile in Japan. Further Manchu dynastic outrages, such as the disastrous decision in 1900 to support the Boxers and their mob violence against foreigners and Chinese with foreign connections, only intensified the outspokenness and iconoclasm of Chinese literati. These disasters provoked a strong desire among the literati to understand what key factors had been preventing China from keeping pace with the growth in "wealth and power" (*fu-ch'iang*) of the West and modern Japan.

In a 1902 essay, "Lun hsiao-shuo yü ch'ün-chih chih kuan-hsi" (On the Relationship Between Fiction and Popular Government), Liang Ch'i-ch'ao came up with an influential if bookish suggestion on how to strengthen China in response to a multitude of threats at home and abroad. Claiming that traditional Chinese fiction had abused its great potential for societal betterment by playing a hugely destructive role in propagating such social ills as superstition and lawlessness, Liang argues for the inculcation of a truly public-spirited and educated citizenry through "New Fiction" (*hsin hsiao-shuo*), which was also the title of the journal he founded at that time (see chapter 38). Because traditional Chinese fiction seemed deficient in the kind of enlightened didactic novels that Liang and other reformers called for, and in the wake of heightened curiosity about the international scene, Chinese translations of European and American fiction were churned out so rapidly that they outpaced homegrown fiction by 1907.

While hindsight indicates that the sort of Western-style reformist fiction championed by Liang Ch'i-ch'ao could not work the kind of socially transformative wonders that he envisioned, this fiction did have some ameliorative effects. For instance, its illustration of more equitable alternatives to China's arranged-marriage system did stimulate much debate among Chinese literati and probably hastened the decline of concubinage and arranged marriages in twentieth-century China. Chinese women's status in the twentieth century doubtless improved more because of fairer marriage laws than because of reform-minded novelists' efforts, but this period's unprecedented growth in the proportion of female novelists relative to their male counterparts suggests that Chinese women enjoyed far more opportunities in this realm than during previous centuries.

Despite Liang Ch'i-ch'ao's arguments to the contrary, the status of traditional Chinese vernacular fiction as a secondary model for twentieth-century Chinese fiction improved with increasing research in this field during and after the late Ch'ing. For instance, the famous literary scholar Wang Kuo-wei (1877–1927) asserted that the eighteenth-century novel *Hung-lou meng* (A Dream of Red Towers), by Ts'ao Hsüeh-ch'in (c. 1724–1764), stands alone among traditional vernacular masterpieces as the only thoroughgoing tragedy in the history of premodern Chinese fiction and drama. Ts'ao's masterpiece strongly colors the fiction of writers like Chang Ai-ling (Eileen Chang; 1920–1995), who knew the novel by heart. Writers such as Wu Tsu-hsiang (1908–1994) adopted *A Dream of Red Towers* as a kind of textbook of masterly vernacular phraseology, while even disparagers of Ts'ao Hsüeh-ch'in's novel, such as Wu Chien-jen (1867–1910), viewed it as a standard against which contemporary novels were invariably compared.

The status of fiction also increased at the expense of classical prose and poetry, which gradually lost the backing of the state. The decline and debasement of the civil service examination system during the 1890s and its final abolition in 1905 removed a key incentive for the study of classical poetry and prose and provided a corresponding stimulus to the development of vernacular fiction in the twentieth century. The accompanying eclipse in the standing of Confucianism among most Chinese literati led to greater interest in rival systems of thought, including imports from Japan and the West that were often explored in fictional works and criticism. The gradual internationalization of twentieth-century Chinese fiction was not an unmixed blessing, but it did stimulate a greater variety of authorial style and topical range than was found in most earlier centuries.

Vernacular fiction quickly gained respectability when adopted as the genre of choice by early-twentieth-century writers as divergent as Liu O (1857–1909), the discoverer of the ancient Shang dynasty oracle-bone script, and Lu Hsün (pseudonym of Chou Shu-jen; 1881–1936), whose 1918 story "K'uang-jen jih-chi" (Diary of a Madman) was a key prelude to the outpouring of fiction of social reform and protest that emerged with the May Fourth New Culture movement beginning in 1919. When the victorious allies at the 1919 Versailles Peace Conference decided to transfer Germany's extraterritorial privileges in Shantung province to Japan, rather than abolish these privileges as an infringement upon China's sovereignty, students and many other Chinese urbanites organized large-scale protests and lengthy boycotts. These slights by the international community were blamed on China's weakness, which in turn seemed to originate from China's anachronistic cultural traditions. Fiction was the preferred vehicle for change in the ensuing New Culture movement, which repeated Liang Ch'i-ch'ao's call for a new type of writing that would self-consciously contribute to cultural and societal advancement.

Vernacular fiction also achieved broader acceptance throughout society than the more experimental genres like vernacular poetry, which several leading fiction writers, including Lu Hsün and Yü Ta-fu (1896–1945), avoided in favor of classical poetry. Similarly, the new nonoperatic *hua-chü* (spoken drama), a form derived from Euro-American models, violated the traditional formalistic expectations of Chinese theater audiences much more severely than the new vernacular fiction confounded its readership with unfamiliarity (see chapter 42). In part for this reason, a surprisingly large number of the century's leading Chinese fiction writers who had a dramatic flair for crafting vivid and memorable dialogue did not write even a single *hua-chü*.

China's fictional output and variety suffered heavy blows during World War II (in China called the War of Anti-Japanese Resistance; 1937–1945), during the Chinese civil war that followed in its wake (1946–1949), and especially during the three subsequent decades of unprecedentedly stringent political controls on literature in the People's Republic of China (PRC) by the ruling Chinese Communist Party (CCP). Fortunately, some countervailing factors mitigated the damage.

In spite of the fact that the average annual number of new mainland Chinese novel titles dropped from about a hundred and fifty before 1949 to no more than seven (an astonishingly small figure for a nation of China's size) during the three subsequent decades of Maoist rule, translations of foreign literature increased in variety and quality. The availability of relatively high-quality translated novels allowed readers and writers to hone their literary sensibilities in anticipation of the day when the CCP's controls on Chinese fiction would be eased, thereby permitting the publication of less tendentious novels than the ones that appeared in the 1950s and 1960s.

Translations were not subject to such strict Maoist political controls as fiction and other literature, but there were other ways of eluding the censor's scissors. Uncensored hand-copied novels and stories were widely read and circulated during the Maoist era (1949–1976). Although these popular works were often melodramatic and poor in overall literary quality, they at least helped prevent many Chinese readers from giving up on their country's contemporary literature altogether. Furthermore, the PRC's lack of control over publishers and writers in Hong Kong, Singapore, and especially Taiwan allowed fiction there to develop along largely independent lines and to improve significantly in quality in these Chinese-speaking territories. Much of this fiction and the fiction of expatriates abroad made its way back to mainland China, often through unofficial channels, and became a stimulus in the PRC for more creative approaches to fiction writing. By the mid- to late 1980s, authors on both sides of the Taiwan Strait were publishing a broad array of contemporary fiction from the "other side" of the strait—something that had been rare to nonexistent for most of the previous thirty-five years.

As heavy as the controls on fiction were during the Maoist period, they were less stringent than government restrictions on films. Because films reached a broader audience than did fiction, CCP elders deemed cinema to have a wider and thus more worrisome influence on political attitudes among the populace. Sharp criticism of the status quo in a novel or story was toned down or even excised in the cinematic version of the work. Beginning in the 1980s, Chinese filmmakers won more latitude for implementing their projects through such means as joint productions with foreign studios, which in turn provided alternative distribution channels for these films.

Even though both Mao Tse-tung (1893–1976) and Chiang K'ai-shek (1887–1975), mid-century strongmen who led the People's Republic of China on the mainland and the Republic of China on Taiwan, respectively, imposed repressive political controls on writers whose obedience they doubted, the heavy-handed measures they often took to silence unwelcome writers worked in favor of these writers in the long run. Readers often shrewdly assumed that any novel that the paramount leader found infuriating enough to denounce must be well worth taking the trouble to read. Many writers have wryly pointed to an angry and vengeful political leader as their best publicist. Some political leaders even resurrected a centuries-old novel in order to make a contemporary political point. In 1975, Mao Tse-tung and his followers made a noisy if indirect assault upon Teng Hsiao-p'ing's (1904–1997) relatively pragmatic economic ideas through headline-grabbing denunciations of the rebel leader Sung Chiang of the Ming novel *Shui-hu chuan* (Water Margin; see chapter 35). Insisting that Sung Chiang was a "capitulationist" who had sold out his band of virtuous outlaws to the corrupt imperial court, Mao implied that Teng's support for using some material incentives in economic production amounted to a sellout to capitalism. Mao's attempt to thwart the growth of Chinese economic pragmatism would fail miserably in the end, but this eleventh-hour gambit unwittingly underscored the significant public role that fiction has been widely thought to play in the twentieth century.

After Mao Tse-tung died in 1976, the stage was set for a cultural thaw reminiscent of the Soviet Union's cultural regeneration in the wake of Stalin's death in 1953. By 1980, China's cultural thaw had brought about dramatic improvements in the quality and quantity of PRC fiction. The deepening of stylistic variety and broadening of novelistic vistas continued apace throughout the final two decades of the century, in spite of periodic government crackdowns on writers for their alleged role in spreading "spiritual pollution" (*ching-shen wu-jan*) in 1983–1984 and "counterrevolutionary turmoil" (*fan-ko-ming tung-luan*) in 1989.

Since the late 1970s, occasional attempts by zealous Communist bureaucrats to turn the clock back to an earlier age replete with made-to-order legends of selfless Communist "boy scouts" like the People's Liberation Army (PLA) sapper Lei Feng (1939–1962) simply did not work. Instead, the formerly yawning gap in literary quality between mainland fiction and the far less political fiction of Taiwan continued to narrow. By 1990, Taiwan had become a primary publishing market for aspiring PRC writers and critics to break into, thereby presenting an alternative and a challenge to the largely state-controlled PRC publishing industry. Unfortunately, the lack of even a single Nobel Prize in literature for a

Chinese writer—until its presentation to the expatriate Kao Hsing-chien (1940–) in 2000—continued to be a vexing issue on both sides of the Taiwan Strait. At the end of the twentieth century, Chinese novelists had yet to achieve the degree of international acclaim already won by their compatriots in filmmaking. Still, these fiction writers' achievements are so multifarious as to make the following survey far from comprehensive, as many deserving novels and authors must go unmentioned in order to provide a reasonably informative account of the works included—particularly among novelists in the latter half of the century, on which far less scholarly consensus exists as to their relative merit.

A SURVEY OF SOME REPRESENTATIVE TWENTIETH-CENTURY NOVELS AND STORIES

The first period of twentieth-century fiction, 1897–1916, begins with the cultural ferment in the wake of China's mid-1890s debacle in the struggle with Japan and ends in 1916, the year before the systematic vernacularization of the literary language was inaugurated. The collapse of China's last imperial dynasty in 1911 and the founding of the Republic of China shortly thereafter were of immense political import but had relatively little direct impact on the development of fiction. Because the first few years of the Republic represent a continuity in literary development with the late Ch'ing, this two-decade period could be called the "extended late Ch'ing." Many patterns in the popular fiction of this period continued largely unbroken throughout the remainder of the century, but the late 1910s mark a watershed in the literature by and for the elite intelligentsia.

Scholars generally consider the extended late Ch'ing a transitional period between earlier fiction of a traditional type and the increasingly foreign-colored varieties of fiction in subsequent decades. As in earlier fiction from the nineteenth century, the extended late Ch'ing favored the novel over the short story, featured traditional *chang-hui* (linked-chapter) novels that were relatively loose and episodic in structure, mustered at least an indirect affirmation of certain Confucian values, and continued the two-track development of fiction in either the vernacular or the classical idiom. Extended late Ch'ing fiction's innovative developments include an emphasis on contemporary sociohistorical phenomena, wandering protagonists whose Chineseness tends to overshadow any regional sensibility, a great expansion of semiautobiographical narration, an absorption with sentiment and the psychology of key characters, and more personalized varieties of descriptive prose and interior monolog.

In many ways, the vast sweep of China's literary inheritance has undoubtedly been a boon to Chinese writers of recent vintage. Yet these latter-day writers have enjoyed such a broad array of ready-made descriptive phrases from which to choose that their own descriptive passages often amount to little more than rearrangements of hackneyed classical phraseology, most typically of four characters in a four-syllable rhythmic unit (see chapter 12). The drab predictability of an excessively parallel prose rhythm has compounded the dearth of originality and freshness in numerous latter-day descriptive passages. One sad result of this approach to narrative description has been a sort of studio art that has often cocooned itself away from the direct observation of either nature or the writer's social milieu, including popular oral performances.

Liu O rejected this bookish studio approach, instead emphasizing prose description based on personal observation. His memorable and compelling descriptions of drum-singer performances and natural landscapes in *Lao Ts'an yu-chi* (The Travels of Lao Ts'an; 1908) allow for a more personalized diction and expressiveness than most earlier Chinese novelists could muster in their descriptive passages. Although *Travels* is the only novel Liu O ever wrote, many literary historians have viewed it as the first truly great novel of twentieth-century China, praising it as a model of unclichéd narrative description. Hu Shih (1891–1962), the famous scholarly champion of vernacular Chinese literature over its classical-language counterpart, edited a well-received 1925 Chinese edition of *Travels* that greatly furthered this novel's ascendancy to the status of a textbook prose model for aspiring novelist and ordinary student alike.

Liu O's highly unorthodox career resonates with his rejection of traditional Chinese patterns of prose description. He probably could have followed the conventional route to officialdom, for his father had served as a high official, and Liu O himself proved his mettle by directing a successful government flood-control project along the notoriously flood-prone Yellow River. Yet Liu O turned aside from the luxurious drudgery of official life to develop talents that led him in many different directions. For instance, he pioneered the collection of Shang dynasty oracle-bone writing specimens and plunged into risky business ventures in railroads and mining. His impressive knowledge of traditional Chinese medicine allowed him to make a living for a while as a traditional house-call doctor. Eventually, China's stunning humiliation in the Sino-Japanese War of 1894–1895 and the Boxer Rebellion of 1900 imparted a sense of urgency to Liu O's reformist inclinations. As China came to be known by the epithet of "the sick man of East Asia" around the turn of the twentieth century, it seemed that the once-proud Celestial Empire desperately needed individuals like Liu O who had enough intelligence and imagination to make a try at diagnosing China's illnesses and prescribing potent remedies.

Travels embodies a search for the golden mean between the extremes of xenophobic traditionalism, as represented by the Boxers, and wholesale Westernization, as promoted by the various Chinese revolutionaries of that time. Liu O begins his novel with an imaginative allegory of a huge but crowded and leaky sailing vessel, whose commanding officers stubbornly reject the wise and well-intentioned advice offered by the middle-aged bachelor protagonist, Lao Ts'an ("Old Derelict"), and other educated reformist friends who have rowed a small boat alongside the huge ship. Details involving the ship's length and the number of its masts are far from coincidental; rather, they indicate that the vessel unmistakably stands for China in the author's allegorical scheme. An earnest desire to persuade influential officials to keep the well-being of ordinary people uppermost in their minds colors Lao Ts'an's actions throughout much of the novel, even though he is retiring by nature and actively avoids officials who think they would be doing him a favor to elevate him to a position in the bureaucracy.

The allegory so prominent in chapter 1 mostly recedes to the background in favor of the novel's dominant mode of a moderately satiric realism. This process occurs while Lao Ts'an assists and befriends effective and just officials who value his talents and advice—and endeavors to undo the harm perpetrated by cruel and ambitious officials like Kang Pi and Yü Hsien.

The only important variation from the dominant mode of realism in the novel after the first allegorical chapter occurs near the middle of the novel during a series of often abstruse philosophical discourses deep within a mountain retreat. This idyllic interlude functions largely to articulate the author's convictions about the many benefits of philosophical syncretism. In this view, a selective synthesis of key ideas from the three main strains of traditional Chinese thought since the Han dynasty (206 B.C.E.–220 C.E.)—Confucianism, Taoism, and Buddhism—allows China to lay the soundest foundation upon which Western innovations can be effectively built. Both the author's semiautobiographical protagonist and the sagacious hermit Yellow Dragon strongly disapprove of the emotional antiforeignism of the Boxers and reactionary officials, on the one hand, and the unreflective aping of the West by overzealous Chinese revolutionists, on the other.

As an illustration of Lao Ts'an's support for selective rather than wholesale Westernization of China, he believes his country needs to develop the legal incentives for technological invention that Western patent law provides. After describing the ingenious design of a Chinese opium lamp whose inventor never emerged from anonymity, Lao Ts'an argues that, even where controversial issues like opium addiction are involved, China's prospects for development and prosperity will remain cloudy if the inventor of such a device wins no recognition or patent rights for his invention.

Liu O's emotional restraint and equanimity during satirical episodes of his novel contrast favorably with the practice of many lesser late Ch'ing dynasty satirical novelists, who tended to indulge in hyperbole and vent so much bitterness that Lu Hsün disparaged their work as "novels of condemnation" (*ch'ien-tse hsiao-shuo*). As an example, among more than a hundred officials portrayed in Li Po-yüan's (Li Pao-chia; 1867–1906) episodic exposé *Kuan-ch'ang hsien-hsing chi* (Exposure of the World of Officials; 1906), not even one is untainted by corruption. Liu O understood well the seriousness of government bribery and influence peddling, but he believed that an overemphasis on these kinds of official wrongdoing diverted attention from an equally grave betrayal of the public trust: the incorruptible official who strives for promotion and fame rather than monetary gain and who sees nothing wrong in gaining a reputation for tough decisiveness by forcing draconian measures upon the unfortunate populace under his authority.

Both of Liu O's two key targets of satire, Kang Pi and Yü Hsien, are "upright" officials of this careerist bent. In order to redress the grievances caused by these two officials' gross miscarriages of justice, Lao Ts'an must draw upon his personal contacts with wiser and more humane officials and sally forth on Holmesian detective gambits. As an ordinary commoner without an official degree, Lao Ts'an risks his life when standing up to Kang Pi and Yü Hsien, yet he enjoys great success in seeking justice and a return to normalcy for these officials' innocent victims of torture and imprisonment.

Although *Travels of Lao Ts'an* recounts many harrowing incidents resulting from rampaging floods and the two officials' cruel punishment of various innocents, the novel is comic overall. Besides bringing about a reversal of the most unjust verdicts passed down by the two officials, Lao Ts'an and his amiable friend Huang Jen-jui both rescue young female flood victims of good family from a grim life of prostitution by marrying them at the conclusion of the novel. Sadly, Liu O did not himself survive the hardships of exile inflicted on him in 1909 by vengeful late Ch'ing officials like the would-be emperor Yüan Shih-k'ai (1859–1916); Liu O died later that same year in the distant wastes of Chinese Turkestan. Ironically, the most genial satire of the late Ch'ing came from the pen of a man who would soon encounter the cruelest fate suffered by his generation of leading novelists.

Another key masterpiece of late Ch'ing fiction that recounts arduous trials and the protagonist's resourcefulness and moral fiber is Wu Chien-jen's *Hen hai* (The Sea of Regret; 1906), the most famous short novel of its day. Instead of focusing on a scholarly reformist like Lao Ts'an, Wu Chien-jen provides a compelling and intimate portrayal of Chang Ti-hua, an urbane young woman from Kwangtung province whose ingrained Confucian sense of duty to her mother and fiancé is sorely tested by a series of catastrophes resulting from the Boxer Rebellion of 1900. Ti-hua is fleeing Peking for Tientsin with her ailing mother, her fiancé, Ch'en Po-ho, and some servants, when she and her mother get separated from Po-ho amid crowds of panicked refugees. Although Ti-hua modestly blames herself for not having better handled matters such as her mother's worsening illness, she exemplifies filial devotion by going so far as to cut out and cook a small piece of flesh from her arm as a tonic for her mother. Much later, after Ti-hua learns that Po-ho has sunk into debauchery, indulging in a brief marriage with a notorious prostitute and developing an addiction to opium, she nonetheless holds fast to her original engagement vows. Po-ho's dissolute ways prove too ingrained for even her to change, but as his health fails she stays by his sickbed, nursing him day and night. After he dies, she insists on keeping her engagement vows by shaving her head and taking up permanent residence in a Buddhist nunnery.

In *The Sea of Regret,* Wu Chien-jen defends Confucian mores and the traditional arranged-marriage system from the growing ranks of Chinese intellectuals who preferred the Western practice of letting youth of marriageable age decide such matters for themselves. Even readers who find Ti-hua overly self-critical and straitlaced must admit that her internal monologues are psychologically compelling and artfully conceived. These deft internal monologues constitute a major advance in the Chinese vernacular novel's ability to represent character psychology and are even more innovative than the first-person narration with which Wu Chien-jen famously experimented in *Erh-shih nien mu-tu chih kuai hsien-chuang* (Strange Scenes Witnessed in the Past Twenty Years; 1905–1910).

Many of the most wildly popular novels of the late Ch'ing and subsequent periods ennobled the sufferings of passionate but virtuous young protagonists, who encounter one obstacle after another in search of an ideal union in "tales of brilliant scholars and beautiful girls" (*ts'ai-tzu chia-jen*). One such novel in classical Chinese is Hsü Chen-ya's (1889–1937?) *Yü li hun* (The Soul of the Jade Pear Flowers; 1912), which unfolds a kind of ill-fated love triangle that has fascinated so many novelists of bittersweet sentimentality and their giant readership. A talented but frustrated tutor named Ho Meng-hsia falls in love with his pupil's mother, the beautiful and kindly widow poetess Lady Pear Flower (*Li-niang*). She responds sympathetically but very obliquely to his entreaties, for the two seldom meet. Similar to Student Chang and Ts'ui Ying-ying of Yüan Chen's "Ying-ying chuan" (Story of Ying-ying) and Wang Shih-fu's "Hsi-hsiang chi" (Romance of the Western Chamber), Ho and Lady Pear Flower communicate mainly through letters and poems in an ornately parallelistic classical idiom. She would like to marry Ho, but feels that she cannot break her vow of chastity to her late husband, so instead arranges for her sister-in-law to marry him, over the initial objections of both Ho and the sister-in-law.

Doom begins to engulf the central characters as Lady Pear Flower realizes that Ho will remain frustrated as long as she is alive. Lady Pear Flower thereupon decides to do away with herself, and does so gradually by refusing all food and medicine. The sister-in-law subsequently becomes very ill after finding out about Lady Pear Flower's ultimate sacrifice and dies in turn. Distraught at these two women's deaths, Ho departs to join the revolutionary army. He dies heroically in combat at Wuhan, a decisive conflict in the revolutionary army's defeat of the Ch'ing forces in 1911.

Although this novel's flower-burying scene is but one of its many echoes of *Dream of Red Towers* and its traditional love-triangle quandary, Hsü's heavy use of interior monologue to reveal complex character psychology sets this novel apart from its premodern counterparts. All in all, *The Soul of the Jade Pear Flowers* appealed to the reader who wanted to explore escalating tensions between individual yearning and traditional pieties, yet not discard those pieties or the literary conventions for articulating them.

The inauguration of the Vernacular Literature movement (1917) and the subsequent May Fourth New Culture movement had a wide-ranging influence on fiction written by and for the elite intelligentsia, but in the popular realm of best-selling fiction achieved little more than hastening both the vernacularization of popular fiction and the importation of foreign popular literature and film. Later generations of popular novelists wrote in the vernacular instead of Hsü Chen-ya's classical idiom, but continued to draw heavily upon his preferred formulas like the bittersweet "tales of brilliant scholars and beautiful girls" and the self-sacrificing spirit of knight-errantry represented by Ho's impetuous eleventh-hour leap into the thick of armed revolutionary struggle.

Chang Hen-shui succeeded in writing one of the three or four most popular novels of the century, *Fate in Tears and Laughter* (1929–1930), precisely by skillfully combining features of "knight-errantry fiction" (*wu-hsia hsiao-shuo*) with the "tales of brilliant scholars and beautiful girls." In a plot full of twists and turns, an educated young man in Peking named Fan Chia-shu becomes enmeshed in a love triangle with the humble but beautiful ballad singer Shen Feng-hsi and the wealthy and gorgeous society girl Ho Li-na. Feng-hsi's unscrupulous uncle sells her into concubinage with a sadistic general, whose harshness toward her drives her insane. Fan's two knight-errant friends, a father-and-daughter martial arts duo, get revenge on the wicked general and also free Fan from kidnappers, enabling him to reunite with Ho Li-na in a comic finale. The couple's joy is tinged with their grief in mourning the knight-errant father and daughter, who have just died in one of China's many internecine battles in the first half of the century.

Fate in Tears and Laughter contains some references to 1920s' Hollywood films familiar to the novel's Shanghai-based readership. Nevertheless, Chang's novel resembles most other novels in the knight-errant and scholar-beauty genres in drawing largely on indigenous literary patterns. For instance, Chang admits having fashioned his dashing young female knight-errant directly on the young heroine Thirteenth Younger Sister (*Shih-san-mei*) in Wen K'ang's (1798–1872) *Erh-nü ying-hsiung chuan* (Tales of Boy and Girl Heroes; 1878?).

By contrast, leading Chinese detective novelists in Chang Hen-shui's generation like Ch'eng Hsiao-ch'ing (1893–1977) and Sun Liao-hung (1897–1958) closely followed Western models of this popular genre. Ch'eng Hsiao-ch'ing's master sleuth, Huo Sang, is directly modeled after Arthur Conan Doyle's Sherlock Holmes, while Sun Liao-hung's debonair con man–turned–detective, Lu P'ing, is fashioned closely on Maurice Leblanc's Arsène Lupin. Although indigenous traditions of literary detection from Judge Pao stories (based on legends about the sagacious and incorruptible Pao Cheng [999–1062]) and the like contributed something to these twentieth-century Chinese detective novels, the foreign influence loomed much larger.

Foreign cultural influences are particularly noticeable in fiction by and for the intelligentsia in the wake of the vernacular literature movement and May fourth New Culture movement, which lasted from 1917 to 1937. In Lu Hsün's bombshell story of 1918, "Diary of a Madman," he borrowed the title and diary format directly from Nikolai Gogol. At the same time, the Chinese setting and cultural contexts of this and most other intelligentsia fiction indicate this kind of fiction's propensity for sociocultural critique. For instance, Lu Hsün published this innovative story in *Hsin ch'ing-nien* (La Jeunesse; New Youth), the same avidly reformist journal that had published Hu Shih's and Ch'en Tu-hsiu's (1879–1942) polemics for a new vernacular literature during the previous year. Moreover, the catalyst for the protagonist's madness is his foreboding sense that China's moralistic classics have the words "eat people" (*ch'ih jen*) here and there on the margins of the pages, and that the town locals would apparently like to kill and eat him, too. Although the protagonist's brother breaks into the narration to assure us that his paranoid brother was later cured of his madness, the author no doubt suggests that the protagonist could develop sensitivity to the inhumane and cruel aspects of traditional Chinese culture only during his seemingly demented estrangement from the other townsfolk and their folkways. Depictions of almost matter-of-fact cannibalism can indeed be found in many premodern novels like *Water Margin*, and many young, disaffected intellectuals seized upon this story's linking of cannibalism with China's cultural inheritance to emphasize the urgency of drastic cultural change.

Lu Hsün continued to write short stories in this outspokenly critical spirit in the late 1910s and early 1920s, and before long published them in two influential collections, *Na-han* (Battlecry; 1923) and *P'ang-huang* (Hesitation; 1926). Among all these pieces, "Ah Q cheng-chuan" (The True Story of Ah Q) was his most influential story both in China and abroad. The satirized protagonist Ah Q is a sort of ne'er-do-well Everyman, whose many serious flaws in character represent common shortcomings in what Lu Hsün conceived as the "Chinese national character." Ah Q's misadventures reveal such flaws in the "national character" as fearing the strong while bullying the weak, rationalizing defeats as spiritual victories, and delighting in the misery of one's fellow human beings (*Schadenfreude*).

In a Rousseauist manner, Lu Hsün more than once expressed his hope that Chinese children could be "saved" from the "degeneration" of the civilization that had long since corrupted their elders—the closing line of "Diary of a Madman" exhorts the reader to "save the children." Yet in stories like "Ku-hsiang" (My Old Home; 1921), the semiautobiographical middle-aged narrator's fond memories of a lively boyhood friend collide with the grim reality of the superstitious, status-conscious, and care-burdened farmer the friend has grown up to become. Having lost hope in the social efficacy of his fiction with a contemporary setting, Lu Hsün abandoned it around 1926 in favor of other types of writing, primarily barbed polemical essays.

Lu Hsün is widely regarded as the greatest Chinese writer of the twentieth century. At his birth he was called Chou Shu-jen, a name that has almost been forgotten, along with his 139 pen names other than Lu Hsün. The details of his life, many of which can be gleaned from his own writings and the writings of his acquaintances, reveal the origins and depth of his passionately patriotic desire to change China. Although he never completed a full-length novel, the sum total of his short stories, essays, translations, letters, and miscellaneous pieces is impressive, and their impact on Chinese society at large is unsurpassed by that of any other twentieth-century Chinese author.

Besides being an outstanding creative writer and perceptive critic, Lu Hsün was also a solid scholar of Chinese literature. His *Chung-kuo hsiao-shuo shih-lüeh* (Brief History of Chinese Fiction), written in classical Chinese and first published in 1923–1924 by Peking University, and *Han wen-hsüeh shih kang-yao* (Outline of the History of Chinese Literature), as well as the vernacular appendix of the former, "Chung-kuo hsiao-shuo pien-ch'ien shih" (History of the Development of Chinese Fiction), plus his invaluable anthology of old fiction culled from various more or less obscure sources published under the title *Ku hsiao-shuo kou-ch'en* (1910/1938), are all still used as basic reference books by serious sinologists who specialize in traditional Chinese fiction.

Finally, it should be noted that Lu Hsün was an ardent advocate of language reform. Scattered throughout his essays are vitriolic attacks on the difficulty of learning and using Chinese characters. He even makes subtle complaints about the unwieldiness of the script in several of his short stories. The booklet cleverly titled *Men-wai wen t'an* (A Layman's View of [the Chinese] Script) is a learned, witty masterpiece that clearly and accurately analyzes the history, formation, nature, function, and limits of the characters, together with their—in his opinion—detrimental effect on the Chinese nation. *A Layman's View of (the Chinese) Script* is essential reading for anyone who is serious about understanding the medium of Chinese writing and its effects upon Chinese society.

Not long after Lu Hsün's death in 1936, Chinese Communist leaders and cultural cadres began the long process of canonizing him as a sort of infallible literary patron saint, even though Lu Hsün had feuded bitterly with prominent Communist functionaries like Chou Yang (1908–1989) during the 1930s.

A second pioneer of the May Fourth era short story was Yü Ta-fu, whose first collection of short stories, *Ch'en-lun* (Sinking; 1921), appeared even before Lu Hsün's *Battlecry*. Like Lu Hsün, he hailed from the wealthy lower Yangtze province of Chekiang and had studied in Japan for several years. But Yü Ta-fu was far more romantic in bent, emphasizing self-absorbed individual confession at the expense of sociocultural critique. All three stories in *Sinking* are semiautobiographical and feature self-pitying, sickly, and sexually frustrated Chinese students in Japan.

The protagonist in the story for which the collection is named, "Sinking," experiences extreme mood swings between the ecstasy of reciting romantic nature rhapsodies and agonizing guilt over his compulsions to masturbate and peep at the innkeeper's daughter undressing for a bath. Fortunately, the narrator's ironic comments on the protagonist's erratic behavior prevent this romantic amalgam of Rousseauist confession and Wertherian *Weltschmerz* from descending into bathos. Moreover, in a scene like the protagonist's ridiculously clumsy encounter with a Japanese prostitute, the story presents a curious tension between such trivial happenings and the grandiosity of the young man's excuse for his failure: it is China's greatly diminished stature in the world that is to blame for this, not his personal shortcomings! This failure to distinguish between the realms of the individual and the nation-state was not unusual among Yü Ta-fu's largely romantic generation of writers and was a polarizing force among the literary intelligentsia.

Unlike Yü Ta-fu, most romantic writers of his generation eventually gravitated toward Marxism and other types of political radicalism. The Szechwanese Kuo Mo-jo's (1892–1978) "Ma-k'o-ssu chin K'ung miao" (Marx Enters the Confucian Temple; 1923) takes a mockingly adversarial stance toward traditional Confucian values, presenting Marx as superior in every way. Similarly, Kuo Mo-jo's "Han-ku kuan" (The Han-ku Pass; 1923) burlesques Lao Tzu by having the originator of Taoism abjectly confess to having cut open the veins of his ill-fated ox and drunk all its blood in order to stave off thirst in the western desert. The gatekeeper at the Han-ku Pass had formerly admired Lao Tzu and his philosophy, but now indignantly decides to follow Lao Tzu's shamefaced advice to burn his copy of *Tao te ching* (Classic of Integrity and the Way). Ironically, during his later career as a powerful PRC establishment intellectual and cultural bureaucrat, Kuo Mo-jo would adopt the same self-flagellating tactic in the chaotic early phase of the Cultural Revolution (1966–1976); he adroitly deflected Red Guard denunciations by hurriedly announcing that all his literary writings were so flawed that they should at once be burned.

In contrast to the May Fourth romantics' Creation Society (Ch'uang-tsao she), the Literary Research Society (Wen-hsüeh yen-chiu hui) advocated literary realism and a more dispassionate approach to literary expression; its leading members included Yeh Sheng-t'ao (pseudonym of Yeh Shao-chün; 1894–1988), Mao Tun (pseudonym of Shen Yen-ping; 1896–1981), and Hsü Ti-shan (1893–1941). Yeh-Sheng-t'ao excelled in individual character portraiture; his "Ma-ling kua" (Horse-Bell Melons; 1923) is an early Chinese experiment with the rarely used inadequate narrator. A schoolboy serves as the wide-eyed participant narrator, who is trying to pass the civil service examination on the eve of that decaying selection system's abolition in 1905. Yeh Sheng-t'ao was disillusioned by the Nationalist leader Chiang K'ai-shek's abrupt break with the Communists in 1927, and expressed the sense of futility felt by much of the urban intelligentsia in his 1930 novel *Ni Huan-chih* (the protagonist's name).

As an early but secret convert to communism, Mao Tun preferred a broader canvas that could portray the "inevitable" debacle in store for China's traditional rural economy and urban capitalist sector. His story "Ch'un ts'an" (Spring Silkworms; 1932) suggests that even a model rural family working day and night at rice farming and sericulture will surely bankrupt itself under the existing global economic order. His later novel *Tzu-yeh* (Midnight; 1933) injects a similar sense of inevitability into the portrayal of how a clever and hard-working business tycoon is brought down by an inexorable combination of forces, including restive workers and foreign financial support for his competitors. Like Yeh Sheng-t'ao and Kuo Mo-jo, Mao Tun took high positions in the PRC literary bureaucracy and stopped writing fiction after 1949.

Although also a long-standing member of the Literary Research Association, Hsü Ti-shan tempered his reformist leanings with an unusual amount of independent and original thinking—and also had a strong interest in religions, such as Buddhism and Christianity. Instead of portraying women as passive or victimized objects of sympathy, he specialized in heroines resourceful enough to challenge patriarchal restrictions in pragmatic ways. In the story "Ch'un-t'ao" (1934), the married heroine of that name eventually starts cohabiting with her business partner, Hsiang-kao, for her husband was forcibly impressed into the military on their wedding night, and she has heard nothing from him since. Ch'un-t'ao repeatedly turns down Hsiang-kao's marriage proposals, since she still considers her first marriage valid. When Ch'un-t'ao's husband suddenly shows up one day, now crippled and begging for a living, Ch'un-t'ao suggests that all three of them can get along fine together in the same household. Each of the two men objects and offers to be the one to depart, but Ch'un-t'ao eventually convinces both of them to stay. They do in fact wind up all living together on reasonably amicable terms; pragmatic flexibility proves more effective than windy ideology in challenging traditional family norms. Hsü Ti-shan's novella *Yü-kuan* (1939) also provides a believable portrait of a barely educated and occasionally obtuse heroine, the title character, who is nonetheless capable of formulating and implementing solutions to problems too thorny for others to solve.

Beginning in the late 1910s and especially the 1920s, some female fiction writers achieved prominence. In spite of having played an even more marginal role as writers of traditional vernacular fiction than they had played as classical poets and essay writers, female story writers and novelists would henceforth remain an essential part of the twentieth-century Chinese literary scene. Two of the most distinguished female May Fourth writers were Ling Shu-hua (1900–1990) and Ping Hsin (pen name of Hsieh Wan-ying; 1900–1999), both of whom excelled academically and focused mostly on the domestic sphere in Peking. Ling Shu-hua employed a deft ironic touch in "Hsiu chen" (Embroidered Pillows; 1925), a story about how a soiled pillow inspires a young lady to put aside her long-cherished dreams of marrying into the top political elite. "Chung-ch'iu-chieh yi-ko wan shang" (One Night During the Mid-Autumn Festival; 1928) artfully portrays how minor misunderstandings between a married couple can snowball into an irreparable rupture when neither party is willing or able to understand the other's special points of sensitivity. The protagonist of Ping Hsin's "Tung-erh ku-niang" (The Winter Girl; 1933) is somewhat reminiscent of Hsü Ti-shan's resourceful heroines of humble background, but the account of her triumph over adversity is narrated by her widowed mother in a colloquial style very different from Hsü's.

As a stylist, Ting Ling (pseudonym of Chiang Ping-chih; 1904–1986) fell far short of Ling Shu-hua and Ping Hsin, but she was one of the first Chinese female writers to address female sexuality with frankness. Her "Sha-fei nü-shih jih-chi" (Ms. Sophie's Diary; 1928) explores the erotic and occupational expectations that many urban Chinese women were now more openly expressing, even if society was continuing to frustrate most of those expectations. Ting Ling's wartime stories like "Wo tsai Hsia-ts'un te shih-hou" (When I Was in Hsia Village; 1941) and "Tsai yi-yüan chung" (In the Hospital; 1941) satirize misogynous villagers and incompetent party-state functionaries in northwestern Communist-controlled "liberated areas" during the civil war. To punish Ting Ling for such politically unflattering stories and for pointing to continuing unfair treatment of women in Mao Tse-tung's wartime capital of Yenan, Mao publicly rebuked her and forced her to write an abject self-criticism during the notorious "rectification" of 1942. During her long career, Ting Ling alternated between toeing the party line and dissenting from it. She spent most of the final two decades of the Maoist era behind bars when she was not doing forced labor in the frigid far north.

Leftist writers with a penchant for organizing formed the Shanghai-based League of Left-Wing Writers (Tso-yi tso-chia lien-meng) in 1930. Having realized that May Fourth fiction's influence had not spread much beyond the rather tiny urban intelligentsia it had been written by and for, the League called for a leftist fiction with more popular appeal. Many League members turned to proletarian novels as the answer, launching numerous heated debates about what characteristics this type of novel should have, but very little significant proletarian fiction actually got written. An early attempt at proletarian fiction that predated the League and its debates came from the romantic revolutionary novelist Chiang Kuang-tz'u (1901–1931). Chiang's *Shao-nien p'iao-po-che* (The Youthful Drifter; 1926) sports a picaresque structure in which the young hero drifts from village to town and city through an unbelievably varied series of jobs, experiencing both oppression and humiliation as a farmer, factory worker, petty clerk, tutor's assistant, and many others. The defiant Byronic hero whom Chiang imagined he had created actually behaves more like a self-pitying and clumsy Pierrot, and the novel borders on unintentional self-parody in its maudlin superficiality.

Far more interesting attempts at proletarian fiction came from nonleftist writers outside the League. The leading representative of the Shanghai "Neo-impressionists" (Hsin kan-chüeh p'ai), Mu Shih-ying (1912–1940), contrasts a formidable and intimidating lumpen-proletarian narrator with a weak and timid intellectual listener in the story "Tsan-men te shih-chieh" (Our World; 1930). Although Lu Hsün scolded Mu Shih-ying for having written such an ideologically incorrect story, the famous essayist and scholar Chu Tzu-ch'ing (1898–1948) recognized Mu's skill at writing a type of natural vernacular that avoids the common May Fourth problem of sounding like a translated foreign novel. Mu Shih-ying returned to the proletarian theme in his satirical story "Pierrot" (1934), which features a naïve short story writer who decides to abandon literature for full-time labor agitation and other assorted assignments from "the Organization," a secretive underground revolutionary party. The erstwhile writer is jailed for leading a giant strike and refuses to divulge any information about the Organization even when the police interrogators apply sadistic torture, leaving him with a permanent limp. Yet after the writer finally reports back to the higher-ups in the Organization upon his release from prison, they suspiciously keep demanding that he admit what he divulged to the enemy interrogators and dismiss his protestations of innocence as a stubborn fabrication. In the story's comic finale, the disillusioned writer and would-be proletarian indignantly walks out on the Organization to resume his career as a fiction writer, which does not seem so bad after all.

China's most famous proletarian novel was written by Lao She (pseudonym of Shu Ch'ing-ch'un; 1899–1966), a Manchu and Peking local-colorist who became one of the greatest Chinese novelists of the century. *Lo-t'o Hsiang-tzu* (Camel Hsiang-tzu, or Rickshaw Boy; 1937), one of his many novels rich in humorous banter in the Peking dialect, relates a burly orphan peasant boy's uphill struggle for a dignified livelihood as an independent rickshaw puller in that ancient city. Entranced by the colorful sights, sounds, and smells of Peking, Hsiang-tzu cannot imagine returning to the drab routine of farming in the countryside. Unfortunately, he cannot anticipate the many dangers that city life holds in store for him.

At the outset, Hsiang-tzu works harder and saves more of his earnings than the other pullers, and after more than a year of denying himself all the gratifications in which most other rickshaw men indulge now and then, he can finally stop renting a rickshaw and buy his own instead. Yet his carelessness and mistaken sense of invincibility during an incursion of an undisciplined army results in the confiscation of his rickshaw by some soldiers. Later, a nest egg Hsiang-tzu has saved up for the purchase of a replacement rickshaw is seized by a crooked police detective, and a series of such reversals leads to Hsiang-tzu's moral exhaustion. The pitiful spectacle of an old independent rickshaw puller too poor to buy medicine for his dying grandson especially demoralizes Hsiang-tzu. He abandons his original dream of using his hard-earned savings from manual labor to get married and raise a family, instead betraying his friends and becoming a shiftless bum and unscrupulous police informer. Lao She's narrator finally loses his sympathy for Hsiang-tzu at this point, criticizing the failed rickshaw puller's excessive individualism, which blinded him to the necessity of organizing with other pullers to better their lot as a group. However, Lao She's satirical portraits of communists and leftist students in this work and many of his earlier novels suggest that he favored incremental changes like labor laws over violent insurrection.

Another leading novelist of the period was Pa Chin (pseudonym of Li Feikan; 1904–), whose leftism took the form of a maverick anarchism that many organization-minded League members severely frowned upon. Pa Chin grew up in a wealthy Szechwanese family with many servants. His novels, such as *Chia* (Family; 1931), reflect the rebellious dissatisfaction that the author felt for the traditional family hierarchy, particularly the sad lot of some servants. Like the author himself, the young protagonist of *Family* is frustrated by the discord between his partially Europeanized values and the seemingly immutable ways of his traditional family. Both wind up heading east for a seaport like Shanghai, where more like-minded young intellectuals are congregating.

For all their popularity with educated urban youth of his day, Pa Chin's novels of 1929 and the 1930s are sophomoric in conception and rough and sometimes slapdash at the sentence level. Pa Chin cherished spontaneity to the point where he generally refused to revise his manuscripts, rashly assuming that his first phrasing of an idea or incident was bound to be better than any subsequent modification. By all accounts, Pa Chin's most esthetically mature novel is *Han yeh* (Cold Nights; 1947), which was set in the wartime nationalist capital of Chungking. A tubercular man who has lost his job through no fault of his own must depend on his wife's salary to support his entire household, which includes his mother and son. As the only breadwinner in the family, the protagonist's wife chafes at the old tradition of showing great deference to the mother-in-law; tensions between the two women escalate, with the protagonist caught in the middle, often taking the blame himself in order to smooth things over. Eventually, the protagonist's wife walks out on him once and for all, revealing a new fragility in the traditional stem family when the wife's job nets as much or more income than the husband's.

China's most serious contender for the Nobel Prize for literature until the mid-1980s, the Hunanese Shen Ts'ung-wen (1902–1988), would have probably received the honor if political pressures had not forced him to abandon fiction writing and turn to museum curating around mid-century. Although he had been a close personal friend of leftist literati like Ting Ling and her communist husband, Hu Yeh-p'in, as early as the 1920s, his unwillingness to focus on society's down-and-out or portray provincial China as hellishly exploitative infuriated many leftist cultural figures. Lu Hsün blackballed Shen Ts'ung-wen's work from appearing in some key 1930s literary anthologies, and Shen became a *persona non grata* on China's literary scene during the three decades before the cultural thaw in the wake of Mao's death. Afterward, Shen Ts'ung-wen's massive oeuvre reemerged as probably the most distinguished single body of short and medium-length fiction in twentieth-century China.

Shen Ts'ung-wen wrote affectionately about life in the west Hunanese countryside and always considered himself one of the "country folk." Nevertheless, his literary bent for varieties of the pastoral did not lead to a formulaic approach bereft of ambiguity and ambivalence. The provincial family in "San-san" (1931) embodies many standard virtues of country folk, yet their unusually keen adaptability to rapidly changing social circumstances undercuts their "rooted" quality and the almost timeless continuity of rural life's rhythms typical in the genre. "Fu-fu" (The Lovers; 1929) goes much further in the direction of ambivalence by illustrating a truly menacing imperfection in an ostensibly idyllic rural setting: a pair of newlyweds caught making love outdoors amid the lush springtime greenery far from their own village suffer the indignities of interrogation by a crowd of self-righteous and hypocritical villagers. The villagers are preparing to take violent punitive measures against the couple that very day; it is only through the intervention of a broad-minded urban official on holiday that the couple manage to escape harm and return home physically untouched. Although Shen's village society is more socially cohesive and his provincial characters much more dynamic and psychologically complex than the norm in modern Chinese fiction, enough conflict and ill will exist in Shen's rural settings to prevent them from slipping into vapid idealizations of the countryside.

Shen's best-known and most highly regarded masterpiece is the novella *Pien-ch'eng* (Bordertown; 1934), in which an orphaned adolescent girl is being raised by her old grandfather, a village ferryboat operator. He hopes to arrange her marriage with a local boy who has courted her in the Miao (Hmong) montagnard pattern of linked folk singing, but some complications arise, including the grandfather's failing health. "Ching" (Quiet; 1932) expertly combines aural and visual imagery of a village's serenity to accentuate the pathos of a traveling family's anxious wait there for the return of the family head, who, unbeknownst to them, has just been killed in battle. Shen's experimentation with narrative approaches ranged from army-camp diary narration in "Wo te chiao-yü" (My Education; 1929) to a polyphonic modernist idyll in "K'an hung lu" (Gazing at Rainbows; 1941).

Another renowned specialist in rural fiction was Wu Tsu-hsiang, a southern Anhui regionalist writer whose fiction evinces a rare intimacy with all classes of the village society in which he grew up. In "Huang-hun" (Twilight; 1933), most of the major characters do not even put in an appearance, but are instead overheard by the narrator during a hot summer evening spent in his village courtyard; speech rhythms and characteristic turns of phrase nevertheless give each of these unseen characters an unmistakable identity. "Yi-ch'ien-pa-pai tan" (Eighteen Hundred Bushels; 1934) stresses finely crafted dialogue even further, dispensing with all but the barest outlines of summary or straight narration in evoking a drama of conflict and intrigue among the clan elders of Wu's village. "Lu chu shan-fang" (The Verdant Bamboo Hermitage; 1933) is a self-reflexive and neo-Gothic story in which various boundaries between life and art dissolve.

"Kuan-kuan te pu-p'in" (Little Lord Kuan-kuan's Tonic; 1932) generates powerful irony from its colorful but laughably inadequate narrator. "Wan-tzu chin-yin hua" (Splay-Petaled Honeysuckle; 1933) reveals a Proustian psychological insight into the recovery of dormant childhood memories that makes Lu Hsün's "My Old Home" seem rather mechanical by comparison. Finally, a traditionally narrated account of a rural family's desperate struggle to eke out an existence during the depression, "T'ien-hsia t'ai-p'ing" (The World at Peace; 1934), adroitly shifts to the fantastic mode in order to capture the protagonist's last moments of fleeting consciousness.

Chinese fiction often took on the propagandistic contours of forced optimism during World War II, but there were some notable exceptions. In "Hua Wei hsien-sheng" (Mr. Hua Wei; 1938), the famous satirist Chang T'ien-yi (1906–1985) pilloried the kind of hypocritical party official who hurries from meeting to meeting making pompous speeches about resisting Japanese aggression, but whose actual concerns do not extend much beyond his creature comforts and career ambitions. In Ai Wu's "Ch'iu shou" (Autumn Harvest; 1941), a young village woman whose husband is away fighting at the front grows to fear and resent the presence of wounded soldiers recuperating in her village. A few of the more mischievous of these soldiers have made a point of singing bawdy limericks within earshot of the village women laundering clothes by the riverside; the women respond with a general mistrust and contempt for the men, overcharging them for local foodstuffs. Frank portrayals of such tensions on the home front were uncommon, and the patriotism of writers like Chang T'ien-yi was heatedly called into question at times.

Some of the finest writings of the wartime period and its immediate aftermath came from writers living under Japanese occupation in Shanghai. Chang Ai-ling wrote a psychologically intricate portrait of a resentful and corrupting personality in her famous novella *Chin so chi* (The Golden Cangue; 1943). Ch'ien Chung-shu's (1910–1999) ironic presentation of a "free" marriage made over the parents' strong objections, "Chi-nien" (Souvenir; 1946), is set in wartime Chungking. An unhappy young university graduate turned housewife manages to keep her anticlimactic affair with a skirt-chasing air force pilot hidden from her dimwitted but kindly husband, but the memories of her dalliance have already started to intrude upon her otherwise peaceful existence, particularly in connection with the "souvenir" she is carrying to term. Ch'ien Chung-shu's acclaimed novel *Wei ch'eng* (The Besieged City; 1947) is an erudite satire of a broad variety of self-absorbed and half-baked intellectuals and other white-collar poseurs. Just as the besiegers of a city want to get in while those within the city hope to get out, Ch'ien Chung-shu's protagonist repeatedly alternates between wanting to enter into a romantic liaison or get a job and later hoping to leave that very liaison or workplace.

Chinese fiction generally grew more politicized during the 1950s in the wake of the Communist victory in the civil war of 1946–1949 and the retreat of the defeated Nationalist government to Taiwan. Even originally apolitical novelists like Chang Ai-ling addressed the human costs of government policies, in as her devastating critiques of communist policies in *Yang ko* (The Rice-Sprout Song; 1954) and *Ch'ih-ti chih lien* (Love in Redland, later retitled *Naked Earth*; 1954), both of which were published in Hong Kong.

PREMIER DECADES FOR FICTION: TAIWAN IN THE 1970S AND THE PRC IN THE 1980S

After an uncertain period of literary and political adjustment following the imposition of Nationalist control in Taiwan under Generalissimo Chiang K'ai-shek, fiction gradually began to thrive there. One of Taiwan's most distinguished and controversial novels is Wang Wen-hsing's (1939–) *Chia pien* (Family Catastrophe; 1972–1973). The novel consists of more than 150 sections, which vary in length from a couple of lines to several pages. The bachelor protagonist, Fan Yeh, dominates most of the narrative present with his reactions to the mysterious disappearance of his elderly father, especially during his extended journeys in search of the old man. Yet the numerous short sections of the novel facilitate cinematic flashbacks to various episodes from Fan Yeh's childhood that flesh out his ambivalent feelings toward his parents, particularly his father. Emotionally, Fan Yeh oscillates between heartfelt concern for his father and impatience, even disgust, with the old man. The harsher emotions appear to prevail, for Fan Yeh finally launches an outspoken attack on the Confucian obligations of filial piety, bitterly vowing to cut off the family line by avoiding marriage and childrearing as entanglements of suffering.

On the second anniversary of his father's mysterious disappearance, Fan Yeh and his mother have tacitly abandoned their search for the old man and appear content and even refreshed by this release from their burden of searching for him. In allegorical terms, the eclipse of the Confucian paternal authority figure has become a process of relief and emotional unburdening to the remaining family members, who no longer perceive a need for a central figure of familial authority. Aside from this allegorical dimension, the novel dramatizes many typical stresses on the modern family in Taiwan, including fierce wifely jealousy over the husband's real or imagined infidelity, sky-high parental expectations of generous financial support in their old age from their sons, and stubborn parental illusions about keeping even their grown-up children emotionally dependent on the elders.

The most vital and vibrant movement in fiction around this time in Taiwan was that of *hsiang-t'u wen-hsüeh* (native literature). This was a rural, roots-oriented kind of fiction that arose as a reaction against the urban-centered, modernist trends that came from "outside." The young authors who participated in the *hsiang-t'u* movement, such as Ch'en Ying-chen (pseudonym of Ch'en Yung-shan; 1936–), Huang Ch'un-ming (1939–), and Wang Chen-ho (1940–

1990), often ran afoul of the authorities because of their deep sympathy with the local, underprivileged elements of society.

On the mainland, the same Teng Hsiao-p'ing who ironically extended an olive branch to writers and sanctioned the post-Mao cultural thaw of the late 1970s and early 1980s also launched a bloody and inconclusive war with Vietnam in 1979. No PRC literary work on this war with Vietnam achieved as much public recognition as Li Ts'un-pao's (1946–) novel *Kao-shan hsia te hua-huan* (The Wreath at the Foot of the Mountain; 1982), which subsequently reached even larger audiences as a film. Li marshals considerable narrative skill in evoking the breathless pace of a forced-march infantry assault without letting character development or the human cost of war fall by the wayside.

The novel focuses on Company 9, the force within the Chinese army selected to lead the sudden attack across the Red River deep into Vietnamese territory that spring. Most of the company consists of peasant recruits, including its commander, who has worked his way up through the ranks. Lacking connections in high places, these "hayseed" soldiers have little choice but to accept the role of cannon fodder if they are ordered to lead an infantry assault on the formidable Vietnamese. The two exceptions to this rule are soldiers whose fathers are both generals—the two young men would have been able to remove themselves from the perilous front lines early in the game if they had exercised their "back-door" connections in the manner so often winked at in the Leninist PRC bureaucracy. One of the pair never even contemplates dodging action at the front lines and is shot dead while trying to bazooka yet another Vietnamese blockhouse, having already destroyed a few. The other soldier of privileged background, named Chao, had used his back-door connections to arrange a transfer away from the war zone, but shamefacedly turns down the transfer after his fellow soldiers begin to shun him as a coward.

Chao compensates for his loss of stature in the company by taking courageous risks during the attack on Vietnam, but winds up in the minority of company soldiers who somehow make it back to their base camp alive. Chao's ensuing case of survivor's guilt worsens when he meets the mother, widow, and child of the company commander, an exemplary figure who had died after destroying the last Vietnamese blockhouse targeted during the raid. The obvious poverty of these bereaved peasants moves Chao to tears after they insist on paying all the debts left by the late commander. In a curious variation on the typical deathbed scene in formulaic Maoist war novels, the dying commander's final action had not been to hand over his last wad of cash and gasp that it was for his Communist Party dues; instead, the commander's trembling hand had held out a bloodstained list of debts incurred while he was assisting needy relatives over the years.

Many 1980s' PRC novels turned backward in time to critique the darkest period for the PRC and its intellectuals, the two decades from the antirightist crackdown of 1957–1958 to the culmination of the Cultural Revolution in 1976 with Mao's death. Occasionally, such novels blunt the harshness of those two decades by injecting a motif like that of the "romantic prison," in which a discouraged prisoner regains hope through the affections of the wife or daughter of a warden or guard. In Ts'ung Wei-hsi's (1933–) novel *Feng lei yen* (Eyes Tearful in the Wind; 1985), the protagonist, named So, is an intellectual who has been sentenced to a long term of hard labor in the countryside on trumped-up political charges. While alone tending the lime kiln in the camp one day, the half-starved inmate has his dinner of two hardtack buns snatched away by a famine refugee. He chases after the refugee, a raggedly dressed woman about twenty years old, and threatens to shoot her if she does not return the buns. Not realizing that he is merely bluffing, she panics: stooping down to grab a handful of lime dust, she whirls around and hurls it into So's face. He flinches, but it is too late: the lime has gotten into his eyes and stings terribly. From that point on in his life, his left eye will be hypersensitive to wind, watering whenever a breeze grazes it.

The famine refugee, named Li Ts'ui-ts'ui, attempts to make amends for what she has done, leading the squinting and stumbling inmate to a stream where she can wash the lime dust from his painful eyes. It finally dawns on him how many peasants in north China have starved to death during the recent famine there, and his anger at Ts'ui-ts'ui soon dissipates. Moved by the story of the hardships she faced in jumping one train after another to reach this mining region, So offers her most of what little money he has and urges her to buy some food.

So and Ts'ui-ts'ui gradually come to know each other better, and, after she finds out that he is still a bachelor, she proposes settling down to live together with him, even going so far as to make a sexual advance at him. Although So is tempted by her offer, he pulls himself away from her, noting that his status as a thought criminal and forced laborer puts him at the very bottom of the social hierarchy, even lower than that of "rovers" (*mang-liu*) from the countryside like Ts'ui-ts'ui.

Their special friendship continues, nevertheless, even after Ts'ui-ts'ui meets and receives a marriage proposal from So's overseer, the labor camp section chief, Cheng. Ts'ui-ts'ui regularly drops by the lime kiln to slip So food to supplement his meager rations. More important, she has a moderating influence on Cheng, who used to treat So and the other convicts very harshly. In fact, with Cheng's support, So's "hat" (crime) is finally removed from his record, and he is formally transferred to an ordinary work unit in the vicinity of the camp. Yet he soon discovers that life in this work unit of ex-prisoners and "rovers" who have settled down in the district is only slightly better than his existence as an inmate. In some ways it is even worse, since many of the ruffians in the work unit feel no compunction about bullying newcomers in ways that would apparently seldom be tolerated within the camp. So is just beginning to get roughed up on his first day there when Ts'ui-ts'ui shows up to use Cheng's authority to defend So from the bullying roughnecks.

Other PRC novels from this period harken back even further in time to the pre-Communist period, producing legendary portrayals with accents of Latin American "magical realism." The army writer Mo Yen's (1956–) *Hung kao-liang chia-tsu* (Red Sorghum Clan; 1986) celebrates a sort of heroic rural primitivism. To many readers, this seemed a welcome departure from decades of repetitious official condemnation of "backwardness" and "feudalism," vague code words for various disagreeable patriarchal and autocratic features of traditional Chinese culture. While a schoolboy in the remote Shantung county of Kao-mi, Mo Yen thrilled to village elders' lively oral accounts of old-time bandits and guerrilla resistance to Japanese invaders of the 1930s and 1940s. Many years later, after he had successfully used a long stint in the army to escape a life of obscurity in the countryside, the "magical realism" of Gabriel Garcia Marquez inspired Mo Yen to throw restraint to the winds in his writing and let his imagination aggressively reshape the oral accounts contained within his memory. The young writer now determinedly emphasized lyricism at the expense of clarity and plausibility, insistently blurred distinctions between dream and actuality, and repeatedly turned aside from the ordinary and typical in life to focus on human behavior *in extremis*.

Red Sorghum Clan creates the backdrop for mythic heroism and primitivist vitality through the exotically portrayed setting of Shantung's lush sorghum fields, which seem to exist in a pristine and primitive state of eternal summer and constant growth, since throughout the novel hardly a word is said about the long and grueling winters of the northeast Asian mainland. Sorghum literally animates the main characters, who eat sorghum gruel, drink sorghum wine, ambush Japanese invaders under the cover of tall sorghum plants, and conceive children such as the narrator's father from within the privacy of dense stands of sorghum. Figuratively, the reddish seedheads of ripe sorghum form a link with the passionate blood of the local inhabitants, which flows and gushes out at regular intervals within this novel of incessant strife and vendettas, such as during the meticulously described skinning alive of the grandmother's most loyal assistant. The author even personifies sorghum on many occasions, directly comparing the way sorghum stalks and humans are cut down by slashing swords or speeding bullets.

Through his thinly disguised alter-ego narrator, the author compensates for what he sees as the mundane and unheroic contours of his own generation by portraying the generations represented by his parents and especially his grandparents in heroic, larger-than-life terms. Mo Yen sought the primitive alternative to an "ultrastable" or stagnant Chinese cultural heritage in a kind of blood cult, in which the primacy of feeling and impulse that animates the rebellious grandparents in *Red Sorghum Clan* challenges Chinese cultural conventions based on conformity, compromise, and moderation. Even the all but universally condemned vestige of Chinese tradition since the Sung dynasty, the customary binding of women's feet, is transformed by Mo Yen into a furtherance of rebellious, impulsive, and thus authentic action: the narrator's grandfather, originally a lowly sedan chair bearer for the narrator's grandmother, decides to "make a woman of her" and free her from an inauspicious arranged marriage largely because of his entrancement with her tiny bound feet.

Red Sorghum Clan is only one of the novels of recent decades that has achieved not merely tremendous success in China but critical international acclaim as well. The world of fiction in China and Taiwan continued to thrive in the 1990s and the early twenty-first century. Particularly noticeable were the increasing commercialization of fiction as a lucrative, salable product and the crossing of political and cultural boundaries in short stories and novels. Just as it had proved to be an accurate index of the radical changes that swept through China at the end of the Ch'ing dynasty and the beginning of the Republic, so does fiction seem to herald fundamental transformations at the dawn of the twenty-first century.

Philip F. C. Williams

Chapter 40

CHINA, HONG KONG, AND TAIWAN DURING THE 1980S AND 1990S

CULTURE OF THE 1980S AND 1990S AND THE PERIPHERY

After the post–Cultural Revolution relaxation of the draconian constraints of Mao Tse-tung's People's Republic of China (PRC), where writers were disaccustomed to taking an interest in any problems not related to China, intellectuals now extended their sights to a "Greater China," with all its peripheral cultures. The term "Cultural China" (*wen-hua Chung-kuo*) has been increasingly used to denominate the expanded entity that reaches far beyond the geographical boundaries of the PRC. The situation in the PRC changed rapidly during this period, leading to an ever-widening gap (social, economic, and cultural) between the coastal cities and the rural towns and villages. Hong Kong, whose stewardship was returned to China in 1997 and which was therefore beset with a multitude of political and economic anxieties and adjustments, also faced the question of its own regional cultural identity. After the election of Chiang Ching-kuo (son of Chiang K'ai-shek; 1910–1988) as president in 1978, Taiwan eagerly took advantage of the new liberties afforded by democratization to define its own identity and—in the watershed year of 2000—elected its first president who was not a member of the Kuomintang (KMT; Nationalist Party), Chen Shui-bian, and its first female vice president, Lü Hsiu-lien—both of them ethnic Taiwanese—sending shock waves through the mainland. In the longer term, strong majority forces on Taiwan hoped to safeguard regional independence and to clarify relationships with China—both with traditional culture and with the realities of a "demanding" motherland, which again seemed to be suffering the labor pains of imminent changes. The influence and the cultural self-confidence of the élites of Chinese origin in Southeast Asia, especially in Singapore and Malaysia, played an increasingly visible role. Additional ethnic group audiences and markets very much in line with Pierre Bourdieu's concept of the cultural field came into play.

At the same time, a small but influential group of Chinese intellectuals in the United States and, to a lesser extent, in Europe was having an increasing impact on China. People who had lived abroad for many years were being welcomed with open arms by China's students and intelligentsia in general. The huge, chaotic, and uncontrollable network of cultural communication, which embraced the whole gamut of opinion voiced by Chinese intellectuals in exile, colored and in some instances shaped the picture of China in the 1990s.

As a primary frame of reference for the quickening pace of cultural reconfiguration, literature appeared to have taken on new functions and facets, but also to have forfeited some of the influence it once had, according to the poet Yang Lien (b. 1954) and the playwright-painter Kao Hsing-chien (b. 1940), who addressed their readers from Paris. Alternative and dissident artists created untraditional forms of expression in their paintings and other works that were parallel to those presented by writers. During the 1990s New Chinese Film, which in many respects had its roots in literature, and its regional variants in Taiwan and Hong Kong, became even more influential than the literature of the 1980s, both nationally and internationally. During the 1980s, furthermore, the Chinese public was inundated with mass culture products. Popular culture evolved, from film to television, from journals to the products of innumerable publishing houses, which tended to dominate the new realities of cultural consumption.

Here, given the fundamental upheavals in all areas of cultural life that were occurring in China, only a few developments can be mentioned as examples. In particular, this chapter takes into consideration the naiveness and the limitations of the literature of the 1980s, and references the élitist literature, painting and art of the absurd, of postmodernism, and of the avant-garde in China. Literary texts and paintings by the avant-garde stood in sharp contrast to the products of the all-embracing mass culture. The respective audiences opted for very different perceptions of the role of literature and art. The sneers of a new brand of cynicism, paralleled by an unaccustomed and somewhat spurious mood of fin-de-siècle jadedness, were phenomena that made sense neither to the nouveaux riches among top Chinese cadres and functionaries nor to many literary scholars and China pundits in the West. Although sophisticated readers found Wang Shuo (b. 1958) and his devil-may-care, in-your-face, vagabond literature simply irritating, his writings were a riotous revelation for China's youth for several years.

Alongside the diverse forms of mass literature on the big screen and on television, a tendency toward critical self-portrayal and self-examination arose. A new generation of Chinese literary and media critics, both at home and abroad, began commenting on important new developments in the field of Chinese art. For the first time, these Chinese critics were defining their own position with merciless accuracy and an impressive awareness of global trends and developments.

The Limited Experiments of the 1980s

After three years of agonizing transition between 1976, the year of Mao's death, and 1979, the 1980s were filled with the hopeful mood of a new beginning in literature such as China had not seen since the May Fourth movement of the 1920s. Post-Mao China embarked on a series of economic and political reforms, and literature became a playground for many impatient would-be actors wishing to pave the way, on a symbolic level, for the anticipated reforms. Most of the authors who now rushed to put pen to paper or finally found their way back to literary creation after years of repression had lost touch with tradition; they had to start from scratch. Yet the conventions of Maoist socialist realism and its Soviet Russian role models continued to have a—rarely noticed—subconscious impact on China's "new era literature" (*hsin shih-ch'i wen-hsüeh*).

Several dozen anthologies, especially of prose and poetry, that documented this literary reawakening became available in the West almost immediately. More than a hundred book translations were produced during this period, and specialized periodicals provided an overview of developments. We may now look back on some of the key features of this experimental literature and comment retrospectively on several important authors of the 1980s, a number of whom have since become silent—perhaps because they went too far and too fast.

It would not be inaccurate to characterize the literature of the 1980s as eruptive efforts "to come to terms with the past" (*fan-ssu*; German, *Vergangenheitsbewültigung*) and, at the same time, as a rather clumsy retraining in the literary *métier.* Some writers, like Chang Chieh (b. 1937), author of the novel *Ch'en-chung te ch'ih-pang* (Heavy Wings; 1981), or Chiang Tzu-lung (b. 1941) in his stories about a reform manager-cadre, produced some rather unsophisticated stories and novels, which, as in the past, were interpreted and presented by the Chinese Communist Party (CCP) as propaganda in support of their economic reform policy. A whole series of reportage documentaries brought back vivid memories of the horrors suffered by individual Chinese, especially women, during the previous decades. One example is Yü Lo-chin's (b. 1946) autobiography, which was the target of excessive official and bureaucracy-inspired semiofficial criticism. Journalists like Liu Pin-yen (b. 1925) used reportage literature to expose social injustice. They and other critics felt obliged to spell out the moral of their stories to ensure that even the least sophisticated of their readers could understand.

Uncompromising critics of the regime's political blunders, like Wang Jo-wang (b. 1918), who had challenged paramount leader Teng Hsiao-p'ing (1904–1997) personally, even in this euphoric phase of reform were made to pay for their outspoken essays and reporting. They were subjected to all sorts of harassment, even harsh prison sentences.

Restless talents, such as the prose author and dramatist Chang Hsin-hsin (b. 1953) in her book *Pei-ching jen* (Chinese Lives; 1985), presented realistic portraits that contrasted sharply with the embellished picture of society as depicted in party propaganda. Attempts "to come to terms with the past" remained linked to the themes of the Cultural Revolution, as Feng Chi-ts'ai (b. 1942) demonstrated in his somewhat superficial and glowing stories, and especially in an ambitious reportage literary project, which, in the end, he was unable to complete and publish because of the changed political atmosphere. Tai Hou-ying (b. 1938 and murdered in 1996), herself originally a misguided radical leftist and later a fervent advocate of "humanism," gave a remorseful account—in her novel *Jen a jen* (Man, ah Man, or Stones of the Wall; 1980), written from Shanghai—of the fate suffered by the intellectuals at China's universities and the seduction of an entire generation of young people by radicals close to the aging chairman Mao Tse-tung.

Writers who had spent twenty years in the camps and rehabilitated "rightist elements" like Ts'ung Wei-hsi (b. 1933) made some hesitant attempts to create prison literature. But they camouflaged their message in verbose and ideological passages and, in the end, pledged their unshaken gratitude to the party, which had allegedly extricated itself from responsibility for the excesses of the past by pointing to the successful efforts at reforming its organization. The writer Chang Hsien-liang (b. 1936) probably attracted the most attention because he drew shattering literary portraits of the psychological destruction and sexual repression of the detainees and former "rightists"; he impressed his audience as a shaken witness of the irreparable harm that had been done to them.

Many victims of the mass political campaigns like Lu Yen-chou (b. 1928), Pai Hua (b. 1930), or Ku Hua (b. 1942) published rather simplistic retrospections and lachrymose, "safe" accusations of a general nature. Only a few writers, the erudite Tsung P'u (b. 1928) and Yang Chiang (b. 1911) being notable examples, managed to provide a deeper insight into the existential trauma they had suffered. Yang, a dramatist famous in the cosmopolitan Shanghai of the 1940s and acknowledged as a highly skilled translator, described, with inimitable understatement, absurd scenes in the rural camps involving China's most brilliant intellectuals (*Kan-hsiao liu chi* [Six Chapters from a Cadre School; 1981]). Poets like Pei Tao (b. 1949) and narrator-novelists like Ah Ch'eng (pen name of

Chung A-ch'eng; b. 1949) spoke out in their early works on behalf of China's protesting youth, who in their hearts had abandoned Chinese communism. Major transformations were also apparent in the development of Wang An-yi (b. 1954) as a dedicated chronicler of Shanghai and portrayer of the youth of her day. She was a typical representative of China's new women's literature, differentiating and adapting her style in a rapid succession of experimental steps.

The 1980s also produced a number of authors who attempted to square the circle, writers who attempted to combine politics and literature. Servile fixation on high-placed politicians, their moods, and sociopolitical inclinations eventually proved the undoing of Shen Jung (b. 1936) and others who, for a time, had artfully "sailed" with the political winds. Wang Meng (b. 1934), tolerated by the regime as Minister of Culture only until 1989, made his imprint with remarkable essays that helped further the cause of aspiring young writers by cautiously testing the limits of acceptability. Ironically, Wang's noncommittal stance (e.g., when he likened himself to a "butterfly" that cannot be pinned down by the terms "modernist," "avant-garde," or anything else) was also the reason that his stories and novels, which tended to paper over many complexities of the situation in China, had only a limited impact at home. An example of his chameleonic skills is his novel *Huo-tung pien-jen-hsing* (Moveable Parts; 1987). Otherwise ordinary or even mediocre talents like the former teacher Liu Hsin-wu (b. 1942) excelled in essays in which they criticized with an admirable sense of justice the social outrages that had been committed by destructive mass political campaigns. The genre of the cultural-political essay, so dear to Chinese literary tastes, reestablished itself prominently with several collections of such texts by the critic Liu Tsai-fu (b. 1941), former director of the Institute of Literature of China's Academy of Social Sciences. Written in the United States and modeled partly on the essays of Lu Hsün (Chou Shu-jen; 1881–1936; see chapter 39), Liu's string of short pieces combines an honest revelation of the predicament of Chinese intellectuals in exile with a sober re-examination of the fundamental problems affecting Chinese society in the twentieth century.

Chinese critics and authors have occasionally complained that some Western Sinologists prefer to regard modern Chinese literature basically as a commentary on the country's social and political development in the early reform years. But there were reasons for this attitude. The limitations of China's literary experiment of these years, which was launched without much knowledge of the Chinese situation in a global context and thus without much understanding of the outside world, meant that important literary works with a global impact could not be written at the time. The only goal that could be achieved was to provide a literary commentary on social injustices in China: a description of the often unsuccessful attempts by harassed and marginalized individuals to survive the chaos of a society thrown into turmoil by constant political campaigns.

"New Wave" and "Avant-Garde" Literature in the 1990s

From about 1984, writers and intellectuals began to reignite the debate of the 1920s, asking to what extent Confucian culture and tradition had been responsible for dooming China's attempts at modernization. Many authors, like Ah Ch'eng, Han Shao-kung (b. 1953), Cheng Wan-lung (b. 1944), and Cheng Yi (b. 1947), then initiated a literature of "Searching for Roots" (*hsün-ken*) in an attempt to revitalize Chinese culture. They looked beyond traditional and modern mainstream culture, searching in rural China and among non-Han local cultures for an untouched elemental culture outside the recognized norms of Chinese civilization. This approach could easily be misinterpreted as a literature of escape from urgent social problems and thus be dismissed as a "diversion" into a blind alley of just another romanticizing Chinese attempt at "self-strengthening," recalling the movement that took place from 1861 to 1895 after China's humiliating defeat at the hands of the European powers in the Opium Wars. The emerging avant-garde (*hsien-feng*) literature, first referred to tentatively as "New Wave" (*hsin-ch'ao*) literature, can be seen as a peculiar artistic reaction to the chaos of present-day China.

It was at this point that New Chinese Film successfully took off and irritating, colorful new styles of painting emerged. Rock music by stars like Ts'ui Chien (b. 1961) also evolved into a subculture subscribed to by youth with few illusions and became, for some years, a further powerful expression of protest.

In the mid-1980s Chinese publishers were forced to become financially responsible or autonomous for the first time (though they were not permitted ideological independence). To generate revenues, many of them turned to publishing Western popular literature in translation, which was warmly received by China's reading public. In addition, they flooded the market with reprints of love stories and popular novels as well as *wu-hsia* (knight-errant) cloak-and-dagger romances from Taiwan and Hong Kong. At the same time, intellectuals began to discuss the character of Chinese culture. In 1987 a new dimension was added by the debate over the television series "Ho-shang" (Ode of the River, or River Elegy; 1988), which employed techniques of pseudo-reportage. The series introduced colorful images of China's cultural crisis as a topic of discussion to an audience of some 600 million viewers. For the first time since 1949, and perhaps for the first time in Chinese history, the foundations of Chinese civilization were subjected to massive, critical public scrutiny. The Chinese Communist Party leadership was astonished by the depth of resentment against the past revealed by "River Elegy." The series arguably was one of the main catalysts of the massive protests that erupted in T'ien-an-men Square in Peking in May and June 1989.

Ordinary readers soon lost much of their initial interest in the literature of "coming to terms with the past," and the authors of more demanding and sophisticated literature suddenly found themselves out in the cold. Many of them left the cause, stopped writing, or adapted; key impulses now increasingly emanated from a younger generation of writers born in the 1960s. This "New Wave" literature can be broken down into the narrative prose of the Lost Generation, the "Searching for Roots" movement, and "avant-garde" literature. Stories by Liu So-la (b. 1955) and Ch'en Chien-kung (b. 1949) were seen as reflecting the mood and the thoughts of the Lost Generation. They had a precursor in *Po-tung* (Waves), an early novel by the poet Pei Tao in which young survivors of the generation formed (or deformed) by the Cultural Revolution have a fateful encounter of hesitating, skeptical affection. "Roots Literature" covers a wide range of works, from Ah Ch'eng's *San wang* (Three Kings) ("Ch'i wang" [King of Chess], "Shu wang" [King of Trees], and "Hai-tzu wang" [King of Children], 1985) to the plays and prose of Nobel laureate (2000) Kao Hsing-chien (1940–), a novelist, playwright, painter, and calligrapher who went into exile in Paris. His root-searching novel *Ling-shan* (Mountain of Souls; 1990) caused a great stir in 1995–1996 when it appeared in French translation. Among those associated with the avant-garde movement are the talented Ma Yüan (b. 1953), who, meanwhile, Rimbaud-like, has given up writing to go into business (a fate that has overtaken many PRC writers and intellectuals); Ts'an Hsüeh (b. 1953), who has delved into every absurd atrocity; and, to some extent, the "anarchist" Wang Shuo, who quickly became a wealthy media star directing his own company. His writings are a marketplace of postmodernist defiance and cynical truths; he has smashed any remaining illusions of a shining future.

The works of Chinese avant-garde literature, in contrast to the descriptive realism of the 1990s, have so far been included in only a few anthologies and are accessible through just a handful of translations, perhaps in part because they are so difficult to comprehend and render. Li Jui (b. 1950) has depicted wild scenes from the changing rural society that will never have a place in state-prescribed textbooks. Mo Yen's (b. 1956) novels present baroque heroes who would be at home in the furious battle scenes of the seventeenth-century picaresque novel *Simplicissimus*, by Hans Jakob von Grimmelshausen, but his novels in fact are directly inspired by Gabriel Garcia Marquez, Jorge Luis Borges, and the magical realism of other Latin American models.

This period of "cultural reorientation," to use the term coined by the critic Henry Chao (Chao Yi-heng), was essentially subversive, the tenor of the texts being clearly anticulture; examples include *Huang-ni chieh* (The Muddy Street), by Ts'an Hsüeh, and "Ni pieh wu hsüan-tse" (You Have No Choice), a story by Liu So-la. These authors were rebelling against the existing norms as reflected, for example, in Wang An-yi's *Shan shang te shih-chi* (The Century on the Hill) or in many stories by Han Shao-kung; and the existing value system was mercilessly ridiculed in Yeh Chao-yen's (b. 1957) *Wu-yüeh te huang-hun* (The Dusk of May) and *Tsao-shu te ku-shih* (The Story of the Date Tree) and in To To's (b. 1951) *Tsui-hou te yi shou ko* (The Last Song). Authors were feeling their way back to "eternal values" outside the narrow confines of mainstream culture. This trend is seen in Ah Ch'eng's "The King of Chess" and Mo Yen's novel *Hung kao-liang* (Red Sorghum). Among the earliest works of the avant-garde was the narrative prose of such writers as Su T'ung (b. 1963), *Yi-chiu san-ssu te t'ao-wang* (The Escape of 1934). Stories like "Ming-yün" (Fate), by Shih T'ieh-sheng (b. 1951), and "Mi chou" (The Lost Boat), by Ko Fei (b. 1964), depict the tragedy of the individual who cannot survive in such a disoriented society. Esoteric and bizarre messages are conveyed in stories like "Yu-ch'ai lai te hsin" (The Letter from the Postman), by Sun Kan-lu (b. 1959), or "Pai niao" (The White Bird), by Ho Li-wei (b. 1954).

One important avant-garde writer after 1987 is Yü Hua, who wrote *Hsien-shih yi-chung* (One Kind of Reality), in which he presents a ludicrous example of brutality in a Chinese family. A murder of revenge at the end of the story is again reminiscent of a scene in *Simplicissimus:* a small dog causes a fatal fit of hysterical laughter by licking the feet of the victim.

For the young egoists among the Chinese writers born in the 1960s, the Cultural Revolution and its repercussions had, at long last, lost significance. The evolving avant-garde literature could no longer be viewed as a simple variant of the "service trade" commodity, as Rudolph Wagner has called the politically correct products of Chinese socialist realism, as well as the only partly successful prose experiments of the 1980s. For the first time, there was no single correct interpretation. A new élite had mounted the stage, an élite that was molding and living the new anticulture, for which the time was now right. Not surprisingly, these authors were both curious and enthusiastic about their own cultural history, which had been withheld from them, dating back to the May Fourth movement of the 1920s and earlier. Their works, moreover, were clearly influenced in many ways by Western literature. Several novels and stories were modeled on Salinger's *Catcher in the Rye*, Marquez's *Hundred Years of Solitude*, and the novels of Borges.

Female Writers of the 1990s

Many female writers left an imprint on the literature of the 1990s. Two of the most prominent were Fang Fang (b. 1955) and Ch'ih Li (b. 1957), from Wu-han, whose writings reflect their attempts at a new realism. Fang Fang exposes the lives of transport workers and urban intellectuals in *Tsu-fu tsai fu-ch'in hsin-chung* (Grandfather in Father's Heart; 1992). Ch'ih Li, in stories like "Lü-shui ch'ang-liu" (The Flow of Clear Water; 1993), portrays the relationship of couples in ill-matched marriages and, in the satire *Ni yi-wei ni shih shei* (Who Do You Think You Are?; 1995), depicts the trials and tribulations of everyday life. Chang Hsin (b. 1954), who hails from Canton, has made her impact with texts like *Chüeh fei ou-jan* (Absolutely No Coincidence; 1995) and *Ai yu ju-ho* (It's Love, So What?; 1995) about women's struggles for acceptance in China's cities.

Female avant-garde writers include Ch'en Jan (b. 1962), from Kwangsi province, and Lin Pai (b. 1958), from Peking. Lin gained recognition with her novel of childhood reminiscences entitled *Ch'ing-t'ai* (Moss; 1995), and Ch'en with stories like "Tsui-ch'un li te yang-kuang" (Sunshine Between the Lips; 1992), in which she explores how to reach a love and mutual understanding that will remain after decades of political struggles and cynicism. Since 1994 authors in Peking have written "novels of new experience" (*hsin t'i-yen hsiao-shuo*), a genre created by Pi Shu-min (b. 1952) and others, with unusual stories, some of them treating rather banal topics like getting rich and encountering death.

"Anarchist" Wang Shuo and the Postmodern Disillusion of the 1990s

One feature of the narrative style employed by writers born in the 1960s, which distinguishes them from the subtle idealistic "protestors" of Pei Tao's generation, is a pervasive cynicism—a negation of practically all values, of society, even of the meaning of their own existence. Wang Shuo soon took center stage, with stories like "Wan-chu" (Leader of the Gang; 1987), "Yi-pan shih huo-yen, yi-pan shih hai-shui" (Hot and Cold, Measure for Measure; 1988), "Wan te chiu-shih hsin-t'iao" (Living Dangerously; 1988), and "Ch'ien-wan pieh pa wo tang chen" (Don't Take Me Seriously; 1989). In these tales, Wang developed and became a virtuoso in the art of juxtaposing two different worlds of expression, the fossilized language of the declining system and its ideology against the urban slang of China's disillusioned youth. Finally, he and his generation wrote about sexual matters with an unprecedented openness.

Wang criticizes Chinese intellectuals as pitifully ineffective. He has only contempt for their hollow ramblings about a "new cultural revolution" and prefers instead to live without ideals and without master strategies for the future. He dismisses the somber attempts of Chang Ch'eng-chih, for example, in *Hsin-ling shih* (History of the Soul) and in his other narrative prose to establish a system of new values.

It was not until Wang's "lifestyle" began to be accepted by a wider public through television adaptations and the filming of his stories (four in one year alone) that the literary watchdogs among cadres and propagandists felt the need to intervene. Most semiofficial literary critics had initially dismissed Wang as nothing but a harmless writer of popular literature.

Wang throws his readers straight into the culture of the *liu-mang* (riffraff and out-of-work adolescents), a peculiar world indeed. The *liu-mang* fears no one, in a way that is reminiscent of the heroes of both the traditional vernacular *hsiao-shuo* novel and modern *wu-hsia* adventure romances.

The author himself had served a jail sentence for his involvement in youth gang warfare, scraped along as a salesman, and, after his military service in the marines, lived off a succession of women—the secretary of a party youth organization, a stewardess, and a dancer. The antiheroes of his love stories are *liu-mang*, *p'i-tzu* (ruffian) anarchists, and inveterate *wan-chu* (gambler) types.

In the screen version of "Hot and Cold, Measure for Measure," the protagonist is an escapee from the prison camps, quite the opposite of the egocentric and often theatrical figures of Chang Hsien-liang or Tai Hou-ying. Masquerading as a police officer, he makes a living out of blackmailing and procuring prostitutes for visitors from Hong Kong. In "Don't Take Me Seriously," a group of *liu-mang* is fighting for survival in chaotic circumstances. Shaken up by Taiwan author Po Yang's (b. 1920) diatribe *Ch'ou-lou te Chung-kuo-jen* (The Ugly Chinaman), Wang uses this political satire to "avenge" a defeat suffered at an international sporting event in Sapporo. A member of a *kung-fu* martial arts team is selected, who naturally ends up as world champion in this discipline—satirically celebrated in an absurd competition of Chinese self-effacement.

The humorous story "Wo shih ni pa-pa" (I Am Your Dad; 1991) shows the absurdity of the attempts by different generations to live together in harmony. The father, a divorcé who works in a bookstore, fails miserably in his attempt to bridge or to ignore the generation gap. His son, in exasperation, demands a return to the observation of boundaries between the generations.

In short, Wang Shuo has depicted disillusioned urban youth as alienated elements among the intellectuals. Wang demands that everyone should have the right to his or her own world and disparages Chinese "modernism" for assuming new forms as if they were new clothes, without adjusting the underlying structures. In his own erratic way, buffoon Wang ridicules the aberrations of such worn-out clichés as a China striving for "total Westernization." Small wonder that Wang Shuo has become both role model and artistic endorsement for the rootless *p'o-p'i* (rascally) or *lai-p'i* (roguish) school of painters (referred to as "cynical realism" in English-language art criticism), many of whose members have achieved extraordinary commercial success.

Not least because of his huge commercial success, following his decision to become a private cultural entrepreneur (*wen-hua ko-t'i-hu*) and to operate from his Sea Horse Movie and Video Production Center in Peking, Wang has had numerous imitators, several of them women. But the blasé cynicism in the works of Hung Ying (b. 1962), for example, is much less harsh, and her fashionable depiction of extreme situations seems somewhat contrived. In the story "K'ang-nai-hsin chü-lo-pu" (Club of Carnations; 1994), Hung portrays a group of young girls with lesbian inclinations hunting down men who have committed serious offenses against women.

The uproar caused by the phenomenon of the "cultural anarchists" continued until the mid-1990s. Younger, rather self-righteous critics joined in a concerted attack on all those writers and critics, including the senior figure Wang Meng, who tolerated the Wang Shuo phenomenon and who accepted such cheap entertainment literature on a par with the serious art for which they themselves were striving. During 1996 and early 1997, Wang Shuo became a scapegoat in the struggle of the party against "spiritual pollution."

Regained Self-Assurance: China's New Cultural Critics

The two decades of the 1980s and 1990s finally saw the emergence of new literary and cultural critics who appeared able to cope with their task as intellectuals. They displayed the same self-assurance witnessed in several other Southeast Asian and East Asian countries during the early 1990s.

Some of these critics were active from within China, for example, Chi Hung-chen (b. 1955) and Ch'en Hsiao-ming (b. 1959), as well as Ch'en P'ing-yüan (b. 1954), a literary historian from Peking University. With silent contempt for any further constructions of orthodoxy, Ch'en P'ing-yüan attempted to elaborate new methods of looking at modern narrative literature along the lines of a genre history of early-modern narrative literature: methodically sound, brilliant in the display of details, and open to new solutions.

Other critics, among them Henry Chao, joined in the international literary debate from outside China. The reflections of these intellectuals on recent developments in China are presented in such a way that Western literary critics and literary historians have begun to take notice and to listen again for the first time in many decades. China's new critics have been guiding scholars, translators, publishers, and readers cautiously (and in the face of political pressures) to important new works and developments. They have been reassuming—with an understandable degree of pride—the role of native interpreter, which since the 1950s had to be relinquished because of the party's claim be the sole arbiter of interpretation, much as had occurred with regard to the interpretation of China's history and the study of contemporary political developments.

Henry Chao, as a representative of this new generation of critics, studied abroad (at the University of California at Berkeley) and, like the Republican author Lao She (pseudonym of Shu Ch'ing-ch'un; 1899–1966) or Taiwan's Ma Sen (b. 1932), spent many years at the School of Oriental and African Studies in London. Chao comments on contemporary cultural developments, both in English and in Chinese. As a critic close to Pei Tao's émigré journal *Chin-t'ien* (Today), which is published separately in Chinese and, in abridged form, in English, Chao has strengthened the position of the aforementioned young PRC literary scholars and critics by compiling various anthologies, among which is his collection of avant-garde literature *Mi chou* (The Lost Boat; 1993), which, as the editor emphasizes, was compiled strictly from a literary viewpoint. Other collections include Chao's *T'ien-hsia ti-hsia* (Under Sky Under Ground; 1994) and his outstanding volume of essays *Pi-yao te ku-tu* (The Need for Solitude; 1995), which is devoted on the surface to a formal analysis of narrative discourse, but in reality treats "inevitable loneliness" as an essential condition for the leading literati of the avant-garde—and possibly also for most other contemporary Chinese intellectuals.

Chao documents the absurd texts of the "new literary start" by the writers of the 1990s that seemed to come from nowhere. His perception of recent Chinese developments, departing clearly from the Maoist cultural "desert" of abandoned traditions, fits anew into the overall scheme of Chinese cultural evolution down through the centuries. He sees the present phase of transition above all as a creative element in a cultural reorientation that is taking place in ruptures. The emergence of an anticulture—in particular the iconoclastic elements within it—is for him more or less just a metaphor, as they existed within the new literature of the May Fourth movement after 1919. In reality, the foundations have now been laid for a new contemporary culture of China.

Chao, therefore, is essentially optimistic about China's cultural future. It remains to be seen, however, whether he is trying to provoke a new self-awareness, simply encouraging Chinese writers, or actually commenting on facts. Whatever the case, critic Chao Yi-heng advises patience. He sees such reorientation phases in the Chinese context as complex, somewhat mysterious processes, and he appeals to all those who have raised the alarm about China's cultural crisis:

> More than one hundred years have passed, with still no immediate prospect of success. Yet history tells us that the reorientation of Chinese culture always took much longer than one century. If that is the case, my pessimistic friends should perhaps be less worried.

Literature and the Authorities: Developments Leading Up to the Fifth Writers' Congress of 1996

Tensions between the authorities and writers are a perennial theme of cultural life in authoritarian societies of leftist as well as rightist persuasion. The literary historian's job is to record the effects of repression on the creative efforts of the country's intellectuals and writers. There is much to be learned from such a record, and in the case of China even more so if parallels are drawn with the Soviet or Russian situation: Leninist (1918–1924), Stalinist (1925–1953), late Soviet (1954–1984), Perestroika (1985–1991), and Post-Perestroika (1991–1996) developments have their parallels in early Maoist, Cultural Revolution, early reform, and post-1989 China. The years from the mid-1970s to the mid-1980s have been recorded in Ho Yü-huai's analysis *Chien-so ho fang-sung te hsün-huan: 1976 chih 1986 nien ch'i-chien Chung-kuo cheng-chih yü wen-hsüeh te kuan-hsi* (translated into English as *Cycles of Repression and Relaxation: Politico-Literary Events in China*; 1992), and the following years in, for example, *Ta-lu tang-tai ming-jen p'ing-chuan* (Biographies of Famous Cultural Personalities from China Mainland—Creators of a Civil Society; 1995). In 1996 and early 1997 Chinese intellectuals in the cultural field faced tension in their relations with the authorities, the extent of which became an issue of debate among Chinese critics outside the PRC.

Strictly speaking, the struggle is only about creating the *preconditions* of literature. Liberation from repression, when the freedom of the press is guaranteed for the creative intellectual—as seems to have been the case in Taiwan since 1987—does not in itself guarantee that literary art works of excellence will be produced. The test of this in China remains to be seen.

After the Chinese Communist Party convened the sixth plenum of its fourteenth Central Committee (October 7–10, 1996), Chai T'ai-feng, together with the party secretary of the Chung-kuo (or, in the 1950s, Chung-hua ch'üan-kuo) wen-hsüeh yi-shu chieh lien-ho-hui (referred to as "Wen-lien" for short; [All-] China Federation of Literary and Art Circles), Kao Chan-hsiang, and other party collaborators, organized the fifth congress of their organization on December 16–20, 1996, parallel with the fifth plenum of the Chung-kuo tso-chia hsieh-hui (Chinese Writers' Federation), which had been held on May 27–31, 1996. The literary and arts congress was the first meeting of its kind since December 1984 because of the upheavals and uncertainties of 1989, in particular the protests at T'ien-an-men Square. The December 1996 event opened with attacks on the previous congress, which had been conducted under the guidance of then Secretary General of the CCP, Hu Yao-pang (1915–1989), whose death had incited demonstrations culminating in the protests at T'ien-an-men. The 1984 congress was cited as one of the direct reasons for all the "liberalization" (*tzu-yu-hua*) of 1987 and the crises of 1989.

During the CCP Central Committee plenum in 1979, Chief of the General Staff, Teng Hsiao-p'ing, had called in his address for a cautious relaxation in the cultural field. President Chiang Tse-min, in his conservative programmatic talk at the sixth plenum of the CCP's fourteenth Central Committee in 1996, attempted to strengthen his authority on ideological questions and propagated a new orthodox nationalism directed against the "infiltration of (Western) colonial culture."

The 1996 congress proved uneventful in resolving differences between the forces of the party that wished to keep literature in check and those authors who were seeking an enhanced role in social and cultural change. As they had done in the past, the congress's organizers used the venerable writer Pa Chin, now ninety-two, as a mere figurehead. They reserved all influence within the Federation for the party committees. The chairpersons, elected from among the writers at the central and provincial levels, were assigned no active role whatsoever. Dramatist Ts'ao Yü (1910–1996), designated to remain the head of the Federation, died suddenly a few days before the event; the former acting minister of culture Chou Wei-chih (b. 1916), a composer, was moved in as the second figurehead in this farce, alongside Pa Chin. Prominent exile writers and journalists like Liu Pin-yen, Liu Tsai-fu, and Ko Yang (b. 1916?) were ousted from the Federation, as also were other critics, including the outspoken translator Yang Hsien-yi (b. 1915) and the scholar Wu Tsu-kuang (b. 1917). The Shanghai writer Pai Hua had already been removed earlier through intrigues in the spring of 1996, ahead of the "elections" of the local branch of the Federation.

In the run-up to the congress, Chai and his deputy party secretaries visited and wooed a dozen veteran leftist writers and critics, including Lin Mo-han (b. 1913), Tsang K'o-chia (b. 1905), Yao Hsüeh-yin (b. 1910), and the dethroned Mongolian author Malcinkuu (Ma-la-ch'in-fu; b. 1930), as well as a few liberal authors and poets like Ping Hsin (pen name of Hsieh Wan-ying; 1900–1999), Pa Chin, Ai Ch'ing, Shao Yen-hsiang (b. 1933), and the cultural bureaucrat Ch'en Huang-mei (1913–1996), who had supported some liberal causes. At the same time, a new kind of campaign was launched against Wang Meng, who barely succeeded in defending his position as one of the deputy chairmen and who now appears to have become a symbol of the cultural liberalization so detested by the hard-liner cadres. After earlier attacks, which had triggered a lawsuit brought by Wang Meng before they petered out, he was again attacked in 1996 and early 1997 because in the past he had welcomed Wang Shuo and his nonchalant *p'i-tzu* texts as refreshing literary innovations of the 1990s. Mo Yen too drew renewed criticism for his novel *Feng-ju fei-t'un* (Full Breasts and Fat Asses; 1995) about superficial consumerism and, in 1996, was forced to halt the distribution of the book. The sex scenes in the novel were used as a pretext to attack him politically. The message was clear: disillusionment and cynicism of the kind propagated by Wang Shuo, which had swept the country through the tens of millions of copies of his books, were now to be eschewed; politically unreliable cultural figures like Mo Yen and Wang Meng were no longer to be left alone. Wang Shuo, the voice of a disillusioned generation because he had had the audacity to stand in the way of the government efforts to raise the nation's level of "spiritual civilization," was in serious trouble: during the summer of 1996, the Propaganda Department of the CCP ordered a halt to new printings of Wang's collected works; he was accused of having ridiculed China's noble values. Two movie projects were scrapped, television scripts failed to pass the censors, and a screenplay based on his story "I Am Your Dad" was banned. Wang was accused of "promoting the worship of money, hedonism, and extreme individualism."

In addition to the criticisms of Mo Yen and the two Wangs, which by implication included writers like Ts'an Hsüeh and the entire avant-garde, new attacks were directed against *Kao-pieh ko-ming* (A Farewell to Revolution; 1996), a dialog between Li Tse-hou (b. 1930), a historian of Chinese philosophy, and Liu Tsai-fu, a literary scholar. Ironically, the book—itself an attack on radicalism written by Li and Liu while in exile in the United States and a plea for gradual reforms in a future China—had already drawn some negative commentary from a very different direction: the younger generation of PRC intellectuals living abroad.

Outrage at international criticism of China's political system and the various forms of cultural repression did not produce reactions from the government alone. Both young intellectuals and the general public responded with a new kind of political and cultural nationalism, reminiscent of earlier calls for a kind of neoauthoritarianism. From such nationalist positions, many young scholars, writers, and journalists launched counterattacks on all criticisms of China—whether from inside the country or from abroad. Suggestions that this kind of hollow nationalism and patriotism had once before proved a trap for Chinese intellectuals (ultimately ordered to act "as cogs in the state machine," as Kao Hsing-chien put it) were ignored.

Dissident Harry Wu (Wu Hung-ta; b. 1937), for example, was vilified as a phony careerist for his exposure of the Chinese gulag in the international media and in his English-language book *Laogai: The Chinese Gulag* (1992). The best-seller *Chung-kuo k'o-yi shuo pu: Leng-chan hou-shih-tai te cheng-chih yü ch'ing-kan chüeh-tse* (China Can Say No! Options for Politics and Emotions in the Post–Cold War Period; 1996) by a group of malcontent young journalists, whose publication was tacitly approved by the Chiang leadership, and similar book-length attacks on China's "enemies" have been analyzed in the West with too much emphasis on the political angle: only the attacks on the superpower America and an economically and politically threatening Japanese empire were registered and emphasized, as well as the desire for a new strategic alliance with Russia. But these books can also be read as a rather revealing cultural commentary and protest: castigation of the lack of international recognition, as demonstrated by an alleged "reticence" to consider a Chinese author for the Nobel Prize in literature theretofore. Seen from a psychoanalytical angle, national reactions to irritating rapid changes, disturbance or crisis, and more personal, even sexual, emotions of perplexity and inadequacy seem to have been unacceptably mixed and were compensated for, as they were in early Republican literature in such works as Yü Ta-fu's story "Ch'en-lun" (Sinking; 1921).

What appears absent in China is a sober analysis of real cultural accomplishments since 1980 and the clear definition of an official cultural policy that seeks international recognition for such accomplishments. Many Chinese critics in the mid- to late 1990s seemed to feel frustrated on many fronts. In this climate of new irritations, any hopes for a debate on the role of literature in cultural advancement, any improvement in the cultural field through help from the political side, any expectation of a reasonable representation of the contemporary Chinese cultural scene by the authorities and their designated critics had to be temporarily abandoned.

The reshaping of the writers' and artists' federation was largely ignored abroad. At the CCP's sixth plenum of the fourteenth Central Committee, Chiang Tse-min delivered his speech "Chung-kung chung-yang kuan-yü chia-ch'iang she-hui-chu-yi ching-shen wen-ming chien-she jo-kan chung-yao wen-t'i te chüeh-yi" (Decisions of the Central Committee of the Communist Party on Some Important Questions Regarding Strengthening the Building of Socialist Spiritual Culture), the implications of which were clearly intended for dissemination to writers and artists. Manipulation of the writers' and artists' federation inspired ironic commentaries even among cadres, as it proved incapable of opening up new roads: a reversion to yesterday's solutions and double standards widened the gap between media language and reality; too many futile attempts were made to revive old recipes of Maoist-socialist campaigning. It is likely that all the verbiage of the 1996 congress, with the concomitant propaganda efforts, was forgotten the moment it was uttered.

HONG KONG: BELATED SEARCH FOR REGIONAL IDENTITY

It is remarkable that an international city like Hong Kong, which can justifiably take pride in its long tradition of relatively unrestricted freedom of the press, has produced so few literary testimonies of self-contemplation. Only a handful of writers have reflected on their own situation and its evolution in pre- and postwar Hong Kong and on the role of the colony during the years of exciting affluence after the Cultural Revolution in the late 1970s and the 1980s. In the main, the West's image of Hong Kong has been generated through Western works and films like Richard Mason's *The World of Suzie Wong* (1957), Han Suyin's *A Many-Splendored Thing* (1952), or other commercially successful novels like James Clavell's *Tai Pan* (1966). These depictions usually capture the world of British-Chinese big business and Hong Kong's glittering high society.

What Is Representative of Hong Kong Literature?

Literary scholars in Hong Kong have compiled a few surveys of Hong Kong's regional literature. But these studies, instead of being historical accounts of fascinating local cultural developments, seem more like chagrined appeals for such a literature. In an accompanying climate of scholarly indifference, only Lo Wai-luen (Lu Wei-luan; b. 1939) has spent years of painstaking reconstruction work to revive the memory of those noteworthy Chinese writers who, like Yü Ta-fu, Hsiao Hung (1911–1942), or Chang Ai-ling (Eileen Chang; 1920–1996), had at some time passed through Hong Kong or lived in the colony for a period of time. We are told about literature *in* and *from* Hong Kong, but definitely not about literature *of* Hong Kong. Only in the last few years before 1997, when control of the colony was returned to China, was there an unprecedented search for the roots of Hong Kong identity and a monumental documentary effort by William Tay (Cheng Shu-sen; b. 1948) and others to present and preserve what long ago should have been unearthed and critically re-evaluated from Hong Kong–related literature and culture.

Shih Shu-ch'ing (b. 1945), sister of the Taiwanese female author Li Ang (b. 1952), who lived in Hong Kong for more than a decade with her British banker husband, published excellent portraits of PRC writers of the 1980s in Taiwan's *Shih-pao* (China Times). However, her cycle of novellas about life in Hong Kong's upper stratum fails to go beyond the level of entertainment. In a trilogy of novels published beginning in 1995, she made a second attempt to portray Hong Kong in anticipation of the year 1997, before eventually moving back to Taiwan.

At the same time, official Chinese channels are making last-ditch efforts, through middlemen and fellow travelers, to establish some kind of Chinese Hong Kong literature acceptable to PRC standards. These include, for example, the activities of the journalist and writer Liu Yi-ch'ang (b. 1918), and his journal *Hsiang-kang wen-hsüeh* (Hong Kong Literature), as well as initiatives by a group of Peking-friendly local writers. Tolerated until 1997 in a gray area, "immigrant" postmodernist PRC Chinese writers like Ma Chien (b. 1953), however, were publishing their works, for example, in an oppositional literary journal, *Wen-yi pao* (News from Literature and the Arts; 1995–1996), disrespectfully appropriating the name of the official national literary journal. Hsi Hsi (b. 1938), more urbane and sophisticated than most writers in the realm of "cultural China," ultimately found more readers in Taiwan than in Hong Kong, where the media clearly failed to take her seriously as a local author and cultural symbol of the city.

The restless climate of the 1990s tempted young scholars to reject the idea of defining a so-called Hong Kong identity through such undistinguished literature. These intellectuals prefer to pursue the concept of popular culture, which they believe can define and express the true nature of Hong Kong culture much more aptly. Popular culture embraces television, film, video, karaoke, fashion, pop music, lifestyle in general, and much more—together, they claim, all these give the city its unique identity. Taking this approach, intellectuals are finding vestiges of local postmodern instability and rootlessness, evidence of dissent and critical inquiry, in clear contrast to the enforced adaptation that for decades has been indispensable for Chinese in the PRC. Likewise, these scholars find themselves confronted in Hong Kong with a preemptive cultural submissiveness toward the new rulers, who, they fear, will be under orders from Peking to bring the former British colony into line.

REGIONALISM IN JEOPARDY: TAIWAN'S LITERARY SCENE

Taiwan's uncertainties with respect to its cultural identity remain of a different nature. In contrast to the situation in Hong Kong, the island's democracy still has a chance—albeit jeopardized both from inside and outside—to move toward a more stable cultural consciousness and to establish an unchallenged local Taiwanese identity. Taiwan's literature is noteworthy in terms of both artistic value and cultural policy, because of the particular forms and special ways in which it has developed over almost a century, in contrast to the other Chinese regional and provincial literatures. Taiwan's writers have been motivated primarily by the spirit of resistance against foreign rule; occasionally, however, there emerges a touch of melancholic self-limitation and a preoccupation with the central question of Taiwan's identity.

Taiwan's New Literature originates in the early 1920s, after rather marginal and insignificant classical-literary-language beginnings in the seventeenth century in this southern haven of immigrants (mostly from Fukien province) or, as it later became, the outermost province of the last Chinese imperial dynasty. Politically, the New Literature was molded and often distorted by increasing repression under Japanese colonial rule (1895–1945) and, subsequently, by the mainland Chinese occupation mentality of the early KMT regime on the island. It was not until the end of the 1980s, when the democratization process started in earnest on Taiwan, that the literature of the colonial period could be rediscovered or "excavated," as it were. Only since that time have forces been mobilized in an effort to "come to terms with the past" and to define Taiwan's vacillating identity. Politically and culturally, there are two opposing positions: while one side is striving for gradually increasing independence, the other continues to see Taiwan in the context of China. These positions appear so irreconcilable that no compromise seems likely or even conceivable. This underlying tension between "Taiwan consciousness" or Taiwanese nativism or regionalism, on the one hand, and "China consciousness," on the other, has in any case prevented the creation of a balanced platform from which Taiwanese scholars might have presented the long-awaited literary history of Taiwan as a cornerstone of the new cultural identity. In times of "nation building," such as during the first few years of the German empire under Bismarck, the public longs for a solid foundation of cultural identity. The fact that attempts in this direction have been made in Taiwan for three decades now and that such an identity-creating work for the field of literature has so far not been written must be taken in itself as symptomatic of Taiwan's inner crisis at the turn of the twenty-first century.

In the PRC, surprisingly, Taiwan literature was conspicuously brought to the reader during the 1980s. Although this "presentation" was dictated by the regime, it was nevertheless handled with remarkable foresight by the PRC scholars entrusted with the task. They published several literary history surveys, which—as relations between Peking and Taipei showed signs of relaxing—even found their way into Taiwanese bookstores both in the original and as reprints.

Taiwanese Authors of the Japanese Period Rediscovered

Taiwan's most important authors from the Japanese period did not generally come to be known until the 1990s and only then began to gain increasing recognition by literary scholars in the West. A detailed knowledge of their background and their ideas is vital to an understanding and a characterization of Taiwanese regionalism.

Ch'en Hsü-ku (1891–1965), like Ts'ai Ch'iu-t'ung (1900–1984), wrote short stories giving a satirical account of the arrogance of the Japanese colonials, especially the role of the Japanese police on Taiwan and the often slavish servility of many Taiwanese. Yang Shou-yü (1905–1959), a close friend of Lai Ho (1894–1943), the most significant author of the time, was a very prolific fiction writer in the Japanese period who also gained a reputation as a poet. Among the subjects of his many stories were the lives of the lower social classes, the street traders, the unemployed, and women. Wang Shih-lang (1908–1984) was a member of prominent literary groups in Taiwan and for a time edited *T'ai-wan hsin wen-hsüeh* (Taiwan's New Literature), the journal founded by Yang K'uei (1905–1985), the second most important author of the period. After 1946, Wang was an influential journalist. He is probably best known for his short story "Yeh-yü" (Night Rain), which describes the breakup of a family after an unsuccessful strike by printing workers.

Chang Wen-huan (1909–1978) wrote stirring novels and short stories. He attended middle school and university in Japan, where he was cofounder of the journal *Formosa*, which aimed at creating "a genuine Taiwanese literature." Chang wrote only in Japanese, and one of his short novels became very popular with Japanese readers. Lung Ying-tsung (1911–1999) belonged to the group of authors who were increasingly influenced by Japan. It is thus no coincidence that he and Chang Wen-huan represented Taiwan at the notorious First Conference on the Literature of Greater East Asia in Tokyo, in November 1942. The Japanese government used this conference to consolidate Japan's cultural supremacy in the colonies and in newly acquired territories by honoring collaboration-inclined authors. Finally, one of the most talented writers of the Japanese period was the author and literary critic Lü Ho-jo (1914–1947), from Taichung.

Anti-Communist Narrative Writing of the 1950s

A number of authors from the Japanese period have recently been brought to light again by major cultural "excavation efforts," including such prominent representatives as the physician Lai Ho and the leftist activist Yang K'uei, who tragically spent much of his life in the prisons of the Japanese and especially the KMT. The literature that emerged in Taiwan after 1949 has also been "revisited" in recent years. Younger literary critics have found that the literature of the 1950s and early 1960s needs to be re-examined, re-evaluated, and reinterpreted.

Indeed, a kind of nostalgia for the four postwar decades appeared to permeate society in the mid-1990s, and publications in this vein, for example, from the *China Times* Press under feature editor and poet Yang Tse (b. 1954), presented a new and enlightening interpretation of the past. The writers of the Japanese colonial period mentioned above were isolated or ousted from the literary stage after that period ended in 1945 with the Japanese defeat in World War II, and the direction was now determined by young intellectuals from the mainland, supporters of the KMT. They in turn were required by the KMT to present a literature of strict ideological subordination and militant anti-Communism.

Chiang Kuei (1908–1980) was one of the most prominent representatives of anti-Communist narrative literature in Taiwan during the 1950s. Chiang's biography is available in English (published by Timothy A. Ross in 1974), as is his best-known novel, *Hsüan-feng* (Whirlwind; 1957). Chu Hsi-ning (b. 1926 in Shantung province) is an intellectual and popular writer who came to prominence from the camp of the KMT military. P'eng Ko (b. 1926), a versatile journalist, was active in Taiwan in the service of the KMT and for many years worked as editor-in-chief of the official KMT newspaper *Chung-yang jih-pao* (Central Daily News). P'eng published more than two dozen nonfiction works, translations, pieces of narrative prose, and essays. P'an Jen-mu (b. 1920) was one of the most popular female members of this group of authors.

Taiwanese Modernism

During the late 1950s and early 1960s, a group of young writers in Taiwan, most of them belonging to the second generation of mainland immigrants, was deeply influenced by modern Western literature. Their models were Camus and Sartre, Faulkner and Joyce. It is important to remember that at this time Taiwan was a "cultural desert" that had been cut adrift both from the lively literary scene in China during the 1930s and from more recent postwar developments on the mainland. Some of these writers left Taiwan and emigrated to the United States and elsewhere in order to retain their intellectual freedom. Because they continued to influence literary circles in Taiwan and also influenced writing on the mainland after the late 1970s, they are sometimes referred to as "semi-emigrants." The best known is Pai Hsien-yung (b. 1937), who taught at the University of California (Santa Barbara) for many years and who portrayed the uprooted military and administrative élite of the KMT in Taiwan (*T'ai-pei jen* [People from Taipei; 1971]). Another is Wang Wen-hsing (b. 1939), author of the two modernist novels *Chia-pien* (Family Catastrophe; 1972) and *Pei-hai te jen* (Backed Against the Sea; 1981). The forces of cultural nativism, however, were such that these authors and intellectuals, who still typified Taiwanese literature abroad to a certain extent in the 1990s, gradually began to take second place behind the more important *hsiang-t'u* (nativist) writers for most readers in Taiwan, who were more attuned to such local-based and local-oriented literature.

Authors of Nativist Literature

In the 1970s, local Taiwanese writers again joined together to form a group that was primarily opposed to the then-dominant modernists, who had largely ignored Taiwanese reality, and also to the rigid KMT establishment. These writers achieved success with what became known as nativist literature, which evolved into the literary mainstream on Taiwan for the next several years.

Li Ch'iao (b. 1934) spent twenty years teaching in rural Taiwan, staying well away from Taipei, the northern "capital of the mainlanders." He authored a trilogy on the history of Taiwan and, in 1995, a fictionalized account of the February 1947 massacre of the local population by the KMT army. Yang Ch'ing-ch'u (b. 1940 in a village near Tainan), who worked at many jobs, both as a laborer and as a white-collar worker, gained recognition as an unsophisticated writer of the working classes, recounting what he himself had experienced. Yang also established a cultural center and a publishing company. Another nativist writer, Wang T'o, and Yang paid for their convictions with long prison sentences; even after they stopped writing creatively, both remained actively involved in cultural policy and general political issues.

Lin Huai-min (b. 1947 in Chiayi) studied in Iowa and took up ballet in New York. He wrote numerous short stories about the search of Taiwan's youth for a new identity. He established a modern Taiwanese ballet, the Cloud Gate Ensemble (Yün-men wu-chi), with both a national and local Chinese repertoire. Lin Shuang-pu (b. 1952), who like Li Ch'iao opted for the life of a teacher in rural Taiwan, away from the "polluted" city of Taipei, has been one of the most outspoken of the local Taiwanese authors. The productive Lin has collected his thoughts and creative ideas—often written in great haste for journals and newspapers—in more than two dozen books. The radical nativist author Sung Tse-lai (b. 1952) changed course many times. Following Oswald Spengler, he pessimistically forecast the downfall not only of the West but also of East Asia; he then, for a decade, sought salvation in local forms of Zen (Ch'an) Buddhism, represented a "literature of human rights," and wrote a bestseller about the murderous environmental destruction on Taiwan. In 1996, he returned to literature as editor of a radical nativist journal, *T'ai-wan hsin-wen-hsüeh chi-k'an* (New Taiwanese Literature Quarterly), mercilessly attacking every literary production close to semiofficial cultural viewpoints and introducing a host of young talents. Wu Chin-fa (b. 1954), a journalist from the idyllic village of Mei-nung near Kaohsiung, has portrayed the tormented search of the Taiwanese for an identity of their own in contrast to culture that had been imposed on them, first by the Chinese empire, then by the Japanese, and more recently by the KMT, which had fled the mainland. Particularly noteworthy are Wu's keen psychological observations and his use of the narrative techniques of the "absurd." The second important theme of this radical author, who sympathizes so compassionately with his fellow Taiwanese, is the history and culture of Taiwan's displaced aboriginal peoples.

Women's Literature on Taiwan

In the 1980s, many female writers who were able to build on the foundations laid by their predecessors came to the fore. Lin Hai-yin (b. 1919) had gone to

Peking to study and worked there as a journalist before returning to Taiwan in 1948. Many of her writings on the subject of women and the family are based on her own experience of life on the mainland. This is particularly true of her autobiographical novel *Ch'eng-nan chiu-shih* (Memories of Peking: Southside Stories; 1960), which is available in English translation. As feature editor of *Lien-ho pao* (United Daily), she had great influence on the literary scene in Taiwan for several years. Yü Li-hua (b. 1931), who emigrated from Taiwan to the United States, pioneered "foreign students' literature," which in the 1960s reflected the often traumatic experiences of the students from Taiwan living abroad. Author Ou-yang Tzu (b. 1939), a "modernist" who in 1962 left Taiwan to settle in the United States, was considered to excel at drawing psychological portraits, especially of women. Liao Hui-ying (b. 1948), from Taichung, who pursued a career in business after graduating from college, has portrayed, in a series of short stories and more recently in novels, the problems of the new type of modern Taiwanese woman, especially the independent businesswoman. Su Wei-chen (b. 1954) belongs to the camp of regime-friendly intellectuals, as she was educated at the party cadre academy in the milieu of the army. She is among those female writers who sought, stylistically, to emulate the precocious Shanghai author Chang Ai-ling, who in Taiwan had become something of a mythical literary paragon *in absentia*, though she lived in the United States. Su gained recognition with both short stories and novels; as editor of the feature section of the conservative *United Daily*, she too was able to influence Taiwan's literary scene considerably. Chu T'ien-hsin (b. 1958), the daughter of the army writer Chu Hsi-ning, since the end of the 1980s has portrayed in her narrative writings young female protagonists who play an active part in defining their changed role in society and whose attitude toward sexuality is extremely liberal by any standards. Chu T'ien-hsin's sister, Chu T'ien-wen (b. 1956), is even more famous, having written *Huang-jen shou-chi* (Notes of a Desolate Man) and other prize-winning novels.

On the Development of Taiwanese Poetry

Like narrative prose, poetry on Taiwan changed course many times, from the experiments in the spirit of the May Fourth movement, a style of modernism that was heavily influenced by the West and also by Japanese lyrical prototypes, to a new and deeply committed Taiwanese poetry with a strong local flavor. Taiwan's mainland poets and writers paved the way for this development.

Ya Hsien (b. 1932) rose to prominence as an experimental modernist who influenced the literary climate in Taiwan not only through his own poetry but also, until the mid-1990s, through his position as senior editor of the influential *United Daily* feature section. Lo Fu (b. 1928) is one of several poets and narrative writers to come from the military. At the end of the 1980s, he renewed contact with contemporary poets on the mainland through his journal *Ch'uang-shih-chi* (Creation). His restless artistic self-consciousness caused him to vacillate between the pride he and his fellow poets felt as the real precursors of the *meng-lung* (misty, obscure; see Introduction) poets in the PRC and the melancholy they experienced knowing that, as representatives of a provincial literature, they would never receive adequate recognition either in China or elsewhere. In 1996, both Ya and Lo—despite their strong attachment to Taiwan—ironically made arrangements for their retirement in Canada. Yü Kuang-chung (b. 1928), who came to Taiwan from southern China, made a lasting impression on the lyrical scene in the 1960s and 1970s. However, as a close supporter of the KMT regime's cultural policy, he polemically opposed nativist literature, a position that lost him many young readers. An otherwise highly respected university professor, he wrote a great deal of poetry and essays and acted as a translator and publisher with an international perspective. Yale University senior lecturer Cheng Ch'ou-yü (b. 1933), whose poetry is widely read, can, like Pai Hsien-yung, be seen as a representative of mainland writers who emigrated to the United States. Younger regional Taiwanese poets include the Kaohsiung physician Cheng Chiung-ming (b. 1948) and the versatile Li Min-yung (b. 1947). Li is a frequent contributor to the press and an expert on cultural policy. He has written several volumes of poetry and essays and published impressive collections of social and political analysis.

Popular and Mass Literature

Until the 1960s, Taiwan had been a closed society. The mass literature that had spread through the island from Taipei, with its maudlin pseudo-traditionalism and cynical disregard for suppression, had functioned as an expedient diverting attention from political dictatorship and the manifold social taboos. As Taiwan opened up increasingly in the 1980s, an all-pervading popular literature, which was influenced particularly by the United States and by Japan and was consistent with a noisy, volatile television culture, eventually created books that were commercially successful. At the same time, these developments largely displaced most serious attempts at creating literary works.

Kuo Liang-hui (b. 1926) wrote countless sentimental love stories that found their way to the mainland. With her apolitical accounts of life in the Sahara and other far-off places, San Mao (1943–1991) caught the imagination of Taiwan's 1970s youth, who felt increasingly caged in on the island. Ch'iung Yao (b. 1938) wrote more than fifty tear-jerking best-sellers about love and marriage. When her books became available in the PRC, her popularity with schoolchildren and students there was so overwhelming that a "Ch'iung Yao storm" swept over the mainland. Chao Shu-hsia (Susie Ch'en; b. 1931), who settled in Switzerland, is one of the few popular Chinese writers living in Europe to have achieved some success both in Taiwan and on the mainland with sentimental and patriotic subjects. A film was made based on her novel about the courtesan Sai Chin-hua and her liaison with Count Waldersee, the German commander of the allied troops that suppressed the Boxer Rebellion in 1900.

The Significance of Cultural Regionalism in Taiwan

Literature, like movies, must be considered an indispensable element of the new Taiwanese consciousness for this island, with its own particular colonial and postcolonial development. It will take generations of Taiwanese scholars to "excavate" the country's cultural heritage after decades of forced obscurity and suppressed history. Only then will they be able fully to define and establish a new Taiwanese identity.

The problem of defining or redefining one's own personal and regional identity—which, in this case, also means breaking free of colonial consciousness and facing the postcolonial situation—has global significance. The loss of leading figures in Taiwan's fight for cultural freedom, the psychological and physical annihilation of intellectuals through persecution and long terms of imprisonment, the elemental uneasiness from collaborating with the ruling groups of the day, the sensitive question of how much opportunism is permissible before it irreparably compromises one's character and integrity—these are all experiences and challenges found throughout the world. Nor does life in exile present problems that are unique to Taiwan.

The significance of the Taiwan paradigm—indeed the essence of Taiwan's regional literary development—from a global perspective lies in such common elements, in similar challenges, and in comparable responses, both on the individual level and seen from the perspective of a vigorous, creative local society.

THE PROSPECTS FOR GREATER CHINA

The different cultural manifestations of regional development in China, Hong Kong, and Taiwan, as mapped out above, as well as the equally challenging realities of "Cultural China" in Southeast Asia, and more marginally in North America, incorporate the broadest range of theoretical possibilities of cultural interaction. But the crux of the matter seems to be less in effectively constructing theoretical models of "Greater China" that seek to explain the complex interaction between the many different regions of "Cultural China." Rather, it is in the interplay of the unpredictable actual forces of rejuvenation and adaptation, from postcolonial premises, to a globalized cultural situation, as shown above for the mid-1990s and preceding years. China is often insufficiently aware that the old pose of cultural unity and superiority, even in a more moderate modern disguise, tends to create strong anxieties among regional partners. The pressures from the center and the consequences of protest and conformism in cities, in regions, and in the hearts of individuals are strong enough to trigger further tragedies; likewise, such interaction may surprise the world with fascinating new cultural products, activities, and visions.

Helmut Martin

PART V

Drama

Chapter 41

TRADITIONAL DRAMATIC LITERATURE

Since this chapter is part of a history of Chinese literature, it does not aim to provide a detailed survey of the development of Chinese theater through the ages. Instead it will focus on dramatic literature, that is, those texts that were distributed and appreciated as literature in premodern or modern times. This means that this chapter will mainly deal with the texts of *tsa-chü* and *ch'uan-ch'i* plays. *Tsa-chü*, a relatively short form, emerged as a major theatrical genre by the middle of the thirteenth century in northern China; its heyday on the stage was over by the middle of the fifteenth century. *Ch'uan-ch'i*, a much longer form, developed out of *hsi-wen*, a theatrical genre that had come into being in the course of the thirteenth century in Wenchow and from there had spread over the region of the lower Yangtze River (customarily known as Kiangnan); it was fully developed by the middle of the fourteenth century, but the period of its greatest productivity comprised the sixteenth and seventeenth centuries. As *ch'uan-ch'i* established itself as a minor branch of literature in the course of the sixteenth century among Kiangnan literati, *tsa-chü* in its wake also achieved that status.

Tsa-chü and *ch'uan-ch'i* developed out of earlier and simpler forms of theater that have left us hardly any textual materials. Alongside *tsa-chü* and *ch'uan-ch'i* there always existed other genres of theater of varying degrees of sophistication. Modern scholars distinguish more than three hundred different genres of traditional Chinese theater (some of which originated only in the twentieth century), and the number may be increased if one also includes the various forms of puppet plays. Many of these genres utilize scripts, but none of them achieved a literary status comparable to that of *tsa-chü* or *ch'uan-ch'i*. This also holds true for the numerous preserved libretti of Peking opera (*ching-hsi*), a genre of traditional Chinese theater that took shape in Peking starting in the last quarter of the eighteenth century and spread to other places beginning in the later decades of the nineteenth century. To the extent that these scripts and libretti are studied, they are studied almost exclusively as documents of theater history or of traditional ritual practices and religious beliefs. For many genres these scripts and libretti have been retrieved only in recent years through extensive efforts to document the surviving traditions of local drama, so it is quite possible that, in the future, when these texts have been studied in more detail, a broader range of texts will be included in the canon of dramatic literature.

However, as the shape of all dramatic texts has been determined by the conventions of performance, the theatrical practices that shaped the plays must be examined. This holds for any discussion of dramatic literature, but it is even more urgent in the Chinese case, as the performance practices of the traditional theater were (and, depending upon the genre, still are) in important aspects different from the performance practices of contemporary theater in the West. Two issues in particular deserve attention: (1) the boundaries between theater and other forms of stage performances, and (2) the interrelations between theater and (exorcistic) ritual (both in its distant origin and in its actual performance).

DRAMA AND OTHER FORMS OF PERFORMANCE

For practical purposes a play is defined here as any performance in which two or more persons, who are dressed for the part, mimic an action while engaging in dialog. This may seem straightforward enough, but problems abound. We may have only one actor or actress on stage engaged in a dramatic monologue. Plays that were written for just one actor or actress are very rare but do exist, for example, "Ch'iao-ying" (Portrait in Disguise), a one-act play by the nineteenth-century female playwright Wu Tsao (1799–1862). Moreover, the Chinese stage knows many skits that may be performed by a single player—as a prelude, an interlude, or an independent vaudeville item. At least from the sixteenth century onward, moreover, it was a quite common practice to perform highlights from longer plays that might feature only a single player. Such single scenes, then, were often filled out to make them into independent program items. These highlights are known as *che-tzu-hsi* (one-act plays). Plays may also contain extensive sections in which not a word is spoken, on occasion even complete scenes; such scenes were traditionally designated as *ya tsa-chü* (dumb shows).

In any genre of theater, a player may directly address the audience in an aside. The Chinese theater also freely makes use of this possibility, not only for asides but also for extensive and reliable self-introductions by players upon their first entrance, when they announce their identity and aims to the public before engaging in interaction with the other characters. This very economic feature of the traditional Chinese theater has often been interpreted as a remnant of the influence of storytelling on the development of drama. Although this seems questionable inasmuch as characters in storytelling do not introduce themselves but are introduced by the narrator, there exist theatrical genres in which use is made of pre-existing texts of prosimetric ballads as libretti. In the Yüan dynasty (1260–1368) villagers and soldiers banded together in order to "act out ballads" (*pan tz'u-hua*). In many varieties of so-called *No-hsi* (exorcistic drama) documented in recent years, numerous concrete examples of this practice have been recorded. In these modern cases, the text of the ballad is divided among the characters in the play in such a way that a specific actor speaks, recites, or sings not only the words spoken by the character in the ballad but also those lines of the ballad in which the actions of that character are narrated from a third-person perspective, in this way intermingling theater and storytelling. Such a use of ready-made ballad texts by simply cutting them up and dividing the lines among the characters in the play should be distinguished from the adaptation of the story of a ballad into another genre, for instance, one of the many genres of drama.

On the other hand, storytelling contains many theatrical elements. Although a single storyteller cannot dress the parts of all the different characters in his or her story, he or she will act out the different roles in his or her tale by intonation, accent, posture, and gesture. In some varieties of storytelling it was quite common to divide the text of the ballad to be performed among several performers, so that each of the performers would take on one or more specific characters. In such circumstances, the performance of a ballad closely approaches the public reading of a play, and one could easily see how such a performance might develop into a full-fledged dramatic performance as soon as the performers don costume and leave their seats.

Another modern genre of vaudeville that very closely approaches drama is *hsiang-sheng* (comic dialog or cross-talk), in which two performers engage in a quick exchange of witty, often satirical dialog. Usually they assume specific roles, if only those of two "concerned citizens," and the one thing that is lacking to turn their performance into a playlet is costume. Many scholars have noted the correspondences between *hsiang-sheng* and *ts'an-chün-hsi* (adjutant plays), comic dialogs between two or more performers that formed an important element in the court entertainment of the T'ang (618–907) and Sung (960–1279) dynasties; this genre of entertainment is considered one of the major precursors of the later full-fledged dramatic genres.

Theater and Ritual

It is often difficult not only to demarcate the boundaries between theater and other forms of entertainment but also to differentiate theatrical performance from ritual performance. The ultimate origins of Chinese theater must be sought in ritual performance. Furthermore, traditional Chinese theater retained many ritual functions even into the twenty-first century. One of the major features of Chinese popular religion, from the palace to the village, from the dawn of Chinese civilization to the present, consists of exorcistic rites, in which a specialist in religious affairs cleanses the local community (a house, a palace, a village, a city) of all evil by ritually turning himself into a god and killing or chasing away all demons—the demons may be represented by effigies or by assistants who act the part, while the religious specialist may be assisted by hosts of ghostly soldiers of his own, not only in his imagination but also in the flesh. The best-known of these rites was the great *No* (Exorcism) ceremony celebrated at the end of each year, as recorded since the time of Confucius. These rites were conspicuous for their terrifying chants, deafening music, colorful costumes, and spectacular action. The many martial plays in the repertoire of the traditional Chinese theater, in which great heroes of the past (who, often at the same time, are venerated as gods, e.g., Kuan Yü) massacre multitudes of enemies and drive off foreign foes, can be seen as a direct continuation of this exorcistic tradition. Stage characters such as Chung K'uei to this day perform primarily as exorcists. Some other types of plays are related to yet other types of rituals. The insistence on a happy ending in full plays can be seen as a reflection of the restoration of cosmic order that concludes many rituals.

Plays also were (and are) primarily performed on ritual occasions, as part of the ritual. The play can constitute the ritual by itself or can be tied to the occasion in other ways. The overwhelming majority of the population attended theatrical performances only on such occasions. Plays were performed at certain yearly festivals of a community (a family, a lineage, a neighborhood, a village) and whenever such a community felt a special need for divine assistance; plays might also be mounted to thank the gods for favors shown. Most major temples were provided with their own fixed stage, located opposite the main temple hall because the deity was the prime spectator. When such a fixed stage was not available, a temporary stage of fitting proportions was erected for performances, and if this could not be positioned opposite the main hall of the temple, the statue of the god might be moved to a temporary seat of honor. While the play was performed outside by the actors, other ritual specialists performed their ritual inside the temple. When the occasion called for it, a theater troupe might also be invited to perform at the house of the sponsors. This Chinese tradition of communal religious drama can in many ways be fruitfully compared to the late medieval European tradition of communal religious drama.

Commercial Theaters and the Acting Profession

Commercial theaters did eventually develop; actually this happened twice in Chinese history. From the late eleventh to the early fifteenth century, the capitals and other major urban centers featured commercial theaters. These offered a varied program of vaudeville and drama that one could watch after having paid an entrance fee—the performers might also make the rounds of the audience collecting donations. These early commercial theaters did not survive beyond the fifteenth century. By the late seventeenth century, large teahouses in the capital and other major cities started to add theater performances to their attractions, and in time these teahouses evolved once again into full-fledged commercial theaters. However, commercial theaters were always restricted to the largest urban centers, and they remained only one of the performance venues for the local actors.

Very rich households might support their own household troupe for the entertainment of the master of the house and his friends. The last century of the Ming was the heyday of such private troupes, when many wealthy theater aficionados instructed their household companies in the performance of plays of their own composition. If a family was as wealthy as the imperial family, it might even provide its private quarters with permanent stages. During the Ch'ing dynasty (1644–1911), the various imperial palaces in Peking and its environs were fitted out with many stages, including three-tiered stages that allowed for the performance of elaborate pageants composed expressly for this format. However, since performances at the palace were meant primarily as private entertainment for the imperial family, these extravaganzas played only a very limited role in the general development of drama. Traditional China did not know a court culture comparable to that of continental Europe during the sixteenth to eighteenth centuries, which played such an important role in the development of Western theater.

At court, eunuchs might be trained to serve as actors, but the Court Entertainment Bureau could also command performances by actors and actresses from outside the palace. In society at large acting usually was a family profession, as sons and daughters followed in the footsteps of their parents. Other new members might be recruited into the profession by purchase of young children. Training was a long and arduous process that could take many years. Occasionally gifted amateurs would "dive into the sea" and join the profession on their own initiative. Professional acting companies were all male, all female, or mixed, depending on local custom, a sponsor's taste, or legal rules. Professional actors and actresses had a very low social status. Until the early eighteenth century, their status was legally that of "base people" (i.e., social outcasts). Until well into the twentieth century, the acting profession had a highly unsavory reputation. In many areas of China, however, plays at local festivals were performed by regular members of the local community. In such cases no stigma was attached to taking part in the performance. On the contrary, playing one's role in such cases was a duty and an honor. In some villages, specific role(s) in these play(s) were handed down in locally established families for tens of generations.

The Prehistory of Chinese Theater

Although ritual was one source of traditional Chinese theater (and a very important one), it certainly was not the only tradition of performance that fed into full-fledged Chinese drama as it emerged into view in the thirteenth century. Song and dance are probably as old as the human race. Documents from the Chou dynasty (c. 1027–256 B.C.E.) inform us not only about the *No* ceremony but also about many other rituals involving song and dance. Many of these performances had a narrative content, for example, the military dances commemorating the victory of the Chou over the Shang (c. 1600–c. 1027 B.C.E.). From the Han dynasty (206 B.C.E.–220 C.E.) we have extensive descriptions (and pictorial evidence) of the *pai-hsi* (hundred games), displays of martial and acrobatic skills, ranging from wrestling and mock combat to tightrope walking and fire-spitting. Also included under this term were elaborate and spectacular pageants. Some of these performances had a certain narrative content, one of them being the Old Man of Tung-hai (Eastern Sea): the old man had once been a powerful magician whose charms could dominate tigers, but his advanced age and his drinking habits diminished his powers, and he ended up being eaten by a tiger he had tried to charm. Many of the skills involved in the performance of *pai-hsi* were elaborated and incorporated in later drama (the skit of the Old Man of Tung-hai also survived into later drama). From the centuries following the Han, we have short descriptions of comical skits involving song and dance (one concerning a woman who reviles her husband for his alcoholism) and references to the use of masks in narrative dance.

Sources from the T'ang dynasty and later become more detailed. At court two forms of theatrical entertainment were most prominent: *ko-wu-chü* (song and dance plays) and *ts'an-chün-hsi* (adjutant plays). Song and dance plays could be elaborate affairs in which large numbers of richly costumed dancers danced out one or more stories narrated in choral songs sung to the music accompanying the dances. Emperor Hsüan-tsung (r. 712–756) was a great aficionado of such spectacles and established a conservatory, the Pear Garden, where three hundred singers and dancers were trained. The name Pear Garden (Li-yüan) has been claimed by actors and actresses ever since as a designation of their profession, and in some places Emperor Hsüan-tsung is venerated as the patron god of the acting profession (he shares that honor with some others, including the last emperor of the Later T'ang dynasty [923–936], yet another theater buff). Most of our evidence links the adjutant plays to the court, but some sources prove that they were also performed outside the palace, in the capital, and throughout the empire, while some of them might involve a large cast and deal with a relatively complicated story. The T'ang dynasty was a cosmopolitan period in Chinese history, and the enriching influences from Central Asia are well documented, at least in the field of music. In many other areas of the performing arts, Central Asian and Indian influences can be seen—a conspicuous example being the lion dance.

Telling stories is a human characteristic that may be as old as song and dance. Just as music, song, and dance flourished during the T'ang period, so did storytelling. The T'ang dynasty witnessed both the flowering of the short story in the classical language (*ch'uan-ch'i*; see chapter 33) and the emergence of longer narrative texts in the vernacular, in prose, in rhyme, or in a mixture of both (the prosimetric tales known as *pien-wen*; see chapter 48). The short stories in the classical language later became extremely important to the development of dramatic literature because they provided the plots of some of the best-loved plays. The emergence of *pien-wen* stimulated the written use of the spoken language while also contributing to the development of longer narratives. The importance of both elements for the eventual emergence of a dramatic literature needs no elaboration. However, the manuscripts discovered at Tun-huang (see chapter 48) probably already provide us with the text of at least one proper playlet or miniplay, "Ch'a-chiu lun" (Discourse Between Tea and Wine). This text concerns a dispute between Tea and Wine as to their respective merits and their relative ranking. On both sides praise of one's own qualities soon turns into a revilement of the other's faults. Eventually the fight between the two parties has to be settled by the intercession of Water. In some of the preserved manuscripts of this witty little piece the stage directions are clearly distinguished from the main text by being written in smaller characters.

The amount of available information on the performing arts becomes still more plentiful in the Sung dynasty. *Tung-ching meng hua lu* (Dreams of Splendor of the Eastern Capital), by Meng Yüan-lao (preface dated 1147), is a nostalgic memoir describing the sights and smells of the Sung capital Kaifeng in the first decades of the twelfth century, before the city was captured by the Chin (Jurchen; 1115–1234). It includes a description of the entertainment quarters, detailing the genres available and listing the most famous performers. For Hangchow, the capital of the Southern Sung dynasty, we have four comparable works, dating from the late twelfth to early fourteenth centuries. These works mention more genres, are more elaborate in their descriptions, and list more performers by name. The surveys cover martial arts and acrobatics, song and dance and instrumental music, various classes of professional storytelling, and five different types of puppet plays. Also included are *chu-kung-tiao* (all keys and modes; medley) and *tsa-chü* (farce). The "all keys and modes" (see below) was a genre of prosimetric storytelling that derived its name from the fact that the rhymed sections did not have a fixed line length (as, for example, in *pien-wen* and most of the later forms of prosimetric literature of the Ming and Ch'ing dynasties), but were written to tunes or suites of tunes that each stipulated their own verse form, while every tune or suite of tunes was in a different key or mode from the one before. The "all keys and modes" was an important precursor of Yüan dynasty *tsa-chü*, because the genre developed the organization of individual tunes into modal suites and so prepared the groundwork for the musical organization of the pre-eminent form of drama during the Mongol period.

Sung dynasty *tsa-chü*, the direct predecessor of Yüan *tsa-chü*, was a much simpler affair. It was performed both at court and in the capital commercial theaters. From Southern Sung times, there exists a long list of titles of stage routines, farces, and skits (probably also including some more elaborate items), but it is not quite clear whether this list refers to the court repertoire or to the repertoire of the genre in general. A comparable, even longer list of titles emanates from the domain of the Chin dynasty, where the same genre went by the name of *yüan-pen* (texts of the [acting] guild). Available Sung dynasty sources point out that roles in *tsa-chü* were divided among a limited number of role-types, many of which are re-encountered in later genres of drama. They further point out that a full performance was introduced by an eye-catching prelude (*yen-tuan*) and that the main action consisted of two scenes, whereupon the show might be concluded with a skit featuring country yokels. In Kaifeng, during the seven days preceding the holiday celebrating Buddhist All Souls, the actors also participated in a theatrical version of the story of Mu-lien's rescue of his mother from hell. In Hangchow, the actors participated in the celebration of the end-of-the-year *No* ceremony, one of them in the role of Chung K'uei.

Common Characteristics of Traditional Chinese Theater

By the beginning of the thirteenth century, all elements were in place for the emergence of traditional Chinese theater as we know it from the texts of Yüan dynasty *tsa-chü* and *hsi-wen*. These two genres, one emerging in the north, the other in the south, share some characteristics that have remained distinctive for traditional Chinese theater throughout its later continuous development. First, all genres of traditional Chinese theater are a form of musical theater: the action on stage is continually accompanied by the music of a small orchestra that also accompanies the arias of the players. Traditionally, the musicians share the stage with the actors and actresses, because the leader of the orchestra (the drummer) needs to have eye contact with the singing actor or actress in order to set the tempo for his fellow musicians (traditional Chinese theater until recently did not have a director [or conductor] in command of the total performance who gives the performance his or her individual stamp).

However, traditional Chinese theater cannot be compared directly to Western genres of musical theater, whether opera or musical. In the Western tradition since the seventeenth century, the music is newly composed for each individual play. Usually the name of the composer is well known, but not often the name of the person who wrote the text (libretto). Only in the case of the ballad-opera is pre-existing music utilized. In the Chinese case, the texts of the plays are always written to pre-existing music. Genres are defined not by issues of plot and character (as in the traditional Western definitions of tragedy and comedy) and not by issues of the relation between music and texts (as in the definitions of opera versus musical), but on the basis of the utilized corpus of pre-existing tunes and related musical conventions (including the dialect in which the texts are sung). The basic defining characteristic of *tsa-chü*, therefore, is that it made use of "northern tunes," a circumscribed group of a few hundred melodies that were current in China north of the Huai River, while *hsi-wen* (and later *ch'uan-ch'i*) made use of a circumscribed body of a few hundred "southern tunes." As time went by, different performance traditions of these southern tunes resulted in different regional styles that eventually established themselves as independent genres of theater.

But whereas *tsa-chü* and *ch'uan-ch'i* both relied on a body of a few hundred melodies, each dictating its own verse form to the playwright, many other genres of theater eventually came to rely on only a single basic melody. In the latter case, the arias have a fixed line length of seven or ten syllables, and the basic melody extends over two lines of text. This basic melody is continuously repeated, but monotony is avoided by endless artful variation. Such a type of theatrical music is known as *pan-ch'iang-t'i* (beat-and-tune style) or *pan-shih pien-hua t'i* (change-of-rhythm style). Its best-known modern-day representative is Peking opera, which employs not just one basic melody but two (*erh-huang* and *hsi-p'i*). Many other forms of modern regional theater also employ this type of music, which started to attract the attention of literate Chinese observers in the eighteenth century. However, the tradition of *pan-ch'iang-t'i* music may well go much further back in time: it is a reasonable hypothesis to assume that the Yüan dynasty villagers and soldiers who "acted out prosimetric ballads" already relied on such a type of music to sing their lines.

Yet another common feature of traditional Chinese theater is that the major roles in each play are distributed over a limited number of role-types. In Yüan dynasty *tsa-chü* the basic role-types are male (*mo*), female (*tan*), and scoundrel (*ching*; villain or clown). This basic setup may be complicated by the addition of supporting roles in each category and by the addition of certain fixed types, such as the emperor and the judge. In *ch'uan-ch'i* the basic role-types are male (*sheng*), female, scoundrel, and fool (*ch'ou*). This four-part division of roles was also adopted in Peking opera and many other forms of regional drama. To these basic role-types could be added such supporting roles as each particular play might require; the basic role-types also were increasingly subdivided according to age (old versus young), status (high versus low), and qualifications (civil versus military).

Actors and actresses were trained from a very early age for a specific role-type. It was not uncommon for women to specialize in a male role-type (e.g., civil leading man, often playing the role of handsome and brilliant young students in love) and for men to specialize in female roles, since young boys were trained to perform as *tan*. In all-male and all-female troupes such cross-dressing was simply unavoidable. Role-types had their own costume and makeup (or face painting). These dazzling costumes and elaborate face paintings compensate for the almost always practically bare stage. The qualities of the role-types inevitably exerted a strong influence on characterization on stage and in dramatic literature. The system of role-types can be compared in some measure to both the way of working in a nineteenth-century stock company, with its fixed types, and the training of opera singers. It also has its counterparts in other Asian traditions of drama, e.g., that of India. In the Chinese case, troupes were expected to be able to perform on command any of the many plays in their repertoire, which precluded the possibility of long rehearsals before each performance: each player always had to be ready to perform all of his or her roles.

The Texts of Plays

The actors knew (their part in) these many plays by heart. An excellent memory was a prerequisite for becoming a star performer. As the long "prehistory" of Chinese dramatic literature makes abundantly clear, the theater has no intrinsic need for written-out texts. It is possible to have a tradition not only of musical theater without composers but also of drama without playwrights. In the West, the commedia dell'arte remained popular for centuries as actors and actresses simply relied on basic plot outlines, a good memory, and a talent for improvisation. In many genres of traditional Chinese theater too, the plots of the plays and the parts for each of the roles were orally transmitted by the teacher to his/her pupils, while for certain role-types a talent for improvisation was at a premium. In the case of *tsa-chü* and *hsi-wen* the intricacy of the verse forms dictated by the arias may well have provided an important stimulus in committing the texts to writing. In the case of *tsa-chü* one can also surmise that the constant demand of the burgeoning commercial theater for new plays contributed to the rise of the playwright.

There are, however, many different reasons why one might want to write (out) a play, and these reasons determine the shape of the text. The earliest preserved printings of *tsa-chü* suggest that they are based on role texts, in this case texts providing the leading male or leading female with the text of his or her arias, an outline of the entrances and exits of his or her fellow players, and the cue lines, so that he or she will know when to speak or to sing. (One early fifteenth-century grave of an actor also contained his favorite role text, that of Ts'ai Po-chieh in the famous *ch'uan-ch'i* play "P'i-p'a chi" [The Story of the Lute].) At the Ming court (1368–1644), the censor insisted on inspecting a complete text of each play before its performance, with the result that the manuscripts of *tsa-chü* emanating from the Ming palace occasionally repeat information *ad nauseam*, whereas other versions simply say "explain what happened earlier." In general, playwrights wrote out what was new in their plays. Where it contained set routines, they limited themselves to noting the nature of those routines, adding "ad lib," and trusting the actors to do their job. Many *ch'uan-ch'i* plays contain, for example, an extensive examination scene, which was customarily performed in a highly conventionalized manner. If the playwright thought that sufficient for his purpose, he might limit himself to the indication "as usual"; if not, he could try to achieve novelty by giving his own twist to that scene, which required that he write out the text.

Not only are there different reasons for writing out a text, but there are also different reasons for distributing it, in print or otherwise. One of the main reasons throughout the centuries for printing play texts probably has been to assist the audience in understanding the lyrics. In view of the great variation of languages and dialects in China, an important segment of the public in commercial theaters in the various capitals may have experienced difficulty in understanding the text of the play, especially the text of the arias, which tended to be more literary in nature than the spoken parts. In this respect it is interesting to note that the overwhelming majority of Yüan dynasty printings of *tsa-chü* are not from the north but from Hangchow in the south. In nineteenth-century Peking there existed a brisk trade in Peking opera libretti for the benefit of the merchants and officials who flocked to the capital from all over the empire. In such cases, the printed versions focused on the arias and were short on the prose dialogs. Spectators may also have wanted to buy play texts as a memento of a memorable performance, especially if it were a special or one-time affair. Playwrights may, of course, have wanted to impress their friends and relations with their works and taken the initiative in distributing copies of them. This may well have been the motive behind the remarkable publication activities of Chu Yu-tun (1379–1439), who had all thirty-one of his *tsa-chü* privately printed. Sponsors of a performance might be interested in obtaining a copy of the text of the play in order to check on the company that they had engaged to perform a certain item.

The existence of a written-out text, in manuscript or in print, does not automatically mean that the text of the play was fixed for good. As long as a play remained in the repertoire, its text was subject to continual revision in order to adapt it to circumstances, such as political censorship, new theatrical conventions, and changes in literary taste. The low status of theater as entertainment only stimulated the frequency and extent of arbitrary changes by players and editors alike. The texts of plays achieved a fixed form only when they had achieved a certain status as literature and were edited and read as the work of an individual author. For *ch'uan-ch'i* and *tsa-chü* this process gained momentum in the sixteenth century and achieved its culmination in the early seventeenth century with the appearance of large and beautifully produced anthologies, which until recently provided the definitive editions of these works for the general reader and scholar alike.

As the status of drama as a genre of literature increased, more and more plays that were never performed came to be composed. Many *ch'uan-ch'i* were written by ambitious authors with little or no practical experience of the theater and as a result do not lend themselves to performance, unless heavily adapted. Many plays also were written with no thought of performance at all. Chinese literature has a long tradition of closet drama (dramatic texts intended for reading rather than for performance). No genre of literature was ever completely abandoned in traditional China, so even for centuries after *tsa-chü* had disappeared from the stage new plays in that genre continued to be written.

PERFORMATIVE LITERATURE OF THE SUNG AND CHIN DYNASTIES

The most important genre of performative literature of this period with extant texts is the *chu-kung-tiao*. According to modern taxonomy, this genre belongs to *shuo-ch'ang wen-hsüeh* (sing and speak [chantefable] literature), if the manner of performance is considered, and to prosimetric literature, if we look at the form of the texts. However, accounts of the twelfth to fourteenth centuries usually discuss the "all keys and modes" in the context of song, stressing its satirical content. And Chung Ssu-ch'eng (c. 1279–c. 1360) in his *Lu-kuei pu* (Register of Ghosts), the earliest preserved catalog of playwrights and their works, places the most prominent author of the genre, Tung Chieh-yüan (Master Tung; active c. 1190–1208), at the head of his list of *san-ch'ü* (see chapter 17) and *tsa-chü* authors. Modern studies often follow the lead of Chung Ssu-ch'eng by discussing the "all keys and modes" as a precursor of northern drama, since it marks an important stage in the development of song, viz., in the change from *tz'u* to (northern) *ch'ü*.

The most popular form of song in the eleventh and twelfth centuries was the *tz'u* (lyric; see chapter 15). Lyric tunes most often consisted of two stanzas, but a few very popular lyric tunes consisted of only one stanza, while a still smaller number of tunes consisted of three stanzas. Longer suites were created by repeating, according to a fixed scheme, the same tune over and over again, repetition of the same tune bringing along variation in melody and tempo. One of the forms created in this manner was the *ku-tzu-tz'u* (drum lyrics). Many texts in this form were written to accompany ballets. However, the form could also be used for narrative purposes by interspersing the songs with prose. Dating from the final years of the Northern Sung (960–1127) is an adaptation of the T'ang poet Yüan Chen's (779–831) "Ying-ying chuan" (Story of Ying-ying) in this format by Chao Ling-chih (1051–1134). One other later example of narrative drum lyrics has been preserved in an early collection of *hua-pen*. It has been argued that it may have been composed originally as a prelude to a (lost) *hsi-wen* or *ch'uan-ch'i*.

The twelfth century witnessed the advent of new forms of suite formation that allowed for the combination of different tunes (in the same key or mode) into one suite. If the suite consisted of an introductory song, one or more other songs, and a coda (*wei* [tail]), the suite was known as *ch'an-ling* (intertwined tunes); if, following the introductory songs, two tunes were used alternately several times before the suite was ended by the coda, the suite was known as a *ch'an-ta*. In all these cases, the text of the coda consisted of three lines of seven syllables each and probably was intended to provide the suite with a witty conclusion and punch line. The only *ch'an-ling* that has been preserved as an independent work is a description of the Sung dynasty game of "football."

The medley (all keys and modes) made full use of these new developments in contemporary song culture. The genre is said to have originated with K'ung San-chuan (Erudite K'ung), who brought the genre to Kaifeng from P'ing-yang in southeastern Shansi province in the early years of the twelfth century and "made fun of students" (*shua hsiu-ts'ai*) in the capital's entertainment district (some scholars read *shua hsiu-ts'ai* as the name of another performer: Student Shua). We have no information on the format of these early medleys, but perhaps K'ung San-chuan's innovation consisted of the addition of a coda to single lyrics.

The earliest (partly) preserved medley is the anonymous "Liu Chih-yüan chu-kung-tiao" (The Medley on Liu Chih-yüan), which may date from the second quarter of the twelfth century. Fragments of a printed edition that was probably produced at P'ing-yang (Shansi province) were discovered in the beginning of the twentieth century by the expedition of the Russian explorer Petr Kuzmitch Koslov among the ruins of Karakhoto (Hei-shui-ch'eng, in Kansu province on the western bank of the Hei-shui River). The original work was in twelve chapters; chapters 1, 2, and 12 have been preserved in their entirety, together with the opening pages of chapter 3 and most of chapter 11. The story deals with the life and loves of Liu Chih-yüan, the founder of the short-lived Later Han state (947–950). Both as an impecunious farmhand and as a simple soldier, Liu Chih-yüan is pursued by eager maidens who have seen signs of his future greatness and insist on marrying him. This extremely popular story later also was dealt with in *Wu-tai shih p'ing-hua* (The Plain Tale of the History of the Five Dynasties), in a lost *tsa-chü*, and in a famous early *ch'uan-ch'i*, "Pai-t'u chi" (The Story of the White Hare).

In the medley, the story is told in an alternation of suites of songs and short connecting prose passages. Each new suite of songs is indeed in a different key or mode from the one before it. Many suites, however, still consist of only a single two-stanza lyric concluded by a coda (in two keys, not even a coda is used). The preserved chapters include a few examples of longer suites marked as *ch'an-ling* in the text. In the printed version, much care has been taken to bring out the formal features of the text as an aid to the performer. Each suite starts at the top of a new column, and the text of the songs is preceded by the name of the key and melody concerned (printed in white in a black cartouche). The two stanzas of each song are clearly separated, while the concluding coda again starts at the top of a new column and is clearly marked as such. Each chapter (one day's performance?) ends with a cliffhanger, and each chapter is interrupted at yet another high point of suspense for the performer to make the rounds of the audience to collect donations. This point is marked in the text by a formulaic question and the note "ad lib."

A medley that has not been preserved dealt with the story of Shuang Chien and Su Hsiao-ch'ing. This story was immensely popular from the twelfth to the early fifteenth century and was repeatedly adapted for the stage, but none of these many versions has been preserved either. The student Shuang Chien and the courtesan Su Hsiao-ch'ing fall in love, to the chagrin of her madam. After he has left to take part in the examinations in the capital, the madam forges a letter to the effect that the student has died on the way and sells her "daughter" to a rich but old and ugly Kiangsi tea merchant, who has wooed Hsiao-ch'ing for a long time. He takes her with him on his tea-trading boat back to Nan-ch'ang (in Kiangsi province). When they pass by the famous Chin-shan monastery (on a little island in the Yangtze, opposite Chen-chiang), they visit this holy place and Su Hsiao-ch'ing leaves a poem on one of the temple walls bemoaning her fate. In the meantime, Shuang Chien has succeeded in the examinations and been appointed as magistrate of Lin-ch'uan (Kiangsi), one of the districts of Nan-ch'ang prefecture. Passing by Chin-shan monastery and visiting it, he finds Hsiao-ch'ing's poem and immediately departs in pursuit of her husband's boat. When he catches up with it, Hsiao-ch'ing elopes with him under the cover of night. And when the tea merchant tries to reclaim his expensively bought concubine in the prefectural court, the prefect rules against him and assigns Su Hsiao-ch'ing to Shuang Chien. Numerous *tsa-chü* have been preserved from later years that are based on the same configuration of brilliant student, beautiful courtesan, greedy madam, and fabulously wealthy merchant, and all these plays assume that the audience will be acquainted with the tale of Shuang Chien and Su Hsiao-ch'ing.

The only medley that has been preserved in its entirety (in several late Ming editions) is "'Hsi-hsiang chi' chu-kung-tiao" (Medley of the "Romance of the Western Chamber"), by Tung Chieh-yüan. About the author nothing is known beyond the fact that he was active around 1200 in the domain of the Chin; he may have hailed from southern Shansi province. His work is a much-elaborated adaptation of Yüan Chen's *ch'uan-ch'i* story "Story of Ying-ying," now provided with a happy ending: Student Chang returns to the monastery and with the help of the monk Fa-ts'ung the lovers elope and are happily married. This is quite unlike the sad conclusion of the T'ang tale where each of the lovers ends up marrying someone else

"Medley of the 'Romance of the Western Chamber'" is a much more ambitious work than "The Medley on Liu Chih-yüan." The work consists of eight chapters that easily double the length of the chapters in the earlier work. Song-suites consisting of a single two-stanza song with (or without) coda are now very rare, as the overwhelming majority of suites consist of numerous songs. The special nature of such complicated suites is rarely noted, and most of the tunes in these suites now consist of only a single stanza, as is the normal pattern with *ch'ü* in later *san-ch'ü* and *tsa-chü*. But, whereas the prose passages between the suites in "The Medley on Liu Chih-yüan" were written in an outspoken vernacular language (a direct predecessor of the modern northern dialects), here the prose passages are composed mostly in a simple Classical Chinese. The songs in both works make full use of the many new possibilities offered to a poet by the northern vernacular.

For the first six chapters of his work, Tung Chieh-yüan followed the plot of the story as provided by the "Story of Ying-ying." However, his much larger format allowed him ample room to develop incidents that were mentioned in his source only briefly. His second chapter, for example, is devoted almost completely to a (farcical) description of the siege of the monastery by a band of rebel troops who are countered by warrior monks. Tung Chieh-yüan also developed Student Chang's attempt to seduce Ying-ying by playing the zither at great length, drawing upon the widely popular romance of the dashing young poet Ssu-ma Hsiang-ju (179–117 B.C.E.; see chapter 12) and the rich young widow Cho Wen-chün. His larger scope also allowed Tung Chieh-yüan to develop some of the characters. Not only the main characters benefit, but also some of the subsidiary figures in the tale. Ying-ying's girl servant Hung-niang (Red Maid) even becomes one of the major figures in Tung Chieh-yüan's treatment. His treatment of Student Chang fully bears out the earliest characterization of the genre as "making fun of students": as a victim of his passion, this epitome of Chinese manhood is reduced to putty in the hands of the manipulating women around him.

For the conclusion of his work, Tung Chieh-yüan had to rely on his own imagination. After Student Chang's departure from the monastery for the capital in order to take part in the examinations, he is visited at night in his inn by Ying-ying, who is shortly afterward hauled away by soldiers for crossing the pass leading to the capital without warrant—but her visit turns out to be only a dream. Following success in the examinations and an official appointment, Student Chang returns to the monastery in order to claim his bride, only to discover that in the meantime her original fiancé, Cheng Heng, has arrived. Cheng Heng is described as an ugly boor, who flaunts his riches and his inherited status and has the sympathy of Ying-ying's mother. Student Chang is desperate, but the monk Fa-ts'ung intervenes and sees to it that the couple elopes that very night to the safe haven of the yamen (government office) of Tu Chüeh, Chang's friend and the officer who earlier relieved the siege of the monastery. There the couple celebrate their marriage, and when Cheng Heng arrives to claim his fiancée he is sent away. The work concludes with his suicide.

"Medley of the 'Romance of the Western Chamber'" is not only a moving love story but an extremely effective social satire. One critic has argued that it can also be read as an allegory on the "arts of the bedchamber." Chung Ssu-ch'eng's treatment of Tung Chieh-yüan in his *Register of Ghosts* testifies to the contemporary appreciation of his work. Roughly a century after its original composition "Medley of the 'Romance of the Western Chamber'" was adapted, quite faithfully, for the stage by Wang Shih-fu as a (highly exceptional) five-*tsa-chü* cycle entitled "Hsi-hsiang chi" (Romance of the Western Chamber). This play eventually was to become China's most popular love comedy, both on stage and in print. By the early fourteenth century, however, people who knew how to sing "Medley of the 'Romance of the Western Chamber'" had already become a rarity.

Sometime in the second half of the thirteenth century the playwright Wang Po-ch'eng composed "T'ien-pao yi-shih chu-kung-tiao" (Medley on the Anecdotes of the T'ien-pao Period [742–756]), an adaptation of the celebrated romance between Emperor Hsüan-tsung (r. 713–756) and his beloved consort Yang Kuei-fei (d. 756). This voluminous work has not been preserved in its entirety, but some fifty song-suites have been recovered from various anthologies and other sources, enough to show that the emperor was portrayed as an old fool, besotted with lust for the physical charms of his plump daughter-in-law, who does not hesitate to carry on an affair with the "fat foreigner" An Lu-shan (the Turko-Sogdian commander of a T'ang frontier army whose rebellion in 755 almost brought down the dynasty; 703–757). Many suites are also devoted to a description of Hsüan-tsung's fabled dream visit to the Moon Palace. The organization of song suites in this work, however, conforms to the contemporary practices in *san-ch'ü* and *tsa-chü*.

DRAMATIC LITERATURE FROM THE THIRTEENTH TO SIXTEENTH CENTURIES (C. 1250–C. 1550)

Political history is not always the best guide to developments in the history of literature. Although it is common to associate the heyday of *tsa-chü* and *hsi-wen* with the Yüan dynasty, both genres may well have appeared on the stage before the formal inauguration of that dynasty. *Tsa-chü* remained the most prestigious form of drama throughout the Yüan and the first century of the Ming: not only was it staged in the commercial theaters of the urban centers of northern China and of Hangchow, but it was performed in the imperial palace as well. After the establishment of the Ming dynasty in 1368, the new rulers also adopted *tsa-chü* as court drama. The founding Hung-wu emperor (r. 1368–1398) took the unprecedented step of erecting an imperial theater outside the palace, while his third son, later the Yung-le emperor (r. 1403–1424), actively patronized *tsa-chü* authors. In the early years of the fifteenth century at least two princes of the imperial house became active as playwrights and drama critics themselves, both writing *tsa-chü*.

As for *hsi-wen* (also referred to as *nan-hsi* [southern plays]), our meager sources suggest that it was performed primarily at temple festivals, either by professional actors or by members of *shu-hui* (writing clubs). These writing clubs originated in the urban centers of southern China from groups of students who studied together in preparation for the examinations but later developed into organizations that practiced the various emergent forms of the new vernacular literature. (From the south the phenomenon of *shu-hui* also spread to the north, where its members also wrote *tsa-chü*, but after the fifteenth century the *shu-hui* disappear from the record.) The Hung-wu emperor reportedly had high praise for Kao Ming's "Story of the Lute," but the anecdote concerned is preserved only in a sixteenth-century source (Hsü Wei's *Nan-tz'u hsü-lu* [An Account of Southern Lyrics]) and most likely reflects the later popularity of the play (and the genre it belongs to) rather than its contemporary status.

The Textual Transmission of Plays

Although some 160 *tsa-chü* of the seven hundred known titles from the Yüan dynasty may have come down to us in one form or another, only thirty of these plays have been preserved in a Yüan dynasty printing. None of these plays carries the name of the author, and in none of these cases can we assume that the author had any hand in the publication of his text(s). Actually, while the majority of the plays concerned appear to have northern authors, the overwhelming majority of these editions seem to be from fourteenth-century Hangchow and to betray traces of textual adaptations necessitated by the local, more southern dialect. These texts present our closest approximation to the texts of the plays as they were actually performed during the lifetime of their authors, yet so far they have been largely ignored in the literary study of early drama because they only present either the arias of the leading player or the arias and other information needed by the leading player. The stage directions concerning the other role-types always are minimal, while the stage directions for the leading player may at times be remarkably detailed. The stage instructions in Kuan Han-ch'ing's (second half of the thirteenth century) "Pai-yüeh t'ing" (Courtyard of Praying to the Moon) even repeatedly instruct its leading lady to act out two or three conflicting emotions at the same time! These Yüan dynasty printings clearly do not intend to present the full text of the play but are based on role-texts and as such may be very complete indeed for a given role. Still, they do not make for easy reading. Literary scholarship therefore has preferred to deal with the editions of Yüan and early Ming *tsa-chü* that were produced during the last decades of the Ming dynasty, starting from the Wan-li reign-period (1573–1620), and that provide a full version of each play. However, these editions as a rule incorporate extensive modifications because of the different uses and different publics of these texts.

The overwhelming majority of these late Ming editions are based directly or indirectly on the *tsa-chü* manuscripts kept at the Ming imperial palace in Peking. When *tsa-chü* was adopted as court drama, it became subject to various pressures. First, express prohibitions of the early Ming did not allow the portrayal on stage of "any emperor, king, empress, or concubine of any era, neither loyal minister nor ardent man of valor, neither prior sage nor prior worthy nor the image of the Buddha." Emperors do not like to be offended for their own amusement. However, no fewer than thirteen of the thirty *tsa-chü* that have been preserved in a Yüan-era printing include an emperor or king among their roles; often the treatment of these characters is frankly irreverent. Such plays were rewritten in case they were incorporated in the court repertoire, but many titles that we know from early catalogs apparently were beyond redemption and were lost forever. The same ideologically inspired selection may well have worked against the survival of other plays that by all accounts were once extremely popular. Whenever a play was included in the court repertoire, the censors saw to it that strident social criticism was deleted and the power of the state as final arbiter in all matters was stressed.

Still other factors affected the form and content of the plays that had been deemed fit for performance at court. One of the most outstanding characteristics of *tsa-chü* is that all songs of the play are assigned to a single role-type, the leading male or the leading female. This fitted in with theatrical conditions in the Yüan dynasty, when most companies were small family troupes that featured only one star performer. He or she played the leading roles, while the other members of the troupe performed the bit parts or performed as musicians. The basic musical structure of a *tsa-chü* consisted of four suites of song, each in a different musical key (each of these suites might be preceded by one or two songs, called a "wedge," while the final suite might be followed by a final demi-suite; on the basis of these suites and wedges, later editors divided the plays into acts and wedges). This musical structure made *tsa-chü* into a highly asymmetrical form, as only one of the parties in each dramatic conflict was allowed to give full expression to his or her feelings. At the Ming court there was no lack of performers, so the pressure to provide a more even distribution of lines in each *tsa-chü* is evident in the texts that have passed through the palace: the prose dialog of all the players is greatly expanded, and their text is further fleshed out by poems and other texts to be recited. The basic musical structure of the genre is maintained, but the number of songs in each suite is cut, in this way diminishing the prominence of the leading male or leading female. It is also obvious that some stage routines have been cut. On the Yüan and early Ming stage, actors and actresses who as part of their performance traveled on horseback rode hobbyhorses, but sometime during the Ming this practice disappeared and was replaced by the convention of carrying a horsewhip to symbolize this action.

The earliest printed editions of Yüan and early Ming *tsa-chü* of the Wan-li period rather faithfully reproduced the texts as they found them. However, the most important editor of this period, Tsang Mao-hsün (1550–1620), heavily edited the one hundred plays he included in his highly successful *Yüan-ch'ü hsüan* (Anthology of Yüan Plays) of 1616–1617. Whereas the manuscripts from the Ming palace were production copies (they often include long lists of the costumes needed for each act), Tsang Mao-hsün published his beautifully produced selection as refined leisure reading for sophisticated Kiangnan literati.

Tsang's editorial changes were quite extensive. He regularized the editorial conventions by formally marking the division into acts and "wedges." He revised dialog and stage directions, adding, cutting, and rewriting as he saw fit. He changed the names of tune titles he deemed faulty and corrected scribal errors and omissions. He reorganized the plots in many dramas in order to bring about a tighter resolution, often resulting in an extraordinary expansion of the final acts; more than half of the 222 arias of his own composition that Tsang added to his texts are found in the fourth acts. This desire to provide the plays with a neat and tidy ending clearly shows the strong influence of southern plays that end with a grand reunion scene. Tsang also revised many of the arias so that his texts would appeal more to the intended readership as poetry, and he rejected at least 142 arias in eighty-five plays. These combined changes of wording and plot also greatly affected the ideological contents of the plays, giving them a much more orthodox Confucian colorization.

The extent of Tsang Mao-hsün's changes can be gauged from a comparison of the two preserved printings of the play "Chao-shih ku-erh" (The Orphan of the House of Chao), by Chi Chün-hsiang (second half of the thirteenth century), a playwright from Ta-tu (modern-day Peking). This play is preserved both in a printed form from Yüan times that consists of only four suites of arias and in an edition in the *Anthology of Yüan Plays* that exceptionally consists of five acts. The latter version has the distinction of being the first Chinese play to have been translated into a European language. A French translation by the Jesuit missionary Joseph-Henri-Marie de Prémare was included in the voluminous *Déscription de la Chine* of 1735. Prémare, however, translated only the prose dialogs of the play, omitting all the arias. His version, which reached Europe during the height of eighteenth-century *chinoiserie*, enjoyed an immediate success and was adapted for the stage in various languages and theatrical genres. The most famous of these reworkings is, of course, Voltaire's "L'orphelin de la Chine" (1755), which left its mark on European theater history because it was one of the first successful plays in which actors dressed in "authentic" costumes.

The plot of "The Orphan of the House of Chao" deals with the power struggles in the ancient state of Chin in the sixth century B.C.E. as narrated by Ssu-ma Ch'ien (c. 145–c. 86 B.C.E.) in his *Shih-chi* (Records of the Historian). The all-powerful minister of war, T'u-an Ku, has exterminated all three hundred members of the rival Chao clan. When the wife of the last representative of the family, who has already earlier committed suicide, gives birth to a baby boy, an old family retainer, the herbalist Ch'eng Ying, smuggles the baby out of the palace compound. He does so with the connivance of the officer guarding the palace, Han Chüeh, who thereupon also commits suicide. When T'u-an Ku finds out that the baby has escaped, he declares that he will kill all infants within the borders of the state unless the baby is given up. Ch'eng Ying, who has just become the father of a son himself, takes his own son to another client of the Chao clan, the retired elderly statesman Kung-sun Ch'u-chiu. The two agree that Ch'eng Ying will accuse Kung-sun Ch'u-chiu with T'u-an Ku of hiding the Orphan of Chao. After Kung-sun Ch'u-chiu has given up the false orphan (Ch'eng Ying's own son), Ch'eng Ying will be able to raise the true Orphan, who later may take revenge.

Ch'eng Ying proceeds as agreed, and as a result Kung-sun Ch'u-chiu is tortured and the false Orphan is discovered and killed. As a reward, T'u-an Ku raises Ch'eng Ying's "son" (the actual Orphan) as his own. Eighteen years later, when T'u-an Ku is about to overthrow the ineffective duke of Chin and occupy the throne for himself, Ch'eng Ying carefully discloses his true identity to the Orphan, who is immediately filled with a desire to take revenge for all three hundred members of his clan. Here the Yüan dynasty printing of the play ends. The edition in *Anthology of Yüan Plays* has a further fifth act, in which the Orphan reports T'u-an Ku's planned rebellion to the throne and requests permission to take revenge for his family. When this permission is granted, he proceeds, together with General Wei Chiang, to capture and execute T'u-an Ku.

Although the sequence of the songs in each of the first four acts of the play is basically the same in both versions, the text of each of these songs shows extensive and important changes. Whereas, for instance, in the Yüan printing the Orphan at the beginning of the fourth suite of songs is quite willing to take part in the rebellion of his adoptive father, he is turned into a model of moral rectitude in the *Anthology of Yüan Plays* version. The extensive prose dialogs show all the signs of being the work of Ming dynasty palace functionaries. In brief, whereas the earlier version dramatizes a tale of revenge and counterrevenge of feuding clans, the later edition stresses the exclusive power of the state to settle such conflicts, not only in its added fifth act but also throughout the play.

In all cases where a comparison can be made between subsequent versions of early *tsa-chü* in their various editions, the same tendencies can be observed, so we may assume that those plays that are preserved only in *Anthology of Yüan Plays* all went through the same process of intensive rewriting and editing. However, as in many cases we have only such very late editions at our disposal, we cannot but make use of them in our discussion of Yüan and early Ming *tsa-chü*. Those plays, however, that consisted of *tsa-chü* cycles had a different publication history. There is an independent printing from the early fifteenth century of Liu Tui's two-*tsa-chü* cycle "Chiao Hung chi" (Story of Chiao-niang and Fei-hung), an adaptation of Sung Yüan's (fl. 1300) once very popular long classical tale *Chiao Hung chuan* (The Tale of Chiao-niang and Fei-hung) on the tragic love of two cousins. There are fragments of a printed edition of Wang Shih-fu's five-*tsa-chü* cycle "Romance of the Western Chamber" from about the same years, while a fully illustrated deluxe edition of this play of 1498 has also been preserved. "Romance of the Western Chamber" was repeatedly reprinted in the course of the sixteenth century, and dozens of editions have been preserved from the Wan-li reign and later, when a publishing boom overtook China in the Kiangnan area.

As for the texts of southern drama, the situation is still worse. We know the titles of two hundred *hsi-wen* of the thirteenth and fourteenth centuries, and many more plays were written during the first two centuries of the Ming dynasty. To the extent that these plays have been preserved, they have come down to us, with very rare exceptions, in editions of the late sixteenth century and beyond. *Yung-le ta-tien* (Yung-le Encyclopedia; 1409) devoted twenty-seven of its more than ten thousand volumes to *hsi-wen*, but only the very last volume of these has been preserved and the representativeness of the three plays it contains is questionable. Of the three preserved plays, two are rather short and faithful adaptations of *tsa-chü*, while the third is perhaps best appreciated as an extensive parody on the genre. Recent archeological discoveries in fifteenth-century graves have yielded other materials, including a printed version of "The White Hare." These materials, early formularies and anthologies, and the extreme diversity exhibited by the earliest preserved printings of both famous and lesser-known plays all make it abundantly clear that, in the centuries after their initial composition, these plays, as popular production texts, were constantly revised and adapted to the changing needs of locality and period. In pre–sixteenth-century editions, plays often declare themselves to be the work of a *shu-hui*. When they carry the name of an author in some later edition, he more often than not is only one of the many revisers of the text at a later date. Even Kao Ming (d. 1359), the author of "The Story of the Lute" and the most famous author of early southern drama, produced only a revised version of an earlier play, and his own redaction in turn has come down to us in a great number of highly divergent renditions.

The Subject Matter of Tsa-chü

The subject matter of *tsa-chü* was extremely varied. Despite its limited length and asymmetrical structure, the genre managed to deal with almost every conceivable plot and accommodated characters drawn from all walks of life. This was already noted by observant contemporaries at the time of its first emergence:

> Plays by actors change with the predilections of the age. In recent times we have, apart from the *yüan-pen* of the Court Entertainment Bureau, by a further change also *tsa-chü* [mixed plays]. As they are called "mixed,"

> there is no creature whose emotions are not caught and whose postures are not exhausted. These range from, on the one hand, the successes and failures in political administration by ruler and ministers at court, to, on the other hand, sincerity and betrayal between father and son, elder brother and younger brother, husband and wife, and friends and companions in the streets and alleys of towns and neighborhoods, even extending to the affairs and dealings of physicians and herbalists, oracle experts, monks and priests and all kinds of merchants, and the differences of customs and languages of faraway regions and strange lands.

This capsule description of *tsa-chü* by Hu Chih-yü (1227–1293) aptly characterizes the contents of typical plays in this genre, which was still new in his time. The authors of *tsa-chü* derived their plots and characters from Chinese history, classical tales and anecdotes, performative literature, religious legends and popular lore, and, last but not least, from contemporary gossip and scandal. However, on the basis of shared plot or shared characters, many plays cluster into a small number of groups. It is obvious, of course, that a listing of such groups can never be exhaustive of the richness and variety of the genre.

First, many plays deal with famous episodes from Chinese history. They cover the full range of Chinese history from the foundation of the Shang dynasty to the events of the Southern Sung dynasty. Playwrights showed a great preference for periods of dynastic change, with their brutal warfare and cunning intrigues. A period that was highly popular with Yüan dynasty playwrights was the period from the collapse of the Ch'in dynasty to the founding of the Han dynasty and its aftermath. This period provided not only such stirring subjects as the clash between the heroic Hsiang Yü and the boorish Liu Pang, ending in the latter's victory, but also the grisly murders, following that victory, by his wife Empress Lü of some of Liu Pang's most deserving generals and of his paramour.

The Ming court was not amused by plays on these topics (so that few have been preserved) and showed a great partiality to plays dealing with the wars of the final decades of the Han dynasty, resulting in the establishment in 220 C.E. of the three kingdoms of Wei, Wu, and Shu-Han, as these gave a prominent role to the heroic loyalty of Kuan Yü. As a result, plays dealing with this period had a greater survival rate and many new plays were added to the repertoire in the Ming. Stories on the "Tripartition" (*san-fen*) of the Later Han dynasty were already a favorite with professional storytellers in the Northern Sung capital, Kaifeng. The authors of *tsa-chü* followed the lead of Chu Hsi (1130–1200) in considering Liu Pei, the founder of the Shu-Han dynasty, the legitimate heir to the Han throne. Accordingly, Ts'ao Ts'ao, the warlord who dominated northern China (and whose son Ts'ao P'i founded the Wei dynasty), became the villain of their pieces, while the southeastern warlord Sun Ch'üan, the founder of the state of Wu, is an unreliable ally of Liu Pei. Throughout his long career,

Liu Pei is assisted by his two sworn brothers, Kuan Yü and Chang Fei. Both are redoubtable warriors: Chang Fei is distinguished by his bulky physique and his impulsive violence, while Kuan Yü is set off by his imposing stature and overbearing self-confidence. Later Liu Pei also acquires the services of the wise statesman and cunning wizard Chu-ko Liang.

Two fine examples of early Three Kingdoms plays are Kuan Han-ch'ing's "Tan-tao hui" (The Single-Sword Meeting) and "Hsi-Shu meng" (The Dream of Western Shu). The two plays share a remarkable structural similarity and may well have been written as a contrasting pair. The first of them deals with the last act of arrogant bravery by Kuan Yü before his death, when he scares off by his imposing presence alone the enemy troops that have ambushed him. The second play takes place immediately after the violent deaths of the hero and his sworn brother Chang Fei and features their impotent ghosts, who, thirsting for vengeance, pay a final visit to Liu Pei in his dream. In "The Single-Sword Meeting" the *mo* (male lead) plays the role of Kuan Yü only in the last two acts, while he plays other roles in the first two acts. In "The Dream of Western Shu" the *mo* plays the role of (the ghost of) Chang Fei, but again only in the last two acts, while he plays two other roles in the first two acts. As these plays show, *tsa-chü* allowed the leading actor or actress to switch roles between acts. The playwright could make use of this possibility when his plot required him to do so or when he wanted to provide the leading performer with a vehicle to display virtuosity by giving him or her an opportunity to play quite different roles in one and the same play.

Yet another period that offered the playwright many materials was the period of the collapse of the Sui dynasty in 618 and the foundation of the T'ang dynasty, centering on the exploits of Li Shih-min (later the T'ang emperor T'ai-tsung) and his generals. Some of these plays deal with the campaigns of the T'ang on the Korean peninsula and feature the hero Hsüeh Jen-kuei (614–683). The collapse of the T'ang dynasty, the following fifty years of warfare that saw the rise and fall of five dynasties in northern China in quick succession, and the subsequent wars of the Sung dynasty against the Khitan (Liao) dynasty during the tenth and eleventh centuries also were mined by playwrights for materials. They could draw not only upon written sources but also on an oral tradition, as the "Five Dynasties" was already one of the favored subjects of Kaifeng storytellers. In their version of the events of the wars between the Sung and the Liao, these storytellers gave a prominent part to the generals of the Yang family who loyally served the Sung at the risk of their own lives. In "Hao-t'ien t'a" (Pagoda of the Vast Heaven) the ghost of Yang Yeh appears to his son Yang Liu-lang, who is commanding the border troops. Yang Yeh, the patriarch of the family, had committed suicide rather than surrender when he was surrounded by Khitan troops and the Chinese commander-in-chief refused to come to his rescue. The Khitan now daily humiliate the remains of their once most formidable foe, and Yang Yeh asks his son to save him from further indignity. Yang

Liu-lang eventually succeeds in this dangerous mission in enemy territory, but only because of the help of his sworn brother Meng Liang.

The story-cycles dealing with the collapse and foundation of dynasties later were all developed into novels. That also happened with the stories of the noble bandits of the Liang-shan marshes (in present-day Shantung province) who were active under the leadership of Sung Chiang during the last years of the reign of Emperor Hui-tsung (r. 1101–1125) of the Sung dynasty. Long before the stories came together in the novel *Shui-hu chuan* (Water Margin), however, they were already popular with storytellers and playwrights. Some early playwrights showed a conspicuous predilection for these materials. The Shantung playwright Kao Wen-hsiu devoted no fewer than eight titles to the adventures of Black Whirlwind Li K'uei. Li K'uei was very popular with the first generations of *tsa-chü* playwrights. In the later novel the character would develop into the personification of unrestrained physical violence, but the playwrights preferred to explore the dialectics between Li K'uei's huge physical bulk and awesome power, on the one hand, and his childlike naïveté and easily aroused indignation, on the other hand.

Remarkably enough, the story of only one of the many early *tsa-chü* devoted to the merry adventures of the members of the Liang-shan band was incorporated in the later novel. This is K'ang Chin-chih's "Li K'uei fu-ching" (Li K'uei Carries Thorns). In this play Li K'uei comes into conflict with Sung Chiang because an innkeeper tells him that his only daughter has been abducted by his chief. When it becomes clear that the real perpetrator of this ignoble act had been an impostor, Li K'uei makes amends by capturing the scoundrel and humiliating himself before Sung Chiang.

Crime and its eventual punishment is another major topic of early *tsa-chü*. The emphasis in this type of play is not on the detection of the culprit of the crime (that often is enacted before the audience at the outset of the play). As the criminals are often persons with high connections, the central character of these plays usually is the incorruptible magistrate who is not swayed by money or power and sees to it that justice is done. In most crime and punishment plays the stern judge is Pao Cheng. The historical Pao Cheng (999–1062) served as a local and metropolitan official during the eleventh century. His biography in the *Sung shih* (History of the Sung Dynasty) depicts him as an exemplary administrator: as a local magistrate he was a clever detective, as metropolitan prefect he was willing to stand up to imperial relatives and high officials who broke the law. His deeds quickly captured the popular imagination. As Clear Sky Pao (Pao Ch'ing-t'ien) he was (and is) believed to judge the living by day and the dead by night. Since he is utterly honest, wronged ghosts do not hesitate to appeal to him. In one anonymous play, "P'en-erh kuei" (The Ghost in the Pot), even the ghost of a man who has been killed by potters—who have pounded his bones to dust, mixed it with their clay, and baked it into a chamber pot—seeks Pao Cheng's assistance. In order to accentuate the character of the good judge, his final verdict is often preceded by the wrong judgment of a corrupt official. Many of the cases of Judge Pao would later be retold in *tz'u-hua* (doggerel tales), in novels and stories, and in many forms of prosimetric literature.

One of the finest Judge Pao plays from Yüan times is the anonymous "Ch'en-chou t'iao-mi" (Selling Rice at Ch'en-chou). When Ch'en-chou is ravaged by a drought, the court dispatches high metropolitan officials to the area to provide relief by selling grain from the ever-full granaries (state reserves). The officials use this opportunity to enrich themselves. In order to document their crooked dealings, Judge Pao changes places with his servant, and he even becomes the donkey-driver of a madam. In Li Hsing-tao's "Hui-lan chi" (The Chalk Circle), Judge Pao has to decide a case in which two women both claim to be the mother of the same young boy. He has a circle drawn on the floor and orders the women each to pull at one arm, telling them that he will award the child to the woman who will pull the child to her side. The verdict is the opposite: the child is awarded to the real mother, as she is afraid to hurt the child. This play was translated as early as 1860 and influenced Bertold Brecht in his conception of "Der Kaukasische Kreidekreis" (The Caucasian Chalk Circle).

Life does not consist only of politics and warfare, crime and justice, so love is naturally one of the major topics of *tsa-chü*. The male protagonist usually is a handsome and brilliant student who is destined for a great career but has not yet succeeded in attracting the attention of the court. The heroine is either a well-born and beautiful young lady or an accomplished courtesan. Plays dramatizing a love affair of a student and a courtesan are usually variations of the tale of Shuang Chien and Su Hsiao-ch'ing. In one interesting variation on this theme, "Tzu-yün t'ing" (Purple Clouds Courtyard), by the P'ing-yang playwright Shih Chün-pao (second half of the thirteenth century), the young man is the son of a high Jurchen (Chin) official, while his paramour is a *chu-kung-tiao* performer. When the boy's father grounds the young man and banishes the girl from his jurisdiction, the young man runs away from home. He teams up with his lover to form a duo of strolling performers. Eventually the father gives the couple his blessing. Shih Chün-pao also dramatized Pai Hsing-chien's classical tale *Li Wa chuan* (An Account of Li Wa) as "Ch'ü-chiang ch'ih" (Serpentine Pond). Classical tales of the T'ang dynasty often provided materials for plays on love between young men and women of high birth. A particularly successful work in this category was Cheng Kuang-tsu's "Ch'ien-nü li-hun" (Ch'ien-nü's Soul Leaves Her Body), which was based on Ch'en Hsüan-yu's "Li-hun chi" (Record of the Disembodied Soul).

One group of plays shares not only a specific set of characters and a specific plot structure but also a specific function: the deliverance plays written to be performed at major anniversaries in the life of important individuals, inasmuch as these plays expressed the wish for longevity. It comes as no surprise that these works form an important part of the oeuvre that has been preserved of the court-connected playwrights of the first century of the Ming. Deliverance plays were also written by the first generations of *tsa-chü* authors. In a typical deliverance play, one of the heavenly deities, such as Hsi Wang-mu (Queen Mother of the West) or her male counterpart, Tung-hua ti-chün (Lord of the East), decides the time has come to deliver somebody on earth. The person concerned is usually a former inhabitant of heaven who has been banished to earth for some worldly thought and whose period of punishment has come to an end. One of the immortals is instructed to convert the person concerned to a religious life so that he or she may achieve immortality. When the immortal, usually in the guise of a physically repulsive mendicant monk, appears before his convert-to-be and tells his message of the vanity of all earthly glories, he is indignantly rejected because the convert-to-be enjoys life to the full and trusts in his or her riches and connections.

Only when a sudden twist of fate, if need be engineered by the teacher, makes him or her aware of the impermanence of this-worldly existence does the convert-to-be see the light and then become willing to cut all ties to the world and devote him- or herself to a life of religious exercises. After a suitable period of austerity, immortality is achieved, and the teacher takes his pupil to see the deity and assume his or her place in the heavenly ranks. Because of the asymmetrical structure of *tsa-chü*, the four suites are assigned either to the teacher or to the pupil. In many deliverance plays, the master is one of the Eight Immortals (legendary Taoist paragons), while his pupil is one of the other members of the group. Some of the deliverance plays feature the patriarchs of the Ch'üan-chen sect (see chapter 10) of Taoism that had originated under the Chin dynasty and achieved great popularity during the Yüan. A few deliverance plays are Buddhist in character. The converts-to-be come from all walks of life, including the despised professions of butcher and courtesan, as if to stress that life eternal is available to everyone who sees the light and is reborn. In an anonymous *tsa-chü* entitled "Lan Ts'ai-ho," the main character and convert-to-be, Lan Ts'ai-ho, is even a professional actor.

One of the best-known deliverance plays is "Huang-liang meng" (Yellow Millet Dream). This play is a dramatization of the T'ang dynasty classical tale "Chen-chung chi" (Record of the World Within a Pillow), by Shen Chi-chi (c. 740–c. 800). The names of the protagonists, however, have been changed. The Taoist priest Lü of the classical tale is now identified as Chung-li Ch'üan, the first of the Eight Immortals, while the student on his way to the capital (surnamed Lü) is now identified as Lü Tung-pin, the second of the Eight Immortals. The play is often discussed as one of the works of Ma Chih-yüan, a leading playwright in the second half of the thirteenth century and a minor official. Actually, he contributed only one of the four suites of songs; the other three suites were composed by another playwright and two professional actors with high positions in the Court Entertainment Bureau. This suggests that the play may have been composed for performance at court.

The Major Playwrights

The main centers for the production of *tsa-chü* during the second half of the thirteenth century were the major urban centers of northern China: Ta-tu (modern-day Peking), Chen-ting (in modern-day Hopei province), Tung-p'ing (in modern-day Shantung province), Kaifeng, and P'ing-yang (in modern-day Shansi province). In the first half of the fourteenth century Hangchow also became an important center for the production of *tsa-chü*, but the genre probably did not make much headway in southern China beyond this metropolitan outpost, with its large contingent of resident northerners. Our information on most of the playwrights is very meager, because the earliest catalogs provide little data beyond their place of origin and a list of their titles. Although many of them obviously were men of some education, only a few held an official post, and rarely one of any importance.

It has often been stated that the Chinese intellectuals of the Yüan dynasty turned to the writing of vernacular literature because the abolition of the examination system by the Yüan rulers denied them a chance to participate in the administration, and that they used the genre to vent their anti-Mongol frustration. But it is difficult to find explicit expressions of anti-Mongol sentiments in plays of that period. This does not mean, however, that the genre shied away from the exploration of the relations between Chinese and barbarian, indigenous and foreign, or that these plays remained silent about contemporary abuses. Social ills were decried with passionate vehemence, but such passages were often toned down considerably by the Ming court censors, who preferred their emperors to believe that the whole world was at peace.

The most famous author of *tsa-chü* is Kuan Han-ch'ing (c. 1220–c. 1307), whose name has already been encountered many times. He is also said to have been the originator of the genre, but this claim is hard to substantiate. However, it is clear that he was by far the most productive playwright. He is credited with authorship of some sixty titles, of which four have been preserved in Yüan dynasty printings. Modern editions of his complete works usually include eighteen plays in various editions and fragments of three more, but in some cases the ascription is questionable. Kuan Han-ch'ing had some connection to the medical profession, but it is not quite clear of what nature, and it certainly did not prompt him to paint a rosy picture of the medical profession. In his best-known play, "Kan t'ien tung ti: Tou Ŏ yüan tsa-chü" (Moving Heaven and Earth: Injustice to Tou Ŏ), a doctor tries to murder the woman from whom he had earlier borrowed some money. Kuan Han-ch'ing was active in Ta-tu, and some contemporary anecdotes connect him with the fashionable fringe of the capital elite. He also was involved with the courtesan-cum-actress Chung-tu-hsiu. However, in an anecdote in Chu Ch'üan's *T'ai-ho cheng-yin p'u* (Formulary for the Correct Sounds of Great Harmony; preface dated 1398, but the book was probably completed later) he strongly dissociates himself from the ranks of professional actors.

The plays now preserved under the name of Kuan Han-ch'ing are highly uneven in quality. His best plays stand out for their sympathetic portrayal of spirited young women. His most famous play in this respect is "Injustice to Tou Ŏ." The available late Ming editions of the play have an opening wedge and four acts. In the opening wedge, the student Tou T'ien-chang hands his young daughter over to old lady Ts'ai as a future bride for her son. In return she provides him with the money he needs to travel to the capital in order to sit for the examinations. The first act takes place eighteen years later. By that time Tou Ŏ has been a widow for three years. After her mother-in-law is saved from strangulation at the hands of one of her debtors (a physician) by two scoundrels, father and son, the pair follow her home and demand to marry the two women. To the disgust of Tou Ŏ, her mother-in-law gives in to their demands, but Tou Ŏ adamantly refuses to comply. The father and son then attempt to frame Tou Ŏ in a plot to poison her mother-in-law, but the plan backfires when the father accidentally eats the poisoned soup, leading the son to accuse Tou Ŏ of murdering his father.

In the second act, Tou Ŏ is brought before the magistrate. She refuses to confess, but when the magistrate threatens to torture her mother-in-law, she gives in for the sake of the old woman. The third act is devoted to Tou Ŏ's walk from the prison to the execution ground. After a tearful final parting from her mother-in-law, she cries out against heaven because of the injustice she has suffered and vows that if she dies innocently, her blood will stream upward, snow will fall in midsummer, and the district will suffer a drought for three years. As soon is she is beheaded, the first two vows are fulfilled. The final act takes places three years later, after the district has been laid waste by a continuous drought. When the inspecting censor Tou T'ien-chang reviews the files of the death penalty cases, the ghost of his daughter places her own file on top of the pile until her father eventually reads it, becomes aware of the injustice she has suffered, and restores her good name.

The songs in this *tsa-chü* are assigned to the female lead, who plays the part of Tou Ŏ; she changes costume between the third and fourth acts. Although the outline of the action is the same in both preserved editions of the play, Tsang Mao-hsün's edition in *Anthology of Yüan Plays* underlines Tou Ŏ's filial virtue, while downplaying elements of sex and money. "Injustice to Tou Ŏ" is by all accounts a very moving play. It has remained in the repertoire, in a revised form, of many kinds of regional theater. For its status in the history of Chinese literature, however, it is very much indebted to China's first modern history of theater and dramatic literature, *Sung Yüan hsi-ch'ü k'ao* (Research on the Drama of the Sung and Yüan Dynasties; 1912), by the erudite scholar Wang Kuo-wei (1877–1927). Wang Kuo-wei, who was aware of the high status of tragedy in Western literature, selected "Injustice to Tou Ŏ" together with "The Orphan of the House of Chao" as Chinese examples of that Western genre.

"Injustice to Tou Ŏ" was selected because the sufferings of the heroine are due not to coincidence but to her own choices (to refuse to remarry and to confess, rather then see her mother-in-law suffer torture). Ever since then, "Injustice to Tou Ŏ" has been celebrated as Kuan Han-ch'ing's most representative work. Kuan Han-ch'ing's writing of "Injustice to Tou Ŏ" eventually became itself a subject of drama in 1958, when the famous modern dramatist T'ien Han wrote his "Kuan Han-ch'ing."

Another play that shows Kuan Han-ch'ing at his best in the portrayal of spirited young women is his "Chiu Feng-ch'en" (The Rescue of a Courtesan). In this play the heroine is a courtesan who, at first unsuccessfully, tries to dissuade a colleague from marrying a boorish bully, and later, when her friend finds married life unbearable, comes to the rescue by seducing the husband. Already discussed above are Kuan Han-ch'ing's two plays on Kuan Yü and Chang Fei, which show his talents in portraying male heroic characters.

Kuan Han-ch'ing may be the most famous author of *tsa-chü*, but the most famous play in the genre is Wang Shih-fu's five-*tsa-chü* cycle "Romance of the Western Chamber." Almost no data are available on Wang Shih-fu. His other preserved works are rather undistinguished. During the Ming dynasty, when the currently available information on Yüan dynasty playwrights and their works was hardly known, it was widely believed that the play was by Kuan Han-ch'ing. Later the received wisdom held that the first four plays in the series had been written by Wang Shih-fu, while the final play was the work of Kuan Han-ch'ing. This view is still supported by some modern scholars, also because many of them find the final play of less literary or ideological quality than the preceding four plays. However, the play as a whole is a rather close adaptation for the stage of Tung Chieh-yüan's "Medley of the 'Romance of the Western Chamber,'" and there are no positive proofs whatsoever of a dual authorship.

One major change by Wang Shih-fu is that the character of the monk, Fa-ts'ung, is split in two: the monk Fa-ts'ung, who is Student Chang's guide and friend in the monastery, and the monk Hui-ming, who fights his way through the massed rebels besieging the monastery in order to deliver the letter of Student Chang to his friend Tu Chüeh. Another change in the plot is that at the end Student Chang and Ying-ying do not elope to the safe haven of the yamen of Tu Chüeh, but the latter comes to the monastery to congratulate his friend and sees to it that the lovers are united in wedlock.

Wang Shih-fu's "Romance of the Western Chamber" departs from the general rules for *tsa-chü* not only in being a cycle of five plays, containing twenty-one suites of songs, but also in having more than one actor or actress sing these arias. Whereas Hui-ming sings one relatively short suite of songs, the remaining suites are divided among the *mo*, who plays the part of Student Chang, the *tan* (female lead), who plays the part of Ying-ying, and the actress who plays the part of Hung-niang. In this way, the character of the saucy servant girl is still further developed. In some later versions of the play in local theater genres, she even becomes the central character of the whole play, which is then often named after her.

Among the earliest generations of *tsa-chü* authors Pai P'u (1226–after 1306) stands out because of his elite background. He was brought up by the famous poet Yüan Hao-wen (1190–1257), and after he grew up he enjoyed the patronage of Shih T'ien-tse (1202–1275), who ruled Shantung province on behalf of the Mongol conquerors, and his own sons were to serve the Yüan dynasty as officials. Pai P'u's best-known play is "Wu-t'ung yü" (Rain on the Plantain), his dramatization of Pai Chü-yi's "Ch'ang-hen ko" (Song of Everlasting Regret). This play has been preserved in a number of late Ming editions. The leading role is given to the male lead, who plays the part of Emperor Hsüan-tsung. The play focuses on the passion of the emperor for Yang Kuei-fei, who, upon her first entrance on the stage (in all editions except the one in *Anthology of Yüan Plays*), confesses to her affair with An Lu-shan. After the emperor has sworn eternal fidelity to Yang Kuei-fei in the first act, he is rudely awakened from his dream of happiness in the second act by the announcement of An Lu-shan's rebellion. His happiness is completely destroyed in the third act, when the guards accompanying the emperor on his flight to distant Chengtu (in the present-day southwestern province of Szechwan) demand the death of his favorite consort. The final act is given over to the outpourings of grief of the aged emperor, still a victim of his passion, after his return to the capital. The ornate beauty of the songs in this play has always attracted great praise.

Pai P'u's "Rain on the Plantain" has an equally famous counterpart in "Han-kung ch'iu" (Autumn in the Han Palace), by Ma Chih-yüan, who is otherwise best known for his deliverance plays. Ma's "Autumn in the Han Palace" deals with the tragic love of Emperor Yüan (r. 48–33 B.C.E.) of the Han dynasty for his concubine Wang Chao-chün. The historical Wang Chao-chün was given as a bride to Hu-han-yeh, a chieftain of the northern nomadic Hsiung-nu, whom she bore two children; upon his death she married his son (by his first wife) and successor. Later legend insisted that Emperor Yüan had portraits made of all his concubines and chose his bedmates by their painted looks. But Wang Chao-chün, trusting in her natural beauty, had refused to bribe the painter Mao Yen-shou, who thereupon blemished her portrait. Consequently, she was neglected by the emperor, but was selected when the Hsiung-nu leader requested a Chinese princess as wife to seal the friendship between his people and the Chinese empire. Emperor Yüan became aware of the mistake only at the moment he saw her off.

Through the ages this story has continued to inspire Chinese poets and painters, and it was also written up as a *pien-wen* (transformation text) that is preserved among the Tun-huang manuscripts. In the dramatization of this story by Ma Chih-yüan, the songs are assigned to Emperor Yüan. In the first act he discovers the charms of Wang Chao-chün, with whom he immediately falls in love. In the second act, however, the court receives the request for Wang Chao-chün from Hu-han-yeh, who has deviously been informed of her beauty by Mao Yen-shou. To the indignation of the emperor, his officials urge him to accede to this request, as it will maintain peace between the two nations. The third act is given over to a tearful farewell scene. However, as soon as Wang Chao-chün has crossed the border river into the domain of the Hsiung-nu, she commits suicide by jumping into the river. The final act is again devoted to the extended description of the emperor's grief.

Whereas Yang Kuei-fei is depicted as a loose woman who is only intent on her own position, Wang Chao-chün is portrayed as an obedient servant who accepts the mission imposed on her. Although Emperor Hsüan-tsung by his indulgence in his own passion wrecks the empire, Emperor Yüan ensures continued peace by his willingness to sacrifice the woman he loves. "Autumn in the Han Palace" is the opening play of *Anthology of Yüan Plays* and was translated into English as early as 1829.

Among the preserved plays of Ma Chih-yüan are several deliverance plays and some plays on the adversities suffered by brilliant scholars. An example of the latter category is his "Ch'ing-shan lei" (Tears on the Blue Gown), which dramatizes Po Chü-yi's banishment to Chiu-chiang, where he wrote his famous ballad "P'i-p'a hsing" (Ballad of the Balloon Lute).

By the first half of the fourteenth century, the center of *tsa-chü* production had shifted to Hangchow and its immediate surroundings, at least as far as known authors are concerned. Of course, our perception is shaped by the nature of our most important source of information, Chung Ssu-ch'eng's *Register of Ghosts*. Chung Ssu-ch'eng was himself a practicing playwright, but his own works have been lost. Most of the authors he records for this period (many of whom were his personal friends) had only a very limited oeuvre. The most highly regarded playwrights of this period are Kung T'ien-t'ing and Ch'iao Chi. Kung T'ien-t'ing served in various educational posts; his two surviving plays are adaptations of moralistic historical anecdotes. Ch'iao Chi (d. 1345) hailed from Taiyuan but ended his life in Hangchow. His three extant plays are all romantic comedies set in the T'ang dynasty. One of these is devoted to the loves of the poet Tu Mu (803–852); another includes the brilliant Li T'ai-po (Li Po; 701–762) in its cast. The third play, entitled "Liang-shih yin-yüan" (A Karmic Bond for Two Generations), dramatizes an anecdote from *T'ai-p'ing kuang-chi* (Extensive Records from the Reign of Great Tranquility) about the love of a mighty late-eighth-century Governor of Chengtu (Szechwan), Wei Kao (745–805), for Yü-hsiao, the adopted sister of a friend—the young maiden dies soon after their first meeting but is reborn as a girl and becomes a concubine of Wei Kao when she has reached a fitting age.

One of the most remarkable playwrights of this period (though not included in *Register of Ghosts*) was Yang Tzu. He was the son of a high Southern Sung military commander who had timely surrendered to the Mongols. As a reward he and his descendants were given high positions, including the supervisorate of international trade at Hai-yen, Hangchow's ocean port. The Yangs also participated in foreign trade themselves and amassed a tremendous fortune that allowed them to maintain their own private theatrical company. In 1327, Yang Tzu took part in the Yüan campaign against Eastern Java. Yang Tzu wrote three plays on historical themes that all deal with the issue of loyalty. In each case, the hero of the play shows a conspicuous loyalty to his lord, risking his life or sacrificing his family. In each case, however, the hero has first left an undeserving master. One is tempted to read these plays as apologies by Yang Tzu for the behavior of his father, in defense of the family honor in a local society where anti-Mongol sentiment ran high.

For information on authors of the second half of the fourteenth century and the first decades of the fifteenth, we have to rely on Chu Ch'üan's *A Formulary for the Correct Sounds of Great Harmony* and on a sequel to *Register of Ghosts* that is believed to have been written by Chia Chung-ming. Chia Chung-ming (1343–after 1424) is one of the most prominent of the court-connected playwrights of the first fifty years of the Ming dynasty; six plays by him have been preserved, among which there are two deliverance plays. The deliverance plays of these decades tend to be more elaborate affairs than those of earlier times. As to literary style, the authors of this period particularly admired the works of Ma Chih-yüan. The writer most admired for his style from the early Ming is Ku Tzu-ching. Ku's only surviving play, entitled "Ch'eng-nan liu" (Willow South of the Wall), is a deliverance play in which Lü Tung-pin shows a willow tree the road to enlightenment. Chia Chung-ming's sequel to *Register of Ghosts* also lists a certain Lo Kuan-chung, whom he credits with three plays, one of which is still extant. However, Chia remains silent about Lo Kuan-chung's dabblings in vernacular fiction (see chapter 35).

Of the two early Ming imperial relatives who wrote *tsa-chü*, Chu Ch'üan (1378–1448), as the seventeenth son of the Hung-wu emperor, the prince of Ning at Nan-ch'ang, is nowadays best remembered in drama studies for his *Formulary for the Correct Sounds of Great Harmony*, the earliest preserved formulary of northern *ch'ü*. The formulary part of the work is preceded by sundry information on *tsa-chü*, including fanciful etymologies of the names of the role-types, some anecdotes, and a catalog of playwrights and their works. Two of Chu Ch'üan's own *tsa-chü* have been preserved. One of these may kindly be characterized as an elaborate but stylistically undistinguished deliverance play, while the other play is an adaptation of the romance of Ssu-ma Hsiang-ju and Cho Wen-chün. As a playwright he pales into insignificance next to his extremely productive and versatile nephew, the Exemplary Prince of Chou, Chu Yu-tun. Chu Yu-tun was the eldest son and successor of the fourth son of the Hung-wu emperor, the only full brother of the Yung-le emperor, and as the prince of Chou at Kaifeng the richest prince of the realm. Chu Yu-tun's conspicuous interest in drama may have been inspired in part by a desire to manifest his disinterest in politics, as his father had been accused of plotting rebellion and barely escaped execution on several occasions.

Chu Yu-tun's thirty-one plays, which have all come down to us in his own private printings, can for the most part be divided into two groups. The first group consists of a large number of court pageants, which usually require a sizable cast, elaborate costumes, and special effects. Many of these plays are tied to a specific occasion, such as the prince's birthday (traditional and reformed deliverance plays) or other yearly festivals (e.g., a scenario in the format of a *tsa-chü* for the year's-end *No* ceremony, in which Chung K'uei is the main exorcist, and a scenario for the lion's dance on New Year's Day). We also have plays that were written as entertainment at flower-viewing parties and celebrated the flowers concerned, such as the peony. In many of these pageants Chu Yu-tun broke with the established rules of the genre by allowing more than one actor or actress to sing.

Chu Yu-tun's remaining plays are not tied to any specific occasion for their performance and as a rule conform rather closely to the established conventions of the genre. Many of these plays deal with the love of a beautiful courtesan for a brilliant student and can be read as an affirmation of the author's loyalty to the emperor. The same theme of loyalty is also stressed in Chu Yu-tun's only play on a historical subject, an episode in the life of Kuan Yü. Two of his plays adopt their characters from the stories about the righteous bandits of the Liang-shan marshes. In the first of these, Li K'uei takes the place of the bashful bride in the sedan chair, when a corrupt and lecherous official covets a poor farmer's daughter, and proceeds to give that scoundrel a sound beating; the play concludes with the band's honorable surrender to the authorities. The second play focuses on Lu Chih-shen, a former monk, who in this play tries to escape from the permanent danger of a bandit's life by once again entering a monastery. After the pleadings of his wife and little son fail to change his mind or persuade him to "return to the laity," he is convinced to rejoin the band when his old mother is carried off by bandits as part of a plot by Sung Chiang to return him to his senses.

Chu Yu-tun's most farcical play is "Fu lo-ch'ang" (Becoming a Singsong Girl Again). This play turns the conventional student-and-courtesan romance on its head. The Kaifeng courtesan-cum-actress Liu Chin-erh, who plays the clown on stage, is eager to marry any customer, however ugly he may be, so long as he has money, but drops the husbands she acquires in this way as soon as she perceives a better prospect. She fails her duties as a housewife completely. Eventually, when she applies for a divorce in Nan-ch'ang, she is sent back to Kaifeng and her original pimp-husband.

Throughout his oeuvre Chu Yu-tun shows himself to be an expert versifier and at times a gifted lyricist. He also writes lively dialogs that are much more vernacular in style than the prose sections found in late Ming editions of *tsa-chü*. During the Ming dynasty, Chu Yu-tun's works enjoyed a continuing popularity, but as none of his plays was included in *Anthology of Yüan Plays* they have unduly suffered neglect ever since. Chu Yu-tun also provided most of his plays in print with a short, dated preface in which he discussed the sources of the play concerned and its function and message. At times he also compared his own work to that of predecessors and discoursed on the general requirements of plays. This makes him the first major drama critic.

While southern drama extended its influence throughout the fifteenth century and started to make inroads in the north, the tradition of *tsa-chü* in Nanking was maintained by Ch'en To (also called Ch'en Ta-sheng; 1488?–1521?), three of whose plays have been preserved. Two of these works are *tsa-chü* and slight but witty comedies. The third work is a rare example of a *yüan-pen* skit. In the north the most notable playwrights after 1500 were some retired officials who wrote *tsa-chü* for their own household troupes, such as K'ang Hai (1475–1541) and Wang Chiu-ssu (1468–1551). Both dramatized the tale of the Wolf of Chung-shan as "Chung-shan lang": after a wolf has been saved from hunters by a traveling scholar who hides him in his book chest, the hungry wolf wants to devour his benefactor because ingratitude is the way of the world; the scholar protests, and they agree to submit their quarrel to the judgment of three old men. The apricot tree, which will shortly be chopped down as firewood since it does not bear fruit anymore and the old buffalo—which is to be slaughtered after many years of faithful service—both side with the wolf, but the third expert (identified as the local god of the earth by Wang Chiu-ssu) first wants to see proof that the big wolf really fits into the book chest. As soon as the wolf is in the chest again, he is killed. K'ang Hai's work has the form of a regular four-act *tsa-chü*, but Wang Chiu-ssu's work consists of only one act.

An important transitional author in the north was Li K'ai-hsien (1501–1568). He collected *san-ch'ü*, wrote skits (*yüan-pen*), and published a collection of revised editions of earlier *tsa-chü*. However, he also had a hand in the revision of "Pao-chien chi" (The Precious Sword), a *ch'uan-ch'i* play that dramatizes the adventures of the officer Lin Ch'ung, whose wife is coveted by a high metropolitan official; hounded by his superiors, Lin Ch'ung eventually has no way out but to join the bandits of the Liang-shan marshes.

In the course of the sixteenth century, *tsa-chü* quickly disappeared from the stage outside the imperial palace, and even there the influence of southern drama made itself felt to a greater extent. However, new *tsa-chü* continued to be written at court up to the Wan-li era, one of the most notable works being a six-*tsa-chü* cycle, "Hsi-yu chi" (Journey to the West), dealing with the exploits of the monk Hsüan-tsang and his supernatural helpers Monkey and Pigsy during their pilgrimage to the Western Paradise (authorship of this work has been credited to Wu Ch'ang-ling of the early Yüan and to Yang Na of the early Ming). Yet another of these late works deals with the early Ming expeditions of Chinese fleets led by the eunuch Cheng Ho (1371–1433) to the Western Ocean (i.e., the countries bordering the Indian Ocean).

Early Southern Drama

The earliest preserved texts of southern drama are the three *hsi-wen* that form the contents of one of the surviving volumes of the gigantic collectanea called the *Yung-le Encyclopedia*. However, this does not automatically mean that these are the earliest southern plays that have been transmitted. It is quite conceivable that some of the early southern plays that have come down to us in much later editions may initially have been composed at an earlier date than the three texts from the *Yung-le Encyclopedia*, even though the available editions show traces of centuries of continuous rewriting. The three preserved *hsi-wen* from the *Yung-le Encyclopedia*, however, contain no internal evidence that allows one to date them more precisely. As the two shorter plays are adaptations of *tsa-chü*, they probably date from the fourteenth century. The longest play, "Chang Hsieh chuang-yüan" (Top-Graduate Chang Hsieh), may have been written at any time during the thirteenth or fourteenth century.

Of the two *tsa-chü* adaptations, "Huan-men tzu-ti ts'o li-shen" (The Scion of an Official Family Opts for the Wrong Career) must be an adaptation of one of the three lost *tsa-chü* of the same title. The story concerns a son of a high Jurchen (Chin dynasty) official who falls in love with a Chinese actress and elopes with her. The plot of the play is practically identical to that of Shih Chün-pao's "Purple Clouds Courtyard," except that the girl does not perform *chu-kung-tiao* but, rather, *tsa-chü*. The other play, "Hsiao Sun t'u" (Little Sun the Butcher), tells a story of two brothers. The elder marries a courtesan despite his younger brother's warnings. During the absence of the younger brother on a pilgrimage, the former prostitute kills the maidservant with the help of her lover, a government clerk; together they frame her husband for the murder. When the younger brother returns, he willingly takes all the blame. He is ready to be executed, when the perspicacious Judge Pao, with some ghostly assistance, becomes aware of the truth of the matter and has the real culprits executed, while the two brothers are reunited forever.

These two translations into another genre clearly bring out the differences between the two genres. *Hsi-wen* are distinguished from *tsa-chü* not only by the fact that southern tunes are used instead of northern *ch'ü* but also by the fact that all the role-types may sing and therefore need songs assigned to them, greatly expanding the bulk of the text. There is no fixed modal organization of tunes (though there are conventions that govern their use, such as which tune is more suitable for which role-type and the fact that the sequence of songs is not random), and the play can consist of any number of scenes. Although the two plays discussed above are very short for southern drama, "Top-Graduate Chang Hsieh" approaches the usual length, with its fifty-three scenes.

"Top-Graduate Chang Hsieh" features one of the most popular characters of early southern drama, the ungrateful student. Chang Hsieh leaves his hometown to travel to the capital in order to sit for the examinations. While en route, he is robbed of all his belongings. A destitute girl who lives in a derelict temple takes care of him, becomes his wife, and even sells her hair to enable him to travel on. Chang Hsieh succeeds in the examinations with highest honors and is appointed as a district magistrate. Now an official, he despises the poor girl, and on his way to his post he stops at the derelict temple and stabs her. The poor girl survives and is later adopted as a daughter by an official who happens to be Chang Hsieh's superior. When the official notices that the recent top-graduate is still a bachelor (so Chang claims), he proposes a marriage to his adopted daughter, and to his great surprise Chang Hsieh finds himself married all over again to the woman he tried to murder. And so all's well that ends well.

The play opens with an introductory scene in which the *mo* sets out to narrate the outline of the story to be enacted. Such introductory scenes occur in all later texts of *ch'uan-ch'i* but usually are a rather simple affair, in which first a summary of the play is presented, next its moral message is stressed, and finally the young male lead (*sheng*) is invited to enter upon the stage and start the play proper. These introductory scenes are usually called *chia-men*. In "Top-Graduate Chang Hsieh" the introductory scene is exceptionally long and is presented in (a mockery of) the format of an "all keys and modes" (i.e., medley), the most unlikely genre of literature to be incorporated into southern drama. This *mo* never finishes his presentation of the outline, because after a while he is interrupted by voices from backstage who want to get the play proper started. The introduction sets a tone for the play as a whole that is remarkable not only for its bizarre plot but also for its extensive scenes of foolish clowning. One is tempted to read the whole play as a parody of the genre to which it belongs. That might well explain its place in the final volume of *hsi-wen* texts in the *Yung-le Encyclopedia*.

The unfaithful student also makes his appearance in Kao Ming's "The Story of the Lute." In a predecessor to Kao's play, the male protagonist, Ts'ai Yung (Po-chieh), leaves his young wife, Chao Wu-niang, to take care of his aged parents while he sets out for the capital. After he has succeeded in the examination with top honors, he eagerly marries the daughter of Prime Minister Niu and refuses to recognize his first wife. As a punishment for his wicked deeds, he is struck dead by a thunderbolt. Kao Ming set out to turn Ts'ai Yung into the very model of a filial son. In his version, Ts'ai Yung sets out for the capital only at the express order of his father, whom he cannot disobey as a filial son. As soon as he has passed the examinations, he sends a letter home to announce his success, but the letter is never delivered. When Prime Minister Niu offers him his daughter's hand in marriage, he protests that he is already married, but to no avail: an imperial edict makes him the live-in son-in-law of the all-powerful minister.

In the meantime, his home district is stricken by disaster. Chao Wu-niang sacrifices herself in taking care of her in-laws by giving them all the remaining rice while herself eating chaff. After her husband's parents have died despite her efforts, she sells her long, beautiful hair in order to provide them with a decent burial. She then travels to the capital, begging for food while performing a ballad of her woes to the accompaniment of her lute. In the capital she attracts the attention of Prime Minister Niu's daughter, who soon realizes that she is her husband's original wife and immediately cedes first place to her. A tearful reunion scene follows, and the emperor allows Ts'ai Yung to return with his two wives to his hometown in order to sacrifice at his parents' tomb.

If this play has a hero, the summary makes clear that it is its heroine. Chao Wu-niang not only is the very model of a patiently suffering wife, but also shows great determination and inventiveness. Despite Kao Ming's efforts, the character of Ts'ai Yung remains unconvincing to most readers; he is at best viewed as a well-intentioned but weak-spined young man. A man of real character would not have accepted the prime minister's daughter as his wife, however dire the consequences might be. Such a faithful young man is portrayed in another early southern play that remained a stage favorite for centuries, "Ching-ch'ai chi" (The Thorn-Hairpin). When the prime minister wants the top graduate, Wang Shih-p'eng, to marry his daughter, Wang steadfastly refuses out of loyalty to his wife, Ch'en Yü-lien, and the prime minister thereupon has him appointed to a distant post. Only after many adventures are Wang Shih-p'eng and his wife eventually reunited—after each believes the other to be dead and offers a sacrifice for the benefit of the other's soul in the same temple. Yet another example of a faithful top-graduate is provided by Liu Wen-lung, the male protagonist in "Chin-ch'ai chi" (The Gold Hairpin), a play that has been preserved in a 1431 manuscript discovered only in 1975 in a grave. When Liu Wen-lung refuses to marry the daughter of the prime minister, that villain has him dispatched to the Hsiung-nu nomads beyond the northern frontier. The Hsiung-nu leader, the khan, takes a liking to him and marries him to his daughter. Only after twenty-one years does Liu escape, with the help of his second wife. During these long years, his first wife has remained loyal to him and resisted all pressure to remarry. Liu arrives back home just in time to save her from committing suicide by drowning.

"The Thorn-Hairpin" is often mentioned in the same breath with three other early plays that enjoyed an equal popularity. These plays are "Pai-yüeh chi" (Praying to the Moon), "Sha kou chi" (Killing a Dog), and "The White Hare." Each of these plays dramatizes a story that also had been treated in *tsa-chü*. "Praying to the Moon" claims in the *chia-men* in one of its earliest editions to be based on a *tsa-chü* from the capital, most likely "Courtyard of Praying to the Moon," by Kuan Han-ch'ing. The action of the very complicated plot is set during the chaotic years of the first onslaught of the Mongols against the Chin dynasty, which resulted in the transfer of the Chin capital to Kaifeng from what is now Peking. The plot involves various mistaken identities, but eventually concludes with the celebration of two marriages. "Killing a Dog" is another tale of brotherly estrangement and reconciliation. Again, the brothers are surnamed

Sun. This time the elder brother is under the influence of bad friends and turns his poor younger brother away from his door. The sensible wife of the elder brother conspires with her brother-in-law to teach her husband a lesson about the unreliability of his friends: they kill a dog and skin it, dress the corpse as a man, and during the night place it on the front steps of the elder brother's house. When the elder brother, drunk as usual, comes home in the middle of the night and finds the corpse, his friends refuse to help him to dispose of it, and eventually he has to appeal to his younger brother, who willingly accepts the charge. The same tale was dramatized in an anonymous *tsa-chü* entitled "Sha kou ch'üan fu" (Admonishing One's Husband by Killing a Dog).

"The White Hare" dramatizes the story of the early career of Liu Chih-yüan, a topic taken up earlier in a (partially preserved) *chu-kung-tiao* and a (lost) *tsa-chü*. The poor and wandering Liu Chih-yüan is taken in by a rich squire who is impressed by his countenance and marries him, over the opposition of her elder brothers, to his daughter Li San-niang. After the old man's death, his sons make life so miserable for Liu that he decides to leave his pregnant wife and become a soldier. When he signs up, Liu's commander and his daughter recognize the signs of future greatness, and the commander orders Liu, despite his protests, to marry his daughter. While Liu pursues his army career, his first wife, who has refused to remarry, suffers the abuse of her brothers, who make her undertake the most menial tasks, such as turning the mill. When it is time for her to have her baby, she does so without any assistance, so she has to bite through the umbilical cord herself. She has the baby taken to Liu, who hands the boy over to his second wife. This woman raises the boy as her own, and even when he has reached the age of twelve he still does not know the identity of his birth mother.

After his father, now the commander, returns from a campaign the victor, the boy is allowed to go hunting. A white hare leads him to a village well, where a haggard woman tells him the story of her life. The boy is surprised to hear that the name of her good-for-nothing husband who has run away to join the army is the same as that of his father and promises her that he will inquire about her husband with his father. When he does so upon his return, Liu realizes the boy has met his mother, and he decides to test Li San-niang's fidelity by visiting her disguised as a common soldier. When he meets her outside the village, she berates him at length for his long absence and enumerates the abuses she has suffered for his sake, but when her brothers appear on the scene, Liu has to flee (in the *chu-kung-tiao* the couple makes love under the open sky before the appearance of her brothers, and that incident also figures in the title of the lost *tsa-chü*, but it is omitted from the southern play). Liu, impressed by her fidelity, returns the next day at the head of his troops to claim his long-lost bride, and his second wife cedes to her the position of first wife.

The list of preserved titles of *hsi-wen* shows that early southern drama dealt with pretty much the same subjects as contemporary *tsa-chü*. This is exemplary of a general tendency in traditional drama: the different genres freely borrowed each other's plots and textual materials. Southern drama, however, often managed to stretch the same plots used in *tsa-chü* into much longer texts. This was due in part to the necessity to provide all roles with a fitting number of songs and in part to the inclusion of some stereotypical scenes and the much greater role allowed to the comic characters. The prevalence of farcical elements, especially in performance, apparently inspired the production of "Wu-lun ch'üan-pei chi" (All Moral Relationships Fulfilled), a southern play devoted to the portrayal of Confucian virtues within a single family. This play was traditionally attributed to the famous Confucian scholar and statesman Ch'iu Chün (1420–1495), but this attribution is highly questionable, as is the case with practically all southern plays from this period whenever an author is mentioned. For all its moralism, "All Moral Relationships Fulfilled" enjoyed considerable popularity on the stage during the fifteenth and sixteenth centuries and had the distinction of being adopted as a textbook for teaching vernacular Chinese in contemporary Korea.

DRAMATIC LITERATURE FROM THE SIXTEENTH TO NINETEENTH CENTURIES (C. 1550–C. 1850)

By the early sixteenth century, the economic and cultural center of China had shifted to the Kiangnan region. Its economic prosperity greatly stimulated theatrical activity. Southern drama was performed in an ever-increasing geographical area, and it also became popular in the north, where its influence was felt even within the palace walls. By the early seventeenth century the performance of traditional *tsa-chü* was a dying art. In the homeland of southern drama different traditions of performance were now distinguished. These differences mainly affected the musical aspects, the style in which the arias were sung. The two most outstanding traditions were the Yi-yang style, which was popular in Kiangsi, and the K'un-ch'ü style, which was perfected by Wei Liang-fu in Soochow around the middle of the sixteenth century. K'un-ch'ü also incorporated many northern melodies in its repertoire, but the delivery of these songs was, of course, adapted to its own characteristics. The play that, more than any other, marked the emergence of K'un-ch'ü as an independent style of performance was Liang Ch'en-yü's (1520–1593) "Huan-sha chi" (Washing Silk), a dramatization of the legend of the beauty Hsi Shih.

As Soochow was the economic and cultural center of the Kiangnan region, its preferred style of performance—K'un-ch'ü—came to be widely imitated in other places too. Because of K'un-ch'ü's refined music and its emphasis on song, it became widely popular with elite audiences. K'un-ch'ü was also the style that was adopted by most of the private troupes, a conspicuous feature of theatrical life during the last century of the Ming dynasty. A different pattern of urbanization and urban culture by the early sixteenth century had resulted in the disappearance, for the time being, of the commercial theater, even in the prosperous and populous towns of Kiangnan. However, the tax regime of the Ming dynasty allowed for the emergence of huge private fortunes that were heavily concentrated there. Many of these wealthy households maintained a private theatrical company, in most cases all-female troupes. Whereas regular professional companies usually performed full plays, such private companies preferred shorter fare for the entertainment of the master of the house and his male guests. Beginning in this period the performance of *che-tzu-hsi*, single scenes from well-known plays, became popular. Many of the owners of private troupes also tried their hands at writing plays, which they then had performed by their own players.

The demand for shorter plays, mentioned above, probably also explains the rise of a new genre of short plays that are also designated as *tsa-chü* but are not bound by the rules of the earlier genre of that name. The new *tsa-chü* of the second half of the sixteenth century and beyond consist of from one to ten acts, employ both northern and southern tunes, and assign songs to more than one role-type. The initiator of the new genre was the maverick poet and painter Hsü Wei (1521–1593); his collection *Ssu-sheng-yüan* (Four Shrieks of the Gibbon) consists of four short plays, one of one act, two of two acts, and one of four; while the first three plays feature northern songs, the last one uses southern melodies.

By the last quarter of the sixteenth century the growing prosperity of Kiangnan also resulted in a publishing boom. Publishers published more and more works of vernacular literature, both fiction and drama, in increasingly luxurious editions. Whereas for earlier periods the original text is usually not available, but only a repeatedly and heavily rewritten version of the play, at this time it became increasingly common for plays to be printed during the lifetime of the author. Many of these editions were prepared under the supervision of the author himself and include prefaces by him and his friends. As a result, the authorship of plays from this period forward is in general well established. Although Li K'ai-hsien's contribution to "The Precious Sword" is a matter of dispute and Wang Shih-chen's (1526–1590) authorship of "Ming-feng chi" (The Crying Phoenix) is questionable, there is no doubt that T'ang Hsien-tsu (1550–1617) wrote "Mu-tan t'ing" (The Peony Pavilion). Plays continued to be adapted for performance and some of such later adaptations were printed, but, although these adaptations may be of great importance for the history of performance, they are usually ignored in the literary study of drama because the author's own work is accessible. Many successful playwrights of the sixteenth century and beyond were preeminent members of China's cultural elite of the time and left not only plays but also voluminous collections of prose and poetry in the classical language.

Not only did publishers put out individual plays, they also marketed anthologies. Initially, these anthologies focused on highlights. The earliest preserved example is the *Feng-yüeh chin-nang* (The Brocade Bag of Breeze and Moonlight; 1553), which has survived in a single copy in the Escorial in Spain. This edition is an expanded reissue of a work that may have been compiled as early as 1421. However, after the commercial success of Tsang Mao-hsün's *Anthology of Yüan Plays*, anthologies of *ch'uan-ch'i* were also published. Eventually the most successful venture in this respect was the *Liu-shih chung ch'ü* (Sixty Plays), a collection of fifty-nine *ch'uan-ch'i* and Wang Shih-fu's "Romance of the Western Chamber." *Sixty Plays* was published in six installments around the middle of the seventeenth century by the famous bibliophile and publisher Mao Chin (1599–1659). The editions of individual plays and the anthologies of excerpts still may be related to performance, but these large and deluxe collective editions of plays are definitely meant for the study. The texts of the individual plays were once again heavily edited with that purpose in mind in order to provide the sophisticated Kiangnan literatus with leisure reading that would not offend his literary and ethical sensibilities. As such, these heavily edited texts were quite removed from the sorts of playscripts that would have been used by actors and actresses. In short, they were more literary and less dramatic.

The establishment of drama as literature was followed by the emergence of literary criticism of drama. There always had existed a body of technical literature for the writing of plays, focusing on the composition of arias and consisting of rhyming dictionaries and song formularies. This tradition of handbooks for the writing of plays culminated in the work of Li Yü (also called Li Li-weng; 1610/11–1680), who in *Hsien-ch'ing ou-chi* (Casual Expressions of Idle Feelings) provided a detailed dramaturgical theory based on extensive practical experience as a playwright and manager. The extensive literary analysis of a play in the form of introductory essays and interlinear commentary, however, was a new phenomenon. The genre was established with Chin Sheng-t'an's (1608–1661) edition of the "Romance of the Western Chamber." The growing theatrical and literary sophistication of drama contributed to the qualities of K'ung Shang-jen's (1648–1718) "T'ao-hua shan" (Peach Blossom Fan) and Hung Sheng's (1645–1704) "Ch'ang-sheng tien" (Palace of Eternal Life). Both famous plays try, each in its own way, to come to grips with the collapse of the native Ming dynasty and testify to the high seriousness that drama had achieved as an art.

The developments sketched out above reached their high point by the middle of the seventeenth century. The devastations of the Manchu conquest, a different fiscal system, and a return to orthodox Neo-Confucianism by both the new state and the disillusioned Chinese literati all contributed to the fading of the golden age of *ch'uan-ch'i*. Theater continued to be important as ritual and as entertainment, and new plays continued to be written throughout the eighteenth century, but few of these authors had the preeminence of their late Ming/early Ch'ing predecessors. Eventually, the most important theatrical developments during the eighteenth century were the reemergence of the commercial theater and the growing importance of the *pan-ch'iang* genres that usually relied on anonymous texts, often orally transmitted. The most conspicuous phenomenon at that time, however, was the addiction to theatrical entertainments of the Ch'ien-lung emperor, who had his major palaces provided with three-tiered stages. In order to make full use of these, huge pageants were composed that each took ten full days to perform.

Ch'uan-ch'i *Plays*

Whereas earlier southern plays usually are referred to as *hsi-wen*, later southern plays are usually designated as *ch'uan-ch'i*. Scholars battle over the definitions of these two terms and over the moment in time when the first term should give way to the other. Actually, the two terms refer to one and the same genre but in different phases of its development. All one can say is that the *ch'uan-ch'i* of the sixteenth century and beyond in printed versions manifest a much larger degree of uniformity in matters of presentation and contents than the earliest *hsi-wen*—but then these works, as discussed above, hardly are representative of the genre during its first century or so of existence.

Although in general any topic is fit for presentation in *ch'uan-ch'i*, the masterplot is often provided by a melodramatic love story. Some examples of this, as mentioned above, are "Top-Graduate Chang Hsieh," "Story of the Lute," and "The White Hare." A young man and a young woman, either just married or otherwise romantically attached, become separated and after many adventures and tribulations, during which he may acquire other wives but she must remain steadfastly loyal to him alone, eventually are happily reunited. A *ch'uan-ch'i* therefore usually ends with a large reunion scene (*t'uan-yüan*), in which all lovers and relatives are reunited and all remaining contradictions are happily resolved. A full-length *ch'uan-ch'i* as a rule took two days to perform, and the text therefore is usually divided into two *chüan* (scrolls, but actually no longer literally in scroll format by this time); the first of these is also concluded by a preliminary *t'uan-yüan*.

A *ch'uan-ch'i* is opened by a *chia-men* scene, after which the second scene is given over to the introduction of the male lead, while the third scene is given over to the introduction of the female lead. The action of the play is then initiated in the fourth scene, often by the hero leaving home in order to pursue a civil or military career. The separation of the male and female leads provides the opportunity for many scenes in which they express their lonely longings. Many early *ch'uan-ch'i* also feature in one of their earlier scenes the manifestation of a god who is the guardian deity of the hero or heroine, but later *ch'uan-ch'i* prefer dream scenes for their supernatural episodes. Other scenes that recur in many plays include garden outings and battles. One recurrent scene, the capital examination, was so conventionally acted on stage that many printed editions of plays in which it occurs do not even provide a text but simply write "as usual" after the title of the scene. Only authors who wanted to achieve some novelty even in this stock scene took the trouble to write out their text.

In some cases the melodramatic master-plot is little more than a device to organize the voluminous materials of the play while the main interest lies elsewhere. This is the case in, for example, "The Crying Phoenix" (c. 1570), a play that celebrates the self-sacrificing protests of the metropolitan official Yang Chi-sheng (1516–1555) and others against the abuses of the all-powerful dictator Yen Sung (1480–1565) and his son Yen Shih-fan (1513–1565). The play concludes with the downfall of Yen Sung and his son, who both returned in many later plays as incarnations of greed and abuse of power.

In other cases, however, the melodramatic plot is the perfect expression of the theme of the play. The finest example here is provided by "Peony Pavilion," by T'ang Hsien-tsu. T'ang hailed from Lin-ch'uan in Kiangsi province and earned the *chin-shih* degree at the age of thirty-four, thereupon serving for a while in low-ranking posts. He retired from public service in 1598 and devoted the remainder of his life to dramatic literature. His first *ch'uan-ch'i*, entitled "Tzu-hsiao chi" (The Purple Flute), was a dramatization of Chiang Fang's classical tale "Huo Hsiao-yü chuan" (An Account of Huo Hsiao-yü). T'ang Hsien-tsu later rewrote the play as "Tzu-ch'ai chi" (The Purple Hairpin). T'ang's masterpiece is his "Peony Pavilion" (also known as "Huan-hun chi" [The Return of the Soul]). This work, a brilliant comedy that glorifies passion as the very basis of life, is by far the finest play of its age, if not China's greatest play of all time. After writing "Peony Pavilion," T'ang Hsien-tsu created two other *ch'uan-ch'i:* one an adaptation of Shen Chi-chi's "Chen-chung chi" (Record of the World Within a Pillow) entitled "Han-tan chi" (The Tale of Han-tan), the other an adaptation of Li Kung-tso's "Nan-k'o t'ai-shou chuan" (The Story of the Prefect of South Branch) entitled "Nan-k'o chi" (The Tale of South Branch). Collectively, these four plays are known as the *Lin-ch'uan ssu-meng* (Four Dreams of Lin-ch'uan) because in each of these plays dreams play a pivotal role in the plot.

"Peony Pavilion" dramatizes the tale of the passion of Liu Meng-mei and Tu Li-niang. Liu Meng-mei hails from Kwangsi province and is presented as a descendant of Liu Tsung-yüan (773–819), the famous T'ang poet and essayist. A brilliant young student, he leaves his hometown in order to take part in the examinations. Tu Li-niang is the daughter of prefect Tu, a staunch Confucianist and conscientious administrator. Her father has her taught by a pedantic scholar. One fine spring day she and her servant girl escape from the boring classroom to visit the flower garden behind the prefect's residence. There the flowers are in full bloom. Filled with thoughts of spring, Tu Li-niang falls asleep in the garden and, in her dream, is deflowered by a brilliant young student whose name she does not know. Afterward, she pines away, but before dying she paints her self-portrait. Her parents have her buried in the flower garden, and her portrait is enshrined in a chapel dedicated to her memory and cared for by an old nun. Soon Prefect Tu is transferred to another post.

On his way to the capital, Liu Meng-mei comes to the town where Tu Li-niang lived and died, and he decides to stay there for a while to study. He rents a room in the garden, and when he sees the portrait, he falls in love with the beauty depicted. Tu Li-niang appears to him in a dream, just as he is the man she saw in her own dream in the garden. Meanwhile, in the underworld she faces King Yama and reclaims her life. After her wish is granted, she instructs Liu Meng-mei how to proceed in order to exhume her remains and bring her back to life. Afterward, they travel to the capital, where Liu Meng-mei takes the examinations. When the couple present themselves to prefect Tu, however, he refuses to recognize his daughter and takes Liu for an impostor. Only after the examination results are announced and Liu Meng-mei turns out to be the top graduate does the father turn around, and at last the final reunion and reconciliation can be played out.

As so often in *ch'uan-ch'i,* the character of the heroine is much more interesting than that of the male protagonist. The passion induced by spring in Tu Li-niang is not only so great that it kills her, it is even so great that it makes her reclaim her life from the king of the underworld and return to her earthly existence. T'ang Hsien-tsu's arias for this passionate character are of an exceptional lyrical intensity. This lyrical intensity is set off by the hilarious and at times bawdy humor of some of the other scenes, especially in the first half of the play. Not surprisingly, several scenes from the play have been stage favorites ever since, while the text has remained consistently in print as a lovers' bible. T'ang Hsien-tsu's glorification of passion was very much in line with developments in late Ming philosophy, which stressed intuition and emotion over principle and ritual. However, T'ang Hsien-tsu was not a philosopher, and it would be wrong to scrutinize the play as a fable to illustrate a scholarly thesis on ethics or psychology. It is a passionately conceived vision of love as the foundation of human life and a humane existence transcending all limitations of class, period, and culture. T'ang Hsien-tsu's later plays, which preach the impermanence of all phenomena, however well written, conspicuously lack this passion and appeal.

T'ang Hsien-tsu wrote his plays in Kiangsi, just when in Soochow K'un-ch'ü already had become the cry of the town through the efforts of Wei Liang-fu and Liang Ch'en-yü. In "Washing Silk," which he probably completed around 1560, Liang Ch'en-yü had dramatized a tale that was closely connected with the ancient history of Soochow as the capital of the kingdom of Wu and had been celebrated ever since the Warring States period (481–221 B.C.E.) in story and song. In the course of the wars between the ancient kingdom of Wu and its neighbor, Yüeh (whose capital was in the area of modern-day Shao-hsing), of the sixth and fifth centuries B.C.E., the king of Yüeh, Kou-chien, was once captured by his adversary, the king of Wu. The latter did not kill him, but kept him and his wife as slaves for many years and had them perform the most menial tasks before allowing them to return to Yüeh.

Kou-chien plotted revenge and shared the toils of his people in preparation for a future campaign. In order to sap the strength of the kingdom of Wu he decided to send the king of Wu the most beautiful girl in the world. After searching throughout Yüeh, his minister Fan Li discovered Hsi Shih while she was washing her silk in the Ju-yeh River. Hsi Shih was carefully groomed for her mission by Fan Li and trained in all the arts of seduction. When the king of Yüeh wanted to present her to the king of Wu, the latter was advised to reject her by his loyal adviser Wu Tzu-hsü but urged to accept her by the venal chancellor Po P'i, who had accepted huge bribes from Fan Li. The king of Wu had Wu Tzu-hsü executed and foolishly accepted Kou-chien's present.

Hsi Shih accomplished her mission most successfully: as soon as she entered the palace of the king of Wu, he succumbed to her charms and neglected his duties in order to enjoy her company, and he spared no effort to please her. When this led to widespread discontent and unrest in the state of Wu, Kou-chien attacked and easily achieved his revenge by killing the Wu king. As to what happened to Hsi Shih afterward, later legends varied. One legend held that Kou-chien, aware of the danger she represented to himself if he kept her, had her killed on the spot; another version insisted that he took her home with him, was bewitched by her beauty, and finally lost his kingdom. Yet a third legend told that Hsi Shih sailed off with Fan Li, who had actually been her lover since the moment he found her, and that they happily roved as merchants over the lakes and rivers of Kiangnan until their death of old age. This last ending of the story was adopted by Liang Ch'en-yü for his "Washing Silk," because it allowed him to provide his play with a happy ending.

Another playwright active in Soochow during the sixteenth century was Chang Feng-yi (1527–1613). Of his seven known *ch'uan-ch'i*, five have survived, together with fragments of yet another play. His most popular work was "Hung-fu chi" (Red Duster), a dramatization of the T'ang dynasty classical tale "Ch'iu-jan-k'o chuan" (An Account of the Curly-Bearded Stranger). Among the many other playwrights active in the second half of the sixteenth century were Cheng Jo-yung (c. 1480–c. 1565) and Kao Lien (fl. 1580). Cheng is best remembered for "Yü-chüeh chi" (The Broken Jade Ring), Kao for "Yü-tsan chi" (The Jade Hairpin).

The very strict musical requirements of K'un-ch'ü demanded from the authors who wrote their plays for this style of performance a meticulous attention to the aural qualities of the wording of their songs. The Soochow playwright who for later generations became the very embodiment of this search for tonal euphony is Shen Ching (1553–1610). In his voluminous writings on prosody, he stressed the close relationship between the music and the words, yet in his own plays he was unbound by the strict rules he prescribed to others. One of his best-known plays is "Yi-hsia chi" (The Righteous Hero), a dramatization of the story of Wu Sung (see chapter 35), who in this telling, as the hero of a *ch'uan-ch'i*, acquired a fiancée. Shen Ching's final work is "Po-hsiao chi" (For Laughs), which presents itself as a *ch'uan-ch'i* but actually consists of a series of ten little farces that each take two to four scenes. In a bow to the genre requirements of *ch'uan-ch'i*, the series opens with a *chia-men*, and both the first and the last farce include a *sheng* and a *tan* among their role-types, while the final farce ends in a wedding, allowing for a *t'uan-yüan*.

In the first half of the seventeenth century, K'un-ch'ü developed in two slightly divergent directions. On the one hand, Soochow was home to some popular and extremely productive playwrights such as Li Yü (1591–1671?), Chang Ta-fu (fl. 1553), and Chu Hu (Su-ch'en; fl. 1644) and his brother Chu Tso-ch'ao (fl. 1644), who adapted popular stories and contemporary events for the stage. On the other hand, the city played host to elite playwrights such as Wu Ping (d. 1646) and Juan Ta-ch'eng (1587–1646), who were heavily indebted to T'ang Hsien-tsu and produced artful and witty comedies.

One of Li Yü's best-known plays is "Yi-p'eng hsüeh" (A Handful of Snow), named after a priceless jade vase in the possession of a certain Mo Huai-ku (the surname and name can be interpreted as "Don't Cherish the Past"). This antique is coveted by Yen Shih-fan; Mo thereupon presents him with an imitation, but when he later reveals this secret to a friend, the latter promptly informs Yen Shih-fan. This results in the ruin of Mo's family, and only after many tribulations can his son take revenge. One of the famous scenes from this play, "Hao-yen" (The Lavish Banquet), involves the performance of a potted version of "Wolf of Chung-shan" as entertainment for the guests.

Chu Hu's best-known play is "Shih-wu kuan" (Fifteen Strings of Cash), an adaptation of a *hua-pen* found in Feng Meng-lung's (1574–1646) *San-yen* (see chapter 34) about the misadventures of a young merchant who is unjustly suspected of having killed a man, robbed him of his money, and stolen his concubine. Li Yü, Chu Hu, and their colleagues freely plundered the storehouse of materials that became available with the publication of *San-yen* and other collections of vernacular stories. For instance, Li Yü adapted "Mai-yu lang tu chan hua-k'uei" (The Oil Vendor and the Courtesan) for the stage as "Chan hua-k'uei" (Conquering the Queen of Flowers). Feng Meng-lung himself was active as an editor not only of vernacular fiction but also of *ch'uan-ch'i*. He collected fourteen *ch'uan-ch'i* plays he had extensively revised in *Mo-han-chai ting-pen ch'uan-ch'i* (Musical Plays as Edited by the Ink-Silly Studio), including Feng's version of "Peony Pavilion" and two of his own dramatic compositions.

In contrast to the productive playwrights mentioned above who had no official career to speak of, both Wu Ping and Juan Ta-ch'eng held high government posts. Wu Ping starved himself to death as he refused to serve the Manchus, while Juan Ta-ch'eng's reputation was tarnished by his association with the eunuch dictator Wei Chung-hsien (1568–1627) and his role in the corruption-ridden Southern Ming court at Nanking (1644–1645). Wu Ping left five *ch'uan-ch'i*. His most successful work is probably "Lü mu-tan" (The Green Peony), which has been described as a brilliant comedy of errors that ruthlessly ridicules the pseudo-intellectuals of the day. Two wealthy but barely literate students try to bluff their way into favorable marriages by asking a talented friend to compose poetry and essays for them. But their schemes are foiled by the shrewd and observant girls they woo. Another play by Wu Ping is "Liao-tu-keng" (The Medicine to Cure Jealousy), a dramatization of the story of Hsiao-ch'ing, a poetically gifted concubine, who is terrorized by her husband's first wife. This story was extremely popular in the seventeenth century and repeatedly adapted for the stage. Wu contrived to provide the tale with a happy ending.

Of the many authors of witty comedies of the final decades of the Ming, Juan Ta-ch'eng is perhaps the most outstanding. Juan had held office during the ascendancy of the notorious eunuch Wei Chung-hsien and had to give up his post after the fall of his patron. In defense of his behavior he composed a play entitled "Ch'un teng-mi" (Spring Lantern Riddles), but to no avail. However, he managed to become one of the most influential officials at the Southern Ming court in Nanking. The Prince of Fu, who presided over the Nanking court, was very much addicted to the theater, and one of Juan's comedies, "Yen-tzu chien" (The Swallow's Love Note; 1645), was given a very lavish palace production. Juan's political affiliations and his role in the collapse of the Nanking regime have greatly damaged his reputation in the eyes of later Chinese readers, who often only grudgingly acknowledge the wit of his plays. "Spring Lantern Riddles" and "The Swallow's Love Note," in fact, are often mentioned together in later literature as emblematic of the hedonistic corruption of the Nanking court, for example by Cheng Hsieh (1691–1764) in "Tao-ch'ing shih-shou" (Ten Songs of Taoist Sentiment). There is also a tradition that Juan's "The Swallow's Love Note" was actually written by his daughter and that Juan only slightly revised the text. The play has a very complicated plot, involving switched portraits and a love note by a minister's daughter who has fallen in love with a handsome young man on a painting—the note is delivered to the brilliant student concerned by a swallow.

Not all elite playwrights of the late Ming limited themselves to comedies, as a look at the oeuvre of Meng Ch'eng-shun (1600–1682) shows. Meng Ch'eng-shun was born into a family of officials in Shao-hsing but never advanced beyond the *chü-jen* degree himself. He started out by writing *tsa-chü*, both love comedies and historical allegories of contemporary events. His first attempt at *ch'uan-ch'i* was his "Story of Chiao-niang and Fei-hung," yet another stage adaptation of Sung Yüan's *Tale of Chiao-niang and Fei-hung*. This play, in which the heroine is determined to choose her own marriage-partner irrespective of her parents' opinion, has in recent years been hailed as one of China's greatest tragedies. Because of various misunderstandings, the lovers are never united and the heroine commits suicide after her beloved dies, so only a heavenly *t'uan-yüan* can be arranged for them.

By contrast, in "Chen-wen chi" (The Chaste Poetess), Meng Ch'en-shun portrayed the late Sung/early Yüan poetess Chang Yü-niang, who insists on marrying a fiancé she has never seen. Meng Ch'eng-shun wrote this *ch'uan-ch'i* after having served for a few years as Assistant Instructor at the Sung-yang county school (in Chekiang province). In Sung-yang he learned the legends surrounding Chang Yü-niang's life. In Meng's treatment, the young lady is turned into the very model of maidenly modesty and chastity. When her parents renege on her engagement to a cousin, she insists she will marry him, even though she has never set eyes on the boy and even refuses to see him when she has a chance. Eventually her cousin dies and she follows him to the grave, joined in turn by her two servant-girls and her parrot. This play, written after the fall of the Ming dynasty, clearly was written as an expression of Ming loyalist sentiment, in praise of those Ming officials who preferred to commit suicide rather than compromise their integrity by serving the Manchus.

The tradition of the witty comedy was continued in the early decades of the Ch'ing dynasty by Li Yü (not to be confused with the prolific Soochow playwright Li Yü who wrote "A Handful of Snow"). At one stage in his long and varied career, Li Yü maintained his own troupe of actresses. With these actresses he visited high officials of the new regime and entertained them with performances of his own and other plays. Li Yü wrote sixteen plays, of which ten have survived. These works exemplify the principles of playwriting, on which he expounded in *Casual Expressions of Idle Feelings*. They have well-made plots and the language of their arias and dialog aims for clarity. Although Li Yü maintained the melodramatic master-plot, he aimed for novelty in his subject matter. Some of his plays are adaptations of the same materials he used in his fiction and display the same risqué wit, dealing with such taboo subjects as male and female homosexual love (e.g., in "Lien-hsiang-pan" [Women in Love]). One of his best-known plays is "Feng-cheng wu" (The Mistake with the Kite), a comedy of mistaken identity. In "Nai-ho-t'ien" (You Can't Do Anything About Fate), three beautiful women adapt themselves to a marriage with an extremely ugly husband. "Shen-chung lou" (The Illusory Tower) is based largely on Li Ch'ao-wei's tale of Liu Yi's meeting with a dragon princess (see chapter 33). "Pi-mu-yü" (Sole Mate, or The Flounder) is set in the milieu of the theater world.

While Li Yü provided entertainment to the officials of the new dynasty, other authors pondered the reasons for the Ming downfall. Some authors attempted a dramatization of the events leading up to the fall of Peking to the rebels led by Li Tzu-ch'eng (1605–1645) and the suicide of the Ch'ung-chen emperor, very much in the style of the plays on contemporary events of the final decades of the Ming dynasty. One of these plays is "Hu-k'ou yü-sheng" (Escape from the Tiger's Maw), which has been attributed to Ts'ao Yin (1658–1712), the grandfather of the famous novelist Ts'ao Hsüeh-ch'in (c. 1724–1764), author of *Hung-lou meng* (Story of the Stone, or Dream of Red Towers). This play focuses on the heroic but ineffective resistance against Li Tzu-ch'eng's rebels by some Ming officers and palace ladies. Other writers looked for the roots of the Ming collapse in Wei Chung-hsien's reign of terror, for example, the Soochow playwright Li Yü in "Ch'ing-chung p'u" (A Roster of the Pure and Loyal), which dramatizes the Soochow protest of Chou Shun-ch'ang (1584–1626) against Wei Chung-hsien's "personality cult."

The most successful of these historical plays was "Peach Blossom Fan" (1699) by K'ung Shang-jen. K'ung hailed from Ch'ü-fu (in Shantung province) and was a sixty-fourth-generation descendant of Confucius. When the K'ang-hsi emperor visited the Master's birthplace in 1684, K'ung Shang-jen was selected to give him a presentation. He was thereupon called to the capital and, after years of river conservation work, served in various official functions in Peking until he was dismissed in 1699, probably for reasons unrelated to the contents of "Peach Blossom Fan." In this play, which is based on careful and exhaustive historical documentation, K'ung Shang-jen inquires into the reasons for the collapse of the Southern Ming court in Nanking in 1645.

All scenes of the play are dated by year and month. Starting in the second month of 1643, the action of the play concludes in the seventh month of 1645, while the epilogue is set in the ninth month of 1648. The major events of the period are all covered, and the protagonists are called by their real names. All the attempts to organize effective resistance are foiled by the inefficiency and corruption of the Nanking court, which is dominated by officials such as Ma Shih-ying and Juan Ta-ch'eng, whose energy is absorbed by the production of "The Swallow's Love Note." Loyal generals like Shih K'o-fa (d. 1644) are left with no choice but to seek death after they fail to stop the advance of the Manchus on Nanking.

The master-plot of the play is provided by the love affair of the student Hou Fang-yü and the courtesan Li Hsiang-chün. Hou Fang-yü eventually turns out to be less intransigent in his opposition to the evil officials of the Nanking court than Li Hsiang-chün. When Juan Ta-ch'eng tries to win Hou Fang-yü over to his faction by providing him with the means to marry his love, this offer is indignantly rejected by Li Hsiang-chün. Later she refuses all pressure to marry a certain T'ien Yang, a high official in the new regime. When Ma Shih-ying and Juan Ta-ch'eng order her violent abduction from her mansion, she falls to the floor and spatters her white fan with her blood and is saved only because her madam takes her place in the bridal sedan chair. Yang Wen-ts'ung, an intermediary between Hou Fang-yü and Juan Ta-ch'eng, turns the bloodstained fan into a painting of peach flowers. Eventually Li Hsiang-chün is drafted into service in the inner court, while Hou Fang-yü continues his efforts on behalf of the resistance. After the fall of Nanking, the lovers have one final meeting at a Buddhist monastery. But the collapse of the dynasty prevents any permanent reunion, and, in a sharp reversal of the *t'uan-yüan* convention, K'ung Shang-jen had both his lovers become religious acolytes.

Other authors who pondered the reasons for the downfall of the Ming looked for parallels in history. The defeat of the Southern Sung by the Mongols and the defeat of the Northern Sung by the Jurchen were obvious choices. An example of this is Chang Ta-fu's play "Ju-shih kuan" (The Way It Should Have Been), in which the heroic general Yüeh Fei is revived and with his sons retakes northern China and frees the captured emperors from their Jurchen prison. The famous poet Wu Wei-yeh (1609–1672) chose the demise of the Southern T'ang dynasty as the background for the romance of his "Mo-ling ch'un" (Nanking Spring). Whereas his male protagonist, Hsü Shih, is portrayed in the play as the son of the early Sung scholar Hsü Hsüan (917–992), the historical Hsü was a nephew of Hsü Hui-yen (d. 1128), a Sung dynasty general who died in battle against the Jurchen. In this play the spirit of Li Yü, the last ruler of the Southern T'ang, acts as the protecting deity of the lovers.

However, by far the most important example here is Hung Sheng's "Palace of Eternal Life" (c. 1684), a detailed dramatization of the love affair of Emperor Hsüan-tsung and Yang Kuei-fei, brutally ended by the rebellion of An Lu-shan. Hung Sheng hailed from Hangchow, but he lived in Peking for a long time as a student of the Imperial Academy. His "Palace of Eternal Life" was praised by the K'ang-hsi emperor, but in 1689 Hung was dismissed from the academy after his play was performed during a period of imperial mourning. He lived out his remaining years in Hangchow, in increasing poverty. Hung Sheng treats Emperor Hsüan-tsung and Yang Kuei-fei sympathetically and concludes his play with their final reunion in heaven.

Hung Sheng and K'ung Shang-jen tower far above all later Ch'ing dynasty playwrights. None of the many *ch'uan-ch'i* authors of the eighteenth century or later even began to approach their fame despite their considerable productivity and the contemporary success of some of their works. The most important eighteenth-century playwrights were T'ang Ying and Chiang Shih-ch'üan. T'ang Ying (1682–c. 1755) was from Shenyang (Mukden). He served for more than two decades as the director of the famous Ching-te-chen porcelain works in Kiangsi province. T'ang left a collection of seventeen plays, six of which are *ch'uan-ch'i*. Chiang Shih-ch'üan (1725–1785) was from Nan-ch'ang. He passed the *chin-shih* examination in 1757, but, after serving for some years as an official, he requested leave in 1763 to take care of his mother. A lifelong friend of Yüan Mei, he was one of the most important poets of his time. Many of his plays deal with the careers of poets: "Ts'ai-shih chi" (The Colored Stone Jetty) was devoted to the life of Li Po, "Ssu-hsien ch'iu" (Four-Stringed Autumn; 1772) dramatizes Po Chü-yi's "Ballad of the Balloon Lute," "Lin-ch'uan meng" (A Dream of Lin-ch'uan; 1774) celebrated his fellow-townsman T'ang Hsien-tsu, and "Tung-ch'ing shu" (The Evergreen Tree; 1781) was devoted to the Sung patriot Wen T'ien-hsiang (1236–1282). The celebrated Hangchow legend of the White Snake (who masqueraded as an attractive young widow but was exorcised by the abbot Fa-hai) was adapted for the stage by Huang T'u-pi (b. 1700) as

"Lei-feng t'a" (Thunderpeak Pagoda; 1738); a revised version of this play by Fang Ch'eng-p'ei was published in 1771.

Tsa-chü

Although the traditional *tsa-chü* survived into the seventeenth century behind the walls of the imperial palace in Peking, Kiangnan literati created a new kind of *tsa-chü*, starting in the second half of the sixteenth century. *Tsa-chü* here serves as the designation of independent short plays; occasionally the old name *yüan-pen* is revived to set these plays off from the much longer *ch'uan-ch'i* and from the *che-tzu-hsi*, highlights from *ch'uan-ch'i*. These new-style *tsa-chü* could vary in length from one to ten acts, either northern or southern tunes might be used, alone or in combination, and the songs might be assigned to more than one role-type. Some of these plays met with considerable success on the stage, while others were written primarily as closet drama.

The originator of this new genre of short plays was the maverick poet and painter Hsü Wei. He wrote four short plays that were collectively published under the title *Four Shrieks of the Gibbon*. The date of composition of these plays is a matter of dispute, but most likely the series was completed around 1580. The common element in all of these plays is "playacting." The first play of the series, "K'uang ku-shih" (The Mad Drummer), consists of only one act and takes place in the underworld, where the eccentric poet Mi Heng (172–208) reenacts the famous scene of his cursing the tyrant Ts'ao Ts'ao (155–220). Since both are now ghosts, Mi Heng has the opportunity to revile Ts'ao Ts'ao for all the sins he committed during his lifetime. In "Yü ch'an-shih" (Zen-master Yü-t'ung), a common courtesan feigns being a virtuous widow in order to seduce a holy monk; when he is reborn as the courtesan Hung-lien in the second act of this two-act play, his former colleague Yüeh-ming reenacts the scene of the seduction as a mime (alternately playing the part of the monk and the courtesan) in order to enlighten him/her. The third play in the series, another two-act play, "Tz'u Mu-lan" (A Female Mu-lan), dramatizes the ballad of Mu-lan, a girl who joins the army dressed as a man when her father becomes too old to serve. The first act is given over to a lengthy description of her transformation from woman to man before she sets out, while the second act is devoted to her virginal return and describes the reverse process. All these three plays use northern music.

The final play in *Four Shrieks of the Gibbon*, however, uses southern music. This play in five scenes, entitled "Nü chuang-yüan" (A Female Top Graduate), dramatizes the story of Huang Ch'ung-ku. This story is found in *Extensive Records from the Reign of Great Tranquility*: during the regime of the Early Shu dynasty (903–925) in Szechwan, Chou Hsiang discovers in his clerk Huang Ch'ung-ku a promising official, but when he offers Huang his daughter's hand in marriage, Huang confesses that "he" is actually a "she." In the play, the first scene presents Huang Ch'ung-ku as a young woman who, out of economic necessity, dresses as a man in her father's gown in order to participate in the examinations. After her success in these examinations in the second scene, she proves herself a capable judge in the third scene and an accomplished poet, calligrapher, and painter in the fourth scene. But when Chou Hsiang wants to give her his daughter as bride, she has to confess her true sex in the fifth and final act. However, Chou Hsiang also has a son who has become the military top graduate, and after Huang Ch'ung-ku changes back into female costume, the play ends with their marriage.

The last two plays have been read, both in traditional and modern times, as paeans to the talents of women by a daring and unconventional author. However, it makes more sense to read the series as an expression of frustration and as a satire on contemporary society. It is no coincidence that the first play of the series has remained the most popular. The series had a great impact on later readers and playwrights and initiated a craze for writing sets consisting of four short plays. A later example is Hung Sheng's *Ssu ch'an-chüan* (Four Lovely Ladies), comprising four one-act plays, each devoted to a scene from the life of a famous female artist (the *shih*-poet Hsieh Tao-yün, the calligrapher Lady Wei, the *tz'u*-poet Li Ch'ing-chao, and the bamboo-painter Kuan Tao-sheng).

In the seventeenth century and later, many playwrights wrote both *ch'uan-ch'i* and the new-style *tsa-chü*. This trend is exemplified by the high officials Ch'en Yü-chiao (1544–1611) and Yeh Hsien-tsu (1566–1641). Ch'en's best-known *ch'uan-ch'i* is "Ying-wu chou" (Parrot Isle), an adaptation of the tale of Wei Kao, a historical figure who in real life was said to have killed nearly half a million Tibetans during his twenty-one years as Governor of Szechwan, and his betrothed, Yü-hsiao. Shortly after they are engaged, Wei is summoned by the emperor. He tells Yü-hsiao that he will come back for her in seven years. Before he returns, however, she pines away for him and dies. Moved by her devotion, Heaven grants that she will be reborn and, thirteen years later, have the chance to meet Wei again. The play has a convoluted counterplot in the affair of the T'ang poet Yüan Chen and the poet-courtesan Hsüeh T'ao (770–830). While Wei Kao spurns the advances of Hsüeh T'ao, she has a relationship with the much younger but fickle poet, who presents her with a copy of his recently completed "Story of Ying-ying." By the end of the play, Hsüeh T'ao has become a Taoist nun who acts as the teacher of the reborn Yü-hsiao. This pupil puts the former courtesan in her place when she refuses to be instructed in passionate poetry and prefers moralistic readings instead. Ch'en Yü-chiao's *tsa-chü* include "Chao-chün ch'u sai" (Chao-chün Crosses the Border) and "Wen-chi ju sai" (Ts'ai Yen Returns to China). Both are one-act plays that closely follow the canonical historical sources concerning these two Chinese women and their marriage to a barbarian. Yeh Hsien-tzu wrote many *ch'uan-ch'i* but only two survive: "Luan-pi chi" (The Barb of Love), which depicts the love affair between the poet Wen T'ing-yün (812?–866) and the poetess Yü Hsüan-chi (840–868), and "Chin-so chi" (The Golden Cangue), an adaptation of "Injustice to Tou Ŏ." In addition, he wrote twenty-four *tsa-chü*, of which eleven survive. One of the finest of these is "Yi-shui han" (The River Yi Is Cold), which recounts the assassin Ching K'o's failed attempt on the life of China's first emperor, Ch'in Shih Huang-ti. Recall that Meng Ch'eng-shun started his career as a playwright by trying his hand at *tsa-chü*. His finest work in this genre is probably "T'ao-hua, jen-mien" (Peach Blossoms, Pink Cheeks), a dramatization of a well-known romantic anecdote from Meng Ch'i's (fl. 841–886) *pi-chi* (cf. chapter 31) collection entitled *Pen-shih shih* (The Original Incidents of Poems).

Many of the new-style *tsa-chü* of the first half of the seventeenth century were collected in Shen T'ai's *Sheng Ming tsa-chü* (*Tsa-chü* of the Great Ming; 1629) and *Sheng Ming tsa-chü erh-chi* (*Tsa-chü* of the Great Ming, Second Collection; 1641), which each contain thirty plays. These deluxe anthologies were followed by the *Tsa-chü san-chi* (Third Collection of *Tsa-chü*; 1660/1661). Some of the plays in these collections still adhere strictly to the traditional rules for *tsa-chü*. Ling Meng-ch'u (1580–1644), nowadays better known as the compiler of two collections of vernacular stories (see chapter 34), explored the asymmetry of the traditional *tsa-chü* form by writing three adaptations of the "Account of the Curly-Bearded Stranger," in each play assigning all four suites of songs to a different character in the same story: Li Ching, the young student and later general; Hung-fu, the young girl who recognizes his talents and elopes with him; and the Curly-Bearded Stranger (only the last two plays have been preserved).

For the second half of the seventeenth century the polymath Yu T'ung (1618–1704) is probably the most important practitioner of the genre. He wrote five *tsa-chü*, no fewer than three of which feature famous poets as their protagonists. "Tu 'Li-sao'" (Reading "Encountering Sorrow") portrays the life of Ch'ü Yüan. After Ch'ü commits suicide by drowning, he is received by the dragon king in his palace under the water. "T'ao-hua yüan" (Peach-Blossom Spring) presents the life of T'ao Yüan-ming and ends with his disappearance into the utopian Peach Blossom Grotto, where he achieves immortality. Both are four-act plays. The one-act "Ch'ing-p'ing-tiao" (A Pure and Plain Mode) allows Li T'ai-po to become a top graduate. Yu's plays, especially "Reading 'Encountering Sorrow,'" were highly appreciated by the first two Manchu emperors. He also wrote a *ch'uan-ch'i* play entitled "Chün-t'ien le" (The Pleasures of Heaven), in which all politically thwarted scholars are compensated in heaven for the positions they failed to obtain during their lifetime. These plays make abundantly clear that drama, especially the shorter forms, once it had been adopted by literati as a minor form of writing, increasingly became yet another vehicle of self-expression for scholars. Some playwrights, for instance Liao Yen (1644–1704), even went so far as to give their protagonists their own names.

During the eighteenth century the most outstanding practitioner of the new *tsa-chü* was Yang Ch'ao-kuan (1710–1788). After he had obtained his *chü-jen* degree, he served in sixteen different posts as a district magistrate, ending his long career in civil administration with the rank of prefect. He left a collection of thirty-two one-act *tsa-chü*, entitled *Yin-feng-ko tsa-chü* (*Tsa-chü* from the Hall of Singing in the Wind). For most of these playlets he derived his subject matter from Chinese history, while for others he derived his materials from legend. Each of these playlets is preceded by a short preface, in the tradition of Po Chü-yi's *Hsin-yüeh-fu* (New Ballads), in which the author explains the aim of his satire. Many pieces have famous poets as their protagonists: Yang Ch'ao-kuan shows us Tung-fang Shuo (c. 140–87 B.C.E.) stealing the peaches of immortality (and chiding the Queen Mother of the West for begrudging these life-giving drugs to us mortals), Juan Chi (210–263) cursing the God of Wealth for the moral corruption caused by money, Han Yü (768–824) being met at Indigo Pass (Lan-kuan) by his nephew Han Hsiang-tzu (one of the Eight Immortals), and Su Shih (Su Tung-p'o; 1037–1101) achieving final enlightenment during his banishment to Hainan island by becoming a butterfly.

Local Theater

Literati usually limited their activities as writers to the elite genres of *ch'uan-ch'i* and *tsa-chü*. However, many localities also had their own local form of drama. Occasionally, a local scholar would develop an interest in such drama and even write scripts for it. From Shantung province, we have some early Ch'ing scripts for a local genre of theater that are traditionally attributed to the short story writer P'u Sung-ling (1640–1715; see chapter 37). As is the case with the many prosimetric ballads credited to him, it is very difficult at this remove in time to determine the reliability of these ascriptions.

Li Fang-kuei (also known as Li Shih-san; 1748–1810), from Wei-nan district in Shensi province, is one of the rare known authors of puppet theater scripts. Even if Li Fang-kuei was slightly more successful in the examinations than P'u Sung-ling (he achieved the *chü-jen* degree in 1786), his career is otherwise comparable to that of P'u, as he spent most of his life teaching. He left ten longer and shorter plays for a local variety of shadow theater that continued to be performed into modern times.

Female Playwrights

If we overlook the possible contribution of Juan Ta-ch'eng's daughter to "The Swallow's Love Note," all the playwrights discussed so far were men. Not until the seventeenth century, which witnessed such a spectacular growth of literary activities by women, do female playwrights appear. However, only the names of twenty-odd female playwrights (some of them courtesans) have survived for the period 1600–1900, and only in a few of these cases has their work been preserved. None of these women playwrights achieved in traditional times a reputation comparable to that of Li Ch'ing-chao in the tradition of *tz'u* or even that of Hsüeh T'ao in the tradition of *shih*. A conspicuous feature in the work of many women playwrights is the fact that their protagonist, who usually is but a thinly disguised alter ego, appears in the guise of a man.

The earliest recorded female playwright whose work has been preserved is Yeh Hsiao-wan (1613–1660?). Her mother, Shen Yi-hsiu, was a niece of Shen Ching and a well-known female poet. So were Hsiao-wan's sisters, Wan-wan (1610–1633) and Hsiao-lan (1616–1632). Yeh Hsiao-wan wrote "Yüan-yang meng" (A Dream of Mandarin Ducks), a four-act *tsa-chü*, in memory of her two sisters, who had died at a very early age. The play describes how three female servants of goddesses are sent down to earth to be reborn as men after they have sworn brotherhood. After their rebirth on earth, the three young men become sworn brothers again, but two of them soon die. The remaining one is enlightened by the Taoist sage Lü Tung-pin as to the impermanence of all earthly phenomena, and eventually all three return to heaven to resume their original identities.

Yeh Hsiao-wan may have preferred male personae for herself and her sisters because doing so allowed her to express her attachment to them more freely than would be possible otherwise. Other female playwrights, however, chose a male persona as their alter ego because they felt restricted by their female gender and believed that their talents equaled those of the finest male writers. In Wang Yün's "Fan-hua meng" (A Dream of Splendor; 1768), a *ch'uan-ch'i* in twenty-five scenes, the *sheng* enters the stage in female costume as Wang Meng-lin, a girl who bemoans the contradiction between her sex and her talent. In a dream she is transformed into a young man, who soon becomes a top graduate and collects three beautiful wives, living a life of luxury and happiness. Only at the very end of the play does our heroine stir from her dream, to be immediately enlightened by the immortal Ma-ku, who makes her realize that both men and women should awaken to the vanity of all earthly forms.

The best-known female playwright of premodern times is Wu Tsao, who lived in the first half of the nineteenth century. She also wrote poetry, both *shih* and *tz'u*, and in 1826 became a disciple of the Hangchow literatus Ch'en Wen-shu (1775–1845), a champion of women's literature. Her only play, "Portrait in Disguise," consists of one act and appeared in print in 1825, after it had been publicly performed with great success. In this drama, the *sheng* plays the part of the young woman Hsieh Hsü-ts'ai (the name refers back to Hsieh Tao-yün), who likes to dress as a man and who contemplates a portrait she has painted of herself while reading Ch'ü Yüan's "Li sao" (Encountering Sorrow) in male dress. The short play is devoted to a long lament over frustrated talent and unfulfilled ambition. The protagonist expresses her desire for a vital life of cosmic activity, such as she credits to the great poets and mystics of China's past, but realizes the impossibility of attaining this wish because of her sex. In yet another short play of the early nineteenth century, Ho P'ei-chu's "Li-hua meng" (Pear Blossom Dream; c. 1840), the female protagonist is played by a *hsiao-sheng* (young male role-type) in male attire. This play focuses on the intense attachment of a young bride for her female friends during the days before her marriage.

Women playwrights also wrote plays celebrating the virtues of devoted wives. In the earliest preserved play by a female author of the Ch'ing dynasty, Chang Fan's "Shuang-k'ou hun" (Double Request at the Palace Gate; 1766), the wife of a competent but unjustly persecuted official appeals to the Wan-li emperor for justice by presenting at the palace gate a memorial written in her own blood. As a result her husband is reinstated to his position and even promoted, and when their sons have succeeded in the metropolitan examinations, the play comes to an end in the *t'uan-yüan* scene.

Drama Theory and Criticism

As early as the fourteenth century, works were compiled to assist the aspiring playwright. The first of these works is Chou Te-ch'ing's *Chung yüan yin-yün* (Rhymes and Sounds of the Central Plains; 1324), a rhyming dictionary for those who intended to compose northern *ch'ü*, whether *san-ch'ü* or *tsa-chü*. Another indispensable aid was the song formulary, a compilation of exemplary lyrics to each of the tunes in the repertoire, illustrating the verse form required by the tune and indicating the preferred tone for each syllable and the ending rhymes. Such handbooks, known as *tz'u-p'u*, also existed for the practitioners of *tz'u* poetry. Formularies for *ch'ü* accordingly became known as *ch'ü-p'u*. The earliest preserved example of the genre is *A Formulary for the Correct Sounds of Great Harmony*, which is credited to Chu Ch'üan and carries a preface dated 1398 but probably is considerably later. Often such handbooks also contain sundry information on the genre they deal with as appended materials. Soon there also appeared formularies for those who intended to write southern *ch'ü*. These early formularies are often very important for the historian of drama, as they contain many arias of plays that have otherwise been lost or that are known only in heavily edited later versions. As time went on, the *ch'ü-p'u* became more and more detailed and voluminous.

From the fourteenth and fifteenth centuries, we also have various lists of authors and their works. These are Chung Ssu-ch'eng's *Register of Ghosts* and its sequel, possibly by Chia Chung-ming, and the list included in the *Formulary for the Correct Sounds of Great Harmony*. These lists pertain only to *tsa-chü*. The earliest catalog of *hsi-wen* and *ch'uan-ch'i* is the mid-sixteenth-century *Nan-tz'u hsü-lu* (Catalog of Southern Plays), which is usually credited to Hsü Wei, but on questionable grounds. In later years, lists of titles often took the form of evaluative classifications, or *p'in* (cf. chapter 45). As in other works of this kind, the titles included are often divided into three classes (upper, middle, and lower), each of which is again subdivided into the same three classes. The author occasionally explained his judgment about the quality of the play in a few words appended to each title. Examples of this genre for the Ming dynasty are *Ch'ü-p'in* (Classification of Plays; 1610, rev. 1613), by Lü T'ien-ch'eng (1573–1619), and *Yüan-shan-t'ang chü-p'in* (Classification of Drama from the Far Mountain Hall) and *Yüan-shan-t'ang ch'ü-p'in* (Classification of Plays from the Far Mountain Hall), both by Ch'i Piao-chia (1602–1645). Lü T'ien-ch'eng's work deals with ancient and modern *ch'uan-ch'i,* whereas the works of Ch'i Piao-chia classify and evaluate Ming dynasty *tsa-chü* and *ch'uan-ch'i* respectively.

Many late Ming literati, often practicing playwrights at the same time, discussed the works of earlier masters and contemporary authors in their *pi-chi.* These remarks on drama were often placed together in a section by itself, which then might be published as a separate work. Comments and comparisons easily shaded off into prescriptions and rules. The most outstanding work in this respect of the early seventeenth century was Wang Chi-te's *Ch'ü-lü* (Rules for Plays). Little is known of the life of Wang Chi-te (1560–1623). A native of Shaohsing, he was a student of Hsü Wei. He traveled extensively in the Kiangnan area and spent considerable time at Peking. Wang made good use of his knowledge of the spoken language of the north in his fine and amply annotated edition of "Romance of the Western Chamber." He also compiled a collection of *tsa-chü* that appeared as *Ku tsa-chü* (Ancient *Tsa-chü*). Of his own dramatic compositions only one *ch'uan-chi* and one *tsa-chü* survive. The latter play, "Nan wang-hou" (The Male Queen), has attracted some attention in recent years because of its subject matter.

Wang Chi-te started writing *Rules for Plays* in 1610. Still working in the tradition of *ch'ü-p'u,* which considered the writing of lyrics for songs the main technical hurdle in the composition of plays, Wang discusses the requirements of song lyrics in *ch'uan-ch'i* at great length. However, his discussion also treats other aspects of play composition, admittedly often in a laconic or even apodictic manner. Moreover, he also engages in the comparative criticism of plays by earlier playwrights from the Yüan and early Ming dynasties and by contemporary masters. Wang Chi-te opposed both an excessive attention to verbal decoration and an exclusive concern with theatrical success, demanding that a good play should be suited both to the stage and to the study. Like many writers on drama before him, he demanded that plays exhibit *pen-se* ("true color"; authenticity). However, also like his predecessors, Wang Chi-te left this essential term rather ill defined, for it can refer to the language of the play (in particular its songs), the characterization of its characters, or the expression of its author's intent.

The tradition of dramaturgical handbooks culminated in premodern times in the work of Li Yü. In the chapters on drama in *Casual Expressions of Idle Feelings,* which he wrote shortly before 1670, he drew on his own extensive experience as a practicing playwright and manager of a theatrical troupe and provided a systematic treatise on the writing of plays, starting not from the composition of individual lyrics but from the concept of the play as an integrated whole and taking into account the nature of a largely illiterate audience. As a result, he demanded clearly constructed plots that integrate convention with novelty and insisted that the language of the play, in both its songs and dialogs, strive for clarity. He also discussed the performance of plays at length.

As a practicing playwright and producer, Li Yü had little interest in the literary criticism of drama. When vernacular literature, including drama, came to be printed in ever-increasing amounts during the Wan-li period and beyond, these works were often provided with a *p'ing-tien* (evaluative comments and emphatic punctuation)-style commentary: the editors provided the text with appreciative comments in the upper margin of the page and drew attention to fine lines by placing dots or little circles alongside the characters concerned. Printed editions of "Romance of the Western Chamber," moreover, often had extensive annotations, starting with the edition of 1498. Wang Chi-te and his contemporaries frequently compared the qualities of different plays, citing chapter and verse. These various traditions of annotation, appreciative comments, and comparative evaluation were fused by Chin Sheng-t'an in his massively detailed commentary on the 1656 version of "Romance of the Western Chamber," which he published more than ten years after his epochal commentary on the vernacular novel *Water Margin*.

The format of Chin Sheng-t'an's commentary on "Romance of the Western Chamber" followed that of his commentary on *Water Margin*. The play was preceded by numerous introductory prefaces and essays, while each act was preceded by its own introductory essay. The text of each act was commented upon almost line by line in his voluminous interlinear commentary. Chin Sheng-t'an restrained himself in modifying the original text of "Romance of the Western Chamber" much more than he did in his edition of *Water Margin*, but he did not refrain from tampering with it either. One of his strategies was to downplay the explicitly sexual references that occasionally occur in earlier versions. This was in line with his overall approach to the text, which he defended against charges that it was "a book teaching debauchery." Chin Sheng-t'an argued that the behavior of Ying-ying was perfectly defensible, as her mother had promised her in marriage to Student Chang. Chin Sheng-t'an's edition presented the full text of the play, but he insisted that the last play of the series was a later addition of inferior quality. The original play had ended, in his opinion, with Student Chang's dream vision of Ying-ying after his departure from P'u-chou for the capital. In this way the play was made to serve Chin Sheng-t'an's contention that life and love are but a dream.

Chin Sheng-t'an's edition of "Romance of the Western Chamber" soon became the most popular edition. Continually reprinted throughout the Ch'ing dynasty, this version shaped Ch'ing readers' conception of the play. It inspired the production of other commentary editions of famous dramas. To give two examples, Mao Tsung-kang and Mao Lun published a commentary edition of "The Story of the Lute" (prefaces dated 1665 and 1666), which became very popular, and Wu Wu-shan (1647–after 1704) in 1694 published an edition of "Peony Pavilion" with an extensive commentary that had been written, so he claimed, by his three successive wives (unfortunately, he added, their original manuscript had been destroyed by fire).

THE HEYDAY OF *LUAN-T'AN* (NINETEENTH AND TWENTIETH CENTURIES)

As K'un-ch'ü increasingly appealed only to an elite, the popular stage was taken over by local genres of theater that sang their arias to *pan-ch'iang*-style music. In the late eighteenth century, when elite authors first deigned to comment on these popular entertainments, they dubbed them *luan-t'an* (cacophonous strummings). However, performed at temple fairs and in the reemerging commercial theaters of the big cities, these various genres met with great popular success and continued to proliferate all through the nineteenth and twentieth centuries. K'un-ch'ü, by contrast, suffered a severe setback when the T'ai-p'ing t'ien-kuo (Heavenly Kingdom of Great Tranquility) rebellion (1849–1864), led by Hung Hsiu-ch'üan (1814–1864), who believed that he was the younger brother of Jesus Christ, laid waste its original heartland, the Kiangnan area.

In the various genres of local theater, including Peking opera, the actor reigned supreme. Texts were borrowed wherever one could find them and, more often than not, were orally transmitted. Literati who were attracted to Peking opera as a rule showed more interest in the physical charms of the boy-actors who performed in the female role-type of *tan* than in the texts of their plays. In place of evaluative classifications of plays there were now evaluative classifications of *tan*. A panoramic overview of the various relationships between patrons and boy-actors in Peking in the early decades of the nineteenth century is sketched by Ch'en Sen in his sixty-chapter novel *P'in-hua pao-chien* (A Precious Mirror for Judging Flowers; 1849).

Both *ch'uan-ch'i* and *tsa-chü* continued to be written in the nineteenth and early twentieth centuries, but hardly any of these achieved a lasting reputation. During the final decade of the Ch'ing dynasty, there was an upsurge in productivity as literati tried to make use of the vernacular forms of literature in order to stimulate their countrymen's reformist zeal and revolutionary fervor. In earlier centuries, too, plays had been written for the purpose of instilling certain values in the audience. In general, however, the moralistic intent of traditional Chinese theater is often overstressed. As is true of most literature worldwide, traditional Chinese drama usually deals with moral issues. In premodern times these moral issues were unavoidably phrased in the shared concepts of the Three Religions (Confucianism, Taoism, and Buddhism). However, these concepts provide the protagonists in the plays with a language to discuss their predicaments, not with ready-made solutions for their dilemmas.

The interest of the play hinges on the element of ethical choice, and suspense is created by the audience's uncertainty as to whether a character will indeed opt for the straight and narrow when faced with the temptations of power, riches, and sex—all graphically described and convincingly defended. In general the characters in traditional Chinese drama are at least as "round" as the characters in preromantic Western literature. However, because the terminology of the ethics concerned is that of not only a different period but also a different culture, it may strike a modern reader as conspicuously intrusive and coercive.

Moralistically inclined traditional authors might propagate quite specific aspects of traditional morality. While some wanted to stress the secular ethics of the Confucian Five Relationships (*wu lun*: father-son, ruler-subject, husband-wife, elder brother-younger brother, friend-friend), characterized respectively by the Five Constants (*wu ch'ang*: *jen* [humaneness], *yi* [justice], *li* [propriety] or *pieh* [separateness], *chih* [wisdom] or *hsü* [precedence], and *hsin* [trust]), others wanted to illustrate the vanity of all earthly glory and preached a religious message of detachment. While some sought to strengthen their message by bringing the courts of the underworld to the stage, others sought to teach the message of the ultimate emptiness of all phenomena. Although certain playwrights supported the cult of a specific deity, for example Kuan-yin (the bodhisattva of compassion), others battled against sins such as adultery and the slaughter of buffaloes for consumption.

The introduction of Western thought in the late nineteenth and early twentieth centuries was accompanied, however, by a new belief in the power of vernacular literature, both fiction and drama, to effect great and lasting, even revolutionary changes in the thought and behavior of the public. This belief was fueled in part by the conviction that fiction and drama had played important roles in the preparation of revolutionary movements of late-eighteenth- and nineteenth-century Europe. The most important spokesman for the importance of dramatic and fictional literature in the enlightenment of his countrymen was Liang Ch'i-ch'ao (1874–1930), who also tried his own hand at fiction and drama. The belief in the importance of fiction and drama for social change would only be strengthened by the subsequent introduction of Marxism in China.

Many of the *ch'uan-ch'i* and *tsa-chü* produced during the first decade of the twentieth century detailed the lives of national heroes who had sacrificed their lives in a heroic struggle against foreign invaders, such as Yüeh Fei, who had fought the Jurchen, Wen T'ien-hsiang, who had fought the Mongols, and Shih K'o-fa, who had fought the Manchus. Other plays tried to present foreign nationalistic heroes and heroines who might serve as examples to the Chinese. Yet other plays dealt with the discrimination suffered by Chinese overseas. However, the incident that inspired more plays than any other was the execution by beheading in 1907 of the feminist revolutionary Ch'iu Chin (1875–1907). This incident resulted in at least eight plays before the end of the Ch'ing dynasty. Other plays stressed the equal contribution women and men could make to the revolution, and the tale of woman-warrior Mu-lan was dramatized once again. In one play a girl lays plaint before the king of the underworld because of the senseless suffering women have to endure for the sake of their tiny bound feet.

Perhaps the only playwright deserving mention by name among these authors, who are more commendable for their patriotic sentiments than for their literary sophistication, is Wu Mei (1884–1939), one of the authors of a play on the death of Ch'iu Chin. A great connoisseur of K'un-ch'ü, Wu Mei came from Soochow. He left a small collection of plays that is still in print, but he is better remembered as one of the pioneer modern scholars of traditional Chinese drama. In this role he exerted a great influence both through his publications and by teaching at many institutions.

Increased contacts with the West also made Chinese intellectuals aware of the existence of another tradition of drama that not only enjoyed great prestige in its own culture but also was different from Chinese theater in many respects. Until the late nineteenth century, Chinese playwrights, actors, and audiences had experienced traditional Chinese theater as a perfectly normal way to mimic human action on stage. The contrast with Western drama made them suddenly aware of the cultural specificity of Chinese theater and its artifice. For better or worse, they focused on the Western spoken drama as the counterpart to *hsi-ch'ü* and not on any of the many Western forms of musical theater. Western drama was represented in their eyes primarily by classical Greek drama, the works of Shakespeare, and the social problem plays by authors such as Ibsen and Shaw. Chinese intellectuals also encountered Western drama during the heyday of realistic, even naturalistic, staging.

While some modern intellectuals set out to provide China with its own tradition of spoken drama on contemporary themes that was to be acted realistically, other equally modern intellectuals set out to transform traditional Chinese drama into an art form that would be the very counterimage of Western drama. The most important figure here was Ch'i Ju-shan (1877–1962), who closely collaborated with, and composed at least forty plays for, the young and rising Peking opera actor Mei Lan-fang (1894–1961), who had been trained as a *tan*. In contrast to the Western predilection for realistic staging, Ch'i Ju-shan stressed the symbolic and conventionalized nature of Chinese acting. He devoted his lifetime to meticulous research on almost every conceivable aspect of Peking opera and summarized the essence of its art in four pithy phrases: every sound should be song; every movement should be dance; no real objects should be used; and no action should imitate reality.

As a result of the efforts of Ch'i Ju-shan and Mei Lan-fang, Peking opera was turned from a popular entertainment into an elite art, its conventions were turned into norms, and its performers were changed into gentlemen—Mei Lan-fang practiced painting and calligraphy and grew a mustache during the Japanese occupation of Peking. Ch'i Ju-shan and Mei Lan-fang also toured the United States (in 1929) and the Soviet Union (1935). There they showed a program that perfectly illustrated their conceptions of what Peking opera should be like and greatly impressed some of the leading directors and playwrights of those years, such as Thornton Wilder and Bertolt Brecht.

As a form of art that had become conscious of its specifically Chinese nature, Peking opera, which in the early years of the twentieth century had experimented with the incorporation of Western elements, soon shut itself off from obvious Western influences. However, neither the modern spoken drama nor the reformed Peking opera exerted much influence outside the major urban centers during the first half of the twentieth century. In the countryside the traditional local forms of theater continued to flourish, and some of these were much more receptive to Western influences, for example in matters of music (tunes and instruments), costumes, and special effects. The continued mass appeal of the traditional theatrical genres made even some propagators of spoken drama try their hand at the composition of plays for the traditional theater.

The situation changed drastically after 1949. After the Chinese Communist Party came to power on the mainland, it set out to reorganize the whole of Chinese society. Because it was a major venue of propaganda, theater became one of the areas most directly affected. Private companies now became state companies, and the repertoire was screened for offensive elements. Plays that were found to contain "feudal" or "superstitious" elements had to be rewritten in order not to be banned, and ritual performances were outlawed. Performances were limited in time to two or two and a half hours, an evening's entertainment. The building of Soviet-style theaters, with large stages and elaborate stage machinery, greatly affected the staging of the remaining repertoire. The training of young actors was institutionalized with the large expansion of theater schools.

The acme of government involvement in theater was reached during the Cultural Revolution (1966–1976), when only eight model operas (*yang-pan-hsi*) were performed. These collectively created plays started out as revolutionary Peking operas, that is, plays written for Peking opera that took their subject matter from modern history, especially the armed struggles of the Chinese Communist Party against the Japanese and the Kuomintang (Nationalist Party); although they adhered to many of the acting techniques of Peking opera, the costumes were realistic and the music was partly modernized. These plays were then adapted in practically every form of local theater. Although in terms of the sheer number of performances these plays may well be the world's most often acted works, no one has yet claimed great literary merit for their scripts.

The early 1980s, when the old repertoire could be played again, was a period of great prosperity for traditional theater. However, in the big cities the audiences soon turned to other forms of entertainment. In the mid-1980s, many companies found themselves in dire financial straits when the government cut their funding and demanded that the companies make greater efforts to increase their own earnings. Many companies responded with a flurry of experimentation. In those regions (mainly in the south) where the traditional forms of theater had maintained their close links with religion and revived their ritual repertoire, the theatrical companies did much better economically.

On Taiwan, Peking opera was, after 1949, initially strongly cultivated as "national opera." However, many of the factors that affected Peking opera on the mainland had an impact in Taipei as well. The local Taiwanese forms of traditional theater met with many obstacles after 1949, until the growing interest in manifestations of Taiwanese culture in the 1970s and 1980s resulted in increased status and even government subsidies.

Traditional theater, both in urban China and on Taiwan, survives primarily as a protected form of cultural heritage. Cut off from its social and ritual contexts, it is performed mainly in modern theaters (often as an exotic attraction for tourists). In the countryside, some forms of theater have maintained or reestablished their links to community ritual, but even there it remains to be seen how long these forms will be able to survive. Traditional dramatic literature, however, will survive, if only because it has been incorporated since the 1920s in the canon of classical literature as taught in high schools and universities. Whereas in its own days it was at best regarded as entertainment, it is now venerated as an inalienable part of the Chinese literary heritage.

Wilt L. Idema

Chapter 42

TWENTIETH-CENTURY SPOKEN DRAMA

THE ORIGINS OF MODERN DRAMA IN CHINA

Chinese spoken drama (*hua-chü*) was a modern invention by May Fourth men of letters who imitated Western dramatic conventions as an alternative to traditional operatic theater, which was then viewed as too constraining for expressing the sentiments and concerns of an increasingly modern world. In contrast to traditional Chinese operatic theater, which combines singing, speaking, acting, and acrobatics, spoken drama, like its Western counterpart, consists mostly of speaking and acting, although dramatists in the later periods experimented with music, singing, and dancing in an attempt to combine the traditions of both East and West. Originally a vehicle for Chinese dramatists to introduce Western theater in order to reform and modernize China, spoken drama has in the course of time developed into a dynamic genre of its own, playing an important role in the cultural construction of knowledge, power, subject identity, nation/state, and Chinese national characteristics in the twentieth century. Although in no way suggesting a clearly definable and easily separable chronology of such a complex genre, the trajectory of modern Chinese drama can be roughly divided into the following seven periods: (1) the formative years (1866–1918); (2) the May Fourth period (1918–1928); (3) the 1930s (1928–1937); (4) the War of Resistance against Japan (1937–1945): (5) the first seventeen years of the People's Republic of China (PRC; 1949–1966); (6) the Cultural Revolution period (1966–1976); and (7) the post-Mao years (1976–present).

The beginning of modern Chinese drama can be traced back to the year 1866, when, as a direct result of Western imperialism and cultural expansion, the Amateur Dramatic Club of Shanghai (Shang-hai hsi-jen yeh-yü chü-t'uan) was established by foreign residents, who built the Lyceum Theater (Lan-hsin hsi-yüan) for their own entertainment. It was in this theater later on that a few Chinese men of letters, such as Cheng Cheng-ch'iu and Hsü Pan-mei, were initiated into Western dramatic forms. At the same time, Western-sponsored missionary schools in urban centers such as Peking, Shanghai, Tientsin, and Canton promoted student amateur performances of biblical stories and other Western plays in order to teach more effectively the Christian spirit and the English language. These theatrical experiences effectively paved the way for Chinese-language plays, at a later point, to be developed on campuses and in other elitist circles in major cities.

Despite these early contacts with Western drama, however, spoken drama in the true sense of the term developed somewhat later, around the turn of the twentieth century. In June 1907, a group of overseas students successfully performed "Hei-nu yü-t'ien lu" (The Black Slave Cries Out to Heaven), a full-fledged dramatic adaptation of Harriet Beecher Stowe's novel *Uncle Tom's Cabin,* in Tokyo. This early piece embodies in itself the paradoxical story of the development of modern Chinese drama. While influenced by the American founding fathers' conception of equality and using this as an argument against the Confucian tradition, the first generation of Chinese dramatists was nevertheless attracted to *Uncle Tom's Cabin* for its powerful critique of black slavery and for the subsequent liberal critique exposing the hypocrisy of the founding principles of the United States.

Who could have imagined that Lin Shu's (1852–1924) 1901 Chinese translation of Stowe's novel, on which the drama adaptation was based, was actually inspired by the translator's indignation over news reports on the cruel treatment of Chinese coolies overseas by the American "white race"? It was this same "white race," Lin Shu claimed, that oppressed both the "black race" and the "yellow race," reminding his audience that it was racial discrimination and oppression abroad that aroused his passion for introducing this play to the Chinese people. Thus the issues of racial conflict, national identity, and resistance to foreign oppression took center stage in modern Chinese drama from its origin. These issues would be further developed in subsequent dramas during the War of Resistance against Japan, when the Japanese, the same "yellow race," and yet an ethnic "other," became the enemy of the Chinese nation, both onstage and offstage, in theater and in real life.

Indeed, the war period saw the most mature and popular productions to date of Chinese drama, which was then seen as a more effective genre than fiction or poetry in mobilizing war efforts and in raising the national consciousness of the Chinese people against Japanese invaders in a time of national crisis. It is ironic that Japan—where Western spoken drama had already been established during the Meiji period (1868–1912)—was host to the first Chinese dramas publicly performed by overseas Chinese students such as Ou-yang Yü-ch'ien (1888–1962) and Lu Ching-jo, who had already established their own drama club in Tokyo in 1906, known as the Spring Willow Society (Ch'un liu she). Putting into practice their knowledge of Western dramatic conventions, these students also drew from Japanese theater reformers, whose political orientations thus helped shape the central concerns of Chinese drama at this early stage of development.

While Chinese overseas students made their debut in Tokyo, back home in Shanghai other young dramatists established the Spring Sun Society (Ch'un yang she) in September 1907 and performed their own version of *Uncle Tom's Cabin* at the Lyceum Theater, thus marking the theater's first opening to the Chinese general public for a drama performance. Together with the Spring Willow and Spring Sun societies, the Evolution Troupe (Chin-hua t'uan)—the first professional modern Chinese drama troupe, established in Shanghai in 1910—played an important part in developing the early form of spoken drama known as "civilized drama" (*wen-ming hsi*), otherwise referred to as "new drama" (*hsin-chü*) in contrast to the "old drama" (*chiu-chü*) of the operatic tradition. Unlike the Western neoclassical rules of the "three unities" of time, place, and plot, which were themselves a source of inspiration for the young generation of Chinese dramatists, many civilized dramas, as best represented in the Evolution Troupe's productions, were nevertheless characterized by an open structure with many acts in diverse locations, in a form known as *mu-piao-chih*. This dramatic form was characterized by improvised dialogs and spontaneous speeches addressing current political events, which were based on sketchy scripts with only outlines of the main plots and dialogs for each act.

Historians of Chinese drama view this style of improvisation as partly related to the radical nature of many civilized dramas that responded to the social concerns of the times, especially to the main political events surrounding the Republican revolution of 1911, which aimed at overthrowing the Ch'ing dynasty. This political orientation of theater accounts for the rapid development of "new drama" in the coastal cities of Shanghai, Canton, Tientsin, and Hong Kong. In 1908 in Canton, for instance, the Roaring-Heaven Spoken Drama Troupe (Chen-t'ien-sheng pai-hua chü-she) performed several "new dramas" with revolutionary themes in the local language (Cantonese), and the troupe was warmly received by Dr. Sun Yat-sen (Republican leader and founding father of modern China; 1866–1925) in Singapore during its overseas tour of Southeast Asia.

Other plays expressed similar political and social concerns. Set in the Meiji Restoration of 1868 in Japan, "Hsüeh-so-yi" (Blood-Stained Straw Cape; 1911), produced by the Evolution Troupe in Nanking in 1911, depicted the struggle of Japanese parliamentarians against imperial monarchists, a clear reference to Chinese revolutionaries' efforts to end imperial rule in China. Similarly, "Tung-ya feng-yün" (The Storms of East Asia; 1911), also produced by the Evolution Troupe in the same season, dramatized the story of An Chung Keun, a Korean national hero who in 1909 assassinated Itō Hirobumi, the Japanese resident-general of Korea, who was responsible for planning the Japanese wars against China and Korea. Imitating the main plot of Alexandre Dumas fils' *La Dame aux camélias*, "Hsin Ch'a-hua" (New Camille; 1911) also featured an overseas student who fought against foreign invaders, having been inspired by the patriotic feelings of a loving prostitute.

These plays represent a trend in civilized drama that utilized the prototypes of foreign "others" to comment on the social problems of contemporary China. Dramatists and performers used the heroic deeds of foreigners to help construct certain positive aspects of Chinese national characteristics. Furthermore, the portrayal of overseas students as carriers of revolutionary messages from abroad and as participants in national revolutionary events anticipated a long tradition of diaspora drama yet to come, in terms of both dramas depicting the experience of overseas students and the fact that many of the dramatists themselves had gone overseas, where they had been inspired by foreign theaters. Well-known examples include Hu Shih (1891–1962), Hung Shen (1894–1955), Hsiung Fo-hsi (1900–1965), Sung Ch'un-fang (1892–1938), and Yü Shang-yüan (1897–1970), who studied in the United States, together with Ou-yang Yü-ch'ien, Pai Wei (1893–1987), Ch'en Ta-pei (1887–1984), and T'ien Han (1898–1968), who lived in Japan. Not coincidentally, all of them were active participants in establishing the Chinese repertoire of the May Fourth period. This second major period of Chinese drama could be seen as having begun with the 1918 publication of a special issue on Ibsen in *Hsin ch'ing-nien* (New Youth), the leading literary journal and a main forum for the May Fourth movement, and as having ended in 1928 with the publication of Ou-yang Yü-ch'ien's "Hui-chia yi-hou" (Homecoming), a play that, among other things, challenged the very ideology of the May Fourth movement.

DEVELOPMENTS DURING THE MAY FOURTH MOVEMENT

The May Fourth movement was an intellectual and literary revolution initially triggered by student demonstrations in T'ien-an-men Square on May 4, 1919, to oppose Chinese officials' signing of the Treaty of Versailles, according to which territorial rights to Shantung province would have been ceded to Japan. Characterized by an anti-imperialist and antitraditionalist agenda, this cultural movement saw in Western powers models for a progressive and modern China. Dramatists of the period used both the form and the content of Western models as weapons against traditional Chinese operatic theater and the ideology it expressed. In a series of critical debates on the future orientation of Chinese theater, for instance, Ch'ien Hsüan-t'ung (1887–1939) called for the abolition of the obsolete operatic theater, which was dominated by the gentry class, in order to promote a "real drama" (*chen-hsi*), which by his definition could only be found in Western realist plays. In a similar way, Chou Tso-jen (1885–1969) repudiated operatic theater as "a dehumanized literature" (*fei-jen te wen-hsüeh*) and argued instead for the promotion of "humanized literature" (*jen te wen-hsüeh*) on the modern Chinese stage.

Even those who advocated the reform, rather than the abolition, of operatic theater invariably also stressed the political implications of the "old drama." Sung Ch'un-fang, for example, argued for the preservation of a "national" theater on the ground that the new drama, the product of European and American ideologies, could undermine traditional cultural values and consequently lead to social corruption. Yet in spite of his attempt to preserve what he considered the useful part of traditional theater, Sung Ch'un-fang was himself very active in introducing Western drama to Chinese culture, as evidenced by his earlier teaching career (he was the first to teach Western drama at Peking University, in 1916) and by the publication in 1918 of an essay in which he recommended to Chinese readers more than one hundred "famous foreign plays" by fifty-eight playwrights from thirteen countries.

Himself an intellectual leader of the May Fourth literary movement, Hu Shih went so far as to list Western subgenres such as the problem play, the symbolist play, the psychological play, and the satirical play as diverse possibilities for creating a "new drama" on the Chinese stage. Putting theory into practice, Hu Shih published his own drama, "Chung-shen ta-shih" (The Greatest Event of One's Life; 1919), in imitation of Ibsen's "A Doll's House," a play that Hu Shih had introduced to Chinese readers in *New Youth* in 1918 as a quintessential example of "Ibsenism," the promotion of individualism and the pursuit of love and freedom. Although primitive in terms of dramaturgy, Hu Shih's one-act play depicts the brave action of one T'ien Ya-mei, who elopes with her Japanese-educated lover against her parents' will. With this play, Hu Shih pioneered a long tradition in Chinese spoken drama, a tradition that would witness numerous Nora-like characters struggling to leave their homes, whether the homes of their parents or of their husbands, in order to find out, as Nora asks in Ibsen's play, "Who is right—society or me?"

Lien-ku in T'ien Han's "Huo-hu chih yeh" (The Night a Tiger Was Captured; 1924) is another early prototype of the Nora-like character, whose dilemma lies in her entrapment in a cold and ignorant patriarchal family. Isolated in a rural village in southern China, where Confucian doctrines demand total obedience to parental will, Lien-ku is told that if a tiger is captured that night, it will be used for her dowry in order to marry her off to a well-to-do family. The seriously wounded "tiger" they "capture" in the mountain trap, however, turns out to be her secret lover, who kills himself in protest against Lien-ku's father, who forbids his daughter to tend to her lover's wounds the night before her wedding day.

Similar to the use of the "trapped tiger" image to characterize the tragic fate of an innocent girl from rural China, "Ta-ch'u yu-ling-t'a" (Breaking Out of Ghost Pagoda; 1928), written by Pai Wei, a female playwright, depicts the large family of a rich landlord as a prisonlike house from which a brave, Nora-like concubine finally breaks out in search of her own freedom. Her story, however, is only a subplot to set off a more tragic story, in which a loving mother and a courageous daughter wage a fierce yet unsuccessful battle against patriarchal society, a society symbolized either by domineering and lustful domestic fathers or by new-nationalist fathers already corrupted by the revolution that aimed to eliminate Confucian fathers. The death of the daughter in her mother's arms at the conclusion of Pai Wei's play symbolizes the sheer difficulty, if not the impossibility, of breaking free of tradition.

Ou-yang Yü-ch'ien's "P'o-fu" (A Shrewish Woman; 1922) seems to address the question the great author Lu Hsün (Chou Shu-jen; 1881–1936) would ask in 1924: "What will happen to Nora after she leaves home" in a society that does not allow women financial freedom? Although married for love instead of by parental arrangement, Yü Su-hsin, the protagonist, finds herself "trapped" by her once modern-minded husband, who now has regressed, acquiring a concubine of his own. Yü Su-hsin's leaving home in this play can be understood as a satire on many of the May Fourth elite who departed from, and even betrayed, the very battle against Confucianism they themselves had initiated in the first place. Unlike Ibsen's Nora, who still needs to find out "who is right," the "shrew woman" can be seen as a mature "Nora" who perceives her own home-leaving as a necessity in carrying out the struggle for women's liberation on her own terms, without having to depend on the male members of the society, who, on earlier occasions, had perceived women's problems as a source of inspiration for their antiofficial discourse against the Confucian establishment.

From an entirely different angle, however, Ou-yang Yü-ch'ien's next play, "Hui-chia yi-hou" (Homecoming), further complicated the May Fourth concern of women's liberation and the entire genre of the "Nora play." The play revolves around a single event: the homecoming of Lu Chih-p'ing, a Chinese student who had gone to study in the United States, to the rural area of Hunan province. "Homecoming" focuses on Lu Chih-p'ing's emotions, torn as they are between his newly acquired Chinese-American "wife," an educated woman from abroad, and his virtuous wife through an arranged marriage. After an agonizing process of soul-searching, the ending of the play suggests that Lu Chih-p'ing is more attracted to his homebound, filial, and understanding Chinese wife than to his "shrew woman" from the West. This play represents a sobering, yet problematic, moment when Chinese dramatists were reflecting on the negative impact of Western education while still trying to come to terms with some of the traditional Chinese values. In "Homecoming," China has been transformed into a peaceful, utopia-like countryside where a daughter-in-law happily sacrifices herself for the members of the patriarchal family. The once-trapped and miserable "Noras" in Hu Shih's, T'ien Han's, and Pai Wei's plays are now replaced by a contented daughter-in-law who patiently waits at home for her estranged husband to come back, never desiring to leave home herself. "Homecoming" became, therefore, an important early piece in the genre of diaspora drama, which focuses on the experience of overseas Chinese, except for the fact that the story was told from the other side of the ocean. As a typical dramatist who was at one point himself an overseas student in Japan, Ou-yang Yü-ch'ien presented in "Homecoming" a self-reflective play on the pros and cons of diaspora experience itself and on the image of the Western "other" that helped construct many of the Chinese national characteristics, which as seen in this play were based on oppositional values: country versus city, traditional versus modern, Asian woman versus her Western counterpart.

Such a homecoming theme in diaspora drama can be traced back to an earlier work by Hsiung Fo-hsi, another important dramatist of the May Fourth period. Written in New York in 1926, while he was studying Western literature, "Yang chuang-yüan" (Foreign Graduate) depicts the homecoming of a native son who feels so privileged as an overseas Chinese, with a foreign degree and a foreign wife, that he is even annoyed by his own mother until she respectfully addresses him with a foreign title such as "Doctor." Considered one of Hsiung Fo-hsi's best plays, "Foreign Graduate" addressed the anti-imperialist theme inherent in the origins of modern Chinese drama, a theme developed concurrently with the anti-Confucian theme of the May Fourth movement. It could be argued that the dramatist's own concern with the negative impact of the West prompted his portrayal of the overseas Chinese graduate as a cowardly and shallow man—a portrayal that consequently became part of a series of negative Chinese national characteristics that Lu Hsün, the quintessential May Fourth fiction writer, was instrumental in critiquing in his famous piece "Ah Q cheng-chuan" (The True Story of Ah Q; 1921).

Hsiung Fo-hsi's engagement with the image of a foreign "other" was a thematic concern of an earlier play entitled "Yi-p'ien ai-kuo hsin" (A Patriotic Heart; 1925), in which a sixteen-year-old girl, born to a Chinese father and a Japanese mother, rebels against her mother, who has persuaded her son to sign a contract in which he ceded the rights to a Chinese mine to the Japanese. The father's promise to take the mother back to Japan, where they first fell in love, out of respect for her patriotic feelings, and the moving reconciliation scene between mother and daughter, both of whom had suffered emotionally and physically, highlight the seemingly irreconcilable national conflict between China and Japan, a conflict that has victimized people from both countries.

In contrast to the above-mentioned plays, which describe contemporary life in 1920s China, Kuo Mo-jo's (1892–1978) trilogy "San ko p'an-ni te nü-hsing" (Three Revolutionary Women) reversed the standard conception of three legendary ancient women, reinterpreting their stories as indictments of the traditional threefold obligations of women to their fathers, husbands, and sons. In the first play, "Cho Wen-chün" (1923), the title character elopes with her lover, Ssu-ma Hsiang-ju, thereby challenging both the strong will of her father and Confucian ideology as a whole, which expects a widow never to remarry, in order to be chaste and faithful to the memory of her late husband. In a similar manner, the trilogy's second play, "Wang Chao-chün" (1923), depicts the heroine as a dignified courtesan who rejects the "love" of the Han emperor by willingly marrying an outsider from a "barbarous" tribe. Kuo Mo-jo's characterization of Wang Chao-chün as a female rebel against the Han imperial court was a radical departure from past historical accounts, which portrayed her as a submissive courtesan who waited patiently all her life for the occasional favor of the Han emperor.

In a way more politically relevant to the reality of 1920s China, Kuo Mo-jo's third play, "Nieh Ying" (1925), presents the title character as a martyr who stands by her patriotic brother against outside invaders. It is important to note that this play was written one month after the outbreak of the May Thirtieth movement of 1925 (initiated when British police officers fired on demonstrators in the International Settlement in Shanghai who were protesting the shooting of striking workers at a Japanese-owned factory) and was enthusiastically applauded as a powerful antiofficial and anti-imperialist play. Kuo Mo-jo's father figures—the domestic "father" in "Cho Wen-chün," the imperial "father" in "Wang Chao-chün," and the imperialist "father" in "Nieh Ying"—show the connections between the racial/national theme in civilized drama and the anti-Confucian theme in May Fourth drama.

All these themes were most skillfully combined and explored in Kuo Mo-jo's "history plays," a new subgenre developed during the period of the War of Resistance against Japan, the early PRC, and the post-Mao period, in which history was rewritten to convey contemporary messages. A significant piece in the May Fourth period, Ou-yang Yü-ch'ien's "P'an Chin-lien" (1927), best combines characteristics of the Nora play with the history play by reversing the misogynist image of the fictional character P'an Chin-lien in *Shui-hu chuan* (Water Margin) as the source of evil into a contemporary image of the May Fourth woman, a woman who courageously fights for self-respect and freedom of love. This is but one notable instance of how a dramatic piece in the modern period is able to reverse the perception of a much-hated figure in a "masterpiece" of traditional fiction.

In addition to the development of new genres and new thematic concerns, the May Fourth period also witnessed significant progress in stage performance. Drama historians frequently cite as examples of progress the establishment in Shanghai in May 1921 of the People's Drama Society (Min chung she), which advocated "noncommercial theater" and "small theater" to carry out its task of "popular education." This occurred after Wang Yu-yu's (1888–1937) expensive yet unsuccessful performance in October 1920 of Bernard Shaw's "Mrs. Warren's Profession," a play that was recommended in *New Youth* as an exemplary realist modern drama from the West. Wang Yu-yu's failed attempt to produce faithfully an elitist play from the West, according to its dramatic conventions, convinced him that it was necessary to adapt to the popular taste of Chinese audiences, who were still accustomed to the familiar expectations of operatic theater. Well-known dramatists such as Ch'en Ta-pei and P'u Po-ying (1875–1935), who pursued their dramatic experiments in Peking, joined Wang Yu-yu in promoting "amateur theater" (*ai-mei chü*) in the 1920s, further popularizing theater activities as both educational and artistic experiences.

The term *ai-mei*, coined by Ch'en Ta-pei as a partial transcription with semantic overlay, best conveyed the twofold emphasis of such a theatrical movement. Whereas "amateur" refers to noncommercial performances by unpaid actors, *ai-mei*, which literally means "love for beauty," emphasizes "art for art's sake." The best artistic achievement of amateur theater can be found in the April 1924 production of Oscar Wilde's well-made play "Lady Windermere's Fan" (1892), directed by Hung Shen, an event that drama historians viewed as the beginning of a realistic performing art on the Chinese stage, with its emphasis on the script, stage design, the role of director, and its translation of the local flavor of Shanghai life into a Chinese style of acting, while still adhering to the spirit of the foreign original. Hung Shen's 1929 production of Hu Shih's "The Greatest Event of One's Life" also marked a significant event, in which actresses, for the first time in modern drama history, performed together with actors on stage.

Also worth noting in this period is the 1925 founding of the Drama Department of the Peking School of Arts (Kuo-li Pei-ching yi-shu chuan-men hsüeh-hsiao), the first art institution sponsored by the government. Chao T'ai-mou and Yü Shang-yüan, its chief architects, were instrumental in promoting "national drama" (*ko-chü*; literally, "song-drama" or "operatic drama"), which was perceived as a "pure art" that "transcends reality" and as a critique against the radical political orientation of many May Fourth plays. Among their more enduring concepts, however, is their exploration of the "suggestive nature of Chinese opera" (*hsi-chü te hsieh-yi t'e-hsing*), which they believed could be best combined with Western realist art for the creation of a truly unique national drama, a theory that was to be further developed in 1962 and popularized in the post-Mao period by Huang Tso-lin (1906–1994). The future orientation of the ideal Chinese theater, Huang Tso-lin argued later, should be toward a combination of three divergent views of theater: those of illusionist theater, or the Stanislavsky school, which believed in the "fourth wall"; those of the "alienation effect," or the Brechtian school, which wanted to demolish the "fourth wall"; and those of Mei Lan-fang (1894–1961; see chapter 41), for whom such a wall did not exist. According to the last view, Chinese theater had always been so highly conventionalized that it could not be seen as having set out to create an illusion of real life for the audience. Elaborating the point of his predecessors four decades later, Huang Tso-lin concluded that realism is the keynote of

Western art and suggestiveness that of Chinese art. Seen in this light, Huang Tso-lin's return to traditional operatic theater can be seen as a response to the radical nature of many May Fourth dramatists, who sought inspiration for theatrical reform almost exclusively in the Western "other."

FROM THE LATE 1920S TO THE 1930S

Such a formation of a distinctively Chinese dramatic theory, of course, was evidently too advanced in 1928, when May Fourth dramatists were still struggling to reform civilized drama, already in decline, while seeking for innovative ways to promote their "new drama" in various forms. Yet the year 1928 also marks a turning point. That year dramatists gathered in Shanghai to hold a seminar in commemoration of the hundredth anniversary of Ibsen's birth, during which Hung Shen's suggestion of replacing the term "new drama" with "spoken drama" was accepted with the unanimous support of Ou-yang Yü-ch'ien and T'ien Han. This watershed event can be seen as the beginning of the third period in the development of modern Chinese drama: the drama of the 1930s, which can itself be further divided into at least four significant movements: (1) the Southern Society (Nan kuo she; 1927–1930); (2) "leftist drama" (Tso-yi hsi-chü; 1930–1934); (3) the major dramas (1934–1936) of Ts'ao Yü (1910–1996), which by most drama historians' accounts placed Chinese drama "on par with masterpieces in world theater"; and (4) "defense drama" (*kuo-fang hsi-chü*; 1936–1937), the forerunner of the theater of the War of Resistance against Japan (1937–1945).

Indeed, by 1927, dramatic activities were gathering momentum in Shanghai, when T'ien Han formed the Southern Society, a name derived from *Nan-kuo pan-yüeh-k'an* (Southern Biweekly), a popular journal initiated by T'ien Han and his wife, Yi Shu-yü, in 1924 that was dedicated to the promotion of literature, film, music, drama, and the fine arts. The most representative work in the early period of the Southern Society can be found in T'ien Han's "Ming-yu chih ssu" (The Death of a Famous Actor), which premiered in Shanghai in 1927. Based in part on the true story of a famous Peking opera singer, the play focuses on the character of Liu Chen-sheng, who dies of fatigue and illness after having been abused by the relentless media and betrayed by Liu Feng-hsien, his once-promising student whose initial success as a rising star nevertheless lures her into pursuit of a luxurious life, at the expense of her dramatic art. Liu Feng-hsien provides an example of a Nora-like character hitherto unseen, a character who, after leaving home, is trapped once again by the whole society as a "plaything" and, as the play suggests, would most likely return to another patriarchal home in search of material comfort. Economic independence, which was seen by many as the only way to help many Chinese Noras survive in the public arena, could be viewed in this play as just another obstacle, if not a trajectory to another disaster.

Based on his own experience as a dramatist struggling in Shanghai, his knowledge of operatic theater, and his expertise in modern spoken drama, T'ien Han was in the best position to have developed a new subgenre that can be called "drama of the theater," a genre that, among other things, recreated on stage the true stories of those in the theater community. Indeed, such a feature had already emerged in his earlier theatrical and film works. In "Huai/Fan-o-lin yü ch'iang-wei" (Violin and Rose; 1920), the first play he had ever written, T'ien Han dramatized the tragic love story of a folklore performer, whereas in a screenplay entitled *Li-yüan ying-lieh* (A Hero in the Pear Garden; 1948), he represented the courageous death of a patriotic opera singer at the hands of Japanese invaders. In these two pieces alone, T'ien Han was able to tell the personal stories of theater performers in the larger contexts of social environment and national crisis.

The impact of T'ien Han on drama of the theater in the years to come can be seen in well-known plays such as Wu Tsu-kuang's (b. 1917) "Feng-yü yeh-kuei-jen" (Return on a Snowy Night; 1942), written during the period of the War of Resistance against Japan; T'ien Han's own "Kuan Han-ch'ing" (1958), written during the PRC period; and Su Shu-yang's (b. 1938) "T'ai-p'ing hu" (T'ai-p'ing Lake; 1986), written during the post-Mao period. Whereas "Return on a Snowy Night" narrates the tragic love, poverty, and death of a once-famous Peking opera singer in lyrical prose and with an open structure characterized by a fluidity of time and space, "Kuan Han-ch'ing" uses a unique structure of an inner and an outer play to recreate the life of the title character. The inner play, "Kan t'ien tung ti: Tou Ŏ yüan tsa-chü" (Moving Heaven and Earth: Injustice to Tou Ŏ), was supposedly written by Kuan Han-ch'ing, the thirteenth-century Yüan dynasty playwright who depicted an innocent woman wrongly accused and executed, the victim of a false witness and a corrupt officer. The outer play, T'ien Han's "Kuan Han-ch'ing," relates how Kuan Han-ch'ing wrote his play in the thirteenth century as a criticism of the corruption of his own times, and how, as a consequence, he was imprisoned and exiled by enforcers of the ruling ideology, who viewed him as a threat to society. Both the inner and outer plays of "Kuan Han-ch'ing" are, of course, not just stories about a particular dramatist; they also address the issue of the subversive nature of play writing, censorship, and theater in general.

It is ironic to note that, together with his other plays, T'ien Han's "Kuan Han-ch'ing" was accused during the Cultural Revolution of drawing on historical figures and legends to attack the Chinese Communist Party's policy on literature and art. In a denouement that would have seemed (outside China) more the stuff of drama than real life, T'ien Han, the foremost "leftist" writer before 1949 and a widely acclaimed playwright/critic after 1949 in the People's Republic of China, was tortured to death in prison in 1968, in a fashion not unlike the fate of his dramatic character from the Yüan dynasty.

Although the death of T'ien Han has never been dramatized on the Chinese stage, Lao She (pseudonym of Shu Ch'ing-ch'un; 1899–1966), his contemporary and another well-known playwright in the PRC, fared better. "T'ai-p'ing Lake," written in 1986 in post-Mao China on the occasion of the twentieth anniversary of Lao She's death, depicts Lao She's last day, August 24, 1966, when he drowned himself in the lake as a protest against his brutal beating and humiliation at the hands of the Red Guards. In the course of the play, Lao She wanders around T'ai-p'ing Lake for a day and a night, meditating on the paradox of his past devotion to the party and the present antiparty charges imposed on him. Puzzled and confused, he engages in conversation with the living—people who still fondly remember his plays—and also with the dead—his dramatic characters who committed suicide to protest the "miserable old society" before 1949 that did not allow even the most patently innocent people to live. If this genre of drama of the theater was first initiated with T'ien Han's earlier pieces criticizing the prejudice against artists in the "old society," it ends with an even harsher critique of the injustice and unfair treatment of artists in Maoist China, a "new society" for which T'ien Han and his contemporaries, in their leftist dramas of the 1930s, had once provided the blueprints.

Drama historians from the PRC credited T'ien Han with being instrumental in orienting the drama world toward leftist theater under the influence of the Chinese Communist Party (CCP), whose ideology called for promoting a class-oriented "proletarian drama" that would depict the unjust oppressions of the working class. One significant event in this regard can be seen in the Southern Society's production of "K'a-men" (Carmen; 1930), adapted from the fiction version of the same title by the French man of letters Prosper Mérimée (1846). The character of Carmen, the gypsy girl who in the original text flirts with and later deserts Don José, a Spanish officer, was now reinterpreted by T'ien Han and his contemporaries as a social rebel against feudal monarchy and as a symbol of their "limited choices" at that time: they had to borrow a foreign story to express their revolutionary sentiments in order to bring about changes in Chinese reality. According to PRC drama historians' accounts, Carmen so offended the ruling Kuomintang (KMT; Nationalist Party) government that it was banned after only three performances, with the dire consequences of the Southern Society being prohibited from dramatic activities in 1930 and the young actor who had played the part of Don José being arrested and subsequently executed in Nanking. Once again, Chinese theater offers an example of how a foreign other, in the forms of both the original text and the dramatic image, was reconstructed on stage in order to construct the Chinese dramatists' vision of what their society was all about; what happened on stage, in turn, directly affected the lives of these dramatists and performers off stage.

An equally significant event with regard to leftist theater can also be found in Ou-yang Yü-ch'ien's 1930 production in Canton of "Nu-hou pa, Chung-kuo!" (China Roars), written by the Soviet playwright Sergei Mikhailovich Tretiakov. This play, which premiered in his homeland in 1926, was occasioned by the British imperialist acts that Tretiakov witnessed in a visit to China in 1924. Leftist theater thus became part of an international stage as productions of the same play appeared in leftist circles in Germany, the United States, and Japan. Such an anti-imperialist thrust at the very inception of Chinese drama had by now become one of the most predominant thematic concerns. It was further complicated, on another front, by the widespread rejection of "imperialist cultural aggression" as the result of Hung Shen's being held in police custody in 1930 after his protest against the Shanghai release of Hollywood's *Shanghai Express* (the Chinese title was *Pu p'a ssu* [Don't Be Afraid to Die]), a film viewed as insulting to the Chinese for giving a derogatory depiction of them. Hollywood's representation of China, in turn, further helped construct Chinese dramatists' perception of the West and their advocacy of anti-imperialist themes in the leftist theater.

With the establishment of the Chinese League of Left-Wing Dramatists (Chung-kuo tso-yi hsi-chü-chia lien-meng) in 1931, a subgroup of the Chinese League of Left-Wing Writers (Chung-kuo tso-yi tso-chia lien-meng) founded in Shanghai in 1930, leftist theater also spread to other parts of China, such as Peking, Tientsin, and Nanking. It was in Nanking that another ironic event occurred: in the production of Ibsen's "A Doll's House" by the People's Theater (Ta-chung chü-she), Wang P'ing, the actress who had successfully played the part of Nora, was nevertheless detained at home by her angry parents while at the same time fired by her employer at an elementary school for her "improper" and "immoral" behavior of acting on the stage. It was not until a public protest by her fellow dramatists and supporters that Wang P'ing was finally given permission to perform again. The reopening of Ibsen's play on March 8, International Women's Day, therefore, marked a celebratory occasion for members of the Nanking Branch of the League of Left-Wing Dramatists, who had committed themselves to carrying out the antitraditional and anti-Confucian agenda of the May Fourth movement.

The May Fourth theme of women's pursuit of free love and independence, however, could not find a more vibrant expression in 1930s theater than in Ts'ao Yü's "Lei-yü" (Thunderstorm; 1933), a watershed play that, by many drama historians' accounts, signified the maturity of modern Chinese drama. Written when Ts'ao Yü was twenty-three, after having buried himself in Western traditions such as Greek theater and the plays of Shakespeare, Ibsen, O'Neill, and Chekhov, in addition to Chinese classics, "Thunderstorm" is a well-structured play with four acts and two scenes that revolves around the dramatic conflicts of two families with a secret, entangled history of thirty years, all of which is unfolded and resolved within a matter of twenty-four hours. With the single event of Lu Ma's arrival at the rich household of the Chou family, where Lu Ssu-feng, her daughter, works as a maid, it is revealed, to her horror, that her daughter is in love with Chou P'ing, her own illegitimately conceived son left behind in the Chou family thirty years earlier. In a strikingly similar way, Lu Ma found her daughter repeating her own tragic story from many years earlier, when Lu Ma, herself also a maid, fell in love with Chou P'u-yüan, the master of the house, who had kicked her out after she had given birth to his two children. Such an incest story is made even more complicated by another "incest" story in which Chou P'ing, a few years earlier, had an affair with Chou Fan-yi, his stepmother, who had been married to Chou P'u-yüan after Lu Ma's departure, but was nevertheless alienated by her husband's indifference and cruelty. The play ends with the tragic deaths of Lu Ssu-feng, Chou P'ing, and Chou Ch'ung, his younger brother, and with a mentally ill Chou Fan-yi and a grief-stricken Lu Ma, who has nothing else to live for.

In a way not unlike Ibsen's "A Doll's House," the play ends with a lonely patriarch on an empty stage, signifying the emptiness of a broken "home" that was never there. Unlike Nora, whose courageous act of leaving home is celebrated, however, both Chou Fan-yi and Lu Ma epitomize the very trap for Chinese women of leaving home: Lu Ma's leaving home thirty years earlier and her determination "never to see the Chous again" only led her to the dreadful realization that her daughter had ended up being trapped in the same home she had tried so hard to escape. In the case of Chou Fan-yi, leaving her parents' home thirty years earlier with the hope of finding true love only sent her back to a prisonlike home, with no chance of leaving again. Her desperate act of trying to trap Chou P'ing in Lu Ssu-feng's house in order to seek revenge on him, and her pitiful begging for him to take her with him, along with Lu Ssu-feng, merely point up her despair and her hopeless longing to have a home of her own.

The deep sense of homelessness expressed by these characters is indeed reminiscent of Ibsen's "A Doll's House," a play dear to the heart of Ts'ao Yü, who at the age of eighteen in 1928, while still a student in Tientsin, was said to be the first one ever to play the role of Nora in China (at a time when it was customary for male actors to play female parts). Ts'ao Yü's "Thunderstorm," written under the influence of Ibsen and other Western dramatists, was successfully premiered in Tokyo, where the earlier generation of Chinese dramatists had first initiated modern Chinese drama. The trajectory of modern Chinese drama, at least geographically speaking, seemed to have come full circle.

Ts'ao Yü's "Thunderstorm" was among the most frequently performed plays in Chinese theater, as evidenced by popular productions in the 1930s by the China Traveling Troupe (Chung-kuo lü-hsing chü-t'uan), the first professional spoken-drama performing group not sponsored by the government, as well as in the PRC period, when it was canonized as one of the best modern Chinese plays depicting the evils of a "big family" in the "old society." Ts'ao Yü himself, on different occasions, later validated this official line of interpretation, despite the original description of his "authorial intention" as expressed in the preface to "Thunderstorm" in 1934, where he stated that the play was motivated by an emotional force, a longing for an explanation of the many mysterious forces in the universe that had captured him and prompted him to write about the fate of individuals. In the PRC revision of the play, moreover, Ts'ao Yü changed part of the ending: in this version Lu Ta-hai, Lu Ma's second son with Chou P'u-yüan, is determined to go back to the mines to lead a workers' strike, thus accentuating the theme of the proletarian drama and class struggle pertinent to the PRC ideology.

Perhaps because of a long and complex history of literary reception, Ts'ao Yü's second play, "Jih-ch'u" (Sunrise; 1936), is regarded by some drama historians as an even better play than "Thunderstorm." Shifting between the scene of a luxurious hotel room and that of a third-class brothel in Shanghai in the 1930s, "Sunrise" tells the story of Ch'en Pai-lu, whose status is somewhere between a prostitute, a courtesan, and a "daughter" to a rich businessman who pays all the expenses for her high-class lifestyle. Her resentment of this parasitic way of life, however, finds expression in her attempts to save a teenage girl named Hsiao Tung-hsi (Little Shrimp) from being trapped in a brothel. Once again, like other Nora-like characters, Ch'en Pai-lu feels trapped in the city after having divorced her husband, a poet whose passionate love for her could not relieve the boredom of marriage. After rejecting a marriage proposal from a childhood friend, who came to Shanghai to take her back home to the countryside, and feeling disillusioned by "free love," Ch'en Pai-lu commits suicide to avoid paying exorbitant hotel bills. At least in this play, the failure to obtain both emotional and financial independence accounts for the ultimate tragedy of a Chinese woman who has left home—both her parents' and her husband's homes.

Because of the potential interpretation of this play as an exposé of the corrupt and decadent life in "old" Shanghai, it is not difficult to understand why "Sunrise" has also been ranked among the most performed plays. Ch'en Pai-lu's dying words—"The sun is risen, and the darkness is left behind"—accompanied by the sound of workers constructing a foundation for a new building, were naturally interpreted in the PRC reception of the play as a call for a better society.

Almost concurrent with Ts'ao Yü's success was the emergence of "defense drama" in the period from 1935 to 1936. With the impending national crisis of a Japanese invasion, the Friendly Association of Shanghai Dramatic Circle (Shang-hai hsi-chü lien-yi-hui) was organized in 1936 to replace the dissolved League of Left-Wing Dramatists and League of Left-Wing Writers. According to the "Declaration of Defense Drama" by the Association of Shanghai Dramatists (Shang-hai chü-tso-che hsieh-hui) in February 1936, "defense drama" aimed at uniting dramatists of diverse political and ideological backgrounds to promote a drama of national resistance to Japanese imperialist aggression. The most popular pieces in this regard are Hsia Yen's "Sai Chin-hua" (1935) and "Shang-hai wu-yen hsia" (Under Shanghai Eaves; 1937), each play representing two distinct subgenres, the history play and the contemporary realist play. "Sai Chin-hua," which premiered in November 1936, is a retelling of the story of the title character, a famous Ch'ing dynasty courtesan who won over important Western men and persuaded them to reduce their demands on China during the 1900 antiforeign Boxer Rebellion. According to PRC drama historians, this play's obvious allusion to the KMT government's nonresistance policy toward the Japanese as reminiscent of the corrupt and cowardly Chinese officials' "kowtowing to Western powers" in the Ch'ing dynasty made the play a popular hit, with a record twenty-two full-house performances. Its censorship and banning by the KMT government and the subsequent public uproar (known as the " 'Sai Chin-hua' Incident") seemed only to have confirmed the genius of the playwright, whose allegorical use of history was not lost on either political camp.

In contrast to "Sai Chin-hua," whose seven scenes were set in six different locations, Hsia Yen's (1900–1995) "Under Shanghai Eaves" presents a unique and innovative dramatic structure with only one setting: a cross section of a typical house in Shanghai, occupied by five poor families struggling for survival. In addition to its diverse and colorful characters—an unwilling prostitute, a discontented primary school teacher, an unemployed clerk, and an eccentric old newspaper vendor who dreams about the impossible homecoming of his son, already killed in the war—the play focuses on a single event, the "homecoming" of K'ang Fu, who, upon his release from prison after eight years, finds Yang Ts'ai-yü, his wife, living with (and emotionally attached to) his friend Lin Chih-ch'eng. Although the play has been conventionally interpreted as portraying a group of people who are able to move beyond personal pain and grievances during a period of national crisis, one can also view Yang Ts'ai-yü as another kind of "Nora" character, who breaks away from the comfort of her parents' home in order to follow K'ang Fu in his revolutionary pursuit, only to find herself trapped again in another home with another lover because of political turmoil, which in her case results in her financial dependence on another man. The temporary reunion with Yang Ts'ai-yü, and the inspiration of his daughter as a "little teacher," nevertheless help K'ang Fu gather new courage to leave his wife's present family undisturbed. The act by a male Nora-like character of leaving "home" can be seen as having finally completed the earlier, unsuccessful attempt by his wife. In a larger context, the originally scheduled premiere of "Under Shanghai Eaves" in Shanghai on August 15, 1937, never materialized, because two days earlier, on August 13, the war broke out against Japan throughout the country. Hsia Yen later wrote that, instead of feeling disappointed, he was in fact excited about the dramatic turn of events: the war effort and its eventual victory should bring an end to the sad and unhappy stories in the play. In fact, he wished that the play would never have to be performed again so that Chinese children would never have to be reminded of their parents' past suffering.

FROM THE ANTI-JAPANESE WAR TO THE EARLY PEOPLE'S REPUBLIC

The canceled premiere of "Under Shanghai Eaves" paradoxically suggested the beginning of the fourth period of drama—that of the War of Resistance against

Japan, known to drama historians as the "golden age of Chinese theater," when drama played the most significant and direct role of any genre in promoting war efforts. The best-known performances included that of "Pao-wei Lu-kou-ch'iao" (In Defense of Marco Polo Bridge), a play that represented the heroic national efforts to resist Japanese invasion. In addition to its popularity as a morale booster, the play, which premiered in Shanghai on August 7, 1937, also initiated the tradition of collective writing (*chi-t'i ch'uang-tso*)—a form of play-writing especially popular during the Cultural Revolution, when "revolutionary model theater" was created to replace the "remnants of old culture." "In Defense of Marco Polo Bridge" was the joint effort of seventeen playwrights; its production was made possible with the help of six musicians, nineteen directors, and a cast of close to a hundred actors and actresses.

Such a spirit of collective effort to promote wartime drama reached its peak in August 1937, when twelve national salvation drama troupes (*chiu-wang yen-chü-tui*) were organized in Shanghai to travel to and perform in different parts of China. Their most frequently produced plays included Ch'en Li-t'ing and others' "Fang-hsia ni te pien-tzu" (Putting Down Your Whip; 1931), which depicts a starving daughter being whipped by her helpless, tearful father, who is urged by others to put down his whip and join the national effort to fight Japanese invaders. The stage lines from the actors and actress to incite responses from the audience and the fact that this play was frequently performed outdoors marked it as an important event in the tradition of modern Chinese "street theater."

The most flourishing period in stage production, however, was from 1938 to 1945 in the unoccupied areas of Chungking and Kweilin, when a series of drama festivals and exhibitions helped produce the most successful plays of the war period. During the "misty seasons" from October to May of each year—Chungking, the wartime capital of China and a mountain city surrounded by rivers, was shrouded by heavy mist and hence sheltered from Japanese air raids—a yearly Misty Season Drama Festival was held. In 1944 alone a total of 118 dramas were staged, featuring diverse authors and different drama troops. Among the best-known pieces produced during this period in Chungking were Ts'ao Yü's "T'ui-pien" (Transformation; 1940) and "Pei-ching jen" (Peking Men; 1940) and Kuo Mo-jo's six history plays, including "Ch'ü Yüan." The last play depicts the title character as a tragic poet (c. 340–278 B.C.E.), whose patriotic feelings and heroic spirit in fighting against the corrupt status quo made this drama a hit with audiences.

In the "liberated area" occupied by the CCP—especially in Yenan, the site of its headquarters—dramatists influenced by Mao Tse-tung's famous "Tsai Yen-an wen-yi tso-t'an-hui shang te chiang-hua" (Talks at the Yenan Forum on Literature and Art; 1942) attempted to create a "national form" of theater, which drew inspiration from the life experiences of workers, peasants, and soldiers, and from the heritage of folk dance and drama. A culminating piece of Yenan drama was "Pai-mao nü" (The White-Haired Girl), a folk opera (*ko-chü*) that premiered in April 1945 on the occasion of the seventh congress of the CCP. In this play, Hsi-erh, a poor peasant girl, having escaped from a vicious landlord who had had her father beaten to death for failure to pay his debts, now survives in a mountain cave as a wild person, her hair finally turning white. Not until she is rescued from her ghostly existence by the arrival of the CCP is she able to take revenge on her enemy. With its celebrated theme—how the old society turned a human being into a ghost and the new society turned a ghost into a human being again—"The White-Haired Girl" was said to have been enthusiastically received in the liberated areas during the 1940s. Consequently, it was often performed at mass meetings in order to raise the peasants' "class consciousness" and turn them against such class enemies as the vicious landlord. Indeed, as drama historians have recorded, the popularity of this folk drama seemed unprecedented: wherever the red flags (symbols of Communist predominance) fluttered, the opera would be successfully performed, and loud cries for the revenge of Hsi-erh would be heard everywhere. The play represents another example of Chinese dramatists' creation of a new identity for this quintessential character of a poor woman waiting to be emancipated—from her past, her misery, and her desires—in order to construct the necessity for a new Chinese nation and socialist state with equality and freedom.

The class oppression theme and the representation of the poor peasants' life in "The White-Haired Girl" anticipated many of the trends in the early years after the founding of the PRC. In spite of the conventional claim that PRC drama is characterized by its radical departure from the pre-1949 past, there are also continuities with the earlier traditions. The legendary story of Hsiung Fo-hsi's tenacious efforts to produce "peasant theater" (1932–1937), among the peasants in rural areas of Hopei province, for example, could be seen as one of the origins of this subgenre. The peasant drama would be fully developed in the PRC, with its fundamental belief in a peasant revolution as an important part of the Communist revolution.

The emphasis on peasant revolution in the official ideology of the PRC finds its perfect expression in several peasant plays popular at the beginning of the 1950s, plays that cleverly combined this new concern with the May Fourth theme of women's pursuit of free love and independence. Chin Chien's one-act play "Chao Hsiao-lan" (1950), for instance, dramatizes one woman's courage in her fight for free love against the will of her parents, in sharp contrast with the tragic story of her sister, who has suffered greatly from an arranged marriage. Unlike Hu Shih's May Fourth play, "The Greatest Event of One's Life," which blames conservative parents and Confucian ideology for the grievances of the new generation, "Chao Hsiao-lan" and other similar plays stress the need for a "new society" after 1949, a society now glorified for its power to eliminate the remnants of the "old society," which confines women to their private sphere.

In PRC drama, the fate of women is usually narrated in the larger context of "socialist revolution and socialist construction," which, according to the predominant PRC ideology, provide women with a perfect stage for public performance. Such a feature can be found in Hu K'o's (b. 1921) "Huai-shu chuang" (Huai-shu Village; 1959), a typical 1950s play that dramatizes the story of Mother Kuo, a prototype of a unique and loving "earth mother" now transformed into the new image of a "revolutionary mother," yet in some respects continuing the long tradition of heroic, self-sacrificing mothers stretching back to Mencius's mother in the fourth century B.C.E. The loss of her only son to the Korean War effort merely reinforces her tenacious effort to take the lead in the numerous political events occurring in the countryside: the land reform movement (1950), the movement to support the Korean War (1950–1953), the various movements aimed at collectivizing farming, and, finally, the disastrous "Great Leap Forward," whose goal was to boost agricultural and industrial productivity with backyard steel furnaces, large-scale public works projects, and other impractical schemes (1958). Such an image of a revolutionary mother playing a central role in the public domain becomes almost a parody in characters of the 1960s and 1970s, in the revolutionary model theater of the Cultural Revolution, as seen in Mother Tu in "Tu-chüan shan" (The Red Azalea; model play version by Wang Shu-yüan and others; 1973), Grandmother Sha in "Sha-chia-pang" (model play version collectively revised by the Peking Opera Troupe of Peking; 1970), and Grandmother Li in "Hung-teng chi" (The Red Lantern; model play version collectively revised by the China Peking Opera Troupe, 1970). All these characters are quintessential nurturers of the "one big revolutionary family" during the war period. In keeping with this spirit, almost all such plays were collectively authored.

In spite of such emphasis on the collective experience of the subaltern class, however, the most popular—and therefore, in some cases, most controversial—"peasant plays" depict love stories in a new context. Yang Lü-fang's (b. 1925) "Pu-ku-niao yu chiao le" (Cuckoo Sings Again; 1957), for example, dramatizes the story of T'ung Ya-nan, an educated young woman in the countryside who finds herself singing again only after having left her possessive boyfriend. Although belonging to the same "family" as the May Fourth Nora-like characters—a tradition that the PRC claimed to have continued—T'ung Ya-nan was nevertheless criticized as an "unhealthy" character during the antirightist movement in 1957, a political campaign that persecuted many intellectuals who dared to express their criticism of bureaucracy and corruption within the CCP. Among other things, the play was attacked for overemphasizing the importance of the "individualist pursuit of love and personal happiness"—a "bourgeois sentiment"—while at the same time presenting negative images of village party leaders as indifferent and uncaring.

If "Cuckoo Sings Again" was viewed as controversial for its romantic story, the triangular relationship in Yüeh Yeh's (b. 1920) "T'ung-kan kung-k'u" (Joys and Sorrows; 1956) between a CCP official and his two women was, not surprisingly, considered even more problematic. Set in contemporary times, the play focuses on the single event of the "homecoming" of Liu Fang-wen, Meng Shih-ching's ex-wife, who brings their son to visit his father. The dramatic event unfolds when Meng Shih-ching realizes that he is more attracted to his ex-wife from an arranged marriage in the countryside—whom he had already divorced on the grounds that she was "ignorant, backward, and unlovely"—than Hua Yün, his educated wife, whom he married out of "free love" after having shared "similar experience" during the revolutionary war period.

As in Ou-yang Yü-ch'ien's May Fourth play "Homecoming," Liu Fang-wen, on the one hand, resembles Wu Tzu-fang as the virtuous and sacrificing wife from the countryside; facing a situation worse than that of Wu Tzu-fang, Liu Fang-wen takes care of her mother-in-law, whom she has kept in the dark about her divorce in order to protect the old woman from such heartbreaking news. On the other hand, the differences between the two female characters cannot be more striking: as if to testify to the importance of the CCP agenda of women's liberation, Liu Fang-wen is now dramatized as a new woman, who has transformed herself from a victim of an arranged marriage in the "old society" into an educated CCP member and a dynamic leader in the collective farming movement in her home village. Most important, she seems to have perfectly combined the virtue and devotion of traditional woman with the active public role of a modern revolutionary woman, thus becoming a more charming lady for Meng Shih-ching than his nagging and, therefore, truly "unlovely" wife.

Liu Fang-wen's embodiment of the CCP's ideal image of an emancipated woman, however, paradoxically critiques the characterization of Meng Shih-ching, the very image of the CCP official, whose changing taste in women disqualifies him as an exemplary party representative who is thus expected to be faithful to his wife. Yet as shown in the most ingenious part of the plot, Meng Shih-ching's dramatic action fits the very profile of a good party official: his position as the deputy director of the Department of Agriculture in a provincial committee of the CCP makes it natural for him to feel drawn to Liu Fang-wen, whose enthusiasm for bringing changes to her home village and report on the difficulties of organizing local peasants into collective farming opens his eyes to the reality of rural areas and provides him with new visions for his own leadership role. Their common interests and rural roots—a theme that would have been acceptable under normal circumstances without a complex triangular relationship—nevertheless did not prevent the play from being criticized as a "rightist play" for its "attack on the party and its officials" in spite of—or perhaps even because of—its popular productions by many theater groups throughout the country. On one level, however, such a campaign against this unconventional play was on target: Liu Fang-wen's final departure from Meng Shih-ching, after she has rejected his proposal for remarriage, does not simply repeat the home-leavings of earlier Nora-like characters on the Chinese stage; she rejects a party official of high rank who is supposed to continue to lead the battle for women's liberation, rather than trapping them once again in a patriarchal home.

This extreme view of theater as an avenue for ideological education culminated during the Cultural Revolution. In order to provide new models for creating "proletarian and revolutionary art" to break away from the remnants of the "old cultures," the purveyors of the official Maoist ideology promoted what were then known as the "eight model plays" (later on increased to thirteen), which consisted of five "revolutionary modern Peking operas," two "revolutionary modern ballets," and one "revolutionary symphony." At the height of the Cultural Revolution, with only a few exceptions, such as in the case of some radical novels, "model theater" dramas were the only available works in all genres of literature and art, and almost everyone was compelled to see these theatrical pieces repeatedly for the sake of political education. To no one's surprise, peasant themes became a significant part of model theater, as shown in the ballet versions of "The White-Haired Girl" and in "Hung-se niang-tzu-chün" (The Red Detachment of Women; model ballet version 1970), in which Wu Ch'ing-hua, a slave girl of a rich landlord who, after having escaped from her miserable existence, finds herself transformed into a dedicated and resourceful "woman warrior."

From a different angle, "Lung-chiang sung" (The Song of the Dragon River; model play version 1972), a Peking opera added to the existing series of "model theater" at a later point in the Cultural Revolution, portrayed the heroic deeds of the peasants in the "new society," a theme that had already become predominant among peasant plays in the 1950s and 1960s. Set in 1963 rural China, "The Song of the Dragon River" depicts the dilemma of peasants from the Dragon River Brigade, who must abide by the county party committee's decision to dam the Dragon River in order to save a drought-ridden area. In so doing, the peasants are asked to flood their own land in order to channel water into the drought-ridden area. The dramatic conflict develops around the collective interest of one peripheral local community, whose members have repeatedly been asked to relinquish personal aspirations and dreams for the good of the nation. To achieve this end, the opera uses the narrative of a "bitterness story" about the "old society" to contrast with the "loving and caring government" of socialist China, whose demand for sacrifice in one local community is justified for the sake of helping out another local community. In this way, as presented in the opera, China can, when built up as a strong nation by local communities' willing sacrifices, ultimately take the lead in supporting revolutionary movements in Third World countries, where the remote "brothers and sisters" of the oppressed classes can draw inspiration from the Chinese revolution. In this opera, in an interesting and paradoxical way, the most isolated and rural part of China was most intimately linked to the outside world when the local aims of the Cultural Revolution were justified by the need to continue world revolution.

THE THEATER AFTER MAO

If the peasant plays from the 1950s and 1960s, taken to the extreme in the model theater, seem to validate the glory of a new socialist countryside, post-Mao theater— from 1976 to the present—presented a relatively dark and pessimistic view of the countryside. When Mao Tse-tung died in 1976, theater was among the first media to react enthusiastically against the Maoist tradition with its productions of a series of very popular plays against the Gang of Four, the most prominent supporters of Chairman Mao's Cultural Revolution. One famous example is Tsung Fu-hsien's (b. 1947) "Yü wu-sheng-ch'u" (In a Land of Silence; 1978), which dramatizes the historic April Fifth movement (Ssu-wu yün-tung) of 1976, during which tens of thousands of people gathered in T'ien-an-men Square to pay homage to the late Premier Chou En-lai (popularly viewed as benign) and to protest against the Gang of Four and its radical ideology during the Cultural Revolution.

During the next few years, "peasant theater" caught up with other subgenres in its own staging of popular plays such as Chin Yün's "Kou-erh yeh nieh-p'an" (The Nirvana of Grandpa Doggy; 1986), which can be viewed as an attempt to rewrite the history of the countryside after 1949. Mounted in 1986 by the Peking People's Art Theater (Pei-ching jen-min yi-shu chü-yüan), the play covers the period from 1949 to the present while dramatizing the tragic story of Kou-erh Yeh, a poor peasant whose happiness in finally being able to own his own piece of land after the land reform movement is soon dashed when he feels pushed to join the collective, thus losing his newly acquired land. Heartbroken and disoriented to the point of insanity, Kou-erh Yeh lives in a dream world, where he continues to till his own land without being affected by the political events occurring in his village and elsewhere in the country.

Such subversive rewriting of history for peasants is also seen in "Sang-shu-p'ing chi-shih" (The Story of Sang-shu-p'ing; 1988), by Ch'en Tzu-tu et al., a theatrically innovative play known for its successful experimentation with Greek-style theater. Set in Sang-shu-p'ing, an isolated village in northwestern China, the play represents the sorrow, tragedy, and daily events of this small village, which remained unchanged for thousands of years with regard to its poverty, ignorance, illiteracy, sexual suppression, primitive lifestyle, and brutal patriarchal structure. The sense of futility in attempting to bring about any changes finds its best expression in a bare, revolving stage that alternates between different geographical spaces characteristic of the "yellow earth plateau"—uphill, downhill, and the cave between. As some theater critics have pointed out, the revolving stage, with its many different angles, not only expands theatrical space but also provides the play with a continuously moving performance space, with chorus members singing and dancing as villagers harvest wheat or participate in local rituals. The revolving stage also helps illustrate the insignificance of the individuals in the flow of time: no one, no matter how tragic his or her story may be, amounts to anything more than a passenger on an empty stage, who comes and goes without being able to leave any lasting mark on the course of history.

As part of the literary and dramatic trend known as "reflection on the historical and cultural past" (*li-shih wen-hua fan-ssu*), in its post-Mao attempt to trace the roots of political upheavals such as the Cultural Revolution, this play presents, in the words of its directors, a "living fossil" embodying the cultural and historical sediments of the previous five thousand years in order to call for real changes in contemporary China. Such a call for change was in the first place achieved by creating a space that is changeless. Li Chin-tou, a CCP production team leader, is presented as no different from a local despot in pre-1949 theater, at once a "slave" to his immediate superior and a "tyrant" to the villagers he now rules as a patriarch of a clan. Nowhere in this play is the familiar story of classic socialist theater in which people living in poverty (before 1949) wait to be liberated by their long-expected CCP saviors. The "sea of bitterness and misery of the poor people before liberation" is there in the landscape of contemporary China, only to be worsened with the unfolding events of the Cultural Revolution, the setting of the play.

This play also subverts the CCP feminist rhetoric of the first seventeen years of the PRC. Entirely isolated from the outside world, villagers still arrange marriages for their children, a "feudal" practice supposedly banned by the party. A twelve-year-old girl has to be sold in exchange for a wife for her insane brother, who abuses his wife and finally drives her to suicide. An eighteen-year-old widow throws herself into a T'ang dynasty well in protest against Li Chin-tou, her father-in-law, who forces her to marry his second son after her husband's death, a striking image of a Nora-like female character in post-Mao theater who is not even given a chance to leave home.

Just as important as the subgenre of peasant theater during the first seventeen years of the PRC and its extreme development in the Cultural Revolutionary model plays were the "workers' plays." Like the other subgenres, the workers' plays can be traced back to the period before 1949; for example, T'ien Han's "Mei-yü" (The Rainy Season; 1931), a one-act play that depicts a poor worker's family and its efforts to bring about a better life. Such stories became more popular in the first seventeen years of the PRC, as exemplified in "Hung-se feng-pao" (The Red Storm), which recounted the famous Peking-Hankow railroad workers' strikes that were brutally suppressed by the warlord Wu P'ei-fu and his foreign supporters on February 7, 1923. The following legendary story illustrates theater artists' dedication to and enthusiasm for workers' plays: Chin Shan (1911–1982)—himself functioning at once as the playwright, director, and lead actor in the "unforgettable" role of Shih Yang, the "great and magnificent lawyer" who had supported the workers' strikes—spent only seventy-two hours rehearsing the play before its successful premiere by the China Youth Theater (Chung-kuo ch'ing-nien yi-shu chü-yüan) in 1958, a record-breaking event with unprecedented ticket sales.

The 1960s theme in the workers' plays, however, shifted dramatically to a focus on the education of the younger generation of workers "never to forget" such a revolutionary history and "never to forget the class struggle," as expressed in the title of Ts'un Shen's (b. 1928) play "Ch'ien-wan pu-yao wang-chi" (Never Forget). First mounted by the Harbin Theater (Ha-erh-pin hua-chü-yüan) in 1964, and soon staged throughout the country, "Never Forget" depicts a young worker whose desire for a better material life is criticized as a negative example of a worker's family being "eroded" by bourgeois ideology.

This constant need to remind the Chinese people of their "bitter past" and of the revolutionary heritage of the working class was showcased in the model opera "The Red Lantern." Set in the 1930s, during the anti-Japanese war, "The Red Lantern" tells the story of Li Yü-ho, a poor railway worker who adopted a mother and orphan girl, whose family members had been murdered during the Peking-Hankow railway workers' strikes. Unlike "The Red Storm," however, which depicts an epic scene of masses of workers participating in the strikes, "The Red Lantern" focuses on the history of a single family: Li Yü-ho and his adopted mother were captured, tortured, and finally executed by a Japanese police chief for not revealing information entrusted to them by the guerrillas. Carrying out the last wishes of her father and grandmother, Li T'ieh-mei (Li Yü-ho's adopted daughter) finally succeeds in sending secret codes to the CCP guerrillas.

With this simple story line, "The Red Lantern" ingeniously denied blood relationships—the basis of families in all cultures—while extending its hierarchical and cohesive structure to the creation of "one big revolutionary family" whose members share a "common class interest" in the fight against their "common enemies." On a different level and yet with a similar strategy, "Hai-kang" (On the Dock; model play version 1972) constructed a global discourse of "world revolution" in its portrayal of the working class in cosmopolitan Shanghai, whose daily work of loading and unloading oceangoing ships to and from the outside world was said to have been closely related to the liberation of the oppressed Third World peoples suffering from the exploitation of Western imperialism and colonialism. The heroes and heroines in those model plays were transformed and idealized as "role models" for the proper behavior of the "revolutionary masses" during the height of the Cultural Revolution.

If Maoist theater from 1949 to 1976, in its various stages of development, presented a gradual progression toward the necessity of "class struggle" in workers' theater, post-Maoist theater distinguishes itself by challenging such views. Known as one of the earliest and most popular anti–Gang-of-Four plays, Ts'ui Te-chih's (b. 1927) "Pao ch'un hua" (Winter Jasmine), first performed by the Liao-ning People's Art Theater (Liao-ning jen-min yi-shu chü-yüan) in 1979, for instance, recounts the discrimination suffered by Pai Chieh, a young female worker in a textile factory, because of her "politically incorrect" family origins: her father had at one time been declared a "counterrevolutionary" for having worked for the KMT government before 1949, and her mother had been declared a "rightist" for having challenged the CCP's radical policies in 1957. The very introduction of Pai Chieh to the Chinese stage marked a historic occasion, for, even before the Cultural Revolution, when the party's policies were less rigid and dogmatic, there had never been a postrevolutionary play in which the protagonist came from a "questionable" class background; the proscription against such a class background extended to all works of literature and art in order, it was said, to serve the best interests of the party, the working people, and the proletarian revolutionary course.

"Winter Jasmine" was followed by a whole series of anti–Gang of Four plays, such as Hsing Yi-hsün's "Ch'üan yü fa" (Power Versus Law; 1979), in which the wife and daughter of a "rightist" are protected by a party secretary newly assigned to his post after the overthrow of the Gang of Four, but this is a party secretary with a difference, for he sees it as his own mission to expose corruption and crimes within the party system itself. Such a positive portrayal of a party representative, however, is challenged in another highly controversial play entitled "Chia-ju wo shih chen-te" (If I Were for Real; 1979), by Sha Yeh-hsin et al., in which a young man from a worker's family without any connection to the privileged and the powerful has no choice but to impersonate the son of an important party official in order to get permission to return to his home city to marry his pregnant girlfriend before she delivers the baby. The play's setting in post-Mao China made it suspect: its critique of the party's corruption was obviously not limited to the Gang of Four, who were no longer in power. It was therefore permitted only forty-six performances in Shanghai for "controlled audiences," audiences that usually consisted of theater critics and officials from various levels of the party hierarchy who were trusted not to be influenced by the play's potential "harmful content."

Among many anti–Gang of Four plays are what theater historians call "plays about revolutionary leaders," which depict the wartime stories of high-ranking CCP and army officials, some of whom, in real life, had been persecuted during the Cultural Revolution, such as Ch'en Yi (1901–1972), Ho Lung (1896–1976), Chu Te, and Liu Shao-ch'i (1898–1969). Indeed, such a tradition of wartime drama, which can be generally grouped under the subgenre of "plays about soldiers," can be traced back to Hung Shen's "Chao Yen-wang" (Yama Chao) in 1922, a play that dramatizes the ordeal of an orderly in a warlord's army from which he has attempted unsuccessfully to escape. The meaninglessness of fighting in a corrupt army in Hung Shen's play, however, was naturally reversed in 1933, when the Soldier's Drama Troupe (Chan-shih chü-she) of the Red Amy in the "Soviet Area" of Jui-chin, Kiangsi province—location of the CCP headquarters—performed "Pa-yi Nan-ch'ang ch'i-yi" (August First Uprising in Nanch'ang; 1933), by Nieh Jung-chen and others, and Li Cho-jan's "Lu-shan chih hsüeh" (The Snow on Lu Mountain; 1933), plays that portrayed revolutionary war experiences as heroic and epoch-making events. Although both plays were representations of real battles won by the CCP troops against the KMT, the performance of the latter was a more unusual theater experience, with high-ranking military commanders such as Nieh Jung-chen, Lin Piao (1907–1971), and Lo Jung-huan (1902–1963) playing their own real-life roles in the CCP army, whereas Lo Jui-ch'ing (1906–1978), another top CCP commander, played the part of their dread enemy Chiang K'ai-shek, the generalissimo of the KMT. Such an event, known in theater history as "soldiers playing soldiers and commanders playing commanders" (*ping yen ping, chiang yen chiang*), was said to have greatly raised the morale of the Red Army and helped shape a dramatic tradition that became part of the revolutionary war experience itself.

These soldiers' plays or wartime dramas had their most popular productions in the first seventeen years of the PRC, for example in Hu K'o's "Chan-tou li ch'eng-chang" (Growing up in the Battlefield; 1950), which tells of a poor peasant's transformation into an army official and his final reunion with his father, who happens to be another "soldier" in the same army unit. Such a family drama built around the twists and turns of the war drama found a new form in Ch'en Ch'i-t'ung's (b. 1916) "Wan-shui ch'ien-shan" (Rivers and Mountains; 1954), an epic play narrating the most difficult journeys during the Long March (the successful retreat of the CCP army from KMT encirclement in the Kiangsi Soviet to Yenan in Shensi [October 1934–October 1935]).

In contrast to the soldiers' plays of the 1950s that emphasized war experience, "Ni-hung teng-hsia te shao-ping" (Soldiers Under Neon Light), by Shen Hsi-meng (b. 1919) et al., which premiered in 1962, represents the soldier's changing life in a "peaceful" China, when the call to the "battlefield" has been transformed into the call to resist corruption by "bourgeois influence." Situated in cosmopolitan Shanghai immediately after its "liberation" around 1949, "Soldiers Under Neon Light" represents the tenacious effort of a company in the People's Liberation Army (PLA) to keep their simple lifestyle and revolutionary spirit intact while resisting the temptations of materialism during their patrols on Nanking Road, the busiest commercial street in Shanghai, hence the stronghold of imperialist and bourgeois influence. Among other diverse soldier characters on stage is Chun-ni, another kind of "Nora" character in 1960s China, who, after a brief reunion with her husband in the army unit, returns to her home village with a broken heart, leaving behind a letter to the company's commander in which she expresses her sadness over her husband's transformation from a brave soldier during the revolutionary war to a petty and weak man tempted by a bourgeois lifestyle in Shanghai. As in the classics of socialist drama, the act of home-leaving on the part of Chun-ni, however, expresses hope: she is confident that she will soon find a new sense of belonging in pursuing her own dream back home in the countryside, where, as part of a new revolutionary family, she will have a fulfilling life with a bright future. If part of the 1960s theme in the soldiers' plays is to resist corruption and to represent a model unit as incorruptible, however, Mo Yen (b. 1956) and Hsiao Yü-tse's "Sung chih-tao-yüan te jih-chi" (The Diary of Instructor Sung), a post-Mao play first presented in 1982, goes in the opposite direction, with a dramatic eyewitness account of how much corruption is indeed occurring within both the army and the party, as filtered through the diary of Instructor Sung, who almost single-handedly fights against this corruption.

Such a play is, of course, a direct reaction against the Maoist tradition of the soldiers' play, which had culminated in the model theater. The subject of the Peking opera "Sha-chia-pang" (the title is the name of an area of lakes and marshes in Kiangsu; model play version 1970), for instance, is an "armed struggle" during the War of Resistance against Japan in which Kuo Chien-kuang, a political instructor of the New Fourth Army (CCP army based in Shantung and Kiangsu that was nearly wiped out in January 1941), and seventeen wounded soldiers defeat KMT troops who are collaborating with the Japanese invaders. The Peking opera "Ch'i-hsi pai-hu-t'uan" (Raid on the White Tiger Regiment; model play version 1972) depicts the "War to Resist the United States and Aid Korea," during which Yen Wei-ts'ai, leader of a scout platoon of the Chinese People's Volunteers, overthrows the "invincible" White Tiger Regiment of the South Korean army, advised by U.S. military personnel. In the Peking opera "Chih-ch'ü wei-hu-shan" (Taking Tiger Mountain by Strategy; model play version 1970), Yang Tzu-jung, a PLA scout, ventures into enemy headquarters in an effort to liberate the poor people. These dramas provided "model plays" with theatrical means by which the Maoist memory of a past Communist revolution was invoked in order to promote a "continuous revolution," the Cultural Revolution, in post-1949 Chinese society.

Intricately related to wartime experience is the dramatization of women's roles in such experiences, which is also epitomized in model theater, where women characters were transformed from subalterns into revolutionary warriors and party leaders. Portrayed as lacking families or attraction to the opposite sex, women in "model plays" were deprived of womanhood, motherhood, and the intimacy of family life. In this "Cultural Revolutionary feminism," the issue of woman's exploitation and inequality is exploited for the consolidation of political and state power. The "worker-peasant-soldier model women"—depicted onstage in order ultimately to be imitated in real life—were fundamentally reduced to the status of the "revolutionary masses," whose only reason for being was to celebrate the "political correctness" of the Communist Party and Mao.

As reactions against such an inherently antifeminist tradition, early post-Mao women's theater finds its best examples in the trilogy written by Pai Feng-hsi (b. 1934), a female playwright whose writing experience had benefited greatly from her earlier career as a successful actress. "Ming-yüeh ch'u-chao jen" (First Bathed in Moonlight; 1981) has as its protagonist Fang Jo-ming, the director of the Provincial Women's Federation, a key position in the socialist state apparatus that regulates the life of women from all walks of life. Excited by the post-Mao regime's call to realize the "Four Modernizations" (agriculture, industry, science and technology, and defense), Fang Jo-ming devotes herself to solving marital disputes in the remote, isolated countryside, where women in poverty are sold into marriages for economic gain. Such attempts to help other, less fortunate women, however, lead her to realize that she is also part of the conspiracy against women: her daughter has yet to gain her approval for her boyfriend from the countryside, whose sister has been forced into an arranged marriage so that his family can afford a wedding for their only son. The portrayal of Fang Jo-ming as both a positive and negative party official in charge of the task of "women's liberation" made the play both a hit with audiences—who sent the playwright more than three hundred letters expressing their enthusiasm and support—and a controversy among theater critics, who argued for a more optimistic view of the figure of the women's leader in socialist China. In a way similar in thematic concern and dramatic style, Pai Feng-hsi's two other plays, "Feng-yü ku-jen lai" (An Old Friend Comes at a Stormy Time; 1983) and "Puchih ch'iu-ssu tsai shui chia" (Where Is Longing in Autumn; 1986), focus on dynamic and challenging mother/daughter relationships among intellectuals and their new identity formation in the post-Mao market economy.

Whereas Pai Feng-hsi's trilogy continued the May Fourth tradition of Pai Wei, who depicted loving mothers and courageous daughters waging a fierce struggle against the patriarchal society, while challenging the Maoist myth of "women's liberation" in socialist China, other female playwrights, such as Chang Li-li (b. 1956), as shown in her play "Lü-se ying-ti" (Green Barracks; 1992), continued to be fascinated with the soldiers' play, especially that of "women warriors." Making use of national allegories, national-identity themes, and the national discourse of post-Maoist China, her women's plays paradoxically revived, if they did not actually empower, the seemingly "old-fashioned" image of women warriors. The women warriors portrayed in post-Maoist theater nevertheless are not mere copies of the Maoist "liberated women" as a collective female body. They fundamentally challenged the plight of the mythical women warriors and attempted to reclaim female subjectivity within the limited space of the PLA, the most male-dominated and restrictive domain in the public arena. To a large extent, then, women warriors were recovered for the public stage by female playwrights who felt deeply the sense of lost self-esteem and identity experienced by women during a tidal wave of economic reforms. In the early post-Mao period, when female playwrights, confronted with the swift expansion of new forms of social organization, capitalism, and urbanization, initially attempted to reclaim the private and familial domains as a means of forging individual connections to the social and public spheres, they met with disappointing results. This historical regression from discontented mother and wife to vibrant woman warrior and leader in post-Mao women's theater illustrates the reflexive, self-evaluating process in which contemporary Chinese women, as masters of their own fate, refuse to be signified as negative reference points from which to ground male positivity. Once again they long to be able to "hold up half of the sky" and to be equal with their male counterparts both at home and in the public sphere.

In spite of its intimate relationship to public life, the story of modern Chinese drama is not only about national and personal identities, or about race, class, and sexual politics. Indeed, most of the popular plays known for their formalistic features from the inception of modern Chinese drama, especially during the early post-Mao period when drama experienced a "renaissance," can be seen as developments of what could be called "the six traditions" of modern Chinese theater: (1) illusionist theater, as seen in Pai Feng-hsi's women's trilogy, Kuo Mo-jo's history plays, and most of the realist plays and history plays; (2) indigenous theater, as seen in Peking-style plays like "The Nirvana of Grandpa Doggy"; (3) modernist theater, as seen in Kao Hsing-chien's (b. 1940) "Ch'e-chan" (Bus Stop; 1983); (4) epic theater, as seen in the Brechtian "If I Were for Real"; (5) suggestive theater, as seen in "Chung-kuo meng" (China Dream; 1987) by William H. Sun and Faye C. Fei; and (6) Greek theater, as seen in "The Story of Sang-shu-p'ing" by Ch'en Tzu-tu and others. These traditions, either separately or combined, represent Chinese dramatists' attempts to avail themselves of what they considered the most appropriate formalist features from both the Oriental and the Occidental traditions.

COMING TO TERMS WITH THE SPECTER OF LAO SHE

Among these traditions, the most uniquely "Chinese" style can be found in a group of indigenous Peking-style plays initiated by Lao She's scripts and perfected by the "second creation" in stage performance by artists from the Peking People's Art Theater. Using the local vernacular language and dialectal expressions unique to the old Peking culture, "Lung-hsü-kou" (Dragon Beard Ditch; 1950) dramatizes the life story of the poor Peking citizen—such as the folklore performer, the rickshaw puller, the bricklayer, and the mother and daughter who live around Dragon Beard Ditch (the stinking slum street that for generations has trapped poor people in the old society)—and the government efforts to rebuild the neighborhood soon after the "liberation" of Peking in 1949. As a result of the successful performance of "Dragon Beard Ditch," Lao She was awarded the title of "people's artist" by the CCP Municipal Committee of Peking, the only such honor ever given to any artist in Maoist China.

In a similar style, "Ch'a-kuan" (Teahouse), Lao She's second "masterpiece," which premiered in 1958, represents on stage more than sixty vivid characters—old Peking citizens including an imperial wrestler, a eunuch, a prostitute, a pimp, a birdlover, a fortuneteller, two KMT secret agents, two deserters, an industrialist, a property owner—as they go in and out of a teahouse, from 1898 to 1945, after the defeat of the Japanese. While alluding to many crucial historical events, the play focuses on the rise and fall of the teahouse and the struggles and sorrows experienced by the shopkeeper's family and friends. In spite of Lao She's intention to satirize the three declining political regimes and their failure to bring Peking citizens a decent life in order to celebrate a "new society," "Teahouse," written in 1957 at the height of the antirightist movement, was deemed controversial because it allegedly expressed the playwright's sympathy for the property-owner shopkeeper in the old society rather than depicting the "heroic deeds" of the common people in the Great Leap Forward movement then under way.

The haunting memory of Lao She's suicide in 1966 during the Cultural Revolution to protest his unfair treatment as a dramatist was finally brought to an end with the watershed 1979 revival of "Teahouse" by the Peking People's Art Theater. Such an event became, in a way typical of the nature of the entire history of modern Chinese drama, an act of real-life theater against the status quo in a national arena, in which scene after scene of political drama was rehearsed and reinvented on the smaller stage of the theater itself. The culminating act of such theater in the broader sense finds its denouement in "Teahouse"'s successful tours in Germany, France, Switzerland, Japan, Canada, and Hong Kong in the 1980s, tours that marked the first instance of the "export" of modern Chinese spoken drama to the international stage—hence, the admission of one of China's most indigenous dramas as a "masterpiece" of world theater. In a way most relevant to the central concerns of this chapter, "Teahouse"'s journey to the outside world simultaneously completes the "journey home," a journey that was undertaken at the very beginning of the twentieth century, when the first generation of Chinese dramatists traveled to Japan and to the West in search of an "elixir" for reviving Chinese theater—and thereby the Chinese nation.

Xiaomei Chen

PART VI

Commentary, Criticism, and Interpretation

Chapter 43

THE RHETORIC OF PREMODERN PROSE STYLE

Among the manifestations of China's culture, Chinese literary style is surely one of the most distinctive. One might say that a comprehensive study of the evolution and metamorphoses of this style would constitute, in a sense, a history of Chinese literature. It is well, furthermore, to recognize the importance of style not only as a vehicle, but as a shaping factor, of philosophical attitudes and concepts.

—Yoshikawa Kōjirō, "The *Shih-shuo hsin-yü* and Six Dynasties Prose Style," in John L. Bishop, ed., *Studies in Chinese Literature* (Cambridge: Harvard University Press, 1965), p. 166.

The difficulty in describing the culture of Chinese rhetoric is compounded by the proliferation of rhetorical subtraditions. Thus at least three profoundly distinct groups must be distinguished: (1) the popular folkloric traditions; (2) the jejune professional scientific traditions; and (3) the literary traditions. These three literary cultures in China interacted only to a limited extent. The compressed algebraic prose of the Mohist scientists (see chapter 3) in the third and fourth centuries, for example, owes as little to the high literary conventions that already informed the emerging Confucian *Lun-yü* (Analects) as do some of the nonliterary and less hermetically inaccessible plain professional medical treatises. However, the vernacular tales of China never aspired to any of this scientific plainness or the concise parallelism of ornate artistic prose. Because of the inherent limitations in the stylistic registers of Western languages like English when compared to Chinese, this immense variety inherent in Chinese literary culture is radically reduced in European translations. Certain simplifications are inevitable when surveying this vast landscape of rhetorical variety in China.

This chapter considers the rhetoric of classical Chinese prose style from three distinct but intimately related perspectives.

First, what did the premodern Chinese traditions of rhetorical thought have to say about their ideals of prose style? This chapter presents an overview of relevant classical Chinese views on rhetoric.

Second, we must ask about traditional Chinese rhetorical practices. We must inquire into the basic conventions of literary communication, the artistic principles and the history of classical Chinese artistic prose styles. This chapter proposes some basic hypotheses on the nature and evolution of classical Chinese prose style.

Third, how did classical Chinese prose style compare to, for example, classical Latin and classical Greek prose style, and what were the specific features of the Chinese case? To seek an answer, it is useful to explore rhetorical analysis in the Western tradition, which is conveniently systematized in standard handbooks. In a comparativist spirit, one may consider the range of rhetorical figures and tropes prominent in Western rhetoric since Aristotle, Cicero, and Quintilian, and go on to ask how prominent they are in classical Greek and Latin compared to classical Chinese artistic prose. More important, one should compare the basic features in the ethnography of literary communication in classical Chinese versus Greek and Latin.

The typological and the comparative characterization of classical Chinese prose style cannot be summarized at this stage. At best it can be intuitively and tentatively characterized on the basis of existing pioneering work, in the hope that such a preliminary characterization will spark the kind of detailed research needed to make intuitions into informed hypotheses.

TRADITIONAL CHINESE VIEWS ON RHETORIC

Confucius maintained that when words get their message across, one should stop (*Analects* 15.41). What was admired in Confucius was his flair for *wei-yen* (subtle speech), which, without being *yin* (hidden, arcane, riddlelike), achieved that peculiar subtle variety of *ming* (translucence, perspicuousness) which became so essential to the classical Chinese esthetic. It was of the essence of this translucent, limpid effect that it was preferably achieved with an austere economy of stylistic means, an apparent sparseness of effort, a naturalness, the elegant light touch.

This ideal of translucence and perspicuousness, then, is not an intellectual clarity brought about by elaborate explicitness or definiteness of meaning. The text is designed to inspire in the reader the congenial but active and even creative production of artistic sense. The texts do not impose meaning; rather, they are designed to inspire the creation of sense. The creation of this sense is a social act, part of the anthropological space into which written documents inscribe themselves in China. Ideally, classical Chinese texts sow the seeds of meaning in the reader rather than transmitting explicitly the fruits of thought. Thus ancient Chinese texts cultivate an implicit mutual understanding. They tend to be pregnant with a socially constructed meaning, rather than directly expressive of a meaning exclusively imposed on the reader by the writer. Under these circumstances, literary meaning in artistic prose does not typically purport to be the product of an individual writer. It presents itself as a product of a hermeneutic process in which the reader plays an important creative part.

Thus the reading technique made proverbial by the poet T'ao Yüan-ming (365–427)—which consists in not aiming for a deep explanation (*pu ch'iu shen chieh*)—is congenial to the rhetorical conventions of the language in the sense that preciseness aimed at getting the author's meaning exactly has a false ring to it in the context of the preferred Chinese rhetoric, insofar as the text ideally should leave the reader free to develop its suggestiveness. The fact that many kinds of Chinese literature do not aim for this suggestiveness does not disprove the point. It only goes to show that not all Chinese prose aimed for the preferred ornate rhetoric of the culture. Indeed the *k'ao-cheng* school (School of Philological Inquiry) during the Ch'ing dynasty (1644–1911) was almost maniacally dedicated to making very precise indeed all the meanings in the classics, and this school was only carrying to extremes tendencies toward explicitness that are present in earlier commentarial literature.

The Greeks were known in antiquity as loquacious and contentious people, and Greek texts are also semantically pugnacious: through definition and explicitness, they push the reader around, aim to force an intended meaning on him or her, and compel him or her to acknowledge an objective truth that the text sets out to make explicit; in short, they aim to appear to give a complete picture of a certain reality.

The preferred rhetoric of Chinese texts eschews mundane pugnaciousness: the philosopher Hsün Tzu (c. 300–c. 219 B.C.E.) is a striking exception when he hammers home the philosophical point that man is by nature evil, and his point was not generally well received. The pontificating, repetitive, itemized dogmatism in some parts of the book *Mo Tzu* (c. fourth century B.C.E.) may have been a delight for Western interpreters of Chinese philosophy, but it was rhetorically marginal in Chinese literary culture. Wang Ch'ung's (27–c. 97 C.E.) plain persistence of style was despised throughout the millennia. Such exceptions show the pluralism in Chinese rhetorical practice. But below all this pluralism, there is an underlying general esthetic core of what was perceived to be elegant. This core must be explored before other subjects can be discussed.

The ornate classical Chinese text does not tend to bully the reader pugnaciously through argument; neither does it coerce the reader by imposing meaning on him. Chinese texts tend to lay out in harmonious patterns points that cajole rather than compel. These texts suggest rather than impose meaning, and they may suggest certain kinds of conclusions to be drawn from this. They leave the reader a peculiar inner fertile space of freedom (*yü ti*) in which the energy of the pregnant thought expressed in the text is designed to take root and gain a life of its own, inspired by and in the spirit of the harmoniously patterned text, which allows the reader to breathe freely. The preferred kind of stylistic beauty is not the flashy kind, but the superficially bland, limpid kind in which the deep esthetic-cum-intellectual energy is all the more powerful through being imperceptible. The texts, as it were, use suggestive watercolor in preference to heavy oil pigments. Thus classical Chinese prose is often stylistically coterminous with poetry.

A useful concept to capture the special genius of Chinese prose style is that of polite and gentle tentativeness, as opposed to the fundamentally more direct and aggressive assertiveness that is the default mode of Latin or Greek prose style. The cantankerous bluntness of ancient Greek comedy is uncongenial to mainstream Chinese literary culture, though not completely absent. So is the compelling and searching emotional explicitness of ancient Greek tragedy. And so is the relentlessly probing, flippantly aggressive persistence of Plato's Socrates, as well as the comprehensively domineering, magisterial explicitness of an Aristotle or a Sextus Empiricus.

To traditional Chinese stylistic sensibilities, all such forms are *ts'u* (crude), without the pregnant inner energy of the noncoercive discourse that is *wei* (subtle). The overexplicitness of the Greek stylistic modes of comedy, tragedy, and so on has something gross and uncouth about it: sexual explicitness is just one symptom of a perceived general inability to leave to the imagination what is much more potent when left to the imagination.

Chinese texts do not normally aspire to capture a reality through some sort of *mimēsis*. Rather, they gesture toward inspiring features of a more hidden reality, sowing these seeds of inspiration in the docile and acquiescent minds of the intended audience, which expects to grow through this experience. In this context "text" is esoteric through an inner cultural logic, not by cultural coincidence: the text requires a docile audience ready for esthetic human growth.

Again, it is by an inner cultural logic that the esthetic and intellectual seeds that are to grow in the audience must have the implicit, unreleased dynamism of *wei* (subtlety). What is crudely explicit is acquired by accretion, not integration. It can never enter as such into the core of human sensibilities. If what is crudely explicit enters the human mind on a large scale, it may grow very big, like a large intellectual excrescence, but it will not affect that core "spiritual" or intellectual orientation. Things will be merely *chih* (understood), but not *t'i* (embodied).

"Much learning [*polumathiē*] does not teach sense," said Heraclitus, with shadowy wisdom. He could not quite have made that caustic comment in these terms for China, where the *chih-nang* (sack of knowledge) is traditionally despised by common consent, and where the presumed and sometimes even superimposed rhetoric of texts to be studied (*hsüeh*) is designed primarily for edification rather than for information, according to Chinese literary values.

Chinese writers were often positively obsessed with getting the facts and dates right. But what is informative and correct without purporting to be ultimately edifying morally and politically will, for this very reason, "never ascend the hall of elegant significance" (*pu shang/teng ta ya chih t'ang*). The heady, bland, explicit, and analytical style of writing did develop in China and was, of course, crucial for the development of the sciences, but it was not cultivated as artistic prose, as was the style of Plato in Athens or that of Tacitus in Rome.

If one surveys classical Greek and Latin literature as well as the Christian literary tradition insofar as it was shaped by this classical heritage, there is no doubt that in traditionalist Chinese eyes these suffer from chronic, obsessive overexplicitness and thus ultimately esthetic and rhetorical crudeness. It is not that one could not be subtle and discreet in the Western tradition, but one can forgive a learned traditional Chinese if, after the necessary intensive study of these literatures in the original Greek and Latin languages, he comes to feel that subtlety in Western literature, by Chinese standards, has a disastrous tendency to be itself elephantine in its overexplicit theoretical pomposity and doctrinaire in its theoretical underpinning. The core of traditional Chinese rhetorical esthetics is the ethereal, intellectual light touch, the esthetic and reflective pinch of cultural salt, an acute sense of what is inevitably left unsaid.

The virtue of this subtle indirectness is not due to some "genius of the Chinese language" or culture: it was born of necessity when one was writing in an environment where it was highly dangerous to write the wrong thing. To be sure, there are limitations to what one can write and say everywhere. Aristophanes was taken to court for what he wrote, and Socrates was condemned to death for what he said. But the degree to which writers wrote in fear of the authorities breathing coldly down their necks varied significantly. In a highly hierarchical and authoritarian society like that of traditional China, indirect discourse may well have originated as a safety measure and was perhaps only later and incidentally estheticized, making a virtue of necessity. One can merely say that it did indeed become a crucial virtue of Chinese literary style, giving this style a peculiar unreleased potency and power that is rare in what in this perspective appears as the rather crude classical European literary tradition.

Thus it is not a coincidence that the ethereal art of calligraphy and the rarefied spirituality of Chinese landscape painting have no counterpart in the West. It is as if we are witnessing an esthetic syndrome: it is as if the tremendous, quintessentially unreleased, inner potential of ethereal, rarified, evanescent sensibility cultivated to excess in Chinese calligraphy and landscape painting, and manifesting itself also in the best of Chinese prose style, was not a spiritual mode particularly cultivated in classical European literature.

And it is in the art of Chinese poetry that these ethereal sensibilities are fully celebrated for their own sake—to the point even of becoming something of an ethereal routine. Thus, in a peculiar sense, Chinese prose style at its best has something profoundly poetic about it, indeed verges on the poetic—just as Chinese poetry, at its best, is often like a "crude," linguistic sound–bound premeditation for the appreciation of the elusive spirituality of the best of Chinese calligraphy and painting.

What strikes us as elusiveness here is in fact a Chinese version of Roman *urbanitas,* which consists essentially in a rhetorical pose that politely presupposes a high culture of sensibility in the audience, where artistic prose, far from presuming to shape the thinking of the audience, limits itself to subtly stimulating what is politely assumed to be already there and to stimulating this in what necessarily aspires to be a congenial way. The text invites the readers to tease out the meaning and significance from the text. The high point of this rhetorical technique of subtlety is the evanescent semantics of the art of calligraphy, which celebrates the ethereal learned sensibility per se.

Whatever is decorative in this subtle art is incidental, and manifest, attractive decorativeness tends toward vulgarity in the learned Chinese perception of calligraphy. So far as we know, there is nothing whatever to compare to this even remotely in the European calligraphic tradition, for the very essence of Western calligraphy is esthetic and decorative, rather than "spiritual" and personally expressive. (Arabic calligraphy likewise has much stronger decorative elements than the Chinese.) In any case, the absence of anything whatever to compare to Chinese calligraphy in the European tradition is not just a historical coincidence; it is a telling symptom of a deep difference in the dominant communicative structures in these civilizations.

Even today, the stylistic difference is manifested in such genres as that of the love letter: surveys show that modern Chinese love letters are significantly more reticent, discreet, and indirect than their European counterparts. Like Classical Chinese texts, they tentatively leave to the imagination what Western rhetoric encourages us to make more definite and explicit.

From the fourth century C.E. to the present, calligraphy has been an endemic esthetic obsession of the Chinese people. Through this obsession, the culture celebrates a reticent esthetic mode that was a central strain in the formation of Chinese rhetorical sensibilities.

ORNATE PROSE RHYTHM

The preferred length of a colon (breath group) in ornate prose rhythm was four characters; cola of six and seven characters are also fairly common, cola of three or five characters can occur as well but only as exceptional rhythms. Other cola are extremely unusual and found only in special circumstances.

In ornate prose, the preferred rhythm is pairs of similar or corresponding units in which the natural "default" emphasis is on the second member of the pair. In the simplest case, the unit is simply a breath group or colon, but the correspondence can also be between larger units like a complex period (a group of two or more cola). Learning to understand Chinese artistic prose is learning to hear these rhythmic units and their modulated parallelisms as well as contrasts.

The structure of the ornate prose style can be basically described as consisting of two parts of unequal prosodic weight, LIGHT HEAVY, in which both the light and the heavy may again consist of complex structures of the same LIGHT HEAVY type. This simple rule explains a vast number of ornate passages in ancient Chinese literature long before the flourishing of *p'ien-t'i wen* (parallel prose) in the early sixth century and also long before the extensive, deliberate use of parallelism in poetry and prose from around 100 C.E. onward (see chapter 12).

If four lines are mostly parallel but one deviates slightly, the deviating line is regularly the third line. Even in what we would call prose, there often is rhyme. If there are four rhyming lines in prose, of which one rhyme is imperfect (or even absent), the imperfect line is again regularly the third line. In longer sequences, the general rule is that when there is deviation of any kind—semantic, rhythmic, or phonetic—the penultimate line is the deviating one. It is as if the penultimate deviation prepares the reader for the end of a sequence.

Unpatterned, nonparallel rhythms are allowable, of course, even in ornate prose, and especially in short direct speech. But as soon as such direct speech becomes long and argumentative, it tends to conform to the general preferred patterns of prose style.

A special feature that gave an extraordinary richness to much of post-Buddhist Chinese artistic prose is a varying but pervasive tendency to switch between vernacular and classical styles within a given piece of writing, even within a given sentence or phrase. The style of commentarial literature from the Later Han dynasty onward is of special interest because it occasionally allows us conveniently to compare the classical originals to their often more colloquial later paraphrases and literary expansions. A fine early example of this is the commentary by Chao Ch'i (d. 201 C.E.) on *Meng Tzu* (Mencius). Chao writes in a meticulously overexplicit, belabored prose style that is perhaps wrongly identified as Late Han colloquial Chinese but that certainly draws on important features of Late Han colloquial speech. Striking later examples of standard colloquial Chinese translations of the classics are such Yüan dynasty (1260–1368) works as *"Ta-hsüeh" yao lüeh* (A Summary of the "Great Learning"), *"Chung-yung" chih chieh* (Direct Explanation of the "Doctrine of the Mean"), and *"Hsiao-ching" chih chieh* (Direct Explanation of the *Classic of Filial Piety*). These translations are kept in a deliberately jejune "official," standard colloquial style, as indeed is *Yüan tien chang* (The Legal Code of the Yüan Dynasty). Texts like these represent an officially sanctioned, unadorned vernacular prose style, promoted and cultivated, in part, no doubt, for easy comprehension by non-Chinese Mongol readers of Chinese.

These styles are in marked contrast to the more subcultural use of colloquial styles in narrative prose especially from the T'ang (618–907) and Sung (960–1279) dynasties as well as from the Ming (1368–1644) and Ch'ing (1644–1911) eras. Here the colloquialism of style, which always thrives on ample admixture of classical literary elements, was intended for a rising Han bourgeoisie.

Indeed, one of the crucial rhetorical features of traditional Chinese literature is that so much of it thrives on switching between grammatically distinct linguistic registers. In pre-Han times, the literary style could naturally switch to archaisms or abruptly introduce colloquial elements, but there is little evidence of a neat grammatical break between literary and colloquial forms. The historian Ssu-ma Ch'ien (c. 145–c. 86 B.C.E.) judiciously deploys occasional colloquial forms to characterize some parts of his dialog. However, even at this rare level of stylistic sophistication, the contrast exploited is more one of style than of grammatical structure.

In a deliberate act of stylistic and rhetorical revolution, the early Buddhist translators and propagators of that religion, which was directed toward the populace at large, gradually came to move from their outlandish and often awkward, colloquial-inspired "translationese" Buddhist hybrid style to a more indigenous, polished vernacular language with a markedly different grammar from the literary language used in secular Chinese contexts that basically purported to maintain the grammar and style of the Warring States (403–221) classics. *Shih-shuo hsin-yü* (New Account of Tales of the World), by Liu Yi-ch'ing (403–444), shows an awareness of Buddhism in many places, and his work is written in a prose style that elegantly moves from the vernacular to literary styles. This book thus sets the scene for a long tradition of "informal" Chinese literature in which the grammar is not homogeneous and where the switching from one stylistic code to a grammatically different one becomes endemic. The effect of this code-switching may be compared to the language mixing in much European Renaissance literature: Martin Luther switched from German to Latin in his *Table Talk* in the same way that informal Chinese writers in the Sung period *yü-lu* (recorded sayings) tradition came to switch from the classical to the colloquial language within one sentence. Thus the long series of Zen (Ch'an) Buddhist *yü-lu* became a crucial factor in the expansion of the range of mixed traditional Chinese prose style.

The predominantly Buddhist *pien-wen* (transformation texts) from the T'ang dynasty are not written in purely vernacular Chinese: they developed the art of weaving together colloquial and classical elements into a highly sophisticated pattern, which gave this literature an extraordinarily energetic depth of stylistic dynamism that came to inform the Chinese tradition first of the short story and then of the novel. In all these media, the author was free to use elements of vernacular Chinese without being constrained from including highly classical styles.

By the time of *Chu-tzu yü-lei* (Classified Conversations of Master Chu), the recorded conversations of the Neo-Confucian thinker Chu Hsi (1130–1200) compiled by Li Ching-te in 1270, this mixed colloquial-classical style had not only been perfected to very considerable rhetorical and artistic effect but had also entered the realm of serious "philosophical" literature. Ch'en Ch'un (1159–1223), in *Pei-hsi tzu yi* (The Meanings of Words by Ch'en Ch'un), went so far as to write a whole book on the semantics of philosophical terms in a heavily colloquial mixed style, which otherwise tended to be associated with informal traditions of narrative fiction and folk literature. The rhetorical message of Ch'en Ch'un's stylistic choice was clear enough: he aimed to preserve in his philosophical disquisitions something of the informal, intimate, and personal touch for which Chu Hsi's discourses had become so famous. It would be possible to reproduce some of this mixed style if one were to blend Italian and Latin, as one could do in Renaissance times. But in modern Europe writers have largely lost this option.

A demonstratively personal rather than merely public and political version of Confucianism was advocated by Wang Yang-ming (1472–1529); his *Ch'uan hsi lu* (Instructions for Practical Living, or A Record of Instruction and Practice) is also written in that highly attractive mixed style where the colloquial mode enlivens stiff classicalism. There are ninety-nine instances of the colloquial word *che* (this) in that fairly short book. Unfortunately, in translation this *che* will end up sounding exactly like the totally different, standard classical *tz'u* (this). Consequently, it is extremely difficult to convey in English translation this type of code-switching between vernacular and classical registers within the same text.

Yüan dynasty drama has a distinctive rhetorical style all its own, and it cultivates a highly estheticized variety of demonstratively colloquial style. For the newcomer to this demanding kind of literature, Chung-wen Shih provides a singularly helpful bilingual introduction in *Injustice to Tou O* (*Tou Ŏ yüan*): *A Study and Translation* (Cambridge: Cambridge University Press, 1972). In this important play, the prose style is predominantly vernacular and seems positively to delight in the unruly quirks of Yüan dynasty argot. Early editions of Yüan plays show an even more vernacular style throughout, as compared with Chung-wen Shih's Ming version. Such an estheticizing celebration of stylized vulgarity was not yet part of the earlier Buddhist experimentation with vernacular styles.

Thus the rhetorical style of such plays is in neat contrast to that of vernacular prose narrative of Sung, Yüan, and Ming times, with its tendency toward a much milder mixture of fairly straightforward standard *koinē* (common dialect, or lingua franca), classical Chinese, and a seasoning of occasional popular argot. For a novel like *Chin P'ing Mei* (Gold Vase Plum), this characterization still holds, although the mimetic popular seasoning has become notoriously prominent in that novel (see chapter 35).

The prose style of the Ming and Ch'ing narrative varies from the almost purely classical *Liao-chai chih yi* (Strange Tales from Make-Do Studio), which has only highly localized brief slips into the colloquial medium but purports to be pure oral folklore, and novels like *Shui-hu chuan* (Water Margin), which is written in a judicious mixture of vernacular and classical styles, with the former clearly setting the overall tone. The difference in effect between the classical and the vernacular is not necessarily one between the formal and the informal—*Strange Tales from Make-Do Studio* is in many ways every bit as unconventional, erotic, and informal as *Water Margin*—but between the classical reticence and pregnancy of diction and the vernacular loquacity, not to mention clear grammatical distinctions.

Commentaries on the classics written in the classical mode can be long-winded and distant. In rhetorical style these classical commentaries are thus rather different from the vernacular ones, which give more scope for personal reaction to a text in addition to scholarly elucidation. In particular, the *k'ou yi* (oral meaning) commentaries, which see themselves in the tradition of the *p'ing* (appreciation) tradition, provide good examples of this.

Not surprisingly, it turns out that the history of Chinese rhetoric cannot be separated from the detailed history of Chinese literary genres, since many rhetorical features are genre-specific, yet many other rhetorical features appear to be remarkably general and applicable right across the literary tableau.

RHETORICAL IDEALS

Let us turn to a more mundane survey of Chinese discourse about their rhetorical ideals. Ever since Confucius, the achievement of *yüeh* (conciseness) and *chien* (simplicity, conciseness) of diction and the cultivation of *wei* (subtlety, discreetness, indirectness of communication) have remained the dominant stylistic ideal throughout the long history of classical Chinese literature. However, even on this basic point there was no shortage of disagreement among traditional scholars. For example, Ku Yen-wu (1613–1682), following Ou-yang Hsiu (1007–1072), argued straightforwardly and famously: "The main point in literary expression is getting things across, and one is not concerned with wordiness or conciseness." In this unorthodox opinion, Ku Yen-wu was supported by such outstanding scholars as Ch'ien Ta-hsin (1728–1804) in his very scientific attitude to style. It is no coincidence that this stylistic stance went along with a hard-nosed intellectual skepticism toward traditional scholarship as well as traditionalist stylistic ideals. Indeed, Chang Hsüeh-ch'eng (1738–1801) made a famous list of *ku-wen shih pi* (ten flaws in ancient prose style), which includes many points of direct relevance to rhetoric.

It is important to realize that Chinese prose style was a controversial and fairly widely discussed issue in Chinese civilization even within given genres, not an automatic practice. There was no single, uncontested rhetoric of Chinese prose style. In considering the summary of Chinese stylistic and rhetorical ideals below, one must also always keep in mind that, in a large and complex culture like that of China, whatever norms there were are bound to have been inadvertently or deliberately contravened or even argued against somewhere by someone. Endemic rhetorical discourse patterns are not unbreakable laws of literary culture. This makes all the more interesting any restraints on classical Chinese rhetoric that seem to be observed with absolute *rigueur* and what distinguishes them from other constraints, which are occasionally broken in marginal cases.

According to the prevalent view, what gives writings permanent value is *wen* (an esthetic pattern); in its absence, words will not travel far, it was said in an old commentary. Chinese writers aimed at ensuring the reach and the longevity of their works inspired by this maxim.

Patterns are achieved through *li* (harmonious balancing), which is the structural essence of *mei* (beauty). Thus the parallelism that Liu Hsieh (465?–520?; see chapter 45) called *li-yen* (harmoniously balanced words) became the core of classical Chinese prose style. A vast range of subtle rhetorical analyses was tied, in the course of Chinese literary history, to the varied phenomenon collectively described as "parallelism." The renowned commentator K'ung Ying-ta (574–648) seems to have been the first to use the key expression *hu-wen* (corresponding term), which refers to the crucial phenomenon that, in corresponding words in corresponding parallel sentences, causes them to be interpreted in such a way that they are felt to relate clearly to each other or harmonize with each other. This notion must be carefully distinguished from a range of other *tui-wen* (corresponding expressions).

One important kind of such corresponding expressions is the *pien-wen* (varied expression), also due to K'ung Ying-ta, which is close to what in Western rhetoric is called *variatio* and refers to the very common and even grammatically important practice whereby one may use words with subtly different meanings indiscriminately in parallel sentences simply for variation, in order to avoid repetition. In such contexts it would be wrong to take the second, semantically differing word to be more than a synonymous stand-in for the first. (This stylistic device, called *pien-wen*, though written with the same graphs, is entirely different from the popular Buddhist prosimetric narrative form known as *pien-wen* [see chapter 48].)

Classical Chinese words and phrases crop up in texts a bit like cobras: whenever we spot one, we do well to look for a corresponding mate not too far away. Chinese prose is pervasively patterned through echoes and resonances with the past, on the one hand, and through echoes and resonances within any passage, on the other. Traditional European literature, of course, contains plenty of parallelism, but no variety of European prose shares the cobralike quality that so pervades nearly all the widely different varieties of mainstream classical Chinese literature from the earliest times.

Apart from this penchant for parallelism, another special form of *wen* commonly discussed and widely cultivated is that of *sheng-wen* (ellipsis) in the second of two parallel sentences, which—like *variatio*—can be seen as a device to avoid the cacophony of repetition under these circumstances. (In general, classical Chinese is more tolerant of repetition than Latin or Greek.) The subcommentaries to the classics by K'ung Ying-ta are a rich source of a wide variety of what today might retrospectively be called rhetorical analysis from a time when rhetorical analysis was still very far from established as a formal discipline in China.

Words, it was felt, needed to be harmoniously balanced in another sense: they needed to find a balance between *chih* (substantial informative content) and *wen* (esthetic patterns), and this esthetic patterning was ideally achieved by natural and balanced parallelism. At least this was the Confucian ideal. During the Warring States period, the prosaic Mohists as well as the hard-nosed Legalists, both highly pragmatic, naturally argued for informative substance at the expense of esthetics. The Eastern Han rationalist Wang Ch'ung was the first to argue *in extenso* in favor of plain unadorned communicativeness in prose style—and was duly disregarded by nearly everyone in the esthetic community throughout history. The Taoists, by contrast, tended to cultivate *wen* as an end in itself, and through their example (notably the *Chuang Tzu*), they exercised a pervasive overt and covert influence over literary standards in China.

We can easily see that in China, as in the West, stylistic ideals were controversial in many ways. Nonetheless, a great deal was above—or below—controversy. In order to qualify as *ya-yen* (dignified words, ornate words) and to be truly beautiful, the harmony achieved and the means by which it is achieved have to appear to be *tzu-jan* (spontaneous, uncontrived, self-driven, natural).

Originating in the "Taoist" tradition, this notion of spontaneity became an integral part of the common esthetic heritage of the Chinese. It is through the notion of the natural in style and the link of this naturalness to what is natural in nature that stylistic beauty, in the Chinese conception of things, attains a cosmic dimension of significance. Stylistic beauty becomes coterminous with cosmic beauty. Ch'en Yi-tseng (Yüan dynasty) was among the literary critics who became famous for continuing the advocacy of spontaneity as a standard for literary excellence. Huang T'ing-chien (1045–1105) focused on the possibility of making elegant, elevated use of vulgar elements.

Related to the stylistic ideal of naturalness is that of concreteness of reference, as when the philosopher Mencius says that, by speaking of what is near, one's meaning should reach far.

The renowned bibliographer and editor Liu Hsiang (79–8 B.C.E.) was the first to note explicitly that, in order to achieve all these esthetic effects, "formulations must be deliberately cultivated" (*tz'u pu k'o pu hsiu*) and that by such effort what was acquired was "the art of literary composition" (*wei tz'u chih shu*). The desired effect was a natural flair of effortlessness that was ironically achieved through strenuous efforts of literary and esthetic self-cultivation—in ancient times as in modern times.

Ssu-ma Ch'ien, the first great historian of China, saw the energy of inner emotion and of *tzu-hsien* (self-expression) through writing as the underlying factor making for great literature. To him, the purity of *chih* (moral aspiration) gave a "fragrance" (*fang*) to one's use of words.

The prosaic explanation of comparison (that it arises when straightforward expression does not make things clear enough) was supplemented by an elaborate subclassification of the esthetics of comparison.

There was a general prejudice against what was *hua* (elaborate, overelaborate) and in favor of the *p'u* (plain, unpretentious).

In prose style the standard rhetorical pose to strike was that of *shu erh pu tso* (transmitting and not creating) what one wrote, a maxim attributed to Confucius. But here again, the situation is far from simple. Already in the first century C.E. Wang Ch'ung opposes plagiarism or traditionalism of formulation and recommends originality not only of thought but also of literary formulation. The literary theoretician Lu Chi (261–303), in a more poetic mode, recommends freshness and originality of diction in place of the rehearsal of the old. He is even afraid (*k'ung*) that what he genuinely feels in his breast may be a rehash of something old and that it therefore may need to be rejected. This feeling about plagiarism was continued by such famous literary figures as Han Yü (768–824) and Li Ao (c. 772–c. 841). The Buddhist monk Chiao-jan (720–805?), in *Shih-p'ing* (A Critique of Poetry), castigates three types of literary thievery: stealing a phrase, stealing an idea, and the less manifest stealing of a literary mode (*t'ou shih*).

The first Chinese book that as a whole is of some persistent interest from the perspective of the history and theory of Chinese rhetoric is *Wen-hsin tiao-lung* (The Literary Mind and Carving of Dragons), by Liu Hsieh. This book deals also in some detail with such rhetorical devices as comparison (*pi-yü*), hyperbole (*k'ua-shih*), quotation and allusion (*shih lei*), comic effects (*hsieh yin*), and indirect suggestive meaning (*yin hsiu*), and it distinguishes between (1) *yen-tui* (verbal parallelism) and *shih-tui* (parallelism of facts); and (2) *cheng-tui* (straight parallelism) and *fan-tui* (inverse parallelism) between opposites.

Liu Hsieh was already well aware that different genres have different stylistic ideals. But the first author to have made a persistent and extensive attempt to define the rules for one particular genre is Liu Chih-chi (661–721), in what must count as one of the world's first book-length studies of historiography, *Shih t'ung* (An Understanding of History). For historiography, Liu emphasizes the need for conciseness, the need to be concrete and unadorned in one's diction, the need to use current, plain language and to avoid outmoded expressions (*hsi-yen*), the use of precise terminology and the consistent and well-considered use of terminology of moral approval or disapproval, the need to avoid parallelism and hyperbole, and the judicious observance of taboos.

Ch'en K'uei (1128–1203), however, in *Wen-tse* (Principles of Literature) moved considerably closer than Liu Hsieh to a focus on rhetorical topics. Understandably, this book is regarded as the first classic of traditional Chinese rhetoric. Systematically, and basing himself on earlier rhetorical literature, Ch'en Kuei distinguishes and exemplifies no fewer than ten types of comparisons that can be drawn, thus inaugurating an orgy of such classifications. With similar meticulousness, Ch'en goes on to classify the various uses of quotation and the poetic effects of *tao yü* (inverted ways of speaking). In all this Ch'en only elaborates existing rhetorical notions. In his discussion of *ts'eng-ti* (climax), Ch'en is more original. He distinguishes three types: (1) from small to large; (2) from subtle to unsubtle (anticlimax!); and (3) from large to small.

Another important stylistic device on which Ch'en dwells in some detail is that of *chiao ts'o* (emphatic repetition of the same word or phrase). Of particular interest is his highly suggestive notion of *t'ung mu* (repetition of keywords) as a stylistic device to keep a text together. In general, Ch'en believed that "expressions may be slow or fast, light or heavy, but they all derive from meaning."

Wen-ching mi-fu lun (Treatise of the Secret Treasury of the Literary Mirror; Japanese, *Bunkyō hifuron*), by the Japanese monk Kōbō Daishi, better known as Kūkai (774–835), is an extremely important source for Six Dynasties (220–589) and T'ang literary criticism and rhetorical analysis. One crucial observation that is first mentioned in this work is the crucial one of *shuang-kuan* (double entendre), a stylistic device that deploys a word with one main meaning as well as other, secondary meanings.

For prose writings like the novel, the Ming dynasty commentator Yeh Chou (d. 1624) offered special rhetorical advice in his endnote to chapter 53 of *Water Margin:* "In all writing in the world, intrinsic esthetic interest is the most important thing. So long as something holds esthetic interest, what need is there for descriptions to correspond to the facts, for the people described to be the real people?" Indeed, the commentaries in the *p'ing* (appreciations) throughout the ages are a vast reservoir of (often delightfully informal) traditional Chinese rhetorical analysis that has not been studied in any detail, except for the part of this tradition that concerns the classical novels of China (see chapters 35 and 46).

Throughout Chinese history down to the early twentieth century, the respectable medium of literary communication was the classical language. But, even so, a wide range of poets and critics have recommended the incorporation of colloquial and "vulgar" (*su*) elements into this medium, although a slogan like that promoted by the diplomat and poet Huang Tsun-hsien (1848–1905) to the effect that "my hand writes what my mouth says" (*wo shou hsieh wo k'ou*)—followed to a limited degree by many proponents of the colloquial medium of vernacular Chinese—was never quite advocated as a revolutionary movement opposed to the predominant use of classical Chinese. It would seem that Huang's provocative slogan owed something crucial to Western—Luther-inspired—stylistic as well as intellectual influence.

HOW TO DO THINGS WITH BOOKS: TOWARD AN ETHNOGRAPHY OF WRITTEN COMMUNICATION IN TRADITIONAL CHINA

Let us now consider the anthropology of the use of the kinds of documents handed down by the tradition in ancient China as a decisive factor shaping rhetorical principles and rhetorical practice. What was the natural forum for the presentation of these ancient Chinese texts? What was the nature of the public they were intended for? On what occasions would these texts be used? What are the significant constraints on what they describe? (The "hard" texts recovered by archeologists raise a host of separate problems that are beyond the scope of this chapter [but see chapters 3, 4, and 5].) The following discussion pro ceeds in a comparativist mode by mirroring Chinese practices against Greek preferences.

One striking feature of classical Chinese rhetorical practice is the absence of basic phrases for "good morning," "good evening," "good night," "hello," "goodbye," "oh, excuse me," "thank you very much," "how is your wife?" and "how are you today?" Phatic communion (speech intended to promote sociability rather than to impart information) must have been common in ancient China, but it is not recorded in Classical Chinese. Classical Chinese rhetoric eschews the ephemeral and inconsequential. The rhetoric of Classical Chinese excludes such small talk, whereas the rhetoric of Homer encourages it.

A Greek book was often designed to represent speech directly, in a mimetic fashion. Demosthenes probably gave speeches like the ones he wrote, just as direct evidence indicates that Cicero wrote down public speeches that he intended to give in the Senate in precisely that form, with plenty of "natural" infelicities of spontaneous speech written into the manuscript. The written document was intended for public oral performance. Public performers existed in ancient China, as did court jesters and other entertainers for whom there is a varied specific nomenclature even in pre-Buddhist Chinese. But what these performers performed was at best only indirectly connected with the traditionally transmitted books.

Many speeches from ancient China are extant, especially in early classics like *Shang shu* or *Shu-ching* (Classic of Documents) and in *Tso chuan* (The Tso Commentary). *Kuo-yü* (Discourses of the States) is devoted to examples of rhetoric, and *Chan-kuo ts'e* (Intrigues of the Warring States) is predominantly about the use of oral rhetoric. But in none of these sources, or later ones, do we find ancient Chinese documents composed and written down by their authors for the purpose of public recitation and performance. Moreover, there is no sign of a custom, in ancient China, of a mixed audience gathering for the public reading of these books. The books themselves give every impression of having been written primarily for depository purposes and secondarily for oral exposition and explanation to a captive, nonhostile audience. Here is a fundamental difference between China and Greece that needs careful interpretation.

What oral performance there was of the known texts appears to have been directed at very small, docile audiences, primarily of a master's disciples, who were intent on learning the text by heart, with a given oral explanation.

Greek manuscripts, by contrast, were designed to be read aloud to a conceivably hostile or even cynical listening public, even when they were not designed to be read by the author himself on any given occasion. They were performance texts even when they did not belong to the realm of performance literature like comedy or tragedy. They were competitive texts even when they happened not to be part of the literary contests that were so important to the Greeks.

The case of drama is paradigmatic here. The manuscript of a play is designed to form the basis for a public, and publicly financed, performance of a certain kind. (One can use it for silent reading, but, for all we know, silent reading was not practiced anywhere or at any time in classical Greece. Even private reading involved the use of the voice. It was reading aloud to oneself. One can use the script of a play for public reading, and there is evidence that Greek plays were used in this way.) Thus nondramatic texts, in the Greek milieu, were enacted and dramatized through more or less public readings.

Against this Greek background, our question now is simply this: what were ancient Chinese manuscripts used for, physically and socially? How did they enter social life?

The available evidence, though slender and indirect, indicates that they were documentary records—some of which were memorized—written down for depository purposes. A text, in pre-Ch'in (221–207 B.C.E.) times, was primarily something that one would recite to oneself, study, and learn to interpret with a master, and certainly learn by heart.

Texts of any size were often kept in *mi-fu* (secret repositories) for archival purposes and not intended for widespread reading. When, during the reign of Emperor Ch'eng (r. 32–7 B.C.E.), a prince wanted to consult the famous historical work *Shih-chi* (Records of the Historian) and applied for permission to use it, that permission was denied by the emperor himself.

In none of the extant prefaces to all sorts of ancient Chinese books is there evidence that they were written for public performance to a listening audience. The heterogeneous Taoist work *Huai-nan Tzu* (139 B.C.E.) as well as the earlier eclectic compilation *Lü-shih ch'un-ch'iu* (Springs and Autumns of Master Lü; 249 B.C.E.) were never said to have been read aloud to the public: they were said to have been displayed as physical objects by the city gates of the capital. The rhyme-prose poetry of Ssu-ma Hsiang-ju (179–117 B.C.E.) was not recited to the emperor, but handed up as text to be read. (There was, of course, a tradition of recitation for shorter poetry—especially lyric poetry—but that is quite different from the recitation of prose under consideration here.)

For the rhetoric of these kinds of texts, the nature of their intended social use makes all the difference. By the time oral performances of texts are mentioned, the reference is to paraphrastic or exegetical elaborations involving actual translation into the vernacular idiom; they were not public readings.

The rhetorical consequences of all this are profound: the Greek writer, like his Roman counterpart, wrote out of fear that he might at any time lose his audience's attention, that their minds might wander, that they might find him insufficiently engaging or interesting. Ancient Chinese books seem to indicate that the classical Chinese writer did not need to have any such qualms, since he wrote ultimately as an archivist, recording what needed to be recorded, for the archival record of a philosophical school or, very often, for the imperial archival record. His purpose was typically depository. The writing was for consultation by those who felt the need to consult the work and for those who were inclined to study it and learn from it. Entertainment or public declaration did not form a significant part of the purpose of writing. When these prose texts are entertaining, it is incidental: their real purpose is archival or didactic. Their rhetoric is ultimately designed toward this didactic end, even when they are overtly archival.

There is no evidence that pre-Buddhist writers in China competed with one another for public acclaim in any literary competition. Royal or official approval was the primary goal. By contrast, the consummate polish of Greek tragedy and comedy texts may be due in part to such competition. In a sense, the extraordinary polish of Plato's writings can be explained by the fact that he was writing philosophical plays; in other words, he was a philosophical playwright. Chinese philosophical texts were thus not so directly in a purely literary or philosophical competition. Such competition as there was tended to be for royal approval. There was no discussion anywhere in pre-Buddhist China, so far as is known, on whether Mo Tzu (480?–400? B.C.E.) or Mencius (c. 372–c. 289 B.C.E.) was the better writer. It is not likely that there could be such a discussion, if only because neither Mo Tzu nor Mencius was a writer, for all we know. Neither, apparently, consciously aspired to literary excellence in the way that Plato did in his surviving dialogs and Aristotle in his dialogs, which are lost to us but were much admired by Cicero.

There was no general public to which to appeal, simply because Chinese texts were not performance texts: they were designed to be respectfully learned and memorized, not to be listened to critically by an ancient Chinese general intellectual public. Mencius's criticism of Mo Tzu never gives the impression that it is based on a close study of a publicly available book. There is no detailed discussion of any extensive passages. The intended audience is one of adherents of Confucius who need to be confirmed in their opposition to the pernicious views of the Mohists.

Consider, in any case, a book like the *Mo Tzu*. Suppose that it were read to an audience of patient listeners. No matter how Mohist they may have been, they must have complained that the text is intolerably repetitive: it preserves up to three versions of a given chapter in many cases. This is tedious in the extreme. What the compilers of that text did was to collect three versions for the record.

There are the dialectical chapters, most of which are utterly incomprehensible to any but the most abjectly esoteric listener. Clearly, these were included purely for the record, not for any public reading sessions. The canons are not comprehensible without the explanations, and the explanations are not comprehensible without the canons. Whoever compiled the book never thought of it as anything other than a repository of material for an archive. In no sense did these texts try to compete in attractiveness with non-Mohist books. This is not even to raise the issue of whether the literary language at the time had already diverged from the spoken languages so much that it would have made recitation of the texts virtually unintelligible to anyone who had not previously committed them to memory. Thus the nature of such texts was not that of performance texts in public competition with other performance texts; rather, they were primarily and quintessentially records.

Geoffrey Lloyd is right when he emphasizes the agonistic spirit of Greece, with its Olympic contests, in contrast with China. He touches a nerve. However, one must keep in mind the fascination for moral ranking of people in the *Han shu* (History of the Han Dynasty) of the first century C.E., as well as for poetic ranking in later treatises on poetry such as *Shih-p'in* (An Evaluation of Poetry); and here, as so often, the difference between East and West is not one of kind but degree.

What, then, is the driving force behind the extraordinary sophistication of early Chinese verse and prose style, if it was not competition for public acclaim? Recalling that all the surviving literature is court literature—that is, it sought primarily the approval of royalty or of (perhaps politically disenchanted) princely patronage—the competition was for royal favor and approval, for princely acclaim. Alternatively, it may have sought the more estheticizing approval of disgruntled circles around the court—as perhaps, in the case of such texts as *Chuang Tzu*. That is why the study of medieval European literature is so eminently useful for those who study traditional China: the court literature of Europe is quite naturally suitable for comparison to Chinese court literature. The sociology of rhetoric in medieval Europe has been so ably studied that it affords ample direct inspiration for sinological research.

The pre-Buddhist texts were not competing for approval by "free citizens" or connoisseurs of literature. There was nothing like a free literary market economy in pre-Buddhist China. Literary estheticism grew in China, from the third century onward, as personal expression together with fine arts like calligraphy and painting. We need to study the development of the literary public one could aim to write for in China, both before and after the advent of Buddhism.

Greek texts, as part of a literary market economy, read as if they were written for a general critical intellectual, and quite probably that is the kind of public for whom these texts were publicly recited and performed: a skeptical, potentially rebellious, and even quite literally impatient audience. The great Roman writers, such as Seneca or Cicero, wrote with an explicit concern for audience reaction. Pre-Buddhist Chinese texts, however, read as if one were eavesdropping on a discourse directed at a ruler and oblivious to the natural reactions of a general reading (much less listening) public.

When they are not written for a ruler or prince, Chinese texts read as if they were written primarily for a captive audience of disciples, for the record and as records, without any notion of a general critical intellectual public. They rarely take account of the possibility of critical, unreceptive readings. Recalling this helps to clarify the underlying dynamics of Chinese prose style.

CONSTRAINTS ON CLASSICAL CHINESE PROSE STYLE

Classical Chinese prose style has many features that were not the focus of the conscious Chinese rhetorical tradition itself, but that are nonetheless crucial. The case of puppetry is instructive in an attempt to understand the nature of authorship in ancient China: the puppeteer's role is like that of the ancient Chinese writer. Like a puppeteer, the ancient Chinese writer enacts roles, but never speaks as the puppeteer himself, only as the impersonal, omnipresent narrator. If he spoke in his own voice, he would be abandoning his culturally predefined role as a writer of prose.

The puppeteer is the actor of the performance, the producing agent. His personality is never the subject of the performance. He never enters the performance as his own person. His person is no more than the underlying hidden agent of the performance, but never part of the object/subject described in the performance. By definition he has no voice of his own and cannot have a voice of his own. Having a voice of his own would go beyond his culturally predefined role as the "puppeteer."

The role of a puppeteer is subject to dynamic, historical change. He can become a masked and thus still hidden actor, or he can become an overt, undisguised actor, until finally he speaks in his own voice—not the voice of his role, but his own voice as an actor commenting on what he enacts or records. Then, he might speak as a person, not as the actor, but still commenting on the play. Finally, he may speak no more of the content of the play, but may purport to speak of his own feelings and opinions, at which point he begins to stage himself. He needs a choreography for his own self-presentation; he has to invent a self for presentation and to ritualize a literary choreography for that self, with all the complexities of rhetoric that this implies.

Part of the fascination of Chinese literature is that it allows one to trace the development of the conventions that dominate—but never quite constrain—

the scribal acts in that culture from an early phase. Like the puppeteer, the scribe is a craftsman who enacts the work of others on a stage where, like the masked actor, he presents a stylized immobile public surface that he knows his public realizes is not his own. On this stage the scribe emerges as a person—shows his own face, as it were. He is still enacting and inscribing the messages of others, but taking overt responsibility for the way in which those messages are written. Such an overt act of taking responsibility is involved in overtly indirect speech, and such overtly indirect, attributed speech remains surprisingly sparse throughout Chinese literary history. In pre-Buddhist times there are some precious and syntactically simple examples showing that indirect speech was not totally alien to pre-Buddhist literature. It is abundantly clear, however, that indirect speech is not a part of the grammatical-rhetorical repertoire of writers of Chinese in the sense that it is an integral part of basic Latin grammar. This primarily grammatical observation concerns a basic feature of the scribal act in ancient China.

The first decisive point, then, is that the rhetorical roles of scribe and author tend not to be identical in pre-Buddhist prose literature. The scribe typically poses as reporting on an author who does not himself appear as the originator of the book bearing his name. Very gradually, from the Han period onward, this changes and writing comes to purport to express what writers themselves consider true. But there remains a characteristically strong tendency to speak in writing through the medium of allusion and unacknowledged indirect quotation. Through implicit quotation the writer may inscribe himself into a tradition, but quite frequently a writer presents as apparently his own the formulations of others. *The History of the Han Dynasty*, by Pan Ku (32–92 C.E.), is a good case in point. The overlaps with *Records of the Historian*, by Ssu-ma Ch'ien, are extensive and pervasively unmarked. Remarkably, they also go unnoted in the introductions, except that Pan Ku, with conventionalized (but not therefore less real) modesty, claims only to have transmitted (*shu*), and, unlike Ssu-ma Ch'ien, he nowhere claims to have composed (*tso*) any of his chapters. The significant point is that even Ssu-ma Ch'ien himself compiled his history through extensive use of unacknowledged quotation from sources he found in the imperial repository of written material, many of which are preserved in other books.

In traditional China, then, a majority of mainline prose writers construed and staged themselves as transmitters of a heritage—especially when what they were doing, in fact, was to innovate. The great master of the late classical Chinese short story, P'u Sung-ling (1640–1715; see chapters 29 and 37), describes himself as an *yi shih* (annalist of the strange), and in general he permits himself to speak in his own name only in little notes at the end of his stories. In particular, there are two features of P'u Sung-ling's personal comments at the end of the stories that he pretends merely to have recorded. First, he declares that his stories are about "the strange," and thus he is not ultimately responsible for their ideological implications. Second, and more important, he directly models himself on the scribal practice (*shih*) of Ssu-ma Ch'ien, who had similarly labeled his personal comments at the end of his chapters as being by the "Grand Historian." In other words, P'u Sung-ling, like Ssu-ma Ch'ien before him, wished his reader to understand that he was simply reporting or recording material that he had acquired from others. Like the historian, therefore, the author of short stories tends to pose, in his main text, as an impartial and impersonal purveyor of literature, while the lyrical poet tends to strike a discreetly communicative pose.

Exactly because of this prevailing tendency (which persisted even after the advent of Buddhism), its opposite—the systematic quest for originality of content, style, and subject matter—was an obvious option for the dissenting individual in traditional China. Li Yü (Li-weng; 1610/11–1680) staged himself as such a dissenter in his antinomian works of fiction. He wanted the subjects of his prose writings as well as his perspectives on these subjects to be his and his alone. Even linguistically, he aimed for innovation and originality. By comparison, Shakespeare was deafeningly traditionalist in the choice of subject matter: practically all his plots are based on unacknowledged more or less well-known earlier sources. Shakespeare was not a plagiarizer of plots, but originality in basic plot was not among his aims as a writer.

To understand Li Yü properly is to understand him as a literary libertine. He revels in staging himself as such in his writings. Likewise, the iconoclastic thinker and advocate of popular literature Li Chih (1527–1602) stages himself as an intellectual libertine aiming for intellectual originality and eschewing the menial role of handing down and merely adapting conventional wisdom.

Moreover, for libertines like Li Yü and Li Chih, their very libertinism became a subject for discussion. They were thus commentators on their own culture and on their own role within that culture. As such, they differ sharply from the vast majority, who construed themselves as bearers and continuers of a grand tradition.

However, one did not have to be a libertine to deviate radically from the mainstream rhetorical prose style one wished to call into question. Thus the substantial works that remain from the brush of the rationalist thinker Wang Ch'ung, collected in *Lun-heng* (Authoritative Expositions; literally "The Steelyard of Exposition"; see chapter 45), strike a basic rhetorical pose that can be conveniently symbolized by the title of one of his justly famous pieces, "Yi ku" (Doubting the Ancient).

In any case, the overall self-communicating reticence of prose writers is best illustrated from the history of autobiographical writing in China. The study of such texts abundantly shows the tight limitations of autobiographical self-representation in the literary world of traditional Chinese prose.

But the significance of this autobiographic reticence goes far beyond the autobiographical dimension as such. For example, the scribal convention in ancient China that nonepistolary prose is presented by a writer who poses not as a person "here and now" at a certain point of time but as a more "abstract" generalized "I" that is more elevated and construed as constant over time. Thus a very long time indeed elapses before the appearance of a Chinese author who writes that he has changed his mind. (The philosopher Chu Hsi does!) In reported direct speech, one does, occasionally, hear someone say that originally he had an impression that later turned out to be wrong. But no writer in pre-Buddhist times overtly states that he formerly maintained one point of view but now believes in another. Reporting such a change of mind would presuppose conventions of writing in which the writer, as a here-and-now person, would have to be on stage not only as the source of what is being written but also as a subject to be discussed as the author of such views. The writer would have to invite the reader into the subjectivity of his creative process as personal history. This does not tend to happen in China. In traditional Chinese prose style, writers do not stage themselves as being engaged in a real-time ongoing process of composing the very text they are writing. This characteristic of Chinese authorship and the corollary traits discussed in the following paragraphs are linked to the concept of selfhood and the role of the individual in society. In brief, "self" is less important than "other" and the "individual" is strongly and explicitly subordinated to the "family" (writ large).

In the context of the foregoing, it will not come as a surprise that in pre-Buddhist Chinese there was remarkably little thinking with the brush, that the scribal act was and remained for a very long time an act of summarizing already thought-out ideas. For a general characterization of traditional prose style, this is an absolutely fundamental feature: Chinese writers hardly ever pose as writing down what happens to be currently on their minds. (*Chuang Tzu* 2 provides a remarkable exception to this rule, but then so much of the *Chuang Tzu* stands as an exception to the rule.) Prose writing never poses as mimetic of ongoing thought.

The stylistic consequences of this traditional Chinese prose style are profound and pervasive. Reported speech is very rarely realistically mimetic as in Aristophanic comedy. Direct speech is habitually used in a summarizing fashion in Chinese, so there is no need for indirect speech as a separate mechanism to indicate the summarizing mode. Speech reports in traditional China are predominantly summarizing reports in direct speech. Mimetic transcription of speech occurs, occasionally and for only brief spells, in Classical Chinese prose style. But, according to the conventions of the time, what we call direct reported speech is not mimetic transcription.

The case of writing down one's thoughts is exactly parallel. Writing down one's thoughts is not mimetic of what one would naturally say in an attempt to express them through speech as one is sorting them out for oneself. What one writes down is only what one might say to summarize concisely the gist of one's thoughts. The prose style of concise summary differs interestingly from the style of the natural flow of speech. In that way the style of classical Chinese differs essentially from that of vernacular Chinese.

The proof of this radical difference is easy to find. Greek and Latin prose writers will freely cultivate *aposiōpēsis,* the falling silent abruptly in midsentence or midthought. No one with any experience in Latin is unable to come up with fitting examples, even some from the most polished metrical verses in Latin literature.

There is not a single case of *aposiōpēsis* in pre-Buddhist Chinese literature, and this rhetorical device remains absent throughout the history of classical Chinese literature. By contrast, *pai-hua* (vernacular) literature includes a few instances of this mimetic device in the representation of speech.

Although *aposiōpēsis* apparently remains absolutely alien to the classical Chinese tradition as a representation of an author's own thoughts, it would not be surprising if an example of this turned up in the work of a libertine writer like Li Chih or Li Yü or of an unconventional literary figure like Feng Meng-lung (1574–1646). The dates, here, are significant: late Ming and early Ch'ing times are exceptionally rich in what, in the Chinese context, must count as outrageous stylistic and rhetorical eccentricity.

It is not a coincidence that, if one is looking for a writer purporting spontaneously to express his thoughts as they are going through his head, one always finds oneself examining the same few exceptional writers, rather than all the other mainstream authors. Perhaps such a prejudice is unjustified, but its very plausibility to Chinese and Western scholars alike remains in itself significant.

A veil of polite reticence regarding one's current ongoing thoughts remains the "default mode" of traditional Chinese prose style, in conspicuous contrast to the loquaciousness that is the hallmark of ancient Greek style.

Epistolary and memorial styles differ sharply from general prose style in one crucial way: traditional Chinese prose style does not cultivate the fiction of a dialog with an imagined rebellious, disbelieving, and disrespectful reader, the famous *lecteur rebelle.* Neither does it introduce that pernicious ghost dubbed *malignus genius* (malign spirit) by Descartes in his seminal *Meditationes,* the internalized ethereal and devil's advocate who roams far beyond the conventionalities of received wisdom, opinion, and taste in his vast spaces of logical necessities and conceivabilities. The predominant style of intellectual prose in the West is ignited and provoked by a more or less dimly perceived *malignus genius* throughout. But, even more important, the history of Western prose contains a stylistic *malignus genius,* with his rollicking, hoarse, and haughty laughter (internalized and feared by the author), which triggers a steady stream of—often parenthetic—metalinguistic formulations of all kinds justifying what is being done stylistically against this internalized "enemy from within." Long before Descartes, Cicero is notoriously full of such material.

On a more banal level, one can easily confirm that, although practically all of Latin prose literature purports to be addressed to a certain person, the rhetorical mode of traditional Chinese literature is primarily directed politely at an impersonal general audience, an audience positively disposed to the message purveyed. The *malignus spiritus Sinensis*, a rare species in Chinese prose, is a most elusive, allusive creature living a very hidden, subtle life.

Some form of implicit dialog with the reader is introduced by the impersonal formula *huo yüeh* ("someone says; someone might say") or simply by an unmarked question that Ch'en K'uei recognized as an important rhetorical device: *ta wen* (responding to questions). The crucial point is that the questions or remarks so introduced are never clearly attributed to the reader of a book *qua* reader of that book (the intimate "dear reader," who is attendant upon the writing process of so many Western authors). The attribution tends to be more general than that even in post-Buddhist times.

The Buddhist-inspired explicit address to the *tu-che* ("the reader here and now who has reached this particular point of the narrative and may be getting bored, etc.") is of special interest in this regard. This usage is apparently limited to vernacular narrative contexts and does not seem to have spilled over into the classical rhetorical practice of nonfictional prose to any significant extent.

Subjectivity

The problem of the objective versus the subjective mode of writing is again intimately linked to the *post festum* summarizing default mode of traditional Chinese prose style. One may feel culturally obliged to record and explain incidents by, for example, including a fictitious speech by one of the participants in the action or observers of the action at the time in terms of what one perceives as public morality and public perceptions, or one may be predisposed to express a current explicitly and vulnerably subjective attitude toward such incidents, representing the process as a matter of one's own individual subjective perception and personal sensitivity as a writer.

In pre-Buddhist times, the overwhelmingly predominant mode remains the naive objective. From the third century onward the overt mode remains the objective one, and there is no current idiom for the ubiquitous *mihi videtur* (it seems to me) in Latin. The Chinese *fang-fu* (apparently) does not have this specifically and vulnerably subjective nuance and is in no way a dominant, routine, rhetorical signal comparable to the Latin *mihi videtur* or to the equally ubiquitous ancient Greek equivalent *phainetai moi*.

Yi wo kuan chih (as I see it, in my view) still poses an objectively true judgment, not a statement about subjective impression or mere appearance as such. The predominant epistemological mode in traditional and Classical Chinese prose style remains objective down to the twentieth century.

COMPARISONS AND CONSTRAINTS

Languages and their associated artistic prose styles, like people, have personalities. Consciously or unconsciously, interpretation of a foreign literary culture involves comparisons even when one's aim is simple exposition.

Western students of Chinese who are familiar with Latin and Greek learn to bring very different expectations to their Greek and Chinese sources: these are not prejudices or preconceptions, but expectations grown out of extensive experience with thousands of pages of ancient European and Chinese primary sources in the original languages. Greek prose style has an extroverted, communicative loquacity and personal expressiveness that tends to be much more subdued and implicit in Chinese. Extant Classical Chinese sources and the varying ideals of prose style to which they aspire have one prevailing tendency in common: they tend to be fundamentally, personally reticent and somehow delicate almost across the board. The colloquial crudeness of Aristophanes has no parallels anywhere in Chinese literature down to Ming times. Classical Chinese texts often came to retain a touch of reticent delicacy even when they rebelled against this reticent mode. Even pornographic prose tends to be less crudely and freely vernacular in its vulgarity than it is in Aristophanes. A dominant stylistic feature remained a certain gauze veil of *wei-yen* (subtle words).

Traditional Chinese prose style thus differs in nontrivial, philosophically, and anthropologically profound ways from Greek and Roman prose style. These contrasts help to delimit the specificities of traditional Chinese literary culture.

Many scholars have aimed to find examples of a wide variety of rhetorical forms in traditional Chinese literature. These investigations focus on what Chinese and Western rhetoric and style have in common. And there is a great deal of common ground. Parallelism is common in the West as it is endemic in China. *Charientismus*, the clothing of a disagreeable sense with agreeable expressions, is more endemic in Chinese prose than in Latin prose. Climax is more common than anticlimax in both literary traditions, and this was indeed noted by traditional rhetoricians.

But the exciting points are not these common features, which, after all, are only to be expected. The excitement is in the surprising gaps, the points where something is endemic in one culture and seems almost scandalously absent in the other. Consider the case of the parenthesis, the asyntactic insertion of alien material into an ongoing sentence: while Cicero uses parentheses within parentheses within parentheses, within parentheses, all of Chinese literature, vernacular as well as classical, seems clinically free of such parenthetic and asyntactic insertions in midsentence. This points to a significant feature of Chinese stylistic practice; Chinese writers rarely make parenthetical comments on what they are currently saying; they rarely "rise" to the level of stylistic self-consciousness that Cicero—as a highly professional and prolific rhetorical theoretician—overcultivated in his writings and that, in milder forms, has remained endemic in the Western literary tradition (including this chapter [and even this sentence]).

It is not part of Chinese style to comment on one's style as one is using it. This contrasts sharply with the Western practice of stylistic self-assessment in midcourse.

What Cicero interestingly called *Asianismus* of style is not at all well represented in traditional China. Wordy, sentimental pomposity was very rarely the hallmark of anything acknowledged as fine classical Chinese style.

The rhetorical device of addressing inanimate objects as if they were persons (oh, you memories of my youth)—*personification* in the vocative mode of inanimates as well as *personification* quite generally—is more sparse in Chinese than in Western prose style. This is not a superficial observation of no philosophical consequence. The anthropological link between personification of inanimates and abstraction is manifest and constitutes a crucial theme in contrastive East-West intellectual history.

CODA

The following is a ruthlessly shortened list of rhetorical devices that were (and are) current in the West, but that a reader of classical Chinese literature learns not to expect, except in truly exceptional circumstances:

Barbarismus—the use of foreign words where one's own language is insufficient—was rare in pre-Buddhist China and remained marginal in Chinese prose style, except when the things described were themselves foreign. In other words, Chinese prose writers were not in the habit, as was Lucretius, of deploring the insufficiency of their own language.

Cacozēlia—the exaggerated and ridiculous overuse of permitted and recommended literary forms—remains marginal throughout Chinese literature.

Compensatio—compensating for something that one has just said and that one regrets having said in this way—is current in Western prose style but absent in Chinese.

Correctio—correcting what one has just written—is a form that slowly enters Chinese prose style only in the vernacular styles. It seems to remain alien to classical Chinese prose style.

Digressio—the deliberately "spontaneous" and explicitly acknowledged deviation from one's proper subject, "in spite of oneself"—remains marginal in classical literature, but narrative digression acquires a certain conventional status in vernacular literature. This shows a profound difference between vernacular (post-Buddhist) and the ongoing classical traditions in traditional China.

Distinctio—the explicit distinction between differing meanings of a word one is using and the making explicit of the intended meaning—is surprisingly rare in traditional classical Chinese prose, except in commentarial literature, where the form is occasionally found.

Epizeuxis—the spontaneous, multiple repetition of a word beyond reduplication— is rare in Chinese prose style, as is the threefold repetition of a vocative: "Oh mother! mother! mother!"

Ēthopoiia—the extensive dwelling on the description of character beyond the needs of the narrative context, which is common in classical Western literature—is absent in pre-Buddhist literature and remains rare in later traditional literature.

Eucharistia—the profuse ritualized expression of thanks, which is so common in Western classical literatures—is absent in pre-Buddhist literature and remains rare, again, in later literature. Thanks are expressed by the gesture of bowing with folded hands and not by words.

Fictio—deliberate and overt coining of new words—is extremely rare in traditional Chinese literature. (As might be expected, the *Chuang Tzu* is the conspicuous pre-Buddhist exception that proves the rule.)

Hirmus—the periodic sentence in which the sense is suspended until the end—is rare in Chinese.

Hyperbaton—the interposition between two words that grammatically belong together of material that does not belong in this construction—is impossible in Chinese for grammatical reasons: the word order is less free than in Latin.

Improprietas—the deliberate use of a completely inappropriate word—is rare indeed.

Metanoia—the qualification of a statement one has just made by recalling it, self-correction—seems absent in traditional Chinese prose style.

Praeteritio—explicitly passing over something or, rather, seeming to pass over something in order to draw special attention to it—is absent in pre-Buddhist Chinese and remains rare in post-Buddhist times.

Reditus ad propositum—the explicit reverting to one's main subject after a digression ("But I digress. Let me return to my main point")—is rare in classical Chinese literature but characteristically common in post-Buddhist vernacular prose.

Restrictio—the figure of speech whereby, after making a general statement, one takes exception to a part—is rare in traditional Chinese prose style.

Subnexio—the appending of an afterthought to a main thought one has just expressed, as a further reflection on it—is comparatively rare in Chinese texts.

One could continue this confusing list for a very long time. The underlying feature of all this is clear enough: literary Chinese prose style is reticent in many ways, among others, in how it does not encourage authors to comment on the very process of their ongoing literary composition. To a significantly smaller extent than in Greece or Rome, literary Chinese authors become objects of critical attention unto themselves in their texts, as they write these texts. Chinese poetry in particular demonstrates abundantly that these Chinese authors were far from naive, stylistically. Vernacular styles show elaborate conventionalized patterns of authorial self-criticism of the very current act of composition. But in the end, conventional and traditional Chinese artistic prose style remains at bottom an act of artistic summarizing, not an act of the literary dramatization of the complex and often contradictory thinking and feeling processes that go on in the literary mind. On the whole, this dramatization has remained, in China, the domain of poetry, yet without a strong emphasis on an explicit, self-conscious, self-reflective, self-assertive ego.

Hence the immense importance in China not of prose style, but of poetic flair—even in Chinese prose.

Christoph Harbsmeier

Chapter 44

CLASSICAL EXEGESIS

For most of Chinese history, the ability to write classical commentary was nearly identical with literacy. Confucius (550–479 B.C.E.) describes some of his disciples as engaged in *wen-hsüeh* (the study of writings; *Lun-yü* [Analects] 11.3): this was doubtless a course of training in the deciphering and interpretation of legal and historical texts, a necessary qualification for office in the palace bureaucracies of early China and a predecessor to the mastery of what later ages would canonize and stabilize as "the classics." Although, of course, *wen-hsüeh* much later came to be adopted as the modern Chinese term for belles-lettres or imaginative literature, the practical bent of the skills acquired by those early *wen-hsüeh* experts must not be lost from sight. Classical exegesis in one form or another was the mainstay of the livelihoods of nearly all Chinese authors. Demonstrated familiarity with the classics was the entry into the world of administration (and thus the goal of premodern education). Once established as a member of the world of letters, a scholar might take part in the most wide-ranging debates about morality, society, and policy through the glossing and emendation of classical writings; his career might rise or fall according to his choice of commentatorial authorities; and, quite naturally, when he composed poetry or read the poems of others, the models of meaning furnished by classical study guided the respective processes. Exegesis of a set of venerated texts gave Chinese literati their common language and their protocols of understanding as well as the matter of their education.

The development of classical exegesis is therefore inseparable from the history of Chinese literature, although their relationship is at no point simple. A period's classical study was as often the deadening routine against which literary movements arose, as it was the vehicle for new ways of conceiving the purpose of study.

From the pre-Ch'in era (i.e., already in the period before the late third century B.C.E.) onward, the five chief areas of a scholar's training were said to be the Odes (*Shih*), the Ritual (*Li*), the Documents (*Shu*), the Changes (*Yi*), and the Annals (*Ch'un-ch'iu*). The classical texts now corresponding to those categories are largely products of exegesis and commentary, both in the sense that scholarship was needed to establish or recover their wording and that much of their text as it stands is explanatory or accretive in nature. The books with the longest history of classical status are, to use their modern designations, the *Shih-ching* (Classic of Poetry), with its most nearly complete recension being the *Mao shih* (Mao Odes, or Odes According to the Elder Mao); the *Yi-li* (Ceremonies and Rites), *Chou-li* (Rites of Chou), and the *Li-chi* (Record of Ritual); the *Shang-shu* or *Shu-ching* (Classic of Documents); the *Chou-yi* (the Changes of Chou); and finally the *Ch'un-ch'iu* (Springs and Autumns), with their three commentatorial traditions, the *Tso chuan* (Tso Commentary), *Kung-yang chuan* (Kung-yang Commentary), and *Ku-liang chuan* (Ku-liang Commentary). All these works claim a pre-Ch'in origin; in no case is so early a date, or indeed the integrity of the text, secure. Moreover, the set of books accepted as classics (see chapter 4) fluctuated, as can be seen from records of imperial proclamations, appointments to teaching chairs, and standard editions carved on stone.

For exegesis to take place presupposes primary texts that, for some reason, are no longer self-explanatory. In early China, reasons for the obscurity of texts are not hard to find. Literate officials often interpreted texts for their superiors, who may have never taken the trouble to learn reading and writing. Moreover, before the standardization of script carried out under the Ch'in, the frequent use of variants and loan characters created obstacles for readers from distinct regions or educational backgrounds. The condensed style of Chinese written documents leaves the reader to interpret the wording in relation to an often unstated context, and the loss of contextual clues could open the door to widely inconsistent readings. Finally, texts were often designed for ambiguity rather than transparency, as the entire *Classic of Change*, or similarly oracular or gnomic passages in other works, remind us. Conventional historiography describes the short-lived Ch'in dynasty (221–207 B.C.E.) as the tragic break in the Chinese literary tradition, when all books that had not received governmental approval were destroyed; it also tells us that the cultural heritage had to be reconstructed, however imperfectly, by the painstaking efforts of scholars enjoying the patronage of the succeeding Han dynasty (206 B.C.E.–220 C.E.). Differences among these scholars, with different schools or lineages all championing their own reconstituted texts, led to the further fragmentation of the ancient learning. It may be, however, that the supposed unanimity of the pre-

Ch'in tradition was, for many of these texts, a post-Ch'in illusion: the very failure of the Han attempt to bring order to the classics showed how loosely a book's title might be identified with this or that transcript.

Of all the classics, the *Yi-ching* (Classic of Change) owes the most to the exegetical impulse. As Edward Shaughnessy has argued, it appears that successive layers of the work came to be applied, one after another, to previous layers that were no longer intelligible. Most of the moralizing philosophical discourse of the *Classic of Change* as it exists today would have been meaningless to the people who composed its earliest strata, the brief statements of outcome intended for use in divinatory rituals.

The next most commentary-based Classic is the *Springs and Autumns*, the guiding thread of which is a bare chronicle of events in the state of Lu over a 350-year period (722–481 B.C.E.). The original *Springs and Autumns* left so much unstated that the three rival traditions of commentary—the three *chuan* mentioned above (*Tso*, *Kung-yang*, and *Ku-liang*)—sprang up to explain what was meant, what precisely happened, and why it was important; and these commentaries earned the status of classics in their own right. (The *Springs and Autumns* seems to have given rise to the lexical pairing of *ching*, the "primary text" accepted by all schools of thought, and *chuan*, the divergent "commentaries" or "transmissions.") These supplements to the *Springs and Autumns* hardly present themselves as a modest body of footnotes: a few words of text may prompt an explication several hundred characters long, and the *Tso Commentary* in particular is renowned for its characterization, drama, rhetorical brilliance, and integrity of conception, though not necessarily for historical verisimilitude and impartiality.

Considering the emphasis on ritual as a means of social stability in Han China, and the importance of texts in establishing correct rituals, it is appropriate that a chapter of the *Record of Ritual* should include "Ching-chieh" (The Exposition of Classical Texts). The *Record of Ritual* often presents fictional dialogues between Confucius and his disciples as a means of rationalizing the ancient customs—as if to designate exegesis as the very marrow of cultural continuity. Scholars of manuscript traditions are familiar with the problem of passages of commentary creeping into the main text: in the classics as they exist today, such a process has been responsible for many parts of the main text.

Exegesis, then, does not happen to a classic from outside: it is often a prime motivation for the writing of the classic. The *Tso Commentary* offers many scenes of interpretation, when a ruler, hesitating over a decision to be made, asks one of his advisers for clarification of a portent or ancient saying. The adviser's response, as likely as not, comes in the shape of a massive analysis of the obscurity, calling on the many resources of the Chinese language (homophony, character combination, association) to redescribe it, thus building up a complex of interrelated terms around the ruler's problem and pointing toward its solution. Trained on such scenes of exposition, the traditional Chinese reader understood exegesis as an imaginative synthesis among pragmatic situations, precedent, and the reconstructed intentions of the ancients.

Early texts show quotation and explication as stock devices of the educated person. The nobles and envoys of the *Tso Commentary* bandy about lines from the *Classic of Poetry* as a form of diplomatic code; Confucius is shown in the *Analects* discussing the *Classic of Poetry* and the *Classic of Documents* with his students; Mencius (371–289 B.C.E.) counters unorthodox readings of the great texts or elucidates their seeming paradoxes; Hsün Tzu (c. 300?–219? B.C.E.) draws on the classics again and again to clinch a point.

These pre-Han intellectual figures were counselors and debaters who cited commonly known texts to support their arguments. After the naming of Erudites (*po-shih*) in the various classics of the Confucian syllabus by the Han government in 124 B.C.E., a new type of intellectual emerged: the specialist whose textual knowledge was a sufficient end in itself. Now scholars appeared at court to present long-lost (or purportedly so) classical writings. A teacher might make a career out of possessing, transmitting, and explicating a single classic. The rewards could be great. The *Hou Han shu* (History of the Later Han Dynasty) tells the story of Cheng Hsüan (127–200), who joined the more than four hundred disciples of the famed scholar Ma Jung (79–166). Ma "occupied an elevated hall. He sat before a scarlet curtain to teach his students; behind it were his female musicians. The students taught one another in order of seniority; rarely did anyone 'enter his chamber'" (i.e., gain Ma's personal approval and recognition). Cheng spent three years in Ma's school before getting to see the great man. A great scholar's authority resembled a minor prince's and was demonstrated through similar prerogatives.

The style of commentary typical of middle Han textual specialists was known as *chang-chü* explication (analysis "by paragraph and sentence"). Books were unpunctuated, and so the first necessity was to parse the text. The author of *chang-chü* proceeded sequentially through the work, piling up all the available erudition on each phrase; one scholar is said to have composed a hundred thousand words of commentary on the mere title of the "Yao tien" (Canon of Yao) section of the *Classic of Documents* and a further thirty thousand on the chapter's first four syllables.

Traditional exegetical texts from Han to modern times encompass many different genres corresponding to different pedagogical purposes. It may be useful to distinguish them here. The heritage of the *chang-chü* genre is plain in the *glossing* or *lexical commentary*, which provides more familiar or less ambiguous equivalents for the difficult words in a classical text. The early lexicographical works *Erh-ya* (Approaching Elegance) and *Shuo-wen chieh-tzu* (The Explication of Characters, Simple and Complex), by Hsü Shen (55?–149?), draw their definitions from such collections of glosses, and in their definitions the influence of particular classics or passages can often be seen. *Periphrastic commentary* restates the meaning of verses or sentences of the text. *Amplifying commentary* supplements the text with information from other sources, inserts dialogs, speculates on motivations, cites authorities, and issues judgments: the three great *Springs and Autumns* commentaries and Tung Chung-shu's (179–104 B.C.E.) essays on problem passages in the *Springs and Autumns* (his *Ch'un-ch'iu fan-lu* [Luxuriant Dew of the Springs and Autumns]) show this genre at its best. *Prefaces* and *postfaces* (both known as *hsü*) and chronological tables (*p'u*) announce the interpretative framework to which the understanding of a text is subject. The glosses and paraphrases put forth in a given tradition tend to harmonize with its *hsü*—which is not to say that the *hsü* necessarily came first. (In the Mao tradition of the *Classic of Poetry*, for example, it seems that the glossing and paraphrasing *chuan* commentary predates the *hsü* affixed to each poem.) Some *hsü* are objects of long-standing controversy, as they seem to dictate directions to the text rather than take signals from it. Cases in point are the Mao tradition's "Hsiao hsü" (Minor Prefaces) to the *Classic of Poetry* and the [pseudo-]K'ung An-kuo (c. 130–c. 90) prefaces to the chapters of the *Classic of Documents*. Both sets of prefaces peremptorily assign authorship, date, and purport to materials whose origin is far from certain. In their defense, it might be said that the Han exegete's aim was almost surely never to discover the classic's original intended meaning, but to render the work usable in contemporary moral-political debate and eligible for state patronage. The ink spilled attacking the early commentators for their countless "errors" demonstrates the differences between the Han ideal of scholarship and that of later ages.

Cheng Hsüan, whose commentaries on the *Classic of Poetry*, the *Classic of Documents*, and the *Record of Ritual* have been preserved and reprinted constantly since his lifetime, departed from the narrow focus of *chang-chü* learning by cross-referencing his points, applying the readings of one classic to the trouble spots of another. This method often cast darkness rather than light, but its tacit premise, that the classics formed a coherent cultural (if not authorial) whole, was not lost on later interpreters. Early applications of the techniques of classical commentary to works outside the official syllabus are the edition of the *Ch'u tz'u* (The Elegies of Ch'u), ascribed to Wang Yi (c. 89–158), and the commentary added by Wang Pi (226–249) to the *Tao te ching* (Classic of the Way and Integrity). Wang Yi's motive seems to have been to acquire the prestige of classical works for the nearly unknown *Elegies of Ch'u;* Wang Pi's, to bring the pre-Ch'in work into the philosophical discussions of his own time.

The proliferation of variant schools of interpretation, together with a renewed emphasis on classical mastery in the recruitment of officials, prompted the T'ang court to order an omnibus edition of the classics to be overseen by K'ung Ying-ta (574–648). This project, known as the *Wu-ching cheng-yi* (Correct Meanings of the Five Classics), lives on as the core of the standard edition most often reprinted today, the *Shih-san-ching chu-shu* (The Thirteen Classics, Annotated and Explicated), edited by Juan Yüan (1764–1849). Like Cheng

Hsüan's notes, the *Correct Meanings of the Five Classics* treats the classics consistently and interreferentially. For each classic, it adopts one leading commentator, discussing and amplifying this commentator's views in a subcommentary. On the lexicographical front, the *Correct Meanings of the Five Classics* draws meaning- and sound-glosses from *Ching-tien shih-wen* (Textual Explications for the Classical Canon), by Lu Te-ming (556–627). As befits a standard work meant for general use, it uses an impersonal literary style, plodding and redundant but reliably plain.

K'ung Ying-ta's *Correct Meanings of the Five Classics* consigned to oblivion most of its predecessors and rivals—in no small part because the T'ang and Sung governments adopted it as the basis of their examination system. K'ung's work was conceived of in a manuscript culture, in which a work of its scope was both a rarity and a monument of effort. In the Sung dynasty, with the spread of printing, a work like the *Correct Meanings of the Five Classics* could indeed become a universal standard—but wide diffusion of texts meant that it no longer enjoyed sole authority. A Sung scholar like Chu Hsi (1130–1200) could advise his students to read several different editions side by side in order to work out a personal interpretation, advice that only a few decades earlier would simply have rung hollow. Sung commentators could assume K'ung's standard edition as a base, extending it or departing from it as their styles of thinking dictated; commentary thus could afford to become more specialized and individual. In the interpretation of the Ch'eng brothers (Ch'eng Hao [1032–1085] and Ch'eng Yi [1033–1107]), the *Classic of Change* was made into the exposition of a coherent natural philosophy ranging from physics to morals: this was not scholarship that aimed merely at making students literate or resolving difficulties in interpretation. Chu Hsi's series of editions (Chou-yi *pen-yi* [The Original Meaning of the *Changes of Chou*], *"Shih-ching" chuan* [A Collection of Commentaries on the *Classic of Poetry*], *Ssu-shu chi-chu* [The Four Books with a Collection of Notes], and so on) drew from the teachings of numerous contemporary scholars: the Ch'engs, Ts'ai Ch'en (1012–1067), and many others. Chu approached the pre-Han and Han traditions freely, rejecting interpretations that seemed to him forced and unreasonable; he also helped to circulate the skeptical attitudes of recent scholars who had expressed doubts about the authenticity or accuracy of the received interpretations. In his oral teaching, as recorded in *Chu-tzu yü-lei* (Classified Conversations of Master Chu), Chu Hsi described classical study as a process of internalization and discovery, in words that evoked a pursuit of enlightenment. As if to bear Chu Hsi out, the outward, public, social concerns of the classics as read by earlier generations frequently figure in Sung interpretative texts as mere pointers to a process of moral transformation to be undergone by the reader. In this, as in the systematic theorizing of the Ch'engs and Chu, the Sung approach to the classics would doubtless have mystified the scholars of the Han.

Editions of classical texts incorporating the views of the Ch'engs, Chu Hsi, and their inheritors became the standard for examinations under the Ming and the Ch'ing. For unforgiving depictions of the hypocrisy and conformity of the Ch'ing schoolroom and examination hall, see the novels *Hung-lou meng* (A Dream of Red Towers), by Ts'ao Hsüeh-ch'in (1724–1764) and Kao O (1763–1815), and *Ju-lin wai-shih* (The Scholars), by Wu Ching-tzu (1701–1754). Among the classically learned, reactions to "Sung learning" took various forms. Eclecticism (particularly the assimilation of Buddhist themes) was one option frequently exercised under the Ming; another, gaining in influence through the Ch'ing, was a return to the glossing and cross-checking of the Han exegetes (a tendency thus known as "Han learning"). Both eclectics and philologists defined themselves initially against the "Sung learning." The eclectics did so by taking untraditional positions and citing unauthorized precedents. The unconventional career of Li Chih (1527–1602) can here serve as example: he was once a Confucian official, but later embraced Ch'an (Zen) Buddhism and taught that Confucianism, Buddhism, and Taoism were merely facets of a unity. For their part, the philologists demanded interpretations for which empirical proof could be provided and returned the old texts to practical ends in a fashion that Chang Hsüeh-ch'eng (1738–1801) crystallized in his well-known statements that "the Six Classics are all histories" and that "The *tao* ('way') of the former sages and kings can no longer be known, but the still tangible means of their achievements is the Six Classics." While the official syllabus continued to mandate that the classics be understood and applied in the framework of the organic Sung philosophy, unofficial learning pursued its own directions, in the long run infiltrating officialdom as students trained in these new ways of thinking won official places for themselves.

The last imperial civil service examinations were held in 1905. Since then the classics have become the object of academic research—more or less distanced, probably never value-free. Exegesis continues: the ancient works may be bought in modern vernacular translation, with or without the original in parallel, and with or without commentaries; and political formations as well as neotraditional religions seek to claim the message of the classics as their own.

Haun Saussy

Chapter 45

LITERARY THEORY AND CRITICISM

FUNDAMENTAL PRINCIPLES

Some of the most individual and influential voices of Chinese literature expressed themselves in literary theory. Their ideas, their innovative and often magnificent writing, their content, and the personalities assumed to underlie their utterances had the power to instruct, inspire, and even entertain across the centuries. By traditional Chinese standards, a survey of literary theory is very much a survey of personalities, for whatever difficulty might arise in establishing biographical details, the assumption that writing is a mirror of an author's personality is fundamental to the Chinese tradition. Style, content, and persona together create a special genre most significant to literature on a practical level and whose esthetic significance is ineffable.

Literary theory and criticism in China constitute a distinctive esthetic discourse rather than a distinctive literary form. The texts take many forms: prefaces, chapters of the dynastic histories, comments on the biographies of individual poets, personal letters, philosophical discussions and essays, even poems in many styles. The focus is principally on poetry, but metaphysically and often practically the discussion of *wen* (literature) extends to all genres of writing, in poetry and prose. It also extends to other arts, because in principle *wen* includes anything made to express feeling in a work of art. From the "Ta hsü" (Major Preface; first century C.E.) to *Shih-ching* (Classic of Poetry), presumably by Wei Hung and the first work of self-conscious literary theory attributed to a named author, we know that this expressive impulse included poetry, music, and dance.

From earliest times, music always enjoyed close association with poetry. According to an account in the *Tso chuan* (Tso Commentary), the ambassador Cha, emissary of the viscount of Wu, visited the state of Lu and asked to hear selections of music from all the states. He stunned his audience with his ability to discern the political situation of each state by listening to its music and seeing its dances. The study of poetry is credited with the same potential to reveal historically accurate information about other times and places.

Although very little music and dance are preserved from the early period of Chinese culture, poetry survives in abundance. This continuity of actual poems has gone hand in hand with a continuity of thought *about* poetry, comprising not just appreciation but interpretation. Both as a transmission of individual voices and as a window on the past, the continuity of literary thought is inseparable from the continuity of Chinese culture itself.

Early Confucian attitudes toward literature presuppose that the purpose of art is to express the political ethos of a given time. In *Lun-yü* (Analects), poetry (*shih*), especially the poetry of the *Classic of Poetry* (or *Book of Songs*), is described as a useful aid to learning: "If one does not study poetry [i.e., the *Classic of Poetry*], one has not the wherewithal to speak" (*pu-hsüeh shih, wu yi yen*). Through the study of literature one acquires understanding of experience beyond one's own, which in turn can stir others to greater understanding of the ends or uses of learning: "Language must achieve its ends to convey meaning" (*tz'u ta erh-yi-yi*). The literary function of language is to express individual intention directed toward the good of the state, and an educated person is required to cultivate the skill to achieve this. In this sense, the vehicle of language is as important as the meaning it is intended to convey. Therefore, language must, above all, be clear, plain, and straightforward, so that the meaning is transparent. Clear language is a sign of the individual's bona fides and clear mind, allowing others to participate in the inspiration of the author and act on good ideas. Since writing reveals not only the writer's character but the social climate in which the writer lived, a person not capable of good writing is not worthy to serve the state. This is an intentional fallacy of extraordinary power throughout Chinese history, and it had a practical impact on the selection of worthy candidates for political office.

Another axiom of Chinese literary thought is that a text may *signify* more than it *says:* what is written suggests, but does not exhaust, what is meant. The phrase used to describe this—*yen-wai* (literally, "beyond words")—indicates the meanings of utterances beyond the literal levels of texts. It was first used in *Han shu* (History of the Han Dynasty) and became part of the bedrock of hermeneutic criticism.

These two esthetic notions of the nature of literature combined to produce an ideal that simultaneously implied utter transparency and a hermeneutics of interpretation coexisting from the beginning of Chinese literature. Traditional readings of "Li sao" (Encountering Sorrow) by the legendary poet and statesman

Ch'ü Yüan (340–278 B.C.E.), who endured fatal hardship to protect his integrity and recorded his experience and feelings in his poem, are examples of this. Language that achieves such a balance allows the writer to transcend space and time.

The pursuit of political goals and personal fame through literature was looked upon with deep skepticism by the early Taoists, who laid the foundation for an alternative or dissenting literary esthetic. The texts attributed to Lao Tzu (c. 250 B.C.E.?) and Chuang Tzu (355?–275 B.C.E.) show two thinkers very clever with language, yet both stress the limited ability of words to convey meaning and the terrible danger of language as deception and cheat. According to Lao Tzu, "Trustworthy words are not beautiful, and beautiful words are not trustworthy" (*hsin yen pu mei, mei yen pu hsin*). Lao Tzu objected strenuously to political debaters and the use of rhetoric to persuade. Chuang Tzu relates the sad story of Hun-tun (Chaos), whom his friends unintentionally murder when they bore holes in his unadorned body in imitation of their own seven apertures. Principally a metaphor for leaving well enough alone, the story is also a warning of the danger of destroying with language that which has perfect integrity without ornament.

Literary criticism is applied theory. Theory, at least in the Chinese tradition, seldom stands on its own, in part because of an emphasis on the didactic function of literature from the earliest literary discourse. With Wei Hung's "Major Preface," theory and criticism begin to evolve as a genre separate from history and philosophy. Furthermore, Wei Hung is followed in this genre by a list of *authors:* their names are known, as are something of their careers and the purpose of literary criticism in their lives. The writers whose central concern was to articulate the nature of literature are regarded as exemplary of their times, recording their personal preferences and often elevating them to a mystical expression of esthetic appreciation.

The following discusses some of the authors whose work decisively transformed the practice of literature and criticism in later ages. Although they were often poets, historians, or philosophers, their enduring fame rests on their literary theory. From the beginning, two main poles of critical ideology coexist in ironic counterpoint: traditionalist or fundamentalist poetics associated with the Confucian mainstream, and a progressive stream seeking to break away from the strict application of literature only to the betterment of the state. Both streams show the ability to accommodate the iconoclasm of Taoist skepticism and, later, to integrate Buddhist notions of the illusory nature of language. Some of the works that have had such powerful impact on the evolution of literary theory are surprisingly concrete in their stated missions. Seldom does an author conduct his discourse without contextualizing by association with particular texts, and it was taken for granted that the texts would be evaluated. Some of the most important contributions to poetic theory are prescriptive, handbooks of technique and process. Another major aspect of poetic discourse is the compilation and editing of anthologies. The theoretical concepts their editors have handed down are not just presented in the prefaces and afterwords and textual notes they provide with their selections: the structure and content of the selections themselves provide an overarching vision of what literature was, and should be. The texts are not bound together by a particular form, but by the purpose of setting forth the ideals and principles of literature so that they can be appreciated and emulated. Literary criticism is seen as part of the literary world in its broadest sense, not as an independent entity separated from culture, history, or artistic practice.

The golden age and foundational period of literary theory runs from the Later Han dynasty (25–220) through the Wei (220–265), Chin (265–420), and Northern and Southern Dynasties (420–589). These works are described in some detail below. For the later periods, beginning with the T'ang dynasty (618–907), only a few exemplary figures and works are presented here. With some notable exceptions, there is not much innovation beyond the basic forms from the earlier period, but literary criticism undergoes significant evolution, refinement, and expansion and sheds light on the cultural milieu of the time. Literary theory is as much a mirror of its age and its author as lyric poetry.

THE BEGINNINGS OF THE TRADITION

"The Great Preface to Mao's Edition of the *Classic of Poetry*" (*Mao-shih* "hsü"), better known simply as the "Major Preface" is attributed to Wei Hung of the Later Han dynasty. In contrast to the "Hsiao hsü" (Minor Prefaces), which purport to identify the original purpose and provenance of each poem in the anthology, the "Major Preface" is positioned before the particular preface and commentary to the first poem in the *Classic of Poetry* and articulates the critic's sense of the purpose of the anthology as a whole. This essay, though brief, makes a complex statement on the nature of poetic expression, which has been one of the most tenacious and influential in Chinese esthetics. Furthermore, by combining description of the nature of artistic inspiration with prescriptions of genre and technique, it exhibits the balance of theoretical and descriptive poetics which is the traditional ideal of Chinese poetic criticism.

There are two important components of the "Major Preface." The first is the statement on the nature of poetic inspiration. This reflects earlier assumptions of the significance of artistic production as a gauge of the condition of the state, but combines them with a new perspective on individual inspiration and expression. Incorporating the late Han revivals and reforms in Confucian doctrine, the essay attempts to formulate the process whereby poetry combines esthetic quality and ethical substance.

> Poetry is the fulfillment of intent: what dwells in the mind is intent, what comes forth in words is poetry. Emotions move in one's essential being

> and take form in words. When speaking them does not suffice, then one sighs or chants them. If sighing and chanting do not suffice, then one sings out. If singing out does not suffice, then unconsciously one taps them out with the hands, dances to them, treads to their measures and stomps them.
>
> Emotions come forth in sounds, and when the sounds create patterns they are called music. The music of an age of peace is tranquil and inspires feelings of joy: it is ruled by harmony. The music of an age of disorder is dissonant and provokes feelings of anger: its rules are perverted. The music of a kingdom in ruins is mournful and inspires feelings of nostalgia: the people are suffering. Therefore, to keep order in times of success or failure, to move heaven and earth, to touch ghosts and spirits, nothing can hold a candle to poetry. The former kings used this means to guide the conduct of husbands and wives, to inspire filial piety and generosity, to enrich social relations, to enhance education and culture, and to develop manners and customs.

The significance of intent (*chih*) for poetry is to establish the purpose of expression, namely, to communicate inspiration in response to the stimulation of emotion (*ch'ing*). With the assumption that the primary purpose of poetry is to promote ethical excellence, Wei Hung attempts to formulate the nature of artistic inspiration ("in the mind"), the process of expressing it ("if . . . does not suffice"), and the response of the audience. In order to achieve expression of inspiration, an artist must call on all resources: emotional, mental, verbal, and even physical. While expression in words must adjust to the limits of language, meaning is under no such constraint; meaning may go beyond the literal level of the text—literally, "beyond words"—and is limited only by the reader's imagination or capacity for understanding.

The poetic act by definition combines perception and expression. This determines the relationship between the act of composition and the act of reading, an essential link either for the reception of didactic content or lyrical transcendence. The act of reading implies the recreation of the artist's original act of perception, but the method employed by the artist to ensure this re-creation will largely define the mode of expression and thus the experience of the reader. The re-creation of this original act of perception is also regarded as a window on the historical reality of the artist's time. The assumption that the personal, emotional elements of poetry are grounded in history is essential to the traditional interpretation of poetry.

The second major critical contribution of the "Major Preface" is the statement of the "six principles" (*liu-yi*) of the composition of the *Classic of Poetry*. These principles are further subdivided into two categories. Three of the principles, *feng* ("airs"), *ya* ("odes"), and *sung* ("hymns"), mark distinctions of genre among the poems and provide the titles of the main divisions of the anthology, further organized in sections identified by the country of origin. The other three principles—"enumeration," (*fu*, sometimes rendered "narration"), "comparison" or "simile" (*pi*), and "affective image" (*hsing*)—are not rhetorical figures but, rather, techniques whereby the artist organizes language to create certain effects. As principles of structure, enumeration organizes and integrates a fixed sequence of at least three expressive units in proper order, comparison coordinates two units, and an affective image presents a single, self-referential unit of meaning. These in turn correspond to different modes of reception on the part of the audience, according to the desired effects.

The "Major Preface" definitely reflects Confucian attitudes toward literature. The statement "poetry is the fulfillment of intent" (*shih yen chih*) has been interpreted by traditionalists as absolute confirmation of the value of poetry to reflect and sustain the ideals of society. Because of the emphasis on the notion that the experience of reading recreates metaphorically, if not actually, the experience of the author, the "Major Preface" also confirms that a poem both reflects its own age and recreates that age in the mind of the reader. Works of literary theory influenced by the "Major Preface" through the Han and Six Dynasties (220–589) largely reflect this interpretation of Confucius's attitude toward the role of literature in human affairs.

DEVELOPMENTS DURING THE HAN DYNASTY

As representatives of the Han dynasty's concretely Confucian notion of criticism as moral discourse by individual authors, two figures stand out: the poet and statesman Yang Hsiung (53 B.C.E.–18 C.E.), and the historian Pan Ku (32–92). In their statements on the nature of literature, they identified certain principles that were vital to later theorists and influenced later criticism. Yang Hsiung, one of the premier poets of rhymeprose or rhapsody (*fu*), became disenchanted with the dazzling style of his own genius and ultimately rejected it. He came to believe that the luxuriant language typical of the genre was incompatible with the purpose of literature to enlighten and instruct. In his essay *Fa-yen* (Discourses on Method), he laments that the principle of *fu* as practiced in the *Classic of Poetry* took its beauty from its power to set forth right principles in proper order with clarity and confidence, while the principle, and the genre which was its embodiment in literature, had deteriorated in the hands of later generations, including his own. He mounts an attack on the greatest poet of the preceding generation, Ssu-ma Hsiang-ju (179–117 C.E.), for putting meretricious motives and delight in his own brilliant use of words ahead of a courtier's duty to enlighten his sovereign. Yang deplores his own work as "insect carving" (*tiao-ch'ung*), condemning ornate poetry as being deficient not only as art but as craft. He asserts the absolute correspondence between words and the person who writes them, saying, "Words are the tones of the heart; writing is the image of the heart. When words and image are formed, they may reveal a superior man, or a scoundrel."

Pan Ku included some poetic commentary in the *History of the Han Dynasty*, mainly for the purpose of identifying political exemplars. His " 'Li sao' hsü" (Preface to "Encountering Sorrow") took its example from Wang Yi's (c. 89–158) "Preface" to his edition of *Ch'u tz'u chang-chu* (Elegies of Ch'u, with Supplemental Commentary; second century C.E.), but goes beyond the focus on Ch'ü Yüan as individual to make the exemplary poet into a poetic exemplar. Wang Yi's preface is biographical, not intended as literary criticism. He confidently assumed that the experience described in "Encountering Sorrow" reflected the personal experience of the poet and legendary statesman Ch'ü Yüan and was essential to the brilliance of his poem. In order to legitimize his fame, the poem is compared in excellence and significance to the poetry of the *Classic of Poetry*—typical elements of traditionalist criticism. Pan Ku discusses how the poem reveals Ch'ü Yüan as a paragon of Confucian rectitude in word and deed. The *History of the Han Dynasty* also included Pan Ku's essay on the poetic genres of his time, "Yi-wen chih shih-fu lüeh" (Outline of the Purpose of Literary Esthetics in Poetry and Rhymeprose).

Wang Ch'ung (29–c. 97) was a Han philosopher who dealt with principles in literary criticism as esthetics in a more abstract fashion. His *Lun-heng* (Authoritative Expositions; literally "The Steelyard of Exposition") is an integrated work of philosophy in eighty-five chapters, including several touching on literary theory. Following his own convictions on the superiority of plain and clear style, he emphasizes that literature must be constructive, displaying a purpose to prove truth. A critic should always try to restore literature to a strictly true context. Writing is a manifestation of the natural order. A literary composition that aspires to meaning beyond its immediate context must nevertheless be grounded in truth. The written word may function as a sign for something beyond itself; however, all that words signify is ultimately grounded in the physical world. Thus poetry should be read as strictly rather than metaphorically true, even if the reader must be led to that truth through the device of metaphor. In other words, poetic truth should be real in the sense that it speaks directly to something recognizable in human nature and experience, rather than some purely abstract or intellectual form beyond human nature and experience. The irony for the reader is that if language is inherently metaphorical, then description of the physical world is already a symbolic act, rather than a concrete one.

The Han dynasty was a period in which the interests of state and culture seemed to be at one. Its long stability appeared to fulfill all the dreams of antiquity for political unity, which in turn ensured the flourishing of artistic culture. The Chien-an reign-period (196–219) saw the collapse of this order (see chapter 13), and a reunified Middle Kingdom became a dream that would require several centuries to realize. The confidence of the Han was replaced by doubt on all levels. The spiritual void created by the political uncertainty of the time inspired an unprecedented questioning of values and norms (political, social, esthetic), and the place of individual psychology in the greater world became a subject for serious consideration. Perhaps significantly, it was precisely at this crucial moment in Chinese cultural history that Buddhism, with its sophisticated philosophical and esthetic discourse, began to make its impact. This period saw the beginnings of many new forms of literature, and poetry especially began to assume the forms that would dominate until at least the end of the T'ang dynasty.

Because of the new focus on the individual, and because of the political chaos of the time, the study of literature shook loose from its mooring to the concerns of the state and began more overtly to privilege individual creativity and expression. This trend is also reflected in the themes of literature of the age, as the personal world of emotion starts to prevail over concerns of state. Poems on themes like the uncertainty of life, the sorrow of separation, old age, and love are still assumed to be transparent windows on the past and on the cultural and political moment in which the poet wrote. This transparency, however, is no longer equated with the poet's primary responsibility to reflect and uphold the state. The period of disunion presaged by the Chien-an period, which included the Wei, Chin, and the Northern and Southern Dynasties, saw the greatest flowering of Chinese literary criticism as an independent form of discourse.

THE ESTHETIC SEA CHANGE OF THE SIX DYNASTIES

The literary thought of two imperial brothers of the Wei dynasty, Ts'ao P'i (187–226) and Ts'ao Chih (192–232), pointed to the bridge from traditional literary ideology to a new field of literary esthetics. The sons of Ts'ao Ts'ao (155–220) intended to fulfill their father's dynastic aspirations, but each had his own intentions, which sometimes conflicted with those of the other. In their literary criticism, both expend much energy criticizing their contemporaries and speculating on their own abilities to transcend their age through literature. Ts'ao Chih was regarded as more brilliant and was certainly far and away the more outstanding poet, but fell from favor and spent the rest of his life fearing his brother's wrath for his presumption. His literary disquisitions took the form of personal letters in which his own disappointed political ambitions threaten to undermine his transcendent poetic talent. His letter to his friend Yang Hsiu, "Ts'ao Tzu-chien yü Yang Te-tsu shu" (Letter from Ts'ao Tzu-chien to Yang Te-tsu), is a strange mixture of mock-humble arrogance and ardent desire to restore literature to its normative function as mirror of the state.

The poetically less-gifted brother not only took the throne but proved the more enduring theorist. The extant "Lun wen" (Essay on Literature) was a section in Ts'ao P'i's twenty-chapter *Tien lun* (Normative Essays). Ts'ao P'i took both his critical and stylistic cue from the "plain style" of Wang Ch'ung; however, the "Essay on Literature" is a far more idiosyncratic, and ultimately more influential, work. Ts'ao P'i wrote of his conviction that literature was ultimately "the great enterprise for managing a state" (*ching kuo chih ta-yeh*). While he shuns unnecessary ornamentation, he asserts that "poetry and rhymeprose should be beautiful," as esthetic beauty will ensure that what endures of a state is worthy of it.

Ts'ao P'i discusses the notion of individual style or spirit (*ch'i*) in writing, which he regards as inborn, a gift of talent obvious in music or literature, where even those equal in skill may not necessarily be equal in achievement. The genre chosen by a writer to some extent defines this talent and so is a significant feature of the reader's appreciation of the poet's character and intent.

"Wen fu" (Rhapsody on Literature), written during the Western Chin dynasty in the late third century by Lu Chi (261–303), is unique and unprecedented in form, language, and critical focus. Using the rhymeprose form for the exposition itself, "Rhapsody on Literature" is divided into nineteen stanzas with distinctive rhyme patterns and includes a prose preface. This is a brilliant poem by any standard. It is a hymn of praise for the craft and art of writing and a specific, prescriptive handbook for the writer. In the preface, Lu Chi declares that, in spite of the infinite variety of poetry, the student of literature can still evaluate its merits and thus enhance the experience of reading. The poem ranges over the topics of inspiration, which comes and goes beyond control of the writer, and the pleasure of writing, which is no less than the harnessing of the transcendent power of the mind as the home of both idea and consciousness (*yi*). The poet is a special manifestation of humanity as microcosm of the universe, whose sympathetic resonance with nature allows journeys throughout the cosmos by the use of the imagination. In this sense, whatever form is used, the poet participates in the experience and genius of Ch'ü Yüan. By choosing the rhymeprose form of his symbolic mentor for his exposition, Lu Chi takes his own place in the tradition and offers the possibility of joining the stream to his readers.

According to the "Rhapsody on Literature," all writing will inevitably, to some degree, be unique because all individual experience is different. Language has limitations: words are fixed things in a physical world in constant flux; therefore, words cannot exhaust the meaning of experience. But words used in writing become evocative: there is no such thing as a "static" text. The act of reading allows the recreation of the flux of the world as imagined by the author. Lu Chi believes that literature is the subtle expression of a unique state of mind, a perfect correlation of inner and outer reality. On the cosmic level, writing creates being from nonbeing; on the human level, readers can divine poets' emotions from reading their words and understand the people behind them. Sitting at his desk ready to write, Lu Chi imagines literature as infinity on a sheet of white silk.

Lu Chi particularly advises on the appropriate choice of genre and the purpose of style. His emphasis on writing as craft is dramatized by his use of an extended metaphor of weaving and his explicit discussion of faults. In this he does not exempt himself, lamenting the gap between his imaginative vision and execution in his poem. But in spite of the emphasis on instructing the reader in the art of writing, no other poet is named for comparison or evaluation. The focus is on the craft and art of writing in and of itself.

The Chin dynasty produced two other critics: a contemporary of Lu Chi, Chih Yü (d. 311), and Li Ch'ung (fourth century), whose work exerted enduring influence. Both were anthologists, and although their anthologies are lost and only fragments of their essays and comments remain, their contributions lie in the authoritative structure they gave to their selections. Chih Yü compiled a collection of early writings divided according to genre, called *Wen-chang liu-pieh chih* (Collection on Development and Change in Literary Genres), accompanied by his critical evaluation, "Wen-chang liu-pieh chih-lun" (Discourse on Development and Change in Literary Genres). Literary genres have different functions in manifesting the patterns of the universe, and he asserts that even popular poetry, seemingly concerned with individual experience, is actually about the affairs of state. Rhymeprose receives his highest praise, but he follows Yang Hsiung in deploring meretricious ornamentation.

Li Ch'ung's *Han-lin lun* (Discourse on the Foremost Writings) appeared in the Eastern Chin dynasty (317–420). He divided literature into four major categories: classics (*ching*), histories (*shih*), philosophy (*tzu*), and collections of creative writing (*chi*), a system of categorization that has been used even down to the present.

The poet Tso Ssu (c. 253–c. 307) was an important adherent of the theory that verisimilitude in literature represents learning and truth. In his "Preface" to his masterwork, "San tu fu" (Rhapsody on the Three Capitals), he describes his scrupulous reconstruction of knowledge of the ancient cities as a counterweight to the fantasies of other authors. His reader can reconstruct the experience of the poet by reconstructing, through reading, the object of the poem—in this case not an object of the poet's personal experience, but a historical object of value because of the poet's particular interpretation of its significance. This explicitly freed the poet from the burden of depending on personal experience for the material of a poem.

The Northern and Southern Dynasties saw the greatest flowering of Chinese literary criticism. Until this point, although many individual voices can be identified whose fame rests on their innovative literary criticism, the writers thought of themselves primarily as writers of other genres: poetry, philosophy, historiography. In this period authors began to identify themselves specifically as literary critics, and criticism becomes an enterprise in its own right, not just a concomitant of other forms. The first specialist books devoted to literary theory appear and represent an extraordinary pluralism in critical viewpoints and approaches. There are works of genre classification and criticism, of literary history, handbooks of technical criticism—in short, literature as an enterprise spawns its own discourse, which in turn gives tremendous energy to the creative and individual aspects of literary production.

These works may be distinguished as traditionalist (or fundamentalist) and progressive (or decadent), as many of their writers so identified themselves. Their authors also felt a great duty to preserve and classify the works of their age, perhaps with a view to gaining perspective on their historical situation and leaving documents that might help later ages gain it if they could not. The intellectual circle of the royal family of the Liang dynasty (502–557), and members of the imperial family themselves, made some of the most important contributions to this effort. It is fair to say that without the anthology compiled by Hsiao T'ung, Prince Chao-ming (501–531), *Wen hsüan* (Literary Selections), also titled *Chao-ming wen-hsüan* (Selections of Refined Literature by Prince Chao-ming), the greatest works of the Han, Wei, and Chin dynasties might very well have been lost, including many seminal works of literary theory.

Hsiao T'ung's preface explains that it was his intention to save his readers from leafing through sheaves of mediocre works to find the most worthy specimens of previous ages. It also presents his sophisticated and inspired notion of literature as distinct from other forms of writing. Literature articulates profound human experience and insight in beautiful form. Hsiao T'ung distinguishes it from history, which is concerned with enumerating and analyzing facts, and from philosophy, which is concerned with ideas but not particular experience. The works in his anthology are selected for exquisitely crafted language and form and for their self-contained integrity. They are also the embodiment of the critical values expressed in the work of a close associate of Hsiao T'ung, Liu Hsieh's (465?–520? C.E.) *Wen-hsin tiao-lung* (The Literary Mind and Carving of Dragons; see below). Together, the theoretical masterpiece and the anthology define the Liang as one of the pinnacles of Chinese artistic culture.

Hsiao Kang (503–551) was Hsiao T'ung's younger brother, and reigned as Emperor Chien-wen for the last two years of his life. He is most famous for his association with the rise of "palace style" (*kung-t'i*) and notorious for his fervent embrace of literary decadence (*t'ui-fei*). He was a thorough radical in poetry and thought, setting poetry apart from other literary arts as the domain of the individual. In a letter to another brother, Hsiao Yi ("Yü Hsiang-tung Wang shu"), Hsiao Kang makes a complete break with traditionalists. He declares that in order for literature to carry on from antiquity, new forms, language, and styles are essential. He attacked the use of archaic models as stifling to individual creativity and as avoiding the realities of a new age. While new kinds of literature may be different, they are not necessarily inferior to the old. The traditional forms were new in their time, reflected those realities, and spoke to their ages. These are circumstances that cannot be resuscitated. He deplores the fundamentalist tendency to jumble the expressive purpose of poetry with other genres, particularly history and philosophy, which do not have a primary duty to be true to the individual writer but, rather, to the state. To this end, he paraphrases Wei Hung's "Major Preface," declaring that the function of poetry that makes it unique is to "sing of one's feelings" (*yin-yung ch'ing-hsing*). Hsiao Kang makes no apology for self-referentiality and even uses the sensual language that is his poetic trademark in his exposition.

The enterprise of classifying poetry allowed critics to include notions from both traditionalist and progressive criticism. *Shih-p'in* (An Evaluation of Poetry), by Chung Jung (469?–518), originally titled *Shih-p'ing* (A Critique of Poetry), is the first work systematically to filiate authors and literary history. Chung Jung's work has two main purposes. First, he classified poets of the Later Han through Liang dynasties who wrote *shih* poetry using the pentasyllabic—or five-character (*wu-yen*)—line according to three grades, both for the quality of their poetry and their presumed suitability for government service. Second, he sought to trace their poetic lineage. His judgments as to which poets should occupy which grade—upper, middle, or lower—have been endlessly debated, not least because, even though he is at pains to discuss individual characteristics of the 120-odd poets selected, his criteria for assessing quality and standards of judgment are not clear. Perhaps his most notorious critical gaffe is the consignment of T'ao Ch'ien (365–427), later much celebrated as the greatest bucolic poet of the Chinese tradition, to the second rank. Issues of the legitimacy of such rankings aside, the fact that the rankings were made, and their justice upheld and contested as his technique of classification was imitated by later critics, shows the influence of this work.

The poetic lineages reflect Chung Jung's more successful attempt at exposition of the history of Chinese poetry and the evolution of pentasyllabic verse up to his own time, which he regards as the most elegant form of poetry and most effective for conveying emotion and individual purpose. His elevation of pentasyllabic verse as the premier form of expression was a radical step, made acceptable to traditionalists by his meticulous filiations of the work of individual poets to sources in the *Classic of Poetry*, especially the "Kuo-feng" (Airs of the States) and "Ta ya" (Greater Elegantiae), and the *Elegies of Ch'u*. For example, the earliest extant poems in pentasyllabic form, the "Ku-shih shih-chiu shou" (Nineteen Old Poems), are explicitly linked to the "Airs of the States," thereby confirming that the beauty of the poems participates in the accepted, high moral purpose of the Confucian classic.

Wen-hsin tiao-lung (The Literary Mind and the Carving of Dragons), by Liu Hsieh, is generally regarded as the masterpiece of Chinese literary criticism. The work is structured as a collection of essays, in the tradition of works such as Wang Ch'ung's *Authoritative Expositions*, but, unlike such previous collections, it is written entirely in magnificent parallel prose. Liu Hsieh combines the two critical streams of traditionalist and progressive poetics in a unified analysis of the nature and purpose of literature. Read chapter by chapter, it appears full of contradictions. For example, one sees that the ancients hand down a precedent that literature must change with the needs of the times, then that a poet must beware of innovation for its own sake, as the ancient models are correct and efficacious in all ages.

The Literary Mind and the Carving of Dragons consists of forty-nine chapters, plus the author's afterword. The analysis may be divided into two main parts. The first begins with four chapters of polemical discussions on the origin of the Tao and literature as its manifestation, the nature of the sage (*sheng*), the Confucian classics (*ching*), and the apocryphal texts (*wei*) attached to them. The classics are seen as the sources of all genres, which return to antiquity and participate in the Confucian belief in literature's first function as a cultural and political force. Chapters 5 though 25 then discuss the history of characteristics of the major genres of literature. Liu Hsieh is inclusive and exhaustive, ranging from poetry (*sao, fu, shih, yüeh-fu,* and sacrificial odes) to inscriptions, laments, humor, historiography, persuasions, proclamations, memorials, debates, and letters.

The second part begins with chapter 26. In the subsequent chapters, Liu Hsieh discourses on concepts of literary theory, the essential terms and vocabulary of literary criticism in China. The terms themselves are evocative, and they are set forth in a style that elicits the esthetic transcendence to which their use in writing aspires. They have become key to the vocabulary of literary criticism. To describe the character of writing in general, Liu Hsieh invokes, according to the titles of his chapters, "Inspiration" (*shen-ssu;* chapter 26), "Form and Nature" (*t'i-hsing;* chapter 27), "Wind and Bone" (*feng-ku,* that is, the affective potency of a work as it evokes canonical principles; chapter 28), and "Continuity and Transformation" (*t'ung-pien;* chapter 29). Chapter 30 concerns "Choosing Style" (*ting-shih*). Thereafter follow several chapters concerning how to balance expressive concerns with technical considerations: 31: "Shades of Emotion" (*ch'ing-ts'ai*); 32: "Casting and Cutting" (*jung-ts'ai*); 33: "Principles of Sound" (*sheng-lü*); and 34: "Paragraph and Line" (*chang-chü*). Poetic devices are dealt with in chapters 35: "Parallelism" (*li-tz'u*); 36: "Comparison and Affective Image" (*pi-hsing*); 37: "Hyperbole" (*k'ua-shih*); 38: "Factual and Textual Allusion" (*shih-lei*); and 39: "Philology and Word Choice" (*lien-tzu*). More general considerations of quality and character are addressed in chapters 40: "Hidden and Manifest" (*yin-hsiu*); 41: "Literary Flaws" (*chih-hsia*); 42: "Nurturing Creative Energy" (*yang-ch'i*); and 43: "Organization and Coherence" (*fu-hui*). The final chapters are concerned with the question of "what is literature?" in all its aspects: 44: "Discussion of Technique" (*tsung-shu*); 45: "Literary Development Through Time" (*shih-hsü*); 46: "Sensual Phenomena" (*wu-so,* referring to the perception of physical objects of the phenomenal world); 47: "Talented Practitioners" (*ts'ai-lüeh*); 48: "The Perfect Listener" (*chih-yin,* literally, "one who understands the tone"); and 49: "The Volume of a Container" (*ch'eng-ch'i,* a discussion of a writer's need to cultivate practical applications of genius in order to achieve fame and serve the state).

Liu Hsieh's personal view of literature and his apologia for his work are contained in his afterword (*hsü-chih*) rather than a preface, another allusion to the structure of Wang Ch'ung's *Authoritative Expositions*. Liu's metaphor of "carving dragons" validates works of lavish ornamentation and artfulness, but also sounds a cautionary note as a counterweight to the "insect carving" deplored by Yang Hsiung. It may be difficult to achieve true greatness, but Liu believes it can be achieved and aspires to it himself. Fulfilling artistic potential requires extraordinary effort, all the while striving to make the results seem effortless. Liu sees literary criticism as a full part of literary art, an avenue to cultural immortality that requires as much artistry as any of the genres discussed in the body of his work. While he deprecates the efforts of his predecessors, his work fully resonates with theirs. In a sense, by taking the pose of a writer standing alone, he focuses literary theory as a genre and enterprise in its own right and establishes the tradition that he sought to transcend.

P'ei Tzu-yeh (469–530) wrote *Tiao-ch'ung lun* (Treatise on Insect Carving)—part playful riposte to Liu Hsieh, part earnest admonition—in a deliberately clumsy style. Yang Hsiung is his explicit literary ancestor, and it is a feature of the extraordinary fertility and variety of the Liang dynasty that the court that produced the foremost practitioner and defender of "decadent" poetry and poetics should also accommodate P'ei's forthright attack on literary progressivism in all its forms. His metaphor of carving for the writing of poetry is not a compliment: Liu Hsieh may hope for dragons, but P'ei sees the young writers of his time as expending their energy and talent on a fruitless enterprise, which will yield neither enlightened leadership for the state nor personal immortality for themselves.

The first poetic anthology produced during this period, by contrast with the more inclusive *Literary Selections*, was Hsü Ling's (507–583) *Yü-t'ai hsin-yung* (New Songs from a Jade Terrace). The anthology is distinctive in that its selection focused generically on popular-style poetry. It includes many outstanding examples of anonymous folk poems and poems in folk style and is thematically focused on love in its many aspects, including eroticism. Not surprisingly, the collection was commissioned by Hsiao Kang. Hsü's "ten books of love songs" is accompanied by a poetic "Preface," which maintains a light and even humorous tone as it enumerates famous ladies of past and present as the subject and inspiration of his selection. Their skills in self-adornment and the arts are the metaphors of poetic production, as artifice replaces spontaneity in his esthetics. Hsü reminds his readers that the "Airs" from the *Classic of Poetry* included similar themes, and so the content of his anthology may not be so scandalous after all. This suggests that there is still some hint of unease in all the banter, as the editor is clearly aware of the gap between his materials and the contents of the classic. But his dazzling language symbolically distracts him from traditionalist constraints, and certainly our appreciation of early popular poetry would be much diminished without this record of the sensual side of Chinese poetry.

A direct confrontation of these decadent poetics came from Yen Chih-t'ui (531–591) in his collection of essays, *Yen-shih chia-hsün* (The Admonitions of

Master Yen). This is a survey of the social and cultural milieu of the Northern and Southern Dynasties, which he presents as a struggle between the relative austerity of northern culture and the tendency to decadence and detachment of southern culture. This is a characterization that had been latent in earlier works, but here takes a form that has allowed the debate to flourish into this century. The section titled "Wen-chang" (Essay on Literature) is unapologetically didactic, while adhering rather closely to the theory of literature presented in *The Literary Mind and the Carving of Dragons.* Yen charges that the poems of his time are "frivolously ornate; their style competing with substance and reason" (*shuai to fu-yen, tz'u yü li-ching*). Like P'ei Tzu-yeh, he regarded this literature as a definite decline from the writings of ancient times and urged a "return to antiquity" (*fu-ku*) in standards.

These writers form the heart of literary criticism in China, and the style and content of their works of literary theory are the implicit standards for all later works. In a sense, later literary criticism is a dialogue with these early masters, and, even in ages of great social stability and political complacency, writers engage the anxieties and uncertainties about the content and purpose of art that underlay the production of the Late Han through the Northern and Southern Dynasties.

THE T'ANG TRANSITION

In the Sui (581–618) and T'ang dynasties, and indeed ever after, the practice of literary criticism became almost an inevitable concomitant of a literary career. In addition to the self-conscious attention given to the subject by creative writers, commentary and critique of literature became a standard subject for scholar-officials in the practice of their official duties. The example set by Pan Ku was followed by the historians who prepared the dynastic histories of the Wei, Chin, and Northern and Southern dynasties (i.e., the Six Dynasties), each work having its own sections devoted to literature. The evaluation of literature as reflection of previous dynasties took its place, in minor but nevertheless significant form, as an integral part of official historiography.

Although the T'ang dynasty is often hailed as the golden age of Chinese poetry and abounds in literary commentary, surprisingly little literary theory in its own right survives from the era. A minor example is by a Buddhist monk, Chiao-jan (720–805?), who compiled a critical survey of formal rules in *Shih-shih* (Designs of Poetry).

One of the most important collections of writings on Chinese poetics and prosody was actually compiled by a Japanese Buddhist monk named Kūkai (774–835) who visited China from 804 to 806. This is *Bunkyō hifuron* (Treatise [*Śāstra*] on the Secret Treasury of the Literary Mirror). Most of the texts preserved in *Bunkyō hifuron* were later lost in China; thus it is extremely valuable for understanding the history of literary criticism and theory in China. Among the unique works preserved in Kūkai's collection are some of the earliest discussions on the "four tones" (*ssu-sheng*) and "eight defects" (*pa-ping*) of the Liang dynasty lay Buddhist poet Shen Yüeh (441–513). These vital rules describing and governing tonal euphony, which led to the preeminent T'ang poetic form known as "regulated verse" (*lü-shih*) and "recent-style verse" (*chin-t'i shih*), have now been shown to derive directly from Sanskrit models. A major work of literary criticism that has been recovered from *Bunkyō hifuron* is the *Shih-ko* (The Framework of Poetry) of Wang Ch'ang-ling (c. 690–c. 756), an outstanding poet of the first half of the eighth century. *The Framework of Poetry* is an extraordinary achievement in many respects. In contrast to the often abstruse, ornate, and difficult works of literary criticism, *The Framework of Poetry* is written in an engaging, informal style and semivernacular language.

The mainstream of T'ang literary discourse carried on traditionalist ideals. The most influential figure of literary ideology and esthetics in this period is Han Yü (768–824). He did not identify himself primarily as a literary theorist; rather, he was a universal cultural critic, whose criticism vitally influenced Chinese esthetics and artistic practice. Literature was a crucial vehicle for his ideas, but literary theory was incidental to his larger vision of "return to antiquity" in style, expression, and thought. He was before all a servant of the state, with an unquenchable energy to use his talents for its betterment. Han Yü's personal ideology of "returning to antiquity" was manifest in his writing as "ancient prose" (*ku-wen;* in his terms, "writing with the force of antiquity behind it").

For Han Yü, literature was a vehicle of political reform. The prose style he adopted was deliberately "eccentric" (*ch'i* [strange]). It involved the heavy use of archaisms, strange grammar, and long phrases, and he was not afraid of deforming conventional syntax for effect. He drew also upon a rich sense of humor, not always appreciated, in his use of rhetoric to achieve political goals. Polemical essays were his specialty, and he eschews clichés in his drive to direct attention to the issues that energized his writing. Although it had the power to shock at first, his innovative style of argument, and its unusual structure, came to be widely imitated. In essays like "Yüan-tao" (Essentials of the Moral Way) and "Shih-shuo" (Discourse on Teachers), Han Yü inverts the usual order of argument: he comes right out with his statement in the opening passages, phrased so abruptly as almost to offend, then conducts his proof and argues the legitimacy of his assertion. He revived obscure meanings of words, even changing their usual semantic values, a strategy frequently used in poetry but not expected in prose. He also used imitation and parody, and his tactics in these essays evoke the prose of Chuang Tzu far more than that of his hero, Confucius. His "Mao Ying chuan" (Biography of Mao Ying) is a parody of the biographies of Ssu-ma Ch'ien (c. 145–c. 86 B.C.E.), as he muses on the political significance of the matters in which his writing brush has dabbled.

In addition to his immense gifts as a poet, Han Yü expanded the realm of prose to categories where rhymeprose and poetry had previously been used. Strictly speaking, this is a contribution not so much to literary criticism as to literary history; however, he inspired writers to see expressive possibilities in prose consistent with traditionalist ideals.

The T'ang dynasty was an age of unprecedented poetic innovation, resulting in an explosion of genres, styles, and the bounds of poetic language, but in the realm of literary theory, there is really only one figure in the tradition of Lu Chi or Liu Hsieh. This is Ssu-k'ung T'u (837–908), also known as a poet. Although he had a successful career as an official, a dark sense of the fragility of the failing T'ang dynasty informed his poetry and his criticism. Toward the end of his life, he likened the dynasty to a reflection in the water, which may in return reflect on the abstruseness and abstraction of his writing on the nature of art.

Indeed, the level of abstraction in *Erh-shih-ssu shih-p'in* (Twenty-four Varieties of Poetic Experience) is such that it is impossible to see Ssu-k'ung T'u's terms as referring to poetry alone. The elusive quality of the text was certainly intended, enhanced by the dense rhythm of the tetrasyllabic (*ssu-yen*) meter employed by the author. The level of abstraction must have been at least as intended. The subject, and object, of *Twenty-four Varieties of Poetic Experience* is to define ultimate categories of esthetic experience, for the poet and for the reader. If we remember that, according to the ancients and the ideals associated with them, artistic expression emulates the patterns of nature, then literature is by no means the only form this expression may take. Ssu-k'ung T'u's title elevates poetry above all other art forms, but such an esthetic construction implicitly extends itself to all the arts.

Twenty-four Varieties of Poetic Experience embraces multiple influences in the history of literary theory, yet is profoundly, thoroughly innovative. To begin with, it takes its title from Chung Jung's *Evaluation of Poetry*, yet Ssu-k'ung T'u classifies no poetry, ranks no poets; indeed, names no names. Nor can the twenty-four verses of *Twenty-four Varieties of Poetic Experience* be considered just a list of styles. The expectations of classification are blocked, for the work far more closely evokes, both in its use of poetry for its exposition and in its subject matter, the "Rhapsody on Literature" of Lu Chi. The mode of exposition may be linked to Liu Hsieh's *Literary Mind and the Carving of Dragons*, although the link is to Liu's enigmatic verse summations of his chapters rather than to his expositions. Ssu-k'ung T'u's vocabulary and his use of the tetrasyllabic line link the work to a completely different mode of discourse, the "abstruse utterances" (*hsüan-yen*) of Eastern Chin (317–420) Taoist philosophical poetry. All these links are tantalizing, and the poet was certainly aware of them. None alone is sufficient to explain the evocative power of this mysterious text, for *Twenty-four Varieties of Poetic Experience* is unique, idiosyncratic, and probably deliberately impenetrable.

Perhaps Ssu-k'ung T'u's intention is not to explain poetry, which, after all, is only a partial reflection of the patterns of the universe, but to remind his readers of the scope of the patterns of the universe even beyond the edges of imagination. Read as a mystical work, *Twenty-four Varieties of Poetic Experience* might awaken his readers to the potential of language to evoke the infinite flux of the universe, even as language defeats this attempt through its own limitations. In human experience, all that appears to be random is in fact the natural pattern of the universe. Language is merely humanity's attempt to evoke that metaphorically, for it is insufficient to express the scope of these patterns. To look at it another way, Ssu-k'ung T'u's poetics follow his own dictum from section 11, "Han-hsü" (Concealed and Implied): "Though not a word is said outright, the elegant style fulfills all" (*pu-chu yi-tzu, chin te feng-liu*). *Twenty-four Varieties of Poetic Experience* attempts nothing less than to give literary theory the mental and emotional resonance of lyric poetry. As one reads about the principles of poetry, one recreates within oneself the experience of poetry in its essence, its totality. The process of passing through the twenty-four "experiences" leads the reader to an epiphany of the nature and scope of poetry itself. One must rely on intuition to enter and integrate with the experience of the poet's creation. The act of reading will reveal all to the initiated; what remains abstruse is a sign of the gap between the reader and esthetic transfiguration.

But Ssu-k'ung T'u's work is usually read as the prime example of metaphorical criticism. His views on the nature of poetry reflect late T'ang esthetics. Two aspects of these esthetics are central concerns throughout the text. First is the notion of flavor (or meaning) that lies "beyond the flavor (or meaning)" (*wei-wai*). Full experience of poetry requires intuition of the words beyond the level of language, an almost experiential integration with the moment. He also makes it clear that poetry should be flexible, not bound to one style, but should contain subtle variations, like food or perfume. If a poet is too attached to any one style, the quality of expression will be diminished because awareness of the conventions of form will obscure clarity of intuition and its expression. A poet should not be controlled by style, but must take control of it, step outside form and convention to achieve full artistic expression. In tune with contemporaries like Li Shang-yin (811?–859) and Tu Mu (803–852), Ssu-k'ung T'u privileges poetry as an art form without obligations to better society, whose ultimate purpose is to combine beautiful language with meaning beyond the literal level of the words (*yen-wai chih yi*). It may be easiest to contemplate the beauty of the language and let the possibility of particular meaning take care of itself.

There are allusions to *Twenty-four Varieties of Poetic Experience* in later periods, notably Su Shih's lament that its value was not sufficiently recognized, but the work did not really come into its own until the Ch'ing dynasty (1644–1911), when it was debated, exalted, and admired by imitation (Yüan Mei [1716–1797] wrote his own version with forty-eight categories). Perhaps its emphasis on the nature of artistic experience and inspiration, its stress on intuition and insight, and its apparently total indifference to the efficacy of literature in ameliorating the problems of the waning dynasty did not appeal. Certainly the Sung dynasty (960–1279) saw a fundamental change in the orientation of theoretical criticism, away from the creative process and individual genius and toward technical criticism. In that sense, Ssu-k'ung T'u's *Twenty-four Varieties of Poetic Experience* is the last major work of literary theory. In the Sung dynasty, technical criticism comes into its own. It is also the age of a more informal, though thoroughly self-conscious, personal voice in literary discourse, a convention of a more relaxed approach to literary criticism.

NEW IDEAS AND APPROACHES IN THE SUNG PERIOD

The Sung genre of literary criticism par excellence is "remarks on poetry" (*shih-hua*). *Shih-hua* are musings on any sort of literary issue, ranging from principles of selection, historical contexts, and analyzing lines or couplets to evaluating and comparing the merits of various poets. The first *shih-hua* appear in a collection of twenty-eight short pieces by Ou-yang Hsiu (1007–1072). The subjects range from personal anecdotes and records of intellectual discussions with friends to evaluations of poems. The personal voice here is quite conversational. The remarks open with a general statement on a certain issue, pose an example, and then offer some chatty comment. The casual tone of these passages seems antitraditionalist; however, light tone does not necessarily mean light content. Reading *shih-hua* makes one recognize the distance the oral style of discourse has come from the *Analects*. The *Analects* are supposed to record the discussions of Confucius and sound the tone of the sage. *Shih-hua* are very similar in form, but preserve the speech of their writers in a much more lively and immediate way. The sense of individual personality is key to their appeal. Ou-yang Hsiu's remarks seem random, providing a sense of spontaneity. This informality of style became a convention in itself, as seen in the "responses" to Ou-yang Hsiu's remarks written by Ssu-ma Kuang (1019–1086), *Hsü shih-hua* (Continuing Remarks on Poetry).

As the genre proliferated, firm structures of organization began to appear. Instead of the casual voice, *shih-hua* took on much more the tone of pronouncements. Ou-yang Hsiu's anecdotes seem touching artifacts of a time when literary discussion was a serious yet enjoyable part of social intercourse, like deep night discussions of literature over coffee for the university students of our time. *Shih-hua* had their own esthetic of casualness, which was later criticized as showing insufficient reverence for the canonical functions of poetry. This seems a shame, since the collections are full of provocative insights not only into the literature of their time but also into their contemporary culture. To take a comment from Ou-yang Hsiu's eighth remark slightly out of context: "It is regrettable that one word [originally] meant as a joke can influence the way things are ever after."

Ou-yang Hsiu's remarks did carry that kind of weight. The very specificity of his anecdotes provides models for evaluating and cherishing small moments of experience, while revealing their more wide-ranging significance. Instead of fixing them as moments of personal history in time, separate from the reader, readers respond to them as to lyrical vignettes, integrating themselves into the experience, which, because of its very quotidian tone, becomes almost universal.

Most collections of Sung period *shih-hua* were relatively short, some of them only a few pages long. As the genre developed, however, they grew in size until, in the eighteenth century, Yüan Mei could put together his *Sui-yüan shih-hua* (Poetry Talks from the Sui Garden), which was 800 pages long. In this work, Yüan Mei was strongly opposed to the piling up of artistic edifice, insisting instead on the poet's own character and spirit (*hsing-ling*).

The most influential work of Sung criticism ostensibly takes the *shih-hua* form, Yen Yü's (c. 1195–c. 1245) *Ts'ang-lang shih-hua* (Ts'ang-lang's Remarks on Poetry). The tone is discursive and personal; however, the text is systematically arranged and builds a provocative argument for the affinity of poetry and Ch'an (Zen) Buddhism. While Buddhism had influenced Chinese poetry and poetics for several hundred years, this is the first disquisition explicitly to assimilate the esthetic experience of lyric poetry to the experience of Buddhist enlightenment.

The text is organized in three parts, beginning with his theoretical statement, then describing the basis of his technical criticism, and finally commenting on literary history and individual poets. In the first chapter, "Shih-pien" (Discernment of Poetry), Yen Yü compares poetic inspiration with Ch'an intuition in a way that makes language an explicit vehicle for spiritual awakening: "One should speak of poetry as one speaks of Ch'an. . . . Just as the essence of Ch'an is marvelous illumination [*miao-wu*], the essence of poetry is likewise marvelous illumination." Although Ch'an teaching rejects language on the most radical level, poetry is elevated among artifacts of language because the nature of inspiration in traditional Chinese poetics has strong affinities with Ch'an intuition. The Ch'an emphasis on spontaneity was esthetic as well as religious, and this formed the bridge between Buddhist thought and poetics. This opening section puts forth a general theory of the essential identity of inspiration and the right way to discriminate quality in poetry. In following sections he proposes qualities and expressive purposes to aid the reader in attaining this.

Yen Yü lays out five "rules" or "dharmas" (*fa*) of poetry: (1) construction of form (*t'i-chih*); (2) structural strength (*ko-li*); (3) embodiment of energy (*ch'i-hsiang*); (4) rousing excitement (*hsing-ch'ü*); and (5) tone and rhythm (*yin-chieh*). He then lists nine "varieties of poetic experience" (*p'in*): (1) the lofty (*kao*); (2) the ancient (*ku*); (3) the profound (*shen*); (4) the distant (*yüan*); (5) the lengthy (*ch'ang*); (6) potent flux (*hsiung-hun*); (7) drifting above it all (*p'iao-yi*); (8) fortitude in affliction (*pei-chuang*); and (9) bittersweet grief (*chi-wan*). *P'in* is translated here as per Ssu-k'ung T'u's work because many of these categories echo his terms, emphasizing the affective aspect of poetry, which in turn complements the comparison with Ch'an experience. These principles may describe, but do not encompass, the nature of poetry. Although he advocates poetry as a vehicle of transcendence, however, he does not denigrate the vehicle itself: "Poetry has distinctive material that has nothing to do with what is written . . . [but] one should not drop into the fish-trap of words." This phrase alludes to a passage from the *Chuang Tzu*, "to forget the fish-trap when you have caught the fish" (*te yü erh wang ch'üan*). Ideally, after the vehicle (fish-trap or language) has performed its function, it can be discarded; however, the philosopher then goes on to lament his inability to discuss the process of transcendence with someone who has achieved it. As a Ch'an practitioner with literary ambitions, Yen Yü limns a gentle irony: if poetry leads one to intuition beyond words, should one not consider the vehicle with appreciation?

The second chapter, "Shih-t'i" (Forms of Poetry), presents Yen Yü's categories of styles. The third chapter is the heart of the *shih-hua*, "Shih-fa" (Rules of Poetry). It ranges widely through quotes and comments on many poets. Yen Yü valorizes the poetry of the High T'ang, especially Tu Fu's (712–770), and rejects the poetry of his own age as superficial by comparison. While his juxtaposition of Ch'an insight and poetic transcendence might seem to favor poetry as personal expression, rather than as a vehicle of social reform, he deplores literary self-indulgence as counterproductive to spiritual progress. Yen Yü was a hero of orthodox criticism for the scholars of the Ming dynasty (1368–1644). He certainly had the final word on the rankings and order of literary history, for his judgments were never questioned by Ming neoclassicists.

A critic of a very different sort from Yan Yü is Yüan Hao-wen (1190–1257), the most celebrated literary figure of the Chin (Jurchen) dynasty (1115–1234). The chief body of Yüan's literary criticism is found in three series of poems on poetry that he wrote, especially his "Lun shih san-shih shou" (Thirty Poems on Poetry). Perhaps reflecting Neo-Confucian sentiments, Yüan emphasizes sincerity, purity, and decorum. His critical stance set the tone for many later writers who preferred discipline, propriety, and heroism over intuition and innovation.

OUTSTANDING EXEMPLARS OF THE MING AND CH'ING PERIODS

A towering figure of the late Ming who struck out in quite a different direction was Yüan Hung-tao (1568–1610). Inspired by the lush, passionate images and verbiage of ancient Ch'u culture, he favored southern virtues (he was from Hunan province) over northern qualities (Yüan Hao-wen hailed from Shansi province). His emphasis on the self and his experimentation with spoken language make him a person of truly "modern" consciousness who came long before his time.

Wang Fu-chih (1619–1692) was one of many intellectuals who straddled the transition from the Ming to the Ch'ing dynasty. A dedicated loyalist, he removed himself from mainstream society after the Manchu conquest and worked endlessly in many scholarly fields—history, philosophy, classical literature—almost as if he saw himself as the last hope of preserving Chinese intellectual culture. His opinions are idiosyncratic, to say the least, but his breadth of scholarship was comparable to Han Yü's, and his judgments are seldom challenged.

In literary criticism, Wang Fu-chih was a revisionist and fundamentalist. He deplored the trends of writers like Yen Yü, who accepted that poetry could come from the imagination and be removed from actual experience. His works of literary criticism are many and varied. For commentary, there is his *Shih kuang-chuan* (Broad Commentary on the *Classic of Poetry*). He produced anthologies on three periods: pre-T'ang, T'ang, and Ming. There are also writings that are more personal in tone, such as *Hsi-t'ang yung-jih hsü-lun* (Discussions to While Away the Days at Evening Hall), *Shih-yi* (Deliberations on Poetry), and his own *Chiang-chai shih-hua* (Discussions of Poetry from the Ginger Studio). Throughout his oeuvre, he asserted that the affective power of poetry depends on the genuine experience of the poet underlying the experience of the poem. In a lyric poem, this means that the inspiring *ch'ing* (emotion) and *ching* (scene) are not just mutually dependent, but become one: "Although there would seem to be distinctions between *ch'ing* and *ching* as they exist in the mind and as they exist in the phenomenal world, in fact *ching* gives rise to *ch'ing*, and *ch'ing* gives rise to *ching*. . . . *Ch'ing* and *ching* are in name two things, but in reality they cannot be separated." In Wang Fu-chih's thinking, there are no true oppositional pairs. Even the underlying principle of the universe, *Tao*, is the complement, not the opposite, of its "concrete manifestations" (*ch'i*). A great poem uses images of nature to embody the inner life of the poet. That is the most important manifestation of the poet's intent (*chih*) and assures perfect resonance between poet and reader, past and present. The vast range of subject matter of poetry reflects the vast range of human experience.

Yeh Hsieh (1627–1703) wrote *Yüan-shih* (On the Origin of Poetry) in 1686. It is the first attempt at a comprehensive statement of literary poetics since *The Literary Mind and the Carving of Dragons*—a fact of which the author is thoroughly aware, as he chastises Liu Hsieh for falling short in his ability to "sustain an argument" (*ch'ih-lun*). The text is divided into two sections, "inner" (*nei*) and "outer" (*wai*), which are further divided into main and supplementary sections. Yeh Hsieh is basically an adherent of expressive theories of poetry, although he elevates intellectual capacity and moral character over emotional capacity or esthetic sense.

He begins his exposition with an unusual proposition: that the failure of poetry to sustain its vitality from its zenith in the T'ang is due to the failure of literary critics to organize its principles adequately and speak with a unified voice. Although there are plenty of methodological critiques of Chinese poetry and literary history, to place the blame for decline in poetry on the shoulders of poetry's critics is a novel stance. Yeh Hsieh asserts the need for a unified theory of poetry in order to reinvigorate poetry and respond to cultural crisis.

Although poetry is ultimately the expression of the heart, and indeed cannot be made to oppose the heart, expression itself is subject to the laws of the structure of the universe. The three features of the universe, "principle" (*li*), "event" (*shih*), and "manner" (*ch'ing*), determine the experience to which poetry is the heart's response. In order to apprehend and express the essential quality of this experience, the poet must draw on four personal qualities: "talent" (*ts'ai*), "courage" (*tan*), "judgment" (*shih*), and "strength" (*li*). Without these qualities, the mind's "spiritual illumination" (*shen-ming*), however profound, cannot be expressed.

As Yeh Hsieh conceives these metaphysical categories, they are explicitly prescriptive. Poetic intent cannot reach expression without cultivation of these qualities, and the writer in possession of them will not only achieve expression but evoke meaning beyond the words (*yen-wai*). Instead of emptying one's mind to be receptive to inspiration, one must be primed and ready to act on it when it strikes.

Following in the spirit of Ssu-k'ung T'u of the T'ang and Yen Yü of the Sung was the great seventeenth-century poet and critic Wang Shih-chen (1634–1711; to be distinguished from the sixteenth-century author with a similar name who lived from 1526 to 1590), an advocate of the elusive notion of *shen-yün* (spiritual expressionism/resonance). His ideas and practices are explored within the context of his forebears and his contemporaries in chapter 21.

The most remarkable development in the literary criticism of the Ch'ing period was the emergence of eccentric individuals such as Chin Sheng-t'an (1608–1661) and Li Yü (1610/11–1680), who began to take creative works of fiction and drama seriously and who wrote extensive commentaries on them. This marked a radical transformation in the history of Chinese literary theory, which heretofore had been devoted solely to poetry. The views and achievements of these revolutionary critics are discussed in other chapters (e.g., chapters 41 and 46).

These are just a few of the critics of the Ch'ing dynasty, during which there was a frenzy of reappraisals of literary history and esthetics, including the reintegration of texts, compilation of vast anthologies, and printing of texts on an unprecedented scale. There were also passionate partisan groups representing extremes of esthetic and political interests. It is possible that more literary critics wrote during the Ch'ing dynasty than during all the rest of Chinese history. Their activities form a microcosm of Chinese literary history up to their time and provided those who followed them with systematic bases for the study of Chinese literature.

THE TWENTIETH CENTURY AND BEYOND

Traditional Chinese literary criticism continued through the twentieth century, reaching its culmination in the *Kuan-ch'ui pien* (Pipe-Awl Chapters, or Limited

Views: Essays on Ideas and Letters) of Ch'ien Chung-shu (1910–1999). Ch'ien offers a dazzling display of erudition that goes far beyond the cultural and linguistic foundations of China, yet is firmly anchored in the past. Whereas Ch'ien may be said to have brought a close not only to a century but also to more than a millennium of literary theorizing and critiquing, he was preceded in this pivotal enterprise by the fabulously learned Wang Kuo-wei (1877–1927). It was Wang who initiated the seamless amalgamation of Eastern and Western, ancient and modern, classical and vernacular in such intellectually scintillating works as his "*Hung-lou meng* p'ing-lun" (A Critique of A *Dream of Red Towers*). Wang's interests ranged widely, from the origins and interpretation of drama to the esthetics of *tz'u* (lyrics). His contributions to the study of *tz'u*, as presented in his epochal *Jen-chien tz'u-hua* (Remarks on Lyric Poetry from the Human World), are seminal and include such endlessly cited concepts as *ching-chieh* (realm) and *pu-ko* (unobstructed). *Remarks on Lyric Poetry from the Human World* was the culmination of a long tradition of commentary on *tz'u* (see chapter 15) and *ch'ü* (see chapter 17) that began with Wang Cho's *Pi-chi man-chih* (Random Notes from Pi-chi; preface 1149).

At the present juncture, contemporary Chinese criticism and theory have been fully integrated into international discourse on literature. Every movement or method known in Europe or America has a counterpart in China, and every literary theoretician anywhere in the world has advocates and opponents within China. Yet echoes of earlier ages and orientations still surface sporadically, so that it is essential to be familiar with them and to understand how they were incorporated in the new explanations of the meaning, nature, function, and value of literature.

Dore J. Levy

Chapter 46

TRADITIONAL FICTION COMMENTARY

From the seventeenth century into the twentieth century, the reader of Chinese fiction, especially vernacular fiction, read it with commentary attached. During that period, at least partly under the influence of such commentary, there was a movement from weak or nonexistent assertions of authorship to strong ones, from editors who denied their editorial work to those who paraded it, from the idea of commentary as supplementary in nature to a conception of it as an integral part of the text, and from fairly naïve readers interested in the plot to sophisticated readers who conceived of themselves as locked in a contest of wits with the author when they read.

P'ING-TIEN COMMENTARY

The kind of commentary involved was mostly situated quite close to the text proper and presented so as to interfere with or control the reading of the text. For example, let us mentally examine a page, which can be described in detail. The page comes from a very influential fiction commentary, Chin Sheng-t'an's (1608–1661) edition of *Shui-hu chuan* (Water Margin), published in 1641. The page contains part of the famous description of Wu Sung's killing of a tiger bare-handed.

On this page the main text of the novel is printed in large characters. There are comma-like dots and circles to the right of some of them. Sometimes these merely delineate sentences or phrases, but at other times they are used for emphasis, similar to the use of italics or underlining. Both the regular and emphatic punctuation were added by Chin Sheng-t'an as part of his general attempt to control the reading of the text by drawing attention to certain parts of it rather than others. This kind of emphatic punctuation was called *ch'üan-tien* (circles and dots).

On this same page, the commentary is written in smaller characters and printed in double columns immediately under the passages on which it comments. The ratio of commentary to text approaches one to one. The comments draw attention to many things, but most particularly to the club carried by Wu Sung, which—contrary to the reader's expectations—will turn out to be of no use against the tiger. Not readily apparent from looking at any page of Chin Sheng-t'an's commentary edition is the fact that he edited the text of the novel rather radically, even though he claimed that those changes were actually all found in the copy of an old edition (*ku-pen*) of the novel that he had come across.

While perhaps the bulk of the comments in traditional Chinese fiction commentary took the form of interlinear comments like these, they could and did appear in a wide variety of forms, ranging from prefaces and prefatory essays to chapter and marginal comments. As can be imagined, the text in these editions can sometimes be almost buried by the commentary. The comments themselves were called *p'i-p'ing*. To reflect the importance of both comments and punctuation, this style of commentary was referred to as *p'ing-tien* or, sometimes, *p'i-tien*. This is interpretative commentary and presents itself as concerned with the deeper meaning of the text, as opposed to lexical or exegetical commentary, which would be concerned mainly with the meaning of the letter of the text.

THE HISTORICAL DEVELOPMENT OF *P'ING-TIEN* COMMENTARIES FOR FICTION

Punctuation is first mentioned in China as a kind of pedagogical exercise. Students were given unpunctuated texts to divide into clauses and sentences; their understanding of the texts was judged according to how well they did this. It was and still is common for readers of unpunctuated Chinese texts to add punctuation as they read. It is then but a simple step to start recording comments about the text in the upper margin as marginal notes or in between the lines of the text as interlinear comments. Mao Tse-tung reportedly said, "If you don't move your pen, you're not really reading."

The earliest textual commentaries in China were written for canonical works such as the Confucian classics or for works in esteemed literary genres, such as poetry. Emphatic punctuation developed in the T'ang dynasty (618–907) but the first extant examples are preserved in Sung dynasty (960–1279) printed editions, which include the first commentary editions of literary works stressing the literary nature of their texts, which can be called *p'ing-tien* commentary.

During the late Ming dynasty (1368–1644) boom in publishing, one way that booksellers tried to sell new editions of old texts was to bring out *p'ing-tien* editions of them. *P'ing-tien* editions of the Confucian classics, famous historical works, and winning examination essays appeared, and the literary nature of these texts was stressed. An example is Ling Chih-lung's 1576 *Shih-chi p'ing-lin* (Forest of Comments on the *Records of the Historian*).

It is no accident that the first *p'ing-tien* editions of Chinese fiction date from this period, since they were written in imitation of *p'ing-tien* commentaries on classical works. Publishers of these early fiction commentaries, such as Yü Hsiang-tou (c. 1550–after 1637), were clearly interested in borrowing prestige from genres more highly respected than fiction. The titles of editions of *San-kuo yen-yi* (Romance of the Three Kingdoms) and *Water Margin* by Yü contain the words *p'ing-lin* (forest of comments). The commentary in such editions almost always took the form of brief unattributed marginal comments, but Yü did conceive of his work as publisher and commentator to include the editing of the texts he published. Some changes he made silently, while others he admitted and tried to justify.

After the turn of the seventeenth century, a new type of fiction commentary appeared. The majority of these commentaries were published under the name of Li Chih (1527–1602), the iconoclast who slit his throat in prison and whose writings were banned. Most of these commentaries were probably actually written by one man, Yeh Chou (d. 1624). Although Li Chih wrote a commentary on *Water Margin* that he wanted to publish, none of the numerous "Li Chih" commentary editions of fiction (or drama) extant appears to be authentic. The attribution of the commentary to Li Chih in their titles is given as much prominence as the title of the work itself.

The commentator in the "Li Chih" fiction commentaries is sure that he could have done a better job than the authors of the novels. He makes many specific complaints and marks off sections to be excised. The impression given is that fiction is worth commenting on, but is still a genre from which you cannot expect too much.

The next—and very significant—development was for fiction commentators to excise, or recontextualize through commentary, passages deemed substandard by earlier commentators or by the commentator himself. Chin Sheng-t'an's commentary edition of *Water Margin* is a prime example. He cut the final third of the novel, made editorial changes on almost every page, and added sections of his own devising—all of which he attributed to the original author of the novel, whom he decided to call Shih Nai-an. He asserted that Lo Kuan-chung, the other popular candidate for the authorship of this novel, authored the parts of the popular editions that he did not like, while he elevated Shih Nai-an to the status of a genius (*ts'ai-tzu*) and worked his name into the title of his edition.

Following Chin Sheng-t'an's lead, standard editions with commentary for the other three of the "four masterworks of the Ming novel" appeared. These are the Huang Chou-hsing and Wang Hsiang-hsü 1663 edition of *Hsi-yu chi* (Journey to the West), the 1680 Mao Lun and Mao Tsung-kang edition of *Romance of the Three Kingdoms*, and the 1695 Chang Chu-p'o edition of *Chin P'ing Mei* (Gold Vase Plum). Claiming to present long-lost original versions of these novels, these commentators also asserted that the mere addition of their commentary had fundamentally altered them.

Fiction commentary's success was also the beginning of its downfall. Later commentators tended mechanically to apply the models and techniques of earlier commentators. Although fiction commentary succeeded in elevating the status of fiction and inspiring new readers to consider fiction commensurate with several of the more respected genres, some of these new readers insisted on using commentarial techniques more appropriate to those respected genres in their fiction commentaries. The results included a commentary on *Journey to the West* insisting that it be read as one big examination essay and one on the *Hung-lou meng* (A Dream of Red Towers), which read that novel as a fictional version of the core Confucian texts, the *Ssu-shu* (Four Books). Commentators became entirely too clever, finding coded meanings in unlikely and unbelievable places. Advocates of the *so-yin* (search for the hidden) school of commentary turned complex artistic works into reductionist *romans à clef*.

In the first decades of the twentieth century, vernacular fiction was valorized as a model for the new kind of literary language being called for, but reprinted without the commentary that had accompanied it for so long. This was done in part because of the power of these commentaries to direct readers' responses in unwanted directions. It is also possible that Chinese intellectuals realized that this was not how Westerners read their fiction.

In recent decades, precisely this perception that reading and writing *p'ing-tien* commentaries on fiction is unique to China has fed renewed interest in the phenomenon. Several histories have been published, as well as modern applications of *p'ing-tien* commentary to premodern and modern works of fiction.

Is fiction commentary of this type really unique to China? Medieval commentaries on classical works such as Virgil's *Aeneid* often included attention to rhetorical features. Particularly in the period in which writing narratives in the vernacular languages instead of Latin began to spread, authors such as Dante, Boccaccio, Spenser, and maybe Chaucer wrote commentary for their own works. The once-prevalent marginal gloss, however, did not survive the transition from manuscript to print culture. Instead, a new form of commentary, the footnote, arose. Edgar Allan Poe published his marginalia, and modernists and postmodernists have experimented with extratextual commentary, but almost always with tongue in cheek.

The major differences, then, between fiction commentary in China and in the West are that in China the tradition matured after the spread of printing, remained strong into the twentieth century, and is enjoying a "renaissance"; in the West, however, after fictional commentary served its purpose in the establishment of the vernacular traditions, the idea of writing commentary to accompany fiction was approached with a kind of irony generally lacking in traditional China.

CREATING NEW AUTHORS AND READERS

Fiction commentaries in China trained readers how to read and future authors how to write. These goals were explicitly stated in the commentaries. For instance, Chang Chu-p'o warned his readers that if they did not write better after reading his commentary edition of *Chin P'ing Mei*, they should lay down their brushes and take up the plow instead. Both later commentary and works of fiction show evidence of lessons learned from reading fiction commentary. Even expedient solutions dreamed up by individual commentators to justify specific features of individual texts were generalized and applied universally.

One thing that readers of fiction commentary learned was that fiction was a respectable genre at which a proper literatus might try his hand. One problem faced by early commentators was the lack of a clear authorial persona (implied author) in the texts on which they were commenting. This was a problem in a culture that conceived of literature as a means for authors to attain literary immortality and for readers to come into contact with those immortals. Early vernacular fiction was cobbled together from disparate oral and written sources with weak editorial control (hence the "Li Chih" commentator's complaints). This made it difficult for readers to conceive of their authors as someone worth meeting or emulating.

Chin Sheng-t'an took steps to solve this problem, including concocting an intimate preface by Shih Nai-an (whom he promoted to be the "fifth genius" of the literary canon after Chuang Tzu, Ch'ü Yüan, Ssu-ma Ch'ien, and Tu Fu) and continually referring to him in his commentary. Later commentators followed suit. Many took advantage of the obscurity of the authors of their texts to model the implied authors they created in their commentaries after themselves, as Chin Sheng-t'an had done.

In traditional Chinese vernacular fiction, the narrator is almost always fashioned on a professional oral storyteller, while the implied reader is a member of the storyteller's audience. This conceit was used not because the texts were "prompt books" or records of actual performances, but because this was one way to naturalize the idea rather strange, at the time, of reading stories written in vernacular Chinese. (All proper, worthy writing in China was traditionally done in the literary, book language.) The narrators address questions to their "audience" and repeat questions supposedly offered up by doubting members of that audience. The kinds of questions the narrator asks and represents his audience as asking of him are restricted mostly to the immediate context and details of the plot. They are designed to help the reader follow the story, rather than contemplate it as a constructed discourse.

The addition of textual commentary immediately changes this, making the fabricated nature of the text inescapable. The commentators invite real readers to emulate their own broader and more sophisticated view of things, challenge them with the prospect that more is going on in the text than meets the eye, but promise that the "crafty" author is following standard and regular literary techniques that will be explicated by the commentator.

Besides editing *Water Margin*, Chin Sheng-t'an revalorized some features of vernacular fiction about which earlier commentators had only complained. Early, long novels like *Water Margin* were rather repetitious. Certain set sequences are repeated over and over again. Chin Sheng-t'an argued that the author of *Water Margin* was doing something difficult and risky. Stressing the similarities between these sequences, he also claims that the skilled reader will note subtle distinctions between them. So what was probably just a product of editorial sloppiness is turned into a refined artistic feature that also unifies the text by forcing the reader to think of both passages at once.

Repetitious use of similar character types also occurs in early vernacular fiction, and the method employed by Chin Sheng-t'an and other fiction commentators was, again, to reinterpret the phenomenon positively. They claimed that characters of similar types were inserted by the author to force readers to notice subtle differences between pairs of characters that meaningfully contrast with each other.

Another problem was that many major characters in early vernacular fiction are presented as paragons of one virtue or another but tend to come off as hypocritical. Although one can argue that this was deliberate, it is perhaps simpler to explain this as a result of the way these texts were cobbled together from disparate sources. But while the "Li Chih" commentator was content to complain about inconsistencies and absurdities in characterization, Chin Sheng-t'an and his followers chose to see these as signs of the author's genius.

For instance, instead of trying to smooth over inconsistencies in the main character in *Water Margin*, Sung Chiang, Chin Sheng-t'an exacerbated them in his edition and called them keys to both Sung Chiang's real nature (hypocritical and duplicitous) and the author's ultimate purpose (to expose Sung Chiang).

Chin Sheng-t'an further argued that the author purposely contrasts Sung Chiang with a supposedly guileless member of the band, Li K'uei. This idea of authors focusing their narratives on contrasting pairs of duplicitous and guileless characters caught on. Interestingly enough, readers sometimes disagreed violently about who was duplicitous and who guileless in such pairs.

These developments turned the reader's attention away from the plot toward characterization. But Chin Sheng-t'an and other fiction critics also had an impact on the structure of Chinese fiction. Instead of a linear reading of narrative, they promoted a "spatial" one focused on the way noncontiguous parts of the narrative were linked together to make an organic whole. Subtlety was preferred to straightforwardness. The more distant and unobtrusive the links, the better.

AUTHORIAL REACTION TO COMMENTARY

Beginning in Chin Sheng-t'an's time, if not earlier, fiction commentators presented themselves as uncovering the hitherto unrecognized artistic intentions and accomplishments of their authors, but justified their interpretations on rather transparently specious claims about long lost original editions or the idea that they were cleverer than everyone else. Many examples could be cited of more or less complete attempts to replace the original authors of their texts with themselves.

Other than writing fiction according to the models advocated in fiction commentaries, how did new writers of fiction react to the challenge of this phenomenon of publishing fiction with commentary? At least three different solutions were tried, excluding sheer indifference and combinations of the three: (1) writing one's own commentary; (2) stealing some of the commentators' thunder by modeling one's narrators after them, incorporating their topics, vocabulary, terminology, and tone; and (3) writing so as to force the reader to produce a commentary in his head as he reads, but designing the holes in the text so that the commentary produced to fill them will be conditioned by them. The first solution creates auto-commentary, the second creates narrator-commentators, and the third creates latent commentary.

Auto-Commentary

Auto-commentary in traditional Chinese fiction contains a great deal of self-congratulation. Auto-commentators could not seem to resist applying to themselves the kind of fulsome praise for the author's abilities that fills regular fiction commentaries. But even in Chin Sheng-t'an's case, praise of the author for a particular technique is often a sign that the feature in question was edited into the text by Chin himself. Auto-commentators often tried to disguise the authorship of their commentaries by attributing them to someone else or leaving them unattributed, but this was a fairly transparent "fig leaf" to hide behind.

Rudimentary auto-commentary was written by both Feng Meng-lung (1574–1646) and Ling Meng-ch'u (1580–1644) for their important collections of vernacular stories, but of more interest is Tung Yüeh's (1620–1686) *"Hsi-yu" pu* (Supplement to *Journey to the West*), published in 1641. This difficult novel traces Sun Wu-k'ung's (a.k.a. Monkey) dream of wandering through an allegorical landscape until he realizes that his dream is being produced by the temptation of Ch'ing-yü (Mackerel Demon), an allegorical figure for the concept of desire. For most of the novel, Sun Wu-k'ung is bewildered by what he sees; this finally throws him into sensory and mental overload and leads to his enlightenment. To allow the reader to experience this process as closely as possible, the traditional storyteller-narrator is allowed to go on holiday and the narrative is presented mostly through Sun Wu-k'ung's consciousness. To keep the reader from missing the point, however, the author provided a prefatory piece as well as chapter and interlinear comments.

About twenty years later, Ch'en Ch'en (1614–after 1666) wrote a sequel to *Water Margin* clearly indebted to Chin Sheng-t'an's commentary on that novel. He made use of the additional voice of his own extratextual commentary to undercut the achievement of a kind of utopia in the narrated world of his novel by bringing the reader's attention back to the less than perfect world that prompted his writing of it in the first place.

Much of the serialized fiction published in magazines toward the end of the Ch'ing dynasty (1644–1911) appeared with what seems to be auto-commentary. In most cases, however, the commentaries peter out before the serialization is completed, and the comments were not included when these works came out in book form.

Narrator-Commentators

Patrick Hanan has identified three coordinate modes in traditional Chinese vernacular fiction. One of these is a commentarial mode, in which the storyteller-narrator comments on the story and its characters directly or through quotation of poems or other material. Both this intratextual commentary and the extratextual commentary discussed earlier are species of commentary, but their content was originally very different. Extratextual commentary talks about authors and readers, recognizes the story as a text, compares it with other texts, shows how apparently unrelated parts of the narrative are really related, and how the true meaning differs from the surface one. Intratextual commentary originally did none of these things. Under the influence of fiction commentaries, however, narrators begin to share some of these features with extratextual commentators.

The narrators in the fiction of Li Yü (1610/11–1680) are good examples of this, as is the narrator in the sequel to *Chin P'ing Mei* written by Ting Yao-k'ang (1599–1669), but the clearest case is Wen K'ang's (1798–1872) *Erh-nü ying-hsiung chuan* (Tales of Boy and Girl Heroes), from the middle of the nineteenth century. This novel circulated with commentary by Tung Hsün (1807–1892), longtime president of the Board of Revenue (how fiction has come up in the world!). Tung Hsün praises the novel for explaining itself, explicitly teaching writing, and for including substantial amounts of discourse on "writing" as opposed to "affairs." Although many extratextual commentators claimed to show readers the "needles" or techniques used to complete the "embroideries" or texts that they commented on, Tung Hsün claimed that Wen K'ang's narrator did this.

The author of a preface to the novel (Wen K'ang himself?) describes how other novels were lucky to find commentators such as Chin Sheng-t'an and Chang Chu-p'o, but they also needed extratextual commentary to be understood. *Tales of Boy and Girl Heroes*, he claims, does not need extratextual commentary, because there is no disjunction between its surface and real meaning. One could also argue that it is less in need of extratextual commentary because its narrator provides his own. This narrator speaks of the author of the novel as distinct from himself, compares his text to other texts, and uses much of the terminology and set habits of fiction commentators.

Latent Commentary

Turning the narrator into a narrator-commentator involved making the narrator even more prominent than before. Reducing the narrator to a minimal presence also happened, as in the case of *Supplement to "Journey to the West."* In that work, some of the commentarial functions of the narrator were transferred to extratextual commentary. In the case of latent commentary, the commentarial function was transferred to the reader. Readers could now be trusted to produce the right kind of commentary themselves because they had been taught how to do so by reading fiction commentaries.

The general animus against the storyteller-narrator in fiction commentaries such as Chin Sheng-t'an's also made it likely that authors would cut down on his functions. Chin Sheng-t'an and other commentators were in competition with these storyteller-narrators for control of the meaning of the narratives on which they commented. They reduced the independence of the storyteller-narrator's voice by alternately cutting his comments or recontextualizing them by surrounding them with their own.

Fiction commentators were also generally very negative about the stoptime set-piece descriptions in parallel prose that occur so frequently in early vernacular fiction (the mode of description, in Patrick Hanan's terminology). Chin Sheng-t'an excised all this material from his edition of *Water Margin.* In this line of development, as opposed to that which produced commentator-narrators, the result was narratives that relied heavily on direct presentation of the action and dialog (Hanan's mode of presentation).

An example of latent commentary is the *Ju-lin wai-shih* (The Scholars), by Wu Ching-tzu (1701–1754). It is perhaps the most extreme development of the suppression of the traditional narrator, its composition was clearly influenced by Chin Sheng-t'an's commentary edition of *Water Margin* (its prolog is modeled after that of Chin's edition), and premodern comments on the novel show that readers versed in traditional fiction criticism did not have the kinds of problems with the novel that modern readers alienated from or ignorant of that tradition have had.

That "good" readers produce a running commentary in their heads as they read should be a familiar idea. Even bad readers, to make sense of what they are reading, produce suppositions as they read that are then confirmed or negated by their further reading. It is a complicated business to try to prove that Wu Ching-tzu intended to provoke a particular form of running commentary in his readers' minds. The first-time reader was in no position to produce a decent commentary on a narrative organized spatially. After fiction commentary had raised the standards of what constituted good fiction and good reading, the first reading of a novel was only preparatory to future readings, in which the reader would be able to see how widely separated portions of the narrative worked with one another. One function of fiction commentary was to help first-time readers skip this stage. Could Wu Ching-tzu depend on his readers to be re-readers? What we know of how actual readers of the novel reacted to it tells us that yes, he could.

It is easy to prove that commentator-narrators were produced in reaction to fiction commentary because of evidence like borrowed terminology. In the case of latent commentary, the argument can only be suggestive rather than conclusive. Any examination of *The Scholars* shows that there are holes in the text that cry out to be filled in by the reader. Furthermore, these holes are such that they can be filled fairly easily and regularly by readers trained by traditional Chinese fiction commentary, as can be proved by the basic level of agreement about the novel in the extant commentaries on it, on the one hand, and through the bewilderment of readers who bring modern Western expectations of how a novel should work to their reading of it, on the other.

CONCLUSION

Fiction commentators often succeeded in getting their radical reinterpretations of earlier novels accepted and in usurping the author's place in the texts they commented on. They did not escape social censure, of course. Some considered Chin Sheng-t'an's and Chang Chu-p'o's premature deaths as heavenly retribution for their editorial and commentarial work. In any case, the writings of earlier commentators were also not immune to distortion and misunderstanding by later commentators.

Authors, however, also asserted themselves. They countered the encroachment of fiction commentators by appropriating ideas from them but, by so doing, made the understanding and appreciation of their own works dependent on an understanding of the commentarial tradition. That is one reason the re-evaluation of traditional Chinese fiction in the last two decades of the twentieth century was so beholden to the rediscovery of this native form of fiction criticism.

David L. Rolston

PART VII

Popular and Peripheral Manifestations

Chapter 47

BALLADRY AND POPULAR SONG

The anonymous popular ballad and southern song were two of the most important genres to emerge during the late classical and early medieval era (c. 50–c. 400 C.E.). They constitute two separate repertoires of anonymous popular expression, and each has its later tradition of literary imitation. Both repertoires had an enduring and profound influence on the ode (*shih*), the lyric (*tz'u*), and dramatic verse arias written by famous poets, musicians, playwrights, and novelists, up to the eighteenth century.

DEFINITION OF TERMS

The repertoire of ballads and southern song composed first by anonymous makers and later by named literary authors from the first century C.E. to the twelfth century C.E. has been known traditionally by the generic term *yüeh-fu*. Yüeh-fu (Music Bureau) was the name of the government office from which the earliest ballads were believed to have historically emerged. Because of conflicting textual evidence, there is considerable disagreement among scholars on the question of when and by whom this office was established. What is clear is that c. 121–113 B.C.E., in the middle of the reign of the early Han emperor Wu (r. 141–87 B.C.E.), the Music Bureau was completely reoriented and radically reformed in terms of concept, function, and scope, mainly in order to encompass the emperor's personal preference for popular secular music.

The usage of the term *yüeh-fu* to designate anonymous popular verse is not seen until the early fourth century and late fifth century C.E., when two passing references to it occur in *Wen-chang liu-pieh chi* (Collection on Development and Change in Literary Genres), by the literary historian Chih Yü, and an essay by the poet, historian, and musicologist Shen Yüeh (441–513). By the mid-sixth century, *yüeh-fu* as the name of the genre became attached to specific ballads in two early medieval imperial anthologies, *Yü-t'ai hsin-yung* (New Songs from a Jade Terrace) and *Wen hsüan* (Literary Selections). From then on, the generic term became fixed and was attached to an increasing variety of anonymous songs. By the early twelfth century, *yüeh-fu* compositions formed a vast repertoire of 5,290 texts anthologized by Kuo Mao-ch'ien.

The term *yüeh-fu* covers a repertoire characterized by generic diversity. It includes many forms, which each have their own subgeneric titles. For example, there are anonymous song-texts (*ko-tz'u*); songs (*ko*); song-pieces (*ko-ch'ü*); balladic suites (*hsing*); lay (*yin*); lament (*yin*); melodic words (*ch'ü-tz'u*); folksongs (*p'ien*); miscellaneous pieces (*tsa-ch'ü*); and song-texts for miscellaneous ditties (*tsa ko-yao tz'u*). In addition, there are the subgenres of the hymns (*chiao-ssu ko*) of successive dynasties, "concerted" (*hsiang-ho*) songs, songs in the Ch'ing-shang mode (*Ch'ing-shang ch'ü-tz'u*), and songs for the *nao*-bell, in addition to songs written for dances and early prophetic songs.

PERIODIZATION OF THE TWO REPERTOIRES OF BALLADRY AND SOUTHERN SONG

The presence of orality in a cultural tradition presents the inherent problem of the dating of the repertoire. In the case of oral pieces, the circumstances of their composition or first performance cannot always be known. Among the criteria for dating are four factors: (1) when their song-text became fixed in a datable classical work; (2) when their title and content are confirmed by paraphrastic accounts in datable works; (3) when their first performance is recorded in a datable text; and (4) when a literary poet, whose dates are known, imitates an oral piece, and so provides a terminus ad quem (latest limiting point) for date of circulation of the oral text.

The first phase of popular expression in ballad and song occurs in the three centuries from c. 50 to c. 200 C.E. This can be characterized as the product of the northern metropolitan region, although some pieces are believed traditionally to have been collected from other regions of the Han empire. This early repertoire consists of about 115 *anonymous* texts. Some are datable by internal or contextual evidence, such as thirty-six early Han hymns, eighteen songs for the *nao*-bell, and miscellaneous verse lampoons. The remainder are traditionally assigned to the Han, despite the lateness of their textual sources. For example, sixteen pieces in Shen Yüeh's collection are not labeled by him as of

Han origin, yet some of them were already being imitated by poets in the later decades of the Han era, especially the poets of the Ts'ao royal family, whose death dates fall within or just after the end of the Eastern (Later) Han (25–220).

The second phase of balladic expression occurs between c. 200 and 550. This period spans the Han and Wei (220–265) era of the north and the post-exile era of the Southern Dynasties, from 317 to c. 550 C.E. This phase is characterized by the inception and continuation of the *balladic imitative mode*, in which named poets reworked anonymous ballads and folksongs and invested them with new literary values. The imitative mode developed primarily under court patronage. First were the royal patrons of the Ts'ao family, who came to prominence toward the end of the Han and throughout the Wei. Second were the royal patrons of the southern courts, especially the Liu and Hsiao families of the Liu-Sung (420–479) and Liang (502–557) dynasties.

The third phase coincides with the early years of the exile of the northern court of Ch'ang-an and Lo-yang to the southeastern region of the Yangtze. This phase, which dates between c. 270 and c. 400 C.E., is marked by an entirely new form of *anonymous popular expression* that was native to the region where the court settled in exile, especially the old region of Wu, centered in the area of modern-day Nanking. Its culture was informed by urban, mercantile values that were very different from the culture of the north.

The fourth phase reflects the *literary response to the popular southern song* when émigré literati imitated the new style, which was termed "modern" (*chin-tai*), to differentiate it from the older balladic tradition of the north. This phase spans the period from c. 400 to c. 589. As during the second phase, it was the patronage of the royal Liu and Hsiao families that prompted the imitation of the native idiom of anonymous popular song.

The fifth phase of balladic and song composition occurs in the T'ang dynasty (618–907), especially from c. 730 to 850, when Li Po (701–762) and Po Chü-yi (772–846) *utilized both traditions*, the repertoire of the Han ballads and their imitations, and the repertoire of southern song and its literary imitations. Although Li Po drew for inspiration on traditional themes, Po Chü-yi developed a new concept for the old tradition in what he termed his "New Balladry" (*hsin yüeh-fu*), which focused primarily on narrative ballads or contemporary issues.

By the early twelfth century, a new song form, the *tz'u* lyric of the Sung dynasty (960–1279), had displaced the older forms of the ballad and southern song. By this time, the genre of *yüeh-fu* was regarded as a spent force, which had enjoyed a brief renaissance in the T'ang. Thereafter, in literary history the trend becomes evident of the homogenization of the genre of *yüeh-fu* with that of the formal literary poem, the *shih*. In the minds of literary critics and practicing poets, the ballad and southern song merged with formal verse to the extent that, in Ming (1368–1644) and Ch'ing (1644–1911) poetry collections, *yüeh-fu* pieces were arranged chronologically with *shih* poetry.

SOURCES OF BALLADIC AND SONG TEXTS

Sources of the Anonymous Han Balladic Tradition

The earliest sources of *yüeh-fu* song-texts are historical. Thirty-six early Han hymns are preserved in the "Li yüeh chih" (Treatise on Ritual and Music) and numerous verse lampoons in the "Wu-hsing chih" (Treatise on the Five Elements), both of which are from Pan Ku's (32–92 C.E.) *Han shu* (History of the Han Dynasty), dating from the late first century C.E. A later historical source preserved another collection of lampoons believed to date from the second century C.E.—the *Hsü Han shu* (Continuation of the History of the Han), by Ssu-ma Piao (240–306), cited in *Hou Han shu* (History of the Later Han [Dynasty]), by Fan Yeh (398–446). All these pieces, unless a date is ascribed to them, date at the latest from the texts that preserved them.

A specialist musicological text, "Yüeh chih" (Treatise on Music), constitutes the most important source for song-texts that are more recognizably balladic. It appears in Shen Yüeh's *Sung shu* (History of the [Liu] Sung Dynasty), dating from 488 C.E. Shen preserved the texts of sixteen ballads that he called "Concerted" pieces, dating from an earlier period, now known to belong at least in part to the Han, and eighteen texts entitled "Han nao-ko shih-pa shou" (Eighteen Han Songs for the *Nao*-Bell), which preserved some of the most primitive balladic material.

Another source is imperial anthologies of the early medieval period, notably *New Songs from a Jade Terrace*, compiled c. 534–545, which preserved seventeen old balladic texts and five old lampoons, and *Literary Selections*, c. 520–526, which preserved just three texts, under the title of *yüeh-fu*.

A fourth source, and the most important for its comprehensive collation of balladic and song texts, is the monumental collection of Kuo Mao-ch'ien, *Yüeh-fu shih chi* (Collection of Ballad Poetry), compiled around 1126 C.E. This brought together texts in earlier sources, in addition to many newly culled texts, from 160 sources in all.

Sources for the Tradition of Southern Song

The major source for the early anonymous texts of southern song is Kuo's anthology. It has preserved a large collection of 733 texts, which comprise 485 anonymous compositions of oral origin organized under a variety of title groupings, and 248 later literary imitations. A parallel source that predates Kuo's anthology for 150 of these texts is the last chapter of *New Songs from a Jade Terrace*.

Sources for Literary Imitations of Anonymous Ballads and Southern Song

The earliest sources for literary imitations of the repertoires of ballads and southern song are the two early medieval imperial anthologies, the collected works of individual poets, and, above all, Kuo's anthology. Kuo's collection is particularly valuable because he devised the organizing principle of combining anonymous texts and imitations chronologically within his musical categories. He also placed versions of old texts together, recognizing the value of conserving textual variation.

Sources for Balladic and Song Imitations in the T'ang

The primary source for T'ang *yüeh-fu* is Kuo's anthology, which preserved 429 "New Balladry" pieces alone, in addition to the large number of imitations by T'ang poets of traditional ballads and songs. For the more famous T'ang poets whose poems have been collected and preserved, their collected works constitute another major source.

The corpus of 5,290 texts in Kuo's anthology, while it includes all the traditional categories of ballad and song, contains texts that are of only peripheral literary interest. The balladic and song texts that are of greatest literary interest in Kuo's collection are: 256 texts in "Ku-ch'ui ch'ü-tz'u" (Words for Percussion and Wind Pieces), 303 texts in "Heng-ch'ui ch'ü-tz'u" (Words for Horizontal Flute Pieces), 831 texts in "Hsiang-ho ko-tz'u" (Words for Concerted Songs), 733 texts in "Ch'ing-shang ch'ü-tz'u" (Words for *Ch'ing-shang* Pieces), and 429 texts in "Hsin yüeh-fu tz'u" (Words for New *Yüeh-fu*). This constitutes a corpus of 2,552 texts in the two repertoires of the balladic and southern song traditions. The 319 "Tsa ko-yao tz'u" (Miscellaneous Songs) texts make a total of 2,871.

MAJOR SOURCES FOR MUSICOLOGICAL DATA

Although, by Kuo's time, the music to the old ballads and popular songs had long been lost, a great deal of information about the music had been written by music specialists and theorists from the third to the eleventh centuries. Much of this data was incorporated by Kuo into the introductory essays to each of his twelve categories of *yüeh-fu* and into his prefaces to groups of *yüeh-fu* titles.

Among the 160 such works consulted and cited by Kuo concerning the musical history and contextual background to the balladic and song repertoire, the most important are the following.

1. *Hsün-shih lu* (The Record of Mr. Hsün), by Hsün Hsü, third century C.E. No longer extant, much of this important early work is cited by later music specialists, including Kuo. A court musician of the Wei dynasty (220–265), Hsün is said by Shen Yüeh to have revised Han song-texts and was instrumental in their transmission.

2. Shen Yüeh's "Treatise on Music," 488 C.E. This is the first complete document to survive that treated seriously the subject of old and new song-texts. In this work, Shen preserved sixteen old balladic texts, most of which (though not labeled as such) may be assigned to the Han, as well as eighteen song-texts for the *nao*-bell, which he designated as being of Han origin. Shen organized

his material into four musical categories that were derived in part from earlier Han systems of categorization, but also newly devised by him, such as his crucial balladic group, Concerted Pieces, *Ch'ing-shang* Pieces, Major Pieces (*ta ch'ü*), and Ch'u Mode Pieces (*Ch'u tiao*).

3. Chih Chiang's *Ku chin yüeh lu* (Record of Ancient and Modern Music), c. 570 C.E., is much valued by traditional and modern specialists in early music for its contextual information on the ballads and songs that were once set to music.

4. Wu Ching's authoritative *Yüeh-fu ku-t'i yao chieh* (Explanations of the Old Titles of *Yüeh-fu*), c. 700 C.E. Wu organized balladic titles into nine musical categories, with valuable data on their content and context, often paraphrasing song-texts.

5. Kuo Mao-ch'ien's introductory essays to his twelve major categories, and his prefaces to many individual balladic and song titles, constitute the culmination of musicological research of the preceding thousand years. His control and organization of such a wealth of data, drawn from 160 sources, demonstrate his specialist knowledge of the subject and bear witness to his artistic and scholarly genius.

THE NATURE OF THE EARLY TRADITION OF THE HAN BALLAD

Although it is important to keep in mind the traditional musical categories of the early anonymous ballads and songs of the Han era, the repertoire can also be clarified and classified into thematic groups. There are the moving and colorful hymns, for which readers must imagine the ritual and musical context, such as the seasonal carol of spring sowing, "Lien shih jih" (We Have Chosen a Timely Day). An amusing group, which contains some of the most corrupt texts, are the fables in verse. There are ballads on the elixir of immortality and several *carpe diem* pieces. Burial songs form one group, another is political broadsides, such as "Ch'eng-shang wu" (Crows on City Walls). Much-copied antiwar ballads, such as "Yin ma ch'ang-ch'eng k'u hsing" (Watering Horses at the Long Wall Hole, a Ballad; They Fought South of the Wall), and narratives of family strife are two important themes. The pastoral narrative "Mo shang sang" (Mulberry Up the Lane), which inspired numerous imitations, shows an interweaving of complex themes. The most accessible themes for modern readers are the introspective and humorous lyrical ballads on the theme of love, a group that also includes a rare homoerotic piece, "Yüeh-jen ko" (Song of the Yüeh Boatman), and the perennial theme of nostalgia for home.

Many features that are characteristic of Western balladry are present in most anonymous Han ballads and songs. These can be summarized as follows: oral origin; performance oriented; some metrical irregularity; unpolished art form; colloquialisms, direct speech, and nonsense words; some earthy expressions and topics; rustic expression and rural point of view; commonplace expressions and formulaic verse structure; universality of representation; stereotypical characterization; impersonality; some incoherent and abrupt verse transitions; some dialogue; refrain and repetition; familiar material; and musical background or accompaniment.

Another group of poems should be considered in evaluating the balladic tradition of the Han period. That is the "Ku-shih shih-chiu shou" (Nineteen Old Poems) ascribed to the first and second centuries C.E. Although anonymous, their texts indicate that some were reworkings of older balladic material by literary, but unknown, poets. This set of poems in the *shih* style that have strong balladic echoes profoundly influenced numerous famous poets in the later tradition. Old Poem 15, "Sheng nien pu man pai" (Man's Years Do Not Amount to a Hundred), shows strong affinities with the ballad "Hsi men hsing" (West Gate), an anonymous Han ballad; ten of the old text's lines are reworked into six lines of Old Poem No. 15. Moreover, Old Poem No. 2, "Ch'ing-ch'ing ho pan ts'ao" (Green, Green, Riverside Grass), is treated as an old anonymous ballad by generations of poets. Its subject is a professional female singer, and its expression can be read as an autobiographical account of an anonymous Han performer of balladry.

BALLADIC IMITATIONS BY LITERARY POETS

The success of this early balladic form that had its origins in anonymous, popular, oral expression can be measured by the promptness with which it was taken up by the top echelons of society. Royal patronage by the Ts'ao family from the period 200 to about 265 C.E. ensured the preservation of some of the repertoire. The most famous exponent of the form was Ts'ao Chih (192–232), who invested the narrative ballad with a deeper social significance and introduced a new introspection into lyrical ballads. A poet of the following Chin dynasty (265–420), Fu Hsüan (217–278), is now best known for his balladic imitations. In some, he used the feminine voice to express a new theme of the inequality of woman in the institution of marriage, such as in the ballad "K'u hsiang p'ien" (Bitter Fate), also subtitled "Yü-chang hsing" (A Yü-chang Ballad).

The most valuable literary document that records the historical evolution of the ballad, from its popular, oral origins to its apogee as a polished literary construct during the five centuries from c. 50 to c. 550, is the imperial anthology *New Songs from a Jade Terrace*. For example, it contains no fewer than seven literary imitations of "Green, Green, Riverside Grass" and five of "Ch'i hsi" (Seventh Night), besides several imitations of the balladic title "Hsing lu nan" (The Road Is Hard), of which the set by Pao Chao (414–466) is the most famous.

The corpus of 115 texts that constitutes the balladic repertoire of the early Han period essentially represents a northern tradition. It was preserved in texts and imitated by poets, much of whose work has survived, who belonged to the northern culture, such as Ts'ao Chih and Fu Hsüan, and also to the southern culture, such as Pao Chao and his sister Pao Ling-hui (fl. c. 464), besides Shen Yüeh, Ho Hsün (d. 517), and the two royal poets, Hsiao Yen (464–549) and Hsiao Kang. Those southern poets, and many more, responded equally enthusiastically to the vibrantly new form of anonymous popular song, that is, the native song tradition of southeastern China.

THE POPULAR TRADITION OF SOUTHERN SONG

The preservation and transmission of the Southern songs of early medieval China are literary processes that are better documented than the early balladic tradition. By one of the quirks of cultural history, in the early years of exile beginning in c. 317 C.E., the urban centers of the south witnessed an explosion of popular songs and popular music. Mostly love songs, they are characterized by multiregionalism, intimate expression, conversational idiom, and local slang and dialectal words, by frivolity and playfulness, and by colorfully erotic language. Historical documents of this era record how the court in exile quickly adopted the new song style and how both the court and the songmakers and performers interacted with the two cultures of literacy and orality.

The process of preservation and transmission is evident in five main ways: (1) through *royal performance*, when songs were performed at royal banquets; (2) through *royal imitation*, when imitations of southern song were composed by emperor-poets; (3) through *royal recorders and song collectors*, when members of the royal family, appointed to regional posts in the Yangtze area, took an interest in the indigenous musical idiom and recorded in writing the texts of songs they heard and began to form small song collections; (4) through *royal attribution*, when attractive anonymous songs were fallaciously ascribed to named members of the royal family by palace archivists; and (5) through *deposit in the palace archive*, when a song-text was attributed to a royal poet or senior official and deposited in the Music Bureau of the palace, thus entering the literary canon. In these five ways, indigenous song was promoted and accepted as orthodox literature.

The definitive textual source for southern song is Kuo Mao-ch'ien's *Collection of Ballad Poetry*. Eight chapters out of one hundred are devoted to this form, believed to date from the fourth century C.E. They preserve the texts of 485 anonymous songs of oral origin and 248 later literary limitations, all listed under Kuo's sixth category of song-texts, "Songs in the Ch'ing-shang Mode." The anonymous songs fall into two groups: (1) Songs Set to Wu Music (*Wu sheng ko-ch'ü*) in twenty-six title categories, deriving from the metropolitan area (the region of modern Nanking); and (2) Western Songs (*Hsi-ch'ü ko*) in thirty-four title categories, traditionally believed to derive from the central Yangtze area (west of the capital). Among the Wu Music titles are five including the designation "Girl of the Night" (*Tzu-yeh*); within these five titles, the most important and numerically larger groups are the forty-two "Girl of the Night Songs" (*Tzu-yeh ko*) and seventy-five "Girl of the Night Four Seasons Songs" (*Tzu-yeh ssu shih ko*). These two groups constitute 25 percent of the anonymous oral song-texts. The singer's voice is primarily female in all of them.

The evidence for the oral composition and popular origin of the songs can be subsumed under seven types, which also underscore the typical features of the songs as a genre: (1) Its song form immediately differentiates the genre from its northern balladic counterpart. The songs are predominantly *pentasyllabic quatrains*, each consisting of only twenty syllables or words (a few compounds occur). Such a brief form suggests verse that is easily composed and readily memorized by the songmaker or singer. (2) *Emphatic use of rhyme*, both end-rhyme and internal rhyme in every quatrain, contributes to its mnemonic function in oral expression. By rhyme is meant not the phonetic categories of Western rhyme, but the tonal rhyme categories of traditional Chinese verse. Since some songs were sung without musical accompaniment, this emphatic use of end-rhyme and internal rhyme would have served as essential metrical devices. (3) There is a heavy use of *punning* for ludic and erotic emphasis, such as the puns cloth/mate (*p'i*), lotus root/mate (*ou*), passion/lotus (*lien*), and silk thread/erotic love (*ssu*). These were phonetic puns, written with different graphs. (4) *Chromatic effects* are used for contrast, decoration, and humor, so that the song's meaning is projected through brilliant sensory effects. (5) *Simple, homespun expression* introduces familiar details into the songs, drawn from everyday life, such as a charcoal stove, a night watchman's drum, and references to eating or not eating. (6) Most songs employ the *conversational mode*, through question-and-answer formulae and direct address by the use of personal pronouns. For example, of a vocabulary of 460 words in southern songs, the southern dialect word *nung* (I or me) occurs 87 times, and *lang* (you or lover) occurs 76 times, while the intimate use of the word *pu* (don't) occurs 199 times. Interrogative and reflexive words also sustain the conversational mode. (7) The celebration of local place names is another indicator of indigenous regionalism in oral expression. There are few such references in the "Girl of the Night" titles but numerous references in the titles of other categories. The place names mark the river routes and urban centers of the Yangtze River basin and estuary, such as "Shih-ch'eng yüeh" (Stone City Music), "Ch'ien-hsi ko" (Ch'ien-hsi River Song), and "Hsün-yang yüeh" (Hsün-yang Music). Some of the references occur within the song-text. Many other place names occur in the song titles, such as Hsiang-yang, Chiang-ling, and Tan-yang, which are precious indicators of the regional source of the song-text so-named.

No single feature in itself proves orality, but, when taken together, these seven types of evidence are strong arguments for the oral origin and indigenous composition of southern song. It is also important to recall that this local form of song was already current at least half a century before the advent of educated, literary émigrés from the north. The social origins of many of the Southern Dynasties' emperors constitutes another crucial factor; being commoners, they preferred popular culture to that of the elite orthodoxy. Without the literary intervention of members of the royal families of the south, much of this oral tradition would have been lost forever.

When this tradition is compared to the pre-exile balladic tradition of the north, it is shown that a new value system was introduced into Chinese culture, achieved through the phenomenon of mercantile trade and business in southeast China. Indigenous popular song of the south voices these values with its language of desire, a desire to please, and its materialism, the erotic materialism of the expensive bed, silk clothing, and feminine jewels. Its mercantile values contrast most strongly, for example, with those of the northern ballad dating from about the fifth century, "Mu-lan shih" (The Ballad of Mulan). This expresses the heroic military ethos typical of the balladic tradition continued in the north and separate from literary developments in the south. "The Ballad of Mulan" represents a woman enacting the masculine code of militarism and, in its gender transposition and theme of cross-dressing, provides an interesting, if unique, example of transgressive writing in early medieval China that prefigures the subject of the warrior heroine in later novels.

THE LATE BALLADIC AND SONG TRADITION IN THE T'ANG ERA

Two poets predominate in the late balladic tradition of the T'ang era, Li Po and Po Chü-yi. A literary divide is perceptible between the balladic practice of these two poets. Li Po reworked traditional balladic themes already refashioned by early medieval poets, such as Pao Chao, while stamping them with his own artistic and imaginative individuality. By contrast, Po Chü-yi introduced more modern concepts into the genre, already by then of a thousand-year vintage.

Of the extant oeuvre exceeding a thousand poems by Li Po, more than 160 are *yüeh-fu*. The most typical example is "Tui chiu" (Bring On the Wine), and his most famous is "Shu tao nan" (The Way to Shu Is Hard), written in conscious imitation of Pao Chao's imitation of an early balladic title, while the title that bears rewarding comparison with its early anonymous balladic prototype is "Watering Horses at the Long Wall Hole." Li also wrote in the style of southern song, such as his "Girl of the Night Song, No. 3" and "Yang P'an-erh."

When Po Chü-yi made a selection of fifty of his balladic imitations, he wrote a preface for it in which he stated his literary aims. Although he consciously drew on a long tradition of folk verse from *Shih-ching* (Classic of Poetry) of c. 600 B.C.E., and of balladry through imitations by Li Po, Tu Fu, and Han Yü, he made a deliberate break with that tradition by renaming his selected ballads "New Ballads." He emphasized that what he intended for his modern concept of the ballad was that it should relate real events, rather than rework age-old story lines, and that it was designed to be prescriptive, to instruct and educate his contemporary society about crucial issues of the day. In these ballads his new poetic voice is satirical and condemnatory. Po Chü-yi identified with people who lived their lives on the margins of society, in such narrative ballads as "Mai t'an weng" (The Old Charcoal Seller), "Hsin-feng che pi weng" (The Old Man with the Broken Arm from Hsin-feng), and "Hung hsien t'an" (The Red Embroidered Carpet). In his titles for them, Po specified the social injustice at which his ballad was directed, such as the government's confiscation policies, militarism, or excessive luxury.

RECENT RESEARCH ON BALLADS AND POPULAR SONGS

During the past half-century, many valuable investigations on balladic literature have been carried out. Beyond merely calling attention to this hitherto-neglected genre, scholars have elucidated themes, formulaic language, and performance techniques. They have also provided analytical translations of core texts. A major development has been the demonstration of the cross-fertilization of diction, theme, and voice between the anonymous ballad and early anonymous literary poems. Furthermore, comparative study of the pastoral mode of Chinese ballads and their counterparts in medieval French songs has revealed important cultural parallels (themes, structures, diction, etc.). Specialized monographs have been written on Ts'ao P'i, Fu Hsüan, and various aspects of southern song. Others have applied modern techniques of literary criticism to the problem of commonplace expression and literary quotation in balladic art. The repertoire of the early anonymous ballads has been brought together and organized into thematic categories. Translation of the assembled texts has been provided, together with contextual discussions and explanations of the technical musicological features of the genre. These primarily Western contributions to the study of the two generic repertoires are indebted to major research publications of earlier Chinese and Japanese scholars, which clarified basic questions about the corpus, discussed the historical development of the genre, and elaborated various classificatory schemes. Through the combined efforts of Western and Eastern scholars, *yüeh-fu* has taken its rightful place in the serious study of Chinese literature.

Anne Birrell

Chapter 48

TUN-HUANG LITERATURE

INTRODUCTION TO TUN-HUANG AND ITS MANUSCRIPTS

Along the Silk Road, in the far northwestern corner of China, lies the oasis of Tun-huang, with its nearby collection of Buddhist cave temples and grottoes known as "The Caves of the Thousand Buddhas" (*Ch'ien fo tung;* also "Caves of Unparalleled Heights" [*Mo-kao k'u*]). This sacred site, with its wealth of paintings and sculptures, flourished as a center of worship and pilgrimage from the fourth to the fifteenth centuries. In the twentieth century, the Caves of the Thousand Buddhas again became a flourishing site, though this time for scholarship and tourism. The impetus for this change came around 1900 with the discovery of a large cache of manuscripts by a self-appointed caretaker and self-styled Taoist, Wang Yüan-lu, a find that would prove revolutionary for our understanding of the development of Chinese literature and medieval Chinese culture and society as a whole. This hidden library, sealed up not long after the year 1000 C.E. in a small chapel, contained thirty thousand to forty thousand manuscripts and fragments dating from the fifth to the eleventh centuries. Many of these manuscripts were damaged and others rendered superfluous with the advent of printing; rather than being destroyed or used for disreputable purposes by the profane, possibly by marauding Tanguts (tribes related to Tibetans who built the powerful state of Hsi Hsia [1038–1227] in the region that is now Kansu and Ninghsia provinces and Inner Mongolia), these scrolls became a kind of sacred hoard, sealed behind the wall of a cave until "Taoist" Wang's discovery. Within a few years, word of this find reached the British explorer Aurel Stein and later the French scholar Paul Pelliot, both of whom, over a period of years and repeated expeditions, carted away the majority of the manuscripts to London and Paris respectively. Their initial visits were followed by those of Japanese, Russian, and Danish scholar-explorers, while what texts remained were sent to Peking. As a result, the cache of manuscripts is dispersed and now conserved in museums and libraries throughout the world.

By virtue of their sheer number and breadth of contents, these manuscripts represent one of the greatest finds in Chinese archeology. The nature of the manuscripts reflects above all the crucial role of Tun-huang and the Caves of the Thousand Buddhas as a Buddhist cultural center on the Chinese frontier, linked by the Silk Road east to central China and west to Central Asia. The majority of the texts are Buddhist scriptures in Chinese, but numerous sacred texts in Tibetan, Khotanese, Sogdian, Sanskrit, and Uyghur exist as well. Other religious writings include Confucian, Taoist, and popular religious texts, as well as Manichean and Nestorian works. Nonscriptural texts are also abundant, embracing a variety of local economic and legal documents, monastic records of daily life, official and private correspondence, and finally literature of both popular and belletristic nature. This highly diverse corpus of texts from Tun-huang provides an incomparable resource for the study of all aspects of medieval Chinese culture, language, and literature, while the manuscripts themselves furnish a unique source for research on calligraphy, paper, xylography, and the early development of the printed text.

The uniqueness of the literature found near Tun-huang is due in part to the singular concealment of the manuscripts and their conservation, time capsule–like, over the centuries of flux in Chinese history and esthetic tastes. The location of the find, which drew from monasteries at or near these Buddhist cavern-sanctuaries on the periphery of the Chinese empire, further defines much of the literature as uniquely local yet fully within the sphere of Chinese cultural influence. Many manuscripts were copied elsewhere in the Chinese empire and brought to Tun-huang by merchants and pilgrims, who offered them as donations. Yet all these texts and manuscripts were culled from local Buddhist monasteries that functioned as schools of proselytization and worship for lay and clergy alike and as centers for training students in the literate culture common to all China. Literacy and access to the collective written culture, it must be remembered, provided the definition of what was civilized and what was Chinese, crucial in the frontier context of Tun-huang.

Because of the role of these monasteries as centers of both learning and religious proselytizing, the corpus of Tun-huang literature is largely popular in nature. With the exception of the literary anthology *Wen hsüan* (Literary Selections), a text used in preparation for the civil service examinations (see below), no prestigious literary work exists in significant quantities. Numerous manuscripts do exist containing exercises in writing and calligraphy as copied by lay students (*hsüeh-shih-lang*). Monasteries provided lay students with the education to acquire literacy and prepare for the civil service examinations, and the copying of texts was an inherent part of the curriculum. These mostly secular texts, varying from doggerel verse and popular narratives to primers such as *Ch'ien-tzu wen* (The Thousand Character Primer) and *T'ai-kung chia-chiao* (The Family Instructions of the Grand Duke), necessarily correspond to the variety of interests and needs of these students and to their levels of comprehension and ability. The resulting manuscripts are a fascinating record of the educational process in medieval China and are invaluable for their preservation of popular literature. Texts of a more religious and technical nature, Buddhist sutras, sutra lecture texts, treatises on calendars, medicine, and so on, were copied by novices, monks, and professional scribes who were more literate. Other aspects of time and place determined which texts were preserved: the scarcity and expense of paper, most notably during the Tibetan occupation of Tun-huang (781–848), required the reuse and preservation of manuscripts that otherwise would have been discarded—thus allowing the survival of jottings, poems, and even doodles scribbled in the margins or on the verso by lay students, monks, and scribes. In their effort to gain merit, pious donors from a variety of socioeconomic backgrounds commissioned copies of scriptures and made donations of others, the result being multiple examples of particular sutras and an indication of which texts were current during specific periods. Narratives and liturgical texts used by proselytizing monks, most notably in popular lectures (*su-chiang*), attest to the popular level of both the audience and the literature.

The corpus of texts from Tun-huang composed by and directed to a cross-section of society represents the largest collection of popular literature from medieval China and provides many of the earliest examples of certain genres and styles. Chinese popular literature is often defined generally in terms of audience and more specifically in terms of form. The Buddhist doctrine of *fang-pien* (skillful means; Sanskrit, *upāya*), that is, adjusting the level of discourse to the abilities of the audience, necessitated a flexibility in style and in form and had a profound influence on Chinese literature and language. In the context of Buddhist proselytization, it was more pragmatic to reach as wide an audience as possible, and numerous manuscripts from Tun-huang provide unique and invaluable evidence (for example, in the form of notations and marginalia or through supplementary descriptions) that certain written texts were performed before a diverse audience on either religious or social occasions, often organized by lay religious societies (*she-yi*). Although it is difficult to ascertain the precise nature of the audience of Tun-huang literature, it is clear that many of these works span the divide between educated and uneducated in terms of their composition. Stylistic and linguistic elements define much of the literature from Tun-huang as popular: the pervasiveness of colloquial elements in syntax and lexical items, formulaic phrases, repetitions, and a pronounced dramatic quality all contrast with the style of contemporaneous classical Chinese literature. The theatricality of Tun-huang popular literature is most apparent in the frequent employment of direct discourse and dialog, most notably in the form of oppositional structure or contests between characters (as, for example, in "Ch'a-chiu lun" [Discourse Between Tea and Wine], "Yen-tzu fu" [Rhapsody on the Swallow], "K'ung-tzu Hsiang T'o hsiang wen-shu" [Colloquy Between Confucius and Hsiang T'o], and "Hsiang-mo pien-wen" [Transformation Text on the Subduing of Demons]). Indeed, the establishment of a distinct genre grounded in vernacular conversations and teachings of Ch'an (Zen) masters, known as *yü-lu* (recorded sayings; for example, *Liu-tsu t'an-ching* [The Platform Scripture of the Sixth Patriarch] and *Pang Chü-shih yü-lu* [Recorded Sayings of Layman P'ang]) attests to the popularity and success of such dialog formats. The conversational tone of many secular and religious works from Tun-huang, together with the use of questions and exhortations aimed at the audience, give this literature a distinct directness and immediacy, evoking the oral milieu from which much of it originated.

Another characteristic of popular literature from Tun-huang is its anonymous nature—few of these works are attributed to any author. Numerous colophons (*t'i-pa*) found on Tun-huang manuscripts do, however, give an indication of the copyists and reasons for the production of certain manuscripts and their importance. Colophons usually provide the exact date of copying, the name of the scribe, and rationale for the duplication. Dated Tun-huang manuscripts of all kinds range from 406 to 1002 C.E., and copyists tend to correspond to the level and content of material: scribes, novices, and monks duplicated explicitly religious works and formal documents, while lay students, though usually affiliated with a monastery, treated less exacting secular material, such as exercises in calligraphy and compositions in the form of primers, model letters, narratives, and poems. Generally, in the colophon of student manuscripts where no rationale for the copying is given, these are clearly learning exercises complete with corrections and emendations. Manuscripts by scribes, monks, and novices (especially religious texts) are usually copied as acts of religious merit, often solicited in the form of a prayer given in the colophon. Merit was gained by the person commissioning the copy and, in typical Chinese fashion, was frequently directed (*hui-hsiang* [transferred]; Sanskrit, *pariṇāmanā*) to improve the fate of one's kin, living or dead, or of the community. All these colophons are vital material for understanding the significance of Tun-huang literature and its audience.

The use of literature as writing exercises indicates certain texts' currency and popularity among the literate and semiliterate populace. The wide variation among specific works that lay students' manuscripts exhibit—both at the lexical level (including orthographic errors and homophones) and in terms of style, form, and even genre—is not only an indication of the individual's abilities but a reflection of the noncanonical, popular nature of much of this literature. Characteristics such as form and genre commonly used to distinguish literary works in the West are problematic when applied to Chinese literature in general and Tun-huang literature in particular. The basic literary forms of poetry and prose are blurred in such a genre as prose-poem, rhymeprose, or rhapsody (*fu*), in the use of metrical and rhythmic prose, or in nonrhyming parallel prose (*p'ien-t'i wen*), while the combination of prose and verse is fundamental to popular genres such as transformation texts (*pien-wen*) and Buddhist narratives about karma (*yüan-ch'i*). Even a seemingly clear and determinative textual feature such as genre marker or genre status can be highly elusive among these texts (see, for example, the discussion of *tz'u*, *tz'u-wen*, and *pien-wen* below). Notions of genre are, of course, operative among Tun-huang texts but remain less standardized than in the high culture of central China, as the actual context of use and immediate function take precedence over the scholar/cataloger's desire to classify and edit. As an integral part of an ever-changing common culture both religious and secular, this literature was less prone to the defining tastes of an elite group of esthetic arbiters. The fact that much of this literature was not preserved elsewhere demonstrates the literati's low regard for it; it was simply excluded from their collections and anthologies. The uniqueness and diversity of Tun-huang literature can thus be seen as a reflection of its former vitality. The remainder of this chapter, though a discussion of form and genre, supplemented by the rich body of documentation that Tun-huang manuscripts and their context provide, offers a consideration of individual works.

PROSE WORKS

Given the monastic and educational setting of Tun-huang literature, it is understandable that the exemplary biography, religious and secular, should figure so prominently as a literary form. Ever since Ssu-ma Ch'ien's (c. 145–c. 86 B.C.E.) *Shih-chi* (Records of the Historian), which established their style and format, biographies have been a standard narrative form in China highly valued for their didactic content (see chapters 26 and 27). Accordingly, within Tun-huang literature, biographies constitute the majority of prose narratives. Originating in historiography, biographies are "transmitted [accounts]" (*chuan* or *chuan-chi*) of notable deeds illustrating moral principles for the benefit of posterity. In addition to serving the didactic purposes of traditional dynastic historiography, biographies also function as vehicles for religious traditions. In both secular and religious contexts, the historiographical roots, style, and format of this genre provide the legitimizing framework necessary to establish the truth and authority of its contents. Exemplary biographies often drew on such substantial documents as historical records, stelae inscriptions, and "accounts of conduct" (*hsing-chuang*; a summary of the deceased's life, usually for ancestral rituals), and then shaped them according to their moral function or purpose.

Thus, among the Tun-huang manuscripts are a large body of biographical narratives portraying not only the lives of well-known historical characters and paragons of virtue but also those of Buddhist and Taoist figures. Narrated in simple classical or semivernacular Chinese, these stories served as popular educational texts and were read by individuals rather than performed. Two texts in the secular mode of exemplary biography are *Hsiao-tzu chuan* (Accounts of Filial Sons) and "Ch'ien Han Liu-chia t'ai-tzu chuan" (The Account of the Crown Prince of the House of Liu During the Former Han). The first, also entitled *Shih-sen* (Forest of Affairs), is a selection of short biographies that drew upon authoritative sources (*Hsiao-ching* [Classic of Filial Piety], dynastic histories, etc.) illustrating the filial acts of virtuous sons. The second concerns the Crown Prince of the Former (or Western) Han dynasty (206 B.C.E.–8 C.E.), recounting his flight from court during the Wang Mang interregnum (9–23 C.E.). Typical of standard biographical accounts, both texts use well-known figures from the past, together with precise historical information to establish their authority, and then focus on a limited set of events (often supramundane), rather than a survey of the main character's life, to illuminate their didactic message. These accounts, and the ones that follow, demonstrate that the boundary between Chinese biography and hagiography is porous.

Another secular type of exemplary biography also employs this format and values, but to a different end. Once common in medieval China, *chia-chuan* (family biographies) functioned as genealogies of prominent lineages in narrative form, rather than in detailed lists as with later family pedigrees (*chia-p'u*). Only one such complete text exists, *Tun-huang Fan-shih chia-chuan* (The Family Biography of the Fan Clan of Tun-huang), written in simple classical prose. The first part of the text traces the family back to its mythical founder Chi, brother of the great sage king Yao, while the second part consists of eleven exemplary biographies of members of the Fan clan. The manuscript is fascinating not only as an example of a lost genre and for what it tells us about Tun-huang society but also as an instance of a once common type of local historical writing, in which exemplary biography and its values legitimate the claims to authority and status of a clan.

Tun-huang manuscripts furnish another kind of biographical account in prose specifically detailing the authority and efficacy of religious belief and devotion. These short narratives are generally termed "miracle tales" and became popular as a form of apologetic literature in early medieval China. Manuscripts from Tun-huang use several different genre markers to label this general group of stories: (1) "accounts of numinous response" or "accounts of evidential miracles" (*ling-yen chi*, *ying-yen chi*, and *chuan-yen chi*); (2) "accounts of the [karmic] circumstances of . . . " (*yin-yu chi* or *yin-yüan chi*); (3) "accounts of merit" (*kung-te chi*); and (4) simply "[transmitted] accounts" (*chuan* or *chuan-chi*). These narratives all illustrate exemplary behavior and its rewards and serve to confirm the truth of Buddhist doctrine through evidential anecdotes of specific individuals and objects (stupas, statues, sutras, and so on) rooted in a particular time and place. In addition, as is true of the exemplary biographies, rather than portray a complex life story, these tales foreground the value system by focusing on a single or small set of extraordinary events that determine an individual's well-being or karmic destiny. The miraculous nature of the events and the wonder they inspire draw on another Chinese narrative tradition, *chih-kuai* (tales of anomaly; see chapters 6 and 29). The term "evidential miracles" (for example, *ling-yen, ying-yen*) found in the genre markers above is indicative of the underlying doctrine of all these narratives, Buddhist and Taoist. Using the basic Chinese concept of stimulus (*kan*) and response (*ying*) common in tales of anomaly, Buddhist miracle tales provide evidence of or witness to (*yen*) the truth of the hidden sacred order, the ineluctable law of karma. Most typically, these tales depict miraculous events or devotional acts by lay people and members of the sangha (Buddhist monastic community) that result in their improved well-being. Thus, for example, the believer's pious act of reciting or copying a sutra elicits a sympathetic response of the production of merit or, in times of distress, intervention by a bodhisattva. Numerous stories circulated recounting the efficacy of such beliefs and practices, often in compilations centered on a particular theme, sutra, or bodhisattva. Among the manuscripts from Tun-huang are portions of two well-known collections, *Yüan-hun chih* (Accounts of Ghosts with Grievances; also entitled *Huan-yüan chih* [Accounts of Requiting Vengeance]), by Yen Chih-t'ui (531–591), and *Sou-shen chi yi-pen* (In Search of the Supernatural, One Volume), modeled after the work by Kan Pao (fl. 320).

Tun-huang literature also provides miracle tales not found elsewhere, in addition to important documentation regarding the use and dissemination of the genre. These tales and their conceptual role become more clearly delineated when compared to another type of Buddhist karmic narratives from Tun-huang. An example of miracle accounts serving as a form of devotional literature is *Ch'ih-sung Chin-kang ching kung-te chi* (Accounts of the Numinous Responses and Merit Gained from Upholding and Reciting the Diamond Scripture). This collection of nineteen evidential narratives written in simple classical prose immediately precedes a copy of the scripture itself. The dedication on the manuscript furnishes valuable background information on the use of these narratives: the text, composed by Chai Feng-ta as an act of merit and completed on May 11, 908, is to encourage others to read or recite the *Diamond Scripture* itself and benefit from it. Other Tun-huang manuscripts confirm this use of miracle tales to legitimate and exemplify the virtues of a particular scripture and the merit of its propagation, as with the "Huang Shih-ch'iang chuan" (Account of Huang Shih-ch'iang), which prefaces *P'u-hsien p'u-sa shuo cheng-ming ching* (Scripture of Evidence Preached by the Bodhisattva Samantabhadra) in numerous copies. The account concerns Huang Shih-ch'iang's return-from-death experience during which he descends into hell, sees its horrors, and is advised to copy the *Scripture of Evidence* to escape such punishments in the future.

Miraculous tales include all levels of Chinese society, even the emperor of China, as in "T'ai-tsung ju-ming chi" (provisional title: Account of Emperor T'ai-tsung's Descent to the Underworld), where he is convinced to practice such pious acts as copying *Ta-yün ching* (Scripture on the Great Cloud). For the Buddhist concerned about his afterlife or the well-being of his ancestors, the Tun-huang manuscripts offer a variety of miracle tales with testimony of the horrors that await in hell, together with the exemplary ritual or behavior necessary to avoid them, from small acts of piety to profound changes in lifestyle. Confession of transgressions was one means advocated, as in the story of Chang Chü-tao's inadvertant journey to hell, "Ch'an-hui mieh-tsui Chin-kuang-ming chuan" (Account of Confession to Eliminate Transgressions [in connection with] the Scripture of the Golden Light), which, analogous in form and content to the "Account of Huang Shih-ch'iang" above, precedes the scripture itself. Joining the sangha was another means, as in "Liu Sa-ho ho-shang yin-yüan chi" (Account of the Circumstances of the Monk Liu Sa-ho). This is one version of several accounts of the well-known monk and cult figure Liu Sa-ho and his becoming a monk on seeing the torments of hell.

Although all these exemplary biographies and miracle-tale narratives discuss the workings of karma and the efficacy of Buddhism, they exist as a separate genre from the other major group of Tun-huang Buddhist narratives, accounts of [karmic] circumstances (*yüan-ch'i* or [*yin-*] *yüan*; Sanskrit, *avadāna, nidāna*), which also describe the workings of karma in a biographical context. Stories of karmic circumstances are discussed in depth below, but a brief comparison of these two genres of Buddhist stories reveals their fundamental differences in form, content, and function. The miracle tales discussed above are primarily an attempt to sinify Buddhism in an authoritative and well-understood narrative mode. They use a standard historiographical format to capture anecdotal evidence of the diversity of the Chinese experience with Buddhism's efficacy and power. Likewise, the operative principle of the natural order, karma, and its moral implications are conceptualized in explicitly Chinese terms. These features contrast sharply with the other, contemporaneous group of Tun-huang Buddhist narratives, stories on circumstances (*avadāna* and *nidāna* literature). These didactic stories elaborate the doctrine of karma, but do so as Chinese adaptations of Indian Buddhist literature. In both content and form, Chinese narratives on karmic circumstances maintain a close affinity with their Indian and Central Asian predecessors, *jātaka* (birth stories), *avadāna*, and *nidāna* tales.

The majority of Tun-huang stories on circumstances take place on the Gangetic plain (in north India), usually around the time of the historical Buddha or in the distant past, and depict the karmic deeds of Indian believers. In terms of style, they use a prosimetric (alternating between prose and verse) format common to Buddhist scriptures, while their language is Buddhist Hybrid Chinese with colloquial elements and abundant use of religious terminology. In contrast, miracle tales are entirely in prose, use simple classical Chinese, and avoid specialized terms. The proximity in form and style of stories on circumstances to Buddhist scriptures makes sense when one realizes that these stories were performed in the liturgical context of popular lectures (*su-chiang*; see below). No evidence exists from Tun-huang that miracle tales functioned in this manner. Yet the two genres complement each other: both serve as substantiation of Buddhist doctrine; miracle tales with their authority of the Chinese historical tradition depict accounts in local and familiar recent settings, whereas stories of karmic circumstances, with their legitimacy linked to scriptures and their sacred origins in India, expand the horizons of Buddhism in time and place.

Another type of vernacular and semivernacular prose narrative from Tun-huang is the *hua* (tale), which prefigures the later *hua-pen* (short story) and *p'ing-hua* (plain tale) of the Sung (960–1279), Yüan (1260–1368), and Ming (1368–1644) dynasties. As is true of their successors, the genre marker of these Tun-huang texts, *hua*, simply means "story" or "tale" and has no specific connotation of "promptbooks" used by storytellers, as sometimes argued by twentieth-century scholars. Although these Tun-huang narratives may have been recited, they bear none of the typical features of contemporaneous performed literature, such as mixed prose and verse, verse introductory formulas, exhortations directed at the audience, or other signature marks of orality found in transformation texts and Buddhist narratives on karmic circumstances. Tun-huang vernacular prose stories include: "Han ch'in-hu hua-pen" (provisional title: The Story of Catch-Tiger Han), "Lu-shan Yüan-kung hua" (The Story of Master Yüan of Lu Mountain), and "Yeh Ching-neng hua" (The Story of Yeh Ching-neng). The first is the account of how Catch-Tiger Han became a general in the army of Wen-ti, founder of the Sui dynasty (581–618), and then chief clerk of the Court of the Underworld. Hui-yüan's (334–416) story recounts the circumstances that led him to become a monk and various episodes of his life up to his death. It provides vivid descriptions of sutra lectures delivered before large audiences. The final narrative concerns the Taoist monk or wizard Yeh Ching-neng of the early T'ang dynasty (618–907) and his life of miraculous achievements. Like the miracle tales and exemplary biographies above, these prose stories concern the determinative events, often miraculous, in the life of a single individual. However, in contrast to tales and biographies, Tun-huang *hua* depict a sequence of episodes that span the individual's life. In doing so, these stories significantly elaborate the plot, character development, and the overall dramatic quality of the narrative. These stories also foreshadow later semivernacular prose narratives of the Yüan and Ming known as *p'ing-hua* (plain tales), being written in semivernacular prose with occasional verse and possessing an episodic or extended sequential structure. In addition, "The Story of Catch-Tiger Han," according to a note at the end of the text, may originally have been accompanied by illustrations, as was often the case with *p'ing-hua*. Tun-huang *hua* narratives, however, differ from *p'ing-hua*, as the latter recount episodes of an extended period of history with a variety of central characters.

Tun-huang semivernacular prose narratives, as unique examples of this genre from medieval China, provide invaluable material for further investigations into the development of later narrative genres such as *hua-pen* and *p'ing-hua*.

POETRY

Tun-huang manuscripts provide a fascinating cross-section of verse forms from medieval China and attest to the enormous popularity of poetry during this period as well as to the variety of functions it served in society. One major genre of poetry, *fu* (see chapter 12), is notable for its diversity of content and peculiarity of form, blurring the distinction between prose and verse in its use of sometimes rhymed, metrical prose. Rhapsodies from Tun-huang manuscripts range from numerous well-known works anthologized in the prestigious collection *Literary Selections* to popular compositions marked by extensive use of colloquialisms, dramatic dialog, and direct expression of emotion.

One stylistic feature common to nearly all these works, literary and popular, and indeed to many other genres of Tun-huang popular literature, is the ubiquity of parallel prose. The prevalence of this style (four- or six-character lines fixed in metrical correspondence, which establish syntactic parallelism; see chapter 12) was due in part to its obvious utility in establishing syntactic and semantic intelligibility and in part to the influence of *Literary Selections*, which was the basis for the literary portion of the civil service examination during the medieval period. More specifically, examinations at various levels required the composition of a prose-poem on a set rhyme and theme (*lü-fu* [regulated prose-poem]), and this literary anthology served as the major treasury of parallel prose and rhapsodies. This close interconnection between *Literary Selections*, Tun-huang rhapsodies, and the role of monasteries as places of secular education is evident from the manuscripts themselves. As noted above, *Literary Selections* is the only major compilation of high literature extant in large numbers among the manuscripts. Rhapsodies, nearly all on secular themes, are usually written several to a manuscript in mediocre calligraphy, accompanied by corrections, and often followed by other educational texts, such as *The Thousand Character Primer* and *Hsin-chi yen-fu chiao* (The Newly Compiled Teachings of a Stern Father). The majority of these manuscripts contain colophons giving the date and name of the lay student who copied them. No doubt as inspiration, the names of the authors (usually from the region) who composed the rhapsody that follows are also noted along with their degrees or positions. Thus these manuscripts offer a fascinating record of the educational process and the role of literature in the daily lives of the local inhabitants.

From a literary viewpoint, Tun-huang rhapsodies are important as popular examples of prose-poems in both narrative and dialog format. They differ from the dominant form of T'ang prose-poem, the *lü-fu* with its strictly parallel lines and rhyme pattern, in their extensive use of colloquialisms, irregular lines, frequent lack of rhyme, and vivid dialog. These features tend to be less pronounced, understandably, in prose-poems composed for examinations, as indicated by a writer's name and credentials. In spite of such differences, popular rhapsodies from Tun-huang continue in the tradition of earlier examples of the genre, which, beginning with works such as Mei Ch'eng's (d. 140 B.C.E.) "Ch'i fa" (Seven Stimuli), served as persuasive pieces of rhetoric (*shui*) in dialog form aimed at the moral edification of their audience. The common device of a contest between opponents creates a dramatic and exhortative setting for the ideas in these prose-poems. For example, "Rhapsody on the Swallow" is a political satire on the excesses and abuse of power couched in a tale about a quarrel between a sparrow and a swallow, adjudicated by a phoenix. In "Discourse Between Tea and Wine," a debate held between the two beverages to determine which is superior is decided by and in favor of water as fundamental to both. (Slightly more sophisticated in style and language than the other works mentioned here, this composition was the work of a successful examination candidate, as duly noted: "Composed by Wang Fu, Graduate of the third Provincial Examination.") "Colloquy Between Confucius and Hsiang-t'o" uses this same oppositional structure to frame an exchange of questions and riddles between Confucius and a boy named Hsiang T'o, ending with Confucius's acknowledgment of the boy's intelligence. Tun-huang literature also contains popular prose-poems on historical themes using a narrative format and extensive dialog. The "Rhapsody on Yen-tzu" recounts the anecdote of Yen Ying (sixth century B.C.E.), prime minister of the state of Ch'i, and his encounter with the king of Liang. "Han P'eng fu" (Rhyme-prose on Han P'eng) is a retelling of the tale of Han P'eng, found in Kan Pao's collection of anomaly tales *In Search of the Supernatural*. The work tells the story of Han P'eng, who loses his wife to the prince of Sung. The couple die separately, and, because they could not be buried together, two trees grow over their graves with branches intertwined, symbolizing their mutual devotion.

Among the several genres of poetry found at Tun-huang, one in particular, the *ch'ü-tzu-tz'u* (song lyric; also known as *ch'ü* [songs] or *tz'u* [lyrics]), has provided crucial information about the development of poetry in medieval China. The song lyric developed during the Six Dynasties (220–589) period, the Sui, and early T'ang as a popular form, further evolving in literary circles in the latter half of the T'ang and the Five Dynasties (907–960) period. Like previous verse forms, poetry such as that found in the *Shih-ching* (Classic of Poetry) and *Ch'u tz'u* (Elegies of Ch'u) and poems of the Music Bureau (*yüeh-fu*) were initially written as poetic texts accompanied by music. Like its predecessors, the song lyric was adopted by the literati and redefined in terms of their literary, stylistic, and thematic concerns. The anthologizing and canonization of the elite creations resulted in the loss of more colloquial examples of the song lyric, obscuring the popular and performative origins of this genre. Fortunately, preserved among the variety of texts and literary genres at Tun-huang were a wide range of song lyrics. These poems provide documentation clarifying the earlier stages of the genre's development with its manifold styles and themes and clearly indicate the popular milieu out of which the genre arose.

The discovery of early and diverse examples of the song lyric has revised our understanding of the origins of the genre and its development as a whole. Early-twentieth-century scholars, following the opinion of Hu Shih (1891–1962) and previous critics, held that the song lyric was a derivation of the dominant T'ang style of poetry, the *lü-shih* (regulated verse), and specifically the *chüeh-chü* (quatrain). It was thought that in order to adapt the regulated verse to newly introduced music from Central Asia, interjections and words were added (*fan-sheng* [floating words]), creating a derivative form. Hu and others attributed this origin of the song lyric to the literati poets of the Middle T'ang (766–836), such as Liu Yü-hsi (772–842) and Po Chü-yi (772–846). Consequently, earlier poems in this style by Li Po (701–762) and others of the Early and High T'ang (618–766) were declared forgeries. However, recent research on Tun-huang song lyrics indicates that this theory is incorrect. Lyrics from Tun-huang provide prototypical examples of the genre dating from the early eighth century, characterized by a combination of oral style and written form and by a diversity of secular and religious themes. This points to the song lyric developing from a long and complex tradition of popular songs influenced by recently arrived Central Asian music (*hu-yüeh*) and Buddhist songs (*fa-ch'ü* or *Fo-ch'ü*) and by the exigencies of actual performance. The interaction between popular, largely female, entertainers, their literati patrons, and the imperial courts, notably through the Palace Music School (*chiao-fang*) of Emperor Hsüan-tsung (r. 712–756), further shaped this genre. Song lyrics were taken up by the elite and written for entertainers and courtesans. Only later did scholar-officials acknowledge the composition of songs specifically for themselves. As a whole, these poems represent a continuum of techniques and styles. Not only do lyrics in a popular style exist side by side with more literary examples, but several compositions combine a variety of poetic conventions. The manifold nature of Tun-huang song lyrics demonstrates the genre's wide circulation among all levels of society and the porous divisions between social strata.

The study of Tun-huang song lyrics is made difficult by the lack of a unified corpus. These poems were written mostly in the margins and unused spaces of manuscripts, no doubt because of the scarcity and value of paper. They exist as examples of practice writing and mnemonic aids by scribes who were perhaps monks but more likely lay students. Depending on the criteria used to define the song lyric (the number of stanzas that constitute a song, isolated *tsa-ch'ü* [independent stanzas] or *lien-chang* [linked stanzas]; the inclusion of Buddhist songs [*Fo-ch'ü*]; differentiation according to genre markers [*tz'u*, *ch'ü*, or *ch'ü-tzu-t'zu*]; and so on), the total number of poems varies from 545 to more than 1,200 depending on how they are counted. Yet the structure and content of these songs distinguish them from other Tun-huang poetic genres, such as *fu*, *tz'u-wen* (lyric texts), and *shih* (poems). In contrast to the dominant poetic style of the T'ang, regulated verse, whose form consists of lines of fixed length (either pentasyllabic or heptasyllabic verse) structured as a series of rhyming couplets, song lyrics vary the number of lines in a poem as *ch'ang-tuan chü* (long and short lines). Rather than a balance of rhyming couplets, the composition of each lyric is based on a specific song or tune pattern (*tz'u-tiao* or *tz'u-p'ai*), with set rhymes and particular tonal conventions. These diverse tune patterns (Tun-huang manuscripts cite roughly sixty) encouraged the use of mixed tonal prosody, which contrasts with a limited number of fixed, recurring patterns in regulated verse. The majority of Tun-huang song lyrics were composed as occasional pieces for public performance accompanied by the popular music of the period (*yen-yüeh* [entertainment music]) and sometimes dance.

A comparison of the two earliest extant collections of song lyrics, *Hua chien chi* (Among the Flowers; 940), compiled by a minor official named Chao Ch'ung-tso (fl. 934–965), and *Yün-yao chi* (Cloud Songs; 922) from the manuscripts, highlights the diverse content of the Tun-huang works, as well as their unique stylistic and linguistic characteristics. The five hundred songs, by eighteen named literati, in *Among the Flowers* mostly concern love described in highly allusive and refined terms. Their canvas-like depiction, elegant language, and indirect expression of emotions contrast sharply with the dramatic and narrative quality used to represent the varied subject matter of the Tun-huang collection, *Cloud Songs*. The popular song lyrics of the latter anthology, all by anonymous authors, portray daily life and its hardships through such themes as the pain of separation due to military conscription, the wanderings of a merchant (see "Ch'ang hsiang-ssu" [Eternal Longing]), and war and patriotic sacrifice, as well as amorous elegies, descriptions of the countryside, music, etc. In contrast to the more lyrical mode of *Among the Flowers*, the explicit expression of new emotions, use of direct dialog (often in the form of questions and answers; see "Ch'üeh t'a chih" [Magpie on the Branch]), and colloquial language all establish the dramatic tenor of these popular songs. This dramatic quality is further enhanced by linking several stanzas together in a quasi-narrative sequence.

The general corpus of Tun-huang lyric songs is characterized to an even greater degree by these popular features found in *Cloud Songs*, the songs in the latter being somewhat refined stylistically in comparison. *Cloud Songs*, however, is not representative of the longer song cycles found at Tun-huang, the majority of which are on Buddhist themes.

Song cycles recovered from Tun-huang contrast with the isolated or independent stanzas both in form and content. These longer works link several stanzas together with the use of the same melody throughout and with the initial repetition of a set term or terms, often in chronological order. Examples are poems in the form of "Wu-keng chuan" (Five Watches of the Night), each stanza of which begins with the number of the watch. Other chronological sequences include the twelve hours of the day, the twelve months of the year, and the hundred years of human life. These sequences in turn serve as the basis for elaborating specific themes, many of which are Buddhist. Thus titles include "Ch'an-men shih-erh-shih" (Twelve Hours of Meditation), "Tzu-men pai-sui p'ien" (One Hundred Years of a Monk), and "T'ai-tzu wu-keng chuan" (Five Watches of the Prince [Siddārtha's Departure]). Song cycles include secular themes such as "T'an pai-sui" (Lament on [the Passing of a] Hundred Years) and "Shih-erh shih hsing-hsiao" (Twelve Hours of the Practice of Filial Piety). There are also more secular sequences such as "Pai-sui p'ien" (One Hundred Years) on men (*chang-fu*) and women (*nü-jen*). The sequential structure of these songs, together with their extended narrative form, potential for thematic development, and repetitions, render these poems both didactic and entertaining, making them useful tools for proselytizing.

Another type of song sequence from Tun-huang is the *ta-ch'ü* (grand song), which was sung accompanied by music and dance in a large-scale spectacle. The five sets of grand songs from Tun-huang (only twenty stanzas of which are extant) would have been performed in a set format, usually consisting of an instrumental introduction, followed by a sequence of songs set to music with a steady beat, and finally music, dance, and occasionally singing at a heightened tempo. None of the extant grand songs are complete. If they had survived intact, they would have between ten and sixteen stanzas. Tun-huang grand songs, all anonymous, issue from the same diverse cultural matrix as the lyric songs and possess similar popular characteristics and a diversity of themes and styles. One grand song is on the hardships of separation in the format of the "five watches" (of the night), another on the hardships of life on the frontier presented in sequential structure, and so on. Like certain lyric songs, several grand songs preserved at Tun-huang date from the seventh century and indicate an anterior stage in the development of this style unknown until the discovery of the manuscripts.

Many Tun-huang songs can be grouped loosely under the rubric "eulogy" or "song of praise" (*tsan*, *tsan-sung*). The variety of poems in this general category combine features of two distinct traditions, one Indian and the other Chinese. *Sung* and *tsan* are translations of the Sanskrit *stotra*, meaning "hymn" or "eulogy," which were commonly sung in unison for religious ceremonies and during liturgies. Introduced to China, these Buddhist liturgical hymns and songs developed in response to the needs of proselytization. The eulogy, as a Chinese literary genre, dates back to a section of the earliest collection of poetry, the *Classic of Poetry* ("Chou-sung" [Hymns/Eulogies of the Chou], nos. 266–296), and evolves to embrace a variety of secular and religious themes, typically using quatrains of five- or seven-syllable verse with variable rhyme schemes. Tun-huang manuscripts provide several distinct types of this genre.

One example from Tun-huang of a more traditional Chinese form of this genre is the "portrait eulogy" (*miao-chen tsan*, *hsiang-tsan*, *chen-jung tsan*, and others). Roughly ninety such songs are extant, dating from the eighth to the eleventh centuries. These were written as panegyrics of prominent individuals, near death or recently deceased, to accompany their painted portraits. They are thus similar to eulogies composed as epitaphs (*mu-chih ming*), but differ in that the portraits were hung within the household temporarily for the deceased's family and acquaintances. Originally sung to music, portrait eulogies, like lyric songs, became divorced from music and could be read as literary creations. These eulogies typically had a four-part structure: a title stating the name of the individual together with his or her profession and status; the poet's name and his position; the eulogy on the individual's life and accomplishments, written in regular, usually tetrasyllabic, verse; and the date and place of composition, followed by the name of the poet. The majority of eulogies concern individuals from Tun-huang and, as such, provide unique and concrete documentation on their lives and activities in the community.

Among the manuscripts from Tun-huang is a large body of Buddhist hymns detailing religious practices and beliefs. These *tsan* stem from a tradition of Buddhist psalmody known as *fan-pai* (Brahmic sounds; *fan* is derived from the Sanskrit *brahm*—having the general sense of things sacred from India—and *pai* comes from *bhaṇ-*, the Sanskrit root "to recite" or "to say"). Tradition holds that Buddhist hymns (*fan-pai*) were first composed in China by the poet Ts'ao Chih (192–232). More likely is that literate Chinese collaborated with monks and musicians from Central Asia to compose the works. Hymns, which became known as *pai-tsan* ([Brahmic] songs) or *Fo-ch'ü* (Buddhist songs), were in time differentiated from the practice of reciting sutras (*chuan-tu*). As hymns, the former covered a wide range of topics and practices, usually introducing a particular ceremony or service to the accompaniment of music. Verses taken from scriptures (that is, *gāthā* [*chi* or *chi/ch'ieh-t'o*, a stanza in four lines]) were also employed as hymns of praise, and because of their analogous function the two were sometimes used interchangeably (as indicated by the genre markers *chieh-sung* or *chieh-tsan*).

Tun-huang manuscripts provide numerous examples of hymns and verses performed in ceremonies and as liturgies (*li-tsan-wen*), documenting the ritual and daily practices of both monks and laymen. Many of these works praise the life of Śākyamuni Buddha, such as "Hsi-ta t'ai-tzu ju Hsüeh-shan hsiu tao tsan" (Hymn on Prince Siddhārtha Entering the Himalayas to Cultivate the Way), which was recited to the sequential format "Five Watches of the Night." Buddhas, bodhisattvas, and even Śākyamuni's mother are subjects of hymns. An integral component of liturgies, eulogies were used in such ubiquitous rites as popular lectures (see below) and confessions (*ch'an-hui*). Examples of practices include "San-hua tsan" (Hymn for Scattering Flowers [as offerings]), "Jan-teng tsan" (Hymn for Lighting Lamps), and "Hsing-hsiang chi-wen" (Text of Verses [*gāthā*] on Burning Incense). The majority of these hymns are composed in pentasyllabic and heptasyllabic verse, often in quatrains, while their language is Buddhist Hybrid Chinese. One final collection of hymns that merits interest is a Chinese translation of Nestorian Christian songs entitled "Ta Ch'in Ching-chiao san-wei meng-tu tsan" (Hymns on the Holy Trinity of the Great Roman Nestorian Religion Who Saves the Ignorant). Written in simple and direct language employing Buddhist terminology and composed of quatrains (*gāthā*) of heptasyllabic verse, these hymns clearly demonstrate Buddhist literary and ideological influences. Their preservation among the manuscripts from Tun-huang underscores the important role of this oasis as a religious and transportation center on the Silk Route.

In addition to the forms of Tun-huang poetry discussed above (prose-poems, lyric texts, lyric songs, hymns, and so forth) is a large body of verse generally termed *shih*. These poems, in the tradition of *ku-t'i shih* (old-style poetry) and *hsin-t'i shih* (new-style poetry; also *lü-shih* [regulated verse]), embrace both popular and literary styles and a variety of secular and religious themes. Scattered throughout the manuscripts as isolated stanzas or grouped together in a variety of collections, roughly three thousand poems preserve material otherwise lost to posterity.

The largest group of *shih* poems are Buddhist, characterized by Buddhist themes and doctrine. As works directed at explaining and propagating doctrine, many of these poems elaborate abstract religious concepts in popular terms often using the enumerative folk format mentioned above. One such example is "Shih-erh yin-yüan liu tzu ko-tz'u" (Hexasyllabic Poem on the Twelve Links of Dependent Origination), by Wei Yüan-sung of the Northern Chou dynasty (557–581), which uses simple allegory and concrete images to explain in twelve eight-line stanzas the Buddhist doctrine of causation (*yin-yüan* or *yüan-ch'i*; Sanskrit, *pratītyasamutpāda*). Another example of linked verse on a single doctrinal theme is "Chiu hsiang-kuan shih" (Poem on the Nine Visualizations). This poem illustrates the Buddhist concept of impermanence (*wu-ch'ang*; Sanskrit, *anitya*), describing an individual's birth, growth, death, and decay through nine stages (nine stanzas of twelve pentasyllabic verses). This is a less gruesome version of the nine stages or nine reflections (*chiu-hsiang*; Sanskrit, *navāpriya-samjñā*) of a rotting corpse, which was a frequent subject of meditation. Both these poems' sequential structure of linked stanzas, common among many didactic poems from Tun-huang, permits an extended narrative of cause and effect to elaborate two important Buddhist doctrines in concrete terms.

Poems exhorting the reader or listener to practice virtuous behavior (*ch'üan-shan*) based on Buddhist doctrine are also prevalent at Tun-huang. An example of general practices rendered in poetic form are the ten bodhisattva precepts in the poem "Ho p'u-sa chieh wen" (Harmonizing [Oneself] with the Bodhisattva Precepts). This anonymous work enumerates these ten basic moral instructions for believers. Each of the ten stanzas, consisting of octets of hexa- and heptasyllabic verse, details the often-dire consequences that ensue from not following a given precept. Another compilation, the collection of anonymous poems entitled *Hsin-hai chi* (Ocean of the Mind; originally 118 stanzas, of which only 95 survive), is directed at calming the mind through Ch'an (Zen) meditational practices. These *gāthā*, in both pentasyllabic and hexasyllabic verse, explain in simple terms the necessity of overcoming the distractions of the world to achieve spiritual attainment.

Of particular interest among the Tun-huang manuscripts are the Buddhist poems attributed to "Brahmacārin Wang," or Wang Fan-chih. These poems are remarkable for the consistent use of vernacular language in their presentation of a variety of Buddhist themes. Although it was very popular from the T'ang to the Sung dynasty, the colloquial character of the verse excluded it from literary canonization in such collections as *Ch'üan T'ang shih* (Complete T'ang Poems). Another reason these poems were not preserved may be the elusive nature of the poet himself. Although one Chinese tradition dates Wang Fan-chih to the Sui dynasty as an inhabitant of Honan province, several factors point to "Wang Fan-chih" being a fictive person rather than an actual historical individual. The poet's name–*Wang* (literally "king"; also a Chinese family name comparable in its commonness to "Smith" in English), who aspires to (*chih*) the sacred (*fan*)—intimates the legendary nature of this figure. The second character of the name, *fan*, consists of two elements, *lin* (forest), on top, and *fan* (common or ordinary [person]), on the bottom; together they mean the "sacred [of Indian origin]" or, in Sanskrit, *brahma*. These three semantic elements accord with one legend that has Wang born from a tree in the Western Regions (Hsi-yü, that is, India or Central Asia). Another factor indicating that the poetry of Wang Fan-chih represents a category of verse rather than the work of a single hand is its parallel with the largely Buddhist poetry of the layman or, perhaps more accurately, group of laymen known as Han-shan (Cold Mountain). Although Wang's poetry is more colloquial and didactic than that of Han-shan, both bodies of verse, each said to number three hundred poems (a traditional figure probably traceable to the *Classic of Poetry*), vary stylistically and appear to be by more than one hand. As is the case with Han-shan, no definitive documentation verifies Wang's existence; the events, times, and places of both their lives remain elusive. Nonetheless, it is possible to view the two bodies of poetry as wide-ranging yet very personalized expressions of Buddhist quests for spiritual attainment.

The style of Wang Fan-chih's poems intentionally directs this quest at the broadest audience possible. The preface to one collection of poems states that, rather than using the style of the classics, its verse employs the vernacular. These poems are preserved in some thirty manuscripts from Tun-huang, whose contents vary from simple morality concerning filial piety and self-restraint to profound reflections on death and the transience of life. Numerous poems depict society and its injustices, often elaborating the differences between rich and poor in terms of karma and personal responsibility. Like the language, the imagery is direct and without ambiguity, geared for ease of comprehension.

Their use as didactic tools is evident from the fact that many of the poems were copied by lay students as writing exercises. Although some verse is heptasyllabic, the majority of poems are written in five-syllable lines, mostly quatrains, many of which follow the conventions of "broken verse" (*chüeh-chü*, i.e., quatrains). They generally use the same rhyme throughout, found in the even lines. The corpus of Wang Fan-chih's poetry is an invaluable literary, social, and religious document. The explicit use of vernacular language provides a point of comparison for understanding the use of the colloquial in the works of other T'ang dynasty poets, while the poems reflect fundamental values and concerns held by both the semiliterate and literate.

Although the majority of religious poetry from Tun-huang is Buddhist in inspiration, numerous individual poems and two significant compilations of Taoist verse have been preserved. Particularly interesting are the two Taoist collections, *Hsüan-ko* (Songs of Mystery) and *She-tao shi* (Poems on Entering the Way). The first, *Songs of Mystery*, was appended to *Hua-hu ching* (Scripture on the Conversion of the Barbarians). This popular Taoist scripture, by the Taoist master Wang Fu of the fourth century C.E., reveals the numerous transformations of Lao Tzu through the ages. He traveled west and, appearing as the Buddha, converted the barbarians. He later returned to China and presented Confucius with his teachings on rites; still later, he developed the doctrines of Manicheism. The anonymous poems appended to this scripture, forming a collection numbering 318 stanzas, are organized in four sections according to events described in the preceding scripture. In pentasyllabic verse and in simple language, the poems praise Lao Tzu and his achievements in his many manifestations. The second collection of Taoist poetry, *Poems on Entering the Way*, is by the otherwise unknown late T'ang poet Li Hsiang. The collection consists of twenty-eight poems in heptasyllabic, regulated verse, which are divided thematically into three sections: fifteen poems on famous Taoist sites; seven poems on various Taoist gods; and six poems presented as epistolary gifts. These works are in the style of Six Dynasties Taoist verse, notably "poetry of mysterious discourse" (*hsüan-yen shih*), "poetry summoning the recluse" (*chao-yin shih*), and "landscape poetry" (*shan-shui shih*). Although sophisticated in style and language, they were not anthologized in such collections as the *Complete T'ang Poems*, and their preservation thus is due to their chance inclusion among the manuscripts from Tun-huang.

Verse in the *shih* form from Tun-huang also contains a large body of secular works remarkable for their variety. They range from literary works by well-known T'ang poets excluded from anthologies such as the *Complete T'ang Poems* and its predecessors, to striking examples of verse detailing the difficulties of life on the frontier by local literati.

"Ch'in-fu yin" (The Lament of the Lady of Ch'in), by Wei Chuang (836?–910), was lost for nearly a thousand years until its discovery among the manuscripts at Tun-huang. This lengthy poem of 238 lines in heptasyllabic verse is an extended narrative about the life of a resident of Ch'ang-an, the "lady of Ch'in," after the sack of the city by Huang Ch'ao and his rebel forces in 882. Through the voice of the woman as recounted by the narrator, the poem details in graphic terms the destruction of the city and countryside, and the suffering caused by the rebels. The woman goes on to tell of her life among the rebels and her flight from the capital toward Lo-yang, where she meets the narrator. The work is considered a masterpiece of Chinese narrative poetry in terms of its integration of stylistic devices with a narrative defined by actions and voices rather than explicit sequential structure (as in various linked poems discussed above). Writing only several years after the events and critical of the ruling class, Wei Chuang chose not to include the poem in his collected works. Fortunately, manuscripts from Tun-huang provided the material to reconstruct the text in its entirety (see chapter 14).

The Tun-huang manuscripts preserve the works of other T'ang dynasty literati poets, some of which were otherwise lost in China. These include compilations of assorted poems by Li Chiao (c. 645–714) in the collection *Li Chiao tsa-yung* (Miscellaneous Poems by Li Chiao); *Kao Shih shih-chi* (The Collected Works of Kao Shih [716–765]); and a small collection of Po Chü-yi's work (*Po Hsiang-shan shih-chi*). In addition to individual poems scattered throughout various manuscripts, numerous anthologies exist of "selected T'ang poets" (*T'ang-jen hsüan T'ang shih*). By supplementing existing anthologies with previously unknown works and by providing variants for extant poems, these manuscripts offer invaluable material for research on T'ang dynasty poetry.

PROSIMETRIC LITERATURE

Transformation texts (*pien-wen*) are perhaps the best-known genre of popular literature from Tun-huang, valued as the earliest written examples of a storytelling and performance tradition that was to shape the development of Chinese literature and fiction profoundly during the following centuries. Although transformation texts, with their prosimetric form and extensive use of colloquialisms, were indeed highly influential in the evolution of Chinese literature, twentieth-century scholars' fascination with this hitherto-unknown genre and the frequent use of the term *pien-wen* as a catchall for a variety of Tun-huang popular literature has unnecessarily obscured this genre's form and function. Moreover, this lack of rigor has slighted the study of similar prosimetric genres from Tun-huang, both as independent genres and as critical elements in the overall development of Chinese literature. In fact, transformation texts are only one of the three distinct prosimetric genres found at Tun-huang, the others being Buddhist narratives on karmic circumstances (*yüan-ch'i*) and "sutra lecture texts" (*chiang-ching wen*). A fourth genre, "lyric texts" (*tz'u-wen*), is written largely in verse but contains occasional lines of prose. It is important as the earliest example of the later prosimetric genre called *tz'u-hua* (doggerel story; see chapters 49 and 50) and as the model for a Buddhist genre unique to Tun-huang, "seat-settling texts" (*ya-tso wen*). These genres share certain stylistic, rhetorical, and thematic features that appear highly similar; yet, when examined in terms of function and performance, their differences become clear. As narrated texts, individually and generically, they are intimately keyed to their performative contexts: the liturgy and popular sutra lecture for narratives of karmic circumstances and sutra lecture texts, and storytelling, either professional or casual, for transformation texts and lyric texts. Mutual comparison of Tun-huang Buddhist literature substantiates the differences among the various genres, but simultaneously asserts their commonalities as popular literature written for performance. With these genres and their constituent texts, Tun-huang provides the earliest examples of a vibrant tradition of popular storytelling in China, which continued, in some cases remarkably unchanged, for another five centuries. The anteriority and origins of these performative genres, together with their continued influence, clearly indicate that Buddhist literature was instrumental in shaping Chinese popular storytelling and the vernacular literature of subsequent dynasties.

Transformation texts, narratives of karmic circumstances, and sutra lecture texts are distinguished above all by their prosimetric format. The feature of alternating prose and verse was sufficiently conspicuous in Sung dynasty China to constitute a line of division between storytelling genres, that is, narratives in a prosimetric format and those in prose alone. The development of new genres using mixed prose and verse coincides with the introduction and assimilation of Buddhism in China. As a fundamental stylistic feature of Buddhist scriptures, alternating prose and verse became diffused through proselytizing and popular storytelling and was to have a profound impact on Chinese narrative and performance literature, as well as on the short story and novel.

The influence of the prosimetric format extended beyond style to affect the conceptual role of narrative as well. Implicit in the Buddhist doctrine of *upāya* (*fang-pien;* expedient means or skillful means) is the acknowledgment of a diversity of abilities and viewpoints. A prosimetric format, with its flexibility of style, together with the doctrine of skillful means, legitimated a variety of discourses and registers beyond the historiographically centered, singular worldview manifest in the exemplary biographies found at the beginning of this chapter (see also chapter 27). The shift from classical prose to vernacular mixed prose and verse was profound: it opened Chinese narrative literature to a previously unknown pluralism in both content and form. It was in this expanded imaginative space of prosimetric narrative that Chinese fiction began to blossom. Yet the flow of ideas and influence was not unilateral. An examination of Tun-huang prosimetric narratives, transformation texts, narratives of karmic circumstances, and lyric texts, together with related genres of sutra lecture texts and seat-settling texts, displays a fascinating picture of Buddhist literature's adaptation to the exigencies of Chinese culture and the adaptation of Chinese literary forms to the needs of Buddhism.

One of the primary vehicles for the introduction and assimilation of Buddhism in China was edifying stories or parables, which as an expedient means illustrated the workings of karma and rebirth to diverse audiences. These stories—primarily Chinese translations of the Indian Buddhist genres *jātaka* (*pen-sheng*), *avadāna* (*p'i-yü*), and *nidāna* (*yüan-ch'i*) tales—functioned either in a scriptural or a performative (liturgy or storytelling) setting as explanatory devices. As narratives, they provide the auditor with model situations or events based on Buddhist values and beliefs for comparison to one's own circumstances. Appropriately, these stories were termed *p'i-yu* or *pi-yu* (comparison; by extension, "metaphor" and "parable"—much like the Greek *paraballein* [put next to each other or compare]). During the Six Dynasties and early T'ang periods, the most popular types of proselytizers were itinerant monks (*ch'ang-tao-shih*), who recited these stories while preaching to diverse crowds. The prevalence and importance of karmic narratives in the promulgation of Buddhism are indicated by numerous compilations assembled and translated into Chinese during this period (*Chuan-chi pai yüan ching* [*Avadānaśataka*], *Tsa-pao tsang-ching* [*Saṃyuktaratnapiṭaka-sūtra*?], etc.). Unfortunately, little is known about the precise techniques of storytelling, the performative contexts, or the formal features such karmic narratives employed during this period.

Tun-huang manuscripts furnish not only numerous examples of karmic narratives actually used in performance but an abundance of documentation on the context of performance—the popular lecture (*su-chiang*) of the T'ang and Five Dynasties periods. Karmic narratives from Tun-huang, *yüan-ch'i* or *[yin-] yüan*, are a direct continuation of the tradition of Indian Buddhist literature (*jātaka*, *avadāna*, and *nidāna*). The terms *yüan-ch'i* and [*yin-*]*yüan*, derived from the doctrine of dependent origination (Sanskrit *pratītyasamutpāda*; the concept that a set of causal conditions or circumstances together give rise to a result), reflect the underlying theme of these narratives: karma. Examples from Tun-huang include "Ch'ou-nü yüan-ch'i" (The Circumstances of the Ugly Girl), which describes the karmic consequences after a girl testily makes an offering to an arhat (or, in some versions, *pratyekabuddha*). For the offering she is reborn into an aristocratic family, but for her irascibility she is born ugly. "Nan-t'o ch'u-chia yüan" (The Circumstances of Nanda Becoming a Monk) recounts how the Buddha converts his half-brother Nanda through expedient journeys to view the pleasures of heaven and the horrors of hell. Another karmic narrative is "Mu-lien yüan-ch'i" (The Circumstances of Mu-lien), which relates the story of Mu-lien's search for his mother in the underworld. This version contains fewer narrative elaborations and is more moralizing in focus than the "Transformation Text on Mu-lien" (see below), highlighting the didactic function of *yüan-ch'i* narratives.

As stated above, karmic narratives differ from indigenous miracle tales in form, content, and function. Several features mark Tun-huang karmic narratives as a distinct genre of performed literature: like other types of Tun-huang popular literature (transformation texts, lyric texts, and sutra lecture texts), they are prosimetric, employing mostly heptasyllabic verse, and use tonal prosody as the primary means of establishing euphony. However, a verse introductory formula, "at that time, what did he say?" (*tang erh chih shih, shuo ho yen-yü;* or simply "what did he say?" [*tao ho yen-yü*]) is unique to this genre of narrative. Furthermore, the verse portions of karmic narratives often contain marginalia specifying the exact method of reciting the verse. The prose portions, by contrast, are occasionally truncated, marked "and so on" (*yün-yün*), indicating the narrator's ability to elaborate if necessary.

That karmic narratives share certain affinities with another genre of prosimetric literature from Tun-huang, sutra lecture texts, is indicative of a common performative context, the popular sutra lecture. During the T'ang dynasty, the Five Dynasties, and the early Sung dynasty, these religious services were held on seasonal and official occasions to propagate Buddhism through the exegesis of sutras, usually concentrating on a particular scripture. These lectures to the laity were conducted by a "dharma master" (*fa-shih*) who performed the service, and, according to Tun-huang manuscripts that record the procedure for giving a popular lecture, involved invocations, "seat-settling texts" (see below), karmic narratives (*yüan-ch'i*), and sutra lecture texts, among other liturgical works. Sutra lecture texts explain the sutra in question, for example the *Vimalakīrti sutra* or the *Lotus Sutra,* line by line, first in prose and then restated in verse, usually heptasyllabic. They also have a characteristic verse formula, "please sing" (*ch'ang-chiang-lai*), directed to the cantor (*tu-chiang*) to commence the explanation of the passage in question. Another genre of popular religious literature, the "seat-settling text" (*ya-tso-wen*), is interesting for its use in the popular sutra lecture but also as a sort of introit that was employed in different performative contexts.

Seat-settling texts functioned as a kind of prolog to the sutra lecture text, in effect inciting interest in the lecture and allowing people to take their places. These works consist almost entirely of heptasyllabic verse, with the occasional line of prose. The verse has a caesura (break or pause) after the fourth character and generally employs either a single rhyme throughout or mixed rhyme. The language is highly colloquial, and the manuscripts are marked by numerous corrections. These prologs recount elements found in the sutra lecture that follows. For example, "Pa-hsiang pien ya-tso wen" (Seat-Settling Text for the Eight Aspects [of the Life of the Buddha]) in several lines describes the Buddha's life, starting with his descent from Tuṣita Heaven through to his enlightenment. Seat-settling texts then usually end with the phrase "Please sing the title of the sutra" (*ching-t'i ming-mu ch'ang-chiang-lai*), thereby introducing the sutra lecture that follows. Seat-settling texts as popular verse compositions are in fact highly similar to another genre of Tun-huang popular literature, the "lyric text" (*tz'u-wen*). These predominantly verse works use heptasyllabic verse with prose occasionally interjected and, like seat-settling texts, were chanted, as opposed to being sung to a particular tune (*tiao*). The most notable example from Tun-huang, "Chi Pu ma-chen tz'u-wen" (The Lyric Text on Chi Pu Shouting Abuses at the Battlefront), relates the story, set in the chaos at the end of the Ch'in dynasty (221–207 B.C.E.), of Chi Pu (a swashbuckling hero of Ch'u; third–second century B.C.E.) and his tirade against Liu Pang (founder of the Han dynasty; 247–195 B.C.E.). Another is the story of Tung Yung and his act of filial piety, selling himself as a slave to pay for his parents' coffins. It, too, is characterized by its heptasyllabic verse, use of a single rhyme scheme, and vernacular diction. Some scholars hold that lyric texts are in the popular ballad (*yüeh-fu*) tradition of the Six Dynasties period, such as "K'ung-ch'üeh tung-nan fei" (A Peacock Southeast Flew) and "Mu-lan tz'u" (or "Mu-lan shih"; The Ballad of Mu-lan). What is certain, however, is that these compositions from Tun-huang are the earliest-known examples of the same genre that was to flourish nearly five hundred years later during the Ming dynasty under the name of "lyric story" (also translated as "doggerel story" or "chantefable"; *tz'u-hua*; see chapters 49 and 50). Their subject matter ranges from historical tales to Buddhist cautionary tales. Like lyric texts, these later prosimetric narratives use seven-syllable verse mixed with prose, a single rhyme, and stock phrases. As was much of the Tun-huang literature above, these later works were written compositions, but reflect the conventions of oral performance. These performance traditions, though overlapping at times, were distinguished by their pragmatic function. Thus, although the heptasyllabic verse, single-rhyme format of lyric texts was also used in a religious context as seat-settling texts, these latter texts are clearly differentiated by their genre marker (*ya-tso-wen*) and their relative brevity. Furthermore, as noted on a Tun-huang manuscript, performers of lyric texts consciously distinguished themselves as such, that is, as "lyricists" (*tz'u-jen*).

The determinative factor of how a text is keyed to its performative context is crucial for understanding the final genre of prosimetric literature, transformation texts. As stated above, the mislabeling of texts under the general rubric of *pien-wen* (transformation texts) has led to obfuscation of the overall typology of Tun-huang literature and impeded research both on genres and on specific texts. Transformation texts are remarkably close in form and style to the genre of popular prosimetric stories known as karmic narratives (*yüan-ch'i* or [*yin-*] *yüan*), and a comparison of the two is instructive. Both genres embrace examples of performed prosimetric stories written in semivernacular Chinese, using mainly heptasyllabic verse and a verse-introductory formula, are of similar length, and may even present the same story (e.g., the tale of Mu-lien). Their differences, however, are indicative of their distinctive performative contexts and functions: transformation texts consistently employ a variation of the verse-introductory formula "[Please look at the] place [where XX happens]; how [should I] describe [it]" (*[ch'ieh k'an]* XX *ch'u, jo-wei ch'en-[shuo]*). This verse-introductory formula, together with additional information from Tun-huang manuscripts and paintings, confirms the customary connection between this genre and illustrations. Although karmic narratives have their own slightly variable verse-introductory formula, "At that time, what did he say?" (*tang erh-chih-shih, tao ho yen-yü*), and may well have been used in conjunction with pictures, no formal or textual feature indicates a necessary link between the narratives and illustrations. The place of performance and the narrators also differ: no external evidence exists for the performance of transformation texts in popular sutra lectures or specifically by monks, a point reconfirmed by their contrast with the pervasive use of religious terminology and the didactic tone of karmic narratives. Indeed, some scattered anecdotal evidence (mostly from non-Buddhist sources) clearly indicates that *pien* were performed by lay entertainers (often women) in secular settings. Transformation texts have their roots in Buddhist literature, and most probably karmic narratives (the choice of the genre marker *pien* [transformation], with its overtly Buddhist doctrinal connotations, is strikingly analogous functionally to *yüan-ch'i* [circumstances]); yet their secularization, apparent in the variety and nature of their contents, also defined them as a genre apart (Sung dynasty storytellers were commonly differentiated according to the content or themes of their narratives). Thus, although the largest number of copies of a single transformation text is that on Mu-lien (Maudgalyāyana), who saved his mother from the sufferings of hell, and another popular narrative is the "Transformation Text on the Subduing of Demons," which recounts the supernatural exploits of another Buddhist saint, Śāriputra, yet narratives from *Han shu* (History of the Han Dynasty), such as "Han chiang Wang Ling pien" (Transformation of the Han General, Wang Ling), the story of Wang Chao-chün (see chapter 42), and the story of Li Ling (see chapter 13) are also extant. Of particular interest are two transformation texts recounting the achievements of contemporaneous local heroes, Chang Yi-ch'ao and his nephew Chang Huai-shen. The first tells in vivid colors how Chang Yi-ch'ao conquered the Tibetans occupying Tun-huang and the surrounding area in 848, while the second recounts the military accomplishments of Chang Huai-shen and his loyalty to the emperor. Transformation texts are, like karmic narratives, popularizations. These texts relate material found elsewhere (e.g., Buddhist doctrine or national and local history), and rather than summarizing or following the authoritative or canonical document, these stories add variants and elaborations (in language, style, and format), which make the message more enjoyable and understandable to a wide audience.

A good example of just how vital the Tun-huang manuscripts are for understanding the development of medieval and later Chinese literature is the obscure text entitled "Ya-ch'ia shu" (Tale of the Headstrong Woman [or Nag / Virago / Scold / Shrew]), which is little known even to Tun-huang specialists. Yet this humble work of popular literature from a frontier town—which exists not just in a single, unique manuscript but in three separate copies—is clearly ancestral to one of the most colorful and entertaining vernacular stories of the late fourteenth or early fifteenth century, the rowdy, raucous, resounding "K'uai-tsui Li Ts'ui-lien chi" (The Shrew: Sharp-Tongued [or Fast-Talking] Li Ts'ui-lien; see chapter 34 and especially chapter 49). What remains to be determined are the complex dynamics of the interrelationship between this early-modern gem of a prosimetric story from central China and its late medieval precursor from a distant Silk Road monastic and trading town.

Tun-huang manuscripts offer a wealth of material unparalleled for understanding the culture and society of medieval China. The manuscripts themselves provide a variety of literary genres, styles, and individual works no longer elsewhere extant, opening new vistas or filling in lacunae in the complex development of Chinese literature. Equally important is the context of use supplied by the body of texts; the performance context of much of this literature is crucial to understanding its significance and the literature that follows in subsequent dynasties.

Socially grounded in the specifics of time and place, the range of Tun-huang literature is representative of the heterogeneity and permeable boundaries of medieval Chinese culture—secular and religious, and across social strata. The Tun-huang caves may have been located at the edge of the Chinese empire, but the manuscripts they yielded have come to play a central role in research on the history of Chinese literature during the last two millennia.

Neil Schmid

Chapter 49

THE ORAL-FORMULAIC TRADITION

DEFINITION OF TERMS

The oral-formulaic tradition in China refers to expressive genres that rely on oral culture either for their performance milieu or as a model for the written text. The outstanding quality of the oral-formulaic tradition in China is the all-inclusive nature of its participation. Storytelling, ballads, wedding and funeral lamentations, and village ritual dramas, all reliant to a degree on specific oral-formulaic traditions, involved the active participation of all sectors of society, from the humblest villager to the emperor at court, from the rustic illiterate to the learned scholar. Men and women contributed equally to China's rich oral expressive culture, and in borderlands non-Han peoples often exerted a powerful influence over the development of particular genres. Popular mythologies created by oral transmission served as a unifying factor in disseminating powerful cultural symbols across China's vast territory; at the same time, the very specificity of local traditions emphasized the empire's incredible diversity and geographic range. Between the oral tale of the village storyteller and the sophisticated narratives of the literati lay a considerable esthetic and linguistic distance. On closer examination, however, it appears that both the oral and the written traditions in China defined themselves in relation to each other. In the relationship between these two dichotomous traditions lies the central importance of China's oral-formulaic culture.

In this chapter a distinction is drawn between two related forms: "oral-formulaic performance" and "prosimetric narratives." By "oral-formulaic performance" is meant oral genres that the performers learn primarily from oral transmission. These genres are associated with a transmitting community instead of an author, are recreated anew with each performance, and are characterized by the manipulation of stereotypical material and a high level of formulism. In the Chinese experience, oral-formulaic performance is often assisted by texts, particularly manuscripts that record one particular character role and that the participant memorizes before a performance. Examples include manuals used by professional storytellers, prosimetric scripts circulating among village men performing New Year's plays of exorcism, and laments and narratives recorded in Women's Script (*nü-shu*) from Chiang-yung county, Hunan province. The oral-formulaic tradition thus refers to works derived from the oral milieu and composed specifically to record or assist with performance.

Prosimetric narratives, by contrast, are composed in writing but are modeled after or derived from a particular performance genre. Some prosimetric narratives are highly formulaic and appear derivative of the oral tradition, although they were written for reading rather than performance. Others, such as the "little drum lyric" (*ku-tzu-tz'u*) composed for performance at court, are written by known authors who appropriated elements of the classical tradition to form a hybrid genre for an elite audience. Both oral-formulaic genres and prosimetric narratives relate stories in prose and verse (sometimes in verse only), and both are named after oral performance genres. However, prosimetric narratives, as defined here, cross the oral-written divide to become primarily fictional stories that imitate certain aspects of the oral model. Prosimetric narratives range from the very simple to the highly sophisticated. At one end of the spectrum are found the colloquial song-prose tales (*shuo-ch'ang-pen*), and, at the other, elaborate narratives with song-suites utilizing complex rhyming and tonal schemes.

At the formal level, what are termed here oral-formulaic and prosimetric traditions share a characteristic format of verse (or song) with interspersed prose. For this reason, any piece with a recognizable verse-prose format has been generally regarded as prosimetric, that is, as belonging to the category of prosimetric narratives (*chiang-ch'ang wen-hsüeh* or *shuo-ch'ang wen-hsüeh*), which in turn is regarded as a subsection of a plethora of oral arts called *ch'ü-yi*. Traditionally, prosimetric forms have been placed within a complex taxonomy arranged in line with particular melodic and formal characteristics. The major distinction is between genres with suites of songs to set melodies requiring strict tonal patterning and rhyme schemes (*yüeh-ch'ü*), and song-prose forms where the song section is composed in lines of seven or ten syllables; it is not based on a particular melody and can be recited, chanted, or sung (*shih-tsan*). Within this taxonomy, the courtly *ku-tzu-tz'u* coexists with the medley (*chu-kung-tiao*) performed in brothels because both rely on melodic suites; the chantefable (*tz'u-hua*) of the blind storyteller is seen as allied to the chantefable written by literati because both are composed in alternating verse and prose. This taxonomy is useful in distinguishing different prosimetric forms, especially those with song-suites, as opposed to those with simpler verse forms, but it is deficient in distinguishing between expressive genres that are primarily oral in composition and performance, and those written ab initio, which have made the transition from oral performance to a text to be read.

The oral-formulaic and prosimetric traditions hold a distinctive place within Chinese literature for the following reasons:

1. In most cases prosimetric genres circulated both as oral performance and as text. For example, the medley could refer both to an oral performance and to a literary text that might be read rather than performed. Written summaries could serve as props to assist even the semiliterate. Villagers who performed prosimetric narrative genres as part of New Year's festivities kept tattered manuscripts recording their own character roles. This ambiguous performance/textual status is also shared by Chinese dramatic genres.

2. Prosimetric genres often circulated in distinct forms in different contexts and social settings. The strummed lyric (*t'an-tz'u*), for example, was composed both as elegant reading material and in simpler form for actual performance. The drum ballad was performed both as village entertainment for illiterate audiences and in more sophisticated form in urban teahouses by professional artists.

3. Chinese oral-formulaic narratives not only entertained their audiences but enacted a powerful ritual function in village life and were often the centerpiece of festival occasions such as New Year's exorcism rites or the Buddhist festival of Yü-lan-p'en (All Souls), where the story of Mahāmaudgalyāyana (Mu-lien) was performed. In the textual tradition, Buddhist prosimetric texts known as precious scrolls (*pao-chüan*) flourished from the fifteenth century onward and came to include many of the attributes of fictional texts. Precious scrolls were particularly popular with female audiences and were often performed by Buddhist nuns.

4. In contrast to literary composition in general, China's rich oral-formulaic and prosimetric tradition did not require one to read or write in order to participate. Performers ranged from village amateurs to blind professional storytellers and literati authors composing for their peers. Oral art forms were usually transmitted by word of mouth and remained relatively untouched by written traditions, but there were exceptions. One example is the prosimetric pieces composed by members of the literati as an act of philanthropy. These were taught by oral transmission to the blind in order to allow them to earn a living as itinerant performers.

5. Amateur performances in the oral-formulaic tradition are intimately tied to regional contexts, are performed in the spoken language of the locality, and play a specific function in the community. To a much greater extent than more literary genres, the oral-formulaic tradition takes on a regional hue and transmits

the cultural lore of its respective milieu. In some cases, oral-formulaic works are even gender specific. Two cases discussed here are the exorcism plays of village men, where they take on the spirit of *yang* heroes in order to exorcise the negative influence of *yin* sicknesses and disorders, and the wedding laments and narratives of the women of Chiang-yung county. The ethos of heroism and sacrifice that one finds in plays of exorcism performed by male villagers is paralleled by the cult of female suffering and stoicism implicit in the laments and narratives inscribed in Women's Script by the female villagers of Chiang-yung county.

6. Oral-formulaic traditions and their associated manuscripts often define themselves with reference to genres composed in classical Chinese, which circulated at elite levels. For example, popular chantefables of the Ming dynasty (1368–1644) and Hong Kong *ma-ko* ballads of the twentieth century contain homely injunctions reminiscent of the Family Instructions (*chia-chiao* or *chia-hsün*) composed by patriarchs for the correct governance of their families. The Twenty-four Paragons of Filial Piety were defined in a canonical text by a known author, but the same notion was popularly disseminated in divergent forms in tomb murals and chantefables. Key items of cultural knowledge, such as the "San-ts'ung" (Three Obediences) and "Ssu-te" (Four Feminine Virtues) taught to women, circulated in parallel and somewhat divergent traditions in both classical formulations and chantefable stories.

Many oral-formulaic forms can best be understood as the counterpart to genres in the classical tradition, as oral ritualists sought to imitate the success of literate specialists at the village level. Similarly, some literary prosimetric works draw their sparkle from a parody of oral-formulaic genres. One example discussed here is the vernacular prosimetric tale, "K'uai-tsui Li Ts'ui-lien chi" (The Shrew: Sharp-Tongued Li Ts'ui-lien), which has a strong but little-known relation to wedding lamentations. In the latter, brides were allowed by tradition to demonstrate their eloquence and histrionic flair to an audience of family and neighbors.

7. The proliferation of manuscripts associated with performance conditioned Chinese receptivity to emerging fictional genres in print. China's earliest vernacular or semivernacular fictional forms, such as the plain tale (*p'ing-hua*), the chantefable (*shuo-ch'ang tz'u-hua*), and the short story (*hua-pen*), all relied to an extent on the oral model. In some cases, this was due to derivation of the story material from a specific oral genre, but it is also likely that authors included verse that could be memorized or sung because of the expectation of their audience that the text was meant in some sense to be "performed," including vocalization to oneself or to an audience. The formulae of prosimetric storytelling quickly became a convention in China's first works of fiction. In the same fashion, the stereotypical material of the oral storyteller was reshaped by literati editors into the fictional masterpieces of the Ming period.

SOURCES AND CORPUS

Origins

Chinese prosimetric forms are barely known before the T'ang dynasty (618–907), although some scholars trace song-prose texts back to the renditions of blind musicians of antiquity and to literary genres such as the *fu* (rhapsody) or *p'ien-[t'i] wen* (parallel prose form). Classical sources, however, are tantalizingly vague and insubstantial. Furthermore, there is no evidence that pre-Buddhist genres relied on the regular alternation of clearly differentiated prose and verse (song) sections to advance a narrative. The general consensus is that the Indian genres used in Buddhist preaching either were the ultimate source of Chinese prosimetric forms or, at the very least, provided a vital creative stimulus in the development of Chinese prosimetric arts. The conventional view holds that Chinese song-prose styles originated during the T'ang period, when Buddhism flourished in China, from a form of preaching known as *su-chiang* (expounding in the vulgar language, or popular lectures). Some texts used in or derived from Buddhist preaching, such as *chiang-ching-wen* (sutra lecture texts), *yüan-ch'i* (Buddhist narratives about karma), and *pien-wen* (transformation texts), are all composed more or less in song-prose form. Many of these genres relate elaborate tales of the supernatural and are composed in Buddhist Hybrid Sinitic/Chinese with vernacular elements. The verse sections are generally composed in heptasyllabic lines and chanted to a Buddhist liturgical tune. However, the attempt to translate the characteristics of the original Sanskrit results in a form metrically distinct from the song form of later Chinese prosimetric literature.

An indigenous influence on prosimetric forms is also possible. Some scholars argue that certain ancient ritual forms influenced both Buddhist genres and later prosimetric literature. From the Han dynasty (206 B.C.E.–220 C.E.) onward, rituals to propitiate the gods of the earth and the five grains included imprecations in repeated units of three-syllable and seven-syllable lines. By the T'ang period, the same form was used for popular songs and Buddhist preaching genres, such as the sutra lecture texts. According to this view, the three-seven-syllable metrical pattern was the precursor of the type of ballad verse used in the *shih-tsan* (nonmelodic prosimetric narrative) forms. Because of its popularity, it was adopted by Buddhist preachers and incorporated into sutra recitations. This verse form can be found today in certain exorcism plays (*No-hsi*), such as that of Meng Chiang-nü from Kuei-ch'ih, Anhwei province. It appears that, while Buddhist (essentially Indian) genres stimulated the rapid development of prosimetric genres in China, preachers may have adapted pre-existing ritual and popular forms in order to attract an audience. Whatever the exact origins of China's rich prosimetric tradition, it has flourished in diverse forms for well over a millennium and greatly enriched China's popular and literary culture.

The Corpus

The corpus of "texts" (including oral performances) in the oral-formulaic and prosimetric traditions can be usefully divided into five categories, ranging across the spectrum from oral to written culture. No category belonged entirely to the oral or the written sphere: village rituals often relied on much-thumbed promptbooks, and sophisticated literary works in prosimetric style referred implicitly to an oral model. Nonetheless there are huge differences in the esthetics, the social function, and the class provenance of the categories outlined below.

First were the festival and ritual performance modes in prosimetric style performed by amateurs on specific occasions such as New Year's. The "text" is either transmitted orally or, in the case of literate amateurs, memorized with the help of handwritten promptbooks. Examples include the Offerings to the Gods (*feng-wen-shu*) of Hai-yen, located on the coast of Chekiang province, the exorcism plays (*No-hsi*) of Kuei-ch'ih and elsewhere, and the verse tales (*ch'ang-pen*) written in Women's Script from Chiang-yung county, Hunan province. Many of the extant examples have been collected in mainland China in the post-Mao period and have been relatively little studied. English translations are generally unavailable, except for a few examples from the Women's Script corpus. Many of the above are structured as sung narratives; even the quasi-dramatic forms are often related in the third-person mode. Nonnarrative forms include ritual songs used in home-building (*shang-liang wen*; laying on the top rafters), *hun-sang yi-shih ko* (lamentations on marriage and at funerals), agricultural calendars in verse, and works of prognostication.

It is characteristic of the above ritual and festival genres that the village participants call down the gods to witness the ceremony and bring blessings on the community. The explicit intention of the performance of narrative stories is thus to entertain the gods and ensure that they carry out their role in protecting the community from sickness and calamity. The Offerings to the Gods, for example, is performed in the third and ninth months (spring and autumn), at weddings, at funerals, or in fulfillment of vows. The gods of the upper world are called on by name (the Jade Emperor, Ju-lai Buddha, Kuan-yin, and so on) and invited to attend a banquet. Next come obeisances to the gods of the middle world (T'ai-sui, Hua-kuang, Kuan-ti), and songs are performed about them. Finally the lower gods are entertained. Stories are in song-prose form and include well-known tales drawn from the Three Kingdoms cycle (see chapter 35) or *Feng-shen yen-yi* (The Investiture of the Gods; see chapter 6). The Offerings to the Gods of Hai-yen are related mostly in third-person narrative, but dramatic roles are sometimes added in standard roles such as *sheng* (male lead or young male), *tan* (female lead), *ching* (butt or comic villain), and *ch'ou* (clown). The village amateurs rely on verse tales, which are passed down and recopied with each generation. Performances are accompanied by percussion instruments such as drums and cymbals. Musically, Offerings to the Gods has songs set to specific melodies and rhyming schemes and is said to be related to the southern play (*nan-hsi*; see chapter 41). In cases where the participants have been influenced by the classical tradition, famous poems and material from primers such as *Ch'ien-tzu wen* (The Thousand Character Classic) and *San-tzu ching* (Trimetrical Classic) are also included.

Second are the religious texts, performed by Buddhist and Taoist preachers, but also circulated as devotional texts for the laity. Often these forms contain fictional content derived from popular entertainment. Examples include sung tales of retribution (*shuo-ch'ang yin-yüan*), Taoist tales (*tao-ch'ing*), precious scrolls, and wooden-fish tales (Mandarin, *mu-yü*; Cantonese, *muk-yu*). The last circulated in Kwangtung province and derived their curious name from the wooden fish-shaped instrument used to tap out the rhythm of the chanted narrative. In these cases, the text, where it exists, is at once an aid to performance and to devotion. The copying, printing, and circulation of these religious texts are believed to bring religious merit to the believer.

Third were commercial entertainment genres performed in entertainment districts, marketplaces, or by itinerant performers. There is a plethora of genres from the Sung dynasty (960–1279) onward. The major source of information about these commercial entertainments is the series of guidebooks to the Sung capitals of Kaifeng and Hangchow setting out the main artistic genres, the names of performers, and their location within the pleasure precincts. Generally professional genres can be distinguished by the region of dissemination, rural or urban provenance, the major occupation of the performer (courtesan, beggar, peddler, medical quack, would-be "monk" or "priest"), their delivery mode (melodic or chanted verse, musical accompaniment, song type, topolect group), and so on.

Texts that directly relate to these oral performances are largely lacking, with the exception of the medley (*chu-kung-tiao*; Chin-Yüan period [1115–1368]) for which several early examples are extant (see chapter 41). A storyteller's manual from the Yüan dynasty (1271–1368), *Tsui-weng t'an-lu* (Notes of an Old Tippler), includes the titles of a vast horde of stories narrated in contemporary oral arts. Sometimes dramatic scripts contain examples drawn from beggars' chants (*lien-hua-lao*) and the peddler's narratives (*huo-lang-erh*). When available, scripts tend to be written with elements of the local language; for example, the strummed lyrics transcribed in Soochow dialect were designed for the performer.

Fourth is reading material for the unlearned, which consists of texts by anonymous authors based on prosimetric forms but designed primarily as reading material for the less educated—for example, some transformation tales (T'ang period), some chantefables (*shuo-ch'ang tz'u-hua*) of the Ming period, and some strummed lyrics of the late Ming and Ch'ing (1644–1911) periods aimed at female readerships. Before the modern era, these texts were not collected or preserved in the libraries of the literati. Early extant examples have been saved from destruction by great good fortune. They include the treasure trove of manuscripts discovered in the caves of Tun-huang (see chapter 48), a medley discovered in the desert at Karakhoto, and the cache of chantefable texts recovered from a late-fifteenth-century tomb in Chia-ting county, outside Shanghai. These manuscripts and printed texts were presumably designed for emerging, semiliterate audiences. For most of these readers, "reading" the text was probably more a matter of reciting, chanting, and singing the text, either to oneself or to an audience of friends or family.

Fifth are literary prosimetric forms. Song-prose texts recognized as "literary" include examples in the *hua-pen* (short story) collections compiled and edited by literati. *Ch'ing-p'ing shan-t'ang hua-pen* (Vernacular Short Stories from the Clear and Peaceful Mountain Studio) and Feng Meng-lung's well-known *San-yen* (Three Words) trilogy contain some examples (see chapter 34). An early edition of the famous *Chin P'ing Mei* (Gold Vase Plum) narrative was termed a "chantefable" (*tz'u-hua*) and did in fact include a great deal of verse material as well as vivid descriptions of chantefable performances by "nuns" for women of relatively affluent households. The literary prosimetric form, while based on performance genres in oral transmission, developed into sophisticated vernacular texts for private reading circles of aficionados. Examples include Master Tung's "'Hsi-hsiang chi' chu-kung-tiao" or "Tung 'Hsi-hsiang'" (Medley of the "Romance of the Western Chamber"). Sometimes men of letters tried their hand at writing popularized history in prosimetric mode, for example, "Ta T'ang Ch'in-wang tz'u-hua" (Chantefable About Prince Ch'in of the Great T'ang Dynasty), by Chu Sheng-lin of the late sixteenth century.

Although the number of literary prosimetric forms was not large, elements of song-prose performance were incorporated into early Chinese drama (*tsa-chü*), and tales of the storyteller or performer were commonly included as topoi in drama and novels. For example, Liu Ching-t'ing (c. 1590–1669) was a well-known professional storyteller of his era who appears in "T'ao-hua shan" (Peach Blossom Fan), a popular play by K'ung Shang-jen (1648–1718). When dealing with politically sensitive events, a dramatist might well retell a sensational current event in the words of a storyteller. Chu Ching-fan (fl. early seventeenth century), for instance, in the aftermath of the execution of the hated eunuch Wei Chung-hsien (1568–1627), related the story of Wei's persecution of Tung-lin Academy members in a chantefable that he inserted into his play "Feng-liu yüan" (House of Romance).

PERFORMANCE AND TEXTUAL ASPECTS

The Prosimetric Tradition and Early Chinese Drama

Scholars trace the roots of ancient Greek drama back to harvest rituals performed to propitiate the deities. Some evidence suggests that the development of Chinese drama followed a similar trajectory. In contemporary China, in regions such as Kuei-ch'ih, Anhwei province, and An-shun, Kweichow province, one can still find traces of ancient shamanistic dramas where masked village participants call on deified heroes to enter their bodies and engage in ritual dramas. Before the Northern Sung dynasty (960–1127), these harvest rituals were religious ceremonies based on various cultic figures. The greater commercialization of the Southern Sung dynasty (1127–1279) and the development of professional urban entertainment led to the growth of itinerant performers who brought more sophisticated oral arts to rural areas. Village rituals of the time were also enriched by traveling Taoist priests, who promoted rites dedicated to the ten categories of Lonely Ghosts (military heroes, loyal ministers, those who died on the battlefield but had not been properly buried, others who had died of violence, and so on). Many of the figures worshiped at this time were historical figures who later became the heroes of fictional tales, novels, and plays. Examples include Hsüeh Jen-kuei, the common soldier who saved the T'ang emperor, or the wily strategist of the Three Kingdoms (220–265) Chu-ko Liang (181–234). Some of the deities promoted at this time became national figures, such as Kuan Ti (Emperor Kuan), who was actually a historical figure, Kuan Yü, of the Three Kingdoms period.

The main intention of the agricultural rituals, performed during the New Year's rites and after the autumn harvest, was to propitiate the Lonely Ghosts, ensure a good harvest, and expel noxious influences and sicknesses from the community. From the tenth to the thirteenth centuries, village harvest rituals gradually came to include quasi-dramatic performances in which masked villagers took on the spirits of the heroes and worshiped and enacted stories celebrating their achievements. Remnants of these early plays of exorcism (*No [-hsi]* or *No-t'ang-hsi*), which may have preceded China's earliest known drama, remain today in remote villages. Exorcism plays begin with invocations to the gods and praise of the emperors of the past, and often involve lengthy battles between opposing forces. Usually an altar is set up on both sides of a rough stage or open space. Play enactments are only one section of the whole performance, which includes a complex series of exorcistic rituals. A central characteristic of *No* village plays is the predominant use of prosimetric third-person narrative, rather than dramatic forms. For example, in An-shun a chorus narrates the tale in songs of seven syllables to a line, typical *shih-tsan* style, while the village actors come on stage and carry out the designated actions. In Kuei-ch'ih, a Master of Ceremonies chants the story in third-person narrative composed in the standard prosimetric style. In certain An-shun and Kuei-ch'ih *No* plays, which some scholars believe reflect the earliest, most primitive form, the masked villagers simply mime their roles and enter and exit the stage as required by the Master of Ceremonies, who narrates the whole story from a prompt book. In other cases there is a mixture of third-person narrative and dramatic voice, sometimes using arias to set melodies. In these cases, the story is partly narrated by the Master of Ceremonies and partly enacted by the village participants. In surviving manuscripts from Kuei-ch'ih, one finds an amalgam of dramatic voice, third-person narrative, and arias drawn from local opera. Villagers who were literate relied on manuscripts to learn their role, while others learned their parts from oral transmission. Character roles were passed down from father to son, and the script was kept within the family and recopied when necessary. It appears that the underlying third-person narrative mode, with its formulaic *shih-tsan* verse, made it possible for illiterate or semiliterate villagers to organize these elaborate dramatic performances.

There are many intriguing parallels between *No* dramas and prosimetric forms that circulated as printed tales during the late imperial period. For example, some chantefables (*shuo-ch'ang tz'u-hua*) published in the late fifteenth century, presumably for a reading audience, have startling textual correspondences with some *No* scripts from Kuei-ch'ih. It is now clear that there is a shared textual tradition between the printed chantefable and prosimetric *No* drama. At this preliminary stage of research, the exact relationship between them is uncertain; however, the current consensus is that prosimetric tales were performed as quasi-dramas within agricultural rituals by the late Southern Sung period and that these chantefables may well derive from *No* prosimetric plays.

One can get an impression of the story content of the *No* ritual plays from the chantefable "Hua Kuan So" (which is available in English translation), from the Ch'eng-hua period (1465–1487) of the Ming dynasty. This chantefable employs lengthy verse sections and an admixture of prose to relate familiar tales in formulaic language. Generally one main rhyme scheme is employed (that is, endings in *-en, -eng, -ien, -in, -ing,* and so on). In "Hua Kuan So" the rhyme endings accord with the phonology of the Wu region, where the text was discovered. Chantefables are generally composed in hepta- or decasyllabic *shih-tsan* narrative style but employ other verse types from the written tradition as well. Examples include history verse (*yung-shih shih*), which were jingles about events in Chinese history memorized by schoolboys, and quatrains in classical Chinese (*shih*) and "eulogistic verse" (*tsan*), which were used for elaborate descriptions.

"Hua Kuan So" relates the tale of a legendary son of the famed hero Kuan Yü. It is remarkable for its divergence from the mainstream Three Kingdoms story-cycle as known in *San-kuo yen-yi* (Romance of the Three Kingdoms). The chantefable of Hua Kuan So and a *No* play script from Kuei-ch'ih both include an extraordinary variant on the classic tale of the oath of brotherhood made by the three heroes at Peach Garden. In this variant, Liu Pei bemoans the fact that his sworn brothers are burdened by families who will surely impede their enterprise of reunifying the Chinese state. Kuan Yü and Chang Fei then decide to slaughter each other's families to prove their dedication to the cause. The massacre is described in detail. Kuan's wife, pregnant with the young Kuan So, narrowly escapes death. The young hero's childhood is also remarkable. He is lost at the Lantern Festival (a common story motif) but later found and adopted by a man called So. As a youth, he is given as an apprentice to a Taoist master and becomes a Taoist adept. As an adult, Kuan So is devoted to proving himself worthy of recognition by his illustrious father and is responsible for reinvigorating the failing enterprise after his father's death. The rise of the younger generation that takes the place of the old is also one of the central themes of the tale of Hsüeh Jen-kuei, who is likewise the subject of *No* theatricals and chantefables. Tales of the wise and incorruptible Judge Pao (a historical figure, Pao Cheng; 999–1062; see chapter 41) are also common to both genres. In *No* plays and chantefables, Pao plays an unusually strong role in upholding the rights of commoners against villainous officials close to the emperor.

The Kuei-ch'ih *No* plays, in common with Chinese exorcism plays generally, are gender-specific rituals. They are performed only by men, who, representing the forces of *yang*, call down powerful deities to take on mortal form in order to expel the *yin* forces of pestilence and misfortune from their communities. Men play all female roles, including even that of the faithful wife, Meng Chiang-nü, who went to seek her husband's body at the Great Wall during the reign of the tyrannous first emperor. Women are not allowed to touch the masks and props or take part in the preparations, although they are allowed to watch performances of *No*. In keeping with their origins in agricultural rituals and their exorcistic function, *No* plays do not deal with tales of romance but, rather, with historical personages who have become cult figures, such as Judge Pao, or with military heroes, such as Kuan So and Hsüeh Jen-kuei.

The Oral Culture of Chinese Women

The village plays of exorcism reflect aspects of Chinese ritual culture that are dominated by male or *yang* forces. The female counterparts are the verse stories and rituals performed and recorded by women in parts of rural China. The best-studied example is the Women's Script (*nü-shu*) culture of Chiang-yung county, Hunan. A substantial corpus of items from the women of Chiang-yung has now been collected, including correspondence, wedding laments, festival material, popular tales, and autobiographical stories. The manuscripts were used by sworn sisters to correspond with one another after marriage, when they moved to another village. Scripts also served as prompts during performances held at women's festivals such as the Girls' Festival (Ku-niang chieh) and the Cold Wind Festival (Ch'ui-liang chieh), which was held in a cool place in the village during midsummer. Most of the extant corpus was recorded during the twentieth century, although some tales derive from the nineteenth century. One such tale relates the hardships suffered during the occupation of the region by the Taiping rebels during the mid-nineteenth century. The most salient characteristic of the Women's Script corpus is that it is composed in the heptasyllabic verse generally characteristic of Chinese prosimetric genres. Extant texts provide a fascinating insight into women's oral culture, which is otherwise a little-known aspect of Chinese life. Much of the Women's Script material deals with the sorrows of women on departing from their natal home on marriage: "Once I lived in the inner chambers with my parents / In tears I got married away from home, my heart as if cut with a knife."

The prevalence and significance of women's orally transmitted genres cannot be denied. Jung Chang, in *Wild Swans*, recalls the life of her grandmother in Harbin in the 1930s:

> Every now and then she and her friends would put on an old Manchu performance for themselves, playing hand drums while they sang and danced. The tunes they played consisted of very simple, repetitious notes and rhythms, and the women made up the lyrics as they went along. The married women sang about their sex lives, and the virgins asked questions about sex. Being mostly illiterate, the women used this as a way to learn about the facts of life. Through their singing, they also talked to each other about their lives and their husbands, and passed on their gossip.

Most of this female line of oral transmission was never recorded; the Women's Script corpus is a striking exception to the norm (for the nature of the script, see chapter 1). The corpus deals overwhelmingly with female grievances, a notion that lies behind local stories about the origin of the curious sloping syllabary reminiscent of women's needlework. In popular mythology, the invention of Women's Script is attributed to an educated beauty, Hu Yü-hsiu, who was selected to be an imperial concubine. When she fell from favor but remained locked away in the palace, she recorded her grief in a secret script in order to avoid discovery by court eunuchs. Women of her region then competed to master the new script and passed it down to each new generation. Local women named the ingenious script, which could effectively record the sounds of their local language and was infinitely easier and simpler to learn than the sinographs (*han-tzu*), Women's Script. They did this in order to distinguish it from Chinese character script, which they called Men's Script (*nan-shu*). The gender distinctions and nature of these two scripts are strikingly similar to those for the Japanese *kana* syllabary and the *kanji* (sinographs), when the former were radically simplified from the latter around a thousand years ago.

Although the story about the origin of Women's Script cannot be substantiated by historical data, it is undoubtedly regarded by its practitioners as a medium to communicate a sense of female grievance and injustice. Much of the extant corpus deals with the pain of forced marriage or of separation from one's husband and resistance to forced remarriage. Although women's misery is a constant theme, Women's Script is not anti-male just as *No* exorcist rituals, dedicated as they are to the expulsion of noxious *yin* influences, are not anti-female. In fact, one of the most popular *No* plays features the dedicated wife Meng Chiang-nü weeping at the Great Wall. In some respects the male domain of *No* and the female domain of lamentations and ballads are akin to the "men's business" and "women's business" of the Australian aborigines and other gender-specific folk genres, although in the Chinese experience there is no taboo on one side's appreciating the activities of the other. For example, women who excel in Women's Script and have many sworn sisters with whom they correspond are praised by men and women alike as "talented," a term also applied to men who win achievement in the world of Chinese letters. Male and female "talent" are two sides of the same coin. Men's exorcism rituals, designed to protect the village, and women's sung narratives, aimed at consolidating bonds of sisterhood, share in common a code of endurance and bravery in the face of adversity, together with a fatalistic belief in the inevitability of suffering. The two forms reflect the complementary and relational nature of Chinese ritual, where gender-specific genres can be accommodated within a complex whole. It could also be argued that both define themselves relative to the other as the masculine defines itself against the feminine. Meanwhile, the feminine emulates aspects of the masculine while never challenging the separation of the two spheres.

Prosimetric genres that made the transition to printed fictional forms, such as Ming chantefables, included material common to both *No* drama and women's oral culture. For example, the Ch'eng-hua period chantefables from the late fifteenth century include a tale that is related in the Women's Script corpus as "Mai-hua nü" (The Flower Seller). The central theme is the abduction and enforced concubinage of women. In the Women's Script version, the son of a merchant marries a woman named Chang, who comes up with a plan to save the family from destitution after the merchant loses his thirteen shops in a fire and his boats in a storm. She decides to make paper flowers and sell them in the city of Kaifeng, the capital during the Northern Sung period. The husband, in a traditional injunction, begs her not to venture outside the home: "Virtuous wife, listen to what I have to say / It is better to starve to death at home / Than to go out and expose your face." Nonetheless, she goes to Kaifeng, where she is abducted by the villainous noble Ts'ao, a relative of the empress. She resists his advances and is cruelly put to death in a press while being whipped with bamboo. Ts'ao has her ritually buried in order to minimize the risk that she will return as a vengeful ghost. This ritual burial, however, does not deter Chang's ghost from seeking help from Yamarāja, god of the underworld. She appears to her husband in a dream and bids him to go to Kaifeng to put her case to the Chinese Solomon, the good Judge Pao. Unfortunately, the husband is promptly imprisoned by Ts'ao before he has a chance to seek Judge Pao's assistance. Wife Chang manifests herself in ghostly form to Pao, who then sets in train the events that will eventually bring Ts'ao to justice. In the Women's Script version, Pao also has the power to bring the husband and wife back to life. Needless to say, this ensures that the ending is a happy one!

A very similar tale appears in a text from the Ch'eng-hua period corpus called "[Hsin-k'an shuo ch'ang] Pao Lung-t'u tuan Ts'ao kuo-chiu kung-an chuan" (Judge Pao Solves the Case of Imperial Kinsman Ts'ao). The major difference is that Pao's detective work is featured in the latter story and the wife's activities are given less prominence. The greater role afforded the leading woman in "The Flower Seller" reflects the community context in which this variant circulated, in this case the peasant women of Chiang-yung county. Stories about Judge Pao were regarded not as fictional tales but as actual examples of his power as a cult figure. Throughout Chiang-yung county, "Iron-Faced Judge Pao" (an epithet referring to his impartiality) is honored in temples and features in the "processions of the gods," where statues of deities are carried around the village. Tales about the good Judge Pao also transmitted popularized notions of the law and the rights of the common people. In the earlier chantefable, Pao alone argues against the proposition that the law of the monarch is above that of any individual. He even destroys the imperial pardon awarded Ts'ao by the emperor on the grounds that the emperor holds sway only within the capital, not outside it. Centuries later, in Women's Script tales, the heroines themselves use the kind of legal arguments put forward by Pao in earlier versions. In "The Flower Seller" wife Chang tells her abductor, "The law of the monarch does not spare anyone." There is some evidence that during the late imperial period the women of Chiang-yung county increasingly contested their marriage rights. In some villages, women were able to divorce their husbands and take their dowry with them. Women's Script culture was often particularly strong in areas where oppression of women was most marked. For example, in Chiang-ho village, even wealthy families would not educate their daughters, and it is from this area that the Women's Script tale "The Flower Seller" was collected. One could conclude that women's oral culture generally, and its transcription in Women's Script, provided an alternative form of "education," including notions of legal rights, to some of the most deprived groups in China.

The male-dominated *No* plays laud heroines such as Meng Chiang-nü and the faithful wives of the military heroes but exclude romantic concerns from the repertoire. Similarly, Women's Script culture deals primarily with female grievances and is not used to record the love songs of the region. However, the corpus also includes tales of blighted romances such as the tragic love story of Liang Shan-po and Chu Ying-t'ai. In this and similar stories, it is the raunchy details that most delight the audience. In the Women's Script version of this well-known tale, a young woman, Chu Ying-t'ai, runs away from her family and dresses up as a male scholar in order to obtain an education. She becomes best friends with a young man, Liang Shan-po, who fails to realize that his handsome companion is actually a young woman. The episode where she sleeps with him on the same couch while still preserving her virginity is the pièce-de-résistance in this tale, which, according to tradition, must end in the death of both. Salacious episodes of this kind were a popular feature of the Liang-Chu story. The

Women's Script version presents a wonderfully comic scene where Chu relies on her keen wits to keep the young man in the dark about her sex. Liang calls on her to strip her clothes and sleep in the nude. On the first evening, she refuses to take off her exquisitely tailored gown. On the second evening, she places four bowls of cold water around her bed and declares that if any drops of water spill during the night he will receive forty strokes of the rod. At this, the terrified young man dare not turn his head no matter what. At midnight, Chu has to answer the call of nature. She squats on a chamber pot, declaring to her bemused companion: "If you stand up to pee, you're just like horses and oxen / But those who squat low are true lads of heaven." The following morning, she washes herself, exposing a fine pair of "milk-smooth breasts, white as frost." This time she tells Liang that big breasts in men are a sign of good fortune and indicate she will have an official career. Liang is "convinced" by the force of her eloquence, at least for the time being.

In elite versions, the Liang-Chu love story is refashioned to demonstrate the maiden Chu's "proper" conduct in preserving her virginity. By the early twentieth century, under the influence of Western feminist movements, Chu Ying-t'ai was reconstructed as a heroine who stood up to the harsh restrictions of traditional propriety (*li-chiao*). The Women's Script tale above, however, reflects the "vulgar" renditions observed by some scholars in Chinese villages of the 1920s. The oral culture of Chinese women, and occasionally printed prosimetric tales based on these, present a more woman-centered view than is common in Chinese culture generally. For example, the story of Hsüeh Jen-kuei, a common soldier who leaves his wife Liu to serve the T'ang emperor, is told in both Kuei-ch'ih *No* plays and a fifteenth-century chantefable. In both versions Liu bids farewell to her husband with a series of injunctions, urging him not to spend time with prostitutes and to return home safely. This was a traditional topos in prosimetric narratives and fiction. Another example is "Chih-yüan pieh San-niang T'ai-yüan t'ou-shih" (How Liu Chih-yüan Bade San-niang Good-bye and Joined the Army in Taiyuan), from "Liu Chih-yüan chu-kung-tiao" (The Medley on Liu Chih-yüan, or Ballad of the Hidden Dragon). In this chantefable, the wife's discourse is more developed. Liu advises her husband that, just as *yang* belongs to Heaven and *yin* to Earth, so men and women marry. This is the fundamental way of the world and the root of human governance. Just as *yang* and *yin* aspects are evenly balanced, so marriage must be based on fidelity and mutual love and respect. This elaborate discourse on male-female equality in marriage is unique to the chantefable among all known versions of this tale.

Prosimetric Genres and Early Chinese Vernacular Fiction

Prosimetric forms were adapted by men of letters to form China's earliest vernacular fiction. One of these is the delightful story "K'uai-tsui Li Ts'ui-lien chi" (The Shrew: Sharp-Tongued Li Ts'ui-lien), composed by an unknown author in the late fourteenth or early fifteenth century. The Shrew is a capable but extremely loquacious young woman who expresses herself in prosimetric-style verse. When she reaches the marriageable age, her parents match her with a young man called Wolf from a neighboring village. Her parents give her repeated injunctions to hold her tongue after marriage, but the irrepressible Ts'ui-lien abuses both the matchmaker and the astrologer who presides over the ceremony of the bridal chamber. She then proceeds to insult each member of the family in turn.

This literary man's reworking of a familiar tale (going back to the Tun-huang "Ya-ch'ia shu" (Tale of the Headstrong Woman [or Nag / Virago / Scold / Shrew]) is best understood as a parody of a particular oral complex relating to women's wedding lamentations. The wedding lamentation (*k'u-chia ko*) is an oral-formulaic genre that was widely prevalent in rural China during the imperial period. In China, a bride married into her husband's family, which in most cases meant that she left her natal village and spent her life in another region, far away from her own family. It was thus a time of mourning for the bride, as she parted from her natal family and village. Weddings were arranged by both sets of parents through a matchmaker, and the young people concerned had minimal or no choice. The ceremony known as "wedding lamentations" took place at the bride's home before she departed from her family. In contemporary China, some examples of this ritual have been recorded and transcribed. Lamentation verse is chanted in a single melodic line, repeated with variations. There is no rhyme, set line length, or tonal requirements, nor is there any musical accompaniment. The songs are quasi-autobiographical in nature and rely on stock formulae, prosaic images, and folk sayings (see chapter 8). There is a set structure to lamentations, which last for one to three days before the bride departs. Women learn how to lament from working together with other women in such tasks as picking cotton, spinning, weaving, and making clothes. Young girls learn how to lament after they reach the age of twelve (at puberty) and watch performances by brides for several years before they themselves perform.

In the wedding lamentations of Nan-hui, now a county in the Shanghai region, the first stage is a dialog between the mother and the bride known as "placing the trousseau in the box." This is sung as family members place coverlets, bolts of cloth, and clothing in ritual order in ceremonial wicker baskets and boxes for the bride to take with her as her trousseau. The mother begins the lamentation by bidding her daughter to obey her in-laws and learn to adapt to their ways. Here are the opening lines of a mother's injunction to her daughter in a contemporary example from Nan-hui:

> Daughter,
> You must always be like the newly rising sun, like the sky born anew,
> Once you change your household, you must learn to follow their ways.

You must not compare your new home with our life here.
The bride, for her part, responds:

Mother,
From birth I have borne my father's [family] name,
As fixed and certain as the nail knocked into the weighing scales
I am just poor merchandise like the shells purchased during the "moldy" season [June/July in this region]
Or like wet cigarette butts.

The bride goes on to thank her mother for raising her, describes her daily labor on behalf of the family, compares her current poverty with the supposed luxury of the groom's family, and complains that they will despise her because her trousseau is too paltry. This section of the ritual, which can go on for eight to ten hours, is watched by the whole family and even the neighborhood. From time to time, the participants, overcome with emotion, will sob rather than chant. A moving performance brings tears to the eyes of the onlookers and may result in additions to the trousseau. At the very least, a good performance will result in an enhancement of the bride's status as well as that of her family. Over a period of days, the bride gives ritual thanks to her father, grandfather, mother's brother, aunts, and the matchmaker. The last is frequently an abusive "thank you," in which the bride implies that the go-between has misrepresented the relative wealth of the two families. Before her departure, the bride is provided with a bowl of rice called "rice given at parting" (*lin-pieh fan*). This ritual parallels that afforded a dying family member, who is also given a few morsels of rice at death. The bride's thank-you to her older brother (or mother's brother if she has no brother) is of particular significance. If she is mistreated in the groom's home, it is to her brother or maternal uncle that she will first turn. There are specific lamentations as the bride departs on the sedan chair, when she steps into the bridal boat, and at the point where she first views the groom's house. All lamentations must cease before she arrives at the groom's house, because any further wailing will bring bad luck. From this moment until after the ceremony, the bride will say nothing.

Lamenters interviewed in Nan-hui and the Hong Kong New Territories often claim that their aim is to ward off the demons of misfortune and bring good luck on themselves and their families; in other words, lamenting serves a particular ritual function. One woman in Nan-hui declared: "I am getting rid of evil influences by lamenting." Since women played only a minimal role in ancestral rituals and the cardinal Confucian festivals, such as Ch'ing-ming (the spring grave-sweeping festival), it is only in wedding and funeral lamentations that women could exercise significant ritual power. It is also interesting that lamentations were apparently specific to lower-class women in rural areas.

Women of the elite did not participate in lamentations because "proper" women did not expose themselves in public. A Buddhist "precious scroll" text collected in the modern-day Wu topolect region forbids "good" women from participating in laments: "It is forbidden to expose your body and perform lamentations" (*ko-ch'ang k'u-ch'i*). Lamentation culture thus presented a direct challenge to the Confucian notion of the virtuous silent woman.

"The Shrew" is a literary man's interpretation of the dilemma presented by the eloquent woman. Ts'ui-lien is both capable and virtuous, but, alas, she is incurably bossy and talkative. She is clearly the product of the same kind of oral context that nurtured the lamentation rituals of lower-class women. In the course of the tale, Ts'ui-lien stresses her contributions to the home economy and her many feminine skills. She weeps on leaving her parents and expresses her gratitude to them for rearing and suckling her. Just as the lamenting woman could get in a sly dig at anyone who had slighted her, Ts'ui-lien criticizes her father's sister, who arrives late for the ceremony. Her prayer to the ancestors that her husband's family will be prosperous and that she will live with them in harmony parallels the mother's injunction to her daughter in the wedding lamentation. Needless to say, Ts'ui-lien's wish that the whole lot would die in three years and leave her all their property is a comic invention of the author! Even telling details such as the mouthful of rice at departure are recorded in this rendition. Ts'ui-lien's abuse of the matchmaker for her "lies" is completely in accordance with a similar tradition in wedding lamentations. The astrologer declares of this abuse: "There is no precedent for such behavior in a bride," but in fact contemporaries would have been aware that there was every precedent for a bride's verbal abuse of the matchmaker. Ts'ui-lien notes further that, if harmed by the groom's family, she will call on her brother to assist her and, if she is killed, she will turn into an avenging ghost. In the end she renounces the world, and the author notes that, although she might not become a bodhisattva (deified savior), she could at least be Buddha's handmaid. In traditional Buddhist thinking, women could not become bodhisattvas, which are construed as male beings. However, in the oral-formulaic tradition women could indeed become bodhisattvas. One Women's Script tale relates the story of Wife Wang, who, because of her heroic virtue, is reborn as a successful examination candidate (*chuang-yüan*) and then attains the status of a bodhisattva. To the modern reader, the irony of a story like "The Shrew" is that the literati author, in seeking to satirize and suppress the oral culture from which the eloquent woman emerged, has actually succeeded in rendering it visible.

Courtesan Culture and the Story of Ying-ying

"The Shrew" provides an excellent example of the interrelationship between the elite and popular traditions. In this case the literary adaptation of what is essentially a misogynistic tale about a talkative woman gains its true significance in contradistinction to lamentation culture, which celebrated the histrionic abilities of the bride. With this and other prosimetric forms, it is always important to understand the context of their derivation and development. Love stories, for example, are often associated with courtesan culture. One important example is the famous story of Ying-ying and her seduction by Chang Sheng (Scholar Chang). The earliest known exemplar of this tale is a semiautobiographical *ch'uan-ch'i* (classical style) story entitled "Ying-ying chuan" (The Story of Ying-ying; see chapter 33), attributed to the famed poet Yüan Chen (779–831). In this tale, the hero, Chang Sheng, is a refined young man, yet to fall in love and lose his virginity, who lodges in a monastery during his travels. Here he comes across a widow called Mrs. Ts'ui who is distantly related to him. During a mutiny of some imperial troops, Chang uses his connections to save the Ts'ui family from plunder. He immediately falls in love with the beautiful daughter, Ying-ying, and seeks advice to cure his lovesickness from her maid, Hung-niang (Red Maiden). The latter tells him that her mistress enjoys reciting poetry and urges him to "seduce her with a love poem." He composes some verse, and the quick-witted Ying-ying responds with a poem of her own that hints at a romantic assignation. But when Chang visits her bed chamber, she gives him a tongue-lashing, accusing him of seeking to ravish her. After this Chang loses all hope. Unaccountably, a few days later Ying-ying visits his bed chamber. The liaison then continues for some months in her room, known as the western wing. Eventually Chang departs to undertake the imperial examinations necessary to win an official position. After a year has gone by, he fails in the examination and sends her an explanatory letter. She writes back a very touching letter which seeks to move his heart, while at the same time she abstains from condemning him for abandoning her. Chang then passes around her letter to his literary friends, who express their appreciation in poems tacked on to the end of the story. In the poems Ying-ying is described as a goddess and likened to a Taoist perfected being (*chen-jen*), a term that was also a common euphemism for a courtesan. Chang Sheng adds his own comments, which, while in keeping with the Confucian proprieties, appear harsh and misogynistic when compared with later interpretations of the story. He likens Ying-ying to the femmes fatales of old who brought down the rulers of antiquity and declares that he has "resolutely suppressed my love" in order to resist her "evil influence." Both Chang and Ying-ying marry other partners. Chang requests to see Ying-ying once more, but she only sends him a message that reminds him poignantly of the pain of her abandonment while stoically accepting his marriage to an upper-class partner.

The story of Ying-ying, which is believed to be based on a love affair of the author, Yüan Chen, rapidly became popular in the entertainment quarters. In the mid-Northern Sung period, entertainment complexes called *kou-lan* flourished in the capital of Pien-ching (modern-day Kaifeng). The *kou-lan* was basically a theater with stage, backstage room, and seats for the audience, but it also included a tavern area and courtesans' quarters. During the Southern Sung period, when the capital was in modern-day Hangchow, a hierarchy of courtesans' houses emerged; some catered exclusively to high officials and literati, while others were favored by affluent merchants. Courtesans favored by the upper class were often highly educated and could recite and compose poetry. Po Chü-yi's (772–846) poem about the tragic romance of the consort Yang Kuei-fei and the T'ang emperor Hsüan-tsung (r. 712–756), "Ch'ang-hen ko" (The Song of Everlasting Regret), was particularly popular with the courtesans. During the Yüan dynasty courtesans performed *tsa-chü* (variety plays), farces, and prosimetric genres such as medleys. It is in this ambiance that Yüan Chen's famous tale circulated. Chao Ling-chih (1051–1134) noted that men of letters enjoyed reading "The Story of Ying-ying" and that courtesans and female entertainers (*ch'ang yu nü-tzu*) could all recite the gist of the tale. Chao rearranged the original text to render it suitable for musical performance in a prosimetric genre he called "drum lyric" (*ku-tzu-tz'u*). He added twelve songs set to the melody "Tieh lien hua" (Butterflies in Love with Flowers) to Yüan Chen's rearranged text. In contrast to mainstream prosimetric genres, the songs in this drum lyric do not further the narrative but, instead, seek to add emotional intensity to the presentation.

The only other major change was in the climax to the story. Chao felt that the original tale betrayed a lack of sympathy for the heroine. He deleted Chang's rationalizing words about Ying-ying as a femme fatale and, by way of ending, added an exchange between himself and a scholar. The latter calls for an ending that explains Chang's abandonment of Ying-ying in terms of his inability to marry her with propriety and calls for "moral exhortations" to be added. In his response to the scholar, Chao rejects this advice and instead leaves the audience to reflect on Ying-ying's innocence and suffering.

In later renditions, the troublesome ending is entirely rewritten to offer something to delight the broader audiences of the *kou-lan*: Chang Sheng and Ying-ying undergo many trials but in the end unite in marriage. A shadowy figure known only as Master Tung (Tung Chieh-yüan; fl. c. 1190–1208) adapted the story of Ying-ying to form a masterpiece of the medley genre known as "Medley of the 'Romance of the Western Chamber'" or "Tung 'Hsi-hsiang'" (Master Tung's "Romance of the Western Chamber"). Medleys were narrated and sung by one performer to musical accompaniment, usually stringed instruments, and were commonly performed in the *kou-lan*. They consisted of dramatic dialog, narrative, and, above, all, arias (*ch'ü*) with different melodies that belonged to various modes (*kung-tiao*). Complex rules governed the arrangement of song suites: the tunes in each verse section must all belong to the same mode, and the same rhyme is used throughout the verse section. The medley thus makes considerable demands on both the composer and the singer. One early extant medley discovered in Karakhoto is the highly vernacular "Medley on Liu Chih-yüan." This fragment is one of the earliest Chinese vernacular printed texts in existence. It was probably designed for semiliterate performers. Master Tung's medley, however, is a literary masterpiece for the sophisticated performer. It is composed mainly in the vernacular of the twelfth century, but also contains lines in the classical language for added refinement.

In this extensively elaborated version of Yüan Chen's tale, many changes are made and intricate subplots added. Chang Sheng is now a poor scholar not related to the Ts'ui family, who have much higher status. This makes his later marriage to Ying-ying less socially perilous, at least on his side. The battle scene is now much more significant and is attributed to the known rebel Sun Fei-hu (Flying Tiger Sun), who poses a direct threat to Ying-ying's safety. Chang Sheng's role in saving Ying-ying is thus much more prominent. The role of maid Hung-niang as go-between offers much comedy in this rendition. Ying-ying's decision to give herself to Chang is afforded a much more convincing rationale in the medley than in Yüan's original tale, which avoided this issue. Ying-ying is greatly moved by Chang's seductive poetry and takes pity on him when he becomes ill from love-longing. Finally, a subplot about an affianced suitor is added to create more suspense. "Master Tung's 'Romance of the Western Chamber'" represents a prosimetric genre rooted in literati culture, particularly the domain of the educated man and the courtesan. Technically it is highly sophisticated. The songs, for example, are often identical to those found in *tz'u* poetry (see chapter 15), which was also commonly associated with courtesans and with female poets such as Li Ch'ing-chao (1084–c. 1151), some of whose poetry is echoed here. As recreated by Master Tung, this medley is ideally suited to convey a full gamut of emotions, from the drama of the rebels in battle to the erotic intensity of the young couple's lovemaking.

INTERACTION OF POPULAR AND ELITE CULTURES

In the past millennium, there was a high level of interaction between popular and elite cultures in both the oral-formulaic and the prosimetric traditions. In some cases, the borrowing is direct. It is possible that the quasi-dramatic prosimetric dramas performed by village men during the New Year's festival were recorded and printed to form an early vernacular fictional genre known in the Ming period as chantefable (*shuo-ch'ang tz'u-hua*). The reading audience for chantefables included lower official families, such as the Hsüan family of Chia-ting county, which buried the chantefables in a marital tomb. In this case, the process seems to have been from village ritual to printed text for an affluent audience. Other prosimetric genres represent the opposite process. Chao Ling-chih inserted musical attributes into a classical story about Ying-ying so that it could be performed by courtesans and entertainers as a drum ballad. A century later, Master Tung produced a much more successful medley based on both tale and drum ballad, which blended sophisticated musical forms, classical

Chinese, and earthy vernacular. His achievement paved the way for the creation of the famous play "Hsi-hsiang chi" (Romance of the Western Chamber, or The Story of the Western Wing), composed by Wang Shih-fu (c. 1250–1300).

In accounting for the widespread influence of prosimetric forms in Chinese society, one must consider the proliferation of manuscripts used as aides-mémoires in performance by people of all social classes during the late imperial period. Ritual texts in classical Chinese were in common use, and many dating from the T'ang period were retrieved from the Tun-huang caves. Some of these are works of household instruction written by patriarchs; others are ceremonial texts such as blessings for newborns and auguries based on dreams or calendars. Many villages had one or two men with some education who became the "literate specialists" for their fellow villagers. Side by side with ritual texts in the classical language there developed an orally transmitted tradition of similar sorts of rituals (household injunctions, ceremonial songs such as "Laying the Rafters," and so on) which were occasionally recorded in the vernacular in manuscript form to assist the semiliterate practitioner. Scripts for exorcism plays were also recorded in this fashion. Occasionally dramatists would collect manuscripts circulating in villages and adapt them to compose plays. One example is Chang Chih-chen's (fl. 1582) version of the famous Mu-lien story cycle. He collected the local version of this tale from a village in his native Anhwei and rewrote it as a play entitled "Ch'üan shan chi" (Encouragement to Do Good). The common partial reliance on manuscript and textual versions allowed for greater intermingling of genres and traditions. It could also account for a certain homogeneity of content in genres that differ greatly in space and time, such as the chantefables discovered in the wealthy Kiangnan (lower Yangtze River valley) area in the fifteenth century and Women's Script performances from remote villages in mid-twentieth-century Hunan province. It is highly significant that these late Ming chantefables were usually "fully illustrated" (*ch'üan-hsiang*) and distinguished by the trappings of performance, such as directions for when to sing and when to recite. Thus although they were texts meant for reading, the printed chantefables clearly were intended to evoke dramatic visualization and vocalization.

Women's oral culture, presumably because women were less likely to be literate and thus to rely on manuscripts, was much less apt to be collected and reinterpreted by literati, who by definition were male. Even today, when Chinese ritual culture is being explored as never before, it is the culture of Chinese men that is most likely to be examined. This is primarily because woman's culture is fundamentally an oral one; it is conveyed in the local language, and scripts are not usually available for scholars to collate and analyze. Even where a woman's line of oral transmission was recorded in writing, as was the case with the Women's Script corpus, the manuscripts were usually burned on the death of the owner and did not circulate beyond the community of women. These were intensely private texts, not for public consumption. Indeed, until it came to be studied for scholarly purposes in recent years, males never became conversant with the Women's Script. Women's oral culture, unlike that of their male counterparts, could make an impact only in its oral form or when mentioned briefly in the written tradition by (almost always unsympathetic) male observers. The local dignitaries of Chiang-yung in the late imperial period, for example, failed to notice or at least chose not to record the phenomenon of Women's Script in their local region. But one should not infer from this that oral culture did not have a pervasive influence on the elite tradition. Women's lamentations offer the interpretive context for stories such as "The Shrew," which seek to satirize exactly the type of intelligent, loquacious woman celebrated in the popular tradition. Similarly, in the twentieth century, the author Pa Chin (b. 1904), in his well-known novel *Chia* (Family), has his "progressive" characters express scorn for the chanting and wailing of female mourners at a funeral. The new "modern" woman is to be redefined in contrast to the emotional, histrionic "traditional" woman of the past.

The relationship between certain oral-formulaic traditions and non-Han peoples is an intriguing topic that awaits further investigation. The very linguistic status of the texts written in the Women's Script is ambivalent. Although the language appears to be constituted on a primarily Sinitic base, it is also characterized by so many non-Sinitic features that it defies convenient classification. Furthermore, much of Women's Script culture and the vibrant, expressive, and festival culture with which it is inextricably linked, together with somewhat unusual marriage arrangements, are possibly derivative in part from the Yao tribal groups that inhabit the southern boundaries of Chiang-yung. Wedding lamentations, once popular throughout rural China, are also a feature of some ethnic minorities such as the T'u-chia people of the adjacent Hupei province. In case studies that have come to light so far, it appears that, as Han peoples gradually moved farther southward, beginning especially around the middle of the fourth century, they assimilated some local marriage and ritual practices from non-Han peoples. Generally speaking, it is Han women rather than Han men who have preserved more of these indigenous practices and incorporated them into gender-specific folk genres.

Prosimetric genres, particularly the printed forms such as plain tales, medleys, and chantefables, which developed from the twelfth century onward, left an indelible impression on the earliest Chinese fiction. The earliest type of vernacular fiction in China often imitated prosimetric features. If not designed for performance by a professional entertainer, these genres were at the very least intended to be "performed" (vocalized or chanted) by their intended readership. The pre-existence of a flourishing prosimetric culture in both oral and written transmission conditioned the reception of early vernacular publishing in China. The reading public expected that a popular text would include verse or song to recite, chant, or sing. The earliest vernacular texts, such as *Shui-hu chuan* (Water Margin), *Hsi-yu chi* (Journey to the West), and the short stories of Feng

Meng-lung (1574–1646), were related mainly in prose but contain copious amounts of verse, presumably because this suited the expectations and reading practices of their target audience for performative, dramaturgic renderings of tales with which they were already familiar from storytellers and local theater.

Another prosimetric influence can be observed in the style of the omniscient storyteller of Chinese vernacular fiction. Chinese novels are serial in nature, each chapter ending with a moment of suspense and an injunction to the reader as audience to "listen in to the next session." The narrative is replete with a form of "storyteller's rhetoric," a simulated context of performance including moralistic exhortations from the narrator, who purports to be a storyteller. The derivation of these rhetorical formulae, together with a vast number of popular sayings, motifs, and story material, can be traced back to prosimetric genres such as plain tales, medleys, and chantefables.

The sheer ubiquity and popularity of prosimetric forms made it very tempting for literati and officials to harness these oral art forms for a political or reformist agenda or simply to express divergent opinions. Chia Ying-ch'ung (1590–1674) was an eccentric scholar-official who preferred writing and composing drum ballads to his official duties. His lengthy "Mu-p'i-san-jen ku-tz'u" (Drum Ballad of "The Tree Bark Idler") was admired in his own era and still chanted in his native Shantung province centuries later. After Western encroachments, Chinese reformers turned their hands to the composition of prosimetric tales that could disseminate new notions to the unlearned. One example deals with the antiforeign Boxer Rebellion in 1900: Li Pao-chia's (1867–1906) "Keng-tzu kuo-pien t'an-tz'u" (Strummed Ballad on the Disturbances of the Year Keng-tzu [1900]). This lengthy narrative in six volumes describes the perfidy of the Ch'ing imperial court in handling the Boxer insurgents and the suffering of the commoners of Peking. Ch'iu Chin (1875–1907), the female revolutionary who was executed by the court, left a fragmentary strummed lyric entitled "Ching-wei shih" (Stones of the Ching-wei Bird). The Ching-wei was a mythical bird that was a reincarnation of the ancient female goddess Nü-wa. It was her laborious task to fill in the Eastern Sea with stones carried in her beak. Ch'iu Chin's strummed lyric dealt with reformist issues concerning the education of the new modern woman.

Starting in the early 1930s, talented Communist writers such as Ch'ü Ch'iu-pai (1899–1935) wrote prosimetric ballads for performance and memorization by those living in areas ruled by the Chinese Communist Party (CCP). Drum ballads were also composed to steel the nerves of soldiers during the anti-Japanese resistance war of the late 1930s and 1940s. After the establishment of the People's Republic of China in 1949, the composition of prosimetric forms (known in contemporary China as *ch'ü-yi* [oral arts]) to promote a particular campaign or popularize government policy, such as the state's policy on birth control, continued well into the 1980s, the reformist era of Teng Hsiao-p'ing (1904–1997) and his successors. One CCP leader, Ch'en Yün (1905–1995), took a particular interest in prosimetric performance (known generally as *p'ing-t'an*) and was often invoked in publications as a kind of "patron saint" of oral art forms. Whether official *p'ing-t'an* will continue after his demise remains to be seen.

INFLUENCE AND SIGNIFICANCE FOR CHINESE LITERATURE/INTERCULTURAL COMPARISONS

Prosimetric literature comprises a significant part of world oral literature generally. Some well-known examples beyond China are the Mongol, Turkish, Arabic, and Indian traditions. Mongol epics in song and prose are sung by bards, often to the accompaniment of a stringed instrument. In content they often deal with military themes and the supernatural. Mongol regions influenced by Sinitic culture are noted for their "book epics," which are essentially popular novels rewritten in epic form. Stories of Hua Kuan So, for example, circulate in Mongolia in epical genres. These may have been adapted from Chinese chantefables, such as the tale of the same name in the Ch'eng-hua period corpus. The medieval Turkish *Book of Dede Korkut* includes the epic stories of the Oghuz or Turkmen, the ancestors of the Turkish people. As is true of the Mongol examples, this deals with the heroic age of the Oghuz Turks and their battles against the infidel. In the *Book of Dede Korkut*, the narrative is composed mostly in prose and the dialog in verse. The Arabic folk epics styled *al sira* known both in oral performance and in chapbooks were called "yellow books." Looked down upon by the upper classes, the "yellow books" are composed in prose and verse in a form of Middle Arabic. The material is usually epic in nature and deals with the mass migration of Arabic populations, battles, and adventure. Many Indian oral epics are also composed in prose and song, and some, like the oral epics of Rajasthan, are embedded in a cultic context similar to the Chinese tradition, for example, performances to cure the sick or propitiate the gods.

In the Mongol "book epics," the written tradition serves as an important model for the oral form and as a source of story material. The oral and the written are also closely related in Chinese prosimetric forms. The Chinese oral-formulaic and prosimetric traditions, perhaps because they originated well after the development of a flourishing written culture, are much more closely allied to texts than are the epic traditions best known in the West, such as the Homeric epics. The oral tale is often conceived of as related to a canonical version in a book, although it may diverge considerably from any such source. The very word "storytelling" (*shuo-shu*) means literally "telling [tales from] books." Any analysis of Chinese oral-formulaic and prosimetric traditions must take into account the prevalence of manuscripts used as aides-mémoires. Even blind musicians were sometimes taught their repertoire from text-based sources.

In sum, China's oral-formulaic and prosimetric traditions are best considered an intrinsic part of China's "performance culture," in which, in premodern times, virtually everyone could participate, whether literate or illiterate. China's dramatic and festival culture centered on amateur performance, although in literary studies exemplars created by men of letters have traditionally received the most prominence. What is termed here China's oral-formulaic tradition (plays of exorcism, lamentation, and so on) is essentially ritual culture that provides a structured framework for the operation of functions significant to the community. Two such ritual functions discussed in this chapter are the exorcism of the *yin* forces of pestilence and disorder and the ritual claims women bring to bear on their natal family on the eve of their marriage. These ritual oral arts combine narrative with laments, praise, prayers, proverbs, and curses, and are inseparable from the community that nurtures them. The oral-formulaic tradition, then, is significant less because of its esthetics than because of the ritual power it can exert in safeguarding the health of the community.

Prosimetric genres, as distinct from oral-formulaic performance, are of two major types. Some derive from or are modeled on the oral-formulaic tradition (for example, Ming chantefables), while others are a literary man's recreation of an item from the classical repertoire in a popular performance genre for entertainers and a broader audience. The latter can be appraised with a truly literary esthetic. The outstanding example is "Master Tung's 'Romance of the Western Chamber.'" But even lesser forms, such as the chantefable, strummed ballads, and drum ballads, were immensely popular with contemporary audiences and provided an endless reservoir of stock material that was reworked by men of letters into China's rich stream of vernacular fiction. Moving beyond aspects of derivation and source material, China's oral-formulaic and prosimetric traditions are of crucial importance in understanding the relationship between oral and written culture and between the popular and elite traditions. Each defined itself in reference to the other in a complex relationship of emulation, tension, and occasionally resistance.

Anne E. McLaren

Chapter 50

REGIONAL LITERATURES

In Chinese literary history, the notion of "regional literature" could apply in some sense to a great deal of the traditional elite canon of poetry and to the less-esteemed genres of drama and vernacular fiction. The earliest Confucian collections of songs and anecdotes are filled with references to locale, and the assumption that local cultures varied from one another is pervasive in these writings. Fascination with parts of China other than one's own prompted the exoticization of large parts of the country, particularly by those northern elites who found fascination in the lands of the Yangtze delta and farther south. The poetry of the borderlands to the north prompted a whole genre of lyrics written about life in exile on the frontier demarcated by the Great Wall. Collections of stories and tales from the T'ang dynasty (618–907), written in Classical Chinese, often concerned strange or unusual local phenomena and events from all over China.

Vernacular fiction with localized content appeared by the fifteenth century from writers such as Feng Meng-lung (1574–1646), whose stories, many seemingly collected from other written and oral sources, largely depict the societies of the lower Yangtze delta in the canal-linked cities of Yangchow, Soochow, and Hangchow. Vernacular novels, ranging from works such as *Chin P'ing Mei* (Gold Vase Plum, or The Golden Lotus) in the sixteenth century, to later works from the eighteenth and nineteenth centuries, such as *Fu-sheng liu-chi* (Six Chapters of a Floating Life), by Shen Fu, *Chiu-wei kuei* (The Nine-Tailed Turtle), and even the *yüan-yang hu-tieh p'ai* (mandarin ducks and butterflies—

the traditional Chinese symbols for a pair of lovers) fiction of urban Shanghai in the 1920s, present life in the Yangtze delta cities with great attention to local color, sometimes mixed with snatches of local Wu topolects.

Regional operatic traditions—literally known as "local opera" (*ti-fang hsi*) and dating to the period of the Mongol occupation of China (the Yüan dynasty 1260–1368 C.E.)—grew up in many areas, particularly in the Yangtze delta and points south into Fukien province and beyond to Canton and westward up the Yangtze into Szechwan province. Written scriptbooks became popular locally by the sixteenth century, as the capabilities of the Chinese publication industry increased. In the case of Ch'ao-chou Opera, a local opera in the Ch'ao-chou region of Kwangtung province, libretti were published in limited editions well into the twentieth century, often circulating among literate women in the community. In many cases, local publishers produced versions of standard collections of poems and stories, such as *T'ang-shih san-pai shou* (Three Hundred T'ang Poems), and editions of the great prose romances such as *San-kuo yen-yi* (Romance of the Three Kingdoms), *Hsi-yu chi* (Journey to the West), and *Hung-lou meng* (A Dream of Red Towers). Many editions of poetry and jottings (*pi-chi*; see chapter 31) by local literati were also published in limited editions all over China. Poets across the country wrote poems in classical style, which often involved references to local history, places, and customs.

Aside from these better-known literary traditions, which received more than local attention during the dynastic period, there exist remnants of regional traditions that were poorly known outside their area of creation and appreciation. Some were printed or handwritten employing a mixture of standard Chinese graphs and specialized characters used to represent local Sinitic languages. Others were written in vernacularized Classical Chinese but, by content, form, tradition, and factors of audience and transmission, were enjoyed locally. In one remote county of Hunan province, a secret "Women's Script" (*nü-shu*) was used to record stories and songs, and known only by women (see chapters 1 and 49). The wealth of ethnic-minority regional literatures is dealt with in chapter 51.

Like most Chinese vernacular literature, many of the regional narrative traditions were, to use John Miles Foley's term, "oral-connected" in the sense that stylistically they share features with oral traditions. In some instances, texts were based on the performances of actual storytellers, and sometimes were compiled by literate storytellers themselves. In certain locales, texts were printed for use by patrons and audiences of performing narratives, who often employed the texts somewhat as opera libretti were used in Europe. Possibly the majority of texts, however, were written in a quasi-oral style, employing conventions of oral traditions such as the mixing of passages of verse, prose, and sometimes dialog. Handwritten or small printed editions were circulated among friends, in some instances networks of literate or partially literate women. The texts could be read silently, aloud to oneself, or recited and sung to one's circle of acquaintances. Frequently such texts were illustrated with woodblock prints, which served to make them more readily understood and more vivid for readers.

These regional works began to receive scholarly recognition only after the intellectual ferment of the May Fourth era (c. 1919–1927), which prompted demotically minded young scholars to explore China's folk and popular culture. Often placed in the general category of "vernacular literature" (*su-wen-hsüeh*), and sometimes described in Chinese sources as literature in local dialects or patois (*t'u-yin*), these vernacular narratives are predominantly prosimetric in form. Below, several of these "speaking and singing" (*shuo-ch'ang*) traditions are examined as examples of major regional literatures in China.

THE "SPEAKING AND SINGING" TRADITIONS

Seeping slowly out of India, across forbidding mountains and the barrens of the Central Asian deserts, and into the northwest gates of China, Buddhism entered East Asia by the first century C.E., rising to great prominence on the continent, the Korean peninsula, and finally Japan by the sixth century. Sutras in Sanskrit carried by monks were translated into Chinese at translation centers in the ancient capital of Ch'ang-an, now known as Sian (Hsi-an), and other regional locations. The effects of the new religion, and the forms of Indian and Central Asian cultures that came with it, were to have a tremendous influence on the societies of East Asia as they syncretized the elements born on the old trans-continental trade route known as the Silk Road with native practices. Sculpture, painting, temple architecture, music, dance, drama, culinary arts, and costume were all influenced at elite and popular levels of society. By the end of the third century C.E., the grand Han empire (206 B.C.E.–220 C.E.), which had been contemporaneous with the Roman empire, lay in shambles. Northern China became a series of kingdoms, often run by leading clans founded by men of Central Asian blood. In this time of constant flux, as the kingdoms rose and fell, Buddhism found fertile ground for expansion among a populace seeking solace and refuge during unstable times.

One method of propagating the exciting, illuminating Buddhist tales among popular audiences was the use of a performance style employing alternating passages of prose and poetry, accompanied by some sort of percussive or stringed instruments. In the early twentieth century, the Hungarian-British Indologist-explorer Aurel Stein and the nonpareil French Sinologist Paul Pelliot made their now-famous recovery of manuscripts that had been immured for nearly nine hundred years in a side chamber of one of the caves at Tun-huang, several hundred miles northwest of Sian. More than thirty thousand manuscripts written in Chinese, Tibetan, Uyghur, Sogdian, Khotanese, and other languages were uncovered, written or occasionally printed on paper scrolls and sheets, and rarely in the form of booklets. The vast majority of these manuscripts are Buddhist sutras, but there are also social and economic documents as well as a wide variety of other types of invaluable texts that are virtually unknown elsewhere in China from such an early period. For students of Chinese popular literature, among the most exciting discoveries is a group of about a hundred manuscripts that can be divided into fewer than half a dozen distinct genres. These are the earliest and most bountiful examples of early prosimetric narrative in Chinese literary history. Twentieth-century Chinese, Japanese, and Western scholars theorize that the prosimetric style spread far and wide across East Asia during the period of Buddhist propagation from the first century C.E. onward (see chapter 48 for a more detailed treatment of Tun-huang literature).

The theory is that Buddhist prosimetric texts of the types found at Tun-huang stimulated the growth of many other styles of local narrative, nearly all in prosimetric form, some possibly created by disenfranchised monks in times of religious persecution as the Chinese government moved to break up the monopolies on precious metals and slaves that the richer monasteries enjoyed. Whatever the case, by the tenth century, styles of prosimetric narrative seem to have developed in regions throughout China. Hard evidence of specific forms dates only to the fifteenth century, however, because of the nature of transmission of oral performance traditions and the low value placed on vernacular written narratives by learned society.

In 1967, a cache of prosimetric texts dating from the late Ming dynasty (1368–1644) was found near the town of Chia-ting, close to Shanghai. Buried in the grave of a lady from a prosperous family, the texts provide early evidence of the prosimetric tastes among literate women in the region. These texts were written in a format called *tz'u-hua* (verse story or chantefable)—a term applied to several styles of vernacular fiction. The titles included tales of early emperors and generals such as "Pai-t'u chi" (The Story of the White Hare) and "Hua Kuan So" (The Story of Hua Kuan So). These texts have helped to fill in some of the blanks in the history of local literatures in China, though the situation is still very murky because of the low survival rate of texts little valued by the literary elite and the general lack of information on the context of usage or authorship of such works (see chapter 49 for more extensive discussion of the Chia-ting chantefables).

The era of greatest popularity for such regional literatures spanned the late Ming through the Ch'ing (1644–1911), and in some cases even into the early decades of the twentieth century. The textual traditions include *pao-chüan* (precious scrolls, or precious volumes), religious narratives popular in many areas, especially eastern China, several types of narrative called *t'an-tz'u* (plucking lyrics) from the Yangtze delta, *ku-tz'u* (drum ballads), the Manchu *tzu-ti-shu* (bannermen's stories) from north and northeast China, and the *mu-yü* (wooden fish) books (see chapter 49). The names of these local traditions should be understood in a rather general way, for no strict canon of style or terminology developed for any of these various bodies of texts. This is due in part to the popular (hence unregulated) nature of such literature and to the circulation of texts from one area in other areas—especially northern drum ballads and *tzu-ti-shu* texts in the southern regions. Studies describing these traditions often differ widely with regard to how the varying texts in a given corpus should be named and categorized; sorting through the conflicting terminology and classification schemes for this type of regional literature is often an extremely confusing business.

These texts seem to have attracted largely urban readers in the lower to mid-level scholar-official and merchant classes, though they were also popular in some rural areas. As noted above, growing evidence suggests that audiences for many of these traditions were women, especially in the south. In the Yangtze delta, women were active in writing and editing prosimetric narratives.

Some of the major regional narrative traditions are described below.

The T'an-tz'u *Traditions of the Lower Yangtze Delta*

The term *t'an-tz'u* (literally "plucking lyrics" or "strummed lyrics") has been used to describe several types of sometimes very different prosimetric narratives once popular in the lower Yangtze delta and farther south. The term is far from exact, and classification of *t'an-tz'u* texts continues to prove troublesome to scholars. The term *t'an-tz'u* was in use as early as the twelfth century, as shown by a reference to a version of the "Hsi-hsiang chi" (Romance of the Western Chamber) dating from the Chin dynasty (1115–1234). The eighteenth and nineteenth centuries, however, seem to have been the heyday of *t'an-tz'u* production, whatever the style.

Although some Ming dynasty texts dealt with Chinese imperial history, the majority of stories concern love affairs between gifted scholars and talented beauties (*ts'ai-tzu chia-jen*). *T'an-tz'u* were still being written in the early twentieth century, sometimes on nationalistic and political themes, including women's liberation. During the second quarter of the twentieth century and into the 1950s, Chinese scholars such as Cheng Chen-to, Ah Ying (Ch'ien Hsing-ts'un), Li Chia-jui, and Chao Ching-shen offered various theories about the evolution of the early prosimetric forms such as transformation texts (*pien-wen*), "medleys" (*chu-kung-tiao*), and the later Ming and Ch'ing dynasty *t'an-tz'u*, yet no clear genetic relationships have been established among them.

The texts referred to explicitly as *t'an-tz'u* (often in their titles) can be divided into two main types or, more correctly, genres. One type is written in Mandarin, utilizing to some degree quasi-oral conventions. The other is written at least partially in one or another of the Wu topolects, often the Soochow dialect. The Wu topolect texts are associated with a tradition of oral performance still common in the delta region, though what that oral tradition was like before the twentieth century, when many of the Wu topolect texts were published, is unclear. Therefore, these local Wu topolect texts can at best be considered somehow "connected" to performance.

Of the texts in the Mandarin corpus, the "women's *t'an-tz'u*" of the lower Yangtze region have shown the greatest endurance and popularity historically, many having been reprinted in numerous editions before 1949 on the mainland

and others reissued since the 1980s. These texts were a part of literate women's culture in the lower Yangtze during the late imperial period and were written, edited, and published by women of elite households in cities such as Soochow and Hangchow. Some of these works exceed a million words and several took decades to complete. The subject matter consists of the standard scholar-beauty romances and stories featuring women cross-dressing as males in order to become officials or, occasionally, women-warriors. Written in a vernacular idiom influenced by Classical Chinese, the texts consist of long series of seven- and ten-character lines of verse interspersed with brief paragraphs of prose. One of the earliest works attributed to a woman author is "T'ien yü hua" (Flowers Under the Rain of Heaven), which concerns the fates of several loyalist families in the Ming dynasty.

Hou Chih (pen-name of Hou Hsiang-yeh, b. 1766), an accomplished writer and editor, prepared the works of other women for publication. Most famous of these is the text of "Tsai-sheng yüan" (Love Reincarnate), written by Ch'en Tuan-sheng (1751–1796?) and completed decades later by Liang Te-sheng. In her foreword (written in 1821), Hou explains that for years she had devoted her time to writing Confucian prose essays, but later turned to writing and editing prosimetric works for publication and consumption by elite women and "other urbanites and merchants." Hou believed that, although poetry "expresses feeling" and "history records events," the purpose of publishing vernacular histories and *t'an-tz'u* was, in part, to preserve entertaining but enlightening stories for future generations. Further along in the foreword, she notes that the text of "Love Reincarnate" had circulated in handwritten form for many years and was only now being formally published for future generations to enjoy.

Ch'en Tuan-sheng, the author of "Love Reincarnate," was born into an official's family in 1751 near the present-day city of Hangchow. There is some evidence that she may have learned the art of writing *t'an-tz'u* from her mother, who may be the anonymous author of an earlier *t'an-tz'u* entitled "Yü-chuan yüan" (Romance of the Jade Bracelet). Set in the Yüan dynasty, "Love Reincarnate" concerns characters who are the reincarnations of characters in the former romance.

The main plot of Ch'en Tuan-sheng's work recounts the relationship between Huang-fu Shao-hua, the handsome son of a military family in Yunnan province (an exotic locale in southwest China where several officials in Ch'en's family were posted during their careers), and Meng Li-chün, a "female genius" of another garrison leader's family. In the course of her marriage arrangements, things go awry, and Meng is engaged to another official's son, Liu K'uei-pi, known far and wide as a rake. Believing that she is rightfully engaged to Huang-fu Shao-hua, she orders her childhood companion and maidservant, Su Ying-hsüeh, to masquerade as herself (Meng) and marry in her stead. Meng then dresses as a young man and escapes with another maidservant. Meng is adopted by a local official whose son has recently drowned. Taking the name Li Chün-yü, Meng soon sits for the various levels of the imperial civil service examinations and eventually becomes the top graduate among that year's candidates. A grand party is held in the capital, and the still-disguised Meng is engaged to a lovely young woman who has recently been adopted by the powerful Liang family.

On Meng's wedding night "he" discovers that "his" bride is none other than "his" former maidservant, Su Ying-hsüeh, who escaped from the unwanted marriage by stabbing Liu K'uei-pi with a pair of scissors and jumping in apparent suicide into Lake Kun-ming, only to be saved by a supernatural wind that pushed her near the pleasure boat of one Madame Liang, who, after the rescue, took her as a daughter. After confronting each other in the marriage chamber, the former mistress and maid decide to continue their charade in the hope that Meng can somehow be reunited with Huang-fu Shao-hua.

A few lines from this scene in which the two women are telling their respective stories since parting will give some sense of the general style of the lyric passages in Mandarin *t'an-tz'u* and similar prosimetric traditions. The first line is in prose dialog, while the succeeding ones are in verse. Meng Li-chün (whose personal name literally means "Beautiful Gentleman") is speaking to her former maidservant, Su Ying-hsüeh. She alludes at the beginning to the archery match in which Liu K'uei-pi took the rightful prize from the true winner, Huang-fu Shao-hua:

"Goodness, my maiden Su, today it has been fated that we should
  meet again."
An arrow striking a willow that decided my marriage;
And thus refused the honor of a match made by imperial decree.
Painting my portrait to leave as a keepsake,
  I then dressed as a male to depart my home.
That Liu K'uei-pi could be so horrid, I never imagined;
  thus I suggested to my parents that you act in my stead.
Who could have known you were in fact unwilling,
  and thus plunged yourself into the clear lake waters, to forgo your
    very own life.
Later, when outside the home, I learned of this news—
  it nearly killed me;
I had taken a beautiful girl and in one day destroyed her life.
I never thought that in this existence
  I would see you again.
Yet, who could know that today we would meet,
  able to speak of our feelings since parting . . . .

The scene ends with a prose passage, which follows the moving speeches in verse by the "married couple":

> With great happiness, Chün-yü said softly: "You may just take the pretense as real, as if I actually am a genuine male—for who would know why I am called 'Beautiful Gentleman'? It is already past midnight, and the light of the candles is lowering. Dear, dear, won't you hurry and become husband and wife with me?" Miss Su giggled bashfully, and spoke very softly: "Miss, you shouldn't trick people anymore." After that, the two grasped hands and prepared to sleep, the netting and the quilting smelling of orchids and musk. The pair slept on one pillow, upon which were embroidered Mandarin ducks. They were just like two lotuses blossoming from the same rootstalk. They spoke together until the fourth watch, when they began to tire. Then they pulled up their covers to sleep. But in their dreams, it still seemed as if they were speaking of their feelings over their long parting. Falling asleep so late, the "spring night" seemed to them to be very short. When they got up the next morning the sun was already high and the shadows of shrubs covered the courtyard. The husband and wife combed their hair and put on makeup in one mirror, and washed their faces together. Then slowly, step by step, they walked out of the door of their room.

Later, Meng Li-chün cures the emperor's mother of a life-threatening disease. Advising the emperor to make use of all talent in the face of an invasion from Korea, Meng is able to have Huang-fu Shao-hua, who has taken refuge in the mountains of southern China, commanded to the capital to join the imperial army. The Liu family is eventually punished, and the Meng family name is cleared. However, Meng Li-chün, still in disguise, eventually arouses the suspicions of the emperor, who attempts to discover the real identity and sex of his talented minister by inviting "him" to a drinking party, where he hopes to remove "his" shoes and discover the tell-tale bound feet. Ch'en Tuan-sheng stopped writing after the seventeenth chapter, leaving Meng still undecided over whether to reveal her identity and take her place in the emperor's harem or continue on as a powerful official in the hope of clearing her family's name and reuniting with her destined husband, Huang-fu Shao-hua. The final three chapters, supplied by another woman, Liang Te-sheng, more than twenty years after Ch'en's death, conclude with the emperor discovering Meng's fraud, sentencing her to death, recanting the sentence, and allowing her to marry Huang-fu Shao-hua, with the maidservant Su Ying-hsüeh joining them as a concubine.

In her foreword, Hou Chih stresses that the story must be assessed not only in terms of entertainment but "within the bounds of loyalty, filial behavior, purity, and righteousness, in accord with the standards of moral conduct." Although Meng's running away from the marriage arrangement was certainly an unfilial act against her parents, her steadfastness in her commitment to Huang-fu Shao-hua (and her own happiness) is filial behavior of another sort, reflective of the life dilemmas of principled late-imperial women. In the 1950s and early 1960s, prominent critics including Ch'en Yin-k'o and Kuo Mo-jo described Meng Li-chün's actions as those of a progressive woman, a theme that has been explored in various ways by different generations of critics and commentators both in China and elsewhere.

Numerous works on similar themes and sequels to the Meng Li-chün story were written by women in the nineteenth century. These include "Pi-sheng hua" (Elegant Words of the Brush), by Chiu Hsin-ju, and Hou Chih's "Tsai-tsao t'ien" (Heaven Recreated), the story of Meng Li-chün's daughter. A *t'an-tz'u* with a more pronounced martial theme featuring cross-dressing is "Shih-li chin-tan" (Ten Golden Pellets), by an anonymous Ch'ing author. Set in the Northern Sung dynasty, the story relates the intrigues surrounding a young woman from an elite family whose marriage to a high military official is stymied by an imperial edict. Dressing as a military officer, she later has an unlikely meeting with her lost fiancé, who is masquerading as a woman.

Unlike the Mandarin *t'an-tz'u* of the lower Yangtze, which were easily readable by literate audiences in other parts of China, another narrative tradition, also called *t'an-tz'u*, was produced and circulated in the same region. These texts were written in a style that mixed Mandarin graphs with specialized graphs used only in writing the Wu topolects, particularly the Soochow dialect. Such texts were wholly accessible only to audiences familiar with this unique writing code.

These written Wu topolect *t'an-tz'u* are related to the orally performed art known as Soochow *t'an-tz'u* (for convenience, they are referred to here as Soochow chantefables) and similar performance traditions in the region (particularly Yangchow and Hangchow). In these oral forms, serial narratives were performed over many days or weeks and presented in a mixture of passages of dialog, singing, and narrative speech. Although it is not very clear what the oral performances were like even in the late nineteenth century, it seems that, some decades earlier, a style of dialog, evidently borrowed from the local *k'un-ch'ü* opera (see chapter 41), enlivened the genre, making it into a kind of dramatic narrative. One or two storytellers would perform the narratives, playing the three-stringed Chinese banjo (*san-hsien*) and the balloon lute (*p'i-p'a*) to accompany their singing. These lengthy narratives were performed in many contexts, including private homes, teahouses, and special storyhouses. At present, Soochow chantefable is still popular among older audiences in Shanghai, Soochow, Wu-hsi, and other cities of the region.

Many of the written Wu topolect *t'an-tz'u* have parallels in the oral performance tradition. Most concern love affairs between scholars and beauties. The best-known stories in both the written and oral mediums are: "San-hsiao yin-yüan" (The Three Smiles Romance), "Chen-chu t'a" (The Pearl Pagoda), "Yü ch'ing-t'ing" (The Jade Dragonfly), "Pai-she chuan" (The Story of the White Snake), "Miao-chin feng" (The Etched Gold Phoenix), "Wo p'ao" (The Japanese Cloak), and "Yang Nai-wu yü Hsiao Pai-ts'ai" (Yang Nai-wu and Little Cabbage). Some of the topolect texts have been attributed by publishers of the era to specific performers. The most extensively studied *t'an-tz'u* is "Three Smiles Romance," a comic story concerning the love affairs of the talented T'ang dynasty literatus T'ang Po-hu (styled T'ang Yin).

Ma Ju-fei was the son of a storyteller from Soochow who performed "Pearl Pagoda," a story that had already appeared in print during the reign of the Ch'ien-lung emperor (1736–1795) in the late eighteenth century. As a youth, Ma was trained in the classics and poetry in preparation for the civil service examinations, which he passed at the county level. He later learned storytelling from a cousin and made numerous innovations in the narrative, lyrics, and music of "Pearl Pagoda," which describes the romance between a poor young scholar named Fang Ch'ing and his lovely, talented, and wealthy cousin. Ma's name appears on several printed versions of the story. He was active in the Soochow storyteller's guild known as Kuang-yü she (Brilliant Abundance Society) and was also the author/editor of a collection of more than three hundred ballads (*k'ai-p'ien*) published in 1886. In performances of Soochow chantefable, these lyrical ballads were sung as warmup pieces before the telling of the main story. Written mostly in Mandarin (*kuan-hua*, a local southern style of which was spoken by officials from the region), these ballads were also sung by young women in teahouses. In some cases (such as the title of Ma's collection), they were also called *nan-tz'u* (southern lyrics), another term that has been used to describe several prosimetric styles in southern China. Like the Wu topolect *t'an-tz'u*, these ballads often reflected a strong influence of the higher literary genres, especially classical poetry.

Several written versions of stories told by contemporary storytellers in Yangchow and Soochow have been published since the late 1950s, some in Mandarin and a few in Soochow dialect. These more recent texts are very different in form from the earlier printed topolect *t'an-tz'u*, reflecting changes both in the performing and written art and in publishing conventions. They include "Wu Sung," which describes the tiger-taming exploits of a colorful character in the famous traditional novel *Shui-hu chuan* (Water Margin), based on the oral version of the Yangchow storyteller Wang Shao-t'ang. This text represents a style of storytelling called *p'ing-hua* (straight talk or plain tale), which includes little if any music and is usually performed by one storyteller. "Love Reincarnate," a Soochow chantefable version of the original eighteenth-century Mandarin *t'an-tz'u* by Ch'en Tuan-sheng, appeared in 1981. This text was based on the oral performances and notes of the Soochow storyteller Ch'in Chi-wen. The text was published in Mandarin to appeal to a larger audience than a Soochow dialect version could reach (though many locals believe that such translations from the language in which they were first performed and written lose the flavor of the original texts).

A version of the "Etched Gold Phoenix," based on the performances of Chang Ju-chün and Liu Yün-jo, was published in 1990 (earliest extant printed version, 1876). Set partly in Soochow during an unusually cold winter during the Ming dynasty, the story concerns the marriage of a once poor young scholar named Hsü Hui-lan to the daughter of an all-too-human fortuneteller named Ch'ien Chih-chieh. In this short passage (in this instance, spoken rather than sung), Ch'ien is returning home after a night in a well-known tavern district, where he has just betrothed his daughter to a local merchant. It is an engagement that must eventually be terminated (with some difficulty) so that his daughter may marry Hsü Hui-lan, with whom she has secretly fallen in love and to whom she has given an etched gold phoenix as a token. The use of place names localizes the story for anyone familiar with the streets and canals of old Soochow. Such descriptive detail is common in many topolect *t'an-tz'u*, both written and oral.

> In the Lung-hsing district, Ch'ien Chih-chieh had got rotten drunk and during a banquet engaged his daughter to Wang Hsüan, a pot of wine being the matchmaker. At the crack of dawn, he prepared to go home and sleep. By now the snow had stopped, and the way was frozen and slippery. He lived outside Pan Gate, by the Wu Gate Bridge. But because he was drunk he didn't turn where he should have turned and took the wrong road. He came out at Hsi Gate, then walked down to the Hsi Gate ferry head. Now, in the Chia-ching period [1522–1566] of the Ming dynasty, there was no bridge there. Yet Ch'ien Chih-chieh had mistaken the place for Pan Gate. He stood there alone, wondering about where the Wu Gate bridge had gone. In a high voice, he called out: "Bri-i-dge!, bri-i-i-dge!"
>
> Suddenly from the opposite bank a voice returned:
>
> "He-e-y!"
>
> Ch'ien Chih-chieh felt odd—how can a bridge speak?
>
> "Bri-i-dge, where are you?"
>
> "I'm over here!"
>
> "Well, hurry up and come over!"
>
> "I'm coming."
>
> Was it really a bridge that was answering from the other side? No. On the other side was a ferry boat, and the rowers were a pair of brothers, Big T'ao and T'ao the Second.

CANTONESE WOODEN FISH TRADITIONS

In the Cantonese-speaking regions of southeast China (present-day Kwangtung province and the Kwangsi Chuang Autonomous Region), printed and handwritten texts of oral and performance-related prosimetric narratives called "wooden-fish songs" or "wooden-fish stories" date to the end of the Ming and early Ch'ing dynasties. The earliest known text is dated 1713. In Cantonese, the term "wooden fish" is pronounced *muk-yu* (in Mandarin, *mu-yü*).

Two basic types of these narratives have been identified, though many terms, some more or less obscure, are associated with printed narratives and oral forms of very similar style. The major types are "dragon-boat" songs (Cantonese, *leung-jau go*; Mandarin, *lung-chou ko*) and "southern tone" (Cantonese, *naam-yam*; Mandarin, *nan-yin*) stories. The former are ballads of up to several hundred lines of irregular length. They seem to have been performed since the late Ming and early Ch'ing dynasties by blind female singers, sometimes on the street, and by singing girls on boats and in teahouses in the entertainment *demimondes* of the Cantonese cities. Some street performers used gongs and drums, while those in the entertainment districts used a variety of stringed instruments such as the *p'i-p'a* (lute), *san-hsien* (three-stringed banjo), and the *erh-hu* (two-stringed fiddle). In rural areas, singing *muk-yu* was engaged in by performers who sang recreationally for fellow villagers. Some accounts indicate that women sometimes engaged blind singers to perform for them at festivals. In some areas, women seem to have had traditions of reading the texts aloud to one another. This is reminiscent of the performance contexts of the late Ming *tz'u-hua* chantefables (see chapter 49).

The term "wooden fish" suggests that at some point the wooden fish-shaped block used in Buddhist ceremonies may have been adopted as part of the performance tradition, but the relationship of this percussive instrument to the wooden-fish songs is still unclear, despite much conjecture by scholars. In the *naam-yam* tradition, the stories are much longer, some consisting of many bound volumes. The basic line is seven characters long, with length varied by the use of extra "pillow words" (*ch'en-tz'u*) to create variety. Some texts are very close in form to the *t'an-tz'u* of the lower Yangtze. For instance, one *naam-yam* version of "Heaven Recreated," published in Canton in the mid-1800s, is said to be a nearly word-for-word reproduction of a *t'an-tz'u* version of that story (see above). Moreover, although a sizable portion of the repertoire is of local origin, many stories have obviously been adapted or taken over wholesale from other narrative traditions, a widespread phenomenon in Chinese regional literatures.

The relationship between *naam-yam* and performance is unclear, though some evidence suggests that oral singers occasionally expanded their repertoires by adapting written *naam-yam* texts. It seems that, if a tradition of performance based on written *naam-yam* texts ever existed, the music and pace were less lively than those of the dragon-boat songs. Some dragon-boat songs were printed or handwritten in vernacular Cantonese (using some local versions of Chinese characters), and others even appeared in parallel Mandarin and local-language versions. The *naam-yam* texts, however, usually were written in Mandarin. If these were performed, they would have required extemporaneous translation into Cantonese. In some *naam-yam* texts, dragon-boat songs are also included, suggesting that in certain cases the two may have been performed together (the dragon-boat ballads perhaps serving as warmup pieces), or that they were considered as related traditions and could thus be published together.

The origin of the wooden-fish songs is unclear, but the term has been traced back to the fifteenth century. A common, but unlikely, attribution of origin is to the legendary song goddess Third Sister Liu (Liu San-chieh) who lived in Kwangsi (west of Kwangtung province) during the T'ang dynasty. She is said to have created numerous styles of antiphonal folksongs, fishermen's songs, and ballads, including wooden-fish songs. The Third Sister Liu legend is very widespread in the Cantonese-speaking regions of China, so it is not surprising that she should be named as the source. Other explanations for the origin of wooden-fish songs connect them with the influx of Manchu officials during the Ch'ing dynasty, some scholars even suggesting that the songs were imitations of the northern *tzu-ti-shu* drum songs. While it seems that certain more northern genres of prosimetric narrative, local opera, and vernacular fiction did influence the repertoire of wooden-fish songs, the form most likely grew out of a combination of Cantonese oral traditions and the same or similar prosimetric traditions that influenced the singing and speaking narratives in other parts of China.

Glen Dudbridge has made a study of the content of one wooden-fish song entitled "Ch'en-hsiang t'ai-tzu" (Prince Ch'en-hsiang). He has identified printed versions by at least three publishers in the region of Canton and suggests that the earliest printed versions (now lost) may have appeared in the Ming dynasty. Rich in detail of social custom and convention, the tale is set in the Sung dynasty and takes place over a wide area in north and south China.

The main thread of the story involves the interaction of the world of the spirits with that of humankind and centers on various kin relationships, particularly between supernatural mother and mortal son. The tale begins with an aged official, his wife, and an unmarried daughter, Jui-hsien, who is eventually possessed by spirits. The minister bankrupts himself trying to cure his daughter by employing ritual specialists at all levels of expertise—even the emperor becomes involved—and matters only become worse. Finally, it is the Goddess of Mount Hua-yüeh (Hua-yüeh san-niang), who, in return for making the young woman her sworn sister, rids her of the evil spirits. Her father is required to build a great temple with an image of the goddess inside. Later, the family's wealth is regained thanks to the alms given at the temple. Eventually, a young student, Liu Hsi, passes by the temple on the way to the civil service examinations. Tricked by the goddess in disguise, he has a three-year marriage with her, which results in a son. Subsequently, under decree from the Lord of Heaven, the son is raised by his father, who by now has passed the examinations. The goddess then decides that her mortal husband should marry her sworn sister, who also has a son. Later, the goddess gives her son divine writings and a magic sword, and he overthrows rebels who have seized the throne and becomes emperor himself. A short excerpt from the early part of the tale illustrates the style of the wooden-fish texts:

In all our life we have given birth but to this daughter alone:
I beseech you, Forebears, to preserve her—
Preserve her to escape from the evil demons,
so that she can carry on the fragrant lamp of the ancestral line.
If anything should happen to this precious girl,
All the ancestors in our shrine will be lonely souls.

DRUMSONGS AND MANCHU *TZU-TI-SHU* IN THE NORTH

Three general types of performance-related prosimetric vernacular narrative became popular in north and northeast China in about the sixteenth century. All are types of "drumsongs" (*ku-tz'u*), although only one style goes by that name. As with the *t'an-tz'u* tradition, it is not clear exactly how all of these texts were connected to performance, though certainly many were utilized by readers and oral performers to suit their own needs. As with other forms of Chinese vernacular fiction employing the conceit of an oral performer as narrator, many stories may have only imitated (in some cases, indirectly) the oral styles. The three categories of narrative (and these are general, as some works defy strict categorization) are known as *ku-tzu-t'zu* (songs of the drum), Manchu *tzu-ti-shu* (bannermen's stories), and *k'u-tz'u* (drumsongs). Although the written styles are similar, and stories were often adapted from one style to another, there are significant differences between them in form and history.

According to Chao Ching-shen, a major feature of the drumsong traditions is that they were current in northern China, particularly in the northeast from the area of Peking into former Manchuria. The term *ku-tz'u* seems to be older than *ku-tzu-t'zu*, also known as *kur-tz'u* (the retroflex *r* is a common ending for nouns in the Peking dialect). Since both terms mention drums, it has been assumed that percussion instruments were part of the early regional performance traditions, which may have involved one or more musicians and a singer/storyteller. These traditions may have been similar to performances of *ta-ku* (big drum), a living oral tradition still maintained in northern China.

The drumsong repertoire can be divided into two formal categories. One is the "big stories" (*ta-shu*), lengthy texts such as "Hu-chia chuan" (The Story of the Hu Family), "Hui-lung chuan" (Return of the Dragon), and "Erh-tu Mei" (The Second Rescue of Mei), which combine passages of prose with those of song. These texts tend to be very long and involved, with many chapters. The second category are the "short passages" (*hsiao-tuan*), which tend to be brief, lively stories or select passages from the longer works. The former category is claimed to be closer to the living traditions of drumsongs in terms of textual style, though the longer written texts could be adapted into the living drumsong traditions, as were stories from other styles of vernacular fiction and opera. Although different styles of oral drumsong performance are marked by unique musical styles and delivery, written texts of *ku-tz'u* and *ta-ku* libretti are often hard to tell apart, and classification is sometimes difficult.

A popular drumsong story, which is still in the living *ta-ku* tradition, is "Ch'ang-pan p'o" (The Slopes of Ch'ang-pan). The narrative recounts the story of a badly wounded Lady Ni, who decides that she must abandon her child, the princeling A-tou, on the battlefield in General Chao Tzu-lung's care, realizing that her wounds make her a burden. She then commits suicide so that General Chao may survive and defeat the enemy forces. This version of the story is based on the works of Liu Pao-ch'üan (1869–1942), a famous Peking drumsinger, who adapted it from texts of Manchu *tzu-ti-shu*. The story is also found in the *ku-tz'u* textual tradition. Kate Steven's English translation is based on a version of the Liu story performed by Chang Ts'ui-feng (1909–1975), one of Liu's female students active in the early decades of the twentieth century. The language of the text is quite literary, Liu having changed very little of the original *tzu-ti-shu* wording. Stevens notes that aside from employing the "common lexicon" of the vernacular narrative arts, performers could count on at least some audience members already being familiar with the stories from having heard other versions or even from renting texts from copyists at local temple fairs. In addition, it was a custom among some drumsong performers to make lengthy introductions concerning the content of the pieces they were about to perform. This selection is therefore a well-documented example of the often complex and varied interplay between the written and oral traditions in China.

See the lady, A-tou at her breast, sit with drooping head;
So pitiful, disheveled hair and streaked face take away her beauty.
Chao Tzu-lung hurried from his saddle, spear in ground, tied up his horse;
Hastened forward to kneel with a flourish and perform obeisance.
As he kowtowed, Chao said, "Milady has been affrighted, is the young prince safe?
The blame must rest with me, Chao Yün; your general has failed you."
The Lady Ni, joy and sorrow intertwined, said, "Does my lord still live?"
Tzu-lung replied, "He broke through enemy lines, headed straight east."
The lady said, "This is our nation's fortune, good fortune for the world,"
And asked again, "Who goes with him?"

The *tzu-ti-shu* tradition of the Manchus was a major form of entertainment for the communities of Manchu military bannermen who took to urban life as officials in the capital in Peking and nearby cities after the conquest of China in 1644. Although *tzu-ti-shu* is similar to *ku-tz'u* in form, its outstanding characteristic is that it was a Manchu form, performed and (in the early phases of development) sometimes written in Manchu. In later phases, texts in Chinese, or occasionally a mixture of Chinese and Manchu, predominate. It is unclear, however, whether the Manchu drumsong tradition was brought to China by the Manchus or was inspired by an early Chinese drumsong tradition. The indigenous and still thriving drumsong tradition of Korea (*p'ansori*), linked with Korean shamanic traditions, indicates that vernacular narratives accompanied by drums were common on both the Chinese and Korean borders of Manchuria. Drums, though of a rather different kind from those of *tzu-ti-shu*, were standard instruments in Manchu shamanic ceremonies. It is likely, therefore, that the well-attested Tungusic (Manchu) and Korean drumsong traditions, both Altaic and both intimately tied to widespread, enduring shamanic rituals, arose independently of Chinese *ku-tz'u*. They (or their ancestral forms) may, indeed, have provided the ultimate inspiration for northern Chinese drum singing, whose origins are otherwise obscure.

During the flourishing of the *tzu-ti-shu* tradition in the eighteenth and early nineteenth centuries, there seem to have been parallel written and oral forms, but, as in the other drumsong traditions, this relationship was complex and certainly included influences moving in both directions from oral to written traditions and vice versa. In performance style, there were two major tune traditions, the "Eastern City Tune" (*Tung-ch'eng-tiao*) and the "Western City Tune" (*Hsi-ch'eng-tiao*).

Many Manchu drumsongs have known authors. Among the most accomplished was a Manchu literatus named Lo Sung-ch'uang, who lived during the Ch'ien-lung era in the mid-eighteenth century. About twenty texts attributed to him survive. Han Hsiao-ch'uang, who was active during the Chia-ch'ing era of the late eighteenth century, was another Manchu intellectual, known for adapting scenes from the great Ch'ing dynasty novel *A Dream of Red Towers* into *tzu-ti-shu* format. His corpus is said to have numbered around five hundred texts, of which several dozen survive. According to the modern scholar of late-imperial popular literature Kuan Te-tung, the golden age of Manchu drumsong textual production was from the period of these two authors until the mid-nineteenth century. Presumably, both the written and the oral counterparts achieved their richest and fullest forms in this period. As noted, texts were printed in Manchu, occasionally in a mixture of Manchu and Mandarin, and later in Mandarin, the language of most surviving texts. Hand-copied texts were the norm, but, by the late eighteenth century, demand was great enough that a few published versions appeared, most issued by the Wen-ts'ui T'ang publishing house, the earliest surviving edition dating to 1795. Of the four hundred extant *tzu-ti-shu* texts, only about twenty are in printed form.

An example of a drumsong mixing the Manchu and Han languages, "Katuri jetere juben i bithe" (The Crab Story), dates from the late eighteenth century. It is a humorous story about a newlywed couple who purchase some crabs in the market, yet really do not know what to do with the strange creatures. In the first passage, one of the crabs attacks the Han Chinese wife, while the Manchu husband races around trying to pull it off. In the second section, the wife's elder sister, alerted by a maid, dresses up and provocatively strolls down the street, attracting male stares all along the way. Later, she explains to the couple how to eat crabs and scolds her sister for being a foolish bumpkin. The italic words represent the original Manchu, while the rest is the Chinese.

> The beauty was both clever and good with words.
> In less than half a year *she could speak* it, the *Manchu tongue.*
> She was a merry woman, fond of jokes,
>   and thus became a half-Manchu, half-Han *spirited woman.*
> *Who would know but that during that year,* there was a drought.
> Food and clothing *became very hard to get.*
> *In despair,* the couple had to move into town,
> *Living* not far, just on *the main street.*
> *One day the husband was mocked for doing nothing,* so he left the house,
> And he *brought home* with him *a few pounds of crabs.*
> *He came into the house* and put them in a pot.
> *The spirited wife* quickly asked, "My goodness, *what on earth are they?*"
> *Our brother* answered *with a laugh,* "*As for this,* don't ask me.
> *I'm also puzzled,* as I've never seen such a thing before."
> The couple *wondered between themselves,* guessing what they might be.
> The crabs *jumped and struggled,* then began crawling outside the pot.
> Then the beauty *cried out,* "Where do you think you're going?"
> Rolling up her sleeves, *she hurried* to capture the crabs, but *two claws* tightly
>   grabbed her hand.
> The *spirited* woman screamed, "*Little wretches,* you're pinching me so tight!"
> The pain was *unbearable,* so she pulled back her delicate hand,
>   but the crab *pinched even tighter* with the help of its legs;
> *Our brother,* seeing this, exclaimed, "My goodness," and went over to help.

CONCLUSION

These are but a few of the regional oral, oral-connected, and performing arts that flourished at various times and in various parts of China. Although the genres described here achieved some sort of written form, it is clear from historical records and eyewitness reports that there were many other local performance traditions. Few of them, however, have ever been written down in a manner that authentically conveys their original linguistic features. In those rare cases where a regional performance genre did develop a written tradition, it was invariably heavily Mandarinized and classicized. In this sense, despite the existence of numerous Sinitic languages and topolects throughout the length and breadth of China, there has been little flowering of written regional literatures comparable to, say, that of Hindi, Urdu, Bengali, Gujarati, Oriya, Nepali, Marathi, Tamil, and Telegu in South Asia or the many thriving written vernacular national and regional languages of Europe.

Mark Bender

Chapter 51

ETHNIC MINORITY LITERATURE

In the early 1950s, the new government of the People's Republic of China (PRC) carried out a census to determine the size of the population it was to administer and, following the model of the Soviet Union, to determine the ethnic makeup of the country. Criteria of language-group affinity, local customs, historical area of inhabitation, and sense of ethnic identity were factored into decisions that led to the recognition of what today number fifty-six ethnic nationalities, reduced from a pool of applicants exceeding four hundred. The largest ethnic group, made up of the different peoples speaking various Sinitic languages and dialects, is the Han nationality, now comprising slightly less than 91 percent of the population. The remaining fifty-five groups, called "minority nationalities" (*shao-shu min-tsu*), consist of people of non-Han ethnicity. Members of some nationalities, such as the He-chen, Oroqen, Ewenki, Tatar, and Chi-no, number in the thousands, while those of others, such as the Chuang, Manchu, Mongol, Tibetan, Uyghur, Miao, and Yi, number in the millions. Many of the minority nationalities have numerous subgroups, often with differing names, sometimes making the ethnic categories rather wide nets covering smaller groups of more or less related peoples.

One such group, for instance, is the Yi nationality of southwest China, which researchers claim comprises more than eighty local groups who speak dialects of Yi and follow distinct local customs. In their individual ethnonyms, none of the groups call themselves Yi (see later). The name was proposed by Chinese authorities in the late 1950s, accepted by Yi leaders, and personally approved by Mao Tse-tung. Although the word "Yi" has a sound like that of a written character once used to refer to the various non-Han "savages," the present character was chosen because the elements forming it include the grain and silk radicals, symbols of prosperity. Thus this ostensibly neutral name was stipulated by the Chinese government so that no one subgroup's own ethnonym would take precedence over any of the others. A similar situation exists with regard to the Miao (literally "sprouts"), a word that is actually a rather inadequate Mandarin transcription for an ethnonym found across wide areas of southern China and Southeast Asia (Hmong or Hmu[b]).

Although the government's classifications are sometimes less than exact in ethnological terms, the recognition accorded minority nationalities by the central government has given political legitimacy to many peoples formerly unrecognized as even existing or considered merely as uncivilized (i.e., un-Confucianized) savages. Today, most members of those nationalities live in more than a hundred "autonomous" areas—some as large as provinces, others as small as townships—located along most of China's inland borders. The larger areas include the Inner Mongolian Autonomous Region in northern China, the Kwangsi Chuang Autonomous Region in the south, the Sinkiang Uyghur Autonomous Region in the far northwest, and the Tibetan Autonomous Region in the Tibetan highlands. Yunnan province, located to the southwest on the borders of Myanmar (Burma) and Laos, is home to twenty-eight recognized minority nationalities in autonomous prefectures, counties, and townships.

The written literatures of the minority nationalities (most of which have rich oral traditions), like the regional literatures of the Han Chinese, had little circulation outside their home areas. The best-known literary traditions of these peoples were created by the Tibetans, Mongols, Manchus, Uyghurs, and Koreans (living in northeast China) in their respective written scripts. Among other nationalities, such as the Na-hsi (or Na-khi), Yi, and Chuang, indigenous writing systems (usually syllabaries, but occasionally lexigraphies) or systems employing localized versions of Han Chinese characters, were used primarily by shaman-priests or other specialists. The situation with the Tai is somewhat different. The Tai possess several alphabetic writing systems that are spread, as are the Tai themselves, over southwest China, Burma, Laos, northern Thailand, and northwest India. Two of these scripts overlap into China. Literacy among Tai speakers in Sipsongbanna (Hsi-shuang-pan-na), Yunnan, was estimated at 30 to 50 percent during the nineteenth century and likely was higher among Tais elsewhere. Reading ability among Tais was by no means restricted to professional monks, but extended to most adult males in varying degrees.

Members of many nationalities, or Han individuals who were intimately involved with them, also produced works of poetry, essays, and fiction in Literary Sinitic but, after the seventeenth century, more often in vernacular Mandarin (see chapter 1). Among the best known is Ts'ao Hsüeh-ch'in (c. 1724–1764), who—while not of Manchu descent—grew up in a family that had long and close relationships with the Manchus and was the author of the great eighteenth-century novel, *Hung-lou meng* (A Dream of Red Towers). An ethnic Manchu, Wen K'ang (1798–1872), wrote the popular vernacular novel entitled *Erh-nü ying-hsiung chuan* (Tales of Boy and Girl Heroes). Shen Ts'ung-wen (1902–1988), well known for having written *Pien-ch'eng* (The Bordertown) and other works in the 1930s and 1940s, was a native of the Miao and T'u-chia areas of northwest Hunan. Lao She (pseudonym of Shu Ch'ing-ch'un; 1899–1966), of Manchu heritage, was an internationally known novelist who penned *Lo-t'o Hsiang-tzu* (Camel Hsiang-tzu, or Rickshaw Boy) and *Ku-shu yi-jen* (The Drumsingers) during the same period. Many writers and poets from minority groups have been active since the 1950s, some of them concentrating on ethnic themes, others on broader subject matter. Tashi Dawa, head of the Tibetan Writers Association, and Li T'o, a Daur who is one of China's most respected contemporary literary critics, both write exclusively in Mandarin. Several other examples are given below.

In the wake of the May Fourth movement (see chapter 39) of the 1920s, and increasing dramatically in the 1950s and again in the 1980s, works from the oral traditions of many nationalities have been rendered into printed form. In some cases, written works with very circumscribed audiences (such as texts used by the shaman-priests) have been brought to the attention of a wider public through translation, publication, and research. Together with the literary texts, these volumes, which number in the hundreds, if not thousands, have essentially created a new genre in Chinese literature: ethnic minority literature in translation. This was undertaken as part of a larger state effort to document, categorize, and "develop" minorities. Folklore collection was rarely done directly in minority languages. Instead, in most cases (especially after the early 1950s) only Mandarin translations were given and these were often highly adulterated.

The folkloric texts that appeared between 1949 and the early 1980s were (like Han folklore texts) subject to strict guidelines concerning editing and revision for proper political content. References to "feudal superstitions" (including Buddhism and other religions), interethnic strife and prejudice, criticisms of the government or the Chinese Communist Party, and unflattering images of the minority nationalities and lower classes were routinely altered or expunged. Some texts from the period were less severely altered than others, though some were rewritten almost beyond recognition. During the Cultural Revolution (1966–1976), the literatures of the national minorities were repressed even more severely than those of the various Han peoples, and many precious scholarly works and transcriptions of performances were destroyed. As China began to change direction in the late 1970s, many minority texts began to appear in bookstores again. Several texts published in the 1950s and early 1960s were reissued, along with much unpublished material that had lain dormant in researchers' hands during the years of chaos, often hidden from destruction at great personal risk. In the 1980s and 1990s, editorial demands periodically loosened and many texts that had previously been published in the *nei-pu* (internal circulation) press for privileged eyes only were made public.

This chapter concentrates on the traditional literatures of selected ethnic groups. The preference is for groups that historically have employed writing, sometimes as a major literary form, sometimes as supportive of oral performances. However, texts based on the rich oral traditions of virtually all of the minority groups have appeared in recent years. Fine examples are *Hxak Hmub* (Ancient Songs of the Miao), an antiphonally sung creation epic collected by the linguist Ma Hsüeh-liang and the Miao folklorist Chin Tan, and the many hero (*mergen*) tales of smaller northeastern minorities such as the He-chen, Oroqen, and Daur. In addition, many modern literary works have emerged from these and other ethnic groups, written mostly in Mandarin. Only a few representative examples of these oral tradition collections and modern works will be examined below.

SOUTHWEST CHINA

The numerous ethnic groups living in the southwestern provinces and in autonomous areas of southwest China are part of a complex web of migrations, invasions, and varied cultural interactions. Languages spoken in the area include those in the Tai-Kadai language family, others from the Miao-Yao group, and many from the Tibeto-Burman family. The southwest topography ranges from broken uplands, limestone karst peaks, and the rare flat land along river valleys to mountains in the foothills of the Himalayas. Compact communities of ethnic-minority peoples are scattered widely within this varied landscape. Literatures in these regions were produced by shaman-priests, storytellers and their patrons, Buddhist monks, and officials. Many texts were written in local scripts; others were written in Chinese or in a mixture of conventional and variant Chinese characters.

The local script traditions fostered by the shaman-priests are outstanding. In the past, such ritual specialists employed various script systems to record chants, epics, histories, and other cultural data, including astronomy and herbal cures. Today, only a few such specialists can read the texts, which are sometimes skeletal, and it is often (but not always) the case that only the specialist and his or her disciples can decipher them. Many accounts written by researchers of their attempts to translate these texts into French, English, Chinese, or other languages note that it was necessary to involve the ritual specialists themselves in order to make sense of the writings. To complicate matters, the written script systems often lack standardization, sometimes to the point that a script or corpus of scripts in a particular area can be read only locally.

The Chuang

Numbering over 15 million, the Chuang are China's largest minority nationality and live mostly in the Kwangsi Chuang Autonomous Region and surrounding provinces. The Chuang language belongs to the Tai-Kadai language family. Most Chuang traditionally have been rice farmers. Although the Chuang and Han peoples of Kwangsi have mutually influenced each other over several centuries of contact, certain features of architecture, local customs, and language distinguish the Chuang from the neighboring Han people and the ten other minority nationalities in Kwangsi, which include the Yao, Miao, Tung, and Mulam. The most famous figure of Chuang culture to enter the popular imagination in modern China is Third Sister Liu (Liu San-chieh), a legendary folksinger of the T'ang dynasty (618–907) who was persecuted by local landlords after ridiculing their singers in a song contest. This phenomenon may be related to the widespread Southeast Asian practice of song-dueling, in which singers improvise vigorous put-downs and compete with one another for official patronage. Courtship singing is a related genre that survives among the Tai, Bulang, Miao, and others.

Some ritual specialists (locally a sort of Taoist priest-shaman called *shih-kung*) among the Chuang traditionally used written texts to record the outlines of mythic epics and historical epics. These narratives, sometimes lasting for hours, were performed at huge song festivals (*ko-hsü*) held at various times during the lunar calendar year and at social events such as house raisings and weddings. The texts were usually written in *t'u-su-tzu*—Chinese characters employed to represent Chuang pronunciations without regard for their semantic significance. Several of these texts were translated and edited in the 1950s and again in the early 1980s after the Cultural Revolution. According to the folklorist Ch'en Chu, some Chuang and Han scholars, including Huang Yung-sha and Lan Hung-en, collected a large number of texts in the form of handwritten chapbooks in the 1950s, and then selected several texts to translate.

The major mythic tale on which they worked concerns Pu-po, a mythic giant who fights with the sons of the Thundergod to make life on earth better for humans. In the process of compiling a text for publication, they combined several versions of the story in order to flesh out the plot. The names of several gods and characters were listed at the beginning of the story. The researchers put the presentation of these names in the format of the antiphonal singing once common among rural Chuang people, in which small groups of singers ask and answer questions in song. Certain other alterations were made to increase the artistic power of the narrative while preserving the essential content. The narrative was also enhanced by consulting Chuang ritual specialists on the texts and reviewing oral versions of the story.

Another narrative based on several written texts and oral versions is "Ch'ang li-luan" (Song of Parting). It is performed at song festivals in the Kuei-hsi area of the autonomous region and takes several hours to complete. The narrative, concerning a pair of parted lovers, is based on historical events in Kwangsi between 1499 and 1528, during the Ming dynasty (1368–1644). As a response to upheavals in the land tenure system that began after the arrival of Ti Ch'ing's troops during the Sung dynasty (960–1279), Chuang peasants were often conscripted by local Chinese garrisons to fight warlords intent on regional expansion and to put down uprisings of other minority groups. Conscripts lost status within their communities and the conscripted "bandits" were often parted from their loved ones for years. The narrative is sung in a style known as *liao-ko* (*liao* songs), in which the final sounds in each stanza are "*liao*."

After the founding of the PRC, the Chuang were provided with a romanized script, which has been widely used for newspapers, journals, teaching materials, and literary works.

The Yi

The Yi nationality is a conglomerate of more than eighty subgroups in Yunnan, Szechwan, and Kweichow provinces in southwest China who speak dialects in the Burmese-Moso branch of the Tibeto-Burman language family. Possibly descendants of the majority population of the ancient Nan-chao kingdom, a long-lasting regional rival of the T'ang dynasty and ancient Tibet, the Yi number over 7 million and locally go by ethnonyms such as Nuosu, Nesu, Nasu, Lolop'o, Lip'o, and Gni. Most Yi live in Yunnan province, though the group that has received the most ethnographic attention are the fiercely independent people formerly known as the "Black Lolo" who maintained an isolated kingdom in the Greater Cool Mountains of southwest Szechwan province into the early 1950s. Although the Yi are farmers and herders by tradition, many cities in the Yi autonomous prefectures and counties have allowed local people to take up other occupations in recent years.

One of the many Yi creation stories relates that, during the great flood, the heavenly spirit sent three *pi-mo* (shaman-priests) to save humankind. They came through the waters, each riding a yellow cow, with the sacred writings tied to the animal's horns. When the *pi-mo* finally made it to land, they hung the soaked books on a green tree to dry. Eagles came and perched in the branches, tearing some of the texts, then bits and pieces of the books stuck to the limbs when they were removed. Thus the Yi writings are incomplete, and this is why there are gaps in the story. Therefore, when a *pi-mo* (in some areas) reads the scriptures he will carry a cow horn, have some eagle claws and a special bamboo hat as equipment, and hold a green staff to indicate that the texts (and his knowledge of them) is not complete.

According to historical guesswork, the ritual texts of the Yi (with the exception of some texts in Han Chinese) were written in a unique script that dates to at least the Ming dynasty, if not considerably earlier, to the T'ang. Today the script is often described as a syllabary (previously it was thought to be pictographic) and utilizes thousands of graphs which are quite unlike standard Chinese characters. Unfortunately, because of the lack of standardization among the older symbols, texts from one region or even from an individual family may be unreadable in another locale. Traditionally, each text was learned with the aid of a ritual specialist (*pi-mo*) who handed down the reading conventions to his disciples. More than eight hundred derivations of these symbols were standardized in the creation of a modern Yi script, which was formalized in 1975 and has gained some popularity among the Yi in Szechwan.

Many Yi texts survive, though most are in the hands of research institutes or private individuals. In the late 1950s some texts began to be edited and translated into Chinese. A few of these translations, the result of concerted efforts by regional scholars and students, became well known in China and constitute an important part of the Yi ethnic profile in the public mind.

The most famous of these works is the story of Ashima (A-shih-ma), published under that name in 1954 in local newspapers, then nationally as a book. Originally a folk creation of the Sani people of Lu-nan county in southern Yunnan, the tale has often been taken to represent the literature of all the Yi peoples. Several written and oral versions of the text were consulted during the translation and editing process. The Chinese text was eventually translated into English by Gladys Yang and was for decades the most widely available Yi text in the world. The story concerns a young woman named Ashima, who is kidnapped by an evil landlord. She and her loyal brother, Ahei, are eventually killed, and she turns into stone. At the popular tourist site called Shih-lin (Stone Forest) is a small peak said to be the valiant young heroine.

Less known, but with richer content, are two other works dating from the same period. A Chinese translation, based on an Yi text collected in the Shuang-po area of the Ch'u-hsiung Yi Nationality Autonomous Prefecture and translated in the late 1950s by the *pi-mo* Shih Hsüeh-sheng, is *Ch'a-mu* (Origins). The text details various stages of creation of the local Yi universe, beginning with the creation of heaven and earth, followed by three ages of proto-humans: the age of the one-eyed people, the age of the vertical-eyed people, and the age of the horizontal-eyed people. In this last age are the stories of the great flood, the brother and sister emerging from a floating calabash and marrying to produce the first humans, who, in turn, intermarry among themselves, thus accounting for the origin of the various regional ethnic groups. These latter motifs concerning the flood and the calabash are pervasive in the creation myths of the southern nationalities. Later chapters include stories of the origins of hemp and cotton, silks and satins, the various metals, paper and brushes, books, and the elixir of immortality.

The translation of the text was not easy. It is said that although Shih Hsüeh-sheng was fluent in the local Yi dialect and could read the Yi text, it was necessary to tutor him in Mandarin in order for him to complete the initial translation. This text was based on his textual notes and a word-for-word oral translation with the aid of members of the Ch'u-hsiung folklore investigation team that sponsored the project. This group, founded in 1955 by members of the Kunming Chinese Writers Association and the Kunming Teachers College, was one of many such groups in the late 1950s that carried out folklore fieldwork projects throughout the rural areas of China. The translation was published in the *nei-pu* press and finally published publicly in 1981 by the Yunnan People's Publishing House after numerous revisions by members of the Kunming branch of the Chinese Writers Association.

A second text, based on oral tradition, was the result of folksong collections made in the vicinity of Yao-an and Ta-yao in the Ch'u-hsiung Yi Nationality Autonomous Prefecture around the same time as *Ch'a-mu* was collected. The area is the home of an Yi subgroup calling themselves Lipo. The team of Han and Yi collectors recorded by hand a large corpus of folksongs dealing with the creation of the world and traditional Yi customs. Three old shaman-priests (locally called *to-hsi*) were the main singers. Translation was so difficult that sign language and miming were at times necessary. Members of the Kunming Chinese Writers Association also aided in the editing of this text. The final product, in polished form, was called *Mei-ko*, named after a local folk tune.

Although certain passages were edited or deleted in the course of preparation for publication, many of the customs described in the collection more or less accurately reflect local Yi lifestyles. Individual sections of the work are devoted to such traditional pursuits as silkworm production, hunting with nets, and salt boiling. The artistic quality of the Chinese translation is quite high, care having been taken not to overembellish the lyrics or overtly politicize them, as is the case with some folkloric texts from this period. Many of the mythic motifs in the creation tale in *Mei-ko* are echoed in written texts from other Yi regions, though differing in detail by locale. In the *Mei-ko* version, all the living things of this age of the earth were created from the body parts of a giant tiger (considered the totem of many Yi groups and claimed by some to be the meaning of the Lolo ethnonym). The work has been called the "encyclopedia" of Yi culture and compared to the Finnish *Kalevala*.

As noted, the Yi written texts were read only by the *pi-mo* ritual specialists. On festive occasions, however, the *pi-mo* would perform them publicly, sometimes from memory, sometimes chanted from the books themselves. Training of *pi-mo* took three to five years. A student would perform chores for the teacher during the day and study the texts at night. A common process was for the *pi-mo* to recite passages of the texts that the student would commit to memory. Only after the student had completed his course of study would he be allowed to copy the teacher's texts, which the student had already memorized. Moreover, texts were usually buried or burned with the owner. Nevertheless, in the late 1940s, Ma Hsüeh-liang, a well-known linguist, collected more than two thousand *pi-mo* texts in northern Yunnan. Many hundreds more were collected in the 1950s by provincial and local researchers. However, both *pi-mo* and their texts were classed as undesirable elements during the Cultural Revolution, and many texts were destroyed. Hundreds of texts, however, were hidden by individual *pi-mo* and their families, who sometimes wrapped them in oiled paper or leaves and hid them in caves or buried them in ceramic roof-tiles. One family in Lu-feng county, Yunnan, alone saved more three hundred volumes in this manner.

In the mid-1980s and early 1990s, many epic narratives from various Yi areas appeared in print. Some of the most interesting are those translated by Nieh-nu Pa-hsi of the Hung-ho Cultural Bureau in south-central Yunnan, a region of mixed Yi and Hani culture. Pa-hsi is descended from a line of five generations of *pi-mo* and learned the local Yi script from old tradition bearers hiding deep in the mountains during the Cultural Revolution. One of the most intriguing of the texts is *Nan-chao kung-teng* (The Palace Lamp of the Nan-chao Kingdom). The text is thought to be a product of the early Ming dynasty, though the date of the version Pa-hsi worked with is unclear. The translation tells the story of one of the kings of the ancient Nan-chao kingdom that ruled southwest China and parts of Southeast Asia during the T'ang dynasty but was later supplanted by the Ta-li kingdom, which fell to the Mongols in 1253 C.E.

Aside from these more literary narrative poems, funeral chants of great length and detail survive. These works, sung in a complex series during funerals, are performed to soothe the dead and guide them on their way to the afterworld. Several have been translated into Mandarin, both by local researchers and at the national institutes. Most of these chants have appeared only in the "internal circulation" press, though restrictions against "superstitious" publications have been relaxed in recent years.

A collection of translations from the Yi in western Kweichow province, entitled *Hsi-nan Yi-chih hsüan* (Annals of the Southwest Yi), was translated by the Kweichow Province Nationalities Research Center and the Pi-chieh Area Yi Literature Translation Group and published in 1982. Based on a collection of Yi written works collected between 1664 and 1729 from the Ta-fang county area, the Chinese translation contains selections from dozens of Yi writings, which include creation narratives, ancestral histories of six Yi clans, expositions on geography, astronomy and astrology, and philosophy; narrative chants about the origins of various cultural phenomena such as iron pots, buckwheat, and the twelve types of grain crops; and songs recalling special cows, horses, and dogs. In the course of the translation and editing, local *pi-mo* priests were consulted, as the texts are filled with obscure names of people, customs, and places. A few lines from the "Origin of the Twelve Grains" are typical of the style of the various Yi texts (in this and other collections):

Great Hoof descended from the Heavenly Palace down to a high mountain peak.
He ordered nine monkeys to plow the earth; and thus the grains were scattered.
They grew into crops and people had food to sustain themselves.
Where that official stayed, the wastelands were opened, and the various grains were planted.
A celestial wind sent rain and there were deep pools along the rivers.
Everywhere grew stalks of rice, flowers turned to fruits all about, and the rice grew into husks for harvest.

The Nakhi

Living in northwest Yunnan province, the Nakhi are found in and around the ancient city of Li-chiang, today a tourist site known for its ancient wooden and stone buildings. Their forebears, like other Tibeto-Burman-speaking peoples, may have migrated from the steppes of Central Asia millennia ago. They maintained a separate kingdom until they were conquered by the Mongols in the thirteenth century. During the Ming and Ch'ing dynasties, the central government recognized them as a sort of tributary state within the borders of the realm. The Mu were the leading aristocratic clan, whose descendants still live beneath Jade Dragon Mountain (Yü-lung shan), a snowy peak that dominates the Nakhi landscape. Li-chiang was an important trading center on the way to Tibet and a market for goods of the local farmers, herbalists, and mountaineers.

The Nakhi and their unique pictographs came to world attention in the 1920s and 1930s thanks to the writing of J. F. Rock, an Austrian explorer and botanist who for decades stayed in a villa outside Li-chiang collecting and translating the religious literature of the ritual specialists known as the *tung-pa*. Research on the Nakhi written tradition is still carried out at the Tung-pa Writing Research Institute in Li-chiang.

Followers of shamanistic beliefs derived from the Bon religion of ancient Tibet (which predates the arrival of Buddhism there in the eighth century), the *tung-pa* priests utilized a style of pictographically written texts that seem to have served as memory aids for the shaman-priests and their disciples, who would recite them aloud during ceremonies and performances at various folk events. The characters are cartoon-like symbols written in sequences of pictographs from left to right. Themes in the writings include ritual chants, creation myths, histories of Nakhi clans, and stories of supernatural beings, such as mountain-dwelling dragons.

One of their major creation myths describes the creation of heaven and earth and humans. In the narrative, various early gods are created from the separation of the dark and light elements of the original chaos. One goddess turns into a white chicken, which lays a white egg. From the egg hatch nine males and seven females, while another egg produces cows. These beings are given the task of propping up the heavens and stabilizing the earth. Later, through a series of transformations, the primal white vapors and beautiful sounds become dewdrops, which change to a sea, from which the first humans are formed. However, these early people eventually incur the wrath of a powerful god on high after they violate the incest taboo against brother and sister marriage. A great flood wipes out all but one human, who survives with the aid of other gods and a crude cowskin boat. He falls in love with the daughter of the heavenly god, who violently opposes the match. Eventually, however, through calling on various spirit allies, the young man marries the god's daughter, and they have three children. Each child speaks a different language, and from these three arose the three major ethnic groups in the traditional Nakhi universe: the Tibetans, the Pai, and the Nakhi themselves. The themes of stabilizing heaven and earth, incest between brothers and sisters, the great flood (often involving a calabash as a lifeboat), and the origins of the local peoples and their languages, are common in the creation myths of many ethnic groups in southwest China.

The Pai

The Pai, once known to the neighboring Chinese as the Min-chia ("common people"), live in the area of Erh-hai lake in northern Yunnan, southwest of Li-chiang. The main city, Ta-li, was once the capital of the ancient Nan-chao kingdom, which lasted from the eighth century until it succumbed to the Mongols in 1253. Ta-li, one of the few walled cities remaining in China, is a popular regional tourist spot. Numbering well over a million, many Pai are Mahayana Buddhists yet worship various ancestral village gods known as *pen-chu*. Farming, fishing, and trading are traditional pursuits. The language of the Pai has tentatively been placed by Chinese linguists in the Tibeto-Burman family, though it may be unrelated to any area languages. Their origins are unknown.

Long influenced by Han Chinese culture, the literature of the Pai consists of early texts from stone steles written in an obsolete script once used in the Nan-chao kingdom and a substantial corpus of poetry and prose, dating mostly from the Ming and Ch'ing dynasties, written in Han Chinese. A form of prosimetric narrative called *ta-pen-ch'ü* (big-volume melodies) in Mandarin is sung by storytellers accompanied by a three-stringed banjo (*san-hsien*). Many of the stories are written using specially adapted Chinese characters (as was common among several ethnic groups in southwest China) in chapbooks that are consulted by the storytellers, sometimes during performances. One of the most popular tales in this and other Pai oral narrative and dramatic traditions is the story of the burning of the Sung-hua Palace in the T'ang dynasty, an event recorded in Chinese histories. The story of Liang Shan-po and Chu Ying-t'ai, a well-known romance from the Han tradition, is a popular *ta-pen-ch'ü* theme. Yang Han, born in the late nineteenth century, was among the best-known singers and authors of *ta-pen-ch'ü* in recent times. Despite having no formal schooling, he cooperated with literate helpers to compose many chapbooks for his use in performance and trained a number of his descendants in the art.

The Tai

The Tai homeland is in the Hsi-shuang-pan-na (in Tai, Sipsongbanna) Tai Autonomous Prefecture in southern Yunnan province. The Tai speak a language called Tai Lüe, which is related to Thai. Both Thai and Tai-Lüe are members of the Tai group, which is spread throughout Assam (India), Burma, Laos, Thailand, and southwest China. The Tai are devout Theravada Buddhists. Their writing, in which are recorded Buddhist sutras, local histories, narrative and lyric poems, medical texts, astronomy, and literary criticism, consists of four major local styles, all based at some remove on an ancient Pali script. Many long narrative poems have been published, beginning in the mid-1950s. Among these narratives are "Suwanna and Her Son" (Mandarin title "Su-wen-na ho t'a erh-tzu"), which tells of a common woman impregnated by the Moon Prince who gives birth to a son who later becomes a Tai ruler, and "O-ping yü Tsang-lo" (O-ping and Tsang-lo), a tragic 1,600-line poem relating the tale of young lovers who unsuccessfully flaunt the constraints of an arranged marriage. A translation of a Tai narrative poem entitled "Not a Dog, An Ancient Tai Ballad," appeared in English in 1962. The text, translated by the New Zealander Rewi Alley (one of the few foreigners other than embassy personnel to stay in China after the 1949 revolution), was based on an oral version (presumably with written counterparts) collected by students of the class of 1956 in the Chinese department at Yunnan University. This was part of the postrevolution effort to nurture and collect "folk literature."

The story, selected for its politically illustrative theme, depicts a place called Meaung Balanasi (in folklore, a name both for utopia and for Sipsongbanna), which was beset by an evil tyrant who was killed after coveting all the melons in the area during a famine. After his death, however, the melon vines run rampant, further threatening the populace. Finally, a hero named Sitaga subdues the melon vines. He is asked to stay and rule the kingdom, but many years pass and he is still without an heir. He decides that the young man and woman who can each eat one thousand crabs at a sitting will take the throne on his death, but no one dares take up the gustatory challenge. Finally, a young commoner named Gamesi is summoned to the palace and made queen, causing the king's councilors and six concubines to begin intricate palace intrigues to destroy their new rival. When Gamesi finally gives birth—to a hundred sons and one daughter—they are thrown over a wall and replaced by a puppy covered with the young woman's own blood. Later, the babies are rescued by an old couple and, in the end, the young queen foils the evil courtiers and leaves the palace to live among the common people.

Although the poem was certainly edited for the purposes of the new Chinese government, its stanzaic form and much of its metaphorical content reflect to some degree the style of Tai narrative poetry, which has been strongly influenced thematically and stylistically by Indic traditions. Such texts with clear political messages (in this case, class struggle in feudal Tai society) were commonly published by the Peking Foreign Languages Press until the early 1980s, when less politically profiled texts began to appear in several Chinese presses serving the foreign markets. As is the custom, names from minority languages are usually sinicized when printed in Chinese translations and, unfortunately, that rendering is commonly adopted in translations into other languages instead of the original names.

THE WESTERN AND NORTHERN BORDERLANDS

At various moments in history, the cultures of the western and northern borderlands have been linked to China because of conquest or as tributary states, sometimes to Han Chinese rulers, often to the overlords of other groups. Although Tibetan forays into China declined greatly after they had briefly seized the capital, Ch'ang-an, in the eighth century, only to be expelled with the help of the Uyghurs, the Khitan (likely ancestors of today's Daur nationality), Mongols, and Manchus ruled over all or part China for the majority of the period from the tenth to the early twentieth century. The early years of the Sung and Ming dynasties were the only times in this period under Han Chinese rule. Today, Tibet has been incorporated into the PRC. The Inner Mongolian Autonomous Region forms a large part of the modern border between China and the Republic of Mongolia. The Manchus, after losing China in 1911, are in the process of reviving a sense of ethnicity, countering claims that they were wholly acculturated by the Han. Descendants of the ancient Uyghur kingdom, founded in the seventh century, inhabit the Sinkiang Uyghur Autonomous Region, which encompasses much of old Chinese Turkestan.

The Tibetans

The height of Tibetan power as an aggressive presence in Central Asia was in the seventh and eighth centuries, a period in which kings such as Srong-btsan Sgampo held sway over a region that included parts of China, Nepal, and Central Asia. The largest body of extant early Tibetan literature forms part of the horde of texts found in the Tun-huang caves of what is now northwest China. Dating from the seventh to the ninth centuries, a sizable quantity of texts in Tibetan script, derived from Indian scripts, and texts with both Chinese and Tibetan were found in the early twentieth century. These writings are largely translations of Buddhist texts, but there are also some extremely important social, historical, and geographical documents (see chapter 48).

Nearly all Tibetan writing is religious, and the themes of the early shamanistic Bon religion and the later schools of Buddhism permeate the written and oral genres, including literary epics, poetry, and the few Tibetan works of prose that approach Western notions of "fiction." A huge tradition of religious writings and translations, especially from Indian Buddhist stories and sutras, was amassed by generations of Buddhist monks, who made up the bulk of the literate population in traditional Tibet.

Foremost among the popular literature—based on an oral tradition much stronger than the written one—is the story of King Gesar of Ling, claimed to be the longest epic in history. The story is known all over Tibet (and bordering lands such as Ladakh and Nepal) and to other nationalities in China today including the Mongols, T'u, Yugur, and Nakhi. Apparently created sometime around the eleventh to thirteenth centuries but with roots going back much further, Gesar's story circulated via oral tradition in many versions, parts of which were written down by hand at various times and places in Tibetan, Mongolian, Turkish and, in recent years, also printed in Chinese translation. The entire cycle has never been recorded, though it is estimated that there are more than a hundred discrete sections.

The story centers on the exploits of Gesar of Ling, a legendary warrior chief who lived sometime in the seventh or eighth century, in a part of what is likely the region of Kham in easternmost Tibet. The tale, which exists as a series of narrative songs connected by the theme of Gesar's battles against enemies of the dharma (Buddhist law or doctrine) who are incarnated in several regional kings, shows influence of the early Bon shamanistic beliefs of Tibet in addition to Indian Buddhism. Basic themes of the saga include Gesar's supernatural birth and early life, as well as his acquiring of supernatural weapons, armor, horse, beautiful wife, and tutelary gods. A major event is a horse race in which he establishes his power. Other episodes include tales of the wars with evil kings.

Gesar, as a great warrior chief, is thus seen as the protector of religion, the proper codes of life, and of Tibet itself. Alexandra David-Neel, who spent many years in the Kham region in the 1920s, reports that in some places she witnessed Tibetans reciting passages of the Gesar epic to gain protection when passing through unsafe areas in the mountains and that some epic singers appeared to be in trance while performing, under the muse of Gesar. One singer, who performed in her presence for six weeks, six hours a day, and still covered only a portion of Gesar's battles with the kingdom of Hor, was reputed to be the incarnation of Dikchen Shenpa, King Gesar's chief minister.

The Gesar epic is a treasure trove of Asian folklore, legend, myth, and history, and its study is relevant not merely to Tibet. The complex origins of the epic can be seen from the fact that the hero's name is derived from the Latin word *caesar*.

Among the most influential and best-loved Tibetan poets was Milarepa, literally, "Mila the Cotton-Clad" (1039–1122). According to legend, the young Mila was deprived of his inheritance by evil relatives and was sent to study with various practitioners of spells and charms. It is said that he was soon able to cause hailstorms and other unfortunate events. He soon tired of this, however, and, after searching among many teachers, he finally was apprenticed to Marpa, who was known as the "Translator." Later, after gaining a deep knowledge of the Kargyupa sect of Buddhism, which had been introduced to Tibet by Marpa, Milarepa retreated to the mountains, where, through prolonged meditation, he developed the ability to generate "psychic heat" (Sanskrit, *tapas*) and could withstand great extremes of temperature.

Milarepa is often depicted in sculpture and painting sitting on a leopard skin, one hand cupped to his ear, and wearing a simple cotton garment. His compendium of poems, which number in the thousands, is called the *mGur-Bum* (The Hundred Thousand Songs). Milarepa's poems are in a language simple enough to be understood by all, and his works became popular in both written and oral form throughout Tibet and neighboring regions. The poems describe the beauties of the high mountain glaciers and include conversations with the Dakinis, or sky spirits. Some poems depict his conversations with various demonesses who provide challenges on his path of development.

In 1947, when Tibet sent a trade commission to the United States, one of the gifts was a copy of Milarepa's poems, printed with red edges indicating that it was produced in the Tibetan capital, Lhasa. The text was deposited in an archive at Columbia University and later translated, in part, by Antoinette K. Gordon under the title *The Hundred Thousand Songs: Selections from Milarepa, Poet-Saint of Tibet*.

Another popular poet was the sixth Dalai Lama (spiritual and temporal ruler of the theocratic Tibetan state), Tsangyang Tshomo Gyatso (r. 1683–1706), who in his poetry fancied himself as the "Turquoise Bee," which gives a hint of his libertine tendencies. Born in the early 1660s, he had the unusual fate of following the great fifth Dalai Lama, Ngawang Lobsang Gyatso, whose death was kept secret for fifteen years by an able regent, a ruse that, when discovered, enraged both influential Mongol princes, who were ardent supporters of Tibetan Buddhism, and the Manchu K'ang-hsi emperor (r. 1662–1722) of China, who considered Tibet a subject state. As it was, the young incarnation did not begin formal training as a lama until age twelve, many years later than normal. When he grew to adulthood, his interest in poetry increased along with an interest in what went on in the secular world outside the Potala Palace, the magnificent seat of the Dalai Lamas, built during the reign of the revered "Great Fifth." It is said that he would often sneak out in disguise to frequent the drinking establishments in old Lhasa, finding there pleasures of the flesh, which became important sources of inspiration in his poems. He also found women of the upper classes fascinating. Many of his poems, mostly four-line lyrics in the style of Tibetan folk songs, concern a young man captivated by the intricacies of his relations with women, an awareness of the dharma, and the beauties, freshness, and lessons of life. The following lyric illustrates the use of traditional folksong motifs in describing his attitude toward an ephemeral love affair:

> Enchanted with the marsh,
> The geese want to stay awhile—
> But their minds are already resigned
> To the ice freezing over water.

According to legend, the sixth Dalai Lama's nighttime rovings were halted when a servant followed footprints in the snow leading to the back of the Potala Palace and discovered what he was up to. In the end, the Dalai Lama's indiscretions led to his decision (under pressure from his advisers, of course) to quit the monkhood, though he retained his position as Dalai Lama and his worldly lifestyle. Lozang Khan, a Mongol prince intent on gaining influence over Tibet, allied with the Manchus against a rival Mongol faction and forced the sixth Dalai Lama to surrender after a prolonged artillery attack on his monastic retreat. The great poet and lover died en route to Peking under military escort in 1706.

From the early eighteenth century comes *Gzon nu zla med kyi gtam rgyud* (The Tale of the Incomparable Prince), a novel written by the famous man of letters and politics mDo mkhar Tshe ring dbang rgyal (1697–1763). As was the norm in his day, the author was schooled in Sanskrit poetics and prose conventions. His "novel," the first of its kind in Tibet, was written for the enlightenment and entertainment of the religious and political elite of Tibetan society. It was influenced structurally by the Hindu epic *Rāmāyaṇa* and by stories of the life of Gautama Buddha.

The story concerns the life of Prince Kumāradvitīya, born to the king and queen of the kingdom of the Joyous Grove, who prayed to the gods for a child. The young prince is engaged to Manohari, a princess who is already betrothed to an evil prince. After much intrigue and bloodshed, the young prince wins his bride, but then, in doubt of her chastity, tests her virtue. Meanwhile, at home, his father has been enthralled by a young beauty, who later tests the character of the young prince in an attempted seduction. He is subsequently exiled because of her scheming, and Manohari becomes lost in the forest searching for him. She finds him and his loyal friend in a remote Buddhist hermitage. At the end of his exile, the prince returns home. On the way, he saves the life of his friend, though sacrificing a limb in the process. The prince thus becomes a bodhisattva (savior) and, upon his return to his father's kingdom, spreads the teachings of the Buddha. The work is thus illustrative in many ways of Buddhist virtues and of how to handle the evils and temptations of mundane life.

Another form of written literature, best appreciated in performance, are the Tibetan masked dramas or mystery plays. They are performed during festivals, especially at harvest time, and are adaptations of classic Indian tales or stories of early Tibet, such as the tale of the great empire builder Srong-btsan-sgam-po of the first half of the seventh century.

The Uyghur

Most of the 7 million Uyghur in China live in the Sinkiang Uyghur Autonomous Region in the far northwest. Their language belongs to the Turkic branch of the Altaic family. The height of their power as an empire was in the eighth century, when the Uyghurs controlled a large portion of the northern (steppe) Silk Road and were important to the T'ang dynasty in China as a supplier of horses and sometimes as a military ally. From the ninth through eleventh centuries, although Buddhism was the main religion among the Uyghurs, Nestorian Christianity and the Persian religion Manicheism were concurrently adopted by some; between the twelfth and fifteenth centuries, Islam became the dominant religion in the region through military conquest and political control.

Written literature in Uyghur is extensive, including religious, historical, and literary writings. The earliest writing of the Uyghur empire is found on a few stone steles in the Orkhon Valley (western Mongolia), dating from the eighth and ninth centuries. The inscriptions on these steles detail the reign of the second Uyghur khan, Moyunchur (Mo-yen-ch'o), and touch upon the introduction of the Manichean religion. The inscriptions are engraved in runic Old Turkish, Chinese, and Sogdian written with a form of the Syriac Aramaic script known as Estrangelo. The Uyghurs adopted the Aramaic script and modified it for their own use. Eventually it was taken over from the Uyghurs by the Mongols and from the Mongols by the Manchus. By the late eleventh and twelfth centuries, however, as Islam spread from western Sinkiang eastward, the Arabic script was gradually imposed along with Islam. Although ill suited for conveying Turkic phonology, a reformed version of the Arabic script is currently employed for writing Uyghur in China, but Cyrillic is used to write Uyghur in various Central Asian republics of the former Soviet Union where Uyghurs reside; the Latin alphabet has at times also been used for Uyghur in both areas.

Many histories, sometimes written in a romantic style suggesting legends, survive from as early as the eleventh century, with several texts dating from between the fifteenth and eighteenth centuries. The earliest compendium of poetry is the didactic work of Yusup Khass Hajib, written in 1069. The collection, *Kutadgu Bilig* (The Wisdom That Leads to Regal Glory), consists of 6,500 couplets and is a didactic text concerned with lessons in the correct conduct of rulers.

Since 1949, writings by Uyghur authors have appeared both in Uyghur and in Mandarin. One of the most outstanding figures in the post-1949 era is Abdurrehim Utkur, the author of a series of novels on the history of Sinkiang in the first half of the twentieth century. Written in Uyghur, the novels include the 1985 work *Iz* (Traces of the Explorer) and the two-volume *Oyghangan Zimin* (The Awakened Land), which appeared in 1988 and 1994. These novels, which chronicle the numerous uprisings in Sinkiang before 1949, have gained a sizable readership in the Turkic world outside China but are comparatively little known in China beyond Sinkiang.

There is little doubt that the best-known literature of the Uyghurs among the general Chinese populace are the stories of Äpändi (translated into Mandarin as *A-fan-t'i te ku-shih*). Äpändi (cf. Turkish *efendi* [gentleman], which derives from Greek), literally meaning "Mister," "teacher," or "funny, eccentric person," is actually a comic, low-class theologian shared by many Muslim peoples. He is called Mullah Nasroddin in Persian, Nasreddin Hoca in Turkish, Juḥā in Arabic, and Mushfiqī in Tajik. Sometimes he is presented in the guise of a Sufi dervish or royal adviser, and his character combines shrewdness with silliness. With his clever, down-to-earth, folkish humor, he is adept at deflating mystical blather and absolutist pretensions. A typical Äpändi story is as follows:

> One day Äpändi was walking along the street. On his head he wore a scholar's cap. A man came up to him and said, "Sir, would you please write a letter for me?" Äpändi replied, "Why do you want me to write a letter for you?" To which the man responded, "Since you are wearing a scholar's cap, you certainly can write a letter." Whereupon Äpändi took off his cap and placed it on the man's head, saying to him, "Sir, now you can write your own letter."

The Mongols

The Mongol invasions and rule over China lasted from the twelfth to fourteenth centuries. They began with the formidable Chingghis Khan (Genghis; 1162–1227), founder of the Mongol empire. Under Chinggis Khan's grandson Khubilai (Qubilai; 1215–1294), who ruled from 1260 to 1294 as emperor of the Yüan dynasty (1260–1368), drama, poetry, and the performing arts flourished (see chapters 17–19 and 41). Little, however, remains of the Mongol literary heritage, since most of it was destroyed in purges during the early Ming dynasty (1368–1644) as Chinese rule reasserted itself.

The major Mongol literary work—at least in any written tradition before modern times—is the famous *Manggol'un niuca tobcaan* (Secret History), which details in vivid prose the rise to power of Temüjin, who would later be given the title of Chinggis Khan. The story of his life was commissioned by one of his sons, Ögödei. At a convention of Mongol leaders in 1240, thirteen years after Chinggis Khan's death in 1227, Ögödei commanded that the story of his father's rise to power and the details of his steppe government and military organization be recorded in writing for secret consultation by ensuing generations of Mongol overlords. The resulting text was the *Secret History*. The original text may have been written in a variant of the Old Uyghur script used before the development (on the same model) of written Mongolian. Because few Mongols were literate at the time, it has been suggested that the unknown author may have been a Uyghur working under the guidance of a Mongol overseer, possibly the principal lawgiver of the empire, Prince Shigikutuku. Whatever the case, no such early Mongol version has survived.

Under Khubilai Khan's reign, a new Mongol script was invented. This so-called 'Phags-pa script was based on written Tibetan and could be oriented in vertical lines like Chinese characters (and unlike the horizontal Old Uyghur script), thus enabling its easy use in bilingual documents. A 'Phags-pa version of the *Secret History* may have existed, but the only extant texts are in a system of writing that uses Chinese characters strictly for their phonetic value in transcription. Compiled late in the Yüan dynasty, these texts may have escaped destruction because they appeared to be in Chinese, rather than Mongolian. The Mongolian text was later reconstructed by various Russian and European scholars of the late nineteenth and early twentieth centuries from the Chinese transcription and Mongolian fragments and with the help of early Middle Eastern and European historical sources.

The story, told in colorful and poetic language, relates how Temüjin, grandson of a Mongol chieftain, overcame hardship and rose to prominence. When Temüjin was still young, his father was poisoned, causing the boy's mother and her few followers to become outcasts from their tribe. As Temüjin grew, he learned skillfully to extend his power over the many tribes and peoples of the steppes, gaining followers in acts of daring revenge, until he assumed the mantle of khan. The narrative not only relates the history of the Mongol leader's rise (though with a certain legendary nuance) but also illustrates Mongol values, especially loyalty and the consequences of keeping or breaking oaths and allegiances.

In recent years many traditional epic poems generally similar to the Tibetan epic of Gesar and sharing commonalities with the tale of Chinggis Khan have appeared in Chinese translation. A major theme in these epics is that of a hero who battles and defeats a multiheaded ogre, called a *manggus*, which captures and enslaves humans. Similar heroic epics from the Kazakhs and Kirghiz have also been issued in print, both in their original languages and in Chinese.

The Manchus

The Manchus are primarily descendants of the Jurchen people who ruled areas of northeast China once known as Manchuria. Since antiquity, the region was controlled by various tribes, some related to Siberian peoples, others to those in Central Asia, Mongolia, and Korea. The Manchus arose as an aggressive force in the early seventeenth century, squeezed by the Chinese Ming dynasty to the southwest and the Yi dynasty of Korea to the east. They were first led in their rise to conquest by the chieftain Nurgaci (or Nurhaci), whose father and grandfather were killed on the Liaotung peninsula by Chinese forces. Well versed in Chinese and Mongol culture and history, Nurgaci established a multiethnic military and administrative system known as the Eight Banners. The Manchus conquered the Ming capital in 1644 and over the ensuing centuries expanded the borders of China to their greatest extent in its history. By the time the Manchu dynasty, named the Ch'ing, collapsed in 1911, the Han and Manchu cultures had merged to such an extent in northeast China that only in the most remote regions and in the imperial court were clearly Manchu customs and language still in use. But the cultural influence went both ways: Chinese culture, especially in the north, had been marked in lasting ways by Manchu customs, dress, and language.

The literature of the Manchus was written in Manchu script and in Chinese. The Manchu script derived from written Mongolian, which itself was based on an earlier Uyghur script of the eighth century, which in turn had Semitic roots farther west along the Silk Road (see the section on the Uyghurs above). Many works from the Chinese literary tradition were translated into Manchu until the eighteenth century, when Chinese began to be the most popular written medium even for Manchus, though court documents and some literary works were still written in Manchu. Because of the existence of numerous Manchu translations of Chinese texts by bilingual Manchu scholars, during the nineteenth century it was *de rigeur* for European sinologists to learn Manchu, which is grammatically more explicit than written Chinese (especially in its more literary forms) usually is. Chinese poetry and essay styles were learned by Manchu literati and officials, while popular narrative traditions, such as the Manchu drumsongs (*tzu-ti-shu*; discussed in chapter 50), were written largely in Chinese.

Among the most famous Manchu texts is the story of the Nisan (sometimes written as Ny Dan, Nizan, or Nyudan) Shamaness, a powerful female medium who is ordered by a king to descend to the underworld to retrieve the soul of his recently killed son. This story was recounted by shamans in many versions and known to many peoples of the old northeast, including the Daur, Sibe, and the various Tungusic-speaking peoples such as the Oroqen, He-chen, and Ewenki. The tale of Princess Pari in the Korean shamanic tradition is to some extent a parallel tale, dealing with a filial princess who travels to the underworld in order to supply her aging in-laws with an elixir of immortality.

The Koreans

Early Korean kingdoms, in particular Koguryo (37 B.C.E.–668 C.E.), controlled much of what is now northeast China. Today, however, only a few regions along the Chinese border with North Korea are ethnically Korean. The largest concentration (numbering more than two million), is found in the Yen-pien Korean

Autonomous Prefecture straddling Kirin and Heilungkiang provinces. Groups of Koreans began entering China from the state of Koryo during the Mongol occupation of China in the thirteenth century. Later groups arrived during and after the invasion of the Ming dynasty by the Manchus in the 1600s. Some immigrated to escape harsh conditions in Korea, others came as prisoners of war or slaves, and thousands more came as soldiers in the Manchu banners. Major migrations of refugees escaping poverty or colonial rule by the Japanese occurred in the latter half of the nineteenth century and especially in the first half of the twentieth century.

These sizable movements of Koreans into northeast China during the nineteenth century and earlier brought with them a narrative singing tradition that is quite similar to Peking *ta-ku* (big drum; see chapter 50) and may have influenced the growth of the latter genre.

The literature of the Korean immigrants was essentially that of their forebears in Korea until 1949. After the establishment of the People's Republic of China, the course of literary development and production was similar to that in other areas of China. Poets, novelists, and dramatists appeared who wrote on "revolutionary" themes, and a literary journal, *Yonbyon munyu* (Yen-pien Literary Arts), was started. The Yen-pien branch of the Chinese Writers' Association was established in August 1956. Various committees and projects were formed or undertaken in all areas of the arts, including the collecting of oral literature. This period of growth and activity came to a sudden end in 1966 with the onset of the Cultural Revolution. During those ten years of chaos, Korean minority literature suffered repression and setbacks similar to those in the rest of the country, recovering gradually only in the late 1970s and early 1980s. The process of healing began with the rejuvenation of *Yonbyon munyu* (which changed its name to *Ch'onji* [Heavenly Pond] in 1985) and the birth of several other literary journals.

As was the case in national and local literary circles all over China, Korean poems, novels, and plays recalling the injustices of the Cultural Revolution soon formed a local body of "scar literature" (see Introduction). Later, longer novels began to explore the roots of Korean experience and identity in terms of culture and history. Works appeared in both Chinese and Korean, the latter printed in the Hangul syllabary developed during the reign of the celebrated King Sejong in the fifteenth century.

WRITINGS OF LOCAL SCHOLAR-OFFICIALS

In many ethnic minority areas, some individuals became literate enough in Chinese to pass various levels of the civil service examinations and to compose classical Chinese poetry, essays, and memorials. Among these scholar-officials are members of what are now called the Manchu, Tung, T'u-chia, Miao, Pai,

Nakhi, Yi, Chuang, Pu-yi, Tibetan, Hui, Uyghur, Kazakh, Mongol, Daur, Sibe, and Korean (north and northeast China) minority nationalities.

Such scholars began to emerge among the Tung people of Kweichow, Hunan, and Kwangsi provinces in the late Ming dynasty. Records from various counties in Kweichow indicate that local academies (*shu-yüan*) for the civil service examinations were set up as early as 1225 in the late Sung dynasty (960–1279) and continued in the Ming and Ch'ing dynasties. One such academy was established in Li-p'ing county during the reign of the Chia-ching emperor (1522–1566). Records from the late Ming indicate that several dozen Tung candidates passed various levels of the exams, though few of their literary creations have survived. During the Ch'ing dynasty, the numbers of such officials increased. According to *San-chiang hsien-chih* (Annals of San-chiang County) from a region by that name in northern Kwangsi province, the number of such local scholar-officials of various ranks exceeded three hundred. Poetic works of note were produced by such local scholar-officials as Yao Hsia-tan (1824–1917) of Hunan province, who, after acting as a lower official for many years, returned to his native village to teach any students, regardless of background, who were willing learners. Among them were Yang T'ing-fang of Yung-chiang county, Kweichow, and Yang Chao-min from the T'ian-chu area of southeast Kweichow. All left behind classical-style verse, as did comparable scholar-officials in the other groups mentioned above. One of Yao Hsia-tan's poems (from a pair that include references to Buddhist temples) is "Ch'un hsiao wang Chin-pi shan" (In Spring Light Gazing on Gold-Jade Mountain):

> Morning light through the mulberry branches,
> the Gold-Jade Mountain so clear.
> Snow on the peaks shows spring's not here,
> as mountain clouds arise from the crags.
> In the shade of trees, people crowd,
> from the temple comes a bell sound.
> Even better is the sunset;
> its rays sincere, spread everywhere.

This is only one small example of a largely unexplored legacy of writings in poetry and prose by local ethnic minority scholars.

CONCLUSION

Just as the regional Sinitic (Han) literatures of China are vastly undeveloped and understudied, so too are the literatures of the many non-Sinitic peoples of China in dire need of research, both diachronically and synchronically. Little reliable information is available about the history of the individual traditions, and scholarly treatments of specific works are few and far between. Most desperately lacking are philologically sound investigations and publications of works in their original languages, instead of in approximative Mandarin translations. Also urgently desired are thorough examinations of the cross-cultural borrowings of themes, motifs, and other literary elements and linguistic features to and from the Sinitic and non-Sinitic languages and literatures of China. After these desiderata are achieved, a welcome light will have been shed on the complex and subtle interrelationships among all the various threads of the Chinese tapestry.

Mark Bender

Chapter 52

THE TRANSLATOR'S TURN: THE BIRTH OF MODERN CHINESE LANGUAGE AND FICTION

The late nineteenth and early twentieth centuries ushered in an era of linguistic and literary revolution in China that exerted a profound influence on the social, cultural, and political life of the Chinese public. The significance of this revolution may well suggest a close parallel to an earlier chapter of Chinese history, when Buddhism first arrived on Chinese soil during the Han dynasty (206 B.C.E.–220 C.E.) and engaged the native scholars in centuries of systematic translating and study of the sacred texts written in Sanskrit. It also invites comparison with the Jesuit missionary activities in the Ming (1368–1644) and early Ch'ing (1644–1911) dynasties that had exposed the imperial courts and the Chinese literati to rudimentary knowledge of the West and of modern science. Despite these obvious parallels, however, there are significant differences between China's earlier contacts with foreign religions and the more recent encounter with the modern West.

TRANSLATION AND CULTURAL ENCOUNTER

When late Ch'ing and modern Chinese intellectuals undertook the work of translation and desired to learn from the West, they did so within the global context of imperialism and nation-building; as a result, their interest in Western knowledge was almost exclusively secular and thus fundamentally different from that of the Buddhist monks and scholars of an earlier time. More important, the modern-era East-West encounters produced structural relationships among countries and societies unlike any that could have emerged from the previous contacts, including, perhaps, the Jesuits' attempt to influence the imperial court and members of the literati starting in the second half of the sixteenth century. These new global structural relationships, which, to some extent, have continued to shape the world, are the historical products of centuries of European colonial exploitation, capital accumulation, and imperialist expansion. They constitute the modern world system and have helped bring about new national identities and new historical sensibilities in many parts of the world.

With regard to late Ch'ing China, the Opium War (1839–1842), the Sino-Japanese War (1894–1895), and the humiliating experience of semicolonialism made the nation's intellectual elite painfully aware of the importance of nation building and of the need to borrow science, technology, and a new vocabulary from the West. The 1911 revolution and the subsequent collapse of the Manchu empire hastened a modernizing process that had already gained some ground in the Manchu court and among the Chinese intellectual elite, leading to the first successful legitimation of *ko-ming* (revolution) in twentieth-century China. Indeed, it is worth noting that the two graphs *ko* and *ming* did not have the meaning "revolution" until the Japanese assigned it to them in modern times. Instead, the traditional meaning of *ko-ming* was "remove the [heavenly] mandate," a concept approved by the Confucian thinker Mencius (371–289 B.C.E.).

The birth of *pai-hua wen* (modern written vernacular; see chapters 1, 38, and 39) was a major event in the Chinese revolution and in China's search for a new national identity. The term should not, however, be confused with an already existing written vernacular as used, for example, in the popular literature of the previous dynasties that had produced classics like *Shui-hu chuan* (Water Margin), *Hsi-yu chi* (Journey to the West), and *Hung-lou meng* (A Dream of Red Towers, or The Story of the Stone). Nor does *pai-hua wen* exactly bear out the familiar image of the speech of ordinary citizens that Hu Shih (1891–1962) and other adherents of the New Culture movement (Hsin wen-hua yün-tung; the predecessor of the May Fourth movement [Wu-ssu yün-tung], which broke out in 1919; see chapters 32, 38, 39, and 42) had envisioned when they advocated language reform in the early Republican era after 1911. This new medium of writing is, in fact, an extraordinary hybrid form deriving from at least four main sources: (1) *wen-yen* (Classical Chinese); (2) premodern written vernacular Chinese (based on the northern dialects of the past); (3) contemporary colloquial speech (Mandarin or northern dialects); and (4) European and Japanese loanwords, neologisms, and syntactical structures. On that basis, modern *pai-hua wen* can be taken to refer to a rich variety of linguistic and stylistic innovations in modern Chinese and to forms of writing that attempt to embody modern, and largely urban, experience in a hybridized language of native and foreign sources.

A notable feature of this new written vernacular is the presence of an unprecedented number of neologisms and loanwords of Japanese and European origin. Although these imported elements have been completely naturalized in the language to the extent that a native speaker may not recognize them as such, modern Chinese stylistics depends precisely on the degree, the manner, and the skill with which the diverse elements, native and foreign, are brought together and put to use. Among the best-known literary works written in this new medium, for example, one may identify a broad spectrum of stylistic experiments from Lu Hsün's (1881–1936) more or less succinct prose style interlaced with Classical Chinese phraseology to Ting Ling's (1904–1986) highly Europeanized syntax, to Eileen Chang's (Chang Ai-ling; 1920–1996) ingenious reinvention of the premodern vernacular in the spirit of metropolitan colloquialism. To give a few more examples, Shen Ts'ung-wen (1902–1988) and his student Wang Tseng-ch'i (1920–1997) are deservedly called master stylists of modern Chinese. Paradoxically, while Shen and Wang did not shun foreign loanwords or imported syntactical structures, they managed to convey in modern Chinese prose a remarkable sense of classical esthetic sensibilities. In contrast, the works by Yü Ta-fu (1896–1945), Pa Chin (pseudonym of Li Fei-kan; b. 1904), Mao Tun (pseudonym of Shen Yen-ping; 1896–1981), and many others represent the opposite pole of the Chinese-Japanese-European hybrids. They are often characterized by the eminent translatability of their Chinese prose and literary sensibility; and, in most cases, these May Fourth writers were themselves able translators of foreign literature.

The story of how the modern written vernacular became an important part of the social agenda in the Chinese revolution cannot be told in isolation from the larger context of modern translations or, more to the point, the history of what happened when the Chinese languages first encountered modern European languages. How did the speakers of such different languages manage to understand one another when bilingual dictionaries were not yet readily available? A century or more later, people could afford to assume a certain level of translatability between Chinese, modern Japanese, and modern European languages, but such was not the case in the middle of the nineteenth century. For example, we now know that the term *ch'üan-li* is a Chinese equivalent of "rights." But when the missionary W. A. P. Martin (1827–1916) first started to render Henry Wheaton's *Elements of International Law* into Chinese as *Wan-kuo kung-fa*, in 1864, he and his fellow Chinese translators had great difficulty in trying to come up with suitable Chinese equivalents for "rights" and other terms. Unable to find an appropriate existing term to match the meaning of the English word, they decided to adopt a makeshift compound, *ch'üan-li*, out of the characters *ch'üan* (authority, power) and *li* (interest, benefit), glossing its meaning as "rights," as was explained in an apologetic note to their translation of another book of international law. The remarkable thing is that thousands of neologisms entered Chinese either this way or via Japanese *kanji* (Chinese character) loanwords from the middle of the nineteenth century through the turn of the twentieth century. Each of these words has a fascinating story to tell and deserves a full chapter or even a monograph.

The desire in the nineteenth century to overcome the enormous barriers between languages that had had very little previous contact gave rise to a growing number of makeshift compounds and syntactical structures in Chinese—many of which became widespread through newspapers and the popular press and, eventually, found their way into the modern written vernacular. However, the significance of these initial attempts toward a level of expedient translatability or equivalence between Chinese and modern European languages goes beyond the mere introduction of loanwords and neologisms. It represents an epistemic leap, one of the few in human history, that has profoundly changed people's understanding of their own civilizations and those of the others as they tried to learn to speak in one another's languages and to transform one language on the model of another. This phenomenon provides us with a new way of asking an old question: how did these major world civilizations, Chinese and European, begin to talk to each other in public discourse for the first time? Once such talk began, it could not be stopped and has not stopped. This is what is meant by an epistemic leap. The leap takes people's earlier curiosity about exotic cultures—wherein one would describe an unfamiliar land to one's home audience—to the next stage of mutual discovery and mutual interpretation, the result being that one culture becomes seriously involved in the affairs of another. Indeed, in the sixteenth and seventeenth centuries, the Jesuits did try to have a similar effect on the imperial court and on a handful of the intellectual elite with whom they came into contact, but full-fledged translations of Western culture and its texts were not made in China until the nineteenth century.

THE MISSIONARY ENTERPRISE

The initial moment of such involvement, if one must pinpoint an exact date, can be traced to Robert Morrison's (1782–1834) arrival in China in 1807. Morrison, assigned by the London Missionary Society to work in China, was the first Protestant missionary to enter China. After his arrival and especially after the Opium Wars, which opened several treaty ports and inland areas to foreign trade and missionary work, a large number of Protestant missionaries arrived and began the systematic work of biblical translation and publishing in the nineteenth century. Liang Ah-fa, a Christian convert and Morrison's assistant, wrote and published *Ch'üan-shih liang-yen* (Good Words to Exhort the World), a popular Chinese rendering of the New Testament based on Morrison's Classical Chinese edition of the Bible. Through a series of coincidences, albeit with major historical consequences, Liang's book became the sacred text for Hung Hsiu-ch'üan, the self-proclaimed brother of Jesus who led the famous Taiping Rebellion (1851–1864) in the name of God. By the mid-nineteenth century, numerous Chinese editions of the Bible appeared in print in what the missionaries themselves called high *wen-li* (Classical Chinese) and easy *wen-li*, a popularized (easier) variant of Classical Chinese. At the same time, Western missionaries also brought out a large number of biblical translations in local Chinese languages, some printed in Chinese characters and others in romanized representations of the Cantonese or Fukienese topolects.

The aspect of the missionary work to which the Chinese intellectual elite responded with enthusiasm was not the religious spirit that had inspired the Taiping Rebellion but secular translations that covered a broad range of subjects, including world geography, medicine, popular science and technology, economics, politics, and international law. W. A. P. Martin, the missionary translator mentioned above, translated and published the first Western book on international law, *Wan-kuo kung-fa* (literally, Public Law of Ten Thousand Countries), in 1864 under the sponsorship of Prince Kung and his Tsungli Yamen (Foreign Office). This book, after being adopted as the official diplomatic manual, represented a crucial turning point in China's diplomatic relationship with the outside world. In 1865, barely a year after the book's publication, the Japanese brought out a *kambun* (Japanese-style Classical Chinese) edition of Martin's *Wan-kuo kung-fa* and put it to unexpected use in the Korean affair (the Tonghak Rebellion) and during the ensuing Sino-Japanese War of 1894–1895. One of Martin's Chinese assistants who helped him with several translation projects was Wang Feng-tsao, who became the first Chinese ambassador to Japan and was directly involved in negotiations with Japan during the Sino-Japanese War.

Although missionary translators had a hidden religious agenda when they engaged in secular translation projects and publications, their religious message often went unheeded as educated Chinese readers sought Western knowledge in the areas of science, technology, and other secular subjects. W. A. P. Martin, John Fryer (1839–1928), and Young John Allen (1836–1907) were among the best-known missionary translators of the time who worked with written Chinese. They each initiated numerous translation projects to popularize and legitimize Western knowledge and the notion of progress. Fryer, who was a senior translator for the Kiangnan Arsenal in Shanghai and later became the first chair professor in the Department of Oriental Languages at the University of California (Berkeley), was responsible for translating hundreds of Western books into Chinese, including creating the Chinese character equivalents of Western terms for the chemical elements and many other neologisms of science and technology that have survived in the modern written vernacular to this day. The Indiana-born Young John Allen was the founder of *Chiao-hui hsin-pao* (Church News) and its reincarnation in *Wan-kuo kung-pao* (World News), which was read avidly by such prominent late Ch'ing reformers as K'ang Yu-wei (1858–1927) and Liang Ch'i-ch'ao (1874–1930).

As early as the mid-nineteenth century, missionaries had begun experimenting with the written vernacular and formed several vernacular societies devoted to publishing religious periodicals in *pai-hua wen*. Soon, newspapers responded by seeking to reach a wider audience through the use of this written medium. For example, when *Shen pao* (Shanghai News) began publication in 1872, the editors announced that they would serve not only the educated but also "peasants, laborers, businessmen, and merchants." In 1876 *Shen pao* created a supplement for women and working men called *Min pao* (People's News), which was probably the first newspaper adopting a full-fledged written vernacular. But it must be pointed out that both Classical Chinese and the written vernacular underwent considerable changes in the course of the nineteenth century and absorbed many neologisms and loanwords into their vocabularies.

SINO-JAPANESE-EUROPEAN HYBRIDS

The Sino-Japanese War and the Hundred Days' Reform (1898, see below) began to change the situation. To the surprise of many, including Europeans on the scene, the Chinese navy was defeated by the Japanese. This turn of events shook the self-confidence of the Chinese not only because China had heretofore regarded Japan as its inferior cultural disciple but, more important, because the Chinese government had tried to modernize its naval forces by purchasing expensive warships from the West and training its military staff with advanced Western knowledge. The defeat led to a great deal of soul-searching and self-reflection. Reform-minded intellectuals began to see China's own political and social system as the main cause of the nation's feeble state. The success story of the Meiji Restoration of 1868 and subsequent far-reaching reform in Japan inspired these intellectual elite to emulate the Japanese and led them to champion the famous Hundred Days' Reform, spearheaded by K'ang Yu-wei, Liang Ch'i-ch'ao, T'an Ssu-t'ung (1865–1898), and Yen Fu (1853–1921). After the sudden crackdown on the reforms by the Empress Dowager Tzu-hsi (1835–1908), some of the intellectuals fled to Japan and started radical publications there. Liang Ch'i-ch'ao closely followed the public discourse that was current among Japanese intellectuals and urged immediate translation of Japanese works.

In the late nineteenth century, the Japanese were still using many *kanji* (Chinese-character) words in their own writing and in the translations of Western works, which made it relatively easy for the Chinese to get the gist of a text's content without actual knowledge of Japanese. It was also a time when the first generation of Chinese students (beginning in 1896) went to Japan to study Western science, technology, medicine, economy, and political science. (In the 1906–1907 academic year, the estimated number of Chinese students in Japan exceeded ten thousand.) The encounter with Japanese translations of Western texts quickly familiarized these students with the Japanese *kanji* rendering of European texts and, as they themselves started preparing and reproducing these works for publication in *Yi-shu hui-pien* (Collected Translations), they introduced a whole new vocabulary to the spoken and written Chinese languages.

Thus the turn of the century saw a major shift in the production of translated Western knowledge. The shift was from the direct participation of Western missionaries to secondhand publication of Japanese renderings of Western texts. Of course, the missionaries in China continued their work as mediators of cultures, but that role began to yield to a significant number and wide range of secondhand translations and publications that began to flood in from publishing houses big and small. Liang Ch'i-ch'ao, while in exile in Japan, encouraged the printing of secondhand Chinese translations of Western books and saw it as an expedient way of mastering knowledge from and about the West. The journal *Collected Translations*, which was published in Japan by Chinese students at the turn of the century, played a seminal role in making available to Chinese readers a large body of works by influential German, French, English, American, and Japanese political thinkers and economists, all (except those originally written in Japanese) taken secondhand from Japanese translations.

These secondhand translations proved a convenient way of appropriating and disseminating Western knowledge from a third party and quickly outpaced missionary translations from the originals. They also introduced a sizable vocabulary in modern Chinese that might be termed Sino-Japanese-European hybrids, which started to compete with the terms coined earlier by missionary translators and grew in popularity. For example, *wan-kuo* (literally, ten thousand [i.e., a myriad] countries), an earlier Chinese translation of "international," became *kuo-chi* from the Japanese *kokusai; fu-kuo ts'e* (literally, stratagem for enriching the country), an earlier rendering of the word "economy," came to be replaced by *ching-chi*, derived from the Japanese compound *keizai*. This Sino-Japanese-European hybrid ultimately prevailed in the press and became the standard term in the language of late Ch'ing journalism.

Sino-Japanese-European hybrids suggest a highly mediated process of translation involving at least three languages at a time: Chinese, Japanese, and one of the European languages. It was a phenomenon unique to East Asian societies, where, in the past, Classical Chinese had been the universal written medium used by the Chinese, Japanese, Koreans, Vietnamese, and others alike (playing a role similar to that of Latin in Europe before the Reformation). In the nineteenth century, when the Japanese took Chinese characters and coined *kanji* compounds to translate European works, they reinvented the Chinese words in terms of their presumed European equivalents and thus converted them into Sino-Japanese-European hybrids. The words that resulted from this process were no longer purely Chinese words by etymology but hybridizations of Chinese, Japanese, and European words. These hybrids, in turn, were reimported by the Chinese as part of their own vocabulary. Such hybrids that have survived in today's journalism and ordinary speech or writing (excluding the professional vocabulary of science, technology, and medicine) are estimated to total as many as 1,800.

Lexical borrowing or loan translation is unique neither to China nor to modern times. The Japanese had long borrowed from Classical Chinese before the two-way and reverse process began at the turn of the twentieth century. Calques, semantic borrowings, and other loans from Central Asian, Arabic, and North Asian sources found their way into Chinese as early as the Han dynasty (206 B.C.E.–220 C.E.). As mentioned above, the translation of the Buddhist canon introduced a fairly large number of neologisms in classical and vernacular Chinese. Even though the influx of neologisms was not unprecedented, the degree of penetration and the impact of the encounter with European languages and modern Japanese were, nonetheless, unique to modern Chinese. In fact, the Sino-Japanese-European hybrids altered Chinese languages so thoroughly that expelling the "foreign" elements would have been tantamount to undermining their intelligibility.

YEN FU AND LIN SHU

The decline of Classical Chinese as a universal prose language seemed inevitable in retrospect. However, the finest translators of the late Ch'ing period wrote and excelled in this language. Yen Fu and Lin Shu (1852–1924), both from Fukien province, were deemed masters of Classical Chinese prose. Their elegant translations set a higher standard than was expected of missionary works for the appreciation of Western learning and were instrumental in cultivating a level of respect for Western philosophical and literary achievements among educated Chinese.

Yen Fu came from a scholar-gentry family in the village of Yang-ch'i, Hou-kuan prefecture, Fukien. His formal training in the English language and Western science began in 1866 at the naval school of the Foochow Shipyard. In 1877–1879, he was sent to England to study naval sciences, first at Portsmouth and then at Greenwich. The burning question Yen Fu had brought with him to England was "What is the secret of Western wealth and power?" Since Great Britain was the supreme exemplar of wealth and power at that time, Yen Fu was particularly eager to find out about British political, economic, and social institutions and contemporary British thought. Upon his return to China in 1879, Yen Fu became a teacher at the Foochow Arsenal School and was soon summoned by the renowned statesman and diplomat Li Hung-chang (1823–1901) to be a dean at the newly established Pei-yang Naval Academy in Tientsin. The Sino-Japanese War, which broke out in 1894, marked a turning point in Yen Fu's career. It was then that he began the historic enterprise of translating the works of eighteenth- and nineteenth-century European thinkers.

T'ien-yen lun (On Evolution) was Yen Fu's translation of Huxley's Romanes Lectures on "Evolution and Ethics" (1893). Completed in 1896 and published in 1898, the translation was essentially a rewriting of the original text interlaced with Yen Fu's commentaries and footnotes. Its immediate success established Yen Fu's reputation as the foremost translator and stylist of the time. In the same year, Yen Fu also published the first volume of *Yüan-fu* (On Wealth), a translation of Adam Smith's classic text *An Inquiry into the Nature and Causes of the Wealth of Nations*. A full translation of Smith's classic text was not completed until 1900. Other major Western works Yen Fu translated between 1898 and 1909 were John Stuart Mill's *On Liberty* (as *Ch'ün-chi ch'üan-chieh lun*) and A *System of Logic* (as *Mu-le ming-hsüeh*), Herbert Spencer's *Study of Sociology* under the Chinese title *Ch'ün-hsüeh yi-yen*, Montesquieu's *Spirit of the Laws* (as *Fa-yi*), Edward Jenks's *History of Politics* (as *She-hui t'ung-ch'üan*), and William S. Jevons's *Primer of Logic* (as *Ming-hsüeh ch'ien-shuo*).

Yen Fu's influence as a translator and theorist of translation was enormous and long-lasting. To the Chinese literati who were undergoing a series of existential crises after their nation had been defeated by the Western powers and Japan, the publication of his translations could not have come at a better time. The defeat in the Sino-Japanese War was a particularly harrowing experience because the Chinese government was forced to sign treaties ceding to Japan the Liaotung peninsula, Formosa (Taiwan), and the Pescadores, and to pay an indemnity of two hundred million taels of silver (one tael = 1 1/3 ounces or 37 grams). There was a pervasive sense of the imminent extinction of the Chinese as a race and a civilization. Yen Fu's interpretation of evolutionary philosophy and social Darwinism seemed to provide an answer to the unexpected changes that had taken place in China and the world and to the question of why and how China had fallen into such a sorry state. Nationalists and social reformers such as Liang Ch'i-ch'ao, Ts'ai Yüan-p'ei (1868–1940), Lu Hsün, Hu Shih, and Mao Tse-tung (1893–1976) were avid readers of Yen Fu's translations and were all persuaded at one time or another by his argument of "survival of the fittest." Although Lu Hsün and the others were to criticize Yen Fu for his "conservative" politics in the Republican era, almost all of them grew up reading his iconoclastic works.

In undertaking those translations, Yen Fu was profoundly concerned with the secrets of Western military, economic, and political power; but, unlike many of his predecessors and contemporaries with similar concerns, he was also profoundly interested in what Western intellectuals had to say about these matters. The significance of Yen Fu's work in the context of modern Chinese intellectual history and world history is that he was arguably the first member of the Chinese literati who studied modern Western sociopolitical thought so seriously and thoroughly.

The far-reaching significance of Yen Fu's intellectual enterprise in the areas of philosophical thinking and social reform was paralleled only by his contemporary and friend Lin Shu's spectacular success as a translator of foreign literature. Unlike Yen Fu, however, Lin Shu had no knowledge of foreign languages and worked exclusively in what might be called a "reverse missionary translation mode," that is, he worked in close collaboration with language informants. Already before Lin Shu had begun his translation enterprise, Western missionaries often served as language informants themselves and relied on the natives to write out or polish their Chinese renderings. Although the "Chinese assistants" were occasionally acknowledged, the missionaries often claimed credit for being the sole translator. Lin Shu copied but reversed this relationship between the translator and his language informant. Typically, Lin Shu's informant would give him an oral rendering of a novel while he recorded and wrote out the story in elegant *ku-wen* (ancient prose). Alexandre Dumas fils' *La Dame aux camélias* (known in English as *Camille*) under the Chinese title *Pa-li ch'a-hua nü yi-shih* (1899) was his first and most popular translation, which he did in collaboration with a friend and French-language informant named Wang Tzu-jen. The success of this novel launched Lin Shu's extremely productive career of literary translations. Between 1894 and 1924, he translated 181 foreign literary works (including eighteen unpublished titles) from eleven different countries and was the first Chinese translator of Balzac and Charles Dickens.

Lin Shu's and his language informants' choice of subject matter favored novels that had powerful emotional and moral appeal. Often, the translator himself was moved to tears by the story of human suffering and injustice in the works he was translating. A famous anecdote recounts that, while Lin Shu and Wang Tzu-jen were working on *La Dame aux camélias*, they wept profusely over the protagonist Marguerite Gautier's misfortune. The sounds of their sorrow were reportedly heard even outside the house. Lin Shu's world of sentiment (*ch'ing*), however, was never just a sentimental world, but was always intimately linked to Confucian *li* (propriety). In this spirit, Lin Shu translated five Dickens novels (*The Old Curiosity Shop*, *David Copperfield*, *Oliver Twist*, *Nicholas Nickleby*, and *Dombey and Son*) and works of eighteen other British writers, including bestselling authors such as H[enry] Rider Haggard (Lin rendered twenty-five of Haggard's novels into Chinese). His sentimental-moralistic rendering of Dickens and other authors raises important questions about the place of moral sentiment in the original works.

Next to sentimental and moralistic novels, detective fiction and adventure novels also comprise a significant portion of Lin Shu's works. His renderings of *Robinson Crusoe*, *Further Adventures of Robinson Crusoe*, and seven novels by Arthur Conan Doyle (author of the Sherlock Holmes series) aroused a new interest in adventure stories and detective fiction. Although these works were hugely entertaining and helped raise the status of the popular genres, Lin Shu seemed to approach them with far more seriousness than granted by his readers: he finds a common predatory motive underlying all Western adventure narratives, from individual acts of robbery to pillaging on the larger scale of countries and continents. The adventure novel, in his view, demonstrated the imperialist nature of the Western nations, beginning with early spying and exploration to Columbus's conquest of America and the more recent aggressive moves toward China. He warned his readers: "We should know that, since the white man could annex America, he can also swallow up China and Asia." In his preface to a translation of Haggard's stories dedicated to Liang Ch'i-ch'ao, Lin Shu observed that these adventure tales encouraged the white man's death-defying spirit of exploration in search of advantages to be extracted from "barbarian regions." Lin Shu went on to show how China had disregarded its own interests and yielded them to foreigners and how it invited the foreign guests to humiliate the hosts and to subject a multitude of 400 million people to the mercy of a few white men.

Lin Shu lived in a time of foreign encroachments and domestic unrest. Foreigners were in charge of China's own Maritime Customs, and foreign steamships roamed the inner waters of China. At the age of thirty-two, Lin Shu witnessed the Sino-French War (1884) in the nearby seas and the destruction of the Chinese naval forces and shipyards by French warships at Foochow. He was angered by the inept Chinese military officers and boldly submitted a letter of protest to Tso Tsung-t'ang (1812–1885), the outstanding statesman and military commander who was responsible for operations against the French and for building the Foochow dockyards. When he was sitting for his last *chin-shih* degree examination in Peking in 1895, he sent a memorial to the Ch'ing court protesting its cession of Taiwan and the Liaotung peninsula to Japan. Like Yen Fu, Lin Shu turned toward translation after the Sino-Japanese War in an attempt to understand and improve China's condition. He would not oppose Yen Fu's promotion of China's national wealth and state power, but neither would he accept the latter's rationalization of how the West became wealthy and powerful. His moral vision led to a profound suspicion of evolutionism and Social Darwinism. For instance, Lin Shu saw white racism as the cause of human suffering in many parts of the world. In a preface to his much acclaimed rendering of Harriet Beecher Stowe's *Uncle Tom's Cabin* (as *Hei-nu yü-t'ien lu*; 1901), Lin Shu drew a parallel between the black slaves and the Chinese laborers in America who had been victimized by the Chinese Exclusion Act and warned that what had happened to the people of Africa would happen to the people of Asia if they did not learn the lesson and resist. In Lin Shu's nationalism, there is a persistent thread of sympathy for the weak and moral repugnance for the powerful.

By an ironic turn of events, Lin Shu's fear of China's being conquered by the West became a different kind of reality when Classical Chinese—the very language that he used in translating Western literature and for which his works won many an admirer—came under attack by language reformers within China as they promoted the vernacular as a more progressive written medium and even called for the use of the roman alphabet to render Chinese on the model of European languages. In fact, before the language reformers came on the scene, late Ch'ing intellectuals had already tried using the written vernacular in journalism and education. For example, Lin Shu himself was responsible for creating a vernacular-language journal even though he preferred to use Classical Chinese in literary writing. Nevertheless, there was a growing need for a more flexible language that would be useful for communication, written and oral, in both literary and nonliterary fields. This led to the formulation of the modern concept of *kuo-yü* (national language) by the Central Congress of Pedagogues, held in Peking a few months before the 1911 Revolution broke out.

During the dramatic unfolding of the events in the New Culture movement and the May Fourth movement (1919), Yen Fu and Lin Shu were relegated to the ranks of the "conservative" by a new and radical generation of intellectuals clustered around the journal *Hsin ch'ing-nien* (New Youth) at Peking University. Fueled by nationalism and internationalism, May Fourth intellectuals, led by Hu Shih, Ch'en Tu-hsiu (1879–1942), and Lu Hsün, vehemently rejected Classical Chinese and searched for new intellectual resources to revitalize their culture and raise its international standing. Once again, they turned to foreign literature, as Lin Shu had done before them, and started a new wave of translating English, French, German, Russian, Japanese, and other foreign works. In so doing, they developed a "Europeanized" written vernacular (*pai-hua wen*), which they then applied to their own creative writing (*hsin wen-hsüeh*). In that sense, the modern written vernacular owes as much to translations from Western literature as to modern Chinese literature both in its origins and in its subsequent evolvement.

Lydia H. Liu

Chapter 53

THE RECEPTION OF CHINESE LITERATURE IN KOREA

Literary Chinese was the primary model for literature on the Korean peninsula. It remained the dominant paradigm for writing until the twentieth century because a viable indigenous script for representing the Korean language, *hangŭl,* did not emerge until the fifteenth century and did not find acceptance as a medium for intellectual discourse until the late nineteenth century. Little survives of the literature produced in the Three Kingdoms—Kuguro or Koguryŏ (37 B.C.E.–668 C.E.), Paekche (18 B.C.E.–660 C.E.), and Silla (57 B.C.E.–935 C.E.)—that vied for military and cultural control of the Korean peninsula in the fourth through seventh centuries C.E.. There are records indicating that, as early as 372, Koguryŏ established a national Confucian academy, so no doubt there was considerable literary production in all three kingdoms, granted little has survived the intervening wars and other crises.

The earliest extant poems in Chinese from Korea date to the Koguryŏ period and include such works as "Hwangcho ga" (Song of the Yellow Bird) attributed to King Ryuri (d. 18), written in four lines with four characters per line; this poem most likely is a later composition. There also exist scattered poems such as "Yŏng gosŏk" (Tribute to a Solitary Stone) (written in eight lines, five characters per line), attributed to Chŏngbŏpsa in unregulated verse drawing upon pre-T'ang Chinese poetic models. Although Koguryŏ had more interaction with China than did Silla in the south, and most likely produced a substantial corpus of literature, little remains of it.

In 621 Silla established direct ties with China, then under the rule of the T'ang dynasty (618–907). After the T'ang emperor T'ai-tsung (r. 626–649) increased the size of the National Academy (T'ai-hsüeh) in 640, Silla encouraged its scholars to study in China, allowing students from Paekche, Silla, and Koguryŏ to work alongside the brightest Chinese literati. In 650, a poem drafted by Queen Chindŏk of Silla in five-character *ku-shih* (ancient-style poetry) form was sent to China along with assorted fabrics. Thereafter a significant number of Korean intellectuals studied in T'ang China, and many passed the civil service examination there. There is even one poem written in Chinese, "Fen-yüan shih" (A Poem of Indignation), by the Silla scholar Wang Kŏ-in, selected for inclusion in the Chinese anthology *Ch'üan T'ang shih* (Complete T'ang Poems). Poems of the Silla and later Koryŏ dynasties adhere closely to the delicate (*ch'i-li*) model of Six Dynasties (220–589) poetry, and prose adheres to the Six Dynasties model of parallel prose (*p'ien-ti wen;* Korean, *pyŏrryŏ-mun*), both of which remained central in the T'ang examination system. Because *Wen hsüan* (Literary Selections) was the dominant model for composition in China, it was by far the most influential collection of the time in Korea as well. Laments on the failures of the public official (*hui-hen*) and remembrances of the past (*huai-ku*) are dominant in these poems. There is also evidence for the influence of late T'ang poetics on poetry through the Koryŏ period.

The most important poet of the Silla Kingdom was Ch'oe Ch'i-wŏn (b. 857), who traveled to China at the age of twelve and passed the civil service examination in 874 before being assigned as an official to Hsüan-chou, China. Ch'i-wŏn spent more than thirty years in China, writing an enormous amount of parallel prose and poems in the *chin-t'i shih* (modern-style verse) and *ch'i-yen lü-shih* (heptasyllabic regulated verse) modes. His collected works, *Kyewŏn p'ilgyŏngjip* (Collection of Jottings from the Cassia Garden), is the largest source for parallel prose composition and poetry surviving from the era. He had a strong preference for quatrains (*chüeh-chü*), although he is best known for his *ch'i-yen lü-shih.* The poet Ch'oe Sŭng-no (927–989) also studied in China and composed a significant corpus of poems. Although Chinese learning increased significantly during the Silla period, there is reason to believe that indigenous forms of song, such as *hyangga,* continued to maintain a dominant role in society, although few have been preserved to the present day.

In the Koryŏ (918–1392) kingdom, the full impact of poetry from the Sung dynasty (960–1279), especially as represented by Su Shih (Su Tung-p'o; 1037–1101), was felt in the decades after Su's death. This was particularly the case as the collection of Su Shih's writings entitled *Tung-p'o wen-chi* circulated in Korea, where it became an important model for poetic composition. The general awareness of Sung poetics during this period was concomitant with the discovery of the high tradition of T'ang poetry.

Such major poets as O Se-jae (b. 1133) and Yi In-no (1152–1220) promoted the poetry of Tu Fu (712–770) and Han Yü (768–824) as well as Sung poetics. Yi In-no formed a poetry society called "The Refined Gathering of the Bamboo Grove" (Chukim kohoe), which embodied the literati ideal of esthetic sensibility associated with Su Shih. Although both these poets saw poetry as a world apart from politics, there is no doubt that interest in Sung poetics was related directly to the rise of Sung Confucian learning, particularly after the Mongol occupation of Korea in 1231. Yi Che-hyŏn (1287–1367) composed poems in accordance with Sung poetics while he attempted to give Korean indigenous song legitimacy as literature by translating it into Chinese in an anthology based on the Chinese *yüeh-fu* (ballad) collections entitled *So akbu* (Minor Ballads).

The tales of bizarre lands found in *Shan hai ching* (Classic of Mountains and Seas) was introduced into the state of Paekche in the third century C.E. Combined with Chinese Six Dynasties anthologies of stories of the strange (*chih-kuai*), it provided an early literary model for proto-fiction. Some sections from the early historical narrative by Pak Il-lyang (d. 1096) entitled *Sui chŏn* (Records of the Strange and Unusual) survived in later anthologies. Pak Il-lyang employed Chinese schemata and plot constructions to relate strange events in Korea.

The Koryŏ historian Kim Pu-sik (1075–1151) was one of the earliest scholars to adopt Chinese *ku-wen* (ancient-style prose) in his historical writings, such as *Sanguk sagi* (Historical Records of the Three Kingdoms; 1146). Kim Pu-sik, as a scholar of the exclusive Harrim (= Chinese, Han-lin) Academy, used the literary style of Su Shih in his attempt to come to terms with the complex history of the Korean peninsula. Kim Pu-sik employed the rhetorical schema of historical judgment established by the Han dynasty (206 B.C.E.–220 C.E.) historian Ssu-ma Ch'ien (c. 145–c. 86) in *Shih-chi* (Records of the Historian) in this major historical work.

The Sung dynasty anthology of literary tales that would become the major source for plots and motifs in Chinese narrative, *T'ai-p'ing kuang-chi* (Extensive Records from the Reign of Great Tranquility; 978), was already in circulation in Korea by the twelfth century, as was the Chinese collection of supernatural tales *Sou-shen chi* (Search for the Supernatural). An important collection of Korean tales of the strange inspired by these Chinese models is *P'a hanjip* (Collection for Dispelling Boredom; 1214), by Yi In-no.

The term *p'aegwan* is generally employed to denote such informal histories and stories of the strange. *P'aegwan* is the Korean reading of the Chinese *pai-kuan*, a term originating in the "Yi-wen-chih" (Bibliographic Treatise) of the *Han shu* (History of the Han Dynasty) that referred to low-ranking officials who gathered stories from among the commoners as a means for rulers to understand their needs. The term was later used in both China and Korea as a general term for popular fiction. A major anthology of literary Chinese essays and popular stories surviving from the Koryŏ dynasty is *Paegun sosŏl* (Tales of White Clouds; 1214), traditionally attributed to Yi Kyu-bo (1168–1241).

In the Koryŏ period, archaic prose was employed primarily by officials at the court, where it competed for legitimacy with parallel prose. Careful mastery of Chinese prose became an important subject for intellectuals, particularly as aristocratic background ceased to determine the careers of officials. Yi Kyu-bo published Su Shih's collected works in his native Chŏnju in order to introduce Su's rich vocabulary and sophisticated use of language. Yi Kyu-bo took Han Yü's theoretical writings seriously as well in his general promotion of T'ang and Sung learning. Yi Kyu-bo's disciple Ch'oe Cha (1188–1260) employed Han Yü's prose as a model in his *Pohanjip* (Collection of Writings for Filling Free Time).

The Yüan occupation introduced Sung Neo-Confucian learning of the Chu Hsi (1130–1200) school and its more rigid interpretation of the interrelationships among scholarship, literature, and ideology, especially as reinforced through the civil service examinations. The scholar Yi Che-hyŏn (1287–1367) advocated *komun chi hak* (learning of archaic prose) and reevaluated the Korean narrative tradition in those terms. Yi Che-hyŏn rejected, however, a narrow Sung Confucian definition of literature, finding much of his inspiration in Buddhism and Taoism, best represented by *Yŏgong p'aesŏl* (Popular Fiction from the Useless Old Man). It consists of essays, jottings, literary criticism, and poetry employing the full range of Chinese idioms available.

Yi Saek (1328–1396) wrote in a style of archaic prose employing vocabulary closer to the Chinese semivernacular found in *Chu-tzu yü-lei* (Classified Conversations of Master Chu). The more creative and supernatural aspects of the Korean tradition that did not fit official historiography, such as etymologies, stories of the strange, and hortative tales, were recorded with some literary sophistication in *Samguk yusa* (Residual History of the Three Kingdoms), compiled by the monk Ilyŏn during the reign of King Ch'ungyŏ (1275–1308).

During the Chosŏn period (1392–1910), the Chinese classical tradition as understood through the filter of Sung Confucian thought took on absolute centrality as the mandate to rule for the *yangban* aristocracy. *Yangban* originally signified two groups of high-ranking civil and military officials, but by the time under discussion it had come to mean simply the aristocracy. The *yangban* justified their rule in terms of their own moral and intellectual superiority; hence alternatives to the Sung Confucian orthodoxy were particularly threatening, with the result that the Chinese canon was much restricted.

By the authority of the official National Confucian Academy (Sŏnggyun'gwan), Ch'eng Yi's (1033–1107) conception of "using literature to transmit the way [of government]" (*wen yi tsai tao*) was vigorously promoted. During the Chosŏn period, the need for official correspondence with China kept parallel prose alive in the academy, particularly in the Hall of Worthies (Chiphyŏnjŏn), even as archaic prose gained authority within intellectual circles and the composition of formal essays in archaic prose took a central position in the civil service examination. Inscriptions (*piji*), prefaces, political treatises, and bibliographies also were major genres. The licentiate examinations tested composition in Chinese *shih* poetry, the rhapsody (*fu*), documentary prose (*piao*), and formulaic essay (*ts'e*), thus ensuring their continued production in the Chosŏn dynasty.

Sŏ Kŏ-jŏng (1420–1488) made a major contribution with his editorship, along with twenty-two other scholars, of *Tongmunsŏn* (Selection of Refined Literature from Korea; 1478), a massive anthology in 130 volumes of Korean literature in Chinese. *Tongmunsŏn* includes a wide range of literary genres with a preponderance of inscriptions and formal essays covering five hundred authors in fifty-five genres of Chinese writing from the Silla dynasty to early Chosŏn. Following the model of *Literary Selections*, *Tongmunsŏn* includes everything from poems and essays to examination compositions (*toryangmun*); the ratio is four parts prose, particularly parallel prose, to one part poetry. *Tongmunsŏn* reflected the refined compositions of Korean aristocrats in the ornate prose and poetry inspired by the Chinese Six Dynasties model. For this reason, it was later criticized as a compendium rather than a selection of models for composition by Kim Chong-jik (1431–1492), who placed the composition of literature within the framework of serving as "an instrument to support the way [of government]" (*chaedo chi ki*).

Koreans continued to compose both *chin-t'i shih* (modern-style [i.e., regulated] poetry) and *ku-t'i shih* (ancient-style poetry) throughout the Chosŏn period. There were arguments about the merits of T'ang poetry, as represented by Li Po (701–762) and Tu Fu, and of Sung poetry, as represented by Su Shih, that follow basically the same lines as such debates in late imperial China. Sung poetics dominated, so that Korean intellectuals came to know more about the specifics of contemporary Chinese poetics. The groups participating in poetic composition also grew and diversified, including many nonaristocrats and a significant number of women from the seventeenth century. The indigenous poetic form of *shijo* adopted themes and poetic language from the Chinese poetic tradition into the composition of Korean song, thus making them accessible to female authors.

An indigenous Korean poetic form in Chinese known as *Chosŏn-p'ung* (Chosŏn-style poetry) that ignored formal rhyme schemes and employed place names from Korea while introducing elements of Korean folk songs established itself as a separate genre in the eighteenth century. The urban poet from outside the ranks of the *yangban* class increased his visibility in this poetic form through such collections as *Sodae p'ungyo* (Folk Songs of a Glorious Age), which features the writings of non-*yangban*, *chung-in* (middle people). Kim Ch'ang-hyŏp (1651–1708) was famous for his advocacy of poetry describing the actual environment of Korea known as "true poetry" (*chinsi*). Sin Kwang-su (1712–1775) produced *Kwansan yungma* (Caparisoned Horses at the Mountain Pass), an extended poem in regulated prosodic song (*yul-ch'ang*), based on episodes taken from the poetry of Tu Fu, which represents the expansion of Chinese poetics into the Korean idiom.

Poets such as Chŏng Sa-ryŏng (1491–1570) evinced a strong interest in Chinese poetics of the Sung dynasty outside the narrow range of Su Shih and his followers, particularly the ornate and experimental *ch'i-yi* poetics of the Sung master Huang T'ing-chien (1045–1105). There was some room for the poetry of Yüan Hung-tao (1568–1610) and other advocates of *hsing-ling* (spiritually inspired) poetry of the late Ming dynasty (1644–1911).

During the reign of King Yŏngjo (1724–1776), the poets Yi Sŏ-gu (1754–1825), Yi Tŭk-mu (1741–1793), Yu Tük-gong (b. 1749), and Pak Che-ga (1750–1805) established themselves as four masters of poetry. All of them saw their poetry in the context of political reform within the central government academy and *shirhak* (practical studies). In addition to their work in formal Chinese poetry, they took an interest in *chu-ji-sa,* an intermediate poetic form in which popular Korean songs were transcribed in literary Chinese. Yi Tŏk-mu modeled himself after the early Ch'ing poet Wang Shih-chen (1634–1711). Yu Tŭk-gong wrote an anthology of Chinese poems entitled *Yishipil tohoe kosi* (Twenty-one Poems on Capitals in the Ancient Style).

The late Chosŏn poet Kang Wi (1820–1884), also of "middle-person" status, modeled his work after that of Huang Tsun-hsien (1848–1905) of contemporary China. He expressed deep respect for Su Shih as a poet and studied the painting and calligraphy of the late Ming literatus Tung Ch'i-ch'ang (1555–1636).

Kim T'aek-yŏng (1850–1927) was the last great figure in the Korean classical tradition; deeply conversant with late Ch'ing dynasty archaic writing, he was a great admirer of the Ming poet and prose master Kuei Yu-kuang (1506–1571). He later drew direct inspiration from the late Ch'ing reformer Liang Ch'i-ch'ao (1874–1930). His selected anthology of the Korean poetic tradition in Chinese, *Yŏhan shipka munch'o* (Selections from the Writings of Ten Great Masters of Korean Literature; 1921), has an introduction by Liang Ch'i-ch'ao. *Yŏhan shipka munch'o* established a canon of Korean literature with all the seriousness of the Chinese literary tradition just at the moment that the Chinese tradition was losing its authority after the annexation of Korea to Japan.

Literature outside of government remained restricted in the early Chosŏn dynasty. With the emergence of the independent Confucian literati group known as Sarim during the rule of King Chungjong (1506–1544), a freer interpretation of literature emerged, and the traces of a more expansive style of narrative based on the vernacular record (*yü-lu*) tradition of the Sung dynasty gained prominence, although archaic prose maintained its eminent authority. Writings on philosophical topics inspired by Sung Confucianism, travelogs (*sansu yugi*), dream records (*mongyurok*), and personal bibliographies emerged in larger numbers in the Chosŏn period, especially in the regional Confucian academies, or *sŏwŏn*.

A great range of registers for narrative expression was available, from parallel prose based on the Four-Six Chinese model (see chapter 12) to archaic prose modeled on the compositions of Sung dynasty writers. The examination system required a distinct style of literary Chinese prose that followed Korean conventions known as *kwamun* (examination prose). In the nineteenth century, the scholar Ro Kyŏng compiled an anthology of examination prose called *Han-*

wŏnjip (Han Source Collection), thus giving legitimacy to *kwamun* as a genre. Although archaic prose continued to have the highest status, a large amount of writing survives in examination prose, as well as in scribal prose (*imun*) that integrates usage and syntax from the Korean language in Chinese writing and was employed for daily communications.

In the early sixteenth century, the scholar Yu Hŭi-ch'un (1513–1577) presented the following texts, among others from China, as essential to mastering written Chinese: the Sung anthology *Wen-chang kuei-fan* (Models for Literary Composition), *Ku-wen chen-pao* (Reliable Treasures of Archaic Prose), and *Chien-teng hsin-hua* (New Stories for Trimming the Lampwick) from the early Ming dynasty. Yu's inclusion of Ch'ü Yu's (1347–1433) *Chien-teng hsin-hua,* a popular collection of romantic tales, is unusual in that such tales were often considered corrupting. Yet it still served as a model for literary composition.

The publication in Korea of the early archaist poet Li Tung-yang's (1447–1516) anthology *Ni-ku yüeh-fu* (Archaistic Ballads) during the reign of King Myŏng-jong (1545–1567) and the later publication in 1580 of a selection of his poems for a Korean readership by Yun Kŭn-su made Ming dynasty theories of archaism accessible to Korean writers. Ming archaism, as put forth by the influential literary critics Wang Shih-chen (1526–1590) and Li P'an-lung (1514–1570), distinguished itself from Sung dynasty archaism in its emphasis on *ku-wen-tz'u* (ancient prose style). The approach suggested that the key to literary composition was the perfect internalization of the deep structure of archaic writing (Han prose and T'ang poetry) in the writer. The archaist movement (see chapters 20 and 21) severely restricted the canon of what could be considered literature, but presented how-to manuals that rendered any man capable of composing the highest literature merely by connecting the dots. The major advocate in Korea of the Ming version of archaic prose was Ch'oe Rip (1539–1612), a scholar who established himself primarily through his literary ability. Ch'oe Rip's annotations of Han Yü and his translations into Korean of Chinese classical poetry earned him fame. Ch'oe's conception of literature as rooted firmly in prose style (*munjang chimun*) was best expressed in his annotated anthology of model selections from *Han shu* (History of the Han Dynasty) entitled *Hansa yŏljŏnch'o*. Emphasis fell on the sophisticated command of archaic language and the resulting laconic, spare style.

King Chŏngjo's (1776–1800) ascent to the throne resulted in the reaffirmation of a narrow model for legitimate prose style and in criticism of nonstandard composition, both of which he saw as a means of preserving the legitimate Confucian tradition and rectifying the realm. King Chŏngjo established a new national Confucian academy to set forth these principles for scholarship and style, the Kyujanggak Academy. He also launched a thoroughgoing attack on what he considered aberrant forms of literature, a literary reformation known as the *munch'ae panjŏng* (rectification of textual style), because of a deep concern about the flood of unorthodox texts pouring into Korea from China. Such heterodox writings included the *hsiao-p'in* (refined essay; see Introduction) of the late Ming and other informal essays. Chŏngjo established serious restrictions on the importation of Ming and Ch'ing prose, popular fiction, and Western writings in translation because he regarded the Chinese classics as the root of all written expression.

The author Kim Si-sŭp (1435–1493) compiled a collection of tales of the supernatural entitled *Kŭmo sinhwa* (New Stories of the Golden Turtle [Mount Kŭmo]), of which five stories survive in an anthology preserved in Japan. Kim Si-sŭp wrote of Korean *yangban* gentrymen who encountered supernatural beings and had occasion to display their learning and cultured sensitivity through Chinese poetry. Romantic love involving supernatural women is a theme in three of the stories. *Kŭmo sinhwa* was modeled after the early Ming collection *Chien-teng hsin-hua*, which was immensely popular throughout East Asia. Although the stories in *Kŭmo sinhwa* show signs of direct borrowing in their language, they are all reset in a Korean context, unlike other novels written in Korean in later centuries, which are often set exclusively in China. Kim Ki-sŭp crafted the poetry in *Kŭmo sinhwa* more carefully than did the Chinese author of *Chien-teng hsin-hua*. This work was an opportunity for a literatus banished to Mount Kŭmo to display his skills.

A distinct Korean narrative tradition emerged from the middle of the seventeenth century that focused on family relationships and the skillful manipulation of the rules of propriety. The focus on propriety in these Korean narratives derives from their primary function as reading material for *yangban* gentrywomen. It served as a source of information on the proper resolution of familial conflict through the careful enactment of etiquette. Most of these narratives survive in both a literary Chinese and a Korean version; they were widely circulated, but exclusively in manuscript form.

In addition to plot elements taken from contemporary Chinese *ts'ai-tzu chia-jen* (brilliant scholars and beautiful girls) fiction (see chapter 36), these narratives employ elements taken from Chinese narratives such as *Lieh-nü chuan* (Biographies of Eminent Women; reportedly first introduced in 1404), *Hsiao-ching* (Classic of Filial Piety), *Shih-chi*, and other Chinese historical works. The content of these narratives consists largely of the resolution of complex familial conflicts through the creative interpretation of the Chinese classical precedents for proper behavior. The most notable novels in this genre are *Ch'angsŏn kamŭi rok* (A Record of the Manifestation of Goodness and the Gratification of Emotional Bonds) from the late seventeenth century and *Wanwŏlhoe maengyŏn* (Alliance Formed at the Wanwŏl Pavilion) from the mid-eighteenth century. The latter is an enormous narrative of several thousand pages written entirely in *hangŭl* that describes the massive conflicts within a family concerning the line of succession and the attempts of women to achieve control through their sons. The vocabulary is quite difficult, assuming a subtle knowledge of the Chinese tradition on the part of its female readers.

Wanwŏlhoe maengyŏn alludes explicitly to such Chinese novels as *Shui-hu chuan* (Water Margin) and *San-kuo chih yen-yi* (Romance of the Three Kingdoms).

The scholar Kim Man-jung (1637–1692) wrote the most famous Korean novel, *Kuun mong* (Dream of Nine Clouds), supposedly in order to amuse his ill mother. Like most premodern Korean novels, it exists in both a Korean and a literary Chinese version and is set in China. *Kuun mong* describes the process by which the central figure, the monk Sŏngjin, is banished from paradise to the vulgar world, along with eight fairies, for the crime of flirtation. Sŏngjin is reincarnated in a scholarly family and does phenomenally well in the civil service examination. The eight fairies, however, are reincarnated into every possible social class from princess to courtesan. The bulk of the novel involves the complex negotiations by which Sŏngjin manages to marry all eight of the women simultaneously, according to the rules of propriety despite class differences. The elaborate negotiations regarding propriety (*ye*) are in part derived from *ts'ai-tzu chia-jen* stories of the early Ch'ing dynasty. Although *ts'ai-tzu chia-jen* novels involve the joining of a male protagonist with several females he meets during his adventures, the marriage of one scholar to eight women in *Kuun mong* is a tour de force. The supernatural frame story and other passages find their origin in *Hsi-yu chi* (Journey to the West); there are also elements borrowed from other *ch'uan-ch'i* tales.

Beginning in the late seventeenth century, Chinese vernacular novels circulated widely in Korean translation among *yangban* gentrywomen. One remarkable cache of these novels survived in the Naksŏnjae library of the royal palace, where they had been the reading material of palace ladies. This collection of more than forty translations, including some Chinese novels that do not survive in China, are largely stories from the *ts'ai-tzu chia-jen* tradition relating the struggles of women to overcome barriers to a proper marriage. Most of these translations, although technically in Korean, include a high percentage of transcribed Chinese vocabulary and required a significant knowledge of Chinese.

After King Chŏngjo banned the importation of Chinese fiction in 1786, there was probably a reduction in the number of Chinese narratives entering Korea. Most Chinese novels were informally imported by translators and merchants who traveled on regular tribute missions to China. As early as 1423, a primer for Chinese language entitled *Pak-t'ongsa* (Interpreter Pak) employed a passage from *Hsi-yu chi* as an example of Chinese vernacular usage. Chinese vernacular narratives were not printed in either Chinese or Korean translation in Korea until the nineteenth century; they were most likely widely, but secretly, read.

Dramatic performances based on Chinese narrative probably existed throughout the later Chosŏn period, although records are scarce. One source describes a professional storyteller called a *chŏngisu* who wandered through Seoul reciting popular Chinese fiction in Korean. The dramatic recitations known as *p'ansori* include renderings of scenes such as the Battle at the Red Cliff from *San-kuo chih yen-yi.*

The most famous narrative in Korean traditional fiction today is *Ch'unhyang jŏn* (The Tale of Ch'unhyang), which is found in so many versions (literary Chinese, Korean narrative, and *p'ansori* recitation) that it is impossible to identify an original text. Ch'unhyang is a virtuous courtesan who gains the attention and respect of a young *yangban* scholar through her remarkable strength of personality and understanding of propriety and then remains faithful to him as a proper wife, despite the efforts of the evil governor to coerce her into serving him as a courtesan. The tale describes the heroic effort of a courtesan to redefine her own class status through the careful manipulation of moral roles. *Ch'unhyang jŏn* includes elements from the Chinese play "Hsi hsiang-chi" (Romance of the Western Chamber), the *ch'uan-ch'i* narrative of the righteous courtesan Li Wa, "Li-wa chuan" (An Account of Li Wa), and assorted references to moral tales of Chinese women. Perhaps the most interesting version of *Ch'unhyang jŏn* is a rendering into vernacular Chinese with a sophisticated commentary by an anonymous scholar entitled *Kwanghanru gi* (Tale of the Kwanghan Pavilion; 1845). The annotator employed the Ch'ing scholar Chang Chu-p'o's approach to appreciating Chinese vernacular fiction, *p'ing-tien* (see chapter 46), in his comments on this Korean classic.

The great nineteenth-century Korean novel is *Ongnu mong* (Dream of the Jade Chamber), written in the 1840s by Nam Yŏng-no (1810–1858). *Ongnu mong* integrates elements from *ts'ai-tzu chia-jen* narratives with elements from *Hung-lou meng* (A Dream of Red Towers) and references to Korean indigenous narratives such as *Kuun mong.* The detailed trips to imagined foreign countries in *Ongnu mong* suggest some relationship to the contemporary Chinese novel *Ching hua yüan* (Flowers in the Mirror, A Romance), by Li Ju-chen (c. 1763–1830). Another novel from the nineteenth century, *Kuun gi* (A Record of Nine Clouds), integrates elements from *Kuun mong* with characters and events borrowed from *Hung-lou meng.*

The eighteenth-century intellectual Pak Ch'i-wŏn (1737–1805) devoted his efforts to the study of Ch'ing dynasty institutions and scholarly principles as part of the larger Pukhak (Northern Studies) movement of the mid-eighteenth century. He thought deeply about the literary writings of such innovative late Ming theorists as Yüan Hung-tao and Li Chih (1527–1602) and was a voracious reader of Chinese popular narratives. To a degree unusual in Korea, Pak Ch'i-wŏn set out to develop his own narrative voice by employing a wide range of idiomatic expressions culled from the entire classical Chinese tradition, including such works of history as *Tso-chuan* (Tso Commentary) and *Shih-chi.* His vivid tales feature great mimetic resolution and a stylistic precision that sets him apart from the general literature of his age. His carefully constructed tales concern immediate social issues in Korea; they are born of a personal concern with expanding the horizons of Koreans and improving his country. Pak Ch'i-wŏn's experimental narrative, *Yŏlha ilgi* (A Diary of the Je-ho River), includes passages written in a style of Chinese based on popular fiction.

The late-seventeenth-century figure Hŏ Kyun (1569–1618) took a strong interest in Chinese vernacular fiction as part of his larger critique of Korean society and its rigid class structure. Hŏ Kyun wrote a now-lost story in literary Chinese about a contemporary bandit king, Hong Kil-dong. The surviving version in Korean, *Hong Kil-dong chŏn* (Tale of Hong Kil-dong), is most likely by a late-eighteenth-century anonymous author. *Hong Kil-dong chŏn* includes elements of the fantastic taken from *Hsi-yu chi* and descriptions of military conquest and strategy indebted to *Shui-hu chuan* and *San-kuo chih yen-yi*.

The otherwise unknown *yangban* scholar Hong Hŭi-bok (1794–1859) translated the baroque late Ch'ing novel *Ching hua yüan* (1828) into Korean under the title *Chaeil kiŏn* (The Greatest Novel in Korean) in 1838. Hong Hŭi-bok reveals in his preface, which happens to be the earliest surviving example of literary criticism drafted in *hangŭl* script, a theory of the novel that relies on both Chinese and Korean works. Hong Hŭi-bok posits himself as a literary reformer trying to introduce both greater realism and moral purpose into the Korean narrative tradition through the translation of this Chinese novel.

Among the Chinese narratives translated into Korean in the mid-nineteenth century are *t'an-tz'u* (strummed lyrics) verse ballads such as "Tsai-sheng yüan" (Love Reincarnate; see chapter 50). These popular ballads on the travails of women were aimed at a female readership. Around 1884, as part of a move to modernize Korea along a Chinese model, the scholar Yi Chong-t'ae (1850–1908) supervised a massive translation project that produced, among other works, a highly accurate translation of *Hung-lou meng* intended for the consumption of the palace ladies. Contemporary records speak of Korean translations of *Hung-lou meng* and all its sequels as being readily available at lending libraries in manuscript form. Selections from *San-kuo chih yen-yi* were extracted and rewritten as the "tales" (*chŏn*) of individuals and published as cheap paperbacks in the early twentieth century. *San-kuo chih yen-yi* circulated in the early twentieth century in Korean translation (*ŏnt'o*).

China continued to be a model for modernization for Korea throughout the early twentieth century. A movement to reform Korean society by reforming its fiction, known as the *Sinsosŏl* (New Novel) movement, quickly developed at the turn of the century. The *Sinsosŏl* movement was directly inspired by the writings, both theoretical and literary, of Liang Ch'i-ch'ao and other reform writers of the late Ch'ing dynasty. The aim was to present models for proper behavior and denounce "feudal" practices in favor of modernization. Although such novels claimed an absolute break with the past, their strong didactic and prescriptive strategy continued the Korean narrative tradition. Yi Hae-jo (1869–1927), among his many narratives based on Chinese models, wrote an exposé novel entitled *Ku'magŏm* (A Sword to Chase Off Devils) that was based directly on the late Ch'ing reformist novel *Sao-mi chou* (A Broom to Sweep Away Ignorance), by the pseudonymous Chinese author Chuang-che ("Strongman").

In the next generation, Yang Paek-hwa (1889–1944) translated Chinese novels such as *Hung-lou meng* (1918) and *Shui-hu chuan* (1926) into readily accessible Korean, in addition to introducing contemporary Chinese authors. After the end of World War II, in a period of extraordinary American influence, interest in Chinese fiction, so strongly associated with an imagined backward past, declined precipitously as Western literature poured into Korea. Since the 1990s, however, Chinese literature has begun to reclaim its previous status: translations into Korean of *San-kuo chih yen-yi* and *Shui-hu chuan* have become massive bestsellers.

Emanuel Pastreich

Chapter 54

THE RECEPTION OF CHINESE LITERATURE IN JAPAN

It is not clear when Chinese writing, and with it Chinese literature, was first transmitted to Japan. Most likely it passed first through Korea and then to Japan, where initially it was not well understood because the Japanese had no previous writing system of their own. Later Japanese records mention learned advisers on cultural affairs, from the Korean state of Paekche, who arrived at the Japanese court in the late fourth century. They brought the Chinese classics with them and served as scribes to the emperor for official documentation. This class of Korean intellectuals formed a hereditary clan of scribes assigned to the emperor; outside their ranks literacy remained marginal in Japan. Implements bearing written inscriptions survive in Japan from the early fifth century, although there is some ambiguity as to whether they were actually produced in Japan or carried over from the Korean peninsula.

The unification of the continent by the Sui dynasty (581–618) in 589 brought greater cultural prestige to the Chinese empire and made travel to China possible for the Japanese. The unification of the Korean peninsula by the state of Silla in 668 resulted in the flight of many educated literati from the defeated state of Paekche to Japan. These cultural transplants, known as *kikajin* (naturalized persons/citizens), played a critical role in introducing and nurturing the practical technologies, Chinese culture, and Buddhism in Japan. The Japanese court of the Asuka period (552–645) had accepted Buddhism as an official religion in 587 and made efforts to integrate Chinese learning into the activities of the new aristocratic administration, going so far as to send missions to China from 630 on. The annotations on three Buddhist sutras entitled *Sangyōgisho*—traditionally attributed to Prince Shōtoku (574–622)—that survive from this period demonstrate a sophisticated grasp of Chinese by a Japanese writer. The Chinese central system of government was adopted to a large degree during the Taika reforms of 645, although it is not certain that all the reforms that exist on paper from this time were fully implemented.

The establishment in 710 of an imperial capital at Nara with the full trappings of a Chinese court resulted in a spate of texts in Chinese. The first history of Japan in Classical Chinese, *Nihon shoki* (Official Records of Japan; 720), employs theories of *yin* and *yang* and Confucian moral judgments along the lines of the *Shih-chi* (Records of the Historian) in its records of past emperors, but at the same time it contains indigenous myths and legends at considerable remove from Chinese historiography. The emotional, violent, or irrational side of Japanese myth so well represented in the *Kojiki* (Record of Ancient Events; 712?), which was written in a mixture of literary Chinese and Japanese, is presented in terms of exalted Confucian ideals; hints of the ancient cults and a matriarchal society are toned down, as the authors carefully imposed the Chinese schema of proper history. Also produced during this period, after the first command of Empress Genmei in 713, were the *Fudoki* (gazetteers), inspired by Chinese models of the Six Dynasties period (220–589) that recorded the topography and local lore of each province. These gazetteers defined and recorded the specifics of Japanese landscape and customs in Classical Chinese (although some Japanese passages exist within these texts).

Increasing literacy among the aristocracy in the late seventh century and the growth of the Buddhist clergy fostered the practice of *kanshi* (Chinese poetry), outside the official transactions of government. Chinese poetry gave cultural legitimacy to its practitioners as a supreme expression of cultural sophistication within the Sinic realm, but it also had a practical role as a *de rigeur* part of diplomatic exchanges with the states of the Korean peninsula or diplomatic missions to T'ang dynasty (618–907) China. Classical Chinese was the *lingua franca* of statecraft in East Asia and Chinese literature the legitimating language that transformed the subject it transmitted.

The performative poetic productions of Nara aristocrats during the eighth century are known through the compilation of 120 Chinese poems by an unknown anthologist in 751 entitled *Kaifūsō* (Remembering the Manners of the Past; 751). The contributors to *Remembering the Manners of the Past* included monks, nobles, and princes of considerable social rank. The collection consists entirely of Chinese old-style *shih* poems, most of which are five-character *wu-yen shih* (pentasyllabic poems) eight lines long, but it also includes several extended poems. The introduction is in Four-Six parallel prose (see chapter 12). The poems feature many *tui-chü* (antithetical) lines and ornate language. Most likely the poetry of the Ch'i (479–502) and Liang (502–557) dynasties served as a model. There is no sign of influence on *Remembering the Manners of the*

Past from the emerging regulated *shih* poetry of contemporary T'ang China. Perhaps regulated *shih* poetry had not yet reached the critical mass of production within China itself to have significant influence abroad. The poems of *Remembering the Manners of the Past* are dominated by concern with rhetorical expression, witty replies within a social context, and the refined manipulation of Chinese idioms culled from *Wen hsüan* (Literary Selections) or *Yü-t'ai hsin-yung* (New Poems from a Jade Terrace). *Remembering the Manners of the Past* stands out as a unique collection that did not inspire direct imitations.

Most of the poems are set at social occasions, such as banquets, often involving ministers and the emperor. The contributors were established aristocrats of considerable influence, and the poetry gatherings were closely related to contemporary politics. Poems adhere closely to Chinese models, leaving little space for personal expression. The verse features obligatory allusions to the classics and familiar tropes of Chinese poetry among the poems on Confucian, Taoist, and Buddhist themes; little hint of indigenous Japanese culture can be spotted in the collection. Inasmuch as the poems of *Remembering the Manners of the Past* imposed a clear intellectual order on the world through their rhetoric of parallelism and reinforced the status of the ruler through their acceptance of his status, they are quite close in social function to similar poetry in China.

Some of the later poems from early Nara (early eighth century) include examples of personal expression, and the poems written under the patronage of Nagaya no Ōkimi (684–729) show elements from early T'ang poetry, particularly evidence of the influence of the early T'ang poets Lo Pin-wang (c. 619–c. 687) and Wang Po (649–676). Isonokami no Otomaro (d. 750) wrote poems of considerable complexity using more elaborate vocabulary, some of which had been taken from "Yu-hsien k'u" (Grotto of Playful Transcendents), the T'ang *ch'uan-ch'i* (classical-language short story; see below) then in circulation in Japan. Nagaya's poem on his exile has a poignancy not found in earlier works.

The *Man'yōshū* (Collection of Ten Thousand Leaves; compiled some time after 759) is the first collection of *waka* (songs in Japanese) to be anthologized with the legitimacy previously reserved for *shih* poetry. In contrast to *Remembering the Manners of the Past,* which focused on the highest levels of secular power, *Collection of Ten Thousand Leaves* is a product of the efforts of the Ōtomo clan, particularly the anthologist Ōtomo no Yakamochi, a line of scholars in political decline who asserted their significance within the literary realm. *Collection of Ten Thousand Leaves* is loosely based on *Literary Selections,* although it lacks a firm organizational structure. The poems are in a hybrid language. They contain both ancient turns of phrase that date back to the mythical and magical preliterate world in which the use of *kotodama* (the efficacious power of language in religious ritual) was primary and embellished rhetorical conceits and parallelisms taken directly from Chinese Six Dynasties poetics. *Collection of Ten Thousand Leaves* contains thousands of *waka* poems from the ritual and mythical songs of antiquity, anonymous folk songs, and explicitly literary compositions by Kakinomoto no Hitomaro. Hitomaro integrates poetic themes based on *Literary Selections* precedents perfectly into a Japanese context so that they lose all foreignness for the Japanese reader. Yamanoue no Okura (660–733) was born in the Korean state of Silla and traveled to T'ang China as a member of the 701 embassy. His poetic portraits of individuals and his laments show familiarity with Chinese poetic conventions and most likely the poetry of T'ao Ch'ien (365–427).

Exposure to Chinese literary anthologies inspired Japanese to take their own songs seriously to a degree that did not happen in either Vietnam or Korea. A new literary realm evolved for the Japanese *waka* that absorbed the rhetoric and topics of the Chinese *shih* poetry tradition but kept the actual Chinese language at a distance. Japanese writers established an elaborate analogy between the Japanese *waka* and *shih* poetry wherein Japanese *waka* remained independent, in that the vocabulary of Chinese poetry did not pass directly into Japanese *waka*, but Chinese modes of literary expression were allowed to flow into *waka* through a semipermeable stylistic membrane. Chinese poetic expressions such as *hsüeh-lei* (tears of blood) did not enter *waka* poetry directly as foreign terms; instead, new expressions consisting entirely of native Japanese words were formulated to translate those expressions. *Chi no namida* is the direct translation into Japanese of *hsüeh-lei* that emerged in the *waka* tradition. It is a term that had not previously existed in Japanese, but it did not draw undue attention to itself as an import from China.

Japanese song was transformed into poetry when it acquired the undergirding of the *shih* poetic tradition. In addition, although *makura no kotoba* (pillow words) and *jo* (prefatory ornamental phrases) affixed to significant words in *waka* find their origins in magic incantations from preliterate Japan, they were not dropped from the *waka* tradition as it was sinicized but, rather, were transformed into ornamental and literary expressions analogous to the turns of phrase in Six Dynasties poetics.

One other contributor to the assessment of native Japanese *waka* as poetry is Fujiwara no Hamanari (724–790), who in 772 wrote a treatise on poetic rules for composition entitled *Uta no shiki* (also known as *Kakyō hyōshiki*; Regulations of Song), in which he applied Chinese concepts of rhyme and structure to Japanese *waka* based on eight flaws of poetic composition. These eight flaws were clearly inspired by the eight defects (*pa ping*) enumerated by the Chinese and the *pa ping*, in turn, were derived from the concept of *doṣa* in Indian prosodic theory (see chapter 13). *Regulations of Song* is the earliest surviving work of Japanese literary criticism.

The Heian period (794–1185) was ushered in by Emperor Saga (786–842), who made T'ang culture and institutions the centerpiece of his rule. The forty years between the reigns of Saga (809–823) and Nimmyō (833–850) are the undisputed peak of Chinese poetry in Japan. Under Emperor Saga's patronage the poet Ono no Minemori (778–830) compiled the first of three *chokusenshi* (imperial anthologies of Chinese poetry), entitled *Ryōunshū* (Collection of Poems that Float up to the Clouds; 814). This collection was a compilation of Chinese *shih* poetry by Japanese poets that served as a legitimating mechanism for Emperor Saga's rule and therefore includes many tributes to him. Most of the poems are the written traces of public performative outings including the imperial family and high courtiers. The collection contains poems based on T'ao Ch'ien's works and *yüeh-fu* (ballad) themes, as well as laments written from a woman's perspective typical of a certain strain within T'ang poetry.

The second imperial anthology compiled under the patronage of Emperor Saga, *Bunkashūreishū* (Anthology of Literary Beauties; 818), collected poems not included in *Collection of Poems That Float up to the Clouds*. The poems are organized not by author, but by theme, in closer imitation of Chinese anthologies such as *Literary Selections*. The themes are more esthetic and less concerned with the direct representation of imperial power. The poems combine diction from contemporary T'ang *shih* poetry, Six Dynasties poetry, and contemporary Chinese vernacular usages. The collection contains seven-character *shih* poems and even examples in the *fu* (rhapsody) mode.

The last of the imperial anthologies is *Keikokushū* (Anthology for Governing the Nation; 827), the title of which refers to the political function of poetry as a mechanism for supporting the state taken from the writings of Emperor Wen (r. 220–226) of Wei (187–226). The preface gives a brief account of *shih* poetry in Japan that reveals a new historical awareness of this type of poetry as an indigenous genre. In addition to the poems produced at court gatherings, new specialized genres of poetry, such as *feng-shih* (presentation verse) of the sort employed in the T'ang examination system, also appear in this collection. In keeping with the patronage of the imperial house, the largest number of poems are attributed to Emperor Saga.

The poetry and prose of the T'ang poet Po Chü-yi (772–846), as they were known through the widely circulated collection *Hakushi monjū* (Collected Works of Mister Po; in Chinese, *Po-shih wen-chi*), found a large audience among Japanese poets. The first record of *Collected Works of Mister Po* in Japan concerns its presentation to Emperor Ninmyō (r. 833–850) in 838. Since Po's works were an accessible form of Chinese poetry that dealt concretely with immediate events without the embellishment of previous poetry, they had immense appeal in Japan, and this collection rapidly became the most influential Chinese anthology in Japanese literature. Po's poems dominated in the poetic *dai* (assigned themes) for Heian poetry exchanges in both *waka* and *shih* poetry from the ninth century on. Sacrifices were even offered to him as a god. Allusions to Po Chü-yi and his poetry abound in the poems of major Heian writers such as Sugawara no Michizane (845–903) as well as in such Japanese-language narratives as *Genji monogatari* (Tale of Genji), which takes its inspiration in part from Po's "Ch'ang-hen ko" (Song of Everlasting Regret). *Literary Selections*, which became the elementary text of instruction at the national university from 798 on, and *Collected Works of Mister Po* became the two greatest traditional sources for poetic composition in Japan.

Kūkai (774–835), the founder of the Shingon sect of Esoteric Buddhism in Japan, was an independent-minded monk who traveled to China in 804 to study Buddhism in Ch'ang-an. During his time in China, Kūkai absorbed an immense amount of knowledge about Chinese language and literature, in particular with regard to rhyme, tones, and grammar, as part of his studies of the *siddham* teachings on Sanskrit language. Later, after his installation as the abbot of a temple that received the direct patronage of Emperor Saga, Kūkai compiled a series of theoretical works on religion and language. In *Bunkyō hifuron* (Treatise on the Secret Treasury of the Literary Mirror; 820), Kūkai made available a great range of Chinese critical works on literature from the Six Dynasties period. Although the introduction of *Treatise on the Secret Treasury of the Literary Mirror* is original with Kūkai, the bulk of the text is culled from a variety of contemporary Chinese theoretical writings, with particular stress on the linguistic aspect of poetic production. Many of the Six Dynasties and T'ang texts Kūkai cities *in extenso* do not survive anywhere else, making *Treatise on the Secret Treasury of the Literary Mirror* an exceedingly valuable source for the reconstruction of the history of Chinese literary theory and praxis. Circulation of this impressive collection of theoretical and critical writings was largely limited to Buddhist monks interested in linguistic study as part of their Buddhist activities and did not circulate widely in Kūkai's age. Kūkai's poetry and prose are collected in *Henjōhokkiseireishū* (Henjō's Collection for Giving Free Rein to the Spirit; 835), which includes sophisticated *p'ien-t'i-wen* (parallel prose) essays and epistles as well as poetry on philosophical topics (he moves away from strict tonal regulations in these works).

The ill-fated literatus Sugawara no Michizane (845–903), who became the patron saint of Chinese studies in Japan, rose quickly in the imperial bureaucracy by dint of his literary abilities, becoming a professor of literature in 877. He was called upon to greet foreign embassies as part of his duties. Michizane gained the trust of Emperor Uda (r. 887–897) because of his bureaucratic and literary ability, but, being from a scholarly family, he lacked the backing to resist the political machinations of the powerful Fujiwara clan. Michizane fell from power and spent his last days in exile at Dazaifu in Kyūshū. Although appointed ambassador to China, he opposed the embassies to China and had them canceled.

Most of Michizane's poetry is known through the collection of his family's (his grandfather's, his father's, and his own) writings, entitled *Kanke bunsō* (Jottings from the Sugawara Family; 900). *Jottings from the Sugawara Family* consists of five-syllable and seven-syllable *chin-t'i shih* (regulated verse) poems. Although Michizane wrote many banquet poems, his corpus also contains inscriptions for paintings and laments, as well as lyric and seasonal poems. His dense and allusive poems reveal a considerable familiarity with late T'ang poetry, but at the same time the large number of Japanified phrases in his poetry suggest a poet who wrote within what he saw as a Japanese idiom. There are many performative works, such as exchanges with foreign embassies, and poems celebrating the glory days of Emperor Uda's reign. What is new in Michizane's poetry is the creation of a sequential literary history of the self in the manner of Li Po (701–762) or Tu Fu (712–770). Michizane made his fall from power and his laments on his personal misfortunes in exile the explicit content of his anthology, which had such literary power that it determined his image for the rest of history. Through his poetic tropes, Michizane established himself as a major icon of the Japanese cultural tradition.

Fujiwara no Akihira (989?–1066) was another noted intellectual whose achievements in literature compensated for his failures in the bureaucracy. He compiled an anthology of later Japanese *shih* poetry and literary Chinese essays entitled *Honchō monzui* (The Essence of Literature in Our Age; 1037), in which he featured the poems of educated scholars, such as Sugawara Michizane, who had served in the Kanrin (= Chinese, Han-lin) Academy and omitted almost all poetry by high-ranking courtiers from the previous imperial anthologies. He divided poems and essays by topic into thirty-nine categories. *Shih* poems based on the late T'ang style of Liu Tsung-yüan (773–819) and Po Chü-yi are conspicuous in the collection. There is also a good selection of belle-lettres and political reports in *p'ien-t'i-wen* style.

The most influential collection of *waka* poetry of the Heian period was *Kokin(waka) shū* (Collection of Songs from the Past and the Present; 905), a collection covering the entire history of Japanese *waka* poetry, but concentrating on poems written after compilation of the three imperial anthologies of *shih* poetry. The preface of *Collection of Songs from the Past and the Present,* written by its compiler, Ki no Tsurayuki (868?–945?), quotes the "Ta hsü" (Major Preface" of the *Shih-ching* (Classic of Poetry) directly as a means of legitimating the literary production of *waka.* The emphasis on the elegant and graceful as well as the decorative and the witty indicates a fuller reception of the entire range of Six Dynasties and early T'ang poetry by this time. The subjects of *waka* poetry in *Collection of Songs from the Past and the Present* are often approached indirectly with typical late Six Dynasties *yi-p'ang* (obliquity). A poem does not directly describe an object but, rather, offers other elements that suggest the true subject, which is never explicitly mentioned.

Fujiwara no Kintō's (966–1041) *Wakan rōeishū* (Poems in Japanese and Chinese for Recitation; 1013) was a new form of poetic anthology that paired poems from the Japanese *waka* tradition with ones from the Chinese *shih* tradition to create a new level of complex interplay between literary motifs in the separate but equal realms of *waka* and *kanshi* (Chinese-style) poetry. The collection features some *shih* poetry by Yüan Chen (779–831) and much by his friend Po Chü-yi; one section of the collection forms an extended tribute to the latter.

The anthology is organized around the seasons in the first part and includes miscellaneous topics in the second. *Poems in Japanese and Chinese for Recitation*, which also includes a large number of *kanshi* by Japanese authors, became a major source of poetic inspiration for later writers.

NARRATIVES AND MISCELLANIES

The indigenous Japanese narrative form of *monogatari* (tale) demonstrates considerable thematic similarity to Chinese tales of the strange from the *chih-kuai* (records of anomalies) tradition, such as found in *T'ai-p'ing kuang-chi* (Extensive Records from the Reign of Great Tranquility), that suggest possible borrowing. For example, "Taketori monogatari" (Tale of the Bamboo Cutter; c. 880) relates the exile of a princess who is banished from the moon to live in the human realm because of a transgression she committed in heaven. She eventually returns to the moon, leaving her tearful adoptive parents behind, in a scene taken from Chinese *chih-kuai*.

The Chinese *ch'uan-ch'i* narrative of a scholar's visit to the grotto of a fabulous goddess where he carries on an amorous exchange, "Grotto of Playful Transcendents," had immense influence on Japanese narrative and poetry even though the text was soon lost in China and survived only in Japan. "Grotto of Playful Transcendents" features a refined male protagonist who reveals his cultural talents through exchanges of poetry with a series of cultivated courtesans. The first signs of its influence in poetry can be detected in the *Collection of Ten Thousand Leaves*, particularly in the poems of Yamanoue no Okura, but it is alluded to in *Poems in Japanese and Chinese for Recitation* and many other works. The use of a first-person narrative style and the careful descriptions of clothing found in "Grotto of Playful Transcendents" offered a new model for Japanese writers. The format of a narrative punctuated at critical moments by witty exchanges of poems taken from "Grotto of Playful Transcendents" formed the core of Japanese *monogatari* narratives from *Ise monogatari* (Tales of Ise; c. 915) onward.

The climax of traditional narrative comes with Murasaki Shikibu's masterpiece *Tale of Genji* (c. 1005), a richly intricate plot constructed around political, emotional, and familial conflicts of a distinctly Japanese cast. *Tale of Genji* integrates elements from Chinese narratives, such as the *ch'uan-ch'i* "Jen-shih chuan" (The Story of Miss Jen) and *Lieh-nü chuan* (Biographies of Illustrious Women), as well as lines and topics from Po Chü-yi's poetry. In the opening, *Tale of Genji* consists of an expansion of the plot of Po Chü-yi's "Song of Everlasting Regret" within the setting of the Japanese court. "Song of Everlasting Regret" recounts the rise of the consort Yang Kuei-fei to a position in the court above her proper social status because of the Emperor Hsüan-tsung's deep love for her (see chapters 11 and 14). Although *Tale of Genji* plays on the theme of human affection and ineluctable social barriers taken from this poem for its entire fifty-four chapters, it leads in new directions because Murasaki, as a female writer, fleshes out the traumas and contradictions in the thinking of the female protagonist and her rivals that remain opaque in Po Chü-yi's writing; the full elaboration of the court struggles for the emperor's affection in *Tale of Genji* gives the reader a sense of what Yang Kuei-fei and her rival consorts may have thought to themselves, but was not revealed within the original poem of Po Chü-yi.

The late Heian literatus Ōe no Masafusa (1041–1111) wrote miscellanies about the popular culture of his age in literary Chinese that took their inspiration from similar Chinese texts in circulation in Japan. His record of the pleasure quarters of his time, *Yūjo ki* (Records About Prostitutes; 1090), draws on a variety of Chinese sources, including the *ch'uan-ch'i* tale "Grotto of Playful Transcendents."

As the aristocratic class that had dominated cultural activities since the Heian period lost its political and economic power to the rising samurai class throughout the Kamakura (1185–1333), Warring States (1482–1558), and Momoyama periods (1573–1603), and military conflicts between rival factions grew to such intensity that they eventually destroyed the capital of Kyoto, the monasteries of Japan became the bearers of Chinese learning. The new dominance of temples in cultural life coincided with an increase in communications with the continent from the thirteenth century best represented by the introduction of Zen (Chinese, Ch'an) Buddhism into Japan from Sung dynasty China. Individual warrior families patronized the monasteries and they became cultural centers of the medieval period. The Gozan (five mountain) monasteries of Kyoto and Kamakura, officially established in 1342, became the new centers of Sinic culture. Large numbers of Japanese novices traveled to China for training during the Yüan dynasty, and Chinese monks took up residence in Japan during this period of unprecedented exchange. In contrast to the Tokugawa period (1603–1868), when the study of China took place at a distance, in the Kamakura and Muromachi periods direct exchanges with Chinese monks were far more frequent.

In the realm of Confucianism, the Sung Neo-Confucian learning of the Chu Hsi (1130–1200) school (see chapter 43) was brought back to Japan along with Zen Buddhism during the fourteenth century by monks who visited China. Confucian learning coexisted with Buddhist study in the Gozan temples. The monks of the Gozan temples produced a variety of Buddhist essays, *fa-yü* (Japanese, *hōgo*); vernacular records, *yü-lu* (Japanese, *goroku*); and parallel prose compositions, *ssu-liu shu* (Japanese, *shirokuso*), on Buddhist and metaphysical subjects. Collections of verse such as *San-t'i shih* (Three Poetic Modes), consisting largely of late T'ang poetry, were introduced for the first time during this period. Chinese poetry played a central role in both the intellectual life and the daily exchanges of the temples. Much of the surviving poetry from the Kamakura period focuses on Buddhism.

Under the patronage of the Ashikaga warrior family, the Gozan temple culture flowered in the fourteenth century during the period known as the Kitayama culture of Kyoto, a period of intense Chinese influence that produced several talented monastic poets who took their poetry outside the realm of Buddhism. Poetry became more intellectually involved and less Buddhist as monks explored every variety of contemporary Chinese poetry; they were becoming literary figures in their own right. For example, Musō Soseki (1275–1351) worked to introduce other styles of *shih* poetry from outside the domain of Buddhism and metaphysics. Sesson Yūbai (1290–1346) traveled to China at the age of eighteen to study and, because of worsening relations between Japan and the Mongols, could not return for ten years. The collection of his poems, *Mingashū* (Min River and Omei Mountain Collection; 1324–1328), completely Chinese in usage and style, was written during his stay.

Musō Soseki's student Zekkai Chūshin (1336–1405) spent nine years at two temples in Ming dynasty (1368–1644) China before returning to Japan to expand the realm of practiced *shih* poetry. Zekkai's collection of poems entitled *Shōkenkō* (Drafts by the Man of the Way of Plantain Strength; 1403), which includes many compositions from his stay in Ming China, consists of pentasyllabic and heptasyllabic *lü-shih* (regulated verse) plus heptasyllabic *chüeh-chü* (quatrains) and *so* (epistles in parallel prose).

An important poet of the late Muromachi period who lived through the Ōnin war of 1467 that destroyed Kyoto and its delicate culture was Ikkyū Sōjun (1394–1481). Ikkyū expressed in his poetry a paradoxical Buddhist philosophy of embracing the material world while pursuing enlightenment. He wrote of sexual adventures in brothels and other physical excesses as part of his Buddhist quest for understanding. Ikkyū experimented with aspects of Sung poetry, including colloquialisms. His collection of poems, *Kyōunshū* (Crazy Cloud Collection), consists almost entirely of heptasyllabic *chüeh-chü*. In his poetry, Ikkyū alternates between expressing desire for Buddhist salvation and blasphemous words and arrogance. Ikkyū carefully constructed a persona for himself as an untrammeled figure that contrasts with the detached metaphysical stance of earlier poets and points toward the later development of persona in the poetry of the Tokugawa period.

The rich variety of popular music, mime magic, song and stunts from the T'ang dynasty generally known as *san-yüeh* (dispersed music) found its way in the eighth century through Korea and directly from the continent into Japan, where it received imperial patronage and a role at Buddhist events (captured in illustrations). Although the imperial office of *sangaku* (the Japanese reading of *san-yüeh*) music was abolished during the Nara period, *sangaku* continued to find a strong following among the general population. *Sangaku* later took the form of humorous farces when it was integrated into the Japanese tradition as part of popular entertainment at temple and *jinja* (Shinto shrine) events. *Sangaku* is often referred to as *sarugaku* (monkey music) in its later incarnation, perhaps because of phonetic confusion between the two names. The playwright and dramaturgist Zeami Motokiyo (1364?–1443) shaped the traditions of *sangaku* and *gagaku* court music (Chinese, *ya-yüeh*) into the Japanese dramatic form of Nō theater. *Gagaku* (elegant music) had also been imported from China at the same time as *sangaku*. Nō dramas were presented for the shogun Ashikaga Yoshimitsu. A popular form of entertainment regarded with contempt by intellectuals thus acquired a new legitimacy. The texts of Nō plays by Zeami and his followers integrated elements from the Chinese poetic and intellectual tradition, above all allusions to Po Chü-yi, in order to give the subject being treated a new, high seriousness. Often the play would consist of a form of elaborate annotation on a single quotation from a Chinese literary text mentioned at the outset of the work.

The reception of Chinese literature in the Tokugawa period showed a new concern with, on the one hand, the proper and accurate apprehension of the Chinese tradition as one foreign to Japan and, on the other, the creative integration of elements from the Chinese tradition into distinctly Japanese literary expression. Japanese readers of Chinese became more sensitive to registers of language in Chinese literature and the distinction between vernacular and literary writing as they were exposed to an unprecedented number of imported books from the eighteenth century on.

The founder of the Tokugawa Confucian tradition, Fujiwara Seika (1561–1619), made poetry a large part of his intellectual activities, but his advocacy of Chu Hsi thought did move him out of the stylistic amalgam of T'ang and Sung poetics that he inherited from the Gozan tradition. Seika's student Hayashi Razan (1583–1657) laid down a strict moral definition of the role of poetry in society that relegated it to the margins of intellectual activity. But the spread of printing and the ready accessibility of Chinese poetic collections and sourcebooks, which included those drafted by Japanese hands by the late seventeenth century, allowed the practice of Chinese poetry, or *kanshi*, to spread unregulated outside Razan's academy. Ishikawa Jōzan (1583–1672), an associate of Razan's, dedicated himself to poetry after retiring to the mountains outside Kyoto, where he built a shrine devoted to the great poets of China. The Buddhist monk Genzei (1623–1668) studied Chinese poetry with a Ming émigré and thereafter devoted his efforts to developing an expressive style of poetry modeled on that of the Ming poet Yüan Hung-tao (1568–1610). According to legend, Genzei read Yüan Hung-tao's collection through repeatedly, then, having internalized its doctrine of free expression, burned it. Both figures were forerunners of later writers who worked outside the strict adherence to moral principles of Confucianism seen in the writings of Seika and Razan.

Itō Tōgai (1670–1736) was an early Confucian scholar who advocated the free, nondogmatic expression of human emotions in poetry and allowed stylistic flexibility at his Kyoto academy. In particular, Tōgai's essay on the *Classic of Poetry*, *Tokushiyōryō* (Essentials for Reading the Classic of Poetry), stressed the origins of poetic expression in the common thoughts and words of the people, thus suggesting that poetry had a more universal and less heuristic social function. Tōgai's theories on poetry loosened the restrictions on subject matter in poetry and shifted the emphasis to self-expression.

In the capital of Tokugawa Japan, Edo, the Confucian scholar Ogyū Sorai (1666–1728) promoted the newly introduced poetic theories of the Ming archaists Wang Shih-chen (1526–1590) and Li P'an-lung (1514–1570), both of whom took High T'ang poetics as a model in their radical stylistic conservatism (see chapters 20 and 21). Despite this approach, Sorai viewed poetic composition as a method for internalizing the Chinese language and not as an expression of moral intentions in the manner one finds in previous Confucian writers. The simple rules set down by Sorai for imitating *ku-wen-tz'u* (ancient prose; Japanese, *kobunji*), borrowed from the Ming archaists, allowed an increasing number of writers into the poetic circle, while at the same time giving aspiring poets the intellectual high ground: they professed to be writing in the pure High T'ang style that had been unknown to previous ignorant poets. The wide circulation after Sorai of Li P'an-lung's anthology of T'ang poetry, *T'ang-shih hsüan*, made it the dominant poetic model for the rest of the Tokugawa period. Sorai's most famous student, Hattori Nankaku (1683–1759), integrated the composition of poetry with painting and other cultural pursuits as a form of esthetic appreciation in his own distinctive *bunjin* (literati) way of life. Although Nankaku may have lived a refined life as defined by his archaic poetry, unlike previous poets he was constantly aware of his status as a published author with a large audience.

In the 1770s, the *haikai* (or haiku) genre of Japanese poetry, which took a focused and immediate depiction of the close-at-hand as its ideal, started to spill over into the production of Chinese poetry. *Haikai* poetry employed an often highly vernacular version of the Japanese language in its description of a much wider range of topics than had previously been possible in *shih* poetry. The emphasis on mixing both the refined and the vulgar advocated in Matsuo Bashō's (1644–1694) theories of *haikai* poetry was revived and promoted by such poets as Yosa Buson (1716–1738) at exactly the same time that the dogmatic adherence to formal rules for composition and content of poetry advocated by Sorai's *kobunji* movement lost momentum. Sung dynasty *shih* poetry was perceived as possessing the gritty expressiveness High T'ang poetry lacked and quickly overwhelmed the poetics of the *kobunji* movement.

The poet-priest Rikunyo (1734–1801) introduced Sung poetics and a new mimetic realism best exemplified in a poem describing the unheard-of topic of watching flies climbing on the outside of a window. The promotion of Sung poetry merged together with the esthetic framing of the quotidian and overly familiar in the lens of poetry derived from *haikai* poetics. The theories of unbridled poetic expression of the contemporary eighteenth-century Chinese poet Yüan Mei (1716–1797) also fed this trend. As a whole, the move toward a greater level of mimetic description led to the introduction of vocabulary and topics entirely alien to the Chinese tradition.

The largest school of Chinese poetry at the end of the eighteenth century was the Kōkosha (Rivers and Lakes) Society in Edo headed by Ichikawa Kansai (1794–1820), a strong promoter of free expression in the Sung poetic tradition. By the turn of the nineteenth century, Edo had displaced Kyoto as locus for the largest concentration of readers of Chinese poetry. At the same time, important schools devoted to the study of poetry emerged throughout western Japan; many rivaled Confucian academies in their scale. Some of these academies emerged in rural areas; the largest of them was that of Kan Chazan (1748–1827) in Kanabe.

A new generation of traveling *kanshi* poets who moved between various wealthy patrons and academies arose as the safety of domestic travel increased in the early nineteenth century. Women took on a significant role in poetic activity primarily as students at the schools of poetry, and some, such as Ema Saikō (1787–1861), established themselves in their own right. By the 1830s Chinese poetry had displaced *haikai* and *waka* as the most vital poetic form in Japan. Sophisticated poets with a fine sense of Chinese poetic diction and even of Chinese phonetics, such as Yanagawa Seigan (1789–1858) of the Gyokuchiginsha (Jade Pond Recitation Society) poetry school in Edo, stayed abreast of contemporary Ch'ing (1644–1911) poetics and produced works in no way inferior to those of China. Chinese poetry remained a vital literary tradition in Japan through the end of the nineteenth century.

The early Ming collection of tales of the supernatural *Chien-teng hsin-hua* (New Stories for Trimming the Lampwick) gained a wide audience among Japanese readers from the seventeenth century on, both in the original and in adaptations into Japanese. The most famous adaptation of *New Stories for Trimming the Lampwick* is *Otogibōko* (Fairy Maid, or the Protective Doll; 1666), which introduced the tales in an accessible Japanese idiom to an audience unfamiliar with literary Chinese. So thoroughly did the author of *Fairy Maid*, Asai Ryōi (d. 1691), adapt the plots of *New Stories for Trimming the Lampwick* to a Japanese context that most readers were unaware that the origin of these sixty-eight tales was Chinese. Asai Ryōi was a popular writer and moralist with no great literary ambitions; his activities were never far from Buddhist circles, and his purpose remained merely to delight and instruct. As a result of Ryōi's translations, *New Stories for Trimming the Lampwick* tales became an integral part of popular culture, showing up repeatedly in *ukiyo-zōshi* popular tales, *yomihon* narratives, and *kabuki* plays.

The increased trade with China through the port of Nagasaki, especially from the turn of the seventeenth century, introduced many works of vernacular Chinese fiction such as *Shui-hu chuan* (Water Margin), *San-kuo chih yen-yi* (Romance of the Three Kingdoms), *Chin P'ing Mei* (Gold Vase Plum), and others previously unknown to Japanese readers. As the Japanese scholarly community reached a higher level of sophistication, thanks to the one hundred and fifty years of peace that had allowed them to rebuild their intellectual infrastructure, they became increasingly dissatisfied with both the limitations of formally simplistic *ukiyo-zōshi* tales and the rigid morality of early Tokugawa Chu Hsi scholarship, which excluded many registers of Chinese narrative from serious consideration. Chinese vernacular fiction found a ready audience in Japan.

The Edo scholar Ogyū Sorai gave unprecedented prominence to the study of Chinese vernacular language as part of his program of teaching his students to understand Chinese properly as a foreign language. Sorai held that spoken Chinese offered an unmediated understanding of the Chinese cultural tradition. The study of vernacular Chinese, which previously had been but a mere curiosity, was given new intellectual legitimacy by Sorai and evolved into a major field of academic research.

Sorai employed the Nagasaki scholar-translator Okajima Kanzan (1674–1728) in his academy to teach Chinese using Chinese vernacular narratives as texts. In 1724 Kanzan left Edo for Kyoto, where he produced a series of primers and glossaries for Chinese vernacular narrative aimed at allowing the emerging audience of educated Japanese intellectuals outside the Confucian academies to read for themselves the exciting new works of Chinese narrative then coming into circulation. In addition, Kanzan translated the Japanese historical classic *Taiheiki* (Chronicle of the Great Peace) into vernacular Chinese in a style modeled after that of *Water Margin* under the title *Taiheiki engi* (Romance of the Chronicle of the Great Peace; 1719). This historical narrative allowed readers to see the Japanese tradition through the lens of Chinese-style narration. *Taiheiki engi* was an important forerunner for the adaptations of Chinese vernacular works in the context of Japanese history that would dominate late-eighteenth-century narrative. Examples of a Chinese plot (*shukō*) set in a Japanese environment (*sekai*) abound from this period.

In the early eighteenth century the head of the Kogidō academy in Kyoto, Itō Tōgai, also included vernacular Chinese literature in his teachings and produced several students who devoted themselves to the promotion of Chinese fiction. The most notable of those students was Oka Hakku (1692–1767), whose annotated editions of the Ming *hua-pen* collections of vernacular short stories such as *Shōsetsu seigen* (Essential Short Stories; 1743) and *Shōsetsu kigen* (Strange Short Stories; 1753) made Chinese vernacular fiction accessible to nonexperts. Whereas vernacular Chinese, with its unfamiliar colloquialisms, had initially been too difficult for the average Japanese reader, now it received greater circulation and appreciation.

When the study of Chinese narrative expanded beyond the Confucian academies, it found an audience in such figures as the Osaka doctor and self-taught scholar of Chinese Tsuga Teishō (1718–1794), who had no interest in either learning to speak Chinese or properly apprehending the Chinese classics.

Teishō was drawn to Chinese fiction as an end in itself unrelated to a Confucian project. He rewrote a series of Nō dramas and *jōruri* puppet plays as Yüan-style *tsa-chü* plays in a collection entitled *Shimeisen* (The Cicada That Calls Four Times; 1771). *Shimeisen* was a sophisticated literary experiment, for Teishō aimed at a discriminating audience. Although Chinese drama did not find a significant readership in Tokugawa Japan, adaptations of famous Chinese vernacular narratives such as *Water Margin, Hsi-yu chi* (Journey to the West), and *Romance of the Three Kingdoms* as *jōruri* and *kabuki* plays remained popular through the late nineteenth century.

Tsuga Teishō also combined Chinese classical and vernacular tales with elements of Japanese folklore and history to produce two collections of short stories, *Hanabusa zōshi* (Flowery Tales; 1749) and *Shigeshige yawa* (Expansive Anecdotes; 1766). Teishō wrote these stories in a hybrid literary language that combined vernacular and literary expressions from both Chinese and Japanese. This literary language would later form the stylistic basis of the dominant popular genre of the late eighteenth century, the *yomihon*.

Teishō's most noted student was the writer Ueda Akinari (1734–1809), who not only had no connection to the Confucian academies but was a follower of the Kokugaku (nativist) scholar Kamo Mabuchi (1697–1769). Mabuchi advocated a total rejection of the entire Chinese tradition as part of his literary ideology. Akinari seamlessly integrated the plots and some vocabulary from Chinese *hua-pen* tales with fragments of Japanese narrative and Nō dramatic texts to form haunting tales of the supernatural of considerable literary complexity in his collection entitled *Ugetsu monogatari* (Tales of the Rain and Moon; 1776). Akinari had completely domesticated the Chinese vernacular narrative so that it fit his own project of understanding Japan.

At the same time that Teishō and Akinari were working elements of Chinese narrative into delicately imbricated texts as part of their larger literary activities, professional translators such as Nishida Korenori (d. 1765) were producing straightforward, transparent translations of such works as *Journey to the West* (1758) aimed at a less discriminating audience. It was only at the turn of the nineteenth century that Takizawa Bakin (1767–1848) in Edo produced numerous extended translations and adaptations of Chinese vernacular fiction and narrative in literary Chinese that were aimed at a general reading audience but were produced with the high literary seriousness for which Teishō and Akinari were known. Bakin is most famous for *Nansō Satomi hakken den* (The Legend of the Eight Dogs of Satomi in Nansō; 1814), a historical novel 106 *satsu* (fascicles) long based loosely on *Water Margin*, but he also adapted *P'ing-yao chuan* (The Quelling of Demons), *Shui-hu hou-chuan* (Water Margin: Later Traditions), *Golden Vase Plum*, and many other novels into Japanese. Bakin wrote critical appraisals of earlier translators of Chinese fiction, thus indicating his awareness that he worked within a tradition of Japanese authors rewriting Chinese themes. Bakin's chief rival in Edo, Santō Kyōden (1761–1816), not to be outdone in either profligacy or erudition, also produced a series of similar adaptations including *Chūshin Suikoden* (The Loyal Vassal's Water Margin; 1799), a resetting of *Water Margin* in the context of a popular *jōruri* play. By the turn of the nineteenth century, much of the vocabulary and conventions of Chinese fiction had become familiar to the Japanese readership, a readership that consisted increasingly of women. Chinese vernacular expressions that had once been unintelligible to Japanese readers became so familiar that they were used to gloss newly imported Western vocabulary.

Not only were Chinese narratives themselves translated into Japanese, but Chinese theories about vernacular fiction by such Ch'ing scholars as Chin Sheng-t'an and Chang Chu-p'o gained currency in Japan (see chapter 46). In the middle of the eighteenth century, the Kyoto scholar Seida Tansō (1719–1785) wrote a short criticism of the *Tale of Genji* in which he applied Chin's structural critique to that masterpiece of the Japanese classical tradition. He was followed in the nineteenth century by Hagiwara Hiromichi (1815–1863), whose careful reading of the *Tale of Genji* within the schema of Chinese narratology entitled *Genji monogatari hyōshaku* (Critical and Explanatory Notes on *The Tale of Genji*; 1861) brought a new emphasis, inspired by Chinese critical approaches, to the structural organization of *Tale of Genji* and the question of authorial intention.

Ch'ing dynasty accounts of the pleasure quarters also produced their share of imitations in Japan such as Terakado Seiken's (1796–1868) history of prostitution and its dependent industries, *Edo Hanjōki* (An Account of the Prosperity of Edo; 1832–1836). *Edo Hanjōki* employs Chinese language, for the most part literary Chinese but with occasional vernacular Chinese and Japanese usages inserted, as a means of reconceiving overly familiar social phenomena with a new detachment.

Chinese narrative was the most familiar form of foreign literature in the late nineteenth century. As Western literature entered Japan after the Meiji Restoration (1868), the novelist Tsubouchi Shōyō (1859–1935) fell back on Chinese models of narrative in his attempt to introduce the theories of the Western novel in his *Shōsetsu shinzui* (The Quintessence of Fiction; 1885). Famous Japanese authors, such as Natsume Sōseki (1867–1916) and Mori Ōgai (1862–1922), resorted to the vocabulary and plot structures of Chinese vernacular and literary works in their attempt to render Western literature into Japanese. Authors such as Izumi Kyōka (1873–1939) and Nagai Kafū (1879–1959) made extensive borrowings from Chinese literature in their writings from the early twentieth century. After the end of World War II, Inoue Hisashi (1934–) wrote novels on Chinese themes with extensive allusions to the Chinese classical tradition. Above all, Japanese scholarship on all aspects of Chinese literature is among the very best in the world. During the twentieth century, Japanese Sinologists made available to the Japanese reading public expert translations of the whole range of literature in China, both with and without extensive commentaries and glosses. It may safely be said that Chinese literature is better known in Japan than anywhere else outside China.

Emanuel Pastreich

Chapter 55

THE RECEPTION OF CHINESE LITERATURE IN VIETNAM

The area that is now northern Vietnam was the ancient independent nation of Nam Viet until 111 B.C.E., when it fell under Chinese rule after being conquered by the armies of the Han dynasty. As a result, despite whatever indigenous traditions may have existed before the imposition of Chinese sovereignty, Vietnamese culture as it developed during the first millennium was inextricably linked to that of China. The Vietnamese adopted Chinese customs and no doubt composed Chinese literature from this time until Vietnam won independence from China in 939. There were some Vietnamese who traveled to China during the T'ang dynasty (618–907) and passed the Chinese civil service examinations; most notable among them is Khuong Cong Phu, who became a minister in the Chinese court. Chinese remained the primary written language of the state even after it gained independence from China.

The Ly dynasty that controlled Vietnam from 1009 to 1225 is often said to have established a centralized state, based on Confucian principles, that was governed using a standardized examination system based on the Chinese model, although the nature of the Vietnamese state during that period was much more complex than can be accounted for by a simple transplantation of Chinese institutions. Nonetheless, the Vietnamese exam required a sophisticated understanding of Literary Chinese and it continued to be employed with some interruptions until 1919, when French colonial administrators assumed control of education in Vietnam. In the same year, the Chinese themselves finally decisively rejected Literary Chinese in favor of vernacular writing. As a result, Vietnam had a steady population of scholars well versed in the Chinese classics for the entirety of its premodern history. The kings of the Tran dynasty (thirteenth to fourteenth centuries) were active as poets and as major patrons of Chinese poetry. Yet almost all the texts produced in Vietnam or introduced from China during the early period of its history vanished in subsequent years. The Chinese occupation of Vietnam from 1407 to 1428 during the early Ming dynasty (1368–1644) resulted in the systematic destruction of the written word in Vietnam.

Both *ku-feng* (old-style) and *lü-shih* (regulated verse) poetry were employed by poets in Vietnam; the composition of the latter was reinforced by obligatory practice mandated by the civil service examination. Later Vietnamese poets introduced indigenous folk prosody into Chinese verse, particularly the double-seven (*song-that*) doublet from Vietnamese song, thus modifying poetic composition in Literary Chinese *shih* poetry. The poet Nguyen Huy Oanh, in the eighteenth century, and the poet Dinh Nhat Than, in the nineteenth century, produced extensive poems in classical Chinese that adopted the Vietnamese meters of "six-eight" (*luc-bat*) and double-seven six-eight; these poems are the exception, however.

The poet best known for his attempt to establish a Vietnamese style of regulated verse is Nguyen Thuyen, who was active in the second half of the thirteenth century. He saw his great cultural mission as reforming poetry in Vietnam. With the king's permission, he adopted the surname Han in honor of Han Yü (768–824), the great Chinese archaist of the T'ang dynasty. Nguyen Thuyen introduced Vietnamese rhyme schemes into Chinese regulated poetry to create a new metric form known as *Han luat*. The exact nature of attempts to develop a Vietnamese verse form out of the regulations of classical *shih* poetry is largely unknown because of the systematic destruction of books by the invading Ming armies under direct orders from the Chinese emperor, Ch'eng-tsu (r. 1403–1424).

Typological similarities between Chinese and Vietnamese language, other than borrowed Sinitic vocabulary, made the adaptation of Chinese rhyme to Vietnamese poetry easier than was the case elsewhere in East Asia. Both Chinese and Vietnamese are tonal languages, with the corresponding interplay of level and oblique tones in song. Since both languages have many single-syllable morphemes, they can be pared down to verbs and nouns without the intervention of particles in poetic composition. Chinese vocabulary was largely kept in place even in poetic writings in Vietnamese using *chu nom* (adapted from the sinographs) phonetics. Chinese poetic forms could be maintained without the radical restructuring required by translation to a foreign syntax required in Japan or Korea.

A major moment in the evolution of Vietnamese literature was the establishment of the Tao-dan academy of poets under the patronage of King Le Thanh Tong (1442–1497; r. 1460–1497). The most famous product of that illustrious group is *Hong-duc quoc am thi tap* (Anthology of Verse in the National Language from the Hong-duc Reign), attributed to King Thanh Tong and his court. The anthology contains 328 works organized under the headings of heaven and earth, the conduct of men, landscape, plants and animals, and miscellaneous topics. The collection was meant as a celebration of Vietnamese cultural independence from China, although most of the themes remain within the Chinese poetic tradition. Nonetheless, the *Anthology of Verse* includes poems, such as a tribute to the betel nut, that stray considerably from the traditional motifs of Chinese poetry and represent an attempt to domesticate poetry.

The term "national language" (*quoc am*) refers to the *chu nom* script, employing Chinese characters chiefly for their phonetic value, which served as the only means of writing vernacular Vietnamese before the introduction of the Roman alphabet in the nineteenth century. As developed in Vietnam, *chu nom* also includes hundreds of characters made in Vietnam specifically for Vietnamese morphemes. Poetic composition in *chu nom* script, as opposed to Chinese, remained the exception through the end of the nineteenth century. Even in verse recorded in *chu nom*, much of the vocabulary is imported directly from the Chinese poetic tradition and not translated into vernacular Vietnamese. Many Chinese characters continued to be used for their semantic value. Given the nature of the *chu nom* script as a whole, if we wish to retain the identity categories of "Vietnamese" and "Chinese" with regard to it at all, then we would have to say that the Sinitic graphs, words, and terms in it have all been "Vietnamized" (i.e., vernacularized).

Modern patriotic critics and historians claim that there is a strong preference for military and nationalistic themes in Vietnamese poetry, ostensibly due to Vietnam's status as an object of constant violence. While in actuality there are probably no more such themes in Vietnamese poetry than in the poetry of other nations, certain poems are attributed to heroes in the struggle against Chinese domination such as Nguyen Trai (1380–1442), who was a major strategist in the victory over the Ming and establishment of the Le dynasty (1428–1789) in Vietnam. His poem "Binh Ngo dai cao" (Proclamation of Victory over the Wu) became famous in the Vietnamese tradition because it celebrates Vietnamese independence from China. Many of the poems attributed to national heroes may well be later compositions from the period of nineteenth-century nation-building under King Tu Duc (1847–1883).

Dang Tran Con (1710–1745), an investigator in the Censorate who lived in a time of immense strife during which government forces of the Le dynasty and rebels battled for control of the country, wrote the famous poem "Chinh phu ngam khuc" (Song of a Soldier's Wife). Written from the perspective of the abandoned wife of a soldier, the poem is full of Chinese place names and allusions to the classical Chinese tradition; as a poetic trope it is based directly on T'ang models, such as the famous "Ch'in-fu yin" (Lament of the Lady of Ch'in), by Wei Chuang (c. 836–910; see chapters 14 and 48). The surviving version in Vietnamese is written in the double-seven six-eight form and is most likely the work of Phan Huy Ich (1750–1822). The poem was frequently translated into Vietnamese, and at least seven different versions survive.

Poems by male authors employing the voice of a wronged woman were a popular genre in Vietnam. Nguyen Gia Thieu (1741–1798), a high-ranking northern aristocrat, composed another famous lament from the female perspective, entitled "Cung oan ngam khuc" (Plaint Inside the Royal Harem). The poem relates the tale of a royal consort who has lost the favor of the emperor, a frequent trope in poetry for a minister who cannot get the ear of the ruler. "A Plaint Inside the Royal Harem" survives in a Vietnamese version, but the preponderance of classical allusions renders it all but unintelligible to a reader without a strong background in Chinese literature.

Tran Te Xuong (1870–1907) was Confucian scholar born late in the classical tradition, who was unable to find employment in an age during which French colonial rule and modernization made his scholarly training useless. His caustic verse in Literary Chinese questioned the common sense of the era. He assumed the pose of a playboy dilettante as a literary response to his marginal social position.

Precious little in the way of narrative fiction survives from the early period of Vietnamese literary history. The oldest surviving text is a collection of tales of the strange modeled on Chinese precedents entitled *Viet dien u linh tap* (Anthology of the Unseen Powers of the Land of Viet; 1329), written by Ly Te Xuyen. It relates twenty-seven legends in bibliographic form.

The earliest surviving extended fictional work produced in Vietnam, *Truyen ky man luc* (Expansive Record of Wondrous Legends; oldest surviving edition dated 1712), by Nguyen Du, dates to the beginning of the sixteenth century. Scion of a distinguished family of intellectuals, Nguyen Du lived through a period of intense strife caused by both internal revolts and a palace coup. He wrote *Truyen ky man luc* after he retired to the countryside to escape from the chaos of the age. *Expansive Record of Wondrous Legends* is modeled on the Chinese collection of literary tales of the supernatural by Ch'ü Yu (1347–1433), *Chien-teng hsin-hua* (New Stories for Trimming the Lampwick). In *Expansive Record*, Nguyen Du weaves details from Vietnamese history together with fabulous elements and plot structures from the Chinese collection. Poetry plays an important role in these stories. The stories feature strong moralistic themes; for example, in one story a fox changes into a scholar-official and presents himself to the king to lecture him on moral principles.

There also survives an edition of *Expansive Record* dated 1783 that employs *chu nom* annotations on the text, thus implying a wide readership among those not conversant with Chinese literature. A sequel to *Expansive Record*, entitled *Truyen ky tan pha* (New Assortment of Wondrous Tales [*ch'uan-ch'i*]), is attributed to Doan Thi Diem (1705–1748), a female author who is also known for translations of Chinese poetry into *chu nom*.

Vietnamese readers had a particular penchant for the *ts'ai-tzu chia-jen* (brilliant scholars and beautiful girls) narratives that relate the efforts of a handsome young man to pass the examinations and make a perfect match with a beautiful young woman despite various obstacles. These romances were also immensely popular with Chinese readers through the eighteenth century and continued to find an audience in Vietnam because of the similar examination culture. Ly Van Phuc (1785–1849) translated the famed *ts'ai-tzu chia-jen* novel *Yü Chiao Li* (Jade Charming Pear, or A Tale of Hong-yü, Wu-chiao, and Lu Meng-li) into Vietnamese in six-eight meter under the title *Ngoc kieu le tan truyen.* In Vietnam the audience for translations of Chinese fiction remained substantially Vietnamese, as opposed to the rest of Southeast Asia, where the readership for Malay translations of Chinese fiction in Malaysia or the Indonesian archipelago was primarily ethnic Chinese.

Little is known about how novels actually circulated in Vietnam, although a 1734 decree in Trinh (northern Vietnam) requiring that books be printed locally suggests that there was a large trade with China. There were close ties with Kwangtung publishers and sometimes joint publications between them and Saigon publishing houses—some *chu nom* works were even published in Kwangtung for export to Vietnam. The degree to which ethnic Chinese living in Vietnam may have been involved in the translation and importation of Chinese fiction remains unknown. The *chu nom* writing system was not frequently employed before the eighteenth century, but during that period there was an explosion of translations from the Chinese employing *chu nom* aimed at a general audience.

Probably in the eighteenth century, and certainly in the nineteenth century, a wide variety of Chinese novels circulated in Vietnamese translation (using *chu nom* script) in both manuscript and xylographically printed booklets. These works are generally known as *truyen* (tales) and were in most cases rendered into verse rather than prose. There were two major verse forms in these narratives: *luc bat* (six/eight-foot verse) and *song that luc bat* (seven/seven, six/eight verse). These extended verse novels enjoyed great popularity in Vietnam into the modern era. The features of Vietnamese verse narrative may very well be related to the popularity of *t'an-tz'u* (strummed lyrics) ballad forms of Chinese fiction that circulated in south China and formed the basis of much of the popular reception of Chinese narrative in the late eighteenth and early nineteenth centuries (see chapter 50). For example, there is the Vietnamese verse narrative *Hoa tien Truyen* (Tale of the Flowery Note Paper), by the distinguished literatus Nguyen Huy Tu (1743–1790), which is based on the Cantonese anthology of *t'an-tz'u* entitled *Hua-chien chi* (Record of Flowery Note Paper). Unlike their peers in Korea and Japan, Vietnamese male authors took an active interest in this genre, which in China was considered feminine.

The famous *truyen* tales often take the relationship of China to its cultural margins as their explicit themes and thereby recapitulate issues of Vietnam's status relative to the Chinese great tradition in their content. The earliest surviving *truyen*, *Vuong Tuong Truyen* (The Tale of Vuong Tuong, which may have origins before the eighteenth century, although its authorship is uncertain), relates the fate of Wang Chao-chün, a Chinese princess who is married to the chief of the northern Hsiung-nu nomads during the Han dynasty and sent off tearfully to the border region. *The Tale of Vuong Tuong* appears to be a cobbling together of various versions of Wang Chao-chün's tragic fate, perhaps including the Yüan drama by Ma Chih-yüan (1260–1325), "Han-kung ch'iu" (Autumn in the Han Palace), or it may be based on some yet unidentified Chinese tale. By playing on the transplantation of a figure from the center of Chinese cultural authority to its margins, the Vietnamese author brings up the Vietnamese condition without ever mentioning Vietnam. A similar theme animates *To Cong phung su* (Su Wu Carries Out His Duties), which appears to derive entirely from an entry in the *Han shu* (History of the Han Dynasty). This verse narrative relates the adventures of Su Wu, a Chinese envoy held in captivity by the Hsiung-nu from 99 to 81 B.C.E.

The Chinese novel that gained the greatest fame in Vietnam was *Chin Yün-ch'iao chuan* (The Tale of Chin Yün-ch'iao), a *ts'ai-tzu chia-jen* novel of the early eighteenth century widely known in its Vietnamese translation as a long narrative poem in six-eight verse entitled *Kim Van Kieu* (known in English as the *Tale of Kieu*). The Vietnamese version is attributed to Nguyen Du (1765–1820; not the same person as the author with the homophonous name discussed above), a vice-minister in the Nguyen dynasty who served on a diplomatic mission to China in 1813. The oldest surviving edition of *The Tale of Kieu* was published in Hanoi around 1815 and circulated widely.

This tragic tale of a woman forced into a morally ambiguous position between greater powers came to be viewed as the essence of Vietnamese historical experience. Many Vietnamese down to the modern age were capable of reciting the text from memory. The heroine of *The Tale of Kieu*, Vuong Thuy Kieu (in Chinese, Wang Ts'ui-ch'iao), is forced to sell herself into prostitution in order to redeem her wrongly imprisoned brother and father. She ends up the concubine of Tu Hai (in Chinese, Hsü Hai), a piratical rebel controlling the coast of south China. The local governor asks Thuy Kieu to persuade Tu Hai to surrender to the authorities; she does so, unaware that the command is a ruse to have him killed.

Nguyen Du reduces the number of incidents in the long plot and creates a relatively compact narrative poem. The protagonist, Kieu, employs Chinese verse, including *chüeh-chü* and *ku-shih* poems, throughout the novel as a means of self-expression. There are more than sixty allusions to Chinese poems in the work, including the poetry of the T'ang courtesan Hsüeh T'ao (770–830). Nguyen also altered the original Chinese plot so as to make Vuong Thuy Kieu and Tu Hai the clear heroes of the story.

Vuong Thuy Kieu's unwitting role in the destruction of her own husband at the hands of the Chinese had deep political resonance for the Vietnamese reader of the nineteenth century. The courtesan torn between the Chinese commander and the pirate brigand who must negotiate between the political center and the marginal rebel was read as an allegory for the cultural status of Vietnam with regard to the cultural and political encroachment of China and, later on, of France. Kieu represented a righteous Vietnamese who is tricked into betraying her country.

Such, at least, is the typical modern nationalist interpretation of this long poem, although other subtle and more nuanced readings of *The Tale of Kieu* are possible.

In the nineteenth century, Vietnamese writers seized on the narrative form presented by the vernacular Chinese novel as a register of language appropriate for relating the history of Vietnam's battle against China for political independence. Interestingly enough, although these novels take a nationalistic perspective, they were not written in vernacular Vietnamese but, rather, in an often highly vernacular Chinese language. These historical novels probably date from the reign of King Tu Duc.

One example of such a narrative is the anonymous and undated nineteenth-century work *Hoang Viet xuan thu* (Spring and Autumn Annals of Imperial Vietnam), a history that relates the conflicts between Vietnam and Ming China in the period 1400 to 1428. Another such vernacular Chinese narrative from the nineteenth century is *Viet-nam khai quoc chi truyen* (Record of the Founding of the Nation of Vietnam), by Nguyen Bang Trung. *Record of the Founding of the Nation of Vietnam* covers the years 1567 through 1802, the date of the establishment of the name Vietnam. The novel is written in a highly vernacular Chinese language, but includes interlinear annotations with the Vietnamese terms for Chinese words supplied. All the standard storyteller's conventions of the Chinese vernacular novel are employed. Both stories attempt to build a mythology of national unity in the period of imminent threat from French expansion. China, however, and not France, is the explicit alien power depicted.

The format of the Chinese historical record was seized on by Vietnamese as a means of filling the large lacunae in their history. Nguyen Van Danh wrote *Dai Nam hanh nghia liet nu tryuen* (A Record of the Virtuous Acts of the Women of the Great Kingdom of Vietnam) in 1846 to fill just such a gap in the historical record: the lack of writings on virtuous Vietnamese women. *A Record of the Virtuous Acts of the Women of the Great Kingdom of Vietnam* is one of the few premodern narratives that focuses exclusively on women.

The golden age of translation from Chinese fiction into Vietnamese came at the turn of the twentieth century when the Roman alphabet, introduced originally by the French, gained acceptance as a national script, known as *quoc ngu* to Vietnamese, and had little association with imperialism. In fact, *quoc ngu* became a powerful tool of nationalistic resistance against the French, who first invaded Vietnam in 1858 and controlled the entire country by 1884. Since the Roman alphabet was far better suited for rendering Vietnamese than the previous *chu nom* system, it quickly displaced the latter. Hundreds of Chinese novels were rendered into Vietnamese in *quoc ngu* for the first time and published from the turn of the century through the 1930s. There is thus a poignant irony in the fact that the new script based on the Roman alphabet was decidedly more effective for translating Chinese novels into Vietnamese than was the old script modeled on the sinographs. The scholar of classical Chinese Phan Ke Binh (1875–1921) rendered many Chinese novels into Vietnamese, including *San-kuo yen-yi* (Romance of the Three Kingdoms). In the 1920s Ly Ngoc Hung (most likely an ethnic Chinese) translated a wide variety of *wu-hsia* (knight-errant) novels for the growing urban population of Saigon and Hanoi. There was also a large market for translations of the *yüan-yang hu-tieh* (mandarin ducks and butterflies—the traditional Chinese symbols for a pair of lovers) romantic Chinese novels of the early twentieth century (see chapter 38). Many of the translators were journalists.

There is a vital tradition of satirical drama in Vietnam, known as *hat cheo,* that one source traces back to a Chinese actor hired by the Vietnamese king in 1005 to teach theater in Vietnam. The classic opera of Vietnam, known as *hat boi,* was directly patronized by the emperor and scholars and performed in the court. The surviving works are based on Chinese opera. Chinese opera was reportedly first introduced when a troupe arrived in Vietnam with the invading Mongol army in 1285. Supposedly the actors' lives were spared in return for teaching their skills to the Vietnamese. There is another record from 1350 of a Chinese performer who served at the northern court of Vietnam. Although originally limited to the royal court, *hat boi* opera was made part of popular entertainment by Dao Huy(?) Tu in the sixteenth century. The surviving works of *hat boi* date mostly from an intense attempt to import Chinese drama during the reign of King Tu Duc. Vietnamese perceived Chinese culture as more modern and advanced. Although performed in Vietnamese, *hat boi* featured many Chinese loanwords. Operas in *hat boi* are classified as military or domestic. *The Romance of the Three Kingdoms* was a popular subject for *hat boi* theater.

In 1919 the French colonial powers took over the school system and started the long process of erasing Vietnam's old Chinese-oriented cultural heritage. The deep influence that Chinese literature had in Vietnam before World War II has been all but obliterated by intensely nationalist approaches to literature stressing the originality of Vietnamese folk traditions and attributing all literature to indigenous origins. Many scholars have dismissed writing in Literary Chinese as unworthy of serious consideration. Massive archives of texts in Chinese remain in Vietnam that are overseen by librarians who cannot read Chinese. Until they are properly studied, our understanding of the Vietnamese tradition will remain incomplete. Chinese martial-arts tales and Chinese ideas of modernity in literature have continued to seep into Vietnam, however, to the present day, but they are now all presented in Vietnamese rendered in the Roman alphabet.

The experience of Vietnam vis-à-vis the Chinese literary tradition in many respects resembles that of Japan and Korea. First came a stage of tutelage and emulation, primarily in Literary Chinese. Gradually, however, a transition was made to increasingly vernacular styles of writing, mirroring a process that occurred in China itself. Next came a period of linguistic shift to literature written in native languages and with indigenous (non-sinographic) scripts. Then, with the coming of the West to East Asia, still more radical adjustments were made in vocabulary, grammar, style, genre, and content. However, now that China is beginning to exercise its economic, political, and cultural muscles once again, it remains to be seen how its literary influence will be felt, not only by its East Asian neighbors, but throughout the world.

Emanuel Pastreich

SUGGESTIONS FOR FURTHER READING

The following list of readings is by no means intended to constitute a complete bibliography for the study of the history of Chinese literature, much less for Chinese literature in general. Here are listed only selected items, primarily in West European languages, that are of particular relevance to the chapters in this volume and that are considered to be both relatively accessible and generally reliable. The serious student should be aware that there is a vast amount of excellent scholarship on Chinese literature in East European languages (especially Russian), Chinese, and Japanese. For a much more complete and frequently updated database of relevant works, the interested reader is invited to consult the online bibliography at **http://ccat.sas.upenn.edu/chineselitbib.**

For ease of access, the list below is divided into the following sections:

General Anthologies
Poetry
- Classical Poetry
- Lyrics and Arias
- Elegies and Rhapsodies
- Folk and Folklike Songs, Ballads, and Narrative Verse
- Modern
- Poetry and Painting

Prose
- Premodern
- Modern

Fiction
  Classical
  Vernacular
  Modern
Drama
  General
  Chu-kung-tiao and Other Early Forms
  Tsa-chü
  Ch'uan-ch'i, with Its Predecessors and Successors
  Peking Opera
  Local and Regional Theater
  Puppet and Shadow Theater
  Modern Plays; Film
Classics
Thought
Myth and Generalized Religion
Buddhism
Taoism
Commentary, Criticism, and Theory
Oral and Performing Arts; Popular Narratives; Proverbs
Travel Literature and Sketches
Ethnic and Regional Literature
Gender
Language and Script
Handbooks and Encyclopedias

N.B.: Several of the entries might well have been listed under two or more of the sections but are given only once.

GENERAL ANTHOLOGIES

Birch, Cyril, ed. *Anthology of Chinese Literature*. 2 vols. New York: Grove, 1965, 1972.

Giles, Herbert A., ed. and trans. *Gems of Chinese Literature*. 1st ed., Shanghai: Kelly and Walsh, 1923; 2nd rev. ed. in 2 vols., London: Quaritch, 1926.

Knechtges, David R., trans. and annot. *Wen xuan, or Selections of Refined Literature*. 3 vols. (8 projected). Princeton: Princeton University Press, 1982, 1986, 1996.

Mair, Victor H., ed. *The Columbia Anthology of Traditional Chinese Literature*. New York: Columbia University Press, 1994.

———. *The Shorter Columbia Anthology of Traditional Chinese Literature*. New York: Columbia University Press, 2000.

Minford, John, and Joseph S. M. Lau, ed. *Classical Chinese Literature: An Anthology of Translations*. Vol. 1. *From Antiquity to the Tang Dynasty*. New York: Columbia University Press; Hong Kong: Chinese University Press, 2000.

Owen, Stephen, ed. *An Anthology of Chinese Literature*. New York: W. W. Norton, 1996.

Zach, Erwin von. *Die chinesische Anthologie*. 2 vols. Cambridge: Harvard University Press, 1958.

POETRY

Classical Poetry

Birrell, Anne. *Chinese Love Poetry: New Songs from a Jade Terrace; A Medieval Anthology*. 1st ed., 1982, 1986; 2nd ed., London: Penguin Books, 1995.

Cai, Zongqi. *The Matrix of Lyric Transformation: Poetic Modes and Self-Presentation in Early Chinese Pentasyllabic Poetry*. Ann Arbor: Center for Chinese Studies, University of Michigan, 1996.

Chan, Marie. *Kao Shih*. Boston: Twayne, 1978.

Chang, H. C., ed. and trans. *Chinese Literature*. Vol. 2. *Nature Poetry*. Edinburgh: Edinburgh University Press, 1977.

Chang, Kang-i Sun. *Six Dynasties Poetry*. Princeton: Princeton University Press, 1986.

Chaves, Jonathan, ed. and trans. *The Columbia Book of Later Chinese Poetry: Yüan, Ming, and Ch'ing Dynasties (1279–1911)*. New York: Columbia University Press, 1986.

———. *Mei Yao-ch'en and the Development of Early Sung Poetry*. New York: Columbia University Press, 1976.

———. *Pilgrim of the Clouds: Poems and Essays from Ming China*. New York and Tokyo: Weatherhill, 1978.

———. *Singing of the Source: Nature and God in the Poetry of the Chinese Painter Wu Li*. Honolulu: University of Hawaii Press, 1993.

Chou, Chih-p'ing. *Yüan Hung-tao and the Kung-an School*. Cambridge: Cambridge University Press, 1988.

Chou, Eva Shan. "Allusions and Periphrasis as Modes of Poetry in Tu Fu's 'Eight Laments.'" *Harvard Journal of Asiatic Studies*, 45 (1991): 5–53.

———. *Reconsidering Tu Fu: Literary Greatness in a Cultural Context*. Cambridge: Cambridge University Press, 1995.

———. "Tu Fu's Social Conscience: Compassion and Topicality in His Poetry." *Harvard Journal of Asiatic Studies*, 51 (1985): 77–128.

Davis, A. R. *T'ao Yüan-ming (A.D. 365–427): His Works and Their Meaning*. 2 vols. Cambridge: Cambridge University Press, 1983.

Davis, A. R., ed.; Robert Kotewall and Norman L. Smith, trans. *The Penguin Book of Chinese Verse*. Harmondsworth: Penguin, 1962.

Duke, Michael S. *Lu Yu*. Boston: Twayne, 1977.

Eide, Elling O. "On Li Po." In Arthur Wright and Denis Twitchett, ed., *Perspectives on the T'ang*, pp. 367–403. New Haven: Yale University Press, 1973.

Frankel, Hans H. *The Flowering Plum and the Palace Lady*. New Haven: Yale University Press, 1976.

Frodsham, J. D. *The Murmuring Stream: The Life and Works of the Chinese Nature Poet Hsieh Ling-yun (385–433), Duke of K'ang-lo*. 2 vols. Kuala Lumpur: University of Malaya Press, 1967.

Frodsham, J. D., trans. *The Poems of Li Ho (791–817)*. Oxford: Oxford University Press, 1970.

Frodsham, J. D., and Ch'eng Hsi, trans. *An Anthology of Chinese Verse: Han Wei Chin and the Northern and Southern Dynasties*. Oxford: Oxford University Press, 1967.

Fuller, Michael. *The Road to East Slope: The Development of Su Shi's Poetic Voice*. Stanford: Stanford University Press, 1990.

Goldin, Paul Rakita. "Reading Po Chü-i." *T'ang Studies*, 12 (1996): 57–95.

Graham, A. C., trans. *Poems of the Late T'ang*. Harmondsworth: Penguin, 1965.

Hawkes, David. *A Little Primer of Tu Fu*. Oxford: Oxford University Press, 1967.

Hightower, James R., trans. and annot. *The Poetry of T'ao Ch'ien*. Oxford: Oxford University Press, 1970.

Holzman, Donald. *Poetry and Politics: The Life and Works of Juan Chi,* A.D. *210–263*. Cambridge: Cambridge University Press, 1976.

Hsieh, Daniel. "The Origin and Nature of the 'Nineteen Old Poems.'" *Sino-Platonic Papers*, 77 (January 1998): 1–49.

Hung, William. *Tu Fu: China's Greatest Poet*. 2 vols. Cambridge: Harvard University Press, 1952.

Kroll, Paul W. "Lexical Landscapes and Textual Mountains in the High T'ang." *T'oung Pao*, 84.1–3 (1998), 62–101.

———. *Meng Hao-jan*. Boston: Twayne, 1981.

Kubin, Wolfgang. *Das lyrische Werk des Tu Mu (803–852): Versuch einer Deutung*. Wiesbaden: Otto Harrassowitz, 1976.

Kwong, Charles Yim-tze. *Tao Qian and the Chinese Poetic Tradition: The Quest for Cultural Identity*. Ann Arbor: Center for Chinese Studies, University of Michigan, 1995.

Levy, Dore J. *Chinese Narrative Poetry: The Late Han Through T'ang Dynasties*. Durham: Duke University Press, 1988.

Lin, Shuen-fu, and Stephen Owen, ed. *The Vitality of the Lyric Voice:* Shih *Poetry from the Late Han to the T'ang*. Princeton: Princeton University Press, 1986.

Liu, James J. Y. *The Art of Chinese Poetry*. Chicago: University of Chicago Press, 1962.

———. *The Poetry of Li Shang-yin, Ninth-Century Baroque Chinese Poet*. Chicago: University of Chicago Press, 1967.

Liu, Wu-chi, and Irving Y. C. Lo, ed. *Sunflower Splendor: Three Thousand Years of Chinese Poetry*. Bloomington: Indiana University Press, 1975.

Lo, Irving Y. C., and William Schultz, ed. *Waiting for the Unicorn: Poems and Lyrics of China's Last Dynasty, 1644–1911*. Bloomington: Indiana University Press, 1986.

Lynn, Richard John. *Kuan Yün-shih*. Boston: Twayne, 1980.

———. "Orthodoxy and Enlightenment: Wang Shih-chen's (1634–1711) Theory of Poetry and Its Antecedents." In W. T. deBary, ed., *The Unfolding of Neo-Confucianism*, pp. 215–269. New York: Columbia University Press, 1975.

———. "Tradition and the Individual: Ming and Ch'ing Views of Yüan Poetry." *Journal of Oriental Studies* (University of Hong Kong), 15 (1977): 1–19.

———. "Traditional Chinese Poetry Societies: A Case Study of the Moon Spring Society (Pujiang, Zhejiang, 1286/7)." In Léon Vandermeersch, ed., *La société civile face à l'état dans les traditions chinoise, japonaise, coréenne et vietnamienne*, pp. 77–108. Paris: École Française d'Extrême-Orient, 1994.

Mair, Victor H. *Four Introspective Poets: A Concordance to Selected Poems by Roan Jyi, Lii Bor, Chern Tzyy-arng, and Jang Jeouling*. Monograph Series, 20. Tempe: Arizona State University Center for Asian Studies, 1987.

———. "Scroll Presentation in the T'ang Dynasty." *Harvard Journal of Asiatic Studies*, 38 (1978): 35–60.

Mair, Victor H., and Tsu-Lin Mei. "The Sanskrit Origins of Recent Style Prosody." *Harvard Journal of Asiatic Studies*, 51.2 (1991): 375–470.

Marney, John. *Beyond the Mulberries: An Anthology of Palace-Style Poetry by Emperor Chien-wen of the Liang Dynasty*. Asian Library Series, 17. San Francisco: Chinese Materials Center, 1982.

———. *Chiang Yen*. Boston: Twayne, 1981.

———. *Liang Chien-wen Ti*. Boston: Twayne, 1976.

Mather, Richard B. *The Poet Shen Yüeh (441–513): The Reticent Marquis*. Princeton: Princeton University Press, 1988.

McCraw, David R. *Du Fu's Laments from the South*. Honolulu: University of Hawaii Press, 1992.

Mei, Tsu-Lin, and Yu-kung Kao. "Tu Fu's 'Autumn Meditations': An Exercise in Linguistic Criticism." *Harvard Journal of Asiatic Studies*, 28 (1968): 59–67.

Mote, Frederick W. *The Poet Kao Ch'i, 1336–1374*. Princeton: Princeton University Press, 1962.

Nienhauser, William H., Jr. *P'i Jih-hsiu*. Boston: Twayne, 1979.

Owen, Stephen. *The End of the Chinese "Middle Ages": Essays in Mid-Tang Literary Culture*. Stanford: Stanford University Press, 1996.

———. *The Great Age of Chinese Poetry: The High T'ang*. New Haven: Yale University Press, 1981.

———. *Poetry of the Early T'ang*. New Haven: Yale University Press, 1977.

———. *The Poetry of Meng Chiao and Han Yü*. New Haven: Yale University Press, 1975.

Palandri, Angela Jung. *Yüan Chen*. Boston: Twayne, 1977.

Rouzer, Paul. *Writing Another's Dream: The Poetry of Wen Tingyun*. Stanford: Stanford University Press, 1993.

Schmidt, J. D. *Stone Lake: The Poetry of Fan Chengda (1126–1193)*. Cambridge: Cambridge University Press, 1992.

———. *Within the Human Realm: The Poetry of Huang Zunxian, 1848–1905*. Cambridge: Cambridge University Press, 1994.

———. *Yang Wan-li*. Boston: Twayne, 1976.

Scott, John. *Love and Protest: Chinese Poems from the Sixth Century* B.C. *to the Seventeenth Century* A.D. London: Rapp and Whiting; New York: Harper and Row, 1972.

Stimson, Hugh M. *Fifty-five T'ang Poems: A Text in the Reading and Understanding of T'ang Poetry*. New Haven: Yale University Press, 1976.

Tu, Kuo-ch'ing. *Li Ho*. Boston: Twayne, 1979.

Wagner, Marsha L. *Wang Wei*. Boston: Twayne, 1981.

Waley, Arthur. *The Life and Times of Po Chü-i, 772–846* A.D. London: George Allen and Unwin, 1949.

———. *The Poetry and Career of Li Po, 701–762* A.D. London: George Allen and Unwin, 1950.

Watson, Burton. *Chinese Lyricism:* Shih *Poetry from the Second to the Twelfth Century, with Translations*. New York: Columbia University Press, 1971.

———. *The Columbia Book of Chinese Poetry from Early Times to the Thirteenth Century*. New York: Columbia University Press, 1984.

Wong, Shirleen S. *Kung Tzu-chen*. Boston: Twayne, 1973.

Yates, Robin D. S. *Washing Silk: The Life and Selected Poetry of Wei Chuang (834?–910)*. Cambridge: Harvard University Press, 1988.

Yoshikawa, Kōjirō. *Gen Min shi gaisetsu* (General History of Classical Verse During the Yüan and Ming Eras). Translated by J. Timothy Wixted as *Five Hundred Years of Chinese Poetry*. Princeton: Princeton University Press, 1989.

Yu, Pauline. *The Poetry of Wang Wei: New Translations and Commentary*. Bloomington: Indiana University Press, 1980.

Zach, Erwin von, trans. *Han Yü's Poetische Werke*. Cambridge: Harvard University Press, 1952.

———. *Tu Fu's Gedichte*. 2 vols. Cambridge: Harvard University Press, 1952.

Lyrics and Arias

Bryant, Daniel. *Lyric Poets of the Southern T'ang: Feng Yen-ssu, 903–960, and Li Yü, 937–978*. Vancouver: University of British Columbia Press, 1982.

Chang, Kang-i Sun. *The Evolution of Chinese* Tz'u *Poetry: From Late T'ang to Northern Sung*. Princeton: Princeton University Press, 1980.

Chu, Madeline Men-lin. *Expanded Lyricism: Ch'en Wei-sung's (1626–1682)* Tz'u *Poems*. Amherst: Asian Studies Committee of the University of Massachusetts, 1988.

Ch'üan Yüan san-ch'ü (The Complete Yüan *san-ch'ü*). Sui Shu-shen, ed. 2 vols. Peking: Chung-hua, 1964, 1981.

Crump, James I. *Song-Poems from Xanadu: Studies in Mongol-Dynasty Song-Poetry (San-ch'ü)*. Ann Arbor: Center for Chinese Studies, University of Michigan, 1993.

———. *Songs from Xanadu*. Ann Arbor: Center for Chinese Studies, University of Michigan, 1983.

Dolby, William. "Kuan Han-ch'ing." *Asia Major*, 16 (1971): 1–60.

———. "'Tea-Trading Ship' and the Tale of Shuang Chien and Su Little Lady." *Bulletin of the School of Oriental and African Studies*, 60.1 (1997): 47–63.

Fong, Grace S. *Wu Wenying and the Art of Southern Song* ci *Poetry*. Princeton: Princeton University Press, 1987.

Fu, Sherwin. "Ma Chih-yuan's San Ch'ü." *Tamkang Review*, 4.1 (1975): 1–17.

Fusek, Lois. *Among the Flowers: The* Hua-chien chi. New York: Columbia University Press, 1982.

Hightower, James R., and Florence Chia-ying Yeh. *Studies in Chinese Poetry*. Cambridge: Harvard University Asia Center, 1998.

Hoffmann, Alfred. *Die Lieder des Li Yü, 937–978, Herrscher der Südlichen T'ang Dynastie, Als Einführung in die Kunst der chinesisichen Lieddichtung aus dem Urtext vollständig übertragen und erläutert*. Cologne: Greven, 1950.

Hu Pin-ching. *Li Ch'ing-chao*. New York: Twayne, 1965.

Jao, Tsong-yi. *Airs de Touen-houang (Touen-houang k'iu): Textes à chanter des VIIIe-Xe siècles*. Paul Demiéville, trans. Mission Paul Pelliot. Documents conservés à la Bibliothèque nationale, 2. Paris: Editions du Centre National de la recherche scientifique, 1971.

Johnson, Dale R. *Yuan Music Drama: Studies in Prosody and Structure and a Complete Catalogue of Northern Arias in the Dramatic Style*. Ann Arbor: Center for Chinese Studies, University of Michigan, 1980.

Lin, Shuen-fu. *The Transformation of the Chinese Lyrical Tradition: Chiang K'uei and Southern Sung* Tz'u *Poetry*. Princeton: Princeton University Press, 1978.

Liu, James J. Y. *Major Lyricists of the Northern Sung, A.D. 960–1126*. Princeton: Princeton University Press, 1974.

Lo, Irving Yucheng. *Hsin Ch'i-chi*. New York: Twayne, 1971.

Lynn, Richard John. "Some Attitudes of Yüan Critics Toward the San-ch'ü." *Literature East and West*, 16.3 (September 1972): 950–960.

McCraw, David R. *Chinese Lyricists of the Seventeenth Century*. Honolulu: University of Hawaii Press, 1990.

Metzger, Charles R., and Richard F. S. Yang. *Fifty Songs from the Yuan*. London: George Allen and Unwin, 1967.

Picken, L. E. R. "Secular Chinese Songs of the Twelfth Century." *Studia Musicologica Academiae Scientiarum Hungaricae*, 8 (1966): 125–146.

Schlepp, Wayne. *San-ch'ü: Its Technique and Imagery*. Madison: University of Wisconsin Press, 1970.

———. "Sanqu." In Chan Sin-wai and David E. Pollard, ed., *An Encyclopaedia of Translation: Chinese-English/English-Chinese*, pp. 807–826. Hong Kong: Chinese University Press, 1995.

Wagner, Marsha. *The Lotus Boat: The Origins of Chinese* Tz'u *Poetry in T'ang Popular Culture*. New York: Columbia University Press, 1984.

Waley, Arthur. "The Green Bower Collection." In Waley, *The Secret History of the Mongols*, pp. 89–107. London: George Allen and Unwin, 1963.

Wixted, John Timothy. *The Song-Poetry of Wei Chuang (836–910 A.D.)*. Tempe: Center for Asian Studies, Arizona State University, 1979.

Yu, Pauline, ed. *Voices of the Song Lyric in China*. Berkeley and Los Angeles: University of California Press, 1994.

Elegies and Rhapsodies

Erkes, Eduard. "*Shen-nü-fu*, The Song of the Goddess." *T'oung Pao*, 25 (1928): 387–402.

Fusek, Lois. "The 'Kao-t'ang *Fu*.'" *Monumenta Serica*, 30 (1972–73): 392–425.

Graham, William T., Jr. *The Lament for the South: Yu Hsin's "Ai Chiang-nan fu."* Cambridge: Cambridge University Press, 1980.

Gulik, R. H. van, trans. and annot. *Hsi K'ang and His Poetical Essay on the Lute*. Tokyo: Sophia University, 1941.

Hawkes, David, trans. and annot. *Ch'u-tz'u: The Songs of the South; An Ancient Chinese Anthology*. Oxford: Clarendon, 1959; rev. ed. as *The Songs of the South: An Anthology of Ancient Chinese Poems by Qu Yuan and Other Poets*. Harmondsworth: Penguin, 1985.

Hervouet, Yves. *Le chapitre 117 du* Che-ki *(Biographie de Sseu-ma Siang-jou)*. Paris: Presses Universitaires de France, 1972.

———. *Un poète de cour sous les Han: Sseu-ma Siang-jou*. Paris: Presses Universitaires de France, 1964.

Hightower, James R. "Chia I's Owl *Fu*." *Asia Major*, 7 (1959): 125–130.

———. "Ch'ü Yüan Studies." In *Silver Jubilee Volume of the Zinbun-Kagaku-Kenkyusyo*, pp. 192–223. Kyoto: Kyoto Daigaku, Jinbun Kagaku Kenkyūjo, 1954.

———. "The *Fu* of T'ao Ch'ien." *Harvard Journal of Asiatic Studies*, 17 (1954): 169–230. Also in John L. Bishop, ed., *Studies in Chinese Literature*, pp. 45–106. Cambridge: Harvard University Press, 1965.

Hughes, E. R. *Two Chinese Poets: Vignettes of Han Life and Thought*. Princeton: Princeton University Press, 1960.

Knechtges, David R. *The Han Rhapsody: A Study of the* Fu *of Yang Hsiung (53 B.C.–A.D. 18)*. Cambridge: Cambridge University Press, 1976.

———. "To Praise the Han: The Eastern Capital *Fu* of Pan Ku and His Contemporaries." In Wilt L. Idema and E. Zürcher, ed., *Thought and Law in Qin and Han China*, pp. 118–139. Leiden: E. J. Brill, 1990.

———. "Riddles as Poetry: The '*Fu* Chapter' of the *Hsün-tzu*." In Tse-tsung Chow, ed., *Wen-lin*, Vol. 2. *Studies in the Chinese Humanities*. Madison: University of Wisconsin Press, 1989.

———. "Ssu-ma Hsiang-ju's 'Tall Gate Palace Rhapsody.'" *Harvard Journal of Asiatic Studies*, 41 (1981): 47–64.

Knechtges, David R., trans. *The* Han-shu *Biography of Yang Xiong*. Tempe: Center for Asian Studies, Arizona State University, 1982.

Kopetsky, Elma C. "Two *Fu* on Sacrifices by Yang Hsiung: 'The *Fu* on Kan-ch'üan' and 'The *Fu* on Ho-tung.'" *Journal of Oriental Studies*, 10 (1972): 85–118.

Kroll, Paul W. "Seven Rhapsodies of Ts'ao Chih." *Journal of the American Oriental Society*, 120.1 (2000): 1–13.

Mair, Victor H. *Mei Cherng's "Seven Stimuli" and Wang Bor's "Pavilion of King Teng": Chinese Poems for Princes*. Calligraphy by Jiang Chunbin; Plastercuts and Woodcuts by Daniel Heitkamp. Studies in Asian Thought and Religion, 2. Lewiston/Queenston: Edwin Mellen, 1988.

Waley, Arthur. *The Nine Songs: A Study of Shamanism in Ancient China*. London: George Allen and Unwin, 1955.

Waley, Arthur, trans. *The Temple and Other Poems*. London: Allen and Unwin, 1923.

Waters, Geoffrey R. *Three Elegies of Ch'u: An Introduction to the Traditional Interpretation of the Ch'u-tz'u*. Madison: University of Wisconsin Press, 1985.

Watson, Burton. *Chinese Rhyme-Prose: Poems in the* Fu *Form from the Han and Six Dynasties Periods*. New York: Columbia Press, 1971.

Whitaker, K. P. K. "Tsaur Jyr's *Luoshern Fuh*." *Asia Major*, 4 (1954): 36–56.

Folk and Folklike Songs, Ballads, and Narrative Verse

Allen, Joseph R. *In the Voice of Others: Chinese Music Bureau Poetry*. Ann Arbor: Center for Chinese Studies, University of Michigan, 1992.

Birrell, Anne. "Mythmaking and Yüeh-fu: Popular Songs and Ballads of Early Imperial China." *Journal of the American Oriental Society*, 109.2 (1989): 223–235.

———. *Popular Songs and Ballads of Han China*. 2nd ed. Honolulu: University of Hawaii Press, 1993.

Diény, Jean-Pierre. *Aux origines de la poésie classique en Chine: Étude sur la poésie lyrique à l'époque des Han*. Leiden: E. J. Brill, 1968.

———. *Pastourelles et Magnanarelles: Essai sur un thème littéraire chinois*. Geneva: Librairie Droz, 1977.

Evans, Marilyn Jane Coutant. "Popular Songs of the Southern Dynasties: A Study in Chinese Poetic Style." Ph.D. dissertation, Yale University, 1966.

Frankel, Hans H. "The Chinese Ballad 'Southeast Fly the Peacocks.'" *Harvard Journal of Asiatic Studies*, 34 (1974): 248–271.

———. "The Formulaic Language of the Chinese Ballad 'Southeast Fly the Peacocks.'" *Chung-yang yen-chiu-yüan, Li-shih yü-yen yen-chiu-so chi-k'an* (Bulletin of the Institute of History and Philology, Academia Sinica), 39 (1969): 219–244.

———. "The Relation Between Narrator and Characters in *Yuefu* Ballads." *Chinoperl Papers*, 13 (1984–85): 107–127.

———. "*Yüeh-fu* Poetry." In Cyril Birch, ed., *Chinese Literary Genres*, pp. 69–107. Berkeley and Los Angeles: University of California Press, 1974.

Hartman, Charles. "Stomping Songs: Word and Image." *Chinese Literature: Essays, Articles, Reviews*, 17 (1995): 1–49.

Holzman, Donald. "Folk Ballads and the Aristocracy." *Études chinoises*, 13.1–2 (1994): 345–360.

Hsieh Sheau-mann. "The Folk Songs of the Southern Dynasties (318–589 A.D.)." Ph.D. dissertation, University of California at Los Angeles, 1973.

Kern, Martin. "In Praise of Political Legitimacy: The *miao* and *jiao* Hymns of the Western Han." *Oriens Extremus*, 39 (1996): 29–67.

Knechtges, David R. "A New Study of Han *Yüeh-fu*." *Journal of the American Oriental Society*, 110.2 (1990): 310–316.

Mayhew, Lenore, and William McNaughton. *A Cold Orchid: The Love Poems of Tzu Yeh*. Rutland, VT: Charles E. Tuttle, 1972.

Modern

Acton, Harold, and Ch'en Shih-hsiang, trans. *Modern Chinese Poetry*. London: Duckworth, 1936.

Birch, Cyril. "English and Chinese Metres in Hsü Chih-mo." *Asia Major*, 8 (1960): 258–293.

Cheung, Dominic. *Feng Chih*. Boston: Twayne, 1979.

Cheung, Dominic, trans. and ed. *The Isle Full of Noises: Modern Chinese Poetry from Taiwan*. New York: Columbia University Press, 1987.

Haft, Lloyd, ed. *A Selective Guide to Chinese Literature, 1900–1949*. Vol. 3. *The Poem*. Leiden: E. J. Brill, 1989.

Hsu, Kai-yu, trans. *Twentieth-Century Chinese Poetry: An Anthology*. Garden City, NY: Doubleday, 1963; reprint, Ithaca: Cornell University Press, 1970.

———. *Wen I-to*. Boston: Twayne, 1980.

Lee, Gregory. *Dai Wangshu: The Life and Poetry of a Chinese Modernist*. Hong Kong: Chinese University Press, 1989.

Lin, Julia C. *Modern Chinese Poetry: An Introduction*. Seattle: University of Washington Press, 1972.

Morin, Edward, ed. *The Red Azalea: Chinese Poetry Since the Cultural Revolution*. Fang Dai, Dennis Ding, and Edward Morin, trans. Honolulu: University of Hawaii Press, 1990.

Palandri, Angela Jung, trans. *Modern Verse from Taiwan*. Berkeley and Los Angeles: University of California Press, 1972.

Payne, Robert, ed. *Contemporary Chinese Poetry*. London: Routledge, 1947.

Yeh, Michelle, ed. and trans. *Anthology of Modern Chinese Poetry*. New Haven: Yale University Press, 1992.

———. *Modern Chinese Poetry: Theory and Practice since 1917*. New Haven: Yale University Press, 1991.

Poetry and Painting

Bickford, Maggie. *Ink Plum: The Making of a Chinese Scholar-Painting Genre*. Cambridge and New York: Cambridge University Press, 1996.

Bush, Susan. *The Chinese Literati on Painting: Su Shih (1037–1101) to Tung Ch'i-ch'ang (1555–1636)*. Cambridge: Harvard University Press, 1971.

Bush, Susan, and Hsio-yen Shih, ed. *Early Chinese Texts on Painting*. Cambridge: Harvard University Press, 1985.

Chaves, Jonathan. "Reading the Painting: Levels of Poetic Meaning in Chinese Pictorial Art." *Asian Art*, 1.1 (Fall/Winter 1987–88): 7–29.

Egan, Ronald C. *Word, Image, and Deed in the Life of Su Shi*. Harvard-Yenching Institute Monograph Series, 39. Cambridge: Council on East Asian Studies Publications, Harvard University, 1994.

Hartman, Charles. "Literary and Visual Interactions in Lo Chih-ch'uan's 'Crows in Old Trees.'" *Metropolitan Museum Journal*, 28 (1993): 129–167.

Levy, Dore J. "Transforming Archetypes in Chinese Poetry and Painting: The Case of Ts'ai Yen." *Asia Major*, 3rd series, 2 (1993): 147–168.

Murck, Alfreda, and Wen C. Fong, ed. *Words and Images: Chinese Poetry, Calligraphy, and Painting*. New York: Metropolitan Museum of Art, 1991.

Murray, Julia K. *Ma Hezhi and the Illustrations of the* Book of Odes. Cambridge and New York: Cambridge University Press, 1993.

Silbergeld, Jerome. "Back to the Red Cliff: Reflections on the Narrative Mode in Early Literati Landscape Painting." *Ars orientalis*, 25 (1995): 19–38.

Wu, Hung. *Monumentality in Early Chinese Art and Architecture*. Stanford: Stanford University Press, 1995.

———. *The Wu Liang Shrine: Ideology of Early Chinese Pictorial Art*. Stanford: Stanford University Press, 1989.

PROSE

Premodern

Allen, Joseph Roe, III. "An Introductory Study of Narrative Structure in the *Shi ji*." *Chinese Literature: Essays, Articles, Reviews (CLEAR)*, 3 (1981): 31–66.

Bokenkamp, Stephen R. "The Peach Flower Font and the Grotto Passage." *Journal of the American Oriental Society*, 106 (1986): 65–77.

Chang, H. C. *Chinese Literature*. Vol. 3. *Tales of the Supernatural*. New York: Columbia University Press, 1984.

Chavannes, Édouard. *Les Mémoires historiques de Se-ma Ts'ien*. 6 vols. 1st ed., 1895–1905; reprint, Paris: Adrien-Maisonneuve, 1967–69.

Chen, Yu-shih. *Images and Ideas in Chinese Classical Prose*. Stanford: Stanford University Press, 1988.

Connery, Christopher Leigh. *The Empire of the Text: Writing and Authority in Early Imperial China*. Lanham, Boulder, New York, Oxford: Rowman and Littlefield, 1998.

Crump, James, trans. *Chan-kuo ts'e*. Oxford: Oxford University Press, 1970.

———. *Intrigues: Studies of the Chan-kuo Ts'e*. Ann Arbor: University of Michigan Press, 1964.

DeWoskin, Kenneth J. *Doctors, Diviners, and Magicians of Ancient China: Biographies of* Fang-shih. New York: Columbia University Press, 1983.

Dubs, Homer H. *The History of the Former Han Dynasty by Pan Ku*. 3 vols. Baltimore: Waverley, 1938–55.

Durrant, Stephen W. *The Cloudy Mirror: Tension and Conflict in the Writings of Sima Qian*. Albany: State University of New York Press, 1995.

Egan, Ronald. *The Literary Works of Ou-yang Hsiu (1007–72)*. Cambridge: Cambridge University Press, 1984.

———. "Narrative in the *Tso chuan*." *Harvard Journal of Asiatic Studies*, 37 (1977): 323–352.

Frankel, Hans H. "T'ang Literati: A Composite Biography." In Arthur Wright and Denis Twitchett, ed., *Confucian Personalities*, pp. 65–83. Stanford: Stanford University Press, 1962.

Gardner, Charles S. *Chinese Traditional Historiography*. Cambridge: Harvard University Press, 1938.

Giles, Lionel, trans. *A Gallery of Chinese Immortals*. London: John Murray, 1948.

Güntsch, Gertrud, trans. *Das* Shen-hsien chuan *und das Erscheinungsbild eines Hsien*. Würzburger Sino-Japonica, 16. Frankfurt: Peter Lang, 1987.

Hartman, Charles. *Han Yü and the T'ang Search for Unity*. Princeton: Princeton University Press, 1986.

Henricks, Robert G. *Philosophy and Argumentation in Third-Century China: The Essays of Hsi K'ang*. Princeton: Princeton University Press, 1983.

Hightower, James R. "Han Yü as Humorist." *Harvard Journal of Asiatic Studies*, 44.1 (June 1984): 5–27.

———. "Some Characteristics of Parallel Prose." In Søren Egerod and Elsa Glahn, ed., *Studia Serica Bernhard Karlgren Dedicata*, pp. 60–91. Copenhagen: Ejnar Munksgaard, 1959. Also in John Lyman Bishop, ed., *Studies in Chinese Literature*, pp. 108–139. Cambridge: Harvard University Press, 1965.

Holzman, Donald. *La vie et pensée de Hi K'ang (223–262 A.D.)*. Leiden: E. J. Brill, 1957.

Johnson, David. "Epic and History in Early China: The Matter of Wu Tzu-hsü." *Journal of Asian Studies*, 40.2 (February 1981): 255–271.

Kaltenmark, Max, trans. *Le Lie-sien tchouan*. Peking: Université de Paris, Publications du Centre d'Études sinologiques de Pékin, 1953.

Knechtges, David R. "Han and Six Dynasties Parallel Prose." *Renditions* (Special Issue: Classical Prose), 33–34 (1990): 63–110.

Lewis, Mark Edward. *Writing and Authority in Early China*. Albany: State University of New York Press, 1999.

Liu, Shih Shun. *Chinese Classical Prose: The Eight Masters of the T'ang-Sung Period*. A *Renditions* Book. Hong Kong: Chinese University Press, 1979.

Mair, Victor H. "Li Po's Letters in Pursuit of Political Patronage." *Harvard Journal of Asiatic Studies*, 44 (1984): 123–153.

Maspero, Henri. "Historical Romance and History." Frank Kierman, Jr., trans. In Maspero, *China in Antiquity*, pp. 357–365. Amherst: University of Massachusetts Press, 1978.

Moloughney, Brian. "From Biographical History to Historical Biography: A Transformation in Chinese Historical Writing." *East Asian History*, 4 (1992): 1–30.

Nienhauser, William H., Jr. "Literature as a Source for Traditional History: The Case of Ou-yang Chan." *Chinese Literature: Essays, Articles, Reviews (CLEAR)*, 12 (1990): 1–14.

Nienhauser, William H., Jr., et al. *Liu Tsung-yüan*. New York: Twayne, 1973.

Nivison, David S. "Aspects of Traditional Chinese Biography." *Journal of Asian Studies*, 21 (1962): 457–463.

Olbricht, Peter. "Die Biographie in China." *Saeculum*, 8 (1957): 224–235.

Paper, Jordan D. *Guide to Chinese Prose*. Boston: G. K. Hall, 1973.

Pulleyblank, E. G. "Chinese Historical Criticism: Liu Chih-chi and Ssu-ma Kuang." In E. G. Pulleyblank and W. G. Beasley, ed., *Historians of China and Japan*, pp. 135–166. London: Oxford University Press, 1961.

Ssu-ma Ch'ien. *The Grand Scribe's Records*. Vol. 1. *The Basic Annals of Pre-Han China*. Vol. 7. *The Memoirs of Pre-Han China*. William H. Nienhauser, Jr., ed.; Tsai-fa Cheng, Zongli Lü, William H. Nienhauser, Jr., and Robert Reynolds, trans. With Chiu-ming Chan. Bloomington: Indiana University Press, 1994.

Twitchett, Denis. C. "Biography." In Twitchett, *The Writing of Official History Under the T'ang*, pp. 62–83. Cambridge: Cambridge University Press, 1992.

———. "Chinese Biographical Writing." In Pulleyblank and Beasley, ed., *Historians of China and Japan*, pp. 95–114.

Wang, John C. Y. "Early Chinese Narrative: The *Tso-chuan* as Example." In Andrew Plaks, ed., *Chinese Narrative: Critical and Theoretical Essays*, pp. 3–20. Princeton: Princeton University Press, 1977.

Watson, Burton. *Early Chinese Literature*. New York: Columbia University Press, 1962.

———. *Records of the Grand Historian of China, Translated from the* Shih chi *of Ssu-ma Ch'ien*. 2 vols. New York: Columbia University Press, 1961; rev. and enlgd. ed. in 3 vols., Hong Kong and New York: *Renditions*–Columbia University Press, 1993.

———. *Ssu-ma Ch'ien: Grand Historian of China*. New York: Columbia University Press, 1958.

Wright, Arthur F. "Biography and Hagiography: Hui-chien's *Lives of Eminent Monks*." In *Silver Jubilee Volume of the Zinbun-Kagaku-Kenkyusyo*, pp. 383–432. Kyoto: Kyoto University, Jinbun Kagaku Kenkyūjo, 1954.

Wu, Pei-yi. *The Confucian's Progress: Autobiographical Writings in Traditional China*. Princeton: Princeton University Press, 1990.

Yang, Lien-sheng. "The Organization of Chinese Official Historiography: Principles and Methods of the Standard Histories from the T'ang through the Ming." In Pulleyblank and Beasley, ed., *Historians of China and Japan*, pp. 31–43.

Yu, Anthony C. "History, Fiction and the Reading of Chinese Narrative." *Chinese Literature: Essays, Articles, Reviews (CLEAR)*, 10 (1988): 1–19.

Zurndorfer, Harriet. "Biography in China: Past and Present." In Zurndorfer, *China Bibliography*, pp. 137–169. Leiden: E. J. Brill, 1995.

Modern

Barmé, Geremie, and John Minford, ed. *Seeds of Fire: Chinese Voices of Conscience*. New York: Hill and Wang, 1988; Noonday (Farrar, Straus, and Giroux), 1989.

Berninghausen, John, and Ted Huters, ed. *Revolutionary Literature in China: An Anthology*. White Plains, NY: M. E. Sharpe, 1976.

Gunn, Edward. *Rewriting Chinese: Style and Innovation in Twentieth-Century Chinese Prose*. Stanford: Stanford University Press, 1991.

Hsia Tsi-an. *The Gate of Darkness: Studies on the Leftist Literary Movement in China*. Seattle: University of Washington Press, 1968.

Hsu, Kai-yu, and Ting Wang, ed. *Literature of the People's Republic of China*. Bloomington: Indiana University Press, 1980.

Larson, Wendy. *Literary Authority and the Modern Chinese Writer: Ambivalence and Autobiography*. Durham: Duke University Press, 1991.

Lau, Joseph S. M., and Howard Goldblatt, ed. *The Columbia Anthology of Modern Chinese Literature*. New York: Columbia University Press, 1995.

Lee, Leo Ou-fan, ed. *Lu Xun and His Legacy*. Berkeley and Los Angeles: University of California Press, 1985.

Liu Kuo-hui and Ts'ao Fu-chih, ed. *Chin-wen kuan-chih* [Pinnacles of the Modern Essay]. 2 vols. Shenyang: Shenyang ch'u-pan-she, 1993.

Martin, Helmut, and Jeffrey C. Kinkley, ed. *Modern Chinese Writers: Self-Portrayals*. Armonk, NY: M. E. Sharpe, 1992.

Nieh, Hualing, ed. *Literature of the Hundred Flowers*. Vol. 1. *Criticism and Polemics*. Vol. 2. *Poetry and Fiction*. New York: Columbia University Press, 1981.

Pollard, David. *A Chinese Look at Literature: The Literary Values of Chou Tso-jen in Relation to the Tradition*. Berkeley and Los Angeles: University of California Press, 1973.

Pollard, David, ed. and trans. *The Chinese Essay*. New York: Columbia University Press, 2000.

Siu, Helen F., ed. *Furrows; Peasants, Intellectuals, and the State: Stories and Histories from Modern China*. New Haven: Yale University Press, 1990.

Soong, Stephen C., and John Minford, ed. *Trees on the Mountain: An Anthology of New Chinese Writing*. Hong Kong: Chinese University Press, 1984.

Wagner, Rudolf. *Inside a Service Trade: Studies in Contemporary Chinese Prose*. Cambridge: Harvard University Press, 1992.

Wolff, Ernst. *Chou Tso-jen*. New York: Twayne, 1971.

FICTION

Classical

Barr, Allan H. "Pu Songling and *Liaozhai zhiyi*: A Study of Textual Transmission, Biographical Background, and Literary Antecedents." Ph.D. dissertation, Oxford University, 1983.

Campany, Robert Ford. *Strange Writing: Anomaly Accounts in Early Medieval China.* Albany: State University of New York Press, 1996.

Chan, Leo Tak-hung. *The Discourse on Foxes and Ghosts: Ji Yun and Eighteenth-Century Literati Storytelling.* Hong Kong: Chinese University Press, 1997.

Chang, H. C., trans. *Chinese Literature.* Vol. 3. *Tales of the Supernatural.* New York: Columbia University Press, 1984.

Cohen, Alvin P. *Tales of Vengeful Souls: A Sixth-Century Collection of Chinese Avenging Ghost Stories.* Variétés Sinologiques, n.s. 68. Taipei: Institut Ricci; Chinese Materials Center, 1982.

DeWoskin, Kenneth J. "The Six Dynasties *Chih-kuai* and the Birth of Fiction." In Andrew Plaks, ed., *Chinese Narrative: Critical and Theoretical Essays,* pp. 21–52. Princeton: Princeton University Press, 1977.

DeWoskin, Kenneth J., and J. I. Crump, Jr., trans. *In Search of the Supernatural: The Written Record.* Stanford: Stanford University Press, 1996.

Dudbridge, Glen. *Religious Experience and Lay Society in T'ang China: A Reading of Tai Fu's* Kuang-i chi. Cambridge: Cambridge University Press, 1995.

———. *The Tale of Li Wa, Study and Critical Edition of a Chinese Story from the Ninth Century.* London: Ithaca Press, 1983.

Edwards, E. D., trans. *Chinese Prose Literature of the T'ang Period.* 2 vols. London: Probsthain, 1937–38.

Kao, Karl S. Y. *Classical Chinese Tales of the Supernatural and the Fantastic: Selections from the Third to the Tenth Century.* Bloomington: Indiana University Press, 1985. (See also Victor H. Mair's review in *CLEAR,* 9 [1986]: 99–102.)

Levy, Howard S., trans. *China's First Novelette: The Dwelling of the Playful Goddesses by Chang Wen-ch'eng (ca. 657–730).* Tokyo: Dai Nippon Insatsu, 1965.

Louie, Kam, and Louise Edwards, trans. *Censored by Confucius: Ghost Stories by Yuan Mei.* Armonk, NY: M. E. Sharpe, 1996.

Ma, Y. W., and Joseph S. M. Lau, ed. *Traditional Chinese Stories: Themes and Variations.* New York: Columbia University Press, 1978.

Mair, Victor H. "The Narrative Revolution in Chinese Literature: Ontological Presuppositions." *Chinese Literature: Essays, Articles, Reviews (CLEAR),* 5 (1983): 1–28.

Mair, Victor H., and Denis Mair, trans. *Strange Tales from Make-Do Studio.* Peking: Foreign Languages Press, 1989.

Mather, Richard B., trans. *Shih-shuo hsin-yü: A New Account of Tales of the World by Liu I-ch'ing, with Commentary by Liu Chün.* Minneapolis: University of Minnesota Press, 1976.

Nienhauser, William H., Jr. "The Origins of Chinese Fiction." *Monumenta Serica,* 38 (1988–89): 191–219.

Rotours, Robert des. *Courtisans chinois à la fin des T'ang, entre circa 789 et le 8 janvier 881; Pei-li tche (Anecdotes du quartier du Nord) par Souen K'i.* Paris: Presses Universitaires de France, 1968.

Spring, Madeleine. *Animal Allegories in T'ang China.* New Haven: American Oriental Society, 1993.

Yang, Hsien-yi, and Gladys Yang, trans. *The Dragon King's Daughter: Ten T'ang Dynasty Stories.* Peking: Foreign Languages Press, 1954.

———. *The Man Who Sold a Ghost: Chinese Tales of the 3rd–6th Centuries.* Peking:

Foreign Languages Press, 1958; Hong Kong: Commercial Press, 1974.
Yu, Anthony C. "'Rest, Rest, Perturbed Spirit!': Ghosts in Traditional Chinese Fiction." *Harvard Journal of Asiatic Studies*, 47 (1987): 397–434.
Zeitlin, Judith T. *Historian of the Strange: Pu Songling and the Chinese Classical Tale*. Stanford: Stanford University Press, 1993.

Vernacular

Barr, Allan H. "The Wanli Context of the 'Courtesan's Jewel Box' Story." *Harvard Journal of Asiatic Studies*, 57.1 (June 1997): 107–141.
Berry, Margaret. *The Chinese Classic Novels: An Annotated Bibliography of Chiefly English-Language Studies*. New York: Garland, 1988.
Birch, Cyril. "Feng Meng-lung and the *Ku-chin hsiao-shuo*." *Bulletin of the School of Oriental and African Studies*, 18.1 (1956): 64–83.
———. "Some Formal Characteristics of the *Hua-pen* Story." *Bulletin of the School of Oriental and African Studies*, 17.2 (1955): 346–364.
Birch, Cyril, trans. *Stories from a Ming Collection: Translations of Chinese Short Stories Published in the Seventeenth Century*. Bloomington: Indiana University Press, 1958.
Bishop, John Lyman. *The Colloquial Short Story in China: A Study of the San-yen Collections*. Cambridge: Harvard University Press, 1956.
Brandauer, Frederick W. *Tung Yüeh*. Boston: Twayne, 1978.
Buck, Pearl S., trans. *All Men Are Brothers (The Water Margin; Shui-hu chuan)*. 2 vols. New York: John Day, 1933; reprint, New York: Grove, 1957.
Carlitz, Katherine. *The Rhetoric of* Chin p'ing mei. Bloomington: Indiana University Press, 1986.
Chang, Shelley Hsüeh-lun. *History and Legend: Ideas and Images in the Ming Historical Novels*. Ann Arbor: University of Michigan Press, 1990.
Crawford, William Bruce. "'The Oil Vendor and the Courtesan' and the *Ts'ai-tzu chia-jen* Novels." In William H. Nienhauser, Jr., ed., *Critical Essays on Chinese Literature*, pp. 31–42. Hong Kong: Chinese University of Hong Kong Press, 1976.
Dolby, William, trans. *The Perfect Lady by Mistake and Other Stories by Feng Menglong (1574–1646)*. London: P. Elek, 1976.
Dudbridge, Glen. *The* Hsi-yu chi: *A Study of the Antecedents to the Sixteenth-Century Chinese Novel*. Cambridge: Cambridge University Press, 1970.
Egerton, Clement, trans. *The Golden Lotus*. 4 vols. London: Routledge, 1939; reprint, New York: Paragon, 1962.
Hanan, Patrick. "The Authorship of Some *Ku-chin hsiao-shuo* Stories." *Harvard Journal of Asiatic Studies*, 29 (1969): 190–200.
———. *The Chinese Short Story: Studies in Dating, Authorship, and Composition*. Cambridge: Harvard University Press, 1973.
———. *The Chinese Vernacular Story*. Cambridge: Harvard University Press, 1981.
———. "The Early Chinese Short Story: A Critical Theory in Outline." *Harvard Journal of Asiatic Studies*, 27 (1967): 168–207.
———. "The Making of *The Pearl-sewn Shirt* and *The Courtesan's Jewel Box*." *Harvard Journal of Asiatic Studies*, 33 (1973): 124–153.
———. "Sources of the *Chin P'ing Mei*." *Asia Major*, n.s. 10.2 (1963): 23–67.

———. "Sung and Yüan Vernacular Fiction: A Critique of Modern Methods of Dating." *Harvard Journal of Asiatic Studies*, 30 (1970): 159–184.

———. "The Text of the *Chin P'ing Mei*." *Asia Major*, n.s. 9.1 (1962): 1–57.

———. "The *Yün-men chuan*: From *Chantefable* to Short Story." *Bulletin of the School of Oriental and African Studies*, 36.2 (1973): 299–308.

Hanan, Patrick, trans. *The Carnal Prayer Mat*. New York: Ballantine, 1990.

Hawkes, David, trans. *The Story of the Stone: A Chinese Novel by Cao Xueqin*. 5 vols. Harmondsworth: Penguin, 1973–86. (Vol. 5 trans. John Minford.)

Hegel, Robert. *The Novel in Seventeenth-Century China*. New York: Columbia University Press, 1981.

Hsia, C. T. *The Classic Chinese Novel: A Critical Introduction*. New York: Columbia University Press, 1968; Ithaca: Cornell University Press, 1996.

———. "Society and Self in the Chinese Short Story." In Hsia, *The Classic Chinese Novel*, pp. 299–321. Bloomington: Indiana University Press, 1980.

Huang, Martin. *Literati and Self-Re/Presentation: Autobiographical Sensibility in the Eighteenth-Century Chinese Novel*. Stanford: Stanford University Press, 1995.

Idema, Wilt L. *Chinese Vernacular Fiction: The Formative Period*. Leiden: E. J. Brill, 1974.

Irwin, Richard G. *The Evolution of a Chinese Novel:* Shui-hu chuan. Cambridge: Harvard University Press, 1953.

———. "Water Margin Revisited." *T'oung Pao*, 58 (1960): 393–415.

Jenner, W. J. F., trans. *Journey to the West*. 3 vols. Peking: Foreign Languages Press, 1982–86.

Lévy, André. *Le Conte en langue vulgaire du XVIIe siècle: vogue et déclin d'un genre narratif de la littérature chinoise*. Lille: Université de Lille, Service de reproduction des thèses, 1974; Paris: Collège de France, 1981.

———. *Études sur le conte et le roman chinois*. Paris: École Française d'Extrême-Orient, 1971.

———. "Études sur trois recueils anciens de contes chinois." *T'oung Pao*, 52.1–3 (1965): 110–137.

Levy, Dore J. *Ideal and Actual in* The Story of the Stone. New York: Columbia University Press, 1999.

Li, Wai-yee. *Enchantment and Disenchantment*. Princeton: Princeton University Press, 1993.

Li, Yu. *Silent Operas* (Wusheng xi). Patrick Hanan, trans. and ed. Hong Kong: Chinese University of Hong Kong Press, 1990.

———. *A Tower for the Summer Heat*. Patrick Hanan, trans. New York: Ballantine Books, 1992.

Lin Tai-yi, trans. *Flowers in the Mirror* [Ching hua yüan]. Berkeley and Los Angeles: University of California Press, 1965.

Liu, Ts'un-yan. *Buddhist and Taoist Influences on Chinese Novels*. Vol. 1. *The Authorship of the* Feng Shen Yen I. Wiesbaden: Otto Harrassowitz, 1962.

Lu, Hsiao-peng. "The Fictional Discourse of *pien-wen*: The Relation of Chinese Fiction to Historiography." *Chinese Literature: Essays, Articles, Reviews (CLEAR)*, 9 (1987): 49–70.

Lu Hsün. *A Brief History of Chinese Fiction*. Yang Hsien-yi and Gladys Yang, trans. Peking: Foreign Languages Press, 1959.

Ma, Y. W. (Yau-Woon). "The Knight-errant in *Hua-pen* Stories." *T'oung Pao*, 61 (1975): 266–300.

———. "The Textual Tradition of Ming *Kung-an* Fiction: A Study of the *Lung-t'u kung-an*." *Harvard Journal of Asiatic Studies*, 35 (1975): 266–300.

———. "Themes and Characterization in the *Lung-t'u kung-an*." *T'oung Pao*, 59.1–5 (1973): 179–202.

Mair, Victor H. "Parallels Between Some Tun-huang Manuscripts and the Seventeenth Chapter of the Kōzanji *Journey to the West*." *Cahiers d'Extrême-Asie*, 3 (1987): 41–54.

———. "Suen Wu-kung = Hanumat? The Progress of a Scholarly Debate." *Chung-yang yen-chiu-yüan ti-erh-chieh kuo-chi Han-hsüeh hui-yi lun-wen-chi* [Papers from the Second International Conference on Sinology at Academia Sinica], pp. 659–752. Taipei: Chung-yang yen-chiu-yüan, 1989.

McLaren, Anne E., trans. *The Chinese Femme Fatale: Stories from the Ming Period*. University of Sidney East Asian Series, 8. Broadway, NSW: Wild Peony, 1994.

McMahon, Keith. *Causality and Containment in Seventeenth-Century Chinese Fiction*. Leiden: E. J. Brill, 1988.

Nyren, Eve Alison, trans. *The Bonds of Matrimony,* Hsing-shih yin-yüan chuan: *A Seventeenth-Century Chinese Novel*. Lewiston, ME: Edwin Mellen, 1995.

Plaks, Andrew. *Archetype and Allegory in the Dream of the Red Chamber*. Princeton: Princeton University Press, 1972.

———. *The Four Masterworks of the Ming Novel*. Princeton: Princeton University Press, 1987.

Plaks, Andrew, ed. *Chinese Narrative: Critical and Theoretical Essays*. Princeton: Princeton University Press, 1977.

Průšek, Jaroslav. *Chinese History and Literature: Collection of Studies*. Dordrecht, the Netherlands: D. Reidel, 1970.

Roberts, Moss, trans. *The Three Kingdoms: A Historical Novel, Attributed to Luo Guanzhong*. Berkeley and Los Angeles: University of California Press, and Peking: Foreign Languages Press, 1991.

Roddy, Stephen J. *Literati Identity and Its Fictional Representations in Late Imperial China*. Stanford: Stanford University Press, 1998.

Ropp, Paul S. *Dissent in Early Modern China:* Ju-lin wai-shih *and Ch'ing Social Criticism*. Ann Arbor: University of Michigan Press, 1981.

Roy, David T., trans. *The Plum in the Golden Vase, or Chin P'ing Mei*. Vol. 1. *The Gathering*. Princeton: Princeton University Press, 1993.

Rushton, Peter H. *The* Jin Ping Mei *and the Nonlinear Dimensions of the Traditional Chinese Novel*. Lewiston, ME: Edwin Mellen, 1994.

Scott, John, trans. *The Lecherous Academician and Other Tales by Master Ling Men-chu*. London: Rapp and Whiting, 1973.

Seaman, Gary. *Journey to the North: An Ethnohistorical Analysis and Annotated Translation of the Chinese Folk Novel* Pei-yu chi. Berkeley and Los Angeles: University of California Press, 1987.

Shang, Wei. "Ritual, Ritual Manuals, and the Crisis of the Confucian World: An Interpretation of *Rulin waishi*." *Harvard Journal of Asiatic Studies*, 58.2 (1998): 373–424.

Shapiro, Sidney, trans. *Outlaws of the Marsh*. 3 vols. Peking: Foreign Languages Press, 1980.
Waley, Arthur, trans. *Monkey*. London: John Day, 1942.
Wang, Chi-chen, trans. *Traditional Chinese Tales*. New York: Columbia University Press, 1944; reprint, New York: Greenwood, 1968.
Wang, Jing. *The Story of Stone: Intertextuality, Ancient Chinese Stone Lore, and Stone Symbolism in* Dream of the Red Chamber, Water Margin, *and* Journey to the West. Durham: Duke University Press, 1992.
Widmer, Ellen. *The Margins of Utopia:* Shui-hu hou-chuan *and the Literature of Ming Loyalism*. Cambridge: Council on East Asian Studies, Harvard University, 1987.
Wivell, Charles J. "The Term 'Hua-pen.'" In David Buxbaum and Frederick W. Mote, ed., *Transition and Permanence: Chinese History and Culture—A Festschrift in Honor of Dr. Hsiao Kung-ch'üan*, pp. 295–306. Hong Kong: Cathay, 1972.
Wong, Timothy C. *Wu Ching-tzu*. Boston: Twayne, 1978.
Yang, Hsien-yi, and Gladys Yang, trans. *The Courtesan's Jewel Box: Chinese Stories of the Tenth–Seventeenth Centuries*. Peking: Foreign Languages Press, 1957.
———. *A Dream of Red Mansions*. 3 vols. Peking: Foreign Languages Press, 1978–80.
———. *Lazy Dragon: Chinese Stories from the Ming Dynasty*. Hong Kong: Joint Publishing Company, 1981.
———. *The Scholars* (Ju-lin wai-shih). Peking: Foreign Languages Press, 1957.
Yang, Winston L. Y., Peter Li, and Nathan K. Mao. *Classical Chinese Fiction: A Guide to Its Study and Appreciation; Essays and Bibliographies*. Boston: G. K. Hall, 1978.
Yen, Alsace. "The Parry-Lord Theory Applied to Vernacular Chinese Stories." *Journal of the American Oriental Society*, 95 (1975): 403–416.
Yu, Anthony C., trans. and annot. *The Journey to the West*. 4 vols. Chicago: University of Chicago Press, 1977–83.
———. *Rereading the Stone: Desire and the Making of Fiction in* Dream of the Red Chamber. Princeton: Princeton University Press, 1997.

Modern

Anderson, Marston. *The Limits of Realism: Chinese Fiction in the Revolutionary Period*. Berkeley: University of California Press, 1990.
Birch, Cyril. "Change and Continuity in Chinese Fiction." In Merle Goldman, ed., *Modern Chinese Literature in the May Fourth Era*, pp. 385–404. Cambridge: Harvard University Press, 1977.
———. *Chinese Communist Literature*. New York: Praeger, 1963.
Doleželová-Velingerová, Milena, ed. *The Chinese Novel at the Turn of the Century*. Toronto: University of Toronto Press, 1980.
———. "Narrative Modes in Late Qing Novels." In Doleželová-Velingerová, ed., *The Chinese Novel at the Turn of the Century*, pp. 57–75.
———. "The Origins of Modern Chinese Literature." In Goldman, ed., *Modern Chinese Literature in the May Fourth Era*, pp. 17–35 (see Birch entry above).
———. "Typology of Plot Structures in Late Qing Novels." In Doleželová-Velingerová, ed., *The Chinese Novel at the Turn of the Century*, pp. 38–56.
———. "Understanding Chinese Fiction 1900–1949." In Doleželová-Velingerová, ed., *A Selective Guide to Chinese Literature, 1900–1949*. Vol. 1. *The Novel*, pp. 3–45. Leiden: E. J. Brill, 1988.

Duke, Michael S. *Blooming and Contending: Chinese Literature in the Post-Mao Era*. Bloomington: Indiana University Press, 1985.

Duke, Michael S., ed. *Worlds of Modern Chinese Fiction*. Armonk, NY: M. E. Sharpe, 1991.

Egan, Michael. "Characterization in *Sea of Woe*." In Doleželová-Velingerová, ed., *The Chinese Novel at the Turn of the Century*, pp. 165–176.

Faurot, Jeannette L., ed. *Chinese Fiction from Taiwan: Critical Perspectives*. Bloomington: Indiana University Press, 1980.

Feuerwerker, Yi-tsi. *Ding Ling's Fiction: Ideology and Narrative in Modern Chinese Literature*. Cambridge: Harvard University Press, 1982.

Fong, Gilbert Chee Fun. "Time in *Nine Murders*: Western Influence and Domestic Tradition." In Doleželová-Velingerová, ed., *The Chinese Novel at the Turn of the Century*, pp. 116–128.

Gálik, Marian. "On the Influences of Foreign Ideas on Chinese Literary Criticism, 1898–1904." *Asian and African Studies* (Bratislava), 2 (1966): 38–48.

Gibbs, Donald A. *Subject and Author Index to Chinese Literature Monthly (1951–1976)*. New Haven: Far Eastern Publications, 1978.

Gibbs, Donald A., and Yun-chen Li. *A Bibliography of Studies and Translations of Modern Chinese Literature, 1918–1942*. Cambridge: Harvard University Press, 1975.

Goldblatt, Howard. *Hsiao Hung*. Boston: Twayne, 1976.

Goldblatt, Howard, ed. *Chairman Mao Would Not Be Amused: Fiction from Today's China*. New York: Grove, 1995.

———. *Worlds Apart: Recent Chinese Writing and Its Audiences*. Armonk, NY: M. E. Sharpe, 1990.

Gunn, Edward. *Unwelcome Muse: Chinese Literature in Shanghai and Peking, 1937–1945*. New York: Columbia University Press, 1980.

Hagenaar, Elly. *Stream of Consciousness and Free Indirect Discourse in Modern Chinese Literature*. Leiden: Centre of Non-Western Studies, 1992.

Hanan, Patrick, trans. *Two Turn-of-the-Century Chinese Romantic Novels:* Stones in the Sea *by Fu Lin and* The Sea of Regret *by Wu Jianren*. Honolulu: University of Hawai'i Press, 1995.

He, Yuhai. *Cycles of Repression and Relaxation: Politico-Literary Events in China, 1976–1989*. Bochum: Universitätsverlag Dr. Brockmeyer, 1992.

Hinrup, Hans J. *An Index to* Chinese Literature, 1951–1976. London: Curzon, 1978.

Holoch, Donald. "A Novel of Setting: *The Bureaucrats*." In Doleželová-Velingerová, ed., *The Chinese Novel at the Turn of the Century*, pp. 76–115.

———. "*The Travels of Laocan*: Allegorical Narrative." In Doleželová-Velingerová, ed., *The Chinese Novel at the Turn of the Century*, pp. 129–149.

Hsia, C. T. *A History of Modern Chinese Fiction*. 1st ed., New Haven: Yale University Press, 1961; 2nd ed., 1971; 3rd ed., Bloomington and Indianapolis: Indiana University Press, 1999.

———. "Yen Fu and Liang Ch'i-ch'ao as Advocates of New Fiction." In Adele Austin Rickett, ed., *Chinese Approaches to Literature from Confucius to Liang Ch'i-ch'ao*, pp. 221–257. Princeton: Princeton University Press, 1978.

Hsia, C. T., and Joseph S. M. Lau, ed. *Twentieth-Century Chinese Stories*. New York: Columbia University Press, 1971.

Huters, Theodore. "A New Way of Writing: The Possibilities for Literature in Late Qing China, 1895–1908." *Modern China*, 14.3 (July 1988): 243–276.

———. *Qian Zhongshu*. Boston: Twayne, 1982.

James, Jean M., trans. *Rickshaw: The Novel* Lo-t'o Hsiang Tzu. Honolulu: University of Hawaii Press, 1979.

Jenner, W. J. F., ed. *Modern Chinese Stories*. London: Oxford University Press, 1970.

Kinkley, Jeffrey C., ed. *After Mao: Chinese Literature and Society, 1978–1981*. Cambridge: Harvard University Press, 1985.

———. *Chinese Justice, the Fiction: Law and Literature in Modern China*. Stanford: Stanford University Press, 2000.

———. *The Odyssey of Shen Congwen*. Stanford: Stanford University Press, 1987.

Král, Oldrich, et al. *Contributions to the Study of the Rise and Development of Modern Literatures in Asia*. 3 vols. Prague: Academia, 1965, 1969, 1970.

Lancashire, Douglas. *Li Po-yuan*. Boston: Twayne, 1981.

Lang, Olga. *Pa Chin and His Writings: Chinese Youth Between the Two Revolutions*. Cambridge: Harvard University Press, 1967.

Larson, Wendy, and Anne Wedell-Wedellsborg, ed. *Inside Out: Modernism and Postmodernism in Chinese Literary Culture*. Aarhus: Aarhus University Press, 1993.

Lau, Joseph S. M., ed. *The Unbroken Chain: An Anthology of Taiwan Fiction Since 1926*. Bloomington: Indiana University Press, 1983.

Lau, Joseph S. M., C. T. Hsia, and Leo Ou-fan Lee, ed. *Modern Chinese Stories and Novellas, 1919–1949*. New York: Columbia University Press, 1981.

Lee, Leo Ou-fan, ed. *Lu Xun and His Legacy*. Berkeley and Los Angeles: University of California Press, 1985.

———, ed. *The Lyrical and the Epic: Studies of Modern Chinese Literature*. Bloomington: Indiana University Press, 1980.

———. *The Romantic Generation of Modern Chinese Writers*. Cambridge: Harvard University Press, 1973.

———. *Voices from the Iron House: A Study of Lu Xun*. Bloomington: Indiana University Press, 1987.

Lee, Peter. "The Dramatic Structure of *Nie hai hua*." In Doleželová-Velingerová, ed., *The Chinese Novel at the Turn of the Century*, pp. 150–164.

Link, Perry. *Mandarin Ducks and Butterflies: Popular Fiction in Early Twentieth-Century Chinese Cities*. Berkeley and Los Angeles: University of California Press, 1981.

———. "Traditional-Style Popular Urban Fiction in the 'Teens and Twenties.'" In Goldman, ed., *Modern Chinese Literature in the May Fourth Era*, pp. 327–349 (see Birch entry above).

Liu, Lydia H. *Translingual Practice: Literature, National Culture, and Translated Modernity—China, 1900–1937*. Stanford: Stanford University Press, 1995.

Liu T'ieh-yün. *The Travels of Lao Ts'an*. Harold Shadick, trans. Ithaca: Cornell University Press, 1952, 1966.

Liu Wu-chi. *Su Man-shu*. New York: Twayne, 1972.

Louie, Kam. *Between Fact and Fiction: Essays on Post-Mao Chinese Literature and Society*. Broadway, NSW: Wild Peony, 1989.

Louie, Kam, and Louise Edwards, ed. *Bibliography of English Translations and Critiques of Contemporary Chinese Fiction, 1945–1992*. Taipei: Center for Chinese Studies, 1993.

Lundberg, Lennart. *Lu Xun as a Translator: Lu Xun's Translation and Introduction of Literature and Literary Theory, 1903–1936*. Stockholm: Orientaliska Studier, Stockholm University, 1989.

Lyell, William A., Jr. *Lu Hsün's Vision of Reality*. Berkeley and Los Angeles: University of California Press, 1976.

Mao, Nathan K. *Pa Chin*. Boston: Twayne, 1978.

Martin, Helmut. "A Transitional Concept of Chinese Literature, 1897–1917: Liang Ch'i-ch'ao on Poetry Reform, Historical Drama and Political Novel." *Oriens Extremus*, 20 (1973): 175–217.

McDougall, Bonnie S., and Kam Louie. *The Literature of China in the Twentieth Century*. New York: Columbia University Press, 1997.

Nieh, Hua-ling. *Shen Ts'ung-wen*. New York: Twayne, 1972.

Perng, Ching-hsi, and Chiu-kuei Wang, ed. *"Death in a Cornfield" and Other Stories from Contemporary Taiwan*. Hong Kong: Oxford University Press, 1994.

Průšek, Jaroslav. "The Changing Role of the Narrator in Chinese Novels at the Beginning of the Twentieth Century." *Archiv Orientálni*, 38 (1970): 169–178.

———. "Lu Hsün's 'Huai Chiu': A Precursor of Modern Chinese Literature." *Harvard Journal of Asiatic Studies*, 29 (1969): 169–176.

———. *The Lyrical and the Epic: Studies of Modern Chinese Literature*. Leo Ou-fan Lee, ed. Bloomington: Indiana University Press, 1980.

Qian, Zhongshu. *Fortress Besieged*. Jeanne Kelly and Nathan K. Mao, trans. Bloomington: Indiana University Press, 1979.

Semanov, V. I. *Lu Sin' i ego predshestvenniki* (Lu Hsün and His Predecessors). Moscow: Nauka, 1967; English translation by Charles J. Alber. White Plains, NY: M.E. Sharpe, 1980.

Slupski, Zbigniew. *The Evolution of a Modern Chinese Writer: An Analysis of Lao She's Fiction with Biographical and Bibliographical Appendices*. Prague: Czechoslovak Academy of Science, 1966.

Slupski, Zbigniew, ed. *A Selective Guide to Chinese Literature, 1900–1949*. Vol. 2. *The Short Story*. Leiden: E. J. Brill, 1988.

Tsau, Shu-ying. "The Rise of 'New Fiction.'" In Doleželová-Velingerová, ed., *The Chinese Novel at the Turn of the Century*, pp. 18–37.

Vohra, Ranbir. *Lao She and the Chinese Revolution*. Cambridge: Harvard University Press, 1974.

Wang, C. C., trans. *Contemporary Chinese Stories*. New York: Columbia University Press, 1944.

Wang, David Der-wei. *Fictional Realism in Twentieth-Century China: Mao Dun, Lao She, Shen Congwen*. New York: Columbia University Press, 1992.

———. *Fin-de-Siècle Splendor: Repressed Modernities in Late-Qing Fiction, 1849–1911*. Stanford: Stanford University Press, 1997.

Wang, David Der-wei, and Jeanne Tai, ed. *Running Wild: New Chinese Writers*. New York: Columbia University Press, 1994.

Wang, Jing, ed. *China's Avant-Garde Fiction: An Anthology*. Durham: Duke University Press, 1998.

———. *High Culture Fever: Politics, Aesthetics, and Ideology in Deng's China*. Berkeley and Los Angeles: University of California Press, 1996.

Widmer, Ellen, and David Der-wei Wang, ed. *From May Fourth to June Fourth: Fiction and Film in 20th-Century China*. Cambridge: Harvard University Press, 1993.

Williams, Philip F. *Village Echoes: The Fiction of Wu Zuxiang*. Boulder: Westview Press, 1993.

Yang, Hsien-yi, and Gladys Yang, trans. *Selected Works of Lu Hsun*. 4 vols. Peking: Foreign Languages Press, 1956–60.

Yang, Winston, and Nathan Mao, ed. *Modern Chinese Fiction: A Guide to Its Study and Appreciation: Essays and Bibliographies*. Boston: G. K. Hall, 1981.

Zhang Yingjin. *The City in Modern Chinese Literature and Film: Configurations of Space, Time, and Gender*. Stanford: Stanford University Press, 1996.

Zhao, Henry Y. H., ed. *The Lost Boat: Avant Garde Fiction from China*. London: Wellsweep, 1993.

———. *The Uneasy Narrator: Chinese Fiction from the Traditional to the Modern*. Oxford: Oxford University Press, 1995.

DRAMA (SEE ALSO ORAL AND PERFORMING ARTS; POPULAR NARRATIVES; PROVERBS BELOW)

General

Chang, H. C. *Chinese Literature*. Vol. 1. *Popular Fiction and Drama*. Edinburgh: Edinburgh University Press, 1973.

Chu Kun-liang. *Les aspects rituels du théâtre chinois*. Paris: Collège de France, 1991.

Dolby, William. *Eight Chinese Plays*. London: Paul Elek, 1978.

———. *A History of Chinese Drama*. London: Paul Elek, 1976.

Gimm, Martin. *Das Yüeh-fu Tsa-lu des Tuan An-chieh: Studien zur Geschichte von Musik, Schauspiel und Tanz in der T'ang Dynastie*. Wiesbaden: Otto Harrassowitz, 1966.

Hung, Josephine Huang. *Ming Drama: Drama of the Ming Dynasty*. Taipei: Heritage Press, 1966.

Idema, Wilt, and Stephen H. West. *Chinese Theater 1100–1450: A Source Book*. Wiesbaden: Franz Steiner, 1982.

Johnson, David, ed. *Ritual Opera, Operatic Ritual: "Mulian Rescues His Mother" in Chinese Popular Culture*. Berkeley: Institute for East Asian Studies, 1989.

Judd, Ellen R. "Ritual Opera and the Bounds of Authority: Transformation and Transcendence." In Bell Yung, Evelyn S. Rawski, and Ruby B. Watson, ed., *Harmony and Counterpoint: Ritual Music in a Chinese Context*, pp. 226–246. Stanford: Stanford University Press, 1996.

Kuzay, Stefan. *Dan Nuo von Guichi: Eine Untersuchung zu religiösen Maskenspielen im südlichen Anhui*. Frankfurt: Peter Lang, 1995.

Lopez, Manual D. *Chinese Drama: An Annotated Bibliography of Commentary, Criticism and Plays in English Translation*. Metuchen, NJ: Scarecrow Press, 1991.

Lu, Tina. *Persons, Roles, and Minds: Identity in "Peony Pavilion" and "Peach Blossom Fan."* Stanford: Stanford University Press, 2001.

Mackerras, Colin. *Chinese Drama: A Historical Survey*. Peking: New World Press, 1990.

———. *Chinese Drama: From Its Origin to the Present Day*. Honolulu: University of Hawaii Press, 1983.

Riley, Jo. *Chinese Theatre and the Actor in Performance*. Cambridge: Cambridge University Press, 1997.

van der Loon, Piet. "Les origines rituelles du théâtre chinois." *Journal Asiatique*, 265 (1977): 141–163.
Wang, Kefen. *The History of Chinese Dance*. Peking: Foreign Languages Press, 1985.

Chu-kung-tiao and Other Early Forms

Chen, Fan Pen. "Yang Kuei-fei in *Tales from the T'ien-pao Era: A Chu-kung-tiao*." *Journal of Sung-Yuan Studies*, 22 (1990–92): 1–22.
Ch'en, Li-li. "Outer and Inner Forms of *Chu-kung-tiao*, with Reference to *pien-wen*, *tz'u* and Vernacular Fiction." *Harvard Journal of Asiatic Studies*, 32 (1972): 124–149.
———. "Some Background Information on the Development of *Chu-kung-tiao*." *Harvard Journal of Asiatic Studies*, 33 (1973): 224–237.
Doleželová-Velingerová, Milena, and J. I. Crump, trans. *Ballad of the Hidden Dragon* (Liu Chih-yüan chu-kung-tiao). Oxford: Oxford University Press, 1971.
Idema, Wilt L. "Data on the *Chu-kung-tiao*: A Reassessment of Conflicting Opinions." *T'oung Pao*, 79 (1993): 69–112.
———. "Performance and Construction of the *Chu-kung-tiao*." *Journal of Oriental Studies*, 16 (1978): 63–78.
———. "Satire and Allegory in All Keys and Modes." In Hoyt C. Tillman and Stephen H. West, ed., *China Under Jurchen Rule*, pp. 238–280. Albany: State University of New York Press, 1995.
West, Stephen H. *Vaudeville and Narrative: Aspects of Chin Theater*. Wiesbaden: Franz Steiner, 1977.

Tsa-chü

Besio, Kimberly. "Zhang Fei in Yuan Vernacular Literature: Legend, Heroism, and History in the Reproduction of the Three Kingdoms Story Cycle." *Journal of Sung-Yuan Studies*, 27 (1997): 63–98.
Crump, James I. *Chinese Theater in the Days of Kublai Khan*. Tucson: University of Arizona Press, 1981.
Crump, James I., trans. "Wang Chiu-ssu: The Wolf of Chung Shan." *Renditions*, 7 (1977): 29–38.
Dolby, A. E. W. "Kuan Han-ch'ing." *Asia Major*, 16 (1971): 1–60.
———. "Wang Shifu's Influence and Reputation." *Ming-Qing yanjiu*, 3 (1994): 19–45.
Du, Wenwei. "*The Chalk Circle* Comes Full Circle: From Yuan Drama Through the Western Stage to Peking Opera." *Asian Theater Journal*, 12.2 (1995): 307–325.
Forke, Alfred, trans. *Chinesische Dramen der Yuan-Dynastie*. Wiesbaden: Franz Steiner, 1978.
Hart, Henry H., trans. *The West Chamber: A Medieval Drama*. Stanford: Stanford University Press, 1936.
Hayden, George A., trans. *Crime and Punishment in Medieval Chinese Drama: Three Judge Pao Plays*. Cambridge: Harvard University Press, 1978.
Hsiung, S. I., trans. *The Romance of the Western Chamber* (Hsi Hsiang Chi). London: Methuen, 1935; reprinted (with a preface by C. T. Hsia), New York: Columbia University Press, 1968.
Idema, W. L. *The Dramatic Oeuvre of Chu Yu-tun, 1379–1439*. Leiden: E. J. Brill, 1985.

———. "Emulation Through Readaptation in Yüan and Early Ming *tsa-chü*." *Asia Major*, 3rd series, 3 (1990): 113–128.

———. "The Orphan of Zhao: Self-Sacrifice, Tragic Choice and Revenge, and the Confucianization of Mongol Drama at the Ming Court." *Cina*, 21 (1988): 159–190.

———. "Why You Never Have Read a Yuan Drama: The Transformation of *zaju* at the Ming Court." In S. M. Carletti, M. Sacchetti, P. Santangelo, ed., *Studi in onore di Lanciello Lanciotti*, pp. 765–791. Naples: Istituto Universitorio Orientale, Dipartimento di Studi Asiatici, 1996.

———. "*Yüan-pen* as a Minor Form of Dramatic Literature in the Fifteenth and Sixteenth Centuries." *Chinese Literature: Essays, Articles, Reviews (CLEAR)*, 6 (1984): 20–42.

Liu, Wu-chi. "Kuan Han-ch'ing: The Man and His Life." *Journal of Sung-Yuan Studies*, 22 (1990–92): 163–188.

———. "The Original Orphan of China." *Comparative Literature*, 5 (1953): 193–212.

Panish, Paul Z. "Trembling Pearls: The Craft of Imagery in Po P'u's 'Rain on the Wu-t'ung Tree.'" *Monumenta Serica*, 12 (1976): 355–373.

Shih, Chung-wen. *The Golden Age of Chinese Drama: Yüan Tsa-chü*. Princeton: Princeton University Press, 1976.

———. *Injustice to Tou O* (Tou O yuan): *A Study and Translation*. Cambridge: Cambridge University Press, 1972.

Wang, Pi-twan H., trans. "The Revenge of the Orphan of Chao, by Chi Chun-hsiang." *Renditions*, 9 (1978): 103–131.

Wang, Shifu. *The Moon and the Zither: The Story of the Western Wing*. Stephen H. West and Wilt L. Idema, ed. and trans. Berkeley and Los Angeles: University of California Press, 1991; reissued by the same publisher in 1995 as *The Story of the Western Wing*.

West, Stephen H. "Jurchen Elements in the Northern Drama *Hu-t'ou-p'ai*." *T'oung Pao*, 63 (1977): 273–295.

———. "A Study in Appropriation: Zang Maoxun's Injustice to Dou E." *Journal of the American Oriental Society*, 111.1 (1991): 283–302.

Yang, Hsien-yi, and Gladys Yang, trans. *Selected Plays of Kuan Han-ch'ing*. Shanghai: New Art and Literature Publishing House, 1958; reprinted as *Selected Plays of Guan Hanqing* (Peking: Foreign Languages Press, 1979).

Yen, Yuan-shu. "Yellow Millet Dream: A Translation" and "Yellow Millet Dream: A Study of Its Artistry." *Tamkang Review*, 6 (1975): 205–249.

Yu, Shao-ling. "Tears on the Blue Gown, by Ma Chih-yuan (fl. 1251)." *Renditions*, 10 (1978): 131–154.

Ch'uan-ch'i, with Its Predecessors and Successors

Birch, Cyril, trans. *The Peony Pavilion* (Mudan Ting). Bloomington: Indiana University Press, 1980.

———. *Scenes for Mandarins: The Elite Theater of the Ming*. New York: Columbia University Press, 1995.

Chang, Chun-shu, and Shelley Hsüeh-lun Chang. *Crisis and Transformation in Seventeenth-Century China: Society, Culture and Modernity in Li Yü's World*. Ann Arbor: University of Michigan Press, 1992.

Chen Shih-hsiang, Harold Acton, and Cyril Birch, trans. *The Peach Blossom Fan*, by K'ung Shang-jen. Berkeley and Los Angeles: University of California Press, 1976.

Hanan, Patrick. *The Invention of Li Yü*. Cambridge: Harvard University Press, 1988.

Henry, Eric P. *Chinese Amusement: The Lively Plays of Li Yu*. Hamden, CT: Archon Books, 1980.

Leung, K. C. *Hsu Wei as Drama Critic: An Annotated Translation of the* Nan-tz'u hsü-lu. University of Oregon, Asian Studies Program, no. 7. Eugene: University of Oregon, 1988.

Mao, Nathan, and Wu-chi Liu. *Li Yu*. Boston: Twayne, 1979.

Martin, Helmut. *Li Li-weng über das Theater*. Heidelberg: privately printed, 1966; reprinted, Taipei: Mei Ya, 1968.

Mulligen, Jean, trans. *The Lute: Kao Ming's* P'i-p'a chi. New York: Columbia University Press, 1980.

Strassberg, Richard E. *The World of K'ung Shang-jen: A Man of Letters in Early Ch'ing China*. New York: Columbia University Press, 1983.

Struve, Lynn A. "History and *The Peach Blossom Fan*." *Chinese Literature: Essays, Articles, Reviews (CLEAR)*, 2.1 (1980): 55–72.

———. "'The Peach Blossom Fan' as Historical Drama." *Renditions*, 7 (1977): 99–113.

Yang, Hsien-yi, and Gladys Yang, trans. *Fifteen Strings of Cash*, by Chu Su-chen. Peking: Foreign Languages Press, 1957.

———. *The Palace of Eternal Youth*, by Hung Sheng. Peking: Foreign Languages Press, 1955.

Zbikowski, Tadeusz. *Early Nan-hsi Plays of the Southern Sung Period*. Warsaw: Wydawnictwa Universytetu Warszawskiego, 1974.

Peking Opera

Arlington, L. C. *The Chinese Drama from the Earliest Times Until Today: A Panoramic Study of the Art in China, Tracing Its Origin and Describing Its Actors (in Both Male and Female Roles) . . . Concluding with Synopses of Thirty Chinese Plays*. Shanghai: Kelly and Walsh, 1930.

Cosdon, Mark. "'Introducing Occidentals to an Exotic Art': Mei Lanfang in New York." *Asian Theater Journal*, 12.1 (1995): 175–189.

Hsu, Tau-Ching. *The Chinese Conception of the Theater*. Seattle: University of Washington Press, 1985.

Jones, Irmgard. "The Reform of Peking Opera in Taiwan." *China Quarterly*, 57 (January–March, 1974): 140–146.

Mackerras, Colin P. *The Rise of the Peking Opera, 1770–1870: Social Aspects of the Theatre in Manchu China*. Oxford: Oxford University Press, 1972.

Pan Xiafeng. *The Stagecraft of Peking Opera: From Its Origins to the Present Day*. Peking: New World Press, 1995.

Schönfelder, Gerd. *Die Musik der Peking Oper*. Leipzig: Deutscher Verlag für Musik, 1972.

Scott, A. C. *The Classical Theatre of China*. London: Allen and Unwin, 1957.

———. *Traditional Chinese Plays*. 3 vols. Madison: University of Wisconsin Press, 1967, 1969, 1975.

Wichmann, Elizabeth. *Listening to Theater: The Aural Dimension of Beijing Opera*. Honolulu: University of Hawaii Press, 1991.

Wichmann, Elizabeth, trans. *The Phoenix Returns to Its Nest: A Beijing Opera Created by Mei Lanfang*. Peking: New World Press, 1986.

Yang, David Shih-p'eng. *An Annotated Bibliography of Materials for the Study of Peking Opera*. Madison: University of Wisconsin Press, 1967.

Yang, Hsien-yi, and Gladys Yang. *Selected Plays of Kuan Han-ch'ing*. Peking: Foreign Languages Press, 1958.

Zung, Cecilia. *Secrets of the Chinese Drama: a Complete Explanatory Guide to Actions and Symbols as Seen in the Performance of Chinese Dramas, with Synopses of Fifty Popular Chinese Plays and 240 Illustrations*. London: G. G. Harrap, 1937.

Local and Regional Theater

Chan, Sau Y. *Improvisation in a Ritual Context: The Music of Cantonese Opera*. Hong Kong: Chinese University Press, 1991.

Gamble, Sidney D., ed. *Chinese Village Plays from the Ting Hsien Region*. Amsterdam: Philo Press, 1970.

Johnson, David, ed. *Ritual Opera: Operatic Ritual: "Mu-lien Rescues His Mother" in Chinese Popular Culture*. Publications of the Chinese Popular Culture Project, 1. Berkeley: IEAS Publications, University of California, 1989.

Kalvadova, Dana. "The Origin and Structure of Szechwan Theatre." *Archiv Orientálni*, 34 (1966): 503–523.

Mair, Victor H., and Li-ching Chang, trans. and intro. "*The Wall*, A Folk Opera, by Pu Songling." *Chinoperl Papers*, 14 (1986): 97–152.

Mark, Lindi Li. "*Kunqu* and Theater in the Transvestite Novel *Pinhua Baojian* [Mirror of Flowered Ranks]." *Chinoperl Papers*, 14 (1986): 37–59.

Sutton, Donald S. "Ritual Drama and Moral Order: Interpreting the God's Festival Troupes of Southern Taiwan." *Journal of Asian Studies*, 41 (1990): 535–554.

van der Loon, Piet. *The Classical Theatre and Art Song of South Fukien: A Study of Three Anthologies*. Taipei: Southern Materials Center, 1992.

Ward, Barbara E. "Regional Operas and Their Audiences: Evidence from Hong Kong." In David Johnson, Andrew J. Nathan, and Evelyn S. Rawski, ed., *Popular Culture in Late Imperial China*, pp. 161–187. Berkeley and Los Angeles: University of California Press, 1985.

Yung, Bell. *Cantonese Opera: Performance as Creative Process*. Cambridge: Cambridge University Press, 1989.

Puppet and Shadow Theater

Broman, Sven. *Chinese Shadow Theatre*. Stockholm: Etnografiska Museet, 1981.

———. "Eight Immortals Crossing the Sea." *Bulletin of the Museum of Far Eastern Antiquities*, 50 (1978): 25–48.

———. "Notes on Chinese Puppetry." *Bulletin of the Museum of Far Eastern Antiquities*, 55 (1983): 89–163.

Cohen, Alvin P. "A Taiwanese Puppeteer and His Theater." *Asian Folklore Studies* (Nagoya), 50.1 (1981): 33–49.

Dolby, William. "The Origins of Chinese Puppetry." *Bulletin of the School of Oriental and African Studies*, 41 (1978): 97–120.
Grube, Wilhelm, et al. *Chinesische Schattenspiele*. Munich: Verlag der Königlichen Bayerischen Akademie der Wissenschaften, 1916.
March, Benjamin. *Chinese Shadow-Figure Plays and Their Making*. With three Pieces from the Chinese: Visiting Li Er Ssu, Fox Bewitchment, The Exorcism, ed. with notes by Paul McPharlin. Detroit: Puppetry Imprints, 1938.
Obraztsov, Sergei. *The Chinese Puppet Theatre*. London: Faber and Faber, 1961.
Pimpaneau, Jacques. *Des poupés à l'ombre: Le théâtre des ombres et de marionettes en Chine*. Paris: Université Paris VII, Centre de Publication Asie Orientale, 1977.
Schipper, K. M. "The Divine Jester: Some Remarks on the Gods of the Chinese Marionette Theater." *Chung-yang yen-chiu-yüan, Min-tsu-hsüeh yan-chiu-so chi-k'an* (Bulletin of the Institute of Ethnology, Academia Sinica), 21 (1966): 81–96.
Stalberg, Roberta Helmer. *China's Puppets*. San Francisco: China Books, 1984.

Modern Plays; Film

Berry, Chris. *Perspectives on Chinese Cinema*. London: British Film Institute, 1991.
Brown, Nick, et al., ed. *New Chinese Cinemas: Forms, Identities, Politics*. Cambridge: Cambridge University Press, 1994.
Chow, Rey. *Primitive Passions: Visuality, Sexuality, Ethnography, and Contemporary Chinese Cinema*. New York: Columbia University Press, 1995.
Clark, Paul. *Chinese Cinema, Culture and Politics Since 1949*. Cambridge: Cambridge University Press, 1987.
Eberstein, Bernd. *Das chinesische Theater im 20. Jahrhundert*. Wiesbaden: Otto Harrassowitz, 1983.
———. *A Selective Guide to Chinese Literature, 1900–1949*. Vol. 4. *The Drama*. Leiden: E. J. Brill, 1990.
Ehrlich, Linda C., and David Dresser, ed. *Cinematic Landscapes: Observations on the Visual Arts of China and Japan*. Austin: University of Texas Press, 1994.
Gunn, Edward M. *Twentieth-century Chinese Drama: An Anthology*. Bloomington: Indiana University Press, 1983.
Guo, Moruo. *Five Historical Plays*. Fumin Peng, Bonnie S. McDougall, Yang Xianyi, and Gladys Yang, trans. Peking: Foreign Languages Press, 1984.
Holm, David L. *Art and Ideology in Revolutionary China*. Oxford: Oxford University Press, 1991.
Hu, John Y. H. *Ts'ao Yü*. New York: Twayne, 1972.
Lao She. *Teahouse: A Play in Three Acts*. John Howard-Gibbon, trans. Peking: Foreign Languages Press, 1980.
Lau, Joseph S. M. *Ts'ao Yü, The Reluctant Disciple of Chekhov and O'Neill: A Study in Literary Influence*. Hong Kong: Hong Kong University Press, 1970.
Levenson, Joseph R. *Revolution and Cosmopolitanism: The Western Stage and the Chinese Stages*. Berkeley and Los Angeles: University of California Press, 1971.
Leyda, Jay. *Dianying/Electric Shadows: An Account of Films and the Film Audience in China*. Cambridge: MIT Press, 1972.
Mackerras, Colin. *The Chinese Theatre in Modern Times: From 1840 to the Present Day*. London: Thames and Hudson, 1975.

Meserve, Walter J., and Ruth I. Meserve, ed. *Modern Drama from Communist China*. New York: New York University Press, 1970.

Mitchell, John D., ed. *The Red Pear Garden: Three Great Dramas of Revolutionary China*. Boston: David R. Godine, 1973.

Roy, David T. *Kuo Mo-jo: The Early Years*. Cambridge: Harvard University Press, 1971.

Semsel, George S., Chen Xihe, and Xia Hong. *Film in Contemporary China: Critical Debates, 1979–1989*. Westport, CT: Praeger, 1993.

Su, Xiaokang, and Wang Luxiang. *Deathsong of the River: A Reader's Guide to the Chinese TV Series "Heshang."* Richard W. Bodman and Pin P. Wang, trans. Cornell East Asia Series. Ithaca: East Asia Program, Cornell University, 1991.

Tay, William, ed. *Filming Modern Chinese Literature*. Special issue, *Modern Chinese Literature*, 7.2 (1993).

Wagner, Rudolf G. *The Contemporary Chinese Historical Drama: Four Studies*. Berkeley and Los Angeles: University of California Press, 1990.

Yan, Haiping, ed. *Theater and Society: An Anthology of Contemporary Chinese Drama*. Armonk, NY: M. E. Sharpe, 1998.

CLASSICS

Note: More information on all the works in this section can be found in Michael Loewe, ed., *Early Chinese Texts: A Bibliographical Guide*, Early China Special Monograph Series, 2. Berkeley: Society for the Study of Early China; Institute of East Asian Studies, University of California, 1993. See also the review article of *Early Chinese Texts* by E. Bruce Brooks, "The Present State and Future Prospects of Pre-Han Text Studies," *Sino-Platonic Papers*, 46 (July 1994): 1–74.

Principal Translations of the Thirteen Classics (arranged by approximate order of original appearance)

Chou I or *I-ching*

Legge, James, trans. *The Yi King*. Vol. 2 of *The Sacred Books of China*. 2nd ed. The Sacred Books of the East, 16. Oxford: Clarendon, 1899; reprint (as *The I-ching*), New York: Gramercy, 1996.

Wilhelm, Richard, trans. *The I-ching or Book of Changes*. Trans. from the German into English by Cary F. Baynes. 3rd ed. Bollingen Series, 19. 2 vols. Princeton: Princeton University Press, 1977.

Lynn, Richard John, trans. *The Classic of Changes: A New Translation of the I Ching as Interpreted by Wang Bi*. New York: Columbia University Press, 1994.

Shaughnessy, Edward L., trans. *I Ching: The Classic of Changes: The First English Translation of the Newly Discovered Second-Century B.C. Mawangdui Texts*. New York: Ballantine, 1996.

Wilhelm, Richard, trans. *I Ging: Text und Materialien*. 22nd ed. Gelbe Reihe, 1. Munich: Diederichs, 1998.

Shang-shu or *Shu-ching*

Legge, James, trans. *The Shoo King or the Book of Historical Documents*. Vol. 3 of *The Chinese Classics*. 2nd ed. Oxford: Clarendon, 1895; reprint, Taipei: Southern Materials Center, 1992.

Couvreur, S., trans. *Chou King*. 4th ed. Sien Hien: Mission catholique, 1934; reprint, Paris: Cathasia, 1950.

Karlgren, Bernhard, trans. *The Book of Documents. Bulletin of the Museum of Far Eastern Antiquities*, 22 (1950): 1–81; reprint, Göteborg: Elanders, 1950.

Mao shih or *Shih-ching*

Legge, James, trans. *The She King or the Book of Poetry*. Vol. 4 of *The Chinese Classics*.

Couvreur, S., trans. *Cheu King*. 3rd ed. Sien Hien: Mission catholique, 1934.

Waley, Arthur, trans. *The Book of Songs*. Boston and New York: Houghton Mifflin, 1937; reprint (ed. Joseph R. Allen), New York: Grove, 1996.

Karlgren, Bernhard, trans. *The Book of Odes. Bulletin of the Museum of Far Eastern Antiquities*, 16–17 (1944–45); reprint, Stockholm: Museum of Far Eastern Antiquities, 1950.

Pound, Ezra, trans. Shih-ching: *The Classic Anthology Defined by Confucius*. Cambridge: Harvard University Press, 1954.

Chou-li

Biot, Edouard, trans. *Le Tcheou-li ou Rites des Tcheou*. 3 vols. in 2. Paris: Imprimerie Nationale, 1851; reprint, Taipei: Ch'eng-wen, 1975.

I-li

Steele, John, trans. *The I-Li, or Book of Etiquette and Ceremonial*. 2 vols. Oriental Series, 8–9. London: Probsthain, 1917.

Couvreur, S., trans. *Cérémonial*. 2nd ed. Sien Hien: Mission catholique, 1928; reprint, Paris: Cathasia, 1951.

Li-chi

Legge, James, trans. *The Li Ki*. Vols. 3 and 4 of *The Sacred Books of China*. The Sacred Books of the East, 27–28.

Couvreur, S., trans. *Li Ki ou Mémoires sur les bienséances et cérémonies*. 2nd ed. 2 vols. Ho Kien Fou: Mission catholique, 1913; reprint, Paris: Cathasia, 1950.

Wilhelm, Richard, trans. *Li Gi: Das Buch der Riten, Sitten und Bräuche*. Gelbe Reihe, 31. 2nd ed. Munich: Diederichs, 1994.

Ch'un-ch'iu Tso chuan

Couvreur, S., trans. *Tch'ouen ts'ieou et Tso tchouan*. 3 vols. Ho Kien Fou: Mission catholique, 1914; reprint, Paris: Cathasia, 1951.

Legge, James, trans. *The Ch'un Ts'ew with the Tso Chuen*. Vol. 5 of *The Chinese Classics*.

Watson, Burton, trans. *The Tso chuan: Selections from China's Oldest Narrative History*. New York: Columbia University Press, 1989.

Ch'un-ch'iu Kung-yang chuan and *Ch'iu-ch'iu Ku-liang chuan*

Malmqvist, Göran. "Studies on the Gongyang and Guuliang Commentaries I–III." *Bulletin of the Museum of Far Eastern Antiquities*, 43 (1971): 67–222; 47 (1975): 19–69; 49 (1977): 33–215.

Lun-yü

Legge, James, trans. *Confucian Analects, the Great Learning, and the Doctrine of the Mean*. Vol. 1 of *The Chinese Classics*.

Giles, Lionel, trans. *The Sayings of Confucius: A Translation of the Confucian Analects*. London: John Murray, 1907; reprint, Twickenham, Middlesex, UK: Tiger Books International, Senate, 1998.

Couvreur, S., trans. *Entretiens de Confucius et de ses disciples*. In *Les quatre livres*. 3rd ed. Sien Hien: Mission catholique, 1930; reprint, Paris: Cathasia, 1949.

Waley, Arthur, trans. *The Analects of Confucius*. London: George Allen and Unwin, 1938; reprint, New York: Vintage, 1989.

Lau, D. C., trans. *Confucius: The Analects*. New York: Penguin, 1979.

Huang, Chichung, trans. *The Analects of Confucius*. New York and Oxford: Oxford University Press, 1997.

Leys, Simon. *The Analects of Confucius*. New York and London: W. W. Norton, 1997.

Brooks, E. Bruce, and A. Taeko Brooks, trans. *The Original Analects: Sayings of Confucius and His Successors*. New York: Columbia University Press, 1998.

Hsiao-ching

Legge, James, trans. *The Hsiao King*. Vol. 1 of *The Sacred Books of China*. The Sacred Books of the East, 3.

Wilhelm, Richard, trans. *Hiau Ging: das Buch der Ehrfurcht*. Kleine Bücher, 6. Peking: Pappelinsel, 1940.

Makra, Mary Lelia, trans. *The Hsiao ching*. Paul K. T. Sih, ed. Asian Institute Translations, 2. New York: St. John's University Press, 1961.

Erh-ya

None

Meng Tzu

Legge, James, trans. *The Works of Mencius*. Vol. 2 of *The Chinese Classics*.

Couvreur, S., trans. *Oeuvres de Meng Tzeu*. In *Les quatre livres*.

Wilhelm, Richard, trans. *Mong Dsï: Die Lehrgespräche des Meisters Meng K'o*. Gelbe Reihe, 42. 2nd ed. Jena: Eugen Diderichs, 1921; reprint, 1982, and Munich: Diderichs, 1994.

Ware, James R., trans. *The Sayings of Mencius*. New York: Mentor, 1960.

Dobson, W.A.C.H., trans. *Mencius*. Toronto: University of Toronto Press, 1963.

Lau, D. C., trans. *Mencius*. Harmondsworth and New York: Penguin, 1970.

Studies

Broman, Sven. *Studies on the* Chou li. Stockholm: Museum of Far Eastern Antiquities, 1961.

Creel, H. G. *Confucius: The Man and the Myth*. New York: John Day, 1949; reprint (as *Confucius and the Chinese Way*), New York: Harper and Row, 1960.

Ess, Hans van. *Politik und Gelehrsamkeit in der Zeit der Han: Die Alttext/Neutext Kontroverse*. Wiesbaden: Harrassowitz, 1993.

Fingarette, Herbert. *Confucius—The Secular as Sacred.* New York: Harper and Row, 1972.

Gardner, Daniel K. *Chu Hsi and the* Ta-hsüeh*: Neo-Confucian Reflections on the Confucian Canon.* Harvard East Asian Monographs, 118. Cambridge: Harvard University Press, 1986.

Granet, Marcel. *Fêtes et chansons anciennes de la Chine.* Bibliothèque de l'École des Hautes Études: Sciences réligieuses, 34. Paris: Ernest Leroux, 1919.

Hightower, James Robert. Han Shih wai-chuan*: Han Ying's Illustrations of the Didactic Application of the* Classic of Songs. Cambridge: Harvard University Press, 1952.

———. "The *Han-shih wai-chuan* and the *San chia shih.*" *Harvard Journal of Asiatic Studies*, 11 (1948): 241–310.

Jensen, Lionel. *Manufacturing Confucianism: Chinese Traditions and Universal Civilization.* Durham: Duke University Press, 1997.

Karlgren, Bernhard. "The Authenticity and Nature of the *Tso Chuan.*" *Göteborgs Högskolas Årsskrift*, 32.3 (1926): 1–65.

———. "The Early History of the *Chou Li* and *Tso Chuan* Texts." *Bulletin of the Museum of Far Eastern Antiquities*, 3 (1931): 1–59.

———. *Glosses on the Book of Documents.* Göteborg: Elanders, 1970.

———. *Glosses on the Book of Odes.* Stockholm: Museum of Far Eastern Antiquities, 1964.

Maspero, Henri. "La composition et la date du *Tso tchouan.*" In *Mélanges chinois et bouddhiques.* Brussels: Institut Belge des Hautes Études Chinoises, 1931–32. I, 137–215.

Nylan, Michael. *The Shifting Center: The Original "Great Plan" and Later Readings.* Nettetal, Germany: Steyler, 1992. [A study of the "Hung-fan," a chapter of the *Shu-ching*]

Peterson, Willard J. "Making Connections: 'Commentary on the Attached Verbalizations' of the *Book of Changes.*" *Harvard Journal of Asiatic Studies*, 42.1 (1982): 67–116.

Queen, Sarah A. *From Chronicle to Canon: The Hermeneutics of the* Spring and Autumn, *According to Tung Chung-shu.* Cambridge: Cambridge University Press, 1996.

Shaughnessy, Edward. *Before Confucius: Studies in the Creation of the Chinese Classics.* Albany: State University Press of New York, 1997.

Shchutskii, Iulian K. *Researches on the I Ching.* William L. MacDonald and Tsuyoshi Hasegawa, trans., with Hellmut Wilhelm. London and Henley: Routledge and Kegan Paul, 1980.

Smith, Kidder, Jr., et al. *Sung Dynasty Uses of the* I Ching. Princeton: Princeton University Press, 1990.

Waley, Arthur. "The Book of Changes." *Bulletin of the Museum of Far Eastern Antiquities*, 5 (1933): 121–142.

Wang, C. H. *The Bell and the Drum:* Shih Ching *as Formulaic Poetry in an Oral Tradition.* Berkeley and Los Angeles: University of California Press, 1974.

Wilhelm, Hellmut. *Change: Eight Lectures on the I ching.* Trans. Cary F. Baynes. London: Routledge and Kegan Paul, 1961.

———. *Heaven, Earth and Man in the* Book of Changes. Seattle: University of Washington Press, 1977.

THOUGHT

Bol, Peter K. *"This Culture of Ours": Intellectual Transitions in T'ang and Sung China*. Stanford: Stanford University Press, 1992.

Chan, Wing-tsit. *A Source Book in Chinese Philosophy*. Princeton: Princeton University Press, 1963.

Creel, Herrlee G. *Chinese Thought from Confucius to Mao Tse-tung*. Chicago: University of Chicago Press, 1953.

de Bary, Wm. Theodore, and Irene Bloom, ed. *Sources of Chinese Tradition*. Vol. 1, 2nd ed. New York: Columbia University Press, 1999.

de Bary, Wm. Theodore, and Richard Lufrano, ed. *Sources of Chinese Tradition*. Vol. 2. 2nd ed. New York: Columbia University Press, 2000.

de Bary, Wm. Theodore, Wing-tsit Chan, and Burton Watson, ed. *Sources of Chinese Tradition*. 2 vols. New York: Columbia University Press, 1960.

Denma Translation Group. *The Art of War: A New Translation*. Boston and London: Shambhala, 2001.

Elman, Benjamin. *From Philosophy to Philology: Intellectual and Social Aspects of Change in Late Imperial China*. Cambridge: Council on East Asian Studies, Harvard University, 1984.

Forke, Alfred, trans. and annot. *Lun-hêng. Part I. Philosophical Essays of Wang Ch'ung. Part II. Miscellaneous Essays of Wang Ch'ung*. 1st ed., 1907; reprint, New York: Paragon, 1962.

Fung, Yu-lan. *A History of Chinese Philosophy*. Derk Bodde, trans. 2 vols. Peking, 1937; reprint, Princeton: Princeton University Press, 1953.

———. *A Short History of Chinese Philosophy*. Derk Bodde, ed. New York: MacMillan, 1948.

Goldin, Paul Rakita. *Rituals of the Way: The Philosophy of Xunzi*. Chicago and La Salle: Open Court, 1999.

Graham, A. C. *The Book of Lieh-tzu*. London: John Murray, 1960.

Henricks, Robert, trans. and annot. *Lao Tzu: Te Tao Ching*. New York: Ballantine, 1989.

Knobloch, John. *Xunzi: A Translation and Study of the Complete Works*. 3 vols. Stanford: Stanford University Press, 1988, 1990, 1994.

Liao, W. K., trans. *The Complete Works of Han Fei Tzu*. 2 vols. London: Arthur Probsthain, 1939.

Mair, Victor H., ed. *Experimental Essays on Chuang-tzu*. Honolulu: University of Hawaii Press, 1983.

Mair, Victor H., trans. *Tao Te Ching: The Classic Book of Integrity and the Way*. New York: Bantam, 1990.

———. *Wandering on the Way: Early Taoist Tales and Parables of Chuang Tzu*. New York: Bantam, 1994; Honolulu: University of Hawaii Press, 1998.

Moore, Charles A. *The Chinese Mind: Essentials of Chinese Philosophy and Culture*. Honolulu: University of Hawaii Press, 1967.

Mote, Frederick W. *Intellectual Foundations of China*. New York: Alfred A. Knopf, 1971.

Nivison, David. *The Ways of Confucianiam: Investigations in Chinese Philosophy*. Bryan W. Van Norden, ed. Chicago and La Salle: Open Court, 1996.

Nylan, Michael. "Confucian Piety and Individualism in Han China." *Journal of the American Oriental Society*, 116.1 (1996): 1–27.
Richards, I. A. *Mencius on the Mind: Experiments in Multiple Definition*. New York: Harcourt, Brace, 1932.
Schwartz, Benjamin. *In Search of Wealth and Power: Yen Fu and the West*. Cambridge: Harvard University Press, 1964.
Watson, Burton. *The Complete Works of Chuang Tzu*. New York: Columbia University Press, 1968.

MYTH AND GENERALIZED RELIGION

Allan, Sarah. *The Heir and the Sage: Dynastic Legend in Early China*. San Francisco: Chinese Materials Center, 1981.
Birrell, Anne. *Chinese Mythology: An Introduction*. Baltimore: Johns Hopkins University Press, 1993.
———. "The Four Flood Myth Traditions of Classical China." *T'oung Pao*, 83 (1997): 213–259.
———. "Studies on Chinese Myth Since 1970: An Appraisal." Part I, *History of Religions*, 33.4 (1994): 389–393; Part II, *History of Religions*, 34.1 (1994): 70–94.
Birrell, Anne, trans. *The Classic of Mountains and Seas*. London: Penguin, 1998.
Bodde, Derk. *Festivals in Classical China: New Year and Other Annual Observances During the Han Dynasty, 206 B.C.–A.D. 220*. Princeton: Princeton University Press, 1975.
———. "Myths of Ancient China." In Samuel Noah Kramer, ed., *Mythologies of the Ancient World*, pp. 367–408. Garden City, NY: Anchor Books, Doubleday, 1961.
Boltz, William G. "Kung Kung and the Flood: Reverse Euhemerism in the *Yao tien*." *T'oung Pao*, 67.3–5 (1981): 141–153.
Cahill, Suzanne E. *Transcendence and Divine Passion: The Queen Mother of the West in Medieval China*. Stanford: Stanford University Press, 1993.
Greatrex, Roger. *The Bowu Zhi: An Annotated Translation*. Stockholm Skrifter utgivna Föreningen för Orientaliska Studier, 20. Stockholm: Orientaliska Studier, 1987.
Groot, J. J. M. de. *The Religious System of China, Its Ancient Forms, Evolution, History and Present Aspect: Manners, Customs, and Social Institutions Connected Therewith*. 6 vols. Leiden: E. J. Brill, 1892–1910.
Hansen, Valerie. *The Changing Gods of Medieval China*. Princeton: Princeton University Press, 1990.
Holzman, Donald. "Songs for the Gods: the Poetry of Popular Religion in Fifth-Century China." *Asia Major*, 3rd series, 1 (1990): 1–20.
Horman, André d'. *Guoyu: Propos sur les principautés*. I: *Zhouyu*. Compléments par Rémi Mathieu. Mémoires de l'Institut des Hautes Études Chinoises, 25.1. Paris: Collège de France, 1985.
Karlgren, Bernhard. "Legends and Cults in Ancient China." *Bulletin of the Museum of Far Eastern Antiquities*, 18 (1946): 199–365.
Le Blanc, Charles, and Rémi Mathieu, ed. *Mythe et philosophie à l'aube de la Chine impériale: Études sur le* Huainan Zi. Montreal: Presses de l'Université de Montreal; Paris: De Boccard, 1992.
Loewe, Michael. *Chinese Ideas of Life and Death*. London: Allen and Unwin, 1982.

Lopez, Donald S., Jr., ed. *Religions of China in Practice*. Princeton: Princeton University Press, 1996.

Mathieu, Rémi. *Anthologie des mythes et légendes de la Chinese ancienne: textes choisis, présentés, traduits et indexés*. Paris: Gallimard, 1993.

———. *Étude sur la mythologie et l'ethnologie de la Chine ancienne: traduction annotée du* Shanhai jing. 2 vols. Mémoires de l'Institut des Hautes Études Chinoises, 22.1–2. Paris: Institut des Hautes Études Chinoises, 1983.

———. *Le Mu Tianzi zhuan: traduction annotée, étude critique*. Paris: Collège de France, 1978.

Porter, Deborah Lynn. *From Deluge to Discourse: Myth, History, and the Generation of Chinese Fiction*. Albany: State University of New York Press, 1996.

Shahar, Meir, and Robert Weller, ed. *Unruly Gods: Divinity and Society in China*. Honolulu: University of Hawaii Press, 1996.

Tu, Wei-ming. *Centrality and Commonality: An Essay of Confucian Religiousness*. Albany: State University of New York Press, 1989.

Ware, James. *Alchemy, Medicine, Religion in the China of* A.D. *320: The* Nei P'ien *of Ko Hung* (Pao-p'u tzu). Cambridge: MIT Press, 1966.

Werner, E. T. C. A *Dictionary of Chinese Mythology*. Shanghai: Kelly and Walsh, 1932; numerous reprints.

Williams, C. A. S. *Encyclopedia of Chinese Symbolism and Art Motives*. 3rd ed. Shanghai: Kelly and Walsh, 1941; numerous reprints.

Yearley, Lee. *Mencius and Aquinas: Theories of Virtue and Conceptions of Courage*. Albany: State University of New York Press, 1990.

Yü, Ying-shih. "O Soul, Come Back! A Study in the Changing Conceptions of the Soul and Afterlife in Pre-Buddhist China." *Harvard Journal of Asiatic Studies*, 47 (1987): 363–395.

Yuan, Ke. *Dragons and Dynasties: An Introduction to Chinese Mythology*. New York: Penguin, 1993.

BUDDHISM

Bantly, Francisca Cho. "Buddhist Allegory in *Journey to the West*." *Journal of Asian Studies*, 49 (1989): 512–524.

Chavannes, Édouard, trans. *Cinq cents contes et apologues*. 4 vols. Paris: Librairie Ernest Leroux, 1910–34.

Ch'en, Kenneth K. S. *Buddhism in China: A Historical Survey*. Princeton: Princeton University Press, 1964.

———. *The Chinese Transformation of Buddhism*. Princeton: Princeton University Press, 1973.

Demiéville, Paul. *L'oeuvre de Wang le Zélateur (Wang Fan-tche), suivi des Instructions domestiques de l'aiëul (T'ai-kong kia-kiao). Poèmes populaires des T'ang (VIIe–Xe siècles), édités, traduits et commentés d'après des manuscrits de Touen-houang*. Paris: Collège de France, 1982.

———. "Le Tch'an et la poésie chinoise." *Hermès*, 7 (1970): 123–136. Also included in Demiéville, *Choix d'études bouddhiques*, pp. 456–469. Leiden: E. J. Brill, 1973.

Dudbridge, Glen. *The Legend of Miao-shan*. London: Ithaca Press, 1978.

Gjertson, Donald E. "The Early Chinese Buddhist Miracle Tales: A Preliminary Survey." *Journal of the American Oriental Society*, 101 (1981): 287–301.

———. *Ghosts, Gods, and Retribution: Nine Buddhist Miracle Tales from Six Dynasties and Early T'ang China*. Asian Studies Committee Occasional Papers Series, 2. Amherst: University of Massachusetts, 1978.

Grant, Beata. *Mount Lu Revisited: Buddhism in the Life and Writings of Su Shih*. Honolulu: University of Hawaii Press, 1994.

Hurvitz, Leon. *Scripture of the Lotus Blossom of the Fine Dharma. Translated from the Chinese of Kumārajīva*. New York: Columbia University Press, 1976.

Jenner, William J. F. *Memories of Loyang: Yang Hsüan-chih and the Lost Capital (493–534)*. Oxford: Oxford University Press, 1981.

Kroll, Paul W. *Dharma Bell and Dhāraṇī Pillar: Li Po's Buddhist Inscriptions*. Kyoto: Italian School of East Asian Studies, 2001.

Mair, Victor H. "Lay Students and the Making of Written Vernacular Narrative: An Inventory of Tun-huang Manuscripts." *Chinoperl Papers*, 10 (1981): 5–96.

———. "A Partial Bibliography for the Study of Indian Influence on Chinese Popular Literature." *Sino-Platonic Papers*, 3 (March 1987): i–iv, 1–214.

Mather, Richard B. "The Landscape Buddhism of the Fifth-Century Poet Hsieh Ling-yün." *Journal of Asian Studies*, 18 (1958): 67–79.

———. "Wang Chin's 'Dhuta Temple Stele Inscription' as an Example of Buddhist Parallel Prose." *Journal of the American Oriental Society*, 83 (1963): 338–359.

Mensikov, Lev N. "Les paraboles bouddhiques dans la littérature chinoise." *Bulletin de l'École française d'Extrême-Orient*, 67 (1980): 303–336.

Nielsen, Thomas P. *The T'ang Poet-Monk Chiao-jan*. Tempe: Center for Asian Studies, Arizona State University, 1972.

Overmyer, Daniel L. *Precious Volumes: An Introduction to Chinese Sectarian Scriptures from the Sixteenth and Seventeenth Centuries*. Cambridge: Harvard University Asia Center, 1999.

Red Pine. *Han-shan: The Collected Songs of Cold Mountain*. Port Townsend, WA: Copper Canyon Press, 1983.

Robinson, Richard, trans. *Chinese Buddhist Verse*. London: John Murray, 1954.

Shih, Robert, trans. *Biographies des moines eminents (Kao Seng Tchouan) de Houei-kiao*. Première partie: *Biographies des premiers traducteurs*. Bibliothèque du Muséon, 54. Louvain: Institut Orientaliste—Bibliothèque de l'Université, 1968.

Teiser, Stephen F. "'Having Once Died and Returned to Life': Representations of Hell in Medieval China." *Harvard Journal of Asiatic Studies*, 48 (1988): 433–464.

———. *The Scripture of the Ten Kings and the Making of Purgatory in Medieval Chinese Buddhism*. Honolulu: Kuroda Institute Studies in East Asian Buddhism, University of Hawai'i Press, 1994.

Tsai, Kathryn Ann, trans. *Lives of the Nuns: Biographies of Chinese Buddhist Nuns from the Fourth to Sixth Centuries*. Honolulu: University of Hawaii Press, 1994.

Waley, Arthur, trans. *Ballads and Stories from Tun-huang*. London: Allen and Unwin, 1960.

Wang Yi-t'ung, trans. *A Record of Buddhist Monasteries in Lo-yang*. Princeton: Princeton University Press, 1984.

Watson, Burton, trans. *The Lotus Sutra*. New York: Columbia University Press, 1993.

Wright, Arthur F. *Buddhism in Chinese History*. Stanford: Stanford University Press, 1959.

TAOISM

Bokenkamp, Stephen R., with Peter Nickerson. *Early Daoist Scriptures*. Berkeley: University of California Press, 1997.

Boltz, Judith M. *A Survey of Taoist Literature, Tenth to Seventeenth Centuries*. China Research Monograph, 32. Berkeley: Institute of East Asian Studies, 1987; reprint (with Corrigenda), 1995.

Cadonna, Alfredo. *"Quali Parole vi Aspettate che Aggiunga?": Il* Commentario al Daodejing *di Bai Yuchan, Maestro Taoista del XIII Secolo*. Orientalia Venetiana, 9. Florence: Leo S. Olschki, 2001.

Creel, Herrlee G. *"What Is Taoism?" and Other Studies in Chinese Cultural History*. Chicago and London: University of Chicago Press, 1970, 1977.

Girardot, N. J. *Myth and Meaning in Early Taoism: The Theme of Chaos* (hun-tun). Berkeley, Los Angeles, London: University of California Press, 1983.

Hansen, Chad. *A Daoist Theory of Chinese Thought: A Philosophical Interpretation*. New York, Oxford: Oxford University Press, 1992.

Kohn, Livia, ed. *Daoism Handbook*. Handbook of Oriental Studies (Handbuch der Orientalistik), Section 4: China, Vol. 14. Leiden, Boston, Cologne: Brill, 2000.

Kroll, Paul W. "Body Gods and Inner Vision: The Scripture of the Yellow Court." In Donald S. Lopez, Jr., ed., *Religions of China in Practice*, pp. 149–155. Princeton: Princeton University Press, 1996.

———. "In the Halls of the AzureLad." *Journal of the American Oriental Society*, 105.1 (1985): 75–94.

———. "Li Po's Purple Haze." *Taoist Resources*, 7.2 (1997): 21–37.

———. "The Light of Heaven in Medieval Taoist Verse," *Journal of Chinese Religions*, 27 (1999): 1–12.

———. "Seduction Songs of One of the Perfected." In Lopez, ed., *Religions of China in Practice*, pp. 180–187.

———. "Spreading Open the Barrier of Heaven." *Asiatische Studien*, 40.1 (1986): 22–39.

———. "Szu-ma Ch'eng-chen in T'ang Verse." *Society for the Study of Chinese Religions Bulletin*, 6 (1978): 16–30.

Lagerwey, John. *Wu-shang pi-yao, somme taoïste du VIe siècle*. Paris: École Française d'Extrême-Orient, 1981.

Maspero, Henri. *Taoism and Chinese Religion*. Frank A. Kierman, Jr., trans. Amherst: University of Massachusetts, 1981.

Needham, Joseph, and Lu Gwei-Djen. *Science and Civilisation in China*. Vol. 5. *Chemistry and Chemical Technology: Spagyrical Discovery and Invention*, Part 5: *Physiological Alchemy*. Cambridge: Cambridge University Press, 1983.

Robinet, Isabelle. *La révélation du Shangqing dans l'histoire du taoïsme*. 2 vols. Paris: École Française d'Extrême-Orient, 1984.

———. *Taoism: Growth of a Religion*. Phyllis Brooks, trans. Stanford: Stanford University Press, 1997.

Schafer, Edward. *Mirages on the Sea of Time: The Taoist Poetry of Ts'ao T'ang*. Berkeley: University of California Press, 1985.

Schipper, Kristofer M. *Concordance du Houang-t'ing king*. Paris: École Française d'Extrême-Orient, 1975.

———. *L'empereur Wou des Han dans la légende taoïste*. Paris: École Française d'Extrême-Orient, 1965.

———. *Indexe du Yunji qiqian*. 2 vols. Paris: École Française d'Extrême-Orient, 1981–82.

———. *The Taoist Body*. Karen C. Duval, trans. Berkeley: University of California Press, 1993.

Seaton, Jerome P. *The Wine of Endless Life: Taoist Drinking Songs from the Yuan Dynasty*. Buffalo: White Pine Press, 1985.

Seidel, Anna K. "Chronicle of Taoist Studies in the West, 1950–1990." *Cahiers d'Extrême-Asie*, 5 (1989–90): 223–347.

———. *La divinisation de Lao Tseu dans le Taoïsme des Han*. Paris: École Française d'Extrême-Orient, 1969; reprint, 1992.

Strickmann, Michel. *Le taoïsme du Mao Chan: chronique d'une révélation*. Paris: Collège de France, 1981.

———. "The Mao Shan Revelations: Taoism and the Aristocracy." *T'oung Pao*, 63 (1977): 1–64.

van der Loon, Piet. *Taoist Books in the Libraries of the Sung Period: A Critical Study and Index*. Oxford Oriental Institute Monograph, 7. London: Ithaca Press, 1984.

Verellen, Franciscus. *Du Guangting (850–933): taoïste de cour à la fin de la Chine médiévale*. Paris: Collège de France, 1989.

———. "Taoism." In "Chinese Religions: The State of the Field (Part II)." *Journal of Asian Studies*, 54.2 (1995): 322–346.

Waley, Arthur, trans. *The Travels of an Alchemist: The Journey of the Taoist Ch'ang-ch'un from China to the Hindukush at the Summons of Chingiz Khan*. London: George Routledge and Sons, 1931.

Welch, Holmes, and Anna Seidel, ed. *Facets of Taoism: Essays in Chinese Religion*. New Haven: Yale University Press, 1979.

Weng Tu-chien, comp. *Tao-tsang tzu-mu yin-te* (Combined Indices to the Authors and Titles of Two Collections of Taoist Literature). Harvard-Yenching Institute Sinological Index Series, 25. Peking: Yenching University Library, 1935; reprint, Taipei: Ch'eng-wen, 1966. Cited as "HY" in chapter 10 of this volume.

COMMENTARY, CRITICISM, AND THEORY

Bailey, Alison. "Microstructure and Macrostructure: Mao Zonggang's Critical Discourses on *The Romance of the Three Kingdoms*." *Poetics East and West*, 4 (1988–89): 159–168.

Bawden, Charles R. "The First Systematic Translation of *Hung-lou meng*: Qasbuu's Commented Mongolian Version." *Zentralasiatische Studien*, 15 (1981): 241–306.

Bonner, Joey. *Wang Kuo-wei: An Intellectual Biography*. Cambridge: Harvard University Press, 1986.

Bush, Susan, and Christian Murck, ed. *Theories of the Arts in China*. Princeton: Princeton University Press, 1983.

Cai, Zongqi, ed. *A Chinese Literary Mind: Culture, Creativity, and Rhetoric in* Wenxin diaolong. Stanford: Stanford University Press, 2001.

Campbell, Duncan M. "The Techniques of Narrative: Mao Tsung-kang (fl. 1661) and *The Romance of the Three Kingdoms*." *Tamkang Review*, 16.2 (1985): 139–161.

Chan Hing-ho. *Le* Honglou meng *et les commentaires de Zhiyanzhai*. Paris: Collège de France, 1982.

Chen, Xiaomei. *Occidentalism: A Theory of Counter-Discourse in Post-Mao China*. New York: Oxford University Press, 1995.

Debon, Günther. *Ts'ang-lang's Gespräche über die Dichtung: Ein Beitrag zur chinesischen Poetik*. Wiesbaden: Harrassowitz, 1962.

Denton, Kirk A., ed. *Modern Chinese Literary Thought: Writing on Literature, 1893–1945*. Stanford: Stanford University Press, 1996.

Ding, Naifei. "Tears of Resentment; or Zhang Zhupo's *Jin Ping Mei*." *positions: east asia cultures critique*, 3.3 (Winter 1995): 663–694.

Doleželová-Velingerová, Milena. "Pre-modern Chinese Fiction and Drama Theory." In Michael Groedon and Martin Kreisworth, ed., *The Johns Hopkins Guide to Literary Theory and Criticism*, pp. 132–129. Baltimore: Johns Hopkins University Press, 1994.

———. "Seventeenth-Century Chinese Theory of Narrative: A Reconstruction of Its System and Concepts." *Poetics East and West*, 4 (1988–89): 137–157.

———. "Traditional Chinese Theories of Drama and the Novel." *Archiv Orientálni*, 59.2 (1991): 132–139.

Egan, Ronald C. "On the Origins of the 'Yu Hsien K'u' Commentary." *Harvard Journal of Asiatic Studies*, 36 (1976): 135–146.

Fang, Achilles. "Rhyme-Prose on Literature: The *Wen-fu* of Lu Chi." *Harvard Journal of Asiatic Studies*, 14 (1951): 527–566.

Feng, Liping. "*The Scholars* and Its Qing Commentators." *Discours social/Social Discourse*, 1.1 (1988): 59–67.

Fenollosa, Ernest F. *The Chinese Written Character as a Medium for Poetry*. 1st ed., 1936; reprint, San Francisco: City Lights Books, 1968.

Führer, Bernhard. *Chinas erste Poetik: Das* Shipin (Kriterion Poietikon) *des Zhong Hong (467?–518)*. Edition Cathay, 10. Dortmund: Projekt, 1995.

Gálik, Marián. *The Genesis of Modern Chinese Literary Criticism (1917–1930)*. London: Curzon, 1980.

Gibbs, Donald A. "Liu Hsieh, Author of the *Wen-hsin tiao-lung*." *Monumenta Serica*, 29 (1971): 117–141.

Henderson, John B. *Scripture, Canon, and Commentary: A Comparison of Confucian and Western Exegesis*. Princeton: Princeton University Press, 1991.

Hightower, James. "The *Wen Hsüan* and Genre Theory." *Harvard Journal of Asiatic Studies*, 20 (1957): 512–533.

Holzman, Donald. "Literary Criticism in China in the Early Third Century A.D." *Asiatische Studien/Études asiatiques*, 28.2 (1974): 113–149.

Huang, Martin W. "Author(ity) and Reader in Traditional Chinese *Xiaoshuo* Commentary." *Chinese Literature: Essays, Articles, Reviews (CLEAR)*, 16 (1994): 41–67.

Hughes, E. R. *The Art of Letters: Lu Chi's "Wen Fu." A.D. 203: A Translation and Comparative Study*. New York: Pantheon, 1951.

Jahshan, Shaun Kelly. "Reader-Oriented Polyphony? Zhang Zhupo's Commentary on the *Jin Ping Mei*." *Modern Language Quarterly*, 56 (March 1995): 1–29.

Jones, Andrew. "The Poetics of Uncertainty in Early Chinese Literature." *Sino-Platonic Papers*, 2 (December 1986): 1–45.

Jullien, François. *La Valeur Allusive: des catégories originales de l'interprétation poétique dans la tradition chinoise (contribution à une reflexion sur l'altérité interculturelle)*. Paris: École Française d'Extrême-Orient, 1985.

Liu, David Jason. "The Chih-yen Chai Commentary: An Analysis in the Perspectives of Western Theories of Literature." *Tamkang Review*, 10.4 (1980): 471–494.

Liu, David Palumbo. *The Poetics of Appropriation: The Literary Theory and Practice of Huang Tingjian*. Stanford: Stanford University Press, 1993.

Liu, James J. Y. *Chinese Theories of Literature*. Chicago: University of Chicago Press, 1975.

———. *The Interlingual Critic: Interpreting Chinese Poetry*. Bloomington: Indiana University Press, 1982.

Lu, Sheldon Hsiao-peng. *From Historicity to Fictionality: The Chinese Poetics of Narrative*. Stanford: Stanford University Press, 1994.

McDougall, Bonnie S. *The Introduction of Western Literary Theories into Modern China, 1919–1925*. Tokyo: Center for East Asian Cultural Studies, 1971.

———. *Mao Zedong's "Talks at the Yan'an Conference on Literature and Art": A Translation of the 1943 Text with Commentary*. Ann Arbor: Center for Chinese Studies, University of Michigan, 1980.

McMullen, David. "Historical and Literary Theory in the Mid-Eighth Century." In Arthur Wright and Denis Twitchett, ed., *Perspectives on the T'ang*, pp. 307–342. New Haven: Yale University Press, 1973.

Miao, Ronald C., ed. *Studies in Chinese Poetry and Poetics*. San Francisco: Chinese Materials Center, 1978.

Owen, Stephen. *Readings in Chinese Literary Thought*. Cambridge: Harvard University Press, 1992.

———. *Traditional Chinese Poetry and Poetics: Omen of the World*. Madison: University of Wisconsin Press, 1985.

Plaks, Andrew H. "The *Chongzhen* Commentary on the *Jin Ping Mei*." *Chinese Literature: Essays, Articles, Reviews (CLEAR)*, 8.1–2 (1986): 19–30.

———. "Conceptual Models in Chinese Narrative Theory." *Journal of Chinese Philosophy*, 4.1 (1977): 25–47.

Rickett, Adele Austin, ed. *Chinese Approaches to Literature from Confucius to Liang Ch'i-ch'ao*. Princeton: Princeton University Press, 1978.

———. *Wang Kuo-wei's* Jen-chien Tz'u-hua: *A Study in Chinese Literary Criticism*. Hong Kong: Hong Kong University Press, 1994.

Robertson, Maureen. " . . . Convey What Is Precious: Ssu-k'ung T'u's Poetics and the *Erh-shih-ssu Shih P'in*." In David C. Buxbaum and Frederick W. Mote, ed., *Transition and Permanence: A Festschrift in Honor of Dr. Hsiao Kung-ch'üan*, pp. 321–357. Hong Kong: Cathay Press, 1972.

Rolston, David L. "'Point of View' in the Writings of Traditional Chinese Fiction Critics." *Chinese Literature: Essays, Articles, Reviews (CLEAR)*, 15 (1993): 113–141.

———. *Traditional Chinese Fiction and Fiction Commentary: Reading and Writing Between the Lines*. Stanford: Stanford University Press, 1997.

Rolston, David L., ed. *How to Read the Chinese Novel*. Princeton: Princeton University Press, 1990.

Roy, David T. "Chang Chu-p'o's Commentary on the *Chin P'ing Mei*." In Andrew Plaks, ed. *Chinese Narrative: Critical and Theoretical Essays*, pp. 115–123. Princeton: Princeton University Press, 1977.

Saussy, Haun. "The Prestige of Writing: *Wen*[2]: Letter, Picture, Image, Ideography." *Sino-Platonic Papers*, 75 (February 1997): 1–40.

———. *The Problem of a Chinese Aesthetic*. Stanford: Stanford University Press, 1993.

Shan Te-hsing. "The Aesthetic Response in *Chin-p'i Shui-hu*: An Iserian Reading of Chin Sheng-t'an's Commentary Edition of the *Shui-hu chuan*." In John Wang, ed., *Chinese Literary Criticism of the Ch'ing Period*, pp. 171–209. Hong Kong: Hong Kong University Press, 1993.

———. "A New Approach to *Hsiao-shuo p'ing-tien: Hsiao-shuo p'ing-tien* and Aesthetic Response." *National Chengchi University Journal*, 55 (1987): 39–60.

Shih, Vincent Yu-cheng, trans. and annot. *The Literary Mind and the Carving of Dragons*. New York: Columbia University Press, 1959; rev., bilingual ed., Hong Kong: Chinese University Press, 1983.

Tokei, Ferenc. *Genre Theory in China in the 3rd–6th Centuries*. Budapest: Academie Kiado, 1971.

Van Zoeren, Steven. *Poetry and Personality: Reading, Exegesis and Hermeneutics in Traditional China*. Stanford: Stanford University Press, 1991.

Waley, Arthur. *Yüan Mei: Eighteenth-Century Chinese Poet*. London: George Allen and Unwin, 1956.

Wang, John C. Y. "The *Chih-yen Chai* Commentary and the *Dream of the Red Chamber*." In Rickett, ed. *Chinese Approaches to Literature: From Confucius to Liang Ch'i-ch'ao*, pp. 189–220.

———. *Chin Sheng-t'an*. New York: Twayne, 1972.

Widmer, Ellen. "*Hsi-yu cheng-tao shu* in the Context of Wang Ch'i's Publishing Enterprise." *Chinese Studies*, 6.1 (1988): 37–64.

Wixted, John Timothy. "The *Kokinshū* Prefaces: Another Perspective." *Harvard Journal of Asiatic Studies*, 43.1 (1983): 215–238.

———. *Poems on Poetry: Literary Criticism by Yuan Hao-wen (1190–1257)*. Wiesbaden: Franz Steiner, 1982.

Wong, Shirleen. *Kung Tzu-chen*. Boston: Twayne, 1975.

Wong, Siu-kit. *Early Chinese Literary Criticism*. Hong Kong: Joint Publishing Company, 1983.

Wu, Fusheng. *The Poetics of Decadence: Chinese Poetry of the Southern Dynasties and Late Tang Periods*. Albany: State University of New York Press, 1998.

Wu, Hua L. "The Concept of Parallelism: Jin Shengtan's Critical Discourses on *The Water Margin*." *Poetics East and West*, 4 (1988–89): 169–179.

Wu, Laura Hua. "From *Xiaoshuo* to Fiction: Hu Yinglin's Genre Study of *Xiaoshuo*." *Harvard Journal of Asiatic Studies*, 55.2 (December 1995): 339–372.

Wu, Shih-ch'ang. *On the Red Chamber Dream: A Critical Study of Two Annotated Manuscripts of the XVIIIth Century*. Oxford: Clarendon, 1961.

Wu, Yenna. "Repetition in *Xingshi yinyuan zhuan*." *Harvard Journal of Asiatic Studies*, 51.1 (1991): 55–87.

Yu, Pauline. *The Reading of Imagery in the Chinese Tradition*. Princeton: Princeton University Press, 1987.

———. "Ssu-k'ung T'u's *Shih-p'in*: Poetic Theory in Poetic Form." In Miao, ed., *Studies in Chinese Poetry and Poetics*, pp. 81–103.

Yu, Pauline, Peter Bol, Stephen Owen, and Willard Peterson, ed. *Ways with Words: Writing About Reading Texts from Early China*. Berkeley and Los Angeles: University of California Press, 2000.

ORAL AND PERFORMING ARTS; POPULAR NARRATIVES; PROVERBS

Bordahl, Vibeke. *The Eternal Storyteller: Oral Literature in Modern China*. Richmond: Curzon, 1999.

———. *The Oral Tradition of Yangzhou Storytelling*. Richmond: Curzon, 1996.

Ch'en, Li-li. *Master Tung's Western Chamber Romance* (Tung Hsi-hsiang chu-kung-tiao). Cambridge: Cambridge University Press, 1976; reprint, New York: Columbia University Press, 1994.

Eberhard, Wolfram. "Notes on Chinese Storytellers." *Fabula*, 11 (1970): 1–31.

———. "Proverbs in Selected Chinese Novels." *Proverbium*, 2 (1985), 21–57.

Hrdličková, Věra. "The Professional Training of Chinese Story-Tellers and the Story-Tellers' Guilds." *Archiv Orientální*, 33 (1965): 225–248.

Hung, Chang-tai. *Going to the People: Chinese Intellectuals and Folk Literature, 1918–1937*. Cambridge: Harvard University Press, 1985.

Josephs, H. K. "The Chanda: A Sung Dynasty Entertainment." *T'oung Pao*, 62 (1976): 167–198.

King, Gail, trans. *The Story of Hua Guan Suo*. Tempe: Center for Asian Studies, Arizona State University, 1989.

Lévy, André. "Un document unique sur un genre disparu de la littérature populaire." In Lévy, *Études sur le conte et le roman chinois*, pp. 187–210. Paris: École Française d'Extrême Orient, 1971.

Link, Perry, ed. *Stubborn Weeds: Popular and Controversial Chinese Literature After the Cultural Revolution*. Bloomington: Indiana University Press, 1983.

Link, Perry, Richard Madsen, and Paul C. Pickowicz, ed. *Unofficial China: Popular Culture and Thought in the People's Republic*. Boulder: Westview, 1989.

Ma, Yau-woon. "The Beginnings of Professional Storytelling in China: A Critique of Current Theories and Evidence." In *Études d'histoire et de littérature chinoises offertes au Professeur Jaroslav Průšek*, pp. 227–245. Bibliothèque de l'Institut des Hautes Études chinoises, 24. Paris: Presses Universitaires de France, 1976.

Mackerras, Colin. *The Performing Arts in Contemporary China*. London: Routledge and Kegan Paul, 1981.

Mair, Victor H. "The Contributions of T'ang and Five Dynasties Transformation Texts (*pien-wen*) to Later Chinese Popular Literature." *Sino-Platonic Papers*, 12 (August 1989): 1–71.

———. *Painting and Performance: Chinese Picture Recitation and Its Indian Genesis*. Honolulu: University of Hawaii Press, 1988

———. "The Prosimetric Form in the Chinese Literary Tradition." In Joseph Harris and Karl Reichl, ed., *Prosimetrum: Cross-cultural Perspectives on Narrative in Prose and Verse*, pp. 365–385. Cambridge: D. S. Brewer, 1997.

———. *T'ang Transformation Texts: A Study of the Buddhist Contribution to the Rise of Vernacular Fiction and Drama in China*. Cambridge: Council on East Asian Studies, Harvard University, 1989.

Mair, Victor H., trans. and annot. *Tun-huang Popular Narratives*. Cambridge: Cambridge University Press, 1983.

McDougall, Bonnie S., ed. *Popular Chinese Literature and Performing Arts in the People's Republic of China 1949–1979*. Berkeley and Los Angeles: University of California Press, 1984.

McLaren, Anne E. *Chinese Popular Culture and Ming Chantefables*. Leiden: E. J. Brill, 1998.

———. "Women's Voices and Textuality: Chastity and Abduction in Chinese *Nüshu* and Prosimetric Narratives." *Modern China*, 22.4 (October 1996): 382–416.

Pai, Hua-wen. "What Is *pien-wen*?" Victor H. Mair, trans. *Harvard Journal of Asiatic Studies*, 44.2 (1984): 493–514.

Pimpaneau, Jacques. *Chanteurs, conteurs, bateleurs: littérature orale et spectacles populaires en Chine*. Paris: Université Paris 7, Centre de publication Asie orientale, 1977.

Rohsenow, John S. *ABC Chinese-English Dictionary of Proverbs*. Honolulu: University of Hawai'i Press, 2001.

———. *Chinese-English Dictionary of Enigmatic Folk Similes (Yanyu)*. Tucson: University of Arizona Press, 1991.

Smith, Arthur H. *Proverbs and Common Sayings from the Chinese*. Shanghai: American Presbyterian Mission Press, 1902; New York: Paragon, 1965.

Ting, Nai-tung. *A Type Index of Chinese Folktales in the Oral Tradition and Major Works of Non-Religious Classical Literature*. Helsinki: Suomalainen Tiedeakatemia, 1978.

Ting, Nai-tung, and Lu-hsia Hsu Ting. *Chinese Folk Narratives: A Bibliographical Guide*. San Francisco: Chinese Materials Center, 1975.

TRAVEL LITERATURE AND SKETCHES

Bodman, Richard. "[On a UFO]." In Victor H. Mair, ed., *The Columbia Anthology of Traditional Chinese Literature*, p. 593. New York: Columbia University Press, 1994.

Bol, Peter K. "A Literary Miscellany and Sung Intellectual History: The Case of Chang Lei's *Ming-tao tsa-chih*." *Journal of Sung-Yuan Studies*, 25 (1995): 121–151.

Boulton, Nancy Elizabeth. "Early Chinese Buddhist Travel Records as a Literary Genre." 2 vols. Georgetown University, Ph.D. dissertation, 1982.

Chang, Chun-shu, and Joan Smythe, trans. *South China in the Twelfth Century: A Translation of Lu Yu's Travel Diaries, July 3–December 6, 1170*. Hong Kong: Chinese University Press, 1981.

Chaves, Jonathan. "The Yellow Mountain Poems of Ch'ien Ch'ien-i (1582–1664): Poetry as *Yu-chi*." *Harvard Journal of Asiatic Studies*, 48.2 (December 1988): 465–492.

Franke, Herbert. "Some Aspects of Chinese Private Historiography in the Thirteenth

and Fourteenth Centuries." In E. G. Pulleyblank and W. G. Beasley, ed., *Historians of China and Japan*, pp. 115–134. London: Oxford University Press, 1961.
———. "Sung Embassies: Some General Observations." In Morris Rossabi, ed., *China Among Equals: The Middle Kingdom and Its Neighbors, 10th–14th Centuries*, pp. 116–148. Berkeley and Los Angeles: University of California Press, 1983.
Franke, Wolfgang. *An Introduction to the Sources of Ming History*, pp. 98–118. Kuala Lumpur: University of Malaya Press, 1968.
Fu Daiwei. " A Contextual and Taxonomic Study of the 'Divine Marvels' and 'Strange Occurrences' in the *Mengxi bitan*." *Chinese Science*, 11 (1993–94): 3–35.
Hargett, James M. *On the Road in Twelfth-Century China: The Travel Diaries of Fan Chengda (1126–1193)*. Stuttgart: Franz Steiner, 1989.
———. "Some Preliminary Remarks on the Travel Records of the Song Dynasty (960–1279)." *Chinese Literature: Essays, Articles, Reviews (CLEAR)*, 7 (1985): 67–93.
Legge, James, trans. *A Record of Buddhist Kingdoms; Being an Account by the Chinese Pilgrim Fâ-hsien of His Travels in India and Ceylon (A.D. 399–414) in Search of the Buddhist Books of Discipline*. Oxford: Clarendon, 1886.
Li Chi, trans. *The Travel Diaries of Hsü Hsia-k'o*. Hong Kong: Chinese University of Hong Kong, 1974.
Ma, Y. W. "Pi-chi." In Nienhauser et al., ed., *The Indiana Companion to Traditional Chinese Literature*, pp. 650–652 (see last section of bibliography).
Mirsky, Jeannette. *The Great Chinese Travelers*. Chicago and London: University of Chicago Press, 1964.
Naquin, Susan, and Chün-fang Yü, ed. *Pilgrims and Sacred Sites in China*. Berkeley and Los Angeles: University of California Press, 1992.
Strassberg, Richard E., trans. *Inscribed Landscapes: Travel Writings from Imperial China*. Berkeley and Los Angeles: University of California Press, 1994.

ETHNIC AND REGIONAL LITERATURE

Alley, Rewi, trans. *Not a Dog: An Ancient Tai Ballad*. Compiled by Students of the Chinese Department of Yunnan University (Class of 1956). Peking: New World Press, 1962.
Bender, Mark. *Seventh Sister and the Serpent: A Narrative Poem of the Yi People*. Peking: New World Press, 1982.
David-Neel, Alexandra, and the Lama Yongden. *The Superhuman Life of Gesar of Ling*. New York: Claude Kendall, 1934.
Dudbridge, Glen. "The Goddess Hua-yüeh San-niang and the Cantonese Ballad *Ch'en-hsiang T'ai-tzu*." *Chinese Studies*, 8.1 (June 1990): vol. 2, 627–646.
Duncan, Marion H. *Harvest Festival Dramas of Tibet*. Hong Kong: Orient, 1955.
Eberhard, Wolfram. *China's Minorities: Yesterday and Today*. Belmont, CA: Wadsworth, 1982
Fields, Rick, Brian Cutillo, and Mayumi Oda. *The Turquoise Bee: Love Songs of the Sixth Dalai Lama*. New York: HarperCollins, 1993.
Gordon, Antoinette K., trans. *The Hundred Thousand Songs: Selections from Milarepa, Poet-Saint of Tibet*. Rutland, VT: Charles E. Tuttle, 1961.
Johnson, David, Andrew J. Nathan, and Evelyn S. Rawski, ed. *Popular Culture in Late Imperial China*. Berkeley and Los Angeles: University of California Press, 1985.

Li, Shuijiang, and Karl W. Luckert. *Mythology and Folklore of the Hui, a Muslim Chinese People*. New York: State University of New York Press, 1994.

Lister, R. P. *Genghis Khan*. New York: Barnes and Noble, 1993.

Mackerras, Colin. *China's Minority Cultures: Identities Since 1912*. New York: St. Martin's Press, 1995.

Mackerras, Colin, trans. and ed. *The Uighur Empire: According to T'ang Dynastic Histories*. Columbia: University of South Carolina Press, 1972.

Nowak, Margaret, and Stephen Durrant. *Tale of the Nisan Shamaness, a Manchu Folk Epic*. Seattle: University of Washington Press, 1977.

Olson, James S. *An Ethnohistorical Dictionary of China*. Westport, CT: Greenwood, 1998.

Rossabi, Morris. *Khubilai Khan: His Life and Times*. Berkeley and Los Angeles: University of California Press, 1988.

Schwarz, Henry G. *The Minorities of Northern China*. Studies on East Asia, 17. Bellingham, WA: Western Washington University, Center for East Asian Studies, 1984.

Stein, R. A. *Tibetan Civilization*. J. E. Stapleton Driver, trans. London: Faber and Faber, 1972.

Stevens, Kate. "*The Slopes of Changban*, A Beijing Drumsong in Liu Style." *Chinoperl Papers*, 15 (1990): 69–83.

Tshe ring dbang rgyal. *Tale of the Incomparable Prince*. Beth Neuman, trans. New York: HarperCollins, 1996.

Yang, Gladys, trans. *Ashima*. Peking: Foreign Languages Press, 1957.

Zhao, Chengri. "An Overview of Contemporary Korean Literature in China." In Daesook Suh and Edward J. Schultz, ed., *Koreans in China*, pp. 144–163. Honolulu: Center for Korean Studies, University of Hawaii, 1990.

GENDER

Barlow, Tani, ed. *Gender Politics in Modern China: Writing and Feminism*. Special issue, *Modern Chinese Literature*, 4 (1988). Durham: Duke University Press, 1993.

Birrell, Anne. "In the Voice of Women: Chinese Love Poetry in the Early Middle Ages." In Lesley Smith and Jane H. M. Taylor, ed., *Women, the Book and the Worldly: Selected Proceedings of the St. Hilda's Conference* (Oxford, 1993), pp. 49–59. Cambridge: D. S. Brewer, 1995.

———. "The Psychology of the Couple: An Assessment of Early Medieval Chinese Love Poetry with Comparative References to Christine's [de Pizan] *Le Livre des Trois Vertus*." In Bernard Ribémont, ed., *Études Christiniennes*, pp. 13–24. Paris: Honoré Champion, 1998.

Chang, Kang-i Sun. *The Late Ming Poet Ch'en Tzu-lung: Crises of Love and Loyalism*. New Haven: Yale University Press, 1991.

Chang, Kang-i Sun, and Haun Saussy, ed. *Women Writers of Traditional China: An Anthology of Poetry and Criticism*. Stanford: Stanford University Press, 1999.

Chen, Yu-shih. "The Historical Template of Pan Chao's *Nü chieh*." *T'oung Pao*, 82.4–5 (1996): 229–257.

Chow, Rey. *Women and Chinese Modernity: The Politics of Reading Between West and East*. Minneapolis: University of Minnesota Press, 1991.

Duke, Michael S., ed. *Modern Chinese Women Writers: Critical Appraisals*. Armonk, NY: M. E. Sharpe, 1989.

Edwards, Louise P. *Men and Women in Qing China: Gender in* The Red Chamber Dream. Leiden: E. J. Brill, 1994.

Frankel, Hans H. "Cai Yan and the Poems Attributed to Her." *Chinese Literature: Essays, Articles, Reviews (CLEAR)*, 5 (1983): 133–156.

Hu, Ying. *Tales of Translation: Composing the New Woman in China, 1898–1918*. Stanford: Stanford University Press, 2001.

Idema, Wilt. *Vrouwenschrift: Vriendschap, huwelijk en wanhoop van Chinese vrouwen, opgetekend in een eigen schrift* (Women's Script: Friendship, Marriage, and Despair of Chinese Women, Recorded in a Script of Their Own). Amsterdam: Meulenhoff, 1996.

Larsen, Jeanne. *Brocade River Poems: Selected Works of the Tang Dynasty Courtesan Xue Tao*. Princeton: Princeton University Press, 1987.

Lin, Julia, trans. *Women of the Red Plain: An Anthology of Contemporary Chinese Women's Poetry*. Peking: Chinese Literature Press and Penguin, 1992.

Lu, Tonglin, ed. *Gender and Sexuality in Twentieth-Century Chinese Literature and Society*. Albany: State University of New York Press, 1993.

———. *Misogyny, Cultural Nihilism, and Oppositional Politics: Contemporary Chinese Experimental Fiction*. Stanford: Stanford University Press, 1995.

Mann, Susan. *Precious Records: Women in China's Long Eighteenth Century*. Stanford: Stanford University Press, 1997.

McMahon, Keith. *Misers, Shrews, and Polygamists: Sexuality and Male-Female Relations in Eighteenth-Century Chinese Fiction*. Durham and London: Duke University Press, 1995.

McLaren, Anne, and Chen Qinjian. "The Oral and Ritual Culture of Chinese Women: Bridal Lamentations of Nanhui." *Asian Folklore Studies*, 59 (2000), 205–208.

Nan Nü: *Men, Women and Gender in Early and Imperial China*. A Journal. Leiden: Brill, 1999– .

O'Hara, Albert Richard. *The Position of Women in Early China According to* Lieh nü chuan. 1st ed., 1945; 2nd ed., Hong Kong: Orient Publishing, 1955.

Rexroth, Kenneth, and Ling Chung, trans. *Li Ch'ing-chao: Complete Poems*. New York: New Directions, 1979.

Ropp, Paul S. "Love, Literacy and Laments: Themes of Women Writers in Late Imperial China." *Women's History Review*, 2.1 (1993): 107–141.

Schafer, Edward H. *The Divine Woman: Dragon Ladies and Rain Maidens in T'ang Literature*. Berkeley and Los Angeles: University of California Press, 1973.

Silber, Cathy. "From Daughter to Daughter-in-law in the Women's Script of Southern Hunan." In Christina K. Gilmartin, et al., ed., *Engendering China: Women, Culture and the State*, pp. 47–68. Cambridge: Harvard University Press, 1994.

Swann, Nancy Lee. *Pan Chao: Foremost Woman Scholar of China, First Century A.D.: Background, Ancestry, Life, and Writings of the Most Celebrated Chinese Woman of Letters*. New York: Century, 1932.

Walls, Jan W. "The Poetry of Yü Hsüan-chi: A Translation, Annotation, Commentary and Critique." Ph.D. dissertation, Indiana University, 1972.

Wang, Jiaosheng. "The Complete *Ci*-poems of Li Qingzhao: A New English Translation." *Sino-Platonic Papers*, 13 (October 1989): i–xii, 1–122.

Widmer, Ellen. "Martyred Matrons, Martial Maidens, and the Woman Reader: Some Sino-Japanese Comparisons." *International Journal of Social Education*, 6.1 (Spring 1991): 60–82.

Widmer, Ellen, and Kang-i Sun Chang, ed. *Writing Women in Late Imperial China*. Stanford: Stanford University Press, 1997.

Wu, Yenna. *The Chinese Virago: A Literary Theme*. Cambridge: Council on East Asian Studies, Harvard University, 1995.

———. *The Lioness Roars: Shrew Stories from Late Imperial China*. Ithaca: Cornell University East Asia Series, 1995.

———. "Venturing Beyond the Domestic Sphere: Suggestions of Proto-Feminist Thought in Ming-Qing Fiction." *Journal of the Chinese Language Teachers Association*, 32.1 (February 1997): 61–94.

LANGUAGE AND SCRIPT

Books

Boltz, William G. *The Origin and Early Development of the Chinese Writing System*. American Oriental Series, 78. New Haven: American Oriental Society, 1994.

Chen, Ping. *Modern Chinese: History and Sociolinguistics*. Cambridge: Cambridge University Press, 1999.

Chiang, William W. *"We Two Know the Script; We Have Become Good Friends": Linguistic and Social Aspects of the Women's Script Literacy in Southern Hunan, China*. Lanham, MD: University Press of America, 1995.

DeFrancis, John. *The Chinese Language: Fact and Fantasy*. Honolulu: University of Hawaii Press, 1984.

———. *Nationalism and Language Reform in China*. Princeton: Princeton University Press, 1950. New York: Octagon (Farrar, Straus, & Giroux), 1972 rpt.

———. *Visible Speech: The Diverse Oneness of Writing Systems*. Honolulu: University of Hawaii Press, 1989.

Hannas, Wm. C. *Asia's Orthographic Dilemma*. Honolulu: University of Hawaii Press, 1997.

Karlgren, Bernhard. *Philology and Ancient China*. Oslo: H. Aschehoug; Cambridge: Harvard University Press, 1926.

———. *Sound and Symbol in Chinese*. London: Oxford University Press, 1929; rev. ed., Hong Kong: Hong Kong University Press, 1962.

Liu, Lydia, ed. *Tokens of Exchange: The Problem of Translation in Global Circulations*. Durham: Duke University Press, 1999.

Masini, Federico. *The Formation of Modern Chinese Lexicon and Its Evolution Toward a National Language: The Period from 1840 to 1898*. Journal of Chinese Linguistics Monograph Series, 6. Berkeley: Project on Linguistic Analysis, University of California, 1993.

Norman, Jerry. *Chinese*. Cambridge Language Surveys. Cambridge: Cambridge University Press, 1988.

Ramsey, S. Robert. *The Languages of China*. Princeton: Princeton University Press, 1987.

Wang, William S-Y., ed. *The Ancestry of the Chinese Language*. Journal of Chinese Linguistics Monograph Series, 8. Berkeley: Project on Linguistic Analysis, University of California, 1995.

Journals and Serials (some of these also issue important monographs)

Cahiers de Linguistique Asie Orientale
International Review of Chinese Linguistics
Journal of Chinese Linguistics
Journal of the Chinese Language Teachers' Association
Linguistics of the Tibeto-Burman Area

Bibliographies

Wang, William S-Y., and Antaole Lyovin, comp. *CLIBOC: Chinese Linguistics Bibliography on Computer*. Cambridge: Cambridge University Press, 1970.

Yang, Paul Fu-mien. *Chinese Dialectology: A Selected and Classified Bibliography*. Hong Kong: Chinese University Press, 1981.

———. *Chinese Lexicology and Lexicography: A Selected and Classified Bibliography*. Hong Kong: Chinese University Press, 1985.

———. *Chinese Linguistics: A Selected and Classified Bibliography*. Hong Kong: Chinese University of Hong Kong, 1974.

HANDBOOKS AND ENCYCLOPEDIAS

Dillon, Michael. *China: A Cultural and Historical Dictionary*. Richmond, Surrey, UK: Curzon, 1998.

Feifel, Eugen. *Bibliographie zur Geschichte der chinesischen Literatur*. Hildesheim, Zurich, New York: Georg Olms, 1992.

Hightower, James Robert. *Topics in Chinese Literature: Outlines and Bibliographies*. Harvard-Yenching Institute Studies, 3. Cambridge: Harvard University Press, 1950; rev. 1971.

Lynn, Richard John. *Chinese Literature: A Draft Bibliography in Western European Languages*. Canberra: Faculty of Asian Studies in association with the Australian National University Press, 1979.

Nienhauser, William H., Jr., ed. *Bibliography of Selected Western Works on T'ang Dynasty Literature*. Taipei: Center for Chinese Studies, 1988.

Nienhauser, William H., Jr., ed.; Charles Hartman, Y. W. Ma, and Stephen H. West, assoc. ed. *The Indiana Companion to Traditional Chinese Literature*. 2 vols. Bloomington: Indiana University Press, 1986, 1998.

Perkins, Dorothy. *Encyclopedia of China: The Essential Reference to China, Its History and Culture*. Chicago, London: Fitzroy Dearborn, 1999.

Wilkinson, Endymion. *Chinese History: A Manual*. Harvard-Yenching Institute Monograph Series, 46, 52. Cambridge: Harvard University Asia Center, 1998; rev. and enlgd., 2000.

Wylie, A. *Notes on Chinese Literature: with Introductory Remarks on the Progressive Advancement of the Art; and a List of Translations from the Chinese into Various European Languages*. 1st ed. Shanghai, 1867; reprint, New York: Paragon, 1964.

PRINCIPAL CHINESE DYNASTIES AND PERIODS

Hsia (not fully verified)	c 2100–c. 1600 B.C.E.
Shang or Yin (largely verified)	c. 1600–c. 1045
Chou	c. 1045–256
Western Chou	c. 1100–771
Eastern Chou	c. 770–256
Spring and Autumn period	722–481/403
Warring States period	481/403–221
Ch'in	246/221–207
Han	206 B.C.E.–220 C.E.
Western or Former Han	206 B.C.E.–8 C.E.
Hsin (New)	9–23
Liu Hsüan (Han)	23–25
Eastern or Later Han	25–220
Three Kingdoms	220–265
Wei (North China)	220–265
Shu (Szechwan)	221 –263
Wu (Lower Yangtze Valley)	222–280
Chin	265–420
Western Chin	265–316
Eastern Chin	317–420

Note: B.C.E. and C.E. stand for Before the Common Era and the Common Era. They coincide with B.C. and A.D.

Southern and Northern Dynasties	420–589
Sixteen Kingdoms (North China)	304–439
Northern Dynasties[1]	386–581
Northern Wei (Tabgatch)	386–534
Eastern Wei	534–550
Western Wei	535–557
Northern Ch'i	550–577
Northern Chou	557–581
Southern Dynasties[2]	420–589
Sung (Former or Liu)	420–479
Ch'i	479–502
Liang	502–557
Ch'en	557–589
Sui	581–618
T'ang	618–684, 705–907
Chou (Empress Wu)	(684) 690–705
Five Dynasties[3]	907–960
Later Liang	907–923
Later T'ang	923–936
Later Chin	936–946
Later Han	947–950
Later Chou	951–960
Sung (Later or Chao)	960–1279
Northern Sung	960–1127
Southern Sung	1127–1279
Liao (Khitan)	916–1125
Western Liao	1125–1201
Western Hsia (Tangut)	1032–1227
Chin (Jurchen)	1115–1234
Yüan (Mongol)	1260–1368
Ming	1368–1644
Ch'ing (Manchu)	1644–1911 C.E.

1. The Northern Dynasties were dominated by non-Sinitic groups.
2. Wu and Eastern Chin plus the Southern Dynasties are collectively known as the Six Dynasties.
3. The Five Dynasties, dominated by non-Sinitic peoples, coexisted with a series of smaller and even more ephemeral Ten Kingdoms.

ROMANIZATION SCHEMES FOR MODERN STANDARD MANDARIN

Wade-Giles	*Pinyin*	*Wade-Giles*	*Pinyin*
a[h]	a	chi	ji
ai	ai	ch'i	qi
an	an	chia	jia
ang	ang	ch'ia	qia
ao	ao	chiang	jiang
cha	zha	ch'iang	qiang
ch'a	cha	chiao	jiao
chai	zhai	ch'iao	qiao
ch'ai	chai	chieh	jie
chan	zhan	ch'ieh	qie
ch'an	chan	chien	jian
chang	zhang	ch'ien	qian
ch'ang	chang	chih	zhi
chao	zhao	ch'ih	chi
ch'ao	chao	chin	jin
che	zhe	ch'in	qin
ch'e	che	ching	jing
chei	zhei	ch'ing	qing
chen	zhen	chiu	jiu
ch'en	chen	ch'iu	qiu
cheng	zheng	chiung	jiong
ch'eng	cheng	ch'iung	qiong

Wade-Giles	*Pinyin*	*Wade-Giles*	*Pinyin*
cho	zhuo	hai	hai
ch'o	chuo	han	han
chou	zhou	hang	hang
ch'ou	chou	hao	hao
chu	zhu	hei	hei
ch'u	chu	hen	hen
chü	ju	heng	heng
ch'ü	qu	ho	he
chua	zhua	hou	hou
ch'ua	chua	hsi	xi
chuai	zhuai	hsia	xia
ch'uai	chuai	hsiang	xiang
chuan	zhuan	hsiao	xiao
ch'uan	chuan	hsieh	xie
chüan	juan	hsien	xian
ch'üan	quan	hsin	xin
chuang	zhuang	hsing	xing
ch'uang	chuang	hsiu	xiu
chüeh	jue	hsiung	xiong
ch'üeh	que	hsü	xu
chui	zhui	hsüan	xuan
ch'ui	chui	hsüeh	xue
chun	zhun	hsün	xun
ch'un	chun	hu	hu
chün	jun	hua	hua
ch'ün	qun	huai	huai
chung	zhong	huan	huan
ch'ung	chong	huang	huang
e[h], ĕ	e	hui	hui
ei	ei	hun	hun
en	en	hung	hong
erh	er	huo	huo
fa	fa	i[1]	ji
fan	fan	jan	ran
fang	fang	jang	rang
fei	fei	jao	rao
fen	fen	jeh	re
feng	feng	jen	ren
fo	fo	jeng	reng
fou	fou	jih	ri
fu	fu	jo	ruo
ha	ha	jou	rou

1. The slightly modified Wade-Giles romanization used in this book substitutes *yi* for *i* and replaces A with *Ah* in names.

Wade-Giles	*Pinyin*
ju	ru
juan	ruan
jui	rui
jun	run
jung	rong
ka	ga
k'a	ka
kai	gai
k'ai	kai
kan	gan
k'an	kan
kang	gang
k'ang	kang
kao	gao
k'ao	kao
ke, ko	ge
k'e, k'o	ke
ken	gen
k'en	ken
keng	geng
k'eng	keng
kou	gou
k'ou	kou
ku	gu
k'u	ku
kua	gua
k'ua	kua
kuai	guai
k'uai	kuai
kuan	guan
k'uan	kuan
kuang	guang
k'uang	kuang
kuei	gui
k'uei	kui
kun	gun
k'un	kun
kung	gong
k'ung	kong
kuo	guo
k'uo	kuo
la	la
lai	lai
lan	lan
lang	lang

Wade-Giles	*Pinyin*
lao	lao
le[h]	le
lei	lei
leng	leng
li	li
lia	lia
liang	liang
liao	liao
lieh	lie
lien	lian
lin	lin
ling	ling
liu	liu
lo, luo	luo
lou	lou
lu	lu
lü	lü, lyu
luan	luan
lüan	lüan, lyuan
lüeh	lüe, lyue
lun	lun
lün	lün, lyun
lung	long
ma	ma
mai	mai
man	man
mang	mang
mao	mao
me	me
mei	mei
men	men
meng	meng
mi	mi
miao	miao
mieh	mie
mien	mian
min	min
ming	ming
miu, miou	miu
mo	mo
mou	mou
mu	mu
na	na
nai	nai
nan	nan

Wade-Giles	*Pinyin*
nang	nang
nao	nao
ne	ne
nei	nei
nen	nen
ni	ni
niang	niang
niao	niao
nieh	nie
nien	nian
nin	nin
ning	ning
niu	niu
no	nuo
nou	nou
nu	nu
nü	nü, nyu
nuan	nuan
nüeh	nüe, nyue
nung	nong
o, ŏ, e	e
ou	ou
pa	ba
p'a	pa
pai	bai
p'ai	pai
pan	ban
p'an	pan
pang	bang
p'ang	pang
pao	bao
p'ao	pao
pei	bei
p'ei	pei
pen	ben
p'en	pen
peng	beng
p'eng	peng
pi	bi
p'i	pi
piao	biao
p'iao	piao
pieh	bie
p'ieh	pie

Wade-Giles	*Pinyin*
pien	bian
p'ien	pian
pin	bin
p'in	pin
ping	bing
p'ing	ping
po	bo
p'o	po
p'ou	pou
pu	bu
p'u	pu
sa	sa
sai	sai
san	san
sang	sang
sao	sao
se	se
sen	sen
seng	seng
sha	sha
shai	shai
shan	shan
shang	shang
shao	shao
she	she
shei	shei
shen	shen
sheng	sheng
shih	shi
shou	shou
shu	shu
shua	shua
shuai	shuai
shuan	shuan
shuang	shuang
shui	shui
shun	shun
shuo	shuo
so	suo
sou	sou
ssu, szu	si
su	su
suan	suan
sui	sui

Wade-Giles	Pinyin
sun	sun
sung	song
ta	da
t'a	ta
tai	dai
t'ai	tai
tan	dan
t'an	tan
tang	dang
t'ang	tang
tao	dao
t'ao	tao
te	de
t'e	te
tei	dei
teng	deng
t'eng	teng
ti	di
t'i	ti
tiao	diao
t'iao	tiao
tieh	die
t'ieh	tie
tien	dian
t'ien	tian
ting	ding
t'ing	ting
tiu	diu
to	duo
t'o	tuo
tou	dou
t'ou	tou
tsa	za
ts'a	ca
tsai	zai
ts'ai	cai
tsan	zan
ts'an	can
tsang	zang
ts'ang	cang
tsao	zao
ts'ao	cao
tse	ze
ts'e	ce

Wade-Giles	Pinyin
tsei	zei
tsen	zen
ts'en	cen
tseng	zeng
ts'eng	ceng
tso	zuo
ts'o	cuo
tsou	zou
ts'ou	cou
tsu	zu
ts'u	cu
tsuan	zuan
ts'uan	cuan
tsui	zui
ts'ui	cui
tsun	zun
ts'un	cun
tsung	zong
ts'ung	cong
tu	du
t'u	tu
tuan	duan
t'uan	tuan
tui	dui
t'ui	tui
tun	dun
t'un	tun
tung	dong
t'ung	tong
tzu	zi
tz'u	ci
wa	wa
wai	wai
wan	wan
wang	wang
wei	wei
wen	wen
weng	weng
wo	wo
wu	wu
ya	ya
yai	yai
yang	yang
yao	yao

Wade-Giles	*Pinyin*	*Wade-Giles*	*Pinyin*
yeh	ye	yü	yu
yen	yan	yüan	yuan
yin	yin	yüeh	yue
ying	ying	yün	yun
yu	you	yung	yong

GLOSSARY OF TERMS

The dates, brief identifications, and limited definitions that appear after certain entries in these glossaries are intended primarily for the purpose of distinguishing homographs or for cross-referencing

ai ("lament")	哀
ai-chi	哀祭
ai-mei chü	愛美劇
an-chien	按鑒
ancient style prose (see *ku-wen*)	
ancient style prose movement (see *ku-wen yün-tung*)	
avant-garde literature (see *hsien-feng p'ai wen-hsüeh*)	
Beautiful Island Incident (Mei-li tao shih-chien)	美麗島事件
BP-chi	BP 機
bunjin	文人
cha ("letter")	札
cha-chi	札記
Ch'a-ling p'ai	茶陵派
ch'a-na	刹那
chaedo chi ki	載道之器
chai-ming	齋名
Ch'an (Zen)	禪
ch'an-hui	懺悔
ch'an-ling	纏令
ch'an-ta	纏達
chang	章
chang-chü	章句
chang-hui hsiao-shuo	章回小說
Ch'ang	常
ch'ang	長
ch'ang-chiang-lai	唱將來
ch'ang-pen	唱本
ch'ang-tao shih	唱導師
ch'ang-tuan chü	長短句
ch'ang yu nü-tzu	娼優女子
"changing iron into gold" (*tien t'ieh ch'eng chin*)	點鐵成金
chao	兆

chao ("proclamation")	詔
Chao-hsia ch'u yü; wan-hsia ch'u ch'ing.	朝霞出雨，晚霞出晴
chao-ling	詔令
chao-yin shih	招隱詩
ch'ao	嘲
ch'ao-chia	抄家
ch'ao-tzu-jan	超自然
ch'ao-yüan	抄園
che	這
Che-hsi p'ai	浙西派
che-tzu-hsi	折子戲
Ch'e tao shan ch'ien, pi yu lu.	車到山前必有路
chen	眞
chen ("admonition," memorial genre)	箴
chen-chia	眞假
Chen chin pu p'a huo lien.	眞金不怕火煉
chen-ch'üan	眞詮
chen-hsi	眞戲
chen-jen	眞人
chen-ju	眞儒
chen-jung tsan	眞容讚
chen-ming	箴銘
chen shan mei	眞善美
chen-tz'u	枕詞
ch'en-cho t'ung-k'uai	沉着/著痛快
ch'en-wei	讖緯
cheng ("correct," "orthodox")	正
cheng ("govern")	政
cheng-chih hsiao-shuo	政治小說
cheng-chih shih	政治詩
cheng-ming	正名
cheng-tao	証道
cheng-tui	正對
cheng-t'ung	正統
Cheng-yi	正義
cheng-yi	正義
Ch'eng-chai t'i	誠齋體
ch'eng-ch'i	程器
Ch'eng-hua	成化
ch'eng-yü	成語
chi ("charge")	檄
chi ("collection")	集
chi ("gāthā")	偈
chi ("records," "memorandum")	記
chi ("requiem")	祭
chi-chuan	紀傳
chi-chuan t'i	記傳體
chi huan wu chen	即幻悟眞
chi-li	肌理
chi shih	記事
chi-t'i ch'uang-tso	集體創作
chi-t'o	寄托 (託)
chi yen	記言
ch'i ("breath," "spirit"; "concrete manifestations")	氣
ch'i (memorial genre)	啓
ch'i ("strange")	奇
ch'i ("vessel," "implement")	器
ch'i-chen	七眞
ch'i-fu shih	棄婦詩
ch'i-hsiang	氣象
ch'i-hsiang yen-yü	氣象諺語
ch'i-jen	奇人
ch'i-ko shen-wen	氣格深穩
ch'i-li	綺麗
ch'i-lin	麒麟
ch'i-shu	奇書
ch'i-wan	淒婉
ch'i-yen ku-shih	七言古詩
ch'i-yen lü-shih	七言律詩
ch'i-yi	奇異
chia-chiao	家教
chia-chieh	假借
chia-chuan	家傳
chia-hsün	家訓
chia k'o	嘉客
chia-ku-wen	甲骨文
chia-men	家門
chia-p'u	家譜
chiang ("Yangtze")	江
chiang-ch'ang wen-hsüeh	講唱文學
chiang-ching wen	講經文
chiang-shih	講史
Chiang-tso san feng	江左三鳳
chiao ("collation")	校
chiao ("instruction")	教

chiao-fang 教坊
chiao-ssu ko 郊祀歌
chiao ts'o 交錯
Ch'iao fu nan wei wu mi chih ch'ui. 巧婦難爲無米之炊
ch'iao hsiao 巧笑
ch'iao-p'i hua 俏皮話
chieh ("columnar inscription") 碣
chieh ("explanation") 解
chieh (sigh) 嗟
chieh ("street") 街
chieh ("warning") 戒
chieh-chüeh 孑孓
chieh-yi 結義
[*ch'ieh k'an*] XX *ch'u, jo-wei ch'en-*[*shuo*] [且看] XX 處, 若爲陳 [說]
ch'ieh-t'o 伽陀
chien ("letter") 箋
chien ("letter") 簡
chien ("report") 牋
Chien-an ch'i tzu 建安七子
chien-hsiung 奸雄
Ch'ien li sung o-mao; li ch'ing, jen-yi chung. 千里送鵝毛, 禮輕人意重
ch'ien-tse hsiao-shuo 譴責小說
ch'ien-wa 瓩 = 千瓦
chih ("aspiration," "intent," "aim," "will") 志
chih ("essays") 誌
chih ("knowledge") 智
chih ("necrology") 誌
chih ("substance"; "plain") 質
chih ("understand," "know") 知
chih-chu 蜘蛛
chih-hsia 指瑕
chih-kuai 志怪
chih-kuai (*hsiao-shuo*) 志怪 (小說)
chih-nang 智囊
chih-shih 指事
chih-shih lei-ch'ing 指事類情
chih-ts'e 制策
chih-yin 知音
ch'ih-han 尺翰
ch'ih jen 吃人
ch'ih-lun 持論
ch'ih-tu 尺牘
chin-hua 進化
chin-shih 進士
chin-tai 近代
chin-t'i 近體
chin-t'i shih ("current style poetry") 今體詩
chin-t'i shih ("recent style poetry") 近體詩
ch'in ("cicada") 螓
ch'in ("zither") 琴
China Consciousness (see *Chung-kuo yi-shih*)
ching ("pure") 淨
ching ("realm") 境
ching ("scene") 景
ching ("scripture," "sūtra") 經
ching-chi 經濟
ching-chieh ("exposition of a classic") 經解
ching-chieh ("realm") 境界
ching-hsi 京戲
ching kuo chih ta-yeh 經國之大業
Ching-ling pa yu 景陵八友
ching-shen wu-jan 精神污染
ching-shih 經世
ching-t'i ming-mu ch'ang-chiang-lai 經題名目唱講來
ching-t'u 淨土
ch'ing ("feelings," "emotions," "sentiments," "love") 情
ch'ing ("pure[ly]") 清
ch'ing-ching 清靜
ch'ing-chiung pa-su 清迥拔俗
ch'ing-hsü sao-ya 清虛騷雅
ch'ing-kang 清剛
ch'ing-ken 情根
ch'ing-kuan 清官
ch'ing-kuo 傾國
ch'ing-li 清麗
Ch'ing-ming 清明
Ch'ing-Shang 清商

ch'ing-ts'ai	情采
ch'ing-yüan	清遠
ch'ing-yüeh	清樂
Chinsi	眞詩
chiu	酒
chiu-chü	舊劇
Chiu ting	九鼎
chiu-wang yen-chü-tui	救亡演劇隊
ch'iu-li	遒麗
Ch'iung-kuei	窮鬼
cho ("clumsiness")	拙
chokusenshi	敕撰詩
chŏn	傳
Chosŏn-p'ung	朝鮮風
ch'ou	丑
ch'ou-lou te Chung-kuo-jen	醜陋的中國人
chu ("note," "commentary")	注
chu ch'eng hsüeh	珠成血
chu-ji-sa	竹枝詞
chu-kung-tiao	諸宮調
Chu-lin ch'i hsien	竹林七賢
chu nom	[illegible]喃
chü-jen	舉人
chü-yi	聚義
ch'u ("in the beginning," "originally")	初
Ch'u *ko*	楚歌
Ch'u *sheng*	楚聲
Ch'u-T'ang ssu-chieh	初唐四傑
ch'ü ("aria"; vernacular song)	曲
ch'ü ("atmosphere")	趣
ch'ü ("to go")	去
ch'ü-p'u	曲譜
ch'ü-tzu	曲子
ch'ü-tzu-tz'u	曲子詞
ch'ü-tz'u	曲辭
ch'ü-yi	曲藝
chuan	傳
chuan-chi	傳記
chuan-chu	轉注
chuan-chuang	傳狀
chuan-tu	轉讀
chüan	卷
ch'uan-ch'i	傳奇
ch'uan-shuo	傳說
ch'üan	權
ch'üan-hsiang	全相
ch'üan-li	權利
ch'üan-tien	圈點
chuang ("obituary")	狀
chuang-yüan	狀元
ch'uang-tsao	創造
ch'uang-tso t'an	創作談
chüeh-chü	絕句
ch'ui-liang chieh	吹涼節
chün-tzu	君子
chün-yung ch'ao-yi	雋永超詣
chung ("central")	中
chung ("loyalty")	忠
chung-in	中人
Chung-kuo-hua	中國話
Chung-kuo yi-shih	中國意識
Chung-wen	中文
Chung yen ni erh, li yü hsing; liang yao k'u k'ou, li yü ping.	忠言逆耳利於行; 良藥苦口利於病
chung-yi	忠義
Cultural China (see *wen-hua Chung-kuo*)	
dai	題
daigaku	大學
decree examination (see *chih-ts'e*)	
Early (Ch'u) T'ang	初唐
eight-legged essay (see *pa-ku-wen*)	
Erh-erh-pa shih-chien	二二八事件
erh-hu	二胡
erh-huang	二黃
erh-p'ai	二拍
erh-shih	二十
erh-shih-wu shih	二十五史
"exchanging the bones, snatching the embryo" (*huan ku to t'ai*)	換骨奪胎
fa	法
fa-chia	法家
fa-ch'ü	法曲

Fa-hsiang 法相
fa-k'an tz'u 發刊詞
fa-shih 法師
fa-yü 法語
fan ("reverse") 反
fan-an 翻案
fan-ch'ieh 反切
fan ko-ming tung-luan 反革命動亂
fan-pai 梵唄
fan-pen 返本
fan ssu 反思
fan-tui 反對
fang ("fragrant") 芳
fang ("house," "building") 房
fang, pang, p'ang, and *peng* 方
fang-chien 房間
fang-chih 方志
fang-fu 仿佛
fang-k'uai-tzu 方塊字
fang-pien 方便
fang-shih 方士
fang-tzu 房子
fang-yen 方言
The February 28th Incident (see Erh-erh-pa shih-chien)
fei-jen ti wen-hsüeh 非人的文學
fen ("indignation," "zeal") 憤
fen ("powder") 粉
feng ("admonish," "satirize"; "intone") 諷
feng ("instruction"; "wind"; "airs" [section of *Shih-ching*]") 風
feng-huang 鳳凰
feng-ku 風骨
feng-shih 奉詩
feng-tz'u 諷刺
feng-wen shu 奉文書
fo-ch'ü 佛曲
Four Outstanding Talents of Wu-chung (see *Wu-chung ssu-chieh*)
"four-six" style (see *ssu-liu wen*)
fu ("commission") 符
fu ("description") 賦
fu ("rhapsody," "rhyme-prose") 賦
fu che ku-shih chih liu 賦者古詩之流
fu-ch'iang 富強
"Fu-en" 復恩
fu-ho-tz'u 複合詞
fu-hui 附會
fu-ku 復古
fu-kuo ts'e 富國策
fu-mo 付末, 副末
fu-yin-tz'u 複音詞
gagaku (see *ya-yüeh*)
goroku (see *yü-lu*)
Greater China (see *ta Chung-kuo*)
Gwoyeu Romatzyh 國語羅馬字
haikai 俳諧
haiku 俳句
Han-hsüeh p'ai 漢學派
Han-lin 翰林
Han-lin academician (see Han-lin hsüeh-shih)
Han-lin hsüeh-shih 翰林學士
Han luat 韓律
han-tzu 漢字
Han-tzu pu mieh, Chung-kuo pi wang! 漢字不滅, 中國必亡!
Han-yü 漢語
hao 號
Hao chieh, hao huan, tsai chieh pu nan. 好借, 好還, 再借不難
hao-chü 豪舉
hao-fang 豪放
hao-han 好漢
hao pi.... 好比
Hao shih to mo. 好事多磨
heng te yi-chih 橫的移植
High (Sheng) T'ang 盛唐
History Bureau (see Shih kuan)
Ho-shang ta san; wu fa, wu t'ien. 和尚打傘, 無法 (髮) 無天

ho-wen 合文
hōgo (see *fa-yü*)
horizontal transplants (see *heng te yi-chih*)
Hou 后
Hou ch'i tzu 後七子
Hou-shan chih hou 後山之後
hsi ("analysis") 析
hsi (breath particle) 兮
hsi ("forty") 卌/卌/卌
hsi ("summons to war") 檄
Hsi-ch'eng-tiao 西城調
hsi-chü te hsieh-yi t'e-hsing 戲劇的寫意特性
Hsi-k'un 西崑
hsi-p'i 西皮
hsi-wen 戲文
hsi-yen 昔言
hsiang-ho 相和
hsiang-hsing 象形
hsiang-hua 想化
hsiang-sheng[a] ("cross-talk") 相聲
hsiang-sheng[b] ("imitative sounds") 象聲
hsiang-tang yü yi ke yü-tsu 相當於一個語族
hsiang-tsan 像讚
hsiang-t'u 鄉土
hsiang-t'u wen-hsüeh 鄉土文學
hsiang-t'u wen-hsüeh yün-tung 鄉土文學運動
hsiao 笑
hsiao-ch'en 小臣
hsiao-chuan 小篆
hsiao-fu 小賦
"*hsiao-hsü*" 小序
hsiao-hsüeh 小學
hsiao-ling 小令
hsiao-p'in(-wen) 小品 (文)
hsiao shih-min 小市民
hsiao-shuo 小說
hsiao-shuo chieh ko-ming 小說界革命
hsiao-shuo chih cheng-tsung 小說之正宗
hsiao-shuo chih shih-chih 小說之實質
hsiao-tuan 小段
hsiao-tzu 小子
hsiao tz'u 小詞
hsiao-yi 小義
hsieh ("prosodic harmony") 諧
hsieh ("write, sketch") 寫
hsieh ch'ing hsiao-shuo 寫情小說
hsieh-hou-yü 歇後語
hsieh yin 諧隱
hsien ("immortals") 仙
hsien ("serenely") 閑
hsien-feng p'ai wen-hsüeh 先鋒派文學
Hsien-tai p'ai 現代派
hsien-tai shih lun-chan 現代詩論戰
hsien-yüan 閑遠
hsin ("heart," "mind") 心
hsin ("new") 新
hsin ("trust," "letter") 信
Hsin-ch'ao wen-hsüeh 新潮文學
hsin-chü 新劇
hsin hsiao-shuo 新小說
hsin-hsüeh 心學
Hsin-ju-chiao 新儒教
hsin kan-chüeh p'ai 新感覺派
hsin-sheng tai 新生代
hsin shih 新詩
hsin shih-ch'i te wen-hsüeh 新時期的文學
hsin-t'i shih 新體詩
hsin t'i-yen hsiao-shuo 新體驗小說
hsin-t'i yüeh-fu 新題樂府
hsin wen-hsüeh 新文學
Hsin wen-hua yün-tung 新文化運動
hsin wen-t'i 新文體
hsin yen pu mei, mei yen pu hsin 信言不美，美言不信
hsin-yüan yi-ma 心猿意馬
hsin yüeh-fu 新樂府
Hsin-yüeh p'ai 新月派
hsing ("balladic verse") 行
hsing ("metaphor") 興
hsing ("nature," "disposition") 性
hsing-ch'ing chih ling 性情之靈
hsing-ch'ü 興趣

hsing-chuang 行狀
hsing-ling 性靈
Hsing-ling p'ai 性靈派
hsing-sheng 形聲
hsing-shu 行書
hsing-ssu 形似
Hsing-tso shih-she 星座詩社
hsiu-hsin 修心
hsiu-hsin lien-hsing 修心鍊性
hsiu-ts'ai 秀才
hsiung-hun 雄渾
hsü ("preface") 序
hsü-chih 序志
hsü-pa 序跋
Hsü wu tzu 續五子
hsüan-tse 選擇
hsüan-yen 玄言
hsüan-yen shih 玄言詩
hsüeh ("jest," "banter") 謔
hsüeh ("learn," "study") 學
hsüeh-lei 血淚
hsüeh-shih 學士
hsüeh-shih-lang 學仕郎
hsün-ken 尋根
"Hsün-li" 循吏
hu chia hu wei 狐假虎威
hu hsi 瓠犀
hu-sun 胡孫 // 猢猻
hu-tieh 蝴蝶
hu-wen 互文
hu-yüeh 胡樂
hua ("flower") 花
hua ("flowery"; "China") 華
hua ("speech") 話
hua chi 畫記
hua-chi (see *ku-chi*)
hua-ching 化境
hua-chü 話劇
hua-pen 話本
hua-tsan 畫讚
hua-yü 華語
huai-chiu 懷舊
huai-ku 懷古
huan-lei 還淚
Huang 皇
Huang-Lao 黃老
huang-ti 皇帝
hui 詼
hui-hen 悔恨
hui-hsiang 迴向
hui-yi 會意
hun-miao chih ching 渾妙之境
hun-sang yi-shih ko 婚喪儀式歌
Hun-tun 渾沌
hung-shui 洪水
huo-lang-erh 貨郎兒
huo yüeh 或曰
hyangga 鄉歌
imun 吏文
jen ("appoint") 任
jen ("person") 人
jen te wen-hsüeh 人的文學
jih-chi 日記
jōruri 淨琉璃
ju ("Confucianists") 儒
ju ("enter") 入
ju Ch'an 入禪
ju-chiang 儒將
ju-hua 入話
ju shen 入神
ju-shih 儒士
jung-ts'ai 鎔裁
kabuki 歌舞伎
k'ai-ho pien-kuai 開闔變怪
k'ai-p'ien 開篇
k'ai-shu 楷書
kakumei 革命
kan 感
kan-ka 尲尬 / 尲尬 / 尷尬 / 尷尬 / 尷尬
kan-pu 邗 = 幹部
kan-shih 感時
kan-ying 感應
k'an ("critical comparison," "collation") 勘
kanbun (or *kambun*) 漢文
k'ang-chan pa-ku 抗戰八股
k'ang-k'ai 慷慨
kanji 漢字
kanshi 漢詩
kao ("high," "tall") 高

kao ("order," "admonition") 誥
k'ao cheng 考證
k'ao-cheng hsüeh 考證學
k'ao-yi 考異
keizai 經濟
kikajin 帰化人
ko ("framework") 格
ko ("song") 歌
ko-ch'ang k'u-ch'i 歌唱哭泣
ko-chü 歌劇
ko-ch'ü 歌曲
ko-hsü 歌圩
ko-li 格力
ko-ming 革命
ko-t'i chieh shan 各體皆善
ko-tiao 格調
ko-tz'u 歌辭
ko-wu-chü 歌舞劇
ko-yen 格言
ko-yi 格義
k'o-chü 科舉
k'o-hsüeh hsiao-shuo 科學小說
kobunji (see *ku-wen-tz'u*)
kokugo 國語
kokusai 國際
komun chi hak 古文之學
kou-lan 勾欄
k'ou yi 口義
k'ou-yü 口語
ku 古
ku-chi (*hua-chi*) 滑稽
ku-feng 古風
ku jen yün: 古人云
ku-lu 轂轆
ku-niang chieh 姑娘節
ku-pen 古本
ku-shih ("incident of past times") 故實
ku shih ("old-style poem") 古詩
ku-shih ("story") 故事
ku-tan hsien-yüan 古澹閑遠
ku-t'i 古體
ku-t'i shih 古體詩
ku-tzu-tz'u 鼓子詞
ku tz'u 鼓詞
ku-tz'u 古辭
ku-wen 古文
ku wen shih pi 古文十弊
ku-wen-tz'u 古文辭
ku-wen yün-tung 古文運動
k'u-chia ko 哭嫁歌
kua-tz'u 卦辭
k'ua-shih ("embellish[-ment]") 夸飾
k'ua-shih ("exaggerate") 誇飾
kuai 怪
kuan ("observe"; "belvedere") 觀
kuan ("official") 官
kuan-hua 官話
Kuang wu tzu 廣五子
kuei ("ghost") 鬼
kuei (indicates a supplement) 癸
kuei-ssu 閨思
kuei-ts'ai 鬼才
k'uei 夔
ku'er-tz'u 孤兒詞
K'un-ch'ü 昆曲
Kung-an 公安
kung-an 公案
kung-an hsiao-shuo 公案小說
kung-ch'ou 公仇
kung-ming fu-kuei 功名富貴
kung-sheng 貢生
kung-t'i 宮體
kung-t'i shih 宮體詩
kuo-chi 國際
kuo-fang hsi-chü 國防戲劇
kuo-ts'ui 國粹
kuo-tzu-chien 國子監
kuo-tzu hsüeh 國子學
kuo-yü 國語
kwamun 科文
lai-p'i 賴皮
lang 郎
"Late T'ang" style (*wan T'ang t'i*) 晚唐體
lei ("category," "type") 類
lei ("dirge") 誄
lei-chuan 類傳
lei-fa 雷法

lei-shu	類書
lei-t'ing fa	雷霆法
li ("beautiful")	麗
li ("benefit," "profit")	利
li ("ceremony," "ritual")	禮
li ("principle")	理
li ("strength," "force")	力
li ("tricent")	里
li-chiao	禮教
li-hsüeh	理學
li-shih wen-hua fan-ssu	歷史文化反思
li-shu	隸書
li-tsan-wen	禮讚文
li-tz'u	麗辭
li-yen	麗言
Li-yüan	梨園
liang-p'ai	兩拍
liao-ko	嘹歌
lieh-chuan	列傳
lieh-fu	烈婦
lieh-nü	列女
lien ("lotus")	蓮
lien ("love")	戀
lien-chü	連句
lien-hua lao	連花落
lien-mien-tzu	連綿字
lien-tzu	練字
lin-pieh fan	臨別飯
ling ("command")	令
ling ("spirit")	靈
ling-chü tzu	領句字
Ling-pao	靈寶
ling-yen	靈驗
Liu-erh Mi-hou	六耳獼猴
liu-mang	流氓
liu shih	六詩
liu-yi	六義
lo-ts'ao	落草
lou-fang	樓房
Lou-tung *t'i*	婁東體
Lu kung erh-shih-ssu yu	魯公二十四友
lü	律
lü-fu	律賦
lü-shih	律詩
luan	亂
luan-t'an	亂彈
luc-bat	六八
lun ("disquisition")	論
lun-pien	論辨
lung	龍
lung-chou ko	龍舟歌
ma-ko	麻歌
magic realism (see *mo-huan hsien-shih chu-yi*)	
mai	麥
man-tz'u	慢詞
mao-chen tsan	貌眞讚
May Fourth movement (see *Wu-ssu yün-tung*)	
mei	美
mei-hsüeh	美學
mei-jen huo-shui	美人禍水
Mei-li tao shih-chien	美麗島事件
mei-shu	美術
mei te chih-tso	美的製作
Mei-ts'un *t'i*	梅村體
men	門
meng-lung shih	朦朧詩
mi	蜜
mi-fu	秘府
miao	妙
miao-ho	妙合
miao-wu	妙悟
Middle (Chung) T'ang	中唐
mien-li	緜麗
Min-chia	民家
ming ("bright," "clear")	明
ming ("inscription")	銘
ming ("name")	名
ming ("order")	命
Ming ch'ien ch'i tzu	明前七子
ming-ching	明經
ming-hsin chien-hsing	明心見性
ming-shih	名士
Misty Poetry (see *meng-lung shih*)	
Mo	墨
mo	末
Mo-che	墨者
Mo-chia	墨家

mo-fang	模彷
mo-huan hsien-shih chu-yi	魔幻現實主義
Mo wu tzu	末五子
Modern Poetry Debate (see *hsien-tai shih lun-chan*)	
Modernist School (see Hsien-tai p'ai)	
monogatari	物語
mou-yi	厶乙 = 某乙
mu-chih ming	墓志銘
mu-piao-chih	幕表制
mu-yü [shu]	木魚 [書]
munch'ae panjŏng	文體反正
munjang chimun	文章之文
nan-hsi	南戲
nan-shu	男書
nan-tz'u	南詞
nan-yin	南音
nao-ko	鐃歌
native literature (see *hsiang-t'u wen-hsüeh*)	
Native Literature movement (see *hsiang-t'u wen-hsüeh yün-tung*)	
nei	內
nei-chuan	內傳
nei-ko	內閣
nei-pu	內部
nei-tan	內丹
Neng-che to lao.	能者多勞
new era literature (see *hsin shih-ch'i te wen-hsüeh*)	
new poetry (see *hsin-shih*)	
New Policies (*hsin fa*)	新法
New Wave Literature (see *Hsin-ch'ao wen-hsüeh*)	
The Newborn Generation (see *hsin-sheng tai*)	
nieh	孽
nieh-p'an	卅/卌 = 涅槃
nien	卄/𠦃/廿
ning (k'o) . . . pu	寧可 . . . 不
ning chih	凝脂
Ning wei yü sui, pu wei wa ch'üan.	寧爲玉碎, 不爲瓦全
No	儺
Nō	能
no-hsi	儺戲
no-[t'ang]-hsi	儺 [堂] 戲
novels of new experience (see *hsin t'i-yen hsiao-shuo*)	
nu	弩
Nu-lo tao	奴樂島
Nü	女
nü-huo	女禍
nü-shu	女書
nung	儂
nung-yen	農諺
O (Lady-like [female deity name])	娥
O (Sublime [female deity name])	阿
Old Phraseology (see *ku-wen-tz'u*)	
ŏnt'o	諺吐
ou ("lotus root")	藕
ou ("mate")	偶
Pa	魃
pa-ku-wen	八股文
pa-ping	八病
pa-ta-fang-yen	八大方言
pa-tzu	八字
p'aegwan	稗官
pai-chia cheng-ming	百家爭鳴
pai-hsi	百戲
pai-hua	白話
pai-hua hsiao-shuo	白話小說
pai-hua shih	白話詩
pai-hua-wen	白話文
pai-hua wen-hsüeh yün-tung	白話文學運動
pai-hua yün-tung	白話運動
pai-se k'ung-pu	白色恐怖
pai-shih	稗史
pai-tsan	唄讚
Pai wen pu ju yi chien.	百聞不如一見

p'ai-lü	排律
pan ("board")	板
pan-ch'iang-t'i	板腔體
pan-shih pien-hua t'i	板式變化體
pan tz'u-hua	搬詞話
p'an ("judgement")	判
p'ang ("side"), *pang, peng, p'eng*	旁
pao	報
pao-chüan	寶卷
pao-kao wen-hsüeh	報告文學
Pao Kung an	包公案
pao-lu wen-hsüeh	暴露文學
parallel prose (see *p'ien-t'i wen*)	
pei ("epitaph")	碑
pei ("threnody")	悲
pei-chih	碑誌
pei-chuang	悲壯
Pei-kuo shih-yu	北郭十友
Pei-yang	北洋
pen-chi	本紀
pen-se	本色
pen-sheng	本生
peng	甭
pi ("simile")	比
pi-chi	筆記
Pi-chieh	畢節
pi-hsing	比興
pi-mo	畢摩
pi-t'an	筆談
pi-yü	比喻
p'i ("annotation")	批
p'i (measure word for cloth; "mate")	匹
p'i-p'a ("kumquat")	枇杷
p'i-p'a ("pear-shaped lute")	琵琶
"P'i-p'a hsien shang shuo hsiang-ssu"	琵琶弦上說相思
p'i-p'ing	批評
p'i-tien	批點
p'i-tzu	痞子
p'i-yü	譬喻
piao (memorial genre)	表
piao ("table," "chart")	表
piao ch'i ching hsiu	標奇競秀
p'iao-yi	飄逸
pieh	別
pieh-chuan	別傳
pien	變
pien-hsiang	變相
pien-sai shih	邊塞詩
pien-wen ("varied expression"; "transformation text")	變文
pi'en ("ode," "chapter," "page")	篇
p'ien-li(-wen)	駢麗/儷(文)
p'ien-t'i-wen	駢體文
p'ien-wen	駢文
piji	碑誌
p'in ("chapter")	品
P'in-yin	拼音
ping-shih chih ko-tz'u	病世之歌詞
ping yen ping, chiang yen chiang	兵演兵, 將演將
p'ing ("appraisal")	評
p'ing ("equal," "flat")	平
p'ing-hua	平/評話
p'ing-lin	評林
p'ing-tan	平淡/澹
p'ing-t'an	評彈
p'ing-tien	評點
po	博
po-hsüeh hung-tz'u	博學弘詞
po-shih	博士
"Po" style (*Po-t'i*)	白體
p'o-p'i	潑皮
p'o-yin	破音
"poetic community" (*shih-she*)	詩社
Poetry Revolution (see *shih chieh ko-ming*)	
political poetry (see *cheng-chih shih*)	
pu (negative)	不
pu-ch'ing	不情
pu ch'iu shen chieh	不求甚解
pu-chu yi-tzu, chin te feng-liu	不著一字, 盡得風流
pu hao-se	不好色

pu-hsüeh shih, wu yi yen	不學詩, 無以言
pu-ju	不如
pu-ko	不隔
pu-k'o ts'ou-po	不可湊泊
pu shang/teng ta-ya chih t'ang	不上 / 登大雅之堂
pu-yi shih	布衣詩
pu-yung	不用
p'u ("register," "manual," "musical score")	譜
p'u ("unworked," "simple")	樸
p'u-hsü	鋪敘
p'u-sa	井 = 菩薩
p'u-shih	樸實
p'u-t'i	蓵 / 苻 = 菩提
p'u-t'ung-hua	普通話
pyŏrryŏmun	駢儷文
quoc am	國音
"Rivers and Lakes" poets (*chiang-hu shih-p'ai*)	江湖詩派
sa	卅 / 丗 / 𠦄
Salim	士林
San chia shih	三家詩
san-chiao	三教
san-ch'ü	散曲
san-chüeh	三絕
san-hsien	三弦
San jen t'ung hsing, pi yu wo shih.	三人同行, 必有我師
san-mei	三昧
san-shih	三十
san-ts'ai	三彩
San-tsang	三藏
san-ts'ung	三從
San-tung	三洞
san-wan	三萬
san-wen	散文
san-yen	三言
san-yüeh	散樂
sao	騷
satsu	冊
Scar Literature (see *shang-hen wen-hsüeh*)	
se	色
sekai	世界
"Shan-hai ching *so yu kuai wu yü pu kan yen yeh.*"	山海經所有怪物余不敢言也
shan-hu	珊瑚
shan-shui shih	山水詩
shan-yao p'ai	山藥派
Shan-yao-tan p'ai	山藥蛋派
shang	上
Shang-ch'ing	上清
shang-hen wen-hsüeh	傷痕文學
shang liang wen	上梁文
shao-shu min-tsu	少數民族
she-hui-chu-yi	礻乂 = 社會主義
she-yi	社邑
shen ("deep")	深
shen ("smile")	哂
shen ("spirit," "divine talent")	神
Shen-hsien	神仙
shen-hua	神話
shen-jen	神人
shen-ming	神明
shen-mo hsiao-shuo	神魔小說
"*Shen shou P'an ch'ou ho jih hsiu*"	沈瘦潘愁何日休
shen-ssu	神思
shen-yu ku-ch'iao	深幽孤峭
shen-yün	神韻
sheng ("abundant," "full")	盛
sheng ("live"; "unripe"; "student")	生
sheng ("panpipes")	笙
sheng ("sage")	聖
sheng-lü	聲律
"Sheng nien pu man pai"	生年不滿百
sheng-t'ai	聖胎
sheng-wen	省文
shih ("act," "do," "make," "bestow," "grant")	施
shih ("address")	誓
shih ("configuration")	勢
shih ("corpse")	尸
shih ("event")	事
shih ("judgement")	識
shih ("poetry")	詩
shih ("scholar")	士

shih ("scribe"; "scribal practice"; "history," "historian")	史
shih (type of poetry)	詩
shih-chia	世家
Shih Ch'iang P'an	史牆盤
shih chieh ko-ming	詩界革命
shih chung wu wo	詩中無我
shih chung yu wo	詩中有我
shih-hsü	時序
shih-hua	詩話
shih-jen hua	士人畫
Shih kuan	史館
shih-kung	師公
shih-lei	事類
shih-ming	室名
shih-she	詩社
shih-tiao	詩調
Shih ts'ai-tzu	十才子
shih-tsan	詩讚
shih-tui	事對
shih-tzu	獅子
shih-wen	詩文
shih-wu-fa	十五伐
shih yen chih	詩言志
shih-yi	釋義
shih yi ta hsing	詩以達性
shijo	詩調
shirhak	實學
shirokuso (see *ssu-liu shu*)	
shōgaku	小學
shu ("letter")	書
shu ("subcommentary")	疏
shu ("transmit")	述
shu-ch'ing	抒情
shu erh pu tso	述而不作
shu-hui	書會
shu-mien-yü	書面語
shu-shih	術士
shu-shuo	書說
shu-yü	熟語
shu-yüan	書院
shua hsiu-ts'ai	耍秀才
shuai to fu-yen, tz'u yü li-ching	率多浮艷,辭與理競
shuang kuan	雙關
shukō	趣向
shuo	說
shuo-ch'ang	說唱
shuo-ch'ang-pen	說唱本
shuo-ch'ang tz'u-hua	說唱詞話
shuo-ch'ang wen-hsüeh	說唱文學
shuo-ch'ang yin-yüan	說唱因緣
shuo-shu	說書
Sinsosŏl	新小說
so	疏
so-yin	索隱
song-that	雙七
song that luc bat	雙七六八
Sŏnggyun'gwan	成均館
Sŏwŏn	書院
ssu (phonophoric root of *shih* "poetry")	寺
ssu ("silk thread")	絲
ssu ("think of")	思
ssu-ch'ou	私仇
ssu-ch'ou chih lu	絲綢之路
ssu chung li	四種力
Ssu-fu	四輔
ssu-liu shu	四六疏
ssu-liu t'i	四六體
ssu-liu wen	四六文
ssu-sheng	四聲
ssu-shih	四十
ssu-ta ch'i-shu	四大奇書
ssu-te	四德
ssu-wen	斯文
Ssu-wu yün-tung	四五運動
ssu-yen	四言
su ("vulgar")	俗
su-chiang	俗講
su-fu	俗賦
su-wen-hsüeh	俗文學
su-yü	俗語
sui-pi	隨筆
sung ("hymn")	頌
sung ("reproach," "dispute")	訟
Sung shih-hui	宋十回
sung-tsan	頌贊
T-hsü ("T-shirt")	T 恤
ta-ch'ü	大曲
ta-chuan	大篆
ta Chung-kuo	大中國

ta-fu 大夫
ta-hsüeh 大學
ta k'o 答客
ta-ku 大鼓
Ta K'uai-chi 大會計
ta-pen-ch'ü 大本曲
ta-p'en-t'i 打噴嚏
Ta-sheng 大乘
ta-shu 大書
ta shui 大水
ta tz'u-tien 大辭典
ta wen 答問
ta-yi 大義
t'ai-hsüeh 太學
t'ai-ko-t'i 臺閣體
T'ai-shih-kung 太史公
T'ai-shih-kung yüeh 太史公曰
T'ai-wan yi-shih 台灣意識
Taiping (T'ai-p'ing) 太平
Taiwan Consciousness (see *T'ai-wan yi-shih*)
tan ("cinnabar") 丹
tan ("female lead in drama") 旦
tan ("gall"; "courage") 膽
t'an ("exclaim") 歎
t'an ("sigh") 嘆
t'an-t'e 忐忑
t'an-tz'u 彈詞
Tang erh chih shih, shuo ho yen-yü? 當爾之時說何言語
tanka 短歌
Tao 道
Tao-chia 道家
Tao-chiao 道教
tao-ch'ing 道情
tao-hsüeh 道學
tao-t'ung 道統
tao yü 倒語
t'ao-shu 套數
te (adverbial) 地
te (complement) 得
te (possessive) 的
te yü erh wang ch'üan 得魚而忘筌
Ten Friends near the Northern City-wall (see *Pei-kuo shih-yu*)
Ten Talented Ones (see *Shih ts'ai-tzu*)
"ten thousand things" (*wan hsiang*) 萬象
teng kao neng/pi fu 登高能 / 必賦
The Third Generation (see Ti san tai)
Ti 帝
ti-fang-chih 地方志
ti-fang hsi 地方戲
Ti san tai 第三代
t'i ("form") 體
t'i ("lifting") 提
t'i ("sprouts"; "tare") 荑
t'i ("topic"; "title") 題
t'i-chih 體制
t'i-hsing 題性
t'i-hsüeh fu-shih 提學副使
t'i-hua shih 題畫詩
t'i-hua wen-hsüeh 題畫文學
t'i-pa ("colophon") 題跋
t'i-pa ("promote," "elevate") 提拔
t'i-t'ien hsing-tao 替天行道
tiao ("condolence") 弔
tiao-ch'ung 雕蟲
t'ieh-t'i 鐵體
tien 典
tien-chung 典重
tien-ku 典故
tien t'ieh ch'eng chin 點鐵成金
t'ien ("heaven/sky") 天
t'ien-hua 天花
t'ien-hua-fen 天花粉
t'ien-hua-pan 天花板
t'ien-kan ti-chih 天干地支
t'ien-ming 天命
t'ien-shu 天書
T'ien-t'ai 天台
t'ien-yüan 田園
t'ien-yüan shih 田園詩
ting-pen 定本
ting-shih 定勢
to-hsin 多心
to-yin 多音
t'o-la-chi 拖拉機

torjangmun 道場文
t'ou shih 偷勢
t'ou shu chi ch'i 投鼠忌器
truyen 傳
tsa 雜
tsa-ch'ao 雜抄
tsa-chi 雜記
tsa-chia 雜家
tsa-chü 雜劇
tsa-ch'ü 雜曲
tsa ko-yao tz'u 雜歌謠辭
tsa shih 雜詩
tsa-wen 雜文
tsai-sheng 再盛
ts'ai ("ability," "talent") 才
ts'ai ("wealth") 財
ts'ai-lüeh 才略
ts'ai-tzu 才子
ts'ai-tzu chia-jen 才子佳人
ts'ai-tzu chia-jen hsiao-shuo 才子佳人小說
tsan ("appreciation") 讚 / 贊
tsan-sung 讚頌
ts'an-chün-hsi 參軍戲
ts'ang-ku 蒼鶻
ts'ao-shu 草書
Ts'ao-tung 曹洞
tse ("oblique" [tone]) 仄
tse ("standard"; a conjunction) 則
ts'e ("fascicle") 冊
ts'e ("formulaic essay") 策
tseng-hsü 贈序
tseng-ta 贈答
tseng-ta shih 贈答詩
ts'eng-ti 層遞
tso ("compose") 作
tso-yi hsi-chü 左翼戲劇
tsou (memorial genre) 奏
tsou ("proposal") 奏
tsou-shu chi 奏書集
tsou-yi 奏議
tsou-yi chi 奏議集
ts'u 粗
ts'un-hsin yang-hsing 存心養性
tsung-heng chia 縱橫家
tsung-shih 宗師
tsung-shu 總書
tsung te chi-ch'eng 縱的繼承
ts'ung-cha 叢札
Ts'ung shan ju teng; ts'ung o ju peng. 從善如登, 從惡如崩
ts'ung-shu 叢書
ts'ung-t'an 叢談
tu ("letter") 牘
tu ("poison"; "vicious") 毒
tu che 讀者
tu-chiang 都講
tu-hsing 獨行
t'u-shu-kuan 圕 / 囯 = 圖書館
t'u-su-tzu 土俗字
t'u-yin 土音
tuan-p'ien hsiao-shuo 短篇小說
t'uan-yüan 團圓
tui-ts'e 對策
tui wen 對文
t'ui-fei ("literary decadence") 頹廢
Tung-chen 洞眞
Tung-ch'eng-tiao 東城調
Tung-lin 東林
tung-pa 東巴
Tung-ya ping-fu 東亞病夫
T'ung-ch'eng p'ai 桐城派
T'ung-ch'eng school (see T'ung-ch'eng p'ai)
t'ung-hsin 童心
t'ung-ling 通靈
t'ung-ling pao-yü 通靈寶玉
t'ung mu 同目
t'ung-pien 通變
t'ung yao ("young boy's songs") 童謠
t'ung-yi 通易
tzu ("son," "master") 子
tzu ("style [name]") 字
tzu hsien 自見
tzu-jan 自然
tzu-ti-shu 子弟書
tz'u ("elegy") 辭
tz'u ("song lyric") 詞
tz'u ("this") 此
tz'u-fu 辭賦

tz'u-hua 詞話
tz'u-jen 詞人
tz'u-p'ai 詞牌
tz'u pu k'o pu hsiu 辭不可不修
tz'u ta erh yi yi 辭達而已矣
tz'u-tiao 詞調
tz'u-wen 詞文
The Ugly Chinese (see *ch'ou-lou te Chung-kuo-jen*)
ukiyo-zōshi 浮世草紙 (草子)
Vergangenheitsbewaltigung (see *fan ssu*)
vernacular poetry (see *pai-hua shih*)
vertical inheritance (see *tsung te chi-ch'eng*)
wai ("external") 外
wai-chuan 外傳
wai-tan 外丹
waka 和歌
wan 晚
wan-chu 頑主
wan hsiang 萬象
wan-yüeh 婉約
wei ("coda"; "tail") 尾
wei ("false") 僞
wei ("tiny," "slight") 微
wei ("weft," "woof") 緯
wei tz'u chih shu 爲辭之術
wei-wai 味外
wei yen 微言
wei-yi ("winding"; "meandering"; and over a dozen other meanings) 逶迤 (and over a dozen dozen other related sinographic forms)
wen 文
wen-chang 文章
wen-chi 文集
wen-chieh ko-ming 文界革命
wen-chüan 溫卷
wen-fang ssu-pao 文房四寶
wen-fu 文賦
wen-hsing ch'u-ch'u 文行出處
wen-hsüeh 文學
wen-hsüeh chih tsui shang sheng 文學之最上乘
wen-hsüeh tzu-chüeh te shih-tai 文學自覺的時代
wen-hua 文化
wen-hua Chung-kuo 文化中國
wen-hua fan-ssu 文化反思
wen-jen 文人
wen-li 文理
wen-ming 文明
wen-ming hsi 文明戲
wen-shen 文身
Wen shih 溫室
wen-shih 文士
wen-t'i 问 = 問題
wen-tzu 文字
wen-tzu yü 文字獄
wen-ya 溫雅
wen-yao 文妖
wen-yen 文言
wen-yen hsiao-shuo 文言小說
wen-yen-wen 文言文
wen-yi 文藝
wen yi tsai tao 文以載道
wen-yüan 文苑
White Terror (see *pai-se k'ung-pu*)
wo-men 我們
Wo *p'ao* 倭袍
Wo shou hsieh wo k'ou. 我手寫我口
wu ("be enlightened"; "realize") 悟
wu ("dance") 舞
wu ("error," "mistake") 誤
wu ("mage") 巫
wu ("military") 武
wu ("noon") 午
wu ("thing") 物
wu-ch'ang 五常
Wu-chung ssu-chieh 吳中四傑
wu fa wu t'ien 無髮無天
wu-hsia 武俠
wu-hsia hsiao-shuo 武俠小說
wu-hsing 五行

wu-lei fa 五雷法
wu-lun 五倫
wu-se 物色
Wu Shih-hui 武十回
Wu shou shu wu k'ou 吾手書吾口
Wu-ssu hsin wen-hua yün-tung 五四新文化運動
Wu-ssu yün-tung 五四運動
wu-tsu 五祖
wu-t'ung 梧桐
wu-yen 五言
wu-yen-shih 五言詩
X-*kuang* X光
ya ("elegance") 雅
ya-cheng 雅正
ya tsa-chü 啞雜劇
ya-tso wen 押座文
ya yen 雅言
ya-yüeh 雅樂
yang 陽
yang-ch'i 養氣
Yang-chou pa-kuai 揚州八怪
Yang-hsien p'ai 陽羨派
yang-pan-hsi 樣板戲
yangban 兩班
yao 妖
yao-hsien 妖仙
yao tz'u (line texts of the *Chou-yi*) 爻辭
yao-yen 謠諺
ye 禮
yeh 也
yeh-shih 野史
yen ("attractive"; "gorgeous") 艷
yen ("examine"; "verify") 驗
yen ("speech") 言
yen chih wu wen, hsing erh pu yüan 言之無文, 行而不遠
yen-hui shih 宴會詩
yen-tuan 艷段
yen-tui 言對
yen-wai 言外
yen-wai chih yi 言外之意
yen-yi 演義
yen yi wen yüan 言以文遠
yen-yü 諺語
yen yüeh: 諺曰
yen-yüeh 燕樂
yen yün: 諺云
yi ("appropriate") 宜
yi ("consciousness," "intentions," "meaning") 意
yi ("different"; "alien") 異
yi ("justice"; "righteousness") 義
yi ("lose"; "bequeath") 遺
yi ch'an yü shih 以禪喻詩
yi-ch'i 義氣
yi ch'ing wu tao 以情悟道
yi-chü 義舉
yi ku 疑古
yi-ma hsin-yüan 意馬心猿
yi-min ("hermit") 逸民
yi-min ("loyalist") 遺民
yi-p'ang 倚傍
yi shen 一身
yi shih ("annalist of the strange") 異史
yi-shih ("anecdotes") 佚事
yi-shih ("honorably releases") 義釋
yi-tai shih-shih 一代詩史
yi-to 義奪
yi wen wei shih 以文爲詩
yi wo kuan chih 以我觀之
yi-yin 意淫
yin ("ditty," "lay") 引
yin ("female principle"; "shady") 陰
yin ("hidden"; "concealed") 隱
yin ("lament") 吟
yin-chieh 音節
yin-hsiu 隱秀
yin-kuo 因果
yin privilege 廕
yin-she 吟社
yin-shih-she 吟詩社
yin-yang 陰陽
[*yin-*]*yüan* [因] 緣
yin-yung ch'ing-hsing 吟詠情性
ying 應
ying-erh pen-lun 嬰兒本論
ying-lien 應憐

ying-t'ien(-shih)	營 = 營田(使)	*yü ti*	餘地
ying-yen	應驗	*yü-tsu*	語族
yomihon	讀み本	*yü-yen*	寓言
yu ("swim"; "rove about"; "ornament hanging from banner")	斿	*yüan*	遠
yu-chi	游 (遊) 記	*yüan-ch'i*	緣起
yu-chi wen-hsüeh	游 (遊) 記文學	*yüan-chih*	原旨
yu-chin teng-k'u	油盡燈枯	*yüan-ch'ing*	緣情
yu-hsien shih	游 (遊) 仙詩	*yüan heng li chen*	元亨利貞
yu-lan shih	遊覽詩	*yüan-nü shih*	怨女詩
yu-mo	幽默	*yüan-pen*	院本
yu-yen	幽艷	Yüan-yang hu-tieh p'ai	鴛鴦蝴蝶派
yü ("desire")	欲	*yüeh*	約
yü ("in," "at," "on," "by," "from")	於	*yüeh-ching*	月經
yü ("jade")	玉	*yüeh-ch'ü*	樂曲
yü-chih	語支	*yüeh-fu*	樂府
yü-hsi	語系	*yul-ch'ang*	律唱
Yü-lan-p'en	盂蘭盆	*yün-yün*	云云
Yü liang ta-ti	禹量大地	*yung*	詠
yü-lu	語錄	Yung-chia ssu ling	永嘉四靈
yü-shih-t'ai	御史臺	*yung-huai*	詠懷
		Yung-ming *t'i*	永明體
		yung-shih shih	詠史詩
		yung-wu	詠物
		yung-wu fu	詠物賦
		yung-wu shih	詠物詩

GLOSSARY OF NAMES

Ah Ch'eng	阿城
Ah-hei	阿黑
Ah-li Hsi-ying	阿里西瑛
Ah-lu Wei	阿魯威
Ah Ying	阿英
Ai, Duke of Lu	魯哀公
Ai Ch'ing	艾青
Ai-na Chü-shih	艾衲居士
Ai Wu	艾蕪
An Chi	安驥
An-hui (Anhwei)	安徽
An Hung-chien	安鴻漸
An-le, Princess	安樂公主
An Lu-shan	安祿山
An Shih-kao	安世高
An-shun	安順
An-ta	俺答
Anhwei (An-hui)	安徽
Ao Ao	翱翱
Aoki Masaru	青木正兒
Asai Ryōi	淺井了意
Ashikaga Yoshimitsu	足利義滿
Bamboo Hat Poetry Club (see Li shih-she)	
Beijing (Pei-ching, Peking)	北京
Blue Star Poetry Club (see Lan-hsing shih-she)	
Central Plain (Chung-yüan)	中原
Cha	札
Cha Shen-hsing	查慎行
Chai Feng-ta	翟奉達
Chai T'ai-feng	翟泰豐
Chai Yung-ming	翟永明
Ch'ai Yüan-kao	柴元皋
Chan Fang-sheng	湛方生
Chan Ping	詹冰
Chan-shih chü-she	戰士劇社
Chan Tzu-ch'ien	展子虔
Ch'an	禪
Chang, Eileen (Chang Ai-ling)	
Chang	張
Chang Ai-ling (Chang, Eileen)	張愛玲
Chang Ch'ao	張潮
Chang Cheng-ch'ang	張正常
Chang Ch'eng-chih	張承志
Chang Chi	張籍

Chang Chi-hsien	張繼先
Chang Ch'i	張琦
Chang Chieh	張潔
Chang Ch'ien	張騫
Chang Ch'ien-niang	張倩娘
Chang Chih-tung	張之洞
Chang Ch'ing	張清
Chang Chiu-ch'eng	張九成
Chang Chiu-ling	張九齡
Chang Cho	張鷟
Chang Chu	張翥
Chang Chu-p'o	張竹坡
Chang Chün	張浚
Chang Chün-fang	張君房
Chang Erh	張耳
Chang Fan	張蘩
Chang Fei	張飛
Chang Feng-yi	張鳳翼
Chang Hen-shui	張恨水
Chang Heng	張衡
Chang Hsi-kuo	張系國
Chang Hsiao-hsiang	張孝祥
Chang Hsieh	張協
Chang Hsien	張憲
Chang Hsien-liang	張賢亮
Chang Hsin	張欣
Chang Hsin-hsin	張辛欣
Chang Hsüeh-ch'eng	章學誠
Chang Hu	張祜
Chang Hua	張華
Chang Huai-shen	張淮深
Chang Hui	張輝
Chang Hui-yen	張惠言
Chang Ju-chün	張如君
Chang Kai	張蓋
Chang K'o-chiu	張可久
Chang K'un-te	張坤德
Chang Kuo-hsiang	張國祥
Chang Lei	張耒
Chang Li-li	張莉莉
Chang Liang	張梁
Chang Lu	張魯
Chang Ming-shan	張鳴善
Chang Mo	張默
Chang Po-tuan	張伯端
Chang Shao	張召
Chang Sheng	張生
Chang Ssu-ch'eng	張嗣成
Chang-sun Wu-chi	長孫無忌
Chang Ta-fu	張大復
Chang Tai	張岱
Chang T'ai-yen	章太炎
Chang Tan	張丹
Chang Tao-ling	張道陵
Chang T'ien-yi	張天翼
Chang Tsai	張載
Chang Tsao	張棗
Chang Ts'o	張錯
Chang Ts'ui-feng	張翠鳳
Chang-tsung	章宗
Chang Tsung-nan	張宗柟
Chang Tzu-ch'iao	張子僑
Chang Wen-huan	張文環
Chang Wen-t'ao	張問陶
Chang Wo-chün	張我軍
Chang Yang-hao	張養浩
Chang Yen	張演
Chang Yi	張揖
Chang Yi-ch'ao	張議潮
Chang Yü	張羽
Chang Yü-ch'u	張宇初
Chang Yü-niang	張玉娘
Chang Yüeh	張說
Ch'ang-an	長安
Ch'ang-ch'i	昌褀
Ch'ang Chien	常建
Ch'ang-chou	常州
Ch'ang-hsi	常羲
Ch'ang-ning, Princess	長寧公主
Ch'ang-sha	長沙
Ch'ang-shu	常熟
Ch'ang-te	常德
Chao	趙
Chao, Henry (Chao Yiheng)	趙毅衡
Chao (Duke of Lu)	昭
Chao Chi	趙佶
Chao Ch'i	趙岐
Chao Chih-hsin	趙執信
Chao Ching-shen	趙景深
Chao Hsiang	趙象
Chao Hsü	趙須
Chao Kou	趙構

Chao K'uang-yi 趙匡義
Chao K'uang-yin 趙匡胤
Chao Ling-chih 趙令畤
Chao Meng-fu 趙孟頫
Chao-ming 昭明
Chao Ming-ch'eng 趙明誠
Chao P'an-erh 趙盼兒
Chao Pi 趙弼
Chao Po-ts'ung 趙伯琮
Chao P'u-chai 趙樸齋
Chao Shan-liao 趙善璙
Chao Shao 張召
Chao Shih-hsiu 趙師秀
Chao Shou-yi 趙受益
Chao Shu-hsia (Susie Ch'en) 趙淑俠
Chao Shu-li 趙樹理
Chao T'ai-mou 趙太侔
Chao Tao-yi 趙道一
Chao Te-ch'ang 趙德昌
Chao T'ien-yi 趙天儀
Chao-tsung 昭宗
Chao Tzu-lung 趙子龍
Chao Wu-niang 趙五娘
Chao Yen-wei 趙彥衛
Chao Yi 趙壹
Chao Yi-chen 趙宜眞
Chao Yi-heng (Chao, Henry) 趙毅衡
Chao Yu-ch'in 趙友欽
Chao Yü-chü 趙與莒
Chao Yün 趙雲
Ch'ao-chou 潮州
Ch'ao Pu-chih 晁補之
Ch'ao Yüan 晁源
Che-chiang (Chekiang) 浙江
Che-hsi 浙西
Che-tsung 哲宗
Chekiang (Che-chiang) 浙江
Chen Pao-yü 甄寶玉
Chen Shih 眞氏
Chen Shih-yin 甄士隱
Chen-t'ien-sheng pai-hua chü-she 振天聲白話劇社
Chen-ting 眞定
Chen-tsung 眞宗
Chen-wu 眞武
Ch'en, Susie (Chao Shu-hsia) 趙淑俠
Ch'en 陳
Ch'en Chen-hui 陳貞慧
Ch'en Ch'en 陳忱
Ch'en Chi-ju 陳繼儒
Ch'en Ch'i 陳起
Ch'en Ch'i-t'ung 陳其通
Ch'en Ch'iao 陳樵
Ch'en Chien-kung 陳建功
Ch'en Chih-ch'ao 陳智超
Ch'en Chih-hsü 陳致虛
Ch'en Ching-chi 陳敬濟
Ch'en Ching-jung 陳敬容
Ch'en Chü 陳駒
Ch'en Ch'un 陳淳
Ch'en Fu 陳孚
Ch'en Hsi 陳喜
Ch'en Hsiao-ming 陳曉明
Ch'en Hsien-chang 陳獻章
Ch'en Hsü-ku 陳虛谷
Ch'en Hsüan-yu 陳玄祐
Ch'en Huang-mei 陳荒煤
Ch'en Hui-hua 陳慧樺
Ch'en Hung 陳鴻
Ch'en Jan 陳染
Ch'en K'uei 陳騤
Ch'en Kung-yin 陳恭尹
Ch'en Li-t'ing 陳鯉庭
Ch'en Liang 陳亮
Ch'en Lin 陳林
Ch'en Lü 陳旅
Ch'en Nan 陳楠
Ch'en Pai-lu 陳白露
Ch'en P'ing 陳平
Ch'en P'ing-yüan 陳平原
Ch'en Sen 陳森
Ch'en She (Sheng) 陳涉 (勝)
Ch'en Shih-tao 陳師道
Ch'en Shou 陳壽
Ch'en Ta-pei 陳大悲
Ch'en T'ien-hua 陳天華
Ch'en T'ing-cho 陳廷焯
Ch'en To (Ta-sheng) 陳多 (大生)
Ch'en Ts'ao-an 陳草庵

Ch'en Tu-hsiu	陳獨秀
Ch'en Tuan-sheng	陳端生
Ch'en T'uan	陳摶
Ch'en Tzu-ang	陳子昂
Ch'en Tzu-liang	陳子良
Ch'en Tzu-lung	陳子龍
Ch'en Tzu-tu	陳子度
Ch'en Wang-tao	陳望道
Ch'en Wei-sung	陳維崧
Ch'en Yi	陳毅
Ch'en Yi-tseng	陳繹曾
Ch'en Yin-ch'üeh/k'o	陳寅恪
Ch'en Ying-chen	陳映真
Ch'en Yü	陳餘
Ch'en Yü-chiao	陳與郊
Ch'en Yü-lien	陳玉蓮
Ch'en Yü-yi	陳與義
Ch'en Yüan	陳垣
Ch'en Yün	陳雲
Ch'en Yung-shan	陳永善
Cheng, clan of Ying-yang	滎陽鄭氏
Cheng (state)	鄭
Cheng Chen	鄭珍
Cheng Chen-to	鄭振鐸
Cheng Cheng-ch'iu	鄭正秋
Cheng Ch'i	鄭棨
Cheng Chih-chen	鄭之珍
Cheng Chiung-ming	鄭炯明
Cheng Ch'ou-yü	鄭愁予
Cheng Ch'u-hui	鄭處誨
Cheng Heng	鄭恒
Cheng Ho	鄭和
Cheng Hsieh	鄭燮
Cheng Hsüan	鄭玄
Cheng Jo-yung	鄭若庸
Cheng Ku	鄭谷
Cheng Kuang-tsu	鄭光祖
Cheng Min	鄭敏
Cheng Shan-fu	鄭善夫
Cheng-shih	正始
Cheng Shu-sen (William Tay)	鄭樹森
Cheng Ssu-hsiao	鄭思肖
Cheng-te	正德
Cheng-t'ung	正統
Cheng Wan-lung	鄭萬隆
Cheng Wen-cho	鄭文焯
Cheng Yi	鄭義
Cheng-yi	正一
Cheng Yin	鄭隱
Cheng Yü	鄭嵎
Cheng Yü-ch'ing	鄭餘慶
Ch'eng, Emperor	成帝
Ch'eng, Emperor of Han	漢成帝
Ch'eng, Madame	程
Ch'eng, Master	程
Ch'eng brothers	程氏
Ch'eng chai	誠齋
Ch'eng-chih	成之
Ch'eng Chu	程朱
Ch'eng Hao	程顥
Ch'eng Hsiao-ch'ing	程小青
Ch'eng-hua	成化
Ch'eng-p'u (battle)	城濮
Ch'eng Shan-chih	程善之
Ch'eng-ti	成帝
Ch'eng T'ing-kuei	成廷珪
Ch'eng-tsu	成祖
Ch'eng-tu (Chengtu)	成都
Ch'eng Wei-yüan	程偉元
Ch'eng Yi	程頤
Ch'eng Ying	程嬰
Chengtu (Ch'eng-tu)	成都
Chi (Lu clan)	季
Chi Chen-yi	季振宜
Chi-chou	吉州
Chi Chün-hsiang	紀君祥
Chi Hsi	朱熹
Chi Hsien	紀弦
Chi Hsien-lin	季羨林
Chi-hu	畸笏
Chi Hung	季紅
Chi Hung-chen	季紅真
Chi K'ang	嵇康
Chi Li	季歷
Chi-lin	吉林
Chi-nan (Tsinan)	濟南
Chi-nan san-ts'ai-tzu	幾南三才子
Chi-no	基諾
Chi Pu	季布
Chi-she	幾社
Chi Wen-tzu	季文子

Chi Yi	姬翼
Chi Yu-kung	計有功
Chi Yün	紀昀
Ch'i, Lady	戚姬
Ch'i (school of *Shih-ching* interpretation)	齊
Ch'i (state)	齊
Ch'i-chi	齊己
Ch'i-hsia	棲霞
Ch'i Hsieh	齊諧
Ch'i Huan	齊桓
Ch'i Ju-shan	齊如山
Ch'i Piao-chia	祁彪佳
Ch'i-sung	契嵩
Ch'i-wu Ch'ien	綦毋潛
Chia, Empress	賈后
Chia, Mr.	夾氏
Chia Chen	賈珍
Chia-ching	嘉靖
Chia Chung-ming	賈仲明
Chia Ch'ung	賈充
Chia Hsi-ch'un	賈惜春
Chia Jui	賈瑞
Chia Jung	賈蓉
Chia Lien	賈璉
Chia Mi	賈謐
Chia Pao-yü	賈寶玉
Chia Shan-hsiang	賈善翔
Chia She	賈赦
Chia Ssu-tao	賈似道
Chia Tan	賈耽
Chia T'an-ch'un	賈探春
Chia Tao	賈島
Chia-ting	嘉定
Chia Yi	賈誼
Chia Ying-ch'un	賈迎春
Chia Ying-ch'ung	賈應寵
Chia-yu	嘉佑
Chia Yü-ts'un	賈雨村
Chia Yüan-ch'un	賈元春
Chiang-chai	薑齋
Chiang Ching-kuo	蔣經國
Chiang Ch'un-lin	蔣春霖
Chiang Fang	蔣防
Chiang Hai-ch'eng	蔣海澄
Chiang Ho	江河
Chiang-hsi (Kiangsi)	江西
Chiang-hu (River and Lakes) School	江湖派
Chiang Kai-shek	蔣介石
Chiang Kuang-tz'u	蔣光慈
Chiang Kuei	姜貴
Chiang K'uei	姜夔
Chiang-ling	江陵
Chiang-nan (Kiangnan)	江南
Chiang-ning	江寧
Chiang Ping-chih	蔣冰之
Chiang Shih-ch'üan	蔣士銓
Chiang Shu-yü	蔣叔輿
Chiang-su (Kiangsu)	江蘇
Chiang Te-yin	姜德隱
Chiang Tse-min	江澤民
Chiang-tso san-ta-chia	江左三大家
Chiang Tzu-lung	蔣子龍
Chiang Yen	江淹
Chiang Ying-k'o	江盈科
Chiang Yü-han	蔣玉菡
Chiang-yün lou	絳雲樓
Chiang-yung	江永
Chiao-jan	皎然
Chiao Na	嬌娜
Ch'iao Chi	喬吉
Chieh Hsi-ssu	揭傒斯
Chien-an (modern Nanking)	建安
Chien-ch'ang	簡長
Chien-hsing	建興
Chien-k'ang	建康
Chien-mei	兼美
Chien-wen, Emperor of Liang	梁簡文帝
Chien-wen ti	簡文帝
Ch'ien Ch'i	錢起
Ch'ien Ch'ien-yi	錢謙益
Ch'ien Chih-chieh	錢志節
Ch'ien Chung-shu	錢鍾書
Ch'ien fo tung	千佛洞
Ch'ien Han	前漢
Ch'ien-hou ch'i-tzu	前後七子
Ch'ien-hsi	前溪
Ch'ien Hsi-yen	錢希言
Ch'ien Hsing-ts'un	錢杏村

Ch'ien Hsüan	錢選
Ch'ien Hsüan-t'ung	錢玄同
Ch'ien-kuo, Lady of	汧國夫人
Ch'ien-lung	乾隆
Ch'ien Ta-hsin	錢大昕
Ch'ien-t'ang	錢塘
Ch'ien Ts'ai	錢采
Ch'ien Wei-yen	錢惟演
Chih (Robber)	盜跖
Chih Chiang	智匠
Chih-ch'ien	支謙
Chih-lou-chia-ch'an	支婁迦讖
Chih-na	支/脂那
Chih-nü	織女
Chih-p'an	志磐
Chih-tun	支遁
Chih-yen Chai	脂硯齋
Chih-yi	智顗
Chih Yü	摯虞
Ch'ih Li	池莉
Ch'ih-pi	赤壁
Ch'ih-tao jen	癡道人
Ch'ih Yu	蚩尤
Chin (Jurchen)	金
Chin (state; 1115–1234)	金
Chin (state; 265–420)	晉
Chin, Eastern	東晉
Chin, Western	西晉
Chin-chiang	晉江
Chin Chien	金劍
Chin-ch'uan	金釧
Chin Ho	金和
Ch'in (dynasty)	秦
Chin-hua t'uan	進化團
Chin-kung	金公
Chin Lien	錦連
Chin-lien	金蓮
Chin-ling	金陵
Chin Shan	金山
Chin Sheng-t'an	金聖嘆
Chin Sung-ts'en	金松岑
Chin Tan	今丹
Chin T'ien-ho	金天翮
Chin Ts'ui-lien	金翠蓮
Chin Wen-ch'ing	金雯青
Chin Yu-tzu	金幼孜
Chin Yün	錦雲
Ch'in, First Emperor of	秦始皇帝
Ch'in (state)	秦
Ch'in Chi-wen	秦紀文
Ch'in Chia	秦嘉
Ch'in Chih-an	秦志安
Ch'in Ch'ing	秦青
Ch'in-chou	沁州
Ch'in Chung	秦鍾
Ch'in K'o-ch'ing	秦可卿
Ch'in Kuan	秦觀
Ch'in Kuei	秦檜
Ch'in Ming	秦明
Ch'in Shu-pao	秦叔寶
Ch'in-tsung	欽宗
Ch'in Tzu-hao	覃子豪
Chindŏk	眞德
Ching	荊
Ching (Prince)	荊
Ching, Duke	景公
Ching-chou	荊州
Ching-huan	警幻
Ching K'o	荊軻
Ching-ling	竟陵
Ching-lung	景龍
Ching-ming Tao	淨明道
Ching-ti	景帝
Ching-tsung	敬宗
Ching Yüan	荊元
Ch'ing (dynasty)	清
Ch'ing (Manchu)	清
Ch'ing-ch'ih fan-cheng tao-jen	情癡反正道人
Ch'ing-ho	清河
Ch'ing-keng	青埂
Ch'ing-lan	慶蘭
Ch'ing-li	慶曆
Ch'ing Pu	黥布
Ch'ing-seng	情僧
Ch'ing-wei	清微
Ch'ing-wen	晴雯
Ch'ing-yang Kung	青羊宮
Ch'ing-yü	鯖魚
Chiphyŏ jŏn	集賢殿
Chiu-chiang	九江
Chiu-mo-lo-shih	鳩摩羅什

Chiu-yeh p'ai	九葉派
Ch'iu Chin	秋瑾
Ch'iu-chü	秋菊
Ch'iu Ch'u-chi	邱處機
Ch'iu Chün	丘濬
Ch'iu Hsin-ju	邱心如
Ch'iu Hu	秋胡
Ch'iu-jung	秋容
Ch'iu Wei-ai	邱惟薆
Ch'iung Kuei	窮鬼
Ch'iung Yao	瓊瑤
Cho-yüan-t'ing Chu-jen	酌元亭主人
Ch'oe Cha	崔滋
Ch'oe Ch'i-wŏn	崔致遠
Ch'oe Rip	崔岦
Ch'oe Sŭng-no	崔承老
Chŏng Sa-ryŏng	鄭士龍
Chŏngbŏpsa	定法師
Chŏngjo	正祖
Chŏnju	全州
Chosŏn	朝鮮
Chou, Duke of	周公
Chou (dynasty)	周
Chou Chi (late Ming Hangchow scholar)	周楫
Chou Chi (1781–1839)	周濟
Chou Chin	周進
Chou Ch'o	周逴
Chou Ch'ung	周沖
Chou En-lai	周恩來
Chou Fan-yi	周繁漪
Chou Hsiang	周庠
Chou Ju-ch'ang	周汝昌
Chou Kuei-sheng	周桂笙
Chou Li	周禮
Chou Meng-tieh	周夢蝶
Chou Mi	周密
Chou Nan	周南
Chou Pang-yen	周邦彥
Chou P'ing	周萍
Chou P'u-yüan	周樸園
Chou Shao-liang	周紹良
Chou Shou-chüan	周瘦鵑
Chou Shou-chung	周守忠
Chou Shu-jen	周樹人
Chou Shun-ch'ang	周順昌
Chou Te-ch'ing	周德清
Chou Tso-jen	周作人
Chou Tun-yi	周敦頤
Chou Wei-chih	周巍峙
Chou Yung	周顒
Chu Ching-chien	竺淨檢
Chu Ching-fan	朱京藩
Chu Ch'o	朱綽
Chu Ch'üan	朱權
Chu Fa-hu	竺法護
Chu Hsi	朱熹
Chu Hsi-ning	朱西寧
Chu Hsiang-hsien	朱象先
Chu Hsiao-tsang (Tsu-mo)	朱孝藏 (祖謨)
Chu Hu (Su-ch'en)	朱㿥 (素臣)
Chu K'ai	朱凱
Chu-ko Liang	諸葛亮
Chu Lien-hsiu	珠簾秀
Chu Pa-chieh	豬八戒
Chu Sheng-lin	諸聖鄰
Chu Shu-chen	朱淑眞
Chu Shu-lan	竺叔蘭
Chu Ta (Pa-ta shan-jen)	朱耷 (八大山人)
Chu Te	朱德
Chu Ti	朱棣
Chu T'ien-hsin	朱天心
Chu T'ien-wen	朱天文
Chu Tso-ch'ao	朱佐朝
Chu Tsu-mou	朱祖謀
Chu T'ung	朱仝
Chu Tzu-ch'ing	朱自清
Chu Tz'u	朱泚
Chu Yi-tsun	朱彝尊
Chu Ying-t'ai	祝英臺
Chu Yu-tun	朱有燉
Chu Yüan-chang	朱元璋
Chu Yün-ming	祝允明
Ch'u	楚
Ch'u Ch'ing	楚卿
Ch'u-hsiung	楚雄
Ch'u Jen-huo	褚人穫
Ch'u Kuang-hsi	儲光羲
Ch'u Liang	褚亮
Ch'u Shao-sun	褚少孫

Ch'u-yün	楚雲
Ch'ü Ch'iu-pai	瞿秋白
Ch'ü Ta-chün	屈大均
Ch'ü Yen	瞿琰
Ch'ü Yu	瞿佑
Ch'ü Yüan	屈原
Chuan-hsü	顓頊
Ch'üan-chen	全眞
Chuang	壯
Chuang, Duke	莊公
Chuang, King	莊王
Chuang-che	壯者
Chuang Chi	莊忌
Chuang Chou	莊周
Chuang Shao-kuang	莊紹光
Chuang Tzu	莊子
Ch'uang-shih-chi shih-she	創世紀詩社
Ch'uang-tso she	創作社
Chui Feng	追風
Chukim kohoe	竹林高會
Chün	俊
Ch'un liu she	春柳社
Ch'un-mei	春梅
Ch'un-ni	春妮
Ch'un T'ao	春桃
Ch'un yang she	春陽社
Ch'un-yü Fen	淳于棼
Chung Ah-ch'eng	鍾阿城
Chung Hsi shu-chü	中西書局
Chung Hsing	鍾惺
Chung-hua shu-chü	中華書局
Chung Jung	鍾嶸
Chung K'uei	鍾馗
Chung-kung chung-yang shih-ssu chieh liu chung ch'üan-hui	中共中央十四屆六中全會
Chung-kuo ching-chü t'uan	中國京劇團
Chung-kuo ch'ing-nien yi-shu chü-yüan	中國青年藝術劇院
Chung-kuo lü-hsing chü-t'uan	中國旅行劇團
Chung-kuo Tao-chiao hsieh-hui	中國道教協會
Chung-kuo tso-chia hsieh-hui	中國作家協會
Chung-kuo tso-yi hsi-chü-chia lien-meng	中國左翼戲劇家聯盟
Chung-kuo tso-yi tso-chia lien-meng	中國左翼作家聯盟
Chung-kuo (Chung-hua ch'üan-kuo) wen-hsüeh yi-shu chieh lien-ho-hui	中國(中華全國)文學藝術界聯合會
Chung-li Ch'üan	鍾離權
Chung-nan	終南
Chung-shan	中山
Chung Ssu-ch'eng	鍾嗣成
Chung-tsung	中宗
Chung-tu-hsiu	忠都秀
Chung-yüan (see Central Plain)	
Ch'ung-chen	崇禎
Ch'ung-ch'ing (see Chungking)	
Ch'ung-erh	重耳
Chungjong	中宗
Chungking (Ch'ung-ch'ing)	重慶
Ch'ungyŏl	忠烈
Confucius (K'ung Tzu)	孔子
Constellations Poetry Club (see Hsing-tso shih-she)	
Crescent School (see Hsin-yüeh p'ai)	
Dang Tran Con	鄧陳琨
Daur (Ta-wo-erh)	達斡爾
Dinh Nhat Than	丁日慎
Doan Thi Diem	段氏點
Dragon Race Poetry Club (see Lung-tsu shih-she)	
Ema Saiko	江馬細香
Epoch Poetry Club (see Ch'uang-shih-chi shih-she)	
Erh-hsien An	二仙庵
Fa-hai	法海
Fa-hsien	法顯
Fa-hu (Chu Fa-hu)	竺法護
Fa-shih	法始
Fa-ts'ung	法聰

Fan Ch'eng-ta 范成大
Fan Chin 范進
Fan Chung-yen 范仲淹
Fan Li 范蠡
Fan-liang Village 樊良鎮
Fan P'eng 范梈
Fan Po-ch'ün 范伯群
Fan Shih 范式
Fan-shih 氾氏
Fan Sui 范雎
Fan Yeh 范曄
Fan Yi 范懌
Fan Yün 范雲
Fang Ch'eng-p'ei 方成培
Fang Ch'ing 方卿
Fang Fang 方昉
Fang Hsüan-ling 房玄齡
Fang Jo-ming 方若明
Fang Ju-hao 方汝浩
Fang Kan 方干
Fang-kuan 芳官
Fang La 方臘
Fang Pao 方苞
Fang-shan 房山
Fang Shu-pao 房叔豹
Fang Weng 放翁
Fei, Faye C. (Fei Ch'un-fang) 費春放
Fei, Master 費
Fei Ch'un-fang 費春放
Feng Chi-ts'ai 馮驥才
Feng Chih 馮至
Feng Meng-lung 馮夢龍
Feng Ming-ch'i 鳳鳴岐
Feng Nai-ch'ao 馮乃超
Feng Tzu-chen 馮子振
Feng Tzu-k'ai 豐子愷
Feng Wei-min 馮惟敏
Feng Yen 封演
Feng Yen-ssu 馮延巳
Feng-ch'e shih-she 風車詩社
Feng-yüeh pao-chien 風月寶鑑
Five Dynasties (Wu-tai) 五代
Fo-chiao 佛教
Fo-kuang 佛光
Foochow (Fuchow, Fu-chou) 福州
Fou-ch'iu Po 浮丘伯
Fou-yün 浮雲
"Four Scholars of Mr. Su's Gate" (Su-men ssu hsüeh-shih) 蘇門四學士
Fu, Prince 福
Fu-ch'ai 夫差
Fu-chien (Fukien) 福建
Fu-chou (Foochow, Fuchow) 福州
Fu-hsi 伏羲
Fu Hsüan 傅玄
Fu Liang 傅亮
Fu-pai Chu-jen 浮白主人
Fu-she 復社
Fu Sheng 伏勝 / 生
Fu Ts'ai-yün 傅彩雲
Fu-yang 阜陽
Fuchow (Fu-chou, Foochow) 福州
Fujieda Akira 藤枝晃
Fujiwara Akihira 藤原明衡
Fujiwara Kintō 藤原公任
Fujiwara no Hamanari 藤原浜成
Fujiwara Seika 藤原惺窩
Fukien (Fu-chien) 福建
Fukui Fumimasa (Bunga) 福井文雅
Genmei 元明
Genzei 元政
Gozan 五山
Grape Orchard Poetry Club (see P'u-t'ao-yüan shih-she)
Gyokuchiginsha 玉池吟社
Ha-erh-pin hua-chü-yüan 哈爾濱話劇院
Ha-ha Tao-shih 哈哈道士
Ha-ni 哈尼
Hagiwara Hiromichi 荻原宏道
Hai-feng 害風
Hai Tzu 海子
Hai-yen 海鹽
Han (battle) 韓
Han (dynasty) 漢
Han (school of *Shih-ching* interpretation) 韓
Han Ch'in-hu 韓擒虎
Han Chü 韓駒
Han Chüeh 韓厥
Han Fei Tzu 韓非子
Han Hsiao-ch'uang 韓小窗

Han Hsin 韓信
Han-ku 函谷
Han-lin (yüan) 翰林 (院)
Han Liu 韓流
Han Pang-ch'ing 韓邦慶
Han P'eng 韓朋
Han P'ing (character in *chih-kuai* story) 韓馮
Han P'ing (character in Tun-huang prose-poem) 韓憑/凭
Han-shan 寒山
Han Shao-kung 韓少功
Han Su-yin 韓素音
Han-tan Ch'un 邯鄲淳
Han Tung 韓東
Han Wo 韓偓
Han Wu-ti 漢武帝
Han Yi 韓翊
Han Ying 韓嬰
Han Yü 韓愈
Hang Yüeh-ho 杭約赫
Hangchow (Hangkou, Hang-chou) 杭州
Hao Ching 郝經
Hao Ta-t'ung 郝大通
Harrim 翰林
Hattori Nankaku 服部南郭
Hayashi Razan 林羅山
Hei-shui-ch'eng 黑水城
Heng-shan 衡山
Heng-yang 衡陽
Ho-chen 赫眞
Ho Ch'i-fang 何其芳
Ho Chih-chang 賀知章
Ho Chih-yüan 何志淵
Ho-ching Hsien-sheng ("Tranquil Gentle-man") 和靖先生
Ho Ching-ming 何景明
Ho Chu 賀鑄
Ho Hsin 何心
Ho Hsün 何遜
Hŏ Kyun 許筠
Ho-lan Chin-ming 賀蘭進明
Ho Li-wei 何立偉
Ho Liang-chün 何良俊
Ho-lu 闔盧
Ho Lung 賀龍
Ho Lung-hsiang 賀龍驤
Ho Meng-ch'un 何孟春
Ho Pang-o 和邦額
Ho-pei 河北
Ho P'ei-chu 何佩珠
Ho-shang Kung 河上公
Ho-shuo 河朔
Ho Yen 何晏
Ho Yü-feng 何玉鳳
Ho Yü-huai 何與懷
Hong Hui-bok 洪羲福
Hou Chi 后稷
Hou Chih 侯芝
Hou Ching 侯景
Hou Chou 後周
Hou Fang-yü 侯方域
Hou-kuan 侯官
Hou Po 侯白
Hou T'u 后土
Hsi-an (Sian) 西安
Hsi Chin 西晉
Hsi-chou 希晝
Hsi Chou sheng 西周生
Hsi Ch'uan 西川
Hsi-erh 喜兒
Hsi-ho 羲和
Hsi Hsi 西西
Hsi Hsia 西夏
Hsi-hu (West Lake) 西湖
Hsi K'ang 嵇康
Hsi Lang-hsien (Lang-hsien) 席浪仙
Hsi-ling 西泠
Hsi-men Ch'ing 西門慶
Hsi-shan 西山
Hsi Shih 西施
Hsi-shuang-pan-na 西雙版納
Hsi-tsang 西藏
Hsi Tso-ch'ih 習鑿齒
Hsi-tsung 僖宗
Hsi wang-mu 西王母
Hsi-yü 西域
Hsia 夏
Hsia Ching-ch'ü 夏敬渠
Hsia Ching-kuan 夏敬觀

Hsia-hou Tsao 夏侯灶
Hsia Kuei 夏珪
Hsia Tseng-yu 夏曾佑
Hsia Wan-ch'un 夏完淳
Hsia Yen 夏衍
Hsia Yü 夏宇
Hsiang (River) 湘
Hsiang, Duke 襄公
Hsiang, King of Wei 魏襄王
Hsiang Ch'u 項楚
Hsiang Hung-tso 項鴻祚
Hsiang K'ai 襄楷
Hsiang Liang 項梁
Hsiang-ling 香菱
Hsiang T'o 項託
Hsiang-yang 襄陽
Hsiang Yü 項羽
Hsiao 蕭
Hsiao, Prince (Liu Wu) 梁孝王
Hsiao Ch'en 蕭琛
Hsiao-ch'ing 小青
Hsiao ch'iu hsi hsiao shih t'an 小丘西小石潭
Hsiao-hsiao Hsien-sheng 笑笑先生
Hsiao Hsieh 小謝
Hsiao Hung 蕭紅
Hsiao-jan yü-sheng 蕭然鬱生
Hsiao Kang 蕭綱
Hsiao-ko 孝哥
Hsiao Niang 蕭娘
Hsiao Shih-ho 蕭時和
Hsiao-shih Tao-jen 小石道人
Hsiao-shuo lin 小說林
Hsiao Tao-ch'eng 蕭道成
Hsiao T'ing-chih 蕭廷芝
Hsiao-ts'ui 小翠
Hsiao-tsung 孝宗
Hsiao Tung-hsi 小東西
Hsiao T'ung 蕭統
Hsiao Tzu-liang 蕭子良
Hsiao Yen 蕭衍
Hsiao Yi 蕭繹
Hsiao Ying-shih 蕭穎士
Hsiao Yü-tse 肖玉澤
Hsieh Ao 謝翺
Hsieh Chao-che 謝肇淛
Hsieh Chen 謝榛
Hsieh Chin 解縉
Hsieh Chou 謝晝
Hsieh Fang-te 謝枋得
Hsieh Hsi-ssu 揭傒斯
Hsieh Hsiao-o 謝小娥
Hsieh Hsü-ts'ai 謝絮才
Hsieh Hun 謝混
Hsieh Kuei 謝珪
Hsieh Kuo-chen 謝國禎
Hsieh Ling-yün 謝靈運
Hsieh Shou-hao 謝守灝
Hsieh T'iao 謝朓
Hsieh Wan-ying 謝婉瑩
Hsien, Prince of Ho-chien 河間獻王
Hsien-pei 鮮卑
Hsien-ti, Emperor of the Han 漢獻帝
Hsien-t'ien 先天
Hsien-tsung 憲宗
Hsien-yang 咸陽
Hsien-yü Pi-jen 鮮于必仁
Hsin-ch'eng 新城
Hsin Ch'i-chi 辛棄疾
Hsin-chiang (Sinkiang) 新疆
Hsin-hsing shu-chü 新興書局
Hsin-k'ai-hu 新開湖
Hsin Ti 辛笛
Hsing-chao 行肇
Hsing Feng 邢鳳
Hsing Yi-hsün 邢益勛
Hsing-tso shih-she 星座詩社
Hsiu T'ao 秀陶
Hsiu-wen kuan 修文館
Hsiung Fo-hsi 熊佛西
Hsiung Lung-feng 熊龍峰
Hsiung-nu 匈奴
Hsü Chao 徐照
Hsü Chen 徐震
Hsü Chen-ch'ing 徐禎卿
Hsü Chen-ya 徐枕亞
Hsü Chi 徐璣
Hsü Chia 徐嘉
Hsü Chih-mo 徐志摩
Hsü Ch'ih 徐摛
Hsü Ching-tsung 許敬宗

Hsü-chou 徐州
Hsü Chün 許俊
Hsü Chung-hsing 徐中行
Hsü Chung-lin 許仲琳
Hsü Fang 徐芳
Hsü Feng-en 許奉恩
Hsü Hai (Tu Hai) 徐海
Hsü Hsia-k'o 徐霞客
Hsü Hsien 徐咸
Hsü Hsüan 徐鉉
Hsü Hsün (fl. c. 358?) 許詢
Hsü Hsün (239–292/374?) 許遜
Hsü Hui 許翽
Hsü Hui-lan 徐惠蘭
Hsü Hun 許渾
Hsü Hung-tsu 徐宏祖
Hsü Kan 徐幹
Hsü K'un 徐昆
Hsü Ling 徐陵
Hsü Mi 許謐
Hsü Nien-tz'u 徐念慈
Hsü Pan-mei 徐半梅
Hsü Pen 徐賁
Hsü Ping 徐冰
Hsü Shao 許邵
Hsü Shen 許慎
Hsü Shih 徐適
Hsü Shou-hsin 徐守信
Hsü Ti-shan 許地山
Hsü Tsai-ssu 徐再思
Hsü Ts'an 許燦
Hsü Tsung 許總
Hsü Tzu-yün 徐紫雲
Hsü Wei 徐渭
Hsü Yao-tso 許堯佐
Hsü Yen-po 徐彥伯
Hsüan 宣
Hsüan-ch'eng 宣城
Hsüan-chou 宣州
Hsüan-chüeh 玄覺
Hsüan-chung Kuan 玄中觀
Hsüan Nü 玄女
Hsüan-ti 宣帝
Hsüan Ting 宣鼎
Hsüan-tsang 玄奘
Hsüan-tsung 玄宗
Hsüan-wu 玄武
Hsüeh Ang-fu 薛昂夫
Hsüeh Hui 薛蕙
Hsüeh Jen-kuei 薛仁貴
Hsüeh Ku 薛瑕
Hsüeh P'an 薛蟠
Hsüeh Pao-ch'ai 薛寶釵
Hsüeh-shan 雪山
Hsüeh Shao-wei 薛紹微
Hsüeh Su-chieh 薛素姐
Hsüeh Sung 薛嵩
Hsüeh T'ao 薛濤
Hsüeh T'iao 薛調
Hsüeh Tzu-hsien 薛紫賢
Hsün Ch'ing/K'uang 荀卿 / 況
Hsün Hsü 荀勗
Hsün Tzu 荀子
Hsün-yang 潯陽
Hsün Yüeh 荀悅
Hu Chen-heng 胡震亨
Hu Chi-ch'en 胡寄麎
Hu Chih-yü 胡祇遹
Hu-chou 湖州
Hu Ch'üan 胡銓
Hu-han-yeh 呼韓邪
Hu Hui-ch'ao 胡慧超
Hu Ju-chia 胡汝嘉
Hu K'o 胡可
Hu-nan 湖南
Hupei 湖北
Hu-pi-lieh Han 忽必烈汗
Hu San-niang 扈三娘
Hu Shih 胡適
Hu Tao-ching 胡道靜
Hu Te-sheng 胡得生
Hu-t'u 滬土
Hu Yao-pang 胡耀邦
Hu-yen Cho 呼延焯
Hu Ying-lin 胡應麟
Hu Yü-hsiu 胡玉秀
Hua-ch'ing kung 華清宮
Hua-chou 滑州
Hua Hsi-jen 花襲人
Hua-jui Fu-jen 花蕊夫人
Hua-jung 花榮
Hua Kuan So 花關索

Hua-kuang 華光
Hua T'o 華陀
Hua Tzu-hsü 花子虛
Hua-yüeh San-niang 華嶽三娘
Hua Yün 華雲
Huai-ku 懷古
Huai-nan 淮南
Huai-nan Wang 淮南王
Huai-yang 淮陽
Huan, Duke 桓公
Huan Fu 桓夫
Huan Shao-chün 桓少君
Huan-ti 桓帝
Huang Ch'ao 黃巢
Huang Chen-yüan 黃振元
Huang-chiang Tiao-sou 荒江釣叟
Huang Chieh 黃節
Huang Ching-jen 黃景仁
Huang-chou 黃州
Huang Chou-hsing 黃周星
Huang Ch'un-ming 黃春明
Huang Ch'ung-ku 黃崇嘏
Huang-fu Fang 皇甫汸
Huang-fu Mei 皇甫枚
Huang-fu Mi 皇甫謐
Huang-fu Shao-hua 皇甫少華
Huang-ho (Yellow River) 黃河
Huang-ho lou 黃鶴樓
Huang Ho-sheng 黃荷生
Huang Hsiang 黃翔
Huang Hsing-tseng 黃省曾
Huang Jen 黃人
Huang Kung-wang 黃公望
Huang Mo-hsi 黃摩西
Huang O 黃娥
Huang-p'o 黃婆
Huang-p'u River 黃埔
Huang Sheng-fu 黃生富
Huang Shih-ch'iang 黃仕強
Huang Shih-hui 黃石輝
Huang Ssu-ch'eng 黃思騁
Huang Ti 黃帝
Huang T'ing-chien 黃庭堅
Huang Tso-lin 黃佐臨
Huang Tsun-hsien 黃遵憲
Huang Tsung-hsi 黃宗羲
Huang T'u-pi 黃圖珌
Huang-tzu Kao-ao 皇子告敖
Huang Wen-ping 黃文炳
Huang Yüan-chi 黃元吉
Huang Yung-sha 黃勇刹
Hui (Muslim) 回
Hui, King 惠王
Hui-chan 慧湛
Hui-chiao 慧皎
Hui-chüeh 慧覺
Hui-ch'ung 惠崇
Hui-ming 惠明
Hui-neng 慧能
Hui-sheng 惠生
Hui-tsung 徽宗
Hui-yüan 慧遠
Hun-yüan Lao Tzu 混元老子
Hunan 湖南
Hung-chih 宏治
Hung-fu 紅拂
Hung Ho 紅河
Hung Hsiu-ch'üan 洪秀全
Hung Liang-chi 洪亮吉
Hung-lien 紅蓮
Hung Mai 洪邁
Hung-niang 紅娘
Hung P'ien 洪楩
Hung Shen 洪深
Hung Sheng 洪昇
Hung-wen kuan 弘文館
Hung Ying 虹影
Hung-yü 紅玉
Huo Ch'ü-ping 霍去病
Huo Hsiao-yü 霍小玉
Huo Huan 霍桓
Huo Shih-hsiu 霍世休
Hupei 湖北
Ichikawa Kansai 市河寛斎
Ikkyū Sōjun 一休宗純
Ilyŏn 一然
Inoue Hisashi 井上靖
Iriya Yoshitaka 入矢義高
Ishikawa Jōzan 石川丈山
Isonokami no Otomaro 石上乙麻呂
Itō Hirobumi 伊藤博文
Itō Tōgai 伊藤東涯

Izumi Kyōka	泉鏡花
Jao-chou	饒州
Jao Tsung-yi	饒宗頤
Jen, Ms. (fox fairy)	任氏
Jen An	任安
Jen Fang	任昉
Jen-tsung	仁宗
Jen Yü	任昱
Ju-chiao	儒教
Ju-chih (Yüeh-chih)	月支
Ju-lai	如來
Juan Chi	阮籍
Juan Ta-ch'eng	阮大成
Juan Yü	阮瑀
Juan Yüan	阮元
Jui-chin	瑞金
Jui-hsien	瑞仙
Jui T'ing-chang	芮挺璋
Jui-tsung	睿宗
Jung-chiang	榕江
Kai K'uan	蓋寬
K'ai-chou	開州
K'ai-feng (Kaifeng)	開封
K'ai-ming	開明
K'ai-yüan	開元
Kaifeng (K'ai-feng)	開封
Kakinomoto no Hitomaro	柿本大麻呂
Kamo Mabuchi	賀茂眞淵
Kan Chazan	菅茶山
Kan-chiang	贛江
Kan Ch'ing	干慶
Kan-ho	泔河
Kan Pao	干寶
Kanaoka Shōkō	金岡照光
Kang Wi	姜瑋
K'ang, King	康王
K'ang Chin-chih	康進之
K'ang Hai	康海
K'ang-hsi	康熙
K'ang-le, Duke of	康樂公
K'ang-li	康里
K'ang Pai-ch'ing	康白情
K'ang Seng-hui	康僧會
K'ang Yu-wei	康有爲
Kanrin	翰林
Kao-an	高安

Kao Chan-hsiang	高占祥
Kao Ch'i	高啓
Kao Chung-wu	高仲武
Kao E	高鶚
Kao Hsing-chien	高行健
Kao Lien	高濂
Kao Ming	高明
Kao Ping	高棅
Kao Shih	高適
Kao-tsu	高祖
Kao-tsung	高宗
Kao Wen-hsiu	高文秀
Kao-yang pu-ts'ai-tzu	高陽不才子
Kao-yu	高郵
Kawaguchi Hisao	川口久雄
Keng Ch'ü-ping	耿去病
Keng Lang	耿郎
Khuong Cong Phu	姜公輔
Ki no Tsurayuki	紀貫之
Kiangnan (Chiang-nan)	江南
Kiangsi (Chiang-hsi)	江西
Kiangsi School (Chiang-hsi shih-she)	江西詩社
Kiangsu (Chiang-su)	江蘇
Kim Ch'ang-hyŏp	金昌協
Kim Chong-jik	金宗直
Kim Man-jung	金萬重
Kim Pu-sik	金富軾
Kim Si-sup	金時習
Kim T'aek-yŏng	金澤榮
Kitayama	北山
Ko Ch'ao-fu	葛巢甫
Ko Fei	格非
Ko Hsüan	葛玄
Ko Hung	葛洪
Ko-tsao	閤皀
Ko Yang	戈揚
K'o-ch'in	克勤
K'o-ch'ing	可卿
K'o Chiu-ssu	柯九思
Kōbō Daishi	弘法大師
Kogidō	古義堂
Koguryŏ	高句麗
Kojō Tandō (Teikichi)	古城坦堂 (眞吉)
Kōkosha	江湖社

Kokugaku	国学
Koryŏ	高麗
Kou-chien	勾踐
Kou-erh Yeh	狗兒爺
K'ou Chun	寇准
Ku (knight-errant)	古
Ku Chen-kuan	顧貞觀
Ku Ch'eng	顧城
Ku Chieh-kang	顧頡剛
Ku Hua	古華
Ku Jo-p'u	顧若璞
Ku K'ai-chih	顧愷之
Ku K'uang	顧況
Ku-liang Hsi	穀梁喜
Ku Lin	顧璘
Ku-shan	孤山
Ku Ssu-li	顧嗣立
Ku T'ai-ch'ing (Ch'un)	顧太清 (春)
Ku Tzu-ching	谷子敬
Ku Yen-wu	顧炎武
Ku Ying	顧瑛
Ku Yüan-ch'ing	顧元慶
K'u Ling	苦苓
Kua-ts'ang	括蒼
Kuan Chieh-ming	關傑明
Kuan-chung	關中
Kuan Chung (Kuan Tzu)	管仲
Kuan Han-ch'ing	關漢卿
Kuan-hsiu	貫休
Kuan-ko	官哥
Kuan Kung	關公
Kuan Ta-ju	管達如
Kuan Te-tung	關德棟
Kuan-ti	關帝
Kuan-ting	灌頂
Kuan Tzu (Kuan Chung)	管子
Kuan-yin	觀音
Kuan Yü	關羽
Kuan Yün-shih	貫雲石
Kuang-chou (Kuangchow)	廣州
Kuang-hsi (Kwangsi)	廣西
Kuang-hsü	光緒
Kuang-tsung	光宗
Kuang-tung (Kwangtung)	廣東
Kuang-yü she	光裕社
K'uang Ch'ao-jen	匡超人
K'uang Chou-yi	況周頤
K'uang Fu	匡復
Kuangchow (Kuang-chou)	廣州
Kuei-chi	會稽
Kuei-ch'ih	貴池
Kuei-chou (Kweichow)	貴州
Kuei Chuang	歸莊
Kuei-lin (Kweilin)	桂林
Kuei Yu-kuang	歸有光
K'uei	夔
Kūkai	空海
Kun	鯀
K'un-lun	崑崙
K'un-ming (Kunming)	昆明
K'un-P'eng	鯤鵬
Kung (Ch'in-wang)	恭 (親王)
Kung, Prince of Lu	魯共王
Kung-an	公安
Kung Hsiang-lin	龔祥麟
Kung K'uei	貢奎
Kung-kung	共工
Kung Sheng-yü	龔聖予
Kung-sun Ch'u-chiu	公孫杵臼
Kung T'ien-t'ing	宮天挺
Kung Ting-tzu	龔鼎孳
Kung Tzu-chen	龔自珍
Kung-yang Kao	公羊高
Kung-yang Shou	公羊壽
Kung Yi-cheng	龔頤正
K'ung An-kuo	孔安國
K'ung-chiao	孔教
K'ung Jung	孔融
K'ung-k'ung tao-jen	空空道人
K'ung Mei-yü	孔梅玉
K'ung San-chuan	孔三傳
K'ung Shang-jen	孔尚仁
K'ung T'ien-yün	孔天允
K'ung Tzu (Confucius)	孔子
K'ung Ying-ta	孔穎達
Kunming (K'un-ming)	昆明
Kuo Chien-kuang	郭建光
Kuo Ch'iu-sheng	郭秋生
Kuo-chü	國劇
Kuo Hsiang	郭象
Kuo Hsieh	郭解
Kuo-hsüeh fu-lun she	國學扶輪社

Kuo Jo-hsü	郭若虛	Li, Empress	李后
Kuo-li Pei-ching yi-shu chuan-men hsüeh-hsiao	國立北京藝術專門學校	Li Ang	李昂
		Li Ao	李翺
		Li Ch'ao-wei	李朝威
Kuo Liang-hui	郭良蕙	Li Chen	李禎
Kuo Lu-sheng	郭路生	Li Ch'i	李頎
Kuo Mao-ch'ien	郭茂倩	Li Chia-jui	李家瑞
Kuo Mo-jo	郭沫若	Li Chia-yu	李嘉祐
Kuo P'u	郭璞	Li-chiang	灕江
Kuo Ssu-chiu	郭思九	Li Chiao	李嶠
Kuo-tien	郭店	Li Chiao-erh	李嬌兒
Kuo T'uan	郭彖	Li Ch'iao	李喬
Kuomintang	國民黨	Li Chih	李贄
Kwangchow (Kuang-chou)	廣州	Li Chih-ch'ang	李志常
		Li Chih-jou	李志柔
Kwangsi (Kuang-hsi)	廣西	Li Chih-kuang	李志光
Kwangtung (Kuang-tung)	廣東	Li Chin-fa	李金髮
Kweichow (Kuei-chou)	貴州	Li Chin-kuei	李金桂
Kweilin (Kuei-lin)	桂林	Li Chin-tou	李金斗
Kyujanggak	奎章閣	Li Ching	李靖
Lai-chou	萊州	Li Ching-te	黎靖德
Lai Ho	賴和	Li Ch'ing-chao	李清照
Lai-yang	萊陽	Li Ch'ing-ch'en	李慶辰
Lan Ho-shang	懶和尚	Li Cho-jan	李卓然
Lan-hsin hsi-yüan	藍心戲院	Li Ch'u-yi	李楚儀
Lan-hu she	蘭湖社	Li Chün-yü	酈君玉
Lan-hsing shih-she	藍星詩社	Li Ch'ün-yü	李群玉
Lan Hung-en	蘭鴻恩	Li Ch'ung	李充
Lan-ling hsiao-hsiao sheng	蘭陵笑笑生	Li Erh	李耳
		Li Fang	李昉
Lan-t'ien	藍田	Li Fang-kuei (Shih-san)	李芳桂 (十三)
Lang-hsien (Hsi Lang-hsien)	浪仙	Li Fei-kan	李芾甘
Lao She	老舍	Li Fu-jen	李夫人
Lao Ts'an	老殘	Li Fu-yen	李復言
Lao Tzu	老子	Li Hai-kuan	李海觀
Latter (Hou) Chou	後周	Li Ho	李賀
Le	黎	Li Hsiang	李翔
Le Moulin Poetry Club (see Feng-ch'e shih-she)		Li Hsiang-chün	李香君
		Li Hsiang-nien	李祥年
		Li Hsiao-kuang	李孝光
Le Thanh Tong	黎聖宗	Li Hsien-min	李獻民
Lei Feng	雷峰	Li Hsing-tao	李行道
Lei Heng	雷橫	Li Hua	李華
Leng	冷	Li Hui	李彙
Leng Yü-ping	冷于冰	Li Hung	李弘

Li Hung-chang	李鴻章
Li Ju-chen	李汝珍
Li Jui	李銳
Li K'ai-hsien	李開先
Li K'ang-ch'eng	李康成
Li Kuang	李廣
Li Kuang-t'ien	李廣田
Li K'uang	力匡
Li Kuei-chieh	李桂姐
Li K'uei	李逵
Li Kung-lin	李公麟
Li Kung-tso	李公佐
Li Lin-fu	李林甫
Li Ling	李陵
Li Liu-fang	李流芳
Li Mei-yung	李每勇
Li Meng-yang	李夢陽
Li Min-yung	李敏勇
Li O	厲鶚
Li Pai-ch'uan	李百川
Li Pai-yao	李百藥
Li P'an-lung	李攀龍
Li Pao-chia	李寶嘉
Li P'eng	李彭
Li P'in	李頻
Li P'ing-erh	李瓶兒
Li Po	李白
Li Po-yüan	李伯元
Li San-niang	李三娘
Li Shan (commentator)	李善
Li Shan (mountain)	驪山
Li Shang	酈商
Li Shang-yin	李商隱
Li Shen	李紳
Li-shih (character in later classical tale)	李氏
Li Shih (663–711)	李適
Li Shih-min	李世民
Li shih-she	笠詩社
Li Shu	林紓
Li Shu-t'ung	李叔同
Li Tao-ch'ien	李道謙
Li Tao-ch'un	李道純
Li T'ao	李燾
Li Te-yü	李德裕
Li T'ieh-mei	李鐵梅
Li T'ing	李庭
Li T'o	李陀
Li Tse-hou	李澤厚
Li Ts'un-pao	李存葆
Li-tsung	理宗
Li Tuan	李端
Li Tung-yang	李東陽
Li Tzu-ch'eng	李自成
Li Wa	李娃
Li Wen	李雯
Li Yen (character in *ch'uan-ch'i*)	李弇
Li Yen (150–177)	酈炎
Li Yen-nien	李延年
Li Yi[1]	李乂
Li Yi[2]	李益
Li Yi-chi	酈食其
Li Yü (937–978)	李煜
Li Yü (1591–1671?)	李玉
Li Yü (Li-weng) (1611–1680)	李漁 (笠翁)
Li Yü-ho	李玉和
Liang (state)	梁
Liang Ah-fa	梁阿發
Liang Ch'en-yü	梁辰魚
Liang Ch'i-ch'ao	梁啓超
Liang P'ei-lan	梁佩蘭
Liang-shan	梁山
Liang Shan-po	梁山伯
Liang Shih-ch'iu	梁實秋
Liang Te-sheng	梁德生
Liang Tsung-tai	梁宗岱
Liang Yi-su	梁夷素
Liang Yu-yü	梁有譽
Liao (Khitan)	遼
Liao Hui-ying	廖輝英
Liao-ning jen-min yi-shu chü-yüan	遼寧人民藝術劇院
Liao Yen	廖燕
Liaotung	遼東
Lien-chou	連州
Lien-hsiang	蓮香
Lien-ku	連姑
Lien Pu	廉布
Lin-chi Yi-hsüan	臨濟義玄
Lin Chih-ch'eng	林志成

Lin Chih-yang	林之洋
Lin-ch'uan	臨川
Lin Ch'uan-chia	林傳甲
Lin Ch'ung	林沖
Lin Hai-yin	林海音
Lin Heng-t'ai	林亨泰
Lin Huai-min	林懷民
Lin Hung	林鴻
Lin Keng	林庚
Lin Ling	林泠
Lin Mo-han	林默涵
Lin Pai	林白
Lin Piao	林彪
Lin Pu	林逋
Lin Shih-mao	林時茂
Lin Shu	林紓
Lin Shuang-pu	林雙不
Lin Tai-yü	林黛玉
Lin Tse-hsü	林則徐
Lin Wei-fu	林偉夫
Lin Yao-te	林燿德
Lin Yi-liang	林以亮
Lin Yü-t'ang	林語堂
Ling, Emperor of Han	漢靈帝
Ling Chih-lung	凌稚隆
Ling Hsing-te	凌性德
Ling-hsiu	靈秀
Ling Hsüan	伶玄
Ling-hu Chang	令狐彰
Ling-hu Ch'u	令狐楚
Ling-hui	靈暉
Ling Meng-ch'u	凌濛初
Ling-nan	嶺南
Ling-pao	靈寶
Ling-shu	靈舒
Ling Shu-hua	凌叔華
Ling-yüan	靈淵
Liu	劉
Liu, Ms.	劉
Liu An	劉安
Liu Chang	劉璋
Liu Chang-ch'ing	劉長卿
Liu-ch'ao	六朝
Liu Chen	劉楨
Liu Chen-sheng	劉振聲
Liu Ch'en-weng	劉辰翁

Liu Ch'eng	劉承
Liu Chi	劉基
Liu Chih-chi	劉知幾
Liu Chih-hsüan	劉志玄
Liu Chih-yüan	劉知遠
Liu Chin-erh	劉金兒
Liu Ching-t'ing	柳敬停
Liu-chou	柳州
Liu Ch'u-hsüan	劉處玄
Liu Ch'ung-yüan	劉崇遠
Liu E	劉鶚
Liu Fang-wen	劉芳紋
Liu Feng-hsien	劉鳳仙
Liu Fu (Liu Pan-nung)	劉復
Liu Fu (late eleventh-century scholar)	劉斧
Liu Ho	柳和
Liu Hsi (author of *Shih-ming*, c. 200 C.E.)	劉熙
Liu Hsi (student in wooden-fish song)	劉錫
Liu Hsiang	劉向
Liu Hsieh	劉勰
Liu Hsien	劉憲
Liu Hsin	劉歆
Liu Hsin-wu	劉心武
Liu Ju-shih	柳如是
Liu Ju-yi	劉如意
Liu K'o-chuang	劉克莊
Liu K'o-hsiang	劉克襄
Liu K'uei-pi	劉奎璧
Liu K'un	劉琨
Liu Kuo	劉過
Liu lao-lao	劉姥姥
Liu Ling-hsien	劉令嫻
Liu Meng-mei	柳夢梅
Liu O	劉鶚
Liu Pan-nung	劉半農
Liu Pang	劉邦
Liu Pao-ch'üan	劉寶全
Liu Pei	劉備
Liu Piao	劉表
Liu Pin-yen	劉賓雁
Liu Ping-chung	劉秉忠
Liu P'o-hsi	劉婆惜
Liu Sa-ho ho-shang	劉薩訶和尙

Liu San-chieh 劉三姐
Liu Shao-ch'i 劉少奇
Liu Shen-hsü 劉昚虛
Liu Shih (Ju-shih) 柳是 (如是)
Liu Shih-chung 劉時中
Liu So-la 劉索拉
Liu Su (*fl.* 740) 劉餗
Liu Su (*fl.* 807) 劉肅
Liu Sung 劉宋
Liu Ta-k'uei 劉大櫆
Liu Ta-pin 劉大彬
Liu Te 劉德
Liu Tsai-fu 劉再復
Liu Ts'ao 劉操
Liu Tsung-yüan 柳宗元
Liu Tui 劉兌
Liu Tung-shan 劉東山
Liu Wen-lung 劉文龍
Liu Wu 劉武
Liu Wu-shuang 劉無雙
Liu Ya-tzu 柳亞子
Liu Yeh-ch'iu 劉葉秋
Liu Yen 劉晏
Liu Yi 劉毅
Liu Yi-ch'ang 劉以鬯
Liu Yi-ch'ing 劉義慶
Liu Yin 劉因
Liu Yü (1257–1308) 劉玉
Liu Yü (d. 422) 劉裕
Liu Yü-hsi 劉禹錫
Liu Yüan-ting 劉元鼎
Liu Yün 劉筠
Liu Yün-jo 劉韻若
Liu Yung 柳永
Lo Ch'ing 羅青
Lo Fu 洛夫
Lo Jui-ch'ing 羅瑞卿
Lo Jung-huan 羅榮桓
Lo Kuan-chung 羅貫中
Lo Ma 羅馬
Lo Mao-teng 羅懋登
Lo Pin-wang 駱賓王
Lo Sung-ch'uang 羅松窗
Lo-yang 洛陽
Lo Yeh 羅燁
Lo Yin 羅隱
Lou 婁
Lou Kuan 樓觀
Lou-tung 婁東
Loyang 洛陽
Lo-yi 洛邑
Lu (state and school of *Shih-ching* interpretation) 魯
Lu (young man in "Record of the World within a Pillow") 盧
Lu, Duke of 魯公
Lu, Mount (Lu-shan) 廬山
Lu Chao-lin 盧照鄰
Lu Chi 陸機
Lu-chiang 廬江
Lu Chih (1234–1300) 盧摯
Lu Chih (754–805) 陸贄
Lu Chih-p'ing 陸治平
Lu Chih-shen 魯智深
Lu Ching-jo 陸鏡若
Lu Ch'ui 陸倕
Lu Chün-yi 盧俊義
Lu Heng 盧恆
Lu Hsiu-ching 陸修靜
Lu Hsün 魯迅
Lu Hung 盧鴻
Lu Jen-lung 陸人龍
Lu Kao 陸杲
Lu Kuei-meng 陸龜蒙
Lu-ling 廬陵
Lu Lun 盧綸
Lu Ma 魯媽
Lu-shan 廬山
Lu Shu-sheng 陸樹聲
Lu Ssu-feng 魯四鳳
Lu Ta (Lu Chih-shen) 魯達 (魯智深)
Lu Ta-hai 魯大海
Lu Te-ming 陸德明
Lu Ts'ai 陸采
Lu Ts'an 陸粲
Lu Ts'ang-yung 盧藏用
Lu Wan 盧綰
Lu Wei-luan 盧瑋鑾
Lu Yen-chih 陸延枝

Lu Yen-chou 魯彥周
Lu-yi 鹿邑
Lu Yi-shih 路易士
Lu Yu 陸游
Lu Yün 陸雲
Lü (Tung-pin) 呂 (洞賓)
Lü An 呂安
Lü Ho-jo 呂赫若
Lü-hou 呂后
Lü Hsiung 呂熊
Lü Pen-chung 呂本中
Lü Pu-wei 呂不韋
Lü Shang 呂尚
Lü Ssu-mien 呂思勉
Lü T'ien-ch'eng 呂天成
Lü Tung-pin 呂洞賓
Lü Yen 呂巖
Lung-hsing 隆興
Lung-hu 龍虎
Lung-men 龍門
Lung-shuo 龍朔
Lung-tsu shih-she 龍族詩社
Lung Ying-tsung 龍瑛宗
Ly 李
Ly Te Xuyen 李濟川
Ly Van Phuc 李文馥
Ma Chien 馬建
Ma Chih-yüan 馬致遠
Ma Ch'un-shang 馬純上
Ma Chün-wu 馬君武
Ma Hsüeh-liang 馬學良
Ma Ju-fei 馬如飛
Ma Jung 馬融
Ma-la-ch'in-fu 馬拉沁夫
Ma Lang 馬朗
Ma-ming 馬鳴
Ma Sen 馬森
Ma Shih-ying 馬士英
Ma Tai 馬戴
Ma Tsu-ch'ang 馬祖常
Ma-tsu Tao-yi 馬祖道一
Ma-wang-tui 馬王堆
Ma-wei 馬嵬
Ma Yao-woon 馬幼垣
Ma Yü 馬鈺
Ma Yüan (b. 1953) 馬原
Ma Yüan (14 B.C.E.–49 C.E.) 馬援
Makita Tairyō 牧田諦亮
Man 蠻
Man-chou 滿洲
Mang, Mount 邙山
Mang K'o 芒克
Mao Ch'ang 毛萇
Mao Chin 毛晉
Mao Heng 毛亨
Mao Hsiang 毛襄
Mao Hsien-shu 毛先舒
Mao K'un 茅坤
Mao Lun 毛綸
Mao School 毛傳
Mao shan 茅山
Mao Tse-tung 毛澤東
Mao Tsung-kang 毛宗崗
Mao Tun 茅盾
Mao Yen-shou 毛延壽
Matsuo Bashō 松尾芭蕉
May Fourth movement (Wu-ssu yün-tung) 五四運動
Mei Ch'eng/Sheng 枚乘
Mei Kao 枚皋
Mei Lan-fang 梅蘭芳
Mei-nung 美濃
Mei Sheng/Ch'eng 枚乘
Mei Ting-tso 梅鼎祚
Mei Tse 梅賾
Mei Ts'un 梅村
Mei Tzu-yü 梅子玉
Mei Yao-ch'en 梅堯臣
Mei Ying-tso 梅膺作
Mencius (Meng Tzu) 孟子
Meng 蒙
Meng (actor) 優孟
Meng Ch'eng-shun 孟稱舜
Meng Chiang-nü 孟姜女
Meng Chiao 孟郊
Meng Chu 孟珠
Meng Hao-jan 孟浩然
Meng Hsien-chung 孟獻忠
Meng Hsü 孟昶
Meng Huo 孟獲
Meng K'o 孟軻

Meng Lang	孟浪
Meng-li	夢梨
Meng Li-chün	孟麗君
Meng Liang	孟良
Meng Shih-ching	孟蒔荊
Meng Tzu (Mencius)	孟子
Meng Yü-lou	孟玉樓
Meng Yüan-lao	孟元老
Mi Heng	禰衡
Mi-lo River	汨羅江
Miao	苗
Miao Shan-shih	苗善時
Miao-yü	妙玉
Min	閩
Min chung she	民衆社
Min-shan	岷山
Ming	明
Ming, Emperor of Wei	魏明帝
Ming-ti	明帝
Mo Ch'i-yen	莫起炎
Mo-chieh	摩詰
Mo Huai-ku	莫懷古
Mo-kao k'u	莫高窟
Mo-le	磨勒
Mo Ti	墨翟
Mo Tzu	墨子
Mo Yen	莫言
Mori Ōgai	森鷗外
Mou Tzu	牟子
Mu	穆
Mu, Duke of Ch'in	秦穆公
Mu-lan	木蘭
Mu-lien	目連
Mu-mu	木母
Mu Mu-t'ien	穆木天
Mu Shih-ying	穆時英
Mu Tan	穆旦
Mu T'ien-tzu	穆天子
Musō Soseki	夢窓疎石
Myŏng-jong	明宗
Na-hsi	納西
Na-lan Hsing-te	納蘭性德
Na-lan Mingju	納蘭明珠
Nagai Kafū	永井花風
Nagaya no Ōkimi	長屋王
Naksŏnjae	樂善齋
Nalan Singde	納蘭性德
Nam Viet	南越
Nam Yŏng-no	南永魯
Nan-ch'ang	南昌
Nan-chao	南詔
Nan-ch'ao	南朝
Nan-ching	南京
Nan Cho	南卓
Nan-hai	南海
Nan-hui	南匯
Nan kuo she	南國社
Nan-pei ch'ao	南北朝
Nan-pei-ti shih-she	南北笛詩社
Nan-she	南社
Nan T'ang	南唐
Nan-t'o	難陀
Nan-tsung	南宗
Nanking (Nan-ching)	南京
Natsume Sōseki	夏日漱石
Nguyen Du	阮攸
Nguyen Gia Thieu	阮嘉韶
Nguyen Huy Oanh	阮輝瑩
Nguyen Huy Tu	阮輝似
Nguyen Thuyen	阮詮
Nguyen Trai	阮廌
Ni Tsan	倪瓚
Nieh Jung-chen	聶榮臻
Nieh-mo-sheng (Kāśyapa-Mātaṅga)	攝摩勝
Nieh-nu pa-hsi	涅努巴西
Nieh Ying	聶嫈
Nien-ch'ang	念常
Nimmyō	仁明
Ning-hai	寧海
Ning Shih-ch'ang	寧師常
Nishida Korenori	西田維則
Niu Hsiu	鈕琇
Niu Seng-ju	牛僧孺
North and South Flute Poetry Club (see Nan-pei-ti shih-she)	
Northern (Pei) Sung	北宋
Nü Tsung	女宗
Nü-wa	女娃
Nü-wa/kua	女媧
O-mei-shan	峨眉山

O Se-jae	吳世才
Ōe no Masafusa	大江匡房
Ogyū Sorai	荻生徂徠
Oka Hakku	丘白駒
Okajima Kanzan	岡島冠山
Ōmura Masuo	大村益夫
Ōnin	應仁
Ono Minemori	小野岑守
Ou Wai-ou	鷗外鷗
Ou-yang Chiang-ho	歐陽江河
Ou-yang Chiung	歐陽炯
Ou-yang Ho	歐陽紇
Ou-yang Hsiu	歐陽修
Ou-yang Hsün	歐陽詢
Ou-yang Tzu	歐陽子
Ou-yang Yü-ch'ien	歐陽予倩
Pa Chin	巴金
Pa-ta shan-jen	八大山人
Paekche	百濟
Pai Chieh	白潔
Pai Ch'iu	白萩
Pai Feng-hsi	白峰溪
Pai Hsien-yung	白先勇
Pai Hsiu-ying	白秀英
Pai Hua (b. 1956)	柏樺
Pai Hua (b. 1930)	白樺
Pai Niang-tzu	白娘子
Pai Pi	白賁
Pai P'u	白樸
Pai Wei	白薇
Pai Yü-ch'an	白玉蟾
Pai-yün Kuan	白雲觀
Pak Che-ga	朴齊家
Pak Ch'i-wŏn	朴趾源
Pak Il-lyang	朴寅亮
Pan Chao	班昭
Pan Chieh-yü (Lady Pan)	班婕妤
Pan Ku	班固
Pan Piao	班彪
P'an	潘
P'an Ch'iao-yün	潘巧雲
P'an Chih-heng	潘之恒
P'an Chin-lien	潘金蓮
P'an Jen-mu	潘人木
P'an-ku	盤古
P'an Lang	潘閬
P'an Ni	潘尼
P'an Yüeh	潘岳
P'ang Ch'un-mei	龐春梅
Pao-ch'ang	寶唱
Pao Chao	鮑照
Pao Cheng	包拯
Pao Ch'ing-t'ien	包清天
Pao-hsien	保暹
Pao Hsüan	鮑宣
Pao Kung	包公
Pao Ling-hui	鮑令暉
Pao Su	鮑蘇
Pao T'ien-hsiao	包天笑
Pao T'ing-hsi	鮑廷璽
Pao-yü (Chia Pao-yü)	寶玉 (賈寶玉)
Pei-ching (Peking, Beijing)	北京
Pei-ching ching-chü t'uan	北京京劇團
Pei-ching jen-min yi-shu chü-yüan	北京人民藝術劇院
Pei Chou	北周
Pei Tao	北島
Pei Tao (Chao Chen-k'ai)	北島 (趙振開)
P'ei	沛
P'ei, Prince	沛王
P'ei Hsing	裴鉶
P'ei Kuei	裴珪
P'ei Sung-chih	裴松之
P'ei Ti	裴迪
P'ei Tzu-yeh	裴子野
Peking (Pei-ching, Beijing)	北京
Pen-chüeh	本覺
P'eng-ch'eng	彭城
P'eng Ko	彭歌
P'eng-lai	蓬萊
P'eng Shih-tu	彭師度
P'eng Sun-yü	彭孫遹
P'eng Ting-ch'iu	彭定求
P'eng Yüeh	彭越
Phan Huy Ich	潘輝益
Pi (battle)	邲
Pi-ho-kuan chu-jen	碧荷館主人

Pi-she-hu	甓社湖
Pi Shu-min	畢淑敏
P'i-chih fo-hsien	辟支佛現
P'i Hsi-jui	皮錫瑞
P'i Jih-hsiu	皮日休
Pieh-ling	鼈靈
Pieh-shih	別士
Pien-chi	辯機
Pien Chih-lin	卞之琳
Pien Kung	邊貢
Pien Shao	邊韶
Pin-chou	邠州
Ping Hsin	冰心
P'ing	平
P'ing, King	平王
P'ing-ch'üan	平泉
P'ing-yang	平陽
Po Chü-yi	白居易
Po Hsing-chien	白行簡
Po P'i	伯嚭
Po Yang	柏楊
Po-yang	波陽
Po-yi	伯夷
P'o-fu	潑婦
Pu-hu-mu	不忽木
Pu-k'ung	不空
Pu-po	布伯
Pu-yi	布依
P'u-chiang Chekiang	浦江, 浙江
P'u-ching	普淨
P'u-chou	蒲州
P'u Po-ying	蒲伯英
P'u Sung-ling	蒲松齡
P'u-t'ao-yüan shih-she	葡萄園詩社
Qubilai Qan (Hu-pi-lieh Han)	忽必烈汗
Rikunyo	六如
Ro Kyŏng	盧兢
Ryuri	琉璃
Sa-ni	撒尼
Sa-tu-la (Sadula)	薩都剌 / 拉
Saeki Tomi	佐伯富
Saga	嵯峨
Sai Chin-hua	賽金花
San chia Shih	三家詩
San-hsia	三峽
San-kuo	三國
San Mao	三毛
Santō Kyōden	山東京伝
Sasagawa Rinpū (Tanerō)	笹川臨風 (種郎)
Sasagawa Taneo	笹川種郎
School of Nine Leaves (see Chiu-yeh p'ai)	
Seida Tansō	清田儋叟
Seng-chao	僧肇
Seng-ts'an	僧璨
Seng-yu	僧祐
Sesson Yūbai	雪村友梅
Sha Yeh-hsin	沙葉新
Shan	山
Shan T'ao	山濤
Shan-yang	山陽
Shan-yin	山陰
Shang	商
Shang Ch'in	商禽
Shang-ch'ing	上清
Shang-hai chü-tso-chia hsieh-hui	上海劇作家協會
Shang-hai hsi-chü lien-yi-hui	上海戲劇聯誼會
Shang-hai hsi-jen yeh-yü chü-t'uan	上海西人業餘劇團
Shang-kuan Wan-erh	上官婉兒
Shang-kuan Yi	上官儀
Shanghai	上海
Shantung	崠 = 山東
Shao-hao	少昊
Shao-hsing	紹興
Shao Hsün-mei	邵洵美
Shao Nan	召南
Shao Pao	邵寶
Shao Pin-ju (Shao Chi-t'ang)	邵彬儒 (邵紀棠)
Shao Po-wen	邵伯溫
Shao Yen-hsiang	邵燕祥
Shao Yung	邵雍
Shen Chi-chi	沈既濟
Shen Ch'i-feng	沈起鳳
Shen Ch'ien	沈謙
Shen Ching	沈璟
Shen Ch'iung-chih	沈瓊芝

Shen Chou 沈周
Shen Chu-hung 沈袾宏
Shen Ch'üan-ch'i 沈佺期
Shen Fu 沈復
Shen Han-kuang 申涵光
Shen Hsi-meng 沈西蒙
Shen-hsiao 神霄
Shen Jung 諶容
Shen Kua 沈括
Shen Man-yüan 沈滿願
Shen Nung 神農
Shen P'ei 申培
Shen T'ai 沈泰
Shen Te-ch'ien 沈德潛
Shen Te-fu 沈德符
Shen-tsung 神宗
Shen Ts'ung-wen 沈從文
Shen Ya-chih 沈亞之
Shen Yen-ping 沈雁冰
Shen Yin-mo 沈尹默
Shen Yüeh 沈約
Shenyang 瀋陽
Shiba Shirō 柴四郎
Shih Che-ts'un 施蟄存
Shih-ch'eng 石城
Shih Ch'eng-chin 石成金
Shih Chieh 石介
Shih-chien 石澗
Shih Chien-wu 施肩吾
Shih Chih 食指
Shih-ch'uan shan 石船山
Shih Chün-pao 石君寶
Shih Ch'ung 石崇
Shih En 施恩
Shih Hsiang-yün 史湘雲
Shih Hsüeh-sheng 施學生
Shih Jun-chang 施閏章
Shih K'o-fa 史可法
Shih Nai-an 施耐庵
Shih-ning 始寧
Shih-san Mei 十三妹
Shih Shu-ch'ing 施淑青
Shih Ta-tsu 史達祖
Shih T'ai 石泰
Shih-t'ao (Tao-chi) 石濤 (道濟)
Shih T'ieh-sheng 史鐵生
Shih-tsung 世宗
Shih Tzu 世子
Shih Yang 施洋
Shih Yen-nien 石延年
Shina 支那
Shingon 眞言
Shu 蜀
Shu-ch'i 叔齊
Shu Ch'ing-ch'un 舒慶春
Shu-Han 蜀漢
Shu Kuang 疏廣
Shu Shou 疏受
Shu T'ing 舒婷
Shuang Chien 雙漸
Shui-hu-ti 睡虎地
Shui Ping-hsin 水冰心
Shui Yin-p'ing 水蔭萍
Shun 舜
Shun-chih 順治
Shun-p'ing Hou 順平侯
Shun-ti 順帝
Shun-tsung 順宗
Sian (Hsi-an) 西安
Silla 新羅
Sin Kwang-su 申光洙
Sinkiang (Hsin-chiang) 新疆
Six Dynasties (Liu-ch'ao) 六朝
So 索
Sŏ Kŏ-jŏng 徐居正
Song Yü 宋玉
Sŏnggyun'gwan 成均館
Sŏngjin 性眞
Soochow (Su-chou) 蘇州
Southern (Nan) Han 南漢
Southern (Nan) Sung 南宋
Southern (Nan) T'ang 南唐
Ssu-ch'uan (Szechwan) 四川
Ssu-k'ung T'u 司空圖
Ssu-ma Chao 司馬昭
Ssu-ma Chen 司馬眞
Ssu-ma Ch'eng-chen 司馬承禎
Ssu-ma Ch'ien 司馬遷
Ssu-ma Hsi 司馬喜
Ssu-ma Hsiang-ju 司馬相如
Ssu-ma Kuang 司馬光
Ssu-ma Lun 司馬倫
Ssu-ma Piao 司馬彪
Ssu-ma T'an 司馬談

Ssu-ma Yen	司馬炎
Ssu-ma Yi	司馬懿
Su	蘇
Su Ch’e	蘇轍
Su Ch’ing	蘇卿
Su-chou (Soochow)	蘇州
Su Hsiao[-hsiao]	蘇小[小]
Su Hsiao-ch’ing	蘇小青
Su Hsün	蘇洵
Su Man-shu	蘇曼殊
Su-men ssu hsüeh-shih (“Four Scholars of Mr. Su’s Gate”)	蘇門四學士
Su Nü	素女
Su-o	素娥
Su San-lao	蘇三老
Su Shih	蘇軾
Su Shu-yang	蘇叔陽
Su Shun-ch’in	蘇舜欽
Su T’ing	蘇頲
Su-tsung	肅宗
Su Tung-p’o	蘇東坡
Su T’ung	蘇童
Su Wei-chen	蘇偉貞
Su Wu	蘇武
Su Ying-hsüeh	蘇映雪
Su Yü-ch’un	蘇育春
Sugawara no Michizane	菅原道眞
Sui	隋
Sui Ching-ch’en	睢景臣
Sui Shu-sen	隋樹森
Sui-yüan	隨園
Sui-yüan hsia-shih	隋緣下士
Sun, William Hui-chu (Sun Hui-chu)	孫惠柱
Sun Ch’ang-wu	孫昌武
Sun Ch’i	孫棨
Sun Ch’o	孫綽
Sun Chu	孫洙
Sun Ch’üan	孫權
Sun Ch’ung	孫崇
Sun Fei-hu	孫飛虎
Sun Hsüeh-o	孫雪娥
Sun Hui-chu (William Sun)	孫惠柱
Sun Kan-lu	孫甘露
Sun Liao-hung	孫了紅
Sun Pu-erh	孫不二
Sun-shu Ao	孫叔敖
Sun Shu-yü	孫述宇
Sun Tzu	孫子
Sun Tzu-ch’u	孫子楚
Sun Wu-k’ung	孫悟空
Sun Yat-sen	孫逸仙
Sung	宋
Sung, Madame	宋
Sung Cheng-yü	宋征輿
Sung Ch’i	宋祁
Sung Chiang	宋江
Sung-chiang	松江
Sung Chih-wen	宋之問
Sung-Chin	宋金
Sung Chiung	宋褧
Sung Ch’un-fang	宋春舫
Sung Hui-lien	宋蕙蓮
Sung Lien	宋濂
Sung Lo	宋犖
Sung Mao-ch’eng	宋楙 (懋) 澄
Sung Pen	宋本
Sung Te-fang	宋德方
Sung Ting-po	宋定伯
Sung Tse-lai	宋澤萊
Sung Wan	宋琬
Sung Wu	宋無
Sung-yang	松陽
Sung Yü	宋玉
Sung Yüan	宋遠
Sung-Yüan	宋元
Sung Yün	宋雲
Szechwan (Ssu-ch’uan)	四川
Ta Chi	妲己
Ta-chung chü-she	大衆劇社
Ta fang	大方
Ta-kuan	大觀
Ta-kuan yüan	大觀園
Ta-li (kingdom)	大理
Ta-li (reign period)	大曆
Ta-te	大德
Ta-tu	大都
Ta-t’ung	大同
Ta Wa-wu shan	大瓦屋山
Ta-yao	大姚
Tai	傣
Tai Chin	戴進

Tai Hou-ying	戴厚英
Tai Shu-lun	戴叔倫
Tai Te	戴德
Tai T'ien	戴天
Tai-tsung	代宗
Tai Wang-shu	戴望舒
T'ai-ch'ing	太清
T'ai-ch'ing Kung	太清宮
T'ai-chou	泰州
T'ai-hang	太行
T'ai-k'ang	太康
T'ai-kung Wang	太公望
T'ai-p'ing t'ien-kuo	太平天國
T'ai-po (style of Li Po)	太白
T'ai-po (temple)	泰伯
T'ai-po (of Wu)	太伯
T'ai shan	泰山
T'ai-shang Lao-chün	太上老君
T'ai-sui	太歲
T'ai-ts'ang	太倉
T'ai-tsu, Emperor of the Sung	宋太祖
T'ai-tsung, Emperor of the Sung	宋太宗
T'ai-tsung, Emperor of T'ang	唐太宗
Taika Reform	大化改新
Taiyuan (T'ai-yüan)	太原
Takizawa Bakin	滝沢馬琴
Tan-yang	丹陽
Tan Ying	淡瑩
T'an Ch'u-tuan	譚處端
T'an K'ai	談愷
T'an-luan	曇鸞
T'an Shao-wen	譚紹聞
T'an Ssu-t'ung	譚嗣同
T'an Yüan-ch'un	譚元春
T'ang (state and dynasty)	唐
T'ang Ch'i	唐祈
T'ang Hsien-tsu	湯顯祖
T'ang Lin	唐臨
T'ang Po-hu	唐伯虎
T'ang Sai-erh	唐賽兒
T'ang Shih	湯式
T'ang Shun-chih	唐順之
T'ang-Sung pa ta chia	唐宋八大家

T'ang Yin	唐寅
T'ang Ying	唐英
Tao-an	道安
Tao-chia	道家
Tao-chiao	道教
Tao-hsin	道信
Tao-hsüan	道宣
Tao-shih	道世
Tao-tan	騷壇
Tao-yen	道衍
Tao-yüan	道原
T'ao Chen-huai	陶貞懷
T'ao Ch'ien (Yüan-ming)	陶潛 (淵明)
T'ao Fu	陶輔
T'ao Han	陶翰
T'ao Hsüeh-liang	陶學良
T'ao-hua yüan	桃花源
T'ao Hung-ching	陶弘景
T'ao Tsung-yi	陶宗儀
T'ao-yeh	桃葉
T'ao Yüan-ming (T'ao Ch'ien)	陶淵明 (陶潛)
Tay, William (Cheng Shu-sen)	鄭樹森
Te-hung	德洪
Te-tsung	德宗
Teng Ch'un	鄧椿
Teng Hsiao-p'ing	鄧小平
Teng T'ing-chen	鄧廷楨
Teng T'o	鄧拓
Teng Tzu-chin	鄧子晉
Teng Wen-yüan	鄧文原
Teng Yü-pin	鄧玉賓
Terakado Seiken	寺門靜軒
Ti Ch'ing	狄青
Ti Hsi-ch'en	狄希陳
Ti K'u	帝嚳
Ti-wu-tz'u ch'üan-kuo tai-piao ta-hui	第五次全國代表大會
T'ieh Chung-yü	鐵中玉
T'ieh-ya/yai	鐵崖
T'ien-an-men	天安門
T'ien-ch'ang	天長
T'ien Ch'eng-ssu	田承嗣
T'ien-ch'i	天啓
T'ien-chin (Tientsin)	天津

T’ien Han 田漢
T’ien Hsi 田錫
T’ien-hsin 天心
T’ien Hu 田虎
T’ien Ju-ch’eng 田汝成
T’ien-pao 天寶
T’ien-shih 天師
T’ien-shih tao 天師道
T’ien-t’ai 天台
T’ien Tan (3rd c. B.C.E. petty official of Ch’i) 田單
T’ien Tan (3rd c. B.C.E. sovereign of Ch’i) 田儋
T’ien Tzu-lin 田子琳
T’ien Ya-mei 田亞梅
T’ien Yang 田仰
Tientsin (T’ien-chin) 天津
Ting Hsien-hsien 丁仙現
Ting Ling 丁玲
Ting P’eng 丁澎
Ting Yao-k’ang 丁耀亢
T’ing-chi 廷紀
To-hsi 多西
To-mu kuai 多目怪
To To 多多
T’o-pa 拓跋
Tou O 竇娥
Tou T’ien-chang 竇天章
Tran 陳
Tran Te Xuong 陳濟昌
“Tranquil Gentleman” (Ho-ching Hsien-sheng) 和靖先生
Trinh 鄭
Ts’ai Ch’en 蔡沈
Ts’ai Chih-yi 蔡志頤
Ts’ai Ching 蔡京
Ts’ai Ch’iu-t’ung 蔡秋桐
Ts’ai Sung-nien 蔡松年
Ts’ai T’ao 蔡絛
Ts’ai Yen 蔡琰
Ts’ai Yü 蔡羽
Ts’ai Yüan-fang 蔡元放
Ts’ai Yüan-p’ei 蔡元培
Ts’ai Yung 蔡邕
Ts’ai Yung (Po-chieh) 蔡邕 (伯喈)
Tsan-ning 贊寧
Ts’an Hsüeh 殘雪
Tsang K’o-chia 臧克家
Tsang Mao-hsün 藏懋循
Ts’ao (state) 曹
Ts’ao Chan (Ts’ao Hsüeh-ch’in) 曹霑 (曹雪芹)
Ts’ao Chih 曹植
Ts’ao Erh-k’an 曹爾堪
Ts’ao Fang 曹芳
Ts’ao Hsien 曹憲
Ts’ao Hsüeh-ch’in 曹雪芹
Ts’ao Jui 曹叡
Ts’ao Mao 曹髦
Ts’ao P’i (Wen Ti, Emperor of the Wei) 曹丕 (魏文帝)
Ts’ao Piao 曹彪
Ts’ao Shuang 曹爽
Ts’ao T’ang-ts’un 曹棠村
Ts’ao Ts’ao 曹操
Ts’ao Yeh 曹鄴
Ts’ao Yin 曹寅
Ts’ao Yü 曹禺
Ts’en Shen 岑參
Tseng Chi 曾幾
Tseng Ch’i 曾棨
Tseng Ch’ing-ying 曾慶瑛
Tseng Hsiao-hsü 曾孝序
Tseng Jui 曾瑞
Tseng Kung 曾鞏
Tseng Kuo-fan 曾國藩
Tseng P’u 曾樸
Tseng Shen 曾參
Tseng-t’ou-shih 曾頭市
Tseng Ts’ao 曾慥
Tseng Tzu 曾子
Tseng Yen-tung 曾衍東
Tsinan (Chi-nan) 濟南
Tso Ch’iu-ming 左丘明
Tso Fen 左芬
Tso Ssu 左思
Tso Tsung-t’ang 左宗棠
Tso Tz’u 左慈
Tsou, Mr. 鄒氏
Tsou Chih-mo 鄒祗謨
Tsou Yang 鄒陽

Tsou Yen 鄒衍
Tsu-hsiu 祖琇
Tsubouchi Shōyō 坪內逍遙
Tsuga Teishō 都賀庭鐘
Ts'ui (young man) 崔
Ts'ui, Madame 崔
Ts'ui Chien 崔健
Ts'ui Chiu-wan 崔九萬
Ts'ui Chü 崔莒
Ts'ui Chuan 崔篆
Ts'ui Hao 崔顥
Ts'ui Hsien 崔銑
Ts'ui Jung 崔融
Ts'ui Kuo-fu 崔國輔
Ts'ui Pao 崔豹
Ts'ui Po-yi (Kung-tu) 崔伯易 (公度)
Ts'ui Shih 崔湜
Ts'ui Shu 崔述
Ts'ui Te-chih 崔德志
Ts'ui Ying-ying 崔鶯鶯
Tsukamoto Zenryū 塚本善隆
Tsung Ch'en 宗臣
Tsung-chien 宗鑑
Tsung Fu-hsien 宗福先
Tsung-li ya-men 總理衙門
Tsung-mi 宗密
Tsung-ping 宗炳
Tsung P'u 宗璞
Ts'ung Shen 叢深
Ts'ung Wei-hsi 從維熙
Tu Ch'in-yen 杜琴言
Tu Ch'üeh 杜確
Tu Duc 嗣德
Tu Erh-wei 杜而未
Tu Fu 杜甫
Tu Hai 徐海
Tu Heng 杜衡
Tu Hsün-ho 杜荀鶴
Tu Jen-chieh 杜仁傑
Tu Kang 杜綱
Tu Kuang-t'ing 杜光庭
Tu Kuo-ch'ing 杜國清
Tu Li-niang 杜麗娘
Tu Ma-ma 杜媽媽
Tu Mu 杜牧
Tu Shao-ch'ing 杜少卿
Tu Shen-yen 杜審言
Tu Te-k'ang 杜德康
Tu Wei 杜韋
Tu Yeh 渡也
Tu Yü 杜預
Tu Yün-hsieh 杜運燮
T'u 土
T'u-an Ku 屠岸賈
T'u-chia 土家
T'u Lung 屠隆
T'u-mu (battle of) 土木
T'u-mu (Earth Mother) 土母
Tuan Ch'eng-shih 段成式
Tuan Chih-chien 段志堅
Tun-huang 敦煌
Tung-ch'ang 東昌
Tung Ch'i-ch'ang 董其昌
Tung Chieh-yüan 董解元
Tung Chin 東晉
Tung Cho 董卓
Tung Chung-shu 董仲舒
Tung-fang Shuo 東方朔
Tung-hai 東海
Tung-hai chüeh-wo 東海覺我
Tung Hsün 董恂
Tung Hu 董狐
Tung-hua ti-chün 東華帝君
Tung-lu Ku-k'uang sheng 東魯古狂生
Tung-men 東門
Tung-ming 東明
Tung Pai (Hsiao-wan) 董白 (小宛)
Tung-p'ing 東平
Tung-shan Liang-chieh 洞山良价
Tung Shao-nan 董邵南
Tung-wu 東武
Tung Wu ta-hsüeh 東吳大學
Tung Yüeh 董說
Tung Yung 董永
T'ung 侗
T'ung Chi-chieh 童寄姐
T'ung-meng hui 同盟會
T'ung Shu-yeh 童書業
T'ung wen kuan 同文館
T'ung Ya-nan 童亞男
Tzu-chüan 紫鵑

Tzu-hsia	子夏
Tzu-kung	子貢
Tzu-ssu	子思
Tzu-yeh	子夜
Tz'u-hsi	慈禧
Ueda Akinari	上田秋成
Vuong Thuy Kieu (Wang Ts'ui-ch'iao)	王翠翹
Wa-la	瓦剌
Wa-wu-shan	瓦屋山
Wan-chu	玩珠
Wan-li	萬曆
Wan Shou-ch'i	萬壽祺
Wang	王
Wang An-shih	王安石
Wang An-yi	王安憶
Wang Ao	王鏊
Wang Ch'ang-ling	王昌齡
Wang Chao-chün	王昭君
Wang Chao-yün	王兆雲
Wang Che	王嚞
Wang Chen-ho	王禎和
Wang Chi	王績
Wang Chi-te	王驥德
Wang Ch'i-sun	王芑孫
Wang Chia	王嘉
Wang Chien	王建
Wang Chih	王直
Wang Chih-chin	王志瑾
Wang Ch'in-jo	王欽若
Wang Ching-hsien	王靖獻
Wang Ch'ing	王慶
Wang Chiu-ssu	王九思
Wang Chou	王宙
Wang Ch'u-yi	王處一
Wang-ch'uan	輞川
Wang Chung	汪中
Wang Chung-min	王重民
Wang Ch'ung	王充
Wang Fan-chih	王梵志
Wang Feng-tsao	汪鳳藻
Wang Fu (4th c. C.E.)	王浮
Wang Fu (8th or 9th c. C.E.)	王敷
Wang Fu-chih	王夫之
Wang Ho-ch'ing	王和卿
Wang Hsi-feng	王熙鳳
Wang Hsiang-hsü	汪象旭
Wang Hsien	王械
Wang Hsien-chih	王獻之
Wang Hsien-k'o	王仙客
Wang Hsing	王行
Wang Hsüan	汪宣
Wang Jo-wang	王若望
Wang Jun-hua	王潤華
Wang Jung	王融
Wang K'ai-yün	王闓運
Wang K'ang-chü	王康琚
Wang Kŏ-in	王巨仁
Wang Kuo-wei	王國維
Wang Ling	王陵
Wang Liu-erh	王六兒
Wang Mang	王莽
Wang Meng	王蒙
Wang Meng-lin	王夢麟
Wang Mien	王冕
Wang Ming-ch'ing	王明清
Wang Pao	王褒
Wang P'eng-yün	王鵬運
Wang Pi	王弼
Wang Pi-chiang	汪辟疆
Wang P'ing	王蘋
Wang Po	王勃
Wang Po-ch'eng	王伯成
Wang Shao-t'ang	王少堂
Wang Shih	王適
Wang shih	王氏
Wang Shih-chen (1526–1590)	王世楨
Wang Shih-chen (1634–1711)	王士禛
Wang Shih-fu	王實甫
Wang Shih-lang	王詩琅
Wang Shih-lu	王士祿
Wang Shih-p'eng	王十朋
Wang Shih-wei	王實味
Wang Shou-jen (Yang-ming)	王守仁 (陽明)
Wang Shu-wen	王叔文
Wang Shu-yüan	王樹元
Wang Shuo	王朔
Wang Ssu-jen	王思任
Wang Tao-k'un	汪道崑

Wang T'ao	王韜
Wang Ting-pao	王定寶
Wang T'ing-hsiang	王廷相
Wang T'o	王拓
Wang Ts'an	王粲
Wang Tse	王則
Wang Tseng-ch'i	汪曾祺
Wang Ts'ui-ch'iao (Vuong Thuy Kieu)	王翠翹
Wang Tu	王度
Wang Tu-ch'ing	王獨清
Wang Tuan	汪端
Wang Tun	王敦
Wang T'ung	王通
Wang T'ung-kuei	王同軌
Wang Tzu-jen	王子仁
Wang-tzu yeh chih shih	王子夜之尸
Wang Wei	王維
Wang Wei (1323–1374)	王褘
Wang Wei-yi	王惟一
Wang Wen-hsing	王文興
Wang Yang-ming	王陽明
Wang Yen (b. 1113 C.E.)	王炎
Wang Yen (fl. c. 500 C.E.)	王琰
Wang Yen-shou	王延壽
Wang Yi	王逸
Wang Yi-chung	王頤中
Wang Yi-fang	王義方
Wang Yi-sun	王沂孫
Wang Ying	王英
Wang Ying-lin	王應麟
Wang Yu-yu	汪優游
Wang Yü-ch'eng	王禹偁
Wang Yü-hui	王玉輝
Wang Yüan-heng	王元亨
Wang Yüan-liang	汪元量
Wang Yüan-lu	王圓籙
Wang Yün (1236–1304)	王惲
Wang Yün (early Ch'ing)	王筠
Wei (kingdom)	魏
Wei (river)	渭
Wei (state)	衛
Wei, Empress	韋后
Wei, Madame	韋
Wei, Master	韋
Wei Ao	韋敖
Wei Cheng	魏徵
Wei Ch'eng	韋逞
Wei Chiang	魏絳
Wei Chih-yi	韋執誼
Wei Ch'ing	衛青
Wei Chuang	韋莊
Wei Chung-hsien	魏忠賢
Wei Chung-kung (Tuan-li)	魏仲恭 (端禮)
Wei-feng	維鳳
Wei Hsiu-jen	魏秀仁
Wei Hsün	韋絢
Wei Hu	韋縠
Wei Hua-ts'un	魏華存
Wei Hung	衛宏
Wei Kao	韋皋
Wei Ku	韋固
Wei Liang-fu	魏良輔
Wei Pao	魏豹
Wei River	渭河
Wei Ssu-li	韋嗣立
Wei Tzu-an	魏子安
Wei Yeh	魏野
Wei Yin	韋崟
Wei Ying-wu	韋應物
Wei Yüan	魏源
Wei Yüan-sung	衛元嵩
Wen	文
Wen, Duke	文公
Wen, Duke of Chin	晉文公
Wen, Emperor (of T'o-pa Wei)	文帝
Wen, Emperor of Sung	宋文帝
Wen, Emperor of Wei	魏文帝
Wen, King of Chou	周文王
Wen-chao	文兆
Wen Cheng-ming	文徵明
Wen Ch'iung	溫瓊
Wen-chou (Wenchow)	溫州
Wen Hsiao-ts'un	文曉村
Wen-hsüeh kuan	文學館
Wen-hsüeh yen-chiu hui	文學研究會
Wen K'ang	文康
Wen-lien	文聯
Wen Su-ch'en	文素臣
Wen-teng	文登

Wen-ti	文帝
Wen T'ien-hsiang	文天祥
Wen T'ing-shih	文廷式
Wen T'ing-yün	溫庭筠
Wen-ts'ui T'ang	文粹堂
Wen Wang	文王
Wen Yen-po	文彥博
Wen Yi-to	聞一多
Wen Ying	文瑩
Wenchow (Wen-chou)	溫州
Weng Chüan	翁卷
Weng Fang-kang	翁方綱
West Lake (Hsi-hu)	西湖
Wo Fo-shan jen	我佛山人
Wu (district; state)	吳
Wu, Emperor of Chin	晉武帝
Wu, Emperor of Han	漢武帝
Wu, Emperor of Liang	梁武帝
Wu, Empress	武后
Wu, Harry (Wu Hung-ta)	吳宏達
Wu Ch'ang-ling	吳昌齡
Wu Chao-ch'ien	吳兆騫
Wu Chen	吳鎮
Wu Ch'eng-en	吳承恩
Wu Ch'i (1619–1694)	吳綺
Wu Ch'i (ancient military strategist)	吳起
Wu Chia-chi	吳嘉紀
Wu-chiang	吳江
Wu Chien-jen	吳趼人
Wu Chih-chen	吳之振
Wu Chin-fa	吳錦發
Wu Ching	吳兢
Wu-ching	悟淨
Wu Ching-tzu	吳敬梓
Wu Ch'ing-hua	吳清華
Wu Chü	伍舉
Wu Chün	吳均
Wu Han	吳晗
Wu Hou	武后
Wu-hsi	無錫
Wu Hsi-ch'i	吳錫麒
Wu Hsiao-ju	吳小如
Wu Hsiao-ling	吳曉鈴
Wu-hsing	吳興
Wu-hsing Yao-shen	吳興妖神
Wu Hung-ta (Harry Wu)	吳宏達
Wu Hung-tao	吳弘道
Wu Jui	吳芮
Wu K'o-chi	吳克己
Wu K'uan	吳寬
Wu Kuang-chien	伍光建
Wu Kung-yeh	武公業
Wu-k'ung	悟空
Wu Kuo-lun	吳國倫
Wu Lai	吳萊
Wu Li	吳歷
Wu Liang	武梁
Wu-ling	武陵
Wu Lung-han	吳龍翰
Wu Mei	吳梅
Wu-men Hui-k'ai	無門慧開
Wu Meng	吳猛
Wu-neng	悟能
Wu P'ei-fu	吳佩孚
Wu-pen	無本
Wu Ping	吳炳
Wu Shang	伍尚
Wu She	伍奢
Wu-shuang	無雙
Wu-ssu yün-tung (May Fourth movement)	五四運動
Wu Sung	武松
Wu Ta	武大
Wu Ta-chen	吳大震
Wu Ta-lang	武大郎
Wu-tai (Five Dynasties)	五代
Wu T'ai-po	吳泰伯
Wu-t'ai-shan	五臺山
Wu-tang	武當
Wu Tao-tzu	吳道子
Wu T'ao	吳檮
Wu-ti, Emperor of the Han	漢武帝
Wu-ting	武丁
Wu Tsao	吳藻
Wu Tse-t'ien	武則天
Wu Tsu-hsiang	吳組緗
Wu Tsu-kuang	吳祖光
Wu Tzu-fang	吳自芳
Wu Tzu-hsü	伍子胥
Wu Tzu-mei	吳子美
Wu Wang	武王

Wu-wei	武威
Wu Wei-yeh	吳偉業
Wu Wen-ying	吳文英
Wu Wo-yao	吳沃堯
Wu Wu-shan	吳吳山
Wu-yi	武夷
Wu Ying-t'ao	吳瀛濤
Wu Yü	吳虞
Wu Yü-pi	吳與弼
Wu Yüan-t'ai	吳元泰
Wu-Yüeh	吳越
Wu Yüeh-niang	吳月娘
Wu Yün	吳筠
Ya-chou	雅州
Ya Hsien	瘂弦
Ya Mo	啞默
Yama	閻王
Yamanoue no Okura	山上憶良
Yanagawa Seigan	柳川星巖
Yang	煬
Yang Chao-min	楊昭敏
Yang Chao-ying	楊朝英
Yang Ch'ao-kuan	楊潮觀
Yang Cheng-jun	楊正潤
Yang Chi	楊基
Yang Chi-sheng	楊繼盛
Yang-ch'i	陽崎
Yang Chiang	楊絳
Yang Chih-ho	楊致和
Yang Ch'ih-ch'ang	楊熾昌
Yang Ch'ing-ch'u	楊青矗
Yang Chiung	楊炯
Yang-chou (Yangchow)	揚州
Yang Ch'ung-yi	楊崇義
Yang Erh-tseng	楊爾曾
Yang Han	楊漢
Yang Hsi	楊羲
Yang-hsien	陽顯
Yang Hsien-yi	楊憲益
Yang Hsiu	楊修
Yang Hsiung	揚雄
Yang Hsüan-chih	楊衒之
Yang Hsün-chi	楊循吉
Yang Hua	楊華
Yang Jung	楊榮
Yang Kuan	陽關
Yang K'uan	楊寬
Yang Kuei-fei	楊貴妃
Yang K'uei	楊逵
Yang Lien	楊煉
Yang Ling-yeh	羊令野
Yang Liu-lang	楊六郎
Yang Lü-fang	楊履方
Yang Mu	楊牧
Yang Na	楊訥
Yang Paek-hwa	梁白華
Yang P'u	楊溥
Yang Shen	楊愼
Yang Shih-ch'i	楊士奇
Yang Shih-tao	楊師道
Yang Shou-yü	楊守愚
Yang-ti	煬帝
Yang T'ing-fang	楊庭芳
Yang T'ing-ho	楊廷和
Yang Tsai	楊載
Yang Ts'ai-yü	楊彩玉
Yang Tse	楊澤
Yang Tzu	楊梓
Yang Tzu-jung	楊子榮
Yang Wan-li	楊萬里
Yang Wei-chen	楊維楨
Yang Wen-ts'ung	楊文驄
Yang Yao	楊么
Yang Yeh	楊業
Yang Yi	楊億
Yangchow (Yang-chou)	揚州
Yangtze River	揚子江
Yao (legendary sage ruler)	堯
Yao (tribal group)	瑤
Yao Ho	姚合
Yao Hsia-tan	姚夏旦
Yao Hsüan	姚鉉
Yao Hsüeh-yin	姚雪垠
Yao Kuang-hsiao	姚廣孝
Yao Nai	姚鼐
Yao Ssu-lien	姚思廉
Yao Sui	姚燧
Yeh	鄴
Yeh (singer)	葉
Yeh Chao-yen	葉兆言
Yeh Ching-neng	葉淨能
Yeh Chou	葉晝

Yeh Fa-shan	葉法善	Yi Kyu-bo	李奎報
Yeh Hsiao-wan	葉小紈	Yi Saek	李穡
Yeh Hsieh	葉燮	Yi-shan	夷山
Yeh Hsien-tsu	葉憲祖	Yi Shu-yü	易漱瑜
Yeh-lü Ch'u-ts'ai	耶律楚材	Yi Sŏ-gu	李書九
Yeh Ni	葉泥	Yi Tŏk-mu	李德懋
Yeh Shan	葉珊	Yi Tsu	乙祖
Yeh Shao-chün	葉紹鈞	Yi-yang	弋陽
Yeh Sheng-t'ao	葉聖陶	Yin Chih-p'ing	尹志平
Yeh Shih	葉適	Yin-ch'üeh-shan	銀雀山
Yeh Wei-lien	葉維廉	Yin Fan	殷璠
Yellow River (Huang-ho)	黃河	Yin Hsi	尹喜
Yen	燕	Yin Wen-ts'ao	尹文操
Yen-an (Yenan)	延安	Yin Yüeh	殷岳
Yen Chi-tao	晏幾道	Ying	英
Yen Chih-t'ui	顏之推	Ying-lien	英蓮
Yen-ching	燕京	Ying-ning	嬰寧
Yen Fu	嚴復	Ying Po-chüeh	應伯爵
Yen Jo-ch'ü	閻若璩	Ying River	潁水
Yen Li	嚴力	Ying-tsung	英宗
Yen-pien	延邊	Ying Yang	應瑒
Yen P'o-hsi	閻婆惜	Ying-ying, [Ts'ui]	鶯鶯 [崔]
Yen Sheng-sun	嚴繩孫	Yŏngjo	英祖
Yen Shih-fan	嚴世蕃	Yosa Buson	與謝蕪村
Yen Shih-ku	顏師古	Yoshida Kenkō	吉田兼好
Yen Shu	晏殊	Yoshikawa Kōjirō	吉川幸次郎
Yen Sung	嚴嵩	Yu Erh-chieh	尤二姐
Yen Ti	炎帝	Yu Hui-ch'un	柳希春
Yen Tzu	晏子	Yu-hsi Chu-jen	游戲主人
Yen Wei-ts'ai	嚴偉才	Yu San-chieh	尤三姐
Yen-yen	艷艷	Yu Tŏk-gong	柳德恭
Yen Yen-chih	顏延之	Yu T'ung	尤侗
Yen Ying	晏嬰	Yü	禹
Yen Yü	嚴羽	Yü-chao	宇昭
Yenan (Yen-an)	延安	Yü Chi (Taoist magician)	于吉
Yi	彝	Yü Chi (1272–1348)	虞集
Yi (the Archer)	羿	Yü Chien	于堅
Yi (Po-yi)	翳 (伯翳)	Yü Chien-wu	庾肩吾
Yi Che-hyŏn	李齊賢	Yü Ch'ien	于謙
Yi-chen	儀眞	Yü Ch'ing-t'ing	玉蜻蜓
Yi-ching	義淨	Yü Ch'un-hsi	虞淳熙
Yi Chong-t'ae	李鍾泰	Yü Hsia	禹夏
Yi Fen-erh	一分兒	Yü Hsiang-tou	余象斗
Yi Hae-jo	李海朝	Yü-hsiao	玉簫
Yi-hsing	宜興	Yü Hsin	庾信
Yi In-no	李仁老	Yü Hsüan-chi	魚玄機

Yü Hua	余華	Yüan Hung-tao	袁宏道
Yü Hung-chien	俞鴻漸	Yüan K'ai	袁凱
Yü Jun-ch'i	于潤崎	Yüan K'o	袁珂
Yü-kuan	玉官	Yüan K'o-chia	袁可嘉
Yü Kuang-chung	余光中	Yüan-kung	遠公
Yü Li-hua	於梨華	Yüan Mei	袁枚
Yü Lo-chin	遇羅錦	Yüan-Ming	元明
Yü-lung Kuan	玉隆觀	Yüan Shih-k'ai	袁世凱
Yü-lung shan	玉龍山	Yüan-shih t'ien-tsun	元始天尊
Yü Ming-chen	俞明震	Yüan Tsung-tao	袁宗道
Yü p'ai	余派	Yüan-yu	元祐
Yü P'ing-po	俞平伯	Yüan Yü-ling	袁于令
Yü School (see Yü p'ai)		Yüeh	越
Yü Shang-yüan	余上沅	Yüeh, King of	越王
Yü Shao-yü	余邵魚	Yüeh-chih (Ju-chih)	月支
Yü Shih-nan	虞世南	Yüeh-ch'üan yin-she	月泉吟社
Yü Su-hsin	于素心	Yüeh Chün	樂鈞
Yü Ta	俞達	Yüeh Fei	岳飛
Yü Ta-fu	郁達夫	Yüeh-fu	樂府
Yü Tao-hsien	于道顯	Yüeh-ming	月明
Yü-t'ung	玉童	Yüeh Yeh	岳野
Yü Wan-ch'un	俞萬春	Yugur (Yü-ku)	裕固
Yü-yao	餘姚	Yun Kun-su	尹根壽
Yü Ying-shih	余英時	Yün-chien	雲間
Yü Yü-te	虞育德	Yün-chüan	雲娟
Yü Yüeh	俞樾	Yün-men wu-chi	雲門舞集
Yüan	元	Yün-nan (Yunnan)	雲南
Yüan, King	元王	Yün Shou-p'ing	惲壽平
Yüan Chen	元稹	Yung, Prince	永王
Yüan-chia	元嘉	Yung-chia	永嘉
Yüan-chia chieh	袁家渴	Yung-chia ssu-ling	永嘉四靈
Yüan Chiao	袁郊	Yung-chou	永州
Yüan Chieh	元結	Yung-p'ing	永平
Yüan Ching	元兢	Yunnan (Yün-nan)	雲南
Yüan Chüeh	袁桷	Zeami	世阿見
Yüan Chung-tao	袁中道	Zeami Motokiyo	世阿弥元清
Yüan Hao-wen	元好問	Zekkai Chūshin	絕海中津
Yüan Hung	袁宏	Zen (Ch'an)	禪

GLOSSARY OF TITLES

A-mi-t'o ching (*O-mi-t'o ching*)	阿彌陀經
A-p'i-ta-mo ta-p'i-p'o-sha-lun	阿毗達磨大毗婆沙論
A-shih-ma	阿詩瑪
"Ah Q cheng-chuan"	阿Q正傳
"Ai Chiang-nan fu"	哀江南賦
"Ai Chiang-t'ou"	哀江頭
"Ai ni wen"	哀溺文
Ai-tzu tsa-shuo	艾子雜說
"Ai wang-sun"	哀王孫
An-ya t'ang chi	安雅堂集
Analects (*Lun-yü*)	論語
"Ao hsiang-kung yin-hen Pan-shan t'ang"	拗相公飲恨半山堂
"Binh Ngo dai cao"	平吳大誥
Bunkashūreishū	文華秀麗集
Bunkyō hifuron	文鏡秘府論
"Ch'a-chiu lun"	茶酒論
"Ch'a-kuan"	茶館
Ch'a-mu	查姆
Chaeil kiŏn	第一奇諺
"Chan hua-k'uei"	占花魁
Chan-kuei chuan	斬鬼傳
Chan-kuo ts'e	戰國策
"Chan-tou li ch'eng-chang"	戰鬥里成長
Ch'an-chen hou-shih	禪眞後史
Ch'an-chen yi-shih	禪眞逸史
Ch'an-hui mieh-tsui Chin-kuang-ming chuan	懺悔滅罪金光明傳
"Ch'an-men shih-erh shih"	禪門十二時
Ch'an-yüan chu-ch'üan-chi tu-hsü	禪源諸詮集都序
"Chang Hsieh chuang-yüan"	張協狀元
"Chang Kuo"	張果
"Chang Tao-ling ch'i shih Chao Sheng"	張道陵七試趙昇
"Chang Yi-ch'ao [pien-wen]"	張義潮 [變文]
"Ch'ang-an ku-yi"	長安古意
Ch'ang-ch'un chen-jen hsi-yu chi	長春眞人西遊記
"Ch'ang-hen ko"	長恨歌
"'Ch'ang-hen ko' chuan"	長恨歌傳
"Ch'ang hsiang-ssu"	長相思

Ch'ang li-luan 唱離亂
"Ch'ang-mao hsiao kou" 長毛小狗
"Ch'ang-pan p'o" 長板坡
"Ch'ang-sheng tien" 長生殿
Ch'ang-shih chi 嘗試集
Ch'angsŏn kamŭi rok 彰善感義錄
"Chao-chün ch'u-sai" 昭君出塞
(Chao) Fei-yen wai-chuan (趙) 飛燕外傳
"Chao Hsiao-lan" 趙小蘭
"Chao hun" 招魂
"Chao P'an-erh feng-yüeh chiu feng-ch'en tsa-chü" 趙盼兒風月救風塵雜劇
"Chao pei-k'o wen" 招北客文
"Chao-shih ku-erh" 趙氏孤兒
Chao-shih pei 照世杯
"Chao Wu-hu ho-chi t'iao chia-hsin, Mo Ta-lang li-ti san shen chien" 趙五虎 合計挑家釁莫大郎立地散神奸
Chao-yang ch'ü-shih 昭陽趣史
"Chao Yen-wang" 趙閻王
"Chao yin-shih" 招隱士
"Chao-yin shih" 招隱詩
"Ch'ao-jan t'ai chi" 超然臺記
Ch'ao-yeh ch'ien-tsai 朝野僉載
"Che chiu-nien fu" 謫九年賦
Che-hsi liu-chia tz'u 浙西六家詞
"Ch'e-chan" 車站
"Chen chien-sheng lang t'un mi-yao, Ch'un-hua nü wu hsieh feng-ch'ing" 甄監生浪呑秘藥春花女誤洩風情
Chen-chu t'a 珍珠塔
"Chen-chung chi" 枕中記
Chen kao 眞誥
"Chen-wen chi" 貞文記
"Ch'en-chou t'iao-mi" 陳州糶米
Ch'en-chung te ch'ih-pang 沉重的翅膀
"Ch'en Hsi-yi ssu tz'u ch'ao ming" 陳希夷四辭朝命
Ch'en-hsiang T'ai-tzu 沉香太子
"Ch'en-lun" 沉淪
Ch'en-lun 沉淪
Ch'en shu 陳書
"Ch'en to-shou sheng-ssu fu-ch'i" 陳多壽生死夫妻
"Ch'en yü-shih ch'iao k'an chin ch'ai tien" 陳御史巧勘金釵鈿
"Cheng ch'i ko" 正氣歌
Cheng-ho wan-shou Tao-tsang 政和萬壽道藏
"Cheng-tao ko" 證道歌
Cheng-t'ung Tao-tsang 正統道藏
"Ch'eng ch'ao-feng tan yü wu t'ou fu, Wang t'ung-p'an shuang hsüeh pu ming yüan" 程朝奉單遇無頭婦王通判雙雪不明冤
"Ch'eng chiu fu" 懲咎賦
Ch'eng-nan chiu-shih 城南舊事
"Ch'eng-nan kan-huai ch'eng Yung-shu" 城南感懷呈永叔
"Ch'eng-nan kuei chih ta feng hsüeh" 城南歸値大風雪
"Ch'eng-nan liu" 城南柳
"Ch'eng-p'ei" 成配
"Ch'eng-shang wu" 城上烏
Ch'eng-tsan ching-t'u fo-she-shou ching 稱讚淨土佛攝受經
"Ch'eng Yüan-yü tien-ssu tai ch'ang ch'ien, Shih-yi niang Yün-kang tsung T'an hsia" 程元玉店肆代償錢十一娘雲崗縱譚俠
"Chi ch'ing-jen" 寄情人
Chi-hai tsa-shih 己亥雜詩
Chi-hsüan chi 極玄集
Chi-ku lu pa-wei 集古錄跋尾
"Chi nien" 紀念
"Chi Pu ma-chen tz'u-wen" 季布罵陣詞文
"Ch'i ai shih" 七哀詩
Ch'i-chen chi 攲枕集
Ch'i-chen nien-p'u 七眞年譜
"Ch'i fa" (Seven Methods) 七法
"Ch'i fa" (Seven Stimuli) 七發
"Ch'i fu p'ien" 棄婦篇
"Ch'i hsi" 七夕
"Ch'i-hsi Pai-hu-t'uan" 奇襲白虎團
"Ch'i-kai fu ch'ung p'ei luan ch'ou" 乞丐婦重配鸞儔

Ch'i-lu teng	歧路燈
Ch'i lüeh	七略
Ch'i-meng	啓蒙
Ch'i nü-tzu chuan	奇女子傳
"Ch'i T'ui nü"	齊推女
Ch'i-tung yeh-yü	齊東野語
Ch'i wang	棋王
Ch'i-yen lu	啓顏錄
"Ch'i-yüeh"	七月
Chia	家
Chia-jen ch'i-yü	佳人奇遇
"Chia-jen lien shang hei-chih"	佳人臉上黑痣
"Chia-ju wo shih chen-te"	假如我是眞的
Chia-ling tz'u ch'üan-chi	迦陵詞全集
Chia pien	家變
Chia-yü	家語
"Chia Yün-hua huan-hun chi"	賈雲華還魂記
Chiang-chai shih-hua	薑齋詩話
"Chiang chin chiu"	將進酒
"Chiang Ch'u kung hua chiao ying ko"	姜楚公畫角鷹歌
"Chiang-chung wang yüeh"	江中望月
"Chiang-hsi shih she tsung-p'ai t'u"	江西詩社宗派圖
"Chiang Hsing-ko ch'ung-hui chen-chu shan"	蔣興哥重會珍珠衫
Chiang-hu chi	江湖集
"Chiang-nan"	江南
"Chiang-nan yü T'ien-pao yüeh-sou"	江南遇天寶樂叟
"Chiang-ts'un ch'ang-ho tz'u"	江村唱和詞
"Chiang-tu shih hsiao-fu t'u shen"	江都市孝婦屠身
"Ch'iang-ts'un"	羌村
Chiao-hui hsin-pao	教會新報
"Chiao Hung chi"	嬌紅記
Chiao Hung chuan	嬌紅傳
"Chiao nü shih"	嬌女詩
"Chiao-ssu ko"	郊祀歌
"Ch'iao Yen-chieh yi ch'ieh p'o chia"	喬彥傑一妾破家
"Ch'iao-ying"	喬影
"Chieh ch'ao"	解嘲
"Chieh-chih-erh chi"	戒指兒記
"Chieh Chih-t'ui huo-feng tu-fu"	介之推火封妒婦
Chieh-ts'un-chai lun-tz'u tsa-chu	介存齋論詞雜著
Ch'ieh-chieh T'ing tsa-wen erh-chi	且介亭雜文二集
Ch'ieh-chung chi	篋中集
Chien-hsia chuan	劍俠傳
"Chien-hu yeh-fan chi"	鑑湖夜泛記
"Chien-ko fu"	劍閣賦
Chien-teng hsin-hua	剪燈新話
Chien-teng lu	剪燈錄
Chien-teng yü-hua	剪燈餘話
"Ch'ien Han Liu-chia t'ai-tzu chuan"	前漢劉家太子傳
Chien-wu chi	漸悟集
Ch'ien-chia shih	千家詩
"Ch'ien-hsi ko"	前溪歌
"Ch'ien-nü li-hun"	倩女離魂
Ch'ien-tzu wen	千字文
Ch'ien wan pieh pa wo tang jen	千萬別把我當人
"Ch'ien-wan pu-yao wang-chi"	千萬不要忘記
Chih-chen yü-lu	至眞語錄
"Chih-chi"	知幾
"Chih-chih fu"	知止賦
"Chih-ch'ü Wei-hu-shan"	智取威虎山
Chih-nan hou lu	指南後錄
Chih-nan lu	指南錄
Chih-nang	智囊
"Chih-sung chin-kang ching kung-te chi"	持頌金剛經功德記
"Chih-yüan pieh San-niang T'ai-yüan t'ou-shih"	知遠別三娘太原投事
"Ch'ih ch'ü ch'üan Mao Lieh lai yüan ch'ien, shih huan hun ya k'uai so sheng ming"	遲取券毛烈賴原錢失還魂牙儈索剩命
"Ch'ih-pi fu"	赤壁賦
Ch'ih p'o-tzu chuan	癡婆子傳
Ch'ih-ti chih lien	赤地之戀

“Chin-ch’ai chi” 金釵記
“Chin chüeh lou” 今覺樓
“Chin-hsiang k’o mang k’an *Chin-kang ching*, ch’u yü seng ch’iao wan fa hui fen” 進香客莽看金剛經出獄僧巧完法會分
Chin-hsiang t’ing 金香亭
“Chin-hsüeh chieh” 進學解
Chin Hung-chou Hsi-shan Shih-erh Chen-chün chuan 晉洪州西山十二眞君傳
Chin-kang po-je ching chi-yen chi 金剛般若經集驗記
Chin-ku ch’i-kuan 今古奇觀
Chin-lien cheng-tsung chi 金蓮正宗記
Chin-lien cheng-tsung hsien-yüan hsiang-chuan 金蓮正宗仙源像傳
“Chin-ling yi” 金陵驛
Chin P’ing Mei 金瓶梅
Chin P’ing Mei te yi-shu 金瓶梅的藝術
Chin P’ing Mei tz’u-hua 金瓶梅詞話
“Chin Sheng-t’an p’i hsiao-shuo shuo” 金聖嘆批小說說
Chin shu 晉書
“Chin-so chi” 金鎖記
Chin so chi 金鎖記
Chin-so ho fang-sung te hsün-huan: 1976 chih 1986 nien ch’i-chien Chung-kuo cheng-chih yü wen-hsüeh te kuan-hsi 緊縮和放鬆的循環 — 1976至1986年期間中國政治與文學的關係
Chin-tan ta-ch’eng chi 金丹大成集
Chin-t’ien 今天
Chin-wen kuan-chih 今文觀止
Chin wu meng 金屋夢
“Chin-yang men” 津陽門
“Chin Yü-nu pang ta po-ch’ing lang” 金玉奴棒打薄情郎
Chin Yün-ch’iao chuan 金雲翹傳
“Ch’in-chung yin” 秦中吟
“Ch’in-fu yin” 秦婦吟
“Ch’in-huai tsa-shih” 秦淮雜詩
“Ch’in meng chi” 秦夢記
“Ching” 靜
“Ching-ch’ai chi” 荊釵記
“*Ching-hsi chi* hsü” 荊溪集序
Ching hua yüan 鏡花緣
Ching-lung wen-kuan chi 景龍文館記
Ching-ming chung-hsiao ch’üan-shu 淨明忠孝全書
“Ching-shih” 警世
Ching-shih t’ung-yen 警世通言
Ching-te ch’uan-teng lu 景德傳燈錄
Ching-tien shih-wen 經典釋文
Ching-t’u lun-chu 淨土論註
Ching-wei shih 精衛石
Ch’ing-an Ying-ch’an-tzu yü-lu 清庵瑩蟾子語錄
“Ch’ing-ch’eng yin-che chi” 青城隱者記
“Ch’ing-ch’ing ho p’an ts’ao” 青青河畔草
“Ch’ing-ch’iu-tzu ko” 青丘子歌
“Ch’ing-ch’ou” 情仇
“Ch’ing-chung p’u” 清忠譜
“Ch’ing-feng ko chi” 清風閣記
Ch’ing-ho chen-jen pei-yu yü-lu 清和眞人北游語錄
Ch’ing-hsiang 傾向
Ch’ing-lou meng 青樓夢
Ch’ing-meng t’uo 情夢柝
Ch’ing-mo min-ch’u hsiao-shuo shu-hsi 清末民初小說書系
Ch’ing-ni lien-hua chi 青泥蓮花記
Ch’ing-p’ing shan t’ang hua-pen 清平山堂話本
“Ch’ing-p’ing-tiao” 清平調
“Ch’ing po p’ien” 輕薄篇
“Ch’ing-shan lei” 青衫淚
“Ch’ing-shang” 清商
“Ch’ing-shang ch’ü-tz’u” 清商曲辭
“Ch’ing shih” 情詩
Ch’ing-shih 情史
Ch’ing shih-hua 清詩話
Ch’ing-shih lei-lüeh 情史類略
Ch’ing-so kao-yi 青瑣高議
Ch’ing-t’an wan-hsüan 清談萬選
Ch’ing-tsun lu 清尊錄
Ch’ing-yeh chung 清夜鍾
Ch’ing-yi pao 清議報

"Chinh phu ngam khuc" 征婦吟曲
"Chiu Feng-ch'en" 救風塵
"Chiu hsia chiu Chao ni-ao mi hua, chi chung chi Chia hsiu-ts'ai pao yüan" 酒下酒趙尼媼迷花機中機賈秀才報怨
"Chiu hsiang-kuan shih" 九相觀詩
"Chiu huai" 九懷
"Chiu ko" 九歌
Chiu ming ch'i yüan 九命奇冤
"Chiu mo ts'ai Yü Chiao ssu o, kuei tui an Yang Hua chieh shih" 酒謀財于郊肆惡鬼對案楊化借屍
"Chiu pien" 九辯
"Chiu ssu" 九思
"Chiu t'an" 九歎
Chiu T'ang shu 舊唐書
Chiu tsa p'i-yü ching 舊雜譬喻經
Chiu-wei kuei 九尾龜
Ch'iu-chia chi 秋笳集
"Ch'iu feng tz'u" 秋風辭
"Ch'iu hsing" 秋興
"Ch'iu-jan k'o chuan" 虬髯客傳
"Ch'iu-jih teng Hung-fu T'eng-wang ko chien-pieh hsü" 秋日登洪府滕王閣餞別序
"Ch'iu-liu shih" 秋柳詩
"Ch'iu-shan fu" 囚山賦
"Ch'iu-sheng fu" 秋聲賦
"Ch'iu shou" 秋收
"Ch'iu-ssu" 秋思
Ch'iu-teng ts'ung-hua 秋燈叢話
"Ch'iu yü" 秋雨
"Ch'iung Ma Chou tsao chi mai tui ao" 窮馬周遭際賣䭔媼
"Cho Wen-chün" 卓文君
Ch'o keng lu 輟耕錄
"Chou chung tsa-yung" 舟中雜詠
"Chou-chung yeh ch'i" 舟中夜起
Chou-kuan 周官
Chou-li 周禮
Chou-yi 周易
Chou yi pen-yi 周易本義
"Chou yü" 周語
"Ch'ou Chu shih-san hsiu-ts'ai" 酬祝十三秀才
"Ch'ou-hsi p'ien" 疇昔篇
"Ch'ou lang-chün p'a chiao p'ien te yen" 醜郎君怕嬌偏得艷
"Ch'ou-lou te Chung-kuo-jen" 醜陋的中國人
"Ch'ou-nü yüan-ch'i" 醜女緣起
"Chu-chih tz'u" 竹枝詞
Chu-ch'un yüan hsiao-shih 駐春園小史
"Chu-fu" 祝福
Chu-lin yeh-shih 株林野史
"Chu p'in" 逐貧
"Chu shan" 珠衫
Chu-shu chi-nien 竹書紀年
Chu-tzu yü-lei 朱子語類
Chu-tzu yü-lu 朱子語錄
Chu-ying hsüeh-shih chi 珠英學士集
Chu-yü 麈餘
"Chü sung" 橘頌
Ch'u-hsüeh chi 初學記
Ch'u-k'o p'ai-an ching-ch'i 初刻拍案驚奇
Ch'u san-tsang chi chi 出三藏記集
"Ch'u tiao" 楚調
Ch'u tz'u 楚辭
Ch'u Tz'u chang-chu 楚辭章注
"Ch'ü-chiang-ch'ih" 曲江池
"Ch'ü Feng-nu ch'ing ch'ien ssu kai" 瞿鳳奴情愆死蓋
Ch'ü-lü 曲律
Ch'ü-p'in 曲品
"Ch'ü-t'u Chung-jen k'u sha chung-sheng, Yün-chou ssu-ma ming ch'üan nei-chih" 屈突仲任酷殺衆生鄆州司馬冥全內姪
"Ch'ü Yüan" 屈原
Chuan-chi pai yüan ching 撰集百緣經
Chuan-chi wen-hsüeh shih-kang 傳記文學史綱
"Chuan yün han yü ch'iao Tung-t'ing hung, Po-ssu hu chih p'o t'o-lung k'o" 轉運漢遇巧洞庭紅波斯胡指破鼉龍殼
Ch'uan hsi lu 傳習錄
Ch'uan-shan ch'üan-shu 船山全書
Ch'uan-shan yi-shu 船山遺書

Ch'üan-hsiang San-kuo chih p'ing-hua 全相三國志平話
"Ch'üan shan chi" 勸善記
Ch'üan-shih liang-yen 勸世良言
Ch'üan Sung shih 全宋詩
Ch'üan Sung-tz'u 全宋詞
Ch'üan T'ang shih 全唐詩
Ch'üan T'ang shih pu-pien 全唐詩補編
Ch'üan T'ang wen 全唐文
"Ch'üan yü fa" 權與法
Ch'üan Yüan san-ch'ü 全元散曲
Chuang Lin hsü Tao-tsang 莊林續道藏
"Chuang shih p'ien" 壯士篇
Chuang Tzu 莊子
Ch'uang-shih-chi 創世紀
Ch'uang-tso t'an 創作談
"Chüeh hsin-k'eng ch'ien-kuei ch'eng ts'ai-chu" 掘新坑慳鬼成財主
"Ch'üeh t'a chih" 雀踏枝
Chūgoku zuihitsu sakuin 中國隨筆索引
Chūgoku zuihitsu zatcho sakuin 中國隨筆雜著索引
"Ch'ui-lao pieh" 垂老別
Ch'ui-wen chih-yü 炊聞卮語
Ch'ui-wen tz'u 炊聞詞
"Chün-t'ien le" 鈞天樂
Ch'un-ch'iu 春秋
Ch'un-ch'iu fan-lu 春秋繁露
Ch'un-ch'iu san chuan 春秋三傳
"Ch'un hsiao" 春曉
"Ch'un hsiao wang Chin-pi shan" 春曉望金碧山
"Ch'un-ssu fu" 春思賦
"Ch'un teng-mi" 春燈謎
Ch'un-teng mi-shih 春燈迷史
"Ch'un ts'an" 春蠶
"Ch'un wang" 春望
Ch'un-yang chen-jen hun-ch'eng chi 純陽眞人渾成集
Ch'un-yang ti-chün shen-hua miao-t'ung chi 純陽帝君神化妙通紀
Ch'ün-chi ch'üan-chieh lun 群己權界論
Ch'ün-hsüeh yi-yen 群學肄言
Chung-ching chuan tsa p'i-yü 衆經撰雜譬喻
Chung-ch'ing li-chi 鍾情麗集
"Chung-ch'iu chieh yi-ko wan-shang" 中秋節一個晚上
"Chung-ch'un chiao-wai" 仲春郊外
Chung-ho chi 中和集
Chung-hsing chien-ch'i chi 中興間氣集
Chung-hua hsiao-shuo chieh 中華小說界
"Chung-kung chung-yang kuan-yü chia-ch'iang she-hui-chu-yi ching-shen wen-ming chien-she jo-kan chung-yao wen-t'i te chüeh-yi" 中共中央關於加強社會主義精神文明建設若干重要問題的決議
Chung-kuo chin-tai hsiao-shuo ta-hsi 中國近代小說大系
Chung-kuo chin-tai wen-hsüeh ta-hsi 中國近代文學大系
Chung-kuo chuan-chi wen-hsüeh shih 中國傳記文學史
Chung-kuo hsiao-shuo pien-ch'ien shih 中國小說變遷史
Chung-kuo hsiao-shuo shih lüeh 中國小說史略
Chung-kuo hsin-shih 中國新詩
Chung-kuo k'o-yi shuo pu: leng-chan hou shih-tai te cheng-chih yü ch'ing-kan te chüeh-tse 中國可以說不——冷戰後時代的政治與情感的抉擇
"Chung-kuo meng" 中國夢
Chung-kuo shih-pao 中國時報
Chung-kuo wen-hsüeh shih 中國文學史
Chung-nan shan Shuo-ching T'ai li-tai chen-hsien pei-chi 終南山說經臺歷代眞仙碑記
Chung-nan shan tsu-t'ing hsien-chen nei-chuan 終南山祖庭仙眞內傳
"Chung-shan lang" 中山狼
"Chung-shen ta-shih" 終身大事
Chung-yang jih-pao 中央日報
Chung-yi shui-hu chuan 忠義水滸傳

Chung-yüan yin-yün 中原音韻
"Chung-yung" 中庸
Chung-yung chih chieh 中庸直解
"Ch'ung tseng Lu Ch'en" 重贈盧諶
Ch'ung-yang chen-jen chin-kuan yü-so chüeh 重陽眞人金關玉鎖訣
Ch'ung-yang chiao-hua chi 重陽教化集
Ch'ung-yang ch'üan-chen chi 重陽全眞集
Ch'ung-yang fen-li shih-hua chi 重陽分梨十化集
Ch'ung-yang li-chiao shih-wu lun 重陽立教十五論
Ch'ung-yang shou Tan-yang erh-shih-ssu chüeh 重陽授丹陽二十四訣
Ch'unhyang jŏn 春香傳
Chūshin Suikoden 忠臣水滸伝
"Cung oan ngam khuc" 宮怨吟曲
Edo Hanjōki 江戶繁昌記
Erh-hsiang t'ing tz'u 二鄉亭詞
Erh-k'o p'ai-an ching-ch'i 二刻拍案驚奇
Erh-nü ying-hsiung chuan 兒女英雄傳
Erh-shih lu 耳食錄
Erh-shih nien mu-tu chih kuai hsien-chuang 二十年目睹之怪現狀
Erh-shih-ssu shih-p'in 二十四詩品
Erh-t'an 耳譚
Erh-t'an lei-tseng 耳譚類增
Erh-tu Mei 二度梅
Erh-ya 爾雅
Erh-yu 耳郵
Fa-tsin kei [*Hua-chien chi*] 花箋記
Fa-yen 法言
Fa-yi 法意
"Fa ying-t'ao shu fu" 伐櫻桃樹賦
Fa-yüan chu-lin 法苑珠林
"Fan chao-yin" 反招隱
"Fan Ch'iu-erh shuang ching ch'ung yüan" 范鰍兒雙鏡重圓
"Fan-hua meng" 繁華夢
"Fan-o-lin yü ch'iang-wei" 梵峨琳與薔薇
"Fang-hsia ni-te pien-tzu" 放下你的鞭子
Fang yen 方言
Fei-hua yung 飛花詠
"Fen-yüan shih" 憤怨詩
"Feng" 風
"Feng-cheng wu" 風箏誤
Feng-huang ch'ih 鳳凰池
Feng-ju fei-t'un 豐乳肥臀
Feng lei yen 風淚眼
"Feng-liu yüan" 風流院
Feng-shen yen-yi 封神演義
Feng-shih wen-chien chi 封氏聞見記
Feng-su t'ung-yi 風俗通義
"Feng Yen chuan" 馮燕傳
"Feng-yü ku-jen lai" 風雨故人來
"Feng-yü yeh-kuei-jen" 風雨夜歸人
"Feng-yüeh chin-nang" 風月錦囊
Feng-yüeh pao-chien 風月寶鑒
Fo-kuo chi 佛國記
Fo pen-hsing chi ching 佛本行集經
Fo-shuo ta-sheng wu-liang-shou chuang-yen ching 佛說大乘無量壽莊嚴經
Fo so hsing tsan ching 佛所行讚經
Fo-tsu li-tai t'ung-tsai 佛祖歷代通載
Fo-tsu t'ung-chi 佛祖統記
Fu-chang lu 拊掌錄
"Fu-ch'ing-nung chuan" 負情儂傳
"Fu-feng ko" 扶風歌
"Fu-fu" 夫婦
"Fu-jung chin-chi t'u" 芙蓉錦雞圖
"Fu-lo-ch'ang" 復落娼
"Fu Lo-yang tao chung tso" 赴洛陽道中作
"Fu niao fu" 鵩鳥賦
"Fu ping hsing" 婦病行
Fu-p'u 賦譜
Fu-sheng liu-chi 浮生六記
"Fu yün lou" 拂雲樓
Fudoki 風土記
Gen Min shi gaisetsu 元明詩概說
Genji monogatari 源氏物語
Genji monogatari hyō-shaku 源氏物語評釈

Hai-ch'iung ch'uan-tao chi	海瓊傳道集
Hai-ch'iung Pai chen-jen yü-lu	海瓊白眞人語錄
Hai-ch'iung wen-tao chi	海瓊問道集
"Hai-kang"	海港
Hai kuo t'u chih	海國圖志
Hai-shang ch'i-shu	海上奇書
Hai-shang hua-lieh-chuan	海上花列傳
Hai-tzu wang	孩子王
Hakushi monjū (*Po-shih wen-chi*)	白氏文集
Han chi	漢紀
"Han chiang Wang Ling pien"	漢將王陵變
"Han Ch'in-hu hua-pen"	韓擒虎話本
"Han-ch'ing pu fu lao"	漢卿不伏老
Han Fei Tzu	韓非子
"Han hsiu-ts'ai ch'eng luan p'in chiao-ch'i, Wu t'ai-shou lien ts'ai chu yin-pu"	韓秀才乘亂聘嬌妻吳太守憐才主姻簿
Han-hsü	含蓄
"Han-kung ch'iu"	漢宮秋
Han-lin hsüeh-shih chi	翰林學士集
Han-lin lun	翰林論
"Han nao-ko shih-pa shou"	漢鐃歌十八首
"Han P'eng fu"	韓朋賦
Han Shih wai-chuan	韓詩外傳
Han shu	漢書
"Han-tan chi"	邯鄲記
Han t'ien-shih shih-chia	漢天師世家
Han-t'ing shih-hua	寒廳詩話
Han Wei Liu-ch'ao chuan-chi wen-hsüeh shih-kao	漢魏六朝傳記文學史稿
Han wen-hsüeh shih kang-yao	漢文學史綱要
Han Wu-ti nei-chuan	漢武帝內傳
Han yeh	寒夜
Han-yüan chi	漢園集
"Han-yüan tien fu"	含元殿賦
Hanabusa zōshi	英草紙
Hansa yŏljŏnch'o	漢史列傳抄
Hanwŏnjip	漢源集
Hao-ch'iu chuan	好逑傳
"Hao li hsing"	蒿里行
"Hao-t'ien t'a"	昊天塔
"Hao-yen"	豪宴
Hei-ch'ao chi	黑潮集
Hei-nu yü-t'ien lu	黑奴籲天錄
Hen hai	恨海
"Heng-ch'ui ch'ü-tz'u"	橫吹曲辭
Henjōhokki seireishū	遍照発揮性靈集
"Ho-chien chuan"	河間傳
"Ho Hsiao Hsi-ma Tzu-hsien 'Ku yi' liu shou"	和蕭洗馬子顯古意六首
"Ho kuei lou"	鶴歸樓
"Ho p'u-sa chieh wen"	和菩薩戒文
"Ho-shang"	河殤
Ho-yüeh ying-ling chi	河嶽英靈集
Hoa tien Truyen	花箋傳
Honchō monzui	本朝文戦
Hong-duc quoc am thi tap	洪德國音詩集
Hong Kil-dong chŏn	洪吉童傳
"Hou Chiung"	侯迵
Hou Han shu	後漢書
"Hou-kuan hsien lieh-nü chien-ch'ou"	侯官縣烈女殲仇
Hou "Shui-hu chuan"	後水滸傳
"Hsi Ch'ang-an hsing"	西長安行
Hsi-ching tsa-chi	西京雜記
"Hsi ch'ü ko"	西曲歌
"Hsi-hsiang chi"	西廂記
"Hsi-hsiang chi chu-kung-tiao"	西廂記諸宮調
"Hsi Hsiao Niang"	戲蕭娘
"Hsi hsin fu"	洗心賦
Hsi-hu chia-hua	西湖佳話
Hsi-hu erh-chi	西湖二集
"Hsi-hu kan-chiu"	西湖感舊
Hsi Kuan-shih-yin ying-yen chi	繫觀世音應驗記
Hsi-k'un ch'ou-ch'ang chi	西崑酬唱集
"Hsi-men hsing"	西門行
Hsi-nan Yi-chih hsüan	西南彝志選
"Hsi-Shu meng"	西蜀夢
"Hsi-ta t'ai-tzu ju hsüeh-shan hsiu tao tsan"	悉達太子入雪山修道讚
Hsi-t'an lu	嘻談錄

Hsi-t'ang yung-jih hsü-lun	夕堂永日緒論
"Hsi-tzu chuan"	喜子傳
"Hsi wan liang"	溪晚涼
Hsi-yu chi	西遊記
Hsi-yu pu	西遊補
Hsi-yü chi	西域記
"Hsia yi lou"	夏宜樓
"Hsiang chün"	湘君
"Hsiang-chung yüan chieh"	湘中怨解
"Hsiang Fu-jen"	湘夫人
"Hsiang-ho"	相和
"Hsiang-ho ko-tz'u"	相和歌辭
Hsiang-kang wen-hsüeh	香港文學
"Hsiang Min-kung yüan-hsiao shih tzu, Shih-san lang wu-sui ch'ao t'ien"	襄 敏公元宵失子十三郎五歲朝天
"Hsiang-mo pien"	降魔變
"Hsiang-mo pien-wen"	降魔變文
Hsiao-ching	孝經
Hsiao-ching chih chieh	孝經直解
Hsiao-fu	笑府
"Hsiao hsü"	小序
Hsiao-lin	笑林
Hsiao-lin kuang-chi	笑林廣記
Hsiao-p'in chi	效顰集
Hsiao-p'in po-je po-lo-mi ching	小品般若波羅蜜經
"Hsiao shui-wan t'ien-hu yi shu"	小水灣天狐貽書
"Hsiao-shuo hsiao hua"	小說小話
Hsiao-shuo lin	小說林
"*Hsiao-shuo lin* fa k'an tz'u"	《小說林》發刊詞
"*Hsiao-shuo lin* yüan-ch'i"	《小說林》緣起
Hsiao-shuo ming-hua ta-kuan	小說名畫大觀
Hsiao-shuo shih-pao	小說時報
Hsiao-shuo ta-kuan	小說大觀
Hsiao-shuo ts'ung-hua	小說叢話
Hsiao-shuo ts'ung-pao	小說叢報
"Hsiao-shuo yüan-li"	小說原理
Hsiao-shuo yüeh-pao	小說月報
"Hsiao Sun t'u"	小孫屠
Hsiao-tao	笑倒
"Hsiao tao-jen yi chao jao t'ien-hsia, nü ch'i-t'ung liang chü chu chung-shen"	小道人一著饒天下女棋童兩局注終身
Hsiao tou-p'eng	小豆棚
Hsiao-tzu chuan	孝子傳
Hsiao-ya	小雅
"Hsieh lu hsing"	薤露行
Hsieh-to	諧鐸
"Hsieh Tzu-jan shih"	謝自然詩
"Hsien chih shih"	見志詩
"Hsien-ch'ing ou-chi"	閑情偶記
Hsien-ch'üan chi	峴泉集
Hsien-le chi	仙樂集
Hsien-shih yi-chung	現實一種
Hsien-tai	現代
Hsien-tai p'ing-lun	現代評論
Hsien-tai-shih chi-k'an	現代詩季刊
Hsien-yü ching	賢愚經
Hsien-yüan chi-shih	仙媛紀事
"Hsin-an li"	新安吏
"Hsin Ch'a-hua"	新茶花
Hsin-chi yen-fu chiao	新集嚴父教
Hsin chi-yüan	新紀元
Hsin chiao-cheng Meng-hsi pi-t'an	新校正夢溪筆談
Hsin ching	心經
Hsin ch'ing-nien	新青年
Hsin Chung-kuo wei-lai chi	新中國未來記
"Hsin-feng che pi weng"	新豐折臂翁
Hsin-hai chi	心海集
Hsin hsiao-shuo	新小說
"Hsin-hsin ming"	信心銘
Hsin hsü	新序
"Hsin huai shuang"	心懷霜
"Hsin-hun pieh"	新婚別
"[Hsin-k'an shuo-ch'ang] Pao Lung-t'u tuan Ts'ao Kuo-chiu kung-an chuan"	[新刊說唱]包龍圖斷曹國舅公案傳
Hsin lieh-kuo chih	新列國志
Hsin-ling shih	心靈史
Hsin shih-t'ou chi	新石頭記
Hsin ta-lu shih shuang-yüeh-k'an	新大陸詩雙月刊

Hsin T'ang shu 新唐書
Hsin-wen pao 新聞報
Hsin Wu-tai shih 新五代史
Hsin Yüeh-fu 新樂府
"Hsing-hsiang chi-wen" 行香偈文
Hsing-hua t'ien 杏花天
"Hsing lu nan" 行路難
Hsing-meng p'ien-yen 醒夢駢言
Hsing-shih heng-yen 醒世恒言
Hsing-shih yin-yüan chuan 醒世姻緣傳
Hsing-tao jih-pao 星島日報
"Hsing-tz'u hsi-chiao tso yi-pai yün" 行次西郊作一百韻
"Hsing ying shen" 形影神
"Hsiu chen" 繡枕
Hsiu-chen shih-shu 修眞十書
"Hsiu-chu p'ien" 修竹篇
Hsiu-hsiang hsiao-shuo 繡像小說
Hsiu-ku ch'un-jung 繡谷春容
Hsiu-p'ing yüan 繡屏緣
Hsiu-t'a yeh-shih 繡榻野史
Hsiu-t'zu-hsüeh fa-fan 修辭學發凡
"Hsiu-wen she-jen chuan" 修文舍人傳
"Hsü Chiang-shih chuan" 續江氏傳
Hsü Chin P'ing Mei 續金瓶梅
Hsü-ching ch'ung-ho hsien-sheng Hsü Shen-weng yü-lu 虛靖沖和先生徐神翁語錄
Hsü Ch'u tz'u 續楚辭
Hsü Han shu 續漢書
Hsü Hsüan-kuai lu 續玄怪錄
Hsü Kao-seng chuan 續高僧傳
Hsü Kuang-shih-yin ying-yen chi 續光世音應驗記
"Hsü lao-p'u yi fen ch'eng chia" 徐老僕義憤成家
"Hsü lien chi erh-shih yung" 續奩集二十詠
Hsü shih-hua 續詩話
Hsü t'ai-shih chen-chün t'u-chuan 許太史眞君圖傳
Hsü Tao-tsang ching 續道藏經
Hsü tzu-chih t'ung-chien ch'ang-pien 續資治通鑑長編
Hsü tz'u hsüan 續詞選
Hsü Yi-chien chih 續夷堅志
Hsüan-feng 旋風
Hsüan-feng ch'ing-hui lu 玄風慶會錄
"Hsüan-ko" 玄歌
Hsüan-kuai lu 玄怪錄
"Hsüan-niao" 玄鳥
Hsüan-p'in lu 玄品錄
Hsüan-yen chi 宣驗記
Hsüeh-ch'uang t'an-yi 雪窗談異
"Hsüeh Liu Kung-kan t'i wu shou" 學劉公幹體五首
"Hsüeh lu-shih yü fu cheng hsien" 薛錄事魚服證仙
"Hsüeh-shan tsan" 雪山讚
"Hsüeh-so-yi" 血蓑衣
Hsüeh-t'ao-ko chi 雪濤閣集
"Hsüeh T'ao P'eng-tse t'i" 學陶彭澤體
Hsüeh-yü t'ang wen-chi 學餘堂文集
Hsün-shih lu 荀氏錄
Hsün Tzu 荀子
"Hsün-yang yüeh" 潯陽樂
Hu-chia chuan 胡家傳
"Hu chia shih-pa p'ai" 胡笳十八拍
Hu-hai hsin-wen Yi-chien hsü-chih 湖海新聞夷堅續志
Hu-hai-lou tz'u-chi 湖海樓詞集
"Hu-k'ou yü-sheng" 虎口餘生
Hu-mei ts'ung-t'an 狐媚叢談
Hu-tieh mei 蝴蝶媒
Hu-tieh meng 蝴蝶夢
Hua-chien chi 花間集
Hua-hu ching 化胡經
Hua-kai shan Fou-ch'iu Wang Kuo san chen-chün shih-shih 華蓋山浮邱王郭三眞君事實
"Hua-shan nü" 華山女
"Hua-teng chiao Lien-nü ch'eng Fo chi" 花燈轎蓮女成佛記
Hua-ts'ao meng-shih 花草蒙拾
"Hua Wei Hsien-sheng" 華威先生
Hua-ying chi 花影集
Hua-yüeh hen 花月痕
"Huai-chiu" 懷舊
Huai-ch'un ya-chi 懷春雅集
"Huai-ku" 懷古
"Huai Li Shu-t'ung Hsien-sheng" 懷李叔同先生
Huai-nan Tzu 淮南子

“Huai-o-lin yü ch’iang-wei” 壞珴琳 (環娥琳) 與薔薇
“Huai sha” 懷沙
“Huai-shu-chuang” 槐樹莊
Huan-hsi yüan-chia 歡喜冤家
“Huan-hun chi” 還魂記
“Huan-men tzu-ti ts’o li-shen” 宦門子弟錯立身
“Huan-sha chi” 浣紗記
“Huan shan-chai” 還山齋
Huan-ying (San-k’o p’ai-an ching-ch’i) 幻影
Huan-yüan chih 還冤志
“Huang chung sha/wei” 黃鍾煞 / 尾
“Huang hun” 黃昏
Huang-jen shou-chi 荒人手記
“Huang-liang meng” 黃粱夢
Huang-Ming shih-hsüan 皇明詩選
Huang-ni chieh 黃泥街
“Huang Shih-ch’iang chuan” 黃仕強傳
Huang-t’ing ching 黃庭經
“Huang t’u-ti” 黃土地
“Hui-chia yi-hou” 回家以後
“Hui-lan chi” 灰欄記
Hui-lung chuan 回龍傳
Hui-t’ou k’an 回頭看
Hui t’u Lieh nü chuan 繪圖列女傳
“Hun-t’ien fu” 渾天賦
Hun-yüan sheng-chi 混元聖紀
“Hung fan” 洪範
“Hung-fu chi” 紅紼記
“Hung-hsien” 紅線
“Hung hsien t’an” 紅線毯
Hung kao-liang 紅高粱
Hung kao-liang chia-tsu 紅高粱家族
Hung-lou meng 紅樓夢
Hung-lou meng hsin-cheng 紅樓夢新證
“*Hung-lou meng* p’ing-lun” 《紅樓夢》評論
“*Hung-lou meng* te liang-ko shih-chieh” 紅樓夢的兩個世界
Hung-ming chi 弘明集
“Hung-se feng-pao” 紅色風暴
“Hung-se niang-tzu-chün” 紅色娘子軍
“Hung-teng chi” 紅燈記
Hung-tu chi 洪度集
“Huo Hsiao-yü chuan” 霍小玉傳
“Huo-hu chih yeh” 獲虎之夜
Huo-tung pien-jen hsing 活動變人形
“Hwangcho ga” 黃鳥歌
Ise monogatari 伊勢物語
“Jan-teng tsan” 燃燈讚
Je-tai-yü (Nettaigyo) 熱帶魚
Jen a jen 人啊人
Jen-chien shih 人間世
Jen-chien tz’u-hua 人間詞話
Jen-chung hua 人中畫
Jen-jen wen-hsüeh 人人文學
“Jen-shih chuan” 任氏傳
“Jih-ch’u” 日出
“*Jih-pen shu-mu chih* chih yü” 《日本書目志》識語
“Jih yü” 日喻
Jou p’u-t’uan 肉蒲團
Ju-lin wai-shih 儒林外史
“Ju-shih kuan” 如是觀
Ju Shu chi 入蜀記
“Ju Shu ch’iu-yeh su chiang-chu” 入蜀秋夜宿江渚
Ju-yi chün chuan 如意君傳
Juan-t’ing shih-yü 阮亭詩餘
Jun-chi 閏集
“Jung-ch’un chi” 融春集
“K’a-men” 卡門
“Kai-hsia ko” 垓下歌
K’ai-p’i 開辟
K’ai T’ien ch’uan-hsin chi 開天傳信記
K’ai-yen lu 開顏錄
Kaifūsō 懷風藻
Kajin no kigū 佳人之奇遇
Kakyō hyōshiki 歌経標式
“Kan-chiu fu” 感舊賦
“Kan ch’üan fu” 甘泉賦
Kan-hsiao liu chi 幹校六記
Kan-lan shu 橄欖樹
“Kan liu wang” 感流亡
Kan-shui hsien-yüan lu 甘水仙源錄
“Kan t’ien tung ti: Tou Ŏ yüan” 感天動地竇娥冤
“Kan-yü” 感遇
“K’an hung lu” 看虹錄
“K’an p’i-hsüeh tan cheng Erh-lang shen” 勘皮靴單證二郎神

Kanke bunsō	菅家文草
Kao-pieh ko-ming	告別革命
Kao-seng chuan	高僧傳
Kao-shan hsia te hua-huan	高山下的花環
Kao-shih chuan	高士傳
Kao Shih shih-chi	高適詩集
"Kao-t'ang fu"	高唐賦
Keikokushū	経国集
Ken-shih	亘史
Keng-ssu (?chi) pien	庚巳 (?己) 編
"Keng-tzu kuo-pien t'an-tz'u"	庚子國變彈詞
Kim Van Kieu	金雲翹
"Ko-che Yeh chi"	歌者葉記
Ko-lien hua-ying	隔簾花影
"Ko Ling-kung sheng yi nung chu-erh"	葛令公生遺弄珠兒
Kojiki	古事記
Kokin (waka) shū	古今和歌集
"Kou-erh Yeh nieh-p'an"	狗兒爺涅槃
"Ku-an man pi"	觚庵漫筆
Ku-chang chüeh-ch'en	鼓掌絕塵
Ku-chin chu	古今註
Ku-chin hsiao-shuo (Yü-shih ming-yen)	古今小說
Ku-chin shih-jen hsiu-chü	古今詩人秀句
Ku-chin shuo-hai	古今說海
Ku-chin t'an-kai	古今譚概
Ku-chin t'u-shu chi-ch'eng	古今圖書集成
Ku-chin yen	古今諺
Ku chin yüeh lu	古今樂錄
"Ku-ching chi"	古鏡記
"Ku-ch'ui ch'ü-tz'u"	鼓吹曲辭
"Ku feng"	古風
"Ku hsiang"	故鄉
Ku hsiao-shuo kou-ch'en	古小說鉤沉
Ku-liang chuan	穀梁傳
Ku Lou Kuan tzu-yün yen-ch'ing chi	古樓觀紫雲衍慶集
Ku-sheng	觚賸
Ku-shih hsüan	古詩選
Ku-shih kuei	古詩歸
Ku shih pien	古史辯
"Ku-shih shih-chiu shou"	古詩十九首
Ku-shih wen-fang hsiao-shuo	顧氏文房小說
Ku shih yüan	古詩源
Ku-shu yi-jen	鼓書藝人
Ku T'ing-lin shih-chi	顧亭林詩集
Ku tsa-chü	古雜劇
Ku-wen chen-pao	古文眞寶
"K'u hsiang p'ien [Yü-chang hsing]"	苦相篇 [豫章行]
"K'u je hsing"	苦熱行
"Kua-fu she-chi chui hsin-lang, chung mei ch'i-hsin to ts'ai-tzu"	寡婦設計贅新郎眾美齊心奪才子
"K'uai-huo ko"	快活歌
"K'uai-tsui Li Ts'ui-lien chi"	快嘴李翠蓮記
K'uai-yüan	獪園
Kuan-ch'ang hsien-hsing chi	官場現形記
"Kuan-chü"	關雎
Kuan-chui p'ien	管錐篇
"Kuan Han-ch'ing"	關漢卿
"Kuan-kuan te pu-p'in"	官官的補品
"Kuan Li Ku ch'ing ssu-ma ti shan-shui t'u san shou"	觀李固清司馬弟山水圖三首
Kuan Tzu	管子
Kuan wu-liang-shou (Fo) ching	觀無量壽 (佛) 經
"Kuan-yüan sou wan feng hsien-nü"	灌園叟晚逢仙女
Kuang hsiao-fu	廣笑府
Kuang Hung-ming chi	廣弘明集
Kuang-shih-yin ying-yen chi	光世音應驗記
Kuang Yen-yi pien	廣艷異編
"K'uang-jen jih-chi"	狂人日記
"K'uang ku-shih"	狂鼓史
"K'uang t'ai-shou tuan ssu hai-erh"	況太守斷死孩兒
"Kuei-ch'ü-lai tz'u"	歸去來辭
"Kuei-t'ien fu"	歸田賦
Kuei t'ien lu	歸田錄
Kuei-tung	鬼董

"Kuei yüan t'ien chü" 歸園田居
K'uei-ch'e chih 睽車志
Ku'magŏm 驅魔劍
Kŭmo sinhwa 金鼇新話
"K'un-lun nu" 崑崙奴
"Kung wu ch'u men" 公無出門
Kung-yang chuan 公羊傳
"Kung-yen shih" 公宴詩
K'ung An-kuo Shang-shu 孔安國尚書
"K'ung-ch'üeh tung-nan fei" 孔雀東南飛
K'ung Tzu chia-yü 孔子家語
"K'ung-tzu Hsiang T'o hsiang-wen shu" 孔子相託相問書
"Kuo feng" 國風
Kuo-hsiu chi 國秀集
Kuo-se t'ien-hsiang 國色天香
Kuo shih 國史
Kuo-wen pao 國聞報
Kuo-yü 國語
"Kuo Yüan-chen" 郭元振
Kuun gi 九雲記
Kuun mong 九雲夢
Kwanghanru gi 廣寒樓記
Kwansan yungma 關山戎馬
Kyewŏn p'ilgyŏngjip 桂苑筆耕集
Kyōunshū 狂雲集
Lai-nan lu 來南錄
Lan-p'ei lu 攬轡錄
"Lan Ts'ai-ho" 藍采和
"Lan-yün wo" 懶雲窩
Lao-hsüeh-an pi-chi 老學菴筆記
"Lao-jen hsing fu" 老人星賦
"Lao men-sheng san-shih pao-en" 老門生三世報恩
Lao Ts'an yu-chi 老殘遊記
Lao Tzu 老子
Lao Tzu ming 老子銘
"Lei-feng t'a" 雷峰塔
Lei-feng t'a ch'uan-ch'i 雷峰塔傳奇
"Lei-yü" 雷雨
"Lei yü hsing" 雷雨行
Li 禮
Li-ch'eng 里乘
Li-chi 禮記
"Li Chiao tsa-yung" 李嶠雜詠
"Li-chih fu" 荔枝賦
"Li Ch'ih chuan" 李赤傳
Li-feng lao-jen chi 離峰老人集
"Li Feng-niang k'u tu tsao t'ien-ch'ien" 李鳳娘酷妒遭天譴
"Li Fu-jen ko" 李夫人歌
"Li-hua chüan" 梨花卷
"Li-hua meng" 梨花夢
"Li-hun chi" 離魂記
"Li-huo lun" 理惑論
"Li K'uei fu-ching" 李逵負荊
Li-pai-liu 禮拜六
"Li sao" 離騷
"Li sao hsü" 離騷序
Li-shih chen-hsien t'i-tao t'ung-chien 歷史眞仙體道通鑑
Li-tai ch'ung-tao chi 歷代崇道記
Li-tai pi-chi kai-shu 歷代筆記概述
"Li Tao-jen tu pu Yün-men" 李道人獨步雲門
"Li Wa chuan" 李娃傳
Li Yu-ts'ai pan-hua 李有才板話
"Li Yü-ying yü chung sung yüan" 李玉英獄中訟冤
"Li-yüan ying-lieh" 梨園英烈
"Li yüeh chih" 禮樂志
Liang Chin yen-yi 兩晉演義
"Liang kua Kao Hsing" 梁寡高行
"Liang-shih yin-yüan" 兩世姻緣
Liang shu 梁書
"Liang ts'o jen Mo ta-chieh ssu-pen, tsai ch'eng-chiao Yang erh-lang cheng-pen" 兩錯認莫大姐私奔再成交楊二郎正本
Liao-chai chih-yi 聊齋志異
Liao-shih 遼史
"Liao-tu keng" 療妒羹
Liao-tu yüan 療妒緣
"Liao-yang hai-shen chuan" 遼陽海神傳
Lieh-ch'ao shih-chi 列朝詩集
Lieh-ch'ao shih-chi hsiao-chuan 列朝詩集小傳
Lieh-hsien chuan 列仙傳
Lieh-kuo chih-chuan 列國志傳

Lieh-nü chuan	列女傳
Lieh-shih chuan	列士傳
Lieh Tzu	列子
Lieh-yi chuan	列異傳
“Lien-ch’ang kung tz’u”	連昌宮詞
Lien-ch’eng pi ch’üan-chi	連城璧全集
Lien-ho pao	聯合報
“Lien-hsiang-pan”	憐香伴
“Lien shih jih”	練時日
“Lin-an li Ch’ien P’o-liu fa-chi”	臨安里錢婆留發跡
Lin-chi lu	臨濟錄
“Lin-ch’uan meng”	臨川夢
“Lin-ch’uan ssu-meng”	臨川四夢
Lin-erh pao	麟兒報
Lin-Lan-Hsiang	林蘭香
Ling-pao ling-chiao chi-tu chin-shu	靈寶領教濟度金書
Ling-pao wu-liang tu-jen shang-p’in miao-ching	靈寶無量度人上品妙經
Ling-shan	靈山
“Liu Chih-yüan chu-kung-tiao”	劉智遠諸宮調
“Liu chün-tzu t’u”	六君子圖
Liu Pin-k’o chia-hua lu	劉賓客嘉話錄
“Liu Sa-ho ho-shang yin-yüan chi”	劉薩訶和尚因緣記
Liu-shih chia hsiao-shuo (Ch’ing-p’ing-shan t’ang hua-pen)	六十家小說
“Liu-shih chuan”	柳氏傳
Liu-shih chung ch’ü	六十種曲
Liu-tsu t’an-ching	六祖壇經
Liu-tu chi-ching	六度集經
“Liu Tung-shan k’ua chi Shun ch’eng men, shih-pa hsiung tsung ch’i ts’un chiu ssu”	劉東山誇技順城門十八兄蹤奇村酒肆
Liu-ya wai-pien	柳崖外編
“Liu Yi”	柳毅
“Liu yi shih”	六憶詩
Liu-yi shih-hua	六一詩話
“Lo-shen fu”	洛神賦
Lo-t’o Hsiang-tzu	駱駝祥子
Lo-yang ch’ieh-lan chi	洛陽伽藍記
“Lu Ch’iu chieh fu”	魯秋潔婦
“Lu chu shan-fang”	菉竹山房
Lu Hsün ch’üan chi	魯迅全集
Lu-kuei pu	錄鬼簿
“Lu-shan chih hsüeh”	廬山之雪
“Lu-shan shan hsing”	魯山山行
“Lu-shan Yüan-kung hua”	廬山遠公話
“Lu t’ai-hsüeh shih chiu ao wang hou”	盧太學詩酒傲王侯
Lü-ch’uang nü-shih	綠窗女史
“Lü-mao pieh”	綠毛鱉
“Lü-men pai-sui p’ien”	緇門百歲篇
“Lü mu-tan”	綠牡丹
“Lü-se ying-ti”	綠色營地
Lü-shih ch’un-ch’iu	呂氏春秋
Lü Tsu chih	呂祖志
Lü-yeh hsien-tsung	綠野仙蹤
“Lü-yi shih-che chuan”	綠衣使者傳
“Luan-pi chi”	鸞鎞記
Luan-tu chih lien	亂都之戀
“Lun fei-o p’o-lai ying-kai huan-hsing”	論費厄潑賴應該緩行
“Lun Fo-ku piao”	論佛骨表
Lun heng	論衡
“Lun hsiao-shuo yü ch’ün-chih chih kuan-hsi”	論小說與群治之關係
“Lun hsieh-ch’ing hsiao-shuo yü hsin she-hui chih kuan-hsi”	論寫情小說與新社會之關係
Lun shih san-shih shou	論詩三十首
“Lun tuan-p’ien hsiao-shuo”	論短篇小說
Lun wen	論文
“Lun wen-hsüeh shang hsiao-shuo chih wei-chih”	論文學上小說之位置
“Lun wen-jen”	論文人
Lun-yü (Analects)	論語
“Lung-chiang sung”	龍江頌
Lung-hsing Fo-chiao pien-nien t’ung-lun	隆興佛教編年通論
“Lung-hsü-kou”	龍須溝
Lung-hu shan chih	龍虎山志
“Ma-feng nü Ch’iu Li-yü”	痲瘋女邱麗玉

"Ma-k'o-ssu chin K'ung miao"	馬克斯進孔廟
"Ma-ling kua"	馬鈴瓜
"Ma-nao lei fu"	瑪瑙勒賦
"Ma shih-ch'ung wen"	罵尸蟲文
Ma-tsu yü-lu	馬祖語錄
"Mai-hua nü"	賣花女
"Mai t'an weng"	賣炭翁
"Mai-yu lang tu chan hua-k'uei"	賣油郎獨占花魁
"Man-chiang hung"	滿江紅
Man-chou shih-lu	滿洲實錄
"Man-t'ing fang"	滿庭芳
"Mang shu-sheng ch'iang t'u yüan-lü"	莽書生強圖鴛侶
Manyōshū	万葉集
Mao shan chih	茅山志
Mao-shih	毛詩
"Mao Ying chuan"	毛穎傳
"Mei-jen fu"	美人賦
Mei-ko	梅葛
"Mei nan-tzu pi huo fan sheng yi"	美男子避惑反生疑
"Mei-yü"	梅雨
Men-wai wen-t'an	門外文談
Mencius (*Meng Tzu*)	孟子
"Meng"	氓
"Meng chiao-kuan ai nü pu shou pao, ch'iung hsiang-sheng chu shih te ling chung"	懵教官愛女不受報窮庠生助師得令終
Meng-hsi pi-t'an	夢溪筆談
"Meng liang tao ku"	孟良盜骨
Meng Tzu (*Mencius*)	孟子
"Mi-chou"	迷舟
Mi-teng yin-hua	覓燈因話
Miao-chin feng	描金鳳
Miao-fa lien-hua ching	妙法蓮華經
"Mien-tui tzu-chi"	面對自己
Min-ch'üan pao	民權報
Min-kuo jih-pao	民國日報
Min pao	民報
"Min sheng fu"	閔生賦
Ming-Ch'ing pi-chi t'an-ts'ung	明清筆記談叢
"Ming-fei ch'ü ho Wang Chieh-fu tso"	明妃曲和王介甫作
"Ming-feng chi"	鳴鳳記
Ming-ho yü-yin	鳴鶴餘音
Ming-hsiang chi	冥祥記
Ming-hsüeh ch'ien-shuo	名學淺說
Ming-huang tsa-lu	明皇雜錄
"Ming-jen chang-hui hsiao-shuo"	明人章回小說
"Ming-kuei"	明鬼
Ming-pao chi	冥報記
Ming shih	明史
Ming-shih chuan	名士傳
Ming-shih kao	明史稿
"Ming-t'ang fu"	明堂賦
Ming-tao p'ien	明道篇
Ming-tao tsa-chih	明道雜志
"Ming tu p'ien"	明都篇
"Ming-wu Ch'an-shih kan Wu-chieh"	明悟禪師赶五戒
"Ming-yu chih ssu"	名優之死
"Ming-yüeh ch'u-chao jen"	明月初照人
Ming-yün	命運
Mingashū	岷峨集
Mo-han-chai ting-pen ch'uan-ch'i	墨憨齋定本傳奇
Mo-ho chih-kuan	摩訶止觀
"Mo-ling-ch'un"	秣陵春
"Mo shang sang"	陌上桑
Mo Tzu	墨子
Mongyurok	夢遊錄
Mu-chai ch'u-hsüeh chi	牧齋初學集
"Mu-lan chai"	木蘭柴
"Mu-lan shih"	木蘭詩
"Mu-lan tz'u"	木蘭詞
Mu-le ming-hsüeh	穆勒名學
"Mu-lien"	目連
"Mu-lien pien-wen"	目連變文
"Mu-lien yüan-ch'i"	目蓮緣起
"Mu-p'i-san-jen ku-tz'u"	木皮散人鼓詞
"Mu-tan"	牡丹
"Mu-tan t'ing"	牡丹亭
Mu t'ien-tzu chuan	穆天子傳
Na-han	吶喊
"Nai-ho-t'ien"	奈何天
Nan-chao kung-teng	南詔宮燈
Nan-fang pao	南方報

Nan-hai chi-kuei nei-fa chuan 南海寄歸內法傳
Nan-hua ching 南華經
"Nan-k'o chi" 南柯記
"Nan-k'o t'ai-shou chuan" 南柯太守傳
Nan-kuo pan yüeh k'an 南國半月刊
Nan-lei shih-li 南雷詩曆
"Nan Meng-mu chiao ho san ch'ien" 男孟母教合三遷
"Nan p'u" 南浦
"Nan-t'o ch'u-chia yüan" 難陀出家緣
Nan-tz'u hsü-lu 南詞敘錄
"Nan wang-hou" 男王后
Nan-yu chi 南游記
Nansō Satomi hakken den 南総里見八犬伝
"Nao yin-ssu Ssu-ma Mao tuan yü" 鬧陰司司馬貌斷獄
"Nei-p'ien" 內篇
"Nei yeh" 內業
Nettaigyo (*Je-tai-yü*) 熱帶魚
Ngoc kieu le tan truyen 玉嬌梨新傳
"Ni 'Hsing lu nan'" 擬行路難
Ni Huan-chih 倪煥之
"Ni-hung-teng hsia te shao-ping" 霓虹燈下的哨兵
Ni-ku yüeh-fu 擬古樂府
Ni pieh wu hsüan-tse 你別無選擇
Nieh-hai hua 孽海花
Nihon shoki 日本書記
"Niu fu" 牛賦
"Nu-hou pa, Chung-kuo!" 怒吼吧, 中國!
"Nü Ch'en P'ing chi sheng ch'i ch'u" 女陳平計生七出
"Nü chieh" 女誡
"Nü chuang-yüan" 女狀元
Nü-hsien wai-shih 女仙外史
"Nü-shih chen t'u" 女史箴圖
"Nü tse" 女則
"O ch'uan-chia chi chuan chia shih yin, hen p'u-jen wu t'ou chen ming chuang" 惡船家計賺假屍銀狠僕人誤投眞命狀
O-mi-t'o ching (*A-mi-t'o ching*) 阿彌陀經
"O-p'ang kung fu" 阿房宮賦
O-ping yü Sang-lo 娥並與桑洛
Ongnu mong 玉樓夢
Otogibōko 伽婢子
Ou Mei ming-chia tuan-p'ien hsiao-shuo ts'ung-k'o 歐美名家短篇小說叢刻
"Ou t'i" 偶題
Pa-li ch'a-hua nü yi-shih 巴黎茶花女遺事
"Pa-sheng Kan-chou" 八聲甘州
Pa-tuan chin 八段錦
Pa tung-t'ien 八洞天
"Pa-yi Nan-ch'ang ch'i-yi" 八一南昌起義
Paegun sosŏl 白雲小說
P'ahanjip 破閑集
Pai-chia kung-an 百家公案
"Pai-ho fang chiang wu tso yu" 百和坊將無作有
Pai-hua wen-hsüeh shih 白話文學史
Pai-kuei chih 白圭志
"Pai ma p'ien" 白馬篇
"Pai-mao nü" 白毛女
Pai-mo tz'u 百末詞
"Pai niang-tzu yung chen Lei-feng t'a" 白娘子永鎮雷峰塔
Pai-niao 白鳥
Pai nien yi chiao 百年一覺
Pai-she chuan 白蛇傳
"Pai-t'u chi" 白兔記
Pai-yü ching 百喻經
"Pai-yüan chuan" 白猿傳
"Pai-yüeh chi" 拜月記
"Pai-yüeh-t'ing" 拜月亭
P'ai-an ching-ch'i (*Ch'u-k'o p'ai-an ching-ch'i*) 拍案驚奇
Pak-t'ongsa 朴通使
"P'an Chin-lien" 潘金蓮
P'an-hsi chi 磻溪集
P'an-ku 盤古
P'an shan yü-lu 盤山語錄
"P'an Wen-tzu ch'i-ho yüan-yang chung" 潘文子契合鴛鴦塚
P'ang Chü-shih yü-lu 龐居士語錄
P'ang-huang 徬徨

“Pao-chien chi” 寶劍記
“Pao ch’un hua” 報春花
Pao-kuang chi 葆光集
Pao-p’u Tzu 抱朴子
“Pao-wei Lu-kou-ch’iao” 保衛蘆溝橋
“Pei cheng” 北征
Pei-ching chih ch’un 北京之春
“Pei-ching jen” 北京人
Pei-ching jen 北京人
“Pei fen shih” 悲憤詩
Pei-hai te jen 背海的人
Pei-hsi tzu yi 北溪字義
“Pei hui feng” 悲回風
Pei-li chih 北里志
“Pei-ying” 背影
Pei-yu chi 北游記
“P’ei Chin-kung yi huan yüan-p’ei” 裴晉公義還原配
P’ei-wen yün-fu 佩文韻府
“Pen-kuan fu-yin shuo-pu yüan-ch’i” 本館復印說部緣起
“P’en-erh-kuei” 盆兒鬼
“P’eng-tang lun” 朋黨論
Pi-cha hua-liang 筆札華梁
“Pi-ch’eng” 碧城
Pi-chi hsiao-shuo ta-kuan 筆記小說大觀
Pi-chi hsiao-shuo ta-kuan so-yin 筆記小說大觀索引
Pi-ch’iu-ni chuan 比丘尼傳
Pi-chou hsüan sheng-yü 敝帚軒剩語
“Pi-mu-yü” 比目魚
Pi-p’o ts’ung-ts’o 筆坡叢脞
“Pi-sheng hua” 筆生花
“Pi shuo” 筆說
Pi-yen lu 碧巖錄
“P’i-p’a chi” 琵琶記
“P’i-p’a hsing” 琵琶行
“P’i-shuang po” 砒霜鉢
“Piao yi-che Kuo Ch’ang” 表醫者郭常
“Pieh-ch’ing” 別情
Pien-ch’eng 邊城
Pien erh ch’ai 弁而釵
“Pien Li sao” 變離騷
“Pien wang lun” 辨亡論
P’in-hua pao-chien 品花寶鑑
Ping-chu ch’ing-t’an 秉燭清談
“P’ing fu” 瓶賦
P’ing-Shan-Leng-Yen 平山冷燕
P’ing yao chuan 平妖傳
Po Hsiang-shan shih-chi 白香山詩集
“Po-hsiao-chi” 博笑記
Po-hsiao chu-chi 博笑珠璣
Po-hsüeh hung-tz’u 博學宏詞
Po-je-po-lo-mi-to-hsin-ching 般若波羅蜜多心經
Po-shih wen-chi (*Hakushi monjū*) 白氏文集
Po-tung 波動
Po-wu chih 博物志
Pohanjip 補閑集
“Pu-chih ch’iu-ssu tsai shui chia” 不知秋思在誰家
“Pu chü” 卜居
“Pu Fei-yen” 步飛煙
“Pu fu lao” 不伏老
“Pu-hsü” 步虛
Pu-hsü ching 步虛經
“Pu-ku-niao yu chiao le” 布穀鳥又叫了
“Pu p’a ssu” 不怕死
P’u-hsien p’u-sa shuo cheng-ming ching 普賢菩薩說証明經
P’u-sa tu-jen ching 菩薩度人經
P’u-t’ung pai-k’o hsin ta tz’u-tien 普通百科新大辭典
P’u yao ching 普曜經
Ryōunshū 凌雲集
“Sai Chin-hua” 賽金花
Samguk yusa 三國遺史
San-chiang hsien-chih 三江縣志
San-chiao chu-ying 三教珠英
“San-fen” 三分
San-hsiao yin-yüan 三笑姻緣
“San-hua tsan” 散花讚
“San ko p’an-ni te nü-hsing” 三個叛逆的女性
San-k’o p’ai-an ching-ch’i (*Huan-ying*) 三刻拍案驚奇
San-kuo chih 三國志
San-kuo yen-yi 三國演義
San-li 三禮

"San liang"	三良
San-miao chuan	三妙傳
San-pao t'ai-chien hsi-yang chi t'ung-su yen-yi	三寶太監西洋記通俗演義
"San-san"	三三
San-shih tai t'ien-shih Hsü-ching chen-chün yü-lu	三十代天師虛靜眞君語錄
San-t'i shih	三體詩
San-t'i shih-ching	三體石經
"San tu fu"	三都賦
San-tung ching-shu mu-lu	三洞經書目錄
San-tzu ching	三字經
San wu li chi	三五歷紀
San-yen	三言
"San yüeh san jih Ch'ü shui shih hsü"	三月三日曲水詩序
"Sang-shu-p'ing chi-shih"	桑樹坪記事
Sanguk sagi	三國史記
Sangyō gisho	三経義疏
Sansu yugi	山水遊記
Sao	騷
Sao-mi-chou	掃迷帚
"Sha-chia-pang"	沙家浜
"Sha-fei nü-shih jih-chi"	莎菲女士日記
"Sha-kou chi"	殺狗記
"Sha-kou ch'üan-fu"	殺狗勸夫
Shan-chung yi-hsi	山中一夕
Shan hai ching	山海經
"Shan hsing chien ku t'ung"	山行見孤桐
"Shan-kuei"	山鬼
"Shan-shang hua tsan"	扇上畫贊
Shan shang te shih-chi	山上的世紀
"Shan tsai hsing"	善哉行
"Shang Chang Ch'in Ch'ing tsan"	尙長禽慶贊
Shang-ch'ing hou-sheng tao-chün lieh-chi	上清後聖道君列紀
"Shang ch'un"	傷春
"Shang-hai wu-yen hsia"	上海屋檐下
"Shang-lin fu"	上林賦
"Shang shih"	傷逝
Shang-shu	尙書
Shang-yang-tzu chin-tan ta-yao	上陽子金丹大要
Shao-nien p'iao-po-che	少年漂泊者
Shao-shih chien-wen lu	邵氏見聞錄
Shao-shih shan-fang pi-ts'ung	少室山房筆叢
She-hui t'ung-ch'üan	社會通銓
"She-tao shih"	涉道詩
"Shen chiang-shih san-ch'ien mai hsiao ch'ien, Wang ch'ao-yi yi-yeh mi-hun chen"	沈將仕三千買笑錢王朝議一夜迷魂陣
Shen-chou ching	神咒經
"Shen-chung-lou"	蜃中樓
"Shen Hsiao-hsia hsiang hui ch'u-shih piao"	沈小霞相會出師表
"Shen Hsiao-kuan yi niao hai ch'i ming"	沈小官一鳥害七命
"Shen-hsien ch'ü"	神絃曲
Shen-hsien chuan	神仙傳
Shen-hsien hui	神仙會
Shen-lou chih	蜃樓志
"Shen-nü fu"	神女賦
Shen pao	申報
"Shen t'ou chi hsing yi-chih mei, hsia tao kuan hsing san mei hsi"	神偷寄興一枝梅俠盜慣行三昧戲
Sheng Ming tsa-chü	盛明雜劇
Sheng Ming tsa-chü erh-chi	盛明雜劇二集
"Sheng wo lou"	生我樓
"Sheng-yang tien ku-chih"	昇陽殿故址
Shigeshige yawa	繁野話
Shih	詩
Shih ch'ang t'an	釋常談
"Shih-ch'eng yüeh"	石城樂
Shih-chi	史記
Shih chi chuan	詩集傳
Shih-chi p'ing-lin	史記評林
"Shih-chi wen"	釋疾文
Shih-chia chih shuo	詩家直說
"Shih-chia fo fu"	釋迦佛賦

Shih-chieh fan-hua pao	世界繁華報
Shih-ching	詩經
"Shih-chung shan chi"	石鍾山記
Shih-erh lou	十二樓
"Shih-erh shih hsing-hsiao"	十二時行孝
"Shih-erh yin-yüan liu-tzu ko-tz'u"	十二因緣六字歌詞
Shih-fa	詩法
"Shih-hao li"	石壕吏
"Shih hua"	詩話
"Shih-jen"	碩人
Shih-ko	詩格
"Shih ku ko"	石鼓歌
Shih kuang-chuan	詩廣傳
"Shih li"	十離
Shih-li	士禮
Shih-li chin-tan	十里金丹
Shih ling-t'u	詩領土
Shih-men cheng t'ung	釋門正統
Shih ming	釋名
"Shih pi"	試筆
"Shih-pien"	詩辯
Shih p'in	詩品
Shih-p'ing	詩評
Shih-san ching	十三經
Shih-sen (Hsiao-tzu chuan)	事森
Shih-shih	詩式
Shih-shih lei-yüan	時事類苑
Shih-shih t'ung-chien	釋氏通鑑
"Shih-shuo"	師說
Shih-shuo hsin-yü	世說新語
Shih sou	詩藪
Shih-ssu-hang chi	十四行集
Shih sui-nao	詩髓腦
"Shih t'ai-tzu tso"	侍太子坐
"Shih-t'i"	詩體
Shih tien t'ou	石點頭
"Shih ting lien-chü shih hsü"	石鼎聯句詩序
Shih-t'ou chi (Hung lou meng)	石頭記(紅樓夢)
Shih t'ung	史通
Shih Tzu	尸子
Shih-tzu hou	獅子吼
"Shih-wu-kuan"	十五貫
Shih wu pao	時務報
"Shih-wu ts'ung-chün cheng"	十五從軍征
"Shih yi"	十翼
Shih-yi	詩譯
Shih-yi chi	拾遺記
Shimeisen	四鳴蟬
Shina bungaku shi	支那文學史
Shōkenkō	蕉堅藁
Shōsetsu kigen	小說奇言
Shōsetsu seigen	小說精言
Shōsetsu shinzui	小說眞髓
"Shou-yang shan Shu-ch'i pien-chieh"	首陽山叔齊變節
Shu	書
"Shu chi"	書記
Shu-ching	書經
"Shu-erh"	述而
"Shu huai"	述懷
"Shu so chien"	書所見
"Shu tao nan"	蜀道難
Shu-wang	樹王
Shu-wang pen-chi	蜀王本紀
Shu yüan chui t'an	菽園贅談
"Shuang-k'ou-hun"	雙叩閽
"Shuang tiao ch'ing"	雙雕慶
Shuang-tzu-hsing jen-wen shih-k'an	雙子星人文詩刊
Shui-hu chuan	水滸傳
Shui-hu chuan te lai-li hsin-t'ai yü yi-shu	水滸傳的來歷心態與藝術
Shui-hu hou-chuan	水滸後傳
Shui-hu lun-heng	水滸論衡
"Shui-tiao ko-t'ou"	水調歌頭
Shui-yün chi	水雲集
"Shun tien"	舜典
"Shun-tzu chih-hsiao pien-wen"	舜子至孝變文
Shuo-fu	說郛
"Shuo hsiao-shuo"	說小說
Shuo-ling	說鈴
Shuo T'ang yen-yi ch'üan chuan	說唐演義全傳
Shuo-t'ing	說聽

Shuo-wen chieh-tzu 說文解字
Shuo yüan 說苑
Shuo Yüeh ch'üan chuan 說岳全傳
So akbu 小樂府
Sodae p'ungyo 昭代風謠
Sou-shen chi 搜神記
Sou-shen chi yi-pen 搜神記一本
Sou-shen hou-chi 搜神後記
Sou-yü hsiao-chi 搜玉小集
"Ssu-chai shui ch'i" 寺齋 睡起
"Ssu ch'an-chüan" 四嬋娟
"Ssu ch'ou shih" 四愁詩
"Ssu-hsien ch'iu" 四線秋
"Ssu hsüan fu" 思玄賦
"Ssu huan ch'un fu" 思還淳賦
"Ssu kan" 斯干
Ssu-k'u ch'üan-shu 四庫全書
Ssu-k'u ch'üan-shu tsung-mu t'i-yao 四庫全書總目提要
Ssu min yüeh ling 四民月令
Ssu-ming shih-hua 四溟詩話
Ssu-pu hsü-kao 四部續稿
Ssu sheng p'u 四聲譜
"Ssu-sheng-yüan" 四聲猿
Ssu shih 四史
"Ssu-shih t'ien-yüan tsa-hsing" 四時田園雜興
Ssu shu 四書
Ssu-shu chi-chu 四書集注
Ssu-wu lun-t'an 四五論壇
Ssu-yu chi 四遊記
Su-hua ch'ing-t'an 俗話傾談
"Su Tung-hsiao Kung" 宿洞霄宮
Su-wen-na ho t'a erh-tzu 蘇文娜和她兒子
Sui chŏn 殊異傳
Sui shih yi-wen 隋史遺文
Sui shu 隋書
Sui T'ang chia-hua 隋唐嘉話
Sui T'ang yen-yi 隋唐演義
Sui Yang-ti yen-shih 隋煬帝豔史
"Sung" 頌
"Sung Chih-tao-yüan te jih-chi" 宋指導員的日記
"Sung Ch'ing chuan" 宋清傳
"Sung ch'iung wen" 送窮文
"Sung feng-po" 訟風伯
Sung Kao-seng chuan 宋高僧傳
Sung-kuei t'ang ch'üan-chi 松桂堂全集
Sung-shih ch'ao 宋詩鈔
Sung-shih chi-shih 宋詩紀事
Sung shu 宋書
Sung ssu-chia tz'u-hsüan 宋四家詞選
"Sung Ssu-kung ta nao Chin-hun Chang" 宋四公大鬧禁魂張
Sung-tai pi-chi yen-chiu 宋代筆記研究
Sung-yin man-lu 淞隱漫錄
"Sung Ying shih" 送應氏
Sung Yüan hsi-ch'ü k'ao 宋元戲曲考
Ta-an-pan shou-yi ching 大安般守意經
"Ta chao" 大招
"Ta-chieh hun yu wan su-yüan, hsiao-yi ping ch'i hsü ch'ien-yüan" 大姊魂遊完宿願小姨病起續前緣
"Ta Ch'in ching-chiao san-wei meng-tu tsan" 大秦景教三威蒙度讚
Ta Ch'ing yi-t'ung-chih 大清一統志
"Ta-ch'u yu-ling-t'a" 打出幽靈塔
"Ta ch'ü" 大曲
"Ta chuan" 大傳
"Ta feng ko" 大風歌
"Ta hsü" 大序
"Ta-hsüeh" 大學
Ta-hsüeh yao lüeh 大學要略
"Ta-jen fu" 大人賦
"Ta-jen Hsien-sheng chuan" 大人先生傳
"Ta-lieh fu" 大獵賦
Ta-lu tang-tai ming-jen p'ing-chuan 大陸當代名人評傳
Ta Ming Hsüan-t'ien shang-ti jui-ying t'u-lu 大明玄天上帝瑞應圖錄
Ta Ming Tao-tsang ching 大明道藏經
"Ta-mu-ch'ien-lien ming-chien chiu-mu pien-wen" 大目乾連冥間救母變文
"Ta-nan" 大男
"Ta-p'eng niao fu" 大鵬鳥賦
Ta-p'in po-je po-lo-mi ching 大品般若波羅蜜經

"Ta-shuo" 大說
Ta Sung hsüan-ho yi-shih 大宋宣和遺事
Ta Sung t'ien-kung pao-tsang 大宋天宮寶藏
Ta Tai Li-chi 大戴禮記
"Ta T'ang Ch'in-wang tz'u-hua" 大唐秦王詞話
Ta T'ang hsi-yü chi 大唐西域記
Ta T'ang hsin-yü 大唐新語
Ta-tung chen-ching 大洞眞經
"Ta wai shih erh-shou" 答外詩二首
"Ta ya" 大雅
"Ta yü" 大魚
Ta-yün ching 大雲經
Tai-ching t'ang shih-hua 帶經堂詩話
"Tai K'u je hsing" 代苦熱行
Tai shih 岱史
T'ai-chi Ko hsien-kung chuan 太極葛仙公傳
T'ai-ho cheng-yin p'u 太和正音譜
T'ai-ku chi 太古集
T'ai-kung chia-chiao 太公家教
T'ai-pei jen 台北人
"T'ai-p'ing hu" 太平湖
T'ai-p'ing kuang-chi 太平廣記
T'ai-p'ing kuang-chi ch'ao 太平廣記鈔
T'ai-p'ing-yang pao 太平洋報
T'ai-p'ing yü-lan 太平御覽
T'ai-p'ing yüeh-fu 太平樂府
"T'ai-shan feng-kuang" 泰山風光
"T'ai-shih" 泰誓
T'ai shih 太誓
"T'ai-shih kung tzu-hsü" 太史公自序
"T'ai-tsung ju-ming chi" 太宗入冥記
T'ai-tzu jui-ying pen-ch'i ching 太子瑞應本起經
"T'ai-tzu wu-keng chuan" 太子五更傳
T'ai-wan ch'ing-nien 台灣青年
T'ai-wan hsin wen-hsüeh 台灣新文學
T'ai-wan hsin-wen-hsüeh chi-k'an 台灣新文學季刊
T'ai-wan min-pao 台灣民報
Taiwanese Youth (see *T'ai-wan ch'ing-nien*)
Taiheiki 太平記
Taiheiki engi 太平記演義
Tainan shimpō (*T'ai-nan hsin-pao*) 臺南新報
"Tan-k'o pan-shu chiu huan, fu-weng ch'ien-chin yi hsiao" 丹客半黍九還富翁千金一笑
"Tan-tao-hui" 單刀會
Tan-yang chen-jen chih-yen 丹陽眞人直言
Tan-yang chen-jen yü-lu 丹陽眞人語錄
Tan-yang chi 丹陽集
Tan-yang shen-kuang ts'an 丹陽神光燦
"T'an Ch'u-yü hsi-li ch'uan-ch'ing, Liu Miao-ku ch'ü chung ssu-chieh" 譚楚玉戲裏傳情劉藐姑曲終死節
"T'an-lan han liu yüan mai feng-liu" 貪婪漢六院賣風流
T'an lung lu 談龍錄
"T'an pai-sui" 嘆百歲
T'an-so 探索
Tang-k'ou chih 蕩寇志
"T'ang chieh-yüan yi hsiao yin-yüan" 唐解元一笑姻緣
T'ang chih yen 唐摭言
T'ang-hsien san-mei chi 唐賢三昧集
T'ang-jen hsiao-shuo 唐人小說
T'ang pai-chia shih-hsüan 唐百家詩選
T'ang-shih chi-shih 唐詩紀事
T'ang-shih hsüan 唐詩選
T'ang-shih kuei 唐詩歸
T'ang-shih pieh-tsai chi 唐詩別載集
T'ang-shih p'in-hui 唐詩品彙
T'ang-shih san-pai-shou 唐詩三百首
T'ang Sung pa-ta chia wen-ch'ao 唐宋八大家文鈔
T'ang-tai san-pai shih 唐代三百詩
T'ang wen ts'ui 唐文粹
T'ang wu-shih-chia shih-chi 唐五十家詩集
T'ang Yeh chen-jen chuan 唐葉眞人傳
T'ang-yin t'ung-ch'ien 唐音通籤
Tao-chia chin-shih lüeh 道家金石略
Tao-chiao wen-hsien 道教文獻
"Tao-ch'ing shih-shou" 道情十首
Tao-fa hsin-chuan 道法心傳
Tao-fa hui-yüan 道法會元

"Tao-kuan nei po-shu fu" 道觀內柏樹賦
"Tao lien-nü" 悼伶女
Tao-men shih-kuei 道門十規
Tao shu 道樞
Tao te ching 道德經
Tao-tsang chi yao 道藏輯要
"Tao wang shih" 悼亡詩
"T'ao-hua jen-mien" 桃花人面
"T'ao-hua shan" 桃花扇
T'ao-hua ying 桃花影
"T'ao-hua yüan" 桃花源
"T'ao-hua yüan chi" 桃花源記
"Te Tao ko" 得道歌
"Teng chen fu" 登眞賦
"Teng-lou fu" 登樓賦
"Teng-t'u Tzu hao-se fu" 登徒子好色賦
"Teng Yi-ch'eng ku-ch'eng fu" 登宜城古城賦
"Teng Yüeh-yang lou" 登岳陽樓
"T'eng ta-yin kuei tuan chia-ssu" 滕大尹鬼斷家私
Ti-ch'i shang-chiang Wen t'ai-pao chuan 地祇上將溫太保傳
"Ti-shih fu" 砥石賦
"Ti-tzu ko" 帝子歌
T'i-hsiao yin-yüan 啼笑姻緣
T'i-hsüan chen-jen hsien-yi lu 體玄眞人顯異錄
"Tiao Ch'ü Yüan wen" 弔屈原文
Tiao-ch'ung lun 雕蟲論
"Tiao Kao Ch'ing-ch'iu" 弔高青丘
"T'iao Chang Chi" 調張籍
"Tieh chü ch'i Ch'eng k'o te chu, san chiu o hai-shen hsien ling" 疊居奇程客得助三救厄海神顯靈
"Tieh lien hua" 蝶戀花
T'ieh-wei shan ts'ung-t'an 鐵圍山叢談
Tien lun 典論
Tien-lun "Lun wen" 典論論文
Tien-shih-chai hua-pao 點石齋畫報
Tien shih-chieh 電世界
T'ien-chin jih-jih hsin-wen pao 天津日日新聞報
"T'ien-hsia t'ai-p'ing" 天下太平
"T'ien-pao yi-shih chu-kung-tiao" 天寶遺事諸宮調
"T'ien shang yao" 天上謠
"T'ien-she weng shih-shih ching-li, mu-t'ung erh yeh-yeh tsun-jung" 田舍翁時時經理牧童兒夜夜尊榮
"T'ien-t'ai fang-yin lu" 天台訪隱錄
T'ien ts'ou ch'iao 天湊巧
"T'ien wen" 天問
"T'ien wen hsün" 天文訓
T'ien-yen lun 天演論
"T'ien yü hua" 天雨花
T'ien-yüan ch'i-yü 天緣奇遇
Ting-ch'ing jen 定情人
"Ting-hun tien" 定婚店
To Cong phung su 蘇公奉使
"T'o-pei chi" 馱背妓
Tokushi yōryō 読詩要領
Tongmunsŏn 東文選
Tou Ŏ yüan 竇娥怨
Tou-p'eng hsien-hua 豆棚閒話
T'ou-hsia lu 投轄錄
Truyen ky man luc 傳奇漫錄
Truyen ky tan pha 傳奇新譜
"Tsa-chü san-chi" 雜劇三集
"Tsa ko-yao tz'u" 雜歌謠辭
Tsa-pao-tsang ching 雜寶藏經
Tsa p'i-yü ching 雜譬喻經
"Tsa-p'ien" 雜篇
"Tsa shih" 雜詩
"Tsa-shuo" 雜說
"Tsai sheng yüan" 再生緣
"Tsai t'i Po fu shih" 再題白傅詩
"Tsai-tsao t'ien" 再造天
"Tsai Yen-an wen-yi tso-t'an hui shang te chiang-hua" 在延安文藝座談會上的講話
"Tsai yi-yüan chung" 在醫院中
"Ts'ai Jui-hung jen ju pao ch'ou" 蔡瑞虹忍辱報仇
Ts'ai-kuei chi 才鬼記
"Ts'ai-lien fu" 采蓮賦
"Ts'ai-shih-chi" 采石磯
Ts'ai-tiao chi 才調集

“Tsan-men te shih-chieh” 咱們的世界
Tsang-wai tao-shu 藏外道書
Ts’ang-lang shih-hua 滄浪詩話
Ts’ang-shan kao wai-pien 藏山稿外編
“Tsao-kao te T’ai-wan wen-hsüeh-chieh” 糟糕的台灣文學界
Tsao-shu te ku-shih 棗樹的故事
“Ts’ao-t’ang shih chih t’u” 草堂十志圖
“Ts’ao Tzu-chien yü Yang Te-tsu shu” 曹子建與楊德祖書
“Tse tzu shih” 責子詩
Ts’e-mao tz’u 側帽詞
“Tseng fu shih” 贈婦詩
“Tseng hsiung hsiu-ts’ai ju-chün” 贈兄秀才入軍
“Tseng Hsü Kan” 贈徐幹
“Tseng Pai-ma wang Piao” 贈白馬王彪
Tso chuan 左傳
“Ts’o jen shih” 錯認屍
“Tsou Meng K’o Mu” 鄒孟軻母
Tsu-t’ang chi 祖堂集
Tsui-ch’a chih-kuai 醉茶志怪
Tsui-hou te yi shou ko 最後的一首歌
Tsui hsing shih 醉醒石
Tsui-weng t’an-lu 醉翁談錄
“Tsui-weng t’ing chi” 醉翁亭記
“Ts’ui niao shih” 翠鳥詩
“Ts’ui Tai-chao sheng-ssu yüan-chia” 崔待詔生死冤家
“Ts’ui ya lou” 萃雅樓
“Ts’ui Ying-ying” 崔鶯鶯
“Tsung ch’iu lun” 縱囚論
“Ts’ung-chün hsing” 從軍行
“Ts’ung-chün shih” 從軍詩
Ts’ung-shan shih-hsüan 聰山詩選
Ts’ung-shan wen-chi 聰山文集
Tsurezure-gusa 徒然草
“Tu-ch’i shou yu fu chih kua, no-fu huan pu ssu chih hun” 妒妻守有夫之寡懦夫還不死之魂
“Tu-chüan shan” 杜鵑山
“Tu Hung-chien chuan” 杜鴻漸傳
“Tu Li-sao” 讀離騷
“Tu *Shan hai ching* shih-san shou” 讀山海經十三首
Tu she ch’üan 毒蛇圈
“Tu Shih-niang nu ch’en pai-pao hsiang” 杜十娘怒沉百寶箱
Tu-shu hou 讀書後
“Tu Tzu-ch’un” 杜子春
“Tu Tzu-ch’un san ju Ch’ang-an” 杜子春三入長安
“T’u-tsan” 圖讚
Tuan-hung ling-yen chi 斷鴻零雁記
“Tui chiu” 對酒
“T’ui-pien” 蛻變
“Tun hsiu-ts’ai yi chao chiao-t’ai” 鈍秀才一朝交泰
Tun-huang Fan-shih chia-chuan 敦煌氾氏家傳
Tun-huang pien-wen chi 敦煌變文集
“Tung ching fu” 東京賦
Tung-ching meng hua lu 東京夢華錄
“Tung-ch’ing-shu” 冬青樹
Tung-Chou lieh-kuo chih 東周列國誌
“Tung-erh Ku-niang” 冬兒姑娘
“Tung-fang Shuo pieh-chuan” 東方朔別傳
Tung-fang tsa-chih 東方雜誌
Tung Hsi-hsiang 董西廂
“Tung-hsiao chi” 洞簫記
Tung-hsüan chin-yü chi 洞玄金玉集
Tung-p’o chih-lin 東坡志林
Tung-p’o wen-chi 東坡文集
Tung-shan ch’ou-ho chi 東山酬和集
Tung-shan yü-lu 洞山語錄
“Tung-t’ing ling-yin chuan” 洞庭靈姻傳
Tung-tu chi 東度記
“Tung-ya feng-yün” 東亞風雲
“Tung-yang yeh-kuai lu” 東陽夜怪錄
Tung-yu chi 東遊記
T’ung-chien kang-mu 通鑒綱目
T’ung chih t’ang chi 通志堂集
“T’ung-ch’uang yu jen chia tso chen, nü hsiu-ts’ai yi-hua chieh-mu” 同窗友認假作眞女秀才移花接木
“T’ung-kan kung-k’u” 同甘共苦

“T’ung-kuan li” 潼關吏
“T’ung sheng ko” 同聲歌
T’ung-t’ien lo 通天樂
Tuo-hsin ching 多心經
“Tzu-ch’ai chi” 紫釵記
Tzu-chih t’ung-chien 資治通鑑
“Tzu-hsiao chi” 紫簫記
“Tzu hsü fu” 子虛賦
Tzu pu yü 子不語
“Tzu-shu” 自述
“Tzu tse” 自責
Tzu Yeh 子夜
“Tzu Yeh ko” 子夜歌
“Tzu Yeh ssu shih ko” 子夜四時歌
“Tzu yi” 緇衣
“Tzu-yün-t’ing” 紫雲庭
Tz’u hsüan 詞選
“Tz’u-lun” 詞論
“Tz’u Mu-lan” 雌木蘭
“Tz’u shih chi hsieh fu” 刺世疾邪歌
Tz’u-tsung 詞綜
Uta no shiki 歌の式
Viet dien u linh tap 粵甸幽靈集
Vuong Tuong Truyen 王嬙傳
“Wai-p’ien” 外篇
Wakan Rōeishū 和漢朗詠集
Wan-chin ch’ing-lin 萬錦情林
Wan Ch’ing hsi-ch’ü hsiao-shuo mu 晚清戲曲小說目
Wan Ch’ing hsiao-shuo shih 晚清小說史
Wan Ch’ing wen-hsüeh ts’ung-ch’ao: hsiao-shuo hsi-ch’ü yen-chiu chüan 晚清文學叢鈔: 小說戲曲研究卷
Wan-chu 玩主
“Wan-fa kuei-yi ko” 萬法歸一歌
Wan Ju Yüeh 宛如約
“Wan-ku-ch’ou ch’ü” 萬古愁曲
Wan-kuo kung-fa 萬國公法
Wan-kuo kung-pao 萬國公報
“Wan-lien chi erh-shih yung” 紈奩集二十詠
Wan-ling chi 宛陵集
“Wan-shui ch’ien-shan” 萬水千山
“Wan-tzu chin-yin hua” 卍字金銀花
“Wan yen shu” 萬言書
“Wang An-shih san nan Su hsüeh-shih” 王安石三難蘇學士
“Wang Chao-chün” 王昭君
Wang ch’uan chi 輞川集
“Wang Hsin-chih yi ssu chiu ch’üan chia” 汪信之一死救全家
“Wang Pen-li t’ien-ya ch’iu fu” 王本立天涯求父
Wang Yi-shang shih-chi 王貽上詩集
Wan’r chiu-shih hsin-t’iao 玩兒就是心跳
Wanwŏlhoe maengyŏn 玩月會盟宴
“Wei ch’ao-feng hen-hsin p’an kuei ch’an, Ch’en hsiu-ts’ai ch’iao-chi chuan yüan fang” 衛朝奉狠心盤貴產陳秀才巧計賺原房
“Wei-ch’i fu” 圍棋賦
“Wei Feng lu-shih chai kuan Ts’ao chiang-chün hua ma t’u ko” 韋諷錄事宅觀曹將軍畫馬圖歌
“Wei Fu-jen chuan” 魏夫人傳
Wei-mo-chieh ching 維摩詰經
“Wei Shih-yi niang chuan” 韋十一娘傳
“Wei tu fu” 魏都賦
Wei-yü 微雨
Wen-chang kuei-fan 文章規範
Wen-chang liu-pieh chi 文章流別集
“Wen-chang liu-pieh chih-lun” 文章流別志論
“Wen-ch’ang ssu lien ts’ai man chu lu-chi” 文昌司憐才慢注祿籍
“Wen-chi ju sai” 文姬入塞
Wen-ching mi-fu lun 文鏡秘府論
“Wen fu” 文賦
Wen-hsin tiao-lung 文心雕龍
Wen hsüan 文選
“Wen-hsüeh kai-liang ch’u-yi” 文學改良芻議
“Wen-hsüeh ko-ming lun” 文學革命論
“Wen kuo lou” 聞過樓
Wen-ming hsiao-shih 文明小史
Wen tse 文則
Wen-yi hsin-ch’ao 文藝新潮

Wen-yi pao 文藝報
Wen-yüan ying-hua 文苑英華
"Wo chih chieh-lieh kuan" 我之節烈觀
"Wo shih ni pa-pa" 我是你爸爸
"Wo te chiao-yü" 我的教育
"Wo tsai Hsia-ts'un te shih-hou" 我在霞村的時候
"Women" 我們
"Wu Chen-chün" 吳眞君
Wu-chen p'ien 悟眞篇
"Wu-chia pieh" 無家別
"Wu chiang-chün yi fan pi ch'ou, Ch'en Ta-lang san-jen ch'ung hui" 烏將軍一飯必酬陳大郎三人重會
"Wu-chieh Ch'an-shih ssu Hung-lien chi" 五戒禪師私紅蓮記
Wu chin-yü chuan 五金魚傳
Wu-ching cheng-yi 五經正義
Wu-ch'uan lu 吳船錄
"Wu-hsing chih" 五行志
"Wu-hsing p'ien" 五行篇
"Wu-keng chuan" 五更傳
Wu-liang-shou ching 無量受經
"Wu-liu hsien-sheng chuan" 五柳先生傳
"Wu-lun ch'üan-pei chi" 伍倫全備記
Wu-men kuan 無門關
"Wu Pao-an ch'i-chia shu-yu" 吳保安棄家贖友
"Wu pei" 五悲
"Wu-p'ing ling-kuai lu" 武平靈怪錄
Wu-se shih 五色石
Wu-shang huang-lu ta-chai li-ch'eng yi 無上黃籙大齋立成儀
Wu-shang pi-yao 無上祕要
Wu-sheng hsi 無聲戲
Wu-sheng hsi erh-chi 無聲戲二集
"Wu sheng ko" 吳聲歌
"Wu sheng ko-ch'ü" 吳聲歌曲
"Wu-shuang chuan" 無雙傳
"Wu-tai-shih p'ing-hua" 五代史平話
"Wu teng lun" 五等論
"Wu-t'i" 無題
Wu-t'o-pang yu-chi 烏托邦遊記
Wu tsa-tsu 五雜組
"Wu-t'ung yü" 梧桐雨
Wu wang fa Chou p'ing-hua 五王伐紂平話
Wu-yin ts'ao 戊寅草
Wu-yüeh te huang-hun 五月的黃昏
Wu yün li-nien chi 五運歷年記
"Ya-ch'ia shu" 齖齣書
Ya-hsüeh 雅謔
"Yang Chiao-ai she ming ch'üan chiao" 羊角哀捨命全交
"Yang Chuang-yüan" 洋狀元
Yang-ch'un pai-hsüeh 陽春白雪
Yang ko 秧歌
"Yang-liu-chih tz'u" 楊柳枝詞
Yang Nai-wu yü Hsiao Pai-ts'ai 楊乃武與小白菜
"Yang P'an-erh" 楊叛兒
"Yang sheng lun" 養生論
"Yao Ti-chu pi hsiu je hsiu, Cheng Yüeh-o chiang ts'o chiu ts'o" 姚滴珠避羞惹羞鄭月娥將錯就錯
"Yao tien" 堯典
"Yeh Ching-neng shih" 葉淨能詩
"Yeh shang Shou-hsiang ch'eng wen ti" 夜上受降城聞笛
Yeh-sou p'u-yen 野叟曝言
"Yeh su Tung-chu fang ko" 夜宿東渚放歌
Yeh-t'an sui-lu 夜譚隨錄
"Yeh t'ing chi" 夜聽妓
"Yeh tso" 夜坐
"Yeh yin" 夜吟
Yeh yü 夜雨
Yeh-yü ch'iu-teng lu 夜雨秋燈錄
"Yen-an wen-yi tso-t'an-hui chiang-hua" 延安文藝座談會講話
Yen-chou shan-jen ssu-pu kao 弇州山人四部稿
"Yen-chung chih chih" 煙中之志
"Yen ko hsing" 豔歌行
Yen-po tz'u 衍波詞
Yen-shih chia-hsün 顏氏家訓
Yen Tan Tzu 燕丹子
"Yen-tzu-chien" 燕子箋

Yen Tzu ch'un-ch'iu	晏子春秋
"Yen-tzu fu"[1]	燕子賦
"Yen-tzu fu"[2]	晏子賦
"Yen-yen"	燕燕
Yen-yi pien	豔異編
Yi	易
"Yi-ch'i huan-ch'ieh kuei shen ch'i"	移妻換妾鬼神奇
Yi-chien chih	夷堅志
Yi-chien shang-hsin pien	一見賞心編
"Yi-ch'ien-pa-pai tan"	一千八百擔
Yi-ching	易經
Yi-chiu-san-ssu te t'ao-wang	一九三四的逃亡
"Yi Fo chi"	移佛記
Yi hang	一行
"Yi-hsia chi"	義俠記
"Yi-k'u kuei lai tao-jen ch'u kuai"	一窟鬼癩道人除怪
Yi-li	儀禮
Yi-lin	易林
"Yi-meng lu"	異夢錄
"Yi-niao lu"	誼鳥錄
Yi-pan shih huo-yen, yi-pan shih hai-shui	一半是火焰, 一半是海水
"Yi-p'eng hsüeh"	一捧雪
"Yi-p'ien ai-kuo hsin"	一片愛國心
Yi-p'ien ch'ing	一片情
Yi-sheng ch'u-chi	依聲初集
Yi-shu hui-pien	譯書匯編
"Yi-shui han"	易水寒
"Yi wen ch'ien hsiao hsi tsao ch'i yüan"	一文錢小隙造奇冤
"Yi-wen chih"	藝文志
Yi-wen chih shih-fu lüeh	藝文志詩賦略
Yi-wen lei-chü	藝文類聚
"Yi-yin cheng-chih hsiao-shuo hsü"	譯印政治小說序
Yi-yüan chih yen	藝苑卮言
"Yin chiu"	飲酒
"Yin chiu tu 'Sao'"	飲酒讀騷
"Yin-feng-ko tsa-chü"	吟風閣雜劇
"Yin hu-shang ch'u ch'ing hou yü"	飲湖上初清後雨
"Yin ma ch'ang-ch'eng k'u hsing"	飲馬長城窟行
Yin mou	陰謀
Yin-shui tz'u	飲水詞
"Ying ch'an-shih fang kuan shan-hai t'u"	瑩禪師房觀山海圖
Ying-ch'uang yi-ts'ao	螢窗異草
Ying-hsiung p'u	英雄譜
"Ying k'an an ta-ju cheng hsien-ch'i, kan shou hsing hsia-nü chu fang-ming"	硬勘案大儒爭閒氣甘受刑俠女著芳名
Ying-mei-an yi-yü	影梅庵憶語
"Ying-wu chou"	鸚鵡洲
"Ying-ying chuan"	鶯鶯傳
Yishipil tohoe kosi	二十一都懷古詩
Yŏgong p'aesŏl	櫟翁稗說
Yŏhan shipka munch'o	麗韓十家文抄
Yŏlha ilgi	熱河日記
"Yŏng gosŏk"	詠孤石
Yu-ch'ai lai te hsin	郵差來的信
Yu Ch'ung-chen kuan nan-lou tu hsin chi-ti t'i-ming	遊崇眞觀南樓覩新及第題名
"Yu Feng-tu Hu-mu Ti yin-shih"	遊酆都胡母迪吟詩
"Yu-hsia p'ien"	遊俠篇
"Yu-hsien"	遊仙
"Yu-hsien chi"	遊仙記
"Yu-hsien k'u"	遊仙窟
"Yu-hsien shih"	遊仙詩
"Yu-hsien shih, ch'i shih"	遊仙詩 (其十)
Yu-hsüan chi	又玄集
Yu-kuai shih-t'an	幽怪詩談
"Yu-lieh shih"	遊獵詩
Yu-lung chuan	猶龍傳
Yu-ming lu	幽明錄
"Yu Nan-shan wang Pei-shan ching hu chung chan-t'iao"	於南山往北山經湖中瞻眺
"Yu Pao-ch'an-shan chi"	游褒禪山記
"Yu Pei-shan fu"	遊北山賦
"Yu Shan-hsi ts'un"	遊山西村

"Yu so ssu"	有所思
Yu-t'ai hsien-kuan pi-chi	右台仙館筆記
"Yu T'ao-yüan"	遊桃源
"Yu T'ien-t'ai shan fu"	遊天台山賦
"Yu-t'ing wu-meng"	郵亭午夢
"Yu Tung-t'ien"	遊東田
"Yu t'ung fu"	幽通賦
Yu-yang tsa-tsu	酉陽雜俎
"Yü ch'an-shih"	玉禪師
"Yü-chang hsing: K'u hsiang p'ien"	豫章行: 苦相篇
"Yü chia ao"	漁家傲
Yü Chiao Li[1]	玉嬌李
Yü Chiao Li[2]	玉嬌梨
"Yü chieh yüan"	玉階怨
"Yü chih hsiao-shuo kuan"	余之小說觀
Yü-chou feng	宇宙風
Yü Ch'u chih	虞初志
Yü Ch'u hsin-chih	虞初新志
Yü-ch'uan yüan	玉釧緣
"Yü-chüeh chi"	玉玦記
"Yü-fu"	漁夫
Yü-hai	玉海
Yü Hsia	禹夏
"Yü Hsiang-tung Wang shu"	與湘東王書
Yü-hu ch'ing-hua	玉壺清話
Yü-hua hsiang	雨花香
Yü-kuan	玉官
Yü Kuo-fan Hsi-yu chi lun-chi	余國蕃西遊記論集
"Yü-lan-p'en fu"	盂蘭盆賦
Yü-lan shih	御覽詩
Yü li hun	玉梨魂
Yü-lou ch'un	玉樓春
Yü-mu hsing-hsin pien	娛目醒心編
"Yü-shan fu"	虞山婦
"Yü-shan shen-nü tz'u ko erh shou: sung shen ch'ü"	魚山神女祠歌二首, 送神曲
Yü-shih ming-yen (*Ku-chin hsiao-shuo*)	喻世明言
Yü-t'ai hou-chi	玉臺後集
Yü-t'ai hsin-yung	玉臺新詠
"Yü-t'ang-ch'un lo nan feng fu"	玉堂春落難逢夫
"Yü-tsan chi"	玉簪記
Yü-wai hsiao-shuo chi	域外小說集
"Yü wu-sheng-ch'u"	於無聲處
Yü-yi chih	于役志
"Yüan-cheng fu"	元正賦
Yüan-chien lei-han	淵鑑類函
Yüan-ch'ü hsüan	元曲選
Yüan-fu	原富
"Yüan hsing"	原性
"Yüan-hu ch'ü"	鴛湖曲
"Yüan hui"	原毀
Yüan-hun chih	冤魂志
Yüan jen lun	原人論
"Yüan ko hsing"	怨歌行
Yüan-pen Chin P'ing Mei	原本金瓶梅
"Yüan pieh-li"	遠別離
"Yüan-p'u fan kuei"	遠浦帆歸
Yüan-shan-t'ang chü-p'in	遠山堂劇品
Yüan shih	元史
Yüan shih	原詩
Yüan-shih hsüan	元詩選
Yüan-shih yen-chiu	元詩研究
"Yüan Tan-ch'iu ko"	元丹丘歌
"Yüan-tao"	原道
Yüan tien chang	元典章
Yüan-yang chen	鴛鴦針
Yüan-yang-meng	鴛鴦夢
"Yüan yu"	遠游
"Yüan-yüan ch'ü"	圓圓曲
"Yüeh-chi"	樂記
"Yüeh chih"	樂志
Yüeh-ch'iu chih-min-ti	月球殖民地
Yüeh-fu	樂府
Yüeh-fu ch'ün-yü	樂府群玉
Yüeh-fu hsin-sheng	樂府新聲
Yüeh-fu ku-t'i yao chieh	樂府古題要解
Yüeh-fu pu-t'i	樂府補題
Yüeh-fu shih chi	樂府詩集
"Yüeh-jen ko"	越人歌
"Yüeh k'o"	約客
"Yüeh-ling"	月令
Yüeh-wei ts'ao-t'ang pi-chi	閱微草堂筆記

"Yüeh yeh" 月夜
Yüeh-yüeh hsiao-shuo 月月小說
"*Yüeh-yüeh hsiao-shuo* hsü" 《月月小說》序
Yūjo ki 遊女記
Yün-chai kuang-lu 雲齋廣錄
Yün-chi ch'i-ch'ien 雲笈七籤
Yün-kuang chi 雲光集
Yün-shan chi 雲山集
Yün-yao chi 雲謠集
Yung-ch'eng chi-hsien lu 墉城集仙錄
"Yung Ching K'o shih" 詠荊軻詩
"Yung-chou pa chi" 永州八記
"Yung erh Shu" 詠二疏
"Yung-ho kung-tz'u" 永和宮詞
"Yung hua-chang" 詠畫障
"Yung hua p'ing-feng shih erh-shih-ssu shou" 詠畫屏風詩二十四首
"Yung-huai" 詠懷
"Yung-huai shih" 詠懷詩
Yung-le ta-tien 永樂大典
"Yung-ming chiu nien ts'e hsiu-ts'ai wen" 永明九年策秀才文
"Yung-shih shih" 詠史詩
"Yung shou" 詠手
"Yung ta hu-tieh" 詠大蝴蝶
"Yung wu-chi" 詠舞妓

INDEX

A-p'i-ta-mo-p'i-p'o-sha lun (*Abhidharma-mahāvibhāṣā-śāstra*), 164
Acton, Harold, 455
Aeneid (Virgil), 943
aesthetics. *See* esthetics
Ah Ch'eng (Chung A-ch'eng), 761–65
Ah-li Hsi-ying, 380
Ah-lu Wei, 380
"Ah Q cheng-chuan" (The True Story of Ah Q; Lu Hsün), 54, 744, 854
Ah Ying (Ch'ien Hsing-ts'un), 698, 722, 1019
ai-chi (lament and requiem), 5, 528
"Ai Chiang-nan fu" (Rhapsody Lamenting the South; Yü Hsin), 241, 242, 273, 288
"Ai chiang-t'ou" (Lament by the Stream; Tu Fu), 299
Ai Ch'ing (Chiang Hai-ch'eng), 456, 463, 771
ai-mei chü (amateur theater), 856
Ai-na chü-shih, 596, 616–17, 619
"Ai ni wen" (Lamenting a Death by Drowning; Liu Tsung-yüan), 305
Ai-tzu tsa-shuo (Master Mugwort's Miscellany), 136
"Ai wang-sun" (Lament for a Royal Scion; Tu Fu), 299
Ai Wu, 752
Ai yu ju-ho (It's Love, So What; Chang Hsin), 765
al sira ("yellow books;" Arabic folk epics), 1013
alchemy, 546, 608, 610, 665; in *Journey to the West*, 633, 634, 635; and Taoism, 175, 186, 189
All Men Are Brothers. See *Shui-hu chuan*
Allen, Young John, 1059
Alley, Rewi, 1043
allusion (*tien-ku*), 28, 151, 242, 243, 245, 262, 322, 323, 331, 377, 893, 894, 900
Altaicization, 22, 33, 39
Amoghavajra, 164
an-chien (based on the *Mirror*), 622
An Chung Keun, 851
An Hung-chien, 137–38
An-le, Princess, 292
An Lu-shan, 800, 814
An Lu-shan rebellion, 202, 303, 339, 341, 476, 525, 586, 589; in drama, 126; and Emperor Hsüan-tsung, 485, 814, 834; and Hsiao Ying-shih, 301; and Tu Fu, 299, 358; and Wang Wei, 295
An Shih-kao, 162
An-ya t'ang chi (Collection from the Hall Where One Finds Solace in Literary Elegance; Sung Wan), 420
Analects. See *Lun-yü*
ancestor worship, 102, 103, 104, 494, 529
Andreyev, L. N., 720
anecdotes, 137–38, 675–78, 687
animals, 66, 114–15, 117, 119–20, 536. See also *yao*

anitya (impermanence), 169
anthologies, 179, 183, 185–90, 284, 286, 291, 296, 610, 614; Ch'ing, 533; compilation of, 918–19; of drama, 803, 804, 812, 814, 815, 817, 824, 825; of fiction, 745; Japanese, 1083; of lyrics, 373, 426, 438; Ming, 533; of poetry, 279–82, 294, 295, 301, 307, 313, 331, 337, 338, 353, 373, 383–85, 401, 407, 409, 412, 415–16, 425, 431, 1083, 1090; prose, 533; Sung, 338, 385, 438, 1069; T'ang, 279–82, 407, 412, 424, 425, 431, 533, 1090; Taoist, 190; Vietnamese, 1098, 1099
antirightist movement (1957), 866
Ao Ao (Chang Ts'o; Dominic Cheung), 458
"Ao hsiang-kung yin-hen Pan-shan t'ang" (The Stubborn Prime Minister; Feng Meng-lung), 601
Aoki Masaru, 467
Äpändi (A-fan-t'i te ku-shih), 1049
April Fifth movement (Ssu-wu yün-tung; 1976), 869
Arabic language, 29, 1013
archaism, 381, 390, 399, 407–9, 430, 432, 433, 1073, 1097. See also *fu-ku* movement; *ku-wen-tz'u*
Archetype and Allegory in the "Dream of the Red Chamber" (Plaks), 650
Aristophanes, 885, 902, 905
Aristotle, 884, 895
Around the World in Eighty Days (Verne), 719
art of the absurd, 15, 759, 778
Ashikaga Yoshimitsu, 1089
Ashima (A-shih-ma), 1038
astrology, 543
Aśvaghoṣa (Ma-ming), 172
Auden, W. H., 455
Austroasiatic, 22, 39
Austronesian, 21, 22, 26, 39
author, 498, 503–4, 568, 570, 900; collective, 866; implied, 322; Ssu-ma Ch'ien as, 504–7
autobiography, 8, 434, 538, 738, 901–2
avadāna (*p'i-yü*; parables), 117, 171–72, 523, 539, 580, 984
Avalokiteśvara (Kuan-yin), 164, 171, 524, 597, 994; in *Journey to the West*, 128, 129, 632, 633, 636
avant-garde (*hsien-feng*) literature, 15, 759, 763–65, 768–69

Bakhtin, Mikhail, 641
ballads, 953–63; act-out, 787; dragon boat, 1026, 1027; drum, 990, 991, 1009, 1012, 1014, 1018, 1019, 1027; forms of, 954, 992, 1024; Korean, 1069; and Li Po, 277, 307, 955, 962, 975; literary imitations of, 955, 956–57, 959–60; and opera, 787, 793; and oral tradition, 954, 989; periodization of, 954–55; and Po Chü-yi, 838, 955; and poetry, 277; and sayings, 156; sources of, 956–57; strummed, 1012, 1014; and vernacular song, 953, 955; and women, 198–99, 200, 205, 959, 1077. See also *yüeh-fu*
Balzac, Honoré de, 1064
bandits, 621, 628, 663, 808, 817, 818. See also *Shui hu chuan*
Barr, Allan H., 675–96
Bayan, 340
Beckett, Samuel, 463
Bellamy, Edward, 718
Bender, Mark, 1015–31, 1032–54
Berg, Daria, 659–74
Bhagavad-Gita (Song of the Blessed One), 78
Bible, 86, 91, 500, 511, 1058–59
"Binh Ngo dai cao" (Proclamation of Victory over the Wu; Nguyen Trai), 1098
biographies, 267, 960; and annals, 503, 507, 509, 521; of authors, 231, 506, 931, 968; of Buddha, 161, 162, 171, 172, 985; Buddhist, 522, 523–24; character in, 512–16; and *ch'uan-ch'i* tales, 579, 580, 581, 592, 681, 690; and classical tales, 693; collections of, 416, 469, 471; Confucian, 518, 524–25; didacticism in, 513, 518, 520, 521; of dynastic founders, 509; early, 511–26; esoteric, 522, 580; and essays, 536, 540, 574–75; family, 969; and fiction, 511, 522, 526, 625, 626, 632, 643; and funerary writing, 529; and history, 503, 508, 511, 579; and *hua-pen*, 598; and humor, 134; of humorists, 140, 141, 143; idealized, 592; of monks, 121, 164–65; of nuns, 165; pseudo-, 581; romance form of, 512; separate, 521, 580; in *Shih-chi*, 507, 513–22, 525, 658; Six Dynasties period, 164–65; and supernatural tales, 549; Taoist, 175, 179–80, 184–85, 522–23; terms for, 513, 528, 580; of transcendents, 121, 508, 522, 523, 550, 554, 580; and Tun-huang literature, 968–69, 971, 983; types of, 513, 579; of women, 134, 165, 197–98, 212, 218, 469, 471, 508, 517–18, 522, 524–25, 550, 1074, 1086. *See also* autobiography
Birrell, Anne, 58–69, 194–220, 953–63
Boccaccio, 943
Bodhidharma, 191
bodhisattvas, 163, 164, 171, 970, 971, 979
Bokenkamp, Stephen, 10
Boltz, Judith, 173–92
Book of Dede Korkut, 1013
Borges, Jorge Luis, 764, 765
Bourdieu, Pierre, 759
Boxer Rebellion, 450, 657, 658, 673, 698, 734, 780, 863, 1012; in twentieth-century fiction, 739, 740, 741
Branner, David Prager, 22
Brecht, Bertold, 809, 846, 876
Breton, André, 457
Britain, 701, 1062
Bronze Age, 2, 12, 21
bronze inscriptions, 49, 56, 97, 108, 474, 475; Chou, 36–37,

41, 467, 495; as historical records, 495, 496; and language study, 46, 47
Brooks, A. Taeko, 94, 95
Brooks, E. Bruce, 94, 95
Bryant, Daniel, 399–409, 429–43
Buddha, 290, 523, 978, 981, 1006, 1047; Amitābha, 163; biographies of, 161, 162, 171, 172, 985; *jātaka* (birth stories) of, 161, 171, 473–74, 971; in *Journey to the West*, 129; Ju-lai, 994; portraits of, 473, 802; and Taoism, 183, 191
Buddhacarita (Aśvaghoṣa), 172
Buddhism, 160–72; and art, 161, 473; and biography, 522, 523–24; Central Asian, 160, 1048; and *ch'uan-ch'i*, 582; and Confucianism, 165, 166, 169, 533; converts to, 271, 295; doctrines of, 112, 983; and drama, 57, 161, 172, 792, 810, 843; festivals of, 991; in fiction, 168, 632, 641, 642, 651, 654, 658, 662, 665, 670, 699, 722, 740, 742, 747; and folklore, 1034; Han, 1055; and *hua-pen*, 596, 598, 601, 603, 616, 617; and humor, 136; hymns of, 977, 978; Indian, 317, 1045; influence of, 5, 6, 9–12, 161, 923; introduction to China of, 166, 253, 428, 473, 898, 901, 983, 1017, 1055; Japanese, 1017, 1079, 1080, 1081, 1087–88; in *Journey to the West*, 128–29, 633, 634, 635, 636, 663; Kargyupa, 1046; Korean, 1017, 1070; and language, 23, 40–41, 45, 56–57, 918; and literary theory, 405, 707; and literati, 163, 169–70, 411–12; and literature, 161, 165–66, 983–84, 993, 1018, 1026; Mahāyāna, 163, 177, 582, 1042; and miracle tales, 162, 165, 168, 171, 551, 582, 969–72; and myth, 59; and oral tradition, 51, 153–54; patrons of, 270; persecution of, 478; and poetry, 163, 169, 170, 289–90, 935; and poets, 268, 289, 290, 298, 302, 306, 312–13, 351, 353, 365, 408, 411, 431, 439, 442, 539, 540; polemical literature of, 165–66; and proverbs, 153; Pure Land (Ching-t'u), 10, 163, 166, 169, 478; and Sanskrit, 241, 270, 965; scriptures of, 86, 161–62, 164, 985, 987, 995, 1045; Shingon sect of Esoteric, 1084; Six Dynasties, 170, 585, 726; and songs, 315, 317; Sung, 362; and supernatural, 110, 113, 114, 115, 121, 123, 170–71, 549, 550–51; T'ang, 11, 170; Tantric, 164, 550; and Taoism, 160, 161, 163, 165, 166, 173, 176, 177; Theravada, 1043; in Three Teachings, 411–12, 612; Tibetan, 1041, 1045, 1046; and travel literature, 556, 558; at Tun-huang, 166, 170, 474, 478, 964, 969, 970, 971–72, 979, 983; and vernacular, 29–30, 32, 34, 888, 889, 980; and women, 1006; Yogācāra, 165. See also *pien-wen*
Bulwer-Lytton, Edward George, 707
bunjin (literati), 1090
Bunkashūreishū (Anthology of Literary Beauties), 1083
Bunkyō hifuron (Treatise on the Secret Treasury of the Literary Mirror; Kūkai), 270, 930–31, 1084
bureaucracy, 1–2, 8, 78, 528–29, 534, 556, 702; Ch'ing, 52, 698; Eastern Chou, 71–72; in fiction, 698, 740; and historical writing, 494, 501–2, 509; supernatural, 112, 113. *See also* civil-service examinations; scholar-officials
Byron, George Gordon, 727

calligraphy, 48–49, 466, 481, 482, 485, 490, 885, 886, 898; Han Yü on, 534; Ou-yang Hsiu on, 539; styles in, 49; of Su Shih, 540; and Tun-huang literature, 965, 966, 967
Camus, Albert, 777
Cantonese language, 31, 35, 39, 56, 619, 1025–28
Carlitz, Katherine, 641
The Carnal Prayer Mat. See *Jou p'u-t'uan*
Catcher in the Rye (Salinger), 765
Catholicism, 428
"The Caucasian Chalk Circle" (Brecht), 809
Central Asia, 14, 22–23, 160, 975, 1048
Ceylon (Sri Lanka), 165
cha-chi. See *pi-chi*
Cha Shen-hsing, 434
"Ch'a-chiu lun" (Discourse Between Tea and Wine; Wang Fu), 166, 791
"Ch'a-kuan" (Teahouse; Lao She), 876–77
Ch'a-ling school, 403
Ch'a-mu (Origins; Ch'i Hsüeh-sheng), 1038, 1039
chaedo chi ki (an instrument to support the way), 1071
Chaeil kiŏn (The Greatest Novel in Korean; trans. Hong Hŭi-bok), 1077
Chai Feng-ta, 970
Chai T'ai-feng, 770–71
Chai Yung-ming, 463
Ch'ai Yüan-kao, 190
Chan Fang-sheng, 266
"Chan hua-k'uei" (Conquering the Queen of Flowers; Li Yü), 830
Chan-kuei chuan (Tale of Beheading Ghosts; Liu Chang), 130
Chan-kuo ts'e (Intrigues of the Warring States), 139, 153, 198, 225, 500, 502, 503, 513, 895
Chan Ping, 461
Chan-shih chü-she (Soldier's Drama Troupe; Red Army), 872
"Chan-tou li ch'eng-chang" (Growing up in the Battlefield; Hu K'o), 873
Chan Tzu-ch'ien, 487

Ch'an (Zen) Buddhism, 10, 11, 190, 707, 778, 1087; and Confucianism, 556, 915; and painting, 479, 480; and poetry, 170, 295, 354, 363, 421, 422–23, 425, 935, 936, 980; recorded sayings of, 168–69, 888, 967
Ch'an-chen hou-shih (Later Tales of the True Way, The Latter History of Buddhists; Fang Ju-hao), 661
Ch'an-chen yi-shih (Lost Tales of the True Way, The Forgotten History of Buddhists; Fang Ju-hao), 661
ch'an-hui (confessions), 978
"Ch'an-hui mieh-tsui Chin-kuang-ming chuan" (Account of Confession to Eliminate Transgressions . . . the Scripture of the Golden Light; Chang Chü-tao), 971
ch'an-ling (intertwined tunes), 797–98
ch'an-ta (alternate tunes), 797
ch'an-wei (prognosticatory apocrypha), 546
Ch'an-yüan chu-ch'üan-chi tu-hsü (General Preface to the Collected Explanations of the Origins of the Zen Sect; Tsung-mi), 166
Chang, K'ang-i Sun, 14
Chang Ai-ling (Eileen Chang), 735, 752–53, 773, 779, 1057
Chang Ch'ao, 690
Chang Cheng-ch'ang, 179
Chang Ch'eng-chih, 766
Chang Chi, 124, 307, 308, 352
Chang Chi-hsien, 179, 180
Chang Ch'i, 438
Chang Chieh, 760
Chang Ch'ien, 555
Chang Chih-chen, 1010
Chang Chih-tung, 710
Chang Chiu-ch'eng, 168
Chang Chiu-ling, 293, 294, 424, 425
Chang Cho, 581, 583
Chang Chu, 387
Chang Chu-p'o, 638, 640, 943, 944, 948, 949, 1076, 1094
chang-chü learning, 912, 913
Chang Chü-tao, 971
Chang Chün, 364
Chang Chün-fang, 177–78
Chang Erh, 516, 519
Chang Fan, 840
Chang Fei, 621, 807, 813
Chang Feng-yi, 829
chang-fu (men), 977
Chang Hen-shui, 733, 743
Chang Heng, 105, 233, 234, 235, 251, 263
Chang Hsi-kuo, 55
Chang Hsiao-hsiang, 325
Chang Hsieh, 260, 267, 268
"Chang Hsieh chuang-yüan" (Top-Graduate Chang Hsieh), 819–20, 826
Chang Hsien, 387
Chang Hsien-liang, 761, 767
Chang Hsin, 765
Chang Hsin-hsin, 761
Chang Hsüeh-ch'eng, 622, 890, 915
Chang Hu, 310
Chang Hua, 120, 260, 261, 263, 471, 548, 549
Chang Huai-shen, 987
chang-hui (linked chapter), 738
chang-hui hsiao-shuo (full length vernacular fiction), 621
Chang Hui-yen, 333, 334, 335, 438, 449
Chang Ju-chün, 1025
Chang Kai, 413
Chang K'o-chiu, 373, 377, 379, 380
Chang Ku, 313
Chang K'un-te, 719
Chang Kuo-hsiang, 178, 180
Chang Lei, 351–53, 564
Chang Li-li, 875
Chang Liang, 516
Chang Lu, 253
Chang Ming-shan, 374–75, 376
Chang Po-tuan, 189–90, 191
Chang Shao, 520–21, 580, 666
Chang Ssu-ch'eng, 184
Chang-sun Wu-chi, 283
Chang Ta-fu, 830, 834
Chang Tai, 7
Chang T'ai-yen, 712
Chang Tan, 414
Chang Tao-ling, 176, 180
"Chang Tao-ling ch'i shih Chao Sheng" (Feng Meng-lung), 601
Chang T'ien-yi, 752
Chang Tsai, 260, 263
Chang Tsao, 463
Chang Ts'o (Ao Ao; Dominic Cheung), 458
Chang Ts'ui-feng, 1029
Chang-tsung, Emperor, 178
Chang Tsung-nan, 424
Chang Tzu-ch'iao, 233
Chang Wen-huan, 776
Chang Wen-t'ao, 436
Chang Wo-chün, 458
Chang Yang-hao, 373, 379
Chang Yen, 171, 241, 432, 447, 448, 449
Chang Yi, 95
Chang Yi-ch'ao, 987
"Chang Yi-ch'ao pien-wen" (Transformation Text on Chang Yi-ch'ao), 168
Chang Yü, 181, 395, 397, 398
Chang Yü-ch'u, 178, 179, 182
Chang Yü-niang, 832
Chang Yüeh, 243, 293, 583
"Ch'ang-an ku-yi" (Old-time Thoughts of Ch'ang-an; Lu Chao-lin), 288
Ch'ang-ch-un chen-jen hsi-yu chi (The Journey to the West of the Perfected Ch'ang-ch'un; Li Chih-ch'ang), 185
Ch'ang Chien, 295
Ch'ang-chou school, 333, 335, 417–18, 437–38, 449, 450
"Ch'ang-hen ko" (Song of Everlasting Regret; Po Chü-yi), 14–15, 202, 308–9, 310, 485, 586, 814, 1008, 1083, 1086
"'Ch'ang-hen ko' chuan" (An Account of the Story of the "Song of Everlasting Regret"; Ch'en Hung), 586
Ch'ang-hsi (goddess), 61
"Ch'ang li-luan" (Song of Parting), 1036–37
"Ch'ang mao hsiao kou" (The Little Dog with Long Hair; Wang Ho-ch'ing), 376

Ch'ang-ning, Princess, 292
"Ch'ang-pan p'o" (The Slopes of Ch'ang-pan), 1029
ch'ang-pen (verse tales), 994
"Ch'ang-sheng tien" (Palace of Eternal Life; Hung Sheng), 126, 825, 834
Ch'ang-shih chi (Experiments; Hu Shih), 454
ch'ang-tao-shih (itinerant monks), 984
ch'ang-tuan chü (long and short lines), 976
ch'ang yu nü-tzu (female entertainers), 1008
Ch'angsŏn kamŭi rok (A Record of the Manifestation of Goodness and the Gratification of Emotional Bonds), 1074
chantefables (*shuo-ch'ang tz'u-hua*), 796, 809, 983, 986, 990, 1009; and *hua-pen*, 598; Ming, 992, 995, 996, 998, 1001, 1003, 1009, 1010, 1012, 1014, 1018, 1026; of Soochow, 1023, 1024; and vernacular fiction, 1018, 1023
chao (omens), 111
Chao, Duke of Lu, 3–4
Chao, Henry (Chao Yi-heng), 764, 768–69
Chao, state of, 13
Chao Ch'i, 96, 468–69, 887
Chao Chih-hsin, 421, 425, 432–33
Chao Ching-shen, 1019, 1028
"Chao-chün ch'u sai" (Chao-chün Crosses the Border; Ch'en Yü-chiao), 836
"Chao Hsiao-lan" (Chin Chien), 865
"Chao hun" (Summons of the Soul; *Ch'u tz'u*), 117, 118, 124, 228, 300
Chao K'uang-yi, 339
Chao K'uang-yin (Emperor T'ai-tsu), 338, 339, 348
chao-ling (edicts and orders), 528
Chao Ling-chih, 796, 1008, 1009
Chao Meng-fu, 386, 394, 487
Chao-ming, Prince (Hsiao T'ung), 926
Chao Ming-ch'eng, 209
Chao-ming wen-hsüan (Selections of Refined Literature by Prince Chao-ming), 926, 1068, 1081. See also *Wen hsüan*
"Chao P'an-erh feng-yüeh chiu feng ch'en tsa-chü" (Chao P'an-erh's Sexy Ploy to Rescue a Whore; Kuan Han-ch'ing), 212–13
"Chao pei-k'o wen" (Text to Summon Back a Visitor from the North; Ts'en Shen), 300
Chao Pi, 681–82
Chao Po-ts'ung, 360
Chao Shan-liao, 142
Chao Shih-hsiu (Ling-hsiu), 365
"Chao-shih ku-erh" (The Orphan of the House of Chao; Chi Chün-hsiang), 803, 812
Chao-shih pei (The Cup That Reflects the World; Cho-yüan-t'ing chu-jen), 147, 615
Chao Shu-hsia (Susie Ch'en), 780
Chao Shu-li, 157
Chao T'ai-mou, 856
Chao Tao-yi, 191
Chao Te-ch'ang (Emperor Chen-tsung), 343, 344
Chao T'ien-yi, 461
Chao-tsung, Emperor, 312
"Chao Wu-hu ho-chi t'iao chia-hsin, Mo Ta-lang li-ti san shen chien" (The "Five Tigers of Chao" Conspire to Provoke a Family Dispute; Ling Meng-ch'u), 609
Chao-yang ch'ü-shih (Delightful Stories from the Chao-yang Palace; Master Yen-yen of Hangchow), 666
"Chao Yen-wang" (Yama Chao; Hung Shen), 872
Chao Yen-wei, 680
Chao Yi, 251, 434, 436
Chao Yi-chen, 191
Chao Yi-heng (Henry Chao), 764, 768–69
"Chao yin-shih" (Summoning the Recluse), 229, 263
chao-yin shih (summoning the recluse) poetry, 261, 262, 263, 265, 268, 981
Chao Yu-ch'in, 190
ch'ao (laugh at), 135
"Ch'ao-jan t'ai chi" (Tower of Transcendence; Su Shih), 539
Ch'ao Pu-chih, 351, 353, 479
ch'ao-tzu-jan (supernatural), 110
Ch'ao-yeh ch'ien-tsai (A Complete Record of the Court and the Outlying Areas; Chang Cho), 581
Char, René, 457
characters: authors as, 506; in *Chin P'ing Mei*, 642; in Ch'ing-Republican fiction, 721, 724, 727; in *ch'uan-ch'i* tales, 593; in drama, 844; in historical writing, 498, 503–4; in twentieth-century fiction, 738, 742, 746; in vernacular fiction, 603, 945, 1015
chariots, 13, 35, 71
Chaucer, Geoffrey, 943
che (this), 889
"Che chiu-nien fu" (Being Banished Nine Years; Liu Yü-hsi), 306
Che-hsi liu-chia tz'u (Lyric Poems by Six Poets of Western Chekiang; comp. Kung Hsiang-lin), 432
Che-hsi (western Chekiang) school, 427, 431, 432, 437, 438, 448, 450, 452
Che-tsung, Emperor, 339
che-tzu-hsi (scenes, one-act plays), 786, 824, 835
"Ch'e-chan" (Bus Stop; Kao Hsing-chien), 876
Chekhov, Anton, 720, 860
chen (admonition), 4, 238, 291
chen (authenticity, reality, truthfulness), 414, 422, 475–76, 477, 713
Chen, Xiaomei, 848–77

chen-chia (truth and fiction), 652
"Chen chien-sheng lang t'un mi-yao, Ch'un-hua nü wu hsieh feng-ch'ing" (Death by Aphrodisiac; Ling Meng-ch'u), 610
Chen Ch'ou-yü, 780
"Chen-chu t'a" (The Pearl Pagoda), 1023, 1024
chen-ch'üan (true interpretation), 633
"Chen-chung chi" (Record of the World Within a Pillow; Shen Chi-chi), 123, 583–84, 585, 592, 810, 827
chen-hsi (real drama), 852
chen-jen (Taoist perfected being; euphemism for courtesan), 1007
chen-ju (true Confucian scholar), 645
Chen kao (Declarations of the Perfected; T'ao Hung-ching), 177
chen-ming (admonition), 528
Chen Shih, 381
Chen Shui-bian, 758
Chen-t'ien-sheng pai-hua chü-she (Roaring-Heaven Spoken Drama Troupe; Canton), 850
Chen-tsung, Emperor (Chao Te-ch'ang), 178, 343, 344
Chen Wan-lung, 763
"Chen-wen chi" (The Chaste Poetess; Meng Ch'eng-shun), 832
Ch'en Chen-hui, 417
Ch'en Ch'en, 628, 663, 947
Ch'en Chi-ju, 7
Ch'en Ch'i, 366
Ch'en Ch'i-t'ung, 873
Ch'en Ch'iao, 387
Ch'en Chien-kung, 764
Ch'en Chih-ch'ao, 179
Ch'en Chih-hsü, 190
Ch'en Ching-jung, 457
ch'en-cho t'ung-k'uai (powerful expressiveness), 425
"Ch'en chou t'iao-mi" (Selling Rice at Ch'en-chou), 809
Ch'en Ch'un, 888–89
Ch'en-chung te ch'ih-pang (Heavy Wings; Chang Chieh), 760
Ch'en dynasty, 252, 272, 273, 282, 283
Ch'en Fu, 387
Ch'en Hsi, 506
"Ch'en Hsi-yi ssu tz'u ch'ao ming" (Ch'en T'uan; Feng Meng-lung), 601
"Ch'en-hsiang t'ai-tzu" (Prince Ch'en-hsiang), 1027
Ch'en Hsiao-ming, 768
Ch'en Hsien-chang, 399–400
Ch'en Hsü-ku, 776
Ch'en Hsüan-yu, 584, 809
Ch'en Huang-mei, 771
Ch'en Hung, 586
Ch'en Jan, 765–66
Ch'en Jen-huo, 669
Ch'en K'uei, 893–94, 904
Ch'en Kung-yin, 415
Ch'en Li-t'ing, 864
Ch'en Liang, 325
Ch'en Lin, 234, 254
Ch'en Lü, 387, 388
"Ch'en-lun" (short story; Sinking; Yü Ta-fu), 772
Ch'en-lun (collection; Sinking; Yü Ta-fu), 745–46
Ch'en Nan, 189
Ch'en P'ing, 515
Ch'en P'ing-yüan, 768
Ch'en Sen, 657, 672, 843
Ch'en She, 515, 516, 519
Ch'en Shih-tao, 355, 356, 357, 363, 443
Ch'en Shou, 261, 508, 622–24
Ch'en shu (History of the Ch'en Dynasty), 283
Ch'en Ta-pei, 851, 856
Ch'en Ta-sheng (Ch'en To), 818
Ch'en T'ing-cho, 329
Ch'en To (Ch'en Ta-sheng), 818
"Ch'en to-shou sheng-ssu fu-ch'i" (The Couple Bound in Life and Death), 604
Ch'en Tu-hsiu, 453–54, 458, 567, 744, 1066
Ch'en Tuan-sheng, 211, 1020, 1024
Ch'en T'uan, 189
Ch'en Tzu-ang, 290, 291, 298, 301, 398, 477
Ch'en Tzu-liang, 284
Ch'en Tzu-lung, 332, 333, 412–13, 414, 416, 444–45, 448
Ch'en Tzu-tu, 869
ch'en-tz'u (pillow words), 1026
Ch'en Wang-tao, 156
Ch'en Wei-sung (Chia-ling), 325, 333, 432, 446, 448; lyrics of, 332, 416, 417–18, 420
Ch'en Wen-shu, 839
Ch'en Yi, 872
Ch'en Yi-tseng, 892
Ch'en Yin-k'o (Ch'en Yin-ch'üeh), 7, 1023
Ch'en Ying-chen (Ch'en Yung-shan), 753
Ch'en Yü, 516
Ch'en Yü-chiao, 836
"Ch'en yü-shih ch'iao k'an chin ch'ai tien" (Censor Ch'en Ingeniously Solves the Case of the Golden Hairpins; Feng Meng-lung), 602
Ch'en Yü-yi, 357
Ch'en Yüan, 179
Ch'en Yün, 1012
cheng (governance), 341
cheng (orthodox), 385
Cheng, Robert, 31
Cheng, state of, 107, 500
Cheng Chen, 438, 439
Cheng Chen-to, 11, 1019
Cheng Cheng-ch'iu, 849
Cheng Ch'i, 581
"Cheng ch'i ko" (Song of the Rectifying Force; Wen T'ien-hsiang), 367
cheng-chih hsiao-shuo (political fiction), 707, 710, 717
cheng-chih shih (political poetry), 375, 462, 593
Cheng Chiung-ming, 780
Cheng Ch'ou-yü, 461, 464
Cheng Ch'u-hui, 581
Cheng Ho, 632, 818
Cheng-ho wan-shou Tao-tsang (Taoist Canon of Cheng-ho Era Longevity), 178
Cheng Hsieh, 434, 435, 448, 449, 831

Cheng Hsüan, 92, 100, 912, 913–14
Cheng Jo-yung, 829
Cheng Ku, 133
Cheng Kuang-tsu, 126, 145, 809
Cheng Min, 456
cheng-ming (rectification of names), 148
Cheng Shan-fu, 406
Cheng-shih period (Wei), 257–60, 265
Cheng Ssu-hsiao, 368
cheng-tao (illumination of the Way), 633
"Cheng-tao ko" (Song of Realization of the Way; Hsüan-chüeh), 170
Cheng-te, Emperor, 403
cheng-tui (straight parallelism), 893
cheng-t'ung (legitimate mandate), 623
Cheng-t'ung Tao-tsang (*Ta Ming Tao-tsang ching*; Scriptures of the Taoist Canon of the Great Ming), 178
Cheng Wen-cho, 451
Cheng Yi, 763
cheng-yi (orthodox interpretations), 283
cheng-yi (upright and righteous), 629
Cheng-yi (Authentic Unity) school (Taoism), 10, 176–77, 180, 182
Cheng Yü-ch'ing, 581
Ch'eng, Emperor, 249–50, 471, 580, 896
Ch'eng-chai (Studio of Sincerity), 364. *See also* Yang Wan-li
Ch'eng-chai style of poetry, 364
"Ch'eng ch'ao-feng tan yü wu t'ou fu, Wang t'ung-p'an shuang hsüeh pu ming yüan" (The Headless Woman; Ling Meng-ch'u), 608
Ch'eng-chih. *see* Lü Ssu-mien
"Ch'eng chiu fu" (Reprehending My Faults; Liu Tsung-yüan), 305
Ch'eng-Chu orthodoxy, 246–47
Ch'eng Hao, 364, 414, 914
Ch'eng Hsiao-ch'ing, 743
Ch'eng-hua period, 1013
Ch'eng-nan chiu-shih (Memories of Peking: Southside Stories; Lin Hai-yin), 779
"Ch'eng-nan kan-huai ch'eng Yung-shu" (South of the City Wall, Stirred Thoughts, Shown to Yung-shu; Su Shun-ch'in), 347
"Ch'eng-nan kuei chih ta feng hsüeh" (Returning from South of the City Wall, Encountering Heavy Snow and Strong Wind; Su Shun-ch'in), 347
"Ch'eng-nan liu" (Willow South of the Wall; Ku Tzu-ching), 816
"Ch'eng p'ei" (Mating; Yang Wei-chen), 393
Ch'eng-p'u, battle of, 499
Ch'eng Shan-chih, 730
"Ch'eng-shang wu" (Crows on City Walls;), 958
Ch'eng T'ing-kuei, 387
Ch'eng-tsu, Emperor, 178, 182, 632, 1097
Ch'eng Wei-yüan, 648
Ch'eng Yi, 89, 168, 364, 414, 914, 1070
ch'eng-yü (four-character phrases), 139, 150–51, 157, 158, 502, 738–39
"Ch'eng Yüan-yü tien-ssu tai ch'ang ch'ien, Shih-yi niang Yün-kang tsung T'an hsia" (Wei Eleventh-Maiden; Ling Meng-ch'u), 607
Cheung, Dominic (Ao Ao; Chang Ts'o), 458
chi (accounts; to record; collections), 383, 538, 560, 925
Chi Chen-yi, 281
"Chi ch'ing-jen" (To My Beloved; Wang Shih), 381
chi-chuan (annals and biographies), 503, 507, 509, 521
Chi-hai tsa-shih (Miscellaneous Poems of the Year Chi-hai; Kung Tzu-chen), 439
Chi Hsien (Lu Yi-shih), 456, 457, 460
Chi Hsien-lin, 12
"Chi-hsüan chi" (anthology of poetry; comp. Yao Ho), 307
Chi-hu (Crooked Tablet), 647
chi huan wu chen (reality is apprehended through illusion), 652
Chi Hung, 457
Chi Hung-chen, 768
Chi K'ang (Hsi K'ang), 7, 258, 259, 265
Chi-ku lu pa-wei (Colophons on Ancient Inscriptions; Ouyang Hsiu), 539
Chi Li, 646
chi-li (substance and order), 433, 434
Chi-nan san-ts'ai-tzu (Three Talents of Southern Chihli), 413
"Chi-nien" (Souvenir; Ch'ien Chung-shu), 752
Chi Pu, 986
"Chi Pu ma-chen tz'u-wen" (The Lyric Text on Chi Pu Shouting Abuses at the Battlefront), 986
Chi-she (Incipiency Society), 413
chi shih (recording events), 496
chi-t'i ch'uang-tso (collective playwriting), 864
chi-t'o (topical allegory), 334–35
chi yen (recording words), 496
Chi Yi, 188
Chi Yu-kung, 281
Chi Yün, 130, 543, 694
ch'i (breath, energy, spirit), 76, 634, 924; belief in, 116; and five phases, 80; in *Huai-nan Tzu*, 82–83
ch'i (concrete manifestations), 937
ch'i (eccentric), 931
ch'i (hostility), 186
ch'i (surprise and wonder), 646
Ch'i, Lady, 580
Ch'i, state of, 195, 501
"Ch'i ai shih" (Seven Sadnesses; Wang Ts'an), 256
ch'i-chen (Seven Perfected), 184

Ch'i-chen chi (Leaning on the Pillow Collection), 598
Ch'i-chen nien-p'u (A Chronicle of the Seven Perfected; Li Tao-ch'ien), 185
Ch'i-chi, 312–13
Ch'i dynasty, 240, 241, 242, 252, 269–73, 1080
"Ch'i fa" (Seven Stimuli; Mei Ch'eng), 232, 974
"Ch'i fu p'ien" (The Discarded Wife; Ts'ao Chih), 199
"Ch'i hsi" (Seventh Night), 959
"Ch'i-hsi pai-hu-t'uan" (Raid on the White Tiger Regiment; model play version), 874
ch'i-hsiang yen-yü (weather proverbs), 152, 158
Ch'i Huan, 457
ch'i-jen (extraordinary characters), 646
Ch'i Ju-shan, 845
"Ch'i-kai fu ch'ung p'ei luan ch'ou" (The Beggar Woman; Hsi Lang-hsien), 605
ch'i-ko shen-wen (personal character both profound and sturdy), 420
ch'i-li (delicate), 1068
Ch'i-Liang school, 246, 287, 290
ch'i-lin (unicorn), 115
Ch'i-lu teng (Lamp at the Crossroads; Li Hai-kuan), 670–71
Ch'i lüeh (Seven Summaries), 175
Ch'i-meng (Enlightenment; underground journal), 462
Ch'i nü-tzu chuan (Tales of Remarkable Women), 688
Ch'i Piao-chia, 841
Ch'i school (of *Shih-ching* interpretation), 90, 99
ch'i-shu (masterpieces), 710
Ch'i-sung, 170
"Ch'i T'ui nü" (Ch'i T'ui's Daughter; Niu Seng-ju), 588
Ch'i-tung yeh-yü (Words of a Retired Scholar from the East of Ch'i; Chou Mi), 142
"Ch'i wang" (King of Chess; Ah Ch'eng), 764–65
Ch'i-wu Ch'ien, 295
ch'i-yen ku-shih (heptasyllabic ancient-verse), 416
ch'i-yen lü-shih (heptasyllabic regulated verse), 1068
ch'i-yi poetics, 1071
Chia (Family; Pa Chin), 750, 1011
Chia, Empress, 261
Chia, Mr. (commentator on *Ch'un-ch'iu*), 92
chia-chiao (*chia-hsün*; Family Instructions), 902
Chia-ch'ing emperor, 383, 406, 1030, 1053
chia-chuan (family biographies), 969
Chia Chung-ming, 816, 840
Chia Ch'ung, 204
"Chia jen lien shang hei chih" (To a Pretty Girl with a Mole on Her Cheek; Pai P'u), 379
"Chia-ju wo shih chen-te" (If I Were for Real; Sha Yeh-hsin et al.), 872, 876
chia k'o (honored guest), 201
chia-ku-wen. *See* oracle bones
Chia-ling tz'u ch'üan-chi (The Complete *Tz'u* of Chia-ling), 418
chia-men (introductory scene), 820, 821, 826, 830
Chia Mi, 239, 261–64
Chia pien (Family Catastrophe; Wang Wen-hsing), 753, 777
chia-p'u (family pedigrees), 969
Chia Shan-hsiang, 183
Chia Ssu-tao, 325, 329, 330
Chia Tan, 591, 593
Chia Tao, 306–7, 312, 365
Chia Yi, 10, 224, 230
Chia Ying-ch'ung, 1012
Chia-ying Yeh Chao, 335
"Chia Yün-hua huan-hun chi" (The Return of the Soul of Chia Yün-hua; Li Chen), 681
Chiang-chai shih-hua (Discussions of Poetry from the Ginger Studio; Wang Fu-chih), 419, 937
chiang-ch'ang wen-hsüeh (*shuo-ch'ang wen-hsüeh*; prosimetric narratives), 11, 990, 1018, 1027, 1042
"Chiang chin chiu" (Bring on the Drink; Li Po), 255
Chiang Ching-kuo, 569, 758
chiang-ching-wen (sūtra lecture texts), 167, 982, 983, 985, 993
"Chiang Ch'u kung chiao ying ko" (A Song on a Goshawk Painted by Chiang, Duke of Ch'u; Tu Fu), 476
Chiang Ch'un-lin, 449, 450
"Chiang-chung wang yüeh" (Gazing at the Moon in the Yangtze"; Lu Chao-lin), 288
Chiang Fang, 585, 827
Chiang Ho (Jiang He), 462
"Chiang-hsi shih she tsung-p'ai t'u" (Chart of the Branches of the Kiangsi Poetic Community; Lü Pen-chung), 356, 360
"Chiang Hsing-ko ch'ung-hui chen-chu shan" (Chiang Hsing-ko Re-encounters the Pearl Shirt; Feng Meng-lung), 600, 602
Chiang-hu (Rivers and Lakes poets), 366, 392
Chiang-hu chi (Rivers and Lakes; poetry collection), 366
Chiang-hu school of poetry, 392
Chiang K'ai-shek, 157, 569, 572, 736, 746, 753, 758, 873
Chiang Kuang-tz'u, 748
Chiang Kuei, 777
Chiang K'uei, 328–29, 330, 432, 447, 448
"Chiang-nan yü T'ien-pao yüeh-sou" (Meeting an Old Musician from the T'ien-pao Era in Chiangnan), 308
Chiang Ping-chih, 748
chiang-shih (telling of historical stories), 621
Chiang Shih-ch'üan, 436, 834
Chiang Shu-yü, 182

Chiang-su (Kiangsu; journal), 725
Chiang Tse-min, 770, 772
Chiang-tso san feng (Three Phoenixes Left of the River), 416
Chiang-tso san-ta-chia (Three Great Masters from Left of the River), 415
"Chiang-ts'un ch'ang-ho tz'u" (River Village Offer and Response Lyrics; Wang Shih-lu), 427
"Chiang-tu shih hsiao-fu t'u shen" (A Filial Daughter-in-Law Offers Her Body to Be Butchered; Hsi Lang-hsien), 604
Chiang Tzu-lung, 760
Chiang Yen, 474, 475
Chiang Ying-k'o, 678
Chiang-yün lou (Puce Gauze Cloud Lodge), 415, 416
"Ch'iang-ts'un" (Ch'iang Village; Tu Fu), 299–300
chiao-fang (Palace Music School), 975
Chiao-hui hsin-pao (Church News), 1059
"Chiao Hung chi" (*Chiao Hung chuan*; The Story of Chiao-niang and Fei-hung; Sung Yüan), 679, 681, 805; stage adaptation of, 831
"Chiao Hung chi" (*tsa-chü*; Story of Chiao-niang and Fei-hung; Liu Tui), 804
Chiao-jan, 169, 302, 893, 930
"Chiao nü shih" (Darling Daughters; Tso Ssu), 263
chiao-ssu ko (hymns), 954, 958
chiao ts'o (emphatic repetition), 894
Ch'iao Chi, 373, 377, 380, 815
ch'iao-hsiao (cunning smile), 195
ch'iao-p'i-hua (witticisms), 152
"Ch'iao Yen-chieh yi ch'ieh p'o chia" (One Concubine Destroys a Household; Feng Meng-lung), 600
"Ch'iao-ying" (Portrait in Disguise; Wu Tsao), 786, 839
chieh (exclamations), 108
"Chieh ch'ao" (Dissolving Ridicule; Yang Hsiung), 233
"Chieh-chih-erh chi" (The Ring; Hung P'ien), 599
"Chieh Chih-t'ui huo-feng tu-fu" (Chieh Chih-t'ui Traps His Jealous Wife in an Inferno; Ai-na chü-shih), 615
Chieh Hsi-ssu, 386
Chieh "Shui hu chuan" (Conclusion of *Water Margin*; Yü Wan-ch'un), 629
Chieh-ts'un-chai lun-tz'u tsa-chu (Miscellaneous Writings on Song Lyrics from the Chieh-ts'un Studio), 438
chieh-yi (form bonds of righteousness), 629
Ch'ieh-chung chi (anthology of verse; comp. Yüan Chieh), 301
chien (simplicity, conciseness), 890
Chien-an ch'i tzu (Seven Masters of the Chien-an Period), 253
Chien-an period (Han), 234, 253–66, 269, 397, 922, 923
Chien-hsia chuan (Tales of Chivalrous Swordsmen; comp. Wang Shih-chen), 688
chien-hsiung (deviant hero), 623
"Chien-hu yeh-fan chi" (A Night Outing on Mirror Lake; Ch'ü Yu), 680
Chien-k'ang (Nanking), 252
"Chien-ko fu" (Li Po), 298, 300
Chien-so ho fang-sung te hsün-huan: 1976 chih 1986 nien ch'i-chien Chung-kuo cheng-chih yü wen-hsüeh te kuan-hsi (Cycles of Repression and Relaxation: Politico-Literary Events in China; Ho Yü-huai), 769
Chien-teng hsin-hua (New Stories for Trimming the Lampwick; comp. Ch'ü Yu), 679, 681–85, 1073, 1074, 1091, 1099
Chien-teng lu (Records by the Trimmed Lamp; comp. Ch'ü Yu), 679, 681–85
Chien-teng yü-hua (Supplementary Tales by the Trimmed Lamp; Li Chen), 680–85, 682
Chien-wen, Emperor of Liang. *See* Hsiao Kang
Chien-wu chi (Anthology of Gradual Awakening), 187
Ch'ien Ch'i, 300–301
Ch'ien-chia shih (Poems of a Thousand Authors), 205
Ch'ien Ch'ien-yi, 281, 413–23, 434, 559, 678; influence of, 416, 417, 421; marriage to Liu Shih, 413, 415, 448; on poetry, 398, 414, 422, 423
Ch'ien Chung-shu, 366, 566, 573, 752
Ch'ien fo tung (The Caves of the Thousand Buddhas), 964, 965
"Ch'ien Han Liu-chia t'ai-tzu chuan" (The Account of the Crown Prince of the House of Liu During the Former Han), 969
Ch'ien Hsi-yen, 678
Ch'ien Hsing-ts'un (Ah Ying), 698
Ch'ien Hsüan, 485, 486
Ch'ien Hsüan-t'ung, 454, 851–52
Ch'ien-lung emperor, 175, 431, 433, 573, 826, 1024, 1030
"Ch'ien-nü li-hun" (Ch'ien-nü's Soul Leaves Her Body; Cheng Kuang-tsu), 126, 145, 809
Ch'ien Ta-hsin, 890
Ch'ien T'ien-hua, 726
Ch'ien Ts'ai, 628
ch'ien-tse hsiao-shuo (novels of indictment), 657, 697, 740
Ch'ien-tzu wen (The Thousand Character Primer), 966, 973, 995
"Ch'ien-wan pieh pa wo tang chen" (Don't Take Me Seriously; Wang Shuo), 766–67

"Ch'ien-wan pu-yao wang-chi" (Never Forget; Ts'un Shen), 871
Ch'ien Wei-yen, 344
chih (intent, aspiration), 892, 920, 937
chih (personal ambition), 412
chih (*shu*; topical essays or treatises), 503
chih (substantial informative content), 892
chih (understood), 884
Chih-chen yü-lu (Discourse Record on Ultimate Perfection; Liu Ch'u-hsüan), 188
"Chih chi" (Knowing Things to Come; Pai P'u), 379
Chih Chiang, 958
Chih-ch'ien, 162, 172
"Chih-chih fu" (Knowing Where to Stop; Li Te-yü), 306
Chih-ch'ing tsa-shuo (Miscellaneous Stories of Chih-ch'ing), 676
"Chih-ch'ü wei-hu-shan" (Taking Tiger Mountain by Strategy; model play version), 874
chih-kuai (tales of the strange; records of anomalies), 117, 119–22, 170–71, 261, 520, 542–54, 579–94, 610, 970; and Buddhism, 120, 121, 549, 550–51; in classical Chinese, 675; and drama, 125; and historical writing, 494, 499; humor in, 146; illustrations for, 121; in Japan, 1086; in Korea, 1069, 1070; in periodicals, 130–31; and *pi-chi*, 560, 562, 563–64; of Six Dynasties period, 119, 121, 544, 579–80, 581, 1069; and *Strange Tales from Make-Do Studio*, 130; and Su Shih, 540; and Sung ancient-style prose, 537; of T'ang dynasty, 119, 121, 548, 580; and Taoism, 119, 120–21, 548, 580; in Vietnam, 1099
Chih-na (China), 46, 54
Chih-nan hou lu (Latter Record of the Compass; Wen T'ien-hsiang), 367
Chih-nan lu (Record of the Compass; Wen T'ien-hsiang), 367
Chih-nang (Sack of Wisdom; comp. Feng Meng-lung), 688
chih-nang (sack of knowledge), 884
Chih-nü (Weaver Girl), 68
Chih-p'an, 167
chih-shih lei-ch'ing (designate affairs and draw categorical correspondences between situations), 334
Chih-tun, 169, 473
Chih-yen chai (Red Inkstone Studio), 647, 649, 651, 652
Chih-yi, 170
Chih Yü, 925, 954
"Chih-yüan pieh San-niang T'ai-yüan t'ou-shih" (How Liu Chih-yüan Bade San-niang Good-bye and Joined the Army in Taiyuan), 1003
"Ch'ih ch'ü ch'üan Mao Lieh lai yüan ch'ien, shih huan hun ya k'uai so sheng ming" (The Deceitful Accomplice; Ling Meng-ch'u), 608
ch'ih jen (eat people), 744
Ch'ih Li, 765
ch'ih-lun (sustain an argument), 937
Ch'ih-pi (Red Cliff), 245, 540; Battle of, 621, 624
"Ch'ih-pi fu" (Rhapsody on the Red Cliff; Su Shih), 245, 624
Ch'ih p'o-tzu chuan (The Story of the Deluded Woman), 640
Ch'ih-sung Chin-kang ching kung-te chi (Accounts of the Numinous Responses and Merit Gained from Upholding and Reciting the Diamond Scripture), 970
Ch'ih-tao jen (Man of the Crazy Way), 665
Ch'ih-ti chih-lien (Love in Redland; Chang Ai-ling), 753
Ch'ih Yu (God of War), 66
"Chin-ch'ai chi" (The Gold Hairpin), 821
Chin Chien, 865
"Chin chüeh lou" (House of Awakening; Shih Ch'eng-chin), 617
Chin (Jurchen) dynasty. *See* Jurchens
Chin dynasty (265-420), 508, 523, 560; court of, 473; Eastern, 22, 252, 264, 265–69, 551, 925, 932; and *fu*, 6; histories of, 549; imitation of ballads in, 959; literary criticism in, 924–25, 930; literary theory in, 919, 923, 926; parallel prose in, 239, 246; poetry of, 234, 240, 265; in *Romance of the Three Kingdoms*, 621; and T'ai-kang reign-period, 545; Western, 239, 258, 260, 262, 264, 272, 274, 924; and women, 206
Chin dynasty (1115–1234): court of, 362, 363; drama in, 144, 819; Kaifeng in, 791; literary criticism in, 936; and Mongols, 340, 821; performative literature of, 796; poetry of, 328, 386; and Sinitic, 22; and Southern Sung, 339, 359, 360, 371; strummed lyrics of, 1019; and Taoism, 810; *yüan-pen* (texts of the guild) of, 792
Chin dynasty (sixth century BCE), 803
Chin Ho, 438–39
"Chin-hsiang k'o mang k'an *Chin-kang ching*, ch'u yü seng ch'iao wan fa hui fen" (The Manuscript of *The Diamond Sutra*; Ling Meng-ch'u), 607
Chin-hsiang t'ing (Pavilion of Embroidered Fragrance), 669
"Chin-hsüeh chieh" (Analysis of Advancing in Learning, or Progress in Learning; Han Yü), 304, 533
chin-hua (transformative evolution), 713
Chin-hua t'uan (Evolution Troupe; Shanghai), 850, 851

Chin Hung-chou Hsi-shan shih-erh chen-chün chuan (Traditions of the Twelve True Lords on Western Mountain in Hung-chou During the Chin Dynasty; Hu Hui-ch'ao), 582
Chin-kang po-je ching chi-yen chi (Collected Wisdom of Diamond-Wisdom-Sutra Miracles; Meng Hsien-chung), 582
Chin-ku ch'i-kuan (Remarkable Stories New and Old), 610, 692
Chin Lien, 461
Chin-lien cheng-tsung chi (An Account of the True Lineage of the Golden Lotus; comp. Ch'in Chih-an), 184
Chin-lien cheng-tsung hsien-yüan hsiang-chuan (An Illustrated Biographical Account of the Transcendent Origins of the True Lineage of the Golden Lotus; Liu Chih-hsüan), 184
Chin-ling, Eight Masters of, 240
"Chin-ling yi" (Chin-ling Post-Station; Wen T'ien-hsiang), 367–68
Chin P'ing Mei (Gold Vase Plum, The Golden Lotus), 214–15, 618, 647, 652, 657, 659, 665, 669–70, 682, 709, 889, 996; Chang Chu-p'o edition of, 943, 944; in Japan, 1091, 1093; sequels to, 642–43, 662, 947; sexuality in, 637–43
"Chin P'ing Mei" te yi-shu (The Art of *Chin P'ing Mei*), 642
"Chin P'ing Mei" tz'u-hua (The Prosimetric *Chin P'ing Mei*), 638
Chin Shan, 870
Chin Sheng-t'an, 627, 631, 708, 710; commentaries of, 842, 938, 944, 946, 949, 1094; edition of *Romance of the Western Chamber*, 825; edition of *Water Margin*, 842, 940–41, 942, 943, 945, 947, 948
"Chin Sheng-t'an p'i hsiao-shuo shuo" (On Chin Sheng-t'an's Critical Discourses on Fiction; Ch'iu Wei-ai), 710
chin-shih (Presented Scholar; Metropolitan Graduate) degree, 1, 2, *passim*
Chin shu (The History of Chin Dynasty), 551
"Chin-so chi" (The Golden Cangue; Yeh Hsien-tzu), 837
Chin so chi (The Golden Cangue; Chang Ai-ling), 752
Chin Sung-ts'en (Chin T'ien-ho), 709, 725
chin-tai (modern), 955
Chin Tan, 1035
Chin-tan ta-ch'eng chi (Anthology on the Great Completion of the Golden Enchymoma; Hsiao T'ing-chih), 189
chin-t'i shih (*hsin-t'i shih*; new-style poetry), 270, 276, 289, 300, 304, 311, 312, 404, 415, 931, 979, 1068, 1071, 1084. See also *p'ai-lü*; Yung-ming *t'i*
chin-t'i shih (regulated verse) poems, 1084
Chin-t'ien (Today; journal), 462, 463, 464, 768
Chin T'ien-ho (Chin Sung-ts'en), 709
Chin-wen kuan-chih (Pinnacles of the Modern Essay), 569
Chin wu meng (Dream of Golden Chambers), 662
"Chin-yang men" (The Chin-yang Gate; Cheng Yü), 310
Chin Yu-tzu, 401
"Chin Yü-nu pang ta po-ch'ing lang" (Chin Yü-nu; Feng Meng-lung), 601–2
Chin Yün, 869
Chin Yün-ch'iao chuan (The Tale of Chin Yün-ch'iao), 1101
ch'in (cicada), 195
ch'in (zither), 646, 655–56
Ch'in, state of, 93, 107, 580. *See also* Ch'in dynasty
Ch'in Chi-wen, 1024
Ch'in Chia, 204, 251
"Ch'in-chung yin" (Odes from Ch'in; Po Chü-yi), 308
Ch'in dynasty, 21, 249, 504, 515, 806, 910–11, 986; and classics, 99; fall of, 507; First Emperor of, 49, 89, 311, 519, 837; language in, 37, 41; and Legalism, 82
"Ch'in-fu yin" (The Lament of the Lady of Ch'in; Wei Chuang), 313, 981–82, 1098
"Ch'in-huai Poems" (Wang Shih-chen), 422
"Ch'in-huai tsa-shih" (Miscellaneous Poems on the Ch'in-huai River; Wang Shih-chen), 422
Ch'in Kuan, 319, 320, 321, 327, 332, 351–52
Ch'in Kuei, 339, 360, 602
"Ch'in meng chi" (Record of a Dream of Ch'in; Shen Ya-chih), 592, 593
Ch'in Shih Huang-ti (First Emperor of Ch'in), 49, 89, 311, 519, 837
Ch'in Shu-pao, 626
Ch'in-ting ssu-k'u ch'üan-shu tsung-mu t'i-yao (Authorized by His Majesty, General Catalog of the Four Treasures Complete Library, With Summary Critiques). See *Ssu-k'u ch'üan-shu tsung-mu t'i-yao*
Ch'in-tsung, Emperor, 628
China, cultural. See *wen-hua Chung-kuo*
China, Greater, 758–81; literature in, 759–60
China, People's Republic of (PRC), 569, 574, 634, 640, 747, 754–57, 760–62; censorship in, 736–37, 758, 769–73; *Chin P'ing Mei* in, 640, 642; drama in, 848, 855, 857, 859, 861–65; establishment of, 459, 1012; ethnic minorities of, 1032–54; feminist rhetoric

of, 870; and Hong Kong, 774; post-Mao period in, 848, 855, 858, 859; proverbs in, 157–58; reforms in, 760; simplified characters in, 53–54; and Taiwan, 758–59, 775, 780; women in, 865–66
China, Republic of (ROC), 459; founding of, 156, 738. *See also* Taiwan
China Federation of Literary and Art Circles (Chung-kuo wen-hsüeh yi-shu chieh lien-ho-hui), 770, 772–73
China Times (newspaper), 776
China Traveling Troupe (Chung-kuo lü-hsing chü-t'uan), 861
China Youth Theater (Chung-kuo ch'ing-nien yi-shu chü-yüan), 870
Chindŏk, Queen (Silla, Korea), 1068
Chinese Communist Party (CCP), 157, 453, 567, 859, 876, 1012, 1034; censorship by, 736–37, 772–73; and literary criticism, 768; and literature, 5, 568, 746, 750, 760, 761; and Lu Hsün, 745; and politicization of fiction, 752–53; and "River Elegy," 763; seventh congress of, 865; and Taiwan, 776–77; and theater, 846, 848, 858, 864, 866, 868–72, 874; and Wang Shuo, 767
Chinese language. *See* Sinitic
Chinese League of Left-Wing Dramatists (Chung-kuo tso-yi hsi-chü-chia lien-meng), 860, 862
Chinese League of Left-Wing Writers (Chung-kuo tso-yi tso-chia lien-meng), 860, 862
Chinese Writers Association, 1039, 1052
Chinese Writers Federation (Chung-kuo tso-chia hsieh-hui), 770
The Chinese Written Character as a Medium for Poetry (Fenollosa), 3
"Ching" (Quiet; Shen Ts'ung-wen), 751
ching (*ch'ou*; clown role), 144, 994
ching (classics; sūtras; scriptures), 86–87. *See also* classical texts
ching (scene), 358, 419, 937
Ching, Duke of Ch'i, 501
Ching, Duke of Chin, 500
"Ching-ch'ai chi" (The Thorn-Hairpin), 821
ching-chieh (boundedness, realm; Sanskrit: *viṣaya, gocara*), 12, 442, 939
ching-hsi. See Peking opera
Ching-hsi chi (Ching Stream Collection; Yang Wan-li), 363
Ching hua yüan (Flowers in the Mirror; Li Ju-chen), 69, 120, 213–14, 545, 655–57, 719, 721–22, 1076; humor in, 147–48; Korean translation of, 1077; satire in, 130, 655; supernatural in, 127, 128
Ching K'o, 273, 506, 580, 587, 837
ching kuo chih ta-yeh (the great enterprise for managing a state), 924
Ching-ling pa yu (Eight Companions of Ching-ling), 270, 271
Ching-ling school, 412, 414
Ching-lung period (T'ang), 291, 292
Ching-lung wen-kuan chi (record of scholars at Chung-tsung's court), 291
Ching-ming chung-hsiao ch'üan-shu (Complete Writings on the Loyalty and Filiality of Ching-ming; comp. Huang Yüan-chi), 190
Ching-ming Tao (Way of Purity and Radiance), 190
ching-shen wu-jan (spiritual pollution), 737
"Ching shih" (Cautionary Verses; Wang Yüan-heng), 380
Ching-shih t'ung-yen (Common Words to Warn the World; Feng Meng-lung), 127, 597, 598, 600
Ching-te ch'uan-teng lu (Records of the Transmission of the Lamp from the Ching-te Period; Tao-yüan), 169
Ching-ti, Emperor (Han), 99
Ching Ti, Emperor (Tai Tsung; Ming), 400, 807
Ching-tien shih-wen (Textual Explications for the Classical Canon; Lu Te-ming), 283, 914
Ching-tsung, Emperor, 311
Ching-t'u (Pure Land) Buddhism, 10, 163, 166, 169, 478
Ching-t'u lun-chu (Commentary and Discourses Regarding the Pure Land; T'an-luan), 166
"Ching-wei shih" (Stones of the Ching-wei Bird; Ch'iu Chin), 1012
ch'ing (feelings, romance, love), 341, 342, 348, 412, 413, 419, 601, 648, 652–53, 657, 920, 937, 1064
ch'ing (manner), 427, 938
ch'ing (purely), 426
Ch'ing-an Ying-ch'an-tzu yü-lu (Discourse Record of Ying-ch'an-tzu; comp. Ch'ai Yüan-kao), 190
"Ch'ing-ch'eng yin-che chi" (The Record of the Ch'ing-ch'eng Recluse; Chao Pi), 681
Ch'ing-ch'ih Fan-cheng Tao-jen (Man of the Way Who Turned Over a New Leaf After Being Crazed with Passion; Li Yü), 664
ch'ing-ching (pure quiescence), 187
"Ch'ing-ch'iu-tzu ko" (Song of the Green Hill Master; Kao Ch'i), 396
ch'ing-chiung pa-su (pure-and-distant and transcending all vulgarity), 415

"Ch'ing ch'ou" (Enmity from Love), 610
"Ch'ing-chung p'u" (A Roster of the Pure and Loyal; Li Yü), 833
Ch'ing dynasty, 410, 509, 528, 552, 559, 564, 612; anthologies of, 533; archaism in, 440, 441, 1072; auto-commentary in, 947; and Boxer Rebellion, 1012; Buddhism in, 641, 642, 662, 670, 699, 722; bureaucracy in, 52, 698; civil-service examinations in, 52, 431, 531, 668, 914–15; classical tales in, 690–96; compilers of, 279; Confucianism in, 52, 662, 670, 671, 672, 721, 726; culture of, 717; detective stories in, 722–25, 729; drama in, 144; early, 613–17; essays in, 708; expository prose in, 541; fall of, 52, 440, 442, 450, 850, 1051; fictional characters in, 721, 723, 724, 726; formalist poetry of, 429–33, 717; genres of, 6; and Han learning, 915; historical writing in, 669–70, 697–98; *hua-pen* in, 595; and Hui people, 34; humor in, 134, 135, 832; and Japan, 863, 1094; language in, 22, 32, 33, 430, 1062; late, 697–731, 704–5, 738–43; literary criticism in, 933, 936–38; literati in, 4; literature of, 704–5; local academies of, 1053; lyrics in, 326, 331, 332, 333, 429–32, 437, 439, 441, 442, 444–52; mid, 617–19; and modernity, 697, 700, 721; novels of, 697, 716–17, 720–25; pageants in, 789, 826; painter-poets of, 435; parallel prose in, 224, 236, 243, 246–47; poetry and painting in, 489; poetry of, 338, 390, 393, 429–43, 717, 724, 1091; prestige of fiction in, 732–33; prosimetric literature of, 792; proverbs in, 153, 155; scholar-beauty romances in, 666–69; scholar-officials of, 383; sexuality in, 662, 664–66, 669, 672–73; *shih* poetry of, 427, 429, 430, 432, 436, 437, 439, 440, 441, 445; study of classics in, 883; and Sung poetry, 368; supernatural literature in, 131, 544; Taiwan in, 458; *t'an-tz'u* of, 995, 1019; Taoism in, 662, 664, 665, 666, 670, 672; transition from Ming to, 332, 413, 415, 416, 421, 426, 427, 428, 446, 610–13, 936; vernacular in, 52, 659, 660, 665, 671, 673, 698, 700, 724, 730, 843, 887; and the West, 669, 670, 721, 725, 731, 1055, 1056; women in, 210, 218, 840; wooden fish stories of, 1026, 1027
"Ch'ing feng ko chi" (Pure Winds Pavilion; Su Shih), 539
Ch'ing-ho chen-jen pei-yu yü-lu (Discourse Record on the Northern Journeys of the Perfected Ch'ing-ho; comp. Tuan Chih-chien), 188
Ch'ing-hsiang (*Tendency*; journal), 464
ch'ing-hsü sao-ya (pure and empty; poetic and elegant), 330
ch'ing-kang (purity and strength), 414
ch'ing-ken (roots of desire), 648
ch'ing-kuan (incorruptible officials), 658
ch'ing-kuo (beauty who topples the state), 202
Ch'ing-lan, 694
ch'ing-li (refined), 374
Ch'ing-li period (Sung), 345
Ch'ing-lou meng (Dream of the Blue Chamber; Yü Ta), 657
Ch'ing-meng t'o (Awakened from the Love Dream), 669
Ch'ing-mo min-ch'u hsiao-shuo shu-hsi (A Compendium of Short Stories from the Late Ch'ing and Early Republican Era; ed. Yü Jun-ch'i), 730
Ch'ing-ni lien-hua chi (Accounts of Lotus Blossoms in the Mire; comp. Mei Ting-tso), 688
Ch'ing-p'ing shan-t'ang hua-pen (Vernacular Short Stories from the Clear and Peaceful Mountain Studio; Hung P'ien), 597, 996
"Ch'ing-p'ing-tiao" (A Pure and Plain Mode; Yu T'ung), 837
"Ch'ing po p'ien" (Frivolity; Chang Hua), 262
Ch'ing Pu, 516, 519
"Ch'ing-shan lei" (Tears on the Blue Gown; Ma Chih-yüan), 815
Ch'ing-shang ch'ü-tz'u (songs in the Ch'ing-shang mode), 954, 958
"Ch'ing shih" (Love Poems; Chang Hua), 262
Ch'ing-shih (Anatomy of Love; comp. Feng Meng-lung), 688
Ch'ing-shih lei-lüeh (Classified Outline of the Anatomy of Love; Feng Meng-lung), 610
Ch'ing-so kao-yi (Lofty Judgements from the Green Lattice; comp. Liu Fu), 679, 685
Ch'ing-t'ai (Moss; Lin Pai), 766
ch'ing-t'an (pure conversation), 549
Ch'ing-t'an wan-hsüan (Myriad Selections of Casual Talk), 682
Ch'ing-tsun lu (Records of the Clear and Honorable; Lien Pu), 675
Ch'ing-wei (Clarified Tenuity) school, 181, 191
Ch'ing-yeh chung (Alarum Bell on a Still Night), 612
Ch'ing-yi pao (The China Discussion; journal), 707, 718
Ch'ing-yü (Mackerel Demon; *Journey to the West*), 946
ch'ing-yüan (purity and distance), 424, 425, 426
ch'ing-yüeh (pure music), 314

Chinggis Khan (Genghis Khan; Temujin), 176, 185, 188, 509, 1049, 1050
"Chinh phu ngam khuc" (Song of a Soldier's Wife; Dang Tran Con), 1098
chinsi (true poetry; Korea), 1071
Chiphyŏnjŏn (Hall of Worthies; Korea), 1070
"Chiu chang" (Nine Pieces), 228
chiu-chü (old drama), 850, 852
"Chiu Feng-ch'en" (Rescue of a Courtesan; Kuan Han-ch'ing), 145, 813
"Chiu hsia chiu Chao ni-ao mi hua, chi chung chi Chia hsiu-ts'ai pao yüan" (The Nun's Trick and Licentiate Chia's Revenge; Ling Meng-ch'u), 609
chiu-hsiang (nine reflections), 979
"Chiu hsiang-kuan shih" (Poem on the Nine Visualizations), 979
"Chiu huai" (Nine Regrets), 229
"Chiu ko" (Nine Songs; *Ch'u tz'u*), 117, 118, 199, 226, 227, 229, 233, 249
Chiu ming ch'i yüan (The Strange Case of the Nine Murders; Wu Chien-jen), 723
Chiu-mo-lo-shih. *See* Kumārajīva
"Chiu mo ts'ai Yü Chiao ssu o, kuei tui an Yang Hua chieh shih" (The Ghost's Possession; Ling Meng-ch'u), 609
"Chiu pien" (Nine Changes), 228
"Chiu ssu" (Nine Longings; Wang Yi), 230
"Chiu t'an" (Nine Laments), 229
Chiu Ting (Maker of the Nine Cauldrons), 65
Chiu tsa p'i-yü (Old Canonical Scripture of Miscellaneous Parables), 171
chiu-wang yen-chü-tui (national salvation drama troupes), 864
Chiu-wei kuei (The Nine-Tailed Turtle), 1015
"Chiu yeh p'ai" (School of Nine Leaves), 457
Ch'iu-chia chi (Collection of Sounds of the Autumn Frontier Woodwind; Wu Chao-ch'ien), 417
Ch'iu Chin, 335, 844, 845, 1012
Ch'iu Ch'u-chi, 176, 178, 185, 188
Ch'iu Chün, 683, 823
"Ch'iu feng tz'u" (Autumn Wind; Emperor Wu), 249
Ch'iu Hsin-ju, 211, 1023
"Ch'iu hsing" (Autumn Sentiments; Tu Fu), 300
"Ch'iu-jan k'o chuan" (An Account of the Curly-Bearded Stranger; Tu Kuang-t'ing), 182, 587, 829, 837
"'Ch'iu-jih teng Hung-fu T'eng-wang ko chien-pieh' hsü" (Preface to "Ascending the Gallery of Prince T'eng of Hung-fu for a Parting Feast on an Autumn Day"; Wang Po), 289
ch'iu-li (forceful beauty), 387
"Ch'iu-liu shih" (Autumn Willows Poems; Wang Shih-chen), 422
"Ch'iu-shan fu" (The Imprisoning Hills; Liu Tsung-yüan), 305
"Ch'iu-sheng fu" (Rhapsody on the Sounds of Autumn; Liu Yü-hsi), 306
"Ch'iu-sheng fu" (Rhapsody on the Sounds of Autumn; Ou-yang Hsiu), 245, 540
"Ch'iu shou" (Autumn Harvest; Ai Wu), 752
"Ch'iu ssu" (Autumn Thoughts; Ma Chih-yüan), 378
Ch'iu-teng ts'ung-hua (Collected Tales by the Autumn Lamp; Wang Hsien), 695
Ch'iu Wei-ai, 710
"Ch'iu yü" (Autumn Rain; Cheng Ssu-hsiao), 368
"Ch'iung Ma Chou tsao chi mai tui ao" (The Impoverished Ma Chou; Feng Meng-lung), 601
Ch'iung Yao, 780
Cho Wen-chün, 799, 816
Cho-yüan-t'ing chu-jen, 615, 619
Ch'o keng lu (Records After Plowing; T'ao Tsung-yi), 374
Ch'oe Cha, 1070
Ch'oe Ch'i-wŏn, 1068
Ch'oe Rip, 1073
Ch'oe Sŭng-no, 1068
chokusenshi (imperial anthologies of Chinese poetry), 1083
chŏn (tales), 1077
Chŏng Sa-ryŏng, 1071
chŏngisu (professional storyteller; Korea), 1075
Chŏngjo, King, 1073, 1074, 1075
Chosŏn-p'ung (Chosŏn-style poetry), 1071
Chou, Duke of, 89, 91, 95, 102
Chou, King of, 512
Chou Chi (1781–1839), 334–35, 438
Chou Chi (late Ming Hangchow scholar), 612
Chou Ch'o. *See* Lu Hsün
"Chou chung tsa yung" (Shipboard Songs; Yüan Chüeh), 394
"Chou-chung yeh ch'i" (Aboard Boat, Rising at Night; Su Shih), 350
Chou dynasty, 21, 471, 496, 509, 511, 522, 545; bronze inscriptions of, 36–37, 41, 467, 495; and *Chou-li*, 91; and Confucius, 3, 74; Eastern, 70–73, 338, 555; and five phases, 80; and history, 494, 632; as ideal, 72, 73, 78, 79; myths of, 60, 65; and *Shih-ching*, 97, 102, 104–5; and *shih* poetry, 338; song and dance in, 790; Western, 3, 71, 72, 73, 79, 89, 660; and women, 195; and *Yi-ching*, 88, 89. *See also* Northern Chou dynasty

Chou dynasty (of Empress Wu), 285, 292
Chou En-lai, 403, 869
Chou Ju-ch'ang, 652
Chou Kuei-sheng, 704, 710, 720, 729
Chou Li, 682
Chou-li (Rites of Chou), 88, 91, 93, 101, 910
Chou Meng-tieh, 461
Chou Mi, 142, 330, 335
Chou Nan, land of, 104–5
Chou Pang-yen, 321, 322, 327, 328–29, 438
Chou Shao-liang, 12
Chou Shou-chüan, 704, 729–30
Chou Shou-chung, 153
Chou Shu-jen, 745. *See also* Lu Hsün
Chou Shun-ch'ang, 833
Chou Te-ch'ing, 372, 374, 381, 840
Chou Tso-jen, 454, 568, 571, 720, 729, 852
Chou Tun-yi, 707
Chou Wei-chih, 770
Chou Yang, 745
Chou-yi. See *Yi-ching*
"Chou yü" (Discourses of Chou; *Kuo-yü*), 64, 65
Chou Yung, 270
ch'ou (clown), 994
"Ch'ou Chu shih-san hsiu-ts'ai" (In Response to Graduate Chu; Hsüeh T'ao), 209
"Ch'ou-hsi p'ien (Times of Yesteryear; Lo Pin-wang), 288
"Ch'ou lang-chün p'a chiao p'ien te yen" (An Ugly Husband Fears a Pretty Wife but Marries a Beautiful One; Li Yü), 613
Ch'ou-lou te Chung-kuo-jen (The Ugly Chinaman; Po Yang), 572, 767
Christianity, 428; Nestorian, 9, 170, 1048
chu (commentaries), 8, 87
chu ch'eng hsüeh (pearls turned to blood), 201
"Chu-chih tz'u" (Bamboo-Branch Lyrics; Liu Yü-hsi), 305–6
Chu Ching-chien (Pure Example), 524
Chu Ching-fan, 996
Chu Ch'o, 182
Chu Ch'üan, 811, 816, 840
Chu-ch'un yüan hsiao-shih (The Garden of Spring Residence), 668
Chu Fa-hu, 162
"Chu fu" (Benediction; Lu Hsün), 570
Chu Hsi, 9, 168, 404, 608, 622–23, 707, 806, 902, 914; and classics, 88, 92, 95, 96; and Neo-Confucianism, 414, 888, 889, 1070, 1087, 1089, 1092
Chu Hsi-ning, 777, 779
Chu Hsiang-hsien, 183–84
Chu Hsiao-tsang (Tsu-mou), 450–51
Chu Hu, 830
chu-ji-sa (intermediate poetic form; Korea), 1072
Chu K'ai, 145
Chu-ko Liang, 127, 508, 621–22, 624–25, 631, 807, 997
chu-kung-tiao (medley), 595, 822, 990, 991, 1012; as early prosimetric form, 796–97, 1019; masterpiece of, 1008–9; in plays, 809, 819, 820; of Sung dynasty, 791–92; texts of, 995
Chu Lien-hsiu, 380, 381
Chu-lin ch'i hsien (Seven Sages of the Bamboo Grove), 258, 259
Chu-lin yeh-shih (Unofficial History of the Bamboo Grove; Ch'ih-tao jen), 665
chu nom (adapted from sinographs) script (Vietnamese), 1097, 1098, 1099, 1100, 1103
Chu Pa-chieh (Pigsy; *Journey to the West*), 69, 129, 147, 633, 634, 635
"Chu p'in fu" (Rhapsody on Expelling Poverty; Yang Hsiung), 233
"Chu shan" (The Pearl Vest; Sung Mao-ch'eng), 600, 689
Chu Shu-chen, 209–10, 217
Chu-shu chi-nien (Bamboo Annals), 93, 522
Chu Shu-lan, 163
Chu Ta (Pa-ta shan-jen), 427, 428, 490
Chu Te, 872
Chu Ti, 400, 401
Chu T'ien-hsin, 779
Chu T'ien-wen, 779
Chu Tso-ch'ao, 830
Chu Tsu-mou, 335
Chu Tzu-ch'ing, 456, 574–75, 749
Chu-tzu yü-lei (Classified Conversations of Master Chu; Chu Hsi; comp. Li Ching-te), 888, 914, 1070
Chu Tz'u, 587
Chu Yi-tsun, 331, 333, 415, 427, 432, 446–47, 448, 559
Chu Yu-tun, 145–46, 399, 795, 816–18
Chu-yü (Whisk Remnants; comp. Hsieh Chao-che), 678
Chu Yü-ming, 677
Chu Yüan-chang, 396, 397, 398, 400, 509, 644, 682
Chu Yün-ming, 402, 404
"Chü sung" (In Praise of the Orange Tree), 228
chü-yi (gather in righteousness), 629
ch'u (in the beginning, originally), 497
Ch'u, King of, 140, 514, 515, 516
Ch'u, state of, 61, 117, 226, 228, 273, 301, 373, 468, 936, 986; and Chou, 104; manuscripts from, 98–99, 100, 101; and *Shih-ching*, 97, 98, 99–100, 101; and women, 199–200, 216. See also *Ch'u tz'u*
Ch'u Ch'ing, 709
Ch'u-hsüeh chi (Records for Elementary Studies; comp. Chang Yüeh), 293
Ch'u Jen-huo, 626
Ch'u-k'o p'ai-an ching-ch'i (Slapping the Table in Amazement, First Collection; Ling Meng-ch'u), 605
Ch'u Kuang-hsi, 295
Ch'u Liang, 284

Ch'u san-tsang chi chi (Collection of Records on the Translated Tripiṭaka; Seng-yu), 164
Ch'u Shao-sun, 141
Ch'u-T'ang ssu-chieh (Four Elites of Early T'ang), 287
Ch'u tiao (Ch'u mode pieces), 958
Ch'u tz'u (Elegies of Ch'u), 60–61, 223, 225–30, 232, 263, 396, 431; "Chiu ko" (Nine Songs) in, 117, 118, 199, 226, 227, 229, 233, 249; and Ch'u Songs, 249, 251; and Ch'ü Yüan, 276, 420; commentary on, 419, 913; and humor, 135; imagery of, 226, 227, 228, 233; as model, 415, 927; poetry of, 264, 353, 385, 974; and *sao*-style, 224, 229–30; as source of *fu*, 225, 235, 289, 300, 310; and supernatural, 117–18, 122, 124, 227. *See also* "Li sao"; "T'ien wen"
Ch'u tz'u chang-chu (Elegies of Ch'u, with Supplemental Commentary), 922
ch'ü (arias; vernacular songs), 14, 32, 392, 444, 801, 939, 953, 974; in exorcism plays, 997, 998; in medleys, 799, 1008; northern, 816, 819, 840; and separate songs (*san-ch'ü*), 370, 373; writers of, 406, 452, 803; Yüan, 274, 331, 391, 399
ch'ü (atmosphere), 397
"Ch'ü-chiang ch'ih" (Serpentine Pond; Shih Chün-pao), 809
Ch'ü Ch'iu-pai, 568, 570, 1012
"Ch'ü Feng-nu ch'ing ch'ien ssu kai" (Ch'ü Feng-nu; Hsi Lang-hsien), 605
Ch'ü-lü (Rules for Plays; Wang Chi-te), 841
Ch'ü-p'in (Classification of Plays; Lü T'ien-ch'eng), 841
ch'ü-p'u (handbooks for *ch'ü*), 840, 841
Ch'ü Ta-chün, 414–15
"Ch'ü-t'u Chung-jen k'u sha chung-sheng, Yün-chou ssu-ma ming ch'üan nei-chih" (The Hunter; Ling Meng-ch'u), 608
ch'ü-tzu (songs), 316
ch'ü-tzu-tz'u (song lyrics), 974–75. See also *tz'u*
ch'ü-yi (oral arts), 15, 990, 1012, 1013, 1014
Ch'ü Yu, 679–83, 1073, 1099
Ch'ü Yüan, 118, 211, 227, 233, 240, 289, 506–7, 837, 922, 924, 944; works attributed to, 228, 276, 415, 420, 839, 917–18. *See also* "Li sao"
"Ch'ü Yüan" (Ch'ü Yüan; Kuo Mo-jo), 864
chuan, chuan-chuang (biographies, commentaries, accounts), 528, 580, 911, 968
Chuan-hsü (Sky God), 66, 68, 69
chuan-tu (reciting sūtras), 978
"Chuan yün han yü ch'iao Tung-t'ing hung, Po-ssu hu chih p'o t'o-lung k'o" (The Tangerines and the Tortoise-shell; Ling Meng-ch'u), 606, 607
chüan (volumes, chapters), 493, 509, 510
ch'uan-ch'i plays, 579, 786, 796, 818, 820, 826–34, 835; anthologies of, 825; classification of, 840–41; earliest catalog of, 840; and literati, 838; in nineteenth and early twentieth centuries, 843, 844; origin of, 785; role types in, 793; in seventeenth century, 418, 836; supernatural in, 126; texts of, 794, 795; women writers of, 839
ch'uan-ch'i (classical-style) tales, 182, 525, 579–83, 589–91, 675, 791, 797, 1007, 1075, 1076, 1081, 1086, 1087, 1099; didacticism in, 592–93; humor in, 146; as mainstream of T'ang tales, 582; poetry in, 122, 681, 685; and proverbs, 154; and *Strange Tales from Make-Do Studio*, 130; Sung-Ming, 679–90; supernatural in, 121, 122–23
Ch'uan hsi lu (Instructions for Practical Living, or a Record of Instruction and Practice; Wang Yang-ming), 889
ch'uan-shuo (historical tradition), 68
Ch'üan-chen (Complete Perfection) school, 10, 175–76, 184–88, 189, 191
ch'üan-hsiang (fully illustrated), 1010
Ch'üan-hsiang San-kuo chih p'ing-hua. See *San-kuo chih p'ing-hua*
ch'üan-li (rights), 1057
ch'üan-shan (virtuous behavior), 979
"Ch'üan shan chi" (Encouragement to Do Good; Chang Chih-chen), 1010
Ch'üan-shih liang-yen (Good Words to Exhort the World; Liang Ah-fa), 1058
Ch'üan Sung shih (Complete Sung Poems), 337
Ch'üan Sung tz'u (Complete Lyrics of the Sung Dynasty), 373
Ch'üan T'ang shih (Complete T'ang Poems), 11, 125, 134, 278–79, 373, 980, 981, 1068
Ch'üan T'ang wen (Complete T'ang Prose; comp. Wu Hsi-ch'i), 246, 278–79
ch'üan-tien (circles and dots), 941
"Ch'üan yü fa" (Power Versus Law; Hsing Yi-hsün), 872
Ch'üan Yüan san-ch'ü (Complete Yüan *san-ch'ü*), 374
Chuang, Duke of Cheng, 499, 512–15
Chuang, King of Ch'u, 140, 514
Chuang Chi, 232
Chuang Chou. *See* Chuang Tzu
Chuang Lin hsü Tao-tsang (Supplementary Taoist Canon of Chuang and Lin; pub. Saso), 179

Chuang peoples, 1036–37
"Chuang shih p'ien" (Braveheart; Chang Hua), 262
Chuang Tzu, 10, 76–77, 173, 503, 535–36, 548, 918, 931, 944; and myth, 62; and poetry, 261, 323, 324, 334, 351; on supernatural, 117
Chuang Tzu (text), 10, 76–77, 173, 175, 188, 522, 547, 892, 898, 902, 907, 936; as classic, 87; and humor, 138, 139; and myth, 60, 61; and poetry, 267, 298, 354, 419; supernatural in, 118
Ch'uang-shih-chi (Creation; journal), 779
ch'uang-tsao (creation), 716
Ch'uang-tsao she (Creation Society), 746
ch'uang-tso t'an (discussion of fiction composition), 573
chüeh-chü (regulated verse quatrains), 269; Japanese, 1088; Korean, 1068; and lyrics (*tz'u*), 318; of Sung dynasty, 349; of T'ang dynasty, 271, 273, 276, 292, 295, 298, 300, 303, 311, 975, 976; in Tun-huang literature, 981; in Vietnamese novels, 1101
Chüeh fei ou-jan (Absolutely No Coincidence; Chang Hsin), 765
"Chüeh hsin-k'eng ch'ien-kuei ch'eng ts'ai-chu" (The Miser Makes a Fortune from New Pits; Cho-yüan-t'ing chu-jen), 615
Chūgoku zuihitsu sakuin (Index to Chinese Miscellaneous Writings; 1954; Saeki Tomi), 564
Chūgoku zuihitsu zatcho sakuin (Index to Chinese Miscellaneous Writings and Essays; 1961; Saeki Tomi), 564
Chui Feng, 458
Ch'ui-wen tz'u (Lyrics to Hear Around the Cooking Fire; Wang Shih-lu), 427
Chukim kohoe (The Refined Gathering of the Bamboo Grove; Korean poetry society), 1068
Chün (god), 64, 66
"Chün-t'ien le" (The Pleasures of Heaven; Yu T'ung), 837
chün-tzu (noble man, gentleman), 5, 341, 344, 498, 505, 525
chün-yung ch'ao-yi (lingering flavor and transcendent profundity), 424
Ch'un-ch'iu (Springs and Autumns; Confucius), 74, 83, 92–94, 496, 497, 500, 624, 913; commentaries on, 88, 93–94, 910, 911
Ch'un-ch'iu fan-lu (Luxuriant Dew of the Springs and Autumns; Tung Chung-shu), 913
Ch'un-ch'iu san chuan (Springs and Autumns with Three Commentaries), 92
"Ch'un hsiao" (Daybreak in Spring; Meng Hao-jan), 294
"Ch'un hsiao wang Chin-pi shan" (In Spring Light Gazing on Gold-Jade Mountain; Yao Hsia-tan), 1053
Ch'un liu she (Spring Willow Society; drama club), 850
"Ch'un-ssu fu" (Springtime Longings; Wang Po), 289
"Ch'un-t'ao" (Hsü Ti-shan), 747
"Ch'un teng-mi" (Spring Lantern Riddles; Juan Ta-ch'eng), 831
Ch'un-teng mi-shih (Dream Story Under the Spring Lamp), 669
"Ch'un ts'an" (Spring Silkworms; Mao Tun), 747
"Ch'un wang" (Spring Prospects; Tu Fu), 299
Ch'un-yang chen-jen hun-ch'eng chi (Anthology of the Perfected Ch'un-yang on Arising from Turbulence; comp. Ho Chih-yüan), 185
Ch'un yang she (Spring Sun Society; Shanghai), 850
Ch'un-yang ti-chün shen-hua miao-t'ung chi (Annals of the Wondrous Communications and Divine Transformations of the Sovereign Lord Ch'un-yang; Miao Shan-shih), 185
Ch'ün-chi ch'üan-chieh lun (On Liberty; trans. Yen Fu), 1063
Ch'ün-hsüeh yi-yen (A Study of Sociology; trans. Yen Fu), 1063
chung (central; Chinese), 12–13
chung (loyalty), 627
Chung A-ch'eng (Ah Ch'eng), 761–65
Chung-ching chuan tsa p'i-yü (Various Parables from All Sūtras), 171
Chung-ch'ing li-chi (A Graceful Account of Profound Love; Ch'iu Chün), 683
"Chung-ch'iu-chieh yi-ko wan shang" (One Night During the Mid-Autumn Festival; Hsieh Wan-ying), 747–48
"Chung-ch'un chiao-wai" (Outside the Suburbs in Mid-Spring; Wang Po), 289
Chung-ho chi (Anthology of Focused Harmony; comp. Ts'ai Chih-yi), 190
Chung Hsing, 7, 412
Chung-hua hsiao-shuo chieh (The World of Chinese Fiction; journal), 705, 715, 729
Chung-hua shu-chü, 565
chung-in (middle people), 1071, 1072
Chung Jung, 118, 260, 898, 927, 932
Chung K'uei, 817
Chung-kuo chin-tai hsiao-shuo ta-hsi (A Treasury of Early Modern Chinese Fiction), 730
Chung-kuo chin-tai wen-hsüeh ta-hsi (A Treasury of Early Modern Chinese Literature), 730
Chung-kuo ch'ing-nien yi-shu chü-yüan (China Youth Theater), 870

"Chung-kuo hsiao-shuo pien-ch'ien shih" (History of the Development of Chinese Fiction; Lu Hsün), 745
Chung-kuo hsiao-shuo shih-lüeh (Brief History of Chinese Fiction; Lu Hsün), 126, 745
Chung-kuo hsin shih (New Chinese Poetry; journal), 457
Chung-kuo hua (Chinese language), 26. *See also* Sinitic
Chung-kuo k'o-yi shuo pu: Leng-chan hou-shih-tai te cheng-chih yü ch'ing-kan chüeh-tse (China Can Say No! Options for Politics and Emotions in the Post-Cold War Period), 772
Chung-kuo lü-hsing chü-t'uan (China Traveling Troupe), 861
"Chung-kuo meng" (China Dream; Sun and Fei), 876
Chung-kuo shih-pao (China Times), 461
Chung-kuo Tao-chiao hsieh-hui (Chinese Association of Taoism), 176
Chung-kuo tso-chia hsieh-hui (Chinese Writers Federation), 770
Chung-kuo tso-yi hsi-chü-chia lien-meng (Chinese League of Left-Wing Dramatists), 860, 862
Chung-kuo tso-yi tso-chia lien-meng (Chinese League of Left-Wing Writers), 860, 862
Chung-kuo wen-hsüeh shih (A History of Chinese Literature; Huang Jen), 712–13
Chung-kuo wen-hsüeh shih (History of Chinese Literature; Lin Ch'uan-chia), 711–13
Chung-kuo wen-hsüeh yi-shu chieh lien-ho-hui (China Federation of Literary and Art Circles), 770, 772–73
Chung-li Ch'üan, 184, 191, 810
Chung-nan shan Shuo-ching T'ai li-tai chen-hsien pei-chi (An Epigraphic Record of Successive Generations of Perfected Transcendents at the Pavilion for Explaining Scripture on Mount Chung-nan; Chu Hsiang-hsien), 183
Chung-nan shan tsu-t'ing hsien-chen nei-chuan (An Inside Account of the Transcendent Perfected of the Ancestral Hall of Mount Chung-nan; comp. Li Tao-ch'ien), 185
"Chung-shan lang" (Wolf of Chung-shan), 818
"Chung-shen ta-shih" (The Greatest Event of One's Life; Hu Shih), 852, 856, 865
Chung Ssu-ch'eng, 796, 800, 815
Chung-tsung, Emperor, 291, 292
Chung-tu-hsiu, 811
Chung-wen (Chinese language), 26. *See also* Sinitic
Chung-wen Shih, 889
Chung-yang jih-pao (Central Daily News; newspaper), 777
chung-yi (loyalty and righteousness), 626
Chung-yi "Shui hu chuan" (Loyal and Righteous *Water Margin*), 627
Chung yüan yin-yün (Sounds and Rhymes of the Central Plain; Chou Te-ch'ing), 372, 840
"Chung-yung" (Application of the Mean; *Li-chi*), 92, 104
Ch'ung-chen, Emperor, 832
Ch'ung-erh (Wen, Duke of Chin), 93, 512
"Ch'ung tseng Lu Ch'en" (Again, Presented to Lu Ch'en; Liu K'un), 264
Ch'ung-yang chen-jen chin-kuan yü-so chüeh (Lessons of the Perfected Ch'ung-yang on the Jade Lock of the Golden Gateway), 186
Ch'ung-yang chiao-hua chi (Anthology on the Proselytism of Ch'ung-yang), 186
Ch'ung-yang ch'üan-chen chi (Ch'ung-yang's Anthology of Complete Perfection; comp. Wang Che), 185–86
Ch'ung-yang fen-li shih-hua chi (Anthology of Ch'ung-yang on the Ten Transformations of Sectioning a Pear), 186
Ch'ung-yang li-chiao shih-wu lun (Fifteen Discourses on the Teachings Set Forth by Ch'ung-yang), 186
Ch'ung-yang shou Tan-yang erh-shih-ssu chüeh (Twenty-four Lessons Conveyed to Tan-yang by Ch'ung-yang), 186
Chungjong, King (Korea), 1072
Ch'ungyŏ, King, 1070
Ch'unhyang jŏn (The Tale of Ch'unhyang), 1076
Churchill, Winston, 443
Chūshin Suikoden (The Loyal Vassal's Water Margin; Santō Kyōden), 1094
Cicero, 895, 897, 899, 903, 905–6
Circassian language, 28
civil-service examinations: abolition of, 441, 702, 734, 735, 811; academies for, 1053; Ch'ing dynasty, 52, 431, 531, 668, 915; and Confucian classics, 88; criticism of, 692; degrees in, 1–2, 290, 309; and fiction, 713, 746; in fiction, 122, 605, 612, 643–44, 655, 656, 664, 684, 694, 799, 812, 819, 820, 826–27, 828, 835–36, 840, 1007, 1021, 1027, 1075; humor about, 147; Korean, 1068, 1072; and Literary Sinitic, 50, 567; and memorizing, 323; Ming dynasty, 397, 659–60; and monasteries, 966; and official service, 296, 349, 1052; and poetry, 176, 291, 338; and prose, 8, 528, 531, 573; special, 299, 303, 349, 417, 418, 420, 427, 432, 540; and storytellers, 1024; Sung dynasty, 330–31, 340, 1070; suspension of, 388, 391; Vietnamese, 1096,

1097; and women, 209, 211, 214, 215, 219, 836
class, 212, 661, 729; in *ch'uan-ch'i* tales, 691; and drama, 789; in *hua-pen*, 596, 599; and humor, 137; and language, 32; and proverbs, 149, 159
The Classic Chinese Novel (C.T. Hsia), 630, 634
Classic of Change. See *Yi-ching*
Classic of Documents. See *Shang-shu*
Classic of Mountains and Seas. See *Shan hai ching*
Classic of Odes. See *Shih-ching*
Classic of Poetry. See *Shih-ching*
Classical Chinese. *See* Literary Sinitic
classical tales. See *wen-yen hsiao-shuo*
classical texts (*ching*), 28, 161, 282, 283, 342, 925; Ch'in, 99; Ch'ing, 883; and Chu Hsi, 88, 92, 95, 96; Confucian, 3–4, 87–88, 411, 912, 927, 941, 942; Han, 83–84, 910–14; and historical writing, 510; in Korean, 1073, 1074, 1077; and literary theory, 707, 708; Ming, 942; and Mongols, 887; and myth, 60–62, 67–68; and prose, 528, 530; Six Classics, 718; Yüan, 887. *See also particular works*
Clavell, James, 773
Coblin, South, 22
colonialism, 781, 1096, 1099
commedia dell'arte, 144
commentary: amplifying, 913; authorial reaction to, 946–49; auto-, 946–47; and footnotes, 943; latent, 948–49; narrator-, 947–48; periphrastic, 912–13; *p'ing-tien*, 940–44, 1076; on poetry, 941; *so-yin* school of, 943; traditional, on fiction, 940–49
Communism. *See* Chinese Communist Party
La Condition humaine (Man's Fate; Malraux), 157
Confucianism (Juism), 6, 9, 399, 501, 556, 612, 849, 889; and biography, 518, 524–25; and Buddhism, 165, 166, 169; and Ch'ing dynasty, 52; and Ch'ing fiction, 670, 671, 672, 721, 726; classical texts of, 3–4, 87–88, 411, 912, 927, 941, 942; and cosmology, 79–80; and didacticism, 507–8; and drama, 803, 823, 843, 852, 853, 855; and emperor, 87–88; festivals of, 1005; Five Relations of, 844; Han, 83–84; and Han Yü, 535; and heavenly mandate, 96, 1056; and historical writing, 494, 509, 510, 632; and *hua-pen*, 598, 601, 603, 604, 616, 618; and humor, 133, 136, 138, 139–40, 147, 148; in Japan, 1080, 1081, 1087, 1089, 1090, 1091; in *Journey to the West*, 633, 634, 635; in Korea, 1067, 1070, 1072, 1073; and Legalism, 78; and literary theory, 707; and literature, 13, 917, 921, 922, 1015, 1064; in Ming-Ch'ing novels, 662; in Ming novels, 660–61; and minorities, 1033; and modern fiction, 735, 738, 740, 741, 742, 746, 747, 753, 763; and Mohism, 897; and myth, 59, 62, 65; New (*Hsin ju-chiao*), 52; opposition to, 374; origins of, 73–75; and painting, 480; and parallelism, 530, 892; and poetry, 282, 285, 304, 325, 333, 344–58, 382, 386, 404, 407, 431, 438; proprieties of, 1007; and prose, 528, 530, 533, 572; reforms in, 919; revivals of, 531; and *Romance of the Three Kingdoms*, 624, 625; in *The Scholars*, 643, 645; scholars of, 469, 915; and self-cultivation, 76; and Shanghai, 702, 704; and *Shih-ching*, 98–99; and Ssu-ma Ch'ien, 507; in *The Story of the Stone*, 654; of Sung dynasty, 340, 342, 343, 348, 351, 358, 362; and supernatural, 66, 543; and "Ta Chuan," 81, 82; and Taoism, 77, 87, 175, 176, 266; in *Travels of Lao Ts'an*, 658; in Tun-huang manuscripts, 965; in Vietnam, 1096; and women, 14, 196, 524–25, 1020. *See also* Neo-Confucianism
Confucius (K'ung Tzu), 9, 73–75, 471, 677, 694, 718, 788, 882, 909, 934; and classics, 3–4, 89, 90, 98–99, 101–2, 102, 498, 912; descendants of, 833; disciples of, 911; in Han, 84; and Han Yü, 931; and historical writing, 494, 498–501; and humor, 139–40, 148; and Lao Tzu, 981; and poetry, 264, 298, 480; and prose, 515, 533, 547, 551, 572; in proverbs, 153; and role of literature, 921; and stylistic ideals, 890; on supernatural, 116, 543; and Taoism, 77, 183; temple of, 505; in Tun-huang literature, 974; works attributed to, 93, 94–95, 496, 893
Connery, Christopher Lee, 223–47
cosmology, 63, 79–82, 545, 546; correlative, 82–83, 84, 92
courtesans, 145, 444, 604, 813, 830; culture of, 1006–9; as poets, 448
Coyajee, J. C., 69
crime, 538; in *hua-pen*, 597, 599; in *tsa-chü*, 808, 812. *See also* bandits; detective stories; *Shui-hu chuan*
Cults and Legends of Ancient Iran and China (Coyajee), 69
Cultural Revolution (1966–1976), 569, 571, 769, 877; end of, 462, 1036; feminism of, 874; and literature of 1980s, 761; and literatures of minorities, 1034–35, 1052; and misty poetry (*meng-lung shih*), 463; and New Wave

literature, 764, 765; and *pi-mo* texts, 1040; and recent PRC fiction, 754–55; and theater, 846, 848, 858, 864, 866, 868, 869, 870, 871, 872, 874; and twentieth-century fiction, 746
culture: as artificial construct, 75, 77, 78, 81, 82, 84–85; Chinese, 2–3, 9, 22, 655, 744, 763, 1079; of Chinese rhetoric, 881, 890–94; commercialization of, 702; and concept of cultural field, 759; continuity of, 428; courtesan, 1006–9; evolution of, 713; examination, 1100; foreign, 717, 726, 905; of Greater China, 758–81; Han Chinese, 12, 1042, 1044; Han dynasty, 922; Japanese, 1088; and language, 25–26; literary, 717, 881, 883, 884, 890; of literati, 1–4, 328, 338, 355, 356, 359, 479, 490, 1009; medieval Chinese, 965–66; minority, 9; modern Chinese, 756–57, 763, 769; omens in, 111; oral, 989–1014; performance, 1013, 1016, 1031; popular, 9, 328, 462, 464, 620, 733, 759, 774, 780–81, 962, 1009–13; print, 323, 329, 337, 338, 400, 914, 943; regional, 21; of Shanghai, 701–5; in Six Dynasties period, 726; in Taiwan, 780–81; urban, 676, 677, 695; Vietnamese, 1096; Western, 714; of women, 999–1003, 1010–11, 1016
Cummings, E. E., 457
"Cung oan ngam khuc" (Plaint Inside the Royal Harem; Nguyen Gia Thieu), 1099
Cutter, Robert Joe, 248–73
Cyrillic script, 34

dai (assigned themes in poetry), 1083
Dai Nam hanh nghia liet nu tryuen (A Record of the Virtuous Acts of the Women of the Great Kingdom of Vietnam; Nguyen Van Danh), 1102
Daily Life in China on the Eve of the Mongol Invasion (Gernet), 565
La Dame aux camélias (Camille; Dumas), 719, 851, 1064
dance, 315, 790, 791, 817, 954, 976; and music, 916–17, 920, 977; revolutionary modern ballet, 868
Dang Tran Con, 1098
Dante Alighieri, 943
Dao Huy Tu, 1103
Daudet, Alphonse, 729–30
David-Neel, Alexandra, 1045
de Maupassant, Guy, 729–30
Dean, Kenneth, 10
deities, 61, 64–69, 112, 115, 126, 547, 632, 994, 1001; and early philosophy, 75, 76, 84; female, 66, 67, 118–19, 181, 196–97, 197, 199–200, 220; in supernatural tales, 118–19, 122, 545; village, 1042
democracy movement (Peking Spring), 463
Demosthenes, 895
"Der Kaukasische Kreidekreis" (The Caucasian Chalk Circle; Brecht), 809
Descartes, René, 903
Déscription de la Chine (de Prémare), 803
Desnos, Robert, 457
detective stories (*kung-an hsiao-shuo*), 718, 719, 722–25, 729, 741, 743
dhāraṇīs (mantras; mystical formulas), 164
dharma (doctrine), 30
Dharmarakṣa (monk), 163, 172
dhyāna (Sanskrit: meditation), 168
dialects, 23–27, 29, 714, 749, 1017, 1031
Diamond Sūtra, 582, 607, 970
diaries, 555–59, 705, 727, 744, 751
Dickens, Charles, 1064
dictionaries, 47, 55, 713, 714
didacticism: in biography, 513, 518, 520, 521; in *ch'uan-ch'i* tales, 592–93; in classical texts, 94, 97–109; as function of literature, 5, 74–75, 84–85; of Han Yü, 533–34; in historical writing, 498, 501, 507–8, 510; in poetry, 254; in prose, 530, 533, 536, 568–69, 570, 610; in Uyghur literature, 1048. *See also* morality
Dinh Nhat Than, 1097
Diplomatists *(tsung-heng chia)*, 502
Disraeli, Benjamin, 707
divination, 36, 80, 88–89, 116, 495, 500, 540, 543; poetry of, 107
Doan Thi Diem, 1099
Doleželová-Velingerová, Milena, 697–731
"A Doll's House" (Ibsen), 852, 853, 860, 861
Doyle, Arthur Conan, 719, 743, 1064
dragons (*lung*), 108, 112, 114–15, 116, 122, 500, 585
drama, 8, 32, 785–879; of 1930s, 848, 857; and acting profession, 789–90; amateur, 856; anthologies of, 824; anti-Gang-of-Four, 869, 871, 872; anti-imperialist themes in, 854, 855, 860; Brechtian school of, 856; and Buddhism, 57, 161, 167–68, 172; characters in, 844; and Chinese Communist Party, 846; civilized, 850, 851, 855, 857; in classical tales, 695; collectively authored, 866; comic dialogs in, 143–44, 787, 790–91; and commercial theater, 789–90, 823–24, 826; and Confucianism, 803, 823, 843, 852, 853; contemporary realist, 862; criticism and interpretation of, 705, 711, 715, 825, 840–43, 939; defense, 857, 862, 863–64; deliverance, 809–10, 814, 815, 816; development of, 371, 392; and diaspora, 854; epic, 876; exorcism in, 787, 788, 992–1001, 1010, 1014; export of

Chinese, 877; and film, 858; genres of, 785–86, 787; golden age of Chinese, 864; Greek, 869, 876; in Harbin, 871; and history, 855, 862, 864, 876; and *hua-pen*, 595, 596, 598, 613, 618; humor in, 132, 136, 143–46; illusionist (Stanislavsky school), 856, 876; indigenous, 876, 877; in Japan, 711, 786, 791, 861, 1091, 1093, 1094; leftist (Tso-yi hsi-chü), 857, 859, 860; and libretti, 793; and literary theory, 711, 713; local, 838; martial, 788; of May Fourth period, 851–57; Ming, 632; modernist, 876; and morality, 843–44; musical, 792–94; national, 852, 856, 864; and noncommercial theater, 855; Nora-like characters in, 852–54, 855, 857, 860–63, 866, 867, 870, 873; and novels, 125, 622, 632, 664, 674, 723; operatic, 15; origins of modern Chinese, 848–51; peasant, 865–70; Peking-style, 876; poetry in, 145; post-Mao, 846, 862, 869–76, 871, 872, 874, 876; proletarian, 859, 870, 871; and prosimetric tradition, 787, 996–99; public reading of, 896; publication of, 824; and puppet theater, 786, 791, 838, 899–900, 1093, 1094; and racial conflict, 849; realist, 876; and reform, 848; about revolutionary leaders, 872; revolutionary model, 864, 866–68, 869, 874; and ritual, 98, 786, 788, 790, 825, 997; and shadow theater, 838; in Shanghai, 702; small, 855; about soldiers, 872–75; and song and dance, 143, 790, 791; southern, 819–23; Southern Society (Nan kuo she), 857, 859; and stages, 788; and street theater, 864; suggestive, 876; and supernatural, 111, 125–26, 128, 543; and Taoism, 168, 191; texts of, 794–96, 801–5; and theater of the absurd, 15; traditional, 785–847; twentieth-century, 735–36, 848–79; vernacular, 111, 399, 442, 566, 889; and vernacular fiction, 620; and War of Resistance against Japan, 848, 849, 855, 857, 862–64; Western, 792–93, 845–46, 848–49, 852, 856–57; without playwrights, 794; and women, 194, 210, 211–13, 218, 836, 844, 845, 854–55, 874; by women, 786, 853; women warriors in, 875–76; Yi-yang style of, 823; Yüan, 391, 632, 792, 793–94, 795, 800–802, 804, 806, 814, 858, 889. *See also particular types*

Dream of the Red Chamber. See *Hung-lou meng*

dreams, 112, 500, 540, 570; and *ch'uan-ch'i* tales, 123, 584; in *hua-pen*, 607; and humor, 137; in *Journey to the West*, 129–30, 637; in novels, 664, 724; and supernatural tales, 117, 118–19, 121, 122

Dudbridge, Glen, 1027

duḥkha (suffering), 169

Dumas, Alexandre, 719, 851, 1064

Dungan script, 34

Durrant, Stephen, 493–510

Eberhard, Wolfram, 155

Edo Hanjōki (An Account of the Prosperity of Edo; Terakado Seiken), 1094

Egan, Ronald, 527–41

Egypt, 35

Ehrenberg, Ilya, 463

"The Elaboration of the Meanings of the *Records of the Three Kingdoms*," 622

Eluard, Paul, 457

Ema Saikō, 1091

emperor, 79–80, 83, 87–88, 176, 529. *See also particular rulers*

Empson, William, 455

encyclopedias, 47, 59, 60, 135, 171, 563, 565

English language, 55, 714

epics, 1013, 1035, 1036, 1040, 1045–46, 1050

Erh-hsiang t'ing tz'u (Lyrics from Two Village Hall), 420

erh-hu (two-stringed fiddle), 1026

erh-huang (basic melody), 793

Erh-k'o p'ai-an ching-ch'i (Slapping the Table in Amazement, Second Collection; Ling Meng-ch'u), 605, 610

Erh-nü ying-hsiung chuan (Tales of Boy and Girl Heroes; Wen K'ang), 656, 671, 743, 947, 948, 1034

Erh pa'i, Liang p'ai ("Two Slappings"; Ling Meng-ch'u), 605–10

Erh-shih lu (Record of the Ears' Repast; Yüeh Chun), 694–95

Erh-shih nien mu-tu chih kuai hsien-chuang (Strange Scenes Witnessed in the Past Twenty Years; Wu Chien-jen), 647, 673, 703, 721–23, 742

Erh-shih-ssu shih-p'in (Twenty-four Varieties of Poetic Experience; Ssu-k'ung T'u), 932, 933, 934; "Han-hsü" (Concealed and Implied) in, 933

Erh-shih-wu shih (twenty-five dynastic histories), 493, 503, 507–9

Erh-t'an (Hearsay Stories; Wang T'ung-kuei), 678

Erh-t'an lei-tseng (Hearsay Stories, Classified and Expanded; Wang T'ung-kuei), 678

Erh-ya (Approaching Elegance), 88, 95, 264, 912

Erh-yü (Hearsay Reports; Yü Yüeh), 695

"Essay on Literature" (Ts'ao P'i), 262

essays, 230, 236, 527, 1073–74; ancient prose, 499; biographies as, 526; character in,

574–75; for civil-service examinations, 713; in Classical Chinese, 700; expository *vs.* lyrical, 570–75; genres of, 570–75; landscape, 535–36, 556; late Ch'ing, 708; and literature of 1980s, 762; narrators in, 569–70; polemical, 744; vernacular in, 566–67
esthetics, 422, 714, 716, 922; in Six Dynasties period, 923–30; and Taoism, 892. *See also* literary criticism; literary theory; literature; painting; *wen*
ethnicity, 9, 12. *See also* minority nationalities
Europe, 24, 25, 29, 31, 706, 712, 716, 898; Chinese emigrés in, 156, 759, 780
Evolution and Ethics (Huxley), 706, 719, 1062
Evolution Troupe (Chin-hua t'uan), 850, 851
examination system. *See* civil-service examinations
expressionism, 410, 414, 419, 422

fa (law; method; normative standards), 349, 354, 356, 405, 419, 422, 423, 424
fa-chia (Legalists), 87
fa-ch'ü (*Fo-ch'ü*; Buddhist songs), 975, 978
Fa-hsiang (Sanskrit: Dharmalakṣana) school, 165
Fa-hsien, 165, 555
Fa-hu, 172
fa-k'an tz'u (inaugural announcements), 708
Fa-shih, 524
fa-shih (dharma master), 985
Fa-yen (Discourses on Method; Yang Hsiung), 233, 921
Fa-yi (Spirit of the Laws; trans. Yen Fu), 1063
"Fa ying-t'ao shu fu" (Felling a Cherry Tree; Hsiao Ying-shih), 301
fa-yü (essays; Japanese: *hōgo*), 1087
Fa-yüan chu-lin (Pearl Gove of the Garden of the Law), 171
fan-an (reverse verdicts), 726
"Fan chao-yin" (Contra Summoning the Recluse; Wang K'ang-chü), 263
Fan Ch'eng-ta, 359, 360, 361–63, 364, 556, 557–59
fan-ch'ieh (reverse cutting or countertomy) spelling, 40–41
"Fan Ch'iu-erh shuang ching ch'ung yüan" (Fan Hsi-chou; Feng Meng-lung), 601
Fan Chung-yen, 345
"Fan-hua meng" (A Dream of Splendor; Wang Yün), 211, 839
fan-ko-ming tung-luan (counterrevolutionary turmoil), 737
Fan Li, 829
fan-pai (Buddhist hymns), 977–78
fan-pen (return to origins), 635
Fan P'eng, 386
Fan Po-ch'ün, 732
fan-sheng (floating words), 975
Fan Shih, 520–21, 580
fan-ssu (come to terms with the past), 760, 761, 763
Fan Sui, 513
fan-tui (inverse parallelism), 893
Fan Yeh, 520, 525, 580, 622, 956
Fan Yi, 185–87
Fan Yün, 270
fang (fragrance), 892
Fang Ch'eng-p'ei, 835
fang-chih, ti-fang-chih (local gazetteers), 153, 565, 701, 1080
Fang Fang, 765
fang-fu (apparently), 904
"Fang-hsia ni te pien-tzu" (Putting Down Your Whip; Ch'en Li-t'ing), 864
Fang Hsüan-ling, 282, 283
Fang Ju-hao, 661
Fang Kan, 313
fang-k'uai-tzu (square-graphs or tetragraphs), 51
Fang La, 627
Fang Pao, 93, 533
fang-pien (skillful means; Sanskrit, *upāya*), 966, 983
Fang-shan, 162
fang-shih (technocrats; magicians; mountebanks), 116, 134, 177
Fang Shu-pao, 590–91
Fang-yen (Topolects; Kuo P'u), 29, 264
fang-yen (dialects; topolects), 23–27, 29, 264, 643, 714, 749, 1017, 1031
Faulkner, William, 777
Fei, Faye C., 876
Fei-hua yung (The Song of Fluttering Flowers), 668
fei-jen te wen-hsüeh (dehumanized literature), 852
Fei-yen wai-chuan (The Unofficial Biography of Fei-yen; Ling Hsüan), 580
fen (anguish and frustration), 628
"Fen-yüan shih" (A Poem of Indignation; Wang Kŏ-in), 1068
"Feng" (Airs). See *Shih-ching*: "Kuo-feng"
feng (airs), 920
feng (instruction), 5
Feng-ch'e shih-she (Windmill Poetry Club), 459
"Feng-cheng wu" (The Mistake with the Kite; Li Yü), 832
Feng Chi-ts'ai, 761
Feng Chih, 456
Feng Chih-wei, 53
feng-huang (phoenix), 115
Feng-huang ch'ih (The Phoenix Pool), 668
Feng-ju fei-t'un (Full Breasts and Fat Asses; Mo Yen), 771
Feng lei-yen (Eyes Tearful in the Wind; Ts'ung Wei-hsi), 755–56
"Feng-liu yüan" (House of Romance; Chu Ching-fan), 996
Feng Meng-lung, 213, 597–605, 610, 619, 625, 631, 665, 685, 688, 903, 946, 996, 1011–12, 1015; as editor of *ch'uan-ch'i*, 830; and humor, 136, 137, 139, 147; and supernatural, 126–28
Feng Nai-ch'ao, 455

Feng-shen yen-yi (Investiture of the Gods; Hsü Chung-lin), 69, 125, 128, 155, 168, 632, 994–95
feng-shih (presentation verse), 1083
Feng-shih wen-chien chi (A Record of What Mr. Feng Saw and Heard; Feng Yen), 581
Feng-su t'ung-yi (Explanations of Social Customs), 63
Feng Tzu-chen, 376, 387
Feng Tzu-k'ai, 569, 574
feng-tz'u (satirical, critical) poetry, 277
Feng Wei-min, 382
feng-wen-shu (Offerings to the Gods), 994, 995
"Feng Yen chuan" (An Account of Feng Yen; Shen Ya-chih), 591, 592, 593
Feng Yen-ssu, 445
"Feng-yü ku-jen lai" (An Old Friend Comes at a Stormy Time; Pai Feng-hsi), 875
"Feng-yü yeh-kuei-jen" (Return on a Snowy Night; Wu Tsu-kuang), 858
Feng-yüeh chin-nang (The Brocade Bag of Breeze and Moonlight), 825
Feng-yüeh pao-chien (Mirror of Love; Ts'ao Hsüeh-ch'in), 649
Fenollosa, Ernest, 3
fiction, 579–784; adventure, 743, 763, 766, 1103; and ancient-style prose, 531, 537; avant-garde, 15, 759, 763–65, 768–69; and biographies, 511, 522, 526, 625, 626, 632, 643; Buddhism in, 632, 641, 642, 651, 654, 658, 662, 665, 670, 699, 722, 740, 742, 747; categories of, 715; characters in, 603, 721, 723, 724, 726, 738, 742, 746, 945, 1015; classical, 675–96; commercialization of, 757; criticism of, 705–16; detective, 718, 719, 722–25, 729, 741, 743, 1064; erotic, 10; and film, 723, 732, 738, 754; and history, 494, 508, 620, 621, 625, 631, 697–98, 718, 739–41, 803, 819; humor in, 132, 146–48; Japanese criticism of Chinese, 710–11; late Ch'ing, 697–731, 738–43; as life experience, 705; and literary theory, 712–13; in Mandarin, 32; martial arts, 128, 671–72; narrators in, 569, 1012; overt, 694; and *pi-chi*, 563; and poetry, 464, 596, 598, 611, 620, 624, 735; political, 707, 710, 717; popular, 1074; publication of, 824; and reality, 476, 712, 715, 727; Republican, 697–731; reworking of, 8; romantic, 709; scholar-beauty, 596, 617, 644, 666–69, 679–90, 742, 743, 798, 817, 1074–76, 1100, 1101; of Shanghai, 1016; supernatural in, 115, 542, 543, 544, 548, 553; Taoist influence on, 10; technology in, 717, 740; theories of, 699–700, 730; Tibetan, 1045; traditional commentary on, 940–49; twentieth-century, 732–57; Western influence on, 743–44; and women, 210, 211, 218; women in, 213–16. *See also* science fiction
fiction, vernacular, 15, 389, 566, 595–674, 816, 881, 940, 943, 987–88; and chantefables, 1018, 1023; characters in, 945, 1015; Chinese, in Japan, 1092, 1093; Chinese theories about, 1094; and classical tales, 692; in fifteenth century, 399; full-length, 620–58; in Korea, 1077; with localized content, 1015; narrator in, 944–45; oral performers of, 992, 1028; and prosimetric genres, 1003–6, 1011, 1014; retribution in, 112; set-piece descriptions in, 948; stories in, 595–619; and supernatural, 111, 125, 126–30; traditional, 734–35; as unofficial history, 621. *See also* novels; short stories
Fifth Writers' Congress (1996), 769–73
filial piety, 69, 189, 469–70, 520, 582, 656; Classic of, 88, 90, 95, 469, 969, 1074; in *hua-pen*, 604, 611, 616, 618; in modern fiction, 724, 741, 753; Twenty-four Paragons of, 992; of women, 212
film, 50, 763; censorship of, 736–37; and fiction, 723, 732, 738, 754; foreign, 743; in Greater China, 759, 760; and Hong Kong, 759, 774; in Taiwan, 759, 780, 781; and Wang Shuo, 766, 767, 771
Fin-de-Siècle Splendor (David Wang), 657
First Conference on the Literature of Greater East Asia (Tokyo; 1942), 776
Five Classics. See *Wu ching*
Five Dynasties period, 168, 209, 339, 342–43, 595, 807, 984; lyrics of, 320, 333, 974
Five Hundred Million Indian Princesses (Verne), 719
Five Masters, 408
five phases (*wu hsing*), 80, 83, 633, 956
"Five Poetesses of Plantain Garden" (Soochow salon), 448
Five Virtues (Five Constants), 482
Five Weeks in a Balloon: A Voyage of Discovery (Verne), 719
Flowers in the Mirror. See *Ching hua yüan*
Fo-kuang (Buddha Light), 558
Fo-kuo chi (Record of Buddhist Kingdoms; Fa-hsien), 165
Fo pen-hsing chi ching (translation of *Buddhacarita*; trans. Jñānagupta), 172
Fo so hsing tsan ching (*Buddhacarita-kāvya-sūtra*), 172
Fo tsu li-tai t'ung tsai (Comprehensive Accounts of the Buddha and the Patriarchs

Under Successive Dynasties; Nien-ch'ang), 167
Fo-tsu t'ung-chi (Comprehensive History of Buddha and the Patriarchs; Chih-p'an), 167
Foley, John Miles, 1016
folk literature, 454, 929, 1034, 1039, 1043
folklore, 9, 508–9, 558, 620
foot-binding, 214, 216, 656, 694, 757
Formosa (journal), 776
Fou-ch'iu Po, 100
four-character phrases (*ch'eng-yü*), 139, 150–51, 157, 158, 502, 738–39
Four Lings of Yung-chia, 365–66, 392
Four Masters, 450, 451
The Four Masterworks of Ming Fiction (Plaks), 630, 634, 637
Four Modernizations, 874
Four-Six style (*ssu-liu t'i, ssu-liu wen*), 236, 239, 242, 244, 245, 246, 277, 527, 530–33, 1072, 1080
fox spirits, 128, 130, 131, 688
France, 701
Friedemann, Käte, 717
Fryer, John, 1059
fu (enumeration; narration), 921
fu (rhapsody; rhyme-prose; prose-poem), 5–6, 56, 188, 200, 266–68, 454, 499, 528, 586, 993; Ch'i-Liang, 242; and civil-service examination, 291, 1070; earliest use of term, 225; of eighth century, 291–303; epideictic, 231, 234, 238; Han, 223, 230–36, 242, 243, 274, 277, 298, 921; influence of, 262; in Japan, 1083; of ninth century, 303–13; objective character of, 231; on objects (*yung-wu*), 240, 242, 250, 251, 292; prose (*wen-fu*), 6, 244, 245, 246, 278, 540; proto-, 224–29; regulated (*lü-fu*), 6, 244, 246, 277, 278, 304, 305, 309, 973; in *sao* style, 225, 230, 232, 233, 234, 235, 239, 288–89, 305; smaller (*hsiao*), 277; T'ang, 274, 276, 277–78, 281–82, 285, 288, 289, 290, 297, 298, 301; topics of, 254, 263; from Tun-huang, 968, 973, 975; verbal excess in, 231, 233, 238. *See also* parallel prose
Fu, Prince, 415, 831
Fu-ch'ai, 515
Fu-chang lu (Record of Clapping Hands), 138
fu-ch'iang (wealth and power), 734
"Fu-ch'ing-nung chuan" (The Faithless Lover; Sung Mao-ch'eng), 600, 689
"Fu-feng ko" (Song of Fu-feng; Liu K'un), 264
"Fu-fu" (The Lovers; Shen Ts'ung-wen), 751
Fu-hsi (mythological figure), 65, 81, 88, 468, 469
Fu Hsüan, 199, 204, 260, 261, 263, 959, 960, 963
"Fu-jung chin-chi t'u" (Golden Pheasant and Hibiscus; painting and poem by Emperor Hui-tsung), 482, 487
fu-ku (archaist, revive antiquity) movement, 243, 402–29, 531, 594, 930, 931; Ch'ing, 440, 441; Ming, 384, 385, 387, 397, 430, 433; opposition to, 409, 411, 435
fu-kuo ts'e (stratagem for enriching the country), 1061
Fu Liang, 171
"Fu lo-ch'ang" (Becoming a Singsong Girl Again; Chu Yu-tun), 145–46, 817
"Fu Lo-yang tao chung tso" (Written on the Road to Lo-yang; Lu Chi), 262
fu-mo (male role), 144
"Fu niao fu" (Rhapsody on an Owl; Chia Yi), 10
Fu-pai Chu-jen, 137
"Fu ping hsing" (Ballad of the Ailing Wife), 199
Fu-p'u (Ledger for the Rhapsody), 309
Fu-she (Restoration Society), 413, 416, 417, 418
Fu Sheng, 89
Fu-sheng liu-chi (Six Chapters of a Floating Life; Shen Fu), 1015
Fu-yang manuscripts, 100
"Fu yün lou" (The Cloud-Scraper; Li Yü), 615
Fudoki (gazetteers), 1080
Fujieda Akira, 12
Fujiwara no Akihira, 1085
Fujiwara no Hamanari, 1082
Fujiwara no Kintō, 1085
Fujiwara Seika, 1089
Fukui Fumimasa (Bunga), 12
Fuller, Michael A., 337–69
funerary writing, 529–30, 534, 977–78

gagaku (elegant music), 1089
Gandhāra, 165
Gang of Four, 869, 871, 872
Gao Xingjian. *See* Kao Hsing-chien
García Lorca, Federico, 457
Garshin, V. M., 720
gazetteers, local (*fang-chih, ti-fang-chih*), 153, 565, 701, 1080
gender, 14, 66, 67, 68
Genghis Khan. *See* Chinggis Khan
Genji monogatari (Tale of Genji; Murasaki no Shikibu), 1083–84, 1086, 1087, 1094
Genji monogatari hyōshaku (Critical and Explanatory Notes on *The Tale of Genji*; Hagiwara Hiromichi), 1094
Genmei, Empress, 1080
Genzei (Buddhist monk), 1089
geography, 545, 546, 555, 559
Gernet, Jacques, 565
Gesar of Ling, 1045
ghosts (*kuei*), 66–67, 112–16, 171, 609, 676, 997; female, 120; in *hua-pen*, 597; humor about, 139; in supernatural tales, 121, 127, 130, 131, 543, 547; in T'ang poetry, 124–25
Giles, Herbert A., 91

Goethe, Johann Wolfgang von, 455
Gogol, Nikolai, 744
Golden Lotus. See *Chin P'ing Mei*
Goldin, Paul Rakita, 86–96
Gordon, Antoinette K., 1046
Gozan (five mountain) monasteries (Japan), 1087–88, 1089
Great Leap Forward, 866, 877
Greece, 70, 71; drama of, 869, 876; literature of, 882–85, 895, 896, 897, 903, 905, 907
"Green, Green, Riverside Grass" (ballad), 959
Grimmelshausen, Hans Jakob von, 764
"Grotto of Playful Transcendents" ("Yu-hsien k'u"), 583, 1086, 1087
Gunavṛddhi, 172
Gyokuchiginsha (Jade Pond Recitation Society) poetry school, 1091
Gzon nu zla med kyi gtam rgyud (The Tale of the Incomparable Prince; Tibetan novel; mDo mkhar Tshe ring dbang rgyal), 1047

Ha Chin (Ha Jin), 54
Ha-erh-pin hua-chü-yüan (Harbin Theater), 871
Ha Jin. *See* Ha Chin
Haggard, Henry Rider, 709, 1064
Hagiwara Hiromichi, 1094
Hai-ch'iung ch'uan-tao chi (Anthology of Hai-ch'iung's Transmission of the Tao), 190
Hai-ch'iung Pai chen-jen yü-lu (Discourse Record of the Perfected Pai Hai-ch'iung), 190
Hai-ch'iung wen-tao chi (Anthology of Hai-ch'iung's Inquiries into the Tao), 190
"Hai-kang" (On the Dock; model play version), 871
Hai kuo t'u chih (Maps and Documents on Maritime Countries; Wei Yüan), 718
Hai-shang ch'i-shu (Marvelous Writings from Shanghai; journal), 733
Hai-shang hua-lieh chuan (Biographies of Shanghai Sing-Song Girls; Han Pang-ch'ing), 657, 673
Hai Tzu, 463
"Hai-tzu wang" (King of Children; Ah Ch'eng), 764
haikai (Haiku) genre, 1090, 1091
Hajib, Yusup Khass, 1048
Han, battle of, 499
Han chi (Annals of the Han; Hsün Yüeh), 509
"Han chiang Wang Ling pien" (Transformation of the Han General, Wang Ling), 987
"Han-ch'ing pu fu lao" (I Refuse to Grow Old; Kuan Han-ch'ing), 212
Han Chü, 357
Han dynasty, 5, 224–38, 502–4, 507, 513, 515, 519, 525, 527, 532, 544, 552; biography in, 181, 250, 267, 546, 580; Buddhism in, 1055; Chien-an period of, 234, 253–66, 269, 397, 922, 923; Ch'u songs of, 249, 257, 273, 953; classics in, 910–14; correlative cosmology of, 92; culture of, 922; end of, 234, 236, 238, 252, 253, 255, 257, 621, 1017; exegesis in, 8; in fiction, 288, 346, 621, 622, 624, 666; founder of, 249, 376, 806, 986; hymns of, 956; language in, 22, 41, 887, 1062; literary theory in, 254, 921–23, 926, 1069; manuscripts from, 98, 467; military in, 790, 1096; music in, 314; old-style verse of, 440; philosophy in, 82–84; picture eulogies of, 468–71, 474, 475; prose in, 527; proverbs in, 152; ritual in, 911, 956, 993; rulers of, 181, 517, 580; scholars of, 509, 913; and *Shih-ching*, 75, 101, 104; *shih* poetry of, 243, 249–51, 254, 255, 959; and songs, 376, 954–55, 956; supernatural in poetry of, 118–19; supernatural tales in, 119, 546–51; and theater, 790, 806, 814; women in, 197, 198–99, 205, 218; writing style in, 900. See also *Han shu*
Han dynasty, Eastern (Later), 234, 235, 242, 250, 518, 520, 523, 546, 892; *fu* of, 225, 229, 230, 232, 233, 240, 245; genres in, 224; Han-Wei period, 236; images and text in, 471; language in, 887; literary theory in, 919; rulers of, 87, 955; *shih* poetry of, 927; Tripartition (San-fen) of, 806. See also *Hou Han shu*
Han dynasty, Western (Former), 306, 507, 544, 546, 563; ballad poetry in, 249, 250; *fu* of, 5, 224, 225, 230–34; literary patronage in, 232–33; and literati culture, 2; officials of, 267; rulers of, 230–32, 249, 953, 969; and *Shih-ching*, 99
Han Fei Tzu, 78, 79, 81, 82
Han Fei Tzu (text), 60, 105, 138, 139, 153
Han Hsiang-tzu, 838
Han Hsiao-ch'uang, 1030
Han Hsin, 506, 516, 519
"Han hsiu-ts'ai ch'eng luan p'in chiao-ch'i, Wu t'ai-shou lien ts'ai chu yin-pu" (The Imperial Decree; Ling Meng-ch'u), 606
Han-hsüeh (Han Learning) school, 418, 428, 915
"Han-ku kuan" (The Han-ku Pass; Kuo Mo-jo), 746
"Han-kung ch'iu" (Autumn in the Han Palace; Ma Chih-yüan), 814, 815, 1101
Han-lin Academy, 4, 529; members of, 244, 379, 394, 416, 417, 418, 420, 440, 1085; officials in, 341, 395, 401, 432, 433
Han-lin hsüeh-shih chi (Anthology of Han-lin Academicians), 279, 284, 286

Han-lin lun (Discourse on the Foremost Writings; Li Ch'ung), 925
"Han nao-ko shih-pa shou" (Eighteen Han Songs for the *Nao*-Bell), 956
Han Pang-ch'ing, 657, 673
Han P'eng/P'ing, 974
Han (Chinese) people, 13, 14, 1011, 1032, 1036
Han P'ing, 581
Han school (of *Shih-ching* interpretation), 90, 99
Han-shan (Cold Mountain), 11, 20, 170, 302, 431, 980
Han Shao-kung, 763, 764
Han shih wai-chuan (External Commentary to the Han Odes), 90, 95
Han shu (History of the Han Dynasty; Pan Ku), 101, 141, 175, 205, 232, 518–19, 523, 686, 898, 900, 917, 922, 987, 1101; biographies in, 250, 267; Korean translation of, 1073; "Li yüeh chih" (Treatise on Ritual and Music) in, 956; "Wu hsing chih" (Treatise on the Five Elements) in, 956; "Yi-wen-chih" (Bibliographic Treatise) in, 1069
Han Suyin, 773
"Han-tan chi" (The Tale of Han-tan; T'ang Hsien-tsu), 827
Han-tan Ch'un, 135
Han t'ien-shih shih-chia (Lineage of the Han Celestial Masters), 179
Han Tung, 463
han-tzu (Chinese characters), 20, 1000. *See also* sinographs
Han-Wei school, 246, 290
Han wen-hsüeh shih kang-yao (Outline of the History of Chinese Literature; Lu Hsün), 745
Han Wen-ti, 50
Han Wo, 313, 393
Han wŏnjip (Han Source Collection), 1072–73
Han Wu-ti. *See* Wu, Emperor (Han)
Han Wu-ti nei-chuan (Esoteric Biography of Emperor Han Wu-ti), 181, 580
Han yeh (Cold Nights; Pa Chin), 750
Han Yi, 584
Han Ying, 90
Han Yü, 11, 124, 166, 306, 424, 425, 434, 530–31, 533–38, 594; influence of, 420, 962, 1068, 1070, 1073, 1097; and Meng Chiao, 303, 307; on plagiarism, 893; in plays, 838; as poet, 304; on poetry, 534; and prose, 354, 931–32; return to antiquity style, 230, 237, 243, 345, 931; as scholar, 937
Han-yü (Chinese language), 22, 26. *See also* Sinitic
Han-yüan chi (The Han Garden; Pien Chih-lin, Ho Ch'i-fang and Li Kuang-t'ien), 455
"Han-yüan tien fu" (Li Hua), 301
Hanabusa zōshi (Flowery Tales; Tsuga Teishō), 1093
Hanan, Patrick, 597, 606, 640, 947, 948
Hang Yüeh-ho, 457
hangŭl (Korean script), 1067, 1074, 1077
Hannic. *See Han-yü*; Sinitic
Hansa yŏljŏnch'o (trans. of *Han shu*; Ch'oe Rip), 1073
Hanwŏnjip (Han Source Collection), 1072
Hao Ching, 386
Hao-ch'iu chuan (The Fortunate Union), 667
hao-chü (generous acts), 645
hao-fang (bold and unfettered) style, 320, 321, 374, 398, 417
hao-han (hero), 630
"Hao-li hsing" (Wormwood Hamlet; Ts'ao Ts'ao), 255
Hao Ta-t'ung, 184, 187
"Hao-t'ien t'a" (Pagoda of Vast Heaven; Chu K'ai), 145, 807
Harbin Theater (Ha-erh-pin hua-chü-yüan), 871
Harbsmeier, Christoph, 881–908
Hargett, James M., 555–65
Harrim Academy (Korea), 1069
Hartman, Charles, 466–90
hat boi (classic opera; Vietnam), 1103
hat cheo (satirical drama; Vietnam), 1103
Hatton Nankaku, 1090
Hayashi Razan, 1089
"Heavenly Questions." *See* "T'ien wen"
Hegel, Georg Wilhelm Friedrich, 712
Hei ch'ao chi (Black Tides; Yang Hua), 459
"Hei-nu yü-t'ien lu" (The Black Slave Cries Out to Heaven; adaptation of *Uncle Tom's Cabin*), 849
Hei-nu yü-t'ien lu (Uncle Tom's Cabin; trans. Lin Shu), 1065
Hen hai (The Sea of Regret; Wu Chien-jen), 673, 721–23, 741–42
heng te yi-chih (horizontal transplants), 460
Henjōhokkiseireishū (Henjō's Collection for Giving Free Rein to the Spirit), 1084
Heraclitus, 884
Herodotus, 497, 505
Herrick, Robert, 323, 324
Hinduism, 9
history, 51, 436, 892; and biography, 511, 579; Buddhist, 165, 166–67; Bureau of, 394, 525; and *ch'uan-ch'i* tales, 594, 679, 681, 686; Confucius on, 73–74; didacticism in, 498, 501, 507–8, 510, 625; and fiction, 494, 508, 620–24, 631, 643, 669–70, 697–98, 718; and funerary writing, 529; and *hua-pen*, 598, 600; humor in, 132, 134, 137–42; and literary criticism, 706; as literature, 493–510, 926; and myth, 67–68; official dynastic, 508, 525–26, 529, 565, 643, 687; in official memorials, 529; and philosophy, 72–74, 501; and *pi-chi*, 563, 565; and poetry, 267, 437; as rec-

ord of events *vs.* words, 496–97, 500, 503, 504; Su Shih on, 540; and supernatural tales, 127, 128, 542–43, 544, 548–49, 551; in travel literature, 555; unofficial, 140, 621; and women, 202–4, 218
History of Chinese Literature (Lin Ch'uan-chia), 713
History of Politics (Jenks). See *She-hui t'ung-ch'üan*
Hitler, Adolph, 443
Hmong peoples, 1033
Ho Ch'i-fang, 455, 456
"Ho-chien chuan" (An Account of Ho-chien; Liu Tsung-yüan), 594
Ho Chih-chang, 298
Ho Chih-yüan, 185
Ho Ching-ming, 404–7, 409, 414
Ho Chu, 321, 327, 352
"Ho Hsiao Hsi-ma Tzu-hsien 'Ku yi' liu shou" (Six Poems Harmonizing with the Royal Equerry Hsiao Tzu-hsien's "Poem on an Old Theme"; Wu Chün), 201
Ho Hsün, 201, 272, 960
"Ho kuei lou" (Homing Crane Lodge; Li Yü), 615
Hŏ Kyun, 1077
Ho-lan Chin-ming, 295
Ho Li-wei, 765
Ho Liang-chün, 406
Ho-lu, king of Wu, 514–15
Ho Lung, 872
Ho Lung-hsiang, 178
Ho Meng-ch'un, 403
Ho Pang-o, 693
Ho P'ei-chu, 839
"Ho p'u-sa chieh wen" (Harmonizing with the Bodhisattva Precepts), 979
"Ho-shang" (River Elegy; television series), 57, 763
Ho-shang Kung, 174
ho-wen (compound graphs), 40
Ho Yen, 301
Ho Yü-huai, 769
Ho-yüeh ying-ling chi (anthology; Yin Fan), 295, 296
Hoa tien Truyen (Tale of the Flowery Note Paper; Nguyen Huy Tu), 1100
Hoang Viet xuan thu (Spring and Autumn Annals of Imperial Vietnam), 1102
Homer, 500, 505, 895
homosexuality, 272, 605, 611, 614, 615, 642, 649, 657, 672
Honchō monzui (The Essence of Literature in Our Age; comp. Fujiwara Akihira), 1085
Hong-duc quoc am thi tap (Anthology of Verse in the National Language from the Hong-duc Reign; comp. King Thanh Tong), 1098
Hong Hŭi-bok, 1077
Hong Kil-dong chŏn (Tale of Hong Kil-dong), 1077
Hong Kong, 35, 736, 763; film in, 759, 774; modernist poets in, 457, 458, 464; regional identity of, 758, 773–74
Hopkins, Gerard Manley, 300
Horace, 324
Hou Chi (Lord Millet), 67, 102, 103
Hou ch'i tzu (Later Seven Masters), 406–9, 411–14, 419, 420, 422, 423, 440
Hou Chih. *See* Hou Hsiang-yeh
Hou Ching, 272
Hou Han shu (History of the Later Han Dynasty; Fan Yeh), 525, 580, 622, 912, 956; "Independent Spirits" chapter from, 520
Hou Hsiang-yeh (Hou Chih), 1020, 1023
"Hou-kuan hsien lieh-nü chien-ch'ou" (The Female Martyr; Hsi Lang-hsien), 604
Hou "Shui-hu chuan" (Sequel to *Water Margin*; Master of the Blue Lotus Chamber), 628, 663
Hou T'u (Sovereign Earth), 67
Hsi, Duke of Lu, 102
"Hsi Ch'ang-an hsing" (Western Ch'ang-an; Fu Hsüan), 260
Hsi-ch'eng-tiao (Western City Tune), 1030
Hsi-ching tsa-chi (Miscellanies of the Western Capital; Ko Hung), 232, 522, 563, 580
Hsi Chou sheng (Scholar of Western Chou), 643, 660
hsi-chü (Chinese opera), 845
hsi-chü te hsieh-yi t'e-hsing (suggestive nature of Chinese opera), 856
"Hsi ch'ü ko" (Songs to Western Tunes), 271, 960
Hsi Ch'uan, 463
Hsi-ho (goddess), 61, 66, 67, 197, 199
Hsi Hsi, 774
Hsi-hsia (Tanguts), 339, 557, 964
"Hsi-hsiang chi" (Romance of the Western Chamber; Wang Shih-fu), 145, 587, 710, 742, 805, 813, 825, 1010, 1019, 1076; annotated editions of, 841, 842
"Hsi-hsiang chi chu-kung-tiao" (Medley on the "Romance of the Western Chamber"; Tung Chieh-yüan), 587, 798, 799, 800, 813, 996, 1008, 1009, 1014
"Hsi Hsiao Niang" (Parody of Hsiao Niang; Shen Man-yüan), 207
"Hsi hsin fu" (Cleansing the Heart; Wu Yün), 302
Hsi-hu chia-hua (Charming Stories of West Lake), 617
Hsi-hu erh-chi (Second Collection of West Lake Stories; Chou Chi), 612
"Hsi-hu kan chiu" (Mulling over the Past at West Lake; T'ang Shih), 375
Hsi K'ang (Chi K'ang), 7, 258, 259, 265
Hsi-k'un ch'ou-ch'ang chi (Collection of Exchanged Poems at Hsi-k'un), 343, 344
Hsi-k'un poetry, 343, 344, 531
Hsi Lang-hsien, 602–5, 619
Hsi-ling school, 414

"Hsi men hsing" (West Gate), 251, 959
Hsi-nan Yi-chih hsüan (Annals of the Southwest Yi), 1040–41
hsi-p'i (basic melody), 793
Hsi Shih (legendary beauty), 350, 616, 823, 829
"Hsi-Shu meng" (The Dream of Western Shu; Kuan Han-ch'ing), 807
"Hsi-ta t'ai-tzu ju Hsüeh-shan hsiu tao tsan" (Hymn on Prince Siddhārtha Entering the Himalayas to Cultivate the Way), 978
Hsi-t'an lu (Ticklish Tales, Record of Jovial Talk), 136
Hsi-t'ang yung-jih hsü-lun (Discussions to While Away the Days at Evening Hall; Wang Fu-chih), 937
Hsi Tso-ch'ih, 623
Hsi-tsung, Emperor, 183, 312
Hsi-tzu, 592
"Hsi-tzu chuan" (Biography of Hsi-tzu; Shen Ya-chih), 591–92
"Hsi-tz'u chuan" (Tradition of the Appended Statements; *Yi-ching*), 89
"Hsi wan liang" (Ravine on a Cold Evening; Li Ho), 124
Hsi Wang-mu (Queen Mother of the West), 66, 810, 838
hsi-wen (*nan-hsi*; southern plays), 785, 793, 796, 801, 826, 995; earliest catalog of, 840; texts of, 792, 794, 805, 819–23
hsi-yen (outmoded expressions), 893
Hsi-yu chi (Journey to the West; Monkey; Wu Ch'eng-en), 12, 69, 188, 399, 543, 545, 632–37, 659, 721, 818, 1011, 1016, 1056, 1075, 1077; and Buddhism, 128–29, 168, 633–36, 663; in drama, 125, 632; humor in, 145, 147, 634, 636, 637; in Japan, 1093; Kuan-yin in, 128, 129, 632, 633, 636; and *pien-wen*, 123; sequels to, 663–64; 1663 edition of, 943; supernatural in, 128–29
"Hsi-yu" pu (Supplement to *Journey to the West*; Tung Yüeh), 129, 637, 663, 946, 948
Hsi-yü chi (Records of the Western Regions; Hsüan-tsang), 588–89
Hsia, C. T., 630–31, 634–35, 641
Hsia, Master. *See* Tzu Hsia
Hsia Ching-ch'ü, 656, 670
Hsia Ching-kuan, 321
Hsia dynasty, 65, 71, 80, 103
Hsia-hou Tsao, 100
Hsia Kuei, 482, 484
Hsia Tseng-yü (Pieh-shih), 454, 706, 708–9, 717
Hsia Wan-ch'un, 412
Hsia Yen, 862, 863
"Hsia yi lou" (The Summer Pavilion; Li Yü), 615
Hsia Yü, 462
Hsiang, king of Wei, 545
Hsiang Ch'u, 12
"Hsiang chün" (Goddess of the Hsiang River; *Ch'u tz'u*), 118, 199
"Hsiang-chung yüan chieh" (An Explanation of the Laments Written in Hsiang; Shen Ya-chih), 122, 591, 592
"Hsiang fu-jen" (The Lady of Hsiang River), 199
hsiang-ho (concerted songs), 954, 956, 958
hsiang-hua (mental transformation), 716
Hsiang Hung-tso (T'ing-chi), 449
Hsiang K'ai, 520
Hsiang-kang wen-hsüeh (Hong Kong Literature; journal), 774
Hsiang Liang, 516
"Hsiang Min-kung yüan-hsiao shih tzu, Shih-san lang wu-sui ch'ao t'ien" (The Kidnapping on the Eve of the Lantern Festival; Ling Meng-ch'u), 609
"Hsiang-mo pien-wen" (Transformation Text on the Subduing of Demons), 123, 167–68
Hsiang of Lu, Sire, 102
hsiang-sheng (comic dialog, cross talk), 143–44, 787, 790–91
hsiang-sheng (seeming-sounds), 144
hsiang-tsan (image eulogy), 473
hsiang-t'u (nativist), 777
hsiang-t'u wen-hsüeh (native literature), 458, 462, 753
Hsiang-t'u wen-hsüeh yün-tung (Native Literature movement; Taiwan), 461, 462
Hsiang Yü, 249, 273, 504–6, 519–20, 806
hsiao (laugh), 135
Hsiao, Prince of Liang (Liu Wu), 231, 232
Hsiao Ch'en, 270
Hsiao-ching (Classic of Filial Piety), 88, 90, 95, 469, 969, 1074
Hsiao-ch'ing (legendary beauty), 617
"Hsiao ch'iu hsi hsiao shih t'an" (Small Rocky Pool West of Little Hillock; Liu Tsung-yüan), 535
hsiao-chuan (small seal) script, 46–47, 49
Hsiao-fu (Treasury of Laughs; Feng Meng-lung), 136, 137
hsiao-hsüeh (minor learning), 45
Hsiao Hung, 773
Hsiao-jan Yü-sheng, 721
Hsiao Kang (Emperor Chien-wen of Liang), 207, 240, 241, 270, 271, 272, 632, 926, 927, 929, 960
Hsiao-lin (Forest of Laughs; Han-tan Ch'un), 135
Hsiao-lin (Grove of Laughter; Fu-pai Chu-jen), 137
Hsiao-lin kuang-chi (Expanded Forest of Laughs), 136
hsiao-ling (single songs; form of *tz'u*), 316, 317, 318, 319, 329, 332, 333, 371

Hsiao-p'in chi (The Contrived Frown Collection; Chao Pi), 681
Hsiao-p'in po-je po-lo-mi ching (abbreviated *Prajñāpāramitā-sūtra*), 6
hsiao-p'in-wen (brief, refined essay), 6–7, 1074
hsiao-sheng (young male role-type), 839
Hsiao Shih-ho, 583
hsiao shih-min (small city dwellers), 702
"Hsiao shui-wan t'ien-hu yi shu" (The Foxes' Revenge; Hsi Lang-hsien), 602
hsiao-shuo ("small talk"; fiction; novels), 117, 388–89, 561, 595, 596, 675, 699, 705, 732, 766; essays on, 714–16; humor in, 146, 147–48. *See also* fiction; novels
hsiao-shuo chieh ko-ming (revolution in fiction), 707, 725
hsiao-shuo chih cheng-tsung (mainstream of fiction), 716
hsiao-shuo chih shih-chih (substance of fiction), 713
"Hsiao-shuo hsiao hua" (Briefly on Fiction), 708, 713
Hsiao-shuo lin (The Grove of Fiction; journal), 702–3, 708, 710, 712, 725, 729
"*Hsiao-shuo lin* fa-k'an-t'zu" (Inaugural Announcement of *The Grove of Fiction*; Huang Jen), 713
"*Hsiao-shuo lin* yüan-ch'i" (Origins of *The Grove of Fiction*; Hsü Nien-tz'u), 712
Hsiao-shuo ming-hua ta-kuan (Illustrated Panorama of Short Stories; comp. Hu Chi-ch'en), 729
Hsiao-shuo shih-pao (Fiction Actualities; journal), 705
Hsiao-shuo ta-kuan (Fiction Panorama; journal), 705, 729–30
"Hsiao-shuo ts'ung-hua" (Colloquy on Fiction; Lü Ssu-mien), 708–10, 715
Hsiao-shuo ts'ung-pao (Collection of Fiction; journal), 704
"Hsiao-shuo yüan-li" (Principles of Fiction), 709
Hsiao-shuo yüeh-pao (Short Story Magazine), 704, 715, 729
"Hsiao Sun t'u" (Little Sun the Butcher), 819
Hsiao Tao-ch'eng, 252
"Hsiao tao-jen yi chao jao t'ien-hsia, nü ch'i-t'ung liang chü chu chung-shen" (The Chess Champions; Ling Meng-ch'u), 606
Hsiao T'ing-chih, 189
Hsiao tou-p'eng (Little Bean Arbor; Tseng Yen-tung), 695
Hsiao-tsung, Emperor, 360, 485
Hsiao T'ung (Prince Chao-ming of Liang), 4–5, 207, 240, 250, 272, 926
Hsiao-tzu chuan (Accounts of Filial Sons), 969
Hsiao Tzu-liang, 270
hsiao tz'u (trifling lyrics), 316. See also *tz'u*
Hsiao Yen (Emperor Wu of Liang), 270, 271, 960
Hsiao Yi, 926
hsiao-yi (petty righteousness), 623
Hsiao Ying-shih, 301
Hsiao Yü-tse, 873
hsieh (jest), 135
hsieh (prosodic harmony), 422
Hsieh Ang-fu, 380
Hsieh Ao, 368
Hsieh Chao-che, 678, 689
Hsieh Chen, 407, 408, 409
Hsieh Chin, 401
hsieh-ch'ing hsiao-shuo (a novel of passion), 724
Hsieh Fang-te, 368
hsieh-hou-yü (folk similes), 150, 151–52, 156, 157
Hsieh Hsi-ssu, 487
Hsieh Hun, 426
Hsieh Kuei, 184
Hsieh Ling-yün, 169, 240, 266, 267–68, 271, 412, 420, 425, 426, 535
"Hsieh lu hsing" (Dew on the Shallots; Ts'ao Ts'ao), 255
Hsieh Shou-hao, 183
Hsieh Tao-yün, 836
Hsieh T'iao, 241, 267, 270, 271, 272, 298, 364, 420
Hsieh-to (The Bantering Bell; Shen Ch'i-feng), 694
"Hsieh Tzu-jan" (Han Yü), 124
Hsieh Wan-ying, 747, 771
Hsieh Wan-ying (Ping Hsin), 747–48, 771
hsieh yin (comic effects), 893
hsien (adepts; immortals; fairies), 112, 113, 115, 121, 124, 125, 129, 265, 547
hsien (serenely), 425–26
Hsien, Prince of Ho-chien (Liu Te), 91, 92, 100
Hsien Chen, 406
"Hsien chih shih" (Poems Expressing My Aims; Li Yen), 251
Hsien-ch'ing ou-chi (Casual Expressions of Idle Feelings; Li Yü), 825, 832, 841–42
Hsien-ch'üan chi (Anthology of Alpine Spring; Chang Yü-ch'u), 179
hsien-feng (avant-garde) literature, 15, 759, 763–65, 768–69
Hsien-le chi (Anthology of Transcendent Joy; Liu Ch'u-hsüan), 188
Hsien-pei tribe (Särbi), 264
Hsien-shih yi-chung (One Kind of Reality; Yü Hua), 765
Hsien-tai (Les Contemporaines; journal), 456, 568
Hsien-tai p'ing-lun (Modern Era Review), 567
Hsien-tai (Modernist) school, 457, 458, 460–61, 464
Hsien-tai shih chi-k'an (Modern Poetry Quarterly), 460
Hsien-tai shih lun-chan (Modern Poetry debate), 461
Hsien-ti, Emperor, 546, 549
Hsien-t'ien period (T'ang), 292
Hsien-tsung, Emperor, 308
Hsien-yü ching (Sūtra of the Wise and the Foolish), 172
Hsien-yü Pi-jen, 380

hsien-yüan (serenity and distance), 424
Hsien-yüan chi-shih (Tales of Immortal Maidens; comp. Yang Erh-tseng), 688
hsin (mind, heart), 170, 414, 633–34, 635
"Hsin Ch'a-hua" (New Camille), 851
hsin-ch'ao (New Wave), 763
Hsin-chi yen-fu chiao (The Newly Compiled Teachings of a Stern Father), 973
Hsin chi-yüan (New Era; Pi-ho-kuan chu-jen), 722
Hsin Ch'i-chi, 322–23, 325, 333, 334, 432, 438; comparisons with, 417, 446, 450; influence of, 328, 450; lyrics of, 324, 326, 333; as model, 445, 449
Hsin chiao-cheng "Meng-hsi pi-t'an" (*Brush Talks from Dream Book*: New Collations and Corrections; Hu Tao-ching), 565
Hsin ching (Heart/Mind Sutra; Sanskrit: *Prajñāpāramitā-hṛdaya sūtra*), 163, 635
Hsin ch'ing-nien (New Youth; journal), 453, 454, 567, 730, 744, 852, 855–56, 1066
hsin-chü (new drama), 850, 852, 857
Hsin Chung-kuo wei-lai chi (The Future of New China; Liang Ch'i-ch'ao), 722, 726
hsin-fa (New Policies), 339, 353, 355, 356
"Hsin-feng che pi weng" (The Old Man with the Broken Arm from Hsin-feng; Po Chü-yi), 730, 963
Hsin-hai chi (Ocean of the Mind), 980
Hsin hsiao-shuo (New Fiction; journal), 702–3, 707–9, 716, 720, 723, 734
hsin hsiao-shuo (new fiction), 707, 720
"Hsin-hsin ming" (Inscription of Faith in Mind; Seng-ts'an), 170
Hsin-hsing shu-chü (publisher), 565
Hsin hsü (New Prefaces; Liu Hsiang), 517
hsin-hsüeh (School of Mind), 414, 635, 642
"Hsin huai shuang" (The Heart Harbors Frost: Yao Ho), 307
Hsin ju-chiao (New Confucianism), 52
Hsin kan-chüeh p'ai (Neo-impressionists), 748
Hsin lieh-kuo chih (New Records of the Various States; Feng Meng-lung), 625
Hsin-ling shih (History of the Soul; Chang Ch'eng-chih), 766
Hsin-sheng tai (the Newborn Generation), 463
hsin-shih (new poetry), 454, 706
hsin shih-ch'i wen-hsüeh (new era literature), 760
Hsin "Shih-t'ou chi" (A New *Story of the Stone*; Wu Chien-jen), 723
Hsin-ta-lu shih shuang-yüeh-k'an (New World Poetry Bimonthly; U.S.journal), 464
Hsin Ti, 457
hsin-t'i shih (*chin-t'i shih*; new-style poetry), 270, 276, 289, 300, 304, 311, 312, 313, 404, 415, 931, 979, 1068, 1071. See also *p'ai-lü*; Yung-ming *t'i*
hsin t'i-yen hsiao-shuo (novels of new experience), 766
hsin wen-hsüeh (creative writing), 1066
Hsin wen-hua yün-tung (New Culture movement), 1056
Hsin-wen pao (The News; newspaper), 733
hsin-wen t'i (new-style writing), 706
Hsin Wu-tai shih (New History of the Five Dynasties), 141
hsin yen pu mei, mei yen pu hsin (Trustworthy words are not beautiful, and beautiful words are not trustworthy), 918
hsin-yüan yi-ma (monkey of the mind, horse of the will), 186, 635
"Hsin-yüeh-fu" (New Ballads; Po Chü-yi), 838, 955
Hsin-yüeh (Crescent) school, 455
hsing (balladic suites), 954
hsing (metaphor), 5, 106–7, 158, 921
hsing (nature), 352, 634
hsing-ch'ing chih ling (spirit that resides in one's personal nature and feeling), 414
hsing-ch'ü (inspired interest), 424
hsing-chuang (accounts of conduct), 525, 968
Hsing Feng, 590
Hsing-hua t'ien (The Paradise of Apricot Blossoms), 669
hsing-ling (native sensibility; spirit), 397, 411, 412, 423, 447, 935, 1072
Hsing-ling (sensibility or inspirational) school, 434
"Hsing lu nan" (The Road Is Hard; Lu Chao-lin), 288
"Hsing lu nan" (The Road Is Hard; Pao Chao), 959
Hsing-meng p'ien-yen (Refined Words to Awaken One from Dreams), 617
Hsing-shih heng-yen (Constant Words to Awaken the World; Feng Meng-lung), 597, 600, 602
Hsing-shih yen (Tales of the World's Exemplars; Lu Jen-lung), 610
Hsing-shih yin-yüan chuan (Marriage Destinies to Awaken the World; Hsi Chou-sheng), 127, 643, 660–61
hsing-shu (running style) script, 49
hsing-ssu (form likeness), 479–80
Hsing-tao jih-pao (Hong Kong Daily), 457
Hsing-te (Na-lan Hsing-te), 417, 418, 447, 452

"Hsing-tz'u hsi-chiao tso yi-pai yün" (One Hundred Rhymes Composed While Traveling Through the Western Suburbs; Li Shang-yin), 311
Hsing Yi-hsün, 872
"Hsing ying shen" (Form, Shadow, Spirit), 266
"Hsiu chen" (Embroidered Pillows; Ling Shu-hua), 747
Hsiu-chen shih-shu (Ten Texts on the Cultivation of Perfection), 189–90
"Hsiu-chu p'ien" (The Tapering Bamboo; Ch'en Tzu-ang), 290
Hsiu-hsiang hsiao-shuo (Fiction Illustrated; journal), 702–3, 709, 718, 724
hsiu-hsin (cultivation of the mind), 635
hsiu-hsin lien-hsing (the accomplishment of cultivating the mind and refining nature), 634
Hsiu-ku ch'un-jung (Spring Complexions from the Embroidered Valley), 684
Hsiu-p'ing yüan (Omen of the Illustrated Screen), 669
Hsiu-t'a yeh-shih (The Unofficial History of the Embroidered Coat; Lü T'ien-ch'eng), 665
Hsiu T'ao, 457
hsiu-ts'ai (licentiate) degree, 1, 2, 643–44
Hsiu-tz'u-hsüeh fa-fan (Introduction to Rhetoric; Ch'en Wang-tao), 156
Hsiu-wen kuan (College for the Cultivation of Literature). *See* Hung-wen kuan
"Hsiu-wen she-jen chuan" (The Tale of the Drafting Secretary; Ch'ü Yu), 680
Hsiung Fo-hsi, 851, 854, 865
Hsiung Lung-feng, 598
Hsiung-nu people, 250, 252, 257, 264, 273, 504, 506, 814, 821, 1101
hsü (preface), 5, 289, 913
Hsü Chao (Ling-hui), 365
Hsü Chen, 666
Hsü Chen-ch'ing, 404, 405, 406
Hsü Chen-ya, 566, 704, 727, 730, 742–43
Hsü Chi (Ling-yün), 365
"Hsü Chiang-shih chuan" ("Pai-yüan chuan"; An Account of the White Monkey), 582–83
hsü-chih (afterword), 928
Hsü Chih-mo, 455
Hsü Ch'ih, 272
Hsü "Chin P'ing Mei" (Sequel to *Chin P'ing Mei*; Ting Yao-k'ang), 642, 662
Hsü-ching ch'ung-ho hsien-sheng Hsü shen-weng yü-lu (Discourse Record of Divine Elder Hsü, Master of Piercing Harmony and Vacant Tranquility), 180
Hsü Ching-tsung, 279, 285, 286
Hsü Ch'u tz'u (Continued *Elegies of Ch'u*; comp. Ch'ao Pu-chih), 353
Hsü Chung-hsing, 407
Hsü Chung-lin, 632
Hsü Erh-t'an (Continued Hearsay Stories), 678
Hsü Fang, 691
Hsü Feng-en, 695
Hsü Han shu (Continuation of the History of the Han), 956
Hsü Hsia-k'o (Hsü Hung-tsu), 556, 559
Hsü Hsien, 142
Hsü Hsüan, 341, 342, 834
Hsü Hsüan-kuai lu (Sequel to Accounts of the Mysterious and Anomalous; Li Fu-yen), 581
Hsü Hsün (239–292/374?), 190
Hsü Hsün (fl.c. 358?), 265
Hsü Hui, 177
Hsü Hui-yen, 834
Hsü Hun, 311
Hsü Hung-tsu (Hsü Hsia-k'o), 556, 559
Hsü Kan, 253, 254
Hsü-kao-seng chuan (Continuation of Lives of Eminent Monks; Tao-hsüan), 165
Hsü Kuan-shih-yin ying-yen chi (Continued Records of Kuan-shih-yin's Responsive Manifestations; Lu Kao), 171
Hsü Kuang-shih-yin ying-yen chi (Further Accounts of Miracles by Avalotiteśvara; Chang Yen), 171
Hsü K'un, 695
"Hsü lao-p'u yi fen ch'eng chia" (Old Servant Hsü; Hsi Lang-hsien), 603
"Hsü lien chi erh-shih yung" (Twenty Supplementary Toilette Box Songs; Yang Wei-chen), 393
Hsü Ling, 207, 217, 241–42, 243, 272, 273, 532, 929
Hsü Mi, 177
Hsü Nien-tz'u (Tung-hai chüeh-wo), 704, 711–12, 715, 720, 729
hsü-pa (preface and colophon), 528
Hsü Pan-mei, 849
Hsü Pen, 395, 398
Hsü Ping, 54
Hsü Shao, 623
Hsü Shen, 46–47, 912
Hsü shih-hua (Continuing Remarks on Poetry; Ssu-ma Kuang), 934
Hsü Shou-hsin, 180
Hsü Shuo-fang, 640
Hsü t'ai-shih chen-chün t'u-chuan (An Illustrated Hagiography of the Perfected Lord, Grand Scribe Hsü), 189
Hsü Tao-tsang ching (Scriptures in Supplement to the Taoist Canon), 178
Hsü Ti-shan, 746–48
Hsü Tsai-ssu, 379
Hsü Ts'an, 448
Hsü Tsung (scholar), 347
Hsü-tsung, Emperor, 203
Hsü tzu-chih t'ung-chien ch'ang-pien (Continuation of the Extended Version of the Mirror for Aiding Government; Li T'ao), 565

Hsü Tzu pu yü (What the Master Did Not Speak Of, Continued; Yüan Mei), 694
Hsü Tzu-yün, 446
Hsü tz'u-hsüan (Chang Hui-yen and Chang Ch'i), 438
Hsü Wei, 7, 146, 407, 411, 435, 801, 824, 835, 840, 841
hsü wu tzu (Continued Five Masters), 408
Hsü Yao-tso, 584
Hsü Yen-po, 292
Hsüan, Emperor, 229
Hsüan-chüeh (Master of Yung-chia), 170
Hsüan-feng (Whirlwind; Chiang Kuei), 777
Hsüan-feng ch'ing-hui lu (Record of a Felicitous Convocation on Sublime Practice; comp. Yeh-lü Ch'u-ts'ai), 188
Hsüan-ko (Songs of Mystery), 981
Hsüan-kuai lu (Accounts of the Mysterious and Anomalous; Niu Seng-ju), 581
Hsüan Nü (Dark Girl), 216
Hsüan-p'in lu (Record of Arcane Ranks; comp. Chang Yü), 181
Hsüan-tang, 632
Hsüan Ting, 695
Hsüan-tsang, 11, 163–65, 555, 589, 632
hsüan-tse (selection), 716
Hsüan-tsung, Emperor, 178, 243, 275, 278, 291, 292, 293, 301, 586, 670; in Ch'ing novels, 670; nostalgia for, 309–10; Palace Music School (*chiao-fang*) of, 975; Pear Garden of, 790; poets of reign of, 280, 295, 299, 301, 302; in supernatural drama, 126; and Yang Kuei-fei, 308–11, 485, 800, 814, 815, 834, 1008, 1086–87
Hsüan-wu (Dark Warrior), 180
hsüan-yen (abstruse utterances), 932
Hsüan-yen chi (Records in Proclamation of Manifestations; Liu Yi-ch'ing), 121, 171, 551
hsüan-yen shih (mysterious discourse poetry), 265, 266, 268, 981
hsüeh (joke), 135
hsüeh (to study), 884
Hsüeh-ch'uang t'an-yi (Conversations about the Strange by the Snowy Window), 682
Hsüeh Hui, 406, 426
Hsüeh Jen-kuei, 807, 997, 999, 1003
hsüeh-lei (tears of blood; Japanese: *Chi no namida*), 1082
"Hsüeh Liu Kung-kan t'i wu shou" (Five Poems Imitating the Style of Liu Kung-kan), 269
"Hsüeh lu-shih yü fu cheng hsien" (Magistrate Hsüeh's Metamorphosis into a Fish; Hsi Lang-hsien), 602, 603
"Hsüeh-shan tsan" (Eulogies on the Snowy Mountain: Chiang Yen), 474
Hsüeh Shao-wei, 719
hsüeh-shih (Academicians), 292
hsüeh-shih-lang (lay students), 966
"Hsüeh-so-yi" (Blood-Stained Straw Cape), 850
Hsüeh Sung, 589
Hsüeh T'ao, 208–9, 217, 312, 836, 839, 1101
Hsüeh-t'ao hsiao-shuo (Snow Billow Stories; Chiang Ying-k'o), 678
Hsüeh-t'ao-ko chi (Snow Billow Pavilion Collection; Chiang Ying-k'o), 678
"Hsüeh T'ao P'eng-tse t'i" (Imitating T'ao P'eng-tse's Style; Pao Chao), 269
Hsüeh T'iao, 587
Hsüeh Tzu-hsien, 189
Hsüeh-yü t'ang wen-chi (Literary Collection from the Hall for Time Extra to Study; Shih Jun-chang), 420
Hsün Hsü, 957
hsün-ken (Searching for Roots), 763, 764
"Hsün-li" (Reasonable Officials), 516
Hsün-shih lu (The Record of Mr. Hsün; Hsün Hsü), 957
Hsün Tzu, 9, 78, 90, 92, 96, 99, 100, 103, 104, 642, 883, 912
Hsün Tzu (text), 60, 225
Hsün Yüeh, 509
Hu Chen-heng, 281
Hu Chi-ch'en, 729
hu chia hu wei (a fox borrows the authority of a tiger), 502
"Hu chia shih-pa p'ai" (Eighteen Cadences for the Barbarian Flute; Ts'ai Yen), 257
Hu Chih-yü, 381, 805–6
Hu Ch'üan, 324
Hu-hai hsing-wen "Yi-chien" hsü-chih (New Reports from Lake and Sea: Sequel to *The Records of the Listener*), 676
Hu-hai-lou tz'u-chi (Collection of Lyrics from the Lakes and Seas Lodge; Ch'en Wei-sung), 418
Hu-han-yeh, 814, 815
hu hsi (melon-seeds), 195
Hu Hui-ch'ao, 582
Hu Ju-chia, 684, 690
Hu K'o, 866, 873
"Hu-k'ou yü-sheng" (Escape from the Tiger's Maw; Ts'ao Yin), 832
Hu-mei ts'ung-t'an (Collected Tales of Fox Fairies; comp. in Wan-li period), 688
Hu Shih, 7, 14, 493, 567, 634, 652, 698, 722, 730, 739, 744, 1063; and literary reform, 156, 453, 1056, 1066; and modern poetry, 453, 454, 458; and new drama, 851, 852, 854, 856, 865; on origin of song lyric, 975
hu-sun (monkey), 635
Hu Tao-ching, 565
Hu-tieh mei (The Butterfly Go-Between), 669
"Hu-tieh meng" (Butterfly Dream), 140, 145
hu-wen (corresponding term), 891

Hu Yao-pang, 770
Hu Yeh-p'in, 750
Hu Ying, 542–54
Hu Ying-lin, 385, 408, 409, 547, 683, 687, 688–89
Hu Yü-hsiu, 1000
hu-yüeh (Central Asian music), 975
hua (flower; flowery, elaborate), 625, 893
hua (tale), 972
hua chi (painting records), 467
hua-chi (*ku-chi*; humor), 134–35
Hua chien chi (Among the Flowers; Chao Ch'ung-tso), 201, 316, 321, 332, 445, 446, 1100
hua-ching (realm of creativity), 425
Hua-ch'ing kung (Palace of Floriate Clarity), 310
hua-chü (spoken drama), 735–36, 848, 857
Hua-hu ching (Scripture on the Conversion of the Barbarians), 981
Hua-jui, Lady, 208–9, 217
Hua-kai shan Fou-ch'iu Wang Kuo san chen-chün shih-shih (A Case History of the Three Perfected Lords Fou-ch'iu, Wang, and Kuo of Mount Hua-kai), 180
"Hua Kuan So" (The Story of Hua Kuan So), 998, 1013, 1018
Hua-kuang (god), 994
hua-pen (vernacular stories), 591, 595–619, 796, 830, 972, 973, 992, 996, 1092, 1093; humor in, 146–47, 596, 606–8, 610, 611, 613, 615, 616; poetry in, 596, 598, 611; and proverbs, 155; supernatural in, 126, 127, 596, 597, 604, 606, 609; themes of, 595, 597; and Three Teachings, 596, 598, 601, 603, 604, 607, 610, 612–18
"Hua-shan nü" (The Girl of Mount Hua; Han Yü), 124
"Hua-teng chiao Lien-nü ch'eng Fo chi" (Lien-nü Attains Buddhahood on the Way to Her Wedding), 599
Hua T'o, 508
hua-tsan (eulogy on a portrait), 467, 468, 475, 478
Hua-ts'ao meng-shih (Blossoming Bushes Plucked by Juvenile Ignorance; comp. Wang Shih-chen), 426
"Hua Wei hsien-sheng" (Mr. Hua Wei; Chang T'ien-yi), 752
Hua-ying chi (The Flower Reflection Collection; T'ao Fu), 681
hua-yü (Mandarin Chinese), 33. *See also* Mandarin, Modern Standard; Sinitic
Hua-yüeh hen (Traces of Flowers and the Moon; Wei Tzu-an), 657, 672–73
Hua Yün, General, 682
"Huai chiu" (Remembrances of the Past; Lu Hsün), 730
huai-chiu (wistful reverie on the past), 571
"Huai/Fan-o-lin yü ch'iang-wei" (Violin and Rose; T'ien Han), 858
"Huai-ku" (Meditation on Antiquity; Wang P'eng-yün), 450
huai-ku (remembrances of the past), 1068
"Huai Li Shu-t'ung Hsien-sheng" (In Memory of Mr. Li Shu-t'ung; Feng Tzu-k'ai), 574
Huai-nan Tzu (comp. Liu An), 10, 61, 63, 64, 82–83, 105, 117, 138, 229, 896
"Huai sha" (Embracing Sands), 228
"Huai-shu chuang" (Huai-shu Village; Hu K'o), 866
Huan, Duke of Ch'i, 97, 139
Huan, Emperor, 182, 625
Huan Fu, 461
Huan-hsi yüan-chia (Antagonists in Love; anthology), 610
"Huan-hun chi" (The Return of the Soul; T'ang Hsien-tsu). *See* Mu-tan t'ing
huan ku to t'ai (exchanging the bones, snatching the embryo), 354
huan-lei (repay a debt of tears), 653
"Huan-men tzu-ti ts'o li-shen" (The Scion of an Official Family Opts for the Wrong Career), 819
"Huan-sha chi" (Washing Silk; Liang Ch'en-yü), 823, 828–29
"Huan shan-chai" (Returning to My Mountain Studio; Yang Shih-tao), 284
Huan Shao-chün, 525
Huan-ying (Illusions), 611
Huan-yüan chih (Accounts of Requiting Vengeance; Yen Chih-t'ui). See Yüan-hun chih
Huang Ch'ao, 183, 312, 313, 982
Huang-chiang tiao-sou, 721
Huang Chieh, 443
Huang Ching-jen, 437
Huang Chou-hsing, 943
Huang Ch'un-ming, 753
"Huang-chung sha/wei" (Yellow Bell, Coda; Kuan Han-ch'ing), 212
Huang-fu Fang, 406
Huang-fu Mei, 589
Huang-fu Mi, 580
Huang Ho-sheng, 457, 461
Huang Hsiang, 463
Huang Hsing-tseng, 406
"Huang-hun" (Twilight; Wu Tsu-hsiang), 751
Huang Jen (Huang Mo-hsi; Man), 704, 712–15
Huang-jen shou-chi (Notes of a Desolate Man; Chu T'ien-wen), 779
Huang Kung-wang, 487, 489
Huang-Lao tradition, 175. *See also* Huang-ti; Taoism
"Huang-liang meng" (Yellow Millet Dream), 810
Huang Ming shih-hsüan, 413
Huang Mo-hsi. *see* Huang Jen
Huang-ni chieh (The Muddy Street; Ts'an Hsüeh), 764
Huang O, 210, 406

"Huang Shih-ch'iang chuan" (Account of Huang Shih-ch'iang; *P'u-hsien p'u-sa shuo cheng-ming ching*), 970, 971
Huang Shih-hui, 458
Huang Ssu-ch'eng, 457
Huang Ti (Yellow Emperor; great god Yellow), 60, 65, 66, 68, 175, 431, 507
Huang T'ing-chien, 230, 327, 351, 353–55, 356, 363, 479, 558, 892; as model, 357, 364, 365, 440, 1072
Huang-t'ing ching (Yellow Court Scripture), 181
Huang Tso-lin, 856, 857
Huang Tsun-hsien, 440–41, 442, 454, 894, 1072
Huang Tsung-hsi, 418, 419
Huang T'u-pi, 834
Huang t'u-ti (Yellow Earth; film), 50
Huang Yüan-chi, 190
Huang Yung-sha, 1036
Hugo, Victor, 720
Hui, king of Liang, 506
Hui-chan, 524
"Hui-chia yi-hou" (Homecoming; Ou-yang Yü-ch'ien), 853, 854, 867
Hui-chiao, 164–65, 523
hui-hen (laments), 1068
hui-hsiang (transferred; Sanskrit: *pariṇāmanā*), 967
"Hui-lan chi" (The Chalk Circle; Li Hsing-tao), 809
Hui-neng, 169, 295
Hui (Muslim) people, 31, 34. *See also* Islam
Hui-sheng, 165
Hui-t'ou k'an (A Retrospect), 718
Hui-tsung, Emperor, 178–79, 339, 357, 481, 482, 627, 628, 808
"Hui-t'u *Lieh-nü chuan*" (Illustrations of the *Biographies of Illustrious Women*), 198
Hui-yüan, 11, 163, 169
humor, 132–48; collections of, 135–38; in essays, 570; in *Flowers in the Mirror*, 656; in historical writing, 502; in *hua-pen*, 146–47, 596, 606–8, 610, 611, 613, 616, 617; in *Journey to the West*, 145, 147, 634, 636, 637; and poetry, 132, 133, 134, 145, 148; in *The Prayer Mat of Flesh*, 665; in twentieth-century fiction, 741, 749, 750; and women, 212, 213
hun-miao chih ching (undifferentiated marvelous), 425
hun-sang yi-shih ko (lamentations on marriage and at funerals), 994
"Hun-t'ien fu" (The Enveloping Sky; Yang Chiang), 290
Hun-tun (chaos), 918
Hun-yüan Lao Tzu, 184
Hun-yüan sheng-chi (A Chronicle of the Sage from the Primordiality of Chaos; Hsieh Shou-hao), 183
Hundred Days' Reform (1898), 441, 450, 698, 706, 717, 734, 1059, 1060
The Hundred Thousand Songs: Selections from Milarepa, Poet-Saint of Tibet (trans. Gordon), 1046
Hundred Years of Solitude (Marquez), 765
Hung-chih, Emperor, 403, 404
"Hung fan" (Glorious Plan; in *Shang shu*), 65
"Hung-fu chi" (Red Duster; Chang Feng-yi), 829
"Hung-hsien" (Hung-hsien; Yüan Chiao), 589
"Hung hsien t'an" (The Red Embroidered Carpet; Po Chü-yi), 963
Hung Hsiu-ch'üan, 843, 1058
Hung kao-liang chia-tsu (Red Sorghum Clan; Mo Yen), 756–57, 765
Hung Liang-chi, 246, 437
Hung-lou meng (A Dream of Red Towers, or The Story of the Stone; Ts'ao Hsüeh-ch'in), 12, 69, 200, 215, 435, 647–55, 657, 659, 672, 693, 707, 709, 716, 723, 735, 742, 832, 915, 1034, 1056; commentary on, 943; Korean translation of, 1077, 1078; as model for Korean novel, 1076; and proverbs, 155; regional versions of, 1016, 1030; supernatural in, 127
"Hung-lou meng hsin-cheng" (New Textual Research on *The Dream of the Red Chamber*; Chou Ju-ch'ang), 652
"*Hung-lou meng* p'ing-lun" (A Critique of *A Dream of Red Towers*; Wang Kuo-wei), 711, 939
"Hung-lou meng te liang-ke shih-chieh" (The Two Worlds of *Hung-lou meng*; Yü Ying-shih), 650
Hung Mai, 122, 476, 557, 564, 676–77, 681, 685
Hung-ming chi (Collection on Propagating and Illuminating Buddhism; Seng-yu), 165, 166
Hung P'ien, 597, 598–99
"Hung-se feng-pao" (The Red Storm), 870, 871
"Hung-se niang-tzu chün" (The Red Detachment of Women; model ballet), 868
Hung Shen, 851, 856, 857, 860, 872
Hung Sheng, 126, 825, 834, 836
"Hung-teng chi" (The Red Lantern; model play), 866, 871
Hung-tu chi (Hung-tu Collection, Brocade River Collection; Hsüeh T'ao), 208
Hung-wen kuan (Hsiu-wen kuan; College for the Enhancement of Literature), 283, 290, 292
Hung-wu, Emperor, 800, 801, 816
Hung Ying, 767
Huntington, Rania, 110–31
"Huo Hsiao-yü chuan" (An Account of Huo Hsiao-yü; Chiang Fang), 585, 593, 827
"Huo-hu chih yeh" (The Night a Tiger Was Captured; T'ien Han), 852

huo-lang-erh (peddler's narratives), 995
Huo Shih-hsiu, 12
Huo-tung pien-jen-hsing (Moveable Parts; Wang Meng), 762
huo yüeh (someone says or might say), 904
Huxley, Thomas, 706, 719, 1062
"Hwangcho ga" (Song of the Yellow Bird; King Ryuri), 1067
Hxak Hmub (Ancient Songs of the Miao), 1035
hyangga (Korean song type), 1068, 1069

Ibsen, Henrik, 845, 852, 853, 857, 860, 861
Ichikawa Kansai, 1091
Idema, Wilt L., 785–847
Ikkyū Sōjun, 1088
Imagists, 3, 700
immortality, 115–16, 139, 166, 177, 258, 602–3; in *Journey to the West*, 633, 635, 637; in Ming-Ch'ing novels, 656, 665, 666; quest for, 118, 546, 665, 666; roaming into, 118, 254, 261, 264–65, 268; and Taoism, 113, 117, 118
Imperial Edict (1903), 713
imun (scribal prose), 1073
India, 70, 71, 167, 474, 588, 704, 794, 1082; Buddhism from, 160, 161; influences from, 11, 13, 114, 168, 172, 632; languages in, 22, 23, 25–26, 29, 30, 31, 48; travel to, 165, 556
Indo-European languages, 22, 23, 26, 39
Injustice to Tou O (Tou O yüan): A Study and Translation (Chung-wen Shih), 889. *See also* "Kan t'ien tung ti"
Inoue Hisashi, 1094
An Inquiry into the Nature and Causes of the Wealth of Nations (Adam Smith), 1063
inscriptions, 4, 539, 1070, 1071; epitaph, 528; on paintings (*t'i-hua wen-hsüeh*), 466, 467–90; and poetry, 467, 474–77, 481, 482, 485, 487, 489. *See also* bronze inscriptions; oracle bones
International Women's Day, 860
internationalism, 1066
Internet, 55–56, 57
Iran, 69, 160
Iriya Yoshitaka, 12
Ise monogatari (Tales of Ise), 1086
Ishikawa Jōzan, 1089
Islam, 9, 1048. *See also* Hui (Muslim) people
Isonokami no Otomaro, 1081
Itō Hirobumi, 851
Itō Tōgai, 1089–90, 1092
Iz (Traces of the Explorer; Abdurrehim Utkur), 1049
Izumi Kyōka, 1094

Jacob, Max, 457
Jade Emperor, 994
James, Henry, 717
Jao Tsung-yi, 12
Japan, 136, 583, 707, 722, 772; Asuka period in, 1079; Buddhism in, 163, 164, 1017, 1079, 1080, 1087; Chinese influence in, 706, 710–11, 1079, 1080; Chinese relations with, 851, 1080; Chinese visitors to, 704, 734, 745, 1060; in fiction, 721, 733, 735, 752; Heian period in, 309, 1082, 1085, 1087; influence of, 45–46, 455, 725; Kamakura period in, 1087, 1088; and Korea, 1052; literature of, 459, 699, 700, 717, 1079–95; in Manchuria, 335; and May Fourth movement, 156; Meiji Restoration in, 441, 706, 733, 850, 1060, 1094; Momoyama period in, 1087; Muromachi period in, 1087, 1088; Nara period in, 1081, 1088; poetry of, 1090; scholars in, 490, 1079, 1093; Taika reforms in, 1080; and Taiwan, 458, 775–76, 778, 779, 780; theater in, 849, 1089; Tokugawa period in, 1087–90, 1092, 1093; War of Resistance against, 456, 568, 573, 752, 846, 848, 849, 855, 857, 858, 863–64, 871, 874, 1012; Warring States period in, 1087
Japanese language, 34, 44, 49, 1000, 1060, 1061
Jaspers, Karl, 70
jātaka (birth stories), 161, 171, 473–74, 971
Jen a jen (Man, ah Man, Stones of the Wall; Tai Houying), 761
Jen An, 7
Jen-chien shih (The Human World; Lin Yü-t'ang), 567
Jen-chien tz'u-hua (Remarks on Lyric Poetry from the Human World; Wang Kuo-wei), 442, 939
Jen-chung hua (Portraits of Society; Ai-na chü-shih), 615
Jen Fang, 241, 270
Jen-jen wen-hsüeh (Everyman's Literature; journal), 457
"Jen-shih chuan" (The Story of Miss Jen; Shen Chi-chi), 122, 146, 584, 1086
jen te wen-hsüeh (humanized literature), 852
Jen-tsung, Emperor, 344, 481
Jenks, Edward, 1063
Jesuits, 23, 31, 57, 803, 1055, 1056, 1058
Jevons, William S., 1063
jih-chi (diaries), 555–59, 705, 727, 744, 751
"Jih-ch'u" (Sunrise; Ts'ao Yü), 862
Jih-pen shu-mu chih (Records of Japanese Book Catalogs; K'ang Yu-wei), 718
"Jih yü" (Parable of the Sun; Su Shih), 539
Jñānagupta, 172
jo (prefatory ornamental phrases), 1082
Joan Haste (Haggard), 709
jōruri puppet plays, 786, 791, 1093, 1094
Jou p'u-t'uan (The Prayer Mat of Flesh; Li Yü), 147, 168, 640, 664–65

Journey to the West. See *Hsi-yu chi*
journeys: spirit, 124; as theme, 633, 637; tradition of, 118; in travel literature, 555
Joyce, James, 777
ju (Confucian scholars), 3, 4, 643
ju Ch'an (enter Ch'an), 424, 425
ju-chiang (Confucian general), 624
ju-hua (entering words, prolog story), 591
Ju-lin wai-shih (The Scholars; Wu Ching-tzu), 215, 388, 643–47, 657, 659, 709, 915, 948, 949; humor in, 147; and proverbs, 155; supernatural in, 127; and vernacular stories, 612, 615, 617
ju shen (enter spirit), 424, 425
Ju-shih (Liu Shih), 332, 333, 413, 415, 416, 448
ju-shih (Confucian scholars), 3
"Ju-shih kuan" (The Way It Should Have Been; Chang Ta-fu), 834
Ju Shu chi (Record of a Trip to Shu; Lu Yu), 557–58
"Ju Shu ch'iu-yeh su chiang-chu" (Passing an Autumn Night on a River Islet on the Way to Shu), 284
Ju-yi chün chuan (The Story of the Ideal Lover), 639
Juan Chi, 242, 258, 259, 265, 273, 298, 554, 581, 838
Juan Ta-ch'eng, 830, 831, 833, 838
Juan-t'ing shih-yü (Juan-t'ing's Lyrics; anthology), 426
Juan Yü, 253, 254, 258
Juan Yüan, 246, 913
Judaism, 4, 9
Judge Pao (Pao Cheng), 8, 142, 145, 743, 808–9, 819, 999, 1001, 1002
Jui T'ing-chang, 280
Jui-tsung, 291
Juism. *See* Confucianism
Jung-ch'un chi (Vignettes of Temperate Spring), 683
Jurchens, 328, 359, 362, 557, 791, 809, 819, 844, 1050; and *Chin P'ing Mei*, 643; and Sinitic, 22; and Sung, 324, 325, 339–40, 834; Taoist canon of, 178; in *Water Margin*, 628. *See also* Chin dynasty (1115–1234)

"K'a-men" (Carmen), 859
kabuki plays, 1091, 1093
"Kai-hsia ko" (Song of Kai-hsia; Hsiang Yü), 249, 273
k'ai-ho pien-kuai (the demonic transformations over which they have natural control), 387
K'ai-ming, Emperor, 518
K'ai-p'i (The Beginning of the World), 69
k'ai p'ien (ballads), 1024
k'ai-shu (regular style) script, 49
K'ai T'ien ch'uan-hsin chi (Records of Accounts of What Really Happened in the K'ai [-yüan] and T'ien[-pao] Eras; Cheng Ch'i), 581
K'ai-yen lu (Record of Cracking Smiles), 139
K'ai-yüan period (T'ang), 178, 292, 303, 424, 581
Kaifūsō (Remembering the Manners of the Past), 1080, 1081
Kajin no kigū (Strange Encounters with the Beauty; trans. Liang Ch'i-ch'ao), 718
Kakinomoto no Hitomaro, 1082
kakumei (Japanese: revolution), 725
Kālidāsa, 172
Kamo Mabuchi, 1093
kan (stimulus), 970
Kan Chazan Academy (Japan), 1091
"Kan-chiu fu" (Remembering Old Times; Ts'en Shen), 300
"Kan ch'üan fu" (Sweet Springs Rhapsody; Yang Hsiung), 233
Kan-hsiao liu chi (Six Chapters from a Cadre School; Yang Chiang), 761
kan-jan-li (contagious emotional power), 712
"Kan liu-wang" (Moved by the Refugees; Wang Yü-ch'eng), 342
Kan Pao, 120, 543, 548, 551–53, 554, 563, 580, 970
kan-shih (being moved by the times), 421
Kan-shui hsien-yüan lu (A Record of the Transcendent Wellsprings at Kan-shui; comp. Li Tao-ch'ien), 185
"Kan t'ien tung ti: Tou Ŏ yüan tsa-chü" (Moving Heaven and Earth: Injustice to Tou Ŏ; Kuan Han-ch'ing), 125, 811, 812, 813, 837, 858
kan-ying (stimulus-response), 83, 111, 112, 117
"Kan-yü" (Empathetic Experiences; Ch'en Tzu-ang), 291, 298
k'an (comparison), 8
"K'an hung lu" (Gazing at Rainbows; Shen Ts'ung-wen), 751
"K'an p'i-hsüeh tan cheng Erh-lang shen" (The Boot That Reveals the Culprit), 598
Kanaoka Shōkō, 12
Kang Wi, 1072
K'ang, king of Sung, 581
k'ang-chan pa-ku (War of Resistance Eight-legged Essay), 573
K'ang Chin-chih, 808
K'ang Hai, 381, 399, 404–7, 818
K'ang-hsi dictionary, 47
K'ang-hsi emperor, 421, 424, 434, 446, 447, 833, 834, 1046
k'ang-k'ai (strength in adversity), 256
"K'ang-nai-hsin chü-lo-pu" (Club of Carnations; Hung Ying), 767
K'ang Pai-ch'ing, 454
K'ang Seng-hui, 163, 171
K'ang Yu-wei, 8, 93, 441, 442, 707, 718; and Hundred Days' Reform, 450, 1059, 1060
Kanke bunsō (Jottings from the Sugawara Family), 1084

kanshi (Chinese poetry; Japan), 1080, 1085, 1086, 1089, 1091
Kant, Immanuel, 442, 711–12
Kao Chan-hsiang, 770
Kao Ch'i, 395–98, 399, 434
Kao Chung-wu, 280
Kao Hsing-chien (Gao Xingjian), 57, 738, 759, 764, 772, 876
Kao Lien, 829
Kao Ming, 801, 805, 820–21
Kao O, 648, 915
Kao-pieh ko-ming (A Farewell to Revolution; Li Tse-hou and Liu Tsai-fu), 771
Kao Ping, 275, 281, 387, 395, 401, 404
Kao-seng chuan (Lives of Eminent Monks; Hui-chiao), 164–65, 523
Kao-shan hsia te hua-huan (The Wreath at the Foot of the Mountain; Li Ts'un-pao), 754
Kao Shih, 295, 296
Kao-shih chuan (Traditions of Lofty-Minded Scholars; Huang-fu Mi), 580
Kao Shih shih-chi (The Collected Works of Kao Shih), 982
"Kao-t'ang fu" (Rhapsody on Mount Kao-t'ang; Sung Yü), 118, 200
Kao-tsu, Emperor (Liu Pang), 249, 282, 284, 376, 504, 515–16, 519–20, 806, 986
Kao-tsung, Emperor, 178, 285, 339, 357, 360, 628
Kao Wen-hsiu, 808
Kao-yang pu-ts'ai-tzu, 722
k'ao-cheng-hsüeh (evidential learning), 57, 670. *See also* Han-hsüeh (Han Learning) school
"K'ao-yi" (Investigations into Differences; Ssu-ma Kuang), 510
Karakhoto, 996, 1008
Karlgren, Bernhard, 59–60, 91, 93, 95
karma, 168, 169, 171, 632, 691; in *hua-pen*, 597, 599, 617, 618; in novels, 641, 643, 651, 660, 661, 662
Kāśyapa Mātaṇga, 523
"Katuri jetere juben i bithe" (The Crab Story), 1030–31
Kawaguchi Hisao, 12
Keats, John, 300
Keikokushū (Anthology for Governing the Nation), 1083
Keiter, Heinrich, 716
Keller, Tony, 716
Ken-shih (Eternal History; comp. P'an Chih-heng), 690
Keng-chi pien. See *Keng-ssu pien*
Keng-ssu pien (A Decade's Jottings; Lu Ts'an), 677
"Keng-tzu kuo-pien t'an-tz'u" (Strummed Ballad on the Disturbances of the Year Keng-tzu; Li Pao-chia), 1012
Khitan people (Liao dynasty), 22, 142, 339, 371, 557, 627, 628, 807–8
Khubilai Khan, 178, 340, 367, 394, 1049, 1050
Khuong Cong Phu, 1096
Ki Pu-sik, 1069
Kiangsi school of poetry, 356–63, 365–67
kikajin (naturalized persons), 1079
Kim Ch'ang-hyŏp, 1071
Kim Chong-jik, 1071
Kim Man-jung, 1075
Kim Pu-sik, 1069
Kim Si-sŭp, 1074
Kim T'aek-yŏng, 1072
Kim Van Kieu (The Tale of Kieu; Nguyen Du), 1101–2
Kingston, Maxine Hong, 55
Kirchmann, J. H. von, 712
Kleeman, Terry, 10
Knechtges, David, 231
knights errant (*wu-hsia*), 657–58, 743, 763, 766, 1103
ko (framework), 397
ko, ke. *See* songs
ko-ch'ang k'u-ch'i (perform lamentations), 1006
Ko Ch'ao-fu, 176
"Ko-che Yeh Chi" (Record of the Singer Yeh; Shen Yachih), 591
ko-chü (folk opera, song-drama, national drama), 856, 864–65
ko-ch'ü (song-pieces), 954
Ko Fei, 765
ko-hsü (song festivals), 1036
Ko Hsüan, 176–77, 182
Ko Hung, 117, 176, 508, 522–23, 580
Ko-lien hua-ying (Flower Shadows Behind the Curtain), 662
"Ko Ling-kung sheng yi nung chu-erh" (General Ko; Feng Meng-lung), 600
ko-ming (revolution), 725, 1056
ko-t'i chieh shan (he excelled at all the forms), 419
ko-tiao (mode; formal style), 334, 431, 434
ko-tz'u (anonymous song texts), 954
ko-wu-chü (song and dance plays), 143, 790
Ko Yang, 770
ko-yen (maxims), 150, 151
ko-yi (matching terms), 160
K'o-ch'in, 169
K'o-ching (goddess), 216
K'o Chiu-ssu, 388
k'o-chü (civil-service examinations), 50
k'o-hsüeh hsiao-shuo (science fiction), 718, 719, 721, 722, 726
Kōbō Daishi. *See* Kūkai
Kogidō Academy, 1092
Kohn, Livia, 10
koine (demotic standard), 20, 25, 32
Kojiki (Record of Ancient Events), 1080
Kojō Tandō, 711
Kokin (waka) shū (Collection of Songs from the Past and the Present; comp. Ki no Tsurayuki), 1085
Kōkosha (Rivers and Lakes) Society, 1091
komun chi hak (learning of archaic prose), 1070
Korea, 733, 866, 1059, 1067–78; Buddhism in, 162, 1017, 1070; Chosŏn period in, 1070–72, 1075; Confucianism in, 1067,

1070, 1072–74; drumsong tradition of, 1030, 1076; eighteenth-century poets of, 1072; *Hsing-shih yen* discovered in, 610; Koguryo period in, 1051–52, 1067, 1068; Koryŏ period in, 1068, 1069; literati culture in, 490; Mongol occupation of, 1069; Paekche period in, 1067–69, 1079; people of, 1051–52; script of, 49; shamanic traditions of, 1030, 1051; Silla period in, 1067, 1068, 1071, 1079; Taoism in, 1070; vernacular Chinese in, 823, 1075, 1076; *yangban* aristocracy in, 1070, 1071, 1074–77; Yi dynasty of, 1051
Korean War, 866, 874
Koslov, Petr Kuzmitch, 797
kotodama (efficacious power of language in religious ritual), 1081–82
Kou-chien, king of Yüeh, 828, 829
"Kou-erh Yeh nieh-p'an" (The Nirvana of Grandpa Doggy; Chin Yün), 869, 876
kou-lan (entertainment complexes), 1007–8
K'ou Chun, 344
k'ou yi (oral meaning) commentaries, 890
k'ou-yü (spoken language), 25. *See also under* language
Kroll, Paul, 10, 274–313
"Ku-an man pi" (Ku-an's Literary Notes; Yü Ming-chen), 710
Ku-chang chüeh-ch'en (Clapping Your Hands to Get Rid of Worldly Dust), 610
Ku Chen-kuan, 417
Ku Ch'eng (Gu Cheng), 462
ku-chi (*hua-chi*; humor), 134–35
Ku Chieh-kang, 68
Ku-chin chu (Commentaries on Antiquity and Today; Ts'ui Pao), 563
Ku-chin hsiao-shuo (Stories Old and New; Feng Meng-lung), 597, 598, 600
Ku-chin shih-jen hsiu-chü (Outstanding Lines from Poets Ancient and Modern; comp. Yüan Ching), 287
Ku-chin shuo-hai (The Ocean of Stories, Past and Present; comp. Lu Chi), 687
Ku-chin t'an-kai (Talks Old and New; comp. Feng Menglung), 136, 139, 688
Ku-chin yen (Ancient and Contemporary Proverbs; Chou Shou-chung), 153
Ku chin yüeh lu (Record of Ancient and Modern Music; Chih Chiang), 958
"Ku-ching chi" (Record of an Ancient Mirror; Wang Tu), 285, 582
"Ku feng" (Old Style Poems; Li Po), 124, 298
ku-feng (old style) poetry, 1097
"Ku-hsiang" (My Old Home; Lu Hsün), 744, 752
Ku hsiao-shuo kou-ch'en (anthology of old fiction; comp. Lu Hsün), 745
Ku Hua, 761
Ku K'ai-chih, 198, 471, 473, 477
Ku K'uang, 583
Ku-liang chuan (Ku-liang Commentary on *Ch'un-ch'iu*), 88, 93, 910, 911
Ku-liang Hsi, 93
Ku Lin, 404, 405, 406
Ku Lou Kuan tzu-yün yen-ch'ing chi (Anthology from the Abundant Felicity of Purple Clouds at the Ancient Tiered Abbey; Chu Hsiang-hsien), 184
ku-pen (old edition), 941
Ku-sheng (Leftover Tablets; Niu Hsiu), 690–91
ku-shih (ancient-style verse). See *ku-t'i shih*
ku-shih (fictional story), 68
ku-shih (precedents), 327
Ku-shih hsüan (Anthology of Ancient-Style Verse; Wang Shih-chen), 425
Ku-shih kuei (Homecoming to Ancient Verse; anthology), 412
Ku-shih pien (Critiques of Ancient History), 68
"Ku-shih shih-chiu shou" (Nineteen Old Poems), 250–51, 254, 927, 959
Ku-shih wen-fang hsiao-shuo (Tales from Mr. Ku's Library; comp. Ku Yü-ch'ing), 687
Ku-shih yüan (Source of Old Poetry; comp. Shen Te-ch'ien), 431
Ku-shu yi-jen (The Drumsingers; Lao She), 1034
Ku Ssu-li, 383, 385, 387, 388
Ku T'ai-ch'ing (Ku Ch'un), 211, 452
ku-tan hsien-yüan (antique-and-placid and serene-and-distant), 425
ku-t'i shih (ancient-style poetry), 250, 251, 263, 412, 416, 425, 979, 1068, 1071, 1101; and ballad verse, 277; Han-Wei, 404, 440; language of, 106–7; of ninth century, 303–5, 312; Sung, 342, 345, 346, 350, 352, 353; T'ang, 276, 288, 296, 298–301; Yüan, 394
Ku T'ing-lin shih-chi (Ku Yen-wu), 419
Ku tsa-chü (Ancient *Tsa-chü*; comp. Wang Chi-te), 841
Ku Tzu-ching, 816
ku-tzu-tz'u (drum lyrics), 796, 990, 991, 1008, 1028. See also *tz'u*
ku-tz'u (drumsongs), 990, 991, 1009, 1012, 1014, 1018, 1028–31
Ku-wen chen-pao (Reliable Treasures of Archaic Prose), 1073
ku-wen shih pi (ten flaws in ancient prose style), 890
ku-wen-tz'u (ancient-style prose; Japanese: *kobunji*), 236, 397, 530–33, 536–38, 594, 706, 890, 931, 1064, 1090; in essays, 499; and fiction, 531, 537; and Korean writers, 1069, 1073; and *pi-chi*, 561; Sung, 537; T'ang-Sung, 243–46, 301, 304, 580, 593
Ku Yen-wu, 418, 419, 890

Ku Ying, 388
Ku Yü-ch'ing, 687
k'u-chia ko (wedding lamentation), 992, 999, 1000, 1004–5
"K'u hsiang p'ien" ("Yü-chang Ballad;" Bitter Fate; Fu Hsüan), 199, 204, 260, 959
"K'u je hsing" (Suffering from Heat; Ts'ao Chih), 269
K'u Ling, 462
"Kua-fu she-chi chui hsin-lang, chung mei ch'i-hsin to ts'ai-tzu" (A Widow Hatches a Plot to Receive a Bridegroom; Li Yü), 614
kua-tz'u (hexagram statement), 88
k'ua-shih (hyperbole), 893
kuai (freaks of nature), 547
"K'uai-huo ko" (Song of Joy; Pai Yü-ch'an), 190
"K'uai-tsui Li Ts'ui-lien chi" (The Shrew: Sharp-Tongued Li Ts'ui-lien; Hung P'ien), 146–47, 598, 988, 992, 1003–4, 1011
K'uai-yüan (Garden of Cunning; Ch'ien Hsi-yen), 678
kuan (looking at; viewing), 475, 480
Kuan-ch'ang hsien-hsing chi (Exposure of the World of Officials; Li Pao-chia), 647, 721–22, 724, 740
Kuan Chieh-ming (John Kwan Terry), 461
Kuan-ch'ui pien (Pipe-Awl Chapters, or Limited Views: Essays on Ideas and Letters; Ch'ien Chung-shu), 939
Kuan Chung, 198, 515, 517
Kuan Han-ch'ing, 125, 145, 212–13, 218, 373, 377, 381, 801; plays of, 807, 811, 812, 821, 858
"Kuan Han-ch'ing" (T'ien Han), 813, 858
Kuan-hsiu, 170, 312–13
kuan-hua (officials' language; Mandarin), 33, 156, 1024. *See also* Mandarin, Modern Standard; Sinitic
"Kuan-kuan te pu-p'in" (Little Lord Kuan-kuan's Tonic; Wu Tsu-hsiang), 752
Kuan Kung. *See* Kuan Yü
Kuan Kung (Kuan Yü), 137
"Kuan Li Ku ch'ing ssu-ma ti shan-shui t'u san shou" (Three Poems upon Viewing a Landscape Painted by the Adjutant at the Request of His Brother Li Ku; Tu Fu), 477
Kuan So, 998–99
Kuan Ta-ju, 715–16
Kuan Tao-sheng, 836
Kuan Te-tung, 1030
Kuan Ti (Emperor Kuan). *See* Kuan Yü
Kuan-ting, 170
Kuan Tzu, 60, 76
Kuan wu-liang-shou Fo ching (Sūtra of Contemplation on the Buddha of Infinite Life), 163
Kuan-yin (Avalokiteśvara), 164, 171, 524, 597, 994; in *Journey to the West*, 129, 633, 636
Kuan Yü (Emperor Kuan; Kuan Kung; Kuan Ti), 508, 621–25, 788, 806, 807, 813, 817, 994, 997
"Kuan-yüan sou wan feng hsien-nü" (The Old Gardener; Hsi Lang-hsien), 602
Kuan Yün-shih (Sewinch Qaya), 373, 379, 380, 387
Kuang hsiao-fu (Expanded Treasury of Laughs; Feng Meng-lung), 136
Kuang-hsü emperor, 441, 734
Kuang-hsüeh hui (Society to Promote Education), 718
Kuang hung-ming chi (Expanded Collection on Propagating and Illuminating Buddhism; Tao-hsüan), 166
Kuang-shih-yin ying-yen chi (Accounts of Miracles by Avalokiteśvara; Fu Liang), 164, 171
Kuang-tsung, Emperor, 183
kuang wu tzu (Expanded Five Masters), 408
Kuang Yen-yi pien (Tales of Glamor and Wonder, Amplified; ed. Wu Ta-chen), 687
Kuang-yü she (Brilliant Abundance Society), 1024
K'uang Chou-yi, 211, 451
"K'uang-jen jih-chi" (Diary of a Madman; Lu Hsün), 730, 735, 744
"K'uang t'ai-shou tuan ssu hai-erh" (Prefect K'uang's Solution of the Case of the Dead Infant), 604
kuei (supplementary), 383
Kuei-ch'e chih (Record of a Carriage Full of Ghosts; Kuo T'uan), 676
"Kuei-ch'ü-lai tz'u" (Let's Return!; T'ao Ch'ien), 267, 354
Kuei Chuang, 418
kuei-ssu (longing of ladies in boudoirs), 427
"Kuei-t'ien fu" (Rhapsody on Returning to the Fields; Chang Heng), 233
Kuei t'ien lu (Notes on Returning to the Farm; Ou-yang Hsiu), 539
kuei-ts'ai (spectral talent), 124
Kuei-tung (A Treasury of Ghost Stories), 676
Kuei Yu-kuang, 7, 418, 1072
"Kuei yüan t'ien chü" (Returning to Live in Garden and Field; T'ao Ch'ien), 267
k'uei (one-legged dragon), 108, 354
Kūkai (Kōbō Daishi), 286, 287, 894, 930, 1084
Ku'magŏm (A Sword to Chase Off Devils; Yi Hae-jo), 1077
Kumārajīva, 163, 171
Kŭmo sinhwa (New Stories of the Golden Turtle; comp. Kim Si-sŭp), 1074
Kun (mythical figure), 65, 66
k'un-ch'ü opera, 715, 823, 828, 829, 830, 843, 845, 1023
"K'un-lun nu" (The K'un-lun Slave; P'ei Hsing), 589, 593
K'un-P'eng, 547
Kung, Prince, 90, 1059

kung-an (Japanese: *kōan*; Zen puzzles), 169
kung-an (law suits), 596
kung-an hsiao-shuo (detective stories), 718, 719, 722–25, 729, 741, 743
Kung-an school, 384, 385, 409, 411, 412, 414, 419, 422, 678
kung-ch'ou (vengeance for the common good), 623
kung-fu (martial arts), 767
Kung K'uei, 386
Kung-kung (mythical figure), 61, 64
kung-ming fu-kuei (success, fame, wealth, exalted position), 644
kung-sheng (senior licentiate) degree, 600, 605
Kung Sheng-yü, 628
kung-t'i shih (Palace-Style Poetry), 200–203, 207–8, 219, 241, 262, 271, 272, 283, 284, 290, 315, 926
kung-tiao (modes), 1008
Kung T'ien-t'ing, 815
Kung Ting-tzu, 415, 447
Kung Tzu-chen, 439–40, 449
"Kung wu ch'u men" (Don't Go Out the Gate; Li Ho), 124
Kung-yang chuan (Kung-yang Commentary), 88, 93, 910, 911
Kung-yang Kao, 93
Kung-yang Shou, 93
"Kung-yen shih" (Lord's Feast; Liu Chen), 255, 256
Kung Yi-cheng, 153
k'ung (afraid), 893
K'ung An-kuo, 90
K'ung An-kuo Shang-shu (K'ung An-kuo's Classic of Documents), 90, 913
"K'ung-ch'üeh tung-nan fei" (A Peacock Southeast Flew), 986
K'ung Jung, 253, 254
K'ung San-chuan (Erudite K'ung), 797
K'ung Shang-jen, 708, 825, 833, 834, 996
K'ung T'ien-yün, 426
K'ung Tzu. *See* Confucius
K'ung Tzu chia-yü (School Sayings of Confucius), 94
K'ung Ying-ta, 87, 283, 891, 913, 914
Kuo Ch'iu-sheng, 458
kuo-fang hsi-chü (defense drama), 857, 862, 863–64
"Kuo-feng." See under *Shih-ching*
Kuo Hsiang, 173
Kuo Hsieh, 506–7
Kuo-hsüeh fu-lun she (Society for Preservation of National Learning), 712, 713
Kuo Jo-hsü, 480
Kuo-li Pei-ching yi-shu chuan-men hsüeh-hsiao (Peking School of Arts), 856
Kuo Liang-hui, 780
Kuo Lu-sheng (Shih Chih), 462
Kuo Mao-ch'ien, 255, 281, 954, 956–58, 960
Kuo Mo-jo, 455, 458, 746–47, 854–55, 864, 876, 1023
Kuo P'u, 29, 68, 118, 260, 261, 264, 265
Kuo-se t'ien-hsiang (Outstanding Beauties, Heavenly Scents), 684
Kuo shih (State History), 175
Kuo-tien manuscripts, 92, 98, 99, 101, 109, 174
kuo-ts'ui (national essence), 706
Kuo T'uan, 676
kuo-tzu-chien (instructor at imperial university), 353
kuo-tzu hsüeh (School for the Scions of State), 4
Kuo-wen pao (National News; newspaper), 706
Kuo-yü (Discourses of the States), 60, 61, 64, 89, 95, 153, 159, 500, 501, 895
kuo-yü (national language; Mandarin), 33, 156, 1066. *See also* Mandarin, Modern Standard; Sinitic
Kuomintang (KMT; Nationalist Party), 35, 157, 459, 462, 753, 758, 859, 863, 874; and literature, 568, 570; and Taiwanese literature, 775–78, 780; and theater, 846, 872–73
Kutadgu Bilig (The Wisdom That Leads to Regal Glory; collection of Uyghur poetry; Yusup Khass Hajib), 1048
Kuun gi (A Record of Nine Clouds), 1076
Kuun mong (Dream of Nine Clouds; Kim Man-jung), 1075, 1076
kwamun (examination prose: Korea), 1072
Kwanghanru gi (Tale of the Kwanghan Pavilion), 1076
Kwansan yungma (Caparisoned Horses at the Mountain Pass), 1071
Kyewŏn p'ilgyŏngjip (Collection of Jottings from the Cassia Garden; Ch'oe Ch'i-wŏn), 1068
Kyōunshū (Crazy Cloud Collection; Ikkyū Sōjun), 1088
Kyujanggak Academy (Korea), 1073

"Lady Windermere's Fan" (Wilde), 856
Lagerwey, John, 10
Lai Ho, 459, 776
Lai-nan lu (Register of Coming South; Li Ao), 556
lai-p'i (roguish), 767
lamentations, 992, 994, 1000, 1004–6
Lan-hsin hsi-yüan (Lyceum Theater), 849, 850
Lan-hu she (Orchid Lake Society), 415
Lan Hung-en, 1036
Lan-ling hsiao-hsiao sheng (The Laughing Scholar of Lan-ling), 638
Lan-p'ei lu (Register of Grasping the Carriage Reins; Fan Ch'eng-ta), 557
"Lan yün wo" (Lazy Cloud Grotto; Ah-li Hsi-ying), 380
land reform movement, 866, 869

language, 19–57; of ancient poetry, 106–7; Arabic, 1013; and bronze inscriptions, 46, 47; and Buddhism, 23, 40–41, 45, 56–57, 918; Chuang, 1036; Circassian, 28; colloquial, 372, 887; English, 55, 714; in Han dynasty, 22, 41, 887, 1062; and humor, 133, 134, 148; in India, 23, 25–26, 29–31, 48; Japanese, 34, 44, 49, 459, 460, 1000, 1060, 1061, 1090, 1094; Korean, 1052; literary function of, 917, 933; Manchu, 435, 1030, 1051; Miao-yao, 1035; Min, 35, 39; neologisms in, 1056–58; Old Turkish, 1048; and reality, 133; Sanskrit, 1046, 1047, 1055, 1084; Sogdian, 1048; spoken, 19–20, 25, 29, 30, 533; "Ta Chuan" on, 82; Tai-Kadai, 1035, 1036; Tai Lüe, 1043; in Taiwan, 31, 33, 35, 53, 56, 458–59; and Taoism, 78; Tibetan, 1044; Tibeto-Burman, 1035, 1037, 1041, 1042; Tungusic, 1051; Turkic branch of Altaic, 1048; Uyghur, 1048–49; Vietnamese, 1104. *See also* Literary Sinitic; Mandarin, Modern Standard; Sinitic; vernacular language

language, written, 19–57, 224, 714, 745, 1052; in bronze inscriptions, 36–37, 41, 46, 47, 49, 56, 97, 108, 467, 474, 475, 495, 496; of Egypt, 35; Japanese, 44, 1000; Korean, 49; and literacy, 33, 44; literary, 25, 27, 31, 223; and literati, 4, 34–35, 49, 50–51; and literature, 50–52; and magic arts, 116; of Manchus, 1048, 1051; of Mesopotamia, 35; of minority nationalities, 1033, 1048; of Mongols, 1048, 1051; morphosyllabic nature of, 40–43; Old Uyghur, 1050, 1051; and oral tradition, 50–51; Phags-pa (Mongol), 1050; phonetic, 34–35, 43–44, 47, 48, 53; prestige of, 50–51, 52; regional, 31–35; romanization of, 31, 34, 48, 53–56, 1104; simplified, 43–44, 53–54; and speech, 19–20, 29; and topolects, 25; vernacular, 25, 28, 29–35, 31, 44, 1056, 1057, 1060, 1066, 1096; Vietnamese, 1097–1100, 1103; Warring States period, 37; and the West, 35–36; women's (*nü-shu*), 33, 34, 990, 992, 994, 999–1003, 1006, 1010–11, 1016. *See also* oracle bones

language reform, 31, 156, 159, 453, 745, 1056–57, 1060, 1063, 1065, 1066

Lao-hsüeh-an pi-chi (Notes from the Retreat on Venerable Knowledge; Lu Yu), 563–64

"Lao-jen hsing fu" (The Old Man Star; Yang Chiung), 290

"Lao men-sheng san-shih pao-en" (The Old Protégé; Feng Meng-lung), 601

Lao She (Shu Ch'ing-ch'un), 32, 156, 749–50, 768, 858, 859, 876–77, 1034

Lao Ts'an yu-chi (The Travels of Lao Ts'an; Liu O), 620–21, 624, 657–58, 708, 721, 739–41

Lao Tzu, 77, 129, 151, 173–78, 181–83, 184, 190, 554, 746, 981

Lao Tzu (text). See *Tao te ching*

Lao Tzu ming (Inscription on Lao Tzu; Pien Shao), 183

Laogai: The Chinese Gulag (Harry Wu), 772

Latin literature, 904, 905; classical style in, 882, 884, 885, 903, 907

Lawrence, D. H., 457

Le Thanh Tong, King (Vietnam), 1097, 1098

Leblanc, Maurice, 743

Legalism, 9, 10, 78, 79–80, 82, 87, 138, 175, 892

Legge, James, 512

legitimacy, political, 72, 82, 546, 623, 625, 626

lei (dirges), 235, 239–40

lei chuan (categorized biographies), 513

Lei Feng, 737

"Lei-feng t'a" (Thunderpeak Pagoda; Huang T'u-pi), 126, 835

lei-shu (classified reference works), 714

lei-t'ing (Thunderclap Rites), 189, 191

"Lei-yü" (Thunderstorm; Ts'ao Yü), 860–62

"Lei yü hsing" (Song of the Thunderstorm; Ch'en Yü-yi), 357

letters (*hsin, ch'ih-han, cha,* etc.), 5, 7–8, 235, 238, 705, 727, 886

Levy, Dore J., 916–39

li (harmonious balancing), 891

li (principle), 411, 427, 938

li (strength), 938

Li, Charles N., 22

Li Ang, 773

Li Ao, 556, 893

Li Ch'ao-wei, 122, 584, 832

Li Chen (Ch'ang-ch'i), 680–83

Li-ch'eng (Neighborhood Gazette; Hsü Feng-en), 695

Li-chi (Record of Ritual, Book of Rites), 83, 88, 91, 95, 102, 133, 150, 910, 913; "Ching-chieh" (Exposition of Classical Texts) in, 911; "Ta-hsüeh" (Great Learning) in, 92, 642; "Tzu yi" in, 92, 99, 101, 109

Li Ch'i, 295

Li Chia-jui, 1019

Li Chia-yu, 302

Li Chiao, 292, 982

li-chiao (traditional propriety), 1003, 1064

Li Chiao tsa-yung (Miscellaneous Poems by Li Chiao), 982

Li Ch'iao, 778

Li Chih, 7, 136, 410–11, 412, 665, 687, 915, 1076; commentaries of, 942, 944, 945; libertinism of, 901, 903

Li Chih-ch'ang, 185

"Li-chih fu" (Rhapsody on the Lichee; Chang Chiu-ling), 293–94
Li Chih-jou, 184
Li Chih-kuang, 397
"Li Ch'ih chuan" (An Account of "Red" Li; Liu Tsung-yüan), 590
Li Chin-fa, 455
Li Chin-tou, 870
Li Ching, 587–88
Li Ching-ch'en, 695
Li Ch'ing-chao, 210, 211, 217, 377, 448; lyrics of, 317, 325–28, 452, 836, 839, 1009
Li Cho-jan, 872
Li Ch'u-yi, 377
Li Ch'ün-yü, 312
Li Ch'ung, 925
Li Erh. *See* Lao Tzu
Li Fang, 136, 342
Li Fang-kuei (Li Shih-san), 838
Li Fei-kan. *See* Pa Chin
Li-feng lao-jen chi (Anthology of Old Man Li-feng; Yü Tao-hsien), 188
"Li Feng-niang k'u tu tsao t'ien-ch'ien" (Jealous and Cruel, Li Feng-niang Suffers from Divine Retribution), 612
"Li fu-jen ko" (Song of Lady Li; Li Yen-nien), 249
Li Fu-yen, 581, 588
Li Hai-kuan, 670–71
Li Ho, 124, 310, 311, 318, 321, 368, 431; as model, 387, 388, 393, 396
Li Hsiao-kuang, 387
Li Hsien-min, 679
Li Hsing-tao, 809
li-hsüeh (study of principles), 340, 414
Li Hua, 301
"Li-hua chüan" (Pear Blossoms; Ch'ien Hsüan), 485, 487
"Li-hua meng" (Pear Blossom Dream; Ho P'ei-chu), 839
Li Hui, 590–91
"Li-hun chi" (Record of the Disembodied Soul; Ch'en Hsüan-yu), 584, 809
Li Hung, 181
Li Hung-chang, 441, 1062
"Li-huo lun" (Discourse Resolving Doubts; Mou Tzu), 165–66
Li Ju-chen, 69, 120, 147–48, 213–14, 655, 656, 1076
Li Jui, 764
Li K'ai-hsien, 377, 382, 407, 818, 824
Li K'ang-ch'eng, 280
Li Kuang, 598
Li Kuang-t'ien, 455
Li K'uang, 457
Li K'uei, 629, 817
"Li K'uei fu-ching" (Li K'uei Carries Thorns; K'ang Chin-chih), 808
Li Kung-lin, 479
Li Kung-tso, 123, 585, 827
Li Li-weng. *See* Li Yü
Li Lin-fu, 301
Li Ling, 250, 264, 987
Li Liu-fang, 7
Li Meng-yang, 381, 403–8, 414, 440
Li Min-yung, 780
Li O, 431, 432, 433, 448–49
Li Pai-ch'uan, 637, 672
Li-pai-liu (Saturday; journal), 704, 729
Li Pai-yao, 284
Li P'an-lung, 407, 408, 414, 1073, 1090
Li Pao-chia (Li Po-yüan), 647, 657, 703, 721, 724, 740, 1012
Li P'eng, 358
Li P'in, 313
Li Po (Li T'ai-po), 57, 255, 271, 279, 296, 302, 304, 478, 558, 568; and balladry, 277, 307, 955, 962, 975; in drama, 815, 834; Han Yü on, 124; and inscription poetry, 475; as model, 307, 345, 364, 377, 387, 395, 396, 398, 401, 414, 415, 423, 424, 437, 1085; Old-Style verse of, 297, 425; prose-poems (*fu*) of, 298, 300; and spirit journeys, 124; and T'ang style, 294, 431, 1071
Li Po-yüan (Li Pao-chia), 647, 657, 703, 720–21, 724, 740, 1012
"Li sao" (Encountering Sorrow; *Ch'u tz'u*), 103, 117, 118, 199, 200, 225–31, 235, 353, 385, 438, 917, 922
"'Li sao' hsü" (Preface to "Encountering Sorrow"; Pan Ku), 922
Li Shan (?–689), 289
Li Shan (Blackhorse Mountain), 310, 311
Li Shang, 516
Li Shang-yin, 244, 310, 311, 321, 344, 421, 531, 933; as model, 393, 440, 447
Li Shen, 308
Li Shih (663–711), 292
Li-shih (character in later classical tale), 692
Li-shih chen-hsien t'i-tao t'ung-chien (Comprehensive Mirror of Successive Generations of Perfected Transcendents and Those Who Embody the Tao; comp. Chao Tao-yi), 191
Li Shih-min. *See* T'ai-tsung, Emperor
Li Shih-san (Li Fang-kuei), 838
Li shih-she (Bamboo Hat; Taiwanese poetry club), 461
li-shih wen-hua fan-ssu (reflection on the historical and cultural past), 870
li-shu (clerical style) script, 49
Li Shu-t'ung, 570, 574
Li-tai ch'ung-tao chi (A Record of Revering the Tao Throughout the Ages; Tu Kuang-t'ing), 183
Li T'ai-po. *See* Li Po
Li Tao-ch'ien, 185
Li Tao-ch'un, 190
"Li Tao-jen tu pu Yün-men" (Yün-men Cave; Hsi Lang-hsien), 602
Li T'ao, 565
Li Te-yü, 306
Li T'o, 1034
li-tsan-wen (liturgies), 978
Li Tse-hou, 771

Li Ts'un-pao, 754
Li-tsung, Emperor (Chao Yü-chü), 366
Li Tuan, 302
Li Tung-yang, 399, 403, 404, 406, 409, 1073
Li Tzu-ch'eng, 832
Li Wa chuan (An Account of Li Wa; Pai Hsing-chien), 586, 593, 594, 809, 1076
Li Wen, 412
Li Yen (150–177), 251
Li Yen (character in *ch'uan-ch'i*), 583
li-yen (harmoniously balanced words), 891
Li Yen-nien, 249
Li Yi (657–716), 292
Li Yi (748–829), 303, 310, 585, 593
Li Yi-chi, 516
Li Yu-ts'ai pan-hua (The Rhymes of Li Yu-ts'ai; Chao Shu-li), 157
Li Yü (937–978; Southern T'ang), 326, 338–39, 418, 447, 834
Li Yü (1591–1671?), 830, 832
Li Yü (1610/11–1680; Li Li-weng), 136, 146, 427, 596, 613–15, 619, 708, 720, 726, 901, 903, 938, 947; dramaturgy of, 825; plays of, 832, 841–42; and *Prayer Mat of Flesh*, 147, 664–65
"Li Yü-ying yü chung sung yüan" (Li Yü-ying Writes Her Defense in Jail; Hsi Lang-hsien), 603
Li-yüan (Pear Garden), 790
Li-yüan ying-lieh (screenplay; A Hero in the Pear Garden; T'ien Han), 858
Liang Ah-fa, 1058
Liang Ch'en-yü, 823, 828, 829
Liang Ch'i-ch'ao, 712, 716–18, 722, 725–26, 734–35; influence of, 844, 1072, 1077; literary theory of, 704, 706–10; poetry of, 441, 442, 454; as reformer, 1059, 1060; and translations of Western books, 1061, 1063, 1064
Liang Chin yen-yi (Romance of the Two Chin Dynasties; Wu Chien-jen), 708
Liang dynasty, 207, 242, 252, 269–73, 289; literary criticism in, 929, 931; official history of, 282, 283; royal patrons in, 240, 926, 955; *shih* poetry in, 241, 927, 1080
"Liang kua Kao Hsing" (Kao Hsing, the Widow of Liang), 198
Liang p'ai, Erh p'ai ("Two Slappings"; Ling Meng-ch'u), 605–10
Liang P'ei-lan, 415
Liang-shan bandits, 808, 817, 818
Liang Shih-ch'iu, 569
"Liang-shih yin-yüan" (A Karmic Bond for two Generations; Ch'iao Chi), 815
Liang shu (History of the Liang Dynasty), 282, 283
Liang Te-sheng, 1020, 1022
"Liang Ti-chu" (The Two Ti-chus; P'an Chih-heng), 690
"Liang ts'o jen Mo ta-chieh ssu-pen, tsai ch'eng-chiao Yang erh-lang cheng-pen" (The Wife Who Eloped; Ling Meng-ch'u), 609
Liang Tsung-tai, 458
Liang Yi-su, 218
Liang Yu-yü, 407
Liao-chai chih-yi (Strange Tales from Make-Do Studio; P'u Sung-ling), 127, 130, 146, 540, 544, 618, 691–95, 709, 889–90
Liao (Khitan) dynasty, 22, 134, 141, 142, 339, 371, 557, 627, 628, 807–8
Liao Hui-ying, 779
liao-ko (*liao* songs), 1037
Liao-ning jen-min yi-shu chü-yüan (Liao-ning People's Art Theater), 871
Liao shih (History of the Liao), 134, 141
"Liao-tu keng" (The Medicine to Cure Jealousy; Wu Ping), 831
Liao-tu yüan (The Cure for Jealousy), 668
"Liao-yang hai-shen chuan" (The Tale of the Liao-yang Sea-Goddess; Ts'ai Yü), 684
Liao Yen, 837
Lieh-ch'ao shih-chi (Collection of Poetry from Successive Reigns; comp. Ch'ien Ch'ien-yi and Liu Shih), 415
Lieh-ch'ao shih-chi hsiao-chuan (collection of critique-biographies), 415–16
lieh-chuan (arrayed traditions; biographies), 503, 514, 516, 517, 520, 522, 626
lieh-fu (chaste woman), 646
Lieh-hsien chuan (Biographies of Transcendents; Liu Hsiang), 121, 522, 523, 550, 554
Lieh-kuo chih-chuan (A Fictionalized History of the States), 128
lieh-nü (virtuous women), 134
Lieh-nü chuan (Biographies of Illustrious Women; Liu Hsiang), 197–98, 212, 469, 471, 508, 517, 518, 524–25, 550, 1074, 1086
Lieh-shih chuan (Biographies of Scholar-Officials; Liu Hsiang), 550
Lieh Tzu, 117, 138
Lieh-yi chuan (Records of Marvels; Ts'ao P'i), 549
"Lien-ch'ang kung tz'u" (Lyric on the Lien-ch'ang Palace; Yüan Chen), 309, 310
Lien-ch'eng pi ch'üan-chi (Priceless Jade; anthology), 614
Lien-ho pao (United Daily; newspaper), 779
"Lien-hsiang-pan" (Women in Love; Li Yü), 832
lien-hua-lao (beggars' chants), 995
Lien Pu, 675
"Lien shih jih" (We Have Chosen a Timely Day; carol of spring sowing), 958
"Lin-an li Ch'ien P'o-liu fa-chi" (Ch'ien Liu; Feng Meng-lung), 600

Lin-chi lu (Recorded Sayings of Master Lin-chi), 169
Lin-chi Yi-hsüan, 169
Lin Ch'uan-chia, 711, 713
"Lin-ch'uan meng" (A Dream of Lin-ch'uan; Chiang Shih-ch'üan), 834
Lin-ch'uan ssu-meng (Four Dreams of Lin-ch'uan; T'ang Hsien-tsu), 827
Lin-erh pao (The Son of Good Fortune), 668
Lin Hai-yin, 778–79
Lin Heng-t'ai, 457, 461
Lin Huai-min, 778
Lin Hung, 275, 401
Lin Keng, 456
Lin Lan Hsiang (The Account of Lin, Lan and Hsiang, The Six Wives of the Wastrel King; Sui-yüan Hsia-shih), 671
Lin Ling, 457
Lin Mo-han, 771
Lin Pai, 765–66
Lin Piao, 873
lin-pieh fan (rice given at parting), 1005
Lin Pu, 343–44
Lin Shu, 703–4, 709, 719, 730, 849, 1063–66
Lin Shuang-pu, 778
Lin Tse-hsü, 718
Lin Wei-fu, 182
Lin Yao-te, 462
Lin Yi-liang (Stephen C. Soong), 457
Lin Yü-t'ang, 567–71
ling (spiritual, numinous), 341, 412, 547
Ling, Emperor (Han), 87, 625
Ling Chih-lung, 942
ling-chü tzu (line-leading words), 319, 322, 329
Ling Hsing-te, 687
Ling Hsüan, 580
Ling-hu Chang, 589
Ling-hu Ch'u, 280
Ling-hui (Hsü Chao), 365
Ling Meng-ch'u, 147, 605–10, 613, 619, 690, 837, 946
Ling-nan school, 414
Ling-pao, 523
Ling-pao ling-chiao chi-tu chin-shu (Golden Script on Salvation Based on the Conveyed Teachings of Ling-pao; comp. Lin Wei-fu), 182
Ling-pao (Numinous Treasure) school, 176, 177, 179–82
Ling-pao wu-liang tu-jen shang-p'in miao-ching (Wondrous Scripture of Supreme Rank on the Infinite Salvation of Ling-pao), 180
Ling-shan (Mountain of Souls; Kao Hsing-chien), 764
Ling Shu-hua, 747
ling-yen (*ying-yen*; evidential miracles), 969, 970
Ling-yün (Hsü Chi), 365
Link, Perry, 699
lion. See *shih-tzu*
literacy, 33, 44, 53–54, 156, 217
literary criticism, 705–16, 881–949, 963; in Chin dynasty, 924–25, 930, 936; in Ch'ing dynasty, 933, 936–38; of drama, 705, 711, 715, 825, 840–43, 939; Japanese, 1082; by Liu Hsieh, 231, 236, 240, 242, 893, 927–29, 932, 937; in medieval period, 257; in Ming dynasty, 936–37; in Republican period, 698–99; in seventeenth century, 420; of *Shih-ching*, 90, 99, 100–103, 106, 108; in Six Dynasties, 894, 930, 1084; in Sung dynasty, 934–36; in T'ang dynasty, 295, 395, 894, 930–34; theory in, 169, 170, 916–39; and translations, 711, 715, 768; in twentieth century, 442, 451, 768–69, 938–39; in Yüan dynasty, 892
literary journals, 457, 464, 699, 702–25, 774, 778; Korean, 1052; in Shanghai, 702–3; short stories in, 704, 714–15, 728–29; and twentieth-century fiction, 732–34, 760
The Literary Mind and the Carving of Dragons (Liu Hsieh). See *Wen-hsin tiao-lung*
Literary Sinitic (LS; *wen-yen*; Classical Chinese), 8, 14, 20, 27–31, 56, 231, 895; and Buddhism, 169; and civil-service examinations, 1–2; in essays, 566–67; and European missionaries, 1058–60, 1061; in fiction, 675–96, 715, 727, 728, 731; and *hua-pen*, 598; humor in, 136; in Japan, 1080; in Korea, 1067; and language reform, 1056–57, 1060, 1065, 1066; late Ch'ing, 430, 698, 700, 724, 730, 1062; and literary criticism, 706; and minority nationalities, 1033; and oral-formulaic tradition, 992; and parallel prose, 238, 243; and poetry, 388, 443, 566, 700, 732–33, 735–36, 998; and political power, 50; prose in, 218, 735, 882–86, 899–904; proverbs in, 149, 151, 154, 158; Republican-period, 727, 728, 731; and rhetoric, 882–83, 894; and scholar-officials, 566–67; and Shanghai writers, 703, 704; and *Shih-san ching*, 86; style of (*wen-yen-wen*), 149, 156, 158; syllables in, 38–39, 42; in Taiwan, 459; T'ang dynasty, 1015; in twentieth-century fiction, 735, 738; and vernacular, 439, 458, 799, 903, 944, 1009–10, 1016, 1065, 1104; in vernacular stories, 595, 596; in Vietnam, 1096; and women, 1020; writing of, 25, 31; and *yü-lu*, 168. See also *ch'uan-ch'i*; *wen-yen hsiao-shuo*
literary societies, 388, 392, 393, 411, 413, 415, 704, 746–47; Korean, 1068–69
literary theory, 699, 706–10, 717, 916–39; and Buddhism, 405, 707; in Chin dynasty (265–420), 919, 923, 926; and Confucianism, 707; and fiction, 712–13; Han, 254, 919, 921–23, 926, 1069; and poetry, 713, 916, 917; and *Shih-*

ching, 916, 917, 922; and vernacular, 707, 708, 709
literati (*wen-yüan, wen-ren*): biographies of, 520; and Buddhism, 163, 169–70, 411–12; and Chinese script, 4, 34–35, 49, 50–51; Ch'ing, 52, 444; as compilers, 271–72, 996; and Confucianism, 340, 348, 351; culture of, 1–4, 328, 338, 355, 356, 359, 392, 479, 490, 1009; and drama, 825, 838, 843; and explication, 912; and expository prose, 528–29; and fiction, 620, 659; and humor, 134; ideal of, 392, 393; as independent artists, 390, 392; and Jesuits, 1056; and language, 28–29, 45, 909; literary competitions of, 292, 897, 898; Ming, 384, 404, 659; narratives of, 989; and Neo-Confucianism, 418–19; as officials, 4–5, 330, 340, 341–42; and painting, 466, 477–81, 485, 490; and poetry, 239, 242, 248, 253, 269–70, 338, 386, 444; and popular literature, 13–14; prosimetric texts of, 991, 996, 1003; and proverbs, 149, 150; and quotation, 912; and ritual culture, 1010; in *The Scholars*, 643–47; in Soochow, 448; Su Shih on, 539; Sung, 341–42, 349, 359, 360, 365, 366, 564; and supernatural tales, 547; T'ang, 291, 292, 302; and twentieth-century fiction, 734, 735, 738, 743, 748; and the West, 1055, 1063; as writers, 838. *See also* scholar-officials
literature: and art, 49; as artificial construct, 84–85; categories of, 4, 8, 51; commentarial, 887, 909–15; court, 898–99; evolution of, 713; experimental, 760–62; folk, 454, 929, 1034, 1039, 1043; foreign, 463, 708, 717–20, 743, 763, 779; genres of, 4–8; informal Chinese, 888; inscription (*t'i-hua wen-hsüeh*), 467–90; internationalization of, 55; mass, 759–60, 780–81; of minority nationalities, 34, 1032–54; native, 458, 459, 460, 461; oppositional structure in, 967, 974; parentheses in Chinese, 905–6; performative, 796–800, 806; popular, 11, 13–15, 134, 135, 148, 167, 302–3, 699, 763, 780, 925, 929, 954, 966–67, 983, 1016, 1018, 1074; proletarian, 157; as propaganda, 157; regional, 1015–31
Liu, Lydia H., 1055–66
Liu An, king of Huai-nan, 60, 82, 117, 229
Liu Chang, 130
Liu Chang-ch'ing, 302, 307
Liu Chen, 253, 254, 269
Liu Ch'en-weng, 325
Liu Ch'eng, 592
Liu Chi, 398
Liu Chih-chi, 525, 581, 594, 893
Liu Chih-hsüan, 184
Liu Chih-yüan, 145, 797, 798, 799, 822
"Liu Chih-yüan chu-kung-tiao" (Medley on Liu Chih-yüan, or Ballad of the Hidden Dragon), 797, 798, 799, 1003, 1008–9
Liu Ching-t'ing, 996
Liu Ch'u-hsüan, 184, 188
"Liu chün-tzu t'u" (The Six Gentlemen: inscribed painting; Ni Tsan), 487–89
Liu Ch'ung-yüan, 403
Liu Fu, 679
Liu Fu (Liu Pan-nung), 454
Liu Hsi, 48
Liu Hsi (student in wooden-fish song), 1027
Liu Hsiang, 121, 175, 197, 224, 225, 229, 233, 469, 502, 508, 517–18, 522, 544, 550, 554, 892
Liu Hsieh, 8, 133, 134, 141, 143, 170, 258, 261, 891; literary criticism of, 231, 236, 240, 242, 893, 927–29, 932, 937; on proverbs, 150, 151
Liu Hsien, 292
Liu Hsin, 91, 93, 175, 224, 544–45
Liu Hsin-wu, 762
Liu Ju-yi, 580
Liu K'o-chuang, 325, 366–67, 369
Liu K'o-hsiang, 462
Liu K'un, 260, 261, 262, 264
Liu Kuo, 325
Liu Ling-hsien, 207–9, 210, 217
liu-mang, p'i-tzu (riffraff, ruffians), 766, 767
Liu O, 657–58, 703–4, 708, 721, 724–25, 735, 739–41
Liu Pan-nung (Liu Fu), 454
Liu Pang. *See* Kao-tsu, Emperor
Liu Pao-ch'üan, 1029
Liu Pei, 508, 521, 621–23, 625, 630, 806
Liu Piao, 234
Liu Pin-k'o chia-hua lu (A Record of the Fine Discourses by the Adviser to the Heir Apparent, Liu; Wei Hsün), 581, 583
Liu Pin-yen, 760, 770
Liu Ping-chung, 381
Liu P'o-hsi, 381
Liu Sa-ho, 971
"Liu Sa-ho ho-shang yin-yüan chi" (Account of the Circumstances of the Monk Liu Sa-ho), 971
Liu San-chieh (Third Sister Liu; song goddess), 1027, 1036
Liu Shao-ch'i, 872
Liu Shen-hsü, 295
Liu Shih (Ju-shih), 332, 333, 413, 415, 416, 448
liu shih (six forms of poetical composition), 101
Liu-shih chia hsiao-shuo (Sixty Stories; Hung P'ien), 597, 598–99
"Liu-shih chuan" (An Account of Ms. Liu; Hsü Yao-tso), 584
Liu Shih-chung, 376
Liu-shih chung ch'ü (Sixty Plays), 825
Liu So-la, 764

Liu Su, 581
Liu Sung dynasty, 252, 550, 552, 955
Liu Ta-k'uei, 533
Liu Ta-pin, 181
Liu Te (Prince Hsien of Ho-chien), 91, 92, 100
Liu Tsai-fu, 762, 770–71
Liu Ts'ao, 184, 189
Liu-tsu t'an-ching (*Platform Sūtra of the Sixth Patriarch*; Hui-neng), 169
Liu Tsung-yüan, 230, 237, 243, 304, 305, 533–36, 556–57, 590, 592, 594, 827, 1085
Liu-tu chi-ching (Canonical Scripture on the Six Perfections; K'ang Seng-hui), 171
Liu Tui, 804
"Liu Tung-shan" (Sung Mao-ch'eng), 689
"Liu Tung-shan k'ua chi Shun ch'eng men, shih-pa hsiung tsung ch'i ts'ung ch'i ts'un chiu ssu" (The Braggart Liu Tung-shan; Ling Meng-ch'u), 606
Liu Wu (Prince Hsiao of Liang), 231, 232
Liu Ya-tzu, 442, 443
Liu-ya wai-pien (Willow Cliff's Informal Collection; Hsü K'un), 695
Liu Yeh-ch'iu, 563
Liu Yen, 589
Liu Yi, 625
"Liu Yi" (Li Ch'ao-wei), 122, 584–85
liu-yi (six principles), 920
Liu Yi-ch'ang, 774
Liu Yi-ch'ing, 6, 121, 171, 522, 548, 550–51, 580
"Liu Yi chuan," 591
"Liu yi shih" (Six Recollections; Shen Yüeh), 271
Liu-yi shih-hua (Remarks on Poetry; Ou-yang Hsiu), 133, 138
Liu Yin, 386
Liu Yü (1257–1308), 190
Liu Yü (d.422), 252
Liu Yü-hsi, 305, 310, 534, 581, 975
Liu Yü-ting, 591
Liu Yün, 344
Liu Yün-jo, 1025
Liu Yung, 316–21, 326, 327
Lloyd, Geoffrey, 898
Lo Ch'ing, 462
Lo Fu, 461, 779–80
Lo Jui-ch'ing, 873
Lo Jung-huan, 873
Lo Kuan-chung, 128, 621, 628, 816
Lo Ma (Shang Ch'in), 457, 461
Lo Mao-teng, 632
Lo Pin-wang, 287, 288, 289, 1081
"Lo-shen fu" (Rhapsody on the Goddess of the Lo River; Ts'ao Chih), 200, 235–36, 473, 474
Lo Sung-ch'uang, 1030
Lo-t'o Hsiang-tzu (Camel Hsiang-tzu, Rickshaw Boy; Lao She), 749–50, 1034
lo-ts'ao (bandits), 621
Lo Wai-luen (Lu Wei-luan), 773
Lo-yang ch'ieh-lan chi (Account of Monasteries and Temples of Loyang; Yang Hsüan-chih), 165
Lo Yeh, 596
Lo Yin, 312
Logician school, 175
Long March, 157, 873
Looking Backward (Bellamy), 718
"L'orphelin de la Chine" (Voltaire), 803
Lotus Sūtra (*Miao-fa lien-hua ching*; *Saddharmapuṇḍarīka-sūtra*), 163
Lozang Khan, 1047
Lu, state of, 3–4, 102, 471, 496, 505, 911, 917
Lu Chao-lin, 287, 288–89, 290
Lu Chi, 200, 239, 260–63, 265, 687, 893, 924, 925, 932
Lu Chih (754–805), 243, 244
Lu Chih (1234–1300), 379, 381
Lu Ching-jo, 850
"Lu Ch'iu chieh-fu" (The Chaste Wife of Ch'iu of Lu), 198
Lu Ch'ui, 270
Lu Heng, 489
Lu Hsiu-ching, 178, 182
Lu Hsiung, 632
Lu Hsün (Chou Shu-jen), 7, 52–54, 156, 254, 454, 564, 566, 568–72, 575, 632, 697, 704, 720, 722, 729, 740, 749–50, 752, 762; *Diary of a Madman*, 730, 735, 744; on *Journey to the West*, 634; and language reform, 1057, 1063, 1066; pseudonyms of, 568, 729, 745; on sexuality, 657; *Story of Ah Q*, 54, 744, 854; on supernatural, 126
Lu Hung, 478, 479
Lu Jen-lung, 610
Lu Kao, 171
Lu Kuei-meng, 312, 403
Lu-kuei pu (Register of Ghosts; Chung Ssu-ch'eng), 145, 796, 800, 815, 816, 840
Lu kung erh-shih-ssu yu (Twenty-four Companions of the Duke of Lu), 239, 261, 262, 264
Lu Lin, 462
Lu Lun, 302
Lu school (of *Shih-ching* interpretation), 90, 99
"Lu-shan chih hsüeh" (The Snow on Lu Mountain; Li Cho-jan), 872
"Lu-shan shan hsing" (Traveling in the Mountains on Mount Lu; Mei Yao-ch'en), 347
Lu Shu-sheng, 7
"Lu t'ai-hsüeh shih chiu ao wang hou" (Lu Nan; Hsi Lang-hsien), 602
Lu Te-ming, 283
Lu Ts'ai, 677, 686
Lu Ts'an, 677
Lu Ts'ang-yung, 292
Lu Wan, 506
Lu Yen-chih, 677
Lu Yen-chou, 761
Lu Yi-shih (Chi Hsien), 456, 457, 460
Lu Yu, 359–63, 366, 367, 416, 420, 434, 556–59, 563–64

Lu Yün, 136, 204, 260, 261
lü (Sanskrit: *vinaya*; rules of conduct), 161–62
Lü, Empress, 197, 580, 806
Lü An, 259
"Lü chu shan-fang" (The Verdant Bamboo Hermitage; Wu Tsu-hsiang), 751
Lü-ch'uang nü-shih (Green Window History of Women), 688
lü-fu (regulated *fu*; prose-poem), 6, 244, 246, 277, 278, 304, 305, 309, 973
Lü Ho-jo, 776
Lü Hsiu-lien, 758
"Lü-mao-pieh" (The Tortoise with Algae on Its Back; Wang Ho-ch'ing), 376
"Lü mu-tan" (The Green Peony; Wu Ping), 831
Lü Pen-chung, 356, 357, 358, 360
Lü Pu-wei, 79, 105
"Lü-se ying-ti" (Green Barracks; Chang Li-li), 875
Lü Shang (T'ai-kung Wang), 522–23
lü-shih (regulated verse), 57, 276, 293, 307, 979, 1068; Ming, 1088; Sung, 342; T'ang, 280, 301, 311, 931, 975; of Tu Fu, 299, 300, 412; Vietnamese, 1097; of Wang Wei, 295
Lü-shih ch'un-ch'iu (Springs and Autumns of Master Lü; Lü Pu-wei), 10, 60, 79, 80, 95, 102, 105, 138, 896
"Lü-shui ch'ang-liu" (The Flow of Clear Water; Ch'ih Li), 765
Lü Ssu-mien, 68, 715–16
Lü T'ien-ch'eng, 841
Lü Tsu chih (A Treatise on Patriarch Lü), 186
Lü Tung-pin, 810, 839
Lü-yeh hsien-tsung (Trails of Immortals in the Green Wilds; Li Pai-ch'uan), 637, 672
Lü Yen, 184–86, 191
"Lü-yi shih-che chuan" (An Account of the Green-Robed Deputy; Chang Yüeh), 583
"Luan-pi chi" (The Barb of Love; Yeh Hsien-tsu), 836
luan-t'an (cacophonous strummings), 843–47
Luan-tu chih lien (Love of a City in Chaos; Chang Wo-chün), 458
luc-bat (six-eight) meter (Vietnamese), 1097, 1099, 1100, 1101
lun (Sanskrit: Abhidharma; moral law), 162
lun, lun-pien (disquisitions, essays), 4, 238, 527, 528
"Lun fei-o p'o-lai ying-kai huan-hsing" (Fair Play Should Be Deferred; Lu Hsün), 571
"Lun Fo-ku piao" (Memorial on the Buddha Bone; Han Yü), 166, 534
Lun-heng (Authoritative Expositions; "The Steelyard of Exposition"; Wang Ch'ung), 901, 922, 927, 929
"Lun hsiao-shuo yü ch'ün-chih chih kuan-hsi" (On the Relationship Between Fiction and Popular Government; Liang Ch'i-ch'ao), 707, 734
"Lun hsieh-ch'ing hsiao-shuo yü hsin she-hui chih kuan-hsi" (On the Relationship Between Romantic Fiction and the New Society; Chin Sung-ts'en), 709
"Lun shih san-shih shou" (Thirty Poems on Poetry; Yüan Hao-wen), 936
"Lun tuan-p'ien hsiao-shuo" (On the Short Story; Hu Shih), 730
"Lun wen" (Essay on Literature; Ts'ao P'i), 236, 257
"Lun wen-hsüeh shang hsiao-shuo chih wei-chih" (The Position of Fiction in Literature; Ch'u Ch'ing), 709
"Lun wen-jen" (On Writers; Ch'ien Chung-shu), 573
Lun-yü (Analects; Confucius), 3, 73, 90, 94–95, 267, 494, 567, 677, 694, 934; and Chinese rhetoric, 881, 882; didacticism of, 97–98, 917; and exegesis, 909, 912; in *Four Books*, 92; and humor, 139–40, 148; and proverbs, 151; and *Shih-ching*, 102; on supernatural, 116, 500; in *Thirteen Classics*, 88; and *yü-lu*, 168
lung. *See* dragons
"Lung-chiang sung" (The Song of the Dragon River; model play version), 868
lung-chou ko (Cantonese: *leung-jau go*; dragon boat songs), 1026
Lung-hsing Fo-chiao pien-nien t'ung-lun (Comprehensive Chronicle of Buddha's Teaching from the Lung-hsing Period; Tsu-hsiu), 166–67
'Lung-hsü-kou" (Dragon Beard Ditch), 876
Lung-hu shan chih (Topography of Mount Lung-hu), 179
Lung-shuo era, 290
Lung-shuo transformation, 286
Lung-tsu shih-she (Dragon Race Poetry Club; Taiwan), 461
Lung Ying-tsung, 776
Luther, Martin, 888, 894
Ly Ngoc Hung, 1103
Ly Te Xuyen, 1099
Ly Van Phuc, 1100
Lynn, Richard John, 383–89, 410–28
lyrics. See *t'an-tz'u*; *tz'u*

Ma, Y. W., 630–31
Ma Chien, 774
Ma Chih-yüan, 373, 377, 378, 810, 814, 815, 816, 1101
Ma Chün-wu, 720
"Ma-feng nü Ch'iu Li-yü" (Leper Girl Ch'iu Li-yü; Hsüan Ting), 695
Ma Hsüeh-liang, 1035, 1040
Ma Ju-fei, 1024

Ma Jung, 912
"Ma-k'o-ssu chin K'ung miao" (Marx Enters the Confucian Temple; Kuo Mo-jo), 746
Ma Lang (Ronald Mar), 457
"Ma ling kua" (Horse-Bell Melons; Yeh Sheng-t'ao), 746
"Ma-nao lei fu" (Rhapsody on an Agate Bridle; Ts'ao P'i), 234
Ma Sen, 768
"Ma shih-ch'ung wen" (Reviling the Corporeal Worms; Liu Tsung-yüan), 305
Ma Shih-ying, 833
Ma Tai, 311
Ma Tsu-ch'ang, 386
Ma-tsu Tao-yi, 168
Ma-tsu yü-lu (Recorded Sayings of Master Ma-tsu), 168–69
Ma-wang-tui manuscripts, 89, 98, 101, 106, 107, 174, 179
Ma Yü, 184, 186–87
Ma Yüan (14 B.C.E–49 C.E.), 520
Ma Yüan (b.1953), 764
MacLeish, Archibald, 457
magic, 115–16, 134
magical realism, 756, 764
Mahānāpanānusmṛti-sūtra (*Ta-an-pan shou-yi ching*), 162
Mahāsattva, 474
"Mai-hua nü" (The Flower Seller), 1001, 1002
"Mai t'an weng" (The Old Charcoal Seller; Po Chü-yi), 963
"Mai-yu lang tu chan hua-k'uei" (The Oil Vendor and the Courtesan), 604, 830
Mair, Victor H., 1–15, 19–57, 160–72
Makita Tairyō, 12, 164
makura no kotoba (pillow talk), 1082
Malaya, 589
Malaysia, 165, 759
Malcinkuu (Ma-la-ch'in-fu), 771
Malraux, André, 157
Malthus, Thomas, 437
Man. *see* Huang Jen
"Man-chiang hung" (River Filled with Red; Wang Shih-lu, Sung Wan, and Ts'ao Erh-k'an), 427
Man-chou shih-lu (The Veritable History of the Manchus), 509
"Man-t'ing fang" (Fragrance Filling the Courtyard), 186
man-tz'u (form of lyric), 316–19, 321, 329, 333. See also *tz'u*
Manchuria, 335, 339, 1030, 1050
Manchus, 1050–51; collapse of empire of, 1056; conquest of China by, 410, 415, 625, 628, 643, 663, 691, 825, 936, 1044, 1052; drumsong tradition of, 1028, 1029–31; in fiction, 625, 628, 642–43, 662, 663; language of, 22, 1048; and literati, 440, 444; and Mongols, 383–84, 1047; as officials, 1027; opposition to, 332, 333–34, 384, 413, 445, 691, 830, 832, 844. *See also* Ch'ing dynasty
Mandarin, Modern Standard (MSM), 22, 24–26, 57, 459, 460, 1056; development of, 32–33; on Internet, 55–56; Japanese influence on, 45; and Literary Sinitic, 31; and minority nationalities, 1033, 1034, 1035, 1039, 1040, 1042, 1049, 1054; and regional literatures, 1019, 1020, 1021, 1023, 1024, 1030; romanization of, 53; syllables in, 38–43; in Taiwan, 33, 35; and writing, 31
Mandarin Ducks and Butterflies: Popular Fiction in Early Twentieth-Century Chinese Cities (Link), 699
Mandate of Heaven (*t'ien-ming*), 73, 75, 96, 111, 543, 546, 1056
Mang Ke (Mang K'o), 462
mang-liu (rovers), 755
"Mang shu-sheng ch'iang t'u yüan-lü" (The Impetuous Student; Hsi Lang-hsien), 604–5
Manggol'un niuca tobcaan (Secret History of the Mongols), 1049–50
Manichaeism, 9, 170, 981, 1048
Mañjuśrī (Kumārabhūta Bodhisattva), 164
Man's Fate (Malraux), 157
Mantarō Hashimoto, 22
manuscripts, 896, 899; Ch'u silk, 467; Fu-yang, 100; Han, 98, 467; Kuo-tien, 92, 98, 99, 101; Ma-wang-tui, 89, 98, 101, 106, 107, 174, 178; Shui-hu-ti, 93; Yin-chüeh-shan, 98. *See also* Tun-huang manuscripts
A *Many-Splendored Thing* (Han Suyin), 773
Manyōshū (Collection of Ten Thousand Leaves), 1081, 1082, 1086
mao (writing brush), 534
Mao Ch'ang, 90
Mao Chin, 825
"Mao chuan" (Mao Commentary to *Shih-ching*), 100, 106–7
Mao Heng, 90
Mao Hsiang, 417, 418
Mao Hsien-shu, 414
Mao K'un, 533
Mao Lun, 621, 623–24, 708, 842, 943
Mao school (of *Shih-ching* interpretation), 100–101, 102, 103, 106, 108
Mao shan chih (Treatise on Mount Mao; Liu Ta-pin), 181
Mao-shih. See *Shih-ching*
Mao Tse-tung, 5, 568–69, 748, 758, 760–61; and censorship, 460, 736; compared with Chu Yüan-chang, 397; death of, 750, 755, 869; and establishment of PRC, 459; on literature and art, 157, 457, 864; poetry of, 336, 443; on textual commentary, 941; and theater, 868, 874; use of proverbs by, 152; and Yen Fu, 1063; and Yi nationality, 1033

Mao Tsung-kang, 621, 623–24, 708, 842, 943
Mao Tun (Shen Yen-ping), 68, 156, 746–47, 1057
Mao Yen-shou, 814, 815
"Mao Ying chuan" (Biography of Mao Ying; Han Yü), 534, 535, 594, 931
Mar, Ronald (Ma Lang), 457
Marquez, Gabriel Garcia, 756, 764–65
martial arts, 128, 671–72
Martin, Helmut, 758–81
Martin, W. A. P., 1057, 1059
Marx, Karl, 746
Marxism, 157, 746, 844
Mason, Richard, 773
Master Yen-yen of Hangchow, 666
Matsuo Bashō, 1090
May Fourth movement (Wu-ssu yün-tung), 458–59, 530, 699; anti-Confucianism in, 852–54, 855, 860; and avant-garde literature, 769; and colloquial writing, 372; and drama, 848, 851–57; and ethnic minority literature, 1034; and fiction, 728, 731, 735, 743, 746; foreign influences on, 744, 749; and *Hsiao-ching*, 95; and individualism, 852, 865; and New Culture movement (Hsin wen-hua yün-tung), 1056, 1066; and Peking opera, 848, 851–52, 856, 857; and poetry, 454, 455, 458, 461, 463, 779; and popular culture, 1017; and proverbs, 156, 157; and short stories, 745; women in, 747–48, 865; writers in, 704, 747–48, 1057, 1066
May Thirtieth movement (1925), 855
māyā (illusion), 169
McCraw, David, 444–52
McLaren, Anne E., 989–1014
mDo makhar Tshe ring dbang rgyal (Tibetan novelist), 1047
Meditationes (Descartes), 903
mei (beauty), 712–13, 891
Mei Ch'eng, 232, 974
mei-hsüeh (*belles lettres*, esthetics), 714
"Mei-jen fu" (Rhapsody on a Beautiful Woman; pseudo-Ssu-ma Hsiang-ju), 106
mei-jen huo-shui (calamity of a beautiful woman), 14
Mei Kao, 233
Mei-ko (folksong collection), 1039
Mei Lan-fang, 845, 856
"Mei nan-tzu pi huo fan sheng yi" (A Handsome Lad Raises Doubts by Trying to Avoid Suspicion; Li Yü), 613–14
mei-shu (fine arts), 714
mei te chih-tso (esthetic construct), 716
Mei Ting-tso, 683, 688
Mei Tse, 90
Mei-ts'un *t'i* (Mei-ts'un style or Lou-tung style), 416
Mei Yao-ch'en, 133, 345, 346, 347, 348, 487
Mei Ying-tso, 47
"Mei-yü" (The Rainy Season; T'ien Han), 870
Meiji Restoration (Japan; 1868), 441, 706, 733, 850, 1060, 1094
Men-wai wen-t'an (Outsider's Chats on Script; Lu Hsün), 52, 745
Mencius (Meng Tzu), 9, 95–96, 506, 518, 533–34, 892, 897, 912, 1056
Mencius (text), 60, 61, 74, 92, 93, 468, 496, 513, 866, 887; and humor, 138, 139; and myth, 62; and *Shih-ching*, 99, 103; in *Thirteen Classics*, 88, 95–96; and women, 196, 198
"Meng" (Vulgar!), 195
Meng Ch'eng-shun, 831, 837
Meng Ch'i, 837
Meng Chiang-nü, 993
Meng Chiao, 303, 307, 368, 431, 534
"Meng chiao-kuan ai nü pu shou pao, ch'iung hsiang-sheng chu shih te ling chung" (The Foolish Official Tutor Receives No Returns for Doting on His Daughters; Ling Meng-ch'u), 607
Meng Chu, 207
Meng Hao-jan, 169, 294, 296, 302, 421, 423, 425, 426
Meng-hsi pi-t'an (Brush Talks from Dream Brook; Shen Kua), 121, 561–64
Meng Hsien-chung, 582
Meng Hsü, emperor of Shu (Five Dynasties), 209
Meng Huo, 624
Meng K'o. *See* Mencius
Meng Lang, 463
Meng Liang, 808
"Meng Liang tao ku" (Meng Liang Steals the Bones; Chu K'ai), 145
meng-lung shih (misty, obscure poetry), 15, 463, 780
Meng Tzu. *See* Mencius
mergen (hero tales), 1035
Mérimée, Prosper, 859
metaphor (*hsing*), 5, 106–7, 158, 921
mGur-Bum (The Hundred Thousand Songs; collection of Tibetan poems), 1046
"Mi chou" (The Lost Boat; Ko Fei), 765
Mi chou (The Lost Boat; comp. Henry Chao), 768
mi-fu (secret repositories), 896
Mi Heng, 835
Mi-teng yin-hua (Inspired Tales of the Searched Lamp), 682
miao (marvelousness), 424
"Miao-chin feng" (The Etched Gold Phoenix), 1023, 1025
Miao-fa lien-hua ching (*Lotus Sūtra*; *Saddharmapuṇḍarīka-sūtra*), 163
miao-ho (fusion), 419
Miao peoples, 1033
Miao Shan-shih, 185
miao-wu (marvelous enlightenment), 423, 935
mien-li (lingering sense of beauty), 421
"Mien-tui tzu-chi" (Facing Oneself; Wang An-yi), 573–74

Milarepa (Tibetan poet), 1045–46
Mill, John Stuart, 1063
Min-ch'üan pao (People's Rights News; newspaper), 715, 727
Min chung she (People's Drama Society), 855
Min-kuo jih-pao (Republic Daily; newspaper), 715
Min language, 35, 39
Min pao (People's News), 1060
"Min sheng fu" (Despairing Over Life; Liu Tsung-yüan), 305
ming (fate), 111, 112
ming (translucence, perspicuousness), 882
Ming, Emperor (r. 57–75), 523–24
Ming, Emperor (Ts'ao Jui; r. 227–239), 254, 257, 259
Ming ch'ien ch'i tzu (Earlier Seven Masters of the Ming), 404–5, 408, 409, 423; archaism of, 411, 419, 440; and High T'ang style, 414, 420; and seventeenth-century poets, 412, 413, 422
ming-ching (examination), 1
Ming-Ch'ing transition, 610–13
Ming dynasty, 401, 508, 543, 552, 559, 1044; anthologies in, 533; archaist movement in, 409, 430, 433, 1073, 1090; Buddhism in, 915; chantefables of, 992, 995, 996, 998, 1001, 1003, 1009, 1010, 1014, 1018, 1026; Ch'eng-hua period of, 998, 1001, 1002; classical tales in, 579, 677–90; drama in, 144–46, 332, 632, 789, 794, 800, 801–5, 816, 823–34, 841; examinations in, 914; fall of, 445, 642–43, 662, 825, 832, 833; in fiction, 625, 663, 1025, 1037; fiction of, 147, 399, 732–33, 972, 986, 992; genres of, 6; humor in, 134, 135, 145–46; and Japan, 1088, 1089; and Jesuits, 1055; literary criticism in, 894, 936–37, 943; local academies (*shu-yüan*) of, 1053; loyalty to, 334, 625, 628, 664, 691; lyrics of, 331, 995, 1019; and Manchus, 822, 1051; Mandarin in, 32, 33; minorities in, 1053; and Mongols, 384, 1050–51; novels of, 69, 659–70; official history of, 509; painter-poets of, 398, 435, 479, 489, 490; philosophy of, 828; poetry in, 333, 372, 390, 393–95, 410, 434, 1072; prose in, 6–7, 246, 541; prosimetric texts of, 792, 1018, 1026; proverbs in, 153, 155; publication during, 599–611, 942; purges of, 1049; storytelling in, 597–98, 1026; style in, 693, 887, 889; and Sung poetry, 338, 368; supernatural tales in, 119, 122; and T'ang poetry, 275, 384, 395; Taoist canon in, 178–81, 184, 189, 192; and Vietnam, 1097, 1102; women in, 210, 218, 332
"Ming-fei ch'ü ho Wang Chieh-fu tso" (Song of Bright Consort, Matching Wang Chieh-fu), 345
"Ming-feng chi" (The Crying Phoenix), 824, 827
Ming-ho yü-yin (Lingering Reverberations of the Calling Crane), 187
Ming-hsiang chi (Accounts of Mysterious Revelations; Wang Yen), 171
ming-hsin chien-hsing (prime concern of illuminating the mind and seeing nature), 634
Ming-hsüeh ch'ien-shuo (Primer of Logic; trans. Yen Fu), 1063
Ming-huang tsa-lu (Miscellaneous Records of Ming-huang; Cheng Ch'u-hui), 581
"Ming-jen chang-hui hsiao-shu" (Chaptered Novels by Ming Writers; Huang Jen), 712
"Ming-kuei" (On Ghosts; Mo Tzu), 543
Ming-pao chi (Records of Miraculous Retribution; T'ang Lin), 582
Ming shih (History of the Ming Dynasty), 509
ming-shih (renowned literatus), 645
Ming-shih chuan (Biographies of Famous Scholars; Yüan Hung), 508
Ming shih kao (Draft History of the Ming Era; Ch'ien Ch'ien-yi), 416
"Ming-t'ang fu" (The Hall of Light; Li Po), 298
Ming-tao p'ien (Folios on Illuminating the Tao; comp. Wang Wei-yi), 191
Ming-tao tsa-chi (Ming-tao Miscellany; Chang Lei), 564
Ming-ti, Emperor, 178, 468
"Ming tu p'ien" (Famous Cities; Ts'ao Chih), 255
"Ming-wu ch'an-shih kan Wu-chieh" (The Enlightened Priest Attempts to Save Five Abstinences; Feng Meng-lung), 600
"Ming-yu chih ssu" (The Death of a Famous Actor; T'ien Han), 857
"Ming-yüeh ch'u-chao jen" (First Bathed in Moonlight; Pai Feng-hsi), 874–75
"Ming-yün" (Fate; Shih T'ieh-sheng), 765
Mingashū (Min River and Omei Mountain Collection; Sesson Yūbai), 1088
minority nationalities (*shao-shu min-tsu*), 9, 19; literature of, 34, 1032–54
miracle tales, 162, 165, 168, 171, 551, 582, 969–72
missionaries, 849, 1058–60, 1061, 1064
Misty Season Drama Festival (Chungking), 864
mo (male lead), 807, 813, 814, 820
Mo Ch'i-yen, 191
Mo-chia (Mohists), 87

mo-fang (assimilation of reality), 716
Mo-han-chai ting-pen ch'uan-ch'i (Musical Plays as edited by the Ink-Silly Studio; comp. Feng Meng-lung), 830
Mo-ho chih-kuan (The Great Cessation and Contemplation; Chih-yi), 170
Mo-kao k'u (Caves of Unparalleled Heights). See *Ch'ien fo tung*
"Mo-ling ch'un" (Nanking Spring; Wu Wei-yeh), 834
"Mo shang sang" (Mulberry Up the Lane), 958
Mo Tzu (Mo Ti), 75, 95, 116, 543
Mo Tzu (text), 60, 95, 883, 897–98. *See also* Mohism
mo wu tzu (Concluding Five Masters), 408
Mo Yen, 756–57, 764–65, 771
modernism, 457, 458, 460–62, 464, 876
modernity, 158, 441, 706, 730, 763, 767, 1056; and Ch'ing fiction, 655, 696, 697, 700, 721; in Korea, 1077; and sexuality, 657; and Shanghai, 701; in Taiwan, 753, 777, 779
Mohamud Sushanlo, 34
Mohism, 75, 76, 81, 82, 84, 87, 175, 881, 892, 897
Möngke, 340
Mongolia, 1044, 1048
Mongols, 391, 400; book epics of, 1013, 1045; and Chin dynasty, 340; and Chinese classics, 887; classical verse (*shih*) of, 383–89; conquest of China by, 331, 367, 368, 392, 485, 816, 821, 1016, 1049–50; conquests of, 814, 833, 1040–42, 1044; expulsion of, 390, 402; in fiction, 622, 628, 662; and Japan, 1088; language of, 22, 1048; and literati culture, 338; and Manchus, 1047; opposition to, 394, 811, 815, 844; and Southern Sung, 328, 330, 386, 834; and Tibetan Buddhism, 1046
mongyurok (dream records), 1072
Monkey. *See* Sun Wu-k'ung
Monkey. See *Hsi-yu chi*
monks, 160, 171; biographies of, 121, 164–65
monogatari (tale), 1086
Montesquieu, Baron de, 1063
Moore, Marianne, 457
morality: in *Chin P'ing Mei*, 640–43; in Ch'ing fiction, 670, 671, 697, 726; in classical tales, 679, 681, 682, 693–94; disquisitions on, 51; in *hua-pen*, 598, 603, 612–13, 616, 617; and humor, 133, 134, 138, 141, 143, 145–48; in *Journey to the West*, 633–35; and literary theory, 707, 710; in Ming-Ch'ing novels, 666; in Ming novels, 660, 661; in periodicals, 131; and proverbs, 153; in *Romance of the Three Kingdoms*, 622, 625; in *The Scholars*, 646–47; secret society, 622, 627; and Shanghai writers, 704; in *Strange Tales from Make-Do Studio*, 130; in supernatural tales, 127; and twentieth-century fiction, 734; in *Water Margin*, 629–31; and women, 198, 219. *See also* didacticism
Mori Ōgai, 1094
Morrison, Robert, 1058
Mou Tzu, 166
Moyunchur (Mo-yen-ch'o), 1048
"Mrs. Warren's Profession" (Shaw), 855–56
Mu, Duke of Ch'in, 255, 592
Mu, Emperor, 264, 544–47, 555, 580
Mu-chai ch'u-hsüeh chi (Literary Collection from the Shepherd's Studio During First Stages of Learning), 416
mu-chih ming (epitaphs), 978
Mu-lan, 845
"Mu-lan chai" (Enclosure for Viewing Magnolia; Wang Wei), 294
"Mu-lan shih" (Ballad of Mu-lan), 68, 960, 986
Mu-le ming-hsüeh (A System of Logic; trans. Yen Fu), 1063
Mu-lien (Mahāmaudgalyāyana), 792, 986, 987, 991, 1010
"Mu-lien pien-wen" (the Mu-lien story; "Ta-mu-ch'ien-lien ming-chien chiu-mu pien-wen"), 123, 125, 168
Mu Mu-t'ien, 455
"Mu-p'i-san-jen ku-tz'u" (Drum Ballad of "The Tree Bark Idler"; Chia Ying-ch'ung), 1012
mu-piao-chih (dramatic form), 850
Mu Shih-ying, 748–49
Mu Tan, 456
"Mu-tan" (Peonies; Ch'en Yü-yi), 358
"Mu-tan t'ing" (Peony Pavilion; T'ang Hsien-tsu), 126, 654, 824, 827–28, 830, 843
Mu t'ien-tzu chuan (Travels of Emperor Mu), 264, 544, 545, 547, 555, 580
mu-yü (Cantonese: *muk-yu*; wooden-fish tales), 995, 1018, 1025–28
mūdras (gestures), 164
munch'ae panjŏng (rectification of textual style), 1073
munjang chimun (prose style), 1073
Murasaki Shikibu, 1086–87
music, 956, 957–58, 975–77; antiphonal singing, 1036; avant-garde, 763; and ballad opera, 793; and Chinese tones, 321; *ch'ü*, 331; and dance, 916–17, 920, 977; in drama, 792–94; elegant (*ya*, *gagaku*), 314, 1089; and emotion, 920; influence of Buddhism on, 161; in *Li-chi*, 92; northern, 793, 835; and poetry, 108–9, 319, 371, 917; popular, 953; revolutionary, 868; ritual, 995; *san-yüeh*

(*sangaku*; *saragaku*; monkey music), 1088–89; in *Shang-shu*, 108; southern, 835; Sung, 791; in *Sung shu*, 956, 957; Western influence on, 846; Wu, 271, 960; Yüan, 331, 371. See also *t'an-tz'u*; *tz'u*
Muslim (Hui) people, 31, 34
Musō Soseki, 1088
Myhre, Karin, 132–48
Myŏng-jong, King, 1073
myth, 3, 51, 58–69; categories of, 62–65; creation, 1037, 1039–42; epic, 1036; historicization of, 59, 61, 62, 64–66; in *Journey to the West*, 663; in literature, 68–69; periodization of, 59–60; and *Romance of the Three Kingdoms*, 622; in *Shan hai ching*, 119–20; sources for, 60–62; and supernatural tales, 544, 545, 548, 552; in T'ang poetry, 124; and women, 196–97, 200

Na-han (Battlecry; Lu Hsün), 744–45
Na-lan Hsing-te (Nara Singde), 333, 417, 418, 447, 449, 452
Na-lan (Nara) Mingju, 417
Nagai Kafū, 1094
nāgas (dragon-kings), 114–15, 585
Nagaya no Ōkimi, 1081
"Nai-ho-t'ien" (You Can't Do Anything About Fate; Li Yü), 832
Nakhi nationality, 1041–42, 1045
Nalan Hsing-te (Nara Singde), 333, 417, 418, 447, 449, 452
Nan-chao kingdom, 1040, 1042
Nan-chao kung-teng (The Palace Lamp of the Nan-chao Kingdom), 1040
Nan Cho, 590, 591
Nan-fang pao (South; journal), 723
Nan-hai chi-kuei nei-fa chuan (Account of Buddhist Practices Sent Home from the Southern Sea; Yi-ching), 165
nan-hsi (southern plays). See *hsi-wen*
Nan-hua ching (Classic of Southern Florescence), 173. See also *Chuang Tzu*
"Nan-k'o chi" (The Tale of South Branch; T'ang Hsien-tsu), 827
"Nan-k'o t'ai-shou chuan" (The Story of the Prefect of South Branch; Li Kung-tso), 123, 146, 585–86, 592, 594, 827
Nan-kuo pan-yüeh-k'an (Southern Biweekly), 857
Nan kuo she (Southern Society), 859
Nan-lei shih-li (A Poetic Chronicle from South of Thunder; Huang Tsung-hsi), 419
"Nan Meng-mu chiao ho san ch'ien" (A Male Mencius's Mother Educates Her Son; Li Yü), 614
Nan-pei-ch'ao period. *See* Southern and Northern Dynasties
"Nan p'u" (South Bank; Wang An-shih), 349
nan-shu (Men's Script), 1000
Nan-tsung (Southern Lineage), 189–91
nan-tz'u (southern lyrics), 1024. See also *tz'u*
Nan-tz'u hsü-lu (An Account of Southern Lyrics; Hsü Wei), 801
"Nan wang-hou" (The Male Queen; Wang Chi-te), 841
nan-yin (Cantonese: *naam-yam*; southern tone stories), 723, 1026
Nan-yu chi (Journey to the South; Yü Hsiang-tou), 129, 664
Nanking, 33
Nanking, Treaty of (1842), 701
Nansō satomi hakken den (The Legend of the Eight Dogs of Satomi in Nansō; Takizawa Bakin), 1093
"Nao yin-ssu Ssu-ma Mao tuan yü" (Ssu-ma Mao; Feng Meng-lung), 602
narration, 700, 706, 707, 716; experiments with, 751; first-person, 673, 723, 726, 730, 731, 742; in historical writing, 496–97, 500, 503, 504; semi-autobiographical, 738
nationalism, 461, 627, 628, 771, 1065, 1066
Natsume Sōseki, 1094
Ne-cha (Naṭa; Investiture of the Gods), 125
nei (inner), 937
nei-chuan (esoteric biographies), 580
nei-ko (Grand Secretariat), 401
"Nei-p'ien" (Inner Chapters; *Chuang Tzu*), 173
nei-pu (internal circulation) press, 1035, 1039, 1040
nei-tan (Inner Alchemy), 186–91, 635
"Nei yeh" (Inner Workings; *Kuan Tzu*), 76
Neo-Confucianism, 9, 351–52, 366, 387, 418–19, 556, 707; Ch'eng-Chu, 246–47, 414; of Chin dynasty, 936; Chu Hsi school of, 414, 888, 1070, 1087, 1089, 1092; and female talent, 447–48; influence of Buddhism on, 161; and Mencius, 96; revivals of, 531, 825; and *yü-lu*, 168. See also *tao-hsüeh*
Nestorian Christianity, 9, 170, 1048
New and Old Text schools, 89–92
New Culture movement. *See* May Fourth movement
new-style poetry. See *chin-t'i shih*
New Wave literature, 763–65
newspapers, 567, 702
Ngawang Lobsang Gyatso (fifth Dalai Lama), 1046
Ngoc kieu le tan truyen (Jade Charming Pear, or A Tale of Hong-yü, Wu-chiao, and Lu Meng-li; trans. from Chinese), 1100
Nguyen Bang Trung, 1102
Nguyen Du, 1101

Nguyen Gia Thieu, 1099
Nguyen Huy Oanh, 1097
Nguyen Huy Tu, 1100
Nguyen Thuyen, 1097
Nguyen Trai, 1098
Nguyen Van Danh, 1102
"Ni 'Hsing lu nan'" (Imitating "The Road Is Hard"; Pao Chao), 269
Ni Huan-chih (Yeh Sheng-t'ao), 746
"Ni-hung teng-hsia te shao-ping" (Soldiers Under Neon Light; Shen Hsi-meng et al.), 873
Ni-ku yüeh-fu (Archaistic Ballads; Li Tung-yang), 1073
"Ni pieh wu hsüan-tse" (You Have No Choice; Liu So-la), 764
Ni Tsan, 387, 388, 392, 394, 487, 488
Ni yi-wei ni shih shei (Who Do You Think You Are; Ch'ih Li), 765
"Ni 'Yung-huai'" (Imitating "Songs of My Soul"; Yü Hsin), 273
nieh (misdeeds), 624
Nieh-hai hua (A Flower in a Sea of Sins; Chin T'ien-ho and Tseng P'u), 657, 709, 721, 724, 725
Nieh Jung-chen, 872, 873
Nieh-mo-sheng (Kāśyapa Mātaṅga), 523–24
Nieh-nu Pa-hsi, 1040
Nien-ch'ang, 167
Nienhauser, William H., Jr., 511–26, 579–94
Nietzche, Friedrich, 442, 711
Nihon shoki (Official Records of Japan), 1080
Nimmyō, Emperor, 1082
Nine Monks, 343
Ninety-three (Hugo), 720
ning chih (congealed fat), 195
Ning Shih-ch'ang, 187
Nisan Shamaness, 1051
Nishida Korenori, 1093
"Niu fu" (The Ox; Liu Tsung-yüan), 305
Niu Hsiu, 690–91
Niu Seng-ju, 581, 588
No (Exorcism) ceremony, 788, 790, 792, 817
Nō dramas, 1093
No-hsi (*No-t'ang-hsi*; exorcism plays), 787, 993, 994, 997–98, 1000–1001
Nobel Prize, 737–38, 750, 764, 772
Norman, Jerry, 22
Northern and Southern dynasties. *See* Southern and Northern Dynasties
Northern Ch'i dynasty (550-577), 252, 282
Northern Chou dynasty (557-581), 252, 273, 282, 979
Northern Sung dynasty, 560, 564, 834, 997; and ancient-style prose, 536–38; Buddhism in, 362; Confucian renaissance of, 350, 359; entertainment complexes (*kou-lan*) in, 1007; in fiction, 643, 1023; humor in, 142; literary ideals in, 359, 365, 392; literati painting of, 477, 479, 480, 481, 485, 490; poetry of, 315, 324, 342, 343–44, 348, 352, 353, 356, 357–58, 393, 395, 478, 482; song forms of, 371, 796; Taoism in, 179, 181. *See also* Southern Sung dynasty; Sung dynasty
Northern Wei dynasty (386–534), 153, 252, 264, 282, 471, 473, 474
"Not a Dog, An Ancient Tai Ballad" (Tai narrative poem), 1043–44
Novalis, 334
novels, 399; adventure, 1064–65; Buddhist influence on, 168; Ch'ing, 697, 717, 720–26; criticism of, 705; European, 722, 723; foreign, 716–20; historical, 210, 499, 713; and *hua-pen*, 595, 619; humor in, 147–48; of indictment (*ch'ien-tse hsiao-shuo*), 657; Japanese criticism of Chinese, 711; Korean, 1052, 1074–76; and literary theory, 711; martial arts, 128, 671–72; Ming, 69; political, 710; proletarian, 748–49; and proverbs, 155; of Republican period, 726–28; and rhetoric, 894, 1012; scholar-beauty, 666–69; as serials, 1012; and short stories, 720, 729; and Taoism, 191; Tibetan, 1047; translations of, 716–20, 1064, 1075, 1102, 1103; twentieth-century, 567, 732, 738; Uyghur, 1049; vernacular, 659–74, 727, 1015, 1075, 1102; Vietnamese, 1100–1103; and women, 210. *See also* fiction
The Novels and Tales (James), 717
"Nu-hou pa, Chung-kuo!" (China Roars; Tretiakov), 859
nu-jen (women), 977
"Nü Ch'en P'ing chi sheng ch'i ch'u" (The Female Ch'en P'ing Saves Her Life; Li Yü), 614, 618
"Nü chieh" (Lessons for Women; Pan Chao), 205
Nü-hsien wai-shih (The Unofficial History of the Woman Immortal; Lu Hsiung), 632
nü-huo (the calamity of women), 14
Nü-kua. *See* Nü-wa
"Nü-shih chen t'u" (Admonitions of the Instructress to the Court Ladies; Chang Hua), 471, 473
"Nü-shih chen t'u" (Admonitions of the Instructress to the Court Ladies; Ku K'ai-chih), 198, 471
nü-shu (Women's Script), 33, 34, 990, 992, 994, 999–1003, 1006, 1010–11, 1016
"Nü tse" (A Model for Women), 205
Nü Tsung (Honored Woman), 524–25
Nü-wa (Nü-kua; goddess), 63, 64, 66, 69, 197, 199, 468, 469, 648

nung-yen (agricultural proverbs), 152–53, 158
Nurgaci (Nurhaci), 1051

"O ch'uan-chia chi chuan chia shih yin, hen p'u jen wu t'ou chen ming chuang" (The Ginger Merchant; Ling Meng-ch'u), 609
O-mi-t'o ching (*Amitābha-sūtra*), 163
"O-p'ang kung fu" (The O-p'ang Palace; Tu Mu), 311
"O-ping yü Tsang-lo" (O-ping and Tsang-lo), 1043
O Se-jae, 1068
ocherkovaia literatura (*pao-kao wen-hsüeh*; reportage), 15, 568, 733, 760, 761, 763
Ōe no Masafusa, 1087
Oghuz Turks, 1013
Ögödei (son of Genghis Khan), 1049–50
Ogyū Sorai, 1090, 1092
Oka Hakku, 1092
Okajima Kanzan, 1092
Ōmura Masuo, 698
O'Neill, Eugene, 860
Ongnu mong (Dream of the Jade Chamber; Nam Yŏng-no), 1076
Ōnin war of 1467, 1088
Ono Minemori, 1083
opera, 15, 154, 210, 553; ballad, 787, 793; folk, 864–65; *k'un-ch'ü*, 828–30, 843, 845, 1023; local, 1016; model, 846; Vietnamese, 1103. *See also* Peking opera
Opium Wars, 335, 763, 1056, 1058
oracle bones (*chia-ku-wen*; SBIs), 35, 49, 56, 442; as historical records, 495, 496; and language study, 47; and Liu O, 735, 739; polysyllabic writing in, 41; and *Yi-ching*, 89
oral tradition, 15, 32, 705, 1052; and ballads, 954, 989; and biography, 511–12, 513, 514, 517; and Buddhist texts, 167–68; and Chinese script, 50–51; and classical tales, 582, 594, 676, 678; and fiction, 211, 620, 622, 739, 756; formulaic, 989–1014; and *fu*, 278; and *hua-pen*, 595, 596; and humor, 134, 135, 137, 138; of minority groups, 1035, 1045; and proverbs, 149, 150, 151, 152, 153; and supernatural tales, 122, 548; and *Tao te ching*, 77
Otogibōko (Fairy Maid, or the Protective Doll; Asai Ryōi), 1091
Ōtomo no Yakamochi, 1081
Ou Mei ming-chia tuan-p'ien hsiao-shuo ts'ung-k'o (Collection of Short Stories by Renowned European and American Writers), 729
"Ou t'i" (Inscribed Perfunctorily; Li Shang-yin), 311
Ou Wai-ou, 456
Ou-yang Chiang-ho, 463
Ou-yang Chiung, 316
Ou-yang Ho, 582–83
Ou-yang Hsiu, 89, 133, 138, 356, 531, 533, 536–40, 557, 558; and Confucianism, 344–48; on inscriptions, 539; lyrics of, 317, 326, 333; on painting and poetry, 481; poems of exile, 358; and poetry, 538, 539, 934; and prose *fu*, 245; style of, 244, 353, 890; and Su Shih, 350; and Su Shun-ch'in, 347; and Wang An-shih, 349; and *wen-jen* ideal, 392
Ou-yang Hsün, 136, 282, 583
Ou-yang Tzu, 779
Ou-yang Yü-ch'ien, 850–59, 867
Owen, Stephen, 319, 322
Oyghangan Zimin (The Awakened Land; Abdurrehim Utkur), 1049

Pa Chin (Li Fei-kan), 156, 750, 770, 771, 1011, 1057
pa-ku wen (eight-legged essay), 236, 244, 246, 247, 531, 644, 713, 734
Pa-li ch'a-hua nü yi-shih (*La Dame aux camélias* ; trans. Lin Shu), 719, 851, 1064
pa ping (eight defects), 270, 276, 931, 1082
"Pa-sheng Kan-chou" (Eight Beats of a Kanchou Song; Liu Yung), 319
pa ta fang-yen (eight major dialects), 23
Pa-tuan chin (Eight Pieces of Brocade), 611
Pa tung-t'ien (Eight Fairylands), 615
"Pa-yi Nan-ch'ang ch'i-yi" (August First Uprising in Nan-ch'ang; Nieh Jung-chen et al.), 872
P'a hanjip (Collection for Dispelling Boredom; Yi In-no), 1069
Paegun sosŏl (Tales of White Clouds; Yi Kyu-bo), 1069
pai-chia cheng-ming (Hundred Schools of Thought Contending), 572
Pai-chia kung-an (The Hundred Cases), 599
Pai Ch'iu, 461
Pai Feng-hsi, 874–75, 876
"Pai-ho fang chiang wu tso yu" (Deception in the Pai-ho Quarter; Cho-yüan-t'ing chu-jen), 615
pai-hsi (hundred games), 790
Pai Hsien-yung, 777, 780
Pai Hua (b.1930), 761, 770
Pai Hua (b.1956), 463
pai-hua hsiao-shuo (vernacular fiction), 716
pai-hua shih (vernacular poetry), 441, 442, 454
pai-hua wen (modern written vernacular), 149, 151, 156, 158, 620, 643, 647, 715, 903, 1056–60, 1066
Pai-hua wen-hsüeh shih (History of Vernacular Literature; Hu Shih), 14
pai-hua yün-tung (Vernacular Literature movement), 384, 453, 743, 744

pai-kuan (Korean: *p'aegwan*; informal histories), 1069
Pai-kuei chih (The Tale of the White Jade Tablet), 668
"Pai ma p'ien" (White Horse; Ts'ao Chih), 256, 262
"Pai-mao nü" (The White-Haired Girl), 864–65, 868
Pai-mo tz'u (Powder from Hundreds of Blossoms Lyrics; Yu T'ung), 418
Pai nationality (Min-chia), 1042–43
"Pai niang-tzu yung chen Lei-feng T'a" (Madam White), 597–98
"Pai niao" (The White Bird; Ho Li-wei), 765
Pai nien yi chiao (A Hundred Years' Sleep; *Looking Backward*; trans. Richard), 718
Pai Pi, 376
Pai P'u, 379, 814
"Pai-she chuan" (The Story of the White Snake), 1023
pai-tsan (Brahmic songs; hymns), 978
"Pai-t'u chi" (The Story of the White Hare), 797, 805, 821, 822, 826, 1018
Pai Wei, 851, 853, 854, 875
Pai Yü-ch'an, 189–91
Pai-yü ching (Canonical Scripture of a Hundred Parables; Gunavṛddhi), 172
"Pai-yüan chuan" ("Hsü Chiang-shih chuan"; An Account of the White Monkey), 582–83
"Pai-yüeh chi" (Praying to the Moon), 821
"Pai-yüeh t'ing" (Courtyard of Praying to the Moon; Kuan Han-ch'ing), 801, 821
P'ai-an ching-ch'i (Slapping the Table in Amazement; Ling Meng-ch'u), 605
p'ai-lü, 276, 284, 291, 293. See also *chin-t'i shih*
painter-poets, 387–88, 402, 415, 466, 480, 487; Ch'ing, 435; Ming, 398, 435, 479, 489, 490; Ming-Ch'ing, 427–28; T'ang, 478, 479, 481, 490; twentieth century, 464
painting, 49, 400, 402, 767; allegorical, 487; artisan, 480; avant-garde, 763; birds and flowers, 485; and Buddhism, 479, 480; Buddhist influence on, 163; and Confucianism, 480; by Emperor Hui-tsung, 482, 487; inscriptions on (*t'i-hua wen-hsüeh*), 466, 467–90, 1084; landscape, 295, 467, 477–79, 487, 490, 885; and literati, 466, 477–81, 485, 490; and poetry, 466–90, 886, 1090; and Taoism, 173, 473, 477
Pak Che-ga, 1072
Pak Ch'i-wŏn, 1076–77
Pak Il-lyang, 1069
Pak-t'ongsa (Interpreter Pak), 1075
Pan, Favorite Beauty (consort of Emperor Ch'eng), 249–50, 471, 473
Pan Chao, 205–6, 217, 507
pan-ch'iang-t'i (beat and tune style), 793, 826, 843
Pan Ku, 175, 205, 233, 501, 506–7, 518–20, 523; and (*fu*), 234, 235, 263, 309; and history writing, 251, 900, 956; and literary criticism, 921, 922, 930; picture eulogies of, 468. See also *Han shu*
Pan Piao, 507
pan-shih pien-hua t'i (change of rhythm style), 793
pan tz'u-hua (act-out ballads), 787
P'an Chih-heng, 685, 689–90
"P'an Chin-lien" (Ou-yang Yü-ch'ien), 855
P'an-hsi chi (Anthology from P'an Tributary; Ch'iu Ch'u-chi), 188
P'an Jen-mu, 777
P'an-ku (creator god), 63, 69
P'an Lang, 343
P'an Ni, 260
P'an shan yü-lu (Discourse Record of Mount P'an; comp. Wang Chih-chin), 187
"P'an Wen-tzu" (Hsi Lang-hsien), 611
"P'an Wen-tzu ch'i-ho yüan-yang chung" (P'an Wen-tzu; Hsi Lang-hsien), 605
P'an Yüeh, 239, 240, 260, 261, 262
P'ang-huang (Hesitation; Lu Hsün), 744
Pāṇini, 30
p'ansori (Korean drumsong tradition), 1030, 1076
pao (retribution), 111, 112, 121, 171, 582, 601, 612, 661, 995. *See also* karma; morality
Pao-ch'ang, 165, 524
Pao Chao, 208, 268–69, 298, 412, 959, 960, 962
Pao Cheng (Judge Pao; Pao-kung), 8, 142, 145, 743, 808–9, 819, 999, 1001, 1002
"Pao-chien chi" (The Precious Sword; Li K'ai-hsien et al.), 818, 824
pao-chüan (Buddhist prosimetric texts; precious scrolls), 12, 641, 991, 995, 1006, 1018
"Pao ch'un hua" (Winter Jasmine; Ts'ui Te-chih), 871, 872
Pao Hsüan, 525
pao-kao wen-hsüeh (reportage literature), 15, 568, 733, 760, 761, 763
Pao-kuang chi (Anthology of Concealed Radiance; comp. Tuan Chih-chien), 188
Pao Kung, 8
Pao Ling-hui, 207–8, 960
pao-lu wen-hsüeh (exposure literature), 15
"Pao Lung-t'u tuan Ts'ao kuo-chiu kung-an chuan" (Judge Pao Solves the Case of Imperial Kinsman Ts'ao), 1002
Pao-p'u Tzu (The Master Who Embraces Simplicity; comp. Ko Hung), 117, 176
Pao Su, 524
Pao T'ien-hsiao, 704, 709, 730
"Pao-wei Lu-kou-ch'iao" (In Defense of Marco Polo Bridge), 864

parables (*p'i-yü*; Sanskrit: *avadāna*), 117, 171–72, 523, 539, 580, 984
Parallel Lives (Plutarch), 517
parallel prose (*p'ien-t'i wen*), 223–47, 499, 527, 530–33, 548, 706, 968, 993; allusion in, 242, 243, 245, 262; and archaic prose, 1069; in Chien-an period, 256; Ch'ing, 224, 236, 243, 246–47; in *ch'uan-ch'i* tales, 583, 680; in early sixth century, 887; epistles in, 1088; in fiction, 620, 739; and *fu*, 236–47, 277–78; in Japan, 1084, 1085, 1087; in Korea, 1068, 1070, 1071, 1072; and literary criticism, 927; and Literary Sinitic, 238, 243; and ornate prose, 881, 887; rhyme in, 247; set-piece descriptions in, 948; of Six Dynasties, 230, 236–40, 244, 1068; Sung, 240, 246; T'ang, 289, 530; and Tun-huang literature, 973
parallelism, 286, 891; and Confucianism, 530, 892; in historical writing, 500; in poetry, 232, 235, 268; straight (*cheng-tui*), 893; syntactic, 276; tonal, 257; verbal, 257, 261, 262, 264, 276, 277; Western, 905
Pastreich, Emanuel, 1067–1104
Patañjali, 30
patronage: of Buddhism, 270; imperial, 181, 182, 232–33, 240, 926, 955, 959; literary, 232–33, 240, 248, 432, 448, 955, 959; of Taoism, 181, 182, 188
Paz, Octavio, 457
peasants, 32, 663, 1037; drama of, 865–70
"Pei cheng" (The Journey North; Tu Fu), 204, 299
pei-chih (epitaph and grave inscription), 528
Pei-ching chih ch'un (Peking Spring; journal), 464
"Pei-ching jen" (Peking Men; Ts'ao Yü), 864
Pei-ching jen (Chinese Lives; Chang Hsin-hsin), 761
Pei-ching jen-min yi-shu chü-yüan (Peking People's Art Theater), 869, 876, 877
"Pei-fen shih" (Poem of Grief and Anger; Ts'ai Yen), 206, 257
Pei-hai te jen (Backed Against the Sea; Wang Wen-hsing), 777
Pei-hsi tzu yi (The Meanings of Words; Ch'en Ch'un), 888–89
"Pei hui feng" (Grieving at the Eddying Wind), 228
Pei-li chi (Record of the Northern Wards; Sun Ch'i), 581
Pei Tao (Bei Dao), 462, 761, 764, 766, 768
"Pei-ying" (With His Back Turned; Chu Tzu-ch'ing), 574–75
Pei-yu chi (Journey to the North; Yü Hsiang-tou), 129, 664
P'ei, Prince, 287
"P'ei Chin-kung yi huan yüan-p'ei" (P'ei Tu; Feng Meng-lung), 600
P'ei Hsing, 579, 589
P'ei Sung-chih, 521, 622
P'ei Ti, 294, 301, 478
P'ei Tzu-yeh, 929, 930
P'ei-wen yün-fu (Storehouse of Quotations Classified by Rhyme from the Pendant to Letters Studio), 434
Peking, 33, 721, 725, 749
Peking opera (*ching-hsi*), 845–46, 866; actors in, 843; basic melodies of, 793; libretti of, 786, 795; and literati, 843; and May Fourth movement, 848, 851–52, 856, 857; reform of, 852; revolutionary modern, 868, 874; on Taiwan, 847
Peking Pedagogical Institute, 713
Peking People's Art Theater (Pei-ching jen-min yi-shu chü-yüan), 869, 876, 877
Peking School of Arts (Kuo-li Pei-ching yi-shu chuan-men hsüeh-hsiao), 856
Peking Spring (democracy movement), 463. *See also* T'ien-an-men Square demonstrations
Pelliot, Paul, 965, 1017
pen-chi (basic annals), 503
pen-chu (ancestral village gods), 1042
Pen-chüeh (monk), 167
"Pen-kuan fu-yin shuo-pu yüan-ch'i" (Announcing Our Policy of Printing a Fiction Supplement; Yen Fu and Hsia Tseng-yü), 706
pen-se (authenticity; true color), 841
pen-sheng tales, 984
Pen-shih shih (The Original Incidents of Poems; Meng Ch'i), 837
"P'en-erh kuei" (Ghost in the Pot), 145, 808
P'eng Ko, 777
P'eng Shih-tu, 416
P'eng Sun-yü, 418
"P'eng-tang lun" (On Factions; Ou-yang Hsiu), 538
P'eng Ting-ch'iu, 178
P'eng Yüeh, 516, 519
People's Drama Society (Min chung she), 855
People's Libertion Army (PLA), 873, 875
People's Theater (Ta-chung chü-she), 860
performance texts, 895–99, 986–88; categories of, 994; and popular storytelling, 983, 1016; *vs.* records, 897–99; verse-introductory formulae in, 985, 987
Phan Huy Ich, 1099
Phan Ke Binh, 1103
philosophy, 557; and history, 501; and humor, 132, 138–40, 146; and literature, 70–85, 926; political, 91; statecraft, 79–80; and women, 218. *See also particular schools*
phonology, 48, 56–57, 91

Pi, battle of, 499
pi, pi-yü (comparison, simile), 5, 150, 151–52, 156, 157, 893–94, 921
Pi-cha hua-liang (The Ornamented Ridgepole of Written Tablets; Shang-kuan Yi), 286
"Pi-ch'eng" (The Walls of Cyan-Blue; Li Shang-yin), 311
pi-chi (*sui-pi*; occasional jottings), 121, 134, 537, 595, 837, 841, 1016; categories of, 563; and *chih-kuai*, 560, 562, 563–64; examples of, 130, 543, 544, 694, 695–96, 939; and humor, 140, 142, 143; Sung, 560–65
Pi-chi hsiao-shuo ta-kuan (The Great Compendium of Pi-chi Fiction), 565
Pi-chi man-chih (Random Notes from Pi-chi; Wang Cho), 939
Pi-ch'iu-ni chuan (Biographies of Nuns; Pao-ch'ang), 165, 524
Pi-chou hsüan sheng-yü (Left-Over Talk from Broken Broom Studio; Shen Te-fu), 142
Pi-ho-kuan chu-jen, 722
pi-mo (shaman-priests), 1035–41
"Pi-mu-yü" (Sole Mate, or The Flounder; Li Yü), 832
Pi-p'o ts'ung-ts'o (Gleanings from the Field of Letters), 682
"Pi-sheng hua" (Elegant Words of the Brush; Chiu Hsin-ju), 1023
Pi Shu-min, 766
"Pi shuo" (Remarks on the Brush; Ou-yang Hsiu), 539
pi-t'an. See *pi-chi*
Pi-yao te ku-tu (The Need for Solitude; Henry Chao), 768
Pi-yen lu (Records from the Emerald Cliff; K'o-ch'in), 169
P'i Jih-hsiu, 312
p'i-p'a (lute), 283, 315, 333, 346, 641, 1023, 1026
"P'i-p'a chi" (The Story of the Lute; Kao Ming), 794, 801, 805, 820–21, 826; commentaries on, 842
"P'i-p'a hsien shang shuo hsiang-ssu" (Longing Told on the Strings of the *P'i-p'a*; Yen Chi-tao), 317
"P'i-p'a hsing" (Ballad of the Balloon Lute; Po Chü-yi), 308, 815, 834
p'i-p'ing (comments), 941
"P'i-shuang po" (Arsenic Bowl; Shao Pin-ju), 619
p'i-tzu, liu-mang (riffraff, ruffians), 766, 767, 771
p'i-yü (Sanskrit: *avadāna*; parables), 117, 171–72, 523, 539, 580, 984
piao (documentary prose), 528–29, 1070
piao (tables), 503
piao ch'i ching hsiu (aiming at the unusual yet striving for the utmost grace), 387
"Piao yi-che Kuo Ch'ang" (In Praise of the Medical Practitioner Kuo Ch'ang; Shen Ya-chih), 592
"Pieh ch'ing" (Parting; Kuan Han-ch'ing), 377
pieh-chuan (separate or distinct biographies), 521, 580
Pieh-ling (Efficacious Turtle; Emperor K'ai-ming), 518
Pieh-shih (Hsia Tseng-yü), 454, 706, 708–9, 717
Pien-ch'eng (Bordertown; Shen Ts'ung-wen), 751, 1034
Pien-chi, 165
Pien Chih-lin, 455, 456
Pien erh ch'ai (Wearing a Cap but Also Hairpins), 611
pien-hsiang (transformation tableau), 478
Pien Kung, 404, 406
"Pien Li sao" (Transformed "Encountering Sorrow"; Ch'ao Pu-chih), 353
pien-sai shih (frontier poetry), 272, 273, 283, 296, 303
Pien Shao, 183
"Pien wang lun" (Treatise on the Fall of a State; Lu Chi), 239
pien-wen (transformation texts), 30, 123, 595, 792, 891; and Buddhism, 993; prose and verse in, 968; and proverbs, 153; T'ang, 888, 995; theories of, 1019; from Tun-huang, 167–68, 814, 972, 982–87
pien-wen (varied expression), 891
p'ien (folksongs), 954, 1039
p'ien-t'i wen. *See* parallel prose
p'ien-wen. *See* parallel prose
"Pierrot" (Mu Shih-ying), 749
Pigsy. *See* Chu Pa-chieh
piji (inscriptions; Korean), 1070, 1071
Pin, state of, 107
p'in (evaluative classifications), 840
P'in-hua pao-chien (A Precious Mirror for Judging Flowers; Ch'en Sen), 657, 672, 843
Ping-chu ch'ing-t'an (Idle Talk by Candlelight; Chou Li), 682, 683
Ping Hsin (Hsieh Wan-ying), 747–48, 771
ping-shih chih ko-tz'u (song words that find fault with the times), 316
ping yen ping, chiang yen chiang (soldiers playing soldiers and commanders playing commanders), 873
P'ing, king of Ch'u, 514
"P'ing fu" (The Wine-Jar; Liu Tsung yüan), 305
p'ing-hua (plain tales), 155, 972, 973, 992, 1012, 1024
p'ing-lin (forest of comments), 942
P'ing-Shan-Leng-Yen (P'ing, Shan, Leng, and Yen; Chang Shao), 666
p'ing-tan (even and bland), 346, 536
p'ing-t'an (prosimetric performance), 1012, 1013

p'ing-tien (evaluative comments and emphatic punctuation), 842
p'ing (appreciation) tradition, 890, 894
P'ing-yao chuan (The Quelling of Demons; ed. Feng Meng-lung), 128, 631, 1093
pinyin (*p'in-yin*; PRC romanization system), 53, 54
Plaks, Andrew, 630, 631, 634–35, 637, 640–42, 650
Platform Sūtra of the Sixth Patriarch (*Liu-tsu t'an-ching*; Hui-neng), 169
Plato, 359, 884, 885, 897
playwrights, 808, 811–18; court-connected, 809–10, 816; female, 838–40, 874; of PRC, 858–59
Plutarch, 517
Po Chü-yi, 7, 11, 14, 202, 208, 279, 586, 587, 730; adaptations to stage of, 814, 834; and archaists, 408, 411; autobiographical poems of, 434; and Buddhism, 169; in Japan, 431, 1083, 1089; as model, 352, 412, 416, 1085–86, 1087; New Balladry of, 955, 962–63; and origin of the song lyric, 975; poems of, 307, 309, 485, 815, 982, 1008; style of, 244, 342, 384, 403, 838; *yüeh-fu* of, 277, 308
Po Hsiang-shan shih-chi (collection of Po Chü-yi's work), 982
"Po-hsiao chi" (For Laughs; Shen Ching), 830
Po Hsing-chien, 586
Po-hsüeh hung-tz'u (For Erudites Whose Writings Carry Far; special examination), 417, 418, 420, 427
Po-je-po-lo-mi-to hsin ching (*Hsin ching*; Heart/Mind Sutra), 635
Po P'i, 829
po-p'o-mo-fo (National Phonetic Symbols), 53
po-shih (Erudites), 2, 4, 912
Po-shih wen-chi (*Hakushi monjū*; Collected Works of Mister Po), 1083–84
Po-t'i style, 342
Po-tung (Waves; Pei Tao), 764
Po-wu chih (A Treatise on Curiosities; Chang Hua), 120, 261, 548, 549–50
Po Yang, 569, 572, 767
Po-yi (Yi), 544–45
"P'o-fu" (A Shrewish Woman; Ou-yang Yü-ch'ien), 853
p'o-yin (split sound) characters, 42
Poe, Edgar Allan, 943
"Poems on History" (Tso Ssu), 263, 264
poet-officials, 394, 395
poetry, 223–490; agrarian, 363; antithesis in, 286; architectural, 301; ascent, 293; competitions in, 292; composition on command in, 232, 234, 241, 283; court-centered, 248, 273, 286, 287, 290; descriptive, 268–69, 304, 474, 475, 487; eighteenth to early twentieth centuries, 429–43; extemporaneous, 234; farewell, 313, 320; feast, 254, 255, 263, 268; and fiction, 464, 596, 598, 611, 620, 624, 735; fifteenth and sixteenth centuries, 399–409; foreign, 454, 455; four essential principles of, 422; fourteenth century, 390–98; function of, 920; genres of, 223–24, 238, 245, 248, 254; group composition of, 229, 232, 233, 234, 238; and history, 267, 437; homosexuality in, 272; and humor, 132–34, 145, 148; imagery in, 226–28, 233, 298; imitation in, 248; inscription, 467, 474–77, 482, 485, 487, 489; interjections in, 109; on Internet, 464; intuitive control in, 423, 425; languages of, 32, 106–7; line length in, 237, 249, 254, 257, 258, 259, 277, 318, 319; and literary theory, 713, 916, 917; lyric, 51, 274, 897, 933; Mao school on, 100; Ming-Ch'ing, 674; modern, 428, 430, 453–65, 730, 760; and music, 108–9, 319, 371, 917; nature, 293–96, 304; on objects, 240, 242, 250, 251, 269–72, 277, 283, 313, 329, 332, 333; official composition of, 232; and painting, 466–90, 886, 1090; Palace-Style, 200–203, 207–8, 219, 241, 262, 271, 272, 283, 284, 290, 315, 926; parallelism in, 232, 235, 268; patriotic, 360, 361, 367; and philosophy, 72, 73; and *pi-chi*, 563; political, 375, 462, 593; popular, 302–3, 925, 929, 954; of presentation and response, 254, 255, 259, 262; quest, 228; realism in, 255, 455; recitation of, 225, 226, 896; rhyme in, 108, 225, 232, 235–39, 319; and riddles, 225, 228; Sanskrit, 241, 270, 276, 931; seventeenth-century, 410–28, 444; on shared topics, 234; and social criticism, 366; and supernatural, 111, 115, 123–25, 543, 549, 553; Tai narrative, 1044; Taiwanese, 779–80; Taoist, 173, 183, 185–86, 188, 192; Tibetan, 1046–47; tones in, 248, 270; topics of, 254; traditionalist ideal of, 430–31; and travel literature, 559; from Tun-huang, 278–80, 302, 313, 315, 327, 973–82; underground, 462–63; vernacular, 441, 442, 454, 735–36; about women, 200–205, 210, 218, 260, 269, 271, 272; by women, 14, 204–5, 249–50, 257, 263, 312, 325–27, 335, 357, 373, 381, 406, 428, 429. *See also particular genres, periods, and schools*
poetry societies (*shih-she*, *yin-shih-she*, *yin-she*), 356, 388, 392, 393, 410, 415; in Korea, 1068–69; of Modernist school, 460–61; in Taiwan, 458, 459

poets: and Buddhism, 268, 289, 290, 298, 302, 306, 312–13, 351, 353, 365, 408, 411, 431, 439, 442, 539, 540; modern, 457, 458, 463–64; role of, 455; and Taoism, 302, 311–13, 353, 394, 408, 411, 442. *See also* painter-poets
Pohanjip (Collection of Writings for Filling Free Time; Ch'oe Cha), 1070
politics, 457, 697, 918; and *ch'uan-ch'i*, 593, 594; and essays, 568–69, 572, 573; and fiction, 707–8; in historical writing, 501, 507–8; and humor, 140–43, 148; legitimacy in, 72, 82, 546, 623–26; and literary theory, 699–700, 707–10; and philosophy, 91; and poetry, 375, 462, 593; and Shanghai writers, 703, 704; and supernatural tales, 543, 546; twentieth-century, 157, 752–53, 762, 769, 772; and women, 197, 202–3, 206. *See also* Chinese Communist Party
post-Mao period, 848, 855, 858, 859
postmodernism, 15, 462, 759, 764, 766–67
Potato School. *See* Shan-yao-tan
Pound, Ezra, 3
Prajñāpāramitā Sūtra (*Po-je po-lo-mi ching*; Perfection of Wisdom scriptures), 6, 163
Prakrit language, 160
The Prayer Mat of Flesh. See *Jou p'u-t'uan*
PRC. *See* China, People's Republic of
Prémare, Joseph-Henri-Marie de, 803
Primer of Logic (Jevons). See *Ming-hsüeh ch'ien-shuo*
printing and publishing, 135, 161, 162, 178, 324, 711, 733; technology of, 702
prologs, 591, 596, 618
prose, 493–575, 716; archaic, 1069–73; Chinese artistic, 882, 883, 886, 887, 908; classical, 218, 735, 884, 885–86; documentary, 528–29, 1070; examination, 1072, 1073; experiments with, 765; expository, 527–41; informal, 561; and Ming-Ch'ing novels, 674; modern, 566–75, 760; personification in, 906; and poetry, 347, 365; premodern style of, 881–908; rhyme in, 108; rhythm of ornate, 886–90; scribal, 1073. *See also* Four-Six style; *ku-wen-tz'u*; parallel prose
prosimetric literature, 11, 57, 167, 168, 982–1014, 1027, 1042; Buddhist, 12, 172, 641, 991, 995, 1006, 1018; Ch'ing, 791; and drama, 787, 996–99; early, 796–97, 1019; and literati, 991, 996, 1003; Ming, 791, 1018, 1026; nonmelodic, 990, 993, 997, 998; and vernacular fiction, 1003–6, 1011, 1014
proverbs, 149–59; agricultural, 152–53, 158; in Literary Sinitic, 149, 151, 154, 158; weather, 152, 158; in written literature, 154–55
Průšek, Jaroslav, 11
"Pu-chih ch'iu-ssu tsai shui chia" (Where Is Longing in Autumn; Pai Feng-hsi), 875
pu-ch'ing (transcendence, negation), 652
pu ch'iu shen chieh (not aiming for a deep explanation), 883
pu-chu yi-tzu, chin te feng-liu (though not a word is said outright, the elegant style fulfills all), 933
"Pu chü" (Divination), 228
Pu Fei-yen, 589
"Pu Fei-yen" (Pu Fei-yen; Huang-fu Mei), 589
"Pu fu lao" (Refusal to Get Old; Kuan Han-ch'ing), 378
pu hao-se (indifference to women), 630
"Pu-hsü" (Pacing the Void; Wu Yün), 302
Pu-hsü ching (Scripture on Pacing the Void), 181
pu-hsüeh shih, wu yi yen (If one does not study poetry, one has not the wherewithal to speak), 917
Pu-hu-mu, 380
pu-ko (unobstructed), 939
pu-k'o ts'ou-po (rational analysis), 424
"Pu-ku-niao yu chiao le" (Cuckoo Sings Again; Yang Lü-fang), 866
Pu p'a ssu (Don't Be Afraid to Die; trans. from *Shanghai Express*), 860
pu shang/teng ta ya chih t'ang (never ascend to hall of elegant significance), 885
pu-yi shih (commoner poetry), 388, 392
p'u (chronological tables), 913
p'u (plain, unpretentious), 893
P'u-hsien p'u-sa shuo cheng-ming ching (Scripture of Evidence Preached by the Bodhisattva Samantabhadra), 970, 971
p'u-hsü (narrative structure), 327
P'u Po-ying, 856
P'u-sa tu-jen ching (Canonical Scripture on Bodhisattvas Leading Men to the Truth), 171
p'u-shih (unadornedly 'real'), 398
P'u Sung-ling, 127, 130, 540, 544, 596, 618, 660, 691–94, 720, 900–901; as Historian of the Strange, 542–43; humor of, 146; and local theater, 838
p'u-t'ung-hua (common speech; Mandarin), 33. *See also* Mandarin, Modern Standard; Sinitic
P'u-t'ung pai-k'o hsin ta tz'u-tien (A New General Encyclopedic Dictionary; Huang Jen), 713
P'u-yao ching (*Lalitavistara*), 172

Puett, Michael, 70–85
Pukhak (Northern Studies) movement (Korea), 1076
puppetry, 786, 791, 838, 899–900, 1093, 1094
pyŏrryŏ-mun. *See* parallel prose

Qubilai. *See* Khubilai Khan
Queen Mother of the West (Hsi Wang-mu), 66, 546, 810, 838
quoc am (national language; Vietnamese), 1098
quoc ngu (national script; Vietnam), 1102–3
Qutugdar (Mongol official), 487

Rāmāyaṇa (Hindu epic), 69, 1047
realism, 459, 475–77, 845; cynical, 767; in fiction, 641, 642, 652, 727, 740; magical, 756, 764; *vs.* modernism, 461–62; and New Wave literature, 764; in poetry, 255, 455; in Republican period fiction, 727; socialist, 157, 456, 760, 765; of Western art, 856–57
rebellion, popular, 116, 251, 374, 436, 621, 624, 631; in drama, 126; in fiction, 128, 663. *See also* Boxer Rebellion; Taiping Rebellion
recent-style poetry. See *chin-t'i shih*
Records of Marvels (Ts'ao P'i), 549
Red Army, 872, 873
Red Cliff (Ch'ih-pi), 245, 540; Battle of, 621, 624
"The Red Detachment of Women" (Hung-se niang-tzu-chün; model ballet), 868
Red Guards, 859
Red Sorghum. See *Hung kao-liang chia-tsu*
Red Turbans, 374
reform: Confucian, 919; in drama, 848; Hundred Days of (1898), 441, 450, 698, 706, 717, 734, 1059, 1060; in Japan, 1080; land, 866, 869; language, 31, 156, 159, 453, 745, 1056–57, 1060, 1065, 1066; literary, 156, 453, 1056, 1066; in PRC, 760, 762; social, 734, 735, 744
reincarnation, 114, 121, 168, 169, 660
religion, 129, 192, 676; Hinduism, 9; and humor, 146; Judaism, 4, 9; messianic, 177, 181, 624, 631; millenarian, 128, 621; popular, 76, 84, 124, 788; and supernatural, 123, 125, 545, 550; Tibetan, 1041, 1045. *See also* Buddhism; Christianity; Confucianism; Islam; Manichaeism; Taoism
reportage literature (*pao-kao wen-hsüeh*), 15, 568, 733, 760, 761, 763
Republican period, 430, 440–42, 1056, 1063; criticism in, 698–700; fiction in, 697–731; phonetic writing systems in, 53; prestige of fiction in, 732–33; supernatural tales in, 131
Rereading the Stone (Anthony Yu), 654
Resurrection (Tolstoy), 720
Revolution of 1911, 850, 1056
rhapsodies. See *fu*
"Rhapsody on the Bright Pearl" (Ts'ui Po-yi), 561
rhetoric: Chinese, 882–86, 905–8; in Classical Chinese, 882–83, 894; devices of, 906–7; of *Tso chuan*, 497; Western, 882, 905–8
rhyme, 225, 232, 235–37, 239, 247, 319, 528, 596, 641, 887, 961; in *Shih-ching*, 107–8
Ricci, Matteo, 52
Richard, Timothy, 718
Richards, I. A., 455
Richthofen, Friedrich von, 559
Richthofen, Manfred von, 559
Rickshaw Boy (*Lo-t'o Hsiang-tzu*; Lao She), 749–50, 1034
Riegel, Jeffrey, 97–109
Rikunyo, 1090
ritual: and drama, 98, 786, 788, 790, 825, 847, 997; in Han dynasty, 911, 956, 993; and historical writing, 494, 495, 501, 502, 510; and language, 1081–82; and literati, 1010; and music, 995; specialists in, 1041; village, 994, 998. See also *Li-chi*
"River Elegy" (Ho-shang; television series), 57, 763
Ro Kyŏng, 1072
Roaring-Heaven Spoken Drama Troupe (Chen-t'ien-sheng pai-hua chü-she), 850
Robinet, Isabelle, 10
Robinson Crusoe, 1064
Rock, J. F., 1041
Rohsenow, John S., 149–59
Die Rolle des Erzählers in der Epik (The Role of the Narrator in the Epic; Friedemann), 716–17
Rolston, David L., 940–49
Der Roman: Geschichte, Theorie und Technik des Romans und der erzählenden Dichtung (The Novel: History, Theory and Technique of the Novel and Narrative Poetry; Keiter and Keller), 716
romance, 709, 826, 828, 858, 1007; in late Ch'ing novels, 722, 723, 724; in recent PRC fiction, 755; in Republican-period fiction, 728; scholar-beauty, 596, 617, 644, 666–69, 679–90, 742, 743, 798, 817, 1074–76, 1100, 1101; and supernatural, 125, 130; translations of, 718
Romance of the Three Kingdoms. See *San-kuo yen-yi*
Romance of the Western Chamber. *See* "Hsi-hsiang chi"
romanticism, 455, 456
Ross, Timothy A., 777
Roy, David, 640–42
Russia, 720, 760, 769, 772. *See also* Soviet Union
Ryōunshū (Collection of Poems that Float up to the Clouds; comp. Ono Minemori), 1083

Sa-tu-la (Sadula), 380–81, 387
Saeki Tomi, 564
Saga, Emperor, 1082–83, 1084
sages, 4, 74–78, 81–84
Sai Chin-hua, 657, 780
"Sai Chin-hua" (play; Hsia Yen), 862–63
"Sai Chin-hua" incident, 863
Salinger, J. D., 463, 765
Samguk yusa (Residual History of the Three Kingdoms; comp. Ilyŏn), 1070
saṃsāra (cycle of rebirth), 169
San chia shih (Three Schools of the *Shih-ching*), 99–100
San-chiang hsien-chih (Annals of San-chiang County), 1053
san-chiao (Three Teachings), 176, 186, 190, 411–12, 612
san-ch'ü poetry, 210, 370–82, 389, 796, 799, 800, 818, 840
san-chüeh (three perfections), 466
"San-hsiao yin-yüan" (The Three Smiles Romance), 1023–24
san-hsien (three-stringed banjo), 1023, 1026, 1042
"San ko p'an-ni te nü-hsing" ([Trilogy of] Three Revolutionary Women; Kuo Mo-jo), 854–55
San-k'o p'ai-an ching-ch'i (Slapping the Table in Amazement, Third Collection), 611
San-kuo chih (History of the Three Kingdoms; Ch'en Shou), 261, 508, 521–22, 622
San-kuo chih p'ing-hua (Illustrated Stories from the Records of the Three Kingdoms), 621, 622
San-kuo yen-yi (Romance of the Three Kingdoms), 218, 499, 508, 621–25, 637–38, 659, 707, 942, 998–99, 1016; and *Chin P'ing Mei*, 637; in Japan, 1091, 1093; and *Journey to the West*, 632; in Korea, 1075, 1076, 1077, 1078; 1680 edition of, 943; supernatural in, 127; in Vietnamese, 1103; and *Water Margin*, 626, 631
San-li (Three ritual Texts), 91
"San liang" (Three Good Men; Ts'ao Chih), 255
San Mao, 780
san-mei (enlightenment), 415, 424, 425
San-miao chuan (The Three Wonders), 683
San-pao t'ai-chien hsi-yang chi t'ung-su yen-yi (Journey to the Western Ocean; Lo Mao-teng), 632
"San-san" (Shen Ts'ung-wen), 751
San-shih tai t'ien-shih Hsü-ching chen-chün yü-lu (Discourse Record of the Thirtieth Generation Celestial Master Perfected Lord of Vacant Tranquility; comp. Chang Yü-ch'u), 179
San-t'i shih (Three Poetic Modes), 1087
San-t'i shih-ching (Three-Font Stone Classics), 90
san-ts'ai (tricolor) mortuary figurines, 589
San-tsang (Sanskrit: *Tripiṭaka*; Three Baskets), 161
"San-ts'ung" (Three Obediences), 992
"San tu fu" (Rhapsody on the Three Capitals; Tso Ssu), 234, 239, 263, 925
San-tung (Three Caves), 161, 180
San-tung ching-shu mu-lu (A Catalog to the Scriptural Writings of the Three Caverns), 178
San-tzu ching (Trimetrical Classic), 995
San wang (Three Kings; Ah Ch'eng), 764
san-wen (*ku-wen*) prose, 236
San wu li chi (Historical Records of the Three Sovereign Divinities and Five Gods), 63
San-yen (Three Words: Feng Meng-lung), 599–602, 604, 830, 996
san-yen (three-word text), 5, 599–602
san-yüeh (*sangaku*; *saragaku*; dispersed, monkey music), 1088–89
"San yüeh san jih Ch'ü shui shih hsü" (Preface to the Winding Stream Poems; Wang Jung), 241
"San yüeh san jih Ch'ü shui shih hsü" (Preface to the Winding Stream Poems; Yen Yen-chih), 240, 241
Sand Monk Wu-ching (*Journey to the West*), 633, 634
"Sang-shu-p'ing chi-shih" (The Story of Sang-shu-p'ing; Ch'en Tzu-tu et al.), 869–70, 876
Sanguk sagi (Historical Records of the Three Kingdoms), 1069
Sangyōgisho (Buddhist sutras), 1080
Sanskrit, 11, 20, 25, 45, 86, 160–61, 164, 993
sansu yugi (travelogs), 1072
Santō Kyōden, 1094
Sao-mi chou (A Broom to Sweep Away Ignorance; Chuang-che), 1078
sao poetry, 223–27, 229–30, 234, 240, 276, 288–89, 353, 396
Sargent, Stuart, 314–36
Sarim (Confucian literary group in Korea), 1072
Sartre, Jean-Paul, 463, 777
Sarvāstivādin school, 162
Sasagawa Rinpū (Sasagawa Taneo), 711, 713
Saso, Michael, 10, 179
śāstras (treatises), 164
satire, 166, 596, 661, 694, 767; in essays, 569, 570, 572, 573; in *Flowers in the Mirror*, 130, 655; in *Journey to the West*, 663; in *The Scholars*, 643, 647; and supernatural, 130; in twentieth-century fiction, 740, 741, 749, 752
Saussy, Haun, 14, 909–15
SBIs. *See* oracle bones

scar literature (*shang-hen wen-hsüeh*), 15, 463, 1052
Schafer, Edward, 10
Schipper, Kristofer, 10
Schlepp, Wayne, 370–82
Schmid, Neil, 964–88
Schmidt-Glintzer, Helwig, 160–72
scholar-officials (*wen-shih*), 4–5, 228, 266, 279, 282, 285, 311, 320, 365; biographies of, 550; Ch'ing, 383; in historical writings, 501; in *hua-pen*, 598, 601; local, 1052–54; Ming, 1012; and painter-poets, 466; and *pi-chi*, 562; and regional literature, 1019; in *The Scholars*, 643–47; Sui, 1, 930; Sung, 489; and suspension of civil-service examination, 388; T'ang, 930; and travel literature, 556, 559; use of classical Chinese by, 566–67. *See also* literati
The Scholars. See *Ju-lin wai-shih*
Schopenhauer, Arthur, 442, 711
science, 885, 1055, 1059, 1060, 1062
science fiction (*k'o-hsüeh hsiao-shuo*), 718, 719, 721, 722, 726
se (form; Sanskrit: *rūpa*), 170, 648
se (lust), 186
Seida Tansō, 1094
Seidel, Anna, 10
Sejong, King (Korea), 1052
sekai (environment), 1092
self-cultivation, 75–76, 79
Seneca, 899
Seng-chao, 169
Seng-ts'an, 170
Seng-yu, 164, 165, 166
Separately Collected Anthologies of Ming and Early Ch'ing Poetry (Shen Te-ch'ien), 431
Sesson Yūbai, 1088
Seven Masters. *See* Chien-an ch'i tzu; Hou ch'i tzu; Ming ch'ien ch'i tzu
Seven Sages of the Bamboo Grove (Chu-lin ch'i hsien), 258, 259
Sextus Empiricus, 884
sexuality, 128, 657, 766, 779; in *Chin P'ing Mei*, 637–43; in *ch'uan-ch'i* tales, 583, 683–84; in *hua-pen*, 599, 610–11; in Ming and Ch'ing novels, 661, 662, 664–66, 669, 672–73; in PRC, 771, 772; in *The Story of the Stone*, 647, 648, 649, 650, 652; and supernatural, 113, 114, 115, 118–19, 124
"Sha-chia-pang" (model play version), 866, 874
"Sha-fei nü-shih jih-chi" (Ms. Sophie's Diary; Ting Ling), 748
"Sha kou chi" (Killing a Dog), 821–22
"Sha kou ch'üan fu" (Admonishing One's Husband by Killing a Dog), 822
Sha Yeh-hsin, 872
Shakespeare, William, 845, 860, 901
shamanism, 9, 227, 1030, 1034–41, 1045; in *Ch'u tz'u*, 117; Korean, 1029, 1051; and supernatural tales, 545; in T'ang poetry, 124; and women, 199
shan (goodness), 713
Shan-chung yi-hsia (One Night in the Mountains; Li Chih), 136
Shan hai ching (Classic of Mountains and Seas), 60–65, 69, 214, 264, 467, 468, 544–53, 580, 1069; Ch'u in, 104; deities in, 66, 67; and *Flowers in the Mirror*, 130; illustrations for, 68, 120; and supernatural tales, 119–20
"Shan hsing chien ku t'ung" (Traveling in the Mountains I See a Solitary Paulownia; Pao Chao), 268–69
"Shan kuei" (Mountain Goddess; *Ch'u tz'u*), 118
"Shan shang hua tsan" (Picture Eulogy on a Fan; T'ao Ch'ien), 470–71
Shan shang te shih-chi (The Century on the Hill; Wang An-yi), 764
shan-shui shih (landscape poetry), 266, 268, 271, 294–95, 302, 313, 344, 388; Six Dynasties, 981; Sung, 346; T'ang, 423, 425, 426
Shan T'ao, 7, 259
"Shan tsai hsing" (Good!; Ts'ao Ts'ao), 255
Shan-yao-tan (Potato) school, 157, 158
"Shang Chang Ch'in Ch'ing tsan" (Eulogy on Shang Chang and Ch'in Ch'ing; T'ao Ch'ien), 471
Shang Ch'in (Lo Ma), 457, 461
Shang-ch'ing hou-sheng tao-chün lieh-chi (Annals of the Lord of the Tao, the Sage-to-Come of Shang-ch'ing), 181
Shang-ch'ing (Supreme Clarity) school, 176–77, 180–82
"Shang ch'un" (Spring Lament; Wen T'ing-shih), 450
Shang dynasty, 21, 71, 80, 96, 496, 509, 522, 790, 806; and Chinese writing system, 36; in fiction, 128, 632; myths of, 60, 65; and *Shih-ching*, 102–3; and *Yi-ching*, 89. *See also* oracle bones
Shang-hai chü-tso-che hsieh-hui (Association of Shanghai Dramatists), 862
Shang-hai hsi-chü lien-yi-hui (Friendly Association of Shanghai Dramatic Circle), 862
Shang-hai hsi-jen yeh-yü chü-t'uan (Amateur Dramatic Club of Shanghai), 849
"Shang-hai wu-yen hsia" (Under Shanghai Eaves; Hsia Yen), 862, 863
shang-hen wen-hsüeh (scar literature), 15, 463, 1052
Shang-kuan Wan-erh, 292, 293
Shang-kuan Yi, 285, 286, 292
shang-liang wen (ritual songs used in home-building), 994
"Shang-lin fu" (Imperial Park Rhapsody; Ssu-ma Hsiang-ju), 231

"Shang shih" (Aching for the Departed; Wei Ying-wu), 302
Shang-shu (*Shu-ching*; Classic of Documents), 74, 83, 96, 99, 496, 532, 895, 910; of K'ung An-kuo, 90, 913; on music, 108; and myth, 60, 61, 62; New and Old Text versions of, 89–90; and *Shih-ching*, 97; in *Thirteen Classics*, 88; "Yao tien" (Canon of Yao) in, 65, 67, 912
Shang-yang-tzu chin-tan ta-yao (Great Principles of the Golden Enchymoma According to Shang-yang-tzu; Ch'en Chih-hsü), 190
Shanghai, 657, 695, 724, 727, 860; in Ch'ing novels, 673, 725; dialect of, 56; drama in, 849, 850, 851, 862; Japanese occupation of, 752; and modern Chinese culture, 701–5, 733, 761, 762; and Western films, 743
Shanghai Dramatists, Association of (Shang-hai chü-tso-che hsieh-hui), 862
Shanghai Museum manuscript, 98–99, 100, 101
Shanghai shih-chieh fan-huo pao (Shanghai Splendor; journal), 724
Shao-hao (God of Light), 65
Shao Hsün-mei, 457
Shao Nan, land of, 104–5
Shao-nien p'iao-po-che (The Youthful Drifter; Chiang Kuang-tz'u), 748
Shao Pao, 403
Shao Pin-ju (Shao Chi-t'ang), 619
Shao Po-wen, 142
Shao-shih chien-wen lu (Record of Things Seen and Heard by Master Shao; Shao Po-wen), 142
Shao-shih shan-fang pi-ts'ung (Collected Jottings from the Shao-shih Retreat; Hu Ying-lin), 688
shao-shu min-tsu (minority nationalities), 9, 19, 34, 1032–54
Shao Yen-hsiang, 771
Shao Yung, 89, 481
Shaughnessy, Edward L., 89, 911
Shaw, George Bernard, 455, 845, 855–56
She-hui t'ung-ch'üan (History of Politics; trans. Yen Fu), 1063
She-tao shi (Poems on Entering the Way; Li Hsiang), 981
she-yi (lay religious societies), 966
Shelley, Percy Bysshe, 573
shen (gods; holy), 66, 112, 115, 419, 425, 547. *See also* deities
Shen Chi-chi, 123, 583–84, 585, 810, 827
Shen Ch'i-feng, 694
"Shen chiang-shih san-ch'ien mai hsiao ch'ien, Wang ch'ao-yi yi-yeh mi-hun chen" (The Gambler; Ling Meng-ch'u), 608
Shen Ch'ien, 414
Shen Ching, 829–30, 839
Shen Chou, 402, 435
Shen-chou ching (Scripture of Spirit Spells), 181
Shen Chu-hung, 617
Shen Ch'üan-ch'i, 291, 292, 293
"Shen-chung lou" (The Illusory Tower; Li Yü), 832
Shen Han-kuang, 414
"Shen Hsiao-hsia hsiang hui ch'u-shih piao" (Shen Hsiao-hsia; Feng Meng-lung), 600–601
"Shen Hsiao-kuan yi niao hai ch'i ming" (One Songbird Causes Seven Deaths), 599
Shen-hsiao (Divine Empyrean) school, 181, 191
Shen-hsien (Divine Transcendence), 175
"Shen-hsien ch'ü" (Tune for Unearthly Strings; Li Ho), 310
Shen-hsien chuan (Biographies of Divine Transcendents; Ko Hung), 508, 522, 580
"Shen-hsien hui" (A Meeting of Immortals; Chu Yu-tun), 145–46
shen-hua (myth), 58–59, 68
Shen Jung, 762
Shen Kua, 121, 481, 561–65
Shen-lou chih (The Mirage of Love), 669
Shen Man-yüan, 207–8, 217
shen-ming (spiritual illumination), 938
shen-mo hsiao-shuo (fiction of gods and demons), 126, 632
"Shen-nü fu" (Rhapsody on the Goddess; Sung Yü), 118–19, 200
Shen Nung (Farmer God), 65, 66
Shen pao (Shanghai News), 131, 702, 733, 1060
Shen P'ei, 99
"Shen shou P'an ch'ou ho jih hsiu?" (Pining and sorrow, when will they end?; Wang Ho-ch'ing), 376
Shen Te-ch'ien, 397, 430–36, 475
Shen Te-fu, 142
"Shen t'ou chi hsing yi-chih mei, hsia tao kuan hsing san mei hsi" (The Master-Thief Lazy Dragon; Ling Meng-ch'u), 607
Shen-tsung, Emperor (Chao Hsü), 339, 349
Shen Ts'ung-wen, 750–51, 1034, 1057
Shen Ya-chih, 122, 590–93
Shen Yen-ping (Mao Tun), 68, 156, 746–47, 1057
Shen Yi-hsiu, 839
Shen Yin-mo, 454
shen-yu ku-ch'iao (profundity and aloofness), 412
Shen Yüeh, 208, 241, 266, 267, 270–72, 276, 686, 957; and balladic imitation, 960; and popular verse, 954; on tonal euphony, 287, 931
shen-yün (spirit resonance; spiritual expressionism), 397, 424, 425, 426, 434, 938
sheng (male lead or young male), 820, 830, 839, 994
Sheng Ming tsa-chü (*Tsa-chü* of the Great Ming; Shen T'ai), 837

Sheng Ming tsa-chü erh-chi (*Tsa-chü* of the Great Ming, Second Collection; Shen T'ai), 837
sheng-t'ai (holy embryo), 635
sheng-wen (ellipsis), 891
"Sheng wo lou" (The House of My Birth; Li Yü), 615
"Sheng-yang tien ku-chih" (Old Site of the Sheng-yang Palace; Su Shun-ch'in), 347
Shiba Shirō, 718
Shigeshige yawa (Expansive Anecdotes; Tsuga Teishō), 1093
Shigikutuku, Prince, 1050
shih (classical verse; poetry), 186, 202, 209–10, 236, 388, 443, 556, 998. See also *shih* poetry
shih (corpse), 67
shih (events), 335, 427, 938
shih (histories), 925
shih (judgment), 938
shih (scribe; scribal practice), 494, 901
Shih, Chung-wen, 889
Shih ch'ang t'an (Explanations of Common Sayings; Kung Yi-cheng), 153
Shih Che-ts'un, 456
Shih Ch'eng-chin, 596, 617, 619
Shih-chi (Records of the Historian or, The Grand Scribe's Records; Ssu-ma Ch'ien), 7, 93, 174, 196–97, 231, 235, 334, 400, 502–6, 509, 896, 900, 968; "Basic Annals of Empress Dowager Lü" in, 580; biographies in, 507, 513–22, 525, 658; and fiction, 580, 626, 646, 686, 693, 710; "Hereditary Families" in, 503, 646; humor in, 134, 140, 141; in Korea, 1069, 1074; as model, 1076, 1080; organization of, 503, 514; proverbs in, 153; speech in, 505; and state of Chin, 803
Shih-chi *p'ing-lin* (Forest of Comments on the *Records of the Historian*; Ling Chih-lung), 942
"Shih-chi wen" (Text to Dispel Illness; Lu Chao-lin), 288
Shih-chia chih shuo (Straight Talk from a Poet; Hsieh Chen), 407
"Shih-chia Fo fu" (Wang Po), 290
"Shih Ch'iang Basin" inscription, 495
Shih Chieh, 344
shih chieh ko-ming (revolution in poetry), 454, 726
"Shih-chien" (Rocky Gorge; Liu Tsung-yüan), 535
Shih Chien-wu, 311
Shih Chih (Kuo Lu-sheng), 462
Shih-ching (*Mao-shih*; Classic of Poetry), 4, 97–109, 195–96, 199, 224, 333, 334, 354, 364, 374, 431, 501, 525; "Ch'i-yüeh" (Seventh Month) in, 105; and Chou dynasty, 97, 102, 104, 105; commentaries to, 106–7, 913, 1089–90; and Confucianism, 98–99; and Confucius, 74, 75; as diplomatic code, 912; divisions of, 91, 101–6; eulogies in, 977; genres in, 5; and Han dynasty, 75, 83, 99, 101, 104; historicization of, 106; "Hsiao ya" (Lesser Odes, Elegantiae) in, 91, 102, 103, 104, 107, 422; "Hsüan niao" (Dark Bird) in, 102–3; influence on poetry of, 226, 230, 232, 249, 256, 346, 347, 385, 927, 980; interpretations of, 90, 99–103, 106, 108, 438; "Kuan-chü" in, 101, 106; "Kuo-feng" (Airs of the States) in, 91, 102, 104–8, 927, 929; language of, 106–7; and literary theory, 916, 917, 922; Mao recension of, 100–103, 106–7, 108, 910, 913, 919; myth in, 65; poetry of, 974; prefaces to, 98, 100, 108–9, 480, 913, 916, 918, 919, 920, 921, 927, 1085; principle of *fu* in, 921; proverbs in, 150; recitation of, 225; rhyme in, 107–8; songs of, 435; as source, 962; and state of Ch'u, 97–101; status of, 910; "Sung" (Hymns) in, 91, 102–3, 105, 107; "Ta ya" (Greater Odes, Elegantiae) in, 91, 102, 103–4, 107, 150, 927; in *Thirteen Classics*, 88, 90–91; "Tsou-yü" in, 105; "Yen-yen" in, 101
Shih Chün-pao, 809, 819
"Shih-chung shan chi" (Record of Stone Bell Mountain; Su Shih), 539, 556–57
shih chung wu wo ("in a poem there is no I"), 433
shih chung yu wo ("in a poem, 'I' am present"), 433
Shih Ch'ung, 262
shih (scholar) class, 3, 71–72, 92. *See also* scholar-officials
Shih-erh lou (Twelve Towers; Li Yü), 147, 615
"Shih-erh yin-yüan liu tzu ko-tz'u" (Hexasyllabic Poem on the Twelve Links of Dependent Origination; Wei Yüan-sung), 979
"Shih-hao li" (The Officer from Shih-hao Village; Tu Fu), 730
Shih Hsüeh-sheng, 1038
"Shih hua" (Poetry Talks; Ou-yang Hsiu), 539
shih-hua (remarks on poetry), 563, 934–35
"Shih jen" (That Stately Person), 195
shih-jen hua (literati painting), 466, 477–81, 485, 490
Shih Jun-chang, 420
Shih-ko (The Framework of Poetry; Wang Ch'ang-ling), 295, 931
Shih K'o-fa, 833, 844
"Shih ku ko" (Song of the Stone Drums; Su Shih), 350
Shih kuang-chuan (Broad Commentary on the *Classic of Poetry*; Wang Fu-chih), 937
shih-kung (Taoist priest-shaman), 1036

shih lei (quotation and allusion), 893, 894, 900
Shih-li. See *Yi-li*
"Shih-li chin-tan" (Ten Golden Pellets), 1023
"Shih li" (Ten Parting) poems (Hsüeh T'ao), 209
Shih ling-t'u (Poetry Territory; journal), 456
Shih-men cheng-t'ung (Correct Sequence of the Buddhist Schools; Wu K'o-chi and Tsung-chien), 167
Shih-ming (Liu Hsi), 48
Shih Nai-an, 628
Shih-pao (China Times), 773
"Shih pi" (Calligraphy Exercises; Ou-yang Hsiu), 539
Shih-p'in (An Evaluation of Poetry; Chung Jung), 118, 260, 898, 927, 932
Shih-p'ing (A Critique of Poetry; Chiao-jan), 302, 893
shih poetry, 107–9, 223, 224, 234–38, 240, 396, 953; in Chien-an period, 260; Ch'ing, 427, 429, 430, 432, 436, 437, 439, 440, 441, 445; of eighth century, 291–303; Han, 243, 249–51, 254, 255, 268, 959; history of, 409, 955; Ho-shuo school of, 413, 414; Hsi-ling school of, 414; and inscriptions on paintings, 466–67; Japanese, 1080, 1081, 1085, 1088, 1090; Japanese compilations of Chinese, 1083, 1085; and Japanese *waka*, 1082, 1083; and licentiate examination, 1070; Literary Chinese, 1097; and literati, 239, 242, 444; Ming, 372, 403, 413, 415; as modern literary form, 443; of ninth century, 303–13; Palace Style of, 241; and *san-ch'ü*, 377; sentences in, 323; of seventeenth century, 416, 418, 419, 420, 423, 427, 445; subgenres of, 262–63; Sung, 337–69, 352, 384, 385, 410, 427, 428; of T'ai-k'ang period, 262; T'ang, 243, 274, 275, 277–79, 285, 288–95, 297, 299–301, 304, 321, 434; from Tun-huang, 976, 979; of women, 428, 429, 839; Yüan, 331, 383–89, 410; and *yüeh-fu*, 955
shih prosody, 241
Shih-san ching (Thirteen Classics), 86–96
Shih-san-ching chu-shu (The Thirteen Classics, Annotated and Explicated; ed. Juan Yüan): *Wu-ching cheng-yi* (Correct Meanings of the Five Classics) in, 913–14
Shih-sen (Forest of Affairs). See *Hsiao-tzu chuan*
Shih-shih (Designs of Poetry; Chiao-jan), 302, 930
Shih-shih lei-yüan (Garden of Contemporary Events Arranged by Category), 323
Shih-shih t'ung-chien (Comprehensive Mirror of the Śākya Clan; Pen-chüeh), 167
Shih Shu-ch'ing, 773–74
"Shih-shuo" (Discourse on Teachers; Han Yü), 533, 931
Shih-shuo hsin-yü (New Account of Tales of the World; Liu Yi-ch'ing), 6, 171, 522, 551, 580, 686, 888
Shih sou (Poetry Oasis; comp. Hu Ying-lin), 409
Shih-ssu hang chi (Sonnets; Feng Chih), 456
Shih sui-nao (The Nous and Pith of Poetry; Yüan Ching), 286
Shih Ta-tsu, 447
Shih T'ai, 189
"Shih t'ai-tzu tso" (Seated in Attendance on the Heir Apparent; Ts'ao Chih), 257
Shih-t'ao (Tao chi), 427, 428
shih-tiao (poetic style), 403
Shih T'ieh-sheng, 765
"Shih tien t'ou" (The Rocks Nod Their Heads; Hsi Lang-hsien), 604
Shih T'ien-tse, 814
"Shih ting lien-chü shih hsü" (Preface to the Linked Verse on a Stone Cauldron; Han Yü), 535
Shih-t'ou chi (The Story of the Stone). See *Hung-lou meng*
Shih ts'ai-tzu (Ten Talented Ones), 395
shih-tsan (nonmelodic prosimetric narrative), 990, 993, 997, 998
Shih-tsung, Emperor (Later Chou), 338
shih-tui (parallelism of facts), 893
Shih t'ung (An Understanding of History; Liu Chih-chi), 525, 594, 893
Shih Tzu, 101
Shih Tzu (text), 60
shih-tzu (lion), 22, 283
Shih-tzu hou (The Lion Roars; Ch'ien T'ien-hua), 726
shih-wen (the prose of our day; eight-legged essay), 531, 713, 733
"Shih-wu kuan" (Fifteen Strings of Cash; Chu Hu), 830
Shih-wu pao (Actualities; journal), 719
"Shih-wu ts'ung-chün cheng" (At Fifteen I Went for a Soldier), 250, 251
shih yen chih (poetry is the fulfillment of intent), 921
Shih Yen-nien, 345
"Shih yi" (Ten Wings; *Yi-ching*), 89
Shih-yi (Deliberations on Poetry; Chiao-jan), 302
Shih-yi (Deliberations on Poetry; Wang Fu-chih), 937
Shih-yi chi (Uncollected Records; Wang Chia), 550
shih yi ta hsing (poetry is for expressing personal nature), 426
shijo (poetic form; Korea), 1071
Shimeisen (The Cicada That Calls Four Times; Tsuga Teishō), 1093
Shimonoseki, Treaty of (1896), 733

Shina bungaku shi (History of Chinese Literature; Kojō Tandō), 711
Shina bungaku shi (History of Chinese Literature; Sasagawa Rinpū), 711, 713
shirhak (practical studies; Korea), 1072
Shklovskij, Viktor, 717
Shōkenkō (Drafts by the Man of the Way of Plantain Strength; Zekkai Chūshin), 1088
short stories: anthologies of, 729, 730, 996; Ch'ing, 697, 700, 717; classical, 698; criticism of, 705; foreign, 729, 730; humor in, 136, 146–47; Japanese, 1092; in literary journals, 704, 715, 728–29; and May Fourth movement, 745; Ming, 399; and novels, 720, 729; and proverbs, 154, 155; Republican-period, 705, 728; revival of, 705, 728–30; twentieth-century, 567, 732, 738, 772; vernacular, 15, 698, 996
Shōsetsu kigen (Strange Short Stories; ed. Oka Hakku), 1092
Shōsetsu seigen (Essential Short Stories; ed. Oka Hakku), 1092
Shōsetsu shinzui (The Quintessence of Fiction; Tsubouchi Shōyō), 1094
Shōtoku, Prince, 1080
"Shou-yang shan Shu-ch'i pien-chieh" (On Mount Shou-yang, Shu-ch'i Switches Loyalties; Ai-na chü-shih), 615
shu (*chih*; topical essays or treatises), 503
shu (subcommentaries), 8, 87
shu (transmitted), 900
Shu, kingdom of, 252, 263, 338, 508, 518, 621, 622, 624
Shu-ching. See *Shang-shu*
Shu Ch'ing-ch'un. *See* Lao She
shu-ch'ing (expressing one's feeling) poetry, 277
shu erh pu tso (transmitting and not creating), 893
"Shu huai" (Expressing Heart-held Thoughts; Wei Cheng), 284
shu-hui (writing clubs), 801, 805
Shu (Shu-Han) kingdom, 623, 806, 835
Shu Kuang, 267
shu-mien-yü (book language), 25
shu-shih (adepts), 116
Shu Shou, 267
shu-shuo (letter and discourse), 528
"Shu tao nan" (The Way to Shu Is Hard; Li Po), 297, 298, 300, 962
Shu T'ing (Shu Ting), 462
"Shu wang" (King of Trees; Ah Ch'eng), 764
Shu-wang pen-chi (Basic Annals of the King of Shu; Yang Hsiung), 518
shu-yü (familiar expressions), 151, 154
shu-yüan (local academies), 1053
Shu yüan chui t'an (Idle Talk from Pulse Garden; Ch'iu Wei-ai), 710
shua hsiu-ts'ai (made fun of students), 797
shuai to fu-yen, tz'u yü li-ching (frivously ornate; their style competing with substance and reason), 930
"Shuang-k'ou hun" (Double Request at the Palace Gate; Chang Fan), 840
shuang-kuan (double entendre), 894
"Shuang tiao ch'ing" (Celebrating the Shooting of Two Vultures), 617
shui (persuasive rhetoric), 974
Shui-hu chuan (Water Margin; Shih Nai-an and Lo Kuan-chung), 197, 213, 399, 499, 622, 626–32, 637–38, 642, 659, 689, 707, 709–10, 737, 744, 889, 890, 894; characters in, 855; and *Chin P'ing Mei*, 637; Chin Sheng-t'an's edition of, 842, 940–41, 942, 943, 945, 947, 948; and drama, 808; humor in, 145, 147; in Japan, 1091, 1092, 1093, 1094; in Korea, 1075, 1077, 1078; and proverbs, 155; and regional literature, 1011, 1024; and *Romance of the Three Kingdoms*, 626, 631; sequels to, 628, 663; supernatural in, 127, 631; as vernacular literature, 1056
"Shui-hu chuan" te lai-li hsin-t'ai yü yi-shu (The Origins, Mentality and Art of *Water Margin*; Sun Shu-yü), 628
Shui-hu hou-chuan (*Water Margin*: Later Traditions; Ch'en Ch'en), 628, 663
Shui-hu hou-chuan (*Water Margin*: Later Traditions; Takizawa Bakin), 1093
Shui-hu lun-heng (Discussions on *Water Margin*; Y. W. Ma), 630
Shui-hu-ti manuscripts, 93
"Shui-tiao ko-t'ou" (Water Music; Chang Hui-yen), 449
Shui-yin-p'ing (Yang Ch'ih-ch'ang), 459
Shui-yün chi (Anthology of Clouds and Water), 187
shukō (plot), 1092
Shun (sage king), 62, 66, 68, 108, 225, 471
Shun-p'ing Hou (Smoothing Pacification Marquis), 521
Shun-tsung, Emperor, 304, 581
"Shun-tzu chih-hsiao pien-wen" (The Boy Shun's Great Filial Piety), 69
shuo (persuasions), 105
shuo (rhetorical anecdote), 68
shuo-ch'ang-pen (song-prose tales), 990
shuo-ch'ang (speaking and singing) tradition, 796, 1017–25
shuo-ch'ang tz'u-hua. *See* chantefables

shuo-ch'ang wen-hsüeh (spoken-sung literature), 11, 796. *See also* chantefables
shuo-ch'ang yin-yüan (sung tales of retribution), 995
Shuo-fu (The Environs of Fiction; T'ao Tsung-yi), 136
"Shuo hsiao-shuo" (Discourse on Fiction; Kuan Ta-ju), 715
Shuo-ling (The Bell of Stories), 691
shuo-shu. *See* storytelling
Shuo T'ang yen-yi ch'üan-chuan (Complete Tradition of T'ang Stories), 626
Shuo-t'ing (Accounts of Things Heard; Lu Yen-chih), 677
Shuo-wen chieh-tzu (Explanation of Simple and Compound Graphs; Hsü Shen), 46–47, 48, 912
Shuo yüan (Florilegea of Persuasion; Liu Hsiang), 517–18
Shuo Yüeh ch'üan chuan (Complete Tradition of Yüeh Fei Stories; Ch'ien Ts'ai), 628
siddham (study of the script and grammar of Sanskrit), 1084
Sienkiewicz, Henrik, 729
Silk Road, 14, 559
similes (*pi*), 5, 150, 151–52, 156, 157, 921
Simplicissimus (Grimmelshausen), 764–65
Sin Kwang-su, 1071
Singapore, 33, 736, 759
Singde, Nara (Nalan Hsing-te), 333, 417, 418, 447, 449, 452
singing girls, 444, 1026
Sinicization, 13
Sinitic (Chinese language), 1037–38, 1042, 1044; and ancient-style prose, 533, 536; Buddhist Hybrid, 11, 971, 979, 993; Cantonese, 31, 35, 39, 56, 618, 1025–28; in Ch'in dynasty, 37, 41; and Chinese writing system, 19–21; in Ch'ing dynasty, 22, 32, 33, 430, 1062; dialects in, 23–27, 29, 714, 749, 1017, 1031; effects on literature of, 1053; future development of, 52–57; homophones in, 39, 46, 48; inscriptions in, 1048; and Internet, 55–56; loanwords, 22–23; Middle, 39; neologisms in, 1056, 1057, 1058, 1059, 1062; in North China, 372; Old (OS), 22, 27, 39; origins of, 21–23; Proto-, 28, 56; spoken, 533; study of, 45–48; tones in, 39, 248, 270, 276, 321, 327, 433, 931; and Vietnamese, 1097; vocabulary expansion in, 37–38. *See also* vernacular language
Sino-French War (1884), 1065
Sino-Japanese War (1894–1895), 458, 733, 738, 739, 1056, 1059, 1060, 1062, 1063, 1065
Sino-Japanese War (1937–1945), 456
sinographs (*han-tzu*; Chinese characters), 20, 37–54, 1000; and language reform, 745; nature of, 39–44; number of, 37, 38; ordering of, 47–48, 55, 714; simplification of, 43–44, 53–54; and Vietnamese, 1097–1100, 1103. *See also* language, written
Sinsosŏl (New Novel) movement (Korea), 1077
Sivin, Nathan, 10
Six Dynasties (Liu-ch'ao) period, 512, 525, 532, 546–51, 554; biographies in, 164–65; Buddhism during, 170, 585, 726; *chih-kuai* in, 119, 121, 544, 579–80, 581, 1069; esthetic changes in, 923–30; fiction in, 689; gazeteers of, 1080; historians of, 594; humor in, 146; literary criticism in, 894, 930, 1084; *Literary Selections* of, 240, 243, 263, 272, 289, 471, 473, 929, 956; literary theory in, 921; as model for poetry, 1071, 1085; painting and poetry in, 470, 474, 478; parallel prose in, 230, 236–40, 244, 1068; poetry of, 6, 230, 241, 242, 270, 275, 277, 393, 406, 440, 475, 974, 981, 986, 1068, 1082, 1083
Skar, Lowell, 10
Smith, Adam, 1063
Snow, Edgar, 152
so (epistles in parallel prose), 1088
So akbu (Minor Ballads), 1069
Sŏ Kŏ-jŏng, 1071
so-yin (search for the hidden), 943
social criticism, 692, 697, 700, 722, 728, 760–61, 762
Social Darwinism, 1063, 1065
Socrates, 885
Sodae p'ungyo (Folk Songs of a Glorious Age; Korea), 1071
Soldier's Drama Troupe (Chan-shih chü-she; Red Army), 872
song-dueling, 1036
song-that (double-seven doublet), 1097
song that luc bat (seven/seven, six/eight verse), 1100
Sŏnggyun'gwan (National Confucian Academy; Korea), 1070
songs (*ko, ke*), 186, 271, 276; anthologies of, 373; and Buddhism, 315, 317, 975; burial, 958, 1040; Ch'ing-shang, 954, 958; of Ch'u, 249, 257, 273, 953; courtship, 1036; and dances, 315, 954; dragon boat, 1026, 1027; drum (*ku-tz'u*), 990, 991, 1009, 1012, 1014, 1018, 1028–31; folk, 314, 315, 394, 454, 954, 1039, 1047, 1071, 1082; Han, 376, 954–55, 956; Japanese, 1081, 1082, 1085, 1091; Korean, 1071; *liao*, 1037; *lien-chang* (linked stanzas) of, 975; literary, 370, 371; lotus-boat, 316; love, 960, 976; Miao, 1035; ninth- and tenth-century, 445; popular, 391, 444, 953–63, 975; and prehistory, 790; single (*hsiao-ling*), 316–19, 329, 332, 333, 371; southern, 953–57, 960–62; Sung, 370; *tsa-ch'ü* (inde-

pendent stanzas) of, 975; Yüan, 370–82. *See also* "Chiu ko"; *ch'ü*; *san-ch'ü*; *tz'u*
Soochow, 398, 402, 448, 490, 823, 828, 829, 830, 1023, 1025
Soong, Stephen C. (Lin Yi-liang), 457
Sou-shen chi (Search for the Supernatural; Kan Pao), 120–21, 548, 551–53, 563, 580, 1069
Sou-shen chi yi-pen (In Search of the Supernatural, One Volume), 970
"Sou-shen" hou-chi (Sequel to Search for the Supernatural; T'ao Ch'ien), 553–54
Southeast Asia, 14, 33, 736, 759, 781. *See also* Vietnam
Southern and Northern Dynasties (Nan-pei-ch'ao), 22, 207, 523, 532, 550, 930, 955, 962; literary criticism in, 919, 923, 925
Southern (Later) Han dynasty, 338
Southern Society (Nan-she), 442
Southern Sung dynasty, 392, 485, 564, 998, 1008; drama in, 791, 806, 997; fall of, 834; music in, 791; poetry of, 324, 325, 330, 331, 333, 339, 340, 357–68, 416, 432, 446, 448, 449; writers of, 360, 363, 447, 450. *See also* Northern Sung dynasty; Sung dynasty
Southern (Later) T'ang dynasty, 326, 338, 339, 403
Southwest United University, 457
Soviet Union, 15, 157, 737, 760, 769. *See also* Russia
sŏwŏn (regional Confucian academies), 1072
speech, 505, 902, 1056; and narrative in historical writing, 496–97, 500, 503, 504. *See also* oral tradition
Spencer, Herbert, 1063
Spengler, Oswald, 778
Spenser, Edmund, 943
Spirit of the Laws (Montesquieu). See *Fa-yi*
Spring and Autumn Annals. See *Ch'un-ch'iu*
Spring and Autumn period, 3, 49, 97, 306, 496, 499, 501, 665
Srong-btsan Sgampo, 1044, 1048
"Ssu-chai shui ch'i" (Waking from Sleep at the Temple Purification Hall; Huang T'ing-chien), 354
Ssu ch'an-chüan (Four Lovely Ladies; Hung Sheng), 836
ssu-chieh (elites), 287
Ssu chou chih (Geography of Four Continents; Lin Tse-hsü), 718
ssu-ch'ou (private vengeance), 623
Ssu-ch'ou chih lu (Silk Road), 14, 559
"Ssu ch'ou shih" (Poem of Four Sorrows; Chang Heng), 251
Ssu-fu (Four Supplements), 180
"Ssu-hsien ch'iu" (Four-Stringed Autumn; Chiang Shih-ch'üan), 834
"Ssu hsüan fu" (Rhapsody on the Contemplation of Mystery; Chang Heng), 233
"Ssu huan ch'un fu" (Longing to Return to Incorruptibility; Wu Yün), 302
"Ssu Kan" (This Mountain Stream), 199
Ssu-k'u ch'üan-shu (Complete Library of the Four Treasuries), 175, 386, 543, 691, 694
Ssu-k'u ch'üan-shu tsung-mu t'i-yao (Annotated General Catalog of the Complete Library of the Four Treasuries), 175, 386
Ssu-k'ung T'u, 421, 424, 932, 933, 935–36, 938
ssu-liu shu (parallel-prose compositions; Japanese: *shirokuso*), 1087
ssu-liu t'i, *ssu-liu wen* (Four-Six style), 236, 239, 242, 244, 245, 246, 277, 527, 530–33, 1072, 1080
Ssu-ma Chao, 258
Ssu-ma Chen, 135
Ssu-ma Ch'eng-chen, 298
Ssu-ma Ch'ien, 7, 228, 237, 250, 502–7, 509, 533, 888, 892, 901, 944, 1069; biographies by, 514–22; biographies of, 931, 968; and fiction, 580, 591, 626, 646, 658, 693, 710; as Grand Historian, 546; and humor, 134, 140, 141, 143; likes and dislikes of, 505; proverbs of, 153; on *Shan hai ching*, 68; and state of Chin, 803. See also *Shih-chi*
Ssu-ma Hsi, 513
Ssu-ma Hsiang-ju, 118, 224, 225, 228, 230, 799, 816, 896–97, 921; biography of, 231; *fu* of, 231–32, 233, 234, 236; pseudo-, 106
Ssu-ma Kuang, 142, 167, 509–10, 622, 934
Ssu-ma Lun, 261, 262
Ssu-ma Piao, 956
Ssu-ma T'an, 174–75, 502–3, 514
Ssu-ma Yen (Emperor Wu of Chin), 258, 625
Ssu-ma Yi, 257
Ssu-min yüeh-ling (Monthly Guidance for the Four Classes of People; Ts'ui Shih), 152
Ssu-ming shih-hua (Remarks on Poetry from Ssu-ming; Hsieh Chen), 407
ssu-sheng (four tones), 931. *See also* Sinitic: tones in
Ssu sheng p'u (Manual on the Four Tones; Chou Yung), 270
Ssu-sheng-yüan (Four Shrieks of the Gibbon; Hsü Wei), 824, 835
"Ssu shih" (Four Histories), 521
"Ssu-shih t'ien-yüan tsa-hsing" (Impromptu Verses on the Four Seasons of the Countryside; Fan Ch'eng-ta), 363

Ssu shu (Four Books), 92, 943
ssu-ta ch'i-shu (*Four Masterworks of Ming Fiction*), 629, 634, 637
"Ssu-te" (Four Feminine Virtues), 992
ssu-wen (this culture), 3
Ssu wu lin-t'an (April Fifth Forum; underground journal), 462
Ssu-wu yün-tung (April Fifth movement; 1976), 869
ssu-yen (tetrasyllabic meter), 932
Ssu-yu chi (Four Journeys; Yang Chih-ho), 637, 664
Stalin, Joseph V., 737
Stein, Aurel, 965, 1017
Stein, Rolf, 10
Stevens, Kate, 1029
Stevens, Wallace, 457
The Story of the Stone. See *Hung-lou meng*
storytelling (*shuo-shu*), 236–37, 984, 989, 1013, 1024, 1035; Buddhist influence on, 163; criticism of, 705; and drama, 787; Indian tradition of, 167; in Korea, 1075; in Ming dynasty, 597–98, 1026; and performance texts, 983, 1016; and proverbs, 153–54, 155; in Shanghai, 702; and singer-storytellers, 1028, 1042; in Sung dynasty, 154, 791, 808, 987; in Yüan dynasty, 595–98
Stowe, Harriet Beecher, 849, 1065
Strange Tales from Make-Do Studio. See *Liao-chai chih-yi*
Strickmann, Michel, 10
A Study of Sociology (Spencer). See *Ch'ün-hsüeh yi-yen*
The Study of the Novel (Whitcomb), 717
su (vulgar), 27, 34, 149, 154, 894
Su Ch'e, 533, 557
su-chiang (popular lectures, sermons), 167, 966, 972, 984, 993
su-fu (folk rhapsody), 6, 278
Su Hsiao-hsiao, 207
Su Hsün, 533, 537
Su-hua ch'ing-t'an (Colloquial Chats; Shao Pin-ju), 619
Su Man-shu, 704–5, 727, 730
Su Nü (White Girl), 216
Su Shih (Su Tung-p'o), 7–8, 348–53, 531, 533, 537, 539–40, 564, 600, 624, 933; on arts, 539; background of, 349; Buddhist influence on, 170; comparisons with, 417, 446, 450; and Confucian renaissance, 350; expression of emotion in, 432; greatness of, 369; and humor, 136; influence of, 451, 1068, 1069, 1070, 1072; inscription writing of, 481, 485; and Kung-an school, 384; lyrics of, 320–21, 324, 326, 328; as model, 325, 357, 386, 408, 411, 412, 445; and painting, 479, 481; in plays, 838; poems of, 350–51, 356, 358, 361, 434, 485; prose *fu* of, 230, 244, 245; as representative of Sung poetry, 1071; students of, 351–53; travel writings of, 556–58; trial of, 480–81; Tu Fu compared to, 480; and Wang Shih-chen, 427; on Wang Wei, 490; and *wen-jen* ideal, 392, 1069
Su Shu-yang, 858
Su Shun-ch'in, 345, 347, 348
Su T'ing, 243
Su-tsung, Emperor, 296, 299
"Su Tung-hsiao Kung" (Spending the Night at Cave Mist Temple; Lin Pu), 343
Su Tung-p'o. *See* Su Shih
Su T'ung, 765
Su Wei-chen, 779
su-wen-hsüeh. *See* vernacular literature
"Su-wen-na ho t'a erh-tzu" (Suwanna and Her Son), 1043
Su Wu, 250, 273, 1101
su-yü (proverbial expression), 150, 151. *See also* proverbs
Sugawara no Michizane, 1083, 1084–85
Sugi (monk), 162
Sui Ching-ch'en, 376
Sui chŏn (Records of the Strange and Unusual; Pak Il-lyang), 1069
Sui dynasty, 252, 270, 273, 282–85, 980; collapse of, 807; and cultural prestige, 1079; in fiction, 626, 661, 669; literary criticism in, 930; music in, 314, 974; painters of, 487; proverbs in, 153; reunification under, 525; scholar-officials of, 1, 930
sui-pi. See *pi-chi*
Sui shih yi-wen (Remnants of Writings on Sui History; Yüan Yü-ling), 626
Sui shu (History of the Sui Dynasty), 282, 284
Sui T'ang chia-hua (Fine Discourses from the Sui and T'ang; Liu Su), 581
Sui T'ang yen-yi (Romance of the Sui and T'ang Dynasties; Ch'u Jen-huo), 626, 669–70
Sui Yang-ti yen-shih (The Merry Adventures of Emperor Yang of the Sui), 669
Sui-yüan Hsia-shih, 671
Sui-yüan shih-hua (Poetry Talks from the Sui Garden; Yüan Mei), 935
Sumerian, 27–28
Sun, William H., 876
Sun Ch'ang-wu, 12
Sun Ch'i, 581
Sun Ch'o, 265
Sun Chu, 281
Sun Ch'üan, 621, 806–7
Sun Ch'ung, 468
Sun Fei-hu (Flying Tiger Sun), 1009
Sun Kan-lu, 765
Sun Liao-hung, 743
Sun Pu-erh, 184, 186–87
Sun-shu Ao, 513, 516–17
Sun Shu-yü, 628, 630, 631, 642
Sun Tzu, 506
Sun Wu-k'ung (Monkey; *Journey to the West*), 69, 125, 128–29, 147, 632–37, 635, 663, 818, 946–47
Sun Yat-sen, 157, 850

sung (hymns), 5, 920. See also under *Shih-ching*
sung (reproach, dispute), 103
Sung, Madame (fourth-century scholar-teacher; mother of Wei Ch'eng), 415
Sung, state of, 102, 524
Sung Cheng-yü, 412
Sung Ch'i, 560
Sung Chiang, 626, 627, 628, 630, 736, 808
"Sung chih-tao-yüan te jih-chi" (The Diary of Instructor Sung; Mo Yen and Hsiao Yü-tse), 873–74
Sung Chih-wen, 291, 292, 294, 475
"Sung Ch'ing chuan" (Biography of Sung Ch'ing; Liu Tsung-yüan), 592
Sung Chiung, 386
"Sung ch'iung wen" (Send Off Poverty or Farewell to Misfortune; Han Yü), 534
Sung Ch'un-fang, 851, 852
Sung dynasty, 162, 323, 787, 972, 1073; academies in, 481–82, 1053; classical tales in, 579, 675–76, 679–90; colloquial style in, 887, 889; Confucian learning in, 915, 1069, 1070, 1072; Confucian renaissance of, 340, 342, 344–58; drama in, 144, 792; examination system of, 914; fall of, 367–68; *fu* of, 6, 243–45, 278; and Han Chinese rule, 1044; history of (*Sung shih*), 808; *hua-pen* in, 146, 595; humor in, 146; inscription poetry of, 477; and Japan, 1087; and Khitan (Liao) dynasty, 807; and Korea, 1068–69; language in, 32; literary criticism of, 933–36; literati-officials of, 330, 340, 341–42; and Mandate of Heaven, 96; minorities in, 1037; and Neo-Confucianism, 1087; New Policies faction in, 352, 353, 355, 356; oral-formulaic tradition in, 995; paintings of, 467, 469, 473, 475, 479–82, 485; parallel prose in, 240, 246; performative literature of, 796–800; *pi-chi* of, 560–65; poetry of, 225, 265–69, 271, 272, 274, 307, 312, 333, 337–69, 372, 384, 386, 397, 398, 401, 402, 427–33, 440, 443, 446, 1088, 1090, 1091; poetry out of prose in, 538; prose of, 509, 526–27, 531, 533, 536, 539; prosimetric format in, 983; proverbs in, 153, 155; punctuation in, 941; *sao* poetry style in, 230; as setting for song, 1027; *shih* poetry in, 337–69; sources for, 337–38; storytelling in, 154, 791, 808, 987; supernatural in, 542, 548; Taoist canon of, 178, 182; *tz'u* in, 13–14, 315, 317, 322, 326, 329, 370, 955; vernacular record tradition of, 1072; women in, 33, 218; *yu-chi* in, 556–59; and *yü-lu*, 168; Yüan-yu faction of, 356. *See also* Northern Sung dynasty; Southern Sung dynasty
"Sung feng-po" (Denouncing the Lord of the Wind; Han Yü), 304
Sung kao-seng chuan (Lives of Eminent Monks Compiled Under the Sung; Tsan-ning), 165
Sung Lien, 387, 396, 398
Sung Lo, 385, 427
Sung Mao-ch'eng, 600, 685, 689–90
Sung Pen, 386
Sung shih (History of the Sung Dynasty), 808
Sung-shih ch'ao (anthology of Sung poetry), 338, 385
Sung-shih chi-shih (Annals of Sung Poetry; Li O), 338, 432
Sung shu (History of the Liu Sung Dynasty; Shen Yüeh), 271, 551, 956, 957
Sung ssu-chia tz'u-hsüan (Anthology of Song Lyrics by Four Sung Poets), 438
"Sung Ssu-kung ta nao chin-hun Chang" (Sung Four Causes Trouble for Miser Chang), 598
Sung Te-fang, 178, 184
Sung Ting-po, 549
sung-tsan (eulogy and appreciation), 528
Sung Tse-lai, 778
Sung Wan, 420–21, 427
Sung Wu, 387
Sung-yin man-lu (Casual Notes by a Shanghai Recluse; Wang T'ao), 695
"Sung Ying shih" (Sending Off Mr. Ying; Ts'ao Chih), 256
Sung Yü, 106, 118, 200, 228
Sung Yüan (Mei-tung), 679, 804–5
Sung Yüan hsi-ch'ü k'ao (Research on the Drama of the Sung and Yüan Dynasties; Wang Kuo-wei), 812
Sung Yün, 165
śūnyatā (emptiness), 168, 169
supernatural, 110–31; and Buddhist literature, 170–71; in *ch'uan-ch'i*, 581, 584–86, 588; in classical tales, 675, 677, 678, 692, 694; in historical writing, 509–10; in *hua-pen*, 126, 127, 596, 597, 604, 606, 609; and poetry, 111, 115, 123–25, 543, 549, 553; in *Tso chuan*, 500; in *Water Margin*, 127, 631. See also *chih-kuai*
surrealism, 459
sūtras (*ching*; scriptures), 11, 86, 161, 162. *See also particular texts*
Symbolists, 700, 720
A System of Logic (Mill). See *Mu-le ming-hsüeh*

Ta-an-pan shou-yi ching (Mahānāpanānusmṛti-sūtra), 162
"Ta chao" (Great Summons; *Ch'u tz'u*), 228
Ta Chi, 128
"Ta-chieh hun yu wan su-yüan, hsiao-yi ping ch'i hsü ch'ien-yüan" (The Younger Sister

Resumes the Older Sister's Marriage Destinies; Ling Meng-ch'u), 606
"Ta Ch'in Ching-chiao san-wei meng-tu tsan" (Hymns on the Holy Trinity of the Great Roman Nestorian Religion Who Save the Ignorant), 979
Ta Ch'ing yi-t'ung-chih (Comprehensive Gazeteer of the Great Ch'ing), 434
"Ta-ch'u yu-ling-t'a" (Breaking Out of Ghost Pagoda; Pai Wei), 853
ta ch'ü (major pieces), 958
ta-ch'ü (grand song), 977
"Ta Chuan" (Great Treatise; *Yi ching*), 80–82
ta-chuan (great seal) script, 49
Ta-chung chü-she (People's Theater), 860
"Ta feng ko" (Song of the Great Wind; Liu Pang), 249
"Ta-hsüeh" (Great Learning; *Li-chi*), 92, 642
ta-hsüeh (major learning), 45
"Ta jen fu" (Rhapsody on the Great Man; Ssu-ma Hsiang-ju), 118
"Ta-jen fu hsü" (Preface to the "Rhapsody on the Great Man"; Lu Chi), 239
"Ta-jen Hsien-sheng chuan" (Biography of a Great Man; Juan Chi), 581
ta-ku (big drum), 1028, 1029, 1052
Ta K'uai-chi (First Assembly of Gods), 65
Ta-kuan yüan (Grand View Garden), 435, 650, 653
Ta-li kingdom, 1040, 1042
"Ta-lieh fu" (The Great Hunt; Li Po), 298
Ta-lu tang-tai ming-jen p'ing-chuan (Biographies of Famous Cultural Personalities from China Mainland–Creators of a Civil Society; Ho Yü-hai), 769
Ta Ming Hsüan-t'ien shang-ti jui-ying t'u-lu (An Illustrated Account of Auspicious Responses to the Great Ming from the Supreme Sovereign of the Dark Celestial Realm), 180
Ta Ming Tao-tsang ching (Scriptures of the Taoist Canon of the Great Ming; ed. Chang Yü-ch'u), 178
"Ta-mu-ch'ien-lien ming-chien chiu-mu pien-wen" (Transformation Text on Mahāmaudgalyāyana's Rescue of His Mother from the Underworld; the Mu-lien story), 123, 168
"Ta-nan" (Big Boy; P'u Sung-ling), 618
ta-pen-ch'ü (big volume melodies), 1042–43
"Ta p'eng-niao fu" (The Great *P'eng*-bird; Li Po), 298
Ta-p'in po-je po-lo-mi ching (full form of *Prajñāpāramitā-sūtra*), 6
Ta-sheng (Mahāyāna) Buddhism, 163, 176, 582, 1042
ta-shu (big story), 1028
ta-shuo (large talk), 732
Ta-Sung Hsüan-ho yi-shih (Events of the Hsüan-ho Era of the Great Sung Synasty), 626
Ta Sung t'ien-kung pao-tsang (Precious Canon of the Celestial Palace of the Great Sung), 178
Ta Tai Li-chi (Record of Ritual of Tai the Elder), 92, 95
"Ta T'ang Ch'in-wang tz'u-hua" (Chantefable About Prince Ch'in of the Great T'ang Dynasty; Chu Sheng-lin), 996
Ta T'ang hsi-yü chi (Accounts of the Western Regions Under the Great T'ang; Pien-chi), 165, 632
Ta T'ang hsin-hua (New Accounts of the Grand T'ang; Liu Su), 581
Ta-te period (Yüan), 375
Ta-tung chen-ching (True Scripture of the Great Cavern), 181
"Ta wai shih erh shou" (Two Poems in Reply to My Husband Who Is Away; Liu Ling-hsien), 208
ta wen (responding to questions), 904
ta-yi (great righteousness), 623, 626
"Ta yü" (The Great Fish; Wang Ho-ch'ing), 376
Ta-yün ching (Scripture on the Great Cloud), 971
Tacitus, 885
Tai Chin, 400
Tai-ching t'ang shih-hua (Discussions of Poetry from the Hall of the Vademecum Classics Scholar; Wang Shih-chen), 424, 426
Tai Hou-ying, 761, 767
"Tai K'u je hsing" (Suffering from Heat, Surrogate Version; Pao Chao), 269
Tai nationality, 1043–44
Tai Pan (Clavell), 773
Tai-shih (A History of Tai), 180
Tai Shu-lun, 302
Tai Te, 92
Tai T'ien, 458
Tai-tsung, Emperor (Ching-ti; Ming), 400, 807
Tai-tsung, Emperor (T'ang), 583
Tai Wang-shu, 456, 457
T'ai-chi Ko hsien-kung chuan (A Biography of Transcendent Lord Ko of the Grand Ultimate; Chu Ch'o), 182
T'ai ch'ing (Grand Clarity) realm, 177, 183
T'ai-ho cheng-yin p'u (Formulary for the Correct Sounds of Great Harmony; Chu Ch'üan), 811, 816, 840
t'ai-hsüeh (Supreme School), 4
T'ai-k'ang period (Chin), 260–65
t'ai-ko t'i (cabinet style), 401, 403
T'ai-ku chi (Anthology of Grand Antiquity; Hao Ta-t'ung), 187

T'ai-kung chia-chiao (The Family Instructions of the Grand Duke), 966
T'ai-kung Wang (Lü Shang), 522–23
T'ai-nan hsin pao (*Tainan shimpō*; T'ai-nan New Daily), 459
T'ai-pei jen (People from Taipei; Pai Hsien-yung), 777
"T'ai-p'ing hu" (T'ai-p'ing Lake; Su Shu-yang), 858, 859
T'ai-p'ing kuang-chi (Extensive Records from the Reign of Great Tranquility), 121, 136, 523, 548, 677, 685, 688, 815, 835, 1069, 1086
T'ai-p'ing kuang-chi ch'ao (Selections from *Extensive Records from the Reign of Great Tranquility*; Feng Meng-lung), 685–87, 688
T'ai-p'ing-yang pao (Shanghai Pacific News), 727
T'ai-p'ing yü-lan (Imperial Digest of the Reign of Great Tranquility), 121, 563
T'ai-p'ing yüeh-fu (The Songs of the Pax Magnifica; comp. Yang Chao-ying), 374
T'ai-po (temple), 645–46
T'ai-po (magazine), 568
T'ai-po of Wu, 505
T'ai-shan feng-kuang (Sights of Mount T'ai; Wu Tsu-hsiang), 572–73
T'ai-shang Lao-chün (Lord Lao the Most High), 176
"T'ai-shih" (Great Declaration; *Shang-shu*), 89–90
T'ai-shih kung tzu-hsü (postface; *Shih-chi*), 506
t'ai-shih kung yüeh (the Lord Grand Historian says), 505
t'ai-shih ling (Prefect Grand Historian), 502
T'ai-sui (god), 994
T'ai-tsu, Emperor (Chao K'uang-yin), 338, 339, 348
T'ai-tsung, Emperor (Li Shih-min), 87, 279, 282–84, 290, 339, 341, 348, 587–88, 633, 807, 1067–68
"T'ai-tsung ju-ming chi" (Account of Emperor T'ai-tsung's Descent to the Underworld), 971
T'ai-tzu jui-ying pen-ch'i ching (Sūtra on the Auspicious Responses of the Prince), 172
T'ai-wan ch'ing-nien (Taiwanese Youth; journal), 458
T'ai-wan hsin wen-hsüeh (Taiwan's New Literature; journal), 776
T'ai-wan hsin-wen-hsüeh chi-k'an (New Taiwanese Literature Quarterly; journal), 778
T'ai-wan min pao (Taiwan People's Daily), 458
Taiheiki (Chronicle of the Great Peace), 1092
Taiheiki engi (Romance of the Chronicle of the Great Peace; trans. Okajima Kanzan), 1092
Taiping Rebellion, 438, 439, 440, 843, 999, 1058, 1059
Taishō Tripiṭaka, 162
Taiwan, 458–62, 572, 774–81; aboriginal peoples of, 778; anti-Communist writing in, 776–77; censorship in, 737, 770; in Ch'ing dynasty, 458; democracy movement in, 462; essays in, 569; fiction in, 736, 753–54; film in, 759, 780, 781; and Japan, 458, 775–76, 778–80, 1063, 1065; language in, 31–32, 33, 35, 53, 56, 458–59; modernist poets in, 457, 458, 464; nativist literature in, 777–78, 780; New Literature in, 775–76; Pai-se k'ung-pu (White Terror) in, 459–60, 462; Peking opera in, 847; poetry clubs in, 458, 460; poets in, 458–61; popular culture in, 763, 780–81; postmodernism in, 462; and PRC, 753, 758–59, 775, 776–77, 780; Taoist texts from, 179. *See also* China, Republic of
"Taketori monogatari" (Tale of the Bamboo Cutter), 1086
Takizawa Bakin, 1093–94
Talks at the Yenan Forum on Literature and Art (Tsai Yen-an wen-yi tso-t'an-hui shang te chiang-hua; Mao Tse-tung), 5, 158, 457, 864
tan (courage), 938
tan (elixir of immortality), 115–16
tan (female lead), 813, 830, 843, 845, 994
Tan, Amy, 55, 57
Tan, Prince of Yen, 580, 587
"Tan-k'o pan-shu chiu huan, fu-weng ch'ien-chin yi hsiao" (The Rich Man and the Alchemist; Ling Meng-ch'u), 608
"Tan-tao hui" (The Single-sword Meeting; Kuan Han-ch'ing), 807
Tan-yang chen-jen chih-yen (Forthright Discourse on the Perfected Tan-yang), 187
Tan-yang chen-jen yü-lu (Discourse Record of the Perfected Tan-yang; Wang Yi-chung), 187
Tan-yang shen-kuang ts'an (Tan-yang's Luster of Hallowed Radiance), 186–87
t'an (sighs), 108
T'an Ch'u-tuan, 184, 187
"T'an Ch'u-yü hsi-li ch'uan-ch'ing Liu Miao-ku ch'ü chung ssu-chieh" (An Actress Scorns Wealth and Honor to Preserve Her Chastity; Li Yü), 614
T'an Kai, 685
"T'an-lan han liu yüan mai feng-liu" (The Brothel Keeper; Hsi Lang-hsien), 605, 618
T'an-luan, 166
T'an lung lu (A Record of Comments on a Dragon; Chao Chih-hsin), 432–33
T'an-so (Exploration; underground journal), 462
T'an Ssu-t'ung, 454, 1060

t'an-tz'u (strummed or plucking lyrics), 211, 991, 995, 1012, 1019–26, 1028, 1100; in Korea, 1077; from Soochow, 1023, 1024; Wu, 1019, 1023, 1024, 1025. See also *tz'u*
T'an Yüan-ch'un, 7, 412
Tang-k'ou chih (Records of the Elimination of Bandits; Yü Wan-ch'un), 629, 663
T'ang, state of, 107
T'ang Ch'i, 457
"T'ang chieh-yüan yi hsiao yin-yüan" (T'ang Yin; Feng Meng-lung), 601
T'ang chih yen (Picked-Up Tales of the T'ang; Wang Ting-pao), 581
T'ang dynasty, 4, 183, 252, 271, 312, 595, 1042; ballads in, 957, 962–63, 1027; Buddhism in, 11, 170, 993; *ch'uan-ch'i* tales of, 130, 579–94, 679, 680, 686–87, 688, 689; and classics, 913; cosmopolitanism of, 589; court entertainment of, 787, 790; in drama, 815; examination system of, 914, 1083; fall of, 371, 807; in fiction, 626, 661, 670; fiction collections of, 1015; founding of, 587, 807; and *fu*, 6, 243–45, 273; histories of, 175, 526; and Japan, 1082, 1085; and Korea, 1067, 1068; language of, 32, 533, 887; literary criticism of, 894, 919, 930–34; as model, 536; music in, 314, 791; painter-poets of, 478, 479, 481, 490; popular lectures in, 984; prose of, 245, 289, 511, 525, 527, 530–31, 533, 536–37, 539; prosimetric forms in, 1010; proverbs in, 153; punctuation in, 941; and song-prose styles, 993; songs in, 955, 974, 975; storytelling in, 791; supernatural tales of, 119, 121, 548, 580; and Taoism, 183; transformation texts from, 888, 995; travel literature in, 556; and the Uyghur, 1048; and Vietnam, 1096; women in, 201–4, 208–9, 218; writers of, 556; and *yü-lu*, 168. *See also* An Lu-shan rebellion; T'ang poetry
T'ang-hsien san-mei chi (Collection of Samādhi of the T'ang; anthology), 424, 425
T'ang Hsien-tsu, 126, 411, 686–87, 824, 827, 828, 830, 834
T'ang-jen hsiao-shuo (Fiction by T'ang Authors; comp. Wang Pi-chiang), 582
T'ang Lin, 582
T'ang pai-chia shih-hsüan (Anthology of One Hundred T'ang Masters; Wang An-shih), 424
T'ang Po-hu (T'ang Yin), 1024
T'ang poetry, 20, 224, 225, 230, 236, 237, 255, 270, 271, 273, 274–313, 923, 936, 1008, 1071; and fourteenth-century poetry, 393, 394, 395, 397, 398; and fifteenth-sixteenth century poetry, 404, 406, 409; and seventeenth-century poetry, 411, 414, 419, 420, 424, 425; and eighteenth-twentieth century poetry, 429, 432, 433, 440, 441, 443; anthologies of, 275, 279–82, 338, 395, 401, 407, 412, 431, 1016, 1090; categories of, 6, 275–78, 363, 395, 475, 1081; court, 241; landscape, 477; as model, 395; and painting, 482; periodization of, 275; regulated, 276, 1081; *shih*-style, 434, 1083; sinographs used in, 38; sources for, 278–82; and Sung poetry, 343, 344, 349, 358, 365, 366, 367, 368; supernatural in, 123–25; and Tun-huang literature, 975, 982; and *tz'u*, 13–14, 333; and Yüan poetry, 372, 386, 387
T'ang Sai-erh, 632
T'ang Shih, 375, 380, 457
T'ang-shih hsüan (Anthology of T'ang poetry; comp. Li P'an-lung), 407, 1090
T'ang-shih kuei (Homecoming to T'ang Verse; anthology), 412
T'ang-shih pieh-tsai chi (Separately Collected Anthology of T'ang Verse; comp. Shen Te-ch'ien), 431
T'ang-shih p'in-hui (Graded Collocation of T'ang Poetry; comp. Kao Ping), 275, 395, 401, 407
T'ang-shih san-pai shou (Three Hundred T'ang Poems), 281, 338, 1016
T'ang shu (T'ang History), 175, 526
T'ang Shun-chih, 407
T'ang-Sung pa ta chia (Eight Great Prose Masters of the T'ang and Sung Dynasties), 566
T'ang Sung pa-ta chia wen-ch'ao (Anthology of Eight Prose Masters of the T'ang and Sung Dynasties; Mao K'un), 533
T'ang Yeh chen-jen chuan (A Biography of Perfected Yeh of the T'ang), 180
T'ang Yin, 402, 404
T'ang Ying, 834
Tanguts (Hsi-hsia), 339, 557, 964
Tao (the Way), 63, 77, 78, 174, 326, 340, 341, 345, 351, 359, 414, 425, 915, 937. See also *Tao te ching*; Taoism
Tao-an, 163
Tao-chia chin-shih lüeh (A Collection of Taoist Epigraphy), 179
Tao-chiao wen-hsien (Literary Resources on Taoism), 178–79
tao-ch'ing (Taoist tales), 375, 379, 995
"Tao-ch'ing shih-shou" (Ten Songs of Taoist Sentiment; Cheng Hsieh), 831
Tao-fa hsin-chuan (Core Teachings on the Rites of the Tao), 191

Tao-fa hui-yüan (Collective Sources on Taoist Rites), 191
Tao-hsüan, 165, 166
tao-hsüeh (learning of the Way), 340, 352, 358, 359, 362, 364, 365, 366, 367. *See also* Neo-Confucianism
"Tao-kuan nei po-shu fu" (A Cypress Tree at a Taoist Abbey; Wei Cheng), 284
"Tao ling nü" (Mourning the Death of an Actress; T'ang Shih), 380
Tao-men shih-kuei (Ten Guidelines on the Taoist Lineage), 182
Tao shu (Pivot of the Tao; Tseng Ts'ao), 189
Tao te ching (Classic of the Way and Integrity; Lao Tzu), 10, 77–78, 173–75, 178, 182, 188, 190, 191, 746, 913, 918; and Buddhism, 163; didacticism of, 98; and *Huai-nan Tzu*, 82; and poetry, 267, 363, 419; proverbs in, 151; and "Ta Chuan," 82. *See also* Taoism
Tao-tsang chi-yao (Collected Essentials of the Taoist Canon; P'eng Ting-ch'iu), 178, 191
tao-t'ung (transmission of the Way), 533–34
"Tao wang shih" (Mourning the Deceased; P'an Yüeh), 261
Tao-yen (Yao Kuang-hsiao), 395
tao yü (inverted ways of speaking), 894
Tao-yüan, 169
T'ao Chen-huai, 211
T'ao Ch'ien (T'ao Yüan-ming), 68, 120, 240, 263, 264, 266–67, 269, 285, 302, 306, 324, 425, 580, 581, 583; classification of, 927; in drama, 837; influence of, 1082; as model, 353, 354, 1083; and picture eulogies, 470, 471; reading technique of, 883; *Sequel to Search for the Supernatural* of, 550, 553–54
T'ao Fu, 681–82
T'ao Han, 295
"T'ao-hua, jen-mien" (Peach Blossoms, Pink Cheeks; Meng Ch'eng-shun), 837
"T'ao-hua shan" (Peach Blossom Fan; K'ung Shang-jen), 825, 833, 996
T'ao-hua ying (In the Peach Blossom Shadow), 669
"T'ao-hua yüan" (Peach Blossom Spring; Yu T'ung), 837
"T'ao-hua yüan chi" (Record of the Peach Blossom Spring; T'ao Ch'ien), 267, 550, 553–54, 580, 583
T'ao Hung-ching, 177
t'ao-shu (song sets), 370
T'ao Tsung-yi, 136, 374, 381
T'ao-yeh (Peach Leaf), 207
T'ao Yüan-ming. *See* T'ao Ch'ien
Taoism, 173–93, 227, 228, 271, 412, 474, 549–50, 580, 915; and biography, 522–23, 582; and Buddhism, 160, 161, 163, 165, 166, 173, 176, 177; canon of, 175–91; Celestial Masters (T'ien-shih tao) of, 175–76, 179–80, 192, 253; in Cheng-shih period, 258, 259; Ch'üan-chen sect of, 810; *vs.* Confucianism, 266; and drama, 168, 839, 843; in Eastern Chin period, 265; Eight Immortals in, 588, 810, 838; and esthetic patterns, 892; in fiction, 662, 664, 665, 666, 670, 672; gods of, 68; and Han Yü, 533, 535; in historical fiction, 631–32; and *hua-pen*, 596, 601, 603, 607, 610, 613, 616, 617; and *Huai-nan Tzu*, 82–83; and humor, 136, 138, 139; influence of, 9–11; in Japan, 1081; in *Journey to the West*, 633, 634, 635, 636; in Korea, 1070; Ling-pao tradition of, 253, 298; and Liu Tsung-yüan, 536; Ming canon of, 179, 180, 181; and myth, 59, 60, 62, 64; origins of, 76–78; and painting, 173, 473, 477; paradises of, 477; and poetry, 124, 173, 183, 185–86, 188, 191–92, 265, 298, 361, 932; and poets, 302, 311, 312, 313, 353, 394, 408, 411, 442; and politics, 918; and religious texts, 995; religious *vs.* philosophical, 174; in *Romance of the Three Kingdoms*, 621, 623, 624, 625; sacred sites of, 175–76, 179, 181, 182–83, 185, 191; schools of, 175–78; and sexuality, 665, 666; Shang-ch'ing tradition of, 248, 253, 298; Southern Lineage of, 188–91; in Southern Sung, 362; and Ssu-ma Ch'ien, 507; in *The Story of the Stone*, 648, 654; and Su Shih, 540; and supernatural, 110, 113–18, 121, 550, 554; transformative images of, 354; traveling priests of, 997; in *Travels of Lao Ts'an*, 658; in Tun-huang manuscripts, 178, 965, 969, 970, 981; and twentieth-century fiction, 740, 746
tapas (psychic heat; Sanskrit), 1046
Tarim Basin mummies, 3
Tashi Dawa, 1034
Tay, William (Cheng Shu-sen), 773
te (marker of possessive case, etc.), 44
Te-hung, 170
"Te tao ko" (Song on Attaining the Tao), 191
Te-tsung, Emperor, 244, 581
te yü erh wang ch'üan (to forget the fish-trap when you have caught the fish), 936
television, 732, 759, 760, 766, 771, 774, 780
Temujin. *See* Chinggis Khan
Tendency (*Ch'ing-hsiang*; journal), 464
"Teng chen fu" (The Ascent to Perfection; Wu Yün), 302
Teng Ch'un, 479
Teng Hsiao-p'ing, 462, 569, 736, 754, 761, 770, 1012

teng kao neng/pi fu ("ascending on high, can/must *fu*"), 5
"Teng-lou fu" (Rhapsody on Climbing the Tower; Wang Ts'an), 235
Teng T'ing-chen, 335
Teng T'o, 569
"Teng-t'u tzu hao-se fu" (Rhapsody on the Lechery of Master Teng-t'u; Sung Yü), 106
Teng Tzu-chin, 373–74
Teng Wen-yüan, 386
"Teng Yi-ch'eng ku-ch'eng fu" (Atop the Olden Walls of Yi-ch'eng; Hsiao Ying-shih), 301
"Teng Yüeh-yang lou" (Climbing Yüeh-yang Tower; Ch'en Yü-yi), 357
"T'eng ta-yin kuei tuan chia-ssu" (Prefect T'eng's Ghostly Solution of a Case of Inheritance; Feng Meng-lung), 602
Terakado Seiken, 1094
Terry, John Kwan (Kuan Chieh-ming), 461
The Theory of Prose (Shklovskij), 717
Thirteen Classics. See *Shih-san ching*
Thomas, Dylan, 457
Three Kingdoms (Korea), 1067
Three Kingdoms period (China), 153, 252, 540, 549, 807, 994, 997. See also *San-kuo yen-yi*
Thucydides, 497, 505
Ti-ch'i shang-chiang Wen T'ai-pao chuan (A Biography of Grand Guardian Wen, Supreme Commander of the Tutelary Deities), 180
Ti Ch'ing, 1037
ti-fang-chih. See gazetteers, local
ti-fang hsi (local opera), 1016
Ti K'u (god), 66, 68
Ti-san tai (the Third Generation), 463
"Ti-shih fu" (The Whetstone; Liu Yü-hsi), 306
"Ti-tzu ko" (Song of the Child of the God; Li Ho), 125
t'i (embodied), 884
t'i (lifting), 707
t'i (literary structure), 715
T'i-hsiao yin-yüan (Fate in Tears and Laughter; Chang Hen-shui), 733, 743
T'i-hsüan chen-jen hsien-yi lu (A Record of the Striking Marvels of the Perfected Who Embodies Sublimity), 185, 187
t'i-hsüeh fu-shih (Education Vice-Commissioner), 402
t'i-hua shih (*shih* poetry inscribed on paintings), 467, 474
t'i-hua wen-hsüeh (inscription literature, writings inscribed on paintings), 467–90
t'i-pa (colophons), 467, 967
t'i t'ien hsing-tao (to realize the Way on behalf of heaven), 629
"Tiao Ch'ü Yüan wen" (Lament for Ch'ü Yüan; Liu Tsung-yüan), 230
tiao-ch'ung (insect carving), 921, 929
Tiao-ch'ung lun (Treatise on Insect Carving; P'ei Tzu-yeh), 929
"Tiao Kao Ch'ing-ch'iu" (Lamenting Kao Ch'i; Chang Yü), 397
t'iao (subsections; items), 562
"T'iao Chang Chi" (Han Yü), 124
Tibet, 1033, 1037, 1041, 1042, 1044–48
Tibeto-Burman, 21, 26, 39
"Tieh chü ch'i Ch'eng k'o te chu, san chiu o hai-shen hsien ling" (The Sea Goddess; Ling Meng-ch'u), 606
t'ieh-t'i (iron style), 387
T'ieh-wei shan ts'ung-t'an (Collection of Talks from the Iron Mountains Surrounding This Mundane World; Ts'ai T'iao), 141
tien (classical diction), 422
tien-chung (classical weightiness), 327
tien-ku (allusion), 28, 151, 242, 243, 245, 262, 322, 323, 331, 377, 893, 894, 900
Tien lun (Normative Essays; Ts'ao P'i), 236, 257, 923–24
Tien-shih-chai hua-pao (Lithography Studio Illustrated; magazine), 131
Tien shih-chieh (Electric World; Kao-yang pu-ts'ai-tzu), 722
tien t'ieh ch'eng chin (changing iron into gold), 354
T'ien-an-men Square demonstrations (1989), 57, 763, 770
T'ien Ch'eng-ssu, 589
T'ien-chin jih-jih hsin-wen pao (Tientsin Daily News), 624
T'ien Han, 851, 852, 854, 857, 858, 859, 870
T'ien Hsi, 342, 351
"T'ien-hsia t'ai-p'ing" (The World at Peace; Wu Tsu-hsiang), 752
T'ien-hsia ti-hsia (Under Sky Under Ground; Henry Chao), 768
T'ien-hsin (Celestial Heart) school, 191
T'ien Hu (*Shui-hu chuan*), 627
T'ien Ju-ch'eng, 685
t'ien-kan ti-chih (heavenly stems and earthly branches), 36
t'ien-ming (Mandate of Heaven), 73, 75, 96, 111, 543, 546, 1056
T'ien-pao period (T'ang), 292, 303, 313, 424, 581
"T'ien-pao yi-shih chu-kung-tiao" (Medley on the Anecdotes of the T'ien-pao Period; Wang Po-ch'eng), 800
"T'ien shang yao" (In Heaven; Li Ho), 124, 125
"T'ien-she weng shih-shih ching-li, mu-t'ung erh yeh-yeh tsun-jung" (The Herdboy; Ling Meng-ch'u), 607
T'ien-shih (Celestial Master) school, 175–76, 179–80, 192, 253
t'ien-shu (heavenly writing), 54

"T'ien-t'ai fang-yin lu" (Record of a Visit to Exiles in T'ien-t'ai; Chü Yu), 681
T'ien-t'ai school, 167, 170
T'ien Tan (3rd c. B.C.E.; petty official of Ch'i), 506
T'ien Tan (3rd c. B.C.E.; sovereign of Ch'i), 516
T'ien ts'ou ch'iao (Predetermined Fortune), 613
"T'ien wen" (Heavenly Questions; *Ch'u tz'u*), 60–61, 62, 63, 65, 117, 199, 226, 228, 468
"T'ien wen hsün" (Treatise on Patterns of Heaven; *Huainan Tzu*), 82–83
T'ien-yen lun (On Evolution; Huxley; trans. Yen Fu), 719, 1062
"T'ien yü hua" (Flowers Under the Rain of Heaven; T'ao Chen-huai), 211, 1020
T'ien-yüan ch'i-yü (Marvelous Assignations Predestined by Heaven), 684
t'ien-yüan (pastoral) poetry, 266, 420
Ting-ch'ing jen (The Tale of Loyal Love), 668
Ting Hsien-hsien, 141
"Ting-hun tien" (The Inn of Betrothal; Li Fu-yen), 588
Ting Ling (Chiang Ping-chih), 748, 750
ting-pen (definitive versions), 282
Ting P'eng, 414
Ting Yao-k'ang, 642, 660, 662, 947
T'ing-chi (Hsiang Hung-tso), 449
To Cong phung su (Su Wu Carries Out His Duties), 1101
To-hsin ching (Sutra of Many Hearts/Minds; *Hsin ching*), 635
To To (Duo Duo), 462, 764
T'o-pa (Tabgatch) people, 264
"T'o-pei chi" (The Hunchbacked Whore), 377
Tokushiyōryō (Essentials for Reading the Classic of Poetry; Itō Tōgai), 1089–90
Tolstoy, L. N., 720, 729
Tonghak Rebellion, 1059
Tongmunsŏn (Selection of Refined Literature from Korea), 1071
topolects, 25, 29, 264
toryangmun (examination compositions; Korea), 1071
Tou Ŏ. *See* "Kan t'ien tung ti"
Tou-p'eng hsien-hua (Idle Talk Under the Bean Arbor; Ai-na chü-shih), 616, 619
T'ou-hsia lu (The Linchpin Tossing Collection; Wang Ming-ch'ing), 675
t'ou shih (stealing a literary mode), 893
townsman poetry, 391–92, 393, 395, 396
Tran Te Xuong, 1099
Translation Publishing House of Western Writing, 711
translations, 1055–66; of Buddhist texts, 160–64, 171, 172, 1055; censorship of, 736; of Chinese works, 760, 1079–95; into Classical Chinese, 1062–66; collections of, 1040; colloquial, 372, 887; from Japanese, 711, 1060–62; into Japanese, 1079–95; into Korean, 1073, 1074, 1077, 1078; and late Ch'ing fiction, 723; and literary criticism, 707, 711, 715, 768; and May Fourth fiction, 749; from minority languages, 1038, 1039; and missionaries, 1055, 1058–60; and modern literature, 729, 730, 733, 734, 763, 764; and neologisms, 1056–58; of novels, 717–20, 1064, 1075, 1102, 1103; secondhand, 1060–62; and Shanghai writers, 703, 704, 705; and vernacular Chinese, 887, 1056–62, 1065–66; into Vietnamese, 1098, 1100–1103; of Western works, 699–700, 703, 707–8, 717–20, 1057–66
travel literature, 535, 555–59, 572, 705; types of, 556–57
Tretiakov, Sergei Mikhailovich, 859
Trigault, Nicolas, 52
Tripiṭaka (*Journey to the West*), 633–37, 663
truyen (tales; Vietnamese), 1100, 1101
Truyen ky man luc (Expansive Record of Wondrous Legends; Nguyen Du), 1099
Truyen ky tan pha (New Assortment of Wondrous Tales; Doan Thi Diem), 1099
tsa (eclectic), 564
tsa-ch'ao. See *pi-chi*
tsa-chi (descriptive accounts and inscriptions), 528
tsa-chia (miscellaneous schools), 561
tsa-chü (drama; variety plays; farce), 394, 418, 626, 791, 797–818, 996, 1008, 1093; sixteenth-eighteenth century, 823, 835–38; nineteenth-early twentieth century, 843, 844; adaptations of, 819, 824; authors of, 796, 808, 810, 811–18, 831, 836–37; centers of production of, 811, 815; collections of, 837, 841; and court entertainment, 802, 817; crime in, 808, 812; humor in, 144; and literati, 838; lost, 822; and northern tunes, 793, 840; role types in, 793–94; subject matter of, 805–10; supernatural in, 125; texts of, 785, 786, 792, 794, 795, 796, 804, 805, 823; Yüan, 389, 792, 793–94, 795, 800–802, 804, 806, 814
Tsa-chü san-chi (Third Collection of *Tsa-chü*; Shen T'ai), 837
tsa-ch'ü (miscellaneous pieces), 954
tsa ko-yao tz'u (song-texts for miscellaneous ditties), 954
Tsa p'i-yü ching (Canonical Scripture of Miscellaneous Parables), 171
"Tsa-p'ien" (Miscellaneous Chapters; *Chuang Tzu*), 174

"Tsa shih" (Miscellaneous Poem; Fu Hsüan), 260
"Tsa shih" (Miscellaneous Poems; Ts'ao Chih), 256
"Tsa-shuo" (Miscellania; Wu Chien-jen), 719
tsa-wen (polemical topical essay), 568, 569, 570, 571–72
"Tsai-sheng yüan" (Love Reincarnate; Ch'en Tuan-sheng), 211, 1020–23, 1024, 1077
"Tsai t'i Po fu shih" (Again Writing About Master Po's Poetry; Fan Ch'eng-ta), 362
"Tsai-tsao t'ien" (Heaven Recreated; Hou Chih), 1023, 1026
"Tsai Yen-an wen-yi tso-t'an-hui shang te chiang-hua" (Talks at the Yenan Forum on Literature and Art; Mao Tse-tung), 5, 158, 457, 864
"Tsai yi-yüan chung" (In the Hospital; Ting Ling), 748
ts'ai (riches), 186
ts'ai (talent), 938
Ts'ai Ch'en, 914
Ts'ai Chih-yi, 190
Ts'ai Ching, 339, 352, 356, 357
Ts'ai Ch'iu-t'ung, 776
"Ts'ai Jui-hung jen ju pao ch'ou" (Ts'ai Jui-hung Bears Humiliation for the Sake of Revenge; Hsi Lang-hsien), 603–4
Ts'ai-kuei chi (Records of Talented Ghosts; comp. Mei Ting-tso), 683, 688
"Ts'ai-lien fu" (Lotus-Picking; Wang Po), 289
"Ts'ai-shih chi" (The Colored Stone Jetty; Chiang Shih-ch'üan), 834
Ts'ai Sung-nien, 325
Ts'ai T'ao, 141
ts'ai-tzu (genius), 942
ts'ai-tzu chia-jen (scholar-beauty) fiction, 596, 617, 644–45, 666–69, 679–90, 742, 743, 798, 817, 1019, 1074–76, 1100, 1101
Ts'ai Yen, 205–6, 217, 257
Ts'ai Yü, 684–85
Ts'ai Yüan-fang, 625
Ts'ai Yüan-p'ei, 1063
Ts'ai Yung, 87, 206, 251, 257
tsan (appreciation, eulogy), 4, 468, 475, 478, 978, 998
"Tsan-men te shih-chieh" (Our World; Mu Shih-ying), 749
Tsan-ning, 165
tsan-sung (song of praise), 977
ts'an-chün-hsi (adjutant plays, comic dialogs), 143, 144, 787, 790–91
Ts'an Hsüeh, 764, 771
Tsang K'o-chia, 771
Tsang Mao-hsün, 803
Tsang-wai Tao-shu (Extracanonical Taoist Texts), 179
ts'ang-ku (gray hawk; straight man in comic dialog), 143, 144
Ts'ang-lang shih-hua (Ts'ang-lang's Remarks on Poetry; Yen Yü), 12, 170, 401, 421, 427, 935–36
Ts'ang-shan kao wai-pien (Mountain-stored Manuscript, Outer Collection; Hsü Fang), 691
Tsangyang Tshomo Gyatso (sixth Dalai Lama), 1046–47
"Tsao-kao te T'ai-wan wen-hsüeh chieh" (The Terrible Taiwanese Literary Scene; Chang Wo-chün), 458
Tsao-shu te ku-shih (The Story of the Date Tree; Yeh Chao-yen), 764
Ts'ao, state of, 107
Ts'ao Chan. *See* Ts'ao Hsüeh-ch'in
Ts'ao Chih, 230, 235, 253–57, 258, 260, 262, 265, 269, 284, 412, 440, 468, 473, 549, 923; and ballads, 959, 960; and Buddhist hymns, 978; women in work of, 199, 200
Ts'ao Erh-k'an, 427
Ts'ao Fang, 257, 258
Ts'ao Hsien, 289
Ts'ao Hsüeh-ch'in (Ts'ao Chan), 69, 215, 720, 723, 735, 832, 915, 1033. See also *Hung-lou meng*
Ts'ao Jui (Emperor Ming), 254, 257, 259
Ts'ao Mao, 258
Ts'ao P'i (Emperor Wen of Wei), 231, 234–36, 252–54, 257, 259, 262, 549, 806, 923–24, 963, 1083
ts'ao-shu (grass style) script, 49
Ts'ao Shuang, 257
"Ts'ao-t'ang shih chih t'u" (Ten Views from My Thatched Lodge; Lu Hung), 478–79
Ts'ao T'ang-ts-un, 654
Ts'ao Ts'ao, 234, 252–55, 257, 521, 549, 621, 623–25, 806, 835, 923
Ts'ao-tung (Sōtō) school, 169
"Ts'ao Tzu-chien yü Yang Te-tsu shu" (Letter from Ts'ao Tzu-chien to Yang Te-tsu), 923
Ts'ao Yeh, 312
Ts'ao Yü, 156, 770, 857, 860, 861, 862, 864
tse (esthetic standards), 422
"Tse tzu shih" (Chiding Sons; T'ao Ch'ien), 263
ts'e (formulaic essay), 1070, 1071
Ts'e-mao tz'u (Lyrics by One Who Wears His Hat Aslant; Nara Singde), 418
Ts'en Shen, 295, 296, 300
Tseng Chi, 357, 359–60
Tseng Ch'i, 401, 680
Tseng Ch'ing-ying, 179
"Tseng fu shih" (Poems for My Wife; Ch'in Chia), 251
"Tseng hsiung hsiu-ts'ai ju chün" (Presented to My Elder Brother the Flourishing Talent on His Entering the Army; Hsi K'ang), 259
tseng-hsü (farewell), 528
"Tseng Hsü Kan" (Presented to Hsü Kan; Ts'ao Chih), 269
Tseng Jui, 380
Tseng Kung, 355, 533
Tseng Kuo-fan, 440
"Tseng Pai-ma wang Piao" (Presented to Piao, Prince of Pai-ma; Ts'ao Chih), 256
Tseng P'u, 657, 703–4, 710–12, 721, 725

Tseng Shen, 95, 469–70
tseng-ta shih (poems of presentation and response), 254, 255, 259, 262
Tseng Ts'ao, 189
Tseng Tzu, 95
Tseng Yen-tung, 695
ts'eng-ti (climax), 894, 905
tso (composed), 900
Tso Ch'ih, 625
Tso Ch'iu-ming, 93
Tso chuan (Tso Commentary on *Ch'un-ch'iu*), 60, 88, 497–505, 512, 515, 522, 525, 625, 895, 910, 911, 912, 917; antecedents of, 499; didacticism of, 93–94, 98; divinatory poetry in, 107; genres of, 498–99; as history, 497–500; and *Hsiao-ching*, 95; humor in, 140; as model, 1076; and poetry, 225, 235, 242, 254; and *Shih-ching*, 102, 104; and Ssu-ma Kuang, 509–10; supernatural in, 113, 116, 500; women in, 196, 499; and *Yi-ching*, 89
Tso Fen, 263
Tso Ssu, 234, 239, 260, 262, 263, 426, 468, 925
Tso Tsung-t'ang, 1065
tso-yi hsi-chü (leftist drama), 857, 859, 860
Tso-yi tso-chia lien-meng (League of Left-Wing Writers), 748
"Ts'o jen shih" (The Wrongly Identified Corpse; Hung P'ien), 600
Tsou, Mr. (commentator on *Ch'un-ch'iu*), 92
"Tsou Meng K'o mu" (The Mother of Meng K'o of Tsou), 198
Tsou Yang, 232, 513–14
Tsou Yen, 80
tsou-yi, tsou-yi chi (*tsou-shu chi*; memorial), 528, 529
Tsu-fu tsai fu-ch'in hsin-chung (Grandfather in Father's Heart; Fang Fang), 765
Tsu-hsiu, 166
Tsu-mou (Chu Hsiao-tsang), 450–51
Tsu-t'ang chi (Collection from the Hall of the Patriarchs), 169
Tsu-yeh ko (Girl of the Night Songs), 961
ts'u (crude), 884
Tsubouchi Shōyō, 1094
Tsuga Teishō, 1092–93
Tsui-ch'a chih-kuai (Tea-tipsy Records of the Strange; Li Ching-ch'en), 695
"Tsui-ch'un li te yang-kuang" (Sunshine Between the Lips; Ch'en Jan), 766
Tsui-hou te yi shou ko (The Last Song; To To), 764
Tsui hsing shih (The Sobering Stone; Tung-Lu Ku-k'uang-sheng), 613
Tsui-weng t'an-lu (Notes of an Old Tippler; Lo Yeh), 596, 995
"Tsui-weng t'ing chi" (Account of the Drunken Old Man's Pavilion; Ou-yang Hsiu), 538
Ts'ui Chien, 763
Ts'ui Chü, 591
Ts'ui Chuan, 107
Ts'ui Hao, 295
Ts'ui Hsien, 404, 406
Ts'ui Jung, 280
Ts'ui Kuo-fu, 295
"Ts'ui niao shih" (Kingfisher; Ts'ai Yung), 251
Ts'ui Pao, 563
Ts'ui Po-yi (Ts'ui Kung-tu), 561
Ts'ui Shih, 152, 292
Ts'ui Shu, 94
"Ts'ui Tai-chao sheng-ssu yüan-chia" (The Jade Kuan-yin), 597
Ts'ui Te-chih, 871
"Ts'ui ya lou" (House of Gathered Refinements; Li Yü), 615
"Ts'ui Ying-ying" (Oriole's Story), 203. *See also* "Ying-ying chuan"
Tsukamoto Zenryū, 164
ts'un-hsin yang-hsing (the learning of preserving the mind and nourishing nature), 634
Ts'un Shen, 871
Tsung Ch'en, 407
Tsung-chien, 167
"Tsung ch'iu lun" (On the Release of Criminals; Ou-yang Hsiu), 538
Tsung Fu-hsien, 869
tsung-heng chia (School of Horizontal and Vertical Alliances), 502
Tsung-mi, 166
Tsung-ping, 169, 477
Tsung P'u, 761
tsung te chi-ch'eng (vertical inheritance), 460
ts'ung-cha. See *pi-chi*
"Ts'ung-chün hsing" (Accompanying the Army; Lu Chi), 255
"Ts'ung-chün shih" (Poems on Accompanying the Army; Wang Ts'an), 255
Ts'ung-shan shih-hsüan (Selected Verse from the Mountain of Acute Hearing; Shen Han-kuang), 413–14
Ts'ung-shan wen-chi (Literary Collection from the Mountain of Acute Hearing; Shen Han-kuang), 414
ts'ung-shu (collectanea), 564
ts'ung-t'an. See *pi-chi*
Ts'ung Wei-hsi, 755, 761
Tsurezuregusa (Essays in Idleness; Yoshida Kenkō), 7
tu-che (the reader), 904
"Tu-ch'i shou yu fu chih kua, no-fu huan pu ssu chih hun" (A Jealous Wife Becomes a Widow While Her Husband Is Still Alive; Li Yü), 615
"Tu-chüan shan" (The Red Azalea; Wang Shu-yüan et al.), 866
Tu Duc, King (Vietnam), 1098, 1102, 1103
Tu Fu, 20, 279, 296, 300, 304, 307, 311, 349, 425, 435, 558–59, 730, 944; and An Lu-shan rebellion, 299, 358;

comparison with, 421, 480; Han Yü on, 124; influence of, 420, 434, 449, 962, 1068; and inscription poetry, 475, 476, 477, 478, 479, 487; as model, 355, 357, 367, 377, 387, 395, 401, 409, 412, 414, 419, 423, 424, 441, 1085; and T'ang poetry, 431, 936, 1071; technique of, 353–54; on women, 204–5
Tu Heng, 456
tu-hsing (independent spirits), 520
Tu Hsün-ho, 313
Tu Hung-chien, 583, 593
"Tu Hung-chien chuan" (An Account of Tu Hung-chien; Hsiao Shih-ho), 583, 593
Tu Jen-chieh, 376
Tu Kang, 596, 618–19
Tu Kuang-t'ing, 182–83, 582, 587
Tu Kuo-ch'ing, 461
"Tu 'Li-sao'" (Reading "Encountering Sorrow"; Yu T'ung), 837
Tu Mu, 245, 310, 311, 317, 431, 815, 933
Tu Pu, 309
"Tu *Shan hai ching* shih-san shou" (On Reading the *Classic of Mountains and Seas*, Thirteen Poems; T'ao Ch'ien), 68, 120, 468
"Tu she chüan" (Coil of Vipers; trans. Chou Kuei-sheng), 720
Tu Shen-yen, 292, 296
"Tu Shih-niang nu ch'en pai-pao hsiang" (Tu Shih-niang Angrily Sinks Her Jewel-Box; Feng Meng-lung), 213, 600, 601, 602
Tu-shu hou (After Reading; Wang Shih-chen), 408
Tu Te-k'ang, 188
"Tu Tzu ch'un" (Li Fu-yen), 588–89
"Tu Tzu-ch'un san ju Ch'ang-an" (Tu Tzu-ch'un; Hsi Lang-hsien), 602–3
Tu Yeh, 54
Tu Yü, 93, 296
Tu Yün-hsieh, 457
T'u-chia people, 1011
T'u Lung, 7, 408, 411
T'u-mu (Earth Mother), 634
T'u-mu, battle of, 400, 402
t'u-su-tzu (Chinese characters employed to represent Chuang pronunciations), 1036
"T'u tsan" (Illustrations; *Shan hai ching*), 68, 120
t'u-yin (local dialects, patois), 1017
Tuan Ch'eng-shih, 581
Tuan Chih-chien, 188
Tuan-hung ling-yen chi (The Lone Swan; Su Man-shu), 727
tuan-p'ien hsiao-shuo (short tales), 729
t'uan-yüan (reunion scene), 826, 830, 831, 833, 834, 840
"Tui chiu" (Bring On the Wine; Po Chü-yi), 962
tui-chü (antithetical) lines, 1080
tui-ts'e (topical replies), 50
tui-wen (corresponding expressions), 891
t'ui-fei (literary decadence), 926
"T'ui-pien" (Transformation; Ts'ao Yü), 864
"Tun hsiu-ts'ai yi chao chiao-t'ai" (The Luckless Licentiate; Feng Meng-lung), 601
Tun-huang Fan-shih chia-chuan (The Family Biography of the Fan Clan of Tun-huang), 969
Tun-huang manuscripts, 11, 14, 964–88, 996, 1010, 1017–18, 1044; Buddhist, 166, 170, 474, 478, 969, 970, 971–72, 979, 983; Ch'an Buddhist, 168, 169; Confucianism in, 965, 974; miracle tales in, 969–72; myth in, 68–69; plays in, 791; poetry in, 278, 279, 280, 302, 313, 315, 327, 973–82; prose works in, 968–73; proverbs in, 153; song cycles in, 976–77; and spoken language of T'ang dynasty, 533; Taoist, 179, 965, 969, 970, 981; transformation texts in, 167–68, 814, 972, 982, 983, 985, 986–87; vernacular in, 30, 278, 533, 972
Tun-huang pien-wen chi (Collection of *pien-wen* from Tun-huang; Wang Chung-min), 167
Tung Chao, 255, 256
Tung-chen (Caverned Perfection), 180
Tung-ch'eng-tiao (Eastern City Tune), 1030
Tung Ch'i-ch'ang, 400, 1072
Tung Chieh-yüan, 587, 796, 800, 1008, 1014
"Tung ching fu" (Eastern Capital Rhapsody; Chang Heng), 105
Tung-ching meng hua lu (Dreams of Splendor of the Eastern Capital; Meng Yüan-lao), 791
"Tung-ch'ing shu" (The Evergreen Tree; Chiang Shih-ch'üan), 834
Tung Chou lieh-kuo chih (Records of the Various States During the Eastern Chou; Ts'ai Yüan-fang), 625
Tung Chung-shu, 83, 93, 913
"Tung-erh ku-niang" (The Winter Girl; Ping Hsin), 748
Tung-fang Shuo, 139, 141, 233, 523, 838
"Tung-fang Shuo pieh-chuan" (The Esoteric Traditions of Tung-fang Shuo), 523
Tung-fang tsa-chih (Eastern Miscellany; periodical), 568
Tung-hai chüeh-wo. *See* Hsü Nien-tz'u
"Tung 'Hsi-hsiang'" (Master Tung's "Romance of the Western Chamber"). *See* "Hsi-hsiang chi chu-kung-tiao"
"Tung-hsiao chi" (The Story of the Flute; Lu Ts'an), 677
Tung-hsüan chin-yü chi (Anthology of the Gold-Jade of Caverned Sublimity), 186

Tung Hsün, 947–48
Tung Hu (legendary historian), 543, 551
Tung-hua ti-chün (Lord of the East), 184, 810
Tung-Lu Ku-k'uang-sheng, 613
tung-pa (ritual specialists), 1041
Tung Pai (Hsiao-wan), 417
Tung peoples, 1053
Tung-p'o chih-lin (East Slope's Forest of Recollections; Su Shih), 540
Tung-p'o wen-chi (collection of Su Shih's writing), 1068
Tung-shan ch'ou-ho chi (Collection of Offer and Response Poems from East Mountain), 416
Tung-shan Liang-chieh, 169
Tung-shan yü-lu (Recorded Sayings of Master Tung-shan), 169
Tung Shao-nan, 534
"Tung t'ing ling-yin chuan" (An Account of the Auspicious Marriage of Tung-t'ing; Li Ch'ao-wei), 584–85
Tung-tu chi (*Tung-yu chi*; Journey to the East; Fang Ju-hao), 661
Tung Wu ta-hsüeh (University of the Eastern Wu Region), 712
"Tung-ya feng-yün" (The Storms of East Asia), 851
"Tung-yang yeh-kuai lu" (Night Apparitions of Tung-yang), 680
tung-yi (understanding the *Changes*), 633
Tung-yu chi (Journey to the East), 129, 661, 664
Tung Yüeh, 129, 637, 663–64, 946
Tung Yung, 986
T'ung-ch'eng school, 246, 533
T'ung-chien kang-mu (Main Principles of the Comprehensive Mirror; Chu Hsi), 622
T'ung chih t'ang chi (Literary Works from the Hall of Realized Ambition; Nara Singde), 418
"T'ung-ch'uang yu jen chia tso chen, nü hsiu-ts'ai yi-hua chieh-mu" (Her Classmate Takes the False for Real, the Lady Licentiate Grafts One Twig on Another; Ling Meng-ch'u), 606
t'ung-hsin (infant's heart/mind), 411
"T'ung-kan kung-k'u" (Joys and Sorrows; Yüeh Yeh), 866–67
t'ung-ling (spiritual realm), 648
t'ung-ling pao-yü (Jade of Numinous Transcendence), 648
T'ung-meng hui (Revolutionary Alliance), 711. *See also* Sun Yat-sen
t'ung mu (repetition of key words), 894
"T'ung sheng ko" (Song of Harmonious Sounds; Chang Heng), 251
T'ung Shu-yeh, 68
T'ung-t'ien le (Understanding Heavenly Pleasures; Shih Ch'eng-chin), 617
T'ung-wen kuan (School of Combined Languages), 718
t'ung yao (Songs of Young Boys; *Tso chuan*), 107
Turkish language, 1013
Twain, Mark, 729
Twenty-four Companions of Chia Mi. *See* Lu kung erh-shih-ssu yu
tzu (philosophy), 925
"Tzu-ch'ai chi" (The Purple Hairpin; T'ang Hsien-tsu), 827
Tzu-chih t'ung-chien (A Comprehensive Mirror for Aid in Government; Ssu-ma Kuang), 167, 509–10, 622
Tzu-hsia (Pu Shang, Pu Tzu), 98, 100
"Tzu-hsiao chi" (The Purple Flute; T'ang Hsien-tsu), 827
tzu-hsien (self-expression), 892
"Tzu hsü fu" (Master Void Rhapsody; Ssu-ma Hsiang-ju), 232
tzu-jan (spontaneous, uncontrived, self-driven, natural), 892
Tzu pu yü (What the Master Did Not Speak Of; Yüan Mei), 693–94
"Tzu shu" (Of Myself; Ch'iao Chi), 377
Tzu-ssu, 99, 101
tzu-ti-shu (bannermen's stories), 1018, 1027, 1028, 1029–31, 1051
"Tzu tse" (I Blame Myself; Chu Shu-chen), 210
Tzu-yeh (Girl of the Night), 207
Tzu-yeh (Midnight; Mao Tun), 747
Tzu-yeh ssu shih ko (Girl of the Night Four Seasons Songs), 961
"Tzu yi" (*Li-chi*), 92, 99, 101, 109
tzu-yu-hua (liberalization), 770
"Tzu-yün t'ing" (Purple Clouds Courtyard; Shih Chün-pao), 809, 819
tz'u (lyrics), 12, 13–14, 32, 185–88, 209–10, 274, 312, 313, 314–36, 370, 396, 968; allusions in, 322, 323, 331, 377; and ballads, 953, 955; birthday, 329; Che-hsi school of, 431–32; and Chinese tones, 321, 327; Ch'ing, 429, 430, 432, 437–39, 441, 442, 444–52; *ch'ü-tzu*, 974–75; drum (*ku-tzu*), 796, 990, 991, 1008, 1028; handbooks of (*tz'u-p'u*), 840; Hsi-ling school of, 414; implied author in, 322; and literary criticism, 327, 442, 939; *man*, 316, 317, 318, 319, 321, 329, 332; Ming, 413; as modern literary form, 443; printing of, 324; quotations in, 321–23; revival of, 444; sentences in, 323; seventeenth-century, 416, 417, 419, 420–21, 426, 427; and *shih* poetry, 320, 322; and song, 953, 1009; southern (*nan*), 1024; Sung, 315–16, 352, 353, 796, 955; trifling (*hsiao*), 316; from Tun-huang, 974–75; by

women, 325–26, 327, 332, 428, 429, 839; writers of, 406
tz'u (this), 889
tz'u-fu (rhapsody), 528
Tz'u-hsi, Empress Dowager, 335, 1060
Tz'u hsüan (Anthology of Song Lyrics; comp. Chang Hui-yen and Chang Ch'i), 438
tz'u-hua. *See* chantefables
tz'u-jen (lyricists), 986
"Tz'u lun" (Discourse on the Lyric; Li Ch'ing-chao), 209, 327
tz'u pu k'o pu hsiu (formulations must be deliberately cultivated), 892
"Tz'u shih chi hsieh fu" (Rhapsody on Satirizing the World and Denouncing Evil; Chao Yi), 251
tz'u ta erh-yi-yi (language must achieve its ends to convey meaning), 917
tz'u-tiao (*tz'u-p'ai*; song or tune pattern), 976
tz'u-wen (lyric texts), 976, 982–83, 985, 986

Uda, Emperor, 1084, 1085
Udyāna, 165
Ueda Akinari, 1093
Ugetsu monogatari (Tales of the Rain and Moon; Ueda Akinari), 1093
ukiyo-zōshi popular tales, 1091, 1092
Uncle Tom's Cabin (Stowe), 849, 850, 1065
United States, 24, 697, 700, 701, 772; Chinese in, 759, 780; and Korean War, 874; and literary criticism, 706, 716; and May Fourth movement, 156; as part of Greater China, 759, 781
The Unofficial History of Officialdom (Wu Ching-tzu). See *Ju-lin wai-shih*
The Unofficial History of Scholars (Wu Ching-tzu), 643
urbanization, 154, 159, 567, 659, 661, 717, 733, 753; and culture, 676, 677, 695
Uta no shiki (*Kakyō hyōshiki*; Regulations of Song; Fujiwara no Hamanari), 1082
Utkur, Abdurrehim, 1048–49
Uyghur people, 39, 1048–49

Vallejo, César, 457
vernacular languages: Japanese, 1090, 1094; regional, 31–35, 665, 671, 673, 692; Vietnamese, 1104
vernacular literature (*su-wen-hsüeh*), 14–15, 50, 811, 824, 842, 908, 1056; Buddhist, 983; drama, 111, 399, 442, 566, 889; in Korea, 1075, 1076; lesser-known, 659–74; and prosimetric form, 1017; regional, 15, 1017; and revolutionary change, 843, 844; in Taiwan, 458–59; tradition of, 399; and Western learning, 442, 844; and writing clubs (*shu-hui*), 801. See also *ch'ü*; fiction, vernacular; *hua-pen*; poetry: vernacular
Vernacular Literature movement (*pai-hua yün-tung*), 384, 453, 743, 744
Vernacular Sinitic (VS), 8, 14, 20, 27–31, 38–44, 399, 442; *vs.* ancient-style prose, 533; in ballads, 953, 955; and Buddhism, 11, 29–30, 32, 34, 169–70, 888, 889, 980; in Ch'ing, 52, 659, 660, 665, 671, 673, 698, 700, 724, 730, 731, 843, 887; in *ch'uan-ch'i* tales, 583, 682; in classical tales, 693; in essays, 566–67; in fiction, 716; on Internet, 56; in Japan, 1092, 1094; in Korea, 823; and Literary Sinitic, 439, 453, 458, 530, 731, 799, 903, 944, 1009–10, 1016, 1065, 1104; and literary theory, 706, 707, 708, 709; and May Fourth movement, 156, 728; modern written (*pai-hua wen*), 149, 151, 156, 158, 384, 453, 620, 643, 646, 715, 903, 1056–60, 1066; in poetry, 980, 981; proverbs in, 149, 151, 158, 159; in Republican period, 727, 731; and Shanghai writers, 703; and supernatural tales, 543, 551, 552; in transformation texts, 167; in Tun-huang manuscripts, 30, 278, 533, 972; and twentieth-century fiction, 735–36, 738, 739, 743, 749; and women, 218; written, 25, 28, 29–35, 44, 1096; at Yenan, 157; and *yü-lu*, 168
Verne, Jules, 718–19
Versailles, Treaty of (1919), 735, 851
Viet dien u linh tap (Anthology of the Unseen Powers of the Land of Viet; Ly Te Xuyen), 1099
Viet-nam khai quoc chi truyen (Record of the Founding of the Nation of Vietnam; Nguyen Bang Trung), 1102
Vietnam, 754, 1096–1104; Chinese relations with, 1096, 1097, 1098; French colonial rule in, 1096, 1099; literature of, 1097, 1100; written language of, 49, 1104
Vimalakīrti, 473
Vimalakīrtinirdeśa-sūtra (*Wei-mo-chieh ching*), 163
vinaya (rules of discipline), 30, 164
Vuong Tuong Truyen (The Tale of Vuong Tuong), 1101

Wagner, Rudolph, 765
wai (outer, external; foreign), 12–13, 937
wai chuan (esoteric, outside biographies), 522, 580
"Wai-p'ien" (Outer Chapters; *Chuang Tzu*), 174
wai-tan (Outer Alchemy), 189
Wai-yee Li, 620–58
waka (songs: Japanese), 1081, 1082, 1085, 1091
Wakan rōeishū (Poems in Japa-

nese and Chinese for Recitation; Fujiwara Kintō), 1085–86
Waldersee, Count, 657, 780
Waley, Arthur, 69, 103, 372, 633, 634
Wan-chin ch'ing-lin (The Forest of Passions in Myriad Hues), 684
Wan Ch'ing hsi-ch'ü hsiao-shuo mu (A Catalog of Late Ch'ing Drama and Fiction), 698
Wan Ch'ing hsiao-shuo shih (A History of Late Ch'ing Fiction; Ch'ien Hsing-ts'un), 698
Wan Ch'ing wen-hsüeh ts'ung-ch'ao: hsiao-shuo hsi-ch'ü yen-chiu chuan (An Anthology of Late Ch'ing Literature: Research Materials on Fiction and Drama), 698
"Wan-chu" (Leader of the Gang; Wang Shuo), 766
"Wan-fa kuei-yi ko" (Song on the Unity Back to Which All Creeds Hearken; Pai Yü-ch'an), 190
wan hsiang (ten thousand images), 363
Wan Ju Yüeh (The Two Wives Well-Met), 668
"Wan-ku-ch'ou ch'u" (Song of Everlasting Sorrow; Kuei Chuang), 418
wan-kuo (ten thousand countries; international), 1061
Wan-kuo kung-fa (Elements of International Law; Wheaton), 1057, 1059
Wan-kuo kung-pao (World News; journal), 718, 1059
Wan-li emperor, 669, 801, 802, 805, 818, 840, 842
Wan-ling chi (The Wan-ling Collection; Mei Yao-ch'en), 133
Wan Shou-ch'i, 427
"Wan-shui ch'ien-shan" (Rivers and Mountains; Ch'en Ch'i-t'ung), 873
"Wan te chiu-shih hsin-t'iao" (Living Dangerously; Wang Shuo), 766
"Wan-tzu chin-yin hua" (Splay-Petaled Honeysuckle; Wu Tsu-hsiang), 752
"Wan yen shu" (Ten Thousand Word Document; Wang An-shih), 8
wan-yüeh (delicate and suggestive) mode, 320, 321, 329, 334
Wang, David, 657
Wang An-shih, 8, 137, 230, 317, 338, 339, 348–49, 353, 363, 424; criticism of, 141, 142; and prose, 533, 556, 601; and *wen-jen* ideal, 392
"Wang An-shih san nan Su hsüeh-shih" (Su Shih; Feng Meng-lung), 601
Wang An-yi, 573–74, 762, 764
Wang Ao, 402
Wang Ch'ang-ling, 295, 931
Wang Chao-chün, 346, 814–15, 987
Wang Chao-yün, 677–78
Wang Che, 176, 184–88, 189
Wang Chen-ho, 753
Wang Chi, 285, 287, 582
Wang Chi-te, 374, 841, 842
Wang Ch'i-sun, 277
Wang Chia, 550
Wang Chien, 308
Wang Chih, 401
Wang Chih-chin, 187
Wang Ch'in-jo, 178
Wang Ching-hsien. *See* Yeh Shan
Wang Chiu-ssu, 381–82, 399, 404, 405, 406, 407, 818
Wang Cho, 939
Wang Ch'u-yi, 184–85, 187
Wang ch'uan chi (Wang River Collection; Wang Wei), 478
Wang Chung, 246
Wang Chung-min, 167
Wang Ch'ung, 116, 508, 883, 892, 893, 901, 922, 923, 927, 929
Wang Fan-chih, 11, 169–70, 302–3, 980, 981
Wang Feng-tsao, 1059
Wang Fu (4th c. C.E.), 981
Wang Fu (8th or 9th c. C.E.), 166
Wang Fu-chih, 419–20, 445–46, 936–37
Wang Ho-ch'ing, 376
Wang Hsiang-hsü, 943
Wang Hsien, 695
Wang Hsien-chih, 207
"Wang Hsin-chih yi ssu chiu ch'üan chia" (Wang Hsin-chih Saves His Whole Family Through His Death; Feng Meng-lung), 600
Wang Hsing, 395
Wang Jo-wang, 761
Wang Jung, 241, 270, 272
Wang K'ai-yün, 440
Wang K'ang-chü, 263
Wang Kuo-wei, 12, 170, 442, 451, 711, 735, 812, 939
Wang Ling, 987
Wang Mang, 91, 233, 471, 507, 546, 969
Wang Meng, 487, 762, 767, 771
Wang Mien, 617, 644
Wang Ming-ch'ing, 675
Wang Pao, 229, 233, 273
"Wang Pen-li t'ien-ya ch'iu fu" (Wang Pen-li; Hsi Lang-hsien), 604
Wang P'eng-yün, 335, 450
Wang Pi, 174, 913
Wang Pi-chiang, 582
Wang P'ing, 860
Wang Po, 287, 288, 289, 290, 1081
Wang Po-ch'eng, 800
Wang Shao-t'ang, 1024
Wang Shih, 381, 534
Wang Shih-chen (1526–1590), 136, 407–8, 409, 413, 687, 688, 824, 1073, 1090
Wang Shih-chen (1634–1711), 396, 397, 413–15, 418, 420–28, 430, 434; influence of, 432–33; as model, 1072; poems of, 426; *shen-yün* of, 433, 938
Wang Shih-fu, 587, 742, 800, 805, 813, 825
Wang Shih-lang, 776
Wang Shih-lu, 427
Wang Shih-wei, 568

Wang Shou-jen. *See* Wang Yang-ming
Wang Shu-wen, 590, 594
Wang Shu-yüan, 866
Wang Shuo, 759, 764, 766–67, 771
Wang Ssu-jen, 7
Wang Tao-k'un, 628
Wang T'ao, 695–96
Wang Ting-pao, 581
Wang T'ing-hsiang, 404, 406
Wang T'o, 778
Wang Ts'an, 230, 234, 235, 253–57
Wang Tse, 631
Wang Tseng-ch'i, 1057
Wang Tu, 285, 582
Wang Tu-ch'ing, 455
Wang Tuan, 210, 218
Wang Tun, 264
Wang T'ung, 285
Wang T'ung-kuei, 678
Wang Tzu-jen, 1064
Wang Wei (701–761), 11, 124, 230, 294–95, 296, 301, 302, 344, 379, 423–26; and Buddhism, 169; as founder of literati painting, 490; and High T'ang style, 431; as model, 421; as painter-poet, 478, 479, 481, 490
Wang Wei (1323–1374), 393; execution of, 396
Wang Wei-yi, 191
Wang Wen-hsing, 753, 777
Wang Yang-ming (Wang Shou-jen), 9, 399, 404, 410–11, 414, 889
Wang Yen (b.1113 C.E.), 360
Wang Yen (fl. c. 500 C.E.), 171
Wang Yen-shou, 301
Wang Yi, 225, 228, 229, 230, 913, 922
Wang Yi-chung, 187
Wang Yi-fang, 289
Wang Yi-shang shih-chi (Wang Shih-chen), 421
Wang Yi-sun, 438, 446
Wang Yin-chih, 103
Wang Ying-lin, 88
Wang Yu-yu, 855, 856
Wang Yü-ch'eng, 342–43
Wang Yüan-heng, 380
Wang Yüan-liang, 368
Wang Yüan-lu, 964
Wang Yün (1236–1304), 386
Wang Yün (early Ch'ing), 211, 839
Wanwŏlhoe maengyŏn (Alliance Formed at the Wanwŏl Pavilion), 1074–75
War of Anti-Japanese Resistance. *See under* Japan
War to Resist the United States and Aid Korea, 874
Ward No. 6 (Chekhov), 720
Warring States period, 3, 72, 78, 80, 97, 146, 467; in Japan, 1087; prose of, 496, 502, 509, 513, 572, 828, 888, 892; supernatural tales in, 544–46; writing system in, 37, 49. See also *Chan-kuo ts'e*
Water Margin. See *Shui-hu chuan*
the Way. See *Tao*
The Wealth of Nations (Adam Smith), 1062
Weber, Max, 96
wei (coda; tail), 797
wei (subtlety), 884, 890
Wei, Empress, 292
Wei, kingdom of (220–265), 93, 107, 195, 523, 560, 806, 955, 957; end of, 258; in fiction, 621–23; literary theory of, 919, 923, 926, 930; poetry of, 242, 245, 252, 253, 258, 261, 263, 265, 269, 272, 440, 468
Wei, Lady, 523, 836
Wei Ao, 591
"Wei ch'ao-feng hen-hsin p'an kuei ch'an, Ch'en hsiu-ts'ai ch'iao-chi chuan yüan fang" (Licentiate Ch'en Regains His House with a Ruse; Ling Meng-ch'u), 607
Wei Cheng, 282, 284
Wei ch'eng (The Besieged City; Ch'ien Chung-shu), 752
"Wei-ch'i fu" (Encirclement Chess; Liu Hsiang), 233
Wei Chih-yi, 581
Wei Ching-sheng (Wei Jing-sheng), 462
Wei Chuang, 280, 313, 318, 445, 981, 982
Wei Chung-hsien, 830, 831, 833, 996
Wei Chung-kung (Tuan-li), 210
"Wei Feng lu-shih chai kuan Ts'ao chiang-chün hua ma t'u ko" (In the Residence of Recorder Wei Feng, I View a Painting of Horses by General Ts'ao Pa; Tu Fu), 476
"Wei fu-jen chuan" (Traditions of Lady Wei; Yang Hsi), 523
Wei Hsiu-jen (Wei Tzu-an), 657, 673
Wei Hsün, 581, 583
Wei Hu, 280
Wei Hua-ts'un (goddess), 181
Wei Hung, 916, 920
Wei Kao, 815, 836
Wei Liang-fu, 823, 828
Wei-mo-chieh ching (*Vimalakīrtinirdeśa-sūtra*), 163
Wei Pao, 516
wei ("phony") poetry, 422
"Wei shih-yi niang chuan" (The Tale of Eleventh Lady Wei; Hu Ju-chia), 684
Wei Ssu-li, 292
"Wei tu fu" (Wei Capital Rhapsody; Tso Ssu), 468
Wei Tzu-an (Wei Hsiu-jen), 657, 673
wei tz'u chih shu (the art of literary composition), 892
wei-wai (beyond the flavor or meaning), 933
Wei Yeh, 343
wei-yen (subtle speech), 882, 905
Wei Ying-wu, 302, 307, 310, 313, 344, 388, 423–26
Wei yü (Light Rain; Li Chin-fa), 455
Wei Yüan, 718
Wei Yüan-sung, 979
Die Welt als Wille und Vorstellung (The World as Intention and Conception; Schopenhauer), 711
wen (esthetic or cultural pattern), 73–74, 75, 246, 340, 341, 348, 891–92

wen (literature; writing; refined), 230, 233, 236, 340, 341, 349, 351, 353, 359, 362, 916; defined, 2–3
Wen, Duke of Chin (Ch'ung-erh), 93, 512
Wen, emperor of Wei. *See* Ts'ao P'i
Wen, king of Chou, 88, 89, 96, 102, 103, 505, 646
Wen, king of Shang, 522
Wen, king of Sung, 267
wen-chang (literary compositions), 1, 340, 352
Wen-chang kuei-fan (Models for Literary Composition), 1073
Wen-chang liu-pieh chi (Collection on Development and Change in Literary Genres; comp. Chih Yü), 954
Wen-chang liu-pieh chih-lun (Discourse on Development and Change in Literary Genres; Chih Yü), 925
"Wen-ch'ang ssu lien ts'ai man chu lu-chi" (Lo Yin), 612
Wen Cheng-ming, 402, 404, 435
wen-chi (collected writings), 340
"Wen-chi ju sai" (Ts'ai Yen Returns to China; Ch'en Yü-chiao), 836
wen chieh ko-ming (revolution in culture and literature), 726
Wen-ching mi-fu lun (Treatise on the Secret Treasury of the Literary Mirror; in *Bunkyō hi-furon*; Kūkai), 286, 295, 894
Wen Ch'iung, 180
wen-chüan (practice scrolls), 593
wen-fang ssu-pao (four treasures of scholar's study), 49
"Wen fu" (Rhapsody on Literature; Lu Chi), 239, 262, 263, 924, 932
wen-fu (prose rhapsodies), 6, 244, 245, 246, 278, 540
Wen-hsin tiao-lung (The Literary Mind and the Carving of Dragons; Liu Hsieh), 8, 11, 258, 262, 893, 926–30, 932, 937; Buddhist influence on, 170; on humor, 133; and parallel prose, 236, 240, 242; on proverbs, 150
wen-hsing ch'u-ch'u (learning, conduct, service, withdrawal), 644
Wen hsüan (Literary Selections; comp. Hsiao T'ung), 4, 207, 240, 527, 530, 926, 954, 956; and civil-service examinations, 965, 973; as model for composition, 1068, 1071, 1081, 1082, 1084; and poetry, 250, 289, 301, 468; and Tun-huang literature, 973. See also *Chao-ming wen-hsüan*
wen-hsüeh (literature; humanities), 6, 706, 713, 714, 909
wen-hsüeh chih tsui shang sheng (the greatest of all literary vehicles), 707
"Wen-hsüeh kai-liang ch'u-yi" (Tentative Suggestions for Literary Reform; Hu Shih), 156, 453
"Wen-hsüeh ko-ming lun" (On Literary Revolution; Ch'en Tu-hsiu), 453
Wen-hsüeh kuan (College of Literary Studies), 283
wen-hsüeh tzu-chüeh te shih-tai (Age of Literary Self-Awareness), 254
Wen-hsüeh yen-chiu hui (Literary Research Society), 746–47
wen-hua (culture), 2
wen-hua Chung-kuo (cultural China), 758, 781
wen-hua fan-ssu (cultural criticism), 572
wen-hua ko-t'i-hu (cultural entrepreneurs), 767
wen-jen (literati), 392, 393
Wen K'ang, 656, 671, 743, 947, 948, 1034
"Wen kuo lou" (Corrigibility House; Li Yü), 615, 617
wen-li (classical Chinese). *See* Literary Sinitic
wen-ming (civilization), 2
wen-ming hsi (civilized drama), 850, 851
Wen-ming hsiao shih (A Brief History of Enlightenment; Li Pao-chia), 647, 721, 724
Wen-ming shu-chü, 729
wen-shen (tattoo the body), 2
wen-shih. *See* scholar-officials
Wen-ti, Emperor (Han), 99
Wen-ti, Emperor (Sui), 972
Wen T'ien-hsiang, 325, 367, 834, 844
Wen T'ing-shih, 335, 450
Wen T'ing-yün, 312, 313, 318, 321, 333, 387, 836
Wen-tse (Principles of Literature; Ch'en K'uei), 893
wen-tzu (graphs; script), 2. *See also* sinographs
wen-tzu yü (literary inquisitions), 644
wen-ya (gentleness and refinement), 412
wen-yao (literary devil), 393
wen-yen (Classical Chinese). *See* Literary Sinitic
wen-yen hsiao-shuo (classical tales), 125–29 *passim*, 600, 605, 675–96. See also *ch'uan-ch'i* tales
Wen Yen-po, 142
wen-yen-wen (classical language style), 149, 156, 158. *See also* Literary Sinitic
wen-yi (the arts), 2
Wen-yi hsin-ch'ao (Literary Current; journal), 457
Wen-yi pao (News from Literature and the Arts; journal), 774
Wen Yi-to, 68, 455, 456, 568
wen yi tsai tao (didactic function of literature), 5, 707, 1070. *See also* didacticism
Wen Ying, 137
wen-yüan. *See* literati
Weng Chüan (Ling-shu), 365
Weng Fang-kang, 433, 434, 436, 437, 438
the West, 86, 120, 650; and CCP, 770, 772; Chinese exiles in, 764; Chinese litera-

ture in, 3, 760; and Ch'ing dynasty, 669, 670, 721, 725, 731, 1055, 1056; drama of, 792–93, 845–46, 848–49, 852, 856–57; encroachment on China by, 559, 733–34; in fiction, 669, 670, 695, 721, 725, 740, 742; films from, 743; historical writing in, 493, 499, 502; and Hong Kong, 773; imperialism of, 437, 871; influence of, 428, 461, 572, 673, 705, 743–44; linguistic influence of, 35–36, 45–46, 57, 1056–62; and literary criticism, 334, 705–6, 711, 712, 716, 768; literature of, 455, 459, 697, 699–700, 717–20, 763, 844, 885, 891, 1066, 1078, 1094; and May Fourth movement, 156; rhetoric of, 882, 905–8; and Taiwanese literature, 777, 778, 779; and twentieth-century literature, 729–30, 731, 733, 735, 736, 738, 739, 762, 765, 767. *See also* translations; United States

Western learning, 439–40, 442, 1055. *See also* Buddhism

Western Paradise, 115, 163, 166, 523

Western Wei dynasty (535–557), 272, 273

Wheaton, Henry, 1057

Whitcomb, Selden, 717

"The White-Haired Girl" ("Pai-mao nü"), 864–65, 868

"The White-Haired Girl" (Pai mao-nü; ballet version), 868

White Lotus Rebellion, 436

Wild Swans, 1000

Wilde, Oscar, 856

Wilder, Thornton, 846

Williams, Philip F. C., 566–75, 732–57

Williams, Wiliam Carlos, 457

Wixted, John Timothy, 390–98

"Wo chih chieh-lieh-kuan" (My Views on Chastity; Lu Hsün), 570

"Wo-men" (Us; play), 54

"Wo p'ao" (The Japanese Cloak), 1023–24

"Wo shih ni pa-pa" (I Am Your Dad; Wang Shuo), 767, 771

wo shou hsieh wo k'ou (my hand writes what my mouth speaks), 441, 894

"Wo te chiao-yü" (My Education; Shen Ts'ung-wen), 751

"Wo tsai Hsia-ts'un te shih-hou" (When I Was in Hsia Village; Ting Ling), 748

women, 194–220; and ballads, 198–99, 200, 205, 959, 1077; biographies of, 134, 165, 197–98, 212, 218, 469, 471, 508, 517–18, 522, 524–25, 550, 1074, 1086; and Buddhism, 1006; CCP liberation of, 867–68; and chantefables, 996, 1018, 1019; in *Ch'u tz'u*, 118; in *ch'uan-ch'i* tales, 122, 684–85, 688; and Classical Chinese, 1020; in classical tales, 692; and Confucianism, 1006, 1020; culture of, 999–1003, 1010–11, 1016; and drama, 786, 793–94, 836, 838, 839, 844, 845, 853, 854–55, 860, 875; and feminism, 462, 844, 870, 874, 875, 1003, 1019; festivals of, 999; in fiction, 148, 630, 643, 653, 655–56, 661, 698, 724, 741, 747, 748; in Han rhapsodies, 118–19; in *hua-pen*, 598–99, 600, 603–5; Japanese, 999, 1091; laments of, 989, 992, 999, 1000, 1004–5, 1007, 1011, 1014, 1083, 1098–99; literary activity among, 412, 413, 838, 1019–20; lyrics by, 325–28, 447, 452, 1020; May-Fourth, 855, 865; in Ming dynasty, 332, 659, 661; in myth, 64, 66, 67; and Neo-Confucianism, 448; networks of literate, 1016; poetry about, 14–15, 260, 269, 271, 272; poetry by, 249–50, 257, 263, 312, 325–26, 327, 335, 357, 373, 381, 406, 416, 428, 429, 448, 452; and poetry groups, 1071; in PRC, 865–66; sexuality of, 128; and silkworms, 552; and supernatural, 113–15, 120, 125–26, 127, 130, 545, 552; and Taiwanese literature, 776, 777, 778–79; and Taoism, 184, 187, 582; in *Tso chuan*, 499; and twentieth-century literature, 734, 741, 747–48, 760, 762, 765–66, 767; as warriors, 607, 657, 671–72, 684–85, 1020; as writers, 14, 15, 205–11, 218, 747–48, 786, 839, 853, 1019–20; of Yüan dynasty, 211, 218. *See also* Women's Script

Women's Script (*nü-shu*), 33, 34, 990, 992, 994, 999–1003, 1006, 1010–11, 1016

The World of Suzie Wong (Mason), 773

World War II, 157, 736, 752

Writers at Work, 573

writing: autobiographical, 901–2; and commentary, 947–48; concision in, 27; as craft, 924–25; exercises in, 967; expressive, 233, 268, 937–38; of local scholar-officials, 1052–54; philosophical, 233; religious, 1045; and social climate, 917; subjective, 904; transgressive, 962; about Vietnamese women, 1102

wu (enlightenment), 422–23, 424, 425

wu (military), 2

wu (wrong), 452

Wu, Emperor (Chin), 258, 260

Wu, Emperor (Han), 91, 139, 141, 229–32, 249, 502, 507, 546, 953

Wu, Emperor (Liang). *See* Hsiao Yen

Wu, Empress. *See* Wu Tse-t'ien, Empress

Wu, Harry (Wu Hung-ta), 772

Wu, king of, 828, 829

Wu, kingdom of, 104, 252, 263, 621, 622, 806, 807, 828, 829

Wu, Yenna, 595–619

Wu and Yüeh, king of, 600

wu ch'ang (Five Constants), 844

wu-ch'ang (impermanence), 979
Wu Ch'ang-ling, 818
Wu Chao-ch'ien, 416–17
Wu Chen, 487
"Wu Chen-chün" (Hu Hui-ch'ao), 582
Wu-chen p'ien (Folios on Apprehending Perfection; Chang Po-tuan), 189, 191
Wu Ch'eng-en, 128, 147, 632
Wu Ch'i, 506, 517–18
Wu Chia-chi, 427
"Wu chiang-chün yi fan pi ch'ou, Ch'en Ta-lang san-jen ch'ung hui" (General Wu; Ling Meng-ch'u), 607
"Wu-chieh ch'an-shih ssu Hung-lien chi" (The Five Abstinences Priest Seduces Red Lotus; Hung P'ien), 599, 600
Wu Chien-jen (Wu Wo-yao), 647, 657, 673, 703–4, 708, 710, 719, 721, 722–24, 729, 735, 741–42
Wu Chih-chen, 385, 427
Wu Chin-fa, 778
Wu chin-yü chuan (The Five Goldfish), 683
Wu Ching, 958
Wu-ching (Five Classics), 87, 90, 282, 283, 342
Wu-ching cheng-yi (Correct Meanings of the Five Classics), 87, 90. See also *Shih-san-ching chu-shu*
Wu Ching-tzu, 147, 215, 643–45, 647, 720, 733, 915, 948, 949
Wu Chü, 514
Wu ch'uan lu (Register of a Boat Trip to Wu; Fan Ch'eng), 557–59
Wu Chün, 201, 241, 272
Wu-chung ssu-chieh (Four Outstanding Talents of Wu-chung, or Soochow), 398
Wu Han, 569
Wu Hsi-ch'i, 246
wu-hsia (knights errant), 656, 657–58, 763, 766, 1103
wu-hsia hsiao-shuo (knight-errantry fiction), 743
Wu Hsiao-ju, 698
Wu Hsiao-ling, 12
wu-hsing (five phases), 80, 83, 633, 956
"Wu-hsing chih" (Treatise on the Five Elements), 956
"Wu-hsing-p'ien" (Essay on the Five Behaviors), 101, 106
Wu Hung-tao, 375
Wu Jui, 519–20
"Wu-keng chuan" (Five Watches of the Night; poem form), 976, 977, 978
Wu K'o-chi, 167
Wu K'uan, 402
Wu Kuang-chien, 720
Wu Kung-yeh, 589
Wu Kuo-lun, 407
Wu Lai, 387
wu-lei-fa (Five Thunder Rites), 189, 191
Wu Li, 427, 428
Wu Liang, 469–70, 471
Wu-liang-shou ching (*Sukhāvatīvyūha, Amitābhavyūha, Aparimitāyuḥ-sūtra*), 163
"Wu-liu hsien-sheng chuan" (Biography of Mr. Five Willows; T'ao Ch'ien), 267, 581
wu lun (Five Human Relationships), 196, 721, 844
"Wu-lun ch'üan-pei chi" (All Moral Relationships Fulfilled), 823
Wu Lung-han, 481
Wu Mei, 845
Wu-men Hui-k'ai, 169
Wu-men kuan (Doorless Gate; Wu-men Hui-k'ai), 169
"Wu Pao-an ch'i-chia shu-yu" (Wu Pao-an Abandons His Family to Ransom His Friend; Feng Meng-lung), 601, 618
"Wu pei" (Five Grievings; Lu Chao-lin), 288
Wu P'ei-fu, 870
Wu Ping, 830–31
"Wu-p'ing ling-kuai lu" (The Spirit Apparitions of Wu-p'ing; Li Chen), 680–81
Wu-se shih (Multicolored Stones), 615
Wu Shang, 514
Wu-shang huang-lu ta-chai li-ch'eng yi (Straightforward Protocols on the Grand Fête of the Incomparable Yellow Register; ed. Chiang Shu-yü), 182
Wu-shang pi-yao (The Essentials of Unsurpassed Arcana), 177
Wu She, 514
Wu-sheng hsi (Silent Operas; Li Yü), 147, 613–14
Wu-sheng hsi erh-chi (Silent Operas, Second Collection; Li Yü), 614
"Wu sheng ko" (Songs to Wu Music), 271
Wu sheng ko-ch'ü (Songs Set to Wu Music), 960
"Wu-shuang chuan" (An Account of Peerless; Hsüeh T'iao), 587
Wu-ssu yün-tung. *See* May Fourth movement
Wu Ta-chen, 687
Wu-tai shih p'ing-hua (The Plain Tale of the History of the Five Dynasties), 797
Wu T'ai-po, 646
Wu-t'ai shan (Sanskrit: Pañcaśīrṣa; Five Terraces Mountain), 164
Wu Tao, 720
Wu Tao-tzu, 479
"Wu teng lun" (Treatise on the Five Classes of Officials; Lu Chi), 239
Wu-ti, Emperor, 686
"Wu-t'i" (Untitled; Li Shang-yin), 311
Wu-ting, king of Shang, 36, 103
Wu-t'o-pang yu-chi (A Journey to Utopia; Hsiao-jan Yü-sheng), 721
Wu tsa-tsu (Five Assorted Offerings; Hsieh Chao-che), 689
Wu Tsao, 210, 452, 786, 839
Wu Tse-t'ien, Empress (Wu-hou), 128, 214, 285, 288, 290, 291, 292, 655, 656, 661

wu-tsu (Five Patriarchs), 184
Wu Tsu-hsiang, 570, 572–73, 735, 751–52
Wu Tsu-kuang, 770, 858
"Wu-t'ung yü" (Rain on the Plantain; Pai P'u), 814
Wu Tzu-hsü, 93, 506, 514, 516, 829
Wu wang fa Chou p'ing-hua (Expository Tale on King Wu's Expedition Against Chou), 128
Wu Wei-yeh, 325, 415–18, 420, 445, 446, 834
Wu Wen-ying, 329, 330, 438, 450
Wu Wo-yao. *see* Wu Chien-jen
Wu Wu-shan, 843
wu-yen (five-character, pentasyllabic) line, 927
wu-yen shih (pentasyllabic poems), 1080
Wu-yin ts'ao (Drafts of Poetry from the *Wu-yin* Year; Liu Shih), 413
Wu Ying-t'ao, 461
Wu Yü, 95, 96
Wu Yü-pi, 399
Wu Yüan-t'ai, 664
Wu-Yüeh, state of, 339
Wu yüeh te huang-hun (The Dusk of May; Yeh Chao-yen), 764
Wu Yün, 124, 302
Wu yün li-nien chi (Chronicle of the Five Cycles of Time), 63

ya (elegance; ode), 5, 27, 103, 149, 154, 920
ya-cheng (proper), 283
"Ya-ch'ia shu" (Tale of the Headstrong Woman), 987, 1004, 1006
Ya Hsien, 458, 461, 779–80
Ya-hsüeh (Elegant Banter), 139
Ya Mo, 463
ya tsa-chü (dumb-shows), 786
ya-tso wen (seat-settling texts), 983, 985, 986
ya-yen (dignified words; ornate words), 892
ya-yüeh (elegant music; court music), 314, 1089
Yamanoue no Okura, 1082, 1086
Yamarāja (god of the underworld), 1001
Yan Li. *See* Yen Li
Yanagawa Seigan, 1091
yang (masculine), 656, 700. See also *yin-yang*
Yang, Emperor, 669–70
Yang, Gladys, 1038
Yang Chao-min, 1053
Yang Chao-ying, 373, 381
Yang Ch'ao-kuan, 837–38
Yang Chi, 387, 395, 398
Yang Chi-sheng, 827
Yang Chiang, 761
"Yang Chiao-ai she ming-ch'üan chiao" (Yang Chiao-ai Gives Up His Life for His Friend; Feng Meng-lung), 601
Yang Chih-ho, 664
Yang Ch'ih-ch'ang (Shui-yin-p'ing), 459
Yang Ch'ing-ch'u, 778
Yang Chiung, 287, 288, 289, 290
Yang-chou pa kuai (Eight Eccentrics of Yangchow), 435, 448
"Yang chuang-yüan" (Foreign Graduate; Hsiung Fo-hsi), 854
Yang-ch'un pai hsüeh (The Snows of Sunny Spring; Yang Chao-ying), 373, 380
Yang Erh-tseng, 688
Yang Han, 1042–43
Yang Hsi, 177, 181, 248, 523
Yang-hsien school, 432, 438, 448
Yang Hsien-yi, 770
Yang Hsiu, 923
Yang Hsiung, 29, 230–34, 236, 921, 925, 929
Yang Hsüan-chih, 165
Yang Hsün-chi, 402
Yang Hua, 459
Yang Jung, 401
Yang ko (The Rice-Sprout Song; Chang Ai-ling), 753
Yang K'uan, 68
Yang Kuei-fei, 14, 203, 308, 310, 485, 586, 1008; in Ch'ing novels, 670; in drama, 126, 800, 815, 834; in Japan, 1086, 1087; and supernatural, 126
Yang K'uei, 776
Yang Lien (Yang Lian), 462, 759
"Yang-liu-chih tz'u" (Willow-Branch Lyrics; Liu Yü-hsi), 306
Yang Liu-lang, 807–8
Yang Lü-fang, 866
Yang Mu. *See* Yeh Shan
Yang Na, 818
"Yang Nai-wu yü Hsiao Pai-ts'ai" (Yang Nai-wu and Little Cabbage), 1024
Yang Paek-hwa, 1078
yang-pan-hsi (model operas), 846
Yang P'u, 401
Yang Shen, 406
"Yang-sheng lun" (On Nourishing Life; Hsi K'ang), 259
Yang Shih-ch'i, 401, 403
Yang Shih-tao, 284
Yang Shou-yü, 776
Yang-ti, 282
Yang T'ing-fang, 1053
Yang T'ing-ho, 406
Yang Tsai, 386
Yang Tse, 776
Yang Tzu, 815–16
Yang Wan-li, 245, 359, 361, 363–65, 366, 367, 435
Yang Wei-chen, 387, 388, 392, 393–94, 396
Yang Yeh, 807
Yang Yi, 343, 344, 531
Yao (sage king), 60, 62, 64, 65, 66, 67, 68, 969
Yao (tribal group), 1011
yao (specters, animal spirits), 112, 114, 115, 116, 126, 128, 547
Yao Ho, 280, 307, 312, 365
Yao Hsia-tan, 1053
yao-hsien (demonic immortals), 637
Yao Hsüan, 281
Yao Hsüeh-yin, 771
Yao Kuang-hsiao (Tao-yen), 395

Yao Nai, 528, 533
Yao Ssu-lien, 283
Yao Sui, 379
"Yao Ti-chu pi hsiu je hsiu, Cheng Yüeh-o chiang ts'o chiu ts'o" (The Double; Ling Meng-ch'u), 608
Yao tribes, 1011
yao-tz'u (line statements), 89, 107
yao-yen (ballads and sayings), 156
ye (propriety), 1075
Yeh, Michelle, 453–65
Yeh Chao-yen, 764
Yeh Chou, 894, 942
Yeh Fa-shan, 180
Yeh Hsiao-lan, 839
Yeh Hsiao-wan, 839
Yeh Hsieh, 427, 937, 938
Yeh Hsien-tsu, 836
Yeh-lü Ch'u-ts'ai, 188
Yeh Shan (Yang Mu; Wang Ching-hsien), 461, 464
"Yeh shang" Shou-hsiang ch'eng wen ti" (Hearing a Barbarian Flute from Atop the Walls of Shou-hsiang Citadel at Night; Li Yi), 303
Yeh Sheng-t'ao (Yeh Shao-chün), 570, 704, 730, 746–47
Yeh Shih, 365, 366
yeh-shih, pai-shih (unofficial histories), 140, 621
Yeh-sou p'u-yen (An Old Rustic's Idle Talk; Hsia Ching-ch'ü), 656, 670
"Yeh su tung-chu fang ko" (Spending the Night at East Isle: Wild Song; Yang Wan-li), 364
Yeh-t'an sui-lu (Evening Conversations Casually Recorded; Ho Pang-o), 693
"Yeh t'ing chi" (Listening to Geishas at Night; Pao Chao), 269
"Yeh tso" (Sitting at Night; Chang Lei), 352
Yeh Wan-wan, 839
Yeh Wei-lien (Wai-lim Yip), 458
"Yeh yin" (Chanting at Night; Lu Yu), 361
"Yeh-yü" (Night Rain; Yang K'uei), 776
Yeh-yü ch'iu-teng lu (Tales Recorded by Evening Rain and Autumn Lamp; Hsüan Ting), 695
Yellow Emperor. *See* Huang Ti
Yellow Turban Uprising, 251, 621
yen (language), 714
yen (voluptuousness), 418
yen (witness to), 970
Yen Chi-tao, 315, 316, 317, 327, 447
Yen Chih-t'ui, 171, 929
Yen-chou shan-jen ssu-pu kao (The Mountain Man of Yen-chou's Manuscripts from the Four Divisions; Wang Shih-chen), 407–8
"Yen-chung chih chih" (A Record of What Happened Amidst the Smoke; Nan Cho), 591
Yen Fu, 706, 708, 717, 719, 1060, 1062–63, 1065, 1066
yen-hui shih (feast poems), 254, 255, 263, 268
Yen Jo-ch'ü, 90
"Yen ko hsing" (Song of Glamorous Beauty; Lu Chi), 200
"Yen ko hsing" (Song of Yen; Kao Shih), 296
"Yen ko hsing" (Song of Yen; Ts'ao P'i), 257
Yen Li (Yan Li), 464
Yen-p'o tz'u (Spreading Waves Lyrics; anthology), 426
Yen-shih chia-hsün (The Admonitions of Master Yen; Yen Chih-t'ui), 929–30
Yen Shih-fan, 827
Yen Shih-ku, 283
Yen Shu, 316, 317, 333
Yen Sung, 827
Yen Tan Tzu (Master Tan of Yen), 580
Yen ti (Fire God), 65
yen-tuan (prelude), 792
yen-tui (verbal parallelism), 893
Yen Tzu, 501, 505–6
"Yen-tzu chien" (The Swallow's Love Note; Juan Ta-ch'eng), 831, 833, 838
Yen Tzu ch'un-ch'iu (Springs and Autumns of Master Yen), 140, 500, 501, 502
yen-wai (beyond literal words), 917, 938
yen-wai chih yi (meaning beyond literal words), 933
Yen Yen-chih, 240, 266
yen-yi (tales of righteousness), 623
Yen-yi pien (Tales of Glamor and Wonder; ed. Wang Shih-chen), 687
Yen Ying, 517
Yen Yü, 12, 170, 275, 401, 404, 421–25, 935–38
yen-yü. *See* proverbs
yen-yüeh (entertainment music), 976
Yenan, 157, 568
Yenan Forum on Literature and Art. *See* "Tsai Yen-an wen-yi tso-t'an-hui shang te chiang-hua"
Yenan Forum on Literature and Art (1942), 5, 158, 457, 864
Yi (Po-yi), 544–45
yi (abnormal or disorderly events), 547
yi (consciousness, thought), 424, 924
yi (meaning), 397
yi (righteousness), 629
yi Ch'an yü shih (Ch'an [Zen] as an analogy for poetry), 422
Yi Che-hyŏn, 1069, 1070
yi-ch'i (meaning and spirit), 479, 480
yi-ch'i (personal loyalty), 623, 631
"Yi-ch'i huan-ch'ieh kuei shen ch'i" (The Spirits Astonish by Switching Wife and Concubine; Li Yü), 614
Yi-chien chih (Records of the Listener; Hung Mai), 122, 564, 598, 676, 677, 681, 685, 688

Yi-chien shang-hsin pien (Instantly Appealing Tales), 687–88
"Yi-ch'ien-pa-pai tan" (Eighteen Hundred Bushels; Wu Tsu-hsiang), 751
Yi-ching (monk), 165, 556
Yi-ching (Classic of Change), 4, 80–82, 83, 97, 107, 150, 187, 364, 625, 633; exegesis of, 910, 911, 914; in *Thirteen Classics*, 88–89
yi ch'ing wu chen (enlightenment through love), 652
yi ch'ing wu tao (enlightenment through love, detachment through attachment), 654
Yi-chiu san-ssu te t'ao-wang (The Escape of 1934; Su T'ung), 765
Yi Chong-t'ae, 1077
yi-chü (righteous deeds), 629
Yi Fen-erh, 381
"Yi Fo chi" (Record of Moving the Buddha; Shen Ya-chih), 590, 592
Yi Hae-jo, 1077
Yi hang (One Line; U.S. journal), 464
"Yi-hsia chi" (The Righteous Hero; Shen Ching), 829
Yi hsing. See *Yi hang*
Yi In-no, 1068
"Yi ku" (Doubting the Ancient; Wang Ch'ung), 901
"Yi-k'u kuei lai tao-jen ch'u kuai" (A Den of Ghosts; Feng Meng-lung), 127
Yi Kyu-bo, 1069, 1070
Yi-li (Ceremonies and Rites), 88, 90, 91–92, 910
Yi-lin (Ts'ui Chuan), 107
yi-ma hsin-yüan (horse of the will and monkey of the mind), 187, 634
"Yi-meng lu" (Account of Dreams of the Extraordinary; Shen Ya-chih), 590, 592
yi-min (Ming loyalists), 413
Yi nationality, 1032–33, 1037–41
"Yi-niao lu" (Account of the Bird of Propriety; Shen Ya-chih), 593
"Yi-pan shih huo-yen, yi-pan shih hai-shui" (Hot and Cold, Measure for Measure; Wang Shuo), 766–67
yi-p'ang (obliquity), 1085
"Yi-p'eng hsüeh" (A Handful of Snow; Li Yü), 830
"Yi-p'ien ai-kuo hsin" (A Patriotic Heart; Hsiung Fo-hsi), 854
Yi-p'ien ch'ing (An Expanse of Love), 611
Yi Saek, 1070
yi-shen (a single person), 414
yi shih (annalist of the strange), 900
yi-shih (anecdotes), 579–80
yi-shih (honorably releases), 623
Yi-shu hui-pien (Collected Translations), 1060, 1061
Yi Shu-yü, 857
"Yi-shui han" (The River Yi Is Cold; Yeh Hsien-tsu), 837
Yi Sŏ-gu, 1072
yi-tai shih-shih (poetic history of the age), 416
Yi the Archer (god), 64
yi to (honorably takes over), 631
Yi Tŭk-mu, 1072
"Yi wen ch'ien hsiao hsi tsao ch'i yüan" (A Single Copper Cash; Hsi Lang-hsien), 603
"Yi-wen chih shih-fu lüeh" (Outline of the Purpose of Literary Esthetics in Poetry and Rhymeprose; Pan Ku), 922
Yi-wen lei-chü (Categorical Medley of Literary Texts; Ou-yang Hsün), 136, 282
yi wen wei shih (turning prose into poetry), 340, 347, 365
yi wo kuan chih (as I see it, in my view), 904
yi-yin (lust of the mind), 650
"Yi-yin cheng-chih hsiao-shuo hsü" (Foreword to the Publication of Political Novels in Translation; Liang Ch'i-ch'ao), 707–8
Yi-yüan chih yen (Apt Words from the Garden of the Arts; Li P'an-lung and Wang Shih-chen), 407
yin (hidden, arcane, riddlelike), 882. See also *yin-yang*
yin (lay; lament), 954
yin (protection), 355, 360, 366
Yin Chih-p'ing, 188
"Yin chiu" (Tippling; T'ao Ch'ien), 266, 267
"Yin chiu tu 'Sao'" (As I Drink Wine, I Read "Encountering Sorrow"; Wu Tsao), 211
Yin-ch'üeh-shan manuscripts, 98
Yin Fan, 280, 295
Yin-feng-ko tsa-chü (*Tsa-chü* from the Hall of Singing in the Wind; Yang Ch'ao-kuan), 838
Yin Hsi, 183
yin hsiu (indirect suggestive meaning), 893
"Yin hu-shang ch'u ch'ing hou yü" (Drinking on the Lake: At First It Was Clear, Then It Rained; Su Shih), 350
yin-kuo (karmic cause and effect), 111, 112, 651
"Yin ma ch'ang-ch'eng k'u hsing" (Watering Horses at the Long Wall Hole, a Ballad; anonymous), 958, 962
Yin mou (Secret Plots; Lü Shang), 522
Yin-shui tz'u (Lyrics of a Water Drinker; Nara Singde), 418
Yin Wen-ts'ao, 184
yin-yang, 79, 81, 83, 175, 335, 633, 634, 1080. *See also* Taoism
yin-yüan. See *yüan-ch'i*
Yin Yüeh, 413
yin-yung ch'ing-hsing (sing of one's feelings), 927
ying (response), 970
Ying, Marquis of, 513
"Ying ch'an-shih fang kuan shan-hai t'u" (Viewing the Painting of Mountains and Seas in the Chamber of the

Ch'an Master Ying; Li Po), 478
Ying-ch'uang yi-ts'ao (Strange Herbs from Firefly Window; Ch'ing-lan), 694
ying-erh pen-lun (the theory of the baby), 635
Ying-hsiung p'u (The Exemplary Records of Heroes), 626
Ying-huan so-chi (Random Sketches of the World; newspaper), 702
"Ying k'an an ta-ju cheng hsien-ch'i, kan shou hsing hsia-nü chu fang-ming" (The Great Confucian; Ling Meng-ch'u), 608
Ying-mei-an yi-yü (Reminiscences of Shadow-Cast Plums Cottage; Mao Hsiang), 417
Ying-tsung, Emperor, 178, 400
"Ying-wu chou" (Parrot Isle; Ch'en Yü-chiao), 836
Ying Yang, 253, 254
"Ying-ying chuan" (Story of Ying-ying; Yüan Chen), 146, 586–87, 593, 679, 742, 796, 798, 799, 836, 1007, 1008
Yishipil tohoe kosi (Twenty-one Poems on Capitals in the Ancient Style), 1072
Yogācāra tradition, 162
Yŏgong p'aesŏl (Popular Fiction from the Useless Old Man), 1070
Yŏhan shipka munch'o (Selections from the Writings of Ten Great Masters of Korean Literature), 1072
Yŏlha ilgi (A Diary of the Je-ho River; Pak Ch'i-wŏn), 1077
yomihon narratives, 1091, 1093
Yonbyon munyu (Yen-pien Literary Arts; Korean literary journal), 1052
"Yŏng gosŏk" (Tribute to a Solitary Stone; Chŏngbŏpsa), 1067
Yŏngjo, King, 1072
Yosa Buson, 1090
Yoshida Kenkō, 7
Yoshikawa Kōjirō, 881
Yu, Anthony, 634, 654
"Yu-ch'ai lai te hsin" (The Letter from the Postman; Sun Kan-lu), 765
yu-chi (travel records), 535, 555–59, 572, 705
yu-chi wen-hsüeh (travel record literature), 555
Yu Chien, 463
yu-chin teng-k'u (when the oil is exhausted, the lamp dries up), 640
"Yu Ch'ung-chen kuan nan-lou tu hsin chi-ti t'i-ming ch'u" (Visiting the South Hall of Ch'ung-chen Temple, I Look at the Names of Recent Examination Graduates; Yü Hsüan-chi), 209
"Yu Feng-tu Hu-mu Ti yin-shih" (Hu-mu Ti; Feng Meng-lung), 602
"Yu-hsia p'ien" (Wandering Hero; Chang Hua), 262
"Yu-hsien" (Roaming to Transcendence; Wu Yün), 302
"Yu-hsien chi" (A Record of Immortals; Ku Kuang), 583
"Yu-hsien k'u" (Grotto of Playful Transcendents; Chang Cho), 583, 1086, 1087
"Yu-hsien shih" (Apotheosis, or Roaming to Transcendence; Wu Yün), 124
"Yu-hsien shih" (Poems on Roaming into Immortality; Kuo P'u), 264
yu-hsien shih (poems of wandering immortals, or roaming into immortality), 118, 254, 261, 264–65, 268
Yu Hŭi-ch'un, 1073
Yu-kuai shih-t'an (Poetic Stories of Mysterious Anomalies), 682
yu-lan shih (sight-seeing poems), 254
"Yu-lieh shih" (Hunting; Chang Hua), 262
Yu-lung chuan (Like unto a Dragon; Chia Shan-hsiang), 183
Yu-ming lu (Records of the Hidden and the Visible Worlds; Liu Yi-ch'ing), 548, 551
yu-mo (humor), 134
"Yu Nan-shan wang Pei-shan ching hu chung chan-t'iao" (Gazing About as I Cross the Lake from South Mountain to North Mountain; Hsieh Ling-yün), 268
"Yu Pao-ch'an-shan chi" (Record of a Trip to Pao-ch'an Mountain; Wang An-shih), 556–57
"Yu pei-shan fu" (Wandering on North Mountain; Wang Chi), 285
"Yu Shan-hsi ts'un" (An Excursion to Shan-hsi Village; Lu Yu), 361
"Yu so ssu" (There Is One for Whom I Long), 260
Yu-t'ai hsien-kuan pi-chi (Notes from Yu-t'ai Lodge; Yü Yüeh), 695–96
"Yu T'ao-yüan" (Roaming to Peach Blossom Spring; Liu Yü-hsi), 306
"Yu T'ien-t'ai shan fu" (Rhapsody on Roaming Mount T'ien-t'ai; Sun Ch'o), 265
"Yu-t'ing wu-meng" (The Dream at the Courier Post; T'ao Fu), 682
Yu Tŭk-gong, 1072
"Yu Tung-t'ien" (Roaming Tung-t'ien; Hsieh T'iao), 271
Yu T'ung, 418, 634, 635, 837
"Yu t'ung fu" (Rhapsody on Communicating with the Hidden; Pan Ku), 233
Yu-yang tsa-tsu (Miscellaneous Delicacies from the South Slope of Mount Yu; Tuan Ch'eng-shih), 581, 686
yu-yen (mysterious voluptuousness), 387
Yü (mythical figure), 62, 64, 65, 66, 124
yü (desire), 648
yü (jade), 648
Yü, King, 544–45

"Yü-chang hsing: K'u hsiang p'ien" ("Yü-chang Ballad;" Bitter Fate; Fu Hsüan), 199, 204, 260, 959
Yü Chi (1272–1348), 372, 386, 388, 394, 395, 487
Yü Chi (Taoist magician), 625
"Yü-chia ao" (Fisherman's Pride; song), 317
Yü Chiao Li (Jade Charming Pear), 667, 1100
Yü Chiao Li (Jade Charming Plum), 662
"Yü chieh yüan" (Jade Steps Plaint; Hsieh T'iao), 271
Yü Chien-wu, 272
Yü Ch'ien, 401–2
"Yü chih hsiao-shuo kuan" (My Views on Fiction; Hsü Nien-tz'u), 712, 729
Yü-chou feng (Wind of the Universe; Lin Yü-t'ang), 567
Yü Ch'u chih (Yü Ch'u's Record), 686–87
Yü Ch'u hsin-chih (New Records of Yü Ch'u; comp. Chang Ch'ao), 690–91
"Yü-chuan yüan" (Romance of the Jade Bracelet), 1020
"Yü-chüeh chi" (The Broken Jade Ring; Cheng Jo-yung), 829
Yü Ch'un-hsi, 682
"Yü fu" (The Fisherman), 228
yü-hsi (language family), 26
Yü Hsia, 65
Yü Hsia (Yü of the Hsia), 69
Yü Hsiang-tou, 129, 664, 942
Yü-hsiao, 815
Yü Hsin, 241, 242, 243, 272, 273, 288, 474–75, 532
Yü Hsüan-chi, 208–9, 217, 312, 313, 836
Yü-hu ch'ing-hua (Elegant Sayings in Yü-hu), 137
Yü Hua, 765
Yü-hua hsiang (Scent of Flowers from Heaven; Shih Ch'eng-chin), 617
Yü Hung-chien, 694
Yü Jun-ch'i, 730
Yü-kuan (Hsü Ti-shan), 747
Yü Kuang-chung, 458, 461, 780
Yü Kuo-fan "Hsi-yu chi" lun-chi (Essays on *Journey to the West*; Anthony Yu), 634
"Yü-lan-p'en fu" (Yang Chiung), 290
Yü Li-hua, 779
Yü li hun (The Soul of the Jade Pear Flower; Hsü Chen-ya), 566, 727, 742–43
Yü liang ta-ti (World Measurer), 65
Yü Lo-chin, 760
Yü-lou ch'un (The Cross-Dressed Scholar's Three Wives), 669
yü-lu (recorded sayings; Japanese: *goroku*), 168–69, 888, 967, 1072, 1087
Yü Ming-chen (Yü Ku-an), 710
Yü-mu hsing-hsin pien (Stories to Delight the Eye and Awaken the Heart; Tu Kang), 618
Yü P'ing-po, 454
"Yü-shan fu" (The Woman of Yü-shan; P'an Chih-heng), 690
"Yü-shan shen-nü tz'u ko erh shou: sung shen ch'ü" (Second Song for the Worship of the Goddess at Yü Mountain: Bidding the Goddess Farewell; Wang Wei), 124
Yü Shang-yüan, 851, 856
Yü Shao-yü, 625
Yü-shih ming-yen (Clear Words to Instruct the World; Feng Meng-lung), 597, 600
Yü Shih-nan, 283, 284
yü-shih-t'ai (Censorate), 401
Yü Ta, 657
Yü Ta-fu, 566, 735, 745–46, 772, 773, 1057
Yü-t'ai hsin-yung (New Songs from a Jade Terrace; comp. Hsü Ling), 68, 200, 207, 241, 272, 929, 954, 956, 959, 1081
"Yü-t'ang-ch'un lo nan feng fu" (Yü-t'ang Ch'un; Feng Meng-lung), 601
Yü Tao-hsien, 188
yü ti (inner space of freedom), 883
"Yü-tsan chi" (The Jade Hairpin; Kao Lien), 829
Yü-wai hsiao-shuo chi (Collection of Stories from Abroad; ed. Chou Tso-jen and Chou Shu-jen), 720, 729
Yü Wan-ch'un, 628, 663
"Yü wu-sheng-ch'ü" (In a Land of Silence; Tsung Fu-hsien), 869
yü-yen (parables), 117, 171–72, 523, 539, 580, 984
Yü-yi chih (Chronicle of Going into Service; Ou-yang Hsiu), 557
Yü Ying-shih, 650
Yü Yüeh, 136, 695
yüan (esthetic distance), 422
Yüan, Emperor, 814, 815
Yüan, king of Ch'u, 99–100
Yüan Chen, 7, 208, 217, 279, 307, 308, 309, 416, 586–87, 1009, 1085. *See also* "Ying-ying chuan"
"Yüan-cheng fu" (New Year's Rhapsody; recovered from Tun-huang; Wang Chi), 285
yüan-ch'i (*yin-yüan*; Buddhist stories of karmic circumstances), 968, 971, 979, 982, 984–85, 986, 993
"Yüan-chia chieh" (Yüan Family Slough; Liu Tsung-yüan), 535
Yüan-chia period (Liu Sung), 266
Yüan Chiao, 589
Yüan Chieh, 280, 301, 307, 556
yüan-chih (original meaning), 633
Yüan Ching, 286
yüan-ch'ing (love) poems, 421
Yüan-ch'ü hsüan (Anthology of Yüan Plays; Tsang Mao-hsün), 803, 804, 812, 814, 815, 818, 825
Yüan Chüeh, 386, 394, 487
Yüan Chung-tao, 7, 409, 411
Yüan dynasty, 246, 559, 816, 995, 1070; *ch'uan-ch'i* tales in, 679, 680; collapse of, 400; drama of, 144, 145, 391, 621, 632, 792–95, 800–802,

804, 806, 814, 858, 889; emperors of, 1049; in fiction, 623, 858, 1020; history of (*Yüan shih*), 396, 509; *hua-pen* in, 146; humor in, 145, 146; inscription poetry of, 469, 477, 478, 479, 485, 487; and Japan, 1087, 1088; language in, 22, 32, 33, 887; literary critics in, 892; literati in, 811; local opera in, 1016; and Mongol script, 1050; music of, 331, 371; oral arts in, 995; poetry of, 274, 330–31, 367, 368, 370–89, 390, 391, 394, 409, 410, 431, 440, 466; popular literature in, 14; proverbs in, 153, 155; songs of, 274, 331, 370–82, 373, 391, 399, 787; storytelling origins in, 595–98; tales of, 972; Taoism in, 178, 182, 810; women of, 211, 218

Yüan-fu (On Wealth; trans. Yen Fu), 1062

Yüan Hao-wen, 325, 386, 396, 434, 440, 676, 814, 936

"Yüan hsing" (Human Nature; Han Yü), 533

"Yüan hui" (Slander; Han Yü), 533

Yüan-hun chih (Accounts of Ghosts with Grievances; Yen Chih-t'ui), 171, 970

Yüan Hung, 508

Yüan Hung-tao, 384, 405, 409, 411, 435, 559, 687, 936, 1072, 1076, 1089

"Yüan jen lun" (On the Origin of Humanity; Tsung-mi), 166

Yüan K'ai, 387

"Yüan ko hsing" (Song of Complaint; Favorite Beauty Pan), 249–50

Yüan K'o-chia, 457

Yüan Mei, 8, 231, 396, 397, 421, 425, 433–37, 559, 693–94; and Chiang Shih-ch'üan, 834; influence of, 436–37; and literary theory, 933, 935, 1090

yüan-nü shih (*ch'i-fu shih*; poems on lonely or abandoned women), 254

yüan-pen (farce skits), 145–46, 792, 805, 818, 835

Yüan-pen "Chin P'ing Mei" (The Original *Chin P'ing Mei*), 638

"Yüan pieh-li" (Distantly Parting; Li Po), 297

"Yüan p'u fan kuei" (Returning Sails; Ma Chih-yüan), 378

Yüan-shan-t'ang chü-p'in (Classification of Drama from the Far Mountain Hall; Ch'i Piao-chia), 841

Yüan shih (History of the Yüan Dynasty), 396, 509

Yüan-shih (On the Origin of Poetry; Yeh Hsieh), 427, 937

Yüan-shih hsüan (Anthology of Yüan Verse; comp. Ku Ssu-li), 383, 384, 385

Yüan Shih-k'ai, 741

Yüan-shih t'ien-tsun (Celestial Worthy of Primordial Commencement), 181

"Yüan Tan-ch'iu ko" (Song of Yüan Tan-ch'iu; Li Po), 297–98

"Yüan-tao" (Essentials of the Moral Way; Han Yü), 533, 931

Yüan Tsung-tao, 409, 411

Yüan-yang chen (A Pair of Needles), 612

yüan-yang hu-tieh p'ai (mandarin ducks and butterflies), 698, 1015–16, 1103

"Yüan-yang meng" (A Dream of Mandarin Ducks; Yeh Hsiao-wan), 839

"Yüan yu" (Distant Journey), 118, 228

Yüan-yu period (Sung), 353, 355

Yüan Yü-ling, 626

yüeh (conciseness), 890

Yüeh, king of, 515

Yüeh, kingdom of, 828–29

"Yüeh-chi" (Records of Music; *Li-chi*), 92

"Yüeh chih" (Treatise on Music; *Sung shu*), 956, 957

Yüeh-ch'iu chih-min-ti (Moon Colony; Huang-chiang tiao-sou), 721

yüeh-ch'ü (song suites set to melodies), 990

Yüeh-ch'üan yin-she (Moon Spring Poetry Society), 388

Yüeh Chun, 694–95

Yüeh Fei, 602, 628, 834, 844

Yüeh-fu ku-t'i yao chieh (Explanations of the Old Titles of *Yüeh-fu*; Wu Ching), 958

yüeh-fu (Music Bureau, or ballad) poetry, 32, 202, 224, 591, 592; ceremonial, 284, 293; Chin, 262, 263, 264, 269; genres of, 954; Han, 249–51, 254, 255, 256, 260, 277, 370, 393, 953; history of, 271, 953–54; in Korea, 1069; of Li Po, 277, 307, 955, 962, 975; and lyric texts, 986; Ming, 396; as model, 387, 1083; and music, 974; new (*hsin*), 277, 307, 308, 312; of Po Chü-yi, 277, 308; research on, 963; *san-ch'ü* compared with, 374; and *shih* poetry, 420, 955; of Six Dynasties, 272, 393; sources of texts of, 956–57; Sung, 353; T'ang, 281, 295, 297, 298, 307, 308, 312, 395

Yüeh-fu pu-t'i (Additional Themes for "Ballads"), 331, 332, 333, 334, 335

Yüeh-fu shih chi (Collection of Ballad Poetry; Kuo Mao-ch'ien), 255, 956, 957, 960

"Yüeh-jen ko" (Song of the Yüeh Boatman;), 958

"Yüeh k'o" (Appointment with a Guest; Chao Shih-hsiu), 365–66

"Yüeh-ling" (Monthly Ordinances; *Li-chi*), 92

Yüeh-wei ts'ao-t'ang pi-chi (Sketches from the Cottage for the Contemplation of Subtleties; comp. Chi Yün), 130, 543, 544, 694

Yüeh Yeh, 866

"Yüeh yeh" (Moonlit Night; Tu Fu), 299

Yüeh-yüeh hsiao-shuo (All-Story Monthly; journal), 702–3, 710, 728–29, 729
"Yüeh yüeh hsiao-shuo hsü" (Preface to *All-Story Monthly*; Wu Chien-jen), 710
Yūjo ki (Records About Prostitutes; Ōe no Masafusa), 1087
yul-ch'ang (regulated prosodic song; Korea), 1071
Yun Kŭn-su, 1073
Yün-chai kuang-lu (Expanded Records of Cloud Studio; Li Hsien-min), 679
Yün-chi ch'i-ch'ien (Seven Lots from the Bookbag of the Clouds; comp. Chang Chün-fang), 177, 523
Yün-chien school, 412, 413, 414
Yün-kuang chi (Anthology of Cloud Radiance; Wang Ch'u-yi), 187
Yün-men wu-chi (Cloud Gate Ensemble; ballet company), 778
Yün-shan chi (Anthology of Cloudy Mountains; Chi Yi), 188
Yün Shou-p'ing, 427
Yün-yao chi (Cloud Songs), 976
yung (describing), 475
Yung, Prince, 296
"Yung-chao pa-chi" (Eight Records of Yung prefecture; Liu Tsung-yüan), 556
Yung-ch'eng chi-hsien lu (Register of the Transcendents Gathered at Yung-ch'eng; Tu Kuang-t'ing), 582
Yung-chia period (Chin), 264, 365
"Yung Ching K'o shih" (Poem on Ching K'o; T'ao Ch'ien), 267
"Yung erh Shu" (Poem on the Two Shus; T'ao Ch'ien), 267
"Yung hua-chang" (Ode on a Painted Screen; Shang-kuan Yi), 286
"Yung hua p'ing-feng shih erh-shih-ssu shou" (Twenty-four Poems Describing Painted Screens; Yü Hsin), 474–75
yung-huai poetry, 260
"Yung-huai shih" (Poems Expressing My Heart, or Songs of My Soul; Juan Chi), 258, 291, 298
Yung-le emperor, 800, 816
Yung-le ta-tien (Yung-le Encyclopedia), 135–36, 805, 819, 820
"Yung-ming chiu nien ts'e hsiu-ts'ai wen" (Five Topics for the 491 C.E. Hsiu-ts'ai Examination; Wang Jung), 241
Yung-ming *t'i* (Yung-ming Style), 240, 270, 271
Yung-p'ing reign, 523
"Yung-shih shih" (Poem on History; Pan Ku), 251, 254
yung-shih shih (history verse), 998
"Yung shou" (On Hands; Ch'iao Chi), 377
"Yung ta hu-tieh" (The Great Butterfly; Wang Ho-ch'ing), 376
"Yung wu chi" (Poem on an Object: The Dancer; Ho Hsün), 201
yung-wu shih (poems on an object), 277, 474; *fu*, 240, 242, 250, 251, 292
Yusup Khass Hajib, 1048

Zeami Motokiyo, 1089
Zekkai Chūshin, 1088
Zen Buddhism. *See* Ch'an (Zen) Buddhism
Zhina (China), 54
Zoroastrianism, 9, 170

CONTRIBUTORS

Allan H. Barr received his doctorate from Oxford University in 1983 and is now Professor of Asian Languages and Literatures at Pomona College. His writings on Ming and Ch'ing literature have appeared in the *Harvard Journal of Asiatic Studies, Late Imperial China, Wenxian*, and elsewhere. Much of his work focuses on classical tales by P'u Sung-ling and other writers of the late Ming and early Ch'ing.

Mark Bender teaches courses on East Asian culture, literature, and folklore at The Ohio State University. His research interests are centered on the oral and oral-related literatures of China, including local and ethnic minority traditions. He has published studies on Soochow *t'an-tz'u* (strummed lyrics) and other professional storytelling traditions, as well as Yi (Ne, Lolo) and Miao (Hmong) nationality folk-songs and epics.

Daria Berg is a Lecturer in Chinese in the Department of East Asian Studies at the University of Durham (United Kingdom). She received her doctorate from the University of Oxford in 1995, with a thesis on the seventeenth-century Chinese novel *Hsing-shih yin-yüan chuan* (Marriage Destinies to Awaken the World). Her research interests include Ming-Ch'ing fiction and history, gender studies, and contemporary Chinese fiction.

Anne Birrell (Clare Hall, University of Cambridge) received her M.A. from the University of Michigan and her Ph.D. from Columbia University. Her teaching positions include those at Cambridge University and the City University of New York. She is the author of *Chinese Love Poetry: New Songs from a Jade Terrace* (1982, 1986, 1995), *Popular Songs and Ballads of Han China* (1988), *Chinese Mythology: An Introduction* (1993, 1999), and *The Classic of Mountains and Seas* (1999). She has published numerous articles applying postmodern theory and gender criticism in *History of Religions*, *New Medieval Literatures* (Oxford), *Journal of the American Oriental Society*, and *T'oung Pao*.

Judith Magee Boltz completed her Ph.D. in the Department of Oriental Languages of the University of California, Berkeley. Her publications include *A Survey of Taoist Literature, Tenth to Seventeenth Centuries* (1987) and articles on various aspects of Taoism. She has held teaching and research positions at the University of Washington and Stanford University.

Daniel Bryant studied with Yeh Chia-ying, Edwin Pulleyblank, and Jan Walls at the University of British Columbia, where he was awarded a doctorate in 1978; his dissertation was on Meng Hao-jan. He has taught since 1976 at the University of Victoria, where he is now Professor of Chinese. His books are *Lyric Poets of the Southern T'ang* (1982) and *Ho Ching-ming ts'ung-k'ao* (Collected Studies of Ho Ching-ming; 1997), as well as a translation, under the title *The Invisible Companion*, of a work by the contemporary novelist Zhang Kangkang (1996). His other scholarly work includes numerous articles, reviews, and translations.

Xiaomei Chen received her Ph.D. in Comparative Literature at Indiana University in 1989. She teaches in the Department of East Asian Languages and Literatures and in the division of Comparative Studies at Ohio State University. She is interested in cultural studies, comparative drama, Chinese American literature, women writers, and modern Chinese drama and fiction, including film, video, and popular culture, especially in the post-Mao period. Among her publications are *Occidentalism: A Theory of Counter-Discourse in Post-Mao China* (1995) and *Acting the Right Part: Political Theater and Popular Drama in Contemporary China—1966–1996* (forthcoming).

Christopher Connery teaches in the Literature Department at the University of California (Santa Cruz), where he is also Codirector of the Center for Cultural Studies and Chair of East Asian Studies. His publications include *Empire of the Text: Writing and Authority in Early Imperial China* (1999) and several journal articles from a work in progress on the Pacific Ocean and its rim as a politico-cultural arena.

Robert Joe Cutter is a professor in the Department of East Asian Languages and Literature at the University of Wisconsin (Madison). He received his Ph.D. from the University of Washington and specializes in early medieval Chinese literature and history, with particular emphasis on Han-Wei literature and *San kuo chih* (Romance of the Three Kingdoms). He is the author of numerous articles, as well as of *The Brush and the Spur: Chinese Culture and the Cockfight* (1989) and (with William G. Crowell) *Empresses and Consorts: Selections from Chen Shou's* Records of the Three States *with Pei Songzhi's Commentary* (1999).

Milena Doleželová-Velingerová is Professor Emerita of Chinese Literature at the University of Toronto and Visiting Professor (1996–2000) at Charles University (Prague), where she was educated. She has published works on the transformation of twentieth-century Chinese fiction, on medieval Chinese storytelling, and on premodern Chinese theory of fiction and drama. Her edited books include *The Chinese Novel at the Turn of the Century* (1980), *A Selective Guide to Chinese Literature 1900–1949*, Vol. 1: *The Novel* (1988), *Poetics East and West* (1988/89), and, with Oldrich Král, *The Appropriation of Cultural Capital: China's May Fourth Project* (2001).

Stephen Durrant is Professor of Chinese literature at the University of Oregon (Eugene). A specialist in early Chinese narrative, he has written numerous articles and two books: *The Book of the Nisan Shamaness: A Manchu Folk Epic* (1976), co-authored with Margaret Nowak, and *The Cloudy Mirror: Tension and Conflict in the Writings of Sima Qian* (1995). He currently serves as Director of the Asian Studies Program at the University of Oregon and is at work on a new translation of the *Tso chuan* (Tso Commentary).

Ronald Egan is Professor of Chinese Literature at the University of California (Santa Barbara). He specializes in poetry and literary-language prose of the T'ang and Sung periods. His publications include *The Literary Works of Ou-yang Hsiu* (1984), *Word, Image, and Deed in the Life of Su Shi* (1994), and a volume of translations entitled *Limited Views: Essays on Ideas and Letters by Qian Zhongshu* (1998).

Michael A. Fuller is Associate Professor of Chinese in the Department of East Asian Languages and Literatures at the University of California (Irvine). His main area of study is the development of the Chinese poetic tradition, and his particular specialty is Sung dynasty poetry. He is the author of *The Road to East Slope: The Development of Su Shi's Poetic Voice* (1990) and *Introduction to Literary Chinese* (1999).

Paul Rakita Goldin teaches Chinese history and philosophy in the Department of Asian and Middle Eastern Studies at the University of Pennsylvania. He is the author of *Rituals of the Way: The Philosophy of Xunzi* (1999) and a forthcoming book on intellectual conceptions of sex and sexuality in ancient China. He is currently compiling, in collaboration with Gilbert L. Mattos, a dictionary of ancient Chinese philosophical terms.

Christoph Harbsmeier read Chinese at Oxford University and took his Ph.D. in Copenhagen. He is now Professor of East Asian Languages and Literatures in the University of Oslo. Concurrently, he holds permanent joint appointments as an advisory professor of Chinese at Peking University, Fudan University, and Shanghai Normal University. His books include *Wilhelm von Humboldt und die philosophische Grammatik des Altchinesischen* (1979); *Aspects of Classical Chinese Syntax* (1981); *Social Realism with a Buddhist Face: The Cartoonist Feng Zikai* (1985); and *Language and Logic* (= *Science and Civilisation in China*, vol. 7.3, 1998). He is currently working on a synonym dictionary of Classical Chinese, which is being undertaken in close collaboration with a number of Chinese and Western scholars.

James M. Hargett earned his Ph.D. degree from Indiana University, where his mentors were Irving Y. C. Lo, Wu-chi Liu, and Eugene Eoyang. Previously he has taught at Middlebury College and the University of Colorado (Boulder). He now teaches at the University at Albany (State University of New York), where he also serves as Chair of the Department of East Asian Studies. He has been editor of the *Journal of Sung-Yüan Studies* for many years. His main research interests are traditional Chinese literature and historical geography.

Charles Hartman is Professor of East Asian Studies at the State University of New York at Albany. He has published *Han Yü and the T'ang Search for Unity* (1986) and served as poetry editor for *The Indiana Companion to Traditional Chinese Literature* (1986, 1998). His academic interests center on the cultural history of medieval China. He is currently at work on a history of literary persecution during the Sung dynasty (960–1279) and a study of the interaction between poetry and painting in traditional China.

Hu Ying is Associate Professor of Chinese Literature at the University of California (Irvine). In addition to having written many papers on Chinese fiction, both traditional and modern, she is the author of *Tales of Translation: Composing the New Woman in Late Qing China* (2000). She is currently preparing a study of women's travel writing.

Rania Huntington is Assistant Professor of Chinese Language and Literature at the University of Illinois at Urbana-Champaign. Her Ph.D. dissertation (Harvard University, 1996) was entitled "Foxes and Ming-Ch'ing Fiction." Her current research focuses on the strange and the exotic in the Chinese literary tradition.

Wilt L. Idema studied sinology at Leiden University, the Netherlands, and received overseas training at Sapporo (Hokkaido), Kyoto, and Hong Kong. From 1970 to 1999 he taught at Leiden University, and since 2000 he has been Professor of Chinese Literature at Harvard University. In a visiting capacity he has also taught at the University of Hawaii and the University of California, Berkeley. He has published extensively in the fields of early Chinese vernacular fiction, early Chinese drama, and Chinese prosimetrical literature. His Dutch-language publications include translations of Classical Chinese poetry from all periods.

Paul W. Kroll is Professor of Chinese at the University of Colorado (Boulder). He has published widely in the areas of medieval literature, religion, and cultural history, with special interests in T'ang poetry, particularly Li Po, and medieval Taoist scriptural verse. His publications include *Meng Hao-jan* (1981), *Dharma Bell and Dhāraṇī Pillar: Li Po's Buddhist Inscriptions* (2001), and more than forty articles. He is currently preparing a translation of the important mid-eighth-century anthology of poetry, *Ho-yüeh ying-ling chi* (The Finest Souls of River and Alp). He is editor of the annual journal *T'ang Studies* and editor-in-chief of the quarterly *Journal of the American Oriental Society*.

Dore J. Levy is Professor of Comparative Literature and East Asian Studies, and Chair of the Department of East Asian Studies, at Brown University. Her research seeks to integrate Chinese into comparative literature and includes interdisciplinary work in art history ("Transforming Archetypes in Chinese Poetry and Painting: the Case of Ts'ai Yen," 1993) and medicine ("Why Baoyu Can't Concentrate: Attention Deficit Disorder in *The Story of the Stone*," 1994). She is the author of *Chinese Narrative Poetry: The Late Han through T'ang Dynasties* (1988) and *Ideal and Actual in* The Story of the Stone (1999).

Wai-yee Li teaches Chinese literature at Harvard University and has previously held positions at Princeton University, the University of Pennsylvania, and the University of Illinois (Urbana-Champaign). She is the author of *Enchantment and Disenchantment: Love and Illusion in Chinese Literature* (1993). She is currently preparing a book manuscript entitled "The Readability of the Past in Early Chinese Historiography."

Lydia H. Liu teaches in the departments of Comparative Literature and East Asian Languages and Cultures at the University of California (Berkeley). She is the author of *Translingual Practice: Literature, National Culture, and Translated Modernity—China, 1900–1937* (1995) and editor of *Tokens of Exchange: The Problem of Translation in Global Circulations* (1999). Among other works, she has published in the fields of popular televisual media in late-twentieth-century China, nineteenth-century translations of international law, and eighteenth-century English fiction and porcelain technology. Her latest research will appear in a forthcoming book entitled *Desire and Sovereign Thinking*.

Richard John Lynn received his Ph.D. from Stanford University and also did graduate work at the University of Washington, the University of Chicago, and Kyoto University. He has taught at various universities in the United States, New Zealand, and Australia, served as Professor of Classical Chinese Studies and Chair, Department of East Asian Studies, University of Alberta (Edmonton, Canada), and is now Professor of Chinese Literature at the University of Toronto. His scholarship ranges across much of the Chinese tradition and deals with a wide variety of issues and figures important in intellectual and literary history. He has published numerous books and articles, including *The Classic of Changes: A New Translation of the I Ching as Interpreted by Wang Bi* (1994) and *The Classic of the Way and Virtue: A New Translation of the Tao-te Ching of Laozi as Interpreted by Wang Bi* (1999). He is currently preparing an annotated translation of Yen Yü's *Ts'ang-lang shih-hua* (Ts'ang-lang's Remarks on Poetry).

Victor H. Mair is Professor of Chinese Language and Literature in the Department of Asian and Middle Eastern Studies (formerly Oriental Studies) at the University of Pennsylvania. He is the editor of *The Columbia Anthology of Traditional Chinese Literature* (1994). Among the many books, articles, and reviews he has written are *T'ang Transformation Texts* (1989), *Painting and Performance* (1988), *Tun-huang Popular Narratives* (1983), *The Tarim Mummies* (with J. P. Mallory; 2000), and "The Sanskrit Origins of Recent Style Prosody" (with Tsu-Lin Mei, 1991). He is the general editor of the ABC Chinese Dictionary Series and the editor of *Sino-Platonic Papers*.

Helmut Martin (1940–1999) was Professor of Chinese Language and Literature at Ruhr University (Bochum) since 1979, having formerly worked at the Hamburg Institute of Asian Affairs. He studied Sinology and Slavistics in Munich, Belgrade, Paris, and Heidelberg, receiving his Ph.D. in Chinese literature at the University of Heidelberg in 1966. Overseas experience included postdoctoral research at National Taiwan University and Kyoto University, research fellowships at the University of Michigan and the University of California (Berkeley), exchange professorships at Tokyo University, a visiting professorship at Tongji University (Shanghai), the Carl Schurz Memorial Professorship at the University of Wisconsin, and research professorships at the National Library of the Republic of China (Taipei) and at the University of Queensland (Brisbane). He was the author of scores of monographs and the editor of numerous volumes and series. His research ranged from premodern drama and poetry to contemporary literature and politics.

David McCraw is Professor of Chinese at the University of Hawaii. He received his Ph.D. from Stanford University and specializes in traditional *shih* and *tz'u* poetry. He especially enjoys making old Chinese poems come alive for modern Western readers. Among his published works are *Du Fu's Laments from the South* (1992) and "Pursuing Zhuangzi as Rhymemaster: A Snark-Hunt in Eight Fits" (1995).

Anne E. McLaren is a Senior Lecturer at the University of Melbourne's Institute of Asian Languages and Societies. She completed her doctoral study at The Australian National University and did postdoctoral work at Harvard University. Her main research interests are vernacular literature of the Ming period, Chinese prosimetric literature, and women's oral culture in China. She is the author of *Chinese Popular Culture and Ming Chantefables* (1998), a volume of translations entitled *The Chinese Femme Fatale: Stories from the Ming Period* (1994), and an edited volume on gender issues in China under the title *Dress, Sex and Text in Chinese Culture* (co-edited with Antonia Finnane; 1999), and many articles on Ming fiction and prosimetric stories.

Karin Myhre has written on dramatic literature and performance in the Sung through Ming periods. Her work traces issues of perception and belief in the context of broader topics of humor and memory. Her forthcoming book, *Appearances of Ghosts in Northern Dramas,* charts the complex cultural origins of ghost characters in a variety of literary, historical, and artistic sources. She is also preparing a series of articles on humor, including a study of jesters in Ssu-ma Ch'ien's *Records of the Grand Historian* and an analysis of political jokes in Sung imperial courts.

William H. Nienhauser, Jr., received his Ph.D. from Indiana University in 1972 after study at the Army Language School and Bonn University (Germany). He taught German at Indiana University for a year before joining the Department of East Asian Languages and Literature at the University of Wisconsin, where he now holds the Halls-Bascom Professorship in Chinese Literature. His publications include *P'i Jih-hsiu* (1979), *The Indiana Companion to Traditional Chinese Literature* (1986, 1998), and the ongoing translation of the *Shih chi* under the title *The Grand Scribe's Records.* Since it was launched in 1979, he has been one of the editors of *Chinese Literature: Essays, Articles, Reviews (CLEAR).*

Emanuel Pastreich is Assistant Professor of Japanese Literature at the University of Illinois (Urbana-Champaign). His present research concerns the reception of Chinese vernacular narrative in Korea and Japan. After completing a degree in Chinese literature at Yale College and spending one year at National Taiwan University, he studied comparative literature at the University of Tokyo for five years. The master's thesis he submitted to the University of Tokyo concerned painting and poetry in Tokugawa Japan. His work on Korean literature took him to Seoul National University for a year while he was completing his Ph.D. at Harvard University. He has published articles in *Monumenta Nipponica, Sino-Japanese Studies,* and the *Harvard Journal of Asiatic Studies,* as well as in Korean and Japanese.

Michael Puett is John L. Loeb Associate Professor of Humanities in the Department of East Asian Languages and Civilizations at Harvard University. Educated at the University of Chicago, his research interests are focused on the intellectual, cultural, and political history of China from the Shang through the T'ang dynasties. His first book, *The Ambivalence of Creation: Debates on Innovation and Artifice in Early China,* was published by Stanford University Press in 2001, and his second book, *To Become a God: Cosmology, Sagehood, and Self-Divinization in Early China,* will be published by Harvard University Press in 2002.

Jeffrey Riegel is Professor of Chinese in the Department of East Asian Languages and Cultures at the University of California (Berkeley). He has written several articles on early Chinese literature, most recently on the *Shih ching,* and, with John Knoblock, has collaborated on a translation of the *Lü-shih ch'un-ch'iu* entitled *The Annals of Lü Buwei* (2000). He has also recently completed the draft of a new translation of the *Mo Tzu.*